The Future Demographic

Global population trends and forecasts to 2020

The Future Demographic

Global Population Trends and Forecasts to 2020

Euromonitor International Plc, 60-61 Britton Street, London, EC1M 5UX

The Future Demographic

Second edition
ISBN: 978-184264-526-0
Researched and published by:

Western and Southern Europe
Euromonitor International - Head Office
60-61 Britton Street, London, EC1M 5UX, United Kingdom
Tel: +44 (0) 20 7251 8024
Fax: +44 (0) 20 7608 3149
email: info@euromonitor.com

North America
Euromonitor International
224 South Michigan Avenue
Suite 1500, Chicago, IL 60604, USA
Tel: + 1 312 922 1115
Fax: +1 312 922 1157
email: insight@euromonitorintl.com

Latin America
Euromonitor International
Avenida Apoquindo 3600, 5th Floor, Las Condes
Santiago C.P. 7550108, Chile
+56 02 7992426
+56 02 4332226

Asia Pacific and Australasia
Euromonitor International
3 Lim Teck Kim Road
#08-01 Singapore Technologies Building, Singapore 088934
Tel: +65 6429 0590
Fax: +65 6324 1855
email: info@euromonitor.com.sg

China
Euromonitor International
Level 21 Unit 06, Tian An Center
No. 338 Nanjing Road (West), Shanghai 200003, China
Tel: +86 21 6372 6288
Fax: +86 21 6372 6289
email: info@euromonitor.com.cn

Middle East and North Africa
Euromonitor International
Building 5E, Block A, office 321, Dubai Airport Free Zone
P.O. Box 54709, Dubai, U.A.E.
Tel: +971 4 609 1340
Fax: +971 4 609 1343
email: info-mena@euromonitor.com

Central and South Africa
Euromonitor International
The Forum, Unit GS04, 6473 Northbank Lane, Century City
Cape Town, 7441, Republic of South Africa
Tel: +27 21 552 0037
Fax: +27 21 552 7071
email: info-africa@euromonitor.com

Central and Eastern Europe
Euromonitor International
Jogailos Street 4, Vilnius, LT-01116, Lithuania
Tel: +370 5 243 1577
Fax: +370 5 243 1599
email: info@euromonitor.lt

Website
http://www.euromonitor.com

British Library Cataloguing in Publication Data

A CIP catalogue record for this book is available from the British Library

Euromonitor International is a member of the Data Publishers Association and the European Association of Directory and Database Publishers

Printed in the United Kingdom

Summary of Contents

Table of Contents

Section two

Introduction

Introduction

Scope of the Handbook

Now in its second edition, ***The Future Demographic: Global Population Trends and Forecasts to 2020*** is a compendium of statistical information from Euromonitor International, featuring an unprecedented wealth of detailed statistics on substantial changes in the demographic structure of the world.

Global businesses are increasingly looking at long-term demographic trends as an indicator of future market potential. Many major markets are reaching maturity in terms of consumer demand and also have static or declining populations. However, each of these markets is characterised by significant changes in the structure of the population, which will present future opportunities and obstacles for companies targeting those groups.

Of equal relevance are the opportunities presented by emerging markets. For emerging markets to offer significant potential, an expanding population has to accompany significant economic improvements. Many emerging markets have faced difficult economic conditions in recent years which have restrained incomes and consumer demand. So big questions arise:

- Which countries are set for the fastest population growth accompanied by fast economic growth?
- What is the size of each demographic market segment in these countries?
- Which are the fastest growing regions, both demographically and economically?
- In mature markets, which demographic segments offer the most potential?

The Future Demographic attempts to answer these questions by providing detailed statistics on population age structure for major regions and countries of the world.

Following this introduction, the book contains five main sections, as follows:

Section One: Regional overviews

Limitations of the book format only allows for the analysis of nine main geographic regions. For the more in-depth study of all 74 major countries featured in this book the reader is referred to ***The Future Demographic Reports***, that may be obtained via our website.

Section Two: Age structure of the population at a glance

Single year age group data enables us to produce these unique contour charts. The reader can chose the age group of interest and quickly track its development over time. Population age structure and its change over time can be compared between different countries and regions at a glance.

Section Three: Rankings

The standardised population database allows for the compilation of a series of unique rankings, showing the relative position for each country within the 74 country matrix measured by a selection of key demographic criteria. Percentage of country total format has been used to further enhance comparability.

Section Four: Cross-country comparisons

This section contains extensive world population data and forms a comprehensive survey of world demographic developments, allowing for easy identification of trends and quick comparisons across countries. It commences with the assessment of key age groups, followed by vital statistics and key economic indicators. It then examines specific marketing segments in detail.

Section Five: Country data

Using the same standardised approach followed in Section Four, this section deals with each of the 74 countries in turn, presenting demographic data under a series of standard headings, thus facilitating the review of key facts and figures on changes in the size of marketing segments within each country. The demographic data is supplemented by key economic trends reflecting income levels and distribution.

Countries and Regions

The handbook focuses on seven geographic regions of the world and examines in detail 74 major countries selected by size of the economy as well as population.

Asia Pacific:	Azerbaijan, China, Hong Kong (China), India, Indonesia, Japan, Kazakhstan, Malaysia, Pakistan, Philippines, Singapore, South Korea, Taiwan, Thailand, Turkmenistan, Vietnam.
Australasia:	Australia, New Zealand.
Eastern Europe:	Belarus, Bosnia-Herzegovina, Bulgaria, Croatia, Czech Republic, Estonia, Hungary, Latvia, Lithuania, Poland, Romania, Russia, Slovakia, Slovenia, Ukraine.
Latin America:	Argentina, Bolivia, Brazil, Chile, Colombia, Costa Rica, Ecuador, Mexico, Peru, Venezuela.
Middle East and Africa:	Algeria, Egypt, Iran, Israel, Jordan, Kuwait, Morocco, Nigeria, Saudi Arabia, South Africa, Tunisia, United Arab Emirates.
North America:	Canada, USA.
Western Europe:	Austria, Belgium, Denmark, Finland, France, Germany, Greece, Ireland, Italy, Netherlands, Norway, Portugal, Spain, Sweden, Switzerland, Turkey, United Kingdom.

Sources and Methodology

Sources

The demographic data included in ***The Future Demographic*** has been compiled following an extensive research programme. Statistical offices of 74 countries around the world were approached by a team of Euromonitor International's researchers in order to obtain the most detailed contemporary data available on population age structure.

A large number of population censuses took place at the brink of the 20th and 21st centuries. The aim of this book was to capture all these latest results. This, however, created problems of compatibility between the latest census results and old data. In a number of occasions structural breaks were discovered in time series provided by National Statistical Offices. In such cases Euromonitor International's demographers used advanced data manipulation techniques to revise the out-of-date series and bring them in line with the latest census information.

The research material was then assembled into a uniform database by applying strict category definitions to standardise the primary data. Data arrangement, availability and definitions varied considerably country by country. Thus painstaking regrouping and adding up of population cohorts had to be carried out to ensure cross-country comparability as well as correct regional aggregations.

For some countries, the quality and availability of the primary data was not sufficient to fit it into this tightly structured database. In such cases United Nations Population Division single year age group estimates were used.

Interpolation

Single year age group data was not available for some of the countries and years. In such cases Sprague multiplier techniques were employed to break down five-year age groups to single-year age groups.

Where data was missing between census or micro-census results, Hermit interpolation was used to fill in these gaps.

Extrapolation and Forecasts

We sought to include population forecasts of National Statistical Offices whenever such data was provided. In most cases, however, we had to resort to our own forecasts, as national data was either not available or the level of detail was not sufficient.

Our forecasts were produced using the cohort-component method. This method is one of the oldest and most widely used procedures for projecting population. In the cohort-component method, the components of population change (fertility, mortality and net migration) are projected separately for each cohort (persons born in a given year). The base population is advanced each year by using projected survival rates and net migration by single year of age and sex. Each year, a new birth cohort is added to the population by applying the projected fertility rates.

The age cohorts determine time interval. The time interval for which an estimate can be made is the length of time it takes all the members of an age cohort (say, 18) to pass on to the next age grouping (the 19 year old group).

Projecting population by the cohort-component method involves a number of steps, each of them utilising the demographer's expert opinion. First, a component projection requires a population properly distributed by sex and age to serve as the base population from the starting date of the projection. Second, assumptions were made regarding the level and patterns of fertility. The level of fertility (total fertility rate) was projected and then a pattern of fertility (age-specific fertility rates) was assumed. A similar process was used to project mortality, where general level of mortality by sex was projected, then age-specific mortality rates assumed. Finally, levels and patterns of net migration were estimated. The projected levels and patterns of the components of population change were applied to the base population to yield the projected population for a given year.

Disclaimer

The compilation of a reference volume of this type involves extracting complex statistical data from numerous sources in different languages. The editors have made every attempt to ensure accuracy but the publishers cannot be held responsible for any errors which may have occurred.

12345

SECTION ONE

Regional Overviews

WORLD

World population will continue to rise in the future but at a decelerating pace. The world's potential labour pool will nearly double between 1980 and 2020. By 2020, the number of those over 50 years of age will make up more than a quarter of world population. Fertility rates in Western Europe and North America have been falling for some time but now appear to have stabilised. In Asia, Africa and Latin America, they are much faster but are still above the replacement level in many countries.

KEY POPULATION TRENDS

Total population

Chart 2.1 – known as a "heat chart", found in section two *"Age structure of the population at a glance"* – depicts changes in the age structure in the world's population over time. Each dot represents the number of people in a specific age group in a given year. Accordingly, a dark red dot represents the largest concentration of people, by age, in a particular year while deep blue dots show the lowest concentrations. A single dark red dot is the equivalent of slightly more than 146.6 million people while each deep blue dot represents almost 6.8 million people and other colour shadings correspond to intermediate population totals (each by age group).

A prominent feature of this chart is the large and expanding area of bright red which is observed in the upper right-hand corner. This area depicts a population boom which first began in the 1980s. By 2020, the oldest people in this boom will be approaching thirty years of age. At the bottom of the chart is a large area of dark blue indicating a relatively sparse number of elderly people. This area is largest during the 1980s and 1990s but over time the dark blue dots are replaced by lighter hues of blues and greens as the number of elderly people increases.

World population has been steadily increasing for several decades and that trend will persist for the foreseeable future. Between 1980 and 2020, the world will add almost 3.2 billion people, pushing its population to nearly 7.6 billion by the end of the four-decade period. The pace of population growth is decelerating however. In 1980-2000, growth averaged 1.61% per year on average but in 2000-2020 the rate will fall to around 1.11% per year.

The working-age population (those between 15 and 64 years) has been growing at an even faster pace but the rate of deceleration is also more rapid. During 1980-2000, the pool of potential workers was increasing at 1.97% per year but in the next two decades the rate will fall to 1.33%. By 2020, the global economy will have a potential labour pool of 5 billion – nearly double the number in 1980.

Chart 1.1 Population Age Shift 2000 and 2020, Each Column Represents a Single Age Group

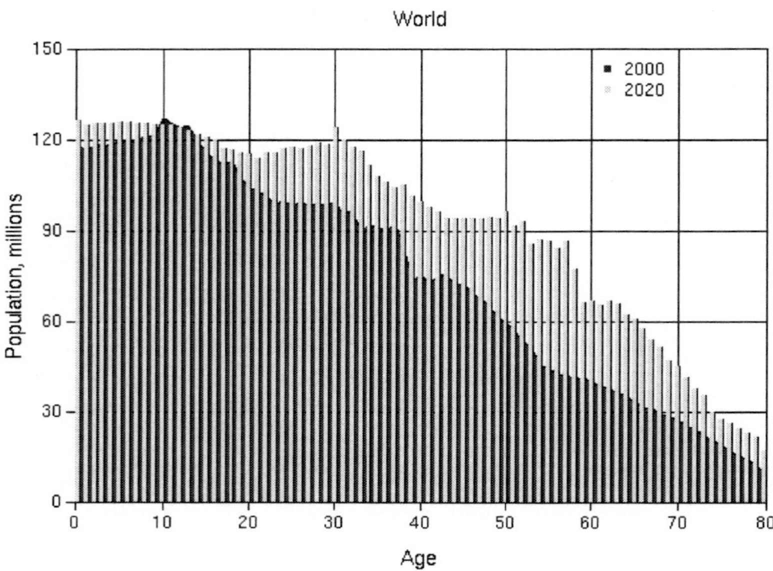

Source: Euromonitor International from National Statistics

Chart 1.1 documents changes in the age structure of the world's population. The number of those between 10 and 13 years will fall between 2000 and 2020 as denoted by the area of bright red. For all other age groups, the population will increase over the two-decade period. Some of the largest proportionate gains will be among those between 50 and 60 years.

— The youth dependency ratio (the number of people 0-14 years relative to the number aged 15-64) will fall from 0.472 in 2000 to 0.374 in 2020;

— The elderly dependency ratio (the number of people over 65 years relative to the number aged 15-64) will rise from 0.110 in 2000 to 0.145 in 2020;

— Between 1980 and 2020, the number of those over 50 years of age will jump from 16.1% to 25.1%.

Chart 1.2 Population Pyramid

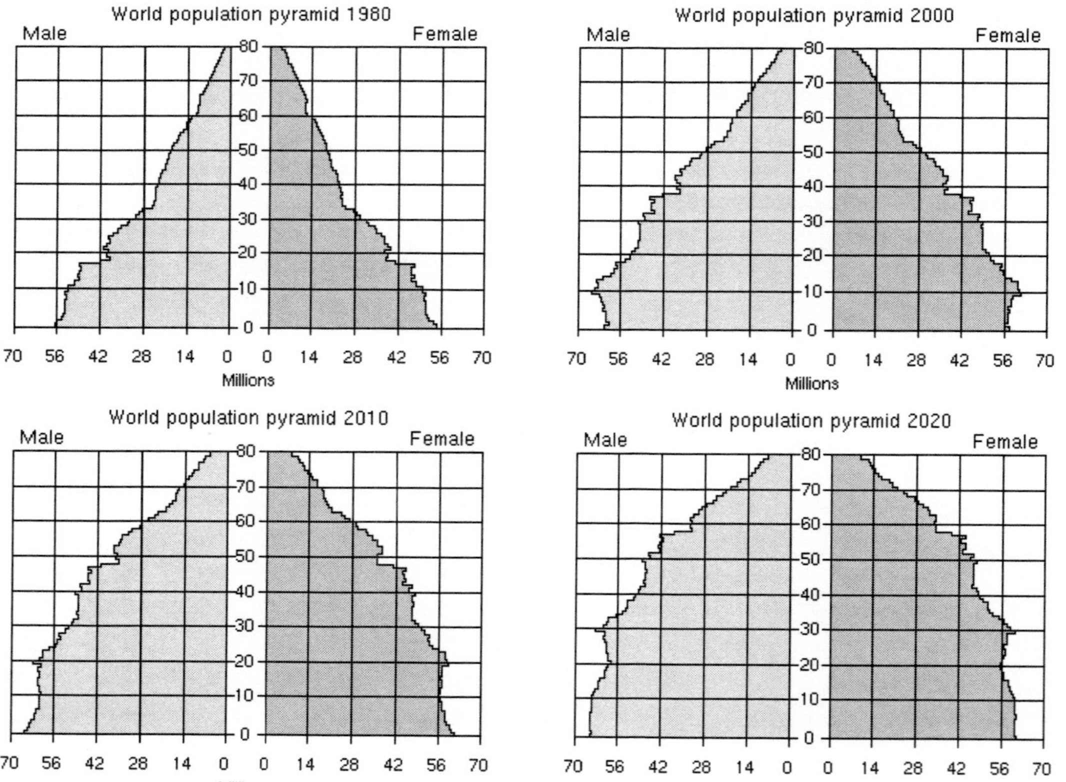

Source: Euromonitor International from National Statistics

Demographic changes by sex are reported in Chart 1.2. The graph for 1980 is very similar to the typical population pyramid but the shape changes over time as society ages. In 2020, the number of males will exceed that of females for all groups less than 52 years of age. Among those over 52 years, the relationship is reversed and the gap widens with age. The number of women over 60 years of age in 2020 will total 567.1 million compared with 485.7 million men.

The gender gap among the elderly is partly due to the longer life expectancy of females. In most parts of the world the incidence of smoking is also higher among males than females. In addition, males suffer more health problems from job-related illnesses than females and generally lead less healthy lifestyles.

The figures in Table 1 provide more details on the demographic structure. The number of children between 0 and 9 years was at a low in 1980 and has been steadily rising over time. The pace of growth will slow in the future but a record high is still expected in 2020. The population of those between 10 and 19 years follows a similar trend.

Among those 20 years and older, each age group has recorded steady increases since 1980 and the upward trend will continue through 2020 when record highs are expected. However, the largest gains will occur in those age groups over 50 years. For example, the population of those in their forties and fifties will more than double between 1980 and 2020 while that of those over 60 years will increase almost threefold.

Table 1.1 **Key Population Trends 1980-2020**

'000

	1980	1985	1990	1995	2000	2005	2010	2015	2020	CAGR %	Period Growth
Total	4,418,995	4,818,701	5,252,486	5,678,752	6,083,607	6,469,261	6,856,153	7,231,004	7,588,242	1.36	71.72
Male	2,222,145	2,426,071	2,645,566	2,854,193	3,059,907	3,256,875	3,453,925	3,645,210	3,826,760	1.37	72.21
Female	2,195,329	2,391,860	2,605,906	2,820,880	3,017,639	3,211,099	3,407,240	3,596,980	3,779,010	1.37	72.14
0-4 yrs	538,902	576,224	621,868	605,761	589,952	605,549	620,108	629,174	627,566	0.38	16.45
5-9 yrs	521,990	527,556	566,947	621,422	601,159	590,461	596,395	614,683	627,055	0.46	20.13
10-14 yrs	495,228	519,303	524,536	570,394	621,745	606,832	588,604	596,958	618,310	0.56	24.85
15-19 yrs	445,455	486,668	512,620	512,790	562,122	597,253	591,076	578,260	590,345	0.71	32.53
20-24 yrs	390,791	438,938	483,532	491,094	507,134	536,183	592,657	587,530	577,787	0.98	47.85
25-29 yrs	356,825	385,446	434,538	474,163	493,870	498,527	536,625	594,838	590,059	1.27	65.36
30-34 yrs	288,389	350,515	381,323	432,253	473,057	486,195	492,129	530,702	589,572	1.80	104.44
35-39 yrs	239,341	283,163	345,550	376,470	431,420	467,295	479,144	485,395	524,239	1.98	119.03
40-44 yrs	226,372	233,661	278,070	343,099	370,684	426,814	465,351	476,314	481,711	1.91	112.80
45-49 yrs	202,820	220,367	227,408	274,841	336,577	366,823	421,593	459,445	470,285	2.12	131.87
50-54 yrs	182,470	195,829	211,359	222,552	267,186	333,272	363,446	415,518	453,747	2.30	148.67
55-59 yrs	152,468	173,667	184,043	202,975	211,398	260,717	325,968	351,736	401,434	2.45	163.29
60-64 yrs	116,349	140,968	158,500	172,818	188,763	202,373	246,892	304,998	327,045	2.62	181.09
65-69 yrs	101,631	102,486	123,129	142,989	153,476	173,081	182,030	220,499	270,512	2.48	166.17
70-74 yrs	74,115	83,870	83,173	104,156	119,267	133,717	148,182	155,438	188,953	2.37	154.95
75-79 yrs	47,318	54,875	61,516	63,041	78,886	94,056	103,175	115,260	121,930	2.39	157.68
80+ yrs	36,446	43,802	52,756	63,602	70,158	88,082	106,978	124,596	144,342	3.50	296.04

Source: *Euromonitor International from National Statistics*

Vital statistics

The number of live births rose throughout most of the 1980s and reached a record high in 1988. The indicator went through several cycles in later years though the secular trend was downward. Since 2005, the long-term trend has been reversed with live births showing gradual increases from year to year. The upward trend is expected to continue until around 2014 when the numbers start to edge downward once again. The birth rate reached a new high in 1982 and has been falling since then. The downward trend will continue through to 2020 when a new low is forecast.

Fertility was at a record high in 1980 (4.4 births per female) and has been steadily falling over time. Presently, the indicator is about 3.1 births per female and it will decline further to around 2.7 by 2020. This will still be well above the replacement level of 2.1 births per female.

- Fertility rates in Western Europe and North America have been falling for some time but there is growing evidence that they have stabilised and may even rise slightly in the future. In Asia, Africa and Latin America they are falling rapidly but are still above the replacement level in many countries. Eastern Europe's fertility rates are especially low;
- The slowdown in births and the fall in fertility are offset to some extent by the increasing number of women of childbearing age (15 to 49 years). In 1980, this group totalled almost 1.1 billion but by 2020 their number will increase to nearly 1.9 billion.

Death rates were at an all-time high in 1980 and have gradually fallen over time. This trend will continue in the future with a record low being expected in 2020. The number of deaths was at a record low in 1980 and have steadily risen as total population grows and societies age. A new high is forecast for 2020.

- In industrialised countries, the primary causes of death among the middle aged and elderly are cancer and heart and vascular disorders. In developing countries HIV/AIDS is a more important cause of death as well as local diseases and the same causes that afflict people in richer countries;
- Life expectancies were at a record low in 1980 and will gradually rising through to 2020 when new highs are expected. The life expectancies of both males and females will increase by just over nine year between 1980 and 2020.

Natural changes in population (defined as the number of births less the number of deaths) have consistently been positive and will continue to be in the future. Net additions to population were rising during the 1980s and reached a record high in 1987. They have gradually fallen in later years and a new low is expected in 2020.

Figures for net migration show a net outflow over time. Net outflows reached a modern high in 1984 (nearly 1.5 million) and fluctuated widely in subsequent years. In the future, net outflows will range between 420,000 and 670,000 per year. The largest numbers of immigrants have come from Asia and Africa but the favoured destinations have varied over time. Demographers estimate that about 9% of all immigrants today are from Africa. Most of these people immigrate in search of better jobs and higher standards of living, though many have also fled from political repression or civil and ethnic strife. There is a general agreement that the broad economic consequences of immigration are positive but the social and emotional issues are much disputed.

Table 1.2 **Vital statistics 1980-2020**

As stated

	1980	1985	1990	1995	2000	2005	2010	2015	2020	CAGR %	Period Growth
Birth rates	20.5	20.4	19.6	17.9	16.6	15.7	15.0	14.2	13.3	-1.08	-35.22
Live births ('000)	122,303.1	132,176.7	137,378.4	134,060.1	132,924.8	133,708.4	135,889.2	136,347.2	133,774.1	0.22	9.38
Death rates	7.7	7.4	7.0	6.9	6.7	6.5	6.4	6.4	6.3	-0.48	-17.44
Deaths ('000)	45,743.7	47,718.0	49,314.8	51,883.2	53,308.0	55,299.0	58,425.6	60,898.8	63,767.5	0.83	39.40
Net migration ('000)	-791.2	-1,261.3	-277.7	-774.0	-532.3	-43.2	-668.4	-579.5	-420.9		

Source: *Euromonitor International from National Statistics*

Note: *Birth and death rates refer to the number per '000 population and fertility rates to the number of children born per female. Age at childbirth refers to average age of women in years.*

Growth of Urban Agglomerations

Chart 1.3 Major cities: 1980, 2000 and 2020

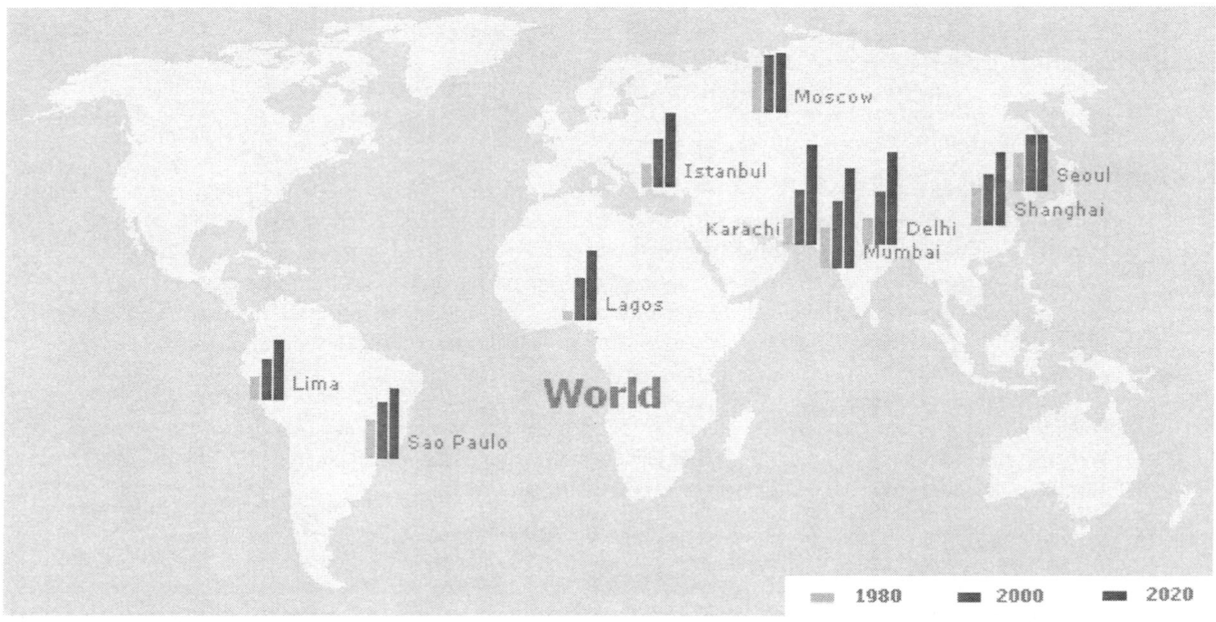

Source: *Euromonitor International from National Statistics*

The world's population density has been steadily rising since 1980 and presently stands at about 52.4 persons per square kilometre. The upward trend will continue in the future and by 2020 the density should be about 58.6 people per square kilometre. Some of the highest population densities are found in parts of Asia, particularly the area from Delhi in India to Dhaka in Bangladesh, the area surrounding Tokyo in Japan and northern China.

The world's population is becoming more urbanised over time. In 1980, 39.5% of the population lived in urban areas and today the figure is 51.5%. The share will slowly rise in the future and by 2020 approximately 55.3% of all people will be living in urban areas. Western Europe is one of the world's most urbanised regions while the African continent is the least urbanised.

Table 1.3 **Population of 10 biggest cities 1980-2020**

'000

	1980	1985	1990	1995	2000	2005	2010	2015	2020	CAGR %	Period Growth
Mumbai	7,396.4	8,527.1	9,710.5	10,839.0	11,854.3	12,915.2	14,199.7	15,699.2	17,551.0	2.18	137.29
Karachi	4,990.7	6,151.4	7,463.9	8,580.8	9,871.5	11,207.5	12,941.8	15,168.7	17,823.4	3.23	257.13
Delhi	4,889.3	5,839.6	6,966.9	8,271.6	9,656.9	11,057.9	12,593.9	14,291.7	16,255.1	3.05	232.46
Shanghai	6,864.9	7,674.2	7,649.7	7,393.0	9,400.0	10,933.4	11,962.3	12,701.6	13,165.5	1.64	91.78
Sao Paulo	7,073.1	8,336.7	9,417.5	10,017.8	10,009.2	10,928.0	11,429.9	11,964.2	12,438.0	1.42	75.85
Istanbul	4,239.6	5,476.0	6,629.4	7,664.6	8,803.5	9,992.4	11,251.6	12,388.1	13,412.9	2.92	216.37
Moscow	8,232.7	8,647.0	9,132.1	9,689.4	10,174.8	10,420.2	10,494.8	10,530.3	10,548.7	0.62	28.13
Lagos	2,033.1	3,322.2	4,874.1	6,306.4	7,547.3	8,749.0	9,925.5	11,129.0	12,365.2	4.62	508.19
Seoul	7,046.2	8,461.9	9,778.8	10,231.2	9,895.2	9,820.2	9,878.1	9,958.3	10,025.6	0.89	42.28
Lima	4,440.8	5,135.0	5,957.0	6,647.7	7,379.9	8,161.5	8,947.6	9,733.3	10,505.7	2.18	136.57
TOTAL	57,207.0	67,571.2	77,579.9	85,641.5	94,592.5	104,185.4	113,625.2	123,564.5	134,091.0	2.15	134.40
% of total population	1.3	1.4	1.5	1.5	1.6	1.6	1.7	1.7	1.8	0.78	36.50

Source: *Euromonitor International from National Statistics*

MARKETING SEGMENTS

Children & teenagers

The number of young children and teenagers has been steadily rising since 1980 and that will continue through to 2020 when a new high is reached. During the forty-year period, the population of this generation will be growing at an average rate of 0.52% per year. In 1980, children and teenagers made up 45.3% of total population and in 2020 their share will be 32.5%.

- In Asia, Africa and Latin America, the issue of child labour is frequently a contentious one. Many children between 8 and 16 years are already at work – usually in the informal sector. Even in industrialised countries, a large proportion of young people do not complete secondary education. As a result, they face considerable penalties in the labour market;
- In Asia and Africa, the percentage of young children not attending schools is higher than in other parts of the world;
- In developing countries, many women marry before the age of 20 and early childbearing is still common;
- As more single-child families emerge, the tendency to invest heavily in education increases.

Families in rich countries spend lavishly on their young children and demand high-quality products. Their teenagers have only modest amounts of earned income but are generously supported by their parents. Many teenagers in developing countries leave school before completing their education. They are often poorly trained and have bleak earning prospects. Typically, they are employed in agriculture or the informal sector or they attempt to immigrate.

Table 1.4 **Children & teenagers 1980-2020**

000

	1980	1985	1990	1995	2000	2005	2010	2015	2020	CAGR %	Period Growth
Babies/infants (0-2)	328,311	350,923	378,866	362,055	353,451	367,725	376,332	379,999	376,440	0.34	14.66
Female	160,470	170,672	184,019	174,962	171,039	177,444	181,532	183,515	182,051	0.32	13.45
Male	167,841	180,251	194,847	187,093	182,413	190,281	194,800	196,484	194,389	0.37	15.82
Kids (aged 3-8)	628,031	649,570	701,289	745,106	715,829	709,746	721,920	743,092	753,377	0.46	19.96
Female	306,732	316,415	341,532	361,046	346,044	342,168	348,904	358,746	364,162	0.43	18.72
Male	321,299	333,154	359,757	384,060	369,785	367,579	373,016	384,346	389,215	0.48	21.14
Tweenagers (9-12)	407,767	415,421	427,188	465,296	498,670	479,957	470,577	480,610	498,564	0.50	22.27
Female	198,986	202,305	208,374	226,494	241,803	231,517	226,952	232,703	240,977	0.48	21.10
Male	208,781	213,115	218,815	238,802	256,867	248,439	243,625	247,907	257,587	0.53	23.38
Teenagers (13-19)	637,466	693,838	718,621	737,902	807,019	842,658	827,352	815,374	834,895	0.68	30.97
Female	312,145	339,050	351,008	360,215	393,393	408,562	399,310	393,825	404,200	0.65	29.49
Male	325,321	354,788	367,613	377,687	413,625	434,095	428,043	421,549	430,695	0.70	32.39

Source: *Euromonitor International from National Statistics*

Young adults

The population of young adults was at a modern-day low in 1980 and has continuously risen over time. That trend will persist through to 2020 when a record high is reached. During these four decades, the population of this generation will nearly double. In 1980, young adults made up 28.9% of total population and in 2020 they will represent about 30.1%.

- In developing countries, unemployment among young adults is especially high. This is due to limited education and the growing demand for greater skills among new job entrants. Many young adults are forced to work in the informal sector for extended periods of time;
- Rapid population growth in many developing countries (for example Brazil, India, Malaysia, Pakistan and the Philippines) means that a large proportion of their populations will soon be under the age of 25. Such trends also put a premium on education and training in order to develop the labour quality needed to compete in international markets. The success of these programmes is questionable in several of the fastest-growing countries;
- There are sharp differences in family size between urban and rural areas. A growing proportion of women in urban areas have only one or two children. In rural areas, the figure is much higher. Thus, rural-to-urban migration seems to be a powerful force in reducing fertility rates;

In developed countries, young adults are the most active borrowers. They have a high propensity to consume and are avid consumers. A similar pattern is emerging among young middle-income adults in many parts of the developing world.

Table 1.5 **Young adults 1980-2020**

'000

	1980	1985	1990	1995	2000	2005	2010	2015	2020	CAGR %	Period Growth
Population aged 20-29	747,616	824,384	918,065	965,252	1,000,999	1,034,706	1,129,281	1,182,369	1,167,846	1.12	56.21
Female	365,950	404,212	450,285	476,963	493,182	510,718	555,699	579,004	569,165	1.11	55.53
Male	381,666	420,172	467,780	488,289	507,817	523,988	573,582	603,365	598,681	1.13	56.86
Population aged 30-39	527,730	633,678	726,868	808,717	904,471	953,484	971,272	1,016,097	1,113,812	1.88	111.06
Female	258,586	311,102	356,568	399,294	447,055	472,387	480,205	500,874	547,250	1.89	111.63
Male	269,144	322,576	370,300	409,423	457,416	481,096	491,067	515,223	566,562	1.88	110.51

Source: *Euromonitor International from National Statistics*

Middle-aged adults

The number of middle agers was at an all-time low in 1980 and has steadily risen over time. The upward trend will continue through to 2020 when a new high is recorded. The average rate of growth between 1980 and 2020 will be about 2.24% per year. In 1980, middle agers represented 19.9% of total population and in 2020 they will account for 28.1%.

- The extent of unemployment and underemployment among the older members of this generation is much higher than among the younger members;
- In industrialised countries, an increasing number of middle agers live in single-person households. The increase is occurring among people between the ages of 45 and 64 – a trend driven by changes in the living habits of baby boomers;

— In developing countries, a growing number of middle-aged women spend much of their working time in unpaid employment. They are most frequently employed in agriculture on the informal market.

Middle agers in industrialised countries have accumulated considerable wealth and are relatively high-income earners. With high levels of discretionary income and ample free time, middle agers are ready consumers of leisure products, luxury goods and household products. In developing countries, the buying habits of middle and upper-income middle agers have come to resemble Western lifestyles but those with sufficient amounts of disposable income are a distinct minority.

Table 1.6 Middle-aged adults 1980-2020

'000

	1980	1985	1990	1995	2000	2005	2010	2015	2020	CAGR %	Period Growth
Population aged 40-64	880,479	964,492	1,059,372	1,216,277	1,374,597	1,589,986	1,823,251	2,008,011	2,134,222	2.24	142.39
Female	442,252	483,858	529,634	609,345	687,681	796,114	915,149	1,008,410	1,072,083	2.24	142.41
Male	438,227	480,634	529,738	606,932	686,916	793,872	908,102	999,601	1,062,140	2.24	142.37

Source: *Euromonitor International from National Statistics*

Older population

The population of those over 65 years has been persistently rising since 1980 and that trend will continue through to 2020 when a modern high is reached. During this period, the total number of elderly will increase almost threefold. This generation accounted for 5.9% of total population in 1980 and their share will be 9.6% in 2020.

— In developing countries, a significant number of all households consist of extended families. Older household members can also be relied upon for child care through informal intra-household arrangements;

— Pension systems in the poorer parts of the developing world are not viable and a large majority of the elderly depend on their families for support;

— In developing countries, the elderly who are able to work are often forced to seek employment in agricultural activities or in the informal sector;

— In many industrialised countries, spending on old age and survivors' benefits is rising by as much as 2% per year;

— In industrialised countries, the elderly will make up around 40% of those living alone in 2010. More than three-quarters of the elderly who live alone are women.

The elderly in industrialised countries are frequent consumers of health products and are very health conscious about their diets. They enjoy travel and will usually have a number of hobbies. Manufacturers are adopting their products and marketing strategies to cater to this generation. In many parts of the developing world, only a minority of the elderly have sufficient wealth or pensions to provide themselves with financial support.

Table 1.7 Older population 1980-2020

'000

	1980	1985	1990	1995	2000	2005	2010	2015	2020	CAGR %	Period Growth
Older generation (65+)	259,510	285,033	320,572	373,787	421,784	488,933	540,365	615,792	725,737	2.60	179.66
Female	149,925	163,948	184,169	212,219	237,076	271,795	299,080	339,477	398,681	2.48	165.92
Male	109,586	121,086	136,402	161,567	184,708	217,138	241,286	276,317	327,058	2.77	198.45

Source: *Euromonitor International from National Statistics*

ASIA PACIFIC

KEY POPULATION TRENDS

Total population

Chart 2.2 – known as a "heat chart", found in section two *"Age structure of the population at a glance"* – depicts changes in the age structure in the Asia-Pacific region over time. Each dot represents the number of people in a specific age group in a given year. Accordingly, a dark red dot represents the largest concentration of people, by age, in a particular year while deep blue dots show the lowest concentrations. A single dark red dot is the equivalent of 75.8 million people while each deep blue dot represents slightly more than 2.6 million people and other colour shadings correspond to intermediate population totals (each by age group).

The most notable feature is the wide band of dark red which begins in the upper left-hand portion of the chart and gradually extends downward from left to right. This area depicts a population explosion which began in the early 1980s and continued until 2005. The bulge created by this boom is somewhat dissipated over time owing to immigration. Another modest jump in population growth is expected during the coming decade as represented by the reappearance of a red area in the upper right-hand corner.

The lower left-hand corner of the chart contains a large area of deep blue which indicates that in the 1980s the number of elderly people was rather sparse. Over time, the colouring changes from blue to green in some places as the population of those over 60 years begins to rise. Over time, the area of dark blue is gradually reduced as the number of those between 60 and 70 years steadily increases.

The total population of the Asia-Pacific region has been steadily increasing over time. In 2020, the region will be home to almost 4.2 billion people, an increase of 1.7 billion over 40 years. The average rate of growth in 1980-2000 was 1.67% per year and during 2000-2020 the rate will fall to 0.99% per year.

The potential workforce (those between 15 and 64 years) will more increasing at an even faster rate during this period, soaring from 1.4 billion in 1980 to nearly 2.9 billion by 2020. The labour pool was growing at an average rate of 2.17% per year in 1980-2000 and the expected rate is 1.29% per year in 2000-2020.

A widespread and accelerating phenomenon is the ageing of Asian society. Several countries – notably China, Japan and Vietnam – will see significant increases in their elderly populations.

Chart 1.4 Population Age Shift 2000 and 2020, Each Column Represents a Single Age Group

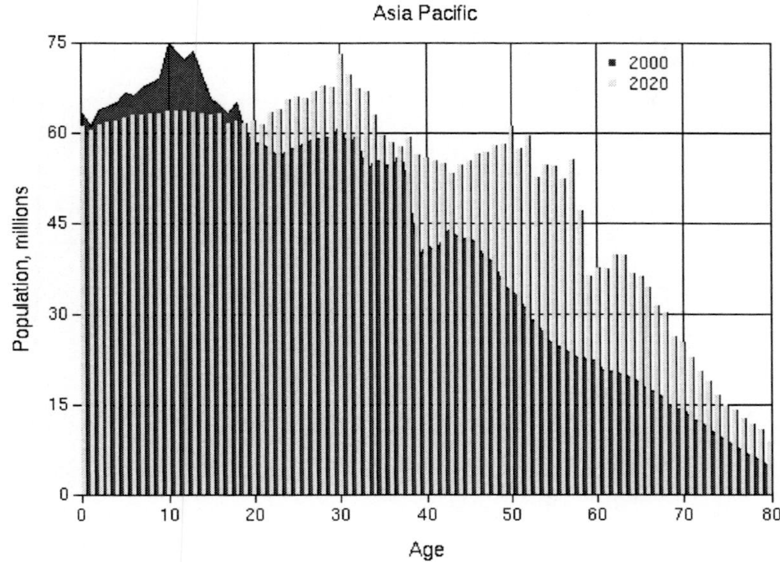

Source: Euromonitor International from National Statistics

Chart 1.4 documents changes in the region's age structure between 2000 and 2020. The area of bright red in the upper left-hand corner of the chart indicates those age groups where the population will decline between 2000 and 2020. The number of those between zero and 18 years of age will fall from 1.28 billion in 2000 to 1.18 billion by 2020. Meanwhile, some of the largest increases during this twenty-year period will occur among those between 55 and 65 years. The population of this age group will jump from 219 million in 2000 to almost 436 million in 2020.

The changing age structure will alter several key demographic indicators:

— The youth dependency ratio (the number of people 0-14 years relative to the number aged 15-64) will fall from 0.460 in 2000 to 0.324 in 2020;

— The elderly dependency ratio (the number of people over 65 years relative to the number aged 15-64) will rise from 0.093 in 2000 to 0.138 in 2020;

— The large increases in elderly population in countries such as China, Singapore and Vietnam will have important implications for spending on healthcare and pose problems for the countries' rudimentary pension systems.

Chart 1.5 Population Pyramid

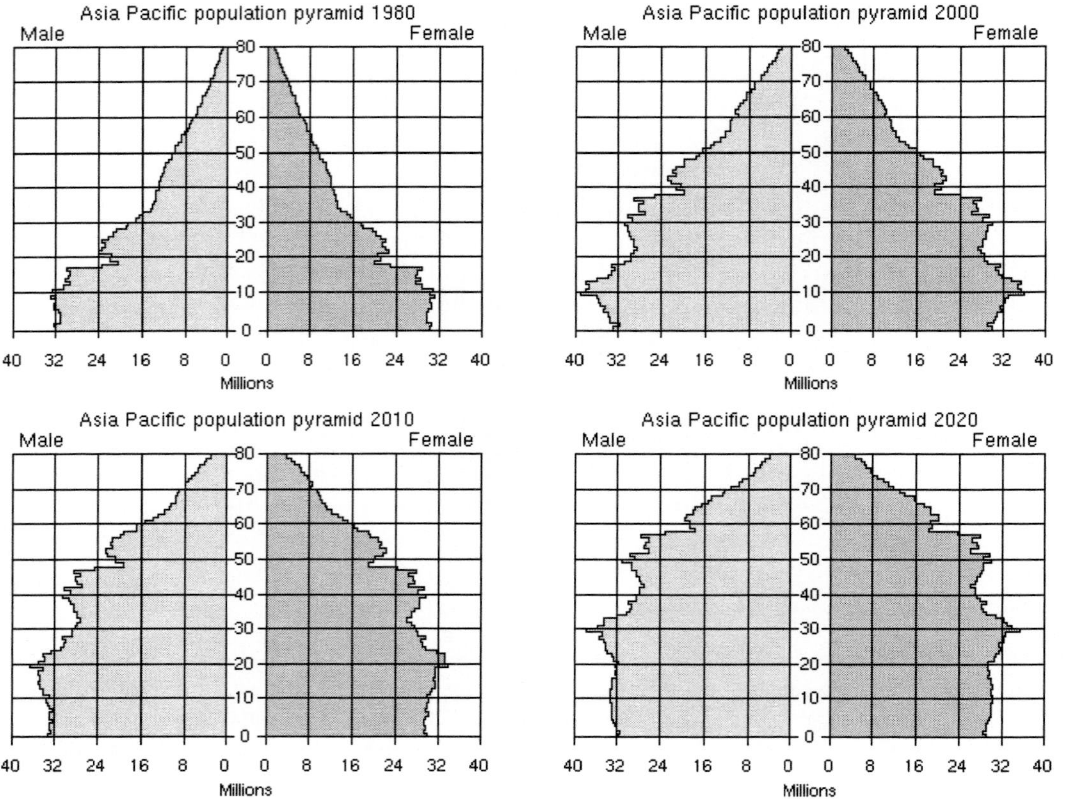

Source: Euromonitor International from National Statistics

Chart 1.5 consists of four population pyramids for selected years. The figure for 1980 bears a close resemblance to a typical pyramid although small population bulges have already emerged between the ages of zero and 30 years. These bulges become more pronounced over time and by 2020 the number of young adults and middle-aged people will exceed the population of children and teenagers.

The male population outnumbers that of females for all ages up to 53 years. Thereafter, the reverse is true. In 2020, the number of females 65 and over will be 211 million while males will total about 185 million. The gender gap is partly due to the longer life expectancy of females. In most Asian countries, the incidence of smoking is much higher for men than women. Males also suffer many more health problems from job-related illnesses and are less likely to seek medical attention when needed.

The figures in Table 1 provide more details on the demographic structure. The number of children between 0 and 9 years reached a high in 1995 and then began a steady decline. The downward trend will continue through to 2020 when a modern-day low is expected. The population of those between 10 and 19 years was at a record low in 1980 and steadily rose over time. The number reached a record high in 2004. Since then, the number of this generation has been dropping and that trend will persist through 2020.

— Fertility rates have been falling but remain well above the replacement level. The downward trend will continue through 2020 but even then fertility will still slightly exceed replacement;

— Japan and Singapore have some of the lowest fertility rates in the region but fertility in most other countries is well above the replacement level;

— Although the number of births per female is falling gradually over time, other demographic changes have the opposite effect. For example, the number of women of childbearing age (15 to 49 years) will increase from 588 million in 1980 to 1.04 billion in 2020.

The population of 20 to 29 year olds was at a low in 1980 and steadily rose over time, reaching a modern high in 2016. Afterwards, the numbers began to edge downward and that trend will continue through 2020. Among those in their thirties, the population has been constantly increasing since 1980. The upward trend will continue through to 2020 when a record high is expected. During this forty-year period the population of this generation will more than double. The number of Asians in older age groups will see an almost constant increase between 1980 and 2020.

— The life expectancy of both sexes has shown slow but steady increases over time. The fact that more people are now living above subsistence level and that many have been able to exchange a harsh life in an agricultural environment for work in services and manufacturing indirectly contributes to these gains;

— As the population in the region ages, the significance of intergenerational transfers (including material support, emotional and practical support and the sharing of skills) will become more important.

Table 1.8 **Key Population Trends 1980-2020**

'000

	1980	1985	1990	1995	2000	2005	2010	2015	2020	CAGR %	Growth Period
Total	2,476,015	2,710,357	2,968,014	3,217,105	3,446,549	3,653,006	3,847,965	4,030,171	4,194,897	1.33	69.42
Male	1,268,157	1,388,897	1,519,850	1,641,282	1,761,082	1,865,882	1,963,392	2,054,611	2,136,173	1.31	68.45
Female	1,207,858	1,321,460	1,448,164	1,575,823	1,685,466	1,787,124	1,884,573	1,975,560	2,058,724	1.34	70.44
0-4 yrs	308,537	325,504	357,259	336,898	317,069	315,189	310,291	309,229	303,142	-0.04	-1.75
5-9 yrs	314,005	303,108	322,106	363,682	338,284	323,387	311,837	310,435	312,043	-0.02	-0.62
10-14 yrs	301,537	312,310	301,114	326,421	364,882	345,677	322,930	313,691	314,992	0.11	4.46
15-19 yrs	260,668	293,926	306,676	290,446	319,236	342,298	331,678	314,102	308,409	0.42	18.31
20-24 yrs	222,078	256,157	292,897	288,170	287,016	295,127	339,251	329,805	315,116	0.88	41.89
25-29 yrs	207,128	218,744	253,972	286,187	292,994	279,943	296,965	343,479	334,201	1.20	61.35
30-34 yrs	160,135	202,242	216,119	252,970	287,320	287,188	275,643	293,800	340,779	1.91	112.81
35-39 yrs	132,179	156,936	199,352	213,225	255,131	284,589	283,454	272,703	291,115	1.99	120.24
40-44 yrs	122,711	128,652	153,977	199,532	210,843	254,306	286,579	284,973	273,395	2.02	122.80
45-49 yrs	110,525	119,521	125,180	153,998	196,746	211,341	253,597	285,372	283,671	2.38	156.66
50-54 yrs	93,702	106,979	114,175	123,607	150,168	198,205	213,014	253,011	284,996	2.82	204.15
55-59 yrs	76,158	89,515	99,697	110,424	117,070	149,003	196,790	207,743	245,407	2.97	222.24
60-64 yrs	59,336	70,406	80,421	94,239	102,278	114,106	141,847	183,351	190,941	2.96	221.80
65-69 yrs	45,413	51,860	59,949	72,842	82,528	94,780	101,593	124,172	158,422	3.17	248.84
70-74 yrs	31,067	36,955	40,787	50,502	59,462	72,670	80,213	85,134	103,792	3.06	234.09
75-79 yrs	18,406	22,424	25,420	30,077	36,524	46,646	54,125	59,800	63,935	3.16	247.37
80+ yrs	12,327	14,998	18,775	23,737	28,837	38,373	47,968	59,166	70,320	4.45	470.45

Source: *Euromonitor International from National Statistics*

Vital Statistics

The number of births was rising throughout most of the 1980s and reached a record high in 1987. The indicator declined until the middle of the present decade and will go through several cyclical fluctuations in the future. Birth rates were at a modern high in 1982 and steadily fell in later years. The downward trend will continue through 2020 when a new low is expected. Fertility was at a modern high in 1980 (4.2 births per female) and steadily declined over time. The indicator will reach a new low in 2020 but even then it will be slightly more than replacement level. Trends in individual countries are markedly different however. Japan and Singapore have extremely low fertility rates. They are much higher in other countries such as China and Vietnam but even there they are dropping rapidly.

— Dramatic social changes are an important reason for the drop in Asia's fertility rates and the declining number of births. Modern families have fewer children, adopt a more egalitarian attitude to both male and female children and invest in the education and health of their children. By contrast, the traditional families favour closer ties between the head of the household and his kin group than with that of his spouse, the birth of sons over daughters, the obedience of women to men and of the young to the aged;

— Strong support for family planning in many Asian countries is another important reason for the declining birth rate.

The number of deaths was at an all-time low in 1980 and has been gradually rising over time. This same trend will continue in the future with a record high expected by 2020. The death rate in the Asia-Pacific region was at a modern-day high in 1980. It has been steadily declining over time and a new low was reported in 2004. Since then, the indicator has been slowly rising as the population of elderly people increases.

Natural changes in population (that is, the number of births less the number of deaths) have consistently been positive for the Asia-Pacific region. They reached an all-time high in 1987 and have been trending downward over time. That same trend will be continued in the future with a record low being expected in 2020.

With regard to net migration, the Asia-Pacific region has long been a net supplier of labour to other parts of the world. Net outflows were at a record low in 1980 – approximately 1.1 million and steadily rose (although with some fluctuations) over the next two decades. The labour exodus reached a record in 1998 (a net outflow of 2 million). This peak roughly coincided with the Asian financial crisis, a downturn which forced many people to leave their home countries in search of economic security.

A "culture of migration" has existed in some countries since the early 1970s. In some countries such as the Philippines this attitude has been encouraged by national policy. For example, Manila facilitates migration, regulates the operations of the recruitment agencies, and looks out for the rights of its migrant workers. Presently, an estimated nine million Filipinos (almost 10% of the country's national population) are working or living abroad in more than 180 countries and territories.

In other parts of the region, war or civil unrest (along with the search for economic security) has spurred migration. Millions of Vietnamese have left their homes in the past for such reasons. Favoured countries of destination are the USA, Australia, Cambodia, Canada, France, Germany, Russia and the UK. Some of these immigrants seek political asylum but many more are illegal residents.

Table 1.9 **Vital Statistics 1980-2020**

As stated

	1980	1985	1990	1995	2000	2005	2010	2015	2020	CAGR %	Growth Period
Birth rates	27.7	27.8	26.5	23.4	20.7	18.9	17.7	16.7	15.4	-1.47	-44.64
Live births ('000)	68,691.2	75,334.2	78,607.8	75,263.9	71,272.1	68,886.6	68,110.6	67,257.7	64,424.8	-0.16	-6.21
Death rates	9.7	9.2	8.6	8.1	7.7	7.5	7.7	7.7	7.9	-0.51	-18.52
Deaths ('000)	23,897.8	24,810.5	25,580.0	26,155.4	26,561.2	27,336.7	29,447.8	31,068.3	32,990.7	0.81	38.05
Net migration ('000)	-1,088.6	-1,416.5	-1,313.5	-1,602.6	-1,373.2	-1,429.1	-1,315.4	-1,251.0	-1,324.6		

Source: *Euromonitor International from National Statistics*
Note: *Birth and death rates refer to the number per '000 population and fertility rates to the number of children born per female. Age at childbirth refers to average age of women in years.*

Growth of Urban Agglomerations

Chart 1.6 Major Cities: 1980, 2000 and 2020

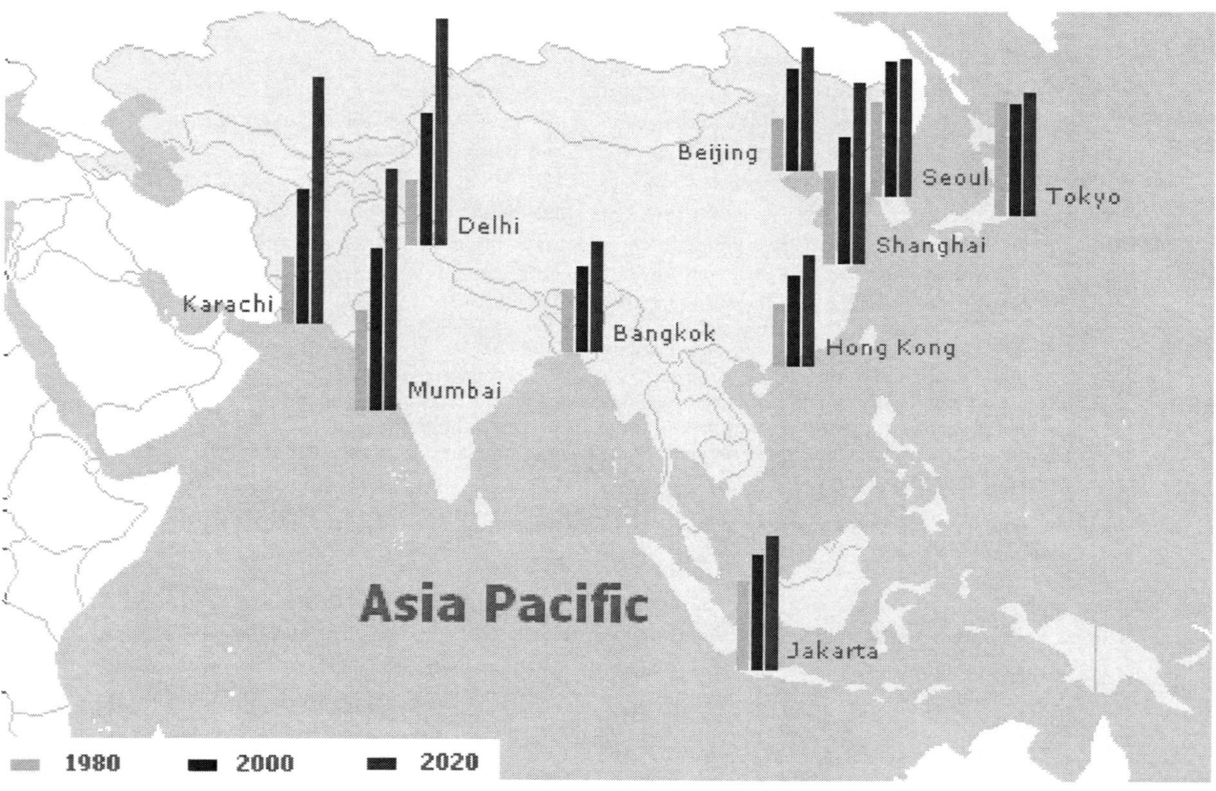

Source: *Euromonitor International from National Statistics*

The population density of the Asia-Pacific region has been steadily rising since 1980. Presently, it stands at 151.4 people per square kilometre, up from 102.0 in 1980. The indicator will continue rising in the future and by 2020 the density should be 166.7 people per square kilometre. The most densely populated areas include the area from Delhi, India to Dhaka in Bangladesh, the area surrounding Tokyo, Japan and northern China.

Unlike most other parts of the world, the Asia-Pacific region is still not highly urbanised. In 1980, just 25.3% of the population lived in urban areas and today the figure is 41.1%. The share will slowly rise in the future and by 2020 approximately 46.3% of all Asians will be living in urban areas. China has seen some of the largest movements of people from rural to urban areas. In part, this migration is in response to government policy which has been focused on the need to secure an adequate and cheap supply of labour for new export-oriented industries. The income gap between urban and rural residents is significant and widening in some Asian countries such as China, and Vietnam.

Several of the region's major cities will see rapid growth over the next couple of decades – particularly Mumbai, Karachi, Delhi, Beijing and Lahore. Mumbai is the economic and commercial of India, accounting for around a quarter of GDP. It is also considered the financial capital of the country. Karachi is the cultural and economic hub of Pakistan and with its two major ports is a centre for transportation. The steady expansion is due both to the high birth rate and high rates of rural-to-urban migration. An estimated 45,000 migrant workers come to the city each month from different parts of Pakistan. More than 1 million Afghan refugees have also taken up permanent residence in and around Karachi. The other major cities in the region have a political or economic prominence that puts them in the world rankings of global agglomerations. Like Mumbai and Karachi, they act as magnets for migrants from rural areas.

Table 1.10 **Population of 10 Biggest Cities 1980-2020**

'000

	1980	1985	1990	1995	2000	2005	2010	2015	2020	CAGR %	Growth Period
Mumbai	7,396.4	8,527.1	9,710.5	10,839.0	11,854.3	12,915.2	14,199.7	15,699.2	17,551.0	2.18	137.29
Karachi	4,990.7	6,151.4	7,463.9	8,580.8	9,871.5	11,207.5	12,941.8	15,168.7	17,823.4	3.23	257.13
Delhi	4,889.3	5,839.6	6,966.9	8,271.6	9,656.9	11,057.9	12,593.9	14,291.7	16,255.1	3.05	232.46
Shanghai	6,864.9	7,674.2	7,649.7	7,393.0	9,400.0	10,933.4	11,962.3	12,701.6	13,165.5	1.64	91.78
Seoul	7,046.2	8,461.9	9,778.8	10,231.2	9,895.2	9,820.2	9,878.1	9,958.3	10,025.6	0.89	42.28
Jakarta	6,569.0	7,433.6	8,222.5	8,662.1	8,389.4	8,540.1	8,833.8	9,201.5	9,626.5	0.96	46.54
Tokyo	8,351.9	8,354.6	8,163.6	7,967.6	8,134.7	8,489.7	8,750.4	8,912.6	9,015.0	0.19	7.94
Beijing	3,975.8	4,831.2	5,715.4	6,525.8	7,509.0	7,935.7	8,339.9	8,684.1	8,950.0	2.05	125.11
Hong Kong	4,632.7	5,077.0	5,603.2	6,156.1	6,665.0	7,040.3	7,448.1	7,826.6	8,164.0	1.43	76.22
Lahore	2,850.9	3,412.2	4,094.0	4,710.3	5,446.4	6,203.4	7,176.9	8,421.1	9,901.3	3.16	247.30
TOTAL	57,567.9	65,763.0	73,368.5	79,337.5	86,822.4	94,143.4	102,124.9	110,865.4	120,477.4	1.86	109.28
% of total population	2.3	2.4	2.5	2.5	2.5	2.6	2.7	2.8	2.9	0.53	23.53

Source: *Euromonitor International from National Statistics*

MARKETING SEGMENTS

Children & Teenagers

The number of children and teenagers in the Asia-Pacific region was at an all-time low in 1980 and steadily rose until 2000 when a record high was reported. The size of this generation has gradually declined since then and that trend will continue through 2020. In 1980, children and teenagers made up 47.9% of the region's total population and in 2020 their share will be 29.5%.

- The percentage of young children not attending schools in the Asia-Pacific region is higher than in other parts of the world;
- The issue of child labour is frequently a contentious one. Many children under the age of 16 are employed. This is particularly the case in the region's larger countries and those experiencing the fastest rates of rural-to-urban migration;
- There are wide variations in the quality of education from one country to another;
- The practice of sex-selective abortion – even in the case of first birth – is still common in many parts of Asia.

With rising disposable income and the rapid development of a middle class, Asian families are increasingly prepared to invest heavily in their children's education, educational toys, nutrition and books etc. The growing number of single-child families re-enforces this trend.

Table 1.11 **Children & Teenagers 1980-2020**
'000

	1980	1985	1990	1995	2000	2005	2010	2015	2020	CAGR %	Growth Period
Babies/infants (0-2)	186,613	197,088	217,622	199,432	187,751	189,497	187,094	186,050	180,640	-0.08	-3.20
Female	90,791	95,042	104,771	95,053	89,602	89,915	88,580	88,232	85,845	-0.14	-5.45
Male	95,822	102,046	112,851	104,379	98,149	99,582	98,514	97,818	94,795	-0.03	-1.07
Kids (aged 3-8)	371,980	371,411	400,565	431,616	398,184	383,066	372,033	371,985	371,921	0.00	-0.02
Female	180,778	179,557	193,567	206,882	189,840	181,511	176,913	176,315	176,591	-0.06	-2.32
Male	191,202	191,854	206,999	224,734	208,344	201,556	195,120	195,671	195,330	0.05	2.16
Tweenagers (9-12)	249,346	246,640	243,111	266,256	290,731	270,679	254,501	248,922	252,029	0.03	1.08
Female	121,029	119,284	117,791	128,568	139,512	128,576	120,668	118,785	119,746	-0.03	-1.06
Male	128,317	127,356	125,320	137,689	151,219	142,102	133,834	130,137	132,283	0.08	3.09
Teenagers (13-19)	376,810	419,708	425,857	420,141	462,804	483,308	463,107	440,500	433,996	0.35	15.18
Female	183,546	203,990	206,785	203,606	223,791	231,493	219,889	209,268	206,927	0.30	12.74
Male	193,263	215,719	219,071	216,536	239,013	251,815	243,219	231,232	227,069	0.40	17.49

Source: *Euromonitor International from National Statistics*

Young Adults

The population of young adults has been constantly rising since 1980 and that trend will persist through 2020. In 1980, this generation made up 29.1% of total population and in 2020 it will account for 30.5%.

— Rapid population growth in countries such as India, Malaysia, Pakistan and the Philippines means that more than half their populations will soon be under the age of 25. This prospect offers a "demographic dividend" not available to countries such as Japan or China. However, such trends also put a premium on education and training in order to develop the labour quality needed to compete in international markets. The success of these programmes is questionable in several of the fastest-growing countries;

— A large number of the new entrants (including even college graduates) are forced to take low-productivity jobs or even work in the informal sector. The number of jobs being created in most countries is far less than the number of new job entrants;

— Though many countries are in the process of creating schemes for family planning, the unmet need for family planning continues to rise. These unmet needs are highest in rural areas and among low-income families;

— It is common practice in many parts of Asia for young adults to reside in the parental home for extended periods of time;

— The gradual decline in the number of young adult households and a decline in the population of young children will have an adverse impact on domestic demand and competitiveness.

Many of those in their mid-to-late twenties live in single-person households or else reside with their parents. They enjoy travelling abroad, sports and leisure activities. This generation spends proportionally large sums on electronic products, media and mobile devices. Those in their thirties have different tastes, spending their disposable income on restaurants, holidays and similar forms of entertainment. They are also big purchasers of home furnishings and electronic products for the home as they begin to marry and form their own families.

Table 1.12 **Young Adults 1980-2020**
'000

	1980	1985	1990	1995	2000	2005	2010	2015	2020	CAGR %	Growth Period
Population aged 20-29	429,206	474,902	546,869	574,357	580,009	575,070	636,215	673,283	649,317	1.04	51.28
Female	207,847	230,629	266,073	282,860	284,445	283,277	311,881	327,219	312,907	1.03	50.55
Male	221,360	244,273	280,796	291,497	295,564	291,793	324,334	346,064	336,411	1.05	51.97
Population aged 30-39	292,314	359,178	415,471	466,195	542,451	571,777	559,097	566,502	631,894	1.95	116.17
Female	140,862	173,831	200,870	228,008	265,914	282,186	275,689	278,265	308,675	1.98	119.13
Male	151,452	185,347	214,602	238,187	276,537	289,591	283,407	288,238	323,219	1.91	113.41

Source: *Euromonitor International from National Statistics*

Middle-aged Adults

The population of this generation was at an all-time low in 1980 and has been constantly rising as Asian society ages. In 1980, middle agers represented 18.7% of the total and in 2020 they will account for 30.5%.

— A growing proportion of the region's workforce consists of middle-aged workers and the percentage will continue to rise for the foreseeable future. This will present a challenge for many economies since older workers are less flexible and adaptable to change;

— Remittances are an important source of income for both middle agers and the elderly;

— The labour force participation rate among middle-aged women is steadily rising.

The rising cost of education (especially with many offspring being sent abroad to attend English-speaking universities) and the high cost of housing absorbs substantial amounts of income and wealth among middle agers. This generation still represents a healthy market for travel and leisure products. They are active and have a growing interest in their appearance.

Table 1.13 **Middle-aged Adults 1980-2020**

'000

	1980	1985	1990	1995	2000	2005	2010	2015	2020	CAGR %	Growth Period
Population aged 40-64	462,432	515,073	573,450	681,799	777,106	926,962	1,091,828	1,214,450	1,278,410	2.57	176.45
Female	224,767	251,122	279,984	335,670	381,413	456,235	540,284	602,793	636,771	2.64	183.30
Male	237,665	263,951	293,466	346,129	395,693	470,727	551,544	611,657	641,640	2.51	169.98

Source: *Euromonitor International from National Statistic*

Older Population

The number of elderly Asians was at an all-time low in 1980 and will steadily rise through 2020. During this forty-year period, the elderly population will more than triple. In 1980, this generation made up 4.3% of total population and in 2020 they will account for 9.5%.

— Most countries in the region lack the social security infrastructure to handle the added pressure of population ageing – particularly when the process is occurring so rapidly in several Asian countries;

— The fiscal burden associated with healthcare will more than double by 2020 in several Asian countries as their populations age;

— It is customary in Asia for adult children to care for their ageing parents. The practice is becoming more difficult as a result of rural-to-urban migration. A change in social values is also occurring as development continues. Currently, there are few homes where the elderly can receive daily care and attention but their numbers are increasing rapidly.

The spending potential of Asian consumers in most countries is huge owing to the high savings ratio over the past several decades. Consumer strategies are expected to shift as the number of elderly increases and the population of young people declines. The demographic shift will give rise to large increases in spending on healthcare and leisure.

Table 1.14 **Older Population 1980-2020**

'000

	1980	**1985**	**1990**	**1995**	**2000**	**2005**	**2010**	**2015**	**2020**	**CAGR %**	**Growth Period**
Older generation (65+)	107,213	126,237	144,931	177,159	207,351	252,470	283,898	328,273	396,469	3.32	269.80
Female	58,187	67,946	78,254	95,102	110,868	133,842	150,572	174,580	211,153	3.27	262.89
Male	49,026	58,291	66,677	82,056	96,483	118,628	133,326	153,692	185,316	3.38	277.99

Source: *Euromonitor International from National Statistics*

AUSTRALASIA

KEY POPULATION TRENDS

Total population

Chart 2.3 – known as a "heat chart", found in section two *"Age structure of the population at a glance"* – depicts changes in the age structure in Australasia over time. Each dot represents the number of people in a specific age group in a given year. Accordingly, a dark red dot represents the largest concentration of people, by age, in a particular year while deep blue dots show the lowest concentrations. A single dark red dot is the equivalent of slightly more than 1.3 million people while each deep blue dot represents around 45,000 people and other colour shadings correspond to intermediate population totals (each by age group).

— One significant feature of the chart is the large expanse of green along the upper boundary. The colouring in this area reflects the rather modest birth rate and the slow rate of increase in the number of young children. Only after 2015 does the colouring change to orange and red as the number of births begins to rise. A second notable characteristic is the series of narrow bands of red which refer to young adults and middle agers. Each of these bands represents a wave of immigration occurring in the 1990s and the early years of the current decade.

— At the bottom of the chart is an area of dark blue indicating a rather sparse number of older people. Over time, this area of dark blue is reduced in size as the number of elderly people rises. Gradually, the area of dark blue is replaced by lighter shades of blue and green, indicating that the population of those over 60 years will be steadily increasing between now and 2020.

— The total number of people in Australasia has been slowly but steadily rising since 1980 and that trend will continue with a record high of 30.0 million expected by 2020. During this forty-year period the region will add around 12.1 million people – many of them as a result of immigration. The region's average rate of growth in 1980-2000 was 1.27% and in 2000-2020 it will rise to 1.33% per year.

— The potential workforce (those between 15 and 64 years) also rose in 1980-2000 but the pace of growth will decelerate in 2000-2020 as the population ages. By 2020, the number of people over 65 years will exceed the population of those less than ten years by more than one million. The region's ageing workforce and low birth rate could eventually slow economic progress. To counter these trends, officials have proposed a series of programmes to boost labour force participation and raise productivity.

Chart 1.7 Population Age Shift 2000 and 2020, Each Column Represents a Single Age Group

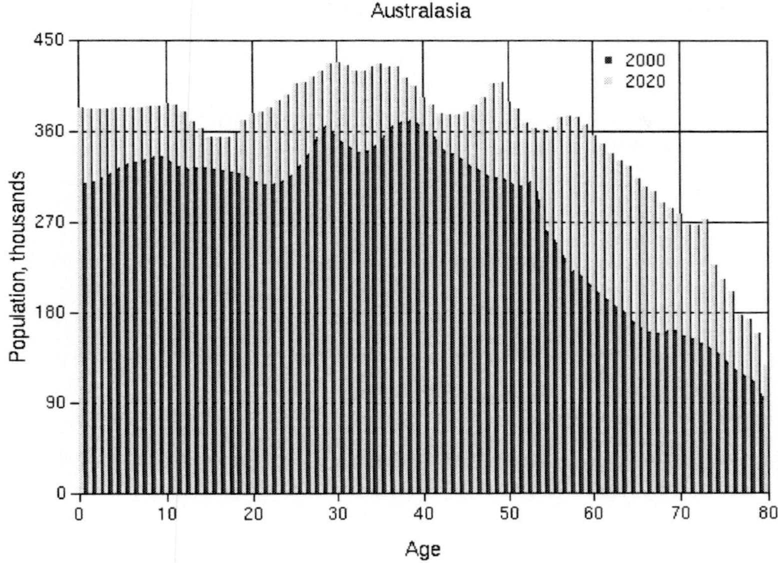

Source: Euromonitor International from National Statistics

Chart 1.7 compares the region's population by age in 2000 and 2020. The population in 2020 will be greater than in 2000 for all age groups. Some of the largest proportionate gains will be among those over 55 years. During this twenty-year period, the number of people over 55 years will jump from 4.9 million to 8.5 million.

— The youth dependency ratio (the number of people 0-14 years relative to the number aged 15-64) will fall slightly from 0.316 in 2000 to 0.296 in 2020;

— The elderly dependency ratio (the number of people over 65 years relative to the number aged 15-64) will rise from 0.185 in 2000 to 0.259 in 2020.

Chart 1.8 Population Pyramid

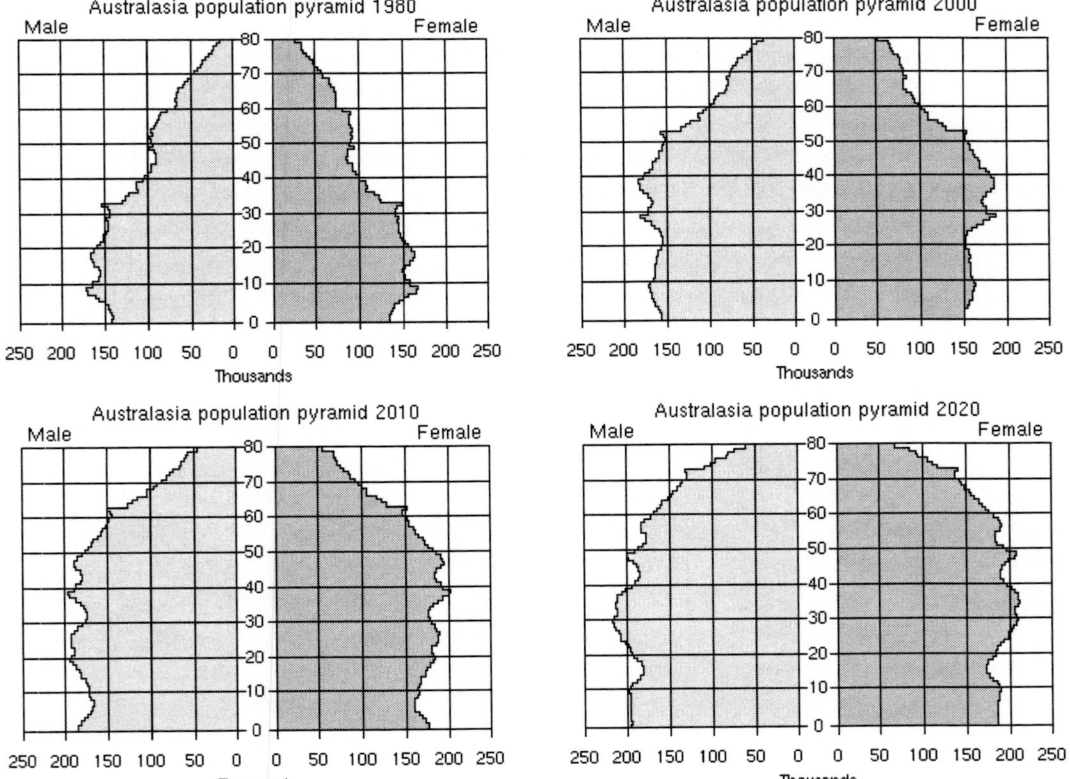

Source: Euromonitor International from National Statistics

Chart 1.8 consists of four population pyramids for selected years. None of these figures resemble the stylised version which would consist of a broad base and narrow, tapering sides to an apex. Population ageing, immigration and relatively low birth rates combine to eventually create a more rectangular shape.

Under the age of 40, males slightly outnumber females but the relationship is reversed among those over 40 and the gender gap widens with age. By 2020, the number of females over the age of 60 will total more than 3.5 million compared with about 3.2 million males. The gender gap is partly due to the longer life expectancy of females. In 2009, the life expectancy of females was about 4.3 years greater than that of males. Men also suffer more health problems from job-related illnesses and generally lead a less healthy lifestyle.

The figures in Table 1 provide more details on the demographic structure. The population of young children between 0 and 9 years hit a low in 1984 and has been constantly rising since then. The same upward trend will continue in the future and a new high is expected in 2020. The population of tweenagers and teenagers rose throughout most of the 1980s before falling back in later years. A modern low was recorded in 1994. Since then, the numbers have been rising and that trend will continue through to 2020 when a new high is expected.

- The region's fertility rate has remained surprisingly stable over time and higher than that of most other parts of the world. It is slightly less than the replacement level of 2.1 children per female and will hover around this benchmark for the foreseeable future. Immigration is a more important contributor to population growth but most of these people are over 20 years when they enter the country;
- The number of women of childbearing age (15 to 49 years) will rise over time, helping to maintain population growth. In 1980, the region had 4.5 million women in this age range and by 2020 the number will be almost 6.9 million.

The population of 20-29 year olds has slowly risen since 1980 and will continue to edge upward in the future, reaching an all-time high in 2020. The number of those in their thirties and forties will follow a similar pattern. Among 50-59 year olds, a modern low was recorded in 1986 and the numbers then rose steadily over time. The population of this generation will continue to edge upward in the future, hitting an all-time high in 2020. As for those 60 years and older, the number has steadily risen and the upward trend will continue through to 2020 when a new high is reached. The population of this generation will more than double over the 40-year period.

- Life expectancies in the region exceed the world average. The life expectancy of males is expected to rise by another 1.8 years between 2009 and 2020 while that of females will increase by 1.3 years;
- The healthcare system in Australasia provides free care for all. The system is predominately financed through public funding along with a small compulsory health insurance levy;
- Immigrants are generally in better health than the locally born. This result stems from the "healthy immigrant effect" which includes stringent eligibility criteria designed to ensure that only healthy immigrants are allowed to enter the region.

Table 1.15 **Key Population Trends 1980-2020**
'000

	1980	1985	1990	1995	2000	2005	2010	2015	2020	CAGR %	Growth Period
Total	17,894	19,124	20,518	21,745	23,011	24,529	26,452	28,186	29,989	1.30	67.60
Male	8,925	9,531	10,210	10,805	11,399	12,153	13,133	14,010	14,919	1.29	67.16
Female	8,968	9,593	10,308	10,941	11,612	12,375	13,319	14,176	15,070	1.31	68.03
0-4 yrs	1,395	1,462	1,537	1,597	1,562	1,570	1,766	1,854	1,913	0.79	37.12
5-9 yrs	1,599	1,437	1,521	1,578	1,652	1,628	1,647	1,823	1,918	0.46	19.92
10-14 yrs	1,566	1,646	1,494	1,561	1,631	1,714	1,698	1,703	1,885	0.47	20.39
15-19 yrs	1,615	1,602	1,698	1,538	1,601	1,706	1,809	1,781	1,791	0.26	10.90
20-24 yrs	1,551	1,646	1,641	1,716	1,545	1,724	1,872	1,949	1,927	0.54	24.24
25-29 yrs	1,458	1,594	1,711	1,658	1,718	1,627	1,885	1,992	2,072	0.88	42.10
30-34 yrs	1,420	1,504	1,670	1,763	1,719	1,809	1,771	2,002	2,114	1.00	48.92
35-39 yrs	1,147	1,467	1,563	1,708	1,817	1,791	1,905	1,853	2,089	1.51	82.14
40-44 yrs	979	1,163	1,497	1,589	1,739	1,866	1,857	1,954	1,909	1.68	95.01
45-49 yrs	898	984	1,173	1,492	1,599	1,761	1,893	1,870	1,973	1.99	119.79
50-54 yrs	933	885	981	1,161	1,496	1,595	1,756	1,875	1,861	1.74	99.37
55-59 yrs	887	913	871	959	1,149	1,474	1,574	1,726	1,852	1.86	108.68
60-64 yrs	720	852	884	850	950	1,127	1,440	1,536	1,694	2.16	135.16
65-69 yrs	641	664	792	824	808	909	1,085	1,386	1,489	2.13	132.35
70-74 yrs	472	561	588	707	753	745	847	1,018	1,311	2.58	177.52
75-79 yrs	314	380	452	484	602	651	657	758	923	2.73	194.05
80+ yrs	298	364	443	559	669	829	991	1,107	1,269	3.69	325.86

Source: *Euromonitor International from National Statistics*

Vital Statistics

Birth rates reached a peak in 1981 and then began a gentle decline. A modern-day low was reported in 2003. Since then, there has been a gradual increase in birth rates although with some fluctuations. The indicator will begin to fall once again during the coming decade. The number of live births was slowly rising during the 1980s and continued its upward rise in later years, albeit with some fluctuations. An all-time high should be reached by 2020. Australasia's fertility rate has hovered just below replacement level since 1980 and will remain near that benchmark for the foreseeable future. The average age at childbirth has been rising since 1980 and the upward trend will continue through 2020. During this period, the indicator will increase by almost four years.

— Ethnic minorities such as Asians and Maoris have higher birth rates than those of European descent;

— The percentage of families with more than three children is steadily falling while the number of children born to women with little or no education is much higher than for those with a college education.

Death rates reached a high in 1985 and gradually fell over the next two decades. The indicator hit an all-time low in 2005 and will slowly rise over time. The number of deaths was at a record low in 1981 and has steadily increased since then. A new high is expected in 2020.

— Australasia's population enjoys good health relative to other regions and the risk of dying is falling for people of all ages. By 2020, the life expectancy of males should reach 80.6 years, an increase of 10.1 years compared with the figure for 1980. Females will have a life expectancy of 84.4 years in 2020 – 7.5 years greater than the average in 1980;

— The major causes of death are heart disease, cerebrovascular disease (stroke), chronic obstructive pulmonary disease, lung cancer and colorectal cancer. A poor diet and a lack of physical activity are the main risk factors.

Natural changes in population (defined as the number of births less the number of deaths) have consistently been positive and that relationship will hold through 2020. Annual additions to population range between 141,000 and 187,000 per year.

Net migration has been volatile, ranging between a low of 42,500 in 1993 and a high of 239,000 in 2007. In the future, net annual additions to population will be between 140,000 and 190,000 per year.

In Australia, government statisticians estimate that 22% of today's residents were born overseas. In addition, another 26% of those born in the country have at least one parent who was born overseas. For a long time the UK and Ireland were the major source of immigrants but more recently there have been successive waves from various non-English speaking countries. The latter groups first came from Eastern Europe followed by waves from the Netherlands, Germany, Italy, Greece, and the Middle East. Since the late 1980s, Asia has been a more important origin of migrants than Europe.

In New Zealand, demographers estimate that almost 24% of all residents were born overseas. Most of those who leave New Zealand choose to go to Australia. Their relocation is facilitated by the Trans-Tasman Travel Arrangement which allows for the free movement between Australia and New Zealand without visas or permits. Presently, more than 445,000 New Zealanders are living in Australia.

Table 1.16 **Vital Statistics 1980-2020**

As stated

	1980	1985	1990	1995	2000	2005	2010	2015	2020	CAGR %	Growth Period
Birth rates	15.4	15.6	15.7	14.4	13.3	12.9	13.7	13.2	12.9	-0.45	-16.53
Live births ('000)	276.1	299.1	322.8	313.9	306.2	317.5	361.1	372.7	386.2	0.84	39.90
Age at childbirth	26.8	27.4	28.1	28.7	29.4	29.9	30.4	30.7	30.8	0.34	14.73
Death rates	7.6	7.6	7.1	7.0	6.7	6.4	6.9	7.1	7.3	-0.08	-3.28
Deaths ('000)	135.4	146.3	146.6	152.9	155.0	157.7	182.7	200.1	219.4	1.22	62.10
Net migration ('000)	64.9	74.6	128.5	106.2	100.0	141.6	144.1	190.6	190.4	2.73	193.24

Source: *Euromonitor International from National Statistics*
Note: *Birth and death rates refer to the number per '000 population and fertility rates to the number of children born per female. Age at childbirth refers to average age of women in years.*

Growth of Urban Agglomerations

Chart 1.9 Major Cities: 1980, 2000 and 2020

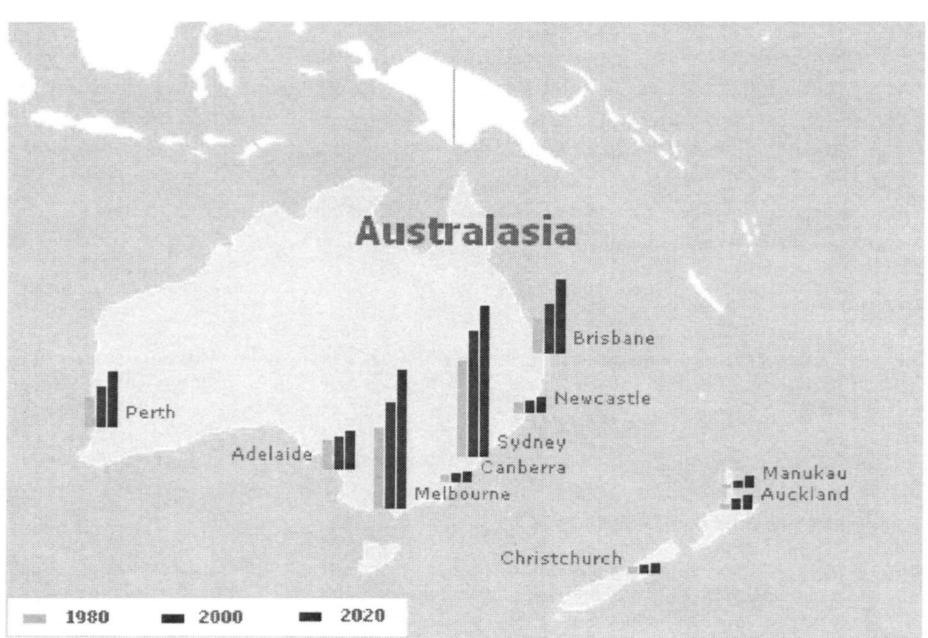

Source: *Euromonitor International from National Statistics*

Australasia's population density is the lowest of any region – 3.3 people per square kilometre in 2009. It has been slowly rising over time and by 2020 is expected to be around 3.8 people per square kilometre. The distribution of population is also somewhat unusual – particularly in Australia. This is due to the fact that much of the central part of the country can support little more than scattered, tiny communities.

The urban share of total population in Australasia has always been comparatively high and has been slowly rising. Urban residents made up 85.4% of the total in 1980 and their share today is 92.5%. By 2020, the share will have risen to 94.1%. Urban migration has been forced on some residents as the result of severe droughts but most settlers and recent immigrants choose to live near the coast. Australia is slightly more urbanised than New Zealand.

Table 1.17 Population of 10 Biggest Cities 1980-2020
'000

	1980	1985	1990	1995	2000	2005	2010	2015	2020	CAGR %	Growth Period
Sydney	2,981.2	3,180.7	3,401.9	3,652.4	3,914.6	4,086.9	4,263.2	4,451.1	4,648.0	1.12	55.91
Melbourne	2,557.4	2,722.2	2,902.9	3,105.0	3,320.7	3,540.9	3,799.1	4,056.2	4,312.0	1.31	68.61
Brisbane	1,116.6	1,203.3	1,303.0	1,420.6	1,553.3	1,717.0	1,933.3	2,139.4	2,336.9	1.86	109.28
Perth	985.2	1,053.8	1,130.6	1,218.7	1,315.2	1,418.8	1,545.5	1,669.2	1,790.3	1.50	81.72
Adelaide	930.1	970.1	1,007.6	1,041.4	1,067.3	1,097.7	1,141.7	1,189.1	1,239.2	0.72	33.23
Newcastle	378.7	400.0	422.4	446.3	469.2	489.0	512.7	537.5	563.1	1.00	48.69
Auckland	246.1	267.4	298.2	339.7	362.3	397.1	431.5	463.1	492.4	1.75	100.06
Christchurch	261.8	273.7	290.7	314.0	321.3	343.3	365.8	386.5	405.8	1.10	55.01
Manukau	187.0	200.8	220.7	249.0	275.9	319.4	364.2	405.5	443.4	2.18	137.17
Canberra	254.4	267.3	280.3	293.5	306.1	326.0	352.1	378.0	403.5	1.16	58.61
TOTAL	9,898.5	10,539.3	11,258.4	12,080.5	12,905.8	13,735.9	14,709.3	15,675.5	16,634.6	1.31	68.05
% of total population	55.3	55.1	54.9	55.6	56.1	56.0	55.6	55.6	55.5	0.01	0.27

Source: *Euromonitor International from National Statistics*

MARKETING SEGMENTS

Children & Teenagers

The number of children and teenagers was falling during the early 1980s and reached an all-time low in 1984. The population of this generation then began to rise and the upward trend will persist through 2020 when a new high is recorded. In 1980, this generation accounted for 34.5% of the total and by 2020 it will make up 25.0%.

— Most children begin their formal education at five years. Compulsory education in New Zealand continues until the age of 15. In Australia, formal education continues to the ages of fifteen to eighteen depending on the state;

— Approximately 20% of all families with children have only one child;

— The region's governments have generous systems of financial support for families with children. Direct cash assistance is provided for most families with children. Child care benefits and a "baby bonus" or maternity allowance is available;

— The growing number of two-income households means that parents have more money to spend on their offspring. Working parents are also forced to spend on childcare.

Middle and upper-income families spend lavishly on their children and demand high-quality products. Low-income families receive considerable government support. Teenagers have only moderate amounts of earned income but are adequately supported by their parents. They are avid consumers of electronic products, mobile phones and other items aimed at the younger generation.

Table 1.18 Children & Teenagers 1980-2020
'000

	1980	1985	1990	1995	2000	2005	2010	2015	2020	CAGR %	Growth Period
Babies/infants (0-2)	828	881	931	951	927	938	1,080	1,112	1,148	0.82	38.62
Female	403	429	454	463	452	456	526	541	559	0.82	38.87
Male	426	452	477	489	476	482	554	570	589	0.82	38.39
Kids (aged 3-8)	1,825	1,723	1,824	1,909	1,951	1,928	1,999	2,214	2,298	0.58	25.97
Female	893	839	889	930	949	940	973	1,079	1,120	0.57	25.45
Male	932	884	936	979	1,002	988	1,025	1,136	1,179	0.59	26.46
Tweenagers (9-12)	1,297	1,243	1,191	1,254	1,320	1,352	1,346	1,370	1,537	0.43	18.52
Female	636	607	580	611	645	658	656	667	749	0.41	17.70
Male	660	636	611	642	676	695	690	703	788	0.44	19.30
Teenagers (13-19)	2,226	2,299	2,304	2,159	2,247	2,399	2,495	2,465	2,524	0.31	13.39
Female	1,095	1,129	1,129	1,053	1,099	1,172	1,215	1,202	1,231	0.29	12.40
Male	1,131	1,170	1,175	1,106	1,148	1,228	1,280	1,262	1,294	0.34	14.34

Source: *Euromonitor International from National Statistics*

Young Adults

The population of young adults will be slowly rising throughout the four-decade period and reach a peak in 2020. In 1980, young adults made up 31.2% of the total and in 2020 they will account for 27.3%

- The proportion of young adults who continue their educational efforts has risen sharply in the past decade;
- The number of young adults who remain in the same household as their parents is steadily increasing;
- Among young adults, a steadily increasing number of births are occurring outside marriage;
- The proportion of young adults who mix work with various types of study programmes is higher than in most other regions of the world.

Young adults are remaining single or childless for longer periods of time. Most have adequate and good earning prospects. They spend freely on entertainment and are attracted to bars, nightclubs, cinemas and types of travel that appeal to this age group. Extended overseas travel is also popular.

Table 1.19 **Young Adults 1980-2020**

'000

	1980	1985	1990	1995	2000	2005	2010	2015	2020	CAGR %	Growth Period
Population aged 20-29	3,009	3,241	3,352	3,374	3,264	3,352	3,757	3,940	3,999	0.71	32.90
Female	1,488	1,603	1,665	1,678	1,629	1,661	1,844	1,923	1,953	0.68	31.24
Male	1,521	1,638	1,686	1,696	1,635	1,691	1,913	2,017	2,046	0.74	34.52
Population aged 30-39	2,567	2,971	3,233	3,472	3,535	3,600	3,677	3,855	4,203	1.24	63.77
Female	1,262	1,474	1,617	1,742	1,787	1,823	1,855	1,928	2,083	1.26	65.02
Male	1,304	1,497	1,616	1,729	1,748	1,777	1,822	1,927	2,121	1.22	62.56

Source: *Euromonitor International from National Statistics*

Middle-aged Adults

The middle-aged population will be increasing throughout the forty-year period. In 1980, this generation will account for 24.7% of the total and by 2020 it will make up 31.0%.

- The earnings gap between men and women is smaller than in most industrialised countries owing to a centralised system of collective bargaining that emphasises equalitarian wage rates;
- Women with a university education are more than twice as likely to be childless as other women;
- The percentage of middle-aged couples who are separated or divorced is steadily rising.

This generation accounts for a large portion of the region's total gross income. Many are "empty-nesters" with ample income to spend on themselves. With high levels of discretionary income and ample free time, they are ready consumers of leisure products, luxury goods and household products.

Table 1.20 **Middle-aged Adults 1980-2020**

'000

	1980	1985	1990	1995	2000	2005	2010	2015	2020	CAGR %	Growth Period
Population aged 40-64	4,417	4,798	5,406	6,051	6,934	7,825	8,519	8,961	9,288	1.88	110.26
Female	2,194	2,370	2,667	3,005	3,465	3,936	4,306	4,546	4,713	1.93	114.81
Male	2,223	2,428	2,739	3,047	3,469	3,889	4,214	4,415	4,575	1.82	105.77

Source: *Euromonitor International from National Statistic*

Older Population

The elderly population will increase almost threefold in 1980-2020. In 1980, the elderly accounted for 9.6% of total population and by 2020 their share will be 16.6%.

- A majority of old-age pensioners are homeowners, most with little or no mortgage debt;
- There is considerable evidence indicating that families are the most significant support network for the elderly. However, the increasing rate of childlessness coupled with family breakdowns and children who relocate domestically or internationally, means that many of the elderly parents will soon be either "functionally" or "actually" childless;
- Health costs are expected to surge in 2015-2020 when a majority of the baby boomers turn 70;
- As a result of population ageing, there will be substantial increases in the number of childless households, one-person households and people living in non-private dwellings;
- The labour force participation rate for older workers is relatively high. This helps to reduce the pressure on pension systems.

The elderly are active and relatively healthy. Most own their own property. The accumulated wealth of the elderly, the reduced amount of time they spend working and their limited financial obligations to their children means they have ample resources and time to devote to leisure pursuits.

Table 1.21 **Older Population 1980-2020**

'000

	1980	1985	1990	1995	2000	2005	2010	2015	2020	CAGR %	Growth Period
Older generation (65+)	1,725	1,968	2,276	2,575	2,833	3,134	3,580	4,268	4,992	2.69	189.37
Female	998	1,141	1,306	1,459	1,587	1,729	1,944	2,288	2,664	2.48	166.82
Male	727	827	970	1,116	1,246	1,404	1,636	1,979	2,328	2.95	220.35

Source: Euromonitor International from National Statistics

EASTERN EUROPE

KEY POPULATION TRENDS

Total population

Chart 2.4 – known as a "heat chart", found in section two *"Age structure of the population at a glance"* – depicts changes in the age structure in Eastern Europe over time. Each dot represents the number of people in a specific age group in a given year. Accordingly, a dark red dot represents the largest concentration of people, by age, in a particular year while deep blue dots show the lowest concentrations. A single dark red dot is the equivalent of almost 11.9 million people while each deep blue dot represents nearly 817,000 people and other colour shadings correspond to intermediate population totals (each by age group).

One significant feature of the chart is the narrow band of bright red which descends diagonally across the chart from left to right. The band represents a brief population boom which began in the 1970s and ended abruptly around 1992. Currently, most of the people involved are between 15 and 25 years of age. Further down the chart is another band of red which depicts a second population boom that began earlier in time and also ended after a brief period.

The upper right-hand corner of the chart consists of light blue and green colours which indicate a sharp and rather drastic decline in the number of young children which began in the 1990s and is expected to accelerate over time.

At the bottom of the chart is an area of dark blue indicating a rather sparse number of older people. Over time, this area of dark blue is reduced in size as the number of elderly people rises. Gradually, this area of dark blue is replaced by lighter shades of blue and green, indicating that the population of those over 60 years will be steadily increasing between now and 2020.

The total number of Eastern Europeans rose during the 1980s and reached an all-time high in 1991 (just over 348 million). The population began to shrink in later years, however, and the downward trend will continue for the foreseeable future. By 2020, the region will have about 319 million people, a decline of almost 11 million compared with the total in 1980. The average rate of growth in 1980-2000 was positive (0.15% per year) thanks to the population growth during the 1980s. However, in 2000-2020, the average rate will be negative (-0.32% per year).

The potential workforce (those between 15 and 64 years) also rose in 1980-2000 but by 2020 will be smaller than it was at the beginning of the forty-year period. In fact, the labour pool will decline by nearly five million over these four decades.

A much more widespread – and accelerating – phenomenon is the ageing of Eastern European society. Virtually all countries will see a steady rise in the median age over time. By 2020, Eastern Europe will have 73.3 million people over the age of 60, an increase of more than 27 million over the figure in 1980.

The cumulative effects of the ageing process in Eastern Europe will significantly alter the macroeconomic landscape.

— Eastern Europe is ageing much faster than most other regions of the world. The long-term effect of this demographic shift will be to slow the pace of growth as the number of workers declines. Rapid gains in productivity will be essential to offset the growing worker scarcity;

— The increasing number of older and elderly consumers will alter patterns of consumption. Spending on categories such as leisure, healthcare and consumer products aimed at older buyers should grow;

— The steadily increasing number of elderly will also put pressure on government budgets. A substantial rise in spending on pensions and health care is inevitable. This will force governments to introduce a variety of pension reforms, or pursue existing reform initiatives more aggressively. Examples include policies to encourage the continued employment of the elderly, greater reliance on private pensions rather than pay-as-you-go methods and more zealous efforts to close the loopholes governing early retirement.

Chart 1.10 Population Age Shift 2000 and 2020, Each Column Represents a Single Age Group

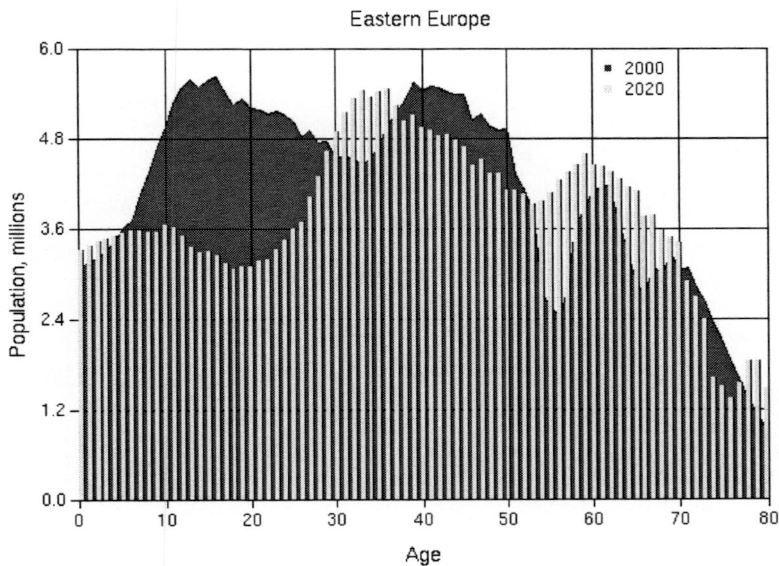

Source: Euromonitor International from National Statistics

Chart 1.10 documents changes in the region's age structure between 2000 and 2020. The areas of bright red indicate age groups where the population will decline between 2000 and 2020. A large drop will occur among those between 5 and 29 years of age. During this two-decade period, the number of those in this age range will decline by 36.8 million. Smaller decrease will occur among those between 38 and 52 years. Finally, the number of those between 71 and 77 years will fall marginally.

— The youth dependency ratio (the number of people 0-14 years relative to the number aged 15-64) will fall from 0.272 in 2000 to 0.243 in 2020;

— The elderly dependency ratio (the number of people over 65 years relative to the number aged 15-64) will jump from 0.187 in 2000 to 0.241 in 2020;

Chart 1.11 Population Pyramid

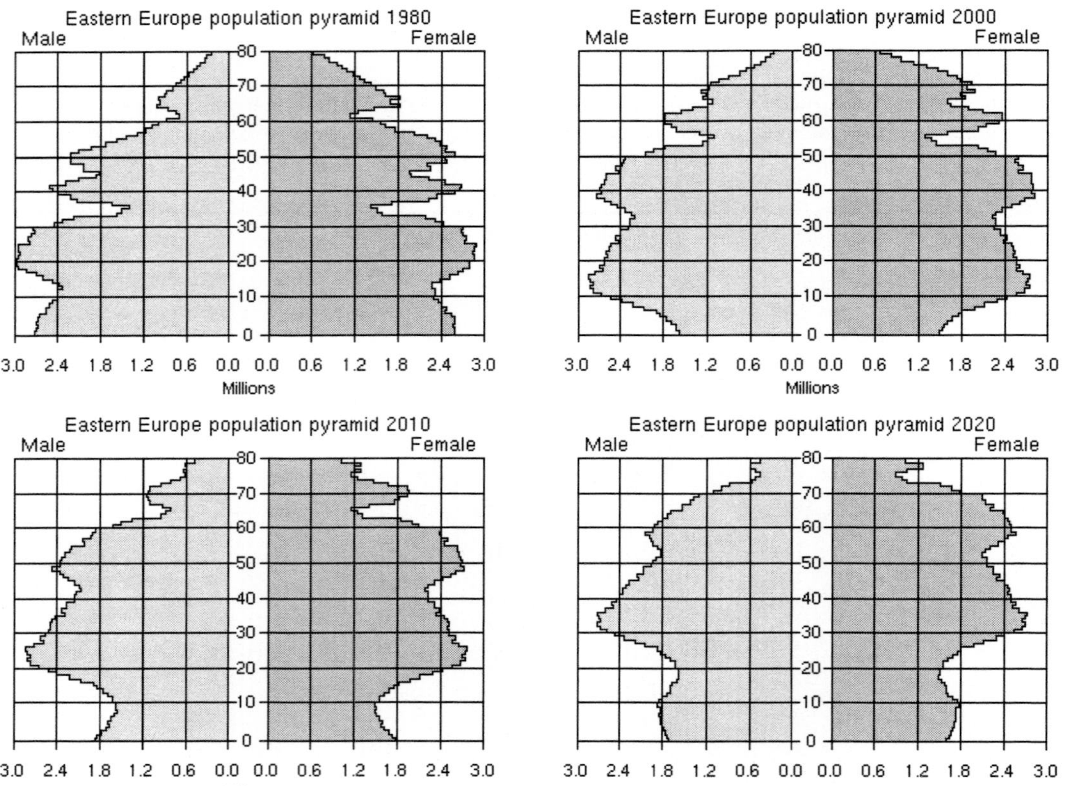

Source: *Euromonitor International from National Statistics*

Chart 1.11 consists of four population pyramids for selected years. None of these figures bear even a remote similarity to the stylistic version which would be with a broad base and narrow, tapering sides to an apex. Over time, the base of each successive pyramid becomes progressively smaller as the region's birth rate declines. At the same time various bulges and irregularities are observed owing to the effects of population ageing.

In 2020, the number of males will exceed that of females among all those under 35 years. However, the reverse will be true for those 35 years and older and the gender gap widens among older people. The widening gender gap is partly due to the longer life expectancy of females. It is also due to the incidence of smoking which is thought to be somewhat higher among males than females. Finally, males also suffer more health problems from job-related illnesses and generally lead a less healthy lifestyle than is true for females.

The figures in Table 1 provide more details on the demographic structure. The number of children between 0 and 9 years was rising throughout most of the 1980s, reaching a record high in 1989. The population of young children then began to decline at an accelerating pace before hitting a modern low in 2006. The number will be gradually edging up in the future but the total in 2020 will still be only around 3 million more than the low reported for 2006. Among those between 10 and 19 years, the number rose until a high was reached in 1999. Afterwards, there was a sharp decline which will continue until 2016 when a new low is expected. Between 1999 and 2016 the number of teenagers will drop by roughly 22 million. The population of this age group will edge upward in the last few years of the coming decade.

- Fertility rates were close to the replacement level during the 1980s but dipped abruptly following the break-up of the former Soviet Union. Some of the lowest rates can be noted for Bulgaria (one of the lowest in the world), Croatia, Poland and Russia. In some parts of the region, the decline has slowed or the indicator will stabilise in the future but the overall impact is still significant;
- In several countries there have been charges of discrimination against women in the work place. Many working women fear that they will lose their jobs if they have children;
- The shrinking population of young children has prompted a number of governments to introduce more family-friendly policies including tax breaks for parents, childcare alternatives and maternity and paternity benefits. These practices will become even more widely accepted in the future.

The population of 20 to 29 year olds was at an all-time high in 1982 and has been steadily dropping since then. The downward trend will continue through to 2020 when a new low is expected. Among those in their thirties, the population was at a record low in 1980 and persistently increased until 1991 when a new high was reported. The numbers then fell for more than a decade but began to rise once again in 2007. A slow but steady increase is expected in the foreseeable future.

The number of Eastern Europeans in their forties was falling rapidly and reached a record low in 1989 before rising until an all-time high was reached in 2001. Since then, the population of this age group has been gradually dropping once again and the downward trend will continue through 2020. The population of 50-59 year olds fell throughout the 1980s and 1990s, reaching a new low in 1999. There was a steady rise in subsequent years which is expected to reach a peak in 2012. Afterwards, the numbers will begin to fall once again. Among the elderly, the population was at a low in 1980 and has been constantly increasing over time. The same trend will continue in the future, with the population of this generation reaching an all-time high in 2020.

— The healthcare offered to middle agers and the elderly deteriorated drastically following the break-up of the former Soviet Union. Gradual improvements began to be introduced around the turn of the century but most countries in the region still lag behind other parts of the developed world;

— The life expectancy of males (though not females) actually fell during the late 1980s and early 1990s. However, both sexes begin to enjoy a steady increase in life spans over the next few years. By 2020, the life expectancy of males should be around 71.3 years compared to a low of just 65.7 years recorded in 1994. Female life expectancy will rise to around 79.0 years by 2020, up from a low of 73.4 years;

— As the society of Eastern Europe ages, the significance of intergenerational transfers will become more important. The increasing co-survival of parents and children means inter-generational financial transfers from children to parents will become much more common.

Table 1.22 **Key Population Trends 1980-2020**

'000

	1980	1985	1990	1995	2000	2005	2010	2015	2020	CAGR %	Growth Period
Total	329,502	338,831	347,536	345,126	339,554	332,515	327,949	323,501	318,795	-0.08	-3.25
Male	155,157	160,162	165,046	163,867	160,810	156,785	154,221	151,886	149,576	-0.09	-3.60
Female	174,346	178,681	182,490	181,259	178,744	175,730	173,729	171,615	169,219	-0.07	-2.94
0-4 yrs	26,414	27,104	26,761	20,391	16,142	15,753	17,317	17,736	17,083	-1.08	-35.33
5-9 yrs	25,030	26,422	27,106	26,682	20,401	16,189	15,761	17,337	17,791	-0.85	-28.92
10-14 yrs	23,444	25,034	26,443	27,072	26,731	20,463	16,219	15,804	17,390	-0.74	-25.83
15-19 yrs	26,647	23,390	25,081	26,051	27,140	26,777	20,457	16,238	15,844	-1.29	-40.54
20-24 yrs	28,967	26,629	23,407	24,536	25,773	27,129	26,675	20,380	16,234	-1.44	-43.96
25-29 yrs	27,740	28,858	26,554	22,858	24,246	25,443	26,931	26,420	20,251	-0.78	-26.99
30-34 yrs	22,519	27,500	28,614	26,086	22,615	23,808	25,177	26,600	26,116	0.37	15.98
35-39 yrs	18,144	22,132	27,150	27,968	25,675	22,185	23,472	24,811	26,227	0.93	44.55
40-44 yrs	24,448	17,777	21,662	26,371	27,211	24,981	21,720	22,982	24,336	-0.01	-0.45
45-49 yrs	20,888	23,710	17,329	20,862	25,408	26,116	24,177	21,051	22,330	0.17	6.91
50-54 yrs	22,581	19,990	22,774	16,416	19,864	24,013	24,911	23,056	20,180	-0.28	-10.63
55-59 yrs	16,468	21,266	18,858	21,271	15,366	18,483	22,505	23,373	21,710	0.69	31.83
60-64 yrs	10,996	15,059	19,586	17,078	19,398	13,964	16,953	20,717	21,600	1.70	96.45
65-69 yrs	13,360	9,517	13,246	17,033	14,927	16,948	12,285	15,118	18,647	0.84	39.58
70-74 yrs	10,081	11,053	7,802	10,863	13,919	12,261	14,167	10,306	12,982	0.63	28.78
75-79 yrs	6,676	7,405	8,283	5,758	8,082	10,307	9,250	11,022	8,123	0.49	21.68
80+ yrs	5,102	5,996	6,881	7,828	6,657	7,694	9,973	10,551	11,950	2.15	134.20

Source: *Euromonitor International from National Statistics*

Vital Statistics

The number of live births reached an all-time high in 1983 and then began to fall at an accelerating pace. A new low was reported in 1999. The indicator has been gently rising since then but will begin to fall once again during the next decade. Birth rates will follow an almost identical trend. These somewhat unusual trends can be attributed to the turmoil following the break-up of the former Soviet Union, civil unrest in various parts of the region and the generally poor quality of natal and pre-natal care in many countries.

The fertility rate hovered around replacement level (2.1 births per female) during the 1980s. A modern-day high of 2.19 was recorded in 1986. However, after the break-up of the former Soviet Union, fertility began a long-term decline and a record low of 1.27 births per female was reached in 2001. A very gradual rise occurred in later years and the same trend is expected to continue for the foreseeable future. However, even by 2020 the indicator will still be well below replacement level.

The average age at childbirth declined very gradually during the 1980s and reached a new low in 1992 (25.5 years). Since then, it has been on the rise and new high is expected by 2020. Women began to postpone birth during the economic transition following the break-up of the Soviet Union.

— An "abortion culture" exists in many parts of the region. The abortion rate has fallen in recent years but is still almost equivalent to the number of live births;

— A sharp drop in the number of second and higher order births has occurred during this decade. The apparent change in preferences contributes to the drop in fertility rates as well as the gradual rise in the age at childbirth;

— The immigration of women of childbearing age has depressed birth rates and the number of live births.

Death rates were at an all-time low in 1986. They fluctuated in later years but the general trend was upward and a record high was reached in 2003. The indicator rose steadily during the present decade and will stabilise in the future. The number of deaths was at a low in the early 1980s and steadily rose until 2003 when a new high was hit. The indicator will go through several cyclical trends in the future.

— Progress on healthcare reforms has been slow and did not make much headway until the beginning of this decade. This weakness probably contributed to the rapid rise in the number of deaths and death rates during the 1990s, as did a shortage of funding;

— Unofficial (under-the-table) payments for healthcare are common in Eastern Europe. They are necessary to gain access to services and indicative of the under-funding which continues to plague the healthcare system today;

— Factors such as a poor diet and the prevalence of smoking are major contributors to the region's relatively high indicators for death.

Natural changes in population (defined as the number of births less the number of deaths) were positive in the 1980s and reached a new high in 1983. The indicator fell in later years and turned negative in 1992. The deficit continued to rise in subsequent years, hitting an all-time low of more than 1.5 million in 2002. Deaths have continued to exceed births in more recent years though the annual totals have been dropping. During the next decade, the annual decline in population will range between 835,000 and 1.1 million per year.

Net migration has been substantial and highly volatile in the past. The number of arrivals exceeded departures throughout most of the 1980s but turned negative in 1989 and net outflows reached a record high in 1991 – more than one million. By the middle of the decade, net migration was once again positive and hit an all-time high (254,000) in 1998. A net inflow was reported throughout most of the present decade. In the future, annual net inflows will range between 31,000 and 120,000 per year and will gradually rise over time. Many of these immigrants are "unofficial" and illegal. Many demographers suspect that the number of illegal immigrants actually exceeds the number of those entering the region legally.

Table 1.23 **Vital Statistics 1980-2020**

As stated

	1980	1985	1990	1995	2000	2005	2010	2015	2020	CAGR %	Growth Period
Birth rates	16.4	16.3	13.6	10.1	9.2	9.9	10.9	11.0	10.3	-1.16	-37.41
Live births ('000)	5,418.6	5,528.3	4,739.7	3,480.5	3,115.3	3,301.1	3,584.1	3,559.6	3,281.1	-1.25	-39.45
Age at childbirth	25.7	25.7	25.6	25.8	26.5	27.2	27.7	28.1	28.2	0.24	10.10
Death rates	10.9	11.3	11.2	13.5	13.5	14.2	13.9	13.9	13.8	0.60	27.01
Deaths ('000)	3,588.9	3,833.1	3,894.4	4,665.7	4,594.5	4,722.9	4,550.7	4,503.4	4,410.3	0.52	22.89
Net migration ('000)	-105.1	202.9	-261.3	-79.7	179.8	72.9	55.4	39.4	118.7		

Source: *Euromonitor International from National Statistics*
Note: *Birth and death rates refer to the number per '000 population and fertility rates to the number of children born per female. Age at childbirth refers to average age of women in years.*

Growth of Urban Agglomerations

Chart 1.12 Major Cities: 1980, 2000 and 2020

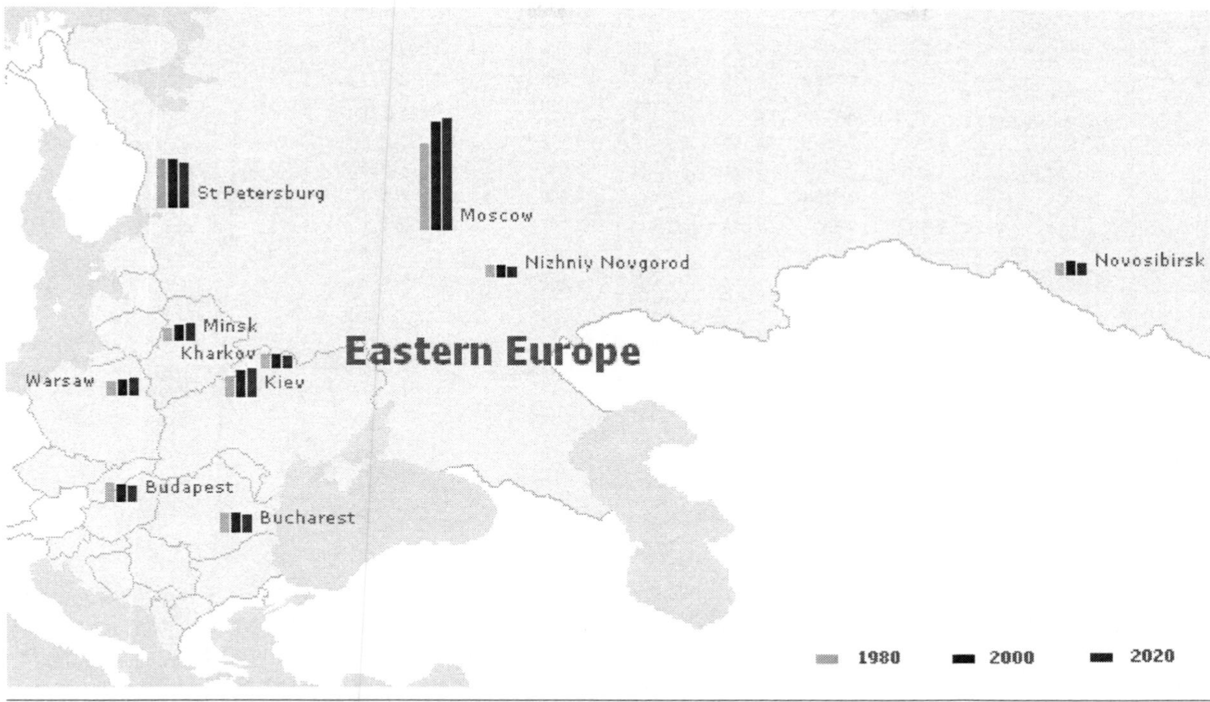

Source: Euromonitor International from National Statistics

Eastern Europe's population density was rising throughout the 1980s and reached a modern high in 1992 (18.7 people per square kilometre). Immigration, a declining fertility rate and a rising death rate has led to declines in the indicator in later years. Population density will steadily fall in the future, reaching a record low of 17.2 people per square kilometre in 2020.

The region is relatively highly urbanised. In 1980, 63.3% of all Eastern Europeans lived in urban areas. Internal migration from rural to urban areas has gradually led to a rise in the urban share over time. That trend will continue in the future and by 2020 roughly 69.9% of total population will live in an urban setting.

Four of the region's largest cities (Moscow, St. Petersburg, Novosibirsk and Nizhniy Novgorod) are in Russia. Moscow – Russia's largest city – is also one of Eastern Europe's fastest-growing cities. Moscow's population increased by around one million per decade in 1980-2000 but the pace will decelerate significantly between now and 2020. Kiev, Minsk and Warsaw are the only other major cities that can expect positive growth between 1980 and 2020.

Kiev is the largest city in the Ukraine. The number of residents was falling during the 1990s but population is forecast to grow by around 0.40% per year on average in 2000-2020. Kiev is an important industrial, scientific, educational and cultural centre for Eastern Europe. It has numerous high-tech industries, several universities and many tourist attractions. Several large engineering firms produce a variety of manufactured items including aircraft, electrical instruments, boats and photographic equipment. Chemicals and various consumer goods are other important industries.

Minsk is the largest city in Belarus and its population will slowly increase between 1980 and 2020. The number of inhabitants grew on average by about 1.3% per year in 1980-2000 and growth in 2000-2020 is expected to be roughly 0.3% per year. Minsk is the industrial centre of the country and unlike many other post-Soviet cities its industrial base did not shrink following the break-up of the Soviet Union. About 40% of the labour force is employed in manufacturing and more than 70% of all goods manufactured in the city are exported, mainly to Russia and other members of the Commonwealth of Independent States.

Table 1.24 **Population of 10 Biggest Cities 1980-2020**
'000

	1980	1985	1990	1995	2000	2005	2010	2015	2020	CAGR %	Growth Period
Moscow	8,232.7	8,647.0	9,132.1	9,689.4	10,174.8	10,420.2	10,494.8	10,530.3	10,548.7	0.62	28.13
St Petersburg	4,639.4	4,869.2	5,036.8	4,905.0	4,723.2	4,548.6	4,421.1	4,344.4	4,299.9	-0.19	-7.32
Kiev	2,195.3	2,429.8	2,613.8	2,668.8	2,616.6	2,666.7	2,776.1	2,821.6	2,831.2	0.64	28.97
Bucharest	2,020.7	2,122.1	2,134.8	2,013.5	1,937.4	1,903.1	1,874.0	1,843.3	1,810.4	-0.27	-10.40
Minsk	1,311.4	1,497.7	1,605.0	1,645.5	1,687.7	1,733.8	1,764.2	1,783.2	1,789.7	0.78	36.47
Warsaw	1,578.6	1,633.9	1,644.9	1,651.5	1,680.5	1,702.0	1,709.3	1,722.8	1,774.9	0.29	12.43
Budapest	2,059.2	2,093.0	2,016.7	1,930.0	1,781.0	1,697.3	1,708.8	1,723.2	1,739.5	-0.42	-15.53
Novosibirsk	1,326.5	1,389.9	1,445.8	1,441.4	1,427.4	1,409.8	1,390.7	1,378.4	1,371.2	0.08	3.37
Kharkov	1,465.1	1,555.0	1,616.0	1,598.2	1,493.4	1,409.0	1,357.5	1,319.5	1,291.0	-0.32	-11.88
Nizhniy Novgorod	1,355.9	1,405.2	1,438.6	1,387.5	1,328.1	1,289.6	1,267.1	1,253.0	1,244.7	-0.21	-8.20
TOTAL	26,184.7	27,642.9	28,684.5	28,930.8	28,850.0	28,780.1	28,763.6	28,719.9	28,701.3	0.23	9.61
% of total population	7.9	8.2	8.3	8.4	8.5	8.7	8.8	8.9	9.0	0.31	13.29

Source: *Euromonitor International from National Statistics*

MARKETING SEGMENTS

Children & Teenagers

The number of children and teenagers in Eastern Europe began to decline in 1990. The downturn coincided with the break-up of the former Soviet Union and will continue until 2015 when a new low is expected. Afterwards, there will be a gentle rise. In 1980, children and teenagers made up 30.8% of the region's total population and in 2020 their share will be 21.4%.

— A large (and probably increasing) number of newborns are born to couples out of wedlock. Analysts attribute this trend to disaffection with marriage, though not towards partnerships in general. Most births outside marriage are to couples in a stable union;

— Today, more families are likely to have only one child rather than two and the incidence of larger families is declining steadily. The lack of adequate housing and the growing array of other options (ranging from education and holidays to the acquisition of consumer products) appears to influence decisions on family size;

— Marriage rates dipped to an all-time low in 1998 but the fall is probably an anomaly owing to the economic and political turmoil following the break-up of the former Soviet Union. The secular trend is clearly downward, however, with marriage rates during the coming decade expected to be significantly lower than the historical average;

— Many births now occur outside marriage. The increase is associated with a growing tendency for cohabitation. Thus, most children born outside marriage still live in a family environment.

Young couples in urban areas are enjoying moderate-to-substantial gains in real income and spend generously on their young children. As the proportion of two-income families rises, the demand for more time-saving products associated with childcare will grow. Parental interest in education is high and tuition costs are modest, even at the university level. More and more teenagers are expected to postpone their entry to the job market in order to continue their education.

Table 1.25 **Children & Teenagers 1980-2020**
'000

	1980	1985	1990	1995	2000	2005	2010	2015	2020	CAGR %	Growth Period
Babies/infants (0-2)	15,839	16,519	15,745	11,358	9,401	9,641	10,711	10,644	10,108	-1.12	-36.18
Female	7,752	8,080	7,690	5,534	4,574	4,687	5,206	5,172	4,912	-1.13	-36.64
Male	8,087	8,439	8,055	5,824	4,828	4,954	5,506	5,472	5,196	-1.10	-35.75
Kids (aged 3-8)	30,771	31,736	32,793	30,256	22,463	18,850	19,282	21,151	21,212	-0.93	-31.06
Female	15,065	15,555	16,078	14,786	10,955	9,186	9,378	10,280	10,304	-0.95	-31.60
Male	15,707	16,181	16,715	15,470	11,508	9,664	9,904	10,871	10,908	-0.91	-30.55
Tweenagers (9-12)	18,999	20,566	21,196	21,980	20,351	14,841	12,523	12,940	14,301	-0.71	-24.73
Female	9,314	10,078	10,404	10,778	9,955	7,250	6,103	6,290	6,947	-0.73	-25.41
Male	9,685	10,488	10,792	11,201	10,396	7,591	6,420	6,650	7,354	-0.69	-24.07
Teenagers (13-19)	35,927	33,130	35,658	36,602	38,199	35,850	27,238	22,380	22,487	-1.16	-37.41
Female	17,600	16,222	17,478	18,000	18,752	17,567	13,309	10,910	10,933	-1.18	-37.88
Male	18,327	16,908	18,180	18,602	19,447	18,282	13,930	11,470	11,554	-1.15	-36.95

Source: *Euromonitor International from National Statistics*

Young Adults

The population of young adults has been falling since 1988 when a modern high was recorded and the downward trend will continue through 2020. In 1980, this generation made up 29.6% of total population and in 2020 it will account for 27.9%.

— Most countries have a rather extensive system of family policies. New mothers generally receive maternity leave and some form of paternity leave is usually available;

— Young people in rural areas are markedly less educated than those in urban areas but the overall standard of education is high;

— Young adults typically command a sizeable portion of national income and their willingness to spend helps to explain a proliferation of shopping malls throughout the region.

Household borrowing and lending rates are steadily rising and young adults are the most active borrowers. They are attracted to the growing number of new, large foreign retailers that have entered the region. The young have a high propensity to consume and are avid purchasers of western products. They are also ready consumers of leisure products, entertainment, travel and clothing.

Table 1.26 **Young Adults 1980-2020**

'000

	1980	1985	1990	1995	2000	2005	2010	2015	2020	CAGR %	Growth Period
Population aged 20-29	56,707	55,487	49,961	47,394	50,018	52,573	53,605	46,800	36,485	-1.10	-35.66
Female	27,931	27,359	24,619	23,347	24,720	26,012	26,454	23,031	17,886	-1.11	-35.96
Male	28,776	28,128	25,342	24,047	25,298	26,561	27,151	23,768	18,599	-1.09	-35.36
Population aged 30-39	40,663	49,632	55,764	54,054	48,290	45,993	48,649	51,411	52,343	0.63	28.73
Female	20,443	24,832	27,860	27,102	24,245	23,097	24,426	25,759	26,124	0.61	27.79
Male	20,220	24,800	27,904	26,952	24,045	22,897	24,223	25,653	26,219	0.65	29.67

Source: *Euromonitor International from National Statistics*

Middle-aged Adults

The population of this generation was at an all-time low in 1980 and has been constantly rising as society ages. The numbers will grow until around 2013 when a new high is expected. In 1980, middle agers represented 28.9% of the total and in 2020 they will account for 34.6%.

— The educational attainment of middle-agers is markedly greater than that of their counterparts in the West or in other large emerging markets. These skills should make it easier to raise productivity provided that investment is available to secure the necessary capital inputs (e.g. machinery and equipment);

— The earnings gap between middle-aged males and females is substantial. The lower pay accorded to females will likely slow the growth in consumption;

— There is a significant degree of underemployment among the older members of this generation. The problem reflects a shortage of investment and the obsolete technologies that exist in many industries. Large pockets of lowly paid middle-aged workers are likely to exist for some time;

— The high mortality rate among males in the economically active age range is a serious concern.

Most members of this generation are willing consumers of new, western products but have limited amounts of discretionary income. However, the middle-aged market will become more attractive as today's younger adults graduate to middle aged status.

Table 1.27 **Middle-aged Adults 1980-2020**

'000

	1980	1985	1990	1995	2000	2005	2010	2015	2020	CAGR %	Growth Period
Population aged 40-64	95,379	97,802	100,208	101,999	107,247	107,557	110,266	111,179	110,157	0.36	15.49
Female	52,576	53,427	53,701	54,199	57,100	57,331	59,043	59,672	58,910	0.28	12.05
Male	42,804	44,376	46,507	47,800	50,147	50,226	51,223	51,507	51,247	0.45	19.73

Source: *Euromonitor International from National Statistics*

Older Population

The number of elderly Eastern Europeans hit a new low in 1986 before beginning a steady rise. The upward trend will continue through 2020 when a record high is anticipated. During this forty-year period, the number of elderly will increase by over 16 million. In 1980, this generation made up 10.7% of total population and in 2020 they will account for 16.2%.

- The pensions of many professionals are below the poverty line even after years of work. Pensions are gradually being raised but the real increases in funding are modest;
- The incidence of poverty among the elderly living in rural areas is nearly twice that of those living in towns and cities;
- Demographers forecast very large increases in age-related expenditure over the next 15 years. This development is expected to raise serious financial concerns for governments in the region;
- The number of households headed by an elderly person is rapidly rising. This is the result of increasing life expectancy and the ageing process;
- Elderly males in rural areas suffer significantly higher mortality rates from cardiovascular disease, respiratory disease and related illnesses than their counterparts in urban areas.
- The gap is explained by differences in medical treatment and facilities. However, mortality rates for both groups are on the rise in rural areas.

The discretionary income of the elderly in most countries is modest and unlikely to grow substantially over the medium term. Pensions are sometimes of little benefit, forcing many to depend on financial assistance from their children. Remittances are another important source of income, again provided mainly by children working abroad.

Table 1.28 **Older Population 1980-2020**

'000

	1980	1985	1990	1995	2000	2005	2010	2015	2020	CAGR %	Growth Period
Older generation (65+)	35,218	33,971	36,212	41,482	43,584	47,210	45,675	46,996	51,701	0.96	46.80
Female	23,665	23,129	24,660	27,513	28,443	30,600	29,810	30,501	33,203	0.85	40.30
Male	11,553	10,842	11,552	13,969	15,141	16,610	15,865	16,495	18,498	1.18	60.12

Source: *Euromonitor International from National Statistics*

LATIN AMERICA

KEY POPULATION TRENDS

Total population

Chart 2.5 – known as a "heat chart", found in section two *"Age structure of the population at a glance"* – depicts changes in the age structure in Latin America over time. Each dot represents the number of people in a specific age group in a given year. Accordingly, a dark red dot represents the largest concentration of people, by age, in a particular year while deep blue dots show the lowest concentrations. A single dark red dot is the equivalent of slightly more than 12.2 million people while each deep blue dot represents 439,000 people and other colour shadings correspond to intermediate population totals (each by age group).

A prominent feature of the chart is the large area of bright red which descends diagonally from the top of the chart from left to right. This area represents a population explosion which began in the early 1980s and will continue with very little abatement until 2020. Currently, most of the people involved are less than 20 years of age. At the bottom of the chart the area of dark blue (indicating a rather sparse number of people) is steadily shrinking over time as it is replaced by lighter shades of blue and greens. The number of those 60 years and over will be steadily rising between now and 2020.

The region's total population will be continuously growing between 1980 and 2020. The average rate of growth in 1980-2000 was 1.82% per year and during 2000-2020 the rate will fall to around 1.16% per year. During the four-decade period, total population will rise by almost 294 million. The potential workforce (those between 15 and 64 years) will be increasing at an even faster rate during the forty-year period. Between 1980 and 2020, the total pool of potential workers will more than double, increasing by more than 233 million.

Chart 1.13 Population Age Shift 2000 and 2020, Each Column Represents a Single Age Group

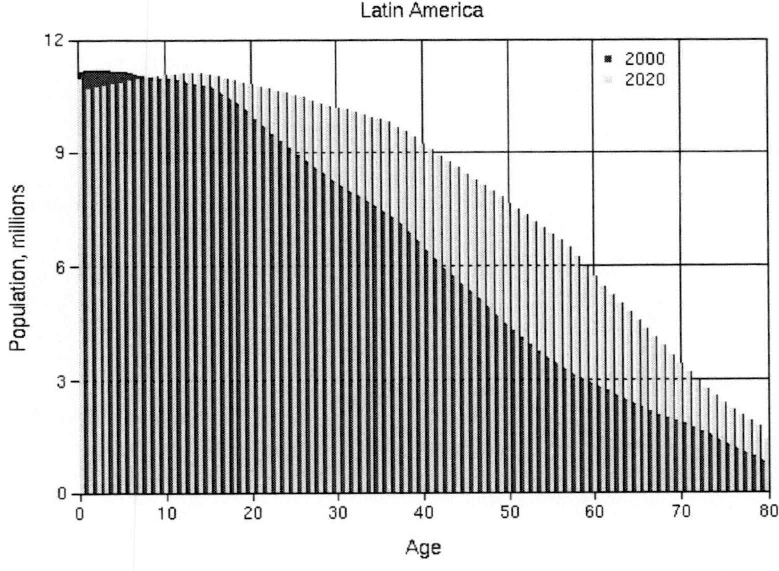

Source: Euromonitor International from National Statistics

Chart 1.13 looks at the country's demographic structure in 2000 and 2020. The small area of bright red indicates a population decline between the ages of zero and eleven years. For all other age groups the numbers will increase between 2000 and 2020. The population of those between 50 and 60 years will see some of the largest proportionate gains.

The consequences of these population shifts are reflected by changes in the region's broad demographic indicators:

— The youth dependency ratio (the number of people 0-14 years relative to the number aged 15-64) will fall from 0.511 in 2000 to 0.372 in 2020;

— The elderly dependency ratio (the number of people over 65 years relative to the number aged 15-64) will rise slightly from 0.092 in 2000 to 0.133 in 2020;

— The population of fifty and sixty-year olds will more than triple between 1980 and 2020, putting increasing pressure on the region's systems of healthcare and its pensions.

Chart 1.14 Population Pyramid

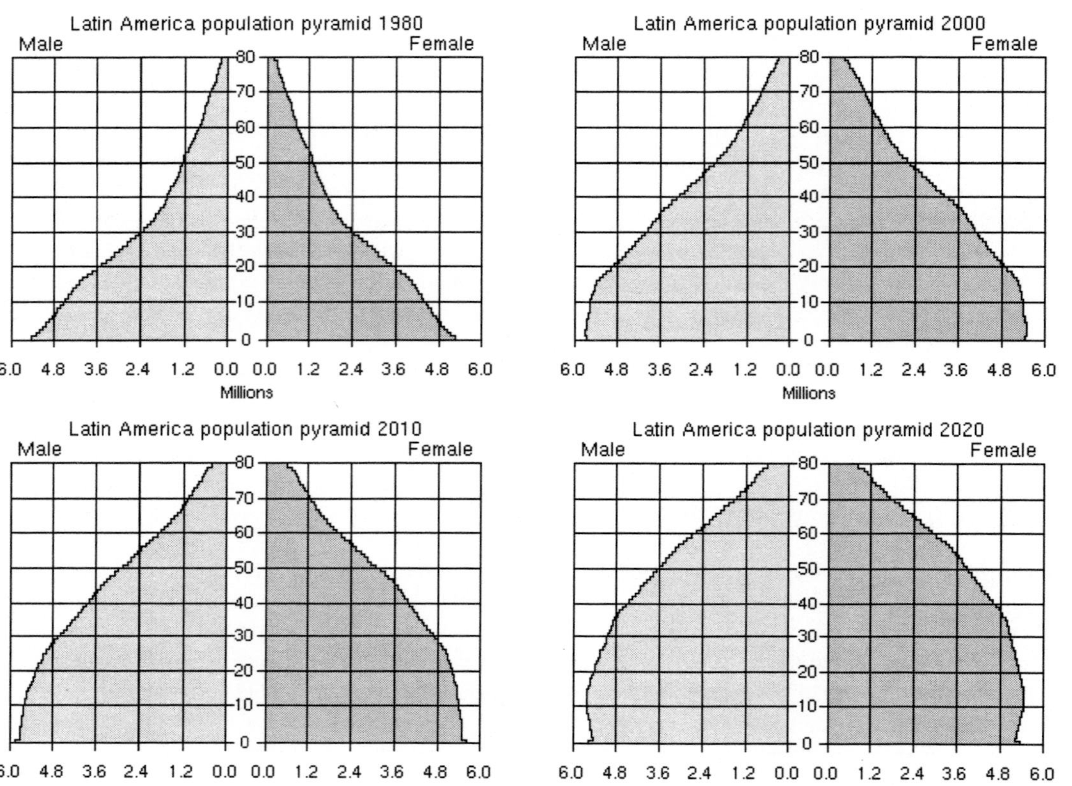

Source: *Euromonitor International from National Statistics*

The figures in chart 1.14 are known as population pyramids because they typically have a wide base with tapering sides rising to an apex. The figure for 1980 matches that description very closely but over time the rapid growth of population produces a much broader base. By 2020, the rate of increase will slow marginally, resulting in a large bulge in the number of those between 20 and 40 years.

The figures also reveal differences in the population of the two sexes. In 2020, the number of males will consistently exceed that of females for all those age groups of 27 years or less. The relationship is reversed, however, among the middle aged and elderly and the gap between females and males widens with age. By 2020, the region will have 63.3 million females over the age of 55 compared with less than 53 million males.

The gender gap is partly due to the longer life expectancy of females. Presently, women live approximately 5.5 years longer than men and by 2020 the difference will still be 5.4 years. The incidence of smoking in Latin America is rather high for both sexes but more males than females are smokers (and this would obviously be a contributing factor). Males also suffer more health problems from job-related illnesses and generally lead an unhealthier lifestyle than females.

More details on the demographic structure are found in table 1. The number of children between 0 and 9 years was at a low in 1980 and rose rapidly over the next two decades. A modern high was recorded in 2000 and the totals have gradually fallen since then. A slow decline is expected over the next decade. The population of those between 10 and 19 years has steadily grown since 1980 and is expected to reach a record high around 2018.

— Fertility rates have been falling but are still well above the replacement level. The downward trend will continue through 2020 but even then fertility will still slightly exceed replacement;

— Although the number of births per female will be gradually falling over time, other demographic changes have the opposite effect. For example, the number of women of childbearing age (15 to 49 years) will nearly double between 1980 and 2020, jumping from 87.2 million to 172.4 million.

The population of 20 to 29 year olds was at a low in 1980 and steadily rose over time. The upward trend will continue through to 2020 when a new high is expected. Much the same sort of steady growth will be occurring among all older age groups between 1980 and 2020. Some of the largest gains will be among those over 50 years of age. For example, in the age range between 50 and 59 years, Latin America's population will increase more than threefold during the forty-year period while among those 65 and over the increase will be nearly fourfold.

— The life expectancy of both sexes has recorded steady increases over time. The two indicators will rise by more than nine years between 1980 and 2020. Improvements in healthcare as well as the fact that more people are now living above subsistence level contribute to these gains;

— Mortality rates and healthy life expectancies have shown the most improvement among middle and upper income households but only limited gains are noted among the region's urban poor and rural population;

— The rate of growth among the elderly population is several times faster than that experienced in industrialised countries. Such rapid gains will put great strains on public services and the extended family system.

Table 1.29 **Key Population Trends 1980-2020**

'000

	1980	1985	1990	1995	2000	2005	2010	2015	2020	CAGR %	Growth Period
Total	364,198	404,261	443,942	483,470	522,396	557,071	592,492	626,504	657,882	1.49	80.64
Male	181,691	201,308	220,663	239,790	258,594	274,861	291,981	308,418	323,553	1.45	78.08
Female	182,508	202,953	223,279	243,680	263,803	282,210	300,511	318,086	334,329	1.52	83.19
0-4 yrs	52,079	55,203	56,008	56,330	56,191	56,149	55,720	54,703	53,387	0.06	2.51
5-9 yrs	47,836	51,003	54,271	55,224	55,653	55,427	55,477	55,192	54,235	0.31	13.38
10-14 yrs	44,166	47,225	50,319	53,658	54,715	54,886	54,923	55,090	54,837	0.54	24.16
15-19 yrs	40,118	43,246	46,177	49,378	52,842	53,234	54,068	54,248	54,480	0.77	35.80
20-24 yrs	33,818	38,808	41,820	44,847	48,066	50,803	51,959	53,003	53,284	1.14	57.56
25-29 yrs	28,137	32,565	37,492	40,539	43,493	46,233	49,648	51,005	52,142	1.55	85.31
30-34 yrs	22,596	27,356	31,762	36,629	39,608	42,574	45,311	48,837	50,263	2.02	122.44
35-39 yrs	18,796	22,057	26,713	31,097	35,940	38,808	41,754	44,606	48,133	2.38	156.09
40-44 yrs	16,254	18,299	21,506	26,094	30,502	35,080	38,066	41,042	43,951	2.52	170.39
45-49 yrs	14,014	15,733	17,732	20,897	25,379	29,599	34,216	37,267	40,226	2.67	187.04
50-54 yrs	12,297	13,395	15,082	17,076	20,188	24,560	28,699	33,270	36,338	2.75	195.50
55-59 yrs	9,966	11,604	12,650	14,301	16,278	19,267	23,520	27,592	32,079	2.97	221.90
60-64 yrs	7,812	9,137	10,706	11,739	13,364	15,234	18,131	22,235	26,175	3.07	235.04
65-69 yrs	6,402	6,931	8,159	9,635	10,661	12,134	13,942	16,693	20,588	2.96	221.57
70-74 yrs	4,503	5,317	5,832	6,949	8,318	9,256	10,620	12,311	14,844	3.03	229.65
75-79 yrs	2,934	3,383	4,084	4,565	5,563	6,747	7,579	8,782	10,288	3.19	250.63
80+ yrs	2,189	2,718	3,344	4,208	5,308	6,735	8,500	10,254	12,248	4.40	459.54

Source: *Euromonitor International from National Statistics*

Vital Statistics

The number of births rose during the 1980s and reached an all-time high in 1990. The number has been declining since then and the downward trend will continue through to 2020 when a record low is expected. Birth rates were at a modern high in 1980 and have fallen continuously over time. The decline will continue in the future and a new low is forecast in 2020. Fertility rates were at a high in 1980 (4.3 births per female) but have been steadily falling over time. The indicator still exceeds replacement level but should continue to fall in the future. The decline in fertility applies to most countries in the region but actual rates vary widely from one country to another.

— Sterilisation and abortion have been widely used methods of birth control in the region but their usage is declining over time;

- Public programmes for family planning have succeeded in broadening the range of options but they are under funded and not widely available;
- The downward trends in birth and fertility rates are an important reason why household size is falling over time. In 1980, there were 4.9 people per household on average and in 2020 that figure will be 3.5.

The number of deaths fell during most of the 1980s and an all-time low was recorded in 1987. Since then, deaths have been rising and that trend will continue as Latin American society ages. The death rate in Latin America was at a record high in 1980 and declined over time. A new low was recorded in 2007 and the indicator will be edging up again in the future.

Natural changes in population (that is, the number of births less the number of deaths) have consistently been positive. The indicator reached a modern high in 1987 (8.7 million) and has been declining very slowly since then. This downward trend will continue through to 2020 when a record low (6.6 million) is expected.

Latin America has long been a net supplier of labour to other parts of the world. Net outflows were at a record low in 1980 (538,000) and steadily rose until the 1990s. Most of the emigration during this period was driven by the poor economic performance of the region's major economies. The total number of emigrants slowed in later years but began to rise again during the present decade with net outflows reaching an all-time high of 1.4 million in 2003. The numbers fell gradually in later years and will total around 600,000 per year over the course of the next decade.

A portion of Latin America's labour flow is made up of intra-regional migration, but the USA and Western Europe have been the primary destinations. In Central America, civil wars and internal strife have been the main reasons for migration. The same is true for a few countries in South America but a majority of emigrants from this part of the region leave for economic motives. Mexico has a long history of emigration to the USA. Washington estimates that approximately 10 million Mexicans are living in the USA today. Almost half of them are undocumented.

Table 1.30 **Vital Statistics 1980-2020**
As stated

	1980	1985	1990	1995	2000	2005	2010	2015	2020	CAGR %	Growth Period
Birth rates	31.9	29.1	26.5	24.2	22.2	20.5	18.9	17.4	16.2	-1.67	-49.07
Live births ('000)	11,610.1	11,767.6	11,772.4	11,697.0	11,600.8	11,420.1	11,219.6	10,931.5	10,681.0	-0.21	-8.00
Death rates	8.4	7.6	7.0	6.4	6.0	5.9	5.9	6.0	6.2	-0.75	-26.09
Deaths ('000)	3,070.2	3,059.6	3,087.1	3,080.3	3,122.2	3,301.0	3,513.9	3,781.9	4,099.0	0.73	33.51
Net migration ('000)	-538.3	-722.7	-761.7	-695.4	-1,146.5	-1,169.2	-701.8	-590.7	-608.5		

Source: *Euromonitor International from National Statistics*
Note: *Birth and death rates refer to the number per '000 population and fertility rates to the number of children born per female. Age at childbirth refers to average age of women in years.*

Growth of Urban Agglomerations

Chart 1.15 Major Cities: 1980, 2000 and 2020

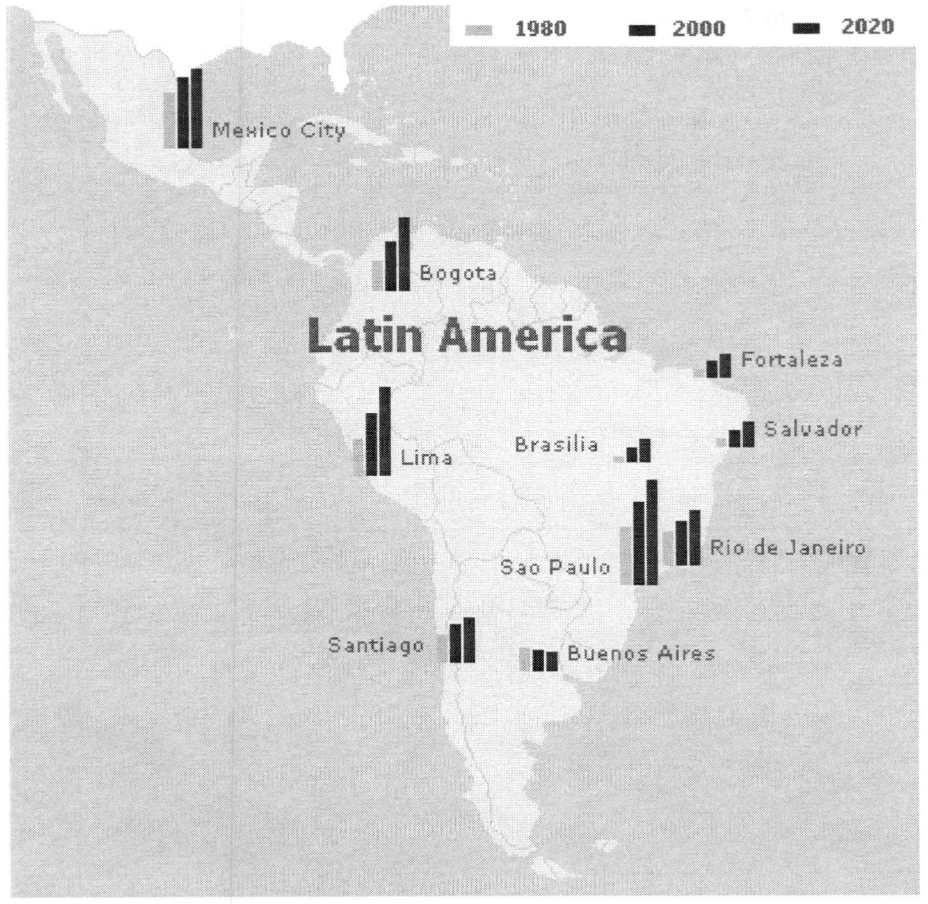

Source: Euromonitor International from National Statistics

Latin America's population density presently stands at 28.9 people per square kilometre, up from 18.0 in 1980. The density will continue to rise over time and by 2020 is expected to about 32.4 people per square kilometre. Brazil is one of the most sparsely settled countries with most of its major cities being located along the coast. Argentina, too, is rather sparsely settled while Colombia and Mexico have densities that are higher than the regional average.

Within the region, rural-to-urban migration has been substantial and the flow from rural areas is expected to continue in the future. Already in 1980, 64.6% of all residents lived in an urban setting and today the share is about 78.6%. The figure will rise further in the future reaching 82.1% by 2020. The steady migration from rural to urban areas has put extreme stress on housing and public services in all major cities.

Table 1.31 Population of 10 Biggest Cities 1980-2020

'000

	1980	1985	1990	1995	2000	2005	2010	2015	2020	CAGR %	Growth Period
Sao Paulo	7,073.1	8,336.7	9,417.5	10,017.8	10,009.2	10,928.0	11,429.9	11,964.2	12,438.0	1.42	75.85
Lima	4,440.8	5,135.0	5,957.0	6,647.7	7,379.9	8,161.5	8,947.6	9,733.3	10,505.7	2.18	136.57
Mexico City	6,870.7	7,615.6	8,092.4	8,270.4	8,391.5	8,463.9	8,796.5	9,188.4	9,594.3	0.84	39.64
Bogota	3,742.8	4,176.8	4,628.6	5,178.5	5,891.5	6,763.3	7,441.9	8,098.3	8,728.7	2.14	133.21
Rio de Janeiro	4,137.1	4,825.7	5,371.9	5,606.5	5,613.9	6,094.2	6,338.5	6,607.6	6,848.8	1.27	65.55
Santiago	3,529.0	3,843.0	4,163.4	4,470.1	4,628.0	4,734.8	4,923.9	5,152.9	5,398.7	1.07	52.98
Salvador	1,343.4	1,656.5	1,986.1	2,262.7	2,331.6	2,673.6	2,893.7	3,103.8	3,283.1	2.26	144.39
Brasilia	1,103.8	1,334.4	1,560.1	1,737.8	2,016.5	2,333.1	2,601.1	2,845.8	3,051.3	2.57	176.42
Fortaleza	1,160.8	1,423.8	1,695.6	1,917.2	2,139.4	2,374.9	2,599.0	2,808.6	2,986.1	2.39	157.25
Buenos Aires	2,922.8	2,988.3	2,999.8	2,910.1	2,803.0	2,679.5	2,568.5	2,468.1	2,377.7	-0.51	-18.65
TOTAL	36,324.5	41,335.7	45,872.5	49,019.0	51,204.5	55,206.8	58,540.6	61,971.1	65,212.4	1.47	79.53
% of total population	10.0	10.2	10.3	10.1	9.8	9.9	9.9	9.9	9.9	-0.02	-0.62

Source: Euromonitor International from National Statistics

MARKETING SEGMENTS

Children & Teenagers

The number of children and teenagers in the Latin American region was at an all-time low in 1980 and will steadily rise until 2010 when a record high is expected. The total will fall gently over the next decade. In 1980, children and teenagers made up 50.6% of the region's total population and in 2020 their share will be 33.0%.

— Most countries have at least eight years of compulsory education. However, desertions rates are sometimes high and laws intended to prevent this are rarely enforced;

— Many women marry before the age of 20 and early childbearing is still common;

— Child labour is a problem and is common among the poor. A substantial number of children between 10 and 14 years hold some type of job;

— Poverty among children and teenagers is common. Their number continues to grow and their average age is falling.

Many teenagers and tweenagers leave school before completing their education. They are poorly trained when they enter the workforce and earn little. Typically, they are employed in agriculture or the informal sector or they attempt to immigrate.

Table 1.32 **Children & Teenagers 1980-2020**
'000

	1980	1985	1990	1995	2000	2005	2010	2015	2020	CAGR %	Growth Period
Babies/infants (0-2)	31,818	33,556	33,839	34,053	33,678	33,846	33,461	32,767	31,932	0.01	0.36
Female	15,640	16,477	16,599	16,692	16,501	16,587	16,383	16,041	15,626	0.00	-0.09
Male	16,178	17,079	17,240	17,361	17,176	17,259	17,077	16,726	16,306	0.02	0.79
Kids (aged 3-8)	58,830	62,778	65,826	66,553	67,131	66,669	66,686	66,065	64,776	0.24	10.11
Female	28,949	30,899	32,374	32,705	32,954	32,742	32,702	32,372	31,731	0.23	9.61
Male	29,881	31,879	33,452	33,847	34,177	33,928	33,984	33,693	33,045	0.25	10.59
Tweenagers (9-12)	36,190	38,660	41,328	43,513	44,034	44,175	44,069	44,201	43,789	0.48	21.00
Female	17,856	19,048	20,374	21,435	21,669	21,740	21,651	21,686	21,466	0.46	20.22
Male	18,334	19,612	20,954	22,079	22,365	22,435	22,418	22,515	22,322	0.49	21.75
Teenagers (13-19)	57,362	61,682	65,782	70,471	74,560	75,007	75,974	76,202	76,444	0.72	33.27
Female	28,562	30,606	32,595	34,932	36,902	37,268	37,529	37,545	37,598	0.69	31.63
Male	28,800	31,076	33,187	35,540	37,658	37,739	38,445	38,657	38,846	0.75	34.88

Source: *Euromonitor International from National Statistics*

Young Adults

The population of young adults has been constantly rising since 1980 and that trend will persist through 2020. In 1980, this generation made up 28.4% of total population and in 2020 it will account for 31.0%.

— Unemployment among young adults is especially high owing to the limited education that many have received and the growing demand for greater skills among new job entrants. Many young adults are forced to work in the informal sector for extended periods of time. They earn low wages and typically live near the poverty line;

— The tempo of childbearing is often disrupted due to the sole migration of a husband or wife but demographers find no evidence of long-term effects on cumulative fertility;

— Many young women opt for part time, low paid jobs in the informal sector in order to balance their work and parenting roles, given a scarcity of childcare options. The high level of employment in the informal sector means that most do not enjoy the right to the childcare benefits;

— Large gains in the population of young adults are driving the housing market in many countries with the demand for mortgages steadily rising.

Income distribution in most countries is inequitable, creating a sharp economic divide among the members of this generation. The middle and upper-income earners will drive consumer spending. Almost all of them live in urban areas, they will have fewer children than their parents and significantly larger amounts of disposable income.

Table 1.33 **Young Adults 1980-2020**
'000

	1980	1985	1990	1995	2000	2005	2010	2015	2020	CAGR %	Growth Period
Population aged 20-29	61,955	71,374	79,312	85,386	91,559	97,037	101,607	104,008	105,427	1.34	70.17
Female	31,130	35,936	39,880	42,881	45,951	48,832	51,096	52,086	52,484	1.31	68.60
Male	30,825	35,438	39,432	42,505	45,609	48,205	50,511	51,922	52,942	1.36	71.75
Population aged 30-39	41,392	49,413	58,475	67,726	75,548	81,382	87,065	93,443	98,396	2.19	137.72
Female	20,786	24,938	29,660	34,476	38,486	41,347	44,261	47,505	49,923	2.21	140.18
Male	20,606	24,476	28,815	33,250	37,063	40,034	42,804	45,939	48,473	2.16	135.24

Source: *Euromonitor International from National Statistics*

Middle-aged Adults

The population of this generation was at an all-time low in 1980 and has been constantly rising as society ages. In 1980, middle agers represented 16.6% of the total and in 2020 they will account for 27.2%.

— In the region's larger economies (Argentina, Brazil, Colombia and Mexico) only about 30% of all workers are covered by social security;

— The earnings gap between middle-aged males and females is substantial. Most females are employed in the informal sector;

— The number of women with three or more children is high by international standards but has been falling steadily over the past two decades.

Middle-agers are becoming an increasingly important market for retailers. Growth of this market, however, is mainly the result of an increase in numbers rather than a significant rise in per capita income. Many had their children at a younger age than their parents and will be "empty-nesters". They will have more income to spend on leisure, health and recreation than their counterparts did at the beginning of this millennium.

Table 1.34 **Middle-aged Adults 1980-2020**
'000

	1980	1985	1990	1995	2000	2005	2010	2015	2020	CAGR %	Growth Period
Population aged 40-64	60,344	68,168	77,676	90,107	105,710	123,740	142,633	161,406	178,769	2.75	196.25
Female	30,750	34,858	39,840	46,348	54,536	64,049	73,973	83,767	92,795	2.80	201.77
Male	29,593	33,310	37,836	43,759	51,175	59,691	68,661	77,639	85,974	2.70	190.52

Source: *Euromonitor International from National Statistic*

Older Population

The number of elderly was at an all-time low in 1980 and will steadily rise through 2020. During this forty-year period, the elderly population will more than triple. In 1980, this generation made up 4.4% of total population and in 2020 they will account for 8.8%.

— A significant number of all households consist of extended families. These households frequently have women or elderly men as household heads;

— Several governments are struggling to improve their fragmented pension systems. Chile has taken the lead in this field;

— Older household members can be relied upon for child care through informal intra-household arrangements. More generous policies of family support would allow many of the elderly to re-enter the work force;

— A majority of the elderly live in urban areas and that proportion is rising faster than the corresponding share for total population. Their motive is to be closer to their family and to have better access to healthcare.

Pension benefits for the elderly are generally meagre and improving only slowly. Those that spent most of their working lives in the informal sector (a sizeable number) have little or no pension. Family ties are strong in most countries, meaning that the elderly can usually rely on the extended family for help and financial assistance when needed.

Table 1.35 Older Population 1980-2020

'000

	1980	1985	1990	1995	2000	2005	2010	2015	2020	CAGR %	Growth Period
Older generation (65+)	16,028	18,349	21,420	25,358	29,850	34,872	40,641	48,042	57,967	3.27	261.66
Female	8,692	10,049	11,813	14,059	16,638	19,470	22,735	26,896	32,511	3.35	274.04
Male	7,336	8,300	9,607	11,299	13,213	15,401	17,906	21,146	25,456	3.16	246.99

Source: *Euromonitor International from National Statistics*

MIDDLE EAST AND AFRICA

KEY POPULATION TRENDS

Total population

Chart 2.6 – known as a "heat chart", found in section two *"Age structure of the population at a glance"* – depicts changes in the age structure in Africa and the Middle East over time. Each dot represents the number of people in a specific age group in a given year. Accordingly, a dark red dot represents the largest concentration of people, by age, in a particular year while deep blue dots show the lowest concentrations. A single dark red dot is the equivalent of almost 41 million people while each deep blue dot represents about 409,000 people and other colour shadings correspond to intermediate population totals (each by age group).

The steadily expanding area of red that eventually covers the entire upper right-hand portion of the chart represents a population explosion that first began in the early 1980s. By 2020, this population growth will apply to all those under 25 years of age. At the bottom of the left side of the chart is an area of deep blue indicating that there were relatively few people over the age of 60 during the 1970s and 1980s. Over time, however, the deep blue dots are replaced by lighter shades of blues and eventually greens which suggest a gradual increase in the elderly population.

The region's population has been steadily rising over time and that trend will persist for the foreseeable future. Between 1980 and 2020, Africa and the Middle East will add almost 947 million, pushing its total population to more than 1.5 billion by the end of the four-decade period. In 1980-2000, total population was increasing at an average rate of 2.78% per year but the pace will decelerate in the future with average growth of 2.19% per year in 2000-2020.

The working-age population (those between 15 and 64 years) is growing at an even faster pace. The pool of potential workers increased at an average rate of 3.05% per year in 1980-2000 and will grow by 2.57% per year in 2000-2020. Altogether, the number of potential workers will jump by more than 602 million during the forty-year period.

A prominent demographic feature throughout the entire region is the extremely high proportion of young people. Africa and the Middle East have the youngest population of all the world's regions. Another common attribute is the high level of unemployment which exists almost everywhere outside the Gulf countries. Growth rates of the economy in most parts of Africa are simply too low to absorb the influx of new workers who enter the work force each year. Unemployment rates of 30-40% are not uncommon.

Chart 1.16 Population Age Shift 2000 and 2020, Each Column Represents a Single Age Group

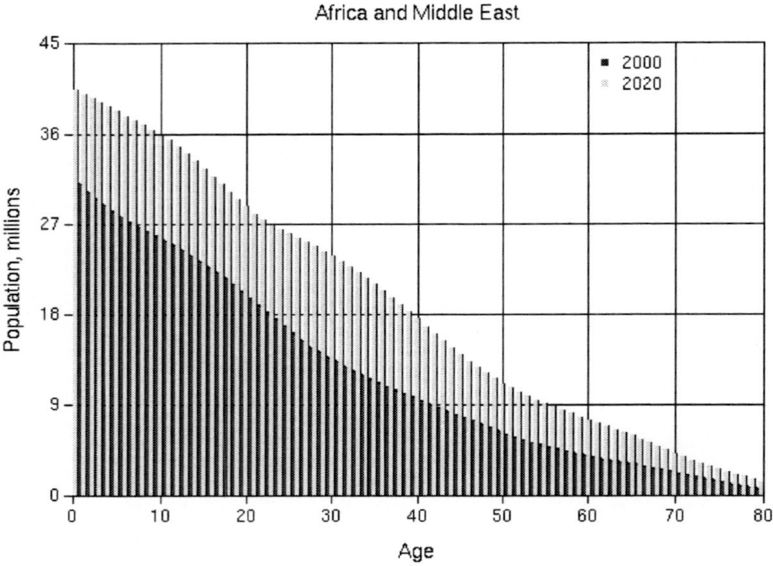

Source: *Euromonitor International from National Statistics*

Chart 1.16 compares the region's population by age in 2000 and 2020. The population in 2020 will be greater than in 2000 for all age groups. Some of the largest proportionate gains will be among those between 30 and 40 years. During this twenty-year period, the number of people in this age range will jump from 116 million to 210 million.

— The youth dependency ratio (the number of people 0-14 years relative to the number aged 15-64) will fall slightly from 0.757 in 2000 to 0.619 in 2020;

— The elderly dependency ratio (the number of people over 65 years relative to the number aged 15-64) will rise from 0.060 in 2000 to 0.068 in 2020;

Chart 1.17 Population Pyramid

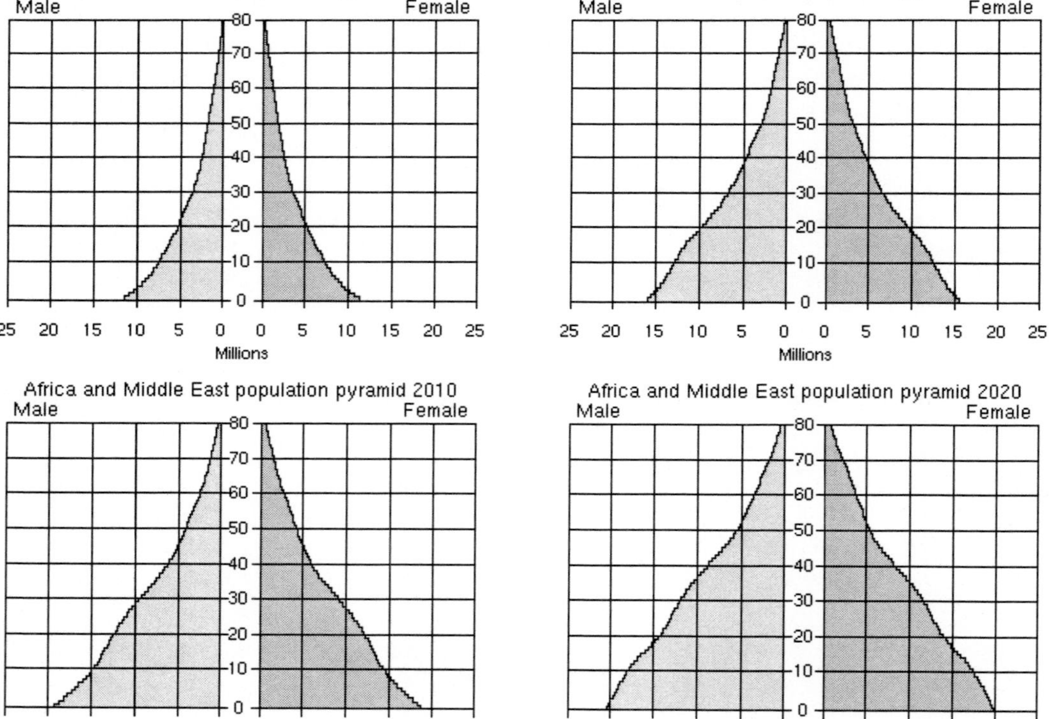

Source: *Euromonitor International from National Statistics*

The figures in chart 1.17 are known as population pyramids because they typically have a wide base with tapering sides rising to an apex. This stylistic description fits well with the graphs in chart 3. Over time, the base becomes progressively broader as the population boom continues although each figure retains its expected shape.

The figures also document differences in the population of the two sexes at all ages. The population of males exceeds that of females among all those 51 years and younger. Among those over 51 years, the relationship is reversed and differences widen with age. By 2020, the region will have approximately 51.5 million women over the age of 60 compared with 43.6 million men. Rates of life expectancy in Africa and the Middle East are lower than in other parts of the world but females still live longer than males, contributing to the gender gap among the elderly. Males also suffer more health problems from job-related illnesses and generally lead a less healthy lifestyle than is true for females.

The figures in Table 1 provide more details on the demographic structure. The number of children between 0 and 9 years has been increasing since 1980 and the upward trend will continue through to 2020 when a record high is expected. In fact, the same relentless rise is expected for all age groups from young children to the elderly. Proportionally, some of the largest gains will occur among those in their fifties and sixties. The population of both these groups will increase about three fold over the forty-year period.

Table 1.36 **Key Population Trends 1980-2020**

'000

	1980	1985	1990	1995	2000	2005	2010	2015	2020	CAGR %	Growth Period
Total	568,893	662,378	763,824	870,953	983,555	1,103,358	1,234,053	1,372,938	1,515,746	2.48	166.44
Male	284,844	332,184	383,148	436,908	493,345	553,903	619,954	690,158	762,278	2.49	167.61
Female	284,049	330,194	380,676	434,045	490,210	549,454	614,098	682,780	753,468	2.47	165.26
0-4 yrs	101,990	118,640	132,116	141,929	150,685	165,179	180,235	191,085	197,291	1.66	93.44
5-9 yrs	82,300	96,516	112,898	125,375	135,536	144,434	159,102	174,620	186,027	2.06	126.04
10-14 yrs	69,739	81,110	95,048	111,044	123,450	133,457	142,514	157,223	172,952	2.30	148.00
15-19 yrs	59,060	68,869	79,619	93,505	109,211	121,365	131,444	140,454	155,207	2.44	162.80
20-24 yrs	49,655	58,061	67,243	77,340	91,687	106,851	119,079	128,983	137,964	2.59	177.84
25-29 yrs	41,501	48,905	56,769	65,257	75,626	89,378	104,271	116,293	126,172	2.82	204.02
30-34 yrs	33,337	40,771	47,728	55,210	63,116	72,961	86,247	100,910	112,959	3.10	238.84
35-39 yrs	27,590	32,572	39,461	46,188	52,986	60,006	69,525	82,612	97,203	3.20	252.32
40-44 yrs	23,775	26,584	31,215	37,917	44,191	50,101	56,692	66,129	79,066	3.05	232.56
45-49 yrs	20,391	22,640	25,237	29,785	36,130	41,680	47,233	53,729	63,011	2.86	209.01
50-54 yrs	17,077	19,184	21,191	23,929	28,060	33,947	39,188	44,602	50,878	2.77	197.93
55-59 yrs	13,757	15,740	17,642	19,720	22,205	25,988	31,566	36,655	41,866	2.82	204.33
60-64 yrs	10,641	12,281	14,019	15,992	17,872	20,064	23,585	28,929	33,796	2.93	217.60
65-69 yrs	7,923	8,936	10,332	12,068	13,818	15,499	17,394	20,734	25,712	2.99	224.54
70-74 yrs	5,279	6,009	6,860	8,085	9,608	11,037	12,473	14,147	17,164	2.99	225.12
75-79 yrs	3,038	3,437	3,960	4,639	5,623	6,766	7,848	9,050	10,393	3.12	242.06
80+ yrs	1,773	2,055	2,415	2,895	3,668	4,558	5,571	6,695	7,992	3.84	350.80

Source: *Euromonitor International from National Statistics*

Vital statistics

The number of live births has been steadily increasing since 1980 and that trend will continue for the foreseeable future. The indicator will reach a new high in 2020. The region's birth rate was at a record high in 1980 and has been gradually falling over time. That trend will be continued in the future and a new low is expected in 2020. Fertility rates have been very high though falling. Presently, fertility is about 4.7 children born per female or more than double the replacement rate. Fertility will continue to fall in the future but even in 2020 it will still be around 3.8 births per female.

— In Africa, fertility is especially high. Today's females of childbearing age can still expect to bear between four and five children on average;

— The use of modern contraceptives in Africa is only around a third of the usage in other developing regions but it is rising at an extremely rapid pace.

The number of deaths was at an all-time low in 1980 and has continuously risen over time. The same pattern will continue in the future and the indicator should reach a record high in 2020. The death rate in Africa and the Middle East has been steadily dropping since 1980 and will reach a new low in 2020.

— Malaria and HIV/AIDS are the main causes of death in Africa;

— Estimates of life expectancy are far lower than in other parts of the world – currently 58.0 years for males and 61.1 years for females. This is largely due to the rudimentary and fragmented systems of healthcare in Africa. Life expectancies in most of the Middle East are close to 80 years or better.

Natural changes in population (defined as the number of births less the number of deaths) have consistently been positive. Net additions to population were at an all-time low in 1980 (16.9 million) and have been slowly rising over time. That trend will continue through to 2020 when a new high of more than 28.9 million is expected.

Net migration was positive during the early 1980s and reached a record high in 1982 – a net inflow of 573,000. The indicator turned negative in later years and net outflows rose substantially over the next two decades, albeit with occasional fluctuations. Net outflows were at a modern high in 2003 (580,000) and fell gradually in later years. A gradual decline is expected in the future with the annual totals for net outflows ranging between 260,000 and 390,000.

Africa is a major source of labour to others parts of the world but the Middle East is a favoured destination. In the latter case, most immigrants are from South Asia while Africans have generally relocated to Europe. In Africa, rapid population growth coupled with the generally erratic performance of the domestic economy, has driven the exodus.

Much of the migration occurring in Africa takes place outside of any regulatory framework, partly because few of these countries have any clear policies on international migration and even fewer are capable of enforcing their laws and regulations. In addition, much of the international migration from Africa is related to forced migration and particularly to the movement of refugees in search of asylum.

— Although Africa's population is growing at a brisk pace, the continent's share of world immigration has actually been declining. Demographers estimate that about 9% of all immigrants today are from Africa, down from approximately 14% in 1980;

— Eastern and Western Africa have the largest numbers of immigrants moving to other parts of the world.

Table 1.37 **Vital Statistics 1980-2020**

As stated

	1980	1985	1990	1995	2000	2005	2010	2015	2020	CAGR %	Growth Period
Birth rates	45.1	43.9	41.0	38.1	36.1	34.9	33.2	30.9	28.4	-1.15	-37.07
Live births ('000)	25,650.2	29,047.8	31,322.1	33,143.8	35,513.6	38,485.3	40,986.2	42,418.5	43,010.4	1.30	67.68
Death rates	15.4	14.1	13.0	12.5	12.1	11.8	11.0	10.0	9.3	-1.25	-39.55
Deaths ('000)	8,755.2	9,315.8	9,949.7	10,843.9	11,919.6	12,985.0	13,516.5	13,769.6	14,101.2	1.20	61.06
Net migration ('000)	444.6	-68.7	-490.0	-370.7	-463.6	-472.2	-389.7	-336.7	-283.2		-163.70

Source: *Euromonitor International from National Statistics*
Note: *Birth and death rates refer to the number per '000 population and fertility rates to the number of children born per female. Age at childbirth refers to average age of women in years.*

Growth of Urban Agglomerations

Chart 1.18 Major cities: 1980, 2000 and 2020

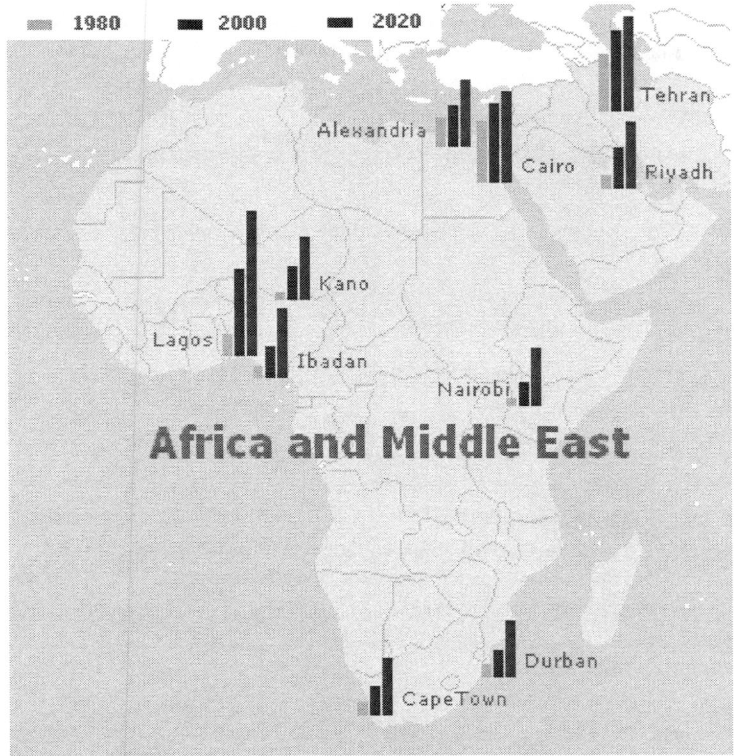

Source: *Euromonitor International from National Statistics*

Relative to other parts of the world, Africa and the Middle East are not densely populated. However, the region's population density has been steadily rising since 1980 and presently stands at about 34.6 persons per square kilometre. The upward trend will continue in the future and by 2020 the density should be approximately 43.5 people per square kilometre. Population density in the Middle East is somewhat higher than on the African continent and is rising rapidly. Much of this area is desert however and the number of residents is highly concentrated along the coast.

Among the larger countries in Africa, Nigeria has the highest population density (around 141 people per square kilometre). Egypt and Morocco are other large countries with relatively high population densities.

Africa and the Middle East are not as highly urbanised as other parts of the world. In 1980, 32.0% of the regional population lived in urban areas and the share today is around 44.6%. Urbanisation will continue in the future, though at a slow pace, and the share of urban residents in 2020 is expected to be around 49.2%. Middle Eastern countries tend to be more highly urbanised than those on the African continent.

Table 1.38 Population of 10 Biggest Cities 1980-2020

'000

	1980	1985	1990	1995	2000	2005	2010	2015	2020	CAGR %	Growth Period
Lagos	2,033.1	3,322.2	4,874.1	6,306.4	7,547.3	8,749.0	9,925.5	11,129.0	12,365.2	4.62	508.19
Tehran	5,007.6	5,886.9	6,412.5	6,712.7	6,942.2	7,054.2	7,358.1	7,794.7	8,248.2	1.26	64.71
Cairo	5,359.7	5,963.4	6,457.8	6,778.9	6,895.7	6,795.1	6,828.7	7,211.4	7,764.4	0.93	44.87
Riyadh	1,351.0	1,925.7	2,567.1	2,999.2	3,624.1	4,201.6	4,740.5	5,272.1	5,791.9	3.71	328.70
Alexandria	2,617.1	2,882.7	3,085.6	3,290.8	3,605.9	4,001.1	4,486.6	5,125.9	5,840.7	2.03	123.18
Ibadan	1,091.9	1,374.2	1,746.5	2,205.2	2,798.0	3,527.5	4,330.9	5,155.3	5,984.0	4.34	448.02
Kano	821.6	1,381.4	2,036.0	2,593.7	3,051.8	3,592.4	4,227.0	4,876.6	5,535.6	4.88	573.72
CapeTown	1,367.7	1,554.8	1,802.2	2,345.9	2,723.6	3,202.1	3,667.9	4,237.0	4,989.4	3.29	264.79
Durban	1,310.3	1,484.3	1,692.6	2,082.8	2,450.4	2,977.3	3,523.1	4,163.2	4,974.8	3.39	279.67
Nairobi	869.3	1,103.6	1,395.4	1,790.5	2,231.3	2,714.9	3,326.9	4,109.7	5,074.4	4.51	483.70
TOTAL	21,829.6	26,879.0	32,069.7	37,106.1	41,870.2	46,815.3	52,415.2	59,075.1	66,568.7	2.83	204.95
% of total population	3.8	4.1	4.2	4.3	4.3	4.2	4.2	4.3	4.4	0.34	14.45

Source: *Euromonitor International from National Statistics*

MARKETING SEGMENTS

Children & Teenagers

The number of young children and teenagers has been steadily rising since 1980 and that will continue through 2020 when a new high is reached. During the forty-year period, the population of this generation will be growing at an average rate of 2.1% per year. In 1980, children and teenagers made up 55.0% of total population and in 2020 their share will be 46.9%.

— Primary school attendance is very high in the Middle East, it is slightly lower in North Africa and only around 60% in southern Africa;

— In many parts of Africa, the poorest families are often forced to send their children to work at eight or nine years of age;

— Currently, more than 50 million children in Africa have either been abandoned or orphaned. Poverty, ethnic strife and the effects of HIV/AIDS are the main causes;

— Up to one-fifth of all women less than 18 years of age have already given birth to at least one child.

Many African children work in the informal sector or in agriculture. Their modest earnings are often essential for survival. Children from professional or two-income families represent a growing consumer market but they are a distinct minority. In the Middle East, families with medium-to high incomes spend lavishly on their children and have substantial amounts of disposable income. The latest types of consumer electronics (for example, iPhones, iPods and computer games) as well as clothing, music and similar items all enjoy healthy and growing markets.

Table 1.39 **Children & Teenagers 1980-2020**

'000

	1980	1985	1990	1995	2000	2005	2010	2015	2020	CAGR %	Growth Period
Babies/infants (0-2)	64,082	74,337	81,595	87,465	92,579	102,491	110,909	116,550	119,723	1.57	86.83
Female	31,698	36,750	40,306	43,193	45,704	50,545	54,700	57,489	59,064	1.57	86.33
Male	32,384	37,587	41,289	44,273	46,875	51,946	56,209	59,061	60,659	1.58	87.31
Kids (aged 3-8)	104,906	122,905	142,337	155,893	167,509	179,283	198,094	215,592	227,338	1.95	116.71
Female	51,945	60,804	70,398	77,048	82,767	88,544	97,793	106,467	112,303	1.95	116.20
Male	52,962	62,101	71,939	78,844	84,742	90,739	100,301	109,125	115,035	1.96	117.20
Tweenagers (9-12)	58,475	68,165	80,110	92,529	101,738	109,169	117,402	130,039	141,928	2.24	142.72
Female	28,938	33,720	39,621	45,747	50,286	53,936	57,982	64,213	70,118	2.24	142.30
Male	29,537	34,445	40,490	46,782	51,453	55,234	59,420	65,826	71,810	2.25	143.12
Teenagers (13-19)	85,626	99,727	115,639	135,966	157,056	173,492	186,889	201,201	222,488	2.42	159.84
Female	42,424	49,319	57,275	67,323	77,729	85,830	92,402	99,439	109,945	2.41	159.16
Male	43,201	50,408	58,364	68,643	79,326	87,662	94,487	101,762	112,543	2.42	160.51

Source: *Euromonitor International from National Statistics*

Young Adults

The population of young adults was at a modern-day low in 1980 and has continuously risen over time. That trend will persist through 2020 when a record high is reached. During these four decades, the population of this generation will more than triple. In 1980, young adults made up 26.7% of total population and in 2020 they will account for 31.3%.

— Unemployment among young adults is very high in most African countries. In the Middle East, many in this generation are employed by their governments but they also have better training than their African counterparts;

— There are sharp differences in family size between urban and rural areas. Up to 40% of women in urban areas still have only two children. In rural areas, the figure is much higher. Thus, rural-to-urban migration seems to be a powerful force in reducing fertility rates;

— Less than 5% of women over the age of 30 are childless;

— There is a significant variation in the age of marriage across regions owing to cultural differences.

Young adult males are much better paid than working females and make most of the decisions regarding consumer spending. Many are unemployed while those holding jobs are careful consumers.

Table 1.40 **Young Adults 1980-2020**

'000

	1980	1985	1990	1995	2000	2005	2010	2015	2020	CAGR %	Growth Period
Population aged 20-29	91,157	106,966	124,012	142,597	167,314	196,229	223,349	245,276	264,136	2.70	189.76
Female	45,343	53,098	61,523	70,989	82,961	97,054	110,495	121,383	130,662	2.68	188.16
Male	45,813	53,868	62,488	71,608	84,353	99,175	112,855	123,892	133,474	2.71	191.34
Population aged 30-39	60,927	73,343	87,190	101,398	116,102	132,967	155,771	183,522	210,162	3.14	244.94
Female	30,622	36,612	43,338	50,344	57,713	65,707	76,504	90,114	103,413	3.09	237.71
Male	30,305	36,731	43,851	51,054	58,389	67,261	79,267	93,409	106,749	3.20	252.25

Source: *Euromonitor International from National Statistics*

Middle-aged Adults

The number of middle agers was at an all-time low in 1980 and has steadily risen over time. The upward trend will continue through to 2020 when a new high is recorded. The average rate of growth between 1980 and 2020 will be about 2.90% per year. In 1980, middle agers represented 15.1% of total population and in 2020 they will account for 17.7%.

— Throughout Africa, women spend nearly half their working time in unpaid employment. They are most frequently employed in agriculture in the informal market. There are restrictions on the employment of women in several Middle Eastern countries;

— The incidence of HIV/AIDS among women under 50 years has been growing at a double-digit rate but the pace has slowed in recent years. Programmes to combat the disease are few and fragmented. Most gains appear to be due to changes in social behaviour;

— Divorce rates are on the rise but are significantly lower than in industrialised countries;

— Employment opportunities for women living in Muslim countries are almost exclusively found in the public sector – mainly in education and health services. In the private sector, less than 5% of employees are Muslim women.

In Africa, the buying habits of middle and upper-income middle agers have come to resemble Western lifestyles but these people are a distinct minority within this generation. In the Middle East, the population of this generation is being swelled by immigration and is rapidly increasing. Many of those entering the country in the future will be skilled workers and thus will have more disposable income than their predecessors.

Table 1.41 **Middle-aged Adults 1980-2020**

'000

	1980	1985	1990	1995	2000	2005	2010	2015	2020	CAGR %	Growth Period
Population aged 40-64	85,641	96,429	109,303	127,343	148,458	171,780	198,263	230,044	268,618	2.90	213.65
Female	43,345	48,887	55,500	64,494	75,376	87,151	100,312	115,570	133,986	2.86	209.11
Male	42,296	47,542	53,804	62,850	73,082	84,629	97,951	114,474	134,631	2.94	218.31

Source: *Euromonitor International from National Statistic*

Older Population

The population of those over 65 years has been persistently rising since 1980 and that trend will continue through 2020 when a modern high is reached. During this period, the total number of elderly will increase more than three fold. This generation accounted for 3.2% of total population in 1980 and their share will be 4.0% in 2020.

— In Africa, very few of the elderly who seek medical attention can obtain it. The most common reason for the lack of care is affordability. In contrast, the elderly living in the Middle East are well cared for;

— Pension systems in Africa are not viable and a large majority of the elderly depend on their families for support. In rural areas, care and financial assistance often extends to the clan;

— The elderly must frequently assume responsibility for the care of their grandchildren who have lost their parents as a result of HIV/AIDS;

— The elderly who are able to work are often engaged in agricultural activities or in the informal sector.

In Africa, the elderly are a sometimes a forgotten generation. Only a minority have sufficient wealth or pensions to provide themselves with financial support. Government programmes for the elderly are limited, leaving many to depend on their children or work in the informal sector. In the Middle East, many of the elderly enjoy at least modest standards of living, both because of their accumulated wealth and the continued operation of the extended family system.

Table 1.42 **Older population 1980-2020**

'000

	1980	1985	1990	1995	2000	2005	2010	2015	2020	CAGR %	Growth Period
Older generation (65+)	18,013	20,438	23,567	27,686	32,718	37,860	43,286	50,625	61,261	3.11	240.09
Female	9,701	10,970	12,680	14,870	17,634	20,646	23,866	28,062	33,931	3.18	249.76
Male	8,312	9,468	10,887	12,817	15,084	17,214	19,420	22,564	27,330	3.02	228.81

Source: *Euromonitor International from National Statistics*

NORTH AMERICA

KEY POPULATION TRENDS

Total Population

Chart 2.7 – known as a "heat chart", found in section two *"Age structure of the population at a glance"* – depicts changes in the age structure in North America over time. Each dot represents the number of people in a specific age group in a given year. Accordingly, a dark red dot represents the largest concentration of people, by age, in a particular year while deep blue dots show the lowest concentrations. A single dark red dot is the equivalent of slightly more than 15.1 million people while each deep blue dot represents almost 813,000 people and other colour shadings correspond to intermediate population totals (each by age group).

A prominent feature is the band of bright red which descends diagonally from left to right all the way across the chart. The band depicts a population boom which began in the early 1960s. By 1980, most of these people were between 15 and 20 years. Two other smaller bands also exist but both of them first appear among teenagers or young adults. These are not the result of any jump in births but immigration. Finally, the upper right-hand corner is also a combination of red and orange dots which suggest that the number of births will be rising after 2015.

At the bottom of the chart is an area of dark blue which indicates a rather sparse population of elderly. Over time, the dark blue area is reduced in size, being replaced in part by lighter shades of blue and green. The change in colouring depicts the ageing of North American society. The population of elderly is gradually rising and this trend will continue through 2020. Proportionally, some of the largest gains in population will occur among those between 50 and 70 years.

Total population is steadily increasing over time. In 1980-2000, total population was growing at an average rate of 1.08% per year and the expected pace in 2000-2020 should be around 0.80%. Between 1980 and 2020, the region will add nearly 115 million people, giving it a total population of 366.8 million by the end of the period.

The potential workforce (those between 15 and 64 years) will also be rising. The region's pool of potential workers was 167.4 million in 1980 and should be about 235.7 million by 2020. Like total population, the average annual rate of growth will be decelerating after 2000.

Chart 1.19 Population Age Shift 2000 and 2020, Each Column Represents a Single Age Group

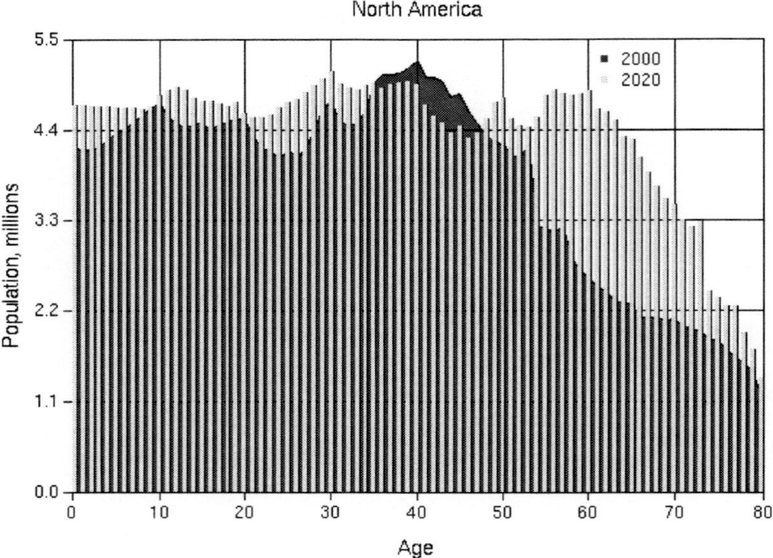

Source: Euromonitor International from National Statistics

Chart 1.19 looks at the region's demographic structure in 2000 and 2020. For the most part, North America's population in 2020 will exceed that in 2000 but there is one small exception. The number of those between 36 and 47 years will be slightly less in 2020 than it was in 2000. In contrast, the population between 55 and 65 years will jump from 27.2 million in 2000 to 47.1 million in 2020.

The consequences of these population shifts are reflected by changes in the country's broad demographic indicators:

- The youth dependency ratio (the number of people 0-14 years relative to the number aged 15-64) will fall from 0.318 in 2000 to 0.301 in 2020;
- The elderly dependency ratio (the number of people over 65 years relative to the number aged 15-64) will moderately increase from 0.187 in 2000 to 0.255 in 2020;
- As demographic ageing proceeds, pressures on age-related public spending will grow. Patterns of consumption will also be altered as older consumers account for a larger share in private consumption.

Chart 1.20 Population Pyramid

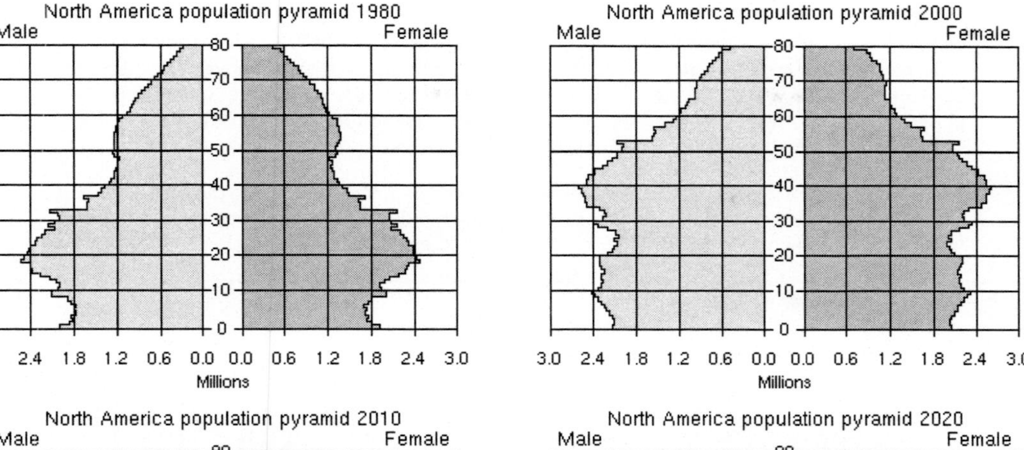

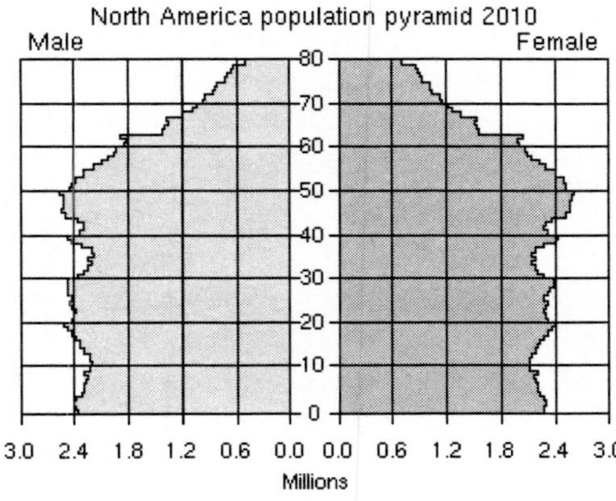

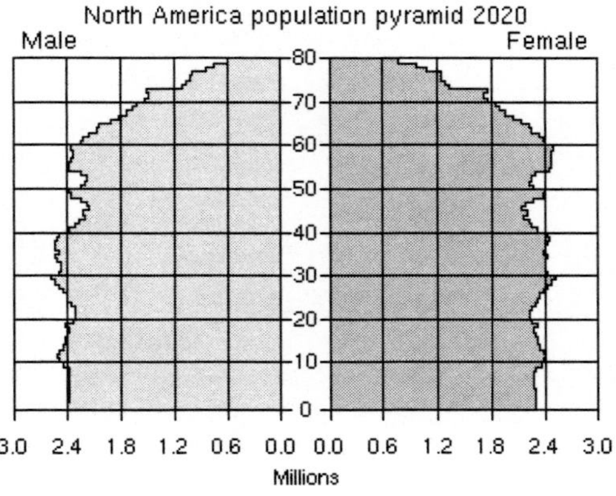

Source: *Euromonitor International from National Statistics*

The figures shown in Chart 1.20 are known as population pyramids which typically have a wide base with tapering sides rising to an apex. That is clearly not the case for North America. Each successive figure gradually becomes more rectangular in shape, reflecting the effects of population ageing and immigration. The figure for 2020 bears no resemblance whatsoever to a pyramid.

The male population slightly outnumbers the female population for all those under the age of 47 but the relationship is reversed among those 47 and over and the gender gap grows with age. For example, by 2020 the number of females 65 and over will total 33.3 million compared with less than 26.7 million males. The gender gap is partly due to the longer life expectancy of females. Males also suffer more health problems from job-related illnesses and generally lead a less healthy lifestyle.

The figures in Table 1 provide more details on the demographic structure. The population of young children between 0 and 9 years was at an all-time low in 1981 and has been steadily increasing over time. The same upward trend will continue for the foreseeable future and a new high should be reached in 2020. The population of tweenagers and teenagers fell during the 1980s and hit a new low in 1989. The numbers rose in later years and the upward trend will continue in the future, albeit with some fluctuations. A record high is expected in 2020.

— The fertility rate in North America has been slightly below replacement level (2.1 children born per female) but has remained remarkably stable over time;

— Although the number of births per female is falling gradually over time, two other factors help to stabilise fertility. First, foreign-born couples have more children than native-born couples. They are in their prime childbearing years and often come from countries where larger families are common. Second, the number of women of childbearing age (15 to 49 years) will increase from 65.3 million in 1980 to 81.6 million in 2020.

The population of 20-29 year olds was rising until 1985 and then began to fall, reaching a record low in 1996. The numbers then began to rise and a modern high is expected in 2014. There will be a gradual decline in subsequent years. Among 30-39 year olds, the population was at a low in 1980 and rose until 1995 when a new high was recorded. Since then, the number has been dropping but a gentle rise is expected in the future. The population of those in their forties was at an all-time low in 1980 and steadily increased until 2005 when a record high was reported. The numbers have been gradually falling since then and the downward trend will continue for the foreseeable future. There has been a persistent rise in the population of people over 50 years and the same trend will continue in the future.

- Life expectancy in the USA is still lower than in many industrialised countries but it is steadily rising. Differences in the mortality of men and women and whites and blacks are also narrowing as a result of improvements in healthcare and a healthier life style;
- Canada has one of the highest life expectancies in the world (currently 80.8 years). The healthy life expectancy at 60 years has also shown substantial gains and currently stands at 17.5 years for 60-year-old males while that for females is 21.3 years. Canada's healthcare system is largely publicly financed. Approximately 70% of all healthcare expenditure occurs in the public sector. The remaining 30% is paid either out-of-pocket or via private insurance;
- The leading causes of death are various forms of cancer and heart disease but the numbers have been slowly dropping over time. The main reasons for the decline are improvements in "lifestyle factors", as well as improvements in the quality of and access to healthcare.

Table 1.43 **Key Population Trends 1980-2020**

'000

	1980	1985	1990	1995	2000	2005	2010	2015	2020	CAGR %	Growth Period
Total	252,243	263,767	277,320	295,580	312,861	327,873	342,830	354,728	366,795	0.94	45.41
Male	123,070	128,561	135,446	144,719	153,655	161,468	169,249	175,329	181,387	0.97	47.39
Female	129,173	135,206	141,875	150,862	159,206	166,404	173,581	179,399	185,407	0.91	43.53
0-4 yrs	18,243	19,688	20,788	21,611	20,978	22,005	23,224	22,919	23,443	0.63	28.51
5-9 yrs	18,415	18,481	20,000	21,430	22,512	21,391	22,406	23,632	23,347	0.60	26.78
10-14 yrs	20,207	18,868	19,090	21,204	22,674	22,932	21,865	22,953	24,275	0.46	20.13
15-19 yrs	23,583	20,745	19,710	20,354	22,355	23,142	23,412	22,471	23,624	0.00	0.17
20-24 yrs	24,014	23,763	21,275	20,310	21,194	23,135	23,771	23,860	22,934	-0.12	-4.50
25-29 yrs	21,998	24,112	23,860	21,865	21,378	22,068	23,927	24,232	24,302	0.25	10.47
30-34 yrs	19,831	22,252	24,475	24,997	22,795	22,176	22,758	24,461	24,779	0.56	24.95
35-39 yrs	15,722	19,616	22,279	25,062	25,343	23,281	22,579	23,032	24,768	1.14	57.53
40-44 yrs	13,075	15,682	19,848	22,525	25,124	25,548	23,426	22,562	23,058	1.43	76.36
45-49 yrs	12,321	12,911	15,429	19,682	22,536	25,072	25,425	23,159	22,359	1.50	81.47
50-54 yrs	12,937	12,103	12,680	15,440	19,817	22,283	24,717	24,884	22,733	1.42	75.72
55-59 yrs	12,787	12,446	11,715	12,476	15,115	19,353	21,739	23,963	24,189	1.61	89.17
60-64 yrs	11,095	12,033	11,805	11,346	12,110	14,509	18,587	20,774	22,958	1.83	106.92
65-69 yrs	9,641	10,233	11,149	11,089	10,659	11,322	13,602	17,349	19,455	1.77	101.80
70-74 yrs	7,457	8,247	8,825	9,846	9,856	9,557	10,219	12,244	15,683	1.88	110.32
75-79 yrs	5,251	6,011	6,755	7,369	8,240	8,284	8,112	8,682	10,479	1.74	99.56
80+ yrs	5,665	6,574	7,639	8,975	10,175	11,815	13,061	13,549	14,407	2.36	154.31

Source: *Euromonitor International from National Statistics*

Vital Statistics

North America's birth rate rose during the 1980s and hit an all-time high in 1989. It began to drop at a rapid pace over the next two decades and will continue to slide downward at a decelerating pace in the future. A new low is expected in 2020. The number of live births was at a record low in 1980 and has slowly risen over time. The upward trend will continue in the future and the indicator will reach a new high in 2020. The average age at childbirth was at a modern low in 1980 and has slowly been rising over time. Presently, it is about 29.0 years. It will continue to rise in the future, reaching a new high in 2020. The age at first childbirth follows a similar trend.

- Among non-Hispanic women, birth rates are falling for women under 25 but rising for older women of childbearing age;
- As women postpone childbirth, the fertility rate of women over 30 years has risen while that of women in their twenties has declined.

The number of deaths was at a low in 1980 and has risen continuously over time. The indicator will continue its rise in the future, reaching a new high in 2020. The death rate rose rapidly in the 1980s and a record high was reported in 1987. The indicator fluctuated over the next couple of decades but the long-term trend was downward and a low was reached in 2006. Death rates will gradually rise again in the future.

- At older ages, Asians and Hispanics tend to have longer life expectancies than Caucasians: At 65 years, Asian and Hispanic men live, on average, about 19 more years – roughly two years longer than white men. Asian and Hispanic women at 65 years should live about 23 more years, or three years longer than white women. Blacks have the shortest life expectancies of all ethnic groups;
- The leading causes of death are various forms of cancer and heart disease but the numbers have been slowly dropping over time.

Natural changes in population (defined as the number of births less the number of deaths) have consistently been positive. Net additions to the population reached a high in 1990 and have gradually been dropping since then. The decline will continue through 2020 when a record low (a net annual gain of about 1.6 million) is expected.

Net migration into North America has long been positive but amounted to less than one million per year during most of the 1980s. Annual inflows began to rise during the 1990s and reached a peak of 1.8 million in 1996. Annual inflows have fallen gradually since then and are expected to range between 700,000 and 800,000 per year during the next decade.

The steady influx of migrants affects virtually all aspects of the North American economy. Inflows to the USA are expected to slow in the future but immigration should still account for almost a third of annual gains in population during the next decade. In addition, the Census Bureau estimates that around 1 million illegal immigrants enter the country each year. On average, the USA accepts 2,600 immigrants per day as legal residents. Another 1,400 enter as unauthorised foreigners. Three-quarters of the foreigners that enter each year come from Asia and Latin America.

The situation in Canada is similar. For example, in 2000-2006 more than 1.2 million immigrants entered the country while the native-born population rose by just 400,000. The Canadian government's emphasis on education and skills as criteria for immigration has been criticised because many highly educated immigrants experience difficulty finding employment commensurate with their training.

Table 1.44 Vital Statistics 1980-2020

As stated

	1980	1985	1990	1995	2000	2005	2010	2015	2020	CAGR %	Growth Period
Birth rates	15.8	15.7	16.4	14.4	14.0	13.8	13.3	13.1	12.9	-0.52	-18.79
Live births ('000)	3,996.4	4,154.2	4,535.7	4,254.4	4,374.4	4,524.2	4,558.1	4,641.9	4,719.1	0.42	18.08
Age at first childbirth	23.4	24.1	24.7	25.1	26.0	26.6	27.2	27.7	27.9	0.44	19.17
Age at childbirth	26.0	26.6	27.1	27.5	28.0	28.5	29.0	29.5	29.6	0.33	14.08
Death rates	8.3	8.6	8.4	8.6	8.4	8.1	8.3	8.3	8.4	0.04	1.77
Deaths ('000)	2,093.0	2,271.8	2,333.0	2,527.7	2,638.4	2,643.0	2,842.3	2,960.1	3,097.3	0.98	47.98
Net migration ('000)	140.2	585.1	1,489.3	1,697.8	1,464.1	1,258.7	612.6	737.5	768.6	4.35	448.28

Source: *Euromonitor International from National Statistics*
Note: *Birth and death rates refer to the number per '000 population and fertility rates to the number of children born per female. Age at childbirth refers to average age of women in years.*

Growth of Urban Agglomerations

Chart 1.21 Major cities: 1980, 2000 and 2020

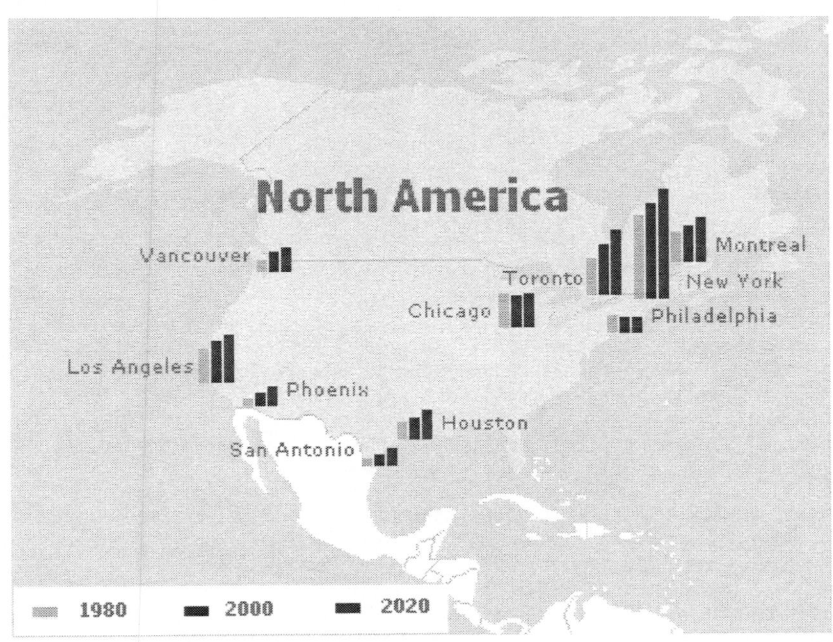

Source: *Euromonitor International from National Statistics*

North America is more sparsely settled than many other parts of the world. Population density is presently 18.6 people per square kilometre, up from 13.8 in 1980. Population density is forecast to rise to about 20.1 people per square kilometre by 2020.

In the USA a majority of the population lives on either the east or west coast but the population in parts of the Gulf coast is also growing rapidly. In the middle of the country, the population density is very low. Most of the country's major cities are also located on or near coastlines.

Like the USA, Canada has one of the lowest population densities in the world – currently just 3.7 people per square kilometre. Most Canadians live within 200 kilometres of the USA. For example, residents in any of the country's three largest cities — Toronto, Montreal and Vancouver — can drive to the American border in less than two hours. In the north, the Yukon Territory, the Northwest Territories and Nunavut are relatively empty, making up 41% of the country's land mass but only 0.3% of its population.

The region is highly urbanised with vast swathes of inland areas being sparsely populated. Currently, an estimated 82.0% of all residents live in urban areas compared with 73.5% in 1980. The urban share in total population will continue to rise in the future, approaching 85% by 2020.

In the USA, urban locales have been steadily expanding into surrounding rural areas since the 1980s. Many of those who are relocating are elderly. In 2000-2010, demographers calculate that 3 million people over the age of 65 will move from rural to urban areas. They are relocating in order to gain easier access to medical facilities, shopping alternatives and companionship.

In Canada, the distribution of population is also unusual owing to the fact that much of the north of the country can support little more than scattered, tiny communities. Canada's urban population is concentrated in just a few specific areas. They include the extended region of southern Ontario; along with Montreal and its environs; British Columbia's Lower Mainland and southern Vancouver Island; and the Calgary-Edmonton corridor. More than half of Canada's total population live in these regions.

Table 1.45 **Population of 10 Biggest Cities 1980-2020**

'000

	1980	1985	1990	1995	2000	2005	2010	2015	2020	CAGR %	Growth Period
New York	7,071.6	7,157.0	7,322.6	7,683.4	8,008.7	8,238.8	8,468.9	8,794.1	9,188.4	0.66	29.93
Toronto	3,136.9	3,334.2	3,576.3	3,846.3	4,290.0	4,683.4	5,000.3	5,285.6	5,563.3	1.44	77.35
Los Angeles	2,968.5	3,202.4	3,485.4	3,638.9	3,694.6	3,768.9	3,886.9	4,045.4	4,232.6	0.89	42.58
Montreal	2,618.2	2,762.9	2,903.5	2,973.5	3,130.3	3,286.1	3,445.1	3,618.4	3,799.7	0.94	45.13
Chicago	3,005.1	2,865.3	2,783.7	2,836.5	2,896.1	2,883.0	2,849.0	2,882.3	2,963.8	-0.03	-1.37
Houston	1,595.1	1,587.1	1,630.6	1,799.3	1,974.2	2,143.2	2,306.4	2,463.2	2,616.3	1.24	64.02
Vancouver	1,173.8	1,260.3	1,389.5	1,577.3	1,792.9	1,938.6	2,026.7	2,126.9	2,232.9	1.62	90.22
Phoenix	789.7	872.9	983.4	1,147.5	1,322.0	1,476.8	1,624.9	1,757.7	1,880.7	2.19	138.15
Philadelphia	1,688.2	1,634.8	1,585.6	1,558.2	1,517.6	1,473.2	1,439.6	1,445.7	1,479.7	-0.33	-12.35
San Antonio	785.9	854.5	935.9	1,045.5	1,160.0	1,276.4	1,398.5	1,509.4	1,612.9	1.81	105.22
TOTAL	24,833.1	25,531.4	26,596.4	28,106.6	29,786.3	31,168.3	32,446.1	33,928.7	35,570.3	0.90	43.24
% of total population	9.8	9.7	9.6	9.5	9.5	9.5	9.5	9.6	9.7	-0.04	-1.50

Source: *Euromonitor International from National Statistics*

MARKETING SEGMENTS

Children & Teenagers

Although the absolute number of members of this generation will rise by 14.2 million over the forty-year period, their share in the total will fall owing to population ageing. Children and teenagers made up 31.9% of total population in 1980 and their share will fall to 25.8% in 2020.

- Education in the USA is mandatory through the primary and secondary (high-school) level. In general, children are required to begin school during the year in which they turn 4 or 5 and attend until the age of 16 to 18, depending on the state;
- In Canada, education is compulsory from the age of six through sixteen years but students are discouraged from leaving school before the age of eighteen;
- Approximately 80% of teenagers hold jobs at some time during their secondary education. Entry into the labour market begins earlier in the USA than in Canada, with about half of youth ages 12 and 13 reporting that they work;
- Americans between 15 and 19 years accounted for 3.5% of gross national income in 1990 and in 2015 their share will be 5.8%. In Canada, teenagers claimed 2.6% of total gross income in 1990 and in 2015 their share will be 3.9%.

The earnings of children and teenagers are modest but they exert considerable influence over the discretionary income of their parents and thus represent a market which far exceeds their own income capabilities. Their purchases are greatly influenced by advertising.

Table 1.46 Children & Teenagers 1980-2020

'000

	1980	1985	1990	1995	2000	2005	2010	2015	2020	CAGR %	Growth Period
Babies/infants (0-2)	11,163	11,815	12,660	12,685	12,495	13,257	14,013	13,779	14,085	0.58	26.18
Female	5,452	5,767	6,182	6,188	6,101	6,473	6,845	6,735	6,886	0.59	26.31
Male	5,711	6,048	6,479	6,496	6,393	6,784	7,168	7,044	7,199	0.58	26.06
Kids (aged 3-8)	21,375	22,775	24,063	26,095	26,337	25,758	27,120	28,123	28,016	0.68	31.06
Female	10,439	11,121	11,746	12,740	12,855	12,589	13,255	13,751	13,704	0.68	31.29
Male	10,937	11,654	12,317	13,354	13,482	13,169	13,865	14,372	14,311	0.67	30.85
Tweenagers (9-12)	16,126	14,411	15,759	16,970	18,436	17,909	17,508	18,444	19,294	0.45	19.65
Female	7,881	7,030	7,683	8,274	8,992	8,736	8,556	9,018	9,438	0.45	19.75
Male	8,245	7,380	8,075	8,697	9,445	9,173	8,953	9,426	9,856	0.45	19.54
Teenagers (13-19)	31,783	28,782	27,106	28,849	31,251	32,546	32,265	31,629	33,293	0.12	4.75
Female	15,584	14,079	13,207	14,032	15,197	15,866	15,743	15,432	16,253	0.11	4.29
Male	16,199	14,703	13,900	14,816	16,054	16,680	16,522	16,197	17,040	0.13	5.19

Source: *Euromonitor International from National Statistics*

Young Adults

Young adults made up 32.3% of total population in 1980 and will account for 26.4% in 2020.

— The percentage of young adults who leave home before the age of 25 – either to live alone or with a partner – is much higher than in other industrialised regions of the world;

— The labour participation rate of young adult women has steadily risen over the past two decades. The educational advances of women are also much greater than those of men;

— A large number of young adults head their own households and they spend freely while saving comparatively little;

— In Canada, young adults claimed 43.3% of total gross income in 1990 and in 2015 their share will be 31.8%. Young American adults earned 46.4% of gross national income in 1990 and the share will fall to 34.3% by 2015. One reason for this is the falling share of young adults in total population. Another is the role of immigration for example, more than two-fifths of all Hispanics living in the USA are between 20 and 40 years and the majority work in menial jobs.

Young adults spend readily on entertainment and travel. The older members of this generation are easily attracted to the latest product novelties. Few have familial obligations, allowing them to spend freely on their careers, entertainment and travel.

Table 1.47 Young Adults 1980-2020

'000

	1980	1985	1990	1995	2000	2005	2010	2015	2020	CAGR %	Growth Period
Population aged 20-29	46,013	47,875	45,135	42,174	42,572	45,202	47,697	48,093	47,236	0.07	2.66
Female	22,909	23,799	22,309	20,827	20,919	22,044	23,222	23,585	23,226	0.03	1.38
Male	23,104	24,076	22,826	21,348	21,652	23,159	24,476	24,507	24,010	0.10	3.92
Population aged 30-39	35,554	41,868	46,754	50,059	48,138	45,457	45,337	47,493	49,548	0.83	39.36
Female	17,919	21,117	23,504	25,034	24,009	22,566	22,374	23,272	24,300	0.76	35.61
Male	17,635	20,751	23,250	25,026	24,129	22,890	22,963	24,221	25,248	0.90	43.17

Source: *Euromonitor International from National Statistics*

Middle-aged adults

Middle-agers made up 24.7% of the North American population in 1980 and will account for 31.4% in 2020.

— More than a quarter of all middle agers live in single-person households. This percentage has been rising for over two decades. Most of this increase is occurring among people between the ages of 45 and 64 – a trend driven by changes in the living habits of baby boomers;

— Three-quarters of middle-aged women who are married use some form of contraception;

— A majority of the older members of this generation have inadequate savings for retirement;

— American middle-agers controlled 42.1% of gross national income in 1990 and in 2015 their share will be 47.0%. In Canada, this generation accounted for 42.9% of total gross income in 1990 and will claim 50.9% of this total in 2015.

This generation spends a substantial portion of their discretionary income on entertainment, eating out and travel. They are more sophisticated than their predecessors and more likely to opt for luxury items. Many have already become home owners and own larger homes than in the past. They allocate a portion of their income to home furnishings and home maintenance. They are frequent purchasers of big-ticket items including cars and home appliances.

Table 1.48 Middle-aged Adults 1980-2020

'000

	1980	1985	1990	1995	2000	2005	2010	2015	2020	CAGR %	Growth Period
Population aged 40-64	62,215	65,175	71,476	81,469	94,703	106,766	113,894	115,344	115,299	1.55	85.32
Female	32,332	33,735	36,749	41,704	48,307	54,385	57,900	58,528	58,277	1.48	80.24
Male	29,883	31,441	34,727	39,765	46,395	52,380	55,994	56,816	57,022	1.63	90.82

Source: *Euromonitor International from National Statistic*

Older population

The ageing of the region's baby boomers will produce a large increase in the number of elderly over the next two decades. Those over 65 years made up 11.1% of total population in 1980 and by 2020 they will account for 16.4%. During this forty-year period, the population of elderly will more than double.

- Unlike younger generations, the elderly are still be a relatively homogeneous group made up predominately of a native-born populace;
- The elderly will account for around two-fifths of all those living alone in 2010. More than three-quarters of the elderly who live alone will be females;
- The labour force participation rate among the elderly has been edging upward for more than two decades;
- In Canada, the elderly accounted for 11.2% of total gross income in 1990 and in 2015 their share is forecast to rise to 13.4%. The American elderly accounted for 8.0% of gross national income in 1990 and in 2015 their share is forecast to be 12.9%. These increasing shares are primarily due to the larger number of elderly in total population and the greater number who are working.

Most of this generation are healthy and have accumulated ample amounts of wealth over their working life. They are frequent consumers of health products and are very health conscious about their diets. They enjoy travel and will usually have a number of hobbies. Manufacturers are adopting their products and marketing strategies to cater to this generation.

Table 1.49 Older Population 1980-2020

'000

	1980	1985	1990	1995	2000	2005	2010	2015	2020	CAGR %	Growth Period
Older generation (65+)	28,013	31,066	34,368	37,279	38,930	40,978	44,994	51,823	60,024	1.92	114.27
Female	16,657	18,558	20,496	22,062	22,825	23,744	25,686	29,078	33,323	1.75	100.05
Male	11,356	12,507	13,873	15,216	16,105	17,234	19,308	22,746	26,701	2.16	135.12

Source: *Euromonitor International from National Statistics*

WESTERN EUROPE

KEY POPULATION TRENDS

Total population

Chart 2.8 – known as a “heat chart”, found in section two *"Age structure of the population at a glance"* – depicts changes in the age structure in Western Europe over time. Each dot represents the number of people in a specific age group in a given year. Accordingly, a dark red dot represents the largest concentration of people, by age, in a particular year while deep blue dots show the lowest concentrations. A single dark red dot is the equivalent of slightly more than 26 million people while each deep blue dot represents almost 1.5 million people and other colour shadings correspond to intermediate population totals (each by age group).

A distinguishing feature of the chart is the band of bright red which descends diagonally from left to right. The band represents a population explosion during the 1960s and spanned about a ten-year period. In recent years the width of the band has widened as the population of baby boomers has been supplemented by an influx of immigrants. Today, most of these people are between 30 and 50 years old and many will be nearing retirement by 2020.

At the top of the chart the colouring gradually changes from bright green to paler shades, suggesting a gentle decline in the number of young people over time. At the bottom left-hand side of the chart there is also a large area of dark blue associated with the population of those 60 years and over. Gradually, this area of dark blue is replaced by lighter shades of blue and green, indicating that the population of elderly people is steadily increasing.

The total number of Western Europeans will be slowly increasing but at a decelerating pace. By 2020, the region will have just over half a billion people, a gain of almost 93 million over 40 years. The potential workforce (those between 15 and 64 years) will also increase by just over 66 million. These totals, however, conceal some divergent trends in different parts of the region. Countries such as Ireland, the Netherlands, Portugal, Spain, Sweden and the UK can expect steady but decelerating population gains, supported in part by migration inflows. However, a few others such as Germany and Italy will actually see their numbers decline over the next decade.

A much more widespread, and accelerating, phenomenon is the ageing of Western European society. Virtually all countries will see a steady rise in the median age. For the region as a whole, the median age will rise from 31.9 years in 1980 to 42.0 years by 2020. At that time Western Europe will have around 250 million people over the age of 42 and many of them will be retired. Western Europe will have over 10 million more people over 65 years in 2020 than there are children under the age of 15.

Although Western Europe’s demographic change is gradual, the cumulative effects will have a significant effect on the macroeconomic landscape.

- Western Europe is ageing much faster than other regions of the world. The long-term effect of this demographic shift will be to slow the pace of growth as the number of workers declines;
- The increasing number of older and elderly consumers will alter patterns of consumption. Spending on categories such as leisure, healthcare and consumer products aimed at older buyers should grow;

— The steadily increasing number of elderly will also put pressure on government budgets. A substantial rise in spending on pensions and health care is inevitable. This will force governments to introduce a variety of pension reforms, or pursue existing reform initiatives more aggressively. Examples include policies to encourage the continued employment of the elderly, greater reliance on private pensions rather than pay-as-you-go methods and more zealous efforts to close the loopholes governing early retirement.

Chart 1.22 Population Age Shift 2000 and 2020, Each Column Represents a Single Age Group

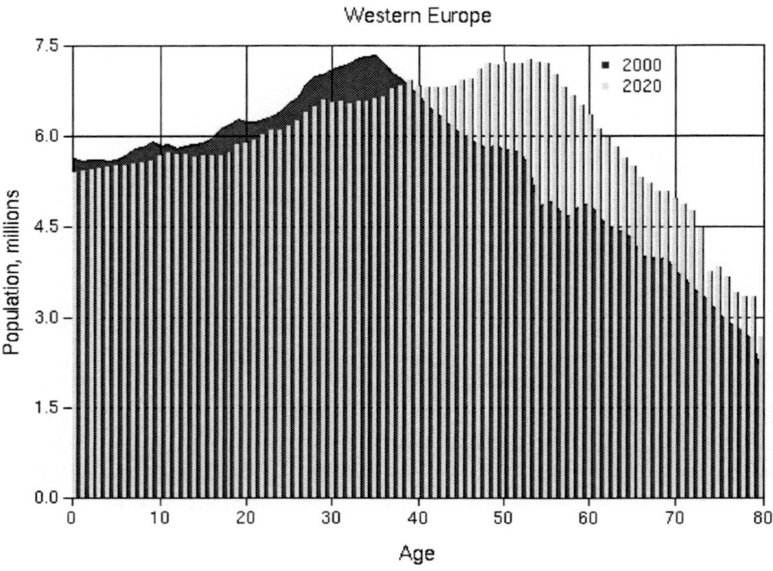

Source: Euromonitor International from National Statistics

Chart 1.22 documents changes in the region's age structure between 2000 and 2020. The area of bright red in the upper left-hand corner of the chart indicates those age groups where the population will decline between 2000 and 2020. The number of those between 0 and 38 years will fall from 246.3 million in 2000 to 231.8 million by 2020. Meanwhile, the population of those 39 and over will rise by 61.8 million.

The changing age structure will alter several key demographic indicators:

— The youth dependency ratio (the number of people 0-14 years relative to the number aged 15-64) will fall from 0.283 in 2000 to 0.254 in 2020;

— The elderly dependency ratio (the number of people over 65 years relative to the number aged 15-64) will jump from 0.220 in 2000 to 0.285 in 2020;

— The growing number of elderly will put pressure on government budgets. A substantial rise in spending on pensions and health care is inevitable. Some of the possible solutions– for example, increasing rates of taxation, reducing pension benefits or raising the retirement age – face considerable resistance, while the immigration of young workers may be politically unpopular in several countries. Increases in growth of productivity and policies to encourage more births will help to alleviate pressure but these can take decades to show results.

Chart 1.23 Population Pyramid

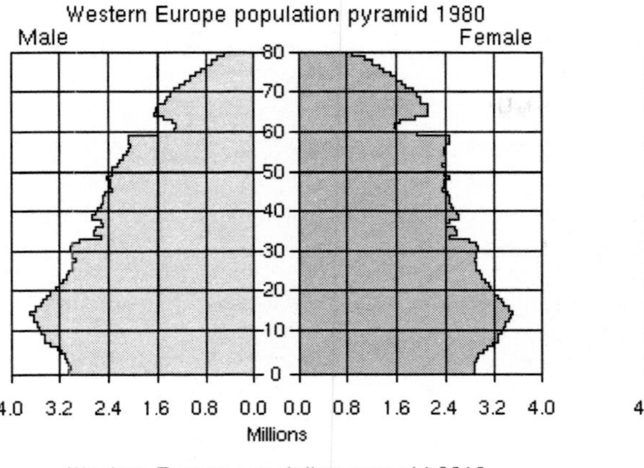

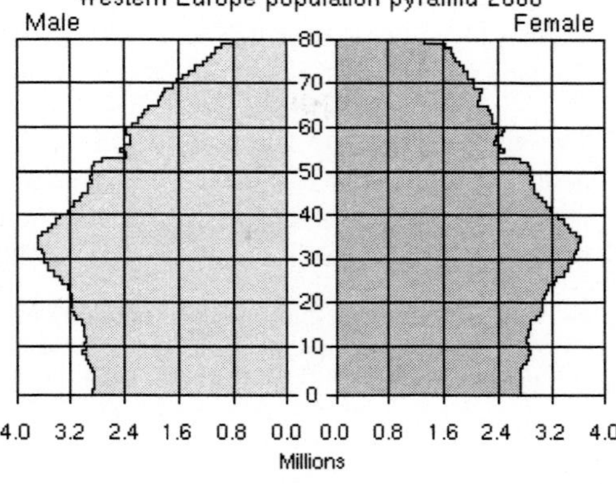

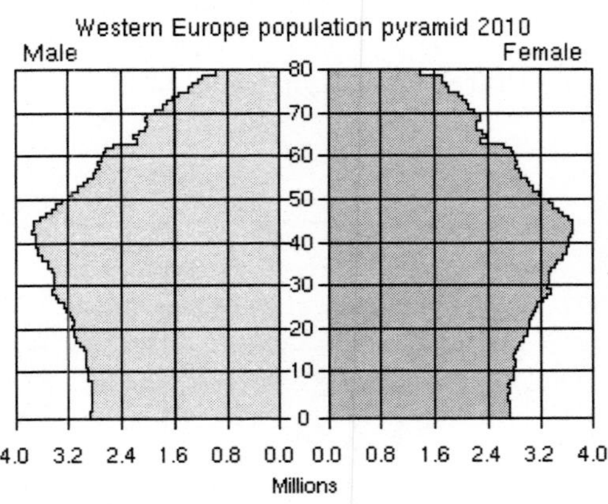

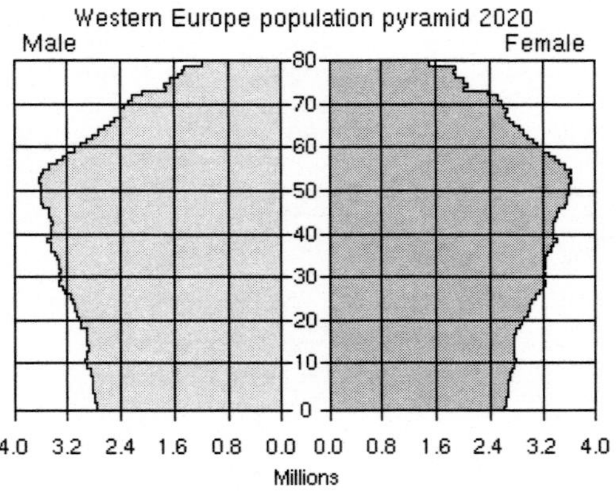

Source: *Euromonitor International from National Statistics*

Chart 1.23 consists of four population pyramids for selected years. The figure for 1980 bears a close resemblance to a typical pyramid, although the shrinking number of young children results in a somewhat narrower base. The effects of the population boom which occurred in the 1960s can also be noted. As this group ages the population bulge becomes more apparent in each subsequent graph.

The male population outnumbers that of females for all ages up to 54 years. Thereafter, the reverse is true. By 2020, the number of females 65 and over will exceed males by about 12.1%. Thus the pyramid is skewed slightly in favour of males in the younger age groups and substantially towards women in the older age groups. This gender difference is a long-standing one which is partly due to the longer life expectancy of females. The incidence of smoking is declining but is still somewhat higher among males (32.1% in 2008) than females (24.0%). Males also suffer more health problems from job-related illnesses and generally lead a less healthy lifestyle.

The figures in Table 1 provide more details on the demographic structure. The number of children between 0 and 9 years has been gently falling since 1980 and will reach an all-time low in 2020. A similar trend can be found among those between 10 and 19 years.

- Fertility rates in Western Europe have been falling since 1980, resulting in the steady decline in the number of young children and teenagers. Fertility rates are below the replacement level (2.1 children per woman) in all countries but inter-country differences are still large. Some of the lowest rates occur in Austria, Italy, Germany, Greece, Spain and a few other countries where fertility is expected to fall to alarmingly low levels. Turkey is the only country where fertility exceeds replacement but that will change in the next decade. In other countries (Ireland, France, the Netherlands, most of Scandinavia and the UK), fertility is already below replacement though not so low as to be viewed with serious concern;
- Although the variations in fertility are considerable, the reasons for the decline are similar throughout the region. They include: increased female participation in the labour force and widespread access to modern means of contraception and abortion;
- The shrinking population of young children has already prompted a number of governments to introduce a number of family-friendly policies such as tax breaks for parents, childcare alternatives and maternity and paternity benefits. These practices will become even more widely accepted in the future and will be supplemented by additional measures designed with the same purpose in mind.

The population of 20 to 29 year olds rose throughout the 1980s and reached an all-time high in 1993. The numbers have been dropping in the years since then and the downward trend will persist through 2020 when a new low is recorded. Among those in their thirties their number rose steadily until 2003 when a modern high was reached. The numbers have been dropping in more recent years and that trend will continue through 2020.

The number of Western European in their forties and fifties will follow similar trends over the 40-year period. The population of those in their forties will peak around 2013 while the number of 50-59 year olds will continue to rise through 2020. Among those 60 and over, the number will be continually rising between 1980 and 2020. The size of this group will almost double between 1980 and 2020.

— Western European countries are spending more on healthcare and employing significantly more resources in the health sector. One result is an increase in life expectancy which has been steadily rising and presently stands at 79.7 years for the total population. By 2020, life expectancy at birth is expected to reach 79.0 years for males and 84.2 years for females;

— The healthy life expectancy of Western Europeans is also rising and in 2007 stood at 17.4 years for 60-year-old males and 20.1 years for females;

— As the population ages, the significance of intergenerational transfers (including material support, emotional and practical support and the sharing of skills) become more important. The increasing co-survival of parents and children means that inter-vivos financial transfers have become much more common.

Table 1.50 **Key Population Trends 1980-2020**

'000

	1980	1985	1990	1995	2000	2005	2010	2015	2020	CAGR %	Growth Period
Total	410,250	419,983	431,332	444,772	455,681	470,903	484,025	494,315	502,938	0.51	22.59
Male	200,213	204,977	210,919	217,904	223,440	231,396	238,244	243,603	248,057	0.54	23.90
Female	210,037	215,006	220,413	226,868	232,240	239,507	245,781	250,713	254,882	0.48	21.35
0-4 yrs	29,888	29,003	28,331	28,554	27,973	27,716	27,650	27,339	26,975	-0.26	-9.75
5-9 yrs	32,539	30,038	29,431	28,749	28,765	28,314	28,064	27,947	27,623	-0.41	-15.11
10-14 yrs	34,891	32,777	30,472	29,978	29,150	29,192	28,701	28,392	28,265	-0.53	-18.99
15-19 yrs	34,620	35,086	33,155	30,980	30,391	29,800	29,677	29,117	28,789	-0.46	-16.84
20-24 yrs	31,622	34,619	35,226	33,642	31,471	31,520	30,647	30,354	29,773	-0.15	-5.85
25-29 yrs	29,636	31,428	34,692	35,775	34,028	32,886	32,719	31,557	31,242	0.13	5.42
30-34 yrs	28,478	29,491	31,620	35,207	36,028	35,122	33,822	33,428	32,247	0.31	13.23
35-39 yrs	25,558	28,185	29,561	31,961	35,284	36,723	35,623	34,181	33,779	0.70	32.17
40-44 yrs	25,247	25,200	28,133	29,644	31,915	35,614	36,925	35,723	34,278	0.77	35.77
45-49 yrs	23,931	24,901	25,011	27,949	29,414	31,946	35,543	36,786	35,593	1.00	48.73
50-54 yrs	23,237	23,368	24,491	24,669	27,486	29,135	31,644	35,160	36,407	1.13	56.68
55-59 yrs	22,428	22,402	22,667	23,887	24,035	26,934	28,579	31,038	34,524	1.08	53.93
60-64 yrs	15,689	21,140	21,267	21,668	22,901	23,171	26,085	27,686	30,119	1.64	91.98
65-69 yrs	18,124	14,259	19,441	19,700	20,211	21,584	21,950	24,820	26,392	0.94	45.62
70-74 yrs	14,962	15,604	12,409	17,184	17,557	18,284	19,701	20,153	22,976	1.08	53.56
75-79 yrs	10,457	11,614	12,476	10,121	14,264	14,809	15,651	17,224	17,720	1.33	69.46
80+ yrs	8,828	10,742	12,837	14,983	14,683	18,014	20,868	23,232	26,055	2.74	195.14
Median age	32	33	34	36	37	38	40	41	42	0.69	31.52

Source: *Euromonitor International from National Statistics*

Vital statistics

Both the number of live births and birth rates has been falling since 1980 and the downward trend will continue through 2020 when modern-day lows are recorded. Fertility was at a high in 1980 (2.0 births per female) but has been dropping over the years. A low was recorded in 2002 (1.6 births per female) but it appears to have stabilised in recent years. No changes in fertility are expected between now and 2020. Trends in individual countries are becoming increasingly divergent with the Dutch, Danes and French experiencing moderate gains (although rates are still less than replacement) while southern European countries report very low rates.

— The number of women having a second child fell steadily during the 1980s and 1990s. However, surveys conducted during the present decade show that the number of women who wish to have a second child have now stabilised;

— Demographic researchers believe that the most important factor leading to a fall in fertility is the growing preference of would-be mothers to postpone birth of the first child;

— Low rates of fertility are associated with high rates of unemployment in those countries where fertility declines have been sharpest;

— The number of women of childbearing age (15 to 49 years) will fall by nearly 2 million between 2000 and 2020. This development, in addition to a long-term decline in marriage rates and a gradual rise in divorce rates, contributes to the decline in births and birth rates;

— In most of Western Europe there has been a large difference in the fertility rates of the educated and the relatively uneducated, with the latter generally being significantly higher. Over time, however, this gap is being reduced.

Both the age at first childbirth and the age at childbirth have been rising and the upward trend will continue for the foreseeable future. In addition, the difference between the two indicators is narrowing over time and by 2020 will amount to just 1.5 years. This trend strongly suggests that the number of children born to each female is declining over time. The growing practice of postponing motherhood coincides with the tendency to delay marriage. Between 1980 and 2020 the average age of women at first marriage will increase by 6.1 years.

Death rates were at a high in 1980 and fell in subsequent years. This indicator recorded an all time low in 2007 and will edge upwards in the future. The number of deaths has fluctuated over time, hitting a low in 2004. Since then, there has been a gradual rise and a new high will be reached in 2020.

— The primary causes of death among the middle aged and elderly are cancer and heart and vascular disorders;

— Western European society has become much healthier over time and healthcare systems are being improved. By 2020, life expectancy at birth is projected to be 81.6 years, an increase of 8.3 years compared to 1980.

Natural changes in population (defined as the number of births less the number of deaths) have consistently been positive. Net additions to population were at a high in 1980 (nearly 2.0 million) and have been slowly falling over time. The downward trend will continue in the future and a new low will be recorded in 2020 of around 840,000.

Net migration has been volatile but positive in most years. A net outflow was recorded in the early 1980s but the numbers soon turned positive and have remained so in later years. A high of almost 1.6 million net immigrants was reported in 2002 but by 2008 the annual net inflow was down to around 900,000. The numbers will drop in the future but Western Europe will still be attracting more than 700,000 net immigrants per year through 2020.

The region has long been a favoured destination for migrants from Central and Eastern Europe and other nearby countries. The post-war economic boom led several countries (notably Austria and Germany) to negotiate bilateral agreements with Turkey and the former Yugoslavia to recruit temporary "guest workers". Hundreds of thousands of migrant workers entered Western Europe during the 1970s and early 1980s. Most were later forced to return to their home countries but some stayed on and their numbers later grew through family reunification policies.

In the 1990s, migration was driven largely by the break-up of the former Soviet Union and the subsequent reunification of Germany. Western Europe's attractiveness as a destination for migrants was further enhanced as the EU expanded its membership to include a number of Central European and Baltic States. Migration from Bulgaria, Poland and Romania reached a peak in the early years of this decade.

Most of these people come to the region in search of better jobs and higher standards of living, though many have also fled from political repression, and civil disruptions in the Balkans and other parts of Eastern Europe. There is general agreement that the broad economic consequences of immigration are positive but the social and emotional issues are much disputed. Immigrants enter the work force, earn and spend wages, pay taxes and use public services. However, their participation slows the growth, or even depresses wages, and boosts profits and the distributional issues are awkward. The unemployed and poorly-educated have to compete directly with immigrants in many unskilled job markets and their earnings probably suffer. Poorly-educated immigrants may also consume more in public services than they produce in their employment.

— Studies of employment trends in Germany and other Western European countries indicate that, on average, a 10% increase in the immigrant share of the workforce results in a 1% decline in the wages of native workers. However, the effects on unskilled and older native workers are somewhat greater;

— The earnings of immigrants are significantly less than those of native workers holding comparable jobs. However, the problems faced by immigrant workers are several. Many do not speak the local language well. Only a small proportion of immigrant children enter a pre-university curriculum and unemployment among foreign-born residents is generally higher than for locals;

- The average age of immigrants tends to be significantly lower than the average age of local workers. Thus, immigration alters the age composition of the work force in a favourable manner;
- Between 2008 and 2020, the net inflow of migrants is forecast to total over 9.7 million. In comparison, net migration in 1980-2007 was around 24.5 million.

Table 1.51 Vital statistics 1980-2020
'000

	1980	1985	1990	1995	2000	2005	2010	2015	2020	CAGR %	Growth Period
Birth rates	15.2	14.0	13.8	12.7	12.5	11.9	11.5	11.1	10.8	-0.86	-29.12
Live births ('000)	6,226.4	5,862.3	5,942.1	5,641.0	5,707.8	5,589.4	5,566.0	5,490.9	5,410.6	-0.35	-13.10
Fertility rates	2.0	1.8	1.8	1.7	1.7	1.7	1.7	1.7	1.6	-0.53	-19.02
Age at first childbirth	24.6	25.4	26.1	27.0	27.6	28.2	28.6	29.0	29.1	0.42	18.28
Age at childbirth	27.3	27.8	28.3	28.9	29.3	29.8	30.1	30.4	30.6	0.28	11.95
Death rates	10.4	10.2	9.8	9.6	9.3	8.9	8.8	8.9	9.1	-0.34	-12.82
Deaths ('000)	4,274.7	4,303.5	4,246.3	4,287.8	4,259.4	4,192.2	4,274.4	4,412.8	4,568.6	0.17	6.88
Net migration ('000)	718.8	269.2	1,193.0	863.6	1,270.1	1,316.5	767.9	717.9	723.5	0.02	0.66

Source: Euromonitor International from National Statistics
Note: Birth and death rates refer to the number per '000 population and fertility rates to the number of children born per female. Age at childbirth refers to average age of women in years.

Growth of Urban Agglomerations

Chart 1.24 Major cities: 1980, 2000 and 2020

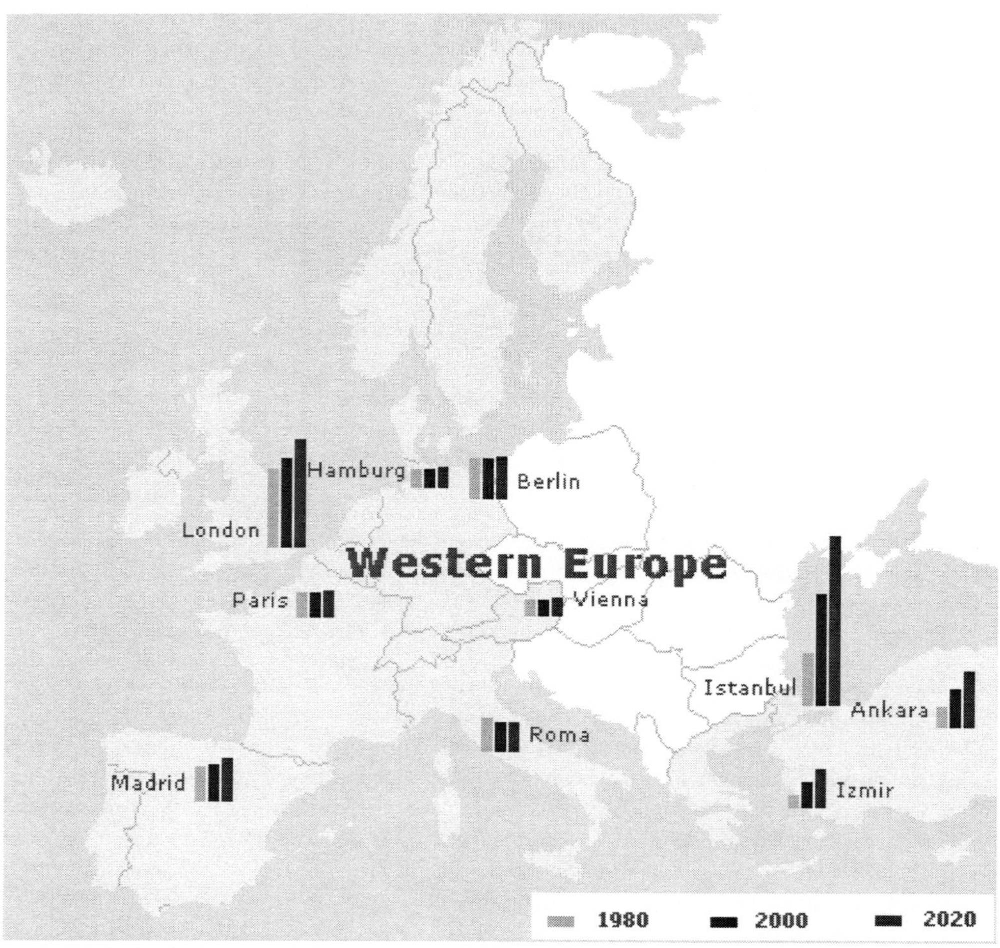

Source: Euromonitor International from National Statistics

Western Europe's population density has been steadily rising since 1980 and presently stands at about 110 people per square kilometre. The upward trend will continue in the future and by 2020 the density will be nearly 116 people per square kilometre. Most of the southern and central parts of the region are densely populated; although, concentrations are much lower in the mountainous areas surrounding the Alps and in central and northern Scandinavia.

Most of the region is highly urbanised. In 1980, 71.6% of the population lived in urban areas and today the figure is 77.3%. The share will slowly rise in the future and by 2020 approximately 80.0% of all Western Europeans will be living in urban areas. Because a majority of the countries are mature economies with very small agricultural sectors, there is only a trickle of rural-to-urban migration. Turkey, with its high rates of migration, is an exception.

Istanbul became Western Europe's largest city in 1990 and is the region's fastest-growing major city over the four-decade period. Istanbul is Turkey's financial and industrial capital, accounting for more than half the country's trade and over a fifth of its GDP. The city employs approximately 20% of Turkey's industrial work force and generates more than a fifth of the country's gross national product. Food processing, textile production, oil products, rubber, metal ware, leather, chemicals, pharmaceuticals, electronics, glass, machinery, automotives, transport vehicles, paper and paper products, and alcoholic drinks are among the city's major industries.

London, Western Europe's second largest city, is slowly growing. It is one of the world's leading business and financial centres and exerts considerable influence on world entertainment, media and fashion. London is also one of the most popular tourist destinations in the world, and its popularity has increased over time. London is home to a wide range of people, cultures, religions, and over 300 different languages. It generates about 20% of the country's GDP. More than half of the UK's top 100 listed companies and over a fifth of Europe's 500 largest companies base their headquarters there.

Ankara, the capital of Turkey, is the region's third largest city and, like Istanbul, is growing rapidly. Ankara is an important commercial and industrial city and a crossroads for trade. It also serves as the marketing centre for the surrounding agricultural area. Rural-to-urban migration is the main reason for the rapid growth of both Istanbul and Ankara. Manufacturing and services are the only activities where new jobs are being generated and they are clustered in and around these two cities.

Bursa, another Turkish city, is the fastest-growing of all Western Europe's major metropolises. Bursa is the centre of the country's automobile industry. The textile and food industry are also prominent. The city is surrounded by a fertile plain and was once an agricultural leader though increased industrialisation has reduced the area of farm land. A steady rise in the inflow of FDI continues to attract more industry and additional workers to the city.

Table 1.52 **Population of 10 biggest cities 1980-2020**

'000

	1980	1985	1990	1995	2000	2005	2010	2015	2020	CAGR %	Growth Period
Istanbul	4,301.0	5,531.7	6,702.6	7,899.7	9,015.9	9,909.1	10,833.8	11,713.7	12,548.7	2.71	191.76
London	6,502.8	6,578.4	6,613.8	6,821.7	7,100.4	7,371.7	7,689.8	7,998.7	8,309.5	0.61	27.78
Ankara	1,916.2	2,406.6	2,804.6	3,131.0	3,513.4	3,895.0	4,285.0	4,657.2	5,008.6	2.43	161.38
Madrid	2,864.1	3,039.1	3,120.7	3,041.0	2,905.8	3,367.6	3,797.3	4,105.7	4,376.8	1.07	52.82
Berlin	3,184.5	3,231.3	3,350.9	3,468.4	3,396.6	3,379.4	3,360.9	3,343.0	3,317.8	0.10	4.19
Izmir	1,416.4	1,792.2	2,113.4	2,399.2	2,711.7	3,005.6	3,306.4	3,595.1	3,866.7	2.54	173.01
Roma	2,835.7	2,840.7	2,790.8	2,687.7	2,566.1	2,547.7	2,523.6	2,502.8	2,489.1	-0.33	-12.22
Paris	2,179.9	2,167.5	2,152.4	2,137.7	2,128.9	2,162.0	2,209.7	2,266.2	2,330.9	0.17	6.93
Bursa	714.8	927.9	1,139.9	1,369.0	1,618.4	1,842.4	2,063.9	2,271.5	2,463.3	3.14	244.59
Barcelona	1,639.4	1,696.0	1,707.3	1,620.6	1,508.2	1,717.4	1,942.3	2,102.9	2,243.9	0.79	36.87
TOTAL	27,554.8	30,211.3	32,496.4	34,576.1	36,465.4	39,198.1	42,012.7	44,556.8	46,955.3	1.34	70.41
% of total population	6.7	7.2	7.5	7.8	8.0	8.3	8.7	9.0	9.3	0.83	39.00

Source: *Euromonitor International from National Statistics*

MARKETING SEGMENTS

Children & teenagers

The number of children and teenagers in Western Europe will decline throughout the four-decade period between 1980 and 2020. In 1980, this group made up 32.2% of total population and in 2020 its share will be 22.2%.

— A larger number of young women complete secondary and post-secondary (non-tertiary) education than men even though their share in total population is slightly smaller. In addition, more young men fail to obtain adequate educational qualifications than women;

— An increasing number of newborns are born to couples out of wedlock. The percentage has been steadily rising for more than a decade. Analysts attribute this trend to disaffection with marriage, though not towards partnerships in general. Most births outside marriage are to couples in a stable union;

— Although there have been significant gains in tertiary education, a large proportion of young people still do not complete secondary education. As a result, they face considerable penalties in the labour market;

— In 1990, teenagers between 15 and 19 years accounted for 5.1% of total gross income and in 2015 their share will still be 4.8%.

Most families spend lavishly on their young children and demand high-quality products. Teenagers have only modest amounts of earned income but are generously supported by their parents. They are avid consumers of electronic products, mobile phones and other products aimed at the younger generation.

Table 1.53 **Children & teenagers 1980-2020**

'000

	1980	1985	1990	1995	2000	2005	2010	2015	2020	CAGR %	Growth Period
Babies/infants (0-2)	17,807	17,153	17,060	17,036	16,793	16,557	16,546	16,360	16,093	-0.25	-9.63
Female	8,665	8,350	8,316	8,312	8,192	8,073	8,064	7,973	7,843	-0.25	-9.48
Male	9,142	8,803	8,744	8,725	8,601	8,484	8,482	8,387	8,249	-0.26	-9.77
Kids (aged 3-8)	37,900	35,767	34,613	34,499	34,042	33,809	33,444	33,292	32,936	-0.35	-13.10
Female	18,468	17,432	16,877	16,827	16,616	16,505	16,312	16,227	16,053	-0.35	-13.08
Male	19,432	18,336	17,736	17,673	17,426	17,304	17,132	17,066	16,884	-0.35	-13.12
Tweenagers (9-12)	27,428	25,363	24,228	23,438	23,371	22,935	22,910	22,561	22,445	-0.50	-18.17
Female	13,384	12,372	11,811	11,426	11,394	11,196	11,183	10,999	10,936	-0.50	-18.29
Male	14,044	12,991	12,418	12,013	11,976	11,739	11,727	11,562	11,510	-0.50	-18.05
Teenagers (13-19)	48,803	48,620	45,480	43,280	42,065	41,712	41,192	40,581	40,177	-0.49	-17.67
Female	23,863	23,769	22,207	21,131	20,528	20,334	20,105	19,808	19,592	-0.49	-17.90
Male	24,940	24,851	23,273	22,148	21,537	21,378	21,088	20,773	20,585	-0.48	-17.46

Source: *Euromonitor International from National Statistics*

Young adults

The population of young adults rose throughout the 1980s and most of the 1990s, reaching an all-time high in 1997. Since then, the numbers have been dropping and the downward trend will continue through 2020. In 1980, this generation made up 28.1% of total population and in 2020 it will account for 25.3%.

— The number of women obtaining a university education is greater than the number of men but the reverse applies in the case of post-graduate degrees;

— The age at which young people leave the family home and start living independently varies widely across the region. In all countries, however, young women leave home at an earlier age than young men. Among the EU member states in Western Europe, more than two-thirds of all young women between the ages of 18 and 24 still live at home while the figure for young men is more than three-quarters;

— The proportion of young people engaged in some form of employment while studying varies widely across the region. It is highest in countries where dual-system apprenticeship programmes are common (Germany, Austria and Denmark) and in other countries such as, the Netherlands and the UK;

— A majority of those who leave home between 18 and 24 years are either living as a couple or as part of a larger household;

— In southern Europe, more than half of all young men live in the parental home throughout their twenties. In Scandinavia, the tendency is for young men to leave home at a much earlier age;

— According to time-use studies conducted in 1998-2004, women between the ages of 15 and 24 spend more than one hour per day on personal care and related activities;

— Young adults claimed 37.5% of total gross income in 1990 and in 2015 their share will be 30.3%.

Young adults who hold white-collar jobs represent an important target market. Many young couples (either married or cohabitating) both hold jobs and have no children or only one child. They are avid travellers and ready consumers of time-saving products, leisure products, entertainment, transportation and clothing.

Table 1.54 **Young adults 1980-2020**

'000

	1980	1985	1990	1995	2000	2005	2010	2015	2020	CAGR %	Growth Period
Population aged 20-29	61,258	66,047	69,913	69,411	65,494	64,401	63,366	61,911	61,014	-0.01	-0.40
Female	30,117	32,538	34,471	34,185	32,295	31,688	31,139	30,383	29,953	-0.01	-0.54
Male	31,141	33,509	35,442	35,226	33,200	32,713	32,228	31,528	31,061	-0.01	-0.26
Population aged 30-39	54,036	57,677	61,176	67,163	71,306	71,839	69,445	67,609	66,026	0.50	22.19
Female	26,643	28,517	30,299	33,243	35,351	35,549	34,309	33,349	32,507	0.50	22.01
Male	27,394	29,160	30,877	33,920	35,955	36,290	35,136	34,260	33,519	0.51	22.36

Source: *Euromonitor International from National Statistics*

Middle-aged adults

The number of middle agers has been rising steadily since 1980 and the upward trend will continue for the foreseeable future. In 1980, this generation represented 26.9% of the total and in 2020 they will account for 34.0%.

— Middle-aged workers in Western Europe tend to work fewer hours than in other parts of the industrialised world. However, they are relatively well equipped with capital and their overall efficiency is comparable to that of other developed regions, in part because these workers are skilled. As a result, labour productivity in most of Western Europe is high;

— Among the working population, a much larger proportion of women than men are employed in services. Retailing, health care, social work and education are the main employers. This pattern prevails throughout Western Europe;

— An estimated 11% of women under the age of 60 live in jobless households while the figure for men is 9%. Almost half the women living alone have at least one child;

— Only 65% of those between 55 and 59 years are still employed and the percentage falls sharply among those between 60 and 64 years;

— Surveys conducted in a number of Western European countries reveal that a majority of those between the ages of 50 and 59 have at least one living parent. In Scandinavia, 56% of women in their fifties have living parents;

— The percentage of women who live alone ranges from 20-21% in the UK, Finland and Germany down to 6% in Spain;

— Middle-agers accounted for 42.4% of total gross income in 1990 and will claim 45.6% of this total in 2015.

Middle agers, especially the baby boomers, have accumulated considerable wealth and are relatively high-income earners. They earn good wages and control a significant portion of gross income. However, their patterns of consumption differ somewhat from their counterparts in other parts of the industrialised world owing to the greater amount of leisure time which is available to them. With high levels of discretionary income and ample free time, middle agers are ready consumers of leisure products, luxury goods and household products.

Table 1.55 **Middle-aged adults 1980-2020**

'000

	1980	1985	1990	1995	2000	2005	2010	2015	2020	CAGR %	Growth Period
Population aged 40-64	110,532	117,010	121,561	127,808	135,741	146,787	158,775	166,392	170,922	1.10	54.64
Female	57,114	60,021	61,520	64,390	68,316	73,825	79,790	83,555	85,688	1.02	50.03
Male	53,418	56,989	60,041	63,418	67,425	72,962	78,985	82,838	85,234	1.17	59.56

Source: *Euromonitor International from National Statistics*

Older population

The elderly population declined briefly, hitting a low in 1984. Their numbers have been increasing since then and that trend is expected to climb through 2020. In 1980, this generation made up 12.8% of total population and in 2020 they will account for 18.5%.

— Co-longevity is increasing the duration of family ties. A substantial number of Western Europeans in their sixties still have living parents. The proportion is highest in France where 23% of those over 60 years have at least one living parent. The figure is almost as high in Greece, Norway, Sweden and Switzerland. Beyond the age of 70, the proportion drops to less than 5% in most countries but is still 8% in Italy and 7% in France;

- Economists predict that total age-related expenditures (that is, pensions, health care and income support) could rise relative to GDP by an average of more than seven percentage points during the first half of this century. The result will be much lower national surpluses or higher fiscal deficits;
- An estimated 22% of the elderly share a home with one of their children or a friend;
- The probability that people over 65 remain in employment is greatest among those having a tertiary education. An estimated 19% of this group are still employed;
- Retired males spend roughly the same amount of time shopping as females but men spend more time on leisure activities than women;
- During this decade, spending on old age and survivors' benefits is rising in Western Europe in real terms by 2% per year;
- In 1990, the elderly accounted for 14.9% of total gross income and in 2015 their share is forecast to be 19.3%.

The elderly are increasingly active and relatively healthy. Most own property and have few financial obligations to their offspring. A growing number will remain in the work force as pension reforms take effect. In general, this group has ample amounts of discretionary income to spend on themselves. They tend to be significant consumers of tourism, sports and wellness products.

Table 1.56 Older population 1980-2020
'000

	1980	1985	1990	1995	2000	2005	2010	2015	2020	CAGR %	Growth Period
Older generation (65+)	52,371	52,220	57,161	61,984	66,712	72,689	78,169	85,428	93,143	1.45	77.85
Female	31,728	31,946	34,842	37,280	39,471	42,251	44,792	48,330	52,220	1.25	64.58
Male	20,643	20,274	22,318	24,705	27,241	30,437	33,378	37,100	40,925	1.73	98.25

Source: *Euromonitor International from National Statistics*

12345

SECTION TWO

Age Structure of the Population at a Glance

World

Chart 2.1 *Age structure of the population at a glance, each dot represents a single age group*

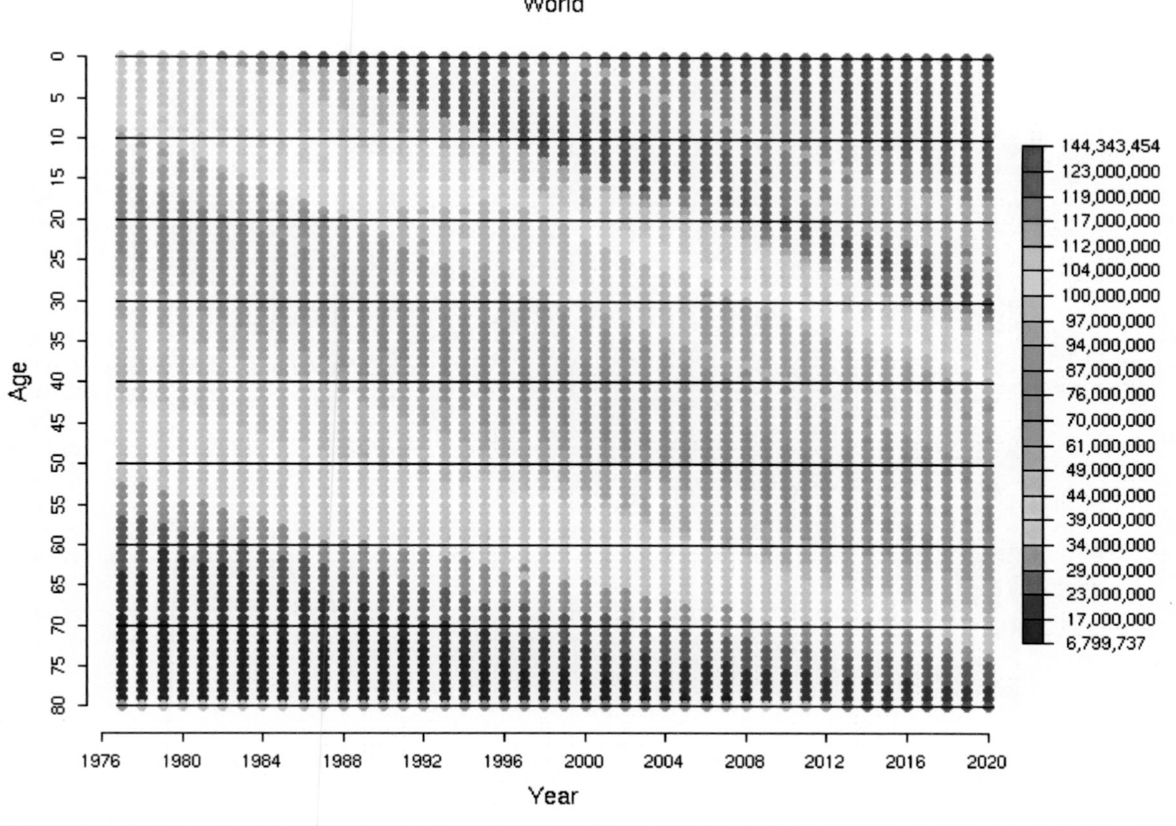

Asia Pacific

Chart 2.2 *Age structure of the population at a glance, each dot represents a single age group*

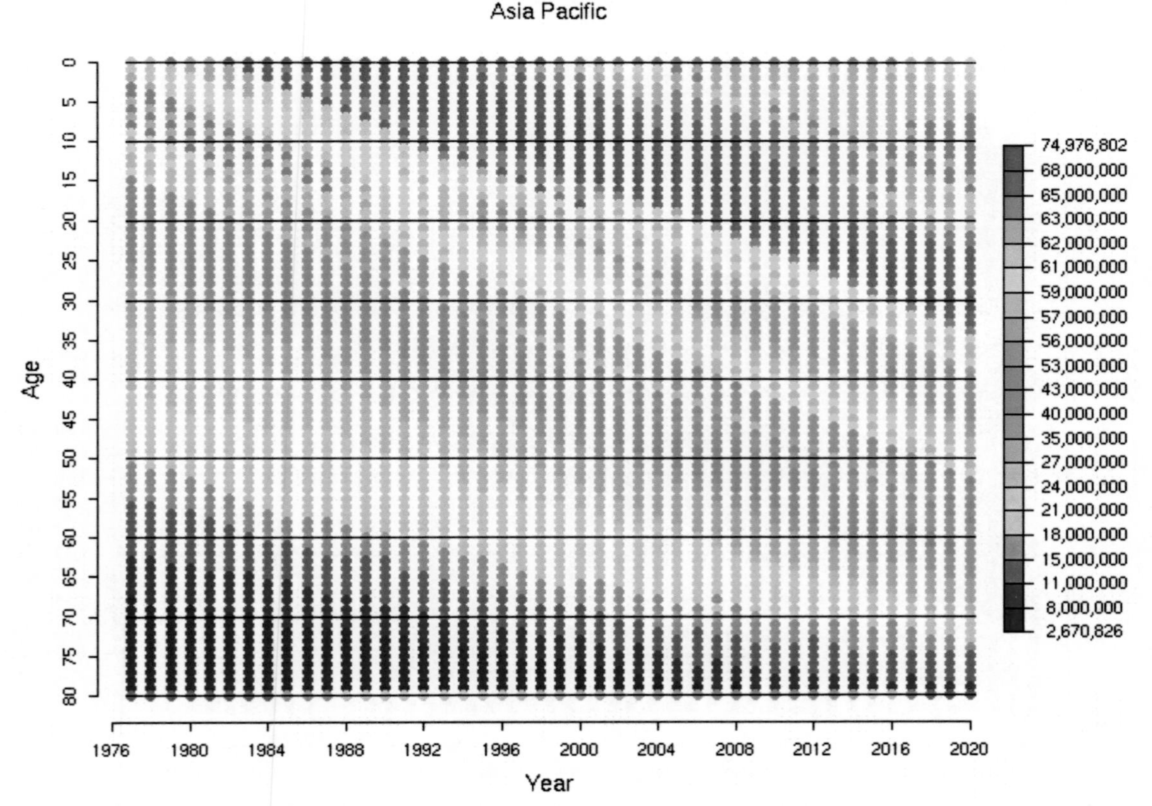

Australasia

Chart 2.3 *Age structure of the population at a glance, each dot represents a single age group*

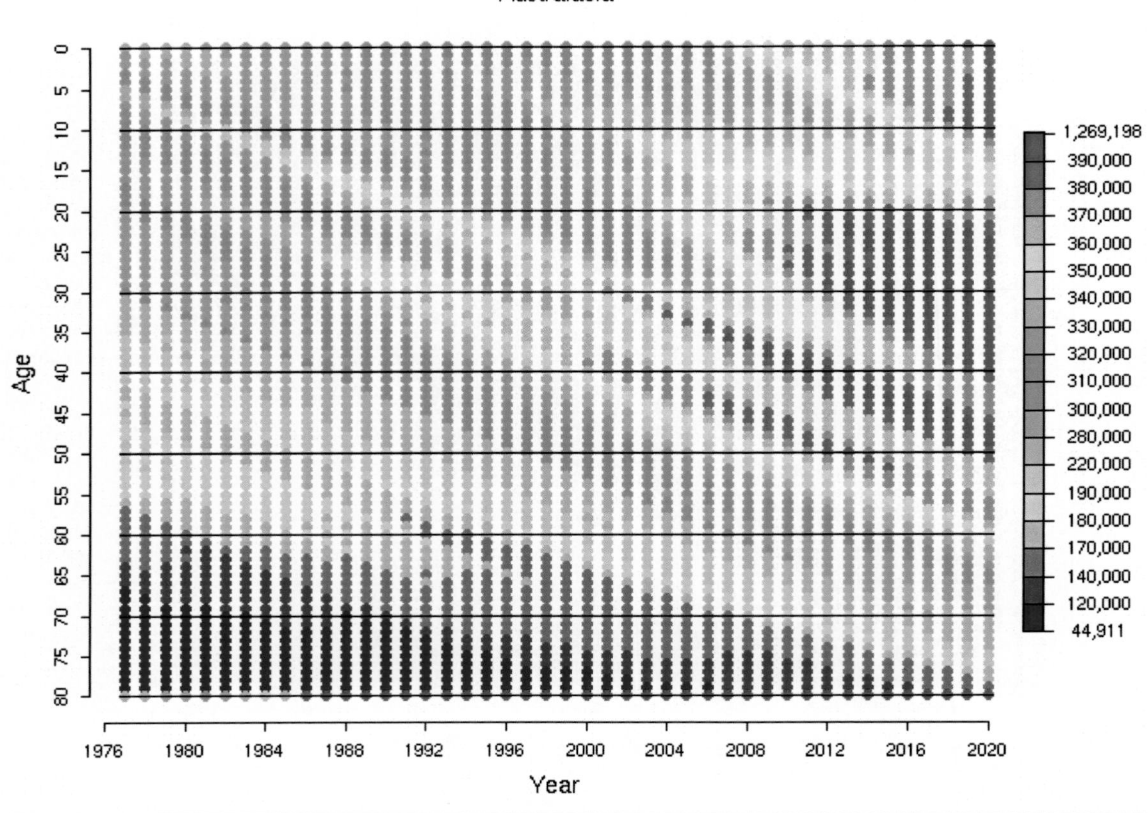

Eastern Europe

Chart 2.4 *Age structure of the population at a glance, each dot represents a single age group*

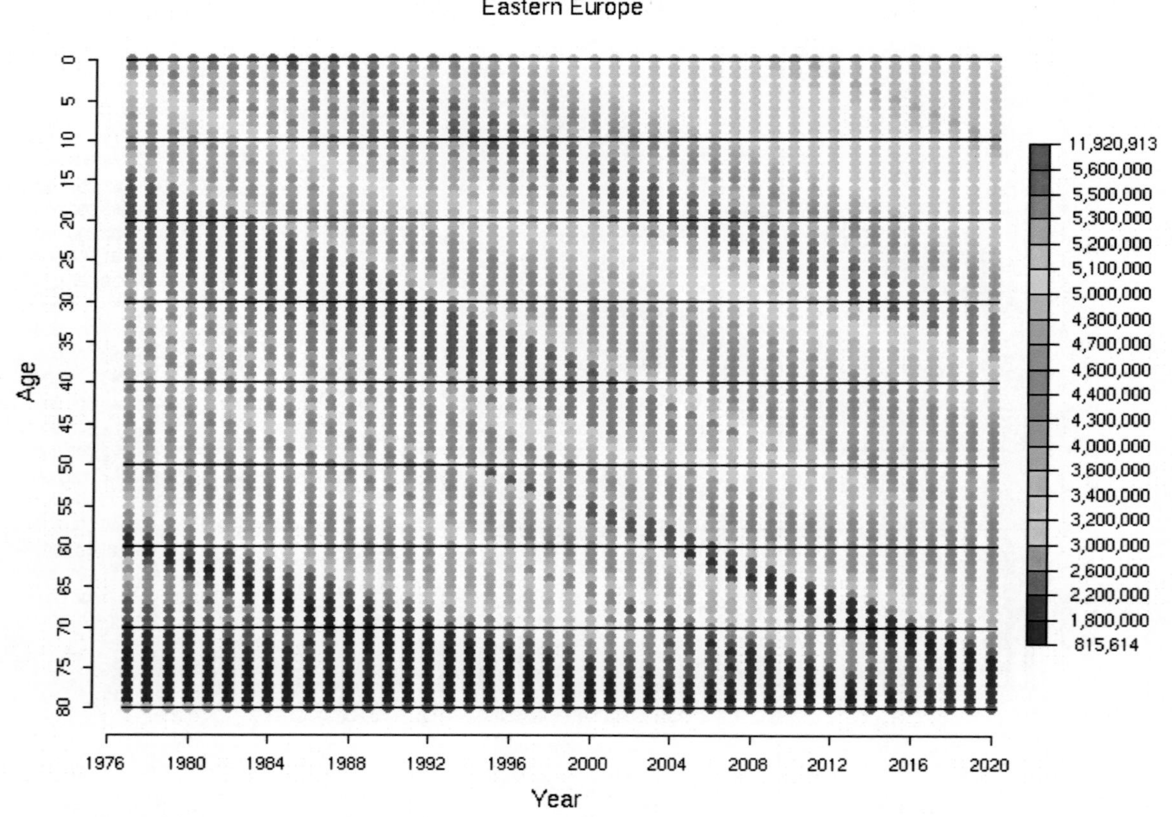

Latin America

Chart 2.5 *Age structure of the population at a glance, each dot represents a single age group*

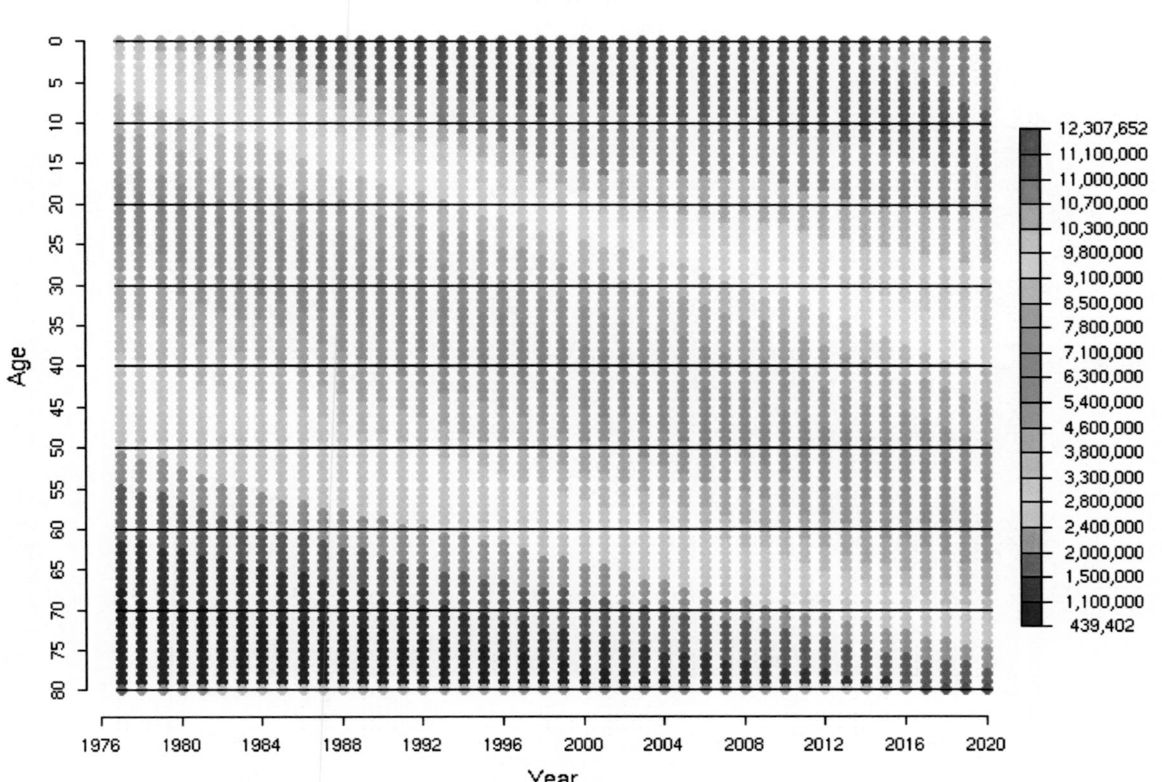

Middle East and Africa

Chart 2.6 *Age structure of the population at a glance, each dot represents a single age group*

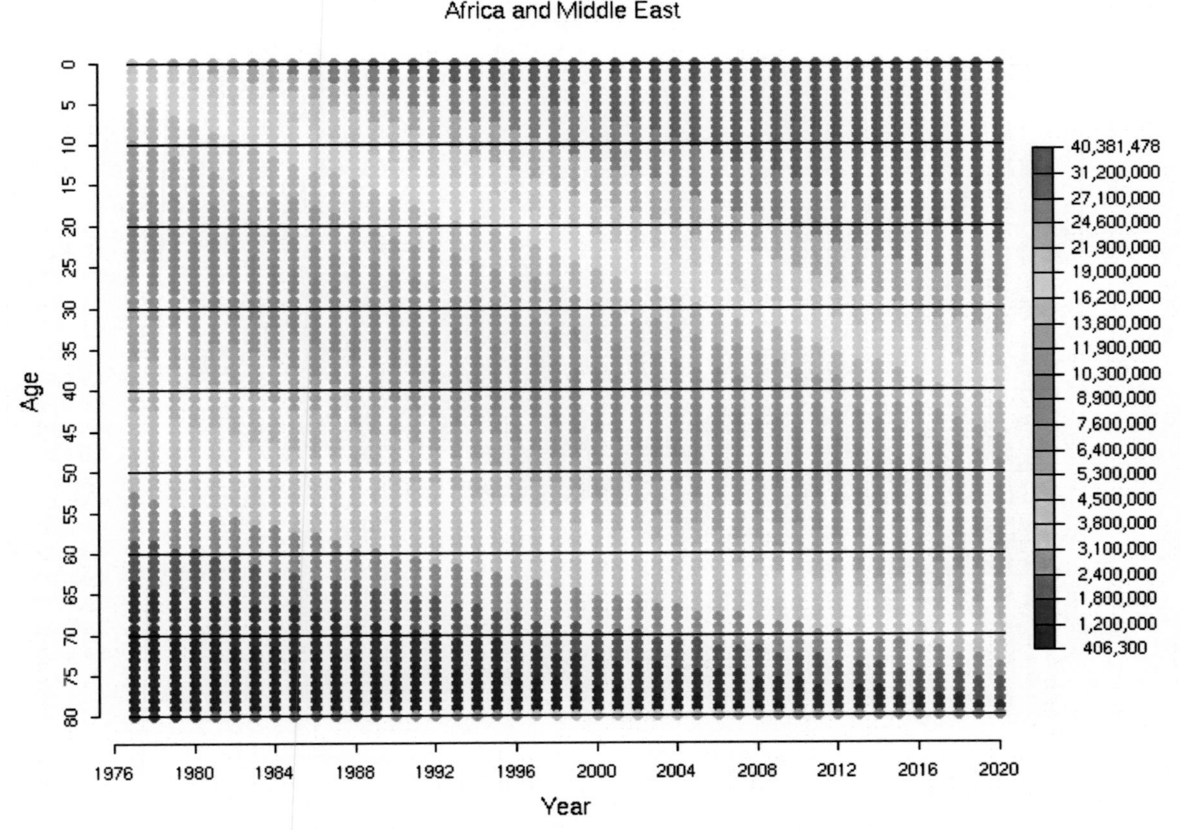

North America

Chart 2.7 *Age structure of the population at a glance, each dot represents a single age group*

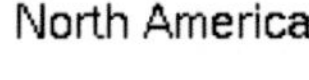

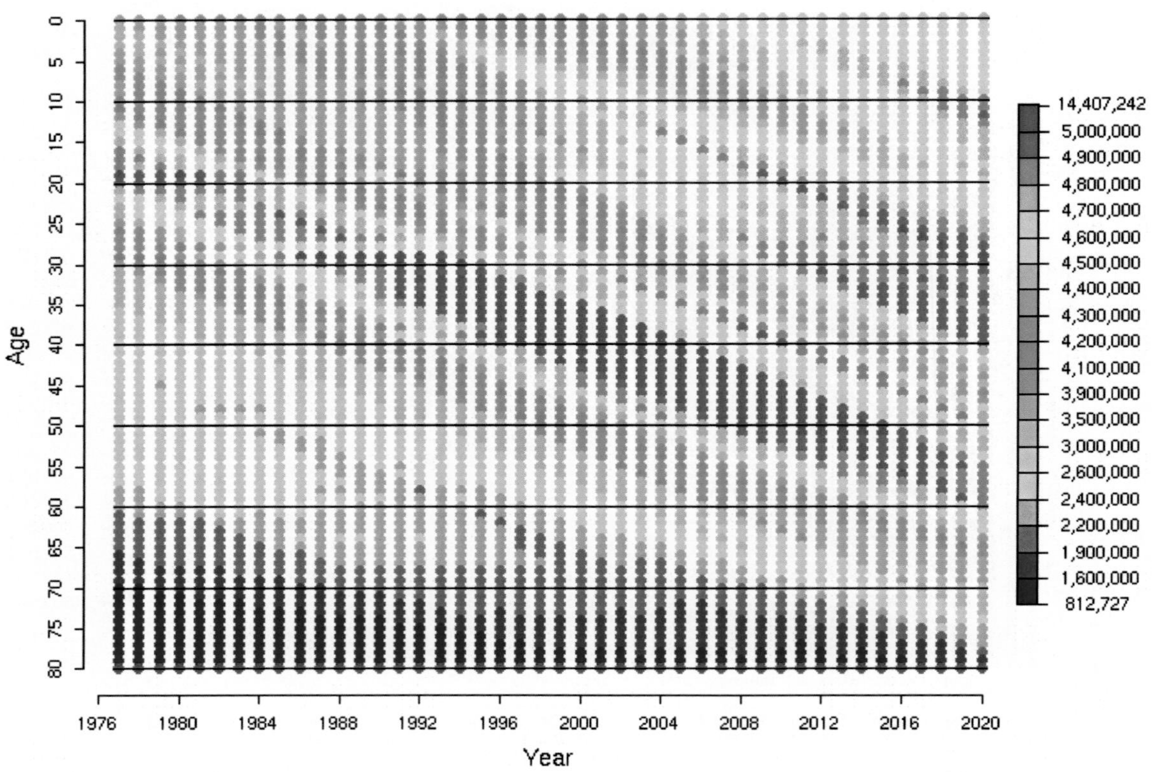

Western Europe

Chart 2.8 *Age structure of the population at a glance, each dot represents a single age group*

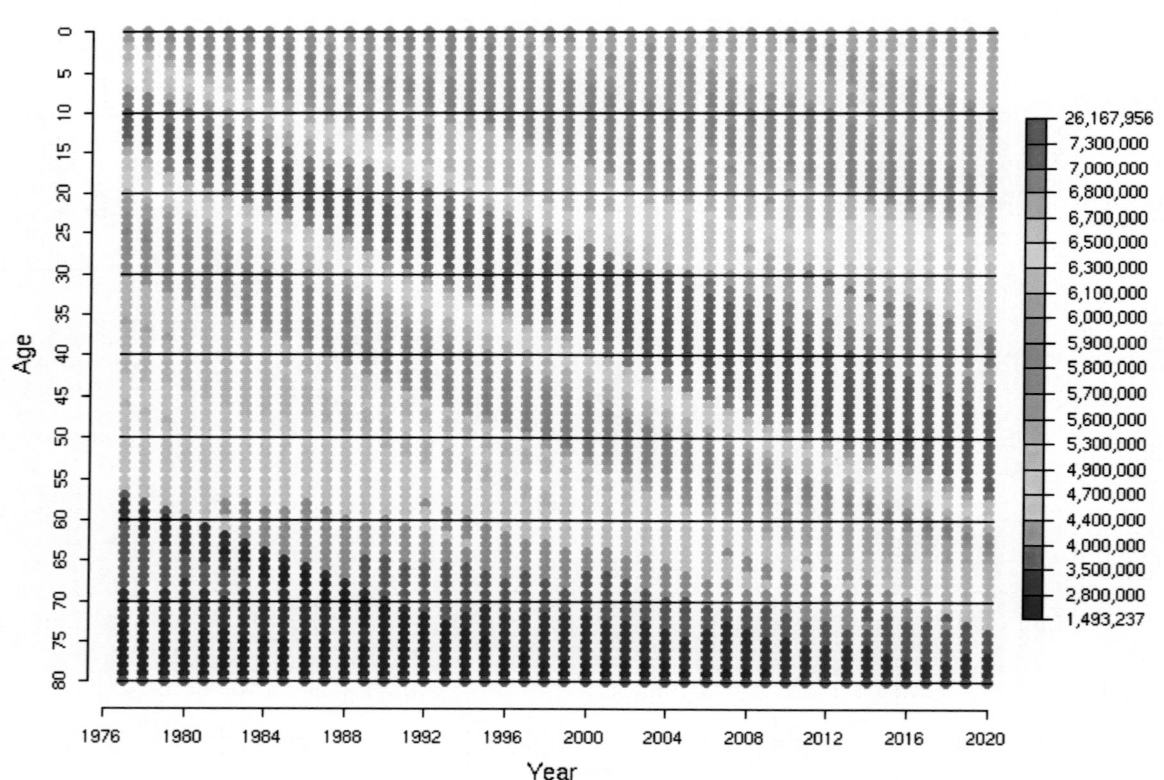

Algeria

Chart 2.9 *Age structure of the population at a glance, each dot represents a single age group*

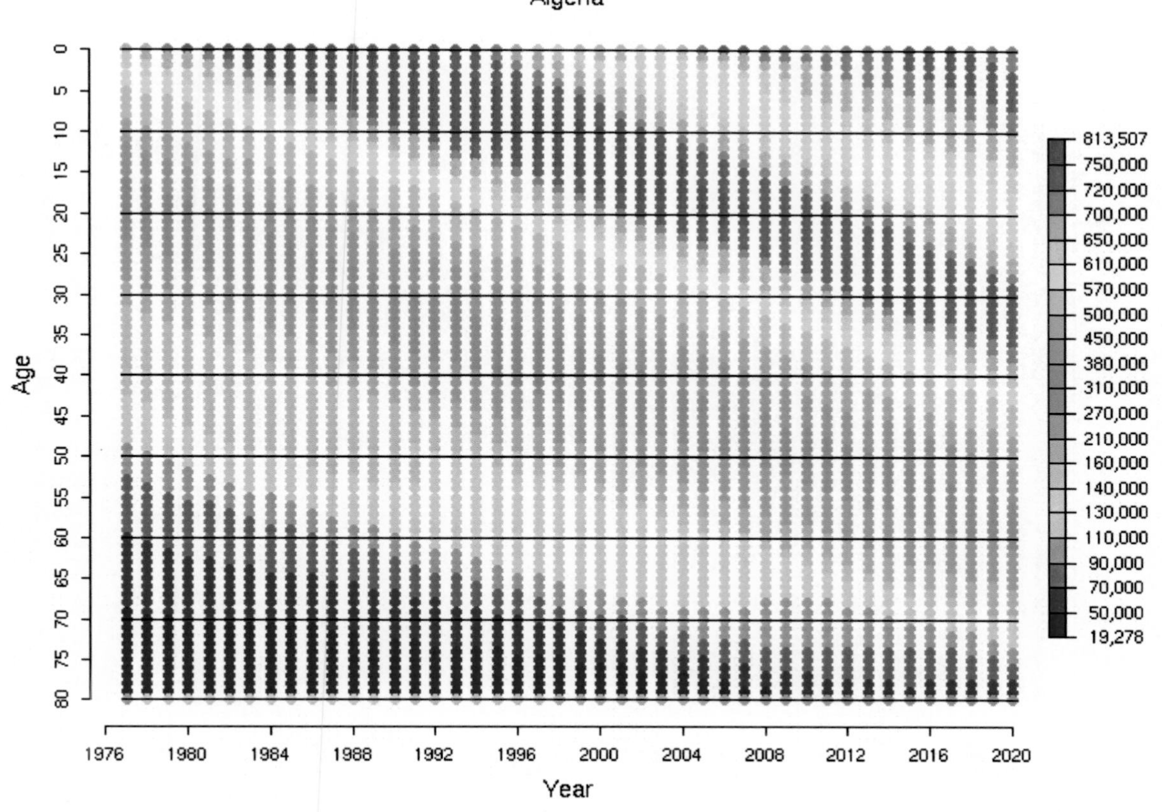

Argentina

Chart 2.10 *Age structure of the population at a glance, each dot represents a single age group*

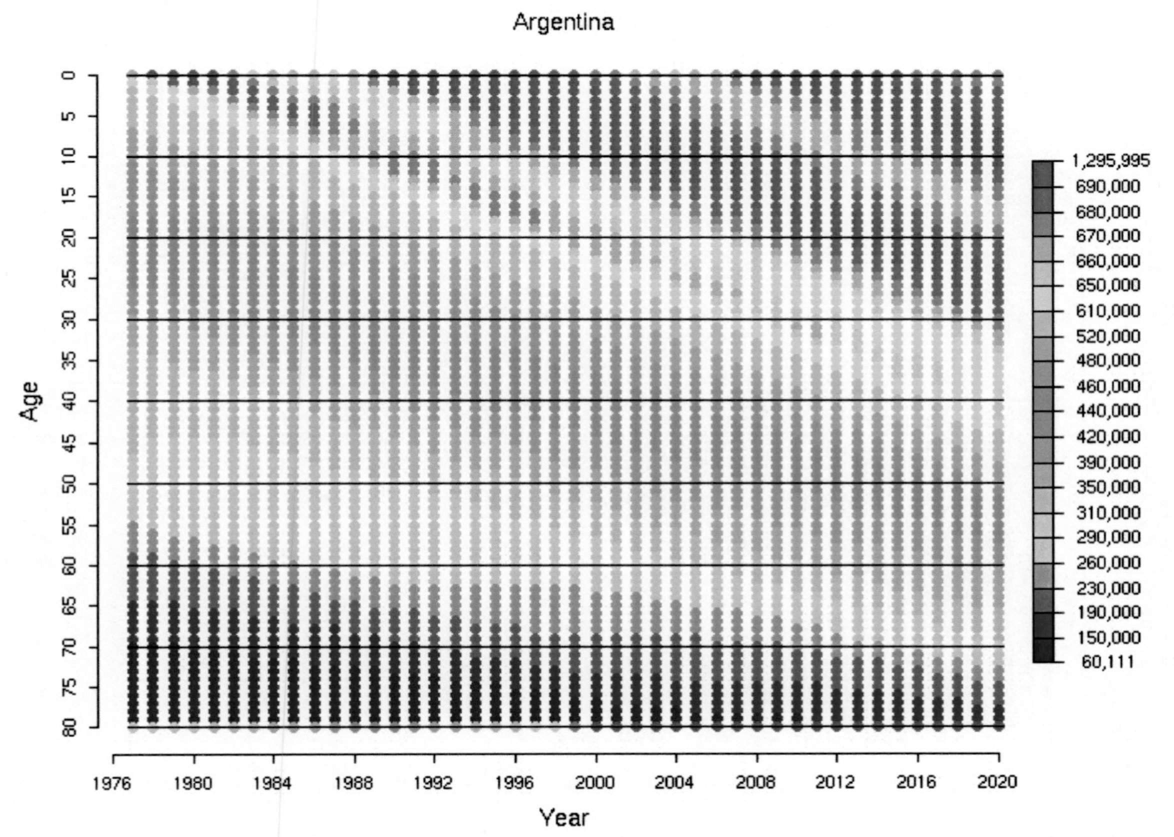

Australia

Chart 2.11 *Age structure of the population at a glance, each dot represents a single age group*

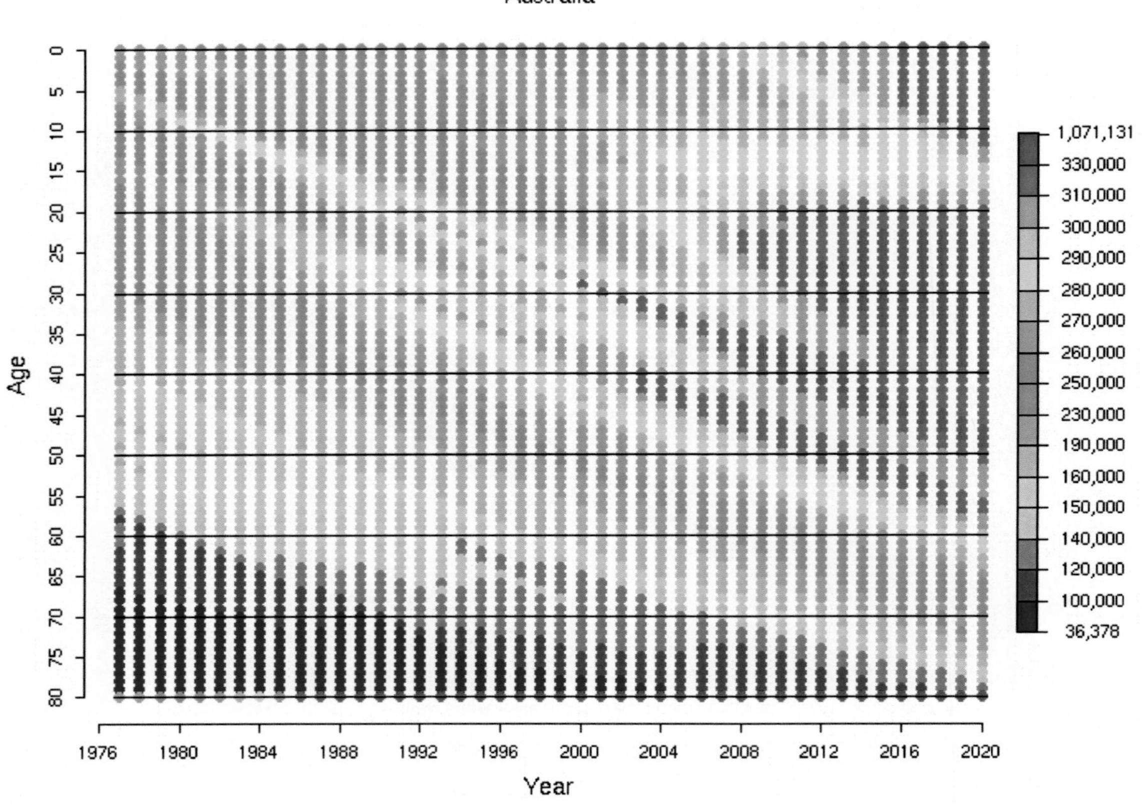

Austria

Chart 2.12 *Age structure of the population at a glance, each dot represents a single age group*

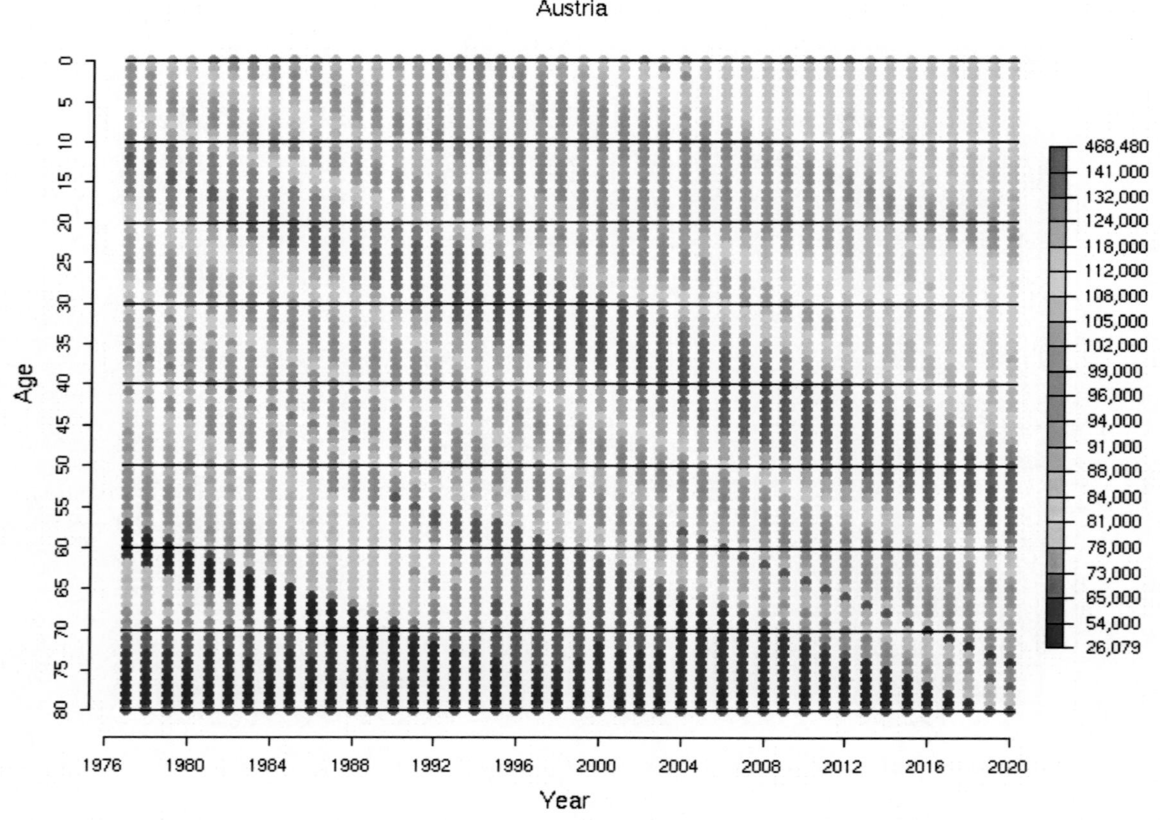

Azerbaijan

Chart 2.13 *Age structure of the population at a glance, each dot represents a single age group*

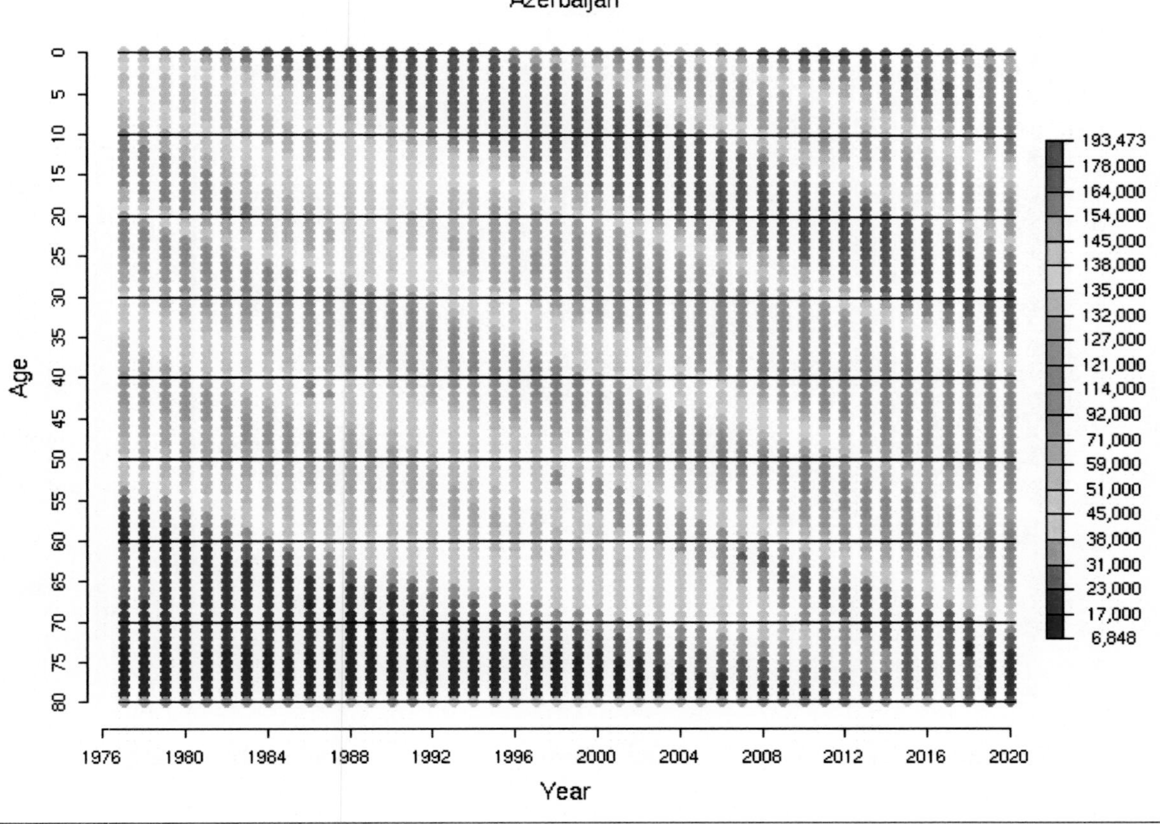

Belarus

Chart 2.14 *Age structure of the population at a glance, each dot represents a single age group*

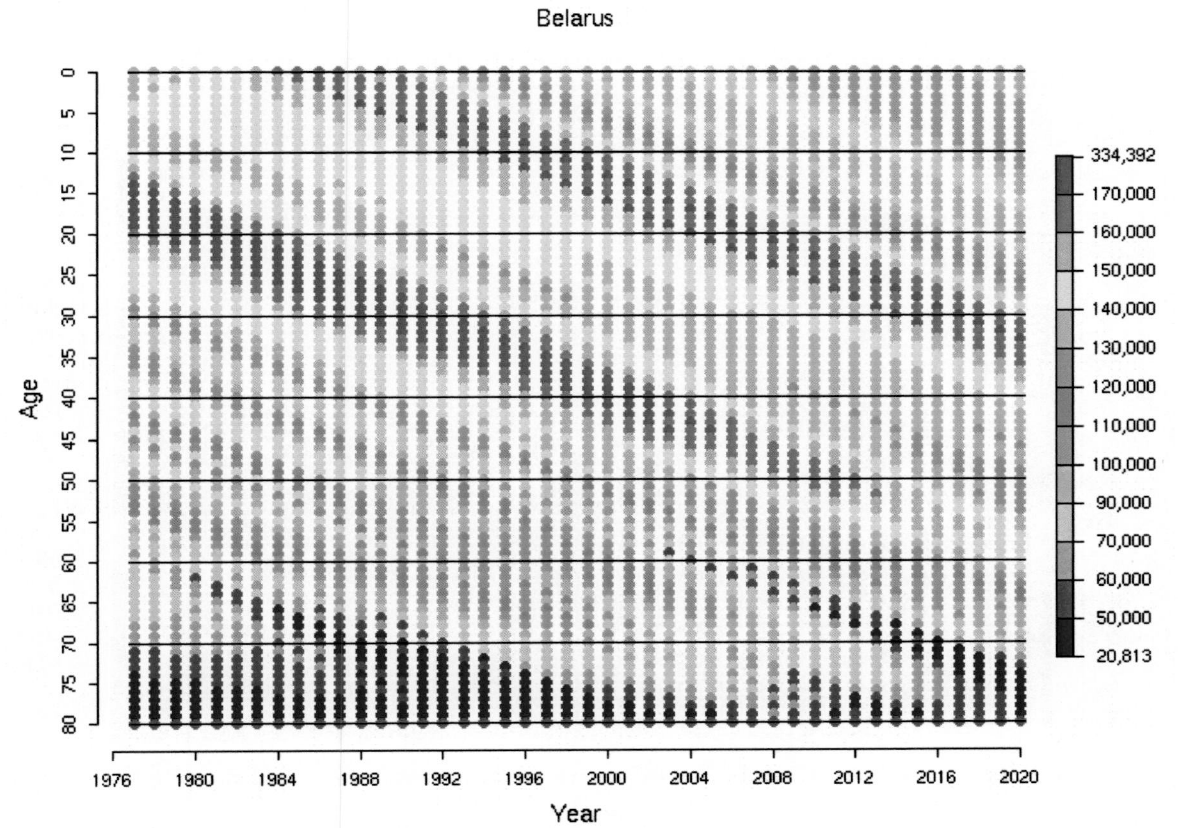

Belgium

Chart 2.15 *Age structure of the population at a glance, each dot represents a single age group*

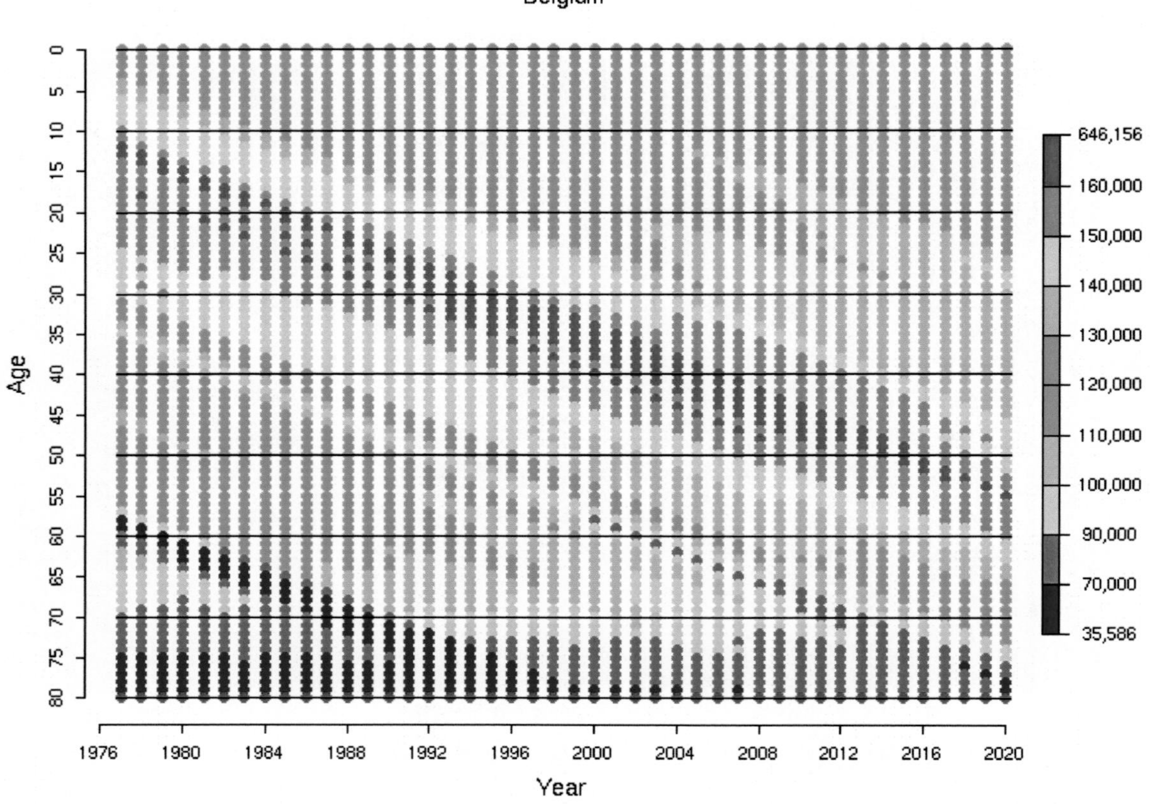

Bolivia

Chart 2.16 *Age structure of the population at a glance, each dot represents a single age group*

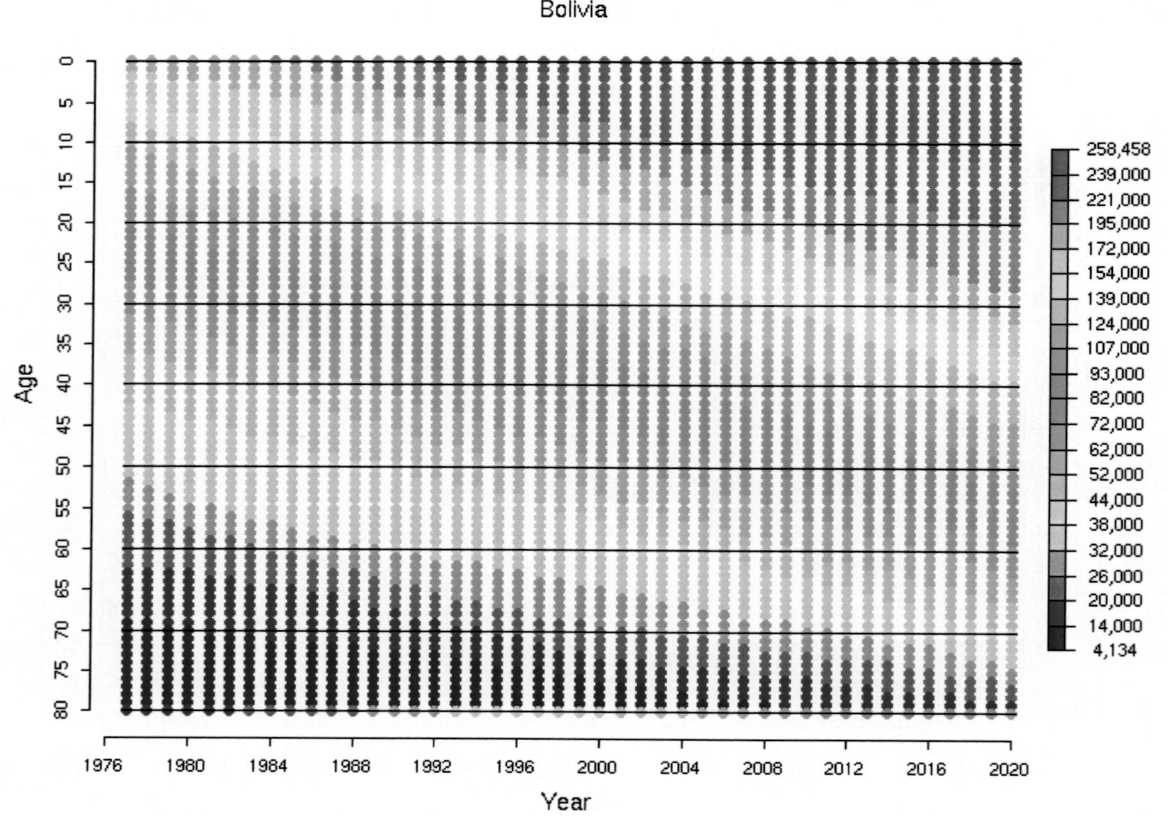

Bosnia-Herzegovina

Chart 2.17 *Age structure of the population at a glance, each dot represents a single age group*

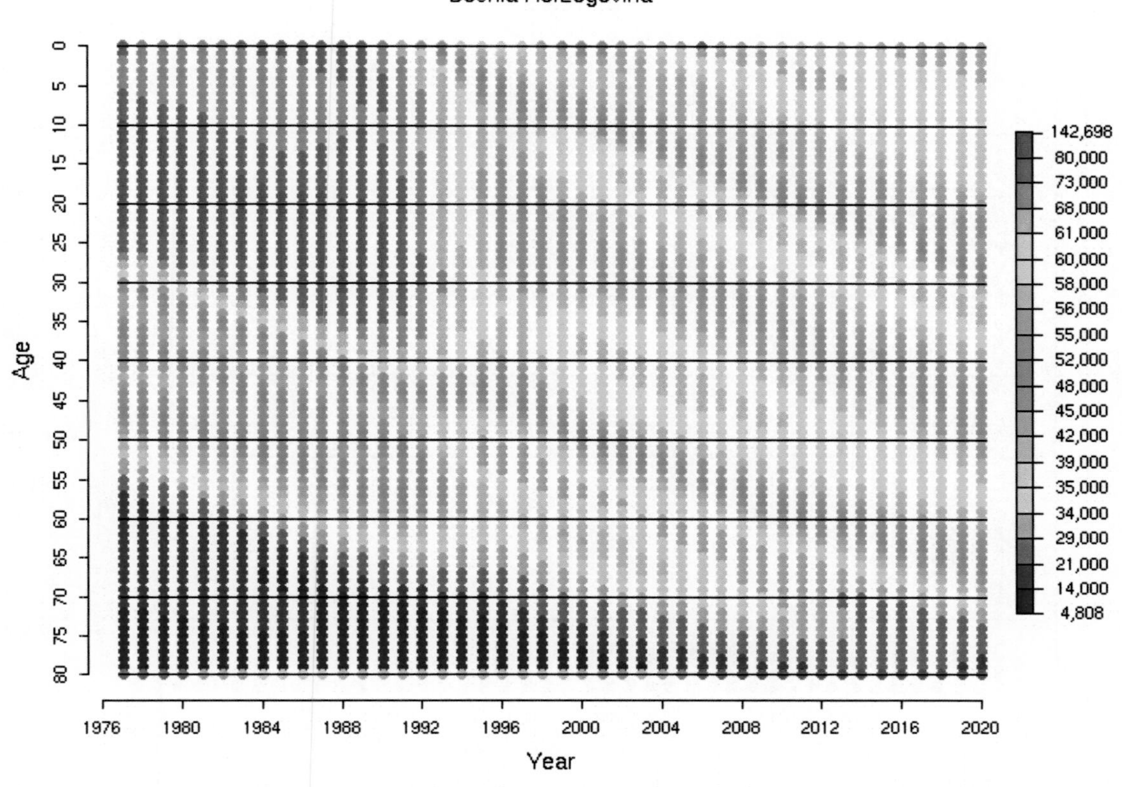

Brazil

Chart 2.18 *Age structure of the population at a glance, each dot represents a single age group*

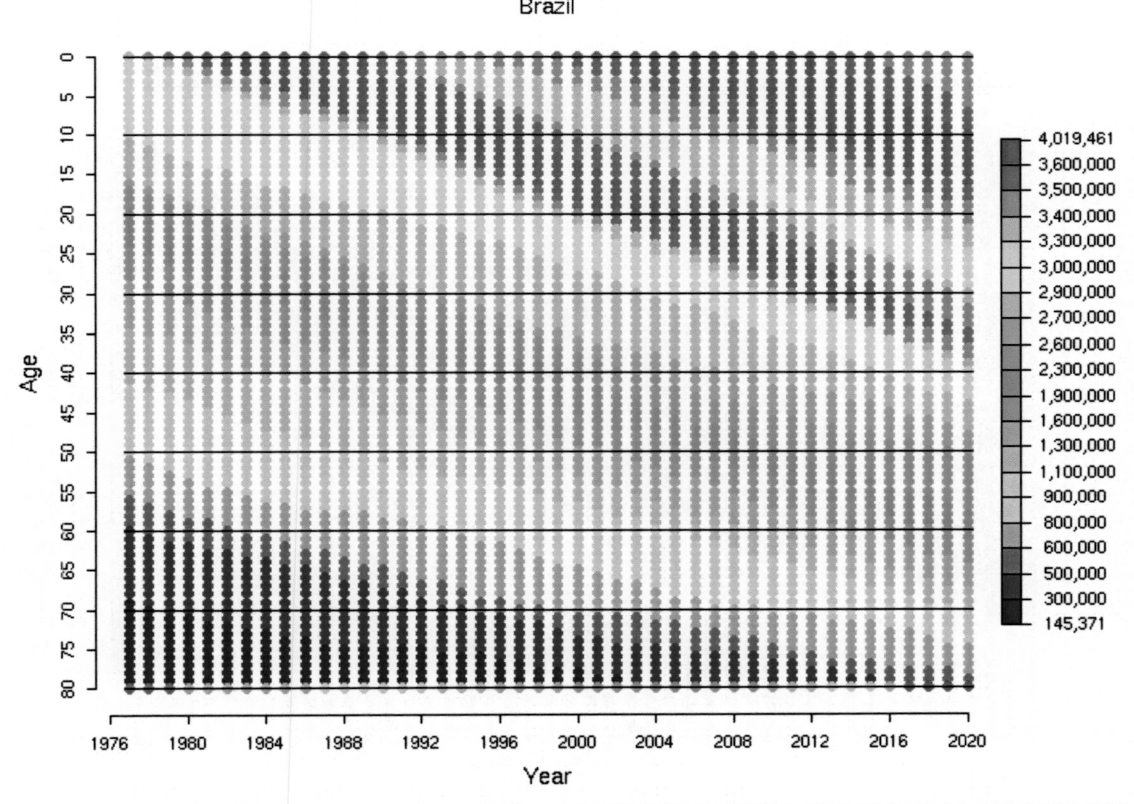

Bulgaria

Chart 2.19 *Age structure of the population at a glance, each dot represents a single age group*

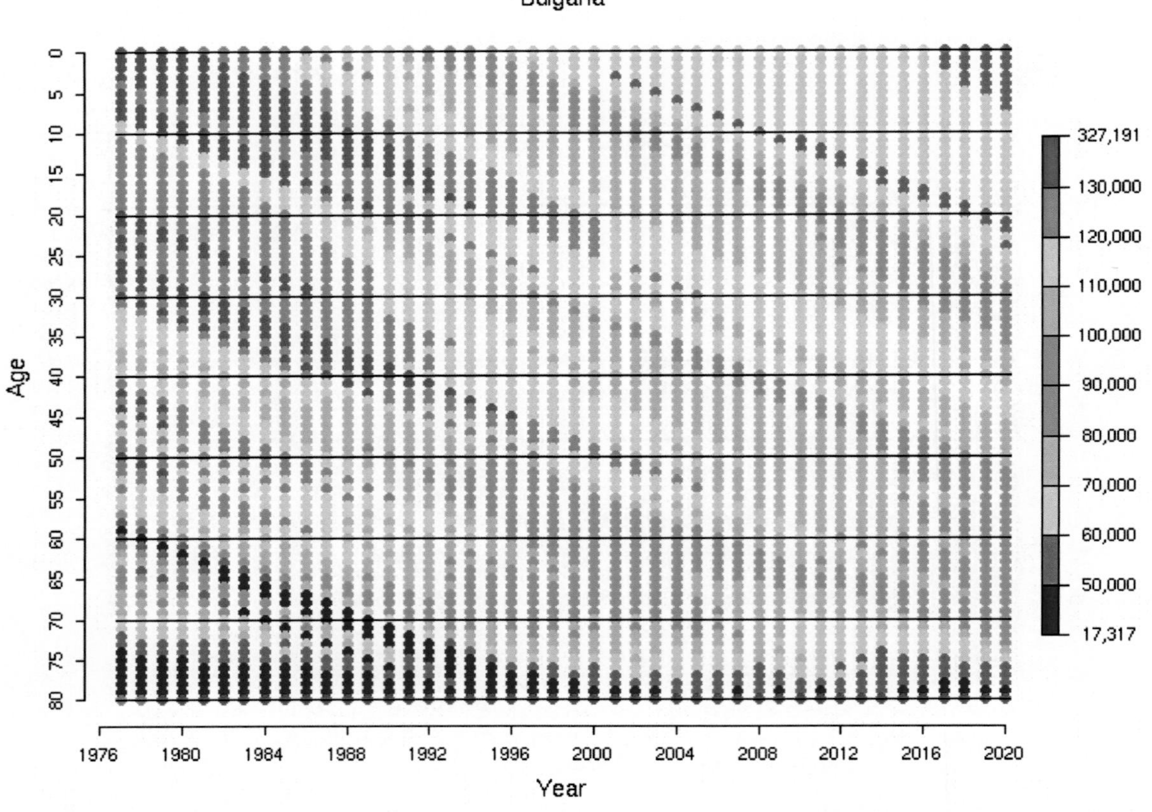

Canada

Chart 2.20 *Age structure of the population at a glance, each dot represents a single age group*

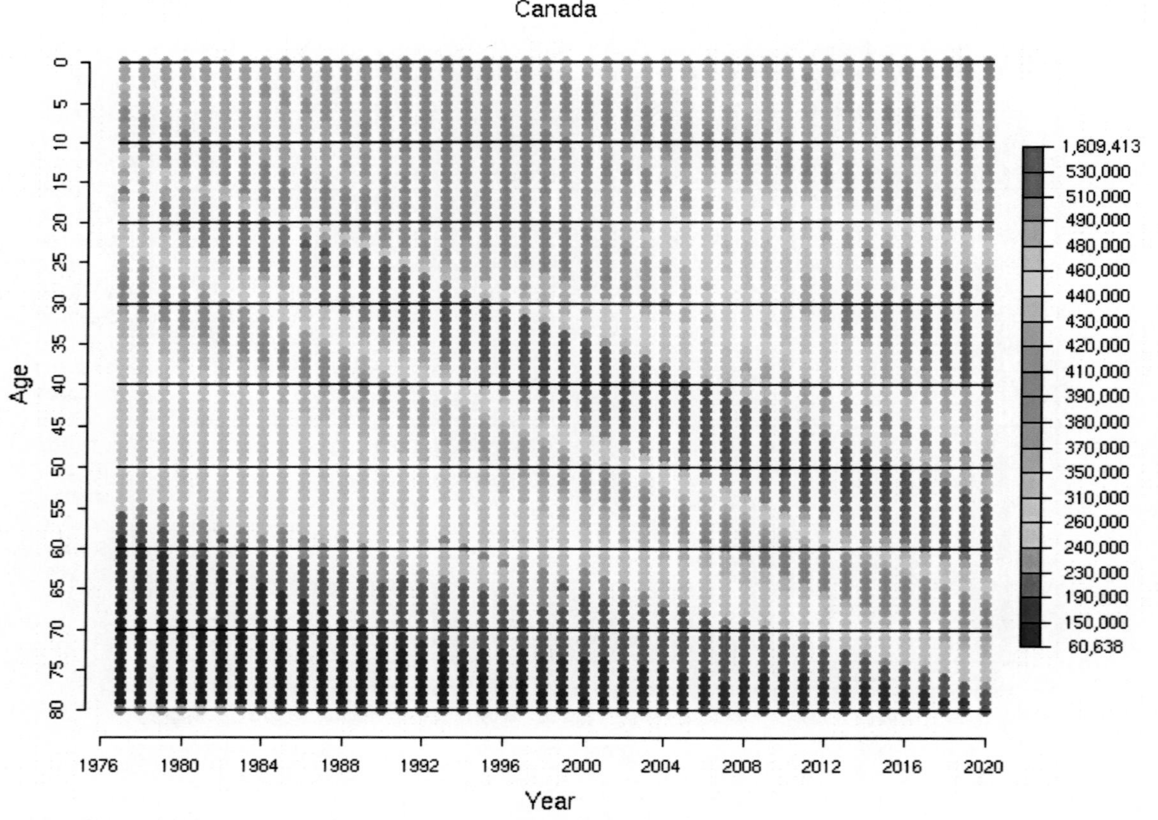

Chile

Chart 2.21 *Age structure of the population at a glance, each dot represents a single age group*

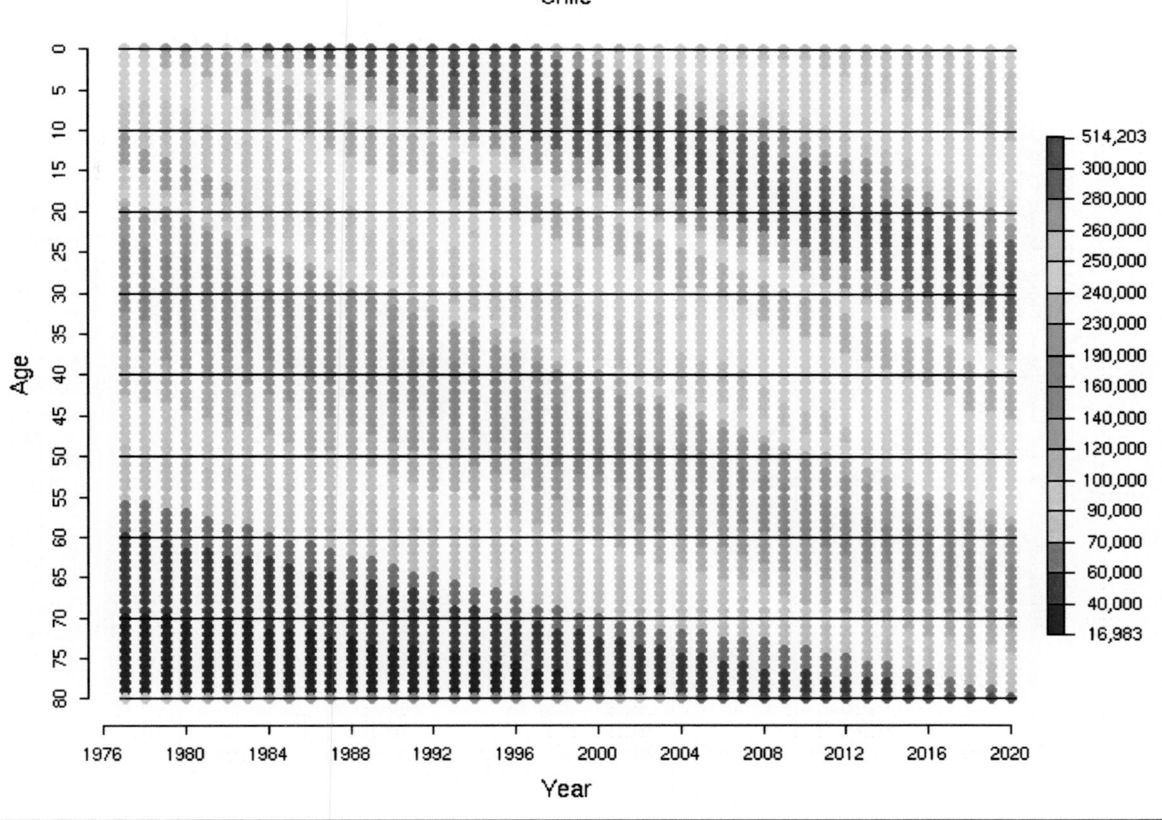

China

Chart 2.22 *Age structure of the population at a glance, each dot represents a single age group*

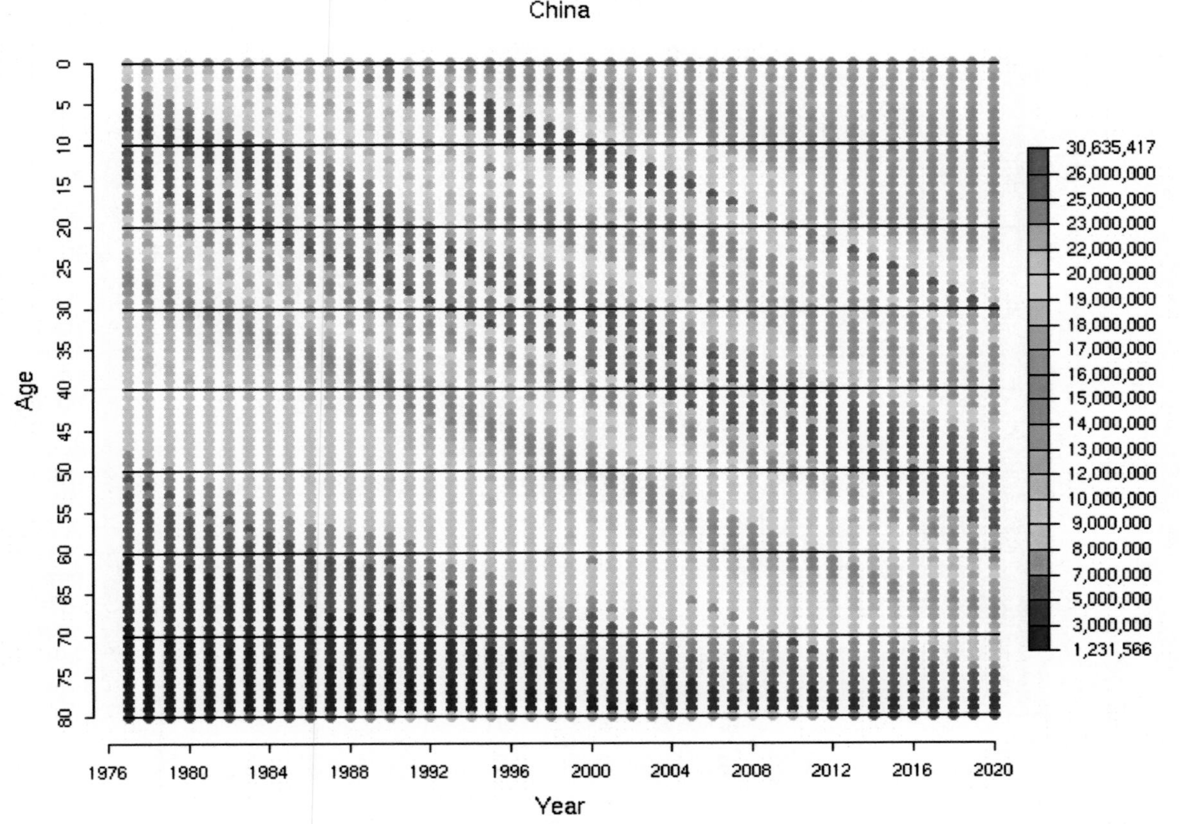

Colombia

Chart 2.23 *Age structure of the population at a glance, each dot represents a single age group*

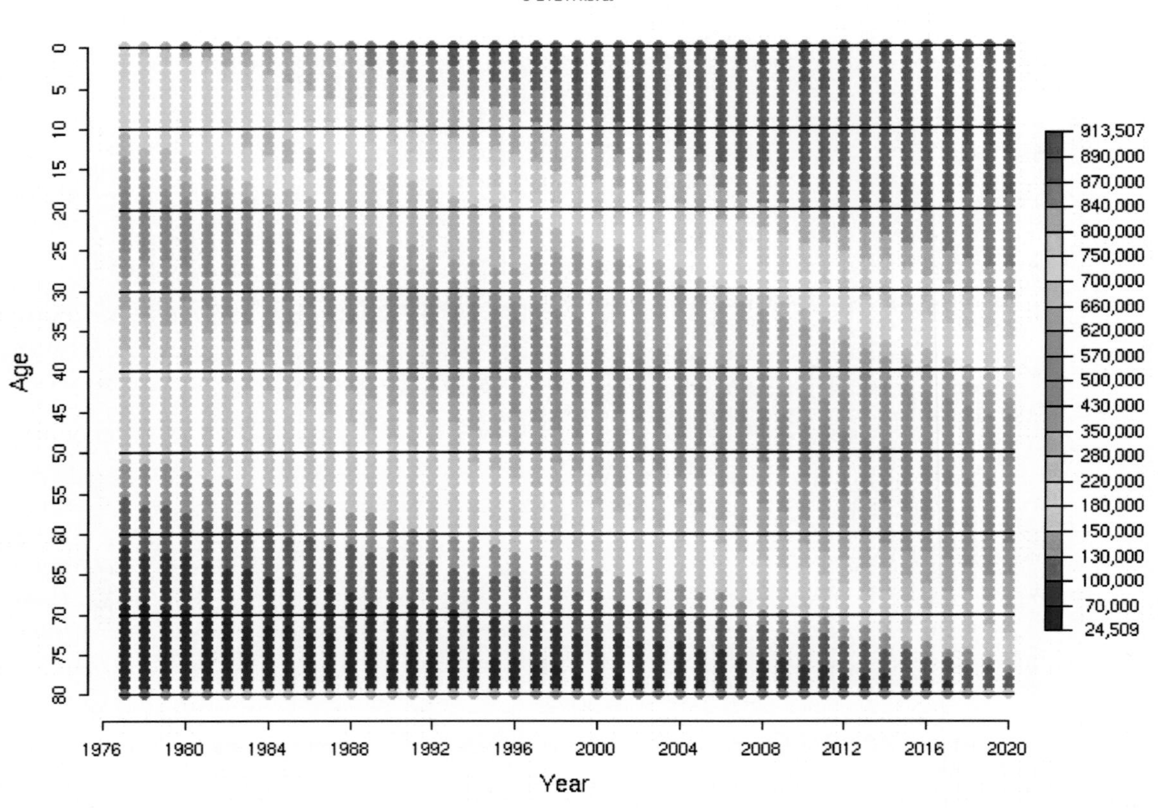

Costa Rica

Chart 2.24 *Age structure of the population at a glance, each dot represents a single age group*

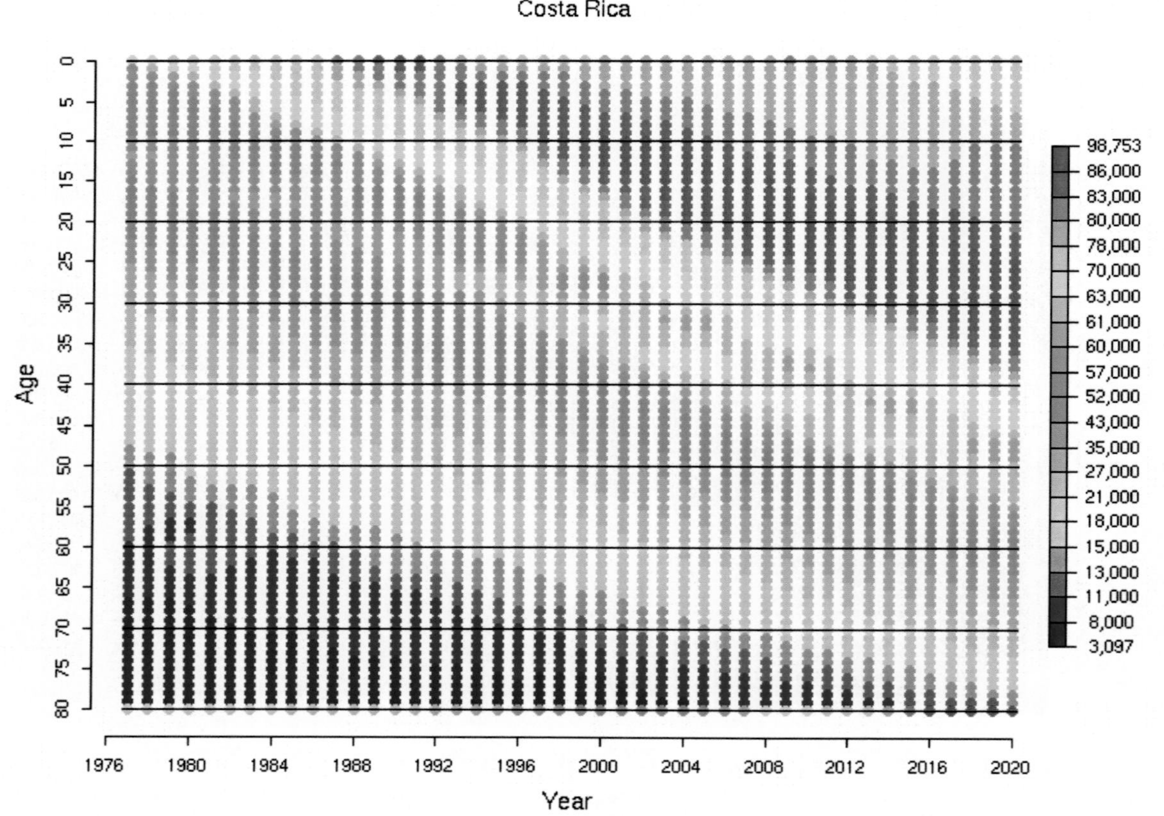

Croatia

Chart 2.25 *Age structure of the population at a glance, each dot represents a single age group*

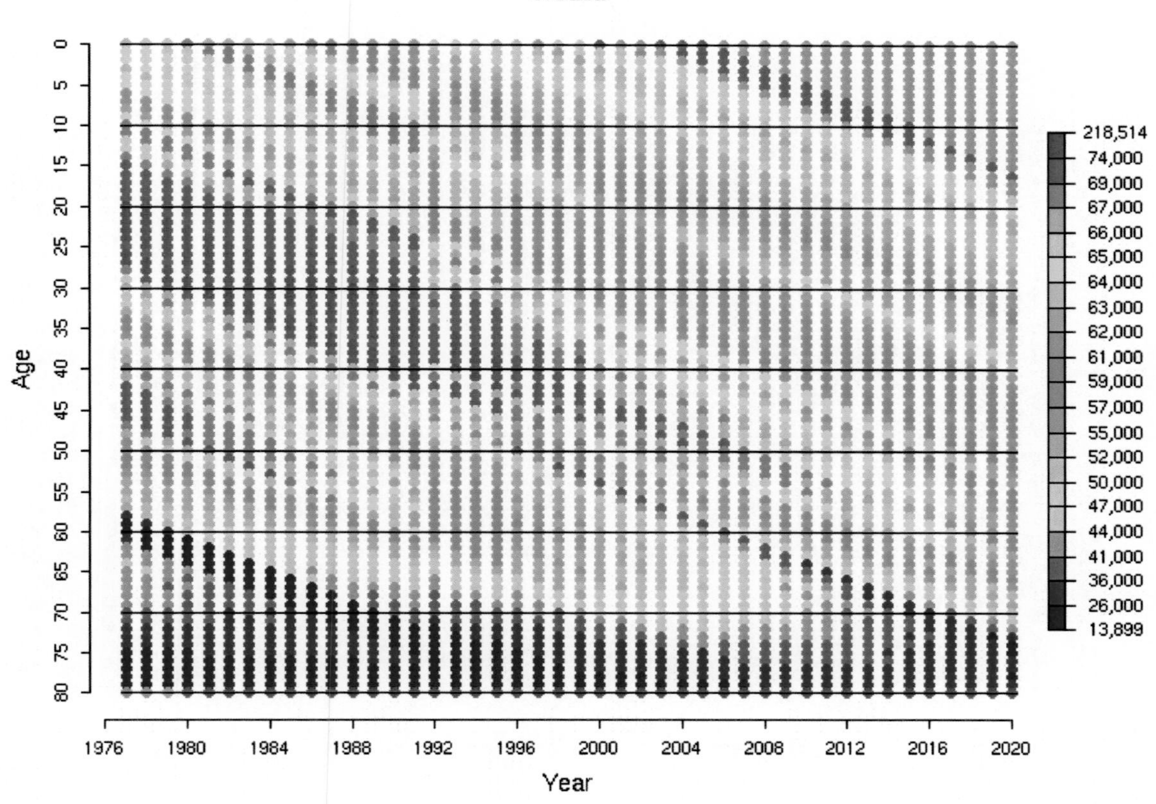

Czech Republic

Chart 2.26 *Age structure of the population at a glance, each dot represents a single age group*

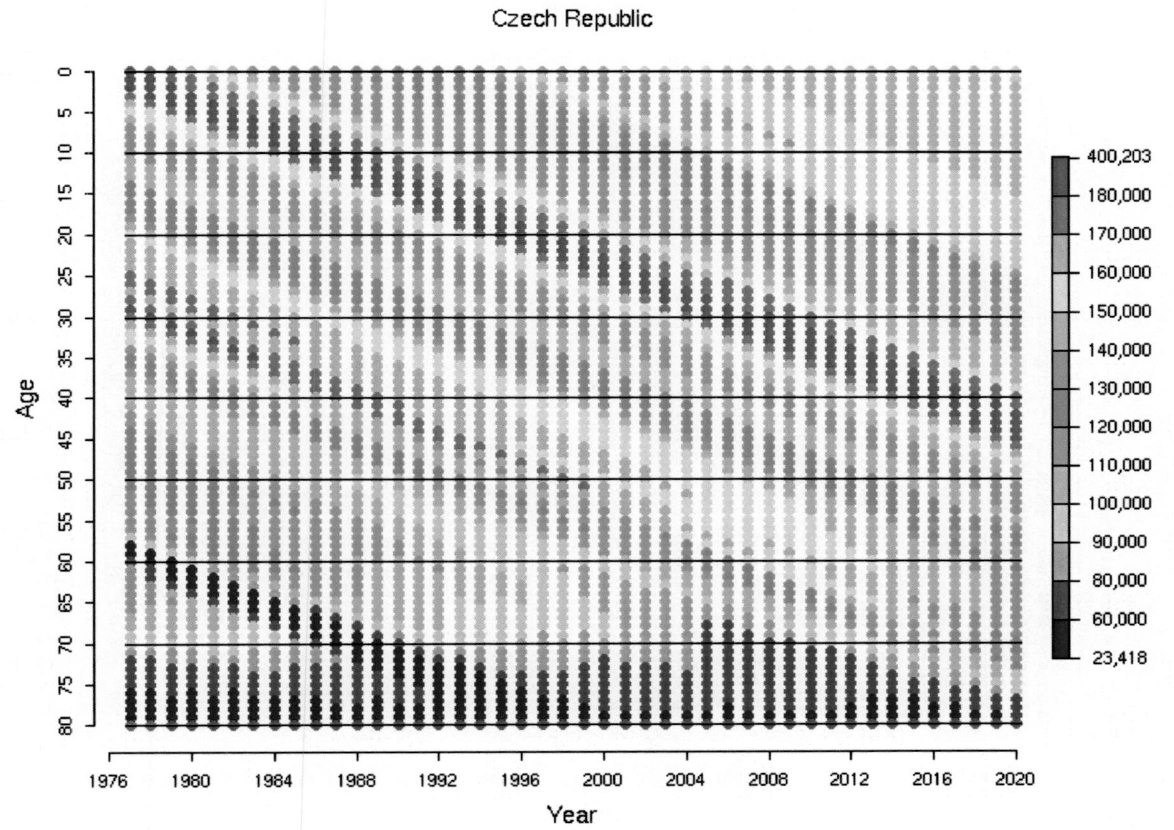

Denmark

Chart 2.27 *Age structure of the population at a glance, each dot represents a single age group*

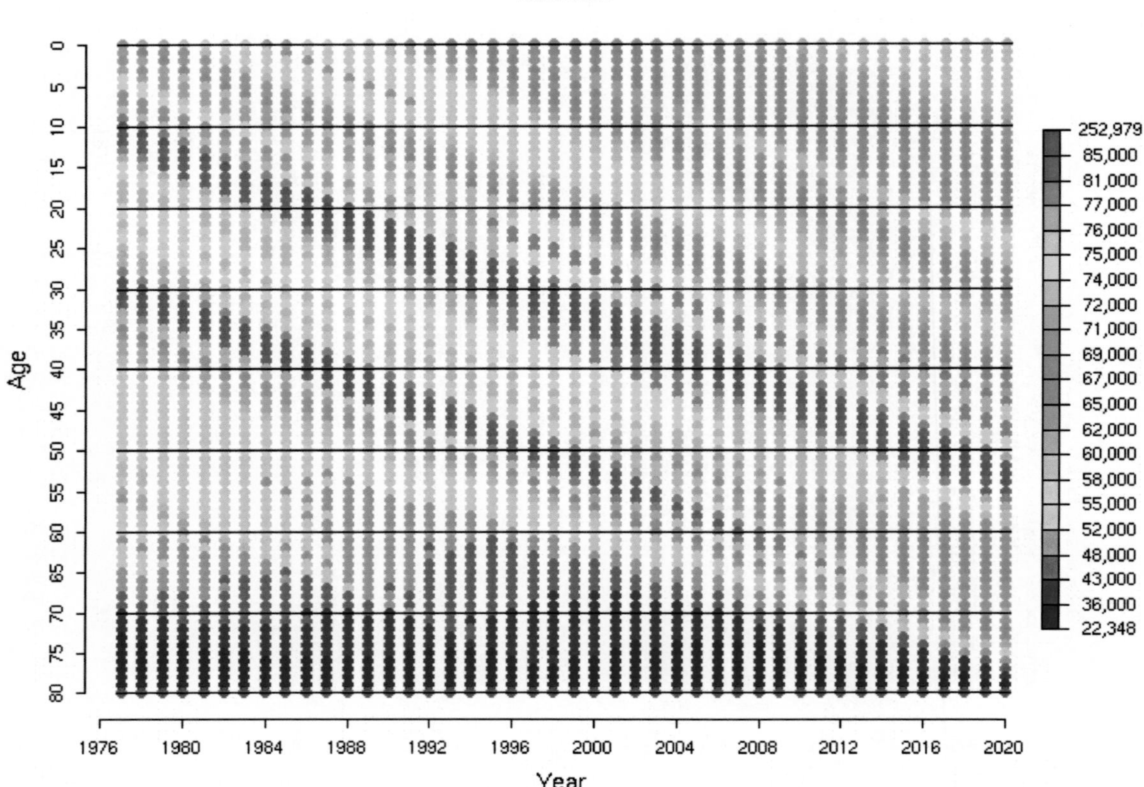

Ecuador

Chart 2.28 *Age structure of the population at a glance, each dot represents a single age group*

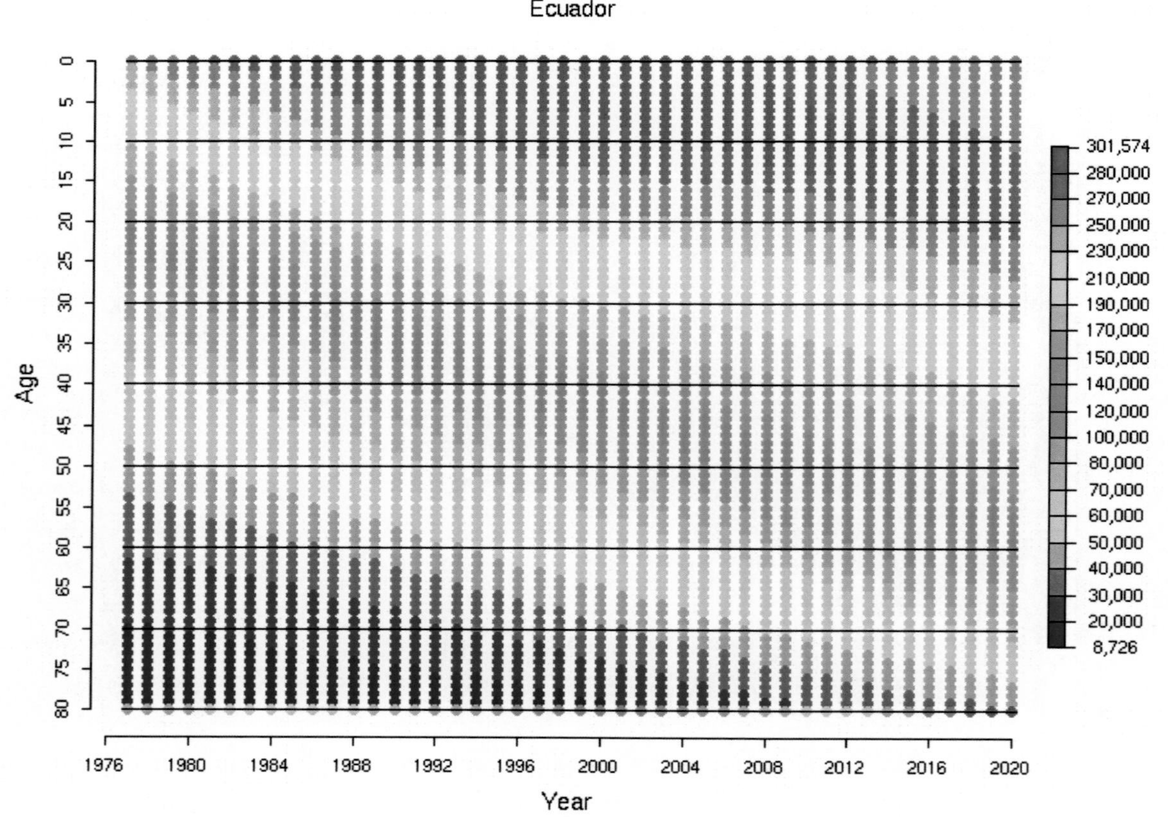

Egypt

Chart 2.29 *Age structure of the population at a glance, each dot represents a single age group*

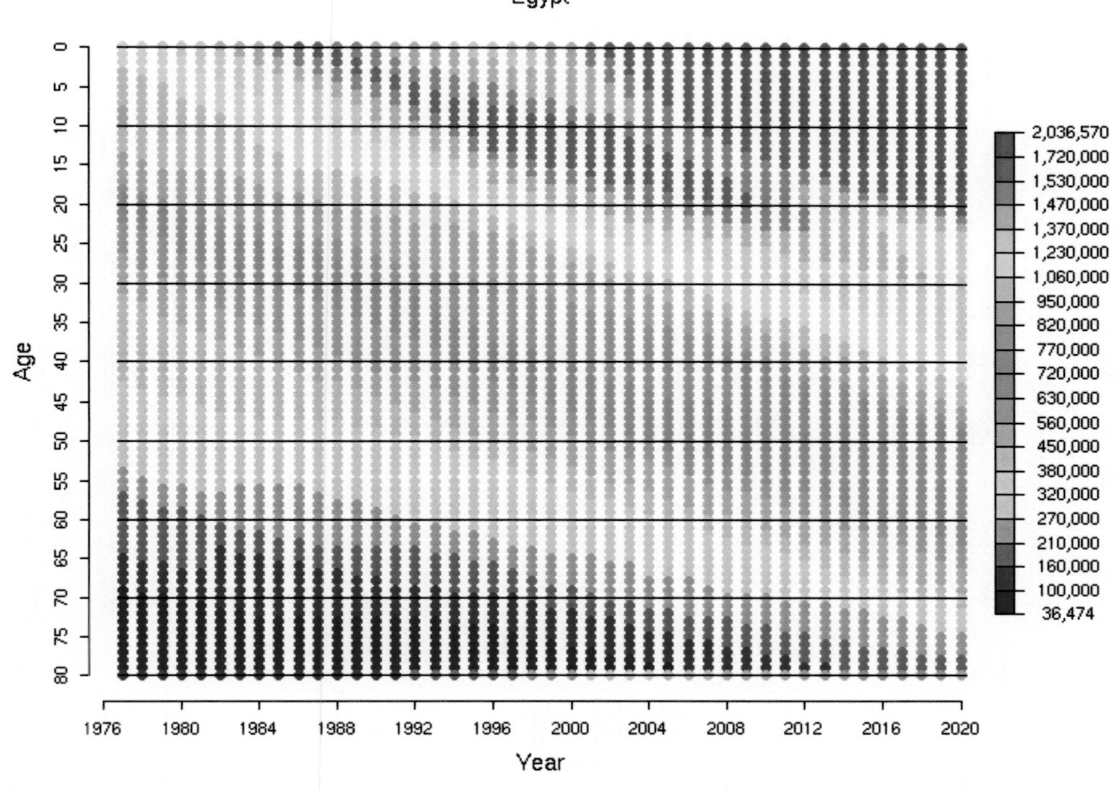

Estonia

Chart 2.30 *Age structure of the population at a glance, each dot represents a single age group*

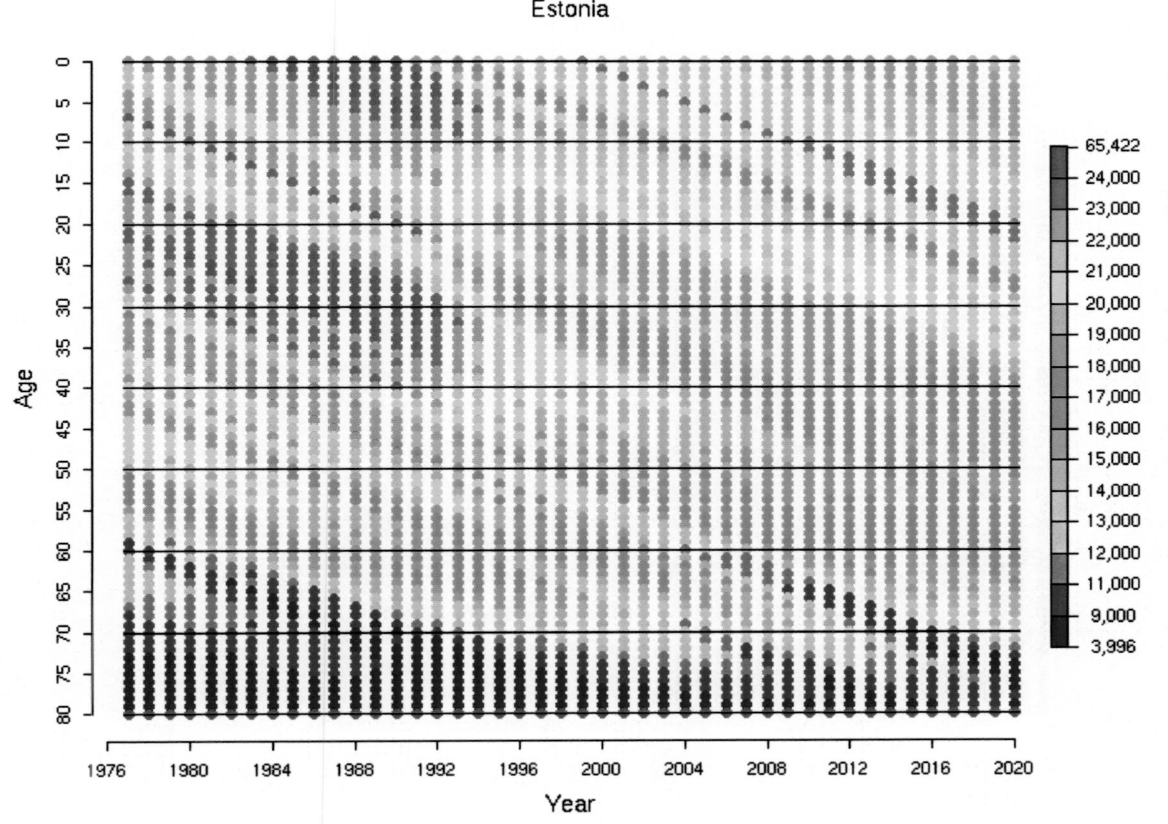

Finland

Chart 2.31 *Age structure of the population at a glance, each dot represents a single age group*

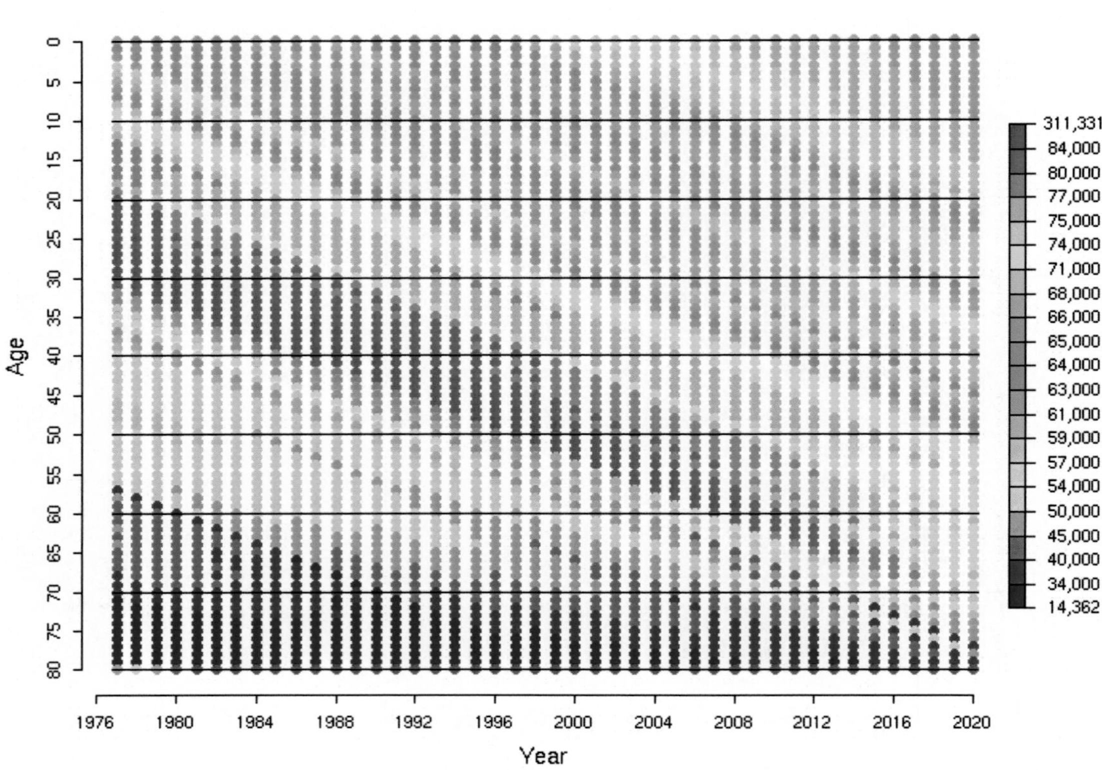

France

Chart 2.32 *Age structure of the population at a glance, each dot represents a single age group*

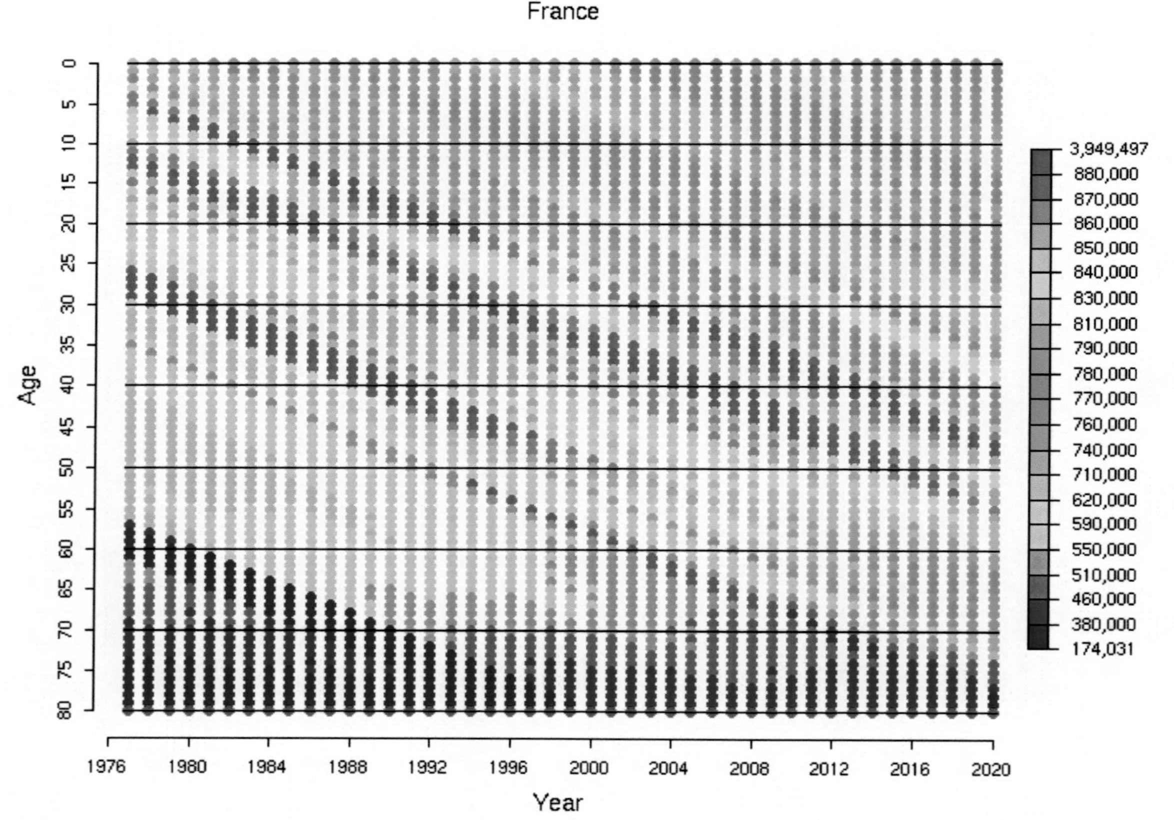

Germany

Chart 2.33 *Age structure of the population at a glance, each dot represents a single age group*

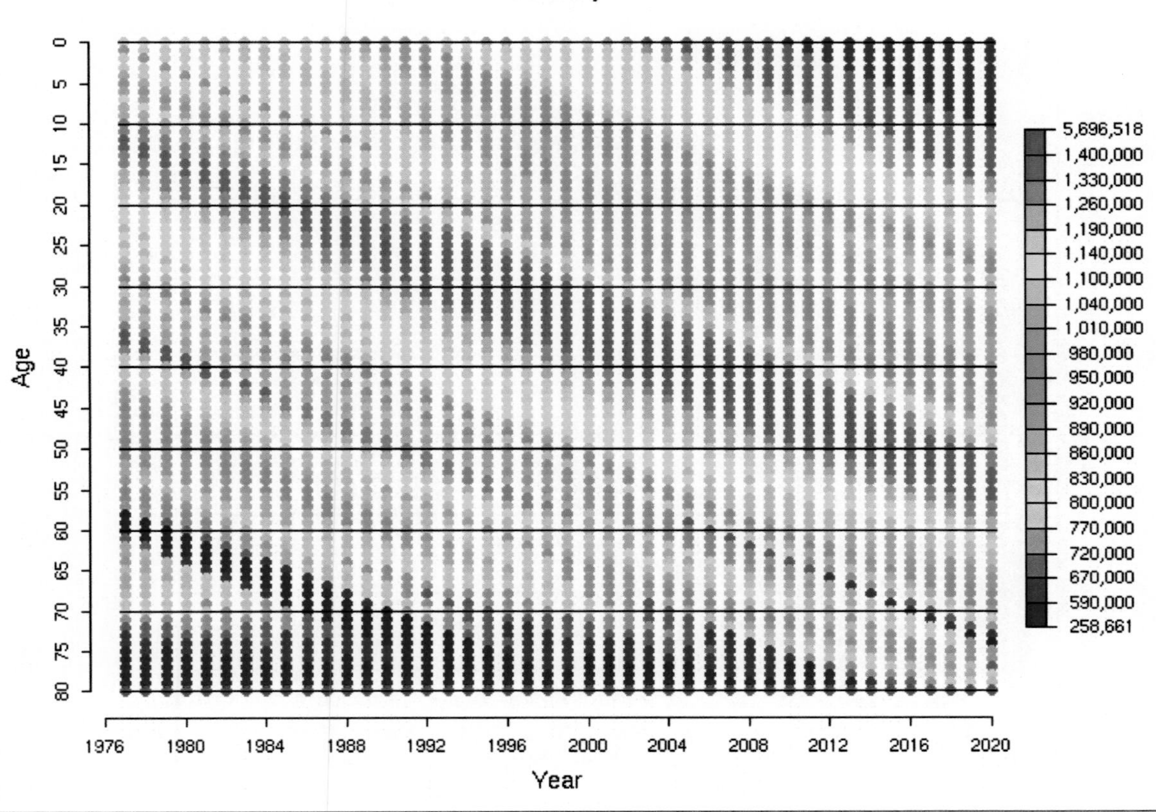

Greece

Chart 2.34 *Age structure of the population at a glance, each dot represents a single age group*

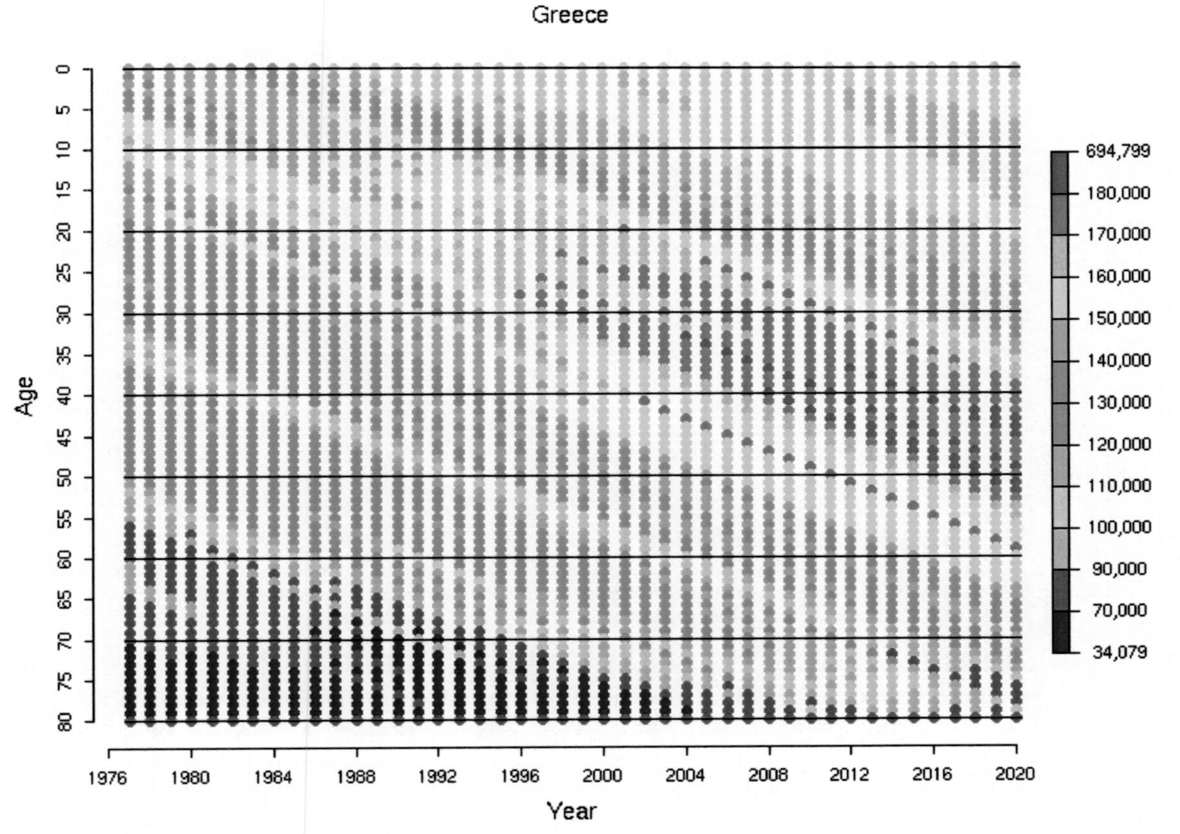

Hong Kong, China

Chart 2.35 *Age structure of the population at a glance, each dot represents a single age group*

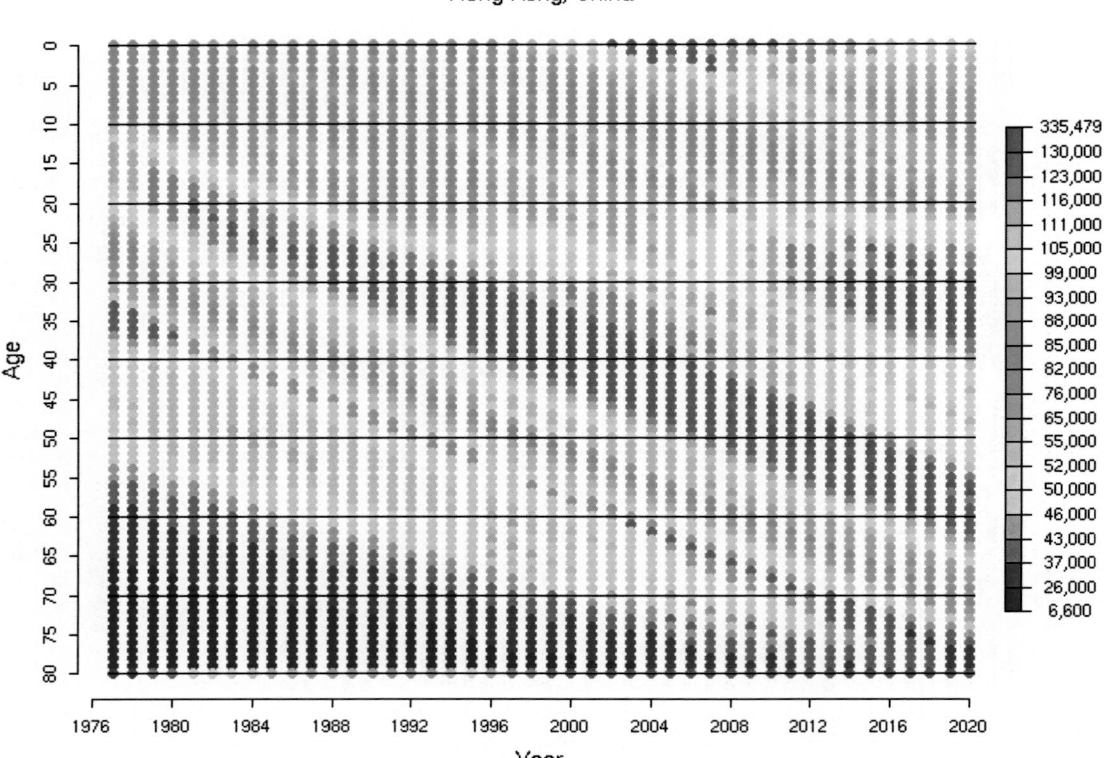

Hungary

Chart 2.36 *Age structure of the population at a glance, each dot represents a single age group*

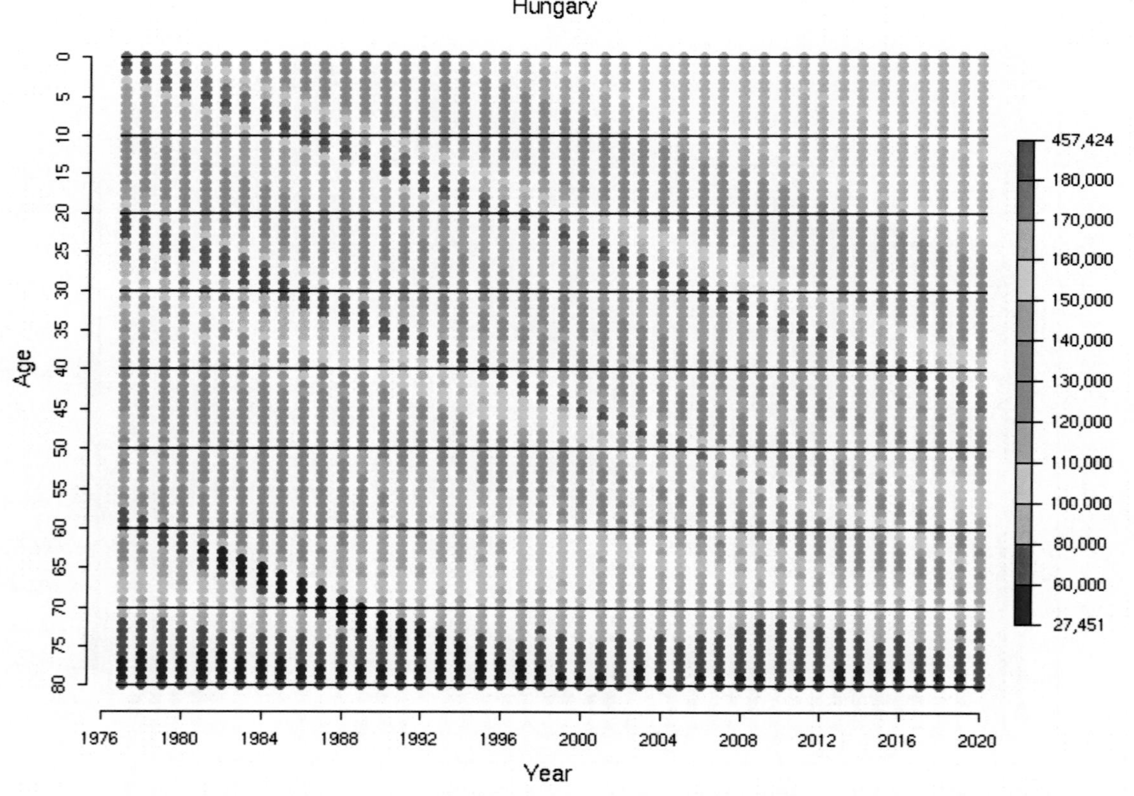

India

Chart 2.37 *Age structure of the population at a glance, each dot represents a single age group*

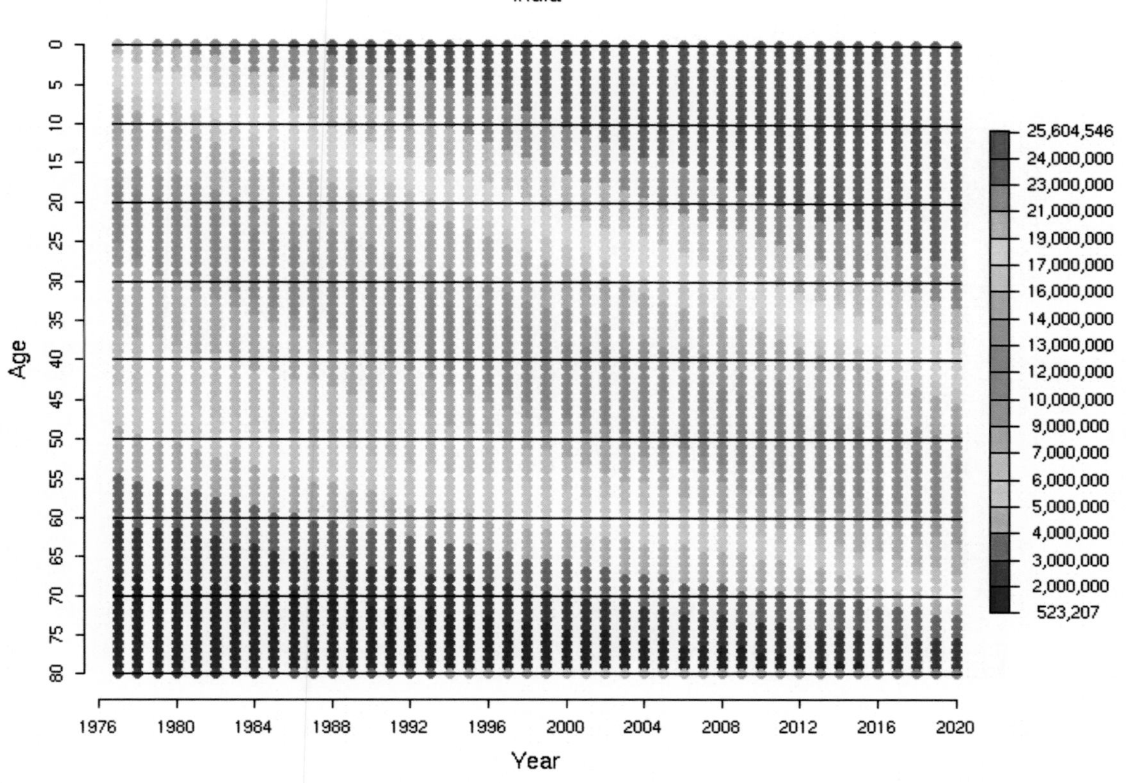

Indonesia

Chart 2.38 *Age structure of the population at a glance, each dot represents a single age group*

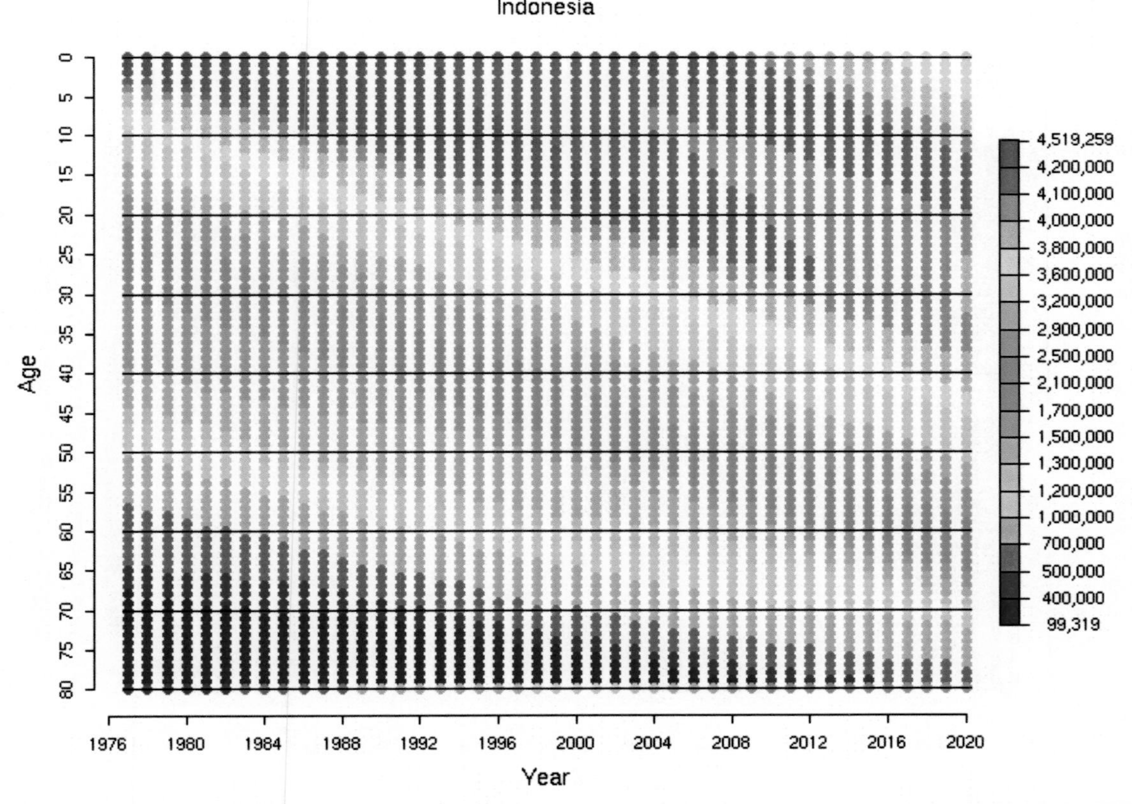

Iran

Chart 2.39 *Age structure of the population at a glance, each dot represents a single age group*

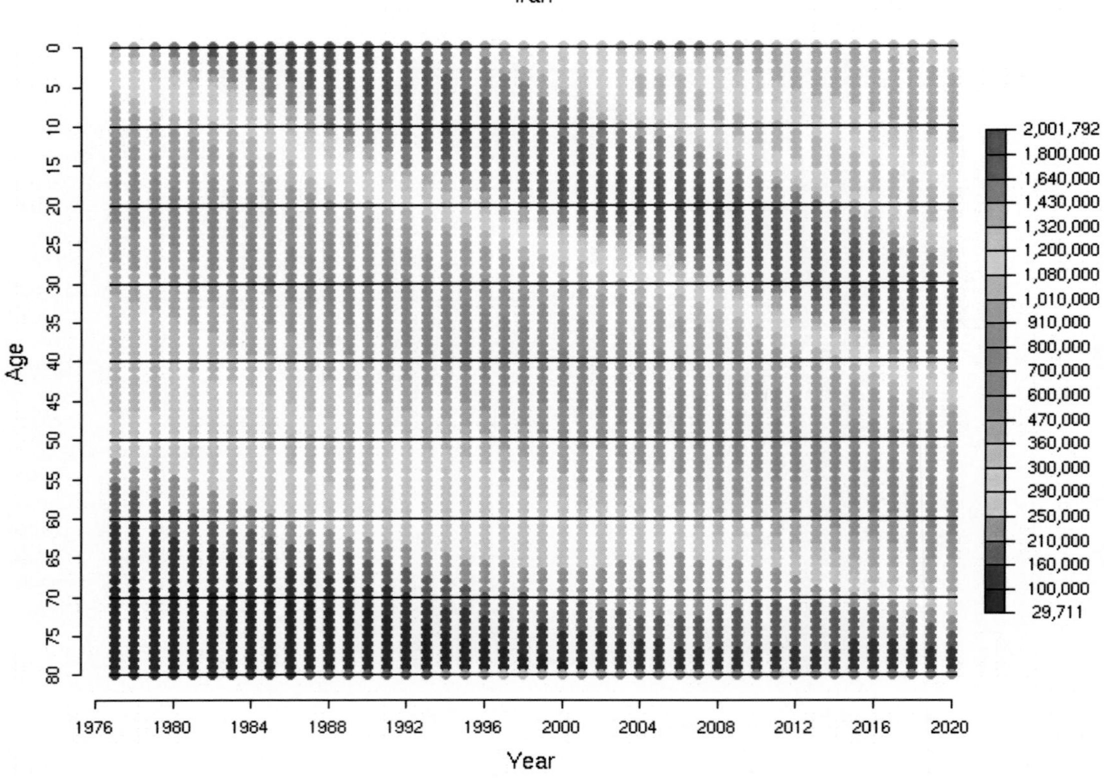

Ireland

Chart 2.40 *Age structure of the population at a glance, each dot represents a single age group*

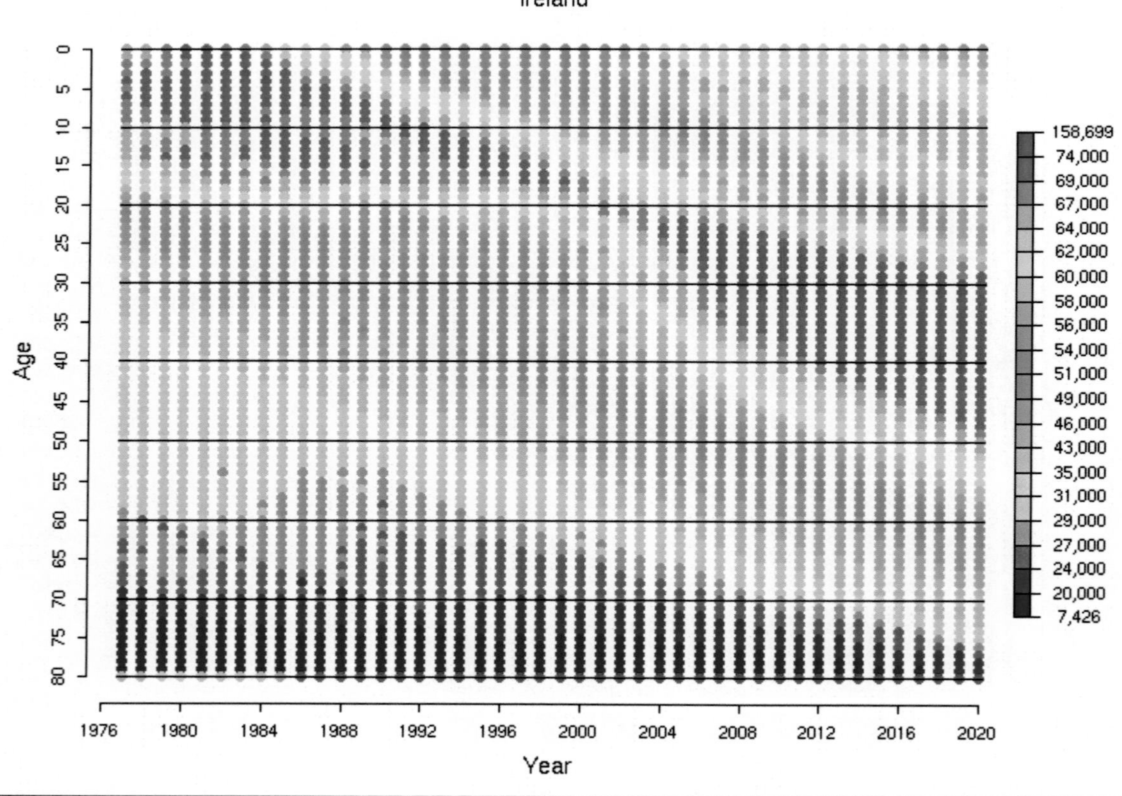

Israel

Chart 2.41 *Age structure of the population at a glance, each dot represents a single age group*

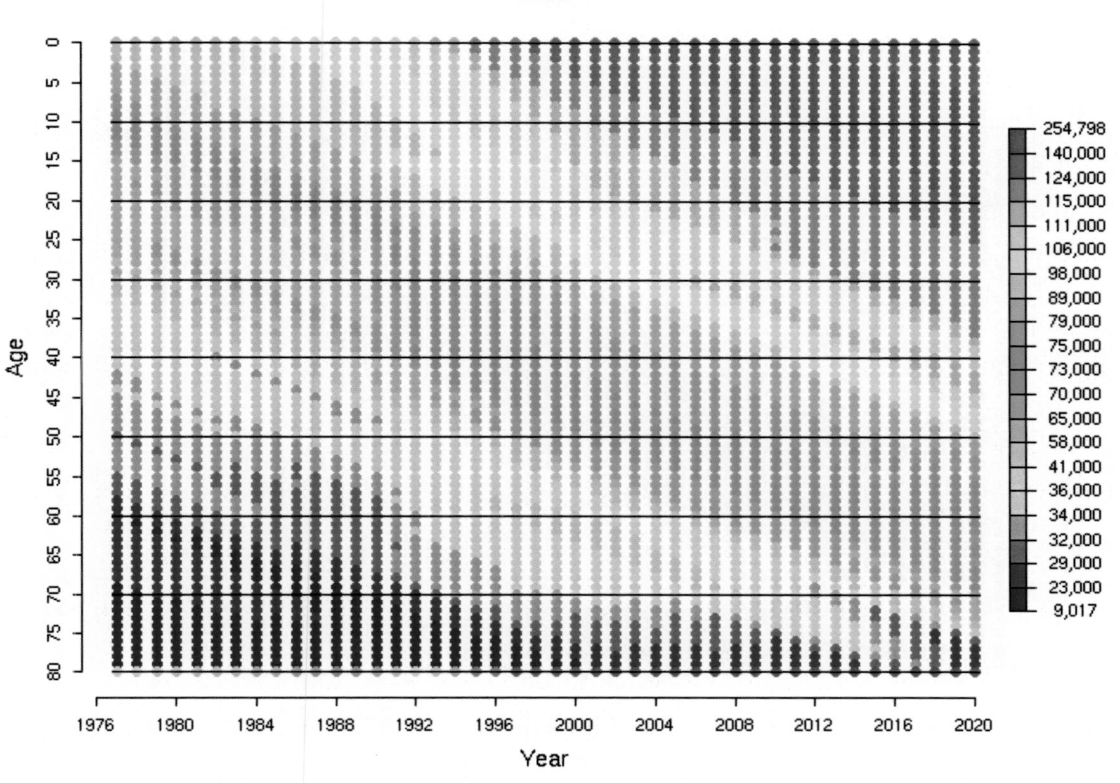

Italy

Chart 2.42 *Age structure of the population at a glance, each dot represents a single age group*

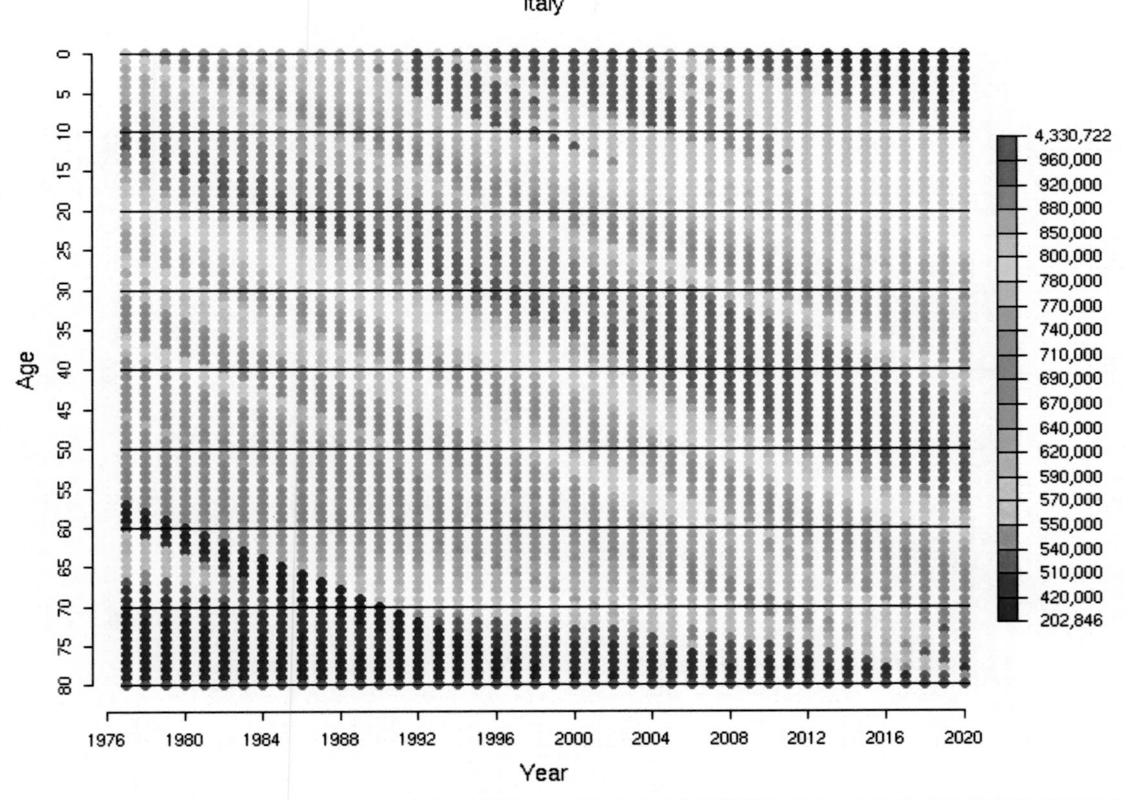

Japan

Chart 2.43 *Age structure of the population at a glance, each dot represents a single age group*

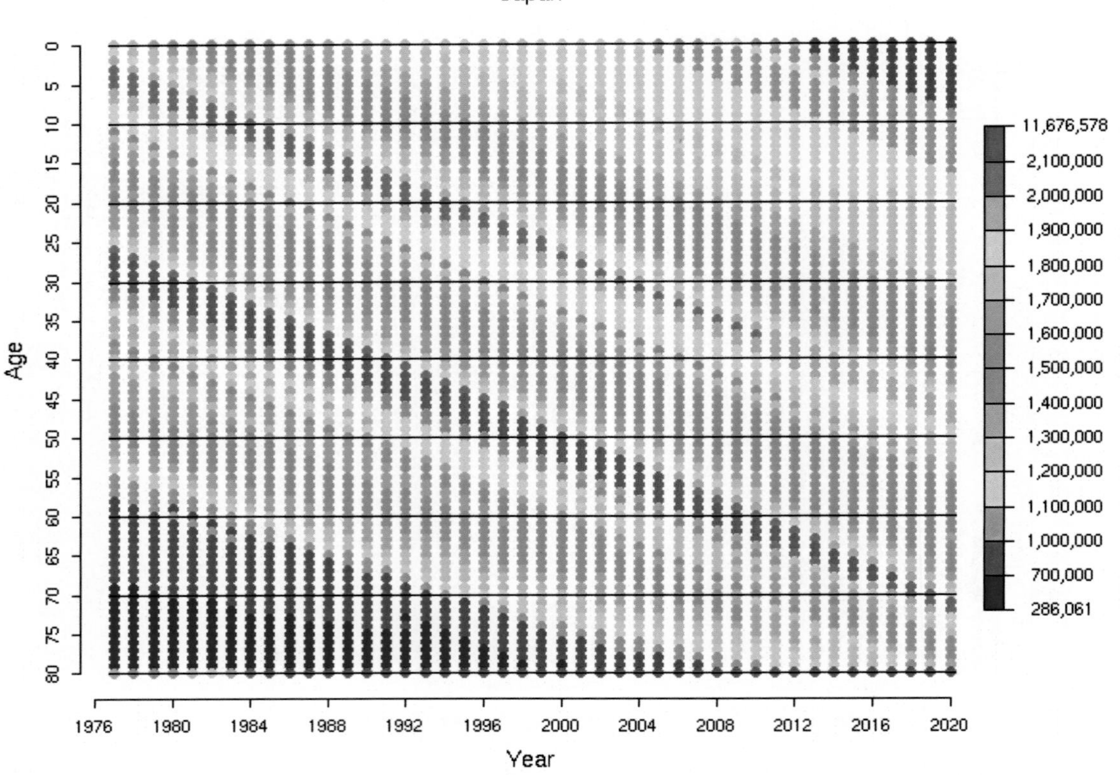

Jordan

Chart 2.44 *Age structure of the population at a glance, each dot represents a single age group*

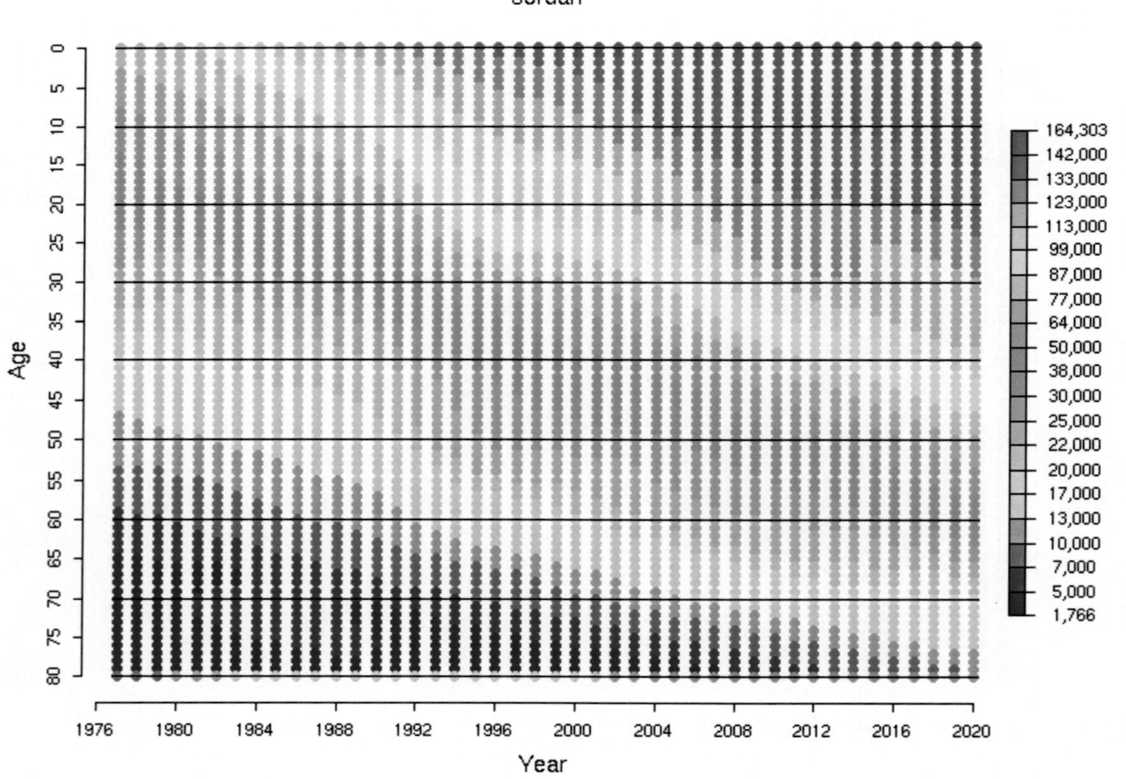

Kazakhstan

Chart 2.45 *Age structure of the population at a glance, each dot represents a single age group*

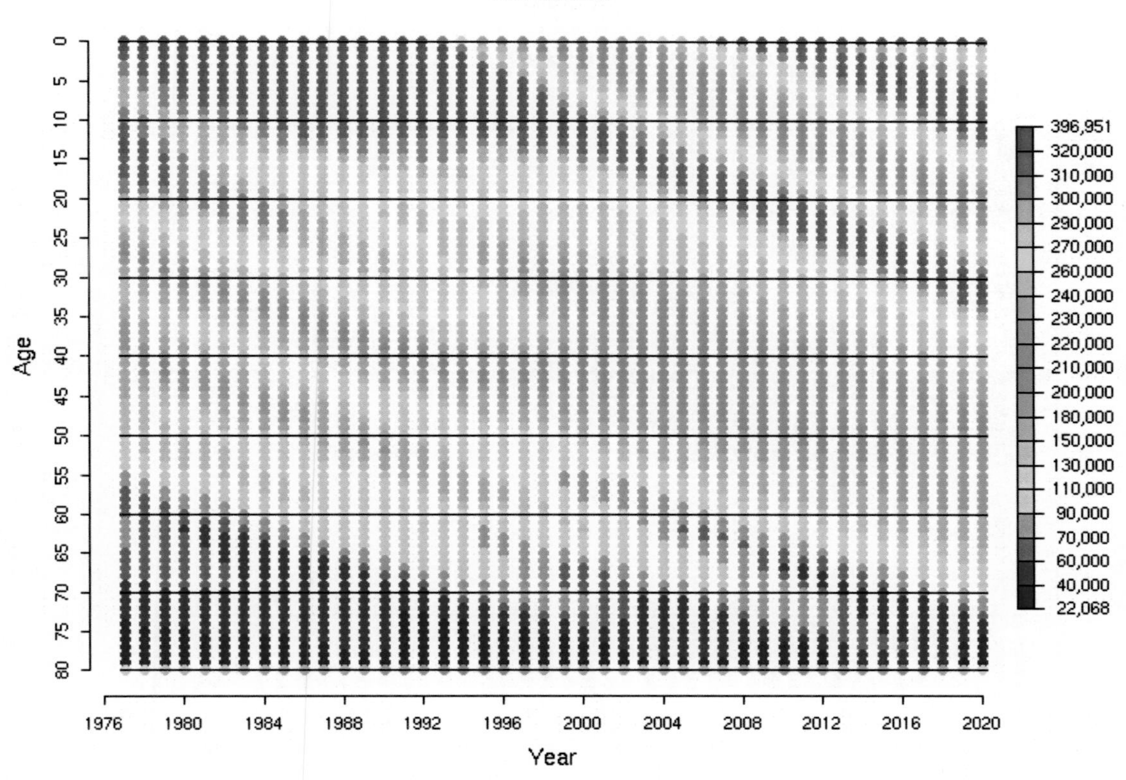

Kuwait

Chart 2.46 *Age structure of the population at a glance, each dot represents a single age group*

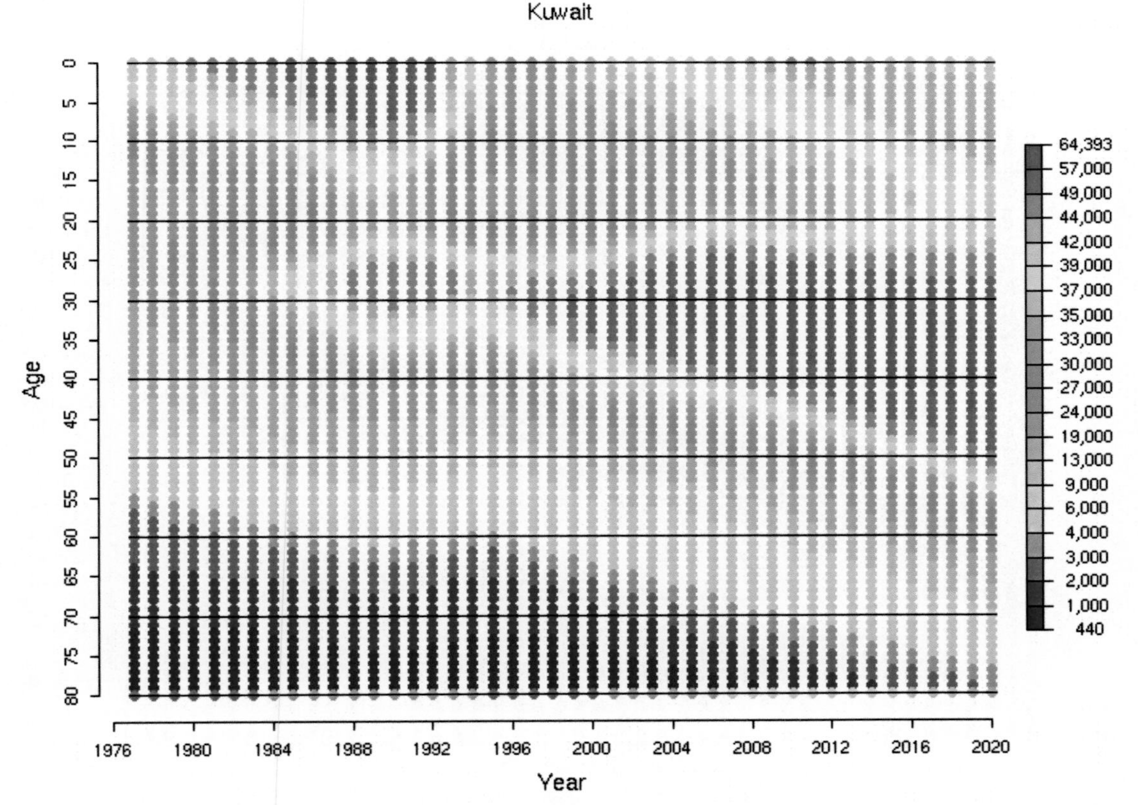

Latvia

Chart 2.47 *Age structure of the population at a glance, each dot represents a single age group*

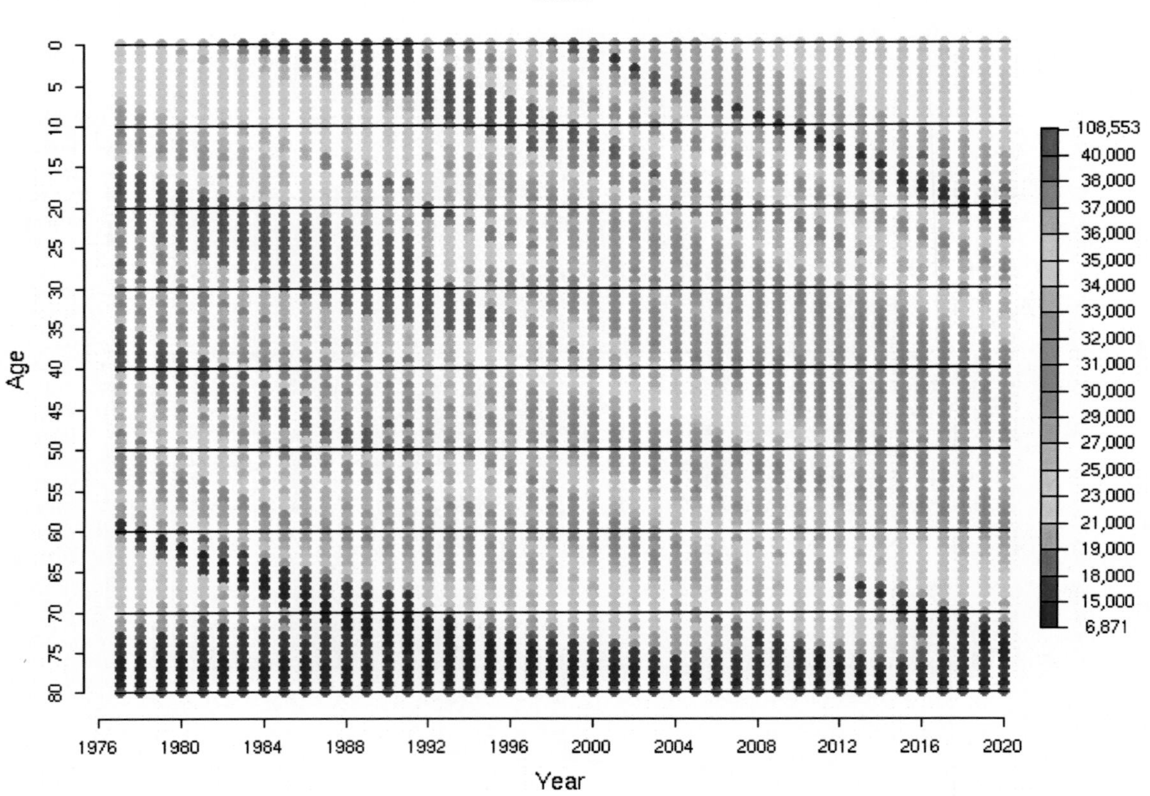

Lithuania

Chart 2.48 *Age structure of the population at a glance, each dot represents a single age group*

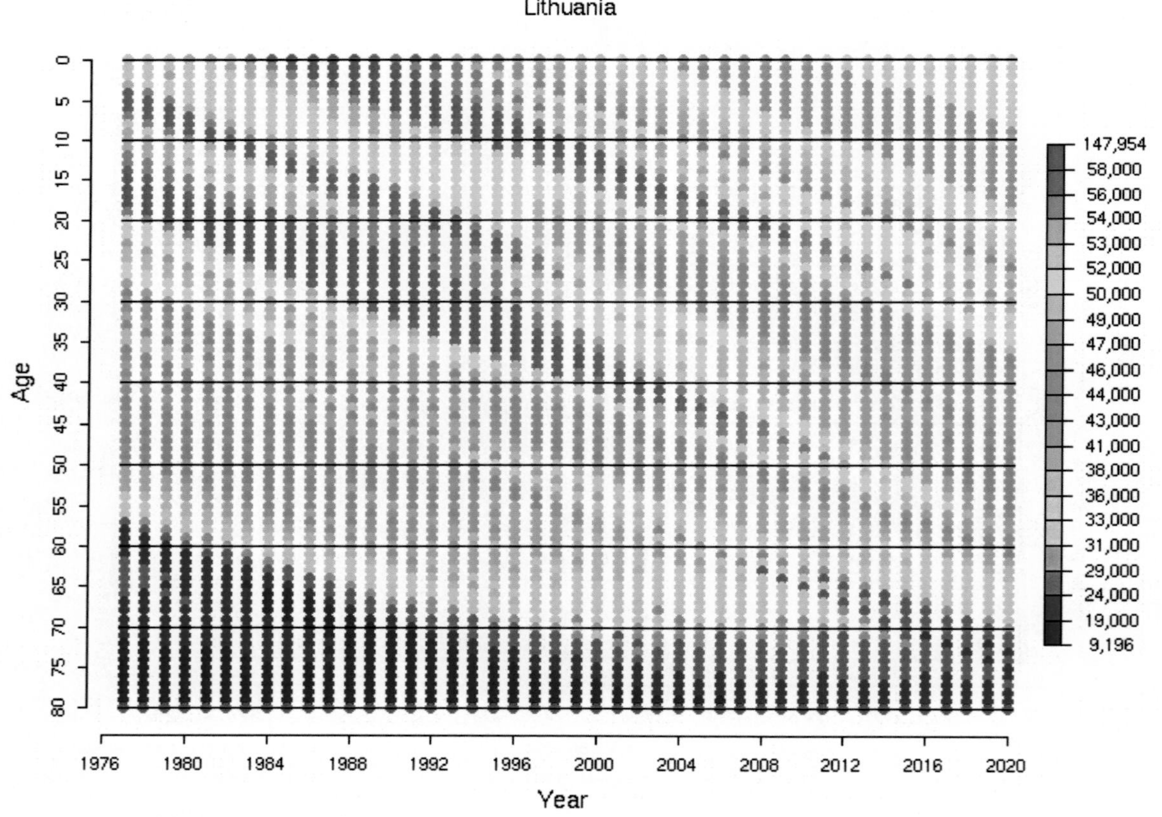

Malaysia

Chart 2.49 *Age structure of the population at a glance, each dot represents a single age group*

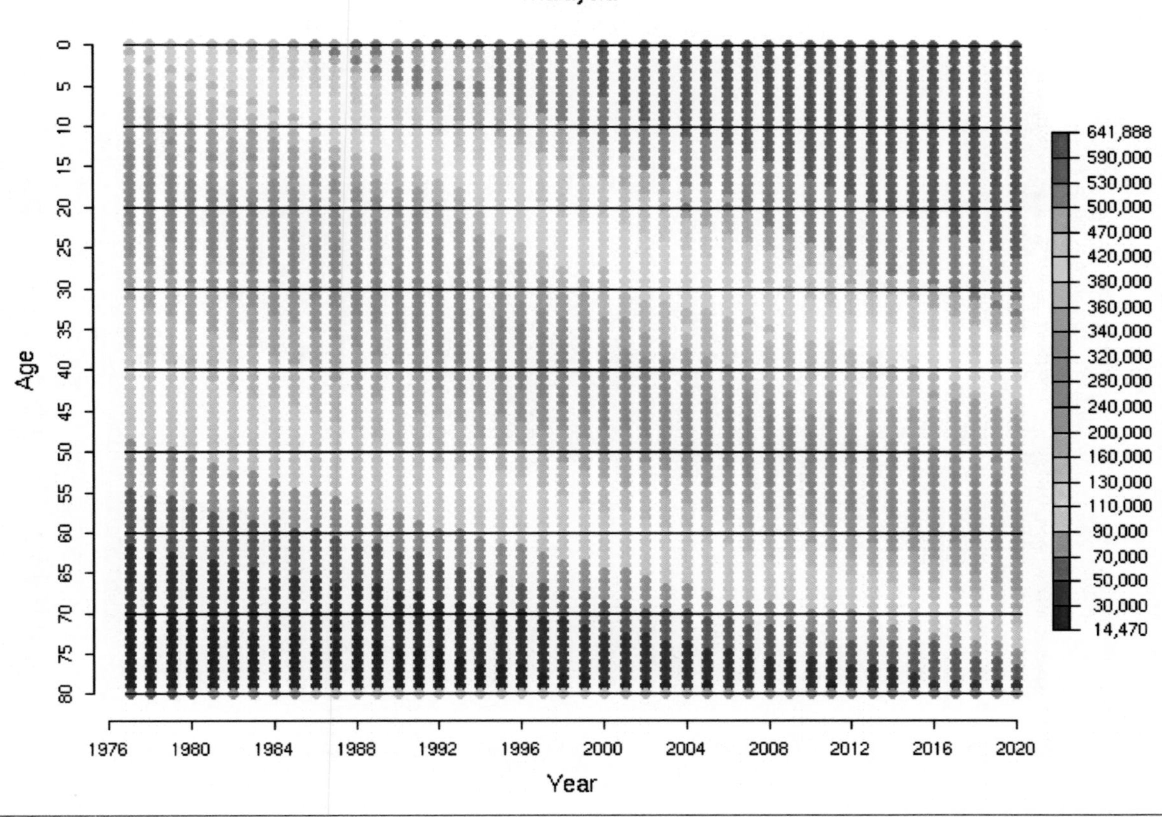

Mexico

Chart 2.50 *Age structure of the population at a glance, each dot represents a single age group*

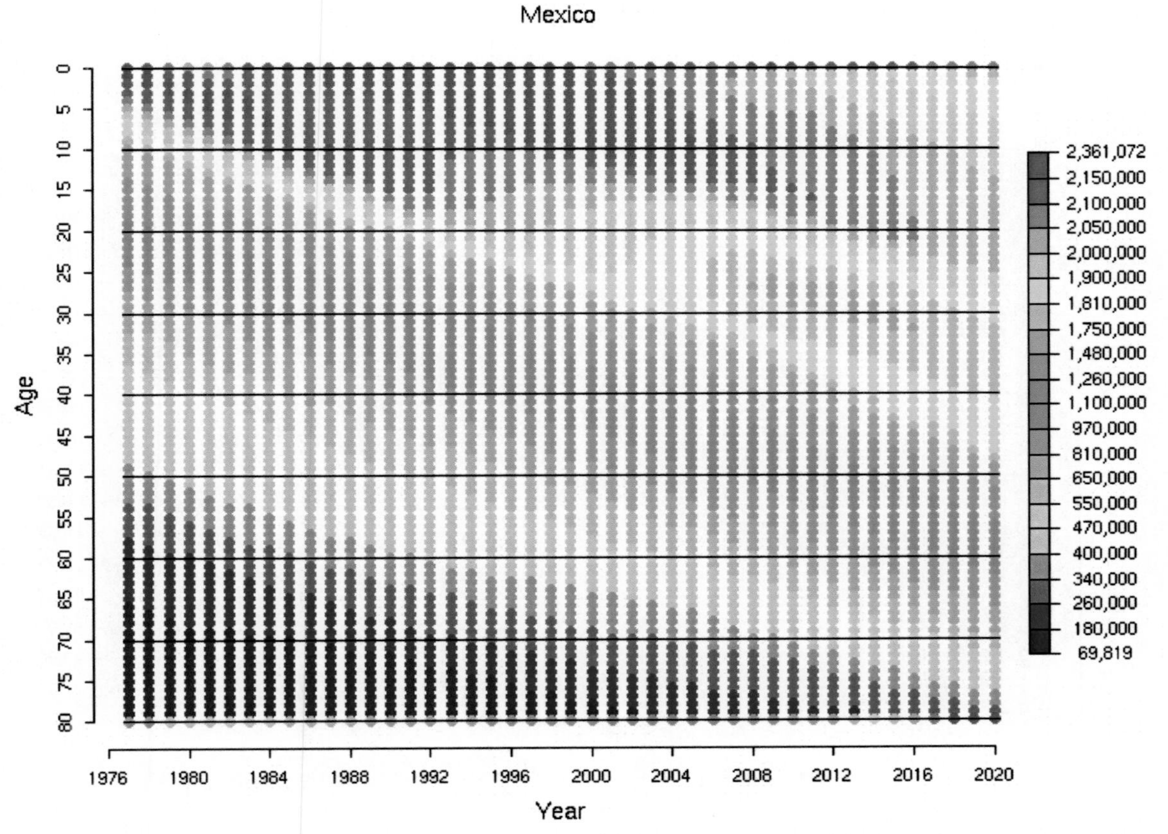

Morocco

Chart 2.51 *Age structure of the population at a glance, each dot represents a single age group*

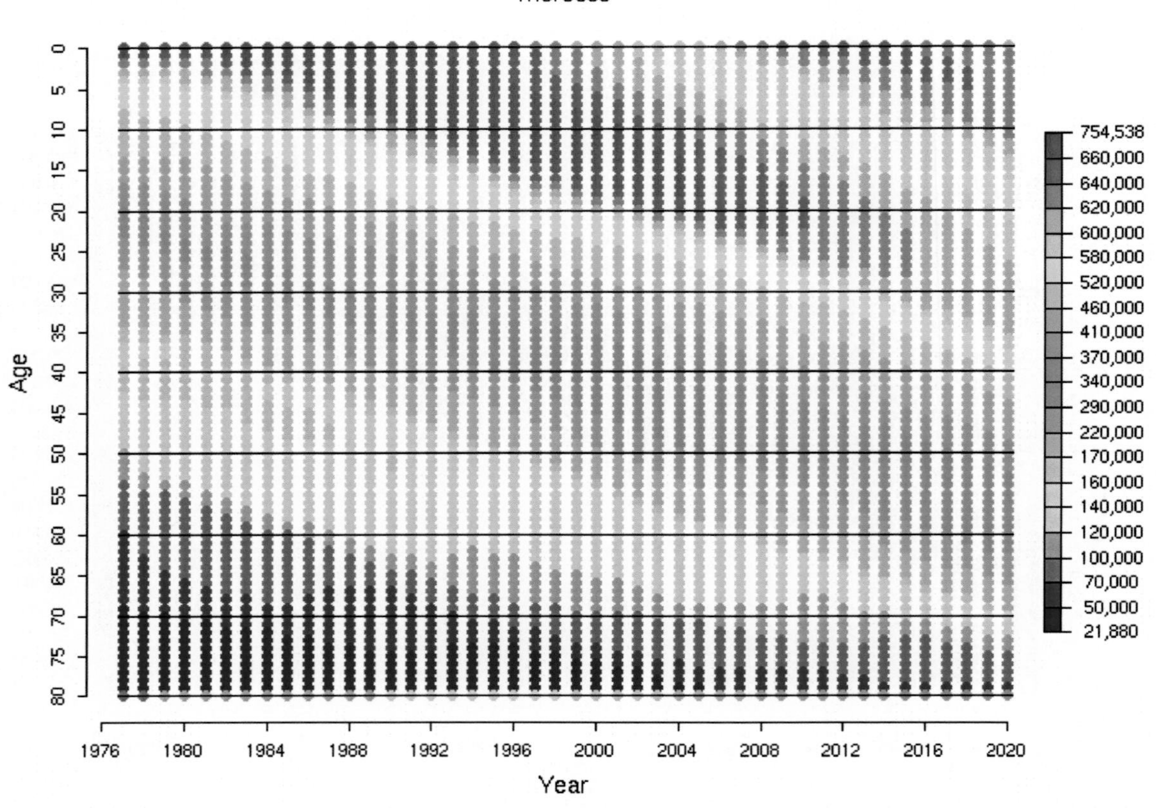

Netherlands

Chart 2.52 *Age structure of the population at a glance, each dot represents a single age group*

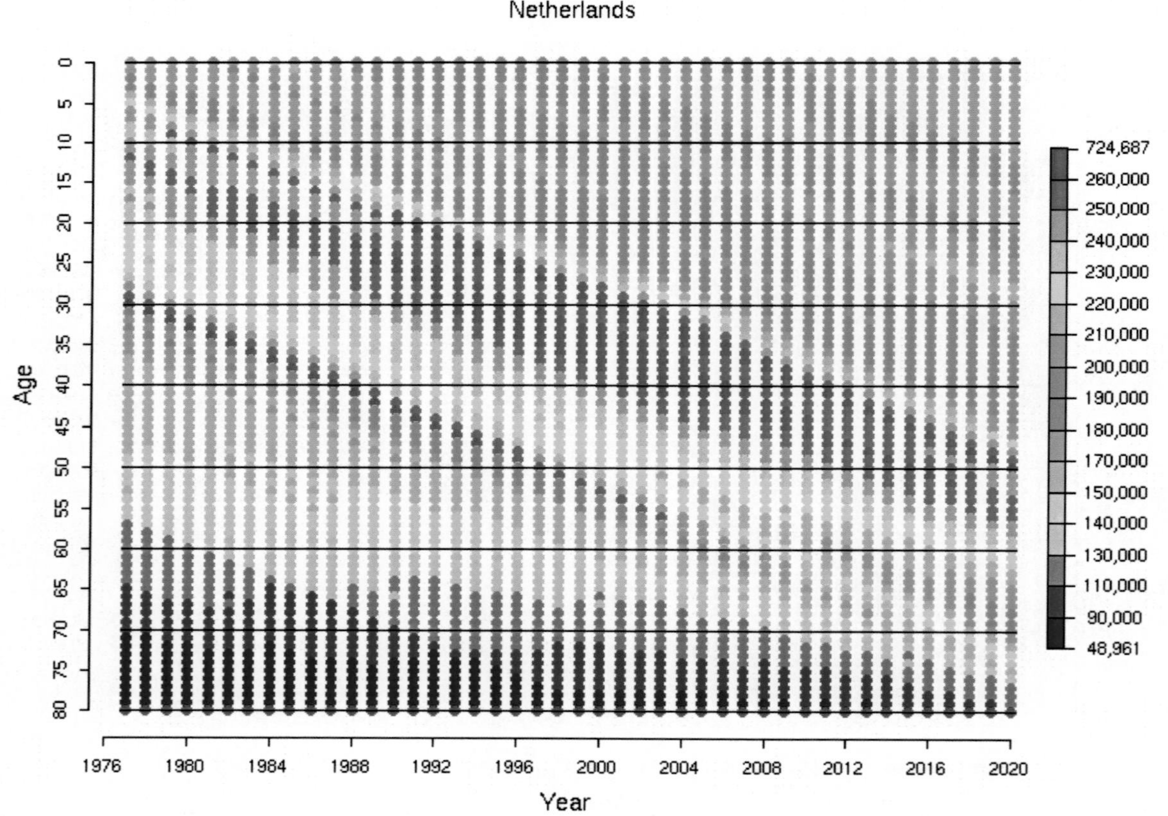

New Zealand

Chart 2.53 *Age structure of the population at a glance, each dot represents a single age group*

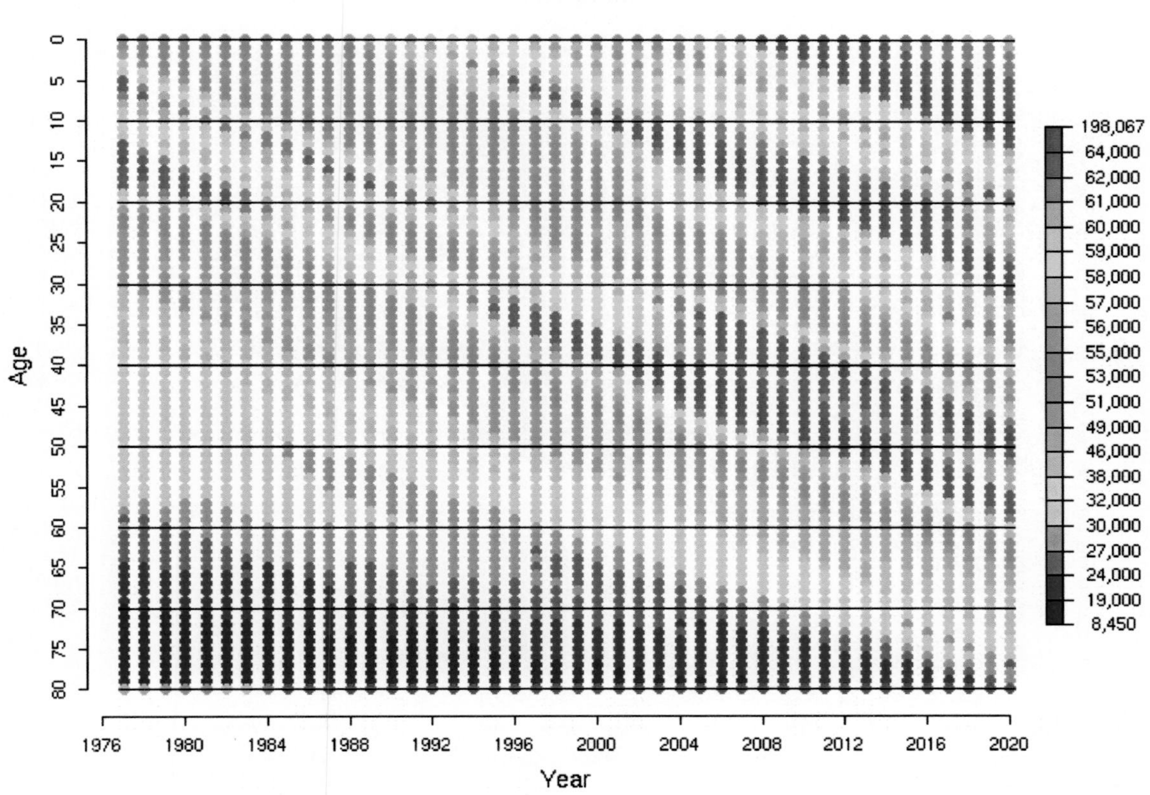

Nigeria

Chart 2.54 *Age structure of the population at a glance, each dot represents a single age group*

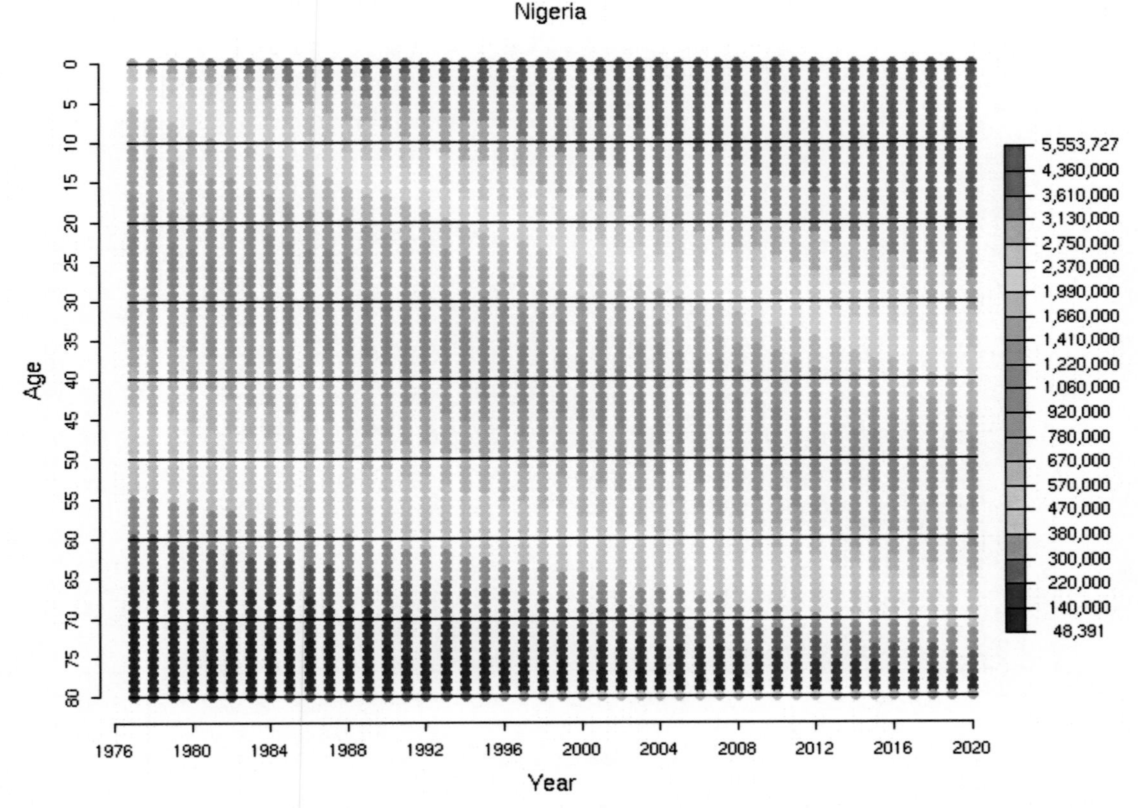

Norway

Chart 2.55 *Age structure of the population at a glance, each dot represents a single age group*

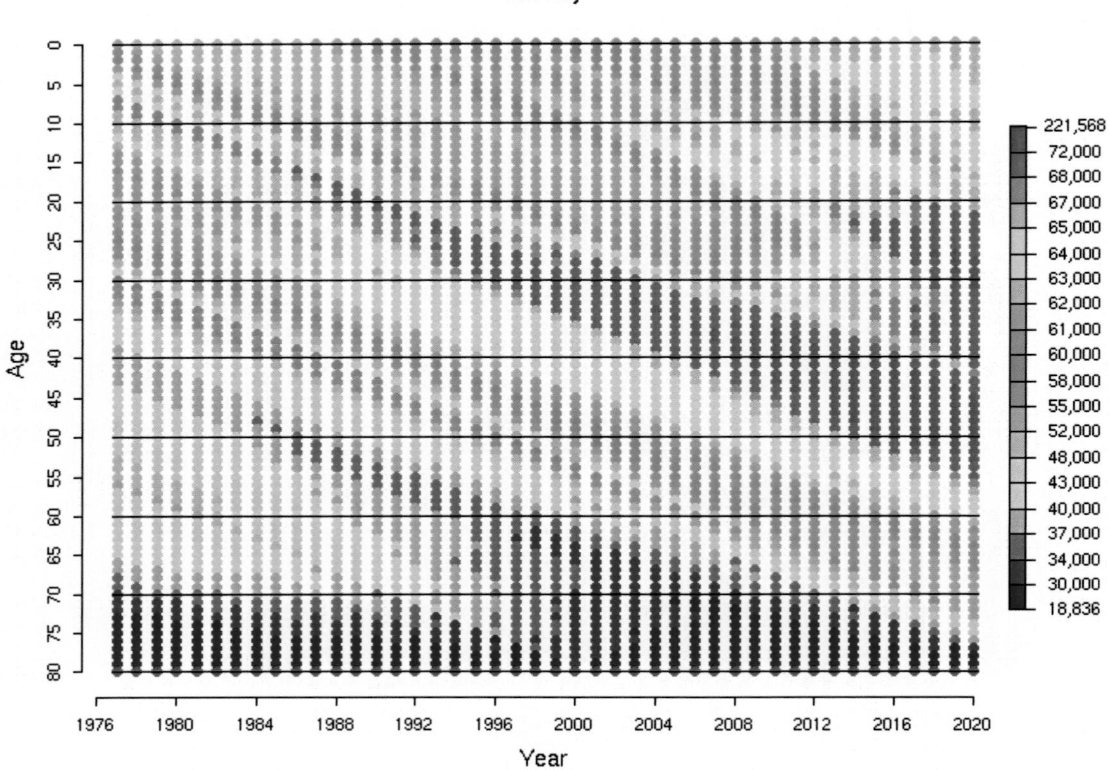

Pakistan

Chart 2.56 *Age structure of the population at a glance, each dot represents a single age group*

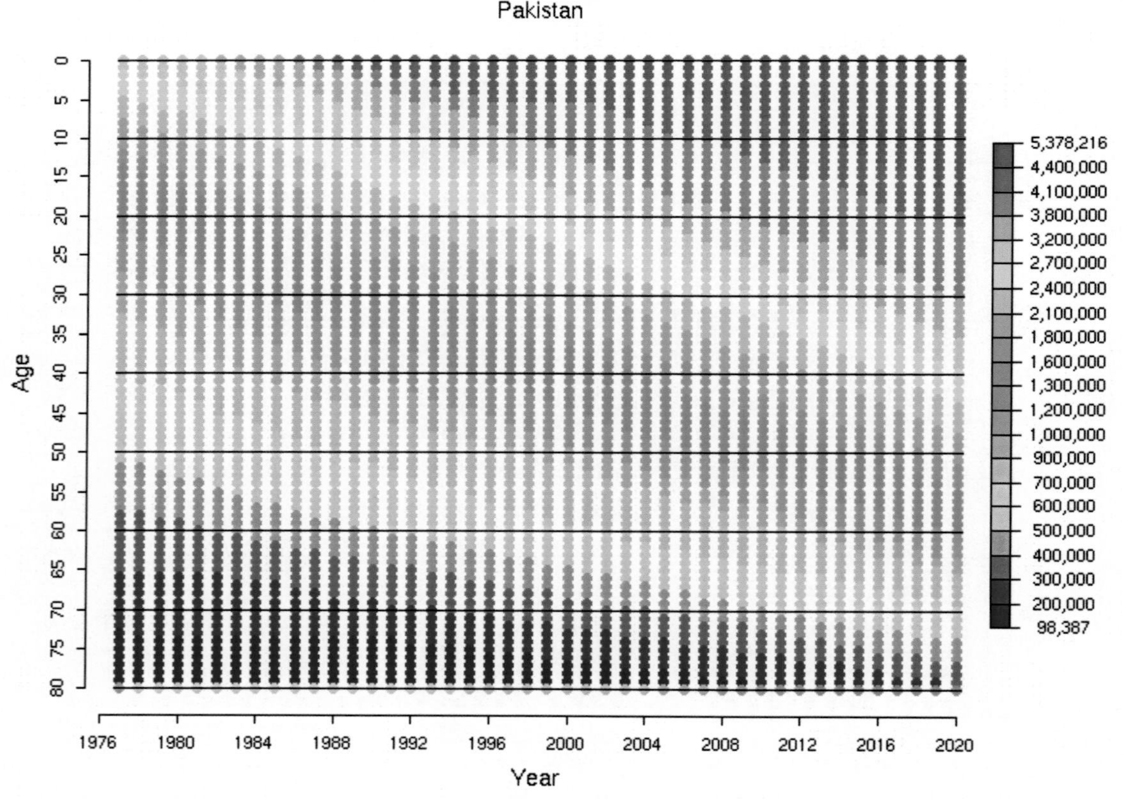

Peru

Chart 2.57 *Age structure of the population at a glance, each dot represents a single age group*

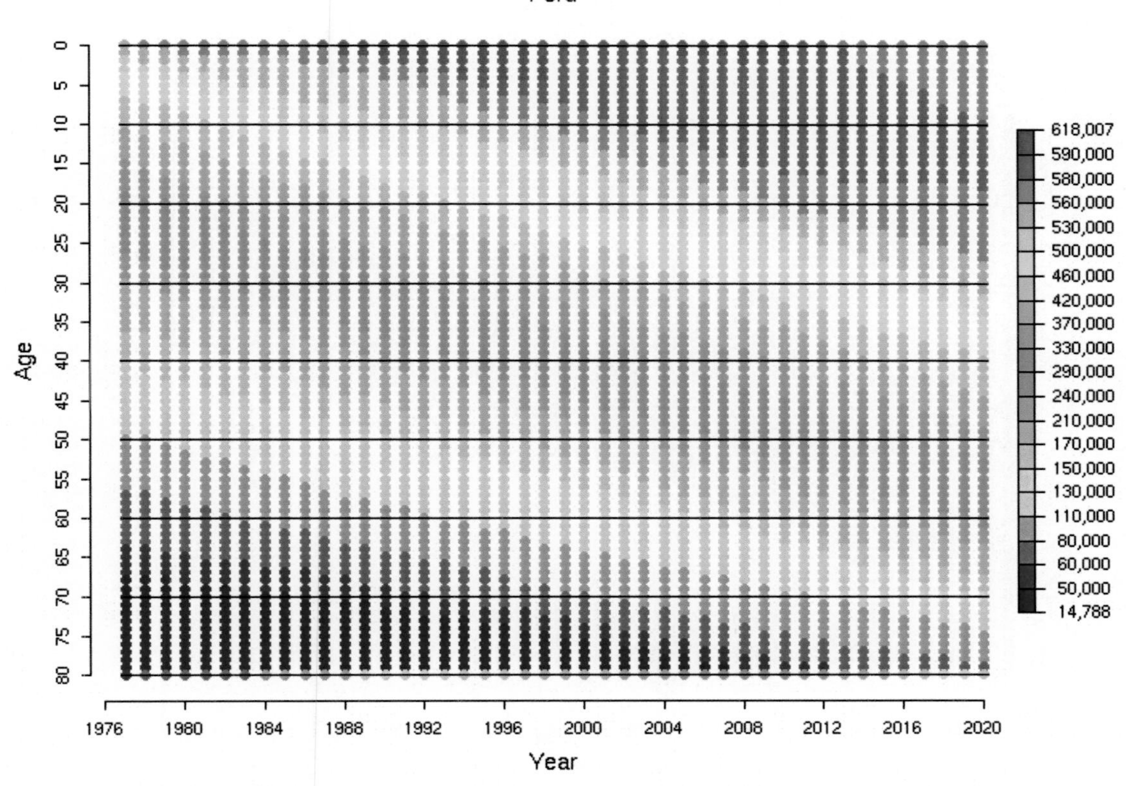

Philippines

Chart 2.58 *Age structure of the population at a glance, each dot represents a single age group*

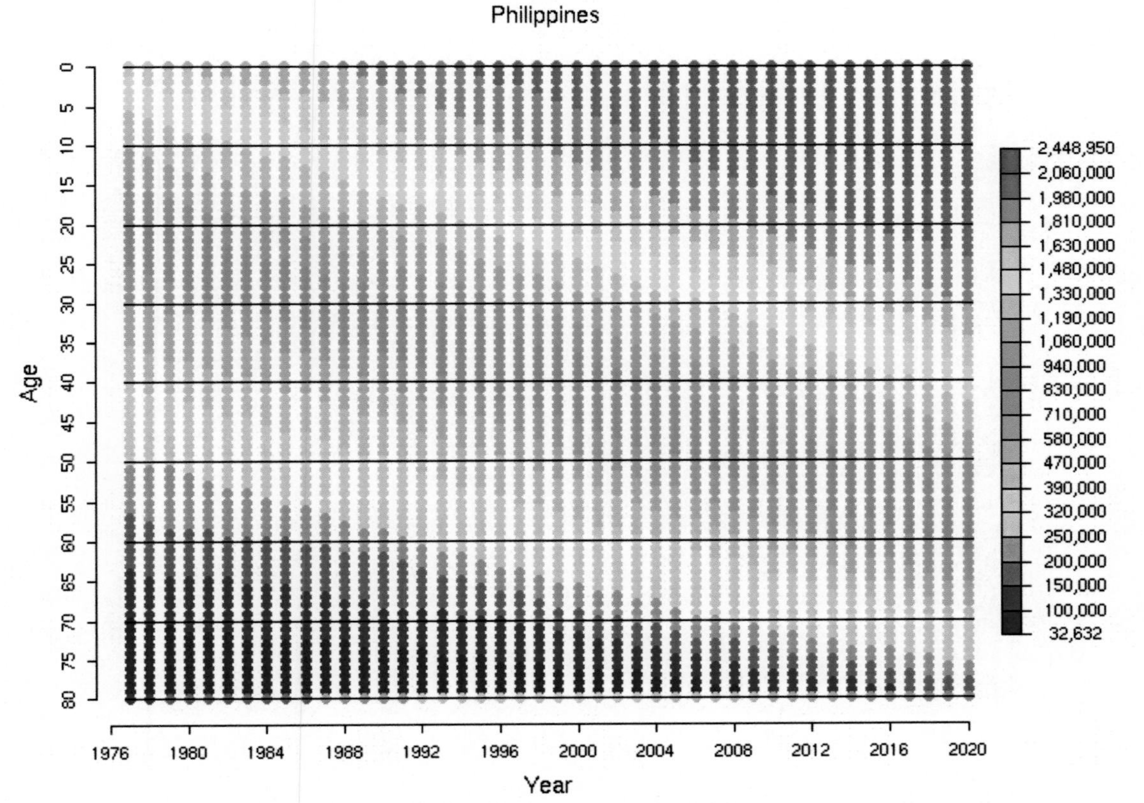

Poland

Chart 2.59 *Age structure of the population at a glance, each dot represents a single age group*

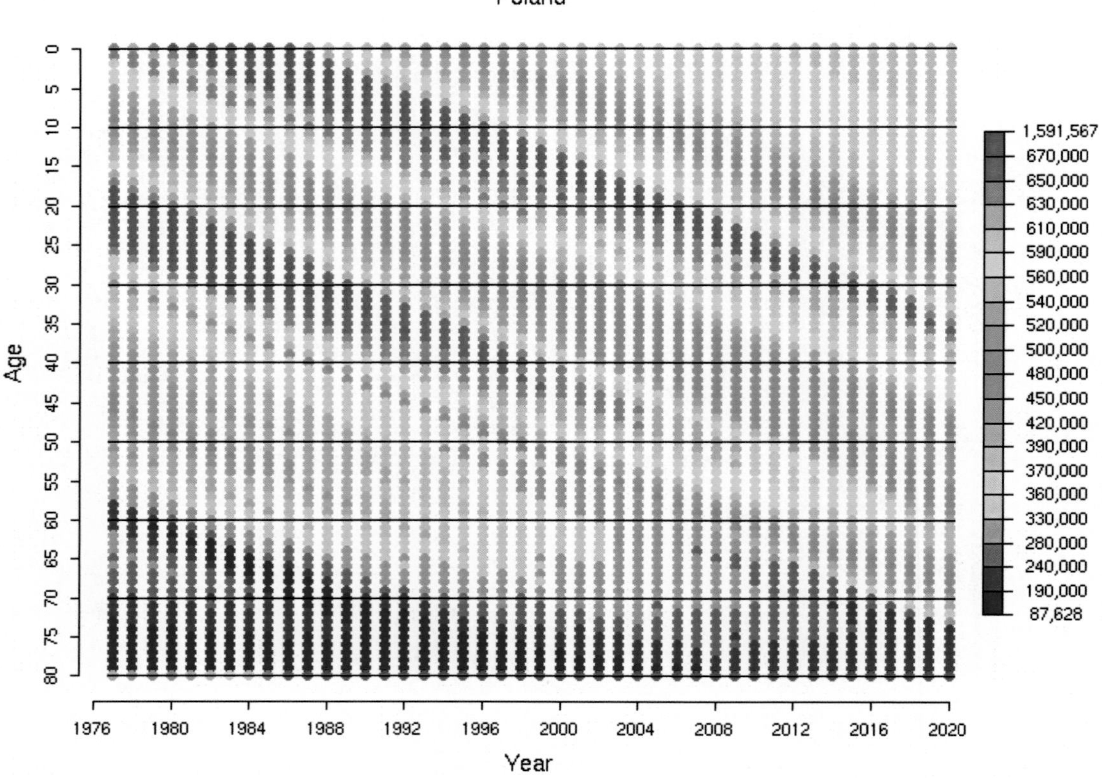

Portugal

Chart 2.60 *Age structure of the population at a glance, each dot represents a single age group*

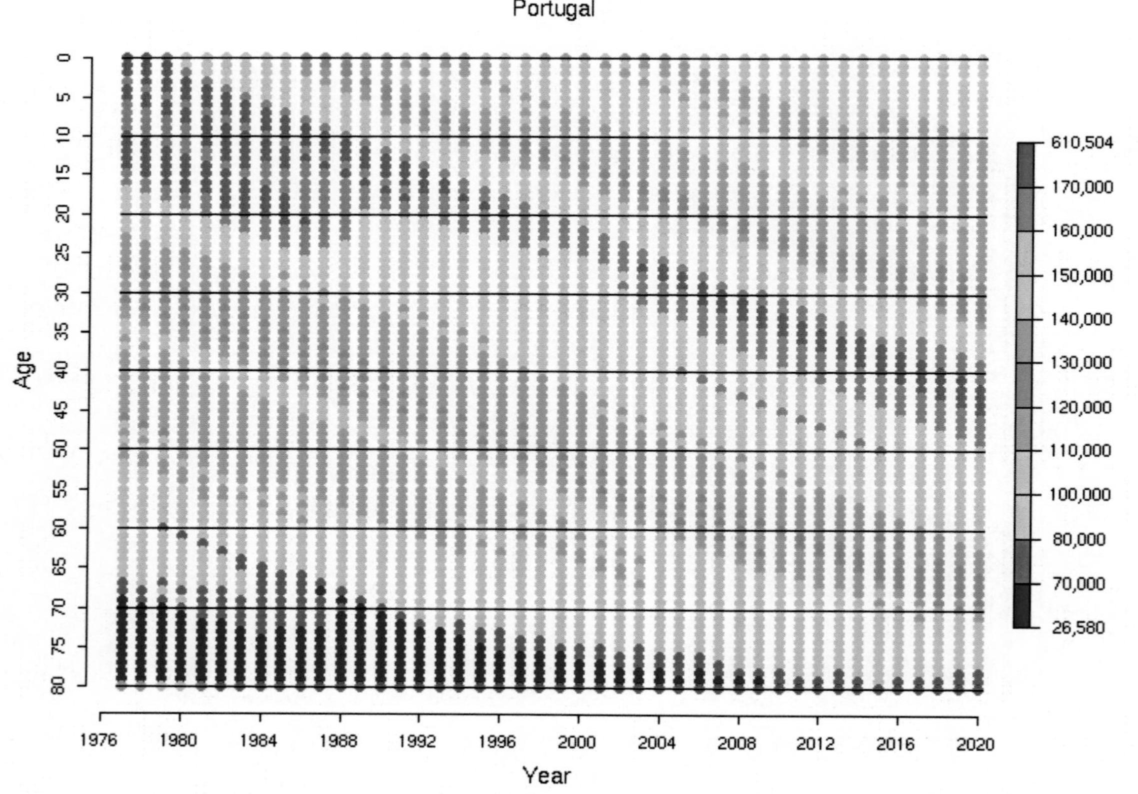

Romania

Chart 2.61 *Age structure of the population at a glance, each dot represents a single age group*

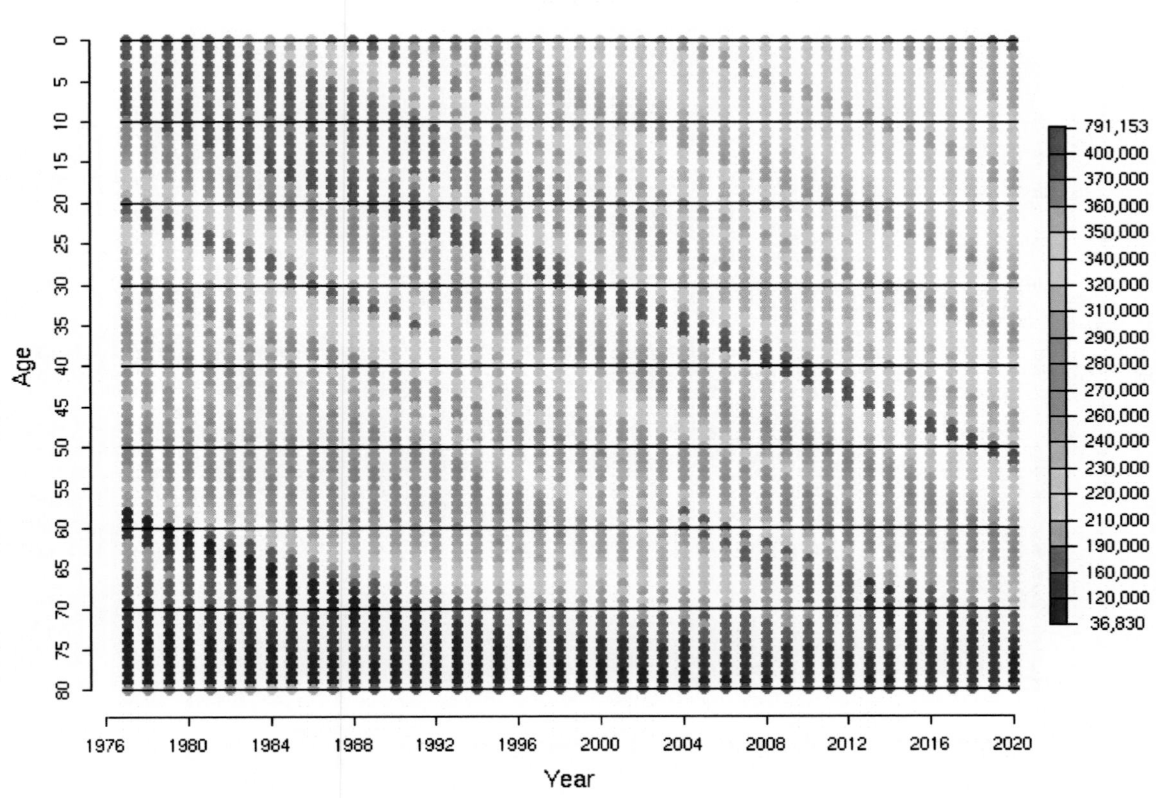

Russia

Chart 2.62 *Age structure of the population at a glance, each dot represents a single age group*

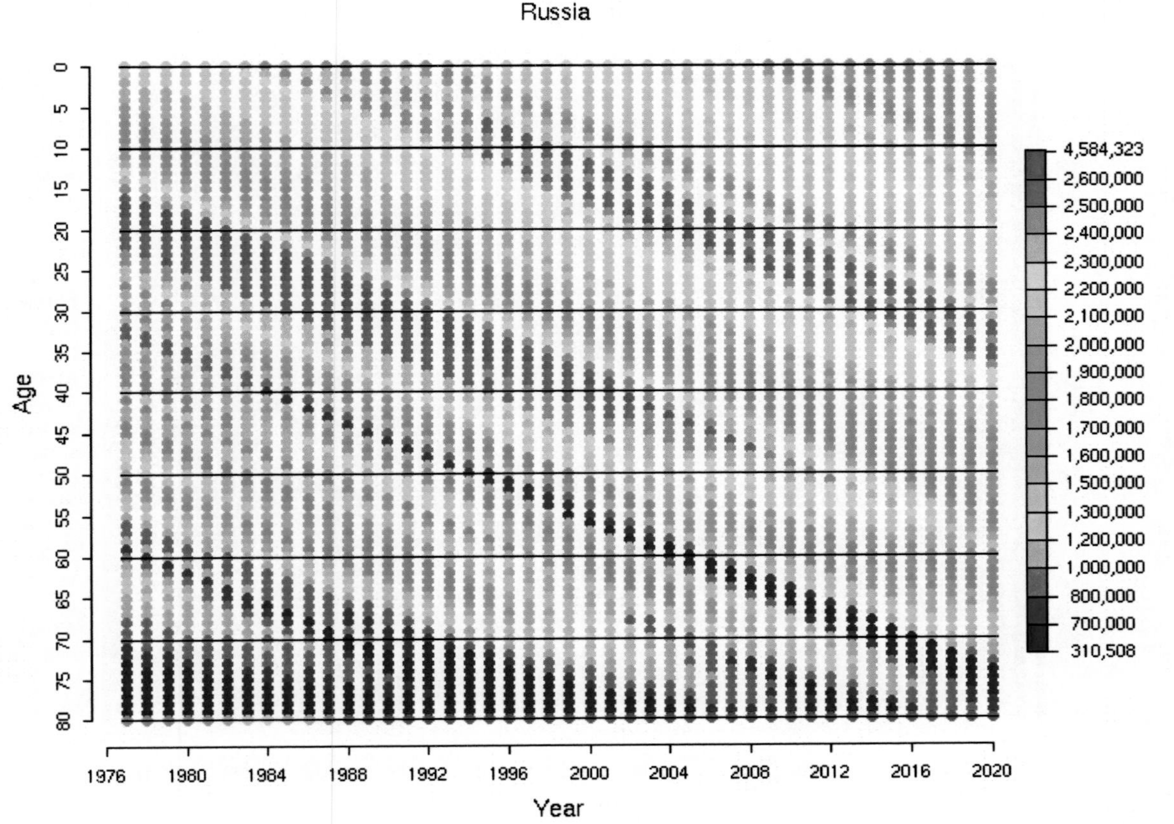

Saudi Arabia

Chart 2.63 *Age structure of the population at a glance, each dot represents a single age group*

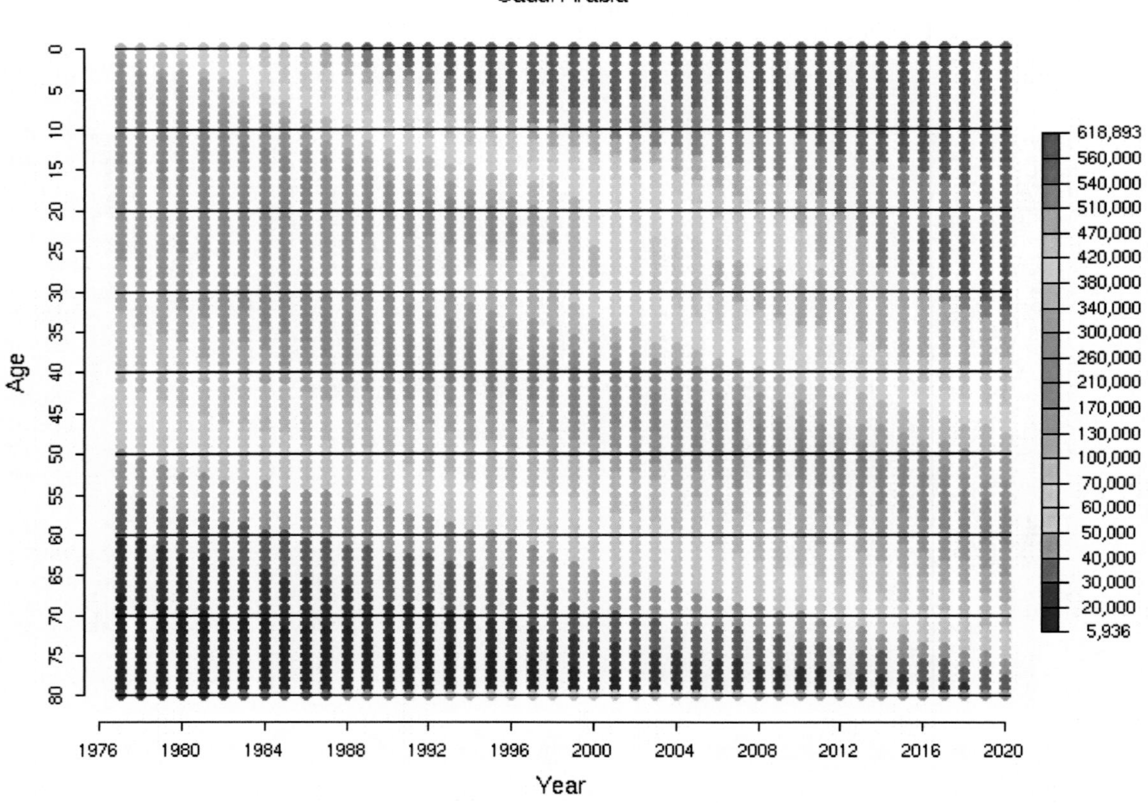

Singapore

Chart 2.64 *Age structure of the population at a glance, each dot represents a single age group*

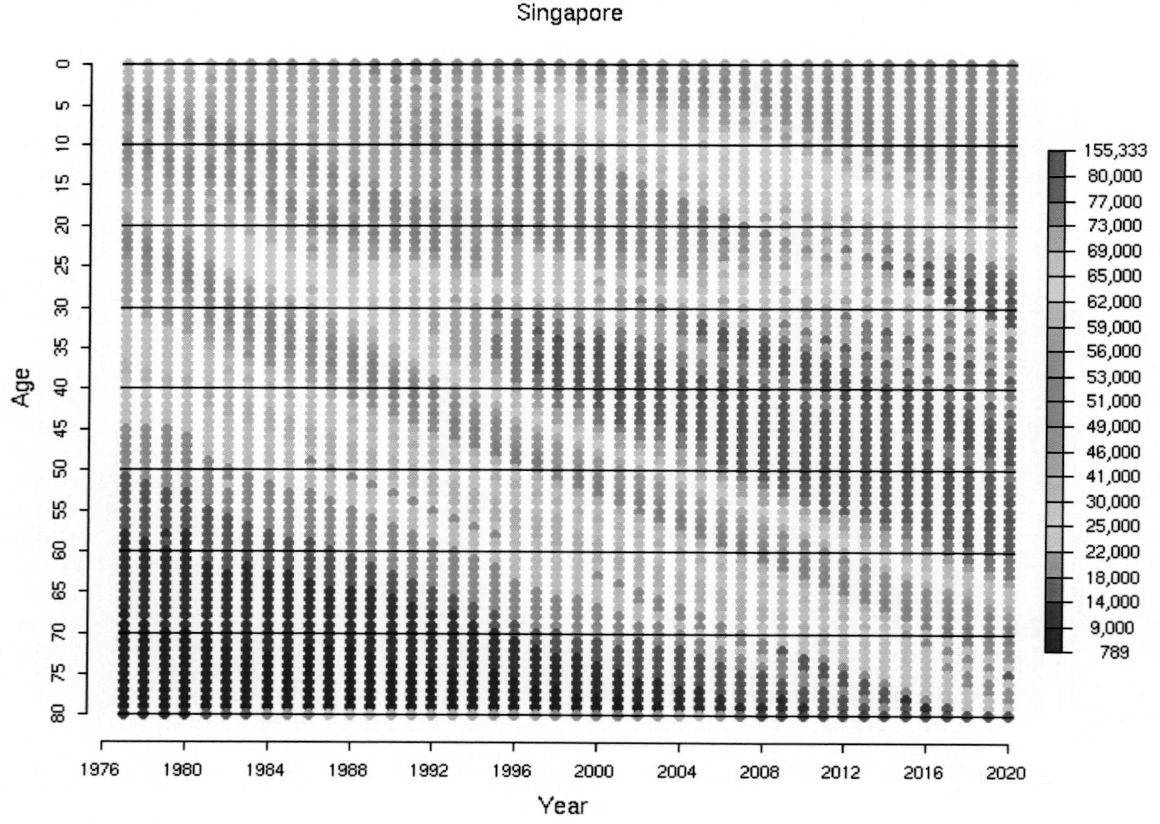

Slovakia

Chart 2.65 *Age structure of the population at a glance, each dot represents a single age group*

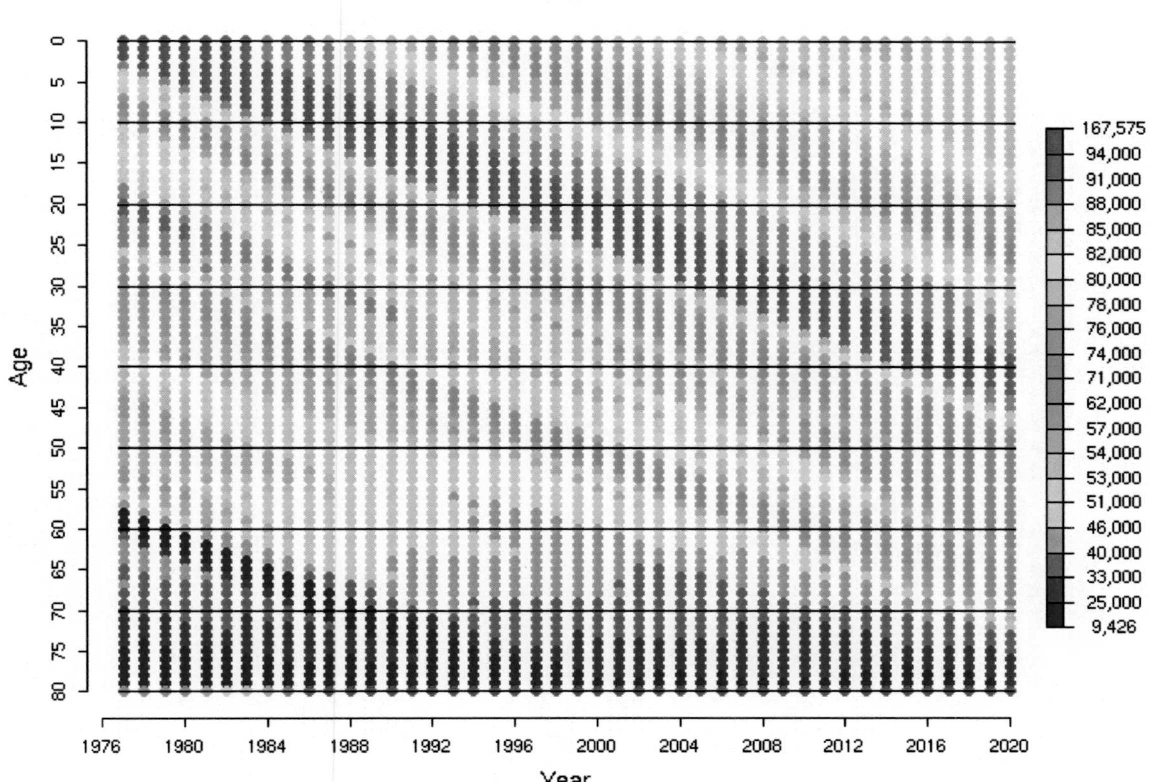

Slovenia

Chart 2.66 *Age structure of the population at a glance, each dot represents a single age group*

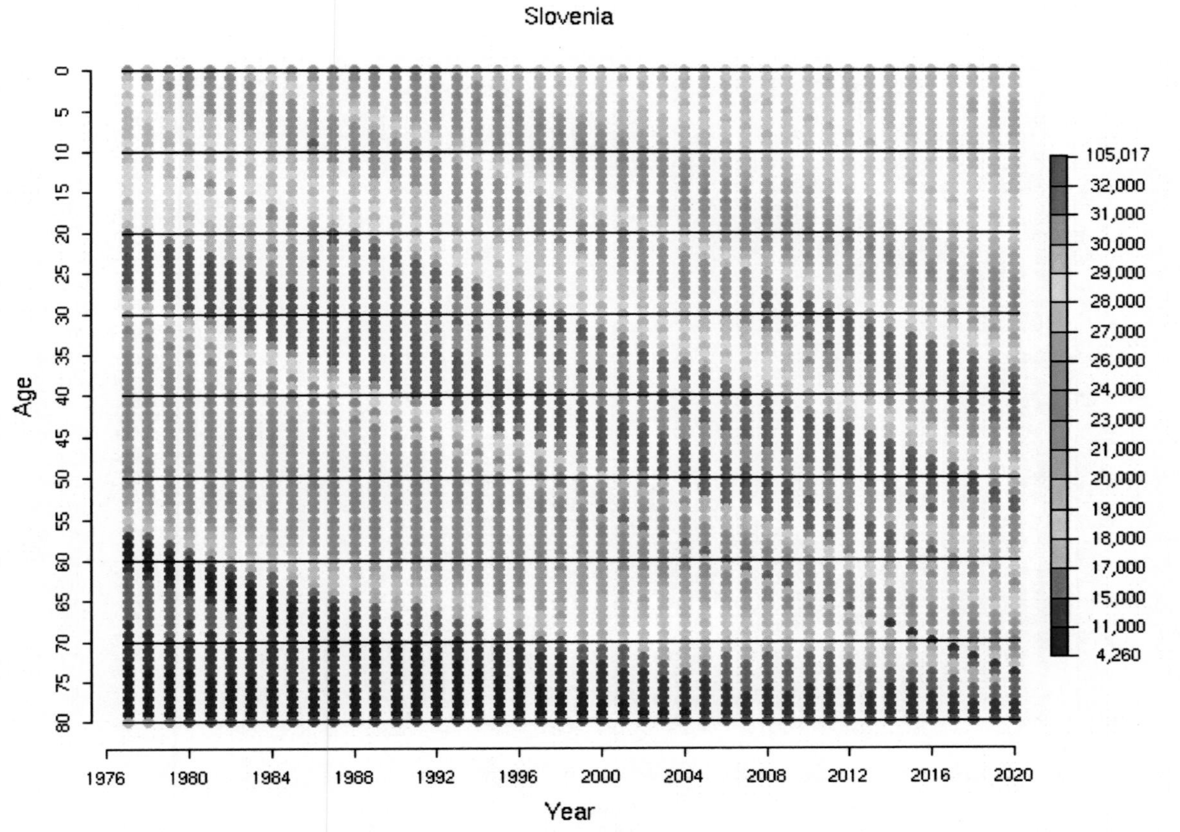

South Africa

Chart 2.67 *Age structure of the population at a glance, each dot represents a single age group*

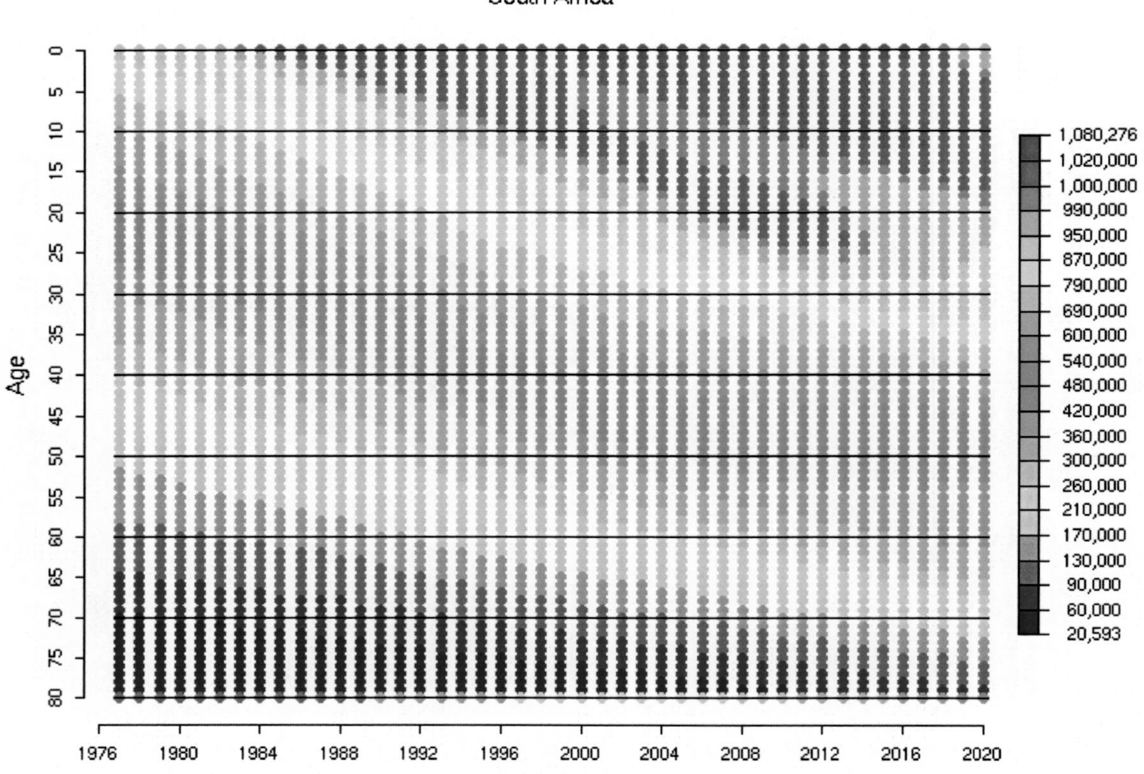

South Korea

Chart 2.68 *Age structure of the population at a glance, each dot represents a single age group*

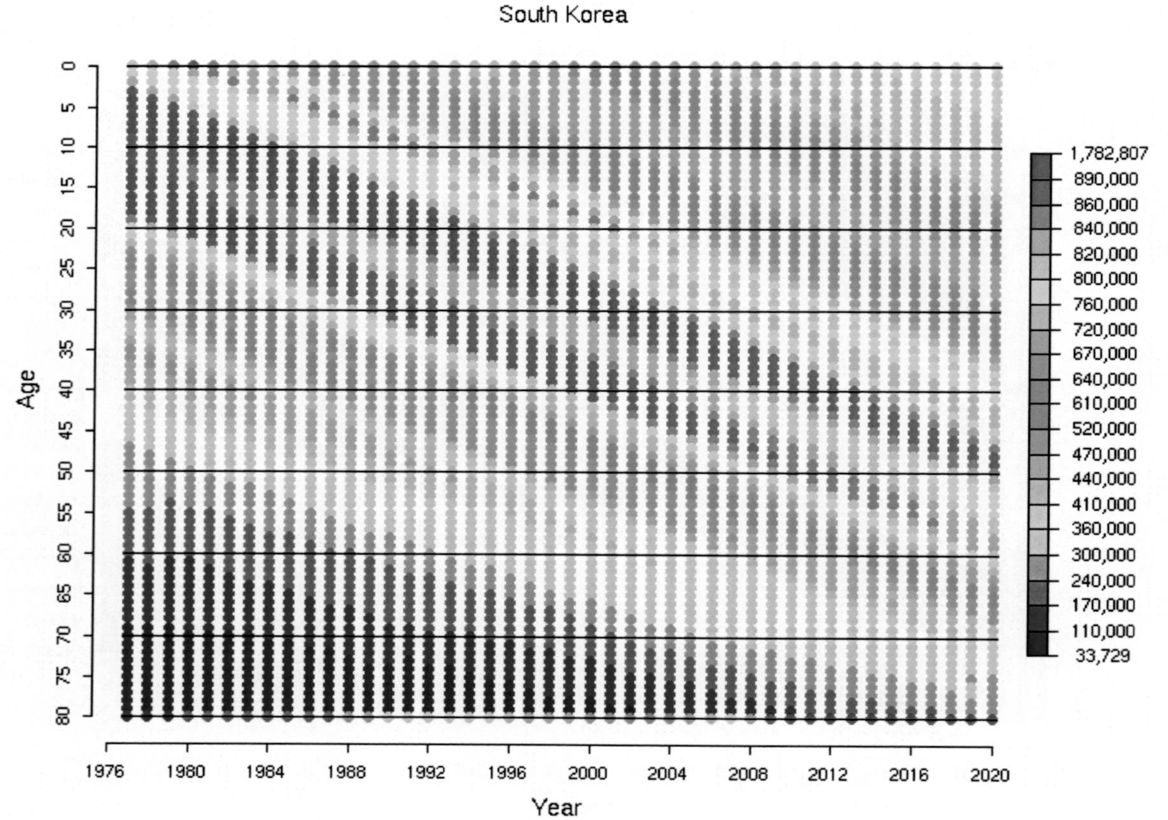

Spain

Chart 2.69 *Age structure of the population at a glance, each dot represents a single age group*

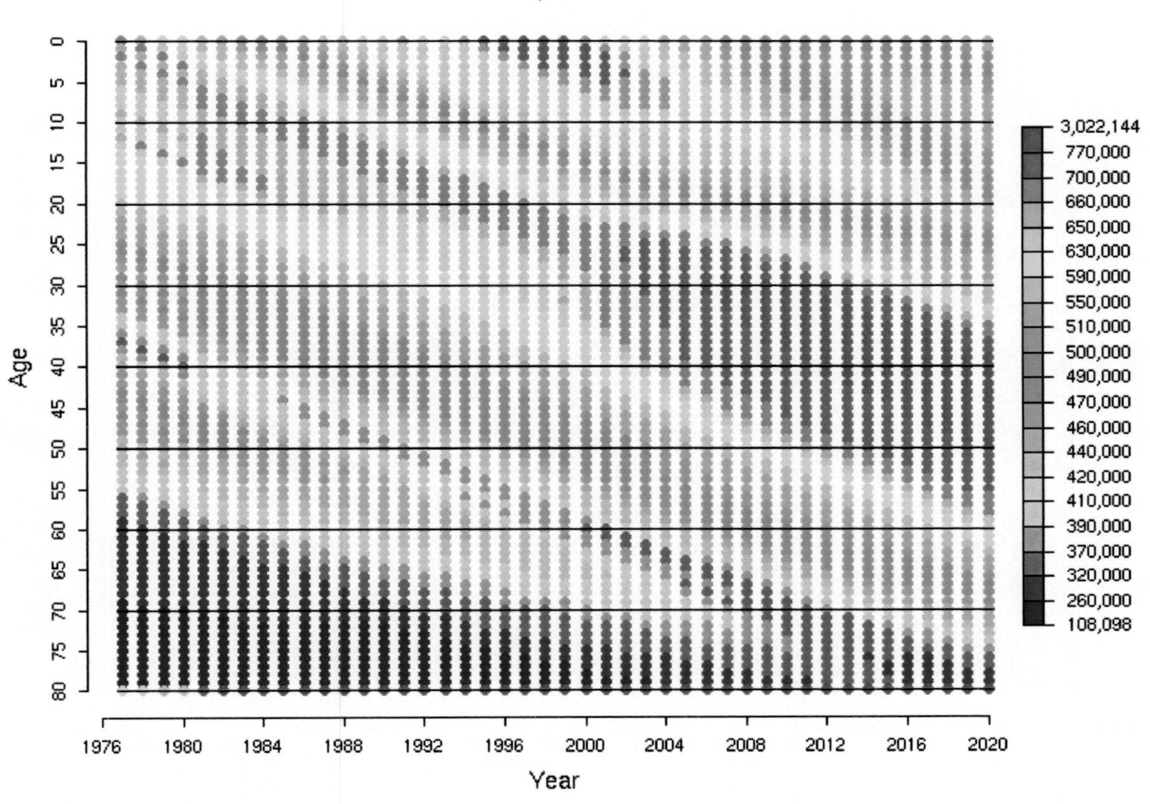

Sweden

Chart 2.70 *Age structure of the population at a glance, each dot represents a single age group*

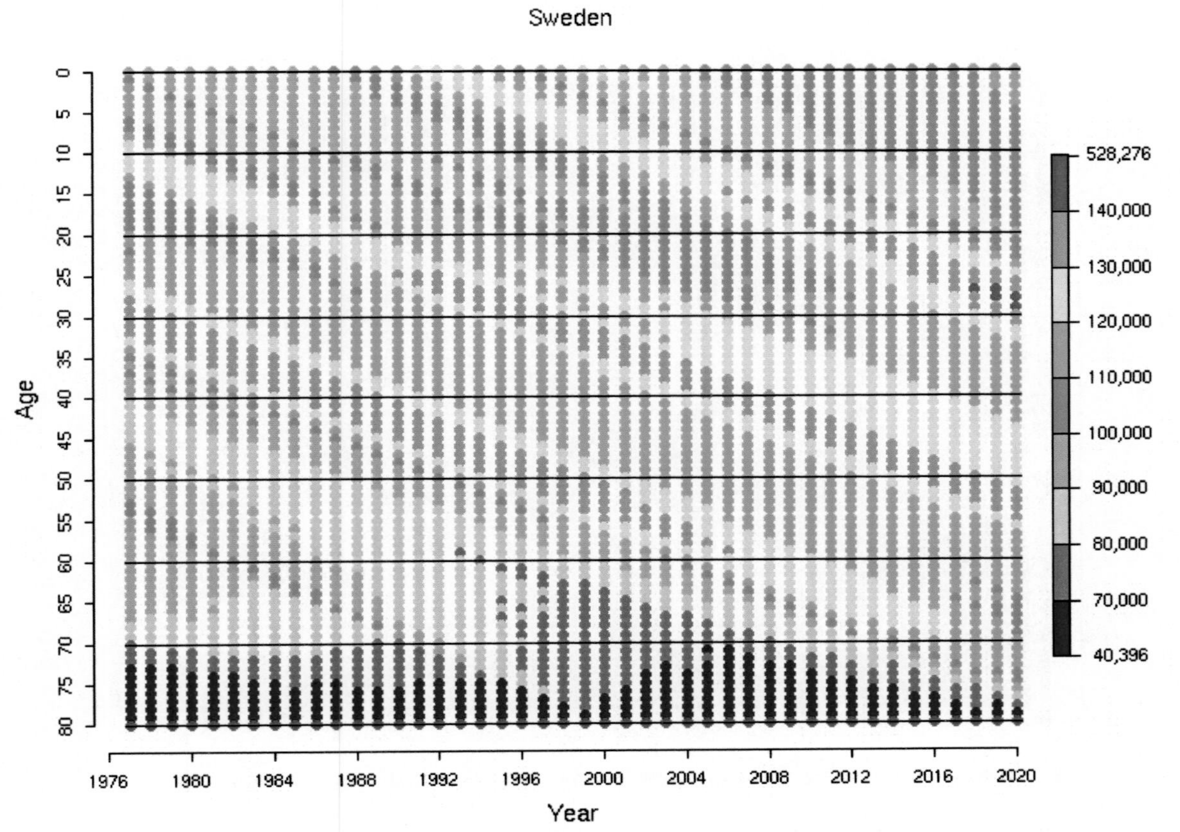

Switzerland

Chart 2.71 *Age structure of the population at a glance, each dot represents a single age group*

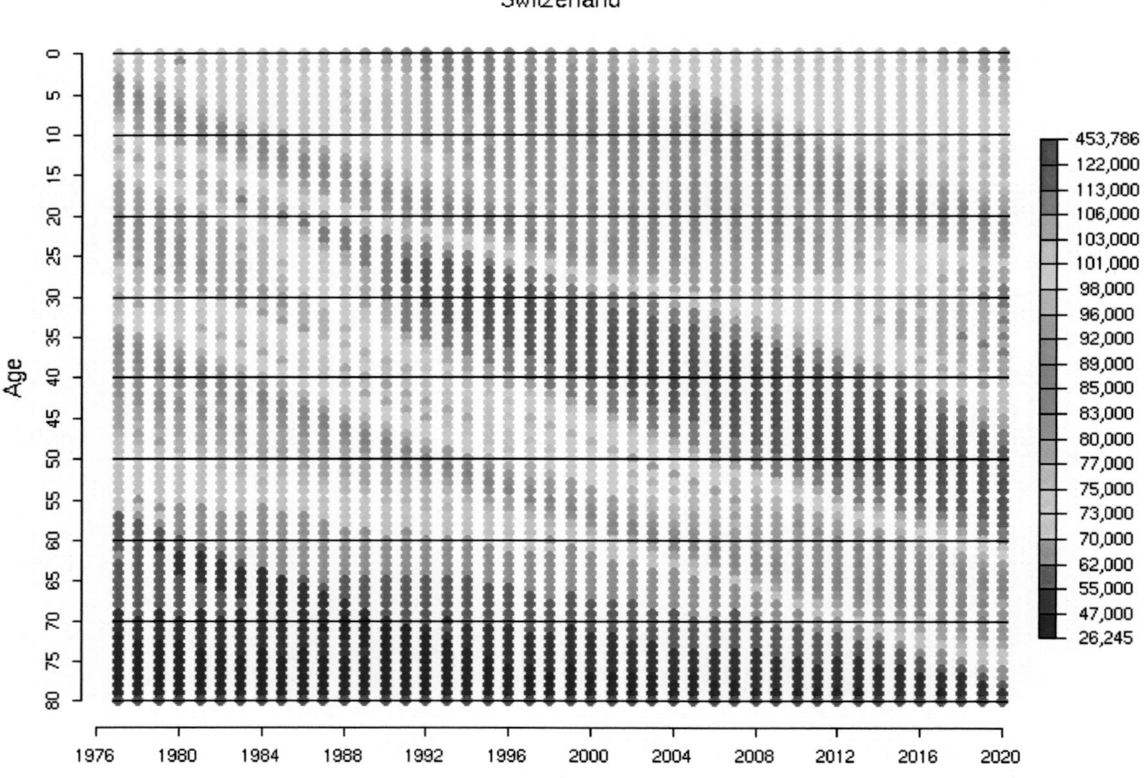

Taiwan

Chart 2.72 *Age structure of the population at a glance, each dot represents a single age group*

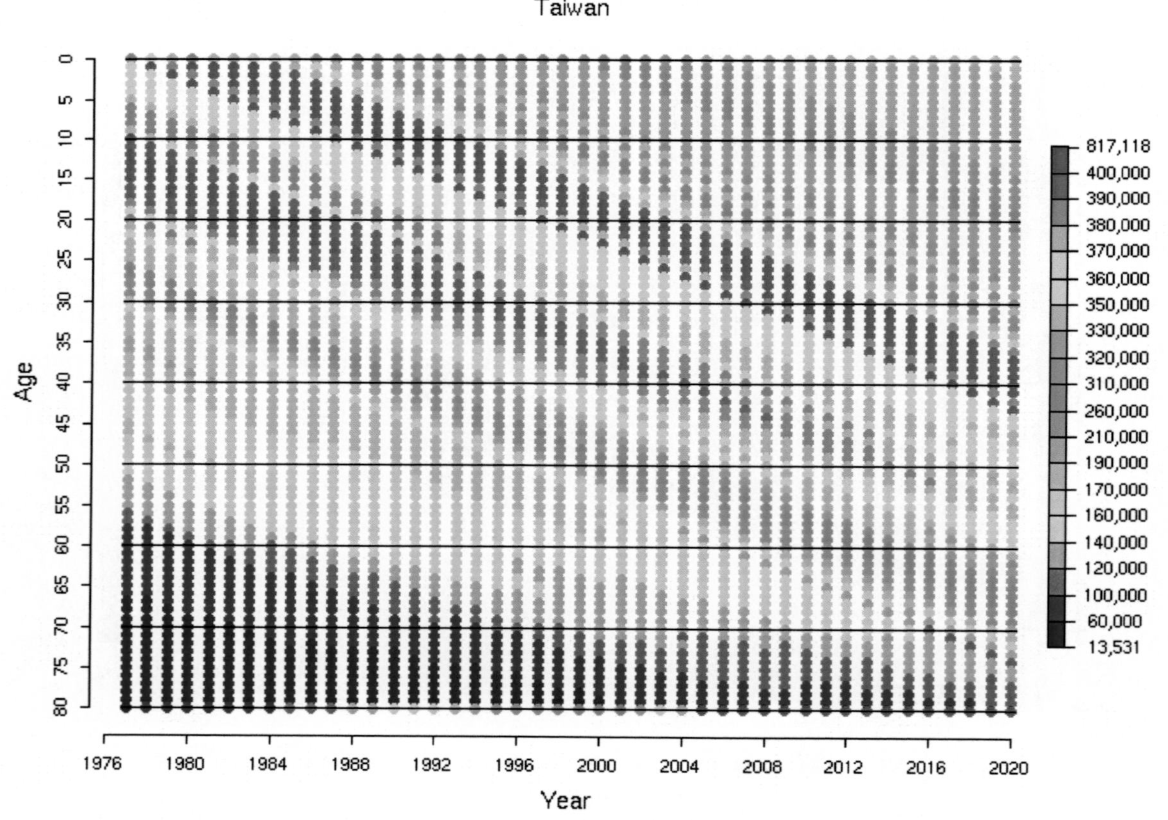

Thailand

Chart 2.73 *Age structure of the population at a glance, each dot represents a single age group*

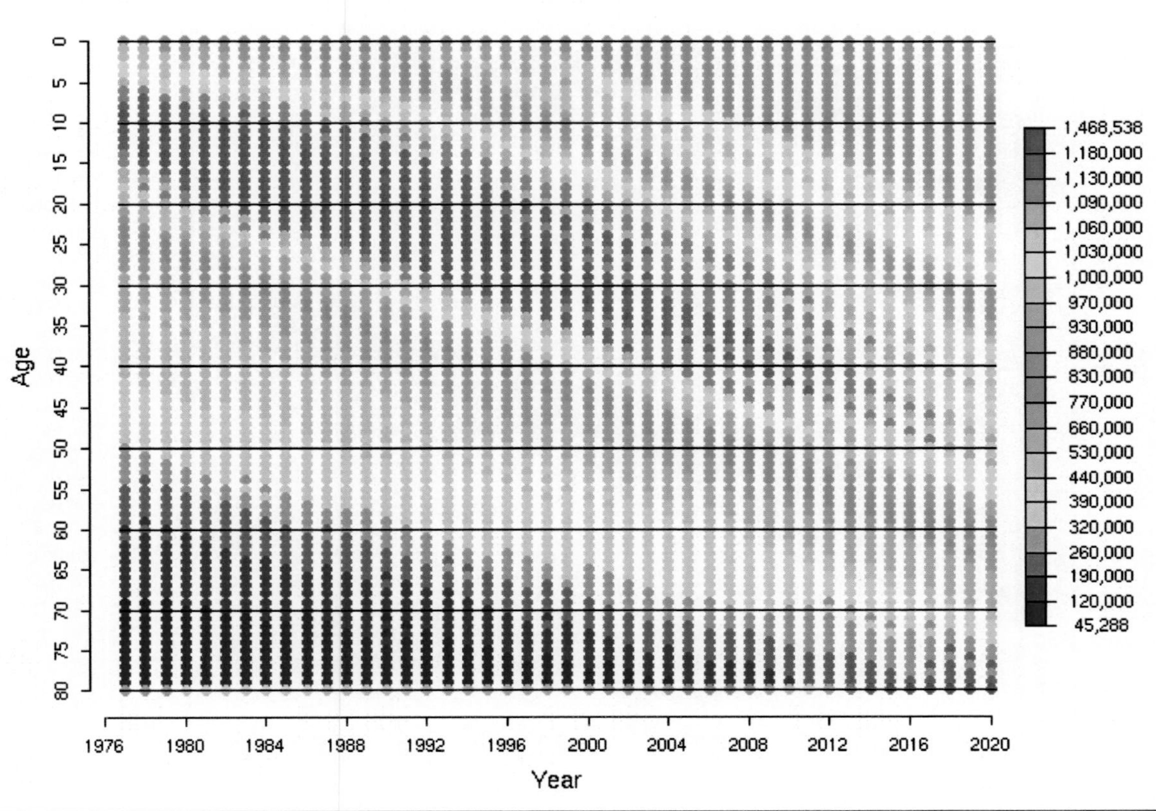

Tunisia

Chart 2.74 *Age structure of the population at a glance, each dot represents a single age group*

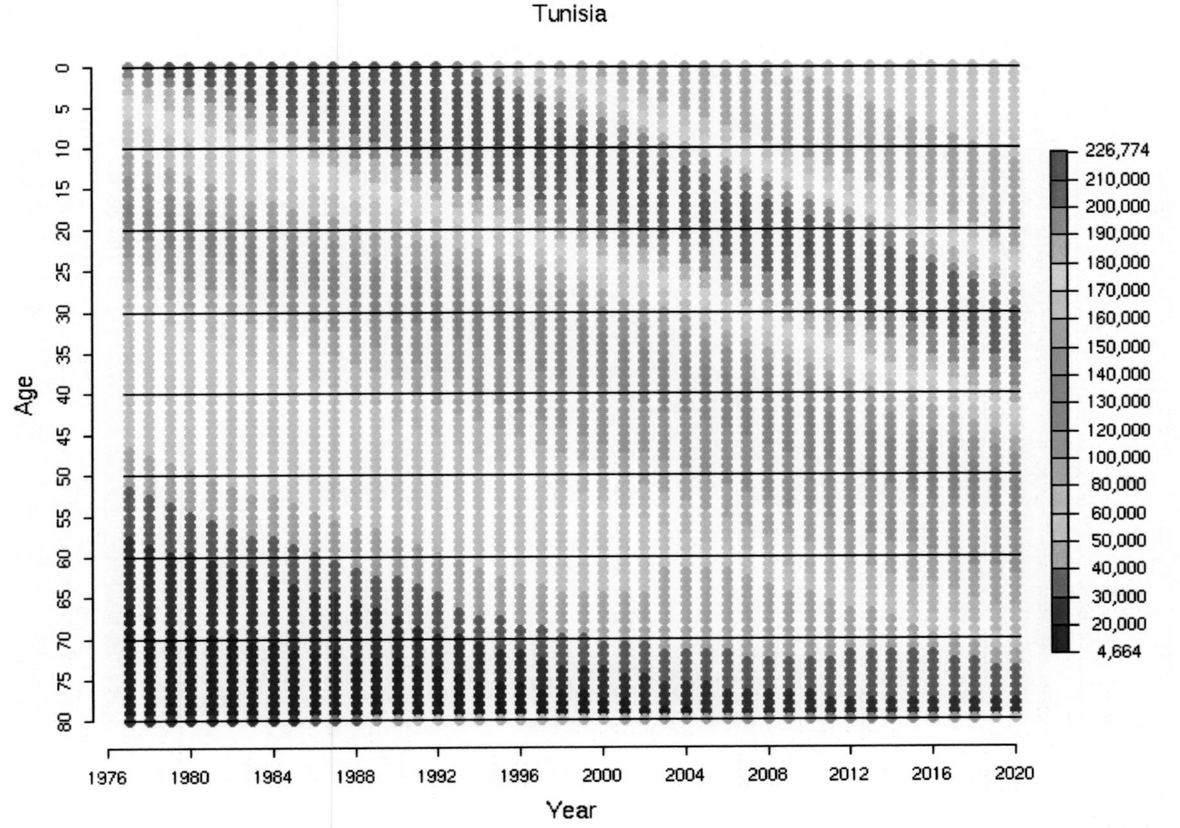

Turkey

Chart 2.75 *Age structure of the population at a glance, each dot represents a single age group*

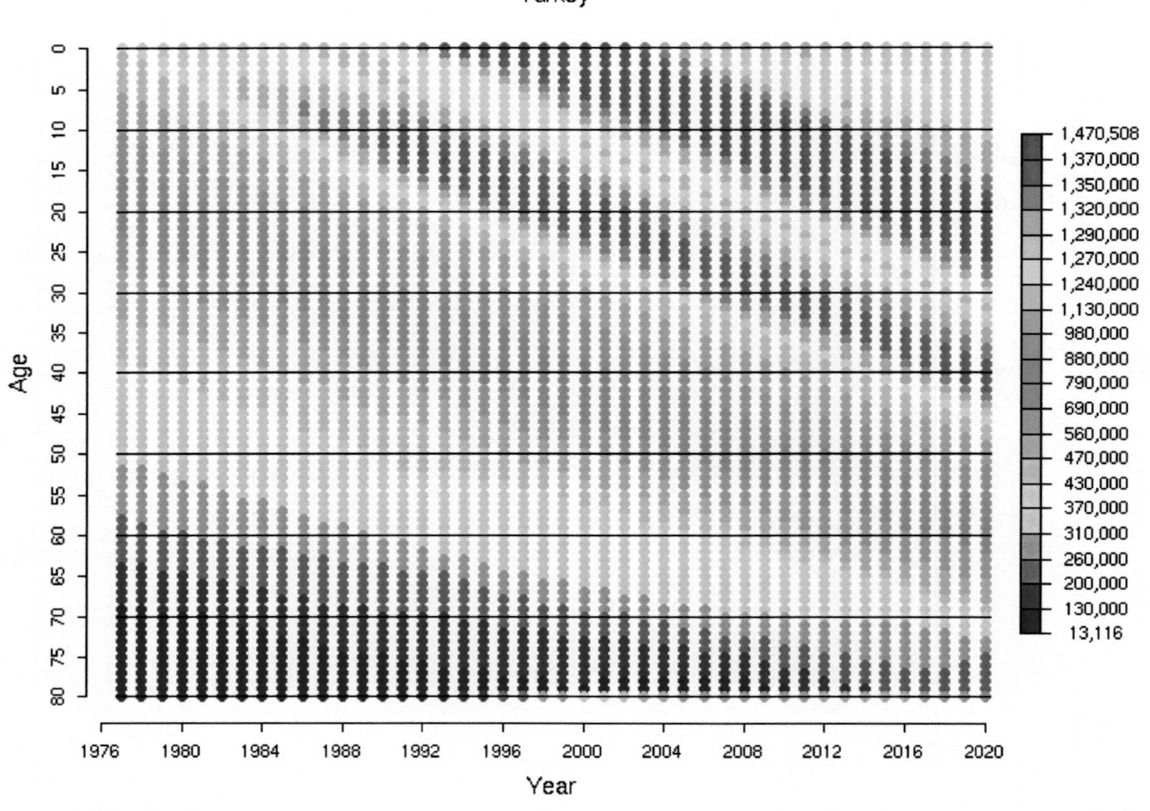

Turkmenistan

Chart 2.76 *Age structure of the population at a glance, each dot represents a single age group*

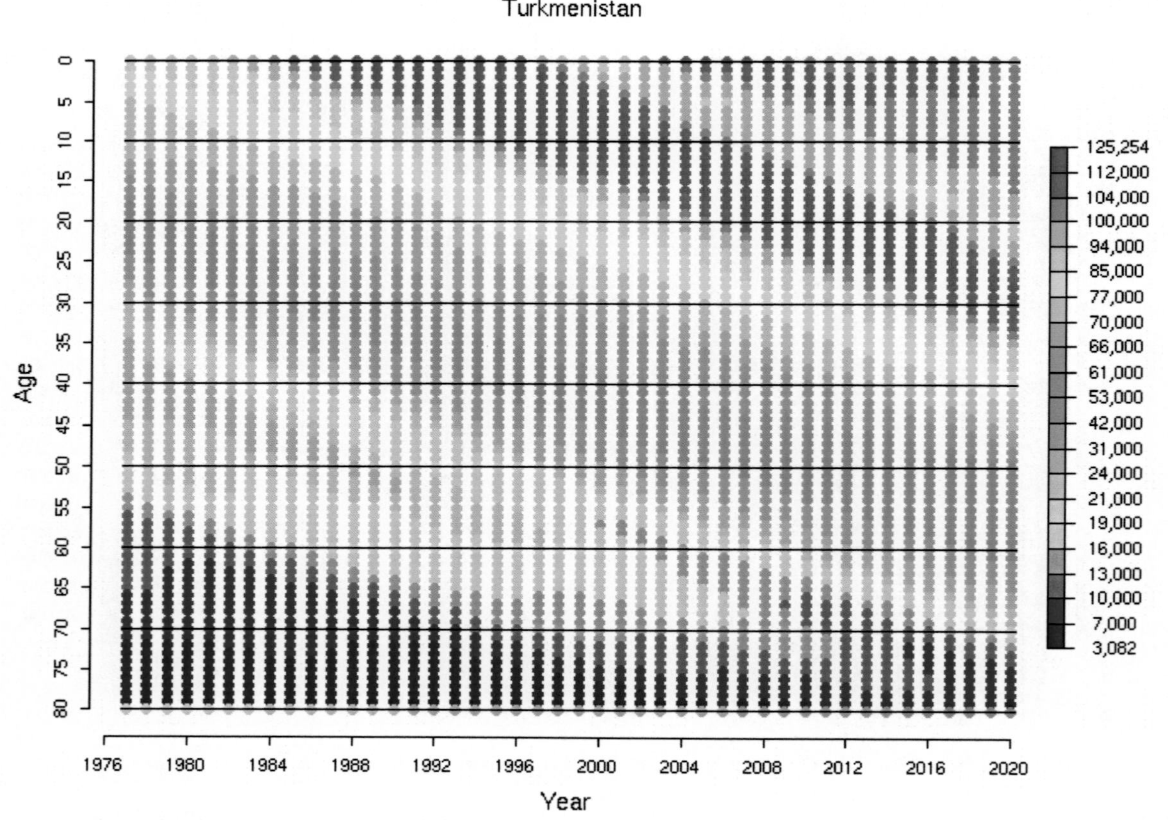

Ukraine

Chart 2.77 *Age structure of the population at a glance, each dot represents a single age group*

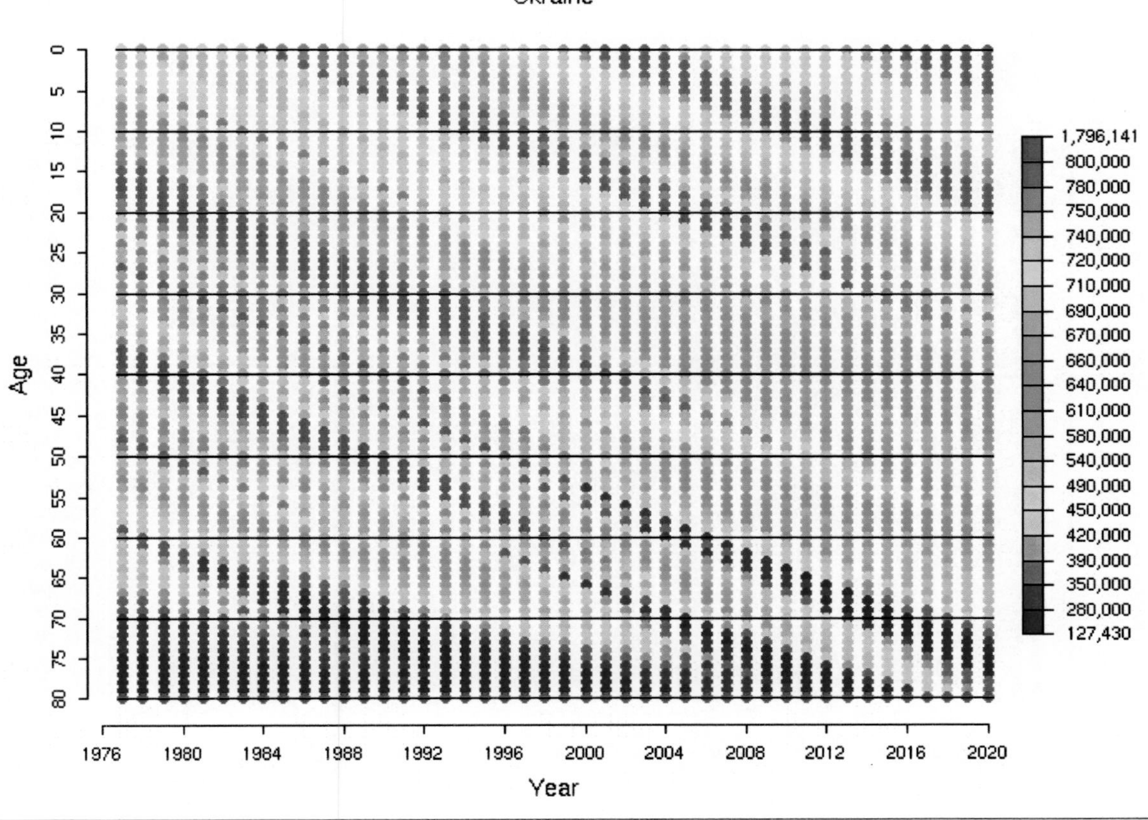

United Arab Emirates

Chart 2.78 *Age structure of the population at a glance, each dot represents a single age group*

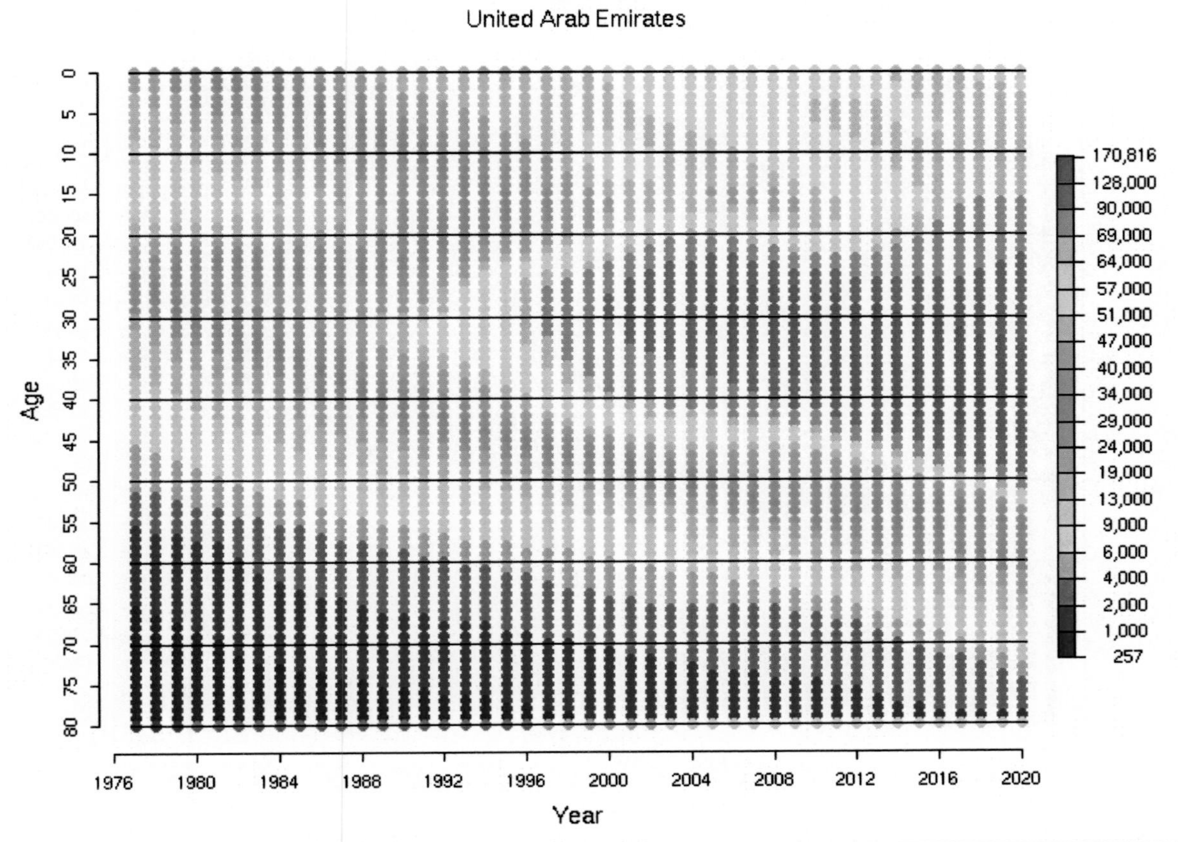

United Kingdom

Chart 2.79 *Age structure of the population at a glance, each dot represents a single age group*

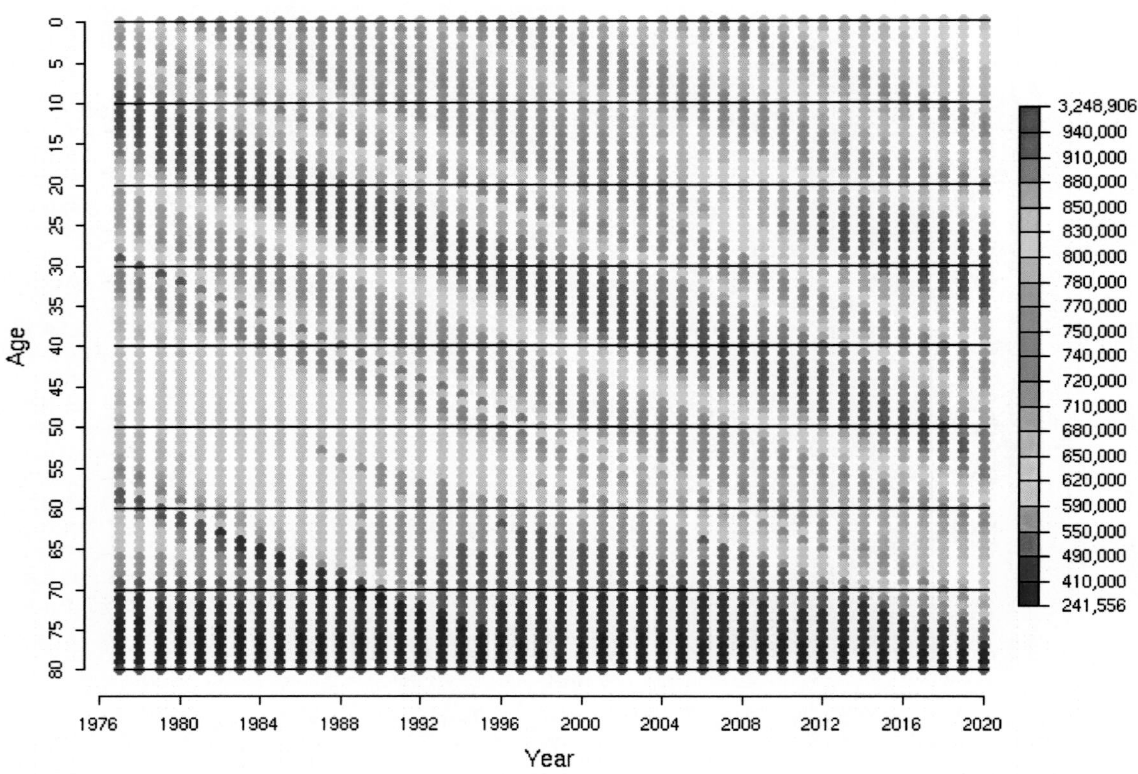

USA

Chart 2.80 *Age structure of the population at a glance, each dot represents a single age group*

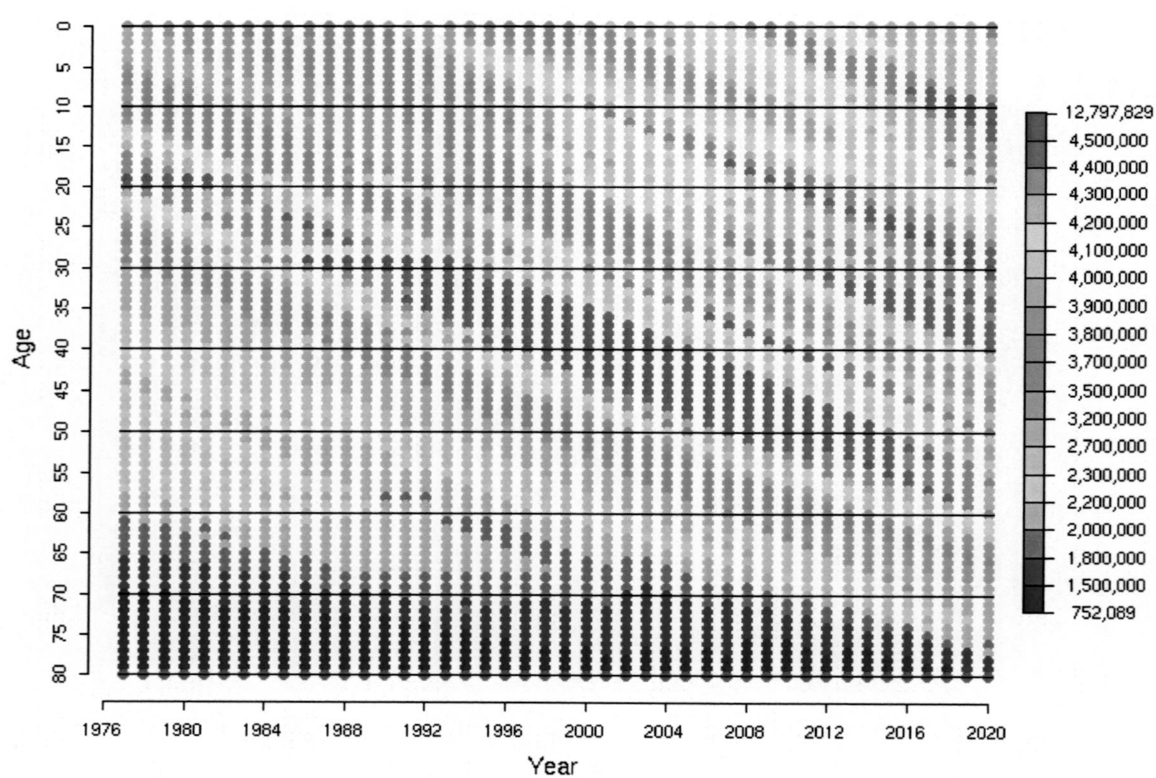

Venezuela

Chart 2.81 *Age structure of the population at a glance, each dot represents a single age group*

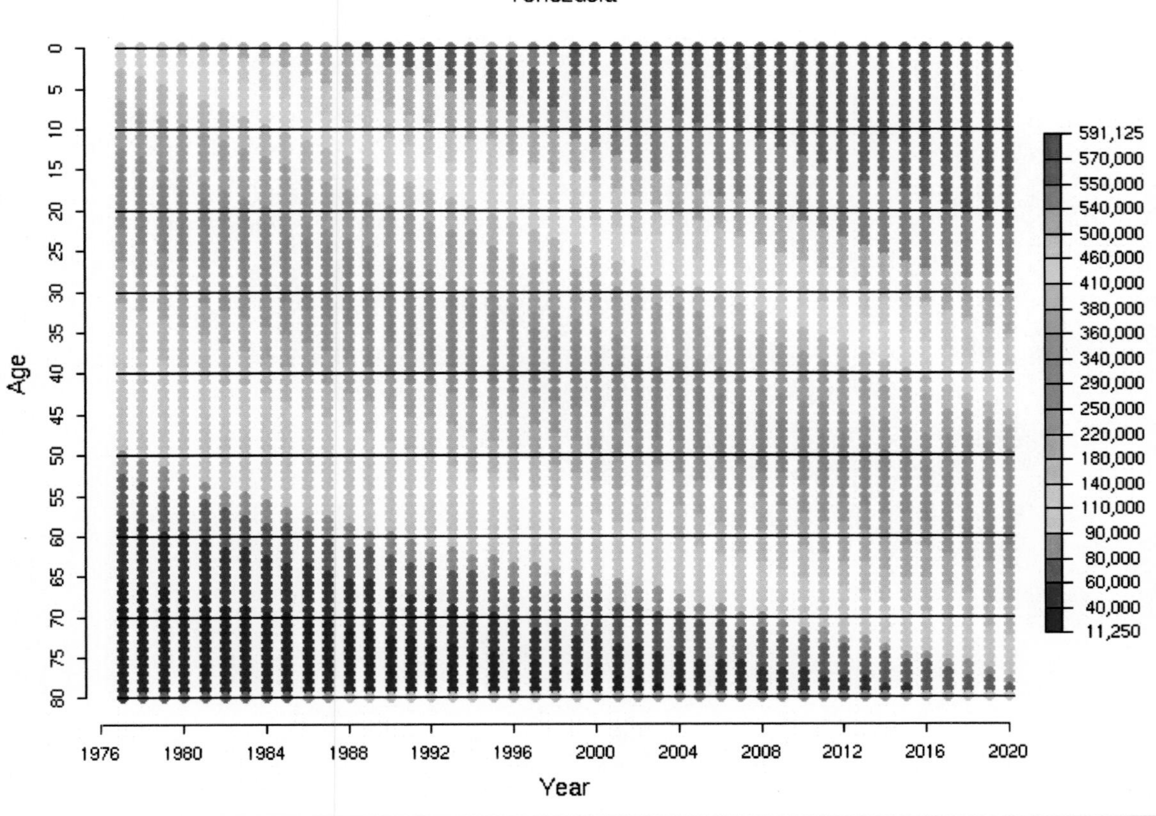

Vietnam

Chart 2.82 *Age structure of the population at a glance, each dot represents a single age group*

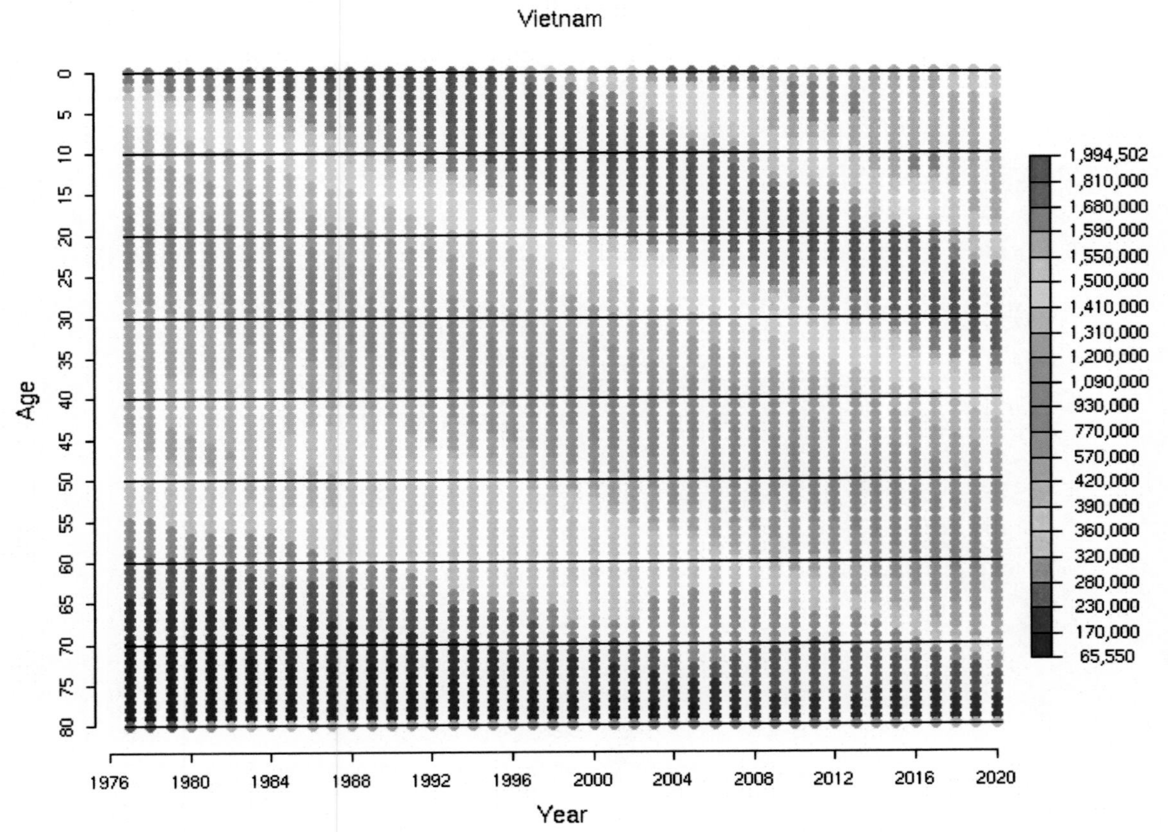

SECTION THREE

Rankings

Population

Table 3.1 Total population

'000

		1985	1990	1995	2000	2005	2010	2015	2020
1	China	1,043,570	1,127,040	1,198,500	1,257,860	1,299,880	1,334,418	1,361,826	1,383,261
2	India	755,878	841,133	929,900	1,017,161	1,103,042	1,184,843	1,262,626	1,333,878
3	USA	237,924	249,623	266,278	282,172	295,561	308,862	319,441	330,206
4	Indonesia	162,348	177,385	191,501	205,280	219,210	232,517	244,191	254,218
5	Pakistan	98,309	115,776	130,397	148,132	165,816	184,753	205,504	226,187
6	Brazil	136,149	149,570	161,692	174,174	186,075	195,423	202,866	209,051
7	Nigeria	85,151	97,338	110,449	124,842	140,879	158,259	175,928	193,252
8	Russia	142,539	147,665	148,460	146,890	143,474	141,786	140,507	139,170
9	Mexico	75,413	83,971	91,725	98,439	103,947	110,199	117,542	124,042
10	Japan	121,049	123,611	125,570	126,926	127,768	127,363	125,846	123,463
11	Philippines	53,829	60,559	68,617	76,504	85,029	93,923	102,896	112,190
12	Vietnam	58,546	65,494	72,363	77,776	83,198	88,744	94,373	99,769
13	Egypt	47,143	52,582	58,130	64,379	71,190	78,160	85,111	91,771
14	Turkey	49,663	55,495	61,204	66,889	71,610	76,157	80,432	84,303
15	Iran	48,418	56,733	62,205	66,903	70,765	75,078	79,454	83,740
16	Germany	77,709	79,113	81,539	82,163	82,501	81,722	80,374	79,003
17	Thailand	50,820	54,291	57,523	60,666	63,003	65,125	66,763	67,990
18	United Kingdom	56,482	57,157	57,943	58,785	60,060	61,966	63,717	65,730
19	France	55,157	56,577	57,753	58,850	60,825	62,772	64,153	65,379
20	Italy	56,588	56,694	56,846	56,929	58,462	59,115	59,216	58,989
21	South Africa	32,959	36,745	41,375	44,872	48,073	50,492	51,684	52,671
22	Colombia	29,997	33,204	36,459	39,773	43,049	46,300	49,385	52,278
23	South Korea	40,806	42,869	45,093	47,008	48,138	48,875	49,277	49,326
24	Spain	38,353	38,826	39,343	40,050	43,038	45,928	47,732	49,268
25	Argentina	30,305	32,581	34,835	36,896	38,747	40,738	42,676	44,486
26	Ukraine	50,648	51,557	51,300	49,115	47,100	45,641	44,187	42,693
27	Algeria	22,097	25,283	28,265	30,506	32,855	35,423	38,088	40,630
28	Poland	37,063	37,988	38,265	38,263	38,174	37,929	37,631	37,385
29	Canada	25,843	27,698	29,302	30,689	32,312	33,968	35,287	36,589
30	Morocco	22,299	24,808	26,951	28,827	30,495	32,381	34,330	36,200
31	Venezuela	17,323	19,741	22,092	24,408	26,726	29,044	31,292	33,412
32	Peru	19,390	21,425	23,444	25,443	27,428	29,403	31,329	33,160
33	Malaysia	15,883	18,102	20,689	23,495	26,128	28,552	30,727	32,745
34	Saudi Arabia	12,867	16,259	18,255	20,808	23,613	26,246	28,933	31,608
35	Australia	15,788	17,065	18,072	19,153	20,395	22,100	23,634	25,254
36	Taiwan	19,069	20,157	21,178	22,092	22,689	23,105	23,376	23,485
37	Romania	22,687	23,211	22,285	21,929	21,659	21,370	20,953	20,389
38	Chile	12,111	13,191	14,410	15,419	16,297	17,135	17,926	18,639
39	Kazakhstan	15,401	16,298	15,957	14,902	15,075	15,985	16,975	17,867
40	Netherlands	14,454	14,893	15,424	15,864	16,306	16,439	16,590	16,726
41	Ecuador	9,103	10,278	11,407	12,310	13,063	13,775	14,596	15,376
42	Bolivia	5,966	6,671	7,484	8,317	9,182	10,031	10,854	11,638
43	Greece	9,919	10,121	10,595	10,904	11,083	11,290	11,437	11,501
44	Tunisia	7,330	8,215	8,935	9,452	9,878	10,374	10,884	11,366
45	Belgium	9,858	9,948	10,131	10,239	10,446	10,699	10,879	11,044
46	Portugal	10,017	9,996	10,018	10,195	10,529	10,694	10,779	10,799
47	Czech Republic	10,302	10,301	10,317	10,236	10,221	10,353	10,361	10,354
48	Hungary	10,657	10,375	10,337	10,222	10,098	10,000	9,871	9,748
49	Sweden	8,343	8,527	8,816	8,861	9,011	9,244	9,466	9,706
50	Azerbaijan	6,622	7,132	7,644	8,016	8,347	8,828	9,292	9,691
51	Belarus	9,929	10,189	10,210	10,019	9,800	9,653	9,515	9,362
52	Austria	7,563	7,645	7,943	8,002	8,207	8,409	8,530	8,634
53	Israel	4,233	4,660	5,545	6,289	6,930	7,518	8,063	8,568
54	Switzerland	6,456	6,674	7,019	7,164	7,415	7,589	7,732	7,879
55	Hong Kong, China	5,456	5,705	6,156	6,665	6,813	7,131	7,443	7,728
56	Jordan	2,706	3,254	4,304	4,853	5,566	6,472	6,957	7,519
57	Bulgaria	8,954	8,767	8,303	7,978	7,728	7,467	7,191	6,885
58	Turkmenistan	3,229	3,668	4,187	4,502	4,843	5,177	5,509	5,816
59	United Arab Emirates	1,379	1,839	2,411	3,236	4,105	4,725	5,213	5,681
60	Denmark	5,111	5,135	5,216	5,330	5,411	5,526	5,602	5,681
61	Finland	4,894	4,974	5,099	5,171	5,237	5,348	5,444	5,520
62	Slovakia	5,140	5,270	5,349	5,379	5,385	5,397	5,398	5,390
63	Norway	4,146	4,233	4,348	4,478	4,606	4,858	5,108	5,352
64	Singapore	2,736	3,047	3,525	4,028	4,342	4,772	5,055	5,276
65	Costa Rica	2,699	3,078	3,479	3,931	4,328	4,640	4,957	5,250
66	Ireland	3,544	3,507	3,598	3,778	4,109	4,507	4,766	4,996
67	New Zealand	3,336	3,453	3,673	3,858	4,134	4,352	4,551	4,736
68	Croatia	4,702	4,778	4,669	4,442	4,444	4,421	4,374	4,315
69	Bosnia-Herzegovina	4,246	4,498	3,523	3,753	3,843	3,844	3,837	3,809
70	Lithuania	3,529	3,694	3,643	3,512	3,425	3,329	3,234	3,150
71	Kuwait	1,697	2,068	1,576	1,883	2,213	2,499	2,767	3,022
72	Latvia	2,570	2,668	2,501	2,382	2,306	2,240	2,172	2,110
73	Slovenia	1,949	1,996	1,989	1,988	1,998	2,029	2,048	2,061
74	Estonia	1,523	1,571	1,448	1,372	1,348	1,326	1,302	1,282

Population

Table 3.2 Population aged 0-14

% of total

		1985	1990	1995	2000	2005	2010	2015	2020
1	Nigeria	45.7	45.8	45.0	43.9	43.1	42.4	41.1	39.1
2	Pakistan	43.4	43.5	43.2	41.3	38.6	36.6	35.2	33.6
3	Egypt	40.0	40.1	38.2	34.5	33.0	33.2	33.2	32.2
4	Bolivia	41.9	40.9	40.6	39.6	38.1	35.8	33.5	31.1
5	Jordan	47.2	46.6	41.4	39.5	37.1	34.0	32.4	30.3
6	Philippines	41.8	40.7	39.5	37.7	35.6	33.5	31.7	30.0
7	South Africa	40.5	38.9	36.0	33.6	31.7	30.3	29.6	28.6
8	Saudi Arabia	42.4	42.0	41.4	38.0	34.6	31.9	29.9	28.0
9	Malaysia	38.3	37.4	35.4	34.1	32.6	31.3	29.6	27.7
10	India	38.7	37.9	36.7	35.0	33.1	30.8	28.7	26.7
11	Turkmenistan	40.5	40.5	39.5	36.2	32.4	29.1	27.9	26.4
12	Venezuela	39.0	38.0	36.0	33.7	31.3	29.5	27.9	26.3
13	Ecuador	41.2	38.9	36.4	34.4	32.6	30.6	28.2	26.1
14	Algeria	45.0	43.0	39.6	34.0	29.7	27.0	26.6	26.0
15	Morocco	41.6	39.8	37.3	33.7	30.3	28.1	26.8	25.9
16	Peru	40.1	38.3	36.2	34.1	32.0	29.9	27.9	25.9
17	Kazakhstan	32.0	31.5	29.8	27.5	24.3	24.1	25.5	25.6
18	Colombia	38.2	36.5	34.8	32.8	30.8	28.8	27.0	25.4
19	Israel	32.6	31.3	29.6	28.6	28.3	27.9	26.6	24.7
20	Azerbaijan	32.8	34.3	34.0	31.1	26.6	24.0	24.1	24.1
21	Iran	44.8	44.9	40.1	32.1	26.5	23.9	24.1	23.6
22	Vietnam	40.1	38.9	37.0	33.5	29.6	26.3	25.0	23.4
23	Mexico	42.1	38.5	35.7	33.1	30.7	28.1	25.5	23.2
24	Argentina	31.0	30.7	29.2	28.0	26.4	25.1	24.0	23.1
25	Indonesia	38.5	35.8	33.0	30.3	28.4	26.7	24.9	22.9
26	Turkey	38.2	35.0	32.1	30.1	28.6	26.6	24.3	22.8
27	Costa Rica	35.9	35.9	34.4	31.7	28.4	25.3	23.4	21.8
28	Tunisia	40.2	38.1	34.3	30.0	25.7	22.9	22.0	21.6
29	Kuwait	37.2	36.4	29.1	25.9	23.8	23.3	22.5	21.2
30	Chile	30.9	29.9	29.6	27.7	24.9	22.3	20.9	20.2
31	Brazil	36.9	35.3	32.8	29.8	27.6	25.6	22.9	20.1
32	New Zealand	24.5	23.1	23.1	22.8	21.5	20.6	20.2	19.9
33	USA	21.7	21.7	21.9	21.4	20.5	20.1	20.0	19.8
34	Australia	23.6	22.0	21.5	20.7	19.7	19.1	18.9	18.9
35	Ireland	29.3	27.4	24.5	21.9	20.7	20.4	19.8	18.5
36	Norway	20.2	18.9	19.4	20.0	19.7	18.9	18.4	18.3
37	United Kingdom	19.3	19.0	19.5	19.1	18.1	17.5	17.6	18.1
38	France	21.4	20.1	19.6	18.9	18.5	18.4	18.4	18.1
39	Russia	22.6	23.0	21.6	18.4	15.2	15.2	16.8	18.0
40	Estonia	22.3	22.3	20.9	18.3	15.4	15.0	16.4	17.4
41	Thailand	30.5	26.8	25.1	23.3	21.7	19.9	18.3	17.4
42	Belgium	18.9	18.1	18.0	17.6	17.2	16.9	17.0	17.1
43	United Arab Emirates	29.7	30.0	27.8	23.7	19.7	19.1	18.6	17.1
44	Sweden	18.2	17.8	18.9	18.5	17.6	16.4	16.7	16.9
45	Denmark	18.6	17.1	17.3	18.4	18.8	18.1	17.3	16.8
46	Finland	19.4	19.3	19.1	18.2	17.5	16.6	16.4	16.6
47	Belarus	22.6	23.1	22.1	18.9	15.6	14.7	15.6	16.3
48	Latvia	21.2	21.4	20.9	18.0	14.8	13.7	15.0	16.0
49	Canada	21.3	20.7	20.4	19.2	17.6	16.4	15.8	15.9
50	Netherlands	19.7	18.2	18.4	18.6	18.5	17.6	16.7	15.8
51	China	30.3	27.7	26.7	23.5	19.6	16.4	15.3	15.3
52	Spain	23.5	20.2	16.9	14.9	14.5	14.9	15.5	15.3
53	Croatia	20.9	19.9	18.4	17.1	16.0	15.2	14.7	15.1
54	Romania	24.9	23.7	21.1	18.8	15.9	15.2	15.2	15.1
55	Czech Republic	23.4	21.7	18.9	16.6	14.9	14.1	14.7	15.0
56	Poland	25.4	25.3	23.1	19.5	16.7	14.9	14.6	15.0
57	Slovakia	26.4	25.5	22.9	19.8	17.1	15.2	14.8	14.9
58	Hungary	21.6	20.5	18.3	16.9	15.6	14.8	14.8	14.9
59	Singapore	24.7	23.0	22.8	21.9	19.9	17.2	15.4	14.8
60	Lithuania	23.1	22.6	21.9	20.2	17.1	14.7	14.3	14.8
61	Switzerland	17.8	17.0	17.6	17.4	16.3	15.1	14.4	14.5
62	Portugal	23.9	20.8	17.9	16.2	15.6	15.4	15.2	14.5
63	Slovenia	22.4	20.9	18.5	16.1	14.4	13.8	14.0	14.3
64	Austria	18.4	17.5	17.8	17.1	16.1	15.0	14.4	14.2
65	Ukraine	21.6	21.5	20.5	17.9	14.8	13.9	14.0	14.1
66	Greece	21.4	19.6	17.5	15.4	14.4	14.2	14.3	14.1
67	Bosnia-Herzegovina	25.1	24.2	22.1	19.8	16.6	15.2	13.9	13.4
68	Bulgaria	21.7	20.5	18.1	15.9	13.8	13.1	13.4	13.0
69	Italy	19.6	16.8	14.8	14.3	14.1	13.9	13.6	12.9
70	Taiwan	30.2	27.5	24.4	21.4	19.3	16.4	14.0	12.6
71	Hong Kong, China	23.4	21.5	19.4	16.9	14.2	12.3	11.8	12.5
72	South Korea	30.2	25.6	23.4	21.1	19.2	16.2	13.7	12.4
73	Germany	16.2	16.0	16.3	15.7	14.5	13.5	12.5	12.0
74	Japan	21.5	18.2	16.0	14.6	13.8	13.3	12.5	11.9

Population

Table 3.3 Population aged 15-64

% of total

		1985	1990	1995	2000	2005	2010	2015	2020
1	United Arab Emirates	68.9	68.8	71.0	75.2	79.2	79.9	80.1	80.8
2	Kuwait	61.5	62.4	69.7	72.7	74.4	74.4	74.4	74.5
3	Taiwan	64.9	66.5	68.2	70.1	71.2	73.0	74.2	72.4
4	South Korea	65.6	69.3	70.7	71.7	71.7	72.9	73.4	72.0
5	China	64.4	66.7	66.6	69.1	71.4	73.9	73.7	71.6
6	Brazil	59.0	60.3	62.3	64.8	66.3	67.6	69.3	70.7
7	Thailand	65.3	68.6	69.7	70.6	71.0	71.9	72.0	70.7
8	Iran	51.9	51.8	55.8	63.2	68.5	71.3	70.8	70.4
9	Singapore	69.8	71.0	70.7	70.9	71.9	73.7	73.0	70.2
10	Hong Kong, China	69.1	70.0	70.8	72.1	73.5	75.1	73.6	70.2
11	Tunisia	55.8	57.3	60.0	63.7	67.7	70.4	70.8	70.0
12	Turkey	57.7	60.5	63.0	64.6	65.5	67.3	69.2	69.8
13	Indonesia	58.0	60.4	62.7	64.8	66.1	67.3	68.5	69.6
14	Vietnam	55.0	56.2	57.9	61.0	64.8	68.1	69.2	69.6
15	Bosnia-Herzegovina	69.2	69.7	69.8	69.1	70.0	70.9	71.1	69.3
16	Belarus	67.2	66.4	65.7	67.8	69.9	71.5	70.9	69.2
17	Costa Rica	59.1	59.2	60.4	62.8	65.8	68.2	69.1	69.2
18	Slovakia	64.2	64.3	66.3	68.8	71.3	72.6	71.6	68.6
19	Turkmenistan	55.6	55.7	56.4	59.4	63.1	66.8	67.9	68.5
20	Azerbaijan	62.2	61.5	61.1	63.2	66.6	69.4	69.6	68.4
21	Ukraine	66.9	66.5	65.9	68.2	69.2	70.4	69.9	68.1
22	Algeria	51.3	53.4	56.7	61.8	65.8	68.3	68.4	68.0
23	Romania	65.7	66.0	66.9	67.8	69.5	70.0	69.5	68.0
24	Saudi Arabia	55.2	55.7	56.2	59.3	62.6	65.1	66.8	67.9
25	Mexico	53.9	57.1	59.6	61.7	63.5	65.4	67.0	67.9
26	Lithuania	66.6	66.6	65.9	66.0	67.8	69.2	69.2	67.8
27	Chile	63.3	63.9	63.7	65.0	67.0	68.5	68.6	67.7
28	Russia	67.6	67.1	66.7	69.3	71.0	72.0	70.2	67.6
29	Ireland	59.9	61.3	64.0	66.8	68.1	68.1	67.5	67.4
30	Morocco	54.4	56.3	58.3	61.6	64.5	66.5	67.3	67.2
31	India	57.6	58.3	59.3	60.7	62.3	64.3	65.9	67.0
32	Poland	65.2	64.8	65.9	68.4	70.1	71.7	70.2	66.8
33	Colombia	57.8	59.2	60.7	62.4	64.2	65.6	66.4	66.6
34	Peru	56.1	57.7	59.5	61.1	62.7	64.1	65.4	66.4
35	Kazakhstan	62.3	62.6	63.2	65.5	67.9	68.9	67.5	66.3
36	Canada	68.5	68.0	67.6	68.3	69.3	69.6	68.3	66.2
37	Latvia	67.0	66.7	65.7	67.2	68.7	69.0	67.5	66.0
38	Austria	67.4	67.6	67.1	67.4	67.9	67.4	66.9	66.0
39	Venezuela	57.5	58.3	59.8	61.7	63.7	64.9	65.5	65.9
40	Croatia	68.7	68.6	68.0	67.2	67.2	67.5	67.6	65.7
41	Spain	64.5	66.3	68.0	68.4	68.7	68.0	66.5	65.6
42	Bulgaria	67.0	66.5	67.0	67.9	69.0	69.3	67.2	65.5
43	Malaysia	58.1	58.9	60.9	62.0	63.1	64.0	65.0	65.5
44	Slovenia	67.5	68.5	69.4	70.0	70.3	69.7	68.2	65.5
45	Jordan	49.2	50.3	56.1	57.7	59.4	62.3	63.6	65.4
46	Hungary	66.2	66.2	67.6	68.1	68.7	68.7	67.7	65.4
47	Switzerland	68.2	68.4	67.7	67.3	67.9	67.9	66.8	65.4
48	South Africa	56.4	57.9	60.6	62.7	64.2	65.1	65.1	65.2
49	Ecuador	54.8	56.9	59.1	60.4	61.5	62.8	64.3	65.1
50	Germany	69.4	69.1	68.3	68.1	66.9	65.9	66.1	65.0
51	Argentina	60.5	60.3	61.3	62.1	63.4	64.4	64.9	65.0
52	Portugal	64.4	66.0	67.3	67.7	67.3	66.8	65.8	65.0
53	Czech Republic	64.8	65.8	68.0	69.6	71.0	70.6	67.5	64.8
54	Greece	65.8	67.0	67.9	68.2	67.5	67.0	65.7	64.7
55	Australia	66.1	66.9	66.6	66.9	67.3	67.3	65.9	64.4
56	Norway	64.2	64.8	64.6	64.8	65.5	66.2	65.4	64.4
57	Philippines	55.0	56.1	57.3	58.8	60.6	62.2	63.5	64.3
58	Netherlands	68.3	69.0	68.4	67.9	67.5	67.1	65.4	64.1
59	USA	66.4	65.8	65.4	66.2	67.1	66.9	65.5	64.0
60	Estonia	66.4	66.1	65.8	66.8	68.0	68.1	66.1	64.0
61	Italy	67.4	68.5	68.7	67.6	66.4	65.6	64.4	63.8
62	United Kingdom	65.6	65.3	64.7	65.1	65.9	66.2	64.9	63.7
63	New Zealand	65.0	65.8	65.4	65.5	66.5	66.3	64.9	63.5
64	Bolivia	54.5	55.3	55.4	56.1	57.4	59.4	61.3	63.1
65	Israel	58.6	59.6	60.9	61.6	61.7	62.4	62.4	62.9
66	Denmark	66.4	67.3	67.4	66.8	66.2	65.5	63.9	62.8
67	Belgium	67.4	67.1	66.2	65.6	65.6	65.8	64.3	62.7
68	Sweden	64.7	64.4	63.7	64.2	65.2	65.3	63.2	61.8
69	Pakistan	52.6	52.8	53.1	55.1	57.6	59.3	60.5	61.8
70	France	65.9	66.0	65.3	65.1	65.1	64.8	63.1	61.7
71	Finland	68.2	67.4	66.8	66.9	66.7	66.4	63.4	61.0
72	Egypt	56.5	56.4	58.3	61.3	62.2	61.6	60.9	60.8
73	Japan	68.2	69.7	69.5	68.1	66.1	63.7	60.7	59.3
74	Nigeria	51.3	51.3	52.1	53.1	53.8	54.5	55.7	57.5

Population

Table 3.4 Population aged 65+

% of total

		1985	1990	1995	2000	2005	2010	2015	2020
1	Japan	10.30	12.08	14.56	17.37	20.17	23.05	26.72	28.89
2	Italy	12.91	14.73	16.49	18.12	19.46	20.44	22.00	23.31
3	Germany	14.47	14.91	15.38	16.25	18.63	20.60	21.35	23.00
4	Finland	12.39	13.30	14.12	14.84	15.87	17.05	20.12	22.40
5	Bulgaria	11.27	12.96	14.85	16.17	17.15	17.66	19.44	21.48
6	Sweden	17.08	17.80	17.47	17.29	17.25	18.30	20.15	21.23
7	Greece	12.77	13.40	14.61	16.42	18.11	18.80	19.95	21.13
8	Portugal	11.74	13.22	14.73	16.04	17.01	17.74	18.98	20.52
9	Denmark	14.99	15.59	15.31	14.83	15.01	16.35	18.76	20.42
10	France	12.79	13.91	15.04	16.01	16.43	16.74	18.50	20.23
11	Slovenia	10.10	10.60	12.07	13.85	15.34	16.53	17.72	20.22
12	Czech Republic	11.80	12.47	13.13	13.80	14.04	15.35	17.83	20.20
13	Belgium	13.70	14.82	15.76	16.75	17.23	17.34	18.67	20.14
14	Switzerland	13.99	14.57	14.70	15.27	15.84	17.05	18.73	20.13
15	Netherlands	11.97	12.80	13.18	13.57	14.04	15.29	17.87	20.06
16	Austria	14.13	14.91	15.07	15.42	15.98	17.61	18.66	19.85
17	Hungary	12.27	13.24	14.11	14.98	15.62	16.49	17.52	19.69
18	Croatia	10.33	11.52	13.62	15.70	16.75	17.30	17.71	19.20
19	Spain	11.92	13.43	15.11	16.74	16.80	17.08	18.02	19.07
20	Estonia	11.29	11.56	13.32	14.96	16.51	16.91	17.51	18.55
21	United Kingdom	15.03	15.72	15.83	15.81	16.01	16.34	17.56	18.18
22	Poland	9.43	9.95	10.94	12.07	13.15	13.46	15.22	18.14
23	Latvia	11.80	11.82	13.45	14.83	16.53	17.29	17.44	17.96
24	Canada	10.25	11.27	11.98	12.55	13.08	14.05	15.87	17.89
25	Ukraine	11.51	11.98	13.57	13.88	15.94	15.72	16.17	17.74
26	Lithuania	10.35	10.81	12.17	13.74	15.09	16.04	16.53	17.40
27	Hong Kong, China	7.45	8.46	9.78	10.94	12.25	12.65	14.58	17.36
28	Norway	15.59	16.32	15.99	15.25	14.71	14.86	16.20	17.31
29	Bosnia-Herzegovina	5.63	6.08	8.14	11.07	13.39	13.92	15.02	17.31
30	Romania	9.46	10.27	12.02	13.36	14.66	14.77	15.27	16.96
31	Australia	10.27	11.10	11.90	12.42	12.93	13.63	15.20	16.65
32	New Zealand	10.41	11.09	11.53	11.76	12.01	13.04	14.83	16.60
33	Slovakia	9.40	10.27	10.80	11.40	11.62	12.23	13.59	16.49
34	USA	11.94	12.52	12.68	12.43	12.43	13.02	14.47	16.20
35	South Korea	4.27	5.12	5.89	7.22	9.07	10.96	12.95	15.61
36	Singapore	5.47	6.01	6.53	7.19	8.21	9.03	11.59	15.00
37	Taiwan	4.85	5.96	7.38	8.44	9.48	10.58	11.80	14.98
38	Belarus	10.19	10.54	12.21	13.30	14.49	13.74	13.55	14.51
39	Russia	9.78	9.87	11.72	12.30	13.72	12.80	12.97	14.35
40	Ireland	10.79	11.39	11.42	11.23	11.15	11.49	12.68	14.06
41	China	5.34	5.58	6.69	7.37	9.06	9.71	10.95	13.13
42	Israel	8.79	9.09	9.53	9.78	9.92	9.72	11.04	12.39
43	Chile	5.85	6.16	6.64	7.29	8.10	9.22	10.52	12.12
44	Thailand	4.18	4.58	5.20	6.15	7.28	8.17	9.63	11.92
45	Argentina	8.51	8.93	9.41	9.88	10.19	10.53	11.11	11.89
46	Brazil	4.07	4.36	4.93	5.44	6.13	6.82	7.83	9.23
47	Costa Rica	5.00	4.98	5.19	5.43	5.83	6.48	7.46	9.00
48	Mexico	3.98	4.34	4.77	5.24	5.78	6.52	7.46	8.89
49	Ecuador	4.05	4.21	4.57	5.14	5.89	6.66	7.50	8.73
50	Tunisia	4.03	4.60	5.75	6.28	6.66	6.73	7.18	8.44
51	Kazakhstan	5.68	5.89	7.08	6.96	7.78	7.00	6.97	8.15
52	Colombia	4.03	4.28	4.49	4.74	5.07	5.61	6.62	8.01
53	Venezuela	3.45	3.73	4.16	4.57	4.98	5.63	6.61	7.80
54	Peru	3.76	3.98	4.35	4.83	5.38	5.97	6.69	7.62
55	Indonesia	3.57	3.81	4.28	4.88	5.52	6.07	6.57	7.51
56	Azerbaijan	4.93	4.23	4.89	5.73	6.75	6.57	6.29	7.47
57	Turkey	4.14	4.53	4.91	5.35	5.82	6.11	6.51	7.42
58	Egypt	3.49	3.51	3.49	4.20	4.80	5.20	5.90	7.06
59	Vietnam	4.90	4.94	5.04	5.45	5.56	5.60	5.84	7.03
60	Malaysia	3.62	3.64	3.65	3.97	4.29	4.62	5.38	6.86
61	Morocco	3.99	3.84	4.31	4.71	5.20	5.40	5.84	6.86
62	India	3.71	3.83	3.99	4.26	4.59	4.91	5.39	6.32
63	South Africa	3.11	3.18	3.37	3.67	4.06	4.61	5.33	6.27
64	Iran	3.24	3.25	4.08	4.67	5.00	4.82	5.04	5.95
65	Algeria	3.72	3.61	3.73	4.19	4.54	4.65	5.01	5.92
66	Bolivia	3.63	3.78	4.07	4.31	4.52	4.78	5.22	5.80
67	Philippines	3.20	3.22	3.25	3.50	3.86	4.29	4.81	5.64
68	Turkmenistan	3.89	3.80	4.10	4.34	4.52	4.17	4.24	5.07
69	Pakistan	4.02	3.72	3.63	3.66	3.82	4.08	4.31	4.64
70	Jordan	3.60	3.14	2.52	2.89	3.47	3.69	4.02	4.30
71	Kuwait	1.21	1.21	1.21	1.37	1.77	2.35	3.13	4.28
72	Saudi Arabia	2.45	2.31	2.41	2.70	2.78	2.96	3.35	4.10
73	Nigeria	2.94	2.95	2.94	2.98	3.05	3.14	3.22	3.40
74	United Arab Emirates	1.41	1.27	1.16	1.09	1.08	1.03	1.37	2.16

Population

Table 3.5 Male population

% of total

		1985	1990	1995	2000	2005	2010	2015	2020
1	United Arab Emirates	64.9	65.4	66.1	67.5	68.0	67.1	66.5	66.3
2	Kuwait	56.8	56.8	60.1	60.8	60.3	59.4	58.8	58.4
3	Saudi Arabia	55.3	55.5	55.8	55.4	55.2	54.7	54.2	53.8
4	China	51.6	51.6	51.1	51.4	51.5	51.5	51.5	51.5
5	India	52.0	52.0	51.9	51.8	51.7	51.6	51.5	51.5
6	Pakistan	52.2	52.0	51.8	51.6	51.5	51.5	51.5	51.4
7	Jordan	52.3	52.1	52.3	51.7	51.4	51.3	51.2	51.1
8	Egypt	51.2	51.2	51.2	51.1	51.1	51.1	51.1	51.0
9	Malaysia	50.6	50.7	51.1	50.9	50.9	50.9	50.8	50.7
10	Costa Rica	50.9	50.9	50.9	50.8	50.8	50.8	50.7	50.6
11	Iran	51.3	51.5	50.9	50.9	51.0	50.8	50.7	50.6
12	Algeria	50.3	50.4	50.4	50.5	50.5	50.5	50.5	50.5
13	Norway	49.4	49.5	49.4	49.5	49.6	50.0	50.2	50.4
14	Philippines	50.2	50.3	50.4	50.4	50.3	50.3	50.3	50.3
15	Nigeria	49.6	49.7	49.8	49.9	50.0	50.1	50.2	50.3
16	Turkey	50.7	50.7	50.6	50.5	50.4	50.4	50.3	50.2
17	Tunisia	50.6	50.5	50.5	50.5	50.3	50.3	50.2	50.2
18	Peru	50.3	50.2	50.2	50.2	50.1	50.1	50.1	50.0
19	South Korea	50.4	50.3	50.4	50.3	50.3	50.2	50.1	50.0
20	Venezuela	50.5	50.4	50.4	50.3	50.3	50.2	50.1	50.0
21	Ireland	50.1	49.7	49.7	49.7	49.8	50.0	50.0	50.0
22	Vietnam	49.7	49.8	49.9	50.0	50.0	50.0	50.0	50.0
23	Canada	49.7	49.6	49.5	49.5	49.5	49.5	49.8	49.9
24	Bolivia	49.4	49.5	49.7	49.8	49.8	49.9	49.9	49.9
25	Ecuador	50.3	50.3	50.2	50.2	50.1	50.1	50.0	49.9
26	Australia	49.9	49.9	49.8	49.6	49.7	49.8	49.8	49.9
27	Sweden	49.4	49.4	49.4	49.4	49.6	49.7	49.8	49.9
28	Indonesia	50.1	50.1	50.1	50.0	50.0	49.9	49.9	49.8
29	Israel	49.9	49.8	49.5	49.3	49.4	49.5	49.7	49.8
30	Azerbaijan	48.8	48.8	48.8	48.9	49.2	49.4	49.6	49.8
31	Taiwan	51.9	51.7	51.5	51.2	50.9	50.4	50.0	49.6
32	Denmark	49.2	49.3	49.3	49.4	49.5	49.6	49.6	49.6
33	Slovenia	48.5	48.5	48.5	48.8	48.9	49.2	49.4	49.6
34	Netherlands	49.5	49.4	49.5	49.5	49.5	49.5	49.5	49.5
35	Spain	49.1	49.0	49.0	49.0	49.2	49.4	49.4	49.5
36	South Africa	49.7	49.5	49.3	49.2	49.2	49.3	49.4	49.5
37	Greece	49.2	49.2	49.5	49.5	49.5	49.5	49.5	49.5
38	United Kingdom	48.6	48.6	48.6	48.7	48.9	49.1	49.3	49.4
39	USA	48.6	48.8	48.9	49.1	49.2	49.3	49.4	49.4
40	Chile	49.3	49.4	49.4	49.5	49.5	49.5	49.4	49.4
41	Germany	47.7	48.2	48.6	48.8	48.9	49.1	49.2	49.2
42	New Zealand	49.4	49.2	49.3	49.1	49.0	49.0	49.1	49.2
43	Turkmenistan	49.1	49.3	49.4	49.4	49.3	49.3	49.2	49.1
44	Singapore	50.7	50.7	50.2	49.9	49.6	49.4	49.2	49.1
45	Finland	48.4	48.5	48.7	48.8	48.9	49.0	49.1	49.1
46	Mexico	49.9	49.8	49.7	49.5	49.3	49.2	49.1	49.1
47	Colombia	49.7	49.6	49.4	49.3	49.3	49.2	49.2	49.1
48	Belgium	48.8	48.9	48.9	48.9	48.9	49.0	49.0	49.1
49	Brazil	49.8	49.7	49.5	49.4	49.3	49.2	49.1	49.0
50	Morocco	50.0	49.9	49.7	49.5	49.2	49.1	49.0	49.0
51	Czech Republic	48.5	48.5	48.6	48.7	48.7	48.8	48.9	48.9
52	Argentina	49.2	49.1	49.0	48.9	48.9	48.9	48.9	48.9
53	Austria	47.4	47.8	48.2	48.3	48.6	48.7	48.8	48.9
54	Italy	48.6	48.6	48.5	48.4	48.5	48.6	48.7	48.8
55	Romania	49.3	49.3	49.1	48.9	48.8	48.7	48.7	48.7
56	Slovakia	49.1	48.9	48.7	48.6	48.5	48.6	48.6	48.6
57	France	48.8	48.7	48.6	48.6	48.6	48.4	48.5	48.6
58	Switzerland	48.7	48.8	48.8	48.9	48.9	48.8	48.7	48.5
59	Portugal	48.2	48.2	48.2	48.2	48.4	48.4	48.5	48.5
60	Bulgaria	49.7	49.3	49.0	48.7	48.5	48.4	48.4	48.5
61	Japan	49.2	49.1	49.0	48.9	48.8	48.7	48.5	48.3
62	Thailand	49.8	49.6	49.5	49.1	48.8	48.6	48.4	48.3
63	Croatia	48.4	48.5	48.1	48.1	48.1	48.2	48.2	48.3
64	Poland	48.8	48.7	48.6	48.5	48.4	48.3	48.3	48.3
65	Bosnia-Herzegovina	49.3	49.4	48.5	48.2	48.1	48.1	48.1	48.1
66	Hungary	48.3	48.0	47.8	47.6	47.5	47.4	47.5	47.5
67	Kazakhstan	48.2	48.4	48.3	48.0	47.8	47.6	47.5	47.4
68	Belarus	46.7	46.9	46.8	46.9	46.8	46.6	46.5	46.5
69	Lithuania	47.1	47.3	47.1	46.8	46.7	46.5	46.4	46.3
70	Latvia	46.2	46.5	46.2	46.1	46.1	46.1	46.1	46.2
71	Russia	46.4	46.8	46.9	46.8	46.4	46.2	46.1	46.0
72	Estonia	46.5	46.8	46.4	46.1	46.1	46.0	45.9	46.0
73	Ukraine	45.9	46.2	46.4	46.3	46.2	46.0	45.9	45.8
74	Hong Kong, China	51.6	51.2	50.1	49.2	47.9	46.7	45.5	44.5

Population

Table 3.6 Mean age of population

years

		1985	1990	1995	2000	2005	2010	2015	2020
1	Japan	35.1	37.0	38.9	40.8	42.6	44.1	45.5	46.7
2	Germany	38.0	38.6	39.1	40.1	41.3	42.7	43.9	45.0
3	Italy	36.6	38.0	39.5	40.7	41.7	42.7	43.8	44.9
4	Bulgaria	35.8	36.7	38.0	39.1	40.5	41.5	42.6	43.8
5	Greece	36.0	37.1	37.9	39.0	40.5	41.6	42.6	43.5
6	Slovenia	34.2	35.1	36.5	38.0	39.6	40.9	42.0	43.1
7	Portugal	34.1	35.8	37.3	38.6	39.6	40.7	41.7	42.8
8	Austria	36.9	37.4	37.7	38.7	39.7	40.7	41.7	42.7
9	Switzerland	37.1	37.8	38.0	38.8	39.8	40.8	41.7	42.5
10	Hong Kong, China	31.0	32.6	34.3	36.1	38.5	40.0	41.3	42.3
11	Spain	34.4	35.9	37.5	39.0	39.7	40.5	41.3	42.3
12	Czech Republic	35.1	35.6	36.4	37.8	39.2	40.2	41.2	42.2
13	Finland	35.8	36.8	37.5	38.5	39.6	40.6	41.4	42.1
14	South Korea	27.0	29.0	30.7	32.5	34.9	37.4	39.8	42.0
15	Croatia	35.3	36.3	37.6	38.7	39.6	40.6	41.3	41.9
16	Bosnia-Herzegovina	30.2	31.4	33.3	35.4	37.4	39.0	40.5	41.8
17	Ukraine	35.7	36.0	36.6	37.8	38.9	39.7	40.7	41.8
18	Hungary	36.1	36.7	37.3	38.4	39.4	40.2	41.0	41.7
19	Netherlands	35.0	36.0	36.7	37.5	38.3	39.5	40.6	41.7
20	Sweden	38.5	38.8	38.7	39.4	40.0	40.5	41.0	41.5
21	Belgium	37.0	37.6	38.2	39.0	39.7	40.3	40.8	41.4
22	Denmark	37.2	37.9	38.2	38.4	38.9	39.5	40.4	41.3
23	Lithuania	34.1	34.4	35.3	36.6	38.1	39.3	40.4	41.2
24	Latvia	35.8	35.7	36.7	38.2	39.4	40.2	40.7	41.2
25	Poland	32.7	33.2	34.2	35.6	37.3	38.8	40.0	41.2
26	Taiwan	27.4	29.2	30.9	32.6	34.7	37.0	39.1	41.2
27	Romania	33.4	33.9	35.4	36.6	37.8	38.9	39.8	40.9
28	Canada	33.4	34.5	35.4	36.6	37.9	39.0	40.0	40.9
29	France	35.6	36.2	37.1	38.0	38.7	39.4	40.1	40.7
30	Estonia	35.0	35.3	36.6	38.0	39.1	39.8	40.3	40.7
31	Slovakia	32.3	32.8	33.7	35.1	36.5	37.9	39.3	40.6
32	Singapore	29.1	30.6	31.8	33.3	35.0	36.8	38.6	40.3
33	China	27.6	28.2	30.3	32.2	35.0	37.2	38.8	39.9
34	Belarus	34.4	34.5	35.3	36.6	37.8	38.6	39.2	39.8
35	United Kingdom	36.9	37.3	37.6	38.2	38.8	39.1	39.5	39.8
36	Norway	36.7	37.1	37.2	37.5	38.0	38.3	38.8	39.4
37	Russia	33.9	34.3	35.3	36.6	37.5	38.2	38.6	38.9
38	Australia	33.1	33.9	34.8	35.9	36.8	37.4	38.0	38.7
39	New Zealand	32.5	33.3	34.0	34.9	35.7	36.6	37.6	38.6
40	USA	34.1	34.6	35.1	35.7	36.4	37.0	37.7	38.4
41	Ireland	31.1	32.1	33.2	34.2	34.8	35.6	36.7	37.9
42	Thailand	26.3	27.9	29.1	30.8	32.7	34.4	36.1	37.8
43	Chile	27.4	28.1	29.0	30.4	32.0	33.5	34.9	36.3
44	Brazil	24.6	25.5	26.7	28.0	29.2	30.8	32.6	34.4
45	Argentina	30.2	30.3	30.6	31.2	32.0	32.7	33.5	34.3
46	Tunisia	23.6	24.6	26.5	28.0	29.6	31.1	32.5	33.9
47	Costa Rica	24.7	25.3	26.2	27.4	28.8	30.5	32.1	33.7
48	Israel	29.0	29.4	30.3	30.9	31.3	31.9	32.7	33.7
49	Mexico	23.0	24.0	25.1	26.4	28.0	29.6	31.3	33.2
50	Azerbaijan	26.4	26.0	26.6	28.0	29.6	30.8	31.8	33.1
51	Indonesia	24.1	25.1	26.2	27.4	28.6	29.9	31.3	32.8
52	Kuwait	23.0	23.3	25.6	27.3	28.1	29.3	31.0	32.7
53	Turkey	24.8	25.7	26.6	27.6	28.8	30.1	31.4	32.7
54	Kazakhstan	27.7	28.3	29.4	30.2	31.0	31.3	31.7	32.6
55	Vietnam	23.8	24.1	24.8	26.2	27.7	29.1	30.7	32.3
56	United Arab Emirates	25.3	25.5	26.1	27.3	28.3	29.6	30.7	32.2
57	Iran	21.9	21.9	23.5	25.7	27.4	28.8	30.3	31.8
58	Colombia	23.6	24.5	25.5	26.6	27.8	29.1	30.5	31.8
59	Ecuador	23.2	24.0	25.0	26.1	27.3	28.7	30.0	31.4
60	Venezuela	23.4	24.2	25.2	26.3	27.5	28.7	29.9	31.2
61	Morocco	23.0	23.6	24.6	26.0	27.4	28.7	29.9	31.2
62	Peru	23.5	24.2	25.0	26.1	27.2	28.4	29.7	31.1
63	Algeria	21.8	22.3	23.4	25.1	26.7	28.1	29.4	30.8
64	Malaysia	23.8	24.3	25.2	26.0	26.9	27.8	29.0	30.2
65	India	24.2	24.6	25.1	25.8	26.7	27.7	28.9	30.1
66	Turkmenistan	23.2	23.3	23.8	25.0	26.1	27.4	28.6	29.9
67	South Africa	23.1	23.7	24.8	25.8	26.6	27.4	28.2	29.0
68	Saudi Arabia	21.5	21.7	22.2	23.4	24.7	26.0	27.4	28.7
69	Egypt	23.7	23.8	24.4	25.7	26.5	27.1	27.7	28.5
70	Philippines	22.4	22.9	23.5	24.3	25.3	26.3	27.3	28.5
71	Bolivia	23.1	23.4	23.6	24.1	24.8	25.6	26.6	27.8
72	Jordan	20.9	20.7	21.8	22.7	23.8	25.0	26.3	27.7
73	Pakistan	22.8	22.5	22.7	23.2	23.9	24.7	25.5	26.5
74	Nigeria	21.6	21.5	21.6	21.8	22.0	22.3	22.8	23.5

Population

Table 3.7 Median age of population

years

		1985	1990	1995	2000	2005	2010	2015	2020
1	Japan	35.2	37.7	39.7	41.5	43.3	44.9	46.6	48.6
2	Germany	36.9	37.6	38.2	39.8	41.8	44.1	46.2	47.8
3	Italy	35.4	36.9	38.5	40.1	41.5	43.4	45.4	47.4
4	Bulgaria	35.1	36.5	38.0	39.1	40.7	41.7	43.3	45.2
5	Greece	34.8	35.9	36.7	38.1	39.9	41.7	43.5	45.2
6	Slovenia	32.5	34.0	36.0	37.8	39.9	41.7	43.1	44.7
7	Austria	35.1	35.6	36.1	37.9	39.8	41.6	43.3	44.5
8	Portugal	31.4	33.9	35.9	37.6	39.2	40.7	42.4	44.4
9	Switzerland	36.0	36.9	37.2	38.5	40.1	41.8	43.1	43.9
10	South Korea	24.3	27.0	29.3	31.8	34.8	38.0	41.0	43.8
11	Spain	31.8	33.4	35.4	37.4	38.6	40.1	41.8	43.8
12	Netherlands	32.9	34.4	35.8	37.3	38.9	40.8	42.6	43.7
13	Czech Republic	33.9	35.1	36.2	37.3	38.7	39.8	41.4	43.5
14	Finland	34.5	36.3	37.7	39.2	40.8	42.0	42.6	43.0
15	Croatia	34.1	35.6	37.5	39.0	40.1	41.4	42.1	42.9
16	Bosnia-Herzegovina	27.9	29.7	32.3	35.0	37.4	39.3	41.0	42.7
17	Denmark	36.0	37.0	37.7	38.2	39.4	40.5	41.7	42.7
18	Belgium	35.2	36.2	37.3	38.7	40.1	41.2	42.1	42.6
19	Hungary	34.9	36.1	37.6	38.5	38.9	39.7	40.8	42.5
20	Hong Kong, China	28.2	31.0	33.6	36.2	39.2	40.6	41.7	42.5
21	Sweden	37.6	38.4	38.4	39.3	40.1	41.1	41.8	42.3
22	Ukraine	34.4	35.0	36.0	37.7	38.8	39.4	40.7	42.1
23	China	23.4	25.2	28.4	31.2	35.4	38.8	41.1	42.0
24	Taiwan	24.6	27.0	29.4	31.6	34.1	36.8	39.3	42.0
25	Romania	31.6	32.6	34.5	34.9	36.4	38.3	39.8	41.8
26	Lithuania	32.0	32.4	33.9	35.8	37.7	39.3	40.6	41.6
27	Latvia	34.7	34.6	36.0	37.9	39.2	40.0	40.8	41.5
28	Singapore	27.2	29.8	31.9	34.0	35.9	37.8	39.8	41.5
29	Canada	31.0	32.9	34.8	36.8	38.5	39.7	40.6	41.4
30	France	33.5	34.7	36.1	37.5	38.8	39.8	40.9	41.3
31	Poland	30.7	32.2	33.7	35.1	36.5	37.8	39.5	41.3
32	Slovakia	30.0	31.2	32.4	33.9	35.3	36.9	39.0	41.2
33	Estonia	33.6	34.2	36.2	37.8	38.8	39.5	40.2	40.8
34	Belarus	32.2	32.8	34.4	36.3	37.6	38.4	39.1	40.0
35	Norway	34.5	35.3	36.0	36.7	37.8	38.6	39.3	39.7
36	United Kingdom	35.3	35.8	36.4	37.5	38.7	39.5	39.6	39.4
37	Russia	32.0	33.1	34.8	36.6	37.3	37.7	38.3	39.0
38	Thailand	23.2	25.4	27.4	29.7	32.2	34.3	36.4	38.5
39	New Zealand	29.6	31.1	32.6	34.3	35.5	36.8	37.5	38.3
40	Ireland	27.2	29.1	30.8	32.4	33.3	34.4	36.1	38.2
41	Australia	30.8	32.1	33.7	35.4	36.5	37.2	37.7	38.2
42	USA	31.4	32.8	34.2	35.4	36.3	37.0	37.4	38.0
43	Chile	24.1	25.7	27.1	28.8	30.5	32.0	33.5	35.2
44	United Arab Emirates	27.0	27.4	27.5	28.6	29.5	31.7	33.2	34.4
45	Kuwait	22.5	23.0	26.8	28.9	29.3	30.6	32.4	34.0
46	Brazil	21.2	22.4	23.9	25.3	26.8	28.8	31.2	33.5
47	Tunisia	19.5	20.7	22.7	24.6	26.8	29.0	31.2	33.5
48	Argentina	27.2	27.1	27.2	27.7	28.8	30.2	31.4	32.6
49	Costa Rica	21.4	22.5	23.5	24.5	26.0	28.1	30.2	32.4
50	Iran	17.5	17.3	19.0	21.8	24.0	26.7	29.5	32.3
51	Indonesia	20.3	21.6	23.1	24.8	26.4	28.2	30.1	32.0
52	Azerbaijan	22.8	23.2	24.1	25.6	27.0	28.3	29.9	32.0
53	Turkey	20.8	21.9	23.3	24.9	26.7	28.6	30.4	31.8
54	Kazakhstan	24.6	26.0	27.0	27.7	28.7	29.3	30.2	31.8
55	Mexico	18.3	19.8	21.4	23.4	25.5	27.5	29.6	31.8
56	Israel	25.4	25.8	26.8	27.6	28.4	29.2	30.2	31.3
57	Vietnam	19.4	20.2	21.3	23.0	24.9	26.8	28.9	31.2
58	Algeria	17.2	18.1	19.5	21.7	24.0	26.2	28.3	30.3
59	Colombia	20.1	21.4	22.6	23.8	25.2	26.7	28.3	29.9
60	Morocco	18.9	19.7	20.8	22.4	24.3	26.2	28.0	29.8
61	Venezuela	20.1	21.0	22.0	23.2	24.6	26.1	27.7	29.3
62	Peru	19.5	20.4	21.5	22.8	24.2	25.6	27.2	28.9
63	Turkmenistan	19.4	19.6	20.2	21.6	23.0	24.7	26.6	28.7
64	Ecuador	19.0	20.1	21.4	22.6	23.9	25.4	27.0	28.7
65	India	20.6	21.1	21.6	22.5	23.6	25.0	26.4	28.1
66	Malaysia	20.5	21.4	22.5	23.3	24.2	25.3	26.5	27.8
67	Saudi Arabia	19.0	19.3	19.4	21.3	23.2	24.6	26.0	27.5
68	South Africa	19.4	20.1	21.7	22.9	23.9	24.9	25.7	26.5
69	Philippines	18.7	19.3	19.9	20.8	21.9	23.1	24.5	25.9
70	Jordan	16.1	16.4	18.7	19.7	20.9	22.7	24.1	25.7
71	Egypt	19.8	19.9	20.4	21.8	23.0	23.8	24.6	24.9
72	Bolivia	18.8	19.2	19.6	20.1	20.8	21.8	23.2	24.7
73	Pakistan	18.1	18.1	18.2	18.9	20.0	21.2	22.5	23.7
74	Nigeria	17.1	16.9	17.2	17.7	18.1	18.5	19.1	20.0

Population

Table 3.8 Urban population

% of total

		1985	1990	1995	2000	2005	2010	2015	2020
1	Hong Kong, China	93.1	98.2	100.0	100.0	100.0	100.0	100.0	100.0
1	Singapore	100.0	100.0	100.0	100.0	100.0	100.0	100.0	100.0
3	Belgium	95.9	96.4	96.8	97.1	97.3	97.4	97.5	97.7
4	Kuwait	93.9	94.9	95.5	96.2	96.4	96.7	96.9	97.1
5	Australia	85.5	85.2	87.6	90.6	92.6	94.0	94.9	95.4
6	Brazil	70.6	74.6	77.7	80.4	83.4	87.5	91.4	94.4
7	Israel	90.0	90.5	91.0	91.5	91.8	92.0	92.3	92.6
8	Venezuela	81.5	83.5	85.4	87.1	88.6	89.8	90.7	91.5
9	Argentina	85.2	86.9	88.3	89.3	89.6	90.1	90.7	91.4
10	Saudi Arabia	71.8	76.3	80.2	86.0	88.9	90.3	91.0	91.4
11	Chile	81.8	83.1	84.5	85.6	86.7	87.9	89.2	90.8
12	United Kingdom	88.5	88.7	88.7	88.9	89.2	89.7	90.2	90.8
13	Germany	84.0	85.3	86.5	87.5	88.5	89.3	90.0	90.7
14	Taiwan	69.6	74.0	77.4	80.0	82.4	84.6	86.7	88.8
15	United Arab Emirates	79.7	78.1	78.3	80.6	83.5	86.2	87.7	88.6
16	Norway	71.3	72.1	73.4	76.1	80.4	83.8	86.3	88.2
17	New Zealand	84.3	85.5	85.5	85.6	86.1	86.5	86.9	87.3
18	Denmark	84.3	84.8	85.1	85.1	85.5	85.4	85.8	86.1
19	Canada	76.4	76.6	77.0	77.9	80.1	82.2	83.9	85.2
20	Sweden	83.1	83.1	83.2	83.3	83.4	83.8	84.3	84.9
21	USA	73.9	75.2	77.1	79.0	80.7	82.3	83.6	84.8
22	South Korea	65.1	73.5	78.0	80.5	80.9	81.9	83.0	84.1
23	Colombia	66.5	69.4	71.7	73.7	75.7	77.7	79.7	81.7
24	Jordan	76.4	77.7	78.2	78.7	78.8	79.1	79.7	81.3
25	France	73.7	74.1	74.9	75.7	76.7	77.8	79.0	80.3
26	Spain	74.2	75.3	75.9	76.3	76.7	77.3	78.1	79.2
27	Mexico	69.0	71.3	73.5	74.6	75.8	76.8	77.9	79.0
28	Peru	66.1	69.6	71.2	72.3	73.7	74.8	75.9	77.0
29	Belarus	64.2	66.8	68.1	70.2	72.3	73.9	75.3	76.3
30	Czech Republic	75.2	75.0	74.5	74.1	74.5	75.2	75.8	76.3
31	Russia	72.6	73.7	72.9	72.9	73.6	74.2	74.8	75.3
32	Bulgaria	65.8	67.1	67.8	68.4	70.7	72.4	73.9	75.2
33	Iran	53.4	56.3	60.2	64.2	66.9	69.5	71.9	74.0
34	Turkey	55.9	59.6	62.1	64.8	67.4	69.7	71.7	73.5
35	Netherlands	59.2	60.0	60.9	63.0	65.3	67.7	70.4	73.5
36	Ecuador	51.4	55.3	59.2	62.7	64.5	67.1	69.8	72.4
37	Malaysia	45.5	50.1	54.7	57.0	60.7	64.4	68.3	72.4
38	Estonia	71.0	71.5	70.0	69.2	69.3	69.6	70.3	72.0
39	Philippines	43.1	48.9	53.9	58.5	62.5	66.1	69.2	71.8
40	Italy	66.8	66.7	66.9	67.2	67.6	68.2	69.3	70.6
41	Hungary	62.8	65.4	65.2	64.5	66.2	67.6	69.0	70.5
42	Ukraine	66.4	67.5	67.8	67.4	67.6	68.2	69.0	70.3
43	Bolivia	47.6	55.6	59.9	62.2	63.7	65.4	67.5	69.7
44	Latvia	68.5	69.0	68.7	68.1	68.0	68.5	69.0	69.5
45	Switzerland	66.4	68.0	67.7	67.6	68.0	68.4	68.9	69.3
46	Costa Rica	45.6	50.7	55.8	59.0	61.7	64.3	66.9	69.3
47	Japan	60.7	63.0	64.5	65.2	65.7	66.5	67.7	69.2
48	Tunisia	57.3	59.6	61.3	62.6	64.4	65.9	67.5	69.2
49	Austria	58.8	63.5	65.7	66.5	67.0	67.4	67.8	68.1
50	Lithuania	65.1	68.1	67.5	67.1	67.1	67.4	67.6	68.0
51	Greece	58.4	58.8	59.3	60.1	61.5	63.2	65.3	67.7
52	Morocco	45.0	48.4	51.9	55.2	58.7	61.9	64.9	67.7
53	Croatia	52.2	54.0	55.8	57.7	59.9	62.2	64.6	67.2
54	Algeria	48.0	51.7	55.8	60.0	59.7	62.0	64.2	66.4
55	Ireland	56.3	56.9	57.9	59.1	60.4	61.9	63.6	65.6
56	Poland	61.2	61.8	61.8	61.8	61.8	62.0	62.8	64.9
57	South Africa	45.8	47.6	53.5	52.9	54.8	57.2	60.1	63.7
58	Portugal	37.5	46.3	50.3	53.1	55.7	58.4	61.0	63.6
59	Finland	56.6	56.8	57.8	60.4	62.2	62.7	63.1	63.3
60	Indonesia	24.7	29.8	35.9	42.0	48.1	53.5	58.3	62.5
61	Kazakhstan	55.4	57.1	55.2	56.3	57.0	57.7	58.7	59.8
62	Slovakia	55.6	56.9	56.3	55.5	55.9	56.9	57.8	58.6
63	Nigeria	30.8	35.0	39.3	44.0	48.5	52.4	55.5	58.2
64	Romania	53.0	54.3	54.9	54.6	54.9	55.1	55.4	56.1
65	Bosnia-Herzegovina	37.6	39.2	41.1	43.2	45.7	48.6	51.8	55.2
66	Slovenia	50.1	50.8	50.8	50.8	50.8	51.2	52.1	53.9
67	Azerbaijan	53.7	53.9	52.8	51.0	50.6	50.9	51.7	53.0
68	China	23.5	26.4	29.0	36.2	42.7	47.2	50.4	52.7
69	Turkmenistan	46.8	45.6	44.7	43.6	44.0	44.9	46.5	49.9
70	Egypt	43.8	43.4	42.9	42.5	42.2	42.9	45.0	47.5
71	Pakistan	29.6	32.1	34.7	33.5	35.2	38.0	40.8	43.6
72	Thailand	28.1	29.4	30.3	31.1	32.3	34.0	36.2	38.9
73	India	24.3	25.5	26.6	27.6	28.7	30.1	31.8	34.1
74	Vietnam	18.9	19.5	20.7	24.2	26.5	28.9	31.2	33.6

Population

Table 3.9 Population density

persons per sq km

		1985	1990	1995	2000	2005	2010	2015	2020
1	Hong Kong, China	5,511.31	5,762.12	6,218.28	6,732.32	6,882.02	7,202.96	7,518.43	7,805.62
2	Singapore	4,083.59	4,547.92	5,260.46	6,011.79	6,301.59	6,926.42	7,336.40	7,657.63
3	South Korea	413.31	434.21	456.73	476.13	487.57	495.03	499.11	499.60
4	Netherlands	426.62	439.57	455.26	468.24	481.27	485.23	489.68	493.68
5	India	254.23	282.91	312.76	342.11	371.00	398.51	424.67	448.64
6	Israel	195.61	215.35	256.23	290.63	320.24	347.40	372.62	395.92
7	Philippines	180.53	203.10	230.13	256.58	285.17	315.00	345.09	376.26
8	Belgium	326.04	329.02	335.06	338.71	345.55	353.90	359.87	365.34
9	Japan	332.00	339.03	344.40	348.22	350.53	349.42	345.26	338.72
10	Vietnam	179.87	201.22	222.32	250.03	268.32	286.61	304.79	322.22
11	Pakistan	127.53	150.19	169.15	192.16	215.10	239.67	266.58	293.41
12	United Kingdom	233.46	236.25	239.51	242.98	248.25	256.13	263.37	271.69
13	Germany	222.81	226.83	233.79	235.58	236.55	234.31	230.45	226.52
14	Nigeria	93.49	106.87	121.27	137.07	154.68	173.76	193.16	212.19
15	Italy	192.41	192.77	193.28	193.57	198.78	201.00	201.34	200.57
16	Switzerland	161.40	166.85	175.48	179.11	185.38	189.73	193.30	196.98
17	Kuwait	95.25	116.04	88.42	105.69	124.21	140.22	155.27	169.61
18	China	111.88	120.83	128.49	134.86	139.36	143.06	146.00	148.30
19	Indonesia	89.62	97.92	105.71	113.32	121.01	128.35	134.80	140.33
20	Czech Republic	133.31	133.29	133.52	132.47	132.29	134.01	134.11	134.02
21	Denmark	120.60	121.15	122.93	125.62	127.54	130.24	132.03	133.88
22	Thailand	99.47	106.27	112.59	118.74	123.32	127.47	130.68	133.08
23	Poland	121.72	124.79	125.71	125.72	124.62	123.56	122.59	121.79
24	France	100.27	102.85	104.99	106.98	110.57	114.11	116.62	118.85
25	Portugal	109.47	109.25	109.48	111.42	115.07	116.88	117.80	118.02
26	Azerbaijan			91.85	97.04	100.98	106.80	112.42	117.23
27	Slovakia	106.90	109.60	111.20	111.82	111.95	112.20	112.22	112.06
28	Turkey	64.53	72.11	79.52	86.91	93.04	98.95	104.51	109.54
29	Hungary	118.57	115.44	115.03	114.06	112.68	111.59	110.15	108.79
30	Austria	91.73	92.72	96.34	97.06	99.53	101.99	103.46	104.72
31	Costa Rica	52.85	60.29	68.13	76.99	84.77	90.87	97.08	102.82
32	Slovenia	96.85	99.22	98.78	98.70	99.19	100.74	101.69	102.33
33	Malaysia	48.34	55.10	62.97	71.51	79.52	86.90	93.52	99.66
34	Spain	76.79	77.74	78.77	80.26	86.22	91.96	95.57	98.65
35	Egypt	47.36	52.82	58.40	64.67	71.52	78.52	85.50	92.19
36	Greece	76.96	78.52	82.20	84.59	85.98	87.59	88.73	89.23
37	Romania	98.50	101.21	97.11	95.46	94.18	92.88	91.06	88.61
38	Jordan	30.67	36.88	48.78	55.00	63.08	73.35	78.84	85.21
39	Morocco	49.96	55.59	60.39	64.59	68.33	72.55	76.92	81.11
40	Croatia	84.08	85.44	83.49	79.43	79.47	79.06	78.21	77.16
41	Bosnia-Herzegovina			68.81	73.30	75.05	75.09	74.94	74.39
42	Ukraine	87.42	88.99	88.55	84.78	81.29	78.77	76.26	73.69
43	Tunisia	47.18	52.88	57.51	60.84	63.58	66.77	70.06	73.16
44	Ireland	51.45	50.91	52.22	54.84	59.65	65.42	69.19	72.52
45	United Arab Emirates	16.50	22.00	28.84	38.71	49.10	56.52	62.36	67.96
46	Mexico	38.79	43.20	47.18	50.64	53.47	56.69	60.47	63.81
47	Bulgaria	80.94	79.25	75.05	72.12	71.13	69.16	66.60	63.77
48	Ecuador	32.88	37.13	41.20	44.47	47.18	49.76	52.72	55.54
49	Iran	29.59	34.67	38.02	40.89	43.25	45.89	48.56	51.18
50	Lithuania	54.46	57.00	58.12	56.03	54.65	53.12	51.60	50.25
51	Colombia	27.04	29.93	32.86	35.85	38.80	41.73	44.51	47.12
52	Belarus	47.86	49.11	49.21	48.29	47.23	46.52	45.86	45.12
53	South Africa	27.14	30.26	34.07	36.95	39.58	41.58	42.56	43.37
54	Venezuela	19.64	22.38	25.05	27.67	30.30	32.93	35.48	37.88
55	USA	25.98	27.25	29.07	30.80	32.26	33.71	34.87	36.04
56	Latvia	41.42	43.00	40.30	38.38	37.03	35.97	34.87	33.87
57	Estonia	36.04	37.16	34.16	32.37	31.79	31.28	30.72	30.24
58	Peru	15.15	16.74	18.32	19.88	21.43	22.97	24.48	25.91
59	Chile	16.17	17.62	19.24	20.59	21.76	22.88	23.94	24.89
60	Brazil	16.09	17.68	19.11	20.59	22.00	23.10	23.98	24.71
61	Sweden	20.33	20.78	21.49	21.60	21.96	22.53	23.07	23.65
62	Finland	16.07	16.33	16.74	16.98	17.19	17.56	17.87	18.12
63	New Zealand	12.45	12.88	13.71	14.40	15.43	16.24	16.98	17.67
64	Norway	13.63	13.91	14.29	14.72	15.14	15.97	16.79	17.59
65	Algeria	9.28	10.62	11.87	12.81	13.79	14.87	15.99	17.06
66	Argentina	11.07	11.91	12.73	13.48	14.16	14.89	15.59	16.26
67	Saudi Arabia	5.99	7.56	8.49	9.68	10.98	12.21	13.46	14.70
68	Turkmenistan	6.87	7.81	8.91	9.58	10.31	11.02	11.72	12.38
69	Bolivia	5.50	6.15	6.90	7.67	8.47	9.25	10.01	10.73
70	Russia	8.44	8.74	9.06	8.97	8.76	8.66	8.58	8.50
71	Kazakhstan	5.77	6.10	5.91	5.52	5.58	5.92	6.29	6.62
72	Canada	2.84	3.05	3.22	3.37	3.55	3.74	3.88	4.02
73	Australia	2.06	2.22	2.35	2.49	2.65	2.88	3.08	3.29

Marketing segments

Table 3.10 Babies (under 12 months)

% of total

		1985	1990	1995	2000	2005	2010	2015	2020
1	Nigeria	4.13	3.97	3.85	3.73	3.64	3.49	3.14	2.85
2	Pakistan	3.78	3.83	3.14	3.05	2.89	2.76	2.62	2.31
3	Philippines	3.22	3.16	2.92	2.65	2.47	2.38	2.27	2.18
4	Bolivia	3.41	3.30	3.27	2.84	2.81	2.47	2.30	2.09
5	Egypt	3.21	2.78	2.30	2.28	2.35	2.28	2.15	1.98
6	Jordan	3.82	3.77	3.12	3.02	2.52	2.54	2.17	1.93
7	Saudi Arabia	3.41	3.57	2.99	2.65	2.51	2.17	2.13	1.93
8	Malaysia	3.10	2.75	2.43	2.51	2.44	2.16	2.07	1.88
9	Kazakhstan	2.45	2.35	1.48	1.37	1.86	2.25	2.10	1.86
10	South Africa	3.11	2.80	2.42	2.31	2.25	2.00	2.00	1.83
11	India	3.02	2.89	2.75	2.43	2.32	2.06	1.93	1.73
12	Venezuela	2.91	2.87	2.43	2.33	2.18	2.03	1.88	1.73
13	Ecuador	3.07	2.76	2.51	2.44	2.13	1.98	1.85	1.73
14	Algeria	3.68	2.89	2.53	1.74	2.19	1.97	1.90	1.72
15	Morocco	3.38	2.67	2.43	2.11	1.96	2.03	1.85	1.71
16	Turkmenistan	3.35	3.41	2.69	1.94	2.42	1.95	1.94	1.71
17	Peru	2.90	2.88	2.54	2.31	2.16	2.02	1.80	1.70
18	Colombia	2.72	2.63	2.49	2.21	2.09	1.97	1.78	1.69
19	Mexico	2.89	2.72	2.56	2.10	2.04	2.00	1.80	1.66
20	Israel	2.33	2.18	2.09	2.13	2.07	1.88	1.71	1.61
21	Azerbaijan	2.63	2.71	2.11	1.47	1.79	1.90	1.78	1.56
22	Argentina	1.97	2.22	2.01	1.84	1.71	1.75	1.59	1.51
23	Turkey	2.54	2.27	2.36	2.18	1.82	1.71	1.60	1.50
24	Vietnam	3.06	3.05	2.45	1.74	2.14	1.71	1.67	1.50
25	Iran	4.13	3.11	2.31	1.78	2.06	1.76	1.64	1.49
26	Tunisia	3.04	2.70	1.98	1.62	1.62	1.59	1.54	1.43
27	Indonesia	2.77	2.37	2.21	2.03	1.97	1.71	1.57	1.41
28	Kuwait	3.04	2.93	2.04	1.96	1.73	1.77	1.48	1.38
29	Costa Rica	2.81	2.75	2.16	1.99	1.80	1.52	1.66	1.36
30	Chile	2.45	2.24	2.02	1.57	1.55	1.50	1.39	1.32
31	USA	1.55	1.60	1.42	1.37	1.39	1.38	1.33	1.31
32	New Zealand	1.60	1.72	1.58	1.47	1.40	1.47	1.35	1.28
33	Australia	1.53	1.50	1.43	1.31	1.26	1.35	1.31	1.28
34	United Kingdom	1.29	1.35	1.28	1.18	1.20	1.29	1.27	1.27
35	Norway	1.21	1.40	1.38	1.33	1.24	1.26	1.23	1.24
36	Brazil	2.83	2.37	2.12	2.05	1.82	1.51	1.31	1.22
37	France	1.35	1.33	1.21	1.26	1.26	1.27	1.21	1.18
38	Sweden	1.12	1.36	1.27	1.00	1.12	1.13	1.13	1.15
39	Russia	1.68	1.44	0.97	0.83	1.04	1.23	1.22	1.14
40	Denmark	1.01	1.19	1.34	1.24	1.20	1.16	1.10	1.12
41	Estonia	1.59	1.53	0.95	0.88	1.03	1.13	1.18	1.12
42	Finland	1.33	1.27	1.27	1.11	1.10	1.11	1.12	1.11
43	Ireland	1.74	1.49	1.34	1.42	1.49	1.39	1.25	1.10
44	Belgium	1.16	1.21	1.14	1.10	1.11	1.16	1.13	1.10
45	Netherlands	1.20	1.26	1.27	1.27	1.19	1.08	1.05	1.07
46	Canada	1.43	1.46	1.30	1.10	1.05	1.07	1.05	1.07
47	Thailand	1.50	1.52	1.54	1.26	1.25	1.20	1.07	1.04
48	Switzerland	1.15	1.21	1.17	1.09	0.98	0.95	0.97	1.03
49	Poland	1.86	1.46	1.23	0.98	0.93	0.97	1.02	1.02
50	Singapore	1.70	1.70	1.55	1.27	1.02	0.98	0.98	1.01
51	Latvia	1.56	1.55	0.96	0.81	0.88	1.03	1.08	1.01
52	Belarus	1.64	1.50	1.06	0.92	0.90	1.12	1.07	1.01
53	United Arab Emirates	2.98	2.75	1.91	1.63	1.56	1.21	1.28	1.01
54	Lithuania	1.65	1.50	1.15	1.03	0.88	0.93	0.98	0.99
55	Croatia	1.34	1.17	1.07	0.89	0.91	0.98	0.99	0.98
56	Slovakia	1.74	1.50	1.23	1.03	0.99	1.00	1.00	0.98
57	Hungary	1.15	1.17	1.10	0.91	0.93	0.97	0.96	0.95
58	Czech Republic	1.31	1.23	1.02	0.87	0.95	1.00	0.99	0.95
59	China	1.82	2.06	1.39	1.11	1.08	1.05	1.01	0.94
60	Slovenia	1.34	1.16	0.97	0.88	0.90	0.94	0.96	0.91
61	Austria	1.17	1.16	1.15	0.98	0.96	0.92	0.92	0.91
62	Spain	1.22	1.03	0.94	0.95	1.05	1.07	1.02	0.91
63	Romania	1.52	1.56	1.06	1.03	0.98	1.02	0.99	0.90
64	Ukraine	1.52	1.33	1.01	0.78	0.90	0.98	0.88	0.87
65	Portugal	1.40	1.15	1.07	1.12	1.03	1.01	0.94	0.86
66	Greece	1.20	1.01	0.99	0.95	0.95	0.97	0.92	0.85
67	Bosnia-Herzegovina	1.83	1.54	0.97	1.37	0.75	0.97	0.87	0.84
68	Bulgaria	1.34	1.26	0.93	0.87	0.87	0.89	0.85	0.78
69	South Korea	1.64	1.53	1.60	1.32	0.94	0.90	0.82	0.77
70	Germany	1.04	1.12	0.94	0.94	0.85	0.81	0.75	0.76
71	Italy	1.04	0.99	0.94	0.93	0.95	0.88	0.81	0.75
72	Taiwan	1.77	1.47	1.39	1.22	0.91	0.83	0.79	0.74
73	Japan	1.18	0.98	0.95	0.92	0.83	0.83	0.74	0.70
74	Hong Kong, China	1.43	1.25	1.20	0.74	0.58	0.60	0.62	0.63

Marketing segments

Table 3.11 Infants (under 24 months)

% of total

		1985	1990	1995	2000	2005	2010	2015	2020
1	Nigeria	8.07	7.76	7.53	7.30	7.13	6.86	6.24	5.66
2	Pakistan	7.36	7.50	6.33	6.01	5.71	5.47	5.20	4.64
3	Philippines	6.40	6.24	5.81	5.30	4.92	4.74	4.44	4.21
4	Bolivia	6.67	6.52	6.46	5.70	5.56	4.95	4.59	4.18
5	Egypt	6.33	5.61	4.65	4.52	4.69	4.58	4.32	4.00
6	Jordan	7.50	7.41	6.18	5.94	5.05	5.00	4.38	3.88
7	Saudi Arabia	6.84	6.97	6.03	5.29	4.96	4.36	4.22	3.86
8	Malaysia	5.98	5.51	4.89	4.96	4.81	4.31	4.11	3.76
9	South Africa	6.15	5.59	4.86	4.59	4.46	4.03	3.99	3.69
10	India	5.99	5.73	5.46	4.88	4.60	4.13	3.85	3.48
11	Venezuela	5.84	5.68	4.90	4.62	4.35	4.07	3.76	3.47
12	Algeria	7.27	5.89	5.07	3.61	4.20	3.95	3.80	3.47
13	Ecuador	6.12	5.51	5.00	4.84	4.30	3.96	3.69	3.45
14	Turkmenistan	6.54	6.71	5.48	4.00	4.64	3.96	3.85	3.45
15	Morocco	6.63	5.44	4.85	4.24	3.90	4.00	3.72	3.43
16	Kazakhstan	4.81	4.68	3.19	2.76	3.55	4.23	3.81	3.42
17	Peru	5.80	5.67	5.09	4.62	4.32	4.03	3.62	3.40
18	Colombia	5.47	5.21	4.96	4.43	4.16	3.93	3.57	3.37
19	Israel	4.65	4.35	4.16	4.23	4.16	3.77	3.44	3.22
20	Mexico	5.74	5.39	5.09	4.27	4.05	3.80	3.41	3.10
21	Azerbaijan	5.15	5.39	4.35	3.05	3.43	3.76	3.51	3.09
22	Argentina	4.07	4.33	4.04	3.70	3.42	3.46	3.21	3.03
23	Vietnam	6.06	5.99	4.99	3.63	4.11	3.47	3.33	3.02
24	Turkey	5.07	4.52	4.63	4.33	3.66	3.40	3.20	3.01
25	Iran	8.09	6.32	4.67	3.56	3.90	3.57	3.32	3.00
26	Tunisia	6.06	5.41	4.08	3.28	3.18	3.16	3.08	2.88
27	Indonesia	5.52	4.78	4.41	4.06	3.92	3.46	3.15	2.84
28	Costa Rica	5.60	5.47	4.42	3.98	3.62	3.08	3.26	2.78
29	Kuwait	6.03	5.80	4.15	3.86	3.45	3.49	3.01	2.75
30	Chile	4.74	4.49	4.07	3.22	3.06	2.98	2.80	2.65
31	USA	3.01	3.12	2.86	2.71	2.77	2.78	2.65	2.61
32	New Zealand	3.18	3.38	3.15	2.91	2.79	2.95	2.71	2.57
33	Australia	3.05	2.98	2.86	2.63	2.51	2.70	2.61	2.55
34	United Kingdom	2.55	2.70	2.58	2.38	2.35	2.58	2.52	2.54
35	Norway	2.41	2.75	2.75	2.64	2.49	2.53	2.46	2.49
36	Brazil	5.62	4.76	4.22	4.07	3.68	3.06	2.63	2.44
37	France	2.67	2.66	2.41	2.49	2.51	2.55	2.42	2.36
38	Russia	3.40	3.00	1.91	1.71	2.05	2.43	2.45	2.31
39	Sweden	2.23	2.68	2.60	2.01	2.23	2.25	2.26	2.30
40	Estonia	3.17	3.09	1.96	1.74	1.99	2.25	2.36	2.27
41	Denmark	2.01	2.34	2.63	2.49	2.40	2.35	2.20	2.24
42	Ireland	3.54	3.07	2.72	2.84	3.00	2.78	2.53	2.22
43	Finland	2.69	2.54	2.54	2.21	2.18	2.23	2.24	2.22
44	Belgium	2.33	2.42	2.33	2.22	2.20	2.32	2.27	2.20
45	Netherlands	2.38	2.51	2.54	2.54	2.42	2.17	2.10	2.14
46	Canada	2.86	2.85	2.63	2.23	2.10	2.15	2.10	2.13
47	Thailand	3.21	3.10	3.18	2.65	2.57	2.45	2.20	2.11
48	United Arab Emirates	5.75	5.42	3.89	3.22	3.07	2.49	2.54	2.07
49	Latvia	3.13	3.13	2.01	1.57	1.78	2.05	2.17	2.05
50	Switzerland	2.28	2.40	2.35	2.19	1.95	1.91	1.93	2.05
51	Poland	3.76	2.98	2.49	1.99	1.84	1.94	2.04	2.04
52	Belarus	3.34	3.12	2.19	1.84	1.80	2.23	2.15	2.03
53	Singapore	3.33	3.59	3.15	2.57	2.09	1.98	1.98	2.03
54	Lithuania	3.29	3.04	2.42	2.07	1.77	1.85	1.96	1.98
55	Croatia	2.71	2.35	2.12	1.93	1.80	1.95	1.99	1.98
56	Slovakia	3.49	3.04	2.58	2.09	1.95	2.00	2.00	1.97
57	Hungary	2.32	2.34	2.22	1.85	1.86	1.95	1.92	1.91
58	Czech Republic	2.62	2.50	2.19	1.74	1.87	2.00	1.99	1.91
59	Slovenia	2.73	2.42	1.96	1.79	1.77	1.87	1.92	1.84
60	Spain	2.47	2.08	1.91	1.86	2.08	2.15	2.05	1.84
61	Romania	2.90	3.15	2.13	2.06	1.95	2.04	1.98	1.83
62	Austria	2.36	2.32	2.35	2.01	1.92	1.86	1.85	1.83
63	China	3.53	4.12	2.60	2.05	2.13	2.01	1.93	1.82
64	Portugal	2.81	2.26	2.18	2.17	2.09	2.03	1.90	1.74
65	Ukraine	3.07	2.77	2.08	1.62	1.76	1.96	1.77	1.74
66	Greece	2.46	2.05	1.97	1.88	1.89	1.94	1.85	1.71
67	Bosnia-Herzegovina	3.59	3.12	2.08	2.61	1.65	1.88	1.77	1.70
68	Bulgaria	2.69	2.56	1.91	1.66	1.73	1.77	1.71	1.57
69	South Korea	3.40	3.02	3.20	2.66	1.94	1.80	1.65	1.54
70	Taiwan	3.75	3.15	2.92	2.43	1.91	1.72	1.63	1.54
71	Germany	2.09	2.26	1.93	1.90	1.72	1.65	1.49	1.53
72	Italy	2.11	1.99	1.90	1.86	1.89	1.78	1.63	1.51
73	Japan	2.41	2.01	1.91	1.85	1.69	1.70	1.50	1.40
74	Hong Kong, China	2.95	2.60	2.43	1.49	1.15	1.20	1.24	1.28

Marketing segments

Table 3.12 Toddlers (1-4)

% of total

		1985	1990	1995	2000	2005	2010	2015	2020
1	Nigeria	14.69	14.25	13.77	13.41	13.16	12.83	12.05	11.01
2	Pakistan	13.40	13.71	12.81	11.49	10.89	10.49	10.08	9.32
3	Bolivia	12.36	12.28	12.21	11.44	10.69	9.93	9.09	8.37
4	Egypt	11.97	11.53	9.75	8.86	9.19	9.27	8.86	8.26
5	Philippines	12.31	11.89	11.37	10.53	9.71	9.24	8.67	8.08
6	Jordan	13.99	13.95	11.91	11.26	10.18	9.48	8.97	7.94
7	Saudi Arabia	13.47	12.85	12.19	10.60	9.56	8.77	8.18	7.70
8	South Africa	11.76	11.06	9.80	9.00	8.67	8.21	7.89	7.53
9	Malaysia	11.25	11.05	9.82	9.55	9.26	8.71	7.93	7.50
10	Algeria	13.74	12.26	10.35	8.10	7.46	7.75	7.56	7.07
11	Turkmenistan	12.05	12.42	11.43	8.94	8.23	8.10	7.60	7.05
12	India	11.46	11.00	10.53	9.75	9.00	8.29	7.64	7.04
13	Venezuela	11.55	10.94	9.99	9.07	8.54	8.07	7.54	6.99
14	Morocco	12.32	11.27	9.77	8.61	7.76	7.60	7.47	6.97
15	Ecuador	11.95	10.90	9.92	9.42	8.78	7.97	7.35	6.90
16	Peru	11.48	10.80	10.14	9.24	8.56	8.02	7.37	6.79
17	Colombia	10.94	10.20	9.70	8.96	8.24	7.76	7.23	6.72
18	Israel	8.99	8.64	8.14	8.14	8.16	7.63	6.95	6.45
19	Kazakhstan	9.07	9.06	7.68	6.01	6.08	7.40	7.26	6.42
20	Azerbaijan	9.53	10.36	9.42	7.08	6.16	6.93	7.05	6.34
21	Iran	14.62	13.08	9.79	7.33	6.54	7.14	6.82	6.19
22	Vietnam	11.63	11.32	10.37	8.23	7.35	7.18	6.66	6.16
23	Argentina	8.79	8.21	8.05	7.52	6.91	6.70	6.50	6.13
24	Turkey	10.23	8.85	8.64	8.47	7.52	6.71	6.34	6.06
25	Mexico	11.34	10.47	9.93	8.91	8.02	7.29	6.53	5.88
26	Tunisia	11.78	10.75	8.86	7.02	6.16	6.11	6.12	5.87
27	Costa Rica	10.82	10.61	9.43	8.09	7.28	6.43	6.18	5.85
28	Indonesia	10.80	9.68	8.72	8.07	7.68	7.13	6.42	5.80
29	Kuwait	11.51	11.16	8.55	7.40	6.81	6.70	6.25	5.58
30	Chile	8.50	8.84	8.30	7.02	6.05	5.81	5.64	5.37
31	USA	5.95	5.96	5.95	5.43	5.48	5.55	5.27	5.20
32	New Zealand	6.27	6.37	6.51	5.87	5.48	5.74	5.52	5.18
33	Australia	6.07	5.87	5.76	5.36	5.04	5.22	5.21	5.09
34	United Kingdom	5.08	5.31	5.33	4.90	4.49	4.89	4.96	5.02
35	Norway	4.92	5.11	5.61	5.43	5.04	4.99	4.95	4.95
36	Brazil	10.90	9.66	8.34	7.92	7.54	6.45	5.45	4.93
37	Russia	6.41	6.51	4.60	3.58	3.75	4.40	4.86	4.81
38	France	5.58	5.36	5.04	4.87	5.05	5.03	4.88	4.75
39	Estonia	6.10	6.19	4.85	3.60	3.81	4.39	4.68	4.68
40	Ireland	7.69	6.63	5.79	5.59	5.71	5.61	5.21	4.64
41	Sweden	4.53	4.97	5.60	4.29	4.27	4.50	4.51	4.58
42	United Arab Emirates	9.90	9.98	8.14	6.26	5.80	5.32	4.95	4.49
43	Belgium	4.86	4.74	4.93	4.53	4.39	4.60	4.61	4.48
44	Finland	5.32	4.95	5.16	4.64	4.32	4.43	4.47	4.46
45	Denmark	4.19	4.40	5.09	5.15	4.87	4.74	4.47	4.42
46	Thailand	7.17	6.05	6.68	6.15	5.18	5.02	4.67	4.33
47	Latvia	5.87	6.27	4.96	3.22	3.48	3.94	4.32	4.30
48	Canada	5.71	5.52	5.47	4.73	4.22	4.29	4.18	4.26
49	Netherlands	4.85	4.97	5.14	4.93	5.01	4.45	4.22	4.22
50	Belarus	6.33	6.46	5.05	3.72	3.66	4.12	4.39	4.21
51	Poland	7.37	6.46	5.35	4.27	3.77	3.82	4.02	4.11
52	Singapore	6.45	6.48	6.64	5.62	4.68	4.09	4.00	4.05
53	Lithuania	6.20	6.40	5.70	4.33	3.63	3.65	3.87	4.01
54	Croatia	5.60	4.89	4.36	4.44	3.74	3.87	3.98	4.00
55	Switzerland	4.56	4.55	4.88	4.51	3.94	3.85	3.81	3.99
56	Slovakia	7.06	6.38	5.62	4.37	3.84	4.00	4.00	3.97
57	Czech Republic	5.51	5.09	4.80	3.56	3.60	4.02	4.01	3.92
58	Hungary	5.07	4.78	4.69	3.99	3.80	3.96	3.91	3.89
59	Spain	5.45	4.36	3.97	3.65	4.00	4.26	4.20	3.88
60	Romania	6.16	6.24	4.71	4.06	3.92	4.07	4.02	3.83
61	Slovenia	5.93	5.11	4.18	3.75	3.58	3.71	3.86	3.81
62	China	7.38	8.25	5.90	4.52	4.27	3.89	3.83	3.76
63	Austria	4.86	4.64	4.80	4.32	3.89	3.80	3.73	3.71
64	Portugal	5.79	4.61	4.40	4.14	4.23	4.08	3.91	3.60
65	Greece	5.50	4.37	4.05	3.84	3.72	3.87	3.80	3.55
66	Ukraine	5.79	5.87	4.73	3.65	3.27	3.89	3.74	3.51
67	Bosnia-Herzegovina	6.78	6.43	5.12	4.58	4.04	3.55	3.60	3.48
68	Taiwan	8.35	6.50	6.18	5.60	4.57	3.56	3.44	3.25
69	Bulgaria	5.45	5.22	4.24	3.28	3.43	3.54	3.47	3.24
70	Italy	4.36	3.95	3.83	3.68	3.73	3.67	3.40	3.12
71	South Korea	7.79	5.94	6.27	5.61	4.34	3.61	3.39	3.12
72	Germany	4.32	4.41	4.20	3.87	3.58	3.34	3.03	3.06
73	Hong Kong, China	6.30	5.33	4.93	3.68	2.67	2.81	2.79	2.91
74	Japan	4.98	4.28	3.83	3.74	3.55	3.42	3.13	2.88

Marketing segments

Table 3.13 Children (2-9)

% of total

		1985	1990	1995	2000	2005	2010	2015	2020
1	Nigeria	25.65	25.43	24.70	24.09	23.72	23.37	22.68	21.26
2	Pakistan	23.89	24.16	24.50	22.27	20.72	19.85	19.19	18.33
3	Egypt	22.05	22.53	20.55	17.95	17.71	18.29	18.07	17.20
4	Bolivia	22.82	22.52	22.44	22.06	20.60	19.48	18.02	16.68
5	Jordan	25.79	25.66	22.58	21.30	20.17	18.15	17.73	16.26
6	Philippines	23.06	22.29	21.70	20.61	19.14	17.93	17.10	16.03
7	South Africa	22.16	21.35	19.55	17.85	16.88	16.39	15.76	15.27
8	Saudi Arabia	24.49	23.26	23.37	20.93	18.57	17.33	15.99	15.13
9	Malaysia	20.81	20.96	19.38	18.36	17.70	17.09	15.74	14.72
10	Turkmenistan	22.04	22.33	22.35	19.64	16.08	15.75	15.00	14.22
11	India	21.33	20.75	20.03	19.12	17.71	16.52	15.27	14.20
12	Algeria	25.02	24.20	21.28	18.00	14.64	14.58	14.65	14.17
13	Venezuela	21.75	20.82	19.79	18.01	16.75	15.87	15.01	14.06
14	Morocco	22.68	22.22	19.98	17.71	15.81	14.70	14.57	14.03
15	Ecuador	22.71	21.26	19.61	18.43	17.65	16.26	14.84	13.85
16	Peru	22.12	20.63	19.72	18.40	17.05	15.97	14.91	13.71
17	Colombia	20.98	19.84	18.83	17.81	16.43	15.35	14.50	13.52
18	Kazakhstan	17.25	17.20	16.73	14.08	11.67	12.92	14.49	13.50
19	Azerbaijan	17.49	19.03	19.17	16.45	12.74	12.48	13.57	13.14
20	Israel	17.63	16.89	15.90	15.42	15.54	15.27	14.16	13.03
21	Iran	25.13	25.52	21.14	16.07	12.37	13.12	13.49	12.72
22	Vietnam	21.94	21.14	20.61	18.13	14.61	14.26	13.33	12.51
23	Argentina	17.61	16.22	15.73	15.11	14.05	13.19	12.91	12.36
24	Turkey	20.84	18.36	16.61	16.38	15.61	13.83	12.73	12.13
25	Mexico	22.71	20.50	19.22	18.08	16.25	14.85	13.44	12.13
26	Indonesia	20.89	19.38	17.51	16.10	15.11	14.40	13.23	12.02
27	Costa Rica	19.86	19.94	19.16	16.78	14.86	13.38	12.14	11.85
28	Tunisia	22.16	20.91	18.66	15.55	12.81	11.89	11.89	11.74
29	Kuwait	20.99	20.53	16.51	14.14	13.05	12.68	12.42	11.37
30	Chile	15.94	16.53	16.41	15.01	12.71	11.54	11.19	10.80
31	New Zealand	12.53	12.20	12.69	12.27	11.16	10.86	11.13	10.58
32	USA	11.50	11.68	11.81	11.34	10.70	10.83	10.75	10.39
33	Brazil	20.25	19.58	17.24	15.54	14.95	13.75	11.76	10.25
34	Australia	11.99	11.79	11.49	11.09	10.34	10.03	10.28	10.15
35	Russia	12.16	12.80	11.70	8.43	7.29	8.07	9.37	9.87
36	Ireland	15.86	14.52	12.44	11.25	11.01	11.13	10.69	9.81
37	United Kingdom	9.79	10.31	10.62	10.22	9.31	9.12	9.70	9.78
38	Norway	10.12	9.84	10.67	11.01	10.45	9.87	9.87	9.78
39	France	10.95	10.89	10.45	9.83	9.84	9.94	9.88	9.59
40	Estonia	11.82	12.11	11.51	8.70	7.40	8.17	9.10	9.47
41	United Arab Emirates	16.49	17.06	15.90	12.53	10.70	10.73	9.82	9.25
42	Belgium	9.80	9.60	9.69	9.48	8.95	8.97	9.25	9.15
43	Thailand	15.80	13.51	12.99	12.88	11.27	10.19	9.78	9.06
44	Sweden	9.31	9.31	10.60	10.14	8.48	8.77	9.00	9.04
45	Finland	10.59	10.26	10.04	9.91	8.95	8.70	8.87	8.92
46	Denmark	9.48	8.50	9.39	10.31	10.02	9.51	9.19	8.82
47	Belarus	11.96	12.74	11.95	8.97	7.50	7.65	8.65	8.79
48	Latvia	11.08	11.76	11.60	8.56	6.73	7.39	8.30	8.77
49	Canada	11.31	11.07	10.95	10.25	9.00	8.45	8.48	8.43
50	Netherlands	9.82	9.67	10.00	9.97	9.83	9.42	8.59	8.34
51	Spain	12.45	9.97	8.36	7.62	7.56	8.20	8.48	8.17
52	Poland	14.10	13.86	11.87	9.81	8.22	7.57	7.82	8.14
53	Croatia	11.32	10.55	9.41	9.02	8.46	7.62	7.93	8.09
54	China	14.95	14.97	15.36	11.07	9.47	8.20	7.99	8.07
55	Czech Republic	12.86	10.62	9.91	8.56	7.12	7.59	8.07	8.01
56	Singapore	12.59	12.12	12.73	12.16	10.43	8.77	8.04	7.98
57	Slovakia	14.65	13.35	11.95	10.10	8.28	7.81	7.99	7.98
58	Romania	13.55	12.07	11.52	8.83	8.07	8.00	8.18	7.97
59	Lithuania	12.00	12.41	12.14	10.28	8.17	7.34	7.59	7.97
60	Hungary	12.00	9.93	9.60	8.90	7.86	7.80	7.97	7.89
61	Slovenia	12.33	10.94	9.46	8.05	7.36	7.29	7.59	7.76
62	Switzerland	9.03	9.05	9.55	9.38	8.41	7.79	7.63	7.72
63	Portugal	12.55	10.38	8.90	8.38	8.27	8.27	8.04	7.60
64	Austria	9.34	9.52	9.45	9.27	8.24	7.77	7.59	7.51
65	Greece	11.57	10.15	8.56	8.00	7.46	7.58	7.74	7.47
66	Ukraine	11.31	11.72	11.00	8.67	7.02	7.19	7.80	7.35
67	Bosnia-Herzegovina	13.08	12.98	11.88	9.42	8.88	7.51	7.23	7.14
68	Bulgaria	11.76	10.51	9.51	7.80	6.71	7.07	7.10	6.80
69	Taiwan	16.84	14.52	12.27	11.75	10.27	8.11	6.98	6.70
70	Italy	9.80	8.32	7.60	7.59	7.39	7.49	7.19	6.65
71	Hong Kong, China	12.45	11.46	9.96	8.95	6.98	6.00	6.53	6.57
72	South Korea	15.75	13.42	11.69	11.77	10.07	7.86	6.98	6.51
73	Germany	8.29	8.66	8.86	8.08	7.53	6.97	6.51	6.15
74	Japan	10.80	9.32	8.09	7.57	7.35	6.91	6.64	6.10

Marketing segments

Table 3.14 **Tweenagers (10-14)**

% of total

		1985	1990	1995	2000	2005	2010	2015	2020
1	Nigeria	12.01	12.59	12.74	12.50	12.27	12.16	12.20	12.20
2	Egypt	11.61	11.96	12.98	12.06	10.59	10.28	10.79	10.97
3	Pakistan	12.13	11.84	12.39	13.02	12.16	11.28	10.79	10.58
4	Bolivia	12.40	11.91	11.67	11.80	11.94	11.36	10.92	10.27
5	Jordan	13.92	13.53	12.65	12.22	11.88	10.90	10.24	10.14
6	Philippines	12.33	12.18	11.95	11.84	11.51	10.80	10.12	9.78
7	South Africa	12.19	11.95	11.60	11.16	10.36	9.89	9.86	9.60
8	Malaysia	11.50	10.95	11.17	10.74	10.11	9.94	9.78	9.17
9	Saudi Arabia	11.03	11.74	11.99	11.74	11.05	10.25	9.69	9.01
10	India	11.34	11.39	11.24	11.04	10.79	10.17	9.60	8.98
11	Peru	12.19	12.00	11.35	11.06	10.59	9.93	9.34	8.82
12	Ecuador	12.33	12.16	11.75	11.17	10.65	10.38	9.64	8.82
13	Venezuela	11.43	11.51	11.33	11.08	10.24	9.54	9.12	8.75
14	Turkmenistan	11.93	11.48	11.68	12.58	11.67	9.35	9.00	8.75
15	Kazakhstan	9.94	9.65	9.84	10.68	9.14	6.92	7.21	8.63
16	Colombia	11.72	11.49	11.06	10.59	10.19	9.50	8.93	8.53
17	Morocco	12.29	12.16	12.51	11.71	10.56	9.35	8.52	8.48
18	Israel	10.28	10.05	9.49	8.94	8.64	8.82	8.99	8.47
19	Algeria	12.66	12.92	13.26	12.43	10.83	8.50	8.18	8.40
20	Indonesia	12.05	11.65	11.12	10.19	9.37	8.82	8.56	8.03
21	Mexico	13.70	12.65	11.37	10.74	10.39	9.47	8.70	7.99
22	Azerbaijan	10.19	9.83	10.46	11.55	10.45	7.75	7.03	7.89
23	Vietnam	12.12	11.75	11.44	11.78	10.92	8.60	8.30	7.89
24	Iran	11.62	13.07	14.31	12.46	10.24	7.16	7.32	7.88
25	Argentina	9.28	10.17	9.48	9.16	8.95	8.41	7.83	7.71
26	Turkey	12.28	12.12	10.89	9.39	9.37	9.38	8.38	7.66
27	Brazil	11.04	10.99	11.33	10.18	8.98	8.78	8.50	7.39
28	Costa Rica	10.45	10.45	10.86	10.96	9.90	8.84	8.02	7.21
29	Kuwait	10.23	10.04	8.44	7.95	7.30	7.12	7.02	7.10
30	Tunisia	11.94	11.77	11.55	11.20	9.69	7.82	7.00	6.99
31	New Zealand	8.84	7.53	7.23	7.60	7.58	6.82	6.40	6.78
32	USA	7.16	6.90	7.21	7.31	7.05	6.44	6.61	6.76
33	Chile	10.19	8.90	9.14	9.51	9.11	7.77	6.91	6.70
34	Ireland	9.89	9.77	9.38	7.85	6.70	6.46	6.61	6.49
35	Thailand	11.47	10.23	8.90	7.75	7.90	7.29	6.36	6.22
36	Australia	8.56	7.23	7.17	6.98	6.87	6.34	5.97	6.19
37	France	7.75	6.59	6.76	6.54	6.11	5.93	6.09	6.13
38	Norway	7.66	6.33	6.00	6.33	6.80	6.50	6.05	6.04
39	Russia	7.02	7.24	7.98	8.29	5.90	4.65	4.98	5.86
40	United Kingdom	7.00	5.95	6.28	6.53	6.41	5.78	5.34	5.81
41	Denmark	7.11	6.30	5.25	5.61	6.39	6.24	5.90	5.77
42	Belgium	6.77	6.09	6.01	5.92	6.04	5.61	5.50	5.76
43	United Arab Emirates	7.50	7.49	8.02	7.95	5.96	5.88	6.21	5.76
44	Estonia	7.32	7.09	7.42	7.83	6.06	4.61	4.96	5.67
45	Sweden	6.69	5.85	5.66	6.35	6.86	5.34	5.40	5.60
46	Finland	6.16	6.55	6.48	6.11	6.33	5.65	5.33	5.49
47	Belarus	7.27	7.22	7.92	8.13	6.32	4.83	4.75	5.48
48	China	11.83	8.61	8.77	10.42	7.98	6.16	5.39	5.43
49	Netherlands	7.52	6.05	5.86	6.05	6.19	5.97	6.01	5.37
50	Canada	7.12	6.78	6.81	6.70	6.53	5.77	5.21	5.33
51	Spain	8.62	8.19	6.65	5.42	4.86	4.57	4.98	5.30
52	Romania	8.41	8.52	7.41	7.93	5.85	5.17	5.03	5.27
53	Latvia	6.96	6.54	7.26	7.84	6.29	4.23	4.54	5.18
54	Portugal	8.54	8.19	6.85	5.68	5.28	5.12	5.24	5.14
55	Czech Republic	7.96	8.63	6.76	6.31	5.94	4.47	4.62	5.11
56	Hungary	7.24	8.26	6.48	6.17	5.93	5.06	4.91	5.10
57	Ukraine	7.21	7.00	7.44	7.58	6.06	4.74	4.39	5.05
58	Croatia	6.92	7.02	6.83	6.16	5.75	5.68	4.80	5.03
59	Slovakia	8.27	9.06	8.36	7.62	6.83	5.39	4.81	4.98
60	Greece	7.38	7.40	6.94	5.55	5.06	4.71	4.72	4.95
61	Poland	7.56	8.44	8.77	7.74	6.65	5.37	4.74	4.84
62	Austria	6.75	5.69	6.04	5.86	5.95	5.34	4.96	4.84
63	Lithuania	7.77	7.13	7.34	7.87	7.14	5.54	4.73	4.79
64	Singapore	8.83	7.25	6.94	7.19	7.41	6.50	5.40	4.78
65	Switzerland	6.48	5.58	5.73	5.87	5.90	5.39	4.86	4.73
66	Slovenia	7.34	7.59	7.11	6.28	5.23	4.64	4.52	4.72
67	Italy	7.74	6.49	5.28	4.88	4.85	4.64	4.77	4.70
68	Bulgaria	7.25	7.47	6.71	6.43	5.39	4.24	4.54	4.66
69	Hong Kong, China	8.03	7.44	7.03	6.48	6.09	5.08	4.01	4.61
70	Bosnia-Herzegovina	8.46	8.13	8.09	7.76	6.10	5.76	4.90	4.59
71	Taiwan	9.61	9.83	9.22	7.25	7.15	6.58	5.36	4.36
72	South Korea	11.01	9.16	8.48	6.66	7.19	6.52	5.04	4.35
73	Japan	8.30	6.92	5.96	5.17	4.73	4.65	4.40	4.35
74	Germany	5.77	5.06	5.51	5.72	5.20	4.84	4.52	4.31

Marketing segments

Table 3.15 Teenagers (13-19)

% of total

		1985	1990	1995	2000	2005	2010	2015	2020
1	Nigeria	14.36	14.99	15.69	15.81	15.55	15.34	15.39	15.63
2	Egypt	14.89	14.60	16.16	16.43	15.20	13.55	13.47	14.26
3	Bolivia	15.27	15.38	14.79	14.75	15.08	15.18	14.59	14.09
4	Pakistan	14.86	14.82	14.90	15.88	16.32	15.23	14.29	13.87
5	Jordan	17.23	17.24	16.50	15.98	15.60	14.79	13.96	13.41
6	South Africa	15.36	15.48	15.19	15.09	14.62	13.82	13.44	13.37
7	Philippines	15.72	15.44	15.35	15.24	15.19	14.71	13.85	13.19
8	Malaysia	15.18	14.27	14.18	14.16	13.66	13.17	13.09	12.91
9	India	14.54	14.49	14.57	14.50	14.35	14.02	13.31	12.64
10	Ecuador	15.60	15.58	15.46	14.95	14.32	13.87	13.50	12.54
11	Peru	15.57	15.49	15.23	14.65	14.37	13.77	12.99	12.32
12	Saudi Arabia	13.68	13.71	14.14	14.11	14.03	13.80	12.97	12.31
13	Venezuela	15.25	14.46	14.67	14.58	14.19	13.19	12.45	12.00
14	Israel	12.83	13.53	12.79	12.24	11.64	11.46	11.82	11.96
15	Turkmenistan	15.29	14.64	14.58	15.57	16.38	14.68	12.24	11.94
16	Colombia	16.30	14.91	14.68	14.21	13.75	13.21	12.41	11.78
17	Indonesia	15.63	15.49	15.09	14.38	13.22	12.30	11.76	11.44
18	Mexico	16.60	17.04	15.68	14.39	13.68	13.19	12.23	11.34
19	Morocco	15.44	15.55	15.85	16.16	15.10	13.61	12.10	11.31
20	Brazil	14.98	14.19	14.55	14.60	13.05	11.95	11.88	11.30
21	Turkey	15.07	16.00	15.53	13.78	12.39	12.57	12.37	11.09
22	Vietnam	15.79	15.26	14.92	15.13	15.37	13.73	11.33	10.99
23	Algeria	15.81	15.85	16.62	17.16	15.92	13.47	10.99	10.88
24	Costa Rica	15.10	13.27	13.72	14.48	14.30	12.92	11.63	10.56
25	Argentina	11.64	12.61	13.32	12.49	12.25	11.90	11.16	10.55
26	Kazakhstan	12.96	12.49	12.75	13.77	14.25	11.57	9.28	10.27
27	Iran	14.61	15.32	17.60	18.74	17.45	12.64	9.43	10.01
28	Azerbaijan	15.01	13.50	12.86	14.45	15.39	13.13	10.01	9.71
29	Tunisia	15.65	15.03	15.11	15.36	14.68	12.45	10.23	9.43
30	Kuwait	12.39	12.30	10.39	10.07	9.92	9.49	9.34	9.37
31	Chile	14.52	12.85	11.67	12.28	12.69	11.89	10.22	9.31
32	USA	10.93	9.78	9.79	10.04	9.99	9.47	9.03	9.27
33	New Zealand	12.60	11.64	10.21	10.01	10.51	10.13	9.23	8.92
34	United Arab Emirates	8.30	9.91	9.92	10.37	8.55	7.38	8.66	8.82
35	Thailand	16.87	15.26	13.50	11.65	10.70	10.91	9.73	8.82
36	Ireland	13.39	13.23	13.26	12.07	10.03	8.69	8.53	8.81
37	France	10.97	10.27	9.29	9.33	8.99	8.38	8.30	8.44
38	Norway	11.23	10.17	8.66	8.33	9.03	9.28	8.84	8.34
39	Australia	11.90	11.15	9.87	9.72	9.63	9.29	8.65	8.32
40	Denmark	10.64	9.84	8.47	7.43	8.11	8.89	8.62	8.20
41	Netherlands	11.84	9.89	8.38	8.24	8.52	8.49	8.41	8.19
42	Belgium	10.26	9.14	8.52	8.33	8.41	8.28	7.80	7.76
43	Sweden	9.78	9.07	8.10	8.11	9.24	9.12	7.45	7.65
44	United Kingdom	11.13	9.31	8.40	8.75	9.22	8.70	7.79	7.49
45	Finland	9.82	8.70	8.97	8.86	8.62	8.60	7.72	7.48
46	Portugal	11.87	11.92	10.91	9.27	7.87	7.33	7.23	7.35
47	Canada	10.76	9.71	9.49	9.50	9.33	8.90	7.85	7.32
48	Romania	11.89	11.56	11.27	10.64	10.54	7.97	7.32	7.27
49	Russia	9.26	9.74	10.33	11.68	11.26	7.94	6.59	7.23
50	Estonia	9.78	9.81	9.78	10.60	10.73	8.04	6.58	7.23
51	China	16.84	14.16	10.98	12.06	11.95	9.47	7.73	7.18
52	Spain	11.99	11.94	10.99	8.93	7.40	6.64	6.51	7.08
53	Taiwan	14.05	12.89	13.13	11.68	9.90	9.80	8.88	7.07
54	Hungary	9.32	10.94	11.01	9.23	8.76	8.18	7.15	7.06
55	Austria	11.28	9.17	8.20	8.41	8.34	8.26	7.42	7.02
56	Singapore	12.79	11.10	9.42	8.98	9.71	9.76	8.48	7.02
57	Belarus	9.99	9.94	10.25	11.44	11.11	8.44	6.87	6.89
58	Croatia	9.76	9.62	9.72	9.37	8.68	8.14	7.76	6.89
59	Greece	10.85	10.48	10.50	9.36	7.59	7.04	6.64	6.80
60	Bosnia-Herzegovina	12.69	11.76	11.15	11.11	10.29	8.46	7.86	6.79
61	Slovakia	10.45	11.62	12.28	11.48	10.66	9.06	7.31	6.79
62	Italy	11.34	10.52	8.65	7.37	6.93	6.76	6.61	6.78
63	Switzerland	10.44	8.75	7.93	8.11	8.26	8.13	7.37	6.77
64	Czech Republic	9.48	11.51	11.42	9.38	8.96	7.80	6.30	6.72
65	Lithuania	10.76	10.38	9.79	10.66	11.08	9.58	7.61	6.71
66	South Korea	15.39	13.99	12.33	10.84	9.33	9.68	8.57	6.69
67	Poland	9.60	10.69	11.70	12.01	10.65	8.94	7.35	6.67
68	Latvia	9.42	9.56	9.28	10.66	10.88	8.17	6.08	6.63
69	Bulgaria	9.78	10.30	10.23	9.51	9.07	7.26	6.14	6.51
70	Ukraine	9.40	9.89	9.87	10.90	10.52	8.30	6.56	6.50
71	Slovenia	10.34	10.23	10.58	9.65	8.51	7.14	6.47	6.42
72	Germany	10.70	7.81	7.45	7.87	8.03	7.19	6.79	6.35
73	Japan	10.74	11.03	9.25	8.07	7.06	6.60	6.55	6.24
74	Hong Kong, China	11.85	10.58	9.74	9.44	8.85	8.38	6.72	5.93

Marketing segments

Table 3.16 Studying age (18-22)

% of total

		1985	1990	1995	2000	2005	2010	2015	2020
1	Nigeria	8.91	9.02	9.54	9.99	10.02	9.87	9.86	10.03
2	Bolivia	9.41	9.69	9.65	9.40	9.50	9.89	9.93	9.60
3	South Africa	9.71	10.01	10.14	10.12	10.28	10.03	9.45	9.31
4	Pakistan	9.15	9.36	9.27	9.62	10.37	10.50	9.75	9.30
5	Jordan	10.01	10.83	11.24	10.91	10.74	10.11	9.61	9.19
6	Philippines	10.13	9.95	9.87	9.92	9.95	9.95	9.64	9.11
7	Ecuador	9.92	10.07	10.10	9.87	9.55	9.26	9.21	8.97
8	India	9.53	9.41	9.47	9.61	9.60	9.60	9.39	8.96
9	Malaysia	10.35	9.44	9.47	9.30	9.34	9.04	8.82	8.90
10	Egypt	9.54	9.29	9.50	10.67	10.42	9.68	8.48	8.80
11	Peru	10.09	10.03	10.11	9.96	9.65	9.54	9.17	8.70
12	Saudi Arabia	9.63	8.94	8.27	9.29	8.97	9.37	9.13	8.62
13	Turkey	9.49	10.07	10.64	10.20	9.05	8.35	8.67	8.43
14	Venezuela	10.44	9.63	9.41	9.66	9.65	9.37	8.72	8.35
15	Colombia	11.09	10.35	9.61	9.65	9.35	9.13	8.80	8.29
16	Brazil	10.41	9.70	9.41	9.83	9.73	8.69	8.19	8.28
17	Israel	8.36	8.65	9.00	8.48	8.20	7.78	7.82	8.17
18	Turkmenistan	10.45	9.55	9.44	9.77	10.55	11.05	9.51	8.12
19	Mexico	9.89	10.71	10.91	10.02	9.13	8.90	8.73	8.11
20	Indonesia	10.08	10.30	10.23	10.04	9.52	8.80	8.29	8.06
21	Morocco	9.76	9.95	10.11	10.45	10.66	9.91	8.91	7.97
22	Costa Rica	11.06	9.45	8.77	9.46	9.92	9.64	8.62	7.88
23	Argentina	7.82	7.87	8.73	8.99	8.44	8.39	8.12	7.60
24	Vietnam	10.45	10.09	9.89	9.95	10.20	10.34	8.94	7.54
25	United Arab Emirates	7.02	7.28	7.94	8.23	8.07	5.74	6.57	7.25
26	Algeria	9.97	10.03	10.32	11.24	11.38	10.40	8.59	7.19
27	Chile	10.59	9.41	8.34	7.88	8.51	8.72	8.00	6.87
28	Tunisia	10.32	9.90	9.77	10.30	10.51	9.87	8.17	6.79
29	Kuwait	8.38	8.45	8.02	7.30	7.90	7.09	6.78	6.61
30	Azerbaijan	11.28	9.55	8.63	8.72	10.13	10.41	8.44	6.54
31	Thailand	11.85	11.40	9.98	8.99	7.78	7.53	7.67	6.53
32	USA	8.50	7.72	6.68	7.07	7.00	7.02	6.56	6.38
33	New Zealand	8.83	8.64	7.61	6.86	7.16	7.38	6.90	6.38
34	Kazakhstan	9.44	8.17	8.53	8.83	9.77	9.65	7.48	6.28
35	Iran	9.40	9.36	10.15	12.37	13.39	11.38	7.81	6.27
36	Australia	8.28	8.33	7.44	6.76	7.00	6.98	6.64	6.21
37	Norway	7.79	7.91	6.98	6.03	5.94	6.54	6.51	6.17
38	Denmark	8.08	7.31	6.97	5.83	5.32	6.00	6.48	6.13
39	Netherlands	8.74	8.35	6.59	5.98	5.89	6.12	6.02	6.09
40	Taiwan	10.49	9.34	8.66	9.02	7.76	6.95	6.87	6.07
41	France	7.89	7.63	6.94	6.59	6.43	6.30	5.83	5.93
42	Ireland	8.61	8.21	8.48	8.60	7.77	6.50	5.71	5.86
43	South Korea	10.42	10.55	9.12	8.55	7.05	6.51	6.82	5.85
44	Singapore	10.48	8.22	7.36	6.33	6.08	7.12	6.69	5.70
45	United Kingdom	8.41	7.70	6.26	6.00	6.49	6.81	6.26	5.63
46	Belgium	7.95	7.18	6.32	6.18	5.94	6.12	5.83	5.59
47	Canada	9.04	7.38	6.74	6.81	6.84	6.77	6.34	5.55
48	Bosnia-Herzegovina	9.72	8.71	7.96	7.56	7.92	7.08	5.90	5.55
49	Croatia	7.28	6.75	6.81	6.94	6.75	6.15	5.83	5.50
50	Finland	7.68	6.65	6.09	6.29	6.30	6.14	6.05	5.38
51	Lithuania	7.95	7.60	7.16	6.89	7.87	7.88	6.51	5.32
52	Romania	5.96	9.29	7.82	8.11	7.53	7.40	5.46	5.31
53	Austria	8.74	7.94	6.38	5.88	6.18	6.09	5.97	5.28
54	Portugal	8.53	8.00	8.32	7.44	6.38	5.52	5.16	5.24
55	Switzerland	8.05	7.24	6.02	5.74	5.85	6.05	5.80	5.23
56	Sweden	7.19	6.83	6.37	5.73	5.86	6.81	6.30	5.21
57	China	11.75	11.34	7.62	7.29	6.42	7.87	5.93	5.11
58	Hungary	6.00	6.88	8.08	7.63	6.50	6.28	5.80	5.08
59	Poland	7.10	6.66	7.74	8.35	8.65	7.32	6.10	5.07
60	Slovakia	7.77	7.14	8.47	8.67	8.22	7.39	6.15	5.06
61	Germany	8.65	7.44	5.42	5.62	5.78	5.93	5.13	5.05
62	Belarus	7.81	6.68	7.06	7.46	8.56	7.79	5.72	4.94
63	Italy	8.24	7.95	7.38	5.93	5.20	5.01	4.84	4.84
64	Japan	6.94	7.76	7.63	6.28	5.61	4.98	4.81	4.82
65	Greece	7.45	7.72	7.62	7.53	6.29	5.29	5.00	4.76
66	Spain	8.44	8.40	8.44	7.62	6.15	5.18	4.70	4.76
67	Hong Kong, China	9.93	7.58	7.05	6.96	6.61	6.66	6.08	4.75
68	Russia	7.46	6.49	7.07	7.63	8.85	7.85	5.26	4.73
69	Estonia	6.90	6.91	6.83	7.07	7.80	7.69	5.27	4.68
70	Slovenia	7.71	7.19	7.40	7.55	6.69	5.97	4.94	4.60
71	Ukraine	7.02	6.55	7.06	7.18	8.24	7.42	5.72	4.58
72	Czech Republic	6.78	6.77	8.65	7.89	6.67	6.37	5.29	4.51
73	Bulgaria	6.75	6.89	7.38	7.35	6.88	6.43	4.87	4.37
74	Latvia	7.12	6.92	6.68	6.88	7.96	7.76	5.33	4.35

Marketing segments

Table 3.17 Young adults (15-29)

% of total

		1985	1990	1995	2000	2005	2010	2015	2020
1	Nigeria	25.4	25.6	26.6	27.7	28.2	28.1	28.1	28.6
2	Bolivia	26.8	27.2	27.1	27.1	27.2	27.9	28.2	28.1
3	South Africa	27.9	28.3	28.9	29.2	29.4	29.3	28.4	27.6
4	Pakistan	25.9	26.3	26.3	27.4	28.8	29.3	28.6	27.4
5	Jordan	27.1	28.8	31.7	30.8	30.5	30.1	28.1	27.0
6	Philippines	28.6	28.4	28.1	28.2	28.4	28.4	27.9	26.9
7	India	27.5	27.2	27.2	27.5	27.7	27.8	27.4	26.6
8	Saudi Arabia	28.9	28.0	26.8	28.0	28.4	27.8	27.4	26.6
9	Turkmenistan	29.7	28.3	27.3	28.2	29.8	30.6	28.7	26.1
10	Ecuador	28.1	28.6	28.9	28.2	27.4	26.7	26.6	26.0
11	Malaysia	29.4	28.1	27.8	27.0	26.8	26.5	26.1	25.9
12	Peru	28.3	28.6	28.8	28.5	28.2	27.5	26.8	25.9
13	Egypt	27.1	26.6	27.2	29.1	29.2	27.7	25.8	24.9
14	Venezuela	29.1	28.2	27.6	27.5	27.8	27.1	26.1	24.9
15	Colombia	30.7	29.8	28.6	27.6	27.2	26.6	25.7	24.7
16	Turkey	27.4	28.7	29.7	29.4	27.5	25.8	25.1	24.5
17	Vietnam	29.1	29.1	28.6	28.8	29.4	29.3	27.0	24.4
18	Morocco	28.4	28.2	28.6	29.5	29.7	29.0	26.8	24.3
19	Brazil	29.3	28.6	27.9	28.1	27.7	26.5	25.1	24.2
20	Mexico	27.9	29.4	30.0	29.4	27.3	25.8	25.0	24.1
21	Costa Rica	31.0	28.5	26.8	26.9	28.1	27.9	26.3	24.0
22	Indonesia	28.6	29.3	29.5	29.1	27.9	26.4	24.9	24.0
23	United Arab Emirates	29.3	26.2	28.7	30.4	31.8	25.2	22.8	23.6
24	Israel	24.6	24.8	25.1	25.1	24.2	23.2	23.1	23.5
25	Algeria	27.4	28.4	29.5	31.5	32.1	30.7	26.6	23.3
26	Argentina	23.1	23.4	24.6	25.3	25.5	24.7	24.0	22.9
27	Azerbaijan	31.6	28.8	26.1	25.7	27.8	28.8	26.1	22.3
28	Tunisia	29.0	28.4	28.0	29.2	30.1	28.9	25.7	22.0
29	Chile	30.2	28.3	25.4	24.2	24.3	24.9	23.9	21.8
30	Iran	26.6	26.5	28.7	32.9	35.5	33.8	27.1	21.7
31	Kuwait	28.2	28.5	29.7	26.9	28.1	25.2	22.6	21.4
32	Kazakhstan	28.0	25.6	24.7	26.0	27.7	27.1	24.2	21.2
33	Thailand	33.4	32.8	30.3	27.3	24.5	22.9	21.8	20.8
34	USA	25.9	23.3	21.2	20.8	20.9	20.8	20.0	19.5
35	Australia	25.2	24.5	22.6	21.2	20.6	21.1	20.3	19.3
36	New Zealand	26.1	25.1	22.7	20.7	20.6	20.9	20.2	19.2
37	Norway	23.2	23.1	21.6	19.6	18.5	19.2	19.5	19.0
38	Denmark	22.7	22.7	21.3	18.8	17.4	17.8	18.5	18.7
39	Taiwan	30.5	28.3	26.7	25.8	24.1	22.3	20.2	18.7
40	Singapore	31.6	27.5	23.4	21.1	20.1	20.5	20.3	18.6
41	United Kingdom	23.5	23.0	20.7	19.1	19.2	20.2	19.9	18.5
42	Ireland	24.7	24.0	24.3	24.6	23.9	21.8	19.1	18.4
43	Netherlands	25.6	24.6	21.8	19.3	18.0	18.1	18.2	18.3
44	South Korea	31.3	30.6	27.9	25.6	22.3	20.9	19.5	18.1
45	Canada	26.9	24.0	21.1	20.3	20.4	20.3	19.3	17.9
46	Sweden	20.7	20.8	19.7	18.3	18.2	19.2	18.8	17.9
47	France	23.3	22.8	21.2	20.1	19.2	18.7	18.1	17.8
48	China	29.7	31.0	26.3	23.9	21.1	21.4	20.8	17.8
49	Lithuania	24.1	23.4	21.9	21.3	22.0	22.6	20.9	17.8
50	Hong Kong, China	30.3	26.4	22.9	21.9	20.4	21.1	19.8	17.4
51	Belgium	23.4	22.3	20.3	19.0	18.3	18.3	17.8	17.4
52	Finland	22.9	20.8	19.4	18.7	18.8	18.7	17.9	17.2
53	Austria	24.8	24.0	21.5	19.0	18.5	18.8	18.0	17.1
54	Bosnia-Herzegovina	28.9	26.3	24.1	22.6	22.7	21.5	19.6	17.0
55	Switzerland	23.2	22.4	20.2	18.3	18.1	18.3	17.9	16.9
56	Slovakia	23.7	22.7	23.6	24.9	24.9	22.9	19.9	16.9
57	Croatia	22.4	21.1	20.6	20.3	20.2	19.3	18.2	16.9
58	Hungary	20.2	19.9	22.1	22.3	21.5	19.5	18.0	16.8
59	Poland	23.3	21.0	21.8	24.0	24.5	23.1	19.7	16.7
60	Belarus	24.1	22.0	20.8	22.2	23.9	23.2	20.0	16.6
61	Romania	22.7	22.5	23.7	23.4	23.8	21.5	19.2	16.3
62	Russia	24.0	21.5	20.6	22.7	24.7	23.3	19.6	16.1
63	Ukraine	21.9	20.9	20.4	21.8	23.1	22.5	19.5	16.1
64	Portugal	24.2	23.7	23.5	22.5	20.4	17.9	16.2	15.9
65	Estonia	22.2	21.2	20.2	21.3	22.5	21.8	18.8	15.8
66	Germany	24.3	22.8	19.9	17.5	17.5	17.5	16.9	15.8
67	Latvia	22.1	21.7	20.3	21.2	22.5	22.2	19.0	15.6
68	Czech Republic	20.2	21.1	23.1	23.5	22.1	19.4	17.0	15.3
69	Greece	22.1	22.2	22.9	22.4	20.0	17.6	15.5	15.0
70	Italy	23.1	23.7	22.4	19.6	17.2	15.6	14.9	14.9
71	Spain	24.1	24.8	24.7	23.1	20.8	17.6	15.3	14.9
72	Slovenia	23.4	22.6	22.2	21.9	21.0	18.8	16.3	14.6
73	Japan	20.7	21.8	21.7	20.3	17.4	15.9	15.0	14.5
74	Bulgaria	20.9	20.4	21.2	21.9	21.2	19.3	16.5	14.3

Marketing segments

Table 3.18 Middle-aged adults (30-59)

% of total

		1985	1990	1995	2000	2005	2010	2015	2020
1	United Arab Emirates	38.8	41.8	41.6	44.0	46.7	53.7	55.6	55.2
2	Kuwait	32.4	33.0	39.0	44.5	45.0	47.4	49.5	49.7
3	China	31.6	32.7	36.8	41.7	46.3	47.4	46.1	47.6
4	Taiwan	31.5	34.7	38.1	41.0	43.5	46.8	47.8	46.7
5	South Korea	31.8	36.0	39.5	42.2	45.5	47.4	48.4	46.4
6	Belarus	38.4	38.6	39.6	39.9	42.1	43.6	45.0	45.7
7	Iran	23.1	23.1	24.9	28.3	31.1	35.2	40.8	45.2
8	Romania	38.2	38.3	37.6	38.8	41.1	43.4	44.0	45.1
9	Bosnia-Herzegovina	37.3	39.0	40.6	41.1	43.0	44.2	44.8	45.1
10	Ukraine	40.0	39.2	40.7	39.6	41.3	42.8	44.0	45.0
11	Slovakia	35.7	37.1	38.4	39.9	42.0	44.4	45.0	44.9
12	Hong Kong, China	35.0	39.5	43.8	46.4	49.6	48.6	47.3	44.9
13	Russia	39.6	39.7	41.3	40.6	42.8	43.9	44.5	44.8
14	Spain	35.6	36.2	37.7	40.4	43.1	45.1	45.8	44.7
15	Singapore	35.5	40.5	44.1	46.4	48.4	48.0	46.5	44.5
16	Bulgaria	40.2	39.9	39.6	40.6	42.2	43.1	43.7	44.2
17	Latvia	40.2	39.5	39.8	39.9	40.5	41.6	42.8	44.0
18	Thailand	29.9	33.2	36.6	40.2	43.4	45.1	45.3	44.0
19	Ireland	31.2	33.4	35.9	38.3	40.0	41.5	43.4	43.9
20	Slovenia	39.6	40.9	41.7	42.9	44.0	45.3	44.8	43.7
21	Lithuania	38.0	38.1	38.8	39.5	40.8	41.7	42.8	43.6
22	Tunisia	24.6	26.4	29.1	31.7	35.0	38.5	41.3	43.5
23	Czech Republic	39.0	39.5	40.0	41.7	43.2	44.1	43.5	43.2
24	Greece	39.0	38.7	38.7	39.9	42.4	43.5	44.1	43.2
25	Poland	37.5	39.0	39.4	39.9	41.7	43.0	43.4	42.9
26	Portugal	35.2	36.9	38.3	39.8	41.7	43.2	43.6	42.7
27	Austria	37.0	38.3	40.9	43.5	43.4	43.2	43.3	42.3
28	Italy	38.6	39.0	40.5	42.0	43.6	43.8	43.4	42.3
29	Hungary	40.2	40.7	40.0	40.7	41.6	43.3	42.6	42.2
30	Switzerland	40.0	41.1	42.6	44.2	44.4	43.6	43.1	42.2
31	Germany	39.7	40.9	43.1	43.8	43.1	43.2	42.8	42.1
32	Brazil	27.6	29.3	32.0	34.0	35.8	37.9	40.5	42.1
33	Estonia	39.6	39.5	40.0	39.4	40.3	40.7	41.2	41.9
34	Croatia	41.2	41.7	41.2	40.9	41.7	42.5	42.5	41.7
35	Canada	37.2	39.8	42.4	43.9	44.2	43.5	42.8	41.5
36	Indonesia	27.3	28.7	30.6	32.9	35.3	38.0	40.2	41.5
37	Algeria	22.2	23.2	25.1	28.2	31.8	35.4	38.8	41.4
38	Vietnam	23.4	24.8	26.9	30.1	33.3	36.6	38.9	41.2
39	Turkey	27.7	29.2	30.6	32.4	35.3	38.5	40.5	41.2
40	Azerbaijan	28.3	29.6	31.8	34.3	36.7	38.5	39.8	41.0
41	Costa Rica	26.0	28.5	31.5	33.7	35.2	37.3	39.1	40.6
42	Chile	30.4	32.7	35.4	37.7	39.2	39.7	40.2	40.6
43	Kazakhstan	31.6	33.4	35.4	35.4	37.7	38.6	39.1	40.4
44	Mexico	24.0	25.6	27.3	30.0	33.8	36.7	38.4	39.8
45	Norway	35.4	36.9	38.8	41.1	42.2	41.0	40.3	39.6
46	United Kingdom	36.4	37.2	39.2	41.1	41.6	39.9	39.6	39.6
47	Australia	36.5	38.1	40.1	41.5	42.1	40.8	40.1	39.5
48	Netherlands	38.0	39.9	42.1	44.0	44.4	42.5	40.9	39.2
49	Japan	43.1	42.4	41.8	41.7	41.9	40.0	39.1	38.9
50	Turkmenistan	23.9	25.0	27.0	29.0	31.7	34.2	36.4	38.9
51	Belgium	38.2	39.2	40.4	41.5	42.5	41.5	40.4	38.9
52	Morocco	24.1	25.8	27.5	29.7	32.6	34.9	37.2	38.7
53	Saudi Arabia	24.8	26.5	28.2	30.0	32.9	35.7	37.2	38.7
54	New Zealand	34.7	36.5	38.9	40.9	41.5	40.2	39.4	38.4
55	USA	35.9	38.2	40.5	41.6	41.8	40.8	39.7	38.4
56	Sweden	38.1	38.5	39.4	41.0	41.0	39.3	38.4	38.1
57	Denmark	38.4	39.8	41.5	43.0	42.8	41.0	39.4	38.0
58	Colombia	25.1	27.4	30.1	32.7	34.6	36.0	37.1	37.9
59	France	37.3	38.0	39.1	40.4	41.6	40.1	38.8	37.8
60	Argentina	33.5	33.0	32.9	33.2	34.2	35.7	36.7	37.8
61	Venezuela	26.5	27.9	30.1	32.1	33.4	34.8	36.0	37.3
62	Finland	40.3	41.5	42.7	43.3	42.7	40.2	38.6	37.3
63	Peru	25.8	26.9	28.4	30.2	32.0	33.9	35.5	37.1
64	India	27.9	28.8	29.7	30.8	32.2	33.9	35.3	36.9
65	Jordan	20.6	19.9	22.7	25.0	27.0	30.3	33.7	36.2
66	Malaysia	26.8	28.9	31.0	32.8	34.0	34.8	35.4	35.7
67	Ecuador	24.8	26.3	28.1	29.9	31.6	33.2	34.3	35.5
68	Israel	30.5	31.5	32.7	33.1	34.6	34.8	34.8	35.2
69	Philippines	24.6	26.0	27.3	28.6	30.0	31.5	32.8	34.3
70	South Africa	26.6	27.7	29.6	31.2	32.3	33.0	33.6	34.2
71	Egypt	27.2	27.7	28.9	29.9	30.6	31.2	31.9	32.2
72	Bolivia	25.6	25.9	26.1	26.9	28.0	29.1	30.5	32.2
73	Pakistan	24.7	24.5	24.9	25.7	26.7	27.9	29.6	31.9
74	Nigeria	24.1	23.8	23.7	23.7	23.9	24.6	25.6	27.0

Marketing segments

Table 3.19 Baby boomers (40-59)

% of total

		1985	1990	1995	2000	2005	2010	2015	2020
1	China	17.2	17.7	21.0	22.9	28.1	32.9	33.9	33.2
2	South Korea	18.0	19.3	20.9	24.1	27.7	30.9	33.1	32.7
3	United Arab Emirates	15.2	17.1	17.7	19.1	19.3	20.8	26.1	31.8
4	Taiwan	17.4	17.5	20.2	23.6	27.3	30.4	30.9	31.4
5	Spain	22.7	22.7	22.8	24.4	26.2	27.8	29.8	31.3
6	Italy	25.0	25.4	25.7	26.0	27.5	29.0	30.6	31.0
7	Kuwait	14.3	14.4	16.1	19.6	20.1	23.1	27.5	30.6
8	Greece	25.6	25.1	24.6	24.9	26.7	28.1	29.4	30.3
9	Singapore	17.6	20.2	23.6	27.7	31.2	32.0	32.0	30.0
10	Bulgaria	25.6	25.7	26.1	27.1	28.2	28.0	28.6	29.9
11	Thailand	15.9	17.1	18.8	21.8	25.5	28.2	29.7	29.9
12	Portugal	22.4	23.3	24.1	25.0	26.6	27.6	28.8	29.9
13	Slovenia	24.4	24.4	26.1	27.5	29.1	30.4	29.8	29.8
14	Czech Republic	22.8	24.5	26.6	28.5	28.5	27.3	27.6	29.6
15	Romania	24.4	23.4	24.4	25.1	25.4	27.3	28.2	29.5
16	Bosnia-Herzegovina	22.0	22.6	23.8	25.5	28.3	29.9	29.8	29.5
17	Austria	23.9	24.1	24.5	26.2	27.6	29.7	30.3	29.2
18	Germany	26.7	26.3	26.7	26.7	28.3	31.0	30.6	29.2
19	Slovakia	20.7	21.0	23.2	25.8	27.6	28.1	28.0	29.0
20	Switzerland	24.7	25.9	26.1	27.4	28.9	29.8	29.8	28.7
21	Belarus	25.0	23.0	23.1	24.8	28.1	29.3	29.3	28.6
22	Ukraine	26.5	24.4	25.5	25.5	27.7	28.4	28.4	28.4
23	Hong Kong, China	18.9	20.2	22.8	27.3	32.8	33.0	31.4	28.3
24	Lithuania	24.6	23.6	23.3	24.2	26.4	28.0	28.8	28.2
25	Hungary	24.8	25.0	26.6	28.0	27.4	27.2	26.8	28.1
26	Croatia	26.2	25.9	26.2	26.8	28.1	28.8	28.2	27.8
27	Latvia	26.6	25.1	25.2	25.7	26.7	27.5	27.9	27.7
28	Ireland	18.1	19.7	21.8	23.6	24.6	24.9	25.8	27.5
29	Japan	26.7	28.8	29.1	28.3	27.4	25.9	26.7	27.5
30	Netherlands	21.9	24.1	25.6	27.4	29.1	29.4	29.2	27.4
31	Russia	24.8	22.9	24.5	25.9	29.1	29.2	28.2	27.4
32	Canada	20.8	22.4	24.7	27.7	30.0	29.7	28.8	27.3
33	Denmark	23.0	25.3	26.8	27.7	28.1	27.7	27.6	26.8
34	Poland	21.6	21.8	23.9	26.7	28.5	28.1	27.0	26.8
35	Belgium	23.6	24.0	24.6	26.2	28.2	28.4	27.9	26.6
36	Norway	20.4	22.2	24.0	26.0	27.0	27.1	27.2	26.5
37	Estonia	25.3	24.5	25.5	25.8	26.9	26.8	26.7	26.3
38	Turkey	15.6	15.8	16.6	17.8	19.6	21.6	23.8	25.9
39	Indonesia	15.7	15.7	16.3	17.7	19.5	21.8	24.0	25.7
40	Tunisia	14.0	13.8	15.4	17.5	20.0	22.2	23.8	25.7
41	Chile	16.8	17.6	18.9	21.4	24.0	25.6	26.3	25.7
42	Sweden	23.0	24.8	25.8	26.9	26.9	26.4	26.3	25.6
43	Brazil	15.0	15.5	16.8	18.5	20.7	22.6	24.1	25.5
44	United Kingdom	22.5	23.6	24.4	25.5	26.8	26.9	26.6	25.5
45	New Zealand	20.0	21.2	22.9	25.2	26.9	27.1	26.8	25.4
46	Mexico	12.9	13.4	14.6	16.2	18.1	20.5	23.3	25.4
47	France	22.0	22.9	24.2	25.8	27.4	27.0	26.5	25.3
48	Australia	20.8	22.2	24.1	26.2	27.4	26.7	26.3	25.3
49	USA	20.1	21.4	23.6	26.3	27.9	27.6	26.4	24.9
50	Finland	22.9	25.5	27.5	29.0	30.0	28.1	25.9	24.8
51	Vietnam	13.0	12.2	13.0	15.2	18.1	21.0	22.9	24.4
52	Azerbaijan	17.3	15.7	15.4	17.5	22.1	25.0	25.3	24.3
53	Costa Rica	13.3	14.0	15.7	18.0	20.7	22.8	23.5	24.1
54	Iran	12.4	11.8	12.7	15.0	17.0	19.3	21.1	23.8
55	Kazakhstan	18.3	17.7	19.5	20.5	23.2	23.9	23.8	23.7
56	Algeria	11.9	11.8	12.6	14.2	16.7	19.2	21.3	23.7
57	Colombia	12.5	13.6	15.4	17.5	19.8	21.5	22.4	23.1
58	Argentina	20.2	19.8	20.0	20.4	20.9	21.1	21.7	23.1
59	Saudi Arabia	10.6	10.9	11.9	13.1	15.5	18.3	20.5	22.4
60	Morocco	13.1	13.0	14.1	16.2	18.6	20.2	21.5	22.4
61	Venezuela	13.5	14.4	15.9	17.5	19.3	20.4	21.2	22.1
62	Peru	14.0	14.4	15.1	16.2	17.6	19.1	20.5	22.0
63	Turkmenistan	13.2	12.0	12.7	14.7	17.6	19.6	20.9	21.9
64	Israel	16.2	17.4	19.4	20.4	21.2	20.6	20.9	21.7
65	India	15.3	15.3	16.2	17.2	18.4	19.5	20.3	21.5
66	Ecuador	13.1	13.5	14.8	16.2	17.8	19.4	20.3	21.2
67	Malaysia	13.9	14.7	16.1	17.8	19.6	20.8	21.2	21.1
68	Jordan	11.5	10.9	11.4	12.1	12.9	15.0	17.7	20.4
69	Philippines	12.7	13.3	14.3	15.4	16.6	17.7	18.6	19.7
70	South Africa	14.2	14.6	15.9	17.1	18.0	18.4	18.4	18.4
71	Bolivia	14.0	14.1	14.2	14.7	15.3	16.0	17.1	18.2
72	Egypt	14.8	15.0	15.7	17.3	18.1	18.0	17.8	18.2
73	Pakistan	13.7	13.4	13.5	13.9	14.4	15.2	16.1	17.2
74	Nigeria	13.1	12.8	12.8	12.8	12.7	12.7	13.0	13.9

Marketing segments

Table 3.20 Pensioners

% of total

		1985	1990	1995	2000	2005	2010	2015	2020
1	Ukraine	21.11	21.31	22.46	23.56	24.03	24.29	25.98	27.24
2	Taiwan	9.96	11.71	13.01	14.04	15.29	17.72	21.69	26.27
3	Belarus	18.46	19.63	20.99	21.41	21.34	21.94	23.70	26.09
4	Bosnia-Herzegovina	8.41	9.67	11.90	14.91	16.96	18.85	21.95	25.78
5	Thailand	9.10	10.04	11.13	12.27	14.29	17.05	20.76	25.42
6	Hungary	21.31	22.05	22.19	19.68	19.83	20.78	22.82	25.37
7	Sweden	21.88	21.86	21.15	21.10	21.82	23.62	24.64	25.36
8	Japan	10.30	12.08	14.56	17.37	19.38	21.02	23.82	25.20
9	Czech Republic	19.19	19.32	19.44	20.19	20.43	20.85	23.07	24.74
10	Russia	17.57	18.71	20.16	20.54	20.33	21.34	23.08	24.62
11	Greece	18.82	20.45	21.89	22.95	23.65	23.73	23.90	24.62
12	Lithuania	15.29	16.31	17.77	19.36	20.55	21.44	22.64	24.59
13	France	18.07	19.02	20.08	20.60	20.22	21.30	22.68	24.23
14	Italy	15.97	17.75	19.65	21.35	21.67	22.02	22.62	23.44
15	Singapore	10.53	11.41	11.61	11.77	14.24	16.62	19.88	23.00
16	Croatia	16.97	18.32	19.42	22.74	21.49	20.54	21.24	22.52
17	Bulgaria	18.74	20.60	22.73	23.29	22.97	20.92	21.56	22.38
18	Finland	12.62	13.53	14.36	15.03	15.88	17.16	20.06	22.13
19	Austria	17.60	17.84	17.56	18.14	18.85	19.57	20.54	21.93
20	Poland	11.95	12.63	13.65	14.68	15.16	15.95	18.25	21.60
21	Latvia	16.78	17.62	19.38	21.25	21.26	19.75	20.24	20.86
22	Romania	12.04	13.03	15.05	16.56	17.44	17.69	18.76	20.60
23	Kuwait	10.43	11.05	11.88	14.80	16.78	16.84	16.63	19.97
24	Turkey	11.97	12.37	12.93	13.33	14.34	15.84	17.59	19.57
25	Slovakia	12.05	12.79	13.21	13.69	13.79	14.56	16.46	19.46
26	Germany	14.47	14.91	15.38	16.25	18.17	19.32	19.30	19.42
27	Slovenia	13.90	14.84	16.57	18.11	18.16	16.40	17.14	19.26
28	United Kingdom	18.12	18.39	18.33	18.33	18.73	19.75	19.63	19.09
29	Netherlands	11.97	12.80	13.18	13.57	13.77	14.63	16.93	18.88
30	Estonia	16.22	16.92	18.49	20.81	20.51	18.47	18.24	18.86
31	Switzerland	15.05	15.61	15.69	16.26	15.87	16.52	17.49	18.14
32	Portugal	11.73	13.12	14.54	16.14	16.65	16.44	16.82	17.62
33	Belgium	15.53	16.58	17.53	18.31	17.48	15.98	16.51	17.58
34	Canada	10.25	11.27	11.98	12.55	12.82	13.35	15.15	17.54
35	Hong Kong, China	7.45	8.46	9.78	10.94	12.23	12.62	14.59	17.47
36	Denmark	13.11	13.66	13.56	13.13	13.01	13.52	15.84	16.98
37	South Korea	6.76	7.74	9.17	10.98	12.23	13.40	14.48	16.51
38	Indonesia	8.66	9.41	10.30	11.10	11.70	12.72	14.39	16.23
39	Australia	11.42	12.19	12.90	13.42	13.40	13.62	14.84	16.23
40	Israel	10.74	10.89	11.25	11.59	11.59	12.40	14.27	15.99
41	Malaysia	8.02	8.20	8.47	8.98	9.79	11.31	13.22	15.21
42	Colombia	7.60	7.87	8.19	8.72	9.66	11.09	12.90	15.01
43	Norway	13.57	14.31	14.30	13.79	13.07	12.67	13.80	14.92
44	Spain	11.92	13.43	15.08	16.65	16.03	14.89	14.51	14.67
45	China	8.10	8.67	10.27	10.93	11.54	11.87	13.47	14.60
46	USA	11.84	12.41	12.63	12.29	11.68	11.59	12.70	14.33
47	New Zealand	10.39	11.07	11.53	11.75	11.59	11.70	12.83	14.03
48	Venezuela	6.36	6.76	7.21	7.88	8.89	10.24	11.77	13.53
49	Chile	7.24	7.63	8.10	8.66	9.49	10.58	11.68	13.41
50	Costa Rica	9.43	9.47	9.72	10.25	8.87	9.27	10.95	13.22
51	Kazakhstan	8.29	8.96	10.15	11.45	11.54	10.96	11.70	13.06
52	Argentina	10.59	11.04	11.00	11.34	11.61	11.77	12.33	13.02
53	Vietnam	8.76	8.72	8.65	8.62	8.64	9.27	10.72	12.76
54	Tunisia	6.17	6.86	7.69	8.33	8.60	9.09	10.40	12.30
55	India	7.77	7.97	8.25	8.63	9.08	9.78	10.81	12.11
56	Ecuador	8.21	8.49	8.97	9.75	8.49	8.70	10.06	11.57
57	Iran	6.64	6.77	7.22	7.39	7.82	8.58	9.79	11.36
58	Algeria	6.74	6.73	6.83	7.00	7.34	8.16	9.37	11.05
59	Ireland	9.84	10.62	10.69	10.50	9.91	9.36	10.01	10.85
60	Brazil	5.14	5.38	5.77	6.26	6.90	7.82	9.08	10.62
61	Turkmenistan	6.36	6.39	6.60	6.90	6.81	7.18	8.36	10.30
62	Morocco	5.54	5.83	6.03	6.52	6.74	7.34	8.53	10.30
63	Egypt	6.25	6.46	6.78	7.09	7.28	7.84	8.81	9.96
64	Azerbaijan	7.88	7.85	8.85	9.51	8.90	7.69	7.67	9.38
65	Philippines	4.84	5.10	5.48	5.96	6.38	6.97	7.87	9.08
66	South Africa	5.18	5.27	5.62	6.06	6.61	6.99	7.49	8.50
67	Jordan	5.99	5.66	5.03	5.75	6.33	6.43	7.09	8.15
68	Pakistan	6.46	6.41	6.53	6.62	6.75	7.05	7.55	8.14
69	Mexico	3.67	3.86	4.19	4.72	5.32	6.03	6.82	7.90
70	Peru	3.69	3.92	4.26	4.76	5.28	5.82	6.52	7.46
71	Saudi Arabia	4.69	4.82	5.28	5.32	5.49	5.71	6.01	6.38
72	Bolivia	3.56	3.68	3.97	4.23	4.47	4.71	5.15	5.71
73	Nigeria	4.06	4.10	4.18	4.32	4.46	4.55	4.81	5.12
74	United Arab Emirates	2.13	2.03	1.79	1.59	1.72	1.93	2.43	3.40

Marketing segments

Table 3.21 Elderly population (60+)

% of total

		1985	1990	1995	2000	2005	2010	2015	2020
1	Japan	14.77	17.55	20.51	23.47	26.88	30.88	33.36	34.76
2	Germany	19.88	20.33	20.69	22.98	24.93	25.87	27.79	30.10
3	Italy	18.59	20.45	22.32	24.07	25.08	26.65	28.07	29.89
4	Finland	17.33	18.39	18.89	19.85	21.08	24.49	27.02	28.90
5	Bulgaria	17.26	19.15	21.12	21.70	22.79	24.51	26.43	28.50
6	Greece	17.43	19.43	20.88	22.28	23.17	24.65	26.05	27.73
7	Slovenia	14.57	15.58	17.50	19.03	20.63	22.06	24.82	27.38
8	Sweden	23.01	22.84	22.06	22.16	23.22	25.08	26.11	27.05
9	Portugal	16.71	18.54	20.20	21.47	22.17	23.45	25.04	26.94
10	Netherlands	16.69	17.29	17.69	18.13	19.09	21.83	24.18	26.73
11	Belgium	19.51	20.43	21.30	21.89	21.96	23.27	24.78	26.68
12	Czech Republic	17.38	17.65	17.99	18.22	19.73	22.35	24.86	26.46
13	Denmark	20.29	20.39	19.90	19.71	20.92	23.09	24.78	26.45
14	Switzerland	19.02	19.46	19.52	20.14	21.32	23.02	24.52	26.41
15	Austria	19.77	20.15	19.74	20.32	21.96	23.02	24.29	26.40
16	Croatia	15.44	17.20	19.86	21.68	22.08	22.98	24.61	26.30
17	France	18.07	19.02	20.08	20.62	20.82	22.75	24.65	26.26
18	Hungary	18.04	18.89	19.52	20.12	21.31	22.40	24.54	26.11
19	Poland	13.77	14.73	15.69	16.55	17.11	19.05	22.25	25.38
20	Hong Kong, China	11.26	12.61	13.91	14.80	15.70	17.95	21.15	25.25
21	Spain	16.83	18.75	20.64	21.62	21.58	22.34	23.39	25.07
22	Estonia	15.92	17.06	18.90	20.96	21.66	22.44	23.58	24.88
23	Ukraine	16.56	18.33	18.43	20.75	20.76	20.81	22.60	24.81
24	Canada	14.61	15.53	16.10	16.64	17.77	19.83	22.11	24.67
25	Bosnia-Herzegovina	8.71	10.43	13.30	16.50	17.71	19.11	21.64	24.56
26	Latvia	16.55	17.40	19.05	20.99	22.18	22.54	23.17	24.38
27	Lithuania	14.80	15.97	17.39	19.03	20.19	20.96	22.02	23.88
28	United Kingdom	20.72	20.82	20.67	20.72	21.11	22.35	22.94	23.75
29	Romania	14.25	15.49	17.57	18.95	19.30	19.94	21.60	23.54
30	Slovakia	14.21	14.75	15.11	15.39	16.02	17.49	20.31	23.22
31	South Korea	6.74	7.82	9.19	11.09	13.07	15.43	18.45	23.14
32	Norway	21.23	21.02	20.13	19.32	19.57	20.85	21.82	23.05
33	New Zealand	14.71	15.31	15.32	15.71	16.42	18.31	20.19	22.45
34	USA	16.53	16.77	16.49	16.28	16.83	18.40	20.28	22.40
35	Australia	14.76	15.42	15.84	16.59	17.56	19.11	20.67	22.26
36	Singapore	8.10	9.05	9.69	10.56	11.59	14.25	17.79	22.10
37	Taiwan	7.85	9.48	10.79	11.83	13.05	14.51	17.97	22.00
38	Belarus	14.86	16.32	17.59	19.01	18.43	18.42	19.41	21.49
39	Russia	13.75	15.75	16.51	18.27	17.33	17.67	19.19	21.06
40	China	8.31	8.59	10.16	10.84	13.00	14.82	17.71	19.25
41	Ireland	14.76	15.23	15.21	15.16	15.31	16.29	17.62	19.23
42	Thailand	6.30	7.08	8.01	9.22	10.40	12.05	14.53	17.87
43	Chile	8.51	9.03	9.56	10.32	11.63	13.14	15.00	17.53
44	Israel	12.42	12.37	12.73	13.14	12.87	14.10	15.51	16.55
45	Argentina	12.45	12.91	13.18	13.51	13.93	14.53	15.34	16.17
46	Brazil	6.21	6.75	7.33	8.12	8.88	9.97	11.56	13.67
47	Costa Rica	7.04	7.15	7.35	7.70	8.30	9.46	11.18	13.51
48	Tunisia	6.27	7.16	8.58	9.04	9.19	9.72	11.09	12.89
49	Mexico	5.97	6.47	6.95	7.46	8.31	9.35	10.98	12.85
50	Kazakhstan	8.37	9.49	10.12	11.08	10.31	10.21	11.24	12.85
51	Azerbaijan	7.18	7.31	8.12	8.94	8.89	8.69	9.97	12.65
52	Ecuador	5.96	6.22	6.70	7.44	8.36	9.46	10.92	12.44
53	Colombia	6.06	6.28	6.52	6.85	7.45	8.58	10.18	12.01
54	Indonesia	5.66	6.19	6.89	7.68	8.34	8.94	10.00	11.65
55	Venezuela	5.33	5.80	6.25	6.73	7.49	8.63	10.01	11.51
56	Turkey	6.76	7.11	7.64	8.17	8.56	9.05	10.10	11.51
57	Peru	5.76	6.11	6.62	7.21	7.86	8.70	9.79	11.10
58	Morocco	5.84	6.23	6.59	7.17	7.48	8.05	9.19	11.00
59	Vietnam	7.33	7.26	7.47	7.57	7.59	7.82	9.10	10.99
60	Malaysia	5.53	5.61	5.75	6.18	6.63	7.36	8.85	10.75
61	Egypt	5.77	5.65	5.78	6.45	7.21	7.97	9.16	10.65
62	India	5.96	6.14	6.36	6.70	7.02	7.56	8.64	9.84
63	South Africa	4.99	5.13	5.48	5.92	6.53	7.33	8.46	9.61
64	Iran	5.50	5.50	6.27	6.69	6.93	7.13	8.04	9.54
65	Algeria	5.48	5.47	5.82	6.26	6.45	6.90	7.94	9.21
66	Philippines	4.93	4.90	5.14	5.52	6.04	6.67	7.64	8.76
67	Turkmenistan	5.88	6.17	6.24	6.55	6.07	6.13	6.99	8.63
68	Bolivia	5.65	6.00	6.24	6.48	6.71	7.18	7.79	8.58
69	Kuwait	2.10	2.11	2.18	2.65	3.14	4.05	5.44	7.68
70	Pakistan	6.04	5.65	5.57	5.66	5.94	6.20	6.56	7.11
71	Saudi Arabia	3.88	3.55	3.65	4.03	4.17	4.61	5.50	6.79
72	Jordan	5.13	4.71	4.17	4.69	5.40	5.54	5.87	6.54
73	Nigeria	4.79	4.76	4.73	4.78	4.87	4.93	5.10	5.34
74	United Arab Emirates	2.21	2.05	1.92	1.86	1.83	2.06	2.94	4.18

SECTION FOUR

Cross-country Comparisons

Key population trends

Table 4.1 Total Population: 2009-2019

'000

	2009	2010	2011	2012	2013	2014	2015	2016	2017	2018	2019	CAGR	Period growth
Algeria	34,895	35,423	35,954	36,489	37,024	37,558	38,088	38,613	39,130	39,640	40,140	1.41	15.03
Argentina	40,338	40,738	41,134	41,526	41,913	42,297	42,676	43,050	43,419	43,781	44,137	0.90	9.42
Australia	21,797	22,100	22,381	22,678	22,988	23,309	23,634	23,959	24,284	24,608	24,931	1.35	14.38
Austria	8,383	8,409	8,434	8,459	8,484	8,507	8,530	8,553	8,574	8,595	8,615	0.27	2.76
Azerbaijan	8,730	8,828	8,923	9,017	9,111	9,203	9,292	9,379	9,463	9,543	9,619	0.97	10.18
Belarus	9,672	9,653	9,626	9,599	9,572	9,544	9,515	9,486	9,457	9,426	9,395	-0.29	-2.87
Belgium	10,661	10,699	10,736	10,773	10,809	10,844	10,879	10,913	10,947	10,980	11,012	0.33	3.30
Bolivia	9,863	10,031	10,198	10,364	10,529	10,692	10,854	11,015	11,173	11,330	11,485	1.53	16.45
Bosnia-Herzegovina	3,844	3,844	3,844	3,843	3,841	3,840	3,837	3,833	3,828	3,823	3,816	-0.07	-0.74
Brazil	193,734	195,423	197,041	198,585	200,064	201,489	202,866	204,200	205,491	206,735	207,923	0.71	7.32
Bulgaria	7,519	7,467	7,415	7,362	7,306	7,250	7,191	7,131	7,070	7,009	6,947	-0.79	-7.60
Canada	33,651	33,968	34,242	34,501	34,763	35,025	35,287	35,549	35,810	36,071	36,331	0.77	7.96
Chile	16,970	17,135	17,297	17,458	17,617	17,773	17,926	18,075	18,221	18,363	18,503	0.87	9.03
China	1,328,020	1,334,418	1,340,213	1,345,773	1,351,256	1,356,624	1,361,826	1,366,802	1,371,489	1,375,824	1,379,763	0.38	3.90
Colombia	45,660	46,300	46,933	47,557	48,173	48,783	49,385	49,981	50,569	51,148	51,718	1.25	13.27
Costa Rica	4,579	4,640	4,702	4,766	4,831	4,894	4,957	5,018	5,077	5,135	5,193	1.27	13.41
Croatia	4,429	4,421	4,413	4,404	4,394	4,384	4,374	4,363	4,351	4,340	4,327	-0.23	-2.28
Czech Republic	10,338	10,353	10,365	10,368	10,367	10,364	10,361	10,358	10,357	10,357	10,356	0.02	0.17
Denmark	5,511	5,526	5,541	5,557	5,572	5,587	5,602	5,617	5,633	5,648	5,664	0.27	2.77
Ecuador	13,625	13,775	13,932	14,096	14,263	14,431	14,596	14,758	14,917	15,073	15,226	1.12	11.75
Egypt	76,761	78,160	79,560	80,958	82,351	83,736	85,111	86,472	87,820	89,152	90,469	1.66	17.86
Estonia	1,331	1,326	1,322	1,317	1,312	1,307	1,302	1,298	1,293	1,289	1,285	-0.34	-3.39
Finland	5,325	5,348	5,369	5,388	5,408	5,426	5,444	5,461	5,477	5,492	5,507	0.34	3.41
France	62,449	62,772	63,056	63,340	63,618	63,889	64,153	64,411	64,662	64,907	65,146	0.42	4.32
Germany	82,002	81,722	81,421	81,148	80,884	80,631	80,374	80,110	79,841	79,568	79,288	-0.34	-3.31
Greece	11,252	11,290	11,325	11,357	11,387	11,414	11,437	11,457	11,473	11,486	11,495	0.21	2.16
Hong Kong, China	7,064	7,131	7,196	7,260	7,322	7,383	7,443	7,502	7,560	7,617	7,673	0.83	8.62
Hungary	10,020	10,000	9,980	9,954	9,926	9,898	9,871	9,844	9,818	9,793	9,770	-0.25	-2.50
India	1,168,784	1,184,843	1,200,772	1,216,547	1,232,138	1,247,508	1,262,626	1,277,475	1,292,044	1,306,314	1,320,264	1.23	12.96
Indonesia	229,965	232,517	234,996	237,403	239,737	241,999	244,191	246,313	248,366	250,359	252,306	0.93	9.72
Iran	74,196	75,078	75,954	76,827	77,699	78,574	79,454	80,340	81,225	82,097	82,940	1.12	11.79
Ireland	4,448	4,507	4,560	4,613	4,665	4,716	4,766	4,815	4,862	4,908	4,953	1.08	11.36
Israel	7,403	7,518	7,630	7,741	7,851	7,958	8,063	8,167	8,270	8,370	8,470	1.35	14.40
Italy	59,052	59,115	59,164	59,198	59,219	59,224	59,216	59,195	59,160	59,114	59,056	0.00	0.01
Japan	127,595	127,363	127,114	126,850	126,551	126,216	125,846	125,441	125,000	124,523	124,010	-0.28	-2.81
Jordan	6,316	6,472	6,599	6,699	6,784	6,866	6,957	7,059	7,169	7,284	7,402	1.60	17.19
Kazakhstan	15,776	15,985	16,184	16,385	16,585	16,782	16,975	17,164	17,348	17,527	17,700	1.16	12.19
Kuwait	2,445	2,499	2,553	2,607	2,661	2,714	2,767	2,819	2,870	2,922	2,972	1.97	21.57
Latvia	2,253	2,240	2,228	2,214	2,199	2,185	2,172	2,159	2,146	2,133	2,121	-0.60	-5.87
Lithuania	3,348	3,329	3,311	3,292	3,272	3,253	3,234	3,216	3,198	3,181	3,165	-0.56	-5.46
Malaysia	28,098	28,552	28,999	29,440	29,874	30,304	30,727	31,145	31,557	31,961	32,357	1.42	15.16
Mexico	108,588	110,199	111,793	113,310	114,762	116,167	117,542	118,894	120,215	121,509	122,782	1.24	13.07
Morocco	31,993	32,381	32,771	33,162	33,553	33,943	34,330	34,715	35,096	35,471	35,839	1.14	12.02
Netherlands	16,410	16,439	16,470	16,501	16,531	16,561	16,590	16,619	16,646	16,673	16,700	0.18	1.77
New Zealand	4,311	4,352	4,394	4,434	4,474	4,513	4,551	4,589	4,627	4,664	4,700	0.87	9.03
Nigeria	154,729	158,259	161,796	165,337	168,876	172,408	175,928	179,433	182,919	186,386	189,830	2.07	22.69
Norway	4,799	4,858	4,913	4,964	5,013	5,061	5,108	5,156	5,205	5,254	5,303	1.00	10.49
Pakistan	180,808	184,753	188,794	192,920	197,104	201,308	205,504	209,679	213,836	217,972	222,089	2.08	22.83
Peru	29,010	29,403	29,793	30,182	30,568	30,951	31,329	31,702	32,072	32,438	32,800	1.24	13.06
Philippines	92,137	93,923	95,709	97,495	99,279	101,080	102,896	104,727	106,573	108,434	110,306	1.82	19.72
Poland	37,990	37,929	37,871	37,813	37,751	37,689	37,631	37,575	37,522	37,473	37,427	-0.15	-1.48
Portugal	10,670	10,694	10,716	10,736	10,752	10,767	10,779	10,788	10,794	10,798	10,800	0.12	1.21
Romania	21,435	21,370	21,302	21,232	21,145	21,056	20,953	20,844	20,733	20,621	20,506	-0.44	-4.33
Russia	141,904	141,786	141,467	141,173	140,935	140,724	140,507	140,275	140,026	139,761	139,477	-0.17	-1.71
Saudi Arabia	25,721	26,246	26,778	27,314	27,853	28,393	28,933	29,471	30,009	30,545	31,078	1.91	20.83
Singapore	4,707	4,772	4,834	4,894	4,950	5,004	5,055	5,103	5,150	5,194	5,236	1.07	11.24
Slovakia	5,395	5,397	5,398	5,398	5,398	5,398	5,398	5,397	5,396	5,395	5,393	0.00	-0.05
Slovenia	2,023	2,029	2,035	2,039	2,042	2,045	2,048	2,051	2,053	2,056	2,059	0.18	1.77
South Africa	50,110	50,492	50,812	51,073	51,292	51,491	51,684	51,878	52,072	52,267	52,467	0.46	4.70
South Korea	48,747	48,875	48,989	49,083	49,163	49,227	49,277	49,312	49,332	49,340	49,338	0.12	1.21
Spain	45,521	45,928	46,305	46,673	47,035	47,388	47,732	48,067	48,391	48,700	48,992	0.74	7.63
Sweden	9,201	9,244	9,288	9,332	9,376	9,421	9,466	9,513	9,561	9,609	9,657	0.48	4.95
Switzerland	7,560	7,589	7,618	7,647	7,675	7,704	7,732	7,761	7,790	7,819	7,849	0.38	3.83
Taiwan	23,034	23,105	23,171	23,232	23,286	23,334	23,376	23,411	23,440	23,462	23,478	0.19	1.93
Thailand	64,732	65,125	65,493	65,838	66,163	66,471	66,763	67,041	67,303	67,549	67,778	0.46	4.71
Tunisia	10,272	10,374	10,476	10,579	10,681	10,783	10,884	10,984	11,082	11,178	11,273	0.93	9.75
Turkey	75,263	76,157	77,039	77,910	78,766	79,607	80,432	81,239	82,030	82,804	83,561	1.05	11.03
Turkmenistan	5,110	5,177	5,243	5,311	5,377	5,444	5,509	5,573	5,637	5,699	5,759	1.20	12.69
Ukraine	45,919	45,641	45,356	45,067	44,774	44,481	44,187	43,892	43,596	43,298	42,997	-0.66	-6.36
United Arab Emirates	4,616	4,725	4,830	4,929	5,025	5,120	5,213	5,307	5,401	5,496	5,589	1.93	21.08
United Kingdom	61,612	61,966	62,260	62,582	62,938	63,325	63,717	64,114	64,514	64,918	65,324	0.59	6.02
USA	306,600	308,862	310,917	312,998	315,138	317,287	319,441	321,599	323,756	325,911	328,062	0.68	7.00
Venezuela	28,583	29,044	29,501	29,955	30,405	30,851	31,292	31,727	32,158	32,582	33,000	1.45	15.45
Vietnam	87,627	88,744	89,868	90,996	92,125	93,252	94,373	95,484	96,585	97,671	98,734	1.20	12.68

Key population trends

Table 4.2 Population Aged 0-14: 2009 (%)

% of total

	0-4 yrs	5-9 yrs	10-14 yrs	Total
Algeria	9.77	8.75	8.85	27.37
Argentina	8.46	8.30	8.54	25.30
Australia	6.50	6.21	6.44	19.15
Austria	4.77	4.90	5.50	15.18
Azerbaijan	8.69	7.37	8.21	24.27
Belarus	5.02	4.67	4.98	14.66
Belgium	5.71	5.52	5.65	16.88
Bolivia	12.64	12.15	11.48	36.27
Bosnia-Herzegovina	4.48	5.07	5.82	15.37
Brazil	8.25	9.01	8.78	26.04
Bulgaria	4.44	4.39	4.28	13.11
Canada	5.33	5.31	5.93	16.57
Chile	7.35	7.33	8.04	22.73
China	4.97	5.41	6.43	16.82
Colombia	9.85	9.66	9.65	29.17
Costa Rica	8.12	8.70	9.02	25.84
Croatia	4.78	4.85	5.73	15.36
Czech Republic	4.97	4.48	4.64	14.09
Denmark	5.93	6.01	6.35	18.29
Ecuador	10.12	10.46	10.46	31.03
Egypt	11.63	11.22	10.23	33.07
Estonia	5.42	4.75	4.69	14.86
Finland	5.53	5.39	5.81	16.73
France	6.27	6.20	5.90	18.37
Germany	4.20	4.53	4.85	13.58
Greece	4.82	4.63	4.78	14.23
Hong Kong, China	3.31	3.88	5.40	12.59
Hungary	4.88	4.80	5.23	14.91
India	10.54	10.44	10.29	31.28
Indonesia	9.03	9.10	8.89	27.02
Iran	8.91	7.61	7.57	24.10
Ireland	7.10	6.87	6.41	20.39
Israel	9.69	9.57	8.75	28.01
Italy	4.62	4.68	4.64	13.94
Japan	4.24	4.46	4.67	13.37
Jordan	12.10	11.33	11.11	34.54
Kazakhstan	9.44	7.26	7.21	23.91
Kuwait	8.49	7.73	7.14	23.36
Latvia	4.83	4.38	4.39	13.60
Lithuania	4.53	4.75	5.67	14.95
Malaysia	11.12	10.60	9.93	31.66
Mexico	9.49	9.51	9.66	28.66
Morocco	9.63	9.19	9.59	28.40
Netherlands	5.63	6.14	5.97	17.74
New Zealand	7.12	6.70	6.92	20.73
Nigeria	16.45	13.94	12.17	42.56
Norway	6.22	6.23	6.56	19.01
Pakistan	13.35	12.16	11.42	36.94
Peru	10.18	10.08	10.06	30.32
Philippines	11.76	11.18	10.95	33.89
Poland	4.75	4.78	5.59	15.12
Portugal	5.11	5.26	5.06	15.42
Romania	5.06	4.99	5.20	15.24
Russia	5.43	4.69	4.77	14.90
Saudi Arabia	11.16	10.87	10.38	32.41
Singapore	5.11	5.90	6.69	17.69
Slovakia	4.99	4.86	5.58	15.43
Slovenia	4.61	4.49	4.74	13.84
South Africa	10.35	10.25	9.93	30.53
South Korea	4.55	5.52	6.71	16.78
Spain	5.30	4.91	4.57	14.79
Sweden	5.63	5.28	5.60	16.51
Switzerland	4.83	4.97	5.49	15.29
Taiwan	4.47	5.73	6.77	16.97
Thailand	6.28	6.49	7.54	20.31
Tunisia	7.70	7.43	8.13	23.26
Turkey	8.54	9.09	9.45	27.08
Turkmenistan	10.24	9.63	9.70	29.57
Ukraine	4.80	4.19	4.96	13.94
United Arab Emirates	6.70	6.66	5.78	19.14
United Kingdom	6.08	5.51	5.90	17.50
USA	6.93	6.65	6.51	20.08
Venezuela	10.23	9.93	9.65	29.81
Vietnam	9.01	8.87	8.95	26.83

Key population trends

Table 4.3 Population Aged 15-64: 2009 (%)

% of total

	15-19 yrs	20-24 yrs	25-29 yrs	30-34 yrs	35-39 yrs	40-44 yrs	45-49 yrs	50-54 yrs	55-59 yrs	60-64 yrs	Total
Algeria	10.35	10.66	10.18	8.63	7.33	6.32	5.18	4.01	3.20	2.14	68.01
Argentina	8.57	8.24	8.06	7.86	6.55	5.83	5.47	5.09	4.64	3.94	64.25
Australia	6.81	7.12	7.16	6.80	7.38	6.99	7.20	6.60	6.00	5.37	67.43
Austria	6.03	6.17	6.58	6.40	7.51	8.55	8.14	6.82	5.87	5.37	67.45
Azerbaijan	10.26	10.22	8.37	6.90	6.68	7.19	7.64	6.05	3.77	1.97	69.06
Belarus	6.88	8.60	8.10	7.21	6.95	7.09	8.31	7.73	6.30	4.13	71.32
Belgium	6.10	5.99	6.32	6.31	6.98	7.44	7.56	7.04	6.38	5.78	65.91
Bolivia	10.71	9.17	7.87	6.92	6.14	5.06	4.25	3.59	2.95	2.36	59.01
Bosnia-Herzegovina	6.37	7.86	7.60	7.18	7.18	7.54	7.93	7.60	6.65	4.89	70.79
Brazil	8.61	9.14	9.07	7.94	7.22	6.88	6.29	5.10	4.00	3.05	67.29
Bulgaria	5.85	6.81	7.16	7.72	7.29	6.72	6.95	7.09	7.22	6.54	69.35
Canada	6.60	6.79	7.00	6.84	6.96	7.39	8.26	7.62	6.55	5.59	69.59
Chile	8.82	8.50	7.54	6.93	7.28	7.34	7.24	6.06	4.73	3.84	68.29
China	7.47	7.58	6.29	6.51	8.89	9.71	7.83	7.50	7.02	4.80	73.58
Colombia	9.49	8.92	8.35	7.60	6.89	6.73	5.85	4.82	3.89	2.84	65.36
Costa Rica	9.57	9.72	8.82	7.63	6.78	6.88	6.40	5.24	3.95	2.86	67.83
Croatia	5.87	6.55	7.11	6.89	6.63	7.07	7.35	7.53	7.01	5.28	67.28
Czech Republic	6.16	6.56	7.32	8.95	7.56	6.77	6.27	7.05	7.41	6.88	70.94
Denmark	6.22	5.73	5.72	6.57	7.01	7.70	7.05	6.59	6.38	6.86	65.82
Ecuador	9.80	8.96	8.06	7.27	6.56	5.88	5.12	4.43	3.67	2.70	62.46
Egypt	9.85	9.68	8.54	7.23	5.79	4.99	4.93	4.50	3.64	2.67	61.82
Estonia	6.73	7.99	7.47	6.92	6.96	6.47	7.09	6.92	6.44	5.14	68.13
Finland	6.26	6.10	6.37	6.27	5.86	6.91	7.10	7.17	7.42	7.07	66.51
France	6.14	6.33	6.42	6.23	7.05	7.01	6.92	6.66	6.58	5.68	65.00
Germany	5.46	6.00	6.11	5.75	6.85	8.60	8.40	7.19	6.54	5.15	66.06
Greece	5.12	5.76	7.15	7.76	7.79	7.71	7.12	6.78	6.10	5.88	67.16
Hong Kong, China	6.20	7.09	7.82	7.73	7.99	8.30	9.44	8.68	6.84	4.79	74.87
Hungary	6.10	6.49	7.28	8.64	7.22	6.50	6.10	7.58	7.07	5.83	68.83
India	10.02	9.28	8.49	7.58	6.64	5.89	5.20	4.54	3.68	2.56	63.88
Indonesia	8.90	8.96	8.88	8.35	7.71	6.88	5.91	4.88	3.70	2.82	67.01
Iran	10.42	12.57	11.68	8.50	6.82	6.11	5.23	4.30	3.23	2.20	71.06
Ireland	6.37	7.18	9.02	8.49	7.75	7.04	6.54	5.88	5.31	4.69	68.26
Israel	8.05	7.77	7.52	7.44	6.70	5.55	5.22	5.01	4.89	4.15	62.30
Italy	4.95	5.08	5.82	7.21	8.03	8.29	7.51	6.64	6.22	6.02	65.77
Japan	4.76	5.43	5.90	6.75	7.62	6.73	6.14	6.07	7.16	7.37	63.92
Jordan	10.57	10.12	9.66	8.17	6.97	5.51	4.00	2.81	2.15	1.87	61.81
Kazakhstan	9.17	9.82	8.48	7.64	6.99	6.46	6.65	5.98	4.81	2.93	68.93
Kuwait	6.77	8.03	11.11	12.91	11.65	9.04	6.33	4.41	2.54	1.63	74.42
Latvia	6.91	8.18	7.46	6.98	7.05	6.83	7.53	6.99	6.12	5.02	69.09
Lithuania	7.58	8.09	7.07	6.58	7.21	7.37	7.96	6.69	5.79	4.69	69.01
Malaysia	9.35	8.97	8.25	7.27	6.71	6.37	5.65	4.82	3.81	2.62	63.82
Mexico	9.45	8.52	8.06	8.28	7.95	6.44	5.30	4.54	3.71	2.74	64.98
Morocco	10.02	10.04	9.23	7.70	6.79	5.92	5.47	4.96	3.59	2.54	66.24
Netherlands	6.14	6.00	5.97	6.08	7.49	7.87	7.74	7.05	6.58	6.36	67.29
New Zealand	7.49	6.94	6.46	6.24	7.15	7.25	7.49	6.59	5.73	5.13	66.46
Nigeria	10.69	9.38	8.07	6.57	5.12	4.08	3.42	2.87	2.33	1.79	54.32
Norway	6.65	6.14	6.30	6.66	7.54	7.50	6.84	6.56	6.11	5.99	66.31
Pakistan	10.98	10.08	8.20	6.83	5.81	4.91	4.09	3.35	2.66	2.12	59.03
Peru	9.90	9.27	8.49	7.86	6.87	6.01	5.15	4.20	3.41	2.67	63.83
Philippines	10.49	9.53	8.39	7.34	6.32	5.53	4.76	4.01	3.21	2.32	61.91
Poland	6.90	8.11	8.51	7.83	6.71	6.18	6.94	7.95	7.25	5.09	71.46
Portugal	5.38	5.89	7.13	7.97	7.63	7.39	7.21	6.63	6.20	5.62	67.05
Romania	6.40	7.97	7.67	8.26	7.90	7.17	6.00	7.19	6.61	4.82	70.00
Russia	6.54	8.87	8.38	7.53	6.95	6.63	8.23	7.88	6.76	4.07	71.83
Saudi Arabia	9.82	9.00	9.05	9.34	8.11	6.90	5.11	3.44	2.34	1.58	64.68
Singapore	7.13	6.51	6.86	7.54	8.67	8.55	8.82	8.10	6.50	4.64	73.31
Slovakia	7.06	7.91	8.48	8.65	7.28	6.79	7.02	7.45	6.83	5.02	72.50
Slovenia	5.40	6.52	7.42	7.60	7.22	7.71	7.67	7.74	7.26	5.23	69.77
South Africa	10.01	10.09	9.32	7.90	6.63	5.60	4.89	4.34	3.54	2.65	64.98
South Korea	6.87	6.45	7.94	7.85	8.94	8.48	8.70	7.66	5.37	4.31	72.57
Spain	4.92	5.76	7.58	8.83	8.50	8.04	7.38	6.42	5.63	5.22	68.28
Sweden	6.94	6.21	5.97	6.28	6.77	7.31	6.51	6.34	6.39	6.87	65.60
Switzerland	5.97	5.99	6.32	6.62	7.46	8.41	8.00	6.99	6.25	5.96	67.97
Taiwan	6.97	7.13	8.66	8.32	7.92	8.16	8.23	7.45	6.17	3.62	72.63
Thailand	7.74	7.34	8.10	8.45	8.63	8.51	7.76	6.51	5.04	3.60	71.67
Tunisia	9.56	10.19	9.61	8.59	7.43	6.58	5.88	5.22	4.14	2.83	70.03
Turkey	8.77	8.38	8.93	8.89	7.89	6.58	5.76	4.95	3.91	2.86	66.92
Turkmenistan	11.18	10.59	8.88	7.70	6.76	6.11	5.65	4.50	3.04	1.82	66.21
Ukraine	6.59	8.27	7.89	7.29	6.97	6.71	7.82	7.34	6.71	4.50	70.10
United Arab Emirates	5.17	7.48	13.81	17.48	14.76	8.84	5.13	3.99	2.23	0.96	79.85
United Kingdom	6.45	6.96	6.75	6.20	7.11	7.64	7.14	6.23	5.87	5.95	66.29
USA	7.00	6.92	7.02	6.51	6.75	6.88	7.47	7.11	6.20	5.16	67.02
Venezuela	9.56	9.29	8.47	7.59	6.64	6.30	5.61	4.56	3.80	2.91	64.72
Vietnam	10.46	10.08	8.93	8.16	7.35	6.64	5.81	4.62	3.40	2.11	67.57

Key population trends

Table 4.4 Population Aged 65+: 2009 (%)

% of total

	65-69 yrs	70-74 yrs	75-79 yrs	80+ yrs	Total
Algeria	1.61	1.39	0.95	0.68	4.63
Argentina	3.22	2.63	2.08	2.52	10.45
Australia	3.99	3.15	2.53	3.74	13.41
Austria	5.78	3.63	3.28	4.68	17.37
Azerbaijan	1.97	2.20	1.48	1.01	6.67
Belarus	3.87	4.12	3.10	2.93	14.02
Belgium	4.32	4.24	3.82	4.82	17.21
Bolivia	1.79	1.35	0.89	0.69	4.72
Bosnia-Herzegovina	4.12	4.36	3.08	2.28	13.84
Brazil	2.33	1.81	1.20	1.32	6.67
Bulgaria	5.17	4.75	3.90	3.72	17.54
Canada	4.13	3.21	2.69	3.81	13.84
Chile	3.04	2.23	1.69	2.02	8.98
China	3.42	2.75	1.88	1.55	9.60
Colombia	1.96	1.43	1.01	1.08	5.47
Costa Rica	2.11	1.60	1.16	1.44	6.32
Croatia	5.10	4.86	3.90	3.50	17.36
Czech Republic	4.91	3.51	3.12	3.43	14.97
Denmark	5.08	3.83	2.86	4.12	15.89
Ecuador	2.16	1.71	1.25	1.38	6.51
Egypt	1.96	1.51	1.01	0.64	5.11
Estonia	5.00	4.58	3.62	3.82	17.01
Finland	4.80	4.09	3.40	4.48	16.77
France	4.02	3.87	3.56	5.18	16.62
Germany	6.26	5.50	3.65	4.94	20.36
Greece	4.80	5.18	4.34	4.28	18.60
Hong Kong, China	3.16	3.30	2.81	3.27	12.54
Hungary	5.04	4.04	3.37	3.81	16.26
India	1.94	1.41	0.86	0.65	4.85
Indonesia	2.37	1.78	1.10	0.73	5.97
Iran	1.61	1.38	1.04	0.81	4.85
Ireland	3.55	2.84	2.20	2.76	11.35
Israel	2.53	2.53	1.91	2.71	9.69
Italy	5.47	4.98	4.20	5.65	20.29
Japan	6.57	5.41	4.55	6.18	22.71
Jordan	1.51	1.02	0.59	0.53	3.65
Kazakhstan	2.25	2.49	1.17	1.25	7.16
Kuwait	1.06	0.65	0.31	0.20	2.21
Latvia	5.40	4.61	3.55	3.76	17.31
Lithuania	4.85	4.26	3.46	3.46	16.03
Malaysia	1.83	1.26	0.72	0.71	4.53
Mexico	2.18	1.62	1.23	1.34	6.36
Morocco	1.94	1.64	1.03	0.75	5.36
Netherlands	4.56	3.67	2.98	3.76	14.97
New Zealand	3.98	3.02	2.43	3.38	12.81
Nigeria	1.36	0.91	0.52	0.33	3.12
Norway	4.12	3.18	2.80	4.58	14.69
Pakistan	1.66	1.11	0.69	0.58	4.03
Peru	2.08	1.61	1.11	1.05	5.85
Philippines	1.75	1.22	0.73	0.50	4.20
Poland	3.71	3.59	3.00	3.12	13.42
Portugal	4.84	4.62	3.80	4.27	17.53
Romania	4.33	4.30	3.23	2.89	14.76
Russia	3.86	4.02	2.72	2.68	13.27
Saudi Arabia	1.13	0.82	0.54	0.42	2.91
Singapore	3.15	2.35	1.68	1.81	8.99
Slovakia	3.89	3.00	2.53	2.65	12.07
Slovenia	4.96	4.20	3.52	3.71	16.39
South Africa	1.93	1.26	0.74	0.55	4.49
South Korea	3.73	3.05	2.05	1.82	10.65
Spain	4.28	4.06	3.73	4.87	16.93
Sweden	5.26	3.98	3.32	5.33	17.89
Switzerland	4.83	3.89	3.28	4.74	16.74
Taiwan	3.31	2.64	2.15	2.30	10.40
Thailand	2.72	2.25	1.59	1.45	8.01
Tunisia	2.21	1.98	1.43	1.09	6.71
Turkey	2.26	1.81	1.07	0.87	6.00
Turkmenistan	1.31	1.35	0.84	0.72	4.23
Ukraine	4.86	4.91	2.97	3.21	15.95
United Arab Emirates	0.40	0.29	0.14	0.18	1.01
United Kingdom	4.53	3.92	3.21	4.55	16.21
USA	3.84	2.93	2.35	3.79	12.91
Venezuela	2.04	1.42	1.01	0.99	5.47
Vietnam	1.75	1.52	1.23	1.10	5.59

Key population trends

Table 4.5 Population Aged 0-14: 2019 (%)

% of total

	0-4 yrs	5-9 yrs	10-14 yrs	Total
Algeria	8.96	8.91	8.37	26.24
Argentina	7.72	7.83	7.72	23.28
Australia	6.39	6.38	6.12	18.89
Austria	4.63	4.72	4.89	14.24
Azerbaijan	8.12	8.41	7.72	24.25
Belarus	5.28	5.64	5.24	16.16
Belgium	5.61	5.80	5.72	17.13
Bolivia	10.64	10.56	10.41	31.61
Bosnia-Herzegovina	4.36	4.52	4.60	13.48
Brazil	6.23	6.72	7.63	20.58
Bulgaria	4.09	4.40	4.67	13.15
Canada	5.31	5.25	5.30	15.86
Chile	6.76	6.82	6.72	20.29
China	4.75	5.17	5.37	15.29
Colombia	8.52	8.59	8.61	25.72
Costa Rica	7.37	7.43	7.31	22.11
Croatia	4.99	5.06	4.95	15.00
Czech Republic	4.92	5.06	5.06	15.03
Denmark	5.52	5.57	5.80	16.89
Ecuador	8.74	8.79	8.96	26.49
Egypt	10.40	11.05	11.00	32.46
Estonia	5.86	5.89	5.56	17.31
Finland	5.58	5.57	5.47	16.62
France	5.96	6.08	6.09	18.13
Germany	3.80	3.92	4.34	12.06
Greece	4.47	4.82	4.92	14.20
Hong Kong, China	3.53	4.30	4.49	12.32
Hungary	4.85	4.98	5.06	14.89
India	8.94	9.03	9.10	27.07
Indonesia	7.35	7.79	8.16	23.30
Iran	7.87	8.15	7.83	23.85
Ireland	5.89	6.41	6.57	18.86
Israel	8.16	8.33	8.61	25.11
Italy	3.92	4.36	4.75	13.03
Japan	3.62	4.01	4.33	11.96
Jordan	10.11	10.48	10.18	30.76
Kazakhstan	8.47	8.82	8.44	25.73
Kuwait	7.08	7.31	7.11	21.51
Latvia	5.38	5.46	5.02	15.86
Lithuania	4.99	4.91	4.75	14.65
Malaysia	9.55	9.15	9.39	28.09
Mexico	7.68	7.85	8.13	23.66
Morocco	8.83	8.85	8.47	26.15
Netherlands	5.27	5.21	5.47	15.95
New Zealand	6.53	6.78	6.69	20.00
Nigeria	14.12	13.22	12.23	39.57
Norway	6.18	6.10	6.02	18.31
Pakistan	11.87	11.44	10.60	33.91
Peru	8.61	8.77	8.94	26.32
Philippines	10.38	10.11	9.86	30.35
Poland	5.13	5.01	4.79	14.94
Portugal	4.54	4.94	5.14	14.62
Romania	4.81	5.10	5.23	15.14
Russia	6.03	6.23	5.65	17.91
Saudi Arabia	9.78	9.46	9.13	28.36
Singapore	5.03	4.95	4.82	14.80
Slovakia	4.97	4.99	4.97	14.94
Slovenia	4.77	4.85	4.68	14.30
South Africa	9.48	9.66	9.66	28.79
South Korea	3.94	4.23	4.38	12.55
Spain	4.89	5.27	5.26	15.42
Sweden	5.71	5.61	5.61	16.93
Switzerland	4.97	4.73	4.76	14.47
Taiwan	4.03	4.29	4.43	12.75
Thailand	5.41	5.92	6.27	17.59
Tunisia	7.39	7.34	6.97	21.69
Turkey	7.65	7.64	7.75	23.04
Turkmenistan	8.95	8.99	8.81	26.76
Ukraine	4.39	4.81	4.98	14.17
United Arab Emirates	5.67	5.89	5.84	17.40
United Kingdom	6.28	6.06	5.71	18.05
USA	6.53	6.54	6.75	19.82
Venezuela	8.86	8.92	8.83	26.61
Vietnam	7.79	7.97	7.97	23.73

Key population trends

Table 4.6 Population Aged 15-64: 2019 (%)

% of total

	15-19 yrs	20-24 yrs	25-29 yrs	30-34 yrs	35-39 yrs	40-44 yrs	45-49 yrs	50-54 yrs	55-59 yrs	60-64 yrs	Total
Algeria	7.54	7.52	8.81	9.11	8.70	7.36	6.22	5.32	4.27	3.20	68.04
Argentina	7.58	7.79	7.80	7.48	7.28	7.08	5.84	5.14	4.74	4.27	65.00
Australia	5.96	6.52	7.05	7.17	6.99	6.44	6.71	6.15	6.17	5.57	64.74
Austria	5.05	5.78	6.41	6.44	6.65	6.36	7.31	8.19	7.67	6.32	66.18
Azerbaijan	6.62	7.27	9.03	8.97	7.33	6.03	5.82	6.20	6.46	4.92	68.64
Belarus	4.88	5.18	7.10	8.77	8.20	7.24	6.88	6.84	7.72	6.79	69.59
Belgium	5.48	5.72	6.26	6.07	6.24	6.12	6.68	7.02	7.03	6.44	63.06
Bolivia	10.06	9.40	8.69	7.45	6.42	5.64	4.96	4.03	3.32	2.74	62.72
Bosnia-Herzegovina	5.12	5.89	6.42	7.93	7.67	7.23	7.19	7.45	7.66	7.16	69.73
Brazil	8.35	8.09	7.90	8.36	8.27	7.20	6.49	6.10	5.46	4.29	70.51
Bulgaria	4.60	4.31	5.76	6.92	7.51	8.10	7.59	6.91	7.04	7.02	65.77
Canada	5.27	6.10	6.89	7.00	7.13	6.74	6.61	6.81	7.44	6.71	66.70
Chile	6.74	7.38	8.08	7.78	6.89	6.32	6.59	6.57	6.38	5.21	67.95
China	5.07	5.79	7.72	7.73	6.01	6.52	9.07	9.79	7.70	6.61	72.03
Colombia	8.45	8.35	8.12	7.61	7.14	6.51	5.89	5.71	4.88	3.91	66.56
Costa Rica	7.82	8.12	8.55	8.61	7.78	6.70	5.91	5.94	5.45	4.36	69.24
Croatia	5.01	5.94	6.13	6.79	7.29	7.03	6.70	7.00	7.11	7.15	66.15
Czech Republic	4.57	4.72	6.23	6.62	7.38	8.97	7.54	6.65	6.00	6.53	65.20
Denmark	5.93	6.46	6.36	5.64	5.57	6.39	6.76	7.29	6.58	6.03	63.00
Ecuador	9.14	8.88	8.13	7.46	6.76	6.14	5.57	4.99	4.31	3.66	65.04
Egypt	9.78	7.97	7.23	7.39	6.79	5.80	4.51	3.84	3.90	3.55	60.75
Estonia	4.85	4.74	6.75	7.97	7.41	6.83	6.77	6.15	6.61	6.29	64.38
Finland	5.30	5.75	6.28	6.13	6.32	6.14	5.67	6.58	6.64	6.58	61.39
France	6.01	5.80	6.10	6.24	6.23	5.98	6.67	6.54	6.37	6.03	61.96
Germany	4.68	5.27	6.11	6.47	6.34	5.86	6.89	8.53	8.22	6.91	65.28
Greece	4.76	4.93	5.30	5.94	7.28	7.83	7.80	7.63	6.95	6.50	64.92
Hong Kong, China	4.14	6.04	7.67	8.48	8.06	6.79	6.63	7.04	8.41	7.70	70.96
Hungary	4.98	5.51	6.50	6.86	7.52	8.76	7.19	6.21	5.61	6.91	66.05
India	9.13	8.97	8.69	8.02	7.30	6.49	5.63	4.90	4.20	3.48	66.81
Indonesia	8.23	7.99	7.93	7.96	7.91	7.45	6.85	6.03	5.05	4.01	69.43
Iran	6.74	6.59	9.13	11.10	10.32	7.47	5.95	5.26	4.39	3.49	70.44
Ireland	6.16	5.78	6.45	7.75	9.06	7.99	7.02	6.28	5.77	5.11	67.37
Israel	8.54	7.77	7.11	6.87	6.67	6.63	5.92	4.74	4.34	4.19	62.77
Italy	4.82	4.83	5.26	5.44	6.08	7.35	8.07	8.25	7.39	6.44	63.94
Japan	4.59	4.91	5.04	5.61	6.01	6.84	7.70	6.75	6.08	5.92	59.46
Jordan	9.48	9.12	8.48	8.12	7.81	6.63	5.65	4.43	3.15	2.12	65.00
Kazakhstan	6.69	6.58	8.35	8.87	7.56	6.73	6.07	5.48	5.45	4.64	66.41
Kuwait	6.56	6.88	8.10	9.42	10.21	10.03	8.68	6.75	4.66	3.20	74.50
Latvia	4.54	4.53	7.12	8.42	7.65	7.07	7.02	6.62	7.05	6.28	66.32
Lithuania	4.95	5.80	7.59	8.08	7.10	6.58	7.14	7.18	7.55	6.14	68.11
Malaysia	9.17	8.61	8.10	7.67	6.92	5.96	5.43	5.17	4.53	3.81	65.38
Mexico	8.24	8.21	7.90	7.29	7.21	7.47	7.15	5.74	4.66	3.89	67.76
Morocco	8.06	8.24	8.46	8.48	7.86	6.58	5.83	5.08	4.63	4.04	67.27
Netherlands	6.07	6.00	6.25	5.97	5.73	5.75	7.18	7.55	7.36	6.57	64.42
New Zealand	6.37	6.44	6.64	6.47	6.39	5.99	6.61	6.51	6.60	5.75	63.77
Nigeria	10.84	9.44	8.18	7.04	5.94	4.76	3.66	2.90	2.39	1.92	57.07
Norway	6.02	6.41	6.76	6.54	6.51	6.54	7.09	6.88	6.14	5.72	64.61
Pakistan	9.78	9.12	8.72	8.01	6.53	5.43	4.59	3.82	3.10	2.42	61.53
Peru	8.87	8.73	8.48	7.88	7.19	6.65	5.79	5.03	4.25	3.39	66.26
Philippines	9.40	9.09	8.59	7.74	6.83	6.01	5.18	4.49	3.79	3.07	64.19
Poland	4.82	5.59	6.81	7.95	8.38	7.71	6.53	5.91	6.52	7.30	67.52
Portugal	5.32	5.12	5.46	5.98	7.19	7.97	7.56	7.25	6.99	6.34	65.19
Romania	5.18	5.30	6.32	7.92	7.75	8.37	7.92	7.07	5.78	6.69	68.30
Russia	4.89	4.97	6.71	8.95	8.36	7.40	6.67	6.16	7.31	6.67	68.09
Saudi Arabia	8.83	8.76	9.20	8.59	7.69	7.24	6.06	5.07	3.71	2.56	67.71
Singapore	5.31	6.30	7.49	7.26	7.13	7.25	8.00	7.54	7.61	6.99	70.88
Slovakia	4.84	5.54	7.01	7.86	8.44	8.57	7.10	6.44	6.52	6.85	69.17
Slovenia	4.52	4.80	5.52	6.66	7.52	7.65	7.20	7.56	7.35	7.21	65.99
South Africa	9.53	9.17	9.02	8.55	7.22	5.68	4.72	4.15	3.77	3.33	65.14
South Korea	5.29	6.47	6.70	6.32	7.77	7.63	8.64	8.19	8.33	7.18	72.53
Spain	4.88	4.71	5.31	6.18	7.69	8.62	8.13	7.56	6.82	5.84	65.75
Sweden	5.30	5.71	7.07	6.34	5.99	6.18	6.53	6.95	6.09	5.82	62.00
Switzerland	4.94	5.68	6.54	6.71	6.71	6.58	7.15	7.92	7.34	6.14	65.71
Taiwan	5.59	6.60	6.88	7.13	8.59	8.13	7.63	7.78	7.75	6.86	72.95
Thailand	6.38	7.32	7.35	6.83	7.45	7.64	7.75	7.65	6.94	5.77	71.08
Tunisia	6.75	7.34	8.61	9.16	8.65	7.71	6.64	5.83	5.10	4.38	70.17
Turkey	8.24	8.54	7.91	7.55	8.03	7.94	6.97	5.72	4.86	4.00	69.76
Turkmenistan	8.44	8.45	9.69	9.13	7.60	6.54	5.65	5.00	4.49	3.41	68.40
Ukraine	4.42	5.25	6.89	8.49	8.03	7.37	6.95	6.57	7.52	6.93	68.41
United Arab Emirates	6.51	7.70	9.16	11.09	13.41	13.37	9.96	4.99	2.46	1.99	80.65
United Kingdom	5.27	6.23	7.25	7.37	6.61	5.81	6.53	6.94	6.40	5.48	63.89
USA	6.54	6.33	6.73	6.71	6.74	6.13	6.21	6.22	6.62	6.15	64.38
Venezuela	8.58	8.31	8.20	7.96	7.24	6.46	5.61	5.26	4.59	3.63	65.83
Vietnam	7.84	7.87	9.18	8.83	7.81	7.12	6.39	5.72	4.93	3.83	69.53

Key population trends

Table 4.7 Population Aged 65+: 2019 (%)

% of total

	65-69 yrs	70-74 yrs	75-79 yrs	80+ yrs	Total
Algeria	2.42	1.46	0.93	0.91	5.72
Argentina	3.72	2.95	2.17	2.88	11.73
Australia	4.95	4.27	2.97	4.17	16.37
Austria	5.30	4.63	4.57	5.08	19.58
Azerbaijan	2.87	1.36	1.16	1.73	7.11
Belarus	5.14	3.09	2.45	3.56	14.25
Belgium	5.69	4.93	3.41	5.79	19.81
Bolivia	2.15	1.58	1.01	0.93	5.67
Bosnia-Herzegovina	6.06	4.12	2.93	3.68	16.79
Brazil	3.21	2.28	1.56	1.87	8.91
Bulgaria	6.80	5.69	3.89	4.71	21.08
Canada	5.58	4.50	3.03	4.33	17.43
Chile	3.91	3.00	2.17	2.68	11.76
China	5.30	3.26	1.96	2.16	12.68
Colombia	3.02	2.05	1.27	1.37	7.71
Costa Rica	3.18	2.17	1.46	1.83	8.65
Croatia	6.34	4.10	3.39	5.02	18.85
Czech Republic	6.59	5.73	3.64	3.81	19.77
Denmark	5.64	5.74	3.89	4.84	20.11
Ecuador	2.95	2.08	1.54	1.91	8.47
Egypt	2.81	1.91	1.20	0.88	6.80
Estonia	5.60	4.16	3.58	4.98	18.31
Finland	6.62	6.06	3.81	5.50	21.99
France	5.82	4.86	3.21	6.02	19.90
Germany	6.11	4.59	5.10	6.85	22.65
Greece	5.72	5.26	3.89	6.00	20.88
Hong Kong, China	5.92	4.03	2.44	4.33	16.71
Hungary	6.18	4.70	3.57	4.61	19.06
India	2.61	1.61	1.01	0.89	6.11
Indonesia	2.85	1.96	1.37	1.10	7.27
Iran	2.46	1.50	0.90	0.85	5.71
Ireland	4.48	3.70	2.47	3.11	13.76
Israel	4.14	3.36	1.67	2.96	12.13
Italy	5.89	5.44	4.54	7.15	23.02
Japan	6.85	6.85	5.72	9.16	28.58
Jordan	1.53	1.21	0.83	0.67	4.24
Kazakhstan	3.42	1.84	1.14	1.45	7.86
Kuwait	1.82	1.10	0.62	0.45	3.99
Latvia	5.20	3.92	3.68	5.02	17.82
Lithuania	5.09	3.89	3.63	4.63	17.24
Malaysia	2.87	1.68	0.93	1.04	6.53
Mexico	3.06	2.13	1.55	1.83	8.58
Morocco	2.75	1.75	1.10	0.99	6.59
Netherlands	6.02	5.70	3.65	4.25	19.63
New Zealand	4.93	4.23	3.02	4.05	16.23
Nigeria	1.44	0.96	0.58	0.38	3.36
Norway	5.14	4.79	3.04	4.12	17.08
Pakistan	1.78	1.26	0.83	0.69	4.56
Peru	2.64	1.92	1.35	1.51	7.42
Philippines	2.31	1.50	0.95	0.71	5.46
Poland	6.41	4.22	2.71	4.20	17.54
Portugal	5.76	4.98	3.90	5.56	20.20
Romania	5.82	3.90	3.03	3.80	16.56
Russia	5.42	3.03	2.37	3.19	14.00
Saudi Arabia	1.73	1.06	0.63	0.51	3.93
Singapore	5.56	3.73	2.22	2.82	14.33
Slovakia	6.12	4.09	2.63	3.06	15.89
Slovenia	6.53	4.42	3.76	5.00	19.71
South Africa	2.54	1.69	1.03	0.81	6.07
South Korea	4.87	3.71	2.90	3.44	14.92
Spain	4.98	4.40	3.34	6.11	18.83
Sweden	5.71	5.86	4.15	5.36	21.08
Switzerland	5.32	5.05	3.82	5.64	19.83
Taiwan	5.48	3.01	2.46	3.36	14.30
Thailand	4.35	2.89	1.99	2.10	11.33
Tunisia	3.30	2.05	1.36	1.43	8.14
Turkey	2.96	1.92	1.51	0.81	7.20
Turkmenistan	2.14	1.15	0.68	0.87	4.84
Ukraine	6.13	3.54	3.67	4.07	17.41
United Arab Emirates	1.05	0.48	0.22	0.21	1.96
United Kingdom	5.01	4.83	3.33	4.90	18.07
USA	5.16	4.05	2.75	3.84	15.81
Venezuela	2.88	2.06	1.30	1.32	7.56
Vietnam	2.69	1.55	1.13	1.37	6.73

Key population trends

Table 4.8 Population Aged 0-4: 2009-2019

'000

	2009	2010	2011	2012	2013	2014	2015	2016	2017	2018	2019	CAGR	Period growth
Algeria	3,408.7	3,444.3	3,479.8	3,515.2	3,549.6	3,580.0	3,603.1	3,616.5	3,620.0	3,613.4	3,597.1	0.54	5.53
Argentina	3,414.5	3,441.7	3,460.9	3,470.4	3,470.6	3,464.1	3,454.3	3,443.5	3,432.4	3,421.4	3,409.6	-0.01	-0.15
Australia	1,416.2	1,452.3	1,477.7	1,501.0	1,518.2	1,530.7	1,541.8	1,554.9	1,567.6	1,580.5	1,593.6	1.19	12.52
Austria	399.9	396.9	396.0	395.4	395.5	396.0	396.7	397.5	398.3	398.9	399.3	-0.02	-0.17
Azerbaijan	758.9	779.5	795.6	810.1	818.8	822.2	820.7	815.1	806.0	794.4	780.8	0.28	2.88
Belarus	485.5	505.5	521.2	529.6	530.9	526.4	519.6	514.8	509.1	502.5	495.6	0.21	2.09
Belgium	608.9	615.8	621.0	624.2	625.7	625.7	624.7	623.2	621.5	619.6	617.7	0.14	1.44
Bolivia	1,246.5	1,243.3	1,240.8	1,239.1	1,238.4	1,237.8	1,236.7	1,234.6	1,231.4	1,227.1	1,222.0	-0.20	-1.97
Bosnia-Herzegovina	172.4	174.0	175.0	175.1	174.4	173.0	171.5	170.0	168.7	167.5	166.2	-0.36	-3.56
Brazil	15,985.7	15,553.6	15,128.4	14,722.4	14,348.4	14,012.4	13,715.8	13,463.5	13,256.4	13,088.6	12,953.1	-2.08	-18.97
Bulgaria	333.8	330.8	328.3	325.4	321.2	316.5	311.0	304.9	298.3	291.4	284.1	-1.60	-14.88
Canada	1,794.8	1,818.6	1,829.8	1,832.9	1,834.7	1,837.1	1,845.1	1,863.6	1,886.6	1,908.3	1,929.1	0.72	7.48
Chile	1,247.3	1,251.9	1,256.0	1,259.0	1,260.7	1,261.1	1,260.3	1,258.6	1,256.1	1,253.1	1,250.1	0.02	0.23
China	66,018.8	65,900.8	66,243.0	66,103.2	66,061.6	65,885.5	65,832.3	65,954.9	66,012.1	65,871.3	65,523.3	-0.08	-0.75
Colombia	4,499.7	4,506.4	4,505.5	4,496.5	4,481.1	4,462.7	4,444.9	4,430.1	4,419.1	4,411.3	4,404.7	-0.21	-2.11
Costa Rica	372.0	368.8	368.8	372.1	377.8	384.0	388.8	391.1	390.3	387.1	382.8	0.28	2.89
Croatia	211.7	214.4	215.3	216.2	216.9	217.5	217.8	217.8	217.5	217.0	216.1	0.21	2.10
Czech Republic	513.6	519.3	520.0	520.1	519.8	519.2	518.5	517.3	515.6	513.1	509.4	-0.08	-0.81
Denmark	326.9	325.9	324.1	320.9	318.3	314.7	312.2	310.7	310.4	311.0	312.5	-0.45	-4.40
Ecuador	1,378.7	1,370.1	1,362.6	1,356.3	1,351.0	1,346.6	1,342.8	1,339.6	1,336.7	1,334.0	1,330.9	-0.35	-3.47
Egypt	8,925.7	9,033.8	9,117.7	9,197.8	9,267.7	9,324.5	9,368.0	9,398.0	9,413.9	9,417.3	9,412.1	0.53	5.45
Estonia	72.1	73.2	74.1	74.8	75.4	75.9	76.2	76.4	76.3	76.0	75.3	0.44	4.47
Finland	294.7	296.7	298.8	299.9	301.5	302.8	304.1	305.3	306.2	306.9	307.4	0.42	4.31
France	3,917.3	3,953.8	3,966.7	3,955.0	3,951.6	3,932.0	3,909.1	3,901.0	3,893.8	3,886.8	3,879.7	-0.10	-0.96
Germany	3,441.3	3,397.2	3,331.9	3,263.2	3,180.2	3,099.0	3,034.1	3,011.1	3,007.2	3,009.7	3,013.2	-1.32	-12.44
Greece	542.7	546.6	548.1	548.1	546.6	543.6	539.4	534.1	527.8	520.8	513.4	-0.55	-5.41
Hong Kong, China	233.9	243.3	246.0	246.2	247.6	250.1	253.7	258.1	262.0	266.5	271.0	1.48	15.86
Hungary	489.2	492.2	492.0	489.0	485.9	482.9	480.4	478.3	476.5	474.9	473.5	-0.33	-3.22
India	123,234.8	122,627.4	122,129.0	121,756.2	121,476.2	121,206.8	120,857.4	120,366.2	119,716.4	118,915.9	118,000.6	-0.43	-4.25
Indonesia	20,758.6	20,549.9	20,339.2	20,134.1	19,934.9	19,733.5	19,519.7	19,285.7	19,034.4	18,779.5	18,543.8	-1.12	-10.67
Iran	6,609.7	6,679.8	6,723.4	6,744.4	6,748.9	6,741.6	6,723.2	6,693.6	6,653.2	6,598.9	6,525.5	-0.13	-1.27
Ireland	315.9	315.4	315.4	314.7	313.3	311.1	308.3	304.8	300.8	296.3	291.7	-0.79	-7.67
Israel	717.1	714.6	711.9	709.0	705.8	702.2	698.8	695.9	693.7	692.1	691.0	-0.37	-3.63
Italy	2,728.2	2,693.6	2,659.5	2,620.4	2,577.9	2,533.3	2,488.0	2,442.9	2,398.9	2,357.0	2,317.9	-1.62	-15.04
Japan	5,415.8	5,411.0	5,358.1	5,270.6	5,150.6	4,995.6	4,875.9	4,766.7	4,667.3	4,576.7	4,493.9	-1.85	-17.02
Jordan	764.3	778.0	786.3	789.0	786.7	781.4	774.9	768.2	761.2	754.6	748.2	-0.21	-2.11
Kazakhstan	1,488.5	1,541.6	1,573.8	1,598.9	1,609.3	1,605.0	1,588.7	1,567.4	1,543.8	1,520.6	1,498.9	0.07	0.69
Kuwait	207.7	211.6	214.3	215.6	215.6	214.9	213.8	212.7	211.7	211.0	210.5	0.14	1.37
Latvia	108.8	111.5	113.3	114.8	115.9	116.8	117.3	117.2	116.8	115.7	114.1	0.48	4.88
Lithuania	151.8	152.5	153.4	154.3	155.3	156.2	157.1	157.7	158.1	158.3	158.1	0.40	4.12
Malaysia	3,124.7	3,101.3	3,077.6	3,052.0	3,045.2	3,054.6	3,072.8	3,090.9	3,101.7	3,101.8	3,090.4	-0.11	-1.10
Mexico	10,310.4	10,239.7	10,125.1	10,043.6	9,965.5	9,882.8	9,795.7	9,705.4	9,612.0	9,519.5	9,431.3	-0.89	-8.53
Morocco	3,080.4	3,120.2	3,153.2	3,177.4	3,192.0	3,198.6	3,199.4	3,196.0	3,188.7	3,177.8	3,162.9	0.26	2.68
Netherlands	923.9	907.7	896.9	887.6	880.9	876.4	874.0	873.4	874.5	876.9	880.6	-0.48	-4.69
New Zealand	306.8	313.5	318.0	319.2	317.4	314.9	312.5	310.5	309.0	307.7	306.9	0.00	0.02
Nigeria	25,458.5	25,817.3	26,114.0	26,346.0	26,517.1	26,637.6	26,719.3	26,771.0	26,798.1	26,806.0	26,799.4	0.51	5.27
Norway	298.5	303.4	308.0	310.5	313.1	314.0	315.5	317.7	320.6	324.1	327.7	0.94	9.81
Pakistan	24,140.3	24,489.2	24,845.3	25,203.1	25,545.7	25,848.7	26,090.7	26,258.5	26,350.4	26,376.8	26,359.8	0.88	9.19
Peru	2,954.3	2,951.1	2,942.6	2,928.8	2,910.9	2,891.4	2,872.5	2,856.0	2,842.5	2,831.8	2,823.0	-0.45	-4.45
Philippines	10,836.3	10,906.6	11,003.2	11,087.5	11,156.7	11,209.3	11,254.1	11,297.1	11,343.0	11,394.0	11,450.0	0.55	5.66
Poland	1,804.8	1,819.7	1,830.6	1,846.3	1,863.6	1,880.5	1,895.2	1,906.7	1,914.7	1,918.9	1,919.2	0.62	6.34
Portugal	544.8	544.9	543.6	540.5	535.9	529.9	522.9	515.1	506.8	498.4	490.0	-1.06	-10.06
Romania	1,083.8	1,087.6	1,084.9	1,079.6	1,071.1	1,061.3	1,049.7	1,036.7	1,022.3	1,005.6	986.3	-0.94	-8.99
Russia	7,708.9	7,979.1	8,205.6	8,426.6	8,542.9	8,571.0	8,544.6	8,580.5	8,577.7	8,516.7	8,413.6	0.88	9.14
Saudi Arabia	2,869.7	2,872.8	2,883.2	2,901.7	2,927.0	2,955.1	2,981.9	3,004.1	3,020.8	3,031.7	3,037.9	0.57	5.86
Singapore	240.6	241.7	243.1	245.1	247.2	249.5	252.0	254.8	257.5	260.3	263.5	0.91	9.48
Slovakia	269.1	269.6	269.5	269.6	269.8	270.0	270.0	269.9	269.6	269.0	268.2	-0.03	-0.32
Slovenia	93.2	94.3	95.4	96.4	97.3	98.1	98.7	99.0	99.0	98.7	98.1	0.51	5.27
South Africa	5,184.1	5,154.7	5,134.2	5,124.2	5,121.9	5,120.8	5,113.6	5,094.7	5,063.0	5,020.8	4,973.8	-0.41	-4.06
South Korea	2,216.9	2,201.5	2,190.8	2,167.5	2,139.1	2,107.1	2,072.8	2,037.3	2,002.3	1,969.7	1,941.9	-1.32	-12.41
Spain	2,414.2	2,450.6	2,481.3	2,493.1	2,499.0	2,498.7	2,490.9	2,476.7	2,457.6	2,429.6	2,395.0	-0.08	-0.80
Sweden	518.2	520.5	523.1	525.7	528.4	531.1	534.1	537.8	542.1	546.6	551.3	0.62	6.38
Switzerland	365.2	364.6	364.5	364.4	365.3	367.1	370.0	373.8	378.6	384.0	390.1	0.66	6.79
Taiwan	1,029.4	1,015.6	1,010.8	1,006.4	1,002.1	996.5	987.1	978.1	967.9	957.9	947.0	-0.83	-8.00
Thailand	4,067.4	4,049.9	4,031.5	4,005.2	3,960.3	3,901.2	3,834.8	3,772.7	3,721.0	3,685.4	3,663.7	-1.04	-9.92
Tunisia	791.0	799.4	807.8	816.0	823.5	829.7	834.2	836.6	836.8	835.3	832.6	0.51	5.26
Turkey	6,426.3	6,415.8	6,421.9	6,422.6	6,417.4	6,400.0	6,383.8	6,396.5	6,404.1	6,400.5	6,388.7	-0.06	-0.58
Turkmenistan	523.2	520.2	518.7	519.1	521.0	523.5	525.3	525.5	523.9	520.5	515.5	-0.15	-1.48
Ukraine	2,202.0	2,221.8	2,234.7	2,201.5	2,156.8	2,101.1	2,042.6	1,987.5	1,941.6	1,908.8	1,885.7	-1.54	-14.36
United Arab Emirates	309.3	308.9	310.1	313.1	317.4	321.9	325.1	326.1	324.7	321.2	316.7	0.23	2.37
United Kingdom	3,746.5	3,833.7	3,886.7	3,928.1	3,950.3	3,958.2	3,965.3	3,999.1	4,034.6	4,070.0	4,103.7	0.91	9.54
USA	21,233.5	21,405.4	21,421.9	21,318.0	21,197.7	21,109.2	21,074.1	21,148.2	21,249.5	21,339.9	21,420.3	0.09	0.88
Venezuela	2,924.4	2,934.6	2,942.2	2,947.2	2,949.7	2,949.9	2,948.0	2,944.2	2,938.6	2,931.7	2,923.6	0.00	-0.03
Vietnam	7,897.4	7,888.4	7,886.7	7,886.5	7,884.4	7,875.5	7,856.5	7,826.0	7,785.5	7,738.1	7,688.5	-0.27	-2.65

Key population trends

Table 4.9 Population Aged 5-9: 2009-2019

'000

	2009	2010	2011	2012	2013	2014	2015	2016	2017	2018	2019	Period CAGR	Period growth
Algeria	3,052.9	3,120.0	3,189.5	3,256.4	3,318.4	3,374.6	3,425.6	3,471.8	3,512.8	3,547.7	3,575.5	1.59	17.12
Argentina	3,346.8	3,340.1	3,344.1	3,358.3	3,379.6	3,403.5	3,425.5	3,442.6	3,453.5	3,458.2	3,457.2	0.32	3.30
Australia	1,354.5	1,359.6	1,373.3	1,396.8	1,429.5	1,467.6	1,505.6	1,534.2	1,559.6	1,578.0	1,590.6	1.62	17.43
Austria	411.1	412.9	412.2	413.7	411.9	411.1	408.1	407.1	406.4	406.3	406.6	-0.11	-1.11
Azerbaijan	643.2	654.4	672.0	694.5	719.7	744.8	767.2	785.2	798.1	805.8	808.6	2.32	25.72
Belarus	451.5	448.7	446.9	453.0	469.0	488.7	508.6	524.1	532.9	534.2	530.3	1.62	17.46
Belgium	588.5	592.0	595.4	602.1	612.1	622.0	628.9	634.3	637.5	639.0	638.9	0.83	8.57
Bolivia	1,198.7	1,207.3	1,213.5	1,217.0	1,218.3	1,218.0	1,217.0	1,215.9	1,214.9	1,213.9	1,212.6	0.12	1.16
Bosnia-Herzegovina	194.8	187.1	181.2	177.2	175.1	174.2	173.9	173.7	173.5	173.1	172.5	-1.21	-11.45
Brazil	17,464.1	17,294.8	17,030.7	16,695.8	16,313.4	15,901.4	15,480.1	15,064.0	14,665.6	14,297.4	13,964.8	-2.21	-20.04
Bulgaria	330.4	329.6	329.2	328.0	327.7	326.5	323.0	319.6	315.5	310.7	305.5	-0.78	-7.53
Canada	1,787.1	1,782.4	1,792.3	1,815.6	1,842.5	1,866.4	1,888.6	1,899.8	1,903.1	1,905.3	1,908.3	0.66	6.78
Chile	1,244.3	1,236.2	1,232.8	1,233.4	1,236.9	1,242.0	1,247.4	1,252.4	1,256.5	1,259.5	1,261.1	0.13	1.36
China	71,876.3	70,358.9	68,966.7	68,488.0	69,054.4	68,951.0	69,362.9	70,182.3	70,592.6	71,042.5	71,378.8	-0.07	-0.69
Colombia	4,412.5	4,419.8	4,430.5	4,443.9	4,457.7	4,469.2	4,475.7	4,475.8	4,469.5	4,458.2	4,444.3	0.07	0.72
Costa Rica	398.3	395.0	390.8	385.8	380.7	376.7	374.6	374.9	377.5	381.6	385.9	-0.32	-3.11
Croatia	214.9	208.7	206.5	207.7	210.2	213.3	216.0	216.8	217.6	218.3	218.8	0.18	1.81
Czech Republic	463.4	474.3	488.5	500.3	510.3	519.2	524.1	524.3	524.3	524.1	523.7	1.23	13.01
Denmark	331.1	329.4	326.8	326.9	327.0	327.3	326.3	324.8	321.7	319.1	315.6	-0.48	-4.67
Ecuador	1,424.6	1,414.2	1,403.2	1,392.2	1,381.6	1,371.6	1,362.6	1,354.6	1,347.8	1,342.2	1,337.6	-0.63	-6.11
Egypt	8,612.2	8,843.1	9,068.9	9,265.1	9,434.5	9,577.4	9,692.9	9,781.7	9,866.6	9,940.7	10,001.0	1.51	16.13
Estonia	63.2	65.0	66.4	68.3	70.0	71.8	72.9	73.8	74.5	75.2	75.7	1.82	19.77
Finland	286.8	287.6	289.2	292.6	296.0	298.9	300.7	302.8	303.8	305.3	306.5	0.67	6.85
France	3,869.2	3,881.9	3,872.2	3,891.3	3,911.3	3,945.8	3,982.3	3,996.3	3,985.1	3,982.0	3,962.6	0.24	2.41
Germany	3,717.0	3,645.6	3,560.2	3,497.9	3,462.3	3,438.9	3,401.0	3,340.4	3,273.9	3,192.2	3,111.3	-1.76	-16.30
Greece	520.9	528.0	534.7	541.7	547.9	553.0	556.9	558.5	558.5	557.0	554.0	0.62	6.36
Hong Kong, China	274.1	270.1	272.4	286.6	298.5	312.5	324.4	328.2	328.5	329.1	330.2	1.88	20.46
Hungary	480.9	482.8	483.2	486.4	489.2	493.3	495.9	495.3	492.2	489.1	486.3	0.11	1.12
India	122,009.0	122,088.6	122,004.5	121,755.2	121,381.1	120,949.2	120,525.7	120,151.9	119,832.3	119,540.5	119,229.5	-0.23	-2.28
Indonesia	20,922.7	20,977.4	20,976.4	20,916.4	20,803.6	20,651.2	20,474.2	20,283.0	20,082.6	19,874.0	19,655.8	-0.62	-6.05
Iran	5,648.4	5,856.2	6,061.3	6,247.2	6,404.5	6,530.2	6,626.0	6,694.7	6,737.9	6,757.6	6,757.1	1.81	19.63
Ireland	305.7	311.9	316.8	322.4	323.7	322.7	321.7	321.7	320.9	319.5	317.3	0.37	3.80
Israel	708.3	717.3	723.7	727.7	726.9	723.2	720.0	716.9	713.5	709.9	705.9	-0.03	-0.34
Italy	2,764.4	2,785.6	2,787.2	2,790.1	2,786.1	2,767.5	2,732.9	2,699.0	2,659.9	2,617.5	2,573.0	-0.71	-6.92
Japan	5,692.7	5,553.2	5,457.2	5,388.5	5,361.5	5,374.4	5,374.0	5,324.7	5,239.4	5,121.2	4,967.6	-1.35	-12.74
Jordan	715.8	720.1	726.5	735.0	744.7	754.6	763.6	770.5	774.7	776.3	775.4	0.80	8.33
Kazakhstan	1,145.3	1,199.2	1,262.9	1,332.7	1,403.0	1,466.7	1,517.9	1,552.3	1,569.0	1,570.3	1,560.8	3.14	36.28
Kuwait	188.9	192.5	196.6	201.1	205.6	209.8	213.2	215.6	217.0	217.5	217.3	1.41	15.04
Latvia	98.8	99.9	101.3	103.6	105.9	107.5	110.1	111.9	113.5	114.8	115.8	1.60	17.18
Lithuania	159.0	153.6	150.6	149.9	150.6	151.0	151.7	152.5	153.5	154.4	155.4	-0.23	-2.27
Malaysia	2,978.4	3,009.6	3,035.0	3,056.3	3,067.9	3,056.9	3,025.6	2,994.5	2,962.6	2,952.0	2,960.2	-0.06	-0.61
Mexico	10,326.8	10,310.4	10,284.9	10,235.2	10,167.7	10,088.8	10,004.2	9,917.4	9,828.6	9,737.0	9,641.8	-0.68	-6.63
Morocco	2,939.2	2,936.4	2,947.6	2,972.0	3,005.9	3,044.0	3,081.2	3,114.0	3,140.4	3,159.9	3,172.3	0.77	7.93
Netherlands	1,008.2	997.7	976.6	957.0	936.7	915.6	899.8	889.2	880.1	873.5	869.3	-1.47	-13.77
New Zealand	288.6	287.4	288.9	295.1	303.5	310.3	317.2	321.7	323.0	321.2	318.8	1.00	10.45
Nigeria	21,571.6	22,029.7	22,488.3	22,941.4	23,378.0	23,784.0	24,147.4	24,460.8	24,722.1	24,933.2	25,099.3	1.53	16.35
Norway	298.9	299.0	298.7	302.1	306.1	310.5	314.6	318.4	320.5	322.9	323.7	0.80	8.28
Pakistan	21,994.3	22,300.6	22,623.6	22,960.8	23,309.4	23,666.6	24,029.4	24,395.0	24,756.1	25,097.3	25,399.6	1.45	15.48
Peru	2,925.0	2,928.5	2,932.4	2,936.1	2,938.4	2,938.0	2,933.7	2,924.8	2,911.7	2,895.4	2,877.4	-0.16	-1.63
Philippines	10,301.8	10,380.8	10,470.9	10,575.0	10,686.4	10,798.0	10,899.7	10,985.5	11,054.0	11,108.1	11,153.7	0.80	8.27
Poland	1,815.5	1,787.3	1,771.5	1,770.7	1,781.7	1,799.1	1,815.1	1,827.1	1,842.8	1,860.0	1,876.5	0.33	3.36
Portugal	561.1	557.4	556.9	554.8	551.0	548.6	548.6	547.3	544.2	539.5	533.5	-0.50	-4.91
Romania	1,068.8	1,057.5	1,051.6	1,057.5	1,068.3	1,076.4	1,078.8	1,074.3	1,066.9	1,057.5	1,046.6	-0.21	-2.08
Russia	6,661.1	6,914.5	7,095.5	7,295.8	7,534.2	7,790.9	8,062.4	8,299.6	8,527.1	8,650.8	8,683.9	2.69	30.37
Saudi Arabia	2,796.6	2,819.6	2,836.0	2,845.7	2,851.0	2,855.5	2,862.9	2,875.4	2,893.2	2,915.1	2,938.5	0.50	5.08
Singapore	277.5	271.2	261.9	258.0	255.1	254.2	254.4	255.1	256.2	257.4	259.0	-0.69	-6.67
Slovakia	262.2	259.9	260.1	263.1	266.5	269.0	269.4	269.2	269.2	269.2	269.3	0.27	2.69
Slovenia	90.8	91.6	91.8	92.7	93.6	95.2	96.1	97.0	98.1	99.0	99.9	0.96	10.07
South Africa	5,138.4	5,158.2	5,163.4	5,154.5	5,135.6	5,113.4	5,094.3	5,081.4	5,074.5	5,071.1	5,066.7	-0.14	-1.40
South Korea	2,691.3	2,517.3	2,364.5	2,279.8	2,230.9	2,193.1	2,177.9	2,167.4	2,144.4	2,116.4	2,084.8	-2.52	-22.54
Spain	2,236.4	2,299.4	2,349.6	2,404.8	2,461.1	2,499.8	2,534.4	2,565.2	2,576.7	2,582.3	2,581.7	1.45	15.44
Sweden	485.7	498.6	509.4	519.7	526.1	529.6	531.9	534.3	536.8	539.2	541.8	1.10	11.55
Switzerland	375.6	371.7	370.7	370.3	369.8	370.1	369.3	369.1	369.0	369.7	371.4	-0.11	-1.10
Taiwan	1,319.8	1,255.3	1,157.3	1,106.9	1,064.9	1,041.3	1,027.5	1,022.8	1,018.0	1,013.3	1,007.6	-2.66	-23.66
Thailand	4,201.0	4,176.8	4,185.5	4,190.8	4,199.1	4,179.0	4,161.7	4,145.5	4,118.4	4,073.1	4,011.8	-0.46	-4.50
Tunisia	763.0	762.4	765.0	770.3	777.6	786.2	795.3	804.4	813.2	821.0	827.4	0.81	8.44
Turkey	6,844.3	6,702.3	6,572.5	6,503.8	6,462.9	6,440.5	6,433.4	6,394.0	6,380.6	6,378.8	6,384.6	-0.69	-6.72
Turkmenistan	492.2	499.9	506.1	510.1	512.1	513.0	513.5	514.3	515.4	516.7	517.8	0.51	5.20
Ukraine	1,922.8	1,955.5	1,991.8	2,070.6	2,133.0	2,172.1	2,187.9	2,196.9	2,162.8	2,119.2	2,066.7	0.72	7.49
United Arab Emirates	307.3	315.7	320.5	322.1	321.4	320.0	319.5	320.3	322.7	325.9	329.1	0.69	7.10
United Kingdom	3,397.4	3,414.6	3,460.7	3,535.3	3,631.0	3,730.2	3,820.6	3,879.3	3,925.0	3,949.4	3,957.8	1.54	16.50
USA	20,376.7	20,623.7	20,754.8	21,045.7	21,339.7	21,561.3	21,743.1	21,771.4	21,671.5	21,551.8	21,464.0	0.52	5.34
Venezuela	2,837.3	2,855.0	2,872.2	2,888.5	2,903.4	2,916.3	2,926.9	2,935.0	2,940.5	2,943.6	2,944.2	0.37	3.77
Vietnam	7,773.8	7,844.0	7,878.4	7,888.6	7,881.8	7,872.0	7,868.8	7,872.7	7,877.5	7,879.6	7,873.5	0.13	1.28

Key population trends

Table 4.10 Population Aged 10-14: 2009-2019

'000

	2009	2010	2011	2012	2013	2014	2015	2016	2017	2018	2019	CAGR	Period growth
Algeria	3,089.2	3,011.9	2,973.2	2,972.7	3,003.5	3,054.4	3,115.2	3,179.1	3,242.5	3,303.2	3,360.1	0.84	8.77
Argentina	3,443.4	3,424.6	3,402.6	3,379.7	3,359.5	3,345.8	3,341.5	3,347.4	3,362.4	3,383.1	3,406.4	-0.11	-1.07
Australia	1,404.3	1,401.5	1,401.8	1,400.5	1,402.0	1,405.4	1,411.9	1,428.2	1,453.4	1,487.0	1,525.7	0.83	8.65
Austria	461.2	449.4	440.9	429.3	424.6	421.2	423.1	422.3	423.7	421.8	420.8	-0.91	-8.74
Azerbaijan	717.1	684.4	659.9	644.5	638.7	641.8	652.9	670.5	693.1	718.2	742.7	0.35	3.57
Belarus	481.2	466.1	460.1	457.7	458.3	454.7	451.7	449.7	456.1	472.2	492.6	0.23	2.37
Belgium	602.1	600.4	601.2	599.4	595.9	595.2	598.7	602.2	609.1	619.3	629.4	0.44	4.53
Bolivia	1,132.2	1,139.2	1,147.7	1,157.4	1,167.7	1,177.1	1,184.9	1,190.5	1,193.8	1,195.3	1,195.6	0.55	5.61
Bosnia-Herzegovina	223.6	221.4	216.9	210.4	202.6	194.7	187.9	182.6	179.1	176.9	175.7	-2.38	-21.44
Brazil	17,005.0	17,155.6	17,305.7	17,418.8	17,462.3	17,407.6	17,246.6	16,989.6	16,660.9	16,283.0	15,873.0	-0.69	-6.66
Bulgaria	321.9	316.3	315.9	316.4	322.4	327.5	326.8	326.6	325.5	325.3	324.1	0.07	0.68
Canada	1,995.4	1,959.4	1,915.2	1,877.8	1,854.7	1,845.5	1,838.4	1,848.2	1,872.3	1,900.4	1,925.6	-0.36	-3.50
Chile	1,365.1	1,332.2	1,303.1	1,279.1	1,260.4	1,247.1	1,238.9	1,235.2	1,235.6	1,238.9	1,243.6	-0.93	-8.90
China	85,438.7	82,137.5	79,373.7	77,310.7	74,561.0	74,518.8	73,450.7	72,482.7	72,514.3	73,650.6	74,087.1	-1.42	-13.29
Colombia	4,405.3	4,400.3	4,396.0	4,393.9	4,394.9	4,399.6	4,408.0	4,419.5	4,432.8	4,445.7	4,455.5	0.11	1.14
Costa Rica	413.1	410.3	408.0	406.0	403.9	401.1	397.4	392.8	387.7	383.0	379.7	-0.84	-8.09
Croatia	253.8	250.9	245.9	235.3	224.7	216.1	210.0	207.6	208.9	211.2	214.3	-1.68	-15.58
Czech Republic	479.5	462.6	457.8	460.1	464.0	469.0	479.1	492.7	504.6	514.7	523.8	0.89	9.24
Denmark	350.1	345.1	341.2	337.9	333.9	332.0	330.4	327.9	328.0	328.2	328.5	-0.63	-6.16
Ecuador	1,424.5	1,429.3	1,430.7	1,428.6	1,423.5	1,415.8	1,406.5	1,396.2	1,385.5	1,374.8	1,364.8	-0.43	-4.19
Egypt	7,849.9	8,035.7	8,237.6	8,456.9	8,691.5	8,935.0	9,179.8	9,418.7	9,625.1	9,802.5	9,951.3	2.40	26.77
Estonia	62.4	61.1	61.1	60.9	61.7	62.8	64.6	65.9	67.9	69.6	71.5	1.37	14.62
Finland	309.3	302.3	296.5	292.4	289.3	289.7	290.4	291.9	295.2	298.5	301.3	-0.26	-2.58
France	3,685.7	3,725.0	3,777.5	3,818.6	3,860.4	3,891.3	3,904.0	3,895.4	3,915.0	3,935.3	3,970.1	0.75	7.72
Germany	3,974.5	3,952.7	3,940.6	3,875.1	3,781.6	3,701.5	3,636.9	3,556.9	3,497.4	3,463.3	3,440.8	-1.43	-13.43
Greece	538.0	531.2	526.7	525.1	526.7	533.1	540.2	547.0	554.1	560.2	565.4	0.50	5.09
Hong Kong, China	381.5	362.1	345.0	322.4	310.7	302.5	298.8	302.0	318.3	330.3	344.3	-1.02	-9.75
Hungary	524.2	505.6	493.8	486.3	484.5	483.2	484.7	484.7	487.9	490.6	494.7	-0.58	-5.64
India	120,302.0	120,440.4	120,628.4	120,856.6	121,078.1	121,228.8	121,254.7	121,133.8	120,880.8	120,539.6	120,167.2	-0.01	-0.11
Indonesia	20,454.0	20,499.3	20,577.5	20,678.2	20,781.6	20,863.4	20,904.2	20,893.4	20,830.5	20,722.5	20,581.0	0.06	0.62
Iran	5,619.6	5,378.9	5,276.4	5,303.6	5,429.8	5,613.1	5,816.4	6,016.5	6,201.5	6,363.2	6,497.0	1.46	15.61
Ireland	285.3	291.2	295.6	298.0	303.1	309.1	314.8	319.6	325.2	326.4	325.3	1.32	14.03
Israel	648.0	662.9	676.8	689.7	703.2	715.7	724.5	730.8	734.8	733.7	729.5	1.19	12.57
Italy	2,740.0	2,743.6	2,762.7	2,773.7	2,786.3	2,803.2	2,824.6	2,826.3	2,829.4	2,825.5	2,807.0	0.24	2.45
Japan	5,955.6	5,925.1	5,897.5	5,851.0	5,768.4	5,674.8	5,540.2	5,447.4	5,380.4	5,354.4	5,368.0	-1.03	-9.87
Jordan	701.6	705.4	706.6	706.4	706.2	707.8	712.5	720.4	730.7	742.2	753.2	0.71	7.37
Kazakhstan	1,137.9	1,106.1	1,092.8	1,099.0	1,124.5	1,166.9	1,223.0	1,289.4	1,361.4	1,432.1	1,494.4	2.76	31.33
Kuwait	174.7	177.9	181.0	184.0	187.1	190.5	194.3	198.5	203.0	207.5	211.4	1.93	21.05
Latvia	98.9	94.8	93.7	93.7	94.9	97.5	98.6	99.9	102.3	104.6	106.5	0.74	7.63
Lithuania	189.8	184.4	177.8	170.8	163.8	158.2	152.8	149.9	149.1	149.8	150.2	-2.31	-20.84
Malaysia	2,791.5	2,837.6	2,880.2	2,920.9	2,948.4	2,976.4	3,004.4	3,026.3	3,044.7	3,053.6	3,039.4	0.85	8.88
Mexico	10,484.3	10,431.3	10,390.5	10,349.2	10,309.2	10,268.3	10,222.7	10,170.5	10,111.3	10,046.1	9,977.4	-0.49	-4.84
Morocco	3,066.7	3,028.1	2,992.0	2,960.9	2,937.6	2,925.4	2,926.1	2,940.1	2,965.5	2,998.8	3,035.0	-0.10	-1.04
Netherlands	979.0	981.0	993.3	1,002.6	1,008.6	1,007.0	997.0	975.9	956.2	935.6	914.3	-0.68	-6.61
New Zealand	298.2	296.7	295.1	293.1	291.5	292.5	291.3	292.8	299.1	307.4	314.4	0.53	5.42
Nigeria	18,823.0	19,237.6	19,663.7	20,101.2	20,549.1	21,005.4	21,466.4	21,927.6	22,381.4	22,816.8	23,221.0	2.12	23.36
Norway	314.8	315.7	315.9	312.9	309.8	309.6	309.0	308.3	311.3	315.0	319.3	0.14	1.44
Pakistan	20,648.0	20,841.0	21,061.4	21,308.0	21,577.9	21,867.1	22,173.1	22,495.0	22,833.1	23,186.1	23,551.3	1.32	14.06
Peru	2,918.0	2,918.3	2,918.8	2,919.9	2,921.8	2,924.5	2,927.6	2,931.0	2,933.8	2,934.8	2,932.7	0.05	0.50
Philippines	10,089.1	10,142.9	10,186.1	10,227.9	10,275.0	10,336.8	10,416.9	10,516.3	10,630.9	10,752.6	10,870.9	0.75	7.75
Poland	2,123.5	2,038.4	1,974.3	1,909.1	1,853.4	1,809.8	1,782.4	1,767.5	1,766.6	1,777.5	1,794.6	-1.67	-15.49
Portugal	539.5	547.2	549.9	555.0	563.0	568.5	564.6	563.9	561.7	557.8	555.2	0.29	2.90
Romania	1,114.4	1,105.4	1,104.4	1,097.4	1,083.5	1,066.5	1,054.9	1,048.7	1,054.0	1,064.5	1,072.1	-0.39	-3.80
Russia	6,773.2	6,593.1	6,483.8	6,452.6	6,566.6	6,741.0	6,991.4	7,177.4	7,378.6	7,620.7	7,881.3	1.53	16.36
Saudi Arabia	2,671.0	2,689.4	2,711.3	2,736.0	2,761.3	2,784.4	2,802.9	2,816.1	2,824.7	2,830.9	2,837.8	0.61	6.24
Singapore	314.7	310.3	306.5	297.6	288.6	280.6	273.0	262.6	257.7	253.9	252.3	-2.19	-19.83
Slovakia	301.1	290.9	283.8	274.6	267.1	262.0	259.6	259.6	262.6	265.8	268.2	-1.15	-10.93
Slovenia	95.9	94.2	93.8	92.7	92.3	91.9	92.6	92.7	93.6	94.7	96.3	0.04	0.37
South Africa	4,978.1	4,993.9	5,015.3	5,039.9	5,063.9	5,083.0	5,094.3	5,096.0	5,089.4	5,078.0	5,066.5	0.18	1.78
South Korea	3,272.2	3,188.1	3,088.1	2,948.7	2,797.8	2,653.6	2,482.2	2,331.6	2,248.3	2,200.2	2,163.0	-4.06	-33.90
Spain	2,080.0	2,101.2	2,140.6	2,193.2	2,247.1	2,314.7	2,375.8	2,425.7	2,481.1	2,537.7	2,576.7	2.16	23.88
Sweden	515.0	493.8	483.4	481.3	487.9	498.2	511.1	521.6	531.8	538.0	541.5	0.50	5.14
Switzerland	414.9	409.1	401.8	393.0	386.4	380.1	376.1	374.9	374.5	373.8	373.9	-1.03	-9.87
Taiwan	1,559.2	1,519.2	1,500.5	1,435.1	1,357.9	1,317.5	1,253.0	1,155.3	1,104.7	1,062.6	1,039.0	-3.98	-33.37
Thailand	4,880.9	4,746.7	4,552.3	4,378.9	4,278.5	4,268.0	4,243.6	4,254.9	4,260.0	4,268.9	4,247.2	-1.38	-12.98
Tunisia	835.2	810.9	791.5	777.2	768.0	763.2	762.2	764.5	769.6	776.8	785.2	-0.61	-5.98
Turkey	7,111.9	7,146.6	7,150.3	7,082.6	6,981.1	6,863.3	6,737.3	6,623.1	6,557.0	6,513.0	6,477.9	-0.93	-8.91
Turkmenistan	495.4	483.9	478.4	478.8	483.3	489.7	496.0	500.9	504.3	506.3	507.6	0.24	2.46
Ukraine	2,277.5	2,162.4	2,062.2	1,968.5	1,922.6	1,909.9	1,938.6	1,970.2	2,043.8	2,103.0	2,141.5	-0.61	-5.97
United Arab Emirates	266.7	277.8	289.3	300.5	310.5	318.3	323.7	326.5	327.3	326.9	326.5	2.04	22.43
United Kingdom	3,637.2	3,582.7	3,519.1	3,448.5	3,395.6	3,382.2	3,402.5	3,453.6	3,531.9	3,629.5	3,729.0	0.25	2.52
USA	19,947.2	19,905.9	20,077.8	20,278.6	20,537.9	20,851.3	21,115.0	21,268.7	21,580.3	21,892.4	22,130.4	1.04	10.95
Venezuela	2,758.7	2,770.5	2,784.5	2,800.4	2,817.5	2,835.3	2,852.9	2,870.1	2,886.3	2,901.1	2,914.0	0.55	5.63
Vietnam	7,842.6	7,634.3	7,547.7	7,565.5	7,652.3	7,753.5	7,828.8	7,868.1	7,882.9	7,879.9	7,872.3	0.04	0.38

Key population trends

Table 4.11 Population Aged 15-19: 2009-2019

'000

	2009	2010	2011	2012	2013	2014	2015	2016	2017	2018	2019	CAGR	Period growth
Algeria	3,611.7	3,528.5	3,420.5	3,295.8	3,169.6	3,060.3	2,982.7	2,944.2	2,944.0	2,975.0	3,026.5	-1.75	-16.20
Argentina	3,455.6	3,464.7	3,467.7	3,464.8	3,456.2	3,442.3	3,423.9	3,402.2	3,379.4	3,359.1	3,343.9	-0.33	-3.23
Australia	1,483.7	1,487.9	1,484.5	1,482.4	1,479.5	1,478.5	1,477.2	1,480.3	1,480.7	1,483.1	1,486.7	0.02	0.20
Austria	505.9	505.5	501.5	495.8	486.8	475.8	464.0	455.4	443.5	438.6	435.0	-1.50	-14.00
Azerbaijan	895.5	867.6	832.0	791.1	749.1	710.0	677.5	653.4	638.7	633.5	637.0	-3.35	-28.87
Belarus	665.9	621.2	579.9	542.8	506.4	484.3	468.9	462.6	460.6	461.0	458.0	-3.67	-31.21
Belgium	650.0	643.9	634.1	624.0	615.5	609.9	608.2	608.9	607.2	603.6	602.9	-0.75	-7.25
Bolivia	1,055.8	1,073.7	1,087.2	1,096.6	1,103.5	1,109.7	1,116.7	1,125.2	1,135.1	1,145.5	1,155.2	0.90	9.41
Bosnia-Herzegovina	244.9	234.8	228.6	225.9	225.1	224.6	222.4	218.0	211.4	203.4	195.4	-2.23	-20.21
Brazil	16,677.2	16,591.1	16,607.0	16,683.4	16,791.0	16,922.9	17,081.2	17,237.8	17,356.7	17,404.5	17,352.0	0.40	4.05
Bulgaria	440.0	411.4	381.4	359.3	335.1	316.6	310.5	309.6	309.6	315.2	319.8	-3.14	-27.31
Canada	2,219.7	2,204.0	2,181.5	2,148.4	2,112.0	2,073.9	2,034.0	1,987.5	1,948.8	1,925.0	1,915.9	-1.46	-13.68
Chile	1,496.6	1,484.1	1,462.7	1,433.7	1,400.1	1,365.3	1,332.4	1,303.5	1,279.5	1,261.0	1,247.8	-1.80	-16.62
China	99,163.0	91,402.7	87,498.2	83,387.1	80,529.3	77,286.2	74,890.0	72,928.4	71,569.8	69,557.3	70,003.7	-3.42	-29.41
Colombia	4,331.9	4,356.0	4,371.1	4,377.8	4,378.3	4,375.1	4,371.0	4,367.6	4,365.8	4,366.8	4,371.3	0.09	0.91
Costa Rica	438.0	433.4	428.9	424.6	420.8	417.5	414.7	412.4	410.5	408.5	405.9	-0.76	-7.34
Croatia	259.9	256.7	254.2	253.5	256.0	254.6	251.7	246.6	236.1	225.5	217.0	-1.79	-16.52
Czech Republic	637.3	617.9	584.8	546.7	515.5	484.7	467.0	461.5	463.9	468.0	473.4	-2.93	-25.71
Denmark	342.9	349.9	354.9	357.0	355.5	353.2	348.4	344.6	341.4	337.5	335.7	-0.21	-2.12
Ecuador	1,335.4	1,344.2	1,355.9	1,369.7	1,383.6	1,395.4	1,403.3	1,406.5	1,405.1	1,400.0	1,392.1	0.42	4.25
Egypt	7,560.9	7,477.7	7,452.3	7,484.9	7,582.3	7,736.0	7,924.0	8,129.4	8,353.8	8,595.1	8,846.7	1.58	17.00
Estonia	89.5	81.2	74.1	69.2	64.5	61.8	60.5	60.5	60.3	61.1	62.3	-3.56	-30.37
Finland	333.1	334.4	331.5	326.7	319.5	311.8	304.7	298.7	294.6	291.5	291.8	-1.32	-12.42
France	3,831.4	3,772.7	3,732.0	3,706.0	3,685.1	3,708.8	3,747.9	3,801.2	3,842.7	3,884.8	3,915.9	0.22	2.21
Germany	4,475.1	4,300.2	4,106.9	4,028.1	3,999.5	3,968.7	3,953.8	3,946.8	3,884.1	3,792.7	3,713.7	-1.85	-17.02
Greece	576.0	574.7	568.7	563.3	557.9	551.8	545.2	540.7	539.2	540.7	547.0	-0.51	-5.03
Hong Kong, China	438.2	434.4	430.8	426.6	413.6	396.5	376.7	359.1	336.8	325.4	317.6	-3.17	-27.53
Hungary	611.4	602.4	588.2	567.9	546.9	528.1	509.4	497.2	489.7	487.9	486.6	-2.26	-20.41
India	117,122.6	118,089.9	118,753.8	119,145.7	119,349.5	119,474.7	119,613.6	119,810.9	120,058.3	120,307.1	120,488.1	0.28	2.87
Indonesia	20,478.0	20,432.4	20,388.2	20,350.9	20,330.9	20,339.7	20,384.8	20,465.7	20,571.8	20,682.3	20,771.7	0.14	1.43
Iran	7,731.0	7,236.4	6,734.9	6,254.6	5,831.6	5,503.4	5,296.5	5,220.4	5,265.2	5,402.7	5,593.3	-3.18	-27.65
Ireland	283.2	279.1	275.0	273.8	276.2	281.6	287.1	291.4	293.9	299.0	304.9	0.74	7.69
Israel	596.2	605.1	615.9	627.3	640.0	654.6	669.6	683.8	697.0	710.8	723.5	1.95	21.36
Italy	2,924.9	2,899.6	2,860.7	2,828.7	2,793.8	2,782.4	2,786.2	2,805.7	2,816.8	2,829.5	2,846.4	-0.27	-2.68
Japan	6,074.6	6,037.5	6,010.2	5,987.9	5,992.3	5,965.1	5,939.7	5,915.9	5,871.5	5,790.6	5,698.2	-0.64	-6.20
Jordan	667.5	677.1	683.4	687.0	688.6	689.4	690.4	691.9	693.9	697.1	702.0	0.50	5.17
Kazakhstan	1,446.7	1,388.6	1,324.6	1,259.3	1,199.2	1,150.9	1,119.5	1,107.3	1,115.0	1,141.6	1,184.9	-1.98	-18.10
Kuwait	165.5	167.9	170.6	173.7	176.8	179.9	182.9	185.8	188.7	191.7	195.1	1.66	17.89
Latvia	155.7	143.3	129.8	116.9	104.9	97.4	93.3	92.2	92.3	93.6	96.4	-4.68	-38.09
Lithuania	253.7	242.0	228.0	213.5	197.9	187.9	182.5	176.0	169.1	162.2	156.8	-4.70	-38.21
Malaysia	2,628.3	2,653.6	2,681.3	2,711.9	2,749.3	2,789.3	2,833.9	2,874.8	2,914.3	2,940.6	2,968.5	1.22	12.94
Mexico	10,257.1	10,344.7	10,397.4	10,403.0	10,374.9	10,329.1	10,279.0	10,231.9	10,189.1	10,150.0	10,112.6	-0.14	-1.41
Morocco	3,205.0	3,174.2	3,140.1	3,103.5	3,065.5	3,027.2	2,989.9	2,954.9	2,924.5	2,901.7	2,889.8	-1.03	-9.84
Netherlands	1,007.7	1,010.4	999.7	989.0	982.6	984.3	986.8	999.6	1,009.1	1,015.0	1,013.4	0.06	0.57
New Zealand	322.9	321.1	316.6	312.2	308.4	305.1	303.6	302.1	300.1	298.6	299.6	-0.75	-7.22
Nigeria	16,538.7	16,886.0	17,245.8	17,618.9	18,005.4	18,405.1	18,817.1	19,240.6	19,674.9	20,119.3	20,572.2	2.21	24.39
Norway	319.2	322.1	323.2	324.7	325.6	325.6	325.9	325.7	322.5	319.4	319.1	0.00	-0.03
Pakistan	19,850.3	19,935.2	20,034.7	20,158.2	20,309.1	20,486.5	20,687.5	20,911.7	21,160.0	21,431.2	21,723.2	0.91	9.43
Peru	2,872.2	2,883.1	2,890.8	2,895.6	2,898.5	2,900.1	2,901.2	2,902.3	2,903.6	2,905.5	2,908.2	0.12	1.25
Philippines	9,667.1	9,784.8	9,880.9	9,960.7	10,026.4	10,083.9	10,135.8	10,185.1	10,235.9	10,294.0	10,365.7	0.70	7.23
Poland	2,621.6	2,528.6	2,416.3	2,306.7	2,207.7	2,115.1	2,030.8	1,967.8	1,902.6	1,846.9	1,803.4	-3.67	-31.21
Portugal	573.6	565.4	558.7	552.3	547.7	546.1	553.7	556.3	561.3	569.3	574.7	0.02	0.19
Romania	1,371.4	1,262.8	1,192.2	1,152.9	1,121.0	1,110.8	1,101.4	1,099.9	1,092.8	1,078.9	1,061.9	-2.53	-22.57
Russia	9,278.5	8,522.0	7,850.9	7,354.2	6,970.3	6,844.1	6,661.8	6,558.5	6,529.8	6,647.4	6,823.8	-3.03	-26.46
Saudi Arabia	2,524.7	2,562.9	2,590.4	2,608.6	2,621.4	2,633.5	2,648.6	2,668.6	2,692.7	2,718.6	2,742.7	0.83	8.63
Singapore	335.4	336.6	333.4	331.2	326.1	318.5	312.9	308.2	297.9	287.4	278.3	-1.85	-17.03
Slovakia	381.0	367.7	350.0	332.5	316.5	300.6	290.3	283.0	273.7	266.1	260.8	-3.72	-31.54
Slovenia	109.3	105.9	102.9	100.4	98.7	97.0	95.2	94.7	93.6	93.3	92.9	-1.60	-14.92
South Africa	5,016.9	4,996.5	4,973.1	4,949.7	4,930.5	4,920.0	4,920.6	4,932.5	4,953.0	4,977.6	5,001.2	-0.03	-0.31
South Korea	3,350.4	3,402.3	3,413.5	3,378.7	3,307.1	3,215.7	3,133.3	3,035.0	2,898.1	2,750.0	2,608.5	-2.47	-22.14
Spain	2,237.5	2,214.7	2,190.0	2,170.5	2,158.9	2,159.6	2,178.9	2,218.1	2,270.4	2,324.1	2,391.4	0.67	6.88
Sweden	638.6	633.5	612.7	585.0	555.4	530.4	508.9	498.1	495.6	501.8	512.0	-2.19	-19.84
Switzerland	451.2	448.4	442.7	437.0	429.3	423.8	417.8	410.2	401.1	394.3	387.7	-1.50	-14.06
Taiwan	1,605.9	1,617.5	1,606.9	1,610.7	1,613.4	1,553.9	1,514.0	1,495.6	1,429.8	1,352.6	1,312.3	-2.00	-18.28
Thailand	5,011.0	5,050.8	5,089.8	5,102.7	5,053.5	4,949.0	4,812.2	4,615.9	4,438.0	4,335.6	4,323.8	-1.46	-13.71
Tunisia	981.9	953.9	923.6	892.0	861.1	832.7	808.4	789.0	774.8	765.6	760.9	-2.52	-22.51
Turkey	6,600.1	6,729.0	6,851.9	6,966.1	7,062.6	7,135.6	7,172.3	7,177.7	7,105.8	7,000.7	6,882.7	0.42	4.28
Turkmenistan	571.1	560.9	545.8	527.3	508.1	491.4	479.9	474.5	475.0	479.6	486.1	-1.60	-14.88
Ukraine	3,026.8	2,849.8	2,685.6	2,534.4	2,391.1	2,269.0	2,154.1	2,053.2	1,959.4	1,912.2	1,898.7	-4.56	-37.27
United Arab Emirates	238.8	244.0	254.9	270.1	287.8	305.6	322.0	336.2	347.9	357.2	364.1	4.31	52.49
United Kingdom	3,974.5	3,927.4	3,856.9	3,787.7	3,734.2	3,685.7	3,634.2	3,575.5	3,508.2	3,456.7	3,443.1	-1.42	-13.37
USA	21,456.2	21,207.8	20,977.5	20,745.2	20,566.3	20,461.4	20,437.5	20,629.4	20,843.8	21,115.0	21,441.0	-0.01	-0.07
Venezuela	2,731.3	2,731.1	2,732.5	2,736.3	2,743.0	2,752.5	2,764.5	2,778.6	2,794.6	2,811.9	2,829.8	0.35	3.60
Vietnam	9,167.5	9,021.7	8,779.9	8,457.3	8,108.2	7,806.2	7,603.4	7,521.8	7,544.1	7,634.6	7,738.1	-1.68	-15.59

Key population trends

Table 4.12 Population Aged 20-24: 2009-2019

'000

	2009	2010	2011	2012	2013	2014	2015	2016	2017	2018	2019	CAGR	Period growth
Algeria	3,720.7	3,709.3	3,692.7	3,668.5	3,630.3	3,571.2	3,486.9	3,378.4	3,253.7	3,128.1	3,020.0	-2.06	-18.83
Argentina	3,324.5	3,356.9	3,387.1	3,413.6	3,435.2	3,451.0	3,460.6	3,464.1	3,461.4	3,452.7	3,438.9	0.34	3.44
Australia	1,551.0	1,567.5	1,582.8	1,600.2	1,615.9	1,624.7	1,630.2	1,629.7	1,629.4	1,627.5	1,626.7	0.48	4.88
Austria	517.5	516.4	518.0	522.6	527.3	529.6	529.2	524.9	519.0	509.6	498.2	-0.38	-3.73
Azerbaijan	892.5	908.0	915.1	913.1	902.3	882.6	854.7	819.7	779.7	738.3	699.7	-2.40	-21.60
Belarus	831.9	817.3	794.5	752.6	716.1	668.3	623.1	581.3	544.6	508.0	486.5	-5.22	-41.52
Belgium	638.9	645.3	655.7	664.1	670.5	669.9	663.7	653.9	643.8	635.3	629.7	-0.14	-1.44
Bolivia	904.2	928.4	953.7	979.2	1,003.6	1,025.2	1,042.8	1,056.2	1,065.7	1,072.8	1,079.3	1.79	19.36
Bosnia-Herzegovina	302.1	295.6	285.2	272.0	257.9	245.1	235.3	229.2	226.5	225.7	224.9	-2.91	-25.56
Brazil	17,698.2	17,433.8	17,182.5	16,930.3	16,712.5	16,547.1	16,471.2	16,495.2	16,578.3	16,690.8	16,825.1	-0.50	-4.93
Bulgaria	511.8	503.8	493.0	473.1	450.4	423.9	394.6	364.0	341.3	317.5	299.4	-5.22	-41.51
Canada	2,285.3	2,310.3	2,334.4	2,359.7	2,378.2	2,375.1	2,355.3	2,330.7	2,295.6	2,257.0	2,216.8	-0.30	-3.00
Chile	1,442.5	1,464.7	1,482.3	1,494.4	1,499.6	1,496.3	1,483.9	1,462.5	1,433.7	1,400.2	1,365.5	-0.55	-5.33
China	100,637.8	110,058.3	111,173.2	108,905.6	105,786.7	99,864.4	91,783.4	88,551.1	84,949.7	82,572.3	79,957.2	-2.27	-20.55
Colombia	4,073.1	4,113.6	4,155.5	4,197.5	4,236.7	4,270.2	4,295.5	4,311.5	4,318.8	4,319.6	4,316.5	0.58	5.98
Costa Rica	444.9	448.6	449.8	448.7	445.8	441.7	437.1	432.6	428.4	424.7	421.7	-0.53	-5.21
Croatia	289.9	282.2	276.5	273.4	267.3	262.5	259.3	256.8	256.0	258.5	257.0	-1.20	-11.37
Czech Republic	677.7	669.8	664.9	661.3	652.9	641.8	621.1	587.2	549.3	518.7	488.6	-3.22	-27.91
Denmark	315.7	322.5	330.4	337.8	348.1	355.2	362.4	367.4	369.4	368.0	365.8	1.48	15.88
Ecuador	1,220.4	1,229.4	1,239.7	1,251.3	1,264.4	1,278.7	1,294.0	1,309.8	1,325.5	1,339.8	1,351.4	1.02	10.73
Egypt	7,431.9	7,465.5	7,449.8	7,386.9	7,270.6	7,130.3	7,016.7	6,966.2	6,979.2	7,063.4	7,209.7	-0.30	-2.99
Estonia	106.3	106.2	105.1	101.4	96.0	88.3	80.0	72.9	68.1	63.5	60.9	-5.41	-42.68
Finland	324.6	323.5	326.7	331.4	337.9	339.0	340.1	337.0	332.1	324.7	316.9	-0.24	-2.39
France	3,949.9	3,980.2	3,994.1	3,983.2	3,960.8	3,899.3	3,841.0	3,801.4	3,775.5	3,754.5	3,777.9	-0.44	-4.35
Germany	4,920.0	4,961.2	5,007.8	4,937.7	4,817.2	4,656.0	4,491.4	4,307.2	4,233.1	4,207.1	4,177.1	-1.62	-15.10
Greece	647.6	624.7	613.2	603.9	600.6	591.1	589.9	584.0	578.6	573.1	567.1	-1.32	-12.44
Hong Kong, China	500.6	503.7	506.0	509.8	508.8	500.2	496.2	492.6	489.2	478.5	463.4	-0.77	-7.42
Hungary	650.0	645.3	638.0	633.8	629.5	621.4	612.1	597.5	577.3	556.5	538.0	-1.87	-17.23
India	108,493.3	110,104.0	111,721.8	113,298.4	114,753.1	115,997.1	116,966.9	117,643.8	118,061.7	118,302.7	118,470.4	0.88	9.20
Indonesia	20,603.8	20,517.0	20,437.9	20,369.6	20,311.2	20,260.5	20,215.3	20,176.1	20,147.7	20,139.2	20,159.8	-0.22	-2.15
Iran	9,327.9	9,141.7	8,864.5	8,508.1	8,088.6	7,626.7	7,142.8	6,655.9	6,190.5	5,780.9	5,463.4	-5.21	-41.43
Ireland	319.3	310.8	304.6	298.8	292.8	287.6	283.4	279.4	278.4	281.0	286.4	-1.08	-10.31
Israel	575.4	578.2	581.1	586.0	593.0	600.0	608.6	619.3	630.7	643.6	658.3	1.35	14.39
Italy	3,001.3	2,982.2	2,981.9	2,994.9	3,013.7	2,994.4	2,969.5	2,931.0	2,899.3	2,864.6	2,853.4	-0.50	-4.93
Japan	6,924.2	6,721.9	6,540.5	6,388.1	6,252.5	6,179.1	6,150.3	6,129.4	6,111.6	6,119.4	6,095.1	-1.27	-11.97
Jordan	639.3	645.2	647.6	647.4	646.4	646.6	649.1	654.1	660.8	668.3	675.4	0.55	5.65
Kazakhstan	1,549.7	1,567.8	1,567.0	1,547.2	1,511.1	1,462.2	1,404.4	1,340.9	1,275.7	1,214.8	1,165.1	-2.81	-24.82
Kuwait	196.3	194.4	193.4	193.5	194.4	195.8	197.3	199.0	200.7	202.6	204.6	0.42	4.27
Latvia	184.4	182.1	179.3	172.7	164.7	153.2	140.9	127.6	115.0	103.4	96.1	-6.31	-47.88
Lithuania	270.8	267.6	264.8	259.2	255.0	247.3	235.8	222.1	208.1	193.2	183.7	-3.80	-32.15
Malaysia	2,520.1	2,547.0	2,569.0	2,585.0	2,608.8	2,630.1	2,652.5	2,677.5	2,706.4	2,743.7	2,784.7	1.00	10.50
Mexico	9,251.5	9,370.2	9,522.5	9,686.1	9,846.6	9,984.8	10,085.0	10,139.6	10,150.2	10,127.1	10,086.0	0.87	9.02
Morocco	3,210.9	3,202.1	3,187.8	3,169.2	3,147.1	3,121.6	3,092.5	3,060.2	3,025.2	2,988.5	2,951.4	-0.84	-8.08
Netherlands	984.6	992.5	1,006.4	1,015.8	1,022.0	1,027.0	1,030.1	1,019.2	1,008.1	1,001.1	1,002.5	0.18	1.81
New Zealand	299.2	304.3	311.2	316.7	319.6	320.1	318.3	313.9	309.6	305.9	302.6	0.11	1.15
Nigeria	14,511.3	14,805.7	15,107.2	15,418.4	15,740.6	16,074.3	16,419.7	16,776.8	17,145.9	17,527.3	17,921.5	2.13	23.50
Norway	294.7	305.6	316.8	326.1	333.0	336.1	337.7	338.1	339.2	339.9	339.8	1.43	15.28
Pakistan	18,221.6	18,689.0	19,045.2	19,295.9	19,464.5	19,584.9	19,689.8	19,800.8	19,929.8	20,082.9	20,262.3	1.07	11.20
Peru	2,689.8	2,724.4	2,755.8	2,783.3	2,806.4	2,825.0	2,839.3	2,849.6	2,856.4	2,860.6	2,863.5	0.63	6.46
Philippines	8,783.9	8,968.8	9,140.3	9,300.3	9,446.9	9,580.4	9,699.2	9,802.6	9,891.2	9,966.8	10,032.3	1.34	14.21
Poland	3,079.7	2,954.6	2,844.1	2,763.2	2,682.1	2,592.5	2,499.9	2,388.9	2,280.9	2,184.0	2,093.9	-3.78	-32.01
Portugal	628.2	609.5	600.0	593.4	588.1	581.5	573.1	566.3	559.7	555.0	553.4	-1.26	-11.90
Romania	1,708.2	1,718.4	1,674.2	1,574.7	1,469.1	1,354.3	1,243.4	1,170.5	1,129.3	1,096.8	1,086.1	-4.43	-36.42
Russia	12,582.2	12,267.4	11,859.0	11,134.7	10,261.5	9,326.3	8,570.4	7,911.4	7,422.1	7,047.2	6,927.4	-5.79	-44.94
Saudi Arabia	2,314.1	2,385.5	2,455.4	2,520.5	2,577.7	2,624.7	2,660.3	2,685.0	2,701.0	2,712.3	2,723.5	1.64	17.69
Singapore	306.6	316.2	332.6	350.1	356.5	354.2	354.0	349.5	345.8	339.0	329.8	0.73	7.59
Slovakia	427.0	417.2	407.3	398.5	389.8	380.0	366.6	348.7	331.0	314.9	298.8	-3.51	-30.03
Slovenia	131.9	129.0	125.6	122.3	116.7	111.3	107.7	104.6	102.0	100.5	98.8	-2.84	-25.05
South Africa	5,053.9	5,067.6	5,058.3	5,029.1	4,986.6	4,939.5	4,895.4	4,858.3	4,830.6	4,814.4	4,811.0	-0.49	-4.81
South Korea	3,145.6	3,113.2	3,118.6	3,173.9	3,252.8	3,326.2	3,378.0	3,389.5	3,355.2	3,284.2	3,193.4	0.15	1.52
Spain	2,622.3	2,549.5	2,492.7	2,449.3	2,414.7	2,386.2	2,360.9	2,336.1	2,316.4	2,304.6	2,305.1	-1.28	-12.10
Sweden	571.6	593.1	617.7	637.9	654.3	657.5	653.6	633.3	606.1	576.3	551.4	-0.36	-3.54
Switzerland	453.1	458.0	464.5	470.3	475.9	474.3	471.5	465.5	459.8	451.8	446.0	-0.16	-1.55
Taiwan	1,642.5	1,589.8	1,587.4	1,605.8	1,617.2	1,602.1	1,613.7	1,603.2	1,606.5	1,608.9	1,549.6	-0.58	-5.65
Thailand	4,751.3	4,749.5	4,802.2	4,895.6	4,971.7	5,021.2	5,062.1	5,104.6	5,117.1	5,066.9	4,958.5	0.43	4.36
Tunisia	1,046.3	1,044.2	1,035.9	1,021.4	1,001.4	976.8	948.7	918.3	886.9	856.0	827.8	-2.32	-20.88
Turkey	6,308.4	6,274.0	6,291.8	6,359.1	6,472.5	6,605.1	6,740.5	6,864.5	6,976.0	7,072.5	7,138.9	1.24	13.16
Turkmenistan	540.9	554.2	564.0	569.6	570.2	565.3	555.0	539.9	521.6	502.7	486.4	-1.06	-10.08
Ukraine	3,799.2	3,684.0	3,557.4	3,376.7	3,200.7	3,008.2	2,832.0	2,668.6	2,519.1	2,377.9	2,258.0	-5.07	-40.57
United Arab Emirates	345.2	330.4	324.7	327.9	338.2	352.7	368.9	385.2	401.0	416.2	430.6	2.24	24.76
United Kingdom	4,288.9	4,337.1	4,372.1	4,401.6	4,394.2	4,358.2	4,311.8	4,243.7	4,175.1	4,120.1	4,068.6	-0.53	-5.13
USA	21,228.2	21,460.3	21,621.4	21,762.3	21,818.7	21,748.6	21,505.1	21,285.9	21,060.0	20,884.9	20,782.0	-0.21	-2.10
Venezuela	2,654.4	2,684.1	2,703.9	2,714.5	2,718.4	2,718.9	2,719.1	2,720.8	2,724.9	2,731.9	2,741.7	0.32	3.29
Vietnam	8,831.9	8,973.8	9,078.4	9,147.3	9,163.7	9,107.6	8,968.7	8,733.5	8,417.0	8,072.6	7,773.6	-1.27	-11.98

Key population trends

Table 4.13 Population Aged 25-29: 2009-2019

'000

	2009	2010	2011	2012	2013	2014	2015	2016	2017	2018	2019	CAGR	Period growth
Algeria	3,552.2	3,620.2	3,664.6	3,687.0	3,691.9	3,685.6	3,672.9	3,655.8	3,631.4	3,593.7	3,535.5	-0.05	-0.47
Argentina	3,252.0	3,240.0	3,241.0	3,256.0	3,282.0	3,314.2	3,347.3	3,377.9	3,404.5	3,425.9	3,441.2	0.57	5.82
Australia	1,561.5	1,602.2	1,630.5	1,649.1	1,660.4	1,677.5	1,695.3	1,713.3	1,732.0	1,748.4	1,756.8	1.19	12.50
Austria	551.4	557.6	555.9	550.4	543.8	541.8	540.5	541.9	546.1	550.4	552.4	0.02	0.18
Azerbaijan	731.1	764.0	796.4	827.0	854.4	876.5	891.8	899.2	898.0	887.9	868.7	1.74	18.81
Belarus	783.2	803.1	816.6	834.8	839.3	829.7	814.7	791.5	750.2	713.8	666.9	-1.59	-14.85
Belgium	673.7	668.1	659.9	655.6	654.3	658.4	664.5	674.9	683.2	689.6	689.0	0.23	2.28
Bolivia	776.2	794.8	814.0	834.0	855.1	877.5	901.4	926.5	952.0	976.3	998.0	2.54	28.57
Bosnia-Herzegovina	292.2	296.5	300.5	303.5	304.4	302.2	296.0	285.8	272.6	258.3	245.2	-1.74	-16.10
Brazil	17,562.0	17,824.6	17,869.9	17,825.5	17,721.5	17,529.1	17,278.2	17,038.5	16,796.7	16,587.3	16,427.2	-0.67	-6.46
Bulgaria	538.7	526.3	517.0	510.0	500.8	493.2	483.5	470.9	449.4	426.6	400.3	-2.93	-25.70
Canada	2,354.7	2,380.6	2,396.5	2,403.3	2,401.8	2,409.7	2,433.0	2,457.7	2,484.4	2,504.2	2,501.7	0.61	6.24
Chile	1,279.8	1,316.5	1,352.0	1,385.1	1,415.1	1,441.3	1,463.5	1,481.1	1,493.3	1,498.5	1,495.4	1.57	16.84
China	83,582.0	84,046.8	87,581.5	92,057.9	98,715.0	106,896.2	116,925.9	118,147.8	115,885.1	112,634.7	106,525.8	2.46	27.45
Colombia	3,812.7	3,849.1	3,884.7	3,920.7	3,958.2	3,997.7	4,039.2	4,082.0	4,124.3	4,163.6	4,196.9	0.96	10.08
Costa Rica	403.7	413.8	423.6	432.7	440.6	446.5	450.1	451.3	450.3	447.5	443.8	0.95	9.92
Croatia	314.9	313.3	309.5	304.5	298.3	292.8	285.1	279.4	276.2	270.2	265.4	-1.70	-15.72
Czech Republic	756.9	725.6	710.0	699.5	687.6	682.2	672.9	666.9	663.4	655.6	645.3	-1.58	-14.74
Denmark	315.1	309.6	307.2	309.8	312.8	319.7	327.9	336.2	343.7	353.5	360.4	1.35	14.37
Ecuador	1,098.6	1,109.9	1,122.9	1,137.3	1,152.6	1,167.9	1,182.7	1,196.8	1,210.3	1,223.9	1,238.0	1.20	12.69
Egypt	6,556.3	6,668.7	6,766.2	6,850.9	6,928.4	6,985.7	7,000.7	6,961.0	6,869.0	6,718.0	6,540.4	-0.02	-0.24
Estonia	99.4	101.5	102.7	103.1	104.2	104.5	104.3	103.1	99.5	94.3	86.8	-1.35	-12.71
Finland	339.3	342.4	342.9	340.8	335.2	332.4	331.2	334.3	338.7	344.9	345.7	0.19	1.89
France	4,008.6	4,014.2	3,986.2	3,977.5	3,976.1	4,023.8	4,054.2	4,069.2	4,058.4	4,035.6	3,973.7	-0.09	-0.87
Germany	5,010.2	5,020.8	4,986.2	4,993.3	5,014.1	5,081.6	5,129.3	5,183.3	5,119.0	5,003.2	4,845.0	-0.33	-3.30
Greece	804.0	784.6	749.4	720.3	687.6	665.5	642.6	631.2	622.0	618.7	609.1	-2.74	-24.24
Hong Kong, China	552.2	568.3	577.9	583.8	589.4	598.6	601.5	603.7	603.6	599.4	588.7	0.64	6.60
Hungary	729.5	703.7	690.2	678.2	669.1	664.0	658.9	651.1	646.8	642.5	634.6	-1.38	-13.02
India	99,196.0	100,843.7	102,447.1	104,019.3	105,584.8	107,167.3	108,776.9	110,402.7	111,998.9	113,484.1	114,765.1	1.47	15.70
Indonesia	20,426.0	20,505.5	20,523.6	20,487.1	20,412.6	20,321.9	20,234.1	20,160.0	20,101.8	20,056.9	20,020.1	-0.20	-1.99
Iran	8,664.7	9,019.5	9,259.0	9,376.1	9,374.6	9,266.2	9,065.4	8,784.4	8,433.0	8,023.4	7,571.7	-1.34	-12.61
Ireland	401.0	393.9	382.2	372.2	360.5	351.0	342.2	336.2	330.5	324.7	319.5	-2.25	-20.32
Israel	556.4	563.0	570.0	575.5	577.9	579.3	581.4	583.9	588.5	595.4	602.1	0.79	8.22
Italy	3,434.7	3,349.3	3,279.4	3,207.4	3,139.8	3,112.3	3,093.7	3,094.0	3,107.5	3,126.3	3,107.1	-1.00	-9.54
Japan	7,529.4	7,439.7	7,364.8	7,280.6	7,144.3	6,968.4	6,775.0	6,600.3	6,452.3	6,320.0	6,248.9	-1.85	-17.01
Jordan	610.0	626.6	633.7	632.4	625.8	618.2	612.8	611.4	613.9	619.8	627.8	0.29	2.92
Kazakhstan	1,338.5	1,381.7	1,429.4	1,478.5	1,524.2	1,559.8	1,580.0	1,581.4	1,563.4	1,527.7	1,477.8	0.99	10.41
Kuwait	271.7	267.7	263.0	258.1	253.3	249.0	245.5	243.0	241.5	240.8	240.8	-1.20	-11.39
Latvia	168.2	172.7	176.1	180.0	182.4	181.4	179.1	176.2	169.9	162.3	151.1	-1.07	-10.16
Lithuania	236.8	244.3	251.6	258.9	263.8	262.3	259.0	256.3	251.0	247.3	240.3	0.15	1.49
Malaysia	2,318.5	2,369.1	2,416.1	2,459.4	2,491.1	2,519.4	2,543.6	2,562.6	2,576.1	2,598.7	2,619.7	1.23	12.99
Mexico	8,753.4	8,747.1	8,764.7	8,798.8	8,857.9	8,946.9	9,067.0	9,215.0	9,380.8	9,547.8	9,697.3	1.03	10.78
Morocco	2,951.9	3,018.5	3,066.8	3,096.7	3,110.5	3,112.4	3,106.1	3,094.0	3,077.4	3,057.0	3,032.9	0.27	2.75
Netherlands	979.3	979.3	975.9	980.0	990.1	1,000.9	1,009.3	1,023.5	1,032.9	1,038.9	1,043.8	0.64	6.58
New Zealand	278.3	282.6	285.4	286.6	288.2	291.0	296.2	303.1	308.6	311.5	312.1	1.15	12.13
Nigeria	12,486.8	12,802.1	13,105.4	13,399.6	13,688.7	13,977.6	14,270.6	14,570.4	14,878.9	15,197.5	15,527.1	2.20	24.35
Norway	302.6	306.4	309.6	313.6	317.2	324.2	332.5	341.6	349.6	355.7	358.4	1.71	18.44
Pakistan	14,826.4	15,419.2	16,060.9	16,727.9	17,378.5	17,964.2	18,447.5	18,813.4	19,069.3	19,240.8	19,364.0	2.71	30.61
Peru	2,462.9	2,485.1	2,514.3	2,550.1	2,590.1	2,631.0	2,669.9	2,704.8	2,734.9	2,760.0	2,780.2	1.22	12.89
Philippines	7,728.2	7,904.0	8,082.8	8,267.2	8,454.5	8,642.8	8,827.4	9,005.0	9,173.2	9,329.0	9,470.1	2.05	22.54
Poland	3,232.5	3,266.4	3,271.7	3,241.6	3,151.8	3,024.5	2,898.9	2,788.7	2,710.0	2,632.9	2,548.5	-2.35	-21.16
Portugal	760.6	742.2	714.7	688.2	659.9	637.4	618.5	608.9	602.2	596.8	590.0	-2.51	-22.43
Romania	1,643.2	1,611.1	1,584.3	1,601.8	1,632.0	1,673.6	1,674.9	1,622.0	1,516.5	1,410.1	1,296.0	-2.35	-21.13
Russia	11,893.4	12,246.9	12,394.6	12,670.5	12,758.4	12,565.9	12,247.3	11,851.7	11,138.4	10,282.3	9,365.6	-2.36	-21.25
Saudi Arabia	2,327.4	2,335.6	2,364.2	2,412.8	2,476.7	2,548.8	2,622.3	2,692.7	2,757.4	2,813.9	2,860.1	2.08	22.89
Singapore	323.1	325.9	323.5	322.6	330.9	350.1	358.7	374.6	391.3	396.1	392.0	1.95	21.31
Slovakia	457.6	450.2	446.6	441.7	433.3	425.9	415.9	405.8	396.8	387.9	378.0	-1.89	-17.41
Slovenia	150.1	146.9	143.4	139.3	136.7	135.0	131.8	128.0	124.6	119.1	113.7	-2.74	-24.27
South Africa	4,671.7	4,748.0	4,805.6	4,843.2	4,861.7	4,863.8	4,852.7	4,830.8	4,800.5	4,765.8	4,731.6	0.13	1.28
South Korea	3,869.6	3,720.6	3,547.5	3,366.5	3,217.8	3,127.8	3,095.6	3,101.0	3,156.1	3,234.8	3,308.1	-1.56	-14.51
Spain	3,452.3	3,320.5	3,183.6	3,057.0	2,942.8	2,845.6	2,767.8	2,710.1	2,666.2	2,631.1	2,602.3	-2.79	-24.62
Sweden	549.7	550.6	554.1	563.8	575.6	595.9	617.2	641.8	662.2	679.3	683.2	2.20	24.29
Switzerland	477.6	480.7	482.2	484.7	486.0	492.0	497.0	503.7	509.7	515.3	513.6	0.73	7.54
Taiwan	1,994.6	1,948.6	1,885.1	1,779.4	1,692.5	1,658.2	1,604.8	1,602.3	1,620.4	1,631.6	1,616.3	-2.08	-18.97
Thailand	5,244.2	5,136.9	5,013.4	4,865.0	4,759.6	4,708.2	4,706.3	4,762.4	4,857.0	4,934.8	4,983.7	-0.51	-4.97
Tunisia	987.0	1,002.6	1,016.5	1,028.1	1,036.2	1,039.7	1,037.4	1,029.0	1,014.5	994.6	970.2	-0.17	-1.71
Turkey	6,718.9	6,654.5	6,575.6	6,482.4	6,384.9	6,311.1	6,280.8	6,297.8	6,364.6	6,474.1	6,606.3	-0.17	-1.68
Turkmenistan	453.6	468.3	484.4	501.4	518.3	533.7	546.7	556.3	561.9	562.8	558.2	2.10	23.05
Ukraine	3,622.9	3,714.0	3,750.9	3,822.5	3,828.0	3,737.8	3,620.6	3,492.9	3,315.8	3,146.0	2,961.4	-2.00	-18.26
United Arab Emirates	637.5	615.8	590.0	562.4	536.1	514.5	499.9	493.1	493.9	500.9	512.1	-2.17	-19.67
United Kingdom	4,156.6	4,269.0	4,368.4	4,472.2	4,583.1	4,669.3	4,716.2	4,752.9	4,783.1	4,774.2	4,734.8	1.31	13.91
USA	21,518.6	21,546.0	21,504.1	21,460.5	21,467.2	21,592.9	21,799.1	21,955.1	22,088.4	22,138.3	22,065.2	0.25	2.54
Venezuela	2,422.1	2,465.4	2,510.8	2,557.1	2,601.4	2,639.9	2,669.8	2,689.8	2,700.7	2,705.0	2,705.9	1.11	11.72
Vietnam	7,827.1	7,982.8	8,166.8	8,370.6	8,577.3	8,763.8	8,911.6	9,022.1	9,096.7	9,118.0	9,065.2	1.48	15.82

Key population trends

Table 4.14 Population Aged 30-34: 2009-2019

'000

	2009	2010	2011	2012	2013	2014	2015	2016	2017	2018	2019	CAGR	Period growth
Algeria	3,011.5	3,116.4	3,225.4	3,334.1	3,435.8	3,522.8	3,589.3	3,633.0	3,655.1	3,660.5	3,655.0	1.96	21.37
Argentina	3,171.3	3,233.1	3,264.1	3,267.9	3,254.4	3,236.6	3,225.6	3,227.3	3,242.4	3,268.3	3,301.8	0.40	4.12
Australia	1,482.8	1,501.6	1,532.3	1,571.6	1,619.5	1,664.4	1,706.3	1,737.4	1,757.9	1,770.1	1,787.4	1.89	20.54
Austria	536.9	531.0	534.3	544.7	557.0	565.4	571.6	569.9	564.2	557.3	555.1	0.33	3.39
Azerbaijan	602.1	615.5	634.1	657.8	685.8	716.8	749.2	781.7	812.7	840.5	862.9	3.66	43.31
Belarus	697.5	706.4	720.1	733.8	751.6	777.6	796.9	809.8	828.4	832.7	824.3	1.68	18.18
Belgium	672.6	673.9	681.0	685.9	686.9	683.9	678.3	670.2	665.9	664.6	668.6	-0.06	-0.60
Bolivia	682.7	694.0	706.9	721.6	737.7	755.1	773.4	792.4	812.4	833.5	855.9	2.29	25.38
Bosnia-Herzegovina	275.9	277.6	280.2	283.6	287.8	292.3	297.0	301.2	304.3	305.1	302.6	0.93	9.69
Brazil	15,380.1	15,750.9	16,198.2	16,636.9	17,022.2	17,374.5	17,646.3	17,701.8	17,667.4	17,572.1	17,386.3	1.23	13.04
Bulgaria	580.3	573.2	563.3	552.5	540.5	529.5	516.5	506.3	498.2	488.6	480.5	-1.87	-17.20
Canada	2,300.2	2,336.6	2,374.6	2,410.9	2,452.8	2,488.7	2,512.8	2,529.0	2,536.2	2,535.0	2,544.0	1.01	10.60
Chile	1,176.8	1,177.2	1,189.1	1,211.8	1,242.8	1,278.4	1,315.0	1,350.4	1,383.4	1,413.3	1,439.5	2.04	22.32
China	86,411.9	83,500.7	81,781.7	84,188.9	83,477.9	83,005.5	83,582.3	87,180.5	91,877.7	98,487.1	106,705.8	2.13	23.49
Colombia	3,468.5	3,542.2	3,606.9	3,661.6	3,707.6	3,747.8	3,785.1	3,821.4	3,857.8	3,895.2	3,934.5	1.27	13.44
Costa Rica	349.3	361.0	372.6	383.6	394.2	404.4	414.3	424.0	433.1	441.1	447.3	2.51	28.07
Croatia	305.1	309.3	313.2	315.0	316.0	315.9	314.4	310.5	305.5	299.3	293.7	-0.38	-3.72
Czech Republic	925.3	908.1	875.4	836.0	799.5	761.4	728.6	712.0	701.6	690.2	685.4	-2.96	-25.93
Denmark	362.1	352.6	340.6	330.8	323.9	315.2	309.6	307.3	309.8	312.8	319.5	-1.24	-11.75
Ecuador	990.8	1,001.9	1,014.2	1,027.8	1,042.3	1,057.5	1,073.1	1,088.8	1,104.5	1,120.0	1,135.1	1.37	14.56
Egypt	5,549.0	5,720.4	5,884.0	6,036.1	6,174.0	6,296.6	6,403.9	6,494.3	6,570.2	6,638.3	6,684.2	1.88	20.46
Estonia	92.1	92.4	93.0	94.0	95.2	97.3	99.2	100.3	100.8	102.0	102.4	1.07	11.22
Finland	333.7	337.2	337.9	337.8	340.8	345.2	348.3	348.6	346.3	340.5	337.4	0.11	1.12
France	3,892.3	3,857.9	3,914.9	3,992.7	4,038.7	4,048.4	4,054.2	4,027.7	4,019.4	4,017.7	4,064.7	0.43	4.43
Germany	4,718.5	4,755.9	4,857.5	4,932.1	5,000.7	5,038.1	5,056.0	5,029.3	5,040.8	5,064.5	5,132.5	0.84	8.77
Greece	873.0	862.1	863.3	852.9	839.5	821.6	802.3	767.2	738.3	705.6	683.4	-2.42	-21.72
Hong Kong, China	545.7	550.9	566.6	578.8	597.4	613.9	629.2	638.0	642.0	644.5	650.3	1.77	19.17
Hungary	866.1	852.7	825.0	797.0	766.8	736.8	710.7	696.7	684.6	675.5	670.6	-2.53	-22.57
India	88,618.9	90,593.2	92,505.0	94,341.5	96,102.3	97,798.3	99,444.5	101,053.3	102,640.7	104,230.3	105,842.0	1.79	19.43
Indonesia	19,209.4	19,439.7	19,661.0	19,865.5	20,039.8	20,169.7	20,245.3	20,264.7	20,234.5	20,170.2	20,091.0	0.45	4.59
Iran	6,309.1	6,723.8	7,190.7	7,687.4	8,175.9	8,611.6	8,957.5	9,192.9	9,310.6	9,312.9	9,209.2	3.85	45.97
Ireland	377.8	396.0	414.4	427.1	435.3	434.5	427.0	415.5	405.5	393.7	384.0	0.16	1.65
Israel	550.8	552.3	550.0	549.5	554.1	560.6	566.8	573.6	578.9	580.9	581.8	0.55	5.63
Italy	4,257.3	4,074.0	3,902.0	3,756.9	3,642.4	3,531.0	3,445.9	3,376.5	3,305.0	3,237.9	3,210.7	-2.78	-24.58
Japan	8,609.0	8,278.9	7,979.9	7,756.9	7,597.7	7,501.4	7,418.6	7,348.8	7,267.6	7,134.0	6,960.3	-2.10	-19.15
Jordan	516.1	535.9	553.8	569.3	582.0	591.8	598.5	602.1	602.9	602.0	601.1	1.54	16.47
Kazakhstan	1,205.3	1,222.5	1,243.1	1,268.1	1,299.5	1,338.1	1,383.5	1,433.9	1,485.8	1,533.2	1,569.3	2.67	30.20
Kuwait	315.7	316.9	315.8	312.7	308.1	302.7	297.2	292.0	287.4	283.4	280.1	-1.19	-11.29
Latvia	157.2	156.4	156.5	157.5	160.1	165.2	169.5	172.9	176.9	179.4	178.7	1.29	13.67
Lithuania	220.2	219.1	219.5	221.2	223.9	230.3	237.5	244.5	251.7	256.8	255.7	1.51	16.13
Malaysia	2,042.4	2,084.1	2,130.1	2,179.8	2,234.9	2,288.2	2,337.2	2,382.4	2,424.2	2,454.3	2,481.6	1.97	21.51
Mexico	8,989.5	8,951.5	8,909.0	8,858.5	8,811.6	8,777.2	8,761.3	8,767.6	8,799.3	8,859.8	8,951.0	-0.04	-0.43
Morocco	2,463.0	2,529.0	2,607.8	2,696.2	2,786.7	2,870.3	2,939.4	2,989.8	3,021.3	3,036.5	3,039.4	2.13	23.40
Netherlands	998.0	981.7	981.8	981.8	979.6	973.8	974.4	971.4	975.9	986.4	997.6	0.00	-0.04
New Zealand	268.8	269.6	273.5	278.6	285.9	291.4	295.8	298.7	300.0	301.5	304.3	1.25	13.20
Nigeria	10,170.9	10,534.7	10,891.7	11,239.7	11,576.7	11,901.3	12,213.2	12,513.2	12,803.5	13,088.4	13,373.0	2.77	31.48
Norway	319.8	318.6	320.3	323.0	328.1	330.7	332.4	334.2	337.2	340.2	346.6	0.81	8.36
Pakistan	12,350.8	12,734.3	13,147.8	13,597.6	14,092.9	14,640.3	15,240.5	15,885.9	16,554.3	17,205.5	17,792.3	3.72	44.06
Peru	2,280.7	2,313.8	2,340.5	2,362.0	2,381.6	2,403.1	2,429.4	2,462.0	2,500.3	2,542.3	2,585.0	1.26	13.34
Philippines	6,763.5	6,940.5	7,108.2	7,270.7	7,431.7	7,597.7	7,771.8	7,955.3	8,146.7	8,342.7	8,538.4	2.36	26.24
Poland	2,973.5	3,024.6	3,065.0	3,074.4	3,116.5	3,176.2	3,206.6	3,209.0	3,180.0	3,094.7	2,973.6	0.00	0.00
Portugal	850.5	838.5	822.4	802.6	785.2	769.4	750.7	723.1	696.5	668.2	645.6	-2.72	-24.09
Romania	1,771.4	1,765.0	1,765.0	1,741.5	1,688.7	1,620.1	1,584.2	1,552.1	1,562.3	1,588.2	1,624.7	-0.86	-8.28
Russia	10,684.8	10,798.6	10,981.7	11,109.7	11,408.9	11,812.4	12,155.2	12,308.7	12,580.6	12,670.0	12,481.9	1.57	16.82
Saudi Arabia	2,402.9	2,432.1	2,443.6	2,441.3	2,433.7	2,431.8	2,444.8	2,477.3	2,528.8	2,594.9	2,668.9	1.06	11.07
Singapore	354.8	355.3	361.3	356.2	361.0	359.1	360.6	356.7	354.3	361.4	380.3	0.70	7.18
Slovakia	466.8	471.0	470.9	466.9	462.9	456.7	449.1	445.3	440.2	431.7	424.0	-0.96	-9.16
Slovenia	153.6	155.8	156.9	156.6	155.5	152.8	149.3	145.5	141.3	138.8	137.1	-1.13	-10.75
South Africa	3,958.8	4,020.4	4,086.1	4,154.3	4,222.5	4,287.4	4,346.2	4,396.9	4,437.6	4,467.0	4,484.5	1.25	13.28
South Korea	3,828.3	3,828.4	3,877.6	3,928.2	3,930.0	3,854.9	3,706.7	3,534.6	3,354.5	3,206.7	3,117.3	-2.03	-18.57
Spain	4,019.5	4,008.8	3,960.9	3,877.0	3,769.0	3,641.7	3,505.5	3,368.7	3,242.0	3,127.6	3,030.1	-2.79	-24.61
Sweden	578.3	568.0	565.4	564.6	565.9	568.1	568.9	571.7	581.1	592.1	612.1	0.57	5.85
Switzerland	500.4	499.0	502.2	505.2	509.0	511.9	515.1	516.6	519.2	520.3	526.4	0.51	5.20
Taiwan	1,917.2	1,978.5	2,025.3	2,020.6	2,038.0	2,014.6	1,968.0	1,903.9	1,796.4	1,708.4	1,673.7	-1.35	-12.70
Thailand	5,470.4	5,457.4	5,402.2	5,335.2	5,287.6	5,176.6	5,066.7	4,942.5	4,789.5	4,681.5	4,626.9	-1.66	-15.42
Tunisia	882.0	904.9	926.3	946.0	964.1	980.8	996.1	1,009.9	1,021.4	1,029.6	1,033.1	1.59	17.14
Turkey	6,687.8	6,752.1	6,784.1	6,788.8	6,766.2	6,720.0	6,659.5	6,580.3	6,487.0	6,387.1	6,309.3	-0.58	-5.66
Turkmenistan	393.3	402.4	411.9	422.1	433.4	446.1	460.5	476.4	493.2	510.0	525.6	2.94	33.63
Ukraine	3,348.4	3,356.2	3,387.0	3,388.7	3,445.4	3,544.7	3,627.8	3,658.6	3,726.0	3,733.4	3,651.4	0.87	9.05
United Arab Emirates	806.8	823.4	824.6	811.7	788.1	758.3	726.5	695.0	665.6	640.1	619.9	-2.60	-23.17
United Kingdom	3,817.3	3,858.9	3,945.2	4,053.0	4,174.3	4,297.7	4,411.2	4,514.5	4,620.4	4,730.9	4,814.9	2.35	26.13
USA	19,966.0	20,421.5	20,989.3	21,421.8	21,771.6	21,929.2	21,948.4	21,916.8	21,877.0	21,883.6	22,007.4	0.98	10.22
Venezuela	2,168.7	2,225.9	2,277.4	2,323.4	2,365.9	2,407.7	2,450.9	2,496.3	2,542.7	2,586.9	2,625.4	1.93	21.06
Vietnam	7,150.1	7,276.3	7,395.2	7,508.4	7,625.7	7,760.7	7,921.5	8,110.5	8,319.0	8,529.8	8,718.8	2.00	21.94

Key population trends

Table 4.15 Population Aged 35-39: 2009-2019

'000

	2009	2010	2011	2012	2013	2014	2015	2016	2017	2018	2019	CAGR	Period growth
Algeria	2,558.9	2,633.0	2,711.7	2,795.8	2,886.2	2,983.5	3,087.0	3,195.1	3,303.3	3,405.0	3,492.3	3.16	36.48
Argentina	2,640.8	2,734.4	2,840.6	2,953.1	3,060.6	3,150.3	3,212.6	3,244.1	3,248.2	3,234.8	3,212.7	1.98	21.66
Australia	1,608.6	1,602.9	1,576.1	1,554.5	1,547.7	1,554.5	1,574.8	1,608.3	1,649.2	1,697.9	1,742.7	0.80	8.34
Austria	629.6	605.9	587.4	568.5	552.9	544.7	538.9	542.2	552.5	564.7	573.0	-0.94	-9.00
Azerbaijan	583.2	580.6	579.1	579.2	582.5	590.1	603.1	621.9	645.8	674.1	705.2	1.92	20.91
Belarus	672.6	678.0	678.6	679.9	681.5	690.3	698.7	711.9	725.8	743.4	770.0	1.36	14.48
Belgium	744.6	729.5	709.2	692.3	680.7	675.8	677.1	684.2	689.1	690.1	687.2	-0.80	-7.71
Bolivia	605.5	621.1	634.3	645.5	655.5	665.6	676.7	689.6	704.2	720.3	737.7	1.99	21.84
Bosnia-Herzegovina	276.0	274.8	274.2	274.1	274.7	276.0	278.1	280.9	284.4	288.4	292.8	0.59	6.09
Brazil	13,985.3	14,124.0	14,306.2	14,538.1	14,829.5	15,183.2	15,560.8	16,013.3	16,456.7	16,846.0	17,200.3	2.09	22.99
Bulgaria	548.4	552.7	557.5	565.2	574.3	573.7	566.3	556.0	544.9	532.7	521.7	-0.50	-4.88
Canada	2,342.2	2,337.8	2,332.5	2,345.1	2,364.9	2,397.8	2,432.7	2,471.8	2,509.6	2,553.6	2,591.6	1.02	10.65
Chile	1,236.1	1,227.8	1,214.6	1,198.4	1,183.3	1,174.0	1,174.5	1,186.4	1,209.1	1,240.0	1,275.4	0.31	3.18
China	118,048.5	109,804.8	103,325.9	95,679.5	90,268.4	86,178.1	83,339.6	81,552.4	84,017.2	83,393.7	82,961.6	-3.47	-29.72
Colombia	3,143.8	3,162.2	3,202.6	3,263.3	3,337.6	3,416.0	3,489.9	3,554.8	3,609.5	3,655.3	3,695.1	1.63	17.54
Costa Rica	310.4	313.2	319.0	327.4	337.7	349.1	360.7	372.1	383.1	393.8	404.2	2.67	30.21
Croatia	293.8	294.7	298.5	300.5	302.7	305.3	309.4	313.2	314.8	315.9	315.7	0.72	7.45
Czech Republic	781.7	832.7	876.4	910.2	929.7	929.0	910.3	876.6	837.3	801.4	763.8	-0.23	-2.29
Denmark	386.2	386.9	388.4	380.8	369.7	362.2	352.7	340.7	331.0	324.1	315.5	-2.00	-18.31
Ecuador	893.9	904.8	916.6	929.4	943.0	957.0	971.3	985.6	1,000.1	1,014.8	1,029.8	1.43	15.20
Egypt	4,447.8	4,635.0	4,824.1	5,014.8	5,202.9	5,385.8	5,561.3	5,727.9	5,881.8	6,020.3	6,142.0	3.28	38.09
Estonia	92.6	92.2	91.4	90.5	90.0	90.1	90.3	90.8	91.9	93.1	95.3	0.29	2.91
Finland	311.8	310.2	313.1	319.6	327.8	337.3	340.7	341.3	341.1	343.9	348.1	1.11	11.64
France	4,402.7	4,359.7	4,261.3	4,120.7	4,004.8	3,903.1	3,869.3	3,927.3	4,005.0	4,050.9	4,060.6	-0.81	-7.77
Germany	5,618.8	5,250.0	4,960.7	4,753.6	4,670.1	4,689.4	4,733.4	4,840.2	4,917.5	4,987.5	5,025.2	-1.11	-10.56
Greece	876.6	882.6	878.0	883.0	885.4	887.7	876.9	878.2	868.0	854.5	836.6	-0.47	-4.56
Hong Kong, China	564.4	561.5	553.8	555.0	549.2	548.9	553.1	568.0	581.2	601.1	618.5	0.92	9.58
Hungary	723.8	753.5	789.5	823.0	846.7	864.6	850.8	822.6	794.8	764.8	735.1	0.15	1.56
India	77,614.9	79,356.0	81,211.2	83,158.7	85,159.2	87,165.5	89,137.8	91,052.9	92,900.5	94,680.1	96,399.4	2.19	24.20
Indonesia	17,730.7	18,013.6	18,279.7	18,531.1	18,771.6	19,004.7	19,232.2	19,452.0	19,656.9	19,834.0	19,968.4	1.20	12.62
Iran	5,059.9	5,200.6	5,382.4	5,612.8	5,900.7	6,252.1	6,666.0	7,132.8	7,629.9	8,119.4	8,555.9	5.39	69.09
Ireland	344.7	352.6	359.3	367.5	377.5	392.2	410.1	428.6	441.4	449.5	448.7	2.67	30.18
Israel	496.2	513.6	529.6	542.5	551.7	557.0	557.9	554.8	553.9	558.3	564.6	1.30	13.77
Italy	4,739.7	4,710.3	4,667.9	4,573.2	4,452.2	4,314.0	4,131.3	3,959.9	3,815.4	3,701.2	3,590.2	-2.74	-24.25
Japan	9,725.2	9,710.2	9,557.9	9,281.1	8,923.4	8,541.8	8,220.7	7,928.5	7,709.2	7,552.7	7,458.1	-2.62	-23.31
Jordan	440.3	457.5	471.1	481.8	491.2	501.5	514.2	529.5	546.5	563.5	578.2	2.76	31.32
Kazakhstan	1,102.9	1,126.9	1,147.6	1,165.0	1,180.8	1,197.3	1,216.4	1,239.2	1,266.4	1,299.1	1,338.1	1.95	21.33
Kuwait	284.9	290.9	296.8	302.4	307.2	310.6	312.4	312.2	310.4	307.3	303.3	0.63	6.46
Latvia	159.0	159.3	158.4	156.6	154.8	153.9	153.1	153.1	154.2	156.9	162.2	0.20	2.03
Lithuania	241.4	236.0	229.5	222.8	217.3	214.4	213.2	213.6	215.3	218.2	224.7	-0.71	-6.90
Malaysia	1,885.9	1,897.1	1,913.8	1,937.0	1,966.0	2,000.3	2,039.5	2,083.4	2,131.9	2,186.8	2,240.5	1.74	18.81
Mexico	8,630.2	8,871.9	9,037.7	9,118.2	9,131.2	9,100.9	9,050.0	8,992.9	8,937.4	8,890.2	8,856.9	0.26	2.63
Morocco	2,172.8	2,216.3	2,257.9	2,299.9	2,346.6	2,402.7	2,471.0	2,551.7	2,641.2	2,732.2	2,816.1	2.63	29.61
Netherlands	1,229.9	1,167.5	1,102.1	1,046.7	1,001.3	978.0	962.3	963.0	963.6	961.9	956.7	-2.48	-22.22
New Zealand	308.2	302.5	293.5	285.4	279.5	277.4	278.3	282.2	287.4	294.7	300.2	-0.26	-2.59
Nigeria	7,915.0	8,216.1	8,539.1	8,880.3	9,233.7	9,591.4	9,946.7	10,295.3	10,634.4	10,962.3	11,278.1	3.60	42.49
Norway	361.8	359.6	356.2	349.7	341.9	338.1	335.6	336.2	338.3	343.0	345.4	-0.46	-4.54
Pakistan	10,513.0	10,827.6	11,151.7	11,486.8	11,835.4	12,201.8	12,590.7	13,006.8	13,457.7	13,953.4	14,501.7	3.27	37.94
Peru	1,993.3	2,038.1	2,085.7	2,134.6	2,182.1	2,225.2	2,261.6	2,290.9	2,314.4	2,335.5	2,358.6	1.70	18.32
Philippines	5,824.0	5,979.0	6,142.3	6,314.9	6,492.8	6,672.6	6,850.1	7,023.4	7,193.2	7,362.7	7,536.0	2.61	29.40
Poland	2,547.6	2,634.1	2,719.8	2,811.9	2,876.2	2,932.5	2,982.0	3,021.0	3,030.6	3,074.1	3,136.1	2.10	23.10
Portugal	814.0	829.9	845.3	856.7	860.9	857.6	845.5	829.3	809.4	791.9	776.1	-0.48	-4.66
Romania	1,694.4	1,669.6	1,663.4	1,683.8	1,712.1	1,750.1	1,741.3	1,738.1	1,711.5	1,657.8	1,588.7	-0.64	-6.24
Russia	9,855.8	10,065.8	10,162.5	10,320.9	10,366.6	10,547.0	10,654.3	10,842.1	10,968.7	11,264.5	11,659.8	1.70	18.30
Saudi Arabia	2,084.9	2,131.4	2,186.1	2,245.6	2,303.1	2,350.4	2,381.6	2,395.1	2,394.7	2,389.0	2,388.9	1.37	14.58
Singapore	408.3	409.7	404.6	398.1	382.4	374.8	374.0	379.2	372.6	376.2	373.1	-0.90	-8.61
Slovakia	393.0	411.2	428.5	445.9	458.0	465.9	470.0	469.7	465.5	461.2	455.0	1.47	15.77
Slovenia	146.0	147.2	150.2	152.7	154.1	155.9	157.8	158.8	158.4	157.4	154.8	0.59	6.04
South Africa	3,323.6	3,350.5	3,373.9	3,396.4	3,422.3	3,457.0	3,504.0	3,564.1	3,634.8	3,711.7	3,788.3	1.32	13.98
South Korea	4,356.3	4,270.2	4,139.3	3,994.1	3,871.6	3,803.0	3,803.7	3,853.1	3,903.7	3,905.8	3,831.4	-1.28	-12.05
Spain	3,869.5	3,944.7	4,016.6	4,081.9	4,127.9	4,148.2	4,134.3	4,086.8	4,003.5	3,896.3	3,769.5	-0.26	-2.58
Sweden	622.7	627.6	626.0	615.6	603.6	591.2	580.4	577.3	576.1	576.9	578.9	-0.73	-7.04
Switzerland	564.1	550.3	537.6	526.2	519.1	515.3	513.9	517.0	520.1	523.7	526.5	-0.69	-6.68
Taiwan	1,823.6	1,801.8	1,787.3	1,840.8	1,871.7	1,921.6	1,982.8	2,029.8	2,024.5	2,041.4	2,017.8	1.02	10.65
Thailand	5,586.6	5,526.9	5,459.4	5,428.3	5,380.5	5,350.8	5,337.1	5,282.7	5,212.7	5,163.6	5,047.8	-1.01	-9.64
Tunisia	763.0	783.1	805.0	828.4	852.3	876.1	898.9	920.1	939.7	957.8	974.5	2.48	27.73
Turkey	5,937.1	6,131.7	6,303.7	6,452.1	6,577.8	6,675.2	6,743.7	6,777.5	6,780.2	6,756.2	6,706.1	1.23	12.95
Turkmenistan	345.4	353.0	360.8	368.9	377.0	385.5	394.3	403.7	413.9	425.1	437.9	2.40	26.79
Ukraine	3,199.2	3,241.8	3,254.1	3,271.4	3,249.9	3,264.7	3,267.9	3,293.4	3,294.0	3,351.4	3,453.3	0.77	7.94
United Arab Emirates	681.4	728.1	765.8	792.9	809.5	816.5	815.2	806.7	792.0	772.3	749.3	0.95	9.96
United Kingdom	4,379.8	4,250.3	4,110.6	3,964.6	3,854.9	3,825.6	3,869.6	3,960.1	4,070.7	4,192.9	4,315.5	-0.15	-1.47
USA	20,680.9	20,241.3	19,778.1	19,658.9	19,796.2	20,147.1	20,598.9	21,173.2	21,609.5	21,962.4	22,125.2	0.68	6.98
Venezuela	1,898.6	1,932.4	1,977.2	2,031.7	2,091.6	2,152.2	2,209.1	2,260.4	2,306.3	2,348.8	2,390.5	2.33	25.91
Vietnam	6,443.9	6,561.4	6,685.2	6,815.7	6,950.0	7,083.9	7,214.8	7,338.3	7,455.9	7,577.0	7,714.5	1.82	19.72

Key population trends

Table 4.16 Population Aged 40-44: 2009-2019

'000

	2009	2010	2011	2012	2013	2014	2015	2016	2017	2018	2019	CAGR	Period growth
Algeria	2,205.9	2,269.8	2,333.2	2,396.9	2,462.4	2,531.0	2,603.9	2,681.9	2,765.5	2,855.8	2,953.1	2.96	33.88
Argentina	2,350.3	2,382.0	2,422.2	2,472.9	2,536.8	2,615.7	2,709.3	2,815.3	2,927.2	3,033.8	3,127.1	2.90	33.05
Australia	1,524.1	1,543.9	1,582.7	1,621.0	1,644.6	1,651.4	1,647.5	1,624.3	1,604.9	1,599.3	1,606.4	0.53	5.40
Austria	716.6	709.4	695.4	678.9	658.9	632.0	608.4	590.1	571.3	555.8	547.6	-2.65	-23.59
Azerbaijan	627.4	609.1	594.2	583.2	575.9	571.3	568.6	567.4	568.0	571.7	579.6	-0.79	-7.63
Belarus	685.7	668.2	663.7	660.2	663.9	662.3	667.2	667.3	669.1	670.5	680.0	-0.08	-0.83
Belgium	793.6	777.3	766.8	759.1	752.2	742.0	727.0	707.0	690.3	678.9	674.1	-1.62	-15.06
Bolivia	499.0	515.8	533.8	552.6	571.2	588.4	603.7	616.8	628.0	638.1	648.3	2.65	29.92
Bosnia-Herzegovina	290.0	285.6	281.9	279.0	277.0	275.6	274.8	274.4	274.3	274.8	275.9	-0.50	-4.87
Brazil	13,336.5	13,404.9	13,475.4	13,550.9	13,640.0	13,753.0	13,900.7	14,090.2	14,328.1	14,623.6	14,978.4	1.17	12.31
Bulgaria	505.3	515.1	525.9	535.7	541.1	539.9	543.8	548.1	555.1	563.8	563.0	1.09	11.42
Canada	2,486.2	2,436.8	2,421.6	2,415.7	2,408.1	2,394.7	2,387.3	2,381.5	2,394.5	2,415.1	2,449.3	-0.15	-1.48
Chile	1,245.3	1,238.9	1,235.4	1,234.3	1,233.4	1,229.8	1,221.6	1,208.5	1,192.5	1,177.6	1,168.5	-0.63	-6.17
China	128,902.1	131,432.4	131,139.7	132,831.1	127,410.1	122,878.1	114,355.8	107,605.5	99,754.6	94,155.1	89,922.9	-3.54	-30.24
Colombia	3,072.1	3,098.3	3,106.4	3,101.7	3,094.2	3,095.6	3,114.8	3,155.6	3,216.2	3,289.9	3,367.3	0.92	9.61
Costa Rica	315.0	314.3	312.7	310.7	309.2	309.4	312.1	317.7	326.1	336.5	348.1	1.00	10.51
Croatia	313.0	309.1	300.6	295.2	293.0	293.0	293.9	297.6	299.5	301.7	304.1	-0.29	-2.85
Czech Republic	700.2	692.9	697.6	713.4	739.8	783.6	833.3	875.9	909.4	929.2	929.1	2.87	32.70
Denmark	424.4	414.4	402.8	391.7	387.7	385.8	386.3	387.7	380.2	369.3	361.9	-1.58	-14.73
Ecuador	801.8	815.8	829.3	842.5	855.3	868.1	880.9	893.9	907.3	920.9	934.7	1.55	16.58
Egypt	3,830.9	3,827.8	3,869.5	3,956.7	4,094.2	4,270.7	4,464.9	4,661.1	4,858.8	5,053.9	5,243.3	3.19	36.87
Estonia	86.1	85.9	87.0	88.7	90.1	90.1	89.6	88.8	88.0	87.6	87.8	0.20	2.03
Finland	368.1	358.7	349.5	338.3	325.7	313.3	311.7	314.4	320.8	328.9	338.2	-0.85	-8.14
France	4,377.7	4,341.3	4,326.4	4,336.4	4,370.0	4,383.7	4,341.2	4,245.2	4,106.8	3,992.6	3,892.5	-1.17	-11.08
Germany	7,050.1	6,852.8	6,597.9	6,306.8	5,951.8	5,543.8	5,189.2	4,910.6	4,709.6	4,629.0	4,648.5	-4.08	-34.06
Greece	867.2	882.1	898.7	897.4	893.7	888.6	894.7	890.2	895.3	897.6	899.9	0.37	3.76
Hong Kong, China	586.3	564.6	553.2	544.1	540.4	536.4	532.5	523.9	525.9	520.6	520.9	-1.18	-11.16
Hungary	651.3	674.2	697.2	711.4	717.4	717.9	746.8	781.7	814.6	838.0	855.9	2.77	31.41
India	68,785.8	70,113.4	71,487.9	72,923.2	74,440.4	76,061.5	77,800.2	79,655.7	81,608.5	83,619.6	85,639.2	2.22	24.50
Indonesia	15,828.8	16,206.9	16,567.1	16,907.2	17,226.7	17,526.5	17,808.6	18,074.4	18,326.5	18,569.0	18,805.4	1.74	18.80
Iran	4,534.7	4,632.9	4,720.1	4,802.1	4,890.0	4,998.4	5,140.3	5,323.9	5,556.4	5,846.1	6,198.3	3.17	36.69
Ireland	313.2	318.3	324.6	331.6	341.1	349.0	356.4	363.0	371.1	381.1	395.6	2.37	26.34
Israel	410.9	424.7	442.4	462.4	482.2	500.5	518.0	534.2	547.2	556.2	561.2	3.17	36.57
Italy	4,894.8	4,870.2	4,833.4	4,806.6	4,787.0	4,764.3	4,735.5	4,693.7	4,599.8	4,479.6	4,342.3	-1.19	-11.29
Japan	8,589.5	8,687.5	9,179.2	9,333.1	9,520.4	9,638.1	9,630.8	9,485.1	9,213.2	8,860.1	8,482.6	-0.13	-1.24
Jordan	347.8	368.1	386.1	402.0	415.9	428.7	440.8	452.6	464.3	476.8	490.5	3.50	41.04
Kazakhstan	1,019.1	1,015.8	1,022.6	1,039.0	1,062.4	1,088.9	1,114.6	1,137.4	1,156.7	1,173.7	1,190.4	1.57	16.81
Kuwait	221.0	231.4	241.5	251.0	260.0	268.4	276.2	283.4	289.6	294.7	298.2	3.04	34.94
Latvia	154.0	152.3	153.3	154.2	154.9	154.5	154.7	153.9	152.2	150.7	150.0	-0.26	-2.58
Lithuania	246.6	242.8	241.4	240.6	238.5	233.8	228.6	222.3	215.9	210.7	208.2	-1.68	-15.56
Malaysia	1,790.9	1,812.8	1,827.5	1,833.0	1,834.8	1,835.9	1,841.1	1,852.5	1,871.4	1,897.2	1,929.3	0.75	7.73
Mexico	6,994.2	7,337.9	7,707.8	8,079.1	8,429.4	8,731.4	8,963.9	9,116.9	9,192.9	9,205.6	9,176.6	2.75	31.20
Morocco	1,893.0	1,932.6	1,977.2	2,025.4	2,075.0	2,123.4	2,169.3	2,212.8	2,255.8	2,302.9	2,359.0	2.23	24.62
Netherlands	1,292.2	1,289.9	1,286.3	1,275.9	1,254.8	1,212.3	1,149.8	1,083.9	1,028.1	982.5	959.5	-2.93	-25.75
New Zealand	312.5	312.7	315.2	317.1	315.9	311.8	306.2	297.3	289.4	283.6	281.6	-1.04	-9.91
Nigeria	6,320.2	6,490.5	6,683.7	6,901.5	7,144.6	7,412.3	7,703.1	8,014.7	8,343.2	8,682.8	9,026.5	3.63	42.82
Norway	359.8	366.1	369.3	372.2	374.4	372.3	369.2	365.3	358.6	350.9	347.0	-0.36	-3.56
Pakistan	8,875.4	9,155.3	9,444.9	9,743.8	10,050.7	10,364.1	10,683.5	11,010.1	11,346.2	11,695.3	12,062.5	3.12	35.91
Peru	1,743.3	1,779.5	1,816.9	1,856.2	1,897.9	1,942.6	1,989.9	2,039.4	2,089.5	2,138.0	2,182.0	2.27	25.16
Philippines	5,095.2	5,222.3	5,348.0	5,476.4	5,610.7	5,755.4	5,912.3	6,081.6	6,261.3	6,447.1	6,634.1	2.67	30.20
Poland	2,346.2	2,327.7	2,341.2	2,374.6	2,433.6	2,502.1	2,587.2	2,671.8	2,763.5	2,828.9	2,887.3	2.10	23.06
Portugal	788.9	785.5	788.6	796.4	807.5	818.0	833.6	848.8	860.0	864.1	860.8	0.88	9.11
Romania	1,538.0	1,673.3	1,791.5	1,887.9	1,784.4	1,668.3	1,642.7	1,635.0	1,653.1	1,680.0	1,716.3	1.10	11.60
Russia	9,401.6	9,184.1	9,206.8	9,258.9	9,491.3	9,634.1	9,834.7	9,937.2	10,092.6	10,140.4	10,316.1	0.93	9.73
Saudi Arabia	1,775.3	1,829.7	1,874.6	1,912.1	1,947.1	1,985.4	2,031.0	2,085.2	2,144.7	2,202.7	2,250.8	2.40	26.79
Singapore	402.3	397.5	395.5	402.3	411.7	419.0	419.7	413.6	405.8	388.3	379.5	-0.58	-5.66
Slovakia	366.2	360.7	359.0	361.9	373.3	390.2	408.4	425.5	442.8	454.6	462.4	2.36	26.26
Slovenia	155.9	154.2	150.7	148.0	147.1	147.7	148.8	151.7	154.2	155.7	157.6	0.11	1.06
South Africa	2,806.1	2,822.7	2,834.4	2,842.0	2,847.6	2,854.0	2,864.3	2,880.3	2,903.4	2,935.7	2,978.8	0.60	6.15
South Korea	4,132.6	4,184.4	4,250.9	4,311.4	4,337.3	4,309.7	4,225.3	4,096.4	3,953.4	3,832.8	3,765.6	-0.93	-8.88
Spain	3,660.3	3,716.0	3,766.3	3,819.0	3,880.7	3,947.9	4,020.1	4,091.4	4,156.5	4,202.4	4,222.8	1.44	15.37
Sweden	672.8	659.1	646.8	638.9	631.8	629.4	634.2	632.4	621.8	609.3	596.6	-1.19	-11.32
Switzerland	635.8	624.4	611.2	597.5	583.3	566.9	552.6	539.4	527.8	520.3	516.2	-2.06	-18.82
Taiwan	1,879.1	1,867.3	1,860.9	1,840.2	1,835.0	1,812.6	1,791.0	1,776.8	1,829.6	1,859.9	1,909.4	0.16	1.61
Thailand	5,507.1	5,505.9	5,543.1	5,543.9	5,452.4	5,426.0	5,364.2	5,297.1	5,263.6	5,214.1	5,181.2	-0.61	-5.92
Tunisia	676.3	691.1	706.2	722.0	738.7	756.9	776.9	798.7	822.0	845.9	869.6	2.55	28.59
Turkey	4,954.6	5,103.2	5,277.6	5,474.8	5,687.1	5,901.6	6,101.0	6,270.4	6,418.3	6,541.0	6,635.6	2.96	33.93
Turkmenistan	312.0	314.5	318.3	323.4	329.5	336.5	343.9	351.7	359.6	367.9	376.4	1.89	20.63
Ukraine	3,083.4	3,018.7	3,035.0	3,050.5	3,090.9	3,101.1	3,138.7	3,147.0	3,163.5	3,146.6	3,167.6	0.27	2.73
United Arab Emirates	408.0	441.3	481.6	526.8	573.9	619.1	659.4	693.1	719.3	737.5	747.5	6.24	83.20
United Kingdom	4,706.5	4,657.2	4,595.0	4,528.3	4,440.8	4,327.3	4,202.6	4,069.8	3,928.8	3,821.7	3,792.6	-2.14	-19.42
USA	21,096.2	20,989.7	21,086.1	21,084.2	20,919.7	20,600.9	20,175.1	19,735.9	19,629.9	19,772.2	20,123.6	-0.47	-4.61
Venezuela	1,800.6	1,815.5	1,827.7	1,839.8	1,855.5	1,878.9	1,912.5	1,957.2	2,011.3	2,071.0	2,131.2	1.70	18.36
Vietnam	5,819.9	5,925.1	6,033.1	6,143.0	6,256.2	6,373.4	6,495.1	6,623.1	6,757.4	6,895.1	7,031.1	1.91	20.81

Key population trends

Table 4.17 Population Aged 45-49: 2009-2019

'000

	2009	2010	2011	2012	2013	2014	2015	2016	2017	2018	2019	CAGR	Period growth
Algeria	1,806.2	1,891.0	1,970.3	2,043.6	2,111.6	2,176.0	2,238.8	2,301.3	2,364.6	2,429.9	2,498.5	3.30	38.33
Argentina	2,208.2	2,229.0	2,248.9	2,268.8	2,290.5	2,316.3	2,348.5	2,388.9	2,439.4	2,502.7	2,578.4	1.56	16.76
Australia	1,570.2	1,569.7	1,557.3	1,542.5	1,532.4	1,537.5	1,558.9	1,600.4	1,640.3	1,664.7	1,671.8	0.63	6.47
Austria	682.7	699.4	710.3	715.0	715.7	713.5	706.5	692.7	676.4	656.6	629.9	-0.80	-7.73
Azerbaijan	667.2	670.8	664.9	651.1	632.5	612.7	594.8	580.6	570.4	563.7	559.5	-1.74	-16.14
Belarus	804.0	781.2	748.7	718.6	690.7	668.4	651.0	646.3	643.3	646.8	646.0	-2.16	-19.65
Belgium	806.2	811.7	813.2	808.5	799.5	785.7	769.6	759.4	751.9	745.2	735.2	-0.92	-8.80
Bolivia	419.3	429.8	441.1	453.4	467.0	482.0	498.4	516.1	534.6	553.0	570.1	3.12	35.97
Bosnia-Herzegovina	304.9	303.5	300.8	297.1	292.7	288.3	284.2	280.7	278.0	275.9	274.3	-1.05	-10.03
Brazil	12,189.3	12,474.6	12,689.7	12,843.5	12,950.9	13,034.5	13,113.0	13,192.6	13,276.4	13,372.3	13,489.7	1.02	10.67
Bulgaria	522.4	518.3	508.1	496.1	488.2	494.6	504.0	514.3	523.5	528.6	527.4	0.09	0.95
Canada	2,779.0	2,776.5	2,729.5	2,660.3	2,574.5	2,496.9	2,444.5	2,428.9	2,423.1	2,415.6	2,402.7	-1.44	-13.54
Chile	1,228.7	1,243.9	1,249.9	1,248.1	1,241.6	1,233.8	1,227.6	1,224.3	1,223.3	1,222.5	1,219.1	-0.08	-0.78
China	103,935.1	115,693.0	129,701.4	130,483.9	130,123.1	131,279.4	133,697.9	133,485.2	135,157.4	129,708.1	125,130.9	1.87	20.39
Colombia	2,670.2	2,756.1	2,837.6	2,911.5	2,973.3	3,018.7	3,045.5	3,054.3	3,050.3	3,043.2	3,044.7	1.32	14.02
Costa Rica	293.0	300.0	305.6	309.5	311.7	312.4	311.7	310.0	308.0	306.7	307.1	0.47	4.82
Croatia	325.3	320.0	318.4	316.7	313.5	309.9	306.2	297.5	292.2	290.0	289.9	-1.15	-10.89
Czech Republic	648.6	674.2	692.4	702.4	707.7	698.3	690.3	694.4	710.1	736.5	780.3	1.87	20.31
Denmark	388.7	399.6	409.2	421.7	426.0	420.4	410.6	399.3	388.6	384.6	382.8	-0.15	-1.52
Ecuador	697.6	714.0	730.8	747.6	764.2	780.1	795.1	809.2	822.5	835.3	847.8	1.97	21.54
Egypt	3,780.7	3,780.5	3,765.8	3,737.4	3,692.6	3,649.1	3,635.1	3,670.2	3,755.0	3,895.3	4,078.4	0.76	7.87
Estonia	94.3	92.3	89.4	86.3	83.7	82.8	82.7	83.7	85.4	86.8	87.0	-0.81	-7.81
Finland	378.0	378.3	376.9	375.0	372.5	366.8	357.4	348.1	337.0	324.6	312.2	-1.89	-17.40
France	4,319.8	4,347.4	4,362.6	4,371.5	4,364.9	4,330.6	4,295.3	4,282.5	4,293.8	4,328.1	4,342.6	0.05	0.53
Germany	6,887.3	7,005.2	7,059.8	7,073.6	7,032.1	6,916.1	6,733.6	6,491.1	6,208.6	5,861.3	5,460.7	-2.29	-20.71
Greece	801.3	807.0	804.4	826.5	851.4	874.9	889.7	906.3	905.1	901.4	896.3	1.13	11.85
Hong Kong, China	667.2	658.9	639.8	619.1	585.1	556.9	534.4	522.1	514.0	512.0	509.1	-2.67	-23.70
Hungary	611.6	601.0	591.5	592.9	613.4	637.2	659.4	681.5	695.5	701.4	702.1	1.39	14.79
India	60,764.7	61,983.3	63,214.8	64,458.3	65,718.3	67,004.0	68,327.8	69,702.5	71,143.4	72,670.6	74,303.1	2.03	22.28
Indonesia	13,600.8	13,987.4	14,380.1	14,777.4	15,174.4	15,564.5	15,941.8	16,302.5	16,644.8	16,968.2	17,273.3	2.42	27.00
Iran	3,877.7	3,997.4	4,117.4	4,236.4	4,351.1	4,457.7	4,554.7	4,643.3	4,728.6	4,820.4	4,932.1	2.43	27.19
Ireland	290.8	296.6	300.8	305.1	308.7	312.9	317.6	323.8	330.8	340.1	347.9	1.81	19.61
Israel	386.4	387.7	390.2	394.2	400.5	410.4	424.1	442.2	462.7	482.8	501.4	2.64	29.76
Italy	4,435.0	4,589.1	4,712.2	4,808.1	4,868.8	4,894.4	4,870.7	4,834.9	4,809.1	4,790.3	4,768.5	0.73	7.52
Japan	7,830.4	8,016.8	7,882.2	8,116.5	8,306.5	8,488.7	8,593.0	9,084.4	9,240.0	9,427.9	9,546.1	2.00	21.91
Jordan	252.5	270.9	288.4	305.3	321.6	337.9	354.4	371.1	387.6	403.5	418.6	5.18	65.76
Kazakhstan	1,049.2	1,046.9	1,037.1	1,022.4	1,007.3	997.1	995.6	1,004.5	1,022.7	1,047.2	1,073.9	0.23	2.35
Kuwait	154.7	163.0	173.0	184.3	196.5	208.8	220.5	231.3	241.1	250.0	258.1	5.25	66.77
Latvia	169.7	165.9	160.2	155.1	150.8	148.0	146.3	147.3	148.3	149.0	148.9	-1.30	-12.23
Lithuania	266.5	262.0	256.0	248.3	241.9	237.7	234.1	232.8	232.1	230.2	226.0	-1.63	-15.17
Malaysia	1,586.4	1,620.4	1,654.6	1,690.3	1,717.8	1,741.2	1,757.6	1,766.2	1,765.4	1,761.2	1,756.9	1.03	10.75
Mexico	5,757.0	5,972.6	6,210.4	6,465.4	6,744.4	7,052.2	7,389.2	7,750.0	8,119.2	8,471.2	8,776.1	4.31	52.44
Morocco	1,750.4	1,756.6	1,769.2	1,789.9	1,818.8	1,855.0	1,896.8	1,943.0	1,991.9	2,041.6	2,089.8	1.79	19.39
Netherlands	1,270.1	1,285.3	1,294.3	1,291.9	1,285.8	1,276.9	1,275.5	1,272.3	1,262.2	1,241.0	1,198.3	-0.58	-5.65
New Zealand	322.9	323.2	320.3	316.1	312.5	311.1	311.3	313.9	315.9	314.8	310.7	-0.39	-3.79
Nigeria	5,293.1	5,400.0	5,511.0	5,629.0	5,757.8	5,902.2	6,066.0	6,251.5	6,460.1	6,692.3	6,947.8	2.76	31.26
Norway	328.4	334.8	342.4	350.4	357.6	365.2	370.8	373.5	376.2	378.3	376.2	1.37	14.55
Pakistan	7,401.5	7,646.1	7,898.8	8,159.6	8,428.1	8,704.1	8,987.1	9,277.8	9,576.5	9,882.8	10,196.0	3.26	37.76
Peru	1,492.8	1,537.1	1,579.2	1,619.2	1,657.5	1,695.2	1,733.0	1,771.7	1,811.7	1,853.9	1,899.0	2.44	27.21
Philippines	4,387.5	4,516.2	4,643.3	4,770.3	4,897.2	5,025.0	5,153.9	5,284.7	5,419.0	5,560.0	5,710.6	2.67	30.16
Poland	2,635.9	2,523.7	2,434.3	2,370.3	2,321.7	2,285.5	2,267.4	2,280.8	2,314.5	2,374.5	2,444.6	-0.75	-7.26
Portugal	769.0	782.2	786.2	787.9	788.7	787.8	784.5	787.5	795.3	806.3	816.7	0.60	6.21
Romania	1,286.2	1,233.7	1,182.7	1,148.1	1,322.8	1,502.6	1,633.7	1,747.1	1,838.7	1,737.5	1,624.2	2.36	26.28
Russia	11,677.1	11,223.5	10,550.6	10,000.5	9,452.8	9,063.7	8,854.9	8,886.5	8,939.7	9,166.1	9,303.5	-2.25	-20.33
Saudi Arabia	1,313.1	1,390.1	1,467.4	1,542.6	1,612.9	1,675.5	1,728.8	1,772.9	1,810.3	1,845.7	1,884.7	3.68	43.53
Singapore	415.0	417.1	419.8	418.2	414.7	405.1	399.2	396.6	403.0	411.8	418.8	0.09	0.90
Slovakia	378.6	379.4	377.1	373.1	368.0	359.7	354.1	352.2	354.9	366.2	383.0	0.12	1.16
Slovenia	155.2	155.9	157.5	158.2	158.0	156.6	154.8	151.1	148.4	147.6	148.3	-0.45	-4.43
South Africa	2,452.6	2,456.9	2,458.3	2,457.8	2,456.1	2,454.6	2,454.3	2,455.7	2,459.3	2,465.6	2,475.3	0.09	0.93
South Korea	4,238.7	4,192.0	4,132.2	4,080.7	4,060.8	4,082.6	4,135.1	4,202.2	4,263.1	4,289.7	4,263.4	0.06	0.58
Spain	3,357.3	3,432.8	3,509.3	3,582.5	3,643.4	3,701.0	3,754.4	3,804.3	3,856.7	3,918.0	3,984.8	1.73	18.69
Sweden	599.0	618.6	639.6	658.6	673.1	674.8	661.2	648.7	640.7	633.4	630.8	0.52	5.31
Switzerland	604.8	620.3	631.0	638.1	638.4	632.5	620.7	607.0	592.9	578.0	561.0	-0.75	-7.24
Taiwan	1,896.3	1,905.3	1,904.9	1,905.9	1,876.0	1,857.6	1,845.9	1,839.8	1,818.9	1,813.3	1,791.1	-0.57	-5.55
Thailand	5,020.1	5,117.4	5,205.4	5,266.9	5,362.3	5,342.0	5,340.1	5,380.1	5,379.3	5,285.0	5,255.5	0.46	4.69
Tunisia	603.7	615.1	627.3	640.4	654.2	668.6	683.3	698.4	714.0	730.7	748.9	2.18	24.04
Turkey	4,336.6	4,437.2	4,542.7	4,649.9	4,762.2	4,891.7	5,042.5	5,216.0	5,407.6	5,618.4	5,827.6	3.00	34.38
Turkmenistan	288.7	293.4	296.4	298.2	299.5	301.0	303.5	307.3	312.4	318.6	325.6	1.21	12.79
Ukraine	3,591.5	3,481.9	3,317.8	3,185.2	3,061.2	2,960.3	2,894.8	2,908.1	2,924.4	2,969.4	2,987.7	-1.82	-16.81
United Arab Emirates	236.8	243.2	255.8	275.2	301.9	335.4	374.9	419.3	466.4	513.4	556.7	8.92	135.11
United Kingdom	4,398.1	4,494.9	4,568.4	4,616.3	4,635.8	4,621.4	4,577.0	4,522.2	4,461.0	4,376.8	4,264.8	-0.31	-3.03
USA	22,895.6	22,648.0	22,200.4	21,701.2	21,221.5	20,811.2	20,714.8	20,823.8	20,831.1	20,676.8	20,372.1	-1.16	-11.02
Venezuela	1,603.2	1,652.7	1,694.4	1,728.0	1,753.9	1,773.5	1,788.5	1,800.8	1,813.1	1,828.9	1,852.3	1.45	15.54
Vietnam	5,092.0	5,254.8	5,396.7	5,521.2	5,633.3	5,740.9	5,850.0	5,961.7	6,075.2	6,191.3	6,310.4	2.17	23.93

Key population trends

Table 4.18 Population Aged 50-54: 2009-2019

'000

	2009	2010	2011	2012	2013	2014	2015	2016	2017	2018	2019	CAGR	Period growth
Algeria	1,400.4	1,455.7	1,522.5	1,599.7	1,683.8	1,769.5	1,852.5	1,930.4	2,002.6	2,069.9	2,134.0	4.30	52.38
Argentina	2,053.6	2,071.9	2,091.9	2,113.7	2,136.4	2,158.9	2,180.4	2,200.7	2,220.8	2,242.4	2,267.9	1.00	10.43
Australia	1,438.8	1,464.6	1,489.3	1,515.8	1,539.9	1,556.5	1,557.9	1,549.0	1,536.5	1,527.9	1,533.4	0.64	6.57
Austria	572.0	593.7	614.8	633.2	653.2	674.1	690.7	701.6	706.4	707.2	705.2	2.12	23.29
Azerbaijan	528.6	560.1	589.0	614.3	634.2	646.7	650.4	645.3	632.5	615.0	596.2	1.21	12.80
Belarus	747.7	765.1	783.8	790.1	788.1	772.4	750.0	718.3	689.9	663.1	642.5	-1.50	-14.07
Belgium	751.0	763.2	771.6	780.5	786.4	792.6	798.3	799.9	795.5	786.8	773.4	0.29	2.99
Bolivia	354.3	363.9	373.3	382.5	391.7	401.3	411.6	422.6	434.8	448.1	462.9	2.71	30.64
Bosnia-Herzegovina	292.0	294.4	296.6	298.5	299.8	300.1	299.1	296.8	293.2	288.8	284.3	-0.27	-2.64
Brazil	9,882.3	10,263.3	10,660.3	11,066.5	11,459.3	11,809.8	12,098.0	12,317.5	12,477.1	12,590.5	12,679.0	2.52	28.30
Bulgaria	533.0	527.4	521.2	515.7	511.2	506.8	502.8	492.8	481.2	473.6	479.8	-1.05	-9.98
Canada	2,565.6	2,615.6	2,667.0	2,698.3	2,731.9	2,756.0	2,749.9	2,702.5	2,633.9	2,549.2	2,473.3	-0.37	-3.60
Chile	1,029.2	1,073.4	1,115.3	1,153.3	1,185.4	1,209.6	1,224.8	1,230.8	1,229.3	1,223.0	1,215.5	1.68	18.10
China	99,549.5	93,745.8	86,489.8	87,693.6	97,803.9	107,300.5	119,405.5	133,799.8	134,601.9	134,168.3	135,104.5	3.10	35.72
Colombia	2,199.1	2,273.2	2,352.0	2,435.2	2,521.5	2,608.5	2,693.5	2,774.2	2,847.2	2,908.1	2,952.7	2.99	34.27
Costa Rica	239.8	250.7	261.4	271.5	280.8	289.0	295.9	301.2	305.1	307.5	308.4	2.55	28.60
Croatia	333.6	330.7	327.8	323.7	321.8	318.4	313.2	311.5	309.7	306.5	303.0	-0.96	-9.19
Czech Republic	728.6	698.0	669.7	645.7	630.0	639.2	663.9	681.3	691.2	696.8	688.3	-0.57	-5.52
Denmark	363.1	364.1	366.8	368.6	373.2	381.8	392.4	401.8	414.0	418.2	412.9	1.29	13.71
Ecuador	603.3	616.3	630.2	645.1	661.0	677.6	694.4	711.3	728.0	744.3	759.9	2.33	25.95
Egypt	3,451.4	3,529.9	3,589.7	3,631.6	3,656.8	3,665.2	3,656.0	3,630.7	3,590.1	3,531.4	3,474.2	0.07	0.66
Estonia	92.1	92.1	91.9	92.0	91.5	89.9	88.0	85.2	82.2	79.8	79.1	-1.50	-14.07
Finland	381.8	378.1	374.8	371.3	370.2	373.5	373.7	372.3	370.5	368.0	362.5	-0.52	-5.06
France	4,159.2	4,172.5	4,185.9	4,203.5	4,206.4	4,242.9	4,271.0	4,288.3	4,298.8	4,293.9	4,261.8	0.24	2.47
Germany	5,899.4	6,034.8	6,196.6	6,366.0	6,529.0	6,712.1	6,838.5	6,900.3	6,917.7	6,879.1	6,766.6	1.38	14.70
Greece	763.0	775.3	794.1	795.2	800.2	803.7	809.4	806.9	828.9	853.5	876.8	1.40	14.91
Hong Kong, China	612.9	632.1	645.1	644.8	653.3	653.7	644.3	624.6	602.7	568.2	540.4	-1.25	-11.83
Hungary	759.8	707.6	665.2	626.4	600.3	582.0	571.2	561.4	562.8	583.2	606.8	-2.22	-20.14
India	53,070.3	54,070.1	55,106.5	56,197.1	57,340.9	58,524.8	59,732.8	60,957.3	62,199.4	63,463.3	64,755.7	2.01	22.02
Indonesia	11,223.1	11,664.4	12,083.1	12,481.2	12,865.5	13,245.8	13,630.2	14,021.7	14,418.9	14,817.1	15,209.6	3.09	35.52
Iran	3,192.1	3,319.7	3,439.7	3,554.0	3,665.6	3,778.0	3,893.3	4,012.4	4,133.1	4,250.8	4,360.5	3.17	36.60
Ireland	261.3	266.7	273.8	279.1	284.1	289.6	294.9	299.1	303.4	306.9	311.1	1.76	19.04
Israel	370.9	373.5	375.8	377.2	378.1	379.0	379.7	381.8	385.5	391.6	401.4	0.79	8.24
Italy	3,922.0	3,994.3	4,077.5	4,176.7	4,282.2	4,412.1	4,566.2	4,689.5	4,785.8	4,847.3	4,873.9	2.20	24.27
Japan	7,739.3	7,628.3	7,562.7	7,597.9	7,647.4	7,699.0	7,889.7	7,761.9	7,996.2	8,186.2	8,368.0	0.78	8.12
Jordan	177.2	189.3	202.0	215.1	228.9	243.5	259.1	275.5	292.6	310.1	327.7	6.34	84.98
Kazakhstan	943.7	962.3	979.4	994.4	1,005.9	1,012.1	1,011.7	1,004.2	991.8	978.4	969.1	0.27	2.69
Kuwait	107.7	115.2	122.4	129.7	137.2	145.5	154.8	165.3	176.8	188.8	200.7	6.42	86.33
Latvia	157.6	159.9	162.0	163.9	163.3	160.6	157.0	151.5	146.8	142.9	140.5	-1.14	-10.81
Lithuania	223.9	234.5	242.0	249.9	254.3	253.7	249.5	243.9	236.7	230.8	227.1	0.14	1.44
Malaysia	1,353.7	1,393.4	1,432.5	1,470.3	1,503.5	1,534.9	1,565.2	1,595.6	1,628.1	1,652.1	1,672.2	2.14	23.53
Mexico	4,929.8	5,081.5	5,241.8	5,407.1	5,582.4	5,772.6	5,981.0	6,209.7	6,461.5	6,740.7	7,050.1	3.64	43.01
Morocco	1,585.7	1,639.5	1,675.7	1,696.2	1,706.0	1,712.1	1,720.5	1,734.8	1,756.4	1,785.5	1,821.4	1.40	14.86
Netherlands	1,157.0	1,176.2	1,194.7	1,214.8	1,233.5	1,252.2	1,268.5	1,278.0	1,275.7	1,269.5	1,260.6	0.86	8.95
New Zealand	284.0	291.2	298.8	306.6	313.8	317.0	317.4	314.6	310.6	307.1	305.8	0.74	7.70
Nigeria	4,444.5	4,535.4	4,627.8	4,722.5	4,819.6	4,919.2	5,021.6	5,127.9	5,240.5	5,363.3	5,500.7	2.16	23.77
Norway	315.0	318.7	321.0	322.6	325.7	329.5	335.4	342.7	350.4	357.5	364.9	1.48	15.87
Pakistan	6,051.6	6,264.8	6,485.0	6,711.9	6,945.0	7,184.2	7,429.3	7,680.8	7,939.6	8,205.9	8,480.0	3.43	40.13
Peru	1,219.3	1,260.7	1,304.9	1,351.3	1,398.7	1,445.5	1,490.5	1,533.0	1,573.1	1,611.4	1,649.1	3.07	35.25
Philippines	3,699.2	3,812.1	3,927.1	4,046.7	4,170.4	4,298.0	4,427.8	4,558.8	4,690.5	4,822.5	4,954.9	2.97	33.94
Poland	3,021.2	2,989.8	2,906.7	2,797.0	2,667.5	2,545.0	2,436.8	2,350.6	2,290.0	2,244.9	2,212.7	-3.07	-26.76
Portugal	707.7	716.5	729.2	745.1	753.6	764.0	777.2	781.2	783.0	784.1	783.3	1.02	10.69
Romania	1,541.0	1,503.2	1,445.2	1,375.8	1,305.6	1,241.7	1,190.9	1,141.4	1,107.6	1,276.9	1,450.7	-0.60	-5.86
Russia	11,187.0	11,225.9	11,404.0	11,416.7	11,296.8	11,027.8	10,597.1	9,974.8	9,461.2	8,951.9	8,590.5	-2.61	-23.21
Saudi Arabia	884.9	941.4	1,003.3	1,070.3	1,141.7	1,216.2	1,292.2	1,368.3	1,442.6	1,512.3	1,574.6	5.93	77.93
Singapore	381.1	391.3	399.0	403.0	407.5	412.5	413.1	414.6	411.3	406.0	394.6	0.35	3.55
Slovakia	402.0	395.4	388.0	379.4	370.7	367.1	367.8	365.4	361.1	355.9	347.4	-1.45	-13.57
Slovenia	156.6	155.6	154.3	153.4	153.4	154.1	154.7	156.2	157.0	156.9	155.6	-0.06	-0.63
South Africa	2,174.4	2,196.3	2,208.1	2,211.0	2,207.3	2,200.4	2,193.1	2,186.8	2,182.2	2,179.4	2,178.2	0.02	0.17
South Korea	3,733.5	3,907.7	4,046.4	4,148.4	4,196.6	4,189.0	4,144.6	4,087.1	4,037.5	4,019.3	4,042.4	0.80	8.28
Spain	2,924.1	3,023.5	3,116.9	3,204.2	3,288.0	3,364.4	3,437.7	3,513.3	3,585.8	3,646.2	3,703.3	2.39	26.65
Sweden	583.1	585.1	584.1	583.0	586.0	596.2	615.7	636.4	655.3	669.6	671.4	1.42	15.14
Switzerland	528.1	540.7	553.7	565.6	578.8	594.9	610.4	621.2	628.3	628.1	621.9	1.65	17.75
Taiwan	1,715.7	1,755.7	1,781.1	1,802.4	1,839.9	1,865.4	1,874.2	1,873.8	1,874.3	1,844.4	1,826.3	0.63	6.45
Thailand	4,212.9	4,337.0	4,424.0	4,567.2	4,714.4	4,856.0	4,954.9	5,046.8	5,108.2	5,205.3	5,182.1	2.09	23.01
Tunisia	536.1	548.9	560.5	571.2	581.6	592.3	603.6	615.7	628.8	642.5	656.8	2.05	22.52
Turkey	3,726.6	3,831.8	3,937.2	4,036.3	4,135.1	4,233.6	4,333.3	4,439.0	4,543.5	4,651.4	4,778.5	2.52	28.23
Turkmenistan	229.8	241.4	251.9	261.2	269.0	275.1	279.6	282.6	284.6	286.0	287.7	2.27	25.19
Ukraine	3,372.1	3,399.8	3,483.8	3,495.7	3,480.1	3,415.6	3,306.6	3,145.8	3,020.5	2,909.5	2,823.1	-1.76	-16.28
United Arab Emirates	184.2	187.9	187.3	183.8	180.0	179.2	184.4	197.1	217.4	245.0	278.6	4.22	51.24
United Kingdom	3,838.1	3,915.3	4,006.1	4,102.4	4,195.4	4,293.0	4,392.6	4,471.9	4,524.4	4,546.6	4,533.1	1.68	18.11
USA	21,799.1	22,101.3	22,340.0	22,375.1	22,356.0	22,364.0	22,134.5	21,715.8	21,242.3	20,785.4	20,396.1	-0.66	-6.44
Venezuela	1,304.4	1,349.1	1,399.9	1,455.2	1,512.2	1,566.7	1,615.4	1,656.6	1,689.9	1,715.7	1,735.2	2.89	33.03
Vietnam	4,052.3	4,229.7	4,418.5	4,613.5	4,807.5	4,990.4	5,155.0	5,299.2	5,426.2	5,540.6	5,649.7	3.38	39.42

Key population trends

Table 4.19 Population Aged 55-59: 2009-2019

'000

	2009	2010	2011	2012	2013	2014	2015	2016	2017	2018	2019	CAGR	Period growth
Algeria	1,117.8	1,176.6	1,226.1	1,268.5	1,308.7	1,353.1	1,406.9	1,472.0	1,547.4	1,629.6	1,713.5	4.36	53.29
Argentina	1,871.5	1,900.4	1,925.0	1,946.0	1,964.8	1,983.1	2,002.2	2,022.8	2,044.7	2,067.3	2,090.2	1.11	11.69
Australia	1,306.7	1,323.3	1,344.9	1,367.5	1,387.9	1,414.3	1,441.6	1,469.1	1,497.4	1,522.5	1,539.4	1.65	17.80
Austria	491.8	494.5	503.6	523.4	540.8	559.7	581.1	601.9	620.2	640.1	660.7	3.00	34.34
Azerbaijan	329.3	367.1	403.8	439.0	472.6	504.8	535.3	563.7	588.8	608.5	621.0	6.55	88.58
Belarus	609.8	614.3	628.9	649.6	670.6	702.1	718.0	735.0	741.2	739.1	725.1	1.75	18.91
Belgium	680.3	688.1	698.0	710.5	720.3	732.3	744.6	753.1	762.1	768.3	774.7	1.31	13.87
Bolivia	290.7	298.9	307.6	316.7	326.0	335.4	344.6	353.7	362.8	371.9	381.3	2.75	31.20
Bosnia-Herzegovina	255.6	264.3	271.2	276.4	280.4	283.6	286.4	288.9	290.9	292.1	292.3	1.35	14.39
Brazil	7,741.3	8,061.7	8,394.0	8,734.8	9,085.8	9,449.3	9,825.1	10,216.3	10,616.3	11,003.0	11,347.6	3.90	46.58
Bulgaria	542.6	531.7	519.9	522.0	517.9	512.4	507.4	502.0	497.2	493.2	489.4	-1.03	-9.81
Canada	2,205.3	2,273.8	2,335.0	2,403.9	2,468.6	2,517.6	2,563.4	2,613.1	2,643.8	2,677.1	2,701.3	2.05	22.50
Chile	802.2	836.2	874.2	915.5	959.0	1,003.2	1,046.5	1,087.6	1,124.9	1,156.5	1,180.4	3.94	47.14
China	93,183.3	98,510.5	102,398.0	104,608.6	105,412.7	100,521.0	94,031.9	86,248.8	87,108.9	97,037.6	106,239.0	1.32	14.01
Colombia	1,775.5	1,849.5	1,919.8	1,987.4	2,054.4	2,123.3	2,196.0	2,273.3	2,354.7	2,438.9	2,523.6	3.58	42.14
Costa Rica	181.1	191.5	202.1	212.9	223.7	234.4	245.0	255.4	265.3	274.6	282.8	4.56	56.18
Croatia	310.4	315.1	318.7	325.9	324.7	323.0	320.2	317.2	313.1	311.2	307.7	-0.09	-0.87
Czech Republic	765.9	763.5	756.0	744.3	729.1	707.0	676.7	649.2	626.1	611.7	621.6	-2.07	-18.84
Denmark	351.5	350.1	349.8	352.5	353.6	353.7	354.9	357.6	359.5	364.0	372.6	0.58	5.99
Ecuador	500.2	521.8	540.4	556.3	570.1	583.0	596.0	609.7	624.4	639.9	656.0	2.75	31.15
Egypt	2,791.4	2,909.2	3,024.2	3,134.7	3,239.2	3,333.4	3,411.3	3,468.5	3,505.8	3,524.9	3,525.5	2.36	26.30
Estonia	85.6	85.2	86.3	86.2	86.1	86.7	86.8	86.6	86.8	86.3	85.0	-0.08	-0.80
Finland	394.9	388.5	384.5	383.9	379.0	373.6	369.9	366.8	363.5	362.5	365.9	-0.76	-7.35
France	4,106.1	4,083.6	4,049.0	4,050.0	4,048.1	4,055.3	4,069.8	4,085.5	4,105.1	4,110.1	4,147.9	0.10	1.02
Germany	5,364.9	5,407.1	5,434.9	5,507.4	5,589.4	5,700.2	5,842.0	6,007.0	6,175.9	6,336.7	6,515.8	1.96	21.45
Greece	686.4	707.6	713.5	728.2	740.7	758.1	770.3	789.0	790.2	795.2	798.7	1.53	16.37
Hong Kong, China	483.1	500.7	525.4	553.8	584.0	606.1	624.4	636.5	636.5	644.9	645.2	2.93	33.54
Hungary	708.9	739.0	753.6	761.4	750.9	720.0	668.1	626.5	589.1	564.6	548.0	-2.54	-22.69
India	43,013.1	44,954.6	46,595.6	47,944.2	49,069.8	50,078.8	51,069.5	52,098.5	53,183.0	54,321.5	55,499.8	2.58	29.03
Indonesia	8,497.8	8,934.3	9,388.0	9,850.0	10,310.1	10,758.8	11,190.0	11,601.0	11,993.7	12,374.9	12,753.5	4.14	50.08
Iran	2,392.9	2,537.9	2,678.7	2,813.8	2,943.1	3,067.2	3,186.8	3,302.9	3,416.4	3,529.2	3,642.8	4.29	52.23
Ireland	236.1	240.2	243.7	248.4	253.1	258.0	263.1	270.1	275.4	280.4	285.9	1.93	21.08
Israel	362.0	365.2	364.4	362.0	360.6	361.3	363.4	365.2	366.3	366.8	367.2	0.14	1.43
Italy	3,674.0	3,670.9	3,683.5	3,737.8	3,806.0	3,874.5	3,947.5	4,031.2	4,130.8	4,236.7	4,366.6	1.74	18.85
Japan	9,129.7	8,624.0	8,220.3	7,857.5	7,633.7	7,557.6	7,456.7	7,398.2	7,436.2	7,487.6	7,540.8	-1.89	-17.40
Jordan	135.5	139.8	145.0	151.4	159.0	168.0	178.5	190.4	203.6	217.9	233.1	5.57	72.02
Kazakhstan	758.4	794.0	824.1	849.3	871.3	891.4	910.8	929.3	945.7	958.3	964.9	2.44	27.23
Kuwait	62.2	68.1	75.1	83.0	91.5	100.0	108.2	115.8	123.1	130.5	138.5	8.34	122.73
Latvia	138.0	137.2	138.8	139.7	142.3	146.4	148.5	150.4	152.2	151.9	149.6	0.81	8.42
Lithuania	193.7	192.9	194.5	197.0	201.4	210.1	220.1	227.2	234.9	239.1	238.8	2.12	23.30
Malaysia	1,069.8	1,124.8	1,175.6	1,221.0	1,260.5	1,297.9	1,335.1	1,371.7	1,407.0	1,437.8	1,467.2	3.21	37.14
Mexico	4,023.4	4,235.4	4,429.2	4,598.9	4,750.9	4,894.9	5,040.0	5,192.1	5,353.8	5,528.1	5,718.2	3.58	42.12
Morocco	1,147.0	1,219.9	1,299.1	1,381.3	1,460.5	1,529.8	1,583.8	1,620.5	1,641.7	1,652.2	1,658.9	3.76	44.62
Netherlands	1,080.1	1,081.0	1,088.6	1,103.2	1,114.2	1,130.9	1,151.1	1,170.3	1,190.9	1,210.0	1,229.3	1.30	13.81
New Zealand	247.1	250.7	256.6	263.0	269.6	277.1	284.3	291.9	299.7	306.8	310.1	2.30	25.49
Nigeria	3,601.2	3,707.9	3,808.1	3,901.9	3,990.7	4,077.1	4,163.4	4,251.3	4,341.3	4,433.4	4,527.9	2.32	25.73
Norway	293.1	295.2	299.0	305.1	308.2	311.4	314.9	317.0	318.6	321.7	325.5	1.05	11.04
Pakistan	4,817.0	4,991.2	5,175.1	5,367.4	5,566.8	5,772.4	5,983.4	6,200.0	6,422.4	6,650.9	6,885.6	3.64	42.95
Peru	988.7	1,024.2	1,059.7	1,095.5	1,132.4	1,171.2	1,212.5	1,256.3	1,302.0	1,348.5	1,394.4	3.50	41.03
Philippines	2,954.5	3,098.5	3,229.3	3,348.6	3,459.9	3,569.2	3,680.9	3,797.6	3,919.8	4,046.7	4,177.0	3.52	41.38
Poland	2,755.3	2,807.3	2,853.7	2,874.6	2,888.0	2,885.8	2,856.8	2,778.5	2,675.0	2,553.3	2,438.8	-1.21	-11.49
Portugal	661.2	667.6	674.4	677.9	686.7	698.5	707.4	720.0	735.9	744.5	754.9	1.33	14.18
Romania	1,417.9	1,420.8	1,441.6	1,464.6	1,468.3	1,467.8	1,432.1	1,377.2	1,311.2	1,244.7	1,184.4	-1.78	-16.46
Russia	9,593.7	9,717.8	9,850.4	10,001.2	10,118.1	10,334.0	10,369.2	10,542.8	10,555.8	10,448.1	10,199.8	0.61	6.32
Saudi Arabia	601.9	644.9	688.5	733.0	779.7	830.0	885.0	945.3	1,010.7	1,080.4	1,153.3	6.72	91.59
Singapore	305.9	319.1	335.7	351.5	364.8	374.9	383.8	390.2	392.6	395.2	398.7	2.68	30.33
Slovakia	368.7	379.7	386.1	389.6	389.2	387.1	380.3	372.7	364.0	355.1	351.3	-0.48	-4.72
Slovenia	146.9	150.7	152.6	155.1	154.8	153.3	152.4	151.0	150.3	150.4	151.2	0.29	2.92
South Africa	1,773.2	1,827.3	1,874.4	1,913.4	1,943.8	1,965.8	1,980.1	1,987.4	1,988.5	1,985.4	1,980.0	1.11	11.67
South Korea	2,618.0	2,805.2	3,023.2	3,233.4	3,448.6	3,658.0	3,830.2	3,968.0	4,069.4	4,118.1	4,112.1	4.62	57.07
Spain	2,561.9	2,605.6	2,656.6	2,726.7	2,813.7	2,907.9	3,004.6	3,096.5	3,182.5	3,265.2	3,340.5	2.69	30.39
Sweden	587.8	576.9	572.9	575.5	576.8	575.7	577.8	576.6	575.5	578.2	588.2	0.01	0.07
Switzerland	472.7	474.6	478.1	488.4	497.9	509.4	522.0	535.0	547.0	560.1	576.2	2.00	21.88
Taiwan	1,421.9	1,497.4	1,572.1	1,607.8	1,636.0	1,675.1	1,714.1	1,739.0	1,759.3	1,795.5	1,820.3	2.50	28.02
Thailand	3,259.8	3,422.2	3,610.6	3,744.3	3,860.1	4,051.2	4,177.4	4,267.9	4,413.1	4,563.2	4,706.0	3.74	44.36
Tunisia	425.6	449.0	470.1	488.6	504.8	519.0	531.7	543.2	553.8	564.2	574.8	3.05	35.07
Turkey	2,941.6	3,087.3	3,222.7	3,348.4	3,464.7	3,575.1	3,681.4	3,782.1	3,878.7	3,972.9	4,064.8	3.29	38.19
Turkmenistan	155.4	167.0	179.0	191.2	203.3	214.9	225.9	236.0	244.9	252.5	258.5	5.22	66.36
Ukraine	3,082.8	3,056.7	3,043.4	3,065.3	3,089.3	3,162.9	3,187.8	3,267.5	3,283.7	3,281.0	3,234.7	0.48	4.93
United Arab Emirates	103.1	111.4	119.9	128.0	134.7	139.0	140.6	139.6	137.2	135.6	137.3	2.91	33.21
United Kingdom	3,615.8	3,575.8	3,564.8	3,591.1	3,646.9	3,717.1	3,796.8	3,892.2	3,991.7	4,086.1	4,183.2	1.47	15.69
USA	19,009.5	19,465.4	19,885.0	20,381.4	20,805.4	21,096.2	21,400.1	21,647.1	21,693.6	21,686.0	21,704.3	1.33	14.18
Venezuela	1,085.2	1,120.4	1,153.7	1,186.4	1,220.7	1,258.9	1,302.6	1,352.2	1,406.3	1,461.9	1,515.2	3.39	39.62
Vietnam	2,978.0	3,210.0	3,414.7	3,597.1	3,765.3	3,933.1	4,110.0	4,298.2	4,492.4	4,685.5	4,867.1	5.04	63.44

Key population trends

Table 4.20 Population Aged 60-64: 2009-2019

'000

	2009	2010	2011	2012	2013	2014	2015	2016	2017	2018	2019	CAGR	Period growth
Algeria	745.4	799.1	860.7	927.4	994.8	1,058.0	1,113.7	1,160.9	1,201.6	1,240.6	1,283.8	5.59	72.22
Argentina	1,589.2	1,627.7	1,666.3	1,704.4	1,740.5	1,773.6	1,802.7	1,827.6	1,848.9	1,867.9	1,885.8	1.73	18.66
Australia	1,171.0	1,210.5	1,242.7	1,239.5	1,254.5	1,274.0	1,292.4	1,316.7	1,341.2	1,362.6	1,389.2	1.72	18.64
Austria	450.4	455.4	479.3	485.6	479.9	476.7	479.7	488.9	508.5	525.7	544.3	1.91	20.85
Azerbaijan	172.1	187.7	210.2	238.6	271.5	306.5	342.0	376.7	410.2	442.2	472.9	10.64	174.76
Belarus	399.4	451.5	501.4	530.7	546.9	553.4	557.6	570.6	589.8	608.8	638.0	4.79	59.74
Belgium	616.0	633.7	651.9	649.6	653.0	656.2	664.4	674.5	687.2	697.3	709.4	1.42	15.17
Bolivia	232.4	240.7	248.7	256.2	263.6	271.2	279.1	287.4	296.2	305.2	314.3	3.07	35.29
Bosnia-Herzegovina	188.0	199.7	211.8	223.9	235.3	245.6	254.2	261.1	266.4	270.2	273.3	3.81	45.35
Brazil	5,908.7	6,154.7	6,411.6	6,681.1	6,963.6	7,260.4	7,571.8	7,894.3	8,225.1	8,565.2	8,916.5	4.20	50.90
Bulgaria	492.0	511.5	527.3	518.6	517.0	512.3	502.8	492.8	495.7	492.5	488.0	-0.08	-0.81
Canada	1,879.4	1,963.1	2,030.9	2,050.7	2,083.9	2,137.4	2,201.0	2,259.7	2,326.4	2,389.2	2,437.2	2.63	29.68
Chile	652.0	671.4	692.2	715.2	740.9	770.1	803.1	839.9	879.9	922.0	964.9	4.00	47.99
China	63,742.2	68,282.2	71,800.7	77,690.2	82,690.0	87,829.8	92,050.0	94,930.6	96,485.3	96,477.3	91,261.0	3.65	43.17
Colombia	1,296.3	1,374.5	1,453.7	1,532.7	1,610.3	1,685.1	1,756.6	1,824.5	1,889.8	1,954.4	2,020.8	4.54	55.89
Costa Rica	130.9	138.6	146.9	155.7	165.0	174.7	184.6	194.8	205.3	215.8	226.4	5.63	72.93
Croatia	233.7	251.3	273.6	281.1	289.3	297.0	301.7	305.1	312.2	311.0	309.3	2.84	32.35
Czech Republic	711.2	725.5	748.6	745.5	736.5	730.0	727.4	720.3	709.7	696.0	676.0	-0.51	-4.95
Denmark	378.1	372.5	363.8	350.7	341.4	338.0	336.9	336.9	339.8	341.1	341.5	-1.01	-9.68
Ecuador	368.5	386.2	407.0	430.2	454.3	477.6	498.5	516.6	531.8	545.1	557.5	4.23	51.29
Egypt	2,049.8	2,167.8	2,286.9	2,408.3	2,531.6	2,655.2	2,777.2	2,896.0	3,009.7	3,116.8	3,212.6	4.60	56.73
Estonia	68.4	73.3	77.0	78.9	79.6	79.4	79.1	80.2	80.1	80.2	80.9	1.68	18.19
Finland	376.3	397.8	402.7	396.3	390.5	381.9	375.8	372.0	371.7	367.1	362.1	-0.38	-3.76
France	3,546.9	3,771.4	3,995.6	4,009.6	3,998.6	3,964.2	3,944.9	3,915.1	3,919.0	3,920.1	3,929.8	1.03	10.79
Germany	4,226.6	4,301.0	4,634.3	4,873.5	5,025.9	5,123.4	5,174.7	5,209.9	5,284.3	5,366.5	5,475.2	2.62	29.54
Greece	661.7	661.4	675.9	670.6	669.9	676.3	697.3	703.4	718.1	730.6	747.7	1.23	12.99
Hong Kong, China	338.3	378.2	412.4	433.3	451.8	471.7	488.8	512.5	539.7	569.0	591.0	5.74	74.68
Hungary	584.0	590.7	619.7	641.9	647.6	663.9	692.9	706.5	714.1	704.3	675.3	1.46	15.62
India	29,901.8	31,363.3	33,132.8	35,135.2	37,230.8	39,252.0	41,065.5	42,609.5	43,893.8	44,982.4	45,970.6	4.39	53.74
Indonesia	6,495.5	6,673.4	6,911.9	7,209.7	7,559.0	7,947.7	8,363.6	8,797.4	9,240.9	9,684.6	10,119.1	4.53	55.79
Iran	1,630.6	1,736.1	1,852.8	1,978.3	2,109.9	2,244.6	2,379.6	2,513.3	2,644.3	2,771.2	2,893.5	5.90	77.45
Ireland	208.7	216.5	221.5	224.5	228.1	231.2	235.1	238.7	243.5	248.2	253.0	1.95	21.27
Israel	307.4	328.8	343.3	348.5	352.2	357.7	360.5	359.2	356.2	354.3	354.6	1.44	15.36
Italy	3,552.7	3,667.1	3,795.3	3,727.1	3,663.4	3,594.3	3,594.0	3,609.0	3,664.6	3,733.7	3,803.0	0.68	7.05
Japan	9,408.6	9,966.8	10,475.4	10,096.5	9,522.3	8,841.3	8,360.4	7,975.6	7,627.5	7,413.8	7,342.8	-2.45	-21.96
Jordan	118.1	119.6	120.7	121.7	123.0	125.3	128.8	133.7	140.1	148.0	157.3	2.90	33.11
Kazakhstan	461.6	512.0	561.9	609.0	652.3	691.2	725.5	755.1	780.3	802.1	821.7	5.94	78.02
Kuwait	39.8	42.7	45.7	49.1	53.1	58.0	63.9	70.8	78.5	86.8	95.0	9.09	138.60
Latvia	113.1	117.6	121.9	125.5	126.4	125.3	124.5	125.9	126.8	129.2	133.2	1.65	17.82
Lithuania	157.1	163.8	166.7	172.7	177.5	178.4	177.7	179.4	181.8	186.1	194.4	2.15	23.70
Malaysia	736.0	780.4	831.7	891.1	950.9	1,010.3	1,065.1	1,115.1	1,159.6	1,197.9	1,234.3	5.31	67.71
Mexico	2,972.0	3,118.5	3,298.0	3,501.4	3,718.2	3,934.0	4,136.8	4,320.6	4,485.1	4,635.0	4,777.8	4.86	60.76
Morocco	811.7	857.7	906.7	959.2	1,016.7	1,080.4	1,151.0	1,227.5	1,306.5	1,382.4	1,448.6	5.96	78.48
Netherlands	1,044.1	1,074.9	1,110.4	1,075.1	1,054.7	1,045.5	1,046.8	1,054.5	1,069.1	1,079.9	1,096.5	0.49	5.02
New Zealand	221.0	229.6	236.1	236.1	237.0	240.3	244.0	249.9	256.2	262.7	270.2	2.03	22.29
Nigeria	2,764.5	2,834.6	2,917.2	3,010.8	3,111.2	3,212.8	3,310.9	3,403.4	3,490.2	3,572.9	3,653.5	2.83	32.16
Norway	287.7	291.2	292.3	286.1	284.6	285.4	287.4	291.1	297.1	300.1	303.4	0.53	5.46
Pakistan	3,829.6	3,919.5	4,027.6	4,154.4	4,298.1	4,455.5	4,623.2	4,799.6	4,984.0	5,175.5	5,373.1	3.44	40.30
Peru	773.4	802.6	833.9	866.8	900.9	935.4	970.0	1,004.5	1,039.3	1,075.0	1,112.5	3.70	43.85
Philippines	2,136.7	2,239.8	2,360.1	2,495.4	2,639.1	2,783.6	2,921.6	3,049.8	3,168.3	3,280.2	3,390.1	4.72	58.66
Poland	1,933.1	2,122.6	2,328.8	2,445.6	2,532.5	2,593.5	2,645.5	2,692.3	2,714.6	2,730.5	2,731.6	3.52	41.31
Portugal	600.2	611.0	619.4	634.4	646.8	646.1	652.7	659.7	663.4	672.4	684.2	1.32	14.00
Romania	1,033.7	1,105.4	1,198.0	1,240.1	1,293.1	1,320.9	1,324.9	1,345.5	1,367.9	1,372.4	1,372.9	2.88	32.81
Russia	5,774.3	6,892.4	7,747.0	8,106.6	8,421.3	8,633.2	8,744.2	8,870.7	9,006.6	9,114.1	9,306.5	4.89	61.17
Saudi Arabia	405.7	434.0	466.2	501.7	539.9	579.5	620.1	661.3	703.7	748.3	796.6	6.98	96.35
Singapore	218.6	249.4	270.5	277.9	288.2	301.0	313.5	329.7	344.9	357.1	366.1	5.29	67.52
Slovakia	270.8	283.9	305.4	326.6	341.1	351.8	362.6	369.0	372.2	371.7	369.4	3.15	36.41
Slovenia	105.9	112.2	124.7	130.9	136.4	141.7	145.3	147.2	149.7	149.6	148.4	3.43	40.15
South Africa	1,329.1	1,372.0	1,419.0	1,469.1	1,520.3	1,570.3	1,616.8	1,658.4	1,694.2	1,723.5	1,745.8	2.76	31.35
South Korea	2,100.6	2,186.7	2,259.1	2,330.2	2,410.2	2,528.3	2,710.9	2,923.3	3,128.2	3,338.1	3,542.6	5.37	68.65
Spain	2,376.5	2,417.6	2,451.3	2,472.2	2,490.6	2,523.6	2,565.8	2,616.0	2,684.9	2,770.2	2,862.5	1.88	20.45
Sweden	632.5	627.6	616.6	599.8	585.9	574.0	563.5	559.6	562.2	563.4	562.5	-1.17	-11.08
Switzerland	450.9	452.9	455.0	450.2	448.9	446.0	447.7	451.0	461.3	470.7	482.0	0.67	6.90
Taiwan	833.5	909.6	1,025.3	1,172.1	1,280.1	1,368.6	1,441.0	1,512.8	1,546.8	1,573.5	1,610.9	6.81	93.27
Thailand	2,332.0	2,526.2	2,677.0	2,835.1	2,996.6	3,106.1	3,271.5	3,465.4	3,601.1	3,719.1	3,912.8	5.31	67.79
Tunisia	290.8	309.8	331.4	355.1	379.6	403.6	426.0	446.3	464.2	479.9	493.8	5.43	69.76
Turkey	2,151.1	2,240.5	2,345.3	2,471.7	2,610.3	2,751.1	2,887.9	3,013.8	3,130.8	3,239.3	3,343.8	4.51	55.44
Turkmenistan	92.8	101.7	111.1	120.7	130.7	141.0	151.7	162.8	174.1	185.3	196.3	7.78	111.47
Ukraine	2,065.1	2,323.3	2,607.5	2,735.6	2,848.6	2,870.8	2,844.5	2,830.2	2,856.1	2,891.4	2,979.5	3.73	44.28
United Arab Emirates	44.2	48.9	54.2	60.0	66.5	73.7	81.6	90.0	98.3	105.7	111.3	9.67	151.70
United Kingdom	3,668.2	3,722.4	3,739.3	3,663.0	3,534.5	3,460.1	3,426.7	3,423.1	3,454.1	3,511.9	3,582.1	-0.24	-2.35
USA	15,822.4	16,623.8	17,418.5	17,417.0	17,720.5	18,125.2	18,573.0	18,988.5	19,473.7	19,887.9	20,175.3	2.46	27.51
Venezuela	831.1	872.9	914.0	954.0	992.2	1,028.4	1,062.3	1,094.6	1,126.3	1,159.5	1,196.6	3.71	43.98
Vietnam	1,848.2	1,969.8	2,142.7	2,359.9	2,603.3	2,847.2	3,072.9	3,272.9	3,451.7	3,616.9	3,781.4	7.42	104.60

Key population trends

Table 4.21 Population Aged 65-69: 2009-2019

'000

	2009	2010	2011	2012	2013	2014	2015	2016	2017	2018	2019	CAGR	Period growth
Algeria	563.2	570.5	585.3	608.3	640.3	681.4	731.0	787.9	849.5	911.9	970.6	5.59	72.34
Argentina	1,300.8	1,328.6	1,359.2	1,392.3	1,427.6	1,464.3	1,501.8	1,539.3	1,576.1	1,611.0	1,643.6	2.37	26.35
Australia	870.3	909.4	951.8	1,023.8	1,084.3	1,124.9	1,165.1	1,199.4	1,198.9	1,215.3	1,235.2	3.56	41.93
Austria	484.4	467.1	426.7	408.6	419.9	429.2	434.5	457.5	463.9	458.9	456.4	-0.59	-5.78
Azerbaijan	172.2	159.0	149.6	145.0	146.1	153.7	167.8	188.3	214.3	244.2	276.1	4.83	60.32
Belarus	374.0	335.7	300.1	289.8	310.1	349.3	394.6	437.5	463.1	477.0	483.1	2.59	29.17
Belgium	460.8	467.1	481.2	524.2	559.3	583.9	601.4	619.4	618.1	622.2	626.1	3.11	35.88
Bolivia	176.1	181.4	187.7	195.0	202.8	210.8	218.6	226.0	233.2	240.3	247.5	3.46	40.56
Bosnia-Herzegovina	158.5	154.7	154.9	159.1	166.7	176.6	187.8	199.3	210.8	221.5	231.1	3.84	45.79
Brazil	4,516.1	4,630.3	4,779.7	4,959.3	5,164.2	5,386.6	5,620.6	5,864.9	6,121.1	6,389.4	6,670.4	3.98	47.70
Bulgaria	389.0	393.6	402.1	421.3	433.6	449.1	467.8	483.3	476.3	475.6	472.2	1.96	21.40
Canada	1,389.8	1,447.9	1,512.0	1,618.6	1,706.8	1,784.7	1,861.2	1,924.5	1,943.4	1,975.3	2,026.7	3.84	45.83
Chile	515.8	537.1	556.9	575.5	593.3	611.0	629.6	649.6	671.5	696.1	724.0	3.45	40.35
China	45,439.1	45,742.4	47,037.4	49,284.4	51,512.1	54,792.4	58,277.4	60,899.2	65,515.4	69,341.2	73,164.8	4.88	61.02
Colombia	895.5	942.4	996.7	1,058.0	1,125.0	1,196.1	1,269.5	1,343.9	1,418.2	1,491.0	1,561.3	5.72	74.35
Costa Rica	96.5	100.7	105.4	110.8	116.9	123.5	130.8	138.6	147.0	155.9	165.1	5.52	71.08
Croatia	226.0	214.9	200.6	201.1	203.6	211.8	229.3	251.3	258.7	266.8	274.4	1.96	21.41
Czech Republic	507.9	540.5	556.6	597.9	638.9	660.8	674.0	695.4	693.5	686.5	682.0	2.99	34.27
Denmark	280.1	298.7	318.5	339.3	351.1	355.0	350.3	342.6	330.8	322.5	319.7	1.33	14.16
Ecuador	294.7	302.7	311.2	320.8	332.1	346.0	362.8	382.5	404.4	427.1	449.1	4.30	52.36
Egypt	1,503.7	1,548.5	1,612.5	1,694.4	1,795.6	1,911.9	2,035.5	2,160.2	2,287.4	2,416.7	2,546.4	5.41	69.34
Estonia	66.5	62.0	58.7	56.5	57.8	61.6	66.1	69.5	71.2	72.0	72.0	0.80	8.24
Finland	255.5	259.0	283.2	298.0	333.4	358.4	378.8	383.6	377.7	372.5	364.6	3.62	42.69
France	2,509.8	2,548.7	2,620.7	2,890.9	3,148.7	3,379.6	3,595.3	3,811.5	3,828.2	3,821.3	3,792.1	4.21	51.09
Germany	5,137.3	4,866.9	4,367.1	4,026.0	3,979.2	3,966.2	4,048.2	4,369.4	4,599.5	4,747.2	4,842.4	-0.59	-5.74
Greece	540.2	543.4	538.1	581.9	615.1	641.3	641.2	655.5	650.9	650.6	657.0	1.98	21.62
Hong Kong, China	223.0	227.6	236.8	265.4	295.4	327.6	365.9	398.6	417.9	435.3	454.4	7.38	103.75
Hungary	505.0	520.3	513.0	511.1	516.3	530.0	535.9	563.5	584.5	588.9	603.6	1.80	19.53
India	22,629.0	23,042.1	23,530.7	24,140.0	24,934.8	25,977.4	27,300.6	28,895.7	30,697.2	32,582.7	34,405.2	4.28	52.04
Indonesia	5,450.4	5,512.6	5,570.0	5,632.1	5,714.0	5,832.6	6,001.0	6,225.1	6,503.5	6,829.7	7,192.6	2.81	31.97
Iran	1,196.1	1,218.1	1,256.2	1,310.9	1,381.4	1,466.2	1,563.8	1,672.5	1,790.3	1,914.4	2,041.4	5.49	70.68
Ireland	157.8	163.6	172.1	182.2	191.3	199.4	206.8	211.8	214.9	218.6	221.9	3.46	40.56
Israel	187.6	193.1	210.9	241.2	273.8	299.8	321.7	336.4	341.5	345.0	350.3	6.45	86.75
Italy	3,228.9	3,141.5	3,031.2	3,153.8	3,280.5	3,419.9	3,532.8	3,658.2	3,596.1	3,538.4	3,475.7	0.74	7.64
Japan	8,377.3	8,198.6	7,780.3	8,102.7	8,577.4	9,017.1	9,560.7	10,051.7	9,693.4	9,147.3	8,497.9	0.14	1.44
Jordan	95.2	98.5	101.0	102.9	104.2	105.3	106.3	107.3	108.6	110.4	113.0	1.73	18.68
Kazakhstan	355.4	324.7	315.8	328.4	358.6	399.4	444.2	488.9	531.5	570.7	605.8	5.48	70.46
Kuwait	25.9	27.8	29.8	32.1	34.5	37.1	39.7	42.6	45.8	49.6	54.1	7.66	109.14
Latvia	121.6	114.6	107.1	100.4	98.1	99.4	103.4	107.0	110.2	111.1	110.2	-0.98	-9.34
Lithuania	162.4	156.2	154.3	148.0	142.2	141.3	147.4	150.2	155.8	160.2	161.2	-0.08	-0.76
Malaysia	514.7	534.4	557.7	583.7	615.2	652.2	696.3	747.9	808.2	869.1	929.6	6.09	80.61
Mexico	2,363.4	2,459.8	2,550.2	2,635.9	2,727.8	2,838.1	2,976.1	3,144.5	3,338.8	3,547.4	3,756.1	4.74	58.93
Morocco	621.6	625.0	638.9	663.1	696.0	735.0	777.8	823.3	871.9	925.1	984.0	4.70	58.32
Netherlands	748.8	778.2	793.8	882.6	956.9	1,005.6	1,037.1	1,073.2	1,036.9	1,015.5	1,005.7	2.99	34.31
New Zealand	171.4	175.5	179.2	189.6	202.9	212.0	220.4	226.8	227.0	228.1	231.5	3.05	35.08
Nigeria	2,102.7	2,150.2	2,194.5	2,237.7	2,283.5	2,336.3	2,399.1	2,472.9	2,556.1	2,645.0	2,735.1	2.66	30.07
Norway	198.0	212.0	226.8	249.0	263.7	273.7	277.1	278.3	272.6	271.5	272.5	3.25	37.63
Pakistan	2,994.5	3,085.6	3,164.8	3,234.9	3,302.2	3,375.0	3,460.2	3,561.7	3,680.3	3,814.3	3,961.0	2.84	32.27
Peru	604.4	621.6	640.8	662.2	685.9	711.8	739.6	769.4	800.6	832.7	865.3	3.65	43.16
Philippines	1,613.5	1,671.7	1,728.5	1,787.2	1,853.1	1,932.2	2,028.4	2,142.4	2,271.4	2,409.0	2,547.0	4.67	57.86
Poland	1,407.5	1,373.3	1,349.3	1,447.4	1,598.9	1,773.9	1,951.5	2,144.3	2,255.4	2,339.2	2,399.2	5.48	70.46
Portugal	516.5	522.0	536.6	548.2	559.2	575.8	586.6	595.1	609.8	622.1	622.0	1.87	20.41
Romania	928.8	899.9	859.1	872.6	888.8	930.5	996.9	1,080.9	1,119.6	1,168.3	1,194.3	2.55	28.58
Russia	5,473.3	4,464.0	3,815.1	3,782.7	4,289.7	5,056.3	6,031.9	6,781.0	7,098.9	7,373.8	7,553.1	3.27	38.00
Saudi Arabia	291.6	305.0	319.9	336.7	355.9	378.2	403.9	433.3	465.9	501.0	537.6	6.31	84.36
Singapore	148.3	139.9	140.2	163.6	188.3	210.0	241.6	262.9	269.4	278.9	291.1	6.98	96.30
Slovakia	209.6	215.4	216.6	221.3	234.1	249.6	262.7	284.0	305.2	319.5	330.1	4.65	57.48
Slovenia	100.4	99.3	94.4	95.3	97.2	99.9	106.0	117.8	123.8	129.2	134.4	2.96	33.85
South Africa	968.2	998.5	1,027.6	1,056.2	1,085.8	1,118.4	1,155.2	1,196.6	1,241.5	1,288.2	1,334.3	3.26	37.82
South Korea	1,819.6	1,811.3	1,812.3	1,840.8	1,903.4	1,988.7	2,071.4	2,141.3	2,210.9	2,289.5	2,404.4	2.83	32.13
Spain	1,947.2	2,020.3	2,107.1	2,186.7	2,244.9	2,295.9	2,335.3	2,368.5	2,389.6	2,408.4	2,441.0	2.29	25.36
Sweden	484.1	516.0	550.4	581.3	599.1	606.3	601.9	591.5	575.7	562.5	551.3	1.31	13.89
Switzerland	364.9	380.9	396.5	409.9	418.1	424.2	426.1	427.9	422.8	421.2	418.0	1.37	14.55
Taiwan	761.7	761.9	733.4	719.7	740.9	783.5	855.6	964.2	1,101.9	1,202.8	1,285.4	5.37	68.76
Thailand	1,761.9	1,779.6	1,835.9	1,893.7	2,024.4	2,158.9	2,356.9	2,511.7	2,672.4	2,837.1	2,947.5	5.28	67.29
Tunisia	227.2	228.5	232.9	240.7	252.0	266.6	284.2	304.3	326.3	349.1	371.5	5.04	63.50
Turkey	1,698.3	1,758.3	1,787.5	1,816.1	1,859.4	1,923.5	2,009.3	2,115.0	2,230.7	2,353.5	2,475.4	3.84	45.76
Turkmenistan	67.0	64.6	65.0	68.1	73.6	80.6	88.4	96.6	105.2	114.1	123.3	6.29	84.09
Ukraine	2,229.4	1,944.8	1,672.2	1,572.6	1,615.5	1,797.6	2,047.1	2,324.9	2,459.7	2,591.1	2,637.3	1.69	18.30
United Arab Emirates	18.6	19.6	21.5	24.3	27.8	31.8	36.1	40.8	46.0	51.8	58.6	12.17	215.45
United Kingdom	2,789.1	2,865.2	2,964.2	3,140.6	3,331.0	3,440.5	3,496.8	3,519.5	3,453.5	3,337.1	3,270.1	1.60	17.25
USA	11,786.9	12,154.2	12,466.0	13,506.0	14,068.6	14,736.0	15,488.1	16,234.8	16,250.8	16,547.0	16,937.0	3.69	43.69
Venezuela	582.7	615.2	650.2	687.3	725.8	765.1	804.4	843.1	880.8	916.9	951.1	5.02	63.24
Vietnam	1,531.4	1,552.2	1,573.4	1,598.8	1,640.3	1,713.9	1,829.9	1,994.0	2,199.6	2,429.9	2,660.5	5.68	73.73

Key population trends

Table 4.22 Population Aged 70-74: 2009-2019

'000

	2009	2010	2011	2012	2013	2014	2015	2016	2017	2018	2019	CAGR	Period growth
Algeria	485.1	485.9	484.5	482.1	480.5	482.1	488.9	502.2	522.8	551.3	587.7	1.94	21.14
Argentina	1,059.5	1,071.1	1,085.8	1,103.6	1,124.6	1,148.6	1,175.3	1,204.4	1,235.7	1,268.8	1,303.3	2.09	23.01
Australia	687.3	710.6	730.5	755.3	779.4	815.1	854.1	896.9	967.4	1,026.2	1,065.8	4.49	55.08
Austria	304.4	342.3	383.4	415.7	433.6	445.7	430.6	393.8	377.9	389.3	398.7	2.73	30.97
Azerbaijan	192.4	189.1	181.5	170.3	157.4	144.5	133.7	126.1	122.5	123.8	130.5	-3.81	-32.17
Belarus	398.4	409.5	404.0	386.2	354.6	308.7	277.0	247.5	240.1	257.7	290.7	-3.10	-27.04
Belgium	452.5	452.6	447.3	432.6	423.8	423.7	430.8	444.9	485.7	519.3	543.0	1.84	20.02
Bolivia	133.3	136.5	139.6	142.6	146.0	150.0	154.9	160.6	167.2	174.3	181.6	3.14	36.17
Bosnia-Herzegovina	167.6	165.1	160.0	153.1	145.8	140.0	137.0	137.5	141.6	148.5	157.4	-0.63	-6.09
Brazil	3,509.3	3,624.2	3,713.8	3,785.6	3,853.1	3,934.8	4,043.7	4,183.3	4,349.1	4,537.0	4,739.9	3.05	35.07
Bulgaria	357.1	341.3	337.2	331.6	333.0	336.9	341.9	350.6	368.7	380.7	395.3	1.02	10.72
Canada	1,078.8	1,101.3	1,131.7	1,172.0	1,222.7	1,273.7	1,324.9	1,383.2	1,481.4	1,562.5	1,633.9	4.24	51.45
Chile	378.3	391.2	407.2	425.7	445.7	466.1	485.7	504.1	521.4	537.9	554.6	3.90	46.59
China	36,554.5	37,153.1	37,306.2	37,295.4	36,970.9	37,982.6	38,069.1	39,020.5	40,745.0	42,399.4	44,951.8	2.09	22.97
Colombia	651.8	673.0	696.4	722.9	753.6	789.9	832.6	881.9	937.4	998.0	1,062.2	5.00	62.96
Costa Rica	73.5	76.1	78.8	81.5	84.5	87.8	91.6	96.0	101.0	106.6	112.8	4.38	53.55
Croatia	215.1	211.9	208.8	202.0	198.1	191.3	180.4	166.2	166.8	169.2	177.3	-1.91	-17.54
Czech Republic	363.0	367.1	383.1	401.0	422.0	451.7	481.1	496.0	534.2	572.3	593.5	5.04	63.50
Denmark	211.1	216.7	223.6	230.0	241.2	254.1	271.7	290.4	309.9	321.2	325.1	4.41	54.01
Ecuador	232.8	240.1	247.2	254.4	261.5	268.7	276.2	284.0	292.9	303.3	316.1	3.10	35.74
Egypt	1,156.6	1,189.9	1,221.4	1,251.3	1,278.0	1,307.5	1,350.3	1,414.2	1,497.8	1,602.6	1,724.1	4.07	49.07
Estonia	60.9	62.7	62.8	63.6	61.1	56.9	53.1	50.3	48.7	50.0	53.5	-1.29	-12.16
Finland	217.7	225.3	223.9	239.7	234.4	236.7	240.2	262.8	277.3	310.3	333.8	4.37	53.33
France	2,416.4	2,395.5	2,361.9	2,305.2	2,301.2	2,332.3	2,371.8	2,442.2	2,698.4	2,943.3	3,162.9	2.73	30.90
Germany	4,511.7	4,715.6	4,877.9	4,952.3	4,825.1	4,664.6	4,431.6	3,984.5	3,681.3	3,645.4	3,641.3	-2.12	-19.29
Greece	582.8	569.1	577.0	547.0	530.8	507.4	511.3	507.8	549.3	580.7	605.2	0.38	3.84
Hong Kong, China	233.3	232.1	228.1	218.6	211.5	210.2	214.9	223.8	251.0	279.2	308.8	2.85	32.40
Hungary	404.4	404.0	411.8	417.1	429.2	435.5	450.3	442.6	440.6	446.0	459.7	1.29	13.65
India	16,453.9	16,864.6	17,240.1	17,585.8	17,915.4	18,253.2	18,627.5	19,066.4	19,608.4	20,307.5	21,214.4	2.57	28.93
Indonesia	4,097.3	4,214.2	4,319.2	4,411.8	4,491.7	4,560.4	4,621.3	4,679.2	4,742.4	4,823.5	4,936.6	1.88	20.48
Iran	1,023.3	1,007.8	994.9	986.9	986.6	996.6	1,019.3	1,055.8	1,106.5	1,170.6	1,247.0	2.00	21.86
Ireland	126.5	129.6	132.0	134.3	138.7	144.0	149.4	157.5	167.0	175.6	183.3	3.78	44.88
Israel	187.6	189.5	187.6	180.9	172.3	168.8	174.2	192.6	224.0	257.8	284.5	4.25	51.66
Italy	2,940.4	3,006.1	3,067.2	3,082.4	3,063.6	3,006.8	2,930.4	2,832.8	2,954.0	3,078.2	3,213.8	0.89	9.30
Japan	6,898.0	6,961.1	7,115.4	7,319.4	7,513.8	7,835.1	7,675.4	7,290.8	7,609.9	8,070.6	8,496.9	2.11	23.18
Jordan	64.1	67.3	70.5	73.7	76.7	79.5	82.1	84.4	86.4	88.0	89.4	3.39	39.50
Kazakhstan	393.2	401.4	388.3	357.6	318.6	282.9	260.1	254.8	266.8	292.5	326.4	-1.84	-16.98
Kuwait	15.8	17.1	18.4	19.8	21.2	22.7	24.4	26.3	28.3	30.5	32.7	7.57	107.46
Latvia	103.8	107.5	108.9	109.3	106.4	101.4	95.5	89.2	83.7	82.0	83.2	-2.19	-19.82
Lithuania	142.5	142.7	141.6	141.0	142.0	140.2	134.9	133.4	128.2	123.4	123.0	-1.46	-13.71
Malaysia	355.4	366.8	377.6	388.1	399.2	413.0	431.0	452.7	477.5	508.2	545.1	4.37	53.39
Mexico	1,754.6	1,820.3	1,900.5	1,990.1	2,084.3	2,177.1	2,264.3	2,345.4	2,424.8	2,511.5	2,616.2	4.08	49.11
Morocco	524.0	533.8	536.1	532.5	527.0	524.4	528.7	541.8	563.6	592.5	626.5	1.80	19.57
Netherlands	602.5	617.6	637.1	649.7	668.8	692.5	722.5	738.2	828.2	903.1	952.1	4.68	58.03
New Zealand	130.1	136.5	144.5	151.7	154.3	159.5	163.6	167.2	177.3	190.0	198.6	4.32	52.65
Nigeria	1,406.1	1,448.9	1,493.0	1,537.7	1,581.7	1,623.7	1,663.1	1,700.5	1,737.4	1,776.8	1,822.1	2.63	29.58
Norway	152.6	157.5	163.3	166.6	173.9	182.9	196.1	210.0	230.7	244.6	254.0	5.23	66.43
Pakistan	2,012.8	2,094.1	2,182.9	2,276.7	2,370.7	2,459.5	2,539.4	2,609.9	2,673.6	2,735.7	2,803.0	3.37	39.26
Peru	465.9	478.7	491.4	504.3	517.7	532.2	548.3	566.1	585.9	607.6	631.2	3.08	35.49
Philippines	1,119.6	1,163.8	1,210.3	1,259.3	1,309.6	1,360.3	1,410.9	1,462.2	1,516.5	1,578.1	1,651.4	3.96	47.50
Poland	1,364.0	1,355.7	1,339.1	1,307.1	1,264.8	1,231.0	1,204.6	1,187.3	1,279.5	1,418.6	1,578.4	1.47	15.72
Portugal	492.7	493.7	486.2	477.9	476.9	478.6	484.8	499.3	510.7	521.7	538.1	0.88	9.21
Romania	921.8	922.4	911.7	874.0	834.8	790.8	768.0	734.3	747.6	763.2	800.7	-1.40	-13.14
Russia	5,709.1	6,140.3	6,225.1	6,095.1	5,380.3	4,454.2	3,638.9	3,131.0	3,140.9	3,583.5	4,220.4	-2.98	-26.07
Saudi Arabia	210.1	216.5	223.9	232.4	241.9	252.4	264.1	277.1	291.9	308.9	328.5	4.57	56.39
Singapore	110.6	117.1	127.3	133.9	134.8	134.4	124.6	124.1	148.0	173.2	195.1	5.84	76.47
Slovakia	162.1	163.4	166.9	171.7	176.8	180.7	186.4	187.6	192.2	204.9	220.3	3.12	35.94
Slovenia	85.0	85.6	86.5	86.8	88.7	90.5	89.6	85.1	86.2	88.2	91.0	0.68	6.99
South Africa	632.7	655.6	679.9	704.9	730.3	755.5	780.2	804.6	829.4	855.6	884.7	3.41	39.83
South Korea	1,485.7	1,526.9	1,571.7	1,621.6	1,653.1	1,658.3	1,653.7	1,658.2	1,688.0	1,749.0	1,830.0	2.11	23.17
Spain	1,848.8	1,794.9	1,750.1	1,741.3	1,781.9	1,823.2	1,892.3	1,974.6	2,050.2	2,106.4	2,155.2	1.55	16.58
Sweden	365.9	379.1	390.2	402.2	423.6	450.2	480.6	512.9	541.9	558.6	565.7	4.45	54.62
Switzerland	294.3	296.8	299.7	307.7	321.8	336.8	352.9	368.6	382.1	390.2	396.1	3.02	34.59
Taiwan	609.1	625.7	645.2	664.2	674.4	685.5	685.5	659.4	646.9	666.6	705.8	1.48	15.87
Thailand	1,456.6	1,488.7	1,497.5	1,547.8	1,526.7	1,554.5	1,571.8	1,629.2	1,687.2	1,820.1	1,956.3	2.99	34.30
Tunisia	203.3	202.7	200.9	198.6	196.5	195.8	197.2	201.4	208.5	218.6	231.6	1.31	13.92
Turkey	1,361.8	1,389.0	1,422.8	1,452.1	1,468.6	1,474.0	1,470.3	1,488.9	1,515.1	1,549.9	1,605.0	1.66	17.86
Turkmenistan	69.2	68.6	66.1	62.1	57.7	54.1	52.3	52.8	55.6	60.2	66.1	-0.46	-4.47
Ukraine	2,254.3	2,455.9	2,519.2	2,482.8	2,212.5	1,870.4	1,597.6	1,335.3	1,250.2	1,314.1	1,521.3	-3.86	-32.51
United Arab Emirates	13.3	13.4	13.6	13.7	14.0	14.8	16.0	18.0	20.5	23.6	27.1	7.38	103.83
United Kingdom	2,413.7	2,438.5	2,437.1	2,432.1	2,461.6	2,523.5	2,599.8	2,698.0	2,866.9	3,048.0	3,152.9	2.71	30.62
USA	8,970.5	9,118.1	9,325.0	9,659.8	10,182.6	10,578.5	10,918.6	11,208.5	12,163.0	12,685.3	13,296.0	4.01	48.22
Venezuela	407.0	422.9	441.4	462.8	487.0	513.9	543.3	575.0	608.7	643.7	679.4	5.26	66.93
Vietnam	1,329.0	1,315.1	1,311.9	1,318.4	1,332.8	1,351.5	1,372.7	1,394.3	1,419.4	1,459.0	1,527.2	1.40	14.91

Key population trends

Table 4.23 Population Aged 75-79: 2009-2019

'000

	2009	2010	2011	2012	2013	2014	2015	2016	2017	2018	2019	CAGR	Period growth
Algeria	329.8	343.2	354.2	362.7	368.5	371.6	372.5	371.7	370.2	369.6	371.9	1.21	12.77
Argentina	839.4	844.3	849.7	856.0	863.8	873.6	885.6	900.0	917.0	936.5	958.4	1.33	14.17
Australia	551.4	551.9	559.0	574.6	592.0	613.8	636.9	657.4	682.1	705.7	739.6	2.98	34.15
Austria	275.1	270.4	264.3	261.3	259.6	265.5	300.2	337.7	367.0	382.9	393.8	3.65	43.14
Azerbaijan	128.9	134.1	139.6	144.5	147.9	148.6	145.8	139.7	131.0	121.0	111.4	-1.44	-13.54
Belarus	300.2	287.0	276.8	286.0	288.2	300.4	307.9	302.9	289.4	265.2	230.6	-2.61	-23.20
Belgium	406.8	406.6	400.0	394.5	391.2	394.3	395.9	392.3	380.3	373.7	375.3	-0.80	-7.76
Bolivia	88.1	90.4	92.9	95.7	98.6	101.4	104.1	106.7	109.5	112.5	116.1	2.80	31.80
Bosnia-Herzegovina	118.2	122.4	126.6	130.4	133.0	133.5	131.6	127.5	121.8	116.1	111.8	-0.56	-5.43
Brazil	2,330.4	2,400.2	2,495.8	2,611.7	2,736.3	2,853.7	2,953.6	3,033.2	3,099.1	3,161.9	3,236.5	3.34	38.88
Bulgaria	293.2	299.2	294.8	295.0	286.3	278.2	267.5	265.8	263.1	265.7	270.1	-0.82	-7.87
Canada	906.7	907.5	908.7	908.5	915.6	932.2	950.4	976.7	1,011.6	1,055.7	1,100.0	1.95	21.31
Chile	287.5	293.7	299.6	305.7	313.0	322.4	334.3	348.9	365.5	383.3	401.2	3.39	39.54
China	24,981.2	25,209.4	26,032.7	26,446.6	26,576.1	26,184.2	26,555.9	26,697.3	26,661.1	26,404.3	27,072.4	0.81	8.37
Colombia	460.0	473.7	488.1	503.3	519.4	536.5	555.1	575.6	598.5	625.2	656.7	3.62	42.75
Costa Rica	53.3	54.9	56.7	58.7	60.9	63.1	65.4	67.7	70.1	72.8	75.8	3.58	42.21
Croatia	172.6	175.1	174.2	173.9	172.8	170.0	166.9	163.9	157.2	153.4	146.7	-1.61	-14.99
Czech Republic	322.4	317.6	309.2	302.0	296.3	297.2	301.6	316.1	332.1	350.7	377.0	1.58	16.95
Denmark	157.5	159.8	162.8	167.4	172.9	179.5	185.0	191.6	197.8	208.2	220.2	3.41	39.85
Ecuador	170.7	177.0	183.3	189.8	196.3	202.7	209.1	215.5	221.8	228.1	234.4	3.22	37.30
Egypt	773.2	811.6	848.0	882.6	916.5	949.4	980.2	1,008.8	1,035.6	1,058.8	1,084.9	3.45	40.32
Estonia	48.2	46.8	46.1	46.1	47.0	48.6	50.2	50.3	51.2	49.3	46.0	-0.48	-4.66
Finland	180.9	179.7	179.7	180.4	183.8	191.3	198.3	197.2	211.7	207.1	209.6	1.48	15.83
France	2,222.3	2,229.7	2,201.7	2,182.6	2,155.4	2,145.6	2,131.0	2,104.3	2,056.9	2,057.4	2,090.1	-0.61	-5.95
Germany	2,994.8	3,086.1	3,216.1	3,401.3	3,613.1	3,873.4	4,064.2	4,217.8	4,290.3	4,182.1	4,047.4	3.06	35.15
Greece	488.3	507.2	498.8	509.7	509.1	508.8	498.1	506.6	480.9	467.3	447.6	-0.87	-8.33
Hong Kong, China	198.5	200.1	201.2	205.1	206.9	206.5	205.5	202.1	193.6	187.6	186.9	-0.60	-5.83
Hungary	338.0	334.6	326.3	321.0	315.2	313.2	313.5	321.7	327.9	340.9	348.4	0.30	3.07
India	10,012.4	10,390.1	10,774.5	11,159.7	11,535.6	11,891.5	12,221.7	12,527.8	12,815.1	13,092.8	13,378.2	2.94	33.62
Indonesia	2,518.5	2,625.1	2,733.7	2,842.8	2,950.1	3,052.7	3,148.6	3,237.1	3,317.9	3,390.2	3,454.3	3.21	37.16
Iran	774.1	775.1	772.5	767.0	759.5	751.2	743.4	737.6	735.2	738.7	750.2	-0.31	-3.09
Ireland	97.9	99.3	100.6	102.5	104.2	106.4	109.2	111.4	113.6	117.7	122.6	2.27	25.21
Israel	141.5	141.8	145.2	151.4	157.8	162.8	164.4	162.0	154.7	145.4	141.5	0.00	-0.01
Italy	2,479.0	2,503.1	2,500.9	2,500.8	2,533.3	2,594.9	2,660.1	2,721.0	2,738.4	2,726.3	2,681.5	0.79	8.17
Japan	5,806.3	5,948.3	6,091.6	6,192.0	6,227.1	6,180.9	6,252.8	6,408.9	6,607.3	6,792.6	7,088.8	2.02	22.09
Jordan	37.4	39.8	42.0	44.1	46.2	48.5	50.9	53.5	56.2	58.9	61.4	5.08	64.19
Kazakhstan	184.5	192.2	212.5	240.6	268.3	286.8	290.2	277.6	253.4	225.0	201.2	0.87	9.02
Kuwait	7.6	8.5	9.5	10.5	11.6	12.7	13.8	14.9	16.0	17.2	18.5	9.27	142.60
Latvia	80.0	77.7	76.3	76.5	77.7	80.1	82.8	83.7	84.0	81.8	78.1	-0.25	-2.47
Lithuania	115.9	115.2	114.7	115.7	115.1	115.2	115.6	115.0	114.8	116.0	114.8	-0.09	-0.92
Malaysia	203.4	211.0	220.4	231.7	242.1	252.3	261.8	270.5	279.1	288.3	300.6	3.98	47.80
Mexico	1,331.6	1,369.9	1,405.9	1,440.5	1,478.9	1,526.2	1,585.5	1,657.2	1,738.3	1,822.9	1,904.9	3.65	43.05
Morocco	327.9	335.6	348.7	365.0	381.4	394.2	401.2	402.2	399.2	395.7	395.4	1.89	20.58
Netherlands	488.4	493.8	496.1	502.0	505.9	520.3	535.6	555.1	567.5	586.5	610.0	2.25	24.91
New Zealand	104.7	104.7	105.3	107.6	110.8	114.8	120.8	128.1	134.8	137.3	142.2	3.11	35.81
Nigeria	808.6	832.8	858.0	884.7	912.9	942.7	974.1	1,006.8	1,040.0	1,072.6	1,103.8	3.16	36.51
Norway	134.6	132.5	129.9	129.3	129.5	132.9	137.5	142.9	146.0	152.7	161.0	1.81	19.63
Pakistan	1,240.2	1,282.5	1,326.7	1,373.9	1,426.0	1,484.6	1,550.3	1,622.5	1,698.9	1,775.2	1,846.8	4.06	48.92
Peru	322.0	335.0	347.7	360.0	372.0	383.7	395.0	406.3	417.7	429.6	442.5	3.23	37.40
Philippines	676.1	712.1	745.3	776.9	808.3	841.6	877.8	917.2	959.1	1,002.1	1,044.8	4.45	54.53
Poland	1,141.1	1,133.3	1,119.2	1,115.5	1,108.8	1,108.2	1,105.4	1,095.9	1,072.9	1,040.9	1,016.1	-1.15	-10.96
Portugal	405.5	412.5	419.5	423.1	423.7	426.5	428.6	423.4	417.4	417.9	420.9	0.37	3.80
Romania	692.7	696.4	694.1	707.9	706.1	714.7	717.2	710.3	682.5	653.7	621.2	-1.08	-10.32
Russia	3,853.2	3,587.8	3,466.3	3,581.9	3,872.6	4,256.2	4,571.1	4,630.8	4,528.5	3,992.6	3,299.5	-1.54	-14.37
Saudi Arabia	139.9	143.5	147.2	151.1	155.3	160.1	165.6	171.9	178.9	186.8	195.5	3.41	39.78
Singapore	79.3	84.5	86.0	84.7	87.0	94.6	100.8	111.0	117.2	117.3	116.3	3.91	46.70
Slovakia	136.3	134.3	131.7	128.1	124.1	123.3	124.5	128.0	132.8	137.8	141.6	0.38	3.89
Slovenia	71.2	71.9	71.4	71.9	71.6	71.7	72.3	73.3	73.8	75.7	77.4	0.85	8.79
South Africa	371.2	385.2	399.4	414.0	429.3	445.6	463.3	482.1	501.9	522.1	542.3	3.86	46.08
South Korea	1,000.2	1,066.9	1,129.7	1,179.5	1,225.7	1,268.6	1,305.8	1,347.4	1,393.8	1,424.1	1,431.1	3.65	43.08
Spain	1,697.7	1,719.5	1,724.9	1,709.5	1,671.4	1,639.5	1,594.9	1,558.8	1,554.7	1,594.5	1,634.6	-0.38	-3.72
Sweden	305.7	304.6	303.7	307.0	312.1	322.5	334.9	345.1	356.4	375.9	400.5	2.74	30.98
Switzerland	248.1	250.8	252.8	255.1	255.2	257.7	260.0	262.8	270.7	284.8	299.8	1.91	20.82
Taiwan	494.3	494.2	493.9	494.4	503.4	513.6	527.8	544.5	560.2	568.5	577.4	1.57	16.82
Thailand	1,028.5	1,067.3	1,132.8	1,163.0	1,215.9	1,255.9	1,287.9	1,296.6	1,346.9	1,324.4	1,351.5	2.77	31.41
Tunisia	146.7	149.5	152.2	154.6	156.4	157.2	157.0	155.9	154.3	153.0	153.0	0.42	4.30
Turkey	803.2	874.7	968.5	1,044.9	1,112.6	1,168.8	1,211.4	1,248.5	1,273.8	1,278.8	1,258.4	4.59	56.67
Turkmenistan	42.7	43.8	45.7	47.9	49.8	50.6	50.0	47.8	44.7	41.5	39.2	-0.87	-8.34
Ukraine	1,365.7	1,262.8	1,237.6	1,353.1	1,592.1	1,860.9	2,056.0	2,120.1	2,101.5	1,871.8	1,577.5	1.45	15.51
United Arab Emirates	6.7	7.0	7.6	8.5	9.4	10.2	10.8	11.1	11.3	11.5	12.1	6.19	82.31
United Kingdom	1,979.0	1,974.7	1,976.2	1,988.3	2,013.5	2,046.8	2,074.7	2,081.3	2,084.1	2,117.0	2,177.8	0.96	10.04
USA	7,204.4	7,204.5	7,229.7	7,279.7	7,419.2	7,590.8	7,731.5	7,922.4	8,221.1	8,685.0	9,034.2	2.29	25.40
Venezuela	289.6	297.2	305.3	314.2	324.2	336.1	350.0	366.2	384.8	405.8	429.1	4.01	48.16
Vietnam	1,076.3	1,100.7	1,108.8	1,103.6	1,090.2	1,076.7	1,068.8	1,069.5	1,078.0	1,092.7	1,110.8	0.32	3.21

Key population trends

Table 4.24 Population Aged 80+: 2009-2019

'000

	2009	2010	2011	2012	2013	2014	2015	2016	2017	2018	2019	CAGR	Period growth
Algeria	235.9	247.1	259.8	273.9	288.6	303.2	317.2	330.4	343.1	354.8	365.1	4.47	54.78
Argentina	1,016.4	1,047.4	1,076.5	1,104.0	1,130.1	1,155.0	1,179.0	1,202.3	1,225.0	1,247.7	1,271.1	2.26	25.06
Australia	814.3	840.5	863.7	882.3	900.3	918.0	936.9	959.9	985.2	1,011.1	1,040.1	2.48	27.73
Austria	392.3	400.9	410.1	416.7	422.2	425.3	426.7	427.4	428.7	430.7	437.8	1.10	11.62
Azerbaijan	88.5	97.4	105.9	113.8	121.4	129.0	136.8	145.0	153.2	160.6	166.2	6.51	87.81
Belarus	283.4	293.9	300.9	304.1	305.8	307.1	310.0	315.4	322.8	329.9	334.4	1.67	17.98
Belgium	514.1	529.4	548.3	565.5	581.2	592.6	602.9	610.8	618.4	626.7	637.4	2.17	23.97
Bolivia	67.8	71.6	75.2	78.7	82.1	85.7	89.4	93.4	97.6	102.0	106.4	4.61	56.94
Bosnia-Herzegovina	87.8	92.9	98.1	103.4	108.8	114.3	119.9	125.6	131.3	136.5	140.5	4.81	59.97
Brazil	2,562.4	2,680.8	2,792.5	2,900.6	3,010.4	3,128.5	3,259.0	3,403.5	3,559.8	3,722.2	3,883.6	4.25	51.56
Bulgaria	279.4	284.7	292.5	296.5	305.4	312.2	320.6	323.2	326.6	327.2	327.0	1.58	17.02
Canada	1,280.9	1,315.7	1,348.3	1,379.3	1,409.1	1,437.2	1,464.2	1,490.1	1,515.7	1,542.8	1,573.5	2.08	22.85
Chile	342.7	358.4	374.1	389.9	405.7	421.2	436.3	450.9	465.3	480.1	496.1	3.77	44.77
China	20,556.0	21,438.9	22,363.4	23,318.3	24,303.3	25,270.2	26,215.9	27,135.2	28,040.4	28,923.6	29,772.0	3.77	44.83
Colombia	491.7	510.1	529.1	548.9	569.4	590.6	612.3	634.9	658.6	683.5	709.8	3.74	44.36
Costa Rica	66.2	68.8	71.4	74.0	76.5	79.1	81.9	85.0	88.2	91.7	95.3	3.71	43.98
Croatia	154.9	162.7	170.4	177.9	185.0	191.8	198.0	203.9	209.4	214.1	217.2	3.44	40.19
Czech Republic	354.8	363.8	373.8	381.4	387.3	389.9	391.2	391.1	390.8	391.2	394.6	1.07	11.21
Denmark	226.9	228.3	230.4	232.7	235.8	239.2	244.1	249.7	256.7	264.8	273.9	1.90	20.74
Ecuador	188.3	197.5	206.9	216.5	226.4	236.5	246.9	257.5	268.3	279.3	290.4	4.43	54.20
Egypt	489.9	515.3	541.1	567.4	594.5	622.9	653.0	685.3	719.9	756.0	792.4	4.92	61.73
Estonia	50.8	52.7	54.7	56.3	57.9	58.4	58.6	59.4	60.5	62.5	64.0	2.34	25.99
Finland	238.6	247.9	256.9	264.2	270.0	273.5	278.2	283.9	288.8	295.0	302.8	2.41	26.91
France	3,233.6	3,336.5	3,446.9	3,545.3	3,636.4	3,702.4	3,770.6	3,816.5	3,860.5	3,893.1	3,921.3	1.95	21.27
Germany	4,054.9	4,168.5	4,284.3	4,359.6	4,412.9	4,458.4	4,615.5	4,804.4	5,001.3	5,200.2	5,431.5	2.97	33.95
Greece	482.0	502.5	542.4	562.3	584.0	607.0	631.6	650.4	667.8	678.0	689.7	3.65	43.10
Hong Kong, China	230.9	242.2	255.6	266.2	278.4	290.9	299.2	308.4	317.2	325.5	332.3	3.71	43.92
Hungary	381.5	390.1	401.6	408.8	416.9	423.9	429.6	434.9	439.1	444.0	450.6	1.68	18.12
India	7,561.1	7,918.5	8,288.7	8,671.4	9,067.2	9,477.6	9,903.1	10,346.3	10,805.8	11,272.9	11,736.0	4.49	55.21
Indonesia	1,669.4	1,763.7	1,859.8	1,958.0	2,059.3	2,165.3	2,276.8	2,394.2	2,516.7	2,642.7	2,770.0	5.19	65.93
Iran	604.0	615.7	628.9	642.9	656.9	669.2	679.0	686.4	692.2	696.8	700.9	1.50	16.04
Ireland	122.6	125.2	127.9	130.6	133.3	136.1	139.2	142.5	146.1	149.8	154.0	2.31	25.63
Israel	200.8	206.5	211.6	216.3	220.7	225.1	229.7	234.8	240.4	246.0	250.9	2.25	24.94
Italy	3,334.4	3,434.2	3,561.3	3,659.5	3,741.8	3,825.1	3,907.0	3,989.5	4,049.7	4,123.8	4,225.3	2.40	26.72
Japan	7,889.5	8,254.3	8,640.5	9,030.1	9,411.6	9,757.6	10,132.1	10,522.4	10,876.7	11,167.4	11,356.3	3.71	43.94
Jordan	33.7	33.4	33.8	34.9	36.4	38.2	40.2	42.3	44.6	47.0	49.7	3.97	47.57
Kazakhstan	196.5	201.3	200.5	195.2	188.5	185.2	188.5	200.2	218.7	239.8	257.4	2.74	31.02
Kuwait	4.8	5.2	5.8	6.3	7.0	7.8	8.7	9.7	10.8	12.0	13.3	10.67	175.63
Latvia	84.7	87.5	90.7	93.2	95.6	96.7	97.1	98.5	100.8	103.9	106.5	2.32	25.81
Lithuania	116.0	119.8	124.6	128.0	132.1	135.2	136.8	139.5	142.4	144.5	146.6	2.37	26.40
Malaysia	198.4	208.3	218.1	228.0	238.7	250.7	264.5	280.5	298.5	317.8	337.0	5.44	69.89
Mexico	1,459.3	1,536.7	1,617.5	1,699.1	1,780.8	1,861.5	1,940.5	2,017.0	2,092.2	2,168.9	2,251.7	4.43	54.30
Morocco	241.5	255.7	266.1	273.4	279.4	286.3	295.8	308.7	324.1	340.5	355.5	3.94	47.21
Netherlands	616.5	624.7	635.9	645.0	655.0	662.2	670.1	678.2	687.3	696.1	709.8	1.42	15.14
New Zealand	145.9	150.6	155.3	159.3	162.8	166.3	170.0	174.1	179.2	184.5	190.4	2.70	30.53
Nigeria	512.2	529.6	547.4	565.7	584.8	604.8	625.8	648.0	671.2	695.7	721.4	3.48	40.84
Norway	219.6	219.8	220.3	220.1	220.0	218.4	216.8	215.4	215.3	216.0	218.3	-0.06	-0.62
Pakistan	1,040.8	1,077.9	1,117.2	1,158.7	1,202.6	1,249.0	1,298.0	1,349.6	1,404.0	1,462.4	1,526.2	3.90	46.64
Peru	304.4	320.9	338.2	356.4	375.3	394.7	414.4	434.4	454.8	475.4	496.1	5.00	62.95
Philippines	460.5	479.6	502.8	530.0	560.4	593.1	627.2	662.5	699.3	738.0	779.0	5.40	69.16
Poland	1,186.6	1,242.4	1,305.2	1,357.0	1,402.1	1,433.7	1,464.8	1,496.8	1,528.2	1,552.6	1,572.5	2.86	32.52
Portugal	456.1	468.5	484.8	501.2	517.6	532.6	546.1	562.9	577.0	588.1	600.2	2.78	31.61
Romania	619.6	637.3	658.2	672.1	695.2	705.7	718.0	730.0	749.3	765.0	779.3	2.32	25.77
Russia	3,796.6	3,962.5	4,167.8	4,164.3	4,202.4	4,065.8	3,977.8	3,990.1	4,079.1	4,291.0	4,450.1	1.60	17.21
Saudi Arabia	106.8	111.6	116.5	121.4	126.4	131.4	136.4	141.5	146.8	152.4	158.4	4.02	48.32
Singapore	85.1	89.5	93.5	99.6	105.1	111.2	119.0	120.2	124.4	134.7	147.6	5.66	73.39
Slovakia	143.2	146.8	150.4	153.8	157.1	158.7	160.0	161.3	162.1	163.1	164.8	1.42	15.12
Slovenia	75.0	78.5	82.8	86.3	89.6	92.4	94.9	97.1	99.5	101.3	103.0	3.23	37.37
South Africa	276.8	288.3	300.5	313.4	327.0	341.2	356.1	371.7	388.1	405.3	423.8	4.35	53.11
South Korea	887.2	951.7	1,023.4	1,099.9	1,180.0	1,262.9	1,349.9	1,438.5	1,525.5	1,612.2	1,698.2	6.71	91.41
Spain	2,214.9	2,308.8	2,407.1	2,504.6	2,599.8	2,690.2	2,778.6	2,855.9	2,916.2	2,955.7	2,995.7	3.07	35.25
Sweden	490.6	491.6	491.7	491.8	490.1	489.5	490.3	493.9	499.3	507.4	518.1	0.55	5.59
Switzerland	358.2	365.8	374.1	382.8	391.7	400.6	409.1	417.2	425.1	433.2	442.6	2.14	23.55
Taiwan	530.1	561.5	594.1	619.7	642.7	666.4	689.9	709.4	733.4	760.9	787.7	4.04	48.59
Thailand	940.3	985.3	1,029.9	1,074.7	1,119.8	1,166.2	1,214.2	1,264.9	1,317.3	1,370.4	1,421.3	4.22	51.16
Tunisia	112.4	117.9	123.3	128.4	133.3	138.2	143.0	147.9	152.7	157.2	161.1	3.67	43.33
Turkey	654.0	628.8	583.1	557.9	540.8	537.0	543.5	554.1	576.0	615.4	677.7	0.36	3.64
Turkmenistan	37.0	38.7	39.8	40.5	41.0	41.6	42.7	44.4	46.5	48.7	50.3	3.12	35.92
Ukraine	1,476.2	1,511.4	1,516.0	1,491.6	1,456.9	1,434.1	1,442.7	1,492.0	1,573.9	1,670.6	1,751.2	1.72	18.63
United Arab Emirates	8.3	8.5	8.6	8.5	8.5	8.5	8.7	9.2	9.9	10.7	11.5	3.33	38.76
United Kingdom	2,805.5	2,848.0	2,889.8	2,928.5	2,960.7	2,988.4	3,018.8	3,057.0	3,100.9	3,149.4	3,200.2	1.32	14.07
USA	11,608.5	11,745.2	11,841.2	11,902.8	11,948.9	11,982.8	12,084.5	12,173.4	12,270.7	12,417.6	12,587.7	0.81	8.44
Venezuela	284.0	298.8	313.3	327.8	342.2	356.7	371.4	386.3	401.5	417.6	435.1	4.36	53.21
Vietnam	965.0	1,004.5	1,050.2	1,100.8	1,152.9	1,201.7	1,243.9	1,278.5	1,306.8	1,330.2	1,351.1	3.42	40.01

Key population trends

Table 4.25 Male Population: 2009-2019

'000

	2009	2010	2011	2012	2013	2014	2015	2016	2017	2018	2019	CAGR	Period growth
Algeria	17,615.8	17,882.2	18,150.6	18,420.6	18,690.9	18,960.2	19,227.1	19,491.0	19,751.1	20,007.0	20,258.1	1.41	15.00
Argentina	19,726.2	19,922.9	20,117.4	20,310.2	20,501.0	20,689.9	20,876.6	21,060.9	21,242.3	21,420.6	21,595.5	0.91	9.48
Australia	10,844.9	10,998.4	11,140.7	11,291.1	11,447.6	11,609.7	11,774.1	11,938.2	12,101.9	12,265.3	12,428.3	1.37	14.60
Austria	4,082.4	4,096.8	4,110.7	4,124.6	4,138.2	4,151.3	4,164.1	4,176.4	4,188.1	4,199.4	4,210.2	0.31	3.13
Azerbaijan	4,311.9	4,364.5	4,415.0	4,465.4	4,515.3	4,564.1	4,611.8	4,657.9	4,702.2	4,744.3	4,784.1	1.04	10.95
Belarus	4,511.7	4,500.2	4,485.7	4,471.4	4,457.1	4,442.7	4,428.3	4,413.7	4,399.0	4,384.1	4,368.8	-0.32	-3.17
Belgium	5,220.8	5,240.6	5,259.9	5,279.0	5,297.8	5,316.3	5,334.5	5,352.4	5,370.0	5,387.4	5,404.5	0.35	3.52
Bolivia	4,918.1	5,002.7	5,086.9	5,170.6	5,253.6	5,335.9	5,417.5	5,498.2	5,578.0	5,656.9	5,734.8	1.55	16.61
Bosnia-Herzegovina	1,849.8	1,849.8	1,849.5	1,848.9	1,848.2	1,847.2	1,845.8	1,843.9	1,841.5	1,838.7	1,835.5	-0.08	-0.77
Brazil	95,406.0	96,198.9	96,955.2	97,674.0	98,360.1	99,019.6	99,656.5	100,273.7	100,870.6	101,444.5	101,990.9	0.67	6.90
Bulgaria	3,642.1	3,615.7	3,589.7	3,563.8	3,536.5	3,509.2	3,481.0	3,452.4	3,423.7	3,394.9	3,366.0	-0.79	-7.58
Canada	16,667.2	16,829.7	16,975.4	17,118.1	17,264.2	17,411.2	17,557.6	17,702.8	17,847.0	17,990.3	18,133.0	0.85	8.79
Chile	8,393.1	8,473.9	8,553.6	8,632.4	8,709.9	8,785.9	8,860.2	8,932.6	9,003.1	9,071.8	9,138.8	0.85	8.88
China	684,037.2	687,411.4	690,463.9	693,381.7	696,243.1	699,022.7	701,691.8	704,217.6	706,569.5	708,719.2	710,646.6	0.38	3.89
Colombia	22,475.5	22,785.1	23,090.7	23,392.4	23,690.1	23,984.4	24,275.2	24,562.6	24,846.2	25,125.5	25,400.3	1.23	13.01
Costa Rica	2,325.5	2,355.8	2,386.9	2,418.7	2,450.8	2,482.6	2,513.6	2,543.7	2,573.2	2,602.1	2,630.5	1.24	13.11
Croatia	2,132.9	2,129.6	2,125.9	2,121.9	2,117.8	2,113.4	2,108.9	2,104.1	2,099.1	2,093.9	2,088.5	-0.21	-2.08
Czech Republic	5,048.0	5,056.6	5,063.2	5,065.9	5,066.6	5,066.6	5,066.3	5,066.2	5,066.7	5,067.6	5,068.2	0.04	0.40
Denmark	2,732.0	2,739.9	2,747.9	2,755.8	2,763.5	2,771.2	2,778.7	2,786.2	2,793.7	2,801.3	2,809.1	0.28	2.82
Ecuador	6,824.9	6,898.0	6,974.8	7,054.7	7,136.5	7,218.4	7,298.9	7,377.7	7,454.9	7,530.5	7,604.6	1.09	11.43
Egypt	39,224.3	39,934.0	40,643.9	41,353.1	42,059.7	42,761.7	43,457.5	44,146.1	44,826.9	45,499.4	46,163.7	1.64	17.69
Estonia	612.1	609.8	607.7	605.2	602.7	600.4	598.2	596.1	594.1	592.3	590.6	-0.36	-3.51
Finland	2,609.6	2,621.4	2,632.4	2,642.7	2,652.8	2,662.6	2,671.9	2,680.6	2,688.9	2,696.8	2,704.1	0.36	3.62
France	30,234.3	30,405.6	30,552.3	30,699.2	30,843.4	30,984.4	31,122.1	31,257.1	31,389.8	31,519.2	31,646.0	0.46	4.67
Germany	40,198.1	40,087.0	39,963.7	39,851.6	39,742.6	39,636.7	39,526.4	39,411.4	39,291.9	39,168.3	39,040.2	-0.29	-2.88
Greece	5,567.8	5,586.0	5,602.7	5,618.3	5,633.0	5,646.1	5,658.0	5,668.2	5,676.5	5,683.3	5,688.4	0.21	2.17
Hong Kong, China	3,313.8	3,328.4	3,342.1	3,355.1	3,367.4	3,379.2	3,390.3	3,401.0	3,411.4	3,421.5	3,431.0	0.35	3.54
Hungary	4,754.4	4,744.3	4,734.5	4,722.4	4,709.8	4,697.3	4,685.3	4,673.5	4,662.3	4,651.7	4,641.7	-0.24	-2.37
India	603,846.4	611,900.9	619,889.0	627,797.3	635,609.4	643,303.2	650,860.1	658,271.0	665,531.0	672,630.2	679,558.8	1.19	12.54
Indonesia	114,807.2	116,062.3	117,279.9	118,460.2	119,604.1	120,713.5	121,790.4	122,834.5	123,845.9	124,828.3	125,786.5	0.92	9.56
Iran	37,727.9	38,153.8	38,579.4	39,005.2	39,431.7	39,859.8	40,289.3	40,720.8	41,151.7	41,575.6	41,984.0	1.07	11.28
Ireland	2,222.6	2,252.5	2,279.7	2,306.5	2,332.9	2,358.7	2,384.0	2,408.6	2,432.4	2,455.5	2,477.7	1.09	11.48
Israel	3,664.0	3,722.5	3,780.3	3,837.4	3,893.7	3,949.1	4,003.7	4,057.5	4,110.6	4,162.9	4,214.4	1.41	15.02
Italy	28,704.2	28,744.7	28,778.1	28,804.2	28,823.6	28,835.8	28,841.5	28,840.7	28,833.5	28,820.5	28,802.3	0.03	0.34
Japan	62,163.8	62,010.2	61,847.0	61,676.5	61,487.8	61,281.7	61,058.5	60,818.2	60,560.7	60,286.0	59,994.1	-0.35	-3.49
Jordan	3,239.3	3,317.5	3,380.7	3,431.1	3,473.3	3,514.5	3,559.8	3,610.6	3,665.3	3,723.0	3,781.6	1.56	16.74
Kazakhstan	7,513.5	7,606.9	7,696.3	7,787.5	7,878.7	7,968.8	8,057.4	8,144.4	8,229.6	8,312.6	8,393.1	1.11	11.71
Kuwait	1,455.7	1,483.5	1,512.1	1,541.2	1,570.5	1,599.6	1,628.2	1,656.2	1,683.8	1,711.2	1,738.2	1.79	19.41
Latvia	1,038.2	1,032.3	1,026.5	1,020.2	1,013.9	1,007.6	1,001.7	996.0	990.4	985.1	980.0	-0.58	-5.61
Lithuania	1,557.7	1,548.1	1,538.6	1,528.8	1,518.9	1,509.1	1,499.8	1,490.9	1,482.3	1,474.1	1,466.5	-0.60	-5.85
Malaysia	14,296.7	14,523.5	14,746.7	14,966.4	15,182.8	15,396.1	15,606.4	15,813.5	16,017.4	16,217.4	16,413.0	1.39	14.80
Mexico	53,395.8	54,169.9	54,939.7	55,675.7	56,382.8	57,069.0	57,741.3	58,402.6	59,049.5	59,681.8	60,301.7	1.22	12.93
Morocco	15,712.2	15,897.2	16,082.9	16,269.6	16,456.6	16,643.3	16,828.9	17,013.0	17,195.0	17,374.3	17,550.3	1.11	11.70
Netherlands	8,117.4	8,133.3	8,149.7	8,166.2	8,182.5	8,198.4	8,213.8	8,228.7	8,243.1	8,257.1	8,270.8	0.19	1.89
New Zealand	2,113.4	2,134.9	2,155.9	2,176.5	2,196.5	2,216.3	2,235.8	2,254.8	2,273.8	2,292.4	2,310.6	0.90	9.33
Nigeria	77,547.5	79,343.4	81,142.6	82,943.7	84,743.5	86,539.4	88,329.3	90,111.2	91,884.0	93,646.3	95,397.6	2.09	23.02
Norway	2,395.1	2,427.8	2,458.3	2,486.6	2,513.6	2,540.0	2,566.1	2,592.2	2,618.3	2,644.5	2,670.7	1.10	11.51
Pakistan	93,101.7	95,115.1	97,181.0	99,293.8	101,438.5	103,593.8	105,743.5	107,881.5	110,008.6	112,124.0	114,229.3	2.07	22.69
Peru	14,540.1	14,734.8	14,928.5	15,121.2	15,312.2	15,501.5	15,688.3	15,873.0	16,055.3	16,235.8	16,414.4	1.22	12.89
Philippines	46,357.8	47,255.4	48,156.0	49,059.2	49,963.2	50,875.3	51,793.6	52,717.9	53,648.1	54,584.3	55,526.5	1.82	19.78
Poland	18,359.2	18,325.9	18,293.9	18,261.7	18,227.6	18,194.2	18,163.8	18,135.0	18,108.2	18,084.1	18,062.6	-0.16	-1.62
Portugal	5,168.2	5,181.0	5,192.6	5,202.9	5,211.8	5,219.5	5,225.7	5,230.5	5,233.8	5,235.8	5,236.5	0.13	1.32
Romania	10,434.4	10,400.6	10,366.2	10,331.6	10,288.6	10,245.5	10,195.7	10,143.4	10,090.2	10,036.5	9,981.6	-0.44	-4.34
Russia	65,641.6	65,544.3	65,356.5	65,184.3	65,041.4	64,915.0	64,789.4	64,660.0	64,525.8	64,386.2	64,238.8	-0.22	-2.14
Saudi Arabia	14,097.8	14,355.0	14,616.9	14,881.9	15,149.0	15,416.4	15,682.7	15,947.8	16,212.0	16,474.8	16,735.7	1.73	18.71
Singapore	2,325.9	2,356.5	2,385.7	2,413.4	2,439.9	2,465.0	2,489.0	2,511.9	2,533.6	2,554.3	2,574.1	1.02	10.67
Slovakia	2,620.6	2,621.8	2,622.8	2,623.4	2,623.9	2,624.2	2,624.2	2,624.1	2,623.8	2,623.3	2,622.5	0.01	0.07
Slovenia	994.3	998.3	1,002.3	1,005.0	1,007.2	1,009.4	1,011.6	1,013.7	1,015.8	1,017.7	1,019.6	0.25	2.55
South Africa	24,705.2	24,902.6	25,067.1	25,202.0	25,315.4	25,419.1	25,522.1	25,626.9	25,733.0	25,841.6	25,953.4	0.49	5.05
South Korea	24,481.5	24,540.3	24,592.5	24,632.7	24,665.7	24,690.0	24,706.8	24,715.0	24,715.5	24,709.2	24,697.2	0.09	0.88
Spain	22,459.9	22,669.2	22,862.2	23,051.3	23,237.2	23,418.7	23,595.3	23,767.4	23,934.4	24,093.2	24,243.7	0.77	7.94
Sweden	4,568.4	4,591.6	4,615.2	4,638.9	4,662.8	4,687.0	4,711.7	4,736.9	4,762.2	4,787.8	4,813.4	0.52	5.36
Switzerland	3,694.7	3,706.5	3,718.1	3,729.4	3,740.6	3,751.8	3,763.0	3,774.3	3,785.7	3,797.2	3,808.8	0.30	3.09
Taiwan	11,624.6	11,639.2	11,652.4	11,662.7	11,671.2	11,676.6	11,679.4	11,680.2	11,677.5	11,673.0	11,665.6	0.04	0.35
Thailand	31,471.5	31,640.6	31,797.9	31,944.8	32,082.2	32,211.7	32,334.5	32,450.7	32,559.6	32,661.0	32,754.6	0.40	4.08
Tunisia	5,165.4	5,215.7	5,266.0	5,316.2	5,366.4	5,416.2	5,465.6	5,514.4	5,562.4	5,609.7	5,656.2	0.91	9.50
Turkey	37,923.5	38,363.8	38,798.4	39,226.9	39,648.1	40,061.2	40,465.3	40,860.1	41,245.6	41,621.9	41,989.4	1.02	10.72
Turkmenistan	2,518.0	2,550.1	2,582.4	2,614.9	2,647.3	2,679.4	2,711.0	2,742.1	2,772.5	2,802.2	2,831.0	1.18	12.43
Ukraine	21,153.7	21,011.6	20,867.0	20,720.7	20,574.0	20,428.1	20,283.2	20,139.4	19,996.3	19,853.6	19,710.6	-0.70	-6.82
United Arab Emirates	3,105.1	3,169.1	3,231.1	3,290.9	3,349.3	3,407.2	3,465.4	3,524.4	3,584.4	3,645.0	3,705.3	1.78	19.33
United Kingdom	30,239.9	30,440.2	30,610.1	30,791.7	30,988.5	31,199.8	31,411.9	31,625.0	31,838.9	32,053.2	32,267.2	0.65	6.70
USA	151,242.7	152,419.5	153,467.6	154,525.0	155,607.1	156,689.7	157,771.2	158,849.8	159,924.3	160,993.6	162,056.6	0.69	7.15
Venezuela	14,349.0	14,575.6	14,800.7	15,023.9	15,245.0	15,463.8	15,680.0	15,893.3	16,103.6	16,310.7	16,514.7	1.42	15.09
Vietnam	43,816.5	44,376.7	44,939.5	45,503.9	46,068.6	46,631.7	47,191.3	47,746.0	48,294.8	48,835.4	49,364.4	1.20	12.66

Key population trends

Table 4.26 Male Population Aged 0-4: 2009-2019

'000

	2009	2010	2011	2012	2013	2014	2015	2016	2017	2018	2019	CAGR	Period growth
Algeria	1,742.7	1,760.7	1,778.6	1,796.5	1,813.9	1,829.4	1,841.1	1,847.9	1,849.7	1,846.4	1,838.2	0.54	5.48
Argentina	1,737.6	1,751.7	1,761.6	1,766.5	1,766.7	1,763.4	1,758.5	1,753.1	1,747.5	1,742.0	1,736.1	-0.01	-0.09
Australia	727.1	745.0	758.3	770.0	778.8	785.2	790.9	797.6	804.1	810.7	817.4	1.18	12.42
Austria	204.6	203.0	202.8	202.5	202.6	202.8	203.2	203.7	204.1	204.5	204.7	0.00	0.03
Azerbaijan	411.4	421.8	430.1	437.6	442.1	443.8	443.0	439.9	434.7	428.1	420.5	0.22	2.21
Belarus	249.3	259.6	267.6	271.7	272.2	270.0	266.8	264.6	261.8	258.6	255.1	0.23	2.31
Belgium	312.4	315.7	318.3	319.9	320.6	320.6	320.1	319.4	318.6	317.6	316.6	0.14	1.37
Bolivia	635.6	634.0	632.8	632.0	631.7	631.5	631.0	630.0	628.4	626.3	623.7	-0.19	-1.87
Bosnia-Herzegovina	89.0	89.8	90.3	90.4	90.0	89.3	88.5	87.8	87.1	86.4	85.8	-0.37	-3.64
Brazil	8,144.7	7,925.1	7,708.9	7,502.6	7,312.5	7,141.8	6,991.3	6,863.5	6,758.7	6,674.0	6,605.7	-2.07	-18.90
Bulgaria	171.2	169.6	168.3	166.8	164.7	162.3	159.4	156.3	152.9	149.4	145.7	-1.60	-14.92
Canada	918.7	930.9	937.2	939.2	940.4	941.8	945.9	955.3	967.0	978.0	988.7	0.74	7.62
Chile	635.3	637.6	639.7	641.3	642.2	642.4	642.0	641.2	639.9	638.4	636.8	0.02	0.25
China	37,301.2	37,260.1	37,544.8	37,347.4	37,257.6	37,111.8	37,067.0	37,112.1	37,116.3	36,989.1	36,729.6	-0.15	-1.53
Colombia	2,297.7	2,301.2	2,300.8	2,296.4	2,288.7	2,279.6	2,270.7	2,263.3	2,257.8	2,253.9	2,250.6	-0.21	-2.05
Costa Rica	190.4	188.8	188.7	190.4	193.3	196.5	199.0	200.2	199.8	198.1	195.9	0.28	2.87
Croatia	108.7	110.0	110.5	110.9	111.3	111.7	111.8	111.9	111.7	111.5	111.1	0.21	2.13
Czech Republic	263.5	266.3	266.7	266.6	266.4	266.1	265.7	265.1	264.2	262.9	261.0	-0.10	-0.97
Denmark	167.5	167.0	166.3	164.5	163.2	161.2	160.0	159.2	159.0	159.4	160.1	-0.45	-4.38
Ecuador	704.1	699.8	696.1	692.9	690.3	688.0	686.1	684.5	683.1	681.7	680.2	-0.34	-3.39
Egypt	4,638.8	4,690.1	4,729.0	4,765.4	4,796.0	4,819.3	4,835.5	4,844.8	4,846.9	4,842.9	4,834.7	0.41	4.22
Estonia	37.2	37.7	38.1	38.5	38.8	39.0	39.2	39.3	39.2	39.0	38.7	0.41	4.16
Finland	150.8	151.8	153.3	154.1	155.0	155.7	156.3	156.9	157.4	157.8	158.0	0.47	4.80
France	1,995.7	2,015.0	2,022.4	2,017.1	2,016.1	2,006.4	1,995.0	1,991.1	1,987.7	1,984.4	1,981.1	-0.07	-0.73
Germany	1,767.8	1,746.5	1,714.3	1,679.3	1,636.9	1,595.2	1,561.8	1,550.0	1,548.0	1,549.3	1,551.2	-1.30	-12.25
Greece	280.4	282.3	283.1	283.0	282.2	280.7	278.5	275.8	272.5	268.9	265.0	-0.56	-5.47
Hong Kong, China	120.7	125.4	125.5	125.6	126.4	127.7	129.5	131.8	134.0	136.4	138.6	1.39	14.78
Hungary	251.4	253.1	252.8	251.2	249.5	248.0	246.6	245.4	244.4	243.5	242.7	-0.35	-3.44
India	64,144.6	63,823.3	63,558.2	63,358.1	63,206.0	63,059.4	62,871.5	62,610.4	62,267.7	61,847.7	61,368.5	-0.44	-4.33
Indonesia	10,586.1	10,479.7	10,372.5	10,268.2	10,167.1	10,065.0	9,956.8	9,838.5	9,711.5	9,582.8	9,464.0	-1.11	-10.60
Iran	3,387.4	3,424.3	3,447.1	3,457.6	3,459.1	3,454.2	3,443.7	3,427.8	3,406.7	3,379.0	3,341.8	-0.14	-1.34
Ireland	162.1	161.9	161.9	161.6	160.8	159.8	158.3	156.5	154.4	152.2	149.8	-0.79	-7.62
Israel	368.0	366.8	365.5	364.0	362.3	360.4	358.7	357.1	355.9	355.1	354.5	-0.37	-3.67
Italy	1,403.0	1,385.7	1,367.5	1,347.5	1,325.7	1,302.9	1,279.6	1,256.5	1,233.9	1,212.4	1,192.4	-1.61	-15.01
Japan	2,776.6	2,776.3	2,749.1	2,703.8	2,642.0	2,562.3	2,500.7	2,444.5	2,393.4	2,346.8	2,304.1	-1.85	-17.02
Jordan	390.7	397.4	401.5	402.9	401.8	399.3	396.1	392.8	389.3	385.9	382.7	-0.21	-2.06
Kazakhstan	762.6	789.8	806.7	819.7	825.0	822.7	814.1	803.0	790.9	779.2	768.3	0.07	0.74
Kuwait	105.3	107.2	108.6	109.2	109.3	108.9	108.3	107.8	107.3	107.0	106.7	0.14	1.38
Latvia	55.9	57.2	58.2	59.0	59.6	60.0	60.3	60.3	60.0	59.5	58.7	0.49	5.03
Lithuania	77.5	77.9	78.4	78.9	79.4	79.8	80.3	80.6	80.8	80.9	80.8	0.42	4.24
Malaysia	1,613.5	1,601.8	1,590.0	1,577.2	1,573.9	1,578.8	1,588.3	1,597.7	1,603.3	1,603.4	1,597.6	-0.10	-0.98
Mexico	5,256.1	5,221.0	5,163.4	5,122.4	5,083.0	5,041.0	4,996.8	4,951.0	4,904.0	4,857.6	4,813.5	-0.88	-8.42
Morocco	1,568.6	1,588.8	1,605.6	1,617.9	1,625.4	1,628.9	1,629.4	1,627.8	1,624.4	1,619.1	1,611.8	0.27	2.76
Netherlands	473.2	465.3	459.8	455.0	451.6	449.2	448.0	447.7	448.2	449.5	451.4	-0.47	-4.61
New Zealand	157.2	160.7	163.1	163.7	162.8	161.5	160.3	159.3	158.5	157.8	157.4	0.01	0.10
Nigeria	12,896.4	13,076.5	13,225.7	13,342.8	13,429.6	13,491.2	13,533.5	13,560.6	13,575.3	13,580.3	13,577.8	0.52	5.28
Norway	152.8	155.5	158.0	159.3	160.6	161.0	161.8	162.9	164.4	166.2	168.1	0.96	9.98
Pakistan	12,407.7	12,588.1	12,772.1	12,956.9	13,133.8	13,290.1	13,414.9	13,501.3	13,548.4	13,561.7	13,552.7	0.89	9.23
Peru	1,507.2	1,505.7	1,501.5	1,494.6	1,485.5	1,475.7	1,466.1	1,457.8	1,451.0	1,445.6	1,441.2	-0.45	-4.38
Philippines	5,542.9	5,579.3	5,629.2	5,672.9	5,709.0	5,736.6	5,760.4	5,783.4	5,808.1	5,835.5	5,865.6	0.57	5.82
Poland	928.3	935.7	941.2	949.1	957.8	966.3	973.7	979.6	983.6	985.7	985.8	0.60	6.19
Portugal	281.6	282.1	281.5	279.9	277.5	274.4	270.8	266.7	262.4	258.0	253.6	-1.04	-9.94
Romania	557.1	559.0	557.6	554.9	550.5	545.4	539.4	532.8	525.3	516.8	506.8	-0.94	-9.03
Russia	3,961.3	4,100.9	4,218.5	4,333.1	4,393.1	4,408.3	4,395.5	4,414.1	4,413.2	4,382.1	4,329.4	0.89	9.29
Saudi Arabia	1,449.8	1,451.5	1,457.0	1,466.7	1,479.9	1,494.5	1,508.5	1,520.0	1,528.8	1,534.5	1,537.9	0.59	6.07
Singapore	123.5	124.3	125.1	126.2	127.3	128.6	129.9	131.4	132.9	134.4	136.2	0.98	10.29
Slovakia	138.3	138.6	138.6	138.6	138.8	138.8	138.9	138.8	138.6	138.3	137.9	-0.03	-0.31
Slovenia	47.8	48.5	49.1	49.6	50.1	50.5	50.8	51.0	51.0	50.8	50.5	0.55	5.60
South Africa	2,612.8	2,597.9	2,587.7	2,583.1	2,582.6	2,582.8	2,580.0	2,571.2	2,555.8	2,535.1	2,511.8	-0.39	-3.87
South Korea	1,149.3	1,141.1	1,136.1	1,123.2	1,108.4	1,091.2	1,073.6	1,053.9	1,035.3	1,017.4	1,002.6	-1.36	-12.76
Spain	1,243.2	1,261.7	1,277.1	1,282.7	1,285.2	1,284.7	1,280.2	1,272.5	1,262.3	1,247.5	1,229.4	-0.11	-1.11
Sweden	265.5	266.6	267.9	269.2	270.6	272.0	273.6	275.5	277.7	280.0	282.4	0.62	6.35
Switzerland	187.1	186.9	186.8	187.0	187.6	188.6	190.1	192.0	194.4	197.3	200.4	0.69	7.14
Taiwan	537.9	530.1	527.9	525.8	523.4	520.8	516.1	511.9	506.3	501.0	495.6	-0.82	-7.87
Thailand	2,076.2	2,067.6	2,056.8	2,042.2	2,018.4	1,987.7	1,953.6	1,921.8	1,895.6	1,877.6	1,867.0	-1.06	-10.08
Tunisia	408.3	412.7	417.1	421.4	425.3	428.5	430.8	432.0	432.2	431.4	430.1	0.52	5.33
Turkey	3,282.4	3,277.0	3,281.1	3,281.1	3,278.9	3,271.5	3,263.2	3,269.8	3,273.9	3,273.6	3,267.7	-0.04	-0.45
Turkmenistan	265.7	264.1	263.4	263.7	264.8	266.2	267.1	267.3	266.5	264.8	262.3	-0.13	-1.26
Ukraine	1,131.0	1,140.9	1,146.7	1,130.1	1,107.2	1,079.0	1,049.6	1,021.9	998.9	982.0	969.8	-1.53	-14.25
United Arab Emirates	158.6	158.3	158.9	160.3	162.4	164.5	166.1	166.6	165.8	164.0	161.6	0.19	1.92
United Kingdom	1,918.3	1,964.7	1,993.8	2,016.7	2,029.4	2,033.9	2,038.0	2,055.8	2,074.5	2,093.1	2,110.9	0.96	10.04
USA	10,862.3	10,947.3	10,954.1	10,898.8	10,835.6	10,789.0	10,769.9	10,806.8	10,857.8	10,903.4	10,944.1	0.07	0.75
Venezuela	1,494.3	1,499.7	1,503.7	1,506.4	1,507.7	1,507.9	1,507.0	1,505.1	1,502.3	1,498.8	1,494.7	0.00	0.03
Vietnam	4,032.9	4,028.7	4,028.2	4,028.4	4,027.6	4,023.4	4,014.0	3,998.7	3,978.3	3,954.5	3,929.4	-0.26	-2.57

Key population trends

Table 4.27 Male Population Aged 5-9: 2009-2019

'000

	2009	2010	2011	2012	2013	2014	2015	2016	2017	2018	2019	CAGR	Period growth
Algeria	1,561.3	1,595.6	1,630.9	1,665.0	1,696.3	1,724.8	1,750.5	1,773.9	1,794.6	1,812.3	1,826.4	1.58	16.98
Argentina	1,701.7	1,698.5	1,700.7	1,708.1	1,719.1	1,731.5	1,742.8	1,751.7	1,757.3	1,759.8	1,759.4	0.33	3.39
Australia	694.2	697.7	704.3	716.7	733.5	752.8	771.7	786.6	799.3	808.7	815.2	1.62	17.44
Austria	210.9	211.8	211.1	211.4	210.5	210.0	208.3	208.1	207.8	207.8	208.0	-0.13	-1.33
Azerbaijan	347.7	355.2	365.5	377.8	391.1	404.1	415.6	424.7	431.2	434.9	436.2	2.29	25.44
Belarus	232.3	230.8	229.7	232.7	240.9	250.9	261.3	269.4	273.9	274.5	272.7	1.61	17.37
Belgium	300.6	302.9	304.9	308.8	314.1	319.4	322.9	325.5	327.1	327.8	327.8	0.87	9.04
Bolivia	610.9	615.2	618.3	620.1	620.7	620.6	620.2	619.7	619.3	618.8	618.3	0.12	1.21
Bosnia-Herzegovina	100.5	96.6	93.5	91.5	90.4	89.9	89.7	89.7	89.5	89.3	89.0	-1.21	-11.42
Brazil	8,889.9	8,804.0	8,669.8	8,499.6	8,305.3	8,096.0	7,882.2	7,671.1	7,469.1	7,282.5	7,113.9	-2.20	-19.98
Bulgaria	169.9	169.6	169.4	168.7	168.2	167.5	165.6	163.8	161.7	159.3	156.6	-0.81	-7.81
Canada	915.0	913.2	918.8	931.8	946.9	960.0	972.2	978.9	981.2	982.6	984.2	0.73	7.57
Chile	633.5	629.4	627.7	628.0	629.8	632.4	635.2	637.8	639.9	641.4	642.2	0.14	1.39
China	39,502.6	38,536.7	37,732.7	37,699.9	38,176.3	38,299.8	38,560.7	39,080.5	39,184.9	39,360.9	39,498.2	0.00	-0.01
Colombia	2,251.5	2,255.3	2,260.9	2,267.8	2,275.0	2,280.9	2,284.3	2,284.5	2,281.5	2,276.0	2,269.1	0.08	0.78
Costa Rica	204.3	202.6	200.4	197.7	195.1	193.0	191.9	192.1	193.4	195.5	197.7	-0.33	-3.23
Croatia	110.1	107.2	106.0	106.6	107.9	109.5	110.7	111.2	111.7	112.1	112.3	0.20	2.00
Czech Republic	238.3	244.1	251.0	257.0	262.0	266.4	268.8	268.8	268.8	268.7	268.5	1.20	12.65
Denmark	169.4	168.6	167.1	167.4	167.3	167.6	167.2	166.5	164.9	163.6	161.7	-0.46	-4.55
Ecuador	726.6	721.3	715.8	710.3	705.0	700.0	695.5	691.6	688.2	685.4	683.0	-0.62	-5.99
Egypt	4,490.5	4,611.0	4,726.5	4,825.2	4,908.4	4,976.7	5,030.3	5,070.5	5,108.1	5,139.8	5,164.2	1.41	15.00
Estonia	32.4	33.4	34.1	35.0	36.0	37.0	37.6	37.9	38.3	38.6	38.9	1.84	19.96
Finland	146.7	147.2	147.7	149.3	151.0	152.8	153.8	155.1	155.9	156.7	157.3	0.71	7.29
France	1,970.1	1,976.1	1,970.2	1,980.1	1,990.2	2,008.8	2,027.7	2,035.6	2,030.6	2,029.6	2,020.0	0.25	2.53
Germany	1,906.3	1,869.4	1,827.5	1,797.0	1,780.2	1,769.9	1,751.8	1,721.7	1,687.7	1,645.7	1,603.9	-1.71	-15.86
Greece	268.5	272.6	276.3	279.5	283.0	285.8	287.8	288.6	288.6	287.8	286.2	0.64	6.61
Hong Kong, China	142.3	139.9	141.3	148.3	154.2	161.4	167.1	167.9	168.0	168.2	168.5	1.70	18.42
Hungary	246.5	247.4	248.1	249.6	251.1	253.1	254.7	254.2	252.6	251.0	249.5	0.12	1.24
India	63,638.8	63,677.6	63,631.5	63,498.9	63,300.2	63,069.9	62,842.0	62,638.4	62,461.8	62,298.8	62,125.4	-0.24	-2.38
Indonesia	10,656.5	10,685.8	10,686.4	10,656.8	10,600.1	10,523.1	10,433.6	10,336.9	10,235.6	10,130.2	10,020.0	-0.61	-5.97
Iran	2,892.2	2,997.6	3,102.6	3,198.6	3,280.4	3,346.1	3,396.1	3,431.7	3,453.7	3,463.2	3,462.3	1.82	19.71
Ireland	155.9	159.3	161.7	165.0	165.7	165.4	165.0	164.9	164.6	163.8	162.7	0.43	4.35
Israel	363.0	367.5	370.7	373.0	372.8	371.0	369.4	367.9	366.2	364.3	362.2	-0.02	-0.22
Italy	1,419.4	1,430.4	1,432.0	1,434.0	1,433.1	1,424.1	1,406.9	1,388.7	1,368.7	1,347.0	1,324.2	-0.69	-6.71
Japan	2,917.9	2,843.4	2,794.1	2,759.5	2,746.2	2,754.6	2,756.5	2,731.2	2,687.0	2,626.1	2,547.2	-1.35	-12.71
Jordan	366.1	368.4	371.7	376.0	380.8	385.7	390.1	393.6	395.7	396.6	396.2	0.79	8.21
Kazakhstan	586.5	614.0	646.6	682.3	718.3	751.1	777.4	795.2	804.0	804.8	800.0	3.15	36.40
Kuwait	95.6	97.4	99.5	101.8	104.2	106.3	108.0	109.2	109.9	110.2	110.1	1.42	15.19
Latvia	50.3	50.9	51.6	53.0	54.2	55.0	56.3	57.3	58.1	58.8	59.3	1.66	17.95
Lithuania	81.9	78.9	77.2	76.8	77.1	77.1	77.5	77.9	78.4	78.9	79.4	-0.30	-2.99
Malaysia	1,536.1	1,554.9	1,569.7	1,581.9	1,588.1	1,582.4	1,566.6	1,550.9	1,534.8	1,529.7	1,534.1	-0.01	-0.13
Mexico	5,240.1	5,232.4	5,220.6	5,196.8	5,164.3	5,126.3	5,085.4	5,043.3	5,000.0	4,955.1	4,908.2	-0.65	-6.33
Morocco	1,494.0	1,492.9	1,498.8	1,511.3	1,528.6	1,548.0	1,566.9	1,583.6	1,597.2	1,607.2	1,613.8	0.77	8.02
Netherlands	516.1	510.6	500.4	490.8	480.6	469.9	462.2	456.8	452.1	448.7	446.5	-1.44	-13.50
New Zealand	147.7	147.2	148.0	151.5	155.8	159.4	162.9	165.3	166.0	165.1	163.8	1.04	10.89
Nigeria	10,942.4	11,175.9	11,408.5	11,637.2	11,856.8	12,060.5	12,242.5	12,399.5	12,530.4	12,636.4	12,719.9	1.52	16.24
Norway	152.7	152.6	152.4	154.2	156.5	159.0	161.1	163.2	164.3	165.5	165.9	0.83	8.67
Pakistan	11,312.2	11,472.2	11,640.4	11,815.7	11,996.6	12,181.5	12,369.0	12,557.6	12,743.6	12,919.2	13,074.5	1.46	15.58
Peru	1,488.9	1,491.1	1,493.4	1,495.7	1,497.2	1,497.2	1,495.2	1,490.9	1,484.4	1,476.2	1,467.2	-0.15	-1.46
Philippines	5,263.0	5,303.9	5,350.5	5,404.4	5,462.1	5,519.9	5,572.6	5,617.3	5,653.1	5,681.6	5,705.8	0.81	8.41
Poland	932.7	919.4	912.0	912.3	917.7	926.5	934.3	940.2	948.1	956.8	965.2	0.34	3.48
Portugal	288.9	287.5	287.8	286.8	284.8	283.5	283.9	283.2	281.6	279.2	276.0	-0.46	-4.46
Romania	548.7	543.1	540.2	543.1	548.8	552.9	554.0	551.6	547.8	542.9	537.2	-0.21	-2.09
Russia	3,414.2	3,546.0	3,641.5	3,747.4	3,873.9	4,006.1	4,147.4	4,271.4	4,389.8	4,454.3	4,472.4	2.74	30.99
Saudi Arabia	1,411.4	1,423.4	1,431.9	1,436.9	1,439.6	1,442.0	1,445.8	1,452.3	1,461.6	1,473.0	1,485.3	0.51	5.24
Singapore	141.6	137.6	132.2	130.1	128.9	128.7	129.1	129.6	130.4	131.1	132.0	-0.70	-6.76
Slovakia	134.3	133.4	133.6	135.0	136.9	138.2	138.4	138.3	138.2	138.3	138.3	0.29	2.92
Slovenia	46.8	47.0	47.1	47.6	48.1	48.8	49.5	49.9	50.5	51.0	51.4	0.95	9.94
South Africa	2,584.5	2,594.6	2,597.3	2,592.7	2,583.1	2,571.9	2,562.5	2,556.4	2,553.6	2,552.7	2,551.3	-0.13	-1.28
South Korea	1,403.4	1,310.3	1,229.2	1,183.5	1,156.9	1,136.6	1,128.6	1,123.6	1,110.9	1,096.3	1,079.3	-2.59	-23.09
Spain	1,149.1	1,182.3	1,208.2	1,238.2	1,267.0	1,286.8	1,304.4	1,319.8	1,325.2	1,327.6	1,326.9	1.45	15.47
Sweden	249.0	255.8	261.0	266.1	269.5	271.2	272.3	273.6	274.8	276.1	277.5	1.09	11.42
Switzerland	192.7	190.3	189.5	189.0	188.4	188.5	188.3	188.3	188.5	189.0	189.9	-0.15	-1.44
Taiwan	689.2	656.2	605.1	579.6	557.8	545.2	537.4	535.5	533.1	530.6	528.0	-2.63	-23.40
Thailand	2,141.6	2,131.5	2,138.2	2,142.9	2,148.1	2,139.2	2,130.9	2,121.3	2,106.7	2,082.8	2,051.3	-0.43	-4.22
Tunisia	393.8	393.4	394.8	397.5	401.3	405.8	410.5	415.3	419.8	423.9	427.3	0.82	8.51
Turkey	3,490.5	3,420.4	3,353.9	3,320.2	3,300.1	3,288.4	3,285.0	3,265.6	3,259.4	3,259.1	3,261.1	-0.68	-6.57
Turkmenistan	249.6	253.5	256.6	258.6	259.6	260.0	260.3	260.8	261.4	262.2	262.9	0.52	5.33
Ukraine	988.6	1,005.6	1,024.1	1,063.2	1,093.9	1,113.6	1,121.4	1,125.5	1,108.6	1,086.2	1,059.4	0.69	7.16
United Arab Emirates	157.9	161.9	163.9	164.1	163.2	162.0	161.2	161.4	162.4	164.0	165.7	0.48	4.91
United Kingdom	1,737.9	1,747.9	1,772.9	1,813.1	1,863.2	1,915.4	1,963.5	1,995.5	2,020.6	2,034.4	2,039.0	1.61	17.33
USA	10,415.6	10,537.9	10,604.5	10,753.1	10,900.8	11,012.4	11,102.6	11,115.6	11,062.7	11,000.1	10,954.1	0.51	5.17
Venezuela	1,448.8	1,457.8	1,466.6	1,475.0	1,482.7	1,489.4	1,494.9	1,499.2	1,502.1	1,503.8	1,504.2	0.38	3.82
Vietnam	3,964.6	4,000.7	4,018.5	4,024.1	4,021.2	4,016.6	4,015.5	4,017.9	4,020.8	4,022.3	4,019.6	0.14	1.39

Key population trends

Table 4.28 Male Population Aged 10-14: 2009-2019

'000

	2009	2010	2011	2012	2013	2014	2015	2016	2017	2018	2019	CAGR	Period growth
Algeria	1,578.7	1,539.4	1,519.8	1,519.6	1,535.4	1,561.4	1,592.4	1,624.9	1,657.0	1,687.8	1,716.6	0.84	8.74
Argentina	1,749.6	1,740.2	1,729.1	1,717.6	1,707.5	1,700.7	1,698.7	1,701.9	1,709.7	1,720.4	1,732.4	-0.10	-0.98
Australia	720.4	718.5	718.3	717.4	717.9	719.9	724.1	732.1	745.4	762.6	782.2	0.83	8.59
Austria	236.0	229.9	225.6	220.0	217.7	215.9	216.8	216.1	216.4	215.4	214.9	-0.93	-8.92
Azerbaijan	374.8	360.0	349.6	343.9	343.1	346.7	354.0	364.3	376.7	390.0	402.7	0.72	7.46
Belarus	247.5	239.8	236.4	235.5	236.0	234.1	232.6	231.5	234.8	243.2	253.7	0.25	2.52
Belgium	308.2	306.9	307.4	306.6	305.0	304.5	306.8	308.9	312.8	318.2	323.7	0.49	5.01
Bolivia	576.9	580.5	584.8	589.7	594.9	599.6	603.5	606.3	608.0	608.8	609.1	0.54	5.57
Bosnia-Herzegovina	115.6	114.4	112.0	108.5	104.5	100.5	97.0	94.3	92.4	91.3	90.7	-2.40	-21.57
Brazil	8,647.4	8,725.7	8,803.5	8,862.1	8,884.9	8,857.6	8,776.0	8,645.7	8,479.1	8,287.4	8,079.5	-0.68	-6.57
Bulgaria	165.0	162.3	162.3	162.6	165.7	168.4	168.3	168.1	167.5	167.0	166.4	0.08	0.80
Canada	1,022.9	1,004.3	982.7	963.9	953.2	950.1	947.7	953.8	967.4	983.2	997.0	-0.26	-2.53
Chile	694.6	677.9	663.1	650.9	641.5	634.8	630.6	628.8	629.0	630.7	633.1	-0.92	-8.85
China	46,978.2	45,364.7	43,843.7	42,538.9	40,797.6	40,559.0	39,804.9	39,230.6	39,486.5	40,275.9	40,706.1	-1.42	-13.35
Colombia	2,245.9	2,243.5	2,241.5	2,240.6	2,241.3	2,243.9	2,248.3	2,254.3	2,261.2	2,267.9	2,272.9	0.12	1.20
Costa Rica	212.5	210.9	209.7	208.5	207.4	205.8	203.9	201.4	198.8	196.4	194.6	-0.87	-8.41
Croatia	129.6	128.3	125.8	120.3	114.9	110.6	107.7	106.5	107.1	108.4	109.9	-1.63	-15.16
Czech Republic	246.1	237.3	235.2	236.5	238.7	241.2	246.6	253.2	259.2	264.3	268.9	0.89	9.26
Denmark	179.6	177.0	174.7	172.9	170.9	169.8	169.0	167.7	167.9	167.9	168.2	-0.65	-6.33
Ecuador	726.0	728.5	729.4	728.4	725.8	721.9	717.2	712.0	706.7	701.4	696.4	-0.42	-4.08
Egypt	4,097.8	4,197.4	4,305.2	4,421.7	4,545.4	4,672.8	4,799.2	4,920.4	5,023.2	5,109.8	5,180.4	2.37	26.42
Estonia	32.0	31.4	31.6	31.5	31.8	32.3	33.2	33.9	34.8	35.8	36.9	1.42	15.13
Finland	157.6	154.1	151.4	149.2	148.0	148.1	148.6	149.0	150.6	152.2	153.9	-0.23	-2.32
France	1,879.5	1,899.9	1,926.6	1,945.7	1,965.4	1,980.3	1,985.9	1,980.5	1,990.7	2,001.0	2,019.7	0.72	7.46
Germany	2,038.8	2,027.4	2,019.7	1,985.7	1,937.9	1,897.0	1,863.6	1,824.4	1,795.2	1,779.1	1,769.1	-1.41	-13.23
Greece	276.2	272.6	269.9	270.4	271.5	274.9	279.0	282.8	286.1	289.5	292.4	0.57	5.86
Hong Kong, China	195.4	185.6	177.3	166.2	160.6	156.2	154.0	155.9	163.9	170.3	177.6	-0.95	-9.13
Hungary	268.7	259.1	252.6	248.9	247.7	247.4	248.2	248.7	250.2	251.8	253.8	-0.57	-5.54
India	62,818.5	62,870.2	62,950.9	63,056.4	63,162.2	63,233.6	63,241.4	63,173.3	63,036.5	62,853.2	62,652.5	-0.03	-0.26
Indonesia	10,404.0	10,428.7	10,470.2	10,523.1	10,577.4	10,620.7	10,642.8	10,638.7	10,607.8	10,553.9	10,482.9	0.08	0.76
Iran	2,886.1	2,761.0	2,706.6	2,719.0	2,782.3	2,875.3	2,978.9	3,081.4	3,176.5	3,259.9	3,329.1	1.44	15.35
Ireland	146.9	149.7	152.0	152.6	154.9	157.7	160.9	163.3	166.5	167.2	166.8	1.28	13.61
Israel	332.2	340.0	347.2	353.6	360.3	366.7	371.2	374.4	376.6	376.3	374.2	1.20	12.65
Italy	1,410.8	1,412.3	1,421.9	1,427.1	1,432.3	1,440.1	1,451.3	1,452.9	1,455.0	1,454.1	1,445.2	0.24	2.44
Japan	3,049.6	3,035.7	3,022.2	2,999.3	2,957.3	2,908.2	2,836.2	2,788.6	2,754.9	2,742.2	2,750.8	-1.03	-9.80
Jordan	358.8	360.4	361.0	360.9	361.0	362.0	364.5	368.5	373.7	379.4	384.9	0.71	7.29
Kazakhstan	583.4	567.3	560.5	563.3	576.0	597.3	625.8	659.7	696.7	733.2	765.4	2.75	31.19
Kuwait	88.9	90.3	91.7	93.1	94.6	96.4	98.3	100.5	102.8	105.1	107.1	1.88	20.43
Latvia	50.7	48.6	47.8	47.6	48.1	49.4	50.0	50.7	52.1	53.3	54.3	0.68	7.05
Lithuania	97.4	94.7	91.5	88.0	84.4	81.5	78.5	76.8	76.4	76.7	76.7	-2.35	-21.20
Malaysia	1,438.1	1,459.5	1,480.2	1,501.0	1,515.8	1,532.1	1,549.3	1,562.4	1,573.1	1,578.1	1,570.8	0.89	9.23
Mexico	5,291.2	5,263.8	5,242.8	5,221.5	5,201.1	5,180.5	5,158.2	5,133.3	5,105.6	5,075.8	5,044.6	-0.48	-4.66
Morocco	1,557.2	1,537.7	1,519.5	1,503.8	1,492.1	1,486.0	1,486.6	1,493.8	1,506.9	1,523.9	1,542.4	-0.10	-0.95
Netherlands	501.4	502.9	509.3	513.6	517.5	517.0	511.6	501.4	491.7	481.3	470.5	-0.63	-6.17
New Zealand	152.9	152.1	151.1	150.1	149.4	149.9	149.4	150.2	153.7	158.0	161.6	0.55	5.68
Nigeria	9,544.3	9,757.1	9,975.9	10,200.3	10,429.6	10,662.4	10,896.8	11,130.1	11,358.8	11,577.5	11,780.1	2.13	23.43
Norway	161.7	162.1	162.0	160.2	158.3	158.1	157.7	157.2	158.9	161.1	163.4	0.11	1.09
Pakistan	10,607.1	10,709.2	10,825.7	10,955.8	11,097.6	11,249.2	11,409.0	11,576.7	11,752.2	11,935.1	12,123.9	1.35	14.30
Peru	1,482.6	1,483.2	1,483.8	1,484.8	1,486.2	1,488.0	1,490.0	1,492.1	1,493.8	1,494.7	1,493.9	0.08	0.76
Philippines	5,148.3	5,176.7	5,199.6	5,221.8	5,246.6	5,278.8	5,320.4	5,371.8	5,431.1	5,494.0	5,555.2	0.76	7.90
Poland	1,087.9	1,045.7	1,014.1	980.7	953.2	931.2	918.3	911.2	911.5	916.9	925.6	-1.60	-14.92
Portugal	276.1	279.7	280.9	284.2	289.3	292.5	290.9	291.2	290.1	287.9	286.6	0.37	3.80
Romania	570.6	566.0	565.7	562.7	555.4	547.3	541.7	538.6	541.2	546.7	550.6	-0.36	-3.52
Russia	3,463.4	3,372.9	3,319.6	3,304.2	3,364.2	3,457.6	3,588.5	3,686.8	3,793.5	3,922.5	4,057.1	1.59	17.14
Saudi Arabia	1,342.4	1,353.2	1,365.6	1,379.0	1,392.4	1,404.5	1,414.1	1,420.9	1,425.3	1,428.5	1,432.1	0.65	6.68
Singapore	161.5	158.9	156.9	151.5	146.2	141.0	136.1	129.8	127.0	125.1	124.4	-2.57	-22.96
Slovakia	154.2	149.1	145.4	140.7	136.8	134.1	133.1	133.2	134.6	136.3	137.5	-1.14	-10.81
Slovenia	49.3	48.5	48.3	47.8	47.6	47.3	47.6	47.6	48.1	48.6	49.4	0.02	0.22
South Africa	2,499.3	2,507.4	2,518.5	2,531.1	2,543.4	2,553.2	2,559.0	2,560.0	2,556.7	2,551.1	2,545.6	0.18	1.85
South Korea	1,721.3	1,670.8	1,613.7	1,540.3	1,461.1	1,383.0	1,291.3	1,211.5	1,166.6	1,140.4	1,120.4	-4.20	-34.91
Spain	1,067.6	1,078.2	1,099.3	1,125.6	1,154.4	1,189.4	1,221.6	1,247.3	1,277.5	1,306.5	1,326.4	2.19	24.24
Sweden	264.0	253.3	248.0	247.3	250.6	255.6	262.4	267.5	272.6	275.8	277.6	0.50	5.15
Switzerland	212.6	209.5	205.7	201.0	197.6	194.2	191.8	190.9	190.4	189.7	189.8	-1.13	-10.75
Taiwan	811.1	790.9	782.6	748.7	709.2	689.3	656.3	605.5	579.7	558.0	545.4	-3.89	-32.76
Thailand	2,483.3	2,416.7	2,319.6	2,233.5	2,185.3	2,180.9	2,171.1	2,179.3	2,184.1	2,189.8	2,180.4	-1.29	-12.20
Tunisia	430.7	418.3	408.4	401.0	396.2	393.8	393.2	394.5	397.1	400.9	405.3	-0.61	-5.91
Turkey	3,617.5	3,635.9	3,639.8	3,606.4	3,556.7	3,498.7	3,436.1	3,379.1	3,346.6	3,323.8	3,306.8	-0.89	-8.59
Turkmenistan	250.6	244.8	242.2	242.4	244.8	248.0	251.2	253.7	255.4	256.4	257.1	0.26	2.60
Ukraine	1,166.4	1,107.5	1,056.8	1,009.5	987.0	981.2	995.9	1,012.0	1,048.5	1,077.3	1,096.3	-0.62	-6.01
United Arab Emirates	137.9	143.7	149.5	155.1	159.8	163.2	165.2	165.9	165.5	164.7	164.0	1.75	18.89
United Kingdom	1,860.4	1,833.2	1,801.3	1,765.7	1,740.6	1,736.2	1,747.7	1,775.3	1,817.4	1,868.4	1,920.7	0.32	3.24
USA	10,207.3	10,185.8	10,269.6	10,369.8	10,499.7	10,657.3	10,788.2	10,866.4	11,025.7	11,182.5	11,302.5	1.02	10.73
Venezuela	1,408.2	1,414.3	1,421.5	1,429.6	1,438.3	1,447.3	1,456.3	1,465.1	1,473.4	1,481.1	1,487.7	0.55	5.65
Vietnam	3,996.2	3,890.5	3,846.8	3,856.1	3,900.5	3,952.3	3,990.9	4,011.3	4,019.3	4,018.3	4,015.0	0.05	0.47

Key population trends

Table 4.29 Male Population Aged 15-19: 2009-2019

'000

	2009	2010	2011	2012	2013	2014	2015	2016	2017	2018	2019	CAGR	Period growth
Algeria	1,843.5	1,801.0	1,745.9	1,682.2	1,617.8	1,562.1	1,522.6	1,503.0	1,503.0	1,519.0	1,545.3	-1.75	-16.18
Argentina	1,754.4	1,758.9	1,760.5	1,759.1	1,754.8	1,747.9	1,738.7	1,727.8	1,716.4	1,706.2	1,698.7	-0.32	-3.18
Australia	762.5	763.7	761.9	760.4	758.9	757.9	756.8	758.1	758.0	759.0	761.1	-0.02	-0.18
Austria	258.5	258.4	256.1	253.1	248.1	242.6	236.6	232.2	226.6	224.2	222.3	-1.50	-14.01
Azerbaijan	461.2	446.9	429.1	409.0	388.7	370.3	355.5	345.3	340.0	339.6	343.4	-2.91	-25.53
Belarus	341.2	318.5	297.6	278.6	259.9	249.1	241.5	238.0	237.3	238.0	236.4	-3.60	-30.71
Belgium	331.6	328.9	323.9	318.6	314.4	311.8	310.4	310.9	310.1	308.5	308.0	-0.74	-7.12
Bolivia	537.1	546.4	553.4	558.3	561.9	565.1	568.6	573.0	578.0	583.2	588.1	0.91	9.50
Bosnia-Herzegovina	125.9	121.1	118.2	116.9	116.5	116.1	114.9	112.5	109.0	104.9	100.8	-2.19	-19.90
Brazil	8,452.5	8,412.7	8,424.2	8,466.0	8,522.9	8,592.0	8,674.4	8,755.9	8,817.9	8,843.4	8,817.7	0.42	4.32
Bulgaria	225.9	211.3	195.6	184.2	172.0	162.4	159.4	159.2	159.2	162.2	164.7	-3.11	-27.11
Canada	1,138.9	1,132.1	1,120.8	1,106.1	1,088.2	1,069.2	1,049.2	1,026.7	1,007.2	996.2	993.1	-1.36	-12.80
Chile	760.8	754.5	743.6	728.9	711.8	694.2	677.6	662.9	650.7	641.3	634.7	-1.80	-16.57
China	54,119.0	50,137.3	48,158.6	45,929.1	44,581.9	42,822.9	41,653.4	40,530.9	39,606.8	38,280.1	38,314.7	-3.39	-29.20
Colombia	2,202.2	2,214.8	2,222.8	2,226.5	2,226.9	2,225.6	2,223.7	2,222.2	2,221.6	2,222.5	2,225.0	0.10	1.04
Costa Rica	225.6	223.2	220.9	218.6	216.6	214.7	213.2	211.9	210.9	209.7	208.3	-0.79	-7.64
Croatia	132.9	131.1	130.0	129.7	130.8	129.9	128.7	126.1	120.6	115.3	111.0	-1.79	-16.50
Czech Republic	326.5	316.9	300.2	280.5	264.4	248.8	239.6	237.2	238.5	240.7	243.5	-2.89	-25.43
Denmark	175.9	179.4	182.0	183.1	182.2	181.0	178.5	176.3	174.5	172.6	171.5	-0.25	-2.47
Ecuador	678.5	683.2	689.5	696.8	704.1	710.3	714.5	716.3	715.6	713.0	709.1	0.44	4.50
Egypt	3,934.8	3,896.3	3,887.6	3,908.8	3,963.1	4,046.1	4,146.5	4,255.9	4,374.7	4,501.7	4,633.0	1.65	17.75
Estonia	46.0	41.7	37.9	35.4	33.1	31.8	31.1	31.3	31.2	31.5	32.0	-3.56	-30.42
Finland	169.9	170.4	168.8	166.6	162.7	158.8	155.3	152.5	150.4	149.1	149.1	-1.30	-12.23
France	1,950.2	1,922.5	1,901.8	1,889.0	1,878.8	1,890.3	1,910.3	1,937.3	1,956.7	1,976.5	1,991.5	0.21	2.12
Germany	2,291.4	2,201.8	2,101.5	2,061.0	2,046.3	2,029.8	2,022.0	2,016.9	1,984.4	1,937.5	1,897.2	-1.87	-17.20
Greece	297.4	296.1	292.8	289.6	286.3	283.4	279.8	277.2	277.7	278.8	282.2	-0.52	-5.11
Hong Kong, China	224.7	222.5	220.1	217.5	210.7	202.1	191.9	183.5	172.5	166.7	162.5	-3.19	-27.69
Hungary	312.1	307.4	300.4	290.2	279.7	270.2	260.6	254.1	250.3	249.2	249.0	-2.23	-20.23
India	61,184.0	61,711.4	62,065.2	62,262.5	62,351.0	62,393.4	62,442.9	62,526.0	62,639.5	62,757.6	62,843.3	0.27	2.71
Indonesia	10,396.5	10,375.0	10,354.2	10,336.8	10,328.4	10,334.7	10,359.8	10,403.2	10,459.5	10,517.9	10,565.3	0.16	1.62
Iran	3,963.4	3,714.7	3,460.4	3,215.3	2,998.3	2,829.0	2,721.4	2,680.2	2,700.8	2,768.8	2,864.4	-3.20	-27.73
Ireland	144.9	142.8	140.7	140.5	141.9	144.7	147.3	149.6	150.2	152.6	155.4	0.70	7.22
Israel	305.2	309.8	315.3	321.4	328.1	335.5	343.4	350.8	357.3	364.1	370.7	1.96	21.45
Italy	1,503.0	1,490.5	1,471.7	1,455.6	1,438.7	1,434.3	1,435.9	1,445.6	1,451.0	1,456.3	1,464.0	-0.26	-2.59
Japan	3,111.1	3,093.4	3,079.2	3,066.2	3,067.9	3,053.7	3,042.4	3,030.8	3,008.9	2,967.8	2,919.3	-0.63	-6.17
Jordan	342.4	347.2	350.2	351.8	352.4	352.6	352.9	353.6	354.7	356.4	359.0	0.48	4.86
Kazakhstan	738.4	709.3	677.3	644.4	614.0	589.5	573.5	567.2	570.9	584.3	606.3	-1.95	-17.89
Kuwait	86.1	87.2	88.4	89.7	91.1	92.3	93.5	94.7	96.0	97.5	99.2	1.43	15.27
Latvia	79.0	72.6	65.9	59.5	53.4	49.7	47.6	46.9	46.7	47.2	48.7	-4.73	-38.41
Lithuania	129.5	123.6	116.6	109.1	101.3	96.4	93.8	90.6	87.1	83.6	80.7	-4.62	-37.68
Malaysia	1,351.1	1,365.3	1,379.7	1,394.7	1,413.4	1,432.5	1,452.8	1,472.4	1,492.5	1,506.9	1,523.4	1.21	12.75
Mexico	5,082.1	5,131.5	5,164.9	5,175.6	5,169.6	5,153.9	5,134.6	5,114.7	5,095.4	5,076.8	5,058.8	-0.05	-0.46
Morocco	1,618.2	1,604.6	1,588.7	1,570.9	1,552.0	1,532.7	1,513.8	1,496.2	1,481.0	1,469.6	1,463.9	-1.00	-9.54
Netherlands	515.1	517.0	511.5	507.0	503.4	504.7	506.5	513.1	517.6	521.4	520.9	0.11	1.12
New Zealand	165.1	164.6	162.5	160.1	158.1	156.3	155.6	154.6	153.6	152.9	153.4	-0.73	-7.05
Nigeria	8,370.2	8,550.0	8,735.6	8,927.5	9,125.8	9,330.7	9,541.9	9,758.9	9,981.3	10,208.5	10,439.3	2.23	24.72
Norway	164.0	165.4	166.2	166.9	167.2	167.2	167.3	167.0	165.1	163.2	163.0	-0.06	-0.59
Pakistan	10,204.6	10,244.6	10,294.0	10,357.7	10,436.9	10,530.7	10,637.1	10,755.4	10,886.1	11,028.3	11,181.0	0.92	9.57
Peru	1,456.5	1,462.4	1,466.5	1,469.4	1,471.2	1,472.5	1,473.5	1,474.4	1,475.5	1,476.9	1,478.8	0.15	1.53
Philippines	4,922.8	4,984.0	5,034.4	5,076.6	5,111.7	5,142.5	5,170.3	5,196.6	5,223.3	5,253.8	5,291.0	0.72	7.48
Poland	1,341.1	1,292.4	1,234.9	1,179.2	1,129.6	1,083.5	1,041.8	1,010.6	977.3	949.8	928.0	-3.61	-30.80
Portugal	292.4	288.5	285.4	282.1	279.8	279.2	282.7	283.8	287.0	292.1	295.3	0.10	0.98
Romania	700.1	645.9	610.2	589.6	574.0	568.8	564.0	563.7	560.8	553.5	545.5	-2.46	-22.08
Russia	4,738.8	4,353.7	4,011.4	3,758.3	3,563.0	3,500.1	3,409.3	3,359.4	3,345.4	3,407.6	3,502.2	-2.98	-26.10
Saudi Arabia	1,253.6	1,274.7	1,290.7	1,302.1	1,310.6	1,318.6	1,327.7	1,339.0	1,352.0	1,365.6	1,378.2	0.95	9.94
Singapore	171.3	171.7	169.7	168.7	165.2	161.0	157.5	154.7	148.4	142.1	136.0	-2.28	-20.59
Slovakia	194.9	188.0	178.7	170.1	162.1	153.8	148.6	144.8	140.1	136.1	133.3	-3.73	-31.61
Slovenia	56.2	54.3	52.8	51.6	50.7	49.9	49.0	48.8	48.3	48.1	47.9	-1.59	-14.80
South Africa	2,515.9	2,505.8	2,493.9	2,482.0	2,472.1	2,466.6	2,466.8	2,472.9	2,483.4	2,496.3	2,508.7	-0.03	-0.29
South Korea	1,781.1	1,807.8	1,812.3	1,789.5	1,744.6	1,690.0	1,640.5	1,584.4	1,512.4	1,434.7	1,358.2	-2.67	-23.74
Spain	1,149.4	1,137.3	1,124.2	1,113.8	1,107.4	1,107.8	1,117.5	1,138.4	1,164.6	1,193.2	1,228.1	0.66	6.85
Sweden	327.7	324.6	314.1	299.4	284.1	271.8	261.0	255.6	254.7	257.8	262.7	-2.19	-19.82
Switzerland	230.4	228.8	225.5	222.4	218.5	215.5	212.4	208.5	203.8	200.2	196.6	-1.57	-14.65
Taiwan	837.3	843.6	836.7	837.8	839.1	809.0	788.9	781.0	746.9	707.6	687.7	-1.95	-17.86
Thailand	2,540.7	2,562.2	2,583.0	2,591.4	2,567.8	2,516.7	2,449.4	2,351.9	2,264.2	2,215.5	2,210.5	-1.38	-12.99
Tunisia	504.6	490.7	475.4	459.5	443.7	429.3	416.9	406.9	399.6	394.9	392.4	-2.48	-22.22
Turkey	3,358.9	3,421.2	3,481.4	3,537.9	3,586.4	3,625.1	3,645.9	3,650.3	3,614.3	3,563.5	3,505.6	0.43	4.37
Turkmenistan	288.3	283.2	275.5	266.2	256.6	248.3	242.6	240.0	240.3	242.7	246.0	-1.58	-14.69
Ukraine	1,550.6	1,460.4	1,376.0	1,298.3	1,224.8	1,161.5	1,102.7	1,051.8	1,004.7	981.6	975.3	-4.53	-37.11
United Arab Emirates	124.5	128.3	136.3	147.5	160.2	172.4	182.9	191.1	197.0	201.0	203.5	5.04	63.51
United Kingdom	2,045.8	2,023.3	1,987.5	1,951.9	1,924.2	1,899.4	1,873.7	1,844.1	1,810.2	1,785.7	1,781.1	-1.38	-12.94
USA	10,988.2	10,856.9	10,738.9	10,621.0	10,529.1	10,475.7	10,463.5	10,557.9	10,665.3	10,801.2	10,965.2	-0.02	-0.21
Venezuela	1,391.0	1,391.2	1,392.2	1,394.4	1,398.0	1,403.0	1,409.2	1,416.5	1,424.7	1,433.5	1,442.6	0.36	3.71
Vietnam	4,661.3	4,588.6	4,466.8	4,303.6	4,126.7	3,973.6	3,870.9	3,829.7	3,841.4	3,887.7	3,940.7	-1.67	-15.46

Key population trends

Table 4.30 Male Population Aged 20-24: 2009-2019

'000

	2009	2010	2011	2012	2013	2014	2015	2016	2017	2018	2019	CAGR	Period growth
Algeria	1,895.5	1,889.7	1,881.3	1,868.8	1,849.2	1,818.9	1,775.8	1,720.3	1,656.7	1,592.8	1,537.7	-2.07	-18.87
Argentina	1,683.5	1,700.8	1,716.7	1,730.4	1,741.5	1,749.5	1,754.4	1,756.2	1,754.9	1,750.7	1,743.9	0.35	3.59
Australia	795.1	805.4	813.8	822.8	830.4	834.4	836.3	836.0	835.5	834.5	833.6	0.47	4.85
Austria	262.4	261.9	262.4	264.7	267.3	268.0	267.9	265.6	262.5	257.4	251.8	-0.41	-4.03
Azerbaijan	458.2	466.5	470.0	468.7	462.7	452.4	438.1	420.5	400.9	381.0	362.9	-2.30	-20.79
Belarus	424.1	416.9	405.9	385.0	366.4	341.9	319.2	298.3	279.6	261.0	250.5	-5.13	-40.95
Belgium	323.5	327.5	333.3	337.5	340.8	340.3	337.5	332.5	327.3	323.1	320.5	-0.10	-0.95
Bolivia	457.5	470.1	483.2	496.4	509.0	520.2	529.4	536.4	541.4	545.1	548.5	1.83	19.89
Bosnia-Herzegovina	152.6	149.6	144.7	138.6	131.9	125.9	121.3	118.5	117.1	116.7	116.2	-2.69	-23.84
Brazil	8,922.6	8,791.2	8,666.4	8,541.7	8,435.3	8,356.0	8,322.2	8,338.7	8,384.6	8,444.9	8,515.8	-0.47	-4.56
Bulgaria	262.3	257.7	252.3	242.5	231.2	217.7	202.6	186.7	175.0	163.0	153.6	-5.21	-41.45
Canada	1,168.1	1,180.8	1,194.5	1,208.8	1,220.2	1,220.9	1,212.9	1,201.0	1,185.5	1,166.4	1,146.3	-0.19	-1.87
Chile	731.6	742.9	751.9	758.2	760.9	759.3	753.1	742.3	727.7	710.8	693.2	-0.54	-5.25
China	50,302.5	55,320.1	56,166.0	55,395.0	54,178.3	51,583.7	47,627.4	46,141.1	44,252.1	43,258.1	41,917.1	-1.81	-16.67
Colombia	2,052.3	2,073.6	2,095.7	2,117.7	2,138.3	2,156.0	2,169.4	2,178.1	2,182.3	2,183.2	2,182.1	0.62	6.33
Costa Rica	228.5	230.5	231.2	230.8	229.4	227.3	225.0	222.7	220.5	218.5	216.9	-0.52	-5.09
Croatia	147.8	143.7	140.8	139.5	136.6	134.1	132.4	131.2	130.9	132.0	131.0	-1.20	-11.36
Czech Republic	346.3	341.9	339.4	337.8	333.8	328.5	318.3	301.3	281.7	265.8	250.5	-3.19	-27.66
Denmark	161.0	164.7	168.8	172.5	177.7	181.2	184.8	187.4	188.5	187.7	186.6	1.49	15.90
Ecuador	617.1	621.8	627.3	633.4	640.3	647.8	655.9	664.2	672.5	680.0	686.1	1.07	11.18
Egypt	3,832.3	3,852.4	3,847.5	3,818.9	3,763.7	3,696.7	3,643.9	3,623.5	3,635.7	3,684.0	3,763.8	-0.18	-1.79
Estonia	54.1	54.2	53.8	51.8	49.1	45.2	40.9	37.2	34.8	32.5	31.2	-5.34	-42.23
Finland	165.9	165.3	167.0	169.1	172.3	172.6	173.0	171.4	169.1	165.1	161.2	-0.28	-2.80
France	1,986.8	2,007.1	2,019.5	2,018.9	2,011.4	1,982.0	1,954.1	1,933.9	1,921.2	1,911.0	1,922.4	-0.33	-3.24
Germany	2,500.7	2,519.0	2,542.1	2,505.1	2,440.8	2,357.0	2,272.9	2,177.1	2,138.8	2,125.3	2,109.3	-1.69	-15.65
Greece	336.3	324.2	317.9	312.4	310.5	304.7	303.4	300.1	297.0	293.7	290.8	-1.44	-13.53
Hong Kong, China	223.6	223.4	224.5	226.9	227.0	222.3	219.6	216.9	214.1	208.1	200.4	-1.09	-10.39
Hungary	329.8	327.9	324.2	322.5	320.3	315.9	311.2	304.0	293.9	283.6	274.3	-1.83	-16.83
India	56,534.6	57,394.6	58,269.1	59,129.6	59,927.5	60,608.8	61,134.2	61,491.3	61,699.1	61,804.2	61,866.4	0.91	9.43
Indonesia	10,401.8	10,364.1	10,328.9	10,297.9	10,271.2	10,248.6	10,229.7	10,214.6	10,205.8	10,207.3	10,223.2	-0.17	-1.72
Iran	4,709.4	4,638.7	4,517.0	4,349.4	4,144.3	3,913.4	3,668.4	3,420.0	3,181.2	2,970.2	2,805.7	-5.05	-40.42
Ireland	161.3	156.9	153.9	150.9	148.1	145.4	143.3	141.2	141.1	142.5	145.4	-1.03	-9.87
Israel	292.6	294.0	295.6	298.2	301.9	305.7	310.2	315.7	321.9	328.6	336.1	1.40	14.87
Italy	1,535.7	1,527.3	1,528.6	1,535.4	1,544.2	1,533.8	1,521.5	1,502.9	1,487.0	1,470.3	1,465.9	-0.46	-4.54
Japan	3,553.3	3,442.9	3,344.1	3,265.2	3,194.6	3,157.3	3,143.3	3,132.0	3,120.9	3,124.2	3,111.3	-1.32	-12.44
Jordan	327.2	330.1	331.3	331.6	331.4	331.8	333.3	335.7	338.9	342.3	345.5	0.55	5.59
Kazakhstan	786.5	795.9	795.7	786.0	768.0	743.6	714.8	683.0	650.5	620.1	595.2	-2.75	-24.32
Kuwait	108.1	106.1	105.1	105.1	105.8	106.6	107.3	107.7	107.8	107.8	107.9	-0.02	-0.19
Latvia	93.7	92.7	90.9	87.7	83.6	77.4	71.1	64.6	58.3	52.5	48.9	-6.30	-47.84
Lithuania	137.6	136.1	134.9	131.9	129.7	126.0	120.1	113.3	106.1	98.7	94.1	-3.73	-31.65
Malaysia	1,282.8	1,299.0	1,312.7	1,323.4	1,338.7	1,351.9	1,364.5	1,377.5	1,391.4	1,410.1	1,429.6	1.09	11.44
Mexico	4,517.5	4,574.5	4,652.0	4,738.8	4,827.3	4,906.9	4,968.7	5,008.5	5,026.0	5,025.2	5,012.2	1.04	10.95
Morocco	1,590.3	1,590.7	1,587.8	1,582.1	1,574.0	1,563.6	1,550.8	1,535.9	1,519.1	1,501.1	1,482.7	-0.70	-6.77
Netherlands	497.9	501.3	508.7	513.8	516.9	519.6	521.8	516.3	511.8	508.0	509.3	0.23	2.29
New Zealand	151.9	155.0	159.2	162.4	164.1	164.6	164.2	162.2	159.7	157.8	156.1	0.28	2.80
Nigeria	7,306.0	7,458.6	7,615.2	7,776.9	7,944.1	8,116.9	8,295.1	8,478.8	8,668.1	8,863.4	9,065.1	2.18	24.08
Norway	150.4	155.8	161.2	165.7	169.6	171.1	172.0	172.5	173.1	173.3	173.2	1.42	15.18
Pakistan	9,395.3	9,633.3	9,812.9	9,937.3	10,019.0	10,076.6	10,127.3	10,182.8	10,249.0	10,329.1	10,423.5	1.04	10.94
Peru	1,359.9	1,377.6	1,393.7	1,407.9	1,420.0	1,429.8	1,437.5	1,443.1	1,447.0	1,449.6	1,451.6	0.66	6.75
Philippines	4,458.3	4,553.6	4,642.3	4,725.5	4,802.0	4,871.8	4,934.2	4,988.7	5,035.7	5,075.9	5,110.9	1.38	14.64
Poland	1,569.7	1,507.0	1,451.5	1,411.2	1,369.0	1,323.4	1,275.1	1,218.4	1,163.7	1,115.2	1,070.6	-3.75	-31.80
Portugal	320.2	310.5	305.6	302.3	299.1	295.7	291.7	288.5	285.1	282.7	282.1	-1.26	-11.92
Romania	872.0	875.9	852.7	802.4	749.0	691.1	635.9	599.3	577.9	562.1	556.7	-4.39	-36.16
Russia	6,368.3	6,217.4	6,019.7	5,659.5	5,220.9	4,749.8	4,367.0	4,032.4	3,784.2	3,594.4	3,535.3	-5.72	-44.49
Saudi Arabia	1,192.4	1,222.2	1,253.7	1,285.1	1,314.2	1,339.1	1,358.5	1,372.4	1,381.8	1,388.5	1,395.1	1.58	17.01
Singapore	154.0	159.1	167.3	175.6	179.0	177.7	177.4	174.6	172.9	168.5	163.5	0.60	6.18
Slovakia	217.5	212.6	207.8	203.3	198.9	194.2	187.1	177.7	168.9	160.9	152.5	-3.49	-29.87
Slovenia	67.7	66.4	64.6	63.0	60.2	57.4	55.4	53.8	52.5	51.6	50.9	-2.82	-24.84
South Africa	2,539.1	2,545.4	2,539.8	2,524.0	2,501.5	2,476.7	2,453.6	2,434.2	2,419.8	2,411.6	2,410.3	-0.52	-5.08
South Korea	1,647.3	1,641.4	1,649.5	1,685.3	1,735.0	1,778.0	1,804.9	1,809.6	1,787.0	1,742.3	1,687.9	0.24	2.47
Spain	1,341.0	1,304.4	1,275.7	1,253.6	1,236.0	1,221.6	1,208.3	1,195.1	1,184.7	1,178.2	1,178.4	-1.28	-12.12
Sweden	291.7	302.6	314.9	325.3	334.2	335.3	332.7	322.5	308.0	292.6	280.3	-0.40	-3.91
Switzerland	228.2	230.1	233.4	236.4	238.8	237.7	236.0	232.8	229.6	225.6	222.5	-0.25	-2.50
Taiwan	845.5	820.0	822.0	834.2	841.7	834.3	840.7	834.2	835.0	836.3	806.5	-0.47	-4.62
Thailand	2,380.1	2,381.4	2,411.6	2,461.5	2,500.8	2,527.9	2,550.1	2,572.7	2,581.2	2,557.4	2,504.6	0.51	5.23
Tunisia	534.4	534.0	530.3	523.4	513.7	501.6	487.6	472.3	456.4	440.8	426.5	-2.23	-20.20
Turkey	3,219.5	3,198.6	3,204.6	3,236.0	3,289.9	3,353.6	3,419.5	3,480.5	3,535.6	3,585.2	3,621.3	1.18	12.48
Turkmenistan	272.7	279.5	284.5	287.2	287.4	284.9	279.7	272.1	262.9	253.5	245.4	-1.05	-10.03
Ukraine	1,939.5	1,881.9	1,818.7	1,727.5	1,637.6	1,539.4	1,449.9	1,366.2	1,289.7	1,217.3	1,155.4	-5.05	-40.43
United Arab Emirates	206.2	196.3	194.4	200.1	211.3	225.3	239.5	252.5	264.0	274.0	282.7	3.20	37.09
United Kingdom	2,190.8	2,204.5	2,217.2	2,229.0	2,223.3	2,206.3	2,184.4	2,150.2	2,115.2	2,087.2	2,061.2	-0.61	-5.91
USA	10,904.3	10,998.2	11,051.4	11,099.8	11,116.6	11,072.4	10,943.9	10,831.9	10,717.8	10,628.2	10,576.1	-0.31	-3.01
Venezuela	1,344.8	1,360.2	1,370.6	1,376.4	1,378.8	1,379.4	1,379.9	1,381.2	1,383.7	1,387.5	1,392.8	0.35	3.57
Vietnam	4,469.7	4,544.5	4,600.2	4,637.5	4,647.9	4,621.3	4,552.4	4,434.3	4,274.5	4,100.5	3,949.3	-1.23	-11.64

Key population trends

Table 4.31 Male Population Aged 25-29: 2009-2019

'000

	2009	2010	2011	2012	2013	2014	2015	2016	2017	2018	2019	CAGR	Period growth
Algeria	1,804.7	1,839.7	1,862.7	1,874.3	1,876.9	1,873.8	1,867.3	1,858.4	1,845.9	1,826.5	1,796.8	-0.04	-0.44
Argentina	1,636.4	1,631.7	1,633.7	1,642.8	1,657.4	1,674.9	1,692.5	1,708.7	1,722.5	1,733.5	1,741.3	0.62	6.41
Australia	791.7	813.1	828.2	838.8	846.0	856.4	867.3	877.0	886.6	894.6	898.3	1.27	13.48
Austria	278.2	280.8	279.9	277.4	274.4	274.0	273.5	274.0	276.2	278.6	279.2	0.03	0.35
Azerbaijan	364.5	383.8	402.5	419.9	435.0	447.0	455.1	458.9	458.0	452.4	442.4	1.96	21.37
Belarus	399.0	408.3	414.0	423.1	425.5	421.4	414.2	403.4	383.0	364.7	340.8	-1.57	-14.60
Belgium	338.7	335.7	332.3	331.0	331.1	333.9	337.8	343.6	347.7	351.0	350.5	0.34	3.47
Bolivia	390.1	399.8	409.9	420.4	431.4	443.0	455.4	468.5	481.6	494.3	505.5	2.63	29.60
Bosnia-Herzegovina	146.4	148.9	151.2	152.8	153.5	152.5	149.7	144.9	138.7	132.0	125.9	-1.50	-14.03
Brazil	8,798.7	8,935.6	8,959.8	8,939.8	8,890.3	8,796.7	8,673.8	8,556.7	8,439.1	8,338.6	8,263.4	-0.63	-6.08
Bulgaria	276.7	270.4	265.6	261.7	256.7	253.1	247.8	241.4	230.9	219.6	206.1	-2.90	-25.50
Canada	1,191.6	1,206.4	1,216.3	1,220.5	1,220.6	1,225.8	1,238.5	1,253.1	1,268.3	1,280.4	1,281.3	0.73	7.53
Chile	646.8	665.6	683.8	700.7	716.0	729.3	740.7	749.7	756.0	758.7	757.2	1.59	17.07
China	41,499.9	41,910.3	43,850.6	46,255.3	49,661.0	53,904.2	59,249.7	60,278.7	59,605.9	58,309.4	55,580.1	2.96	33.93
Colombia	1,896.1	1,915.8	1,935.1	1,954.5	1,974.6	1,995.7	2,017.8	2,040.4	2,062.8	2,083.6	2,101.4	1.03	10.83
Costa Rica	206.6	211.8	216.9	221.7	225.8	229.0	231.0	231.7	231.3	230.0	228.1	0.99	10.41
Croatia	160.0	159.3	157.1	154.6	151.3	148.6	144.6	141.6	140.3	137.4	134.9	-1.69	-15.66
Czech Republic	387.3	371.2	362.8	357.4	351.5	348.2	343.1	340.1	338.5	334.8	330.0	-1.59	-14.80
Denmark	158.2	155.5	154.5	156.1	157.8	161.7	165.9	170.3	173.9	178.9	182.3	1.43	15.24
Ecuador	552.4	558.2	564.9	572.3	580.2	588.1	595.8	603.2	610.3	617.4	624.8	1.24	13.10
Egypt	3,352.9	3,404.0	3,449.7	3,490.7	3,530.4	3,561.4	3,572.0	3,555.2	3,512.8	3,441.5	3,357.7	0.01	0.14
Estonia	50.4	51.2	51.8	52.0	52.7	52.8	52.9	52.4	50.6	47.9	44.3	-1.29	-12.15
Finland	173.8	175.5	175.5	174.5	171.4	169.9	169.3	170.9	172.8	175.9	176.1	0.13	1.30
France	2,008.9	2,011.4	1,997.8	1,993.8	1,995.0	2,023.5	2,043.4	2,056.2	2,055.6	2,047.7	2,018.2	0.05	0.46
Germany	2,534.9	2,540.2	2,522.6	2,526.7	2,537.2	2,571.3	2,593.4	2,620.3	2,586.1	2,524.1	2,441.7	-0.37	-3.68
Greece	418.6	408.3	389.7	373.6	356.2	344.3	332.2	326.0	320.6	318.6	312.8	-2.87	-25.26
Hong Kong, China	236.4	239.3	238.9	234.8	231.9	232.5	231.9	232.6	234.4	233.9	228.9	-0.32	-3.18
Hungary	372.1	357.6	350.0	343.0	338.0	335.8	333.7	329.8	328.1	325.9	321.7	-1.44	-13.53
India	51,630.8	52,487.9	53,320.5	54,137.2	54,954.0	55,787.3	56,644.9	57,521.1	58,389.4	59,201.1	59,899.9	1.50	16.02
Indonesia	10,227.2	10,269.6	10,282.1	10,268.2	10,236.3	10,197.7	10,162.1	10,134.8	10,116.7	10,105.6	10,098.2	-0.13	-1.26
Iran	4,302.6	4,472.8	4,598.9	4,675.5	4,700.1	4,672.8	4,595.7	4,472.3	4,307.0	4,106.5	3,880.4	-1.03	-9.81
Ireland	200.8	196.6	190.6	185.7	180.0	175.5	171.0	168.1	165.3	162.5	159.9	-2.26	-20.40
Israel	281.0	284.7	288.7	291.7	292.8	293.3	294.4	295.8	298.3	302.0	305.7	0.85	8.81
Italy	1,741.6	1,698.5	1,663.3	1,629.1	1,597.6	1,584.8	1,576.6	1,578.3	1,585.1	1,593.9	1,583.5	-0.95	-9.07
Japan	3,847.1	3,809.9	3,779.3	3,740.4	3,669.4	3,575.4	3,469.3	3,373.9	3,297.0	3,228.1	3,191.9	-1.85	-17.03
Jordan	314.8	322.4	325.4	324.2	320.5	316.5	313.8	313.3	314.8	318.1	322.3	0.24	2.39
Kazakhstan	669.7	693.3	718.6	744.1	767.4	785.6	796.0	797.1	788.6	771.4	747.0	1.10	11.54
Kuwait	166.1	162.4	158.3	154.0	149.8	146.2	143.2	141.0	139.5	138.6	138.0	-1.84	-16.92
Latvia	85.4	87.5	89.3	91.1	92.2	91.8	90.8	89.1	85.9	82.1	76.1	-1.14	-10.87
Lithuania	120.4	123.9	127.1	130.8	133.3	132.3	130.8	129.6	126.8	124.9	121.6	0.10	1.05
Malaysia	1,174.3	1,200.9	1,225.9	1,249.3	1,266.3	1,282.4	1,297.3	1,309.7	1,319.1	1,334.1	1,347.4	1.38	14.74
Mexico	4,272.8	4,265.2	4,269.5	4,282.5	4,309.0	4,352.5	4,414.4	4,493.2	4,583.7	4,676.8	4,762.0	1.09	11.45
Morocco	1,423.0	1,460.3	1,488.8	1,508.3	1,519.9	1,525.4	1,526.7	1,524.8	1,520.2	1,513.3	1,504.0	0.56	5.70
Netherlands	490.6	491.2	489.6	492.0	497.4	502.8	506.5	514.2	519.3	522.4	525.2	0.68	7.04
New Zealand	137.2	139.6	141.1	142.3	143.6	145.8	148.9	153.2	156.4	158.2	158.7	1.47	15.66
Nigeria	6,264.3	6,423.6	6,577.6	6,727.8	6,876.3	7,025.3	7,176.8	7,332.1	7,491.9	7,656.8	7,827.1	2.25	24.95
Norway	153.6	155.5	157.1	159.6	161.1	164.4	168.6	173.1	177.0	180.5	181.8	1.70	18.38
Pakistan	7,647.7	7,953.0	8,284.0	8,628.4	8,964.0	9,265.1	9,512.0	9,696.7	9,823.5	9,906.3	9,964.8	2.68	30.30
Peru	1,242.3	1,253.5	1,268.2	1,286.3	1,306.7	1,327.5	1,347.4	1,365.3	1,380.9	1,394.0	1,404.7	1.24	13.07
Philippines	3,906.9	3,996.7	4,088.6	4,183.9	4,281.0	4,378.7	4,474.5	4,566.6	4,653.8	4,734.8	4,808.4	2.10	23.08
Poland	1,638.8	1,656.1	1,660.0	1,645.6	1,600.8	1,537.4	1,474.6	1,419.3	1,380.3	1,340.4	1,297.7	-2.31	-20.81
Portugal	385.0	376.0	362.7	349.5	335.7	324.1	314.3	309.2	305.9	302.6	299.1	-2.49	-22.32
Romania	839.6	822.4	808.6	818.7	833.5	853.3	852.8	825.2	772.0	718.3	660.9	-2.36	-21.28
Russia	5,969.2	6,148.1	6,225.4	6,369.5	6,417.0	6,320.8	6,170.7	5,981.6	5,629.6	5,203.0	4,744.3	-2.27	-20.52
Saudi Arabia	1,298.7	1,291.7	1,295.3	1,309.5	1,332.5	1,361.2	1,392.5	1,424.3	1,455.2	1,483.3	1,507.2	1.50	16.06
Singapore	156.9	158.7	158.4	158.0	162.2	172.2	177.1	185.5	193.6	196.7	194.7	2.18	24.08
Slovakia	233.6	230.0	228.0	225.5	220.8	216.9	211.9	206.9	202.2	197.8	192.9	-1.90	-17.42
Slovenia	77.6	75.7	74.2	71.9	70.5	69.6	68.1	66.1	64.4	61.7	58.8	-2.73	-24.16
South Africa	2,378.9	2,416.8	2,444.0	2,460.2	2,466.3	2,464.0	2,455.3	2,441.7	2,424.4	2,405.5	2,387.3	0.04	0.35
South Korea	1,995.6	1,921.5	1,838.9	1,748.6	1,675.9	1,637.7	1,632.0	1,640.0	1,675.7	1,725.2	1,768.1	-1.20	-11.40
Spain	1,773.8	1,703.2	1,631.1	1,565.1	1,506.1	1,456.5	1,417.3	1,388.2	1,365.9	1,348.1	1,333.5	-2.81	-24.82
Sweden	279.7	280.4	282.3	287.5	293.0	303.5	314.4	326.8	337.3	346.5	348.0	2.21	24.41
Switzerland	236.7	238.8	239.4	240.4	241.1	244.0	246.0	249.5	252.5	255.0	253.7	0.70	7.18
Taiwan	1,009.4	986.0	954.7	901.8	859.8	844.8	819.3	821.8	833.7	841.2	833.9	-1.89	-17.38
Thailand	2,607.5	2,552.1	2,489.1	2,414.9	2,364.8	2,342.8	2,344.3	2,376.4	2,426.9	2,467.2	2,494.0	-0.44	-4.35
Tunisia	502.6	510.4	517.6	523.7	528.3	530.6	530.0	526.3	519.5	509.8	497.8	-0.10	-0.95
Turkey	3,429.7	3,394.4	3,353.7	3,305.2	3,254.1	3,214.4	3,196.0	3,201.8	3,232.9	3,284.1	3,347.3	-0.24	-2.40
Turkmenistan	227.2	234.7	242.9	251.6	260.3	268.2	274.8	279.7	282.5	282.8	280.5	2.13	23.48
Ukraine	1,837.5	1,885.7	1,905.9	1,944.1	1,945.8	1,900.2	1,842.0	1,779.0	1,690.3	1,603.8	1,509.9	-1.94	-17.82
United Arab Emirates	438.9	421.5	402.7	384.1	367.9	355.6	348.6	347.1	350.7	358.2	368.1	-1.74	-16.13
United Kingdom	2,106.6	2,173.7	2,228.1	2,282.8	2,335.9	2,368.6	2,381.8	2,395.5	2,407.9	2,401.7	2,382.9	1.24	13.12
USA	11,057.2	11,090.2	11,076.9	11,037.0	11,005.8	11,036.4	11,112.1	11,162.7	11,207.2	11,220.7	11,175.3	0.11	1.07
Venezuela	1,219.8	1,241.7	1,264.8	1,288.5	1,311.2	1,331.0	1,346.6	1,357.2	1,363.2	1,365.9	1,366.9	1.15	12.06
Vietnam	3,938.2	4,018.8	4,114.4	4,220.4	4,328.3	4,425.8	4,503.6	4,562.2	4,602.5	4,615.6	4,590.8	1.55	16.57

Key population trends

Table 4.32 Male Population Aged 30-34: 2009-2019

'000

	2009	2010	2011	2012	2013	2014	2015	2016	2017	2018	2019	CAGR	Period growth
Algeria	1,525.2	1,578.8	1,634.5	1,690.2	1,742.3	1,786.9	1,821.1	1,843.6	1,855.1	1,857.9	1,855.3	1.98	21.64
Argentina	1,587.6	1,619.1	1,635.4	1,638.2	1,632.5	1,624.9	1,620.8	1,623.2	1,632.3	1,646.9	1,665.0	0.48	4.88
Australia	741.8	752.2	768.7	790.2	815.8	840.0	862.1	878.8	890.4	898.0	908.4	2.05	22.46
Austria	269.3	267.6	269.9	275.2	281.3	285.4	288.0	287.1	284.6	281.5	281.0	0.43	4.35
Azerbaijan	286.8	294.4	305.3	319.4	336.2	354.6	373.6	392.3	409.8	425.2	437.4	4.31	52.53
Belarus	348.9	355.0	363.2	370.8	379.9	393.3	402.5	408.2	417.6	420.3	416.7	1.79	19.45
Belgium	338.1	338.8	341.8	344.2	344.9	343.7	340.7	337.3	336.0	336.1	339.0	0.03	0.26
Bolivia	339.6	345.7	352.6	360.4	369.0	378.1	387.7	397.7	408.1	419.1	430.8	2.41	26.87
Bosnia-Herzegovina	133.7	135.8	138.2	140.8	143.6	146.4	149.0	151.4	153.1	153.7	152.6	1.33	14.16
Brazil	7,664.8	7,845.1	8,068.6	8,289.0	8,484.1	8,663.7	8,805.9	8,836.6	8,823.2	8,779.7	8,691.1	1.26	13.39
Bulgaria	295.9	292.8	288.0	282.6	276.7	271.4	264.8	259.5	255.1	249.9	246.0	-1.83	-16.85
Canada	1,156.2	1,173.2	1,191.2	1,210.5	1,233.6	1,254.4	1,269.4	1,280.0	1,284.7	1,285.0	1,290.7	1.11	11.63
Chile	591.4	592.0	598.4	610.3	626.3	644.5	663.3	681.3	698.2	713.4	726.8	2.08	22.90
China	43,361.1	42,002.8	41,012.2	42,280.2	42,053.8	41,941.2	42,407.7	44,384.5	46,940.7	50,358.4	54,694.5	2.35	26.14
Colombia	1,699.5	1,737.7	1,771.6	1,800.5	1,825.1	1,846.9	1,867.1	1,886.9	1,906.7	1,926.9	1,948.0	1.37	14.62
Costa Rica	178.0	184.1	190.1	195.8	201.3	206.6	211.8	216.8	221.6	225.8	229.1	2.55	28.69
Croatia	154.2	156.5	158.8	159.8	160.3	160.3	159.7	157.4	154.9	151.7	148.9	-0.35	-3.42
Czech Republic	471.2	462.5	446.4	426.5	408.1	389.0	372.2	363.4	358.0	352.3	349.3	-2.95	-25.86
Denmark	181.7	176.8	170.7	165.4	161.9	157.4	154.7	153.6	155.2	156.9	160.6	-1.23	-11.60
Ecuador	495.3	500.8	507.0	513.9	521.3	529.0	537.0	545.0	553.1	561.1	568.9	1.39	14.86
Egypt	2,824.7	2,911.5	2,991.5	3,063.4	3,125.9	3,179.6	3,226.6	3,267.4	3,303.3	3,337.8	3,363.1	1.76	19.06
Estonia	45.9	46.3	46.6	47.3	47.7	48.7	49.5	50.0	50.2	51.0	51.2	1.10	11.51
Finland	171.1	172.9	173.2	173.0	174.8	177.0	178.6	178.6	177.4	174.3	172.6	0.08	0.85
France	1,950.1	1,934.0	1,962.7	2,002.1	2,025.3	2,029.5	2,031.7	2,018.7	2,014.9	2,015.8	2,043.9	0.47	4.81
Germany	2,393.9	2,413.7	2,463.6	2,499.9	2,535.0	2,553.4	2,562.6	2,549.1	2,555.6	2,567.5	2,601.7	0.84	8.68
Greece	452.0	447.4	448.5	443.2	435.8	426.3	416.0	397.6	381.6	364.2	352.3	-2.46	-22.06
Hong Kong, China	229.6	229.1	232.5	235.2	240.0	244.3	246.9	246.1	241.5	238.1	238.4	0.38	3.83
Hungary	441.0	435.1	421.1	406.8	391.8	375.7	361.1	353.3	346.3	341.3	339.2	-2.59	-23.08
India	46,039.4	47,049.6	48,033.8	48,984.5	49,899.2	50,781.0	51,636.1	52,470.5	53,294.3	54,123.5	54,972.0	1.79	19.40
Indonesia	9,575.6	9,688.9	9,797.9	9,898.7	9,985.5	10,051.9	10,093.7	10,110.2	10,104.6	10,084.1	10,057.5	0.49	5.03
Iran	3,234.2	3,418.2	3,624.5	3,844.9	4,064.7	4,266.3	4,434.4	4,559.8	4,637.3	4,663.9	4,638.7	3.67	43.43
Ireland	192.6	201.5	209.7	215.3	218.6	217.4	213.0	207.1	202.1	196.4	191.9	-0.04	-0.37
Israel	276.5	277.1	275.8	275.7	278.7	282.7	286.3	290.2	293.1	294.1	294.4	0.63	6.45
Italy	2,154.7	2,062.7	1,976.2	1,902.3	1,844.3	1,788.3	1,745.4	1,710.4	1,676.5	1,645.4	1,632.7	-2.74	-24.23
Japan	4,369.3	4,202.4	4,052.1	3,940.3	3,866.1	3,823.9	3,790.2	3,762.1	3,724.7	3,655.1	3,562.3	-2.02	-18.47
Jordan	269.4	279.6	288.5	295.9	301.6	305.6	308.2	309.3	309.1	308.3	307.7	1.34	14.23
Kazakhstan	586.7	596.3	608.1	622.6	640.4	661.8	686.3	713.0	740.0	764.6	783.4	2.93	33.53
Kuwait	203.7	203.2	201.2	197.8	193.3	188.4	183.6	179.1	175.3	172.0	169.2	-1.84	-16.92
Latvia	79.2	78.8	79.0	79.5	80.9	83.6	85.5	87.4	89.1	90.3	90.1	1.30	13.75
Lithuania	109.4	109.3	109.9	111.2	112.4	115.6	119.0	122.0	125.6	128.2	127.6	1.55	16.65
Malaysia	1,030.8	1,051.8	1,075.4	1,101.7	1,130.1	1,157.9	1,183.7	1,207.9	1,230.6	1,246.9	1,262.7	2.05	22.50
Mexico	4,419.3	4,397.6	4,373.8	4,346.2	4,320.3	4,300.5	4,289.6	4,289.4	4,301.9	4,329.3	4,373.0	-0.11	-1.05
Morocco	1,155.1	1,189.8	1,231.4	1,278.1	1,326.3	1,371.4	1,409.7	1,439.1	1,459.6	1,472.0	1,478.4	2.50	27.99
Netherlands	498.2	489.6	489.7	488.7	487.9	485.4	486.4	485.0	487.7	493.3	499.1	0.02	0.17
New Zealand	128.7	129.3	131.5	134.4	138.5	141.8	144.2	145.8	147.0	148.3	150.5	1.58	16.97
Nigeria	5,110.0	5,293.9	5,473.7	5,648.2	5,817.0	5,979.9	6,137.0	6,289.1	6,437.2	6,583.5	6,730.2	2.79	31.71
Norway	162.8	162.3	163.5	164.6	167.3	168.7	169.5	170.3	172.2	173.4	176.5	0.81	8.42
Pakistan	6,376.0	6,572.5	6,784.7	7,016.0	7,271.1	7,553.5	7,863.3	8,196.5	8,541.2	8,876.6	9,177.7	3.71	43.94
Peru	1,148.2	1,165.0	1,178.4	1,189.3	1,199.0	1,209.8	1,223.0	1,239.4	1,258.8	1,280.1	1,301.9	1.26	13.38
Philippines	3,408.3	3,498.2	3,583.9	3,667.4	3,750.5	3,836.3	3,926.2	4,020.9	4,119.5	4,220.5	4,321.6	2.40	26.80
Poland	1,504.0	1,529.2	1,549.2	1,553.3	1,574.5	1,604.3	1,619.7	1,622.2	1,608.5	1,566.2	1,506.5	0.02	0.16
Portugal	428.2	422.7	414.3	404.3	395.7	388.4	379.2	365.8	352.5	338.7	327.0	-2.66	-23.63
Romania	906.0	903.5	902.9	888.7	861.3	826.7	807.8	791.6	798.2	810.9	828.2	-0.89	-8.59
Russia	5,282.8	5,340.6	5,432.8	5,500.7	5,662.1	5,877.7	6,052.3	6,133.5	6,275.8	6,325.1	6,233.0	1.67	17.99
Saudi Arabia	1,389.4	1,392.4	1,386.9	1,374.7	1,360.0	1,348.5	1,344.7	1,351.1	1,367.9	1,393.0	1,423.5	0.24	2.45
Singapore	167.6	167.9	171.2	170.5	174.3	174.5	175.9	175.1	174.1	178.0	188.1	1.16	12.20
Slovakia	238.0	239.9	240.2	238.0	236.0	233.1	229.4	227.3	224.6	219.7	215.7	-0.98	-9.37
Slovenia	79.6	80.8	81.4	81.5	81.0	79.3	77.2	75.5	73.2	71.7	71.0	-1.15	-10.89
South Africa	2,052.5	2,091.7	2,129.9	2,166.6	2,200.8	2,231.6	2,258.3	2,280.1	2,296.6	2,307.3	2,312.2	1.20	12.65
South Korea	1,975.4	1,977.2	2,003.4	2,030.5	2,031.2	1,993.2	1,919.3	1,837.0	1,747.1	1,674.6	1,636.7	-1.86	-17.15
Spain	2,082.4	2,076.6	2,050.2	2,004.5	1,945.8	1,877.2	1,804.3	1,732.3	1,666.3	1,607.2	1,557.4	-2.86	-25.21
Sweden	294.0	288.7	287.3	286.6	287.3	288.5	289.2	290.9	296.1	301.1	311.6	0.58	5.97
Switzerland	247.6	246.4	247.6	249.3	250.8	252.2	254.3	255.0	256.0	256.7	259.6	0.47	4.84
Taiwan	961.7	991.5	1,013.5	1,009.7	1,017.8	1,005.4	982.0	951.3	898.3	856.5	841.7	-1.32	-12.48
Thailand	2,699.5	2,697.1	2,672.8	2,640.3	2,616.3	2,559.4	2,503.1	2,440.2	2,364.3	2,313.3	2,290.0	-1.63	-15.17
Tunisia	447.4	460.1	471.5	481.6	490.7	499.0	506.7	513.8	519.9	524.5	526.9	1.65	17.77
Turkey	3,408.0	3,440.2	3,458.2	3,460.5	3,449.1	3,424.4	3,392.3	3,351.2	3,302.1	3,250.0	3,208.5	-0.60	-5.85
Turkmenistan	195.6	200.2	205.0	210.2	215.9	222.3	229.7	237.8	246.5	255.1	263.1	3.01	34.48
Ukraine	1,665.0	1,672.7	1,691.9	1,695.4	1,730.0	1,784.2	1,828.5	1,846.3	1,883.0	1,886.1	1,844.6	1.03	10.79
United Arab Emirates	596.8	604.5	601.0	587.5	567.0	543.2	519.2	496.9	477.4	461.4	449.8	-2.79	-24.62
United Kingdom	1,909.9	1,937.4	1,988.0	2,048.5	2,119.1	2,194.4	2,262.1	2,318.4	2,373.9	2,426.5	2,457.8	2.55	28.69
USA	10,164.0	10,405.2	10,697.5	10,936.2	11,137.5	11,234.7	11,258.4	11,250.6	11,212.8	11,181.3	11,210.6	0.98	10.30
Venezuela	1,087.7	1,116.2	1,141.9	1,164.9	1,186.3	1,207.3	1,229.2	1,252.3	1,276.0	1,298.7	1,318.6	1.94	21.23
Vietnam	3,576.5	3,644.6	3,707.7	3,766.8	3,827.4	3,896.9	3,980.1	4,078.1	4,186.4	4,296.2	4,395.0	2.08	22.89

Key population trends

Table 4.33 Male Population Aged 35-39: 2009-2019

'000

	2009	2010	2011	2012	2013	2014	2015	2016	2017	2018	2019	CAGR	Period growth
Algeria	1,293.4	1,330.8	1,370.7	1,413.3	1,459.2	1,508.7	1,561.5	1,616.7	1,672.1	1,724.2	1,769.1	3.18	36.78
Argentina	1,316.7	1,363.7	1,417.0	1,473.5	1,527.5	1,572.8	1,604.6	1,621.1	1,624.1	1,618.5	1,608.8	2.02	22.18
Australia	799.1	796.3	784.4	774.6	772.3	776.4	787.5	805.4	827.7	853.7	877.9	0.94	9.86
Austria	314.2	301.7	292.4	283.4	276.1	273.1	271.4	273.8	279.0	285.1	289.2	-0.83	-7.97
Azerbaijan	270.9	271.7	272.2	272.8	274.6	278.7	286.1	297.0	311.2	328.1	346.6	2.49	27.94
Belarus	330.5	333.1	333.7	335.2	336.5	341.8	347.8	356.0	363.8	373.0	386.7	1.58	17.01
Belgium	375.7	367.8	357.0	348.5	342.1	339.0	339.7	342.6	345.1	345.8	344.7	-0.86	-8.26
Bolivia	298.3	306.3	313.1	319.0	324.4	329.8	335.8	342.7	350.4	359.0	368.2	2.13	23.40
Bosnia-Herzegovina	127.6	127.8	128.6	129.8	131.5	133.6	135.9	138.4	141.0	143.7	146.4	1.39	14.78
Brazil	6,920.8	6,997.0	7,092.6	7,209.8	7,353.9	7,527.7	7,711.6	7,937.9	8,161.0	8,358.6	8,539.8	2.12	23.39
Bulgaria	278.7	281.0	283.5	287.7	292.4	292.5	289.4	284.5	278.9	273.1	267.7	-0.40	-3.94
Canada	1,178.8	1,176.7	1,174.5	1,180.1	1,189.9	1,206.4	1,223.6	1,242.6	1,263.0	1,287.2	1,309.2	1.05	11.05
Chile	617.9	614.0	607.6	599.9	592.7	588.5	589.1	595.6	607.4	623.3	641.5	0.38	3.82
China	59,174.7	55,081.5	51,835.5	47,945.5	45,434.5	43,415.4	42,088.2	41,029.5	42,331.2	42,150.9	42,045.5	-3.36	-28.95
Colombia	1,519.4	1,529.3	1,550.4	1,581.8	1,620.0	1,660.4	1,698.7	1,732.6	1,761.6	1,786.2	1,807.9	1.75	18.99
Costa Rica	157.8	159.1	162.0	166.3	171.7	177.6	183.7	189.6	195.3	200.8	206.2	2.71	30.67
Croatia	147.7	148.4	150.5	151.5	152.8	154.4	156.7	158.9	159.9	160.4	160.4	0.82	8.54
Czech Republic	399.6	425.1	447.0	464.0	473.5	472.2	462.9	446.3	426.6	408.4	389.7	-0.25	-2.49
Denmark	195.0	194.7	194.9	190.8	185.2	181.2	176.4	170.3	165.1	161.6	157.2	-2.13	-19.35
Ecuador	445.2	450.5	456.3	462.5	469.2	476.2	483.3	490.5	497.8	505.2	512.9	1.42	15.19
Egypt	2,245.7	2,349.7	2,453.1	2,555.5	2,654.9	2,749.8	2,838.1	2,918.9	2,991.0	3,053.1	3,105.8	3.30	38.30
Estonia	45.6	45.4	45.1	44.6	44.5	44.4	44.7	45.0	45.7	46.1	47.2	0.35	3.51
Finland	159.4	158.5	160.4	164.1	168.0	172.7	174.4	174.7	174.4	176.1	178.2	1.12	11.75
France	2,193.2	2,175.4	2,128.8	2,061.2	2,004.8	1,954.6	1,938.5	1,967.6	2,006.8	2,029.9	2,034.0	-0.75	-7.26
Germany	2,864.8	2,672.7	2,524.0	2,417.7	2,375.4	2,386.6	2,409.8	2,462.4	2,500.2	2,536.0	2,554.5	-1.14	-10.83
Greece	449.4	452.9	450.6	454.0	456.4	458.5	453.9	455.0	449.9	442.5	433.0	-0.37	-3.65
Hong Kong, China	240.9	240.8	238.5	237.1	232.4	229.2	228.4	231.4	234.5	239.6	244.0	0.13	1.31
Hungary	367.4	382.5	401.0	418.5	430.5	440.2	434.2	420.1	405.7	390.9	374.9	0.20	2.05
India	40,287.6	41,162.5	42,097.1	43,081.2	44,095.6	45,117.3	46,126.7	47,112.2	48,067.8	48,991.4	49,884.9	2.16	23.82
Indonesia	8,839.9	8,972.6	9,099.0	9,220.1	9,337.4	9,452.1	9,564.6	9,673.8	9,776.3	9,866.2	9,936.6	1.18	12.41
Iran	2,623.9	2,703.3	2,797.1	2,908.6	3,041.7	3,199.9	3,383.9	3,590.6	3,811.5	4,032.0	4,234.1	4.90	61.37
Ireland	174.5	178.9	183.3	187.9	193.1	200.8	209.6	217.9	223.4	226.7	225.5	2.60	29.26
Israel	248.9	258.1	266.4	272.8	277.3	279.6	279.9	278.3	278.0	280.9	284.9	1.36	14.45
Italy	2,394.7	2,379.9	2,358.6	2,312.0	2,250.7	2,182.1	2,090.6	2,004.5	1,931.0	1,873.1	1,817.4	-2.72	-24.11
Japan	4,920.3	4,913.2	4,837.2	4,696.1	4,515.9	4,322.7	4,160.8	4,014.2	3,904.6	3,831.9	3,790.6	-2.57	-22.96
Jordan	228.0	237.1	244.6	250.6	256.1	261.8	268.4	275.9	284.1	291.9	298.5	2.73	30.94
Kazakhstan	530.9	541.4	550.6	558.4	566.0	574.6	585.1	598.2	614.0	632.8	654.7	2.12	23.32
Kuwait	188.2	190.5	192.9	195.3	197.2	198.3	198.3	197.2	195.0	192.1	188.7	0.03	0.29
Latvia	79.1	79.5	79.2	78.6	77.6	77.1	76.7	76.9	77.4	78.9	81.6	0.32	3.22
Lithuania	118.6	115.8	112.6	109.3	106.6	105.2	105.1	105.6	106.9	108.3	111.6	-0.61	-5.90
Malaysia	953.0	957.7	965.3	976.1	990.1	1,006.9	1,026.6	1,049.2	1,074.9	1,103.2	1,131.3	1.73	18.72
Mexico	4,229.7	4,355.8	4,441.9	4,483.1	4,488.9	4,472.0	4,444.4	4,413.6	4,383.8	4,357.9	4,338.5	0.25	2.57
Morocco	1,013.9	1,030.1	1,047.1	1,066.2	1,089.3	1,118.3	1,154.2	1,196.7	1,244.1	1,292.7	1,338.1	2.81	31.97
Netherlands	616.2	582.8	548.2	519.6	496.6	484.6	476.3	476.9	476.3	475.8	473.6	-2.60	-23.14
New Zealand	146.5	143.7	139.7	136.0	133.4	132.5	133.1	135.3	138.3	142.4	145.7	-0.05	-0.54
Nigeria	3,971.3	4,129.2	4,297.0	4,472.7	4,653.3	4,834.9	5,014.4	5,189.8	5,359.9	5,524.4	5,683.1	3.65	43.10
Norway	185.3	184.2	182.4	179.3	175.3	173.3	172.1	172.7	173.5	175.9	177.2	-0.45	-4.37
Pakistan	5,429.4	5,593.3	5,761.7	5,935.1	6,114.9	6,303.5	6,503.4	6,717.1	6,948.8	7,203.6	7,485.9	3.26	37.88
Peru	1,000.3	1,023.1	1,047.3	1,072.1	1,096.2	1,118.0	1,136.4	1,151.1	1,162.9	1,173.4	1,185.0	1.71	18.46
Philippines	2,923.8	3,003.0	3,086.9	3,175.7	3,267.4	3,360.2	3,451.6	3,540.7	3,628.0	3,715.0	3,804.1	2.67	30.11
Poland	1,286.3	1,329.8	1,371.5	1,417.3	1,449.2	1,476.7	1,500.9	1,519.9	1,524.3	1,546.3	1,577.4	2.06	22.63
Portugal	406.6	414.6	422.8	429.0	431.6	430.3	424.6	416.2	406.2	397.5	390.1	-0.41	-4.04
Romania	858.3	847.0	845.8	857.7	873.1	892.5	888.7	886.6	870.8	843.1	808.4	-0.60	-5.81
Russia	4,850.8	4,946.8	4,982.6	5,052.9	5,068.4	5,153.5	5,210.1	5,305.6	5,374.0	5,533.8	5,744.9	1.71	18.43
Saudi Arabia	1,266.0	1,278.5	1,294.8	1,313.5	1,331.2	1,343.9	1,348.5	1,344.5	1,333.8	1,320.7	1,310.7	0.35	3.53
Singapore	196.4	196.9	194.0	189.9	181.9	178.1	177.8	180.7	179.5	182.8	182.4	-0.73	-7.09
Slovakia	198.9	208.5	217.2	226.5	233.2	237.4	239.1	239.3	237.0	234.8	231.8	1.54	16.54
Slovenia	75.2	76.2	77.9	79.1	79.9	81.0	82.1	82.6	82.7	82.2	80.5	0.69	7.12
South Africa	1,698.8	1,729.1	1,757.2	1,783.6	1,809.9	1,838.2	1,869.9	1,905.3	1,943.2	1,981.8	2,018.5	1.74	18.82
South Korea	2,235.0	2,194.3	2,128.5	2,055.2	1,995.1	1,962.9	1,965.1	1,991.4	2,018.6	2,019.5	1,981.9	-1.19	-11.32
Spain	1,995.1	2,038.1	2,078.5	2,114.9	2,140.5	2,151.4	2,143.8	2,117.7	2,072.4	2,014.2	1,946.1	-0.25	-2.46
Sweden	315.9	318.2	317.5	312.1	306.2	299.9	294.3	292.7	291.8	292.3	293.5	-0.73	-7.10
Switzerland	280.0	273.0	266.3	260.2	256.4	254.2	253.0	254.2	256.0	257.4	258.7	-0.79	-7.59
Taiwan	913.1	899.9	890.5	916.1	930.6	954.5	984.1	1,006.3	1,002.3	1,010.4	998.0	0.89	9.30
Thailand	2,714.6	2,689.3	2,661.7	2,652.1	2,632.5	2,622.7	2,620.3	2,596.9	2,563.3	2,538.9	2,479.9	-0.90	-8.64
Tunisia	376.4	389.0	402.5	416.5	430.5	444.1	456.6	468.0	478.1	487.2	495.5	2.79	31.64
Turkey	3,007.9	3,112.1	3,202.6	3,280.0	3,346.3	3,396.9	3,432.6	3,450.2	3,451.9	3,439.5	3,413.0	1.27	13.47
Turkmenistan	171.8	175.1	178.6	182.4	186.4	190.6	195.0	199.8	204.9	210.6	217.1	2.37	26.35
Ukraine	1,567.9	1,589.8	1,595.5	1,605.4	1,596.9	1,606.7	1,612.5	1,629.8	1,633.5	1,668.8	1,724.0	0.95	9.96
United Arab Emirates	526.6	559.0	582.4	596.1	601.0	598.7	591.2	579.8	565.6	549.4	532.3	0.11	1.08
United Kingdom	2,166.6	2,102.8	2,036.2	1,969.5	1,920.2	1,910.9	1,939.6	1,992.3	2,054.1	2,125.1	2,200.0	0.15	1.54
USA	10,420.2	10,207.9	9,995.1	9,950.8	10,040.6	10,233.4	10,469.2	10,764.5	11,005.1	11,207.6	11,307.4	0.82	8.51
Venezuela	949.3	966.0	988.3	1,015.4	1,045.2	1,075.4	1,103.8	1,129.3	1,152.3	1,173.5	1,194.6	2.32	25.84
Vietnam	3,190.3	3,252.1	3,318.5	3,389.7	3,463.3	3,536.3	3,606.7	3,672.2	3,733.5	3,795.9	3,866.7	1.94	21.20

Key population trends

Table 4.34 Male Population Aged 40-44: 2009-2019

'000

	2009	2010	2011	2012	2013	2014	2015	2016	2017	2018	2019	CAGR	Period growth
Algeria	1,115.1	1,146.9	1,178.5	1,210.4	1,243.3	1,277.7	1,314.5	1,353.9	1,396.3	1,442.1	1,491.7	2.95	33.78
Argentina	1,166.2	1,182.5	1,202.9	1,228.3	1,260.3	1,299.8	1,346.6	1,399.6	1,455.7	1,509.2	1,556.1	2.93	33.44
Australia	757.6	767.9	786.5	804.9	816.1	819.6	817.8	807.6	798.9	797.2	801.5	0.56	5.79
Austria	362.7	358.4	350.2	340.8	329.4	314.6	302.2	293.0	284.1	276.9	273.9	-2.77	-24.48
Azerbaijan	284.9	274.9	268.0	264.3	263.1	263.4	264.0	264.6	265.5	267.5	271.7	-0.47	-4.61
Belarus	332.4	324.1	321.6	319.8	321.7	320.9	323.5	324.2	326.0	327.5	333.1	0.02	0.20
Belgium	401.5	393.0	387.2	382.6	378.4	373.1	365.3	354.7	346.3	340.1	337.0	-1.74	-16.08
Bolivia	244.1	252.5	261.6	271.0	280.3	289.1	296.9	303.6	309.5	314.8	320.3	2.76	31.23
Bosnia-Herzegovina	134.6	131.8	129.6	128.1	127.3	127.1	127.5	128.4	129.7	131.3	133.3	-0.10	-0.98
Brazil	6,486.6	6,540.4	6,591.9	6,643.4	6,699.2	6,764.9	6,846.1	6,945.9	7,066.7	7,213.3	7,387.9	1.31	13.89
Bulgaria	254.3	259.8	266.1	271.4	274.9	274.5	276.8	279.2	283.3	287.9	288.0	1.25	13.23
Canada	1,246.4	1,222.1	1,215.1	1,214.0	1,211.9	1,206.1	1,203.3	1,201.4	1,207.3	1,217.6	1,234.7	-0.09	-0.94
Chile	619.6	616.6	615.1	614.7	614.4	612.9	609.1	602.8	595.2	588.1	584.0	-0.59	-5.75
China	65,136.0	66,469.2	66,612.5	67,603.1	64,672.6	62,342.9	58,064.1	54,597.9	50,556.4	47,931.7	45,825.7	-3.46	-29.65
Colombia	1,474.1	1,486.4	1,490.2	1,488.0	1,484.7	1,486.1	1,496.5	1,517.8	1,549.1	1,586.9	1,626.8	0.99	10.36
Costa Rica	160.7	160.2	159.2	158.0	157.0	156.9	158.2	161.1	165.4	170.8	176.8	0.96	9.98
Croatia	156.1	154.3	150.2	148.0	147.1	147.4	148.0	150.1	151.0	152.3	153.8	-0.15	-1.45
Czech Republic	356.8	353.3	355.5	363.5	377.0	399.8	424.5	445.9	462.7	472.3	471.4	2.83	32.13
Denmark	215.8	210.3	204.2	198.4	195.8	194.3	193.9	194.2	190.1	184.6	180.7	-1.76	-16.28
Ecuador	398.2	404.9	411.5	417.8	424.1	430.3	436.5	442.9	449.4	456.1	462.9	1.52	16.26
Egypt	1,931.2	1,930.0	1,954.6	2,005.1	2,083.7	2,183.2	2,291.5	2,399.0	2,505.5	2,608.9	2,707.5	3.44	40.20
Estonia	41.3	41.3	41.9	42.8	43.7	43.8	43.5	43.3	42.9	42.7	42.8	0.35	3.54
Finland	186.8	182.0	177.3	171.6	165.5	159.6	158.6	160.4	164.1	167.9	172.5	-0.79	-7.63
France	2,157.6	2,143.3	2,139.5	2,148.1	2,168.9	2,180.1	2,162.2	2,116.9	2,050.5	1,995.0	1,945.7	-1.03	-9.82
Germany	3,614.2	3,512.1	3,377.9	3,226.7	3,043.1	2,830.8	2,646.4	2,503.4	2,400.5	2,359.7	2,371.0	-4.13	-34.40
Greece	437.3	446.0	456.0	456.6	456.1	454.5	458.0	455.7	459.2	461.5	463.6	0.59	6.01
Hong Kong, China	260.3	247.8	240.0	235.3	232.8	232.8	232.3	229.7	228.1	223.2	219.8	-1.68	-15.58
Hungary	326.4	338.9	351.2	358.9	362.6	363.3	377.9	395.9	413.2	425.0	434.9	2.91	33.22
India	35,632.5	36,292.5	36,978.5	37,697.5	38,459.5	39,275.2	40,151.0	41,086.9	42,073.6	43,092.8	44,120.6	2.16	23.82
Indonesia	7,929.9	8,108.5	8,277.4	8,435.9	8,584.4	8,724.2	8,856.9	8,983.4	9,105.0	9,223.4	9,339.9	1.65	17.78
Iran	2,303.6	2,354.4	2,405.7	2,459.4	2,518.5	2,586.7	2,667.2	2,762.6	2,875.4	3,009.7	3,168.6	3.24	37.55
Ireland	158.0	161.5	164.9	168.4	173.5	177.1	181.2	185.6	190.2	195.3	203.0	2.54	28.51
Israel	203.6	210.7	220.1	230.7	241.1	250.9	260.2	268.6	275.2	279.5	281.7	3.30	38.34
Italy	2,464.8	2,454.3	2,437.6	2,424.7	2,416.6	2,404.7	2,390.4	2,369.4	2,323.3	2,262.6	2,194.6	-1.15	-10.96
Japan	4,324.4	4,373.2	4,621.4	4,699.1	4,793.2	4,855.3	4,852.0	4,779.8	4,641.6	4,464.5	4,274.0	-0.12	-1.17
Jordan	179.9	190.5	199.9	208.0	215.1	221.7	228.2	234.7	241.3	248.3	255.8	3.58	42.18
Kazakhstan	485.5	483.9	486.6	493.5	503.6	515.0	526.3	536.5	545.6	554.1	563.2	1.49	15.99
Kuwait	146.8	153.7	160.1	165.8	170.8	175.3	179.3	182.8	185.8	188.0	189.2	2.57	28.93
Latvia	75.2	74.5	74.9	75.4	76.2	76.1	76.5	76.2	75.7	74.9	74.5	-0.09	-0.91
Lithuania	119.8	117.9	116.9	116.4	115.5	113.5	110.7	107.7	104.6	102.1	101.0	-1.69	-15.69
Malaysia	906.7	916.9	923.0	923.9	923.9	923.4	925.0	929.7	938.2	950.6	966.2	0.64	6.56
Mexico	3,377.6	3,548.3	3,735.5	3,926.5	4,108.5	4,266.4	4,388.1	4,467.9	4,507.1	4,512.8	4,496.8	2.90	33.14
Morocco	895.1	912.3	930.2	948.3	966.3	983.9	1,001.6	1,019.7	1,039.5	1,063.0	1,092.1	2.01	22.01
Netherlands	653.5	651.4	647.8	640.9	627.6	604.1	570.6	535.8	507.1	484.0	472.2	-3.20	-27.74
New Zealand	150.1	149.8	150.5	151.2	150.5	148.3	145.6	141.7	138.0	135.4	134.6	-1.09	-10.36
Nigeria	3,137.1	3,229.5	3,334.3	3,451.9	3,582.2	3,724.4	3,877.3	4,039.4	4,208.8	4,382.5	4,557.3	3.80	45.27
Norway	185.3	188.4	189.8	191.0	192.2	191.3	189.8	187.7	184.4	180.5	178.5	-0.38	-3.72
Pakistan	4,577.0	4,721.9	4,872.9	5,029.6	5,190.8	5,355.2	5,522.1	5,691.7	5,865.4	6,045.0	6,233.6	3.14	36.19
Peru	871.5	889.9	908.8	928.7	949.9	972.4	996.4	1,021.4	1,046.8	1,071.3	1,093.5	2.30	25.47
Philippines	2,545.7	2,610.4	2,675.0	2,741.5	2,811.3	2,886.5	2,967.8	3,055.2	3,147.8	3,243.3	3,339.3	2.75	31.17
Poland	1,179.6	1,170.3	1,177.3	1,193.5	1,223.3	1,257.0	1,299.7	1,340.7	1,386.3	1,418.7	1,447.4	2.07	22.70
Portugal	389.6	389.1	391.5	396.0	401.9	407.1	414.9	422.9	428.8	431.4	430.0	0.99	10.37
Romania	771.9	840.6	900.3	948.5	897.8	841.0	829.5	827.6	838.3	853.1	871.5	1.22	12.90
Russia	4,531.6	4,429.7	4,447.7	4,478.1	4,591.6	4,656.6	4,748.8	4,788.8	4,858.3	4,876.7	4,959.7	0.91	9.45
Saudi Arabia	1,119.4	1,147.2	1,167.6	1,181.9	1,192.8	1,203.6	1,216.9	1,233.7	1,252.8	1,270.9	1,283.9	1.38	14.70
Singapore	199.5	195.7	193.3	195.3	198.6	201.8	202.1	198.6	193.9	184.9	180.5	-0.99	-9.51
Slovakia	183.6	181.1	180.6	182.5	188.4	197.0	206.4	215.1	224.2	230.7	234.8	2.49	27.85
Slovenia	79.1	78.6	77.1	76.0	76.1	76.5	77.4	79.0	80.2	81.1	82.3	0.40	4.05
South Africa	1,373.8	1,391.7	1,410.2	1,429.4	1,449.5	1,471.0	1,494.2	1,519.6	1,547.2	1,577.3	1,610.1	1.60	17.20
South Korea	2,108.4	2,131.5	2,163.5	2,195.4	2,214.2	2,206.4	2,166.7	2,102.2	2,030.2	1,971.4	1,940.1	-0.83	-7.98
Spain	1,858.9	1,892.6	1,924.0	1,956.8	1,993.9	2,033.5	2,074.9	2,114.9	2,151.1	2,176.6	2,187.5	1.64	17.68
Sweden	342.9	335.7	328.6	324.0	319.7	318.4	320.6	319.9	314.5	308.3	301.9	-1.26	-11.94
Switzerland	318.6	311.4	303.8	296.2	288.9	280.4	273.4	266.4	260.2	256.2	254.0	-2.24	-20.27
Taiwan	946.1	938.2	933.4	921.0	915.0	901.8	888.7	879.9	905.0	919.4	943.0	-0.03	-0.34
Thailand	2,639.6	2,640.9	2,660.4	2,662.3	2,622.2	2,614.3	2,588.6	2,561.6	2,551.2	2,531.2	2,520.2	-0.46	-4.53
Tunisia	323.6	331.9	341.0	350.8	361.4	373.0	385.5	398.9	412.8	426.9	440.4	3.13	36.10
Turkey	2,488.3	2,562.8	2,653.5	2,757.7	2,870.6	2,985.8	3,090.7	3,180.2	3,258.3	3,321.7	3,370.6	3.08	35.46
Turkmenistan	153.6	155.7	158.0	160.4	163.1	166.0	169.2	172.7	176.4	180.4	184.7	1.86	20.22
Ukraine	1,477.5	1,448.6	1,460.0	1,470.3	1,490.8	1,497.0	1,517.0	1,522.0	1,532.6	1,527.4	1,540.6	0.42	4.27
United Arab Emirates	308.8	334.1	364.7	398.8	433.7	465.9	493.1	513.9	528.0	535.5	537.0	5.69	73.88
United Kingdom	2,326.5	2,301.0	2,267.8	2,229.9	2,182.6	2,125.5	2,064.3	2,001.3	1,937.1	1,889.2	1,880.1	-2.11	-19.19
USA	10,556.9	10,516.1	10,563.9	10,571.7	10,493.0	10,339.1	10,131.8	9,931.6	9,894.2	9,986.3	10,178.9	-0.36	-3.58
Venezuela	898.0	905.2	911.1	917.0	924.7	936.2	952.9	975.1	1,001.9	1,031.6	1,061.5	1.69	18.20
Vietnam	2,870.5	2,922.9	2,976.9	3,032.0	3,089.3	3,149.6	3,213.5	3,282.0	3,354.9	3,430.1	3,504.1	2.01	22.07

Key population trends

Table 4.35 Male Population Aged 45-49: 2009-2019

'000

	2009	2010	2011	2012	2013	2014	2015	2016	2017	2018	2019	CAGR	Period growth
Algeria	914.3	956.8	996.5	1,033.0	1,066.8	1,098.8	1,130.0	1,161.2	1,192.8	1,225.5	1,260.0	3.26	37.81
Argentina	1,080.3	1,093.7	1,106.1	1,117.9	1,129.9	1,143.6	1,160.1	1,180.5	1,205.8	1,237.4	1,275.1	1.67	18.03
Australia	778.0	778.4	772.8	765.6	760.9	763.3	774.3	794.3	813.4	825.1	828.7	0.63	6.51
Austria	344.9	353.2	358.7	360.7	360.8	359.7	355.5	347.5	338.3	327.1	312.4	-0.98	-9.42
Azerbaijan	318.8	317.5	311.1	300.6	288.1	276.1	266.3	259.8	256.4	255.6	256.0	-2.17	-19.69
Belarus	385.0	373.3	357.0	342.5	328.9	317.6	309.7	307.4	306.0	308.0	307.7	-2.22	-20.08
Belgium	405.3	408.4	409.4	407.4	403.1	395.8	387.4	381.8	377.4	373.3	368.2	-0.96	-9.16
Bolivia	203.6	208.8	214.4	220.6	227.4	234.9	243.1	252.0	261.2	270.4	279.1	3.21	37.09
Bosnia-Herzegovina	145.7	144.2	142.0	139.2	136.2	133.2	130.6	128.5	127.1	126.3	126.0	-1.44	-13.48
Brazil	5,801.9	5,945.0	6,061.3	6,154.2	6,228.5	6,291.8	6,350.8	6,407.2	6,463.3	6,523.2	6,591.7	1.28	13.61
Bulgaria	260.0	258.3	253.5	248.0	244.8	248.5	254.0	260.1	265.4	268.8	268.6	0.33	3.31
Canada	1,393.3	1,393.0	1,370.5	1,335.9	1,292.4	1,253.9	1,229.0	1,222.3	1,221.3	1,219.3	1,213.6	-1.37	-12.90
Chile	608.4	616.0	619.0	618.3	615.2	611.5	608.6	607.2	606.9	606.7	605.3	-0.05	-0.51
China	52,600.0	58,349.0	65,581.9	66,115.9	65,824.1	66,526.2	67,780.9	67,903.8	68,929.6	65,952.7	63,617.4	1.92	20.95
Colombia	1,273.9	1,314.8	1,353.5	1,388.7	1,418.0	1,439.5	1,452.1	1,456.3	1,454.5	1,451.6	1,453.1	1.33	14.07
Costa Rica	149.5	153.0	155.7	157.6	158.7	158.9	158.4	157.4	156.1	155.3	155.3	0.38	3.90
Croatia	161.3	158.7	158.2	157.3	155.9	154.0	152.2	148.1	145.8	145.0	145.2	-1.05	-10.01
Czech Republic	328.1	341.3	350.5	355.8	358.8	354.2	350.4	352.4	360.4	373.8	396.5	1.91	20.87
Denmark	196.7	202.5	207.2	213.6	215.5	212.8	207.5	201.5	195.9	193.4	192.0	-0.24	-2.41
Ecuador	345.5	353.5	361.6	369.7	377.7	385.4	392.6	399.4	405.8	412.0	418.1	1.93	21.01
Egypt	1,936.9	1,933.7	1,923.5	1,906.5	1,881.1	1,857.5	1,851.5	1,873.7	1,924.0	2,005.2	2,109.1	0.86	8.89
Estonia	44.2	43.3	42.0	40.7	39.3	39.0	38.9	39.5	40.4	41.3	41.5	-0.64	-6.20
Finland	190.8	191.0	190.4	189.4	188.0	185.1	180.3	175.7	170.0	164.0	158.1	-1.86	-17.10
France	2,111.5	2,126.3	2,135.6	2,142.2	2,141.1	2,126.9	2,112.9	2,110.2	2,119.5	2,140.6	2,152.1	0.19	1.92
Germany	3,507.3	3,573.3	3,609.0	3,621.0	3,600.9	3,541.9	3,447.8	3,320.5	3,174.2	2,995.0	2,787.1	-2.27	-20.53
Greece	398.7	402.1	402.1	413.6	427.0	439.8	448.4	458.3	458.9	458.4	456.8	1.37	14.59
Hong Kong, China	315.8	306.6	293.8	281.9	265.5	250.5	237.7	229.5	225.2	223.4	223.5	-3.40	-29.24
Hungary	297.8	293.8	290.0	291.8	303.1	315.8	328.0	339.9	347.5	351.2	352.0	1.69	18.20
India	31,394.0	31,993.5	32,600.8	33,215.8	33,840.6	34,479.9	35,140.1	35,827.8	36,550.6	37,318.2	38,139.9	1.97	21.49
Indonesia	6,831.6	7,020.4	7,211.3	7,403.5	7,594.1	7,780.0	7,958.3	8,127.1	8,286.3	8,436.3	8,578.4	2.30	25.57
Iran	1,988.4	2,049.3	2,106.2	2,159.5	2,210.1	2,259.6	2,309.4	2,361.2	2,416.5	2,477.5	2,547.3	2.51	28.11
Ireland	145.1	147.8	150.1	152.9	155.2	158.0	161.3	164.7	168.1	173.1	176.6	1.98	21.69
Israel	187.7	189.1	191.1	193.8	197.4	202.7	209.9	219.3	230.2	240.9	250.8	2.94	33.59
Italy	2,212.1	2,292.6	2,357.9	2,409.8	2,443.3	2,460.5	2,450.6	2,434.5	2,422.2	2,414.7	2,403.4	0.83	8.65
Japan	3,931.8	4,025.3	3,954.7	4,072.0	4,165.2	4,252.9	4,304.9	4,551.8	4,630.2	4,724.3	4,786.3	1.99	21.73
Jordan	129.3	138.9	148.2	157.1	165.8	174.4	183.0	191.6	200.0	208.2	216.0	5.26	67.00
Kazakhstan	486.6	485.6	481.4	475.0	468.4	464.0	463.4	467.4	475.4	486.3	498.1	0.23	2.37
Kuwait	100.1	105.5	112.3	120.4	129.2	138.0	146.1	153.1	159.0	163.9	168.2	5.32	67.96
Latvia	80.6	79.1	76.7	74.4	72.3	71.2	70.5	70.9	71.5	72.3	72.4	-1.08	-10.28
Lithuania	127.0	125.3	123.0	119.4	116.1	113.8	112.1	111.1	110.8	110.1	108.2	-1.59	-14.77
Malaysia	804.8	820.0	835.8	853.0	865.6	876.3	883.5	886.3	883.8	880.7	877.4	0.87	9.02
Mexico	2,778.1	2,877.9	2,988.5	3,108.1	3,241.1	3,390.8	3,558.1	3,740.5	3,929.9	4,112.3	4,271.4	4.40	53.75
Morocco	838.8	834.3	835.9	844.0	857.6	874.7	893.3	912.2	930.9	949.0	966.7	1.43	15.24
Netherlands	640.4	648.6	653.6	652.6	649.5	644.0	642.4	639.1	632.3	619.1	595.6	-0.72	-7.00
New Zealand	156.6	156.4	154.9	152.6	150.7	149.5	149.2	150.0	150.7	150.1	147.9	-0.56	-5.51
Nigeria	2,591.6	2,647.1	2,705.8	2,769.2	2,839.1	2,917.9	3,007.3	3,108.2	3,221.1	3,345.7	3,481.6	3.00	34.34
Norway	168.5	172.1	176.4	180.8	184.5	188.6	191.2	192.4	193.4	194.5	193.6	1.40	14.90
Pakistan	3,825.6	3,947.7	4,074.8	4,207.1	4,344.4	4,486.5	4,633.2	4,784.8	4,941.1	5,101.7	5,265.6	3.25	37.64
Peru	742.4	764.9	786.2	806.4	825.8	844.8	863.9	883.4	903.6	924.8	947.6	2.47	27.63
Philippines	2,181.3	2,245.9	2,310.0	2,374.5	2,439.3	2,504.8	2,571.2	2,638.7	2,708.3	2,781.3	2,859.3	2.74	31.08
Poland	1,306.5	1,252.6	1,210.5	1,179.8	1,155.8	1,138.7	1,129.8	1,136.8	1,153.4	1,183.7	1,218.2	-0.70	-6.76
Portugal	377.1	383.3	385.1	386.2	386.8	387.2	386.6	388.9	393.4	399.2	404.2	0.70	7.19
Romania	635.6	610.2	585.7	569.6	657.3	748.1	814.3	871.2	916.8	867.7	812.9	2.49	27.90
Russia	5,501.5	5,281.5	4,954.1	4,691.0	4,435.6	4,253.4	4,161.0	4,184.8	4,216.6	4,326.2	4,388.3	-2.24	-20.23
Saudi Arabia	840.9	886.0	931.6	976.0	1,017.0	1,052.3	1,080.4	1,101.1	1,115.6	1,126.9	1,138.1	3.07	35.34
Singapore	208.9	209.5	210.2	208.9	206.3	199.8	195.2	192.3	193.9	196.8	199.7	-0.45	-4.38
Slovakia	188.7	189.0	187.6	185.5	183.1	179.0	176.3	175.8	177.5	183.3	191.7	0.16	1.60
Slovenia	79.2	79.4	80.2	80.7	80.2	79.7	79.1	77.4	76.4	76.5	77.0	-0.28	-2.78
South Africa	1,159.4	1,162.1	1,165.0	1,168.5	1,173.7	1,181.6	1,193.1	1,208.3	1,227.0	1,248.6	1,272.3	0.93	9.74
South Korea	2,144.2	2,125.5	2,102.6	2,079.6	2,064.6	2,069.4	2,093.1	2,125.5	2,157.6	2,176.8	2,169.8	0.12	1.19
Spain	1,682.3	1,723.3	1,765.2	1,805.6	1,840.6	1,874.7	1,907.1	1,938.3	1,970.8	2,007.7	2,047.0	1.98	21.68
Sweden	304.5	314.2	325.4	335.2	342.7	342.7	335.8	328.6	324.1	319.8	318.4	0.45	4.55
Switzerland	303.3	311.0	316.3	319.7	318.9	315.1	307.8	300.1	292.2	284.6	275.9	-0.94	-9.03
Taiwan	951.2	955.6	954.1	953.4	938.0	928.4	920.6	916.3	903.9	897.9	885.0	-0.72	-6.96
Thailand	2,392.8	2,436.8	2,473.2	2,499.4	2,541.7	2,533.7	2,535.0	2,556.0	2,557.4	2,516.5	2,507.3	0.47	4.79
Tunisia	290.9	294.6	299.2	304.9	311.6	319.2	327.4	336.4	346.2	356.8	368.3	2.39	26.61
Turkey	2,185.1	2,229.2	2,277.5	2,328.7	2,382.5	2,447.4	2,523.7	2,613.7	2,714.3	2,825.7	2,937.4	3.00	34.43
Turkmenistan	135.6	138.2	140.5	142.5	144.5	146.4	148.5	150.8	153.2	155.9	158.9	1.60	17.15
Ukraine	1,676.5	1,625.2	1,547.1	1,485.2	1,428.6	1,384.4	1,356.2	1,367.6	1,379.8	1,404.3	1,415.4	-1.68	-15.58
United Arab Emirates	169.4	171.7	179.8	194.4	215.3	242.2	273.9	309.1	346.0	381.7	413.0	9.32	143.82
United Kingdom	2,160.2	2,204.6	2,239.3	2,263.7	2,275.3	2,268.4	2,245.5	2,216.2	2,181.2	2,135.7	2,079.4	-0.38	-3.74
USA	11,328.5	11,213.0	11,008.0	10,768.4	10,546.2	10,357.0	10,319.9	10,374.2	10,386.7	10,313.3	10,167.2	-1.08	-10.25
Venezuela	797.5	821.9	842.4	858.9	871.5	880.9	888.2	894.2	900.1	907.9	919.4	1.43	15.28
Vietnam	2,506.1	2,586.0	2,655.7	2,716.9	2,772.3	2,825.6	2,879.9	2,935.6	2,992.4	3,051.1	3,112.3	2.19	24.19

Key population trends

Table 4.36 Male Population Aged 50-54: 2009-2019

'000

	2009	2010	2011	2012	2013	2014	2015	2016	2017	2018	2019	CAGR	Period growth
Algeria	709.6	737.1	770.4	809.0	851.1	894.0	935.5	974.3	1,010.2	1,043.6	1,075.4	4.25	51.55
Argentina	984.9	994.2	1,005.5	1,018.8	1,033.2	1,047.7	1,061.4	1,073.9	1,085.7	1,097.6	1,111.1	1.21	12.80
Australia	712.7	724.5	735.4	748.4	760.6	769.2	770.5	766.7	760.7	756.8	759.3	0.64	6.54
Austria	283.7	295.4	306.8	317.3	327.9	338.5	346.8	352.3	354.4	354.6	353.7	2.23	24.65
Azerbaijan	255.9	270.8	284.0	295.0	302.8	306.4	305.2	299.2	289.4	277.7	266.3	0.40	4.04
Belarus	346.7	355.3	364.3	367.3	366.0	359.4	348.3	333.3	320.0	307.5	297.4	-1.52	-14.24
Belgium	375.8	381.8	386.4	390.6	393.5	396.5	399.7	400.7	398.8	394.7	387.7	0.31	3.17
Bolivia	170.5	175.3	180.0	184.6	189.2	194.0	199.1	204.6	210.6	217.3	224.6	2.80	31.78
Bosnia-Herzegovina	140.9	141.6	142.2	142.6	142.7	142.2	141.0	139.0	136.4	133.4	130.4	-0.77	-7.43
Brazil	4,664.8	4,843.1	5,027.5	5,215.6	5,398.7	5,566.0	5,709.7	5,827.8	5,923.2	6,000.4	6,066.2	2.66	30.04
Bulgaria	259.4	257.1	255.1	253.0	251.3	250.0	248.5	244.0	238.9	236.0	239.7	-0.79	-7.59
Canada	1,275.4	1,302.5	1,330.4	1,349.2	1,368.9	1,384.2	1,383.1	1,360.9	1,326.6	1,283.6	1,245.7	-0.24	-2.33
Chile	506.3	528.1	548.9	567.7	583.6	595.6	603.1	606.2	605.6	602.7	599.2	1.70	18.35
China	50,901.2	48,088.1	44,218.4	44,797.9	50,025.2	54,572.7	60,435.5	67,672.9	68,037.2	67,715.8	68,178.1	2.97	33.94
Colombia	1,041.9	1,077.1	1,114.5	1,154.1	1,195.1	1,236.3	1,276.7	1,314.9	1,349.4	1,378.2	1,399.3	2.99	34.31
Costa Rica	121.9	127.6	133.0	138.1	142.8	146.9	150.3	152.9	154.8	155.9	156.3	2.51	28.18
Croatia	165.0	162.8	160.9	158.9	157.9	156.3	153.7	153.1	152.2	150.8	148.9	-1.02	-9.78
Czech Republic	361.1	347.0	333.8	322.7	315.3	320.8	333.5	342.3	347.6	350.7	346.7	-0.41	-4.00
Denmark	182.7	183.3	184.6	185.4	187.8	192.1	197.6	202.3	208.4	210.4	207.7	1.29	13.69
Ecuador	297.6	304.0	310.8	318.0	325.8	333.8	341.9	350.0	358.0	365.8	373.3	2.29	25.42
Egypt	1,762.7	1,806.1	1,838.0	1,859.1	1,870.0	1,871.1	1,863.1	1,847.5	1,824.5	1,792.5	1,762.6	0.00	0.00
Estonia	41.8	41.9	41.8	41.8	41.7	41.0	40.1	38.9	37.7	36.5	36.3	-1.41	-13.21
Finland	190.7	189.2	187.5	185.6	185.2	187.1	187.3	186.6	185.8	184.4	181.6	-0.49	-4.76
France	2,020.2	2,025.4	2,032.2	2,040.6	2,042.4	2,061.2	2,076.1	2,086.5	2,094.0	2,093.9	2,081.1	0.30	3.01
Germany	2,973.2	3,049.2	3,134.2	3,221.7	3,307.7	3,405.4	3,475.6	3,515.0	3,529.0	3,510.7	3,453.8	1.51	16.16
Greece	376.4	382.4	391.3	392.7	395.3	397.5	400.9	401.0	412.4	425.6	438.1	1.53	16.39
Hong Kong, China	303.3	312.5	317.9	316.0	315.7	311.0	301.4	288.3	275.5	258.5	243.5	-2.17	-19.72
Hungary	360.7	334.9	314.7	296.5	284.2	276.0	271.9	268.1	270.0	281.3	294.0	-2.03	-18.51
India	27,303.8	27,782.2	28,280.9	28,810.0	29,368.8	29,950.1	30,544.8	31,148.9	31,762.9	32,389.4	33,031.7	1.92	20.98
Indonesia	5,639.1	5,853.4	6,057.0	6,251.2	6,439.2	6,625.2	6,812.5	7,002.3	7,193.7	7,384.3	7,570.8	2.99	34.26
Iran	1,608.3	1,675.1	1,740.8	1,805.3	1,868.3	1,929.3	1,987.9	2,044.0	2,097.8	2,149.7	2,200.4	3.18	36.82
Ireland	131.2	133.7	137.2	139.6	141.9	144.6	147.1	149.4	152.1	154.4	157.2	1.83	19.85
Israel	177.9	179.1	180.5	181.3	181.8	182.9	184.0	185.7	188.2	191.8	197.0	1.03	10.77
Italy	1,936.4	1,976.0	2,019.7	2,071.6	2,126.6	2,194.1	2,274.7	2,340.1	2,392.3	2,426.4	2,444.2	2.36	26.23
Japan	3,861.8	3,804.4	3,771.5	3,789.3	3,815.2	3,842.5	3,937.8	3,871.2	3,988.2	4,081.1	4,168.3	0.77	7.94
Jordan	90.1	96.5	103.0	109.7	116.7	124.1	132.2	140.8	149.8	159.1	168.4	6.45	86.84
Kazakhstan	422.7	431.5	439.5	446.3	451.6	454.5	454.6	451.8	447.1	442.0	438.7	0.37	3.77
Kuwait	70.4	74.9	79.3	83.6	88.2	93.5	99.8	107.2	115.4	124.0	132.5	6.52	88.06
Latvia	72.9	74.1	75.2	76.3	75.9	74.6	73.1	70.9	68.8	67.1	66.1	-0.98	-9.35
Lithuania	103.3	108.3	111.8	115.6	118.0	118.4	116.8	114.7	111.5	108.6	106.7	0.32	3.23
Malaysia	690.7	709.4	727.6	744.9	758.9	772.1	785.0	798.6	813.9	824.6	833.6	1.90	20.69
Mexico	2,385.6	2,453.8	2,526.7	2,602.4	2,683.0	2,770.6	2,866.7	2,972.6	3,090.2	3,222.6	3,372.5	3.52	41.37
Morocco	802.6	823.1	832.4	832.2	826.4	819.8	816.7	819.3	828.1	841.9	858.8	0.68	7.01
Netherlands	581.2	590.5	600.5	610.4	620.2	630.3	639.3	644.8	644.1	641.2	635.9	0.90	9.40
New Zealand	139.2	142.6	145.9	149.2	152.3	153.6	153.5	152.1	149.9	148.0	146.9	0.54	5.56
Nigeria	2,148.3	2,193.4	2,239.5	2,287.0	2,336.2	2,387.2	2,440.6	2,497.0	2,557.7	2,624.4	2,699.3	2.31	25.65
Norway	160.0	162.4	163.9	165.1	167.2	169.2	172.5	176.5	180.8	184.3	188.4	1.64	17.70
Pakistan	3,142.9	3,248.8	3,358.0	3,470.5	3,586.4	3,705.6	3,828.4	3,955.0	4,086.0	4,221.8	4,362.5	3.33	38.80
Peru	602.5	623.0	645.0	668.3	692.0	715.5	738.1	759.5	779.6	798.9	817.8	3.10	35.74
Philippines	1,823.3	1,880.8	1,939.4	2,000.2	2,062.9	2,127.4	2,193.0	2,259.3	2,326.0	2,393.0	2,460.6	3.04	34.95
Poland	1,468.9	1,455.7	1,415.3	1,363.0	1,301.7	1,243.5	1,192.4	1,152.7	1,124.2	1,102.8	1,088.3	-2.95	-25.91
Portugal	344.1	348.7	355.6	363.3	367.5	372.4	378.6	380.4	381.5	382.2	382.7	1.07	11.22
Romania	744.7	727.5	700.7	668.6	635.6	605.5	581.5	558.1	542.8	627.2	714.2	-0.42	-4.09
Russia	5,072.8	5,087.1	5,176.0	5,178.7	5,116.5	4,995.0	4,796.5	4,507.0	4,272.4	4,046.0	3,885.1	-2.63	-23.41
Saudi Arabia	569.7	606.0	644.3	684.7	727.0	770.8	815.6	860.6	904.5	945.1	980.2	5.58	72.04
Singapore	191.7	197.2	201.1	202.8	204.7	206.6	206.2	206.1	203.8	200.1	192.4	0.04	0.36
Slovakia	196.6	193.7	190.6	186.6	182.2	180.4	180.5	179.1	176.8	174.2	170.1	-1.44	-13.47
Slovenia	80.1	79.6	78.6	77.9	78.2	78.4	78.5	79.3	79.8	79.4	79.0	-0.14	-1.38
South Africa	1,004.8	1,010.6	1,012.5	1,011.3	1,008.4	1,005.3	1,003.7	1,004.4	1,007.8	1,014.2	1,023.7	0.19	1.89
South Korea	1,882.4	1,965.7	2,030.0	2,077.6	2,101.3	2,099.5	2,082.5	2,061.4	2,039.9	2,026.2	2,032.0	0.77	7.94
Spain	1,447.4	1,497.7	1,545.7	1,591.2	1,635.2	1,675.8	1,715.7	1,757.0	1,797.0	1,831.6	1,865.4	2.57	28.87
Sweden	294.4	295.7	295.2	294.4	296.4	301.9	311.6	322.6	332.4	339.9	340.0	1.45	15.50
Switzerland	265.8	271.9	277.9	282.8	289.0	296.5	304.3	309.6	313.0	312.1	308.0	1.49	15.91
Taiwan	853.3	872.7	884.9	895.4	914.3	926.8	931.0	930.0	929.0	914.0	904.7	0.59	6.02
Thailand	1,984.8	2,044.7	2,086.6	2,155.9	2,225.5	2,287.0	2,331.7	2,369.8	2,396.0	2,439.0	2,429.9	2.04	22.43
Tunisia	268.8	272.8	275.9	278.5	281.0	283.9	287.5	292.2	297.9	304.5	312.0	1.50	16.09
Turkey	1,888.1	1,938.6	1,989.0	2,032.9	2,076.3	2,118.0	2,162.0	2,210.6	2,259.9	2,310.3	2,372.7	2.31	25.66
Turkmenistan	107.5	112.6	117.1	121.0	124.2	127.0	129.5	131.7	133.8	135.8	137.9	2.52	28.24
Ukraine	1,523.2	1,536.5	1,577.1	1,584.4	1,577.0	1,547.4	1,498.3	1,424.3	1,368.3	1,320.4	1,284.6	-1.69	-15.67
United Arab Emirates	141.1	141.1	136.8	129.7	122.2	117.7	119.0	127.5	143.3	165.7	193.0	3.18	36.73
United Kingdom	1,891.7	1,927.3	1,968.7	2,011.7	2,051.9	2,095.2	2,141.2	2,178.8	2,205.4	2,218.4	2,212.1	1.58	16.94
USA	10,693.1	10,846.8	10,965.4	10,988.5	10,977.9	10,988.3	10,882.1	10,692.7	10,467.3	10,257.6	10,080.1	-0.59	-5.73
Venezuela	646.3	668.2	693.0	720.2	748.2	774.9	798.8	819.0	835.2	847.7	857.1	2.86	32.61
Vietnam	1,989.3	2,075.4	2,167.4	2,262.6	2,357.5	2,447.1	2,527.7	2,598.3	2,660.6	2,717.0	2,770.9	3.37	39.29

Key population trends

Table 4.37 Male Population Aged 55-59: 2009-2019

'000

	2009	2010	2011	2012	2013	2014	2015	2016	2017	2018	2019	Period CAGR	Period growth
Algeria	556.1	589.6	617.3	640.0	660.7	682.9	709.4	741.7	779.2	820.2	862.1	4.48	55.01
Argentina	891.6	904.2	914.4	922.8	930.4	938.5	948.1	959.7	972.9	987.2	1,001.8	1.17	12.37
Australia	647.9	655.1	665.6	676.0	685.0	697.7	710.3	722.7	736.6	749.4	758.1	1.58	17.01
Austria	241.1	242.0	246.3	255.9	265.0	274.8	286.3	297.5	307.9	318.3	328.9	3.16	36.43
Azerbaijan	156.9	175.1	192.8	209.8	226.0	241.3	255.5	268.3	279.1	286.9	290.6	6.36	85.26
Belarus	272.4	273.8	279.9	288.8	298.2	312.5	320.2	328.4	331.3	330.2	324.7	1.77	19.19
Belgium	339.6	342.9	347.4	353.4	358.1	364.0	370.0	374.7	379.0	382.0	385.1	1.27	13.42
Bolivia	137.9	141.9	146.1	150.6	155.3	160.0	164.7	169.2	173.7	178.2	182.9	2.86	32.59
Bosnia-Herzegovina	122.2	126.4	129.7	132.0	133.7	134.9	135.8	136.6	137.1	137.2	136.8	1.13	11.92
Brazil	3,615.5	3,758.7	3,910.0	4,067.6	4,231.3	4,400.8	4,575.1	4,755.3	4,939.0	5,118.0	5,281.2	3.86	46.07
Bulgaria	257.1	252.3	247.0	248.5	247.0	244.6	242.8	241.3	239.8	238.5	237.6	-0.79	-7.58
Canada	1,085.4	1,119.1	1,150.5	1,186.5	1,222.2	1,249.4	1,275.3	1,302.9	1,321.5	1,340.9	1,356.2	2.25	24.95
Chile	389.8	406.8	425.6	446.0	467.4	489.2	510.5	530.7	549.0	564.5	576.2	3.99	47.82
China	47,622.9	50,072.3	52,091.0	53,054.4	53,320.3	50,824.9	47,629.7	43,475.4	43,676.6	48,564.7	52,895.9	1.06	11.07
Colombia	833.6	868.3	901.3	933.2	964.8	997.4	1,031.7	1,068.2	1,106.6	1,146.4	1,186.3	3.59	42.32
Costa Rica	90.7	96.1	101.6	107.3	112.9	118.5	124.0	129.2	134.2	138.8	142.9	4.65	57.50
Croatia	152.1	155.2	156.7	159.6	158.5	157.4	155.2	153.3	151.3	150.4	148.7	-0.23	-2.25
Czech Republic	372.0	371.2	368.0	362.9	356.3	345.7	332.0	319.4	309.0	302.4	308.2	-1.86	-17.14
Denmark	175.5	174.7	175.0	176.2	176.9	177.0	177.7	178.9	179.8	182.1	186.4	0.60	6.20
Ecuador	245.6	256.0	265.1	272.8	279.5	285.8	292.1	298.7	305.8	313.3	321.0	2.72	30.74
Egypt	1,398.3	1,458.9	1,518.8	1,577.4	1,634.4	1,686.7	1,729.6	1,760.0	1,778.6	1,786.2	1,783.2	2.46	27.52
Estonia	37.6	37.4	37.8	37.8	37.8	38.0	38.2	38.0	38.1	38.0	37.5	-0.03	-0.29
Finland	196.5	192.5	190.2	189.8	187.2	184.5	183.1	181.5	179.8	179.5	181.4	-0.80	-7.69
France	1,999.7	1,983.3	1,959.7	1,955.8	1,951.6	1,952.0	1,957.9	1,966.1	1,975.7	1,978.8	1,998.5	-0.01	-0.06
Germany	2,657.1	2,675.7	2,694.3	2,737.6	2,787.5	2,852.2	2,931.2	3,017.7	3,104.7	3,189.5	3,284.8	2.14	23.63
Greece	337.2	347.7	350.8	356.6	362.7	370.3	376.2	385.0	386.5	389.1	391.2	1.50	16.02
Hong Kong, China	240.4	248.3	260.3	274.8	289.1	299.5	308.4	313.4	311.3	311.1	306.4	2.46	27.48
Hungary	326.6	341.2	347.8	352.0	347.2	332.2	306.8	287.4	270.5	259.6	253.0	-2.52	-22.52
India	21,880.7	22,886.2	23,723.4	24,397.3	24,946.8	25,430.9	25,904.4	26,398.5	26,923.0	27,477.1	28,052.9	2.52	28.21
Indonesia	4,208.2	4,445.1	4,682.5	4,916.2	5,143.0	5,360.9	5,569.1	5,767.8	5,958.1	6,143.2	6,327.0	4.16	50.35
Iran	1,195.9	1,268.7	1,338.3	1,404.3	1,467.8	1,530.2	1,592.7	1,655.8	1,719.2	1,781.9	1,842.7	4.42	54.08
Ireland	118.7	120.8	122.4	124.6	126.7	129.1	131.5	135.0	137.3	139.7	142.4	1.84	20.04
Israel	173.2	174.6	173.9	172.5	171.7	171.9	172.9	174.0	174.6	174.9	175.6	0.14	1.39
Italy	1,796.4	1,795.0	1,802.6	1,831.6	1,867.7	1,902.8	1,942.9	1,987.0	2,039.2	2,094.5	2,162.1	1.87	20.36
Japan	4,514.8	4,266.0	4,066.1	3,887.2	3,776.5	3,737.2	3,685.8	3,657.2	3,676.4	3,703.5	3,731.6	-1.89	-17.35
Jordan	67.4	69.8	72.7	76.1	80.1	84.8	90.1	96.1	102.8	110.0	117.8	5.74	74.81
Kazakhstan	324.9	339.3	351.9	362.8	372.6	381.9	390.9	399.5	407.1	413.1	416.6	2.52	28.23
Kuwait	39.9	43.7	48.4	53.6	59.2	64.7	69.8	74.5	78.9	83.4	88.5	8.30	121.92
Latvia	60.8	60.6	61.4	61.8	63.3	65.5	66.5	67.4	68.4	68.3	67.2	1.00	10.43
Lithuania	86.0	85.9	86.9	88.0	90.0	93.8	98.4	101.6	105.2	107.6	108.0	2.31	25.59
Malaysia	544.7	571.1	595.5	617.3	636.1	653.5	670.6	687.2	702.9	715.3	727.2	2.93	33.51
Mexico	1,960.6	2,057.1	2,144.7	2,220.7	2,288.5	2,352.8	2,417.8	2,486.5	2,560.1	2,639.7	2,726.7	3.35	39.07
Morocco	582.0	619.9	660.3	701.2	739.0	769.7	790.4	800.3	800.8	795.7	789.9	3.10	35.72
Netherlands	543.9	543.7	546.4	553.4	558.4	566.6	576.6	587.1	597.6	607.9	618.7	1.30	13.75
New Zealand	121.6	123.1	125.9	128.9	131.8	135.4	138.8	142.1	145.4	148.4	149.8	2.11	23.23
Nigeria	1,723.6	1,772.5	1,819.3	1,863.9	1,906.9	1,949.2	1,991.9	2,035.6	2,080.6	2,127.2	2,175.5	2.36	26.22
Norway	148.9	149.8	151.5	154.3	155.9	157.8	160.0	161.3	162.5	164.6	166.6	1.13	11.86
Pakistan	2,487.0	2,582.3	2,680.3	2,780.2	2,881.9	2,985.1	3,090.1	3,197.4	3,307.4	3,420.4	3,536.8	3.58	42.21
Peru	485.5	502.6	519.8	537.2	555.2	574.2	594.5	616.2	638.9	662.0	684.8	3.50	41.07
Philippines	1,445.9	1,512.4	1,574.4	1,632.8	1,688.8	1,744.6	1,801.7	1,861.1	1,922.8	1,986.5	2,051.8	3.56	41.90
Poland	1,304.3	1,329.8	1,353.8	1,366.6	1,374.8	1,375.5	1,364.0	1,327.0	1,279.0	1,223.2	1,170.4	-1.08	-10.26
Portugal	317.4	320.4	323.5	325.4	330.4	336.8	341.4	348.2	355.9	360.1	365.0	1.41	15.01
Romania	670.7	672.4	682.7	693.7	695.6	695.9	680.3	655.6	626.0	595.6	567.9	-1.65	-15.33
Russia	4,167.3	4,209.0	4,249.8	4,310.0	4,359.6	4,448.3	4,463.4	4,547.9	4,552.2	4,500.3	4,394.9	0.53	5.46
Saudi Arabia	363.5	395.3	427.3	459.4	492.0	525.6	561.0	598.2	637.4	678.5	721.2	7.09	98.40
Singapore	155.0	161.7	170.1	178.4	185.0	189.9	194.8	198.2	199.1	200.1	201.3	2.65	29.90
Slovakia	176.2	181.8	184.9	186.6	186.7	185.8	182.8	179.6	175.5	171.0	169.0	-0.41	-4.05
Slovenia	75.0	76.9	77.8	79.2	78.6	77.7	77.2	76.3	75.6	76.0	76.3	0.18	1.80
South Africa	813.9	833.0	848.5	860.1	868.0	872.8	875.1	875.5	874.5	872.9	871.8	0.69	7.11
South Korea	1,302.1	1,395.3	1,504.8	1,611.7	1,720.8	1,824.0	1,905.5	1,968.9	2,016.1	2,040.1	2,039.3	4.59	56.61
Spain	1,253.5	1,275.4	1,300.6	1,335.2	1,378.4	1,425.7	1,474.4	1,521.4	1,566.2	1,609.5	1,649.4	2.78	31.58
Sweden	295.2	289.9	287.6	289.5	290.0	289.5	290.8	290.3	289.5	291.4	296.8	0.05	0.55
Switzerland	234.5	235.1	236.7	242.4	247.5	253.7	259.9	265.9	270.8	276.9	284.4	1.95	21.28
Taiwan	701.7	737.9	774.2	791.4	804.2	823.0	841.7	853.9	863.8	882.1	894.1	2.45	27.41
Thailand	1,519.4	1,590.9	1,678.4	1,739.6	1,793.4	1,884.3	1,945.2	1,988.7	2,058.8	2,129.8	2,191.5	3.73	44.23
Tunisia	217.2	228.5	238.2	246.2	252.5	257.5	261.4	264.5	267.1	269.7	272.6	2.30	25.51
Turkey	1,466.9	1,541.3	1,609.0	1,672.1	1,731.2	1,786.5	1,838.7	1,885.3	1,928.4	1,968.3	2,007.3	3.19	36.83
Turkmenistan	71.3	76.5	82.0	87.6	93.1	98.3	103.1	107.3	111.0	114.2	116.9	5.08	64.06
Ukraine	1,340.8	1,327.5	1,318.8	1,326.7	1,338.1	1,374.1	1,388.1	1,429.2	1,440.9	1,442.1	1,422.5	0.59	6.09
United Arab Emirates	79.2	85.3	91.2	96.6	100.3	101.4	99.7	95.2	89.3	84.0	82.0	0.34	3.47
United Kingdom	1,775.5	1,755.2	1,749.3	1,761.4	1,787.9	1,821.0	1,858.0	1,901.7	1,946.3	1,987.3	2,030.4	1.35	14.35
USA	9,220.9	9,447.7	9,653.1	9,894.8	10,108.7	10,254.5	10,408.3	10,530.7	10,559.8	10,555.5	10,571.3	1.38	14.64
Venezuela	535.6	552.3	568.1	583.7	600.1	618.5	639.7	663.8	690.2	717.3	743.2	3.33	38.77
Vietnam	1,455.9	1,569.7	1,669.6	1,758.0	1,839.2	1,920.1	2,005.5	2,096.8	2,191.2	2,285.2	2,373.7	5.01	63.04

Key population trends

Table 4.38 Male Population Aged 60-64: 2009-2019

'000

	2009	2010	2011	2012	2013	2014	2015	2016	2017	2018	2019	CAGR	Period growth
Algeria	350.8	378.2	411.2	448.2	486.4	522.4	553.8	579.9	601.5	621.3	642.7	6.24	83.20
Argentina	743.4	760.7	778.3	795.8	812.3	827.1	839.7	850.0	858.5	866.3	874.1	1.63	17.59
Australia	584.8	603.1	616.8	613.7	619.6	627.9	636.2	648.2	659.5	669.2	682.0	1.55	16.62
Austria	217.2	220.2	232.1	234.9	231.9	230.4	231.5	235.8	245.3	254.2	263.8	1.97	21.49
Azerbaijan	79.5	86.9	97.5	110.9	126.4	142.9	159.7	176.2	192.0	207.2	221.6	10.79	178.60
Belarus	168.6	191.2	211.5	223.4	229.4	231.5	233.0	238.3	246.3	254.5	267.0	4.70	58.34
Belgium	303.0	312.3	321.6	320.3	322.2	324.1	327.7	332.4	338.4	343.4	349.4	1.43	15.30
Bolivia	109.3	113.2	116.8	120.2	123.6	127.0	130.8	134.8	139.1	143.6	148.1	3.08	35.47
Bosnia-Herzegovina	87.3	92.9	98.9	104.8	110.4	115.4	119.6	122.8	125.1	126.7	127.9	3.90	46.57
Brazil	2,737.4	2,849.3	2,962.9	3,079.6	3,201.1	3,329.7	3,467.0	3,612.0	3,763.0	3,919.5	4,081.1	4.07	49.09
Bulgaria	225.6	234.6	242.1	238.0	237.4	235.6	231.8	227.7	229.6	228.8	227.1	0.07	0.65
Canada	921.9	962.0	994.5	1,003.9	1,019.6	1,046.1	1,078.0	1,108.5	1,143.3	1,177.8	1,204.3	2.71	30.64
Chile	310.4	320.1	330.6	342.1	354.8	369.3	385.5	403.5	423.0	443.6	464.4	4.11	49.63
China	32,567.0	34,964.1	36,506.8	39,394.2	41,907.2	44,352.0	46,210.7	47,633.9	48,271.2	48,123.1	45,481.3	3.40	39.65
Colombia	601.0	637.5	674.4	711.2	747.2	781.9	815.1	846.7	877.2	907.3	938.4	4.56	56.13
Costa Rica	64.5	68.4	72.6	77.1	81.8	86.7	91.8	97.1	102.5	108.0	113.4	5.81	75.83
Croatia	109.2	118.4	130.0	134.4	139.0	143.0	146.0	147.5	150.3	149.3	148.2	3.10	35.70
Czech Republic	335.4	342.6	354.4	353.3	349.5	346.7	346.0	343.2	338.9	333.3	324.0	-0.35	-3.41
Denmark	188.5	185.4	180.5	173.8	169.1	167.3	166.8	167.2	168.6	169.4	169.6	-1.05	-10.04
Ecuador	179.8	188.3	198.4	209.5	221.1	232.3	242.4	251.0	258.4	264.7	270.7	4.18	50.60
Egypt	1,018.1	1,074.9	1,132.9	1,192.5	1,253.7	1,315.7	1,377.8	1,439.1	1,499.1	1,557.3	1,610.6	4.69	58.19
Estonia	28.6	30.6	32.1	32.9	33.2	33.2	33.0	33.5	33.5	33.6	33.8	1.69	18.22
Finland	184.5	195.2	197.5	194.4	191.4	187.0	183.3	181.3	181.1	178.7	176.3	-0.46	-4.47
France	1,726.4	1,833.0	1,937.5	1,939.5	1,928.9	1,905.8	1,891.4	1,871.1	1,869.2	1,867.0	1,869.2	0.80	8.27
Germany	2,078.4	2,116.6	2,279.3	2,392.8	2,463.9	2,507.0	2,530.7	2,553.2	2,597.4	2,647.2	2,710.5	2.69	30.41
Greece	316.2	316.7	323.8	322.9	322.7	327.4	337.6	340.9	346.6	352.6	360.1	1.31	13.88
Hong Kong, China	171.3	190.8	207.3	215.8	223.8	232.5	240.3	251.7	265.5	279.4	289.5	5.39	68.97
Hungary	258.4	261.9	275.8	285.2	287.3	295.0	309.0	315.1	319.2	315.1	301.8	1.56	16.79
India	14,804.3	15,548.2	16,457.8	17,492.4	18,575.6	19,615.9	20,540.5	21,315.8	21,947.9	22,472.3	22,941.3	4.48	54.96
Indonesia	3,043.5	3,148.7	3,289.3	3,462.8	3,662.2	3,877.6	4,100.1	4,323.7	4,544.9	4,760.6	4,968.7	5.02	63.26
Iran	799.1	849.1	906.3	969.3	1,035.8	1,103.5	1,170.4	1,235.4	1,298.4	1,359.7	1,420.2	5.92	77.72
Ireland	104.9	108.5	111.0	112.4	114.0	115.5	117.5	119.1	121.4	123.5	125.9	1.85	20.06
Israel	146.8	156.9	163.9	166.4	168.1	170.8	171.9	170.9	169.2	168.2	168.1	1.37	14.56
Italy	1,718.4	1,774.5	1,837.0	1,803.9	1,772.6	1,741.2	1,741.8	1,751.1	1,780.9	1,817.5	1,853.2	0.76	7.85
Japan	4,601.4	4,875.4	5,120.1	4,929.3	4,645.5	4,313.3	4,080.6	3,893.2	3,724.3	3,620.4	3,584.6	-2.47	-22.10
Jordan	58.5	58.6	58.8	59.1	59.9	61.3	63.3	66.0	69.4	73.5	78.2	2.95	33.68
Kazakhstan	188.6	209.2	228.9	247.0	263.4	278.1	291.3	303.2	313.9	323.6	332.6	5.84	76.33
Kuwait	25.1	27.0	28.9	31.1	33.7	36.9	40.7	45.3	50.4	55.8	61.1	9.31	143.60
Latvia	47.3	49.1	51.0	52.6	52.9	52.5	52.3	52.9	53.4	54.7	56.7	1.82	19.80
Lithuania	66.0	68.6	70.0	72.8	75.0	75.7	75.7	76.6	77.8	79.7	83.2	2.35	26.18
Malaysia	374.3	395.6	420.2	448.6	477.0	505.2	531.1	554.8	575.9	593.9	610.6	5.02	63.13
Mexico	1,454.9	1,525.1	1,609.5	1,703.8	1,803.1	1,901.2	1,992.5	2,074.6	2,147.4	2,213.6	2,276.9	4.58	56.50
Morocco	398.6	423.5	449.8	477.9	508.3	541.5	577.8	616.3	655.1	690.9	719.9	6.09	80.62
Netherlands	524.2	539.8	557.5	539.1	528.5	523.0	523.0	525.9	532.9	537.8	546.0	0.41	4.15
New Zealand	108.6	112.7	115.8	115.7	116.1	117.4	119.0	121.8	124.7	127.6	131.1	1.90	20.75
Nigeria	1,319.9	1,351.3	1,388.0	1,429.4	1,474.0	1,519.5	1,564.1	1,606.9	1,647.8	1,687.5	1,726.8	2.72	30.83
Norway	145.0	146.8	147.5	144.5	143.9	143.9	144.7	146.4	149.1	150.7	152.6	0.51	5.22
Pakistan	1,936.5	1,984.0	2,043.6	2,114.9	2,196.0	2,283.6	2,374.9	2,468.3	2,563.4	2,660.1	2,758.5	3.60	42.45
Peru	376.3	390.3	405.3	421.0	437.3	453.8	470.3	486.8	503.5	520.7	538.9	3.66	43.22
Philippines	1,047.7	1,096.3	1,151.4	1,212.2	1,276.5	1,341.5	1,404.7	1,464.9	1,522.2	1,577.6	1,632.8	4.54	55.85
Poland	883.5	972.1	1,068.2	1,122.7	1,163.6	1,192.9	1,218.3	1,242.4	1,256.3	1,266.1	1,269.1	3.69	43.64
Portugal	279.4	286.2	291.8	300.2	306.3	306.1	309.1	312.3	314.3	319.4	325.6	1.54	16.55
Romania	474.7	508.3	551.2	570.5	594.3	607.2	609.8	620.2	631.0	633.6	634.6	2.95	33.69
Russia	2,374.2	2,823.5	3,165.4	3,302.1	3,420.0	3,491.3	3,528.5	3,566.7	3,618.5	3,663.1	3,737.8	4.64	57.43
Saudi Arabia	219.7	238.9	261.5	287.1	315.0	344.2	374.0	404.0	434.2	465.1	497.1	8.51	126.29
Singapore	108.7	124.5	135.6	140.0	146.3	153.6	160.1	168.3	176.4	182.5	187.0	5.58	72.08
Slovakia	122.5	129.6	140.6	151.4	158.8	164.4	170.0	173.0	174.5	174.6	173.5	3.54	41.63
Slovenia	51.5	55.0	61.4	64.8	67.9	70.9	72.7	73.6	75.0	74.6	73.9	3.67	43.39
South Africa	599.9	616.7	634.5	652.7	670.6	687.5	702.5	715.3	725.6	733.4	738.9	2.11	23.17
South Korea	1,023.1	1,067.8	1,103.7	1,138.9	1,178.3	1,236.2	1,325.8	1,430.8	1,533.5	1,638.3	1,737.6	5.44	69.83
Spain	1,144.0	1,163.9	1,180.7	1,191.8	1,201.8	1,218.7	1,239.9	1,264.9	1,298.8	1,341.1	1,387.1	1.95	21.26
Sweden	316.6	313.4	307.7	299.1	292.2	286.7	281.7	279.5	281.4	281.9	281.6	-1.17	-11.08
Switzerland	221.9	222.4	222.9	220.1	218.9	217.2	217.7	219.2	225.0	229.9	236.1	0.62	6.39
Taiwan	406.4	443.3	499.8	570.6	622.8	665.0	699.1	733.8	749.9	761.9	779.8	6.73	91.87
Thailand	1,075.6	1,165.0	1,232.1	1,303.6	1,374.7	1,424.5	1,497.1	1,586.9	1,648.8	1,703.5	1,795.4	5.26	66.93
Tunisia	144.8	154.8	166.1	178.3	190.7	202.5	213.1	222.3	229.9	235.9	240.8	5.22	66.30
Turkey	1,044.0	1,089.5	1,141.6	1,204.9	1,273.6	1,343.6	1,412.5	1,474.6	1,532.8	1,586.3	1,637.5	4.60	56.85
Turkmenistan	42.1	45.8	49.7	53.8	58.1	62.6	67.3	72.2	77.3	82.3	87.1	7.55	107.01
Ukraine	849.0	962.1	1,086.0	1,143.3	1,190.6	1,198.1	1,187.0	1,180.6	1,192.5	1,211.1	1,254.2	3.98	47.73
United Arab Emirates	31.2	34.5	38.6	43.2	48.6	54.4	60.6	66.8	72.4	76.9	79.4	9.78	154.22
United Kingdom	1,788.0	1,814.6	1,823.0	1,785.9	1,723.2	1,686.3	1,669.6	1,667.7	1,682.2	1,709.8	1,742.8	-0.26	-2.53
USA	7,584.1	7,972.0	8,351.6	8,346.3	8,489.1	8,683.7	8,905.0	9,107.1	9,341.7	9,549.0	9,692.4	2.48	27.80
Venezuela	407.3	427.6	447.4	466.4	484.4	501.3	517.3	532.4	547.3	563.1	580.8	3.61	42.60
Vietnam	892.6	951.5	1,035.8	1,142.2	1,261.4	1,380.6	1,490.5	1,587.3	1,673.4	1,752.5	1,831.3	7.45	105.17

Key population trends

Table 4.39 Male Population Aged 65-69: 2009-2019

'000

	2009	2010	2011	2012	2013	2014	2015	2016	2017	2018	2019	CAGR	Period growth
Algeria	264.2	267.3	273.3	282.8	296.8	316.1	341.1	371.1	404.9	439.7	472.6	5.99	78.85
Argentina	589.2	602.2	616.1	630.8	646.3	662.5	679.1	695.9	712.4	728.0	742.4	2.34	26.02
Australia	431.2	450.4	472.0	507.3	537.1	556.4	575.1	589.9	588.6	595.2	603.9	3.43	40.07
Austria	227.6	219.3	200.0	192.0	197.9	202.7	205.9	217.1	219.9	217.4	216.2	-0.51	-5.00
Azerbaijan	75.9	70.3	66.3	64.5	65.2	68.8	75.4	84.8	96.7	110.4	125.1	5.12	64.76
Belarus	140.6	126.3	113.3	110.2	119.1	134.2	152.2	168.1	177.6	182.4	184.2	2.74	31.08
Belgium	219.2	223.3	230.6	252.2	269.6	281.9	291.0	300.2	299.5	301.8	304.1	3.33	38.74
Bolivia	81.5	84.0	86.9	90.3	93.8	97.4	100.9	104.2	107.4	110.6	113.8	3.40	39.65
Bosnia-Herzegovina	71.8	69.9	70.0	71.9	75.5	80.2	85.5	91.0	96.5	101.7	106.4	4.01	48.10
Brazil	2,045.6	2,092.0	2,157.9	2,240.1	2,334.8	2,436.2	2,540.4	2,646.2	2,755.1	2,868.4	2,987.9	3.86	46.07
Bulgaria	170.7	172.8	176.3	185.2	190.7	197.7	206.2	213.4	210.4	210.3	209.4	2.07	22.71
Canada	671.8	701.1	733.3	785.8	828.8	866.6	903.6	934.0	943.0	958.0	983.2	3.88	46.34
Chile	238.5	248.7	258.4	267.5	276.2	285.0	294.2	304.0	314.8	326.8	340.3	3.62	42.64
China	23,448.9	23,360.7	23,931.4	24,957.0	25,890.3	27,419.5	29,221.5	30,293.9	32,504.1	34,378.3	36,141.6	4.42	54.13
Colombia	406.5	428.1	453.2	481.6	512.5	545.3	579.0	613.1	647.1	680.3	712.4	5.77	75.27
Costa Rica	46.7	48.6	51.0	53.6	56.6	60.0	63.6	67.5	71.7	76.1	80.8	5.65	73.22
Croatia	99.6	94.4	87.8	88.4	90.0	94.8	103.9	115.4	119.8	124.4	128.3	2.56	28.82
Czech Republic	229.0	244.5	251.5	270.9	290.2	301.4	308.0	318.8	318.4	315.9	314.4	3.22	37.25
Denmark	136.6	145.9	156.1	166.7	172.5	174.5	171.9	167.7	161.8	157.7	156.4	1.36	14.51
Ecuador	141.7	145.6	149.7	154.3	159.8	166.4	174.4	183.8	194.2	204.9	215.3	4.27	51.92
Egypt	730.2	755.7	789.8	831.2	880.2	935.3	994.0	1,053.8	1,115.5	1,178.9	1,243.4	5.47	70.28
Estonia	25.8	24.1	22.8	22.0	22.5	23.9	25.7	27.0	27.7	28.0	28.0	0.84	8.68
Finland	120.6	122.9	135.1	142.6	159.8	172.0	182.0	184.2	181.5	179.0	175.0	3.79	45.12
France	1,195.5	1,217.9	1,253.4	1,382.3	1,504.6	1,614.4	1,715.0	1,814.3	1,818.1	1,810.4	1,790.9	4.12	49.80
Germany	2,466.6	2,339.7	2,100.1	1,938.6	1,917.0	1,913.3	1,955.6	2,110.2	2,218.1	2,286.5	2,328.4	-0.57	-5.60
Greece	247.7	249.8	250.2	271.9	288.3	299.7	300.2	307.2	306.6	306.7	311.3	2.31	25.68
Hong Kong, China	117.0	118.2	120.7	133.9	147.5	162.5	181.0	196.7	204.2	211.5	219.7	6.50	87.77
Hungary	209.4	217.0	214.3	213.9	217.2	223.4	226.4	239.4	247.7	248.5	254.7	1.98	21.66
India	10,895.5	11,099.7	11,336.4	11,629.4	12,014.6	12,527.1	13,186.2	13,987.9	14,897.3	15,849.1	16,764.8	4.40	53.87
Indonesia	2,477.2	2,502.6	2,527.8	2,558.5	2,602.9	2,670.2	2,766.9	2,895.5	3,053.6	3,235.0	3,431.0	3.31	38.50
Iran	594.6	600.1	613.4	634.9	664.6	702.4	747.8	800.0	857.7	919.0	981.3	5.14	65.03
Ireland	78.4	81.1	85.2	90.2	94.9	99.0	102.4	104.9	106.4	108.0	109.6	3.40	39.75
Israel	87.4	90.8	99.7	114.4	130.1	142.2	152.6	159.6	162.1	163.7	166.2	6.63	90.08
Italy	1,519.3	1,480.8	1,432.1	1,494.9	1,559.5	1,629.1	1,684.1	1,744.7	1,715.6	1,688.4	1,661.1	0.90	9.33
Japan	4,001.7	3,912.3	3,711.9	3,875.9	4,111.3	4,330.4	4,592.6	4,824.2	4,647.3	4,382.8	4,072.4	0.18	1.77
Jordan	49.5	50.7	51.4	51.5	51.3	51.0	50.9	51.0	51.6	52.6	54.0	0.89	9.22
Kazakhstan	131.5	118.9	115.3	120.5	132.4	148.1	164.9	181.1	196.2	210.0	222.5	5.40	69.20
Kuwait	15.9	17.2	18.5	20.0	21.5	23.2	24.9	26.7	28.8	31.2	34.1	7.91	114.16
Latvia	46.9	44.2	41.3	38.7	38.1	38.6	40.1	41.7	43.0	43.2	43.0	-0.88	-8.48
Lithuania	63.8	61.4	60.6	58.1	56.0	55.8	58.1	59.4	61.9	63.8	64.6	0.13	1.35
Malaysia	256.1	267.0	279.2	292.1	307.2	324.8	345.7	370.2	398.8	427.4	455.9	5.94	78.03
Mexico	1,139.4	1,186.7	1,231.6	1,274.4	1,319.9	1,373.3	1,438.6	1,516.7	1,605.5	1,699.9	1,793.4	4.64	57.40
Morocco	286.5	291.2	300.7	314.9	332.9	353.8	376.4	400.4	425.8	453.3	483.5	5.37	68.75
Netherlands	368.8	384.4	392.6	437.7	474.8	499.5	515.5	533.4	514.4	503.3	497.4	3.04	34.89
New Zealand	83.6	85.6	87.3	92.4	98.8	103.2	107.1	110.1	110.2	110.7	112.0	2.96	33.88
Nigeria	991.9	1,015.0	1,036.3	1,056.6	1,077.7	1,101.4	1,129.1	1,161.5	1,198.0	1,237.1	1,277.0	2.56	28.74
Norway	96.9	104.5	112.1	123.5	131.0	136.2	137.9	138.6	136.0	135.5	135.7	3.42	40.02
Pakistan	1,515.4	1,555.2	1,589.6	1,620.5	1,651.6	1,687.7	1,732.5	1,787.9	1,853.8	1,928.3	2,008.7	2.86	32.55
Peru	289.2	297.4	306.6	316.8	328.0	340.2	353.4	367.4	382.0	397.1	412.4	3.61	42.61
Philippines	762.3	793.0	823.1	853.9	887.3	925.5	970.0	1,021.1	1,077.8	1,137.9	1,198.7	4.63	57.25
Poland	605.8	592.3	583.8	628.9	698.6	778.5	859.0	946.1	996.8	1,035.6	1,064.2	5.80	75.66
Portugal	235.9	237.7	243.8	248.8	253.9	262.1	268.7	274.1	282.1	288.1	288.1	2.02	22.12
Romania	404.9	393.3	375.3	382.4	390.9	409.7	439.9	477.6	494.9	516.2	528.1	2.69	30.42
Russia	2,005.7	1,634.8	1,402.0	1,411.5	1,614.1	1,898.7	2,256.7	2,530.0	2,640.5	2,735.0	2,789.6	3.35	39.08
Saudi Arabia	150.0	157.0	165.2	174.7	186.2	200.4	217.5	237.8	260.9	286.1	312.7	7.62	108.43
Singapore	70.9	67.1	67.8	79.9	92.2	103.7	120.0	131.3	135.3	141.3	148.4	7.68	109.49
Slovakia	88.5	91.2	91.7	94.3	100.9	108.8	115.8	126.8	137.4	144.8	150.3	5.44	69.82
Slovenia	46.3	46.0	43.7	44.1	45.4	47.2	50.4	56.4	59.6	62.6	65.5	3.53	41.45
South Africa	412.5	425.4	437.6	449.1	460.7	472.9	486.3	501.0	516.5	532.2	547.3	2.87	32.67
South Korea	833.1	833.6	839.6	859.5	896.5	942.9	984.6	1,018.5	1,052.3	1,090.3	1,145.6	3.24	37.50
Spain	919.7	954.9	996.2	1,033.5	1,060.9	1,085.0	1,104.3	1,121.1	1,132.5	1,143.1	1,160.0	2.35	26.13
Sweden	239.8	256.4	273.7	289.0	297.2	300.3	297.5	292.3	284.4	278.0	273.0	1.31	13.88
Switzerland	174.0	182.5	191.1	197.9	201.7	204.3	204.7	205.1	202.1	200.8	198.9	1.34	14.29
Taiwan	362.3	363.4	350.0	343.4	354.0	374.6	409.0	461.3	526.3	574.2	612.9	5.40	69.18
Thailand	797.7	805.4	830.0	854.7	915.6	972.5	1,063.3	1,132.0	1,204.5	1,276.7	1,326.8	5.22	66.32
Tunisia	107.5	108.6	111.3	115.6	121.7	129.4	138.5	148.8	159.8	171.1	181.9	5.40	69.25
Turkey	796.5	829.2	842.8	856.2	877.3	908.0	950.0	1,002.3	1,057.8	1,117.6	1,176.7	3.98	47.73
Turkmenistan	29.7	28.6	28.7	29.9	32.1	34.9	38.0	41.4	44.8	48.5	52.4	5.83	76.20
Ukraine	834.1	719.3	606.3	568.7	590.9	673.2	785.0	909.0	971.9	1,030.0	1,048.7	2.32	25.74
United Arab Emirates	12.3	12.9	14.1	15.9	18.2	21.1	24.3	28.0	32.1	36.8	42.3	13.15	244.03
United Kingdom	1,339.8	1,377.3	1,425.4	1,511.0	1,603.9	1,658.0	1,685.5	1,696.7	1,665.3	1,609.5	1,577.0	1.64	17.70
USA	5,515.4	5,695.5	5,848.4	6,355.2	6,627.9	6,946.7	7,305.9	7,657.4	7,662.4	7,801.1	7,987.2	3.77	44.81
Venezuela	279.4	295.3	312.5	330.6	349.3	368.2	386.9	405.2	422.8	439.5	455.3	5.00	62.97
Vietnam	732.8	742.4	751.9	763.3	782.4	817.1	872.6	951.6	1,050.9	1,162.2	1,273.5	5.68	73.78

Key population trends

Table 4.40 Male Population Aged 70-74: 2009-2019

'000

	2009	2010	2011	2012	2013	2014	2015	2016	2017	2018	2019	CAGR	Period growth
Algeria	222.85	222.20	221.21	220.27	219.91	220.77	223.50	228.65	236.89	249.04	265.76	1.78	19.25
Argentina	451.13	457.11	464.54	473.39	483.54	494.76	506.83	519.63	533.09	547.18	561.76	2.22	24.52
Australia	331.40	343.80	354.00	367.02	379.24	397.07	416.18	437.84	472.23	500.98	519.72	4.60	56.83
Austria	136.73	154.98	174.45	189.37	197.36	202.49	195.44	178.55	171.91	177.75	182.53	2.93	33.50
Azerbaijan	81.79	80.06	76.64	71.89	66.47	61.18	56.76	53.71	52.38	53.13	56.21	-3.68	-31.28
Belarus	136.83	139.97	137.13	130.76	119.06	103.71	93.22	83.69	81.95	88.99	100.33	-3.05	-26.67
Belgium	205.49	205.85	203.83	197.55	194.02	194.98	199.44	206.66	226.78	243.10	254.78	2.17	23.99
Bolivia	59.98	61.44	62.85	64.27	65.83	67.66	69.86	72.47	75.40	78.54	81.72	3.14	36.26
Bosnia-Herzegovina	74.63	73.19	70.63	67.31	63.90	61.19	59.80	60.03	61.86	65.02	69.11	-0.77	-7.40
Brazil	1,565.68	1,614.35	1,648.65	1,672.70	1,693.97	1,722.71	1,765.99	1,825.72	1,899.20	1,983.21	2,072.81	2.85	32.39
Bulgaria	149.56	142.53	140.49	138.01	138.38	139.95	142.18	145.71	153.75	158.90	165.32	1.01	10.53
Canada	507.19	518.27	533.08	553.34	578.93	604.43	630.33	659.41	707.08	745.98	779.92	4.40	53.77
Chile	167.52	173.88	181.49	190.18	199.52	208.98	218.13	226.78	234.98	242.91	250.89	4.12	49.77
China	18,533.57	18,910.35	19,053.39	19,035.54	18,873.35	19,389.48	19,255.28	19,693.36	20,503.65	21,220.82	22,442.87	1.93	21.09
Colombia	288.03	297.44	307.88	319.73	333.53	349.86	369.11	391.36	416.40	443.70	472.57	5.08	64.07
Costa Rica	34.76	36.02	37.27	38.55	39.91	41.45	43.25	45.34	47.76	50.49	53.52	4.41	54.00
Croatia	88.73	87.50	86.22	83.27	81.56	78.45	73.33	66.85	67.42	69.07	73.79	-1.83	-16.84
Czech Republic	152.64	154.94	162.83	171.36	181.04	194.62	208.12	214.58	232.00	249.50	260.09	5.47	70.39
Denmark	99.02	102.19	105.78	109.10	115.09	121.43	130.11	139.61	149.45	154.93	157.05	4.72	58.59
Ecuador	109.95	113.34	116.71	120.06	123.41	126.79	130.28	133.99	138.15	143.06	149.04	3.09	35.55
Egypt	514.72	530.59	546.54	563.08	579.32	597.50	621.79	655.27	696.74	746.50	802.92	4.55	55.99
Estonia	21.51	22.06	22.01	22.23	21.41	19.96	18.68	17.71	17.16	17.69	18.89	-1.29	-12.18
Finland	97.60	101.30	100.89	108.68	106.60	108.07	110.33	121.47	128.71	144.36	155.45	4.76	59.26
France	1,087.13	1,083.43	1,075.10	1,054.87	1,059.16	1,078.75	1,101.02	1,135.33	1,254.95	1,368.66	1,471.00	3.07	35.31
Germany	2,074.29	2,175.01	2,256.44	2,297.47	2,242.22	2,171.99	2,067.20	1,859.76	1,721.54	1,706.82	1,708.53	-1.92	-17.63
Greece	258.50	251.49	253.76	240.87	233.92	225.31	227.72	228.92	248.92	263.99	274.29	0.59	6.11
Hong Kong, China	113.92	114.43	113.61	109.65	106.96	106.68	108.00	110.42	122.83	135.49	149.13	2.73	30.91
Hungary	151.51	150.92	154.59	158.46	164.84	169.26	176.67	173.69	172.97	175.61	180.94	1.79	19.42
India	7,647.61	7,829.61	8,003.48	8,169.86	8,331.78	8,496.97	8,676.28	8,882.43	9,135.43	9,464.37	9,897.11	2.61	29.41
Indonesia	1,821.40	1,870.61	1,913.69	1,950.47	1,981.26	2,007.38	2,031.06	2,055.16	2,084.25	2,125.18	2,185.36	1.84	19.98
Iran	517.54	504.29	493.13	485.03	480.90	481.72	488.31	501.22	520.79	547.19	580.22	1.15	12.11
Ireland	60.05	61.86	63.36	64.88	67.20	69.77	72.31	76.15	80.77	85.22	89.03	4.02	48.26
Israel	83.50	84.67	84.14	81.41	77.99	77.07	80.35	89.46	104.74	120.88	133.40	4.80	59.76
Italy	1,327.95	1,362.71	1,394.15	1,403.72	1,396.92	1,372.78	1,341.09	1,300.31	1,361.71	1,424.17	1,490.74	1.16	12.26
Japan	3,189.66	3,223.67	3,299.44	3,396.42	3,488.32	3,634.20	3,556.69	3,378.49	3,539.10	3,764.16	3,972.99	2.22	24.56
Jordan	32.32	34.04	35.77	37.45	38.96	40.21	41.12	41.68	41.91	41.94	41.91	2.63	29.67
Kazakhstan	133.99	134.60	128.13	116.10	101.79	89.18	81.44	79.96	84.45	93.49	105.06	-2.40	-21.59
Kuwait	9.33	10.17	11.01	11.87	12.77	13.74	14.82	16.01	17.31	18.69	20.13	8.00	115.81
Latvia	36.42	37.79	38.21	38.38	37.29	35.51	33.38	31.15	29.25	28.89	29.42	-2.11	-19.22
Lithuania	51.39	51.46	51.07	50.97	51.45	50.79	48.97	48.47	46.55	45.09	45.06	-1.31	-12.31
Malaysia	165.28	171.58	178.05	185.09	192.34	200.88	210.90	222.27	234.47	249.09	266.53	4.89	61.26
Mexico	819.54	856.11	897.87	942.51	988.19	1,032.75	1,074.78	1,114.27	1,153.11	1,195.13	1,244.81	4.27	51.89
Morocco	234.45	236.22	236.07	234.78	233.80	234.84	239.26	247.66	259.86	275.18	292.72	2.24	24.85
Netherlands	282.71	291.38	302.29	309.94	320.84	333.68	349.60	357.86	403.61	441.02	465.89	5.12	64.80
New Zealand	62.18	65.22	69.17	72.66	73.88	76.65	78.60	80.28	85.14	91.16	95.26	4.36	53.21
Nigeria	649.63	670.11	691.36	712.97	734.27	754.56	773.50	791.18	808.34	826.24	846.38	2.68	30.29
Norway	71.08	73.77	77.20	79.06	82.98	87.87	94.87	101.92	112.46	119.35	124.21	5.74	74.75
Pakistan	1,029.65	1,065.75	1,105.31	1,147.01	1,188.57	1,227.54	1,262.33	1,292.90	1,320.90	1,349.49	1,382.44	2.99	34.26
Peru	217.01	223.06	229.03	235.08	241.38	248.18	255.68	263.98	273.14	283.18	294.08	3.09	35.51
Philippines	507.49	526.72	547.98	571.29	595.99	621.47	647.21	673.27	700.44	730.18	764.09	4.18	50.56
Poland	546.98	544.27	538.42	527.54	511.77	500.06	491.06	486.34	527.39	589.14	659.35	1.89	20.54
Portugal	216.16	217.18	214.22	210.76	210.55	211.41	213.55	219.56	224.35	229.42	237.30	0.94	9.78
Romania	381.35	380.29	375.07	359.36	343.42	326.28	317.89	303.98	310.79	318.70	335.03	-1.29	-12.15
Russia	1,939.58	2,065.60	2,076.92	2,015.82	1,762.93	1,453.21	1,188.23	1,028.73	1,051.83	1,212.02	1,424.19	-3.04	-26.57
Saudi Arabia	108.82	110.58	113.16	116.59	120.83	125.87	131.71	138.50	146.57	156.40	168.48	4.47	54.82
Singapore	50.90	54.09	58.70	61.49	62.10	62.44	57.99	58.44	70.78	83.41	95.03	6.44	86.68
Slovakia	62.59	63.03	64.85	67.17	69.50	71.63	74.30	74.75	77.25	83.83	91.64	3.89	46.42
Slovenia	36.26	36.86	37.46	37.83	38.76	39.60	39.37	37.48	37.99	39.32	41.01	1.24	13.12
South Africa	247.03	255.33	264.38	274.00	283.88	293.75	303.41	312.82	322.17	331.83	342.23	3.31	38.53
South Korea	636.51	658.56	682.29	707.41	723.17	727.79	730.17	737.90	757.87	792.82	835.63	2.76	31.28
Spain	834.81	812.67	794.90	793.85	815.54	837.09	870.09	908.67	943.86	970.15	993.29	1.75	18.98
Sweden	173.18	180.53	186.64	193.38	204.87	218.59	234.27	250.37	264.65	272.33	275.51	4.75	59.09
Switzerland	133.67	135.04	136.48	140.91	148.38	156.17	164.71	173.36	180.20	183.94	186.44	3.38	39.48
Taiwan	282.80	288.60	297.17	306.16	311.27	317.07	317.92	306.10	300.29	309.93	328.58	1.51	16.19
Thailand	634.64	647.49	653.02	675.98	665.54	678.50	685.92	711.00	735.75	797.50	854.83	3.02	34.70
Tunisia	94.76	93.34	91.80	90.38	89.41	89.29	90.33	92.73	96.54	101.80	108.42	1.36	14.42
Turkey	621.02	633.36	649.36	664.67	671.21	672.51	670.45	678.75	690.97	708.26	733.65	1.68	18.14
Turkmenistan	28.85	28.55	27.49	25.85	24.05	22.58	21.83	21.99	23.03	24.78	27.02	-0.65	-6.33
Ukraine	815.97	877.23	888.18	864.67	751.35	616.57	511.05	407.13	378.82	412.67	505.61	-4.67	-38.04
United Arab Emirates	8.04	8.29	8.45	8.60	8.82	9.27	10.05	11.25	12.88	14.92	17.36	7.99	115.77
United Kingdom	1,131.31	1,145.67	1,146.55	1,145.48	1,160.45	1,190.86	1,228.09	1,275.10	1,355.73	1,442.85	1,493.82	2.82	32.04
USA	4,061.30	4,138.71	4,240.09	4,399.40	4,648.29	4,834.26	4,998.29	5,138.12	5,595.26	5,844.46	6,131.06	4.20	50.96
Venezuela	189.57	197.03	205.82	216.02	227.60	240.48	254.56	269.69	285.68	302.22	318.96	5.34	68.25
Vietnam	625.21	618.80	617.31	620.32	626.93	635.44	645.01	654.50	665.56	683.38	714.89	1.35	14.34

Key population trends

Table 4.41 Male Population Aged 75-79: 2009-2019

'000

	2009	2010	2011	2012	2013	2014	2015	2016	2017	2018	2019	CAGR	Period growth
Algeria	149.45	155.23	159.31	161.83	163.03	163.33	163.10	162.64	162.19	162.15	163.05	0.87	9.10
Argentina	329.09	331.19	333.66	336.67	340.43	345.15	350.93	357.82	365.76	374.64	384.33	1.56	16.79
Australia	255.37	256.10	260.29	268.03	276.64	287.31	299.38	309.83	322.61	334.41	351.14	3.24	37.50
Austria	114.53	113.01	110.80	110.11	110.19	113.56	129.66	146.70	159.68	166.51	170.90	4.08	49.22
Azerbaijan	53.07	55.20	57.25	58.97	60.00	59.95	58.62	56.04	52.53	48.58	44.81	-1.68	-15.57
Belarus	91.82	86.99	83.96	86.31	87.72	90.73	92.55	90.47	86.28	78.45	68.21	-2.93	-25.72
Belgium	170.24	171.13	169.42	167.93	167.79	169.74	170.85	169.83	165.10	162.88	164.68	-0.33	-3.26
Bolivia	38.23	39.18	40.28	41.48	42.72	43.95	45.13	46.30	47.50	48.84	50.43	2.81	31.93
Bosnia-Herzegovina	50.58	52.34	54.02	55.46	56.32	56.30	55.28	53.31	50.76	48.21	46.32	-0.88	-8.43
Brazil	993.29	1,021.71	1,062.51	1,112.99	1,167.08	1,216.66	1,256.68	1,285.61	1,306.85	1,326.21	1,351.57	3.13	36.07
Bulgaria	117.70	119.41	117.32	116.76	113.00	109.46	105.00	104.18	103.07	104.04	105.86	-1.05	-10.05
Canada	408.07	409.44	411.00	411.38	415.44	423.59	432.67	445.30	462.38	484.00	505.45	2.16	23.87
Chile	119.01	121.99	124.95	128.10	131.77	136.29	141.86	148.47	155.93	163.84	171.76	3.74	44.32
China	12,190.99	12,364.39	12,669.85	12,939.91	13,050.97	12,985.07	13,235.88	13,346.56	13,346.56	13,235.41	13,591.08	1.09	11.48
Colombia	197.23	202.77	208.69	215.02	221.79	229.08	237.02	245.78	255.67	267.21	280.89	3.60	42.42
Costa Rica	24.36	25.02	25.85	26.80	27.83	28.88	29.92	30.96	32.04	33.23	34.59	3.57	42.00
Croatia	64.93	66.10	65.86	66.13	66.28	65.16	63.98	62.72	59.82	58.16	55.10	-1.63	-15.14
Czech Republic	123.95	122.62	120.21	117.99	116.51	117.41	119.79	126.65	133.97	142.28	153.89	2.19	24.15
Denmark	69.36	70.79	72.64	75.30	78.19	81.63	84.67	88.06	91.25	96.74	102.55	3.99	47.86
Ecuador	78.97	81.79	84.68	87.61	90.56	93.50	96.41	99.28	102.14	104.98	107.84	3.17	36.57
Egypt	310.87	318.50	326.92	336.53	348.06	361.20	374.97	388.78	403.18	417.25	433.42	3.38	39.42
Estonia	15.40	14.91	14.66	14.64	14.96	15.35	15.81	15.82	16.07	15.54	14.53	-0.58	-5.66
Finland	73.71	74.15	75.07	75.66	77.66	81.28	84.56	84.35	91.24	89.57	91.11	2.14	23.60
France	920.94	929.74	923.97	922.93	917.67	919.69	918.97	914.11	899.02	905.43	925.31	0.05	0.48
Germany	1,268.88	1,321.38	1,389.64	1,478.89	1,579.19	1,699.67	1,790.79	1,865.48	1,904.23	1,859.88	1,804.55	3.58	42.22
Greece	212.22	219.57	216.90	217.92	217.92	216.71	211.50	214.18	203.61	198.12	191.34	-1.03	-9.84
Hong Kong, China	94.25	94.24	94.41	95.57	96.60	96.32	96.94	96.44	92.99	90.75	90.61	-0.39	-3.85
Hungary	119.02	117.30	113.44	109.90	106.97	105.71	105.97	110.26	114.57	121.17	125.69	0.55	5.60
India	4,570.86	4,711.80	4,858.06	5,008.00	5,158.58	5,306.07	5,448.37	5,585.79	5,718.99	5,849.26	5,981.66	2.73	30.87
Indonesia	1,083.83	1,126.95	1,171.47	1,216.55	1,260.77	1,302.45	1,340.39	1,374.31	1,404.15	1,429.87	1,452.11	2.97	33.98
Iran	402.93	398.07	391.61	384.02	375.83	367.66	360.19	354.02	349.78	348.26	350.30	-1.39	-13.06
Ireland	43.85	44.74	45.39	46.23	47.00	48.21	49.81	51.19	52.60	54.66	56.96	2.65	29.89
Israel	60.16	60.56	62.19	65.11	68.23	70.73	71.69	70.89	67.80	63.98	62.79	0.43	4.38
Italy	1,038.77	1,053.81	1,058.99	1,062.91	1,082.25	1,113.51	1,146.66	1,176.84	1,186.97	1,183.60	1,166.34	1.17	12.28
Japan	2,523.64	2,592.44	2,664.57	2,716.04	2,737.16	2,721.42	2,759.34	2,834.70	2,926.84	3,011.87	3,140.88	2.21	24.46
Jordan	18.67	19.57	20.48	21.42	22.43	23.56	24.81	26.16	27.53	28.80	29.85	4.81	59.91
Kazakhstan	54.96	56.13	60.83	67.61	74.14	77.97	77.61	73.02	65.50	57.18	50.50	-0.84	-8.12
Kuwait	4.09	4.63	5.24	5.89	6.56	7.24	7.91	8.58	9.26	9.99	10.79	10.20	164.09
Latvia	25.10	24.16	23.71	23.62	24.11	24.98	25.87	26.11	26.23	25.51	24.31	-0.32	-3.12
Lithuania	38.19	37.89	37.59	37.97	37.75	37.72	37.88	37.72	37.83	38.35	38.02	-0.04	-0.45
Malaysia	91.73	94.85	98.60	102.98	108.39	113.80	119.23	124.82	131.07	137.59	145.54	4.72	58.66
Mexico	582.36	603.15	624.43	646.18	669.99	697.27	728.84	764.69	803.55	843.22	881.52	4.23	51.37
Morocco	151.13	154.05	157.88	162.16	166.10	168.87	170.07	169.84	168.90	168.45	169.80	1.17	12.35
Netherlands	210.57	215.02	218.13	222.86	226.45	235.12	243.88	254.82	262.37	273.15	285.93	3.11	35.79
New Zealand	48.33	48.70	48.95	49.92	51.64	53.41	56.21	59.79	62.97	64.14	66.65	3.27	37.92
Nigeria	364.42	375.48	387.07	399.31	412.35	426.26	441.01	456.45	472.22	487.76	502.57	3.27	37.91
Norway	59.33	58.73	57.78	57.98	58.46	60.26	62.73	65.80	67.51	71.05	75.48	2.44	27.23
Pakistan	642.87	661.24	680.50	701.21	724.17	750.06	779.11	811.04	844.71	878.11	909.18	3.53	41.42
Peru	144.40	150.23	155.93	161.49	166.90	172.16	177.32	182.42	187.57	192.95	198.74	3.25	37.63
Philippines	295.61	311.93	326.08	338.80	351.15	364.43	379.48	396.53	415.19	434.80	454.71	4.40	53.82
Poland	420.62	418.42	414.11	412.78	411.34	411.19	411.22	408.92	402.52	392.09	384.90	-0.88	-8.49
Portugal	167.39	170.36	173.60	175.04	175.50	177.29	178.77	177.01	174.77	175.26	176.76	0.55	5.60
Romania	274.87	274.74	273.29	277.38	275.51	277.36	277.54	274.56	263.88	253.15	241.53	-1.28	-12.13
Russia	1,151.65	1,071.56	1,035.00	1,067.64	1,155.84	1,257.52	1,336.62	1,342.72	1,301.52	1,137.21	936.80	-2.04	-18.66
Saudi Arabia	73.99	75.63	76.77	77.59	78.34	79.35	80.86	82.99	85.75	89.07	92.94	2.31	25.61
Singapore	34.84	37.05	37.84	37.31	38.29	41.83	44.88	49.46	52.08	52.37	52.40	4.17	50.39
Slovakia	48.39	47.69	46.63	45.07	43.33	42.88	43.29	45.07	47.36	49.65	51.75	0.67	6.93
Slovenia	26.32	26.78	26.97	27.58	27.88	28.30	28.89	29.49	29.92	30.80	31.60	1.85	20.10
South Africa	132.00	135.75	139.58	143.60	148.01	153.00	158.67	165.00	171.83	178.97	186.18	3.50	41.04
South Korea	376.92	410.55	442.50	467.52	490.09	510.90	529.49	550.25	572.51	586.90	591.99	4.62	57.06
Spain	725.16	736.29	740.27	735.07	719.77	707.39	690.86	678.19	679.81	700.77	721.40	-0.05	-0.52
Sweden	135.12	135.39	136.32	138.64	141.98	147.62	154.37	159.99	166.22	176.63	189.05	3.42	39.91
Switzerland	104.46	106.70	108.57	110.01	110.55	112.38	113.69	115.08	119.49	126.97	134.78	2.58	29.02
Taiwan	249.81	241.69	233.30	227.46	227.14	229.24	234.05	241.22	248.42	252.47	257.05	0.29	2.90
Thailand	427.60	442.41	470.13	481.12	504.41	522.34	535.08	540.66	563.60	552.61	565.22	2.83	32.18
Tunisia	69.86	70.56	70.86	70.76	70.30	69.54	68.57	67.53	66.58	66.00	66.10	-0.55	-5.38
Turkey	340.01	373.03	417.64	455.86	488.24	514.67	534.79	554.55	566.31	567.50	558.88	5.10	64.37
Turkmenistan	16.55	16.98	17.69	18.52	19.21	19.50	19.22	18.41	17.25	16.05	15.17	-0.87	-8.35
Ukraine	432.61	399.27	391.93	432.35	519.36	612.37	675.47	691.24	677.10	581.20	463.80	0.70	7.21
United Arab Emirates	3.48	3.72	4.18	4.81	5.49	6.08	6.51	6.75	6.90	7.08	7.45	7.91	114.13
United Kingdom	872.49	877.71	885.43	896.51	912.45	931.38	946.70	951.25	953.99	970.34	999.60	1.37	14.57
USA	3,080.68	3,097.52	3,122.71	3,158.00	3,233.02	3,320.84	3,392.80	3,484.20	3,623.16	3,838.76	3,999.02	2.64	29.81
Venezuela	131.79	135.12	138.65	142.52	146.97	152.26	158.57	165.99	174.53	184.20	194.95	3.99	47.92
Vietnam	494.10	505.21	508.91	506.51	500.43	494.20	490.51	490.63	494.28	500.72	508.55	0.29	2.92

Key population trends

Table 4.42 Male Population Aged 80+: 2009-2019

'000

	2009	2010	2011	2012	2013	2014	2015	2016	2017	2018	2019	CAGR	Period growth
Algeria	88.35	93.07	98.71	105.09	111.79	118.19	123.87	128.76	132.95	136.46	139.34	4.66	57.72
Argentina	322.88	332.41	341.31	349.67	357.62	365.28	372.82	380.24	387.63	395.20	403.28	2.25	24.90
Australia	314.19	327.34	339.27	349.15	358.76	368.25	377.79	389.62	402.34	415.37	429.81	3.18	36.80
Austria	119.84	125.34	131.14	135.77	139.86	142.89	145.08	147.04	149.32	152.00	156.63	2.71	30.70
Azerbaijan	29.75	33.49	37.01	40.32	43.47	46.52	49.53	52.53	55.42	57.95	59.75	7.22	100.87
Belarus	64.52	67.38	69.07	69.67	69.64	69.51	69.76	70.62	71.93	73.19	73.77	1.35	14.34
Belgium	171.75	177.68	185.05	191.94	198.18	203.01	207.30	210.68	213.99	218.02	222.79	2.64	29.72
Bolivia	27.06	28.52	29.91	31.23	32.53	33.86	35.26	36.77	38.36	40.01	41.69	4.42	54.07
Bosnia-Herzegovina	30.95	33.44	35.88	38.22	40.49	42.70	44.84	46.95	48.99	50.74	51.94	5.32	67.85
Brazil	1,053.86	1,097.96	1,138.63	1,177.31	1,216.45	1,259.20	1,307.35	1,361.83	1,421.43	1,483.24	1,543.56	3.89	46.47
Bulgaria	102.20	104.16	106.84	108.22	111.33	113.60	116.38	117.11	118.07	118.17	117.82	1.43	15.29
Canada	467.62	484.54	500.98	517.20	533.08	548.29	562.80	576.65	590.15	604.14	619.58	2.85	32.50
Chile	121.82	127.82	133.82	139.83	145.82	151.74	157.57	163.28	168.94	174.80	181.20	4.05	48.74
China	8,797.40	9,219.77	9,654.46	10,092.52	10,537.95	10,971.98	11,398.97	11,812.00	12,219.68	12,613.78	12,986.91	3.97	47.62
Colombia	194.92	201.50	208.30	215.33	222.61	230.13	237.92	246.07	254.69	263.83	273.55	3.45	40.34
Costa Rica	28.64	29.72	30.73	31.69	32.63	33.62	34.70	35.90	37.21	38.62	40.07	3.42	39.92
Croatia	44.82	47.65	50.41	53.06	55.57	57.95	60.17	62.28	64.25	65.91	67.01	4.10	49.52
Czech Republic	110.10	113.84	117.80	121.04	123.84	125.59	126.77	127.60	128.28	129.42	131.65	1.80	19.57
Denmark	79.63	81.16	82.83	84.64	86.66	89.05	92.02	95.34	99.29	103.54	108.44	3.14	36.19
Ecuador	82.34	86.27	90.27	94.34	98.49	102.71	107.01	111.40	115.87	120.39	124.95	4.26	51.75
Egypt	203.81	213.37	222.75	232.00	241.32	250.98	261.19	272.16	283.87	296.03	308.19	4.22	51.22
Estonia	12.22	12.93	13.66	14.24	14.75	15.03	15.13	15.44	15.82	16.41	16.89	3.29	38.19
Finland	73.24	77.20	81.26	85.09	88.09	90.37	92.98	96.08	98.82	102.05	106.04	3.77	44.78
France	1,080.81	1,122.08	1,165.56	1,204.89	1,242.23	1,270.01	1,300.11	1,321.73	1,344.64	1,363.50	1,381.54	2.49	27.82
Germany	1,259.52	1,333.40	1,407.61	1,464.34	1,511.26	1,554.17	1,643.25	1,744.04	1,846.17	1,948.40	2,062.79	5.06	63.78
Greece	204.73	214.02	229.24	239.36	247.30	256.34	266.68	273.87	279.68	283.13	286.79	3.43	40.08
Hong Kong, China	83.79	89.39	95.48	100.65	106.21	111.66	114.98	118.70	122.75	126.79	130.00	4.49	55.14
Hungary	115.45	118.49	122.42	124.95	127.68	130.19	132.38	134.26	135.33	136.96	139.35	1.90	20.70
India	3,439.08	3,580.19	3,723.34	3,868.79	4,017.35	4,170.36	4,328.79	4,493.82	4,665.10	4,840.29	5,016.06	3.85	45.85
Indonesia	685.02	721.62	758.36	795.31	832.88	871.69	912.13	954.43	998.17	1,042.33	1,085.51	4.71	58.46
Iran	318.37	324.13	329.63	334.63	338.81	341.69	342.98	342.77	341.40	339.16	336.43	0.55	5.67
Ireland	43.48	44.79	46.24	47.73	49.24	50.74	52.37	53.99	55.78	57.56	59.61	3.21	37.11
Israel	76.31	78.08	79.78	81.41	83.04	84.76	86.65	88.82	91.26	93.77	96.07	2.33	25.89
Italy	1,127.20	1,167.57	1,218.22	1,258.03	1,291.39	1,326.67	1,361.42	1,396.86	1,423.02	1,456.24	1,501.34	2.91	33.19
Japan	2,669.21	2,820.36	2,980.10	3,140.51	3,295.98	3,436.52	3,589.41	3,750.19	3,895.32	4,011.21	4,085.57	4.35	53.06
Jordan	16.10	16.18	16.46	16.91	17.50	18.19	18.94	19.76	20.65	21.63	22.71	3.50	41.08
Kazakhstan	40.02	40.50	39.69	37.77	35.50	33.93	33.81	35.53	38.77	42.60	45.68	1.33	14.16
Kuwait	2.17	2.38	2.63	2.93	3.29	3.70	4.18	4.73	5.35	6.02	6.74	12.00	210.49
Latvia	19.57	20.86	22.11	23.26	24.21	24.75	25.08	25.69	26.55	27.67	28.80	3.94	47.14
Lithuania	29.99	31.13	32.68	33.72	34.80	35.75	36.13	37.05	37.90	38.45	39.10	2.69	30.35
Malaysia	82.71	86.25	89.73	93.25	97.01	101.28	106.25	112.09	118.72	125.87	133.02	4.87	60.84
Mexico	589.00	619.88	651.97	684.34	717.10	750.23	783.81	817.72	852.18	888.14	926.87	4.64	57.36
Morocco	102.66	107.81	112.07	115.63	118.76	121.93	125.42	129.41	133.75	138.06	141.81	3.28	38.14
Netherlands	203.37	207.90	213.79	218.84	224.34	228.79	233.60	238.60	244.12	249.34	256.84	2.36	26.29
New Zealand	56.06	58.51	61.15	63.41	65.16	67.11	69.16	71.11	73.65	76.30	79.03	3.49	40.99
Nigeria	216.26	223.99	231.89	239.99	248.37	257.16	266.41	276.14	286.37	297.15	308.58	3.62	42.69
Norway	76.70	78.03	79.52	80.57	81.69	82.13	82.44	82.67	83.55	84.77	86.56	1.22	12.85
Pakistan	564.54	582.06	600.59	620.14	640.71	662.28	684.90	708.46	733.11	759.36	787.91	3.39	39.57
Peru	125.27	131.89	138.89	146.24	153.87	161.69	169.63	177.69	185.86	194.11	202.40	4.91	61.58
Philippines	174.13	182.62	193.26	205.86	219.79	234.13	248.20	261.77	275.10	288.54	302.64	5.68	73.80
Poland	354.31	375.10	398.25	418.11	434.85	447.61	459.82	472.60	485.04	495.45	504.16	3.59	42.29
Portugal	162.03	166.53	172.55	179.12	185.41	191.01	196.04	202.43	207.82	212.07	216.89	2.96	33.86
Romania	223.15	230.37	238.26	243.69	252.62	256.46	260.74	265.09	271.77	277.11	281.62	2.35	26.20
Russia	848.42	915.05	998.17	1,003.88	1,022.79	986.98	968.96	978.26	1,008.41	1,067.02	1,103.82	2.67	30.10
Saudi Arabia	48.09	50.84	53.68	56.57	59.40	62.01	64.30	66.25	67.93	69.49	71.10	3.99	47.86
Singapore	32.75	34.60	36.32	38.95	41.31	43.64	47.11	47.84	49.68	54.19	59.80	6.21	82.62
Slovakia	43.63	44.60	45.60	46.52	47.46	47.87	48.25	48.60	48.80	49.06	49.64	1.30	13.79
Slovenia	20.32	21.69	23.43	24.76	26.03	27.12	28.24	29.39	30.60	31.62	32.58	4.84	60.36
South Africa	80.02	83.32	86.56	89.77	92.98	96.25	99.64	103.16	106.83	110.78	115.17	3.71	43.93
South Korea	266.22	287.32	311.79	338.85	368.61	400.19	433.74	468.08	502.08	536.14	570.15	7.91	114.17
Spain	792.62	830.62	870.32	909.92	948.78	985.45	1,020.62	1,051.58	1,075.47	1,090.38	1,106.45	3.39	39.59
Sweden	179.05	180.09	180.97	182.02	182.42	183.36	185.30	188.25	192.13	197.24	203.59	1.29	13.70
Switzerland	123.17	126.53	130.08	133.78	137.56	141.26	144.86	148.26	151.52	154.92	158.92	2.58	29.02
Taiwan	265.86	279.68	292.49	300.23	305.09	307.62	312.58	310.41	315.41	319.59	323.79	1.99	21.79
Thailand	355.93	368.98	381.34	393.39	405.20	417.32	429.89	443.30	457.32	471.65	485.63	3.16	36.44
Tunisia	49.97	52.05	54.09	56.06	57.91	59.55	60.93	62.05	62.93	63.57	63.96	2.50	28.01
Turkey	279.04	266.99	242.75	226.61	215.56	211.59	211.70	211.80	220.07	237.59	263.37	-0.58	-5.61
Turkmenistan	11.27	12.00	12.53	12.90	13.17	13.49	13.93	14.56	15.31	16.06	16.63	3.97	47.63
Ukraine	357.55	371.35	375.78	371.75	364.13	359.31	362.44	375.82	397.20	421.47	440.42	2.11	23.18
United Arab Emirates	4.02	4.12	4.14	4.08	4.02	4.03	4.19	4.52	5.00	5.57	6.14	4.33	52.78
United Kingdom	1,018.20	1,049.35	1,079.81	1,108.89	1,134.83	1,158.06	1,182.18	1,209.24	1,237.91	1,268.02	1,298.41	2.46	27.52
USA	4,182.81	4,262.84	4,326.55	4,376.11	4,417.32	4,453.97	4,519.15	4,577.30	4,639.43	4,722.54	4,813.99	1.42	15.09
Venezuela	119.60	125.95	132.14	138.21	144.19	150.12	156.05	162.01	168.07	174.43	181.39	4.25	51.67
Vietnam	420.47	436.35	454.84	475.36	496.38	515.79	532.08	544.85	554.64	562.17	568.54	3.06	35.21

Key population trends

Table 4.43 Female Population: 2009-2019

'000

	2009	2010	2011	2012	2013	2014	2015	2016	2017	2018	2019	CAGR	Period growth
Algeria	17,279.7	17,540.4	17,803.4	18,068.1	18,333.4	18,598.2	18,861.1	19,121.7	19,379.2	19,632.9	19,882.2	1.41	15.06
Argentina	20,611.6	20,815.1	21,016.3	21,215.4	21,412.3	21,607.1	21,799.6	21,989.6	22,176.8	22,360.9	22,541.8	0.90	9.37
Australia	10,951.7	11,101.6	11,240.4	11,387.2	11,540.3	11,699.2	11,860.3	12,021.3	12,182.0	12,342.5	12,502.8	1.33	14.16
Austria	4,300.7	4,312.0	4,323.2	4,334.4	4,345.4	4,356.1	4,366.4	4,376.3	4,385.9	4,395.3	4,404.5	0.24	2.41
Azerbaijan	4,418.4	4,464.0	4,507.8	4,551.7	4,595.4	4,638.5	4,680.6	4,721.5	4,761.1	4,798.9	4,835.0	0.90	9.43
Belarus	5,160.3	5,152.5	5,140.5	5,128.0	5,114.9	5,101.3	5,087.2	5,072.6	5,057.5	5,042.0	5,025.9	-0.26	-2.61
Belgium	5,439.7	5,458.0	5,475.9	5,493.6	5,510.9	5,527.8	5,544.5	5,560.7	5,576.6	5,592.3	5,607.7	0.30	3.09
Bolivia	4,944.8	5,028.1	5,111.0	5,193.4	5,275.1	5,356.3	5,436.7	5,516.3	5,595.2	5,673.1	5,750.2	1.52	16.29
Bosnia-Herzegovina	1,994.7	1,994.6	1,994.2	1,993.8	1,993.3	1,992.5	1,991.2	1,989.4	1,987.0	1,984.0	1,980.6	-0.07	-0.70
Brazil	98,327.8	99,224.3	100,086.0	100,911.4	101,704.4	102,469.1	103,209.0	103,926.0	104,620.4	105,290.2	105,932.4	0.75	7.73
Bulgaria	3,877.1	3,851.1	3,825.0	3,798.6	3,769.8	3,740.6	3,709.9	3,678.3	3,646.3	3,614.0	3,581.4	-0.79	-7.63
Canada	16,983.8	17,138.1	17,266.2	17,383.3	17,498.6	17,613.4	17,729.0	17,845.8	17,963.2	18,080.8	18,197.9	0.69	7.15
Chile	8,577.1	8,660.8	8,743.7	8,825.8	8,907.0	8,986.9	9,065.4	9,142.3	9,217.7	9,291.5	9,363.9	0.88	9.17
China	643,982.8	647,006.7	649,749.4	652,391.3	655,013.3	657,601.2	660,134.6	662,584.7	664,919.0	667,105.2	669,115.9	0.38	3.90
Colombia	23,184.2	23,515.1	23,841.8	24,164.5	24,483.2	24,798.3	25,110.0	25,418.1	25,722.4	26,022.4	26,317.7	1.28	13.52
Costa Rica	2,253.5	2,284.0	2,315.4	2,347.4	2,379.7	2,411.8	2,443.2	2,473.8	2,503.8	2,533.4	2,562.5	1.29	13.71
Croatia	2,295.6	2,291.5	2,286.8	2,281.8	2,276.4	2,270.7	2,264.8	2,258.6	2,252.3	2,245.7	2,239.0	-0.25	-2.47
Czech Republic	5,289.9	5,296.9	5,301.7	5,302.1	5,300.4	5,297.7	5,294.9	5,292.2	5,290.3	5,289.0	5,287.7	0.00	-0.04
Denmark	2,779.4	2,786.2	2,793.5	2,801.0	2,808.4	2,815.9	2,823.4	2,831.0	2,838.8	2,846.8	2,855.1	0.27	2.72
Ecuador	6,800.2	6,876.9	6,957.3	7,041.0	7,126.7	7,212.6	7,297.3	7,380.4	7,462.0	7,542.2	7,620.9	1.15	12.07
Egypt	37,537.0	38,226.2	38,915.7	39,604.6	40,291.4	40,974.8	41,653.4	42,326.3	42,992.9	43,652.7	44,305.5	1.67	18.03
Estonia	718.5	716.2	714.1	711.6	709.0	706.5	704.1	701.7	699.3	697.1	694.9	-0.33	-3.29
Finland	2,715.5	2,726.3	2,736.3	2,745.6	2,754.7	2,763.7	2,772.2	2,780.3	2,788.0	2,795.5	2,802.5	0.32	3.20
France	32,214.7	32,366.3	32,503.2	32,640.7	32,775.0	32,904.7	33,030.9	33,153.6	33,272.5	33,388.2	33,500.2	0.39	3.99
Germany	41,804.3	41,634.5	41,457.0	41,295.9	41,141.8	40,994.6	40,847.2	40,698.8	40,549.6	40,399.5	40,247.9	-0.38	-3.72
Greece	5,684.1	5,704.0	5,722.2	5,738.8	5,754.1	5,767.4	5,779.1	5,788.8	5,796.5	5,802.3	5,806.4	0.21	2.15
Hong Kong, China	3,750.3	3,802.6	3,854.0	3,904.7	3,954.7	4,004.0	4,052.9	4,101.3	4,148.9	4,195.7	4,241.9	1.24	13.11
Hungary	5,265.4	5,255.3	5,245.1	5,231.3	5,216.1	5,200.7	5,185.4	5,170.3	5,155.6	5,141.4	5,127.9	-0.26	-2.61
India	564,937.3	572,942.3	580,883.4	588,749.3	596,528.2	604,204.9	611,766.3	619,204.4	626,513.3	633,683.6	640,705.5	1.27	13.41
Indonesia	115,157.5	116,454.5	117,716.4	118,942.9	120,132.7	121,285.4	122,401.1	123,478.7	124,519.7	125,530.4	126,519.5	0.95	9.87
Iran	36,467.8	36,923.7	37,374.3	37,821.4	38,267.0	38,714.2	39,164.6	39,618.7	40,073.3	40,521.8	40,955.9	1.17	12.31
Ireland	2,225.1	2,254.1	2,280.4	2,306.4	2,332.2	2,357.5	2,382.3	2,406.5	2,430.1	2,453.0	2,475.3	1.07	11.25
Israel	3,739.5	3,795.3	3,850.2	3,904.0	3,956.9	4,008.8	4,059.7	4,109.8	4,159.0	4,207.5	4,255.3	1.30	13.79
Italy	30,347.5	30,370.1	30,385.7	30,393.9	30,395.1	30,388.5	30,374.9	30,354.2	30,326.8	30,293.3	30,254.1	-0.03	-0.31
Japan	65,431.2	65,352.9	65,266.5	65,173.9	65,063.0	64,934.2	64,787.5	64,622.6	64,439.0	64,236.8	64,016.0	-0.22	-2.16
Jordan	3,077.2	3,154.9	3,217.9	3,268.2	3,310.4	3,351.8	3,397.2	3,448.2	3,503.3	3,561.4	3,620.5	1.64	17.66
Kazakhstan	8,263.0	8,378.1	8,487.3	8,597.3	8,706.2	8,813.0	8,917.5	9,019.4	9,118.4	9,214.4	9,307.0	1.20	12.63
Kuwait	989.3	1,015.2	1,040.7	1,065.7	1,090.3	1,114.6	1,138.7	1,162.7	1,186.6	1,210.5	1,234.1	2.24	24.75
Latvia	1,215.2	1,208.1	1,201.1	1,193.4	1,185.5	1,177.6	1,170.0	1,162.6	1,155.3	1,148.2	1,141.3	-0.63	-6.08
Lithuania	1,790.3	1,781.4	1,772.5	1,763.1	1,753.5	1,743.9	1,734.5	1,725.2	1,716.1	1,707.1	1,698.5	-0.52	-5.13
Malaysia	13,801.6	14,028.2	14,252.1	14,473.2	14,691.6	14,907.5	15,120.8	15,331.5	15,539.3	15,743.8	15,944.5	1.45	15.53
Mexico	55,192.7	56,029.4	56,853.4	57,634.4	58,378.9	59,097.9	59,800.8	60,491.1	61,165.6	61,827.0	62,480.3	1.25	13.20
Morocco	16,280.4	16,484.1	16,687.9	16,892.1	17,096.1	17,299.4	17,501.6	17,702.1	17,900.5	18,096.3	18,288.8	1.17	12.34
Netherlands	8,292.8	8,306.1	8,320.2	8,334.6	8,348.9	8,363.0	8,376.7	8,390.1	8,403.3	8,416.3	8,429.2	0.16	1.64
New Zealand	2,197.1	2,217.6	2,237.8	2,257.6	2,277.1	2,296.3	2,315.4	2,334.2	2,352.8	2,371.2	2,389.3	0.84	8.75
Nigeria	77,181.4	78,915.6	80,653.4	82,393.4	84,132.6	85,868.4	87,598.5	89,321.3	91,035.3	92,739.4	94,432.8	2.04	22.35
Norway	2,404.2	2,430.3	2,454.7	2,477.3	2,499.0	2,520.6	2,542.2	2,564.1	2,586.4	2,609.1	2,632.1	0.91	9.48
Pakistan	87,706.4	89,638.2	91,612.7	93,625.8	95,665.3	97,714.4	99,760.1	101,797.7	103,827.5	105,848.1	107,859.5	2.09	22.98
Peru	14,470.4	14,668.0	14,864.9	15,061.0	15,255.8	15,449.1	15,640.2	15,829.4	16,016.7	16,202.3	16,386.1	1.25	13.24
Philippines	45,779.2	46,668.1	47,553.5	48,435.9	49,316.0	50,204.4	51,102.0	52,009.2	52,925.3	53,849.3	54,779.6	1.81	19.66
Poland	19,630.7	19,603.6	19,576.7	19,551.2	19,523.3	19,494.7	19,467.3	19,440.1	19,413.6	19,388.4	19,364.2	-0.14	-1.36
Portugal	5,502.1	5,513.5	5,523.7	5,532.8	5,540.7	5,547.6	5,553.1	5,557.4	5,560.5	5,562.4	5,563.3	0.11	1.11
Romania	11,000.8	10,969.3	10,935.7	10,900.6	10,856.0	10,810.5	10,757.2	10,700.7	10,643.1	10,584.5	10,524.6	-0.44	-4.33
Russia	76,262.3	76,241.5	76,110.2	75,988.6	75,893.2	75,808.9	75,717.7	75,614.8	75,500.4	75,375.0	75,237.8	-0.14	-1.34
Saudi Arabia	11,622.8	11,891.0	12,160.7	12,431.6	12,703.7	12,976.5	13,249.8	13,523.4	13,797.0	14,070.1	14,342.5	2.12	23.40
Singapore	2,381.2	2,415.8	2,448.8	2,480.2	2,510.1	2,538.6	2,565.8	2,591.6	2,616.2	2,639.7	2,662.0	1.12	11.79
Slovakia	2,774.7	2,775.0	2,775.1	2,774.9	2,774.6	2,774.1	2,773.6	2,772.9	2,772.1	2,771.2	2,770.2	-0.02	-0.17
Slovenia	1,028.5	1,030.6	1,032.6	1,033.9	1,034.8	1,035.7	1,036.5	1,037.1	1,037.7	1,038.3	1,038.9	0.10	1.01
South Africa	25,404.6	25,589.8	25,744.4	25,871.2	25,977.1	26,071.7	26,162.4	26,251.5	26,338.8	26,425.8	26,513.6	0.43	4.37
South Korea	24,265.2	24,334.2	24,396.4	24,450.5	24,497.1	24,537.5	24,570.2	24,596.8	24,616.9	24,631.1	24,640.8	0.15	1.55
Spain	23,060.8	23,259.1	23,442.8	23,622.1	23,797.7	23,969.6	24,137.0	24,299.3	24,456.7	24,607.1	24,748.5	0.71	7.32
Sweden	4,633.1	4,652.8	4,672.7	4,692.7	4,712.9	4,733.5	4,754.5	4,776.2	4,798.3	4,820.8	4,843.7	0.45	4.55
Switzerland	3,865.2	3,882.6	3,900.0	3,917.2	3,934.4	3,951.7	3,969.1	3,986.6	4,004.4	4,022.3	4,040.5	0.44	4.54
Taiwan	11,409.3	11,465.8	11,519.0	11,569.3	11,614.8	11,657.4	11,696.5	11,730.5	11,762.2	11,789.0	11,812.0	0.35	3.53
Thailand	33,260.6	33,484.1	33,694.7	33,893.4	34,081.1	34,259.2	34,428.8	34,590.2	34,743.1	34,887.5	35,023.1	0.52	5.30
Tunisia	5,106.1	5,158.2	5,210.4	5,262.7	5,315.0	5,366.9	5,418.4	5,469.2	5,519.1	5,568.3	5,616.7	0.96	10.00
Turkey	37,339.1	37,792.9	38,240.9	38,682.8	39,117.9	39,545.8	39,966.4	40,379.2	40,784.3	41,181.8	41,572.0	1.08	11.34
Turkmenistan	2,591.9	2,626.4	2,661.1	2,695.7	2,730.1	2,764.3	2,798.1	2,831.4	2,864.2	2,896.3	2,927.5	1.23	12.95
Ukraine	24,765.3	24,629.3	24,489.3	24,346.0	24,200.4	24,053.1	23,904.0	23,752.8	23,599.5	23,444.0	23,286.1	-0.61	-5.97
United Arab Emirates	1,511.1	1,556.3	1,598.7	1,638.5	1,676.2	1,712.5	1,748.0	1,782.8	1,817.0	1,850.6	1,883.8	2.23	24.66
United Kingdom	31,372.3	31,525.6	31,650.3	31,790.1	31,949.2	32,125.5	32,305.4	32,488.7	32,675.4	32,865.0	33,056.9	0.52	5.37
USA	155,357.6	156,442.7	157,449.2	158,473.3	159,530.6	160,596.9	161,670.2	162,749.0	163,831.9	164,917.8	166,005.4	0.67	6.85
Venezuela	14,234.4	14,467.9	14,700.1	14,930.8	15,159.8	15,386.8	15,611.6	15,834.1	16,054.0	16,271.2	16,485.5	1.48	15.81
Vietnam	43,810.0	44,367.8	44,928.8	45,492.1	46,056.5	46,620.2	47,181.2	47,738.4	48,290.4	48,835.3	49,369.5	1.20	12.69

Key population trends

Table 4.44 Female Population Aged 0-4: 2009-2019

'000

	2009	2010	2011	2012	2013	2014	2015	2016	2017	2018	2019	CAGR	Period growth
Algeria	1,666.0	1,683.6	1,701.2	1,718.7	1,735.7	1,750.7	1,762.0	1,768.6	1,770.3	1,767.0	1,758.9	0.54	5.58
Argentina	1,676.9	1,690.1	1,699.3	1,703.9	1,703.9	1,700.7	1,695.8	1,690.4	1,684.9	1,679.4	1,673.5	-0.02	-0.20
Australia	689.1	707.3	719.4	731.1	739.4	745.5	750.9	757.3	763.5	769.8	776.1	1.20	12.63
Austria	195.3	193.9	193.3	193.0	192.9	193.1	193.5	193.8	194.2	194.4	194.6	-0.04	-0.37
Azerbaijan	347.6	357.7	365.5	372.5	376.7	378.3	377.7	375.3	371.3	366.2	360.4	0.36	3.68
Belarus	236.1	245.9	253.6	257.9	258.7	256.4	252.9	250.2	247.3	244.0	240.5	0.19	1.87
Belgium	296.6	300.0	302.7	304.3	305.1	305.0	304.5	303.8	302.9	302.0	301.1	0.15	1.52
Bolivia	610.9	609.3	608.0	607.1	606.7	606.3	605.8	604.7	603.0	600.8	598.3	-0.21	-2.07
Bosnia-Herzegovina	83.3	84.1	84.7	84.8	84.4	83.7	83.0	82.3	81.6	81.0	80.4	-0.35	-3.47
Brazil	7,841.0	7,628.5	7,419.5	7,219.9	7,035.9	6,870.5	6,724.5	6,600.0	6,497.7	6,414.6	6,347.4	-2.09	-19.05
Bulgaria	162.6	161.3	160.0	158.6	156.5	154.2	151.5	148.6	145.4	142.0	138.4	-1.59	-14.84
Canada	876.1	887.7	892.7	893.8	894.4	895.3	899.2	908.3	919.6	930.2	940.4	0.71	7.34
Chile	612.0	614.3	616.3	617.7	618.5	618.7	618.3	617.5	616.2	614.7	613.2	0.02	0.20
China	28,717.7	28,640.6	28,698.2	28,755.8	28,804.0	28,773.6	28,765.3	28,842.8	28,895.8	28,882.1	28,793.7	0.03	0.26
Colombia	2,202.0	2,205.2	2,204.7	2,200.1	2,192.4	2,183.1	2,174.2	2,166.8	2,161.3	2,157.4	2,154.1	-0.22	-2.17
Costa Rica	181.6	180.0	180.0	181.7	184.4	187.5	189.8	190.9	190.6	189.0	186.9	0.29	2.90
Croatia	103.0	104.5	104.8	105.2	105.6	105.8	105.9	105.9	105.8	105.5	105.1	0.20	2.06
Czech Republic	250.0	253.0	253.4	253.5	253.3	253.1	252.8	252.2	251.4	250.2	248.4	-0.06	-0.63
Denmark	159.4	158.8	157.9	156.4	155.0	153.4	152.2	151.5	151.3	151.6	152.4	-0.45	-4.43
Ecuador	674.7	670.3	666.5	663.3	660.8	658.6	656.7	655.1	653.7	652.2	650.6	-0.36	-3.56
Egypt	4,287.0	4,343.7	4,388.6	4,432.4	4,471.7	4,505.2	4,532.5	4,553.2	4,567.0	4,574.4	4,577.4	0.66	6.77
Estonia	34.9	35.5	36.0	36.3	36.7	36.9	37.1	37.1	37.1	36.9	36.6	0.47	4.80
Finland	143.9	144.8	145.6	145.9	146.5	147.2	147.8	148.3	148.8	149.1	149.3	0.37	3.79
France	1,921.6	1,938.8	1,944.3	1,937.8	1,935.5	1,925.6	1,914.1	1,909.9	1,906.1	1,902.4	1,898.6	-0.12	-1.20
Germany	1,673.5	1,650.7	1,617.6	1,583.9	1,543.3	1,503.8	1,472.3	1,461.1	1,459.2	1,460.4	1,462.1	-1.34	-12.63
Greece	262.4	264.3	265.1	265.0	264.3	262.9	260.9	258.3	255.3	251.9	248.3	-0.55	-5.35
Hong Kong, China	113.1	118.0	120.5	120.6	121.2	122.5	124.2	126.3	128.0	130.2	132.4	1.58	17.02
Hungary	237.8	239.2	239.2	237.8	236.3	235.0	233.8	232.9	232.1	231.4	230.7	-0.30	-2.99
India	59,090.2	58,804.2	58,570.8	58,398.2	58,270.2	58,147.3	57,985.9	57,755.8	57,448.7	57,068.3	56,632.1	-0.42	-4.16
Indonesia	10,172.6	10,070.2	9,966.7	9,865.9	9,767.8	9,668.5	9,562.9	9,447.2	9,322.9	9,196.7	9,079.7	-1.13	-10.74
Iran	3,222.4	3,255.5	3,276.3	3,286.7	3,289.8	3,287.4	3,279.5	3,265.9	3,246.5	3,219.9	3,183.7	-0.12	-1.20
Ireland	153.7	153.5	153.5	153.1	152.4	151.4	150.0	148.3	146.3	144.2	141.9	-0.80	-7.72
Israel	349.0	347.8	346.5	345.0	343.5	341.8	340.2	338.8	337.8	337.0	336.5	-0.37	-3.60
Italy	1,325.2	1,307.9	1,292.0	1,272.9	1,252.2	1,230.5	1,208.4	1,186.4	1,165.0	1,144.6	1,125.5	-1.62	-15.07
Japan	2,639.2	2,634.7	2,609.0	2,566.8	2,508.6	2,433.3	2,375.2	2,322.1	2,273.9	2,229.9	2,189.8	-1.85	-17.03
Jordan	373.6	380.6	384.8	386.1	384.9	382.2	378.8	375.4	371.9	368.6	365.5	-0.22	-2.17
Kazakhstan	726.0	751.8	767.1	779.2	784.3	782.3	774.6	764.4	752.9	741.4	730.6	0.06	0.64
Kuwait	102.4	104.4	105.7	106.4	106.4	106.0	105.4	104.9	104.4	104.1	103.8	0.14	1.36
Latvia	52.9	54.3	55.1	55.8	56.4	56.8	57.0	57.0	56.7	56.2	55.4	0.46	4.73
Lithuania	74.3	74.6	75.0	75.5	75.9	76.4	76.8	77.1	77.3	77.4	77.3	0.39	4.00
Malaysia	1,511.2	1,499.5	1,487.6	1,474.9	1,471.4	1,475.7	1,484.5	1,493.2	1,498.4	1,498.4	1,492.8	-0.12	-1.21
Mexico	5,054.3	5,018.7	4,961.7	4,921.2	4,882.6	4,841.8	4,798.9	4,754.3	4,708.0	4,661.9	4,617.9	-0.90	-8.64
Morocco	1,511.9	1,531.4	1,547.6	1,559.5	1,566.6	1,569.8	1,570.0	1,568.2	1,564.4	1,558.8	1,551.1	0.26	2.60
Netherlands	450.7	442.5	437.1	432.6	429.3	427.2	426.0	425.7	426.2	427.4	429.2	-0.49	-4.77
New Zealand	149.6	152.8	154.9	155.5	154.6	153.4	152.2	151.3	150.5	149.9	149.5	-0.01	-0.06
Nigeria	12,562.1	12,740.7	12,888.2	13,003.2	13,087.5	13,146.4	13,185.9	13,210.4	13,222.8	13,225.7	13,221.6	0.51	5.25
Norway	145.6	147.9	150.0	151.2	152.5	153.0	153.7	154.7	156.1	157.9	159.6	0.92	9.62
Pakistan	11,732.6	11,901.1	12,073.2	12,246.2	12,412.0	12,558.6	12,675.8	12,757.2	12,802.0	12,815.1	12,807.2	0.88	9.16
Peru	1,447.2	1,445.4	1,441.1	1,434.2	1,425.3	1,415.7	1,406.4	1,398.2	1,391.5	1,386.2	1,381.7	-0.46	-4.52
Philippines	5,293.4	5,327.3	5,373.9	5,414.5	5,447.7	5,472.7	5,493.7	5,513.7	5,534.9	5,558.4	5,584.4	0.54	5.50
Poland	876.5	884.0	889.4	897.2	905.8	914.2	921.5	927.2	931.1	933.2	933.3	0.63	6.49
Portugal	263.2	262.8	262.1	260.7	258.4	255.5	252.1	248.4	244.4	240.4	236.4	-1.07	-10.19
Romania	526.6	528.6	527.3	524.7	520.6	515.8	510.2	504.0	497.0	488.9	479.5	-0.93	-8.96
Russia	3,747.6	3,878.3	3,987.0	4,093.5	4,149.8	4,162.6	4,149.2	4,166.4	4,164.6	4,134.6	4,084.2	0.86	8.98
Saudi Arabia	1,419.8	1,421.3	1,426.2	1,435.0	1,447.1	1,460.6	1,473.4	1,484.1	1,492.0	1,497.2	1,500.0	0.55	5.65
Singapore	117.2	117.4	118.0	118.9	119.9	120.9	122.1	123.4	124.6	125.9	127.3	0.83	8.64
Slovakia	130.8	131.0	131.0	131.0	131.1	131.1	131.1	131.1	131.0	130.7	130.4	-0.03	-0.32
Slovenia	45.3	45.7	46.3	46.8	47.2	47.6	47.9	48.0	48.0	47.9	47.6	0.48	4.92
South Africa	2,571.3	2,556.8	2,546.5	2,541.1	2,539.3	2,538.0	2,533.6	2,523.5	2,507.2	2,485.7	2,462.0	-0.43	-4.25
South Korea	1,067.6	1,060.3	1,054.8	1,044.2	1,030.7	1,015.9	999.2	983.4	967.0	952.2	939.2	-1.27	-12.03
Spain	1,171.0	1,188.9	1,204.2	1,210.5	1,213.8	1,214.1	1,210.7	1,204.2	1,195.3	1,182.1	1,165.6	-0.05	-0.46
Sweden	252.7	253.9	255.2	256.4	257.8	259.1	260.5	262.3	264.4	266.6	268.9	0.62	6.41
Switzerland	178.2	177.7	177.7	177.4	177.7	178.5	179.9	181.8	184.1	186.8	189.6	0.63	6.44
Taiwan	491.5	485.5	482.9	480.6	478.7	475.7	471.0	466.2	461.6	456.9	451.4	-0.85	-8.14
Thailand	1,991.1	1,982.3	1,974.8	1,963.0	1,941.9	1,913.5	1,881.2	1,850.9	1,825.4	1,807.7	1,796.8	-1.02	-9.76
Tunisia	382.7	386.7	390.7	394.6	398.2	401.2	403.4	404.5	404.6	403.8	402.5	0.51	5.18
Turkey	3,143.8	3,138.8	3,140.8	3,141.5	3,138.4	3,128.5	3,120.6	3,126.8	3,130.2	3,126.9	3,121.0	-0.07	-0.73
Turkmenistan	257.6	256.1	255.3	255.4	256.3	257.4	258.2	258.2	257.4	255.6	253.2	-0.17	-1.71
Ukraine	1,071.0	1,080.9	1,088.0	1,071.4	1,049.6	1,022.1	993.0	965.5	942.7	926.8	915.9	-1.55	-14.48
United Arab Emirates	150.7	150.6	151.2	152.8	155.0	157.3	159.0	159.6	158.9	157.2	155.0	0.28	2.84
United Kingdom	1,828.2	1,869.0	1,892.9	1,911.4	1,920.9	1,924.4	1,927.4	1,943.4	1,960.1	1,976.9	1,992.8	0.87	9.01
USA	10,371.1	10,458.0	10,467.8	10,419.2	10,362.1	10,320.2	10,304.3	10,341.4	10,391.6	10,436.6	10,476.2	0.10	1.01
Venezuela	1,430.1	1,434.9	1,438.5	1,440.9	1,442.0	1,442.0	1,441.0	1,439.1	1,436.3	1,432.9	1,428.9	-0.01	-0.09
Vietnam	3,864.5	3,859.7	3,858.5	3,858.1	3,856.8	3,852.1	3,842.5	3,827.3	3,807.1	3,783.6	3,759.0	-0.28	-2.73

Key population trends

Table 4.45 Female Population Aged 5-9: 2009-2019

'000

	2009	2010	2011	2012	2013	2014	2015	2016	2017	2018	2019	CAGR	Period growth
Algeria	1,491.6	1,524.5	1,558.5	1,591.5	1,622.0	1,649.8	1,675.1	1,698.0	1,718.2	1,735.4	1,749.1	1.60	17.26
Argentina	1,645.1	1,641.7	1,643.4	1,650.2	1,660.5	1,672.0	1,682.7	1,690.9	1,696.2	1,698.4	1,697.8	0.32	3.20
Australia	660.3	661.9	669.0	680.1	696.0	714.8	733.9	747.6	760.3	769.3	775.4	1.62	17.43
Austria	200.3	201.1	201.1	202.4	201.4	201.2	199.7	199.0	198.6	198.4	198.5	-0.09	-0.87
Azerbaijan	295.5	299.2	306.5	316.7	328.6	340.7	351.6	360.5	366.9	370.8	372.5	2.34	26.04
Belarus	219.2	217.9	217.3	220.3	228.1	237.8	247.3	254.7	259.1	259.6	257.7	1.63	17.55
Belgium	287.9	289.1	290.5	293.3	298.1	302.6	306.1	308.8	310.5	311.2	311.1	0.78	8.08
Bolivia	587.8	592.1	595.2	596.9	597.5	597.3	596.8	596.2	595.6	595.1	594.4	0.11	1.11
Bosnia-Herzegovina	94.3	90.6	87.7	85.8	84.7	84.3	84.1	84.1	84.0	83.8	83.5	-1.21	-11.48
Brazil	8,574.2	8,490.8	8,360.9	8,196.2	8,008.1	7,805.4	7,597.9	7,392.9	7,196.5	7,015.0	6,850.9	-2.22	-20.10
Bulgaria	160.5	159.9	159.8	159.3	159.6	159.0	157.4	155.8	153.7	151.4	148.9	-0.75	-7.23
Canada	872.1	869.2	873.5	883.8	895.6	906.4	916.4	920.9	921.9	922.7	924.0	0.58	5.95
Chile	610.8	606.8	605.1	605.4	607.1	609.6	612.2	614.6	616.7	618.1	618.9	0.13	1.32
China	32,373.7	31,822.2	31,234.1	30,788.1	30,878.1	30,651.2	30,802.2	31,101.8	31,407.8	31,681.6	31,880.5	-0.15	-1.52
Colombia	2,161.1	2,164.5	2,169.6	2,176.1	2,182.8	2,188.3	2,191.4	2,191.3	2,188.0	2,182.3	2,175.2	0.07	0.66
Costa Rica	194.0	192.5	190.4	188.0	185.6	183.7	182.6	182.8	184.1	186.1	188.2	-0.30	-2.98
Croatia	104.8	101.5	100.5	101.1	102.3	103.8	105.3	105.6	105.9	106.2	106.5	0.16	1.61
Czech Republic	225.1	230.1	237.5	243.4	248.3	252.7	255.3	255.4	255.5	255.4	255.2	1.26	13.39
Denmark	161.7	160.8	159.7	159.5	159.7	159.7	159.1	158.2	156.8	155.5	153.9	-0.49	-4.80
Ecuador	698.1	692.9	687.4	681.9	676.6	671.6	667.0	663.1	659.7	656.9	654.5	-0.64	-6.23
Egypt	4,121.7	4,232.1	4,342.3	4,439.9	4,526.1	4,600.7	4,662.6	4,711.3	4,758.4	4,800.9	4,836.8	1.61	17.35
Estonia	30.8	31.6	32.3	33.3	34.0	34.8	35.3	35.8	36.2	36.5	36.8	1.80	19.57
Finland	140.1	140.4	141.5	143.3	145.0	146.1	147.0	147.7	147.9	148.5	149.1	0.62	6.40
France	1,899.1	1,905.8	1,902.0	1,911.2	1,921.0	1,937.0	1,954.6	1,960.7	1,954.5	1,952.3	1,942.6	0.23	2.29
Germany	1,810.6	1,776.2	1,732.7	1,700.9	1,682.1	1,669.0	1,649.3	1,618.6	1,586.2	1,546.5	1,507.4	-1.82	-16.75
Greece	252.4	255.4	258.4	262.3	264.9	267.2	269.1	269.9	269.9	269.2	267.8	0.59	6.09
Hong Kong, China	131.8	130.2	131.1	138.4	144.3	151.1	157.3	160.3	160.5	160.9	161.7	2.06	22.66
Hungary	234.4	235.4	235.1	236.8	238.1	240.2	241.3	241.1	239.6	238.1	236.7	0.10	0.99
India	58,370.2	58,411.0	58,373.0	58,256.3	58,080.9	57,879.4	57,683.7	57,513.5	57,370.5	57,241.8	57,104.1	-0.22	-2.17
Indonesia	10,266.2	10,291.6	10,290.0	10,259.6	10,203.5	10,128.1	10,040.6	9,946.1	9,847.0	9,743.8	9,635.8	-0.63	-6.14
Iran	2,756.2	2,858.6	2,958.7	3,048.6	3,124.1	3,184.1	3,229.9	3,263.0	3,284.2	3,294.4	3,294.8	1.80	19.54
Ireland	149.7	152.6	155.1	157.4	158.0	157.3	156.8	156.8	156.4	155.7	154.6	0.32	3.22
Israel	345.4	349.8	353.0	354.8	354.1	352.2	350.6	349.0	347.4	345.6	343.7	-0.05	-0.48
Italy	1,345.1	1,355.2	1,355.2	1,356.1	1,353.0	1,343.4	1,326.1	1,310.3	1,291.2	1,270.6	1,248.9	-0.74	-7.15
Japan	2,774.7	2,709.8	2,663.1	2,629.0	2,615.2	2,619.8	2,617.5	2,593.5	2,552.4	2,495.0	2,420.5	-1.36	-12.77
Jordan	349.7	351.7	354.8	359.0	363.9	368.9	373.4	376.9	379.0	379.8	379.2	0.81	8.45
Kazakhstan	558.8	585.2	616.4	650.4	684.6	715.6	740.4	757.1	765.1	765.6	760.8	3.13	36.15
Kuwait	93.3	95.1	97.1	99.3	101.5	103.5	105.2	106.4	107.1	107.3	107.2	1.40	14.89
Latvia	48.5	49.0	49.7	50.7	51.7	52.5	53.8	54.6	55.3	56.0	56.4	1.53	16.38
Lithuania	77.1	74.7	73.4	73.0	73.5	73.9	74.2	74.6	75.0	75.5	76.0	-0.15	-1.50
Malaysia	1,442.2	1,454.7	1,465.3	1,474.4	1,479.8	1,474.5	1,459.1	1,443.6	1,427.8	1,422.4	1,426.1	-0.11	-1.12
Mexico	5,086.7	5,078.0	5,064.3	5,038.4	5,003.4	4,962.5	4,918.8	4,874.1	4,828.6	4,781.9	4,733.5	-0.72	-6.94
Morocco	1,445.1	1,443.5	1,448.9	1,460.7	1,477.3	1,496.0	1,514.3	1,530.3	1,543.2	1,552.6	1,558.5	0.76	7.85
Netherlands	492.0	487.1	476.2	466.3	456.1	445.7	437.6	432.4	428.0	424.9	422.9	-1.50	-14.06
New Zealand	140.9	140.2	140.9	143.7	147.7	151.0	154.3	156.4	157.0	156.1	155.0	0.96	9.98
Nigeria	10,629.2	10,853.8	11,079.8	11,304.2	11,521.2	11,723.6	11,904.9	12,061.3	12,191.7	12,296.8	12,379.4	1.54	16.47
Norway	146.3	146.4	146.4	147.9	149.6	151.6	153.5	155.2	156.2	157.3	157.8	0.76	7.87
Pakistan	10,682.0	10,828.4	10,983.2	11,145.1	11,312.9	11,485.1	11,660.4	11,837.4	12,012.5	12,178.2	12,325.1	1.44	15.38
Peru	1,436.1	1,437.4	1,438.9	1,440.4	1,441.2	1,440.8	1,438.4	1,433.9	1,427.3	1,419.2	1,410.3	-0.18	-1.80
Philippines	5,038.8	5,076.9	5,120.4	5,170.6	5,224.3	5,278.1	5,327.0	5,368.2	5,400.9	5,426.5	5,447.9	0.78	8.12
Poland	882.8	867.9	859.5	858.4	864.0	872.6	880.8	886.9	894.7	903.2	911.3	0.32	3.23
Portugal	272.1	269.9	269.1	268.0	266.3	265.0	264.7	264.0	262.6	260.3	257.5	-0.55	-5.38
Romania	520.1	511.4	511.4	514.4	519.5	523.5	524.8	522.7	519.2	514.6	509.3	-0.21	-2.08
Russia	3,246.9	3,368.5	3,454.1	3,548.4	3,660.3	3,784.8	3,914.9	4,028.3	4,137.3	4,196.6	4,211.4	2.64	29.71
Saudi Arabia	1,385.2	1,396.2	1,404.1	1,408.8	1,411.3	1,413.5	1,417.1	1,423.1	1,431.6	1,442.0	1,453.2	0.48	4.91
Singapore	135.9	133.6	129.7	127.9	126.3	125.5	125.3	125.5	125.9	126.3	127.0	-0.68	-6.58
Slovakia	127.9	126.5	126.5	128.1	129.7	130.8	131.0	130.9	130.9	131.0	131.0	0.24	2.45
Slovenia	44.0	44.5	44.7	45.1	45.6	46.3	46.6	47.1	47.6	48.1	48.5	0.98	10.20
South Africa	2,553.9	2,563.6	2,566.1	2,561.8	2,552.5	2,541.5	2,531.8	2,525.0	2,521.0	2,518.5	2,515.4	-0.15	-1.51
South Korea	1,287.9	1,207.0	1,135.3	1,096.3	1,074.0	1,056.5	1,049.3	1,043.8	1,033.4	1,020.1	1,005.5	-2.45	-21.93
Spain	1,087.3	1,117.2	1,141.4	1,166.6	1,194.0	1,213.0	1,230.0	1,245.4	1,251.5	1,254.6	1,254.8	1.44	15.41
Sweden	236.7	242.8	248.4	253.5	256.6	258.4	259.6	260.7	261.9	263.1	264.3	1.11	11.68
Switzerland	182.9	181.4	181.1	181.4	181.4	181.5	181.0	180.8	180.5	180.7	181.5	-0.07	-0.74
Taiwan	630.6	599.1	552.2	527.4	507.1	496.2	490.2	487.3	484.9	482.7	479.6	-2.70	-23.94
Thailand	2,059.4	2,045.3	2,047.3	2,047.9	2,051.1	2,039.8	2,030.8	2,024.1	2,011.7	1,990.2	1,960.5	-0.49	-4.80
Tunisia	369.3	369.0	370.2	372.8	376.3	380.4	384.7	389.1	393.3	397.1	400.1	0.81	8.35
Turkey	3,353.8	3,281.9	3,218.6	3,183.6	3,162.7	3,152.1	3,148.4	3,128.4	3,121.3	3,119.7	3,123.6	-0.71	-6.86
Turkmenistan	242.7	246.4	249.5	251.5	252.5	252.9	253.2	253.5	254.0	254.5	255.0	0.50	5.07
Ukraine	934.2	949.9	967.7	1,007.4	1,039.1	1,058.5	1,066.5	1,071.4	1,054.2	1,033.0	1,007.4	0.76	7.84
United Arab Emirates	149.4	153.8	156.6	157.9	158.2	158.1	158.2	158.9	160.3	161.9	163.4	0.90	9.42
United Kingdom	1,659.5	1,666.7	1,687.8	1,722.2	1,767.8	1,814.8	1,857.1	1,883.8	1,904.4	1,915.0	1,918.8	1.46	15.63
USA	9,961.1	10,085.8	10,150.3	10,292.6	10,438.9	10,548.9	10,640.5	10,655.8	10,608.8	10,551.7	10,509.9	0.54	5.51
Venezuela	1,388.5	1,397.2	1,405.6	1,413.5	1,420.7	1,426.9	1,432.0	1,435.8	1,438.4	1,439.8	1,440.0	0.36	3.71
Vietnam	3,809.2	3,843.4	3,859.9	3,864.5	3,860.7	3,855.4	3,853.3	3,854.8	3,856.7	3,857.3	3,853.8	0.12	1.17

Key population trends

Table 4.46 Female Population Aged 10-14: 2009-2019

'000

	2009	2010	2011	2012	2013	2014	2015	2016	2017	2018	2019	CAGR	Period growth
Algeria	1,510.5	1,472.5	1,453.5	1,453.1	1,468.1	1,493.0	1,522.8	1,554.2	1,585.4	1,615.4	1,643.4	0.85	8.80
Argentina	1,693.8	1,684.4	1,673.4	1,662.0	1,652.0	1,645.1	1,642.8	1,645.6	1,652.7	1,662.7	1,674.0	-0.12	-1.17
Australia	683.9	683.0	683.5	683.1	684.1	685.5	687.8	696.1	708.0	724.4	743.5	0.84	8.71
Austria	225.2	219.5	215.3	209.3	207.0	205.4	206.2	206.2	207.3	206.3	205.9	-0.89	-8.56
Azerbaijan	342.3	324.4	310.3	300.6	295.5	295.1	298.8	306.2	316.5	328.2	340.0	-0.07	-0.68
Belarus	233.7	226.2	223.7	222.3	222.3	220.6	219.2	218.2	221.3	229.0	238.9	0.22	2.21
Belgium	293.9	293.5	293.7	292.8	290.9	290.7	291.9	293.3	296.3	301.1	305.7	0.40	4.03
Bolivia	555.2	558.7	562.9	567.7	572.8	577.5	581.4	584.1	585.7	586.5	586.6	0.55	5.64
Bosnia-Herzegovina	108.0	107.0	104.9	101.8	98.1	94.3	90.9	88.4	86.6	85.6	85.0	-2.37	-21.31
Brazil	8,357.6	8,430.0	8,502.3	8,556.8	8,577.3	8,550.0	8,470.6	8,343.9	8,181.8	7,995.5	7,793.5	-0.70	-6.75
Bulgaria	156.9	154.0	153.6	153.8	156.7	159.0	158.5	158.4	158.0	158.3	157.8	0.05	0.54
Canada	972.5	955.1	932.5	914.0	901.4	895.5	890.7	894.5	904.9	917.1	928.5	-0.46	-4.52
Chile	670.5	654.3	640.0	628.1	618.9	612.4	608.3	606.5	606.6	608.2	610.5	-0.93	-8.95
China	38,460.5	36,772.8	35,530.0	34,771.8	33,763.4	33,959.8	33,645.8	33,252.1	33,027.8	33,374.8	33,381.0	-1.41	-13.21
Colombia	2,159.4	2,156.8	2,154.6	2,153.4	2,153.6	2,155.7	2,159.7	2,165.2	2,171.6	2,177.8	2,182.5	0.11	1.07
Costa Rica	200.6	199.3	198.4	197.5	196.6	195.3	193.5	191.3	188.9	186.7	185.0	-0.80	-7.75
Croatia	124.2	122.6	120.0	115.0	109.8	105.5	102.3	101.2	101.7	102.9	104.3	-1.73	-16.01
Czech Republic	233.4	225.3	222.6	223.6	225.3	227.8	232.4	239.5	245.4	250.4	254.9	0.88	9.20
Denmark	170.5	168.1	166.4	165.1	163.1	162.2	161.4	160.2	160.1	160.3	160.3	-0.61	-5.97
Ecuador	698.6	700.8	701.3	700.3	697.7	693.9	689.3	684.2	678.8	673.5	668.4	-0.44	-4.31
Egypt	3,752.1	3,838.3	3,932.4	4,035.2	4,146.1	4,262.2	4,380.5	4,498.3	4,601.9	4,692.8	4,770.8	2.43	27.15
Estonia	30.4	29.7	29.6	29.4	29.9	30.6	31.4	32.1	33.0	33.8	34.6	1.33	14.08
Finland	151.7	148.2	145.1	143.2	141.3	141.6	141.8	142.9	144.6	146.3	147.4	-0.29	-2.86
France	1,806.2	1,825.0	1,850.9	1,872.9	1,895.0	1,911.0	1,918.1	1,914.9	1,924.3	1,934.3	1,950.4	0.77	7.98
Germany	1,935.7	1,925.3	1,920.9	1,889.4	1,843.7	1,804.5	1,773.3	1,732.4	1,702.1	1,684.2	1,671.7	-1.46	-13.64
Greece	261.8	258.7	256.7	254.7	255.1	258.1	261.2	264.2	268.1	270.7	273.0	0.42	4.28
Hong Kong, China	186.1	176.6	167.7	156.2	150.1	146.3	144.8	146.1	154.3	160.0	166.8	-1.09	-10.39
Hungary	255.6	246.6	241.1	237.4	236.8	235.8	236.5	236.0	237.6	238.8	240.9	-0.59	-5.74
India	57,483.5	57,570.1	57,677.5	57,800.2	57,915.9	57,995.1	58,013.3	57,960.5	57,844.3	57,686.3	57,514.6	0.01	0.05
Indonesia	10,050.0	10,070.6	10,107.3	10,155.1	10,204.2	10,242.8	10,261.3	10,254.7	10,222.6	10,168.6	10,098.1	0.05	0.48
Iran	2,733.5	2,618.0	2,569.7	2,584.6	2,647.5	2,737.9	2,837.5	2,935.1	3,025.0	3,103.3	3,167.9	1.49	15.89
Ireland	138.4	141.5	143.6	145.4	148.1	151.3	154.0	156.4	158.7	159.2	158.5	1.36	14.48
Israel	315.8	322.9	329.5	336.0	343.0	349.0	353.3	356.4	358.2	357.3	355.2	1.18	12.49
Italy	1,329.1	1,331.3	1,340.9	1,346.6	1,354.0	1,363.1	1,373.4	1,373.4	1,374.4	1,371.4	1,361.8	0.24	2.46
Japan	2,906.0	2,889.4	2,875.3	2,851.7	2,811.2	2,766.6	2,704.0	2,658.8	2,625.5	2,612.3	2,617.2	-1.04	-9.94
Jordan	342.8	345.0	345.7	345.5	345.2	345.8	348.0	351.8	357.0	362.8	368.3	0.72	7.45
Kazakhstan	554.5	538.8	532.4	535.7	548.5	569.6	597.3	629.7	664.7	698.9	729.0	2.77	31.47
Kuwait	85.7	87.6	89.3	90.8	92.4	94.1	96.0	98.0	100.2	102.4	104.3	1.98	21.70
Latvia	48.2	46.2	45.9	46.1	46.9	48.1	48.6	49.2	50.2	51.3	52.2	0.79	8.23
Lithuania	92.4	89.6	86.3	82.8	79.4	76.7	74.3	73.1	72.6	73.2	73.5	-2.26	-20.46
Malaysia	1,353.4	1,378.2	1,400.0	1,419.9	1,432.5	1,444.2	1,455.1	1,463.9	1,471.6	1,475.5	1,468.6	0.82	8.51
Mexico	5,193.2	5,167.5	5,147.7	5,127.7	5,108.2	5,087.7	5,064.5	5,037.2	5,005.6	4,970.4	4,932.8	-0.51	-5.01
Morocco	1,509.5	1,490.4	1,472.5	1,457.1	1,445.5	1,439.4	1,439.6	1,446.3	1,458.7	1,474.9	1,492.6	-0.11	-1.12
Netherlands	477.6	478.1	484.1	489.0	491.1	490.1	485.4	474.5	464.5	454.3	443.8	-0.73	-7.08
New Zealand	145.3	144.6	144.0	143.0	142.1	142.6	141.9	142.6	145.4	149.4	152.7	0.50	5.14
Nigeria	9,278.7	9,480.4	9,687.8	9,900.9	10,119.5	10,342.9	10,569.7	10,797.5	11,022.6	11,239.3	11,440.8	2.12	23.30
Norway	153.1	153.6	153.9	152.7	151.6	151.5	151.3	151.0	152.4	154.0	155.9	0.18	1.81
Pakistan	10,040.9	10,131.7	10,235.7	10,352.3	10,480.2	10,617.9	10,764.1	10,918.4	11,080.9	11,251.1	11,427.5	1.30	13.81
Peru	1,435.4	1,435.1	1,435.0	1,435.1	1,435.6	1,436.5	1,437.6	1,438.9	1,440.0	1,440.1	1,438.8	0.02	0.24
Philippines	4,940.8	4,966.2	4,986.5	5,006.1	5,028.5	5,058.0	5,096.5	5,144.4	5,199.8	5,258.6	5,315.7	0.73	7.59
Poland	1,035.6	992.6	960.3	928.3	900.2	878.6	864.2	856.3	855.2	860.6	869.1	-1.74	-16.08
Portugal	263.4	267.5	269.0	270.8	273.7	275.9	273.6	272.8	271.6	269.9	268.6	0.20	1.97
Romania	543.8	539.5	538.7	534.7	528.1	519.1	513.3	510.1	512.8	517.8	521.6	-0.42	-4.09
Russia	3,309.8	3,220.2	3,164.1	3,148.4	3,202.4	3,283.4	3,402.9	3,490.6	3,585.0	3,698.3	3,824.2	1.46	15.54
Saudi Arabia	1,328.7	1,336.2	1,345.7	1,357.0	1,368.8	1,379.9	1,388.8	1,395.2	1,399.4	1,402.4	1,405.7	0.57	5.80
Singapore	153.2	151.4	149.6	146.1	142.4	139.6	137.0	132.8	130.7	128.8	127.9	-1.79	-16.52
Slovakia	146.9	141.8	138.4	133.8	130.3	127.9	126.5	126.4	128.0	129.5	130.6	-1.17	-11.06
Slovenia	46.6	45.6	45.4	44.9	44.7	44.5	45.0	45.1	45.6	46.1	46.9	0.05	0.54
South Africa	2,478.9	2,486.4	2,496.8	2,508.8	2,520.5	2,529.9	2,535.3	2,536.1	2,532.7	2,526.9	2,520.9	0.17	1.70
South Korea	1,550.9	1,517.3	1,474.4	1,408.4	1,336.7	1,270.6	1,190.8	1,120.2	1,081.7	1,059.8	1,042.5	-3.89	-32.78
Spain	1,012.5	1,022.9	1,041.3	1,067.5	1,092.8	1,125.3	1,154.2	1,178.3	1,203.7	1,231.3	1,250.3	2.13	23.49
Sweden	251.1	240.5	235.4	233.9	237.3	242.6	248.7	254.1	259.3	262.2	263.9	0.50	5.13
Switzerland	202.3	199.6	196.1	191.9	188.8	185.9	184.4	184.0	184.2	184.1	184.2	-0.93	-8.95
Taiwan	748.2	728.3	718.0	686.4	648.7	628.2	596.8	549.9	525.0	504.6	493.6	-4.07	-34.02
Thailand	2,397.6	2,330.0	2,232.7	2,145.3	2,093.2	2,087.1	2,072.6	2,075.6	2,075.8	2,079.1	2,066.9	-1.47	-13.80
Tunisia	404.4	392.6	383.1	376.2	371.7	369.4	369.0	370.1	372.5	375.9	380.0	-0.62	-6.05
Turkey	3,494.4	3,510.6	3,510.5	3,476.2	3,424.4	3,364.5	3,301.2	3,244.1	3,210.4	3,189.2	3,171.2	-0.97	-9.25
Turkmenistan	244.9	239.0	236.2	236.3	238.5	241.7	244.8	247.2	248.9	249.9	250.5	0.23	2.31
Ukraine	1,111.1	1,054.9	1,005.5	959.0	935.6	928.7	942.7	958.2	995.3	1,025.7	1,045.2	-0.61	-5.93
United Arab Emirates	128.8	134.1	139.8	145.4	150.7	155.1	158.5	160.6	161.7	162.2	162.6	2.36	26.21
United Kingdom	1,776.8	1,749.5	1,717.9	1,682.8	1,655.0	1,646.0	1,654.8	1,678.3	1,714.6	1,761.1	1,808.3	0.18	1.77
USA	9,739.9	9,720.2	9,808.3	9,908.8	10,038.2	10,194.0	10,326.8	10,402.3	10,554.6	10,709.9	10,827.9	1.06	11.17
Venezuela	1,350.4	1,356.2	1,363.0	1,370.8	1,379.2	1,388.0	1,396.6	1,405.0	1,412.9	1,420.0	1,426.2	0.55	5.61
Vietnam	3,846.4	3,743.7	3,700.9	3,709.4	3,751.8	3,801.2	3,837.9	3,856.8	3,863.6	3,861.5	3,857.3	0.03	0.28

Key population trends

Table 4.47 Female Population Aged 15-19: 2009-2019

'000

	2009	2010	2011	2012	2013	2014	2015	2016	2017	2018	2019	CAGR	Period growth
Algeria	1,768.2	1,727.5	1,674.7	1,613.6	1,551.8	1,498.2	1,460.2	1,441.2	1,440.9	1,456.0	1,481.2	-1.76	-16.23
Argentina	1,701.2	1,705.7	1,707.2	1,705.7	1,701.4	1,694.4	1,685.2	1,674.4	1,663.0	1,652.9	1,645.3	-0.33	-3.29
Australia	721.2	724.2	722.6	722.0	720.6	720.6	720.4	722.2	722.7	724.1	725.6	0.06	0.60
Austria	247.3	247.1	245.3	242.7	238.8	233.2	227.5	223.2	217.0	214.5	212.7	-1.50	-13.99
Azerbaijan	434.3	420.6	402.9	382.1	360.4	339.8	322.0	308.1	298.7	293.9	293.6	-3.84	-32.40
Belarus	324.7	302.7	282.3	264.2	246.4	235.2	227.4	224.6	223.2	223.0	221.6	-3.75	-31.74
Belgium	318.4	315.1	310.3	305.4	301.1	298.1	297.8	298.0	297.1	295.1	294.9	-0.76	-7.38
Bolivia	518.8	527.4	533.8	538.3	541.6	544.6	548.0	552.2	557.1	562.3	567.1	0.89	9.31
Bosnia-Herzegovina	119.0	113.7	110.4	109.0	108.7	108.5	107.6	105.5	102.3	98.5	94.6	-2.27	-20.53
Brazil	8,224.6	8,178.5	8,182.8	8,217.5	8,268.0	8,330.9	8,406.8	8,482.0	8,538.8	8,561.1	8,534.3	0.37	3.77
Bulgaria	214.0	200.2	185.7	175.1	163.1	154.3	151.1	150.4	150.4	153.0	155.1	-3.17	-27.51
Canada	1,080.8	1,071.9	1,060.7	1,042.3	1,023.9	1,004.7	984.7	960.8	941.5	928.7	922.9	-1.57	-14.61
Chile	735.9	729.7	719.1	704.8	688.2	671.1	654.9	640.6	628.8	619.6	613.1	-1.81	-16.68
China	45,044.0	41,265.3	39,339.5	37,458.0	35,947.4	34,463.3	33,236.6	32,397.5	31,963.0	31,277.2	31,689.0	-3.46	-29.65
Colombia	2,129.7	2,141.2	2,148.3	2,151.4	2,151.4	2,149.6	2,147.3	2,145.3	2,144.2	2,144.3	2,146.3	0.08	0.78
Costa Rica	212.5	210.2	208.1	206.0	204.2	202.7	201.5	200.5	199.6	198.8	197.6	-0.72	-7.02
Croatia	127.0	125.5	124.2	123.8	125.2	124.7	123.1	120.5	115.5	110.3	106.0	-1.79	-16.53
Czech Republic	310.8	301.0	284.6	266.3	251.2	236.0	227.4	224.4	225.4	227.3	229.9	-2.97	-26.00
Denmark	167.1	170.6	173.0	173.9	173.3	172.2	169.9	168.2	166.9	165.0	164.1	-0.18	-1.75
Ecuador	656.9	660.9	666.4	672.9	679.5	685.1	688.8	690.3	689.5	686.9	683.1	0.39	3.99
Egypt	3,626.2	3,581.4	3,564.7	3,576.1	3,619.2	3,690.0	3,777.5	3,873.5	3,979.0	4,093.4	4,213.6	1.51	16.20
Estonia	43.5	39.6	36.2	33.8	31.3	30.1	29.4	29.3	29.1	29.6	30.3	-3.55	-30.32
Finland	163.2	164.0	162.7	160.2	156.8	153.0	149.3	146.2	144.3	142.4	142.6	-1.34	-12.63
France	1,881.2	1,850.2	1,830.2	1,817.0	1,806.3	1,818.5	1,837.5	1,863.9	1,886.0	1,908.3	1,924.4	0.23	2.30
Germany	2,183.7	2,098.4	2,005.4	1,967.1	1,953.2	1,938.9	1,931.8	1,929.8	1,899.7	1,855.1	1,816.5	-1.82	-16.82
Greece	278.6	278.6	275.9	273.7	271.6	268.4	265.4	263.4	261.5	261.9	264.8	-0.51	-4.95
Hong Kong, China	213.5	211.9	210.8	209.1	202.9	194.4	184.7	175.6	164.3	158.6	155.1	-3.15	-27.35
Hungary	299.3	295.0	287.8	277.7	267.1	257.9	248.8	243.1	239.4	238.8	237.7	-2.28	-20.59
India	55,938.7	56,378.5	56,688.6	56,883.2	56,998.5	57,081.3	57,170.7	57,284.9	57,418.9	57,549.5	57,644.8	0.30	3.05
Indonesia	10,081.5	10,057.3	10,034.0	10,014.1	10,002.5	10,004.9	10,025.0	10,062.5	10,112.4	10,164.5	10,206.4	0.12	1.24
Iran	3,767.6	3,521.7	3,274.5	3,039.4	2,833.4	2,674.4	2,575.1	2,540.2	2,564.5	2,633.9	2,728.9	-3.17	-27.57
Ireland	138.3	136.3	134.3	133.3	134.4	136.9	139.8	141.8	143.7	146.4	149.6	0.79	8.19
Israel	291.0	295.3	300.5	305.8	312.0	319.1	326.2	333.0	339.6	346.7	352.8	1.95	21.26
Italy	1,422.0	1,409.1	1,389.0	1,373.1	1,355.0	1,348.1	1,350.3	1,360.1	1,365.8	1,373.3	1,382.4	-0.28	-2.78
Japan	2,963.5	2,944.1	2,931.0	2,921.7	2,924.4	2,911.3	2,897.3	2,885.0	2,862.5	2,822.8	2,778.9	-0.64	-6.23
Jordan	325.1	329.9	333.2	335.2	336.2	336.8	337.5	338.2	339.2	340.7	342.9	0.54	5.49
Kazakhstan	708.4	679.2	647.4	615.0	585.2	561.4	546.0	540.1	544.1	557.3	578.6	-2.00	-18.32
Kuwait	79.5	80.7	82.2	83.9	85.8	87.6	89.4	91.1	92.6	94.2	95.9	1.90	20.72
Latvia	76.6	70.7	63.9	57.4	51.5	47.7	45.7	45.3	45.6	46.4	47.7	-4.63	-37.77
Lithuania	124.2	118.4	111.4	104.4	96.6	91.5	88.7	85.4	82.0	78.6	76.0	-4.79	-38.77
Malaysia	1,277.1	1,288.3	1,301.5	1,317.2	1,335.9	1,356.8	1,381.1	1,402.4	1,421.8	1,433.7	1,445.1	1.24	13.15
Mexico	5,175.0	5,213.2	5,232.5	5,227.4	5,205.3	5,175.2	5,144.5	5,117.1	5,093.7	5,073.2	5,053.8	-0.24	-2.34
Morocco	1,586.8	1,569.6	1,551.4	1,532.6	1,513.5	1,494.5	1,476.1	1,458.7	1,443.5	1,432.1	1,425.9	-1.06	-10.14
Netherlands	492.6	493.4	488.2	482.1	479.2	479.5	480.2	486.4	491.5	493.6	492.5	0.00	-0.02
New Zealand	157.8	156.5	154.0	152.1	150.4	148.7	148.1	147.5	146.5	145.6	146.1	-0.76	-7.39
Nigeria	8,168.5	8,336.0	8,510.2	8,691.4	8,879.6	9,074.4	9,275.3	9,481.7	9,693.6	9,910.8	10,132.9	2.18	24.05
Norway	155.3	156.7	157.0	157.8	158.4	158.4	158.6	158.7	157.4	156.2	156.1	0.06	0.56
Pakistan	9,645.7	9,690.6	9,740.6	9,800.5	9,872.2	9,955.8	10,050.5	10,156.3	10,273.9	10,402.9	10,542.2	0.89	9.29
Peru	1,415.7	1,420.8	1,424.2	1,426.3	1,427.3	1,427.7	1,427.8	1,427.9	1,428.1	1,428.6	1,429.4	0.10	0.97
Philippines	4,744.3	4,800.8	4,846.5	4,884.1	4,914.7	4,941.3	4,965.5	4,988.5	5,012.5	5,040.3	5,074.7	0.68	6.96
Poland	1,280.6	1,236.1	1,181.3	1,127.5	1,078.2	1,031.6	989.1	957.2	925.3	897.0	875.4	-3.73	-31.64
Portugal	281.2	276.9	273.4	270.2	267.9	267.0	271.0	272.5	274.3	277.3	279.5	-0.06	-0.62
Romania	671.3	617.0	581.9	563.3	547.0	542.0	537.3	536.2	532.0	525.4	516.4	-2.59	-23.07
Russia	4,539.7	4,168.4	3,839.5	3,595.9	3,407.3	3,343.9	3,252.6	3,199.2	3,184.4	3,239.8	3,321.6	-3.08	-26.83
Saudi Arabia	1,271.2	1,288.3	1,299.7	1,306.5	1,310.8	1,314.9	1,320.9	1,329.6	1,340.7	1,353.0	1,364.5	0.71	7.34
Singapore	164.1	164.8	163.7	162.4	160.9	157.5	155.4	153.4	149.5	145.4	142.2	-1.42	-13.30
Slovakia	186.0	179.7	171.3	162.5	154.4	146.8	141.7	138.2	133.6	130.0	127.5	-3.71	-31.46
Slovenia	53.0	51.6	50.1	48.8	48.1	47.2	46.1	45.9	45.3	45.2	45.1	-1.62	-15.06
South Africa	2,501.0	2,490.7	2,479.1	2,467.7	2,458.5	2,453.4	2,453.8	2,459.6	2,469.5	2,481.4	2,492.5	-0.03	-0.34
South Korea	1,569.3	1,594.4	1,601.1	1,589.3	1,562.5	1,525.7	1,492.8	1,450.6	1,385.7	1,315.2	1,250.3	-2.25	-20.33
Spain	1,088.1	1,077.3	1,065.8	1,056.7	1,051.5	1,051.9	1,061.4	1,079.7	1,105.8	1,130.9	1,163.3	0.67	6.92
Sweden	311.0	308.9	298.6	285.6	271.3	258.6	247.9	242.6	240.9	244.1	249.2	-2.19	-19.85
Switzerland	220.8	219.7	217.1	214.6	210.8	208.2	205.4	201.7	197.4	194.1	191.1	-1.43	-13.44
Taiwan	768.6	773.9	770.1	772.8	774.3	744.9	725.1	714.6	682.9	645.1	624.6	-2.05	-18.74
Thailand	2,470.3	2,488.6	2,506.8	2,511.3	2,485.6	2,432.3	2,362.8	2,263.9	2,173.7	2,120.1	2,113.3	-1.55	-14.45
Tunisia	477.3	463.3	448.1	432.6	417.3	403.4	391.6	382.1	375.2	370.7	368.4	-2.55	-22.80
Turkey	3,241.2	3,307.8	3,370.5	3,428.2	3,476.2	3,510.5	3,526.4	3,527.4	3,491.5	3,437.3	3,377.1	0.41	4.19
Turkmenistan	282.7	277.8	270.3	261.1	251.5	243.1	237.3	234.5	234.7	236.9	240.1	-1.62	-15.08
Ukraine	1,476.1	1,389.4	1,309.5	1,236.2	1,166.3	1,107.5	1,051.3	1,001.4	954.6	930.7	923.4	-4.58	-37.44
United Arab Emirates	114.3	115.7	118.5	122.6	127.6	133.2	139.1	145.1	150.9	156.2	160.6	3.46	40.48
United Kingdom	1,928.8	1,904.1	1,869.4	1,835.8	1,810.0	1,786.3	1,760.5	1,731.4	1,698.0	1,671.0	1,662.1	-1.48	-13.83
USA	10,468.1	10,350.9	10,238.6	10,124.2	10,037.1	9,985.7	9,974.0	10,071.5	10,178.6	10,313.8	10,475.8	0.01	0.07
Venezuela	1,340.3	1,339.9	1,340.3	1,341.9	1,345.0	1,349.5	1,355.2	1,362.1	1,369.9	1,378.4	1,387.2	0.34	3.50
Vietnam	4,506.3	4,433.1	4,313.1	4,153.7	3,981.5	3,832.6	3,732.5	3,692.1	3,702.7	3,746.9	3,797.5	-1.70	-15.73

Key population trends

Table 4.48 Female Population Aged 20-24: 2009-2019

'000

	2009	2010	2011	2012	2013	2014	2015	2016	2017	2018	2019	CAGR	Period growth
Algeria	1,825.2	1,819.5	1,811.4	1,799.7	1,781.1	1,752.3	1,711.1	1,658.1	1,597.0	1,535.4	1,482.2	-2.06	-18.79
Argentina	1,641.0	1,656.2	1,670.5	1,683.2	1,693.7	1,701.5	1,706.2	1,707.9	1,706.5	1,702.0	1,695.1	0.32	3.29
Australia	755.9	762.2	769.0	777.4	785.5	790.3	794.0	793.7	794.0	793.0	793.1	0.48	4.92
Austria	255.1	254.5	255.6	257.8	259.9	261.7	261.3	259.4	256.5	252.2	246.4	-0.35	-3.41
Azerbaijan	434.3	441.5	445.0	444.4	439.6	430.2	416.6	399.1	378.8	357.3	336.8	-2.51	-22.45
Belarus	407.7	400.4	388.5	367.5	349.7	326.3	303.9	283.0	265.0	247.0	236.0	-5.32	-42.12
Belgium	315.4	317.8	322.4	326.5	329.7	329.6	326.2	321.4	316.5	312.3	309.2	-0.20	-1.94
Bolivia	446.7	458.3	470.5	482.8	494.5	504.9	513.4	519.8	524.3	527.7	530.8	1.74	18.82
Bosnia-Herzegovina	149.5	146.0	140.5	133.5	126.0	119.2	114.0	110.8	109.3	109.0	108.7	-3.14	-27.31
Brazil	8,775.6	8,642.6	8,516.0	8,388.5	8,277.2	8,191.1	8,149.0	8,156.5	8,193.7	8,245.9	8,309.3	-0.54	-5.31
Bulgaria	249.6	246.0	240.7	230.6	219.2	206.3	192.0	177.3	166.3	154.5	145.8	-5.23	-41.58
Canada	1,117.1	1,129.5	1,139.9	1,150.9	1,157.9	1,154.3	1,142.4	1,129.7	1,110.1	1,090.6	1,070.6	-0.43	-4.17
Chile	710.9	721.7	730.3	736.2	738.7	737.0	730.8	720.2	705.9	689.4	672.3	-0.56	-5.42
China	50,335.3	54,738.2	55,007.2	53,510.6	51,608.4	48,280.7	44,156.0	42,410.0	40,697.6	39,314.2	38,040.1	-2.76	-24.43
Colombia	2,020.8	2,040.0	2,059.8	2,079.8	2,098.4	2,114.2	2,126.1	2,133.4	2,136.5	2,136.4	2,134.4	0.55	5.62
Costa Rica	216.4	218.1	218.6	217.9	216.4	214.4	212.1	209.9	207.9	206.2	204.8	-0.55	-5.34
Croatia	142.1	138.5	135.7	134.0	130.7	128.4	127.0	125.6	125.2	126.5	126.0	-1.20	-11.38
Czech Republic	331.4	327.9	325.5	323.5	319.2	313.3	302.8	285.9	267.7	252.9	238.0	-3.25	-28.17
Denmark	154.7	157.8	161.5	165.3	170.4	174.0	177.6	180.0	180.9	180.3	179.3	1.48	15.87
Ecuador	603.3	607.5	612.4	617.9	624.1	630.9	638.1	645.6	653.1	659.8	665.3	0.98	10.26
Egypt	3,599.6	3,613.1	3,602.3	3,568.0	3,507.0	3,433.6	3,372.8	3,342.7	3,343.5	3,379.4	3,445.9	-0.44	-4.27
Estonia	52.3	52.0	51.3	49.5	46.9	43.0	39.1	35.7	33.3	30.9	29.7	-5.49	-43.13
Finland	158.7	158.2	159.8	162.3	165.7	166.4	167.1	165.7	163.0	159.6	155.6	-0.20	-1.96
France	1,963.1	1,973.1	1,974.6	1,964.3	1,949.5	1,917.3	1,886.9	1,867.5	1,854.3	1,843.5	1,855.5	-0.56	-5.48
Germany	2,419.3	2,442.1	2,465.7	2,432.6	2,376.4	2,299.0	2,218.6	2,130.1	2,094.2	2,081.7	2,067.8	-1.56	-14.53
Greece	311.3	300.5	295.3	291.5	290.1	286.4	286.5	283.8	281.6	279.4	276.3	-1.19	-11.27
Hong Kong, China	276.9	280.3	281.5	283.0	281.8	277.8	276.6	275.7	275.1	270.4	263.0	-0.51	-5.02
Hungary	320.2	317.4	313.8	311.3	309.2	305.5	301.0	293.5	283.4	272.9	263.7	-1.92	-17.64
India	51,958.8	52,709.4	53,452.8	54,168.9	54,825.6	55,388.3	55,832.7	56,152.4	56,362.6	56,498.5	56,604.0	0.86	8.94
Indonesia	10,202.0	10,152.9	10,109.1	10,071.8	10,040.0	10,011.8	9,985.7	9,961.4	9,941.9	9,931.9	9,936.6	-0.26	-2.60
Iran	4,618.5	4,503.0	4,347.5	4,158.7	3,944.3	3,713.4	3,474.5	3,236.0	3,009.2	2,810.7	2,657.7	-5.38	-42.46
Ireland	158.0	153.8	150.7	147.8	144.7	142.2	140.1	138.2	137.3	138.4	141.0	-1.13	-10.76
Israel	282.8	284.2	285.6	287.9	291.1	294.3	298.4	303.6	308.9	315.0	322.1	1.31	13.91
Italy	1,465.6	1,454.9	1,453.2	1,459.6	1,469.5	1,460.6	1,448.0	1,428.1	1,412.3	1,394.3	1,387.4	-0.55	-5.33
Japan	3,370.9	3,279.0	3,196.3	3,123.0	3,057.8	3,021.8	3,007.1	2,997.4	2,990.7	2,995.2	2,983.8	-1.21	-11.48
Jordan	312.0	315.2	316.2	315.9	315.0	314.8	315.8	318.4	322.0	326.0	329.9	0.56	5.71
Kazakhstan	763.2	771.9	771.2	761.2	743.1	718.6	689.7	657.9	625.2	594.8	569.9	-2.88	-25.32
Kuwait	88.2	88.3	88.3	88.4	88.6	89.1	90.0	91.3	93.0	94.8	96.7	0.93	9.73
Latvia	90.7	89.4	88.3	85.1	81.2	75.7	69.9	63.1	56.7	50.9	47.2	-6.31	-47.91
Lithuania	133.2	131.5	129.9	127.3	125.3	121.4	115.6	108.8	102.0	94.5	89.7	-3.88	-32.67
Malaysia	1,237.3	1,248.0	1,256.2	1,261.7	1,270.2	1,278.3	1,288.0	1,300.0	1,315.0	1,333.6	1,355.1	0.91	9.52
Mexico	4,734.1	4,795.7	4,870.5	4,947.2	5,019.3	5,078.0	5,116.3	5,131.1	5,124.1	5,101.9	5,073.8	0.70	7.18
Morocco	1,620.5	1,611.4	1,600.0	1,587.1	1,573.1	1,558.0	1,541.7	1,524.3	1,506.2	1,487.4	1,468.7	-0.98	-9.37
Netherlands	486.7	491.2	497.7	502.1	505.1	507.4	508.3	502.9	496.4	493.1	493.1	0.13	1.32
New Zealand	147.3	149.3	152.0	154.3	155.4	155.4	154.1	151.7	149.9	148.2	146.5	-0.06	-0.55
Nigeria	7,205.3	7,347.1	7,492.0	7,641.5	7,796.5	7,957.4	8,124.6	8,298.0	8,477.7	8,663.9	8,856.4	2.08	22.92
Norway	144.3	149.8	155.7	160.4	163.4	165.0	165.7	165.6	166.1	166.6	166.6	1.44	15.39
Pakistan	8,826.2	9,055.7	9,232.3	9,358.7	9,445.4	9,508.3	9,562.4	9,618.0	9,680.7	9,753.9	9,838.8	1.09	11.47
Peru	1,329.9	1,346.8	1,362.1	1,375.4	1,386.4	1,395.2	1,401.8	1,406.5	1,409.4	1,411.0	1,411.9	0.60	6.17
Philippines	4,325.7	4,415.2	4,498.0	4,574.8	4,645.0	4,708.6	4,765.0	4,813.9	4,855.6	4,890.9	4,921.4	1.30	13.77
Poland	1,510.0	1,447.6	1,392.6	1,352.0	1,313.1	1,269.1	1,224.8	1,170.5	1,117.3	1,068.8	1,023.3	-3.82	-32.23
Portugal	308.0	298.9	294.4	291.1	288.9	285.7	281.4	277.8	274.6	272.3	271.4	-1.26	-11.89
Romania	836.2	842.5	821.5	772.4	720.1	663.1	607.5	571.2	551.4	534.7	529.4	-4.47	-36.69
Russia	6,213.9	6,050.0	5,839.3	5,475.2	5,040.6	4,576.5	4,203.4	3,879.0	3,637.9	3,452.8	3,392.0	-5.87	-45.41
Saudi Arabia	1,121.8	1,163.3	1,201.7	1,235.4	1,263.6	1,285.6	1,301.8	1,312.6	1,319.3	1,323.8	1,328.4	1.71	18.42
Singapore	152.6	157.2	165.3	174.5	177.5	176.5	176.7	174.9	172.8	170.5	166.3	0.87	9.02
Slovakia	209.5	204.5	199.5	195.3	190.9	185.8	179.5	170.9	162.1	154.0	146.3	-3.53	-30.18
Slovenia	64.2	62.6	61.0	59.3	56.5	53.9	52.4	50.8	49.5	48.8	48.0	-2.87	-25.27
South Africa	2,514.8	2,522.2	2,518.5	2,505.1	2,485.1	2,462.8	2,441.8	2,424.1	2,410.8	2,402.8	2,400.7	-0.46	-4.53
South Korea	1,498.3	1,471.7	1,469.1	1,488.6	1,517.8	1,548.2	1,573.1	1,579.8	1,568.2	1,541.8	1,505.5	0.05	0.48
Spain	1,281.3	1,245.1	1,217.0	1,195.7	1,178.6	1,164.6	1,152.6	1,140.9	1,131.7	1,126.5	1,126.7	-1.28	-12.07
Sweden	279.9	290.5	302.7	312.6	320.1	322.3	320.9	310.8	298.1	283.7	271.0	-0.32	-3.16
Switzerland	224.9	227.9	231.0	233.9	237.1	236.6	235.4	232.8	230.2	226.2	223.5	-0.06	-0.60
Taiwan	797.0	769.8	765.4	771.6	775.5	767.8	773.1	769.0	771.4	772.6	743.2	-0.70	-6.75
Thailand	2,371.2	2,368.1	2,390.6	2,434.1	2,470.8	2,493.3	2,512.0	2,531.8	2,535.9	2,509.5	2,453.8	0.34	3.49
Tunisia	511.9	510.2	505.6	497.9	487.6	475.2	461.1	446.0	430.4	415.2	401.3	-2.40	-21.60
Turkey	3,088.9	3,075.3	3,087.2	3,123.2	3,182.6	3,251.4	3,321.0	3,384.0	3,440.4	3,487.3	3,517.6	1.31	13.88
Turkmenistan	268.2	274.7	279.5	282.3	282.7	280.4	275.4	267.9	258.7	249.2	241.0	-1.06	-10.13
Ukraine	1,859.7	1,802.1	1,738.6	1,649.2	1,563.1	1,468.8	1,382.2	1,302.4	1,229.4	1,160.6	1,102.6	-5.09	-40.71
United Arab Emirates	138.9	134.1	130.3	127.8	126.9	127.4	129.4	132.6	137.0	142.2	147.9	0.63	6.45
United Kingdom	2,098.1	2,132.6	2,154.9	2,172.6	2,170.9	2,151.9	2,127.3	2,093.5	2,059.9	2,032.9	2,007.4	-0.44	-4.32
USA	10,323.9	10,462.1	10,569.9	10,662.5	10,702.1	10,676.2	10,561.2	10,454.0	10,342.2	10,256.7	10,205.9	-0.11	-1.14
Venezuela	1,309.6	1,323.9	1,333.3	1,338.2	1,339.7	1,339.5	1,339.1	1,339.6	1,341.3	1,344.4	1,348.9	0.30	3.00
Vietnam	4,362.3	4,429.3	4,478.3	4,509.8	4,515.8	4,486.3	4,416.3	4,299.2	4,142.4	3,972.1	3,824.3	-1.31	-12.33

Key population trends

Table 4.49 Female Population Aged 25-29: 2009-2019

'000

	2009	2010	2011	2012	2013	2014	2015	2016	2017	2018	2019	CAGR	Period growth
Algeria	1,747.5	1,780.5	1,802.0	1,812.7	1,815.0	1,811.8	1,805.7	1,797.3	1,785.6	1,767.2	1,738.7	-0.05	-0.50
Argentina	1,615.6	1,608.3	1,607.3	1,613.2	1,624.7	1,639.4	1,654.8	1,669.2	1,682.0	1,692.4	1,699.9	0.51	5.22
Australia	769.9	789.2	802.2	810.2	814.4	821.1	828.1	836.3	845.3	853.8	858.4	1.09	11.51
Austria	273.2	276.8	276.0	273.0	269.3	267.8	267.0	267.9	269.9	271.7	273.2	0.00	0.02
Azerbaijan	366.6	380.2	393.9	407.2	419.3	429.5	436.6	440.3	440.1	435.4	426.3	1.52	16.27
Belarus	384.2	394.8	402.6	411.6	413.7	408.3	400.5	388.1	367.2	349.1	326.1	-1.62	-15.11
Belgium	335.0	332.4	327.6	324.6	323.3	324.5	326.8	331.3	335.5	338.6	338.6	0.11	1.07
Bolivia	386.2	394.9	404.1	413.6	423.7	434.5	446.0	458.1	470.3	482.1	492.5	2.46	27.53
Bosnia-Herzegovina	145.8	147.5	149.3	150.6	151.0	149.7	146.3	140.9	133.9	126.2	119.3	-1.99	-18.17
Brazil	8,763.3	8,889.1	8,910.1	8,885.7	8,831.2	8,732.4	8,604.4	8,481.8	8,357.6	8,248.7	8,163.8	-0.71	-6.84
Bulgaria	262.1	255.8	251.4	248.3	244.1	240.2	235.7	229.4	218.6	207.0	194.2	-2.95	-25.91
Canada	1,163.2	1,174.1	1,180.2	1,182.7	1,181.2	1,183.8	1,194.4	1,204.6	1,216.1	1,223.8	1,220.4	0.48	4.92
Chile	633.0	650.9	668.2	684.4	699.1	712.0	722.8	731.4	737.3	739.8	738.1	1.55	16.61
China	42,082.1	42,136.6	43,730.9	45,802.6	49,053.9	52,992.1	57,676.2	57,869.2	56,279.1	54,325.3	50,945.7	1.93	21.06
Colombia	1,916.6	1,933.3	1,949.6	1,966.2	1,983.6	2,002.0	2,021.5	2,041.6	2,061.5	2,080.0	2,095.6	0.90	9.34
Costa Rica	197.1	202.0	206.6	211.0	214.7	217.5	219.1	219.6	219.0	217.6	215.6	0.90	9.40
Croatia	154.9	154.0	152.4	149.9	147.0	144.2	140.6	137.7	136.0	132.7	130.4	-1.70	-15.79
Czech Republic	369.6	354.4	347.2	342.1	336.2	334.1	329.8	326.9	324.9	320.8	315.4	-1.58	-14.68
Denmark	156.9	154.1	152.8	153.7	154.9	158.0	162.0	165.9	169.8	174.6	178.1	1.27	13.49
Ecuador	546.1	551.7	558.0	565.0	572.4	579.8	586.9	593.6	600.0	606.5	613.2	1.16	12.27
Egypt	3,203.4	3,264.7	3,316.5	3,360.1	3,398.0	3,424.3	3,428.8	3,405.8	3,356.2	3,276.5	3,182.7	-0.06	-0.65
Estonia	49.1	50.3	50.9	51.1	51.6	51.7	51.4	50.6	48.9	46.4	42.5	-1.42	-13.29
Finland	165.4	166.9	167.3	166.3	163.7	162.5	161.9	163.4	165.9	169.1	169.6	0.25	2.51
France	1,999.7	2,002.8	1,988.4	1,983.7	1,981.1	2,000.3	2,010.8	2,013.0	2,002.9	1,987.8	1,955.5	-0.22	-2.21
Germany	2,475.3	2,480.7	2,463.7	2,466.6	2,476.9	2,510.3	2,535.9	2,563.1	2,532.9	2,479.1	2,403.3	-0.29	-2.91
Greece	385.5	376.4	359.7	346.7	331.5	321.2	310.4	305.2	301.5	300.0	296.3	-2.60	-23.14
Hong Kong, China	315.9	328.9	339.0	349.0	357.5	366.1	369.6	371.1	369.2	365.5	359.8	1.31	13.91
Hungary	357.4	346.1	340.2	335.2	331.1	328.2	325.2	321.3	318.7	316.6	312.8	-1.32	-12.48
India	47,565.2	48,355.9	49,126.6	49,882.2	50,630.7	51,379.9	52,132.1	52,881.5	53,609.5	54,283.0	54,865.2	1.44	15.35
Indonesia	10,198.8	10,235.9	10,241.5	10,219.0	10,176.4	10,124.3	10,072.1	10,025.2	9,985.1	9,951.3	9,921.9	-0.27	-2.72
Iran	4,362.1	4,546.7	4,660.1	4,700.6	4,674.4	4,593.4	4,469.7	4,312.1	4,126.0	3,916.9	3,691.3	-1.66	-15.38
Ireland	200.2	197.3	191.6	186.5	180.5	175.4	171.1	168.0	165.2	162.2	159.7	-2.24	-20.24
Israel	275.5	278.2	281.3	283.8	285.1	286.0	287.0	288.1	290.2	293.4	296.4	0.74	7.61
Italy	1,693.2	1,650.8	1,616.1	1,578.3	1,542.2	1,527.4	1,517.1	1,515.8	1,522.3	1,532.3	1,523.6	-1.05	-10.02
Japan	3,682.4	3,629.8	3,585.5	3,540.2	3,474.9	3,393.0	3,305.7	3,226.4	3,155.3	3,091.9	3,057.0	-1.84	-16.98
Jordan	295.2	304.1	308.3	308.2	305.3	301.7	299.0	298.1	299.1	301.7	305.4	0.34	3.48
Kazakhstan	668.7	688.4	710.9	734.5	756.8	774.3	784.0	784.3	774.8	756.3	730.8	0.89	9.27
Kuwait	105.7	105.3	104.8	104.1	103.5	102.8	102.3	102.0	102.0	102.2	102.8	-0.27	-2.70
Latvia	82.8	85.2	86.8	89.0	90.2	89.6	88.3	87.2	84.0	80.2	75.0	-0.99	-9.43
Lithuania	116.4	120.5	124.5	128.2	130.5	130.0	128.3	126.7	124.2	122.3	118.7	0.19	1.94
Malaysia	1,144.3	1,168.2	1,190.2	1,210.1	1,224.8	1,237.0	1,246.3	1,253.0	1,257.0	1,264.6	1,272.3	1.07	11.19
Mexico	4,480.6	4,481.8	4,495.1	4,516.4	4,548.9	4,594.3	4,652.6	4,721.8	4,797.1	4,871.0	4,935.3	0.97	10.15
Morocco	1,528.9	1,558.2	1,578.0	1,588.3	1,590.6	1,587.0	1,579.4	1,569.3	1,557.2	1,543.7	1,528.9	0.00	0.00
Netherlands	488.7	488.0	486.4	488.0	492.7	498.1	502.8	509.3	513.6	516.5	518.6	0.59	6.11
New Zealand	141.1	143.0	144.3	144.3	144.6	145.2	147.2	149.9	152.2	153.4	153.4	0.84	8.70
Nigeria	6,222.5	6,378.5	6,527.8	6,671.7	6,812.4	6,952.4	7,093.8	7,238.3	7,387.0	7,540.7	7,700.0	2.15	23.74
Norway	149.0	150.8	152.5	154.1	156.1	159.8	163.8	168.5	172.6	175.1	176.5	1.71	18.50
Pakistan	7,178.7	7,466.3	7,776.9	8,099.5	8,414.5	8,699.0	8,935.5	9,116.7	9,245.9	9,334.5	9,399.2	2.73	30.93
Peru	1,220.5	1,231.6	1,246.1	1,263.7	1,283.4	1,303.5	1,322.5	1,339.4	1,354.0	1,366.0	1,375.5	1.20	12.70
Philippines	3,821.4	3,907.3	3,994.2	4,083.3	4,173.5	4,264.1	4,352.9	4,438.4	4,519.4	4,594.3	4,661.8	2.01	21.99
Poland	1,593.8	1,610.3	1,611.7	1,595.9	1,551.0	1,487.1	1,424.3	1,369.3	1,329.6	1,292.5	1,250.8	-2.39	-21.52
Portugal	375.6	366.2	352.0	338.7	324.3	313.4	304.2	299.7	296.3	294.2	290.9	-2.52	-22.54
Romania	803.6	788.7	775.6	783.0	798.4	820.3	822.2	796.8	744.5	691.8	635.1	-2.33	-20.98
Russia	5,924.2	6,098.8	6,169.1	6,301.0	6,341.5	6,245.2	6,076.5	5,870.1	5,508.7	5,079.4	4,621.3	-2.45	-21.99
Saudi Arabia	1,028.7	1,043.9	1,068.9	1,103.3	1,144.2	1,187.6	1,229.8	1,268.4	1,302.3	1,330.5	1,352.8	2.78	31.50
Singapore	166.2	167.2	165.2	164.7	168.7	177.9	181.6	189.1	197.7	199.4	197.3	1.73	18.70
Slovakia	224.0	220.2	218.5	216.1	212.6	209.0	204.0	198.9	194.6	190.2	185.1	-1.89	-17.40
Slovenia	72.5	71.2	69.2	67.4	66.3	65.3	63.6	61.9	60.2	57.4	54.8	-2.76	-24.38
South Africa	2,292.7	2,331.2	2,361.6	2,383.0	2,395.5	2,399.8	2,397.4	2,389.1	2,376.1	2,360.4	2,344.3	0.22	2.25
South Korea	1,874.0	1,799.1	1,708.6	1,617.8	1,541.9	1,490.0	1,463.6	1,460.9	1,480.4	1,509.6	1,540.0	-1.94	-17.82
Spain	1,678.6	1,617.3	1,552.6	1,491.8	1,436.7	1,389.1	1,350.4	1,321.9	1,300.3	1,283.0	1,268.8	-2.76	-24.41
Sweden	270.0	270.2	271.8	276.3	282.6	292.3	302.8	315.0	325.0	332.8	335.2	2.19	24.17
Switzerland	240.8	241.9	242.8	244.4	244.9	248.0	251.0	254.2	257.2	260.4	259.9	0.76	7.90
Taiwan	985.2	962.7	930.4	877.6	832.7	813.4	785.5	780.5	786.7	790.4	782.4	-2.28	-20.59
Thailand	2,636.7	2,584.9	2,524.4	2,450.0	2,394.8	2,365.4	2,362.0	2,386.0	2,430.1	2,467.6	2,489.7	-0.57	-5.57
Tunisia	484.5	492.2	498.9	504.3	507.9	509.1	507.4	502.7	495.1	484.8	472.4	-0.25	-2.50
Turkey	3,289.1	3,260.1	3,222.0	3,177.2	3,130.7	3,096.6	3,084.8	3,096.0	3,131.7	3,190.0	3,259.0	-0.09	-0.92
Turkmenistan	226.5	233.7	241.5	249.8	258.0	265.5	271.8	276.6	279.5	279.9	277.7	2.06	22.62
Ukraine	1,785.4	1,828.3	1,845.0	1,878.4	1,882.2	1,837.6	1,778.5	1,713.9	1,625.5	1,542.2	1,451.5	-2.05	-18.70
United Arab Emirates	198.5	194.4	187.3	178.2	168.2	158.9	151.3	146.0	143.3	142.7	144.0	-3.16	-27.49
United Kingdom	2,050.0	2,095.3	2,140.3	2,189.5	2,247.1	2,300.6	2,334.4	2,357.4	2,375.2	2,372.6	2,351.8	1.38	14.72
USA	10,461.4	10,455.8	10,427.2	10,423.5	10,461.5	10,556.5	10,687.1	10,792.4	10,881.2	10,917.6	10,889.9	0.40	4.10
Venezuela	1,202.3	1,223.7	1,246.0	1,268.7	1,290.2	1,308.9	1,323.2	1,332.6	1,337.5	1,339.1	1,338.9	1.08	11.36
Vietnam	3,888.9	3,964.0	4,052.5	4,150.2	4,249.1	4,338.0	4,408.0	4,459.9	4,494.2	4,502.4	4,474.4	1.41	15.05

Key population trends

Table 4.50 Female Population Aged 30-34: 2009-2019

'000

	2009	2010	2011	2012	2013	2014	2015	2016	2017	2018	2019	CAGR	Period growth
Algeria	1,486.3	1,537.7	1,590.9	1,643.9	1,693.5	1,735.9	1,768.2	1,789.4	1,800.1	1,802.5	1,799.7	1.93	21.09
Argentina	1,583.7	1,614.0	1,628.7	1,629.7	1,621.9	1,611.7	1,604.8	1,604.1	1,610.1	1,621.5	1,636.8	0.33	3.35
Australia	741.0	749.5	763.6	781.4	803.7	824.4	844.2	858.7	867.5	872.1	879.0	1.72	18.62
Austria	267.6	263.4	264.4	269.6	275.7	280.0	283.6	282.7	279.6	275.8	274.1	0.24	2.42
Azerbaijan	315.4	321.1	328.8	338.3	349.6	362.2	375.6	389.4	403.0	415.3	425.5	3.04	34.92
Belarus	348.6	351.4	356.9	363.0	371.7	384.2	394.4	401.6	410.8	412.5	407.5	1.57	16.90
Belgium	334.6	335.2	339.3	341.8	342.0	340.2	337.6	332.8	329.9	328.5	329.6	-0.15	-1.46
Bolivia	343.1	348.4	354.4	361.2	368.8	377.0	385.6	394.7	404.2	414.3	425.1	2.17	23.90
Bosnia-Herzegovina	142.2	141.8	142.0	142.8	144.2	146.0	147.9	149.8	151.2	151.4	150.0	0.54	5.48
Brazil	7,715.2	7,905.8	8,129.6	8,347.9	8,538.1	8,710.7	8,840.4	8,865.2	8,844.2	8,792.4	8,695.1	1.20	12.70
Bulgaria	284.4	280.4	275.3	270.0	263.8	258.2	251.6	246.8	243.1	238.7	234.5	-1.91	-17.56
Canada	1,144.0	1,163.4	1,183.4	1,200.3	1,219.3	1,234.3	1,243.4	1,248.9	1,251.5	1,250.0	1,253.3	0.92	9.55
Chile	585.5	585.2	590.7	601.6	616.6	633.9	651.7	669.0	685.2	699.9	712.8	1.99	21.74
China	43,050.8	41,498.0	40,769.5	41,908.7	41,424.1	41,064.2	41,174.6	42,795.9	44,936.9	48,128.7	52,011.3	1.91	20.81
Colombia	1,769.0	1,804.5	1,835.3	1,861.1	1,882.5	1,900.9	1,917.9	1,934.5	1,951.1	1,968.3	1,986.5	1.17	12.29
Costa Rica	171.3	176.9	182.4	187.7	192.8	197.8	202.5	207.2	211.5	215.3	218.2	2.45	27.43
Croatia	150.9	152.8	154.4	155.1	155.7	155.6	154.8	153.1	150.6	147.6	144.8	-0.41	-4.04
Czech Republic	454.2	445.7	429.0	409.5	391.5	372.4	356.4	348.7	343.6	337.9	336.1	-2.97	-25.99
Denmark	180.4	175.8	169.9	165.4	162.0	157.8	154.9	153.6	154.5	155.8	158.9	-1.26	-11.91
Ecuador	495.5	501.0	507.2	513.9	521.1	528.5	536.1	543.7	551.4	558.9	566.2	1.34	14.27
Egypt	2,724.3	2,808.9	2,892.5	2,972.7	3,048.1	3,117.0	3,177.3	3,226.9	3,266.9	3,300.5	3,321.0	2.00	21.91
Estonia	46.2	46.1	46.4	46.8	47.5	48.6	49.7	50.3	50.6	51.1	51.2	1.04	10.94
Finland	162.5	164.2	164.7	164.8	166.0	168.2	169.7	170.0	168.9	166.2	164.8	0.14	1.42
France	1,942.2	1,923.9	1,952.2	1,990.6	2,013.4	2,018.9	2,022.5	2,008.9	2,004.5	2,001.8	2,020.9	0.40	4.05
Germany	2,324.6	2,342.3	2,394.0	2,432.1	2,465.7	2,484.7	2,493.4	2,480.1	2,485.3	2,497.0	2,530.8	0.85	8.87
Greece	421.0	414.7	414.8	409.7	403.7	395.3	386.3	369.6	356.6	341.4	331.1	-2.37	-21.36
Hong Kong, China	316.1	321.7	334.1	343.7	357.4	369.6	382.3	391.9	400.5	406.5	411.9	2.68	30.32
Hungary	425.1	417.6	403.8	390.2	374.9	361.1	349.6	343.4	338.3	334.2	331.3	-2.46	-22.05
India	42,579.5	43,543.7	44,471.2	45,357.0	46,203.1	47,017.2	47,808.4	48,582.9	49,346.4	50,106.9	50,870.0	1.79	19.47
Indonesia	9,633.8	9,750.8	9,863.1	9,966.7	10,054.3	10,117.8	10,151.7	10,154.5	10,129.9	10,086.0	10,033.5	0.41	4.15
Iran	3,074.9	3,305.6	3,566.2	3,842.5	4,111.2	4,345.4	4,523.1	4,633.1	4,673.3	4,649.1	4,570.4	4.04	48.64
Ireland	185.2	194.5	204.7	211.8	216.7	217.1	214.0	208.4	203.4	197.3	192.2	0.37	3.75
Israel	274.2	275.3	274.2	273.7	275.4	277.9	280.4	283.3	285.7	286.8	287.4	0.47	4.81
Italy	2,102.6	2,011.3	1,925.8	1,854.6	1,798.1	1,742.7	1,700.5	1,666.1	1,628.5	1,592.6	1,578.1	-2.83	-24.95
Japan	4,239.7	4,076.5	3,927.9	3,816.6	3,731.6	3,677.5	3,628.4	3,586.7	3,542.9	3,478.9	3,398.0	-2.19	-19.85
Jordan	246.7	256.3	265.2	273.4	280.5	286.2	290.3	292.8	293.7	293.7	293.4	1.75	18.92
Kazakhstan	618.6	626.3	635.0	645.5	659.1	676.3	697.2	720.9	745.7	768.6	785.9	2.42	27.04
Kuwait	112.0	113.6	114.6	115.0	114.8	114.3	113.6	112.8	112.1	111.4	110.8	-0.10	-1.04
Latvia	78.0	77.6	77.5	77.9	79.2	81.7	84.0	85.6	87.7	89.1	88.6	1.28	13.60
Lithuania	110.8	109.8	109.6	110.0	111.5	114.7	118.6	122.5	126.1	128.5	128.1	1.46	15.62
Malaysia	1,011.6	1,032.3	1,054.6	1,078.0	1,104.8	1,130.3	1,153.5	1,174.5	1,193.6	1,207.4	1,219.0	1.88	20.50
Mexico	4,570.2	4,553.9	4,535.2	4,512.3	4,491.2	4,476.7	4,471.7	4,478.2	4,497.4	4,530.5	4,578.0	0.02	0.17
Morocco	1,307.9	1,339.2	1,376.4	1,418.1	1,460.4	1,499.0	1,529.7	1,550.7	1,561.8	1,564.5	1,561.0	1.78	19.35
Netherlands	499.8	492.2	492.1	493.1	491.7	488.4	488.0	486.5	488.3	493.1	498.6	-0.02	-0.25
New Zealand	140.2	140.3	142.0	144.2	147.4	149.6	151.6	152.9	153.0	153.2	153.8	0.93	9.75
Nigeria	5,060.9	5,240.7	5,418.0	5,591.5	5,759.7	5,921.4	6,076.1	6,224.1	6,366.3	6,505.0	6,642.8	2.76	31.26
Norway	157.1	156.3	156.8	158.4	160.8	162.0	162.9	163.8	165.0	166.8	170.1	0.80	8.31
Pakistan	5,974.7	6,161.8	6,363.1	6,581.6	6,821.7	7,086.8	7,377.2	7,689.5	8,013.1	8,328.9	8,614.6	3.73	44.18
Peru	1,132.4	1,148.8	1,162.0	1,172.8	1,182.6	1,193.3	1,206.4	1,222.6	1,241.5	1,262.2	1,283.1	1.26	13.31
Philippines	3,355.2	3,442.3	3,524.3	3,603.3	3,681.2	3,761.4	3,845.6	3,934.4	4,027.2	4,122.2	4,216.8	2.31	25.68
Poland	1,469.5	1,495.4	1,515.9	1,521.1	1,541.9	1,571.9	1,586.8	1,586.8	1,571.5	1,528.5	1,467.1	-0.02	-0.16
Portugal	422.3	415.9	408.2	398.2	389.5	381.0	371.5	357.3	343.9	329.5	318.6	-2.78	-24.55
Romania	865.3	861.6	862.1	852.8	827.3	793.4	776.4	760.5	764.2	777.3	796.5	-0.83	-7.95
Russia	5,402.0	5,458.0	5,549.0	5,609.0	5,746.8	5,934.7	6,102.9	6,175.1	6,304.8	6,344.9	6,248.9	1.47	15.68
Saudi Arabia	1,013.5	1,039.6	1,056.7	1,066.7	1,073.7	1,083.4	1,100.1	1,126.2	1,160.9	1,201.9	1,245.3	2.08	22.87
Singapore	187.2	187.4	190.1	185.7	186.7	184.6	184.7	181.7	180.2	183.4	192.2	0.27	2.69
Slovakia	228.8	231.1	230.7	228.9	226.8	223.6	219.7	218.0	215.6	211.9	208.3	-0.93	-8.95
Slovenia	74.0	75.0	75.5	75.1	74.6	73.5	72.1	70.0	68.2	67.1	66.2	-1.11	-10.60
South Africa	1,906.3	1,928.7	1,956.1	1,987.7	2,021.7	2,055.8	2,088.0	2,116.7	2,141.0	2,159.7	2,172.3	1.31	13.95
South Korea	1,852.9	1,851.2	1,874.2	1,897.7	1,898.8	1,861.7	1,787.5	1,697.6	1,607.5	1,532.1	1,480.6	-2.22	-20.09
Spain	1,937.1	1,932.2	1,910.7	1,872.6	1,823.2	1,764.5	1,701.2	1,636.4	1,575.7	1,520.4	1,472.7	-2.70	-23.97
Sweden	284.2	279.4	278.1	278.0	278.6	279.6	279.7	280.8	285.0	290.9	300.5	0.56	5.72
Switzerland	252.7	252.6	254.6	255.9	258.2	259.7	260.8	261.6	263.2	263.7	266.8	0.54	5.56
Taiwan	955.6	987.0	1,011.9	1,010.9	1,020.1	1,009.2	986.0	952.6	898.2	851.8	832.0	-1.38	-12.93
Thailand	2,770.9	2,760.3	2,729.4	2,694.8	2,671.2	2,617.2	2,563.6	2,502.3	2,425.2	2,368.2	2,336.9	-1.69	-15.66
Tunisia	434.6	444.8	454.8	464.3	473.4	481.8	489.4	496.1	501.5	505.1	506.3	1.54	16.49
Turkey	3,279.8	3,311.9	3,325.9	3,328.3	3,317.0	3,295.5	3,267.1	3,229.1	3,184.9	3,137.1	3,100.8	-0.56	-5.46
Turkmenistan	197.7	202.2	206.9	212.0	217.5	223.8	230.8	238.5	246.8	254.9	262.5	2.88	32.79
Ukraine	1,683.4	1,683.5	1,695.1	1,693.3	1,715.4	1,760.5	1,799.3	1,812.3	1,843.0	1,847.4	1,806.8	0.71	7.33
United Arab Emirates	210.1	218.9	223.6	224.2	221.1	215.2	207.3	198.1	188.3	178.6	170.0	-2.09	-19.05
United Kingdom	1,907.4	1,921.6	1,957.2	2,004.5	2,055.2	2,103.3	2,149.1	2,196.1	2,246.5	2,304.4	2,357.1	2.14	23.58
USA	9,802.0	10,016.3	10,291.8	10,485.6	10,634.1	10,694.5	10,690.0	10,666.2	10,664.2	10,702.2	10,796.8	0.97	10.15
Venezuela	1,081.0	1,109.7	1,135.5	1,158.5	1,179.7	1,200.4	1,221.7	1,244.0	1,266.7	1,288.2	1,306.9	1.92	20.89
Vietnam	3,573.7	3,631.7	3,687.5	3,741.5	3,798.3	3,863.8	3,941.5	4,032.5	4,132.6	4,233.6	4,323.8	1.92	20.99

Key population trends

Table 4.51 Female Population Aged 35-39: 2009-2019

'000

	2009	2010	2011	2012	2013	2014	2015	2016	2017	2018	2019	Period CAGR	Period growth
Algeria	1,265.5	1,302.2	1,341.1	1,382.5	1,427.0	1,474.7	1,525.5	1,578.4	1,631.2	1,680.8	1,723.3	3.14	36.17
Argentina	1,324.0	1,370.7	1,423.7	1,479.7	1,533.1	1,577.5	1,608.0	1,623.0	1,624.1	1,616.3	1,603.9	1.94	21.14
Australia	809.5	806.5	791.8	779.9	775.4	778.1	787.3	802.8	821.5	844.2	864.9	0.66	6.85
Austria	315.4	304.2	295.0	285.1	276.8	271.6	267.5	268.4	273.5	279.5	283.8	-1.05	-10.02
Azerbaijan	312.3	308.9	306.9	306.4	307.9	311.4	317.1	324.9	334.6	346.0	358.6	1.39	14.81
Belarus	342.2	344.9	344.9	344.7	345.0	348.5	350.9	355.9	362.1	370.4	383.4	1.14	12.03
Belgium	368.9	361.7	352.2	343.8	338.6	336.8	337.4	341.5	344.0	344.3	342.5	-0.74	-7.15
Bolivia	307.2	314.8	321.2	326.5	331.1	335.8	340.9	346.9	353.7	361.3	369.6	1.87	20.31
Bosnia-Herzegovina	148.4	147.0	145.6	144.3	143.2	142.4	142.2	142.5	143.4	144.7	146.3	-0.14	-1.39
Brazil	7,064.4	7,127.0	7,213.6	7,328.2	7,475.6	7,655.5	7,849.2	8,075.4	8,295.7	8,487.4	8,660.5	2.06	22.59
Bulgaria	269.7	271.7	274.1	277.5	281.9	281.2	276.9	271.5	265.9	259.6	254.0	-0.60	-5.84
Canada	1,163.4	1,161.2	1,158.0	1,165.1	1,175.0	1,191.4	1,209.1	1,229.1	1,246.6	1,266.4	1,282.4	0.98	10.23
Chile	618.2	613.8	606.9	598.5	590.6	585.6	585.4	590.8	601.7	616.7	633.9	0.25	2.54
China	58,873.9	54,723.3	51,490.4	47,734.0	44,833.9	42,762.6	41,251.4	40,522.9	41,686.1	41,242.8	40,916.1	-3.57	-30.50
Colombia	1,624.4	1,632.8	1,652.2	1,681.6	1,717.6	1,755.6	1,791.2	1,822.1	1,847.9	1,869.1	1,887.3	1.51	16.18
Costa Rica	152.6	154.1	157.0	161.0	166.0	171.5	177.1	182.5	187.8	193.0	198.0	2.64	29.73
Croatia	146.0	146.3	148.0	149.1	149.9	150.9	152.7	154.3	154.9	155.5	155.3	0.62	6.35
Czech Republic	382.1	407.7	429.4	446.2	456.3	456.7	447.4	430.2	410.7	392.9	374.1	-0.21	-2.08
Denmark	191.2	192.2	193.4	190.0	184.5	181.0	176.3	170.4	165.9	162.5	158.3	-1.87	-17.24
Ecuador	448.6	454.3	460.3	466.8	473.7	480.8	488.0	495.1	502.3	509.6	516.9	1.43	15.21
Egypt	2,202.1	2,285.3	2,371.1	2,459.3	2,548.0	2,636.0	2,723.2	2,809.0	2,890.8	2,967.2	3,036.2	3.26	37.88
Estonia	47.0	46.8	46.3	45.9	45.6	45.7	45.5	45.8	46.2	47.0	48.1	0.23	2.34
Finland	152.4	151.7	152.7	155.6	159.8	164.6	166.2	166.6	166.6	167.8	169.9	1.10	11.51
France	2,209.6	2,184.3	2,132.5	2,059.5	1,999.9	1,948.5	1,930.8	1,959.7	1,998.2	2,021.1	2,026.6	-0.86	-8.28
Germany	2,754.0	2,577.2	2,436.6	2,335.9	2,294.7	2,302.8	2,323.7	2,377.8	2,417.3	2,451.5	2,470.7	-1.08	-10.29
Greece	427.2	429.7	427.5	429.0	429.1	429.2	423.0	423.1	418.1	412.1	403.7	-0.56	-5.50
Hong Kong, China	323.6	320.7	315.4	318.0	316.8	319.6	324.7	336.6	346.7	361.4	374.5	1.47	15.73
Hungary	356.4	371.0	388.5	404.5	416.2	424.4	416.7	402.6	389.0	373.8	360.1	0.10	1.05
India	37,327.2	38,193.5	39,114.1	40,077.5	41,063.6	42,048.2	43,011.1	43,940.7	44,832.7	45,688.7	46,514.5	2.22	24.61
Indonesia	8,890.8	9,041.1	9,180.7	9,311.0	9,434.2	9,552.6	9,667.5	9,778.1	9,880.6	9,967.8	10,031.8	1.21	12.83
Iran	2,435.9	2,497.4	2,585.2	2,704.2	2,859.1	3,052.2	3,282.1	3,542.2	3,818.4	4,087.4	4,321.8	5.90	77.42
Ireland	170.2	173.8	176.0	179.6	184.4	191.3	200.4	210.7	217.9	222.8	223.2	2.75	31.12
Israel	247.4	255.5	263.2	269.7	274.4	277.3	278.0	276.5	275.8	277.4	279.7	1.24	13.08
Italy	2,345.0	2,330.4	2,309.3	2,261.1	2,201.4	2,131.9	2,040.7	1,955.4	1,884.4	1,828.1	1,772.8	-2.76	-24.40
Japan	4,804.8	4,797.0	4,720.7	4,585.0	4,407.4	4,219.1	4,060.0	3,914.3	3,804.6	3,720.8	3,667.5	-2.66	-23.67
Jordan	212.3	220.4	226.5	231.1	235.1	239.7	245.8	253.6	262.5	271.6	279.7	2.79	31.72
Kazakhstan	572.0	585.5	597.1	606.6	614.8	622.7	631.3	641.0	652.4	666.3	683.4	1.80	19.47
Kuwait	96.8	100.4	103.8	107.1	110.0	112.4	114.1	115.1	115.4	115.2	114.6	1.71	18.44
Latvia	79.9	79.8	79.2	78.0	77.2	76.8	76.4	76.3	76.7	78.0	80.6	0.09	0.85
Lithuania	122.8	120.3	116.9	113.5	110.7	109.2	108.2	108.0	108.3	109.9	113.1	-0.82	-7.87
Malaysia	932.9	939.4	948.5	960.9	975.9	993.4	1,012.9	1,034.3	1,057.0	1,083.6	1,109.2	1.75	18.90
Mexico	4,400.5	4,516.0	4,595.8	4,635.0	4,642.3	4,629.0	4,605.7	4,579.3	4,553.6	4,532.3	4,518.4	0.26	2.68
Morocco	1,158.9	1,186.2	1,210.8	1,233.7	1,257.3	1,284.3	1,316.8	1,355.0	1,397.1	1,439.6	1,478.0	2.46	27.54
Netherlands	613.7	584.7	553.9	527.0	504.7	493.3	485.9	486.2	487.4	486.1	483.1	-2.37	-21.29
New Zealand	161.7	158.8	153.8	149.4	146.1	145.0	145.1	146.9	149.1	152.3	154.5	-0.45	-4.44
Nigeria	3,943.7	4,086.9	4,242.1	4,407.6	4,580.4	4,756.5	4,932.3	5,105.5	5,274.5	5,438.0	5,595.1	3.56	41.87
Norway	176.6	175.4	173.7	170.4	166.6	164.8	163.5	163.6	164.9	167.1	168.2	-0.48	-4.73
Pakistan	5,083.6	5,234.2	5,390.0	5,551.7	5,720.5	5,898.3	6,087.3	6,289.7	6,509.0	6,749.8	7,015.8	3.27	38.01
Peru	993.0	1,015.0	1,038.5	1,062.5	1,085.9	1,107.2	1,125.2	1,139.8	1,151.5	1,162.1	1,173.6	1.69	18.19
Philippines	2,900.2	2,976.0	3,055.5	3,139.2	3,225.3	3,312.4	3,398.5	3,482.7	3,565.3	3,647.7	3,731.9	2.55	28.68
Poland	1,261.2	1,304.2	1,348.3	1,394.5	1,427.0	1,455.8	1,481.2	1,501.1	1,506.3	1,527.8	1,558.7	2.14	23.59
Portugal	407.5	415.3	422.5	427.8	429.3	427.3	420.8	413.1	403.2	394.4	385.9	-0.54	-5.29
Romania	836.1	822.6	817.6	826.1	838.9	857.6	852.6	851.6	840.6	814.6	780.3	-0.69	-6.68
Russia	5,005.0	5,119.0	5,179.9	5,267.9	5,298.2	5,393.5	5,444.2	5,536.4	5,594.7	5,730.6	5,914.8	1.68	18.18
Saudi Arabia	818.9	853.0	891.3	932.1	971.9	1,006.5	1,033.1	1,050.6	1,060.9	1,068.3	1,078.2	2.79	31.67
Singapore	211.9	212.8	210.6	208.2	200.5	196.6	196.2	198.5	193.1	193.4	190.7	-1.05	-10.01
Slovakia	194.1	202.7	211.3	219.4	224.9	228.6	230.9	230.4	228.5	226.4	223.1	1.41	14.98
Slovenia	70.8	71.1	72.3	73.6	74.2	74.8	75.7	76.2	75.8	75.2	74.2	0.48	4.89
South Africa	1,624.8	1,621.4	1,616.7	1,612.8	1,612.4	1,618.8	1,634.1	1,658.8	1,691.6	1,729.9	1,769.8	0.86	8.92
South Korea	2,121.3	2,075.9	2,010.8	1,938.9	1,876.5	1,840.1	1,838.7	1,861.7	1,885.1	1,886.3	1,849.5	-1.36	-12.82
Spain	1,874.4	1,906.6	1,938.1	1,967.0	1,987.5	1,996.9	1,990.5	1,969.1	1,931.2	1,882.1	1,823.5	-0.27	-2.72
Sweden	306.8	309.4	308.5	303.4	297.4	291.3	286.1	284.6	284.3	284.6	285.4	-0.72	-6.98
Switzerland	284.2	277.2	271.3	266.0	262.8	261.1	260.9	262.8	264.1	266.3	267.7	-0.59	-5.78
Taiwan	910.5	901.9	896.8	924.7	941.0	967.2	998.8	1,023.5	1,022.3	1,031.1	1,019.8	1.14	12.00
Thailand	2,872.0	2,837.6	2,797.6	2,776.3	2,748.1	2,728.1	2,716.8	2,685.8	2,649.4	2,624.7	2,567.9	-1.11	-10.59
Tunisia	386.6	394.1	402.6	411.9	421.8	432.0	442.2	452.2	461.7	470.7	479.1	2.17	23.92
Turkey	2,929.2	3,019.7	3,101.1	3,172.2	3,231.5	3,278.3	3,311.1	3,327.3	3,328.3	3,316.8	3,293.1	1.18	12.43
Turkmenistan	173.5	177.9	182.2	186.5	190.7	194.9	199.3	204.0	209.0	214.5	220.8	2.44	27.23
Ukraine	1,631.3	1,652.0	1,658.5	1,666.0	1,653.0	1,658.0	1,655.3	1,663.6	1,660.5	1,682.7	1,729.3	0.59	6.01
United Arab Emirates	154.8	169.1	183.4	196.8	208.5	217.8	224.0	226.9	226.4	222.9	217.0	3.43	40.16
United Kingdom	2,213.3	2,147.5	2,074.4	1,995.2	1,934.7	1,914.7	1,930.0	1,967.8	2,016.6	2,067.8	2,115.5	-0.45	-4.42
USA	10,260.7	10,033.4	9,783.0	9,708.2	9,755.6	9,913.8	10,129.6	10,408.7	10,604.4	10,754.8	10,817.8	0.53	5.43
Venezuela	949.3	966.3	988.9	1,016.3	1,046.4	1,076.8	1,105.4	1,131.1	1,154.0	1,175.2	1,195.9	2.34	25.97
Vietnam	3,253.7	3,309.3	3,366.6	3,426.0	3,486.7	3,547.6	3,608.0	3,666.2	3,722.4	3,781.1	3,847.8	1.69	18.26

Key population trends

Table 4.52 Female Population Aged 40-44: 2009-2019

'000

	2009	2010	2011	2012	2013	2014	2015	2016	2017	2018	2019	CAGR	Period growth
Algeria	1,090.8	1,122.9	1,154.6	1,186.5	1,219.1	1,253.2	1,289.4	1,328.0	1,369.2	1,413.7	1,461.4	2.97	33.98
Argentina	1,184.1	1,199.5	1,219.3	1,244.6	1,276.5	1,315.9	1,362.7	1,415.7	1,471.5	1,524.6	1,570.9	2.87	32.67
Australia	766.4	776.0	796.2	816.1	828.5	831.8	829.8	816.7	806.0	802.1	804.9	0.49	5.02
Austria	353.9	351.1	345.1	338.0	329.5	317.4	306.2	297.1	287.2	278.9	273.7	-2.54	-22.67
Azerbaijan	342.5	334.2	326.2	318.9	312.8	308.0	304.6	302.8	302.6	304.2	307.8	-1.06	-10.14
Belarus	353.3	344.1	342.2	340.4	342.3	341.3	343.7	343.1	343.1	343.1	347.0	-0.18	-1.80
Belgium	392.1	384.3	379.6	376.5	373.9	368.9	361.7	352.3	344.0	338.9	337.2	-1.50	-14.01
Bolivia	254.9	263.3	272.3	281.6	290.8	299.4	306.9	313.2	318.5	323.2	328.0	2.55	28.66
Bosnia-Herzegovina	155.4	153.8	152.3	151.0	149.7	148.5	147.3	146.0	144.7	143.5	142.6	-0.86	-8.24
Brazil	6,849.9	6,864.5	6,883.4	6,907.6	6,940.9	6,988.1	7,054.6	7,144.3	7,261.4	7,410.3	7,590.5	1.03	10.81
Bulgaria	250.9	255.3	259.8	264.2	266.2	265.4	266.9	268.9	271.8	275.9	275.0	0.92	9.59
Canada	1,239.8	1,214.7	1,206.5	1,201.7	1,196.2	1,188.6	1,184.0	1,180.1	1,187.2	1,197.5	1,214.7	-0.20	-2.03
Chile	625.7	622.3	620.4	619.6	618.9	616.9	612.5	605.7	597.3	589.5	584.5	-0.68	-6.58
China	63,766.1	64,963.3	64,527.1	65,228.1	62,737.5	60,535.3	56,291.7	53,007.6	49,198.1	46,223.5	44,097.2	-3.62	-30.85
Colombia	1,598.0	1,611.8	1,616.2	1,613.8	1,609.5	1,609.5	1,618.3	1,637.8	1,667.1	1,702.9	1,740.5	0.86	8.92
Costa Rica	154.2	154.1	153.5	152.7	152.2	152.4	153.9	156.7	160.7	165.8	171.3	1.06	11.07
Croatia	156.9	154.8	150.3	147.2	145.9	145.6	145.9	147.5	148.5	149.3	150.2	-0.43	-4.24
Czech Republic	343.4	339.7	342.1	349.9	362.8	383.9	408.8	430.0	446.7	456.9	457.7	2.92	33.29
Denmark	208.6	204.0	198.6	193.4	191.9	191.5	192.4	193.6	190.1	184.7	181.2	-1.40	-13.13
Ecuador	403.6	410.9	417.9	424.6	431.3	437.8	444.4	451.1	457.9	464.8	471.8	1.57	16.90
Egypt	1,899.7	1,897.8	1,914.9	1,951.6	2,010.5	2,087.4	2,173.5	2,262.0	2,353.3	2,445.0	2,535.8	2.93	33.49
Estonia	44.8	44.7	45.1	45.9	46.4	46.3	46.1	45.5	45.1	44.9	45.0	0.06	0.63
Finland	181.4	176.7	172.2	166.7	160.2	153.7	153.0	154.0	156.8	160.9	165.6	-0.90	-8.68
France	2,220.1	2,198.1	2,187.0	2,188.3	2,201.0	2,203.6	2,179.0	2,128.4	2,056.3	1,997.6	1,946.8	-1.30	-12.31
Germany	3,435.9	3,340.7	3,220.0	3,080.1	2,908.7	2,713.0	2,542.8	2,407.1	2,309.1	2,269.2	2,277.5	-4.03	-33.71
Greece	429.9	436.0	442.7	440.8	437.7	434.1	436.7	434.5	436.1	436.1	436.2	0.15	1.48
Hong Kong, China	325.9	316.8	313.2	308.9	307.6	303.7	300.2	294.3	297.8	297.4	301.1	-0.79	-7.62
Hungary	324.9	335.3	346.0	352.5	354.9	354.7	368.8	385.8	401.4	412.9	421.0	2.63	29.60
India	33,153.3	33,820.9	34,509.4	35,225.8	35,980.9	36,786.4	37,649.2	38,568.9	39,534.9	40,526.7	41,518.6	2.28	25.23
Indonesia	7,898.9	8,098.4	8,289.7	8,471.3	8,642.2	8,802.3	8,951.7	9,091.0	9,221.5	9,345.6	9,465.5	1.83	19.83
Iran	2,231.1	2,278.5	2,314.4	2,342.7	2,371.5	2,411.8	2,473.0	2,561.3	2,681.0	2,836.4	3,029.7	3.11	35.79
Ireland	155.2	156.8	159.7	163.2	167.6	171.9	175.2	177.4	180.9	185.8	192.6	2.19	24.13
Israel	207.3	213.9	222.4	231.8	241.0	249.6	257.7	265.5	272.1	276.7	279.5	3.03	34.83
Italy	2,429.9	2,415.8	2,395.8	2,381.9	2,370.4	2,359.5	2,345.2	2,324.3	2,276.4	2,217.0	2,147.8	-1.23	-11.61
Japan	4,265.1	4,314.3	4,557.8	4,634.0	4,727.2	4,782.8	4,778.8	4,705.4	4,571.6	4,395.6	4,208.6	-0.13	-1.33
Jordan	167.9	177.5	186.3	194.0	200.8	207.0	212.6	217.9	223.0	228.4	234.7	3.41	39.83
Kazakhstan	533.6	531.9	536.0	545.4	558.8	573.8	588.3	600.8	611.1	619.6	627.3	1.63	17.55
Kuwait	74.2	77.7	81.4	85.3	89.2	93.1	96.9	100.5	103.8	106.7	109.0	3.92	46.83
Latvia	78.8	77.8	78.4	78.8	78.7	78.4	78.2	77.7	76.5	75.8	75.5	-0.43	-4.18
Lithuania	126.8	124.9	124.6	124.2	122.9	120.4	117.9	114.6	111.3	108.6	107.2	-1.66	-15.44
Malaysia	884.1	895.9	904.5	909.1	910.9	912.5	916.2	922.8	933.2	946.6	963.1	0.86	8.93
Mexico	3,616.7	3,789.6	3,972.3	4,152.7	4,320.9	4,465.0	4,575.8	4,649.0	4,685.8	4,692.7	4,679.8	2.61	29.40
Morocco	997.9	1,020.3	1,047.1	1,077.1	1,108.7	1,139.5	1,167.8	1,193.0	1,216.3	1,239.9	1,266.9	2.42	26.96
Netherlands	638.7	638.5	638.5	635.1	627.1	608.2	579.1	548.1	521.0	498.5	487.3	-2.67	-23.71
New Zealand	162.4	162.9	164.7	165.9	165.4	163.4	160.6	155.6	151.3	148.1	147.0	-0.99	-9.50
Nigeria	3,183.2	3,261.0	3,349.4	3,449.6	3,562.4	3,687.9	3,825.8	3,975.2	4,134.4	4,300.3	4,469.2	3.45	40.40
Norway	174.5	177.7	179.5	181.2	182.2	181.0	179.5	177.6	174.2	170.4	168.6	-0.34	-3.39
Pakistan	4,298.4	4,433.4	4,572.0	4,714.3	4,859.9	5,008.9	5,161.5	5,318.4	5,480.8	5,650.2	5,828.9	3.09	35.61
Peru	871.8	889.6	908.0	927.4	948.1	970.1	993.5	1,017.9	1,042.7	1,066.6	1,088.4	2.24	24.85
Philippines	2,549.5	2,611.9	2,673.0	2,734.9	2,799.4	2,868.9	2,944.5	3,026.3	3,113.5	3,203.8	3,294.8	2.60	29.23
Poland	1,166.7	1,157.4	1,163.9	1,181.1	1,210.3	1,245.2	1,287.6	1,331.1	1,377.2	1,410.2	1,440.0	2.13	23.43
Portugal	399.3	396.5	397.1	400.4	405.6	410.9	418.6	425.9	431.2	432.7	430.8	0.76	7.88
Romania	766.0	832.7	891.2	939.3	886.6	827.4	813.3	807.4	814.8	827.0	844.8	0.98	10.29
Russia	4,870.0	4,754.3	4,759.1	4,780.8	4,899.7	4,977.4	5,086.0	5,148.3	5,234.2	5,263.8	5,356.4	0.96	9.99
Saudi Arabia	655.9	682.6	707.0	730.2	754.3	781.8	814.1	851.4	891.9	931.9	966.9	3.96	47.42
Singapore	202.8	201.8	202.2	207.1	213.1	217.1	217.6	215.0	212.0	203.4	199.0	-0.19	-1.89
Slovakia	182.6	179.7	178.4	179.4	184.9	193.3	201.9	210.5	218.5	223.9	227.6	2.23	24.66
Slovenia	76.8	75.7	73.6	72.0	71.1	71.2	71.5	72.7	74.0	74.6	75.3	-0.20	-2.03
South Africa	1,432.3	1,431.0	1,424.2	1,412.6	1,398.0	1,383.1	1,370.0	1,360.7	1,356.3	1,358.5	1,368.7	-0.45	-4.44
South Korea	2,024.2	2,052.9	2,087.3	2,116.0	2,123.1	2,103.3	2,058.6	1,994.3	1,923.2	1,861.4	1,825.5	-1.03	-9.82
Spain	1,801.5	1,823.4	1,842.3	1,862.2	1,886.8	1,914.4	1,945.3	1,976.5	2,005.4	2,025.8	2,035.2	1.23	12.98
Sweden	330.0	323.4	318.2	314.8	312.0	310.9	313.6	312.5	307.3	301.0	294.7	-1.12	-10.68
Switzerland	317.3	313.0	307.4	301.4	294.4	286.5	279.2	273.0	267.5	264.0	262.2	-1.89	-17.36
Taiwan	932.9	929.1	927.5	919.2	920.0	910.9	902.3	896.9	924.6	940.5	966.4	0.35	3.59
Thailand	2,867.5	2,865.0	2,882.7	2,881.6	2,830.1	2,811.7	2,775.7	2,735.4	2,712.4	2,682.9	2,661.0	-0.74	-7.20
Tunisia	352.7	359.2	365.2	371.2	377.3	383.9	391.4	399.9	409.2	419.1	429.2	1.98	21.69
Turkey	2,466.3	2,540.5	2,624.1	2,717.0	2,816.5	2,915.8	3,010.3	3,090.2	3,160.0	3,219.3	3,265.0	2.85	32.38
Turkmenistan	158.4	158.8	160.3	162.9	166.4	170.5	174.7	179.0	183.2	187.4	191.7	1.93	21.03
Ukraine	1,605.8	1,570.1	1,575.0	1,580.2	1,600.1	1,604.2	1,621.7	1,625.0	1,630.9	1,619.2	1,627.0	0.13	1.32
United Arab Emirates	99.2	107.2	116.9	128.0	140.2	153.2	166.3	179.2	191.4	202.1	210.5	7.81	112.21
United Kingdom	2,380.0	2,356.3	2,327.2	2,298.4	2,258.2	2,201.8	2,138.3	2,068.5	1,991.7	1,932.4	1,912.6	-2.16	-19.64
USA	10,539.3	10,473.6	10,522.2	10,512.5	10,426.7	10,261.7	10,043.3	9,804.2	9,735.7	9,785.9	9,944.7	-0.58	-5.64
Venezuela	902.6	910.3	916.6	922.8	930.8	942.6	959.6	982.1	1,009.4	1,039.4	1,069.7	1.71	18.52
Vietnam	2,949.4	3,002.1	3,056.2	3,111.0	3,166.9	3,223.8	3,281.6	3,341.1	3,402.5	3,465.0	3,527.0	1.80	19.58

Key population trends

Table 4.53 Female Population Aged 45-49: 2009-2019

'000

	2009	2010	2011	2012	2013	2014	2015	2016	2017	2018	2019	CAGR	Period growth
Algeria	891.9	934.2	973.8	1,010.6	1,044.8	1,077.2	1,108.7	1,140.2	1,171.8	1,204.4	1,238.5	3.34	38.86
Argentina	1,127.9	1,135.3	1,142.8	1,151.0	1,160.6	1,172.7	1,188.4	1,208.4	1,233.6	1,265.3	1,303.3	1.46	15.55
Australia	792.2	791.3	784.5	776.9	771.5	774.3	784.5	806.1	826.9	839.6	843.1	0.62	6.42
Austria	337.8	346.2	351.6	354.3	354.9	353.8	351.1	345.1	338.1	329.5	317.5	-0.62	-6.01
Azerbaijan	348.4	353.3	353.9	350.5	344.3	336.6	328.5	320.8	313.9	308.1	303.5	-1.37	-12.88
Belarus	419.0	407.9	391.7	376.1	361.8	350.8	341.3	338.9	337.3	338.8	338.3	-2.12	-19.26
Belgium	400.8	403.3	403.8	401.1	396.4	389.8	382.2	377.6	374.5	371.9	367.1	-0.88	-8.43
Bolivia	215.7	221.0	226.7	232.8	239.6	247.1	255.3	264.2	273.4	282.5	291.1	3.04	34.91
Bosnia-Herzegovina	159.2	159.3	158.8	157.8	156.5	155.1	153.6	152.2	150.9	149.6	148.3	-0.71	-6.87
Brazil	6,387.3	6,529.6	6,628.4	6,689.4	6,722.5	6,742.7	6,762.2	6,785.3	6,813.1	6,849.1	6,898.0	0.77	7.99
Bulgaria	262.4	260.0	254.6	248.1	243.5	246.1	250.1	254.1	258.1	259.8	258.8	-0.14	-1.38
Canada	1,385.7	1,383.5	1,359.1	1,324.5	1,282.1	1,243.1	1,215.6	1,206.7	1,201.7	1,196.3	1,189.1	-1.52	-14.19
Chile	620.3	627.9	630.9	629.8	626.4	622.3	619.0	617.1	616.4	615.8	613.8	-0.11	-1.05
China	51,335.0	57,343.9	64,119.5	64,368.0	64,299.0	64,753.1	65,917.0	65,581.4	66,227.8	63,755.4	61,513.4	1.83	19.83
Colombia	1,396.4	1,441.4	1,484.1	1,522.9	1,555.3	1,579.2	1,593.3	1,598.0	1,595.8	1,591.6	1,591.6	1.32	13.98
Costa Rica	143.5	147.0	149.8	151.8	153.0	153.5	153.3	152.7	151.9	151.4	151.8	0.56	5.78
Croatia	163.9	161.2	160.2	159.3	157.6	156.0	154.0	149.4	146.3	145.0	144.7	-1.24	-11.75
Czech Republic	320.5	332.9	341.9	346.6	348.9	344.0	339.9	342.0	349.7	362.7	383.8	1.82	19.74
Denmark	192.0	197.1	202.0	208.1	210.4	207.6	203.1	197.8	192.7	191.2	190.8	-0.06	-0.62
Ecuador	352.1	360.5	369.2	377.9	386.5	394.7	402.5	409.8	416.7	423.3	429.8	2.01	22.07
Egypt	1,843.8	1,846.8	1,842.3	1,830.9	1,811.5	1,791.6	1,783.6	1,796.5	1,831.0	1,890.1	1,969.3	0.66	6.81
Estonia	50.1	49.0	47.5	45.7	44.4	43.9	43.8	44.2	45.0	45.5	45.5	-0.96	-9.23
Finland	187.2	187.3	186.6	185.6	184.5	181.7	177.0	172.5	167.0	160.5	154.1	-1.93	-17.71
France	2,208.3	2,221.1	2,227.0	2,229.3	2,223.8	2,203.7	2,182.5	2,172.4	2,174.3	2,187.5	2,190.5	-0.08	-0.81
Germany	3,380.0	3,431.9	3,450.8	3,452.6	3,431.2	3,374.2	3,285.8	3,170.6	3,034.4	2,866.2	2,673.5	-2.32	-20.90
Greece	402.7	404.9	402.3	412.8	424.4	435.2	441.3	448.0	446.2	443.0	439.5	0.88	9.13
Hong Kong, China	351.3	352.3	345.9	337.2	319.6	306.5	296.7	292.7	288.8	288.6	285.6	-2.05	-18.71
Hungary	313.8	307.2	301.4	301.1	310.3	321.3	331.4	341.7	348.0	350.3	350.0	1.10	11.56
India	29,370.7	29,989.9	30,613.9	31,242.5	31,877.7	32,524.0	33,187.7	33,874.8	34,592.8	35,352.3	36,163.3	2.10	23.13
Indonesia	6,769.2	6,967.0	7,168.8	7,374.0	7,580.3	7,784.4	7,983.6	8,175.4	8,358.5	8,531.9	8,694.9	2.54	28.45
Iran	1,889.4	1,948.1	2,011.2	2,077.0	2,140.9	2,198.1	2,245.3	2,282.1	2,312.1	2,342.9	2,384.8	2.36	26.22
Ireland	145.7	148.7	150.6	152.3	153.5	154.9	156.3	159.1	162.7	167.0	171.2	1.63	17.54
Israel	198.7	198.6	199.1	200.5	203.0	207.6	214.2	222.9	232.5	242.0	250.6	2.35	26.15
Italy	2,222.9	2,296.5	2,354.3	2,398.3	2,425.4	2,433.8	2,420.0	2,400.4	2,386.8	2,375.7	2,365.1	0.62	6.40
Japan	3,898.6	3,991.5	3,927.5	4,044.5	4,141.3	4,235.8	4,288.1	4,532.6	4,609.8	4,703.7	4,759.7	2.02	22.09
Jordan	123.2	132.0	140.3	148.2	155.8	163.5	171.4	179.5	187.6	195.4	202.6	5.10	64.46
Kazakhstan	562.6	561.2	555.7	547.4	538.9	533.1	532.2	537.1	547.2	560.9	575.8	0.23	2.34
Kuwait	54.6	57.6	60.6	63.8	67.2	70.8	74.5	78.3	82.1	86.0	89.9	5.11	64.57
Latvia	89.0	86.8	83.5	80.7	78.5	76.8	75.8	76.3	76.8	76.8	76.6	-1.50	-13.99
Lithuania	139.4	136.7	133.0	128.9	125.7	123.8	122.0	121.6	121.3	120.2	117.8	-1.67	-15.54
Malaysia	781.5	800.4	818.8	837.3	852.3	864.9	874.1	879.9	881.6	880.5	879.5	1.19	12.54
Mexico	2,978.9	3,094.7	3,221.9	3,357.3	3,503.3	3,661.4	3,831.1	4,009.5	4,189.3	4,358.8	4,504.7	4.22	51.22
Morocco	911.6	922.3	933.3	945.9	961.2	980.3	1,003.5	1,030.8	1,061.1	1,092.5	1,123.1	2.11	23.20
Netherlands	629.7	636.7	640.7	639.2	636.3	632.9	633.1	633.2	629.9	621.9	602.7	-0.44	-4.28
New Zealand	166.4	166.8	165.4	163.5	161.8	161.6	162.0	163.9	165.1	164.7	162.8	-0.22	-2.17
Nigeria	2,701.6	2,752.9	2,805.2	2,859.8	2,918.7	2,984.3	3,058.7	3,143.3	3,239.0	3,346.6	3,466.2	2.52	28.30
Norway	159.9	162.7	166.1	169.6	173.2	176.6	179.6	181.2	182.8	183.8	182.6	1.33	14.18
Pakistan	3,575.9	3,698.4	3,824.0	3,952.5	4,083.8	4,217.6	4,353.9	4,493.0	4,635.4	4,781.2	4,930.4	3.26	37.88
Peru	750.4	772.2	793.0	812.8	831.8	850.4	869.1	888.3	908.1	929.1	951.5	2.40	26.80
Philippines	2,206.2	2,270.3	2,333.3	2,395.8	2,457.9	2,520.2	2,582.7	2,646.0	2,710.8	2,778.7	2,851.3	2.60	29.24
Poland	1,329.4	1,271.1	1,223.7	1,190.6	1,165.8	1,146.8	1,137.5	1,143.9	1,161.1	1,190.7	1,226.4	-0.80	-7.75
Portugal	391.9	398.9	401.1	401.7	401.9	400.6	397.9	398.6	401.9	407.1	412.5	0.51	5.26
Romania	650.6	623.4	597.0	578.5	665.4	754.5	819.4	875.9	921.9	869.8	811.3	2.23	24.70
Russia	6,175.6	5,942.0	5,596.5	5,309.5	5,017.2	4,810.3	4,693.9	4,701.7	4,723.1	4,839.9	4,915.2	-2.26	-20.41
Saudi Arabia	472.1	504.1	535.8	566.7	595.9	623.2	648.4	671.8	694.7	718.9	746.6	4.69	58.12
Singapore	206.1	207.6	209.6	209.3	208.3	205.3	204.0	204.2	209.1	215.0	219.0	0.61	6.24
Slovakia	189.9	190.4	189.5	187.6	184.9	180.7	177.8	176.5	177.4	182.9	191.2	0.07	0.72
Slovenia	76.0	76.5	77.3	77.5	77.8	76.9	75.7	73.6	72.0	71.1	71.3	-0.63	-6.15
South Africa	1,293.2	1,294.7	1,293.4	1,289.3	1,282.5	1,273.0	1,261.2	1,247.4	1,232.3	1,217.0	1,203.0	-0.72	-6.97
South Korea	2,094.5	2,066.5	2,029.6	2,001.1	1,996.2	2,013.2	2,042.1	2,076.7	2,105.5	2,112.9	2,093.6	0.00	-0.04
Spain	1,675.1	1,709.5	1,744.1	1,776.9	1,802.8	1,826.3	1,847.3	1,866.0	1,885.9	1,910.4	1,937.8	1.47	15.69
Sweden	294.5	304.3	314.2	323.4	330.4	332.0	325.4	320.1	316.6	313.6	312.4	0.59	6.10
Switzerland	301.5	309.2	314.7	318.5	319.4	317.4	312.8	306.9	300.7	293.4	285.1	-0.56	-5.45
Taiwan	945.1	949.7	950.8	952.5	938.0	929.2	925.3	923.5	914.9	915.3	906.1	-0.42	-4.13
Thailand	2,627.3	2,680.6	2,732.2	2,767.5	2,820.6	2,808.3	2,805.2	2,824.1	2,821.9	2,768.5	2,748.1	0.45	4.60
Tunisia	312.9	320.5	328.1	335.5	342.6	349.4	355.8	361.9	367.8	373.9	380.6	1.98	21.64
Turkey	2,151.6	2,207.9	2,265.2	2,321.2	2,379.7	2,444.3	2,518.7	2,602.3	2,693.3	2,792.7	2,890.2	3.00	34.33
Turkmenistan	153.1	155.2	156.0	155.7	155.0	154.6	155.0	156.5	159.1	162.7	166.7	0.86	8.92
Ukraine	1,915.0	1,856.6	1,770.7	1,699.9	1,632.6	1,576.0	1,538.7	1,540.6	1,544.6	1,565.2	1,572.3	-1.95	-17.89
United Arab Emirates	67.4	71.5	76.0	80.9	86.5	93.2	101.1	110.2	120.4	131.7	143.8	7.87	113.21
United Kingdom	2,238.0	2,290.3	2,329.1	2,352.7	2,360.6	2,352.9	2,331.4	2,306.0	2,279.8	2,241.1	2,185.3	-0.24	-2.35
USA	11,567.1	11,435.1	11,192.4	10,932.8	10,675.3	10,454.2	10,394.9	10,449.6	10,444.4	10,363.5	10,204.9	-1.25	-11.78
Venezuela	805.7	830.8	852.0	869.2	882.4	892.5	900.3	906.7	913.0	921.0	932.9	1.48	15.79
Vietnam	2,586.0	2,668.8	2,741.0	2,804.2	2,861.0	2,915.3	2,970.1	3,026.1	3,082.7	3,140.2	3,198.1	2.15	23.67

Key population trends

Table 4.54 Female Population Aged 50-54: 2009-2019

'000

	2009	2010	2011	2012	2013	2014	2015	2016	2017	2018	2019	CAGR	Period growth
Algeria	690.8	718.6	752.1	790.7	832.7	875.5	917.0	956.1	992.4	1,026.3	1,058.6	4.36	53.24
Argentina	1,068.7	1,077.7	1,086.4	1,094.9	1,103.2	1,111.2	1,119.0	1,126.8	1,135.1	1,144.7	1,156.8	0.80	8.25
Australia	726.1	740.2	753.9	767.4	779.3	787.3	787.3	782.4	775.9	771.1	774.0	0.64	6.60
Austria	288.3	298.3	308.0	315.9	325.4	335.6	343.9	349.3	352.0	352.6	351.5	2.00	21.94
Azerbaijan	272.6	289.3	305.1	319.4	331.4	340.3	345.3	346.1	343.1	337.3	329.9	1.93	21.01
Belarus	400.9	409.8	419.5	422.8	422.2	413.0	401.6	385.1	369.9	355.5	345.1	-1.49	-13.92
Belgium	375.1	381.5	385.3	389.8	392.9	396.2	398.6	399.2	396.7	392.1	385.7	0.28	2.81
Bolivia	183.9	188.6	193.3	197.9	202.5	207.3	212.5	218.1	224.1	230.9	238.3	2.63	29.59
Bosnia-Herzegovina	151.2	152.8	154.4	155.9	157.1	157.9	158.1	157.8	156.8	155.5	153.9	0.18	1.83
Brazil	5,217.5	5,420.2	5,632.8	5,850.9	6,060.6	6,243.9	6,388.3	6,489.7	6,553.8	6,590.1	6,612.8	2.40	26.74
Bulgaria	273.6	270.3	266.1	262.7	259.9	256.8	254.3	248.8	242.2	237.6	240.1	-1.30	-12.25
Canada	1,290.2	1,313.1	1,336.6	1,349.2	1,363.0	1,371.8	1,366.7	1,341.7	1,307.3	1,265.6	1,227.6	-0.50	-4.85
Chile	523.0	545.3	566.4	585.6	601.9	614.1	621.7	624.6	623.7	620.3	616.4	1.66	17.86
China	48,648.2	45,657.6	42,271.4	42,895.8	47,778.7	52,727.9	58,970.0	66,126.8	66,564.7	66,452.5	66,926.4	3.24	37.57
Colombia	1,157.3	1,196.1	1,237.4	1,281.1	1,326.4	1,372.1	1,416.9	1,459.3	1,497.8	1,529.9	1,553.5	2.99	34.23
Costa Rica	117.9	123.2	128.4	133.4	138.0	142.1	145.6	148.3	150.3	151.6	152.1	2.58	29.03
Croatia	168.6	167.9	166.9	164.9	163.9	162.2	159.5	158.4	157.5	155.7	154.1	-0.90	-8.61
Czech Republic	367.4	351.0	335.9	323.0	314.7	318.5	330.4	339.0	343.6	346.1	341.6	-0.73	-7.02
Denmark	180.4	180.8	182.2	183.2	185.4	189.8	194.7	199.6	205.6	207.9	205.1	1.29	13.72
Ecuador	305.7	312.3	319.4	327.1	335.3	343.8	352.5	361.3	370.0	378.4	386.6	2.38	26.46
Egypt	1,688.7	1,723.8	1,751.7	1,772.4	1,786.8	1,794.2	1,792.9	1,783.2	1,765.6	1,738.9	1,711.6	0.13	1.35
Estonia	50.3	50.2	50.1	50.2	49.8	48.9	47.8	46.3	44.5	43.3	42.8	-1.59	-14.79
Finland	191.1	188.8	187.3	185.6	185.0	186.5	186.5	185.7	184.8	183.6	180.9	-0.55	-5.35
France	2,139.1	2,147.1	2,153.7	2,162.9	2,164.1	2,181.7	2,195.0	2,201.8	2,204.7	2,200.0	2,180.7	0.19	1.95
Germany	2,926.2	2,985.7	3,062.4	3,144.3	3,221.3	3,306.7	3,362.9	3,385.3	3,388.7	3,368.5	3,312.8	1.25	13.21
Greece	386.6	392.9	402.8	402.5	404.8	406.2	408.4	405.9	416.4	427.9	438.7	1.27	13.47
Hong Kong, China	309.6	319.6	327.2	328.8	337.6	342.6	342.9	336.3	327.3	309.7	296.9	-0.42	-4.10
Hungary	399.1	372.7	350.5	329.9	316.1	306.0	299.3	293.3	292.8	301.9	312.8	-2.41	-21.61
India	25,766.5	26,287.9	26,825.6	27,387.1	27,972.1	28,574.7	29,188.0	29,808.4	30,436.5	31,073.9	31,724.0	2.10	23.12
Indonesia	5,584.0	5,811.0	6,026.1	6,230.0	6,426.3	6,620.6	6,817.7	7,019.4	7,225.2	7,432.8	7,638.8	3.18	36.80
Iran	1,583.8	1,644.6	1,698.9	1,748.7	1,797.3	1,848.6	1,905.5	1,968.5	2,035.3	2,101.1	2,160.1	3.15	36.39
Ireland	130.2	133.0	136.5	139.6	142.2	145.0	147.8	149.7	151.3	152.5	153.9	1.69	18.22
Israel	193.0	194.3	195.3	195.9	196.3	196.1	195.7	196.1	197.3	199.8	204.4	0.58	5.91
Italy	1,985.6	2,018.3	2,057.7	2,105.1	2,155.7	2,217.9	2,291.5	2,349.3	2,393.5	2,420.9	2,429.7	2.04	22.37
Japan	3,877.4	3,823.9	3,791.1	3,808.7	3,832.2	3,856.5	3,951.9	3,890.6	4,008.0	4,105.2	4,199.7	0.80	8.31
Jordan	87.0	92.8	99.0	105.5	112.3	119.4	126.9	134.7	142.8	151.0	159.3	6.23	83.06
Kazakhstan	521.0	530.8	539.9	548.0	554.4	557.7	557.1	552.4	544.7	536.4	530.5	0.18	1.82
Kuwait	37.3	40.2	43.2	46.1	49.0	52.0	55.0	58.1	61.4	64.7	68.2	6.23	83.07
Latvia	84.6	85.8	86.8	87.6	87.4	86.0	83.9	80.6	78.0	75.9	74.4	-1.28	-12.08
Lithuania	120.5	126.2	130.2	134.3	136.3	135.3	132.7	129.1	125.1	122.1	120.4	-0.01	-0.09
Malaysia	663.0	684.0	704.9	725.4	744.7	762.9	780.2	797.0	814.1	827.5	838.6	2.38	26.49
Mexico	2,544.2	2,627.7	2,715.1	2,804.7	2,899.4	3,002.0	3,114.2	3,237.1	3,371.3	3,518.1	3,677.6	3.75	44.55
Morocco	783.1	816.4	843.2	863.9	879.6	892.3	903.8	915.4	928.3	943.6	962.5	2.08	22.91
Netherlands	575.8	585.7	594.2	604.4	613.4	621.9	629.2	633.3	631.6	628.4	624.7	0.82	8.50
New Zealand	144.8	148.5	153.0	157.4	161.5	163.4	163.9	162.5	160.7	159.1	158.9	0.94	9.76
Nigeria	2,296.2	2,342.0	2,388.3	2,435.5	2,483.5	2,532.0	2,580.9	2,630.8	2,682.9	2,739.0	2,801.4	2.01	22.00
Norway	154.9	156.3	157.1	157.4	158.6	160.3	162.9	166.2	169.6	173.2	176.6	1.32	13.98
Pakistan	2,908.7	3,016.0	3,127.0	3,241.4	3,358.7	3,478.6	3,600.9	3,725.8	3,853.6	3,984.2	4,117.5	3.54	41.56
Peru	616.8	637.7	659.8	683.0	706.7	730.0	752.4	773.5	793.4	812.5	831.3	3.03	34.77
Philippines	1,875.9	1,931.3	1,987.8	2,046.5	2,107.5	2,170.5	2,234.7	2,299.5	2,364.5	2,429.4	2,494.3	2.89	32.96
Poland	1,552.3	1,534.2	1,491.4	1,434.0	1,365.8	1,301.6	1,244.4	1,198.0	1,165.7	1,142.1	1,124.4	-3.17	-27.57
Portugal	363.6	367.8	373.6	381.8	386.1	391.5	398.5	400.8	401.5	401.8	400.6	0.97	10.18
Romania	796.2	775.6	744.5	707.2	669.9	636.3	609.4	583.3	564.8	649.7	736.5	-0.78	-7.51
Russia	6,114.2	6,138.8	6,228.0	6,238.0	6,180.3	6,032.9	5,800.6	5,467.8	5,188.8	4,905.9	4,705.4	-2.58	-23.04
Saudi Arabia	315.2	335.4	359.0	385.6	414.7	445.3	476.5	507.7	538.1	567.2	594.4	6.55	88.58
Singapore	189.3	194.1	197.9	200.3	202.8	205.9	206.8	208.5	207.5	205.8	202.2	0.66	6.77
Slovakia	205.4	201.7	197.4	192.8	188.5	186.7	187.3	186.3	184.3	181.6	177.4	-1.46	-13.66
Slovenia	76.5	76.0	75.7	75.5	75.2	75.7	76.2	76.9	77.1	77.5	76.6	0.02	0.16
South Africa	1,169.7	1,185.8	1,195.6	1,199.6	1,198.9	1,195.1	1,189.4	1,182.4	1,174.4	1,165.2	1,154.5	-0.13	-1.30
South Korea	1,851.0	1,942.0	2,016.4	2,070.8	2,095.2	2,089.4	2,062.0	2,025.7	1,997.6	1,993.1	2,010.5	0.83	8.61
Spain	1,476.7	1,525.8	1,571.2	1,613.0	1,652.8	1,688.5	1,722.0	1,756.3	1,788.9	1,814.6	1,837.9	2.21	24.47
Sweden	288.7	289.4	288.9	288.6	289.7	294.3	304.1	313.8	322.9	329.7	331.4	1.39	14.79
Switzerland	262.3	268.8	275.8	282.8	289.8	298.5	306.1	311.5	315.3	316.1	313.8	1.81	19.62
Taiwan	862.4	883.0	896.1	907.0	925.5	938.6	943.1	943.8	945.3	930.4	921.6	0.67	6.87
Thailand	2,228.1	2,292.2	2,337.4	2,411.3	2,488.8	2,569.0	2,623.2	2,676.9	2,712.2	2,766.3	2,752.2	2.13	23.52
Tunisia	267.3	276.2	284.6	292.7	300.6	308.4	316.0	323.5	330.9	338.0	344.8	2.58	28.98
Turkey	1,838.5	1,893.1	1,948.2	2,003.4	2,058.8	2,115.6	2,171.3	2,228.5	2,283.6	2,341.1	2,405.8	2.73	30.86
Turkmenistan	122.3	128.8	134.8	140.2	144.7	148.1	150.1	150.9	150.7	150.2	149.8	2.05	22.51
Ukraine	1,848.8	1,863.3	1,906.7	1,911.3	1,903.1	1,868.2	1,808.2	1,721.5	1,652.2	1,589.1	1,538.5	-1.82	-16.78
United Arab Emirates	43.1	46.8	50.5	54.1	57.8	61.5	65.4	69.5	74.1	79.4	85.6	7.11	98.75
United Kingdom	1,946.4	1,987.9	2,037.4	2,090.7	2,143.5	2,197.8	2,251.5	2,293.1	2,319.0	2,328.2	2,321.0	1.78	19.24
USA	11,106.0	11,254.6	11,374.6	11,386.6	11,378.1	11,375.7	11,252.4	11,023.2	10,775.0	10,527.8	10,316.0	-0.74	-7.11
Venezuela	658.1	681.0	706.8	735.0	764.0	791.7	816.6	837.7	854.7	868.0	878.1	2.93	33.43
Vietnam	2,063.0	2,154.3	2,251.1	2,350.8	2,449.9	2,543.3	2,627.4	2,700.9	2,765.5	2,823.6	2,878.8	3.39	39.54

Key population trends

Table 4.55 Female Population Aged 55-59: 2009-2019

'000

	2009	2010	2011	2012	2013	2014	2015	2016	2017	2018	2019	CAGR	Period growth
Algeria	561.7	586.9	608.8	628.4	648.0	670.3	697.4	730.2	768.2	809.4	851.5	4.25	51.59
Argentina	979.9	996.2	1,010.6	1,023.3	1,034.5	1,044.6	1,054.1	1,063.1	1,071.8	1,080.2	1,088.4	1.06	11.07
Australia	658.9	668.2	679.2	691.5	702.8	716.6	731.3	746.4	760.8	773.1	781.3	1.72	18.58
Austria	250.7	252.5	257.3	267.5	275.9	284.9	294.8	304.4	312.3	321.7	331.8	2.84	32.34
Azerbaijan	172.5	192.0	211.0	229.2	246.6	263.5	279.8	295.4	309.6	321.6	330.4	6.72	91.59
Belarus	337.4	340.5	349.1	360.8	372.4	389.6	397.8	406.6	409.9	408.8	400.4	1.73	18.68
Belgium	340.7	345.2	350.5	357.1	362.2	368.3	374.6	378.5	383.1	386.3	389.5	1.35	14.33
Bolivia	152.7	157.0	161.5	166.0	170.7	175.3	179.9	184.5	189.1	193.7	198.5	2.65	29.94
Bosnia-Herzegovina	133.4	137.9	141.5	144.4	146.8	148.8	150.6	152.3	153.7	154.9	155.6	1.55	16.66
Brazil	4,125.9	4,303.1	4,484.0	4,667.2	4,854.5	5,048.5	5,250.0	5,461.1	5,677.3	5,885.0	6,066.3	3.93	47.03
Bulgaria	285.6	279.4	273.0	273.6	270.9	267.8	264.6	260.7	257.4	254.7	251.8	-1.25	-11.82
Canada	1,119.9	1,154.7	1,184.5	1,217.4	1,246.4	1,268.2	1,288.0	1,310.2	1,322.3	1,336.1	1,345.2	1.85	20.12
Chile	412.4	429.5	448.6	469.5	491.6	514.0	536.0	556.9	575.9	592.0	604.1	3.89	46.50
China	45,560.4	48,438.2	50,307.0	51,554.1	52,092.4	49,696.1	46,402.1	42,773.4	43,432.3	48,472.8	53,343.1	1.59	17.08
Colombia	942.0	981.2	1,018.4	1,054.2	1,089.5	1,125.9	1,164.3	1,205.1	1,248.0	1,292.5	1,337.3	3.57	41.97
Costa Rica	90.3	95.3	100.4	105.6	110.8	115.9	121.1	126.2	131.1	135.7	139.9	4.47	54.85
Croatia	158.3	159.9	162.0	166.4	166.3	165.6	165.0	163.8	161.8	160.8	159.0	0.05	0.46
Czech Republic	393.9	392.3	388.0	381.4	372.8	361.3	344.7	329.8	317.1	309.3	313.4	-2.26	-20.45
Denmark	176.0	175.3	174.8	176.3	176.7	176.7	177.2	178.7	179.7	181.9	186.2	0.56	5.77
Ecuador	254.7	265.8	275.3	283.5	290.6	297.2	303.9	311.0	318.6	326.6	335.0	2.78	31.54
Egypt	1,393.1	1,450.3	1,505.4	1,557.3	1,604.8	1,646.7	1,681.7	1,708.5	1,727.2	1,738.7	1,742.4	2.26	25.07
Estonia	48.0	47.8	48.5	48.4	48.4	48.7	48.7	48.6	48.7	48.3	47.5	-0.12	-1.19
Finland	198.4	196.0	194.2	194.1	191.8	189.1	186.8	185.3	183.6	183.0	184.5	-0.72	-7.01
France	2,106.3	2,100.3	2,089.3	2,094.2	2,096.5	2,103.2	2,111.9	2,119.4	2,129.4	2,131.3	2,149.4	0.20	2.05
Germany	2,707.8	2,731.3	2,740.6	2,769.8	2,802.0	2,847.9	2,910.8	2,989.3	3,071.1	3,147.2	3,231.0	1.78	19.32
Greece	349.1	359.9	362.6	371.6	378.0	387.7	394.1	404.0	403.7	406.1	407.5	1.56	16.71
Hong Kong, China	242.8	252.4	265.1	279.0	294.9	306.7	315.9	323.2	325.1	333.8	338.7	3.39	39.54
Hungary	382.3	397.8	405.7	409.4	403.7	387.8	361.4	339.1	318.7	305.0	295.0	-2.56	-22.84
India	21,132.4	22,068.4	22,872.2	23,546.9	24,123.1	24,647.9	25,165.1	25,699.9	26,260.0	26,844.5	27,446.9	2.65	29.88
Indonesia	4,289.5	4,489.1	4,705.5	4,933.8	5,167.1	5,397.9	5,620.8	5,833.2	6,035.6	6,231.7	6,426.5	4.13	49.82
Iran	1,197.0	1,269.2	1,340.4	1,409.4	1,475.2	1,536.9	1,594.1	1,647.1	1,697.2	1,747.3	1,800.1	4.16	50.39
Ireland	117.4	119.3	121.3	123.8	126.4	128.9	131.5	135.1	138.1	140.7	143.4	2.02	22.13
Israel	188.8	190.7	190.6	189.6	188.8	189.3	190.5	191.2	191.7	191.9	191.6	0.15	1.46
Italy	1,877.6	1,875.8	1,880.8	1,906.1	1,938.3	1,971.7	2,004.6	2,044.1	2,091.6	2,142.2	2,204.5	1.62	17.41
Japan	4,614.9	4,358.0	4,154.2	3,970.2	3,857.2	3,820.4	3,770.9	3,741.0	3,759.8	3,784.1	3,809.1	-1.90	-17.46
Jordan	68.1	70.0	72.3	75.2	78.8	83.2	88.3	94.2	100.8	107.9	115.3	5.40	69.27
Kazakhstan	433.6	454.7	472.2	486.5	498.6	509.5	519.9	529.8	538.6	545.2	548.3	2.38	26.47
Kuwait	22.3	24.3	26.7	29.4	32.3	35.3	38.4	41.3	44.2	47.1	50.0	8.41	124.16
Latvia	77.2	76.5	77.4	77.9	78.9	81.0	82.1	83.0	83.8	83.6	82.5	0.66	6.83
Lithuania	107.7	107.0	107.7	109.1	111.4	116.3	121.7	125.6	129.6	131.6	130.8	1.96	21.46
Malaysia	525.1	553.7	580.1	603.7	624.4	644.4	664.5	684.5	704.1	722.5	740.0	3.49	40.91
Mexico	2,062.7	2,178.3	2,284.6	2,378.2	2,462.4	2,542.2	2,622.2	2,705.6	2,793.8	2,888.5	2,991.5	3.79	45.02
Morocco	565.0	600.0	638.8	680.1	721.6	760.1	793.4	820.3	840.9	856.5	869.0	4.40	53.80
Netherlands	536.2	537.3	542.2	549.8	555.9	564.3	574.5	583.1	593.3	602.1	610.6	1.31	13.87
New Zealand	125.6	127.6	130.7	134.1	137.7	141.7	145.5	149.9	154.3	158.4	160.3	2.47	27.68
Nigeria	1,877.6	1,935.4	1,988.8	2,038.0	2,083.8	2,127.8	2,171.5	2,215.7	2,260.6	2,306.3	2,352.4	2.28	25.29
Norway	144.2	145.5	147.4	150.8	152.3	153.6	155.0	155.7	156.0	157.2	158.9	0.98	10.20
Pakistan	2,329.9	2,409.0	2,494.8	2,587.1	2,685.0	2,787.3	2,893.3	3,002.6	3,115.0	3,230.5	3,348.8	3.69	43.73
Peru	503.3	521.6	539.9	558.3	577.2	597.0	617.9	640.1	663.1	686.5	709.6	3.49	40.99
Philippines	1,508.6	1,586.1	1,654.9	1,715.8	1,771.2	1,824.6	1,879.2	1,936.6	1,997.0	2,060.2	2,125.2	3.49	40.87
Poland	1,451.0	1,477.6	1,500.0	1,507.9	1,513.2	1,510.2	1,492.9	1,451.5	1,396.0	1,330.2	1,268.4	-1.34	-12.59
Portugal	343.8	347.3	350.9	352.5	356.3	361.7	366.0	371.8	380.0	384.5	389.9	1.27	13.41
Romania	747.2	748.3	758.9	770.9	772.7	772.0	751.8	721.5	685.2	649.1	616.6	-1.90	-17.48
Russia	5,426.3	5,508.8	5,600.6	5,691.3	5,758.5	5,885.8	5,905.8	5,994.9	6,003.6	5,947.8	5,804.9	0.68	6.98
Saudi Arabia	238.4	249.6	261.2	273.7	287.8	304.3	324.0	347.1	373.2	401.9	432.1	6.12	81.20
Singapore	150.9	157.4	165.6	173.1	179.8	185.0	189.0	192.0	193.5	195.0	197.4	2.72	30.77
Slovakia	192.6	197.8	201.2	203.0	202.5	201.3	197.5	193.1	188.5	184.1	182.3	-0.55	-5.33
Slovenia	72.0	73.9	74.8	75.9	76.2	75.6	75.2	74.8	74.7	74.4	74.9	0.40	4.09
South Africa	959.2	994.2	1,025.9	1,053.3	1,075.8	1,093.0	1,105.0	1,111.9	1,114.0	1,112.4	1,108.2	1.45	15.53
South Korea	1,315.9	1,409.9	1,518.4	1,621.7	1,727.8	1,834.0	1,924.8	1,999.1	2,053.4	2,078.1	2,072.8	4.65	57.52
Spain	1,308.4	1,330.2	1,356.0	1,391.4	1,435.2	1,482.3	1,530.2	1,575.1	1,616.3	1,655.7	1,691.0	2.60	29.24
Sweden	292.6	286.9	285.3	286.0	286.9	286.2	286.9	286.3	285.9	286.9	291.4	-0.04	-0.41
Switzerland	238.2	239.5	241.4	246.0	250.4	255.7	262.1	269.1	276.2	283.1	291.8	2.05	22.48
Taiwan	720.2	759.5	797.9	816.4	831.8	852.1	872.4	885.1	895.5	913.4	926.2	2.55	28.60
Thailand	1,740.4	1,831.3	1,932.2	2,004.7	2,066.7	2,166.9	2,232.2	2,279.2	2,354.2	2,433.4	2,514.5	3.75	44.48
Tunisia	208.3	220.5	231.8	242.5	252.3	261.5	270.3	278.6	286.7	294.5	302.2	3.79	45.04
Turkey	1,474.6	1,546.1	1,613.7	1,676.2	1,733.4	1,788.6	1,842.7	1,896.8	1,950.3	2,004.6	2,057.5	3.39	39.53
Turkmenistan	84.1	90.5	97.0	103.6	110.2	116.6	122.8	128.6	133.9	138.3	141.6	5.34	68.31
Ukraine	1,742.0	1,729.2	1,724.5	1,738.6	1,751.3	1,788.8	1,799.6	1,838.3	1,842.7	1,838.9	1,812.2	0.40	4.03
United Arab Emirates	23.8	26.1	28.6	31.4	34.4	37.6	40.9	44.4	47.9	51.6	55.3	8.78	132.02
United Kingdom	1,840.2	1,820.6	1,815.5	1,829.6	1,859.0	1,896.1	1,938.8	1,990.5	2,045.4	2,098.8	2,152.8	1.58	16.99
USA	9,788.6	10,017.7	10,231.9	10,486.6	10,696.8	10,841.7	10,991.8	11,116.4	11,133.8	11,130.4	11,132.9	1.30	13.73
Venezuela	549.6	568.2	585.7	602.8	620.6	640.3	662.9	688.4	716.1	744.6	772.0	3.45	40.45
Vietnam	1,522.1	1,640.2	1,745.1	1,839.1	1,926.1	2,013.1	2,104.4	2,201.3	2,301.2	2,400.2	2,493.4	5.06	63.81

Key population trends

Table 4.56 Female Population Aged 60-64: 2009-2019

'000

	2009	2010	2011	2012	2013	2014	2015	2016	2017	2018	2019	CAGR	Period growth
Algeria	394.6	420.9	449.5	479.2	508.4	535.6	559.8	581.0	600.1	619.3	641.1	4.97	62.47
Argentina	845.8	867.0	888.0	908.6	928.3	946.6	963.0	977.6	990.4	1,001.6	1,011.7	1.81	19.61
Australia	586.1	607.4	625.9	625.7	635.0	646.1	656.2	668.5	681.7	693.4	707.2	1.90	20.66
Austria	233.2	235.2	247.2	250.7	248.0	246.4	248.2	253.0	263.2	271.5	280.5	1.86	20.25
Azerbaijan	92.6	100.7	112.6	127.7	145.1	163.6	182.3	200.6	218.1	235.0	251.3	10.50	171.46
Belarus	230.8	260.4	289.9	307.4	317.5	321.8	324.5	332.3	343.5	354.3	371.1	4.86	60.75
Belgium	312.9	321.3	330.2	329.3	330.8	332.2	336.7	342.1	348.7	353.9	360.0	1.41	15.05
Bolivia	123.0	127.6	131.9	136.1	140.1	144.1	148.3	152.6	157.1	161.6	166.2	3.06	35.13
Bosnia-Herzegovina	100.7	106.8	113.0	119.1	124.9	130.2	134.7	138.3	141.2	143.5	145.4	3.74	44.30
Brazil	3,171.3	3,305.4	3,448.7	3,601.4	3,762.5	3,930.7	4,104.8	4,282.3	4,462.1	4,645.7	4,835.3	4.31	52.47
Bulgaria	266.4	276.9	285.2	280.6	279.7	276.6	271.0	265.1	266.0	263.7	260.9	-0.21	-2.06
Canada	957.6	1,001.1	1,036.4	1,046.9	1,064.2	1,091.3	1,122.9	1,151.2	1,183.0	1,211.4	1,232.9	2.56	28.76
Chile	341.6	351.2	361.6	373.1	386.0	400.8	417.6	436.4	456.8	478.5	500.5	3.89	46.51
China	31,175.2	33,318.1	35,293.9	38,296.0	40,782.8	43,477.7	45,839.3	47,296.8	48,214.1	48,354.2	45,779.8	3.92	46.85
Colombia	695.3	736.9	779.2	821.5	863.1	903.2	941.5	977.8	1,012.7	1,047.1	1,082.4	4.53	55.68
Costa Rica	66.4	70.2	74.3	78.7	83.2	87.9	92.8	97.7	102.8	107.9	113.0	5.46	70.11
Croatia	124.5	132.9	143.6	146.7	150.3	154.0	155.7	157.6	161.9	161.7	161.1	2.61	29.42
Czech Republic	375.8	382.9	394.2	392.2	387.0	383.3	381.4	377.1	370.8	362.7	352.0	-0.65	-6.34
Denmark	189.5	187.1	183.3	176.9	172.3	170.6	170.1	169.7	171.2	171.7	171.8	-0.97	-9.32
Ecuador	188.8	197.9	208.6	220.7	233.2	245.3	256.2	265.5	273.5	280.4	286.8	4.27	51.94
Egypt	1,031.7	1,092.9	1,154.0	1,215.8	1,277.9	1,339.5	1,399.4	1,456.9	1,510.6	1,559.5	1,602.1	4.50	55.29
Estonia	39.8	42.7	44.9	45.9	46.4	46.2	46.0	46.7	46.6	46.7	47.1	1.68	18.16
Finland	191.8	202.5	205.2	201.9	199.0	194.8	192.4	190.7	190.6	188.4	185.9	-0.31	-3.08
France	1,820.5	1,938.4	2,058.0	2,070.1	2,069.7	2,058.4	2,053.5	2,044.0	2,049.9	2,053.2	2,060.7	1.25	13.19
Germany	2,148.2	2,184.4	2,355.0	2,480.6	2,561.9	2,616.4	2,644.0	2,656.7	2,686.9	2,719.3	2,764.6	2.55	28.70
Greece	345.5	344.7	352.1	347.7	347.2	348.9	359.7	362.5	371.5	377.9	387.6	1.16	12.18
Hong Kong, China	167.0	187.5	205.1	217.4	227.9	239.2	248.5	260.8	274.2	289.7	301.5	6.09	80.54
Hungary	325.6	328.8	343.9	356.7	360.3	368.8	383.9	391.4	394.9	389.2	373.5	1.38	14.70
India	15,097.5	15,815.1	16,675.0	17,642.8	18,655.2	19,636.1	20,525.1	21,293.7	21,945.9	22,510.1	23,029.3	4.31	52.54
Indonesia	3,452.0	3,524.7	3,622.6	3,746.9	3,896.8	4,070.1	4,263.5	4,473.7	4,696.0	4,924.0	5,150.4	4.08	49.20
Iran	831.5	887.0	946.5	1,009.0	1,074.1	1,141.1	1,209.2	1,277.9	1,345.9	1,411.5	1,473.3	5.89	77.19
Ireland	103.8	108.0	110.5	112.1	114.1	115.8	117.6	119.6	122.0	124.6	127.1	2.05	22.50
Israel	160.6	171.9	179.4	182.1	184.0	186.9	188.6	188.3	187.0	186.1	186.5	1.50	16.09
Italy	1,834.3	1,892.6	1,958.3	1,923.2	1,890.8	1,853.1	1,852.2	1,858.0	1,883.7	1,916.2	1,949.8	0.61	6.30
Japan	4,807.1	5,091.4	5,355.3	5,167.2	4,876.9	4,528.0	4,279.8	4,082.4	3,903.2	3,793.3	3,758.1	-2.43	-21.82
Jordan	59.6	61.0	61.9	62.5	63.1	64.0	65.5	67.7	70.7	74.5	79.0	2.86	32.55
Kazakhstan	273.0	302.8	332.9	362.0	388.9	413.1	434.2	451.9	466.5	478.5	489.1	6.01	79.19
Kuwait	14.7	15.7	16.8	18.0	19.4	21.1	23.1	25.5	28.1	31.0	33.9	8.69	130.09
Latvia	65.8	68.5	70.9	72.9	73.5	72.8	72.1	73.0	73.5	74.5	76.6	1.53	16.39
Lithuania	91.2	95.2	96.7	99.9	102.5	102.6	102.0	102.7	104.1	106.4	111.1	2.00	21.91
Malaysia	361.7	384.8	411.5	442.5	473.9	505.1	534.0	560.3	583.7	604.0	623.8	5.60	72.44
Mexico	1,517.1	1,593.5	1,688.6	1,797.7	1,915.0	2,032.8	2,144.3	2,246.0	2,337.7	2,421.4	2,501.0	5.13	64.86
Morocco	413.1	434.2	456.9	481.4	508.4	538.9	573.2	611.1	651.4	691.5	728.7	5.84	76.41
Netherlands	519.8	535.1	553.0	536.1	526.1	522.5	523.8	528.6	536.3	542.1	550.5	0.57	5.90
New Zealand	112.4	117.0	120.4	120.4	120.9	123.0	125.0	128.1	131.5	135.1	139.1	2.16	23.77
Nigeria	1,444.6	1,483.3	1,529.3	1,581.4	1,637.2	1,693.3	1,746.8	1,796.5	1,842.4	1,885.3	1,926.7	2.92	33.38
Norway	142.7	144.4	144.8	141.6	140.8	141.5	142.7	144.7	148.0	149.5	150.8	0.56	5.71
Pakistan	1,893.1	1,935.6	1,984.0	2,039.4	2,102.1	2,171.9	2,248.4	2,331.4	2,420.6	2,515.4	2,614.7	3.28	38.11
Peru	397.1	412.3	428.6	445.8	463.6	481.6	499.7	517.7	535.8	554.2	573.6	3.75	44.44
Philippines	1,089.0	1,143.5	1,208.7	1,283.2	1,362.7	1,442.1	1,516.9	1,584.8	1,646.1	1,702.6	1,757.3	4.90	61.37
Poland	1,049.7	1,150.5	1,260.6	1,322.8	1,368.9	1,400.6	1,427.2	1,449.9	1,458.3	1,464.4	1,462.6	3.37	39.34
Portugal	320.8	324.8	327.6	334.3	340.5	340.1	343.6	347.4	349.1	353.0	358.5	1.12	11.78
Romania	559.0	597.1	646.8	669.5	698.8	713.7	715.0	725.3	736.9	738.8	738.3	2.82	32.07
Russia	3,400.2	4,069.0	4,581.6	4,804.6	5,001.3	5,141.9	5,215.8	5,303.9	5,388.1	5,451.0	5,568.7	5.06	63.78
Saudi Arabia	186.0	195.1	204.7	214.6	224.9	235.3	246.1	257.3	269.5	283.3	299.5	4.88	61.00
Singapore	109.9	124.8	134.9	137.9	142.0	147.4	153.4	161.4	168.4	174.5	179.1	5.01	63.00
Slovakia	148.3	154.3	164.7	175.2	182.2	187.4	192.6	196.0	197.7	197.1	195.9	2.82	32.10
Slovenia	54.4	57.3	63.3	66.0	68.5	70.8	72.6	73.6	74.6	75.0	74.5	3.20	37.09
South Africa	729.2	755.3	784.5	816.4	849.7	882.7	914.2	943.1	968.6	990.0	1,006.9	3.28	38.08
South Korea	1,077.5	1,119.0	1,155.4	1,191.3	1,231.9	1,292.0	1,385.1	1,492.4	1,594.7	1,699.8	1,805.0	5.30	67.53
Spain	1,232.6	1,253.7	1,270.6	1,280.5	1,288.8	1,304.9	1,325.8	1,351.2	1,386.1	1,429.1	1,475.3	1.81	19.70
Sweden	315.9	314.2	309.0	300.7	293.7	287.3	281.8	280.1	280.8	281.5	280.9	-1.17	-11.07
Switzerland	229.0	230.5	232.1	230.1	230.0	228.9	230.0	231.7	236.4	240.7	245.9	0.72	7.40
Taiwan	427.1	466.3	525.4	601.5	657.3	703.7	741.9	779.1	796.9	811.6	831.2	6.88	94.59
Thailand	1,256.4	1,361.3	1,445.0	1,531.5	1,621.9	1,681.6	1,774.4	1,878.5	1,952.3	2,015.6	2,117.4	5.36	68.53
Tunisia	146.1	154.9	165.3	176.8	188.9	201.1	212.9	224.0	234.3	244.0	253.0	5.65	73.19
Turkey	1,107.1	1,151.0	1,203.7	1,266.9	1,336.7	1,407.5	1,475.3	1,539.2	1,598.0	1,653.0	1,706.2	4.42	54.11
Turkmenistan	50.7	55.9	61.3	66.9	72.6	78.4	84.4	90.5	96.8	103.0	109.2	7.96	115.16
Ukraine	1,216.1	1,361.2	1,521.6	1,592.3	1,658.0	1,672.7	1,657.5	1,649.6	1,663.6	1,680.3	1,725.2	3.56	41.86
United Arab Emirates	13.0	14.4	15.6	16.8	17.9	19.3	21.0	23.2	25.8	28.8	32.0	9.40	145.65
United Kingdom	1,880.2	1,907.8	1,916.3	1,877.1	1,811.4	1,773.8	1,757.1	1,755.5	1,771.9	1,802.2	1,839.3	-0.22	-2.18
USA	8,238.3	8,651.8	9,066.9	9,070.8	9,231.4	9,441.5	9,667.9	9,881.4	10,132.0	10,338.9	10,483.0	2.44	27.25
Venezuela	423.8	445.3	466.7	487.7	507.8	527.0	545.1	562.2	579.0	596.4	615.8	3.81	45.31
Vietnam	955.6	1,018.3	1,106.8	1,217.7	1,341.9	1,466.6	1,582.4	1,685.5	1,778.3	1,864.4	1,950.1	7.39	104.08

Key population trends

Table 4.57 Female Population Aged 65-69: 2009-2019

'000

	2009	2010	2011	2012	2013	2014	2015	2016	2017	2018	2019	CAGR	Period growth
Algeria	298.9	303.2	312.0	325.6	343.5	365.3	389.9	416.7	444.6	472.2	498.0	5.24	66.59
Argentina	711.6	726.4	743.1	761.5	781.3	801.8	822.7	843.5	863.7	883.0	901.1	2.39	26.63
Australia	439.1	459.0	479.9	516.4	547.2	568.5	590.0	609.4	610.4	620.1	631.3	3.70	43.76
Austria	256.7	247.9	226.7	216.6	222.0	226.5	228.7	240.4	244.0	241.5	240.1	-0.67	-6.47
Azerbaijan	96.3	88.7	83.2	80.5	80.9	84.9	92.5	103.5	117.6	133.8	151.0	4.60	56.81
Belarus	233.5	209.4	186.8	179.5	191.0	215.1	242.4	269.4	285.5	294.6	298.9	2.50	28.02
Belgium	241.5	243.8	250.6	272.0	289.7	302.0	310.3	319.2	318.6	320.4	322.0	2.92	33.29
Bolivia	94.6	97.4	100.8	104.7	109.0	113.4	117.7	121.8	125.8	129.7	133.7	3.52	41.34
Bosnia-Herzegovina	86.7	84.8	84.9	87.2	91.3	96.5	102.3	108.3	114.2	119.8	124.8	3.71	43.88
Brazil	2,470.5	2,538.2	2,621.8	2,719.2	2,829.4	2,950.3	3,080.2	3,218.6	3,366.0	3,521.0	3,682.6	4.07	49.06
Bulgaria	218.3	220.8	225.8	236.1	242.9	251.4	261.6	269.9	265.9	265.3	262.8	1.87	20.37
Canada	718.0	746.7	778.6	832.8	878.0	918.0	957.6	990.5	1,000.4	1,017.3	1,043.6	3.81	45.35
Chile	277.3	288.3	298.6	308.1	317.1	326.0	335.4	345.6	356.7	369.3	383.7	3.30	38.37
China	21,990.2	22,381.8	23,106.1	24,327.4	25,621.8	27,372.9	29,055.9	30,605.3	33,011.3	34,962.9	37,023.2	5.35	68.36
Colombia	489.0	514.2	543.4	576.4	612.5	650.8	690.5	730.8	771.1	810.7	848.9	5.67	73.59
Costa Rica	49.9	52.0	54.4	57.2	60.2	63.5	67.2	71.1	75.3	79.7	84.3	5.39	69.08
Croatia	126.4	120.5	112.7	112.7	113.6	117.0	125.4	135.9	138.9	142.5	146.1	1.46	15.58
Czech Republic	278.9	296.1	305.1	327.0	348.6	359.4	366.0	376.6	375.0	370.6	367.6	2.80	31.82
Denmark	143.5	152.8	162.4	172.6	178.7	180.5	178.4	174.9	169.0	164.8	163.3	1.30	13.84
Ecuador	153.0	157.2	161.6	166.5	172.4	179.6	188.4	198.7	210.2	222.2	233.8	4.33	52.77
Egypt	773.5	792.8	822.7	863.2	915.4	976.6	1,041.5	1,106.4	1,171.9	1,237.8	1,303.1	5.35	68.45
Estonia	40.7	37.9	35.9	34.6	35.3	37.7	40.4	42.5	43.6	44.0	43.9	0.77	7.96
Finland	134.9	136.1	148.0	155.4	173.5	186.4	196.8	199.4	196.3	193.6	189.6	3.46	40.52
France	1,314.3	1,330.9	1,367.3	1,508.6	1,644.1	1,765.2	1,880.3	1,997.3	2,010.1	2,011.0	2,001.2	4.29	52.26
Germany	2,670.7	2,527.2	2,267.0	2,087.4	2,062.2	2,052.9	2,092.6	2,259.2	2,381.4	2,460.7	2,513.9	-0.60	-5.87
Greece	292.6	293.6	287.9	310.0	326.9	341.7	341.0	348.4	344.3	343.9	345.7	1.68	18.18
Hong Kong, China	106.0	109.4	116.0	131.5	147.9	165.1	185.0	201.9	213.7	223.8	234.6	8.27	121.40
Hungary	295.6	303.3	298.8	297.1	299.1	306.5	309.5	324.1	336.8	340.4	348.9	1.67	18.02
India	11,733.5	11,942.4	12,194.3	12,510.6	12,920.2	13,450.2	14,114.4	14,907.9	15,800.0	16,733.7	17,640.3	4.16	50.34
Indonesia	2,973.1	3,010.0	3,042.1	3,073.6	3,111.1	3,162.4	3,234.1	3,329.6	3,450.0	3,594.7	3,761.7	2.38	26.52
Iran	601.5	617.9	642.8	676.0	716.8	763.8	816.0	872.5	932.6	995.4	1,060.1	5.83	76.26
Ireland	79.4	82.4	86.9	92.0	96.4	100.4	104.4	106.9	108.5	110.6	112.3	3.52	41.36
Israel	100.2	102.3	111.2	126.8	143.7	157.5	169.1	176.8	179.4	181.3	184.1	6.28	83.85
Italy	1,709.6	1,660.7	1,599.2	1,658.9	1,721.0	1,790.8	1,848.7	1,913.5	1,880.5	1,850.1	1,814.6	0.60	6.14
Japan	4,375.7	4,286.3	4,068.4	4,226.8	4,466.0	4,686.7	4,968.1	5,227.5	5,046.1	4,764.5	4,425.5	0.11	1.14
Jordan	45.8	47.7	49.6	51.4	53.0	54.3	55.4	56.3	57.1	57.9	59.0	2.57	28.92
Kazakhstan	223.9	205.8	200.4	208.0	226.2	251.3	279.3	307.8	335.3	360.7	383.3	5.52	71.20
Kuwait	9.9	10.6	11.3	12.1	13.0	13.9	14.8	15.9	17.0	18.4	20.0	7.24	101.09
Latvia	74.6	70.4	65.8	61.7	60.1	60.7	63.2	65.3	67.2	67.8	67.3	-1.04	-9.88
Lithuania	98.7	94.8	93.6	89.9	86.1	85.5	89.3	90.8	93.9	96.4	96.6	-0.21	-2.12
Malaysia	258.6	267.4	278.5	291.7	308.0	327.4	350.6	377.7	409.4	441.6	473.6	6.24	83.16
Mexico	1,224.0	1,273.1	1,318.6	1,361.5	1,407.9	1,464.8	1,537.5	1,627.9	1,733.3	1,847.5	1,962.7	4.84	60.35
Morocco	335.0	333.8	338.2	348.3	363.0	381.2	401.3	422.9	446.1	471.7	500.6	4.10	49.40
Netherlands	380.0	393.8	401.2	444.9	482.1	506.0	521.7	539.8	522.5	512.1	508.3	2.95	33.75
New Zealand	87.7	89.9	91.9	97.2	104.1	108.9	113.4	116.7	116.8	117.4	119.5	3.14	36.22
Nigeria	1,110.8	1,135.2	1,158.2	1,181.1	1,205.9	1,235.0	1,270.0	1,311.4	1,358.1	1,408.0	1,458.1	2.76	31.26
Norway	101.1	107.6	114.8	125.5	132.8	137.5	139.2	139.7	136.6	136.0	136.8	3.07	35.34
Pakistan	1,479.2	1,530.5	1,575.2	1,614.4	1,650.6	1,687.3	1,727.7	1,773.8	1,826.5	1,886.1	1,952.3	2.81	31.99
Peru	315.2	324.2	334.2	345.5	357.9	371.5	386.3	402.0	418.5	435.6	452.9	3.69	43.67
Philippines	851.2	878.8	905.4	933.3	965.8	1,006.7	1,058.4	1,121.3	1,193.6	1,271.0	1,348.3	4.71	58.40
Poland	801.7	781.0	765.5	818.6	900.2	995.4	1,092.5	1,198.2	1,258.6	1,303.6	1,335.1	5.23	66.52
Portugal	280.6	284.3	292.8	299.4	305.3	313.8	317.9	320.9	327.7	334.0	333.9	1.75	18.97
Romania	523.9	506.5	483.8	490.2	497.9	520.8	556.9	603.3	624.6	652.1	666.1	2.43	27.15
Russia	3,467.6	2,829.2	2,413.1	2,371.2	2,675.6	3,157.6	3,775.1	4,251.0	4,458.4	4,638.7	4,763.5	3.23	37.37
Saudi Arabia	141.6	148.0	154.8	162.0	169.7	177.8	186.4	195.5	205.0	214.8	224.9	4.74	58.86
Singapore	77.5	72.8	72.4	83.7	96.1	106.3	121.6	131.7	134.1	137.7	142.7	6.30	84.23
Slovakia	121.1	124.1	124.9	127.1	133.2	140.8	146.9	157.2	167.7	174.7	179.8	4.03	48.46
Slovenia	54.1	53.4	50.7	51.1	51.7	52.8	55.6	61.4	64.2	66.6	68.9	2.45	27.35
South Africa	555.6	573.1	590.1	607.1	625.1	645.5	668.9	695.6	725.0	756.0	787.1	3.54	41.65
South Korea	986.5	977.8	972.7	981.3	1,007.0	1,045.8	1,086.8	1,122.8	1,158.6	1,199.2	1,258.8	2.47	27.60
Spain	1,027.5	1,065.4	1,110.9	1,153.1	1,184.1	1,210.9	1,231.0	1,247.4	1,257.1	1,265.3	1,281.0	2.23	24.67
Sweden	244.4	259.7	276.8	292.3	301.9	305.9	304.4	299.2	291.3	284.4	278.3	1.31	13.89
Switzerland	190.8	198.4	205.4	212.1	216.5	220.0	221.3	222.8	220.7	220.4	219.1	1.39	14.79
Taiwan	399.4	398.6	383.4	376.2	386.9	408.9	446.6	503.0	575.6	628.5	672.5	5.35	68.39
Thailand	964.2	974.3	1,005.9	1,039.0	1,108.8	1,186.4	1,293.6	1,379.7	1,467.9	1,560.4	1,620.7	5.33	68.10
Tunisia	119.8	119.9	121.7	125.1	130.3	137.2	145.7	155.5	166.5	178.0	189.7	4.70	58.35
Turkey	901.8	929.1	944.8	959.9	982.1	1,015.4	1,059.2	1,112.7	1,172.8	1,235.9	1,298.7	3.71	44.01
Turkmenistan	37.3	36.0	36.3	38.2	41.5	45.7	50.4	55.3	60.4	65.6	71.0	6.65	90.38
Ukraine	1,395.3	1,225.5	1,065.9	1,003.9	1,024.6	1,124.3	1,262.1	1,415.9	1,487.8	1,561.1	1,588.6	1.31	13.85
United Arab Emirates	6.3	6.7	7.4	8.4	9.5	10.7	11.8	12.8	13.8	15.0	16.3	10.01	159.59
United Kingdom	1,449.3	1,487.9	1,538.8	1,629.6	1,727.0	1,782.5	1,811.3	1,822.8	1,788.2	1,727.6	1,693.1	1.57	16.83
USA	6,271.4	6,458.7	6,617.6	7,150.7	7,440.7	7,789.3	8,182.2	8,577.4	8,588.4	8,745.9	8,949.8	3.62	42.71
Venezuela	303.3	319.8	337.7	356.7	376.5	396.9	417.5	437.9	458.0	477.4	495.9	5.04	63.49
Vietnam	798.6	809.8	821.5	835.5	857.9	896.8	957.3	1,042.4	1,148.7	1,267.6	1,387.0	5.68	73.69

Key population trends

Table 4.58 Female Population Aged 70-74: 2009-2019

'000

	2009	2010	2011	2012	2013	2014	2015	2016	2017	2018	2019	CAGR	Period growth
Algeria	262.3	263.7	263.3	261.8	260.6	261.3	265.4	273.6	285.9	302.2	322.0	2.07	22.75
Argentina	608.3	614.0	621.2	630.2	641.1	653.8	668.4	684.8	702.6	721.7	741.5	2.00	21.90
Australia	355.9	366.8	376.5	388.2	400.2	418.0	437.9	459.1	495.1	525.2	546.1	4.38	53.45
Austria	167.7	187.3	208.9	226.3	236.3	243.2	235.1	215.3	206.0	211.5	216.2	2.57	28.91
Azerbaijan	110.6	109.0	104.8	98.5	90.9	83.3	76.9	72.4	70.1	70.7	74.3	-3.90	-32.82
Belarus	261.6	269.6	266.9	255.4	235.5	205.0	183.8	163.8	158.2	168.7	190.4	-3.13	-27.23
Belgium	247.0	246.8	243.5	235.0	229.8	228.8	231.3	238.2	259.0	276.2	288.2	1.56	16.72
Bolivia	73.4	75.1	76.7	78.4	80.2	82.3	85.0	88.2	91.8	95.8	99.9	3.13	36.10
Bosnia-Herzegovina	93.0	91.9	89.4	85.8	81.9	78.8	77.2	77.5	79.7	83.5	88.3	-0.52	-5.05
Brazil	1,943.6	2,009.9	2,065.1	2,112.9	2,159.1	2,212.1	2,277.8	2,357.6	2,449.9	2,553.7	2,667.1	3.21	37.22
Bulgaria	207.5	198.8	196.7	193.6	194.7	196.9	199.7	204.9	215.0	221.7	230.0	1.04	10.86
Canada	571.7	583.0	598.6	618.7	643.8	669.3	694.6	723.8	774.3	816.5	853.9	4.10	49.38
Chile	210.8	217.4	225.7	235.5	246.2	257.1	267.6	277.3	286.4	295.0	303.7	3.72	44.06
China	18,020.9	18,242.7	18,252.8	18,259.9	18,097.5	18,593.1	18,813.8	19,327.2	20,241.3	21,178.5	22,508.9	2.25	24.90
Colombia	363.8	375.6	388.6	403.2	420.1	440.0	463.5	490.6	521.0	554.3	589.7	4.95	62.08
Costa Rica	38.7	40.1	41.5	43.0	44.6	46.3	48.3	50.6	53.2	56.1	59.3	4.35	53.15
Croatia	126.3	124.4	122.6	118.8	116.6	112.9	107.1	99.3	99.3	100.2	103.6	-1.97	-18.03
Czech Republic	210.3	212.2	220.3	229.7	241.0	257.0	273.0	281.4	302.2	322.8	333.4	4.71	58.51
Denmark	112.1	114.5	117.8	120.9	126.1	132.7	141.6	150.8	160.4	166.2	168.1	4.14	49.96
Ecuador	122.9	126.7	130.5	134.3	138.1	142.0	145.9	150.1	154.7	160.2	167.0	3.12	35.90
Egypt	641.9	659.3	674.8	688.2	698.7	710.0	728.5	758.9	801.0	856.1	921.2	3.68	43.52
Estonia	39.4	40.7	40.8	41.4	39.7	37.0	34.5	32.6	31.5	32.3	34.6	-1.29	-12.15
Finland	120.1	124.0	123.0	131.0	127.8	128.6	129.8	141.3	148.6	165.9	178.3	4.03	48.51
France	1,329.2	1,312.1	1,286.8	1,250.4	1,242.0	1,253.6	1,270.8	1,306.9	1,443.4	1,574.6	1,691.9	2.44	27.29
Germany	2,437.4	2,540.6	2,621.5	2,654.8	2,582.9	2,492.6	2,364.4	2,124.7	1,959.7	1,938.6	1,932.7	-2.29	-20.71
Greece	324.3	317.6	323.3	306.1	296.9	282.1	283.6	278.9	300.4	316.7	330.9	0.20	2.03
Hong Kong, China	119.4	117.7	114.5	109.0	104.6	103.5	106.9	113.4	128.2	143.7	159.7	2.96	33.82
Hungary	252.9	253.0	257.2	258.7	264.3	266.2	273.6	268.9	267.6	270.4	278.7	0.98	10.20
India	8,806.3	9,035.0	9,236.6	9,415.9	9,583.6	9,756.2	9,951.2	10,184.0	10,473.0	10,843.2	11,317.3	2.54	28.51
Indonesia	2,275.9	2,343.5	2,405.5	2,461.3	2,510.4	2,553.0	2,590.2	2,624.0	2,658.1	2,698.3	2,751.2	1.91	20.89
Iran	505.8	503.5	501.7	501.9	505.7	514.9	531.0	554.6	585.7	623.4	666.8	2.80	31.83
Ireland	66.5	67.8	68.6	69.4	71.5	74.2	77.1	81.3	86.2	90.4	94.3	3.56	41.83
Israel	104.1	104.9	103.5	99.5	94.3	91.8	93.9	103.1	119.3	136.9	151.1	3.80	45.17
Italy	1,612.4	1,643.4	1,673.1	1,678.7	1,666.7	1,634.0	1,589.3	1,532.5	1,592.3	1,654.0	1,723.1	0.67	6.86
Japan	3,708.3	3,737.4	3,816.0	3,923.0	4,025.4	4,200.9	4,118.7	3,912.3	4,070.8	4,306.5	4,523.9	2.01	21.99
Jordan	31.8	33.3	34.7	36.2	37.7	39.3	41.0	42.8	44.5	46.1	47.5	4.10	49.50
Kazakhstan	259.2	266.8	260.2	241.5	216.8	193.7	178.7	174.9	182.3	199.0	221.3	-1.57	-14.60
Kuwait	6.5	6.9	7.4	7.9	8.4	9.0	9.6	10.3	11.0	11.8	12.6	6.93	95.39
Latvia	67.4	69.8	70.7	70.9	69.1	65.9	62.1	58.0	54.4	53.1	53.8	-2.22	-20.15
Lithuania	91.2	91.3	90.5	90.0	90.6	89.4	85.9	84.9	81.6	78.3	77.9	-1.55	-14.50
Malaysia	190.1	195.2	199.5	203.1	206.8	212.2	220.1	230.4	243.0	259.1	278.6	3.90	46.54
Mexico	935.0	964.2	1,002.6	1,047.6	1,096.1	1,144.4	1,189.6	1,231.2	1,271.7	1,316.3	1,371.4	3.90	46.67
Morocco	289.5	297.6	300.0	297.7	293.2	289.5	289.4	294.2	303.7	317.3	333.8	1.43	15.29
Netherlands	319.8	326.2	334.8	339.7	348.0	358.8	372.9	380.3	424.6	462.1	486.2	4.28	52.04
New Zealand	67.9	71.3	75.3	79.0	80.4	82.8	85.0	87.0	92.1	98.8	103.3	4.29	52.14
Nigeria	756.5	778.8	801.7	824.7	847.4	869.1	889.6	909.3	929.1	950.6	975.7	2.58	28.98
Norway	81.5	83.7	86.1	87.6	90.9	95.0	101.2	108.1	118.3	125.2	129.8	4.76	59.18
Pakistan	983.2	1,028.3	1,077.6	1,129.7	1,182.1	1,231.9	1,277.1	1,317.0	1,352.7	1,386.2	1,420.6	3.75	44.49
Peru	248.9	255.7	262.4	269.2	276.3	284.1	292.6	302.1	312.7	324.4	337.1	3.08	35.47
Philippines	612.1	637.0	662.3	688.0	713.6	738.8	763.7	788.9	816.1	847.9	887.3	3.78	44.97
Poland	817.0	811.4	800.7	779.5	753.0	731.0	713.5	701.0	752.1	829.4	919.0	1.18	12.48
Portugal	276.6	276.5	272.0	267.1	266.4	267.2	271.2	279.7	286.3	292.3	300.8	0.84	8.75
Romania	540.5	542.1	536.6	514.6	491.4	464.6	450.1	430.3	436.8	444.5	465.6	-1.48	-13.85
Russia	3,769.5	4,074.7	4,148.1	4,079.3	3,617.4	3,001.0	2,450.6	2,102.3	2,089.0	2,371.5	2,796.3	-2.94	-25.82
Saudi Arabia	101.2	105.9	110.8	115.8	121.0	126.5	132.4	138.6	145.3	152.5	160.0	4.68	58.07
Singapore	59.7	63.0	68.6	72.4	72.7	72.0	66.6	65.7	77.3	89.8	100.1	5.31	67.75
Slovakia	99.5	100.3	102.1	104.6	107.3	109.1	112.1	112.8	115.0	121.0	128.7	2.61	29.35
Slovenia	48.8	48.7	49.0	49.0	50.0	50.9	50.2	47.7	48.2	48.9	50.0	0.24	2.43
South Africa	385.6	400.3	415.5	430.9	446.4	461.7	476.8	491.8	507.2	523.8	542.4	3.47	40.66
South Korea	849.2	868.3	889.5	914.2	929.9	930.5	923.6	920.3	930.1	956.2	994.3	1.59	17.09
Spain	1,014.0	982.2	955.2	947.4	966.3	986.1	1,022.2	1,065.9	1,106.3	1,136.2	1,162.0	1.37	14.59
Sweden	192.7	198.6	203.6	208.8	218.7	231.6	246.3	262.5	277.3	286.3	290.2	4.18	50.60
Switzerland	160.6	161.8	163.2	166.8	173.4	180.6	188.2	195.2	201.9	206.2	209.6	2.70	30.52
Taiwan	326.3	337.1	348.1	358.1	363.2	368.4	367.5	353.3	346.6	356.6	377.2	1.46	15.60
Thailand	822.0	841.2	844.5	871.8	861.1	876.0	885.8	918.2	951.5	1,022.6	1,101.5	2.97	34.00
Tunisia	108.5	109.3	109.1	108.2	107.1	106.5	106.9	108.6	111.9	116.8	123.2	1.27	13.49
Turkey	740.8	755.6	773.4	787.4	797.3	801.5	799.8	810.2	824.1	841.6	871.3	1.64	17.62
Turkmenistan	40.4	40.1	38.6	36.3	33.6	31.5	30.4	30.8	32.6	35.5	39.1	-0.32	-3.14
Ukraine	1,438.3	1,578.7	1,631.1	1,618.2	1,461.1	1,253.8	1,086.6	928.1	871.4	901.5	1,015.7	-3.42	-29.38
United Arab Emirates	5.2	5.2	5.1	5.1	5.2	5.5	6.0	6.7	7.6	8.6	9.7	6.37	85.46
United Kingdom	1,282.4	1,292.8	1,290.6	1,286.6	1,301.1	1,332.6	1,371.7	1,422.9	1,511.1	1,605.2	1,659.0	2.61	29.37
USA	4,909.2	4,979.4	5,085.0	5,260.4	5,534.3	5,744.2	5,920.3	6,070.4	6,567.8	6,840.8	7,164.9	3.85	45.95
Venezuela	217.4	225.8	235.6	246.8	259.4	273.4	288.8	305.3	323.0	341.5	360.5	5.19	65.78
Vietnam	703.8	696.3	694.6	698.1	705.8	716.0	727.7	739.8	753.9	775.6	812.3	1.44	15.42

Key population trends

Table 4.59 Female Population Aged 75-79: 2009-2019

'000

	2009	2010	2011	2012	2013	2014	2015	2016	2017	2018	2019	CAGR	Period growth
Algeria	180.34	187.93	194.85	200.83	205.43	208.32	209.45	209.11	208.05	207.49	208.86	1.48	15.81
Argentina	510.34	513.11	516.03	519.37	523.39	528.41	534.63	542.20	551.22	561.82	574.04	1.18	12.48
Australia	295.98	295.79	298.72	306.53	315.32	326.44	337.48	347.62	359.51	371.30	388.51	2.76	31.26
Austria	160.57	157.43	153.52	151.21	149.40	151.93	170.58	190.97	207.28	216.43	222.88	3.33	38.80
Azerbaijan	75.82	78.94	82.34	85.58	87.94	88.64	87.21	83.67	78.48	72.47	66.64	-1.28	-12.12
Belarus	208.39	200.01	192.80	199.74	200.49	209.65	215.33	212.40	203.17	186.78	162.35	-2.47	-22.09
Belgium	236.60	235.42	230.54	226.53	223.39	224.55	225.01	222.48	215.16	210.85	210.59	-1.16	-10.99
Bolivia	49.88	51.19	52.66	54.25	55.87	57.46	58.98	60.45	61.96	63.66	65.69	2.79	31.69
Bosnia-Herzegovina	67.66	70.06	72.58	74.93	76.63	77.19	76.34	74.15	71.07	67.88	65.50	-0.32	-3.18
Brazil	1,337.15	1,378.49	1,433.27	1,498.73	1,569.26	1,637.03	1,696.94	1,747.63	1,792.23	1,835.68	1,884.92	3.49	40.97
Bulgaria	175.49	179.81	177.49	178.27	173.32	168.76	162.52	161.60	160.00	161.62	164.24	-0.66	-6.41
Canada	498.66	498.03	497.68	497.07	500.20	508.61	517.73	531.42	549.20	571.67	594.52	1.77	19.22
Chile	168.48	171.68	174.62	177.64	181.28	186.10	192.47	200.40	209.61	219.50	229.40	3.13	36.16
China	12,790.17	12,844.98	13,362.80	13,506.73	13,525.14	13,199.12	13,320.06	13,350.73	13,314.52	13,168.85	13,481.34	0.53	5.40
Colombia	262.81	270.98	279.44	288.29	297.58	307.45	318.11	329.78	342.86	357.99	375.83	3.64	43.00
Costa Rica	28.95	29.84	30.83	31.91	33.05	34.24	35.46	36.72	38.07	39.55	41.22	3.60	42.39
Croatia	107.65	109.03	108.34	107.79	106.57	104.80	102.96	101.15	97.37	95.21	91.61	-1.60	-14.90
Czech Republic	198.42	194.98	188.95	184.03	179.83	179.82	181.86	189.43	198.09	208.42	223.14	1.18	12.46
Denmark	88.13	89.06	90.18	92.15	94.73	97.92	100.33	103.53	106.58	111.50	117.69	2.94	33.55
Ecuador	91.75	95.17	98.64	102.15	105.69	109.22	112.71	116.19	119.65	123.09	126.56	3.27	37.94
Egypt	462.29	493.10	521.06	546.11	568.45	588.16	605.25	620.03	632.45	641.54	651.45	3.49	40.92
Estonia	32.81	31.90	31.46	31.42	32.08	33.22	34.38	34.51	35.13	33.77	31.43	-0.43	-4.20
Finland	107.23	105.58	104.67	104.70	106.13	109.98	113.73	112.87	120.42	117.55	118.47	1.00	10.48
France	1,301.41	1,299.96	1,277.71	1,259.63	1,237.70	1,225.94	1,212.00	1,190.24	1,157.89	1,151.97	1,164.77	-1.10	-10.50
Germany	1,725.91	1,764.72	1,826.47	1,922.43	2,033.94	2,173.73	2,273.36	2,352.37	2,386.10	2,322.23	2,242.89	2.65	29.95
Greece	276.12	287.63	281.85	291.74	291.21	292.09	286.57	292.46	277.28	269.21	256.31	-0.74	-7.17
Hong Kong, China	104.27	105.87	106.76	109.54	110.29	110.14	108.54	105.63	100.65	96.88	96.32	-0.79	-7.63
Hungary	219.02	217.29	212.86	211.15	208.25	207.51	207.51	211.49	213.33	219.70	222.73	0.17	1.69
India	5,441.53	5,678.26	5,916.44	6,151.67	6,377.01	6,585.38	6,773.29	6,942.00	7,096.11	7,243.51	7,396.56	3.12	35.93
Indonesia	1,434.69	1,498.20	1,562.26	1,626.27	1,689.29	1,750.21	1,808.16	1,862.83	1,913.79	1,960.35	2,002.22	3.39	39.56
Iran	371.19	377.03	380.89	383.00	383.70	383.54	383.24	383.55	385.46	390.41	399.93	0.75	7.74
Ireland	54.05	54.52	55.20	56.28	57.16	58.15	59.37	60.25	61.04	63.02	65.62	1.96	21.42
Israel	81.33	81.28	83.00	86.27	89.52	92.06	92.73	91.16	86.91	81.39	78.69	-0.33	-3.25
Italy	1,440.28	1,449.31	1,441.88	1,437.92	1,451.03	1,481.41	1,513.41	1,544.11	1,551.44	1,542.65	1,515.20	0.51	5.20
Japan	3,282.67	3,355.82	3,427.02	3,475.93	3,489.94	3,459.51	3,493.48	3,574.23	3,680.49	3,780.77	3,947.88	1.86	20.26
Jordan	18.74	20.24	21.56	22.73	23.81	24.90	26.06	27.31	28.65	30.08	31.57	5.35	68.46
Kazakhstan	129.54	136.07	151.68	172.99	194.21	208.83	212.55	204.62	187.91	167.79	150.65	1.52	16.30
Kuwait	3.52	3.87	4.25	4.64	5.04	5.45	5.86	6.28	6.71	7.17	7.66	8.09	117.67
Latvia	54.93	53.52	52.61	52.89	53.63	55.12	56.97	57.62	57.76	56.33	53.74	-0.22	-2.18
Lithuania	77.67	77.31	77.13	77.69	77.32	77.52	77.72	77.23	76.95	77.65	76.77	-0.12	-1.16
Malaysia	111.68	116.17	121.79	128.70	133.69	138.50	142.55	145.69	148.06	150.72	155.09	3.34	38.88
Mexico	749.23	766.76	781.50	794.36	808.94	828.90	856.62	892.56	934.77	979.65	1,023.36	3.17	36.59
Morocco	176.80	181.60	190.77	202.87	215.33	225.35	231.09	232.32	230.30	227.23	225.63	2.47	27.62
Netherlands	277.82	278.82	277.95	279.14	279.47	285.20	291.70	300.29	305.16	313.31	324.11	1.55	16.66
New Zealand	56.35	56.03	56.39	57.66	59.20	61.41	64.58	68.35	71.82	73.18	75.50	2.97	34.00
Nigeria	444.18	457.28	470.97	485.35	500.51	516.45	533.10	550.31	567.76	584.88	601.27	3.07	35.37
Norway	75.28	73.72	72.13	71.28	71.07	72.68	74.75	77.08	78.50	81.67	85.55	1.29	13.64
Pakistan	597.29	621.31	646.24	672.72	701.82	734.50	771.14	811.48	854.21	897.08	937.62	4.61	56.98
Peru	177.63	184.77	191.74	198.53	205.10	211.49	217.73	223.91	230.15	236.68	243.74	3.21	37.22
Philippines	380.54	400.21	419.25	438.07	457.17	477.15	498.31	520.72	543.94	567.25	590.12	4.49	55.08
Poland	720.44	714.88	705.11	702.77	697.51	697.02	694.19	687.00	670.37	648.80	631.16	-1.31	-12.39
Portugal	238.08	242.13	245.92	248.08	248.16	249.24	249.80	246.38	242.61	242.60	244.12	0.25	2.54
Romania	417.79	421.66	420.80	430.57	430.62	437.32	439.65	435.74	418.62	400.52	379.65	-0.95	-9.13
Russia	2,701.60	2,516.27	2,431.33	2,514.27	2,716.72	2,998.67	3,234.50	3,288.03	3,227.01	2,855.44	2,362.68	-1.33	-12.55
Saudi Arabia	65.89	67.86	70.41	73.49	76.99	80.77	84.74	88.88	93.20	97.76	102.59	4.53	55.69
Singapore	44.42	47.43	48.17	47.43	48.68	52.76	55.90	61.55	65.09	64.97	63.88	3.70	43.80
Slovakia	87.94	86.59	85.08	83.01	80.77	80.40	81.25	82.96	85.41	88.14	89.88	0.22	2.21
Slovenia	44.86	45.15	44.47	44.32	43.73	43.42	43.46	43.83	43.89	44.90	45.82	0.21	2.15
South Africa	239.21	249.44	259.80	270.35	281.24	292.63	304.60	317.15	330.08	343.14	356.10	4.06	48.86
South Korea	623.24	656.39	687.18	712.02	735.58	757.71	776.31	797.16	821.31	837.20	839.08	3.02	34.63
Spain	972.54	983.23	984.63	974.42	951.66	932.11	904.07	880.58	874.93	893.72	913.18	-0.63	-6.10
Sweden	170.61	169.21	167.39	168.33	170.09	174.90	180.52	185.15	190.16	199.32	211.41	2.17	23.91
Switzerland	143.67	144.08	144.28	145.05	144.68	145.35	146.35	147.67	151.25	157.82	165.02	1.39	14.86
Taiwan	244.49	252.53	260.58	266.89	276.30	284.37	293.79	303.30	311.83	316.04	320.39	2.74	31.05
Thailand	600.89	624.86	662.67	681.89	711.53	733.58	752.78	755.93	783.33	771.83	786.29	2.73	30.85
Tunisia	76.81	78.93	81.34	83.84	86.07	87.66	88.40	88.33	87.72	87.05	86.87	1.24	13.10
Turkey	463.19	501.64	550.85	589.00	624.39	654.17	676.58	693.98	707.45	711.30	699.49	4.21	51.02
Turkmenistan	26.19	26.82	27.97	29.38	30.59	31.13	30.74	29.41	27.48	25.48	24.01	-0.87	-8.33
Ukraine	933.07	863.55	845.70	920.78	1,072.69	1,248.52	1,380.53	1,428.91	1,424.44	1,290.62	1,113.71	1.79	19.36
United Arab Emirates	3.18	3.28	3.46	3.68	3.92	4.12	4.25	4.32	4.36	4.46	4.70	3.97	47.53
United Kingdom	1,106.49	1,096.97	1,090.75	1,091.76	1,101.04	1,115.42	1,128.05	1,130.00	1,130.12	1,146.65	1,178.15	0.63	6.48
USA	4,123.74	4,106.99	4,106.99	4,121.71	4,186.23	4,269.95	4,338.67	4,438.17	4,597.95	4,846.21	5,035.14	2.02	22.10
Venezuela	157.81	162.10	166.66	171.64	177.27	183.80	191.43	200.25	210.29	221.59	234.12	4.02	48.36
Vietnam	582.16	595.49	599.93	597.06	589.81	582.48	578.32	578.85	583.68	592.00	602.21	0.34	3.44

Key population trends

Table 4.60 Female Population Aged 80+: 2009-2019

'000

	2009	2010	2011	2012	2013	2014	2015	2016	2017	2018	2019	CAGR	Period growth
Algeria	147.51	154.00	161.11	168.77	176.82	185.06	193.31	201.68	210.13	218.30	225.74	4.35	53.03
Argentina	693.56	714.99	735.21	754.34	772.47	789.71	806.22	822.04	837.34	852.45	867.84	2.27	25.13
Australia	500.12	513.12	524.45	533.12	541.58	549.79	559.14	570.29	582.89	595.76	610.31	2.01	22.03
Austria	272.43	275.54	278.95	280.89	282.29	282.42	281.61	280.33	279.36	278.69	281.20	0.32	3.22
Azerbaijan	58.74	63.95	68.84	73.44	77.90	82.48	87.29	92.45	97.75	102.65	106.43	6.12	81.19
Belarus	218.91	226.52	231.81	234.47	236.12	237.60	240.21	244.79	250.84	256.75	260.63	1.76	19.06
Belgium	342.36	351.70	363.25	373.61	382.98	389.58	395.57	400.12	404.36	408.69	414.57	1.93	21.09
Bolivia	40.73	43.04	45.28	47.45	49.62	51.85	54.18	56.66	59.26	61.96	64.69	4.74	58.85
Bosnia-Herzegovina	56.86	59.43	62.25	65.22	68.35	71.64	75.04	78.62	82.31	85.77	88.51	4.53	55.67
Brazil	1,508.55	1,582.81	1,653.84	1,723.34	1,793.98	1,869.34	1,951.60	2,041.71	2,138.40	2,239.01	2,340.02	4.49	55.12
Bulgaria	177.20	180.55	185.66	188.32	194.07	198.61	204.24	206.09	208.48	209.02	209.13	1.67	18.02
Canada	813.24	831.19	847.31	862.12	875.99	888.93	901.35	913.44	925.54	938.68	953.94	1.61	17.30
Chile	220.88	230.54	240.27	250.09	259.85	269.42	278.71	287.64	296.35	305.26	314.95	3.61	42.59
China	11,758.62	12,219.14	12,708.98	13,225.78	13,765.32	14,298.27	14,816.93	15,323.15	15,820.70	16,309.80	16,785.10	3.62	42.75
Colombia	296.76	308.55	320.83	333.60	346.83	360.44	374.42	388.86	403.91	419.67	436.23	3.93	47.00
Costa Rica	37.52	39.12	40.69	42.27	43.86	45.50	47.23	49.06	51.01	53.06	55.18	3.93	47.08
Croatia	110.10	115.04	120.01	124.82	129.45	133.81	137.85	141.64	145.16	148.14	150.17	3.15	36.39
Czech Republic	244.71	249.92	256.04	260.36	263.51	264.34	264.39	263.55	262.54	261.77	262.95	0.72	7.45
Denmark	147.23	147.19	147.57	148.11	149.16	150.19	152.07	154.35	157.37	161.22	165.47	1.17	12.39
Ecuador	105.99	111.20	116.59	122.16	127.90	133.80	139.85	146.05	152.41	158.89	165.46	4.55	56.10
Egypt	286.13	301.96	318.35	335.36	353.15	371.91	391.80	413.18	436.08	460.00	484.18	5.40	69.22
Estonia	38.57	39.78	40.99	42.06	43.13	43.36	43.47	43.97	44.72	46.06	47.11	2.02	22.13
Finland	165.35	170.68	175.62	179.11	181.93	183.17	185.24	187.77	189.99	192.95	196.76	1.75	19.00
France	2,152.78	2,214.42	2,281.38	2,340.37	2,394.20	2,432.40	2,470.45	2,494.80	2,515.82	2,529.61	2,539.80	1.67	17.98
Germany	2,795.40	2,835.06	2,876.72	2,895.30	2,901.68	2,904.20	2,972.24	3,060.33	3,155.12	3,251.77	3,368.75	1.88	20.51
Greece	277.26	288.45	313.19	322.92	336.71	350.69	364.96	376.54	388.14	394.87	402.92	3.81	45.32
Hong Kong, China	147.10	152.85	160.10	165.50	172.18	179.23	184.17	189.70	194.46	198.70	202.31	3.24	37.53
Hungary	266.04	271.60	279.13	283.84	289.26	293.69	297.20	300.68	303.78	307.07	311.25	1.58	16.99
India	4,122.06	4,338.33	4,565.35	4,802.58	5,049.87	5,307.23	5,574.29	5,852.53	6,140.71	6,432.62	6,719.92	5.01	63.02
Indonesia	984.36	1,042.06	1,101.39	1,162.68	1,226.46	1,293.60	1,364.68	1,439.79	1,518.52	1,600.35	1,684.48	5.52	71.12
Iran	285.60	291.52	299.23	308.29	318.05	327.53	336.04	343.66	350.81	357.66	364.44	2.47	27.61
Ireland	79.07	80.42	81.67	82.83	84.06	85.36	86.86	88.51	90.37	92.21	94.35	1.78	19.32
Israel	124.48	128.39	131.86	134.90	137.66	140.30	143.01	145.94	149.09	152.18	154.81	2.20	24.36
Italy	2,207.15	2,266.61	2,343.04	2,401.46	2,450.42	2,498.40	2,545.61	2,592.62	2,626.70	2,667.58	2,723.92	2.13	23.41
Japan	5,220.28	5,433.91	5,660.41	5,889.57	6,115.63	6,321.06	6,542.65	6,772.24	6,981.42	7,156.19	7,270.78	3.37	39.28
Jordan	17.58	17.19	17.35	17.95	18.91	20.05	21.26	22.54	23.91	25.40	26.99	4.38	53.51
Kazakhstan	156.47	160.77	160.85	157.40	153.00	151.27	154.71	164.66	179.89	197.17	211.76	3.07	35.33
Kuwait	2.66	2.87	3.12	3.41	3.75	4.12	4.52	4.98	5.47	6.00	6.56	9.47	147.14
Latvia	65.11	66.69	68.62	69.90	71.38	71.97	71.99	72.83	74.26	76.23	77.74	1.79	19.40
Lithuania	85.98	88.64	91.92	94.29	97.35	99.44	100.62	102.48	104.50	106.01	107.49	2.26	25.02
Malaysia	115.68	122.01	128.35	134.79	141.69	149.40	158.22	168.40	179.82	191.97	204.02	5.84	76.36
Mexico	870.25	916.85	965.54	1,014.76	1,063.75	1,111.28	1,156.66	1,199.33	1,239.99	1,280.80	1,324.81	4.29	52.23
Morocco	138.86	147.89	154.00	157.81	160.62	164.37	170.39	179.24	190.33	202.42	213.73	4.41	53.92
Netherlands	413.11	416.83	422.12	426.18	430.63	433.40	436.53	439.57	443.21	446.78	453.00	0.93	9.66
New Zealand	89.82	92.05	94.19	95.93	97.66	99.20	100.84	102.98	105.52	108.25	111.38	2.18	24.01
Nigeria	295.97	305.58	315.49	325.74	336.42	347.62	359.41	371.81	384.84	398.51	412.86	3.38	39.49
Norway	142.93	141.73	140.76	139.56	138.35	136.27	134.36	132.76	131.71	131.28	131.72	-0.81	-7.84
Pakistan	476.22	495.87	516.63	538.60	561.90	586.68	613.14	641.17	670.92	703.03	738.32	4.48	55.04
Peru	179.17	188.99	199.32	210.16	221.42	232.98	244.76	256.74	268.93	281.26	293.67	5.07	63.91
Philippines	286.38	296.96	309.53	324.11	340.64	358.99	379.00	400.71	424.23	449.49	476.38	5.22	66.34
Poland	832.33	867.34	906.92	938.92	967.20	986.13	1,005.00	1,024.23	1,043.12	1,057.15	1,068.36	2.53	28.36
Portugal	294.05	302.00	312.24	322.11	332.18	341.60	350.11	360.47	369.14	376.06	383.34	2.69	30.37
Romania	396.46	406.93	419.89	428.43	442.54	449.22	457.27	464.93	477.58	487.91	497.64	2.30	25.52
Russia	2,948.18	3,047.41	3,169.65	3,160.43	3,179.57	3,078.82	3,008.87	3,011.88	3,070.72	3,224.00	3,346.23	1.27	13.50
Saudi Arabia	58.72	60.79	62.83	64.85	66.98	69.36	72.11	75.29	78.90	82.92	87.31	4.05	48.70
Singapore	52.40	54.89	57.22	60.63	63.79	67.57	71.91	72.32	74.73	80.49	87.84	5.30	67.63
Slovakia	99.56	102.22	104.82	107.28	109.64	110.88	111.74	112.69	113.34	114.00	115.19	1.47	15.70
Slovenia	54.65	56.76	59.36	61.50	63.58	65.30	66.71	67.75	68.86	69.63	70.41	2.57	28.82
South Africa	196.76	204.98	213.94	223.63	234.00	244.96	256.48	268.55	281.23	294.56	308.60	4.60	56.84
South Korea	620.98	664.36	711.61	761.02	811.41	862.72	916.18	970.37	1,023.46	1,076.05	1,128.06	6.15	81.66
Spain	1,422.32	1,478.18	1,536.76	1,594.70	1,651.05	1,704.79	1,757.99	1,804.36	1,840.70	1,865.34	1,889.28	2.88	32.83
Sweden	311.59	311.51	310.69	309.77	307.66	306.11	305.03	305.67	307.12	310.15	314.49	0.09	0.93
Switzerland	235.05	239.31	244.01	248.99	254.17	259.30	264.26	268.98	273.56	278.27	283.66	1.90	20.68
Taiwan	264.23	281.85	301.57	319.51	337.60	358.75	377.31	399.03	418.03	441.28	463.90	5.79	75.57
Thailand	584.37	616.34	648.55	681.28	714.57	748.90	784.28	821.57	860.02	898.76	935.72	4.82	60.12
Tunisia	62.47	65.90	69.18	72.33	75.44	78.67	82.10	85.80	89.73	93.63	97.19	4.52	55.59
Turkey	374.93	361.78	340.39	331.32	325.28	325.44	331.79	342.28	355.88	377.85	414.37	1.01	10.52
Turkmenistan	25.75	26.66	27.24	27.56	27.78	28.13	28.78	29.83	31.19	32.60	33.68	2.72	30.80
Ukraine	1,118.61	1,140.02	1,140.20	1,119.88	1,092.78	1,074.80	1,080.28	1,116.20	1,176.67	1,249.17	1,310.78	1.60	17.18
United Arab Emirates	4.31	4.39	4.44	4.44	4.43	4.45	4.53	4.68	4.90	5.16	5.41	2.31	25.67
United Kingdom	1,787.31	1,798.63	1,810.00	1,819.61	1,825.87	1,830.36	1,836.66	1,847.77	1,862.97	1,881.41	1,901.78	0.62	6.40
USA	7,425.66	7,482.34	7,514.65	7,526.68	7,531.61	7,528.80	7,565.35	7,596.07	7,631.30	7,695.10	7,773.74	0.46	4.69
Venezuela	164.38	172.81	181.19	189.59	198.06	206.62	215.35	224.27	233.48	243.19	253.69	4.43	54.33
Vietnam	544.52	568.15	595.35	625.44	656.51	685.94	711.85	733.70	752.16	768.02	782.58	3.69	43.72

Key population trends

Table 4.61 Mean age of population: 2009-2019

years

	2009	2010	2011	2012	2013	2014	2015	2016	2017	2018	2019	CAGR	Period growth
Algeria	27.8	28.1	28.4	28.7	28.9	29.2	29.4	29.7	30.0	30.3	30.5	0.93	9.69
Argentina	32.6	32.7	32.8	33.0	33.1	33.3	33.5	33.6	33.8	34.0	34.1	0.48	4.86
Australia	37.3	37.4	37.5	37.7	37.8	37.9	38.0	38.2	38.3	38.4	38.6	0.34	3.50
Austria	40.5	40.7	40.9	41.1	41.3	41.5	41.7	41.9	42.1	42.3	42.5	0.49	5.01
Azerbaijan	30.6	30.8	31.0	31.2	31.4	31.6	31.8	32.0	32.3	32.5	32.8	0.71	7.29
Belarus	38.5	38.6	38.7	38.8	38.9	39.0	39.2	39.3	39.4	39.6	39.7	0.31	3.12
Belgium	40.1	40.3	40.4	40.5	40.6	40.7	40.8	40.9	41.1	41.2	41.3	0.29	2.89
Bolivia	25.4	25.6	25.8	26.0	26.2	26.4	26.6	26.8	27.1	27.3	27.5	0.80	8.33
Bosnia-Herzegovina	38.7	39.0	39.3	39.6	39.9	40.2	40.5	40.7	41.0	41.3	41.6	0.71	7.33
Brazil	30.5	30.8	31.2	31.5	31.9	32.2	32.6	33.0	33.3	33.7	34.1	1.12	11.76
Bulgaria	41.3	41.5	41.7	41.9	42.1	42.4	42.6	42.8	43.1	43.3	43.6	0.53	5.48
Canada	38.8	39.0	39.2	39.4	39.6	39.8	40.0	40.2	40.4	40.6	40.7	0.49	4.99
Chile	33.2	33.5	33.8	34.1	34.4	34.6	34.9	35.2	35.5	35.8	36.0	0.82	8.50
China	36.8	37.2	37.6	37.9	38.2	38.5	38.8	39.0	39.3	39.5	39.7	0.76	7.86
Colombia	28.8	29.1	29.4	29.6	29.9	30.2	30.5	30.7	31.0	31.3	31.6	0.91	9.47
Costa Rica	30.2	30.5	30.9	31.2	31.5	31.8	32.1	32.4	32.7	33.0	33.4	1.00	10.50
Croatia	40.5	40.6	40.8	40.9	41.1	41.2	41.3	41.4	41.5	41.7	41.8	0.32	3.27
Czech Republic	40.0	40.2	40.4	40.6	40.8	41.0	41.2	41.4	41.6	41.8	42.0	0.49	5.04
Denmark	39.4	39.5	39.7	39.9	40.0	40.2	40.4	40.6	40.8	40.9	41.1	0.44	4.44
Ecuador	28.4	28.7	29.0	29.2	29.5	29.8	30.0	30.3	30.6	30.9	31.1	0.91	9.51
Egypt	26.9	27.1	27.2	27.3	27.4	27.6	27.7	27.9	28.0	28.2	28.4	0.52	5.32
Estonia	39.7	39.8	39.9	40.0	40.1	40.2	40.3	40.3	40.4	40.5	40.6	0.22	2.22
Finland	40.4	40.6	40.8	40.9	41.1	41.3	41.4	41.6	41.7	41.8	42.0	0.38	3.87
France	39.3	39.4	39.6	39.7	39.8	40.0	40.1	40.2	40.4	40.5	40.6	0.32	3.29
Germany	42.4	42.7	42.9	43.2	43.4	43.7	43.9	44.2	44.4	44.6	44.8	0.55	5.66
Greece	41.4	41.6	41.8	42.0	42.2	42.4	42.6	42.7	42.9	43.1	43.3	0.45	4.58
Hong Kong, China	39.7	40.0	40.3	40.5	40.8	41.0	41.3	41.5	41.7	41.9	42.1	0.59	6.05
Hungary	40.1	40.2	40.3	40.5	40.7	40.8	41.0	41.1	41.3	41.4	41.6	0.38	3.82
India	27.5	27.7	28.0	28.2	28.4	28.6	28.9	29.1	29.4	29.6	29.9	0.83	8.63
Indonesia	29.6	29.9	30.2	30.5	30.7	31.0	31.3	31.6	31.9	32.2	32.5	0.94	9.80
Iran	28.5	28.8	29.1	29.4	29.7	30.0	30.3	30.6	30.9	31.2	31.5	1.00	10.52
Ireland	35.4	35.6	35.8	36.0	36.2	36.4	36.7	36.9	37.1	37.4	37.7	0.62	6.42
Israel	31.8	31.9	32.0	32.2	32.4	32.5	32.7	32.9	33.1	33.3	33.4	0.52	5.28
Italy	42.5	42.7	43.0	43.2	43.4	43.6	43.8	44.0	44.3	44.5	44.7	0.50	5.15
Japan	43.8	44.1	44.3	44.6	44.9	45.2	45.5	45.7	46.0	46.2	46.5	0.60	6.21
Jordan	24.8	25.0	25.3	25.5	25.8	26.0	26.3	26.6	26.8	27.1	27.4	1.02	10.66
Kazakhstan	31.3	31.3	31.4	31.5	31.5	31.6	31.7	31.9	32.0	32.2	32.4	0.36	3.66
Kuwait	29.0	29.3	29.6	29.9	30.2	30.6	31.0	31.3	31.7	32.0	32.4	1.11	11.71
Latvia	40.1	40.2	40.3	40.4	40.5	40.6	40.7	40.8	40.9	41.0	41.1	0.25	2.54
Lithuania	39.1	39.3	39.6	39.8	40.0	40.2	40.4	40.5	40.7	40.9	41.1	0.49	4.96
Malaysia	27.6	27.8	28.1	28.3	28.5	28.7	29.0	29.2	29.5	29.7	30.0	0.82	8.52
Mexico	29.2	29.6	29.9	30.3	30.6	31.0	31.3	31.7	32.1	32.4	32.8	1.16	12.17
Morocco	28.5	28.7	28.9	29.2	29.4	29.6	29.9	30.1	30.4	30.6	30.9	0.83	8.62
Netherlands	39.2	39.5	39.7	40.0	40.2	40.4	40.6	40.9	41.1	41.3	41.5	0.56	5.79
New Zealand	36.5	36.6	36.8	37.0	37.2	37.4	37.6	37.8	38.0	38.2	38.4	0.51	5.24
Nigeria	22.2	22.3	22.4	22.5	22.6	22.7	22.8	22.9	23.1	23.2	23.4	0.51	5.18
Norway	38.3	38.3	38.4	38.5	38.6	38.7	38.8	38.9	39.0	39.1	39.3	0.25	2.50
Pakistan	24.5	24.7	24.8	25.0	25.1	25.3	25.5	25.7	25.8	26.0	26.3	0.68	7.04
Peru	28.1	28.4	28.6	28.9	29.1	29.4	29.7	30.0	30.2	30.5	30.8	0.91	9.47
Philippines	26.0	26.3	26.5	26.7	26.9	27.1	27.3	27.6	27.8	28.0	28.3	0.82	8.49
Poland	38.5	38.8	39.0	39.3	39.6	39.8	40.0	40.3	40.5	40.7	41.0	0.62	6.41
Portugal	40.5	40.7	40.9	41.1	41.3	41.5	41.7	41.9	42.2	42.4	42.6	0.52	5.33
Romania	38.7	38.9	39.1	39.2	39.4	39.6	39.8	40.0	40.2	40.5	40.7	0.50	5.16
Russia	38.1	38.2	38.3	38.4	38.5	38.5	38.6	38.6	38.7	38.8	38.8	0.18	1.86
Saudi Arabia	25.8	26.0	26.3	26.6	26.8	27.1	27.4	27.6	27.9	28.2	28.5	1.00	10.47
Singapore	36.5	36.8	37.2	37.6	37.9	38.3	38.6	39.0	39.3	39.7	40.0	0.94	9.76
Slovakia	37.7	37.9	38.2	38.5	38.7	39.0	39.3	39.5	39.8	40.1	40.4	0.70	7.19
Slovenia	40.7	40.9	41.2	41.4	41.6	41.8	42.0	42.3	42.5	42.7	42.9	0.52	5.30
South Africa	27.3	27.4	27.6	27.8	27.9	28.0	28.2	28.3	28.5	28.6	28.8	0.54	5.57
South Korea	36.9	37.4	37.9	38.4	38.8	39.3	39.8	40.2	40.7	41.1	41.6	1.20	12.62
Spain	40.3	40.5	40.6	40.8	41.0	41.1	41.3	41.5	41.7	41.9	42.1	0.43	4.39
Sweden	40.4	40.5	40.6	40.7	40.7	40.9	41.0	41.1	41.2	41.3	41.4	0.25	2.51
Switzerland	40.6	40.8	40.9	41.1	41.3	41.5	41.7	41.9	42.0	42.2	42.4	0.44	4.46
Taiwan	36.5	37.0	37.4	37.8	38.2	38.7	39.1	39.5	39.9	40.3	40.8	1.10	11.59
Thailand	34.0	34.4	34.7	35.0	35.4	35.7	36.1	36.4	36.8	37.1	37.5	0.97	10.10
Tunisia	30.8	31.1	31.4	31.7	31.9	32.2	32.5	32.7	33.0	33.3	33.6	0.86	8.96
Turkey	29.8	30.1	30.3	30.6	30.9	31.1	31.4	31.6	31.9	32.2	32.4	0.84	8.77
Turkmenistan	27.1	27.4	27.6	27.8	28.1	28.3	28.6	28.8	29.1	29.3	29.6	0.90	9.40
Ukraine	39.5	39.7	39.8	40.0	40.2	40.5	40.7	41.0	41.2	41.4	41.6	0.50	5.16
United Arab Emirates	29.4	29.6	29.9	30.1	30.3	30.5	30.7	31.0	31.3	31.6	31.9	0.83	8.61
United Kingdom	39.1	39.1	39.2	39.3	39.3	39.4	39.5	39.5	39.6	39.7	39.7	0.17	1.68
USA	36.9	37.0	37.2	37.3	37.4	37.6	37.7	37.8	38.0	38.1	38.2	0.35	3.57
Venezuela	28.4	28.7	28.9	29.2	29.4	29.7	29.9	30.2	30.5	30.7	31.0	0.85	8.88
Vietnam	28.8	29.1	29.4	29.7	30.0	30.3	30.7	31.0	31.3	31.6	31.9	1.02	10.73

Key population trends

Table 4.62 Mean age of male population: 2009-2019

years

	2009	2010	2011	2012	2013	2014	2015	2016	2017	2018	2019	CAGR	Period growth
Algeria	27.5	27.7	28.0	28.3	28.5	28.8	29.1	29.3	29.6	29.9	30.2	0.95	9.89
Argentina	31.3	31.4	31.6	31.7	31.9	32.0	32.2	32.3	32.5	32.7	32.9	0.49	4.98
Australia	36.5	36.6	36.8	36.9	37.0	37.2	37.3	37.5	37.6	37.7	37.9	0.36	3.66
Austria	39.1	39.3	39.6	39.8	40.0	40.3	40.5	40.7	40.9	41.1	41.3	0.56	5.75
Azerbaijan	29.2	29.4	29.6	29.8	30.0	30.2	30.3	30.5	30.8	31.0	31.2	0.66	6.78
Belarus	35.9	36.0	36.1	36.2	36.3	36.4	36.5	36.6	36.7	36.8	37.0	0.30	3.00
Belgium	38.9	39.0	39.1	39.2	39.3	39.5	39.6	39.7	39.8	39.9	40.1	0.31	3.10
Bolivia	24.8	25.0	25.2	25.4	25.6	25.8	26.0	26.2	26.4	26.7	26.9	0.81	8.44
Bosnia-Herzegovina	37.5	37.8	38.1	38.4	38.6	38.9	39.2	39.4	39.7	39.9	40.1	0.67	6.93
Brazil	29.7	30.0	30.3	30.7	31.0	31.4	31.7	32.1	32.4	32.8	33.1	1.10	11.59
Bulgaria	39.8	40.0	40.1	40.3	40.5	40.8	41.0	41.2	41.5	41.7	42.0	0.54	5.50
Canada	37.9	38.1	38.3	38.5	38.8	39.0	39.2	39.4	39.5	39.7	39.9	0.51	5.23
Chile	32.3	32.6	32.9	33.2	33.5	33.8	34.1	34.3	34.6	34.9	35.1	0.83	8.60
China	36.2	36.5	36.9	37.2	37.5	37.8	38.0	38.3	38.5	38.7	38.9	0.71	7.38
Colombia	28.0	28.3	28.6	28.8	29.1	29.3	29.6	29.9	30.1	30.4	30.7	0.90	9.37
Costa Rica	29.8	30.2	30.5	30.8	31.1	31.4	31.7	32.0	32.3	32.6	32.9	1.00	10.45
Croatia	38.7	38.9	39.0	39.2	39.3	39.4	39.6	39.7	39.8	39.9	40.0	0.34	3.44
Czech Republic	38.5	38.7	38.9	39.2	39.4	39.6	39.8	40.0	40.2	40.4	40.6	0.54	5.53
Denmark	38.4	38.6	38.8	39.0	39.2	39.4	39.6	39.8	40.0	40.1	40.3	0.48	4.94
Ecuador	28.0	28.2	28.5	28.8	29.0	29.3	29.5	29.8	30.1	30.3	30.6	0.89	9.27
Egypt	26.4	26.5	26.6	26.8	26.9	27.0	27.2	27.3	27.5	27.7	27.9	0.53	5.46
Estonia	36.8	36.9	37.0	37.0	37.1	37.2	37.3	37.3	37.4	37.5	37.5	0.21	2.08
Finland	39.0	39.2	39.4	39.6	39.8	39.9	40.1	40.2	40.4	40.5	40.7	0.42	4.27
France	37.9	38.0	38.2	38.3	38.4	38.6	38.7	38.8	39.0	39.1	39.2	0.35	3.51
Germany	41.1	41.4	41.6	41.9	42.2	42.5	42.8	43.0	43.3	43.5	43.7	0.62	6.43
Greece	40.2	40.4	40.6	40.8	41.0	41.2	41.4	41.6	41.8	41.9	42.1	0.46	4.68
Hong Kong, China	39.5	39.8	40.1	40.4	40.7	40.9	41.2	41.4	41.6	41.8	42.0	0.63	6.49
Hungary	37.9	38.1	38.2	38.3	38.5	38.7	38.8	39.0	39.1	39.3	39.5	0.40	4.08
India	27.2	27.4	27.6	27.8	28.0	28.3	28.5	28.7	29.0	29.2	29.5	0.81	8.41
Indonesia	29.1	29.4	29.7	29.9	30.2	30.5	30.8	31.1	31.4	31.7	32.0	0.94	9.80
Iran	28.4	28.7	29.0	29.2	29.5	29.8	30.1	30.3	30.6	30.9	31.2	0.94	9.83
Ireland	34.7	34.9	35.1	35.3	35.6	35.8	36.0	36.3	36.5	36.8	37.1	0.66	6.82
Israel	30.7	30.9	31.0	31.2	31.4	31.6	31.7	31.9	32.1	32.3	32.5	0.57	5.83
Italy	41.0	41.3	41.5	41.7	41.9	42.2	42.4	42.6	42.8	43.1	43.3	0.54	5.51
Japan	42.4	42.6	42.9	43.2	43.5	43.7	44.0	44.2	44.5	44.7	45.0	0.59	6.10
Jordan	24.8	25.0	25.2	25.5	25.7	25.9	26.2	26.5	26.7	27.0	27.3	0.98	10.29
Kazakhstan	29.3	29.3	29.3	29.4	29.4	29.5	29.6	29.7	29.8	30.0	30.2	0.30	3.01
Kuwait	30.4	30.7	31.1	31.4	31.8	32.1	32.5	32.9	33.3	33.6	34.0	1.11	11.72
Latvia	37.2	37.3	37.5	37.6	37.7	37.8	37.9	38.0	38.1	38.2	38.3	0.28	2.88
Lithuania	36.5	36.8	37.0	37.2	37.4	37.6	37.7	37.9	38.1	38.3	38.4	0.51	5.21
Malaysia	27.3	27.5	27.7	28.0	28.2	28.4	28.6	28.8	29.0	29.3	29.5	0.77	7.99
Mexico	28.7	29.1	29.4	29.8	30.1	30.4	30.8	31.1	31.5	31.8	32.2	1.15	12.11
Morocco	28.0	28.2	28.4	28.6	28.9	29.1	29.3	29.5	29.8	30.0	30.2	0.78	8.11
Netherlands	38.3	38.6	38.8	39.1	39.3	39.6	39.8	40.0	40.3	40.5	40.7	0.61	6.28
New Zealand	35.7	35.8	36.0	36.2	36.4	36.5	36.7	36.9	37.1	37.3	37.5	0.50	5.12
Nigeria	21.9	22.0	22.0	22.1	22.2	22.4	22.5	22.6	22.8	22.9	23.1	0.53	5.43
Norway	37.3	37.4	37.6	37.7	37.8	38.0	38.1	38.2	38.4	38.5	38.7	0.35	3.55
Pakistan	24.5	24.7	24.8	25.0	25.1	25.3	25.5	25.6	25.8	26.0	26.2	0.66	6.77
Peru	27.7	27.9	28.2	28.4	28.7	28.9	29.2	29.5	29.7	30.0	30.3	0.89	9.31
Philippines	25.6	25.8	26.0	26.2	26.5	26.7	26.9	27.1	27.3	27.6	27.8	0.81	8.41
Poland	36.8	37.1	37.3	37.6	37.9	38.1	38.3	38.6	38.8	39.0	39.3	0.65	6.70
Portugal	39.0	39.2	39.4	39.6	39.8	40.0	40.2	40.5	40.7	40.9	41.1	0.53	5.42
Romania	37.2	37.4	37.6	37.8	38.0	38.2	38.4	38.6	38.8	39.0	39.2	0.52	5.31
Russia	35.5	35.6	35.6	35.7	35.8	35.8	35.8	35.9	35.9	36.0	36.0	0.14	1.44
Saudi Arabia	27.0	27.2	27.5	27.8	28.0	28.3	28.5	28.8	29.1	29.3	29.6	0.93	9.72
Singapore	36.0	36.4	36.8	37.1	37.5	37.9	38.2	38.6	39.0	39.4	39.7	0.99	10.30
Slovakia	36.1	36.3	36.6	36.9	37.2	37.4	37.7	38.0	38.3	38.6	38.9	0.75	7.74
Slovenia	39.1	39.4	39.6	39.9	40.1	40.4	40.6	40.8	41.0	41.3	41.5	0.59	6.03
South Africa	26.5	26.6	26.7	26.9	27.0	27.1	27.3	27.4	27.5	27.7	27.8	0.51	5.18
South Korea	35.8	36.3	36.7	37.2	37.7	38.1	38.6	39.1	39.5	40.0	40.4	1.23	12.95
Spain	39.0	39.2	39.4	39.5	39.7	39.9	40.1	40.3	40.4	40.6	40.9	0.46	4.72
Sweden	39.4	39.5	39.6	39.7	39.8	40.0	40.1	40.2	40.3	40.5	40.6	0.31	3.12
Switzerland	39.4	39.6	39.8	40.0	40.2	40.4	40.6	40.8	41.0	41.1	41.3	0.47	4.78
Taiwan	36.1	36.5	36.9	37.2	37.6	38.0	38.4	38.7	39.1	39.5	39.9	1.00	10.48
Thailand	33.1	33.4	33.7	34.0	34.3	34.7	35.0	35.3	35.6	36.0	36.3	0.92	9.60
Tunisia	30.3	30.6	30.9	31.1	31.4	31.6	31.9	32.1	32.4	32.6	32.9	0.81	8.35
Turkey	29.4	29.7	29.9	30.2	30.4	30.7	30.9	31.2	31.4	31.7	31.9	0.84	8.71
Turkmenistan	26.3	26.5	26.8	27.0	27.2	27.5	27.7	27.9	28.2	28.5	28.7	0.90	9.37
Ukraine	36.8	36.9	37.1	37.2	37.4	37.7	37.9	38.1	38.3	38.5	38.7	0.50	5.11
United Arab Emirates	31.2	31.4	31.6	31.8	32.0	32.1	32.3	32.6	32.8	33.1	33.4	0.70	7.19
United Kingdom	38.0	38.1	38.1	38.2	38.3	38.4	38.5	38.5	38.6	38.7	38.8	0.20	2.05
USA	35.8	35.9	36.1	36.2	36.4	36.5	36.7	36.8	37.0	37.1	37.2	0.40	4.02
Venezuela	28.0	28.3	28.5	28.7	29.0	29.2	29.5	29.7	30.0	30.2	30.5	0.83	8.66
Vietnam	28.4	28.7	29.0	29.3	29.6	29.9	30.2	30.5	30.8	31.1	31.4	1.02	10.69

Key population trends

Table 4.63 Mean age of female population: 2009-2019

years

	2009	2010	2011	2012	2013	2014	2015	2016	2017	2018	2019	CAGR	Period growth
Algeria	28.2	28.5	28.8	29.0	29.3	29.6	29.8	30.1	30.3	30.6	30.9	0.91	9.50
Argentina	33.8	33.9	34.0	34.2	34.4	34.5	34.7	34.9	35.0	35.2	35.4	0.47	4.76
Australia	38.0	38.1	38.3	38.4	38.5	38.6	38.8	38.9	39.0	39.2	39.3	0.33	3.36
Austria	41.8	42.0	42.2	42.4	42.5	42.7	42.9	43.1	43.3	43.5	43.6	0.43	4.38
Azerbaijan	31.8	32.1	32.3	32.6	32.8	33.0	33.3	33.5	33.8	34.0	34.3	0.75	7.81
Belarus	40.8	40.9	41.0	41.1	41.2	41.4	41.5	41.7	41.8	41.9	42.1	0.31	3.18
Belgium	41.4	41.5	41.6	41.7	41.8	41.9	42.0	42.2	42.3	42.4	42.5	0.27	2.71
Bolivia	26.0	26.2	26.4	26.6	26.8	27.0	27.2	27.4	27.7	27.9	28.2	0.79	8.23
Bosnia-Herzegovina	39.8	40.1	40.4	40.7	41.1	41.4	41.7	42.0	42.3	42.6	42.9	0.74	7.68
Brazil	31.2	31.6	31.9	32.3	32.7	33.1	33.4	33.8	34.2	34.6	35.0	1.13	11.91
Bulgaria	42.8	43.0	43.2	43.4	43.6	43.9	44.1	44.3	44.6	44.8	45.1	0.53	5.46
Canada	39.7	39.9	40.1	40.3	40.5	40.7	40.9	41.0	41.2	41.4	41.6	0.47	4.80
Chile	34.0	34.3	34.6	34.9	35.2	35.5	35.8	36.1	36.3	36.6	36.9	0.81	8.40
China	37.5	37.9	38.3	38.6	39.0	39.3	39.6	39.9	40.1	40.4	40.6	0.81	8.35
Colombia	29.6	29.9	30.2	30.4	30.7	31.0	31.3	31.6	31.9	32.1	32.4	0.92	9.55
Costa Rica	30.6	30.9	31.2	31.6	31.9	32.2	32.5	32.8	33.1	33.4	33.8	1.01	10.55
Croatia	42.1	42.3	42.4	42.5	42.7	42.8	42.9	43.1	43.2	43.3	43.4	0.31	3.14
Czech Republic	41.4	41.6	41.8	42.0	42.2	42.4	42.6	42.8	42.9	43.1	43.3	0.45	4.62
Denmark	40.3	40.4	40.6	40.7	40.9	41.1	41.2	41.4	41.6	41.7	41.9	0.39	3.99
Ecuador	28.9	29.1	29.4	29.7	30.0	30.3	30.6	30.8	31.1	31.4	31.7	0.93	9.74
Egypt	27.5	27.6	27.7	27.9	28.0	28.1	28.3	28.4	28.6	28.7	28.9	0.51	5.18
Estonia	42.2	42.3	42.4	42.5	42.6	42.7	42.8	42.9	43.0	43.1	43.2	0.23	2.30
Finland	41.8	41.9	42.1	42.2	42.4	42.5	42.7	42.8	43.0	43.1	43.2	0.35	3.53
France	40.6	40.8	40.9	41.0	41.2	41.3	41.4	41.5	41.7	41.8	41.9	0.31	3.12
Germany	43.7	43.9	44.1	44.4	44.6	44.8	45.1	45.3	45.5	45.7	45.9	0.49	4.99
Greece	42.5	42.7	42.9	43.1	43.3	43.5	43.7	43.9	44.0	44.2	44.4	0.44	4.49
Hong Kong, China	39.9	40.2	40.4	40.7	40.9	41.1	41.3	41.5	41.8	42.0	42.2	0.55	5.66
Hungary	42.0	42.1	42.3	42.4	42.6	42.7	42.9	43.0	43.2	43.4	43.5	0.36	3.63
India	27.9	28.1	28.3	28.6	28.8	29.0	29.3	29.5	29.8	30.1	30.3	0.85	8.84
Indonesia	30.1	30.4	30.7	31.0	31.2	31.5	31.8	32.1	32.4	32.8	33.1	0.94	9.79
Iran	28.6	28.9	29.2	29.5	29.8	30.1	30.5	30.8	31.1	31.4	31.8	1.07	11.22
Ireland	36.1	36.3	36.4	36.6	36.8	37.0	37.3	37.5	37.7	38.0	38.3	0.59	6.03
Israel	32.8	32.9	33.0	33.2	33.3	33.5	33.7	33.8	34.0	34.2	34.4	0.47	4.81
Italy	43.9	44.1	44.3	44.6	44.8	45.0	45.2	45.4	45.6	45.8	46.1	0.47	4.85
Japan	45.1	45.4	45.7	46.0	46.3	46.6	46.9	47.1	47.4	47.7	47.9	0.61	6.26
Jordan	24.8	25.1	25.3	25.6	25.8	26.1	26.4	26.7	27.0	27.3	27.6	1.05	11.06
Kazakhstan	33.1	33.2	33.3	33.4	33.5	33.6	33.7	33.8	34.0	34.2	34.4	0.41	4.13
Kuwait	26.9	27.1	27.4	27.7	28.1	28.4	28.7	29.1	29.4	29.8	30.1	1.15	12.09
Latvia	42.5	42.7	42.8	42.9	43.0	43.1	43.2	43.2	43.3	43.4	43.5	0.23	2.31
Lithuania	41.4	41.6	41.8	42.0	42.2	42.4	42.6	42.8	43.0	43.1	43.3	0.46	4.73
Malaysia	27.9	28.1	28.4	28.6	28.9	29.1	29.4	29.6	29.9	30.2	30.4	0.87	9.05
Mexico	29.7	30.1	30.4	30.8	31.1	31.5	31.9	32.2	32.6	33.0	33.4	1.16	12.22
Morocco	28.9	29.2	29.4	29.7	29.9	30.2	30.4	30.7	31.0	31.3	31.5	0.87	9.08
Netherlands	40.2	40.4	40.6	40.8	41.0	41.3	41.5	41.7	41.9	42.1	42.3	0.52	5.34
New Zealand	37.2	37.4	37.6	37.8	38.0	38.2	38.4	38.6	38.8	39.0	39.2	0.52	5.35
Nigeria	22.6	22.6	22.7	22.8	22.9	23.0	23.1	23.3	23.4	23.5	23.7	0.48	4.94
Norway	39.2	39.2	39.3	39.3	39.4	39.4	39.5	39.6	39.7	39.8	39.9	0.15	1.54
Pakistan	24.5	24.7	24.8	25.0	25.2	25.3	25.5	25.7	25.9	26.1	26.3	0.71	7.33
Peru	28.6	28.8	29.1	29.3	29.6	29.9	30.2	30.5	30.7	31.0	31.3	0.92	9.63
Philippines	26.5	26.7	26.9	27.1	27.3	27.6	27.8	28.0	28.3	28.5	28.7	0.83	8.56
Poland	40.1	40.3	40.6	40.9	41.1	41.4	41.6	41.9	42.1	42.3	42.5	0.60	6.15
Portugal	41.8	42.0	42.2	42.5	42.7	42.9	43.1	43.3	43.6	43.8	44.0	0.51	5.26
Romania	40.1	40.3	40.4	40.6	40.8	41.0	41.2	41.4	41.6	41.8	42.1	0.49	5.03
Russia	40.4	40.5	40.6	40.7	40.8	40.9	40.9	41.0	41.1	41.2	41.3	0.21	2.12
Saudi Arabia	24.3	24.6	24.9	25.1	25.4	25.7	26.0	26.3	26.6	26.9	27.2	1.11	11.70
Singapore	37.0	37.3	37.6	38.0	38.3	38.7	39.0	39.3	39.7	40.0	40.4	0.89	9.24
Slovakia	39.2	39.4	39.7	40.0	40.2	40.5	40.7	41.0	41.3	41.5	41.8	0.65	6.71
Slovenia	42.2	42.4	42.7	42.9	43.1	43.3	43.5	43.7	43.8	44.0	44.2	0.46	4.69
South Africa	28.1	28.3	28.4	28.6	28.8	28.9	29.1	29.3	29.4	29.6	29.8	0.58	5.95
South Korea	38.1	38.6	39.1	39.5	40.0	40.5	40.9	41.4	41.9	42.3	42.8	1.17	12.29
Spain	41.5	41.7	41.9	42.0	42.2	42.4	42.5	42.7	42.9	43.1	43.2	0.40	4.11
Sweden	41.4	41.4	41.5	41.6	41.6	41.7	41.8	41.9	42.0	42.1	42.2	0.19	1.96
Switzerland	41.6	41.8	42.0	42.2	42.4	42.6	42.7	42.9	43.1	43.2	43.4	0.41	4.13
Taiwan	37.0	37.5	38.0	38.4	38.9	39.4	39.8	40.3	40.7	41.2	41.7	1.20	12.62
Thailand	34.9	35.3	35.6	36.0	36.4	36.7	37.1	37.5	37.8	38.2	38.6	1.00	10.52
Tunisia	31.3	31.6	31.9	32.2	32.5	32.8	33.1	33.4	33.7	34.0	34.3	0.92	9.55
Turkey	30.2	30.5	30.8	31.0	31.3	31.6	31.8	32.1	32.4	32.6	32.9	0.85	8.83
Turkmenistan	27.9	28.1	28.4	28.7	28.9	29.1	29.4	29.6	29.9	30.2	30.5	0.90	9.41
Ukraine	41.9	42.1	42.2	42.4	42.6	42.9	43.1	43.4	43.7	43.8	44.0	0.50	5.15
United Arab Emirates	25.7	26.0	26.3	26.6	26.9	27.2	27.6	27.9	28.2	28.6	28.9	1.20	12.66
United Kingdom	40.1	40.2	40.2	40.3	40.3	40.4	40.4	40.5	40.5	40.6	40.7	0.14	1.36
USA	38.0	38.1	38.2	38.3	38.5	38.6	38.7	38.8	39.0	39.1	39.2	0.31	3.16
Venezuela	28.9	29.1	29.4	29.6	29.9	30.1	30.4	30.7	30.9	31.2	31.5	0.87	9.09
Vietnam	29.3	29.6	29.9	30.2	30.5	30.8	31.1	31.5	31.8	32.1	32.4	1.03	10.77

Key population trends

Table 4.64 Median age of population: 2009-2019

years

	2009	2010	2011	2012	2013	2014	2015	2016	2017	2018	2019	CAGR	Period growth
Algeria	25.8	26.2	26.6	27.1	27.5	27.9	28.3	28.7	29.1	29.5	29.9	1.51	16.20
Argentina	29.9	30.2	30.4	30.6	30.9	31.1	31.4	31.6	31.9	32.1	32.3	0.79	8.20
Australia	37.1	37.2	37.3	37.4	37.5	37.6	37.7	37.8	37.9	38.0	38.1	0.28	2.79
Austria	41.3	41.6	42.0	42.4	42.7	43.0	43.3	43.6	43.9	44.1	44.3	0.71	7.38
Azerbaijan	28.0	28.3	28.6	28.9	29.2	29.5	29.9	30.3	30.7	31.1	31.5	1.20	12.62
Belarus	38.2	38.4	38.5	38.6	38.7	38.9	39.1	39.3	39.4	39.6	39.8	0.41	4.13
Belgium	41.0	41.2	41.4	41.6	41.8	42.0	42.1	42.3	42.4	42.4	42.5	0.37	3.74
Bolivia	21.6	21.8	22.0	22.3	22.6	22.9	23.2	23.5	23.8	24.1	24.4	1.25	13.26
Bosnia-Herzegovina	38.9	39.3	39.6	40.0	40.3	40.7	41.0	41.4	41.7	42.0	42.4	0.85	8.88
Brazil	28.4	28.8	29.3	29.7	30.2	30.7	31.2	31.6	32.1	32.6	33.1	1.54	16.57
Bulgaria	41.4	41.7	42.0	42.3	42.6	43.0	43.3	43.7	44.0	44.4	44.8	0.78	8.07
Canada	39.5	39.7	39.9	40.1	40.3	40.5	40.6	40.8	41.0	41.1	41.3	0.45	4.55
Chile	31.7	32.0	32.3	32.6	32.9	33.2	33.5	33.8	34.1	34.5	34.8	0.93	9.68
China	38.2	38.8	39.3	39.9	40.3	40.7	41.1	41.4	41.6	41.8	41.9	0.93	9.71
Colombia	26.4	26.7	27.0	27.3	27.7	28.0	28.3	28.6	28.9	29.3	29.6	1.14	12.03
Costa Rica	27.7	28.1	28.5	29.0	29.4	29.8	30.2	30.6	31.0	31.5	31.9	1.44	15.39
Croatia	41.2	41.4	41.5	41.7	41.8	41.9	42.1	42.2	42.4	42.5	42.7	0.36	3.69
Czech Republic	39.5	39.8	40.0	40.3	40.6	41.0	41.4	41.8	42.2	42.7	43.1	0.87	9.00
Denmark	40.3	40.5	40.8	41.0	41.2	41.5	41.7	41.9	42.2	42.4	42.6	0.54	5.57
Ecuador	25.1	25.4	25.7	26.1	26.4	26.7	27.0	27.3	27.7	28.0	28.3	1.21	12.75
Egypt	23.6	23.8	23.9	24.1	24.3	24.4	24.6	24.7	24.8	24.8	24.9	0.52	5.32
Estonia	39.3	39.5	39.6	39.8	39.9	40.1	40.2	40.3	40.4	40.6	40.7	0.34	3.50
Finland	41.8	42.0	42.2	42.4	42.5	42.6	42.6	42.7	42.7	42.8	42.9	0.26	2.62
France	39.6	39.8	40.0	40.3	40.5	40.7	40.9	41.0	41.1	41.2	41.3	0.41	4.14
Germany	43.7	44.1	44.5	45.0	45.4	45.8	46.2	46.6	47.0	47.3	47.5	0.85	8.85
Greece	41.4	41.7	42.1	42.5	42.8	43.2	43.5	43.8	44.2	44.5	44.8	0.81	8.38
Hong Kong, China	40.4	40.6	40.9	41.1	41.3	41.5	41.7	41.9	42.1	42.2	42.4	0.48	4.94
Hungary	39.5	39.7	39.9	40.1	40.3	40.5	40.8	41.1	41.5	41.8	42.2	0.65	6.69
India	24.7	25.0	25.2	25.5	25.8	26.1	26.4	26.7	27.1	27.4	27.7	1.18	12.42
Indonesia	27.9	28.2	28.6	29.0	29.3	29.7	30.1	30.5	30.8	31.2	31.6	1.27	13.45
Iran	26.2	26.7	27.3	27.8	28.4	28.9	29.5	30.1	30.6	31.2	31.7	1.94	21.23
Ireland	34.1	34.4	34.7	35.0	35.3	35.7	36.1	36.5	36.9	37.4	37.8	1.04	10.88
Israel	29.1	29.2	29.4	29.6	29.8	30.0	30.2	30.5	30.7	30.9	31.1	0.66	6.80
Italy	43.0	43.4	43.8	44.2	44.6	45.0	45.4	45.8	46.2	46.6	47.0	0.89	9.22
Japan	44.6	44.9	45.2	45.5	45.9	46.3	46.6	47.0	47.4	47.8	48.2	0.78	8.12
Jordan	22.4	22.7	23.0	23.3	23.6	23.8	24.1	24.4	24.7	25.0	25.4	1.25	13.19
Kazakhstan	29.1	29.3	29.4	29.6	29.7	29.9	30.2	30.5	30.8	31.1	31.5	0.77	7.98
Kuwait	30.3	30.6	30.9	31.3	31.6	32.0	32.4	32.7	33.1	33.4	33.7	1.08	11.39
Latvia	39.9	40.0	40.2	40.3	40.5	40.6	40.8	40.9	41.1	41.2	41.3	0.36	3.70
Lithuania	39.0	39.3	39.6	39.9	40.2	40.4	40.6	40.8	41.0	41.2	41.4	0.60	6.16
Malaysia	25.0	25.3	25.5	25.8	26.0	26.3	26.5	26.7	27.0	27.3	27.5	0.96	10.04
Mexico	27.1	27.5	27.9	28.4	28.8	29.2	29.6	30.0	30.5	30.9	31.3	1.47	15.68
Morocco	25.8	26.2	26.5	26.9	27.3	27.6	28.0	28.4	28.7	29.1	29.5	1.34	14.25
Netherlands	40.4	40.8	41.2	41.6	41.9	42.3	42.6	42.9	43.2	43.4	43.5	0.76	7.88
New Zealand	36.6	36.8	37.0	37.1	37.2	37.4	37.5	37.6	37.8	38.0	38.1	0.42	4.28
Nigeria	18.4	18.5	18.6	18.7	18.8	19.0	19.1	19.3	19.4	19.6	19.8	0.73	7.53
Norway	38.5	38.6	38.8	38.9	39.0	39.2	39.3	39.4	39.4	39.5	39.6	0.28	2.83
Pakistan	21.0	21.2	21.5	21.7	22.0	22.2	22.5	22.7	22.9	23.2	23.4	1.11	11.67
Peru	25.3	25.6	25.9	26.2	26.5	26.8	27.2	27.5	27.9	28.2	28.6	1.23	12.96
Philippines	22.9	23.1	23.4	23.7	23.9	24.2	24.5	24.8	25.1	25.4	25.7	1.15	12.17
Poland	37.5	37.8	38.1	38.5	38.8	39.1	39.5	39.9	40.2	40.6	41.0	0.88	9.12
Portugal	40.4	40.7	41.0	41.4	41.7	42.1	42.4	42.8	43.2	43.6	44.0	0.85	8.81
Romania	38.0	38.3	38.6	38.8	39.1	39.5	39.8	40.2	40.6	41.0	41.4	0.87	9.07
Russia	37.7	37.7	37.9	37.9	38.0	38.1	38.3	38.4	38.5	38.7	38.8	0.31	3.14
Saudi Arabia	24.3	24.6	24.8	25.1	25.4	25.7	26.0	26.3	26.6	26.9	27.2	1.13	11.95
Singapore	37.4	37.8	38.3	38.7	39.1	39.5	39.8	40.1	40.5	40.9	41.2	0.97	10.17
Slovakia	36.6	36.9	37.3	37.7	38.1	38.6	39.0	39.4	39.9	40.3	40.8	1.10	11.55
Slovenia	41.4	41.7	42.0	42.3	42.6	42.9	43.1	43.4	43.7	44.0	44.3	0.70	7.22
South Africa	24.7	24.9	25.1	25.2	25.4	25.6	25.7	25.9	26.1	26.2	26.4	0.67	6.88
South Korea	37.3	38.0	38.6	39.2	39.8	40.4	41.0	41.6	42.1	42.7	43.3	1.48	15.86
Spain	39.8	40.1	40.4	40.8	41.1	41.5	41.8	42.2	42.6	43.0	43.4	0.87	9.03
Sweden	40.9	41.1	41.2	41.4	41.5	41.6	41.8	41.9	42.1	42.2	42.2	0.31	3.16
Switzerland	41.4	41.8	42.1	42.3	42.6	42.9	43.1	43.3	43.5	43.6	43.8	0.55	5.65
Taiwan	36.3	36.8	37.3	37.8	38.3	38.8	39.3	39.8	40.4	40.9	41.5	1.35	14.30
Thailand	33.8	34.3	34.7	35.1	35.5	36.0	36.4	36.8	37.3	37.7	38.1	1.19	12.55
Tunisia	28.6	29.0	29.5	29.9	30.4	30.8	31.2	31.7	32.1	32.6	33.1	1.46	15.59
Turkey	28.3	28.6	29.0	29.4	29.7	30.0	30.4	30.7	31.0	31.3	31.5	1.11	11.62
Turkmenistan	24.3	24.7	25.1	25.5	25.9	26.2	26.6	27.0	27.5	27.9	28.3	1.52	16.32
Ukraine	39.3	39.4	39.6	39.8	40.1	40.4	40.7	41.0	41.3	41.6	41.9	0.64	6.64
United Arab Emirates	31.3	31.7	32.1	32.4	32.7	33.0	33.2	33.5	33.8	34.0	34.2	0.90	9.40
United Kingdom	39.3	39.5	39.6	39.6	39.7	39.7	39.6	39.6	39.5	39.4	39.4	0.01	0.10
USA	36.9	37.0	37.1	37.1	37.2	37.3	37.4	37.5	37.6	37.7	37.9	0.25	2.54
Venezuela	25.8	26.1	26.4	26.7	27.0	27.3	27.7	28.0	28.3	28.6	29.0	1.18	12.42
Vietnam	26.4	26.8	27.2	27.7	28.1	28.5	28.9	29.4	29.8	30.3	30.8	1.53	16.44

Key population trends

Table 4.65 Median age of male population: 2009-2019

years

	2009	2010	2011	2012	2013	2014	2015	2016	2017	2018	2019	CAGR	Period growth
Algeria	25.5	25.9	26.4	26.8	27.2	27.6	28.0	28.4	28.8	29.2	29.6	1.52	16.27
Argentina	28.8	29.0	29.3	29.5	29.7	29.9	30.2	30.4	30.6	30.9	31.1	0.79	8.17
Australia	36.2	36.3	36.4	36.5	36.6	36.7	36.7	36.8	36.9	37.1	37.2	0.27	2.68
Austria	40.1	40.5	40.8	41.2	41.5	41.8	42.0	42.3	42.5	42.7	42.9	0.67	6.89
Azerbaijan	26.3	26.6	26.9	27.2	27.5	27.9	28.2	28.6	29.0	29.4	29.8	1.28	13.52
Belarus	35.2	35.3	35.4	35.6	35.7	35.8	36.0	36.2	36.5	36.7	36.9	0.48	4.93
Belgium	39.8	39.9	40.1	40.3	40.5	40.6	40.7	40.8	40.9	41.0	41.1	0.32	3.25
Bolivia	21.0	21.3	21.5	21.8	22.1	22.3	22.6	22.9	23.2	23.6	23.9	1.29	13.68
Bosnia-Herzegovina	37.4	37.7	38.0	38.2	38.5	38.8	39.1	39.4	39.7	40.0	40.4	0.77	7.96
Brazil	27.6	28.0	28.4	28.9	29.4	29.8	30.3	30.7	31.2	31.6	32.1	1.53	16.38
Bulgaria	39.6	39.9	40.2	40.5	40.8	41.1	41.4	41.8	42.2	42.7	43.1	0.85	8.88
Canada	38.5	38.8	39.0	39.1	39.3	39.5	39.7	39.8	40.0	40.1	40.3	0.45	4.59
Chile	30.8	31.1	31.4	31.6	31.9	32.2	32.6	32.9	33.2	33.6	33.9	0.97	10.09
China	37.7	38.2	38.7	39.2	39.6	40.0	40.2	40.4	40.6	40.6	40.7	0.77	7.96
Colombia	25.5	25.8	26.1	26.4	26.7	27.0	27.3	27.6	27.9	28.2	28.5	1.14	12.00
Costa Rica	27.4	27.8	28.2	28.6	29.0	29.4	29.8	30.3	30.7	31.1	31.6	1.44	15.37
Croatia	39.2	39.3	39.4	39.6	39.8	39.9	40.1	40.2	40.4	40.6	40.8	0.41	4.14
Czech Republic	37.9	38.2	38.5	38.9	39.3	39.7	40.2	40.6	41.0	41.5	41.9	1.00	10.51
Denmark	39.4	39.6	39.9	40.1	40.4	40.6	40.9	41.1	41.3	41.5	41.6	0.55	5.62
Ecuador	24.7	25.0	25.2	25.5	25.9	26.2	26.5	26.8	27.1	27.4	27.7	1.18	12.41
Egypt	23.1	23.3	23.4	23.6	23.7	23.9	24.0	24.1	24.2	24.2	24.3	0.49	4.98
Estonia	35.9	36.0	36.1	36.2	36.4	36.5	36.6	36.7	36.9	37.1	37.3	0.38	3.82
Finland	40.3	40.4	40.6	40.7	40.7	40.8	40.8	40.9	41.0	41.2	41.3	0.26	2.58
France	38.1	38.3	38.5	38.7	38.9	39.1	39.2	39.2	39.3	39.4	39.5	0.35	3.59
Germany	42.5	43.0	43.4	43.9	44.3	44.7	45.1	45.5	45.8	46.1	46.3	0.85	8.80
Greece	40.1	40.4	40.8	41.1	41.5	41.8	42.2	42.5	42.8	43.2	43.6	0.84	8.75
Hong Kong, China	40.9	41.2	41.6	41.9	42.1	42.4	42.7	42.9	43.2	43.4	43.6	0.63	6.51
Hungary	37.1	37.3	37.5	37.8	38.1	38.5	38.8	39.2	39.5	39.9	40.2	0.80	8.31
India	24.4	24.7	25.0	25.2	25.5	25.8	26.1	26.4	26.7	27.0	27.4	1.15	12.14
Indonesia	27.4	27.8	28.1	28.5	28.8	29.2	29.6	29.9	30.3	30.7	31.0	1.25	13.20
Iran	26.1	26.6	27.2	27.7	28.2	28.8	29.3	29.8	30.4	30.9	31.4	1.88	20.45
Ireland	33.6	33.9	34.2	34.6	34.9	35.3	35.7	36.2	36.6	37.0	37.4	1.10	11.57
Israel	28.0	28.2	28.4	28.6	28.8	29.0	29.2	29.4	29.6	29.8	30.1	0.72	7.39
Italy	41.6	42.0	42.4	42.8	43.2	43.6	44.0	44.4	44.8	45.2	45.6	0.91	9.54
Japan	42.8	43.1	43.5	43.9	44.2	44.6	45.0	45.4	45.8	46.2	46.6	0.85	8.89
Jordan	22.5	22.8	23.1	23.4	23.6	23.9	24.1	24.4	24.7	25.0	25.3	1.21	12.82
Kazakhstan	27.1	27.2	27.4	27.6	27.8	28.0	28.3	28.5	28.8	29.1	29.5	0.83	8.62
Kuwait	31.9	32.3	32.7	33.0	33.4	33.9	34.3	34.7	35.1	35.5	35.8	1.16	12.20
Latvia	36.6	36.8	36.9	37.1	37.3	37.4	37.6	37.7	37.8	38.0	38.2	0.44	4.49
Lithuania	36.1	36.4	36.6	36.8	37.0	37.2	37.3	37.5	37.7	37.9	38.1	0.55	5.64
Malaysia	24.7	24.9	25.2	25.4	25.6	25.8	26.1	26.3	26.5	26.8	27.0	0.90	9.36
Mexico	26.5	26.9	27.4	27.8	28.2	28.6	29.0	29.4	29.8	30.2	30.6	1.44	15.40
Morocco	25.1	25.4	25.8	26.1	26.5	26.8	27.2	27.5	27.8	28.2	28.5	1.29	13.69
Netherlands	39.6	40.0	40.4	40.8	41.2	41.5	41.8	42.1	42.3	42.4	42.6	0.72	7.43
New Zealand	35.6	35.7	35.8	35.9	36.0	36.1	36.2	36.3	36.5	36.6	36.8	0.34	3.40
Nigeria	18.1	18.2	18.3	18.5	18.6	18.7	18.9	19.0	19.2	19.4	19.6	0.77	7.94
Norway	37.7	37.9	38.1	38.2	38.4	38.5	38.7	38.8	38.8	38.9	39.0	0.35	3.52
Pakistan	21.0	21.3	21.5	21.8	22.0	22.2	22.5	22.7	22.9	23.2	23.4	1.09	11.40
Peru	24.9	25.2	25.5	25.8	26.1	26.4	26.7	27.1	27.4	27.7	28.1	1.21	12.76
Philippines	22.5	22.8	23.0	23.3	23.5	23.8	24.1	24.4	24.7	25.0	25.2	1.15	12.13
Poland	35.6	36.0	36.3	36.7	37.0	37.4	37.8	38.1	38.5	38.9	39.3	0.97	10.16
Portugal	38.8	39.1	39.5	39.8	40.1	40.5	40.9	41.3	41.7	42.1	42.5	0.91	9.47
Romania	36.4	36.7	36.9	37.3	37.6	38.0	38.4	38.8	39.2	39.6	40.0	0.95	9.89
Russia	34.6	34.7	34.8	34.9	35.0	35.1	35.2	35.4	35.6	35.7	36.0	0.38	3.89
Saudi Arabia	26.6	26.8	27.0	27.2	27.4	27.6	27.8	28.0	28.3	28.5	28.8	0.79	8.18
Singapore	37.2	37.6	38.0	38.5	38.9	39.2	39.5	39.9	40.2	40.5	40.8	0.94	9.86
Slovakia	35.0	35.4	35.8	36.3	36.7	37.1	37.6	38.0	38.5	38.9	39.4	1.20	12.63
Slovenia	39.8	40.1	40.4	40.7	41.0	41.3	41.6	42.0	42.3	42.6	43.0	0.77	7.95
South Africa	24.2	24.4	24.6	24.8	25.0	25.1	25.3	25.4	25.6	25.8	25.9	0.69	7.16
South Korea	36.3	36.9	37.5	38.1	38.6	39.2	39.7	40.3	40.8	41.3	41.8	1.43	15.22
Spain	38.5	38.9	39.2	39.6	39.9	40.3	40.7	41.1	41.5	41.9	42.3	0.93	9.73
Sweden	39.9	40.1	40.2	40.4	40.6	40.7	40.9	41.0	41.1	41.2	41.3	0.33	3.33
Switzerland	40.5	40.8	41.1	41.4	41.6	41.9	42.1	42.2	42.4	42.5	42.6	0.51	5.19
Taiwan	35.7	36.1	36.6	37.0	37.5	37.9	38.5	39.0	39.5	40.0	40.5	1.27	13.47
Thailand	32.8	33.2	33.6	33.9	34.3	34.7	35.1	35.5	35.9	36.3	36.6	1.11	11.70
Tunisia	28.0	28.5	28.9	29.3	29.8	30.2	30.6	31.0	31.5	31.9	32.4	1.44	15.39
Turkey	27.9	28.3	28.7	29.0	29.3	29.7	30.0	30.3	30.6	30.8	31.1	1.08	11.30
Turkmenistan	23.7	24.1	24.4	24.8	25.2	25.6	26.0	26.3	26.8	27.2	27.6	1.53	16.39
Ukraine	35.9	36.1	36.3	36.5	36.7	37.0	37.3	37.6	37.9	38.2	38.5	0.70	7.19
United Arab Emirates	32.8	33.2	33.5	33.8	34.0	34.3	34.6	34.8	35.1	35.3	35.6	0.81	8.44
United Kingdom	38.2	38.3	38.3	38.4	38.3	38.3	38.2	38.1	38.0	38.0	38.1	-0.03	-0.30
USA	35.5	35.6	35.7	35.8	35.9	36.0	36.1	36.3	36.4	36.6	36.7	0.33	3.39
Venezuela	25.3	25.6	25.9	26.2	26.5	26.9	27.2	27.5	27.8	28.1	28.4	1.15	12.12
Vietnam	25.9	26.3	26.8	27.2	27.6	28.0	28.5	28.9	29.3	29.8	30.3	1.55	16.64

Key population trends

Table 4.66 Median age of female population: 2009-2019

years

	2009	2010	2011	2012	2013	2014	2015	2016	2017	2018	2019	CAGR	Period growth
Algeria	26.0	26.5	26.9	27.3	27.8	28.2	28.6	29.0	29.4	29.8	30.2	1.51	16.12
Argentina	31.0	31.3	31.5	31.8	32.1	32.3	32.6	32.9	33.1	33.4	33.6	0.80	8.33
Australia	37.8	38.0	38.2	38.3	38.4	38.5	38.6	38.7	38.8	38.9	39.0	0.30	3.09
Austria	42.4	42.8	43.2	43.5	43.9	44.2	44.5	44.9	45.1	45.4	45.7	0.74	7.64
Azerbaijan	29.8	30.1	30.4	30.7	31.0	31.4	31.7	32.1	32.5	32.9	33.3	1.11	11.69
Belarus	41.2	41.4	41.5	41.6	41.8	41.9	42.2	42.3	42.5	42.7	42.9	0.39	3.99
Belgium	42.2	42.4	42.6	42.8	43.0	43.2	43.4	43.6	43.8	43.9	44.0	0.42	4.24
Bolivia	22.1	22.4	22.6	22.9	23.1	23.4	23.7	24.0	24.3	24.7	25.0	1.22	12.84
Bosnia-Herzegovina	40.2	40.6	41.1	41.5	41.9	42.3	42.7	43.1	43.5	43.9	44.3	0.97	10.14
Brazil	29.2	29.6	30.1	30.6	31.0	31.5	32.0	32.5	33.0	33.5	34.0	1.55	16.64
Bulgaria	43.6	43.8	44.0	44.2	44.5	44.9	45.2	45.6	46.0	46.3	46.7	0.69	7.17
Canada	40.4	40.6	40.9	41.1	41.3	41.5	41.6	41.8	41.9	42.1	42.3	0.45	4.54
Chile	32.7	33.0	33.3	33.6	33.9	34.2	34.5	34.8	35.1	35.4	35.8	0.90	9.36
China	38.7	39.3	39.9	40.5	41.0	41.5	41.9	42.3	42.7	43.0	43.2	1.10	11.58
Colombia	27.4	27.7	28.0	28.3	28.7	29.0	29.3	29.7	30.0	30.3	30.7	1.15	12.06
Costa Rica	28.0	28.5	28.9	29.3	29.7	30.1	30.5	31.0	31.4	31.9	32.3	1.44	15.43
Croatia	43.1	43.3	43.5	43.7	43.9	44.0	44.1	44.2	44.4	44.5	44.7	0.37	3.80
Czech Republic	41.3	41.5	41.7	41.9	42.2	42.5	42.8	43.1	43.5	43.9	44.3	0.70	7.17
Denmark	41.2	41.5	41.7	41.9	42.1	42.3	42.6	42.8	43.0	43.2	43.5	0.53	5.42
Ecuador	25.6	25.9	26.3	26.6	26.9	27.2	27.6	27.9	28.3	28.6	29.0	1.24	13.07
Egypt	24.1	24.3	24.5	24.7	24.8	25.0	25.1	25.3	25.4	25.5	25.5	0.56	5.77
Estonia	42.9	42.9	43.0	43.2	43.3	43.5	43.6	43.8	43.9	44.0	44.2	0.30	3.05
Finland	43.3	43.6	43.8	44.0	44.2	44.3	44.4	44.5	44.6	44.6	44.6	0.29	2.92
France	41.1	41.3	41.5	41.8	42.0	42.2	42.4	42.6	42.8	43.0	43.1	0.46	4.74
Germany	44.8	45.3	45.7	46.1	46.5	46.9	47.3	47.7	48.1	48.4	48.7	0.84	8.69
Greece	42.7	43.1	43.5	43.8	44.2	44.6	44.9	45.2	45.6	45.9	46.2	0.79	8.17
Hong Kong, China	40.0	40.2	40.4	40.6	40.7	40.9	41.0	41.1	41.2	41.4	41.5	0.37	3.81
Hungary	42.1	42.2	42.4	42.6	42.8	43.0	43.2	43.4	43.6	43.8	44.2	0.48	4.91
India	25.0	25.3	25.6	25.9	26.2	26.5	26.8	27.1	27.5	27.8	28.1	1.21	12.74
Indonesia	28.3	28.7	29.1	29.5	29.8	30.2	30.6	31.0	31.4	31.8	32.2	1.29	13.69
Iran	26.2	26.8	27.4	27.9	28.5	29.1	29.7	30.3	30.8	31.4	32.0	2.01	22.04
Ireland	34.7	34.9	35.2	35.5	35.8	36.1	36.5	36.9	37.3	37.7	38.2	0.96	10.07
Israel	30.2	30.4	30.5	30.7	30.9	31.1	31.3	31.5	31.7	31.9	32.1	0.61	6.32
Italy	44.4	44.8	45.2	45.6	46.0	46.4	46.8	47.2	47.6	48.0	48.4	0.86	8.93
Japan	46.3	46.7	47.0	47.4	47.7	48.0	48.4	48.7	49.1	49.5	49.9	0.75	7.76
Jordan	22.3	22.7	23.0	23.3	23.5	23.8	24.1	24.4	24.7	25.0	25.4	1.28	13.59
Kazakhstan	31.2	31.4	31.5	31.7	31.8	32.0	32.3	32.5	32.8	33.1	33.5	0.71	7.28
Kuwait	27.2	27.5	27.8	28.2	28.5	28.8	29.1	29.4	29.7	30.0	30.3	1.06	11.17
Latvia	43.2	43.3	43.5	43.6	43.7	43.8	43.9	44.1	44.2	44.3	44.5	0.29	2.98
Lithuania	41.7	42.1	42.4	42.7	43.0	43.3	43.6	43.9	44.1	44.3	44.5	0.65	6.66
Malaysia	25.3	25.6	25.9	26.2	26.4	26.7	27.0	27.2	27.5	27.8	28.1	1.03	10.76
Mexico	27.6	28.0	28.5	28.9	29.4	29.8	30.2	30.7	31.1	31.6	32.0	1.49	15.97
Morocco	26.5	26.9	27.3	27.6	28.0	28.4	28.8	29.2	29.6	30.0	30.4	1.39	14.79
Netherlands	41.1	41.5	41.9	42.3	42.7	43.0	43.4	43.7	44.0	44.3	44.5	0.78	8.09
New Zealand	37.4	37.7	37.9	38.2	38.4	38.6	38.7	38.9	39.1	39.2	39.4	0.52	5.36
Nigeria	18.7	18.8	18.9	19.0	19.1	19.2	19.4	19.5	19.7	19.8	20.0	0.69	7.13
Norway	39.3	39.4	39.5	39.6	39.7	39.8	39.9	40.0	40.1	40.1	40.2	0.21	2.16
Pakistan	20.9	21.2	21.5	21.7	22.0	22.2	22.4	22.7	22.9	23.2	23.4	1.14	11.95
Peru	25.7	26.0	26.3	26.6	26.9	27.3	27.6	28.0	28.3	28.7	29.1	1.24	13.15
Philippines	23.3	23.5	23.8	24.1	24.3	24.6	24.9	25.2	25.5	25.8	26.1	1.16	12.19
Poland	39.6	39.9	40.1	40.4	40.7	41.0	41.3	41.6	42.0	42.3	42.7	0.76	7.84
Portugal	42.0	42.3	42.7	43.0	43.3	43.6	44.0	44.4	44.7	45.1	45.5	0.80	8.31
Romania	39.4	39.8	40.2	40.5	40.8	41.1	41.4	41.7	42.1	42.5	42.9	0.85	8.80
Russia	40.8	40.8	40.9	41.0	41.0	41.2	41.3	41.4	41.5	41.7	41.8	0.25	2.53
Saudi Arabia	21.7	22.1	22.4	22.8	23.2	23.6	23.9	24.3	24.7	25.1	25.4	1.59	17.08
Singapore	37.6	38.0	38.5	38.9	39.4	39.7	40.1	40.4	40.8	41.2	41.6	1.00	10.45
Slovakia	38.3	38.6	39.0	39.3	39.7	40.1	40.5	40.9	41.4	41.8	42.2	0.97	10.17
Slovenia	42.9	43.3	43.6	44.0	44.3	44.5	44.8	45.1	45.3	45.6	45.9	0.68	6.99
South Africa	25.2	25.4	25.5	25.7	25.9	26.0	26.2	26.4	26.5	26.7	26.8	0.64	6.59
South Korea	38.4	39.0	39.7	40.3	41.0	41.6	42.2	42.9	43.5	44.1	44.7	1.53	16.38
Spain	41.1	41.4	41.7	42.1	42.4	42.7	43.1	43.4	43.8	44.2	44.5	0.81	8.38
Sweden	41.9	42.1	42.3	42.4	42.5	42.6	42.7	42.9	43.0	43.1	43.2	0.30	3.05
Switzerland	42.3	42.7	43.0	43.3	43.6	43.8	44.1	44.3	44.5	44.7	44.9	0.59	6.01
Taiwan	36.9	37.4	38.0	38.5	39.0	39.6	40.1	40.7	41.2	41.8	42.4	1.41	15.03
Thailand	34.9	35.3	35.8	36.2	36.7	37.2	37.7	38.1	38.6	39.0	39.5	1.25	13.20
Tunisia	29.2	29.6	30.1	30.5	31.0	31.5	31.9	32.4	32.8	33.3	33.8	1.48	15.79
Turkey	28.6	29.0	29.3	29.7	30.1	30.4	30.8	31.1	31.4	31.7	32.0	1.13	11.93
Turkmenistan	25.0	25.4	25.8	26.1	26.5	26.9	27.3	27.7	28.2	28.6	29.0	1.51	16.18
Ukraine	42.6	42.8	43.0	43.2	43.4	43.6	44.0	44.3	44.6	44.9	45.1	0.56	5.79
United Arab Emirates	27.0	27.5	27.9	28.4	28.7	29.1	29.4	29.6	29.9	30.1	30.3	1.15	12.11
United Kingdom	40.5	40.6	40.7	40.8	41.0	41.0	41.0	41.0	41.0	40.9	40.8	0.08	0.81
USA	38.3	38.4	38.5	38.6	38.6	38.7	38.7	38.8	38.9	38.9	39.1	0.20	2.05
Venezuela	26.2	26.5	26.8	27.2	27.5	27.8	28.2	28.5	28.8	29.2	29.5	1.20	12.69
Vietnam	26.9	27.3	27.7	28.1	28.6	29.0	29.4	29.9	30.3	30.8	31.3	1.52	16.26

Vital statistics

Table 4.67 Live births: 2009-2019

'000

	2009	2010	2011	2012	2013	2014	2015	2016	2017	2018	2019	CAGR	Period growth
Algeria	723.4	730.8	736.5	740.6	743.1	743.9	742.7	739.6	734.5	727.8	719.5	-0.05	-0.53
Argentina	698.4	699.7	700.1	699.7	698.6	697.0	694.8	692.1	688.9	685.3	681.4	-0.25	-2.44
Australia	297.7	297.8	300.7	303.1	305.7	308.4	311.2	314.0	316.8	319.6	322.3	0.80	8.28
Austria	76.8	76.8	77.0	77.1	77.3	77.5	77.7	77.8	77.8	77.7	77.6	0.10	0.98
Azerbaijan	151.8	150.0	150.9	151.0	150.4	149.1	147.3	145.0	142.2	139.0	135.6	-1.13	-10.71
Belarus	108.9	105.9	105.2	104.3	103.2	101.9	100.5	99.0	97.3	95.6	93.9	-1.47	-13.79
Belgium	123.3	123.6	123.6	123.4	123.2	122.9	122.6	122.3	122.1	121.9	121.8	-0.13	-1.24
Bolivia	262.1	261.3	260.5	259.7	258.8	257.7	256.6	255.4	254.0	252.6	251.2	-0.42	-4.16
Bosnia-Herzegovina	34.7	34.6	34.5	34.4	34.3	34.1	33.9	33.7	33.4	33.0	32.7	-0.61	-5.96
Brazil	3,026.4	2,958.0	2,900.3	2,851.1	2,808.0	2,770.1	2,736.2	2,704.7	2,674.5	2,644.3	2,613.6	-1.46	-13.64
Bulgaria	70.6	69.8	68.9	67.9	66.7	65.4	64.0	62.3	60.6	58.8	57.0	-2.13	-19.35
Canada	367.7	361.7	361.2	366.1	370.3	374.5	378.4	382.2	385.7	388.9	391.7	0.64	6.54
Chile	252.1	252.8	253.2	253.4	253.4	253.1	252.7	252.2	251.7	251.1	250.6	-0.06	-0.62
China	15,999.4	15,714.7	15,687.9	15,752.4	15,781.0	15,764.6	15,691.6	15,558.4	15,370.8	15,139.9	14,874.3	-0.73	-7.03
Colombia	917.3	915.2	912.5	909.6	906.6	903.8	901.2	898.7	896.0	893.1	889.9	-0.30	-2.99
Costa Rica	75.7	76.2	76.8	77.4	77.7	77.8	77.6	77.3	76.9	76.6	76.3	0.08	0.81
Croatia	43.0	43.2	43.3	43.4	43.4	43.3	43.2	43.0	42.7	42.4	42.1	-0.21	-2.05
Czech Republic	100.7	98.9	96.8	95.4	94.3	93.6	93.0	92.6	92.4	92.2	92.0	-0.90	-8.65
Denmark	63.8	62.9	62.1	61.6	61.3	61.2	61.3	61.7	62.2	62.8	63.5	-0.04	-0.43
Ecuador	278.9	277.3	275.9	274.7	273.7	272.8	271.9	271.1	270.2	269.1	268.0	-0.40	-3.92
Egypt	1,855.7	1,863.1	1,867.8	1,869.9	1,869.4	1,866.7	1,861.8	1,855.3	1,847.6	1,839.4	1,831.1	-0.13	-1.33
Estonia	15.1	15.2	15.3	15.3	15.3	15.3	15.2	15.0	14.8	14.5	14.2	-0.65	-6.28
Finland	59.5	59.7	60.0	60.3	60.5	60.8	60.9	61.0	61.0	61.0	61.0	0.24	2.44
France	803.0	786.5	784.1	782.3	780.6	779.1	777.6	776.2	774.6	772.8	770.8	-0.41	-4.01
Germany	665.6	623.4	604.7	598.4	597.2	597.2	597.5	598.0	598.3	598.3	597.5	-1.07	-10.22
Greece	95.8	95.5	95.3	95.1	94.9	94.8	94.7	94.7	94.8	94.9	95.0	-0.08	-0.81
Hong Kong, China	75.3	76.1	76.6	76.9	77.1	77.2	77.2	77.2	77.2	77.3	77.3	0.26	2.64
Hungary	98.0	97.3	96.6	96.0	95.4	95.0	94.6	94.3	94.1	93.7	93.3	-0.48	-4.74
India	26,787.4	26,665.7	26,542.8	26,411.4	26,265.1	26,101.3	25,918.5	25,716.8	25,499.2	25,268.4	25,025.5	-0.68	-6.58
Indonesia	4,174.3	4,126.6	4,076.3	4,023.3	3,968.6	3,913.8	3,861.3	3,813.5	3,772.2	3,738.2	3,712.2	-1.17	-11.07
Iran	1,390.4	1,392.4	1,392.9	1,390.9	1,385.8	1,377.0	1,363.8	1,345.6	1,322.8	1,296.6	1,267.8	-0.92	-8.81
Ireland	66.0	66.0	65.9	65.7	65.4	65.0	64.7	64.3	64.1	64.0	64.1	-0.29	-2.86
Israel	143.8	143.4	142.8	142.2	141.7	141.1	140.6	140.2	139.9	139.7	139.6	-0.30	-2.97
Italy	576.2	567.5	564.4	560.3	555.6	550.8	545.9	541.5	537.4	533.8	530.6	-0.82	-7.91
Japan	1,067.9	1,039.7	1,013.8	990.2	968.8	949.5	932.0	916.1	901.5	887.9	875.4	-1.97	-18.02
Jordan	158.4	159.2	159.4	159.0	158.2	157.0	155.6	154.1	152.5	151.0	149.6	-0.57	-5.54
Kazakhstan	364.7	360.0	362.9	362.7	359.5	355.7	351.5	346.8	341.7	336.1	330.2	-0.99	-9.48
Kuwait	52.1	52.4	52.5	52.5	52.3	52.2	52.0	51.8	51.6	51.4	51.3	-0.16	-1.63
Latvia	22.9	23.2	23.5	23.6	23.7	23.7	23.6	23.4	23.1	22.6	22.1	-0.36	-3.52
Lithuania	31.6	31.9	32.1	32.2	32.4	32.5	32.5	32.5	32.4	32.1	31.8	0.05	0.52
Malaysia	487.8	487.1	486.4	485.6	484.5	483.0	481.1	478.8	476.1	473.1	469.7	-0.38	-3.70
Mexico	2,685.3	2,616.7	2,604.0	2,602.7	2,597.1	2,585.8	2,570.7	2,552.9	2,536.1	2,521.1	2,508.2	-0.68	-6.60
Morocco	651.4	655.2	657.5	658.7	658.9	657.9	655.7	652.4	647.9	642.5	636.4	-0.23	-2.31
Netherlands	178.9	177.7	176.6	176.0	175.8	176.0	176.5	177.3	178.2	179.3	180.4	0.08	0.80
New Zealand	64.0	63.3	62.8	62.4	62.1	61.8	61.6	61.4	61.3	61.3	61.2	-0.45	-4.37
Nigeria	6,080.8	6,119.8	6,144.9	6,158.2	6,161.8	6,157.5	6,146.5	6,130.0	6,109.3	6,085.9	6,061.7	-0.03	-0.31
Norway	54.5	54.5	54.7	55.0	55.4	55.9	56.5	57.1	57.8	58.4	59.0	0.79	8.21
Pakistan	5,403.4	5,464.9	5,518.3	5,561.6	5,593.9	5,614.6	5,624.1	5,623.6	5,615.9	5,603.9	5,589.4	0.34	3.44
Peru	605.1	600.9	596.3	591.8	587.4	583.3	579.6	576.3	573.2	570.3	567.5	-0.64	-6.22
Philippines	2,282.5	2,299.8	2,321.9	2,347.5	2,370.0	2,392.9	2,416.2	2,440.0	2,463.7	2,486.8	2,509.5	0.95	9.94
Poland	374.8	378.4	381.7	384.3	386.1	387.3	387.8	387.6	386.5	384.5	381.6	0.18	1.83
Portugal	118.1	117.0	115.7	114.3	112.9	111.4	110.0	108.7	107.7	107.0	106.6	-1.02	-9.75
Romania	219.5	217.7	215.8	213.6	211.3	208.7	205.5	201.6	196.9	191.6	186.0	-1.64	-15.26
Russia	1,757.3	1,671.2	1,688.8	1,720.9	1,734.3	1,724.4	1,708.3	1,686.2	1,659.3	1,628.5	1,595.5	-0.96	-9.21
Saudi Arabia	593.3	596.7	600.6	604.7	608.6	611.9	614.6	616.5	617.9	618.7	618.9	0.42	4.32
Singapore	38.9	39.3	39.8	40.2	40.7	41.2	41.7	42.2	42.8	43.4	44.0	1.24	13.11
Slovakia	52.3	52.3	52.2	52.1	52.0	51.9	51.7	51.5	51.2	50.9	50.4	-0.37	-3.62
Slovenia	18.9	19.1	19.3	19.4	19.4	19.4	19.3	19.2	19.0	18.7	18.5	-0.22	-2.16
South Africa	1,085.5	1,080.3	1,075.4	1,070.1	1,063.8	1,056.6	1,048.5	1,039.9	1,031.0	1,022.4	1,014.2	-0.68	-6.57
South Korea	474.8	468.9	463.1	457.6	452.8	448.7	445.3	442.5	440.4	438.7	437.1	-0.82	-7.94
Spain	484.3	486.2	486.2	484.7	481.8	477.8	473.1	468.2	457.9	448.4	439.8	-0.96	-9.19
Sweden	107.6	108.2	108.4	108.8	109.4	110.2	111.1	112.1	113.1	114.0	114.9	0.66	6.81
Switzerland	72.1	72.4	72.9	73.6	74.4	75.4	76.4	77.5	78.7	79.8	80.9	1.16	12.18
Taiwan	202.4	201.4	198.3	195.3	193.3	190.2	187.2	185.2	182.2	179.1	175.1	-1.44	-13.50
Thailand	921.2	914.3	906.6	898.4	890.2	882.0	873.9	866.1	858.5	851.1	843.9	-0.87	-8.39
Tunisia	165.3	166.9	168.2	169.3	170.0	170.3	170.3	170.1	169.6	169.0	168.3	0.18	1.80
Turkey	1,362.7	1,363.0	1,361.3	1,357.8	1,353.1	1,347.6	1,342.0	1,336.6	1,331.5	1,326.5	1,321.7	-0.30	-3.01
Turkmenistan	110.9	111.1	111.2	111.1	110.9	110.5	109.8	108.8	107.7	106.3	104.7	-0.58	-5.61
Ukraine	473.7	471.0	466.2	460.1	453.0	445.2	436.9	427.9	418.4	408.5	398.3	-1.72	-15.91
United Arab Emirates	68.6	69.2	69.7	70.1	70.2	70.0	69.7	69.1	68.5	67.9	67.4	-0.18	-1.78
United Kingdom	804.3	784.2	789.3	795.5	802.7	810.4	818.2	825.7	832.3	837.8	841.9	0.46	4.67
USA	4,290.6	4,196.3	4,182.9	4,208.0	4,229.3	4,247.6	4,263.5	4,277.7	4,290.8	4,302.9	4,314.2	0.05	0.55
Venezuela	599.7	600.3	600.5	600.1	599.3	598.2	596.8	595.0	593.1	591.0	588.7	-0.18	-1.83
Vietnam	1,596.0	1,608.5	1,620.4	1,631.5	1,641.6	1,650.1	1,656.4	1,660.0	1,658.5	1,647.9	1,626.6	0.19	1.92

Vital statistics

Table 4.68 Birth rates: 2009-2019

per '000 inhabitants

	2009	2010	2011	2012	2013	2014	2015	2016	2017	2018	2019	CAGR	Period growth
Algeria	20.73	20.63	20.49	20.30	20.07	19.81	19.50	19.15	18.77	18.36	17.93	-1.44	-13.53
Argentina	17.31	17.18	17.02	16.85	16.67	16.48	16.28	16.08	15.87	15.65	15.44	-1.14	-10.84
Australia	13.66	13.48	13.44	13.37	13.30	13.23	13.17	13.10	13.05	12.99	12.93	-0.55	-5.33
Austria	9.17	9.14	9.13	9.12	9.12	9.11	9.10	9.09	9.07	9.05	9.01	-0.17	-1.73
Azerbaijan	17.39	16.99	16.91	16.74	16.50	16.21	15.86	15.46	15.02	14.56	14.09	-2.08	-18.96
Belarus	11.26	10.97	10.93	10.87	10.78	10.68	10.56	10.43	10.29	10.15	9.99	-1.19	-11.24
Belgium	11.57	11.55	11.51	11.46	11.39	11.33	11.27	11.21	11.15	11.10	11.06	-0.45	-4.40
Bolivia	26.57	26.05	25.55	25.06	24.58	24.10	23.64	23.18	22.74	22.30	21.87	-1.93	-17.69
Bosnia-Herzegovina	9.03	9.01	8.98	8.95	8.92	8.88	8.84	8.78	8.71	8.64	8.56	-0.54	-5.26
Brazil	15.62	15.14	14.72	14.36	14.04	13.75	13.49	13.25	13.02	12.79	12.57	-2.15	-19.54
Bulgaria	9.39	9.35	9.30	9.23	9.14	9.03	8.89	8.74	8.57	8.39	8.20	-1.35	-12.71
Canada	10.93	10.65	10.55	10.61	10.65	10.69	10.72	10.75	10.77	10.78	10.78	-0.13	-1.32
Chile	14.86	14.75	14.64	14.51	14.38	14.24	14.10	13.96	13.81	13.68	13.54	-0.92	-8.85
China	12.05	11.78	11.71	11.71	11.68	11.62	11.52	11.38	11.21	11.00	10.78	-1.11	-10.52
Colombia	20.09	19.77	19.44	19.13	18.82	18.53	18.25	17.98	17.72	17.46	17.21	-1.54	-14.36
Costa Rica	16.54	16.43	16.34	16.23	16.08	15.89	15.66	15.41	15.15	14.92	14.70	-1.17	-11.11
Croatia	9.71	9.77	9.81	9.85	9.87	9.88	9.87	9.85	9.82	9.78	9.73	0.02	0.23
Czech Republic	9.75	9.55	9.34	9.20	9.10	9.03	8.98	8.94	8.92	8.90	8.89	-0.92	-8.81
Denmark	11.57	11.37	11.21	11.08	11.00	10.95	10.95	10.98	11.04	11.12	11.21	-0.32	-3.12
Ecuador	20.47	20.13	19.80	19.49	19.19	18.90	18.63	18.37	18.11	17.86	17.60	-1.50	-14.02
Egypt	24.18	23.84	23.48	23.10	22.70	22.29	21.88	21.46	21.04	20.63	20.24	-1.76	-16.28
Estonia	11.36	11.47	11.57	11.63	11.68	11.68	11.66	11.57	11.44	11.25	11.02	-0.30	-2.99
Finland	11.18	11.17	11.18	11.19	11.20	11.20	11.19	11.17	11.15	11.11	11.07	-0.09	-0.94
France	12.86	12.53	12.44	12.35	12.27	12.19	12.12	12.05	11.98	11.91	11.83	-0.83	-7.98
Germany	8.12	7.63	7.43	7.37	7.38	7.41	7.43	7.46	7.49	7.52	7.54	-0.74	-7.15
Greece	8.51	8.46	8.41	8.37	8.34	8.31	8.28	8.27	8.26	8.26	8.27	-0.29	-2.91
Hong Kong, China	10.66	10.68	10.65	10.60	10.53	10.45	10.37	10.29	10.22	10.14	10.07	-0.56	-5.50
Hungary	9.78	9.73	9.68	9.64	9.61	9.59	9.59	9.58	9.58	9.57	9.55	-0.23	-2.30
India	22.92	22.51	22.10	21.71	21.32	20.92	20.53	20.13	19.74	19.34	18.95	-1.88	-17.30
Indonesia	18.15	17.75	17.35	16.95	16.55	16.17	15.81	15.48	15.19	14.93	14.71	-2.08	-18.94
Iran	18.74	18.55	18.34	18.10	17.84	17.53	17.16	16.75	16.29	15.79	15.29	-2.02	-18.43
Ireland	14.84	14.65	14.45	14.24	14.01	13.78	13.57	13.36	13.19	13.05	12.94	-1.36	-12.77
Israel	19.43	19.07	18.72	18.38	18.04	17.73	17.44	17.17	16.92	16.69	16.48	-1.63	-15.18
Italy	9.76	9.60	9.54	9.46	9.38	9.30	9.22	9.15	9.08	9.03	8.98	-0.82	-7.92
Japan	8.37	8.16	7.98	7.81	7.66	7.52	7.41	7.30	7.21	7.13	7.06	-1.69	-15.65
Jordan	25.08	24.60	24.16	23.74	23.32	22.87	22.37	21.83	21.27	20.73	20.21	-2.13	-19.39
Kazakhstan	23.12	22.52	22.42	22.13	21.68	21.20	20.71	20.21	19.70	19.18	18.65	-2.12	-19.32
Kuwait	21.32	20.98	20.57	20.13	19.67	19.22	18.78	18.36	17.96	17.59	17.25	-2.10	-19.08
Latvia	10.15	10.35	10.53	10.68	10.79	10.86	10.89	10.85	10.76	10.60	10.40	0.25	2.49
Lithuania	9.45	9.57	9.68	9.79	9.89	9.99	10.06	10.11	10.12	10.10	10.05	0.62	6.33
Malaysia	17.36	17.06	16.77	16.49	16.22	15.94	15.66	15.37	15.09	14.80	14.52	-1.77	-16.38
Mexico	24.73	23.75	23.29	22.97	22.63	22.26	21.87	21.47	21.10	20.75	20.43	-1.89	-17.39
Morocco	20.36	20.23	20.06	19.86	19.64	19.38	19.10	18.79	18.46	18.11	17.76	-1.36	-12.79
Netherlands	10.90	10.81	10.73	10.67	10.63	10.63	10.64	10.67	10.70	10.75	10.80	-0.10	-0.95
New Zealand	14.86	14.55	14.29	14.07	13.88	13.69	13.52	13.39	13.26	13.15	13.03	-1.30	-12.29
Nigeria	39.30	38.67	37.98	37.25	36.49	35.71	34.94	34.16	33.40	32.65	31.93	-2.05	-18.75
Norway	11.36	11.23	11.14	11.08	11.06	11.05	11.06	11.08	11.10	11.11	11.12	-0.21	-2.07
Pakistan	29.88	29.58	29.23	28.83	28.38	27.89	27.37	26.82	26.26	25.71	25.17	-1.70	-15.79
Peru	20.86	20.44	20.02	19.61	19.22	18.85	18.50	18.18	17.87	17.58	17.30	-1.85	-17.06
Philippines	24.77	24.49	24.26	24.08	23.87	23.67	23.48	23.30	23.12	22.93	22.75	-0.85	-8.17
Poland	9.86	9.98	10.08	10.16	10.23	10.28	10.31	10.31	10.30	10.26	10.20	0.33	3.36
Portugal	11.07	10.94	10.80	10.65	10.50	10.35	10.21	10.08	9.98	9.91	9.87	-1.14	-10.83
Romania	10.24	10.19	10.13	10.06	9.99	9.91	9.81	9.67	9.49	9.29	9.07	-1.21	-11.42
Russia	12.38	11.79	11.94	12.19	12.31	12.25	12.16	12.02	11.85	11.65	11.44	-0.79	-7.63
Saudi Arabia	23.07	22.73	22.43	22.14	21.85	21.55	21.24	20.92	20.59	20.25	19.91	-1.46	-13.67
Singapore	8.27	8.24	8.22	8.22	8.22	8.23	8.25	8.28	8.31	8.36	8.41	0.17	1.68
Slovakia	9.69	9.68	9.67	9.66	9.63	9.61	9.58	9.54	9.49	9.43	9.35	-0.36	-3.57
Slovenia	9.33	9.41	9.47	9.51	9.51	9.48	9.43	9.35	9.24	9.11	8.97	-0.39	-3.84
South Africa	21.66	21.40	21.16	20.95	20.74	20.52	20.29	20.04	19.80	19.56	19.33	-1.13	-10.77
South Korea	9.74	9.59	9.45	9.32	9.21	9.11	9.04	8.97	8.93	8.89	8.86	-0.94	-9.04
Spain	10.64	10.59	10.50	10.38	10.24	10.08	9.91	9.74	9.46	9.21	8.98	-1.68	-15.60
Sweden	11.69	11.71	11.67	11.66	11.67	11.69	11.74	11.78	11.83	11.87	11.90	0.18	1.77
Switzerland	9.54	9.54	9.57	9.62	9.70	9.78	9.88	9.99	10.10	10.21	10.31	0.78	8.04
Taiwan	8.79	8.72	8.56	8.41	8.30	8.15	8.01	7.91	7.77	7.63	7.46	-1.63	-15.13
Thailand	14.23	14.04	13.84	13.65	13.45	13.27	13.09	12.92	12.76	12.60	12.45	-1.33	-12.51
Tunisia	16.10	16.09	16.06	16.00	15.91	15.80	15.65	15.49	15.31	15.12	14.93	-0.75	-7.24
Turkey	18.11	17.90	17.67	17.43	17.18	16.93	16.68	16.45	16.23	16.02	15.82	-1.34	-12.64
Turkmenistan	21.71	21.46	21.21	20.93	20.63	20.29	19.93	19.53	19.10	18.65	18.18	-1.76	-16.24
Ukraine	10.31	10.32	10.28	10.21	10.12	10.01	9.89	9.75	9.60	9.43	9.26	-1.07	-10.20
United Arab Emirates	14.87	14.65	14.44	14.22	13.97	13.68	13.36	13.02	12.68	12.36	12.06	-2.07	-18.88
United Kingdom	13.05	12.66	12.68	12.71	12.75	12.80	12.84	12.88	12.90	12.91	12.89	-0.13	-1.28
USA	13.99	13.59	13.45	13.44	13.42	13.39	13.35	13.30	13.25	13.20	13.15	-0.62	-6.03
Venezuela	20.98	20.67	20.35	20.03	19.71	19.39	19.07	18.75	18.44	18.14	17.84	-1.61	-14.97
Vietnam	18.21	18.12	18.03	17.93	17.82	17.70	17.55	17.39	17.17	16.87	16.47	-1.00	-9.55

Vital statistics

Table 4.69 Deaths: 2009-2019

'000

	2009	2010	2011	2012	2013	2014	2015	2016	2017	2018	2019	CAGR	Period growth
Algeria	171.70	174.08	176.51	179.01	181.62	184.34	187.16	190.08	193.12	196.29	199.64	1.52	16.27
Argentina	308.23	310.83	313.44	316.05	318.67	321.31	323.96	326.66	329.39	332.18	335.05	0.84	8.70
Australia	147.89	153.44	156.33	159.41	162.57	165.80	169.08	172.36	175.69	179.10	182.60	2.13	23.47
Austria	76.06	76.46	76.96	77.52	78.10	78.71	79.25	79.65	79.97	80.24	80.50	0.57	5.84
Azerbaijan	54.31	55.49	56.42	57.34	58.28	59.22	60.16	61.11	62.05	63.01	63.98	1.65	17.81
Belarus	135.82	138.86	138.21	137.49	136.71	135.89	135.05	134.21	133.39	132.57	131.79	-0.30	-2.97
Belgium	105.20	105.87	106.39	106.76	107.12	107.45	107.75	107.99	108.22	108.43	108.64	0.32	3.27
Bolivia	73.40	73.71	74.03	74.36	74.70	75.07	75.45	75.85	76.29	76.75	77.25	0.51	5.25
Bosnia-Herzegovina	34.84	35.55	36.17	36.73	37.30	37.87	38.45	39.04	39.62	40.17	40.69	1.56	16.80
Brazil	1,238.55	1,255.51	1,272.83	1,290.32	1,307.88	1,325.59	1,343.65	1,362.33	1,381.97	1,402.82	1,425.00	1.41	15.05
Bulgaria	111.18	110.42	109.64	108.82	108.01	107.16	106.29	105.40	104.53	103.64	102.82	-0.78	-7.52
Canada	244.71	251.20	254.93	258.11	261.71	265.46	269.32	273.34	277.52	281.84	286.36	1.58	17.02
Chile	93.13	95.50	97.85	100.23	102.66	105.15	107.69	110.28	112.94	115.65	118.42	2.43	27.16
China	9,597.52	9,916.36	10,125.70	10,267.11	10,411.42	10,559.71	10,712.99	10,869.35	11,032.56	11,199.32	11,373.51	1.71	18.50
Colombia	251.31	255.08	259.09	263.38	267.95	272.81	277.95	283.37	289.03	294.91	300.98	1.82	19.77
Costa Rica	19.02	19.51	20.01	20.53	21.07	21.64	22.22	22.83	23.47	24.13	24.83	2.70	30.54
Croatia	52.74	53.19	53.58	53.92	54.21	54.46	54.65	54.81	54.91	54.98	55.03	0.43	4.34
Czech Republic	106.38	107.06	107.85	108.57	109.25	109.90	110.55	111.24	111.99	112.82	113.74	0.67	6.93
Denmark	54.14	53.56	53.11	52.77	52.54	52.42	52.38	52.43	52.56	52.76	53.04	-0.21	-2.04
Ecuador	70.93	72.27	73.65	75.08	76.57	78.13	79.74	81.40	83.10	84.84	86.61	2.02	22.11
Egypt	450.36	455.06	459.76	464.52	469.42	474.47	479.74	485.29	491.23	497.65	504.59	1.14	12.04
Estonia	17.58	17.55	17.51	17.46	17.38	17.30	17.19	17.08	16.95	16.82	16.68	-0.52	-5.09
Finland	49.71	50.38	51.05	51.69	52.31	52.91	53.49	54.04	54.58	55.09	55.60	1.13	11.84
France	549.68	562.21	569.27	576.33	583.20	589.70	595.78	601.40	606.57	611.27	615.49	1.14	11.97
Germany	864.56	875.29	882.22	889.29	896.23	902.96	909.42	915.55	921.35	926.94	932.19	0.76	7.82
Greece	95.58	95.61	95.73	95.97	96.26	96.63	97.11	97.70	98.39	99.17	100.05	0.46	4.67
Hong Kong, China	41.39	42.63	43.87	45.09	46.31	47.53	48.74	49.95	51.16	52.38	53.62	2.62	29.55
Hungary	131.34	130.71	130.16	129.68	129.24	128.85	128.45	128.04	127.62	127.19	126.79	-0.35	-3.47
India	10,012.27	10,053.99	10,096.46	10,142.09	10,193.00	10,250.50	10,315.45	10,388.03	10,467.43	10,553.00	10,644.68	0.61	6.32
Indonesia	1,445.01	1,457.84	1,472.04	1,487.30	1,503.42	1,520.29	1,537.87	1,556.20	1,575.52	1,596.06	1,617.99	1.14	11.97
Iran	420.65	421.96	423.06	424.12	425.34	426.87	428.85	431.32	434.33	437.94	442.29	0.50	5.14
Ireland	33.77	33.76	33.62	33.53	33.52	33.61	33.79	34.06	34.51	35.16	36.02	0.65	6.66
Israel	40.62	41.38	42.15	42.94	43.73	44.52	45.29	46.06	46.83	47.61	48.41	1.77	19.19
Italy	593.03	614.27	621.33	629.05	635.74	643.26	649.69	656.05	663.04	668.71	674.35	1.29	13.71
Japan	1,232.61	1,257.15	1,273.61	1,289.74	1,306.86	1,325.47	1,345.94	1,368.20	1,391.44	1,414.97	1,438.37	1.56	16.69
Jordan	25.89	26.20	26.49	26.77	27.07	27.40	27.77	28.19	28.66	29.17	29.74	1.40	14.89
Kazakhstan	154.84	158.08	159.63	160.26	160.37	160.42	160.46	160.56	160.71	160.88	161.11	0.40	4.05
Kuwait	5.74	6.03	6.34	6.68	7.04	7.42	7.83	8.27	8.74	9.23	9.76	5.45	70.07
Latvia	33.33	33.30	33.24	33.16	33.06	32.94	32.76	32.57	32.35	32.12	31.85	-0.45	-4.45
Lithuania	45.16	45.31	45.44	45.53	45.58	45.59	45.54	45.43	45.29	45.09	44.84	-0.07	-0.71
Malaysia	124.47	127.34	130.43	133.71	137.17	140.78	144.55	148.49	152.60	156.88	161.34	2.63	29.62
Mexico	560.24	578.90	591.88	603.60	614.73	626.24	638.31	650.95	664.18	678.02	692.53	2.14	23.61
Morocco	186.14	188.26	190.43	192.65	194.94	197.28	199.69	202.18	204.77	207.51	210.43	1.23	13.05
Netherlands	141.09	142.99	144.88	146.71	148.57	150.48	152.44	154.49	156.39	158.40	160.52	1.30	13.78
New Zealand	28.92	29.22	29.52	29.82	30.22	30.62	31.02	31.42	31.82	32.22	32.72	1.24	13.15
Nigeria	2,504.81	2,526.70	2,544.02	2,557.04	2,566.16	2,571.70	2,574.18	2,574.29	2,572.89	2,570.84	2,568.71	0.25	2.55
Norway	41.12	41.05	40.96	40.87	40.78	40.70	40.62	40.58	40.56	40.57	40.64	-0.12	-1.16
Pakistan	1,233.86	1,240.59	1,247.28	1,253.99	1,260.80	1,267.80	1,275.12	1,282.88	1,291.24	1,300.33	1,310.25	0.60	6.19
Peru	157.44	159.59	161.89	164.33	166.90	169.57	172.35	175.22	178.20	181.31	184.54	1.60	17.21
Philippines	439.22	445.34	451.81	458.67	465.95	473.68	481.88	490.59	499.83	509.61	519.93	1.70	18.38
Poland	381.23	383.21	385.19	387.17	389.05	390.82	392.38	393.65	394.67	395.52	396.31	0.39	3.96
Portugal	115.19	114.59	113.75	112.80	111.73	110.62	109.51	108.46	107.64	107.00	106.63	-0.77	-7.43
Romania	270.24	270.97	270.88	270.16	268.96	267.85	266.30	264.58	262.64	260.89	258.99	-0.42	-4.16
Russia	2,097.26	2,131.90	2,124.18	2,119.47	2,115.26	2,110.08	2,103.48	2,094.97	2,085.26	2,075.02	2,064.63	-0.16	-1.56
Saudi Arabia	93.23	94.97	96.86	98.90	101.09	103.42	105.92	108.58	111.42	114.44	117.67	2.36	26.21
Singapore	17.82	18.27	18.75	19.25	19.77	20.33	20.93	21.60	22.33	23.14	24.02	3.03	34.80
Slovakia	53.43	53.63	53.83	54.01	54.19	54.34	54.46	54.56	54.65	54.73	54.83	0.26	2.61
Slovenia	19.06	19.28	19.51	19.72	19.94	20.14	20.32	20.48	20.61	20.73	20.84	0.90	9.33
South Africa	761.64	768.07	771.54	772.79	772.62	771.73	770.82	770.38	770.51	771.20	772.56	0.14	1.43
South Korea	258.45	266.11	274.38	283.26	292.68	302.56	312.79	323.27	333.90	344.58	355.23	3.23	37.45
Spain	395.61	400.50	405.34	410.14	414.90	419.58	424.16	428.70	433.10	440.35	447.37	1.24	13.08
Sweden	90.84	90.71	90.58	90.45	90.34	90.24	90.17	90.21	90.38	90.68	91.13	0.03	0.32
Switzerland	62.86	63.56	64.33	65.13	65.96	66.78	67.60	68.41	69.23	70.06	70.91	1.21	12.80
Taiwan	146.01	148.95	150.91	153.85	156.79	158.75	161.69	164.63	167.57	170.51	173.45	1.74	18.79
Thailand	554.62	562.15	570.75	579.86	589.05	598.17	607.16	616.05	625.02	634.20	643.62	1.50	16.05
Tunisia	61.01	61.83	62.66	63.49	64.34	65.20	66.08	66.97	67.89	68.84	69.84	1.36	14.47
Turkey	482.00	492.54	502.72	512.63	522.39	532.00	541.50	550.93	560.42	570.12	580.17	1.87	20.37
Turkmenistan	39.00	39.24	39.41	39.56	39.70	39.85	40.02	40.22	40.45	40.70	40.99	0.50	5.10
Ukraine	757.47	753.67	749.05	743.68	737.66	731.08	724.07	716.73	709.19	701.62	694.15	-0.87	-8.36
United Arab Emirates	7.14	7.34	7.56	7.78	8.03	8.31	8.62	8.96	9.33	9.74	10.20	3.64	42.92
United Kingdom	578.56	593.14	594.46	595.87	597.42	598.99	600.52	602.06	603.69	605.46	607.44	0.49	4.99
USA	2,524.18	2,591.13	2,616.11	2,633.91	2,652.28	2,671.15	2,690.75	2,711.31	2,732.97	2,755.89	2,780.29	0.97	10.15
Venezuela	146.78	149.82	152.97	156.21	159.52	162.91	166.40	169.99	173.70	177.55	181.53	2.15	23.68
Vietnam	438.28	447.54	457.09	467.13	477.79	488.90	500.28	511.67	522.18	530.36	535.52	2.02	22.19

Vital statistics

Table 4.70 **Death rates: 2009-2019**

per '000 inhabitants

	2009	2010	2011	2012	2013	2014	2015	2016	2017	2018	2019	CAGR	Period growth
Algeria	4.92	4.91	4.91	4.91	4.91	4.91	4.91	4.92	4.94	4.95	4.97	0.11	1.08
Argentina	7.64	7.63	7.62	7.61	7.60	7.60	7.59	7.59	7.59	7.59	7.59	-0.07	-0.66
Australia	6.79	6.94	6.99	7.03	7.07	7.11	7.15	7.19	7.24	7.28	7.32	0.77	7.94
Austria	9.07	9.09	9.13	9.16	9.21	9.25	9.29	9.31	9.33	9.34	9.34	0.30	2.99
Azerbaijan	6.22	6.29	6.32	6.36	6.40	6.43	6.47	6.52	6.56	6.60	6.65	0.67	6.92
Belarus	14.04	14.39	14.36	14.32	14.28	14.24	14.19	14.15	14.11	14.06	14.03	-0.01	-0.10
Belgium	9.87	9.90	9.91	9.91	9.91	9.91	9.90	9.90	9.89	9.88	9.87	0.00	-0.03
Bolivia	7.44	7.35	7.26	7.17	7.10	7.02	6.95	6.89	6.83	6.77	6.73	-1.01	-9.61
Bosnia-Herzegovina	9.06	9.25	9.41	9.56	9.71	9.86	10.02	10.18	10.35	10.51	10.66	1.64	17.66
Brazil	6.39	6.42	6.46	6.50	6.54	6.58	6.62	6.67	6.73	6.79	6.85	0.70	7.20
Bulgaria	14.79	14.79	14.79	14.78	14.78	14.78	14.78	14.78	14.78	14.79	14.80	0.01	0.09
Canada	7.27	7.40	7.45	7.48	7.53	7.58	7.63	7.69	7.75	7.81	7.88	0.81	8.39
Chile	5.49	5.57	5.66	5.74	5.83	5.92	6.01	6.10	6.20	6.30	6.40	1.55	16.63
China	7.23	7.43	7.56	7.63	7.70	7.78	7.87	7.95	8.04	8.14	8.24	1.32	14.06
Colombia	5.50	5.51	5.52	5.54	5.56	5.59	5.63	5.67	5.72	5.77	5.82	0.56	5.74
Costa Rica	4.15	4.20	4.26	4.31	4.36	4.42	4.48	4.55	4.62	4.70	4.78	1.42	15.10
Croatia	11.91	12.03	12.14	12.24	12.34	12.42	12.50	12.56	12.62	12.67	12.72	0.66	6.77
Czech Republic	10.29	10.34	10.41	10.47	10.54	10.60	10.67	10.74	10.81	10.89	10.98	0.65	6.74
Denmark	9.82	9.69	9.58	9.50	9.43	9.38	9.35	9.33	9.33	9.34	9.36	-0.48	-4.71
Ecuador	5.21	5.25	5.29	5.33	5.37	5.41	5.46	5.52	5.57	5.63	5.69	0.89	9.28
Egypt	5.87	5.82	5.78	5.74	5.70	5.67	5.64	5.61	5.59	5.58	5.58	-0.50	-4.93
Estonia	13.21	13.24	13.25	13.26	13.25	13.24	13.20	13.16	13.11	13.04	12.98	-0.18	-1.76
Finland	9.33	9.42	9.51	9.59	9.67	9.75	9.83	9.90	9.96	10.03	10.10	0.79	8.16
France	8.80	8.96	9.03	9.10	9.17	9.23	9.29	9.34	9.38	9.42	9.45	0.71	7.34
Germany	10.54	10.71	10.84	10.96	11.08	11.20	11.31	11.43	11.54	11.65	11.76	1.10	11.51
Greece	8.49	8.47	8.45	8.45	8.45	8.47	8.49	8.53	8.58	8.63	8.70	0.24	2.46
Hong Kong, China	5.86	5.98	6.10	6.21	6.33	6.44	6.55	6.66	6.77	6.88	6.99	1.78	19.27
Hungary	13.11	13.07	13.04	13.03	13.02	13.02	13.01	13.01	13.00	12.99	12.98	-0.10	-0.99
India	8.57	8.49	8.41	8.34	8.27	8.22	8.17	8.13	8.10	8.08	8.06	-0.60	-5.88
Indonesia	6.28	6.27	6.26	6.26	6.27	6.28	6.30	6.32	6.34	6.38	6.41	0.20	2.06
Iran	5.67	5.62	5.57	5.52	5.47	5.43	5.40	5.37	5.35	5.33	5.33	-0.61	-5.94
Ireland	7.59	7.49	7.37	7.27	7.19	7.13	7.09	7.07	7.10	7.16	7.27	-0.43	-4.22
Israel	5.49	5.50	5.52	5.55	5.57	5.59	5.62	5.64	5.66	5.69	5.72	0.41	4.19
Italy	10.04	10.39	10.50	10.63	10.74	10.86	10.97	11.08	11.21	11.31	11.42	1.29	13.70
Japan	9.66	9.87	10.02	10.17	10.33	10.50	10.70	10.91	11.13	11.36	11.60	1.85	20.07
Jordan	4.10	4.05	4.01	4.00	3.99	3.99	3.99	3.99	4.00	4.00	4.02	-0.20	-1.96
Kazakhstan	9.81	9.89	9.86	9.78	9.67	9.56	9.45	9.35	9.26	9.18	9.10	-0.75	-7.26
Kuwait	2.35	2.41	2.48	2.56	2.65	2.73	2.83	2.93	3.04	3.16	3.28	3.41	39.89
Latvia	14.79	14.86	14.92	14.98	15.03	15.07	15.09	15.09	15.08	15.06	15.01	0.15	1.50
Lithuania	13.49	13.61	13.72	13.83	13.93	14.02	14.08	14.13	14.16	14.17	14.17	0.49	5.03
Malaysia	4.43	4.46	4.50	4.54	4.59	4.65	4.70	4.77	4.84	4.91	4.99	1.19	12.56
Mexico	5.16	5.25	5.29	5.33	5.36	5.39	5.43	5.48	5.52	5.58	5.64	0.90	9.32
Morocco	5.82	5.81	5.81	5.81	5.81	5.81	5.82	5.82	5.83	5.85	5.87	0.09	0.92
Netherlands	8.60	8.70	8.80	8.89	8.99	9.09	9.19	9.30	9.39	9.50	9.61	1.12	11.80
New Zealand	6.71	6.71	6.72	6.73	6.76	6.79	6.82	6.85	6.88	6.91	6.96	0.37	3.78
Nigeria	16.19	15.97	15.72	15.47	15.20	14.92	14.63	14.35	14.07	13.79	13.53	-1.78	-16.41
Norway	8.57	8.45	8.34	8.23	8.14	8.04	7.95	7.87	7.79	7.72	7.66	-1.11	-10.55
Pakistan	6.82	6.71	6.61	6.50	6.40	6.30	6.20	6.12	6.04	5.97	5.90	-1.45	-13.55
Peru	5.43	5.43	5.43	5.44	5.46	5.48	5.50	5.53	5.56	5.59	5.63	0.36	3.66
Philippines	4.77	4.74	4.72	4.70	4.69	4.69	4.68	4.68	4.69	4.70	4.71	-0.11	-1.12
Poland	10.03	10.10	10.17	10.24	10.31	10.37	10.43	10.48	10.52	10.55	10.59	0.54	5.52
Portugal	10.80	10.71	10.61	10.51	10.39	10.27	10.16	10.05	9.97	9.91	9.87	-0.89	-8.54
Romania	12.61	12.68	12.72	12.72	12.72	12.72	12.71	12.69	12.67	12.65	12.63	0.02	0.18
Russia	14.78	15.04	15.02	15.01	15.01	14.99	14.97	14.93	14.89	14.85	14.80	0.02	0.16
Saudi Arabia	3.62	3.62	3.62	3.62	3.63	3.64	3.66	3.68	3.71	3.75	3.79	0.44	4.45
Singapore	3.79	3.83	3.88	3.93	3.99	4.06	4.14	4.23	4.34	4.45	4.59	1.94	21.18
Slovakia	9.90	9.94	9.97	10.00	10.04	10.07	10.09	10.11	10.13	10.15	10.17	0.26	2.66
Slovenia	9.42	9.50	9.59	9.67	9.76	9.85	9.92	9.99	10.04	10.08	10.13	0.72	7.49
South Africa	15.20	15.21	15.18	15.13	15.06	14.99	14.91	14.85	14.80	14.75	14.72	-0.32	-3.12
South Korea	5.30	5.44	5.60	5.77	5.95	6.15	6.35	6.56	6.77	6.98	7.20	3.11	35.80
Spain	8.69	8.72	8.75	8.79	8.82	8.85	8.89	8.92	8.95	9.04	9.13	0.49	5.05
Sweden	9.87	9.81	9.75	9.69	9.64	9.58	9.53	9.48	9.45	9.44	9.44	-0.45	-4.41
Switzerland	8.32	8.38	8.44	8.52	8.59	8.67	8.74	8.82	8.89	8.96	9.03	0.83	8.64
Taiwan	6.34	6.45	6.51	6.62	6.73	6.80	6.92	7.03	7.15	7.27	7.39	1.54	16.55
Thailand	8.57	8.63	8.71	8.81	8.90	9.00	9.09	9.19	9.29	9.39	9.50	1.03	10.83
Tunisia	5.94	5.96	5.98	6.00	6.02	6.05	6.07	6.10	6.13	6.16	6.20	0.42	4.30
Turkey	6.40	6.47	6.53	6.58	6.63	6.68	6.73	6.78	6.83	6.89	6.94	0.81	8.41
Turkmenistan	7.63	7.58	7.52	7.45	7.38	7.32	7.26	7.22	7.18	7.14	7.12	-0.70	-6.74
Ukraine	16.50	16.51	16.51	16.50	16.48	16.44	16.39	16.33	16.27	16.20	16.14	-0.22	-2.13
United Arab Emirates	1.55	1.55	1.56	1.58	1.60	1.62	1.65	1.69	1.73	1.77	1.82	1.67	18.04
United Kingdom	9.39	9.57	9.55	9.52	9.49	9.46	9.42	9.39	9.36	9.33	9.30	-0.10	-0.97
USA	8.23	8.39	8.41	8.42	8.42	8.42	8.42	8.43	8.44	8.46	8.47	0.29	2.94
Venezuela	5.14	5.16	5.19	5.21	5.25	5.28	5.32	5.36	5.40	5.45	5.50	0.69	7.12
Vietnam	5.00	5.04	5.09	5.13	5.19	5.24	5.30	5.36	5.41	5.43	5.42	0.81	8.44

Vital statistics

Table 4.71 Net migration: 2009-2019

'000

	2009	2010	2011	2012	2013	2014	2015	2016	2017	2018	2019
Algeria	-27.09	-27.46	-26.98	-26.43	-26.65	-27.56	-28.41	-28.45	-27.70	-26.46	-24.81
Argentina	11.79	9.04	7.15	6.23	5.71	5.70	5.90	6.02	6.04	6.05	6.04
Australia	153.63	136.64	152.90	165.88	177.88	182.94	182.91	182.86	182.82	182.77	182.72
Austria	24.93	24.75	24.98	25.08	24.56	24.26	23.81	23.22	22.84	22.46	22.04
Azerbaijan	0.64	-0.20	-0.12	-0.12	-0.13	-0.13	-0.13	-0.13	-0.13	-0.13	-0.13
Belarus	7.60	6.58	6.13	5.74	5.54	5.39	5.43	5.50	5.55	5.57	5.53
Belgium	19.87	19.60	19.50	19.48	19.39	19.37	19.33	19.23	19.17	19.09	19.02
Bolivia	-20.30	-20.07	-19.95	-19.93	-19.93	-19.95	-19.98	-19.98	-19.96	-19.97	-19.98
Bosnia-Herzegovina	0.01	0.27	0.69	1.07	1.24	1.14	0.77	0.58	0.54	0.52	0.52
Brazil	-61.85	-48.63	-46.28	-49.02	-48.34	-43.93	-36.94	-29.58	-24.93	-25.27	-30.30
Bulgaria	-11.75	-11.66	-11.57	-15.28	-15.15	-17.25	-17.83	-17.66	-17.12	-16.72	-16.18
Canada	193.85	163.24	153.43	153.37	153.22	152.99	152.82	152.79	152.80	152.76	152.67
Chile	6.39	6.22	6.36	6.59	6.59	6.36	6.02	5.70	5.50	5.50	5.69
Colombia	-21.91	-23.70	-25.07	-25.76	-25.74	-25.04	-24.17	-23.60	-23.38	-23.38	-23.61
Costa Rica	3.65	4.99	6.36	7.27	7.48	6.96	6.19	5.69	5.49	5.50	5.70
Croatia	2.24	1.67	1.27	0.99	0.79	0.65	0.56	0.49	0.44	0.41	0.38
Czech Republic	21.20	19.50	14.20	12.20	12.20	13.30	14.80	17.20	19.10	20.00	20.00
Denmark	4.96	6.03	6.36	6.40	6.36	6.26	6.17	6.10	6.03	5.97	5.91
Ecuador	-61.26	-51.49	-41.84	-34.06	-29.46	-28.15	-28.66	-29.32	-29.75	-30.00	-29.93
Egypt	-7.68	-8.91	-9.37	-9.59	-10.57	-12.29	-14.18	-15.60	-16.49	-17.01	-17.32
Estonia	-2.05	-2.04	-2.68	-2.88	-2.86	-2.62	-2.47	-2.25	-1.94	-1.53	-1.02
Finland	12.72	11.70	10.65	10.61	10.51	9.95	9.47	8.96	8.96	8.34	8.06
France	69.69	59.30	69.52	72.53	73.24	74.58	75.92	76.75	77.13	77.24	77.11
Germany	-81.86	-48.94	4.30	27.78	45.85	48.10	48.62	48.80	49.31	49.07	49.49
Greece	1.55	-0.60	-2.44	-4.07	-5.47	-6.69	-7.74	-8.66	-9.48	-10.22	-10.87
Hong Kong, China	33.72	32.47	31.65	31.16	30.95	30.96	31.08	31.22	31.35	31.47	31.57
Hungary	13.30	13.27	7.72	5.86	5.84	6.59	7.04	7.72	8.72	10.08	11.80
India	-652.03	-617.32	-594.70	-586.68	-591.30	-606.42	-619.42	-619.79	-612.59	-605.44	-598.89
Indonesia	-143.23	-152.75	-160.81	-165.53	-167.12	-165.97	-166.08	-170.14	-173.73	-171.82	-164.62
Iran	-86.82	-91.43	-95.23	-94.24	-86.77	-72.52	-52.21	-28.75	-9.52	-1.06	-3.95
Ireland	16.18	15.97	15.76	15.47	15.11	14.69	14.24	13.77	13.27	12.75	12.21
Israel	14.07	13.60	13.13	12.66	12.18	11.71	11.24	10.77	10.30	9.82	9.35
Italy	364.51	314.32	280.29	257.87	245.58	238.15	234.51	232.45	231.09	230.42	230.67
Japan	-67.18	-32.10	-3.27	-0.07	3.17	6.12	8.69	10.96	12.97	14.54	16.28
Jordan	36.09	8.23	-19.37	-39.60	-47.62	-43.04	-31.61	-20.08	-11.01	-5.08	-2.80
Kazakhstan	-1.40	-3.36	-2.09	-2.25	-2.29	-2.23	-2.13	-2.06	-2.05	-2.05	-2.09
Kuwait	7.51	7.54	7.87	8.17	8.34	8.30	8.23	8.34	8.55	8.74	8.88
Latvia	-2.66	-2.64	-4.24	-4.75	-4.72	-4.31	-4.06	-3.70	-3.18	-2.49	-1.63
Lithuania	-4.95	-4.92	-5.86	-6.15	-6.12	-5.61	-5.29	-4.83	-4.17	-3.29	-2.20
Malaysia	93.41	90.49	87.90	85.96	84.70	84.11	84.09	84.38	84.55	84.21	83.32
Mexico	-514.15	-443.98	-495.23	-547.37	-577.32	-584.27	-580.78	-580.51	-578.19	-569.87	-555.33
Morocco	-77.42	-77.76	-76.88	-75.13	-73.44	-71.73	-69.83	-67.63	-65.34	-63.20	-61.29
Netherlands	-8.66	-4.23	-0.88	1.33	2.70	3.56	4.29	4.82	5.23	5.65	6.08
New Zealand	6.77	7.48	7.54	7.38	7.40	7.65	7.69	7.73	7.76	7.48	7.55
Nigeria	-52.47	-59.35	-61.63	-60.90	-60.06	-59.67	-59.71	-59.76	-59.57	-59.29	-59.35
Norway	16.05	16.00	16.01	15.99	16.00	16.00	16.01	16.00	16.01	15.99	16.01
Pakistan	-269.24	-231.85	-188.06	-152.67	-138.68	-146.56	-163.10	-174.16	-177.97	-177.01	-171.52
Peru	-54.38	-49.80	-44.78	-40.11	-36.29	-33.49	-31.33	-29.32	-27.16	-24.74	-22.06
Philippines	-57.66	-68.18	-84.33	-103.96	-111.76	-110.97	-110.64	-110.51	-110.60	-110.85	-111.40
Poland	-53.96	-54.00	-54.30	-59.16	-59.03	-54.32	-51.46	-47.19	-41.04	-34.69	-27.26
Portugal	16.58	13.22	10.25	7.67	5.48	3.65	2.20	1.11	0.37	-0.03	-0.08
Romania	-14.64	-14.59	-14.54	-31.10	-30.97	-43.92	-48.03	-47.78	-46.48	-45.57	-44.28
Russia	221.75	141.63	141.67	160.29	170.33	168.90	162.82	160.21	160.98	161.91	162.02
Saudi Arabia	22.70	26.79	30.03	31.72	32.22	31.48	30.52	30.29	30.45	30.44	30.28
Singapore	44.14	41.08	38.17	35.40	32.77	30.27	27.93	25.73	23.68	21.79	20.04
Slovakia	2.52	2.53	2.12	1.98	1.99	2.00	2.00	2.00	2.00	2.00	2.00
Slovenia	6.27	6.28	4.13	3.54	3.54	3.71	3.81	3.96	4.18	4.49	4.87
South Africa	88.67	38.71	-13.41	-56.71	-82.32	-88.88	-83.89	-75.81	-66.03	-53.60	-39.66
South Korea	-82.52	-81.77	-84.37	-87.37	-88.02	-89.01	-90.30	-91.62	-92.24	-91.32	-89.25
Spain	318.86	290.98	287.49	286.97	286.44	285.92	285.40	284.87	284.35	283.83	283.30
Sweden	26.12	26.00	25.85	25.82	25.81	25.77	25.90	25.62	25.38	25.19	25.06
Switzerland	20.00	20.00	20.00	20.00	20.00	20.00	20.00	20.00	20.00	20.00	20.00
Taiwan	14.75	13.90	13.22	12.50	11.58	10.41	9.27	8.42	7.74	6.95	5.88
Thailand	37.68	28.06	20.87	16.78	15.28	16.27	18.22	19.61	20.32	20.62	20.46
Tunisia	-1.96	-2.66	-3.08	-3.28	-3.53	-3.77	-4.03	-4.33	-4.54	-4.54	-4.33
Turkey	13.29	12.17	11.80	11.22	10.30	9.04	7.20	4.78	2.77	1.34	0.48
Turkmenistan	-5.48	-5.07	-4.77	-4.64	-4.65	-4.79	-4.88	-4.78	-4.64	-4.64	-4.77
Ukraine	5.67	-1.91	-6.74	-8.64	-8.54	-8.15	-7.75	-7.56	-7.53	-7.70	-7.99
United Arab Emirates	50.10	44.90	39.81	35.51	33.01	32.22	32.72	33.88	35.05	35.69	35.68
United Kingdom	127.71	103.68	126.57	156.24	182.41	180.55	178.74	176.97	175.24	173.56	171.90
USA	495.45	449.34	514.73	565.32	571.85	578.30	584.70	591.05	597.33	603.57	609.76
Venezuela	8.57	8.20	8.11	8.17	8.18	8.13	8.04	7.96	7.93	7.94	7.98
Vietnam	-42.71	-40.06	-37.49	-35.90	-35.89	-37.48	-39.85	-41.99	-43.24	-43.21	-41.95

Density and urbanisation

Table 4.72 Population density: 2009-2019

persons per sq km

	2009	2010	2011	2012	2013	2014	2015	2016	2017	2018	2019	CAGR	Period growth
Algeria	14.65	14.87	15.10	15.32	15.55	15.77	15.99	16.21	16.43	16.64	16.85	1.41	15.03
Argentina	14.74	14.89	15.03	15.17	15.32	15.46	15.59	15.73	15.87	16.00	16.13	0.90	9.42
Australia	2.84	2.88	2.91	2.95	2.99	3.03	3.08	3.12	3.16	3.20	3.25	1.35	14.38
Austria	101.67	101.99	102.29	102.59	102.89	103.18	103.46	103.73	103.99	104.24	104.48	0.27	2.76
Azerbaijan	105.62	106.80	107.95	109.09	110.22	111.33	112.42	113.47	114.48	115.45	116.37	0.97	10.18
Belarus	46.62	46.52	46.40	46.27	46.13	46.00	45.86	45.72	45.58	45.43	45.28	-0.29	-2.87
Belgium	352.65	353.90	355.14	356.35	357.55	358.72	359.87	361.00	362.11	363.20	364.28	0.33	3.30
Bolivia	9.10	9.25	9.40	9.56	9.71	9.86	10.01	10.16	10.30	10.45	10.59	1.53	16.45
Bosnia-Herzegovina	75.09	75.09	75.07	75.05	75.03	74.99	74.94	74.87	74.78	74.66	74.53	-0.07	-0.74
Brazil	22.90	23.10	23.29	23.48	23.65	23.82	23.98	24.14	24.29	24.44	24.58	0.71	7.32
Bulgaria	69.64	69.16	68.67	68.19	67.67	67.14	66.60	66.04	65.48	64.91	64.34	-0.79	-7.60
Canada	3.70	3.74	3.77	3.79	3.82	3.85	3.88	3.91	3.94	3.97	4.00	0.77	7.96
Chile	22.66	22.88	23.10	23.31	23.53	23.73	23.94	24.14	24.33	24.52	24.71	0.87	9.03
China	142.38	143.06	143.68	144.28	144.87	145.44	146.00	146.53	147.04	147.50	147.92	0.38	3.90
Colombia	41.15	41.73	42.30	42.86	43.42	43.97	44.51	45.05	45.58	46.10	46.61	1.25	13.27
Costa Rica	89.68	90.87	92.10	93.34	94.61	95.85	97.08	98.27	99.43	100.58	101.70	1.27	13.41
Croatia	79.19	79.06	78.91	78.75	78.58	78.40	78.21	78.02	77.81	77.60	77.39	-0.23	-2.28
Czech Republic	133.81	134.01	134.16	134.20	134.19	134.15	134.11	134.08	134.06	134.05	134.05	0.02	0.17
Denmark	129.90	130.24	130.60	130.96	131.32	131.68	132.03	132.39	132.75	133.12	133.49	0.27	2.77
Ecuador	49.22	49.76	50.33	50.92	51.52	52.13	52.72	53.31	53.88	54.45	55.00	1.12	11.75
Egypt	77.11	78.52	79.92	81.33	82.73	84.12	85.50	86.87	88.22	89.56	90.88	1.66	17.86
Estonia	31.39	31.28	31.18	31.06	30.95	30.83	30.72	30.61	30.51	30.42	30.33	-0.34	-3.39
Finland	17.48	17.56	17.63	17.69	17.75	17.81	17.87	17.93	17.98	18.03	18.08	0.34	3.41
France	113.52	114.11	114.63	115.14	115.65	116.14	116.62	117.09	117.55	117.99	118.43	0.42	4.32
Germany	235.12	234.31	233.45	232.67	231.91	231.19	230.45	229.69	228.92	228.14	227.34	-0.34	-3.31
Greece	87.29	87.59	87.86	88.11	88.34	88.55	88.73	88.88	89.01	89.10	89.18	0.21	2.16
Hong Kong, China	7,135.48	7,202.96	7,268.79	7,333.11	7,396.04	7,457.76	7,518.43	7,578.06	7,636.62	7,694.09	7,750.44	0.83	8.62
Hungary	111.82	111.59	111.37	111.08	110.77	110.46	110.15	109.86	109.57	109.29	109.03	-0.25	-2.50
India	393.11	398.51	403.87	409.17	414.42	419.59	424.67	429.66	434.57	439.36	444.06	1.23	12.96
Indonesia	126.94	128.35	129.72	131.05	132.34	133.59	134.80	135.97	137.10	138.20	139.27	0.93	9.72
Iran	45.35	45.89	46.42	46.95	47.49	48.02	48.56	49.10	49.64	50.18	50.69	1.12	11.79
Ireland	64.56	65.42	66.19	66.96	67.72	68.46	69.19	69.89	70.58	71.25	71.90	1.08	11.36
Israel	342.12	347.40	352.61	357.74	362.78	367.74	372.62	377.42	382.14	386.80	391.39	1.35	14.40
Italy	200.78	201.00	201.16	201.28	201.35	201.37	201.34	201.27	201.15	200.99	200.80	0.00	0.01
Japan	350.05	349.42	348.73	348.01	347.19	346.27	345.26	344.14	342.93	341.63	340.22	-0.28	-2.81
Jordan	71.58	73.35	74.78	75.92	76.88	77.81	78.84	80.00	81.24	82.55	83.89	1.60	17.19
Kazakhstan	5.84	5.92	5.99	6.07	6.14	6.22	6.29	6.36	6.43	6.49	6.56	1.16	12.19
Kuwait	137.20	140.22	143.26	146.29	149.31	152.31	155.27	158.19	161.08	163.95	166.80	1.97	21.57
Latvia	36.18	35.97	35.76	35.54	35.31	35.08	34.87	34.65	34.45	34.25	34.06	-0.60	-5.87
Lithuania	53.41	53.12	52.83	52.52	52.21	51.90	51.60	51.31	51.03	50.75	50.49	-0.56	-5.46
Malaysia	85.52	86.90	88.26	89.60	90.93	92.23	93.52	94.80	96.05	97.28	98.49	1.42	15.16
Mexico	55.86	56.69	57.51	58.29	59.04	59.76	60.47	61.16	61.84	62.51	63.16	1.24	13.07
Morocco	71.68	72.55	73.43	74.30	75.18	76.05	76.92	77.78	78.64	79.48	80.30	1.14	12.02
Netherlands	484.36	485.23	486.13	487.04	487.94	488.83	489.68	490.52	491.34	492.13	492.91	0.18	1.77
New Zealand	16.08	16.24	16.39	16.55	16.69	16.84	16.98	17.12	17.26	17.40	17.54	0.87	9.03
Nigeria	169.89	173.76	177.65	181.54	185.42	189.30	193.16	197.01	200.84	204.65	208.43	2.07	22.69
Norway	15.77	15.97	16.15	16.31	16.47	16.63	16.79	16.95	17.10	17.27	17.43	1.00	10.49
Pakistan	234.55	239.67	244.91	250.26	255.69	261.14	266.58	272.00	277.39	282.76	288.10	2.08	22.83
Peru	22.66	22.97	23.28	23.58	23.88	24.18	24.48	24.77	25.06	25.34	25.63	1.24	13.06
Philippines	309.01	315.00	320.99	326.98	332.96	339.00	345.09	351.23	357.42	363.66	369.94	1.82	19.72
Poland	123.76	123.56	123.37	123.18	122.98	122.78	122.59	122.41	122.23	122.07	121.92	-0.15	-1.48
Portugal	116.61	116.88	117.12	117.33	117.51	117.67	117.80	117.90	117.97	118.01	118.03	0.12	1.21
Romania	93.16	92.88	92.58	92.28	91.90	91.51	91.06	90.59	90.11	89.62	89.12	-0.44	-4.33
Russia	8.66	8.66	8.64	8.62	8.60	8.59	8.58	8.56	8.55	8.53	8.51	-0.17	-1.71
Saudi Arabia	11.96	12.21	12.46	12.71	12.96	13.21	13.46	13.71	13.96	14.21	14.46	1.91	20.83
Singapore	6,831.73	6,926.42	7,016.60	7,102.50	7,184.30	7,262.20	7,336.40	7,407.07	7,474.36	7,538.45	7,599.49	1.07	11.24
Slovakia	112.17	112.20	112.22	112.23	112.23	112.23	112.22	112.20	112.18	112.15	112.11	0.00	-0.05
Slovenia	100.44	100.74	101.04	101.23	101.39	101.54	101.69	101.83	101.96	102.09	102.21	0.18	1.77
South Africa	41.26	41.58	41.84	42.05	42.23	42.40	42.56	42.72	42.88	43.04	43.20	0.46	4.70
South Korea	493.74	495.03	496.19	497.15	497.95	498.61	499.11	499.46	499.67	499.75	499.73	0.12	1.21
Spain	91.14	91.96	92.71	93.45	94.18	94.88	95.57	96.24	96.89	97.51	98.09	0.74	7.63
Sweden	22.42	22.53	22.64	22.74	22.85	22.96	23.07	23.18	23.30	23.42	23.54	0.48	4.95
Switzerland	189.00	189.73	190.45	191.17	191.88	192.59	193.30	194.02	194.75	195.49	196.23	0.38	3.83
Thailand	126.70	127.47	128.19	128.87	129.51	130.11	130.68	131.22	131.74	132.22	132.67	0.46	4.71
Tunisia	66.11	66.77	67.43	68.09	68.75	69.41	70.06	70.70	71.33	71.95	72.56	0.93	9.75
Turkey	97.79	98.95	100.10	101.23	102.34	103.44	104.51	105.56	106.58	107.59	108.57	1.05	11.03
Turkmenistan	10.87	11.02	11.16	11.30	11.44	11.58	11.72	11.86	11.99	12.13	12.25	1.20	12.69
Ukraine	79.25	78.77	78.28	77.78	77.28	76.77	76.26	75.76	75.24	74.73	74.21	-0.66	-6.36
United Arab Emirates	55.22	56.52	57.77	58.96	60.11	61.24	62.36	63.48	64.61	65.74	66.86	1.93	21.08
United Kingdom	254.67	256.13	257.35	258.68	260.15	261.75	263.37	265.01	266.67	268.33	270.01	0.59	6.02
USA	33.46	33.71	33.94	34.16	34.40	34.63	34.87	35.10	35.34	35.57	35.81	0.68	7.00
Venezuela	32.41	32.93	33.45	33.96	34.47	34.98	35.48	35.97	36.46	36.94	37.41	1.45	15.45
Vietnam	283.00	286.61	290.24	293.88	297.53	301.17	304.79	308.38	311.94	315.44	318.87	1.20	12.68

Density and urbanisation

Table 4.73 Urban population: 2009-2019

'000

	2009	2010	2011	2012	2013	2014	2015	2016	2017	2018	2019	CAGR	Period growth
Algeria	21,472	21,949	22,462	22,947	23,451	23,949	24,457	24,983	25,466	25,995	26,501	2.13	23.42
Argentina	36,291	36,701	37,098	37,501	37,896	38,304	38,695	39,093	39,498	39,886	40,282	1.05	11.00
Australia	20,430	20,764	21,074	21,398	21,730	22,073	22,418	22,758	23,093	23,426	23,758	1.52	16.29
Austria	5,647	5,669	5,691	5,718	5,739	5,763	5,782	5,807	5,824	5,843	5,863	0.38	3.84
Azerbaijan	4,427	4,491	4,543	4,607	4,671	4,730	4,801	4,866	4,932	4,997	5,072	1.37	14.57
Belarus	7,125	7,135	7,147	7,150	7,155	7,157	7,161	7,159	7,158	7,154	7,147	0.03	0.31
Belgium	10,381	10,420	10,459	10,497	10,534	10,571	10,608	10,645	10,682	10,718	10,754	0.35	3.59
Bolivia	6,418	6,564	6,716	6,862	7,014	7,165	7,322	7,476	7,634	7,793	7,951	2.17	23.89
Bosnia-Herzegovina	1,846	1,869	1,893	1,916	1,940	1,965	1,989	2,013	2,036	2,058	2,080	1.20	12.67
Brazil	165,417	167,973	170,391	172,729	174,963	177,065	179,077	180,953	182,717	184,388	185,998	1.18	12.44
Bulgaria	5,422	5,409	5,397	5,377	5,361	5,340	5,315	5,290	5,261	5,233	5,203	-0.41	-4.05
Canada	27,524	27,915	28,280	28,609	28,943	29,272	29,593	29,911	30,228	30,541	30,855	1.15	12.10
Chile	14,870	15,057	15,244	15,433	15,621	15,811	15,995	16,184	16,368	16,557	16,735	1.19	12.54
China	616,059	629,802	642,523	654,285	665,589	675,963	686,624	696,020	705,004	713,637	721,567	1.59	17.13
Colombia	35,293	35,976	36,659	37,328	38,010	38,680	39,366	40,033	40,701	41,377	42,046	1.77	19.14
Costa Rica	2,922	2,985	3,049	3,115	3,181	3,248	3,314	3,379	3,444	3,509	3,573	2.03	22.29
Croatia	2,733	2,750	2,765	2,781	2,798	2,810	2,826	2,841	2,856	2,872	2,885	0.54	5.57
Czech Republic	7,760	7,787	7,813	7,824	7,837	7,845	7,852	7,860	7,874	7,878	7,892	0.17	1.69
Denmark	4,735	4,754	4,775	4,794	4,814	4,834	4,854	4,875	4,895	4,917	4,939	0.42	4.30
Ecuador	9,070	9,241	9,416	9,609	9,798	9,988	10,182	10,371	10,560	10,753	10,946	1.90	20.69
Egypt	32,771	33,550	34,392	35,299	36,217	37,232	38,279	39,312	40,337	41,399	42,494	2.63	29.67
Estonia	925	923	921	919	917	916	915	915	916	917	919	-0.06	-0.62
Finland	3,336	3,355	3,373	3,388	3,403	3,421	3,434	3,449	3,461	3,472	3,486	0.44	4.50
France	48,453	48,856	49,229	49,587	49,966	50,319	50,676	51,051	51,425	51,790	52,136	0.74	7.60
Germany	73,089	72,961	72,815	72,696	72,568	72,453	72,339	72,203	72,090	71,938	71,805	-0.18	-1.76
Greece	7,059	7,131	7,196	7,263	7,329	7,398	7,465	7,525	7,593	7,660	7,725	0.91	9.43
Hong Kong, China	7,064	7,131	7,196	7,260	7,322	7,383	7,443	7,502	7,560	7,617	7,673	0.83	8.62
Hungary	6,746	6,764	6,780	6,785	6,796	6,806	6,813	6,823	6,835	6,843	6,854	0.16	1.60
India	348,249	356,447	365,180	374,042	383,061	392,427	402,133	412,328	422,437	432,798	443,875	2.46	27.46
Indonesia	120,611	124,387	128,027	131,645	135,250	138,846	142,309	145,767	149,056	152,351	155,496	2.57	28.92
Iran	51,196	52,177	53,158	54,138	55,120	56,107	57,100	58,098	59,098	60,090	61,061	1.78	19.27
Ireland	2,740	2,790	2,838	2,888	2,934	2,985	3,033	3,083	3,131	3,181	3,228	1.65	17.79
Israel	6,809	6,918	7,026	7,132	7,236	7,340	7,442	7,544	7,644	7,741	7,839	1.42	15.12
Italy	40,195	40,327	40,476	40,598	40,726	40,891	41,012	41,152	41,269	41,410	41,514	0.32	3.28
Japan	84,673	84,750	84,860	84,928	85,062	85,180	85,230	85,301	85,408	85,444	85,431	0.09	0.89
Jordan	4,990	5,119	5,224	5,310	5,388	5,462	5,547	5,643	5,749	5,864	5,985	1.83	19.93
Kazakhstan	9,073	9,220	9,369	9,507	9,658	9,798	9,957	10,097	10,245	10,395	10,537	1.51	16.13
Kuwait	2,362	2,415	2,469	2,522	2,575	2,628	2,680	2,732	2,783	2,834	2,884	2.02	22.10
Latvia	1,542	1,534	1,528	1,521	1,514	1,505	1,499	1,492	1,485	1,479	1,473	-0.46	-4.47
Lithuania	2,253	2,244	2,234	2,221	2,212	2,201	2,188	2,178	2,169	2,159	2,151	-0.47	-4.56
Malaysia	17,884	18,384	18,882	19,405	19,912	20,449	20,980	21,515	22,057	22,602	23,159	2.62	29.50
Mexico	83,193	84,657	86,135	87,576	88,923	90,278	91,573	92,877	94,171	95,469	96,719	1.52	16.26
Morocco	19,608	20,048	20,497	20,928	21,380	21,833	22,278	22,733	23,166	23,613	24,051	2.06	22.66
Netherlands	11,029	11,126	11,239	11,346	11,463	11,574	11,685	11,804	11,915	12,039	12,162	0.98	10.27
New Zealand	3,725	3,765	3,804	3,842	3,881	3,918	3,956	3,993	4,029	4,066	4,101	0.97	10.09
Nigeria	79,928	82,877	85,858	88,790	91,744	94,722	97,695	100,714	103,600	106,632	109,427	3.19	36.91
Norway	3,992	4,072	4,144	4,215	4,281	4,346	4,409	4,472	4,536	4,597	4,658	1.55	16.68
Pakistan	67,710	70,227	72,758	75,392	78,183	80,981	83,811	86,639	89,628	92,525	95,491	3.50	41.03
Peru	21,628	21,990	22,352	22,704	23,060	23,419	23,784	24,132	24,494	24,841	25,187	1.53	16.45
Philippines	60,260	62,058	63,858	65,670	67,503	69,316	71,190	73,041	74,883	76,723	78,634	2.70	30.49
Poland	23,548	23,528	23,519	23,534	23,563	23,587	23,621	23,698	23,796	23,902	24,061	0.22	2.18
Portugal	6,172	6,243	6,311	6,377	6,445	6,510	6,575	6,635	6,695	6,755	6,808	0.99	10.32
Romania	11,790	11,770	11,748	11,728	11,691	11,662	11,618	11,578	11,543	11,505	11,468	-0.28	-2.74
Russia	105,160	105,252	105,121	105,090	105,111	105,013	105,072	104,979	104,984	104,953	104,842	-0.03	-0.30
Saudi Arabia	23,162	23,691	24,218	24,753	25,280	25,800	26,327	26,848	27,366	27,876	28,379	2.05	22.52
Singapore	4,707	4,772	4,834	4,894	4,950	5,004	5,055	5,103	5,150	5,194	5,236	1.07	11.24
Slovakia	3,059	3,069	3,079	3,090	3,097	3,107	3,119	3,127	3,135	3,144	3,154	0.30	3.08
Slovenia	1,034	1,040	1,045	1,050	1,054	1,059	1,066	1,073	1,081	1,090	1,099	0.61	6.27
South Africa	28,389	28,866	29,300	29,753	30,172	30,619	31,059	31,535	32,011	32,506	33,033	1.53	16.36
South Korea	39,814	40,017	40,228	40,417	40,579	40,741	40,894	41,032	41,158	41,271	41,371	0.38	3.91
Spain	35,145	35,515	35,868	36,228	36,585	36,945	37,293	37,655	37,999	38,356	38,694	0.97	10.10
Sweden	7,704	7,748	7,793	7,839	7,885	7,933	7,980	8,032	8,082	8,135	8,188	0.61	6.28
Switzerland	5,166	5,194	5,219	5,246	5,273	5,297	5,325	5,350	5,377	5,403	5,433	0.50	5.16
Taiwan	19,388	19,553	19,707	19,855	20,009	20,144	20,277	20,404	20,522	20,643	20,750	0.68	7.02
Thailand	21,743	22,118	22,501	22,894	23,297	23,711	24,138	24,577	25,029	25,492	25,968	1.79	19.43
Tunisia	6,743	6,841	6,943	7,046	7,148	7,250	7,352	7,456	7,559	7,660	7,760	1.42	15.09
Turkey	52,109	53,113	54,049	54,978	55,895	56,792	57,694	58,570	59,463	60,329	61,147	1.61	17.35
Turkmenistan	2,281	2,322	2,367	2,411	2,460	2,510	2,564	2,622	2,684	2,752	2,824	2.16	23.78
Ukraine	31,238	31,117	30,990	30,860	30,740	30,621	30,505	30,386	30,279	30,189	30,099	-0.37	-3.65
United Arab Emirates	3,957	4,071	4,179	4,282	4,381	4,477	4,572	4,666	4,760	4,852	4,944	2.25	24.92
United Kingdom	55,185	55,574	55,893	56,238	56,622	57,039	57,459	57,896	58,327	58,776	59,211	0.71	7.30
USA	251,335	254,090	256,678	259,217	261,844	264,489	267,125	269,695	272,380	275,020	277,551	1.00	10.43
Venezuela	25,611	26,085	26,557	27,023	27,490	27,939	28,391	28,839	29,284	29,718	30,144	1.64	17.70
Vietnam	24,887	25,650	26,392	27,167	27,928	28,697	29,451	30,266	31,107	31,860	32,688	2.76	31.35

Density and urbanisation

Table 4.74 Urban population: 2009-2019 (%)

% of total

	2009	2010	2011	2012	2013	2014	2015	2016	2017	2018	2019	CAGR	Period growth
Algeria	61.5	62.0	62.5	62.9	63.3	63.8	64.2	64.7	65.1	65.6	66.0	0.71	7.30
Argentina	90.0	90.1	90.2	90.3	90.4	90.6	90.7	90.8	91.0	91.1	91.3	0.14	1.44
Australia	93.7	94.0	94.2	94.4	94.5	94.7	94.9	95.0	95.1	95.2	95.3	0.17	1.67
Austria	67.4	67.4	67.5	67.6	67.6	67.7	67.8	67.9	67.9	68.0	68.1	0.10	1.05
Azerbaijan	50.7	50.9	50.9	51.1	51.3	51.4	51.7	51.9	52.1	52.4	52.7	0.39	3.99
Belarus	73.7	73.9	74.2	74.5	74.8	75.0	75.3	75.5	75.7	75.9	76.1	0.32	3.27
Belgium	97.4	97.4	97.4	97.4	97.5	97.5	97.5	97.5	97.6	97.6	97.7	0.03	0.28
Bolivia	65.1	65.4	65.9	66.2	66.6	67.0	67.5	67.9	68.3	68.8	69.2	0.62	6.39
Bosnia-Herzegovina	48.0	48.6	49.2	49.9	50.5	51.2	51.8	52.5	53.2	53.8	54.5	1.27	13.50
Brazil	85.4	86.0	86.5	87.0	87.5	87.9	88.3	88.6	88.9	89.2	89.5	0.47	4.77
Bulgaria	72.1	72.4	72.8	73.0	73.4	73.7	73.9	74.2	74.4	74.7	74.9	0.38	3.85
Canada	81.8	82.2	82.6	82.9	83.3	83.6	83.9	84.1	84.4	84.7	84.9	0.38	3.83
Chile	87.6	87.9	88.1	88.4	88.7	89.0	89.2	89.5	89.8	90.2	90.4	0.32	3.22
China	46.4	47.2	47.9	48.6	49.3	49.8	50.4	50.9	51.4	51.9	52.3	1.21	12.73
Colombia	77.3	77.7	78.1	78.5	78.9	79.3	79.7	80.1	80.5	80.9	81.3	0.51	5.18
Costa Rica	63.8	64.3	64.8	65.3	65.9	66.4	66.9	67.3	67.8	68.3	68.8	0.76	7.83
Croatia	61.7	62.2	62.7	63.1	63.7	64.1	64.6	65.1	65.6	66.2	66.7	0.78	8.03
Czech Republic	75.1	75.2	75.4	75.5	75.6	75.7	75.8	75.9	76.0	76.1	76.2	0.15	1.52
Denmark	85.9	86.0	86.2	86.3	86.4	86.5	86.7	86.8	86.9	87.0	87.2	0.15	1.49
Ecuador	66.6	67.1	67.6	68.2	68.7	69.2	69.8	70.3	70.8	71.3	71.9	0.77	8.00
Egypt	42.7	42.9	43.2	43.6	44.0	44.5	45.0	45.5	45.9	46.4	47.0	0.96	10.02
Estonia	69.5	69.6	69.7	69.8	69.9	70.1	70.3	70.5	70.8	71.1	71.5	0.28	2.86
Finland	62.6	62.7	62.8	62.9	62.9	63.0	63.1	63.2	63.2	63.2	63.3	0.11	1.06
France	77.6	77.8	78.1	78.3	78.5	78.8	79.0	79.3	79.5	79.8	80.0	0.31	3.15
Germany	89.1	89.3	89.4	89.6	89.7	89.9	90.0	90.1	90.3	90.4	90.6	0.16	1.61
Greece	62.7	63.2	63.5	64.0	64.4	64.8	65.3	65.7	66.2	66.7	67.2	0.69	7.12
Hong Kong, China	100.0	100.0	100.0	100.0	100.0	100.0	100.0	100.0	100.0	100.0	100.0	0.00	0.00
Hungary	67.3	67.6	67.9	68.2	68.5	68.8	69.0	69.3	69.6	69.9	70.2	0.41	4.20
India	29.8	30.1	30.4	30.7	31.1	31.5	31.8	32.3	32.7	33.1	33.6	1.21	12.84
Indonesia	52.4	53.5	54.5	55.5	56.4	57.4	58.3	59.2	60.0	60.9	61.6	1.63	17.51
Iran	69.0	69.5	70.0	70.5	70.9	71.4	71.9	72.3	72.8	73.2	73.6	0.65	6.70
Ireland	61.6	61.9	62.2	62.6	62.9	63.3	63.6	64.0	64.4	64.8	65.2	0.56	5.77
Israel	92.0	92.0	92.1	92.1	92.2	92.2	92.3	92.4	92.4	92.5	92.6	0.06	0.63
Italy	68.1	68.2	68.4	68.6	68.8	69.0	69.3	69.5	69.8	70.1	70.3	0.32	3.27
Japan	66.4	66.5	66.8	67.0	67.2	67.5	67.7	68.0	68.3	68.6	68.9	0.37	3.81
Jordan	79.0	79.1	79.2	79.3	79.4	79.6	79.7	79.9	80.2	80.5	80.9	0.23	2.34
Kazakhstan	57.5	57.7	57.9	58.0	58.2	58.4	58.7	58.8	59.1	59.3	59.5	0.35	3.51
Kuwait	96.6	96.7	96.7	96.8	96.8	96.8	96.9	96.9	97.0	97.0	97.0	0.04	0.44
Latvia	68.4	68.5	68.6	68.7	68.8	68.9	69.0	69.1	69.2	69.3	69.4	0.15	1.48
Lithuania	67.3	67.4	67.5	67.5	67.6	67.6	67.6	67.7	67.8	67.9	68.0	0.10	0.96
Malaysia	63.6	64.4	65.1	65.9	66.7	67.5	68.3	69.1	69.9	70.7	71.6	1.18	12.45
Mexico	76.6	76.8	77.0	77.3	77.5	77.7	77.9	78.1	78.3	78.6	78.8	0.28	2.82
Morocco	61.3	61.9	62.5	63.1	63.7	64.3	64.9	65.5	66.0	66.6	67.1	0.91	9.49
Netherlands	67.2	67.7	68.2	68.8	69.3	69.9	70.4	71.0	71.6	72.2	72.8	0.81	8.36
New Zealand	86.4	86.5	86.6	86.6	86.7	86.8	86.9	87.0	87.1	87.2	87.3	0.10	0.97
Nigeria	51.7	52.4	53.1	53.7	54.3	54.9	55.5	56.1	56.6	57.2	57.6	1.10	11.59
Norway	83.2	83.8	84.4	84.9	85.4	85.9	86.3	86.7	87.1	87.5	87.8	0.55	5.60
Pakistan	37.4	38.0	38.5	39.1	39.7	40.2	40.8	41.3	41.9	42.4	43.0	1.39	14.82
Peru	74.6	74.8	75.0	75.2	75.4	75.7	75.9	76.1	76.4	76.6	76.8	0.30	3.00
Philippines	65.4	66.1	66.7	67.4	68.0	68.6	69.2	69.7	70.3	70.8	71.3	0.87	9.00
Poland	62.0	62.0	62.1	62.2	62.4	62.6	62.8	63.1	63.4	63.8	64.3	0.37	3.72
Portugal	57.8	58.4	58.9	59.4	59.9	60.5	61.0	61.5	62.0	62.6	63.0	0.86	8.99
Romania	55.0	55.1	55.2	55.2	55.3	55.4	55.4	55.5	55.7	55.8	55.9	0.17	1.67
Russia	74.1	74.2	74.3	74.4	74.6	74.6	74.8	74.8	75.0	75.1	75.2	0.14	1.43
Saudi Arabia	90.1	90.3	90.4	90.6	90.8	90.9	91.0	91.1	91.2	91.3	91.3	0.14	1.40
Singapore	100.0	100.0	100.0	100.0	100.0	100.0	100.0	100.0	100.0	100.0	100.0	0.00	0.00
Slovakia	56.7	56.9	57.0	57.2	57.4	57.6	57.8	57.9	58.1	58.3	58.5	0.31	3.13
Slovenia	51.1	51.2	51.3	51.5	51.6	51.8	52.1	52.3	52.6	53.0	53.4	0.43	4.43
South Africa	56.7	57.2	57.7	58.3	58.8	59.5	60.1	60.8	61.5	62.2	63.0	1.06	11.13
South Korea	81.7	81.9	82.1	82.3	82.5	82.8	83.0	83.2	83.4	83.6	83.9	0.26	2.66
Spain	77.2	77.3	77.5	77.6	77.8	78.0	78.1	78.3	78.5	78.8	79.0	0.23	2.30
Sweden	83.7	83.8	83.9	84.0	84.1	84.2	84.3	84.4	84.5	84.7	84.8	0.13	1.26
Switzerland	68.3	68.4	68.5	68.6	68.7	68.8	68.9	68.9	69.0	69.1	69.2	0.13	1.29
Taiwan	84.2	84.6	85.0	85.5	85.9	86.3	86.7	87.2	87.6	88.0	88.4	0.49	5.00
Thailand	33.6	34.0	34.4	34.8	35.2	35.7	36.2	36.7	37.2	37.7	38.3	1.32	14.06
Tunisia	65.6	65.9	66.3	66.6	66.9	67.2	67.5	67.9	68.2	68.5	68.8	0.48	4.87
Turkey	69.2	69.7	70.2	70.6	71.0	71.3	71.7	72.1	72.5	72.9	73.2	0.56	5.69
Turkmenistan	44.6	44.9	45.1	45.4	45.7	46.1	46.5	47.1	47.6	48.3	49.0	0.94	9.83
Ukraine	68.0	68.2	68.3	68.5	68.7	68.8	69.0	69.2	69.5	69.7	70.0	0.29	2.90
United Arab Emirates	85.7	86.2	86.5	86.9	87.2	87.5	87.7	87.9	88.1	88.3	88.5	0.31	3.18
United Kingdom	89.6	89.7	89.8	89.9	90.0	90.1	90.2	90.3	90.4	90.5	90.6	0.12	1.20
USA	82.0	82.3	82.6	82.8	83.1	83.4	83.6	83.9	84.1	84.4	84.6	0.32	3.21
Venezuela	89.6	89.8	90.0	90.2	90.4	90.6	90.7	90.9	91.1	91.2	91.3	0.19	1.95
Vietnam	28.4	28.9	29.4	29.9	30.3	30.8	31.2	31.7	32.2	32.6	33.1	1.54	16.57

Key economic trends

Table 4.75 GDP per capita: 2009-2019

US$ per capita, at constant 2010 prices

	2009	2010	2011	2012	2013	2014	2015	2016	2017	2018	2019	CAGR	Period growth
Algeria	4,567	4,667	4,778	4,907	5,042	5,180	5,320	5,466	5,612	5,756	5,892	2.58	29.02
Argentina	7,331	7,351	7,463	7,608	7,737	7,903	7,972	8,011	8,029	8,022	7,983	0.86	8.89
Australia	43,358	43,599	44,468	45,385	46,208	46,919	47,637	48,404	49,208	49,997	50,771	1.59	17.10
Austria	46,263	46,261	46,856	47,665	48,541	49,559	50,637	51,769	52,954	54,189	55,473	1.83	19.91
Azerbaijan	5,525	5,865	6,039	6,001	6,150	6,145	6,220	6,310	6,410	6,516	6,632	1.84	20.04
Belarus	5,283	5,505	5,782	6,085	6,450	6,866	7,321	7,832	8,394	9,038	9,762	6.33	84.79
Belgium	45,057	44,915	45,489	46,240	47,164	48,157	49,152	50,182	51,255	52,366	53,515	1.74	18.77
Bolivia	1,927	1,899	1,904	1,920	1,944	1,964	1,993	2,022	2,052	2,087	2,127	0.99	10.35
Bosnia-Herzegovina	4,559	4,582	4,766	5,053	5,358	5,602	5,843	6,083	6,331	6,603	6,879	4.20	50.90
Brazil	8,542	8,840	9,076	9,322	9,595	9,883	10,181	10,502	10,841	11,181	11,536	3.05	35.06
Bulgaria	6,200	6,088	6,253	6,549	6,930	7,333	7,759	8,229	8,737	9,286	9,871	4.76	59.21
Canada	41,872	42,363	43,518	44,596	45,372	45,987	46,590	47,197	47,821	48,468	49,135	1.61	17.34
Chile	9,088	9,364	9,693	10,103	10,533	11,004	11,505	12,045	12,623	13,243	13,902	4.34	52.97
China	3,635	3,944	4,309	4,713	5,153	5,620	6,119	6,655	7,237	7,861	8,529	8.90	134.64
Colombia	5,304	5,361	5,500	5,700	5,908	6,097	6,299	6,507	6,727	6,962	7,216	3.13	36.05
Costa Rica	6,497	6,559	6,698	6,906	7,168	7,443	7,728	8,012	8,297	8,605	8,951	3.26	37.78
Croatia	14,219	14,304	14,689	15,308	15,955	16,631	17,331	18,069	18,828	19,593	20,334	3.64	43.00
Czech Republic	19,225	19,446	19,910	20,601	21,427	22,290	23,208	24,176	25,187	26,251	27,377	3.60	42.40
Denmark	58,726	59,109	59,834	61,196	62,640	63,901	65,055	66,266	67,536	68,868	70,256	1.81	19.63
Ecuador	4,311	4,328	4,357	4,414	4,493	4,574	4,658	4,742	4,823	4,903	4,983	1.46	15.60
Egypt	2,637	2,707	2,792	2,895	3,017	3,145	3,277	3,410	3,551	3,700	3,855	3.87	46.19
Estonia	14,355	14,033	14,276	14,752	15,359	16,029	16,721	17,426	18,109	18,785	19,468	3.09	35.62
Finland	47,054	47,294	48,051	49,073	50,121	51,322	52,573	53,924	55,345	56,860	58,469	2.20	24.26
France	43,616	43,784	44,352	45,006	45,803	46,666	47,563	48,497	49,463	50,463	51,503	1.68	18.08
Germany	40,421	40,696	41,447	42,311	43,224	44,161	45,120	46,095	47,103	48,141	49,215	1.99	21.76
Greece	31,349	31,223	31,332	31,603	32,011	32,531	33,106	33,726	34,378	35,059	35,768	1.33	14.09
Hong Kong, China	30,204	30,968	31,903	32,992	34,110	35,274	36,502	37,799	39,158	40,584	42,080	3.37	39.32
Hungary	13,947	13,680	14,389	15,387	16,137	16,578	17,201	17,844	18,508	19,194	19,902	3.62	42.70
India	1,065	1,131	1,216	1,308	1,414	1,530	1,632	1,739	1,849	1,965	2,083	6.93	95.52
Indonesia	2,351	2,436	2,531	2,643	2,774	2,921	3,083	3,260	3,453	3,659	3,880	5.14	65.05
Iran	4,807	4,854	4,951	5,051	5,155	5,261	5,370	5,478	5,589	5,704	5,820	1.93	21.09
Ireland	52,190	50,219	50,140	50,724	51,456	52,222	53,025	53,877	54,767	55,707	56,678	0.83	8.60
Israel	25,923	26,429	27,146	27,976	28,770	29,613	30,468	31,321	32,185	33,034	33,885	2.71	30.71
Italy	36,701	36,750	36,992	37,470	38,056	38,776	39,581	40,444	41,361	42,351	43,414	1.69	18.29
Japan	39,986	40,730	41,781	42,839	43,816	44,720	45,615	46,571	47,595	48,697	49,870	2.23	24.72
Jordan	3,714	3,769	3,864	3,996	4,163	4,339	4,514	4,684	4,853	5,022	5,192	3.41	39.81
Kazakhstan	7,480	7,434	7,835	8,110	8,390	8,857	9,387	9,943	10,561	11,261	12,051	4.89	61.12
Kuwait	53,587	54,170	55,344	56,746	58,280	59,812	61,469	63,253	65,169	67,226	69,434	2.62	29.57
Latvia	10,935	10,562	10,780	11,264	11,777	12,331	12,919	13,500	14,068	14,611	15,147	3.31	38.51
Lithuania	10,824	10,448	10,821	11,266	11,786	12,330	12,884	13,450	14,028	14,608	15,175	3.44	40.21
Malaysia	7,499	7,566	7,751	8,055	8,414	8,792	9,206	9,643	10,093	10,566	11,061	3.96	47.50
Mexico	8,495	8,644	8,938	9,303	9,675	10,026	10,370	10,715	11,058	11,392	11,726	3.28	38.03
Morocco	2,866	2,922	3,018	3,131	3,249	3,373	3,503	3,639	3,777	3,921	4,069	3.57	42.01
Netherlands	49,857	50,102	50,320	51,061	52,057	53,319	54,625	55,983	57,391	58,861	60,396	1.94	21.14
New Zealand	26,235	26,557	26,933	27,483	28,099	28,765	29,428	30,066	30,698	31,324	31,919	1.98	21.66
Nigeria	1,111	1,140	1,174	1,217	1,265	1,318	1,372	1,427	1,484	1,540	1,600	3.72	44.04
Norway	83,165	83,204	83,774	84,472	85,361	86,289	87,335	88,425	89,649	90,981	92,351	1.05	11.05
Pakistan	924	931	948	969	996	1,029	1,065	1,104	1,145	1,190	1,239	2.97	34.06
Peru	4,548	4,745	4,939	5,144	5,358	5,583	5,822	6,077	6,345	6,621	6,907	4.27	51.89
Philippines	1,799	1,821	1,855	1,903	1,953	2,005	2,057	2,111	2,167	2,225	2,286	2.42	27.06
Poland	11,144	11,406	11,880	12,367	12,868	13,405	13,950	14,489	15,029	15,559	16,083	3.74	44.32
Portugal	21,363	21,400	21,548	21,789	22,038	22,294	22,571	22,868	23,185	23,520	23,879	1.12	11.78
Romania	7,707	7,768	8,153	8,724	9,360	9,865	10,379	10,884	11,370	11,853	12,348	4.83	60.23
Russia	9,559	9,620	9,845	10,162	10,530	11,015	11,546	12,122	12,736	13,402	14,117	3.98	47.69
Saudi Arabia	16,524	16,847	17,220	17,694	18,202	18,747	19,351	19,998	20,674	21,426	22,247	3.02	34.63
Singapore	38,288	39,312	40,478	41,655	43,079	44,562	46,176	47,930	49,805	51,837	53,978	3.49	40.98
Slovakia	17,224	17,856	18,779	19,596	20,438	21,306	22,190	23,104	24,051	25,033	26,035	4.22	51.16
Slovenia	25,333	25,400	26,277	27,197	28,049	28,926	29,849	30,805	31,783	32,785	33,807	2.93	33.45
South Africa	5,441	5,493	5,667	5,882	6,120	6,370	6,627	6,889	7,158	7,439	7,735	3.58	42.16
South Korea	16,946	17,502	18,369	19,245	20,109	20,995	21,933	22,927	23,996	25,142	26,370	4.52	55.62
Spain	32,656	32,126	32,140	32,346	32,650	33,085	33,527	33,985	34,458	34,948	35,465	0.83	8.60
Sweden	46,979	47,309	48,265	49,480	50,971	52,720	54,525	56,413	58,390	60,519	62,792	2.94	33.66
Switzerland	65,598	65,655	66,061	66,636	67,385	68,143	68,927	69,792	70,752	71,794	72,962	1.07	11.23
Taiwan	16,145	16,688	17,336	18,119	18,981	19,888	20,836	21,828	22,868	23,958	25,106	4.51	55.50
Thailand	4,205	4,335	4,504	4,705	4,962	5,236	5,520	5,816	6,125	6,451	6,795	4.92	61.60
Tunisia	3,935	4,052	4,212	4,405	4,615	4,847	5,091	5,344	5,608	5,882	6,165	4.59	56.69
Turkey	7,562	7,756	7,913	8,099	8,291	8,491	8,701	8,931	9,176	9,430	9,688	2.51	28.12
Turkmenistan	11,679	13,290	14,293	15,323	16,351	17,440	18,634	19,903	21,249	22,635	24,067	7.50	106.07
Ukraine	2,554	2,634	2,783	2,940	3,066	3,240	3,445	3,665	3,898	4,153	4,428	5.66	73.35
United Arab Emirates	52,340	52,336	52,931	54,114	55,649	57,439	59,335	61,341	63,412	65,486	67,581	2.59	29.12
United Kingdom	37,593	37,719	38,476	39,377	40,283	41,192	42,104	43,035	43,990	44,983	46,021	2.04	22.42
USA	46,716	47,078	48,061	48,991	49,872	50,590	51,167	51,708	52,277	52,873	53,486	1.36	14.49
Venezuela	13,353	13,088	12,932	12,794	12,662	12,528	12,399	12,275	12,155	12,038	11,925	-1.12	-10.69
Vietnam	1,125	1,170	1,224	1,288	1,361	1,440	1,521	1,609	1,702	1,802	1,910	5.44	69.77

Key economic trends

Table 4.76 Real GDP growth: 2009-2019

% growth

	2009	2010	2011	2012	2013	2014	2015	2016	2017	2018	2019
Algeria	2.1	3.7	3.9	4.2	4.3	4.2	4.2	4.2	4.0	3.9	3.7
Argentina	-2.5	1.5	2.5	3.0	3.0	3.0	2.9	2.7	2.6	2.5	2.4
Australia	0.7	2.0	3.3	3.4	3.2	3.0	2.9	3.0	3.0	3.0	2.9
Austria	-3.8	0.3	1.6	2.0	2.1	2.4	2.5	2.5	2.5	2.6	2.6
Azerbaijan	7.5	7.4	4.1	0.4	3.5	0.9	2.2	2.4	2.5	2.5	2.6
Belarus	-1.2	1.8	5.2	5.7	6.5	6.9	7.1	7.4	7.5	8.0	8.3
Belgium	-3.2	0.0	1.6	2.0	2.3	2.4	2.4	2.4	2.5	2.5	2.5
Bolivia	2.8	3.4	3.7	3.8	3.7	3.7	3.8	3.7	3.7	3.8	3.9
Bosnia-Herzegovina	-3.0	0.5	4.0	6.0	6.0	4.5	4.2	4.0	4.0	4.1	4.0
Brazil	-0.7	3.5	3.5	3.5	3.7	3.7	3.8	3.9	3.9	3.8	3.8
Bulgaria	-6.5	-2.5	2.0	4.0	5.0	5.0	5.0	5.2	5.3	5.4	5.4
Canada	-2.5	2.1	3.6	3.3	2.5	2.1	2.1	2.1	2.1	2.1	2.1
Chile	-1.7	4.0	4.5	5.2	5.2	5.4	5.5	5.6	5.6	5.7	5.8
China	8.5	9.0	9.7	9.8	9.8	9.5	9.3	9.1	9.1	9.0	8.8
Colombia	-0.3	2.5	4.0	5.0	5.0	4.5	4.6	4.5	4.6	4.7	4.8
Costa Rica	-1.5	2.3	3.5	4.5	5.2	5.2	5.2	5.0	4.8	4.9	5.2
Croatia	-5.2	0.4	2.5	4.0	4.0	4.0	4.0	4.0	3.9	3.8	3.5
Czech Republic	-4.3	1.3	2.5	3.5	4.0	4.0	4.1	4.1	4.2	4.2	4.3
Denmark	-2.4	0.9	1.5	2.6	2.6	2.3	2.1	2.1	2.2	2.3	2.3
Ecuador	-1.0	1.5	1.8	2.5	3.0	3.0	3.0	2.9	2.8	2.7	2.7
Egypt	4.7	4.5	5.0	5.5	6.0	6.0	5.9	5.7	5.8	5.8	5.7
Estonia	-14.0	-2.6	1.4	3.0	3.7	4.0	3.9	3.9	3.6	3.4	3.3
Finland	-6.4	0.9	2.0	2.5	2.5	2.8	2.8	2.9	2.9	3.0	3.1
France	-2.4	0.9	1.8	1.9	2.2	2.3	2.3	2.4	2.4	2.4	2.4
Germany	-5.3	0.3	1.5	1.7	1.8	1.8	1.8	1.8	1.8	1.9	1.9
Greece	-0.8	-0.1	0.7	1.2	1.6	1.9	2.0	2.1	2.1	2.1	2.1
Hong Kong, China	-3.6	3.5	4.0	4.3	4.3	4.3	4.3	4.4	4.4	4.4	4.4
Hungary	-6.7	-0.9	3.2	4.5	4.0	3.5	3.5	3.5	3.4	3.4	3.4
India	5.4	6.4	7.3	7.6	8.0	8.1	7.9	7.8	7.5	7.4	7.1
Indonesia	4.0	4.8	5.0	5.5	6.0	6.3	6.5	6.7	6.8	6.8	6.9
Iran	1.5	2.2	3.2	3.2	3.2	3.2	3.2	3.1	3.1	3.2	3.1
Ireland	-7.5	-2.5	1.0	2.3	2.6	2.6	2.6	2.6	2.7	2.7	2.7
Israel	-0.1	2.4	4.2	4.7	4.4	4.4	4.3	4.2	4.1	3.9	3.8
Italy	-5.1	0.2	0.7	1.4	1.6	1.9	2.1	2.1	2.2	2.3	2.4
Japan	-5.4	1.7	2.4	2.3	2.0	1.8	1.7	1.8	1.8	1.9	2.0
Jordan	3.0	4.0	4.5	5.0	5.5	5.5	5.4	5.3	5.2	5.2	5.1
Kazakhstan	-2.0	2.0	6.0	5.6	5.6	7.5	7.5	7.6	7.8	8.1	8.3
Kuwait	-1.5	3.3	4.4	4.7	4.8	4.7	4.8	4.8	4.9	5.0	5.1
Latvia	-18.0	-4.0	1.5	3.8	3.9	4.0	4.1	3.9	3.6	3.3	3.1
Lithuania	-18.5	-4.0	3.0	3.5	4.0	4.0	3.9	3.8	3.7	3.6	3.4
Malaysia	-3.6	2.5	4.1	5.5	6.0	6.0	6.2	6.2	6.0	6.0	6.0
Mexico	-7.3	3.3	4.9	5.5	5.3	4.9	4.6	4.5	4.3	4.1	4.0
Morocco	5.0	3.2	4.5	5.0	5.0	5.0	5.1	5.0	5.0	4.9	4.9
Netherlands	-4.2	0.7	0.6	1.7	2.1	2.6	2.6	2.7	2.7	2.7	2.8
New Zealand	-2.2	2.2	2.4	3.0	3.2	3.3	3.2	3.0	2.9	2.9	2.7
Nigeria	2.9	5.0	5.2	5.9	6.2	6.3	6.2	6.1	6.0	5.8	5.8
Norway	-1.9	1.3	1.8	1.9	2.0	2.1	2.2	2.2	2.3	2.4	2.5
Pakistan	2.0	3.0	4.0	4.5	5.0	5.5	5.7	5.7	5.8	5.9	6.1
Peru	1.5	5.8	5.5	5.5	5.5	5.5	5.6	5.6	5.6	5.6	5.5
Philippines	1.0	3.2	3.8	4.5	4.5	4.5	4.5	4.4	4.4	4.5	4.5
Poland	1.0	2.2	4.0	3.9	3.9	4.0	3.9	3.7	3.6	3.4	3.2
Portugal	-3.0	0.4	0.9	1.3	1.3	1.3	1.4	1.4	1.4	1.5	1.5
Romania	-8.5	0.5	4.6	6.6	6.8	5.0	4.7	4.3	3.9	3.7	3.6
Russia	-7.5	1.5	3.0	3.7	4.2	5.0	5.0	5.1	5.2	5.2	5.3
Saudi Arabia	-0.9	4.0	4.3	4.8	4.9	5.0	5.2	5.3	5.3	5.5	5.6
Singapore	-3.3	4.1	4.3	4.2	4.6	4.6	4.7	4.8	4.9	5.0	5.0
Slovakia	-4.7	3.7	5.2	4.4	4.3	4.2	4.1	4.1	4.1	4.1	4.0
Slovenia	-4.7	0.6	3.8	3.7	3.3	3.3	3.3	3.3	3.3	3.3	3.2
South Africa	-2.2	1.7	3.8	4.3	4.5	4.5	4.4	4.4	4.3	4.3	4.4
South Korea	-1.0	3.6	5.2	5.0	4.7	4.5	4.6	4.6	4.7	4.8	4.9
Spain	-3.8	-0.7	0.9	1.4	1.7	2.1	2.1	2.1	2.1	2.1	2.1
Sweden	-4.8	1.2	2.5	3.0	3.5	3.9	3.9	4.0	4.0	4.2	4.3
Switzerland	-2.0	0.5	1.0	1.3	1.5	1.5	1.5	1.6	1.8	1.9	2.0
Taiwan	-4.1	3.7	4.2	4.8	5.0	5.0	5.0	4.9	4.9	4.9	4.9
Thailand	-3.5	3.7	4.5	5.0	6.0	6.0	5.9	5.8	5.7	5.7	5.7
Tunisia	3.0	4.0	5.0	5.6	5.8	6.0	6.0	5.9	5.9	5.8	5.7
Turkey	-6.5	3.7	4.0	3.5	3.5	3.5	3.6	3.7	3.8	3.8	3.7
Turkmenistan	4.0	15.3	8.9	8.6	8.1	8.0	8.1	8.1	8.0	7.7	7.4
Ukraine	-14.0	2.7	4.0	5.0	5.4	5.8	6.0	6.2	6.2	6.2	6.2
United Arab Emirates	-0.2	2.4	3.4	4.3	4.8	5.2	5.2	5.2	5.2	5.1	5.0
United Kingdom	-4.4	0.9	2.5	2.9	2.9	2.9	2.8	2.8	2.9	2.9	2.9
USA	-2.7	1.5	2.8	2.6	2.5	2.1	1.8	1.7	1.8	1.8	1.8
Venezuela	-2.0	-0.4	0.4	0.5	0.5	0.4	0.4	0.4	0.4	0.4	0.3
Vietnam	4.6	5.3	6.0	6.5	7.0	7.0	7.0	7.0	7.0	7.1	7.1

Key economic trends

Table 4.77 Disposable income per capita: 2009-2019

US$ per capita, at constant 2010 prices

	2009	2010	2011	2012	2013	2014	2015	2016	2017	2018	2019	CAGR	Period growth
Algeria	2,074	2,128	2,172	2,234	2,308	2,381	2,433	2,508	2,581	2,648	2,700	2.67	30.19
Argentina	3,825	3,888	3,972	4,055	4,123	4,220	4,312	4,401	4,483	4,564	4,649	1.97	21.53
Australia	25,160	25,357	25,832	26,330	26,775	27,188	27,598	28,029	28,494	28,941	29,385	1.56	16.79
Austria	30,880	31,200	31,746	32,518	33,260	34,109	34,969	35,834	36,712	37,613	38,540	2.24	24.80
Azerbaijan	2,415	2,532	2,599	2,564	2,606	2,625	2,626	2,674	2,714	2,767	2,785	1.43	15.30
Belarus	2,893	3,031	3,268	3,520	3,812	4,135	4,479	4,863	5,282	5,756	6,286	8.07	117.29
Belgium	27,367	27,463	27,885	28,406	29,071	29,727	30,405	31,100	31,797	32,508	33,264	1.97	21.55
Bolivia	1,266	1,271	1,275	1,293	1,311	1,327	1,349	1,371	1,397	1,426	1,456	1.41	14.98
Bosnia-Herzegovina	3,854	3,830	3,910	4,097	4,300	4,447	4,597						
Brazil	5,378	5,578	5,771	5,976	6,193	6,419	6,654	6,890	7,138	7,388	7,640	3.57	42.06
Bulgaria	4,682	4,739	4,912	5,187	5,533	5,891	6,262	6,643	7,066	7,514	8,001	5.50	70.87
Canada	25,223	25,385	25,990	26,538	26,926	27,218	27,501	27,776	28,055	28,336	28,618	1.27	13.46
Chile	7,081	7,398	7,708	8,086	8,460	8,863	9,292	9,747	10,234	10,754	11,306	4.79	59.68
China	1,929	2,099	2,296	2,508	2,738	2,973	3,219	3,484	3,772	4,078	4,403	8.60	128.22
Colombia	3,501	3,526	3,594	3,706	3,823	3,932	4,054	4,182	4,320	4,470	4,634	2.84	32.37
Costa Rica	4,827	4,919	5,064	5,251	5,480	5,713	5,942						
Croatia	8,777	8,831	9,052	9,422	9,802	10,197	10,609	11,059	11,518	11,986	12,436	3.55	41.68
Czech Republic	10,631	10,769	11,072	11,540	12,033	12,562	13,117	13,684	14,265	14,893	15,528	3.86	46.06
Denmark	32,851	33,303	33,952	35,008	35,942	36,775	37,504	38,265	39,060	39,857	40,699	2.17	23.89
Ecuador	3,383	3,426	3,447	3,510	3,586	3,657	3,727	3,793	3,852	3,915	3,980	1.64	17.66
Egypt	2,109	2,171	2,241	2,325	2,423	2,525	2,631	2,737	2,851	2,970	3,094	3.91	46.72
Estonia	7,430	7,297	7,395	7,610	7,933	8,269	8,623	8,996	9,354	9,699	10,048	3.07	35.25
Finland	25,229	25,565	26,292	27,098	27,868	28,680	29,485	30,310	31,189	32,093	33,054	2.74	31.02
France	29,556	29,561	29,993	30,293	30,821	31,395	32,016	32,597	33,249	33,803	34,441	1.54	16.53
Germany	28,128	28,162	28,780	29,314	29,971	30,609	31,215	31,936	32,667	33,263	34,070	1.94	21.13
Greece	21,279	21,362	21,557	21,875	22,245	22,683	23,157	23,649	24,154	24,684	25,215	1.71	18.50
Hong Kong, China	24,700	25,083	25,758	26,762	27,453	28,373	29,396	30,540	31,494	32,565	33,855	3.20	37.06
Hungary	6,724	6,750	7,047	7,537	7,938	8,165	8,497	8,844	9,207	9,579	9,961	4.01	48.14
India	646	673	710	750	798	850	896	940	990	1,042	1,097	5.44	69.78
Indonesia	1,555	1,633	1,726	1,823	1,935	2,059	2,194	2,338	2,494	2,662	2,843	6.22	82.82
Iran	2,709	2,758	2,825	2,895	2,968	3,040	3,111						
Ireland	25,702	24,287	23,910	24,000	24,176	24,462	24,736	25,095	25,465	25,879	26,311	0.23	2.37
Israel	15,573	15,822	16,233	16,751	17,305	17,825	18,359	18,894	19,435	19,964	20,496	2.79	31.62
Italy	25,390	25,398	25,711	26,191	26,612	27,182	27,787	28,395	29,049	29,743	30,475	1.84	20.03
Japan	26,084	26,347	26,857	27,428	27,953	28,436	28,938	29,456	30,048	30,699	31,415	1.88	20.44
Jordan	2,851	2,877	2,907	2,974	3,070	3,172	3,274	3,372	3,470	3,568	3,666	2.55	28.59
Kazakhstan	3,329	3,336	3,481	3,629	3,800	4,026	4,289	4,553	4,874	5,188	5,568	5.28	67.23
Kuwait	21,113	21,536	22,073	22,693	23,326	23,894	24,558	25,158	25,847	26,594	27,399	2.64	29.78
Latvia	6,582	6,194	6,177	6,293	6,493	6,720	6,966	7,220	7,481	7,733	7,988	1.96	21.37
Lithuania	7,388	7,038	7,274	7,584	7,952	8,324	8,658	9,040	9,443	9,869	10,232	3.31	38.48
Malaysia	4,099	4,200	4,400	4,670	4,935	5,213	5,505	5,810	6,115	6,440	6,776	5.15	65.29
Mexico	5,818	5,926	6,206	6,495	6,805	7,124	7,414	7,709	7,981	8,259	8,542	3.92	46.82
Morocco	2,006	2,105	2,237	2,359	2,486	2,611	2,735	2,867	2,995	3,124	3,260	4.97	62.49
Netherlands	24,163	24,138	24,318	24,777	25,305	25,986	26,683	27,391	28,109	28,870	29,646	2.07	22.69
New Zealand	14,309	14,631	14,974	15,365	15,807	16,250	16,689	17,105	17,525	17,927	18,309	2.50	27.95
Nigeria	931	1,000	1,038	1,089	1,148	1,209	1,272	1,335	1,396	1,457	1,520	5.02	63.16
Norway	37,540	38,346	38,995	39,719	40,470	41,107	41,918	42,579	43,380	44,094	44,861	1.80	19.50
Pakistan	690	705	727	749	777	808	842	876	913	951	993	3.71	43.88
Peru	2,929	2,997	3,107	3,225	3,336	3,464	3,600	3,747	3,903	4,066	4,234	3.75	44.53
Philippines	1,317	1,337	1,369	1,411	1,452	1,494	1,537	1,579	1,622	1,666	1,713	2.66	30.06
Poland	7,290	7,509	7,853	8,190	8,553	8,919	9,292	9,662	10,032	10,392	10,746	3.96	47.41
Portugal	15,523	15,670	15,867	16,128	16,359	16,586	16,812	17,051	17,296	17,541	17,804	1.38	14.69
Romania	4,766	4,843	5,118	5,484	5,905	6,242	6,581	6,917	7,241	7,561	7,886	5.17	65.47
Russia	5,482	5,642	5,904	6,173	6,489	6,864	7,212	7,643	8,047	8,495	8,972	5.05	63.67
Saudi Arabia	6,142	6,427	6,671	6,939	7,251	7,508	7,812	8,140	8,481	8,816	9,202	4.13	49.82
Singapore	22,265	22,582	22,847	22,977	23,446	24,068	24,671	25,330	26,162	27,053	28,017	2.32	25.83
Slovakia	11,325	11,494	11,979	12,393	12,853	13,347	13,864	14,394	14,937	15,510	16,093	3.58	42.09
Slovenia	16,040	16,151	16,782	17,479	18,098	18,712	19,328	19,977	20,650	21,326	22,032	3.22	37.35
South Africa	3,256	3,331	3,455	3,616	3,775	3,939	4,107	4,277	4,448	4,626	4,811	3.98	47.74
South Korea	10,759	10,970	11,440	11,917	12,376	12,865	13,393	13,944	14,545	15,183	15,865	3.96	47.45
Spain	20,799	20,452	20,401	20,532	20,681	20,908	21,157	21,411	21,664	21,932	22,207	0.66	6.77
Sweden	22,626	22,893	23,431	24,078	24,838	25,714	26,608	27,534	28,502	29,544	30,653	3.08	35.48
Switzerland	40,411	41,009	41,935	42,770	43,582	44,360	45,098	45,848	46,631	47,452	48,323	1.80	19.58
Taiwan	11,413	11,610	12,120	12,771	13,345	14,013	14,728	15,435	16,180	16,948	17,764	4.52	55.65
Thailand	2,355	2,426	2,516	2,624	2,762	2,908	3,067	3,230	3,400	3,583	3,770	4.82	60.11
Tunisia	2,426	2,481	2,562	2,668	2,786	2,917	3,057	3,201	3,352	3,510	3,673	4.24	51.42
Turkey	5,745	5,842	6,009	6,161	6,305	6,462	6,637	6,821	7,014	7,210	7,406	2.57	28.90
Turkmenistan	1,293	1,453	1,533	1,639	1,731	1,833	1,951	2,077	2,211	2,354	2,496	6.80	93.07
Ukraine	1,540	1,578	1,675	1,772	1,885	2,015	2,155	2,308	2,472	2,649	2,837	6.30	84.25
United Arab Emirates	32,856	33,462	34,194	35,259	36,426	37,561	38,656	39,916	41,319	42,723	44,200	3.01	34.53
United Kingdom	24,775	24,667	25,055	25,538	26,059	26,613	27,150	27,732	28,327	28,965	29,634	1.81	19.61
USA	33,922	34,278	34,934	35,633	36,280	36,810	37,260	37,668	38,064	38,496	38,949	1.39	14.82
Venezuela	9,509	9,401	9,383	9,356	9,334	9,239	9,164	9,083	9,006	8,944	8,876	-0.69	-6.66
Vietnam	815	858	906	960	1,021	1,085	1,152	1,223	1,298	1,379	1,465	6.04	79.77

Key economic trends

Table 4.78 Disposable income per household: 2009-2019

US$ per household, at constant 2010 prices

	2009	2010	2011	2012	2013	2014	2015	2016	2017	2018	2019	CAGR	Period growth
Algeria	11,967	12,117	12,200	12,386	12,630	12,862	12,973	13,207	13,420	13,599	13,696	1.36	14.45
Argentina	14,003	14,198	14,460	14,717	14,914	15,206	15,476	15,729	15,949	16,159	16,371	1.57	16.91
Australia	68,181	68,609	69,719	70,939	72,056	73,121	74,190	75,316	76,531	77,698	78,856	1.47	15.66
Austria	71,753	72,143	73,089	74,583	76,023	77,706	79,403	81,092	82,792	84,531	86,319	1.87	20.30
Azerbaijan	10,946	11,435	11,688	11,484	11,631	11,668	11,628	11,795	11,926	12,114	12,145	1.05	10.96
Belarus	6,834	7,129	7,651	8,206	8,854	9,571	10,337	11,195	12,134	13,199	14,394	7.73	110.61
Belgium	63,291	63,255	63,976	64,917	66,186	67,429	68,716	70,036	71,356	72,702	74,144	1.60	17.15
Bolivia	4,936	4,874	4,815	4,811	4,809	4,805	4,824	4,848	4,886	4,933	4,989	0.11	1.08
Bosnia-Herzegovina	12,100	12,001	12,235	12,814	13,447	13,910	14,384						
Brazil	19,121	19,644	20,126	20,637	21,177	21,734	22,306	22,871	23,462	24,045	24,618	2.56	28.75
Bulgaria	12,027	12,110	12,493	13,132	13,949	14,793	15,666	16,562	17,559	18,617	19,766	5.09	64.35
Canada	65,740	65,988	67,304	68,439	69,166	69,648	70,113	70,561	71,022	71,492	71,969	0.91	9.48
Chile	25,513	26,437	27,318	28,420	29,485	30,628	31,835	33,107	34,460	35,893	37,402	3.90	46.60
China	6,587	7,125	7,746	8,411	9,129	9,854	10,611	11,423	12,305	13,236	14,221	8.00	115.90
Colombia	13,374	13,255	13,289	13,477	13,673	13,827	14,014	14,210	14,425	14,668	14,939	1.11	11.70
Costa Rica	17,374	17,543	17,915	18,440	19,115	19,805	20,478						
Croatia	25,764	25,847	26,416	27,414	28,438	29,497	30,597	31,803	33,025	34,263	35,443	3.24	37.57
Czech Republic	24,445	24,670	25,276	26,258	27,295	28,414	29,588	30,790	32,021	33,357	34,708	3.57	41.98
Denmark	70,668	71,447	72,656	74,743	76,574	78,187	79,580	81,041	82,572	84,110	85,743	1.95	21.33
Ecuador	12,267	12,178	12,022	12,022	12,074	12,112	12,154	12,189	12,210	12,249	12,299	0.03	0.26
Egypt	8,551	8,700	8,876	9,103	9,379	9,665	9,959	10,247	10,558	10,884	11,217	2.75	31.18
Estonia	16,804	16,461	16,643	17,093	17,784	18,508	19,270	20,077	20,851	21,598	22,353	2.89	33.03
Finland	53,082	53,547	54,846	56,312	57,709	59,206	60,691	62,220	63,862	65,563	67,383	2.41	26.94
France	68,657	68,307	68,920	69,248	70,106	71,076	72,156	73,151	74,309	75,252	76,385	1.07	11.26
Germany	57,747	57,561	58,573	59,443	60,582	61,703	62,765	64,064	65,389	66,449	67,934	1.64	17.64
Greece	59,842	59,644	59,760	60,209	60,797	61,556	62,402	63,286	64,190	65,145	66,091	1.00	10.44
Hong Kong, China	74,859	75,636	77,286	79,908	81,580	83,917	86,543	89,507	91,895	94,611	97,941	2.72	30.83
Hungary	16,148	16,046	16,598	17,604	18,402	18,799	19,445	20,127	20,848	21,593	22,362	3.31	38.48
India	3,399	3,534	3,715	3,916	4,158	4,416	4,646	4,863	5,108	5,369	5,638	5.19	65.87
Indonesia	5,306	5,490	5,725	5,964	6,246	6,561	6,905	7,271	7,669	8,095	8,553	4.89	61.19
Iran	10,173	10,096	10,107	10,144	10,205	10,279	10,360						
Ireland	70,718	66,064	64,346	63,952	63,841	64,056	64,273	64,742	65,268	65,930	66,660	-0.59	-5.74
Israel	53,758	54,479	55,772	57,423	59,188	60,839	62,528	64,220	65,927	67,587	69,256	2.57	28.83
Italy	61,584	61,161	61,506	62,274	62,923	63,940	65,055	66,189	67,446	68,804	70,262	1.33	14.09
Japan	65,946	66,090	66,861	67,786	68,590	69,285	70,024	70,792	71,736	72,810	74,028	1.16	12.26
Jordan	15,717	15,752	15,810	16,065	16,480	16,917	17,350	17,764	18,168	18,568	18,961	1.89	20.64
Kazakhstan	10,675	10,678	11,125	11,588	12,136	12,860	13,712	14,575	15,625	16,662	17,921	5.32	67.88
Kuwait	146,555	150,069	154,316	159,088	163,907	168,234	173,197	177,685	182,771	188,247	194,118	2.85	32.45
Latvia	18,297	17,116	16,972	17,197	17,654	18,180	18,756	19,351	19,963	20,549	21,143	1.46	15.55
Lithuania	17,766	16,827	17,300	17,950	18,740	19,536	20,245	21,064	21,936	22,859	23,636	2.90	33.04
Malaysia	18,116	18,407	19,124	20,140	21,126	22,154	23,234	24,358	25,474	26,666	27,890	4.41	53.95
Mexico	22,899	23,060	23,888	24,721	25,607	26,503	27,266	28,029	28,689	29,356	30,028	2.75	31.13
Morocco	10,149	10,545	11,098	11,593	12,104	12,596	13,078	13,586	14,070	14,550	15,055	4.02	48.34
Netherlands	54,476	54,200	54,397	55,222	56,209	57,541	58,910	60,305	61,726	63,245	64,798	1.75	18.95
New Zealand	40,835	41,660	42,534	43,536	44,673	45,812	46,939	47,996	49,066	50,081	51,034	2.25	24.98
Nigeria	4,593	4,910	5,069	5,291	5,553	5,816	6,088	6,359	6,613	6,868	7,125	4.49	55.13
Norway	84,859	86,997	88,732	90,579	92,456	94,063	96,071	97,738	99,733	101,535	103,469	2.00	21.93
Pakistan	4,970	5,067	5,219	5,377	5,565	5,783	6,010	6,244	6,494	6,752	7,037	3.54	41.59
Peru	11,975	12,112	12,401	12,705	12,971	13,290	13,626	13,996	14,388	14,795	15,205	2.42	26.97
Philippines	6,365	6,437	6,568	6,742	6,913	7,092	7,268	7,443	7,625	7,812	8,008	2.32	25.82
Poland	19,185	19,548	20,241	20,923	21,676	22,443	23,237	24,032	24,843	25,636	26,435	3.26	37.79
Portugal	40,103	40,216	40,480	40,926	41,312	41,702	42,106	42,553	43,029	43,516	44,053	0.94	9.85
Romania	13,699	13,852	14,568	15,538	16,654	17,525	18,395	19,249	20,064	20,864	21,674	4.69	58.22
Russia	14,738	15,184	15,888	16,621	17,484	18,512	19,469	20,650	21,753	22,975	24,271	5.12	64.69
Saudi Arabia	33,400	34,601	35,573	36,681	38,016	39,059	40,345	41,750	43,216	44,654	46,346	3.33	38.76
Singapore	88,360	88,949	89,404	89,396	90,763	92,763	94,723	96,929	99,822	102,957	106,389	1.87	20.40
Slovakia	27,053	27,257	28,219	29,017	29,924	30,915	31,959	33,037	34,147	35,325	36,529	3.05	35.03
Slovenia	44,150	44,182	45,641	47,268	48,678	50,070	51,462	52,938	54,472	56,009	57,621	2.70	30.51
South Africa	11,950	12,100	12,404	12,811	13,182	13,545	13,897	14,234	14,555	14,873	15,192	2.43	27.13
South Korea	29,457	29,600	30,476	31,394	32,284	33,271	34,378	35,556	36,876	38,299	39,845	3.07	35.27
Spain	54,488	53,244	52,815	52,886	53,027	53,388	53,825	54,292	54,768	55,298	55,856	0.25	2.51
Sweden	45,783	46,300	47,362	48,642	50,149	51,886	53,653	55,483	57,393	59,445	61,628	3.02	34.61
Switzerland	89,673	90,851	92,749	94,440	96,073	97,628	99,087	100,569	102,117	103,742	105,470	1.64	17.62
Taiwan	34,546	34,781	35,945	37,501	38,805	40,356	42,013	43,617	45,304	47,023	48,847	3.52	41.40
Thailand	8,346	8,520	8,755	9,048	9,440	9,856	10,305	10,762	11,236	11,742	12,259	3.92	46.89
Tunisia	10,175	10,288	10,506	10,821	11,176	11,580	12,011	12,448	12,901	13,375	13,858	3.14	36.20
Turkey	23,761	23,966	24,446	24,860	25,226	25,640	26,109	26,604	27,123	27,636	28,140	1.71	18.43
Turkmenistan	8,578	9,605	10,096	10,754	11,313	11,924	12,633	13,374	14,160	14,987	15,790	6.29	84.07
Ukraine	3,532	3,599	3,804	4,012	4,256	4,542	4,849	5,188	5,553	5,945	6,364	6.07	80.21
United Arab Emirates	206,794	211,120	216,159	223,244	230,934	238,432	245,712	254,088	263,419	272,804	282,685	3.18	36.70
United Kingdom	56,161	55,774	56,458	57,378	58,413	59,551	60,655	61,861	63,101	64,442	65,854	1.60	17.26
USA	87,747	88,328	89,651	91,074	92,360	93,347	94,130	94,800	95,440	96,168	96,940	1.00	10.48
Venezuela	42,607	41,813	41,414	40,972	40,560	39,834	39,198	38,541	37,910	37,345	36,758	-1.47	-13.73
Vietnam	3,605	3,779	3,975	4,195	4,441	4,699	4,969	5,252	5,551	5,871	6,211	5.59	72.30

Marketing segments: Young generation

Table 4.79 Babies (under 12 months): 2009-2019

'000

	2009	2010	2011	2012	2013	2014	2015	2016	2017	2018	2019	CAGR	Period growth
Algeria	704.8	698.2	698.9	704.5	712.7	720.0	723.9	723.9	721.2	715.9	708.7	0.06	0.55
Argentina	706.6	712.6	712.0	705.8	696.4	687.0	680.0	676.2	674.5	674.3	673.8	-0.47	-4.64
Australia	295.6	299.4	299.4	302.1	304.4	306.8	309.4	312.0	314.6	317.3	320.0	0.80	8.25
Austria	77.9	77.8	77.8	77.9	78.1	78.4	78.6	78.7	78.8	78.9	78.8	0.12	1.22
Azerbaijan	167.7	167.6	166.2	167.4	167.5	166.8	165.6	163.7	161.3	158.4	155.1	-0.78	-7.50
Belarus	107.3	108.2	105.2	104.8	104.2	103.0	101.7	100.4	98.9	97.4	95.8	-1.12	-10.66
Belgium	123.4	124.0	124.1	124.0	123.8	123.4	123.0	122.7	122.3	121.9	121.5	-0.15	-1.53
Bolivia	249.6	247.5	246.9	247.5	248.6	249.6	249.8	249.2	248.0	246.3	244.5	-0.20	-2.03
Bosnia-Herzegovina	35.7	37.4	37.8	37.1	35.8	34.5	33.5	32.9	32.6	32.5	32.3	-0.99	-9.48
Brazil	3,035.2	2,952.9	2,875.5	2,804.8	2,744.3	2,693.2	2,650.9	2,618.5	2,593.8	2,573.8	2,556.3	-1.70	-15.78
Bulgaria	66.8	66.2	65.5	64.7	63.7	62.7	61.4	60.0	58.5	57.0	55.3	-1.87	-17.18
Canada	363.1	362.5	356.9	356.7	361.9	366.3	370.7	375.0	379.1	383.0	386.6	0.63	6.47
Chile	256.8	256.5	255.8	254.5	252.9	251.2	249.8	248.7	247.8	247.2	246.9	-0.39	-3.86
China	14,041.1	13,955.5	13,692.4	13,649.7	13,694.1	13,705.3	13,686.9	13,621.6	13,508.8	13,353.0	13,162.7	-0.64	-6.26
Colombia	913.5	912.0	907.0	899.1	889.9	881.9	876.8	875.3	876.7	879.5	881.7	-0.35	-3.48
Costa Rica	70.6	70.5	72.1	75.1	78.5	81.2	82.3	81.4	79.0	75.8	72.9	0.32	3.27
Croatia	43.0	43.2	43.3	43.5	43.5	43.6	43.5	43.4	43.2	43.0	42.7	-0.06	-0.57
Czech Republic	103.5	103.6	103.6	103.6	103.5	103.3	103.0	102.5	101.8	100.8	99.7	-0.38	-3.73
Denmark	65.3	64.1	63.1	62.4	61.9	61.6	61.5	61.7	62.0	62.5	63.2	-0.33	-3.29
Ecuador	272.9	272.5	272.0	271.5	270.9	270.4	269.8	269.3	268.6	267.8	266.8	-0.22	-2.22
Egypt	1,769.5	1,785.3	1,798.3	1,809.4	1,818.1	1,824.2	1,827.4	1,827.4	1,824.7	1,820.9	1,818.7	0.27	2.78
Estonia	14.8	15.0	15.1	15.3	15.3	15.4	15.3	15.3	15.2	15.0	14.7	-0.10	-1.00
Finland	59.4	59.6	59.9	60.2	60.4	60.7	60.9	61.1	61.2	61.2	61.2	0.31	3.09
France	797.5	799.4	783.1	780.9	779.1	777.6	776.2	774.8	773.5	772.0	770.3	-0.35	-3.41
Germany	683.0	666.0	624.1	605.7	599.9	599.3	599.7	600.4	601.4	602.2	602.6	-1.24	-11.77
Greece	109.3	109.3	109.0	108.3	107.4	106.3	105.1	103.6	102.1	100.5	98.9	-1.00	-9.55
Hong Kong, China	42.7	42.7	43.0	43.5	44.4	45.3	46.4	47.6	48.1	48.5	48.7	1.33	14.16
Hungary	97.4	96.7	96.1	95.5	95.0	94.6	94.3	94.1	93.8	93.5	93.1	-0.45	-4.40
India	24,607.3	24,418.3	24,347.5	24,365.8	24,424.1	24,449.6	24,390.9	24,232.4	23,994.5	23,705.6	23,408.7	-0.50	-4.87
Indonesia	4,044.8	3,977.5	3,932.5	3,905.1	3,887.0	3,865.6	3,832.3	3,783.9	3,725.1	3,665.3	3,617.7	-1.11	-10.56
Iran	1,352.3	1,322.9	1,307.8	1,302.6	1,304.0	1,306.4	1,305.6	1,301.8	1,296.4	1,287.1	1,271.3	-0.62	-5.99
Ireland	62.7	62.6	62.3	61.9	61.3	60.6	59.8	58.9	57.9	56.9	56.0	-1.13	-10.71
Israel	141.8	141.3	140.6	139.9	139.2	138.6	138.1	137.8	137.7	137.7	137.8	-0.29	-2.82
Italy	530.3	522.2	513.4	504.2	494.9	485.7	476.8	468.3	460.2	452.9	446.6	-1.70	-15.78
Japan	1,114.5	1,058.5	1,029.6	1,003.0	978.8	956.8	936.9	918.9	902.5	887.3	873.2	-2.41	-21.65
Jordan	161.3	164.3	164.3	161.9	158.1	154.0	150.7	148.5	147.0	146.2	145.6	-1.02	-9.74
Kazakhstan	354.2	358.9	354.9	358.2	360.8	360.4	356.3	352.1	347.7	342.8	337.4	-0.49	-4.75
Kuwait	43.5	44.1	44.1	43.4	42.5	41.6	41.0	40.7	40.8	41.0	41.3	-0.51	-5.03
Latvia	22.8	23.1	23.4	23.5	23.6	23.6	23.5	23.3	23.0	22.5	22.0	-0.34	-3.34
Lithuania	30.7	31.0	31.2	31.4	31.5	31.7	31.8	31.8	31.8	31.7	31.4	0.22	2.26
Malaysia	620.6	615.3	615.5	619.8	626.5	632.3	635.2	634.5	631.3	626.4	621.1	0.01	0.07
Mexico	2,220.1	2,202.5	2,147.0	2,136.5	2,135.2	2,130.5	2,121.1	2,108.6	2,094.0	2,080.2	2,067.9	-0.71	-6.86
Morocco	649.8	657.9	659.8	656.3	649.4	641.9	635.8	631.6	628.8	626.4	623.4	-0.41	-4.06
Netherlands	178.9	177.0	175.6	174.7	174.3	174.2	174.5	175.0	175.8	176.7	177.8	-0.06	-0.57
New Zealand	64.3	63.9	63.2	62.7	62.2	61.8	61.5	61.2	61.1	61.0	60.9	-0.54	-5.28
Nigeria	5,468.3	5,518.2	5,545.8	5,553.7	5,547.9	5,536.9	5,527.0	5,520.5	5,516.2	5,513.1	5,509.4	0.07	0.75
Norway	60.7	61.1	61.2	61.3	61.4	62.1	62.8	63.5	64.3	65.0	65.8	0.81	8.40
Pakistan	5,040.3	5,107.6	5,177.0	5,247.3	5,310.5	5,356.3	5,378.2	5,372.4	5,342.9	5,300.7	5,261.2	0.43	4.38
Peru	595.4	592.7	588.1	581.8	574.9	568.8	564.6	562.7	562.7	563.8	564.7	-0.53	-5.15
Philippines	2,256.2	2,231.1	2,247.7	2,268.6	2,292.7	2,313.9	2,335.6	2,358.1	2,381.2	2,404.4	2,427.0	0.73	7.57
Poland	366.2	369.7	373.5	377.3	380.3	382.5	384.2	385.1	385.2	384.6	383.0	0.45	4.59
Portugal	109.1	108.5	107.5	106.3	104.8	103.1	101.4	99.7	98.0	96.3	94.8	-1.40	-13.18
Romania	218.5	217.2	215.5	213.6	211.5	209.3	206.6	203.5	199.6	195.0	189.8	-1.40	-13.13
Russia	1,702.2	1,746.2	1,668.9	1,684.8	1,715.6	1,727.5	1,718.3	1,703.1	1,681.0	1,653.9	1,622.4	-0.48	-4.69
Saudi Arabia	571.1	570.3	575.5	585.4	597.6	608.7	616.0	618.9	618.2	615.0	611.4	0.68	7.05
Singapore	46.2	46.8	47.3	47.9	48.5	49.1	49.8	50.5	51.2	51.9	52.6	1.31	13.88
Slovakia	53.9	54.0	54.0	54.1	54.1	54.1	54.0	54.0	53.8	53.6	53.3	-0.11	-1.08
Slovenia	18.8	19.1	19.3	19.5	19.6	19.7	19.7	19.6	19.5	19.3	19.1	0.14	1.44
South Africa	1,018.4	1,009.4	1,009.5	1,017.0	1,027.5	1,035.1	1,035.4	1,027.0	1,011.7	992.9	975.6	-0.43	-4.20
South Korea	443.0	438.2	432.2	425.5	418.2	410.8	403.5	396.4	390.1	385.2	382.7	-1.45	-13.62
Spain	488.1	491.9	493.6	493.5	491.9	488.9	484.9	480.2	475.2	464.8	455.1	-0.70	-6.75
Sweden	103.5	104.2	104.4	104.8	105.5	106.3	107.2	108.2	109.2	110.2	111.0	0.71	7.30
Switzerland	72.3	72.3	72.6	72.9	73.5	74.2	75.2	76.4	77.7	79.1	80.4	1.06	11.07
Taiwan	191.8	192.5	191.2	190.0	187.8	186.6	183.5	182.5	180.4	178.4	176.3	-0.84	-8.06
Thailand	788.3	783.7	773.6	759.4	743.2	728.5	717.4	711.1	708.3	707.8	707.3	-1.08	-10.27
Tunisia	164.4	165.3	166.2	167.0	167.6	167.9	167.8	167.1	166.0	164.7	163.5	-0.06	-0.56
Turkey	1,303.0	1,304.2	1,303.7	1,301.4	1,297.7	1,293.2	1,288.3	1,283.7	1,279.2	1,275.1	1,271.2	-0.25	-2.44
Turkmenistan	103.6	100.7	100.2	101.5	103.8	105.8	106.8	106.6	105.4	103.5	101.4	-0.21	-2.13
Ukraine	451.7	445.6	436.7	424.5	411.1	398.1	387.8	381.3	377.9	376.5	374.2	-1.86	-17.15
United Arab Emirates	57.8	57.4	58.6	61.0	63.8	66.1	66.9	66.1	64.0	61.2	58.7	0.15	1.49
United Kingdom	794.8	802.4	782.0	786.8	792.7	799.6	807.0	814.5	821.6	828.0	833.1	0.47	4.82
USA	4,305.4	4,273.4	4,180.3	4,168.6	4,195.3	4,217.9	4,237.9	4,255.3	4,271.1	4,285.8	4,299.3	-0.01	-0.14
Venezuela	590.4	591.0	591.1	590.7	589.9	588.8	587.6	586.1	584.5	582.8	581.0	-0.16	-1.59
Vietnam	1,562.9	1,514.1	1,499.2	1,509.8	1,535.5	1,560.2	1,572.3	1,568.8	1,554.2	1,533.0	1,512.2	-0.33	-3.24

Marketing segments: Young generation

Table 4.80 Babies (under 12 months): 2009-2019 (%)

% of total

	2009	2010	2011	2012	2013	2014	2015	2016	2017	2018	2019
Algeria	2.02	1.97	1.94	1.93	1.92	1.92	1.90	1.87	1.84	1.81	1.77
Argentina	1.75	1.75	1.73	1.70	1.66	1.62	1.59	1.57	1.55	1.54	1.53
Australia	1.36	1.35	1.34	1.33	1.32	1.32	1.31	1.30	1.30	1.29	1.28
Austria	0.93	0.92	0.92	0.92	0.92	0.92	0.92	0.92	0.92	0.92	0.91
Azerbaijan	1.92	1.90	1.86	1.86	1.84	1.81	1.78	1.75	1.70	1.66	1.61
Belarus	1.11	1.12	1.09	1.09	1.09	1.08	1.07	1.06	1.05	1.03	1.02
Belgium	1.16	1.16	1.16	1.15	1.15	1.14	1.13	1.12	1.12	1.11	1.10
Bolivia	2.53	2.47	2.42	2.39	2.36	2.33	2.30	2.26	2.22	2.17	2.13
Bosnia-Herzegovina	0.93	0.97	0.98	0.97	0.93	0.90	0.87	0.86	0.85	0.85	0.85
Brazil	1.57	1.51	1.46	1.41	1.37	1.34	1.31	1.28	1.26	1.24	1.23
Bulgaria	0.89	0.89	0.88	0.88	0.87	0.86	0.85	0.84	0.83	0.81	0.80
Canada	1.08	1.07	1.04	1.03	1.04	1.05	1.05	1.05	1.06	1.06	1.06
Chile	1.51	1.50	1.48	1.46	1.44	1.41	1.39	1.38	1.36	1.35	1.33
China	1.06	1.05	1.02	1.01	1.01	1.01	1.01	1.00	0.98	0.97	0.95
Colombia	2.00	1.97	1.93	1.89	1.85	1.81	1.78	1.75	1.73	1.72	1.70
Costa Rica	1.54	1.52	1.53	1.58	1.63	1.66	1.66	1.62	1.56	1.48	1.40
Croatia	0.97	0.98	0.98	0.99	0.99	0.99	0.99	0.99	0.99	0.99	0.99
Czech Republic	1.00	1.00	1.00	1.00	1.00	1.00	0.99	0.99	0.98	0.97	0.96
Denmark	1.18	1.16	1.14	1.12	1.11	1.10	1.10	1.10	1.10	1.11	1.11
Ecuador	2.00	1.98	1.95	1.93	1.90	1.87	1.85	1.82	1.80	1.78	1.75
Egypt	2.31	2.28	2.26	2.23	2.21	2.18	2.15	2.11	2.08	2.04	2.01
Estonia	1.12	1.13	1.15	1.16	1.17	1.17	1.18	1.18	1.17	1.16	1.14
Finland	1.12	1.11	1.12	1.12	1.12	1.12	1.12	1.12	1.12	1.11	1.11
France	1.28	1.27	1.24	1.23	1.22	1.22	1.21	1.20	1.20	1.19	1.18
Germany	0.83	0.81	0.77	0.75	0.74	0.74	0.75	0.75	0.75	0.76	0.76
Greece	0.97	0.97	0.96	0.95	0.94	0.93	0.92	0.90	0.89	0.87	0.86
Hong Kong, China	0.60	0.60	0.60	0.60	0.61	0.61	0.62	0.63	0.64	0.64	0.63
Hungary	0.97	0.97	0.96	0.96	0.96	0.96	0.96	0.96	0.96	0.95	0.95
India	2.11	2.06	2.03	2.00	1.98	1.96	1.93	1.90	1.86	1.81	1.77
Indonesia	1.76	1.71	1.67	1.64	1.62	1.60	1.57	1.54	1.50	1.46	1.43
Iran	1.82	1.76	1.72	1.70	1.68	1.66	1.64	1.62	1.60	1.57	1.53
Ireland	1.41	1.39	1.37	1.34	1.31	1.29	1.25	1.22	1.19	1.16	1.13
Israel	1.92	1.88	1.84	1.81	1.77	1.74	1.71	1.69	1.67	1.65	1.63
Italy	0.90	0.88	0.87	0.85	0.84	0.82	0.81	0.79	0.78	0.77	0.76
Japan	0.87	0.83	0.81	0.79	0.77	0.76	0.74	0.73	0.72	0.71	0.70
Jordan	2.55	2.54	2.49	2.42	2.33	2.24	2.17	2.10	2.05	2.01	1.97
Kazakhstan	2.25	2.25	2.19	2.19	2.18	2.15	2.10	2.05	2.00	1.96	1.91
Kuwait	1.78	1.77	1.73	1.67	1.60	1.53	1.48	1.44	1.42	1.40	1.39
Latvia	1.01	1.03	1.05	1.06	1.07	1.08	1.08	1.08	1.07	1.06	1.04
Lithuania	0.92	0.93	0.94	0.95	0.96	0.97	0.98	0.99	0.99	1.00	0.99
Malaysia	2.21	2.16	2.12	2.11	2.10	2.09	2.07	2.04	2.00	1.96	1.92
Mexico	2.04	2.00	1.92	1.89	1.86	1.83	1.80	1.77	1.74	1.71	1.68
Morocco	2.03	2.03	2.01	1.98	1.94	1.89	1.85	1.82	1.79	1.77	1.74
Netherlands	1.09	1.08	1.07	1.06	1.05	1.05	1.05	1.05	1.06	1.06	1.06
New Zealand	1.49	1.47	1.44	1.41	1.39	1.37	1.35	1.33	1.32	1.31	1.30
Nigeria	3.53	3.49	3.43	3.36	3.29	3.21	3.14	3.08	3.02	2.96	2.90
Norway	1.26	1.26	1.24	1.23	1.23	1.23	1.23	1.23	1.23	1.24	1.24
Pakistan	2.79	2.76	2.74	2.72	2.69	2.66	2.62	2.56	2.50	2.43	2.37
Peru	2.05	2.02	1.97	1.93	1.88	1.84	1.80	1.77	1.75	1.74	1.72
Philippines	2.45	2.38	2.35	2.33	2.31	2.29	2.27	2.25	2.23	2.22	2.20
Poland	0.96	0.97	0.99	1.00	1.01	1.01	1.02	1.02	1.03	1.03	1.02
Portugal	1.02	1.01	1.00	0.99	0.97	0.96	0.94	0.92	0.91	0.89	0.88
Romania	1.02	1.02	1.01	1.01	1.00	0.99	0.99	0.98	0.96	0.95	0.93
Russia	1.20	1.23	1.18	1.19	1.22	1.23	1.22	1.21	1.20	1.18	1.16
Saudi Arabia	2.22	2.17	2.15	2.14	2.15	2.14	2.13	2.10	2.06	2.01	1.97
Singapore	0.98	0.98	0.98	0.98	0.98	0.98	0.98	0.99	0.99	1.00	1.01
Slovakia	1.00	1.00	1.00	1.00	1.00	1.00	1.00	1.00	1.00	0.99	0.99
Slovenia	0.93	0.94	0.95	0.96	0.96	0.96	0.96	0.96	0.95	0.94	0.93
South Africa	2.03	2.00	1.99	1.99	2.00	2.01	2.00	1.98	1.94	1.90	1.86
South Korea	0.91	0.90	0.88	0.87	0.85	0.83	0.82	0.80	0.79	0.78	0.78
Spain	1.07	1.07	1.07	1.06	1.05	1.03	1.02	1.00	0.98	0.95	0.93
Sweden	1.12	1.13	1.12	1.12	1.13	1.13	1.13	1.14	1.14	1.15	1.15
Switzerland	0.96	0.95	0.95	0.95	0.96	0.96	0.97	0.98	1.00	1.01	1.02
Taiwan	0.83	0.83	0.83	0.82	0.81	0.80	0.79	0.78	0.77	0.76	0.75
Thailand	1.22	1.20	1.18	1.15	1.12	1.10	1.07	1.06	1.05	1.05	1.04
Tunisia	1.60	1.59	1.59	1.58	1.57	1.56	1.54	1.52	1.50	1.47	1.45
Turkey	1.73	1.71	1.69	1.67	1.65	1.62	1.60	1.58	1.56	1.54	1.52
Turkmenistan	2.03	1.95	1.91	1.91	1.93	1.94	1.94	1.91	1.87	1.82	1.76
Ukraine	0.98	0.98	0.96	0.94	0.92	0.89	0.88	0.87	0.87	0.87	0.87
United Arab Emirates	1.25	1.21	1.21	1.24	1.27	1.29	1.28	1.25	1.18	1.11	1.05
United Kingdom	1.29	1.29	1.26	1.26	1.26	1.26	1.27	1.27	1.27	1.28	1.28
USA	1.40	1.38	1.34	1.33	1.33	1.33	1.33	1.32	1.32	1.32	1.31
Venezuela	2.07	2.03	2.00	1.97	1.94	1.91	1.88	1.85	1.82	1.79	1.76
Vietnam	1.78	1.71	1.67	1.66	1.67	1.67	1.67	1.64	1.61	1.57	1.53

Marketing segments: Young generation

Table 4.81 Infants (under 24 months): 2009-2019

'000

	2009	2010	2011	2012	2013	2014	2015	2016	2017	2018	2019	CAGR	Period growth
Algeria	1,408.2	1,400.7	1,402.6	1,411.9	1,425.5	1,438.6	1,447.1	1,449.2	1,445.8	1,437.6	1,425.2	0.12	1.21
Argentina	1,396.6	1,410.1	1,413.7	1,408.1	1,395.9	1,381.7	1,369.5	1,361.2	1,356.3	1,353.6	1,351.4	-0.33	-3.24
Australia	584.8	596.1	599.7	602.6	607.8	612.6	617.6	622.8	628.1	633.4	638.7	0.89	9.21
Austria	156.6	156.2	156.2	156.3	156.7	157.1	157.5	157.8	158.1	158.2	158.2	0.10	1.04
Azerbaijan	328.9	332.4	333.0	334.5	333.4	330.4	326.5	321.9	316.9	311.6	305.9	-0.72	-7.00
Belarus	210.4	215.5	213.5	210.1	209.1	207.2	204.7	202.1	199.3	196.4	193.3	-0.84	-8.12
Belgium	246.3	248.0	248.7	248.7	248.4	247.7	247.0	246.2	245.6	244.8	244.0	-0.09	-0.93
Bolivia	500.7	496.9	495.1	495.1	496.3	497.6	498.0	497.1	495.2	492.4	489.4	-0.23	-2.26
Bosnia-Herzegovina	69.3	72.4	73.6	73.1	71.5	69.5	67.8	66.6	65.9	65.5	65.1	-0.63	-6.08
Brazil	6,149.6	5,978.3	5,819.6	5,672.2	5,541.7	5,430.7	5,337.8	5,263.5	5,206.8	5,162.3	5,124.9	-1.81	-16.66
Bulgaria	133.5	132.4	131.1	129.7	127.7	125.6	123.2	120.6	117.7	114.6	111.4	-1.79	-16.53
Canada	726.2	729.7	723.2	717.2	722.1	731.8	740.7	749.4	757.9	765.9	773.5	0.63	6.52
Chile	509.4	509.9	509.6	508.4	506.4	504.0	501.7	499.7	497.9	496.5	495.5	-0.28	-2.73
China	26,820.6	26,837.1	26,507.7	26,231.7	26,260.3	26,325.6	26,341.4	26,275.6	26,120.4	25,877.1	25,557.6	-0.48	-4.71
Colombia	1,819.5	1,818.8	1,812.5	1,800.9	1,786.4	1,772.4	1,762.0	1,756.7	1,756.1	1,758.5	1,760.9	-0.33	-3.22
Costa Rica	143.7	142.9	144.7	148.9	154.2	159.0	161.6	161.3	158.3	153.7	149.0	0.37	3.71
Croatia	85.8	86.2	86.6	86.8	87.0	87.1	87.1	86.9	86.6	86.2	85.8	0.00	-0.05
Czech Republic	207.1	207.4	207.5	207.4	207.2	206.9	206.4	205.6	204.4	202.8	200.6	-0.32	-3.14
Denmark	130.2	129.6	127.5	125.9	124.6	123.8	123.4	123.5	124.0	124.8	126.0	-0.33	-3.24
Ecuador	546.3	544.8	543.4	542.1	540.9	539.7	538.6	537.5	536.4	535.0	533.3	-0.24	-2.38
Egypt	3,548.1	3,583.0	3,612.1	3,636.3	3,656.3	3,671.2	3,680.5	3,683.8	3,681.0	3,674.5	3,668.5	0.33	3.39
Estonia	29.5	29.8	30.1	30.4	30.5	30.6	30.7	30.6	30.4	30.1	29.6	0.05	0.48
Finland	118.4	119.2	119.7	120.3	120.8	121.4	121.8	122.2	122.5	122.6	122.6	0.35	3.55
France	1,581.3	1,598.0	1,583.4	1,565.0	1,561.1	1,557.8	1,554.9	1,552.2	1,549.5	1,546.7	1,543.6	-0.24	-2.39
Germany	1,368.3	1,348.5	1,289.8	1,230.0	1,206.1	1,199.8	1,199.6	1,200.7	1,202.5	1,204.4	1,205.6	-1.26	-11.89
Greece	218.6	218.9	218.5	217.5	216.0	214.0	211.7	209.0	206.0	202.8	199.6	-0.90	-8.67
Hong Kong, China	86.0	85.9	86.2	87.1	88.4	90.1	92.2	94.4	96.9	97.7	98.3	1.34	14.28
Hungary	196.2	195.0	193.8	192.5	191.4	190.5	189.7	189.2	188.6	188.1	187.4	-0.46	-4.48
India	49,320.2	48,948.7	48,746.0	48,692.0	48,720.1	48,728.3	48,627.2	48,375.6	47,986.4	47,497.6	46,967.7	-0.49	-4.77
Indonesia	8,173.7	8,045.4	7,946.0	7,873.5	7,817.9	7,762.6	7,692.8	7,601.3	7,492.8	7,380.5	7,284.2	-1.15	-10.88
Iran	2,722.7	2,682.6	2,656.8	2,643.7	2,639.7	2,638.7	2,634.2	2,624.5	2,610.6	2,590.4	2,559.3	-0.62	-6.00
Ireland	125.4	125.5	125.1	124.3	123.3	122.0	120.5	118.8	116.9	114.9	113.0	-1.04	-9.92
Israel	284.5	283.5	282.3	280.9	279.5	278.2	277.1	276.3	275.9	275.8	275.8	-0.31	-3.06
Italy	1,068.7	1,053.4	1,036.5	1,018.5	1,000.1	981.6	963.5	946.0	929.4	914.1	900.5	-1.70	-15.74
Japan	2,210.4	2,167.4	2,083.0	2,028.0	1,977.4	1,931.4	1,889.7	1,852.0	1,817.7	1,786.2	1,757.0	-2.27	-20.51
Jordan	317.0	323.4	325.2	322.8	317.3	310.8	305.0	300.5	297.2	294.8	293.1	-0.78	-7.52
Kazakhstan	664.2	675.8	673.7	673.7	668.8	659.2	646.4	635.8	628.0	622.3	617.5	-0.73	-7.04
Kuwait	85.9	87.3	87.7	87.1	85.8	84.4	83.2	82.6	82.4	82.6	82.9	-0.35	-3.42
Latvia	45.1	45.8	46.4	46.9	47.1	47.2	47.2	46.8	46.3	45.5	44.5	-0.13	-1.34
Lithuania	61.2	61.6	62.1	62.5	62.8	63.1	63.4	63.6	63.6	63.4	63.0	0.29	2.94
Malaysia	1,246.5	1,231.0	1,225.5	1,229.8	1,240.8	1,253.1	1,261.6	1,263.8	1,259.8	1,251.7	1,241.4	-0.04	-0.41
Mexico	4,225.7	4,183.6	4,106.1	4,074.9	4,054.1	4,031.2	4,003.7	3,972.4	3,938.1	3,904.8	3,875.0	-0.86	-8.30
Morocco	1,277.8	1,295.9	1,304.7	1,304.5	1,297.6	1,287.6	1,278.0	1,270.3	1,264.1	1,258.5	1,252.0	-0.20	-2.01
Netherlands	360.5	356.2	353.0	350.8	349.6	349.0	349.2	350.0	351.2	353.0	355.0	-0.15	-1.52
New Zealand	128.4	128.2	127.2	126.0	124.9	124.1	123.3	122.8	122.4	122.1	121.9	-0.51	-5.02
Nigeria	10,742.5	10,857.6	10,934.6	10,975.3	10,987.4	10,983.2	10,973.9	10,965.0	10,957.0	10,949.6	10,941.0	0.18	1.85
Norway	120.1	122.9	123.3	123.4	123.6	124.4	125.7	127.2	128.7	130.2	131.7	0.92	9.58
Pakistan	9,971.5	10,108.5	10,248.3	10,388.6	10,518.1	10,620.5	10,683.1	10,698.8	10,671.3	10,615.0	10,552.6	0.57	5.83
Peru	1,188.4	1,184.5	1,177.4	1,167.2	1,155.3	1,144.1	1,135.2	1,129.7	1,127.4	1,127.3	1,127.7	-0.52	-5.11
Philippines	4,449.1	4,448.8	4,480.6	4,507.1	4,529.1	4,545.2	4,563.5	4,587.6	4,618.3	4,653.9	4,691.2	0.53	5.44
Poland	729.2	735.2	742.6	750.4	757.1	762.4	766.3	768.9	769.9	769.4	767.1	0.51	5.21
Portugal	218.5	217.5	215.9	213.7	211.0	207.9	204.5	201.1	197.6	194.2	191.0	-1.34	-12.58
Romania	437.0	435.1	432.0	428.5	424.3	420.0	414.9	409.1	402.1	393.7	383.9	-1.29	-12.16
Russia	3,303.4	3,450.7	3,415.6	3,355.0	3,401.5	3,444.9	3,447.3	3,423.1	3,385.7	3,336.5	3,278.2	-0.08	-0.76
Saudi Arabia	1,147.6	1,145.2	1,151.7	1,166.2	1,185.6	1,204.9	1,219.6	1,227.9	1,230.1	1,227.8	1,223.4	0.64	6.61
Singapore	93.5	94.5	95.5	96.5	97.6	98.8	100.0	101.4	102.7	104.0	105.5	1.21	12.77
Slovakia	107.8	107.8	107.9	108.0	108.1	108.1	108.1	107.9	107.7	107.4	106.9	-0.08	-0.84
Slovenia	37.5	38.0	38.5	38.9	39.2	39.4	39.4	39.4	39.2	38.9	38.4	0.26	2.62
South Africa	2,053.7	2,035.0	2,029.3	2,035.7	2,048.5	2,059.3	2,060.8	2,049.4	2,026.3	1,996.0	1,965.6	-0.44	-4.29
South Korea	886.5	878.0	867.2	854.5	840.6	825.9	811.3	797.1	783.7	772.5	765.1	-1.46	-13.70
Spain	978.6	985.7	990.8	992.2	990.3	985.5	978.3	969.4	959.5	943.9	923.6	-0.58	-5.62
Sweden	207.1	208.4	209.4	210.0	211.2	212.6	214.3	216.2	218.2	220.1	221.9	0.69	7.12
Switzerland	145.0	144.8	145.0	145.6	146.5	147.8	149.5	151.7	154.1	156.8	159.5	0.95	9.95
Taiwan	396.0	396.4	395.8	393.3	389.8	386.3	381.9	377.7	374.5	370.2	365.9	-0.79	-7.59
Thailand	1,598.1	1,593.3	1,578.5	1,554.5	1,524.1	1,493.4	1,467.5	1,450.3	1,441.0	1,437.8	1,436.9	-1.06	-10.09
Tunisia	325.7	328.0	330.4	332.5	334.3	335.4	335.7	335.1	333.5	331.4	329.2	0.11	1.07
Turkey	2,585.7	2,587.3	2,596.3	2,583.1	2,581.4	2,577.5	2,576.4	2,569.7	2,560.6	2,555.0	2,548.1	-0.15	-1.46
Turkmenistan	210.1	205.0	203.1	204.2	207.2	210.3	212.3	212.3	210.7	207.8	204.2	-0.28	-2.80
Ukraine	905.5	895.8	880.9	859.7	834.1	807.2	784.1	767.5	757.7	753.2	749.4	-1.87	-17.24
United Arab Emirates	118.9	117.8	119.0	122.3	126.6	130.4	132.5	132.0	129.2	125.1	120.9	0.17	1.72
United Kingdom	1,566.3	1,596.2	1,583.0	1,567.8	1,578.9	1,592.1	1,606.4	1,621.3	1,636.0	1,649.5	1,661.0	0.59	6.05
USA	8,629.0	8,585.9	8,459.4	8,355.1	8,370.3	8,419.1	8,461.9	8,499.0	8,532.0	8,562.6	8,590.5	-0.04	-0.45
Venezuela	1,178.7	1,180.8	1,181.8	1,181.7	1,180.7	1,179.1	1,176.9	1,174.2	1,171.1	1,167.7	1,164.1	-0.12	-1.24
Vietnam	3,141.9	3,076.8	3,056.6	3,069.5	3,101.6	3,131.4	3,143.3	3,133.6	3,108.3	3,073.6	3,039.1	-0.33	-3.27

Marketing segments: Young generation

Table 4.82 Infants (under 24 months): 2009-2019 (%)

% of total

	2009	2010	2011	2012	2013	2014	2015	2016	2017	2018	2019
Algeria	4.04	3.95	3.90	3.87	3.85	3.83	3.80	3.75	3.69	3.63	3.55
Argentina	3.46	3.46	3.44	3.39	3.33	3.27	3.21	3.16	3.12	3.09	3.06
Australia	2.68	2.70	2.68	2.66	2.64	2.63	2.61	2.60	2.59	2.57	2.56
Austria	1.87	1.86	1.85	1.85	1.85	1.85	1.85	1.85	1.84	1.84	1.84
Azerbaijan	3.77	3.76	3.73	3.71	3.66	3.59	3.51	3.43	3.35	3.26	3.18
Belarus	2.18	2.23	2.22	2.19	2.18	2.17	2.15	2.13	2.11	2.08	2.06
Belgium	2.31	2.32	2.32	2.31	2.30	2.28	2.27	2.26	2.24	2.23	2.22
Bolivia	5.08	4.95	4.85	4.78	4.71	4.65	4.59	4.51	4.43	4.35	4.26
Bosnia-Herzegovina	1.80	1.88	1.91	1.90	1.86	1.81	1.77	1.74	1.72	1.71	1.71
Brazil	3.17	3.06	2.95	2.86	2.77	2.70	2.63	2.58	2.53	2.50	2.46
Bulgaria	1.77	1.77	1.77	1.76	1.75	1.73	1.71	1.69	1.66	1.64	1.60
Canada	2.16	2.15	2.11	2.08	2.08	2.09	2.10	2.11	2.12	2.12	2.13
Chile	3.00	2.98	2.95	2.91	2.87	2.84	2.80	2.76	2.73	2.70	2.68
China	2.02	2.01	1.98	1.95	1.94	1.94	1.93	1.92	1.90	1.88	1.85
Colombia	3.98	3.93	3.86	3.79	3.71	3.63	3.57	3.51	3.47	3.44	3.40
Costa Rica	3.14	3.08	3.08	3.12	3.19	3.25	3.26	3.21	3.12	2.99	2.87
Croatia	1.94	1.95	1.96	1.97	1.98	1.99	1.99	1.99	1.99	1.99	1.98
Czech Republic	2.00	2.00	2.00	2.00	2.00	2.00	1.99	1.99	1.97	1.96	1.94
Denmark	2.36	2.35	2.30	2.26	2.24	2.22	2.20	2.20	2.20	2.21	2.22
Ecuador	4.01	3.96	3.90	3.85	3.79	3.74	3.69	3.64	3.60	3.55	3.50
Egypt	4.62	4.58	4.54	4.49	4.44	4.38	4.32	4.26	4.19	4.12	4.05
Estonia	2.22	2.25	2.28	2.31	2.33	2.35	2.36	2.36	2.35	2.33	2.31
Finland	2.22	2.23	2.23	2.23	2.23	2.24	2.24	2.24	2.24	2.23	2.23
France	2.53	2.55	2.51	2.47	2.45	2.44	2.42	2.41	2.40	2.38	2.37
Germany	1.67	1.65	1.58	1.52	1.49	1.49	1.49	1.50	1.51	1.51	1.52
Greece	1.94	1.94	1.93	1.92	1.90	1.88	1.85	1.82	1.80	1.77	1.74
Hong Kong, China	1.22	1.20	1.20	1.20	1.21	1.22	1.24	1.26	1.28	1.28	1.28
Hungary	1.96	1.95	1.94	1.93	1.93	1.92	1.92	1.92	1.92	1.92	1.92
India	4.22	4.13	4.06	4.00	3.95	3.91	3.85	3.79	3.71	3.64	3.56
Indonesia	3.55	3.46	3.38	3.32	3.26	3.21	3.15	3.09	3.02	2.95	2.89
Iran	3.67	3.57	3.50	3.44	3.40	3.36	3.32	3.27	3.21	3.16	3.09
Ireland	2.82	2.78	2.74	2.70	2.64	2.59	2.53	2.47	2.40	2.34	2.28
Israel	3.84	3.77	3.70	3.63	3.56	3.50	3.44	3.38	3.34	3.29	3.26
Italy	1.81	1.78	1.75	1.72	1.69	1.66	1.63	1.60	1.57	1.55	1.52
Japan	1.73	1.70	1.64	1.60	1.56	1.53	1.50	1.48	1.45	1.43	1.42
Jordan	5.02	5.00	4.93	4.82	4.68	4.53	4.38	4.26	4.15	4.05	3.96
Kazakhstan	4.21	4.23	4.16	4.11	4.03	3.93	3.81	3.70	3.62	3.55	3.49
Kuwait	3.51	3.49	3.44	3.34	3.23	3.11	3.01	2.93	2.87	2.83	2.79
Latvia	2.00	2.05	2.08	2.12	2.14	2.16	2.17	2.17	2.16	2.13	2.10
Lithuania	1.83	1.85	1.87	1.90	1.92	1.94	1.96	1.98	1.99	1.99	1.99
Malaysia	4.44	4.31	4.23	4.18	4.15	4.14	4.11	4.06	3.99	3.92	3.84
Mexico	3.89	3.80	3.67	3.60	3.53	3.47	3.41	3.34	3.28	3.21	3.16
Morocco	3.99	4.00	3.98	3.93	3.87	3.79	3.72	3.66	3.60	3.55	3.49
Netherlands	2.20	2.17	2.14	2.13	2.11	2.11	2.10	2.11	2.11	2.12	2.13
New Zealand	2.98	2.95	2.90	2.84	2.79	2.75	2.71	2.68	2.65	2.62	2.59
Nigeria	6.94	6.86	6.76	6.64	6.51	6.37	6.24	6.11	5.99	5.87	5.76
Norway	2.50	2.53	2.51	2.49	2.47	2.46	2.46	2.47	2.47	2.48	2.48
Pakistan	5.51	5.47	5.43	5.38	5.34	5.28	5.20	5.10	4.99	4.87	4.75
Peru	4.10	4.03	3.95	3.87	3.78	3.70	3.62	3.56	3.52	3.48	3.44
Philippines	4.83	4.74	4.68	4.62	4.56	4.50	4.44	4.38	4.33	4.29	4.25
Poland	1.92	1.94	1.96	1.98	2.01	2.02	2.04	2.05	2.05	2.05	2.05
Portugal	2.05	2.03	2.01	1.99	1.96	1.93	1.90	1.86	1.83	1.80	1.77
Romania	2.04	2.04	2.03	2.02	2.01	1.99	1.98	1.96	1.94	1.91	1.87
Russia	2.33	2.43	2.41	2.38	2.41	2.45	2.45	2.44	2.42	2.39	2.35
Saudi Arabia	4.46	4.36	4.30	4.27	4.26	4.24	4.22	4.17	4.10	4.02	3.94
Singapore	1.99	1.98	1.98	1.97	1.97	1.97	1.98	1.99	1.99	2.00	2.01
Slovakia	2.00	2.00	2.00	2.00	2.00	2.00	2.00	2.00	2.00	1.99	1.98
Slovenia	1.85	1.87	1.89	1.91	1.92	1.92	1.92	1.92	1.91	1.89	1.87
South Africa	4.10	4.03	3.99	3.99	3.99	4.00	3.99	3.95	3.89	3.82	3.75
South Korea	1.82	1.80	1.77	1.74	1.71	1.68	1.65	1.62	1.59	1.57	1.55
Spain	2.15	2.15	2.14	2.13	2.11	2.08	2.05	2.02	1.98	1.94	1.89
Sweden	2.25	2.25	2.25	2.25	2.25	2.26	2.26	2.27	2.28	2.29	2.30
Switzerland	1.92	1.91	1.90	1.90	1.91	1.92	1.93	1.95	1.98	2.01	2.03
Taiwan	1.72	1.72	1.71	1.69	1.67	1.66	1.63	1.61	1.60	1.58	1.56
Thailand	2.47	2.45	2.41	2.36	2.30	2.25	2.20	2.16	2.14	2.13	2.12
Tunisia	3.17	3.16	3.15	3.14	3.13	3.11	3.08	3.05	3.01	2.96	2.92
Turkey	3.44	3.40	3.37	3.32	3.28	3.24	3.20	3.16	3.12	3.09	3.05
Turkmenistan	4.11	3.96	3.87	3.85	3.85	3.86	3.85	3.81	3.74	3.65	3.55
Ukraine	1.97	1.96	1.94	1.91	1.86	1.81	1.77	1.75	1.74	1.74	1.74
United Arab Emirates	2.58	2.49	2.46	2.48	2.52	2.55	2.54	2.49	2.39	2.28	2.16
United Kingdom	2.54	2.58	2.54	2.51	2.51	2.51	2.52	2.53	2.54	2.54	2.54
USA	2.81	2.78	2.72	2.67	2.66	2.65	2.65	2.64	2.64	2.63	2.62
Venezuela	4.12	4.07	4.01	3.94	3.88	3.82	3.76	3.70	3.64	3.58	3.53
Vietnam	3.59	3.47	3.40	3.37	3.37	3.36	3.33	3.28	3.22	3.15	3.08

Marketing segments: Young generation

Table 4.83 Toddlers (1-4): 2009-2019

'000

	2009	2010	2011	2012	2013	2014	2015	2016	2017	2018	2019	CAGR	Period growth
Algeria	2,703.9	2,746.2	2,780.9	2,810.8	2,836.9	2,860.0	2,879.3	2,892.6	2,898.8	2,897.4	2,888.4	0.66	6.82
Argentina	2,707.9	2,729.1	2,748.9	2,764.6	2,774.2	2,777.1	2,774.2	2,767.3	2,757.9	2,747.1	2,735.7	0.10	1.03
Australia	1,120.6	1,152.9	1,178.3	1,198.9	1,213.8	1,223.9	1,232.5	1,243.0	1,253.0	1,263.2	1,273.6	1.29	13.65
Austria	322.1	319.2	318.2	317.5	317.4	317.6	318.1	318.8	319.5	320.0	320.5	-0.05	-0.50
Azerbaijan	591.3	611.9	629.4	642.7	651.4	655.4	655.2	651.4	644.7	636.0	625.7	0.57	5.82
Belarus	378.2	397.2	415.9	424.8	426.7	423.4	417.9	414.4	410.2	405.1	399.8	0.56	5.71
Belgium	485.5	491.8	496.9	500.2	501.9	502.3	501.7	500.6	499.2	497.7	496.2	0.22	2.20
Bolivia	996.9	995.8	993.8	991.7	989.7	988.2	986.9	985.4	983.4	980.8	977.5	-0.20	-1.95
Bosnia-Herzegovina	136.6	136.5	137.2	138.0	138.5	138.5	138.0	137.1	136.1	135.0	133.9	-0.20	-2.01
Brazil	12,950.4	12,600.8	12,252.9	11,917.6	11,604.0	11,319.2	11,064.9	10,845.1	10,662.6	10,514.8	10,396.8	-2.17	-19.72
Bulgaria	267.0	264.7	262.8	260.6	257.4	253.9	249.6	244.8	239.8	234.4	228.8	-1.53	-14.31
Canada	1,431.7	1,456.1	1,472.9	1,476.3	1,472.9	1,470.8	1,474.4	1,488.6	1,507.5	1,525.3	1,542.5	0.75	7.74
Chile	990.5	995.4	1,000.2	1,004.5	1,007.9	1,009.9	1,010.5	1,010.0	1,008.3	1,005.9	1,003.2	0.13	1.28
China	51,977.8	51,945.3	52,550.6	52,453.5	52,367.5	52,180.2	52,145.5	52,333.3	52,503.3	52,518.2	52,360.7	0.07	0.74
Colombia	3,586.2	3,594.4	3,598.4	3,597.4	3,591.2	3,580.8	3,568.1	3,554.8	3,542.4	3,531.7	3,523.0	-0.18	-1.76
Costa Rica	301.4	298.2	296.6	297.0	299.3	302.8	306.5	309.6	311.3	311.4	309.8	0.28	2.80
Croatia	168.7	171.2	172.0	172.7	173.4	173.9	174.3	174.4	174.3	174.0	173.4	0.27	2.78
Czech Republic	410.0	415.7	416.4	416.5	416.3	415.9	415.5	414.8	413.9	412.2	409.8	-0.01	-0.07
Denmark	261.6	261.8	261.0	258.5	256.4	253.1	250.7	249.1	248.3	248.5	249.4	-0.48	-4.68
Ecuador	1,105.9	1,097.6	1,090.6	1,084.8	1,080.1	1,076.2	1,073.0	1,070.3	1,068.1	1,066.1	1,064.0	-0.38	-3.78
Egypt	7,156.3	7,248.4	7,319.3	7,388.4	7,449.6	7,500.3	7,540.6	7,570.6	7,589.2	7,596.4	7,593.5	0.59	6.11
Estonia	57.3	58.2	58.9	59.5	60.1	60.6	60.9	61.1	61.1	61.0	60.6	0.57	5.89
Finland	235.3	237.1	238.9	239.8	241.1	242.1	243.2	244.2	245.0	245.7	246.1	0.45	4.61
France	3,119.8	3,154.4	3,183.6	3,174.1	3,172.5	3,154.4	3,132.9	3,126.2	3,120.3	3,114.8	3,109.3	-0.03	-0.34
Germany	2,758.3	2,731.2	2,707.8	2,657.5	2,580.3	2,499.7	2,434.4	2,410.7	2,405.7	2,407.5	2,410.6	-1.34	-12.60
Greece	433.4	437.3	439.2	439.8	439.1	437.3	434.3	430.5	425.8	420.4	414.5	-0.45	-4.37
Hong Kong, China	191.2	200.6	203.0	202.7	203.2	204.9	207.3	210.5	213.9	218.1	222.3	1.52	16.24
Hungary	391.9	395.5	395.9	393.4	390.8	388.3	386.1	384.2	382.7	381.4	380.4	-0.30	-2.93
India	98,627.4	98,209.1	97,781.5	97,390.4	97,052.1	96,757.2	96,466.5	96,133.8	95,721.9	95,210.4	94,591.9	-0.42	-4.09
Indonesia	16,713.9	16,572.4	16,406.6	16,229.0	16,047.9	15,867.9	15,687.3	15,501.8	15,309.3	15,114.2	14,926.0	-1.12	-10.70
Iran	5,257.5	5,356.9	5,415.7	5,441.8	5,444.9	5,435.2	5,417.6	5,391.8	5,356.8	5,311.8	5,254.3	-0.01	-0.06
Ireland	253.2	252.7	253.0	252.8	252.0	250.5	248.5	245.9	242.9	239.4	235.7	-0.71	-6.91
Israel	575.3	573.3	571.3	569.1	566.5	563.6	560.7	558.1	555.9	554.4	553.2	-0.39	-3.83
Italy	2,197.9	2,171.4	2,146.1	2,116.1	2,082.9	2,047.6	2,011.2	1,974.7	1,938.7	1,904.0	1,871.3	-1.60	-14.86
Japan	4,301.4	4,352.5	4,328.5	4,267.6	4,171.8	4,038.8	3,939.0	3,847.8	3,764.8	3,689.4	3,620.6	-1.71	-15.83
Jordan	603.0	613.7	622.0	627.0	628.7	627.4	624.2	619.7	614.2	608.4	602.6	-0.01	-0.07
Kazakhstan	1,134.4	1,182.7	1,218.9	1,240.8	1,248.6	1,244.6	1,232.4	1,215.2	1,196.2	1,177.8	1,161.5	0.24	2.39
Kuwait	164.2	167.5	170.2	172.1	173.1	173.3	172.8	172.0	171.0	170.0	169.2	0.30	3.07
Latvia	86.1	88.4	89.9	91.2	92.3	93.2	93.7	93.9	93.8	93.2	92.1	0.68	7.06
Lithuania	121.1	121.6	122.2	123.0	123.8	124.5	125.3	125.9	126.3	126.6	126.6	0.45	4.60
Malaysia	2,504.0	2,486.0	2,462.1	2,432.2	2,418.7	2,422.3	2,437.6	2,456.3	2,470.4	2,475.4	2,469.4	-0.14	-1.38
Mexico	8,090.3	8,037.1	7,978.1	7,907.1	7,830.3	7,752.3	7,674.6	7,596.8	7,518.0	7,439.3	7,363.5	-0.94	-8.98
Morocco	2,430.6	2,462.3	2,493.5	2,521.0	2,542.6	2,556.7	2,563.6	2,564.3	2,560.0	2,551.4	2,539.5	0.44	4.48
Netherlands	745.0	730.8	721.3	712.8	706.6	702.2	699.5	698.4	698.7	700.1	702.7	-0.58	-5.68
New Zealand	242.5	249.6	254.8	256.5	255.2	253.2	251.0	249.3	247.9	246.8	246.0	0.14	1.42
Nigeria	19,990.2	20,299.1	20,568.2	20,792.3	20,969.2	21,100.8	21,192.3	21,250.5	21,281.9	21,292.9	21,290.0	0.63	6.50
Norway	237.8	242.4	246.8	249.2	251.6	251.9	252.7	254.1	256.3	259.1	262.0	0.97	10.17
Pakistan	19,100.1	19,381.6	19,668.3	19,955.8	20,235.2	20,492.3	20,712.5	20,886.1	21,007.5	21,076.1	21,098.7	1.00	10.46
Peru	2,359.0	2,358.4	2,354.4	2,346.9	2,336.0	2,322.5	2,307.9	2,293.3	2,279.8	2,268.0	2,258.2	-0.44	-4.27
Philippines	8,580.2	8,675.5	8,755.5	8,818.8	8,864.0	8,895.5	8,918.5	8,939.0	8,961.8	8,989.6	9,023.0	0.50	5.16
Poland	1,438.6	1,450.0	1,457.0	1,469.0	1,483.4	1,497.9	1,511.0	1,521.7	1,529.4	1,534.4	1,536.2	0.66	6.78
Portugal	435.7	436.4	436.1	434.3	431.1	426.8	421.5	415.4	408.9	402.1	395.2	-0.97	-9.28
Romania	865.2	870.4	869.4	865.9	859.6	852.0	843.0	833.3	822.7	810.6	796.5	-0.82	-7.95
Russia	6,006.8	6,232.9	6,536.7	6,741.8	6,827.3	6,843.5	6,826.3	6,877.4	6,896.8	6,862.8	6,791.2	1.23	13.06
Saudi Arabia	2,298.5	2,302.5	2,307.7	2,316.3	2,329.3	2,346.5	2,365.8	2,385.2	2,402.6	2,416.7	2,426.5	0.54	5.57
Singapore	194.4	195.0	195.8	197.2	198.7	200.4	202.2	204.3	206.3	208.4	210.8	0.81	8.44
Slovakia	215.2	215.7	215.5	215.6	215.7	215.9	216.0	215.9	215.8	215.4	214.9	-0.01	-0.12
Slovenia	74.4	75.2	76.1	76.9	77.7	78.4	79.0	79.4	79.5	79.4	79.0	0.61	6.23
South Africa	4,165.7	4,145.3	4,124.7	4,107.2	4,094.4	4,085.8	4,078.2	4,067.8	4,051.3	4,027.9	3,998.2	-0.41	-4.02
South Korea	1,773.9	1,763.3	1,758.7	1,742.0	1,721.0	1,696.4	1,669.3	1,640.9	1,612.2	1,584.5	1,559.2	-1.28	-12.10
Spain	1,926.2	1,958.7	1,987.7	1,999.7	2,007.1	2,009.8	2,006.0	1,996.5	1,982.3	1,964.8	1,939.9	0.07	0.71
Sweden	414.8	416.4	418.7	420.8	422.9	424.8	426.9	429.6	432.9	436.5	440.3	0.60	6.15
Switzerland	292.9	292.2	291.9	291.5	291.8	292.9	294.8	297.5	300.9	305.0	309.7	0.56	5.74
Taiwan	837.6	823.1	819.6	816.5	814.2	809.9	803.6	795.5	787.5	779.6	770.7	-0.83	-7.98
Thailand	3,279.1	3,266.2	3,258.0	3,245.8	3,217.1	3,172.7	3,117.4	3,061.6	3,012.7	2,977.6	2,956.4	-1.03	-9.84
Tunisia	626.6	634.1	641.6	649.0	655.9	661.8	666.4	669.4	670.8	670.6	669.1	0.66	6.79
Turkey	5,123.3	5,111.6	5,118.2	5,121.2	5,119.7	5,106.8	5,095.4	5,112.8	5,124.8	5,125.4	5,117.5	-0.01	-0.11
Turkmenistan	419.6	419.5	418.5	417.6	417.3	417.7	418.5	418.9	418.5	416.9	414.1	-0.13	-1.32
Ukraine	1,750.2	1,776.2	1,798.0	1,776.9	1,745.7	1,703.0	1,654.7	1,606.1	1,563.7	1,532.3	1,511.5	-1.46	-13.64
United Arab Emirates	251.5	251.5	251.5	252.1	253.6	255.8	258.2	260.0	260.7	260.0	258.0	0.25	2.57
United Kingdom	2,951.7	3,031.3	3,104.7	3,141.4	3,157.5	3,158.6	3,158.4	3,184.7	3,212.9	3,242.0	3,270.6	1.03	10.80
USA	16,928.0	17,132.0	17,241.6	17,149.4	17,002.4	16,891.3	16,836.2	16,892.9	16,978.4	17,054.1	17,121.0	0.11	1.14
Venezuela	2,334.0	2,343.6	2,351.1	2,356.5	2,359.8	2,361.1	2,360.4	2,358.0	2,354.1	2,348.9	2,342.6	0.04	0.37
Vietnam	6,334.5	6,374.3	6,387.5	6,376.7	6,348.9	6,315.3	6,284.2	6,257.2	6,231.2	6,205.1	6,176.3	-0.25	-2.50

Marketing segments: Young generation

Table 4.84 Toddlers (1-4): 2009-2019 (%)

% of total

	2009	2010	2011	2012	2013	2014	2015	2016	2017	2018	2019
Algeria	7.75	7.75	7.73	7.70	7.66	7.61	7.56	7.49	7.41	7.31	7.20
Argentina	6.71	6.70	6.68	6.66	6.62	6.57	6.50	6.43	6.35	6.27	6.20
Australia	5.14	5.22	5.26	5.29	5.28	5.25	5.21	5.19	5.16	5.13	5.11
Austria	3.84	3.80	3.77	3.75	3.74	3.73	3.73	3.73	3.73	3.72	3.72
Azerbaijan	6.77	6.93	7.05	7.13	7.15	7.12	7.05	6.94	6.81	6.66	6.50
Belarus	3.91	4.12	4.32	4.42	4.46	4.44	4.39	4.37	4.34	4.30	4.26
Belgium	4.55	4.60	4.63	4.64	4.64	4.63	4.61	4.59	4.56	4.53	4.51
Bolivia	10.11	9.93	9.75	9.57	9.40	9.24	9.09	8.95	8.80	8.66	8.51
Bosnia-Herzegovina	3.55	3.55	3.57	3.59	3.61	3.61	3.60	3.58	3.56	3.53	3.51
Brazil	6.68	6.45	6.22	6.00	5.80	5.62	5.45	5.31	5.19	5.09	5.00
Bulgaria	3.55	3.54	3.54	3.54	3.52	3.50	3.47	3.43	3.39	3.34	3.29
Canada	4.25	4.29	4.30	4.28	4.24	4.20	4.18	4.19	4.21	4.23	4.25
Chile	5.84	5.81	5.78	5.75	5.72	5.68	5.64	5.59	5.53	5.48	5.42
China	3.91	3.89	3.92	3.90	3.88	3.85	3.83	3.83	3.83	3.82	3.79
Colombia	7.85	7.76	7.67	7.56	7.45	7.34	7.23	7.11	7.01	6.90	6.81
Costa Rica	6.58	6.43	6.31	6.23	6.20	6.19	6.18	6.17	6.13	6.06	5.97
Croatia	3.81	3.87	3.90	3.92	3.95	3.97	3.98	4.00	4.01	4.01	4.01
Czech Republic	3.97	4.02	4.02	4.02	4.02	4.01	4.01	4.00	4.00	3.98	3.96
Denmark	4.75	4.74	4.71	4.65	4.60	4.53	4.47	4.43	4.41	4.40	4.40
Ecuador	8.12	7.97	7.83	7.70	7.57	7.46	7.35	7.25	7.16	7.07	6.99
Egypt	9.32	9.27	9.20	9.13	9.05	8.96	8.86	8.75	8.64	8.52	8.39
Estonia	4.30	4.39	4.46	4.52	4.58	4.63	4.68	4.71	4.73	4.73	4.72
Finland	4.42	4.43	4.45	4.45	4.46	4.46	4.47	4.47	4.47	4.47	4.47
France	5.00	5.03	5.05	5.01	4.99	4.94	4.88	4.85	4.83	4.80	4.77
Germany	3.36	3.34	3.33	3.27	3.19	3.10	3.03	3.01	3.01	3.03	3.04
Greece	3.85	3.87	3.88	3.87	3.86	3.83	3.80	3.76	3.71	3.66	3.61
Hong Kong, China	2.71	2.81	2.82	2.79	2.78	2.77	2.79	2.81	2.83	2.86	2.90
Hungary	3.91	3.96	3.97	3.95	3.94	3.92	3.91	3.90	3.90	3.90	3.89
India	8.44	8.29	8.14	8.01	7.88	7.76	7.64	7.53	7.41	7.29	7.16
Indonesia	7.27	7.13	6.98	6.84	6.69	6.56	6.42	6.29	6.16	6.04	5.92
Iran	7.09	7.14	7.13	7.08	7.01	6.92	6.82	6.71	6.60	6.47	6.34
Ireland	5.69	5.61	5.55	5.48	5.40	5.31	5.21	5.11	4.99	4.88	4.76
Israel	7.77	7.63	7.49	7.35	7.22	7.08	6.95	6.83	6.72	6.62	6.53
Italy	3.72	3.67	3.63	3.57	3.52	3.46	3.40	3.34	3.28	3.22	3.17
Japan	3.37	3.42	3.41	3.36	3.30	3.20	3.13	3.07	3.01	2.96	2.92
Jordan	9.55	9.48	9.43	9.36	9.27	9.14	8.97	8.78	8.57	8.35	8.14
Kazakhstan	7.19	7.40	7.53	7.57	7.53	7.42	7.26	7.08	6.90	6.72	6.56
Kuwait	6.71	6.70	6.67	6.60	6.51	6.39	6.25	6.10	5.96	5.82	5.69
Latvia	3.82	3.94	4.04	4.12	4.20	4.26	4.32	4.35	4.37	4.37	4.34
Lithuania	3.62	3.65	3.69	3.74	3.78	3.83	3.87	3.91	3.95	3.98	4.00
Malaysia	8.91	8.71	8.49	8.26	8.10	7.99	7.93	7.89	7.83	7.74	7.63
Mexico	7.45	7.29	7.14	6.98	6.82	6.67	6.53	6.39	6.25	6.12	6.00
Morocco	7.60	7.60	7.61	7.60	7.58	7.53	7.47	7.39	7.29	7.19	7.09
Netherlands	4.54	4.45	4.38	4.32	4.27	4.24	4.22	4.20	4.20	4.20	4.21
New Zealand	5.63	5.74	5.80	5.79	5.70	5.61	5.52	5.43	5.36	5.29	5.23
Nigeria	12.92	12.83	12.71	12.58	12.42	12.24	12.05	11.84	11.63	11.42	11.22
Norway	4.95	4.99	5.02	5.02	5.02	4.98	4.95	4.93	4.92	4.93	4.94
Pakistan	10.56	10.49	10.42	10.34	10.27	10.18	10.08	9.96	9.82	9.67	9.50
Peru	8.13	8.02	7.90	7.78	7.64	7.50	7.37	7.23	7.11	6.99	6.88
Philippines	9.31	9.24	9.15	9.05	8.93	8.80	8.67	8.54	8.41	8.29	8.18
Poland	3.79	3.82	3.85	3.88	3.93	3.97	4.02	4.05	4.08	4.09	4.10
Portugal	4.08	4.08	4.07	4.05	4.01	3.96	3.91	3.85	3.79	3.72	3.66
Romania	4.04	4.07	4.08	4.08	4.07	4.05	4.02	4.00	3.97	3.93	3.88
Russia	4.23	4.40	4.62	4.78	4.84	4.86	4.86	4.90	4.93	4.91	4.87
Saudi Arabia	8.94	8.77	8.62	8.48	8.36	8.26	8.18	8.09	8.01	7.91	7.81
Singapore	4.13	4.09	4.05	4.03	4.01	4.00	4.00	4.00	4.01	4.01	4.03
Slovakia	3.99	4.00	3.99	3.99	4.00	4.00	4.00	4.00	4.00	3.99	3.99
Slovenia	3.68	3.71	3.74	3.77	3.81	3.84	3.86	3.87	3.87	3.86	3.84
South Africa	8.31	8.21	8.12	8.04	7.98	7.93	7.89	7.84	7.78	7.71	7.62
South Korea	3.64	3.61	3.59	3.55	3.50	3.45	3.39	3.33	3.27	3.21	3.16
Spain	4.23	4.26	4.29	4.28	4.27	4.24	4.20	4.15	4.10	4.03	3.96
Sweden	4.51	4.50	4.51	4.51	4.51	4.51	4.51	4.52	4.53	4.54	4.56
Switzerland	3.87	3.85	3.83	3.81	3.80	3.80	3.81	3.83	3.86	3.90	3.95
Taiwan	3.64	3.56	3.54	3.51	3.50	3.47	3.44	3.40	3.36	3.32	3.28
Thailand	5.07	5.02	4.97	4.93	4.86	4.77	4.67	4.57	4.48	4.41	4.36
Tunisia	6.10	6.11	6.12	6.14	6.14	6.14	6.12	6.09	6.05	6.00	5.94
Turkey	6.81	6.71	6.64	6.57	6.50	6.42	6.34	6.29	6.25	6.19	6.12
Turkmenistan	8.21	8.10	7.98	7.86	7.76	7.67	7.60	7.52	7.42	7.32	7.19
Ukraine	3.81	3.89	3.96	3.94	3.90	3.83	3.74	3.66	3.59	3.54	3.52
United Arab Emirates	5.45	5.32	5.21	5.11	5.05	5.00	4.95	4.90	4.83	4.73	4.62
United Kingdom	4.79	4.89	4.99	5.02	5.02	4.99	4.96	4.97	4.98	4.99	5.01
USA	5.52	5.55	5.55	5.48	5.40	5.32	5.27	5.25	5.24	5.23	5.22
Venezuela	8.17	8.07	7.97	7.87	7.76	7.65	7.54	7.43	7.32	7.21	7.10
Vietnam	7.23	7.18	7.11	7.01	6.89	6.77	6.66	6.55	6.45	6.35	6.26

Marketing segments: Young generation

Table 4.85 Children (2-9): 2009-2019

'000

	2009	2010	2011	2012	2013	2014	2015	2016	2017	2018	2019	CAGR	Period growth
Algeria	5,053.4	5,163.6	5,266.7	5,359.7	5,442.5	5,516.0	5,581.6	5,639.1	5,686.9	5,723.5	5,747.4	1.30	13.73
Argentina	5,364.8	5,371.8	5,391.3	5,420.6	5,454.3	5,485.9	5,510.3	5,524.9	5,529.7	5,526.0	5,515.3	0.28	2.81
Australia	2,185.9	2,215.8	2,251.3	2,295.2	2,339.9	2,385.8	2,429.8	2,466.4	2,499.2	2,525.1	2,545.5	1.53	16.45
Austria	654.5	653.6	652.1	652.8	650.7	650.0	647.3	646.8	646.6	647.0	647.6	-0.11	-1.05
Azerbaijan	1,073.3	1,101.6	1,134.6	1,170.1	1,205.2	1,236.5	1,261.4	1,278.4	1,287.3	1,288.6	1,283.6	1.81	19.60
Belarus	726.5	738.7	754.6	772.6	790.8	807.9	823.5	836.8	842.7	840.3	832.6	1.37	14.60
Belgium	951.2	959.8	967.7	977.6	989.5	1,000.0	1,006.7	1,011.3	1,013.5	1,013.8	1,012.7	0.63	6.46
Bolivia	1,944.6	1,953.8	1,959.2	1,961.0	1,960.3	1,958.2	1,955.8	1,953.4	1,951.1	1,948.5	1,945.3	0.00	0.03
Bosnia-Herzegovina	297.8	288.7	282.6	279.2	277.9	277.6	277.5	277.1	276.3	275.1	273.6	-0.84	-8.13
Brazil	27,300.1	26,870.1	26,339.5	25,746.0	25,120.1	24,483.1	23,858.1	23,264.0	22,715.2	22,223.7	21,793.0	-2.23	-20.17
Bulgaria	530.7	528.0	526.4	523.7	521.2	517.4	510.7	503.9	496.1	487.5	478.2	-1.04	-9.89
Canada	2,855.7	2,871.2	2,899.0	2,931.4	2,955.1	2,971.6	2,993.1	3,014.0	3,031.8	3,047.6	3,063.8	0.71	7.29
Chile	1,982.1	1,978.1	1,979.1	1,984.0	1,991.2	1,999.1	2,006.0	2,011.3	2,014.7	2,016.1	2,015.7	0.17	1.69
China	111,074.5	109,422.5	108,702.0	108,359.5	108,855.7	108,510.9	108,853.8	109,861.6	110,484.3	111,036.7	111,344.5	0.02	0.24
Colombia	7,092.7	7,107.4	7,123.5	7,139.5	7,152.5	7,159.5	7,158.6	7,149.2	7,132.4	7,111.0	7,088.1	-0.01	-0.06
Costa Rica	626.6	620.9	614.9	609.0	604.3	601.7	601.8	604.6	609.5	615.1	619.7	-0.11	-1.12
Croatia	340.8	336.9	335.2	337.1	340.1	343.6	346.7	347.6	348.5	349.0	349.2	0.24	2.46
Czech Republic	769.8	786.2	801.0	813.0	822.9	831.5	836.1	835.9	835.5	834.4	832.5	0.79	8.14
Denmark	527.8	525.7	523.5	521.9	520.7	518.1	515.1	512.0	508.0	505.3	502.2	-0.50	-4.86
Ecuador	2,257.1	2,239.4	2,222.4	2,206.4	2,191.7	2,178.5	2,166.7	2,156.6	2,148.2	2,141.1	2,135.2	-0.55	-5.40
Egypt	13,989.8	14,293.9	14,574.5	14,826.5	15,045.9	15,230.7	15,380.4	15,495.9	15,599.4	15,683.5	15,744.6	1.19	12.54
Estonia	105.8	108.4	110.3	112.7	114.9	117.1	118.5	119.5	120.4	121.0	121.4	1.38	14.72
Finland	463.0	465.1	468.3	472.2	476.7	480.3	483.0	485.8	487.5	489.6	491.2	0.59	6.08
France	6,205.2	6,237.7	6,255.5	6,281.2	6,301.8	6,320.0	6,336.5	6,345.2	6,329.4	6,322.1	6,298.7	0.15	1.51
Germany	5,790.0	5,694.3	5,602.2	5,531.1	5,436.4	5,338.1	5,235.5	5,150.7	5,078.6	4,997.6	4,918.9	-1.62	-15.04
Greece	845.1	855.7	864.3	872.3	878.4	882.6	884.7	883.7	880.4	875.0	867.8	0.27	2.69
Hong Kong, China	422.0	427.5	432.2	445.8	457.6	472.6	485.9	492.0	493.6	497.9	502.9	1.77	19.17
Hungary	773.9	780.0	781.4	782.9	783.7	785.8	786.6	784.4	780.0	775.9	772.3	-0.02	-0.21
India	195,923.6	195,767.3	195,387.5	194,819.5	194,137.2	193,427.7	192,756.0	192,142.6	191,562.3	190,958.8	190,262.4	-0.29	-2.89
Indonesia	33,507.6	33,481.8	33,369.6	33,177.0	32,920.5	32,622.1	32,301.1	31,967.4	31,624.3	31,273.0	30,915.4	-0.80	-7.74
Iran	9,535.4	9,853.5	10,127.9	10,347.9	10,513.7	10,633.1	10,714.9	10,763.9	10,780.5	10,766.1	10,723.2	1.18	12.46
Ireland	496.1	501.8	507.1	512.7	513.7	511.8	509.5	507.7	504.8	500.9	495.9	0.00	-0.04
Israel	1,140.9	1,148.3	1,153.3	1,155.8	1,153.1	1,147.3	1,141.8	1,136.5	1,131.3	1,126.2	1,121.1	-0.17	-1.74
Italy	4,424.0	4,425.8	4,410.2	4,391.9	4,363.9	4,319.2	4,257.5	4,195.9	4,129.4	4,060.4	3,990.4	-1.03	-9.80
Japan	8,898.1	8,796.8	8,732.3	8,631.2	8,534.6	8,438.6	8,360.2	8,239.4	8,089.0	7,911.7	7,704.5	-1.43	-13.41
Jordan	1,163.2	1,174.7	1,187.6	1,201.2	1,214.2	1,225.2	1,233.5	1,238.1	1,238.8	1,236.0	1,230.5	0.56	5.79
Kazakhstan	1,969.6	2,065.0	2,163.0	2,257.9	2,343.4	2,412.5	2,460.2	2,483.8	2,484.9	2,468.6	2,442.2	2.17	23.99
Kuwait	310.7	316.8	323.2	329.6	335.4	340.3	343.7	345.7	346.3	345.9	344.9	1.05	11.01
Latvia	162.5	165.6	168.2	171.5	174.7	177.1	180.3	182.3	183.9	185.0	185.4	1.33	14.09
Lithuania	249.5	244.5	242.0	241.7	243.0	244.0	245.4	246.7	248.0	249.3	250.4	0.03	0.34
Malaysia	4,856.5	4,879.9	4,887.1	4,878.6	4,872.4	4,858.4	4,836.8	4,821.6	4,804.4	4,802.1	4,809.2	-0.10	-0.97
Mexico	16,411.6	16,366.5	16,303.9	16,203.9	16,079.1	15,940.4	15,796.2	15,650.4	15,502.5	15,351.7	15,198.0	-0.77	-7.39
Morocco	4,741.8	4,760.7	4,796.2	4,844.8	4,900.3	4,955.0	5,002.6	5,039.7	5,065.1	5,079.2	5,083.2	0.70	7.20
Netherlands	1,571.5	1,549.2	1,520.4	1,493.8	1,468.0	1,442.9	1,424.6	1,412.6	1,403.3	1,397.5	1,394.9	-1.19	-11.24
New Zealand	467.1	472.7	479.7	488.4	495.9	501.2	506.4	509.5	509.6	506.9	503.7	0.76	7.85
Nigeria	36,287.6	36,989.3	37,667.6	38,312.1	38,907.7	39,438.4	39,892.8	40,266.9	40,563.2	40,789.6	40,957.7	1.22	12.87
Norway	477.3	479.5	483.5	489.2	495.5	500.2	504.3	508.9	512.4	516.8	519.8	0.86	8.91
Pakistan	36,163.1	36,681.3	37,220.6	37,775.3	38,337.0	38,894.7	39,437.1	39,954.7	40,435.1	40,859.1	41,206.9	1.31	13.95
Peru	4,691.0	4,695.1	4,697.6	4,697.7	4,693.9	4,685.3	4,670.9	4,651.1	4,626.7	4,599.9	4,572.7	-0.25	-2.52
Philippines	16,689.1	16,838.5	16,993.5	17,155.3	17,314.0	17,462.2	17,590.3	17,695.0	17,778.7	17,848.2	17,912.5	0.71	7.33
Poland	2,891.1	2,871.8	2,859.5	2,866.5	2,888.2	2,917.1	2,944.0	2,965.0	2,987.5	3,009.5	3,028.5	0.47	4.75
Portugal	887.4	884.7	884.6	881.7	876.0	870.6	867.0	861.3	853.4	843.7	832.5	-0.64	-6.18
Romania	1,715.6	1,710.0	1,704.5	1,708.6	1,715.1	1,717.7	1,713.5	1,701.9	1,687.1	1,669.4	1,649.0	-0.40	-3.88
Russia	11,066.7	11,442.9	11,885.5	12,367.3	12,675.5	12,917.0	13,159.7	13,457.0	13,719.2	13,831.0	13,819.3	2.25	24.87
Saudi Arabia	4,518.7	4,547.2	4,567.5	4,581.2	4,592.4	4,605.8	4,625.1	4,651.6	4,683.9	4,719.0	4,753.1	0.51	5.19
Singapore	424.6	418.4	409.5	406.6	404.7	405.0	406.4	408.5	411.0	413.7	417.0	-0.18	-1.80
Slovakia	423.5	421.7	421.7	424.7	428.2	430.8	431.3	431.2	431.1	430.9	430.7	0.17	1.68
Slovenia	146.5	147.9	148.7	150.2	151.8	153.9	155.4	156.7	157.9	158.9	159.6	0.86	8.92
South Africa	8,268.9	8,277.9	8,268.3	8,243.1	8,209.1	8,175.0	8,147.1	8,126.8	8,111.2	8,095.9	8,074.9	-0.24	-2.35
South Korea	4,021.6	3,840.8	3,688.1	3,592.7	3,529.4	3,474.3	3,439.3	3,407.7	3,363.0	3,313.5	3,261.5	-2.07	-18.90
Spain	3,672.0	3,764.3	3,840.1	3,905.7	3,969.8	4,013.0	4,047.0	4,072.5	4,074.8	4,068.0	4,053.1	0.99	10.38
Sweden	796.8	810.8	823.1	835.3	843.3	848.2	851.7	855.9	860.7	865.7	871.2	0.90	9.34
Switzerland	595.8	591.5	590.1	589.2	588.6	589.4	589.7	591.3	593.4	596.9	602.0	0.10	1.05
Taiwan	1,953.2	1,874.5	1,772.2	1,720.1	1,677.1	1,651.5	1,632.7	1,623.2	1,611.5	1,601.1	1,588.7	-2.04	-18.66
Thailand	6,670.3	6,633.4	6,638.6	6,641.4	6,635.2	6,586.8	6,529.0	6,467.9	6,398.4	6,320.6	6,238.7	-0.67	-6.47
Tunisia	1,228.4	1,233.7	1,242.5	1,253.9	1,266.9	1,280.4	1,293.7	1,305.9	1,316.5	1,324.9	1,330.9	0.80	8.34
Turkey	10,684.9	10,530.7	10,398.0	10,343.3	10,298.9	10,263.0	10,240.8	10,220.8	10,224.2	10,224.3	10,225.3	-0.44	-4.30
Turkmenistan	805.3	815.1	821.6	824.9	826.0	826.2	826.5	827.4	828.6	829.4	829.1	0.29	2.95
Ukraine	3,219.3	3,281.5	3,345.6	3,412.4	3,455.7	3,466.0	3,446.3	3,416.8	3,346.7	3,274.9	3,203.1	-0.05	-0.50
United Arab Emirates	497.7	506.8	511.6	512.9	512.2	511.5	512.1	514.5	518.1	522.0	524.8	0.53	5.45
United Kingdom	5,577.6	5,652.1	5,764.4	5,895.7	6,002.4	6,096.3	6,179.5	6,257.1	6,323.6	6,369.9	6,400.6	1.39	14.75
USA	32,981.2	33,443.1	33,717.2	34,008.6	34,167.1	34,251.4	34,355.3	34,420.6	34,389.0	34,329.1	34,293.8	0.39	3.98
Venezuela	4,583.0	4,608.8	4,632.7	4,654.0	4,672.3	4,687.1	4,698.0	4,705.0	4,708.1	4,707.5	4,703.7	0.26	2.63
Vietnam	12,529.3	12,655.6	12,708.5	12,705.6	12,664.6	12,616.2	12,582.1	12,565.1	12,554.7	12,544.2	12,522.9	-0.01	-0.05

Marketing segments: Young generation

Table 4.86 Female children (2-9): 2009-2019

'000

	2009	2010	2011	2012	2013	2014	2015	2016	2017	2018	2019	CAGR	Period growth
Algeria	2,469.2	2,523.2	2,573.9	2,619.8	2,660.7	2,697.1	2,729.6	2,758.0	2,781.6	2,799.6	2,811.3	1.31	13.86
Argentina	2,636.3	2,639.5	2,648.8	2,662.9	2,679.2	2,694.5	2,706.2	2,713.2	2,715.4	2,713.5	2,708.2	0.27	2.72
Australia	1,064.7	1,079.0	1,096.4	1,117.7	1,139.5	1,162.1	1,184.1	1,201.7	1,218.0	1,230.6	1,240.6	1.54	16.52
Austria	319.2	318.9	318.3	319.1	318.0	317.7	316.4	315.9	315.7	315.8	316.0	-0.10	-1.00
Azerbaijan	491.2	503.1	518.0	534.7	551.7	567.2	579.6	588.2	592.9	594.0	592.1	1.89	20.53
Belarus	353.1	358.9	366.8	375.8	385.0	393.3	400.6	406.8	409.6	408.3	404.3	1.37	14.53
Belgium	464.4	468.2	471.9	476.3	482.0	486.8	490.2	492.5	493.7	493.8	493.3	0.61	6.22
Bolivia	953.5	958.1	960.7	961.6	961.2	960.1	958.8	957.5	956.2	954.9	953.1	0.00	-0.04
Bosnia-Herzegovina	144.1	139.7	136.7	135.1	134.5	134.4	134.3	134.1	133.7	133.1	132.4	-0.85	-8.15
Brazil	13,400.7	13,189.0	12,928.0	12,636.1	12,328.3	12,014.8	11,707.0	11,414.1	11,143.5	10,900.9	10,688.3	-2.24	-20.24
Bulgaria	258.0	256.7	256.0	254.7	253.9	252.1	248.9	245.6	241.8	237.6	233.0	-1.01	-9.68
Canada	1,393.9	1,400.9	1,413.3	1,427.6	1,437.6	1,444.6	1,454.2	1,463.4	1,471.6	1,479.1	1,486.9	0.65	6.67
Chile	972.9	970.9	971.3	973.7	977.2	981.0	984.4	987.0	988.6	989.3	989.1	0.17	1.67
China	49,414.9	48,727.6	48,317.7	48,036.5	48,156.9	47,867.0	47,998.2	48,388.6	48,792.5	49,128.9	49,347.6	-0.01	-0.14
Colombia	3,473.0	3,480.0	3,487.7	3,495.4	3,501.6	3,504.8	3,504.2	3,499.3	3,490.8	3,480.0	3,468.5	-0.01	-0.13
Costa Rica	305.4	302.7	299.8	297.0	294.7	293.5	293.5	294.9	297.3	300.0	302.2	-0.10	-1.03
Croatia	166.0	164.0	163.2	164.1	165.5	167.2	168.8	169.2	169.6	169.8	169.9	0.23	2.35
Czech Republic	374.2	382.1	389.8	395.7	400.7	405.0	407.4	407.4	407.2	406.7	405.8	0.81	8.45
Denmark	257.8	256.7	255.4	254.6	254.1	252.8	251.2	249.6	247.7	246.3	245.0	-0.51	-4.99
Ecuador	1,105.6	1,096.9	1,088.4	1,080.3	1,073.0	1,066.3	1,060.4	1,055.3	1,051.1	1,047.6	1,044.6	-0.57	-5.52
Egypt	6,704.6	6,853.3	6,992.5	7,120.0	7,233.5	7,332.0	7,414.3	7,479.9	7,540.1	7,591.1	7,630.9	1.30	13.82
Estonia	51.4	52.6	53.6	54.8	55.8	56.8	57.5	58.1	58.5	58.8	59.0	1.39	14.83
Finland	226.4	227.3	229.0	230.7	232.9	234.3	235.6	236.7	237.2	238.1	238.9	0.54	5.52
France	3,045.6	3,062.0	3,071.0	3,082.7	3,092.3	3,100.1	3,107.8	3,111.1	3,102.5	3,098.1	3,086.2	0.13	1.33
Germany	2,819.1	2,771.7	2,723.5	2,687.1	2,639.4	2,590.0	2,538.9	2,496.5	2,461.4	2,422.0	2,383.9	-1.66	-15.44
Greece	409.1	413.8	417.8	422.1	424.7	426.5	427.6	427.2	425.6	423.0	419.5	0.25	2.55
Hong Kong, China	202.9	206.2	209.5	216.6	222.3	229.6	236.5	240.5	241.1	243.2	246.0	1.94	21.24
Hungary	376.9	379.8	380.1	381.0	381.3	382.5	382.7	381.9	379.8	377.8	376.1	-0.02	-0.22
India	93,787.0	93,714.0	93,535.4	93,268.5	92,949.0	92,618.9	92,309.1	92,029.2	91,766.3	91,492.8	91,174.5	-0.28	-2.79
Indonesia	16,435.0	16,420.6	16,364.2	16,268.7	16,142.0	15,994.7	15,836.2	15,671.4	15,501.7	15,327.9	15,150.8	-0.81	-7.81
Iran	4,653.3	4,808.8	4,942.0	5,047.8	5,127.0	5,183.8	5,223.0	5,247.0	5,255.8	5,249.8	5,229.8	1.17	12.39
Ireland	242.5	245.0	247.7	250.1	250.4	249.3	248.2	247.3	245.9	244.0	241.5	-0.04	-0.40
Israel	556.0	559.7	562.1	563.1	561.5	558.6	555.9	553.3	550.8	548.4	545.9	-0.18	-1.81
Italy	2,151.0	2,151.3	2,143.6	2,134.1	2,119.3	2,097.0	2,066.4	2,037.2	2,004.8	1,971.1	1,937.1	-1.04	-9.95
Japan	4,337.6	4,289.1	4,257.7	4,208.1	4,160.7	4,112.3	4,072.1	4,013.4	3,940.7	3,854.6	3,754.0	-1.43	-13.45
Jordan	568.2	573.8	580.2	587.0	593.5	599.1	603.3	605.6	605.9	604.5	601.6	0.57	5.88
Kazakhstan	961.1	1,007.6	1,055.3	1,101.5	1,143.0	1,176.6	1,199.7	1,211.1	1,211.4	1,203.3	1,190.2	2.16	23.84
Kuwait	153.4	156.4	159.5	162.6	165.5	167.8	169.5	170.5	170.8	170.6	170.1	1.04	10.90
Latvia	79.5	81.0	82.2	83.7	85.2	86.4	87.9	88.9	89.6	90.1	90.3	1.28	13.51
Lithuania	121.5	119.2	118.1	118.0	118.7	119.4	120.0	120.6	121.3	121.9	122.4	0.08	0.78
Malaysia	2,349.4	2,358.0	2,359.4	2,353.8	2,350.4	2,343.6	2,332.7	2,325.0	2,316.3	2,314.8	2,317.9	-0.13	-1.34
Mexico	8,074.7	8,050.8	8,017.7	7,965.8	7,901.5	7,830.3	7,756.6	7,682.5	7,607.7	7,531.8	7,454.5	-0.80	-7.68
Morocco	2,330.5	2,339.4	2,356.5	2,380.3	2,407.5	2,434.4	2,457.7	2,475.8	2,488.0	2,494.6	2,496.3	0.69	7.11
Netherlands	767.1	756.0	741.3	727.8	715.1	702.7	693.4	687.5	683.1	680.3	679.0	-1.21	-11.47
New Zealand	227.9	230.5	233.8	237.7	241.4	243.9	246.4	247.8	247.8	246.5	245.0	0.73	7.51
Nigeria	17,886.7	18,232.2	18,567.6	18,887.5	19,184.0	19,448.6	19,675.2	19,861.4	20,008.6	20,120.8	20,203.8	1.23	12.95
Norway	233.4	234.6	236.4	239.1	241.9	244.0	245.9	248.0	249.7	251.8	253.3	0.82	8.51
Pakistan	17,564.8	17,813.5	18,072.8	18,339.9	18,610.8	18,880.1	19,142.5	19,393.3	19,626.5	19,832.6	20,001.9	1.31	13.87
Peru	2,301.5	2,303.1	2,303.8	2,303.4	2,301.2	2,296.6	2,289.3	2,279.3	2,267.2	2,253.8	2,240.3	-0.27	-2.66
Philippines	8,159.9	8,232.2	8,307.0	8,385.1	8,461.4	8,532.6	8,593.9	8,643.8	8,683.3	8,715.8	8,745.5	0.70	7.18
Poland	1,404.8	1,394.5	1,387.9	1,390.7	1,401.6	1,416.0	1,429.6	1,440.1	1,451.3	1,462.1	1,471.4	0.46	4.74
Portugal	429.9	427.8	427.1	425.6	422.9	420.3	418.2	415.5	411.7	407.0	401.7	-0.68	-6.56
Romania	834.4	831.6	828.8	830.9	834.0	835.2	833.4	827.9	820.7	812.2	802.3	-0.39	-3.85
Russia	5,389.4	5,569.5	5,781.8	6,012.0	6,157.7	6,274.1	6,389.7	6,532.2	6,657.7	6,711.0	6,703.8	2.21	24.39
Saudi Arabia	2,237.6	2,251.3	2,261.1	2,267.7	2,273.0	2,279.4	2,288.7	2,301.3	2,316.7	2,333.5	2,349.7	0.49	5.01
Singapore	207.9	205.4	201.6	200.2	199.0	198.8	199.1	199.9	200.9	202.0	203.4	-0.22	-2.19
Slovakia	206.3	205.2	205.0	206.6	208.2	209.4	209.7	209.6	209.6	209.5	209.4	0.15	1.53
Slovenia	71.2	71.9	72.3	73.0	73.8	74.8	75.4	76.0	76.6	77.1	77.4	0.84	8.77
South Africa	4,107.2	4,111.6	4,106.8	4,094.3	4,077.4	4,060.3	4,045.8	4,034.9	4,026.0	4,017.1	4,005.3	-0.25	-2.48
South Korea	1,928.6	1,844.2	1,772.6	1,728.9	1,699.4	1,673.9	1,657.0	1,642.5	1,621.2	1,598.3	1,574.2	-2.01	-18.38
Spain	1,783.6	1,827.6	1,864.6	1,895.1	1,926.7	1,948.0	1,965.0	1,978.1	1,980.0	1,977.4	1,970.8	1.00	10.50
Sweden	388.4	395.2	401.5	407.6	411.5	413.9	415.7	417.7	420.0	422.4	425.1	0.91	9.44
Switzerland	290.4	288.7	288.4	288.1	287.9	288.2	288.2	289.0	289.8	291.3	293.7	0.11	1.15
Taiwan	932.7	894.8	845.9	820.3	799.7	787.2	778.9	773.7	768.0	762.5	756.2	-2.08	-18.93
Thailand	3,267.2	3,246.0	3,247.3	3,247.5	3,244.3	3,219.6	3,191.0	3,162.5	3,129.3	3,091.9	3,051.8	-0.68	-6.59
Tunisia	594.5	597.1	601.2	606.7	612.9	619.4	625.8	631.6	636.7	640.7	643.5	0.80	8.25
Turkey	5,233.3	5,155.5	5,090.4	5,062.2	5,039.1	5,021.2	5,009.9	4,999.6	5,000.4	4,999.2	5,000.4	-0.45	-4.45
Turkmenistan	396.8	401.7	404.9	406.5	407.0	407.1	407.2	407.5	407.9	408.2	407.9	0.27	2.78
Ukraine	1,564.8	1,595.1	1,627.2	1,660.7	1,683.2	1,688.5	1,678.9	1,664.6	1,629.4	1,594.3	1,559.3	-0.03	-0.35
United Arab Emirates	242.2	247.0	249.9	251.1	251.4	251.6	252.3	253.8	255.7	257.6	258.9	0.67	6.91
United Kingdom	2,724.1	2,758.6	2,810.2	2,870.7	2,920.6	2,964.8	3,003.3	3,038.9	3,069.4	3,090.4	3,104.7	1.32	13.97
USA	16,118.4	16,350.1	16,485.4	16,629.3	16,710.5	16,754.3	16,808.6	16,842.6	16,829.6	16,802.2	16,786.3	0.41	4.14
Venezuela	2,242.5	2,255.1	2,266.7	2,277.0	2,285.7	2,292.8	2,297.9	2,301.1	2,302.5	2,302.1	2,300.1	0.25	2.57
Vietnam	6,137.3	6,198.8	6,224.2	6,222.1	6,201.2	6,176.7	6,159.2	6,150.2	6,144.5	6,138.7	6,127.6	-0.02	-0.16

Marketing segments: Young generation

Table 4.87 Male children (2-9): 2009-2019

'000

	2009	2010	2011	2012	2013	2014	2015	2016	2017	2018	2019	CAGR	Period growth
Algeria	2,584.2	2,640.4	2,692.8	2,740.0	2,781.8	2,818.9	2,852.1	2,881.1	2,905.3	2,923.9	2,936.1	1.28	13.62
Argentina	2,728.4	2,732.3	2,742.5	2,757.7	2,775.1	2,791.4	2,804.1	2,811.7	2,814.2	2,812.5	2,807.2	0.28	2.89
Australia	1,121.2	1,136.8	1,154.9	1,177.5	1,200.4	1,223.7	1,245.7	1,264.7	1,281.2	1,294.5	1,305.0	1.53	16.39
Austria	335.3	334.7	333.8	333.7	332.7	332.3	330.8	330.9	330.9	331.2	331.6	-0.11	-1.10
Azerbaijan	582.0	598.4	616.6	635.3	653.5	669.4	681.8	690.2	694.4	694.6	691.5	1.74	18.80
Belarus	373.5	379.7	387.8	396.8	405.8	414.6	422.8	430.0	433.1	432.1	428.3	1.38	14.67
Belgium	486.8	491.6	495.9	501.3	507.4	513.1	516.4	518.7	519.8	520.0	519.4	0.65	6.70
Bolivia	991.1	995.7	998.4	999.4	999.1	998.2	997.0	995.9	994.9	993.7	992.1	0.01	0.11
Bosnia-Herzegovina	153.6	149.0	145.9	144.1	143.4	143.3	143.2	143.0	142.6	141.9	141.2	-0.84	-8.12
Brazil	13,899.5	13,681.1	13,411.5	13,109.8	12,791.8	12,468.3	12,151.2	11,849.8	11,571.7	11,322.8	11,104.7	-2.22	-20.11
Bulgaria	272.6	271.3	270.5	269.0	267.4	265.3	261.8	258.3	254.3	249.9	245.1	-1.06	-10.09
Canada	1,461.8	1,470.4	1,485.7	1,503.8	1,517.5	1,527.1	1,538.9	1,550.6	1,560.2	1,568.5	1,576.9	0.76	7.88
Chile	1,009.2	1,007.3	1,007.8	1,010.3	1,014.0	1,018.0	1,021.6	1,024.3	1,026.1	1,026.8	1,026.6	0.17	1.72
China	61,659.6	60,695.0	60,384.4	60,323.0	60,698.9	60,643.8	60,855.6	61,473.0	61,691.8	61,907.8	61,996.8	0.05	0.55
Colombia	3,619.7	3,627.4	3,635.8	3,644.1	3,650.9	3,654.7	3,654.4	3,649.9	3,641.7	3,631.0	3,619.7	0.00	0.00
Costa Rica	321.3	318.2	315.1	312.0	309.6	308.2	308.3	309.7	312.2	315.1	317.4	-0.12	-1.20
Croatia	174.8	172.9	172.0	173.0	174.6	176.4	177.9	178.4	178.9	179.2	179.3	0.25	2.56
Czech Republic	395.6	404.1	411.3	417.3	422.2	426.5	428.7	428.5	428.2	427.7	426.7	0.76	7.85
Denmark	270.0	268.9	268.1	267.4	266.6	265.3	263.9	262.4	260.3	258.9	257.2	-0.48	-4.74
Ecuador	1,151.4	1,142.6	1,134.0	1,126.0	1,118.7	1,112.2	1,106.4	1,101.3	1,097.1	1,093.6	1,090.6	-0.54	-5.29
Egypt	7,285.2	7,440.6	7,581.9	7,706.6	7,812.4	7,898.7	7,966.0	8,016.0	8,059.3	8,092.4	8,113.7	1.08	11.37
Estonia	54.4	55.8	56.7	57.9	59.0	60.3	61.0	61.4	61.9	62.2	62.4	1.37	14.63
Finland	236.6	237.8	239.4	241.5	243.8	246.0	247.4	249.2	250.3	251.5	252.3	0.64	6.61
France	3,159.6	3,175.7	3,184.5	3,198.5	3,209.4	3,219.9	3,228.7	3,234.0	3,226.9	3,223.9	3,212.5	0.17	1.67
Germany	2,970.9	2,922.6	2,878.7	2,843.9	2,797.0	2,748.1	2,696.6	2,654.2	2,617.2	2,575.6	2,535.0	-1.57	-14.67
Greece	436.0	441.8	446.5	450.2	453.7	456.0	457.0	456.5	454.8	452.0	448.2	0.28	2.81
Hong Kong, China	219.1	221.3	222.7	229.2	235.3	243.0	249.5	251.5	252.5	254.7	256.9	1.61	17.26
Hungary	397.0	400.2	401.3	401.9	402.4	403.3	403.9	402.6	400.2	398.1	396.2	-0.02	-0.20
India	102,136.6	102,053.3	101,852.1	101,551.0	101,188.2	100,808.8	100,446.8	100,113.4	99,796.0	99,466.0	99,087.9	-0.30	-2.98
Indonesia	17,072.6	17,061.2	17,005.3	16,908.3	16,778.5	16,627.4	16,464.8	16,296.0	16,122.5	15,945.1	15,764.7	-0.79	-7.66
Iran	4,882.2	5,044.7	5,186.0	5,300.1	5,386.7	5,449.3	5,491.9	5,516.9	5,524.7	5,516.4	5,493.4	1.19	12.52
Ireland	253.6	256.7	259.4	262.6	263.2	262.5	261.3	260.4	259.0	256.9	254.4	0.03	0.31
Israel	584.9	588.7	591.2	592.7	591.6	588.7	585.9	583.2	580.5	577.8	575.2	-0.17	-1.67
Italy	2,273.0	2,274.6	2,266.6	2,257.8	2,244.6	2,222.2	2,191.0	2,158.7	2,124.6	2,089.2	2,053.4	-1.01	-9.66
Japan	4,560.4	4,507.8	4,474.6	4,423.1	4,374.0	4,326.3	4,288.1	4,226.0	4,148.3	4,057.1	3,950.5	-1.43	-13.37
Jordan	595.0	601.0	607.5	614.2	620.6	626.1	630.2	632.5	632.9	631.6	628.9	0.56	5.69
Kazakhstan	1,008.6	1,057.4	1,107.7	1,156.5	1,200.4	1,235.9	1,260.5	1,272.7	1,273.5	1,265.3	1,252.0	2.19	24.14
Kuwait	157.3	160.4	163.7	167.0	170.0	172.4	174.2	175.2	175.5	175.3	174.8	1.06	11.11
Latvia	83.0	84.6	85.9	87.8	89.5	90.7	92.3	93.5	94.3	94.9	95.1	1.38	14.64
Lithuania	128.1	125.4	123.9	123.7	124.3	124.7	125.4	126.0	126.8	127.4	128.0	-0.01	-0.08
Malaysia	2,507.1	2,522.0	2,527.7	2,524.8	2,522.0	2,514.8	2,504.1	2,496.6	2,488.1	2,487.3	2,491.3	-0.06	-0.63
Mexico	8,336.9	8,315.7	8,286.2	8,238.1	8,177.6	8,110.1	8,039.6	7,967.9	7,894.8	7,819.9	7,743.6	-0.74	-7.12
Morocco	2,411.4	2,421.4	2,439.7	2,464.5	2,492.8	2,520.7	2,544.9	2,563.9	2,577.1	2,584.5	2,587.0	0.71	7.28
Netherlands	804.5	793.2	779.2	765.9	752.9	740.2	731.1	725.1	720.3	717.2	715.8	-1.16	-11.02
New Zealand	239.2	242.2	245.9	250.6	254.5	257.3	260.0	261.7	261.7	260.3	258.7	0.79	8.17
Nigeria	18,400.9	18,757.1	19,100.1	19,424.6	19,723.7	19,989.8	20,217.7	20,405.4	20,554.5	20,668.8	20,754.0	1.21	12.79
Norway	243.8	245.0	247.1	250.1	253.6	256.2	258.4	260.9	262.7	265.0	266.4	0.89	9.28
Pakistan	18,598.3	18,867.8	19,147.8	19,435.4	19,726.3	20,014.6	20,294.6	20,561.3	20,808.6	21,026.5	21,205.0	1.32	14.02
Peru	2,389.4	2,392.1	2,393.8	2,394.3	2,392.8	2,388.7	2,381.7	2,371.8	2,359.6	2,346.0	2,332.4	-0.24	-2.39
Philippines	8,529.2	8,606.3	8,686.5	8,770.2	8,852.6	8,929.6	8,996.3	9,051.2	9,095.4	9,132.5	9,167.0	0.72	7.48
Poland	1,486.3	1,477.3	1,471.6	1,475.8	1,486.6	1,501.2	1,514.4	1,524.9	1,536.3	1,547.4	1,557.2	0.47	4.77
Portugal	457.5	456.9	457.5	456.0	453.0	450.3	448.8	445.8	441.7	436.6	430.8	-0.60	-5.83
Romania	881.1	878.4	875.7	877.7	881.1	882.4	880.1	874.1	866.4	857.2	846.7	-0.40	-3.91
Russia	5,677.3	5,873.3	6,103.7	6,355.2	6,517.8	6,642.9	6,769.9	6,924.8	7,061.5	7,120.0	7,115.5	2.28	25.33
Saudi Arabia	2,281.1	2,295.8	2,306.4	2,313.5	2,319.3	2,326.4	2,336.5	2,350.3	2,367.2	2,385.5	2,403.4	0.52	5.36
Singapore	216.7	213.0	207.9	206.4	205.7	206.2	207.3	208.6	210.1	211.7	213.6	-0.14	-1.42
Slovakia	217.3	216.5	216.7	218.1	220.0	221.4	221.6	221.5	221.5	221.4	221.2	0.18	1.82
Slovenia	75.3	76.0	76.4	77.2	78.0	79.1	80.0	80.6	81.3	81.8	82.1	0.87	9.06
South Africa	4,161.7	4,166.3	4,161.5	4,148.7	4,131.6	4,114.7	4,101.2	4,091.9	4,085.2	4,078.8	4,069.6	-0.22	-2.21
South Korea	2,093.1	1,996.5	1,915.5	1,863.8	1,830.0	1,800.4	1,782.3	1,765.3	1,741.7	1,715.2	1,687.4	-2.13	-19.38
Spain	1,888.4	1,936.7	1,975.5	2,010.5	2,043.1	2,064.9	2,082.0	2,094.4	2,094.8	2,090.6	2,082.3	0.98	10.27
Sweden	408.4	415.6	421.6	427.7	431.8	434.3	436.0	438.2	440.6	443.3	446.1	0.89	9.24
Switzerland	305.4	302.8	301.8	301.1	300.6	301.1	301.5	302.3	303.7	305.6	308.3	0.10	0.96
Taiwan	1,020.4	979.6	926.4	899.7	877.5	864.3	853.8	849.4	843.5	838.5	832.5	-2.01	-18.42
Thailand	3,403.1	3,387.4	3,391.3	3,394.0	3,390.9	3,367.2	3,337.9	3,305.4	3,269.0	3,228.8	3,186.9	-0.65	-6.35
Tunisia	633.9	636.7	641.2	647.2	653.9	661.0	667.9	674.3	679.8	684.2	687.3	0.81	8.43
Turkey	5,451.6	5,375.2	5,307.7	5,281.1	5,259.8	5,241.7	5,230.9	5,221.2	5,223.7	5,225.1	5,224.9	-0.42	-4.16
Turkmenistan	408.5	413.5	416.7	418.4	419.0	419.1	419.4	419.9	420.7	421.2	421.2	0.31	3.11
Ukraine	1,654.5	1,686.4	1,718.4	1,751.7	1,772.5	1,777.5	1,767.5	1,752.2	1,717.3	1,680.5	1,643.7	-0.07	-0.65
United Arab Emirates	255.5	259.8	261.7	261.8	260.8	259.9	259.8	260.7	262.5	264.4	265.9	0.40	4.07
United Kingdom	2,853.5	2,893.5	2,954.2	3,025.0	3,081.8	3,131.5	3,176.2	3,218.2	3,254.2	3,279.5	3,295.8	1.45	15.50
USA	16,862.8	17,093.1	17,231.9	17,379.3	17,456.6	17,497.1	17,546.6	17,577.9	17,559.4	17,526.9	17,507.5	0.38	3.82
Venezuela	2,340.6	2,353.7	2,366.0	2,377.0	2,386.6	2,394.3	2,400.1	2,403.8	2,405.6	2,405.4	2,403.6	0.27	2.69
Vietnam	6,392.0	6,456.8	6,484.3	6,483.5	6,463.4	6,439.5	6,422.9	6,414.9	6,410.2	6,405.5	6,395.2	0.01	0.05

Marketing segments: Young generation

Table 4.88 Children (2-9): 2009-2019 (%)

% of total

	2009	2010	2011	2012	2013	2014	2015	2016	2017	2018	2019
Algeria	14.48	14.58	14.65	14.69	14.70	14.69	14.65	14.60	14.53	14.44	14.32
Argentina	13.30	13.19	13.11	13.05	13.01	12.97	12.91	12.83	12.74	12.62	12.50
Australia	10.03	10.03	10.06	10.12	10.18	10.24	10.28	10.29	10.29	10.26	10.21
Austria	7.81	7.77	7.73	7.72	7.67	7.64	7.59	7.56	7.54	7.53	7.52
Azerbaijan	12.29	12.48	12.72	12.98	13.23	13.44	13.57	13.63	13.60	13.50	13.34
Belarus	7.51	7.65	7.84	8.05	8.26	8.47	8.65	8.82	8.91	8.92	8.86
Belgium	8.92	8.97	9.01	9.08	9.15	9.22	9.25	9.27	9.26	9.23	9.20
Bolivia	19.72	19.48	19.21	18.92	18.62	18.31	18.02	17.74	17.46	17.20	16.94
Bosnia-Herzegovina	7.75	7.51	7.35	7.27	7.23	7.23	7.23	7.23	7.22	7.20	7.17
Brazil	14.09	13.75	13.37	12.96	12.56	12.15	11.76	11.39	11.05	10.75	10.48
Bulgaria	7.06	7.07	7.10	7.11	7.13	7.14	7.10	7.07	7.02	6.96	6.88
Canada	8.49	8.45	8.47	8.50	8.50	8.48	8.48	8.48	8.47	8.45	8.43
Chile	11.68	11.54	11.44	11.36	11.30	11.25	11.19	11.13	11.06	10.98	10.89
China	8.36	8.20	8.11	8.05	8.06	8.00	7.99	8.04	8.06	8.07	8.07
Colombia	15.53	15.35	15.18	15.01	14.85	14.68	14.50	14.30	14.10	13.90	13.71
Costa Rica	13.69	13.38	13.08	12.78	12.51	12.29	12.14	12.05	12.01	11.98	11.93
Croatia	7.70	7.62	7.60	7.65	7.74	7.84	7.93	7.97	8.01	8.04	8.07
Czech Republic	7.45	7.59	7.73	7.84	7.94	8.02	8.07	8.07	8.07	8.06	8.04
Denmark	9.58	9.51	9.45	9.39	9.34	9.27	9.19	9.11	9.02	8.95	8.87
Ecuador	16.57	16.26	15.95	15.65	15.37	15.10	14.84	14.61	14.40	14.21	14.02
Egypt	18.23	18.29	18.32	18.31	18.27	18.19	18.07	17.92	17.76	17.59	17.40
Estonia	7.95	8.17	8.34	8.56	8.76	8.96	9.10	9.21	9.31	9.39	9.44
Finland	8.70	8.70	8.72	8.76	8.82	8.85	8.87	8.90	8.90	8.91	8.92
France	9.94	9.94	9.92	9.92	9.91	9.89	9.88	9.85	9.79	9.74	9.67
Germany	7.06	6.97	6.88	6.82	6.72	6.62	6.51	6.43	6.36	6.28	6.20
Greece	7.51	7.58	7.63	7.68	7.71	7.73	7.74	7.71	7.67	7.62	7.55
Hong Kong, China	5.97	6.00	6.01	6.14	6.25	6.40	6.53	6.56	6.53	6.54	6.55
Hungary	7.72	7.80	7.83	7.87	7.90	7.94	7.97	7.97	7.94	7.92	7.91
India	16.76	16.52	16.27	16.01	15.76	15.51	15.27	15.04	14.83	14.62	14.41
Indonesia	14.57	14.40	14.20	13.97	13.73	13.48	13.23	12.98	12.73	12.49	12.25
Iran	12.85	13.12	13.33	13.47	13.53	13.53	13.49	13.40	13.27	13.11	12.93
Ireland	11.15	11.13	11.12	11.12	11.01	10.85	10.69	10.54	10.38	10.20	10.01
Israel	15.41	15.27	15.11	14.93	14.69	14.42	14.16	13.91	13.68	13.45	13.24
Italy	7.49	7.49	7.45	7.42	7.37	7.29	7.19	7.09	6.98	6.87	6.76
Japan	6.97	6.91	6.87	6.80	6.74	6.69	6.64	6.57	6.47	6.35	6.21
Jordan	18.42	18.15	18.00	17.93	17.90	17.84	17.73	17.54	17.28	16.97	16.62
Kazakhstan	12.48	12.92	13.37	13.78	14.13	14.38	14.49	14.47	14.32	14.08	13.80
Kuwait	12.71	12.68	12.66	12.64	12.61	12.54	12.42	12.26	12.07	11.84	11.60
Latvia	7.21	7.39	7.55	7.75	7.94	8.10	8.30	8.45	8.57	8.67	8.74
Lithuania	7.45	7.34	7.31	7.34	7.43	7.50	7.59	7.67	7.75	7.84	7.91
Malaysia	17.28	17.09	16.85	16.57	16.31	16.03	15.74	15.48	15.22	15.02	14.86
Mexico	15.11	14.85	14.58	14.30	14.01	13.72	13.44	13.16	12.90	12.63	12.38
Morocco	14.82	14.70	14.64	14.61	14.60	14.60	14.57	14.52	14.43	14.32	14.18
Netherlands	9.58	9.42	9.23	9.05	8.88	8.71	8.59	8.50	8.43	8.38	8.35
New Zealand	10.84	10.86	10.92	11.01	11.09	11.11	11.13	11.10	11.01	10.87	10.72
Nigeria	23.45	23.37	23.28	23.17	23.04	22.88	22.68	22.44	22.18	21.88	21.58
Norway	9.94	9.87	9.84	9.85	9.89	9.88	9.87	9.87	9.85	9.84	9.80
Pakistan	20.00	19.85	19.71	19.58	19.45	19.32	19.19	19.06	18.91	18.75	18.55
Peru	16.17	15.97	15.77	15.56	15.36	15.14	14.91	14.67	14.43	14.18	13.94
Philippines	18.11	17.93	17.76	17.60	17.44	17.28	17.10	16.90	16.68	16.46	16.24
Poland	7.61	7.57	7.55	7.58	7.65	7.74	7.82	7.89	7.96	8.03	8.09
Portugal	8.32	8.27	8.25	8.21	8.15	8.09	8.04	7.98	7.91	7.81	7.71
Romania	8.00	8.00	8.00	8.05	8.11	8.16	8.18	8.16	8.14	8.10	8.04
Russia	7.80	8.07	8.40	8.76	8.99	9.18	9.37	9.59	9.80	9.90	9.91
Saudi Arabia	17.57	17.33	17.06	16.77	16.49	16.22	15.99	15.78	15.61	15.45	15.29
Singapore	9.02	8.77	8.47	8.31	8.18	8.09	8.04	8.00	7.98	7.97	7.96
Slovakia	7.85	7.81	7.81	7.87	7.93	7.98	7.99	7.99	7.99	7.99	7.99
Slovenia	7.24	7.29	7.31	7.37	7.43	7.53	7.59	7.64	7.69	7.73	7.75
South Africa	16.50	16.39	16.27	16.14	16.00	15.88	15.76	15.67	15.58	15.49	15.39
South Korea	8.25	7.86	7.53	7.32	7.18	7.06	6.98	6.91	6.82	6.72	6.61
Spain	8.07	8.20	8.29	8.37	8.44	8.47	8.48	8.47	8.42	8.35	8.27
Sweden	8.66	8.77	8.86	8.95	8.99	9.00	9.00	9.00	9.00	9.01	9.02
Switzerland	7.88	7.79	7.75	7.71	7.67	7.65	7.63	7.62	7.62	7.63	7.67
Taiwan	8.48	8.11	7.65	7.40	7.20	7.08	6.98	6.93	6.87	6.82	6.77
Thailand	10.30	10.19	10.14	10.09	10.03	9.91	9.78	9.65	9.51	9.36	9.20
Tunisia	11.96	11.89	11.86	11.85	11.86	11.87	11.89	11.89	11.88	11.85	11.81
Turkey	14.20	13.83	13.50	13.28	13.08	12.89	12.73	12.58	12.46	12.35	12.24
Turkmenistan	15.76	15.75	15.67	15.53	15.36	15.18	15.00	14.85	14.70	14.55	14.40
Ukraine	7.01	7.19	7.38	7.57	7.72	7.79	7.80	7.78	7.68	7.56	7.45
United Arab Emirates	10.78	10.73	10.59	10.40	10.19	9.99	9.82	9.69	9.59	9.50	9.39
United Kingdom	9.05	9.12	9.26	9.42	9.54	9.63	9.70	9.76	9.80	9.81	9.80
USA	10.76	10.83	10.84	10.87	10.84	10.80	10.75	10.70	10.62	10.53	10.45
Venezuela	16.03	15.87	15.70	15.54	15.37	15.19	15.01	14.83	14.64	14.45	14.25
Vietnam	14.30	14.26	14.14	13.96	13.75	13.53	13.33	13.16	13.00	12.84	12.68

Marketing segments: Young generation

Table 4.89 Female children (2-9): 2009-2019 (%)

% of total

	2009	2010	2011	2012	2013	2014	2015	2016	2017	2018	2019
Algeria	7.08	7.12	7.16	7.18	7.19	7.18	7.17	7.14	7.11	7.06	7.00
Argentina	6.54	6.48	6.44	6.41	6.39	6.37	6.34	6.30	6.25	6.20	6.14
Australia	4.88	4.88	4.90	4.93	4.96	4.99	5.01	5.02	5.02	5.00	4.98
Austria	3.81	3.79	3.77	3.77	3.75	3.73	3.71	3.69	3.68	3.67	3.67
Azerbaijan	5.63	5.70	5.81	5.93	6.06	6.16	6.24	6.27	6.27	6.22	6.16
Belarus	3.65	3.72	3.81	3.91	4.02	4.12	4.21	4.29	4.33	4.33	4.30
Belgium	4.36	4.38	4.40	4.42	4.46	4.49	4.51	4.51	4.51	4.50	4.48
Bolivia	9.67	9.55	9.42	9.28	9.13	8.98	8.83	8.69	8.56	8.43	8.30
Bosnia-Herzegovina	3.75	3.63	3.56	3.52	3.50	3.50	3.50	3.50	3.49	3.48	3.47
Brazil	6.92	6.75	6.56	6.36	6.16	5.96	5.77	5.59	5.42	5.27	5.14
Bulgaria	3.43	3.44	3.45	3.46	3.47	3.48	3.46	3.44	3.42	3.39	3.35
Canada	4.14	4.12	4.13	4.14	4.14	4.12	4.12	4.12	4.11	4.10	4.09
Chile	5.73	5.67	5.62	5.58	5.55	5.52	5.49	5.46	5.43	5.39	5.35
China	3.72	3.65	3.61	3.57	3.56	3.53	3.52	3.54	3.56	3.57	3.58
Colombia	7.61	7.52	7.43	7.35	7.27	7.18	7.10	7.00	6.90	6.80	6.71
Costa Rica	6.67	6.52	6.38	6.23	6.10	6.00	5.92	5.88	5.86	5.84	5.82
Croatia	3.75	3.71	3.70	3.73	3.77	3.81	3.86	3.88	3.90	3.91	3.93
Czech Republic	3.62	3.69	3.76	3.82	3.86	3.91	3.93	3.93	3.93	3.93	3.92
Denmark	4.68	4.65	4.61	4.58	4.56	4.52	4.48	4.44	4.40	4.36	4.32
Ecuador	8.11	7.96	7.81	7.66	7.52	7.39	7.26	7.15	7.05	6.95	6.86
Egypt	8.73	8.77	8.79	8.79	8.78	8.76	8.71	8.65	8.59	8.51	8.43
Estonia	3.86	3.97	4.06	4.16	4.25	4.35	4.41	4.48	4.52	4.56	4.59
Finland	4.25	4.25	4.26	4.28	4.31	4.32	4.33	4.33	4.33	4.34	4.34
France	4.88	4.88	4.87	4.87	4.86	4.85	4.84	4.83	4.80	4.77	4.74
Germany	3.44	3.39	3.35	3.31	3.26	3.21	3.16	3.12	3.08	3.04	3.01
Greece	3.64	3.67	3.69	3.72	3.73	3.74	3.74	3.73	3.71	3.68	3.65
Hong Kong, China	2.87	2.89	2.91	2.98	3.04	3.11	3.18	3.21	3.19	3.19	3.21
Hungary	3.76	3.80	3.81	3.83	3.84	3.86	3.88	3.88	3.87	3.86	3.85
India	8.02	7.91	7.79	7.67	7.54	7.42	7.31	7.20	7.10	7.00	6.91
Indonesia	7.15	7.06	6.96	6.85	6.73	6.61	6.49	6.36	6.24	6.12	6.00
Iran	6.27	6.41	6.51	6.57	6.60	6.60	6.57	6.53	6.47	6.39	6.31
Ireland	5.45	5.44	5.43	5.42	5.37	5.29	5.21	5.14	5.06	4.97	4.88
Israel	7.51	7.44	7.37	7.27	7.15	7.02	6.89	6.77	6.66	6.55	6.45
Italy	3.64	3.64	3.62	3.61	3.58	3.54	3.49	3.44	3.39	3.33	3.28
Japan	3.40	3.37	3.35	3.32	3.29	3.26	3.24	3.20	3.15	3.10	3.03
Jordan	9.00	8.87	8.79	8.76	8.75	8.73	8.67	8.58	8.45	8.30	8.13
Kazakhstan	6.09	6.30	6.52	6.72	6.89	7.01	7.07	7.06	6.98	6.87	6.72
Kuwait	6.27	6.26	6.25	6.24	6.22	6.18	6.13	6.05	5.95	5.84	5.72
Latvia	3.53	3.62	3.69	3.78	3.87	3.95	4.05	4.12	4.18	4.23	4.25
Lithuania	3.63	3.58	3.57	3.58	3.63	3.67	3.71	3.75	3.79	3.83	3.87
Malaysia	8.36	8.26	8.14	8.00	7.87	7.73	7.59	7.46	7.34	7.24	7.16
Mexico	7.44	7.31	7.17	7.03	6.89	6.74	6.60	6.46	6.33	6.20	6.07
Morocco	7.28	7.22	7.19	7.18	7.18	7.17	7.16	7.13	7.09	7.03	6.97
Netherlands	4.67	4.60	4.50	4.41	4.33	4.24	4.18	4.14	4.10	4.08	4.07
New Zealand	5.29	5.30	5.32	5.36	5.40	5.40	5.41	5.40	5.36	5.29	5.21
Nigeria	11.56	11.52	11.48	11.42	11.36	11.28	11.18	11.07	10.94	10.80	10.64
Norway	4.86	4.83	4.81	4.82	4.83	4.82	4.81	4.81	4.80	4.79	4.78
Pakistan	9.71	9.64	9.57	9.51	9.44	9.38	9.31	9.25	9.18	9.10	9.01
Peru	7.93	7.83	7.73	7.63	7.53	7.42	7.31	7.19	7.07	6.95	6.83
Philippines	8.86	8.76	8.68	8.60	8.52	8.44	8.35	8.25	8.15	8.04	7.93
Poland	3.70	3.68	3.66	3.68	3.71	3.76	3.80	3.83	3.87	3.90	3.93
Portugal	4.03	4.00	3.99	3.96	3.93	3.90	3.88	3.85	3.81	3.77	3.72
Romania	3.89	3.89	3.89	3.91	3.94	3.97	3.98	3.97	3.96	3.94	3.91
Russia	3.80	3.93	4.09	4.26	4.37	4.46	4.55	4.66	4.75	4.80	4.81
Saudi Arabia	8.70	8.58	8.44	8.30	8.16	8.03	7.91	7.81	7.72	7.64	7.56
Singapore	4.42	4.30	4.17	4.09	4.02	3.97	3.94	3.92	3.90	3.89	3.88
Slovakia	3.82	3.80	3.80	3.83	3.86	3.88	3.88	3.88	3.88	3.88	3.88
Slovenia	3.52	3.54	3.55	3.58	3.61	3.66	3.68	3.71	3.73	3.75	3.76
South Africa	8.20	8.14	8.08	8.02	7.95	7.89	7.83	7.78	7.73	7.69	7.63
South Korea	3.96	3.77	3.62	3.52	3.46	3.40	3.36	3.33	3.29	3.24	3.19
Spain	3.92	3.98	4.03	4.06	4.10	4.11	4.12	4.12	4.09	4.06	4.02
Sweden	4.22	4.28	4.32	4.37	4.39	4.39	4.39	4.39	4.39	4.40	4.40
Switzerland	3.84	3.80	3.79	3.77	3.75	3.74	3.73	3.72	3.72	3.73	3.74
Taiwan	4.05	3.87	3.65	3.53	3.43	3.37	3.33	3.30	3.28	3.25	3.22
Thailand	5.05	4.98	4.96	4.93	4.90	4.84	4.78	4.72	4.65	4.58	4.50
Tunisia	5.79	5.76	5.74	5.73	5.74	5.74	5.75	5.75	5.75	5.73	5.71
Turkey	6.95	6.77	6.61	6.50	6.40	6.31	6.23	6.15	6.10	6.04	5.98
Turkmenistan	7.77	7.76	7.72	7.65	7.57	7.48	7.39	7.31	7.24	7.16	7.08
Ukraine	3.41	3.50	3.59	3.69	3.76	3.80	3.80	3.79	3.74	3.68	3.63
United Arab Emirates	5.25	5.23	5.17	5.09	5.00	4.91	4.84	4.78	4.73	4.69	4.63
United Kingdom	4.42	4.45	4.51	4.59	4.64	4.68	4.71	4.74	4.76	4.76	4.75
USA	5.26	5.29	5.30	5.31	5.30	5.28	5.26	5.24	5.20	5.16	5.12
Venezuela	7.85	7.76	7.68	7.60	7.52	7.43	7.34	7.25	7.16	7.07	6.97
Vietnam	7.00	6.99	6.93	6.84	6.73	6.62	6.53	6.44	6.36	6.29	6.21

Marketing segments: Young generation

Table 4.90 Male children (2-9): 2009-2019 (%)

% of total

	2009	2010	2011	2012	2013	2014	2015	2016	2017	2018	2019
Algeria	7.41	7.45	7.49	7.51	7.51	7.51	7.49	7.46	7.42	7.38	7.31
Argentina	6.76	6.71	6.67	6.64	6.62	6.60	6.57	6.53	6.48	6.42	6.36
Australia	5.14	5.14	5.16	5.19	5.22	5.25	5.27	5.28	5.28	5.26	5.23
Austria	4.00	3.98	3.96	3.95	3.92	3.91	3.88	3.87	3.86	3.85	3.85
Azerbaijan	6.67	6.78	6.91	7.05	7.17	7.27	7.34	7.36	7.34	7.28	7.19
Belarus	3.86	3.93	4.03	4.13	4.24	4.34	4.44	4.53	4.58	4.58	4.56
Belgium	4.57	4.60	4.62	4.65	4.69	4.73	4.75	4.75	4.75	4.74	4.72
Bolivia	10.05	9.93	9.79	9.64	9.49	9.34	9.19	9.04	8.90	8.77	8.64
Bosnia-Herzegovina	4.00	3.88	3.80	3.75	3.73	3.73	3.73	3.73	3.72	3.71	3.70
Brazil	7.17	7.00	6.81	6.60	6.39	6.19	5.99	5.80	5.63	5.48	5.34
Bulgaria	3.63	3.63	3.65	3.65	3.66	3.66	3.64	3.62	3.60	3.57	3.53
Canada	4.34	4.33	4.34	4.36	4.37	4.36	4.36	4.36	4.36	4.35	4.34
Chile	5.95	5.88	5.83	5.79	5.76	5.73	5.70	5.67	5.63	5.59	5.55
China	4.64	4.55	4.51	4.48	4.49	4.47	4.47	4.50	4.50	4.50	4.49
Colombia	7.93	7.83	7.75	7.66	7.58	7.49	7.40	7.30	7.20	7.10	7.00
Costa Rica	7.02	6.86	6.70	6.55	6.41	6.30	6.22	6.17	6.15	6.13	6.11
Croatia	3.95	3.91	3.90	3.93	3.97	4.02	4.07	4.09	4.11	4.13	4.14
Czech Republic	3.83	3.90	3.97	4.03	4.07	4.12	4.14	4.14	4.13	4.13	4.12
Denmark	4.90	4.87	4.84	4.81	4.78	4.75	4.71	4.67	4.62	4.58	4.54
Ecuador	8.45	8.29	8.14	7.99	7.84	7.71	7.58	7.46	7.35	7.26	7.16
Egypt	9.49	9.52	9.53	9.52	9.49	9.43	9.36	9.27	9.18	9.08	8.97
Estonia	4.09	4.21	4.29	4.39	4.50	4.61	4.68	4.73	4.78	4.82	4.85
Finland	4.44	4.45	4.46	4.48	4.51	4.53	4.54	4.56	4.57	4.58	4.58
France	5.06	5.06	5.05	5.05	5.04	5.04	5.03	5.02	4.99	4.97	4.93
Germany	3.62	3.58	3.54	3.50	3.46	3.41	3.36	3.31	3.28	3.24	3.20
Greece	3.87	3.91	3.94	3.96	3.98	4.00	4.00	3.98	3.96	3.94	3.90
Hong Kong, China	3.10	3.10	3.09	3.16	3.21	3.29	3.35	3.35	3.34	3.34	3.35
Hungary	3.96	4.00	4.02	4.04	4.05	4.07	4.09	4.09	4.08	4.07	4.06
India	8.74	8.61	8.48	8.35	8.21	8.08	7.96	7.84	7.72	7.61	7.51
Indonesia	7.42	7.34	7.24	7.12	7.00	6.87	6.74	6.62	6.49	6.37	6.25
Iran	6.58	6.72	6.83	6.90	6.93	6.94	6.91	6.87	6.80	6.72	6.62
Ireland	5.70	5.70	5.69	5.69	5.64	5.57	5.48	5.41	5.33	5.23	5.14
Israel	7.90	7.83	7.75	7.66	7.54	7.40	7.27	7.14	7.02	6.90	6.79
Italy	3.85	3.85	3.83	3.81	3.79	3.75	3.70	3.65	3.59	3.53	3.48
Japan	3.57	3.54	3.52	3.49	3.46	3.43	3.41	3.37	3.32	3.26	3.19
Jordan	9.42	9.28	9.21	9.17	9.15	9.12	9.06	8.96	8.83	8.67	8.50
Kazakhstan	6.39	6.61	6.84	7.06	7.24	7.36	7.43	7.42	7.34	7.22	7.07
Kuwait	6.43	6.42	6.41	6.41	6.39	6.35	6.30	6.21	6.11	6.00	5.88
Latvia	3.68	3.77	3.86	3.97	4.07	4.15	4.25	4.33	4.40	4.45	4.48
Lithuania	3.83	3.77	3.74	3.76	3.80	3.83	3.88	3.92	3.96	4.01	4.04
Malaysia	8.92	8.83	8.72	8.58	8.44	8.30	8.15	8.02	7.88	7.78	7.70
Mexico	7.68	7.55	7.41	7.27	7.13	6.98	6.84	6.70	6.57	6.44	6.31
Morocco	7.54	7.48	7.44	7.43	7.43	7.43	7.41	7.39	7.34	7.29	7.22
Netherlands	4.90	4.83	4.73	4.64	4.55	4.47	4.41	4.36	4.33	4.30	4.29
New Zealand	5.55	5.56	5.60	5.65	5.69	5.70	5.71	5.70	5.66	5.58	5.51
Nigeria	11.89	11.85	11.81	11.75	11.68	11.59	11.49	11.37	11.24	11.09	10.93
Norway	5.08	5.04	5.03	5.04	5.06	5.06	5.06	5.06	5.05	5.04	5.02
Pakistan	10.29	10.21	10.14	10.07	10.01	9.94	9.88	9.81	9.73	9.65	9.55
Peru	8.24	8.14	8.03	7.93	7.83	7.72	7.60	7.48	7.36	7.23	7.11
Philippines	9.26	9.16	9.08	9.00	8.92	8.83	8.74	8.64	8.53	8.42	8.31
Poland	3.91	3.89	3.89	3.90	3.94	3.98	4.02	4.06	4.09	4.13	4.16
Portugal	4.29	4.27	4.27	4.25	4.21	4.18	4.16	4.13	4.09	4.04	3.99
Romania	4.11	4.11	4.11	4.13	4.17	4.19	4.20	4.19	4.18	4.16	4.13
Russia	4.00	4.14	4.31	4.50	4.62	4.72	4.82	4.94	5.04	5.09	5.10
Saudi Arabia	8.87	8.75	8.61	8.47	8.33	8.19	8.08	7.97	7.89	7.81	7.73
Singapore	4.60	4.46	4.30	4.22	4.16	4.12	4.10	4.09	4.08	4.08	4.08
Slovakia	4.03	4.01	4.01	4.04	4.08	4.10	4.11	4.10	4.10	4.10	4.10
Slovenia	3.72	3.75	3.76	3.79	3.82	3.87	3.90	3.93	3.96	3.98	3.99
South Africa	8.31	8.25	8.19	8.12	8.06	7.99	7.94	7.89	7.85	7.80	7.76
South Korea	4.29	4.09	3.91	3.80	3.72	3.66	3.62	3.58	3.53	3.48	3.42
Spain	4.15	4.22	4.27	4.31	4.34	4.36	4.36	4.36	4.33	4.29	4.25
Sweden	4.44	4.50	4.54	4.58	4.61	4.61	4.61	4.61	4.61	4.61	4.62
Switzerland	4.04	3.99	3.96	3.94	3.92	3.91	3.90	3.90	3.90	3.91	3.93
Taiwan	4.43	4.24	4.00	3.87	3.77	3.70	3.65	3.63	3.60	3.57	3.55
Thailand	5.26	5.20	5.18	5.15	5.13	5.07	5.00	4.93	4.86	4.78	4.70
Tunisia	6.17	6.14	6.12	6.12	6.12	6.13	6.14	6.14	6.13	6.12	6.10
Turkey	7.24	7.06	6.89	6.78	6.68	6.58	6.50	6.43	6.37	6.31	6.25
Turkmenistan	7.99	7.99	7.95	7.88	7.79	7.70	7.61	7.53	7.46	7.39	7.31
Ukraine	3.60	3.69	3.79	3.89	3.96	4.00	4.00	3.99	3.94	3.88	3.82
United Arab Emirates	5.54	5.50	5.42	5.31	5.19	5.08	4.98	4.91	4.86	4.81	4.76
United Kingdom	4.63	4.67	4.74	4.83	4.90	4.95	4.98	5.02	5.04	5.05	5.05
USA	5.50	5.53	5.54	5.55	5.54	5.51	5.49	5.47	5.42	5.38	5.34
Venezuela	8.19	8.10	8.02	7.94	7.85	7.76	7.67	7.58	7.48	7.38	7.28
Vietnam	7.29	7.28	7.22	7.13	7.02	6.91	6.81	6.72	6.64	6.56	6.48

Marketing segments: Young generation

Table 4.91 Tweenagers (10-14): 2009-2019

'000

	2009	2010	2011	2012	2013	2014	2015	2016	2017	2018	2019	CAGR	Period growth
Algeria	3,089.2	3,011.9	2,973.2	2,972.7	3,003.5	3,054.4	3,115.2	3,179.1	3,242.5	3,303.2	3,360.1	0.84	8.77
Argentina	3,443.4	3,424.6	3,402.6	3,379.7	3,359.5	3,345.8	3,341.5	3,347.4	3,362.4	3,383.1	3,406.4	-0.11	-1.07
Australia	1,404.3	1,401.5	1,401.8	1,400.5	1,402.0	1,405.4	1,411.9	1,428.2	1,453.4	1,487.0	1,525.7	0.83	8.65
Austria	461.2	449.4	440.9	429.3	424.6	421.2	423.1	422.3	423.7	421.8	420.8	-0.91	-8.74
Azerbaijan	717.1	684.4	659.9	644.5	638.7	641.8	652.9	670.5	693.1	718.2	742.7	0.35	3.57
Belarus	481.2	466.1	460.1	457.7	458.3	454.7	451.7	449.7	456.1	472.2	492.6	0.23	2.37
Belgium	602.1	600.4	601.2	599.4	595.9	595.2	598.7	602.2	609.1	619.3	629.4	0.44	4.53
Bolivia	1,132.2	1,139.2	1,147.7	1,157.4	1,167.7	1,177.1	1,184.9	1,190.5	1,193.8	1,195.3	1,195.6	0.55	5.61
Bosnia-Herzegovina	223.6	221.4	216.9	210.4	202.6	194.7	187.9	182.6	179.1	176.9	175.7	-2.38	-21.44
Brazil	17,005.0	17,155.6	17,305.7	17,418.8	17,462.3	17,407.6	17,246.6	16,989.6	16,660.9	16,283.0	15,873.0	-0.69	-6.66
Bulgaria	321.9	316.3	315.9	316.4	322.4	327.5	326.8	326.6	325.5	325.3	324.1	0.07	0.68
Canada	1,995.4	1,959.4	1,915.2	1,877.8	1,854.7	1,845.5	1,838.4	1,848.2	1,872.3	1,900.4	1,925.6	-0.36	-3.50
Chile	1,365.1	1,332.2	1,303.1	1,279.1	1,260.4	1,247.1	1,238.9	1,235.2	1,235.6	1,238.9	1,243.6	-0.93	-8.90
China	85,438.7	82,137.5	79,373.7	77,310.7	74,561.0	74,518.8	73,450.7	72,482.7	72,514.3	73,650.6	74,087.1	-1.42	-13.29
Colombia	4,405.3	4,400.3	4,396.0	4,393.9	4,394.9	4,399.6	4,408.0	4,419.5	4,432.8	4,445.7	4,455.5	0.11	1.14
Costa Rica	413.1	410.3	408.0	406.0	403.9	401.1	397.4	392.8	387.7	383.0	379.7	-0.84	-8.09
Croatia	253.8	250.9	245.9	235.3	224.7	216.1	210.0	207.6	208.9	211.2	214.3	-1.68	-15.58
Czech Republic	479.5	462.6	457.8	460.1	464.0	469.0	479.1	492.7	504.6	514.7	523.8	0.89	9.24
Denmark	350.1	345.1	341.2	337.9	333.9	332.0	330.4	327.9	328.0	328.2	328.5	-0.63	-6.16
Ecuador	1,424.5	1,429.3	1,430.7	1,428.6	1,423.5	1,415.8	1,406.5	1,396.2	1,385.5	1,374.8	1,364.8	-0.43	-4.19
Egypt	7,849.9	8,035.7	8,237.6	8,456.9	8,691.5	8,935.0	9,179.8	9,418.7	9,625.1	9,802.5	9,951.3	2.40	26.77
Estonia	62.4	61.1	61.1	60.9	61.7	62.8	64.6	65.9	67.9	69.6	71.5	1.37	14.62
Finland	309.3	302.3	296.5	292.4	289.3	289.7	290.4	291.9	295.2	298.5	301.3	-0.26	-2.58
France	3,685.7	3,725.0	3,777.5	3,818.6	3,860.4	3,891.3	3,904.0	3,895.4	3,915.0	3,935.3	3,970.1	0.75	7.72
Germany	3,974.5	3,952.7	3,940.6	3,875.1	3,781.6	3,701.5	3,636.9	3,556.9	3,497.4	3,463.3	3,440.8	-1.43	-13.43
Greece	538.0	531.2	526.7	525.1	526.7	533.1	540.2	547.0	554.1	560.2	565.4	0.50	5.09
Hong Kong, China	381.5	362.1	345.0	322.4	310.7	302.5	298.8	302.0	318.3	330.3	344.3	-1.02	-9.75
Hungary	524.2	505.6	493.8	486.3	484.5	483.2	484.7	484.7	487.9	490.6	494.7	-0.58	-5.64
India	120,302.0	120,440.4	120,628.4	120,856.6	121,078.1	121,228.8	121,254.7	121,133.8	120,880.8	120,539.6	120,167.2	-0.01	-0.11
Indonesia	20,454.0	20,499.3	20,577.5	20,678.2	20,781.6	20,863.4	20,904.2	20,893.4	20,830.5	20,722.5	20,581.0	0.06	0.62
Iran	5,619.6	5,378.9	5,276.4	5,303.6	5,429.8	5,613.1	5,816.4	6,016.5	6,201.5	6,363.2	6,497.0	1.46	15.61
Ireland	285.3	291.2	295.6	298.0	303.1	309.1	314.8	319.6	325.2	326.4	325.3	1.32	14.03
Israel	648.0	662.9	676.8	689.7	703.2	715.7	724.5	730.8	734.8	733.7	729.5	1.19	12.57
Italy	2,740.0	2,743.6	2,762.7	2,773.7	2,786.3	2,803.2	2,824.6	2,826.3	2,829.4	2,825.5	2,807.0	0.24	2.45
Japan	5,955.6	5,925.1	5,897.5	5,851.0	5,768.4	5,674.8	5,540.2	5,447.4	5,380.4	5,354.4	5,368.0	-1.03	-9.87
Jordan	701.6	705.4	706.6	706.4	706.2	707.8	712.5	720.4	730.7	742.2	753.2	0.71	7.37
Kazakhstan	1,137.9	1,106.1	1,092.8	1,099.0	1,124.5	1,166.9	1,223.0	1,289.4	1,361.4	1,432.1	1,494.4	2.76	31.33
Kuwait	174.7	177.9	181.0	184.0	187.1	190.5	194.3	198.5	203.0	207.5	211.4	1.93	21.05
Latvia	98.9	94.8	93.7	93.7	94.9	97.5	98.6	99.9	102.3	104.6	106.5	0.74	7.63
Lithuania	189.8	184.4	177.8	170.8	163.8	158.2	152.8	149.9	149.1	149.8	150.2	-2.31	-20.84
Malaysia	2,791.5	2,837.6	2,880.2	2,920.9	2,948.4	2,976.4	3,004.4	3,026.3	3,044.7	3,053.6	3,039.4	0.85	8.88
Mexico	10,484.3	10,431.3	10,390.5	10,349.2	10,309.2	10,268.3	10,222.7	10,170.5	10,111.3	10,046.1	9,977.4	-0.49	-4.84
Morocco	3,066.7	3,028.1	2,992.0	2,960.9	2,937.6	2,925.4	2,926.1	2,940.1	2,965.5	2,998.8	3,035.0	-0.10	-1.04
Netherlands	979.0	981.0	993.3	1,002.6	1,008.6	1,007.0	997.0	975.9	956.2	935.6	914.3	-0.68	-6.61
New Zealand	298.2	296.7	295.1	293.1	291.5	292.5	291.3	292.8	299.1	307.4	314.4	0.53	5.42
Nigeria	18,823.0	19,237.6	19,663.7	20,101.2	20,549.1	21,005.4	21,466.4	21,927.6	22,381.4	22,816.8	23,221.0	2.12	23.36
Norway	314.8	315.7	315.9	312.9	309.8	309.6	309.0	308.3	311.3	315.0	319.3	0.14	1.44
Pakistan	20,648.0	20,841.0	21,061.4	21,308.0	21,577.9	21,867.1	22,173.1	22,495.0	22,833.1	23,186.1	23,551.3	1.32	14.06
Peru	2,918.0	2,918.3	2,918.8	2,919.9	2,921.8	2,924.5	2,927.6	2,931.0	2,933.8	2,934.8	2,932.7	0.05	0.50
Philippines	10,089.1	10,142.9	10,186.1	10,227.9	10,275.0	10,336.8	10,416.9	10,516.3	10,630.9	10,752.6	10,870.9	0.75	7.75
Poland	2,123.5	2,038.4	1,974.3	1,909.1	1,853.4	1,809.8	1,782.4	1,767.5	1,766.6	1,777.5	1,794.6	-1.67	-15.49
Portugal	539.5	547.2	549.9	555.0	563.0	568.5	564.6	563.9	561.7	557.8	555.2	0.29	2.90
Romania	1,114.4	1,105.4	1,104.4	1,097.4	1,083.5	1,066.5	1,054.9	1,048.7	1,054.0	1,064.5	1,072.1	-0.39	-3.80
Russia	6,773.2	6,593.1	6,483.8	6,452.6	6,566.6	6,741.0	6,991.4	7,177.4	7,378.6	7,620.7	7,881.3	1.53	16.36
Saudi Arabia	2,671.0	2,689.4	2,711.3	2,736.0	2,761.3	2,784.4	2,802.9	2,816.1	2,824.7	2,830.9	2,837.8	0.61	6.24
Singapore	314.7	310.3	306.5	297.6	288.6	280.6	273.0	262.6	257.7	253.9	252.3	-2.19	-19.83
Slovakia	301.1	290.9	283.8	274.6	267.1	262.0	259.6	259.6	262.6	265.8	268.2	-1.15	-10.93
Slovenia	95.9	94.2	93.8	92.7	92.3	91.9	92.6	92.7	93.6	94.7	96.3	0.04	0.37
South Africa	4,978.1	4,993.9	5,015.3	5,039.9	5,063.9	5,083.0	5,094.3	5,096.0	5,089.4	5,078.0	5,066.5	0.18	1.78
South Korea	3,272.2	3,188.1	3,088.1	2,948.7	2,797.8	2,653.6	2,482.2	2,331.6	2,248.3	2,200.2	2,163.0	-4.06	-33.90
Spain	2,080.0	2,101.2	2,140.6	2,193.2	2,247.1	2,314.7	2,375.8	2,425.7	2,481.1	2,537.7	2,576.7	2.16	23.88
Sweden	515.0	493.8	483.4	481.3	487.9	498.2	511.1	521.6	531.8	538.0	541.5	0.50	5.14
Switzerland	414.9	409.1	401.8	393.0	386.4	380.1	376.1	374.9	374.5	373.8	373.9	-1.03	-9.87
Taiwan	1,559.2	1,519.2	1,500.5	1,435.1	1,357.9	1,317.5	1,253.0	1,155.3	1,104.7	1,062.6	1,039.0	-3.98	-33.37
Thailand	4,880.9	4,746.7	4,552.3	4,378.9	4,278.5	4,268.0	4,243.6	4,254.9	4,260.0	4,268.9	4,247.2	-1.38	-12.98
Tunisia	835.2	810.9	791.5	777.2	768.0	763.2	762.2	764.5	769.6	776.8	785.2	-0.61	-5.98
Turkey	7,111.9	7,146.6	7,150.3	7,082.6	6,981.1	6,863.3	6,737.3	6,623.1	6,557.0	6,513.0	6,477.9	-0.93	-8.91
Turkmenistan	495.4	483.9	478.4	478.8	483.3	489.7	496.0	500.9	504.3	506.3	507.6	0.24	2.46
Ukraine	2,277.5	2,162.4	2,062.2	1,968.5	1,922.6	1,909.9	1,938.6	1,970.2	2,043.8	2,103.0	2,141.5	-0.61	-5.97
United Arab Emirates	266.7	277.8	289.3	300.5	310.5	318.3	323.7	326.5	327.3	326.9	326.5	2.04	22.43
United Kingdom	3,637.2	3,582.7	3,519.1	3,448.5	3,395.6	3,382.2	3,402.5	3,453.6	3,531.9	3,629.5	3,729.0	0.25	2.52
USA	19,947.2	19,905.9	20,077.8	20,278.6	20,537.9	20,851.3	21,115.0	21,268.7	21,580.3	21,892.4	22,130.4	1.04	10.95
Venezuela	2,758.7	2,770.5	2,784.5	2,800.4	2,817.5	2,835.3	2,852.9	2,870.1	2,886.3	2,901.1	2,914.0	0.55	5.63
Vietnam	7,842.6	7,634.3	7,547.7	7,565.5	7,652.3	7,753.5	7,828.8	7,868.1	7,882.9	7,879.9	7,872.3	0.04	0.38

Marketing segments: Young generation

Table 4.92 Female tweenagers (10-14): 2009-2019

'000

	2009	2010	2011	2012	2013	2014	2015	2016	2017	2018	2019	CAGR	Period growth
Algeria	1,510.5	1,472.5	1,453.5	1,453.1	1,468.1	1,493.0	1,522.8	1,554.2	1,585.4	1,615.4	1,643.4	0.85	8.80
Argentina	1,693.8	1,684.4	1,673.4	1,662.0	1,652.0	1,645.1	1,642.8	1,645.6	1,652.7	1,662.7	1,674.0	-0.12	-1.17
Australia	683.9	683.0	683.5	683.1	684.1	685.5	687.8	696.1	708.0	724.4	743.5	0.84	8.71
Austria	225.2	219.5	215.3	209.3	207.0	205.4	206.2	206.2	207.3	206.3	205.9	-0.89	-8.56
Azerbaijan	342.3	324.4	310.3	300.6	295.5	295.1	298.8	306.2	316.5	328.2	340.0	-0.07	-0.68
Belarus	233.7	226.2	223.7	222.3	222.3	220.6	219.2	218.2	221.3	229.0	238.9	0.22	2.21
Belgium	293.9	293.5	293.7	292.8	290.9	290.7	291.9	293.3	296.3	301.1	305.7	0.40	4.03
Bolivia	555.2	558.7	562.9	567.7	572.8	577.5	581.4	584.1	585.7	586.5	586.6	0.55	5.64
Bosnia-Herzegovina	108.0	107.0	104.9	101.8	98.1	94.3	90.9	88.4	86.6	85.6	85.0	-2.37	-21.31
Brazil	8,357.6	8,430.0	8,502.3	8,556.8	8,577.3	8,550.0	8,470.6	8,343.9	8,181.8	7,995.5	7,793.5	-0.70	-6.75
Bulgaria	156.9	154.0	153.6	153.8	156.7	159.0	158.5	158.4	158.0	158.3	157.8	0.05	0.54
Canada	972.5	955.1	932.5	914.0	901.4	895.5	890.7	894.5	904.9	917.1	928.5	-0.46	-4.52
Chile	670.5	654.3	640.0	628.1	618.9	612.4	608.3	606.5	606.6	608.2	610.5	-0.93	-8.95
China	38,460.5	36,772.8	35,530.0	34,771.8	33,763.4	33,959.8	33,645.8	33,252.1	33,027.8	33,374.8	33,381.0	-1.41	-13.21
Colombia	2,159.4	2,156.8	2,154.6	2,153.4	2,153.6	2,155.7	2,159.7	2,165.2	2,171.6	2,177.8	2,182.5	0.11	1.07
Costa Rica	200.6	199.3	198.4	197.5	196.6	195.3	193.5	191.3	188.9	186.7	185.0	-0.80	-7.75
Croatia	124.2	122.6	120.0	115.0	109.8	105.5	102.3	101.2	101.7	102.9	104.3	-1.73	-16.01
Czech Republic	233.4	225.3	222.6	223.6	225.3	227.8	232.4	239.5	245.4	250.4	254.9	0.88	9.20
Denmark	170.5	168.1	166.4	165.1	163.1	162.2	161.4	160.2	160.1	160.3	160.3	-0.61	-5.97
Ecuador	698.6	700.8	701.3	700.3	697.7	693.9	689.3	684.2	678.8	673.5	668.4	-0.44	-4.31
Egypt	3,752.1	3,838.3	3,932.4	4,035.2	4,146.1	4,262.2	4,380.5	4,498.3	4,601.9	4,692.8	4,770.8	2.43	27.15
Estonia	30.4	29.7	29.6	29.4	29.9	30.6	31.4	32.1	33.0	33.8	34.6	1.33	14.08
Finland	151.7	148.2	145.1	143.2	141.3	141.6	141.8	142.9	144.6	146.3	147.4	-0.29	-2.86
France	1,806.2	1,825.0	1,850.9	1,872.9	1,895.0	1,911.0	1,918.1	1,914.9	1,924.3	1,934.3	1,950.4	0.77	7.98
Germany	1,935.7	1,925.3	1,920.9	1,889.4	1,843.7	1,804.5	1,773.3	1,732.4	1,702.1	1,684.2	1,671.7	-1.46	-13.64
Greece	261.8	258.7	256.7	254.7	255.1	258.1	261.2	264.2	268.1	270.7	273.0	0.42	4.28
Hong Kong, China	186.1	176.6	167.7	156.2	150.1	146.3	144.8	146.1	154.3	160.0	166.8	-1.09	-10.39
Hungary	255.6	246.6	241.1	237.4	236.8	235.8	236.5	236.0	237.6	238.8	240.9	-0.59	-5.74
India	57,483.5	57,570.1	57,677.5	57,800.2	57,915.9	57,995.1	58,013.3	57,960.5	57,844.3	57,686.3	57,514.6	0.01	0.05
Indonesia	10,050.0	10,070.6	10,107.3	10,155.1	10,204.2	10,242.8	10,261.3	10,254.7	10,222.6	10,168.6	10,098.1	0.05	0.48
Iran	2,733.5	2,618.0	2,569.7	2,584.6	2,647.5	2,737.9	2,837.5	2,935.1	3,025.0	3,103.3	3,167.9	1.49	15.89
Ireland	138.4	141.5	143.6	145.4	148.1	151.3	154.0	156.4	158.7	159.2	158.5	1.36	14.48
Israel	315.8	322.9	329.5	336.0	343.0	349.0	353.3	356.4	358.2	357.3	355.2	1.18	12.49
Italy	1,329.1	1,331.3	1,340.9	1,346.6	1,354.0	1,363.1	1,373.4	1,373.4	1,374.4	1,371.4	1,361.8	0.24	2.46
Japan	2,906.0	2,889.4	2,875.3	2,851.7	2,811.2	2,766.6	2,704.0	2,658.8	2,625.5	2,612.3	2,617.2	-1.04	-9.94
Jordan	342.8	345.0	345.7	345.5	345.2	345.8	348.0	351.8	357.0	362.8	368.3	0.72	7.45
Kazakhstan	554.5	538.8	532.4	535.7	548.5	569.6	597.3	629.7	664.7	698.9	729.0	2.77	31.47
Kuwait	85.7	87.6	89.3	90.8	92.4	94.1	96.0	98.0	100.2	102.4	104.3	1.98	21.70
Latvia	48.2	46.2	45.9	46.1	46.9	48.1	48.6	49.2	50.2	51.3	52.2	0.79	8.23
Lithuania	92.4	89.6	86.3	82.8	79.4	76.7	74.3	73.1	72.6	73.2	73.5	-2.26	-20.46
Malaysia	1,353.4	1,378.2	1,400.0	1,419.9	1,432.5	1,444.2	1,455.1	1,463.9	1,471.6	1,475.5	1,468.6	0.82	8.51
Mexico	5,193.2	5,167.5	5,147.7	5,127.7	5,108.2	5,087.7	5,064.5	5,037.2	5,005.6	4,970.4	4,932.8	-0.51	-5.01
Morocco	1,509.5	1,490.4	1,472.5	1,457.1	1,445.5	1,439.4	1,439.6	1,446.3	1,458.7	1,474.9	1,492.6	-0.11	-1.12
Netherlands	477.6	478.1	484.1	489.0	491.1	490.1	485.4	474.5	464.5	454.3	443.8	-0.73	-7.08
New Zealand	145.3	144.6	144.0	143.0	142.1	142.6	141.9	142.6	145.4	149.4	152.7	0.50	5.14
Nigeria	9,278.7	9,480.4	9,687.8	9,900.9	10,119.5	10,342.9	10,569.7	10,797.5	11,022.6	11,239.3	11,440.8	2.12	23.30
Norway	153.1	153.6	153.9	152.7	151.6	151.5	151.3	151.0	152.4	154.0	155.9	0.18	1.81
Pakistan	10,040.9	10,131.7	10,235.7	10,352.3	10,480.2	10,617.9	10,764.1	10,918.4	11,080.9	11,251.1	11,427.5	1.30	13.81
Peru	1,435.4	1,435.1	1,435.0	1,435.1	1,435.6	1,436.5	1,437.6	1,438.9	1,440.0	1,440.1	1,438.8	0.02	0.24
Philippines	4,940.8	4,966.2	4,986.5	5,006.1	5,028.5	5,058.0	5,096.5	5,144.4	5,199.8	5,258.6	5,315.7	0.73	7.59
Poland	1,035.6	992.6	960.3	928.3	900.2	878.6	864.2	856.3	855.2	860.6	869.1	-1.74	-16.08
Portugal	263.4	267.5	269.0	270.8	273.7	275.9	273.6	272.8	271.6	269.9	268.6	0.20	1.97
Romania	543.8	539.5	538.7	534.7	528.1	519.1	513.3	510.1	512.8	517.8	521.6	-0.42	-4.09
Russia	3,309.8	3,220.2	3,164.1	3,148.4	3,202.4	3,283.4	3,402.9	3,490.6	3,585.0	3,698.3	3,824.2	1.46	15.54
Saudi Arabia	1,328.7	1,336.2	1,345.7	1,357.0	1,368.8	1,379.9	1,388.8	1,395.2	1,399.4	1,402.4	1,405.7	0.57	5.80
Singapore	153.2	151.4	149.6	146.1	142.4	139.6	137.0	132.8	130.7	128.8	127.9	-1.79	-16.52
Slovakia	146.9	141.8	138.4	133.8	130.3	127.9	126.5	126.4	128.0	129.5	130.6	-1.17	-11.06
Slovenia	46.6	45.6	45.4	44.9	44.7	44.5	45.0	45.1	45.6	46.1	46.9	0.05	0.54
South Africa	2,478.9	2,486.4	2,496.8	2,508.8	2,520.5	2,529.9	2,535.3	2,536.1	2,532.7	2,526.9	2,520.9	0.17	1.70
South Korea	1,550.9	1,517.3	1,474.4	1,408.4	1,336.7	1,270.6	1,190.8	1,120.2	1,081.7	1,059.8	1,042.5	-3.89	-32.78
Spain	1,012.5	1,022.9	1,041.3	1,067.5	1,092.8	1,125.3	1,154.2	1,178.3	1,203.7	1,231.3	1,250.3	2.13	23.49
Sweden	251.1	240.5	235.4	233.9	237.3	242.6	248.7	254.1	259.3	262.2	263.9	0.50	5.13
Switzerland	202.3	199.6	196.1	191.9	188.8	185.9	184.4	184.0	184.2	184.1	184.2	-0.93	-8.95
Taiwan	748.2	728.3	718.0	686.4	648.7	628.2	596.8	549.9	525.0	504.6	493.6	-4.07	-34.02
Thailand	2,397.6	2,330.0	2,232.7	2,145.3	2,093.2	2,087.1	2,072.6	2,075.6	2,075.8	2,079.1	2,066.9	-1.47	-13.80
Tunisia	404.4	392.6	383.1	376.2	371.7	369.4	369.0	370.1	372.5	375.9	380.0	-0.62	-6.05
Turkey	3,494.4	3,510.6	3,510.5	3,476.2	3,424.4	3,364.5	3,301.2	3,244.1	3,210.4	3,189.2	3,171.2	-0.97	-9.25
Turkmenistan	244.9	239.0	236.2	236.3	238.5	241.7	244.8	247.2	248.9	249.9	250.5	0.23	2.31
Ukraine	1,111.1	1,054.9	1,005.5	959.0	935.6	928.7	942.7	958.2	995.3	1,025.7	1,045.2	-0.61	-5.93
United Arab Emirates	128.8	134.1	139.8	145.4	150.7	155.1	158.5	160.6	161.7	162.2	162.6	2.36	26.21
United Kingdom	1,776.8	1,749.5	1,717.9	1,682.8	1,655.0	1,646.0	1,654.8	1,678.3	1,714.6	1,761.1	1,808.3	0.18	1.77
USA	9,739.9	9,720.2	9,808.3	9,908.8	10,038.2	10,194.0	10,326.8	10,402.3	10,554.6	10,709.9	10,827.9	1.06	11.17
Venezuela	1,350.4	1,356.2	1,363.0	1,370.8	1,379.2	1,388.0	1,396.6	1,405.0	1,412.9	1,420.0	1,426.2	0.55	5.61
Vietnam	3,846.4	3,743.7	3,700.9	3,709.4	3,751.8	3,801.2	3,837.9	3,856.8	3,863.6	3,861.5	3,857.3	0.03	0.28

Marketing segments: Young generation

Table 4.93 Male tweenagers (10-14): 2009-2019

'000

	2009	2010	2011	2012	2013	2014	2015	2016	2017	2018	2019	CAGR	Period growth
Algeria	1,578.7	1,539.4	1,519.8	1,519.6	1,535.4	1,561.4	1,592.4	1,624.9	1,657.0	1,687.8	1,716.6	0.84	8.74
Argentina	1,749.6	1,740.2	1,729.1	1,717.6	1,707.5	1,700.7	1,698.7	1,701.9	1,709.7	1,720.4	1,732.4	-0.10	-0.98
Australia	720.4	718.5	718.3	717.4	717.9	719.9	724.1	732.1	745.4	762.6	782.2	0.83	8.59
Austria	236.0	229.9	225.6	220.0	217.7	215.9	216.8	216.1	216.4	215.4	214.9	-0.93	-8.92
Azerbaijan	374.8	360.0	349.6	343.9	343.1	346.7	354.0	364.3	376.7	390.0	402.7	0.72	7.46
Belarus	247.5	239.8	236.4	235.5	236.0	234.1	232.6	231.5	234.8	243.2	253.7	0.25	2.52
Belgium	308.2	306.9	307.4	306.6	305.0	304.5	306.8	308.9	312.8	318.2	323.7	0.49	5.01
Bolivia	576.9	580.5	584.8	589.7	594.9	599.6	603.5	606.3	608.0	608.8	609.1	0.54	5.57
Bosnia-Herzegovina	115.6	114.4	112.0	108.5	104.5	100.5	97.0	94.3	92.4	91.3	90.7	-2.40	-21.57
Brazil	8,647.4	8,725.7	8,803.5	8,862.1	8,884.9	8,857.6	8,776.0	8,645.7	8,479.1	8,287.4	8,079.5	-0.68	-6.57
Bulgaria	165.0	162.3	162.3	162.6	165.7	168.4	168.3	168.1	167.5	167.0	166.4	0.08	0.80
Canada	1,022.9	1,004.3	982.7	963.9	953.2	950.1	947.7	953.8	967.4	983.2	997.0	-0.26	-2.53
Chile	694.6	677.9	663.1	650.9	641.5	634.8	630.6	628.8	629.0	630.7	633.1	-0.92	-8.85
China	46,978.2	45,364.7	43,843.7	42,538.9	40,797.6	40,559.0	39,804.9	39,230.6	39,486.5	40,275.9	40,706.1	-1.42	-13.35
Colombia	2,245.9	2,243.5	2,241.5	2,240.6	2,241.3	2,243.9	2,248.3	2,254.3	2,261.2	2,267.9	2,272.9	0.12	1.20
Costa Rica	212.5	210.9	209.7	208.5	207.4	205.8	203.9	201.4	198.8	196.4	194.6	-0.87	-8.41
Croatia	129.6	128.3	125.8	120.3	114.9	110.6	107.7	106.5	107.1	108.4	109.9	-1.63	-15.16
Czech Republic	246.1	237.3	235.2	236.5	238.7	241.2	246.6	253.2	259.2	264.3	268.9	0.89	9.26
Denmark	179.6	177.0	174.7	172.9	170.9	169.8	169.0	167.7	167.9	167.9	168.2	-0.65	-6.33
Ecuador	726.0	728.5	729.4	728.4	725.8	721.9	717.2	712.0	706.7	701.4	696.4	-0.42	-4.08
Egypt	4,097.8	4,197.4	4,305.2	4,421.7	4,545.4	4,672.8	4,799.2	4,920.4	5,023.2	5,109.8	5,180.4	2.37	26.42
Estonia	32.0	31.4	31.6	31.5	31.8	32.3	33.2	33.9	34.8	35.8	36.9	1.42	15.13
Finland	157.6	154.1	151.4	149.2	148.0	148.1	148.6	149.0	150.6	152.2	153.9	-0.23	-2.32
France	1,879.5	1,899.9	1,926.6	1,945.7	1,965.4	1,980.3	1,985.9	1,980.5	1,990.7	2,001.0	2,019.7	0.72	7.46
Germany	2,038.8	2,027.4	2,019.7	1,985.7	1,937.9	1,897.0	1,863.6	1,824.4	1,795.2	1,779.1	1,769.1	-1.41	-13.23
Greece	276.2	272.6	269.9	270.4	271.5	274.9	279.0	282.8	286.1	289.5	292.4	0.57	5.86
Hong Kong, China	195.4	185.6	177.3	166.2	160.6	156.2	154.0	155.9	163.9	170.3	177.6	-0.95	-9.13
Hungary	268.7	259.1	252.6	248.9	247.7	247.4	248.2	248.7	250.2	251.8	253.8	-0.57	-5.54
India	62,818.5	62,870.2	62,950.9	63,056.4	63,162.2	63,233.6	63,241.4	63,173.3	63,036.5	62,853.2	62,652.5	-0.03	-0.26
Indonesia	10,404.0	10,428.7	10,470.2	10,523.1	10,577.4	10,620.7	10,642.8	10,638.7	10,607.8	10,553.9	10,482.9	0.08	0.76
Iran	2,886.1	2,761.0	2,706.6	2,719.0	2,782.3	2,875.3	2,978.9	3,081.4	3,176.5	3,259.9	3,329.1	1.44	15.35
Ireland	146.9	149.7	152.0	152.6	154.9	157.7	160.9	163.3	166.5	167.2	166.8	1.28	13.61
Israel	332.2	340.0	347.2	353.6	360.3	366.7	371.2	374.4	376.6	376.3	374.2	1.20	12.65
Italy	1,410.8	1,412.3	1,421.9	1,427.1	1,432.3	1,440.1	1,451.3	1,452.9	1,455.0	1,454.1	1,445.2	0.24	2.44
Japan	3,049.6	3,035.7	3,022.2	2,999.3	2,957.3	2,908.2	2,836.2	2,788.6	2,754.9	2,742.2	2,750.8	-1.03	-9.80
Jordan	358.8	360.4	361.0	360.9	361.0	362.0	364.5	368.5	373.7	379.4	384.9	0.71	7.29
Kazakhstan	583.4	567.3	560.5	563.3	576.0	597.3	625.8	659.7	696.7	733.2	765.4	2.75	31.19
Kuwait	88.9	90.3	91.7	93.1	94.6	96.4	98.3	100.5	102.8	105.1	107.1	1.88	20.43
Latvia	50.7	48.6	47.8	47.6	48.1	49.4	50.0	50.7	52.1	53.3	54.3	0.68	7.05
Lithuania	97.4	94.7	91.5	88.0	84.4	81.5	78.5	76.8	76.4	76.7	76.7	-2.35	-21.20
Malaysia	1,438.1	1,459.5	1,480.2	1,501.0	1,515.8	1,532.1	1,549.3	1,562.4	1,573.1	1,578.1	1,570.8	0.89	9.23
Mexico	5,291.2	5,263.8	5,242.8	5,221.5	5,201.1	5,180.5	5,158.2	5,133.3	5,105.6	5,075.8	5,044.6	-0.48	-4.66
Morocco	1,557.2	1,537.7	1,519.5	1,503.8	1,492.1	1,486.0	1,486.6	1,493.8	1,506.9	1,523.9	1,542.4	-0.10	-0.95
Netherlands	501.4	502.9	509.3	513.6	517.5	517.0	511.6	501.4	491.7	481.3	470.5	-0.63	-6.17
New Zealand	152.9	152.1	151.1	150.1	149.4	149.9	149.4	150.2	153.7	158.0	161.6	0.55	5.68
Nigeria	9,544.3	9,757.1	9,975.9	10,200.3	10,429.6	10,662.4	10,896.8	11,130.1	11,358.8	11,577.5	11,780.1	2.13	23.43
Norway	161.7	162.1	162.0	160.2	158.3	158.1	157.7	157.2	158.9	161.1	163.4	0.11	1.09
Pakistan	10,607.1	10,709.2	10,825.7	10,955.8	11,097.6	11,249.2	11,409.0	11,576.7	11,752.2	11,935.1	12,123.9	1.35	14.30
Peru	1,482.6	1,483.2	1,483.8	1,484.8	1,486.2	1,488.0	1,490.0	1,492.1	1,493.8	1,494.7	1,493.9	0.08	0.76
Philippines	5,148.3	5,176.7	5,199.6	5,221.8	5,246.6	5,278.8	5,320.4	5,371.8	5,431.1	5,494.0	5,555.2	0.76	7.90
Poland	1,087.9	1,045.7	1,014.1	980.7	953.2	931.2	918.3	911.2	911.5	916.9	925.6	-1.60	-14.92
Portugal	276.1	279.7	280.9	284.2	289.3	292.5	290.9	291.2	290.1	287.9	286.6	0.37	3.80
Romania	570.6	566.0	565.7	562.7	555.4	547.3	541.7	538.6	541.2	546.7	550.6	-0.36	-3.52
Russia	3,463.4	3,372.9	3,319.6	3,304.2	3,364.2	3,457.6	3,588.5	3,686.8	3,793.5	3,922.5	4,057.1	1.59	17.14
Saudi Arabia	1,342.4	1,353.2	1,365.6	1,379.0	1,392.4	1,404.5	1,414.1	1,420.9	1,425.3	1,428.5	1,432.1	0.65	6.68
Singapore	161.5	158.9	156.9	151.5	146.2	141.0	136.1	129.8	127.0	125.1	124.4	-2.57	-22.96
Slovakia	154.2	149.1	145.4	140.7	136.8	134.1	133.1	133.2	134.6	136.3	137.5	-1.14	-10.81
Slovenia	49.3	48.5	48.3	47.8	47.6	47.3	47.6	47.6	48.1	48.6	49.4	0.02	0.22
South Africa	2,499.3	2,507.4	2,518.5	2,531.1	2,543.4	2,553.2	2,559.0	2,560.0	2,556.7	2,551.1	2,545.6	0.18	1.85
South Korea	1,721.3	1,670.8	1,613.7	1,540.3	1,461.1	1,383.0	1,291.3	1,211.5	1,166.6	1,140.4	1,120.4	-4.20	-34.91
Spain	1,067.6	1,078.2	1,099.3	1,125.6	1,154.4	1,189.4	1,221.6	1,247.3	1,277.5	1,306.5	1,326.4	2.19	24.24
Sweden	264.0	253.3	248.0	247.3	250.6	255.6	262.4	267.5	272.6	275.8	277.6	0.50	5.15
Switzerland	212.6	209.5	205.7	201.0	197.6	194.2	191.8	190.9	190.4	189.7	189.8	-1.13	-10.75
Taiwan	811.1	790.9	782.6	748.7	709.2	689.3	656.3	605.5	579.7	558.0	545.4	-3.89	-32.76
Thailand	2,483.3	2,416.7	2,319.6	2,233.5	2,185.3	2,180.9	2,171.1	2,179.3	2,184.1	2,189.8	2,180.4	-1.29	-12.20
Tunisia	430.7	418.3	408.4	401.0	396.2	393.8	393.2	394.5	397.1	400.9	405.3	-0.61	-5.91
Turkey	3,617.5	3,635.9	3,639.8	3,606.4	3,556.7	3,498.7	3,436.1	3,379.1	3,346.6	3,323.8	3,306.8	-0.89	-8.59
Turkmenistan	250.6	244.8	242.2	242.4	244.8	248.0	251.2	253.7	255.4	256.4	257.1	0.26	2.60
Ukraine	1,166.4	1,107.5	1,056.8	1,009.5	987.0	981.2	995.9	1,012.0	1,048.5	1,077.3	1,096.3	-0.62	-6.01
United Arab Emirates	137.9	143.7	149.5	155.1	159.8	163.2	165.2	165.9	165.5	164.7	164.0	1.75	18.89
United Kingdom	1,860.4	1,833.2	1,801.3	1,765.7	1,740.6	1,736.2	1,747.7	1,775.3	1,817.4	1,868.4	1,920.7	0.32	3.24
USA	10,207.3	10,185.8	10,269.6	10,369.8	10,499.7	10,657.3	10,788.2	10,866.4	11,025.7	11,182.5	11,302.5	1.02	10.73
Venezuela	1,408.2	1,414.3	1,421.5	1,429.6	1,438.3	1,447.3	1,456.3	1,465.1	1,473.4	1,481.1	1,487.7	0.55	5.65
Vietnam	3,996.2	3,890.5	3,846.8	3,856.1	3,900.5	3,952.3	3,990.9	4,011.3	4,019.3	4,018.3	4,015.0	0.05	0.47

Marketing segments: Young generation

Table 4.94 Tweenagers (10-14): 2009-2019 (%)

% of total

	2009	2010	2011	2012	2013	2014	2015	2016	2017	2018	2019
Algeria	8.85	8.50	8.27	8.15	8.11	8.13	8.18	8.23	8.29	8.33	8.37
Argentina	8.54	8.41	8.27	8.14	8.02	7.91	7.83	7.78	7.74	7.73	7.72
Australia	6.44	6.34	6.26	6.18	6.10	6.03	5.97	5.96	5.98	6.04	6.12
Austria	5.50	5.34	5.23	5.07	5.01	4.95	4.96	4.94	4.94	4.91	4.89
Azerbaijan	8.21	7.75	7.40	7.15	7.01	6.97	7.03	7.15	7.32	7.53	7.72
Belarus	4.98	4.83	4.78	4.77	4.79	4.76	4.75	4.74	4.82	5.01	5.24
Belgium	5.65	5.61	5.60	5.56	5.51	5.49	5.50	5.52	5.56	5.64	5.72
Bolivia	11.48	11.36	11.25	11.17	11.09	11.01	10.92	10.81	10.68	10.55	10.41
Bosnia-Herzegovina	5.82	5.76	5.64	5.47	5.27	5.07	4.90	4.76	4.68	4.63	4.60
Brazil	8.78	8.78	8.78	8.77	8.73	8.64	8.50	8.32	8.11	7.88	7.63
Bulgaria	4.28	4.24	4.26	4.30	4.41	4.52	4.54	4.58	4.60	4.64	4.67
Canada	5.93	5.77	5.59	5.44	5.34	5.27	5.21	5.20	5.23	5.27	5.30
Chile	8.04	7.77	7.53	7.33	7.15	7.02	6.91	6.83	6.78	6.75	6.72
China	6.43	6.16	5.92	5.74	5.52	5.49	5.39	5.30	5.29	5.35	5.37
Colombia	9.65	9.50	9.37	9.24	9.12	9.02	8.93	8.84	8.77	8.69	8.61
Costa Rica	9.02	8.84	8.68	8.52	8.36	8.20	8.02	7.83	7.64	7.46	7.31
Croatia	5.73	5.68	5.57	5.34	5.11	4.93	4.80	4.76	4.80	4.87	4.95
Czech Republic	4.64	4.47	4.42	4.44	4.48	4.53	4.62	4.76	4.87	4.97	5.06
Denmark	6.35	6.24	6.16	6.08	5.99	5.94	5.90	5.84	5.82	5.81	5.80
Ecuador	10.46	10.38	10.27	10.14	9.98	9.81	9.64	9.46	9.29	9.12	8.96
Egypt	10.23	10.28	10.35	10.45	10.55	10.67	10.79	10.89	10.96	11.00	11.00
Estonia	4.69	4.61	4.63	4.63	4.70	4.81	4.96	5.08	5.25	5.40	5.56
Finland	5.81	5.65	5.52	5.43	5.35	5.34	5.33	5.34	5.39	5.44	5.47
France	5.90	5.93	5.99	6.03	6.07	6.09	6.09	6.05	6.05	6.06	6.09
Germany	4.85	4.84	4.84	4.78	4.68	4.59	4.52	4.44	4.38	4.35	4.34
Greece	4.78	4.71	4.65	4.62	4.63	4.67	4.72	4.77	4.83	4.88	4.92
Hong Kong, China	5.40	5.08	4.79	4.44	4.24	4.10	4.01	4.03	4.21	4.34	4.49
Hungary	5.23	5.06	4.95	4.89	4.88	4.88	4.91	4.92	4.97	5.01	5.06
India	10.29	10.17	10.05	9.93	9.83	9.72	9.60	9.48	9.36	9.23	9.10
Indonesia	8.89	8.82	8.76	8.71	8.67	8.62	8.56	8.48	8.39	8.28	8.16
Iran	7.57	7.16	6.95	6.90	6.99	7.14	7.32	7.49	7.63	7.75	7.83
Ireland	6.41	6.46	6.48	6.46	6.50	6.55	6.61	6.64	6.69	6.65	6.57
Israel	8.75	8.82	8.87	8.91	8.96	8.99	8.99	8.95	8.89	8.76	8.61
Italy	4.64	4.64	4.67	4.69	4.71	4.73	4.77	4.77	4.78	4.78	4.75
Japan	4.67	4.65	4.64	4.61	4.56	4.50	4.40	4.34	4.30	4.30	4.33
Jordan	11.11	10.90	10.71	10.54	10.41	10.31	10.24	10.21	10.19	10.19	10.18
Kazakhstan	7.21	6.92	6.75	6.71	6.78	6.95	7.21	7.51	7.85	8.17	8.44
Kuwait	7.14	7.12	7.09	7.06	7.03	7.02	7.02	7.04	7.07	7.10	7.11
Latvia	4.39	4.23	4.21	4.23	4.32	4.46	4.54	4.63	4.77	4.90	5.02
Lithuania	5.67	5.54	5.37	5.19	5.01	4.86	4.73	4.66	4.66	4.71	4.75
Malaysia	9.93	9.94	9.93	9.92	9.87	9.82	9.78	9.72	9.65	9.55	9.39
Mexico	9.66	9.47	9.29	9.13	8.98	8.84	8.70	8.55	8.41	8.27	8.13
Morocco	9.59	9.35	9.13	8.93	8.76	8.62	8.52	8.47	8.45	8.45	8.47
Netherlands	5.97	5.97	6.03	6.08	6.10	6.08	6.01	5.87	5.74	5.61	5.47
New Zealand	6.92	6.82	6.72	6.61	6.52	6.48	6.40	6.38	6.46	6.59	6.69
Nigeria	12.17	12.16	12.15	12.16	12.17	12.18	12.20	12.22	12.24	12.24	12.23
Norway	6.56	6.50	6.43	6.30	6.18	6.12	6.05	5.98	5.98	6.00	6.02
Pakistan	11.42	11.28	11.16	11.05	10.95	10.86	10.79	10.73	10.68	10.64	10.60
Peru	10.06	9.93	9.80	9.67	9.56	9.45	9.34	9.25	9.15	9.05	8.94
Philippines	10.95	10.80	10.64	10.49	10.35	10.23	10.12	10.04	9.98	9.92	9.86
Poland	5.59	5.37	5.21	5.05	4.91	4.80	4.74	4.70	4.71	4.74	4.79
Portugal	5.06	5.12	5.13	5.17	5.24	5.28	5.24	5.23	5.20	5.17	5.14
Romania	5.20	5.17	5.18	5.17	5.12	5.06	5.03	5.03	5.08	5.16	5.23
Russia	4.77	4.65	4.58	4.57	4.66	4.79	4.98	5.12	5.27	5.45	5.65
Saudi Arabia	10.38	10.25	10.13	10.02	9.91	9.81	9.69	9.56	9.41	9.27	9.13
Singapore	6.69	6.50	6.34	6.08	5.83	5.61	5.40	5.14	5.00	4.89	4.82
Slovakia	5.58	5.39	5.26	5.09	4.95	4.85	4.81	4.81	4.87	4.93	4.97
Slovenia	4.74	4.64	4.61	4.55	4.52	4.49	4.52	4.52	4.56	4.60	4.68
South Africa	9.93	9.89	9.87	9.87	9.87	9.87	9.86	9.82	9.77	9.72	9.66
South Korea	6.71	6.52	6.30	6.01	5.69	5.39	5.04	4.73	4.56	4.46	4.38
Spain	4.57	4.57	4.62	4.70	4.78	4.88	4.98	5.05	5.13	5.21	5.26
Sweden	5.60	5.34	5.21	5.16	5.20	5.29	5.40	5.48	5.56	5.60	5.61
Switzerland	5.49	5.39	5.27	5.14	5.04	4.93	4.86	4.83	4.81	4.78	4.76
Taiwan	6.77	6.58	6.48	6.18	5.83	5.65	5.36	4.93	4.71	4.53	4.43
Thailand	7.54	7.29	6.95	6.65	6.47	6.42	6.36	6.35	6.33	6.32	6.27
Tunisia	8.13	7.82	7.55	7.35	7.19	7.08	7.00	6.96	6.95	6.95	6.97
Turkey	9.45	9.38	9.28	9.09	8.86	8.62	8.38	8.15	7.99	7.87	7.75
Turkmenistan	9.70	9.35	9.12	9.02	8.99	9.00	9.00	8.99	8.95	8.88	8.81
Ukraine	4.96	4.74	4.55	4.37	4.29	4.29	4.39	4.49	4.69	4.86	4.98
United Arab Emirates	5.78	5.88	5.99	6.10	6.18	6.22	6.21	6.15	6.06	5.95	5.84
United Kingdom	5.90	5.78	5.65	5.51	5.40	5.34	5.34	5.39	5.47	5.59	5.71
USA	6.51	6.44	6.46	6.48	6.52	6.57	6.61	6.61	6.67	6.72	6.75
Venezuela	9.65	9.54	9.44	9.35	9.27	9.19	9.12	9.05	8.98	8.90	8.83
Vietnam	8.95	8.60	8.40	8.31	8.31	8.31	8.30	8.24	8.16	8.07	7.97

Marketing segments: Young generation

Table 4.95 Female tweenagers (10-14): 2009-2019 (%)

% of total

	2009	2010	2011	2012	2013	2014	2015	2016	2017	2018	2019
Algeria	4.33	4.16	4.04	3.98	3.97	3.98	4.00	4.03	4.05	4.08	4.09
Argentina	4.20	4.13	4.07	4.00	3.94	3.89	3.85	3.82	3.81	3.80	3.79
Australia	3.14	3.09	3.05	3.01	2.98	2.94	2.91	2.91	2.92	2.94	2.98
Austria	2.69	2.61	2.55	2.47	2.44	2.41	2.42	2.41	2.42	2.40	2.39
Azerbaijan	3.92	3.67	3.48	3.33	3.24	3.21	3.22	3.27	3.34	3.44	3.53
Belarus	2.42	2.34	2.32	2.32	2.32	2.31	2.30	2.30	2.34	2.43	2.54
Belgium	2.76	2.74	2.74	2.72	2.69	2.68	2.68	2.69	2.71	2.74	2.78
Bolivia	5.63	5.57	5.52	5.48	5.44	5.40	5.36	5.30	5.24	5.18	5.11
Bosnia-Herzegovina	2.81	2.78	2.73	2.65	2.55	2.45	2.37	2.31	2.26	2.24	2.23
Brazil	4.31	4.31	4.31	4.31	4.29	4.24	4.18	4.09	3.98	3.87	3.75
Bulgaria	2.09	2.06	2.07	2.09	2.14	2.19	2.20	2.22	2.23	2.26	2.27
Canada	2.89	2.81	2.72	2.65	2.59	2.56	2.52	2.52	2.53	2.54	2.56
Chile	3.95	3.82	3.70	3.60	3.51	3.45	3.39	3.36	3.33	3.31	3.30
China	2.90	2.76	2.65	2.58	2.50	2.50	2.47	2.43	2.41	2.43	2.42
Colombia	4.73	4.66	4.59	4.53	4.47	4.42	4.37	4.33	4.29	4.26	4.22
Costa Rica	4.38	4.30	4.22	4.14	4.07	3.99	3.90	3.81	3.72	3.63	3.56
Croatia	2.81	2.77	2.72	2.61	2.50	2.41	2.34	2.32	2.34	2.37	2.41
Czech Republic	2.26	2.18	2.15	2.16	2.17	2.20	2.24	2.31	2.37	2.42	2.46
Denmark	3.09	3.04	3.00	2.97	2.93	2.90	2.88	2.85	2.84	2.84	2.83
Ecuador	5.13	5.09	5.03	4.97	4.89	4.81	4.72	4.64	4.55	4.47	4.39
Egypt	4.89	4.91	4.94	4.98	5.03	5.09	5.15	5.20	5.24	5.26	5.27
Estonia	2.28	2.24	2.24	2.23	2.28	2.34	2.41	2.47	2.55	2.62	2.70
Finland	2.85	2.77	2.70	2.66	2.61	2.61	2.60	2.62	2.64	2.66	2.68
France	2.89	2.91	2.94	2.96	2.98	2.99	2.99	2.97	2.98	2.98	2.99
Germany	2.36	2.36	2.36	2.33	2.28	2.24	2.21	2.16	2.13	2.12	2.11
Greece	2.33	2.29	2.27	2.24	2.24	2.26	2.28	2.31	2.34	2.36	2.37
Hong Kong, China	2.63	2.48	2.33	2.15	2.05	1.98	1.94	1.95	2.04	2.10	2.17
Hungary	2.55	2.47	2.42	2.39	2.39	2.38	2.40	2.40	2.42	2.44	2.47
India	4.92	4.86	4.80	4.75	4.70	4.65	4.59	4.54	4.48	4.42	4.36
Indonesia	4.37	4.33	4.30	4.28	4.26	4.23	4.20	4.16	4.12	4.06	4.00
Iran	3.68	3.49	3.38	3.36	3.41	3.48	3.57	3.65	3.72	3.78	3.82
Ireland	3.11	3.14	3.15	3.15	3.18	3.21	3.23	3.25	3.26	3.24	3.20
Israel	4.27	4.29	4.32	4.34	4.37	4.39	4.38	4.36	4.33	4.27	4.19
Italy	2.25	2.25	2.27	2.27	2.29	2.30	2.32	2.32	2.32	2.32	2.31
Japan	2.28	2.27	2.26	2.25	2.22	2.19	2.15	2.12	2.10	2.10	2.11
Jordan	5.43	5.33	5.24	5.16	5.09	5.04	5.00	4.98	4.98	4.98	4.98
Kazakhstan	3.51	3.37	3.29	3.27	3.31	3.39	3.52	3.67	3.83	3.99	4.12
Kuwait	3.51	3.50	3.50	3.48	3.47	3.47	3.47	3.48	3.49	3.50	3.51
Latvia	2.14	2.06	2.06	2.08	2.13	2.20	2.24	2.28	2.34	2.40	2.46
Lithuania	2.76	2.69	2.61	2.52	2.43	2.36	2.30	2.27	2.27	2.30	2.32
Malaysia	4.82	4.83	4.83	4.82	4.80	4.77	4.74	4.70	4.66	4.62	4.54
Mexico	4.78	4.69	4.60	4.53	4.45	4.38	4.31	4.24	4.16	4.09	4.02
Morocco	4.72	4.60	4.49	4.39	4.31	4.24	4.19	4.17	4.16	4.16	4.16
Netherlands	2.91	2.91	2.94	2.96	2.97	2.96	2.93	2.86	2.79	2.72	2.66
New Zealand	3.37	3.32	3.28	3.23	3.18	3.16	3.12	3.11	3.14	3.20	3.25
Nigeria	6.00	5.99	5.99	5.99	5.99	6.00	6.01	6.02	6.03	6.03	6.03
Norway	3.19	3.16	3.13	3.08	3.02	2.99	2.96	2.93	2.93	2.93	2.94
Pakistan	5.55	5.48	5.42	5.37	5.32	5.27	5.24	5.21	5.18	5.16	5.15
Peru	4.95	4.88	4.82	4.75	4.70	4.64	4.59	4.54	4.49	4.44	4.39
Philippines	5.36	5.29	5.21	5.13	5.06	5.00	4.95	4.91	4.88	4.85	4.82
Poland	2.73	2.62	2.54	2.46	2.38	2.33	2.30	2.28	2.28	2.30	2.32
Portugal	2.47	2.50	2.51	2.52	2.55	2.56	2.54	2.53	2.52	2.50	2.49
Romania	2.54	2.52	2.53	2.52	2.50	2.47	2.45	2.45	2.47	2.51	2.54
Russia	2.33	2.27	2.24	2.23	2.27	2.33	2.42	2.49	2.56	2.65	2.74
Saudi Arabia	5.17	5.09	5.03	4.97	4.91	4.86	4.80	4.73	4.66	4.59	4.52
Singapore	3.25	3.17	3.09	2.99	2.88	2.79	2.71	2.60	2.54	2.48	2.44
Slovakia	2.72	2.63	2.56	2.48	2.41	2.37	2.34	2.34	2.37	2.40	2.42
Slovenia	2.30	2.25	2.23	2.20	2.19	2.18	2.20	2.20	2.22	2.24	2.28
South Africa	4.95	4.92	4.91	4.91	4.91	4.91	4.91	4.89	4.86	4.83	4.80
South Korea	3.18	3.10	3.01	2.87	2.72	2.58	2.42	2.27	2.19	2.15	2.11
Spain	2.22	2.23	2.25	2.29	2.32	2.37	2.42	2.45	2.49	2.53	2.55
Sweden	2.73	2.60	2.53	2.51	2.53	2.58	2.63	2.67	2.71	2.73	2.73
Switzerland	2.68	2.63	2.57	2.51	2.46	2.41	2.38	2.37	2.36	2.35	2.35
Taiwan	3.25	3.15	3.10	2.95	2.79	2.69	2.55	2.35	2.24	2.15	2.10
Thailand	3.70	3.58	3.41	3.26	3.16	3.14	3.10	3.10	3.08	3.08	3.05
Tunisia	3.94	3.78	3.66	3.56	3.48	3.43	3.39	3.37	3.36	3.36	3.37
Turkey	4.64	4.61	4.56	4.46	4.35	4.23	4.10	3.99	3.91	3.85	3.80
Turkmenistan	4.79	4.62	4.51	4.45	4.44	4.44	4.44	4.44	4.42	4.39	4.35
Ukraine	2.42	2.31	2.22	2.13	2.09	2.09	2.13	2.18	2.28	2.37	2.43
United Arab Emirates	2.79	2.84	2.89	2.95	3.00	3.03	3.04	3.03	2.99	2.95	2.91
United Kingdom	2.88	2.82	2.76	2.69	2.63	2.60	2.60	2.62	2.66	2.71	2.77
USA	3.18	3.15	3.15	3.17	3.19	3.21	3.23	3.23	3.26	3.29	3.30
Venezuela	4.72	4.67	4.62	4.58	4.54	4.50	4.46	4.43	4.39	4.36	4.32
Vietnam	4.39	4.22	4.12	4.08	4.07	4.08	4.07	4.04	4.00	3.95	3.91

Marketing segments: Young generation

Table 4.96 Male tweenagers (10-14): 2009-2019 (%)

% of total

	2009	2010	2011	2012	2013	2014	2015	2016	2017	2018	2019
Algeria	4.52	4.35	4.23	4.16	4.15	4.16	4.18	4.21	4.23	4.26	4.28
Argentina	4.34	4.27	4.20	4.14	4.07	4.02	3.98	3.95	3.94	3.93	3.93
Australia	3.31	3.25	3.21	3.16	3.12	3.09	3.06	3.06	3.07	3.10	3.14
Austria	2.81	2.73	2.67	2.60	2.57	2.54	2.54	2.53	2.52	2.51	2.49
Azerbaijan	4.29	4.08	3.92	3.81	3.77	3.77	3.81	3.88	3.98	4.09	4.19
Belarus	2.56	2.48	2.46	2.45	2.47	2.45	2.44	2.44	2.48	2.58	2.70
Belgium	2.89	2.87	2.86	2.85	2.82	2.81	2.82	2.83	2.86	2.90	2.94
Bolivia	5.85	5.79	5.73	5.69	5.65	5.61	5.56	5.50	5.44	5.37	5.30
Bosnia-Herzegovina	3.01	2.97	2.91	2.82	2.72	2.62	2.53	2.46	2.41	2.39	2.38
Brazil	4.46	4.47	4.47	4.46	4.44	4.40	4.33	4.23	4.13	4.01	3.89
Bulgaria	2.19	2.17	2.19	2.21	2.27	2.32	2.34	2.36	2.37	2.38	2.39
Canada	3.04	2.96	2.87	2.79	2.74	2.71	2.69	2.68	2.70	2.73	2.74
Chile	4.09	3.96	3.83	3.73	3.64	3.57	3.52	3.48	3.45	3.43	3.42
China	3.54	3.40	3.27	3.16	3.02	2.99	2.92	2.87	2.88	2.93	2.95
Colombia	4.92	4.85	4.78	4.71	4.65	4.60	4.55	4.51	4.47	4.43	4.39
Costa Rica	4.64	4.55	4.46	4.38	4.29	4.21	4.11	4.01	3.92	3.82	3.75
Croatia	2.93	2.90	2.85	2.73	2.61	2.52	2.46	2.44	2.46	2.50	2.54
Czech Republic	2.38	2.29	2.27	2.28	2.30	2.33	2.38	2.44	2.50	2.55	2.60
Denmark	3.26	3.20	3.15	3.11	3.07	3.04	3.02	2.98	2.98	2.97	2.97
Ecuador	5.33	5.29	5.24	5.17	5.09	5.00	4.91	4.82	4.74	4.65	4.57
Egypt	5.34	5.37	5.41	5.46	5.52	5.58	5.64	5.69	5.72	5.73	5.73
Estonia	2.41	2.37	2.39	2.39	2.42	2.47	2.55	2.61	2.69	2.78	2.87
Finland	2.96	2.88	2.82	2.77	2.74	2.73	2.73	2.73	2.75	2.77	2.80
France	3.01	3.03	3.06	3.07	3.09	3.10	3.10	3.07	3.08	3.08	3.10
Germany	2.49	2.48	2.48	2.45	2.40	2.35	2.32	2.28	2.25	2.24	2.23
Greece	2.45	2.41	2.38	2.38	2.38	2.41	2.44	2.47	2.49	2.52	2.54
Hong Kong, China	2.77	2.60	2.46	2.29	2.19	2.12	2.07	2.08	2.17	2.24	2.31
Hungary	2.68	2.59	2.53	2.50	2.50	2.50	2.51	2.53	2.55	2.57	2.60
India	5.37	5.31	5.24	5.18	5.13	5.07	5.01	4.95	4.88	4.81	4.75
Indonesia	4.52	4.49	4.46	4.43	4.41	4.39	4.36	4.32	4.27	4.22	4.15
Iran	3.89	3.68	3.56	3.54	3.58	3.66	3.75	3.84	3.91	3.97	4.01
Ireland	3.30	3.32	3.33	3.31	3.32	3.34	3.38	3.39	3.42	3.41	3.37
Israel	4.49	4.52	4.55	4.57	4.59	4.61	4.60	4.58	4.55	4.50	4.42
Italy	2.39	2.39	2.40	2.41	2.42	2.43	2.45	2.45	2.46	2.46	2.45
Japan	2.39	2.38	2.38	2.36	2.34	2.30	2.25	2.22	2.20	2.20	2.22
Jordan	5.68	5.57	5.47	5.39	5.32	5.27	5.24	5.22	5.21	5.21	5.20
Kazakhstan	3.70	3.55	3.46	3.44	3.47	3.56	3.69	3.84	4.02	4.18	4.32
Kuwait	3.64	3.61	3.59	3.57	3.56	3.55	3.55	3.56	3.58	3.60	3.60
Latvia	2.25	2.17	2.15	2.15	2.18	2.26	2.30	2.35	2.43	2.50	2.56
Lithuania	2.91	2.85	2.76	2.67	2.58	2.50	2.43	2.39	2.39	2.41	2.42
Malaysia	5.12	5.11	5.10	5.10	5.07	5.06	5.04	5.02	4.99	4.94	4.85
Mexico	4.87	4.78	4.69	4.61	4.53	4.46	4.39	4.32	4.25	4.18	4.11
Morocco	4.87	4.75	4.64	4.53	4.45	4.38	4.33	4.30	4.29	4.30	4.30
Netherlands	3.06	3.06	3.09	3.11	3.13	3.12	3.08	3.02	2.95	2.89	2.82
New Zealand	3.55	3.50	3.44	3.38	3.34	3.32	3.28	3.27	3.32	3.39	3.44
Nigeria	6.17	6.17	6.17	6.17	6.18	6.18	6.19	6.20	6.21	6.21	6.21
Norway	3.37	3.34	3.30	3.23	3.16	3.12	3.09	3.05	3.05	3.07	3.08
Pakistan	5.87	5.80	5.73	5.68	5.63	5.59	5.55	5.52	5.50	5.48	5.46
Peru	5.11	5.04	4.98	4.92	4.86	4.81	4.76	4.71	4.66	4.61	4.55
Philippines	5.59	5.51	5.43	5.36	5.28	5.22	5.17	5.13	5.10	5.07	5.04
Poland	2.86	2.76	2.68	2.59	2.52	2.47	2.44	2.43	2.43	2.45	2.47
Portugal	2.59	2.62	2.62	2.65	2.69	2.72	2.70	2.70	2.69	2.67	2.65
Romania	2.66	2.65	2.66	2.65	2.63	2.60	2.59	2.58	2.61	2.65	2.68
Russia	2.44	2.38	2.35	2.34	2.39	2.46	2.55	2.63	2.71	2.81	2.91
Saudi Arabia	5.22	5.16	5.10	5.05	5.00	4.95	4.89	4.82	4.75	4.68	4.61
Singapore	3.43	3.33	3.25	3.10	2.95	2.82	2.69	2.54	2.47	2.41	2.38
Slovakia	2.86	2.76	2.69	2.61	2.53	2.48	2.47	2.47	2.49	2.53	2.55
Slovenia	2.44	2.39	2.38	2.34	2.33	2.31	2.32	2.32	2.34	2.36	2.40
South Africa	4.99	4.97	4.96	4.96	4.96	4.96	4.95	4.93	4.91	4.88	4.85
South Korea	3.53	3.42	3.29	3.14	2.97	2.81	2.62	2.46	2.36	2.31	2.27
Spain	2.35	2.35	2.37	2.41	2.45	2.51	2.56	2.60	2.64	2.68	2.71
Sweden	2.87	2.74	2.67	2.65	2.67	2.71	2.77	2.81	2.85	2.87	2.87
Switzerland	2.81	2.76	2.70	2.63	2.57	2.52	2.48	2.46	2.44	2.43	2.42
Taiwan	3.52	3.42	3.38	3.22	3.05	2.95	2.81	2.59	2.47	2.38	2.32
Thailand	3.84	3.71	3.54	3.39	3.30	3.28	3.25	3.25	3.25	3.24	3.22
Tunisia	4.19	4.03	3.90	3.79	3.71	3.65	3.61	3.59	3.58	3.59	3.60
Turkey	4.81	4.77	4.72	4.63	4.52	4.40	4.27	4.16	4.08	4.01	3.96
Turkmenistan	4.90	4.73	4.62	4.56	4.55	4.56	4.56	4.55	4.53	4.50	4.46
Ukraine	2.54	2.43	2.33	2.24	2.20	2.21	2.25	2.31	2.41	2.49	2.55
United Arab Emirates	2.99	3.04	3.10	3.15	3.18	3.19	3.17	3.13	3.06	3.00	2.93
United Kingdom	3.02	2.96	2.89	2.82	2.77	2.74	2.74	2.77	2.82	2.88	2.94
USA	3.33	3.30	3.30	3.31	3.33	3.36	3.38	3.38	3.41	3.43	3.45
Venezuela	4.93	4.87	4.82	4.77	4.73	4.69	4.65	4.62	4.58	4.55	4.51
Vietnam	4.56	4.38	4.28	4.24	4.23	4.24	4.23	4.20	4.16	4.11	4.07

Marketing segments: Young generation

Table 4.97 Teenagers (13-19): 2009-2019

'000

	2009	2010	2011	2012	2013	2014	2015	2016	2017	2018	2019	CAGR	Period growth
Algeria	4,902.8	4,771.6	4,627.5	4,481.6	4,349.7	4,248.0	4,187.7	4,172.4	4,198.5	4,256.6	4,334.2	-1.23	-11.60
Argentina	4,842.9	4,846.7	4,841.9	4,829.2	4,810.0	4,786.5	4,761.3	4,736.8	4,715.5	4,700.6	4,693.6	-0.31	-3.08
Australia	2,054.7	2,053.9	2,048.6	2,046.7	2,047.4	2,048.3	2,044.5	2,046.1	2,050.6	2,060.9	2,079.1	0.12	1.19
Austria	696.9	694.5	687.1	674.8	660.2	646.5	632.8	624.7	614.4	610.3	606.7	-1.38	-12.94
Azerbaijan	1,204.1	1,159.5	1,109.1	1,056.3	1,006.0	962.7	929.9	909.5	901.7	905.7	919.6	-2.66	-23.63
Belarus	873.0	814.5	762.5	724.0	691.4	670.2	653.8	643.2	638.6	639.9	639.4	-3.07	-26.76
Belgium	891.1	885.4	876.8	865.1	854.5	850.0	848.7	846.3	844.1	845.5	850.2	-0.47	-4.59
Bolivia	1,502.0	1,522.6	1,538.9	1,551.7	1,562.5	1,572.9	1,583.8	1,595.7	1,608.2	1,620.3	1,630.9	0.83	8.58
Bosnia-Herzegovina	335.4	325.1	318.1	313.7	310.6	307.0	301.7	294.3	285.3	275.6	266.4	-2.28	-20.59
Brazil	23,391.5	23,347.0	23,415.5	23,564.9	23,754.3	23,942.3	24,104.3	24,207.0	24,230.7	24,154.7	23,954.3	0.24	2.41
Bulgaria	577.9	542.3	504.8	477.0	461.4	448.5	441.3	439.5	438.3	445.8	450.8	-2.45	-22.00
Canada	3,055.7	3,022.2	2,974.5	2,922.7	2,877.7	2,827.4	2,769.6	2,719.6	2,690.9	2,675.0	2,672.5	-1.33	-12.54
Chile	2,063.3	2,036.6	2,001.3	1,959.5	1,914.8	1,871.3	1,832.0	1,799.0	1,773.2	1,754.5	1,742.4	-1.68	-15.55
China	136,218.5	126,310.8	121,233.6	115,378.9	111,555.8	108,523.9	105,263.6	102,158.4	101,057.4	99,810.5	99,498.7	-3.09	-26.96
Colombia	6,094.1	6,117.0	6,129.9	6,134.2	6,132.8	6,129.2	6,126.4	6,126.2	6,129.4	6,136.4	6,146.7	0.09	0.86
Costa Rica	605.6	599.6	593.9	588.9	584.4	580.4	576.5	572.7	568.7	564.4	559.7	-0.79	-7.58
Croatia	360.5	359.7	358.5	354.4	352.4	347.3	339.3	329.7	317.7	307.2	301.2	-1.78	-16.44
Czech Republic	842.8	807.3	769.0	730.8	698.3	667.7	653.3	651.8	657.0	666.1	680.3	-2.12	-19.28
Denmark	487.2	491.4	493.5	493.8	490.5	488.6	482.7	476.0	472.3	469.0	467.0	-0.42	-4.15
Ecuador	1,898.3	1,910.8	1,925.4	1,940.7	1,954.7	1,965.1	1,970.4	1,969.9	1,964.3	1,954.6	1,942.3	0.23	2.31
Egypt	10,605.3	10,587.0	10,630.3	10,740.0	10,924.7	11,173.1	11,460.3	11,767.3	12,093.1	12,432.1	12,773.7	1.88	20.45
Estonia	115.5	106.6	98.7	92.9	88.0	86.6	85.7	85.7	85.9	87.7	90.2	-2.44	-21.92
Finland	463.1	460.1	453.6	445.2	436.4	428.8	420.4	413.6	410.3	409.4	410.9	-1.19	-11.27
France	5,295.9	5,257.8	5,212.6	5,186.7	5,195.3	5,265.2	5,327.1	5,365.0	5,396.3	5,438.9	5,476.7	0.34	3.41
Germany	6,041.1	5,876.5	5,718.4	5,627.1	5,556.5	5,506.7	5,456.7	5,401.6	5,310.7	5,205.6	5,107.5	-1.66	-15.45
Greece	798.2	794.6	784.8	774.4	765.9	762.7	759.0	756.7	758.2	762.2	771.8	-0.34	-3.30
Hong Kong, China	604.7	597.8	583.9	565.8	544.5	526.3	500.0	477.5	456.7	445.3	448.1	-2.95	-25.90
Hungary	835.7	818.3	792.3	763.9	738.3	721.6	705.7	692.0	682.6	679.6	681.7	-2.02	-18.44
India	165,072.4	166,104.9	166,833.6	167,307.2	167,609.5	167,833.3	168,045.4	168,268.4	168,483.0	168,644.4	168,699.5	0.22	2.20
Indonesia	28,634.2	28,589.0	28,561.5	28,556.9	28,580.8	28,635.9	28,720.2	28,825.6	28,936.7	29,031.4	29,086.0	0.16	1.58
Iran	10,145.3	9,487.1	8,874.6	8,341.3	7,918.4	7,631.3	7,492.0	7,497.7	7,629.3	7,850.3	8,114.5	-2.21	-20.02
Ireland	393.3	391.7	390.8	392.8	396.7	401.7	406.5	414.8	423.9	431.1	435.6	1.03	10.77
Israel	847.1	861.5	878.7	896.9	915.4	934.3	952.8	973.1	993.0	1,007.7	1,018.2	1.86	20.20
Italy	4,024.4	3,996.6	3,960.0	3,930.7	3,902.3	3,904.8	3,913.5	3,928.6	3,948.3	3,976.5	3,992.1	-0.08	-0.80
Japan	8,466.0	8,410.2	8,391.2	8,358.8	8,349.2	8,301.9	8,240.4	8,169.2	8,067.3	7,919.9	7,807.8	-0.81	-7.77
Jordan	945.5	957.4	964.8	968.2	969.0	969.5	971.1	974.5	979.8	987.3	997.0	0.53	5.44
Kazakhstan	1,929.3	1,848.9	1,768.5	1,693.8	1,632.4	1,591.0	1,574.5	1,584.2	1,619.7	1,677.2	1,751.1	-0.96	-9.24
Kuwait	233.6	237.2	241.2	245.4	249.7	254.0	258.3	262.7	267.4	272.3	277.6	1.74	18.88
Latvia	199.3	183.1	167.0	152.8	141.4	135.7	131.9	130.7	132.1	133.8	137.2	-3.67	-31.18
Lithuania	333.6	319.1	302.0	285.4	268.5	255.8	246.1	236.1	228.3	221.9	216.4	-4.24	-35.14
Malaysia	3,719.4	3,761.4	3,807.6	3,856.0	3,913.0	3,968.1	4,023.6	4,067.1	4,111.5	4,159.8	4,197.9	1.22	12.86
Mexico	14,466.5	14,535.0	14,569.3	14,554.7	14,507.9	14,445.4	14,379.3	14,315.3	14,253.5	14,193.1	14,132.4	-0.23	-2.31
Morocco	4,453.0	4,405.7	4,354.9	4,301.9	4,249.1	4,199.2	4,155.0	4,118.6	4,092.6	4,079.1	4,080.0	-0.87	-8.38
Netherlands	1,400.0	1,396.5	1,386.5	1,383.2	1,384.0	1,391.5	1,394.9	1,401.7	1,407.6	1,404.7	1,389.3	-0.08	-0.77
New Zealand	445.5	441.1	435.0	429.8	427.1	424.6	420.0	417.0	417.2	417.1	419.4	-0.60	-5.85
Nigeria	23,778.0	24,283.3	24,805.8	25,346.5	25,905.5	26,482.8	27,077.3	27,687.6	28,311.1	28,943.4	29,577.7	2.21	24.39
Norway	446.0	450.7	451.9	451.3	451.9	453.0	451.4	448.3	445.8	444.7	445.1	-0.02	-0.20
Pakistan	27,991.5	28,135.9	28,308.0	28,516.3	28,762.7	29,044.2	29,356.7	29,699.4	30,073.3	30,477.3	30,909.1	1.00	10.42
Peru	4,038.3	4,049.5	4,057.2	4,062.1	4,065.1	4,067.3	4,069.4	4,071.9	4,075.0	4,078.7	4,082.4	0.11	1.09
Philippines	13,674.3	13,817.5	13,932.0	14,026.3	14,105.6	14,180.1	14,255.6	14,337.0	14,428.5	14,534.1	14,656.3	0.70	7.18
Poland	3,522.3	3,391.4	3,247.1	3,101.9	2,975.9	2,867.7	2,765.0	2,677.5	2,598.3	2,544.0	2,513.5	-3.32	-28.64
Portugal	790.0	783.5	775.3	768.6	771.1	772.8	779.5	786.0	791.1	794.3	796.8	0.09	0.85
Romania	1,824.9	1,702.7	1,628.5	1,595.8	1,567.0	1,554.2	1,533.2	1,515.4	1,504.8	1,496.3	1,487.6	-2.02	-18.48
Russia	12,131.8	11,260.1	10,475.0	9,959.9	9,558.4	9,408.6	9,262.5	9,267.8	9,424.7	9,660.1	9,825.6	-2.09	-19.01
Saudi Arabia	3,578.6	3,623.0	3,657.5	3,684.2	3,706.8	3,729.2	3,753.8	3,781.6	3,811.3	3,840.8	3,867.3	0.78	8.07
Singapore	463.9	465.6	460.3	454.1	444.6	438.1	428.7	416.5	403.1	389.5	379.1	-2.00	-18.27
Slovakia	507.9	488.7	467.8	446.8	428.5	410.0	394.8	384.1	375.2	370.5	367.9	-3.17	-27.56
Slovenia	148.7	144.8	141.2	137.7	135.5	134.2	132.5	131.5	130.2	130.4	131.1	-1.25	-11.85
South Africa	7,000.0	6,980.4	6,961.3	6,945.3	6,935.8	6,935.3	6,944.6	6,962.0	6,984.1	7,007.2	7,027.4	0.04	0.39
South Korea	4,718.0	4,732.5	4,695.8	4,614.2	4,522.1	4,400.0	4,225.5	4,029.0	3,840.3	3,650.8	3,471.9	-3.02	-26.41
Spain	3,076.0	3,050.9	3,028.2	3,017.2	3,026.3	3,057.5	3,106.9	3,162.6	3,238.5	3,320.1	3,400.2	1.01	10.54
Sweden	863.9	842.9	810.5	778.1	747.2	724.0	705.7	700.1	705.4	716.8	728.9	-1.68	-15.62
Switzerland	620.4	616.8	609.3	599.9	589.5	579.6	569.8	561.4	551.1	544.2	538.2	-1.41	-13.25
Taiwan	2,252.2	2,263.8	2,251.8	2,200.5	2,162.6	2,141.6	2,075.8	1,997.7	1,902.3	1,797.2	1,737.6	-2.56	-22.85
Thailand	7,070.9	7,105.7	7,049.4	6,927.1	6,822.9	6,679.5	6,498.4	6,301.5	6,151.6	6,071.0	6,040.6	-1.56	-14.57
Tunisia	1,332.0	1,292.0	1,251.0	1,210.7	1,173.0	1,139.9	1,112.9	1,092.5	1,078.9	1,071.5	1,069.5	-2.17	-19.71
Turkey	9,407.0	9,573.1	9,725.0	9,847.0	9,931.3	9,980.7	9,952.7	9,880.0	9,769.2	9,624.9	9,486.1	0.08	0.84
Turkmenistan	777.5	760.1	739.7	718.3	698.6	683.3	674.0	671.2	673.9	680.2	687.8	-1.22	-11.54
Ukraine	4,005.4	3,790.3	3,573.5	3,369.8	3,184.0	3,031.7	2,899.4	2,799.7	2,734.5	2,719.8	2,720.2	-3.80	-32.09
United Arab Emirates	339.5	349.0	364.8	385.5	408.6	431.2	451.3	467.9	480.7	490.2	496.9	3.88	46.34
United Kingdom	5,448.0	5,389.1	5,309.3	5,214.6	5,127.2	5,044.2	4,966.2	4,907.5	4,869.9	4,856.8	4,873.2	-1.11	-10.55
USA	29,598.5	29,243.2	28,943.5	28,716.2	28,613.6	28,747.5	28,859.9	29,065.9	29,397.9	29,749.3	30,153.8	0.19	1.88
Venezuela	3,828.4	3,831.3	3,837.0	3,846.3	3,859.2	3,875.5	3,894.6	3,916.0	3,939.2	3,963.4	3,987.7	0.41	4.16
Vietnam	12,426.7	12,182.0	11,880.2	11,530.6	11,179.3	10,886.5	10,693.7	10,621.6	10,655.5	10,758.3	10,873.6	-1.33	-12.50

Marketing segments: Young generation

Table 4.98 Female teenagers (13-19): 2009-2019

'000

	2009	2010	2011	2012	2013	2014	2015	2016	2017	2018	2019	CAGR	Period growth
Algeria	2,399.7	2,335.5	2,264.9	2,193.4	2,128.7	2,078.8	2,049.2	2,041.7	2,054.4	2,082.8	2,120.7	-1.23	-11.62
Argentina	2,383.8	2,385.7	2,383.2	2,376.9	2,367.3	2,355.5	2,342.9	2,330.6	2,319.9	2,312.4	2,308.7	-0.32	-3.15
Australia	999.2	999.8	997.3	997.0	997.9	998.7	997.1	998.3	1,000.5	1,005.1	1,014.3	0.15	1.51
Austria	340.6	339.4	336.1	330.2	323.4	316.6	309.5	305.5	300.5	298.3	296.8	-1.37	-12.86
Azerbaijan	583.0	560.5	534.8	507.4	480.6	457.0	438.3	425.5	418.8	418.1	422.6	-3.16	-27.50
Belarus	425.2	396.3	371.3	352.3	336.1	325.6	317.0	311.9	309.5	309.7	309.7	-3.12	-27.15
Belgium	435.8	433.1	428.9	423.0	417.9	415.4	415.2	413.8	412.6	412.9	414.9	-0.49	-4.80
Bolivia	737.6	747.5	755.3	761.5	766.8	771.8	777.2	783.1	789.3	795.3	800.5	0.82	8.52
Bosnia-Herzegovina	162.7	157.3	153.6	151.5	150.0	148.4	145.9	142.4	138.1	133.4	128.9	-2.30	-20.76
Brazil	11,526.2	11,499.8	11,529.2	11,599.1	11,689.2	11,779.2	11,856.8	11,905.3	11,915.2	11,876.5	11,776.8	0.22	2.17
Bulgaria	281.7	264.1	245.5	232.1	224.7	218.5	214.7	213.2	212.6	216.4	218.8	-2.49	-22.32
Canada	1,487.9	1,470.3	1,446.5	1,419.2	1,395.7	1,370.1	1,341.2	1,315.2	1,300.0	1,290.2	1,287.5	-1.44	-13.47
Chile	1,014.3	1,001.1	983.7	963.1	941.1	919.6	900.2	884.0	871.2	862.0	856.0	-1.68	-15.61
China	61,929.9	57,081.9	54,471.3	51,808.1	49,839.3	48,549.5	47,193.4	45,910.0	45,625.9	45,208.4	45,198.4	-3.10	-27.02
Colombia	2,993.8	3,004.7	3,010.7	3,012.5	3,011.5	3,009.4	3,007.6	3,007.2	3,008.4	3,011.5	3,016.2	0.07	0.75
Costa Rica	293.8	290.9	288.2	285.9	283.8	282.0	280.2	278.5	276.7	274.7	272.5	-0.75	-7.24
Croatia	176.4	175.8	175.0	173.2	172.4	170.0	165.8	161.0	155.3	149.9	147.0	-1.81	-16.69
Czech Republic	410.8	393.2	374.4	355.9	340.2	324.7	317.6	316.8	319.3	323.5	330.5	-2.15	-19.54
Denmark	237.4	239.4	240.5	240.6	239.3	238.5	235.6	232.4	230.7	229.2	228.5	-0.38	-3.76
Ecuador	933.1	938.9	945.7	952.9	959.5	964.4	966.8	966.4	963.6	958.8	952.6	0.21	2.09
Egypt	5,081.5	5,066.8	5,081.7	5,128.9	5,212.9	5,328.3	5,463.0	5,607.6	5,762.2	5,925.0	6,091.6	1.83	19.88
Estonia	56.3	52.0	48.1	45.2	42.8	42.0	41.5	41.5	41.7	42.6	43.8	-2.48	-22.22
Finland	227.0	225.5	222.6	218.4	214.1	210.0	205.8	202.3	200.9	200.2	201.0	-1.21	-11.47
France	2,599.3	2,577.7	2,554.8	2,542.8	2,547.2	2,581.6	2,613.2	2,632.7	2,650.1	2,672.4	2,691.5	0.35	3.55
Germany	2,946.5	2,866.6	2,790.7	2,746.9	2,711.8	2,689.6	2,666.0	2,639.2	2,595.3	2,543.8	2,495.5	-1.65	-15.31
Greece	386.0	385.6	381.7	376.6	372.7	370.9	368.4	367.7	367.7	369.0	373.3	-0.34	-3.31
Hong Kong, China	294.5	291.9	286.5	277.9	266.7	256.9	244.3	233.5	223.1	216.9	217.5	-2.99	-26.15
Hungary	408.8	400.2	387.0	373.2	360.8	352.7	344.7	338.0	333.3	332.2	332.7	-2.04	-18.61
India	78,838.8	79,317.6	79,667.3	79,909.0	80,078.0	80,213.1	80,341.1	80,470.1	80,590.2	80,680.6	80,717.5	0.24	2.38
Indonesia	14,090.7	14,066.1	14,050.3	14,045.7	14,055.0	14,079.5	14,118.1	14,167.0	14,218.8	14,262.6	14,287.1	0.14	1.39
Iran	4,941.3	4,616.0	4,315.2	4,055.0	3,849.7	3,711.5	3,645.7	3,651.1	3,717.9	3,828.0	3,958.7	-2.19	-19.89
Ireland	191.9	190.8	190.3	191.0	193.1	195.5	198.2	202.4	207.3	210.9	213.2	1.06	11.15
Israel	413.3	420.2	428.5	437.2	446.1	455.2	464.3	474.4	484.1	491.3	496.3	1.85	20.09
Italy	1,955.4	1,941.1	1,922.3	1,907.1	1,893.0	1,893.3	1,897.8	1,906.4	1,916.4	1,930.7	1,938.0	-0.09	-0.89
Japan	4,130.2	4,102.0	4,093.1	4,078.4	4,072.6	4,049.1	4,018.6	3,983.7	3,934.5	3,864.1	3,808.9	-0.81	-7.78
Jordan	460.8	466.9	470.8	472.7	473.4	473.7	474.6	476.3	478.8	482.4	487.1	0.56	5.72
Kazakhstan	943.7	903.5	863.5	826.6	796.4	776.1	768.1	773.1	790.5	818.8	854.9	-0.98	-9.40
Kuwait	112.7	114.7	116.9	119.3	121.8	124.2	126.7	129.1	131.5	134.0	136.6	1.95	21.25
Latvia	97.9	90.0	82.0	75.0	69.5	66.6	64.9	64.4	65.2	66.1	67.7	-3.62	-30.81
Lithuania	163.2	156.1	147.5	139.2	130.7	124.3	119.6	114.7	110.7	107.7	105.2	-4.29	-35.51
Malaysia	1,806.0	1,826.0	1,848.7	1,873.6	1,903.6	1,932.0	1,960.0	1,980.8	2,001.1	2,023.5	2,040.1	1.23	12.96
Mexico	7,267.9	7,296.3	7,306.1	7,290.5	7,258.8	7,220.1	7,181.3	7,145.2	7,111.8	7,079.8	7,047.5	-0.31	-3.03
Morocco	2,201.4	2,176.0	2,149.5	2,122.6	2,096.3	2,071.5	2,049.6	2,031.5	2,018.4	2,011.4	2,011.5	-0.90	-8.63
Netherlands	684.1	681.2	676.6	674.4	674.3	677.8	679.1	681.9	684.9	683.0	675.1	-0.13	-1.31
New Zealand	217.3	214.9	212.0	209.4	208.2	207.0	205.0	203.5	203.4	203.2	204.4	-0.61	-5.95
Nigeria	11,738.1	11,982.4	12,235.8	12,498.4	12,770.5	13,051.9	13,342.0	13,640.2	13,945.5	14,255.9	14,568.2	2.18	24.11
Norway	216.8	219.1	219.6	219.5	220.0	220.5	220.0	218.9	217.9	217.5	217.8	0.04	0.44
Pakistan	13,605.9	13,678.9	13,763.1	13,862.8	13,979.5	14,112.3	14,260.0	14,422.4	14,600.1	14,792.8	14,999.5	0.98	10.24
Peru	1,989.6	1,994.7	1,998.0	1,999.9	2,000.8	2,001.3	2,001.7	2,002.4	2,003.3	2,004.5	2,005.7	0.08	0.81
Philippines	6,707.6	6,776.2	6,830.5	6,874.7	6,911.6	6,946.3	6,981.7	7,020.2	7,063.9	7,114.6	7,173.4	0.67	6.94
Poland	1,721.2	1,656.9	1,585.6	1,514.0	1,451.4	1,397.5	1,345.8	1,301.3	1,261.8	1,234.1	1,218.8	-3.39	-29.19
Portugal	386.6	383.4	379.5	376.1	377.1	377.8	380.8	383.4	385.3	386.4	387.2	0.02	0.15
Romania	892.4	831.9	794.7	779.4	764.8	758.0	747.4	738.3	732.6	728.3	723.3	-2.08	-18.94
Russia	5,935.1	5,506.8	5,121.0	4,868.2	4,669.3	4,593.7	4,520.5	4,519.8	4,591.8	4,702.0	4,778.9	-2.14	-19.48
Saudi Arabia	1,797.5	1,816.8	1,831.1	1,841.6	1,850.2	1,859.1	1,869.6	1,882.1	1,895.9	1,909.9	1,922.6	0.68	6.96
Singapore	226.6	227.8	225.9	222.8	219.0	216.3	213.0	208.3	203.3	197.8	194.0	-1.54	-14.38
Slovakia	248.2	238.7	228.5	218.1	209.1	200.4	192.6	187.3	183.2	180.9	179.7	-3.18	-27.61
Slovenia	72.3	70.4	68.6	66.9	65.8	65.2	64.2	63.7	63.1	63.3	63.7	-1.26	-11.92
South Africa	3,489.0	3,479.0	3,469.5	3,461.7	3,457.1	3,457.0	3,461.6	3,470.1	3,480.8	3,491.8	3,501.2	0.03	0.35
South Korea	2,211.7	2,225.5	2,213.9	2,178.5	2,141.5	2,092.1	2,015.5	1,926.5	1,838.0	1,749.0	1,666.7	-2.79	-24.64
Spain	1,496.2	1,484.6	1,474.1	1,468.6	1,473.5	1,488.3	1,513.2	1,539.4	1,575.5	1,614.3	1,652.7	1.00	10.46
Sweden	420.9	411.0	395.2	379.4	364.6	352.8	343.4	340.9	343.2	348.7	354.9	-1.69	-15.68
Switzerland	303.3	301.8	298.5	294.2	289.2	284.4	279.7	275.7	271.0	268.0	265.2	-1.33	-12.55
Taiwan	1,079.2	1,084.4	1,079.1	1,055.3	1,036.8	1,025.2	993.4	954.1	907.3	855.7	826.5	-2.63	-23.42
Thailand	3,483.2	3,497.9	3,469.3	3,405.7	3,352.4	3,279.5	3,186.6	3,086.5	3,009.8	2,966.8	2,948.5	-1.65	-15.35
Tunisia	647.0	627.0	606.7	586.8	568.3	552.2	539.0	529.0	522.4	518.8	517.8	-2.20	-19.96
Turkey	4,621.5	4,705.8	4,782.3	4,843.0	4,884.7	4,906.9	4,890.3	4,851.9	4,795.7	4,722.3	4,652.2	0.07	0.66
Turkmenistan	384.8	376.2	366.1	355.4	345.6	337.8	333.1	331.6	332.9	336.0	339.7	-1.24	-11.74
Ukraine	1,953.2	1,848.1	1,742.6	1,644.3	1,553.4	1,478.6	1,413.5	1,363.7	1,331.5	1,324.3	1,323.6	-3.82	-32.23
United Arab Emirates	163.1	166.3	171.3	177.8	185.3	193.3	201.2	208.6	215.4	221.1	225.7	3.30	38.41
United Kingdom	2,647.3	2,617.3	2,578.4	2,532.2	2,488.6	2,447.5	2,409.3	2,379.1	2,358.2	2,349.5	2,355.7	-1.16	-11.02
USA	14,439.2	14,272.7	14,126.3	14,013.3	13,963.0	14,031.3	14,091.2	14,194.0	14,357.7	14,532.9	14,734.0	0.20	2.04
Venezuela	1,877.5	1,878.6	1,881.1	1,885.3	1,891.5	1,899.3	1,908.6	1,919.0	1,930.4	1,942.2	1,954.1	0.40	4.08
Vietnam	6,105.4	5,983.5	5,833.8	5,661.0	5,487.7	5,343.2	5,247.9	5,212.0	5,228.2	5,278.2	5,334.4	-1.34	-12.63

Marketing segments: Young generation

Table 4.99 Male teenagers (13-19): 2009-2019

'000

	2009	2010	2011	2012	2013	2014	2015	2016	2017	2018	2019	CAGR	Period growth
Algeria	2,503.1	2,436.1	2,362.6	2,288.2	2,220.9	2,169.1	2,138.5	2,130.8	2,144.1	2,173.8	2,213.4	-1.22	-11.57
Argentina	2,459.1	2,461.1	2,458.7	2,452.3	2,442.7	2,431.0	2,418.4	2,406.1	2,395.6	2,388.2	2,384.9	-0.31	-3.02
Australia	1,055.5	1,054.1	1,051.2	1,049.7	1,049.5	1,049.6	1,047.4	1,047.8	1,050.2	1,055.8	1,064.8	0.09	0.88
Austria	356.2	355.1	351.0	344.6	336.8	329.9	323.3	319.1	313.9	312.1	309.9	-1.38	-13.01
Azerbaijan	621.2	599.0	574.3	549.0	525.3	505.7	491.7	484.0	482.9	487.5	496.9	-2.21	-20.00
Belarus	447.9	418.2	391.2	371.7	355.3	344.7	336.8	331.3	329.1	330.2	329.6	-3.02	-26.40
Belgium	455.3	452.3	447.9	442.1	436.7	434.6	433.5	432.5	431.5	432.6	435.3	-0.45	-4.39
Bolivia	764.4	775.1	783.5	790.2	795.7	801.0	806.6	812.6	818.9	825.0	830.4	0.83	8.63
Bosnia-Herzegovina	172.7	167.8	164.4	162.2	160.6	158.6	155.8	151.9	147.2	142.2	137.5	-2.26	-20.42
Brazil	11,865.3	11,847.3	11,886.2	11,965.8	12,065.0	12,163.0	12,247.5	12,301.7	12,315.5	12,278.3	12,177.5	0.26	2.63
Bulgaria	296.3	278.2	259.3	244.8	236.7	229.9	226.6	226.3	225.7	229.4	232.0	-2.42	-21.71
Canada	1,567.8	1,552.0	1,528.0	1,503.5	1,482.0	1,457.2	1,428.4	1,404.4	1,390.9	1,384.9	1,385.1	-1.23	-11.65
Chile	1,049.1	1,035.5	1,017.6	996.4	973.8	951.7	931.8	915.1	902.0	892.5	886.5	-1.67	-15.50
China	74,288.6	69,228.9	66,762.3	63,570.8	61,716.5	59,974.4	58,070.2	56,248.4	55,431.4	54,602.1	54,300.3	-3.09	-26.91
Colombia	3,100.2	3,112.3	3,119.2	3,121.7	3,121.3	3,119.8	3,118.7	3,119.0	3,121.0	3,124.9	3,130.5	0.10	0.98
Costa Rica	311.8	308.7	305.7	303.0	300.6	298.4	296.3	294.2	292.0	289.7	287.2	-0.82	-7.90
Croatia	184.1	183.9	183.5	181.1	180.0	177.3	173.5	168.6	162.4	157.3	154.3	-1.75	-16.19
Czech Republic	432.0	414.1	394.7	375.0	358.1	343.0	335.7	335.0	337.7	342.6	349.8	-2.09	-19.03
Denmark	249.8	252.0	253.1	253.2	251.3	250.2	247.1	243.6	241.6	239.8	238.5	-0.46	-4.52
Ecuador	965.3	971.9	979.7	987.8	995.2	1,000.7	1,003.6	1,003.5	1,000.7	995.9	989.7	0.25	2.53
Egypt	5,523.8	5,520.2	5,548.6	5,611.2	5,711.8	5,844.7	5,997.3	6,159.7	6,330.9	6,507.1	6,682.1	1.92	20.97
Estonia	59.3	54.6	50.6	47.7	45.2	44.5	44.2	44.2	44.2	45.1	46.4	-2.41	-21.64
Finland	236.0	234.6	231.0	226.8	222.3	218.8	214.6	211.3	209.4	209.3	209.9	-1.17	-11.07
France	2,696.6	2,680.1	2,657.9	2,643.9	2,648.1	2,683.6	2,713.9	2,732.3	2,746.3	2,766.5	2,785.2	0.32	3.29
Germany	3,094.6	3,009.9	2,927.7	2,880.3	2,844.7	2,817.1	2,790.6	2,762.4	2,715.4	2,661.9	2,612.1	-1.68	-15.59
Greece	412.1	409.0	403.1	397.8	393.2	391.9	390.6	389.1	390.5	393.2	398.5	-0.33	-3.30
Hong Kong, China	310.2	305.9	297.4	287.9	277.8	269.4	255.8	244.0	233.6	228.4	230.6	-2.92	-25.66
Hungary	426.9	418.1	405.3	390.7	377.5	368.9	361.0	354.0	349.3	347.4	349.0	-2.00	-18.27
India	86,233.5	86,787.3	87,166.3	87,398.3	87,531.4	87,620.2	87,704.3	87,798.3	87,892.9	87,963.8	87,981.9	0.20	2.03
Indonesia	14,543.5	14,522.9	14,511.2	14,511.2	14,525.8	14,556.4	14,602.1	14,658.6	14,717.9	14,768.8	14,798.9	0.17	1.76
Iran	5,204.0	4,871.1	4,559.4	4,286.4	4,068.7	3,919.8	3,846.2	3,846.6	3,911.5	4,022.3	4,155.8	-2.22	-20.14
Ireland	201.4	200.9	200.6	201.8	203.5	206.2	208.3	212.4	216.6	220.1	222.4	1.00	10.41
Israel	433.8	441.3	450.2	459.7	469.3	479.1	488.6	498.7	508.8	516.4	521.8	1.87	20.31
Italy	2,069.1	2,055.5	2,037.7	2,023.6	2,009.3	2,011.5	2,015.7	2,022.1	2,031.9	2,045.8	2,054.1	-0.07	-0.72
Japan	4,335.8	4,308.1	4,298.1	4,280.5	4,276.6	4,252.9	4,221.9	4,185.5	4,132.7	4,055.8	3,998.9	-0.81	-7.77
Jordan	484.7	490.5	494.0	495.5	495.7	495.7	496.5	498.2	501.0	504.9	509.8	0.51	5.19
Kazakhstan	985.7	945.4	905.0	867.2	836.0	814.9	806.3	811.2	829.1	858.4	896.1	-0.95	-9.08
Kuwait	120.9	122.5	124.3	126.1	127.9	129.8	131.7	133.7	135.9	138.3	141.0	1.55	16.67
Latvia	101.4	93.1	85.0	77.8	72.0	69.1	67.1	66.2	66.9	67.8	69.4	-3.72	-31.52
Lithuania	170.5	163.0	154.5	146.2	137.8	131.5	126.4	121.4	117.7	114.2	111.2	-4.19	-34.79
Malaysia	1,913.4	1,935.3	1,959.0	1,982.4	2,009.4	2,036.1	2,063.6	2,086.3	2,110.4	2,136.3	2,157.7	1.21	12.77
Mexico	7,198.6	7,238.7	7,263.2	7,264.2	7,249.1	7,225.2	7,198.0	7,170.0	7,141.6	7,113.2	7,085.0	-0.16	-1.58
Morocco	2,251.6	2,229.7	2,205.4	2,179.3	2,152.9	2,127.7	2,105.4	2,087.2	2,074.2	2,067.7	2,068.5	-0.84	-8.13
Netherlands	715.9	715.3	709.9	708.8	709.7	713.7	715.8	719.8	722.7	721.7	714.2	-0.02	-0.24
New Zealand	228.1	226.2	223.1	220.4	219.0	217.6	215.1	213.4	213.8	213.9	215.0	-0.59	-5.76
Nigeria	12,039.9	12,300.8	12,570.1	12,848.1	13,135.0	13,430.9	13,735.3	14,047.3	14,365.6	14,687.6	15,009.5	2.23	24.67
Norway	229.2	231.5	232.3	231.8	231.8	232.4	231.4	229.4	227.9	227.2	227.3	-0.08	-0.81
Pakistan	14,385.6	14,457.0	14,544.9	14,653.5	14,783.2	14,931.8	15,096.7	15,277.0	15,473.2	15,684.4	15,909.6	1.01	10.59
Peru	2,048.7	2,054.8	2,059.2	2,062.2	2,064.3	2,066.0	2,067.7	2,069.5	2,071.7	2,074.2	2,076.6	0.14	1.36
Philippines	6,966.7	7,041.3	7,101.5	7,151.5	7,193.9	7,233.8	7,273.9	7,316.7	7,364.6	7,419.6	7,482.9	0.72	7.41
Poland	1,801.2	1,734.6	1,661.4	1,588.0	1,524.5	1,470.3	1,419.2	1,376.1	1,336.5	1,309.9	1,294.7	-3.25	-28.12
Portugal	403.5	400.1	395.8	392.6	394.0	395.0	398.8	402.6	405.8	407.9	409.6	0.15	1.53
Romania	932.5	870.8	833.8	816.4	802.2	796.2	785.8	777.1	772.2	768.0	764.3	-1.97	-18.04
Russia	6,196.7	5,753.3	5,354.0	5,091.8	4,889.1	4,814.9	4,742.0	4,748.0	4,832.8	4,958.1	5,046.7	-2.03	-18.56
Saudi Arabia	1,781.1	1,806.2	1,826.5	1,842.7	1,856.6	1,870.1	1,884.2	1,899.5	1,915.4	1,930.9	1,944.7	0.88	9.19
Singapore	237.3	237.9	234.4	231.2	225.6	221.8	215.8	208.2	199.8	191.7	185.1	-2.45	-21.98
Slovakia	259.7	250.1	239.3	228.7	219.4	209.7	202.3	196.7	192.0	189.6	188.2	-3.17	-27.52
Slovenia	76.4	74.4	72.5	70.9	69.7	69.0	68.3	67.8	67.1	67.1	67.4	-1.25	-11.79
South Africa	3,511.1	3,501.4	3,491.8	3,483.6	3,478.7	3,478.3	3,483.0	3,491.9	3,503.4	3,515.5	3,526.3	0.04	0.43
South Korea	2,506.3	2,507.0	2,481.9	2,435.6	2,380.6	2,308.0	2,209.9	2,102.5	2,002.3	1,901.8	1,805.2	-3.23	-27.97
Spain	1,579.8	1,566.3	1,554.1	1,548.5	1,552.9	1,569.2	1,593.7	1,623.2	1,663.0	1,705.9	1,747.5	1.01	10.62
Sweden	443.0	431.9	415.3	398.7	382.6	371.2	362.2	359.2	362.2	368.2	374.0	-1.68	-15.57
Switzerland	317.1	315.0	310.8	305.7	300.4	295.2	290.1	285.7	280.1	276.2	273.0	-1.49	-13.92
Taiwan	1,173.0	1,179.4	1,172.7	1,145.2	1,125.8	1,116.4	1,082.4	1,043.7	994.9	941.5	911.2	-2.49	-22.32
Thailand	3,587.7	3,607.9	3,580.1	3,521.5	3,470.5	3,400.0	3,311.8	3,215.0	3,141.8	3,104.2	3,092.1	-1.48	-13.81
Tunisia	685.1	665.0	644.3	623.9	604.7	587.8	573.9	563.5	556.5	552.7	551.7	-2.14	-19.47
Turkey	4,785.5	4,867.3	4,942.7	5,003.9	5,046.6	5,073.8	5,062.4	5,028.1	4,973.5	4,902.7	4,833.9	0.10	1.01
Turkmenistan	392.6	383.8	373.6	362.9	353.1	345.5	340.9	339.5	341.0	344.2	348.1	-1.20	-11.34
Ukraine	2,052.3	1,942.3	1,830.9	1,725.5	1,630.6	1,553.1	1,485.9	1,436.0	1,403.0	1,395.5	1,396.6	-3.78	-31.95
United Arab Emirates	176.5	182.6	193.5	207.7	223.2	237.9	250.1	259.2	265.4	269.1	271.2	4.39	53.66
United Kingdom	2,800.7	2,771.7	2,730.9	2,682.5	2,638.6	2,596.7	2,556.9	2,528.4	2,511.7	2,507.3	2,517.5	-1.06	-10.11
USA	15,159.3	14,970.5	14,817.3	14,702.9	14,650.6	14,716.3	14,768.6	14,871.9	15,040.2	15,216.4	15,419.8	0.17	1.72
Venezuela	1,950.9	1,952.7	1,955.9	1,960.9	1,967.7	1,976.2	1,986.0	1,997.0	2,008.9	2,021.2	2,033.6	0.42	4.24
Vietnam	6,321.3	6,198.5	6,046.3	5,869.6	5,691.7	5,543.3	5,445.8	5,409.6	5,427.3	5,480.1	5,539.3	-1.31	-12.37

Marketing segments: Young generation

Table 4.100 Teenagers (13-19): 2009-2019 (%)

% of total

	2009	2010	2011	2012	2013	2014	2015	2016	2017	2018	2019
Algeria	14.05	13.47	12.87	12.28	11.75	11.31	10.99	10.81	10.73	10.74	10.80
Argentina	12.01	11.90	11.77	11.63	11.48	11.32	11.16	11.00	10.86	10.74	10.63
Australia	9.43	9.29	9.15	9.02	8.91	8.79	8.65	8.54	8.44	8.38	8.34
Austria	8.31	8.26	8.15	7.98	7.78	7.60	7.42	7.30	7.17	7.10	7.04
Azerbaijan	13.79	13.13	12.43	11.71	11.04	10.46	10.01	9.70	9.53	9.49	9.56
Belarus	9.03	8.44	7.92	7.54	7.22	7.02	6.87	6.78	6.75	6.79	6.81
Belgium	8.36	8.28	8.17	8.03	7.91	7.84	7.80	7.76	7.71	7.70	7.72
Bolivia	15.23	15.18	15.09	14.97	14.84	14.71	14.59	14.49	14.39	14.30	14.20
Bosnia-Herzegovina	8.73	8.46	8.27	8.16	8.08	7.99	7.86	7.68	7.45	7.21	6.98
Brazil	12.07	11.95	11.88	11.87	11.87	11.88	11.88	11.85	11.79	11.68	11.52
Bulgaria	7.69	7.26	6.81	6.48	6.32	6.19	6.14	6.16	6.20	6.36	6.49
Canada	9.08	8.90	8.69	8.47	8.28	8.07	7.85	7.65	7.51	7.42	7.36
Chile	12.16	11.89	11.57	11.22	10.87	10.53	10.22	9.95	9.73	9.55	9.42
China	10.26	9.47	9.05	8.57	8.26	8.00	7.73	7.47	7.37	7.25	7.21
Colombia	13.35	13.21	13.06	12.90	12.73	12.56	12.41	12.26	12.12	12.00	11.89
Costa Rica	13.23	12.92	12.63	12.36	12.10	11.86	11.63	11.41	11.20	10.99	10.78
Croatia	8.14	8.14	8.12	8.05	8.02	7.92	7.76	7.56	7.30	7.08	6.96
Czech Republic	8.15	7.80	7.42	7.05	6.74	6.44	6.30	6.29	6.34	6.43	6.57
Denmark	8.84	8.89	8.91	8.89	8.80	8.75	8.62	8.47	8.38	8.30	8.24
Ecuador	13.93	13.87	13.82	13.77	13.70	13.62	13.50	13.35	13.17	12.97	12.76
Egypt	13.82	13.55	13.36	13.27	13.27	13.34	13.47	13.61	13.77	13.94	14.12
Estonia	8.68	8.04	7.47	7.05	6.71	6.62	6.58	6.60	6.64	6.80	7.02
Finland	8.70	8.60	8.45	8.26	8.07	7.90	7.72	7.57	7.49	7.45	7.46
France	8.48	8.38	8.27	8.19	8.17	8.24	8.30	8.33	8.35	8.38	8.41
Germany	7.37	7.19	7.02	6.93	6.87	6.83	6.79	6.74	6.65	6.54	6.44
Greece	7.09	7.04	6.93	6.82	6.73	6.68	6.64	6.61	6.61	6.64	6.71
Hong Kong, China	8.56	8.38	8.11	7.79	7.44	7.13	6.72	6.36	6.04	5.85	5.84
Hungary	8.34	8.18	7.94	7.67	7.44	7.29	7.15	7.03	6.95	6.94	6.98
India	14.12	14.02	13.89	13.75	13.60	13.45	13.31	13.17	13.04	12.91	12.78
Indonesia	12.45	12.30	12.15	12.03	11.92	11.83	11.76	11.70	11.65	11.60	11.53
Iran	13.67	12.64	11.68	10.86	10.19	9.71	9.43	9.33	9.39	9.56	9.78
Ireland	8.84	8.69	8.57	8.52	8.50	8.52	8.53	8.61	8.72	8.78	8.80
Israel	11.44	11.46	11.52	11.59	11.66	11.74	11.82	11.91	12.01	12.04	12.02
Italy	6.82	6.76	6.69	6.64	6.59	6.59	6.61	6.64	6.67	6.73	6.76
Japan	6.64	6.60	6.60	6.59	6.60	6.58	6.55	6.51	6.45	6.36	6.30
Jordan	14.97	14.79	14.62	14.45	14.28	14.12	13.96	13.81	13.67	13.55	13.47
Kazakhstan	12.23	11.57	10.93	10.34	9.84	9.48	9.28	9.23	9.34	9.57	9.89
Kuwait	9.55	9.49	9.45	9.41	9.38	9.36	9.34	9.32	9.32	9.32	9.34
Latvia	8.84	8.17	7.50	6.90	6.43	6.21	6.08	6.05	6.15	6.27	6.47
Lithuania	9.97	9.58	9.12	8.67	8.20	7.86	7.61	7.34	7.14	6.97	6.84
Malaysia	13.24	13.17	13.13	13.10	13.10	13.09	13.09	13.06	13.03	13.02	12.97
Mexico	13.32	13.19	13.03	12.85	12.64	12.44	12.23	12.04	11.86	11.68	11.51
Morocco	13.92	13.61	13.29	12.97	12.66	12.37	12.10	11.86	11.66	11.50	11.38
Netherlands	8.53	8.49	8.42	8.38	8.37	8.40	8.41	8.43	8.46	8.42	8.32
New Zealand	10.33	10.13	9.90	9.69	9.55	9.41	9.23	9.09	9.02	8.94	8.92
Nigeria	15.37	15.34	15.33	15.33	15.34	15.36	15.39	15.43	15.48	15.53	15.58
Norway	9.29	9.28	9.20	9.09	9.02	8.95	8.84	8.69	8.57	8.47	8.39
Pakistan	15.48	15.23	14.99	14.78	14.59	14.43	14.29	14.16	14.06	13.98	13.92
Peru	13.92	13.77	13.62	13.46	13.30	13.14	12.99	12.84	12.71	12.57	12.45
Philippines	14.84	14.71	14.56	14.39	14.21	14.03	13.85	13.69	13.54	13.40	13.29
Poland	9.27	8.94	8.57	8.20	7.88	7.61	7.35	7.13	6.92	6.79	6.72
Portugal	7.40	7.33	7.23	7.16	7.17	7.18	7.23	7.29	7.33	7.36	7.38
Romania	8.51	7.97	7.64	7.52	7.41	7.38	7.32	7.27	7.26	7.26	7.25
Russia	8.55	7.94	7.40	7.06	6.78	6.69	6.59	6.61	6.73	6.91	7.04
Saudi Arabia	13.91	13.80	13.66	13.49	13.31	13.13	12.97	12.83	12.70	12.57	12.44
Singapore	9.85	9.76	9.52	9.28	8.98	8.76	8.48	8.16	7.83	7.50	7.24
Slovakia	9.41	9.06	8.67	8.28	7.94	7.60	7.31	7.12	6.95	6.87	6.82
Slovenia	7.35	7.14	6.94	6.76	6.64	6.56	6.47	6.41	6.34	6.34	6.37
South Africa	13.97	13.82	13.70	13.60	13.52	13.47	13.44	13.42	13.41	13.41	13.39
South Korea	9.68	9.68	9.59	9.40	9.20	8.94	8.57	8.17	7.78	7.40	7.04
Spain	6.76	6.64	6.54	6.46	6.43	6.45	6.51	6.58	6.69	6.82	6.94
Sweden	9.39	9.12	8.73	8.34	7.97	7.68	7.45	7.36	7.38	7.46	7.55
Switzerland	8.21	8.13	8.00	7.85	7.68	7.52	7.37	7.23	7.07	6.96	6.86
Taiwan	9.78	9.80	9.72	9.47	9.29	9.18	8.88	8.53	8.12	7.66	7.40
Thailand	10.92	10.91	10.76	10.52	10.31	10.05	9.73	9.40	9.14	8.99	8.91
Tunisia	12.97	12.45	11.94	11.44	10.98	10.57	10.23	9.95	9.74	9.59	9.49
Turkey	12.50	12.57	12.62	12.64	12.61	12.54	12.37	12.16	11.91	11.62	11.35
Turkmenistan	15.21	14.68	14.11	13.53	12.99	12.55	12.24	12.04	11.95	11.94	11.94
Ukraine	8.72	8.30	7.88	7.48	7.11	6.82	6.56	6.38	6.27	6.28	6.33
United Arab Emirates	7.36	7.38	7.55	7.82	8.13	8.42	8.66	8.82	8.90	8.92	8.89
United Kingdom	8.84	8.70	8.53	8.33	8.15	7.97	7.79	7.65	7.55	7.48	7.46
USA	9.65	9.47	9.31	9.17	9.08	9.06	9.03	9.04	9.08	9.13	9.19
Venezuela	13.39	13.19	13.01	12.84	12.69	12.56	12.45	12.34	12.25	12.16	12.08
Vietnam	14.18	13.73	13.22	12.67	12.13	11.67	11.33	11.12	11.03	11.01	11.01

Marketing segments: Young generation

Table 4.101 Female teenagers (13-19): 2009-2019 (%)

% of total

	2009	2010	2011	2012	2013	2014	2015	2016	2017	2018	2019
Algeria	6.88	6.59	6.30	6.01	5.75	5.53	5.38	5.29	5.25	5.25	5.28
Argentina	5.91	5.86	5.79	5.72	5.65	5.57	5.49	5.41	5.34	5.28	5.23
Australia	4.58	4.52	4.46	4.40	4.34	4.28	4.22	4.17	4.12	4.08	4.07
Austria	4.06	4.04	3.99	3.90	3.81	3.72	3.63	3.57	3.50	3.47	3.45
Azerbaijan	6.68	6.35	5.99	5.63	5.28	4.97	4.72	4.54	4.43	4.38	4.39
Belarus	4.40	4.11	3.86	3.67	3.51	3.41	3.33	3.29	3.27	3.29	3.30
Belgium	4.09	4.05	4.00	3.93	3.87	3.83	3.82	3.79	3.77	3.76	3.77
Bolivia	7.48	7.45	7.41	7.35	7.28	7.22	7.16	7.11	7.06	7.02	6.97
Bosnia-Herzegovina	4.23	4.09	4.00	3.94	3.90	3.86	3.80	3.72	3.61	3.49	3.38
Brazil	5.95	5.88	5.85	5.84	5.84	5.85	5.84	5.83	5.80	5.74	5.66
Bulgaria	3.75	3.54	3.31	3.15	3.08	3.01	2.99	2.99	3.01	3.09	3.15
Canada	4.42	4.33	4.22	4.11	4.02	3.91	3.80	3.70	3.63	3.58	3.54
Chile	5.98	5.84	5.69	5.52	5.34	5.17	5.02	4.89	4.78	4.69	4.63
China	4.66	4.28	4.06	3.85	3.69	3.58	3.47	3.36	3.33	3.29	3.28
Colombia	6.56	6.49	6.41	6.33	6.25	6.17	6.09	6.02	5.95	5.89	5.83
Costa Rica	6.42	6.27	6.13	6.00	5.88	5.76	5.65	5.55	5.45	5.35	5.25
Croatia	3.98	3.98	3.97	3.93	3.92	3.88	3.79	3.69	3.57	3.46	3.40
Czech Republic	3.97	3.80	3.61	3.43	3.28	3.13	3.07	3.06	3.08	3.12	3.19
Denmark	4.31	4.33	4.34	4.33	4.29	4.27	4.21	4.14	4.10	4.06	4.03
Ecuador	6.85	6.82	6.79	6.76	6.73	6.68	6.62	6.55	6.46	6.36	6.26
Egypt	6.62	6.48	6.39	6.34	6.33	6.36	6.42	6.48	6.56	6.65	6.73
Estonia	4.23	3.92	3.64	3.43	3.26	3.22	3.19	3.20	3.22	3.31	3.40
Finland	4.26	4.22	4.15	4.05	3.96	3.87	3.78	3.70	3.67	3.64	3.65
France	4.16	4.11	4.05	4.01	4.00	4.04	4.07	4.09	4.10	4.12	4.13
Germany	3.59	3.51	3.43	3.39	3.35	3.34	3.32	3.29	3.25	3.20	3.15
Greece	3.43	3.42	3.37	3.32	3.27	3.25	3.22	3.21	3.21	3.21	3.25
Hong Kong, China	4.17	4.09	3.98	3.83	3.64	3.48	3.28	3.11	2.95	2.85	2.83
Hungary	4.08	4.00	3.88	3.75	3.64	3.56	3.49	3.43	3.39	3.39	3.41
India	6.75	6.69	6.63	6.57	6.50	6.43	6.36	6.30	6.24	6.18	6.11
Indonesia	6.13	6.05	5.98	5.92	5.86	5.82	5.78	5.75	5.72	5.70	5.66
Iran	6.66	6.15	5.68	5.28	4.95	4.72	4.59	4.54	4.58	4.66	4.77
Ireland	4.31	4.23	4.17	4.14	4.14	4.15	4.16	4.20	4.26	4.30	4.31
Israel	5.58	5.59	5.62	5.65	5.68	5.72	5.76	5.81	5.85	5.87	5.86
Italy	3.31	3.28	3.25	3.22	3.20	3.20	3.20	3.22	3.24	3.27	3.28
Japan	3.24	3.22	3.22	3.22	3.22	3.21	3.19	3.18	3.15	3.10	3.07
Jordan	7.29	7.21	7.13	7.06	6.98	6.90	6.82	6.75	6.68	6.62	6.58
Kazakhstan	5.98	5.65	5.34	5.05	4.80	4.62	4.53	4.50	4.56	4.67	4.83
Kuwait	4.61	4.59	4.58	4.58	4.58	4.58	4.58	4.58	4.58	4.59	4.60
Latvia	4.34	4.02	3.68	3.39	3.16	3.05	2.99	2.99	3.04	3.10	3.19
Lithuania	4.87	4.69	4.46	4.23	3.99	3.82	3.70	3.57	3.46	3.38	3.32
Malaysia	6.43	6.40	6.37	6.36	6.37	6.38	6.38	6.36	6.34	6.33	6.31
Mexico	6.69	6.62	6.54	6.43	6.33	6.22	6.11	6.01	5.92	5.83	5.74
Morocco	6.88	6.72	6.56	6.40	6.25	6.10	5.97	5.85	5.75	5.67	5.61
Netherlands	4.17	4.14	4.11	4.09	4.08	4.09	4.09	4.10	4.11	4.10	4.04
New Zealand	5.04	4.94	4.82	4.72	4.65	4.59	4.50	4.44	4.40	4.36	4.35
Nigeria	7.59	7.57	7.56	7.56	7.56	7.57	7.58	7.60	7.62	7.65	7.67
Norway	4.52	4.51	4.47	4.42	4.39	4.36	4.31	4.24	4.19	4.14	4.11
Pakistan	7.53	7.40	7.29	7.19	7.09	7.01	6.94	6.88	6.83	6.79	6.75
Peru	6.86	6.78	6.71	6.63	6.55	6.47	6.39	6.32	6.25	6.18	6.11
Philippines	7.28	7.21	7.14	7.05	6.96	6.87	6.79	6.70	6.63	6.56	6.50
Poland	4.53	4.37	4.19	4.00	3.84	3.71	3.58	3.46	3.36	3.29	3.26
Portugal	3.62	3.58	3.54	3.50	3.51	3.51	3.53	3.55	3.57	3.58	3.58
Romania	4.16	3.89	3.73	3.67	3.62	3.60	3.57	3.54	3.53	3.53	3.53
Russia	4.18	3.88	3.62	3.45	3.31	3.26	3.22	3.22	3.28	3.36	3.43
Saudi Arabia	6.99	6.92	6.84	6.74	6.64	6.55	6.46	6.39	6.32	6.25	6.19
Singapore	4.81	4.77	4.67	4.55	4.42	4.32	4.21	4.08	3.95	3.81	3.70
Slovakia	4.60	4.42	4.23	4.04	3.87	3.71	3.57	3.47	3.39	3.35	3.33
Slovenia	3.58	3.47	3.37	3.28	3.22	3.19	3.14	3.11	3.07	3.08	3.09
South Africa	6.96	6.89	6.83	6.78	6.74	6.71	6.70	6.69	6.68	6.68	6.67
South Korea	4.54	4.55	4.52	4.44	4.36	4.25	4.09	3.91	3.73	3.54	3.38
Spain	3.29	3.23	3.18	3.15	3.13	3.14	3.17	3.20	3.26	3.31	3.37
Sweden	4.57	4.45	4.25	4.07	3.89	3.74	3.63	3.58	3.59	3.63	3.67
Switzerland	4.01	3.98	3.92	3.85	3.77	3.69	3.62	3.55	3.48	3.43	3.38
Taiwan	4.69	4.69	4.66	4.54	4.45	4.39	4.25	4.08	3.87	3.65	3.52
Thailand	5.38	5.37	5.30	5.17	5.07	4.93	4.77	4.60	4.47	4.39	4.35
Tunisia	6.30	6.04	5.79	5.55	5.32	5.12	4.95	4.82	4.71	4.64	4.59
Turkey	6.14	6.18	6.21	6.22	6.20	6.16	6.08	5.97	5.85	5.70	5.57
Turkmenistan	7.53	7.27	6.98	6.69	6.43	6.21	6.05	5.95	5.91	5.90	5.90
Ukraine	4.25	4.05	3.84	3.65	3.47	3.32	3.20	3.11	3.05	3.06	3.08
United Arab Emirates	3.53	3.52	3.55	3.61	3.69	3.78	3.86	3.93	3.99	4.02	4.04
United Kingdom	4.30	4.22	4.14	4.05	3.95	3.86	3.78	3.71	3.66	3.62	3.61
USA	4.71	4.62	4.54	4.48	4.43	4.42	4.41	4.41	4.43	4.46	4.49
Venezuela	6.57	6.47	6.38	6.29	6.22	6.16	6.10	6.05	6.00	5.96	5.92
Vietnam	6.97	6.74	6.49	6.22	5.96	5.73	5.56	5.46	5.41	5.40	5.40

Marketing segments: Young generation

Table 4.102 Male teenagers (13-19): 2009-2019 (%)

% of total

	2009	2010	2011	2012	2013	2014	2015	2016	2017	2018	2019
Algeria	7.17	6.88	6.57	6.27	6.00	5.78	5.61	5.52	5.48	5.48	5.51
Argentina	6.10	6.04	5.98	5.91	5.83	5.75	5.67	5.59	5.52	5.45	5.40
Australia	4.84	4.77	4.70	4.63	4.57	4.50	4.43	4.37	4.32	4.29	4.27
Austria	4.25	4.22	4.16	4.07	3.97	3.88	3.79	3.73	3.66	3.63	3.60
Azerbaijan	7.12	6.78	6.44	6.09	5.77	5.49	5.29	5.16	5.10	5.11	5.17
Belarus	4.63	4.33	4.06	3.87	3.71	3.61	3.54	3.49	3.48	3.50	3.51
Belgium	4.27	4.23	4.17	4.10	4.04	4.01	3.99	3.96	3.94	3.94	3.95
Bolivia	7.75	7.73	7.68	7.62	7.56	7.49	7.43	7.38	7.33	7.28	7.23
Bosnia-Herzegovina	4.49	4.36	4.28	4.22	4.18	4.13	4.06	3.96	3.84	3.72	3.60
Brazil	6.12	6.06	6.03	6.03	6.03	6.04	6.04	6.02	5.99	5.94	5.86
Bulgaria	3.94	3.73	3.50	3.33	3.24	3.17	3.15	3.17	3.19	3.27	3.34
Canada	4.66	4.57	4.46	4.36	4.26	4.16	4.05	3.95	3.88	3.84	3.81
Chile	6.18	6.04	5.88	5.71	5.53	5.35	5.20	5.06	4.95	4.86	4.79
China	5.59	5.19	4.98	4.72	4.57	4.42	4.26	4.12	4.04	3.97	3.94
Colombia	6.79	6.72	6.65	6.56	6.48	6.40	6.32	6.24	6.17	6.11	6.05
Costa Rica	6.81	6.65	6.50	6.36	6.22	6.10	5.98	5.86	5.75	5.64	5.53
Croatia	4.16	4.16	4.16	4.11	4.10	4.04	3.97	3.87	3.73	3.62	3.56
Czech Republic	4.18	4.00	3.81	3.62	3.45	3.31	3.24	3.23	3.26	3.31	3.38
Denmark	4.53	4.56	4.57	4.56	4.51	4.48	4.41	4.34	4.29	4.25	4.21
Ecuador	7.08	7.06	7.03	7.01	6.98	6.93	6.88	6.80	6.71	6.61	6.50
Egypt	7.20	7.06	6.97	6.93	6.94	6.98	7.05	7.12	7.21	7.30	7.39
Estonia	4.45	4.12	3.83	3.62	3.45	3.41	3.39	3.40	3.42	3.50	3.61
Finland	4.43	4.39	4.30	4.21	4.11	4.03	3.94	3.87	3.82	3.81	3.81
France	4.32	4.27	4.22	4.17	4.16	4.20	4.23	4.24	4.25	4.26	4.28
Germany	3.77	3.68	3.60	3.55	3.52	3.49	3.47	3.45	3.40	3.35	3.29
Greece	3.66	3.62	3.56	3.50	3.45	3.43	3.42	3.40	3.40	3.42	3.47
Hong Kong, China	4.39	4.29	4.13	3.97	3.79	3.65	3.44	3.25	3.09	3.00	3.01
Hungary	4.26	4.18	4.06	3.92	3.80	3.73	3.66	3.60	3.56	3.55	3.57
India	7.38	7.32	7.26	7.18	7.10	7.02	6.95	6.87	6.80	6.73	6.66
Indonesia	6.32	6.25	6.18	6.11	6.06	6.02	5.98	5.95	5.93	5.90	5.87
Iran	7.01	6.49	6.00	5.58	5.24	4.99	4.84	4.79	4.82	4.90	5.01
Ireland	4.53	4.46	4.40	4.38	4.36	4.37	4.37	4.41	4.46	4.48	4.49
Israel	5.86	5.87	5.90	5.94	5.98	6.02	6.06	6.11	6.15	6.17	6.16
Italy	3.50	3.48	3.44	3.42	3.39	3.40	3.40	3.42	3.43	3.46	3.48
Japan	3.40	3.38	3.38	3.37	3.38	3.37	3.35	3.34	3.31	3.26	3.22
Jordan	7.67	7.58	7.49	7.40	7.31	7.22	7.14	7.06	6.99	6.93	6.89
Kazakhstan	6.25	5.91	5.59	5.29	5.04	4.86	4.75	4.73	4.78	4.90	5.06
Kuwait	4.94	4.90	4.87	4.84	4.81	4.78	4.76	4.74	4.73	4.73	4.74
Latvia	4.50	4.15	3.82	3.52	3.27	3.16	3.09	3.07	3.12	3.18	3.27
Lithuania	5.09	4.90	4.67	4.44	4.21	4.04	3.91	3.78	3.68	3.59	3.51
Malaysia	6.81	6.78	6.76	6.73	6.73	6.72	6.72	6.70	6.69	6.68	6.67
Mexico	6.63	6.57	6.50	6.41	6.32	6.22	6.12	6.03	5.94	5.85	5.77
Morocco	7.04	6.89	6.73	6.57	6.42	6.27	6.13	6.01	5.91	5.83	5.77
Netherlands	4.36	4.35	4.31	4.30	4.29	4.31	4.31	4.33	4.34	4.33	4.28
New Zealand	5.29	5.20	5.08	4.97	4.90	4.82	4.73	4.65	4.62	4.59	4.57
Nigeria	7.78	7.77	7.77	7.77	7.78	7.79	7.81	7.83	7.85	7.88	7.91
Norway	4.77	4.77	4.73	4.67	4.63	4.59	4.53	4.45	4.38	4.32	4.29
Pakistan	7.96	7.83	7.70	7.60	7.50	7.42	7.35	7.29	7.24	7.20	7.16
Peru	7.06	6.99	6.91	6.83	6.75	6.68	6.60	6.53	6.46	6.39	6.33
Philippines	7.56	7.50	7.42	7.34	7.25	7.16	7.07	6.99	6.91	6.84	6.78
Poland	4.74	4.57	4.39	4.20	4.04	3.90	3.77	3.66	3.56	3.50	3.46
Portugal	3.78	3.74	3.69	3.66	3.66	3.67	3.70	3.73	3.76	3.78	3.79
Romania	4.35	4.08	3.91	3.85	3.79	3.78	3.75	3.73	3.72	3.72	3.73
Russia	4.37	4.06	3.78	3.61	3.47	3.42	3.37	3.38	3.45	3.55	3.62
Saudi Arabia	6.92	6.88	6.82	6.75	6.67	6.59	6.51	6.45	6.38	6.32	6.26
Singapore	5.04	4.98	4.85	4.73	4.56	4.43	4.27	4.08	3.88	3.69	3.54
Slovakia	4.81	4.63	4.43	4.24	4.06	3.88	3.75	3.65	3.56	3.51	3.49
Slovenia	3.78	3.67	3.56	3.48	3.41	3.38	3.34	3.31	3.27	3.26	3.27
South Africa	7.01	6.93	6.87	6.82	6.78	6.76	6.74	6.73	6.73	6.73	6.72
South Korea	5.14	5.13	5.07	4.96	4.84	4.69	4.48	4.26	4.06	3.85	3.66
Spain	3.47	3.41	3.36	3.32	3.30	3.31	3.34	3.38	3.44	3.50	3.57
Sweden	4.81	4.67	4.47	4.27	4.08	3.94	3.83	3.78	3.79	3.83	3.87
Switzerland	4.19	4.15	4.08	4.00	3.91	3.83	3.75	3.68	3.60	3.53	3.48
Taiwan	5.09	5.10	5.06	4.93	4.83	4.78	4.63	4.46	4.24	4.01	3.88
Thailand	5.54	5.54	5.47	5.35	5.25	5.12	4.96	4.80	4.67	4.60	4.56
Tunisia	6.67	6.41	6.15	5.90	5.66	5.45	5.27	5.13	5.02	4.94	4.89
Turkey	6.36	6.39	6.42	6.42	6.41	6.37	6.29	6.19	6.06	5.92	5.78
Turkmenistan	7.68	7.42	7.12	6.83	6.57	6.35	6.19	6.09	6.05	6.04	6.04
Ukraine	4.47	4.26	4.04	3.83	3.64	3.49	3.36	3.27	3.22	3.22	3.25
United Arab Emirates	3.82	3.87	4.01	4.21	4.44	4.65	4.80	4.88	4.91	4.90	4.85
United Kingdom	4.55	4.47	4.39	4.29	4.19	4.10	4.01	3.94	3.89	3.86	3.85
USA	4.94	4.85	4.77	4.70	4.65	4.64	4.62	4.62	4.65	4.67	4.70
Venezuela	6.83	6.72	6.63	6.55	6.47	6.41	6.35	6.29	6.25	6.20	6.16
Vietnam	7.21	6.98	6.73	6.45	6.18	5.94	5.77	5.67	5.62	5.61	5.61

Marketing segments: Young generation

Table 4.103 Studying age (18-22): 2009-2019

'000

	2009	2010	2011	2012	2013	2014	2015	2016	2017	2018	2019	Period CAGR	growth
Algeria	3,717.4	3,685.1	3,637.2	3,570.6	3,484.4	3,381.9	3,270.1	3,158.2	3,057.2	2,979.0	2,932.7	-2.34	-21.11
Argentina	3,388.1	3,416.2	3,438.0	3,453.7	3,463.1	3,466.4	3,463.5	3,454.3	3,439.1	3,419.4	3,398.9	0.03	0.32
Australia	1,525.4	1,543.4	1,557.4	1,564.8	1,569.3	1,568.5	1,568.3	1,566.4	1,565.7	1,564.3	1,567.3	0.27	2.75
Austria	507.4	512.0	516.6	519.1	518.8	514.7	508.9	499.7	488.5	476.5	467.6	-0.81	-7.85
Azerbaijan	920.6	919.3	907.8	886.7	857.6	822.7	784.5	745.3	707.7	674.7	649.3	-3.43	-29.47
Belarus	793.6	751.9	715.5	667.7	623.3	581.3	544.0	507.2	485.5	470.5	464.6	-5.21	-41.45
Belgium	646.4	655.0	661.4	660.9	654.7	644.8	634.7	626.3	620.7	618.9	619.6	-0.42	-4.15
Bolivia	967.2	991.8	1,014.9	1,035.5	1,053.1	1,067.2	1,078.2	1,086.8	1,094.1	1,101.2	1,108.9	1.38	14.65
Bosnia-Herzegovina	283.7	272.1	259.8	248.1	238.2	230.9	226.3	223.7	222.1	220.1	216.7	-2.66	-23.64
Brazil	17,248.2	16,990.4	16,768.3	16,598.7	16,519.0	16,539.8	16,620.9	16,732.8	16,867.9	17,027.8	17,184.0	-0.04	-0.37
Bulgaria	500.3	480.2	458.5	432.7	403.7	373.3	350.5	326.2	307.6	301.6	300.6	-4.97	-39.91
Canada	2,271.8	2,299.5	2,318.5	2,315.9	2,296.6	2,272.2	2,237.8	2,200.3	2,160.9	2,119.4	2,071.2	-0.92	-8.83
Chile	1,483.9	1,494.7	1,498.2	1,493.7	1,481.0	1,460.6	1,433.7	1,402.3	1,368.5	1,335.1	1,305.0	-1.28	-12.06
China	107,266.7	104,997.0	101,548.2	95,694.6	87,788.5	84,435.4	80,772.4	78,318.9	75,579.6	73,519.2	71,765.7	-3.94	-33.10
Colombia	4,186.2	4,225.6	4,261.8	4,293.2	4,318.1	4,335.6	4,345.3	4,348.1	4,345.7	4,340.5	4,335.8	0.35	3.57
Costa Rica	448.0	447.4	444.9	441.1	436.4	431.5	427.0	423.2	420.2	417.8	415.8	-0.74	-7.19
Croatia	275.2	272.0	266.0	261.2	258.0	255.6	254.8	257.2	255.7	252.9	247.8	-1.04	-9.95
Czech Republic	661.6	659.1	652.0	641.3	620.5	586.3	548.0	517.1	486.7	469.3	464.2	-3.48	-29.83
Denmark	325.7	331.7	341.6	348.8	356.1	361.1	363.2	361.7	359.4	354.8	351.1	0.75	7.79
Ecuador	1,268.4	1,276.2	1,286.5	1,299.2	1,313.8	1,329.2	1,344.1	1,357.4	1,368.4	1,376.0	1,379.7	0.85	8.78
Egypt	7,622.0	7,569.7	7,466.1	7,339.6	7,239.4	7,200.0	7,221.6	7,311.4	7,461.0	7,647.1	7,852.1	0.30	3.02
Estonia	105.6	101.9	96.7	88.9	80.6	73.4	68.6	63.9	61.3	60.0	60.1	-5.48	-43.07
Finland	323.9	328.5	335.1	336.2	337.3	334.4	329.6	322.2	314.5	307.3	301.2	-0.72	-6.99
France	3,962.6	3,951.8	3,927.8	3,865.6	3,807.3	3,768.0	3,742.4	3,721.4	3,744.9	3,784.0	3,837.2	-0.32	-3.16
Germany	4,919.9	4,846.7	4,721.0	4,555.6	4,387.5	4,201.3	4,126.6	4,100.2	4,070.2	4,055.7	4,048.7	-1.93	-17.71
Greece	606.9	597.7	594.3	584.7	583.5	577.5	572.2	566.8	560.7	554.0	549.4	-0.99	-9.47
Hong Kong, China	471.4	474.9	474.0	465.4	461.3	457.4	452.8	439.8	424.4	405.4	389.0	-1.90	-17.48
Hungary	632.2	628.3	624.6	616.6	607.3	592.6	572.3	551.4	532.8	514.1	502.1	-2.28	-20.57
India	112,270.4	113,782.5	115,157.7	116,343.1	117,297.9	118,010.2	118,502.3	118,820.4	119,026.4	119,187.3	119,352.6	0.61	6.31
Indonesia	20,545.0	20,468.7	20,402.4	20,344.4	20,294.3	20,255.2	20,232.2	20,231.4	20,257.8	20,313.0	20,392.2	-0.07	-0.74
Iran	8,894.7	8,541.2	8,121.5	7,650.6	7,153.1	6,661.9	6,209.3	5,821.5	5,520.0	5,321.8	5,233.9	-5.16	-41.16
Ireland	298.6	293.0	286.9	281.6	277.3	273.3	272.1	274.7	280.1	285.7	290.1	-0.29	-2.84
Israel	580.1	585.2	592.3	599.5	608.3	618.8	630.2	643.0	657.8	673.1	687.1	1.71	18.44
Italy	2,948.6	2,961.7	2,980.3	2,960.8	2,935.7	2,897.0	2,865.3	2,830.5	2,819.3	2,823.2	2,842.7	-0.37	-3.59
Japan	6,501.9	6,343.6	6,203.6	6,127.6	6,096.6	6,073.9	6,054.8	6,061.7	6,036.5	6,012.7	5,989.9	-0.82	-7.87
Jordan	647.1	654.6	659.4	662.1	663.7	665.6	668.5	672.6	677.2	681.9	686.6	0.59	6.10
Kazakhstan	1,558.2	1,542.0	1,507.3	1,456.9	1,396.2	1,331.7	1,269.2	1,212.6	1,165.5	1,132.4	1,117.1	-3.27	-28.31
Kuwait	177.2	177.2	178.2	180.0	182.4	185.0	187.5	189.9	192.2	194.5	197.0	1.06	11.15
Latvia	180.3	173.8	165.9	154.2	141.9	128.4	115.7	103.9	96.5	92.6	91.6	-6.55	-49.20
Lithuania	267.7	262.2	258.2	250.5	238.6	224.7	210.5	195.2	185.4	180.3	174.0	-4.22	-34.99
Malaysia	2,564.8	2,582.5	2,607.2	2,629.6	2,653.5	2,679.4	2,708.6	2,744.8	2,784.4	2,830.3	2,872.7	1.14	12.01
Mexico	9,660.6	9,804.1	9,952.1	10,079.4	10,177.5	10,239.2	10,262.9	10,252.3	10,215.1	10,163.1	10,108.8	0.45	4.64
Morocco	3,228.8	3,207.5	3,183.3	3,156.5	3,127.0	3,094.7	3,059.5	3,022.0	2,983.3	2,945.5	2,911.4	-1.03	-9.83
Netherlands	997.5	1,006.5	1,012.5	1,017.4	1,020.6	1,010.0	999.2	992.5	994.0	996.3	1,009.0	0.11	1.15
New Zealand	315.8	321.2	324.1	324.5	322.8	318.3	314.0	310.3	307.0	305.6	304.0	-0.38	-3.72
Nigeria	15,302.7	15,612.8	15,934.0	16,268.0	16,614.9	16,974.6	17,346.5	17,730.3	18,125.8	18,533.4	18,953.7	2.16	23.86
Norway	307.1	317.6	325.5	329.1	331.0	331.5	332.7	333.4	333.3	333.6	333.3	0.82	8.55
Pakistan	19,139.3	19,408.0	19,595.1	19,722.0	19,817.8	19,912.6	20,027.3	20,171.4	20,347.2	20,552.6	20,783.3	0.83	8.59
Peru	2,779.0	2,805.6	2,827.3	2,844.4	2,857.3	2,866.7	2,873.2	2,877.4	2,879.8	2,881.2	2,882.6	0.37	3.73
Philippines	9,182.9	9,347.3	9,492.6	9,622.3	9,736.0	9,836.1	9,922.4	9,995.5	10,057.3	10,111.7	10,164.9	1.02	10.69
Poland	2,857.4	2,777.5	2,697.7	2,608.4	2,515.0	2,402.9	2,293.8	2,195.5	2,103.7	2,020.3	1,958.4	-3.71	-31.46
Portugal	596.4	589.9	584.7	578.1	569.8	563.0	556.5	551.9	550.3	557.8	560.3	-0.62	-6.04
Romania	1,681.6	1,581.8	1,478.9	1,365.7	1,256.1	1,184.7	1,143.8	1,110.8	1,099.8	1,090.4	1,089.0	-4.25	-35.24
Russia	11,847.6	11,128.8	10,249.1	9,308.8	8,547.9	7,886.0	7,392.5	7,013.4	6,888.6	6,710.1	6,611.3	-5.67	-44.20
Saudi Arabia	2,392.4	2,458.4	2,514.9	2,560.7	2,596.0	2,622.4	2,642.1	2,657.6	2,671.5	2,686.3	2,703.8	1.23	13.01
Singapore	321.9	339.6	346.5	344.8	345.2	341.1	338.2	332.4	323.8	317.1	311.5	-0.33	-3.24
Slovakia	407.6	398.9	390.2	380.5	367.2	349.3	331.8	315.7	299.6	289.2	281.9	-3.62	-30.85
Slovenia	124.2	121.1	115.8	110.5	106.9	103.8	101.2	99.6	97.9	96.1	95.7	-2.57	-22.91
South Africa	5,071.7	5,062.9	5,037.8	5,000.1	4,956.7	4,915.9	4,884.2	4,864.9	4,858.7	4,864.9	4,881.1	-0.38	-3.76
South Korea	3,125.5	3,180.9	3,260.0	3,333.5	3,385.3	3,396.6	3,362.3	3,291.1	3,200.1	3,118.0	3,020.2	-0.34	-3.37
Spain	2,416.9	2,377.3	2,342.9	2,314.6	2,289.4	2,264.6	2,245.0	2,233.4	2,234.0	2,253.2	2,292.1	-0.53	-5.16
Sweden	609.6	629.6	645.5	648.5	644.2	623.7	596.3	566.4	541.5	519.7	508.7	-1.79	-16.55
Switzerland	453.1	458.9	464.6	463.0	460.2	454.2	448.5	440.7	435.2	429.0	421.1	-0.73	-7.07
Taiwan	1,587.6	1,605.7	1,617.0	1,602.5	1,614.2	1,603.3	1,606.8	1,609.6	1,550.2	1,510.2	1,491.4	-0.62	-6.06
Thailand	4,810.1	4,902.1	4,976.3	5,025.1	5,065.7	5,107.3	5,120.0	5,071.4	4,964.5	4,825.9	4,625.0	-0.39	-3.85
Tunisia	1,037.4	1,023.7	1,004.0	979.3	950.7	920.1	889.2	859.2	831.4	807.0	787.1	-2.72	-24.13
Turkey	6,291.6	6,357.4	6,470.0	6,603.0	6,735.0	6,859.6	6,975.5	7,075.4	7,142.3	7,176.5	7,176.9	1.33	14.07
Turkmenistan	566.6	572.0	571.9	566.1	555.1	540.4	523.9	507.3	492.4	480.9	474.2	-1.76	-16.30
Ukraine	3,567.6	3,386.9	3,211.3	3,020.1	2,843.8	2,677.8	2,527.2	2,384.4	2,263.8	2,149.7	2,049.0	-5.39	-42.57
United Arab Emirates	276.6	271.3	275.1	287.0	304.2	323.5	342.4	359.7	375.1	388.9	401.2	3.79	45.05
United Kingdom	4,184.8	4,216.9	4,207.2	4,168.7	4,121.8	4,055.4	3,988.4	3,935.0	3,885.1	3,832.0	3,771.9	-1.03	-9.87
USA	21,516.6	21,670.4	21,722.0	21,651.7	21,408.2	21,188.4	20,963.8	20,788.0	20,685.9	20,663.9	20,856.8	-0.31	-3.07
Venezuela	2,706.5	2,719.9	2,726.3	2,727.7	2,727.0	2,727.1	2,729.8	2,736.1	2,745.7	2,758.1	2,772.8	0.24	2.45
Vietnam	9,133.3	9,172.5	9,129.9	9,015.8	8,846.4	8,646.5	8,436.7	8,217.3	7,990.7	7,781.0	7,618.5	-1.80	-16.59

Marketing segments: Young generation

Table 4.104 Female studying age (18-22): 2009-2019

'000

	2009	2010	2011	2012	2013	2014	2015	2016	2017	2018	2019	CAGR	Period growth
Algeria	1,821.9	1,806.1	1,782.7	1,750.2	1,708.2	1,658.0	1,603.3	1,548.5	1,498.9	1,460.4	1,437.6	-2.34	-21.09
Argentina	1,669.8	1,683.3	1,693.9	1,701.6	1,706.3	1,707.9	1,706.4	1,701.8	1,694.2	1,684.3	1,674.0	0.03	0.25
Australia	741.0	749.7	756.9	761.0	764.2	763.8	764.1	763.2	763.3	763.1	764.8	0.32	3.22
Austria	249.3	251.6	253.7	255.5	255.3	253.4	250.7	246.6	240.9	234.9	230.4	-0.78	-7.55
Azerbaijan	446.9	446.4	441.1	431.0	416.8	399.5	380.1	359.8	339.8	321.7	307.1	-3.68	-31.27
Belarus	387.6	366.8	349.0	325.8	304.0	283.1	264.8	246.6	235.5	227.9	225.3	-5.28	-41.86
Belgium	317.4	321.7	324.9	324.8	321.4	316.6	311.7	307.5	304.5	304.1	304.3	-0.42	-4.15
Bolivia	476.7	488.5	499.6	509.5	517.9	524.7	530.0	534.1	537.7	541.1	544.9	1.35	14.31
Bosnia-Herzegovina	139.6	133.5	127.0	120.7	115.5	111.6	109.2	108.0	107.2	106.4	104.8	-2.83	-24.94
Brazil	8,533.4	8,403.6	8,290.6	8,203.0	8,159.5	8,166.0	8,202.5	8,254.7	8,318.7	8,395.0	8,469.7	-0.07	-0.75
Bulgaria	244.2	234.1	223.1	210.6	196.5	181.9	170.8	158.8	149.9	146.8	146.1	-5.01	-40.20
Canada	1,108.9	1,121.7	1,129.6	1,126.5	1,114.9	1,102.2	1,083.0	1,064.0	1,044.3	1,023.7	998.8	-1.04	-9.92
Chile	730.5	735.8	737.4	735.1	728.8	718.7	705.5	689.9	673.2	656.8	641.9	-1.28	-12.13
China	51,757.5	50,246.2	48,368.5	45,188.6	41,189.4	39,435.4	37,718.8	36,335.5	35,049.2	33,927.2	33,118.8	-4.37	-36.01
Colombia	2,067.9	2,086.7	2,103.9	2,118.8	2,130.6	2,138.8	2,143.2	2,144.1	2,142.5	2,139.6	2,136.8	0.33	3.33
Costa Rica	217.6	217.2	216.0	214.0	211.7	209.4	207.2	205.4	204.1	203.0	202.1	-0.74	-7.12
Croatia	135.0	133.2	130.0	127.7	126.3	124.9	124.5	125.8	125.3	123.7	121.1	-1.08	-10.28
Czech Republic	323.6	322.3	318.6	313.0	302.4	285.4	267.0	252.0	237.0	228.6	225.8	-3.54	-30.23
Denmark	158.9	161.8	166.8	170.4	174.1	176.5	177.4	176.8	175.7	173.5	171.9	0.79	8.18
Ecuador	625.7	629.3	634.1	640.1	647.0	654.3	661.3	667.7	672.8	676.4	678.1	0.81	8.38
Egypt	3,675.6	3,646.6	3,592.2	3,526.1	3,472.4	3,448.4	3,454.0	3,493.1	3,561.4	3,647.8	3,743.4	0.18	1.84
Estonia	51.5	49.7	47.2	43.3	39.3	35.9	33.5	31.1	29.8	29.2	29.1	-5.55	-43.51
Finland	158.3	160.8	164.2	164.9	165.6	164.3	161.7	158.3	154.4	150.7	147.5	-0.70	-6.80
France	1,958.1	1,947.5	1,931.8	1,899.3	1,868.9	1,849.5	1,836.6	1,825.8	1,837.9	1,857.0	1,883.2	-0.39	-3.83
Germany	2,410.0	2,375.9	2,317.4	2,237.9	2,155.5	2,065.9	2,029.8	2,017.1	2,003.2	1,996.3	1,994.3	-1.88	-17.25
Greece	292.0	288.2	286.8	283.0	283.1	280.4	278.2	276.1	272.9	269.8	267.9	-0.86	-8.25
Hong Kong, China	244.3	245.2	243.9	240.0	238.6	237.1	235.5	229.3	221.6	212.2	203.7	-1.80	-16.63
Hungary	310.4	308.1	306.3	302.6	298.1	290.6	280.5	270.0	260.8	251.7	246.0	-2.30	-20.72
India	53,710.7	54,401.1	55,025.2	55,562.3	55,997.6	56,329.0	56,567.9	56,734.9	56,855.9	56,958.4	57,061.4	0.61	6.24
Indonesia	10,143.3	10,101.3	10,065.4	10,034.6	10,008.0	9,986.6	9,972.5	9,968.6	9,977.6	10,000.8	10,036.0	-0.11	-1.06
Iran	4,366.0	4,175.5	3,958.6	3,722.3	3,477.0	3,237.0	3,016.9	2,829.0	2,683.7	2,589.3	2,549.0	-5.24	-41.62
Ireland	147.0	144.3	141.1	138.5	136.4	134.5	133.5	134.6	137.2	140.1	142.2	-0.33	-3.26
Israel	284.2	286.7	290.0	293.3	297.6	302.6	307.9	314.0	321.3	328.5	335.1	1.66	17.91
Italy	1,434.0	1,440.3	1,450.1	1,441.2	1,428.4	1,408.4	1,392.6	1,374.6	1,367.8	1,370.0	1,379.7	-0.38	-3.78
Japan	3,176.1	3,099.6	3,032.0	2,994.5	2,978.6	2,968.0	2,960.5	2,964.5	2,952.6	2,939.5	2,927.8	-0.81	-7.82
Jordan	315.7	319.4	321.6	322.7	323.4	324.3	325.8	328.0	330.5	333.1	335.6	0.61	6.31
Kazakhstan	765.5	757.2	739.8	714.5	684.3	652.1	621.0	592.9	569.5	553.1	545.5	-3.33	-28.74
Kuwait	82.9	83.4	84.0	84.7	85.7	86.9	88.4	90.1	91.9	93.7	95.5	1.42	15.19
Latvia	88.6	85.4	81.6	76.1	70.2	63.3	57.0	51.1	47.4	45.4	45.1	-6.53	-49.10
Lithuania	131.1	128.6	126.7	122.7	116.9	109.9	103.1	95.3	90.4	87.7	84.5	-4.30	-35.55
Malaysia	1,254.2	1,260.4	1,269.4	1,278.1	1,288.5	1,301.0	1,316.1	1,334.2	1,355.0	1,380.1	1,402.0	1.12	11.79
Mexico	4,923.5	4,993.3	5,061.9	5,117.3	5,156.0	5,175.6	5,176.5	5,161.0	5,133.8	5,101.5	5,070.9	0.30	2.99
Morocco	1,614.8	1,600.4	1,585.2	1,569.4	1,553.1	1,535.8	1,517.6	1,498.5	1,479.1	1,460.2	1,443.2	-1.12	-10.63
Netherlands	490.7	494.8	497.9	500.2	501.1	495.9	489.7	486.6	486.8	487.3	493.4	0.06	0.56
New Zealand	154.6	156.9	158.0	158.0	156.7	154.3	152.4	150.7	149.1	148.4	147.8	-0.45	-4.39
Nigeria	7,580.8	7,729.6	7,884.0	8,045.0	8,212.7	8,387.1	8,567.9	8,754.7	8,947.6	9,146.5	9,351.8	2.12	23.36
Norway	150.0	155.5	159.0	160.9	161.8	161.8	162.4	162.9	162.8	163.0	163.1	0.84	8.73
Pakistan	9,281.1	9,416.0	9,511.3	9,577.1	9,626.9	9,674.8	9,730.9	9,799.9	9,883.2	9,980.1	10,089.0	0.84	8.71
Peru	1,372.3	1,385.2	1,395.6	1,403.6	1,409.6	1,413.8	1,416.7	1,418.3	1,419.0	1,419.2	1,419.4	0.34	3.44
Philippines	4,515.3	4,594.7	4,664.5	4,726.5	4,780.5	4,827.7	4,868.3	4,902.5	4,931.3	4,956.6	4,981.5	0.99	10.33
Poland	1,397.8	1,357.7	1,319.4	1,275.6	1,231.0	1,176.2	1,122.5	1,073.5	1,027.2	985.0	953.6	-3.75	-31.78
Portugal	292.3	289.1	287.0	283.8	279.4	275.9	272.7	270.4	269.4	273.5	275.0	-0.61	-5.95
Romania	824.9	775.6	724.8	668.7	613.8	578.3	558.7	541.8	536.3	531.6	530.5	-4.32	-35.69
Russia	5,823.5	5,463.5	5,026.7	4,560.9	4,186.2	3,861.2	3,618.4	3,431.7	3,368.8	3,278.9	3,227.5	-5.73	-44.58
Saudi Arabia	1,188.6	1,223.6	1,251.9	1,273.4	1,288.8	1,299.6	1,307.3	1,313.4	1,319.1	1,325.6	1,333.6	1.16	12.19
Singapore	158.4	167.9	171.1	170.5	170.9	169.4	167.8	166.0	162.2	159.6	157.2	-0.08	-0.79
Slovakia	199.5	195.3	191.0	185.9	179.6	171.1	162.3	154.2	146.5	141.4	137.8	-3.63	-30.92
Slovenia	60.4	58.8	56.1	53.6	52.0	50.5	49.2	48.5	47.5	46.6	46.4	-2.61	-23.27
South Africa	2,528.0	2,523.8	2,511.7	2,493.5	2,472.6	2,452.9	2,437.7	2,428.4	2,425.4	2,428.3	2,435.7	-0.37	-3.65
South Korea	1,476.3	1,496.0	1,525.6	1,556.2	1,581.1	1,587.6	1,575.8	1,549.3	1,512.7	1,480.1	1,438.3	-0.26	-2.57
Spain	1,178.2	1,158.9	1,141.9	1,128.0	1,116.0	1,104.4	1,095.3	1,090.1	1,090.3	1,099.8	1,117.9	-0.52	-5.12
Sweden	297.9	307.6	314.9	317.0	315.3	305.2	292.4	277.9	265.3	254.4	248.9	-1.78	-16.44
Switzerland	223.4	226.3	229.6	229.1	227.9	225.2	222.7	218.8	216.3	213.3	209.5	-0.64	-6.25
Taiwan	764.8	770.9	774.8	767.6	772.7	768.7	771.2	772.5	743.4	723.2	712.5	-0.71	-6.83
Thailand	2,385.7	2,428.6	2,464.5	2,486.7	2,505.4	2,524.6	2,528.8	2,503.3	2,448.6	2,378.1	2,276.5	-0.47	-4.58
Tunisia	506.2	498.9	488.8	476.2	461.9	446.7	431.4	416.6	403.0	391.0	381.3	-2.79	-24.67
Turkey	3,083.0	3,119.0	3,178.5	3,248.1	3,315.1	3,378.5	3,437.0	3,485.5	3,517.3	3,533.5	3,530.8	1.37	14.53
Turkmenistan	280.6	283.3	283.3	280.5	275.1	267.8	259.6	251.3	243.8	238.0	234.6	-1.77	-16.40
Ukraine	1,742.5	1,652.9	1,567.1	1,473.5	1,387.1	1,306.4	1,233.1	1,163.3	1,104.8	1,049.1	999.3	-5.41	-42.65
United Arab Emirates	122.9	120.5	119.7	120.5	122.8	126.1	130.4	135.5	141.2	147.2	153.2	2.23	24.69
United Kingdom	2,040.4	2,059.6	2,057.0	2,037.0	2,012.4	1,979.5	1,946.9	1,920.9	1,896.4	1,869.7	1,839.7	-1.03	-9.83
USA	10,490.6	10,587.2	10,624.6	10,598.8	10,484.0	10,376.7	10,265.8	10,180.0	10,129.8	10,118.9	10,216.9	-0.26	-2.61
Venezuela	1,332.1	1,338.4	1,341.2	1,341.5	1,340.8	1,340.4	1,341.5	1,344.3	1,348.8	1,354.7	1,361.8	0.22	2.23
Vietnam	4,501.3	4,518.1	4,495.1	4,437.2	4,352.5	4,252.9	4,148.7	4,040.0	3,927.8	3,824.1	3,743.7	-1.83	-16.83

Marketing segments: Young generation

Table 4.105 Male studying age (18-22): 2009-2019

'000

	2009	2010	2011	2012	2013	2014	2015	2016	2017	2018	2019	CAGR	Period growth
Algeria	1,895.5	1,879.0	1,854.5	1,820.4	1,776.3	1,723.9	1,666.8	1,609.7	1,558.3	1,518.5	1,495.1	-2.34	-21.12
Argentina	1,718.3	1,732.9	1,744.1	1,752.1	1,756.9	1,758.6	1,757.1	1,752.5	1,744.9	1,735.1	1,724.9	0.04	0.39
Australia	784.4	793.7	800.5	803.8	805.1	804.7	804.3	803.3	802.4	801.3	802.5	0.23	2.30
Austria	258.1	260.4	262.9	263.6	263.5	261.2	258.2	253.1	247.6	241.5	237.1	-0.84	-8.13
Azerbaijan	473.7	472.9	466.8	455.7	440.7	423.2	404.3	385.5	367.9	353.0	342.2	-3.20	-27.77
Belarus	406.0	385.1	366.4	341.9	319.3	298.3	279.3	260.6	250.0	242.6	239.3	-5.15	-41.05
Belgium	329.0	333.3	336.5	336.1	333.2	328.2	323.0	318.8	316.2	314.8	315.3	-0.42	-4.15
Bolivia	490.6	503.3	515.3	526.0	535.1	542.5	548.2	552.7	556.5	560.1	564.0	1.41	14.98
Bosnia-Herzegovina	144.1	138.6	132.9	127.3	122.7	119.3	117.1	115.8	114.9	113.7	111.8	-2.50	-22.38
Brazil	8,714.7	8,586.8	8,477.7	8,395.7	8,359.4	8,373.9	8,418.4	8,478.0	8,549.2	8,632.8	8,714.3	0.00	-0.01
Bulgaria	256.0	246.1	235.4	222.2	207.2	191.5	179.7	167.4	157.7	154.8	154.5	-4.92	-39.64
Canada	1,162.9	1,177.8	1,188.9	1,189.5	1,181.7	1,169.9	1,154.8	1,136.3	1,116.5	1,095.7	1,072.3	-0.81	-7.79
Chile	753.4	758.9	760.8	758.5	752.2	741.9	728.3	712.4	695.2	678.3	663.1	-1.27	-11.99
China	55,509.2	54,750.8	53,179.7	50,506.0	46,599.1	45,000.0	43,053.6	41,983.4	40,530.4	39,592.0	38,646.9	-3.56	-30.38
Colombia	2,118.2	2,138.9	2,157.9	2,174.3	2,187.5	2,196.8	2,202.2	2,204.0	2,203.1	2,200.9	2,198.9	0.37	3.81
Costa Rica	230.4	230.2	229.0	227.1	224.7	222.2	219.8	217.8	216.1	214.8	213.7	-0.75	-7.26
Croatia	140.2	138.8	136.0	133.5	131.8	130.6	130.3	131.4	130.5	129.3	126.7	-1.01	-9.64
Czech Republic	337.9	336.8	333.4	328.3	318.1	300.9	281.1	265.1	249.7	240.7	238.4	-3.43	-29.45
Denmark	166.8	169.9	174.9	178.4	182.0	184.6	185.8	184.9	183.7	181.3	179.2	0.72	7.42
Ecuador	642.7	646.9	652.4	659.1	666.8	674.9	682.7	689.8	695.6	699.6	701.6	0.88	9.17
Egypt	3,946.4	3,923.0	3,873.9	3,813.5	3,767.0	3,751.6	3,767.6	3,818.4	3,899.5	3,999.3	4,108.7	0.40	4.11
Estonia	54.1	52.2	49.5	45.6	41.3	37.5	35.1	32.8	31.4	30.8	31.0	-5.41	-42.65
Finland	165.6	167.7	170.9	171.3	171.7	170.1	167.9	163.9	160.1	156.5	153.7	-0.74	-7.17
France	2,004.4	2,004.3	1,996.0	1,966.3	1,938.4	1,918.4	1,905.8	1,895.6	1,907.0	1,927.0	1,954.0	-0.25	-2.52
Germany	2,510.0	2,470.8	2,403.6	2,317.7	2,232.0	2,135.4	2,096.8	2,083.1	2,066.9	2,059.4	2,054.4	-1.98	-18.15
Greece	314.9	309.5	307.5	301.7	300.4	297.1	294.0	290.7	287.8	284.2	281.6	-1.11	-10.60
Hong Kong, China	227.0	229.7	230.0	225.4	222.7	220.3	217.3	210.5	202.8	193.1	185.2	-2.01	-18.41
Hungary	321.8	320.3	318.3	314.0	309.2	302.0	291.8	281.5	272.0	262.5	256.1	-2.26	-20.43
India	58,559.7	59,381.4	60,132.5	60,780.8	61,300.3	61,681.3	61,934.4	62,085.5	62,170.5	62,228.9	62,291.2	0.62	6.37
Indonesia	10,401.6	10,367.4	10,337.0	10,309.8	10,286.3	10,268.6	10,259.7	10,262.8	10,280.2	10,312.3	10,356.2	-0.04	-0.44
Iran	4,528.6	4,365.7	4,162.9	3,928.3	3,676.1	3,424.9	3,192.4	2,992.5	2,836.3	2,732.5	2,685.0	-5.09	-40.71
Ireland	151.6	148.7	145.8	143.0	140.9	138.8	138.6	140.0	142.9	145.6	147.9	-0.25	-2.44
Israel	295.9	298.5	302.3	306.2	310.7	316.2	322.3	329.0	336.6	344.6	351.9	1.75	18.95
Italy	1,514.7	1,521.4	1,530.2	1,519.7	1,507.3	1,488.6	1,472.7	1,456.0	1,451.6	1,453.2	1,462.9	-0.35	-3.42
Japan	3,325.7	3,244.0	3,171.6	3,133.1	3,118.1	3,106.0	3,094.3	3,097.2	3,083.9	3,073.2	3,062.1	-0.82	-7.93
Jordan	331.4	335.2	337.8	339.4	340.3	341.3	342.7	344.6	346.6	348.8	351.0	0.58	5.91
Kazakhstan	792.7	784.8	767.5	742.3	711.9	679.6	648.2	619.7	596.0	579.3	571.6	-3.22	-27.89
Kuwait	94.3	93.8	94.2	95.3	96.7	98.1	99.1	99.8	100.3	100.8	101.4	0.74	7.61
Latvia	91.6	88.4	84.3	78.1	71.7	65.0	58.8	52.8	49.1	47.2	46.5	-6.57	-49.29
Lithuania	136.6	133.6	131.5	127.7	121.8	114.8	107.5	99.9	95.1	92.5	89.5	-4.14	-34.46
Malaysia	1,310.7	1,322.1	1,337.8	1,351.6	1,364.9	1,378.4	1,392.5	1,410.5	1,429.4	1,450.3	1,470.7	1.16	12.21
Mexico	4,737.1	4,810.9	4,890.2	4,962.2	5,021.5	5,063.5	5,086.4	5,091.3	5,081.3	5,061.6	5,037.9	0.62	6.35
Morocco	1,613.9	1,607.1	1,598.1	1,587.0	1,574.0	1,558.9	1,541.9	1,523.5	1,504.2	1,485.3	1,468.2	-0.94	-9.03
Netherlands	506.8	511.6	514.6	517.3	519.5	514.0	509.5	505.9	507.2	509.0	515.6	0.17	1.73
New Zealand	161.2	164.3	166.1	166.5	166.1	164.0	161.6	159.6	157.9	157.1	156.2	-0.31	-3.08
Nigeria	7,721.9	7,883.2	8,050.0	8,223.0	8,402.2	8,587.5	8,778.6	8,975.5	9,178.2	9,386.9	9,602.0	2.20	24.35
Norway	157.1	162.1	166.4	168.2	169.2	169.7	170.4	170.5	170.5	170.6	170.2	0.81	8.37
Pakistan	9,858.2	9,992.0	10,083.7	10,144.9	10,190.9	10,237.7	10,296.3	10,371.5	10,464.0	10,572.5	10,694.3	0.82	8.48
Peru	1,406.7	1,420.5	1,431.8	1,440.7	1,447.6	1,452.8	1,456.6	1,459.1	1,460.8	1,462.0	1,463.2	0.39	4.01
Philippines	4,667.7	4,752.6	4,828.1	4,895.8	4,955.5	5,008.3	5,054.1	5,093.0	5,126.0	5,155.1	5,183.4	1.05	11.05
Poland	1,459.6	1,419.8	1,378.3	1,332.8	1,284.0	1,226.6	1,171.2	1,122.0	1,076.4	1,035.3	1,004.8	-3.66	-31.16
Portugal	304.0	300.9	297.7	294.3	290.3	287.2	283.8	281.5	280.8	284.3	285.4	-0.63	-6.13
Romania	856.7	806.2	754.1	697.0	642.3	606.4	585.1	569.1	563.6	558.8	558.5	-4.19	-34.81
Russia	6,024.1	5,665.3	5,222.4	4,747.9	4,361.7	4,024.9	3,774.1	3,581.7	3,519.9	3,431.2	3,383.8	-5.60	-43.83
Saudi Arabia	1,203.8	1,234.9	1,263.0	1,287.3	1,307.2	1,322.8	1,334.8	1,344.2	1,352.4	1,360.7	1,370.2	1.30	13.82
Singapore	163.5	171.8	175.4	174.3	174.2	171.7	170.3	166.4	161.6	157.5	154.3	-0.58	-5.61
Slovakia	208.1	203.5	199.2	194.5	187.6	178.2	169.5	161.5	153.1	147.8	144.0	-3.61	-30.79
Slovenia	63.7	62.2	59.7	56.9	54.9	53.3	52.0	51.1	50.3	49.5	49.4	-2.52	-22.56
South Africa	2,543.8	2,539.1	2,526.1	2,506.6	2,484.1	2,463.0	2,446.6	2,436.5	2,433.3	2,436.7	2,445.4	-0.39	-3.87
South Korea	1,649.2	1,684.9	1,734.4	1,777.3	1,804.2	1,809.0	1,786.4	1,741.8	1,687.4	1,637.9	1,581.9	-0.42	-4.08
Spain	1,238.6	1,218.5	1,201.0	1,186.6	1,173.4	1,160.2	1,149.8	1,143.3	1,143.7	1,153.3	1,174.2	-0.53	-5.20
Sweden	311.7	322.0	330.6	331.6	328.9	318.5	303.9	288.5	276.2	265.3	259.8	-1.80	-16.64
Switzerland	229.7	232.6	235.0	233.9	232.3	229.0	225.8	221.9	218.9	215.6	211.6	-0.82	-7.87
Taiwan	822.8	834.9	842.2	834.9	841.5	834.6	835.5	837.0	806.9	787.1	778.9	-0.55	-5.34
Thailand	2,424.4	2,473.5	2,511.8	2,538.5	2,560.3	2,582.7	2,591.2	2,568.1	2,515.9	2,447.9	2,348.6	-0.32	-3.13
Tunisia	531.2	524.8	515.3	503.0	488.8	473.4	457.8	442.6	428.4	416.0	405.8	-2.66	-23.61
Turkey	3,208.6	3,238.4	3,291.5	3,354.9	3,419.9	3,481.1	3,538.5	3,589.9	3,625.0	3,643.0	3,646.1	1.29	13.63
Turkmenistan	286.0	288.7	288.6	285.6	280.0	272.6	264.2	255.9	248.5	242.9	239.6	-1.75	-16.21
Ukraine	1,825.2	1,733.9	1,644.2	1,546.7	1,456.7	1,371.4	1,294.2	1,221.1	1,159.0	1,100.6	1,049.7	-5.38	-42.49
United Arab Emirates	153.7	150.7	155.4	166.4	181.5	197.4	212.0	224.2	234.0	241.7	248.0	4.90	61.34
United Kingdom	2,144.5	2,157.3	2,150.2	2,131.7	2,109.4	2,075.9	2,041.5	2,014.0	1,988.7	1,962.4	1,932.2	-1.04	-9.90
USA	11,026.0	11,083.1	11,097.4	11,052.9	10,924.2	10,811.8	10,697.9	10,607.9	10,556.1	10,545.0	10,639.9	-0.36	-3.50
Venezuela	1,374.4	1,381.6	1,385.2	1,386.2	1,386.3	1,386.6	1,388.4	1,391.8	1,396.9	1,403.4	1,411.0	0.26	2.66
Vietnam	4,632.0	4,654.4	4,634.8	4,578.6	4,493.9	4,393.5	4,287.9	4,177.4	4,062.9	3,956.9	3,874.8	-1.77	-16.35

Marketing segments: Young generation

Table 4.106 Studying age (18-22): 2009-2019 (%)

% of total

	2009	2010	2011	2012	2013	2014	2015	2016	2017	2018	2019
Algeria	10.65	10.40	10.12	9.79	9.41	9.00	8.59	8.18	7.81	7.52	7.31
Argentina	8.40	8.39	8.36	8.32	8.26	8.20	8.12	8.02	7.92	7.81	7.70
Australia	7.00	6.98	6.96	6.90	6.83	6.73	6.64	6.54	6.45	6.36	6.29
Austria	6.05	6.09	6.13	6.14	6.11	6.05	5.97	5.84	5.70	5.54	5.43
Azerbaijan	10.54	10.41	10.17	9.83	9.41	8.94	8.44	7.95	7.48	7.07	6.75
Belarus	8.20	7.79	7.43	6.96	6.51	6.09	5.72	5.35	5.13	4.99	4.95
Belgium	6.06	6.12	6.16	6.13	6.06	5.95	5.83	5.74	5.67	5.64	5.63
Bolivia	9.81	9.89	9.95	9.99	10.00	9.98	9.93	9.87	9.79	9.72	9.66
Bosnia-Herzegovina	7.38	7.08	6.76	6.46	6.20	6.01	5.90	5.84	5.80	5.76	5.68
Brazil	8.90	8.69	8.51	8.36	8.26	8.21	8.19	8.19	8.21	8.24	8.26
Bulgaria	6.65	6.43	6.18	5.88	5.53	5.15	4.87	4.57	4.35	4.30	4.33
Canada	6.75	6.77	6.77	6.71	6.61	6.49	6.34	6.19	6.03	5.88	5.70
Chile	8.74	8.72	8.66	8.56	8.41	8.22	8.00	7.76	7.51	7.27	7.05
China	8.08	7.87	7.58	7.11	6.50	6.22	5.93	5.73	5.51	5.34	5.20
Colombia	9.17	9.13	9.08	9.03	8.96	8.89	8.80	8.70	8.59	8.49	8.38
Costa Rica	9.78	9.64	9.46	9.25	9.03	8.82	8.62	8.43	8.28	8.14	8.01
Croatia	6.21	6.15	6.03	5.93	5.87	5.83	5.83	5.90	5.88	5.83	5.73
Czech Republic	6.40	6.37	6.29	6.19	5.99	5.66	5.29	4.99	4.70	4.53	4.48
Denmark	5.91	6.00	6.17	6.28	6.39	6.46	6.48	6.44	6.38	6.28	6.20
Ecuador	9.31	9.26	9.23	9.22	9.21	9.21	9.21	9.20	9.17	9.13	9.06
Egypt	9.93	9.68	9.38	9.07	8.79	8.60	8.48	8.46	8.50	8.58	8.68
Estonia	7.93	7.69	7.31	6.75	6.15	5.62	5.27	4.92	4.74	4.65	4.68
Finland	6.08	6.14	6.24	6.24	6.24	6.16	6.05	5.90	5.74	5.59	5.47
France	6.35	6.30	6.23	6.10	5.98	5.90	5.83	5.78	5.79	5.83	5.89
Germany	6.00	5.93	5.80	5.61	5.42	5.21	5.13	5.12	5.10	5.10	5.11
Greece	5.39	5.29	5.25	5.15	5.12	5.06	5.00	4.95	4.89	4.82	4.78
Hong Kong, China	6.67	6.66	6.59	6.41	6.30	6.20	6.08	5.86	5.61	5.32	5.07
Hungary	6.31	6.28	6.26	6.19	6.12	5.99	5.80	5.60	5.43	5.25	5.14
India	9.61	9.60	9.59	9.56	9.52	9.46	9.39	9.30	9.21	9.12	9.04
Indonesia	8.93	8.80	8.68	8.57	8.47	8.37	8.29	8.21	8.16	8.11	8.08
Iran	11.99	11.38	10.69	9.96	9.21	8.48	7.81	7.25	6.80	6.48	6.31
Ireland	6.71	6.50	6.29	6.10	5.94	5.79	5.71	5.70	5.76	5.82	5.86
Israel	7.84	7.78	7.76	7.74	7.75	7.78	7.82	7.87	7.95	8.04	8.11
Italy	4.99	5.01	5.04	5.00	4.96	4.89	4.84	4.78	4.77	4.78	4.81
Japan	5.10	4.98	4.88	4.83	4.82	4.81	4.81	4.83	4.83	4.83	4.83
Jordan	10.24	10.11	9.99	9.88	9.78	9.69	9.61	9.53	9.45	9.36	9.28
Kazakhstan	9.88	9.65	9.31	8.89	8.42	7.94	7.48	7.06	6.72	6.46	6.31
Kuwait	7.25	7.09	6.98	6.91	6.85	6.82	6.78	6.74	6.70	6.66	6.63
Latvia	8.00	7.76	7.45	6.97	6.45	5.88	5.33	4.82	4.50	4.34	4.32
Lithuania	8.00	7.88	7.80	7.61	7.29	6.91	6.51	6.07	5.80	5.67	5.50
Malaysia	9.13	9.04	8.99	8.93	8.88	8.84	8.82	8.81	8.82	8.86	8.88
Mexico	8.90	8.90	8.90	8.90	8.87	8.81	8.73	8.62	8.50	8.36	8.23
Morocco	10.09	9.91	9.71	9.52	9.32	9.12	8.91	8.71	8.50	8.30	8.12
Netherlands	6.08	6.12	6.15	6.17	6.17	6.10	6.02	5.97	5.97	5.98	6.04
New Zealand	7.33	7.38	7.38	7.32	7.21	7.05	6.90	6.76	6.63	6.55	6.47
Nigeria	9.89	9.87	9.85	9.84	9.84	9.85	9.86	9.88	9.91	9.94	9.98
Norway	6.40	6.54	6.62	6.63	6.60	6.55	6.51	6.47	6.40	6.35	6.29
Pakistan	10.59	10.50	10.38	10.22	10.05	9.89	9.75	9.62	9.52	9.43	9.36
Peru	9.58	9.54	9.49	9.42	9.35	9.26	9.17	9.08	8.98	8.88	8.79
Philippines	9.97	9.95	9.92	9.87	9.81	9.73	9.64	9.54	9.44	9.33	9.22
Poland	7.52	7.32	7.12	6.90	6.66	6.38	6.10	5.84	5.61	5.39	5.23
Portugal	5.59	5.52	5.46	5.39	5.30	5.23	5.16	5.12	5.10	5.17	5.19
Romania	7.85	7.40	6.94	6.43	5.94	5.63	5.46	5.33	5.30	5.29	5.31
Russia	8.35	7.85	7.24	6.59	6.07	5.60	5.26	5.00	4.92	4.80	4.74
Saudi Arabia	9.30	9.37	9.39	9.38	9.32	9.24	9.13	9.02	8.90	8.79	8.70
Singapore	6.84	7.12	7.17	7.05	6.97	6.82	6.69	6.51	6.29	6.10	5.95
Slovakia	7.56	7.39	7.23	7.05	6.80	6.47	6.15	5.85	5.55	5.36	5.23
Slovenia	6.14	5.97	5.69	5.42	5.24	5.07	4.94	4.86	4.77	4.67	4.65
South Africa	10.12	10.03	9.91	9.79	9.66	9.55	9.45	9.38	9.33	9.31	9.30
South Korea	6.41	6.51	6.65	6.79	6.89	6.90	6.82	6.67	6.49	6.32	6.12
Spain	5.31	5.18	5.06	4.96	4.87	4.78	4.70	4.65	4.62	4.63	4.68
Sweden	6.62	6.81	6.95	6.95	6.87	6.62	6.30	5.95	5.66	5.41	5.27
Switzerland	5.99	6.05	6.10	6.06	6.00	5.90	5.80	5.68	5.59	5.49	5.36
Taiwan	6.89	6.95	6.98	6.90	6.93	6.87	6.87	6.88	6.61	6.44	6.35
Thailand	7.43	7.53	7.60	7.63	7.66	7.68	7.67	7.56	7.38	7.14	6.82
Tunisia	10.10	9.87	9.58	9.26	8.90	8.53	8.17	7.82	7.50	7.22	6.98
Turkey	8.36	8.35	8.40	8.48	8.55	8.62	8.67	8.71	8.71	8.67	8.59
Turkmenistan	11.09	11.05	10.91	10.66	10.32	9.93	9.51	9.10	8.73	8.44	8.24
Ukraine	7.77	7.42	7.08	6.70	6.35	6.02	5.72	5.43	5.19	4.96	4.77
United Arab Emirates	5.99	5.74	5.70	5.82	6.05	6.32	6.57	6.78	6.95	7.08	7.18
United Kingdom	6.79	6.81	6.76	6.66	6.55	6.40	6.26	6.14	6.02	5.90	5.77
USA	7.02	7.02	6.99	6.92	6.79	6.68	6.56	6.46	6.39	6.34	6.36
Venezuela	9.47	9.37	9.24	9.11	8.97	8.84	8.72	8.62	8.54	8.47	8.40
Vietnam	10.42	10.34	10.16	9.91	9.60	9.27	8.94	8.61	8.27	7.97	7.72

Marketing segments: Young generation

Table 4.107 Female studying age (18-22): 2009-2019 (%)

% of total

	2009	2010	2011	2012	2013	2014	2015	2016	2017	2018	2019
Algeria	5.22	5.10	4.96	4.80	4.61	4.41	4.21	4.01	3.83	3.68	3.58
Argentina	4.14	4.13	4.12	4.10	4.07	4.04	4.00	3.95	3.90	3.85	3.79
Australia	3.40	3.39	3.38	3.36	3.32	3.28	3.23	3.19	3.14	3.10	3.07
Austria	2.97	2.99	3.01	3.02	3.01	2.98	2.94	2.88	2.81	2.73	2.67
Azerbaijan	5.12	5.06	4.94	4.78	4.58	4.34	4.09	3.84	3.59	3.37	3.19
Belarus	4.01	3.80	3.63	3.39	3.18	2.97	2.78	2.60	2.49	2.42	2.40
Belgium	2.98	3.01	3.03	3.02	2.97	2.92	2.87	2.82	2.78	2.77	2.76
Bolivia	4.83	4.87	4.90	4.92	4.92	4.91	4.88	4.85	4.81	4.78	4.74
Bosnia-Herzegovina	3.63	3.47	3.30	3.14	3.01	2.91	2.85	2.82	2.80	2.78	2.75
Brazil	4.40	4.30	4.21	4.13	4.08	4.05	4.04	4.04	4.05	4.06	4.07
Bulgaria	3.25	3.14	3.01	2.86	2.69	2.51	2.38	2.23	2.12	2.09	2.10
Canada	3.30	3.30	3.30	3.26	3.21	3.15	3.07	2.99	2.92	2.84	2.75
Chile	4.30	4.29	4.26	4.21	4.14	4.04	3.94	3.82	3.69	3.58	3.47
China	3.90	3.77	3.61	3.36	3.05	2.91	2.77	2.66	2.56	2.47	2.40
Colombia	4.53	4.51	4.48	4.46	4.42	4.38	4.34	4.29	4.24	4.18	4.13
Costa Rica	4.75	4.68	4.59	4.49	4.38	4.28	4.18	4.09	4.02	3.95	3.89
Croatia	3.05	3.01	2.95	2.90	2.87	2.85	2.85	2.88	2.88	2.85	2.80
Czech Republic	3.13	3.11	3.07	3.02	2.92	2.75	2.58	2.43	2.29	2.21	2.18
Denmark	2.88	2.93	3.01	3.07	3.12	3.16	3.17	3.15	3.12	3.07	3.03
Ecuador	4.59	4.57	4.55	4.54	4.54	4.53	4.53	4.52	4.51	4.49	4.45
Egypt	4.79	4.67	4.52	4.36	4.22	4.12	4.06	4.04	4.06	4.09	4.14
Estonia	3.87	3.75	3.57	3.29	3.00	2.75	2.57	2.40	2.31	2.26	2.26
Finland	2.97	3.01	3.06	3.06	3.06	3.03	2.97	2.90	2.82	2.74	2.68
France	3.14	3.10	3.06	3.00	2.94	2.89	2.86	2.83	2.84	2.86	2.89
Germany	2.94	2.91	2.85	2.76	2.66	2.56	2.53	2.52	2.51	2.51	2.52
Greece	2.59	2.55	2.53	2.49	2.49	2.46	2.43	2.41	2.38	2.35	2.33
Hong Kong, China	3.46	3.44	3.39	3.31	3.26	3.21	3.16	3.06	2.93	2.79	2.65
Hungary	3.10	3.08	3.07	3.04	3.00	2.94	2.84	2.74	2.66	2.57	2.52
India	4.60	4.59	4.58	4.57	4.54	4.52	4.48	4.44	4.40	4.36	4.32
Indonesia	4.41	4.34	4.28	4.23	4.17	4.13	4.08	4.05	4.02	3.99	3.98
Iran	5.88	5.56	5.21	4.85	4.47	4.12	3.80	3.52	3.30	3.15	3.07
Ireland	3.31	3.20	3.10	3.00	2.92	2.85	2.80	2.80	2.82	2.85	2.87
Israel	3.84	3.81	3.80	3.79	3.79	3.80	3.82	3.84	3.88	3.92	3.96
Italy	2.43	2.44	2.45	2.43	2.41	2.38	2.35	2.32	2.31	2.32	2.34
Japan	2.49	2.43	2.39	2.36	2.35	2.35	2.35	2.36	2.36	2.36	2.36
Jordan	5.00	4.93	4.87	4.82	4.77	4.72	4.68	4.65	4.61	4.57	4.53
Kazakhstan	4.85	4.74	4.57	4.36	4.13	3.89	3.66	3.45	3.28	3.16	3.08
Kuwait	3.39	3.34	3.29	3.25	3.22	3.20	3.20	3.20	3.20	3.21	3.21
Latvia	3.93	3.81	3.66	3.44	3.19	2.90	2.62	2.37	2.21	2.13	2.13
Lithuania	3.92	3.86	3.83	3.73	3.57	3.38	3.19	2.96	2.83	2.76	2.67
Malaysia	4.46	4.41	4.38	4.34	4.31	4.29	4.28	4.28	4.29	4.32	4.33
Mexico	4.53	4.53	4.53	4.52	4.49	4.46	4.40	4.34	4.27	4.20	4.13
Morocco	5.05	4.94	4.84	4.73	4.63	4.52	4.42	4.32	4.21	4.12	4.03
Netherlands	2.99	3.01	3.02	3.03	3.03	2.99	2.95	2.93	2.92	2.92	2.95
New Zealand	3.59	3.61	3.60	3.56	3.50	3.42	3.35	3.28	3.22	3.18	3.15
Nigeria	4.90	4.88	4.87	4.87	4.86	4.86	4.87	4.88	4.89	4.91	4.93
Norway	3.13	3.20	3.24	3.24	3.23	3.20	3.18	3.16	3.13	3.10	3.08
Pakistan	5.13	5.10	5.04	4.96	4.88	4.81	4.74	4.67	4.62	4.58	4.54
Peru	4.73	4.71	4.68	4.65	4.61	4.57	4.52	4.47	4.42	4.38	4.33
Philippines	4.90	4.89	4.87	4.85	4.82	4.78	4.73	4.68	4.63	4.57	4.52
Poland	3.68	3.58	3.48	3.37	3.26	3.12	2.98	2.86	2.74	2.63	2.55
Portugal	2.74	2.70	2.68	2.64	2.60	2.56	2.53	2.51	2.50	2.53	2.55
Romania	3.85	3.63	3.40	3.15	2.90	2.75	2.67	2.60	2.59	2.58	2.59
Russia	4.10	3.85	3.55	3.23	2.97	2.74	2.58	2.45	2.41	2.35	2.31
Saudi Arabia	4.62	4.66	4.68	4.66	4.63	4.58	4.52	4.46	4.40	4.34	4.29
Singapore	3.37	3.52	3.54	3.48	3.45	3.39	3.32	3.25	3.15	3.07	3.00
Slovakia	3.70	3.62	3.54	3.44	3.33	3.17	3.01	2.86	2.71	2.62	2.56
Slovenia	2.99	2.90	2.76	2.63	2.55	2.47	2.40	2.36	2.32	2.26	2.25
South Africa	5.04	5.00	4.94	4.88	4.82	4.76	4.72	4.68	4.66	4.65	4.64
South Korea	3.03	3.06	3.11	3.17	3.22	3.23	3.20	3.14	3.07	3.00	2.92
Spain	2.59	2.52	2.47	2.42	2.37	2.33	2.29	2.27	2.25	2.26	2.28
Sweden	3.24	3.33	3.39	3.40	3.36	3.24	3.09	2.92	2.77	2.65	2.58
Switzerland	2.96	2.98	3.01	3.00	2.97	2.92	2.88	2.82	2.78	2.73	2.67
Taiwan	3.32	3.34	3.34	3.30	3.32	3.29	3.30	3.30	3.17	3.08	3.03
Thailand	3.69	3.73	3.76	3.78	3.79	3.80	3.79	3.73	3.64	3.52	3.36
Tunisia	4.93	4.81	4.67	4.50	4.32	4.14	3.96	3.79	3.64	3.50	3.38
Turkey	4.10	4.10	4.13	4.17	4.21	4.24	4.27	4.29	4.29	4.27	4.23
Turkmenistan	5.49	5.47	5.40	5.28	5.12	4.92	4.71	4.51	4.33	4.18	4.07
Ukraine	3.79	3.62	3.46	3.27	3.10	2.94	2.79	2.65	2.53	2.42	2.32
United Arab Emirates	2.66	2.55	2.48	2.45	2.44	2.46	2.50	2.55	2.61	2.68	2.74
United Kingdom	3.31	3.32	3.30	3.26	3.20	3.13	3.06	3.00	2.94	2.88	2.82
USA	3.42	3.43	3.42	3.39	3.33	3.27	3.21	3.17	3.13	3.10	3.11
Venezuela	4.66	4.61	4.55	4.48	4.41	4.34	4.29	4.24	4.19	4.16	4.13
Vietnam	5.14	5.09	5.00	4.88	4.72	4.56	4.40	4.23	4.07	3.92	3.79

Marketing segments: Young generation

Table 4.108 Male studying age (18-22): 2009-2019 (%)

% of total

	2009	2010	2011	2012	2013	2014	2015	2016	2017	2018	2019
Algeria	5.43	5.30	5.16	4.99	4.80	4.59	4.38	4.17	3.98	3.83	3.72
Argentina	4.26	4.25	4.24	4.22	4.19	4.16	4.12	4.07	4.02	3.96	3.91
Australia	3.60	3.59	3.58	3.54	3.50	3.45	3.40	3.35	3.30	3.26	3.22
Austria	3.08	3.10	3.12	3.12	3.11	3.07	3.03	2.96	2.89	2.81	2.75
Azerbaijan	5.43	5.36	5.23	5.05	4.84	4.60	4.35	4.11	3.89	3.70	3.56
Belarus	4.20	3.99	3.81	3.56	3.34	3.13	2.93	2.75	2.64	2.57	2.55
Belgium	3.09	3.12	3.13	3.12	3.08	3.03	2.97	2.92	2.89	2.87	2.86
Bolivia	4.97	5.02	5.05	5.08	5.08	5.07	5.05	5.02	4.98	4.94	4.91
Bosnia-Herzegovina	3.75	3.61	3.46	3.31	3.19	3.11	3.05	3.02	3.00	2.97	2.93
Brazil	4.50	4.39	4.30	4.23	4.18	4.16	4.15	4.15	4.16	4.18	4.19
Bulgaria	3.40	3.30	3.17	3.02	2.84	2.64	2.50	2.35	2.23	2.21	2.22
Canada	3.46	3.47	3.47	3.45	3.40	3.34	3.27	3.20	3.12	3.04	2.95
Chile	4.44	4.43	4.40	4.34	4.27	4.17	4.06	3.94	3.82	3.69	3.58
China	4.18	4.10	3.97	3.75	3.45	3.32	3.16	3.07	2.96	2.88	2.80
Colombia	4.64	4.62	4.60	4.57	4.54	4.50	4.46	4.41	4.36	4.30	4.25
Costa Rica	5.03	4.96	4.87	4.76	4.65	4.54	4.43	4.34	4.26	4.18	4.11
Croatia	3.17	3.14	3.08	3.03	3.00	2.98	2.98	3.01	3.00	2.98	2.93
Czech Republic	3.27	3.25	3.22	3.17	3.07	2.90	2.71	2.56	2.41	2.32	2.30
Denmark	3.03	3.07	3.16	3.21	3.27	3.30	3.32	3.29	3.26	3.21	3.16
Ecuador	4.72	4.70	4.68	4.68	4.67	4.68	4.68	4.67	4.66	4.64	4.61
Egypt	5.14	5.02	4.87	4.71	4.57	4.48	4.43	4.42	4.44	4.49	4.54
Estonia	4.07	3.94	3.74	3.47	3.15	2.87	2.69	2.53	2.43	2.39	2.41
Finland	3.11	3.14	3.18	3.18	3.18	3.14	3.08	3.00	2.92	2.85	2.79
France	3.21	3.19	3.17	3.10	3.05	3.00	2.97	2.94	2.95	2.97	3.00
Germany	3.06	3.02	2.95	2.86	2.76	2.65	2.61	2.60	2.59	2.59	2.59
Greece	2.80	2.74	2.72	2.66	2.64	2.60	2.57	2.54	2.51	2.47	2.45
Hong Kong, China	3.21	3.22	3.20	3.11	3.04	2.98	2.92	2.81	2.68	2.54	2.41
Hungary	3.21	3.20	3.19	3.15	3.11	3.05	2.96	2.86	2.77	2.68	2.62
India	5.01	5.01	5.01	5.00	4.98	4.94	4.91	4.86	4.81	4.76	4.72
Indonesia	4.52	4.46	4.40	4.34	4.29	4.24	4.20	4.17	4.14	4.12	4.10
Iran	6.10	5.81	5.48	5.11	4.73	4.36	4.02	3.72	3.49	3.33	3.24
Ireland	3.41	3.30	3.20	3.10	3.02	2.94	2.91	2.91	2.94	2.97	2.99
Israel	4.00	3.97	3.96	3.96	3.96	3.97	4.00	4.03	4.07	4.12	4.16
Italy	2.57	2.57	2.59	2.57	2.55	2.51	2.49	2.46	2.45	2.46	2.48
Japan	2.61	2.55	2.50	2.47	2.46	2.46	2.46	2.47	2.47	2.47	2.47
Jordan	5.25	5.18	5.12	5.07	5.02	4.97	4.93	4.88	4.84	4.79	4.74
Kazakhstan	5.02	4.91	4.74	4.53	4.29	4.05	3.82	3.61	3.44	3.31	3.23
Kuwait	3.86	3.75	3.69	3.66	3.63	3.61	3.58	3.54	3.49	3.45	3.41
Latvia	4.07	3.95	3.79	3.53	3.26	2.98	2.71	2.45	2.29	2.21	2.19
Lithuania	4.08	4.01	3.97	3.88	3.72	3.53	3.32	3.10	2.97	2.91	2.83
Malaysia	4.66	4.63	4.61	4.59	4.57	4.55	4.53	4.53	4.53	4.54	4.55
Mexico	4.36	4.37	4.37	4.38	4.38	4.36	4.33	4.28	4.23	4.17	4.10
Morocco	5.04	4.96	4.88	4.79	4.69	4.59	4.49	4.39	4.29	4.19	4.10
Netherlands	3.09	3.11	3.12	3.13	3.14	3.10	3.07	3.04	3.05	3.05	3.09
New Zealand	3.74	3.77	3.78	3.75	3.71	3.63	3.55	3.48	3.41	3.37	3.32
Nigeria	4.99	4.98	4.98	4.97	4.98	4.98	4.99	5.00	5.02	5.04	5.06
Norway	3.27	3.34	3.39	3.39	3.38	3.35	3.33	3.31	3.28	3.25	3.21
Pakistan	5.45	5.41	5.34	5.26	5.17	5.09	5.01	4.95	4.89	4.85	4.82
Peru	4.85	4.83	4.81	4.77	4.74	4.69	4.65	4.60	4.55	4.51	4.46
Philippines	5.07	5.06	5.04	5.02	4.99	4.95	4.91	4.86	4.81	4.75	4.70
Poland	3.84	3.74	3.64	3.52	3.40	3.25	3.11	2.99	2.87	2.76	2.68
Portugal	2.85	2.81	2.78	2.74	2.70	2.67	2.63	2.61	2.60	2.63	2.64
Romania	4.00	3.77	3.54	3.28	3.04	2.88	2.79	2.73	2.72	2.71	2.72
Russia	4.25	4.00	3.69	3.36	3.09	2.86	2.69	2.55	2.51	2.46	2.43
Saudi Arabia	4.68	4.70	4.72	4.71	4.69	4.66	4.61	4.56	4.51	4.45	4.41
Singapore	3.47	3.60	3.63	3.56	3.52	3.43	3.37	3.26	3.14	3.03	2.95
Slovakia	3.86	3.77	3.69	3.60	3.47	3.30	3.14	2.99	2.84	2.74	2.67
Slovenia	3.15	3.07	2.93	2.79	2.69	2.61	2.54	2.49	2.45	2.41	2.40
South Africa	5.08	5.03	4.97	4.91	4.84	4.78	4.73	4.70	4.67	4.66	4.66
South Korea	3.38	3.45	3.54	3.62	3.67	3.67	3.63	3.53	3.42	3.32	3.21
Spain	2.72	2.65	2.59	2.54	2.49	2.45	2.41	2.38	2.36	2.37	2.40
Sweden	3.39	3.48	3.56	3.55	3.51	3.38	3.21	3.03	2.89	2.76	2.69
Switzerland	3.04	3.06	3.09	3.06	3.03	2.97	2.92	2.86	2.81	2.76	2.70
Taiwan	3.57	3.61	3.63	3.59	3.61	3.58	3.57	3.58	3.44	3.35	3.32
Thailand	3.75	3.80	3.84	3.86	3.87	3.89	3.88	3.83	3.74	3.62	3.47
Tunisia	5.17	5.06	4.92	4.75	4.58	4.39	4.21	4.03	3.87	3.72	3.60
Turkey	4.26	4.25	4.27	4.31	4.34	4.37	4.40	4.42	4.42	4.40	4.36
Turkmenistan	5.60	5.58	5.50	5.38	5.21	5.01	4.80	4.59	4.41	4.26	4.16
Ukraine	3.97	3.80	3.63	3.43	3.25	3.08	2.93	2.78	2.66	2.54	2.44
United Arab Emirates	3.33	3.19	3.22	3.38	3.61	3.86	4.07	4.22	4.33	4.40	4.44
United Kingdom	3.48	3.48	3.45	3.41	3.35	3.28	3.20	3.14	3.08	3.02	2.96
USA	3.60	3.59	3.57	3.53	3.47	3.41	3.35	3.30	3.26	3.24	3.24
Venezuela	4.81	4.76	4.70	4.63	4.56	4.49	4.44	4.39	4.34	4.31	4.28
Vietnam	5.29	5.24	5.16	5.03	4.88	4.71	4.54	4.37	4.21	4.05	3.92

Marketing segments: Young generation

Table 4.109 Young adults (15-29): 2009-2019

'000

	2009	2010	2011	2012	2013	2014	2015	2016	2017	2018	2019	CAGR	Period growth
Algeria	10,884.6	10,858.0	10,777.9	10,651.3	10,491.8	10,317.0	10,142.6	9,978.4	9,829.1	9,696.8	9,582.0	-1.27	-11.97
Argentina	10,032.1	10,061.6	10,095.8	10,134.3	10,173.4	10,207.5	10,231.8	10,244.2	10,245.3	10,237.6	10,224.0	0.19	1.91
Australia	4,596.2	4,657.7	4,697.8	4,731.6	4,755.8	4,780.7	4,802.8	4,823.3	4,842.1	4,859.0	4,870.1	0.58	5.96
Austria	1,574.7	1,579.5	1,575.3	1,568.8	1,557.8	1,547.3	1,533.8	1,522.2	1,508.6	1,498.6	1,485.6	-0.58	-5.66
Azerbaijan	2,519.2	2,539.6	2,543.5	2,531.3	2,505.8	2,469.1	2,423.9	2,372.3	2,316.5	2,259.7	2,205.5	-1.32	-12.45
Belarus	2,281.0	2,241.5	2,190.9	2,130.1	2,061.8	1,982.3	1,906.7	1,835.4	1,755.4	1,682.8	1,611.4	-3.42	-29.35
Belgium	1,962.6	1,957.3	1,949.8	1,943.6	1,940.3	1,938.2	1,936.4	1,937.7	1,934.2	1,928.6	1,921.7	-0.21	-2.09
Bolivia	2,736.3	2,796.9	2,854.9	2,909.9	2,962.2	3,012.4	3,060.9	3,107.9	3,152.7	3,194.6	3,232.5	1.68	18.13
Bosnia-Herzegovina	839.2	826.8	814.3	801.3	787.5	771.8	753.7	733.0	710.4	687.4	665.5	-2.29	-20.70
Brazil	51,937.4	51,849.6	51,659.4	51,439.3	51,225.1	50,999.1	50,830.6	50,771.6	50,731.8	50,682.7	50,604.3	-0.26	-2.57
Bulgaria	1,490.5	1,441.5	1,391.3	1,342.4	1,286.3	1,233.8	1,188.6	1,144.4	1,100.4	1,059.3	1,019.5	-3.73	-31.60
Canada	6,859.7	6,894.9	6,912.4	6,911.4	6,892.0	6,858.7	6,822.3	6,775.9	6,728.7	6,686.2	6,634.4	-0.33	-3.28
Chile	4,218.9	4,265.3	4,297.0	4,313.2	4,314.7	4,302.9	4,279.9	4,247.2	4,206.5	4,159.6	4,108.7	-0.26	-2.61
China	283,382.9	285,507.8	286,252.9	284,350.6	285,030.9	284,046.9	283,599.3	279,627.3	272,404.6	264,764.3	256,486.7	-0.99	-9.49
Colombia	12,217.6	12,318.7	12,411.3	12,496.0	12,573.2	12,643.1	12,705.7	12,761.0	12,808.9	12,850.0	12,884.8	0.53	5.46
Costa Rica	1,286.6	1,295.8	1,302.3	1,306.1	1,307.1	1,305.7	1,301.9	1,296.3	1,289.2	1,280.8	1,271.3	-0.12	-1.19
Croatia	864.7	852.2	840.3	831.4	821.6	809.9	796.2	782.8	768.4	754.2	739.3	-1.55	-14.50
Czech Republic	2,071.9	2,013.2	1,959.7	1,907.6	1,856.1	1,808.8	1,761.0	1,715.7	1,676.6	1,642.3	1,607.3	-2.51	-22.42
Denmark	973.7	982.0	992.5	1,004.7	1,016.4	1,028.2	1,038.7	1,048.2	1,054.5	1,059.1	1,061.9	0.87	9.05
Ecuador	3,654.4	3,683.4	3,718.5	3,758.3	3,800.6	3,842.1	3,880.0	3,913.1	3,941.0	3,963.7	3,981.5	0.86	8.95
Egypt	21,549.1	21,611.8	21,668.3	21,722.7	21,781.3	21,852.0	21,941.5	22,056.7	22,202.0	22,376.6	22,596.8	0.48	4.86
Estonia	295.3	288.9	281.8	273.7	264.7	254.6	244.8	236.5	227.9	218.9	210.1	-3.35	-28.85
Finland	997.0	1,000.2	1,001.1	998.9	992.6	983.2	975.9	970.1	965.4	961.1	954.3	-0.44	-4.29
France	11,790.0	11,767.1	11,712.3	11,666.8	11,622.0	11,631.9	11,643.1	11,671.8	11,676.6	11,674.8	11,667.5	-0.10	-1.04
Germany	14,405.4	14,282.2	14,100.9	13,959.1	13,830.8	13,706.2	13,574.6	13,437.3	13,236.2	13,002.9	12,735.7	-1.22	-11.59
Greece	2,027.7	1,984.0	1,931.3	1,887.6	1,846.1	1,808.4	1,777.7	1,755.8	1,739.8	1,732.5	1,723.2	-1.61	-15.02
Hong Kong, China	1,491.0	1,506.4	1,514.8	1,520.2	1,511.8	1,495.2	1,474.4	1,455.4	1,429.7	1,403.3	1,369.7	-0.85	-8.14
Hungary	1,990.9	1,951.4	1,916.3	1,879.9	1,845.5	1,813.6	1,780.4	1,745.8	1,713.8	1,686.9	1,659.2	-1.81	-16.66
India	324,812.0	329,037.6	332,922.7	336,463.5	339,687.4	342,639.0	345,357.4	347,857.4	350,118.9	352,094.0	353,723.6	0.86	8.90
Indonesia	61,507.7	61,454.9	61,349.7	61,207.7	61,054.8	60,922.1	60,834.2	60,801.8	60,821.3	60,878.4	60,951.6	-0.09	-0.90
Iran	25,723.6	25,397.6	24,858.4	24,138.8	23,294.8	22,396.3	21,504.7	20,660.8	19,888.7	19,207.0	18,628.4	-3.18	-27.58
Ireland	1,003.5	983.7	961.8	944.7	929.6	920.1	912.6	907.0	902.8	904.7	910.9	-0.96	-9.23
Israel	1,728.0	1,746.3	1,767.0	1,788.8	1,810.9	1,833.9	1,859.7	1,886.9	1,916.2	1,949.8	1,983.9	1.39	14.81
Italy	9,360.9	9,231.1	9,122.1	9,031.0	8,947.3	8,889.1	8,849.4	8,830.7	8,823.6	8,820.4	8,806.9	-0.61	-5.92
Japan	20,528.2	20,199.1	19,915.4	19,656.7	19,389.1	19,112.5	18,865.1	18,645.6	18,435.4	18,230.1	18,042.2	-1.28	-12.11
Jordan	1,916.7	1,948.9	1,964.7	1,966.8	1,960.9	1,954.2	1,952.4	1,957.4	1,968.7	1,985.2	2,005.1	0.45	4.61
Kazakhstan	4,334.9	4,338.1	4,321.1	4,285.1	4,234.6	4,173.0	4,104.0	4,029.6	3,954.1	3,884.1	3,827.8	-1.24	-11.70
Kuwait	633.5	629.9	627.1	625.3	624.5	624.7	625.8	627.8	630.9	635.1	640.5	0.11	1.11
Latvia	508.3	498.1	485.2	469.7	452.1	431.9	413.4	396.1	377.2	359.3	343.6	-3.84	-32.40
Lithuania	761.3	753.9	744.4	731.7	716.7	697.5	677.3	654.3	628.2	602.7	580.8	-2.67	-23.71
Malaysia	7,466.9	7,569.7	7,666.4	7,756.3	7,849.2	7,938.9	8,030.0	8,114.9	8,196.8	8,283.0	8,372.9	1.15	12.13
Mexico	28,262.0	28,461.9	28,684.5	28,887.9	29,079.4	29,260.8	29,431.0	29,586.4	29,720.0	29,824.9	29,896.0	0.56	5.78
Morocco	9,367.8	9,394.8	9,394.7	9,369.4	9,323.1	9,261.1	9,188.5	9,109.2	9,027.2	8,947.1	8,874.1	-0.54	-5.27
Netherlands	2,971.7	2,982.1	2,982.0	2,984.9	2,994.7	3,012.2	3,026.1	3,042.3	3,050.2	3,055.1	3,059.6	0.29	2.96
New Zealand	900.4	907.9	913.2	915.5	916.2	916.1	918.2	919.1	918.3	916.0	914.3	0.15	1.54
Nigeria	43,536.8	44,493.8	45,458.5	46,436.9	47,434.7	48,457.1	49,507.4	50,587.8	51,699.7	52,844.1	54,020.7	2.18	24.08
Norway	916.5	934.1	949.6	964.4	975.8	985.9	996.1	1,005.4	1,011.3	1,015.0	1,017.3	1.05	10.99
Pakistan	52,898.2	54,043.5	55,140.8	56,182.0	57,152.1	58,035.5	58,824.8	59,525.9	60,159.1	60,754.9	61,349.5	1.49	15.98
Peru	8,024.8	8,092.6	8,160.9	8,229.0	8,295.0	8,356.2	8,410.4	8,456.6	8,494.8	8,526.1	8,551.9	0.64	6.57
Philippines	26,179.3	26,657.6	27,104.0	27,528.2	27,927.9	28,307.1	28,662.3	28,992.8	29,300.3	29,589.9	29,868.1	1.33	14.09
Poland	8,933.9	8,749.6	8,532.0	8,311.5	8,041.7	7,732.1	7,429.6	7,145.4	6,893.5	6,663.8	6,445.7	-3.21	-27.85
Portugal	1,962.4	1,917.0	1,873.4	1,833.8	1,795.7	1,765.0	1,745.3	1,731.4	1,723.2	1,721.1	1,718.1	-1.32	-12.45
Romania	4,722.8	4,592.4	4,450.6	4,329.4	4,222.0	4,138.6	4,019.7	3,892.4	3,738.6	3,585.8	3,443.9	-3.11	-27.08
Russia	33,754.2	33,036.3	32,104.5	31,159.4	29,990.2	28,736.3	27,479.5	26,321.6	25,090.3	23,976.9	23,116.7	-3.71	-31.51
Saudi Arabia	7,166.2	7,284.0	7,409.9	7,541.8	7,675.8	7,807.0	7,931.2	8,046.3	8,151.2	8,244.8	8,326.3	1.51	16.19
Singapore	965.1	978.7	989.5	1,003.9	1,013.5	1,022.8	1,025.6	1,032.2	1,034.9	1,022.4	1,000.1	0.36	3.63
Slovakia	1,265.6	1,235.1	1,203.8	1,172.7	1,139.7	1,106.4	1,072.8	1,037.5	1,001.5	968.9	937.6	-2.96	-25.92
Slovenia	391.2	381.8	371.9	361.9	352.2	343.3	334.7	327.3	320.2	312.8	305.5	-2.44	-21.92
South Africa	14,742.5	14,812.0	14,837.0	14,822.0	14,778.9	14,723.4	14,668.7	14,621.6	14,584.0	14,557.9	14,543.8	-0.14	-1.35
South Korea	10,365.6	10,236.1	10,079.5	9,919.1	9,777.7	9,669.7	9,606.9	9,525.5	9,409.3	9,268.9	9,110.0	-1.28	-12.11
Spain	8,312.2	8,084.7	7,866.3	7,676.8	7,516.3	7,391.5	7,307.6	7,264.3	7,253.0	7,259.8	7,298.8	-1.29	-12.19
Sweden	1,759.9	1,777.2	1,784.4	1,786.7	1,785.3	1,783.8	1,779.7	1,773.2	1,763.9	1,757.4	1,746.5	-0.08	-0.76
Switzerland	1,381.8	1,387.1	1,389.3	1,392.1	1,391.2	1,390.0	1,386.3	1,379.4	1,370.6	1,361.4	1,347.4	-0.25	-2.49
Taiwan	5,243.0	5,156.0	5,079.3	4,995.8	4,923.0	4,814.2	4,732.5	4,701.0	4,656.7	4,593.2	4,478.3	-1.56	-14.59
Thailand	15,006.4	14,937.3	14,905.5	14,863.3	14,784.8	14,678.4	14,580.6	14,482.9	14,412.0	14,337.4	14,266.0	-0.50	-4.93
Tunisia	3,015.2	3,000.8	2,975.9	2,941.5	2,898.7	2,849.2	2,794.5	2,736.3	2,676.2	2,616.3	2,558.8	-1.63	-15.14
Turkey	19,627.3	19,657.5	19,719.3	19,807.6	19,919.9	20,051.7	20,193.6	20,340.0	20,446.5	20,547.4	20,627.9	0.50	5.10
Turkmenistan	1,565.6	1,583.4	1,594.2	1,598.2	1,596.5	1,590.4	1,581.5	1,570.7	1,558.5	1,545.0	1,530.7	-0.23	-2.23
Ukraine	10,448.8	10,247.8	9,993.9	9,733.6	9,419.7	9,015.1	8,606.7	8,214.7	7,794.3	7,436.1	7,118.1	-3.77	-31.88
United Arab Emirates	1,221.4	1,190.2	1,169.5	1,160.4	1,162.1	1,172.8	1,190.8	1,214.5	1,242.9	1,274.3	1,306.8	0.68	6.99
United Kingdom	12,420.0	12,533.5	12,597.4	12,661.6	12,711.4	12,713.2	12,662.1	12,572.2	12,466.3	12,351.0	12,246.5	-0.14	-1.40
USA	64,203.0	64,214.2	64,103.0	63,968.0	63,852.2	63,802.8	63,741.7	63,870.4	63,992.2	64,138.2	64,288.3	0.01	0.13
Venezuela	7,807.8	7,880.6	7,947.2	8,008.0	8,062.8	8,111.3	8,153.3	8,189.1	8,220.3	8,248.8	8,277.4	0.59	6.01
Vietnam	25,826.5	25,978.3	26,025.1	25,975.3	25,849.2	25,677.5	25,483.7	25,277.4	25,057.7	24,825.1	24,576.9	-0.49	-4.84

Marketing segments: Young generation

Table 4.110 Female young adults (15-29): 2009-2019

'000

	2009	2010	2011	2012	2013	2014	2015	2016	2017	2018	2019	CAGR	Period growth
Algeria	5,340.9	5,327.5	5,288.1	5,226.0	5,147.9	5,062.3	4,976.9	4,896.6	4,823.5	4,758.6	4,702.1	-1.27	-11.96
Argentina	4,957.8	4,970.1	4,985.0	5,002.1	5,019.8	5,035.2	5,046.2	5,051.5	5,051.5	5,047.3	5,040.2	0.16	1.66
Australia	2,247.0	2,275.6	2,293.9	2,309.6	2,320.5	2,332.1	2,342.5	2,352.2	2,362.0	2,370.9	2,377.2	0.56	5.79
Austria	775.6	778.4	776.9	773.5	768.0	762.7	755.8	750.4	743.4	738.5	732.3	-0.57	-5.58
Azerbaijan	1,235.3	1,242.4	1,241.8	1,233.7	1,219.3	1,199.5	1,175.3	1,147.6	1,117.5	1,086.6	1,056.7	-1.55	-14.45
Belarus	1,116.6	1,097.9	1,073.4	1,043.4	1,009.9	969.9	931.8	895.7	855.5	819.1	783.7	-3.48	-29.81
Belgium	968.7	965.3	960.2	956.5	954.1	952.2	950.8	950.7	949.1	946.1	942.7	-0.27	-2.69
Bolivia	1,351.7	1,380.7	1,408.4	1,434.8	1,459.9	1,484.0	1,507.4	1,530.1	1,551.8	1,572.0	1,590.4	1.64	17.66
Bosnia-Herzegovina	414.3	407.2	400.2	393.1	385.6	377.3	367.9	357.1	345.5	333.7	322.5	-2.47	-22.15
Brazil	25,763.6	25,710.1	25,608.9	25,491.7	25,376.5	25,254.3	25,160.1	25,120.3	25,090.1	25,055.7	25,007.4	-0.30	-2.94
Bulgaria	725.6	702.0	677.9	654.0	626.4	600.7	578.9	557.1	535.2	514.6	495.1	-3.75	-31.77
Canada	3,361.1	3,375.5	3,380.8	3,376.0	3,363.0	3,342.8	3,321.6	3,295.1	3,267.7	3,243.2	3,213.8	-0.45	-4.38
Chile	2,079.7	2,102.3	2,117.6	2,125.5	2,126.0	2,120.1	2,108.5	2,092.3	2,072.0	2,048.8	2,023.5	-0.27	-2.70
China	137,461.4	138,140.1	138,077.7	136,771.2	136,609.7	135,736.1	135,068.7	132,676.6	128,939.8	124,916.7	120,674.8	-1.29	-12.21
Colombia	6,067.1	6,114.5	6,157.8	6,197.4	6,233.4	6,265.9	6,294.9	6,320.3	6,342.2	6,360.7	6,376.2	0.50	5.10
Costa Rica	626.0	630.3	633.3	635.0	635.4	634.6	632.7	630.0	626.6	622.5	618.0	-0.13	-1.27
Croatia	424.0	418.0	412.3	407.7	402.9	397.3	390.6	383.8	376.6	369.5	362.4	-1.56	-14.53
Czech Republic	1,011.8	983.2	957.3	931.9	906.5	883.3	860.0	837.2	818.0	801.0	783.3	-2.53	-22.58
Denmark	478.7	482.5	487.3	493.0	498.7	504.3	509.5	514.2	517.6	519.9	521.5	0.86	8.94
Ecuador	1,806.4	1,820.1	1,836.8	1,855.8	1,876.0	1,895.8	1,913.8	1,929.5	1,942.6	1,953.2	1,961.5	0.83	8.59
Egypt	10,429.2	10,459.1	10,483.5	10,504.2	10,524.2	10,547.8	10,579.1	10,622.0	10,678.8	10,749.4	10,842.3	0.39	3.96
Estonia	144.8	141.8	138.3	134.4	129.9	124.8	119.9	115.6	111.3	106.9	102.6	-3.39	-29.17
Finland	487.4	489.1	489.8	488.8	486.2	481.8	478.3	475.3	473.1	471.0	467.8	-0.41	-4.02
France	5,844.0	5,826.2	5,793.2	5,765.1	5,736.8	5,736.0	5,735.3	5,744.4	5,743.2	5,739.6	5,735.4	-0.19	-1.86
Germany	7,078.4	7,021.2	6,934.7	6,866.3	6,806.5	6,748.1	6,686.2	6,623.0	6,526.9	6,416.0	6,287.6	-1.18	-11.17
Greece	975.4	955.4	930.9	911.9	893.2	876.0	862.2	852.5	844.5	841.3	837.4	-1.51	-14.15
Hong Kong, China	806.3	821.2	831.3	841.0	842.2	838.3	830.9	822.3	808.7	794.5	777.9	-0.36	-3.52
Hungary	976.9	958.5	941.8	924.1	907.5	891.6	874.9	857.9	841.5	828.2	814.2	-1.81	-16.65
India	155,462.6	157,443.7	159,268.0	160,934.2	162,454.8	163,849.5	165,135.5	166,318.9	167,391.0	168,331.1	169,114.0	0.85	8.78
Indonesia	30,482.3	30,446.1	30,384.5	30,304.8	30,218.9	30,141.0	30,082.7	30,049.1	30,039.3	30,047.6	30,064.9	-0.14	-1.37
Iran	12,748.2	12,571.4	12,282.1	11,898.7	11,452.1	10,981.1	10,519.3	10,088.2	9,699.7	9,361.6	9,077.9	-3.34	-28.79
Ireland	496.5	487.4	476.6	467.6	459.6	454.5	451.0	448.1	446.1	447.0	450.3	-0.97	-9.31
Israel	849.2	857.8	867.4	877.5	888.1	899.4	911.7	924.6	938.7	955.0	971.4	1.35	14.38
Italy	4,580.7	4,514.8	4,458.4	4,411.0	4,366.7	4,336.2	4,315.4	4,303.9	4,300.5	4,299.9	4,293.4	-0.65	-6.27
Japan	10,016.8	9,853.0	9,712.8	9,584.9	9,457.2	9,326.1	9,210.1	9,108.9	9,008.5	8,910.0	8,819.7	-1.26	-11.95
Jordan	932.3	949.2	957.8	959.3	956.5	953.3	952.4	954.8	960.2	968.4	978.2	0.48	4.93
Kazakhstan	2,140.3	2,139.6	2,129.5	2,110.7	2,085.1	2,054.3	2,019.7	1,982.3	1,944.1	1,908.4	1,879.3	-1.29	-12.19
Kuwait	273.3	274.3	275.3	276.4	277.8	279.6	281.7	284.4	287.6	291.3	295.5	0.78	8.12
Latvia	250.1	245.3	239.0	231.4	222.9	213.0	203.8	195.6	186.3	177.5	169.9	-3.79	-32.07
Lithuania	373.8	370.3	365.8	359.9	352.4	342.8	332.6	320.9	308.2	295.4	284.4	-2.70	-23.91
Malaysia	3,658.7	3,704.6	3,748.0	3,788.9	3,830.9	3,872.2	3,915.5	3,955.3	3,993.8	4,031.9	4,072.5	1.08	11.31
Mexico	14,389.7	14,490.7	14,598.1	14,691.0	14,773.5	14,847.5	14,913.3	14,969.9	15,014.9	15,046.1	15,062.9	0.46	4.68
Morocco	4,736.2	4,739.2	4,729.4	4,708.1	4,677.3	4,639.5	4,597.2	4,552.3	4,506.9	4,463.2	4,423.5	-0.68	-6.60
Netherlands	1,468.1	1,472.7	1,472.3	1,472.2	1,477.0	1,485.0	1,491.3	1,498.7	1,501.5	1,503.2	1,504.3	0.24	2.47
New Zealand	446.2	448.8	450.3	450.8	450.4	449.4	449.4	449.1	448.7	447.1	446.0	0.00	-0.04
Nigeria	21,596.3	22,061.6	22,530.0	23,004.6	23,488.5	23,984.2	24,493.7	25,018.1	25,558.4	26,115.4	26,689.3	2.14	23.58
Norway	448.6	457.4	465.1	472.2	477.9	483.1	488.2	492.9	496.1	498.0	499.2	1.08	11.29
Pakistan	25,650.6	26,212.5	26,749.8	27,258.7	27,732.1	28,163.1	28,548.4	28,891.0	29,200.5	29,491.2	29,780.2	1.50	16.10
Peru	3,966.1	3,999.2	4,032.4	4,065.4	4,097.1	4,126.4	4,152.1	4,173.8	4,191.4	4,205.6	4,216.9	0.61	6.32
Philippines	12,891.4	13,123.4	13,338.7	13,542.2	13,733.1	13,914.0	14,083.3	14,240.9	14,387.5	14,525.5	14,657.9	1.29	13.70
Poland	4,384.4	4,294.0	4,185.6	4,075.5	3,942.4	3,787.8	3,638.1	3,497.1	3,372.2	3,258.3	3,149.4	-3.25	-28.17
Portugal	964.8	942.0	919.7	899.9	881.1	866.1	856.7	849.9	845.2	843.7	841.8	-1.35	-12.75
Romania	2,311.1	2,248.2	2,179.1	2,118.7	2,065.5	2,025.4	1,967.0	1,904.2	1,828.0	1,751.9	1,680.8	-3.13	-27.27
Russia	16,677.8	16,317.1	15,848.0	15,372.1	14,789.4	14,165.6	13,532.5	12,948.3	12,331.0	11,772.0	11,334.9	-3.79	-32.04
Saudi Arabia	3,421.6	3,495.4	3,570.2	3,645.2	3,718.5	3,788.1	3,852.4	3,910.6	3,962.2	4,007.3	4,045.7	1.69	18.24
Singapore	482.8	489.2	494.2	501.6	507.1	512.0	513.7	517.5	520.0	515.2	505.8	0.47	4.77
Slovakia	619.6	604.4	589.2	573.9	557.9	541.6	525.1	508.0	490.3	474.1	458.8	-2.96	-25.94
Slovenia	189.7	185.3	180.3	175.5	170.9	166.4	162.1	158.5	155.0	151.4	147.9	-2.46	-22.07
South Africa	7,308.5	7,344.1	7,359.2	7,355.8	7,339.0	7,316.1	7,293.0	7,272.8	7,256.3	7,244.6	7,237.6	-0.10	-0.97
South Korea	4,941.6	4,865.3	4,778.8	4,695.6	4,622.3	4,564.0	4,529.5	4,491.4	4,434.2	4,366.7	4,295.8	-1.39	-13.07
Spain	4,048.0	3,939.8	3,835.3	3,744.2	3,666.9	3,605.6	3,564.5	3,542.5	3,537.8	3,540.4	3,558.8	-1.28	-12.08
Sweden	860.8	869.5	873.1	874.5	874.1	873.2	871.6	868.4	864.0	860.5	855.5	-0.06	-0.62
Switzerland	686.5	689.5	690.9	692.9	692.7	692.8	691.8	688.6	684.8	680.7	674.5	-0.18	-1.75
Taiwan	2,550.9	2,506.4	2,465.9	2,422.0	2,382.5	2,326.1	2,283.6	2,264.1	2,241.0	2,208.1	2,150.2	-1.69	-15.71
Thailand	7,478.2	7,441.6	7,421.8	7,395.4	7,351.3	7,291.0	7,236.8	7,181.8	7,139.7	7,097.3	7,056.8	-0.58	-5.63
Tunisia	1,473.6	1,465.7	1,452.6	1,434.8	1,412.9	1,387.7	1,360.1	1,330.8	1,300.7	1,270.7	1,242.1	-1.69	-15.71
Turkey	9,619.2	9,643.3	9,679.7	9,728.6	9,789.5	9,858.6	9,932.2	10,007.4	10,063.6	10,114.6	10,153.7	0.54	5.56
Turkmenistan	777.4	786.1	791.3	793.2	792.1	789.0	784.5	779.0	772.9	766.1	758.8	-0.24	-2.39
Ukraine	5,121.2	5,019.8	4,893.2	4,763.8	4,611.6	4,413.9	4,212.1	4,017.7	3,809.6	3,633.4	3,477.5	-3.80	-32.10
United Arab Emirates	451.8	444.2	436.1	428.6	422.7	419.5	419.7	423.7	431.1	441.1	452.4	0.01	0.14
United Kingdom	6,076.9	6,132.0	6,164.6	6,197.9	6,228.0	6,238.9	6,222.2	6,182.3	6,133.1	6,076.5	6,021.3	-0.09	-0.92
USA	31,253.3	31,268.8	31,235.8	31,210.1	31,200.7	31,218.3	31,222.2	31,317.9	31,402.0	31,488.1	31,571.6	0.10	1.02
Venezuela	3,852.3	3,887.5	3,919.6	3,948.8	3,974.9	3,997.8	4,017.5	4,034.3	4,048.7	4,061.9	4,075.0	0.56	5.78
Vietnam	12,757.5	12,826.5	12,843.8	12,813.7	12,746.3	12,656.8	12,556.8	12,451.2	12,339.3	12,221.5	12,096.2	-0.53	-5.18

Marketing segments: Young generation

Table 4.111 Male young adults (15-29): 2009-2019

'000

	2009	2010	2011	2012	2013	2014	2015	2016	2017	2018	2019	CAGR	Period growth
Algeria	5,543.7	5,530.5	5,489.8	5,425.3	5,344.0	5,254.7	5,165.6	5,081.8	5,005.6	4,938.2	4,879.9	-1.27	-11.98
Argentina	5,074.3	5,091.5	5,110.9	5,132.2	5,153.6	5,172.2	5,185.6	5,192.7	5,193.8	5,190.3	5,183.8	0.21	2.16
Australia	2,349.2	2,382.1	2,403.9	2,422.0	2,435.3	2,448.6	2,460.4	2,471.1	2,480.1	2,488.0	2,493.0	0.60	6.12
Austria	799.1	801.1	798.4	795.3	789.8	784.6	777.9	771.8	765.3	760.2	753.3	-0.59	-5.74
Azerbaijan	1,283.9	1,297.2	1,301.7	1,297.6	1,286.4	1,269.6	1,248.7	1,224.7	1,199.0	1,173.0	1,148.7	-1.11	-10.53
Belarus	1,164.4	1,143.7	1,117.5	1,086.8	1,051.9	1,012.5	974.9	939.7	899.9	863.7	827.7	-3.36	-28.92
Belgium	993.9	992.0	989.5	987.1	986.2	985.9	985.7	987.0	985.1	982.5	978.9	-0.15	-1.50
Bolivia	1,384.6	1,416.3	1,446.5	1,475.1	1,502.3	1,528.4	1,553.5	1,577.8	1,601.0	1,622.6	1,642.1	1.72	18.60
Bosnia-Herzegovina	424.9	419.6	414.1	408.3	401.9	394.5	385.8	375.9	364.9	353.7	342.9	-2.12	-19.29
Brazil	26,173.8	26,139.4	26,050.5	25,947.5	25,848.6	25,744.8	25,670.4	25,651.3	25,641.7	25,627.0	25,596.9	-0.22	-2.20
Bulgaria	764.9	739.4	713.5	688.3	659.9	633.1	609.8	587.3	565.1	544.7	524.3	-3.71	-31.45
Canada	3,498.6	3,519.4	3,531.6	3,535.5	3,529.0	3,515.9	3,500.7	3,480.8	3,461.0	3,443.0	3,420.6	-0.23	-2.23
Chile	2,139.2	2,163.0	2,179.3	2,187.8	2,188.7	2,182.9	2,171.4	2,154.9	2,134.4	2,110.8	2,085.2	-0.26	-2.53
China	145,921.5	147,367.7	148,175.3	147,579.4	148,421.2	148,310.7	148,530.6	146,950.6	143,464.8	139,847.7	135,811.9	-0.72	-6.93
Colombia	6,150.5	6,204.2	6,253.5	6,298.6	6,339.8	6,377.2	6,410.9	6,440.7	6,466.7	6,489.2	6,508.5	0.57	5.82
Costa Rica	660.7	665.6	669.0	671.1	671.8	671.1	669.2	666.3	662.6	658.2	653.3	-0.11	-1.12
Croatia	440.7	434.2	428.0	423.7	418.7	412.6	405.6	399.0	391.8	384.7	376.9	-1.55	-14.47
Czech Republic	1,060.1	1,030.0	1,002.4	975.7	949.6	925.4	901.0	878.5	858.6	841.4	824.0	-2.49	-22.27
Denmark	495.1	499.5	505.3	511.7	517.7	523.9	529.2	534.0	536.9	539.2	540.4	0.88	9.16
Ecuador	1,848.1	1,863.3	1,881.6	1,902.5	1,924.6	1,946.3	1,966.2	1,983.6	1,998.3	2,010.4	2,020.0	0.89	9.30
Egypt	11,120.0	11,152.7	11,184.8	11,218.5	11,257.1	11,304.2	11,362.4	11,434.7	11,523.2	11,627.2	11,754.5	0.56	5.71
Estonia	150.5	147.1	143.5	139.3	134.9	129.8	124.9	120.9	116.6	112.0	107.5	-3.31	-28.55
Finland	509.6	511.1	511.3	510.1	506.3	501.4	497.6	494.8	492.2	490.0	486.4	-0.46	-4.55
France	5,945.9	5,941.0	5,919.1	5,901.7	5,885.2	5,895.9	5,907.8	5,927.5	5,933.5	5,935.2	5,932.1	-0.02	-0.23
Germany	7,327.0	7,261.0	7,166.2	7,092.8	7,024.3	6,958.1	6,888.3	6,814.3	6,709.3	6,586.9	6,448.1	-1.27	-11.99
Greece	1,052.3	1,028.6	1,000.3	975.6	953.0	932.4	915.5	903.4	895.3	891.2	885.9	-1.71	-15.82
Hong Kong, China	684.7	685.2	683.5	679.2	669.6	656.9	643.5	633.0	621.0	608.8	591.7	-1.45	-13.58
Hungary	1,014.0	992.9	974.6	955.7	938.0	922.0	905.5	887.9	872.3	858.7	845.0	-1.81	-16.67
India	169,349.3	171,593.9	173,654.7	175,529.3	177,232.6	178,789.5	180,221.9	181,538.5	182,728.0	183,762.9	184,609.6	0.87	9.01
Indonesia	31,025.4	31,008.7	30,965.1	30,902.9	30,835.9	30,781.0	30,751.5	30,752.7	30,782.0	30,830.8	30,886.7	-0.04	-0.45
Iran	12,975.4	12,826.2	12,576.3	12,240.1	11,842.7	11,415.2	10,985.4	10,572.6	10,189.0	9,845.5	9,550.5	-3.02	-26.40
Ireland	507.0	496.3	485.3	477.1	470.0	465.6	461.6	459.0	456.6	457.6	460.6	-0.96	-9.15
Israel	878.8	888.5	899.6	911.3	922.8	934.5	948.0	962.3	977.5	994.7	1,012.5	1.43	15.22
Italy	4,780.3	4,716.3	4,663.6	4,620.1	4,580.6	4,552.8	4,534.0	4,526.8	4,523.1	4,520.5	4,513.5	-0.57	-5.58
Japan	10,511.4	10,346.1	10,202.6	10,071.8	9,932.0	9,786.4	9,655.0	9,536.7	9,426.8	9,320.1	9,222.5	-1.30	-12.26
Jordan	984.5	999.7	1,006.9	1,007.6	1,004.3	1,000.9	1,000.0	1,002.6	1,008.4	1,016.9	1,026.9	0.42	4.31
Kazakhstan	2,194.6	2,198.5	2,191.6	2,174.4	2,149.4	2,118.7	2,084.3	2,047.3	2,010.0	1,975.8	1,948.4	-1.18	-11.22
Kuwait	360.2	355.7	351.8	348.8	346.7	345.1	344.1	343.4	343.3	343.9	345.1	-0.43	-4.21
Latvia	258.2	252.8	246.2	238.2	229.2	218.9	209.5	200.5	190.9	181.8	173.7	-3.89	-32.72
Lithuania	387.5	383.6	378.6	371.8	364.3	354.7	344.7	333.5	320.0	307.3	296.4	-2.64	-23.51
Malaysia	3,808.2	3,865.1	3,918.4	3,967.4	4,018.4	4,066.8	4,114.6	4,159.5	4,203.1	4,251.1	4,300.4	1.22	12.93
Mexico	13,872.3	13,971.2	14,086.4	14,196.9	14,305.9	14,413.3	14,517.7	14,616.4	14,705.1	14,778.8	14,833.1	0.67	6.93
Morocco	4,631.5	4,655.6	4,665.3	4,661.3	4,645.9	4,621.7	4,591.3	4,556.8	4,520.3	4,484.0	4,450.6	-0.40	-3.91
Netherlands	1,503.6	1,509.5	1,509.7	1,512.7	1,517.7	1,527.2	1,534.8	1,543.6	1,548.7	1,551.9	1,555.4	0.34	3.44
New Zealand	454.1	459.1	462.9	464.7	465.8	466.7	468.7	470.0	469.7	468.9	468.2	0.31	3.10
Nigeria	21,940.5	22,432.2	22,928.5	23,432.3	23,946.2	24,472.9	25,013.8	25,569.8	26,141.3	26,728.7	27,331.4	2.22	24.57
Norway	468.0	476.7	484.5	492.2	497.9	502.7	507.9	512.5	515.2	517.0	518.0	1.02	10.70
Pakistan	27,247.6	27,830.9	28,390.9	28,923.3	29,420.0	29,872.4	30,276.4	30,634.9	30,958.6	31,263.7	31,569.4	1.48	15.86
Peru	4,058.7	4,093.4	4,128.5	4,163.6	4,197.9	4,229.8	4,258.3	4,282.9	4,303.4	4,320.6	4,335.1	0.66	6.81
Philippines	13,287.9	13,534.2	13,765.3	13,986.0	14,194.7	14,393.1	14,579.0	14,751.9	14,912.8	15,064.4	15,210.3	1.36	14.47
Poland	4,549.5	4,455.6	4,346.4	4,236.0	4,099.3	3,944.2	3,791.5	3,648.3	3,521.3	3,405.5	3,296.3	-3.17	-27.55
Portugal	997.6	975.0	953.7	933.9	914.6	898.9	888.6	881.5	878.0	877.4	876.4	-1.29	-12.15
Romania	2,411.7	2,344.2	2,271.5	2,210.7	2,156.6	2,113.2	2,052.7	1,988.2	1,910.6	1,833.9	1,763.1	-3.08	-26.90
Russia	17,076.4	16,719.2	16,256.5	15,787.3	15,200.8	14,570.7	13,947.0	13,373.4	12,759.2	12,204.9	11,781.8	-3.64	-31.01
Saudi Arabia	3,744.6	3,788.6	3,839.7	3,896.6	3,957.3	4,018.9	4,078.8	4,135.7	4,189.0	4,237.5	4,280.6	1.35	14.31
Singapore	482.3	489.5	495.4	502.3	506.5	510.9	511.9	514.8	514.9	507.2	494.3	0.25	2.50
Slovakia	646.0	630.6	614.6	598.8	581.8	564.9	547.6	529.5	511.3	494.7	478.7	-2.95	-25.90
Slovenia	201.5	196.5	191.6	186.5	181.4	176.9	172.5	168.8	165.2	161.4	157.6	-2.43	-21.78
South Africa	7,434.0	7,467.9	7,477.8	7,466.2	7,439.8	7,407.3	7,375.7	7,348.8	7,327.7	7,313.4	7,306.3	-0.17	-1.72
South Korea	5,424.0	5,370.8	5,300.7	5,223.4	5,155.4	5,105.7	5,077.4	5,034.1	4,975.1	4,902.2	4,814.2	-1.19	-11.24
Spain	4,264.2	4,144.9	4,030.9	3,932.5	3,849.5	3,785.9	3,743.2	3,721.8	3,715.2	3,719.5	3,740.1	-1.30	-12.29
Sweden	899.1	907.6	911.3	912.3	911.2	910.6	908.1	904.8	899.9	896.9	891.0	-0.09	-0.90
Switzerland	695.3	697.6	698.4	699.2	698.5	697.2	694.5	690.7	685.9	680.7	672.8	-0.33	-3.23
Taiwan	2,692.1	2,649.6	2,613.4	2,573.8	2,540.6	2,488.2	2,448.9	2,436.9	2,415.7	2,385.1	2,328.1	-1.44	-13.52
Thailand	7,528.3	7,495.7	7,483.7	7,467.9	7,433.4	7,387.4	7,343.8	7,301.1	7,272.3	7,240.1	7,209.2	-0.43	-4.24
Tunisia	1,541.6	1,535.1	1,523.3	1,506.6	1,485.8	1,461.4	1,434.4	1,405.5	1,375.5	1,345.5	1,316.7	-1.56	-14.59
Turkey	10,008.1	10,014.2	10,039.6	10,079.1	10,130.4	10,193.1	10,261.4	10,332.6	10,382.8	10,432.7	10,474.2	0.46	4.66
Turkmenistan	788.2	797.3	802.9	805.1	804.3	801.4	797.1	791.7	785.6	779.0	771.9	-0.21	-2.07
Ukraine	5,327.6	5,228.0	5,100.7	4,969.8	4,808.2	4,601.1	4,394.6	4,197.1	3,984.7	3,802.7	3,640.6	-3.74	-31.67
United Arab Emirates	769.6	746.1	733.4	731.8	739.4	753.4	771.0	790.7	811.7	833.3	854.4	1.05	11.01
United Kingdom	6,343.1	6,401.5	6,432.8	6,463.7	6,483.4	6,474.3	6,439.9	6,389.9	6,333.3	6,274.6	6,225.3	-0.19	-1.86
USA	32,949.7	32,945.3	32,867.2	32,757.9	32,651.5	32,584.5	32,519.5	32,552.5	32,590.2	32,650.1	32,716.7	-0.07	-0.71
Venezuela	3,955.6	3,993.0	4,027.5	4,059.2	4,087.9	4,113.5	4,135.7	4,154.9	4,171.6	4,187.0	4,202.3	0.61	6.24
Vietnam	13,069.1	13,151.9	13,181.3	13,161.5	13,102.9	13,020.7	12,926.9	12,826.2	12,718.4	12,603.7	12,480.7	-0.46	-4.50

Marketing segments: Young generation

Table 4.112 Young adults (15-29): 2009-2019 (%)

% of total

	2009	2010	2011	2012	2013	2014	2015	2016	2017	2018	2019
Algeria	31.2	30.7	30.0	29.2	28.3	27.5	26.6	25.8	25.1	24.5	23.9
Argentina	24.9	24.7	24.5	24.4	24.3	24.1	24.0	23.8	23.6	23.4	23.2
Australia	21.1	21.1	21.0	20.9	20.7	20.5	20.3	20.1	19.9	19.7	19.5
Austria	18.8	18.8	18.7	18.5	18.4	18.2	18.0	17.8	17.6	17.4	17.2
Azerbaijan	28.9	28.8	28.5	28.1	27.5	26.8	26.1	25.3	24.5	23.7	22.9
Belarus	23.6	23.2	22.8	22.2	21.5	20.8	20.0	19.3	18.6	17.9	17.2
Belgium	18.4	18.3	18.2	18.0	18.0	17.9	17.8	17.8	17.7	17.6	17.5
Bolivia	27.7	27.9	28.0	28.1	28.1	28.2	28.2	28.2	28.2	28.2	28.1
Bosnia-Herzegovina	21.8	21.5	21.2	20.9	20.5	20.1	19.6	19.1	18.6	18.0	17.4
Brazil	26.8	26.5	26.2	25.9	25.6	25.3	25.1	24.9	24.7	24.5	24.3
Bulgaria	19.8	19.3	18.8	18.2	17.6	17.0	16.5	16.0	15.6	15.1	14.7
Canada	20.4	20.3	20.2	20.0	19.8	19.6	19.3	19.1	18.8	18.5	18.3
Chile	24.9	24.9	24.8	24.7	24.5	24.2	23.9	23.5	23.1	22.7	22.2
China	21.3	21.4	21.4	21.1	21.1	20.9	20.8	20.5	19.9	19.2	18.6
Colombia	26.8	26.6	26.4	26.3	26.1	25.9	25.7	25.5	25.3	25.1	24.9
Costa Rica	28.1	27.9	27.7	27.4	27.1	26.7	26.3	25.8	25.4	24.9	24.5
Croatia	19.5	19.3	19.0	18.9	18.7	18.5	18.2	17.9	17.7	17.4	17.1
Czech Republic	20.0	19.4	18.9	18.4	17.9	17.5	17.0	16.6	16.2	15.9	15.5
Denmark	17.7	17.8	17.9	18.1	18.2	18.4	18.5	18.7	18.7	18.8	18.7
Ecuador	26.8	26.7	26.7	26.7	26.6	26.6	26.6	26.5	26.4	26.3	26.1
Egypt	28.1	27.7	27.2	26.8	26.4	26.1	25.8	25.5	25.3	25.1	25.0
Estonia	22.2	21.8	21.3	20.8	20.2	19.5	18.8	18.2	17.6	17.0	16.3
Finland	18.7	18.7	18.6	18.5	18.4	18.1	17.9	17.8	17.6	17.5	17.3
France	18.9	18.7	18.6	18.4	18.3	18.2	18.1	18.1	18.1	18.0	17.9
Germany	17.6	17.5	17.3	17.2	17.1	17.0	16.9	16.8	16.6	16.3	16.1
Greece	18.0	17.6	17.1	16.6	16.2	15.8	15.5	15.3	15.2	15.1	15.0
Hong Kong, China	21.1	21.1	21.1	20.9	20.6	20.3	19.8	19.4	18.9	18.4	17.9
Hungary	19.9	19.5	19.2	18.9	18.6	18.3	18.0	17.7	17.5	17.2	17.0
India	27.8	27.8	27.7	27.7	27.6	27.5	27.4	27.2	27.1	27.0	26.8
Indonesia	26.7	26.4	26.1	25.8	25.5	25.2	24.9	24.7	24.5	24.3	24.2
Iran	34.7	33.8	32.7	31.4	30.0	28.5	27.1	25.7	24.5	23.4	22.5
Ireland	22.6	21.8	21.1	20.5	19.9	19.5	19.1	18.8	18.6	18.4	18.4
Israel	23.3	23.2	23.2	23.1	23.1	23.0	23.1	23.1	23.2	23.3	23.4
Italy	15.9	15.6	15.4	15.3	15.1	15.0	14.9	14.9	14.9	14.9	14.9
Japan	16.1	15.9	15.7	15.5	15.3	15.1	15.0	14.9	14.7	14.6	14.5
Jordan	30.3	30.1	29.8	29.4	28.9	28.5	28.1	27.7	27.5	27.3	27.1
Kazakhstan	27.5	27.1	26.7	26.2	25.5	24.9	24.2	23.5	22.8	22.2	21.6
Kuwait	25.9	25.2	24.6	24.0	23.5	23.0	22.6	22.3	22.0	21.7	21.6
Latvia	22.6	22.2	21.8	21.2	20.6	19.8	19.0	18.3	17.6	16.8	16.2
Lithuania	22.7	22.6	22.5	22.2	21.9	21.4	20.9	20.3	19.6	18.9	18.4
Malaysia	26.6	26.5	26.4	26.3	26.3	26.2	26.1	26.1	26.0	25.9	25.9
Mexico	26.0	25.8	25.7	25.5	25.3	25.2	25.0	24.9	24.7	24.5	24.3
Morocco	29.3	29.0	28.7	28.3	27.8	27.3	26.8	26.2	25.7	25.2	24.8
Netherlands	18.1	18.1	18.1	18.1	18.1	18.2	18.2	18.3	18.3	18.3	18.3
New Zealand	20.9	20.9	20.8	20.6	20.5	20.3	20.2	20.0	19.8	19.6	19.5
Nigeria	28.1	28.1	28.1	28.1	28.1	28.1	28.1	28.2	28.3	28.4	28.5
Norway	19.1	19.2	19.3	19.4	19.5	19.5	19.5	19.5	19.4	19.3	19.2
Pakistan	29.3	29.3	29.2	29.1	29.0	28.8	28.6	28.4	28.1	27.9	27.6
Peru	27.7	27.5	27.4	27.3	27.1	27.0	26.8	26.7	26.5	26.3	26.1
Philippines	28.4	28.4	28.3	28.2	28.1	28.0	27.9	27.7	27.5	27.3	27.1
Poland	23.5	23.1	22.5	22.0	21.3	20.5	19.7	19.0	18.4	17.8	17.2
Portugal	18.4	17.9	17.5	17.1	16.7	16.4	16.2	16.0	16.0	15.9	15.9
Romania	22.0	21.5	20.9	20.4	20.0	19.7	19.2	18.7	18.0	17.4	16.8
Russia	23.8	23.3	22.7	22.1	21.3	20.4	19.6	18.8	17.9	17.2	16.6
Saudi Arabia	27.9	27.8	27.7	27.6	27.6	27.5	27.4	27.3	27.2	27.0	26.8
Singapore	20.5	20.5	20.5	20.5	20.5	20.4	20.3	20.2	20.1	19.7	19.1
Slovakia	23.5	22.9	22.3	21.7	21.1	20.5	19.9	19.2	18.6	18.0	17.4
Slovenia	19.3	18.8	18.3	17.8	17.2	16.8	16.3	16.0	15.6	15.2	14.8
South Africa	29.4	29.3	29.2	29.0	28.8	28.6	28.4	28.2	28.0	27.9	27.7
South Korea	21.3	20.9	20.6	20.2	19.9	19.6	19.5	19.3	19.1	18.8	18.5
Spain	18.3	17.6	17.0	16.4	16.0	15.6	15.3	15.1	15.0	14.9	14.9
Sweden	19.1	19.2	19.2	19.1	19.0	18.9	18.8	18.6	18.5	18.3	18.1
Switzerland	18.3	18.3	18.2	18.2	18.1	18.0	17.9	17.8	17.6	17.4	17.2
Taiwan	22.8	22.3	21.9	21.5	21.1	20.6	20.2	20.1	19.9	19.6	19.1
Thailand	23.2	22.9	22.8	22.6	22.3	22.1	21.8	21.6	21.4	21.2	21.0
Tunisia	29.4	28.9	28.4	27.8	27.1	26.4	25.7	24.9	24.2	23.4	22.7
Turkey	26.1	25.8	25.6	25.4	25.3	25.2	25.1	25.0	24.9	24.8	24.7
Turkmenistan	30.6	30.6	30.4	30.1	29.7	29.2	28.7	28.2	27.6	27.1	26.6
Ukraine	22.8	22.5	22.0	21.6	21.0	20.3	19.5	18.7	17.9	17.2	16.6
United Arab Emirates	26.5	25.2	24.2	23.5	23.1	22.9	22.8	22.9	23.0	23.2	23.4
United Kingdom	20.2	20.2	20.2	20.2	20.2	20.1	19.9	19.6	19.3	19.0	18.7
USA	20.9	20.8	20.6	20.4	20.3	20.1	20.0	19.9	19.8	19.7	19.6
Venezuela	27.3	27.1	26.9	26.7	26.5	26.3	26.1	25.8	25.6	25.3	25.1
Vietnam	29.5	29.3	29.0	28.5	28.1	27.5	27.0	26.5	25.9	25.4	24.9

Marketing segments: Young generation

Table 4.113 Female young adults (15-29): 2009-2019 (%)

% of total

	2009	2010	2011	2012	2013	2014	2015	2016	2017	2018	2019
Algeria	15.31	15.04	14.71	14.32	13.90	13.48	13.07	12.68	12.33	12.00	11.71
Argentina	12.29	12.20	12.12	12.05	11.98	11.90	11.82	11.73	11.63	11.53	11.42
Australia	10.31	10.30	10.25	10.18	10.09	10.00	9.91	9.82	9.73	9.63	9.53
Austria	9.25	9.26	9.21	9.14	9.05	8.97	8.86	8.77	8.67	8.59	8.50
Azerbaijan	14.15	14.07	13.92	13.68	13.38	13.03	12.65	12.24	11.81	11.39	10.99
Belarus	11.54	11.37	11.15	10.87	10.55	10.16	9.79	9.44	9.05	8.69	8.34
Belgium	9.09	9.02	8.94	8.88	8.83	8.78	8.74	8.71	8.67	8.62	8.56
Bolivia	13.70	13.76	13.81	13.84	13.87	13.88	13.89	13.89	13.89	13.87	13.85
Bosnia-Herzegovina	10.78	10.59	10.41	10.23	10.04	9.83	9.59	9.32	9.02	8.73	8.45
Brazil	13.30	13.16	13.00	12.84	12.68	12.53	12.40	12.30	12.21	12.12	12.03
Bulgaria	9.65	9.40	9.14	8.88	8.57	8.29	8.05	7.81	7.57	7.34	7.13
Canada	9.99	9.94	9.87	9.79	9.67	9.54	9.41	9.27	9.13	8.99	8.85
Chile	12.26	12.27	12.24	12.17	12.07	11.93	11.76	11.58	11.37	11.16	10.94
China	10.35	10.35	10.30	10.16	10.11	10.01	9.92	9.71	9.40	9.08	8.75
Colombia	13.29	13.21	13.12	13.03	12.94	12.84	12.75	12.65	12.54	12.44	12.33
Costa Rica	13.67	13.58	13.47	13.32	13.15	12.97	12.77	12.56	12.34	12.12	11.90
Croatia	9.57	9.45	9.34	9.26	9.17	9.06	8.93	8.80	8.66	8.51	8.37
Czech Republic	9.79	9.50	9.24	8.99	8.74	8.52	8.30	8.08	7.90	7.73	7.56
Denmark	8.69	8.73	8.79	8.87	8.95	9.03	9.10	9.15	9.19	9.20	9.21
Ecuador	13.26	13.21	13.18	13.17	13.15	13.14	13.11	13.07	13.02	12.96	12.88
Egypt	13.59	13.38	13.18	12.97	12.78	12.60	12.43	12.28	12.16	12.06	11.98
Estonia	10.88	10.70	10.47	10.21	9.90	9.55	9.20	8.91	8.60	8.29	7.98
Finland	9.15	9.15	9.12	9.07	8.99	8.88	8.79	8.70	8.64	8.58	8.50
France	9.36	9.28	9.19	9.10	9.02	8.98	8.94	8.92	8.88	8.84	8.80
Germany	8.63	8.59	8.52	8.46	8.42	8.37	8.32	8.27	8.17	8.06	7.93
Greece	8.67	8.46	8.22	8.03	7.84	7.68	7.54	7.44	7.36	7.32	7.28
Hong Kong, China	11.41	11.52	11.55	11.58	11.50	11.35	11.16	10.96	10.70	10.43	10.14
Hungary	9.75	9.59	9.44	9.28	9.14	9.01	8.86	8.72	8.57	8.46	8.33
India	13.30	13.29	13.26	13.23	13.18	13.13	13.08	13.02	12.96	12.89	12.81
Indonesia	13.26	13.09	12.93	12.77	12.61	12.46	12.32	12.20	12.09	12.00	11.92
Iran	17.18	16.74	16.17	15.49	14.74	13.98	13.24	12.56	11.94	11.40	10.95
Ireland	11.16	10.81	10.45	10.14	9.85	9.64	9.46	9.31	9.18	9.11	9.09
Israel	11.47	11.41	11.37	11.34	11.31	11.30	11.31	11.32	11.35	11.41	11.47
Italy	7.76	7.64	7.54	7.45	7.37	7.32	7.29	7.27	7.27	7.27	7.27
Japan	7.85	7.74	7.64	7.56	7.47	7.39	7.32	7.26	7.21	7.16	7.11
Jordan	14.76	14.67	14.51	14.32	14.10	13.88	13.69	13.53	13.40	13.29	13.22
Kazakhstan	13.57	13.39	13.16	12.88	12.57	12.24	11.90	11.55	11.21	10.89	10.62
Kuwait	11.18	10.98	10.78	10.60	10.44	10.30	10.18	10.09	10.02	9.97	9.94
Latvia	11.10	10.95	10.73	10.46	10.13	9.75	9.39	9.06	8.68	8.32	8.01
Lithuania	11.16	11.12	11.05	10.93	10.77	10.54	10.28	9.98	9.64	9.29	8.99
Malaysia	13.02	12.97	12.92	12.87	12.82	12.78	12.74	12.70	12.66	12.62	12.59
Mexico	13.25	13.15	13.06	12.97	12.87	12.78	12.69	12.59	12.49	12.38	12.27
Morocco	14.80	14.64	14.43	14.20	13.94	13.67	13.39	13.11	12.84	12.58	12.34
Netherlands	8.95	8.96	8.94	8.92	8.93	8.97	8.99	9.02	9.02	9.02	9.01
New Zealand	10.35	10.31	10.25	10.17	10.07	9.96	9.88	9.79	9.70	9.59	9.49
Nigeria	13.96	13.94	13.92	13.91	13.91	13.91	13.92	13.94	13.97	14.01	14.06
Norway	9.35	9.41	9.47	9.51	9.53	9.55	9.56	9.56	9.53	9.48	9.41
Pakistan	14.19	14.19	14.17	14.13	14.07	13.99	13.89	13.78	13.66	13.53	13.41
Peru	13.67	13.60	13.53	13.47	13.40	13.33	13.25	13.17	13.07	12.96	12.86
Philippines	13.99	13.97	13.94	13.89	13.83	13.77	13.69	13.60	13.50	13.40	13.29
Poland	11.54	11.32	11.05	10.78	10.44	10.05	9.67	9.31	8.99	8.70	8.41
Portugal	9.04	8.81	8.58	8.38	8.19	8.04	7.95	7.88	7.83	7.81	7.79
Romania	10.78	10.52	10.23	9.98	9.77	9.62	9.39	9.14	8.82	8.50	8.20
Russia	11.75	11.51	11.20	10.89	10.49	10.07	9.63	9.23	8.81	8.42	8.13
Saudi Arabia	13.30	13.32	13.33	13.35	13.35	13.34	13.32	13.27	13.20	13.12	13.02
Singapore	10.26	10.25	10.22	10.25	10.24	10.23	10.16	10.14	10.10	9.92	9.66
Slovakia	11.48	11.20	10.92	10.63	10.33	10.03	9.73	9.41	9.09	8.79	8.51
Slovenia	9.38	9.13	8.86	8.61	8.37	8.14	7.92	7.73	7.55	7.36	7.18
South Africa	14.58	14.54	14.48	14.40	14.31	14.21	14.11	14.02	13.94	13.86	13.79
South Korea	10.14	9.95	9.75	9.57	9.40	9.27	9.19	9.11	8.99	8.85	8.71
Spain	8.89	8.58	8.28	8.02	7.80	7.61	7.47	7.37	7.31	7.27	7.26
Sweden	9.36	9.41	9.40	9.37	9.32	9.27	9.21	9.13	9.04	8.96	8.86
Switzerland	9.08	9.09	9.07	9.06	9.03	8.99	8.95	8.87	8.79	8.71	8.59
Taiwan	11.07	10.85	10.64	10.43	10.23	9.97	9.77	9.67	9.56	9.41	9.16
Thailand	11.55	11.43	11.33	11.23	11.11	10.97	10.84	10.71	10.61	10.51	10.41
Tunisia	14.35	14.13	13.87	13.56	13.23	12.87	12.50	12.12	11.74	11.37	11.02
Turkey	12.78	12.66	12.56	12.49	12.43	12.38	12.35	12.32	12.27	12.22	12.15
Turkmenistan	15.21	15.19	15.09	14.94	14.73	14.49	14.24	13.98	13.71	13.44	13.18
Ukraine	11.15	11.00	10.79	10.57	10.30	9.92	9.53	9.15	8.74	8.39	8.09
United Arab Emirates	9.79	9.40	9.03	8.69	8.41	8.19	8.05	7.98	7.98	8.03	8.09
United Kingdom	9.86	9.90	9.90	9.90	9.90	9.85	9.77	9.64	9.51	9.36	9.22
USA	10.19	10.12	10.05	9.97	9.90	9.84	9.77	9.74	9.70	9.66	9.62
Venezuela	13.48	13.39	13.29	13.18	13.07	12.96	12.84	12.72	12.59	12.47	12.35
Vietnam	14.56	14.45	14.29	14.08	13.84	13.57	13.31	13.04	12.78	12.51	12.25

Marketing segments: Young generation

Table 4.114 Male young adults (15-29): 2009-2019 (%)

% of total

	2009	2010	2011	2012	2013	2014	2015	2016	2017	2018	2019
Algeria	15.89	15.61	15.27	14.87	14.43	13.99	13.56	13.16	12.79	12.46	12.16
Argentina	12.58	12.50	12.42	12.36	12.30	12.23	12.15	12.06	11.96	11.86	11.74
Australia	10.78	10.78	10.74	10.68	10.59	10.51	10.41	10.31	10.21	10.11	10.00
Austria	9.53	9.53	9.47	9.40	9.31	9.22	9.12	9.02	8.93	8.84	8.74
Azerbaijan	14.71	14.69	14.59	14.39	14.12	13.80	13.44	13.06	12.67	12.29	11.94
Belarus	12.04	11.85	11.61	11.32	10.99	10.61	10.25	9.91	9.52	9.16	8.81
Belgium	9.32	9.27	9.22	9.16	9.12	9.09	9.06	9.04	9.00	8.95	8.89
Bolivia	14.04	14.12	14.18	14.23	14.27	14.29	14.31	14.32	14.33	14.32	14.30
Bosnia-Herzegovina	11.05	10.92	10.77	10.62	10.46	10.27	10.06	9.81	9.53	9.25	8.99
Brazil	13.51	13.38	13.22	13.07	12.92	12.78	12.65	12.56	12.48	12.40	12.31
Bulgaria	10.17	9.90	9.62	9.35	9.03	8.73	8.48	8.24	7.99	7.77	7.55
Canada	10.40	10.36	10.31	10.25	10.15	10.04	9.92	9.79	9.66	9.55	9.42
Chile	12.61	12.62	12.60	12.53	12.42	12.28	12.11	11.92	11.71	11.49	11.27
China	10.99	11.04	11.06	10.97	10.98	10.93	10.91	10.75	10.46	10.16	9.84
Colombia	13.47	13.40	13.32	13.24	13.16	13.07	12.98	12.89	12.79	12.69	12.58
Costa Rica	14.43	14.34	14.23	14.08	13.91	13.71	13.50	13.28	13.05	12.82	12.58
Croatia	9.95	9.82	9.70	9.62	9.53	9.41	9.27	9.15	9.00	8.86	8.71
Czech Republic	10.25	9.95	9.67	9.41	9.16	8.93	8.70	8.48	8.29	8.12	7.96
Denmark	8.98	9.04	9.12	9.21	9.29	9.38	9.45	9.51	9.53	9.55	9.54
Ecuador	13.56	13.53	13.51	13.50	13.49	13.49	13.47	13.44	13.40	13.34	13.27
Egypt	14.49	14.27	14.06	13.86	13.67	13.50	13.35	13.22	13.12	13.04	12.99
Estonia	11.31	11.09	10.86	10.58	10.28	9.93	9.59	9.32	9.02	8.68	8.36
Finland	9.57	9.56	9.52	9.47	9.36	9.24	9.14	9.06	8.99	8.92	8.83
France	9.52	9.46	9.39	9.32	9.25	9.23	9.21	9.20	9.18	9.14	9.11
Germany	8.94	8.89	8.80	8.74	8.68	8.63	8.57	8.51	8.40	8.28	8.13
Greece	9.35	9.11	8.83	8.59	8.37	8.17	8.00	7.88	7.80	7.76	7.71
Hong Kong, China	9.69	9.61	9.50	9.36	9.15	8.90	8.65	8.44	8.21	7.99	7.71
Hungary	10.12	9.93	9.77	9.60	9.45	9.32	9.17	9.02	8.88	8.77	8.65
India	14.49	14.48	14.46	14.43	14.38	14.33	14.27	14.21	14.14	14.07	13.98
Indonesia	13.49	13.34	13.18	13.02	12.86	12.72	12.59	12.49	12.39	12.31	12.24
Iran	17.49	17.08	16.56	15.93	15.24	14.53	13.83	13.16	12.54	11.99	11.51
Ireland	11.40	11.01	10.64	10.34	10.07	9.87	9.69	9.53	9.39	9.32	9.30
Israel	11.87	11.82	11.79	11.77	11.75	11.74	11.76	11.78	11.82	11.88	11.95
Italy	8.10	7.98	7.88	7.80	7.74	7.69	7.66	7.65	7.65	7.65	7.64
Japan	8.24	8.12	8.03	7.94	7.85	7.75	7.67	7.60	7.54	7.48	7.44
Jordan	15.59	15.45	15.26	15.04	14.80	14.58	14.37	14.20	14.07	13.96	13.87
Kazakhstan	13.91	13.75	13.54	13.27	12.96	12.62	12.28	11.93	11.59	11.27	11.01
Kuwait	14.73	14.23	13.78	13.38	13.03	12.72	12.43	12.18	11.96	11.77	11.61
Latvia	11.46	11.28	11.05	10.76	10.42	10.02	9.65	9.29	8.90	8.52	8.19
Lithuania	11.57	11.52	11.43	11.29	11.13	10.90	10.66	10.37	10.01	9.66	9.37
Malaysia	13.55	13.54	13.51	13.48	13.45	13.42	13.39	13.36	13.32	13.30	13.29
Mexico	12.78	12.68	12.60	12.53	12.47	12.41	12.35	12.29	12.23	12.16	12.08
Morocco	14.48	14.38	14.24	14.06	13.85	13.62	13.37	13.13	12.88	12.64	12.42
Netherlands	9.16	9.18	9.17	9.17	9.18	9.22	9.25	9.29	9.30	9.31	9.31
New Zealand	10.54	10.55	10.54	10.48	10.41	10.34	10.30	10.24	10.15	10.05	9.96
Nigeria	14.18	14.17	14.17	14.17	14.18	14.19	14.22	14.25	14.29	14.34	14.40
Norway	9.75	9.81	9.86	9.91	9.93	9.93	9.94	9.94	9.90	9.84	9.77
Pakistan	15.07	15.06	15.04	14.99	14.93	14.84	14.73	14.61	14.48	14.34	14.21
Peru	13.99	13.92	13.86	13.80	13.73	13.67	13.59	13.51	13.42	13.32	13.22
Philippines	14.42	14.41	14.38	14.35	14.30	14.24	14.17	14.09	13.99	13.89	13.79
Poland	11.98	11.75	11.48	11.20	10.86	10.47	10.08	9.71	9.38	9.09	8.81
Portugal	9.35	9.12	8.90	8.70	8.51	8.35	8.24	8.17	8.13	8.13	8.11
Romania	11.25	10.97	10.66	10.41	10.20	10.04	9.80	9.54	9.22	8.89	8.60
Russia	12.03	11.79	11.49	11.18	10.79	10.35	9.93	9.53	9.11	8.73	8.45
Saudi Arabia	14.56	14.43	14.34	14.27	14.21	14.15	14.10	14.03	13.96	13.87	13.77
Singapore	10.25	10.26	10.25	10.26	10.23	10.21	10.13	10.09	10.00	9.77	9.44
Slovakia	11.97	11.69	11.39	11.09	10.78	10.46	10.15	9.81	9.47	9.17	8.88
Slovenia	9.96	9.69	9.42	9.14	8.88	8.65	8.42	8.23	8.05	7.85	7.66
South Africa	14.84	14.79	14.72	14.62	14.50	14.39	14.27	14.17	14.07	13.99	13.93
South Korea	11.13	10.99	10.82	10.64	10.49	10.37	10.30	10.21	10.08	9.94	9.76
Spain	9.37	9.02	8.71	8.43	8.18	7.99	7.84	7.74	7.68	7.64	7.63
Sweden	9.77	9.82	9.81	9.78	9.72	9.67	9.59	9.51	9.41	9.33	9.23
Switzerland	9.20	9.19	9.17	9.14	9.10	9.05	8.98	8.90	8.80	8.71	8.57
Taiwan	11.69	11.47	11.28	11.08	10.91	10.66	10.48	10.41	10.31	10.17	9.92
Thailand	11.63	11.51	11.43	11.34	11.24	11.11	11.00	10.89	10.81	10.72	10.64
Tunisia	15.01	14.80	14.54	14.24	13.91	13.55	13.18	12.80	12.41	12.04	11.68
Turkey	13.30	13.15	13.03	12.94	12.86	12.80	12.76	12.72	12.66	12.60	12.53
Turkmenistan	15.43	15.40	15.31	15.16	14.96	14.72	14.47	14.21	13.94	13.67	13.40
Ukraine	11.60	11.45	11.25	11.03	10.74	10.34	9.95	9.56	9.14	8.78	8.47
United Arab Emirates	16.67	15.79	15.18	14.84	14.71	14.72	14.79	14.90	15.03	15.16	15.29
United Kingdom	10.30	10.33	10.33	10.33	10.30	10.22	10.11	9.97	9.82	9.67	9.53
USA	10.75	10.67	10.57	10.47	10.36	10.27	10.18	10.12	10.07	10.02	9.97
Venezuela	13.84	13.75	13.65	13.55	13.45	13.33	13.22	13.10	12.97	12.85	12.73
Vietnam	14.91	14.82	14.67	14.46	14.22	13.96	13.70	13.43	13.17	12.90	12.64

Marketing segments: Middle aged generation

Table 4.115 Middle-aged adults (30-59): 2009-2019

'000

	2009	2010	2011	2012	2013	2014	2015	2016	2017	2018	2019	CAGR	Period growth
Algeria	12,100.7	12,542.5	12,989.2	13,438.7	13,888.5	14,335.8	14,778.4	15,213.6	15,638.6	16,050.7	16,446.5	3.12	35.91
Argentina	14,295.6	14,550.8	14,792.7	15,022.5	15,243.6	15,460.9	15,678.6	15,899.1	16,122.8	16,349.2	16,578.1	1.49	15.97
Australia	8,931.2	9,006.1	9,082.6	9,173.0	9,271.9	9,378.6	9,487.0	9,588.5	9,686.3	9,782.4	9,881.0	1.02	10.63
Austria	3,629.6	3,633.9	3,645.7	3,663.8	3,678.6	3,689.4	3,697.2	3,698.3	3,691.1	3,681.6	3,671.4	0.11	1.15
Azerbaijan	3,337.8	3,403.2	3,465.2	3,524.5	3,583.4	3,642.4	3,701.5	3,760.5	3,818.3	3,873.4	3,924.4	1.63	17.57
Belarus	4,217.3	4,213.2	4,224.0	4,232.0	4,246.5	4,273.0	4,281.8	4,288.6	4,297.8	4,295.6	4,287.9	0.17	1.67
Belgium	4,448.3	4,443.8	4,439.9	4,436.8	4,426.1	4,412.4	4,394.9	4,373.8	4,354.8	4,334.0	4,313.2	-0.31	-3.04
Bolivia	2,851.5	2,923.5	2,997.0	3,072.2	3,149.1	3,227.8	3,308.5	3,391.3	3,476.7	3,564.8	3,656.3	2.52	28.23
Bosnia-Herzegovina	1,694.4	1,700.2	1,704.8	1,708.7	1,712.3	1,716.0	1,719.6	1,722.8	1,725.0	1,725.1	1,722.3	0.16	1.65
Brazil	72,514.7	74,079.4	75,723.7	77,370.7	78,987.7	80,604.2	82,143.8	83,531.8	84,822.0	86,007.4	87,081.2	1.85	20.09
Bulgaria	3,232.0	3,218.3	3,195.9	3,187.2	3,173.1	3,156.9	3,140.8	3,119.6	3,100.0	3,080.5	3,061.7	-0.54	-5.27
Canada	14,678.5	14,777.1	14,860.4	14,934.4	15,000.8	15,051.7	15,090.5	15,126.8	15,141.1	15,145.6	15,162.3	0.32	3.30
Chile	6,718.3	6,797.5	6,878.5	6,961.5	7,045.5	7,128.8	7,210.0	7,288.0	7,362.5	7,432.8	7,498.4	1.10	11.61
China	630,030.4	632,687.1	634,836.4	635,485.6	634,496.1	631,162.6	628,412.9	629,872.2	632,517.8	636,950.0	646,064.7	0.25	2.54
Colombia	16,329.3	16,681.5	17,025.2	17,360.7	17,688.6	18,009.8	18,324.8	18,633.5	18,935.6	19,230.6	19,518.1	1.80	19.53
Costa Rica	1,688.5	1,730.8	1,773.3	1,815.5	1,857.3	1,898.7	1,939.7	1,980.4	2,020.8	2,060.2	2,097.9	2.19	24.24
Croatia	1,881.2	1,878.9	1,877.2	1,877.0	1,871.9	1,865.5	1,857.3	1,847.3	1,834.7	1,824.4	1,814.0	-0.36	-3.57
Czech Republic	4,550.2	4,569.5	4,567.5	4,552.1	4,535.8	4,518.4	4,503.2	4,489.4	4,475.8	4,465.7	4,468.6	-0.18	-1.79
Denmark	2,276.1	2,267.5	2,257.6	2,246.1	2,234.0	2,219.1	2,206.5	2,194.5	2,183.1	2,173.0	2,165.2	-0.50	-4.87
Ecuador	4,487.6	4,574.5	4,661.5	4,748.6	4,835.9	4,923.3	5,010.8	5,098.6	5,186.8	5,275.1	5,363.3	1.80	19.51
Egypt	23,851.2	24,402.7	24,957.4	25,511.2	26,059.9	26,600.8	27,132.5	27,652.7	28,161.8	28,664.1	29,147.6	2.03	22.21
Estonia	542.8	540.2	539.1	537.7	536.6	536.9	536.5	535.4	535.0	535.7	536.6	-0.12	-1.15
Finland	2,168.3	2,151.1	2,136.7	2,126.0	2,116.0	2,109.9	2,101.7	2,091.6	2,079.2	2,068.4	2,064.3	-0.49	-4.80
France	25,257.7	25,162.4	25,100.1	25,074.7	25,032.9	24,963.9	24,901.0	24,856.6	24,828.8	24,793.3	24,770.1	-0.19	-1.93
Germany	35,538.9	35,305.8	35,107.4	34,939.6	34,773.2	34,599.6	34,392.8	34,178.5	33,970.1	33,758.1	33,549.3	-0.57	-5.60
Greece	4,867.5	4,916.7	4,951.9	4,983.1	5,010.9	5,034.6	5,043.4	5,037.8	5,025.7	5,007.8	4,991.6	0.25	2.55
Hong Kong, China	3,459.6	3,468.7	3,483.9	3,495.8	3,509.5	3,515.9	3,517.8	3,513.2	3,502.3	3,491.4	3,484.3	0.07	0.71
Hungary	4,321.4	4,328.0	4,321.9	4,312.2	4,295.5	4,258.5	4,207.0	4,170.4	4,141.4	4,127.4	4,118.4	-0.48	-4.70
India	391,867.7	401,070.7	410,121.0	419,023.0	427,830.9	436,632.9	445,512.7	454,520.3	463,675.5	472,985.4	482,439.1	2.10	23.11
Indonesia	86,090.6	88,246.3	90,359.0	92,412.4	94,388.0	96,270.0	98,048.1	99,716.3	101,275.3	102,733.4	104,101.2	1.92	20.92
Iran	25,366.4	26,412.3	27,528.9	28,706.5	29,926.4	31,165.0	32,398.6	33,608.2	34,775.2	35,878.9	36,898.9	3.82	45.46
Ireland	1,823.9	1,870.4	1,916.5	1,959.0	1,999.8	2,036.1	2,069.1	2,100.0	2,127.7	2,151.8	2,173.2	1.77	19.15
Israel	2,577.3	2,617.0	2,652.4	2,687.9	2,727.1	2,768.7	2,809.8	2,851.8	2,894.5	2,936.6	2,977.6	1.45	15.54
Italy	25,922.7	25,908.8	25,876.4	25,859.3	25,838.6	25,790.2	25,697.1	25,585.6	25,445.8	25,293.1	25,152.1	-0.30	-2.97
Japan	51,622.9	50,945.7	50,382.1	49,943.0	49,629.1	49,426.5	49,209.6	49,006.9	48,862.4	48,648.6	48,355.8	-0.65	-6.33
Jordan	1,869.4	1,961.4	2,046.4	2,124.8	2,198.7	2,271.4	2,345.4	2,421.1	2,497.5	2,573.8	2,649.3	3.55	41.72
Kazakhstan	6,078.7	6,168.4	6,254.0	6,338.2	6,427.2	6,524.8	6,632.7	6,748.5	6,869.0	6,989.8	7,105.8	1.57	16.90
Kuwait	1,146.3	1,185.5	1,224.6	1,263.1	1,300.5	1,336.1	1,369.3	1,400.1	1,428.4	1,454.6	1,478.9	2.58	29.02
Latvia	935.4	931.0	929.2	927.0	926.2	928.7	929.2	929.1	930.5	930.8	930.0	-0.06	-0.58
Lithuania	1,392.2	1,387.3	1,383.0	1,379.8	1,377.2	1,380.0	1,383.1	1,384.3	1,386.5	1,385.8	1,380.6	-0.08	-0.83
Malaysia	9,729.0	9,932.6	10,134.1	10,331.4	10,517.6	10,698.3	10,875.7	11,051.8	11,228.0	11,389.5	11,547.9	1.73	18.70
Mexico	39,324.1	40,450.7	41,536.0	42,527.1	43,449.9	44,329.3	45,185.4	46,029.2	46,864.1	47,695.5	48,528.9	2.13	23.41
Morocco	11,011.9	11,293.9	11,586.9	11,888.8	12,193.6	12,493.3	12,780.8	13,052.5	13,308.3	13,550.9	13,784.6	2.27	25.18
Netherlands	7,027.3	6,981.7	6,947.8	6,914.2	6,869.2	6,824.1	6,781.5	6,739.0	6,696.5	6,651.3	6,602.0	-0.62	-6.05
New Zealand	1,743.5	1,749.9	1,758.0	1,766.9	1,777.2	1,785.8	1,793.2	1,798.7	1,802.9	1,808.5	1,812.7	0.39	3.97
Nigeria	37,744.9	38,884.6	40,061.4	41,274.9	42,523.1	43,803.5	45,114.0	46,453.8	47,823.1	49,222.7	50,654.0	2.99	34.20
Norway	1,978.0	1,993.0	2,008.0	2,022.9	2,035.9	2,047.3	2,058.4	2,068.9	2,079.3	2,091.6	2,105.7	0.63	6.45
Pakistan	50,009.3	51,619.3	53,303.3	55,067.0	56,919.0	58,866.8	60,914.5	63,061.4	65,296.7	67,593.9	69,918.2	3.41	39.81
Peru	9,718.1	9,953.4	10,186.8	10,418.7	10,650.3	10,882.8	11,117.0	11,353.2	11,591.0	11,829.7	12,068.0	2.19	24.18
Philippines	28,724.0	29,568.6	30,398.3	31,227.7	32,062.7	32,917.8	33,796.8	34,701.4	35,630.5	36,581.6	37,551.0	2.72	30.73
Poland	16,279.8	16,307.2	16,320.7	16,302.7	16,303.4	16,327.1	16,336.8	16,311.7	16,253.6	16,170.5	16,093.0	-0.12	-1.15
Portugal	4,591.3	4,620.3	4,646.1	4,666.7	4,682.7	4,695.3	4,698.8	4,689.9	4,680.1	4,659.2	4,637.5	0.10	1.01
Romania	9,248.7	9,265.6	9,289.5	9,301.7	9,281.7	9,250.7	9,225.0	9,191.0	9,184.5	9,185.1	9,189.0	-0.06	-0.65
Russia	62,399.9	62,215.7	62,155.9	62,107.8	62,134.5	62,419.1	62,465.3	62,492.0	62,598.6	62,641.0	62,551.6	0.02	0.24
Saudi Arabia	9,063.0	9,369.6	9,663.4	9,945.0	10,218.3	10,489.3	10,763.4	11,044.0	11,331.7	11,625.1	11,921.1	2.78	31.54
Singapore	2,267.3	2,290.1	2,315.8	2,329.4	2,342.1	2,345.2	2,350.3	2,350.9	2,339.6	2,338.8	2,344.9	0.34	3.42
Slovakia	2,375.3	2,397.4	2,409.7	2,416.7	2,422.1	2,426.8	2,429.7	2,430.9	2,428.5	2,424.7	2,423.1	0.20	2.01
Slovenia	914.2	919.5	922.3	924.0	923.0	920.4	917.8	914.2	909.7	906.9	904.6	-0.11	-1.05
South Africa	16,488.7	16,674.0	16,835.3	16,974.9	17,099.6	17,219.2	17,342.0	17,471.1	17,605.9	17,744.9	17,885.2	0.82	8.47
South Korea	22,907.5	23,188.0	23,469.7	23,696.2	23,844.9	23,897.2	23,845.6	23,741.3	23,581.6	23,372.4	23,132.2	0.10	0.98
Spain	20,392.7	20,731.4	21,026.7	21,291.3	21,522.7	21,711.1	21,856.7	21,961.1	22,027.0	22,055.7	22,051.0	0.78	8.13
Sweden	3,643.7	3,635.2	3,634.8	3,636.1	3,637.3	3,635.4	3,638.2	3,643.2	3,650.5	3,659.5	3,678.1	0.09	0.94
Switzerland	3,306.0	3,309.3	3,313.8	3,321.2	3,326.6	3,330.9	3,334.6	3,336.3	3,335.2	3,330.6	3,328.1	0.07	0.67
Taiwan	10,653.8	10,805.9	10,931.7	11,017.7	11,096.5	11,147.0	11,176.0	11,163.2	11,103.0	11,062.8	11,038.4	0.36	3.61
Thailand	29,057.0	29,366.7	29,644.6	29,885.7	30,057.2	30,202.7	30,240.5	30,217.1	30,166.4	30,112.6	29,999.5	0.32	3.24
Tunisia	3,886.6	3,992.1	4,095.4	4,196.5	4,295.7	4,393.6	4,490.4	4,586.0	4,679.8	4,770.8	4,857.8	2.26	24.99
Turkey	28,584.3	29,343.3	30,068.1	30,750.3	31,393.1	31,997.1	32,561.3	33,065.4	33,515.3	33,927.1	34,321.9	1.85	20.07
Turkmenistan	1,724.6	1,771.7	1,818.5	1,865.0	1,911.7	1,959.1	2,007.7	2,057.6	2,108.5	2,160.1	2,211.7	2.52	28.24
Ukraine	19,677.4	19,555.1	19,521.0	19,456.7	19,416.8	19,449.4	19,423.5	19,420.4	19,412.0	19,391.4	19,317.9	-0.18	-1.83
United Arab Emirates	2,420.4	2,535.2	2,634.9	2,718.4	2,788.0	2,847.6	2,901.0	2,950.7	2,998.0	3,043.9	3,089.4	2.47	27.64
United Kingdom	24,755.6	24,752.4	24,789.9	24,855.8	24,948.1	25,082.2	25,249.8	25,430.6	25,597.1	25,754.8	25,904.1	0.45	4.64
USA	125,447.3	125,867.2	126,278.8	126,622.7	126,870.3	126,948.7	126,971.8	127,012.5	126,883.4	126,766.4	126,728.8	0.10	1.02
Venezuela	9,860.8	10,096.0	10,330.4	10,564.6	10,799.8	11,037.7	11,279.1	11,523.7	11,769.6	12,013.2	12,249.8	2.19	24.23
Vietnam	31,536.4	32,457.2	33,343.4	34,198.8	35,037.9	35,882.5	36,746.4	37,631.0	38,526.1	39,419.2	40,291.7	2.48	27.76

Marketing segments: Middle aged generation

Table 4.116 Female middle-aged adults (30-59): 2009-2019

'000

	2009	2010	2011	2012	2013	2014	2015	2016	2017	2018	2019	CAGR	Period growth
Algeria	5,987.0	6,202.4	6,421.3	6,642.7	6,865.1	7,086.8	7,306.3	7,522.2	7,732.9	7,937.0	8,132.9	3.11	35.84
Argentina	7,268.3	7,393.4	7,511.5	7,623.0	7,729.6	7,833.6	7,937.0	8,041.1	8,146.2	8,252.6	8,360.2	1.41	15.02
Australia	4,494.1	4,531.7	4,569.1	4,613.3	4,661.2	4,712.4	4,764.5	4,813.0	4,858.6	4,902.3	4,947.2	0.97	10.08
Austria	1,813.6	1,815.6	1,821.3	1,830.5	1,838.1	1,843.3	1,847.0	1,847.0	1,842.7	1,838.0	1,832.3	0.10	1.03
Azerbaijan	1,763.7	1,798.9	1,831.8	1,862.6	1,892.6	1,922.0	1,951.0	1,979.4	2,006.8	2,032.5	2,055.8	1.54	16.56
Belarus	2,201.5	2,198.7	2,204.3	2,207.7	2,215.3	2,227.5	2,229.8	2,231.2	2,233.1	2,229.1	2,221.7	0.09	0.92
Belgium	2,212.3	2,211.1	2,210.7	2,210.1	2,206.0	2,200.3	2,192.2	2,181.9	2,172.2	2,161.9	2,151.6	-0.28	-2.74
Bolivia	1,457.5	1,493.0	1,529.2	1,566.0	1,603.5	1,641.9	1,681.2	1,721.6	1,763.1	1,806.0	1,850.5	2.42	26.96
Bosnia-Herzegovina	889.8	892.6	894.6	896.1	897.4	898.7	899.8	900.5	900.6	899.5	896.8	0.08	0.78
Brazil	37,360.3	38,150.1	38,971.7	39,791.2	40,592.2	41,389.4	42,144.7	42,821.1	43,445.6	44,014.3	44,523.2	1.77	19.17
Bulgaria	1,626.6	1,617.0	1,602.8	1,596.0	1,586.0	1,575.4	1,564.5	1,550.8	1,538.5	1,526.3	1,514.1	-0.71	-6.92
Canada	7,343.0	7,390.5	7,428.1	7,458.2	7,482.0	7,497.3	7,506.8	7,516.7	7,516.6	7,512.1	7,512.3	0.23	2.31
Chile	3,385.0	3,424.0	3,463.9	3,504.7	3,545.9	3,586.7	3,626.2	3,664.2	3,700.2	3,734.1	3,765.5	1.07	11.24
China	311,234.5	312,624.3	313,484.9	313,688.7	313,165.5	311,539.3	310,006.7	310,808.2	312,046.0	314,275.7	318,807.6	0.24	2.43
Colombia	8,487.0	8,667.8	8,843.7	9,014.6	9,180.9	9,343.3	9,501.9	9,656.8	9,807.7	9,954.4	10,096.7	1.75	18.97
Costa Rica	829.9	850.7	871.6	892.3	912.9	933.2	953.4	973.5	993.4	1,012.8	1,031.4	2.20	24.28
Croatia	944.7	943.0	941.9	942.0	939.4	935.8	931.8	926.5	919.5	913.9	908.2	-0.39	-3.87
Czech Republic	2,261.4	2,269.2	2,266.4	2,256.6	2,247.0	2,236.8	2,227.7	2,219.7	2,211.5	2,205.7	2,206.7	-0.24	-2.42
Denmark	1,128.7	1,125.2	1,121.0	1,116.3	1,111.0	1,104.4	1,098.7	1,093.6	1,088.5	1,084.0	1,080.5	-0.43	-4.26
Ecuador	2,260.1	2,304.7	2,349.3	2,393.8	2,438.4	2,482.9	2,527.4	2,572.0	2,616.8	2,661.5	2,706.2	1.82	19.73
Egypt	11,751.6	12,013.0	12,277.9	12,544.2	12,809.7	13,072.8	13,332.2	13,586.1	13,834.8	14,080.4	14,316.3	1.99	21.82
Estonia	286.3	284.6	283.9	282.8	282.0	282.0	281.6	280.7	280.1	280.0	280.1	-0.22	-2.16
Finland	1,073.0	1,064.8	1,057.7	1,052.4	1,047.2	1,043.9	1,039.2	1,034.0	1,027.7	1,022.1	1,019.8	-0.51	-4.96
France	12,825.5	12,774.8	12,741.6	12,724.7	12,698.8	12,659.5	12,621.8	12,590.6	12,567.4	12,539.2	12,514.9	-0.24	-2.42
Germany	17,528.5	17,409.1	17,304.4	17,214.9	17,123.6	17,029.3	16,919.4	16,810.3	16,705.9	16,599.6	16,496.3	-0.61	-5.89
Greece	2,416.4	2,438.2	2,452.8	2,466.4	2,477.7	2,487.7	2,489.9	2,485.2	2,477.1	2,466.6	2,456.5	0.16	1.66
Hong Kong, China	1,869.2	1,883.5	1,901.0	1,915.5	1,933.9	1,948.7	1,962.8	1,974.9	1,986.2	1,997.4	2,008.7	0.72	7.46
Hungary	2,201.4	2,201.7	2,196.0	2,187.7	2,176.1	2,155.3	2,127.1	2,105.8	2,088.3	2,078.1	2,070.3	-0.61	-5.96
India	189,329.8	193,904.3	198,406.4	202,836.8	207,220.4	211,598.5	216,009.6	220,475.6	225,003.2	229,593.0	234,237.2	2.15	23.72
Indonesia	43,066.3	44,157.4	45,234.0	46,286.8	47,304.3	48,275.7	49,193.0	50,051.6	50,851.3	51,595.9	52,290.9	1.96	21.42
Iran	12,412.1	12,943.3	13,516.3	14,124.5	14,755.3	15,393.0	16,023.0	16,634.2	17,217.4	17,764.3	18,267.0	3.94	47.17
Ireland	903.9	926.1	948.9	970.3	990.8	1,009.1	1,025.3	1,040.4	1,054.3	1,066.1	1,076.5	1.76	19.10
Israel	1,309.4	1,328.3	1,344.8	1,361.1	1,379.0	1,397.9	1,416.6	1,435.6	1,455.2	1,474.6	1,493.2	1.32	14.04
Italy	12,963.6	12,948.2	12,923.7	12,907.2	12,889.4	12,857.6	12,802.5	12,739.6	12,661.2	12,576.5	12,497.9	-0.37	-3.59
Japan	25,700.4	25,361.2	25,079.2	24,859.0	24,696.9	24,592.1	24,478.1	24,370.6	24,296.7	24,188.3	24,042.6	-0.66	-6.45
Jordan	905.3	949.0	989.7	1,027.5	1,063.4	1,099.0	1,135.4	1,172.7	1,210.3	1,248.0	1,285.1	3.57	41.95
Kazakhstan	3,241.4	3,290.4	3,335.9	3,379.5	3,424.5	3,473.0	3,525.9	3,582.1	3,639.8	3,696.9	3,751.1	1.47	15.73
Kuwait	397.2	413.8	430.4	446.7	462.6	477.9	492.4	506.1	519.0	531.1	542.5	3.17	36.60
Latvia	487.6	484.4	482.9	481.1	479.9	480.7	480.4	479.5	479.5	479.1	478.2	-0.19	-1.93
Lithuania	728.0	724.9	722.0	720.0	718.5	719.7	721.1	721.5	721.8	721.0	717.4	-0.15	-1.46
Malaysia	4,798.3	4,905.7	5,011.5	5,114.4	5,212.9	5,308.3	5,401.3	5,493.0	5,583.7	5,668.1	5,749.4	1.82	19.82
Mexico	20,173.2	20,760.2	21,324.8	21,840.2	22,319.6	22,776.2	23,220.7	23,658.6	24,091.2	24,520.9	24,950.1	2.15	23.68
Morocco	5,724.4	5,884.4	6,049.6	6,218.8	6,388.8	6,555.5	6,715.0	6,865.1	7,005.4	7,136.7	7,260.6	2.41	26.84
Netherlands	3,493.9	3,475.1	3,461.6	3,448.6	3,429.0	3,409.0	3,389.8	3,370.3	3,351.4	3,330.1	3,307.0	-0.55	-5.35
New Zealand	900.9	904.9	909.5	914.5	920.0	924.7	928.7	931.7	933.5	935.9	937.3	0.40	4.03
Nigeria	19,063.1	19,618.9	20,191.9	20,782.1	21,388.5	22,009.9	22,645.4	23,294.6	23,957.7	24,635.0	25,327.1	2.88	32.86
Norway	967.2	973.9	980.6	987.8	993.6	998.4	1,003.4	1,008.0	1,012.5	1,018.3	1,025.0	0.58	5.98
Pakistan	24,171.2	24,952.8	25,771.0	26,628.6	27,529.6	28,477.5	29,474.0	30,518.9	31,606.8	32,724.8	33,856.1	3.43	40.07
Peru	4,867.6	4,984.9	5,101.2	5,216.8	5,332.2	5,448.0	5,564.6	5,682.2	5,800.4	5,919.0	6,037.4	2.18	24.03
Philippines	14,395.6	14,817.9	15,228.7	15,635.6	16,042.5	16,458.0	16,885.2	17,325.5	17,778.3	18,242.0	18,714.3	2.66	30.00
Poland	8,230.2	8,239.9	8,243.1	8,229.2	8,224.0	8,231.4	8,230.3	8,212.4	8,177.9	8,129.6	8,085.0	-0.18	-1.77
Portugal	2,328.4	2,341.6	2,353.4	2,362.4	2,368.7	2,373.1	2,373.4	2,367.5	2,361.8	2,350.1	2,338.4	0.04	0.43
Romania	4,661.5	4,664.3	4,671.4	4,674.9	4,661.0	4,641.1	4,623.0	4,600.2	4,591.5	4,587.5	4,586.0	-0.16	-1.62
Russia	32,993.2	32,920.9	32,913.1	32,896.4	32,900.7	33,034.6	33,033.3	33,024.2	33,049.2	33,032.9	32,945.6	-0.01	-0.14
Saudi Arabia	3,514.0	3,664.2	3,811.0	3,954.9	4,098.3	4,244.5	4,396.3	4,554.8	4,719.8	4,890.0	5,063.5	3.72	44.09
Singapore	1,148.3	1,161.2	1,176.0	1,183.6	1,191.3	1,194.6	1,198.4	1,199.9	1,195.4	1,196.0	1,200.4	0.44	4.54
Slovakia	1,193.3	1,203.5	1,208.5	1,211.0	1,212.5	1,214.2	1,215.1	1,214.8	1,212.8	1,210.9	1,209.9	0.14	1.40
Slovenia	446.1	448.0	449.2	449.6	449.0	447.7	446.2	444.2	441.8	439.9	438.5	-0.17	-1.69
South Africa	8,385.5	8,455.8	8,511.9	8,555.3	8,589.3	8,618.7	8,647.6	8,677.9	8,709.6	8,742.7	8,776.5	0.46	4.66
South Korea	11,259.9	11,398.4	11,536.8	11,646.2	11,717.7	11,741.8	11,713.5	11,654.9	11,572.2	11,463.9	11,332.4	0.06	0.64
Spain	10,073.1	10,227.7	10,362.4	10,483.1	10,588.3	10,672.8	10,736.5	10,779.5	10,803.3	10,809.0	10,798.2	0.70	7.20
Sweden	1,796.7	1,792.8	1,793.2	1,794.3	1,795.0	1,794.4	1,795.9	1,798.1	1,802.1	1,806.7	1,815.8	0.11	1.06
Switzerland	1,656.2	1,660.3	1,665.1	1,670.6	1,675.1	1,678.8	1,681.9	1,685.0	1,687.0	1,686.6	1,687.4	0.19	1.88
Taiwan	5,326.6	5,410.2	5,481.0	5,530.7	5,576.6	5,607.2	5,627.9	5,625.4	5,600.7	5,582.6	5,572.0	0.45	4.61
Thailand	15,106.3	15,266.9	15,411.5	15,536.3	15,625.6	15,701.2	15,716.5	15,703.7	15,675.4	15,644.0	15,580.6	0.31	3.14
Tunisia	1,962.4	2,015.2	2,067.1	2,118.0	2,168.0	2,217.1	2,265.2	2,312.3	2,357.8	2,401.3	2,442.1	2.21	24.44
Turkey	14,140.0	14,519.1	14,878.2	15,218.3	15,537.0	15,838.1	16,121.2	16,374.2	16,600.5	16,811.6	17,012.5	1.87	20.31
Turkmenistan	889.1	913.3	937.3	960.9	984.6	1,008.4	1,032.7	1,057.5	1,082.7	1,108.0	1,133.1	2.46	27.45
Ukraine	10,426.4	10,354.8	10,330.6	10,289.4	10,255.4	10,255.7	10,222.8	10,201.3	10,173.9	10,142.4	10,086.2	-0.33	-3.26
United Arab Emirates	598.4	639.7	678.9	715.4	748.6	778.4	804.9	828.2	848.5	866.2	882.3	3.96	47.43
United Kingdom	12,525.3	12,524.2	12,540.7	12,571.1	12,611.1	12,666.7	12,739.1	12,822.1	12,899.0	12,972.5	13,044.3	0.41	4.14
USA	63,063.7	63,230.7	63,395.8	63,512.3	63,566.5	63,541.7	63,502.0	63,468.2	63,357.5	63,264.6	63,213.2	0.02	0.24
Venezuela	4,946.4	5,066.2	5,185.5	5,304.5	5,423.9	5,544.4	5,666.4	5,790.0	5,913.9	6,036.5	6,155.5	2.21	24.44
Vietnam	15,947.9	16,406.5	16,847.5	17,272.7	17,689.0	18,106.9	18,533.0	18,968.1	19,407.0	19,843.7	20,268.9	2.43	27.09

Marketing segments: Middle aged generation

Table 4.117 Male middle-aged adults (30-59): 2009-2019

'000

	2009	2010	2011	2012	2013	2014	2015	2016	2017	2018	2019	CAGR	Period growth
Algeria	6,113.7	6,340.1	6,567.9	6,796.0	7,023.4	7,249.1	7,472.1	7,691.4	7,905.7	8,113.6	8,313.6	3.12	35.98
Argentina	7,027.3	7,157.4	7,281.2	7,399.4	7,513.9	7,627.2	7,741.6	7,858.0	7,976.5	8,096.7	8,217.9	1.58	16.94
Australia	4,437.1	4,474.4	4,513.5	4,559.7	4,610.8	4,666.2	4,722.5	4,775.4	4,827.7	4,880.1	4,933.8	1.07	11.20
Austria	1,815.9	1,818.2	1,824.3	1,833.3	1,840.5	1,846.1	1,850.2	1,851.3	1,848.4	1,843.6	1,839.1	0.13	1.28
Azerbaijan	1,574.1	1,604.3	1,633.4	1,661.9	1,690.8	1,720.4	1,750.6	1,781.1	1,811.5	1,841.0	1,868.6	1.73	18.71
Belarus	2,015.9	2,014.6	2,019.7	2,024.4	2,031.2	2,045.5	2,052.0	2,057.3	2,064.7	2,066.5	2,066.2	0.25	2.50
Belgium	2,236.0	2,232.7	2,229.2	2,226.7	2,220.1	2,212.1	2,202.7	2,191.9	2,182.6	2,172.0	2,161.6	-0.34	-3.33
Bolivia	1,393.9	1,430.4	1,467.9	1,506.2	1,545.6	1,585.9	1,627.3	1,669.8	1,713.6	1,758.9	1,805.9	2.62	29.55
Bosnia-Herzegovina	804.6	807.6	810.2	812.6	814.9	817.3	819.9	822.3	824.3	825.6	825.5	0.26	2.60
Brazil	35,154.5	35,929.3	36,752.0	37,579.5	38,395.6	39,214.9	39,999.1	40,710.7	41,376.5	41,993.1	42,558.0	1.93	21.06
Bulgaria	1,605.4	1,601.3	1,593.1	1,591.2	1,587.1	1,581.5	1,576.3	1,568.7	1,561.5	1,554.2	1,547.6	-0.37	-3.60
Canada	7,335.5	7,386.6	7,432.3	7,476.2	7,518.8	7,554.4	7,583.6	7,610.1	7,624.5	7,633.5	7,650.0	0.42	4.29
Chile	3,333.3	3,373.4	3,414.6	3,456.8	3,499.6	3,542.2	3,583.7	3,623.9	3,662.3	3,698.7	3,732.9	1.14	11.99
China	318,795.9	320,062.9	321,351.6	321,796.9	321,330.6	319,623.3	318,406.2	319,064.0	320,471.7	322,674.3	327,257.0	0.26	2.65
Colombia	7,842.3	8,013.6	8,181.5	8,346.1	8,507.7	8,666.5	8,822.9	8,976.8	9,127.9	9,276.2	9,421.4	1.85	20.14
Costa Rica	858.6	880.2	901.7	923.2	944.4	965.5	986.3	1,006.9	1,027.4	1,047.4	1,066.5	2.19	24.21
Croatia	936.5	935.9	935.3	935.0	932.5	929.7	925.5	920.9	915.2	910.6	905.9	-0.33	-3.27
Czech Republic	2,288.8	2,300.3	2,301.2	2,295.5	2,288.9	2,281.6	2,275.6	2,269.8	2,264.3	2,260.0	2,261.9	-0.12	-1.17
Denmark	1,147.4	1,142.4	1,136.6	1,129.8	1,123.0	1,114.7	1,107.8	1,100.9	1,094.6	1,089.1	1,084.6	-0.56	-5.47
Ecuador	2,227.4	2,269.8	2,312.2	2,354.8	2,397.5	2,440.4	2,483.4	2,526.6	2,570.0	2,613.6	2,657.1	1.78	19.29
Egypt	12,099.6	12,389.8	12,679.5	12,967.0	13,250.1	13,528.0	13,800.3	14,066.6	14,327.0	14,583.7	14,831.4	2.06	22.58
Estonia	256.5	255.6	255.2	254.9	254.5	254.9	254.9	254.7	254.9	255.7	256.5	0.00	-0.01
Finland	1,095.3	1,086.3	1,079.0	1,073.6	1,068.9	1,066.0	1,062.5	1,057.5	1,051.5	1,046.3	1,044.5	-0.47	-4.64
France	12,432.2	12,387.6	12,358.5	12,350.0	12,334.1	12,304.4	12,279.2	12,265.9	12,261.4	12,254.1	12,255.2	-0.14	-1.42
Germany	18,010.4	17,896.7	17,803.0	17,724.7	17,649.6	17,570.3	17,473.4	17,368.2	17,264.2	17,158.4	17,053.1	-0.54	-5.32
Greece	2,451.1	2,478.5	2,499.1	2,516.8	2,533.2	2,546.9	2,553.5	2,552.6	2,548.6	2,541.2	2,535.1	0.34	3.43
Hong Kong, China	1,590.4	1,585.2	1,582.9	1,580.3	1,575.5	1,567.2	1,555.0	1,538.3	1,516.2	1,493.9	1,475.6	-0.75	-7.21
Hungary	2,120.0	2,126.3	2,125.9	2,124.5	2,119.4	2,103.2	2,079.9	2,064.6	2,053.1	2,049.3	2,048.1	-0.34	-3.39
India	202,537.9	207,166.4	211,714.6	216,186.2	220,610.5	225,034.4	229,503.1	234,044.7	238,672.3	243,392.3	248,201.9	2.05	22.55
Indonesia	43,024.3	44,088.9	45,125.0	46,125.6	47,083.6	47,994.4	48,855.1	49,664.7	50,424.0	51,137.6	51,810.2	1.88	20.42
Iran	12,954.3	13,469.0	14,012.6	14,582.0	15,171.2	15,772.0	16,375.6	16,974.0	17,557.7	18,114.6	18,631.9	3.70	43.83
Ireland	920.0	944.3	967.6	988.7	1,009.0	1,027.1	1,043.9	1,059.6	1,073.4	1,085.7	1,096.7	1.77	19.20
Israel	1,267.9	1,288.8	1,307.7	1,326.8	1,348.1	1,370.8	1,393.2	1,416.2	1,439.3	1,462.0	1,484.4	1.59	17.08
Italy	12,959.1	12,960.6	12,952.6	12,952.1	12,949.2	12,932.6	12,894.6	12,846.0	12,784.6	12,716.6	12,654.3	-0.24	-2.35
Japan	25,922.5	25,584.5	25,302.9	25,084.0	24,932.1	24,834.4	24,731.5	24,636.4	24,565.7	24,460.3	24,313.1	-0.64	-6.21
Jordan	964.1	1,012.4	1,056.8	1,097.4	1,135.3	1,172.4	1,210.0	1,248.4	1,287.1	1,325.9	1,364.2	3.53	41.50
Kazakhstan	2,837.3	2,878.0	2,918.1	2,958.7	3,002.7	3,051.8	3,106.8	3,166.4	3,229.2	3,292.8	3,354.7	1.69	18.23
Kuwait	749.1	771.6	794.2	816.4	837.9	858.2	876.9	893.9	909.4	923.4	936.3	2.26	24.99
Latvia	447.8	446.6	446.3	446.0	446.2	448.0	448.8	449.7	451.0	451.7	451.8	0.09	0.89
Lithuania	664.1	662.5	661.0	659.8	658.7	660.3	662.1	662.8	664.6	664.9	663.1	-0.01	-0.15
Malaysia	4,930.7	5,027.0	5,122.6	5,217.0	5,304.7	5,390.1	5,474.4	5,558.8	5,644.2	5,721.3	5,798.5	1.63	17.60
Mexico	19,150.9	19,690.5	20,211.2	20,686.9	21,130.3	21,553.1	21,964.7	22,370.6	22,772.9	23,174.6	23,578.9	2.10	23.12
Morocco	5,287.5	5,409.5	5,537.3	5,670.0	5,804.8	5,937.8	6,065.8	6,187.4	6,302.9	6,414.2	6,524.0	2.12	23.39
Netherlands	3,533.4	3,506.6	3,486.2	3,465.6	3,440.3	3,415.0	3,391.6	3,368.7	3,345.1	3,321.2	3,295.0	-0.70	-6.75
New Zealand	842.6	845.0	848.5	852.4	857.1	861.1	864.5	867.0	869.3	872.7	875.4	0.38	3.90
Nigeria	18,681.9	19,265.7	19,869.5	20,492.8	21,134.6	21,793.6	22,468.6	23,159.1	23,865.3	24,587.7	25,326.9	3.09	35.57
Norway	1,010.9	1,019.1	1,027.5	1,035.1	1,042.3	1,048.8	1,055.0	1,060.9	1,066.8	1,073.3	1,080.7	0.67	6.91
Pakistan	25,838.0	26,666.5	27,532.3	28,438.4	29,389.4	30,389.4	31,440.5	32,542.5	33,689.9	34,869.1	36,062.2	3.39	39.57
Peru	4,850.5	4,968.5	5,085.6	5,201.9	5,318.1	5,434.7	5,552.3	5,671.0	5,790.6	5,910.6	6,030.6	2.20	24.33
Philippines	14,328.4	14,750.7	15,169.5	15,592.1	16,020.2	16,459.8	16,911.6	17,375.9	17,852.2	18,339.6	18,836.7	2.77	31.46
Poland	8,049.5	8,067.3	8,077.6	8,073.6	8,079.4	8,095.7	8,106.5	8,099.3	8,075.7	8,040.9	8,008.1	-0.05	-0.52
Portugal	2,262.9	2,278.8	2,292.7	2,304.2	2,314.0	2,322.2	2,325.4	2,322.4	2,318.3	2,309.1	2,299.1	0.16	1.60
Romania	4,587.2	4,601.3	4,618.1	4,626.8	4,620.7	4,609.6	4,602.0	4,590.8	4,592.9	4,597.6	4,603.0	0.03	0.34
Russia	29,406.7	29,294.8	29,242.9	29,211.4	29,233.8	29,384.5	29,432.0	29,467.8	29,549.4	29,608.1	29,606.0	0.07	0.68
Saudi Arabia	5,549.0	5,705.3	5,852.5	5,990.1	6,120.0	6,244.7	6,367.2	6,489.3	6,611.9	6,735.0	6,857.7	2.14	23.58
Singapore	1,119.1	1,128.9	1,139.9	1,145.8	1,150.8	1,150.6	1,151.9	1,150.9	1,144.2	1,142.7	1,144.5	0.23	2.27
Slovakia	1,182.0	1,193.9	1,201.2	1,205.7	1,209.6	1,212.6	1,214.6	1,216.1	1,215.7	1,213.8	1,213.2	0.26	2.64
Slovenia	468.2	471.5	473.1	474.4	474.0	472.7	471.6	470.0	467.9	467.0	466.1	-0.04	-0.44
South Africa	8,103.2	8,218.2	8,323.3	8,419.6	8,510.3	8,600.5	8,694.3	8,793.2	8,896.3	9,002.2	9,108.7	1.18	12.41
South Korea	11,647.6	11,789.6	11,932.9	12,050.1	12,127.3	12,155.4	12,132.1	12,086.4	12,009.4	11,908.5	11,799.8	0.13	1.31
Spain	10,319.6	10,503.7	10,664.3	10,808.1	10,934.4	11,038.3	11,120.1	11,181.6	11,223.7	11,246.7	11,252.8	0.87	9.04
Sweden	1,847.0	1,842.4	1,841.6	1,841.8	1,842.3	1,841.0	1,842.3	1,845.1	1,848.5	1,852.9	1,862.2	0.08	0.83
Switzerland	1,649.8	1,649.0	1,648.6	1,650.6	1,651.4	1,652.1	1,652.7	1,651.3	1,648.2	1,643.9	1,640.7	-0.06	-0.55
Taiwan	5,327.1	5,395.7	5,450.6	5,487.0	5,519.9	5,539.7	5,548.1	5,537.7	5,502.3	5,480.2	5,466.5	0.26	2.62
Thailand	13,950.7	14,099.8	14,233.1	14,349.4	14,431.6	14,501.4	14,523.9	14,513.3	14,491.0	14,468.7	14,418.9	0.33	3.36
Tunisia	1,924.2	1,976.9	2,028.3	2,078.5	2,127.7	2,176.5	2,225.2	2,273.8	2,322.0	2,369.5	2,415.7	2.30	25.54
Turkey	14,444.3	14,824.2	15,189.8	15,531.9	15,856.1	16,159.0	16,440.0	16,691.1	16,914.8	17,115.5	17,309.4	1.83	19.84
Turkmenistan	835.5	858.4	881.2	904.1	927.2	950.7	975.0	1,000.1	1,025.8	1,052.1	1,078.6	2.59	29.09
Ukraine	9,251.0	9,200.3	9,190.5	9,167.3	9,161.4	9,193.7	9,200.7	9,219.1	9,238.1	9,249.0	9,231.7	-0.02	-0.21
United Arab Emirates	1,822.0	1,895.5	1,955.9	2,003.0	2,039.4	2,069.2	2,096.1	2,122.5	2,149.6	2,177.7	2,207.1	1.94	21.14
United Kingdom	12,230.3	12,228.3	12,249.2	12,284.6	12,337.0	12,415.5	12,510.7	12,608.6	12,698.1	12,782.3	12,859.7	0.50	5.15
USA	62,383.6	62,636.6	62,883.0	63,110.4	63,303.8	63,407.0	63,469.8	63,544.4	63,525.9	63,501.8	63,515.6	0.18	1.81
Venezuela	4,914.4	5,029.8	5,144.9	5,260.1	5,376.0	5,493.3	5,612.6	5,733.7	5,855.7	5,976.6	6,094.3	2.18	24.01
Vietnam	15,588.5	16,050.7	16,495.9	16,926.1	17,348.9	17,775.6	18,213.4	18,662.9	19,119.1	19,575.5	20,022.8	2.53	28.45

Marketing segments: Middle aged generation

Table 4.118 Middle-aged adults (30-59): 2009-2019 (%)

% of total

	2009	2010	2011	2012	2013	2014	2015	2016	2017	2018	2019
Algeria	34.7	35.4	36.1	36.8	37.5	38.2	38.8	39.4	40.0	40.5	41.0
Argentina	35.4	35.7	36.0	36.2	36.4	36.6	36.7	36.9	37.1	37.3	37.6
Australia	41.0	40.8	40.6	40.4	40.3	40.2	40.1	40.0	39.9	39.8	39.6
Austria	43.3	43.2	43.2	43.3	43.4	43.4	43.3	43.2	43.1	42.8	42.6
Azerbaijan	38.2	38.5	38.8	39.1	39.3	39.6	39.8	40.1	40.3	40.6	40.8
Belarus	43.6	43.6	43.9	44.1	44.4	44.8	45.0	45.2	45.4	45.6	45.6
Belgium	41.7	41.5	41.4	41.2	40.9	40.7	40.4	40.1	39.8	39.5	39.2
Bolivia	28.9	29.1	29.4	29.6	29.9	30.2	30.5	30.8	31.1	31.5	31.8
Bosnia-Herzegovina	44.1	44.2	44.4	44.5	44.6	44.7	44.8	44.9	45.1	45.1	45.1
Brazil	37.4	37.9	38.4	39.0	39.5	40.0	40.5	40.9	41.3	41.6	41.9
Bulgaria	43.0	43.1	43.1	43.3	43.4	43.5	43.7	43.7	43.8	44.0	44.1
Canada	43.6	43.5	43.4	43.3	43.2	43.0	42.8	42.6	42.3	42.0	41.7
Chile	39.6	39.7	39.8	39.9	40.0	40.1	40.2	40.3	40.4	40.5	40.5
China	47.4	47.4	47.4	47.2	47.0	46.5	46.1	46.1	46.1	46.3	46.8
Colombia	35.8	36.0	36.3	36.5	36.7	36.9	37.1	37.3	37.4	37.6	37.7
Costa Rica	36.9	37.3	37.7	38.1	38.4	38.8	39.1	39.5	39.8	40.1	40.4
Croatia	42.5	42.5	42.5	42.6	42.6	42.6	42.5	42.3	42.2	42.0	41.9
Czech Republic	44.0	44.1	44.1	43.9	43.8	43.6	43.5	43.3	43.2	43.1	43.2
Denmark	41.3	41.0	40.7	40.4	40.1	39.7	39.4	39.1	38.8	38.5	38.2
Ecuador	32.9	33.2	33.5	33.7	33.9	34.1	34.3	34.5	34.8	35.0	35.2
Egypt	31.1	31.2	31.4	31.5	31.6	31.8	31.9	32.0	32.1	32.2	32.2
Estonia	40.8	40.7	40.8	40.8	40.9	41.1	41.2	41.3	41.4	41.5	41.7
Finland	40.7	40.2	39.8	39.5	39.1	38.9	38.6	38.3	38.0	37.7	37.5
France	40.4	40.1	39.8	39.6	39.3	39.1	38.8	38.6	38.4	38.2	38.0
Germany	43.3	43.2	43.1	43.1	43.0	42.9	42.8	42.7	42.5	42.4	42.3
Greece	43.3	43.5	43.7	43.9	44.0	44.1	44.1	44.0	43.8	43.6	43.4
Hong Kong, China	49.0	48.6	48.4	48.2	47.9	47.6	47.3	46.8	46.3	45.8	45.4
Hungary	43.1	43.3	43.3	43.3	43.3	43.0	42.6	42.4	42.2	42.1	42.2
India	33.5	33.9	34.2	34.4	34.7	35.0	35.3	35.6	35.9	36.2	36.5
Indonesia	37.4	38.0	38.5	38.9	39.4	39.8	40.2	40.5	40.8	41.0	41.3
Iran	34.2	35.2	36.2	37.4	38.5	39.7	40.8	41.8	42.8	43.7	44.5
Ireland	41.0	41.5	42.0	42.5	42.9	43.2	43.4	43.6	43.8	43.8	43.9
Israel	34.8	34.8	34.8	34.7	34.7	34.8	34.8	34.9	35.0	35.1	35.2
Italy	43.9	43.8	43.7	43.7	43.6	43.5	43.4	43.2	43.0	42.8	42.6
Japan	40.5	40.0	39.6	39.4	39.2	39.2	39.1	39.1	39.1	39.1	39.0
Jordan	29.6	30.3	31.0	31.7	32.4	33.1	33.7	34.3	34.8	35.3	35.8
Kazakhstan	38.5	38.6	38.6	38.7	38.8	38.9	39.1	39.3	39.6	39.9	40.1
Kuwait	46.9	47.4	48.0	48.5	48.9	49.2	49.5	49.7	49.8	49.8	49.8
Latvia	41.5	41.6	41.7	41.9	42.1	42.5	42.8	43.0	43.4	43.6	43.8
Lithuania	41.6	41.7	41.8	41.9	42.1	42.4	42.8	43.0	43.3	43.6	43.6
Malaysia	34.6	34.8	34.9	35.1	35.2	35.3	35.4	35.5	35.6	35.6	35.7
Mexico	36.2	36.7	37.2	37.5	37.9	38.2	38.4	38.7	39.0	39.3	39.5
Morocco	34.4	34.9	35.4	35.9	36.3	36.8	37.2	37.6	37.9	38.2	38.5
Netherlands	42.8	42.5	42.2	41.9	41.6	41.2	40.9	40.6	40.2	39.9	39.5
New Zealand	40.4	40.2	40.0	39.8	39.7	39.6	39.4	39.2	39.0	38.8	38.6
Nigeria	24.4	24.6	24.8	25.0	25.2	25.4	25.6	25.9	26.1	26.4	26.7
Norway	41.2	41.0	40.9	40.8	40.6	40.5	40.3	40.1	40.0	39.8	39.7
Pakistan	27.7	27.9	28.2	28.5	28.9	29.2	29.6	30.1	30.5	31.0	31.5
Peru	33.5	33.9	34.2	34.5	34.8	35.2	35.5	35.8	36.1	36.5	36.8
Philippines	31.2	31.5	31.8	32.0	32.3	32.6	32.8	33.1	33.4	33.7	34.0
Poland	42.9	43.0	43.1	43.1	43.2	43.3	43.4	43.4	43.3	43.2	43.0
Portugal	43.0	43.2	43.4	43.5	43.5	43.6	43.6	43.5	43.4	43.1	42.9
Romania	43.1	43.4	43.6	43.8	43.9	43.9	44.0	44.1	44.3	44.5	44.8
Russia	44.0	43.9	43.9	44.0	44.1	44.4	44.5	44.5	44.7	44.8	44.8
Saudi Arabia	35.2	35.7	36.1	36.4	36.7	36.9	37.2	37.5	37.8	38.1	38.4
Singapore	48.2	48.0	47.9	47.6	47.3	46.9	46.5	46.1	45.4	45.0	44.8
Slovakia	44.0	44.4	44.6	44.8	44.9	45.0	45.0	45.0	45.0	44.9	44.9
Slovenia	45.2	45.3	45.3	45.3	45.2	45.0	44.8	44.6	44.3	44.1	43.9
South Africa	32.9	33.0	33.1	33.2	33.3	33.4	33.6	33.7	33.8	34.0	34.1
South Korea	47.0	47.4	47.9	48.3	48.5	48.5	48.4	48.1	47.8	47.4	46.9
Spain	44.8	45.1	45.4	45.6	45.8	45.8	45.8	45.7	45.5	45.3	45.0
Sweden	39.6	39.3	39.1	39.0	38.8	38.6	38.4	38.3	38.2	38.1	38.1
Switzerland	43.7	43.6	43.5	43.4	43.3	43.2	43.1	43.0	42.8	42.6	42.4
Taiwan	46.3	46.8	47.2	47.4	47.7	47.8	47.8	47.7	47.4	47.2	47.0
Thailand	44.9	45.1	45.3	45.4	45.4	45.4	45.3	45.1	44.8	44.6	44.3
Tunisia	37.8	38.5	39.1	39.7	40.2	40.7	41.3	41.8	42.2	42.7	43.1
Turkey	38.0	38.5	39.0	39.5	39.9	40.2	40.5	40.7	40.9	41.0	41.1
Turkmenistan	33.7	34.2	34.7	35.1	35.6	36.0	36.4	36.9	37.4	37.9	38.4
Ukraine	42.9	42.8	43.0	43.2	43.4	43.7	44.0	44.2	44.5	44.8	44.9
United Arab Emirates	52.4	53.7	54.6	55.1	55.5	55.6	55.6	55.6	55.5	55.4	55.3
United Kingdom	40.2	39.9	39.8	39.7	39.6	39.6	39.6	39.7	39.7	39.7	39.7
USA	40.9	40.8	40.6	40.5	40.3	40.0	39.7	39.5	39.2	38.9	38.6
Venezuela	34.5	34.8	35.0	35.3	35.5	35.8	36.0	36.3	36.6	36.9	37.1
Vietnam	36.0	36.6	37.1	37.6	38.0	38.5	38.9	39.4	39.9	40.4	40.8

Marketing segments: Middle aged generation

Table 4.119 Female middle-aged adults (30-59): 2009-2019 (%)

% of total

	2009	2010	2011	2012	2013	2014	2015	2016	2017	2018	2019
Algeria	17.2	17.5	17.9	18.2	18.5	18.9	19.2	19.5	19.8	20.0	20.3
Argentina	18.0	18.1	18.3	18.4	18.4	18.5	18.6	18.7	18.8	18.8	18.9
Australia	20.6	20.5	20.4	20.3	20.3	20.2	20.2	20.1	20.0	19.9	19.8
Austria	21.6	21.6	21.6	21.6	21.7	21.7	21.7	21.6	21.5	21.4	21.3
Azerbaijan	20.2	20.4	20.5	20.7	20.8	20.9	21.0	21.1	21.2	21.3	21.4
Belarus	22.8	22.8	22.9	23.0	23.1	23.3	23.4	23.5	23.6	23.6	23.6
Belgium	20.8	20.7	20.6	20.5	20.4	20.3	20.2	20.0	19.8	19.7	19.5
Bolivia	14.8	14.9	15.0	15.1	15.2	15.4	15.5	15.6	15.8	15.9	16.1
Bosnia-Herzegovina	23.1	23.2	23.3	23.3	23.4	23.4	23.4	23.5	23.5	23.5	23.5
Brazil	19.3	19.5	19.8	20.0	20.3	20.5	20.8	21.0	21.1	21.3	21.4
Bulgaria	21.6	21.7	21.6	21.7	21.7	21.7	21.8	21.7	21.8	21.8	21.8
Canada	21.8	21.8	21.7	21.6	21.5	21.4	21.3	21.1	21.0	20.8	20.7
Chile	19.9	20.0	20.0	20.1	20.1	20.2	20.2	20.3	20.3	20.3	20.4
China	23.4	23.4	23.4	23.3	23.2	23.0	22.8	22.7	22.8	22.8	23.1
Colombia	18.6	18.7	18.8	19.0	19.1	19.2	19.2	19.3	19.4	19.5	19.5
Costa Rica	18.1	18.3	18.5	18.7	18.9	19.1	19.2	19.4	19.6	19.7	19.9
Croatia	21.3	21.3	21.3	21.4	21.4	21.3	21.3	21.2	21.1	21.1	21.0
Czech Republic	21.9	21.9	21.9	21.8	21.7	21.6	21.5	21.4	21.4	21.3	21.3
Denmark	20.5	20.4	20.2	20.1	19.9	19.8	19.6	19.5	19.3	19.2	19.1
Ecuador	16.6	16.7	16.9	17.0	17.1	17.2	17.3	17.4	17.5	17.7	17.8
Egypt	15.3	15.4	15.4	15.5	15.6	15.6	15.7	15.7	15.8	15.8	15.8
Estonia	21.5	21.5	21.5	21.5	21.5	21.6	21.6	21.6	21.7	21.7	21.8
Finland	20.1	19.9	19.7	19.5	19.4	19.2	19.1	18.9	18.8	18.6	18.5
France	20.5	20.4	20.2	20.1	20.0	19.8	19.7	19.5	19.4	19.3	19.2
Germany	21.4	21.3	21.3	21.2	21.2	21.1	21.1	21.0	20.9	20.9	20.8
Greece	21.5	21.6	21.7	21.7	21.8	21.8	21.8	21.7	21.6	21.5	21.4
Hong Kong, China	26.5	26.4	26.4	26.4	26.4	26.4	26.4	26.3	26.3	26.2	26.2
Hungary	22.0	22.0	22.0	22.0	21.9	21.8	21.6	21.4	21.3	21.2	21.2
India	16.2	16.4	16.5	16.7	16.8	17.0	17.1	17.3	17.4	17.6	17.7
Indonesia	18.7	19.0	19.2	19.5	19.7	19.9	20.1	20.3	20.5	20.6	20.7
Iran	16.7	17.2	17.8	18.4	19.0	19.6	20.2	20.7	21.2	21.6	22.0
Ireland	20.3	20.5	20.8	21.0	21.2	21.4	21.5	21.6	21.7	21.7	21.7
Israel	17.7	17.7	17.6	17.6	17.6	17.6	17.6	17.6	17.6	17.6	17.6
Italy	22.0	21.9	21.8	21.8	21.8	21.7	21.6	21.5	21.4	21.3	21.2
Japan	20.1	19.9	19.7	19.6	19.5	19.5	19.5	19.4	19.4	19.4	19.4
Jordan	14.3	14.7	15.0	15.3	15.7	16.0	16.3	16.6	16.9	17.1	17.4
Kazakhstan	20.5	20.6	20.6	20.6	20.6	20.7	20.8	20.9	21.0	21.1	21.2
Kuwait	16.2	16.6	16.9	17.1	17.4	17.6	17.8	18.0	18.1	18.2	18.3
Latvia	21.6	21.6	21.7	21.7	21.8	22.0	22.1	22.2	22.3	22.5	22.5
Lithuania	21.7	21.8	21.8	21.9	22.0	22.1	22.3	22.4	22.6	22.7	22.7
Malaysia	17.1	17.2	17.3	17.4	17.4	17.5	17.6	17.6	17.7	17.7	17.8
Mexico	18.6	18.8	19.1	19.3	19.4	19.6	19.8	19.9	20.0	20.2	20.3
Morocco	17.9	18.2	18.5	18.8	19.0	19.3	19.6	19.8	20.0	20.1	20.3
Netherlands	21.3	21.1	21.0	20.9	20.7	20.6	20.4	20.3	20.1	20.0	19.8
New Zealand	20.9	20.8	20.7	20.6	20.6	20.5	20.4	20.3	20.2	20.1	19.9
Nigeria	12.3	12.4	12.5	12.6	12.7	12.8	12.9	13.0	13.1	13.2	13.3
Norway	20.2	20.0	20.0	19.9	19.8	19.7	19.6	19.5	19.5	19.4	19.3
Pakistan	13.4	13.5	13.7	13.8	14.0	14.1	14.3	14.6	14.8	15.0	15.2
Peru	16.8	17.0	17.1	17.3	17.4	17.6	17.8	17.9	18.1	18.2	18.4
Philippines	15.6	15.8	15.9	16.0	16.2	16.3	16.4	16.5	16.7	16.8	17.0
Poland	21.7	21.7	21.8	21.8	21.8	21.8	21.9	21.9	21.8	21.7	21.6
Portugal	21.8	21.9	22.0	22.0	22.0	22.0	22.0	21.9	21.9	21.8	21.7
Romania	21.7	21.8	21.9	22.0	22.0	22.0	22.1	22.1	22.1	22.2	22.4
Russia	23.3	23.2	23.3	23.3	23.3	23.5	23.5	23.5	23.6	23.6	23.6
Saudi Arabia	13.7	14.0	14.2	14.5	14.7	14.9	15.2	15.5	15.7	16.0	16.3
Singapore	24.4	24.3	24.3	24.2	24.1	23.9	23.7	23.5	23.2	23.0	22.9
Slovakia	22.1	22.3	22.4	22.4	22.5	22.5	22.5	22.5	22.5	22.4	22.4
Slovenia	22.1	22.1	22.1	22.1	22.0	21.9	21.8	21.7	21.5	21.4	21.3
South Africa	16.7	16.7	16.8	16.8	16.7	16.7	16.7	16.7	16.7	16.7	16.7
South Korea	23.1	23.3	23.5	23.7	23.8	23.9	23.8	23.6	23.5	23.2	23.0
Spain	22.1	22.3	22.4	22.5	22.5	22.5	22.5	22.4	22.3	22.2	22.0
Sweden	19.5	19.4	19.3	19.2	19.1	19.0	19.0	18.9	18.8	18.8	18.8
Switzerland	21.9	21.9	21.9	21.8	21.8	21.8	21.8	21.7	21.7	21.6	21.5
Taiwan	23.1	23.4	23.7	23.8	23.9	24.0	24.1	24.0	23.9	23.8	23.7
Thailand	23.3	23.4	23.5	23.6	23.6	23.6	23.5	23.4	23.3	23.2	23.0
Tunisia	19.1	19.4	19.7	20.0	20.3	20.6	20.8	21.1	21.3	21.5	21.7
Turkey	18.8	19.1	19.3	19.5	19.7	19.9	20.0	20.2	20.2	20.3	20.4
Turkmenistan	17.4	17.6	17.9	18.1	18.3	18.5	18.7	19.0	19.2	19.4	19.7
Ukraine	22.7	22.7	22.8	22.8	22.9	23.1	23.1	23.2	23.3	23.4	23.5
United Arab Emirates	13.0	13.5	14.1	14.5	14.9	15.2	15.4	15.6	15.7	15.8	15.8
United Kingdom	20.3	20.2	20.1	20.1	20.0	20.0	20.0	20.0	20.0	20.0	20.0
USA	20.6	20.5	20.4	20.3	20.2	20.0	19.9	19.7	19.6	19.4	19.3
Venezuela	17.3	17.4	17.6	17.7	17.8	18.0	18.1	18.2	18.4	18.5	18.7
Vietnam	18.2	18.5	18.7	19.0	19.2	19.4	19.6	19.9	20.1	20.3	20.5

Marketing segments: Middle aged generation

Table 4.120 Male middle-aged adults (30-59): 2009-2019 (%)

% of total

	2009	2010	2011	2012	2013	2014	2015	2016	2017	2018	2019
Algeria	17.5	17.9	18.3	18.6	19.0	19.3	19.6	19.9	20.2	20.5	20.7
Argentina	17.4	17.6	17.7	17.8	17.9	18.0	18.1	18.3	18.4	18.5	18.6
Australia	20.4	20.2	20.2	20.1	20.1	20.0	20.0	19.9	19.9	19.8	19.8
Austria	21.7	21.6	21.6	21.7	21.7	21.7	21.7	21.6	21.6	21.5	21.3
Azerbaijan	18.0	18.2	18.3	18.4	18.6	18.7	18.8	19.0	19.1	19.3	19.4
Belarus	20.8	20.9	21.0	21.1	21.2	21.4	21.6	21.7	21.8	21.9	22.0
Belgium	21.0	20.9	20.8	20.7	20.5	20.4	20.2	20.1	19.9	19.8	19.6
Bolivia	14.1	14.3	14.4	14.5	14.7	14.8	15.0	15.2	15.3	15.5	15.7
Bosnia-Herzegovina	20.9	21.0	21.1	21.1	21.2	21.3	21.4	21.5	21.5	21.6	21.6
Brazil	18.1	18.4	18.7	18.9	19.2	19.5	19.7	19.9	20.1	20.3	20.5
Bulgaria	21.4	21.4	21.5	21.6	21.7	21.8	21.9	22.0	22.1	22.2	22.3
Canada	21.8	21.7	21.7	21.7	21.6	21.6	21.5	21.4	21.3	21.2	21.1
Chile	19.6	19.7	19.7	19.8	19.9	19.9	20.0	20.0	20.1	20.1	20.2
China	24.0	24.0	24.0	23.9	23.8	23.6	23.4	23.3	23.4	23.5	23.7
Colombia	17.2	17.3	17.4	17.5	17.7	17.8	17.9	18.0	18.1	18.1	18.2
Costa Rica	18.8	19.0	19.2	19.4	19.6	19.7	19.9	20.1	20.2	20.4	20.5
Croatia	21.1	21.2	21.2	21.2	21.2	21.2	21.2	21.1	21.0	21.0	20.9
Czech Republic	22.1	22.2	22.2	22.1	22.1	22.0	22.0	21.9	21.9	21.8	21.8
Denmark	20.8	20.7	20.5	20.3	20.2	20.0	19.8	19.6	19.4	19.3	19.1
Ecuador	16.3	16.5	16.6	16.7	16.8	16.9	17.0	17.1	17.2	17.3	17.5
Egypt	15.8	15.9	15.9	16.0	16.1	16.2	16.2	16.3	16.3	16.4	16.4
Estonia	19.3	19.3	19.3	19.4	19.4	19.5	19.6	19.6	19.7	19.8	20.0
Finland	20.6	20.3	20.1	19.9	19.8	19.6	19.5	19.4	19.2	19.1	19.0
France	19.9	19.7	19.6	19.5	19.4	19.3	19.1	19.0	19.0	18.9	18.8
Germany	22.0	21.9	21.9	21.8	21.8	21.8	21.7	21.7	21.6	21.6	21.5
Greece	21.8	22.0	22.1	22.2	22.2	22.3	22.3	22.3	22.2	22.1	22.1
Hong Kong, China	22.5	22.2	22.0	21.8	21.5	21.2	20.9	20.5	20.1	19.6	19.2
Hungary	21.2	21.3	21.3	21.3	21.4	21.2	21.1	21.0	20.9	20.9	21.0
India	17.3	17.5	17.6	17.8	17.9	18.0	18.2	18.3	18.5	18.6	18.8
Indonesia	18.7	19.0	19.2	19.4	19.6	19.8	20.0	20.2	20.3	20.4	20.5
Iran	17.5	17.9	18.4	19.0	19.5	20.1	20.6	21.1	21.6	22.1	22.5
Ireland	20.7	21.0	21.2	21.4	21.6	21.8	21.9	22.0	22.1	22.1	22.1
Israel	17.1	17.1	17.1	17.1	17.2	17.2	17.3	17.3	17.4	17.5	17.5
Italy	21.9	21.9	21.9	21.9	21.9	21.8	21.8	21.7	21.6	21.5	21.4
Japan	20.3	20.1	19.9	19.8	19.7	19.7	19.7	19.6	19.7	19.6	19.6
Jordan	15.3	15.6	16.0	16.4	16.7	17.1	17.4	17.7	18.0	18.2	18.4
Kazakhstan	18.0	18.0	18.0	18.1	18.1	18.2	18.3	18.4	18.6	18.8	19.0
Kuwait	30.6	30.9	31.1	31.3	31.5	31.6	31.7	31.7	31.7	31.6	31.5
Latvia	19.9	19.9	20.0	20.1	20.3	20.5	20.7	20.8	21.0	21.2	21.3
Lithuania	19.8	19.9	20.0	20.0	20.1	20.3	20.5	20.6	20.8	20.9	21.0
Malaysia	17.5	17.6	17.7	17.7	17.8	17.8	17.8	17.8	17.9	17.9	17.9
Mexico	17.6	17.9	18.1	18.3	18.4	18.6	18.7	18.8	18.9	19.1	19.2
Morocco	16.5	16.7	16.9	17.1	17.3	17.5	17.7	17.8	18.0	18.1	18.2
Netherlands	21.5	21.3	21.2	21.0	20.8	20.6	20.4	20.3	20.1	19.9	19.7
New Zealand	19.5	19.4	19.3	19.2	19.2	19.1	19.0	18.9	18.8	18.7	18.6
Nigeria	12.1	12.2	12.3	12.4	12.5	12.6	12.8	12.9	13.0	13.2	13.3
Norway	21.1	21.0	20.9	20.9	20.8	20.7	20.7	20.6	20.5	20.4	20.4
Pakistan	14.3	14.4	14.6	14.7	14.9	15.1	15.3	15.5	15.8	16.0	16.2
Peru	16.7	16.9	17.1	17.2	17.4	17.6	17.7	17.9	18.1	18.2	18.4
Philippines	15.6	15.7	15.8	16.0	16.1	16.3	16.4	16.6	16.8	16.9	17.1
Poland	21.2	21.3	21.3	21.4	21.4	21.5	21.5	21.6	21.5	21.5	21.4
Portugal	21.2	21.3	21.4	21.5	21.5	21.6	21.6	21.5	21.5	21.4	21.3
Romania	21.4	21.5	21.7	21.8	21.9	21.9	22.0	22.0	22.2	22.3	22.4
Russia	20.7	20.7	20.7	20.7	20.7	20.9	20.9	21.0	21.1	21.2	21.2
Saudi Arabia	21.6	21.7	21.9	21.9	22.0	22.0	22.0	22.0	22.0	22.0	22.1
Singapore	23.8	23.7	23.6	23.4	23.2	23.0	22.8	22.6	22.2	22.0	21.9
Slovakia	21.9	22.1	22.3	22.3	22.4	22.5	22.5	22.5	22.5	22.5	22.5
Slovenia	23.1	23.2	23.2	23.3	23.2	23.1	23.0	22.9	22.8	22.7	22.6
South Africa	16.2	16.3	16.4	16.5	16.6	16.7	16.8	16.9	17.1	17.2	17.4
South Korea	23.9	24.1	24.4	24.6	24.7	24.7	24.6	24.5	24.3	24.1	23.9
Spain	22.7	22.9	23.0	23.2	23.2	23.3	23.3	23.3	23.2	23.1	23.0
Sweden	20.1	19.9	19.8	19.7	19.6	19.5	19.5	19.4	19.3	19.3	19.3
Switzerland	21.8	21.7	21.6	21.6	21.5	21.4	21.4	21.3	21.2	21.0	20.9
Taiwan	23.1	23.4	23.5	23.6	23.7	23.7	23.7	23.7	23.5	23.4	23.3
Thailand	21.6	21.7	21.7	21.8	21.8	21.8	21.8	21.6	21.5	21.4	21.3
Tunisia	18.7	19.1	19.4	19.6	19.9	20.2	20.4	20.7	21.0	21.2	21.4
Turkey	19.2	19.5	19.7	19.9	20.1	20.3	20.4	20.5	20.6	20.7	20.7
Turkmenistan	16.4	16.6	16.8	17.0	17.2	17.5	17.7	17.9	18.2	18.5	18.7
Ukraine	20.1	20.2	20.3	20.3	20.5	20.7	20.8	21.0	21.2	21.4	21.5
United Arab Emirates	39.5	40.1	40.5	40.6	40.6	40.4	40.2	40.0	39.8	39.6	39.5
United Kingdom	19.9	19.7	19.7	19.6	19.6	19.6	19.6	19.7	19.7	19.7	19.7
USA	20.3	20.3	20.2	20.2	20.1	20.0	19.9	19.8	19.6	19.5	19.4
Venezuela	17.2	17.3	17.4	17.6	17.7	17.8	17.9	18.1	18.2	18.3	18.5
Vietnam	17.8	18.1	18.4	18.6	18.8	19.1	19.3	19.5	19.8	20.0	20.3

Marketing segments: Middle aged generation

Table 4.121 Baby boomers (40-59): 2009-2019

'000

	2009	2010	2011	2012	2013	2014	2015	2016	2017	2018	2019	CAGR	Period growth
Algeria	6,530.3	6,793.1	7,052.1	7,308.8	7,566.4	7,829.6	8,102.0	8,385.5	8,680.2	8,985.2	9,299.2	3.60	42.40
Argentina	8,483.6	8,583.4	8,688.0	8,801.4	8,928.5	9,074.0	9,240.4	9,427.7	9,632.2	9,846.2	10,063.6	1.72	18.62
Australia	5,839.8	5,901.6	5,974.2	6,046.9	6,104.8	6,159.7	6,205.9	6,242.8	6,279.2	6,314.4	6,350.9	0.84	8.75
Austria	2,463.1	2,497.0	2,524.0	2,550.5	2,568.7	2,579.2	2,586.7	2,586.3	2,574.4	2,559.7	2,543.4	0.32	3.26
Azerbaijan	2,152.5	2,207.1	2,252.0	2,287.5	2,315.2	2,335.5	2,349.2	2,357.0	2,359.7	2,358.9	2,356.3	0.91	9.47
Belarus	2,847.2	2,828.9	2,825.3	2,818.4	2,813.4	2,805.2	2,786.1	2,766.9	2,743.5	2,719.5	2,693.6	-0.55	-5.39
Belgium	3,031.0	3,040.4	3,049.7	3,058.5	3,058.5	3,052.7	3,039.5	3,019.4	2,999.8	2,979.2	2,957.4	-0.25	-2.43
Bolivia	1,563.3	1,608.4	1,655.8	1,705.1	1,755.8	1,807.1	1,858.3	1,909.3	1,960.1	2,011.0	2,062.7	2.81	31.94
Bosnia-Herzegovina	1,142.5	1,147.8	1,150.5	1,151.0	1,149.9	1,147.7	1,144.6	1,140.7	1,136.3	1,131.6	1,126.9	-0.14	-1.37
Brazil	43,149.4	44,204.5	45,219.3	46,195.7	47,136.0	48,046.6	48,936.7	49,816.6	50,697.9	51,589.4	52,494.6	1.98	21.66
Bulgaria	2,103.3	2,092.4	2,075.0	2,069.5	2,058.4	2,053.7	2,058.1	2,057.2	2,056.9	2,059.2	2,059.5	-0.21	-2.08
Canada	10,036.0	10,102.7	10,153.2	10,178.4	10,183.0	10,165.2	10,145.0	10,126.0	10,095.3	10,057.0	10,026.7	-0.01	-0.09
Chile	4,305.4	4,392.4	4,474.8	4,551.2	4,619.4	4,676.4	4,720.5	4,751.2	4,770.0	4,779.5	4,783.5	1.06	11.10
China	425,570.0	439,381.6	449,728.8	455,617.2	460,749.8	461,979.1	461,491.0	461,139.3	456,622.9	455,069.2	456,397.3	0.70	7.24
Colombia	9,717.0	9,977.1	10,215.7	10,435.8	10,643.4	10,846.1	11,049.8	11,257.4	11,468.4	11,680.1	11,888.4	2.04	22.35
Costa Rica	1,028.8	1,056.6	1,081.8	1,104.5	1,125.4	1,145.2	1,164.7	1,184.4	1,204.6	1,225.3	1,246.4	1.94	21.14
Croatia	1,282.3	1,274.9	1,265.4	1,261.5	1,253.1	1,244.4	1,233.4	1,223.7	1,214.4	1,209.3	1,204.6	-0.62	-6.06
Czech Republic	2,843.2	2,828.6	2,815.7	2,805.8	2,806.5	2,828.1	2,864.3	2,900.8	2,936.9	2,974.2	3,019.4	0.60	6.20
Denmark	1,527.8	1,528.1	1,528.6	1,534.5	1,540.4	1,541.7	1,544.2	1,546.5	1,542.3	1,536.2	1,530.1	0.02	0.15
Ecuador	2,602.9	2,667.9	2,730.7	2,791.4	2,850.6	2,908.8	2,966.5	3,024.2	3,082.2	3,140.3	3,198.4	2.08	22.88
Egypt	13,854.4	14,047.3	14,249.2	14,460.3	14,682.9	14,918.4	15,167.4	15,430.5	15,709.7	16,005.5	16,321.4	1.65	17.81
Estonia	358.1	355.6	354.6	353.2	351.4	349.5	347.1	344.3	342.4	340.6	338.9	-0.55	-5.38
Finland	1,522.9	1,503.7	1,485.7	1,468.5	1,447.4	1,427.3	1,412.7	1,401.7	1,391.8	1,384.0	1,378.8	-0.99	-9.46
France	16,962.7	16,944.8	16,923.9	16,961.4	16,989.4	17,012.4	16,977.4	16,901.6	16,804.4	16,724.7	16,644.8	-0.19	-1.87
Germany	25,201.6	25,299.9	25,289.2	25,253.9	25,102.3	24,872.1	24,603.4	24,309.0	24,011.8	23,706.1	23,391.6	-0.74	-7.18
Greece	3,117.9	3,172.0	3,210.6	3,247.2	3,286.0	3,325.2	3,364.1	3,392.4	3,419.4	3,447.7	3,471.6	1.08	11.34
Hong Kong, China	2,349.4	2,356.4	2,363.4	2,361.9	2,362.9	2,353.2	2,335.5	2,307.2	2,279.1	2,245.8	2,215.5	-0.59	-5.70
Hungary	2,731.5	2,721.7	2,707.4	2,692.2	2,682.1	2,657.1	2,645.5	2,651.1	2,662.0	2,687.1	2,712.7	-0.07	-0.69
India	225,633.9	231,121.4	236,404.8	241,522.8	246,569.5	251,669.1	256,930.4	262,414.1	268,134.3	274,075.0	280,197.8	2.19	24.18
Indonesia	49,150.5	50,793.0	52,418.3	54,015.8	55,576.6	57,095.6	58,570.6	59,999.6	61,383.9	62,729.3	64,041.8	2.68	30.30
Iran	13,997.4	14,487.9	14,955.9	15,406.4	15,849.8	16,301.2	16,775.1	17,282.6	17,834.6	18,446.5	19,133.8	3.18	36.69
Ireland	1,101.4	1,121.8	1,142.8	1,164.4	1,187.0	1,209.4	1,232.0	1,255.9	1,280.8	1,308.5	1,340.5	1.98	21.70
Israel	1,530.3	1,551.1	1,572.8	1,595.9	1,621.3	1,651.1	1,685.2	1,723.4	1,761.7	1,797.5	1,831.3	1.81	19.67
Italy	16,925.7	17,124.5	17,306.5	17,529.2	17,744.0	17,945.2	18,119.9	18,249.2	18,325.4	18,353.9	18,351.2	0.81	8.42
Japan	33,288.8	32,956.6	32,844.3	32,905.0	33,108.0	33,383.3	33,570.2	33,729.6	33,885.6	33,961.9	33,937.4	0.19	1.95
Jordan	913.0	968.0	1,021.6	1,073.8	1,125.4	1,178.1	1,232.7	1,289.5	1,348.1	1,408.3	1,470.0	4.88	61.00
Kazakhstan	3,770.5	3,819.0	3,863.3	3,905.0	3,946.9	3,989.5	4,032.8	4,075.4	4,116.9	4,157.5	4,198.4	1.08	11.35
Kuwait	545.6	577.7	612.0	648.0	685.2	722.7	759.8	795.9	830.6	863.9	895.5	5.08	64.12
Latvia	619.3	615.3	614.3	613.0	611.2	609.5	606.6	603.1	599.5	594.5	589.1	-0.50	-4.87
Lithuania	930.6	932.2	934.0	935.8	936.0	935.3	932.4	926.2	919.5	910.9	900.2	-0.33	-3.27
Malaysia	5,800.7	5,951.4	6,090.2	6,214.6	6,316.7	6,409.9	6,499.0	6,585.9	6,671.9	6,748.4	6,825.7	1.64	17.67
Mexico	21,704.4	22,627.3	23,589.3	24,550.4	25,507.1	26,451.1	27,374.1	28,268.6	29,127.4	29,945.6	30,721.0	3.54	41.54
Morocco	6,376.1	6,548.6	6,721.2	6,892.8	7,060.3	7,220.3	7,370.5	7,511.0	7,645.8	7,782.2	7,929.0	2.20	24.36
Netherlands	4,799.4	4,832.4	4,863.9	4,885.8	4,888.3	4,872.3	4,844.8	4,804.5	4,756.9	4,703.0	4,647.7	-0.32	-3.16
New Zealand	1,166.6	1,177.8	1,191.0	1,202.9	1,211.8	1,217.0	1,219.2	1,217.8	1,215.5	1,212.3	1,208.2	0.35	3.57
Nigeria	19,659.0	20,133.8	20,630.6	21,154.8	21,712.7	22,310.8	22,954.1	23,645.4	24,385.1	25,171.9	26,002.9	2.84	32.27
Norway	1,296.3	1,314.9	1,331.6	1,350.3	1,365.9	1,378.5	1,390.4	1,398.5	1,403.8	1,408.3	1,413.7	0.87	9.05
Pakistan	27,145.5	28,057.5	29,003.8	29,982.6	30,990.8	32,024.7	33,083.3	34,168.7	35,284.7	36,435.0	37,624.2	3.32	38.60
Peru	5,444.2	5,601.5	5,760.6	5,922.1	6,086.5	6,254.5	6,425.9	6,600.3	6,776.3	6,951.8	7,124.4	2.73	30.86
Philippines	16,136.4	16,649.1	17,147.7	17,642.1	18,138.2	18,647.5	19,174.8	19,722.6	20,290.6	20,876.3	21,476.6	2.90	33.09
Poland	10,758.7	10,648.5	10,535.9	10,416.5	10,310.8	10,218.5	10,148.2	10,081.7	10,043.0	10,001.7	9,983.4	-0.75	-7.21
Portugal	2,926.8	2,951.9	2,978.3	3,007.3	3,036.6	3,068.3	3,102.6	3,137.5	3,174.3	3,199.0	3,215.8	0.95	9.87
Romania	5,783.0	5,830.9	5,861.0	5,876.4	5,881.0	5,880.5	5,899.4	5,900.7	5,910.7	5,939.2	5,975.6	0.33	3.33
Russia	41,859.4	41,351.3	41,011.7	40,677.3	40,359.0	40,059.7	39,655.8	39,341.3	39,049.2	38,706.5	38,409.9	-0.86	-8.24
Saudi Arabia	4,575.2	4,806.1	5,033.7	5,258.1	5,481.5	5,707.1	5,937.0	6,171.6	6,408.3	6,641.1	6,863.4	4.14	50.01
Singapore	1,504.3	1,525.1	1,550.0	1,575.1	1,598.6	1,611.4	1,615.7	1,614.9	1,612.7	1,601.2	1,591.5	0.57	5.80
Slovakia	1,515.5	1,515.2	1,510.2	1,503.9	1,501.2	1,504.1	1,510.6	1,515.9	1,522.8	1,531.8	1,544.1	0.19	1.89
Slovenia	614.6	616.5	615.1	614.7	613.4	611.8	610.7	610.0	609.9	610.6	612.7	-0.03	-0.31
South Africa	9,206.3	9,303.2	9,375.3	9,424.2	9,454.8	9,474.9	9,491.7	9,510.2	9,533.5	9,566.2	9,612.3	0.43	4.41
South Korea	14,722.8	15,089.3	15,452.8	15,773.9	16,043.3	16,239.3	16,335.2	16,353.7	16,323.4	16,259.9	16,183.5	0.95	9.92
Spain	12,503.7	12,777.9	13,049.1	13,332.3	13,625.8	13,921.2	14,216.9	14,505.6	14,781.5	15,031.8	15,251.3	2.01	21.97
Sweden	2,442.7	2,439.7	2,443.5	2,456.0	2,467.8	2,476.1	2,488.9	2,494.1	2,493.3	2,490.5	2,487.1	0.18	1.82
Switzerland	2,241.5	2,260.0	2,274.0	2,289.7	2,298.4	2,303.7	2,305.6	2,302.7	2,295.9	2,286.5	2,275.2	0.15	1.50
Taiwan	6,913.0	7,025.7	7,119.0	7,156.4	7,186.9	7,210.8	7,225.1	7,229.5	7,282.1	7,313.0	7,347.0	0.61	6.28
Thailand	18,000.0	18,382.5	18,783.0	19,122.2	19,389.1	19,675.2	19,836.7	19,991.8	20,164.2	20,267.6	20,324.8	1.22	12.92
Tunisia	2,241.7	2,304.1	2,364.1	2,422.2	2,479.3	2,536.7	2,595.5	2,656.0	2,718.6	2,783.3	2,850.1	2.43	27.14
Turkey	15,959.4	16,459.5	16,980.2	17,509.3	18,049.1	18,602.0	19,158.1	19,707.5	20,248.1	20,783.8	21,306.5	2.93	33.50
Turkmenistan	985.9	1,016.3	1,045.7	1,074.0	1,101.3	1,127.5	1,152.9	1,177.5	1,201.4	1,224.9	1,248.2	2.39	26.61
Ukraine	13,129.8	12,957.1	12,880.0	12,796.6	12,721.6	12,640.0	12,527.8	12,468.5	12,392.0	12,306.5	12,213.2	-0.72	-6.98
United Arab Emirates	932.2	983.7	1,044.5	1,113.8	1,190.4	1,272.8	1,359.4	1,449.1	1,540.4	1,631.6	1,720.3	6.32	84.54
United Kingdom	16,558.5	16,643.2	16,734.2	16,838.1	16,918.9	16,958.8	16,969.0	16,956.0	16,906.0	16,831.1	16,773.7	0.13	1.30
USA	84,800.4	85,204.4	85,511.4	85,541.9	85,302.6	84,872.4	84,424.6	83,922.6	83,396.9	82,920.4	82,596.1	-0.26	-2.60
Venezuela	5,793.5	5,937.7	6,075.8	6,209.5	6,342.3	6,477.8	6,619.0	6,766.9	6,920.7	7,077.5	7,233.9	2.25	24.86
Vietnam	17,942.3	18,619.6	19,263.0	19,874.8	20,462.3	21,037.9	21,610.1	22,182.1	22,751.2	23,312.5	23,858.4	2.89	32.97

Marketing segments: Middle aged generation

Table 4.122 Female baby boomers (40-59): 2009-2019

'000

	2009	2010	2011	2012	2013	2014	2015	2016	2017	2018	2019	CAGR	Period growth
Algeria	3,235.2	3,362.6	3,489.4	3,616.3	3,744.6	3,876.2	4,012.6	4,154.4	4,301.6	4,453.7	4,610.0	3.60	42.49
Argentina	4,360.6	4,408.8	4,459.2	4,513.7	4,574.7	4,644.4	4,724.2	4,814.0	4,912.0	5,014.8	5,119.4	1.62	17.40
Australia	2,943.7	2,975.7	3,013.8	3,052.0	3,082.1	3,109.9	3,132.9	3,151.5	3,169.5	3,186.0	3,203.3	0.85	8.82
Austria	1,230.7	1,248.0	1,261.9	1,275.8	1,285.6	1,291.6	1,296.0	1,295.9	1,289.6	1,282.7	1,274.5	0.35	3.56
Azerbaijan	1,136.0	1,168.9	1,196.1	1,217.9	1,235.1	1,248.4	1,258.3	1,265.1	1,269.2	1,271.2	1,271.6	1.13	11.94
Belarus	1,510.7	1,502.4	1,502.5	1,500.0	1,498.7	1,494.8	1,484.4	1,473.7	1,460.2	1,446.2	1,430.8	-0.54	-5.28
Belgium	1,508.8	1,514.3	1,519.3	1,524.5	1,525.4	1,523.2	1,517.2	1,507.6	1,498.3	1,489.2	1,479.4	-0.20	-1.95
Bolivia	807.3	829.9	853.6	878.3	903.6	929.1	954.6	979.9	1,005.1	1,030.3	1,055.8	2.72	30.78
Bosnia-Herzegovina	599.2	603.8	607.0	609.1	610.1	610.2	609.6	608.2	606.1	603.4	600.4	0.02	0.21
Brazil	22,580.6	23,117.3	23,628.6	24,115.0	24,578.4	25,023.2	25,455.1	25,880.5	26,305.6	26,734.5	27,167.6	1.87	20.31
Bulgaria	1,072.5	1,065.0	1,053.4	1,048.6	1,040.4	1,036.0	1,036.0	1,032.5	1,029.5	1,028.0	1,025.7	-0.45	-4.37
Canada	5,035.6	5,065.9	5,086.7	5,092.8	5,087.7	5,071.6	5,054.3	5,038.6	5,018.6	4,995.6	4,976.6	-0.12	-1.17
Chile	2,181.3	2,225.0	2,266.3	2,304.6	2,338.7	2,367.2	2,389.2	2,404.3	2,413.3	2,417.5	2,418.8	1.04	10.89
China	209,309.9	216,403.0	221,225.0	224,046.0	226,907.5	227,712.4	227,580.8	227,489.3	225,423.0	224,904.2	225,880.3	0.76	7.92
Colombia	5,093.6	5,230.5	5,356.1	5,471.9	5,580.8	5,686.8	5,792.8	5,900.2	6,008.7	6,117.0	6,222.9	2.02	22.17
Costa Rica	506.0	519.7	532.2	543.5	554.0	564.0	573.8	583.8	594.0	604.5	615.1	1.97	21.57
Croatia	647.8	644.0	639.5	637.8	633.7	629.4	624.3	619.1	614.1	610.8	608.1	-0.63	-6.13
Czech Republic	1,425.2	1,415.9	1,407.9	1,400.9	1,399.2	1,407.7	1,423.8	1,440.8	1,457.2	1,474.9	1,496.4	0.49	5.00
Denmark	757.0	757.2	757.6	761.0	764.5	765.7	767.5	769.6	768.0	765.7	763.4	0.08	0.84
Ecuador	1,316.0	1,349.4	1,381.8	1,413.1	1,443.6	1,473.6	1,503.3	1,533.1	1,563.1	1,593.1	1,623.1	2.12	23.33
Egypt	6,825.3	6,918.7	7,014.3	7,112.2	7,213.6	7,319.8	7,431.7	7,550.2	7,677.1	7,812.7	7,959.0	1.55	16.61
Estonia	193.2	191.8	191.2	190.2	189.0	187.8	186.4	184.6	183.3	182.0	180.8	-0.66	-6.39
Finland	758.1	748.9	740.3	732.1	721.4	711.1	703.3	697.4	692.2	688.1	685.1	-1.01	-9.63
France	8,673.7	8,666.6	8,656.9	8,674.7	8,685.4	8,692.2	8,668.4	8,622.0	8,564.7	8,516.3	8,467.4	-0.24	-2.38
Germany	12,449.9	12,489.6	12,473.8	12,446.9	12,363.2	12,241.8	12,102.4	11,952.3	11,803.3	11,651.2	11,494.8	-0.79	-7.67
Greece	1,568.3	1,593.8	1,610.5	1,627.7	1,644.9	1,663.2	1,680.6	1,692.4	1,702.4	1,713.1	1,721.8	0.94	9.79
Hong Kong, China	1,229.6	1,241.1	1,251.5	1,253.9	1,259.7	1,259.4	1,255.7	1,246.4	1,239.0	1,229.5	1,222.3	-0.06	-0.59
Hungary	1,420.0	1,413.0	1,403.6	1,392.9	1,385.0	1,369.8	1,360.9	1,359.8	1,360.9	1,370.1	1,378.8	-0.29	-2.90
India	109,423.0	112,167.1	114,821.1	117,402.3	119,953.7	122,533.0	125,190.0	127,952.0	130,824.1	133,797.5	136,852.8	2.26	25.07
Indonesia	24,541.7	25,365.6	26,190.1	27,009.0	27,815.9	28,605.3	29,373.8	30,119.0	30,840.9	31,542.0	32,225.7	2.76	31.31
Iran	6,901.3	7,140.3	7,364.9	7,577.8	7,785.0	7,995.4	8,217.8	8,459.0	8,725.7	9,027.8	9,374.7	3.11	35.84
Ireland	548.4	557.8	568.2	578.9	589.7	600.6	610.8	621.3	633.0	645.9	661.1	1.89	20.55
Israel	787.8	797.5	807.4	817.7	829.2	842.6	858.2	875.7	893.6	910.4	926.1	1.63	17.56
Italy	8,516.0	8,606.5	8,688.7	8,791.5	8,889.8	8,983.0	9,061.3	9,118.1	9,148.3	9,155.8	9,147.0	0.72	7.41
Japan	16,656.0	16,487.7	16,430.7	16,457.4	16,557.9	16,695.5	16,789.7	16,869.6	16,949.2	16,988.6	16,977.2	0.19	1.93
Jordan	446.2	472.3	497.9	522.9	547.8	573.1	599.3	626.3	654.1	682.7	712.0	4.78	59.56
Kazakhstan	2,050.8	2,078.6	2,103.8	2,127.4	2,150.7	2,174.0	2,197.5	2,220.1	2,241.7	2,262.1	2,281.9	1.07	11.27
Kuwait	188.4	199.9	211.9	224.6	237.8	251.2	264.8	278.3	291.6	304.6	317.1	5.34	68.29
Latvia	329.7	327.0	326.2	325.1	323.5	322.2	320.0	317.6	315.0	312.0	309.0	-0.65	-6.28
Lithuania	494.5	494.8	495.5	496.4	496.3	495.9	494.3	491.0	487.4	482.5	476.2	-0.38	-3.69
Malaysia	2,853.7	2,934.0	3,008.4	3,075.5	3,132.3	3,184.6	3,234.9	3,284.2	3,333.1	3,377.1	3,421.2	1.83	19.88
Mexico	11,202.5	11,690.3	12,193.8	12,692.8	13,186.1	13,670.6	14,143.3	14,601.1	15,040.2	15,458.1	15,853.6	3.53	41.52
Morocco	3,257.6	3,359.0	3,462.4	3,567.1	3,671.1	3,772.2	3,868.5	3,959.5	4,046.6	4,132.6	4,221.5	2.63	29.59
Netherlands	2,380.4	2,398.2	2,415.6	2,428.5	2,432.6	2,427.3	2,415.9	2,397.7	2,375.8	2,350.9	2,325.3	-0.23	-2.31
New Zealand	599.1	605.8	613.7	620.9	626.5	630.1	632.0	631.9	631.5	630.4	629.0	0.49	4.98
Nigeria	10,058.4	10,291.3	10,531.8	10,783.0	11,048.4	11,332.0	11,636.9	11,965.1	12,316.9	12,692.1	13,089.2	2.67	30.13
Norway	633.5	642.2	650.0	659.0	666.3	671.6	677.0	680.6	682.6	684.5	686.6	0.81	8.38
Pakistan	13,112.9	13,556.8	14,017.9	14,495.3	14,987.4	15,492.4	16,009.5	16,539.8	17,084.8	17,646.1	18,225.7	3.35	38.99
Peru	2,742.3	2,821.1	2,900.7	2,981.5	3,063.7	3,147.5	3,233.0	3,319.8	3,407.4	3,494.8	3,580.7	2.70	30.58
Philippines	8,140.1	8,399.6	8,648.9	8,893.2	9,136.0	9,384.2	9,641.1	9,908.3	10,185.8	10,472.2	10,765.5	2.83	32.25
Poland	5,499.4	5,440.2	5,379.0	5,313.6	5,255.1	5,203.8	5,162.3	5,124.5	5,100.0	5,073.3	5,059.1	-0.83	-8.01
Portugal	1,498.7	1,510.5	1,522.7	1,536.4	1,549.9	1,564.8	1,581.0	1,597.1	1,614.6	1,626.2	1,633.9	0.87	9.02
Romania	2,960.1	2,980.1	2,991.7	2,996.0	2,994.7	2,990.1	2,993.9	2,988.1	2,986.7	2,995.6	3,009.2	0.16	1.66
Russia	22,586.2	22,343.9	22,184.2	22,019.5	21,855.7	21,706.3	21,486.2	21,312.7	21,149.7	20,957.4	20,781.9	-0.83	-7.99
Saudi Arabia	1,681.7	1,771.7	1,863.0	1,956.1	2,052.7	2,154.7	2,263.1	2,378.0	2,498.0	2,619.9	2,739.9	5.00	62.93
Singapore	749.2	761.0	775.2	789.8	804.0	813.3	817.5	819.8	822.1	819.2	817.5	0.88	9.12
Slovakia	770.4	769.6	766.5	762.7	760.9	762.0	764.5	766.4	768.7	772.6	778.5	0.10	1.05
Slovenia	301.3	302.0	301.4	300.9	300.2	299.4	298.5	298.0	297.8	297.6	298.1	-0.11	-1.05
South Africa	4,854.4	4,905.7	4,939.1	4,954.8	4,955.2	4,944.2	4,925.6	4,902.3	4,877.0	4,853.1	4,834.4	-0.04	-0.41
South Korea	7,285.6	7,471.3	7,651.8	7,809.5	7,942.3	8,040.0	8,087.4	8,095.7	8,079.7	8,045.5	8,002.4	0.94	9.84
Spain	6,261.6	6,388.9	6,513.7	6,643.5	6,777.6	6,911.5	7,044.8	7,173.9	7,296.5	7,406.5	7,502.0	1.82	19.81
Sweden	1,205.7	1,204.0	1,206.6	1,212.9	1,219.0	1,223.5	1,230.1	1,232.7	1,232.8	1,231.2	1,229.9	0.20	2.01
Switzerland	1,119.3	1,130.5	1,139.2	1,148.7	1,154.1	1,158.0	1,160.3	1,160.6	1,159.7	1,156.7	1,152.8	0.30	2.99
Taiwan	3,460.6	3,521.3	3,572.3	3,595.1	3,615.4	3,630.9	3,643.1	3,649.3	3,680.3	3,699.7	3,720.2	0.73	7.50
Thailand	9,463.4	9,669.0	9,884.5	10,065.2	10,206.3	10,355.9	10,436.2	10,515.6	10,600.8	10,651.0	10,675.8	1.21	12.81
Tunisia	1,141.2	1,176.3	1,209.8	1,241.8	1,272.8	1,303.3	1,333.6	1,364.0	1,394.6	1,425.5	1,456.8	2.47	27.65
Turkey	7,931.0	8,187.6	8,451.2	8,717.8	8,988.4	9,264.3	9,543.0	9,817.8	10,087.2	10,357.8	10,618.5	2.96	33.89
Turkmenistan	517.9	533.3	548.1	562.5	576.4	589.7	602.6	615.0	627.0	638.5	649.8	2.30	25.48
Ukraine	7,111.6	7,019.3	6,976.9	6,930.0	6,887.1	6,837.2	6,768.2	6,725.5	6,670.4	6,612.4	6,550.1	-0.82	-7.90
United Arab Emirates	233.6	251.7	272.0	294.4	318.9	345.4	373.6	403.3	433.8	464.7	495.3	7.81	112.04
United Kingdom	8,404.6	8,455.1	8,509.1	8,571.4	8,621.2	8,648.7	8,660.0	8,658.1	8,635.9	8,600.4	8,571.7	0.20	1.99
USA	43,001.0	43,180.9	43,321.0	43,318.5	43,176.8	42,933.4	42,682.4	42,393.3	42,088.9	41,807.6	41,598.6	-0.33	-3.26
Venezuela	2,916.0	2,990.2	3,061.1	3,129.8	3,197.8	3,267.2	3,339.4	3,414.8	3,493.2	3,573.1	3,652.7	2.28	25.26
Vietnam	9,120.5	9,465.5	9,793.4	10,105.1	10,404.0	10,695.5	10,983.5	11,269.5	11,552.0	11,829.0	12,097.3	2.86	32.64

Marketing segments: Middle aged generation

Table 4.123 Male baby boomers (40-59): 2009-2019

'000

	2009	2010	2011	2012	2013	2014	2015	2016	2017	2018	2019	CAGR	Period growth
Algeria	3,295.1	3,430.5	3,562.7	3,692.5	3,821.9	3,953.4	4,089.4	4,231.1	4,378.5	4,531.5	4,689.2	3.59	42.31
Argentina	4,123.0	4,174.6	4,228.9	4,287.8	4,353.9	4,429.5	4,516.2	4,613.7	4,720.1	4,831.3	4,944.1	1.83	19.92
Australia	2,896.2	2,925.9	2,960.3	2,994.8	3,022.7	3,049.8	3,073.0	3,091.2	3,109.6	3,128.4	3,147.6	0.84	8.68
Austria	1,232.4	1,249.0	1,262.1	1,274.7	1,283.0	1,287.6	1,290.8	1,290.4	1,284.8	1,276.9	1,268.9	0.29	2.96
Azerbaijan	1,016.5	1,038.2	1,055.9	1,069.6	1,080.0	1,087.1	1,090.9	1,091.9	1,090.5	1,087.7	1,084.7	0.65	6.71
Belarus	1,336.5	1,326.5	1,322.8	1,318.3	1,314.7	1,310.4	1,301.7	1,293.2	1,283.3	1,273.2	1,262.8	-0.57	-5.52
Belgium	1,522.2	1,526.1	1,530.4	1,534.0	1,533.0	1,529.4	1,522.4	1,511.9	1,501.5	1,490.1	1,478.0	-0.29	-2.91
Bolivia	756.0	778.5	802.1	826.8	852.2	878.0	903.7	929.4	955.0	980.7	1,006.9	2.91	33.18
Bosnia-Herzegovina	543.3	544.0	543.4	541.9	539.8	537.4	534.9	532.5	530.2	528.2	526.5	-0.31	-3.10
Brazil	20,568.8	21,087.1	21,590.8	22,080.7	22,557.6	23,023.5	23,481.6	23,936.2	24,392.3	24,854.9	25,327.0	2.10	23.13
Bulgaria	1,030.8	1,027.5	1,021.6	1,020.9	1,018.0	1,017.6	1,022.1	1,024.7	1,027.4	1,031.2	1,033.9	0.03	0.30
Canada	5,000.5	5,036.7	5,066.5	5,085.6	5,095.3	5,093.6	5,090.7	5,087.4	5,076.7	5,061.4	5,050.2	0.10	0.99
Chile	2,124.1	2,167.5	2,208.5	2,246.6	2,280.6	2,309.2	2,331.3	2,346.9	2,356.7	2,362.0	2,364.7	1.08	11.33
China	216,260.1	222,978.6	228,503.9	231,571.2	233,842.2	234,266.7	233,910.3	233,650.1	231,199.9	230,165.0	230,517.0	0.64	6.59
Colombia	4,623.4	4,746.6	4,859.6	4,963.9	5,062.6	5,159.3	5,257.0	5,357.2	5,459.7	5,563.1	5,665.5	2.05	22.54
Costa Rica	522.8	536.9	549.6	561.0	571.4	581.2	590.8	600.6	610.5	620.8	631.2	1.90	20.73
Croatia	634.5	630.9	626.0	623.7	619.4	615.0	609.1	604.6	600.3	598.5	596.6	-0.62	-5.98
Czech Republic	1,418.0	1,412.8	1,407.8	1,405.0	1,407.3	1,420.4	1,440.5	1,460.0	1,479.7	1,499.3	1,522.9	0.72	7.40
Denmark	770.7	770.9	771.0	773.6	775.9	776.1	776.7	776.9	774.3	770.5	766.8	-0.05	-0.51
Ecuador	1,286.9	1,318.4	1,348.9	1,378.4	1,407.0	1,435.2	1,463.1	1,491.1	1,519.1	1,547.2	1,575.4	2.04	22.42
Egypt	7,029.2	7,128.6	7,234.9	7,348.1	7,469.3	7,598.6	7,735.7	7,880.3	8,032.7	8,192.8	8,362.4	1.75	18.97
Estonia	165.0	163.9	163.4	163.0	162.4	161.7	160.7	159.7	159.0	158.6	158.0	-0.43	-4.19
Finland	764.8	754.8	745.4	736.5	726.0	716.3	709.4	704.3	699.6	695.9	693.7	-0.97	-9.29
France	8,289.0	8,278.2	8,267.0	8,286.7	8,304.0	8,320.3	8,309.0	8,279.6	8,239.7	8,208.4	8,177.4	-0.14	-1.35
Germany	12,751.8	12,810.3	12,815.4	12,807.0	12,739.2	12,630.3	12,501.0	12,356.7	12,208.4	12,054.9	11,896.8	-0.69	-6.70
Greece	1,549.6	1,578.2	1,600.1	1,619.5	1,641.1	1,662.1	1,683.6	1,700.0	1,717.0	1,734.6	1,749.8	1.22	12.92
Hong Kong, China	1,119.8	1,115.3	1,111.9	1,108.0	1,103.1	1,093.7	1,079.8	1,060.8	1,040.2	1,016.2	993.2	-1.19	-11.31
Hungary	1,311.6	1,308.7	1,303.7	1,299.3	1,297.1	1,287.3	1,284.6	1,291.3	1,301.1	1,317.1	1,333.9	0.17	1.70
India	116,210.9	118,954.3	121,583.7	124,120.6	126,615.7	129,136.1	131,740.4	134,462.1	137,310.2	140,277.5	143,345.0	2.12	23.35
Indonesia	24,608.8	25,427.4	26,228.2	27,006.7	27,760.7	28,490.4	29,196.8	29,880.6	30,543.1	31,187.2	31,816.2	2.60	29.29
Iran	7,096.2	7,347.5	7,590.9	7,828.6	8,064.8	8,305.8	8,557.3	8,823.6	9,108.9	9,418.8	9,759.1	3.24	37.53
Ireland	553.0	563.9	574.6	585.5	597.3	608.8	621.2	634.6	647.8	662.6	679.3	2.08	22.85
Israel	742.5	753.6	765.5	778.2	792.1	808.5	827.0	847.7	868.2	887.0	905.2	2.00	21.91
Italy	8,409.7	8,518.0	8,617.8	8,737.7	8,854.2	8,962.2	9,058.6	9,131.1	9,177.1	9,198.1	9,204.2	0.91	9.45
Japan	16,632.8	16,468.9	16,413.6	16,447.7	16,550.1	16,687.9	16,780.5	16,860.0	16,936.4	16,973.3	16,960.3	0.20	1.97
Jordan	466.8	495.7	523.7	550.9	577.7	605.0	633.5	663.2	693.9	725.6	758.0	4.97	62.39
Kazakhstan	1,719.7	1,740.3	1,759.4	1,777.7	1,796.2	1,815.4	1,835.3	1,855.2	1,875.2	1,895.4	1,916.6	1.09	11.45
Kuwait	357.2	377.9	400.0	423.4	447.4	471.5	495.0	517.6	539.1	559.3	578.4	4.94	61.91
Latvia	289.6	288.3	288.1	287.9	287.8	287.3	286.6	285.4	284.4	282.5	280.1	-0.33	-3.26
Lithuania	436.1	437.4	438.5	439.4	439.7	439.5	438.0	435.2	432.1	428.4	423.9	-0.28	-2.80
Malaysia	2,947.0	3,017.4	3,081.9	3,139.1	3,184.4	3,225.3	3,264.1	3,301.7	3,338.8	3,371.2	3,404.5	1.45	15.52
Mexico	10,501.9	10,937.0	11,395.5	11,857.6	12,321.1	12,780.5	13,230.8	13,667.6	14,087.2	14,487.4	14,867.3	3.54	41.57
Morocco	3,118.5	3,189.6	3,258.8	3,325.7	3,389.2	3,448.1	3,502.0	3,551.5	3,599.3	3,649.6	3,707.5	1.75	18.89
Netherlands	2,419.0	2,434.2	2,448.3	2,457.3	2,455.7	2,445.0	2,428.9	2,406.8	2,381.1	2,352.2	2,322.3	-0.41	-4.00
New Zealand	567.5	572.0	577.3	582.0	585.3	586.8	587.1	585.8	584.0	581.9	579.3	0.21	2.08
Nigeria	9,600.6	9,842.5	10,098.8	10,371.9	10,664.3	10,978.8	11,317.2	11,680.3	12,068.2	12,479.8	12,913.7	3.01	34.51
Norway	662.8	672.6	681.6	691.2	699.7	706.9	713.4	717.9	721.2	723.9	727.0	0.93	9.69
Pakistan	14,032.6	14,500.7	14,985.9	15,487.4	16,003.4	16,532.4	17,073.8	17,628.9	18,199.9	18,788.9	19,398.5	3.29	38.24
Peru	2,701.9	2,780.4	2,859.8	2,940.6	3,022.9	3,107.0	3,193.0	3,280.5	3,368.9	3,457.0	3,543.7	2.75	31.16
Philippines	7,996.3	8,249.4	8,498.8	8,748.9	9,002.2	9,263.3	9,533.7	9,814.3	10,104.8	10,404.1	10,711.0	2.97	33.95
Poland	5,259.2	5,208.3	5,156.9	5,102.9	5,055.7	5,014.7	4,985.9	4,957.2	4,942.9	4,928.4	4,924.3	-0.66	-6.37
Portugal	1,428.1	1,441.4	1,455.7	1,470.9	1,486.7	1,503.5	1,521.5	1,540.4	1,559.6	1,572.9	1,581.9	1.03	10.77
Romania	2,822.9	2,850.8	2,869.3	2,880.4	2,886.3	2,890.4	2,905.5	2,912.6	2,923.9	2,943.6	2,966.4	0.50	5.08
Russia	19,273.2	19,007.4	18,827.5	18,657.8	18,503.3	18,353.3	18,169.6	18,028.6	17,899.6	17,749.1	17,628.0	-0.89	-8.54
Saudi Arabia	2,893.6	3,034.4	3,170.8	3,301.9	3,428.7	3,552.4	3,673.9	3,793.6	3,910.3	4,021.3	4,123.4	3.61	42.50
Singapore	755.1	764.1	774.7	785.3	794.6	798.0	798.2	795.2	790.6	781.9	774.0	0.25	2.51
Slovakia	745.1	745.6	743.7	741.2	740.4	742.1	746.1	749.5	754.1	759.2	765.7	0.27	2.76
Slovenia	313.4	314.5	313.7	313.8	313.2	312.4	312.2	312.0	312.1	313.1	314.6	0.04	0.40
South Africa	4,351.9	4,397.4	4,436.2	4,469.4	4,499.6	4,530.7	4,566.1	4,607.8	4,656.5	4,713.1	4,777.9	0.94	9.79
South Korea	7,437.2	7,618.0	7,801.0	7,964.4	8,100.9	8,199.3	8,247.8	8,258.0	8,243.7	8,214.4	8,181.2	0.96	10.00
Spain	6,242.1	6,389.0	6,535.5	6,688.8	6,848.1	7,009.7	7,172.1	7,331.6	7,485.0	7,625.3	7,749.3	2.19	24.15
Sweden	1,237.0	1,235.6	1,236.9	1,243.1	1,248.8	1,252.6	1,258.8	1,261.5	1,260.5	1,259.4	1,257.2	0.16	1.63
Switzerland	1,122.2	1,129.5	1,134.8	1,141.1	1,144.2	1,145.6	1,145.4	1,142.1	1,136.2	1,129.9	1,122.4	0.00	0.02
Taiwan	3,452.4	3,504.3	3,546.7	3,561.3	3,571.5	3,579.9	3,582.0	3,580.1	3,601.8	3,613.3	3,626.8	0.49	5.05
Thailand	8,536.6	8,713.4	8,898.5	9,057.0	9,182.8	9,319.3	9,400.5	9,476.2	9,563.4	9,616.5	9,648.9	1.23	13.03
Tunisia	1,100.4	1,127.8	1,154.3	1,180.4	1,206.5	1,233.5	1,261.9	1,292.0	1,324.0	1,357.8	1,393.3	2.39	26.61
Turkey	8,028.4	8,271.9	8,529.0	8,791.5	9,060.7	9,337.7	9,615.1	9,889.8	10,160.8	10,426.0	10,688.0	2.90	33.13
Turkmenistan	468.1	483.1	497.6	511.5	524.9	537.8	550.3	562.5	574.5	586.4	598.4	2.49	27.85
Ukraine	6,018.1	5,937.8	5,903.0	5,866.6	5,834.5	5,802.8	5,759.6	5,743.0	5,721.6	5,694.2	5,663.1	-0.61	-5.90
United Arab Emirates	698.6	732.1	772.6	819.4	871.5	927.3	985.7	1,045.8	1,106.6	1,166.8	1,225.0	5.78	75.35
United Kingdom	8,153.9	8,188.1	8,225.1	8,266.7	8,297.7	8,310.1	8,309.0	8,297.9	8,270.1	8,230.6	8,202.0	0.06	0.59
USA	41,799.4	42,023.5	42,190.4	42,223.4	42,125.7	41,938.9	41,742.2	41,529.3	41,308.0	41,112.8	40,997.5	-0.19	-1.92
Venezuela	2,877.5	2,947.6	3,014.7	3,079.7	3,144.5	3,210.6	3,279.7	3,352.1	3,427.5	3,504.4	3,581.2	2.21	24.46
Vietnam	8,821.8	9,154.1	9,469.6	9,769.6	10,058.3	10,342.4	10,626.6	10,912.7	11,199.2	11,483.4	11,761.1	2.92	33.32

Marketing segments: Middle aged generation

Table 4.124 Baby boomers (40-59): 2009-2019 (%)

% of total

	2009	2010	2011	2012	2013	2014	2015	2016	2017	2018	2019
Algeria	18.7	19.2	19.6	20.0	20.4	20.8	21.3	21.7	22.2	22.7	23.2
Argentina	21.0	21.1	21.1	21.2	21.3	21.5	21.7	21.9	22.2	22.5	22.8
Australia	26.8	26.7	26.7	26.7	26.6	26.4	26.3	26.1	25.9	25.7	25.5
Austria	29.4	29.7	29.9	30.2	30.3	30.3	30.3	30.2	30.0	29.8	29.5
Azerbaijan	24.7	25.0	25.2	25.4	25.4	25.4	25.3	25.1	24.9	24.7	24.5
Belarus	29.4	29.3	29.3	29.4	29.4	29.4	29.3	29.2	29.0	28.9	28.7
Belgium	28.4	28.4	28.4	28.4	28.3	28.2	27.9	27.7	27.4	27.1	26.9
Bolivia	15.9	16.0	16.2	16.5	16.7	16.9	17.1	17.3	17.5	17.7	18.0
Bosnia-Herzegovina	29.7	29.9	29.9	30.0	29.9	29.9	29.8	29.8	29.7	29.6	29.5
Brazil	22.3	22.6	22.9	23.3	23.6	23.8	24.1	24.4	24.7	25.0	25.2
Bulgaria	28.0	28.0	28.0	28.1	28.2	28.3	28.6	28.8	29.1	29.4	29.6
Canada	29.8	29.7	29.7	29.5	29.3	29.0	28.8	28.5	28.2	27.9	27.6
Chile	25.4	25.6	25.9	26.1	26.2	26.3	26.3	26.3	26.2	26.0	25.9
China	32.0	32.9	33.6	33.9	34.1	34.1	33.9	33.7	33.3	33.1	33.1
Colombia	21.3	21.5	21.8	21.9	22.1	22.2	22.4	22.5	22.7	22.8	23.0
Costa Rica	22.5	22.8	23.0	23.2	23.3	23.4	23.5	23.6	23.7	23.9	24.0
Croatia	29.0	28.8	28.7	28.6	28.5	28.4	28.2	28.0	27.9	27.9	27.8
Czech Republic	27.5	27.3	27.2	27.1	27.1	27.3	27.6	28.0	28.4	28.7	29.2
Denmark	27.7	27.7	27.6	27.6	27.6	27.6	27.6	27.5	27.4	27.2	27.0
Ecuador	19.1	19.4	19.6	19.8	20.0	20.2	20.3	20.5	20.7	20.8	21.0
Egypt	18.0	18.0	17.9	17.9	17.8	17.8	17.8	17.8	17.9	18.0	18.0
Estonia	26.9	26.8	26.8	26.8	26.8	26.7	26.7	26.5	26.5	26.4	26.4
Finland	28.6	28.1	27.7	27.3	26.8	26.3	25.9	25.7	25.4	25.2	25.0
France	27.2	27.0	26.8	26.8	26.7	26.6	26.5	26.2	26.0	25.8	25.5
Germany	30.7	31.0	31.1	31.1	31.0	30.8	30.6	30.3	30.1	29.8	29.5
Greece	27.7	28.1	28.3	28.6	28.9	29.1	29.4	29.6	29.8	30.0	30.2
Hong Kong, China	33.3	33.0	32.8	32.5	32.3	31.9	31.4	30.8	30.1	29.5	28.9
Hungary	27.3	27.2	27.1	27.0	27.0	26.8	26.8	26.9	27.1	27.4	27.8
India	19.3	19.5	19.7	19.9	20.0	20.2	20.3	20.5	20.8	21.0	21.2
Indonesia	21.4	21.8	22.3	22.8	23.2	23.6	24.0	24.4	24.7	25.1	25.4
Iran	18.9	19.3	19.7	20.1	20.4	20.7	21.1	21.5	22.0	22.5	23.1
Ireland	24.8	24.9	25.1	25.2	25.4	25.6	25.8	26.1	26.3	26.7	27.1
Israel	20.7	20.6	20.6	20.6	20.7	20.7	20.9	21.1	21.3	21.5	21.6
Italy	28.7	29.0	29.3	29.6	30.0	30.3	30.6	30.8	31.0	31.0	31.1
Japan	26.1	25.9	25.8	25.9	26.2	26.4	26.7	26.9	27.1	27.3	27.4
Jordan	14.5	15.0	15.5	16.0	16.6	17.2	17.7	18.3	18.8	19.3	19.9
Kazakhstan	23.9	23.9	23.9	23.8	23.8	23.8	23.8	23.7	23.7	23.7	23.7
Kuwait	22.3	23.1	24.0	24.9	25.8	26.6	27.5	28.2	28.9	29.6	30.1
Latvia	27.5	27.5	27.6	27.7	27.8	27.9	27.9	27.9	27.9	27.9	27.8
Lithuania	27.8	28.0	28.2	28.4	28.6	28.8	28.8	28.8	28.7	28.6	28.4
Malaysia	20.6	20.8	21.0	21.1	21.1	21.2	21.2	21.1	21.1	21.1	21.1
Mexico	20.0	20.5	21.1	21.7	22.2	22.8	23.3	23.8	24.2	24.6	25.0
Morocco	19.9	20.2	20.5	20.8	21.0	21.3	21.5	21.6	21.8	21.9	22.1
Netherlands	29.2	29.4	29.5	29.6	29.6	29.4	29.2	28.9	28.6	28.2	27.8
New Zealand	27.1	27.1	27.1	27.1	27.1	27.0	26.8	26.5	26.3	26.0	25.7
Nigeria	12.7	12.7	12.8	12.8	12.9	12.9	13.0	13.2	13.3	13.5	13.7
Norway	27.0	27.1	27.1	27.2	27.2	27.2	27.2	27.1	27.0	26.8	26.7
Pakistan	15.0	15.2	15.4	15.5	15.7	15.9	16.1	16.3	16.5	16.7	16.9
Peru	18.8	19.1	19.3	19.6	19.9	20.2	20.5	20.8	21.1	21.4	21.7
Philippines	17.5	17.7	17.9	18.1	18.3	18.4	18.6	18.8	19.0	19.3	19.5
Poland	28.3	28.1	27.8	27.5	27.3	27.1	27.0	26.8	26.8	26.7	26.7
Portugal	27.4	27.6	27.8	28.0	28.2	28.5	28.8	29.1	29.4	29.6	29.8
Romania	27.0	27.3	27.5	27.7	27.8	27.9	28.2	28.3	28.5	28.8	29.1
Russia	29.5	29.2	29.0	28.8	28.6	28.5	28.2	28.0	27.9	27.7	27.5
Saudi Arabia	17.8	18.3	18.8	19.3	19.7	20.1	20.5	20.9	21.4	21.7	22.1
Singapore	32.0	32.0	32.1	32.2	32.3	32.2	32.0	31.6	31.3	30.8	30.4
Slovakia	28.1	28.1	28.0	27.9	27.8	27.9	28.0	28.1	28.2	28.4	28.6
Slovenia	30.4	30.4	30.2	30.1	30.0	29.9	29.8	29.7	29.7	29.7	29.8
South Africa	18.4	18.4	18.5	18.5	18.4	18.4	18.4	18.3	18.3	18.3	18.3
South Korea	30.2	30.9	31.5	32.1	32.6	33.0	33.1	33.2	33.1	33.0	32.8
Spain	27.5	27.8	28.2	28.6	29.0	29.4	29.8	30.2	30.5	30.9	31.1
Sweden	26.5	26.4	26.3	26.3	26.3	26.3	26.3	26.2	26.1	25.9	25.8
Switzerland	29.6	29.8	29.9	29.9	29.9	29.9	29.8	29.7	29.5	29.2	29.0
Taiwan	30.0	30.4	30.7	30.8	30.9	30.9	30.9	30.9	31.1	31.2	31.3
Thailand	27.8	28.2	28.7	29.0	29.3	29.6	29.7	29.8	30.0	30.0	30.0
Tunisia	21.8	22.2	22.6	22.9	23.2	23.5	23.8	24.2	24.5	24.9	25.3
Turkey	21.2	21.6	22.0	22.5	22.9	23.4	23.8	24.3	24.7	25.1	25.5
Turkmenistan	19.3	19.6	19.9	20.2	20.5	20.7	20.9	21.1	21.3	21.5	21.7
Ukraine	28.6	28.4	28.4	28.4	28.4	28.4	28.4	28.4	28.4	28.4	28.4
United Arab Emirates	20.2	20.8	21.6	22.6	23.7	24.9	26.1	27.3	28.5	29.7	30.8
United Kingdom	26.9	26.9	26.9	26.9	26.9	26.8	26.6	26.4	26.2	25.9	25.7
USA	27.7	27.6	27.5	27.3	27.1	26.7	26.4	26.1	25.8	25.4	25.2
Venezuela	20.3	20.4	20.6	20.7	20.9	21.0	21.2	21.3	21.5	21.7	21.9
Vietnam	20.5	21.0	21.4	21.8	22.2	22.6	22.9	23.2	23.6	23.9	24.2

Marketing segments: Middle aged generation

Table 4.125 Female baby boomers (40-59): 2009-2019 (%)

% of total

	2009	2010	2011	2012	2013	2014	2015	2016	2017	2018	2019
Algeria	9.27	9.49	9.71	9.91	10.11	10.32	10.53	10.76	10.99	11.24	11.48
Argentina	10.81	10.82	10.84	10.87	10.91	10.98	11.07	11.18	11.31	11.45	11.60
Australia	13.51	13.46	13.47	13.46	13.41	13.34	13.26	13.15	13.05	12.95	12.85
Austria	14.68	14.84	14.96	15.08	15.15	15.18	15.19	15.15	15.04	14.92	14.79
Azerbaijan	13.01	13.24	13.41	13.51	13.56	13.57	13.54	13.49	13.41	13.32	13.22
Belarus	15.62	15.56	15.61	15.63	15.66	15.66	15.60	15.54	15.44	15.34	15.23
Belgium	14.15	14.15	14.15	14.15	14.11	14.05	13.95	13.81	13.69	13.56	13.43
Bolivia	8.18	8.27	8.37	8.47	8.58	8.69	8.79	8.90	9.00	9.09	9.19
Bosnia-Herzegovina	15.59	15.71	15.79	15.85	15.88	15.89	15.89	15.87	15.83	15.78	15.73
Brazil	11.66	11.83	11.99	12.14	12.29	12.42	12.55	12.67	12.80	12.93	13.07
Bulgaria	14.26	14.26	14.21	14.24	14.24	14.29	14.41	14.48	14.56	14.67	14.76
Canada	14.96	14.91	14.86	14.76	14.64	14.48	14.32	14.17	14.01	13.85	13.70
Chile	12.85	12.99	13.10	13.20	13.28	13.32	13.33	13.30	13.24	13.16	13.07
China	15.76	16.22	16.51	16.65	16.79	16.79	16.71	16.64	16.44	16.35	16.37
Colombia	11.16	11.30	11.41	11.51	11.58	11.66	11.73	11.80	11.88	11.96	12.03
Costa Rica	11.05	11.20	11.32	11.40	11.47	11.52	11.58	11.64	11.70	11.77	11.85
Croatia	14.63	14.57	14.49	14.48	14.42	14.36	14.27	14.19	14.11	14.08	14.05
Czech Republic	13.79	13.68	13.58	13.51	13.50	13.58	13.74	13.91	14.07	14.24	14.45
Denmark	13.74	13.70	13.67	13.69	13.72	13.70	13.70	13.70	13.64	13.56	13.48
Ecuador	9.66	9.80	9.92	10.02	10.12	10.21	10.30	10.39	10.48	10.57	10.66
Egypt	8.89	8.85	8.82	8.79	8.76	8.74	8.73	8.73	8.74	8.76	8.80
Estonia	14.52	14.46	14.47	14.44	14.41	14.37	14.31	14.22	14.17	14.12	14.07
Finland	14.24	14.00	13.79	13.59	13.34	13.10	12.92	12.77	12.64	12.53	12.44
France	13.89	13.81	13.73	13.70	13.65	13.61	13.51	13.39	13.25	13.12	13.00
Germany	15.18	15.28	15.32	15.34	15.28	15.18	15.06	14.92	14.78	14.64	14.50
Greece	13.94	14.12	14.22	14.33	14.45	14.57	14.69	14.77	14.84	14.92	14.98
Hong Kong, China	17.41	17.40	17.39	17.27	17.20	17.06	16.87	16.61	16.39	16.14	15.93
Hungary	14.17	14.13	14.07	13.99	13.95	13.84	13.79	13.81	13.86	13.99	14.11
India	9.36	9.47	9.56	9.65	9.74	9.82	9.92	10.02	10.13	10.24	10.37
Indonesia	10.67	10.91	11.14	11.38	11.60	11.82	12.03	12.23	12.42	12.60	12.77
Iran	9.30	9.51	9.70	9.86	10.02	10.18	10.34	10.53	10.74	11.00	11.30
Ireland	12.33	12.38	12.46	12.55	12.64	12.74	12.82	12.90	13.02	13.16	13.35
Israel	10.64	10.61	10.58	10.56	10.56	10.59	10.64	10.72	10.81	10.88	10.93
Italy	14.42	14.56	14.69	14.85	15.01	15.17	15.30	15.40	15.46	15.49	15.49
Japan	13.05	12.95	12.93	12.97	13.08	13.23	13.34	13.45	13.56	13.64	13.69
Jordan	7.06	7.30	7.55	7.81	8.07	8.35	8.61	8.87	9.12	9.37	9.62
Kazakhstan	13.00	13.00	13.00	12.98	12.97	12.95	12.95	12.94	12.92	12.91	12.89
Kuwait	7.71	8.00	8.30	8.62	8.94	9.26	9.57	9.87	10.16	10.42	10.67
Latvia	14.63	14.60	14.64	14.69	14.71	14.75	14.73	14.72	14.68	14.63	14.57
Lithuania	14.77	14.86	14.97	15.08	15.17	15.24	15.28	15.27	15.24	15.17	15.05
Malaysia	10.16	10.28	10.37	10.45	10.48	10.51	10.53	10.54	10.56	10.57	10.57
Mexico	10.32	10.61	10.91	11.20	11.49	11.77	12.03	12.28	12.51	12.72	12.91
Morocco	10.18	10.37	10.57	10.76	10.94	11.11	11.27	11.41	11.53	11.65	11.78
Netherlands	14.51	14.59	14.67	14.72	14.72	14.66	14.56	14.43	14.27	14.10	13.92
New Zealand	13.90	13.92	13.97	14.00	14.00	13.96	13.89	13.77	13.65	13.52	13.38
Nigeria	6.50	6.50	6.51	6.52	6.54	6.57	6.61	6.67	6.73	6.81	6.90
Norway	13.20	13.22	13.23	13.28	13.29	13.27	13.25	13.20	13.12	13.03	12.95
Pakistan	7.25	7.34	7.42	7.51	7.60	7.70	7.79	7.89	7.99	8.10	8.21
Peru	9.45	9.59	9.74	9.88	10.02	10.17	10.32	10.47	10.62	10.77	10.92
Philippines	8.83	8.94	9.04	9.12	9.20	9.28	9.37	9.46	9.56	9.66	9.76
Poland	14.48	14.34	14.20	14.05	13.92	13.81	13.72	13.64	13.59	13.54	13.52
Portugal	14.05	14.12	14.21	14.31	14.41	14.53	14.67	14.80	14.96	15.06	15.13
Romania	13.81	13.95	14.04	14.11	14.16	14.20	14.29	14.34	14.41	14.53	14.67
Russia	15.92	15.76	15.68	15.60	15.51	15.42	15.29	15.19	15.10	15.00	14.90
Saudi Arabia	6.54	6.75	6.96	7.16	7.37	7.59	7.82	8.07	8.32	8.58	8.82
Singapore	15.92	15.95	16.04	16.14	16.24	16.25	16.17	16.06	15.96	15.77	15.61
Slovakia	14.28	14.26	14.20	14.13	14.09	14.12	14.16	14.20	14.25	14.32	14.44
Slovenia	14.89	14.89	14.81	14.76	14.70	14.64	14.57	14.53	14.50	14.47	14.48
South Africa	9.69	9.72	9.72	9.70	9.66	9.60	9.53	9.45	9.37	9.29	9.21
South Korea	14.95	15.29	15.62	15.91	16.16	16.33	16.41	16.42	16.38	16.31	16.22
Spain	13.76	13.91	14.07	14.23	14.41	14.58	14.76	14.92	15.08	15.21	15.31
Sweden	13.10	13.02	12.99	13.00	13.00	12.99	12.99	12.96	12.89	12.81	12.74
Switzerland	14.81	14.90	14.95	15.02	15.04	15.03	15.01	14.95	14.89	14.79	14.69
Taiwan	15.02	15.24	15.42	15.47	15.53	15.56	15.58	15.59	15.70	15.77	15.85
Thailand	14.62	14.85	15.09	15.29	15.43	15.58	15.63	15.69	15.75	15.77	15.75
Tunisia	11.11	11.34	11.55	11.74	11.92	12.09	12.25	12.42	12.58	12.75	12.92
Turkey	10.54	10.75	10.97	11.19	11.41	11.64	11.86	12.08	12.30	12.51	12.71
Turkmenistan	10.13	10.30	10.45	10.59	10.72	10.83	10.94	11.04	11.12	11.21	11.28
Ukraine	15.49	15.38	15.38	15.38	15.38	15.37	15.32	15.32	15.30	15.27	15.23
United Arab Emirates	5.06	5.33	5.63	5.97	6.35	6.75	7.17	7.60	8.03	8.46	8.86
United Kingdom	13.64	13.64	13.67	13.70	13.70	13.66	13.59	13.50	13.39	13.25	13.12
USA	14.03	13.98	13.93	13.84	13.70	13.53	13.36	13.18	13.00	12.83	12.68
Venezuela	10.20	10.30	10.38	10.45	10.52	10.59	10.67	10.76	10.86	10.97	11.07
Vietnam	10.41	10.67	10.90	11.11	11.29	11.47	11.64	11.80	11.96	12.11	12.25

Marketing segments: Middle aged generation

Table 4.126 Male baby boomers (40-59): 2009-2019 (%)

% of total

	2009	2010	2011	2012	2013	2014	2015	2016	2017	2018	2019
Algeria	9.44	9.68	9.91	10.12	10.32	10.53	10.74	10.96	11.19	11.43	11.68
Argentina	10.22	10.25	10.28	10.33	10.39	10.47	10.58	10.72	10.87	11.04	11.20
Australia	13.29	13.24	13.23	13.21	13.15	13.08	13.00	12.90	12.81	12.71	12.63
Austria	14.70	14.85	14.96	15.07	15.12	15.13	15.13	15.09	14.98	14.86	14.73
Azerbaijan	11.64	11.76	11.83	11.86	11.85	11.81	11.74	11.64	11.52	11.40	11.28
Belarus	13.82	13.74	13.74	13.73	13.74	13.73	13.68	13.63	13.57	13.51	13.44
Belgium	14.28	14.26	14.25	14.24	14.18	14.10	13.99	13.85	13.72	13.57	13.42
Bolivia	7.67	7.76	7.87	7.98	8.09	8.21	8.33	8.44	8.55	8.66	8.77
Bosnia-Herzegovina	14.13	14.15	14.14	14.10	14.05	14.00	13.94	13.89	13.85	13.82	13.80
Brazil	10.62	10.79	10.96	11.12	11.28	11.43	11.57	11.72	11.87	12.02	12.18
Bulgaria	13.71	13.76	13.78	13.87	13.93	14.04	14.21	14.37	14.53	14.71	14.88
Canada	14.86	14.83	14.80	14.74	14.66	14.54	14.43	14.31	14.18	14.03	13.90
Chile	12.52	12.65	12.77	12.87	12.95	12.99	13.01	12.98	12.93	12.86	12.78
China	16.28	16.71	17.05	17.21	17.31	17.27	17.18	17.09	16.86	16.73	16.71
Colombia	10.13	10.25	10.35	10.44	10.51	10.58	10.64	10.72	10.80	10.88	10.95
Costa Rica	11.42	11.57	11.69	11.77	11.83	11.88	11.92	11.97	12.03	12.09	12.16
Croatia	14.33	14.27	14.19	14.16	14.10	14.03	13.93	13.86	13.80	13.79	13.79
Czech Republic	13.72	13.65	13.58	13.55	13.58	13.70	13.90	14.10	14.29	14.48	14.71
Denmark	13.98	13.95	13.91	13.92	13.93	13.89	13.86	13.83	13.75	13.64	13.54
Ecuador	9.44	9.57	9.68	9.78	9.86	9.95	10.02	10.10	10.18	10.27	10.35
Egypt	9.16	9.12	9.09	9.08	9.07	9.07	9.09	9.11	9.15	9.19	9.24
Estonia	12.40	12.36	12.37	12.38	12.38	12.38	12.34	12.31	12.30	12.30	12.29
Finland	14.36	14.11	13.88	13.67	13.43	13.20	13.03	12.90	12.77	12.67	12.60
France	13.27	13.19	13.11	13.08	13.05	13.02	12.95	12.85	12.74	12.65	12.55
Germany	15.55	15.68	15.74	15.78	15.75	15.66	15.55	15.42	15.29	15.15	15.00
Greece	13.77	13.98	14.13	14.26	14.41	14.56	14.72	14.84	14.97	15.10	15.22
Hong Kong, China	15.85	15.64	15.45	15.26	15.07	14.81	14.51	14.14	13.76	13.34	12.94
Hungary	13.09	13.09	13.06	13.05	13.07	13.01	13.01	13.12	13.25	13.45	13.65
India	9.94	10.04	10.13	10.20	10.28	10.35	10.43	10.53	10.63	10.74	10.86
Indonesia	10.70	10.94	11.16	11.38	11.58	11.77	11.96	12.13	12.30	12.46	12.61
Iran	9.56	9.79	9.99	10.19	10.38	10.57	10.77	10.98	11.21	11.47	11.77
Ireland	12.43	12.51	12.60	12.69	12.80	12.91	13.03	13.18	13.32	13.50	13.71
Israel	10.03	10.02	10.03	10.05	10.09	10.16	10.26	10.38	10.50	10.60	10.69
Italy	14.24	14.41	14.57	14.76	14.95	15.13	15.30	15.43	15.51	15.56	15.59
Japan	13.04	12.93	12.91	12.97	13.08	13.22	13.33	13.44	13.55	13.63	13.68
Jordan	7.39	7.66	7.94	8.22	8.52	8.81	9.11	9.40	9.68	9.96	10.24
Kazakhstan	10.90	10.89	10.87	10.85	10.83	10.82	10.81	10.81	10.81	10.81	10.83
Kuwait	14.61	15.12	15.67	16.24	16.82	17.37	17.89	18.36	18.78	19.14	19.46
Latvia	12.85	12.87	12.93	13.01	13.08	13.15	13.20	13.22	13.26	13.24	13.21
Lithuania	13.03	13.14	13.24	13.35	13.44	13.51	13.54	13.53	13.51	13.47	13.39
Malaysia	10.49	10.57	10.63	10.66	10.66	10.64	10.62	10.60	10.58	10.55	10.52
Mexico	9.67	9.92	10.19	10.46	10.74	11.00	11.26	11.50	11.72	11.92	12.11
Morocco	9.75	9.85	9.94	10.03	10.10	10.16	10.20	10.23	10.26	10.29	10.34
Netherlands	14.74	14.81	14.87	14.89	14.85	14.76	14.64	14.48	14.30	14.11	13.91
New Zealand	13.16	13.14	13.14	13.12	13.08	13.00	12.90	12.77	12.62	12.48	12.33
Nigeria	6.20	6.22	6.24	6.27	6.31	6.37	6.43	6.51	6.60	6.70	6.80
Norway	13.81	13.85	13.87	13.92	13.96	13.97	13.97	13.92	13.86	13.78	13.71
Pakistan	7.76	7.85	7.94	8.03	8.12	8.21	8.31	8.41	8.51	8.62	8.73
Peru	9.31	9.46	9.60	9.74	9.89	10.04	10.19	10.35	10.50	10.66	10.80
Philippines	8.68	8.78	8.88	8.97	9.07	9.16	9.27	9.37	9.48	9.59	9.71
Poland	13.84	13.73	13.62	13.50	13.39	13.31	13.25	13.19	13.17	13.15	13.16
Portugal	13.38	13.48	13.58	13.70	13.83	13.96	14.12	14.28	14.45	14.57	14.65
Romania	13.17	13.34	13.47	13.57	13.65	13.73	13.87	13.97	14.10	14.27	14.47
Russia	13.58	13.41	13.31	13.22	13.13	13.04	12.93	12.85	12.78	12.70	12.64
Saudi Arabia	11.25	11.56	11.84	12.09	12.31	12.51	12.70	12.87	13.03	13.17	13.27
Singapore	16.04	16.01	16.03	16.05	16.05	15.95	15.79	15.58	15.35	15.05	14.78
Slovakia	13.81	13.82	13.78	13.73	13.71	13.75	13.82	13.89	13.97	14.07	14.20
Slovenia	15.49	15.50	15.42	15.39	15.34	15.28	15.25	15.21	15.20	15.23	15.28
South Africa	8.68	8.71	8.73	8.75	8.77	8.80	8.83	8.88	8.94	9.02	9.11
South Korea	15.26	15.59	15.92	16.23	16.48	16.66	16.74	16.75	16.71	16.65	16.58
Spain	13.71	13.91	14.11	14.33	14.56	14.79	15.03	15.25	15.47	15.66	15.82
Sweden	13.44	13.37	13.32	13.32	13.32	13.30	13.30	13.26	13.18	13.11	13.02
Switzerland	14.84	14.88	14.90	14.92	14.91	14.87	14.81	14.72	14.59	14.45	14.30
Taiwan	14.99	15.17	15.31	15.33	15.34	15.34	15.32	15.29	15.37	15.40	15.45
Thailand	13.19	13.38	13.59	13.76	13.88	14.02	14.08	14.14	14.21	14.24	14.24
Tunisia	10.71	10.87	11.02	11.16	11.30	11.44	11.59	11.76	11.95	12.15	12.36
Turkey	10.67	10.86	11.07	11.28	11.50	11.73	11.95	12.17	12.39	12.59	12.79
Turkmenistan	9.16	9.33	9.49	9.63	9.76	9.88	9.99	10.09	10.19	10.29	10.39
Ukraine	13.11	13.01	13.01	13.02	13.03	13.05	13.03	13.08	13.12	13.15	13.17
United Arab Emirates	15.13	15.49	16.00	16.62	17.34	18.11	18.91	19.71	20.49	21.23	21.92
United Kingdom	13.23	13.21	13.21	13.21	13.18	13.12	13.04	12.94	12.82	12.68	12.56
USA	13.63	13.61	13.57	13.49	13.37	13.22	13.07	12.91	12.76	12.61	12.50
Venezuela	10.07	10.15	10.22	10.28	10.34	10.41	10.48	10.57	10.66	10.76	10.85
Vietnam	10.07	10.32	10.54	10.74	10.92	11.09	11.26	11.43	11.60	11.76	11.91

Marketing segments: Elder generation

Table 4.127 Pensioners: 2009-2019

'000

	2009	2010	2011	2012	2013	2014	2015	2016	2017	2018	2019	CAGR	Period growth
Algeria	2,779.0	2,891.9	3,011.7	3,138.5	3,273.3	3,416.9	3,570.6	3,734.6	3,908.8	4,093.0	4,287.0	4.43	54.26
Argentina	4,718.3	4,796.8	4,886.7	4,940.7	5,042.9	5,147.7	5,261.1	5,391.2	5,460.6	5,577.8	5,693.4	1.90	20.67
Australia	2,942.6	3,010.1	3,084.7	3,187.1	3,280.5	3,391.5	3,507.1	3,624.4	3,736.2	3,857.0	3,979.2	3.06	35.23
Austria	1,632.2	1,645.8	1,655.9	1,675.0	1,700.1	1,725.3	1,752.4	1,782.1	1,813.6	1,845.4	1,876.0	1.40	14.93
Azerbaijan	690.9	679.2	672.1	667.2	676.9	692.1	713.0	739.7	772.3	811.1	856.6	2.17	23.98
Belarus	2,102.8	2,117.4	2,136.2	2,152.5	2,184.4	2,209.8	2,254.7	2,303.9	2,347.6	2,380.7	2,414.0	1.39	14.80
Belgium	1,705.6	1,709.2	1,712.1	1,731.7	1,751.2	1,772.5	1,796.0	1,820.9	1,847.1	1,879.1	1,910.5	1.14	12.01
Bolivia	458.6	472.5	487.4	503.7	521.1	539.5	558.6	578.3	598.6	619.7	641.6	3.41	39.89
Bosnia-Herzegovina	707.8	724.6	743.9	765.7	789.6	815.3	842.1	869.4	897.4	925.7	954.0	3.03	34.80
Brazil	14,737.8	15,281.5	15,834.0	16,446.1	17,076.3	17,732.2	18,421.8	19,132.0	19,852.2	20,616.1	21,389.5	3.80	45.13
Bulgaria	1,560.2	1,561.8	1,565.4	1,560.1	1,561.6	1,558.9	1,550.5	1,542.8	1,542.3	1,538.8	1,539.5	-0.13	-1.32
Canada	4,438.4	4,533.9	4,645.7	4,817.3	4,988.8	5,160.6	5,344.6	5,534.7	5,728.8	5,943.1	6,174.4	3.36	39.11
Chile	1,758.9	1,812.3	1,862.6	1,915.1	1,970.5	2,029.9	2,094.0	2,163.6	2,238.9	2,320.2	2,407.4	3.19	36.86
China	155,065.6	158,341.8	160,496.8	165,810.0	170,683.8	177,068.1	183,483.7	188,681.7	195,834.6	200,342.2	199,914.1	2.57	28.92
Colombia	4,918.1	5,136.0	5,363.3	5,600.1	5,846.6	6,103.1	6,369.8	6,646.9	6,933.8	7,230.0	7,534.7	4.36	53.20
Costa Rica	411.9	430.0	449.5	470.4	492.9	517.0	542.6	569.9	598.7	629.0	660.7	4.84	60.39
Croatia	905.8	908.1	906.5	908.6	914.8	920.4	928.9	937.4	944.5	952.7	960.4	0.59	6.03
Czech Republic	2,105.1	2,158.5	2,210.3	2,254.2	2,299.1	2,344.2	2,390.7	2,435.6	2,476.9	2,512.6	2,540.1	1.90	20.66
Denmark	730.8	747.0	768.3	794.8	825.3	858.1	887.5	909.7	927.0	942.6	953.9	2.70	30.53
Ecuador	1,156.7	1,198.7	1,245.3	1,296.4	1,351.5	1,409.3	1,468.6	1,528.5	1,589.2	1,651.0	1,714.1	4.01	48.19
Egypt	5,902.5	6,126.4	6,368.4	6,628.0	6,904.5	7,195.9	7,499.6	7,814.1	8,138.2	8,469.9	8,806.3	4.08	49.20
Estonia	250.8	244.9	240.0	235.1	236.1	235.9	237.6	239.6	240.2	241.3	241.7	-0.37	-3.66
Finland	888.7	917.6	953.8	990.9	1,027.3	1,061.3	1,092.0	1,119.0	1,147.6	1,172.7	1,197.8	3.03	34.77
France	13,107.1	13,373.4	13,643.2	13,860.0	14,090.4	14,301.9	14,547.2	14,776.8	15,029.6	15,289.1	15,552.2	1.73	18.66
Germany	15,786.5	15,788.3	15,535.0	15,357.7	15,331.8	15,375.8	15,511.3	15,540.6	15,508.2	15,474.7	15,419.5	-0.23	-2.32
Greece	2,670.1	2,679.6	2,686.5	2,693.6	2,708.1	2,721.4	2,733.9	2,747.5	2,764.0	2,784.8	2,807.1	0.50	5.13
Hong Kong, China	883.2	900.1	919.5	953.2	991.6	1,035.0	1,086.3	1,134.8	1,183.4	1,233.9	1,289.7	3.86	46.03
Hungary	2,049.7	2,078.4	2,105.1	2,135.3	2,171.6	2,200.0	2,252.0	2,316.2	2,372.4	2,424.1	2,449.7	1.80	19.52
India	112,343.0	115,842.1	119,553.4	123,479.7	127,616.1	131,951.6	136,472.9	141,171.6	146,043.0	151,076.4	156,253.5	3.35	39.09
Indonesia	28,658.9	29,576.6	30,568.4	31,636.3	32,768.7	33,941.1	35,129.6	36,318.6	37,506.7	38,709.1	39,953.2	3.38	39.41
Iran	6,229.4	6,442.8	6,674.1	6,923.5	7,190.8	7,475.8	7,777.3	8,095.6	8,429.9	8,778.9	9,140.3	3.91	46.73
Ireland	416.0	421.8	428.4	438.3	450.6	463.5	477.1	490.5	502.5	513.7	528.4	2.42	27.02
Israel	900.7	931.9	970.1	1,014.9	1,060.9	1,104.1	1,150.4	1,197.5	1,242.0	1,284.0	1,325.2	3.94	47.13
Italy	12,971.2	13,018.2	13,047.1	13,114.1	13,199.7	13,304.1	13,396.3	13,484.1	13,555.6	13,655.4	13,741.7	0.58	5.94
Japan	26,681.9	26,768.3	26,713.6	27,502.7	28,397.2	29,290.3	29,974.0	30,422.9	30,689.8	30,845.5	30,927.2	1.49	15.91
Jordan	403.4	416.1	429.4	443.5	458.6	475.0	492.9	512.5	534.1	557.9	584.1	3.77	44.79
Kazakhstan	1,738.3	1,751.5	1,777.3	1,815.9	1,865.5	1,923.0	1,985.5	2,051.2	2,119.6	2,190.2	2,261.9	2.67	30.12
Kuwait	411.0	420.8	429.4	437.4	444.6	452.1	460.3	467.1	471.8	513.2	557.0	3.09	35.52
Latvia	446.0	442.5	441.4	441.6	440.2	439.2	439.5	439.7	440.6	441.1	440.0	-0.14	-1.35
Lithuania	712.1	713.9	716.9	719.4	723.5	727.5	732.2	737.4	745.4	754.0	763.6	0.70	7.23
Malaysia	3,087.4	3,228.2	3,382.0	3,545.0	3,715.6	3,893.1	4,061.6	4,233.5	4,412.9	4,601.2	4,797.4	4.51	55.39
Mexico	6,405.1	6,648.0	6,899.7	7,160.7	7,433.0	7,718.9	8,020.5	8,339.1	8,674.7	9,028.6	9,403.3	3.91	46.81
Morocco	2,293.6	2,375.9	2,466.9	2,567.0	2,676.7	2,796.8	2,928.0	3,070.5	3,224.2	3,387.3	3,556.3	4.48	55.05
Netherlands	2,359.1	2,405.6	2,442.8	2,549.5	2,648.8	2,731.9	2,809.3	2,880.5	2,948.3	3,021.4	3,092.3	2.74	31.08
New Zealand	501.9	509.4	518.3	534.7	551.3	567.3	584.1	600.0	615.8	630.8	647.1	2.57	28.94
Nigeria	6,992.1	7,194.2	7,416.8	7,660.2	7,920.5	8,192.2	8,469.2	8,748.2	9,029.1	9,312.5	9,598.4	3.22	37.28
Norway	608.7	615.5	625.9	641.8	659.7	683.6	705.0	725.1	744.0	762.4	779.5	2.50	28.06
Pakistan	12,609.5	13,026.4	13,471.5	13,945.0	14,444.7	14,966.4	15,505.7	16,060.1	16,629.3	17,212.5	17,808.3	3.51	41.23
Peru	1,654.9	1,711.1	1,770.3	1,832.5	1,898.1	1,967.6	2,041.1	2,119.0	2,201.6	2,288.6	2,379.9	3.70	43.81
Philippines	6,288.7	6,543.0	6,814.7	7,105.4	7,416.1	7,747.5	8,100.2	8,474.9	8,870.5	9,287.6	9,726.9	4.46	54.67
Poland	5,982.4	6,049.4	6,142.0	6,276.1	6,452.8	6,650.5	6,866.7	7,110.2	7,347.0	7,588.2	7,839.2	2.74	31.04
Portugal	1,754.6	1,758.1	1,771.0	1,771.6	1,779.7	1,795.4	1,812.5	1,832.9	1,847.2	1,864.7	1,881.6	0.70	7.23
Romania	3,754.5	3,779.5	3,795.7	3,812.8	3,842.8	3,857.4	3,930.1	4,006.0	4,068.5	4,114.2	4,155.1	1.02	10.67
Russia	29,802.8	30,259.7	30,649.3	31,048.4	31,455.8	31,854.8	32,422.9	33,007.8	33,463.6	33,838.6	34,075.2	1.35	14.34
Saudi Arabia	1,454.5	1,497.9	1,542.9	1,589.3	1,637.4	1,687.2	1,738.5	1,791.2	1,845.5	1,901.2	1,958.6	3.02	34.66
Singapore	755.1	793.3	833.2	876.1	918.8	962.1	1,005.0	1,046.1	1,089.1	1,133.6	1,177.0	4.54	55.88
Slovakia	773.4	785.6	799.1	816.5	838.9	862.1	888.6	920.2	954.0	987.8	1,019.9	2.80	31.86
Slovenia	339.5	332.8	332.6	334.4	338.7	344.3	351.0	359.7	368.3	377.4	387.4	1.33	14.11
South Africa	3,476.7	3,528.1	3,528.3	3,603.2	3,676.3	3,759.1	3,873.1	3,976.7	4,079.0	4,233.0	4,353.9	2.28	25.23
South Korea	6,417.3	6,550.1	6,677.5	6,772.9	6,872.1	7,044.5	7,133.4	7,278.1	7,498.0	7,713.3	7,918.6	2.12	23.39
Spain	6,836.7	6,840.4	6,854.2	6,871.8	6,890.2	6,903.7	6,924.4	6,950.2	6,984.4	7,039.6	7,129.2	0.42	4.28
Sweden	2,141.8	2,183.1	2,219.5	2,251.1	2,277.5	2,304.7	2,332.3	2,356.9	2,383.3	2,410.8	2,437.3	1.30	13.79
Switzerland	1,234.6	1,253.9	1,275.1	1,295.2	1,315.7	1,334.3	1,352.2	1,367.2	1,381.2	1,396.3	1,412.7	1.36	14.42
Taiwan	3,938.5	4,094.7	4,278.0	4,454.7	4,647.6	4,855.2	5,071.2	5,290.9	5,506.1	5,728.7	5,953.3	4.22	51.16
Thailand	10,585.6	11,101.2	11,631.1	12,151.1	12,649.4	13,239.7	13,860.4	14,479.2	15,125.7	15,800.4	16,543.0	4.57	56.28
Tunisia	917.6	942.6	972.1	1,006.2	1,044.6	1,086.9	1,132.2	1,180.4	1,231.2	1,284.6	1,340.4	3.86	46.07
Turkey	11,635.0	12,060.0	12,466.0	12,877.0	13,294.0	13,721.0	14,149.0	14,607.0	15,059.0	15,517.0	15,996.0	3.23	37.48
Turkmenistan	359.9	371.5	385.2	400.9	418.7	438.6	460.7	485.1	511.5	539.8	569.2	4.69	58.17
Ukraine	11,071.2	11,085.5	11,100.9	11,114.6	11,193.7	11,292.0	11,478.1	11,647.3	11,737.1	11,759.7	11,695.3	0.55	5.64
United Arab Emirates	86.5	91.4	96.9	103.1	109.9	117.7	126.9	137.4	149.4	162.6	177.3	7.45	105.06
United Kingdom	12,033.5	12,237.9	12,266.2	12,363.8	12,434.4	12,478.4	12,506.4	12,522.1	12,531.2	12,540.4	12,548.0	0.42	4.27
USA	35,414.7	35,788.6	36,130.3	36,682.3	38,099.4	39,320.5	40,567.6	41,774.7	43,046.0	44,453.2	45,855.2	2.62	29.48
Venezuela	2,845.6	2,975.3	3,108.6	3,245.6	3,386.6	3,532.4	3,683.7	3,840.7	4,003.2	4,170.9	4,343.6	4.32	52.64
Vietnam	7,956.3	8,228.2	8,536.2	8,881.0	9,261.5	9,675.2	10,119.0	10,590.9	11,090.1	11,615.0	12,163.7	4.34	52.88

Marketing segments: Elder generation

Table 4.128 Elderly population (60+): 2009-2019

'000

	2009	2010	2011	2012	2013	2014	2015	2016	2017	2018	2019	CAGR	Period growth
Algeria	2,359.4	2,445.8	2,544.4	2,654.3	2,772.6	2,896.4	3,023.3	3,153.2	3,287.3	3,428.2	3,579.1	4.26	51.70
Argentina	5,805.3	5,919.1	6,037.5	6,160.4	6,286.7	6,415.1	6,544.4	6,673.7	6,802.7	6,931.9	7,062.1	1.98	21.65
Australia	4,094.2	4,222.8	4,347.8	4,475.3	4,610.5	4,745.8	4,885.4	5,030.3	5,174.8	5,321.0	5,470.0	2.94	33.60
Austria	1,906.5	1,936.1	1,963.8	1,987.9	2,015.2	2,042.4	2,071.7	2,105.2	2,145.8	2,187.5	2,231.0	1.58	17.02
Azerbaijan	754.1	767.3	786.6	812.2	844.2	882.3	926.2	975.8	1,031.1	1,091.8	1,157.1	4.37	53.44
Belarus	1,755.5	1,777.7	1,783.1	1,796.9	1,805.6	1,818.8	1,847.0	1,873.8	1,905.3	1,938.8	1,976.8	1.19	12.60
Belgium	2,450.1	2,489.3	2,528.6	2,566.4	2,608.5	2,650.7	2,695.3	2,741.8	2,789.6	2,839.1	2,891.2	1.67	18.00
Bolivia	697.7	720.6	744.1	768.3	793.2	819.1	846.1	874.3	903.7	934.3	965.9	3.31	38.45
Bosnia-Herzegovina	720.2	734.8	751.5	770.0	789.7	810.0	830.5	851.0	871.8	892.9	914.1	2.41	26.92
Brazil	18,826.9	19,490.2	20,193.3	20,938.4	21,727.7	22,564.0	23,448.7	24,379.3	25,354.2	26,375.7	27,446.9	3.84	45.79
Bulgaria	1,810.6	1,830.4	1,853.9	1,863.1	1,875.4	1,888.7	1,900.7	1,915.7	1,930.3	1,941.7	1,952.6	0.76	7.84
Canada	6,535.7	6,735.5	6,931.6	7,129.1	7,338.1	7,565.2	7,801.7	8,034.2	8,278.4	8,525.5	8,771.3	2.99	34.21
Chile	2,176.4	2,251.7	2,330.0	2,412.0	2,498.6	2,590.8	2,689.0	2,793.4	2,903.6	3,019.5	3,140.8	3.74	44.31
China	191,272.9	197,826.0	204,540.5	214,035.0	222,052.3	232,059.2	241,168.4	248,682.8	257,447.1	263,545.7	266,222.0	3.36	39.18
Colombia	3,795.3	3,973.6	4,164.0	4,365.8	4,577.7	4,798.3	5,026.2	5,260.9	5,502.6	5,752.1	6,010.8	4.71	58.37
Costa Rica	420.4	439.1	459.2	480.7	503.7	528.2	554.3	582.1	611.6	642.7	675.4	4.86	60.67
Croatia	1,002.3	1,016.0	1,027.6	1,036.1	1,048.9	1,061.8	1,076.4	1,090.4	1,104.3	1,114.5	1,124.9	1.16	12.24
Czech Republic	2,259.3	2,314.5	2,371.3	2,427.9	2,481.1	2,529.6	2,575.3	2,619.0	2,660.2	2,696.6	2,723.1	1.88	20.53
Denmark	1,253.6	1,276.1	1,299.1	1,320.2	1,342.4	1,365.9	1,388.0	1,411.2	1,434.9	1,457.8	1,480.5	1.68	18.10
Ecuador	1,255.2	1,303.4	1,355.6	1,411.7	1,470.6	1,531.5	1,593.5	1,656.0	1,719.2	1,782.9	1,847.5	3.94	47.19
Egypt	5,973.2	6,233.1	6,509.8	6,804.0	7,116.2	7,446.8	7,796.3	8,164.5	8,550.4	8,950.9	9,360.4	4.59	56.71
Estonia	294.8	297.6	299.3	301.4	303.4	304.9	307.1	309.8	311.8	314.0	316.3	0.71	7.28
Finland	1,269.0	1,309.8	1,346.4	1,378.6	1,412.1	1,441.8	1,471.2	1,499.4	1,527.1	1,552.1	1,572.9	2.17	23.95
France	13,929.1	14,281.8	14,626.8	14,933.5	15,240.3	15,524.2	15,813.5	16,089.7	16,363.0	16,635.3	16,896.2	1.95	21.30
Germany	20,925.3	21,138.0	21,379.8	21,612.7	21,856.2	22,086.0	22,334.1	22,586.0	22,856.7	23,141.5	23,437.8	1.14	12.01
Greece	2,755.1	2,783.5	2,832.2	2,871.5	2,909.0	2,940.9	2,979.4	3,023.8	3,067.0	3,107.2	3,147.3	1.34	14.24
Hong Kong, China	1,224.0	1,280.3	1,334.0	1,388.5	1,444.0	1,506.9	1,574.2	1,645.4	1,719.5	1,796.6	1,873.5	4.35	53.06
Hungary	2,213.0	2,239.6	2,272.4	2,299.9	2,325.3	2,366.4	2,422.2	2,469.3	2,506.2	2,524.1	2,537.6	1.38	14.67
India	86,558.2	89,578.6	92,966.8	96,692.1	100,683.8	104,851.5	109,118.4	113,445.8	117,820.4	122,238.4	126,704.3	3.88	46.38
Indonesia	20,231.1	20,789.0	21,394.6	22,054.4	22,774.1	23,558.6	24,411.2	25,333.0	26,321.4	27,370.7	28,472.7	3.48	40.74
Iran	5,228.0	5,352.7	5,505.2	5,686.1	5,894.3	6,127.8	6,385.1	6,665.6	6,968.4	7,291.7	7,633.0	3.86	46.00
Ireland	713.5	734.2	754.1	774.0	795.6	817.1	839.7	861.9	885.2	909.9	934.8	2.74	31.02
Israel	1,024.9	1,059.8	1,098.7	1,138.3	1,176.7	1,214.2	1,250.5	1,285.0	1,316.8	1,348.3	1,381.8	3.03	34.83
Italy	15,535.3	15,752.0	15,955.9	16,123.6	16,282.6	16,441.0	16,624.2	16,810.4	17,002.7	17,200.4	17,399.4	1.14	12.00
Japan	38,379.7	39,329.0	40,103.2	40,740.6	41,252.2	41,632.0	41,981.3	42,249.5	42,414.8	42,591.7	42,782.7	1.09	11.47
Jordan	348.6	358.5	368.0	377.2	386.6	396.8	408.2	421.2	435.9	452.4	470.8	3.05	35.08
Kazakhstan	1,591.1	1,631.6	1,679.0	1,730.8	1,786.3	1,845.4	1,908.5	1,976.7	2,050.7	2,129.9	2,212.5	3.35	39.05
Kuwait	93.9	101.3	109.2	117.9	127.5	138.3	150.5	164.2	179.4	196.0	213.6	8.57	127.47
Latvia	503.2	505.0	504.9	504.8	504.3	502.8	503.2	504.3	505.5	508.1	511.3	0.16	1.61
Lithuania	693.9	697.7	701.9	705.4	708.8	710.2	712.3	717.4	723.0	730.2	739.9	0.64	6.63
Malaysia	2,007.9	2,100.9	2,205.4	2,322.7	2,446.1	2,578.5	2,718.6	2,866.7	3,022.9	3,181.3	3,346.7	5.24	66.68
Mexico	9,880.8	10,305.2	10,772.2	11,267.2	11,790.0	12,336.9	12,903.1	13,484.9	14,079.2	14,685.7	15,306.7	4.47	54.91
Morocco	2,526.6	2,607.8	2,696.4	2,793.3	2,900.4	3,020.3	3,154.4	3,303.4	3,465.3	3,636.1	3,810.1	4.19	50.80
Netherlands	3,500.2	3,589.2	3,673.3	3,754.5	3,841.3	3,926.2	4,012.1	4,099.1	4,189.1	4,281.1	4,374.2	2.25	24.97
New Zealand	773.0	797.0	820.4	844.2	867.9	893.0	918.8	946.1	974.4	1,002.6	1,032.8	2.94	33.62
Nigeria	7,594.1	7,796.0	8,010.2	8,236.6	8,474.0	8,720.2	8,973.1	9,231.5	9,494.9	9,763.0	10,036.0	2.83	32.15
Norway	992.5	1,012.9	1,032.7	1,051.2	1,071.8	1,093.3	1,114.9	1,137.7	1,161.7	1,185.0	1,209.1	1.99	21.83
Pakistan	11,117.9	11,459.7	11,819.3	12,198.6	12,599.6	13,023.4	13,471.1	13,943.4	14,440.8	14,963.1	15,510.2	3.39	39.51
Peru	2,470.1	2,558.8	2,652.0	2,749.8	2,851.8	2,957.7	3,067.4	3,180.8	3,298.2	3,420.3	3,547.5	3.69	43.62
Philippines	6,006.4	6,267.0	6,547.0	6,848.8	7,170.5	7,510.7	7,865.9	8,234.1	8,614.7	9,007.3	9,412.4	4.59	56.71
Poland	7,032.4	7,227.3	7,441.6	7,672.6	7,907.1	8,140.4	8,371.8	8,616.6	8,850.5	9,081.8	9,297.8	2.83	32.21
Portugal	2,471.0	2,507.7	2,546.5	2,584.8	2,624.2	2,659.7	2,698.8	2,740.3	2,778.3	2,822.2	2,865.3	1.49	15.96
Romania	4,196.6	4,261.4	4,321.0	4,366.7	4,418.0	4,462.6	4,524.9	4,601.0	4,667.0	4,722.5	4,768.2	1.29	13.62
Russia	24,606.6	25,047.0	25,421.3	25,730.8	26,166.2	26,465.6	26,963.9	27,403.6	27,854.0	28,355.1	28,829.6	1.60	17.16
Saudi Arabia	1,154.0	1,210.7	1,273.7	1,343.3	1,419.3	1,501.6	1,590.2	1,685.2	1,787.3	1,897.4	2,016.6	5.74	74.74
Singapore	641.8	680.3	717.6	759.6	803.4	851.2	899.5	948.0	1,003.9	1,061.2	1,116.3	5.69	73.92
Slovakia	922.0	943.8	971.0	1,001.6	1,033.2	1,064.2	1,096.3	1,129.9	1,164.5	1,196.9	1,226.3	2.89	33.00
Slovenia	437.4	447.5	459.8	471.1	483.5	496.2	508.3	520.6	532.9	543.9	554.1	2.39	26.68
South Africa	3,578.0	3,699.6	3,826.3	3,957.6	4,092.6	4,230.9	4,371.6	4,513.5	4,655.0	4,794.7	4,930.9	3.26	37.81
South Korea	7,293.3	7,543.6	7,796.2	8,071.9	8,372.4	8,706.7	9,091.8	9,508.6	9,946.5	10,412.9	10,906.2	4.11	49.54
Spain	10,085.2	10,261.1	10,440.5	10,614.3	10,788.6	10,972.4	11,166.9	11,373.8	11,595.7	11,835.2	12,089.0	1.83	19.87
Sweden	2,278.9	2,318.9	2,352.6	2,382.1	2,410.8	2,442.4	2,471.2	2,503.1	2,535.4	2,567.9	2,598.0	1.32	14.00
Switzerland	1,716.4	1,747.2	1,778.1	1,805.7	1,835.8	1,865.3	1,895.8	1,927.4	1,962.1	2,000.0	2,038.4	1.73	18.76
Taiwan	3,228.7	3,353.0	3,491.8	3,670.1	3,841.6	4,017.5	4,199.8	4,390.4	4,589.3	4,772.2	4,967.3	4.40	53.85
Thailand	7,519.3	7,847.2	8,173.1	8,514.3	8,883.4	9,241.6	9,702.2	10,167.8	10,625.0	11,071.2	11,589.4	4.42	54.13
Tunisia	980.5	1,008.4	1,040.7	1,077.4	1,117.8	1,161.4	1,207.4	1,255.7	1,305.9	1,357.8	1,411.0	3.71	43.91
Turkey	6,668.4	6,891.2	7,107.2	7,342.7	7,591.7	7,854.4	8,122.3	8,420.3	8,726.3	9,036.9	9,360.3	3.45	40.37
Turkmenistan	308.8	317.4	327.6	339.3	352.7	367.9	385.0	404.4	426.1	449.9	475.3	4.41	53.90
Ukraine	9,390.7	9,498.2	9,552.6	9,635.8	9,725.5	9,833.7	9,987.9	10,102.5	10,241.4	10,339.1	10,466.8	1.09	11.46
United Arab Emirates	91.1	97.5	105.5	115.0	126.2	139.0	153.3	169.0	185.9	203.3	220.6	9.25	142.32
United Kingdom	13,655.6	13,848.8	14,006.6	14,152.5	14,301.3	14,459.3	14,616.9	14,778.9	14,959.4	15,163.5	15,383.0	1.20	12.65
USA	55,392.6	56,845.8	58,280.4	59,765.3	61,339.9	63,013.3	64,795.6	66,527.5	68,379.4	70,222.8	72,030.2	2.66	30.04
Venezuela	2,394.3	2,506.9	2,624.3	2,746.1	2,871.6	3,000.2	3,131.4	3,265.3	3,402.2	3,543.6	3,691.3	4.42	54.17
Vietnam	6,749.8	6,942.3	7,187.0	7,481.4	7,819.4	8,190.9	8,588.3	9,009.1	9,455.5	9,928.7	10,431.0	4.45	54.54

Marketing segments: Elder generation

Table 4.129 Female elderly population (60+): 2009-2019

'000

	2009	2010	2011	2012	2013	2014	2015	2016	2017	2018	2019	CAGR	Period growth
Algeria	1,283.7	1,329.8	1,380.8	1,436.1	1,494.7	1,555.6	1,618.0	1,682.1	1,748.8	1,819.5	1,895.7	3.98	47.67
Argentina	3,369.7	3,435.4	3,503.6	3,574.1	3,646.5	3,720.4	3,795.0	3,870.1	3,945.3	4,020.6	4,096.2	1.97	21.56
Australia	2,177.2	2,242.2	2,305.4	2,370.1	2,439.2	2,508.8	2,580.8	2,655.0	2,729.6	2,805.8	2,883.4	2.85	32.43
Austria	1,090.6	1,103.3	1,115.3	1,125.7	1,137.9	1,150.5	1,164.2	1,180.0	1,199.8	1,219.7	1,240.8	1.30	13.77
Azerbaijan	434.0	441.4	451.8	465.6	482.7	502.9	526.2	552.6	582.1	614.6	649.7	4.12	49.68
Belarus	1,153.2	1,165.9	1,168.2	1,176.5	1,180.6	1,189.2	1,206.3	1,222.6	1,241.3	1,261.2	1,283.3	1.07	11.28
Belgium	1,380.4	1,399.0	1,418.1	1,436.5	1,456.7	1,477.0	1,499.0	1,522.1	1,545.8	1,570.0	1,595.4	1.46	15.58
Bolivia	381.5	394.3	407.4	420.9	434.8	449.2	464.1	479.7	495.9	512.8	530.1	3.34	38.94
Bosnia-Herzegovina	404.9	413.0	422.1	432.3	443.1	454.3	465.5	476.9	488.6	500.4	512.4	2.38	26.55
Brazil	10,431.1	10,814.8	11,222.7	11,655.6	12,114.3	12,599.5	13,111.2	13,647.9	14,208.6	14,795.2	15,409.9	3.98	47.73
Bulgaria	1,044.9	1,056.9	1,070.8	1,076.9	1,084.6	1,092.3	1,099.1	1,107.6	1,115.4	1,121.4	1,127.1	0.76	7.87
Canada	3,559.1	3,660.1	3,758.6	3,857.5	3,962.2	4,076.2	4,194.3	4,310.3	4,432.5	4,555.5	4,678.9	2.77	31.46
Chile	1,219.1	1,259.1	1,300.8	1,344.4	1,390.5	1,439.5	1,491.8	1,547.3	1,605.9	1,667.6	1,732.2	3.58	42.09
China	95,735.1	99,006.7	102,724.6	107,615.8	111,792.6	116,941.2	121,846.0	125,903.1	130,601.9	133,974.3	135,578.2	3.54	41.62
Colombia	2,107.7	2,206.3	2,311.5	2,423.0	2,540.1	2,662.0	2,788.0	2,917.8	3,051.6	3,189.7	3,333.0	4.69	58.14
Costa Rica	221.5	231.3	241.8	253.0	264.9	277.6	291.0	305.2	320.3	336.3	353.0	4.77	59.39
Croatia	595.0	601.9	607.3	610.8	616.5	622.5	628.9	635.7	642.7	647.7	652.5	0.93	9.68
Czech Republic	1,308.1	1,336.1	1,364.5	1,393.3	1,420.0	1,443.9	1,466.7	1,488.1	1,508.6	1,526.2	1,539.1	1.64	17.65
Denmark	680.4	690.6	701.3	710.7	721.0	731.9	742.4	753.2	764.6	775.5	786.4	1.46	15.58
Ecuador	662.4	688.1	716.0	745.8	777.3	809.8	843.0	876.5	910.5	944.8	979.6	3.99	47.88
Egypt	3,195.5	3,340.0	3,490.9	3,648.7	3,813.6	3,986.1	4,166.5	4,355.4	4,552.1	4,754.9	4,961.9	4.50	55.28
Estonia	191.3	193.0	194.0	195.4	196.6	197.4	198.8	200.4	201.6	202.8	204.1	0.65	6.72
Finland	719.4	738.9	756.6	772.1	788.4	803.1	818.0	832.0	845.9	858.4	869.0	1.91	20.80
France	7,918.3	8,095.7	8,271.2	8,429.0	8,587.8	8,735.5	8,887.0	9,033.2	9,177.1	9,320.3	9,458.3	1.79	19.45
Germany	11,777.6	11,852.0	11,946.7	12,040.6	12,142.6	12,239.8	12,346.6	12,453.3	12,569.2	12,692.7	12,822.9	0.85	8.88
Greece	1,515.7	1,532.0	1,558.3	1,578.5	1,598.9	1,615.5	1,635.8	1,658.7	1,681.5	1,702.7	1,723.4	1.29	13.70
Hong Kong, China	643.7	673.2	702.5	732.9	762.9	797.2	833.0	871.5	911.2	952.7	994.5	4.45	54.50
Hungary	1,359.2	1,374.0	1,391.9	1,407.5	1,421.3	1,442.8	1,471.7	1,496.6	1,516.4	1,526.7	1,535.1	1.22	12.94
India	45,200.9	46,809.1	48,587.7	50,523.6	52,585.9	54,735.1	56,938.3	59,180.1	61,455.7	63,763.1	66,103.4	3.87	46.24
Indonesia	11,120.1	11,418.6	11,734.0	12,070.7	12,434.1	12,829.3	13,260.6	13,729.9	14,236.4	14,777.8	15,350.0	3.28	38.04
Iran	2,595.5	2,677.0	2,771.1	2,878.2	2,998.3	3,130.8	3,275.5	3,432.2	3,600.4	3,778.4	3,964.5	4.33	52.75
Ireland	382.8	393.1	402.9	412.6	423.2	434.0	445.3	456.6	468.2	480.9	493.7	2.58	28.96
Israel	570.7	588.8	609.0	629.6	649.2	668.6	687.3	705.3	721.8	737.9	755.2	2.84	32.33
Italy	8,803.7	8,912.7	9,015.5	9,100.2	9,179.9	9,257.7	9,349.1	9,440.6	9,534.5	9,630.5	9,726.6	1.00	10.48
Japan	21,394.1	21,904.8	22,327.1	22,682.5	22,973.9	23,196.2	23,402.7	23,568.8	23,682.0	23,801.3	23,926.2	1.12	11.84
Jordan	173.5	179.4	185.2	190.8	196.5	202.6	209.2	216.6	224.8	233.9	244.1	3.47	40.70
Kazakhstan	1,042.1	1,072.3	1,106.0	1,141.8	1,179.1	1,218.2	1,259.4	1,303.8	1,351.9	1,403.1	1,456.2	3.40	39.74
Kuwait	37.3	40.0	42.9	46.1	49.6	53.5	57.9	62.9	68.3	74.3	80.7	8.03	116.40
Latvia	327.9	328.9	328.6	328.3	327.7	326.5	326.4	326.7	327.1	328.0	329.1	0.04	0.38
Lithuania	444.6	447.3	449.9	451.9	453.9	454.5	455.6	458.1	461.0	464.7	469.9	0.55	5.69
Malaysia	1,037.8	1,085.6	1,139.7	1,200.7	1,264.2	1,332.6	1,405.4	1,482.5	1,564.0	1,647.4	1,735.1	5.27	67.19
Mexico	5,295.6	5,514.3	5,756.8	6,016.0	6,291.7	6,582.1	6,884.6	7,196.9	7,517.4	7,845.7	8,183.2	4.45	54.53
Morocco	1,353.3	1,395.1	1,439.9	1,488.0	1,540.6	1,599.3	1,665.5	1,739.8	1,821.9	1,910.2	2,002.4	4.00	47.97
Netherlands	1,910.5	1,950.7	1,989.0	2,026.0	2,066.3	2,106.0	2,146.6	2,188.6	2,231.7	2,276.5	2,322.1	1.97	21.54
New Zealand	414.2	426.3	438.1	450.2	462.3	475.3	488.8	503.1	517.8	532.8	548.8	2.85	32.50
Nigeria	4,052.0	4,160.1	4,275.6	4,398.3	4,527.4	4,661.4	4,799.0	4,939.3	5,082.2	5,227.3	5,374.6	2.87	32.64
Norway	543.5	551.1	558.6	565.5	573.9	583.0	592.3	602.3	613.1	623.6	634.6	1.56	16.78
Pakistan	5,429.0	5,611.5	5,799.8	5,994.9	6,198.5	6,412.3	6,637.4	6,874.8	7,124.9	7,387.8	7,663.5	3.51	41.16
Peru	1,318.0	1,365.9	1,416.3	1,469.2	1,524.3	1,581.7	1,641.1	1,702.5	1,766.1	1,832.2	1,901.0	3.73	44.23
Philippines	3,219.3	3,356.4	3,505.2	3,666.7	3,839.9	4,023.7	4,216.3	4,416.5	4,623.9	4,838.2	5,059.5	4.62	57.16
Poland	4,221.2	4,325.1	4,438.8	4,562.6	4,686.9	4,810.1	4,932.4	5,060.3	5,182.5	5,303.4	5,416.2	2.52	28.31
Portugal	1,410.1	1,429.7	1,450.5	1,471.0	1,492.5	1,511.9	1,532.7	1,554.8	1,574.9	1,598.0	1,620.6	1.40	14.93
Romania	2,437.6	2,474.4	2,507.8	2,533.3	2,561.2	2,585.6	2,618.9	2,659.6	2,694.6	2,723.8	2,747.3	1.20	12.71
Russia	16,287.0	16,536.5	16,743.8	16,929.8	17,190.5	17,377.9	17,684.9	17,957.1	18,233.2	18,540.7	18,837.4	1.47	15.66
Saudi Arabia	553.4	577.7	603.5	630.8	659.5	689.8	721.8	755.7	791.9	831.2	874.3	4.68	57.98
Singapore	343.8	362.9	381.3	402.0	423.2	446.0	469.3	492.6	519.7	547.5	573.6	5.25	66.83
Slovakia	556.4	567.6	581.6	597.1	613.1	628.5	644.6	661.7	679.1	695.0	709.4	2.46	27.51
Slovenia	256.8	261.3	266.8	272.0	277.5	283.1	288.6	294.2	299.8	305.0	309.6	1.89	20.59
South Africa	2,106.5	2,183.1	2,263.8	2,348.4	2,436.4	2,527.5	2,621.1	2,716.3	2,812.1	2,907.5	3,001.1	3.60	42.47
South Korea	4,157.4	4,285.8	4,416.3	4,559.7	4,715.8	4,888.7	5,087.9	5,303.1	5,528.2	5,768.4	6,025.3	3.78	44.93
Spain	5,668.9	5,762.7	5,858.1	5,950.1	6,041.9	6,138.8	6,241.1	6,349.4	6,465.2	6,589.7	6,720.8	1.72	18.55
Sweden	1,235.1	1,253.1	1,267.4	1,280.0	1,292.1	1,305.8	1,318.1	1,332.6	1,346.6	1,361.7	1,375.3	1.08	11.35
Switzerland	959.1	974.1	989.0	1,003.0	1,018.7	1,034.1	1,050.2	1,066.4	1,083.7	1,103.4	1,123.3	1.59	17.11
Taiwan	1,661.5	1,736.3	1,819.0	1,922.2	2,021.3	2,124.1	2,227.1	2,337.6	2,448.9	2,554.1	2,665.2	4.84	60.40
Thailand	4,227.9	4,418.0	4,606.6	4,805.5	5,018.0	5,226.5	5,490.9	5,754.0	6,015.0	6,269.2	6,561.6	4.49	55.20
Tunisia	513.7	529.0	546.6	566.2	587.8	611.1	635.9	662.3	690.2	719.4	749.9	3.86	45.99
Turkey	3,587.8	3,699.1	3,813.1	3,934.5	4,065.9	4,204.0	4,342.7	4,498.3	4,658.3	4,819.7	4,990.1	3.35	39.08
Turkmenistan	180.3	185.4	191.5	198.3	206.1	214.8	224.7	235.9	248.4	262.2	277.0	4.38	53.57
Ukraine	6,101.5	6,168.9	6,204.4	6,255.0	6,309.2	6,374.1	6,466.9	6,538.7	6,623.9	6,682.7	6,754.0	1.02	10.70
United Arab Emirates	32.0	33.9	36.0	38.4	41.0	44.0	47.6	51.7	56.5	62.0	68.1	7.84	112.67
United Kingdom	7,505.7	7,584.1	7,646.4	7,704.7	7,766.4	7,834.8	7,904.8	7,978.9	8,064.3	8,163.0	8,271.4	0.98	10.20
USA	30,968.3	31,679.2	32,391.1	33,130.3	33,924.3	34,773.8	35,674.4	36,563.4	37,517.5	38,466.9	39,406.6	2.44	27.25
Venezuela	1,266.7	1,325.9	1,387.8	1,452.4	1,519.1	1,587.7	1,658.1	1,730.0	1,803.8	1,880.1	1,960.0	4.46	54.73
Vietnam	3,584.6	3,688.1	3,818.2	3,973.8	4,151.9	4,347.8	4,557.6	4,780.2	5,016.7	5,267.7	5,534.2	4.44	54.39

Marketing segments: Elder generation

Table 4.130 Male elderly population (60+): 2009-2019

'000

	2009	2010	2011	2012	2013	2014	2015	2016	2017	2018	2019	CAGR	Period growth
Algeria	1,075.7	1,116.0	1,163.7	1,218.2	1,277.9	1,340.8	1,405.4	1,471.1	1,538.4	1,608.7	1,683.4	4.58	56.50
Argentina	2,435.6	2,483.6	2,533.9	2,586.3	2,640.2	2,694.7	2,749.4	2,803.6	2,857.4	2,911.3	2,965.9	1.99	21.77
Australia	1,917.0	1,980.7	2,042.3	2,105.3	2,171.3	2,237.0	2,304.6	2,375.4	2,445.2	2,515.1	2,586.6	3.04	34.93
Austria	815.9	832.8	848.5	862.1	877.2	892.0	907.5	925.2	946.0	967.9	990.2	1.95	21.36
Azerbaijan	320.0	326.0	334.8	346.6	361.6	379.4	400.0	423.2	449.1	477.3	507.4	4.72	58.55
Belarus	602.3	611.8	614.9	620.4	625.0	629.6	640.7	651.2	664.0	677.6	693.5	1.42	15.14
Belgium	1,069.7	1,090.3	1,110.5	1,129.9	1,151.8	1,173.7	1,196.3	1,219.7	1,243.8	1,269.2	1,295.8	1.94	21.13
Bolivia	316.1	326.3	336.7	347.4	358.4	369.9	381.9	394.5	407.8	421.6	435.8	3.26	37.86
Bosnia-Herzegovina	315.3	321.9	329.4	337.7	346.6	355.8	365.0	374.1	383.3	392.5	401.7	2.45	27.40
Brazil	8,395.8	8,675.4	8,970.6	9,282.7	9,613.4	9,964.5	10,337.4	10,731.4	11,145.6	11,580.5	12,036.9	3.67	43.37
Bulgaria	765.7	773.5	783.1	786.2	790.9	796.4	801.6	808.1	814.9	820.2	825.5	0.75	7.81
Canada	2,976.6	3,075.4	3,172.9	3,271.6	3,375.9	3,489.0	3,607.4	3,723.9	3,845.9	3,970.0	4,092.4	3.23	37.49
Chile	957.3	992.6	1,029.2	1,067.6	1,108.2	1,151.3	1,197.2	1,246.1	1,297.7	1,351.9	1,408.5	3.94	47.14
China	95,537.8	98,819.3	101,815.9	106,419.2	110,259.8	115,118.0	119,322.3	122,779.7	126,845.3	129,571.3	130,643.8	3.18	36.75
Colombia	1,687.6	1,767.4	1,852.5	1,942.8	2,037.6	2,136.3	2,238.2	2,343.0	2,451.0	2,562.4	2,677.8	4.72	58.67
Costa Rica	198.9	207.8	217.4	227.8	238.8	250.7	263.3	276.8	291.2	306.4	322.4	4.95	62.09
Croatia	407.3	414.1	420.3	425.3	432.4	439.3	447.5	454.7	461.6	466.8	472.4	1.49	15.99
Czech Republic	951.1	978.4	1,006.8	1,034.6	1,061.1	1,085.7	1,108.6	1,130.9	1,151.6	1,170.4	1,184.0	2.21	24.48
Denmark	573.1	585.4	597.8	609.5	621.4	633.9	645.5	657.9	670.4	682.3	694.0	1.93	21.10
Ecuador	592.7	615.3	639.7	665.8	693.3	721.7	750.5	779.5	808.7	838.1	867.9	3.89	46.42
Egypt	2,777.7	2,893.1	3,018.9	3,155.3	3,302.6	3,460.7	3,629.7	3,809.2	3,998.4	4,196.0	4,398.5	4.70	58.35
Estonia	103.5	104.6	105.3	106.0	106.8	107.4	108.3	109.4	110.3	111.2	112.2	0.80	8.33
Finland	549.7	570.8	589.8	606.4	623.6	638.7	653.2	667.3	681.3	693.7	703.9	2.50	28.06
France	6,010.8	6,186.1	6,355.6	6,504.5	6,652.5	6,788.6	6,926.5	7,056.5	7,185.9	7,314.9	7,437.9	2.15	23.74
Germany	9,147.7	9,286.1	9,433.1	9,572.1	9,713.7	9,846.2	9,987.5	10,132.7	10,287.5	10,448.8	10,614.9	1.50	16.04
Greece	1,239.3	1,251.5	1,273.9	1,293.0	1,310.1	1,325.5	1,343.7	1,365.0	1,385.5	1,404.6	1,423.8	1.40	14.89
Hong Kong, China	580.3	607.1	631.5	655.6	681.1	709.7	741.2	773.9	808.3	843.9	879.0	4.24	51.47
Hungary	853.8	865.6	880.5	892.4	904.0	923.6	950.5	972.7	989.8	997.4	1,002.5	1.62	17.42
India	41,357.3	42,769.5	44,379.0	46,168.5	48,098.0	50,116.4	52,180.1	54,265.7	56,364.7	58,475.3	60,600.9	3.89	46.53
Indonesia	9,111.0	9,370.4	9,660.7	9,983.7	10,340.0	10,729.3	11,150.6	11,603.1	12,085.0	12,592.9	13,122.6	3.72	44.03
Iran	2,632.6	2,675.7	2,734.1	2,807.8	2,896.0	2,997.0	3,109.6	3,233.4	3,368.1	3,513.3	3,668.4	3.37	39.35
Ireland	330.7	341.0	351.2	361.4	372.4	383.1	394.4	405.3	417.0	429.0	441.1	2.92	33.40
Israel	454.2	471.0	489.6	508.8	527.5	545.6	563.2	579.7	595.1	610.5	626.6	3.27	37.96
Italy	6,731.6	6,839.3	6,940.4	7,023.4	7,102.7	7,183.3	7,275.1	7,369.8	7,468.2	7,569.9	7,672.8	1.32	13.98
Japan	16,985.6	17,424.1	17,776.1	18,058.1	18,278.3	18,435.8	18,578.6	18,680.7	18,732.9	18,790.5	18,856.5	1.05	11.01
Jordan	175.1	179.1	182.8	186.4	190.1	194.2	199.0	204.6	211.1	218.4	226.8	2.62	29.50
Kazakhstan	549.1	559.3	572.9	589.0	607.2	627.2	649.0	672.8	698.8	726.8	756.3	3.25	37.74
Kuwait	56.6	61.3	66.3	71.8	77.9	84.7	92.5	101.3	111.1	121.7	132.9	8.91	134.77
Latvia	175.3	176.1	176.3	176.5	176.6	176.4	176.8	177.6	178.4	180.0	182.2	0.38	3.89
Lithuania	249.3	250.5	252.0	253.5	255.0	255.7	256.8	259.3	261.9	265.5	270.0	0.80	8.32
Malaysia	970.1	1,015.3	1,065.8	1,122.0	1,181.9	1,245.9	1,313.2	1,384.2	1,458.9	1,533.8	1,611.6	5.21	66.13
Mexico	4,585.2	4,790.9	5,015.3	5,251.2	5,498.3	5,754.8	6,018.5	6,287.9	6,561.8	6,840.0	7,123.4	4.50	55.36
Morocco	1,173.3	1,212.7	1,256.5	1,305.3	1,359.9	1,421.0	1,489.0	1,563.6	1,643.5	1,725.9	1,807.7	4.42	54.07
Netherlands	1,589.6	1,638.5	1,684.3	1,728.4	1,775.0	1,820.1	1,865.5	1,910.5	1,957.4	2,004.6	2,052.1	2.59	29.09
New Zealand	358.8	370.7	382.3	394.1	405.6	417.7	430.0	443.0	456.7	469.9	484.1	3.04	34.91
Nigeria	3,542.1	3,635.9	3,734.6	3,838.3	3,946.6	4,058.8	4,174.2	4,292.2	4,412.7	4,535.8	4,661.3	2.78	31.60
Norway	449.0	461.8	474.1	485.7	498.0	510.3	522.6	535.4	548.6	561.4	574.5	2.49	27.95
Pakistan	5,689.0	5,848.2	6,019.5	6,203.7	6,401.1	6,611.2	6,833.7	7,068.6	7,315.9	7,575.3	7,846.7	3.27	37.93
Peru	1,152.1	1,192.9	1,235.7	1,280.6	1,327.4	1,376.0	1,426.3	1,478.3	1,532.1	1,588.1	1,646.5	3.63	42.91
Philippines	2,787.2	2,910.6	3,041.8	3,182.0	3,330.6	3,487.0	3,649.6	3,817.6	3,990.8	4,169.1	4,352.9	4.56	56.18
Poland	2,811.2	2,902.2	3,002.8	3,110.0	3,220.2	3,330.3	3,439.5	3,556.4	3,668.0	3,778.4	3,881.7	3.28	38.08
Portugal	1,060.9	1,078.0	1,096.0	1,113.8	1,131.6	1,147.9	1,166.1	1,185.4	1,203.4	1,224.2	1,244.7	1.61	17.32
Romania	1,759.0	1,787.0	1,813.1	1,833.4	1,856.7	1,877.1	1,905.9	1,941.4	1,972.3	1,998.7	2,020.9	1.40	14.89
Russia	8,319.6	8,510.5	8,677.5	8,801.0	8,975.7	9,087.7	9,279.0	9,446.5	9,620.8	9,814.4	9,992.1	1.85	20.10
Saudi Arabia	600.6	633.0	670.3	712.6	759.8	811.8	868.4	929.5	995.4	1,066.2	1,142.3	6.64	90.20
Singapore	298.0	317.3	336.3	357.6	380.2	405.2	430.1	455.3	484.3	513.7	542.6	6.18	82.09
Slovakia	365.6	376.1	389.4	404.4	420.1	435.6	451.6	468.2	485.4	501.9	516.9	3.52	41.36
Slovenia	180.7	186.2	193.0	199.2	206.0	213.1	219.6	226.4	233.2	238.9	244.5	3.07	35.33
South Africa	1,471.5	1,516.5	1,562.5	1,609.2	1,656.2	1,703.4	1,750.6	1,797.2	1,842.9	1,887.2	1,929.8	2.75	31.14
South Korea	3,135.9	3,257.7	3,379.9	3,512.2	3,656.6	3,818.0	4,003.9	4,205.6	4,418.2	4,644.4	4,880.9	4.52	55.65
Spain	4,416.2	4,498.4	4,582.4	4,664.1	4,746.7	4,833.6	4,925.8	5,024.4	5,130.5	5,245.4	5,368.2	1.97	21.56
Sweden	1,043.7	1,065.8	1,085.2	1,102.1	1,118.7	1,136.6	1,153.1	1,170.4	1,188.8	1,206.2	1,222.7	1.60	17.15
Switzerland	757.2	773.2	789.1	802.6	817.1	831.2	845.7	861.0	878.3	896.6	915.1	1.91	20.85
Taiwan	1,567.2	1,616.7	1,672.8	1,747.9	1,820.3	1,893.5	1,972.6	2,052.8	2,140.4	2,218.2	2,302.1	3.92	46.90
Thailand	3,291.5	3,429.2	3,566.5	3,708.8	3,865.4	4,015.1	4,211.4	4,413.8	4,609.9	4,802.0	5,027.9	4.33	52.75
Tunisia	466.8	479.3	494.1	511.1	530.0	550.3	571.5	593.4	615.7	638.4	661.1	3.54	41.62
Turkey	3,080.6	3,192.1	3,294.1	3,408.1	3,525.9	3,650.4	3,779.5	3,922.0	4,068.0	4,217.2	4,370.2	3.56	41.86
Turkmenistan	128.5	131.9	136.1	141.0	146.6	153.0	160.3	168.5	177.7	187.7	198.3	4.44	54.36
Ukraine	3,289.2	3,329.3	3,348.2	3,380.8	3,416.4	3,459.6	3,521.0	3,563.8	3,617.5	3,656.4	3,712.8	1.22	12.88
United Arab Emirates	59.0	63.6	69.4	76.6	85.2	94.9	105.7	117.3	129.4	141.3	152.6	9.96	158.40
United Kingdom	6,149.9	6,264.6	6,360.2	6,447.8	6,534.9	6,624.6	6,712.1	6,800.0	6,895.1	7,000.5	7,111.6	1.46	15.64
USA	24,424.3	25,166.6	25,889.3	26,635.0	27,415.6	28,239.5	29,121.2	29,964.1	30,861.9	31,755.8	32,623.6	2.94	33.57
Venezuela	1,127.6	1,181.0	1,236.4	1,293.7	1,352.5	1,412.4	1,473.4	1,535.3	1,598.4	1,663.5	1,731.3	4.38	53.54
Vietnam	3,165.2	3,254.2	3,368.8	3,507.6	3,667.5	3,843.1	4,030.7	4,228.9	4,438.8	4,661.0	4,896.8	4.46	54.71

Marketing segments: Elder generation

Table 4.131 Pensioners: 2009-2019 (%)

% of total

	2009	2010	2011	2012	2013	2014	2015	2016	2017	2018	2019
Algeria	7.96	8.16	8.38	8.60	8.84	9.10	9.37	9.67	9.99	10.33	10.68
Argentina	11.70	11.77	11.88	11.90	12.03	12.17	12.33	12.52	12.58	12.74	12.90
Australia	13.50	13.62	13.78	14.05	14.27	14.55	14.84	15.13	15.39	15.67	15.96
Austria	19.47	19.57	19.63	19.80	20.04	20.28	20.54	20.84	21.15	21.47	21.78
Azerbaijan	7.91	7.69	7.53	7.40	7.43	7.52	7.67	7.89	8.16	8.50	8.91
Belarus	21.74	21.94	22.19	22.42	22.82	23.15	23.70	24.29	24.82	25.26	25.70
Belgium	16.00	15.98	15.95	16.07	16.20	16.35	16.51	16.69	16.87	17.11	17.35
Bolivia	4.65	4.71	4.78	4.86	4.95	5.05	5.15	5.25	5.36	5.47	5.59
Bosnia-Herzegovina	18.41	18.85	19.35	19.93	20.56	21.23	21.95	22.68	23.44	24.22	25.00
Brazil	7.61	7.82	8.04	8.28	8.54	8.80	9.08	9.37	9.66	9.97	10.29
Bulgaria	20.75	20.92	21.11	21.19	21.37	21.50	21.56	21.64	21.81	21.95	22.16
Canada	13.19	13.35	13.57	13.96	14.35	14.73	15.15	15.57	16.00	16.48	16.99
Chile	10.36	10.58	10.77	10.97	11.19	11.42	11.68	11.97	12.29	12.64	13.01
China	11.68	11.87	11.98	12.32	12.63	13.05	13.47	13.80	14.28	14.56	14.49
Colombia	10.77	11.09	11.43	11.78	12.14	12.51	12.90	13.30	13.71	14.14	14.57
Costa Rica	9.00	9.27	9.56	9.87	10.20	10.56	10.95	11.36	11.79	12.25	12.72
Croatia	20.45	20.54	20.54	20.63	20.82	20.99	21.24	21.49	21.71	21.95	22.19
Czech Republic	20.36	20.85	21.32	21.74	22.18	22.62	23.07	23.51	23.92	24.26	24.53
Denmark	13.26	13.52	13.86	14.30	14.81	15.36	15.84	16.19	16.46	16.69	16.84
Ecuador	8.49	8.70	8.94	9.20	9.48	9.77	10.06	10.36	10.65	10.95	11.26
Egypt	7.69	7.84	8.00	8.19	8.38	8.59	8.81	9.04	9.27	9.50	9.73
Estonia	18.85	18.47	18.16	17.85	18.00	18.05	18.24	18.46	18.57	18.71	18.80
Finland	16.69	17.16	17.77	18.39	19.00	19.56	20.06	20.49	20.95	21.35	21.75
France	20.99	21.30	21.64	21.88	22.15	22.39	22.68	22.94	23.24	23.56	23.87
Germany	19.25	19.32	19.08	18.93	18.96	19.07	19.30	19.40	19.42	19.45	19.45
Greece	23.73	23.73	23.72	23.72	23.78	23.84	23.90	23.98	24.09	24.25	24.42
Hong Kong, China	12.50	12.62	12.78	13.13	13.54	14.02	14.59	15.13	15.65	16.20	16.81
Hungary	20.46	20.78	21.09	21.45	21.88	22.23	22.82	23.53	24.16	24.75	25.08
India	9.61	9.78	9.96	10.15	10.36	10.58	10.81	11.05	11.30	11.57	11.84
Indonesia	12.46	12.72	13.01	13.33	13.67	14.03	14.39	14.74	15.10	15.46	15.84
Iran	8.40	8.58	8.79	9.01	9.25	9.51	9.79	10.08	10.38	10.69	11.02
Ireland	9.35	9.36	9.39	9.50	9.66	9.83	10.01	10.19	10.34	10.47	10.67
Israel	12.17	12.40	12.71	13.11	13.51	13.87	14.27	14.66	15.02	15.34	15.65
Italy	21.97	22.02	22.05	22.15	22.29	22.46	22.62	22.78	22.91	23.10	23.27
Japan	20.91	21.02	21.02	21.68	22.44	23.21	23.82	24.25	24.55	24.77	24.94
Jordan	6.39	6.43	6.51	6.62	6.76	6.92	7.09	7.26	7.45	7.66	7.89
Kazakhstan	11.02	10.96	10.98	11.08	11.25	11.46	11.70	11.95	12.22	12.50	12.78
Kuwait	16.81	16.84	16.82	16.78	16.71	16.66	16.63	16.57	16.44	17.57	18.74
Latvia	19.79	19.75	19.82	19.95	20.02	20.10	20.24	20.37	20.53	20.68	20.74
Lithuania	21.27	21.44	21.65	21.85	22.11	22.36	22.64	22.93	23.31	23.70	24.13
Malaysia	10.99	11.31	11.66	12.04	12.44	12.85	13.22	13.59	13.98	14.40	14.83
Mexico	5.90	6.03	6.17	6.32	6.48	6.64	6.82	7.01	7.22	7.43	7.66
Morocco	7.17	7.34	7.53	7.74	7.98	8.24	8.53	8.84	9.19	9.55	9.92
Netherlands	14.38	14.63	14.83	15.45	16.02	16.50	16.93	17.33	17.71	18.12	18.52
New Zealand	11.64	11.70	11.80	12.06	12.32	12.57	12.83	13.07	13.31	13.53	13.77
Nigeria	4.52	4.55	4.58	4.63	4.69	4.75	4.81	4.88	4.94	5.00	5.06
Norway	12.68	12.67	12.74	12.93	13.16	13.51	13.80	14.06	14.30	14.51	14.70
Pakistan	6.97	7.05	7.14	7.23	7.33	7.43	7.55	7.66	7.78	7.90	8.02
Peru	5.70	5.82	5.94	6.07	6.21	6.36	6.52	6.68	6.86	7.06	7.26
Philippines	6.83	6.97	7.12	7.29	7.47	7.66	7.87	8.09	8.32	8.57	8.82
Poland	15.75	15.95	16.22	16.60	17.09	17.65	18.25	18.92	19.58	20.25	20.95
Portugal	16.44	16.44	16.53	16.50	16.55	16.68	16.82	16.99	17.11	17.27	17.42
Romania	17.52	17.69	17.82	17.96	18.17	18.32	18.76	19.22	19.62	19.95	20.26
Russia	21.00	21.34	21.67	21.99	22.32	22.64	23.08	23.53	23.90	24.21	24.43
Saudi Arabia	5.66	5.71	5.76	5.82	5.88	5.94	6.01	6.08	6.15	6.22	6.30
Singapore	16.04	16.62	17.23	17.90	18.56	19.23	19.88	20.50	21.15	21.82	22.48
Slovakia	14.34	14.56	14.80	15.12	15.54	15.97	16.46	17.05	17.68	18.31	18.91
Slovenia	16.78	16.40	16.35	16.40	16.58	16.84	17.14	17.54	17.93	18.36	18.82
South Africa	6.94	6.99	6.94	7.05	7.17	7.30	7.49	7.67	7.83	8.10	8.30
South Korea	13.16	13.40	13.63	13.80	13.98	14.31	14.48	14.76	15.20	15.63	16.05
Spain	15.02	14.89	14.80	14.72	14.65	14.57	14.51	14.46	14.43	14.45	14.55
Sweden	23.28	23.62	23.90	24.12	24.29	24.46	24.64	24.78	24.93	25.09	25.24
Switzerland	16.33	16.52	16.74	16.94	17.14	17.32	17.49	17.62	17.73	17.86	18.00
Taiwan	17.10	17.72	18.46	19.17	19.96	20.81	21.69	22.60	23.49	24.42	25.36
Thailand	16.35	17.05	17.76	18.46	19.12	19.92	20.76	21.60	22.47	23.39	24.41
Tunisia	8.93	9.09	9.28	9.51	9.78	10.08	10.40	10.75	11.11	11.49	11.89
Turkey	15.46	15.84	16.18	16.53	16.88	17.24	17.59	17.98	18.36	18.74	19.14
Turkmenistan	7.04	7.18	7.35	7.55	7.79	8.06	8.36	8.70	9.07	9.47	9.88
Ukraine	24.11	24.29	24.47	24.66	25.00	25.39	25.98	26.54	26.92	27.16	27.20
United Arab Emirates	1.87	1.93	2.01	2.09	2.19	2.30	2.43	2.59	2.77	2.96	3.17
United Kingdom	19.53	19.75	19.70	19.76	19.76	19.71	19.63	19.53	19.42	19.32	19.21
USA	11.55	11.59	11.62	11.72	12.09	12.39	12.70	12.99	13.30	13.64	13.98
Venezuela	9.96	10.24	10.54	10.84	11.14	11.45	11.77	12.11	12.45	12.80	13.16
Vietnam	9.08	9.27	9.50	9.76	10.05	10.38	10.72	11.09	11.48	11.89	12.32

Marketing segments: Elder generation

Table 4.132 Elderly population (60+): 2009-2019 (%)

% of total

	2009	2010	2011	2012	2013	2014	2015	2016	2017	2018	2019
Algeria	6.76	6.90	7.08	7.27	7.49	7.71	7.94	8.17	8.40	8.65	8.92
Argentina	14.39	14.53	14.68	14.84	15.00	15.17	15.34	15.50	15.67	15.83	16.00
Australia	18.78	19.11	19.43	19.73	20.06	20.36	20.67	21.00	21.31	21.62	21.94
Austria	22.74	23.02	23.28	23.50	23.75	24.01	24.29	24.61	25.03	25.45	25.90
Azerbaijan	8.64	8.69	8.82	9.01	9.27	9.59	9.97	10.40	10.90	11.44	12.03
Belarus	18.15	18.42	18.52	18.72	18.86	19.06	19.41	19.75	20.15	20.57	21.04
Belgium	22.98	23.27	23.55	23.82	24.13	24.44	24.78	25.12	25.48	25.86	26.25
Bolivia	7.07	7.18	7.30	7.41	7.53	7.66	7.79	7.94	8.09	8.25	8.41
Bosnia-Herzegovina	18.73	19.11	19.55	20.04	20.56	21.10	21.64	22.20	22.77	23.36	23.95
Brazil	9.72	9.97	10.25	10.54	10.86	11.20	11.56	11.94	12.34	12.76	13.20
Bulgaria	24.08	24.51	25.00	25.31	25.67	26.05	26.43	26.86	27.30	27.70	28.10
Canada	19.42	19.83	20.24	20.66	21.11	21.60	22.11	22.60	23.12	23.64	24.14
Chile	12.82	13.14	13.47	13.82	14.18	14.58	15.00	15.45	15.94	16.44	16.97
China	14.40	14.82	15.26	15.90	16.43	17.11	17.71	18.19	18.77	19.16	19.29
Colombia	8.31	8.58	8.87	9.18	9.50	9.84	10.18	10.53	10.88	11.25	11.62
Costa Rica	9.18	9.46	9.77	10.09	10.43	10.79	11.18	11.60	12.05	12.52	13.01
Croatia	22.63	22.98	23.29	23.53	23.87	24.22	24.61	24.99	25.38	25.68	26.00
Czech Republic	21.85	22.35	22.88	23.42	23.93	24.41	24.86	25.28	25.68	26.04	26.29
Denmark	22.74	23.09	23.44	23.76	24.09	24.45	24.78	25.12	25.48	25.81	26.14
Ecuador	9.21	9.46	9.73	10.01	10.31	10.61	10.92	11.22	11.52	11.83	12.13
Egypt	7.78	7.97	8.18	8.40	8.64	8.89	9.16	9.44	9.74	10.04	10.35
Estonia	22.16	22.44	22.64	22.89	23.13	23.33	23.58	23.87	24.11	24.36	24.60
Finland	23.83	24.49	25.08	25.58	26.11	26.57	27.02	27.46	27.88	28.26	28.56
France	22.30	22.75	23.20	23.58	23.96	24.30	24.65	24.98	25.31	25.63	25.94
Germany	25.52	25.87	26.26	26.63	27.02	27.39	27.79	28.19	28.63	29.08	29.56
Greece	24.49	24.65	25.01	25.28	25.55	25.77	26.05	26.39	26.73	27.05	27.38
Hong Kong, China	17.33	17.95	18.54	19.13	19.72	20.41	21.15	21.93	22.74	23.59	24.42
Hungary	22.09	22.40	22.77	23.11	23.43	23.91	24.54	25.08	25.53	25.77	25.97
India	7.41	7.56	7.74	7.95	8.17	8.40	8.64	8.88	9.12	9.36	9.60
Indonesia	8.80	8.94	9.10	9.29	9.50	9.74	10.00	10.28	10.60	10.93	11.28
Iran	7.05	7.13	7.25	7.40	7.59	7.80	8.04	8.30	8.58	8.88	9.20
Ireland	16.04	16.29	16.54	16.78	17.05	17.33	17.62	17.90	18.20	18.54	18.87
Israel	13.84	14.10	14.40	14.70	14.99	15.26	15.51	15.73	15.92	16.11	16.31
Italy	26.31	26.65	26.97	27.24	27.50	27.76	28.07	28.40	28.74	29.10	29.46
Japan	30.08	30.88	31.55	32.12	32.60	32.98	33.36	33.68	33.93	34.20	34.50
Jordan	5.52	5.54	5.58	5.63	5.70	5.78	5.87	5.97	6.08	6.21	6.36
Kazakhstan	10.09	10.21	10.37	10.56	10.77	11.00	11.24	11.52	11.82	12.15	12.50
Kuwait	3.84	4.05	4.28	4.52	4.79	5.09	5.44	5.83	6.25	6.71	7.19
Latvia	22.33	22.54	22.66	22.81	22.93	23.01	23.17	23.36	23.56	23.82	24.10
Lithuania	20.73	20.96	21.20	21.43	21.66	21.83	22.02	22.31	22.60	22.95	23.38
Malaysia	7.15	7.36	7.61	7.89	8.19	8.51	8.85	9.20	9.58	9.95	10.34
Mexico	9.10	9.35	9.64	9.94	10.27	10.62	10.98	11.34	11.71	12.09	12.47
Morocco	7.90	8.05	8.23	8.42	8.64	8.90	9.19	9.52	9.87	10.25	10.63
Netherlands	21.33	21.83	22.30	22.75	23.24	23.71	24.18	24.67	25.17	25.68	26.19
New Zealand	17.93	18.31	18.67	19.04	19.40	19.79	20.19	20.62	21.06	21.50	21.98
Nigeria	4.91	4.93	4.95	4.98	5.02	5.06	5.10	5.14	5.19	5.24	5.29
Norway	20.68	20.85	21.02	21.18	21.38	21.60	21.82	22.06	22.32	22.56	22.80
Pakistan	6.15	6.20	6.26	6.32	6.39	6.47	6.56	6.65	6.75	6.86	6.98
Peru	8.51	8.70	8.90	9.11	9.33	9.56	9.79	10.03	10.28	10.54	10.82
Philippines	6.52	6.67	6.84	7.02	7.22	7.43	7.64	7.86	8.08	8.31	8.53
Poland	18.51	19.05	19.65	20.29	20.95	21.60	22.25	22.93	23.59	24.24	24.84
Portugal	23.16	23.45	23.76	24.08	24.41	24.70	25.04	25.40	25.74	26.14	26.53
Romania	19.58	19.94	20.28	20.57	20.89	21.19	21.60	22.07	22.51	22.90	23.25
Russia	17.34	17.67	17.97	18.23	18.57	18.81	19.19	19.54	19.89	20.29	20.67
Saudi Arabia	4.49	4.61	4.76	4.92	5.10	5.29	5.50	5.72	5.96	6.21	6.49
Singapore	13.64	14.25	14.84	15.52	16.23	17.01	17.79	18.57	19.49	20.43	21.32
Slovakia	17.09	17.49	17.99	18.55	19.14	19.71	20.31	20.94	21.58	22.19	22.74
Slovenia	21.63	22.06	22.60	23.11	23.68	24.26	24.82	25.38	25.95	26.46	26.92
South Africa	7.14	7.33	7.53	7.75	7.98	8.22	8.46	8.70	8.94	9.17	9.40
South Korea	14.96	15.43	15.91	16.45	17.03	17.69	18.45	19.28	20.16	21.10	22.11
Spain	22.16	22.34	22.55	22.74	22.94	23.15	23.39	23.66	23.96	24.30	24.68
Sweden	24.77	25.08	25.33	25.53	25.71	25.93	26.11	26.31	26.52	26.72	26.90
Switzerland	22.70	23.02	23.34	23.61	23.92	24.21	24.52	24.84	25.19	25.58	25.97
Taiwan	14.02	14.51	15.07	15.80	16.50	17.22	17.97	18.75	19.58	20.34	21.16
Thailand	11.62	12.05	12.48	12.93	13.43	13.90	14.53	15.17	15.79	16.39	17.10
Tunisia	9.55	9.72	9.93	10.18	10.47	10.77	11.09	11.43	11.78	12.15	12.52
Turkey	8.86	9.05	9.23	9.42	9.64	9.87	10.10	10.36	10.64	10.91	11.20
Turkmenistan	6.04	6.13	6.25	6.39	6.56	6.76	6.99	7.26	7.56	7.89	8.25
Ukraine	20.45	20.81	21.06	21.38	21.72	22.11	22.60	23.02	23.49	23.88	24.34
United Arab Emirates	1.97	2.06	2.18	2.33	2.51	2.71	2.94	3.18	3.44	3.70	3.95
United Kingdom	22.16	22.35	22.50	22.61	22.72	22.83	22.94	23.05	23.19	23.36	23.55
USA	18.07	18.40	18.74	19.09	19.46	19.86	20.28	20.69	21.12	21.55	21.96
Venezuela	8.38	8.63	8.90	9.17	9.44	9.72	10.01	10.29	10.58	10.88	11.19
Vietnam	7.70	7.82	8.00	8.22	8.49	8.78	9.10	9.44	9.79	10.17	10.56

Marketing segments: Elder generation

Table 4.133 Female elderly population (60+): 2009-2019 (%)

% of total

	2009	2010	2011	2012	2013	2014	2015	2016	2017	2018	2019
Algeria	3.68	3.75	3.84	3.94	4.04	4.14	4.25	4.36	4.47	4.59	4.72
Argentina	8.35	8.43	8.52	8.61	8.70	8.80	8.89	8.99	9.09	9.18	9.28
Australia	9.99	10.15	10.30	10.45	10.61	10.76	10.92	11.08	11.24	11.40	11.57
Austria	13.01	13.12	13.22	13.31	13.41	13.52	13.65	13.80	13.99	14.19	14.40
Azerbaijan	4.97	5.00	5.06	5.16	5.30	5.46	5.66	5.89	6.15	6.44	6.75
Belarus	11.92	12.08	12.14	12.26	12.33	12.46	12.68	12.89	13.13	13.38	13.66
Belgium	12.95	13.08	13.21	13.33	13.48	13.62	13.78	13.95	14.12	14.30	14.49
Bolivia	3.87	3.93	3.99	4.06	4.13	4.20	4.28	4.36	4.44	4.53	4.62
Bosnia-Herzegovina	10.53	10.74	10.98	11.25	11.53	11.83	12.13	12.44	12.76	13.09	13.43
Brazil	5.38	5.53	5.70	5.87	6.06	6.25	6.46	6.68	6.91	7.16	7.41
Bulgaria	13.90	14.15	14.44	14.63	14.84	15.07	15.28	15.53	15.78	16.00	16.22
Canada	10.58	10.78	10.98	11.18	11.40	11.64	11.89	12.13	12.38	12.63	12.88
Chile	7.18	7.35	7.52	7.70	7.89	8.10	8.32	8.56	8.81	9.08	9.36
China	7.21	7.42	7.66	8.00	8.27	8.62	8.95	9.21	9.52	9.74	9.83
Colombia	4.62	4.77	4.93	5.09	5.27	5.46	5.65	5.84	6.03	6.24	6.44
Costa Rica	4.84	4.98	5.14	5.31	5.48	5.67	5.87	6.08	6.31	6.55	6.80
Croatia	13.44	13.61	13.76	13.87	14.03	14.20	14.38	14.57	14.77	14.93	15.08
Czech Republic	12.65	12.90	13.16	13.44	13.70	13.93	14.16	14.37	14.57	14.74	14.86
Denmark	12.35	12.50	12.66	12.79	12.94	13.10	13.25	13.41	13.57	13.73	13.88
Ecuador	4.86	5.00	5.14	5.29	5.45	5.61	5.78	5.94	6.10	6.27	6.43
Egypt	4.16	4.27	4.39	4.51	4.63	4.76	4.90	5.04	5.18	5.33	5.48
Estonia	14.37	14.55	14.68	14.84	14.99	15.11	15.27	15.44	15.59	15.73	15.88
Finland	13.51	13.82	14.09	14.33	14.58	14.80	15.03	15.24	15.44	15.63	15.78
France	12.68	12.90	13.12	13.31	13.50	13.67	13.85	14.02	14.19	14.36	14.52
Germany	14.36	14.50	14.67	14.84	15.01	15.18	15.36	15.55	15.74	15.95	16.17
Greece	13.47	13.57	13.76	13.90	14.04	14.15	14.30	14.48	14.66	14.82	14.99
Hong Kong, China	9.11	9.44	9.76	10.10	10.42	10.80	11.19	11.62	12.05	12.51	12.96
Hungary	13.57	13.74	13.95	14.14	14.32	14.58	14.91	15.20	15.45	15.59	15.71
India	3.87	3.95	4.05	4.15	4.27	4.39	4.51	4.63	4.76	4.88	5.01
Indonesia	4.84	4.91	4.99	5.08	5.19	5.30	5.43	5.57	5.73	5.90	6.08
Iran	3.50	3.57	3.65	3.75	3.86	3.98	4.12	4.27	4.43	4.60	4.78
Ireland	8.61	8.72	8.83	8.94	9.07	9.20	9.34	9.48	9.63	9.80	9.97
Israel	7.71	7.83	7.98	8.13	8.27	8.40	8.52	8.64	8.73	8.82	8.92
Italy	14.91	15.08	15.24	15.37	15.50	15.63	15.79	15.95	16.12	16.29	16.47
Japan	16.77	17.20	17.56	17.88	18.15	18.38	18.60	18.79	18.95	19.11	19.29
Jordan	2.75	2.77	2.81	2.85	2.90	2.95	3.01	3.07	3.14	3.21	3.30
Kazakhstan	6.61	6.71	6.83	6.97	7.11	7.26	7.42	7.60	7.79	8.01	8.23
Kuwait	1.53	1.60	1.68	1.77	1.86	1.97	2.09	2.23	2.38	2.54	2.72
Latvia	14.55	14.68	14.75	14.83	14.90	14.94	15.03	15.14	15.25	15.38	15.52
Lithuania	13.28	13.43	13.59	13.73	13.87	13.97	14.09	14.24	14.41	14.61	14.85
Malaysia	3.69	3.80	3.93	4.08	4.23	4.40	4.57	4.76	4.96	5.15	5.36
Mexico	4.88	5.00	5.15	5.31	5.48	5.67	5.86	6.05	6.25	6.46	6.66
Morocco	4.23	4.31	4.39	4.49	4.59	4.71	4.85	5.01	5.19	5.39	5.59
Netherlands	11.64	11.87	12.08	12.28	12.50	12.72	12.94	13.17	13.41	13.65	13.90
New Zealand	9.61	9.79	9.97	10.15	10.33	10.53	10.74	10.96	11.19	11.42	11.68
Nigeria	2.62	2.63	2.64	2.66	2.68	2.70	2.73	2.75	2.78	2.80	2.83
Norway	11.32	11.34	11.37	11.39	11.45	11.52	11.59	11.68	11.78	11.87	11.97
Pakistan	3.00	3.04	3.07	3.11	3.14	3.19	3.23	3.28	3.33	3.39	3.45
Peru	4.54	4.65	4.75	4.87	4.99	5.11	5.24	5.37	5.51	5.65	5.80
Philippines	3.49	3.57	3.66	3.76	3.87	3.98	4.10	4.22	4.34	4.46	4.59
Poland	11.11	11.40	11.72	12.07	12.42	12.76	13.11	13.47	13.81	14.15	14.47
Portugal	13.22	13.37	13.54	13.70	13.88	14.04	14.22	14.41	14.59	14.80	15.01
Romania	11.37	11.58	11.77	11.93	12.11	12.28	12.50	12.76	13.00	13.21	13.40
Russia	11.48	11.66	11.84	11.99	12.20	12.35	12.59	12.80	13.02	13.27	13.51
Saudi Arabia	2.15	2.20	2.25	2.31	2.37	2.43	2.49	2.56	2.64	2.72	2.81
Singapore	7.30	7.61	7.89	8.22	8.55	8.91	9.29	9.65	10.09	10.54	10.96
Slovakia	10.31	10.52	10.77	11.06	11.36	11.64	11.94	12.26	12.59	12.88	13.16
Slovenia	12.69	12.88	13.11	13.34	13.59	13.84	14.09	14.35	14.60	14.84	15.04
South Africa	4.20	4.32	4.46	4.60	4.75	4.91	5.07	5.24	5.40	5.56	5.72
South Korea	8.53	8.77	9.01	9.29	9.59	9.93	10.33	10.75	11.21	11.69	12.21
Spain	12.45	12.55	12.65	12.75	12.85	12.95	13.08	13.21	13.36	13.53	13.72
Sweden	13.42	13.56	13.65	13.72	13.78	13.86	13.92	14.01	14.09	14.17	14.24
Switzerland	12.69	12.83	12.98	13.12	13.27	13.42	13.58	13.74	13.91	14.11	14.31
Taiwan	7.21	7.51	7.85	8.27	8.68	9.10	9.53	9.99	10.45	10.89	11.35
Thailand	6.53	6.78	7.03	7.30	7.58	7.86	8.22	8.58	8.94	9.28	9.68
Tunisia	5.00	5.10	5.22	5.35	5.50	5.67	5.84	6.03	6.23	6.44	6.65
Turkey	4.77	4.86	4.95	5.05	5.16	5.28	5.40	5.54	5.68	5.82	5.97
Turkmenistan	3.53	3.58	3.65	3.73	3.83	3.95	4.08	4.23	4.41	4.60	4.81
Ukraine	13.29	13.52	13.68	13.88	14.09	14.33	14.64	14.90	15.19	15.43	15.71
United Arab Emirates	0.69	0.72	0.75	0.78	0.82	0.86	0.91	0.97	1.05	1.13	1.22
United Kingdom	12.18	12.24	12.28	12.31	12.34	12.37	12.41	12.44	12.50	12.57	12.66
USA	10.10	10.26	10.42	10.58	10.76	10.96	11.17	11.37	11.59	11.80	12.01
Venezuela	4.43	4.57	4.70	4.85	5.00	5.15	5.30	5.45	5.61	5.77	5.94
Vietnam	4.09	4.16	4.25	4.37	4.51	4.66	4.83	5.01	5.19	5.39	5.61

Marketing segments: Elder generation

Table 4.134 Male elderly population (60+): 2009-2019 (%)

% of total

	2009	2010	2011	2012	2013	2014	2015	2016	2017	2018	2019
Algeria	3.08	3.15	3.24	3.34	3.45	3.57	3.69	3.81	3.93	4.06	4.19
Argentina	6.04	6.10	6.16	6.23	6.30	6.37	6.44	6.51	6.58	6.65	6.72
Australia	8.79	8.96	9.13	9.28	9.45	9.60	9.75	9.91	10.07	10.22	10.37
Austria	9.73	9.90	10.06	10.19	10.34	10.48	10.64	10.82	11.03	11.26	11.49
Azerbaijan	3.67	3.69	3.75	3.84	3.97	4.12	4.30	4.51	4.75	5.00	5.28
Belarus	6.23	6.34	6.39	6.46	6.53	6.60	6.73	6.86	7.02	7.19	7.38
Belgium	10.03	10.19	10.34	10.49	10.66	10.82	11.00	11.18	11.36	11.56	11.77
Bolivia	3.21	3.25	3.30	3.35	3.40	3.46	3.52	3.58	3.65	3.72	3.79
Bosnia-Herzegovina	8.20	8.37	8.57	8.79	9.02	9.27	9.51	9.76	10.01	10.27	10.53
Brazil	4.33	4.44	4.55	4.67	4.81	4.95	5.10	5.26	5.42	5.60	5.79
Bulgaria	10.18	10.36	10.56	10.68	10.82	10.99	11.15	11.33	11.53	11.70	11.88
Canada	8.85	9.05	9.27	9.48	9.71	9.96	10.22	10.48	10.74	11.01	11.26
Chile	5.64	5.79	5.95	6.12	6.29	6.48	6.68	6.89	7.12	7.36	7.61
China	7.19	7.41	7.60	7.91	8.16	8.49	8.76	8.98	9.25	9.42	9.47
Colombia	3.70	3.82	3.95	4.09	4.23	4.38	4.53	4.69	4.85	5.01	5.18
Costa Rica	4.34	4.48	4.62	4.78	4.94	5.12	5.31	5.52	5.74	5.97	6.21
Croatia	9.20	9.37	9.53	9.66	9.84	10.02	10.23	10.42	10.61	10.76	10.92
Czech Republic	9.20	9.45	9.71	9.98	10.24	10.48	10.70	10.92	11.12	11.30	11.43
Denmark	10.40	10.59	10.79	10.97	11.15	11.35	11.52	11.71	11.90	12.08	12.25
Ecuador	4.35	4.47	4.59	4.72	4.86	5.00	5.14	5.28	5.42	5.56	5.70
Egypt	3.62	3.70	3.79	3.90	4.01	4.13	4.26	4.41	4.55	4.71	4.86
Estonia	7.78	7.89	7.96	8.05	8.14	8.22	8.32	8.43	8.52	8.62	8.73
Finland	10.32	10.67	10.99	11.25	11.53	11.77	12.00	12.22	12.44	12.63	12.78
France	9.63	9.85	10.08	10.27	10.46	10.63	10.80	10.96	11.11	11.27	11.42
Germany	11.16	11.36	11.59	11.80	12.01	12.21	12.43	12.65	12.88	13.13	13.39
Greece	11.01	11.09	11.25	11.38	11.51	11.61	11.75	11.91	12.08	12.23	12.39
Hong Kong, China	8.21	8.51	8.78	9.03	9.30	9.61	9.96	10.32	10.69	11.08	11.46
Hungary	8.52	8.66	8.82	8.97	9.11	9.33	9.63	9.88	10.08	10.18	10.26
India	3.54	3.61	3.70	3.80	3.90	4.02	4.13	4.25	4.36	4.48	4.59
Indonesia	3.96	4.03	4.11	4.21	4.31	4.43	4.57	4.71	4.87	5.03	5.20
Iran	3.55	3.56	3.60	3.65	3.73	3.81	3.91	4.02	4.15	4.28	4.42
Ireland	7.43	7.57	7.70	7.84	7.98	8.12	8.27	8.42	8.57	8.74	8.91
Israel	6.13	6.26	6.42	6.57	6.72	6.86	6.98	7.10	7.20	7.29	7.40
Italy	11.40	11.57	11.73	11.86	11.99	12.13	12.29	12.45	12.62	12.81	12.99
Japan	13.31	13.68	13.98	14.24	14.44	14.61	14.76	14.89	14.99	15.09	15.21
Jordan	2.77	2.77	2.77	2.78	2.80	2.83	2.86	2.90	2.94	3.00	3.06
Kazakhstan	3.48	3.50	3.54	3.59	3.66	3.74	3.82	3.92	4.03	4.15	4.27
Kuwait	2.31	2.45	2.60	2.75	2.93	3.12	3.34	3.59	3.87	4.16	4.47
Latvia	7.78	7.86	7.91	7.97	8.03	8.07	8.14	8.23	8.31	8.44	8.59
Lithuania	7.45	7.52	7.61	7.70	7.79	7.86	7.94	8.06	8.19	8.34	8.53
Malaysia	3.45	3.56	3.68	3.81	3.96	4.11	4.27	4.44	4.62	4.80	4.98
Mexico	4.22	4.35	4.49	4.63	4.79	4.95	5.12	5.29	5.46	5.63	5.80
Morocco	3.67	3.75	3.83	3.94	4.05	4.19	4.34	4.50	4.68	4.87	5.04
Netherlands	9.69	9.97	10.23	10.47	10.74	10.99	11.24	11.50	11.76	12.02	12.29
New Zealand	8.32	8.52	8.70	8.89	9.07	9.26	9.45	9.65	9.87	10.08	10.30
Nigeria	2.29	2.30	2.31	2.32	2.34	2.35	2.37	2.39	2.41	2.43	2.46
Norway	9.36	9.51	9.65	9.78	9.93	10.08	10.23	10.38	10.54	10.69	10.83
Pakistan	3.15	3.17	3.19	3.22	3.25	3.28	3.33	3.37	3.42	3.48	3.53
Peru	3.97	4.06	4.15	4.24	4.34	4.45	4.55	4.66	4.78	4.90	5.02
Philippines	3.03	3.10	3.18	3.26	3.35	3.45	3.55	3.65	3.74	3.84	3.95
Poland	7.40	7.65	7.93	8.22	8.53	8.84	9.14	9.46	9.78	10.08	10.37
Portugal	9.94	10.08	10.23	10.38	10.52	10.66	10.82	10.99	11.15	11.34	11.53
Romania	8.21	8.36	8.51	8.63	8.78	8.91	9.10	9.31	9.51	9.69	9.86
Russia	5.86	6.00	6.13	6.23	6.37	6.46	6.60	6.73	6.87	7.02	7.16
Saudi Arabia	2.33	2.41	2.50	2.61	2.73	2.86	3.00	3.15	3.32	3.49	3.68
Singapore	6.33	6.65	6.96	7.31	7.68	8.10	8.51	8.92	9.40	9.89	10.36
Slovakia	6.78	6.97	7.21	7.49	7.78	8.07	8.37	8.68	9.00	9.30	9.58
Slovenia	8.93	9.18	9.49	9.77	10.09	10.42	10.72	11.04	11.35	11.62	11.88
South Africa	2.94	3.00	3.08	3.15	3.23	3.31	3.39	3.46	3.54	3.61	3.68
South Korea	6.43	6.67	6.90	7.16	7.44	7.76	8.13	8.53	8.96	9.41	9.89
Spain	9.70	9.79	9.90	9.99	10.09	10.20	10.32	10.45	10.60	10.77	10.96
Sweden	11.34	11.53	11.68	11.81	11.93	12.07	12.18	12.30	12.43	12.55	12.66
Switzerland	10.02	10.19	10.36	10.50	10.65	10.79	10.94	11.09	11.28	11.47	11.66
Taiwan	6.80	7.00	7.22	7.52	7.82	8.11	8.44	8.77	9.13	9.45	9.81
Thailand	5.08	5.27	5.45	5.63	5.84	6.04	6.31	6.58	6.85	7.11	7.42
Tunisia	4.54	4.62	4.72	4.83	4.96	5.10	5.25	5.40	5.56	5.71	5.86
Turkey	4.09	4.19	4.28	4.37	4.48	4.59	4.70	4.83	4.96	5.09	5.23
Turkmenistan	2.51	2.55	2.60	2.66	2.73	2.81	2.91	3.02	3.15	3.29	3.44
Ukraine	7.16	7.29	7.38	7.50	7.63	7.78	7.97	8.12	8.30	8.44	8.64
United Arab Emirates	1.28	1.35	1.44	1.55	1.69	1.85	2.03	2.21	2.39	2.57	2.73
United Kingdom	9.98	10.11	10.22	10.30	10.38	10.46	10.53	10.61	10.69	10.78	10.89
USA	7.97	8.15	8.33	8.51	8.70	8.90	9.12	9.32	9.53	9.74	9.94
Venezuela	3.94	4.07	4.19	4.32	4.45	4.58	4.71	4.84	4.97	5.11	5.25
Vietnam	3.61	3.67	3.75	3.85	3.98	4.12	4.27	4.43	4.60	4.77	4.96

SECTION FIVE

Country Data

Algeria

Table 5.1 Key population trends

'000

	1980	1985	1990	1995	2000	2005	2010	2015	2020	CAGR	Period growth
Population at January 1st	18,811.2	22,097.3	25,282.5	28,265.3	30,506.1	32,854.5	35,422.6	38,088.3	40,630.0	1.94	115.99
Male	9,439.8	11,112.4	12,735.7	14,257.4	15,392.0	16,583.2	17,882.2	19,227.1	20,503.7	1.96	117.20
Female	9,371.4	10,985.0	12,546.9	14,007.9	15,114.0	16,271.3	17,540.4	18,861.1	20,126.3	1.93	114.76
0-4 yrs	3,365.3	3,849.4	3,829.8	3,640.2	3,002.8	3,169.8	3,444.3	3,603.1	3,571.7	0.15	6.13
5-9 yrs	2,830.0	3,286.2	3,776.8	3,808.5	3,588.9	3,019.7	3,120.0	3,425.6	3,595.5	0.60	27.05
10-14 yrs	2,438.3	2,797.3	3,266.3	3,746.9	3,792.4	3,559.1	3,011.9	3,115.2	3,412.7	0.84	39.96
15-19 yrs	2,045.4	2,423.9	2,769.1	3,237.0	3,711.2	3,751.6	3,528.5	2,982.7	3,088.1	1.04	50.98
20-24 yrs	1,599.1	2,034.2	2,392.8	2,735.7	3,191.6	3,656.7	3,709.3	3,486.9	2,944.1	1.54	84.11
25-29 yrs	1,337.6	1,591.2	2,007.0	2,363.7	2,698.2	3,145.9	3,620.2	3,672.9	3,452.6	2.40	158.12
30-34 yrs	960.5	1,324.4	1,569.2	1,981.8	2,333.0	2,661.2	3,116.4	3,589.3	3,643.4	3.39	279.31
35-39 yrs	747.7	945.8	1,301.9	1,544.8	1,952.4	2,297.9	2,633.0	3,087.0	3,559.5	3.98	376.04
40-44 yrs	740.5	736.0	926.5	1,278.5	1,518.2	1,919.5	2,269.8	2,603.9	3,056.9	3.61	312.79
45-49 yrs	685.5	728.1	719.4	907.8	1,253.8	1,488.6	1,891.0	2,238.8	2,571.5	3.36	275.14
50-54 yrs	531.5	665.8	706.4	699.0	883.1	1,220.2	1,455.7	1,852.5	2,196.6	3.61	313.30
55-59 yrs	421.0	505.1	635.2	675.3	669.1	846.7	1,176.6	1,406.9	1,794.9	3.69	326.34
60-64 yrs	351.6	388.9	470.0	592.7	631.7	627.0	799.1	1,113.7	1,336.0	3.39	280.00
65-69 yrs	278.7	310.7	347.6	421.7	533.6	570.5	570.5	731.0	1,022.4	3.30	266.89
70-74 yrs	225.3	228.5	258.2	290.2	354.0	450.3	485.9	488.9	631.6	2.61	180.39
75-79 yrs	134.9	162.1	167.4	191.3	215.9	266.6	343.2	372.5	378.6	2.61	180.73
80+ yrs	118.4	119.7	138.8	150.3	175.8	203.1	247.1	317.2	373.9	2.92	215.85
Median age of population (years)	16.8	17.2	18.1	19.5	21.7	24.0	26.2	28.3	30.3	1.49	80.97

Table 5.2 Key economic trends

As stated

	1990	1995	2000	2005	2010	2015	2020	CAGR	Period growth
Total GDP (DZD per capita)	246,402.7	223,186.9	240,441.6	283,735.4	301,619.4	343,883.0	389,375.7	1.54	58.0
Disposable income (DZD per capita)	93,896.1	78,321.6	102,854.5	124,567.5	137,553.5	157,241.4	179,436.9	2.18	91.1
Disposable income (DZD per household)	676,410.3	541,980.7	672,141.7	760,077.7	783,187.7	838,490.8	899,433.9	0.95	33.0
Number of households by annual household disposable income ('000)									
Over US$1,000	3,508.7	4,073.3	4,656.6	5,379.4	6,219.7	7,141.6	8,105.3	2.83	131.0
Over US$10,000	1,398.2	476.0	620.3	1,269.8	2,814.9	4,494.0	6,367.3	5.18	355.4
Over US$25,000	261.3	95.1	116.7	212.7	479.2	893.5	1,614.8	6.26	518.0
Over US$75,000	48.1	23.9	30.1	48.6	86.8	137.3	217.0	5.15	350.8
Over US$150,000	20.3	9.9	12.6	20.3	36.5	56.9	88.9	5.04	337.7
Total households	3,509.6	4,084.6	4,668.2	5,384.5	6,221.4	7,142.7	8,105.7	2.83	131.0

Note: Per capita data is shown at constant 2010 prices. Household disposable income bands are shown at current prices.

Table 5.3 Young generation

'000

	1980	1985	1990	1995	2000	2005	2010	2015	2020	CAGR	Period growth
Babies under 12 months	725.2	813.5	731.0	714.7	531.0	719.3	698.2	723.9	700.0	-0.09	-3.47
Infants under 24 months	1,423.6	1,607.5	1,488.0	1,434.3	1,100.4	1,379.2	1,400.7	1,447.1	1,409.5	-0.02	-0.99
Toddlers aged 1-4	2,640.1	3,035.9	3,098.8	2,925.5	2,471.8	2,450.6	2,746.2	2,879.3	2,871.7	0.21	8.77
Children aged 2-9	4,771.7	5,528.1	6,118.7	6,014.4	5,491.4	4,810.4	5,163.6	5,581.6	5,757.7	0.47	20.66
Female	2,339.4	2,708.0	2,992.3	2,940.1	2,684.6	2,350.6	2,523.2	2,729.6	2,816.3	0.46	20.38
Male	2,432.2	2,820.1	3,126.4	3,074.4	2,806.8	2,459.8	2,640.4	2,852.1	2,941.5	0.48	20.94
Tweenagers aged 10-14	2,438.3	2,797.3	3,266.3	3,746.9	3,792.4	3,559.1	3,011.9	3,115.2	3,412.7	0.84	39.96
Female	1,196.0	1,372.9	1,600.5	1,833.1	1,854.4	1,740.6	1,472.5	1,522.8	1,669.4	0.84	39.58
Male	1,242.3	1,424.4	1,665.8	1,913.7	1,938.1	1,818.6	1,539.4	1,592.4	1,743.3	0.85	40.33
Teenagers aged 13-19	2,977.1	3,493.6	4,006.9	4,696.5	5,234.9	5,228.9	4,771.6	4,187.7	4,420.1	0.99	48.47
Female	1,459.1	1,715.5	1,966.8	2,301.8	2,562.8	2,558.9	2,335.5	2,049.2	2,162.9	0.99	48.24
Male	1,518.0	1,778.0	2,040.1	2,394.7	2,672.1	2,670.0	2,436.1	2,138.5	2,257.2	1.00	48.69
Studying age 18-22	1,763.3	2,203.0	2,535.5	2,916.2	3,427.7	3,739.6	3,685.1	3,270.1	2,922.2	1.27	65.72
Female	863.5	1,081.6	1,246.4	1,432.6	1,682.1	1,833.1	1,806.1	1,603.3	1,432.2	1.27	65.87
Male	899.9	1,121.4	1,289.1	1,483.6	1,745.6	1,906.5	1,879.0	1,666.8	1,490.0	1.27	65.58
Young adults aged 15-29	4,982.1	6,049.2	7,168.9	8,336.3	9,601.1	10,554.2	10,858.0	10,142.6	9,484.8	1.62	90.38
Female	2,444.6	2,968.3	3,522.8	4,096.2	4,716.1	5,180.7	5,327.5	4,976.9	4,654.2	1.62	90.39
Male	2,537.6	3,080.9	3,646.1	4,240.1	4,884.9	5,373.5	5,530.5	5,165.6	4,830.6	1.62	90.36

Table 5.4 Middle-aged generation

'000

	1980	1985	1990	1995	2000	2005	2010	2015	2020	CAGR	Period growth
Middle-aged adults 30-59	4,087	4,905	5,859	7,087	8,610	10,434	12,543	14,778	16,823	3.60	311.6
Female	2,108	2,501	2,958	3,555	4,291	5,179	6,202	7,306	8,319	3.49	294.7
Male	1,979	2,404	2,900	3,532	4,318	5,255	6,340	7,472	8,504	3.71	329.7
Baby boomers aged 40-59	2,378	2,635	2,988	3,561	4,324	5,475	6,793	8,102	9,620	3.56	304.5
Female	1,223	1,357	1,544	1,821	2,178	2,730	3,363	4,013	4,769	3.46	290.0
Male	1,156	1,278	1,443	1,740	2,146	2,745	3,431	4,089	4,851	3.65	319.7

Table 5.5 Elderly population

'000

	1980	1985	1990	1995	2000	2005	2010	2015	2020	CAGR	Period growth
Elderly population (60+)	1,108.7	1,209.9	1,382.1	1,646.2	1,911.1	2,117.7	2,445.8	3,023.3	3,742.5	3.09	237.5
Female	586.5	648.0	745.3	882.4	1,030.2	1,146.4	1,329.8	1,618.0	1,978.5	3.09	237.3
Male	522.2	561.9	636.7	763.9	880.9	971.2	1,116.0	1,405.4	1,764.0	3.09	237.8

Table 5.6 Population of biggest cities 1980-2020

'000

	1980	1985	1990	1995	2000	2005	2010	2015	2020	CAGR	Period growth
Algiers	1,534.6	1,523.8	1,476.8	1,475.2	1,585.0	1,847.2	2,147.6	2,460.5	2,768.8	1.49	80.4
Oran	537.9	608.5	644.5	670.7	713.6	788.1	868.5	953.0	1,036.1	1.65	92.6
Constantine	382.2	432.7	448.3	451.0	481.2	562.4	656.4	754.3	850.8	2.02	122.6
Annaba	273.0	298.1	314.0	332.5	364.9	423.2	489.5	558.6	626.7	2.10	129.6
Batna	127.0	167.4	200.0	227.1	255.0	293.9	337.2	382.3	426.7	3.08	236.1
Blida	145.7	163.2	184.5	211.2	237.1	265.7	295.7	327.1	358.1	2.27	145.7
Setif	142.3	162.9	180.4	199.2	222.4	256.9	295.3	335.4	374.8	2.45	163.5
Sidi bel Abbès	126.1	146.4	159.9	171.7	189.0	218.5	250.8	284.6	317.8	2.34	152.1
Biskra	101.5	120.8	139.4	159.2	180.0	207.2	237.4	269.0	300.1	2.75	195.5
Chlef	91.6	119.2	144.7	168.1	187.9	209.0	230.1	252.2	274.0	2.78	199.2

Chart 5.1 Population age shift 2000 and 2020, Each Column Represents a Single Age Group

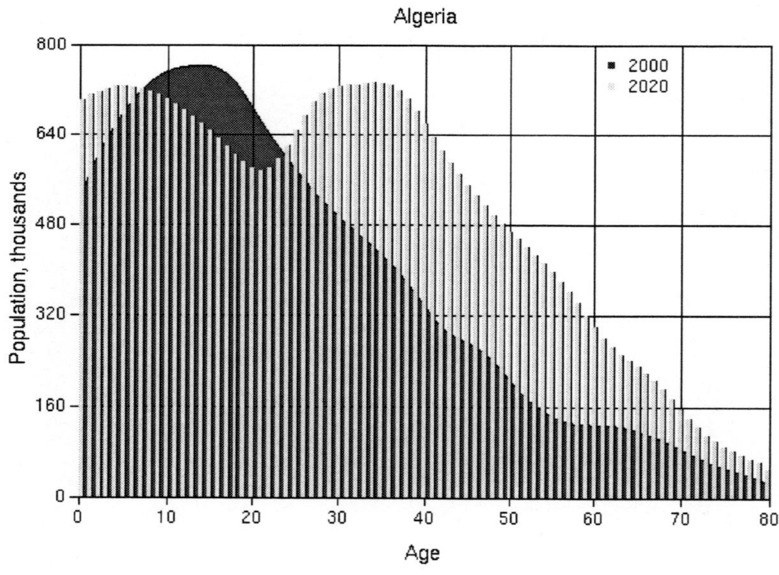

Chart 5.2 Population pyramids, 1980/2000/2010/2020

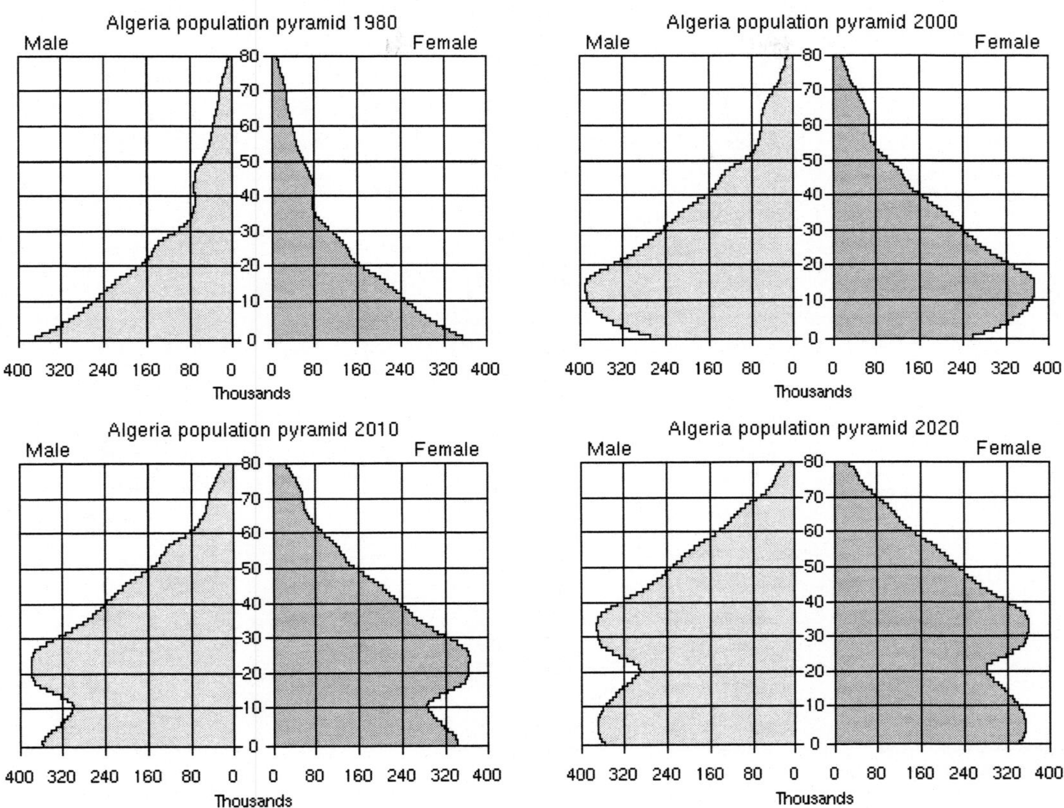

Chart 5.3 Major Cities: 1980, 2000 and 2020

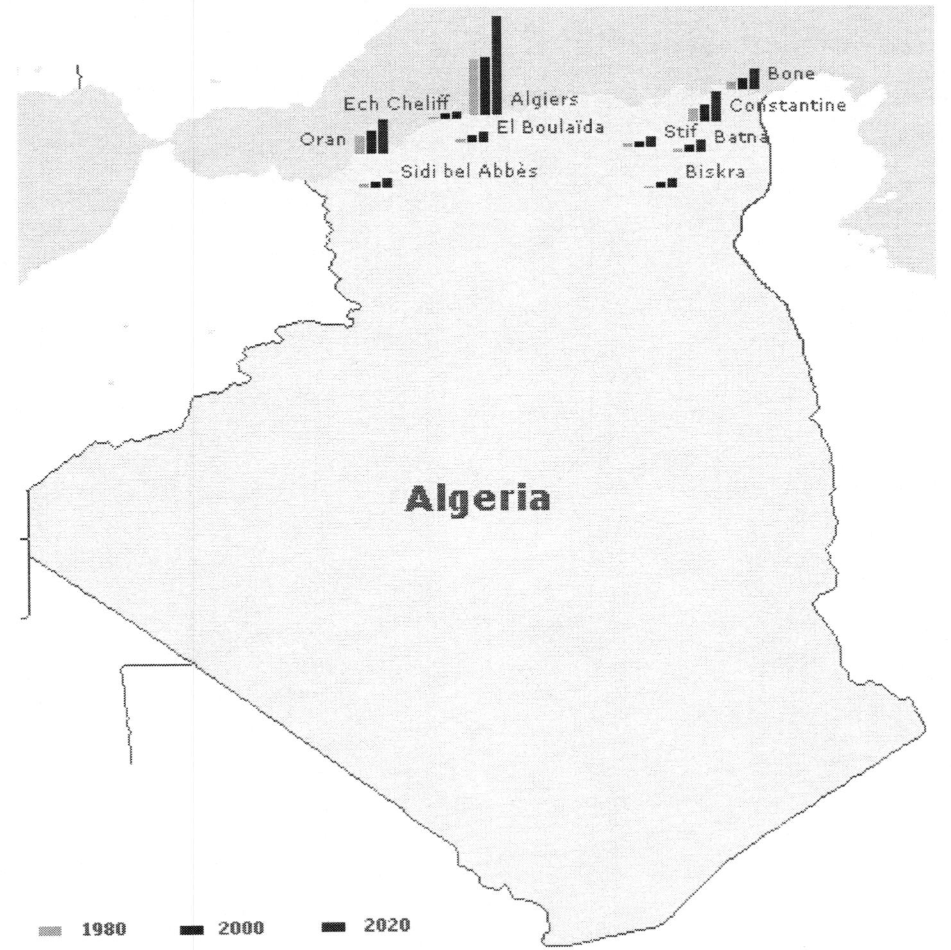

Argentina

Table 5.7 **Key population trends**

'000

	1980	1985	1990	1995	2000	2005	2010	2015	2020	CAGR	Period growth
Population at January 1st	28,093.5	30,305.3	32,580.9	34,834.9	36,895.7	38,747.1	40,738.0	42,676.1	44,486.2	1.16	58.35
Male	13,860.3	14,913.4	15,996.7	17,086.1	18,059.3	18,948.5	19,922.9	20,876.6	21,766.8	1.13	57.04
Female	14,233.2	15,391.9	16,584.2	17,748.8	18,836.4	19,798.6	20,815.1	21,799.6	22,719.4	1.18	59.62
0-4 yrs	3,342.9	3,259.6	3,396.6	3,504.2	3,454.0	3,337.0	3,441.7	3,454.3	3,398.2	0.04	1.65
5-9 yrs	2,791.3	3,310.3	3,299.7	3,382.8	3,487.6	3,431.0	3,340.1	3,425.5	3,450.0	0.53	23.60
10-14 yrs	2,451.7	2,812.8	3,313.4	3,301.0	3,380.8	3,467.7	3,424.6	3,341.5	3,429.9	0.84	39.89
15-19 yrs	2,314.1	2,462.8	2,817.5	3,310.7	3,276.7	3,364.1	3,464.7	3,423.9	3,333.4	0.92	44.05
20-24 yrs	2,218.7	2,323.5	2,464.7	2,811.3	3,278.3	3,252.9	3,356.9	3,460.6	3,423.2	1.09	54.29
25-29 yrs	2,128.9	2,216.6	2,331.7	2,461.3	2,780.2	3,251.2	3,240.0	3,347.3	3,449.6	1.21	62.03
30-34 yrs	1,929.0	2,115.3	2,213.2	2,323.5	2,432.8	2,754.8	3,233.1	3,225.6	3,338.7	1.38	73.08
35-39 yrs	1,718.4	1,912.0	2,094.0	2,195.0	2,294.7	2,407.2	2,734.4	3,212.6	3,187.5	1.56	85.49
40-44 yrs	1,581.4	1,696.0	1,883.6	2,067.9	2,161.9	2,264.4	2,382.0	2,709.3	3,207.4	1.78	102.82
45-49 yrs	1,527.2	1,548.7	1,658.2	1,847.8	2,026.7	2,122.6	2,229.0	2,348.5	2,658.2	1.40	74.06
50-54 yrs	1,464.4	1,478.9	1,496.9	1,609.3	1,795.0	1,972.6	2,071.9	2,180.4	2,302.0	1.14	57.21
55-59 yrs	1,284.9	1,394.8	1,406.0	1,429.8	1,541.5	1,723.3	1,900.4	2,002.2	2,114.0	1.25	64.53
60-64 yrs	1,065.8	1,194.4	1,295.0	1,313.1	1,340.5	1,449.0	1,627.7	1,802.7	1,902.8	1.46	78.53
65-69 yrs	881.7	955.5	1,070.9	1,169.8	1,191.9	1,221.3	1,328.6	1,501.8	1,674.2	1.62	89.90
70-74 yrs	664.4	743.6	808.4	917.1	1,010.4	1,035.4	1,071.1	1,175.3	1,338.1	1.77	101.39
75-79 yrs	431.5	507.8	571.5	632.6	731.6	812.3	844.3	885.6	982.9	2.08	127.80
80+ yrs	297.3	372.6	459.6	557.6	711.0	880.3	1,047.4	1,179.0	1,296.0	3.75	335.87
Median age of population (years)	27.1	27.2	27.1	27.2	27.7	28.8	30.2	31.4	32.6	0.46	20.13

Table 5.8 **Key economic trends**

As stated

	1990	1995	2000	2005	2010	2015	2020	CAGR	Period growth
Total GDP (ARS per capita)	19,122.1	23,814.4	25,534.3	26,831.2	32,029.7	34,732.3	34,493.4	1.99	80.4
Disposable income (ARS per capita)	16,237.8	13,102.8	13,111.4	13,031.3	16,941.0	18,786.0	20,576.2	0.79	26.7
Disposable income (ARS per household)	60,312.3	48,169.2	48,459.8	48,071.3	61,859.0	67,427.5	72,064.1	0.60	19.5
Number of households by annual household disposable income ('000)									
Over US$1,000	8,590.6	9,368.1	9,823.2	10,311.3	10,968.9	11,693.0	12,517.2	1.26	45.7
Over US$10,000	4,200.0	6,471.8	6,589.3	4,160.3	6,347.2	7,025.4	8,241.4	2.27	96.2
Over US$25,000	1,055.3	2,634.2	2,757.7	893.0	2,000.8	2,378.5	3,261.2	3.83	209.0
Over US$75,000	130.1	295.2	334.2	131.1	228.7	273.0	391.1	3.74	200.6
Over US$150,000	55.6	104.8	111.3	56.5	92.2	105.3	134.3	2.98	141.6
Total households	8,771.7	9,475.6	9,982.6	10,503.7	11,156.7	11,890.0	12,702.0	1.24	44.8

Note: Per capita data is shown at constant 2010 prices. Household disposable income bands are shown at current prices.

Table 5.9 **Young generation**

'000

	1980	1985	1990	1995	2000	2005	2010	2015	2020	CAGR	Period growth
Babies under 12 months	719.6	597.2	722.0	701.7	679.4	661.0	712.6	680.0	672.2	-0.17	-6.58
Infants under 24 months	1,414.4	1,232.2	1,411.8	1,407.9	1,365.5	1,324.1	1,410.1	1,369.5	1,348.7	-0.12	-4.65
Toddlers aged 1-4	2,623.3	2,662.4	2,674.6	2,802.5	2,774.6	2,676.0	2,729.1	2,774.2	2,726.0	0.10	3.91
Children aged 2-9	4,719.8	5,337.7	5,284.5	5,479.1	5,576.1	5,443.9	5,371.8	5,510.3	5,499.5	0.38	16.52
Female	2,325.6	2,627.0	2,600.1	2,694.6	2,741.8	2,676.1	2,639.5	2,706.2	2,700.3	0.37	16.11
Male	2,394.1	2,710.6	2,684.4	2,784.6	2,834.3	2,767.8	2,732.3	2,804.1	2,799.2	0.39	16.92
Tweenagers aged 10-14	2,451.7	2,812.8	3,313.4	3,301.0	3,380.8	3,467.7	3,424.6	3,341.5	3,429.9	0.84	39.89
Female	1,209.7	1,388.4	1,637.0	1,627.5	1,663.7	1,706.0	1,684.4	1,642.8	1,685.3	0.83	39.31
Male	1,242.0	1,424.4	1,676.4	1,673.5	1,717.1	1,761.7	1,740.2	1,698.7	1,744.5	0.85	40.46
Teenagers aged 13-19	3,271.1	3,526.1	4,109.9	4,638.9	4,609.4	4,746.7	4,846.7	4,761.3	4,694.3	0.91	43.51
Female	1,624.3	1,742.8	2,033.9	2,293.9	2,276.0	2,337.3	2,385.7	2,342.9	2,308.8	0.88	42.14
Male	1,646.9	1,783.2	2,076.0	2,345.0	2,333.4	2,409.4	2,461.1	2,418.4	2,385.5	0.93	44.85
Studying age 18-22	2,253.9	2,369.1	2,565.3	3,040.5	3,317.6	3,271.8	3,416.2	3,463.5	3,379.4	1.02	49.94
Female	1,133.4	1,175.6	1,271.2	1,507.3	1,645.1	1,616.3	1,683.3	1,706.4	1,664.2	0.96	46.83
Male	1,120.4	1,193.5	1,294.0	1,533.2	1,672.5	1,655.5	1,732.9	1,757.1	1,715.2	1.07	53.08
Young adults aged 15-29	6,661.7	7,002.9	7,613.9	8,583.3	9,335.1	9,868.2	10,061.6	10,231.8	10,206.2	1.07	53.21
Female	3,349.8	3,500.8	3,784.8	4,258.5	4,633.6	4,887.1	4,970.1	5,046.2	5,031.1	1.02	50.19
Male	3,311.9	3,502.1	3,829.1	4,324.8	4,701.5	4,981.1	5,091.5	5,185.6	5,175.1	1.12	56.26

Table 5.10 Middle-aged generation

'000

	1980	1985	1990	1995	2000	2005	2010	2015	2020	CAGR	Period growth
Middle-aged adults 30-59	9,505	10,146	10,752	11,473	12,253	13,245	14,551	15,679	16,808	1.44	76.8
Female	4,810	5,157	5,488	5,854	6,250	6,749	7,393	7,937	8,468	1.42	76.1
Male	4,695	4,989	5,264	5,619	6,003	6,496	7,157	7,742	8,340	1.45	77.6
Baby boomers aged 40-59	5,858	6,118	6,445	6,955	7,525	8,083	8,583	9,240	10,282	1.42	75.5
Female	2,975	3,119	3,298	3,568	3,875	4,164	4,409	4,724	5,224	1.42	75.6
Male	2,883	3,000	3,147	3,387	3,650	3,919	4,175	4,516	5,057	1.42	75.4

Table 5.11 Elderly population

'000

	1980	1985	1990	1995	2000	2005	2010	2015	2020	CAGR	Period growth
Elderly population (60+)	3,341	3,774	4,205	4,590	4,985	5,398	5,919	6,544	7,194	1.94	115.3
Female	1,843	2,112	2,379	2,622	2,877	3,130	3,435	3,795	4,173	2.06	126.4
Male	1,498	1,662	1,826	1,968	2,109	2,268	2,484	2,749	3,022	1.77	101.7

Table 5.12 Population of biggest cities 1980-2020

'000

	1980	1985	1990	1995	2000	2005	2010	2015	2020	CAGR	Period growth
Buenos Aires	2,922.8	2,988.3	2,999.8	2,910.1	2,803.0	2,679.5	2,568.5	2,468.1	2,377.7	-0.51	-18.65
San Justo	949.6	1,034.5	1,115.4	1,176.5	1,242.5	1,297.4	1,345.3	1,386.8	1,422.6	1.02	49.82
Cordoba	970.6	1,066.6	1,153.3	1,208.2	1,259.5	1,298.6	1,332.7	1,361.8	1,386.7	0.90	42.88
Rosario	794.1	860.6	910.1	918.2	911.6	896.4	882.4	869.4	857.2	0.19	7.95
Lomas de Zamora	510.1	546.6	575.5	585.3	591.3	592.2	592.6	592.6	592.2	0.37	16.09
La Plata	459.1	491.9	521.4	540.3	560.7	576.5	590.1	601.8	611.7	0.72	33.26
San Miguel de Tucumán	394.1	432.4	468.6	495.0	522.5	545.0	564.7	581.8	596.5	1.04	51.34
Almirante Brown	331.9	390.1	443.9	479.9	509.6	533.1	553.6	571.3	586.6	1.43	76.74
Mar del Plata	414.7	467.1	511.0	530.7	541.0	545.2	548.6	551.3	553.2	0.72	33.41
Quilmes	446.6	483.7	512.2	519.4	519.9	515.4	511.2	507.1	503.1	0.30	12.66

Chart 5.4 Population age shift 2000 and 2020, Each Column Represents a Single Age Group

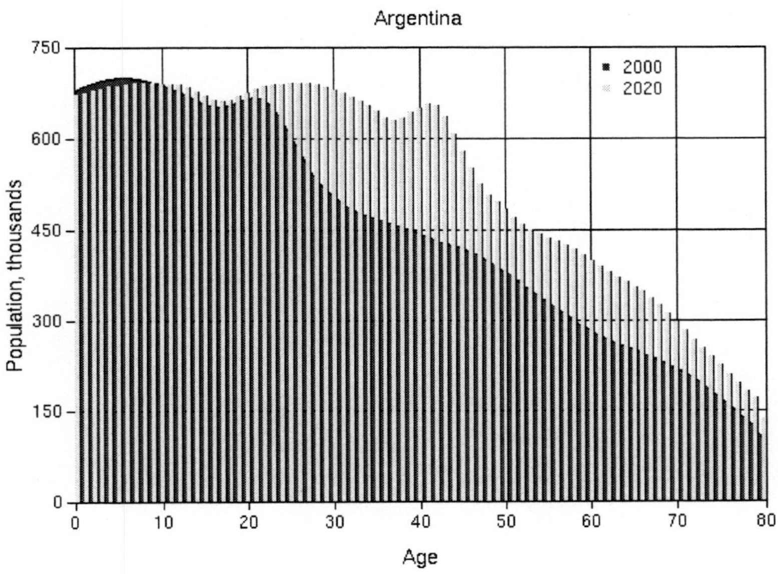

Chart 5.5 Population pyramids, 1980/2000/2010/2020

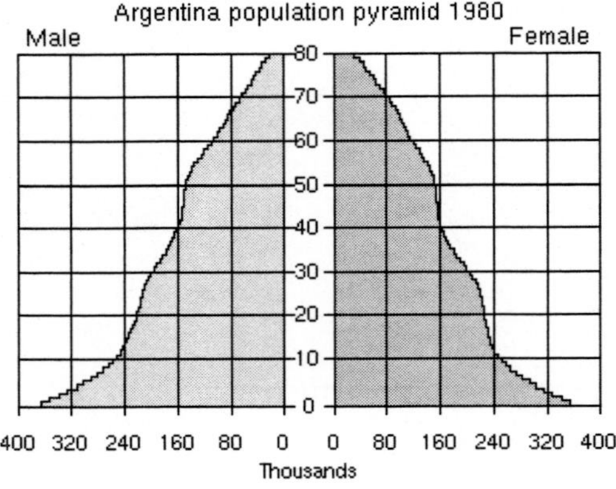

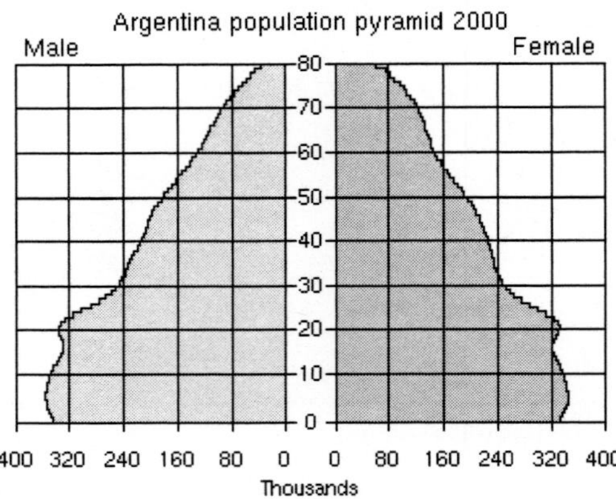

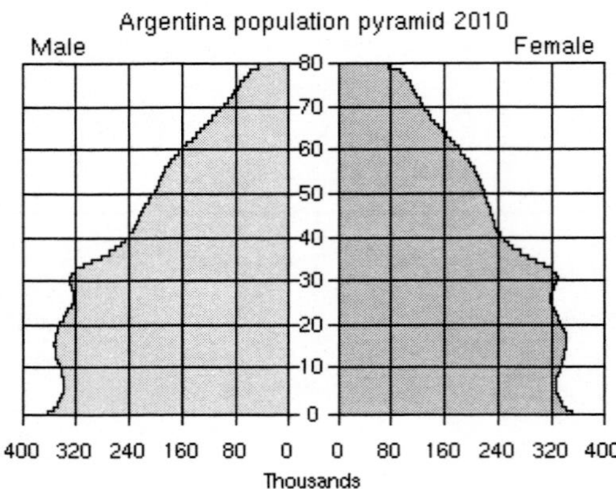

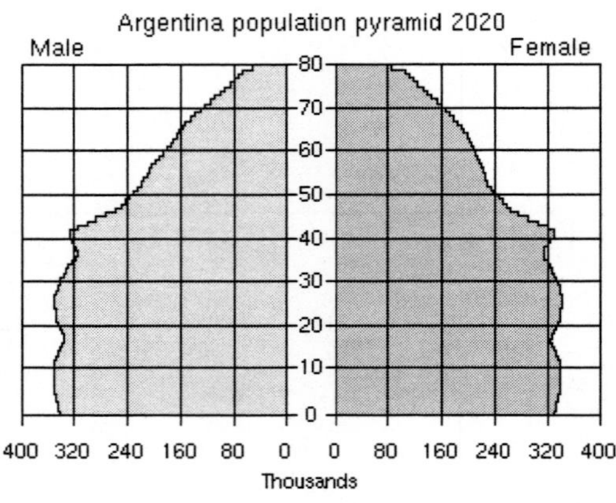

Chart 5.6 Major Cities: 1980, 2000 and 2020

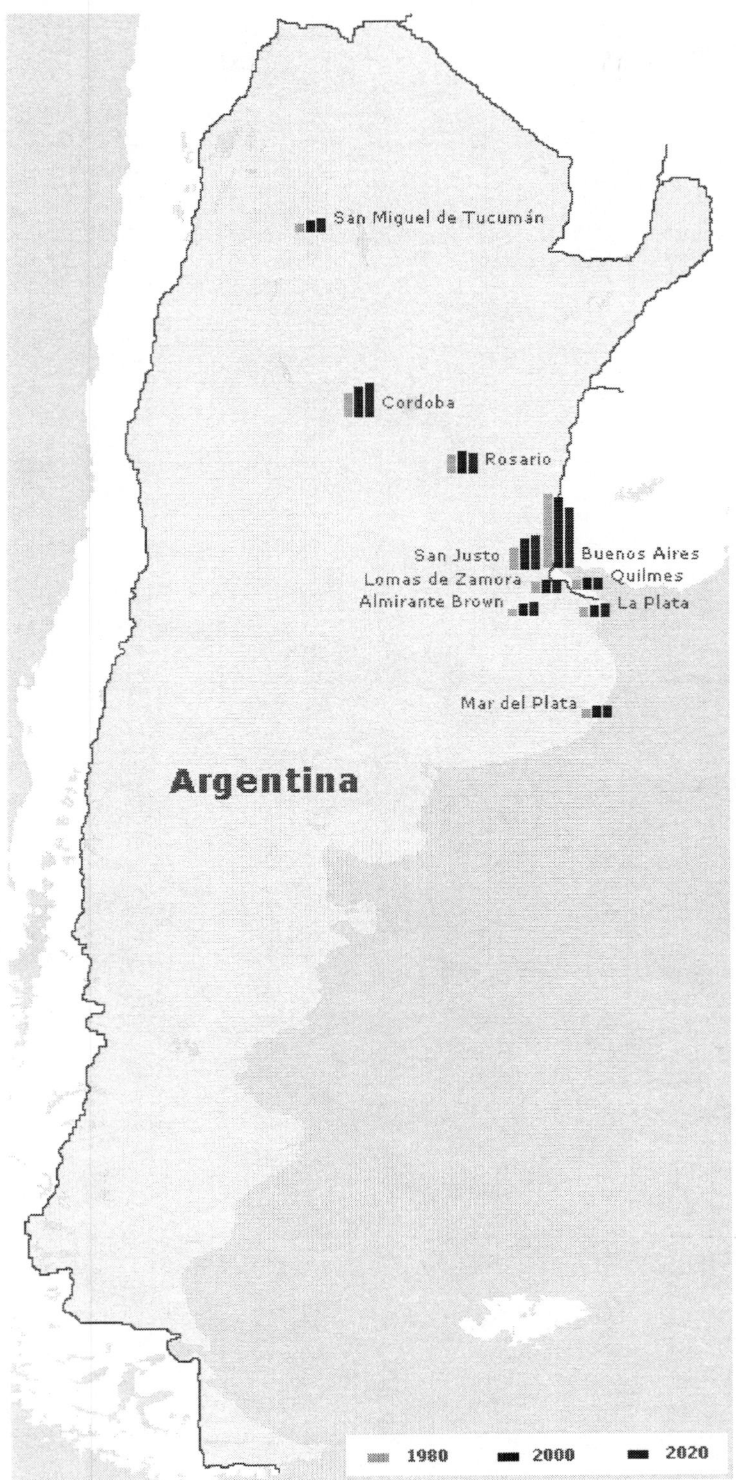

Australia

Table 5.13 Key population trends

'000

	1980	1985	1990	1995	2000	2005	2010	2015	2020	CAGR	Period growth
Population at January 1st	14,695.4	15,788.3	17,065.1	18,071.8	19,153.4	20,394.8	22,100.0	23,634.4	25,253.5	1.36	71.8
Male	7,338.1	7,882.7	8,511.3	8,993.6	9,505.3	10,128.1	10,998.4	11,774.1	12,590.8	1.36	71.6
Female	7,357.3	7,905.6	8,553.9	9,078.2	9,648.0	10,266.7	11,101.6	11,860.3	12,662.7	1.37	72.1
0-4 yrs	1,132.2	1,199.6	1,258.2	1,299.5	1,279.0	1,285.5	1,452.3	1,541.8	1,606.7	0.88	41.9
5-9 yrs	1,306.6	1,175.1	1,262.3	1,292.7	1,349.9	1,335.6	1,359.6	1,505.6	1,601.4	0.51	22.6
10-14 yrs	1,272.2	1,350.9	1,234.5	1,295.9	1,337.2	1,401.0	1,401.5	1,411.9	1,564.0	0.52	22.9
15-19 yrs	1,307.6	1,304.7	1,402.4	1,269.2	1,327.2	1,399.6	1,487.9	1,477.2	1,493.0	0.33	14.2
20-24 yrs	1,269.1	1,349.5	1,358.4	1,429.5	1,291.1	1,435.9	1,567.5	1,630.2	1,625.3	0.62	28.1
25-29 yrs	1,209.9	1,319.5	1,422.6	1,378.8	1,449.2	1,371.6	1,602.2	1,695.3	1,762.0	0.94	45.6
30-34 yrs	1,180.5	1,252.7	1,393.6	1,461.6	1,426.8	1,515.9	1,501.6	1,706.3	1,804.8	1.07	52.9
35-39 yrs	950.5	1,227.6	1,312.8	1,423.2	1,504.8	1,482.7	1,602.9	1,574.8	1,784.1	1.59	87.7
40-44 yrs	809.8	968.5	1,259.2	1,333.3	1,448.7	1,542.6	1,543.9	1,647.5	1,626.5	1.76	100.8
45-49 yrs	741.5	818.7	982.1	1,251.8	1,341.2	1,465.2	1,569.7	1,558.9	1,667.9	2.05	124.9
50-54 yrs	774.5	733.0	821.1	972.2	1,257.6	1,338.5	1,464.6	1,557.9	1,554.5	1.76	100.7
55-59 yrs	736.8	759.0	726.1	802.2	963.7	1,238.6	1,323.3	1,441.6	1,541.0	1.86	109.1
60-64 yrs	590.7	708.5	738.5	710.3	797.7	944.5	1,210.5	1,292.4	1,416.4	2.21	139.8
65-69 yrs	528.6	546.3	662.4	689.4	677.1	762.3	909.4	1,165.1	1,253.8	2.18	137.2
70-74 yrs	385.1	464.3	488.5	593.0	633.2	625.2	710.6	854.1	1,104.6	2.67	186.9
75-79 yrs	254.0	310.3	375.2	402.9	507.3	549.2	551.9	636.9	776.4	2.83	205.6
80+ yrs	245.6	300.0	367.3	466.1	561.6	700.8	840.5	936.9	1,071.1	3.75	336.2
Median age of population (years)	29.4	30.8	32.1	33.7	35.4	36.5	37.2	37.7	38.2	0.66	30.1

Table 5.14 Key economic trends

As stated

	1990	1995	2000	2005	2010	2015	2020	CAGR	Period growth
Total GDP (A$ per capita)	38,680.5	41,593.5	48,278.5	53,025.5	55,027.0	60,123.8	65,053.6	1.75	68.2
Disposable income (A$ per capita)	24,748.4	25,906.8	28,158.4	30,582.1	32,003.4	34,831.9	37,636.4	1.41	52.1
Disposable income (A$ per household)	74,113.1	73,759.4	77,359.3	82,837.7	86,592.6	93,636.4	100,957.2	1.04	36.2
Number of households by annual household disposable income ('000)									
Over US$1,000	5,682.1	6,327.9	6,951.7	7,517.8	8,152.2	8,776.8	9,401.9	1.69	65.5
Over US$10,000	4,974.4	5,566.8	6,031.6	7,034.7	7,532.6	8,184.4	8,907.6	1.96	79.1
Over US$25,000	3,188.2	3,691.2	3,735.3	5,601.8	5,787.8	6,482.7	7,427.9	2.86	133.0
Over US$75,000	528.5	695.3	590.3	1,753.4	1,621.7	2,033.5	2,892.0	5.83	447.2
Over US$150,000	122.6	148.5	142.4	304.2	287.9	361.4	643.3	5.68	424.6
Total households	5,698.5	6,347.4	6,971.7	7,529.4	8,167.8	8,791.8	9,414.4	1.69	65.2

Note: Per capita data is shown at constant 2010 prices. Household disposable income bands are shown at current prices.

Table 5.15 Young generation

'000

	1980	1985	1990	1995	2000	2005	2010	2015	2020	CAGR	Period growth
Babies under 12 months	222.6	241.0	256.6	257.9	251.4	257.6	299.4	309.4	322.5	0.93	44.9
Infants under 24 months	445.5	480.9	507.9	516.5	504.7	512.5	596.1	617.6	643.9	0.93	44.5
Toddlers aged 1-4	909.6	958.5	1,001.6	1,041.6	1,027.6	1,028.0	1,152.9	1,232.5	1,284.1	0.87	41.2
Children aged 2-9	1,993.3	1,893.8	2,012.6	2,075.7	2,124.2	2,108.6	2,215.8	2,429.8	2,564.2	0.63	28.6
Female	974.6	922.8	980.6	1,011.6	1,034.2	1,027.2	1,079.0	1,184.1	1,249.7	0.62	28.2
Male	1,018.7	971.0	1,032.0	1,064.1	1,089.9	1,081.4	1,136.8	1,245.7	1,314.5	0.64	29.0
Tweenagers aged 10-14	1,272.2	1,350.9	1,234.5	1,295.9	1,337.2	1,401.0	1,401.5	1,411.9	1,564.0	0.52	22.9
Female	621.8	659.7	600.5	631.8	652.5	681.7	683.0	687.8	762.7	0.51	22.7
Male	650.5	691.2	634.0	664.1	684.7	719.3	718.5	724.1	801.2	0.52	23.2
Teenagers aged 13-19	1,803.1	1,878.6	1,902.6	1,783.9	1,860.9	1,964.5	2,053.9	2,044.5	2,101.6	0.38	16.6
Female	882.9	918.7	928.3	869.1	909.7	958.3	999.8	997.1	1,024.7	0.37	16.1
Male	920.1	959.8	974.3	914.9	951.2	1,006.2	1,054.1	1,047.4	1,077.0	0.39	17.0
Studying age 18-22	1,307.7	1,306.6	1,422.0	1,344.2	1,295.4	1,428.5	1,543.4	1,568.3	1,567.6	0.45	19.9
Female	644.4	640.4	699.0	658.8	635.4	701.4	749.7	764.1	765.2	0.43	18.7
Male	663.3	666.2	723.0	685.3	660.1	727.1	793.7	804.3	802.4	0.48	21.0
Young adults aged 15-29	3,786.6	3,973.7	4,183.4	4,077.5	4,067.5	4,207.0	4,657.7	4,802.8	4,880.2	0.64	28.9
Female	1,865.5	1,953.1	2,061.6	2,010.1	2,012.3	2,069.9	2,275.6	2,342.5	2,382.6	0.61	27.7
Male	1,921.1	2,020.6	2,121.8	2,067.4	2,055.2	2,137.1	2,382.1	2,460.4	2,497.7	0.66	30.0

Table 5.16 Middle-aged generation

'000

	1980	1985	1990	1995	2000	2005	2010	2015	2020	CAGR	Period growth
Middle-aged adults 30-59	5,194	5,760	6,495	7,244	7,943	8,584	9,006	9,487	9,979	1.65	92.1
Female	2,551	2,831	3,208	3,599	3,974	4,315	4,532	4,764	4,991	1.69	95.6
Male	2,642	2,928	3,287	3,645	3,968	4,269	4,474	4,723	4,988	1.60	88.8
Baby boomers aged 40-59	3,063	3,279	3,789	4,360	5,011	5,585	5,902	6,206	6,390	1.86	108.6
Female	1,506	1,603	1,857	2,156	2,500	2,806	2,976	3,133	3,221	1.92	113.9
Male	1,557	1,676	1,931	2,204	2,512	2,779	2,926	3,073	3,169	1.79	103.5

Table 5.17 Elderly population

'000

	1980	1985	1990	1995	2000	2005	2010	2015	2020	CAGR	Period growth
Elderly population (60+)	2,004.0	2,329.6	2,631.8	2,861.7	3,177.0	3,582.1	4,222.8	4,885.4	5,622.3	2.61	180.6
Female	1,126.9	1,303.7	1,455.5	1,574.1	1,728.5	1,924.4	2,242.2	2,580.8	2,963.4	2.45	163.0
Male	877.0	1,025.9	1,176.4	1,287.6	1,448.5	1,657.7	1,980.7	2,304.6	2,659.0	2.81	203.2

Table 5.18 Population of biggest cities 1980-2020

'000

	1980	1985	1990	1995	2000	2005	2010	2015	2020	CAGR	Period growth
Sydney	2,981.2	3,180.7	3,401.9	3,652.4	3,914.6	4,086.9	4,263.2	4,451.1	4,648.0	1.12	55.9
Melbourne	2,557.4	2,722.2	2,902.9	3,105.0	3,320.7	3,540.9	3,799.1	4,056.2	4,312.0	1.31	68.6
Brisbane	1,116.6	1,203.3	1,303.0	1,420.6	1,553.3	1,717.0	1,933.3	2,139.4	2,336.9	1.86	109.3
Perth	985.2	1,053.8	1,130.6	1,218.7	1,315.2	1,418.8	1,545.5	1,669.2	1,790.3	1.50	81.7
Adelaide	930.1	970.1	1,007.6	1,041.4	1,067.3	1,097.7	1,141.7	1,189.1	1,239.2	0.72	33.2
Newcastle	378.7	400.0	422.4	446.3	469.2	489.0	512.7	537.5	563.1	1.00	48.7
Canberra	254.4	267.3	280.3	293.5	306.1	326.0	352.1	378.0	403.5	1.16	58.6
Hobart	176.8	182.6	187.2	190.1	191.4	198.0	209.9	221.9	234.0	0.70	32.4
Darwin	66.6	72.7	80.0	88.9	98.9	104.6	110.8	117.0	123.3	1.55	85.1

Chart 5.7 Population age shift 2000 and 2020, Each Column Represents a Single Age Group

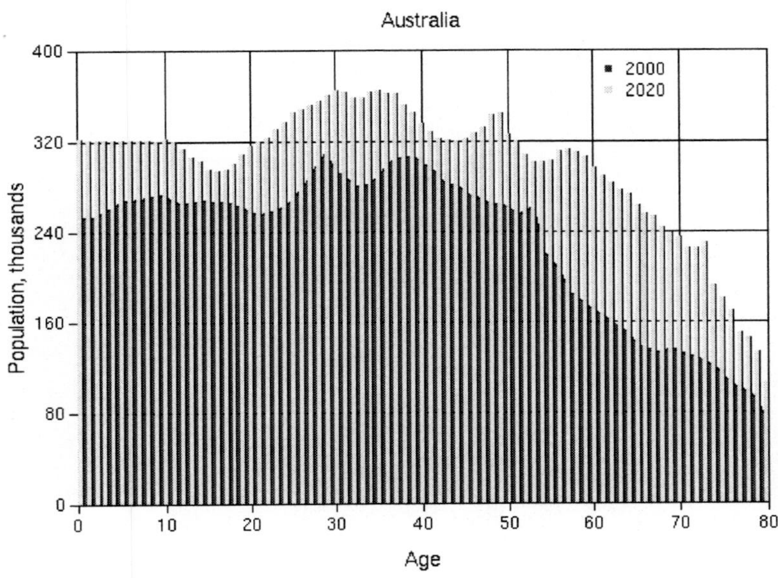

Chart 5.8 Population pyramids, 1980/2000/2010/2020

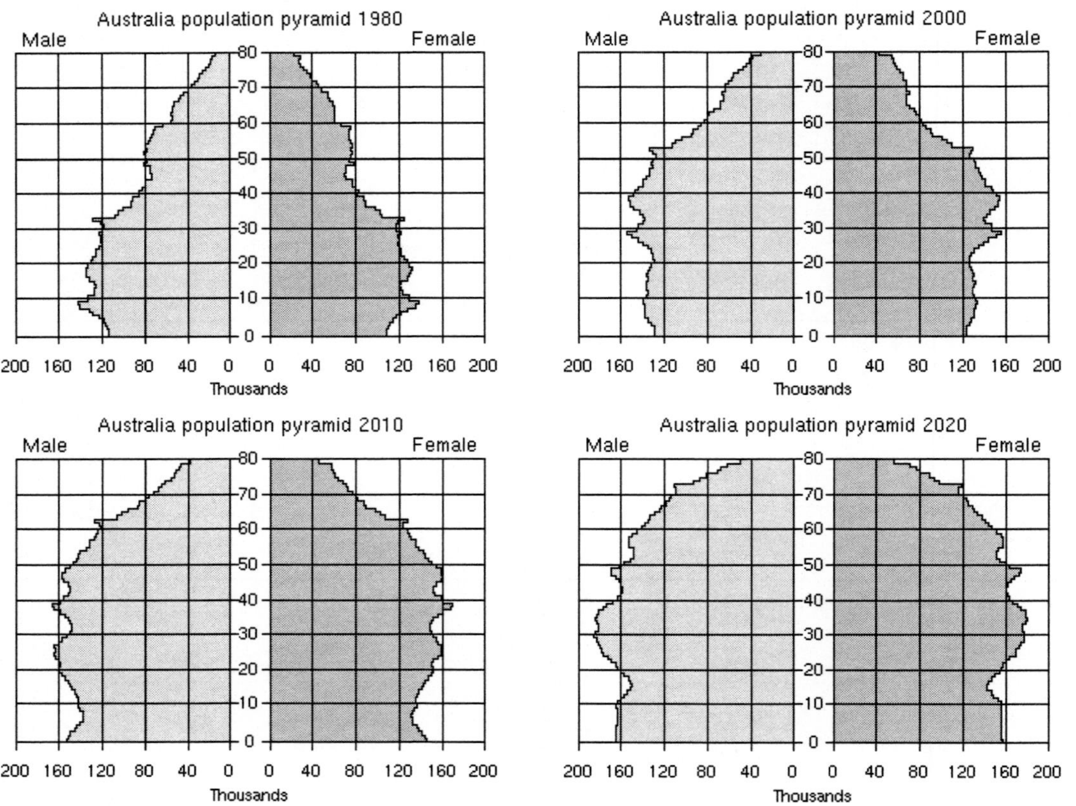

Chart 5.9 Major Cities: 1980, 2000 and 2020

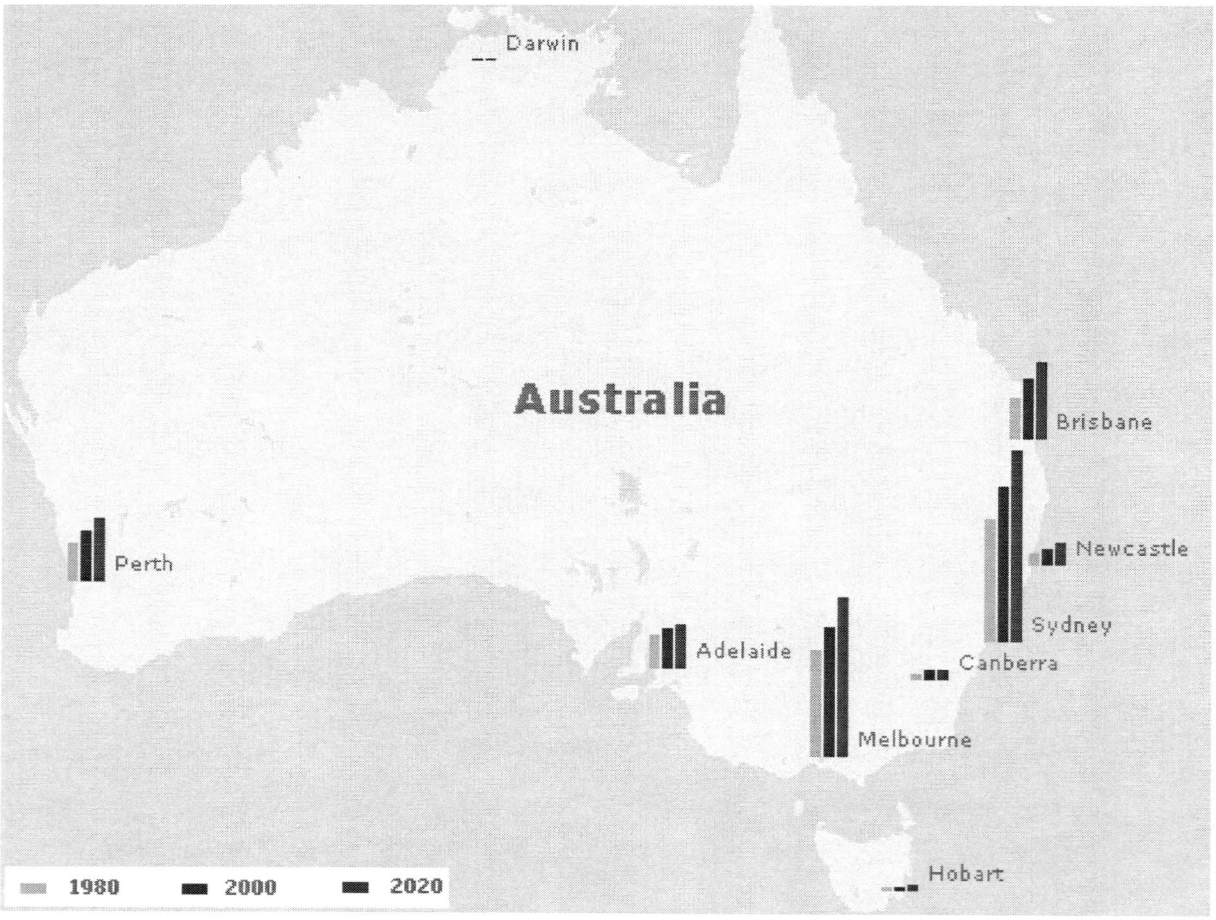

Austria

Table 5.19 Key population trends

'000

	1980	1985	1990	1995	2000	2005	2010	2015	2020	CAGR	Period growth
Population at January 1st	7,545.5	7,563.2	7,644.8	7,943.5	8,002.2	8,206.5	8,408.8	8,530.5	8,633.8	0.34	14.42
Male	3,564.2	3,588.1	3,654.9	3,831.2	3,868.3	3,986.3	4,096.8	4,164.1	4,220.4	0.42	18.41
Female	3,981.4	3,975.1	3,989.9	4,112.3	4,133.9	4,220.2	4,312.0	4,366.4	4,413.5	0.26	10.85
0-4 yrs	429.6	456.4	443.2	473.2	424.5	398.0	396.9	396.7	399.3	-0.18	-7.06
5-9 yrs	506.2	428.2	462.4	464.2	478.1	436.2	412.9	408.1	407.1	-0.54	-19.58
10-14 yrs	622.9	510.6	434.7	479.7	469.2	488.4	449.4	423.1	417.6	-0.99	-32.96
15-19 yrs	654.5	633.1	522.0	458.1	485.6	487.1	505.5	464.0	436.7	-1.01	-33.29
20-24 yrs	580.1	660.0	647.6	558.9	469.0	524.3	516.4	529.2	486.0	-0.44	-16.21
25-29 yrs	507.0	579.7	668.4	692.4	568.2	509.4	557.6	540.5	551.5	0.21	8.78
30-34 yrs	497.9	501.7	583.4	700.2	690.9	592.4	531.0	571.6	553.5	0.27	11.18
35-39 yrs	550.7	491.0	503.9	605.6	693.8	702.3	605.9	538.9	579.0	0.13	5.14
40-44 yrs	440.1	543.3	489.2	515.5	598.7	697.6	709.4	608.4	541.7	0.52	23.09
45-49 yrs	419.8	431.5	535.9	490.7	508.4	597.4	699.4	706.5	606.6	0.92	44.48
50-54 yrs	443.4	407.7	421.9	526.0	480.0	502.8	593.7	690.7	698.4	1.14	57.50
55-59 yrs	453.6	424.6	391.7	410.7	509.4	468.5	494.5	581.1	677.2	1.01	49.30
60-64 yrs	270.0	426.5	400.6	371.5	392.7	490.4	455.4	479.7	565.4	1.87	109.42
65-69 yrs	388.1	245.5	391.7	369.8	344.5	371.5	467.1	434.5	459.7	0.42	18.45
70-74 yrs	337.4	332.1	213.8	345.3	329.3	312.6	342.3	430.6	404.3	0.45	19.82
75-79 yrs	245.3	255.7	263.9	173.3	287.8	280.2	270.4	300.2	381.4	1.11	55.47
80+ yrs	198.9	235.6	270.4	308.4	272.1	347.4	400.9	426.7	468.5	2.16	135.48
Median age of population (years)	34.7	35.1	35.6	36.1	37.9	39.8	41.6	43.3	44.5	0.63	28.34

Table 5.20 Key economic trends

As stated

	1990	1995	2000	2005	2010	2015	2020	CAGR	Period growth
Total GDP (EUR per capita)	24,946.6	26,292.4	30,236.2	31,904.9	32,838.1	35,944.4	40,323.8	1.61	61.6
Disposable income (EUR per capita)	16,035.9	19,078.7	20,458.9	21,053.5	22,146.9	24,822.4	28,034.3	1.88	74.8
Disposable income (EUR per household)	40,917.1	48,403.6	49,565.8	49,715.5	51,209.9	56,363.0	62,581.1	1.43	52.9
Number of households by annual household disposable income ('000)									
Over US$1,000	2,996.1	3,131.0	3,303.0	3,475.3	3,636.6	3,756.8	3,867.7	0.85	29.1
Over US$10,000	2,946.0	3,112.9	3,278.4	3,464.9	3,629.7	3,752.5	3,865.1	0.91	31.2
Over US$25,000	2,104.0	2,759.0	2,619.5	3,214.1	3,462.3	3,650.0	3,811.6	2.00	81.2
Over US$75,000	169.1	447.4	215.7	708.6	1,074.5	1,605.8	2,415.3	9.27	1,328.1
Over US$150,000	64.9	106.1	77.4	143.3	185.0	273.2	539.6	7.32	731.7
Total households	2,996.1	3,131.0	3,303.0	3,475.3	3,636.6	3,756.8	3,867.7	0.85	29.1

Note: Per capita data is shown at constant 2010 prices. Household disposable income bands are shown at current prices.

Table 5.21 Young generation

'000

	1980	1985	1990	1995	2000	2005	2010	2015	2020	CAGR	Period growth
Babies under 12 months	85.4	88.7	88.7	91.6	78.6	78.9	77.8	78.6	78.7	-0.20	-7.86
Infants under 24 months	169.0	178.3	177.7	186.4	160.6	157.6	156.2	157.5	158.0	-0.17	-6.50
Toddlers aged 1-4	344.2	367.7	354.5	381.5	345.9	319.1	319.2	318.1	320.6	-0.18	-6.86
Children aged 2-9	766.8	706.3	727.9	750.9	741.9	676.5	653.6	647.3	648.4	-0.42	-15.45
Female	374.9	344.8	354.9	365.5	362.0	329.7	318.9	316.4	316.3	-0.42	-15.63
Male	391.9	361.5	373.0	385.4	379.9	346.9	334.7	330.8	332.1	-0.41	-15.27
Tweenagers aged 10-14	622.9	510.6	434.7	479.7	469.2	488.4	449.4	423.1	417.6	-0.99	-32.96
Female	305.1	250.1	211.6	234.2	228.6	237.9	219.5	206.2	204.4	-1.00	-33.02
Male	317.7	260.6	223.1	245.5	240.6	250.5	229.9	216.8	213.2	-0.99	-32.91
Teenagers aged 13-19	909.5	853.5	701.2	651.3	672.6	684.8	694.5	632.8	606.0	-1.01	-33.37
Female	448.6	418.6	343.6	317.3	328.6	333.5	339.4	309.5	296.5	-1.03	-33.91
Male	460.9	434.8	357.6	334.0	344.1	351.3	355.1	323.3	309.5	-0.99	-32.85
Studying age 18-22	614.5	660.7	607.4	506.8	470.5	506.9	512.0	508.9	455.6	-0.75	-25.87
Female	304.3	325.8	298.6	250.8	230.8	249.6	251.6	250.7	224.1	-0.76	-26.36
Male	310.2	334.9	308.8	255.9	239.6	257.3	260.4	258.2	231.4	-0.73	-25.39
Young adults aged 15-29	1,741.7	1,872.7	1,838.0	1,709.3	1,522.8	1,520.8	1,579.5	1,533.8	1,474.2	-0.42	-15.36
Female	864.5	925.3	902.7	840.5	754.7	749.5	778.4	755.8	726.4	-0.43	-15.98
Male	877.1	947.5	935.3	868.9	768.1	771.4	801.1	777.9	747.8	-0.40	-14.74

Table 5.22 Middle-aged generation

'000

	1980	1985	1990	1995	2000	2005	2010	2015	2020	CAGR	Period growth
Middle-aged adults 30-59	2,805.5	2,799.8	2,926.1	3,248.7	3,481.2	3,561.0	3,633.9	3,697.2	3,656.4	0.66	30.3
Female	1,448.1	1,413.3	1,466.1	1,616.5	1,735.4	1,778.6	1,815.6	1,847.0	1,825.1	0.58	26.0
Male	1,357.4	1,386.5	1,460.0	1,632.3	1,745.9	1,782.4	1,818.2	1,850.2	1,831.3	0.75	34.9
Baby boomers aged 40-59	1,756.9	1,807.1	1,838.7	1,942.9	2,096.5	2,266.3	2,497.0	2,586.7	2,523.9	0.91	43.7
Female	930.4	919.8	925.5	976.6	1,053.9	1,134.5	1,248.0	1,296.0	1,264.7	0.77	35.9
Male	826.6	887.3	913.2	966.3	1,042.6	1,131.8	1,249.0	1,290.8	1,259.2	1.06	52.3

Table 5.23 Elderly population

'000

	1980	1985	1990	1995	2000	2005	2010	2015	2020	CAGR	Period growth
Elderly population (60+)	1,439.7	1,495.4	1,540.5	1,568.4	1,626.4	1,802.1	1,936.1	2,071.7	2,279.3	1.16	58.3
Female	906.4	954.3	968.3	964.6	975.0	1,048.0	1,103.3	1,164.2	1,264.4	0.84	39.5
Male	533.4	541.1	572.2	603.8	651.4	754.1	832.8	907.5	1,014.9	1.62	90.3

Table 5.24 Population of biggest cities 1980-2020

'000

	1980	1985	1990	1995	2000	2005	2010	2015	2020	CAGR	Period growth
Vienna	1,531.4	1,525.1	1,532.1	1,553.6	1,545.6	1,590.8	1,640.5	1,677.8	1,712.8	0.28	11.85
Graz	243.4	240.6	237.9	233.6	226.1	229.7	234.1	236.9	239.6	-0.04	-1.57
Linz	199.2	202.1	202.9	197.5	185.0	180.5	177.2	173.2	169.6	-0.40	-14.85
Salzburg	138.9	140.7	143.1	145.2	142.8	144.6	147.0	148.5	150.0	0.19	7.95
Innsbruck	117.1	117.4	117.8	117.4	113.6	113.8	114.6	114.8	114.9	-0.05	-1.87
Klagenfurt	87.2	86.7	88.8	95.1	97.5	100.4	103.5	105.9	108.2	0.54	24.09
Villach	52.7	52.8	54.1	56.6	57.5	59.7	62.1	63.9	65.7	0.55	24.67
Wels	51.0	50.9	52.0	54.9	56.3	58.5	60.9	62.7	64.5	0.59	26.50
Sankt Polten	50.5	50.0	49.9	50.2	49.3	49.9	50.7	51.2	51.7	0.05	2.21
Dornbirn	38.5	39.2	40.3	41.8	42.1	43.4	44.8	45.9	46.9	0.50	21.89

Chart 5.10 Population age shift 2000 and 2020, Each Column Represents a Single Age Group

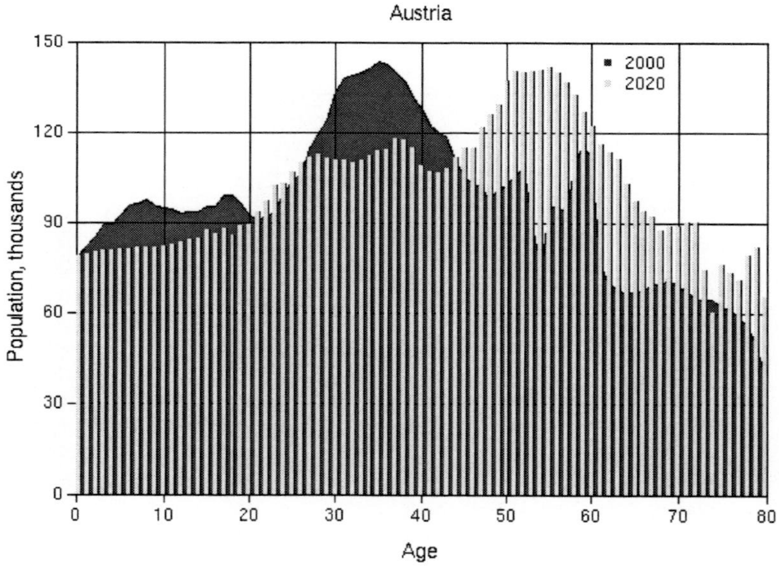

Chart 5.11 Population pyramids, 1980/2000/2010/2020

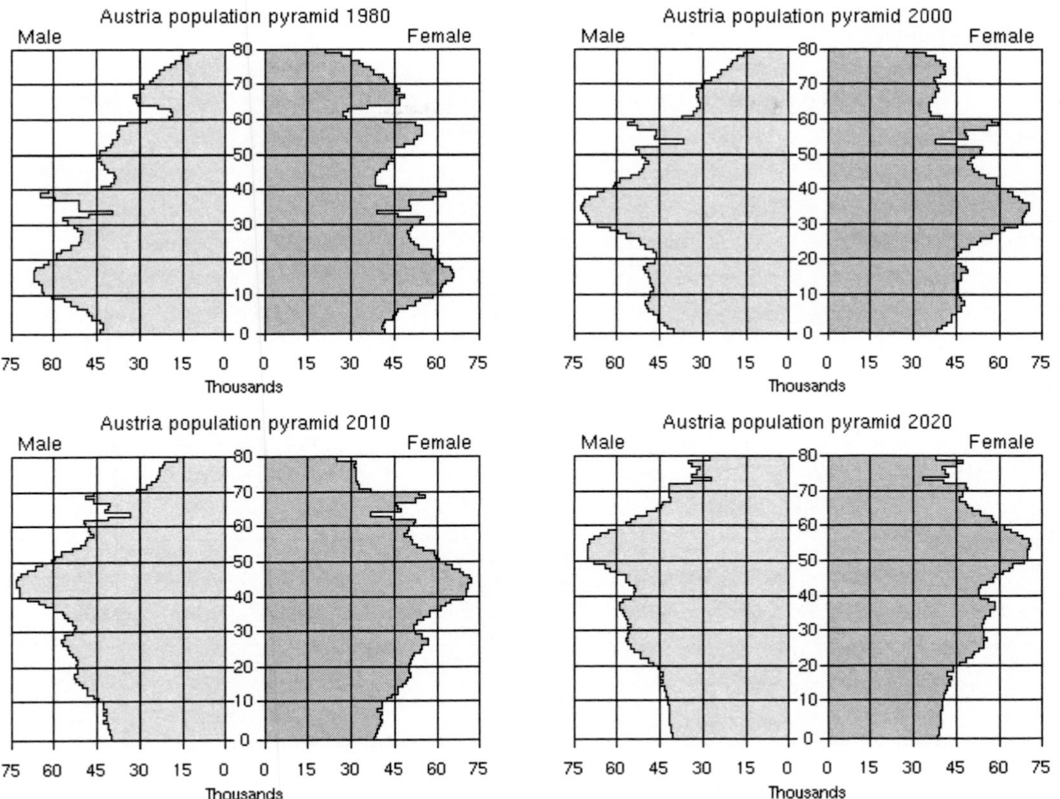

Chart 5.12 Major Cities: 1980, 2000 and 2020

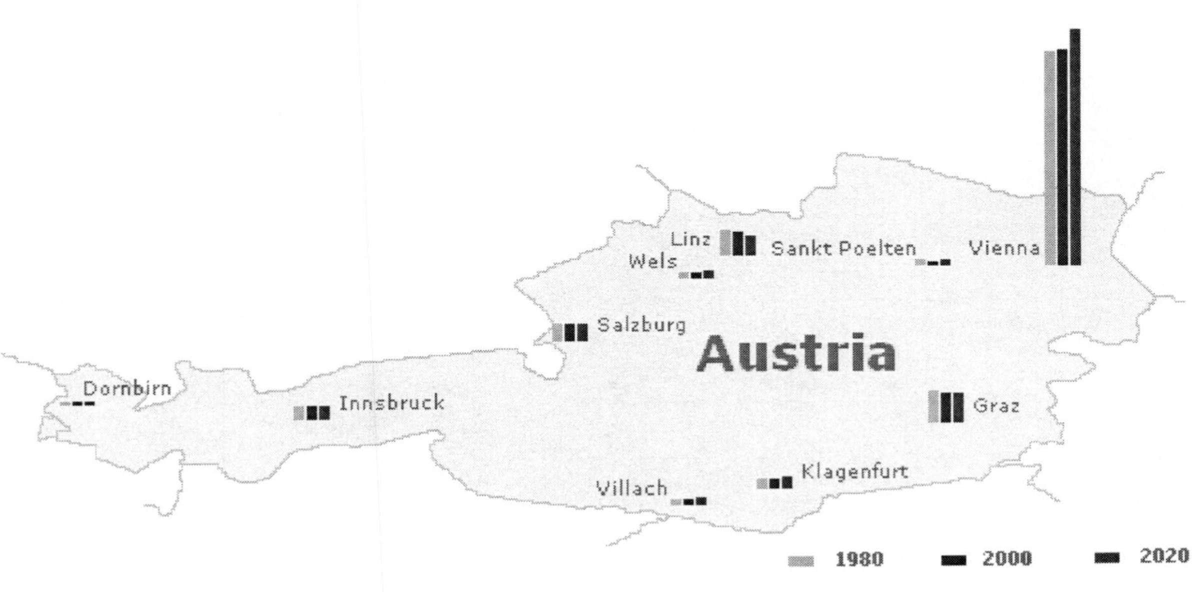

Azerbaijan

Table 5.25 Key population trends

'000

	1980	1985	1990	1995	2000	2005	2010	2015	2020	CAGR	Period growth
Population at January 1st	6,114.3	6,622.4	7,131.9	7,643.5	8,016.2	8,347.3	8,828.5	9,292.4	9,690.5	1.16	58.49
Male	2,981.5	3,229.0	3,477.8	3,728.8	3,918.3	4,103.7	4,364.5	4,611.8	4,821.5	1.21	61.71
Female	3,132.8	3,393.4	3,654.1	3,914.7	4,097.9	4,243.6	4,464.0	4,680.6	4,869.1	1.11	55.42
0-4 yrs	703.6	805.0	932.2	881.4	685.6	663.8	779.5	820.7	765.8	0.21	8.84
5-9 yrs	672.4	694.5	809.4	916.7	878.1	686.0	654.4	767.2	807.4	0.46	20.08
10-14 yrs	740.8	674.9	701.4	799.9	926.1	872.0	684.4	652.9	764.4	0.08	3.18
15-19 yrs	792.6	720.6	688.6	680.6	795.6	918.1	867.6	677.5	648.3	-0.50	-18.21
20-24 yrs	672.4	745.8	679.1	656.3	652.2	776.8	908.0	854.7	667.5	-0.02	-0.72
25-29 yrs	449.0	629.2	686.8	654.6	614.9	627.4	764.0	891.8	841.2	1.58	87.35
30-34 yrs	296.2	439.3	575.1	682.1	638.9	591.7	615.5	749.2	878.4	2.75	196.56
35-39 yrs	222.8	288.8	419.0	576.9	702.1	620.9	580.6	603.1	737.6	3.04	231.01
40-44 yrs	368.3	219.8	258.9	407.8	593.9	685.7	609.1	568.6	592.7	1.20	60.92
45-49 yrs	322.0	361.2	263.3	241.7	400.1	577.1	670.8	594.8	557.1	1.38	72.99
50-54 yrs	273.0	309.7	320.8	234.2	215.7	383.9	560.1	650.4	579.1	1.90	112.15
55-59 yrs	164.5	257.9	275.7	290.4	196.4	201.6	367.1	535.3	625.1	3.39	279.92
60-64 yrs	104.4	149.5	220.2	247.4	257.0	178.7	187.7	342.0	502.0	4.01	381.06
65-69 yrs	108.0	91.4	119.0	183.5	213.9	225.7	159.0	167.8	308.4	2.66	185.48
70-74 yrs	91.1	90.0	79.6	88.1	142.6	175.7	189.1	133.7	142.8	1.13	56.72
75-79 yrs	59.9	67.5	65.6	50.5	57.9	106.2	134.1	145.8	103.6	1.38	72.78
80+ yrs	73.2	77.3	37.3	51.5	45.1	56.1	97.4	136.8	169.2	2.12	131.06
Median age of population (years)	21.0	22.8	23.2	24.1	25.6	27.0	28.3	29.9	32.0	1.06	52.25

Table 5.26 Key economic trends

As stated

	1990	1995	2000	2005	2010	2015	2020	CAGR	Period growth
Total GDP (AZN per capita)		1,076.7	1,437.7	2,409.9	4,728.3	5,014.1	5,445.3		
Disposable income (AZN per capita)		600.9	966.7	1,160.3	2,041.4	2,116.7	2,294.7		
Disposable income (AZN per household)		2,891.6	4,534.7	5,318.7	9,218.3	9,373.8	9,970.2		
Number of households by annual household disposable income ('000)									
Over US$1,000		974.5	1,575.4	1,801.4	1,954.9	2,098.2	2,230.3		
Over US$10,000		17.7	38.3	73.2	483.0	740.7	1,249.6		
Over US$25,000		5.5	12.0	19.3	95.9	149.9	262.1		
Over US$75,000		1.4	3.0	4.9	20.5	29.2	44.8		
Over US$150,000		0.6	1.2	2.1	8.7	12.3	18.6		
Total households	1,404.6	1,588.5	1,708.8	1,821.0	1,955.1	2,098.3	2,230.3	2	59

Note: Per capita data is shown at constant 2010 prices. Household disposable income bands are shown at current prices.

Table 5.27 Young generation

'000

	1980	1985	1990	1995	2000	2005	2010	2015	2020	CAGR	Period growth
Babies under 12 months	150.7	174.0	193.5	161.2	117.8	149.7	167.6	165.6	151.6	0.01	0.60
Infants under 24 months	295.3	341.2	384.5	332.5	244.9	286.6	332.4	326.5	299.6	0.04	1.48
Toddlers aged 1-4	552.9	631.0	738.7	720.1	567.8	514.1	611.9	655.2	614.2	0.26	11.09
Children aged 2-9	1,080.7	1,158.3	1,357.1	1,465.5	1,318.8	1,063.2	1,101.6	1,261.4	1,273.5	0.41	17.85
Female	530.3	564.8	661.3	713.8	640.1	499.2	503.1	579.6	587.9	0.26	10.88
Male	550.4	593.5	695.7	751.7	678.7	564.0	598.4	681.8	685.6	0.55	24.56
Tweenagers aged 10-14	740.8	674.9	701.4	799.9	926.1	872.0	684.4	652.9	764.4	0.08	3.18
Female	363.7	329.8	343.5	392.1	449.9	422.5	324.4	298.8	350.5	-0.09	-3.64
Male	377.1	345.1	357.9	407.8	476.3	449.4	360.0	354.0	413.9	0.23	9.77
Teenagers aged 13-19	1,099.9	993.9	962.9	982.7	1,158.2	1,285.1	1,159.5	929.9	941.1	-0.39	-14.44
Female	538.5	487.9	465.0	486.7	567.8	623.0	560.5	438.3	431.4	-0.55	-19.89
Male	561.5	506.0	497.8	496.0	590.4	662.1	599.0	491.7	509.7	-0.24	-9.21
Studying age 18-22	742.1	747.1	680.8	659.8	699.1	845.9	919.3	784.5	633.5	-0.39	-14.63
Female	366.6	374.9	341.1	325.2	352.3	413.2	446.4	380.1	297.2	-0.52	-18.94
Male	375.4	372.2	339.7	334.6	346.8	432.8	472.9	404.3	336.3	-0.28	-10.43
Young adults aged 15-29	1,914.0	2,095.6	2,054.5	1,991.5	2,062.8	2,322.3	2,539.6	2,423.9	2,157.0	0.30	12.70
Female	952.8	1,055.3	1,044.8	1,010.1	1,045.4	1,154.1	1,242.4	1,175.3	1,029.4	0.19	8.04
Male	961.2	1,040.3	1,009.8	981.3	1,017.3	1,168.1	1,297.2	1,248.7	1,127.6	0.40	17.31

Table 5.28 **Middle-aged generation**
'000

	1980	1985	1990	1995	2000	2005	2010	2015	2020	CAGR	Period growth
Middle-aged adults 30-59	1,646.9	1,876.7	2,112.8	2,433.2	2,747.1	3,060.9	3,403.2	3,701.5	3,969.9	2.22	141.1
Female	855.8	968.1	1,099.0	1,272.9	1,437.3	1,611.0	1,798.9	1,951.0	2,076.1	2.24	142.6
Male	791.0	908.6	1,013.8	1,160.3	1,309.8	1,449.9	1,604.3	1,750.6	1,893.8	2.21	139.4
Baby boomers aged 40-59	1,127.9	1,148.6	1,118.7	1,174.1	1,406.1	1,848.3	2,207.1	2,349.2	2,353.9	1.86	108.7
Female	588.4	594.2	583.8	613.6	725.0	959.7	1,168.9	1,258.3	1,271.3	1.94	116.1
Male	539.5	554.4	534.9	560.5	681.1	888.7	1,038.2	1,090.9	1,082.6	1.76	100.7

Table 5.29 **Elderly population**
'000

	1980	1985	1990	1995	2000	2005	2010	2015	2020	CAGR	Period growth
Elderly population (60+)	436.7	475.6	521.7	621.0	716.5	742.4	767.3	926.2	1,226.1	2.61	180.7
Female	286.0	309.7	318.6	362.4	410.7	426.5	441.4	526.2	687.0	2.22	140.2
Male	150.7	165.9	203.1	258.6	305.8	315.9	326.0	400.0	539.0	3.24	257.6

Table 5.30 **Population of biggest cities 1980-2020**
'000

	1980	1985	1990	1995	2000	2005	2010	2015	2020	CAGR	Period growth
Baku	1,036.8	1,110.7	1,144.3	1,094.2	1,077.7	1,124.0	1,185.5	1,263.4	1,352.1	0.67	30.4
Ganja	235.8	257.7	281.0	292.9	296.7	304.2	315.4	332.1	352.4	1.01	49.5
Sumqayit	193.5	212.6	234.0	247.5	255.8	265.4	276.3	291.8	310.3	1.19	60.4
Mingacevir	61.8	73.7	87.9	97.6	95.6	94.3	98.0	103.3	109.7	1.44	77.5
Nakhichevan	36.0	50.1	61.4	64.1	63.2	67.3	75.2	83.2	91.3	2.36	153.7
Ali-Bajramli	42.8	50.2	60.2	68.4	68.9	68.8	71.4	75.2	79.9	1.57	86.4
Shaki	50.1	53.4	56.9	61.2	61.6	62.0	63.8	66.9	70.7	0.86	41.1
Stepanakert	34.9	40.6	46.6	50.2	51.5	53.6	56.7	60.5	64.9	1.56	85.9
Yevlakh	40.8	50.4	57.3	57.1	53.7	51.3	49.9	50.0	51.2	0.56	25.3
Lankaran	40.8	43.6	46.0	47.3	47.8	48.5	49.1	50.8	53.2	0.66	30.2

Chart 5.13 Population age shift 2000 and 2020, Each Column Represents a Single Age Group

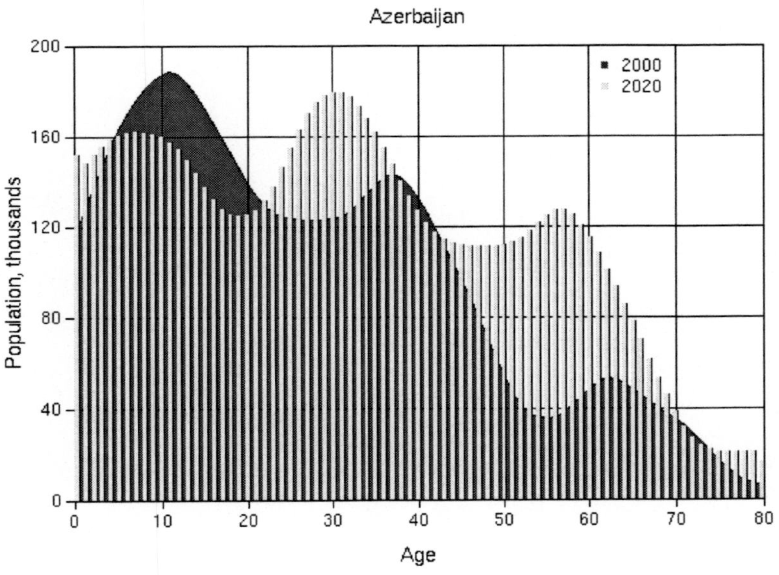

Chart 5.14 Population pyramids, 1980/2000/2010/2020

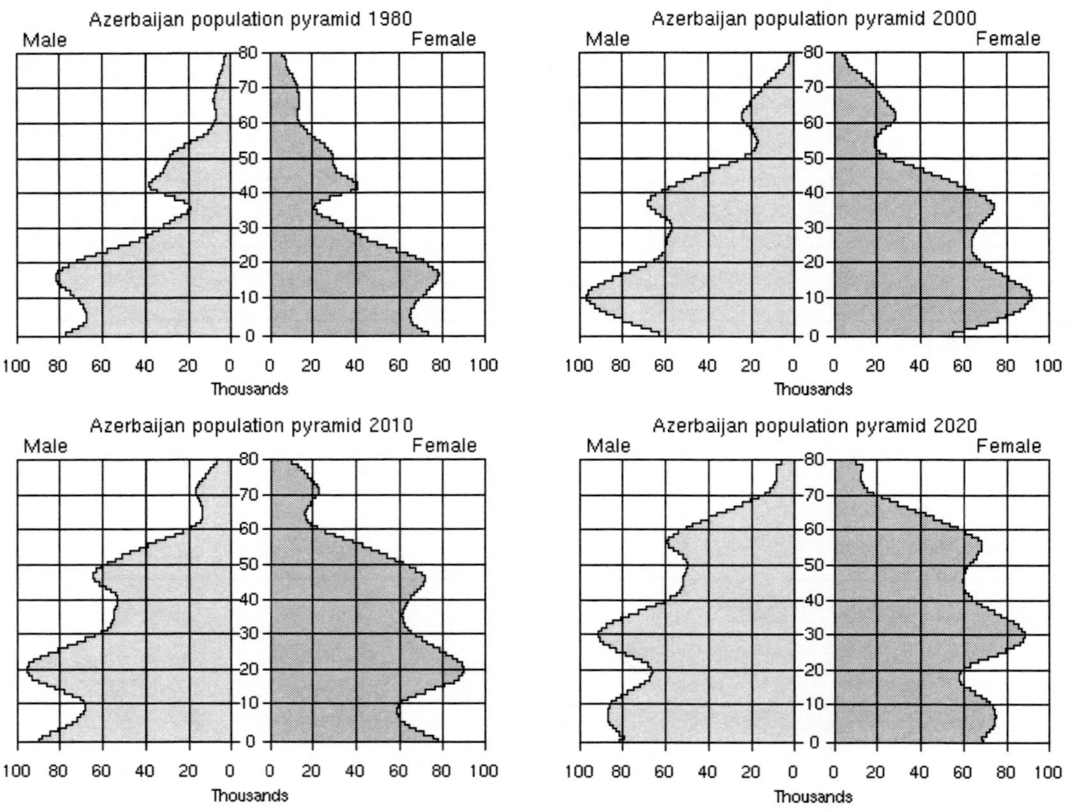

Chart 5.15 Major Cities: 1980, 2000 and 2020

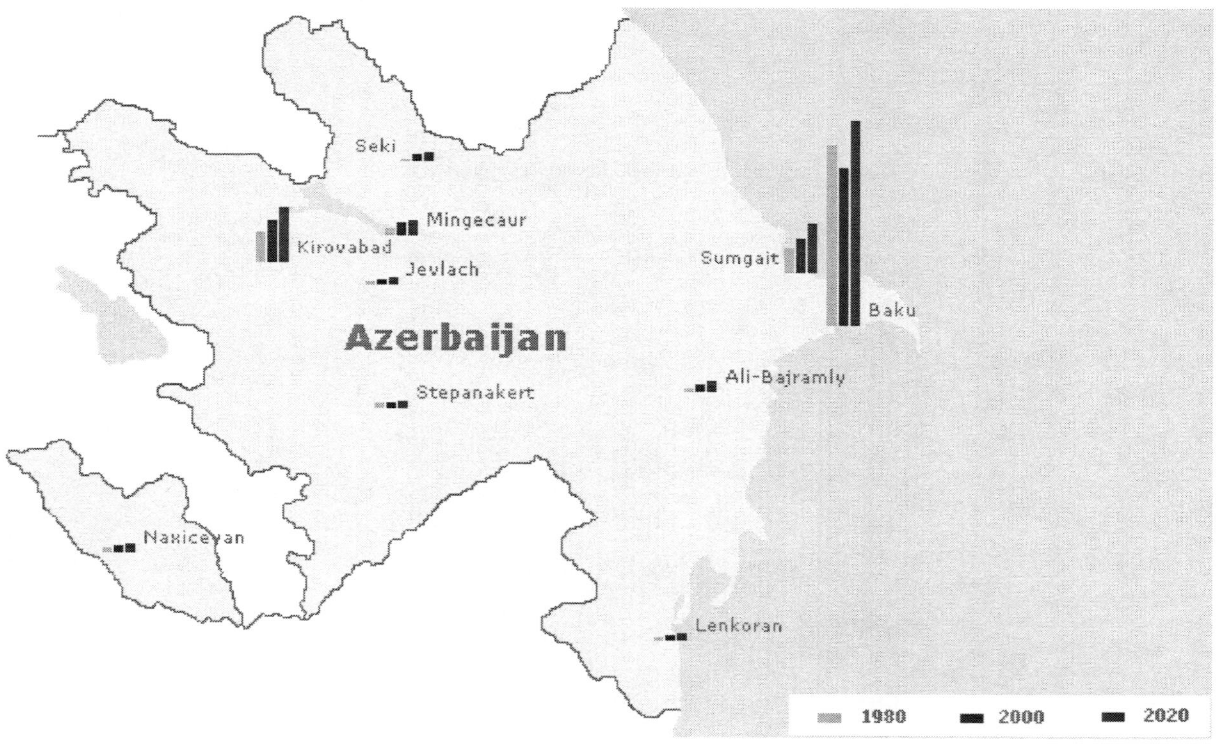

Belarus

Table 5.31 Key population trends

'000

	1980	1985	1990	1995	2000	2005	2010	2015	2020	CAGR	Period growth
Population at January 1st	9,591.8	9,929.0	10,188.9	10,210.4	10,019.5	9,800.1	9,652.7	9,515.4	9,362.3	-0.06	-2.39
Male	4,456.8	4,632.3	4,777.5	4,779.7	4,703.2	4,583.1	4,500.2	4,428.3	4,353.1	-0.06	-2.33
Female	5,135.0	5,296.7	5,411.5	5,430.7	5,316.3	5,217.0	5,152.5	5,087.2	5,009.3	-0.06	-2.45
0-4 yrs	711.0	791.1	811.2	624.3	464.6	447.1	505.5	519.6	488.4	-0.93	-31.31
5-9 yrs	709.4	728.3	804.3	819.5	618.1	464.1	448.7	508.6	524.3	-0.75	-26.09
10-14 yrs	703.7	721.8	735.8	808.5	814.9	618.9	466.1	451.7	513.4	-0.78	-27.03
15-19 yrs	846.9	707.6	720.8	737.3	808.3	816.5	621.2	468.9	455.7	-1.54	-46.19
20-24 yrs	846.0	836.4	689.0	702.4	719.7	807.7	817.3	623.1	471.7	-1.45	-44.24
25-29 yrs	733.4	852.7	836.7	681.7	694.6	713.8	803.1	814.7	622.8	-0.41	-15.08
30-34 yrs	596.7	738.9	854.1	833.6	690.3	687.1	706.4	796.9	810.6	0.77	35.85
35-39 yrs	513.2	593.5	732.9	844.6	820.9	680.8	678.0	698.7	790.4	1.09	54.00
40-44 yrs	700.6	503.1	580.4	716.9	825.2	804.0	668.2	667.2	689.4	-0.04	-1.60
45-49 yrs	663.0	692.9	487.7	560.2	690.2	798.9	781.2	651.0	651.8	-0.04	-1.69
50-54 yrs	677.6	643.7	668.8	463.0	535.5	656.6	765.1	750.0	626.8	-0.19	-7.49
55-59 yrs	515.0	643.5	604.0	622.9	432.3	498.0	614.3	718.0	705.1	0.79	36.90
60-64 yrs	339.7	463.6	589.3	548.9	572.7	386.5	451.5	557.6	653.4	1.65	92.31
65-69 yrs	349.3	272.4	394.3	515.4	475.2	496.0	335.7	394.6	487.8	0.84	39.66
70-74 yrs	290.3	292.3	211.4	326.3	424.9	384.6	409.5	277.0	329.1	0.31	13.36
75-79 yrs	211.0	234.2	233.5	157.2	242.2	314.6	287.0	307.9	207.4	-0.04	-1.73
80+ yrs	185.0	213.0	234.7	247.7	189.9	224.8	293.9	310.0	334.2	1.49	80.63
Median age of population (years)	31.7	32.2	32.8	34.4	36.3	37.6	38.4	39.1	40.0	0.58	26.19

Table 5.32 Key economic trends

As stated

	1990	1995	2000	2005	2010	2015	2020	CAGR	Period growth
Total GDP (BYR per capita)	9,467,814.1	6,093,530.9	8,430,924.6	12,380,415.8	16,297,172.1	21,674,382.8	31,358,086.6	4.07	231.2
Disposable income (BYR per capita)		1,918,546.9	3,166,763.7	5,555,975.9	8,972,918.9	13,259,323.1	20,390,133.4		
Disposable income (BYR per household)		5,246,561.0	8,138,478.2	13,501,489.5	21,104,092.5	30,601,564.9	46,632,164.9		
Number of households by annual household disposable income ('000)									
Over US$1,000		2,838.6	2,753.9	3,963.9	4,092.5	4,121.6	4,093.6		
Over US$10,000		46.9	40.4	197.2	591.7	1,968.5	3,609.3		
Over US$25,000		14.4	12.4	51.3	106.3	308.2	1,146.7		
Over US$75,000		3.5	3.0	12.6	26.5	56.3	130.3		
Over US$150,000		1.4	1.2	5.2	11.0	23.4	52.2		
Total households	3,535.4	3,733.7	3,898.7	4,032.8	4,104.1	4,122.9	4,093.7	0.49	15.8

Note: Per capita data is shown at constant 2010 prices. Household disposable income bands are shown at current prices.

Table 5.33 Young generation

'000

	1980	1985	1990	1995	2000	2005	2010	2015	2020	CAGR	Period growth
Babies under 12 months	144.1	163.1	153.0	108.4	92.1	88.5	108.2	101.7	94.3	-1.05	-34.57
Infants under 24 months	287.0	331.7	317.5	223.5	183.9	176.2	215.5	204.7	190.2	-1.02	-33.72
Toddlers aged 1-4	566.9	628.1	658.2	515.9	372.4	358.7	397.2	417.9	394.1	-0.90	-30.48
Children aged 2-9	1,133.3	1,187.7	1,298.0	1,220.3	898.8	735.0	738.7	823.5	822.5	-0.80	-27.43
Female	556.9	582.4	636.5	597.7	437.5	356.9	358.9	400.6	399.2	-0.83	-28.32
Male	576.4	605.3	661.5	622.6	461.2	378.1	379.7	422.8	423.3	-0.77	-26.57
Tweenagers aged 10-14	703.7	721.8	735.8	808.5	814.9	618.9	466.1	451.7	513.4	-0.78	-27.03
Female	351.0	355.8	361.9	399.1	398.2	301.6	226.2	219.2	248.9	-0.86	-29.08
Male	352.7	366.0	374.0	409.4	416.7	317.3	239.8	232.6	264.5	-0.72	-24.99
Teenagers aged 13-19	1,141.5	991.6	1,012.8	1,046.9	1,146.3	1,088.7	814.5	653.8	645.4	-1.42	-43.46
Female	566.4	497.5	502.4	518.7	560.3	531.7	396.3	317.0	312.4	-1.48	-44.84
Male	575.2	494.1	510.4	528.2	586.0	557.0	418.2	336.8	333.0	-1.36	-42.10
Studying age 18-22	875.7	775.3	681.0	720.7	747.0	838.6	751.9	544.0	462.9	-1.58	-47.14
Female	434.2	386.8	344.7	358.3	364.6	411.4	366.8	264.8	224.1	-1.64	-48.38
Male	441.5	388.5	336.3	362.4	382.5	427.2	385.1	279.3	238.8	-1.53	-45.92
Young adults aged 15-29	2,426.3	2,396.7	2,246.5	2,121.3	2,222.5	2,338.0	2,241.5	1,906.7	1,550.3	-1.11	-36.11
Female	1,201.8	1,192.8	1,121.2	1,061.8	1,096.0	1,147.4	1,097.9	931.8	753.3	-1.16	-37.32
Male	1,224.5	1,203.8	1,125.3	1,059.6	1,126.5	1,190.6	1,143.7	974.9	797.0	-1.07	-34.91

Table 5.34 Middle-aged generation

'000

	1980	1985	1990	1995	2000	2005	2010	2015	2020	CAGR	Period growth
Middle-aged adults 30-59	3,666	3,816	3,928	4,041	3,994	4,125	4,213	4,282	4,274	0.38	16.58
Female	1,966	2,009	2,039	2,096	2,068	2,146	2,199	2,230	2,212	0.30	12.54
Male	1,701	1,807	1,889	1,945	1,926	1,979	2,015	2,052	2,062	0.48	21.25
Baby boomers aged 40-59	2,556	2,483	2,341	2,363	2,483	2,757	2,829	2,786	2,673	0.11	4.57
Female	1,411	1,344	1,246	1,251	1,306	1,454	1,502	1,484	1,417	0.01	0.45
Male	1,145	1,139	1,095	1,112	1,177	1,303	1,326	1,302	1,256	0.23	9.66

Table 5.35 Elderly population

'000

	1980	1985	1990	1995	2000	2005	2010	2015	2020	CAGR	Period growth
Elderly population (60+)	1,375.4	1,475.4	1,663.2	1,795.5	1,904.9	1,806.6	1,777.7	1,847.0	2,011.8	0.96	46.3
Female	919.6	995.0	1,099.3	1,167.1	1,227.3	1,179.2	1,165.9	1,206.3	1,303.4	0.88	41.7
Male	455.7	480.5	563.9	628.4	677.7	627.3	611.8	640.7	708.4	1.11	55.4

Table 5.36 Population of biggest cities 1980-2020

'000

	1980	1985	1990	1995	2000	2005	2010	2015	2020	CAGR	Period growth
Minsk	1,311.4	1,497.7	1,605.0	1,645.5	1,687.7	1,733.8	1,764.2	1,783.2	1,789.7	0.78	36.47
Gomel	400.7	471.1	503.6	495.2	483.9	482.0	479.8	477.5	474.0	0.42	18.27
Mogilev	301.7	343.1	360.6	356.7	356.3	365.8	373.8	379.0	381.1	0.59	26.32
Vitebsk	306.2	338.4	351.2	349.3	347.1	344.6	340.4	336.9	333.1	0.21	8.77
Grodno	204.7	246.2	275.2	290.8	304.2	316.6	325.2	330.8	333.5	1.23	62.97
Brest	187.5	232.0	262.8	276.8	287.9	299.4	307.8	313.3	315.9	1.31	68.50
Bobrujsk	197.8	215.4	221.8	220.9	220.6	219.6	217.2	215.2	213.0	0.18	7.65
Baranovichi	135.2	151.6	160.7	164.3	167.2	168.1	167.4	166.7	165.6	0.51	22.44
Borisov	116.4	134.5	145.4	149.2	150.9	150.3	148.5	147.0	145.3	0.56	24.91
Orsha	114.6	119.8	124.5	132.2	135.4	126.6	115.6	107.7	101.6	-0.30	-11.32

Chart 5.16 Population age shift 2000 and 2020, Each Column Represents a Single Age Group

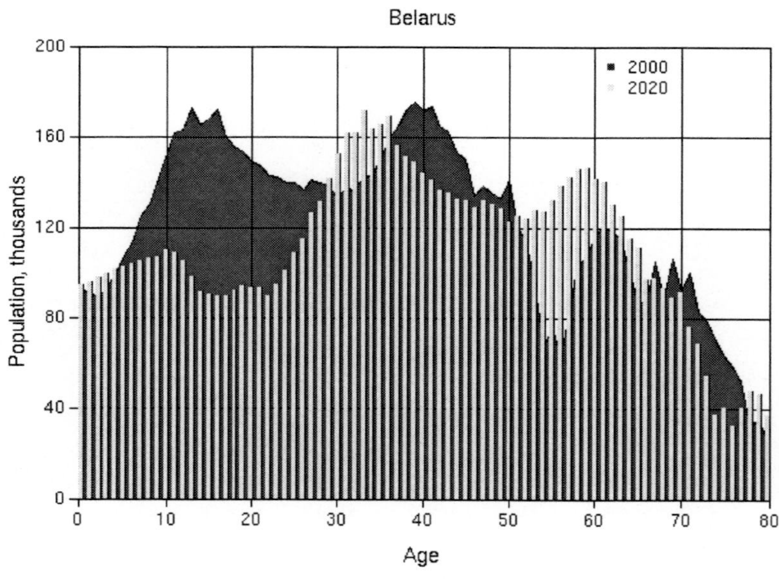

Chart 5.17 Population pyramids, 1980/2000/2010/2020

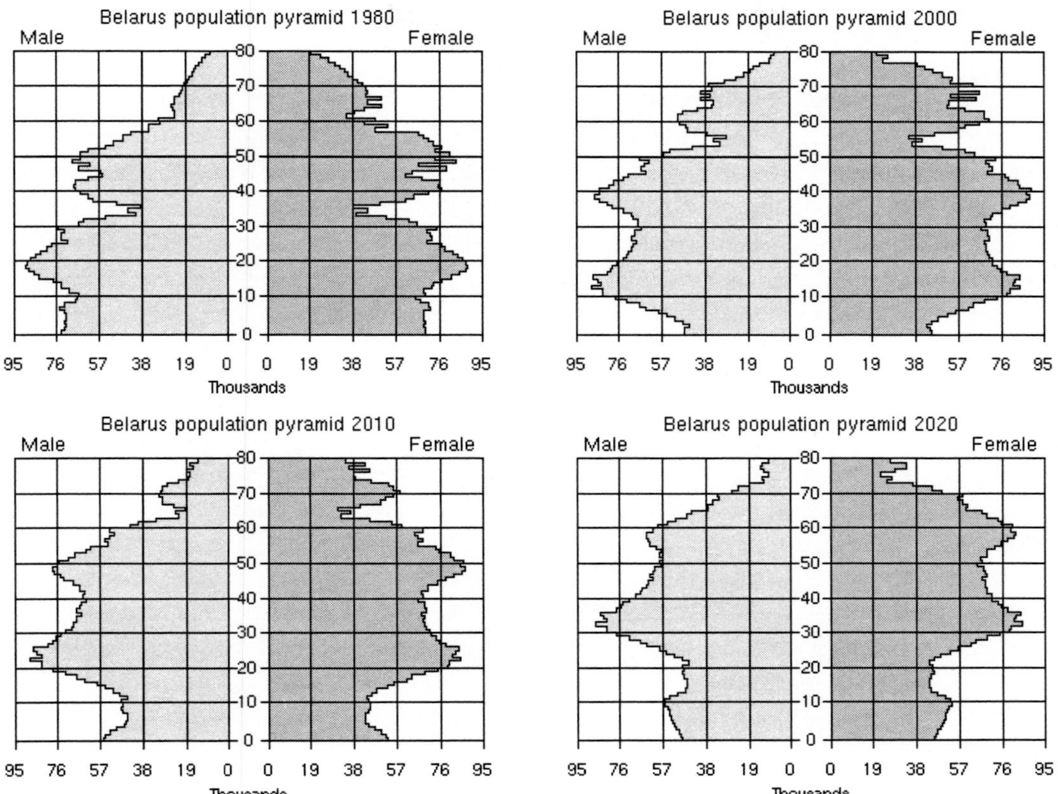

Chart 5.18 Major Cities: 1980, 2000 and 2020

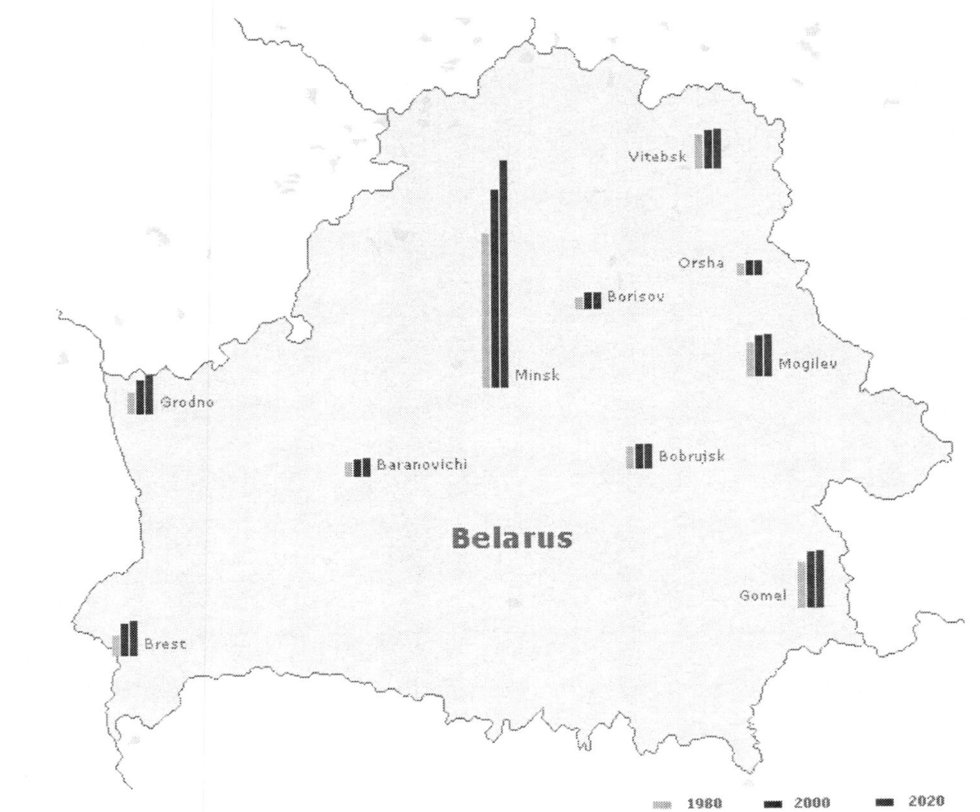

Belgium

Table 5.37 Key population trends

'000

	1980	1985	1990	1995	2000	2005	2010	2015	2020	CAGR	Period growth
Population at January 1st	9,855.1	9,857.7	9,947.8	10,130.6	10,239.1	10,445.9	10,698.5	10,878.9	11,044.3	0.29	12.07
Male	4,818.9	4,811.6	4,860.1	4,954.7	5,006.0	5,111.3	5,240.6	5,334.5	5,421.4	0.29	12.50
Female	5,036.2	5,046.2	5,087.7	5,175.9	5,233.1	5,334.5	5,458.0	5,544.5	5,622.9	0.28	11.65
0-4 yrs	598.6	593.4	591.9	615.1	577.2	574.9	615.8	624.7	615.6	0.07	2.85
5-9 yrs	666.7	602.4	603.5	602.5	621.1	589.1	592.0	628.9	637.9	-0.11	-4.32
10-14 yrs	733.6	667.0	605.8	609.3	606.5	630.9	600.4	598.7	636.4	-0.35	-13.25
15-19 yrs	797.3	731.5	669.9	612.9	615.2	619.2	643.9	608.2	606.5	-0.68	-23.93
20-24 yrs	790.7	796.9	741.4	686.5	628.7	641.8	645.3	663.7	627.9	-0.57	-20.58
25-29 yrs	758.2	781.6	806.5	757.2	698.2	655.8	668.1	664.5	682.8	-0.26	-9.94
30-34 yrs	721.5	731.3	781.8	814.4	760.9	719.5	673.9	678.3	674.8	-0.17	-6.47
35-39 yrs	559.4	700.8	726.5	783.2	811.9	773.7	729.5	677.1	681.7	0.50	21.86
40-44 yrs	591.6	548.4	693.7	723.5	776.6	815.0	777.3	727.0	675.5	0.33	14.18
45-49 yrs	629.9	579.6	539.4	686.9	713.6	772.5	811.7	769.6	720.5	0.34	14.39
50-54 yrs	617.3	610.7	565.8	530.6	673.5	703.5	763.2	798.3	757.8	0.51	22.78
55-59 yrs	610.0	591.3	589.4	550.5	514.7	656.5	688.1	744.6	780.5	0.62	27.96
60-64 yrs	370.3	572.8	558.2	561.7	525.7	494.1	633.7	664.4	721.9	1.68	94.96
65-69 yrs	464.4	335.7	521.5	515.2	521.4	494.0	467.1	601.4	634.7	0.78	36.67
70-74 yrs	393.8	399.0	290.7	459.3	457.8	471.8	452.6	430.8	560.2	0.88	42.25
75-79 yrs	293.9	306.4	316.4	235.9	379.4	386.1	406.6	395.9	383.2	0.67	30.38
80+ yrs	258.0	309.0	345.5	386.3	356.5	447.7	529.4	602.9	646.2	2.32	150.45
Median age of population (years)	33.9	35.2	36.2	37.3	38.7	40.1	41.2	42.1	42.6	0.57	25.65

Table 5.38 Key economic trends

As stated

	1990	1995	2000	2005	2010	2015	2020	CAGR	Period growth
Total GDP (EUR per capita)	24,258.9	26,294.3	29,708.0	31,591.2	31,882.5	34,890.0	38,840.1	1.58	60.1
Disposable income (EUR per capita)	16,079.7	17,815.7	18,502.4	18,519.8	19,494.1	21,582.7	24,158.6	1.37	50.2
Disposable income (EUR per household)	40,405.4	44,078.4	44,704.4	43,574.4	44,900.8	48,777.1	53,671.7	0.95	32.8
Number of households by annual household disposable income ('000)									
Over US$1,000	3,958.5	4,094.4	4,237.6	4,439.4	4,644.6	4,813.5	4,971.1	0.76	25.6
Over US$10,000	3,823.0	4,008.2	4,088.9	4,365.5	4,583.2	4,768.3	4,942.5	0.86	29.3
Over US$25,000	2,699.8	3,267.6	2,716.8	3,759.3	4,091.5	4,408.0	4,711.2	1.87	74.5
Over US$75,000	240.9	481.4	259.2	763.4	1,137.0	1,706.9	2,513.7	8.13	943.6
Over US$150,000	87.0	119.7	90.5	153.7	185.6	268.7	470.7	5.79	440.9
Total households	3,958.8	4,094.6	4,237.8	4,439.7	4,644.9	4,813.7	4,971.2	0.76	25.6

Note: Per capita data is shown at constant 2010 prices. Household disposable income bands are shown at current prices.

Table 5.39 Young generation

'000

	1980	1985	1990	1995	2000	2005	2010	2015	2020	CAGR	Period growth
Babies under 12 months	121.8	114.4	120.6	115.5	112.9	115.9	124.0	123.0	121.0	-0.02	-0.71
Infants under 24 months	241.7	230.1	240.8	236.2	227.5	229.4	248.0	247.0	243.0	0.01	0.54
Toddlers aged 1-4	476.7	479.0	471.3	499.6	464.3	459.0	491.8	501.7	494.7	0.09	3.76
Children aged 2-9	1,023.6	965.7	954.6	981.3	970.8	934.6	959.8	1,006.7	1,010.5	-0.03	-1.27
Female	500.4	471.8	465.3	478.7	474.6	457.3	468.2	490.2	492.2	-0.04	-1.64
Male	523.2	493.9	489.3	502.6	496.2	477.3	491.6	516.4	518.3	-0.02	-0.92
Tweenagers aged 10-14	733.6	667.0	605.8	609.3	606.5	630.9	600.4	598.7	636.4	-0.35	-13.25
Female	359.7	325.7	295.8	297.5	295.6	308.1	293.5	291.9	309.2	-0.38	-14.04
Male	373.9	341.3	310.0	311.8	310.9	322.8	306.9	306.8	327.2	-0.33	-12.49
Teenagers aged 13-19	1,102.5	1,011.8	908.9	863.3	852.9	878.6	885.4	848.7	857.6	-0.63	-22.21
Female	540.4	494.5	444.1	422.5	417.1	429.7	433.1	415.2	418.0	-0.64	-22.65
Male	562.0	517.3	464.8	440.8	435.9	448.8	452.3	433.5	439.6	-0.61	-21.79
Studying age 18-22	794.2	783.4	713.9	639.9	633.0	620.1	655.0	634.7	617.9	-0.63	-22.20
Female	388.8	383.8	350.0	314.2	312.3	306.1	321.7	311.7	303.4	-0.62	-21.97
Male	405.4	399.6	363.9	325.7	320.7	314.0	333.3	323.0	314.5	-0.63	-22.42
Young adults aged 15-29	2,346.2	2,310.1	2,217.9	2,056.6	1,942.2	1,916.7	1,957.3	1,936.4	1,917.3	-0.50	-18.28
Female	1,145.1	1,131.7	1,086.2	1,008.5	957.1	947.4	965.3	950.8	940.2	-0.49	-17.89
Male	1,201.1	1,178.3	1,131.6	1,048.0	985.1	969.4	992.0	985.7	977.1	-0.51	-18.65

Table 5.40 Middle-aged generation

'000

	1980	1985	1990	1995	2000	2005	2010	2015	2020	CAGR	Period growth
Middle-aged adults 30-59	3,730	3,762	3,897	4,089	4,251	4,441	4,444	4,395	4,291	0.35	15.0
Female	1,868	1,877	1,936	2,026	2,107	2,204	2,211	2,192	2,140	0.34	14.6
Male	1,862	1,885	1,960	2,063	2,144	2,237	2,233	2,203	2,151	0.36	15.5
Baby boomers aged 40-59	2,449	2,330	2,388	2,491	2,678	2,947	3,040	3,040	2,934	0.45	19.8
Female	1,241	1,176	1,196	1,240	1,332	1,467	1,514	1,517	1,468	0.42	18.3
Male	1,207	1,153	1,192	1,251	1,347	1,481	1,526	1,522	1,466	0.49	21.4

Table 5.41 Elderly population

'000

	1980	1985	1990	1995	2000	2005	2010	2015	2020	CAGR	Period growth
Elderly population (60+)	1,780.4	1,922.9	2,032.2	2,158.2	2,240.8	2,293.6	2,489.3	2,695.3	2,946.2	1.27	65.5
Female	1,045.3	1,127.7	1,186.7	1,249.7	1,287.7	1,306.0	1,399.0	1,499.0	1,622.8	1.11	55.3
Male	735.1	795.2	845.5	908.5	953.2	987.7	1,090.3	1,196.3	1,323.4	1.48	80.0

Table 5.42 Population of biggest cities 1980-2020

'000

	1980	1985	1990	1995	2000	2005	2010	2015	2020	CAGR	Period growth
Anvers	502.7	482.1	470.3	457.1	446.5	458.5	478.3	489.0	496.9	-0.03	-1.15
Gand	240.2	233.0	230.5	226.8	224.2	231.3	239.7	243.7	246.7	0.07	2.69
Charleroi	220.0	209.7	206.8	206.0	200.8	201.0	201.1	199.5	198.8	-0.25	-9.65
Liege	208.3	200.6	196.8	191.9	185.6	186.4	191.6	194.0	195.9	-0.15	-5.92
Brussels	138.7	136.2	136.7	134.9	133.9	143.1	151.6	156.4	159.8	0.35	15.16
Schaerbeek	106.6	104.6	104.8	103.2	105.7	111.1	118.6	123.2	126.5	0.43	18.73
Bruges	119.6	117.2	117.5	115.1	116.2	117.2	116.6	115.1	114.4	-0.11	-4.31
Namur	102.2	101.5	103.5	105.9	105.4	106.7	108.2	108.3	108.5	0.15	6.21
Anderlecht	93.9	90.9	89.2	88.1	87.8	94.4	101.3	105.2	107.9	0.35	14.93
Mons	91.6	90.7	91.9	92.6	90.9	91.2	90.8	89.7	89.1	-0.07	-2.73

Chart 5.19 Population age shift 2000 and 2020, Each Column Represents a Single Age Group

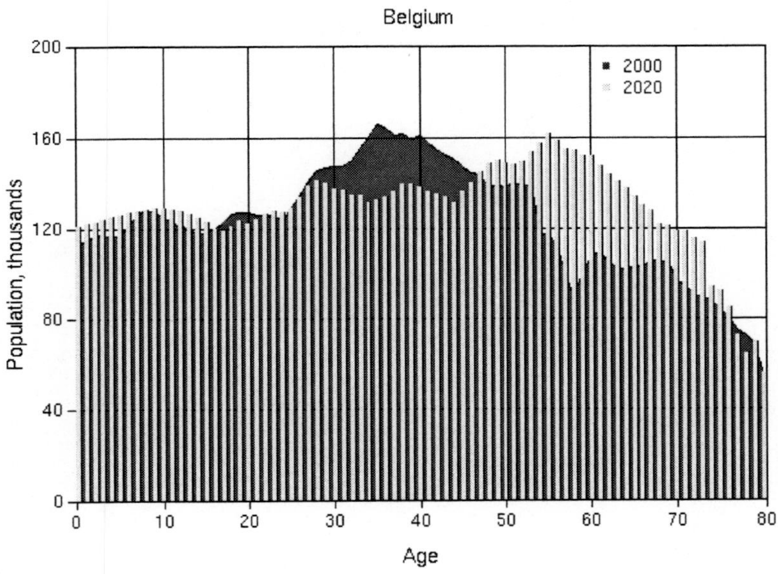

Chart 5.20 Population pyramids, 1980/2000/2010/2020

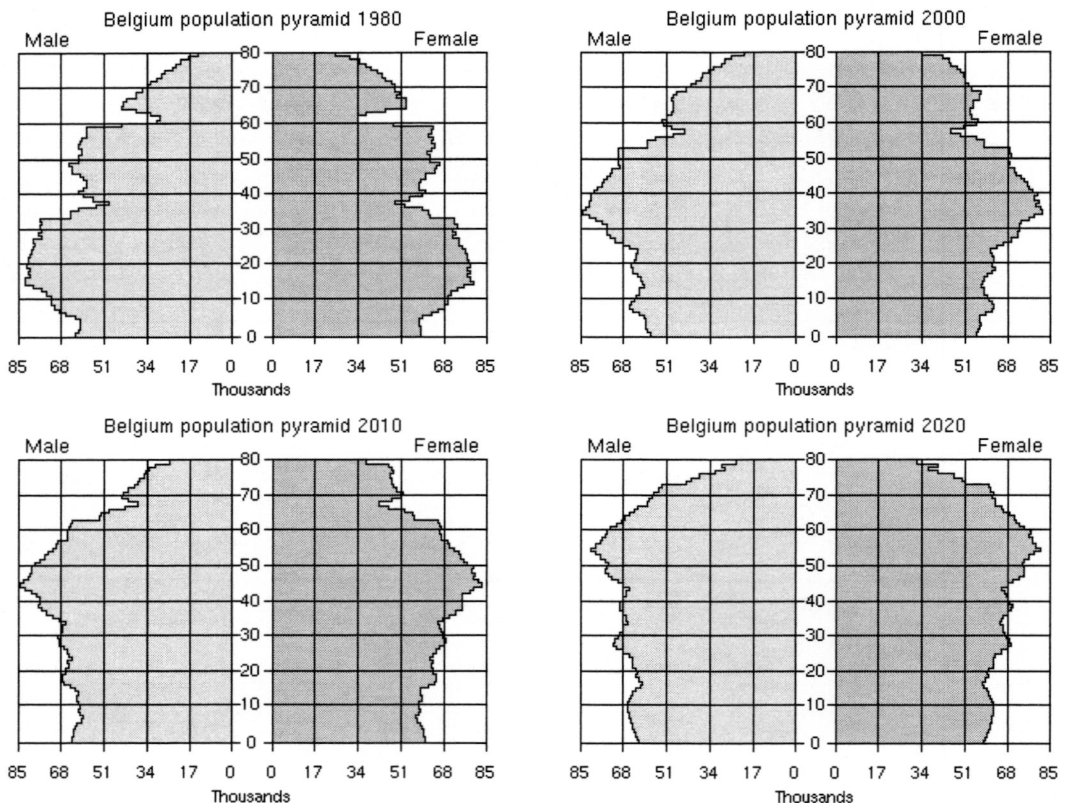

Chart 5.21 Major Cities: 1980, 2000 and 2020

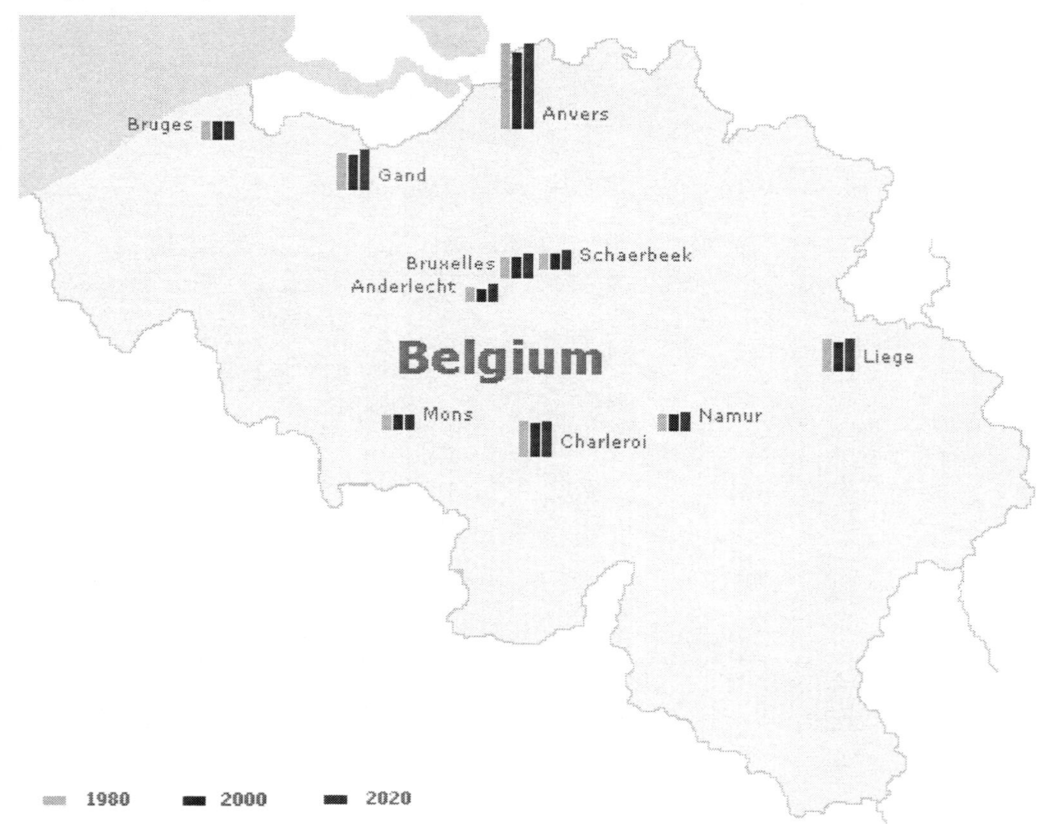

Bolivia

Table 5.43 Key population trends

'000

	1980	1985	1990	1995	2000	2005	2010	2015	2020	CAGR	Period growth
Population at January 1st	5,356.0	5,965.5	6,670.6	7,484.2	8,317.4	9,182.1	10,030.8	10,854.1	11,637.9	1.96	117.3
Male	2,641.2	2,947.3	3,304.3	3,717.2	4,138.4	4,574.8	5,002.7	5,417.5	5,811.7	1.99	120.0
Female	2,714.8	3,018.2	3,366.2	3,767.0	4,178.9	4,607.3	5,028.1	5,436.7	5,826.2	1.93	114.6
0-4 yrs	865.2	940.7	1,039.3	1,158.4	1,187.7	1,239.5	1,243.3	1,236.7	1,216.4	0.86	40.6
5-9 yrs	764.7	818.1	897.6	1,003.9	1,121.7	1,162.0	1,207.3	1,217.0	1,210.9	1.16	58.4
10-14 yrs	648.9	739.6	794.5	873.7	981.8	1,096.4	1,139.2	1,184.9	1,195.4	1.54	84.2
15-19 yrs	555.5	626.6	717.2	771.5	851.8	958.7	1,073.7	1,116.7	1,163.2	1.86	109.4
20-24 yrs	475.3	524.9	596.0	685.8	741.7	821.1	928.4	1,042.8	1,086.5	2.09	128.6
25-29 yrs	398.2	448.4	498.2	568.9	659.6	714.9	794.8	901.4	1,015.8	2.37	155.1
30-34 yrs	333.4	377.5	427.7	477.2	548.6	638.1	694.0	773.4	879.8	2.46	163.9
35-39 yrs	271.5	318.4	362.3	411.8	461.8	531.9	621.1	676.7	756.0	2.59	178.5
40-44 yrs	235.0	258.5	304.8	347.9	397.2	446.0	515.8	603.7	659.5	2.61	180.6
45-49 yrs	203.0	222.7	246.0	290.8	333.4	381.2	429.8	498.4	585.3	2.68	188.4
50-54 yrs	176.1	190.4	209.9	232.2	275.9	316.8	363.9	411.6	479.1	2.53	172.1
55-59 yrs	134.2	162.6	176.9	195.5	217.4	259.0	298.9	344.6	391.4	2.71	191.6
60-64 yrs	104.4	120.8	148.0	162.0	180.2	201.0	240.7	279.1	323.3	2.87	209.6
65-69 yrs	84.2	89.6	105.6	130.9	144.6	161.6	181.4	218.6	255.0	2.81	202.8
70-74 yrs	56.9	66.1	72.1	86.5	108.6	120.9	136.5	154.9	188.7	3.04	231.8
75-79 yrs	31.7	38.3	46.0	51.2	62.8	79.7	90.4	104.1	120.5	3.40	280.5
80+ yrs	17.8	22.4	28.4	35.9	42.7	53.3	71.6	89.4	110.8	4.68	523.1
Median age of population (years)	18.5	18.8	19.2	19.6	20.1	20.8	21.8	23.2	24.7	0.73	33.6

Table 5.44 Key economic trends

As stated

	1990	1995	2000	2005	2010	2015	2020	CAGR	Period growth
Total GDP (Bvs per capita)	9,799.9	10,676.8	11,377.7	11,999.9	13,175.2	13,829.9	15,054.7	1.44	53.62
Disposable income (Bvs per capita)	7,230.4	7,525.2	8,090.3	8,118.1	8,821.0	9,359.0	10,332.2	1.20	42.90
Disposable income (Bvs per household)	35,299.5	35,906.4	37,072.7	34,071.8	33,823.2	33,477.5	35,075.9	-0.02	-0.63
Number of households by annual household disposable income ('000)									
Over US$1,000	1,006.1	1,288.5	1,504.1	1,694.5	2,406.2	2,886.3	3,328.0	4.07	230.78
Over US$10,000	51.9	72.4	99.3	84.8	269.0	465.8	785.6	9.48	1,414.04
Over US$25,000	11.7	16.7	22.5	20.1	56.3	96.1	165.5	9.24	1,315.70
Over US$75,000	3.1	4.4	5.8	5.4	13.0	19.9	30.2	7.89	876.10
Over US$150,000	1.3	1.9	2.5	2.3	5.6	8.6	13.0	7.88	873.10
Total households	1,366.3	1,568.5	1,815.1	2,187.8	2,616.0	3,034.4	3,428.1	3.11	150.90

Note: Per capita data is shown at constant 2010 prices. Household disposable income bands are shown at current prices.

Table 5.45 Young generation

'000

	1980	1985	1990	1995	2000	2005	2010	2015	2020	CAGR	Period growth
Babies under 12 months	178.5	203.2	220.4	244.8	236.2	258.4	247.5	249.8	242.9	0.77	36.1
Infants under 24 months	355.1	397.7	434.7	483.1	474.4	510.3	496.9	498.0	486.3	0.79	37.0
Toddlers aged 1-4	686.7	737.4	818.9	913.6	951.6	981.1	995.8	986.9	973.5	0.88	41.8
Children aged 2-9	1,274.8	1,361.1	1,502.2	1,679.1	1,835.0	1,891.2	1,953.8	1,955.8	1,941.0	1.06	52.3
Female	634.7	674.2	740.2	824.6	899.6	927.0	958.1	958.8	950.9	1.02	49.8
Male	640.0	686.9	762.0	854.5	935.4	964.2	995.7	997.0	990.1	1.10	54.7
Tweenagers aged 10-14	648.9	739.6	794.5	873.7	981.8	1,096.4	1,139.2	1,184.9	1,195.4	1.54	84.2
Female	325.7	369.7	394.8	431.5	483.0	538.1	558.7	581.4	586.4	1.48	80.1
Male	323.2	369.9	399.7	442.2	498.8	558.4	580.5	603.5	609.0	1.60	88.4
Teenagers aged 13-19	802.1	911.0	1,025.7	1,107.2	1,227.1	1,384.8	1,522.6	1,583.8	1,639.2	1.80	104.4
Female	403.8	457.1	512.4	549.6	605.8	681.3	747.5	777.2	804.6	1.74	99.2
Male	398.2	453.9	513.3	557.5	621.3	703.5	775.1	806.6	834.6	1.87	109.6
Studying age 18-22	507.2	561.6	646.5	722.5	781.6	872.7	991.8	1,078.2	1,117.6	1.99	120.4
Female	256.4	283.2	324.7	361.1	388.3	431.3	488.5	530.0	549.1	1.92	114.1
Male	250.7	278.4	321.8	361.4	393.4	441.4	503.3	548.2	568.4	2.07	126.7
Young adults aged 15-29	1,429.1	1,599.8	1,811.3	2,026.1	2,253.0	2,494.7	2,796.9	3,060.9	3,265.5	2.09	128.5
Female	724.2	807.9	911.2	1,014.4	1,122.4	1,236.6	1,380.7	1,507.4	1,606.4	2.01	121.8
Male	704.8	791.9	900.2	1,011.7	1,130.7	1,258.1	1,416.3	1,553.5	1,659.1	2.16	135.4

Table 5.46 Middle-aged generation

'000

	1980	1985	1990	1995	2000	2005	2010	2015	2020	CAGR	Period growth
Middle-aged adults 30-59	1,353.2	1,530.1	1,727.6	1,955.5	2,234.3	2,573.0	2,923.5	3,308.5	3,751.3	2.58	177.2
Female	696.2	788.7	890.4	1,006.6	1,148.0	1,318.9	1,493.0	1,681.2	1,896.6	2.54	172.4
Male	657.1	741.4	837.2	948.9	1,086.2	1,254.1	1,430.4	1,627.3	1,854.7	2.63	182.3
Baby boomers aged 40-59	748.3	834.3	937.6	1,066.4	1,223.9	1,403.1	1,608.4	1,858.3	2,115.4	2.63	182.7
Female	386.9	431.7	485.5	553.0	634.3	726.2	829.9	954.6	1,081.7	2.60	179.6
Male	361.4	402.6	452.0	513.4	589.6	676.9	778.5	903.7	1,033.7	2.66	186.0

Table 5.47 Elderly population

'000

	1980	1985	1990	1995	2000	2005	2010	2015	2020	CAGR	Period growth
Elderly population (60+)	295.0	337.3	400.2	466.6	538.8	616.4	720.6	846.1	998.4	3.10	238.5
Female	159.0	182.1	216.3	253.3	293.6	336.6	394.3	464.1	547.9	3.14	244.6
Male	136.0	155.2	183.9	213.3	245.2	279.8	326.3	381.9	450.5	3.04	231.3

Table 5.48 Population of biggest cities 1980-2020

'000

	1980	1985	1990	1995	2000	2005	2010	2015	2020	CAGR	Period growth
Santa Cruz	331.28	450.71	614.71	827.34	1,064.14	1,316.02	1,582.86	1,855.14	2,126.01	4.76	541.7
El Alto	189.83	259.10	356.30	482.76	618.98	764.73	919.37	1,076.32	1,232.45	4.79	549.2
La Paz	682.56	691.94	701.84	732.33	779.56	821.41	843.46	865.33	888.97	0.66	30.2
Cochabamba	227.08	288.60	363.64	440.72	505.92	552.47	592.53	633.73	675.60	2.76	197.5
Sucre	76.62	95.41	119.84	150.01	185.68	232.51	287.68	344.16	400.23	4.22	422.3
Oruro	139.80	157.93	176.09	190.29	199.03	210.05	221.38	232.95	244.85	1.41	75.1
Tarija	48.08	62.34	81.01	103.92	129.90	161.47	197.20	233.72	270.01	4.41	461.5
Potosi	85.92	95.79	106.88	118.75	130.39	143.81	157.42	171.30	185.31	1.94	115.7
Sacaba	8.78	15.48	28.62	52.66	85.54	120.29	155.98	192.37	228.42	8.49	2,500.3
Montero	34.52	42.65	52.44	63.80	75.72	88.84	102.39	116.17	129.94	3.37	276.4

Chart 5.22 Population age shift 2000 and 2020, Each Column Represents a Single Age Group

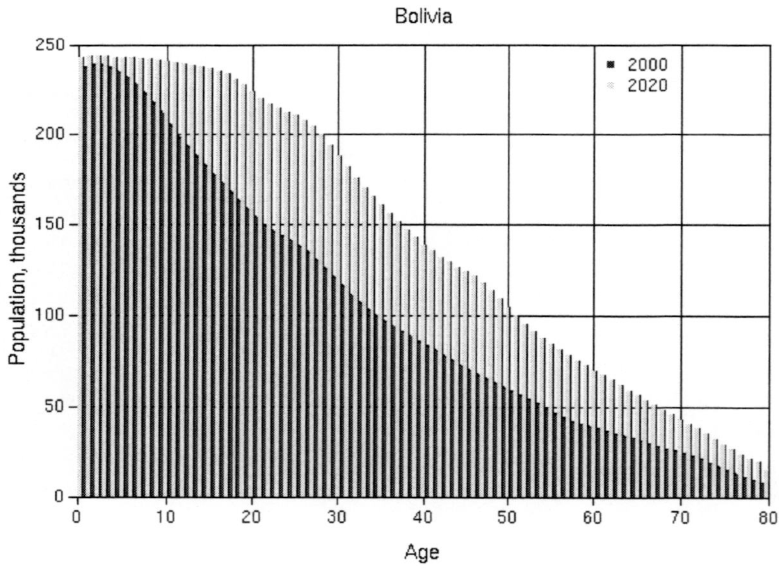

Chart 5.23 Population pyramids, 1980/2000/2010/2020

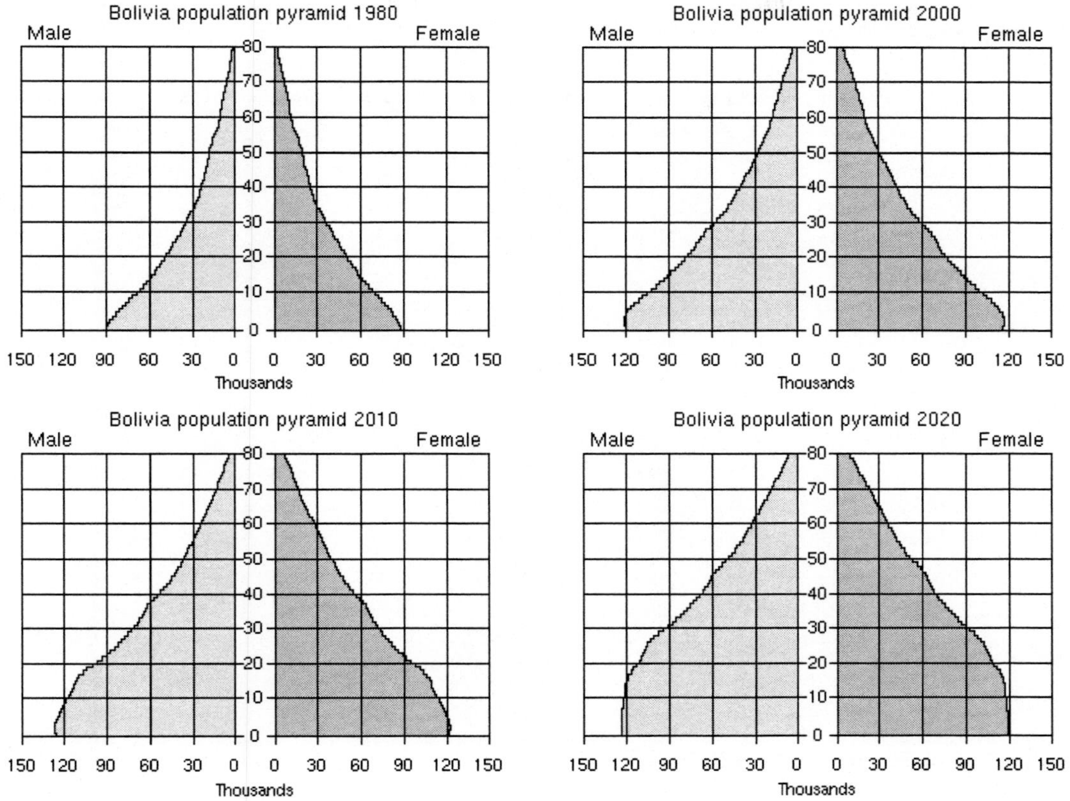

Chart 5.24 Major Cities: 1980, 2000 and 2020

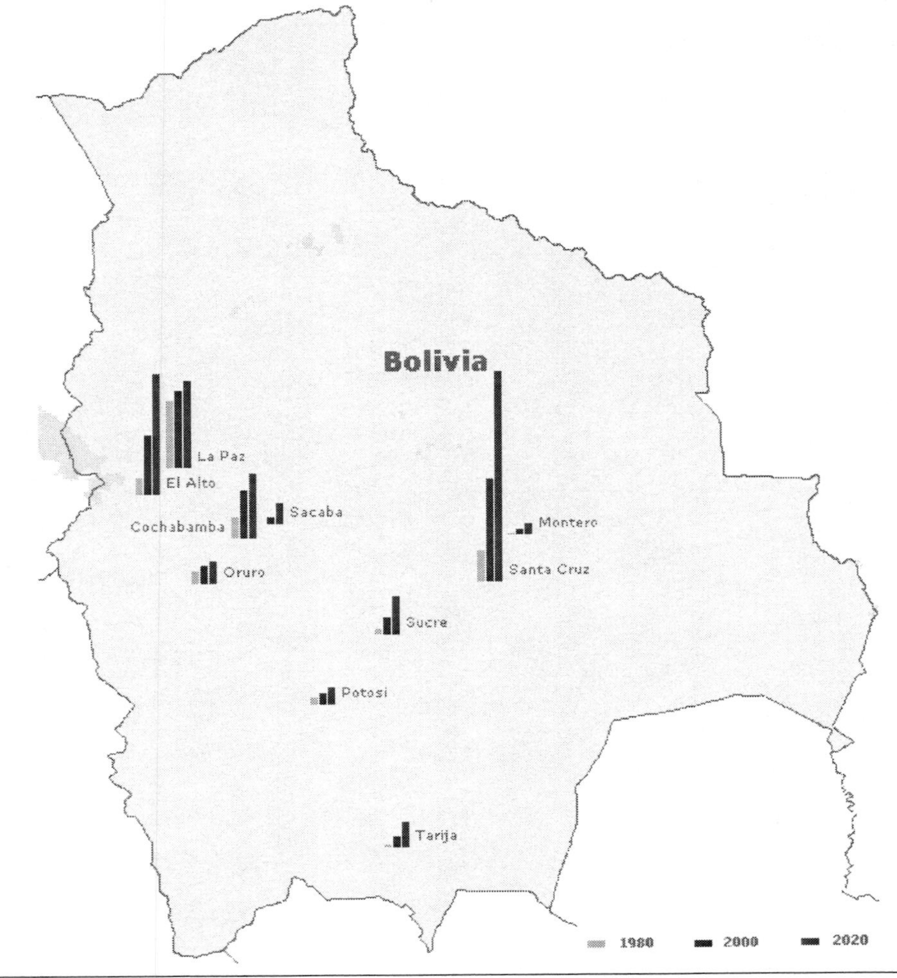

Bosnia-Herzegovina

Table 5.49 Key population trends

'000

	1980	1985	1990	1995	2000	2005	2010	2015	2020	CAGR	Period growth
Population at January 1st	4,040.0	4,245.9	4,498.4	3,523.0	3,753.1	3,842.5	3,844.4	3,837.1	3,808.6	-0.15	-5.73
Male	1,988.5	2,094.3	2,222.9	1,708.5	1,809.0	1,848.8	1,849.8	1,845.8	1,831.9	-0.20	-7.88
Female	2,051.4	2,151.6	2,275.5	1,814.6	1,944.1	1,993.7	1,994.6	1,991.2	1,976.8	-0.09	-3.64
0-4 yrs	346.5	365.4	358.4	214.7	223.3	184.1	174.0	171.5	164.8	-1.84	-52.43
5-9 yrs	360.7	342.5	365.6	277.3	228.1	220.6	187.1	173.9	171.6	-1.84	-52.42
10-14 yrs	394.4	359.1	365.8	285.0	291.4	234.6	221.4	187.9	175.0	-2.01	-55.63
15-19 yrs	426.5	391.9	381.6	279.8	295.5	296.2	234.8	222.4	188.4	-2.02	-55.83
20-24 yrs	420.4	421.3	397.7	281.3	277.8	297.6	295.6	235.3	222.6	-1.58	-47.06
25-29 yrs	380.1	413.2	404.4	286.6	274.0	278.6	296.5	296.0	235.1	-1.19	-38.13
30-34 yrs	281.1	371.9	387.2	299.7	284.0	275.5	277.6	297.0	296.1	0.13	5.36
35-39 yrs	224.4	276.2	351.0	291.5	303.4	286.7	274.8	278.1	297.2	0.70	32.40
40-44 yrs	270.3	221.5	274.2	266.8	298.7	306.2	285.6	274.8	277.8	0.07	2.77
45-49 yrs	258.0	264.0	226.4	204.9	274.2	300.1	303.5	284.2	273.3	0.14	5.93
50-54 yrs	211.6	248.5	267.8	165.0	211.6	273.1	294.4	299.1	280.2	0.70	32.40
55-59 yrs	141.9	200.6	248.9	201.8	171.6	208.7	264.3	286.4	291.3	1.81	105.31
60-64 yrs	80.9	130.9	195.6	181.9	204.1	166.2	199.7	254.2	275.9	3.12	241.15
65-69 yrs	93.6	71.7	121.8	136.7	178.2	189.0	154.7	187.8	239.2	2.37	155.49
70-74 yrs	75.8	76.2	58.6	78.9	125.7	155.7	165.1	137.0	167.3	2.00	120.64
75-79 yrs	46.6	55.2	52.2	31.4	67.2	101.2	122.4	131.6	110.1	2.17	136.12
80+ yrs	27.2	35.8	41.0	39.6	44.2	68.4	92.9	119.9	142.7	4.23	424.97
Median age of population (years)	25.9	27.9	29.7	32.3	35.0	37.4	39.3	41.0	42.7	1.26	65.11

Table 5.50 Key economic trends

As stated

	1990	1995	2000	2005	2010	2015	2020	CAGR	Period growth
Total GDP (BAM per capita)		1,398	3,617	5,529	6,492	8,279	10,157		
Disposable income (BAM per capita)			3,548	5,121	5,427	6,514			
Disposable income (BAM per household)			11,582	16,335	17,004	20,380			
Number of households by annual household disposable income ('000)									
Total households	1,236	1,017	1,150	1,205	1,227	1,226	1,217	0	-2

Note: Per capita data is shown at constant 2010 prices. Household disposable income bands are shown at current prices.

Table 5.51 Young generation

'000

	1980	1985	1990	1995	2000	2005	2010	2015	2020	CAGR	Period growth
Babies under 12 months	69.0	77.8	69.1	34.2	51.4	29.0	37.4	33.5	32.1	-1.90	-53.48
Infants under 24 months	138.3	152.6	140.3	73.4	97.9	63.4	72.4	67.8	64.6	-1.88	-53.27
Toddlers aged 1-4	277.5	287.7	289.2	180.5	171.8	155.1	136.5	138.0	132.7	-1.83	-52.17
Children aged 2-9	568.9	555.3	583.7	418.6	353.4	341.2	288.7	277.5	271.8	-1.83	-52.22
Female	275.9	269.4	285.7	205.7	170.6	165.1	139.7	134.3	131.6	-1.83	-52.31
Male	293.0	286.0	298.0	212.9	182.8	176.1	149.0	143.2	140.3	-1.83	-52.13
Tweenagers aged 10-14	394.4	359.1	365.8	285.0	291.4	234.6	221.4	187.9	175.0	-2.01	-55.63
Female	192.8	174.5	178.8	140.0	143.6	113.6	107.0	90.9	84.7	-2.04	-56.08
Male	201.6	184.5	186.9	145.1	147.8	121.0	114.4	97.0	90.3	-1.99	-55.21
Teenagers aged 13-19	589.1	539.0	529.2	392.8	417.0	395.6	325.1	301.7	258.8	-2.04	-56.08
Female	288.8	263.4	259.8	194.0	206.2	194.5	157.3	145.9	125.2	-2.07	-56.64
Male	300.3	275.6	269.4	198.8	210.8	201.0	167.8	155.8	133.5	-2.01	-55.53
Studying age 18-22	427.0	412.8	391.7	280.4	283.8	304.5	272.1	226.3	211.4	-1.74	-50.50
Female	210.0	202.3	192.0	142.1	141.7	150.9	133.5	109.2	102.3	-1.78	-51.28
Male	217.0	210.5	199.7	138.3	142.0	153.6	138.6	117.1	109.0	-1.71	-49.75
Young adults aged 15-29	1,226.9	1,226.5	1,183.8	847.8	847.4	872.3	826.8	753.7	646.1	-1.59	-47.34
Female	603.0	602.4	581.1	432.6	432.5	436.2	407.2	367.9	312.8	-1.63	-48.13
Male	623.9	624.0	602.7	415.2	414.9	436.1	419.6	385.8	333.3	-1.55	-46.57

Table 5.52 Middle-aged generation

'000

	1980	1985	1990	1995	2000	2005	2010	2015	2020	CAGR	Period growth
Middle-aged adults 30-59	1,387.3	1,582.6	1,755.6	1,429.7	1,543.6	1,650.5	1,700.2	1,719.6	1,715.9	0.53	23.7
Female	722.5	808.3	884.2	731.6	802.6	865.8	892.6	899.8	892.0	0.53	23.5
Male	664.8	774.3	871.4	698.1	741.0	784.7	807.6	819.9	823.9	0.54	23.9
Baby boomers aged 40-59	881.8	934.5	1,017.4	838.5	956.1	1,088.2	1,147.8	1,144.6	1,122.6	0.61	27.3
Female	466.3	486.8	520.4	431.9	492.7	564.6	603.8	609.6	597.3	0.62	28.1
Male	415.4	447.7	497.0	406.6	463.4	523.6	544.0	534.9	525.2	0.59	26.4

Table 5.53 Elderly population

'000

	1980	1985	1990	1995	2000	2005	2010	2015	2020	CAGR	Period growth
Elderly population (60+)	324.2	369.8	469.2	468.6	619.4	680.5	734.8	830.5	935.3	2.68	188.5
Female	190.1	223.1	276.5	270.1	347.0	382.5	413.0	465.5	524.5	2.57	176.0
Male	134.1	146.7	192.7	198.4	272.4	298.0	321.9	365.0	410.8	2.84	206.3

Table 5.54 Population of biggest cities 1980-2020

'000

	1980	1985	1990	1995	2000	2005	2010	2015	2020	CAGR	Period growth
Sarajevo	311.0	364.8	422.9	339.6	371.7	380.0	380.2	374.9	368.1	0.42	18.34
Banja Luka	121.9	133.9	146.2	124.7	148.9	165.1	171.8	172.6	171.0	0.85	40.23
Tuzla	63.5	74.1	85.3	70.4	79.7	84.1	85.8	85.4	84.2	0.71	32.53
Zenica	61.2	77.9	96.6	77.6	83.7	84.3	83.5	81.9	80.2	0.68	31.16
Mostar	62.1	70.0	77.9	60.8	64.3	63.5	62.3	60.8	59.4	-0.11	-4.43
Brcko	30.5	36.1	41.9	36.5	44.0	49.0	51.1	51.4	50.9	1.29	66.86
Bijeljina	30.5	34.1	37.9	32.2	38.1	42.1	43.9	44.1	43.7	0.90	43.26
Bihac	28.7	37.0	46.2	36.8	39.2	38.9	38.3	37.4	36.6	0.61	27.59
Prijedor	28.9	32.2	35.5	28.0	30.2	30.5	30.2	29.7	29.1	0.01	0.59
Trebinje	16.8	19.6	22.6	19.0	22.2	24.0	24.7	24.7	24.4	0.94	45.25

Chart 5.25 Population age shift 2000 and 2020, Each Column Represents a Single Age Group

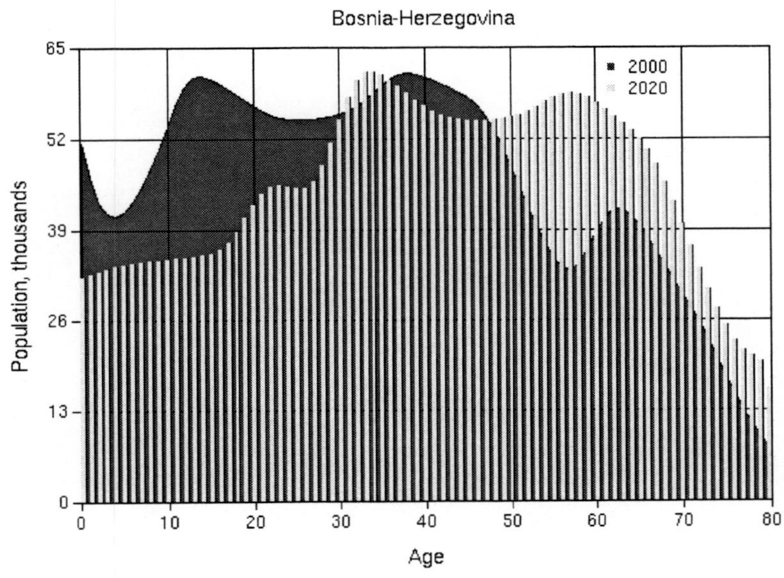

Chart 5.26 Population pyramids, 1980/2000/2010/2020

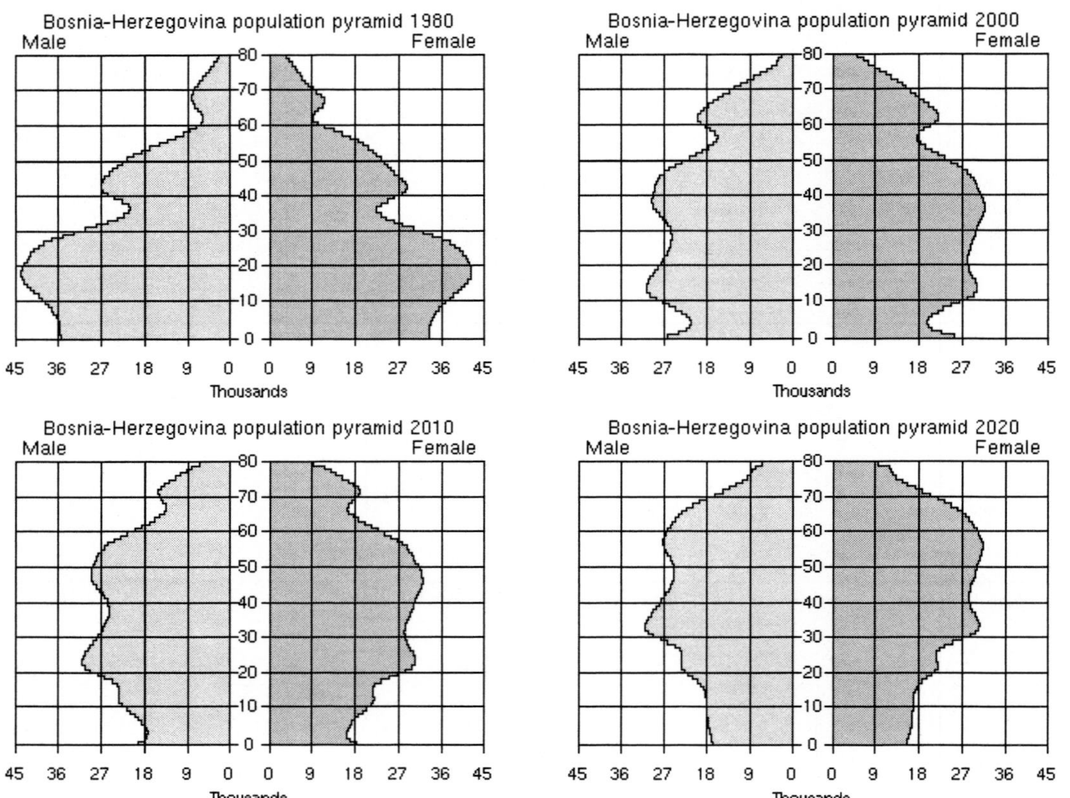

Chart 5.27 Major Cities: 1980, 2000 and 2020

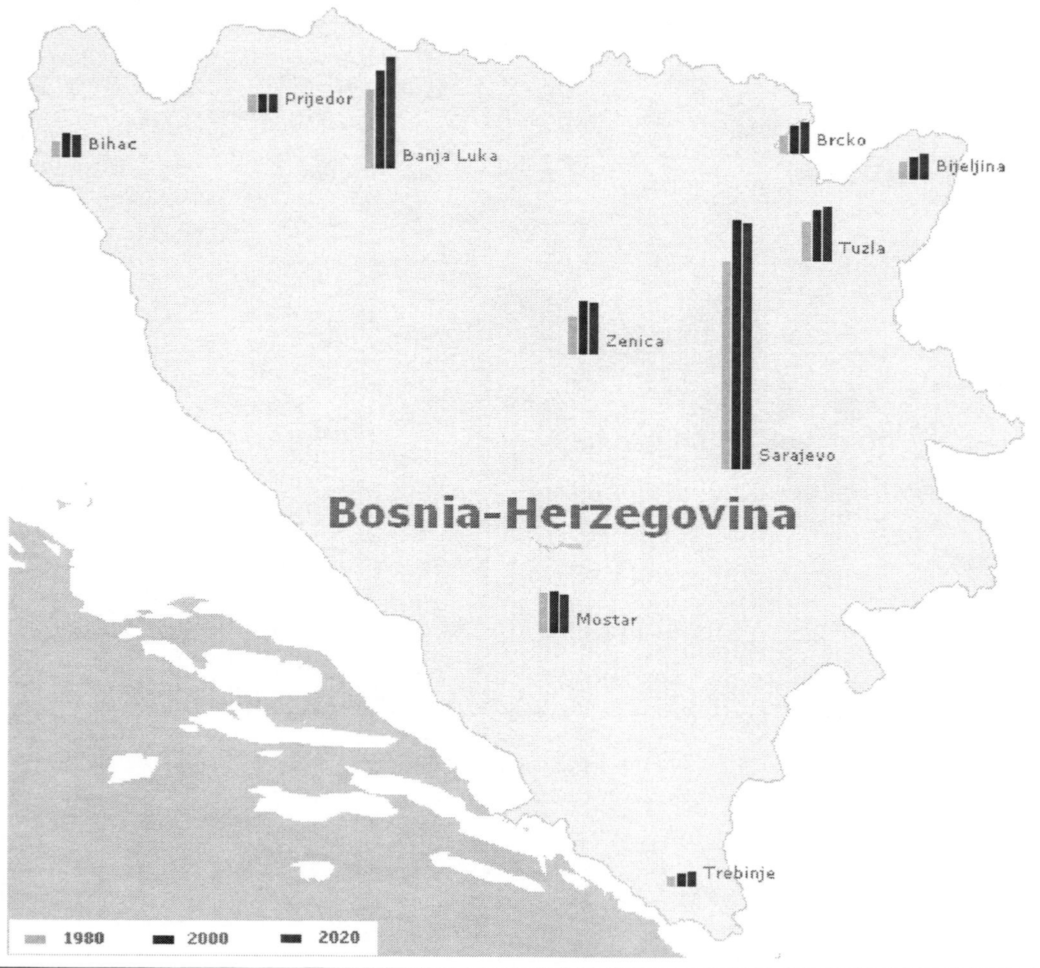

Brazil

Table 5.55 Key population trends

'000

	1980	1985	1990	1995	2000	2005	2010	2015	2020	CAGR	Period growth
Population at January 1st	121,618.4	136,149.4	149,570.5	161,692.0	174,174.4	186,074.6	195,423.3	202,865.5	209,051.1	1.36	71.89
Male	60,676.4	67,797.4	74,304.7	80,110.7	86,090.0	91,780.3	96,198.9	99,656.5	102,506.6	1.32	68.94
Female	60,942.0	68,352.0	75,265.8	81,581.3	88,084.5	94,294.3	99,224.3	103,209.0	106,544.5	1.41	74.83
0-4 yrs	16,804.2	18,686.6	17,990.8	16,914.3	17,374.3	17,427.6	15,553.6	13,715.8	12,843.3	-0.67	-23.57
5-9 yrs	15,129.6	16,543.2	18,418.5	17,780.1	16,776.7	17,243.5	17,294.8	15,480.1	13,668.9	-0.25	-9.65
10-14 yrs	14,591.7	15,027.6	16,437.4	18,322.3	17,723.8	16,706.2	17,155.6	17,246.6	15,451.0	0.14	5.89
15-19 yrs	13,897.9	14,485.7	14,902.2	16,316.1	18,224.7	17,612.9	16,591.1	17,081.2	17,190.3	0.53	23.69
20-24 yrs	11,815.3	13,738.4	14,309.4	14,732.3	16,165.9	18,044.3	17,433.8	16,471.2	16,982.6	0.91	43.73
25-29 yrs	9,690.4	11,614.4	13,530.7	14,104.8	14,556.3	15,967.2	17,824.6	17,278.2	16,352.8	1.32	68.75
30-34 yrs	7,885.7	9,496.9	11,408.0	13,306.3	13,907.9	14,352.2	15,750.9	17,646.3	17,139.2	1.96	117.35
35-39 yrs	6,506.6	7,695.7	9,292.0	11,181.4	13,083.3	13,677.2	14,124.0	15,560.8	17,471.8	2.50	168.52
40-44 yrs	5,846.7	6,319.2	7,486.7	9,061.3	10,941.6	12,810.6	13,404.9	13,900.7	15,354.3	2.44	162.62
45-49 yrs	4,761.0	5,640.1	6,095.4	7,243.3	8,801.0	10,638.1	12,474.6	13,113.0	13,638.7	2.67	186.47
50-54 yrs	4,185.6	4,524.7	5,370.6	5,828.0	6,960.1	8,472.6	10,263.3	12,098.0	12,760.2	2.83	204.86
55-59 yrs	3,208.6	3,921.0	4,233.2	5,047.8	5,512.2	6,602.3	8,061.7	9,825.1	11,630.2	3.27	262.47
60-64 yrs	2,478.2	2,912.1	3,575.9	3,887.5	4,666.1	5,116.5	6,154.7	7,571.8	9,278.3	3.36	274.41
65-69 yrs	2,035.4	2,173.8	2,559.5	3,174.9	3,479.5	4,196.9	4,630.3	5,620.6	6,964.1	3.12	242.15
70-74 yrs	1,319.0	1,666.5	1,789.1	2,148.5	2,699.5	2,982.6	3,624.2	4,043.7	4,952.7	3.36	275.48
75-79 yrs	851.9	952.2	1,233.8	1,374.2	1,688.9	2,150.6	2,400.2	2,953.6	3,333.2	3.47	291.28
80+ yrs	610.6	751.3	937.3	1,269.1	1,612.6	2,073.1	2,680.8	3,259.0	4,039.5	4.84	561.60
Median age of population (years)	20.2	21.2	22.4	23.9	25.3	26.8	28.8	31.2	33.5	1.28	66.40

Table 5.56 Key economic trends

As stated

	1990	1995	2000	2005	2010	2015	2020	CAGR	Period growth
Total GDP (R$ per capita)	12,392.3	13,333.0	13,672.7	14,682.6	16,882.0	19,442.9	22,709.9	2.04	83.3
Disposable income (R$ per capita)	5,784.3	7,760.2	8,572.0	8,850.3	10,652.6	12,705.8	15,058.7	3.24	160.3
Disposable income (R$ per household)	24,910.2	31,647.5	33,010.4	32,612.0	37,512.1	42,596.5	48,036.8	2.21	92.8
Number of households by annual household disposable income ('000)									
Over US$1,000		36,860.4	41,989.2	48,658.0	54,180.7	59,878.5	65,206.3		
Over US$10,000		13,383.4	11,026.1	13,740.4	23,422.6	31,633.2	43,017.5		
Over US$25,000		4,212.7	2,911.6	3,599.6	7,103.5	10,332.9	16,460.5		
Over US$75,000		722.1	500.8	647.3	1,208.4	1,823.7	2,987.9		
Over US$150,000		236.0	190.2	248.6	411.0	608.8	943.5		
Total households	34,731.0	39,648.0	45,229.0	50,497.5	55,496.1	60,511.2	65,533.7	2.14	88.7

Note: Per capita data is shown at constant 2010 prices. Household disposable income bands are shown at current prices.

Table 5.57 Young generation

'000

	1980	1985	1990	1995	2000	2005	2010	2015	2020	CAGR	Period growth
Babies under 12 months	3,585	3,851	3,543	3,428	3,571	3,393	2,953	2,651	2,541	-0.86	-29.12
Infants under 24 months	7,044	7,658	7,124	6,822	7,088	6,845	5,978	5,338	5,092	-0.81	-27.72
Toddlers aged 1-4	13,219	14,836	14,448	13,486	13,803	14,035	12,601	11,065	10,302	-0.62	-22.07
Children aged 2-9	24,890	27,571	29,285	27,872	27,063	27,826	26,870	23,858	21,420	-0.37	-13.94
Female	12,239	13,574	14,415	13,716	13,302	13,663	13,189	11,707	10,504	-0.38	-14.17
Male	12,650	13,998	14,870	14,156	13,761	14,163	13,681	12,151	10,916	-0.37	-13.71
Tweenagers aged 10-14	14,592	15,028	16,437	18,322	17,724	16,706	17,156	17,247	15,451	0.14	5.89
Female	7,235	7,394	8,100	9,028	8,733	8,221	8,430	8,471	7,586	0.12	4.85
Male	7,357	7,633	8,338	9,294	8,991	8,485	8,726	8,776	7,865	0.17	6.91
Teenagers aged 13-19	19,688	20,401	21,218	23,524	25,424	24,289	23,347	24,104	23,627	0.46	20.00
Female	9,884	10,111	10,455	11,609	12,548	11,984	11,500	11,857	11,615	0.40	17.51
Male	9,804	10,290	10,763	11,914	12,876	12,305	11,847	12,248	12,012	0.51	22.52
Studying age 18-22	12,742	14,173	14,502	15,208	17,130	18,108	16,990	16,621	17,300	0.77	35.77
Female	6,435	7,120	7,190	7,515	8,486	8,965	8,404	8,203	8,525	0.71	32.49
Male	6,307	7,053	7,312	7,693	8,644	9,143	8,587	8,418	8,775	0.83	39.12
Young adults aged 15-29	35,404	39,839	42,742	45,153	48,947	51,624	51,850	50,831	50,526	0.89	42.71
Female	17,874	20,034	21,363	22,437	24,281	25,621	25,710	25,160	24,960	0.84	39.65
Male	17,530	19,804	21,379	22,716	24,666	26,004	26,139	25,670	25,566	0.95	45.84

Table 5.58 Middle-aged generation

'000

	1980	1985	1990	1995	2000	2005	2010	2015	2020	CAGR	Period growth
Middle-aged adults 30-59	32,394	37,598	43,886	51,668	59,206	66,553	74,079	82,144	87,994	2.53	171.6
Female	16,295	19,106	22,485	26,641	30,587	34,336	38,150	42,145	44,948	2.57	175.8
Male	16,099	18,491	21,401	25,027	28,619	32,217	35,929	39,999	43,047	2.49	167.4
Baby boomers aged 40-59	18,002	20,405	23,186	27,180	32,215	38,524	44,204	48,937	53,383	2.75	196.5
Female	9,034	10,375	11,896	14,073	16,809	20,176	23,117	25,455	27,591	2.83	205.4
Male	8,968	10,030	11,290	13,107	15,406	18,348	21,087	23,482	25,793	2.68	187.6

Table 5.59 Elderly population

'000

	1980	1985	1990	1995	2000	2005	2010	2015	2020	CAGR	Period growth
Elderly population (60+)	7,295	8,456	10,096	11,854	14,147	16,520	19,490	23,449	28,568	3.47	291.6
Female	3,835	4,481	5,404	6,413	7,706	9,097	10,815	13,111	16,053	3.64	318.7
Male	3,460	3,975	4,692	5,441	6,440	7,422	8,675	10,337	12,515	3.27	261.6

Table 5.60 Population of biggest cities 1980-2020

'000

	1980	1985	1990	1995	2000	2005	2010	2015	2020	CAGR	Period growth
Sao Paulo	7,073.1	8,336.7	9,417.5	10,017.8	10,009.2	10,928.0	11,429.9	11,964.2	12,438.0	1.42	75.8
Rio de Janeiro	4,137.1	4,825.7	5,371.9	5,606.5	5,613.9	6,094.2	6,338.5	6,607.6	6,848.8	1.27	65.5
Salvador	1,343.4	1,656.5	1,986.1	2,262.7	2,331.6	2,673.6	2,893.7	3,103.8	3,283.1	2.26	144.4
Brasilia	1,103.8	1,334.4	1,560.1	1,737.8	2,016.5	2,333.1	2,601.1	2,845.8	3,051.3	2.57	176.4
Fortaleza	1,160.8	1,423.8	1,695.6	1,917.2	2,139.4	2,374.9	2,599.0	2,808.6	2,986.1	2.39	157.2
Belo Horizonte	1,487.0	1,750.7	1,974.6	2,097.3	2,154.2	2,375.3	2,511.3	2,649.2	2,769.6	1.57	86.3
Curitiba	911.1	1,097.2	1,276.1	1,408.5	1,618.3	1,757.9	1,921.7	2,075.1	2,205.2	2.23	142.0
Manaus	653.7	811.4	981.2	1,138.2	1,285.8	1,644.7	1,874.3	2,081.4	2,253.7	3.14	244.8
Recife	970.0	1,134.8	1,268.5	1,329.8	1,388.2	1,501.0	1,579.3	1,660.3	1,731.5	1.46	78.5
Porto Alegre	919.0	1,083.5	1,224.7	1,295.9	1,321.9	1,428.7	1,497.6	1,570.1	1,634.1	1.45	77.8

Chart 5.28 Population age shift 2000 and 2020, Each Column Represents a Single Age Group

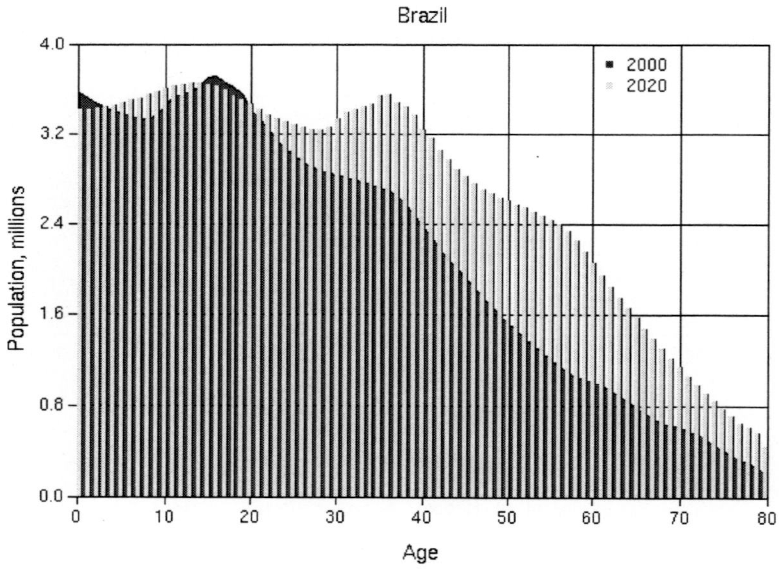

Chart 5.29 Population pyramids, 1980/2000/2010/2020

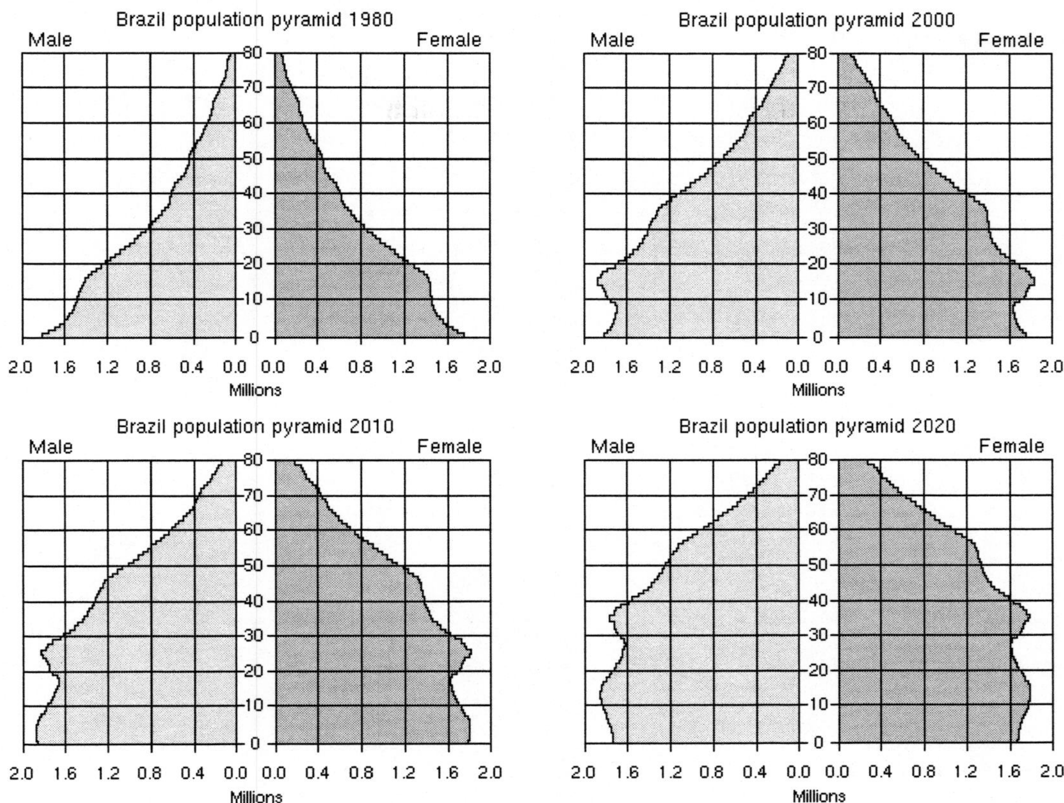

Chart 5.30 Major Cities: 1980, 2000 and 2020

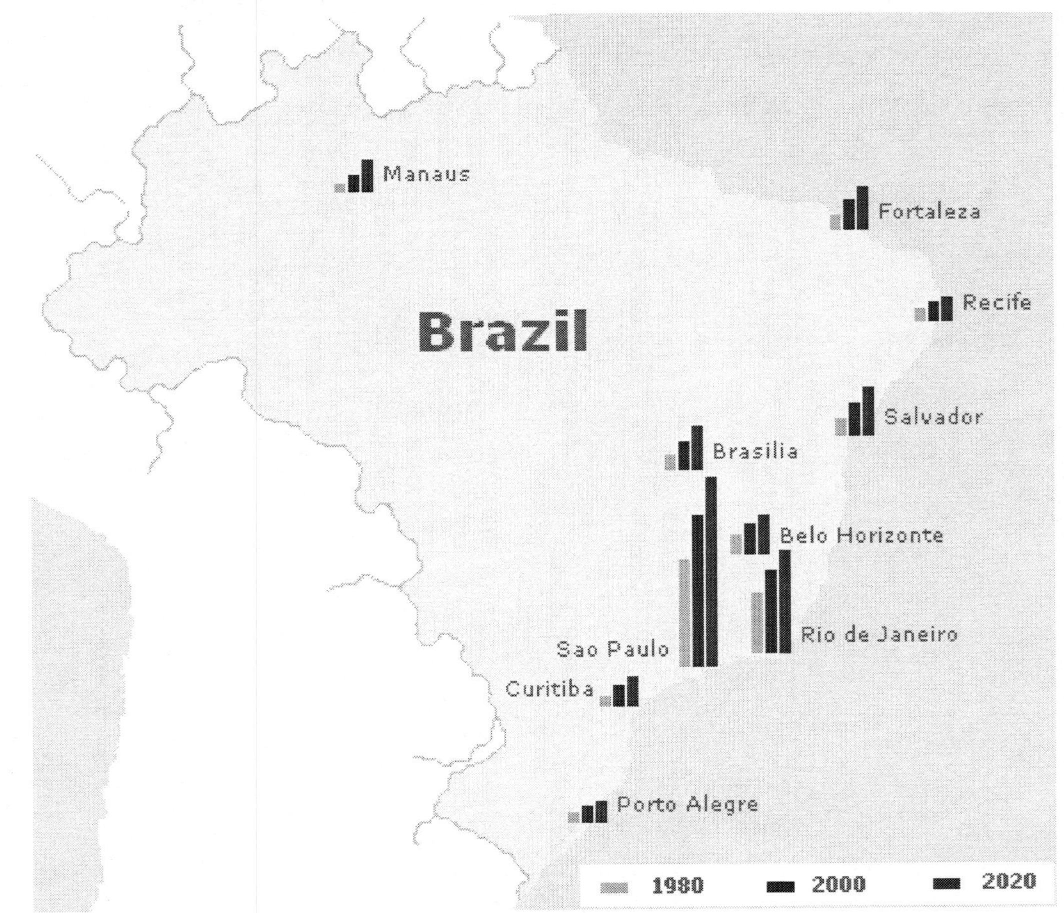

Bulgaria

Table 5.61 Key population trends

'000

	1980	1985	1990	1995	2000	2005	2010	2015	2020	CAGR	Period growth
Population at January 1st	8,835.3	8,953.9	8,767.3	8,303.0	7,978.2	7,728.0	7,466.9	7,190.8	6,885.4	-0.62	-22.07
Male	4,403.6	4,447.8	4,323.8	4,069.0	3,887.5	3,751.6	3,615.7	3,481.0	3,337.0	-0.69	-24.22
Female	4,431.7	4,506.1	4,443.5	4,234.0	4,090.7	3,976.4	3,851.1	3,709.9	3,548.4	-0.55	-19.93
0-4 yrs	688.0	608.0	568.5	429.0	331.4	332.6	330.8	311.0	276.4	-2.25	-59.82
5-9 yrs	650.5	685.3	577.3	519.6	423.0	319.4	329.6	323.0	299.8	-1.92	-53.92
10-14 yrs	618.7	648.8	655.1	557.0	512.8	416.7	316.3	326.8	320.7	-1.63	-48.17
15-19 yrs	624.7	616.6	634.2	621.3	549.4	517.5	411.4	310.5	319.1	-1.67	-48.92
20-24 yrs	633.1	621.7	573.2	591.8	611.9	540.1	503.8	394.6	293.5	-1.90	-53.64
25-29 yrs	658.1	629.6	584.7	544.4	582.4	580.9	526.3	483.5	372.1	-1.42	-43.47
30-34 yrs	658.0	653.8	607.7	549.6	535.2	558.8	573.2	516.5	470.7	-0.83	-28.46
35-39 yrs	555.9	652.4	631.3	570.2	538.9	523.2	552.7	566.3	508.7	-0.22	-8.50
40-44 yrs	562.1	548.7	630.1	596.0	556.1	530.1	515.1	543.8	555.6	-0.03	-1.15
45-49 yrs	628.4	550.8	526.8	595.0	576.3	545.0	518.3	504.0	531.2	-0.42	-15.46
50-54 yrs	612.7	609.7	524.9	492.2	567.7	556.3	527.4	502.8	489.1	-0.56	-20.17
55-59 yrs	578.2	583.3	574.6	483.4	461.8	546.4	531.7	507.4	485.9	-0.43	-15.95
60-64 yrs	327.8	536.2	542.6	520.3	441.1	436.1	511.5	502.8	483.9	0.98	47.60
65-69 yrs	397.4	288.2	479.0	467.1	457.9	400.8	393.6	467.8	464.4	0.39	16.84
70-74 yrs	310.2	327.2	235.4	386.3	383.5	391.3	341.3	341.9	412.8	0.72	33.08
75-79 yrs	198.2	221.8	235.1	168.0	279.4	291.6	299.2	267.5	275.3	0.82	38.89
80+ yrs	133.4	171.9	186.8	211.7	169.7	241.5	284.7	320.6	326.3	2.26	144.67
Median age of population (years)	34.1	35.1	36.5	38.0	39.1	40.7	41.7	43.3	45.2	0.71	32.70

Table 5.62 Key economic trends

As stated

	1990	1995	2000	2005	2010	2015	2020	CAGR	Period growth
Total GDP (BGN per capita)	7,730.5	5,541.0	5,605.6	7,485.9	8,451.6	10,772.5	14,568.6	2.13	88.46
Disposable income (BGN per capita)	10,164.8	4,983.7	4,401.7	5,660.6	6,579.3	8,693.4	11,830.6	0.51	16.39
Disposable income (BGN per household)	29,702.0	14,200.5	12,051.0	14,893.9	16,812.8	21,749.5	29,149.1	-0.06	-1.86
Number of households by annual household disposable income ('000)									
Over US$1,000	2,928.0	2,711.4	2,746.7	2,900.7	2,913.8	2,871.1	2,793.6	-0.16	-4.59
Over US$10,000	234.4	117.9	91.8	543.8	1,560.2	2,164.2	2,510.8	8.23	971.21
Over US$25,000	54.6	31.1	31.2	79.8	277.0	644.7	1,274.9	11.07	2,233.00
Over US$75,000	13.7	7.8	7.7	19.4	43.6	71.4	145.0	8.19	959.34
Over US$150,000	5.7	3.3	3.2	8.1	18.3	29.6	49.2	7.44	760.33
Total households	3,000.4	2,913.9	2,914.1	2,937.1	2,922.0	2,874.2	2,794.5	-0.24	-6.86

Note: Per capita data is shown at constant 2010 prices. Household disposable income bands are shown at current prices.

Table 5.63 Young generation

'000

	1980	1985	1990	1995	2000	2005	2010	2015	2020	CAGR	Period growth
Babies under 12 months	132.5	120.1	110.6	77.0	69.3	67.2	66.2	61.4	53.6	-2.24	-59.55
Infants under 24 months	264.1	240.6	224.2	158.7	132.1	133.3	132.4	123.2	108.1	-2.21	-59.08
Toddlers aged 1-4	555.5	487.9	457.9	352.0	262.0	265.4	264.7	249.6	222.8	-2.26	-59.89
Children aged 2-9	1,074.4	1,052.7	921.6	789.9	622.2	518.6	528.0	510.7	468.1	-2.06	-56.43
Female	522.7	512.4	448.8	385.0	302.7	252.1	256.7	248.9	228.1	-2.05	-56.35
Male	551.8	540.2	472.9	404.8	319.6	266.5	271.3	261.8	240.0	-2.06	-56.51
Tweenagers aged 10-14	618.7	648.8	655.1	557.0	512.8	416.7	316.3	326.8	320.7	-1.63	-48.17
Female	300.6	315.3	319.1	270.4	250.4	202.7	154.0	158.5	156.2	-1.62	-48.04
Male	318.1	333.5	336.0	286.5	262.3	213.9	162.3	168.3	164.5	-1.64	-48.30
Teenagers aged 13-19	860.9	875.6	903.1	849.4	758.9	701.0	542.3	441.3	448.6	-1.62	-47.89
Female	418.3	425.3	440.6	413.5	369.3	341.8	264.1	214.7	217.7	-1.62	-47.96
Male	442.6	450.3	462.5	435.9	389.6	359.2	278.2	226.6	230.9	-1.61	-47.83
Studying age 18-22	623.6	604.0	604.5	612.4	586.7	531.4	480.2	350.5	300.6	-1.81	-51.80
Female	304.4	294.0	296.1	300.8	285.6	258.9	234.1	170.8	146.0	-1.82	-52.03
Male	319.2	310.0	308.4	311.6	301.1	272.6	246.1	179.7	154.6	-1.80	-51.58
Young adults aged 15-29	1,915.9	1,867.9	1,792.1	1,757.6	1,743.7	1,638.5	1,441.5	1,188.6	984.6	-1.65	-48.61
Female	940.8	911.4	880.5	861.8	852.0	798.7	702.0	578.9	477.9	-1.68	-49.21
Male	975.1	956.6	911.5	895.8	891.7	839.7	739.4	609.8	506.8	-1.62	-48.03

Table 5.64 Middle-aged generation

'000

	1980	1985	1990	1995	2000	2005	2010	2015	2020	CAGR	Period growth
Middle-aged adults 30-59	3,595	3,599	3,495	3,286	3,236	3,260	3,218	3,141	3,041	-0.42	-15.41
Female	1,805	1,810	1,766	1,669	1,645	1,648	1,617	1,564	1,502	-0.46	-16.78
Male	1,791	1,788	1,729	1,618	1,591	1,611	1,601	1,576	1,540	-0.38	-14.02
Baby boomers aged 40-59	2,381	2,293	2,256	2,167	2,162	2,178	2,092	2,058	2,062	-0.36	-13.41
Female	1,200	1,159	1,147	1,109	1,112	1,115	1,065	1,036	1,024	-0.39	-14.64
Male	1,181	1,134	1,110	1,058	1,050	1,063	1,027	1,022	1,038	-0.32	-12.16

Table 5.65 Elderly population

'000

	1980	1985	1990	1995	2000	2005	2010	2015	2020	CAGR	Period growth
Elderly population (60+)	1,366.9	1,545.2	1,678.8	1,753.5	1,731.5	1,761.2	1,830.4	1,900.7	1,962.5	0.91	43.6
Female	734.5	839.4	919.6	970.4	975.8	1,009.9	1,056.9	1,099.1	1,131.7	1.09	54.1
Male	632.5	705.8	759.2	783.1	755.7	751.3	773.5	801.6	830.8	0.68	31.4

Table 5.66 Population of biggest cities 1980-2020

'000

	1980	1985	1990	1995	2000	2005	2010	2015	2020	CAGR	Period growth
Sofia	905.4	1,121.8	1,251.2	1,116.8	1,092.3	1,156.8	1,193.7	1,197.7	1,184.7	0.67	30.85
Plovdiv	332.0	343.1	336.9	344.3	338.2	341.7	349.2	351.9	349.4	0.13	5.26
Varna	273.5	302.8	313.3	301.4	307.9	311.9	320.2	324.1	323.0	0.42	18.13
Burgas	166.1	182.9	192.3	199.5	192.0	189.4	188.6	186.2	181.5	0.22	9.25
Ruse	185.1	185.5	172.5	168.1	161.6	157.9	156.7	154.4	150.2	-0.52	-18.87
Stara Zagora	144.6	151.2	149.6	149.7	144.2	141.5	140.4	138.0	134.1	-0.19	-7.27
Pleven	115.2	129.9	135.6	125.0	121.2	114.5	111.9	109.2	105.4	-0.22	-8.52
Sliven	95.0	102.4	105.2	107.0	100.9	95.8	94.1	91.9	88.7	-0.17	-6.61
Dobrich	108.7	109.2	103.4	103.5	99.2	94.0	92.9	91.2	88.5	-0.52	-18.66
Shumen	104.3	100.1	91.0	97.2	90.1	86.6	87.1	86.9	85.4	-0.50	-18.10

Chart 5.31 Population age shift 2000 and 2020, Each Column Represents a Single Age Group

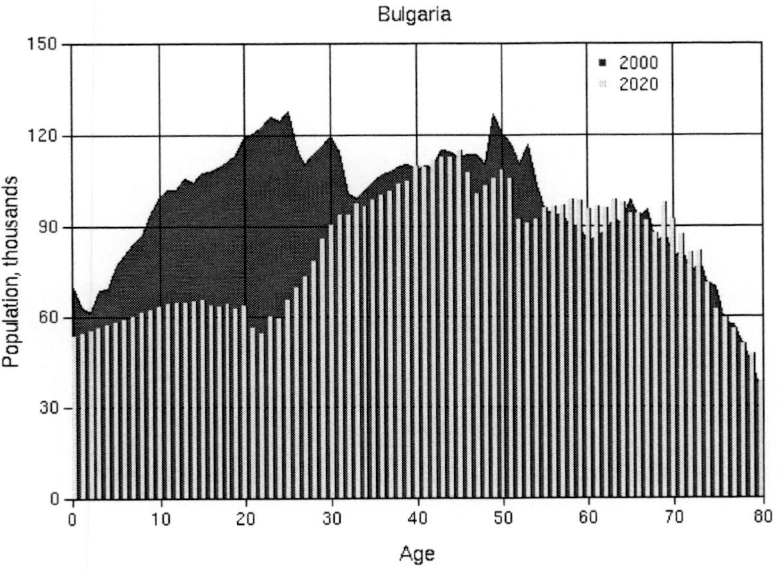

Chart 5.32 Population pyramids, 1980/2000/2010/2020

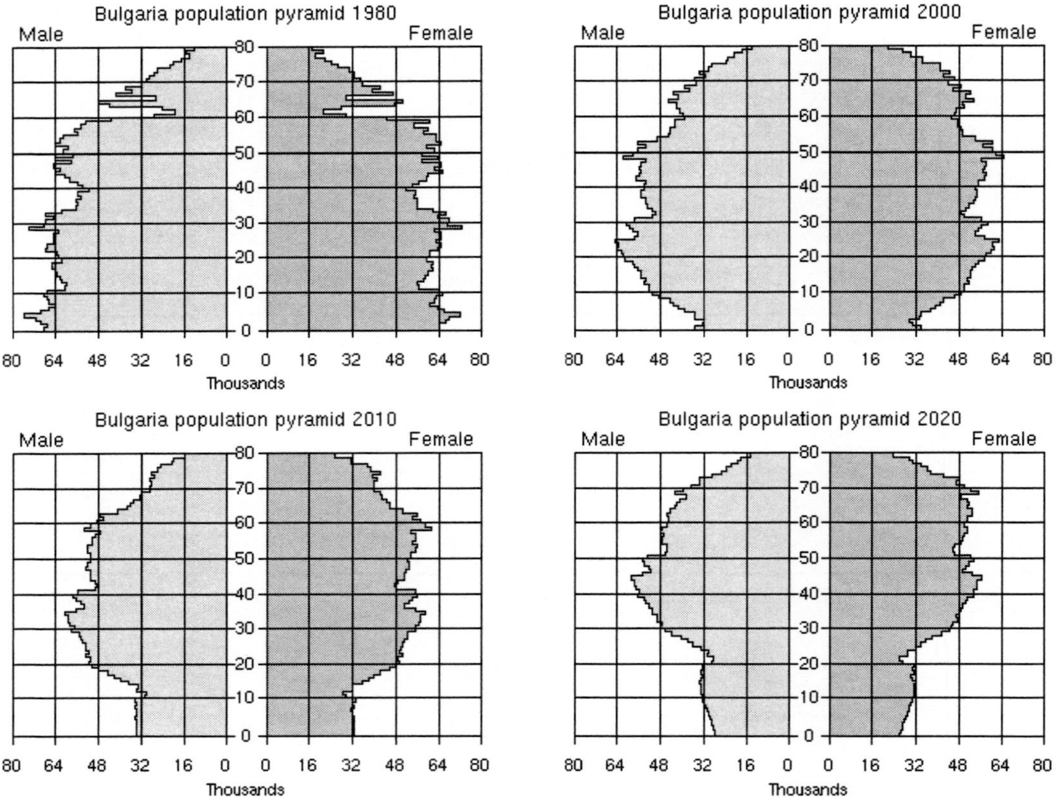

Chart 5.33 Major Cities: 1980, 2000 and 2020

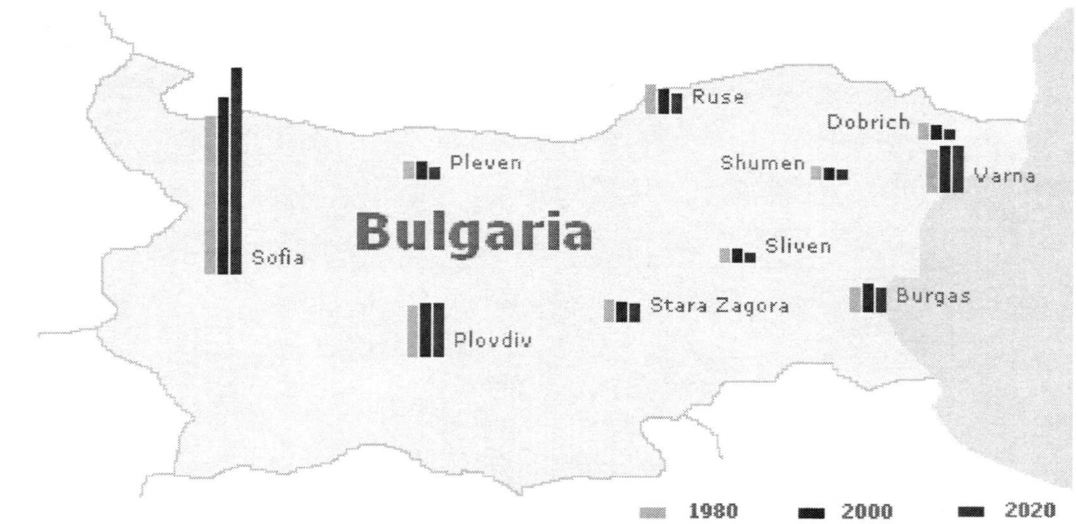

Canada

Table 5.1 Key population trends

'000

	1980	1985	1990	1995	2000	2005	2010	2015	2020	CAGR	Period growth
Population at January 1st	24,516.1	25,842.7	27,697.5	29,302.1	30,689.0	32,312.1	33,967.8	35,286.6	36,588.9	1.01	49.24
Male	12,210.8	12,831.3	13,731.8	14,503.3	15,196.7	16,003.8	16,829.7	17,557.6	18,275.1	1.01	49.66
Female	12,305.2	13,011.5	13,965.8	14,798.8	15,492.3	16,308.3	17,138.1	17,729.0	18,313.8	1.00	48.83
0-4 yrs	1,791.7	1,846.6	1,931.3	1,984.5	1,791.2	1,703.3	1,818.6	1,845.1	1,948.7	0.21	8.76
5-9 yrs	1,812.5	1,816.0	1,923.3	1,991.9	2,036.8	1,885.7	1,782.4	1,888.6	1,916.9	0.14	5.76
10-14 yrs	1,970.3	1,840.5	1,877.4	1,996.7	2,055.6	2,108.6	1,959.4	1,838.4	1,948.8	-0.03	-1.09
15-19 yrs	2,417.7	2,018.2	1,938.1	1,980.1	2,095.7	2,148.3	2,204.0	2,034.0	1,908.5	-0.59	-21.06
20-24 yrs	2,424.5	2,498.5	2,124.4	2,009.5	2,069.9	2,246.4	2,310.3	2,355.3	2,174.3	-0.27	-10.32
25-29 yrs	2,205.9	2,440.9	2,582.7	2,184.9	2,075.7	2,198.6	2,380.6	2,433.0	2,481.2	0.29	12.48
30-34 yrs	2,020.7	2,226.4	2,536.2	2,624.6	2,257.0	2,228.1	2,336.6	2,512.8	2,568.9	0.60	27.13
35-39 yrs	1,602.0	2,012.5	2,288.8	2,570.8	2,684.8	2,367.9	2,337.8	2,432.7	2,617.0	1.23	63.36
40-44 yrs	1,328.0	1,594.2	2,054.6	2,306.1	2,601.1	2,747.5	2,436.8	2,387.3	2,485.4	1.58	87.15
45-49 yrs	1,268.1	1,305.0	1,599.6	2,058.3	2,314.8	2,620.8	2,776.5	2,444.5	2,395.7	1.60	88.93
50-54 yrs	1,241.0	1,249.5	1,301.8	1,583.6	2,043.1	2,302.6	2,615.6	2,749.9	2,421.9	1.69	95.15
55-59 yrs	1,175.3	1,217.9	1,236.7	1,293.6	1,556.6	2,012.8	2,273.8	2,563.4	2,695.6	2.10	129.35
60-64 yrs	952.7	1,127.0	1,181.8	1,208.0	1,253.9	1,515.7	1,963.1	2,201.0	2,481.8	2.42	160.51
65-69 yrs	831.1	890.3	1,070.5	1,112.1	1,141.5	1,194.8	1,447.9	1,861.2	2,087.4	2.33	151.17
70-74 yrs	615.4	731.9	799.5	956.4	1,004.7	1,044.6	1,101.3	1,324.9	1,703.4	2.58	176.78
75-79 yrs	421.0	500.2	607.8	660.9	804.2	865.9	907.5	950.4	1,144.0	2.53	171.75
80+ yrs	438.3	527.1	643.0	780.0	902.5	1,120.7	1,315.7	1,464.2	1,609.4	3.31	267.22
Median age of population (years)	29.1	31.0	32.9	34.8	36.8	38.5	39.7	40.6	41.4	0.88	42.19

Table 5.2 Key economic trends

As stated

	1990	1995	2000	2005	2010	2015	2020	CAGR	Period growth
Total GDP (C$ per capita)	35,898.7	36,967.7	43,217.9	46,582.3	46,621.3	51,272.8	54,838.6	1.42	52.8
Disposable income (C$ per capita)	22,112.4	21,859.4	24,678.4	26,537.4	27,936.6	30,265.2	31,818.9	1.22	43.9
Disposable income (C$ per household)	62,352.4	59,978.9	66,524.3	69,840.8	72,620.3	77,159.9	79,763.3	0.82	27.9
Number of households by annual household disposable income ('000)									
Over US$1,000	9,817.9	10,669.7	11,372.1	12,272.3	13,060.0	13,833.8	14,589.0	1.33	48.6
Over US$10,000	9,230.2	9,770.2	10,453.0	11,770.1	12,489.7	13,349.7	14,160.9	1.44	53.4
Over US$25,000	6,509.3	6,354.0	7,233.6	9,567.9	10,192.5	11,440.3	12,515.5	2.20	92.3
Over US$75,000	765.6	689.0	1,075.1	2,598.2	3,007.0	4,421.7	5,828.0	7.00	661.2
Over US$150,000	221.9	213.0	262.9	470.2	524.6	962.5	1,580.1	6.76	612.0
Total households	9,822.5	10,679.2	11,384.7	12,277.6	13,067.2	13,840.8	14,595.9	1.33	48.6

Note: Per capita data is shown at constant 2010 prices. Household disposable income bands are shown at current prices.

Table 5.3 Young generation

'000

	1980	1985	1990	1995	2000	2005	2010	2015	2020	CAGR	Period growth
Babies under 12 months	365.2	370.3	403.4	381.8	339.0	338.6	362.5	370.7	389.9	0.16	6.74
Infants under 24 months	723.1	739.0	789.4	769.3	683.2	680.1	729.7	740.7	780.4	0.19	7.92
Toddlers aged 1-4	1,426.4	1,476.2	1,527.9	1,602.7	1,452.2	1,364.7	1,456.1	1,474.4	1,558.8	0.22	9.28
Children aged 2-9	2,881.0	2,923.6	3,065.2	3,207.2	3,144.8	2,909.0	2,871.2	2,993.1	3,085.1	0.17	7.09
Female	1,402.3	1,423.2	1,494.1	1,564.1	1,534.2	1,421.1	1,400.9	1,454.2	1,497.2	0.16	6.77
Male	1,478.7	1,500.4	1,571.1	1,643.0	1,610.6	1,487.8	1,470.4	1,538.9	1,587.9	0.18	7.38
Tweenagers aged 10-14	1,970.3	1,840.5	1,877.4	1,996.7	2,055.6	2,108.6	1,959.4	1,838.4	1,948.8	-0.03	-1.09
Female	960.3	898.3	914.2	972.0	1,002.4	1,027.4	955.1	890.7	938.9	-0.06	-2.22
Male	1,010.0	942.2	963.2	1,024.7	1,053.2	1,081.2	1,004.3	947.7	1,009.9	0.00	-0.02
Teenagers aged 13-19	3,242.4	2,780.8	2,689.1	2,779.3	2,916.2	3,014.6	3,022.2	2,769.6	2,678.6	-0.48	-17.39
Female	1,586.2	1,353.1	1,309.2	1,351.4	1,418.1	1,470.0	1,470.3	1,341.2	1,288.8	-0.52	-18.75
Male	1,656.2	1,427.7	1,379.9	1,428.0	1,498.1	1,544.6	1,552.0	1,428.4	1,389.8	-0.44	-16.09
Studying age 18-22	2,462.0	2,335.6	2,043.0	1,976.3	2,089.5	2,210.6	2,299.5	2,237.8	2,031.0	-0.48	-17.51
Female	1,214.7	1,139.9	999.7	965.8	1,018.2	1,077.4	1,121.7	1,083.0	978.9	-0.54	-19.42
Male	1,247.2	1,195.7	1,043.3	1,010.5	1,071.3	1,133.2	1,177.8	1,154.8	1,052.1	-0.42	-15.64
Young adults aged 15-29	7,048.1	6,957.6	6,645.2	6,174.5	6,241.3	6,593.3	6,894.9	6,822.3	6,564.0	-0.18	-6.87
Female	3,483.9	3,416.4	3,261.1	3,030.5	3,052.9	3,230.4	3,375.5	3,321.6	3,175.3	-0.23	-8.86
Male	3,564.2	3,541.2	3,384.2	3,144.0	3,188.4	3,363.0	3,519.4	3,500.7	3,388.7	-0.13	-4.92

Table 5.4 Middle-aged generation

'000

	1980	1985	1990	1995	2000	2005	2010	2015	2020	CAGR	Period growth
Middle-aged adults 30-59	8,635	9,606	11,018	12,437	13,457	14,280	14,777	15,090	15,185	1.42	75.8
Female	4,291	4,782	5,487	6,215	6,726	7,140	7,391	7,507	7,515	1.41	75.1
Male	4,344	4,824	5,531	6,222	6,731	7,140	7,387	7,584	7,669	1.43	76.6
Baby boomers aged 40-59	5,012	5,367	6,193	7,242	8,516	9,684	10,103	10,145	9,999	1.74	99.5
Female	2,507	2,672	3,081	3,632	4,275	4,859	5,066	5,054	4,959	1.72	97.8
Male	2,505	2,694	3,112	3,610	4,240	4,824	5,037	5,091	5,040	1.76	101.2

Table 5.5 Elderly population

'000

	1980	1985	1990	1995	2000	2005	2010	2015	2020	CAGR	Period growth
Elderly population (60+)	3,258	3,777	4,303	4,717	5,107	5,742	6,736	7,802	9,026	2.58	177.0
Female	1,815	2,132	2,424	2,643	2,843	3,158	3,660	4,194	4,806	2.46	164.7
Male	1,443	1,644	1,878	2,075	2,264	2,583	3,075	3,607	4,220	2.72	192.4

Table 5.6 Population of biggest cities 1980-2020

'000

	1980	1985	1990	1995	2000	2005	2010	2015	2020	CAGR	Period growth
Toronto	3,136.9	3,334.2	3,576.3	3,846.3	4,290.0	4,683.4	5,000.3	5,285.6	5,563.3	1.44	77.4
Montreal	2,618.2	2,762.9	2,903.5	2,973.5	3,130.3	3,286.1	3,445.1	3,618.4	3,799.7	0.94	45.1
Vancouver	1,173.8	1,260.3	1,389.5	1,577.3	1,792.9	1,938.6	2,026.7	2,126.9	2,232.9	1.62	90.2
Calgary	622.5	660.1	703.1	749.2	857.2	966.5	1,054.5	1,122.8	1,184.8	1.62	90.3
Edmonton	648.3	681.1	706.5	707.5	767.1	845.5	915.3	971.9	1,024.6	1.15	58.0
Ottawa - Gatineau	661.1	700.4	744.1	779.7	826.0	857.5	885.4	924.9	969.4	0.96	46.6
Quebec	522.7	552.8	584.3	604.6	630.4	654.9	682.0	714.6	749.8	0.91	43.4
Hamilton	495.9	523.9	552.3	570.8	612.5	643.4	669.9	702.0	736.5	0.99	48.5
Winnipeg	559.5	589.4	616.4	621.2	625.7	637.7	660.9	691.3	724.8	0.65	29.5
London	273.6	289.9	308.0	322.0	335.2	349.8	366.5	384.8	404.1	0.98	47.7

Chart 5.34 Population age shift 2000 and 2020, Each Column Represents a Single Age Group

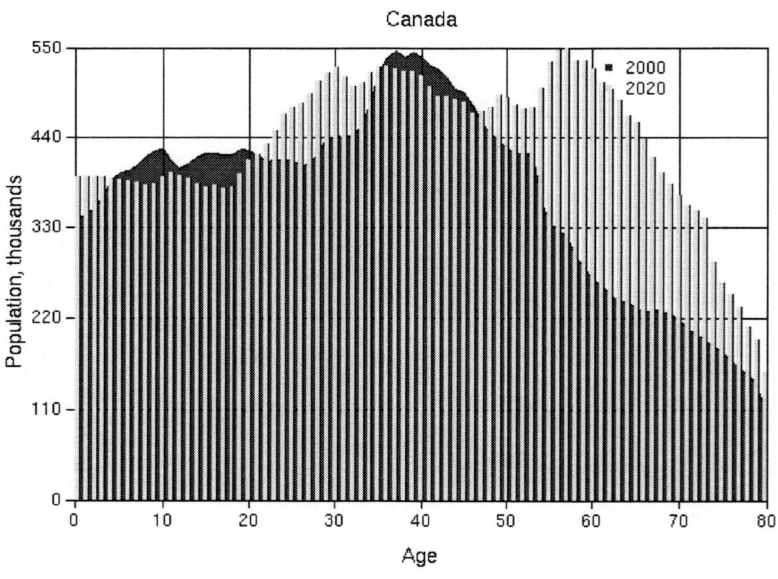

Chart 5.35 Population pyramids, 1980/2000/2010/2020

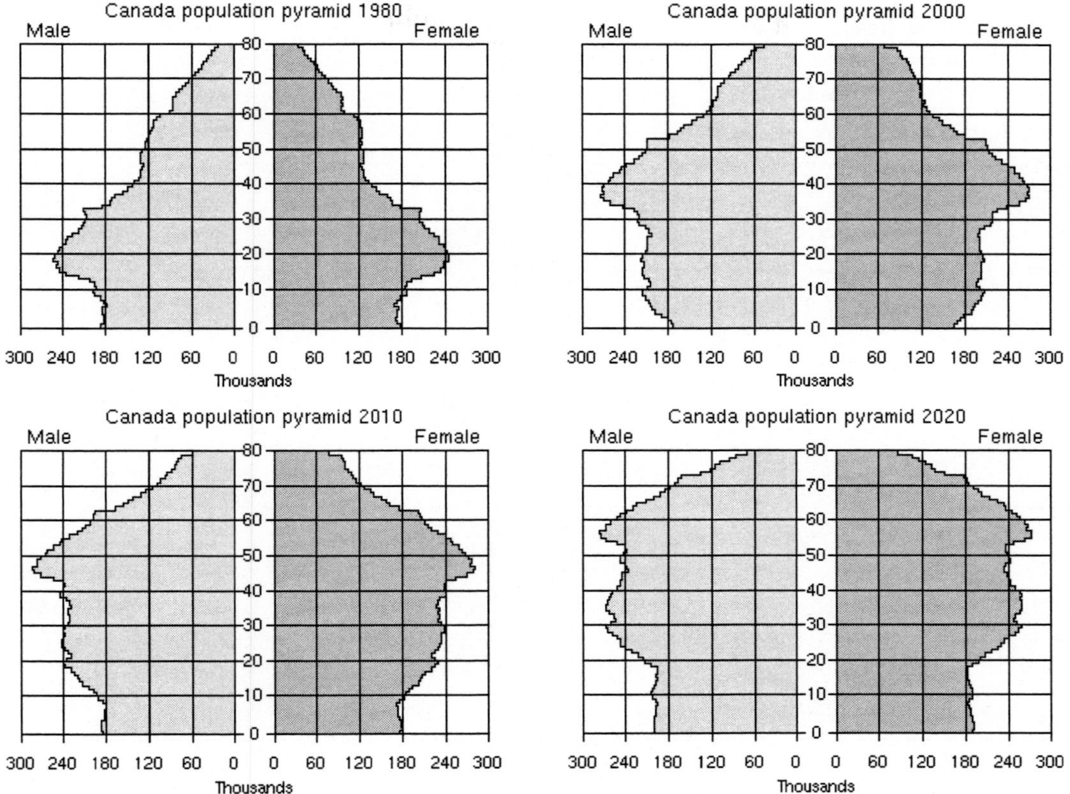

Chart 5.36 Major Cities: 1980, 2000 and 2020

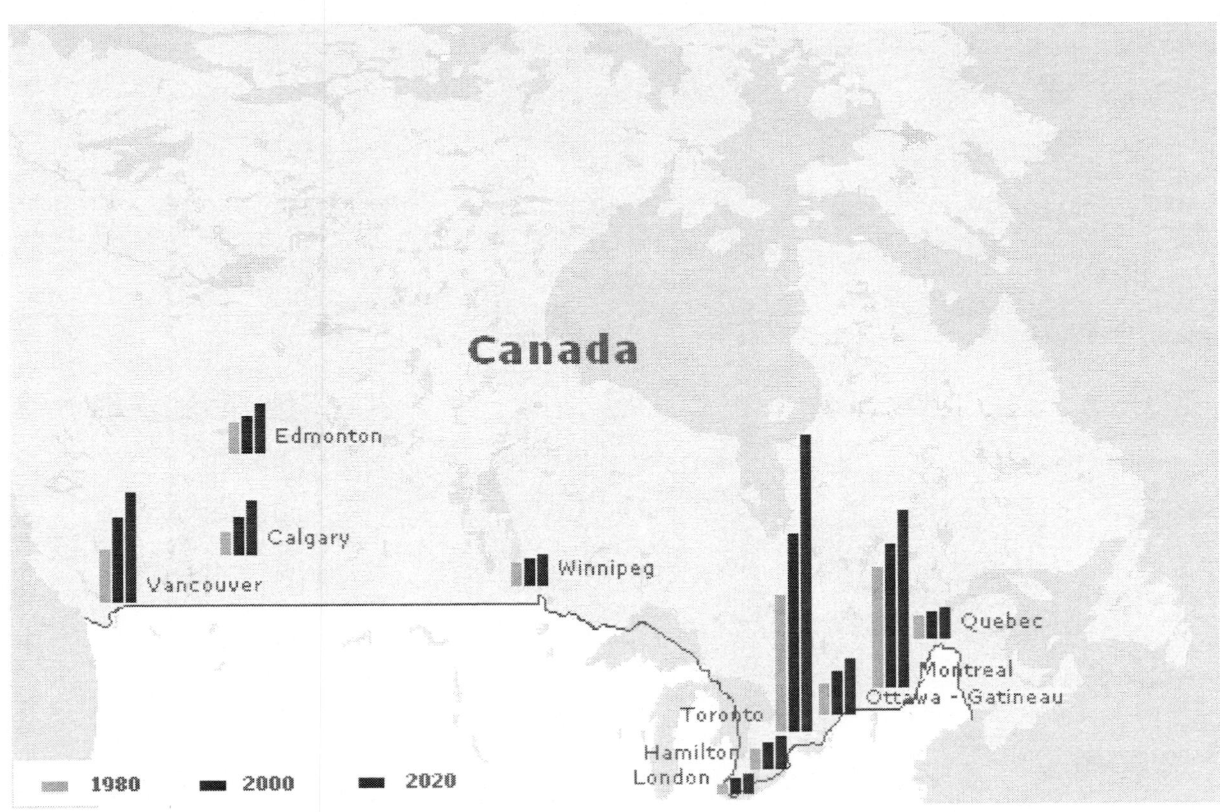

Chile

Table 5.7 Key population trends

'000

	1980	1985	1990	1995	2000	2005	2010	2015	2020	CAGR	Period growth
Population at January 1st	11,181.4	12,110.6	13,190.5	14,410.0	15,418.7	16,297.5	17,134.7	17,925.5	18,639.0	1.29	66.70
Male	5,515.1	5,975.6	6,514.8	7,124.9	7,625.9	8,061.5	8,473.9	8,860.2	9,204.0	1.29	66.89
Female	5,666.2	6,135.0	6,675.7	7,285.1	7,792.8	8,236.0	8,660.8	9,065.4	9,435.0	1.28	66.51
0-4 yrs	1,174.8	1,326.9	1,461.5	1,486.7	1,324.0	1,238.0	1,251.9	1,260.3	1,247.2	0.15	6.16
5-9 yrs	1,244.0	1,177.2	1,311.2	1,463.9	1,486.3	1,332.0	1,236.2	1,247.4	1,261.5	0.03	1.41
10-14 yrs	1,269.4	1,234.4	1,173.7	1,317.1	1,466.2	1,484.4	1,332.2	1,238.9	1,248.8	-0.04	-1.63
15-19 yrs	1,298.9	1,257.8	1,227.3	1,178.0	1,319.3	1,465.6	1,484.1	1,332.4	1,239.7	-0.12	-4.56
20-24 yrs	1,142.3	1,279.2	1,245.5	1,232.3	1,180.7	1,318.0	1,464.7	1,483.9	1,332.9	0.39	16.68
25-29 yrs	912.3	1,119.6	1,263.7	1,250.0	1,234.4	1,178.9	1,316.5	1,463.5	1,483.1	1.22	62.57
30-34 yrs	767.0	896.3	1,107.6	1,266.9	1,250.9	1,231.5	1,177.2	1,315.0	1,461.8	1.63	90.59
35-39 yrs	659.1	752.0	885.0	1,108.6	1,264.9	1,246.1	1,227.8	1,174.5	1,311.9	1.74	99.06
40-44 yrs	537.8	644.3	740.4	882.8	1,103.2	1,256.5	1,238.9	1,221.6	1,169.1	1.96	117.40
45-49 yrs	483.2	522.9	631.3	734.2	874.3	1,091.2	1,243.9	1,227.6	1,211.1	2.32	150.63
50-54 yrs	427.5	465.0	507.6	620.5	721.3	859.0	1,073.4	1,224.8	1,209.7	2.63	182.97
55-59 yrs	347.9	404.3	444.5	491.7	601.5	700.8	836.2	1,046.5	1,195.4	3.13	243.60
60-64 yrs	289.0	321.7	378.2	421.0	467.6	574.7	671.4	803.1	1,007.0	3.17	248.38
65-69 yrs	231.5	258.0	291.0	346.8	388.5	435.0	537.1	629.6	755.5	3.00	226.33
70-74 yrs	178.9	194.2	220.6	253.1	305.2	347.0	391.2	485.7	572.0	2.95	219.69
75-79 yrs	114.4	135.6	151.5	176.6	206.8	256.0	293.7	334.3	418.2	3.29	265.43
80+ yrs	103.2	121.3	150.0	180.1	223.7	282.8	358.4	436.3	514.2	4.10	398.12
Median age of population (years)	22.5	24.1	25.7	27.1	28.8	30.5	32.0	33.5	35.2	1.12	56.14

Table 5.8 Key economic trends

As stated

	1990	1995	2000	2005	2010	2015	2020	CAGR	Period growth
Total GDP (CLP per capita)	2,493,490.5	3,464,997.3	3,988,960.0	4,645,135.4	5,103,144.2	6,270,243.0	7,956,796.5	3.94	219.1
Disposable income (CLP per capita)	1,670,017.7	2,449,498.7	2,689,897.9	3,333,221.0	4,031,787.6	5,064,105.8	6,480,400.7	4.62	288.0
Disposable income (CLP per household)	7,083,320.8	9,888,886.6	10,413,256.3	12,404,881.2	14,408,300.7	17,349,881.0	21,246,565.7	3.73	200.0
Number of households by annual household disposable income ('000)									
Over US$1,000	2,710.6	3,562.4	3,978.8	4,376.2	4,793.5	5,231.7	5,684.9	2.50	109.7
Over US$10,000	507.6	1,475.5	1,806.4	3,096.1	4,103.9	4,954.4	5,562.2	8.31	995.9
Over US$25,000	118.7	348.4	390.2	801.9	1,547.7	2,984.6	4,327.6	12.73	3,544.7
Over US$75,000	19.2	60.2	63.0	99.4	168.5	376.1	777.5	13.13	3,953.6
Over US$150,000	8.5	24.5	26.9	41.8	64.9	112.7	184.0	10.80	2,071.5
Total households	3,109.9	3,569.4	3,982.9	4,379.2	4,794.7	5,232.1	5,685.1	2.03	82.8

Note: Per capita data is shown at constant 2010 prices. Household disposable income bands are shown at current prices.

Table 5.9 Young generation

'000

	1980	1985	1990	1995	2000	2005	2010	2015	2020	CAGR	Period growth
Babies under 12 months	224.1	297.1	295.0	290.5	241.8	252.1	256.5	249.8	246.7	0.24	10.10
Infants under 24 months	455.0	573.9	592.3	585.8	496.5	498.7	509.9	501.7	494.9	0.21	8.75
Toddlers aged 1-4	950.8	1,029.8	1,166.4	1,196.2	1,082.1	985.9	995.4	1,010.5	1,000.5	0.13	5.23
Children aged 2-9	1,963.8	1,930.2	2,180.4	2,364.7	2,313.7	2,071.3	1,978.1	2,006.0	2,013.9	0.06	2.55
Female	968.5	949.9	1,071.2	1,161.5	1,136.2	1,016.9	970.9	984.4	988.2	0.05	2.03
Male	995.3	980.3	1,109.2	1,203.2	1,177.5	1,054.4	1,007.3	1,021.6	1,025.7	0.08	3.05
Tweenagers aged 10-14	1,269.4	1,234.4	1,173.7	1,317.1	1,466.2	1,484.4	1,332.2	1,238.9	1,248.8	-0.04	-1.63
Female	627.9	609.3	578.2	647.5	720.6	729.3	654.3	608.3	613.0	-0.06	-2.37
Male	641.5	625.1	595.6	669.6	745.7	755.2	677.9	630.6	635.7	-0.02	-0.90
Teenagers aged 13-19	1,812.0	1,758.1	1,694.6	1,682.3	1,893.3	2,068.8	2,036.6	1,832.0	1,736.1	-0.11	-4.19
Female	898.2	869.7	836.6	828.8	931.3	1,017.2	1,001.1	900.2	852.8	-0.13	-5.06
Male	913.8	888.4	858.0	853.5	961.9	1,051.6	1,035.5	931.8	883.3	-0.08	-3.34
Studying age 18-22	1,226.7	1,282.5	1,240.7	1,202.3	1,215.6	1,386.8	1,494.7	1,433.7	1,280.0	0.11	4.35
Female	609.0	635.9	614.0	594.5	599.6	683.0	735.8	705.5	629.6	0.08	3.38
Male	617.7	646.6	626.7	607.9	616.0	703.9	758.9	728.3	650.4	0.13	5.30
Young adults aged 15-29	3,353.5	3,656.6	3,736.6	3,660.3	3,734.4	3,962.5	4,265.3	4,279.9	4,055.7	0.48	20.94
Female	1,666.8	1,815.4	1,852.7	1,813.1	1,846.5	1,955.2	2,102.3	2,108.5	1,997.3	0.45	19.82
Male	1,686.7	1,841.2	1,883.9	1,847.3	1,887.9	2,007.2	2,163.0	2,171.4	2,058.4	0.50	22.04

Table 5.10 Middle-aged generation

'000

	1980	1985	1990	1995	2000	2005	2010	2015	2020	CAGR	Period growth
Middle-aged adults 30-59	3,222.4	3,684.8	4,316.4	5,104.6	5,816.1	6,385.1	6,797.5	7,210.0	7,559.0	2.15	134.6
Female	1,656.5	1,886.7	2,197.6	2,585.1	2,938.5	3,220.4	3,424.0	3,626.2	3,794.2	2.09	129.1
Male	1,565.9	1,798.1	2,118.8	2,519.4	2,877.6	3,164.7	3,373.4	3,583.7	3,764.8	2.22	140.4
Baby boomers aged 40-59	1,796.4	2,036.6	2,323.8	2,729.1	3,300.3	3,907.5	4,392.4	4,720.5	4,785.3	2.48	166.4
Female	937.4	1,058.9	1,199.6	1,396.7	1,680.1	1,982.4	2,225.0	2,389.2	2,418.8	2.40	158.0
Male	859.0	977.7	1,124.2	1,332.4	1,620.2	1,925.0	2,167.5	2,331.3	2,366.5	2.57	175.5

Table 5.11 Elderly population

'000

	1980	1985	1990	1995	2000	2005	2010	2015	2020	CAGR	Period growth
Elderly population (60+)	917.1	1,030.7	1,191.2	1,377.5	1,591.7	1,895.5	2,251.7	2,689.0	3,266.8	3.23	256.2
Female	522.7	591.9	685.3	790.4	907.3	1,069.5	1,259.1	1,491.8	1,799.5	3.14	244.3
Male	394.4	438.8	506.0	587.0	684.4	826.0	992.6	1,197.2	1,467.3	3.34	272.0

Table 5.12 Population of biggest cities 1980-2020

'000

	1980	1985	1990	1995	2000	2005	2010	2015	2020	CAGR	Period growth
Santiago	3,529.0	3,843.0	4,163.4	4,470.1	4,628.0	4,734.8	4,923.9	5,152.9	5,398.7	1.07	52.98
Puente Alto	96.3	143.0	216.8	317.4	438.4	566.9	679.9	780.5	870.0	5.66	803.51
Antofagasta	177.2	193.2	214.5	243.0	272.7	303.9	334.9	364.9	393.3	2.01	121.98
Vina del Mar	259.6	271.3	281.0	289.7	289.0	286.7	291.2	299.4	309.7	0.44	19.31
Temuco	152.8	163.7	178.5	198.5	218.8	239.8	261.5	282.9	303.4	1.73	98.53
Valparaiso	260.7	268.4	272.7	275.4	268.5	259.3	257.9	260.9	266.6	0.06	2.24
Concepcion	273.4	241.1	210.1	197.5	203.2	224.7	246.3	267.6	287.7	0.13	5.23
Rancagua	133.4	151.6	171.7	191.1	203.7	213.0	225.0	238.2	251.5	1.60	88.50
Talcahuano	123.5	137.1	152.9	170.4	184.6	197.5	212.0	226.9	241.6	1.69	95.66
Arica	134.7	145.4	156.5	167.7	174.1	178.7	186.4	195.4	205.0	1.05	52.14

Chart 5.37 Population age shift 2000 and 2020, Each Column Represents a Single Age Group

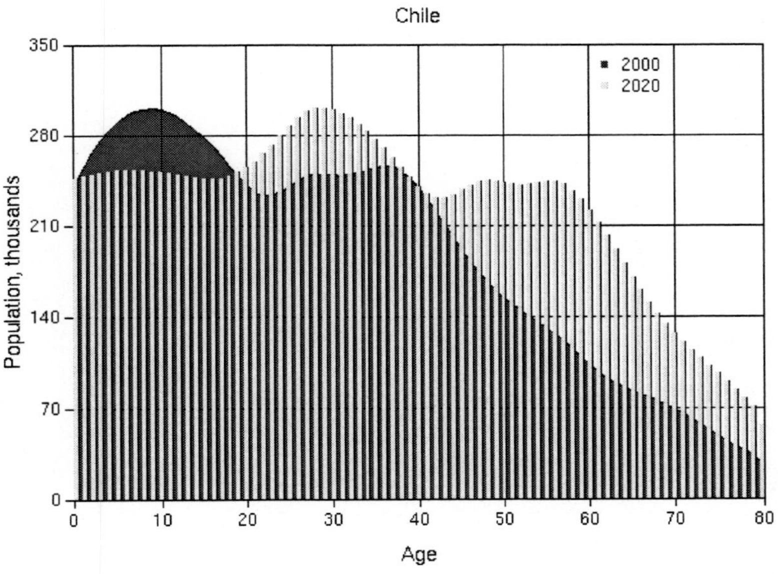

Chart 5.38 Population pyramids, 1980/2000/2010/2020

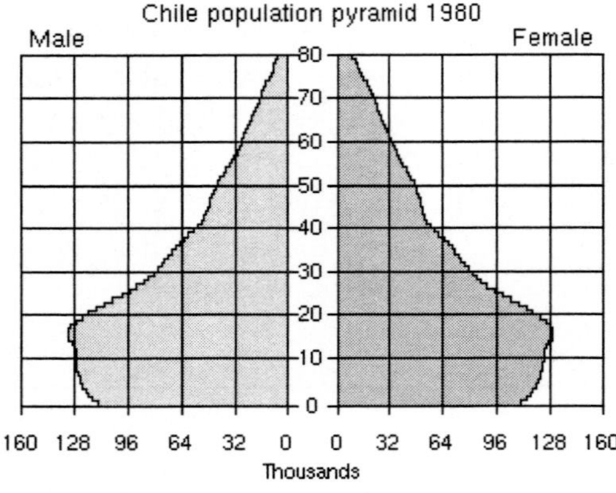

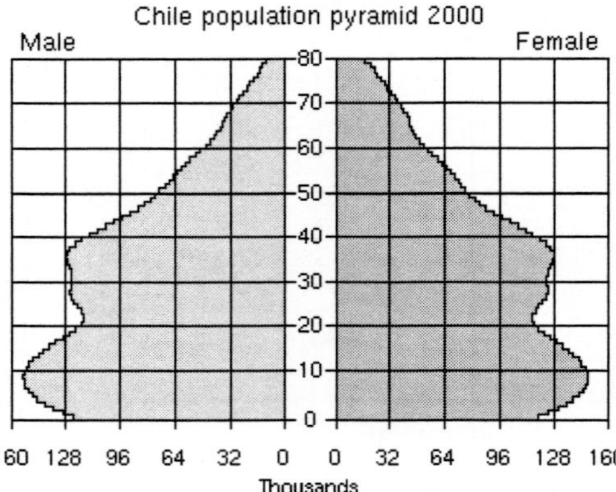

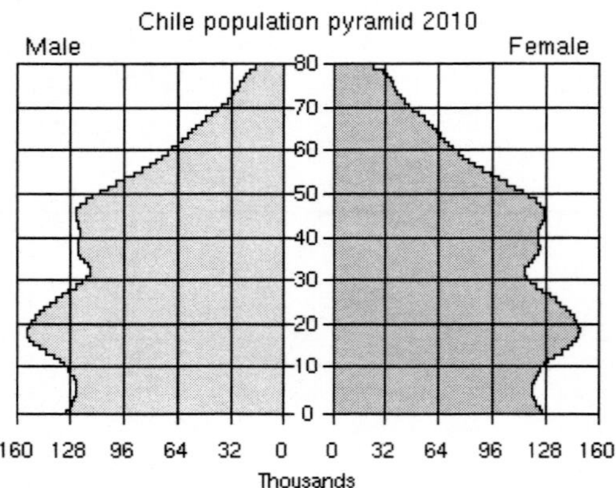

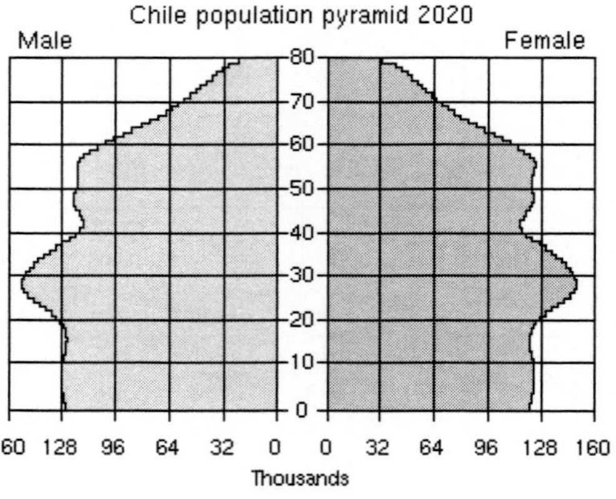

Chart 5.39 Major Cities: 1980, 2000 and 2020

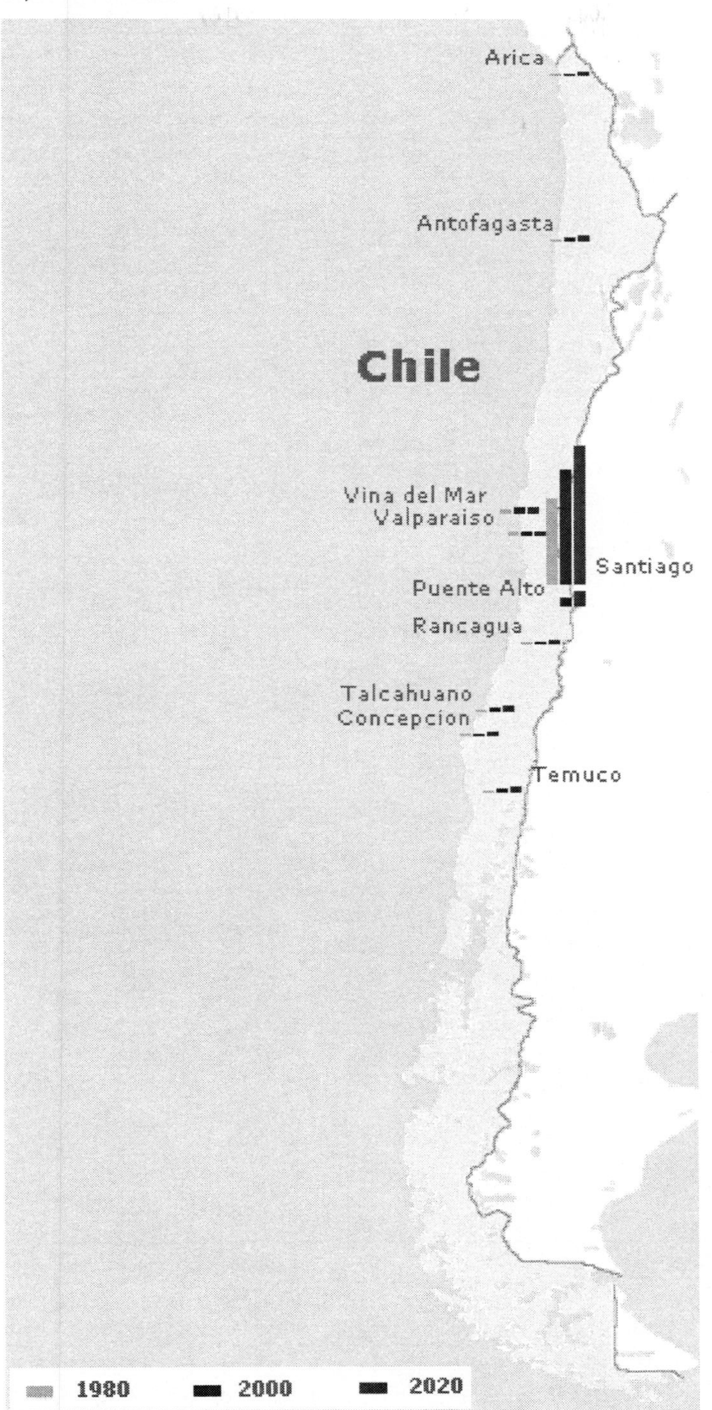

China

Table 5.13 Key population trends

'000

	1980	1985	1990	1995	2000	2005	2010	2015	2020	CAGR	Period growth
Population at January 1st	975,420.0	1,043,570.0	1,127,040.0	1,198,500.0	1,257,860.0	1,299,880.0	1,334,418.0	1,361,826.4	1,383,260.7	0.88	41.81
Male	501,920.0	538,480.0	580,990.0	612,460.0	646,920.0	669,760.0	687,411.4	701,691.8	712,333.3	0.88	41.92
Female	473,500.0	505,090.0	546,050.0	586,040.0	610,940.0	630,120.0	647,006.7	660,134.6	670,927.3	0.88	41.70
0-4 yrs	94,743.4	95,962.2	116,130.2	87,365.7	70,699.6	69,542.5	65,900.8	65,832.3	65,003.6	-0.94	-31.39
5-9 yrs	122,739.3	96,871.0	99,017.2	127,960.1	94,301.1	81,293.2	70,358.9	69,362.9	71,833.0	-1.33	-41.48
10-14 yrs	129,007.1	123,435.5	97,040.3	105,131.3	131,111.1	103,674.9	82,137.5	73,450.7	75,052.9	-1.35	-41.82
15-19 yrs	105,081.4	123,500.6	119,888.0	88,458.1	99,999.1	110,525.1	91,402.7	74,890.0	69,560.5	-1.03	-33.80
20-24 yrs	84,377.9	103,212.2	125,337.6	104,713.0	88,134.3	79,265.7	110,058.3	91,783.4	77,909.7	-0.20	-7.67
25-29 yrs	88,813.0	83,543.4	103,821.9	121,885.2	112,829.4	84,902.0	84,046.8	116,925.9	98,540.0	0.26	10.95
30-34 yrs	65,112.8	86,318.6	83,448.8	105,712.1	125,986.2	110,592.4	83,500.7	83,582.3	116,762.7	1.47	79.32
35-39 yrs	51,033.7	64,118.8	85,946.5	83,283.2	110,658.3	126,319.5	109,804.8	83,339.6	83,596.9	1.24	63.81
40-44 yrs	47,887.3	49,810.5	63,573.2	88,862.6	83,840.0	112,879.9	131,432.4	114,355.8	87,000.2	1.50	81.68
45-49 yrs	44,984.5	47,426.3	48,973.1	66,402.9	89,265.0	87,809.0	115,693.0	133,697.9	116,519.4	2.41	159.02
50-54 yrs	38,161.9	44,693.7	45,473.3	50,797.2	66,140.5	94,651.9	93,745.8	119,405.5	137,638.4	3.26	260.67
55-59 yrs	32,109.2	37,915.0	41,576.1	46,113.0	48,578.1	69,455.2	98,510.5	94,031.9	117,509.0	3.30	265.97
60-64 yrs	25,457.3	31,006.1	33,911.5	41,593.9	43,626.7	51,158.4	68,282.2	92,050.0	84,763.4	3.05	232.96
65-69 yrs	19,466.6	23,185.9	26,279.7	32,736.8	36,689.1	43,172.0	45,742.4	58,277.4	76,238.6	3.47	291.64
70-74 yrs	13,363.2	16,545.2	18,037.9	23,515.6	26,845.3	34,798.7	37,153.1	38,069.1	47,579.0	3.23	256.05
75-79 yrs	8,132.9	10,045.7	10,920.5	13,775.6	16,709.6	22,173.0	25,209.4	26,555.9	27,154.4	3.06	233.88
80+ yrs	4,948.4	5,979.3	7,664.2	10,193.9	12,446.6	17,666.7	21,438.9	26,215.9	30,598.9	4.66	518.36
Median age of population (years)	22.4	23.4	25.2	28.4	31.2	35.4	38.8	41.1	42.0	1.58	87.30

Table 5.14 Key economic trends

As stated

	1990	1995	2000	2005	2010	2015	2020	CAGR	Period growth
Total GDP (RMB per capita)	4,595.4	7,712.0	11,108.0	16,984.7	26,910.3	41,754.4	63,132.0	9.13	1,273.8
Disposable income (RMB per capita)	2,826.4	4,232.1	5,525.0	9,123.7	14,320.7	21,965.0	32,432.6	8.47	1,047.5
Disposable income (RMB per household)	11,503.6	16,029.7	19,948.9	31,887.8	48,612.8	72,404.7	104,264.3	7.62	806.4
Number of households by annual household disposable income ('000)									
Over US$1,000	98,106.4	189,665.1	256,246.3	306,263.6	363,033.0	398,742.2	424,556.5	5.00	332.8
Over US$10,000	2,070.3	3,815.3	6,132.9	18,783.4	57,116.6	121,880.2	221,426.8	16.85	10,595.2
Over US$25,000	649.8	1,203.5	1,969.6	4,126.1	11,422.8	28,469.1	68,307.5	16.79	10,412.8
Over US$75,000	161.9	301.7	504.6	1,095.1	2,322.4	4,590.1	10,494.1	14.92	6,380.8
Over US$150,000	67.4	126.1	213.7	474.2	1,018.7	1,915.9	3,683.7	14.27	5,366.3
Total households	276,911.0	316,423.1	348,371.0	371,918.6	393,101.3	413,128.9	430,279.5	1.48	55.4

Note: Per capita data is shown at constant 2010 prices. Household disposable income bands are shown at current prices.

Table 5.15 Young generation

'000

	1980	1985	1990	1995	2000	2005	2010	2015	2020	CAGR	Period growth
Babies under 12 months	17,628	18,981	23,176	16,703	13,904	13,979	13,955	13,687	12,951	-0.77	-26.53
Infants under 24 months	36,748	36,860	46,466	31,211	25,761	27,683	26,837	26,341	25,190	-0.94	-31.45
Toddlers aged 1-4	77,115	76,981	92,954	70,663	56,796	55,564	51,945	52,145	52,052	-0.98	-32.50
Children aged 2-9	180,735	155,973	168,681	184,115	139,239	123,153	109,423	108,854	111,647	-1.20	-38.23
Female	87,728	74,447	80,671	86,239	63,821	54,603	48,728	47,998	49,548	-1.42	-43.52
Male	93,006	81,526	88,010	97,875	75,418	68,550	60,695	60,856	62,098	-1.00	-33.23
Tweenagers aged 10-14	129,007	123,436	97,040	105,131	131,111	103,675	82,137	73,451	75,053	-1.35	-41.82
Female	62,361	59,294	46,828	50,351	62,293	47,387	36,773	33,646	33,784	-1.52	-45.83
Male	66,646	64,141	50,213	54,781	68,818	56,288	45,365	39,805	41,269	-1.19	-38.08
Teenagers aged 13-19	154,502	175,770	159,630	131,648	151,701	155,308	126,311	105,264	99,305	-1.10	-35.73
Female	75,672	85,498	77,425	63,447	72,788	72,648	57,082	47,193	45,109	-1.28	-40.39
Male	78,831	90,273	82,205	68,201	78,913	82,661	69,229	58,070	54,196	-0.93	-31.25
Studying age 18-22	74,353	122,651	127,825	91,274	91,688	83,489	104,997	80,772	70,752	-0.12	-4.84
Female	36,687	60,308	62,338	45,455	45,165	41,209	50,246	37,719	32,801	-0.28	-10.59
Male	37,666	62,343	65,487	45,819	46,523	42,280	54,751	43,054	37,951	0.02	0.76
Young adults aged 15-29	278,272	310,256	349,048	315,056	300,963	274,693	285,508	283,599	246,010	-0.31	-11.59
Female	135,646	151,083	169,815	156,338	147,852	135,180	138,140	135,069	115,455	-0.40	-14.88
Male	142,626	159,174	179,233	158,718	153,111	139,512	147,368	148,531	130,555	-0.22	-8.46

Table 5.16 Middle-aged generation

'000

	1980	1985	1990	1995	2000	2005	2010	2015	2020	CAGR	Period growth
Middle-aged adults 30-59	279,289	330,283	368,991	441,171	524,468	601,708	632,687	628,413	659,027	2.17	136.0
Female	131,465	157,418	176,134	215,732	255,771	296,053	312,624	310,007	325,055	2.29	147.3
Male	147,824	172,865	192,857	225,439	268,697	305,654	320,063	318,406	333,971	2.06	125.9
Baby boomers aged 40-59	163,143	179,846	199,596	252,176	287,824	364,796	439,382	461,491	458,667	2.62	181.1
Female	76,840	85,048	94,607	122,655	139,335	178,050	216,403	227,581	227,372	2.75	195.9
Male	86,303	94,798	104,989	129,520	148,488	186,746	222,979	233,910	231,295	2.50	168.0

Table 5.17 Elderly population

'000

	1980	1985	1990	1995	2000	2005	2010	2015	2020	CAGR	Period growth
Elderly population (60+)	71,368	86,762	96,814	121,816	136,317	168,969	197,826	241,168	266,334	3.35	273.2
Female	38,522	45,533	50,697	63,169	69,572	84,665	99,007	121,846	135,896	3.20	252.8
Male	32,846	41,229	46,117	58,647	66,745	84,304	98,819	119,322	130,439	3.51	297.1

Table 5.18 Population of biggest cities 1980-2020

'000

	1980	1985	1990	1995	2000	2005	2010	2015	2020	CAGR	Period growth
Shanghai	6,865	7,674	7,650	7,393	9,400	10,933	11,962	12,702	13,165	1.64	91.8
Beijing	3,976	4,831	5,715	6,526	7,509	7,936	8,340	8,684	8,950	2.05	125.1
Guangzhou	2,816	3,128	2,892	2,382	3,695	5,691	6,958	7,782	8,299	2.74	194.7
Chongqing	2,084	2,309	2,265	2,276	3,533	5,130	6,293	7,147	7,731	3.33	271.0
Tianjin	3,722	4,237	4,521	4,803	5,240	5,394	5,988	6,457	6,785	1.51	82.3
Wuhan	2,811	3,158	3,177	3,135	4,239	5,171	5,879	6,429	6,820	2.24	142.7
Nanjing	2,130	2,290	2,114	1,893	2,582	3,473	4,154	4,691	5,084	2.20	138.7
Shenyang	3,158	3,555	3,588	3,441	3,944	4,080	4,134	4,170	4,187	0.71	32.6
Xi'an	2,007	2,192	2,089	1,912	2,428	2,951	3,299	3,556	3,731	1.56	85.9
Harbin	2,299	2,538	2,468	2,272	2,638	2,850	2,976	3,056	3,101	0.75	34.9

Chart 5.40 Population age shift 2000 and 2020, Each Column Represents a Single Age Group

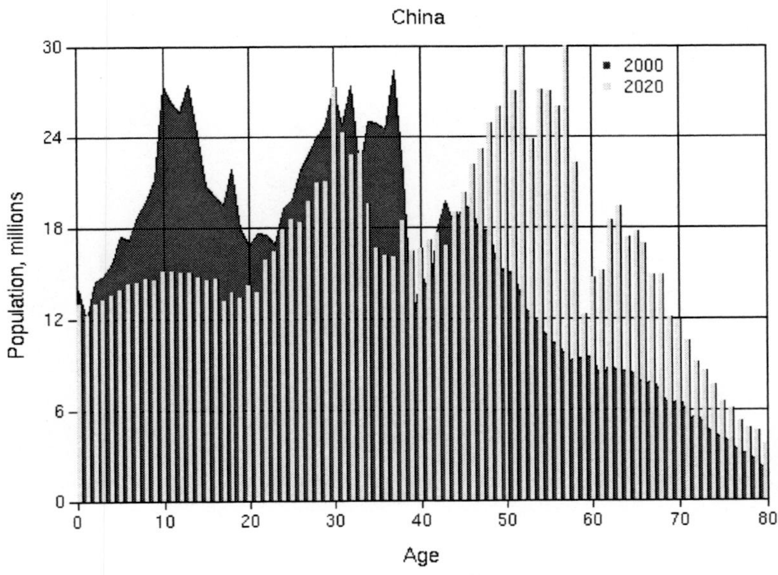

Chart 5.41 Population pyramids, 1980/2000/2010/2020

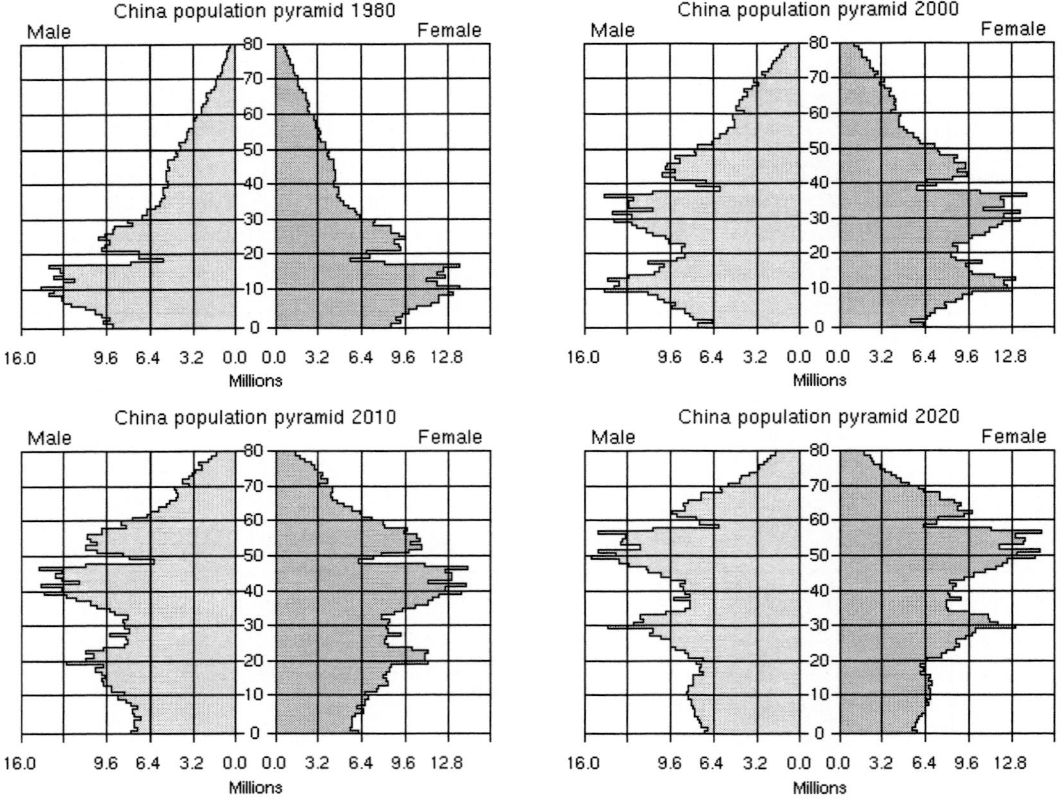

Chart 5.42 Major Cities: 1980, 2000 and 2020

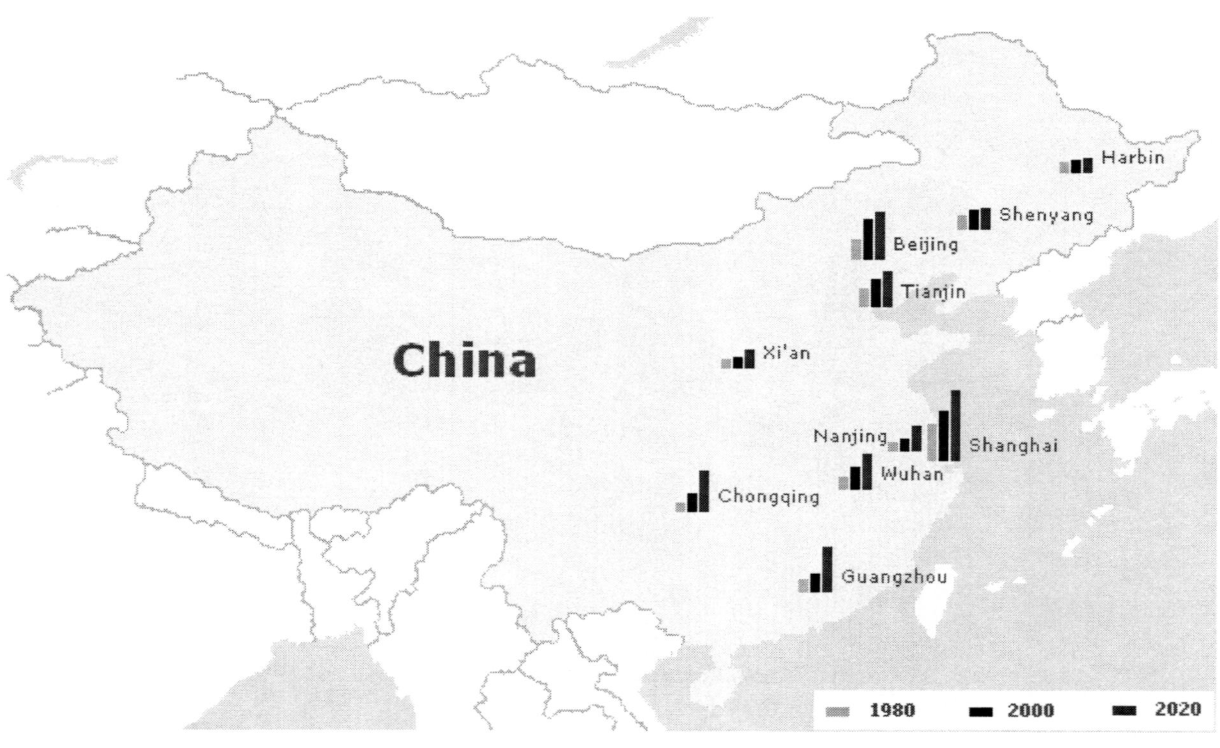

Colombia

Table 5.19 Key population trends

'000

	1980	1985	1990	1995	2000	2005	2010	2015	2020	CAGR	Period growth
Population at January 1st	26,890.7	29,996.7	33,203.8	36,459.0	39,772.9	43,049.2	46,300.2	49,385.2	52,278.4	1.68	94.4
Male	13,389.8	14,912.2	16,475.5	18,025.0	19,625.7	21,212.8	22,785.1	24,275.2	25,670.2	1.64	91.7
Female	13,500.9	15,084.5	16,728.4	18,434.0	20,147.2	21,836.4	23,515.1	25,110.0	26,608.2	1.71	97.1
0-4 yrs	3,916.8	4,098.2	4,257.9	4,445.7	4,439.1	4,443.9	4,506.4	4,444.9	4,396.9	0.29	12.3
5-9 yrs	3,536.7	3,838.2	4,061.9	4,226.6	4,406.6	4,417.8	4,419.8	4,475.7	4,430.1	0.56	25.3
10-14 yrs	3,537.8	3,514.2	3,814.2	4,031.5	4,211.9	4,388.2	4,400.3	4,408.0	4,460.1	0.58	26.1
15-19 yrs	3,208.5	3,496.9	3,470.5	3,764.2	3,995.2	4,178.0	4,356.0	4,371.0	4,379.5	0.78	36.5
20-24 yrs	2,683.5	3,128.3	3,408.8	3,371.7	3,690.0	3,927.4	4,113.6	4,295.5	4,312.5	1.19	60.7
25-29 yrs	2,208.2	2,583.6	3,019.8	3,285.4	3,282.7	3,608.8	3,849.1	4,039.2	4,222.1	1.63	91.2
30-34 yrs	1,694.3	2,129.2	2,498.0	2,920.2	3,207.8	3,215.2	3,542.2	3,785.1	3,975.7	2.16	134.6
35-39 yrs	1,248.9	1,644.1	2,071.1	2,428.5	2,860.3	3,150.1	3,162.2	3,489.9	3,732.2	2.77	198.8
40-44 yrs	1,011.2	1,213.5	1,601.3	2,017.6	2,379.4	2,808.5	3,098.3	3,114.8	3,440.4	3.11	240.2
45-49 yrs	869.5	979.3	1,178.0	1,557.3	1,972.6	2,330.7	2,756.1	3,045.5	3,063.8	3.20	252.4
50-54 yrs	759.5	835.4	943.3	1,137.3	1,512.2	1,919.7	2,273.2	2,693.5	2,979.1	3.48	292.2
55-59 yrs	660.3	717.9	792.4	897.1	1,088.8	1,452.4	1,849.5	2,196.0	2,606.5	3.49	294.8
60-64 yrs	524.6	609.6	666.1	738.4	841.6	1,025.8	1,374.5	1,756.6	2,090.8	3.52	298.6
65-69 yrs	415.9	464.7	544.2	598.6	669.8	768.0	942.4	1,269.5	1,628.5	3.47	291.6
70-74 yrs	295.1	345.1	389.9	461.0	514.0	581.0	673.0	832.6	1,128.6	3.41	282.4
75-79 yrs	179.8	222.1	263.7	302.0	364.3	412.2	473.7	555.1	693.8	3.43	286.0
80+ yrs	139.9	176.3	222.7	275.8	336.5	421.6	510.1	612.3	737.7	4.24	427.2
Median age of population (years)	18.8	20.1	21.4	22.6	23.8	25.2	26.7	28.3	29.9	1.18	59.6

Table 5.20 Key economic trends

As stated

	1990	1995	2000	2005	2010	2015	2020	CAGR	Period growth
Total GDP (Col$ per capita)	8,342,077.3	9,502,796.7	9,117,815.0	10,208,758.0	11,444,877.5	13,447,235.3	15,971,012.6	2.19	91.45
Disposable income (Col$ per capita)	6,403,031.0	5,945,956.2	5,245,381.2	6,816,035.2	7,527,600.0	8,654,322.9	10,261,515.5	1.58	60.26
Disposable income (Col$ per household)	32,752,462.6	28,348,137.6	23,160,426.7	27,757,825.6	28,296,172.2	29,916,420.1	32,495,909.0	-0.03	-0.78
Number of households by annual household disposable income ('000)									
Over US$1,000	5,609.3	6,987.1	7,886.0	9,677.9	11,547.4	13,610.6	15,963.8	3.55	184.59
Over US$10,000	931.1	1,795.4	1,405.1	2,190.8	3,135.0	4,339.0	6,117.2	6.48	556.95
Over US$25,000	198.1	444.4	303.4	489.7	727.7	1,056.7	1,605.1	7.22	710.28
Over US$75,000	36.2	71.3	54.0	79.9	114.8	161.1	238.9	6.49	559.08
Over US$150,000	15.9	29.6	23.7	35.0	49.2	67.5	95.9	6.18	504.00
Total households	6,491.3	7,647.2	9,007.8	10,570.9	12,317.2	14,286.3	16,508.4	3.16	154.32

Note: Per capita data is shown at constant 2010 prices. Household disposable income bands are shown at current prices.

Table 5.21 Young generation

'000

	1980	1985	1990	1995	2000	2005	2010	2015	2020	CAGR	Period growth
Babies under 12 months	858.1	815.9	872.3	908.0	877.4	898.7	912.0	876.8	881.6	0.07	2.75
Infants under 24 months	1,669.0	1,642.1	1,731.3	1,807.3	1,762.8	1,789.9	1,818.8	1,762.0	1,760.5	0.13	5.48
Toddlers aged 1-4	3,058.8	3,282.3	3,385.6	3,537.7	3,561.7	3,545.2	3,594.4	3,568.1	3,515.3	0.35	14.92
Children aged 2-9	5,784.6	6,294.3	6,588.5	6,865.0	7,082.9	7,071.8	7,107.4	7,158.6	7,066.5	0.50	22.16
Female	2,843.7	3,091.8	3,232.2	3,365.4	3,470.1	3,463.7	3,480.0	3,504.2	3,457.6	0.49	21.59
Male	2,940.8	3,202.5	3,356.3	3,499.7	3,612.9	3,608.1	3,627.4	3,654.4	3,608.9	0.51	22.72
Tweenagers aged 10-14	3,537.8	3,514.2	3,814.2	4,031.5	4,211.9	4,388.2	4,400.3	4,408.0	4,460.1	0.58	26.07
Female	1,742.4	1,730.9	1,876.5	1,981.1	2,066.8	2,151.5	2,156.8	2,159.7	2,184.6	0.57	25.38
Male	1,795.4	1,783.2	1,937.7	2,050.4	2,145.1	2,236.7	2,243.5	2,248.3	2,275.4	0.59	26.74
Teenagers aged 13-19	4,611.3	4,889.2	4,951.8	5,353.9	5,653.0	5,918.0	6,117.0	6,126.4	6,159.5	0.73	33.57
Female	2,272.1	2,410.2	2,441.9	2,641.1	2,783.6	2,909.6	3,004.7	3,007.6	3,022.2	0.72	33.01
Male	2,339.2	2,479.0	2,509.9	2,712.8	2,869.5	3,008.5	3,112.3	3,118.7	3,137.3	0.74	34.12
Studying age 18-22	2,892.0	3,325.1	3,436.5	3,502.1	3,838.5	4,027.2	4,225.6	4,345.3	4,333.7	1.02	49.85
Female	1,429.6	1,644.4	1,702.8	1,741.2	1,904.2	1,992.6	2,086.7	2,143.2	2,135.4	1.01	49.37
Male	1,462.4	1,680.7	1,733.7	1,760.9	1,934.2	2,034.6	2,138.9	2,202.2	2,198.3	1.02	50.33
Young adults aged 15-29	8,100.2	9,208.9	9,899.2	10,421.2	10,967.9	11,714.3	12,318.7	12,705.7	12,914.1	1.17	59.43
Female	4,021.3	4,572.1	4,924.1	5,205.8	5,473.1	5,829.3	6,114.5	6,294.9	6,389.0	1.16	58.88
Male	4,078.9	4,636.8	4,975.1	5,215.4	5,494.8	5,885.0	6,204.2	6,410.9	6,525.0	1.18	59.97

Table 5.22 Middle-aged generation
'000

	1980	1985	1990	1995	2000	2005	2010	2015	2020	CAGR	Period growth
Middle-aged adults 30-59	6,244	7,519	9,084	10,958	13,021	14,877	16,681	18,325	19,798	2.93	217.1
Female	3,232	3,894	4,703	5,684	6,763	7,734	8,668	9,502	10,234	2.92	216.6
Male	3,011	3,625	4,381	5,274	6,258	7,142	8,014	8,823	9,563	2.93	217.6
Baby boomers aged 40-59	3,301	3,746	4,515	5,609	6,953	8,511	9,977	11,050	12,090	3.30	266.3
Female	1,724	1,965	2,368	2,942	3,644	4,460	5,231	5,793	6,325	3.30	266.9
Male	1,577	1,781	2,147	2,667	3,309	4,051	4,747	5,257	5,765	3.29	265.6

Table 5.23 Elderly population
'000

	1980	1985	1990	1995	2000	2005	2010	2015	2020	CAGR	Period growth
Elderly population (60+)	1,555.3	1,817.9	2,086.6	2,375.9	2,726.2	3,208.6	3,973.6	5,026.2	6,279.4	3.55	303.7
Female	842.7	990.9	1,145.1	1,312.8	1,511.8	1,782.2	2,206.3	2,788.0	3,481.9	3.61	313.2
Male	712.6	827.0	941.5	1,063.1	1,214.4	1,426.3	1,767.4	2,238.2	2,797.6	3.48	292.6

Table 5.24 Population of biggest cities 1980-2020
'000

	1980	1985	1990	1995	2000	2005	2010	2015	2020	CAGR	Period growth
Bogota	3,742.8	4,176.8	4,628.6	5,178.5	5,891.5	6,763.3	7,441.9	8,098.3	8,728.7	2.14	133.2
Medellin	1,367.7	1,452.4	1,505.3	1,630.3	1,893.3	2,187.4	2,350.3	2,519.8	2,687.9	1.70	96.5
Cali	1,214.0	1,369.3	1,537.6	1,698.3	1,837.2	2,039.6	2,280.4	2,503.0	2,713.6	2.03	123.5
Barranquilla	855.4	917.5	964.0	1,005.9	1,041.8	1,109.1	1,195.0	1,276.6	1,357.2	1.16	58.7
Cartagena	457.0	514.0	575.2	648.7	741.7	845.8	912.0	979.9	1,046.9	2.09	129.1
Cucuta	340.2	383.6	430.5	476.2	517.4	566.2	606.8	648.1	689.4	1.78	102.6
Bucaramanga	316.4	351.7	387.7	423.7	458.4	502.7	533.5	565.2	597.4	1.60	88.8
Ibague	248.0	280.6	316.5	357.8	407.2	465.9	506.5	546.8	586.1	2.17	136.3
Santa Marta	132.7	175.7	233.7	288.3	331.3	384.2	439.7	491.3	539.4	3.57	306.5
Pereira	190.3	241.9	309.7	354.1	350.0	358.7	406.5	448.7	488.2	2.38	156.6

Chart 5.43 Population age shift 2000 and 2020, Each Column Represents a Single Age Group

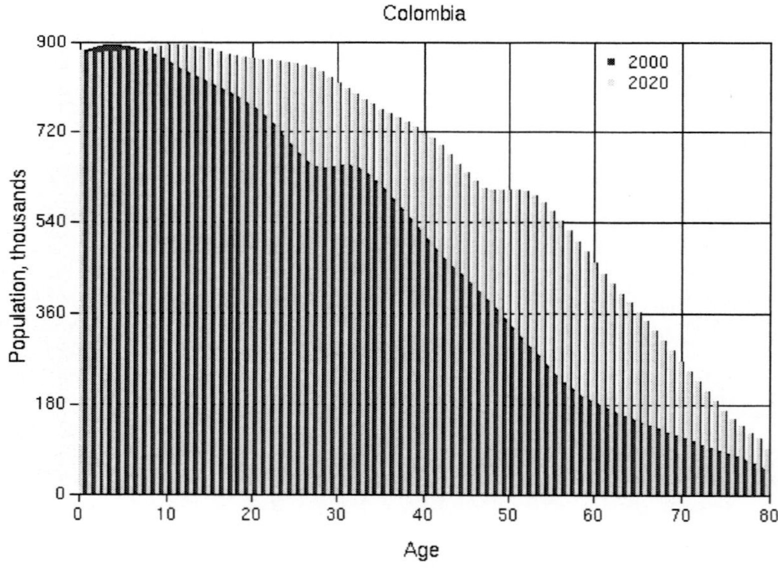

Chart 5.44 Population pyramids, 1980/2000/2010/2020

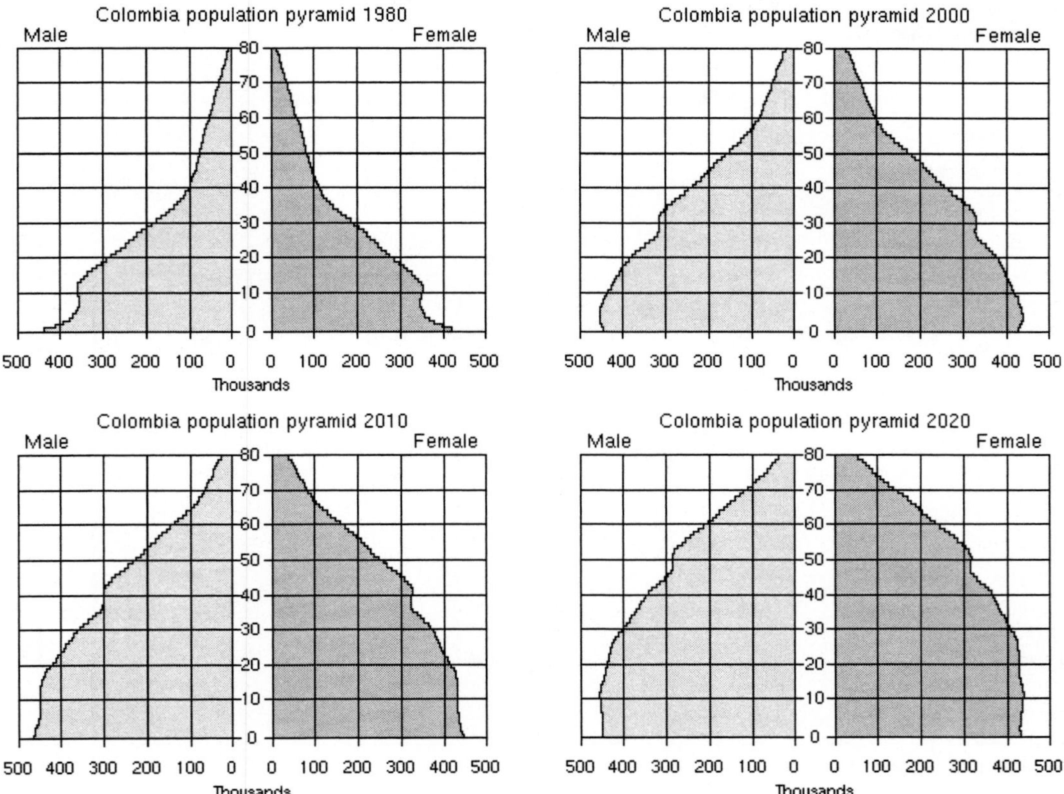

Chart 5.45 Major Cities: 1980, 2000 and 2020

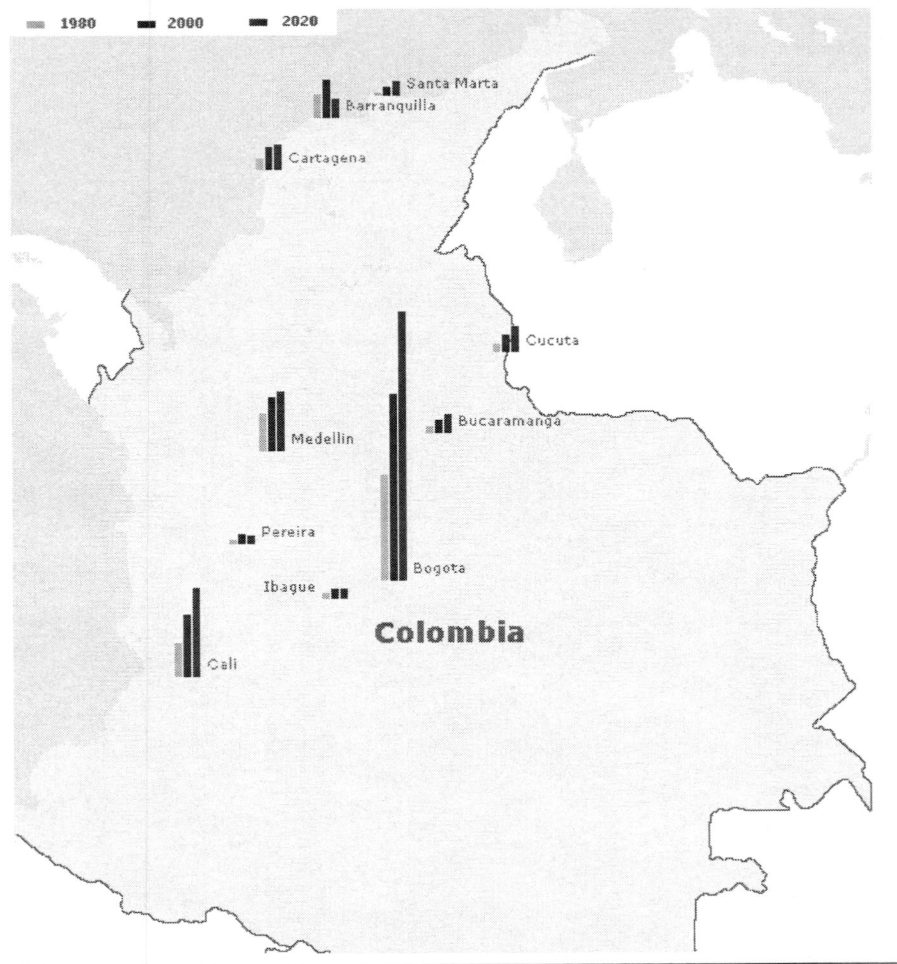

Costa Rica

Table 5.25 Key population trends

'000

	1980	1985	1990	1995	2000	2005	2010	2015	2020	CAGR	Period growth
Population at January 1st	2,348.6	2,698.6	3,078.3	3,478.6	3,930.9	4,328.4	4,639.8	4,956.7	5,249.8	2.03	123.5
Male	1,197.2	1,374.1	1,566.0	1,769.0	1,998.6	2,200.2	2,355.8	2,513.6	2,658.5	2.01	122.1
Female	1,151.5	1,324.5	1,512.3	1,709.6	1,932.3	2,128.1	2,284.0	2,443.2	2,591.3	2.05	125.0
0-4 yrs	320.7	367.6	411.5	403.0	396.1	393.3	368.8	388.8	378.7	0.42	18.1
5-9 yrs	276.3	319.3	370.7	417.2	420.1	406.6	395.0	374.6	389.3	0.86	40.9
10-14 yrs	290.7	281.9	321.8	377.6	430.7	428.7	410.3	397.4	378.4	0.66	30.1
15-19 yrs	287.9	295.5	285.8	332.1	398.6	444.3	433.4	414.7	402.3	0.84	39.8
20-24 yrs	247.4	291.8	298.5	295.1	351.9	411.6	448.6	437.1	419.2	1.33	69.4
25-29 yrs	194.8	250.0	292.9	303.8	307.7	360.0	413.8	450.1	439.5	2.06	125.7
30-34 yrs	146.2	196.2	250.1	296.0	312.4	313.0	361.0	414.3	451.2	2.86	208.5
35-39 yrs	112.9	147.3	195.8	251.8	301.4	315.4	313.2	360.7	414.4	3.30	266.9
40-44 yrs	94.7	113.5	146.7	196.5	254.9	302.5	314.3	312.1	359.8	3.39	280.0
45-49 yrs	81.0	94.9	112.6	146.4	197.5	254.2	300.0	311.7	310.0	3.41	282.8
50-54 yrs	71.4	80.5	93.5	111.7	146.5	195.9	250.7	295.9	307.9	3.72	331.4
55-59 yrs	57.1	70.1	78.3	91.6	110.5	143.8	191.5	245.0	289.7	4.14	407.0
60-64 yrs	54.7	55.0	66.8	75.3	89.1	106.9	138.6	184.6	236.9	3.73	332.9
65-69 yrs	42.5	50.7	50.8	62.4	71.1	84.0	100.7	130.8	174.7	3.60	311.2
70-74 yrs	30.5	37.1	44.4	45.2	56.3	64.4	76.1	91.6	119.6	3.47	291.8
75-79 yrs	20.5	24.2	29.9	36.5	38.0	47.8	54.9	65.4	79.3	3.43	285.9
80+ yrs	19.2	22.8	28.2	36.3	48.1	56.1	68.8	81.9	98.9	4.19	416.6
Median age of population (years)	20.0	21.4	22.5	23.5	24.5	26.0	28.1	30.2	32.4	1.22	62.2

Table 5.26 Key economic trends

As stated

	1990	1995	2000	2005	2010	2015	2020	CAGR	Period growth
Total GDP (CRC per capita)	2,400,887	2,772,264	3,120,684	3,462,582	3,916,218	4,614,017	5,561,113	2.84	131.6
Disposable income (CRC per capita)	1,324,945	2,244,996	2,367,157	2,522,723	2,936,830	3,547,843			
Disposable income (CRC per household)	6,058,119	9,519,022	9,423,587	9,482,333	10,474,406	12,226,827			
Number of households by annual household disposable income ('000)									
Total households	673	820	987	1,152	1,301	1,438	1,562	2.84	132.0

Note: Per capita data is shown at constant 2010 prices. Household disposable income bands are shown at current prices.

Table 5.27 Young generation

'000

	1980	1985	1990	1995	2000	2005	2010	2015	2020	CAGR	Period growth
Babies under 12 months	72.5	75.8	84.8	75.1	78.2	78.1	70.5	82.3	71.3	-0.04	-1.64
Infants under 24 months	140.1	151.1	168.5	153.9	156.5	156.5	142.9	161.6	145.8	0.10	4.09
Toddlers aged 1-4	248.2	291.9	326.8	327.9	317.8	315.2	298.2	306.5	307.4	0.54	23.84
Children aged 2-9	457.0	535.8	613.7	666.3	659.7	643.4	620.9	601.8	622.1	0.77	36.15
Female	223.8	261.9	299.4	324.2	320.6	313.0	302.7	293.5	303.4	0.76	35.60
Male	233.2	273.9	314.3	342.1	339.2	330.3	318.2	308.3	318.7	0.78	36.68
Tweenagers aged 10-14	290.7	281.9	321.8	377.6	430.7	428.7	410.3	397.4	378.4	0.66	30.14
Female	141.2	137.9	157.4	184.2	209.4	207.9	199.3	193.5	184.4	0.67	30.59
Male	149.5	144.0	164.4	193.4	221.3	220.8	210.9	203.9	193.9	0.65	29.71
Teenagers aged 13-19	406.4	407.5	408.5	477.4	569.2	619.0	599.6	576.5	554.6	0.78	36.47
Female	196.8	198.0	199.9	233.2	277.4	300.6	290.9	280.2	270.1	0.79	37.24
Male	209.6	209.5	208.7	244.2	291.8	318.4	308.7	296.3	284.5	0.77	35.75
Studying age 18-22	266.3	298.6	291.0	305.2	371.8	429.2	447.4	427.0	413.6	1.11	55.32
Female	128.8	144.5	141.7	149.3	181.4	208.9	217.2	207.2	201.2	1.12	56.19
Male	137.5	154.0	149.3	155.9	190.4	220.3	230.2	219.8	212.4	1.09	54.51
Young adults aged 15-29	730.0	837.3	877.2	931.0	1,058.1	1,215.9	1,295.8	1,301.9	1,261.0	1.38	72.73
Female	354.3	405.6	426.8	454.4	517.0	592.5	630.3	632.7	613.1	1.38	73.07
Male	375.8	431.7	450.4	476.6	541.2	623.4	665.6	669.2	647.9	1.37	72.40

Table 5.28 Middle-aged generation
'000

	1980	1985	1990	1995	2000	2005	2010	2015	2020	CAGR	Period growth
Middle-aged adults 30-59	563.4	702.6	877.0	1,094.1	1,323.2	1,524.8	1,730.8	1,939.7	2,133.1	3.38	278.6
Female	280.5	349.1	433.6	538.6	650.2	749.3	850.7	953.4	1,048.7	3.35	273.8
Male	282.9	353.5	443.3	555.5	673.0	775.5	880.2	986.3	1,084.4	3.42	283.3
Baby boomers aged 40-59	304.2	359.1	431.0	546.3	709.4	896.4	1,056.6	1,164.7	1,267.5	3.63	316.6
Female	151.6	180.0	216.2	272.2	350.8	441.3	519.7	573.8	625.8	3.61	312.9
Male	152.7	179.1	214.8	274.1	358.6	455.1	536.9	590.8	641.8	3.66	320.4

Table 5.29 Elderly population
'000

	1980	1985	1990	1995	2000	2005	2010	2015	2020	CAGR	Period growth
Elderly population (60+)	167.4	189.9	220.2	255.7	302.7	359.1	439.1	554.3	709.4	3.68	323.7
Female	83.4	96.1	113.0	133.1	158.6	189.0	231.3	291.0	370.4	3.80	344.0
Male	84.0	93.8	107.1	122.7	144.1	170.1	207.8	263.3	339.0	3.55	303.5

Table 5.30 Population of biggest cities 1980-2020
'000

	1980	1985	1990	1995	2000	2005	2010	2015	2020	CAGR	Period growth
San Jose	221.46	245.95	267.82	288.24	309.67	341.14	367.84	392.93	416.08	1.59	87.9
Limon	29.76	35.11	41.39	48.13	55.67	62.29	67.88	72.95	77.51	2.42	160.5
Alajuela	26.29	30.04	34.03	38.17	42.89	48.66	53.67	58.07	61.94	2.17	135.6
San Francisco	8.42	12.90	20.56	29.84	40.84	45.50	49.14	52.54	55.67	4.84	561.4
Cinco Esquinas	24.70	27.72	30.62	33.48	36.63	40.98	44.75	48.15	51.20	1.84	107.2
Desamparados	41.07	43.33	42.44	40.06	36.44	40.68	44.36	47.69	50.69	0.53	23.4
Liberia	9.71	13.38	19.28	26.32	34.47	39.36	43.21	46.64	49.68	4.16	411.4
Puntarenas	26.21	28.74	30.30	31.43	32.46	36.68	40.40	43.68	46.57	1.45	77.7
Paraiso	8.66	11.81	16.85	22.86	30.05	33.49	36.33	38.94	41.32	3.99	377.4
San Vicente	22.62	25.12	27.35	29.43	31.69	33.93	35.84	37.83	39.78	1.42	75.9

Chart 5.46 Population age shift 2000 and 2020, Each Column Represents a Single Age Group

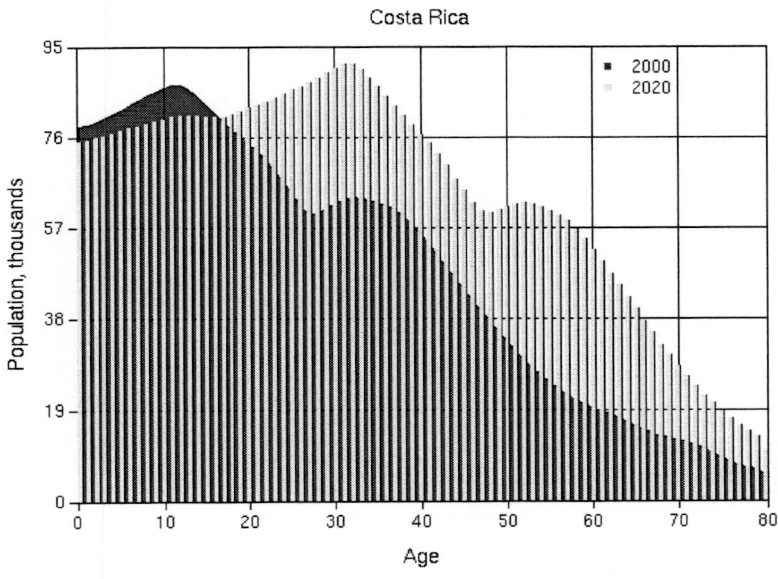

Chart 5.47 Population pyramids, 1980/2000/2010/2020

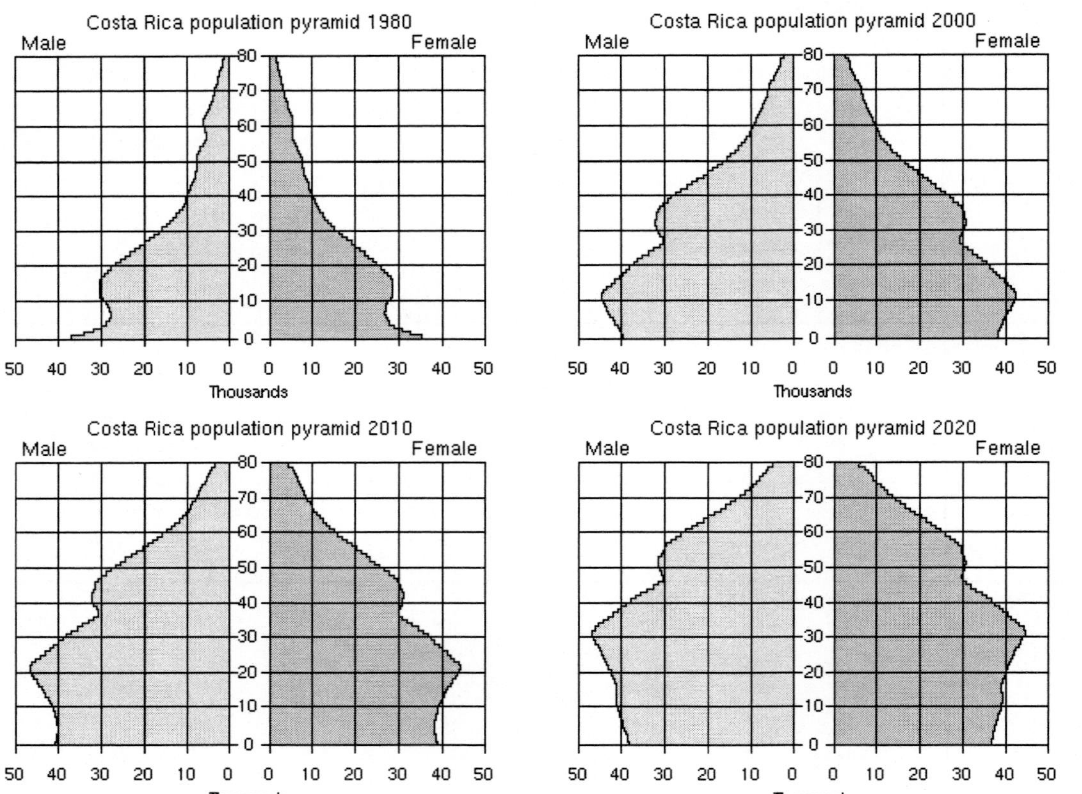

Chart 5.48 Major Cities: 1980, 2000 and 2020

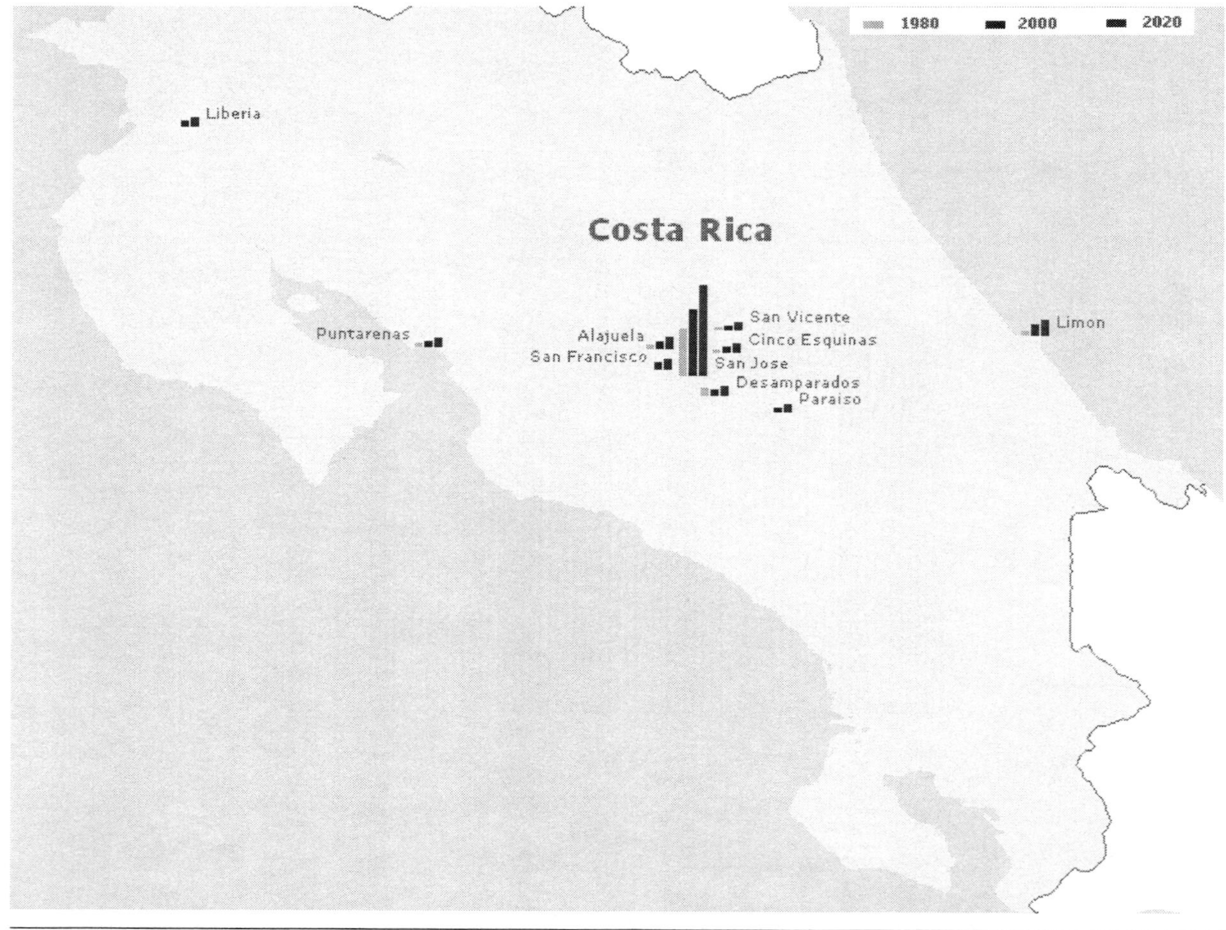

Croatia

Table 5.31 Key population trends

'000

	1980	1985	1990	1995	2000	2005	2010	2015	2020	CAGR	Period growth
Population at January 1st	4,598.1	4,701.7	4,778.0	4,668.8	4,441.7	4,443.9	4,421.0	4,373.6	4,314.9	-0.16	-6.16
Male	2,225.0	2,276.4	2,315.4	2,243.7	2,137.7	2,139.2	2,129.6	2,108.9	2,082.9	-0.16	-6.39
Female	2,373.1	2,425.3	2,462.6	2,425.0	2,304.0	2,304.7	2,291.5	2,264.8	2,232.1	-0.15	-5.94
0-4 yrs	327.8	326.4	289.8	253.8	236.7	206.6	214.4	217.8	215.2	-1.05	-34.36
5-9 yrs	320.3	333.1	326.9	284.8	249.6	249.5	208.7	216.0	219.1	-0.94	-31.59
10-14 yrs	325.6	325.4	335.4	319.0	273.7	255.5	250.9	210.0	217.0	-1.01	-33.36
15-19 yrs	341.1	330.8	327.5	323.9	304.2	279.4	256.7	251.7	211.0	-1.19	-38.15
20-24 yrs	372.5	347.1	333.1	314.1	304.5	310.2	282.2	259.3	254.2	-0.95	-31.76
25-29 yrs	375.9	376.9	349.9	323.1	292.7	307.9	313.3	285.1	262.2	-0.90	-30.25
30-34 yrs	322.2	378.8	377.6	338.8	305.3	294.0	309.3	314.4	286.2	-0.30	-11.16
35-39 yrs	283.9	323.7	378.1	362.6	319.6	309.6	294.7	309.4	314.2	0.25	10.67
40-44 yrs	327.3	283.3	322.1	359.2	338.8	322.8	309.1	293.9	308.2	-0.15	-5.81
45-49 yrs	347.3	322.5	279.7	303.9	331.4	337.3	320.0	306.2	290.8	-0.44	-16.27
50-54 yrs	307.0	336.6	314.1	265.1	277.9	325.4	330.7	313.2	299.3	-0.06	-2.52
55-59 yrs	260.3	291.0	321.9	293.1	244.2	264.3	315.1	320.2	302.6	0.38	16.28
60-64 yrs	140.1	240.6	271.5	291.6	265.6	236.9	251.3	301.7	306.5	1.98	118.74
65-69 yrs	203.1	122.7	217.4	235.6	254.6	247.0	214.9	229.3	279.1	0.80	37.46
70-74 yrs	170.6	163.8	103.6	172.3	194.1	220.7	211.9	180.4	194.8	0.33	14.23
75-79 yrs	103.4	112.3	122.4	116.6	133.8	151.5	175.1	166.9	136.0	0.69	31.56
80+ yrs	69.8	86.6	106.9	111.3	114.8	125.4	162.7	198.0	218.5	2.89	212.90
Median age of population (years)	33.4	34.1	35.6	37.5	39.0	40.1	41.4	42.1	42.9	0.63	28.33

Table 5.32 Key economic trends

As stated

	1990	1995	2000	2005	2010	2015	2020	CAGR	Period growth
Total GDP (HRK per capita)	55,106.4	46,457.6	57,197.3	71,369.4	77,194.8	93,532.2	113,744.7	2.45	106.41
Disposable income (HRK per capita)		23,897.5	28,491.8	45,061.6	47,659.0	57,251.5	69,615.5		
Disposable income (HRK per household)		73,044.0	85,819.7	133,808.3	139,488.8	165,122.4	197,812.8		
Number of households by annual household disposable income ('000)									
Over US$1,000		1,524.9	1,472.4	1,496.4	1,510.5	1,516.4	1,518.5		
Over US$10,000		401.5	319.5	1,103.8	1,325.5	1,452.5	1,498.0		
Over US$25,000		53.5	46.4	184.4	356.7	719.1	1,120.4		
Over US$75,000		13.2	11.4	27.7	40.0	63.4	123.8		
Over US$150,000		5.4	4.7	11.4	16.5	25.1	39.3		
Total households	1,536.4	1,527.5	1,474.6	1,496.5	1,510.5	1,516.4	1,518.5	-0.04	-1.17

Note: Per capita data is shown at constant 2010 prices. Household disposable income bands are shown at current prices.

Table 5.33 Young generation

'000

	1980	1985	1990	1995	2000	2005	2010	2015	2020	CAGR	Period growth
Babies under 12 months	67.6	62.9	56.0	50.1	39.6	40.3	43.2	43.5	42.5	-1.15	-37.10
Infants under 24 months	133.1	127.3	112.5	99.2	85.7	80.1	86.2	87.1	85.3	-1.11	-35.95
Toddlers aged 1-4	260.2	263.5	233.9	203.7	197.1	166.3	171.2	174.3	172.7	-1.02	-33.65
Children aged 2-9	514.9	532.2	504.3	439.4	400.7	376.1	336.9	346.7	349.0	-0.97	-32.23
Female	251.3	259.8	245.9	215.1	195.1	183.4	164.0	168.8	169.8	-0.98	-32.44
Male	263.7	272.5	258.4	224.3	205.6	192.7	172.9	177.9	179.2	-0.96	-32.03
Tweenagers aged 10-14	325.6	325.4	335.4	319.0	273.7	255.5	250.9	210.0	217.0	-1.01	-33.36
Female	159.4	159.0	164.0	156.6	133.7	124.8	122.6	102.3	105.8	-1.02	-33.61
Male	166.2	166.4	171.4	162.4	140.0	130.6	128.3	107.7	111.1	-1.00	-33.12
Teenagers aged 13-19	477.4	459.0	459.6	453.6	416.4	385.5	359.7	339.3	297.4	-1.18	-37.71
Female	234.9	225.2	224.8	223.3	203.3	188.9	175.8	165.8	145.1	-1.20	-38.23
Male	242.5	233.8	234.9	230.3	213.1	196.7	183.9	173.5	152.3	-1.16	-37.20
Studying age 18-22	359.7	342.1	322.5	317.8	308.3	300.0	272.0	254.8	237.5	-1.03	-33.98
Female	177.2	168.9	158.1	157.1	150.7	147.0	133.2	124.5	116.2	-1.05	-34.45
Male	182.4	173.3	164.3	160.7	157.5	153.0	138.8	130.3	121.3	-1.02	-33.53
Young adults aged 15-29	1,089.5	1,054.8	1,010.5	961.1	901.4	897.5	852.2	796.2	727.4	-1.01	-33.24
Female	531.5	519.8	497.8	476.3	442.6	440.6	418.0	390.6	356.3	-1.00	-32.97
Male	558.1	535.0	512.7	484.8	458.8	456.8	434.2	405.6	371.1	-1.01	-33.50

Table 5.34 Middle-aged generation

'000

	1980	1985	1990	1995	2000	2005	2010	2015	2020	CAGR	Period growth
Middle-aged adults 30-59	1,847.9	1,935.9	1,993.5	1,922.7	1,817.3	1,853.4	1,878.9	1,857.3	1,801.3	-0.06	-2.52
Female	951.0	975.9	996.4	970.5	914.0	932.3	943.0	931.8	901.5	-0.13	-5.20
Male	897.0	960.0	997.1	952.2	903.3	921.1	935.9	925.5	899.8	0.01	0.32
Baby boomers aged 40-59	1,241.9	1,233.4	1,237.8	1,221.3	1,192.4	1,249.9	1,274.9	1,233.4	1,201.0	-0.08	-3.29
Female	653.9	634.5	626.4	620.1	602.0	631.2	644.0	624.3	605.7	-0.19	-7.36
Male	588.0	598.9	611.4	601.2	590.5	618.6	630.9	609.1	595.2	0.03	1.23

Table 5.35 Elderly population

'000

	1980	1985	1990	1995	2000	2005	2010	2015	2020	CAGR	Period growth
Elderly population (60+)	687.0	726.0	821.8	927.3	962.9	981.4	1,016.0	1,076.4	1,135.0	1.26	65.2
Female	415.2	449.0	503.8	558.1	577.0	584.7	601.9	628.9	657.2	1.16	58.3
Male	271.8	277.1	318.0	369.2	386.0	396.7	414.1	447.5	477.8	1.42	75.8

Table 5.36 Population of biggest cities 1980-2020

'000

	1980	1985	1990	1995	2000	2005	2010	2015	2020	CAGR	Period growth
Zagreb	649.0	683.7	707.3	707.2	688.3	707.2	723.9	737.3	751.0	0.37	15.72
Split	167.5	179.4	189.0	190.7	187.5	194.2	200.1	205.1	210.0	0.57	25.35
Rijeka	158.6	165.1	168.5	159.5	145.1	139.6	134.2	129.2	124.7	-0.60	-21.39
Osijek	104.7	106.3	105.8	99.8	91.2	88.1	85.1	82.2	79.7	-0.68	-23.94
Zadar	59.0	67.3	75.3	74.2	69.7	69.2	68.7	68.1	67.7	0.34	14.71
Slavonski Brod	46.9	51.4	55.3	57.4	57.9	61.5	64.6	67.4	70.0	1.01	49.24
Pula	55.6	59.4	62.2	61.4	58.6	59.0	59.4	59.6	59.8	0.18	7.62
Sesvete	16.6	24.9	33.7	39.6	43.7	49.7	55.0	60.0	64.3	3.45	287.97
Karlovac	54.6	57.7	60.0	56.0	49.8	46.7	43.8	41.0	38.6	-0.86	-29.23
Varazdin	39.3	41.0	42.0	42.1	41.2	42.5	43.7	44.7	45.7	0.38	16.21

Chart 5.49 Population age shift 2000 and 2020, Each Column Represents a Single Age Group

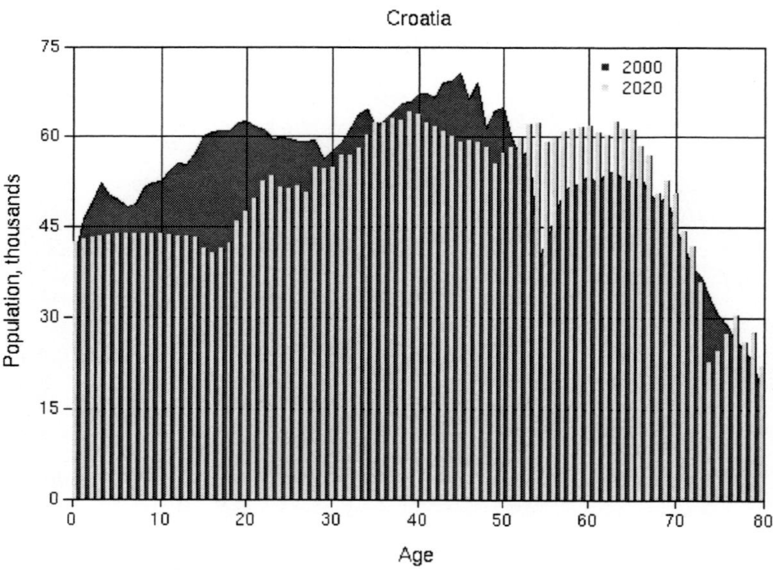

Chart 5.50 Population pyramids, 1980/2000/2010/2020

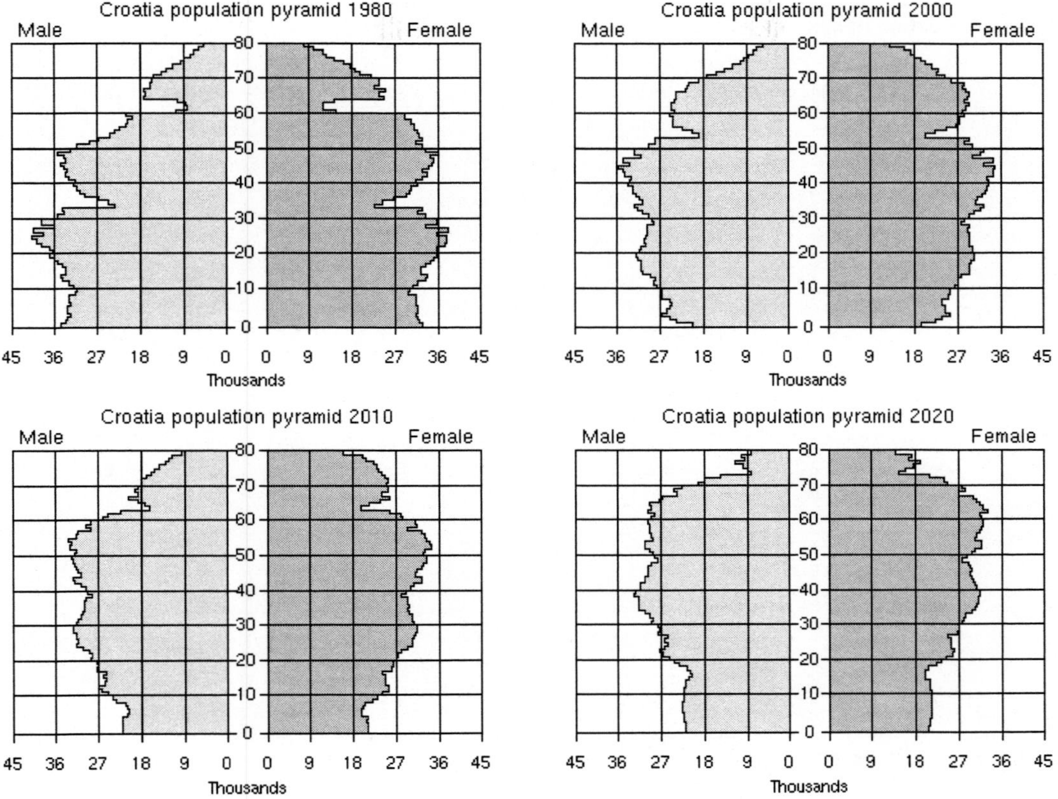

Chart 5.51 Major Cities: 1980, 2000 and 2020

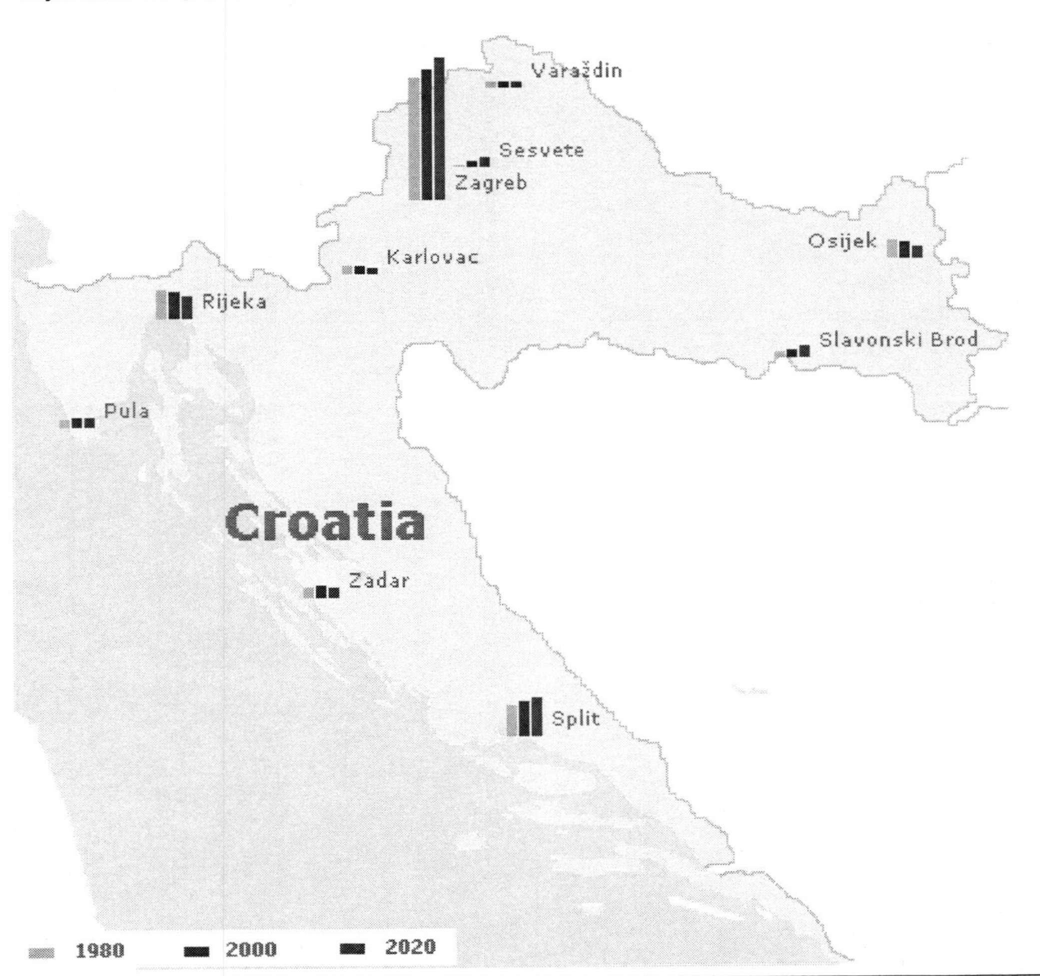

Czech Republic

Table 5.37 Key population trends

'000

	1980	1985	1990	1995	2000	2005	2010	2015	2020	CAGR	Period growth
Population at January 1st	10,276.6	10,302.2	10,300.6	10,316.9	10,236.3	10,220.6	10,353.5	10,361.2	10,354.2	0.02	0.76
Male	4,980.3	4,995.9	4,998.4	5,012.5	4,980.7	4,980.9	5,056.6	5,066.3	5,068.2	0.04	1.76
Female	5,296.2	5,306.2	5,302.2	5,304.3	5,255.6	5,239.7	5,296.9	5,294.9	5,286.0	0.00	-0.19
0-4 yrs	892.9	702.7	650.7	601.3	453.2	465.6	519.3	518.5	504.6	-1.42	-43.49
5-9 yrs	820.9	892.2	699.9	646.3	601.2	453.9	474.3	524.1	523.0	-1.12	-36.29
10-14 yrs	684.4	820.2	888.6	697.4	645.8	607.5	462.6	479.1	529.0	-0.64	-22.71
15-19 yrs	674.2	682.6	816.9	886.6	696.7	657.2	617.9	467.0	483.9	-0.83	-28.23
20-24 yrs	729.6	674.5	681.9	819.4	885.6	708.8	669.8	621.1	471.3	-1.09	-35.40
25-29 yrs	841.7	726.8	675.4	681.0	822.1	891.5	725.6	672.9	625.5	-0.74	-25.69
30-34 yrs	845.9	831.4	722.4	669.5	683.6	819.6	908.1	728.6	676.8	-0.56	-20.00
35-39 yrs	686.3	833.5	823.3	713.4	669.8	683.9	832.7	910.3	731.6	0.16	6.61
40-44 yrs	534.8	674.7	821.1	812.1	709.1	669.9	692.9	833.3	911.1	1.34	70.37
45-49 yrs	590.0	522.3	659.6	806.5	800.7	704.1	674.2	690.3	830.0	0.86	40.67
50-54 yrs	615.8	569.1	504.3	643.1	786.4	783.0	698.0	663.9	681.3	0.25	10.64
55-59 yrs	627.8	582.3	538.3	483.9	616.7	759.1	763.5	676.7	646.6	0.07	3.00
60-64 yrs	333.7	574.4	533.5	502.2	453.0	581.9	725.5	727.4	648.2	1.67	94.21
65-69 yrs	517.1	290.7	500.6	476.9	452.3	414.7	540.5	674.0	681.0	0.69	31.69
70-74 yrs	415.5	416.7	235.1	417.0	404.3	391.9	367.1	481.1	606.9	0.95	46.06
75-79 yrs	273.8	290.3	298.7	175.6	319.5	319.7	317.6	301.6	403.1	0.97	47.23
80+ yrs	191.9	217.9	250.3	284.6	236.3	308.3	363.8	391.2	400.2	1.85	108.55
Median age of population (years)	32.8	33.9	35.1	36.2	37.3	38.7	39.8	41.4	43.5	0.71	32.52

Table 5.38 Key economic trends

As stated

	1990	1995	2000	2005	2010	2015	2020	CAGR	Period growth
Total GDP (CZK per capita)	258,595.2	244,021.1	264,743.2	318,575.0	354,772.3	423,415.1	521,422.6	2.37	101.6
Disposable income (CZK per capita)	139,914.3	148,216.5	154,008.4	170,676.1	196,471.4	239,301.0	295,633.1	2.52	111.3
Disposable income (CZK per household)	357,405.5	368,697.3	370,886.0	399,523.8	450,082.3	539,805.2	659,534.9	2.06	84.5
Number of households by annual household disposable income ('000)									
Over US$1,000	4,019.3	4,146.4	4,250.1	4,366.2	4,519.5	4,593.2	4,641.2	0.48	15.5
Over US$10,000	217.7	816.9	745.5	3,227.7	4,133.9	4,402.7	4,558.1	10.67	1,994.0
Over US$25,000	62.3	129.9	123.7	414.2	1,173.0	1,925.3	2,860.9	13.61	4,492.4
Over US$75,000	15.1	31.5	29.9	75.8	123.2	168.7	256.0	9.89	1,594.6
Over US$150,000	6.2	12.9	12.2	30.9	50.6	67.7	96.8	9.60	1,466.1
Total households	4,032.4	4,147.4	4,250.6	4,366.2	4,519.5	4,593.2	4,641.2	0.47	15.1

Note: Per capita data is shown at constant 2010 prices. Household disposable income bands are shown at current prices.

Table 5.39 Young generation

'000

	1980	1985	1990	1995	2000	2005	2010	2015	2020	CAGR	Period growth
Babies under 12 months	169.2	135.0	126.5	105.7	88.8	97.6	103.6	103.0	98.2	-1.35	-41.92
Infants under 24 months	344.5	270.3	257.1	225.5	178.6	191.5	207.4	206.4	198.0	-1.38	-42.53
Toddlers aged 1-4	723.8	567.7	524.2	495.6	364.4	368.1	415.7	415.5	406.3	-1.43	-43.86
Children aged 2-9	1,369.3	1,324.6	1,093.5	1,022.0	875.8	727.9	786.2	836.1	829.6	-1.24	-39.42
Female	669.4	647.5	533.9	498.3	426.3	353.9	382.1	407.4	404.4	-1.25	-39.58
Male	699.9	677.1	559.6	523.7	449.6	374.0	404.1	428.7	425.2	-1.24	-39.25
Tweenagers aged 10-14	684.4	820.2	888.6	697.4	645.8	607.5	462.6	479.1	529.0	-0.64	-22.71
Female	334.0	400.6	435.3	340.2	315.4	295.8	225.3	232.4	257.6	-0.65	-22.86
Male	350.5	419.6	453.3	357.2	330.4	311.7	237.3	246.6	271.4	-0.64	-22.56
Teenagers aged 13-19	952.5	977.0	1,185.8	1,177.7	959.8	915.8	807.3	653.3	695.8	-0.78	-26.95
Female	464.8	477.8	580.6	575.7	468.5	447.0	393.2	317.6	338.0	-0.79	-27.28
Male	487.8	499.2	605.2	602.0	491.3	468.7	414.1	335.7	357.9	-0.77	-26.64
Studying age 18-22	664.3	698.7	697.3	892.0	808.1	681.5	659.1	548.0	466.8	-0.88	-29.74
Female	324.8	341.7	341.6	436.5	395.0	332.9	322.3	267.0	227.0	-0.89	-30.11
Male	339.5	357.0	355.7	455.5	413.1	348.6	336.8	281.1	239.8	-0.87	-29.38
Young adults aged 15-29	2,245.6	2,083.9	2,174.2	2,387.1	2,404.4	2,257.5	2,013.2	1,761.0	1,580.7	-0.87	-29.61
Female	1,100.0	1,019.9	1,063.1	1,167.5	1,176.5	1,104.8	983.2	860.0	769.8	-0.89	-30.02
Male	1,145.6	1,064.0	1,111.1	1,219.5	1,227.9	1,152.7	1,030.0	901.0	810.8	-0.86	-29.22

Table 5.40 Middle-aged generation

'000

	1980	1985	1990	1995	2000	2005	2010	2015	2020	CAGR	Period growth
Middle-aged adults 30-59	3,901	4,013	4,069	4,129	4,266	4,420	4,570	4,503	4,477	0.35	14.8
Female	1,987	2,030	2,048	2,074	2,137	2,206	2,269	2,228	2,211	0.27	11.3
Male	1,914	1,983	2,021	2,054	2,129	2,213	2,300	2,276	2,266	0.42	18.4
Baby boomers aged 40-59	2,368	2,348	2,523	2,746	2,913	2,916	2,829	2,864	3,069	0.65	29.6
Female	1,229	1,206	1,285	1,393	1,474	1,470	1,416	1,424	1,521	0.53	23.7
Male	1,139	1,142	1,239	1,353	1,439	1,446	1,413	1,440	1,548	0.77	35.9

Table 5.41 Elderly population

'000

	1980	1985	1990	1995	2000	2005	2010	2015	2020	CAGR	Period growth
Elderly population (60+)	1,732.1	1,790.0	1,818.2	1,856.3	1,865.3	2,016.5	2,314.5	2,575.3	2,739.4	1.15	58.2
Female	1,038.1	1,076.5	1,095.8	1,114.1	1,113.6	1,185.9	1,336.1	1,466.7	1,546.1	1.00	48.9
Male	694.0	713.5	722.4	742.2	751.7	830.7	978.4	1,108.6	1,193.3	1.36	72.0

Table 5.42 Population of biggest cities 1980-2020

'000

	1980	1985	1990	1995	2000	2005	2010	2015	2020	CAGR	Period growth
Prague	1,180.4	1,201.2	1,211.5	1,214.6	1,186.9	1,170.6	1,247.7	1,313.7	1,360.5	0.36	15.26
Brno	378.0	384.6	387.7	390.0	383.6	367.7	371.5	374.6	376.5	-0.01	-0.40
Ostrava	325.9	329.1	328.2	325.7	321.3	311.4	306.8	301.4	297.0	-0.23	-8.86
Plzen	173.0	174.4	173.5	171.8	166.8	162.6	166.7	169.2	170.9	-0.03	-1.21
Liberec	102.1	102.9	102.3	100.7	99.6	97.4	101.7	104.9	107.1	0.12	4.91
Olomouc	102.4	104.4	105.7	106.2	103.0	100.8	100.3	99.5	98.9	-0.09	-3.42
Usti nad Labem	98.7	99.9	99.9	97.2	96.1	93.9	95.5	96.0	96.2	-0.06	-2.50
Ceske Budejovice	90.3	93.5	96.7	99.8	98.9	94.6	94.9	94.3	93.8	0.09	3.86
Hradec Kralove	96.4	98.4	99.7	100.7	98.7	94.7	94.4	94.0	93.5	-0.07	-2.94
Pardubice	92.4	94.1	94.9	94.1	92.1	88.2	90.3	92.0	93.2	0.02	0.82

Chart 5.52 Population age shift 2000 and 2020, Each Column Represents a Single Age Group

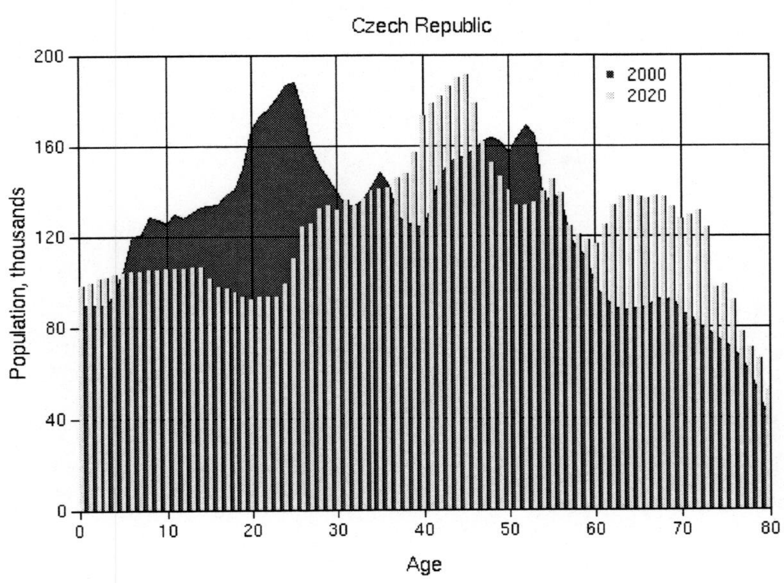

Chart 5.53 Population pyramids, 1980/2000/2010/2020

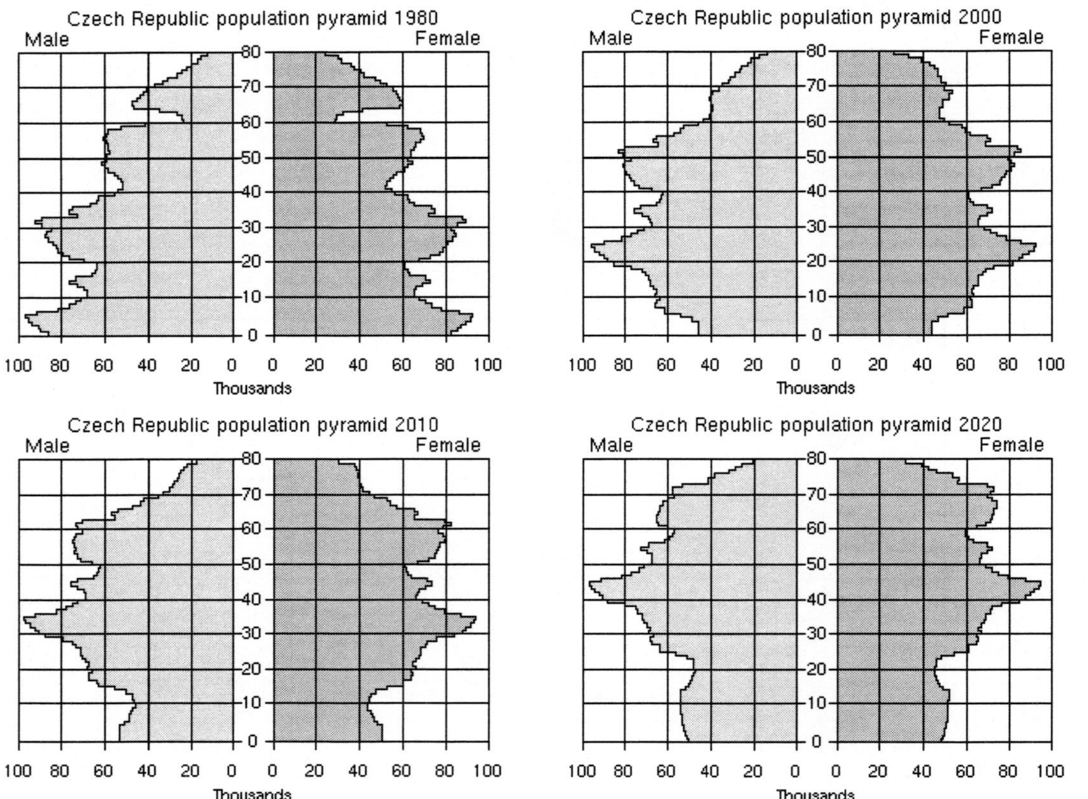

Chart 5.54 Major Cities: 1980, 2000 and 2020

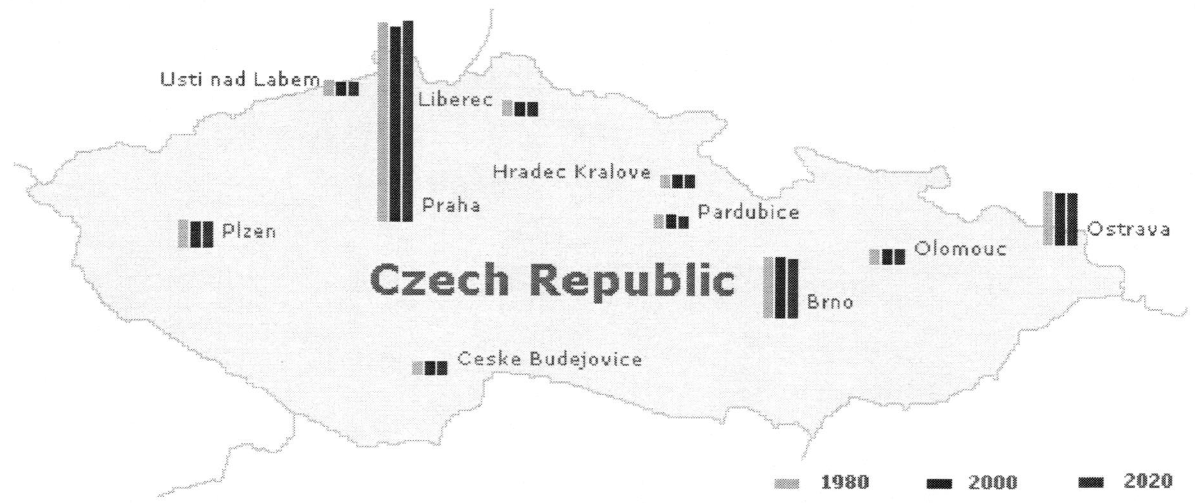

Denmark

Table 5.43 Key population trends

'000

	1980	1985	1990	1995	2000	2005	2010	2015	2020	CAGR	Period growth
Population at January 1st	5,122.1	5,111.1	5,135.4	5,215.7	5,330.0	5,411.4	5,526.0	5,602.1	5,680.6	0.26	10.90
Male	2,529.1	2,517.1	2,530.6	2,573.3	2,634.1	2,677.3	2,739.9	2,778.7	2,817.0	0.27	11.39
Female	2,593.0	2,594.0	2,604.8	2,642.4	2,695.9	2,734.1	2,786.2	2,823.4	2,863.5	0.25	10.43
0-4 yrs	321.3	266.2	287.1	335.1	340.6	328.1	325.9	312.2	314.9	-0.05	-2.00
5-9 yrs	363.4	321.1	269.8	291.9	341.8	344.1	329.4	326.3	313.2	-0.37	-13.81
10-14 yrs	396.8	363.4	323.7	273.9	298.8	346.0	345.1	330.4	327.7	-0.48	-17.41
15-19 yrs	390.8	398.2	366.6	328.4	281.3	304.6	349.9	348.4	334.1	-0.39	-14.51
20-24 yrs	371.7	391.9	402.1	373.9	339.8	292.5	322.5	362.4	361.4	-0.07	-2.80
25-29 yrs	374.8	369.8	396.0	408.3	383.4	345.7	309.6	327.9	367.2	-0.05	-2.02
30-34 yrs	419.0	371.8	371.0	399.0	414.2	384.2	352.6	309.6	327.5	-0.61	-21.84
35-39 yrs	361.3	415.6	370.5	372.3	403.2	413.9	386.9	352.7	310.0	-0.38	-14.19
40-44 yrs	295.4	357.3	412.2	369.3	373.6	401.7	414.4	386.3	352.5	0.44	19.34
45-49 yrs	272.3	290.4	352.1	407.6	366.9	369.9	399.6	410.6	383.4	0.86	40.80
50-54 yrs	274.8	264.9	283.2	344.9	400.8	359.8	364.1	392.4	403.4	0.96	46.77
55-59 yrs	289.6	263.5	253.9	273.5	335.0	389.0	350.1	354.9	382.9	0.70	32.23
60-64 yrs	256.2	270.9	246.9	239.0	260.2	319.4	372.5	336.9	342.8	0.73	33.80
65-69 yrs	245.9	231.5	244.8	224.8	218.5	241.3	298.7	350.3	319.1	0.65	29.76
70-74 yrs	202.3	211.2	199.4	210.9	194.8	191.8	216.7	271.7	321.3	1.16	58.84
75-79 yrs	144.3	159.0	167.7	158.1	168.3	158.6	159.8	185.0	236.2	1.24	63.76
80+ yrs	142.3	164.4	188.4	204.9	208.8	220.9	228.3	244.1	283.1	1.73	98.95
Median age of population (years)	34.1	36.0	37.0	37.7	38.2	39.4	40.5	41.7	42.7	0.56	25.18

Table 5.44 Key economic trends

As stated

	1990	1995	2000	2005	2010	2015	2020	CAGR	Period growth
Total GDP (DKr per capita)	238,935.7	264,207.5	297,623.9	312,011.5	312,223.5	343,632.4	378,795.6	1.55	58.5
Disposable income (DKr per capita)	127,145.1	137,750.2	149,027.9	166,224.6	175,912.1	198,102.7	219,608.3	1.84	72.7
Disposable income (DKr per household)	288,274.7	304,742.8	326,329.1	360,002.1	377,397.2	420,352.6	461,904.3	1.58	60.2
Number of households by annual household disposable income ('000)									
Over US$1,000	2,263.3	2,356.3	2,431.7	2,497.1	2,574.5	2,639.0	2,699.8	0.59	19.3
Over US$10,000	2,064.2	2,219.4	2,212.7	2,386.7	2,476.8	2,558.8	2,635.1	0.82	27.7
Over US$25,000	1,266.5	1,625.0	1,418.0	1,957.5	2,078.3	2,233.0	2,371.1	2.11	87.2
Over US$75,000	122.2	254.2	166.5	581.0	673.6	912.9	1,166.1	7.81	853.9
Over US$150,000	41.9	61.3	49.8	110.1	106.7	188.6	304.9	6.84	627.2
Total households	2,265.0	2,357.6	2,434.1	2,498.6	2,575.8	2,640.1	2,700.8	0.59	19.2

Note: Per capita data is shown at constant 2010 prices. Household disposable income bands are shown at current prices.

Table 5.45 Young generation

'000

	1980	1985	1990	1995	2000	2005	2010	2015	2020	CAGR	Period growth
Babies under 12 months	59.2	51.8	61.2	69.7	66.3	64.7	64.1	61.5	63.9	0.19	7.82
Infants under 24 months	121.4	102.8	120.2	137.4	132.9	129.8	129.6	123.4	127.3	0.12	4.88
Toddlers aged 1-4	262.1	214.4	225.8	265.4	274.3	263.3	261.8	250.7	251.0	-0.11	-4.22
Children aged 2-9	563.3	484.5	436.7	489.6	549.5	542.3	525.7	515.1	500.7	-0.29	-11.10
Female	275.4	237.1	213.5	238.4	267.5	264.5	256.7	251.2	244.3	-0.30	-11.29
Male	287.9	247.4	223.2	251.1	282.0	277.8	268.9	263.9	256.5	-0.29	-10.91
Tweenagers aged 10-14	396.8	363.4	323.7	273.9	298.8	346.0	345.1	330.4	327.7	-0.48	-17.41
Female	193.4	177.7	158.2	134.1	145.5	168.5	168.1	161.4	159.8	-0.48	-17.34
Male	203.4	185.7	165.5	139.8	153.3	177.5	177.0	169.0	167.9	-0.48	-17.48
Teenagers aged 13-19	562.2	544.0	505.1	442.0	396.2	438.7	491.4	482.7	466.1	-0.47	-17.10
Female	274.7	264.9	246.8	216.2	194.1	213.5	239.4	235.6	227.8	-0.47	-17.07
Male	287.5	279.1	258.3	225.8	202.2	225.2	252.0	247.1	238.3	-0.47	-17.14
Studying age 18-22	372.3	412.9	375.5	363.8	310.8	288.1	331.7	363.2	348.1	-0.17	-6.52
Female	182.0	201.1	182.5	178.4	153.0	141.2	161.8	177.4	170.6	-0.16	-6.24
Male	190.3	211.8	193.0	185.3	157.9	146.9	169.9	185.8	177.4	-0.18	-6.78
Young adults aged 15-29	1,137.3	1,159.9	1,164.7	1,110.6	1,004.5	942.8	982.0	1,038.7	1,062.7	-0.17	-6.57
Female	555.4	565.9	566.8	542.8	494.8	464.8	482.5	509.5	521.9	-0.16	-6.02
Male	582.0	594.0	597.9	567.8	509.7	478.0	499.5	529.2	540.7	-0.18	-7.09

Table 5.46 Middle-aged generation

'000

	1980	1985	1990	1995	2000	2005	2010	2015	2020	CAGR	Period growth
Middle-aged adults 30-59	1,912.4	1,963.5	2,042.9	2,166.6	2,293.7	2,318.5	2,267.5	2,206.5	2,159.7	0.30	12.9
Female	952.6	973.8	1,009.4	1,067.5	1,129.5	1,146.8	1,125.2	1,098.7	1,078.3	0.31	13.2
Male	959.8	989.7	1,033.4	1,099.1	1,164.2	1,171.7	1,142.4	1,107.8	1,081.3	0.30	12.7
Baby boomers aged 40-59	1,132.1	1,176.1	1,301.4	1,395.3	1,476.3	1,520.4	1,528.1	1,544.2	1,522.2	0.74	34.5
Female	571.8	588.9	646.5	691.0	730.2	752.8	757.2	767.5	760.1	0.71	32.9
Male	560.2	587.2	654.9	704.3	746.1	767.6	770.9	776.7	762.1	0.77	36.0

Table 5.47 Elderly population

'000

	1980	1985	1990	1995	2000	2005	2010	2015	2020	CAGR	Period growth
Elderly population (60+)	990.9	1,037.0	1,047.2	1,037.7	1,050.6	1,131.9	1,276.1	1,388.0	1,502.5	1.05	51.6
Female	557.0	589.2	598.4	592.6	593.8	626.2	690.6	742.4	797.1	0.90	43.1
Male	433.9	447.7	448.8	445.1	456.8	505.7	585.4	645.5	705.3	1.22	62.6

Table 5.48 Population of biggest cities 1980-2020

'000

	1980	1985	1990	1995	2000	2005	2010	2015	2020	CAGR	Period growth
Copenhagen	498.9	476.0	466.7	471.5	495.7	502.4	513.2	523.9	533.6	0.17	6.96
Arhus	244.8	250.6	261.4	277.3	284.8	295.0	299.6	303.3	307.1	0.57	25.44
Odense	168.5	170.6	176.1	182.6	183.9	185.9	186.8	186.8	187.6	0.27	11.31
Aalborg	153.9	153.3	155.0	158.8	161.2	163.2	165.6	167.3	169.2	0.24	9.90
Frederiksberg	88.3	85.9	85.6	88.0	90.3	91.9	94.1	96.3	98.1	0.26	11.14
Esbjerg	79.3	80.4	81.5	82.7	82.9	82.7	83.4	83.6	84.1	0.15	6.06
Gentofte	67.3	65.4	65.3	66.3	68.0	68.6	69.2	69.5	69.9	0.10	3.90
Kolding	55.8	56.1	57.3	59.4	61.6	63.2	63.5	63.6	63.9	0.34	14.67
Randers	62.5	61.2	61.0	61.7	62.0	62.5	63.0	63.3	63.7	0.05	1.87
Gladsaxe	65.0	62.4	60.9	61.1	61.9	62.2	62.6	62.6	62.9	-0.08	-3.12

Chart 5.55 Population age shift 2000 and 2020, Each Column Represents a Single Age Group

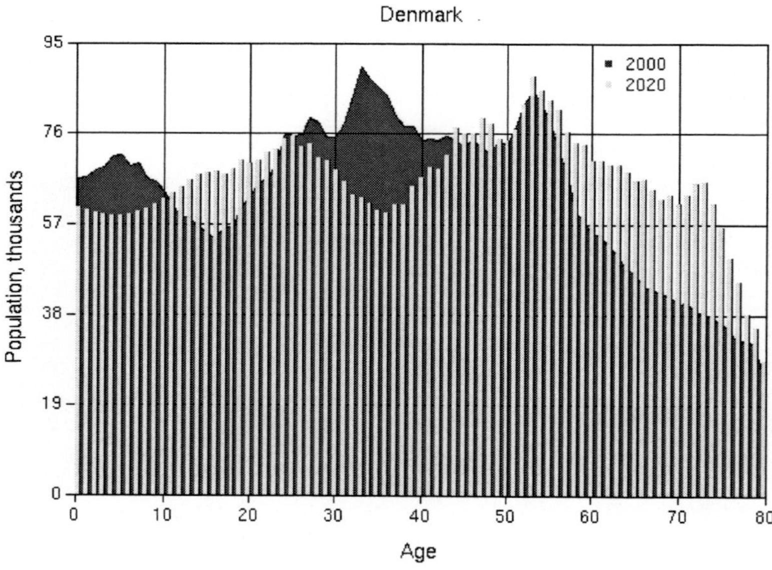

Chart 5.56 Population pyramids, 1980/2000/2010/2020

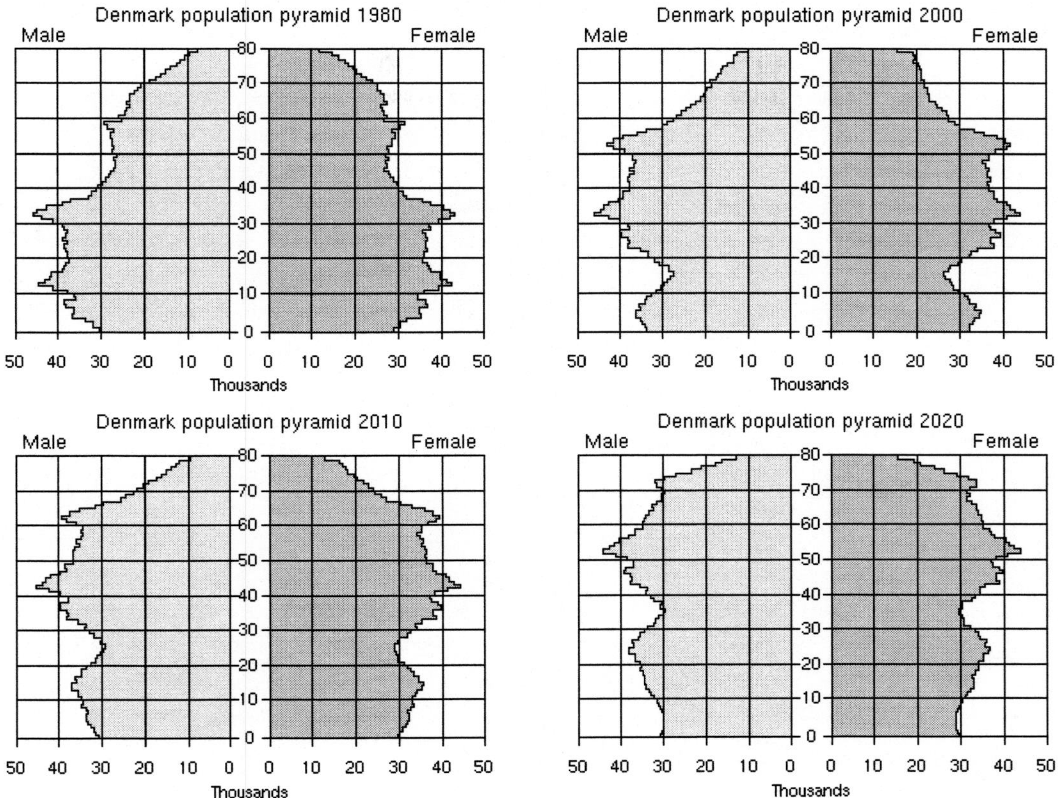

Chart 5.57 Major Cities: 1980, 2000 and 2020

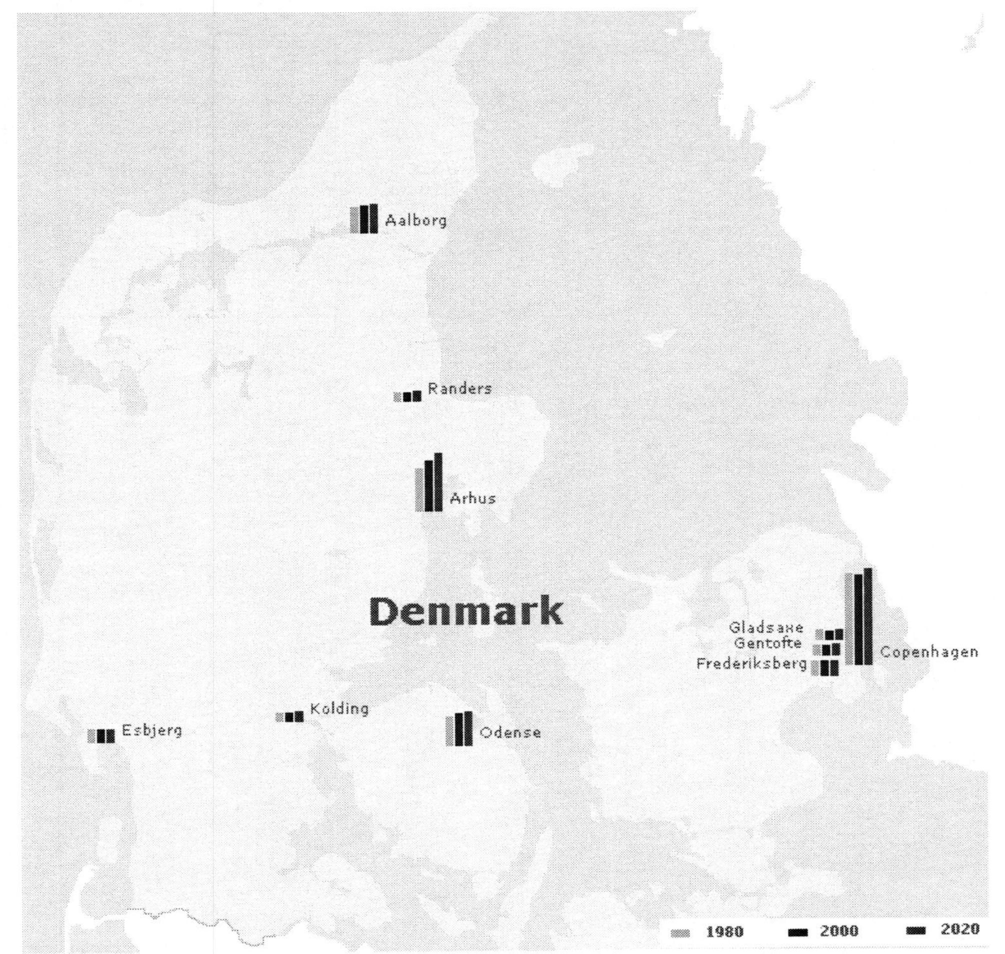

Ecuador

Table 5.49 Key population trends

'000

	1980	1985	1990	1995	2000	2005	2010	2015	2020	CAGR	Period growth
Population at January 1st	7,964.3	9,102.9	10,278.5	11,406.8	12,310.3	13,062.5	13,774.9	14,596.2	15,375.5	1.66	93.06
Male	4,004.8	4,577.5	5,167.3	5,731.1	6,180.2	6,550.0	6,898.0	7,298.9	7,677.2	1.64	91.70
Female	3,959.5	4,525.4	5,111.2	5,675.6	6,130.1	6,512.5	6,876.9	7,297.3	7,698.3	1.68	94.43
0-4 yrs	1,285.0	1,367.2	1,404.2	1,418.1	1,460.1	1,425.2	1,370.1	1,342.8	1,327.0	0.08	3.27
5-9 yrs	1,130.3	1,256.8	1,347.1	1,390.0	1,404.6	1,441.9	1,414.2	1,362.6	1,333.8	0.41	18.00
10-14 yrs	993.8	1,122.3	1,250.2	1,340.5	1,375.5	1,391.7	1,429.3	1,406.5	1,355.8	0.78	36.43
15-19 yrs	853.8	987.6	1,116.3	1,236.8	1,295.7	1,320.8	1,344.2	1,403.3	1,382.7	1.21	61.96
20-24 yrs	727.6	846.7	980.3	1,094.9	1,156.2	1,192.1	1,229.4	1,294.0	1,359.0	1.57	86.78
25-29 yrs	616.8	719.9	838.6	960.5	1,024.1	1,064.5	1,109.9	1,182.7	1,252.9	1.79	103.12
30-34 yrs	468.8	608.9	711.5	821.6	906.1	954.7	1,001.9	1,073.1	1,149.7	2.27	145.26
35-39 yrs	385.0	461.5	600.3	696.3	778.2	851.3	904.8	971.3	1,045.1	2.53	171.44
40-44 yrs	330.9	377.3	453.0	587.0	665.7	740.7	815.8	880.9	948.8	2.67	186.73
45-49 yrs	278.9	322.2	368.3	441.4	563.9	638.5	714.0	795.1	860.5	2.86	208.57
50-54 yrs	231.6	269.3	312.1	356.8	423.7	542.3	616.3	694.4	774.7	3.06	234.50
55-59 yrs	187.6	220.4	257.3	299.2	341.0	406.3	521.8	596.0	672.4	3.24	258.49
60-64 yrs	152.3	174.5	206.4	242.5	282.3	323.2	386.2	498.5	570.2	3.36	274.36
65-69 yrs	125.6	136.4	158.2	189.4	224.8	264.0	302.7	362.8	468.9	3.35	273.30
70-74 yrs	89.3	105.6	117.0	138.6	169.3	203.9	240.1	276.2	331.6	3.33	271.17
75-79 yrs	58.4	67.8	82.9	95.1	117.0	146.4	177.0	209.1	240.9	3.61	312.88
80+ yrs	48.8	58.5	74.6	98.1	122.2	154.9	197.5	246.9	301.6	4.66	517.86
Median age of population (years)	18.3	19.0	20.1	21.4	22.6	23.9	25.4	27.0	28.7	1.13	56.93

Table 5.50 Key economic trends

As stated

	1990	1995	2000	2005	2010	2015	2020	CAGR	Period growth
Total GDP (US$ per capita)	3,151.9	3,360.6	3,263.7	4,004.9	4,328.0	4,658.0	5,066.3	1.59	60.74
Disposable income (US$ per capita)	72,569.0	22,792.9	2,237.9	2,922.4	3,426.3	3,726.7	4,048.4	-9.17	-94.42
Disposable income (US$ per household)	363,870.9	107,995.4	9,849.8	11,594.7	12,178.5	12,154.1	12,364.3	-10.66	-96.60
Number of households by annual household disposable income ('000)									
Over US$1,000	1,937.9	2,304.3	2,420.2	3,215.2	3,830.9	4,439.9	5,010.8	3.22	158.57
Over US$10,000	164.9	319.1	183.5	592.4	979.6	1,371.9	1,935.3	8.56	1,073.80
Over US$25,000	37.5	87.0	49.5	159.9	267.1	379.0	548.6	9.35	1,362.70
Over US$75,000	9.3	18.8	11.4	33.8	55.2	77.0	110.1	8.60	1,088.83
Over US$150,000	4.0	7.6	5.0	13.6	21.4	28.7	40.3	7.99	904.57
Total households	2,049.9	2,407.4	2,796.9	3,292.4	3,875.5	4,475.5	5,034.4	3.04	145.59

Note: Per capita data is shown at constant 2010 prices. Household disposable income bands are shown at current prices.

Table 5.51 Young generation

'000

	1980	1985	1990	1995	2000	2005	2010	2015	2020	CAGR	Period growth
Babies under 12 months	270.6	279.7	283.5	286.0	300.0	278.1	272.5	269.8	265.5	-0.05	-1.89
Infants under 24 months	534.4	557.1	566.0	570.6	595.4	561.0	544.8	538.6	531.0	-0.02	-0.62
Toddlers aged 1-4	1,014.4	1,087.5	1,120.7	1,132.1	1,160.2	1,147.1	1,097.6	1,073.0	1,061.6	0.11	4.65
Children aged 2-9	1,880.9	2,066.9	2,185.3	2,237.4	2,269.4	2,306.1	2,239.4	2,166.7	2,129.8	0.31	13.23
Female	926.7	1,017.7	1,075.0	1,099.4	1,113.5	1,130.1	1,096.9	1,060.4	1,041.9	0.29	12.43
Male	954.2	1,049.3	1,110.3	1,138.0	1,155.8	1,176.0	1,142.6	1,106.4	1,087.9	0.33	14.02
Tweenagers aged 10-14	993.8	1,122.3	1,250.2	1,340.5	1,375.5	1,391.7	1,429.3	1,406.5	1,355.8	0.78	36.43
Female	490.5	553.6	616.3	660.1	676.5	683.4	700.8	689.3	663.9	0.76	35.35
Male	503.3	568.7	634.0	680.3	699.0	708.3	728.5	717.2	691.9	0.80	37.48
Teenagers aged 13-19	1,234.9	1,420.2	1,601.8	1,763.7	1,840.5	1,870.1	1,910.8	1,970.4	1,928.7	1.12	56.19
Female	610.1	701.3	790.4	869.8	907.1	920.4	938.9	966.8	945.9	1.10	55.03
Male	624.8	718.9	811.3	893.9	933.4	949.6	971.9	1,003.6	982.8	1.14	57.32
Studying age 18-22	774.1	903.3	1,034.9	1,152.4	1,214.6	1,247.8	1,276.2	1,344.1	1,379.4	1.45	78.19
Female	382.9	446.6	511.4	569.3	600.3	616.3	629.3	661.3	677.8	1.44	77.01
Male	391.2	456.7	523.5	583.0	614.3	631.5	646.9	682.7	701.5	1.47	79.35
Young adults aged 15-29	2,198.1	2,554.2	2,935.2	3,292.2	3,476.1	3,577.3	3,683.4	3,880.0	3,994.6	1.50	81.73
Female	1,088.3	1,263.8	1,451.6	1,628.1	1,719.7	1,769.7	1,820.1	1,913.8	1,967.5	1.49	80.78
Male	1,109.9	1,290.4	1,483.6	1,664.1	1,756.4	1,807.6	1,863.3	1,966.2	2,027.2	1.52	82.65

Table 5.52 Middle-aged generation

'000

	1980	1985	1990	1995	2000	2005	2010	2015	2020	CAGR	Period growth
Middle-aged adults 30-59	1,882.7	2,259.6	2,702.5	3,202.3	3,678.5	4,133.9	4,574.5	5,010.8	5,451.1	2.69	189.5
Female	940.9	1,130.8	1,353.5	1,605.0	1,846.3	2,078.7	2,304.7	2,527.4	2,750.5	2.72	192.3
Male	941.9	1,128.8	1,349.0	1,597.2	1,832.3	2,055.2	2,269.8	2,483.4	2,700.6	2.67	186.7
Baby boomers aged 40-59	1,028.9	1,189.2	1,390.7	1,684.3	1,994.2	2,327.9	2,667.9	2,966.5	3,256.4	2.92	216.5
Female	516.3	597.9	700.1	848.7	1,005.6	1,175.1	1,349.4	1,503.3	1,652.9	2.95	220.1
Male	512.6	591.3	690.6	835.6	988.7	1,152.8	1,318.4	1,463.1	1,603.4	2.89	212.8

Table 5.53 Elderly population

'000

	1980	1985	1990	1995	2000	2005	2010	2015	2020	CAGR	Period growth
Elderly population (60+)	474.4	542.9	639.2	763.8	915.5	1,092.4	1,303.4	1,593.5	1,913.1	3.55	303.3
Female	250.4	286.0	337.0	403.2	482.7	575.9	688.1	843.0	1,015.1	3.56	305.3
Male	224.0	256.9	302.1	360.6	432.8	516.5	615.3	750.5	898.0	3.53	301.0

Table 5.54 Population of biggest cities 1980-2020

'000

	1980	1985	1990	1995	2000	2005	2010	2015	2020	CAGR	Period growth
Guayaquil	1,125.9	1,300.9	1,508.4	1,775.6	1,991.3	2,108.3	2,247.3	2,426.3	2,615.7	2.13	132.3
Quito	809.8	947.1	1,100.8	1,276.7	1,405.9	1,474.8	1,561.1	1,677.1	1,801.5	2.02	122.5
Cuenca	143.0	165.6	195.0	235.6	275.2	304.0	333.6	367.6	402.0	2.62	181.2
Santo Domingo de los Colorados	60.7	83.9	114.4	155.0	195.9	227.6	258.0	290.4	322.2	4.26	430.5
Machala	97.1	118.4	144.2	176.7	204.1	221.0	239.3	261.3	284.0	2.72	192.4
Eloy Alfaro	45.9	59.6	82.4	123.1	170.3	203.5	234.9	267.5	299.1	4.80	551.9
Manta	94.9	107.4	125.5	154.8	182.7	198.7	215.9	236.3	257.2	2.52	170.9
Portoviejo	95.5	113.0	132.9	155.6	172.2	182.4	194.5	210.0	226.3	2.18	137.0
Ambato	94.5	108.5	124.2	142.7	155.0	161.4	169.9	181.7	194.6	1.82	105.9
Riobamba	70.9	81.6	94.5	111.2	124.9	133.2	142.6	154.5	166.9	2.16	135.3

Chart 5.58 Population age shift 2000 and 2020, Each Column Represents a Single Age Group

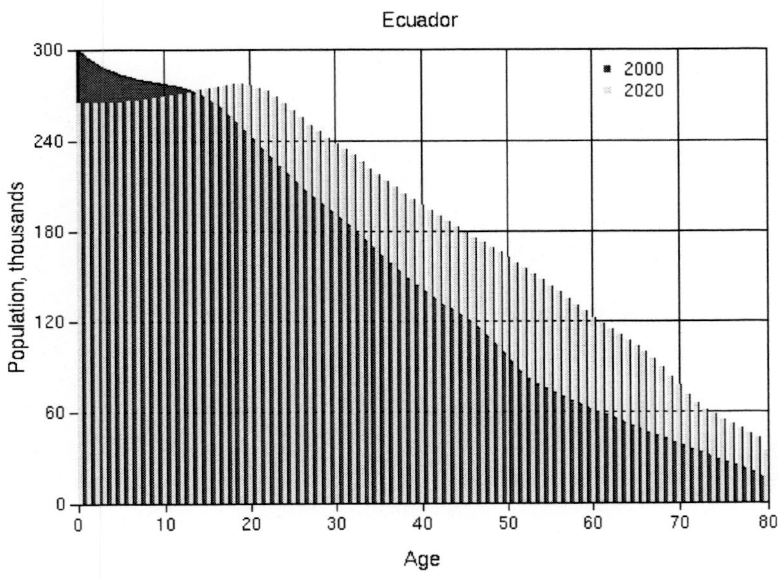

Chart 5.59 Population pyramids, 1980/2000/2010/2020

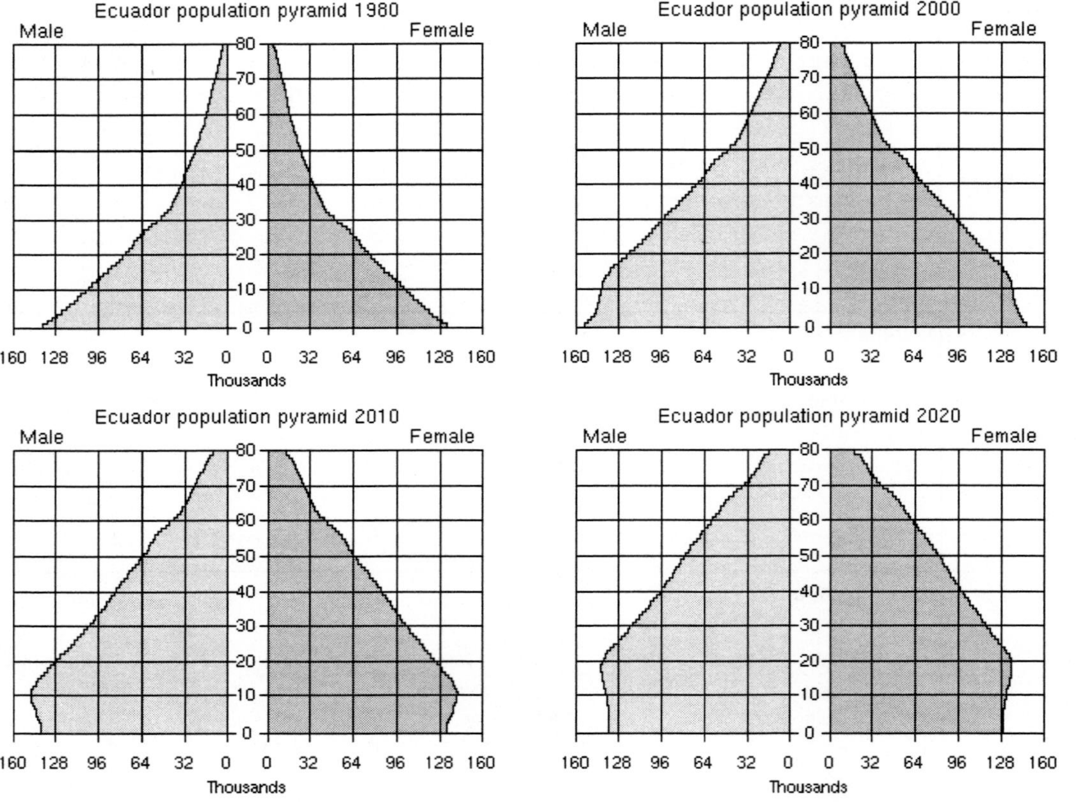

Chart 5.60 Major Cities: 1980, 2000 and 2020

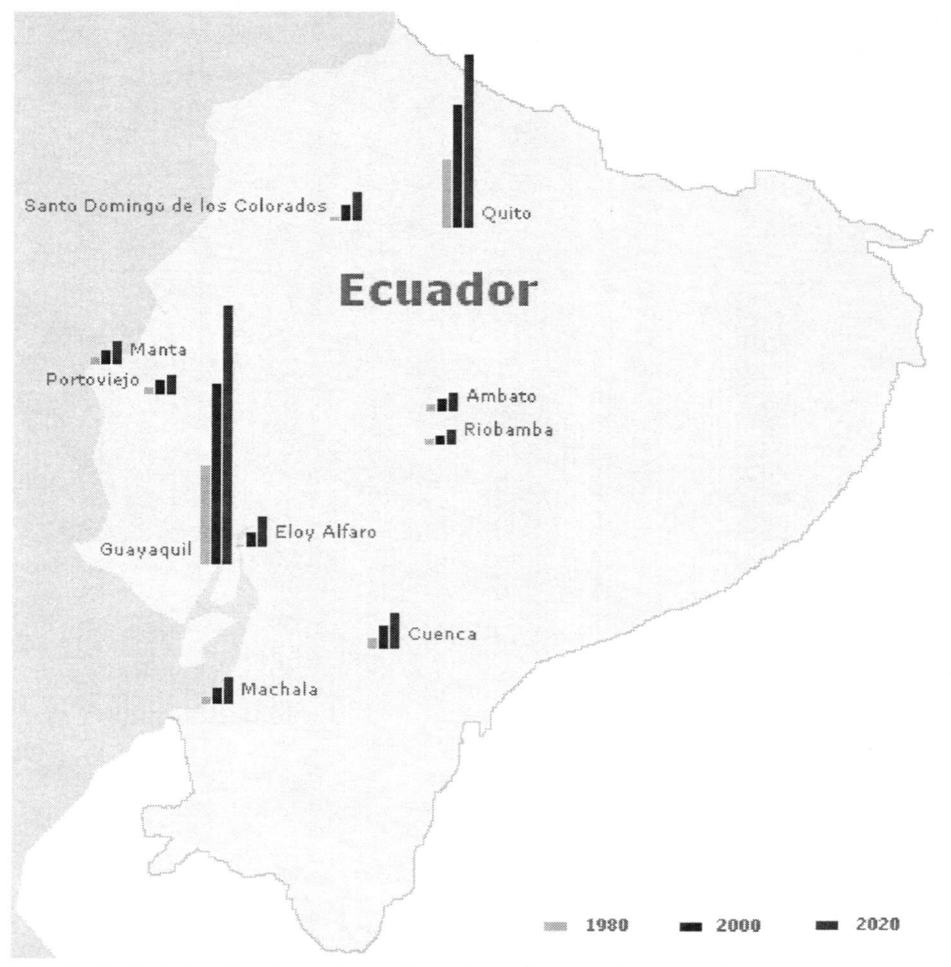

Egypt

Table 5.55 Key population trends

'000

	1980	1985	1990	1995	2000	2005	2010	2015	2020	CAGR	Period growth
Population at January 1st	41,377.9	47,142.5	52,581.9	58,129.5	64,378.7	71,190.4	78,160.3	85,110.9	91,770.5	2.01	121.8
Male	21,134.5	24,134.8	26,928.8	29,750.3	32,927.0	36,393.9	39,934.0	43,457.5	46,819.6	2.01	121.5
Female	20,243.4	23,007.7	25,653.1	28,379.2	31,451.7	34,796.5	38,226.2	41,653.4	44,951.0	2.01	122.1
0-4 yrs	6,120.5	7,155.7	7,527.6	7,004.9	7,166.7	8,217.4	9,033.8	9,368.0	9,404.0	1.08	53.6
5-9 yrs	5,235.3	6,223.7	7,271.6	7,647.3	7,300.1	7,726.4	8,843.1	9,692.9	10,046.9	1.64	91.9
10-14 yrs	4,854.2	5,474.8	6,288.7	7,547.2	7,762.3	7,541.6	8,035.7	9,179.8	10,070.1	1.84	107.5
15-19 yrs	4,558.6	4,896.5	5,288.0	6,460.6	7,460.4	7,754.3	7,477.7	7,924.0	9,099.7	1.74	99.6
20-24 yrs	3,798.0	4,243.0	4,619.7	5,022.5	6,328.4	7,079.5	7,465.5	7,016.7	7,393.6	1.68	94.7
25-29 yrs	3,094.6	3,625.0	4,055.0	4,312.0	4,932.5	5,985.1	6,668.7	7,000.7	6,391.8	1.83	106.5
30-34 yrs	2,647.2	3,085.5	3,595.2	3,979.1	4,186.6	4,812.5	5,720.4	6,403.9	6,683.3	2.34	152.5
35-39 yrs	2,148.5	2,723.7	3,068.6	3,684.1	3,974.3	4,032.6	4,635.0	5,561.3	6,246.8	2.70	190.7
40-44 yrs	2,003.4	2,122.4	2,646.2	3,090.6	3,700.4	3,915.0	3,827.8	4,464.9	5,424.8	2.52	170.8
45-49 yrs	1,771.3	1,914.6	2,022.1	2,561.1	3,098.5	3,623.6	3,780.5	3,635.1	4,281.2	2.23	141.7
50-54 yrs	1,466.9	1,650.5	1,738.4	1,924.7	2,470.7	3,036.5	3,529.9	3,656.0	3,449.3	2.16	135.1
55-59 yrs	1,239.3	1,308.3	1,490.0	1,538.4	1,842.9	2,332.3	2,909.2	3,411.3	3,506.7	2.63	182.9
60-64 yrs	869.5	1,072.8	1,124.2	1,327.4	1,453.7	1,713.3	2,167.8	2,777.2	3,290.4	3.38	278.4
65-69 yrs	737.5	715.9	858.2	930.0	1,193.8	1,377.7	1,548.5	2,035.5	2,674.3	3.27	262.6
70-74 yrs	429.3	523.1	527.3	609.2	787.2	1,024.9	1,189.9	1,350.3	1,853.7	3.72	331.8
75-79 yrs	267.3	261.2	304.7	315.8	454.6	626.9	811.6	980.2	1,125.7	3.66	321.2
80+ yrs	136.3	146.0	156.4	174.6	265.7	390.8	515.3	653.0	828.3	4.62	507.9
Median age of population (years)	19.9	19.8	19.9	20.4	21.8	23.0	23.8	24.6	24.9	0.56	25.1

Table 5.56 Key economic trends

As stated

	1990	1995	2000	2005	2010	2015	2020	CAGR	Period growth
Total GDP (E£ per capita)	9,133.8	9,470.9	11,424.0	12,384.2	15,130.8	18,319.8	22,501.0	3.05	146.3
Disposable income (E£ per capita)	7,170.1	7,543.2	9,109.0	9,657.6	12,135.1	14,706.4	18,047.8	3.12	151.7
Disposable income (E£ per household)	35,393.1	35,566.2	40,869.4	41,075.9	48,634.3	55,674.7	64,755.2	2.03	83.0
Number of households by annual household disposable income ('000)									
Over US$1,000	9,624.6	12,173.3	14,274.7	16,473.2	19,480.5	22,474.6	25,574.8	3.31	165.7
Over US$10,000	262.4	538.0	1,165.8	882.6	4,340.2	9,717.6	17,570.8	15.04	6,594.9
Over US$25,000	83.1	160.1	273.3	240.5	730.1	1,634.0	3,703.2	13.49	4,357.2
Over US$75,000	20.9	39.6	68.1	60.2	166.7	302.4	540.0	11.45	2,481.3
Over US$150,000	8.8	16.4	28.4	25.1	69.8	126.8	224.9	11.42	2,466.3
Total households	10,652.3	12,328.7	14,348.8	16,738.0	19,502.3	22,482.0	25,577.1	2.96	140.1

Note: Per capita data is shown at constant 2010 prices. Household disposable income bands are shown at current prices.

Table 5.57 Young generation

'000

	1980	1985	1990	1995	2000	2005	2010	2015	2020	CAGR	Period growth
Babies under 12 months	1,291	1,514	1,464	1,337	1,465	1,674	1,785	1,827	1,820	0.86	40.9
Infants under 24 months	2,547	2,986	2,952	2,704	2,912	3,337	3,583	3,681	3,667	0.92	44.0
Toddlers aged 1-4	4,829	5,641	6,063	5,668	5,701	6,543	7,248	7,541	7,584	1.13	57.1
Children aged 2-9	8,809	10,393	11,847	11,948	11,555	12,607	14,294	15,380	15,784	1.47	79.2
Female	4,287	5,050	5,757	5,795	5,588	6,054	6,853	7,414	7,660	1.46	78.7
Male	4,521	5,344	6,090	6,153	5,967	6,553	7,441	7,966	8,124	1.48	79.7
Tweenagers aged 10-14	4,854	5,475	6,289	7,547	7,762	7,542	8,036	9,180	10,070	1.84	107.5
Female	2,310	2,603	3,018	3,635	3,743	3,621	3,838	4,381	4,835	1.86	109.3
Male	2,544	2,872	3,271	3,913	4,019	3,921	4,197	4,799	5,235	1.82	105.8
Teenagers aged 13-19	6,478	7,018	7,675	9,391	10,577	10,818	10,587	11,460	13,086	1.77	102.0
Female	3,070	3,306	3,666	4,495	5,094	5,209	5,067	5,463	6,246	1.79	103.4
Male	3,408	3,711	4,009	4,897	5,484	5,609	5,520	5,997	6,840	1.76	100.7
Studying age 18-22	4,117	4,498	4,884	5,523	6,867	7,421	7,570	7,222	8,077	1.70	96.2
Female	1,968	2,133	2,350	2,647	3,298	3,586	3,647	3,454	3,849	1.69	95.6
Male	2,149	2,365	2,534	2,876	3,569	3,835	3,923	3,768	4,228	1.71	96.7
Young adults aged 15-29	11,451	12,764	13,963	15,795	18,721	20,819	21,612	21,941	22,885	1.75	99.8
Female	5,558	6,183	6,744	7,711	9,049	10,066	10,459	10,579	10,970	1.71	97.4
Male	5,894	6,582	7,219	8,084	9,672	10,753	11,153	11,362	11,915	1.78	102.2

Table 5.58 Middle-aged generation

'000

	1980	1985	1990	1995	2000	2005	2010	2015	2020	CAGR	Period growth
Middle-aged adults 30-59	11,277	12,805	14,561	16,778	19,273	21,753	24,403	27,132	29,592	2.44	162.4
Female	5,637	6,386	7,259	8,297	9,578	10,759	12,013	13,332	14,530	2.40	157.8
Male	5,640	6,419	7,301	8,481	9,696	10,994	12,390	13,800	15,062	2.49	167.0
Baby boomers aged 40-59	6,481	6,996	7,897	9,115	11,112	12,907	14,047	15,167	16,662	2.39	157.1
Female	3,222	3,491	3,915	4,462	5,473	6,358	6,919	7,432	8,118	2.34	152.0
Male	3,259	3,504	3,982	4,653	5,640	6,550	7,129	7,736	8,544	2.44	162.1

Table 5.59 Elderly population

'000

	1980	1985	1990	1995	2000	2005	2010	2015	2020	CAGR	Period growth
Elderly population (60+)	2,440	2,719	2,971	3,357	4,155	5,134	6,233	7,796	9,772	3.53	300.5
Female	1,195	1,320	1,432	1,622	2,085	2,697	3,340	4,167	5,172	3.73	332.8
Male	1,245	1,399	1,539	1,735	2,070	2,436	2,893	3,630	4,601	3.32	269.6

Table 5.60 Population of biggest cities 1980-2020

'000

	1980	1985	1990	1995	2000	2005	2010	2015	2020	CAGR	Period growth
Cairo	5,359.7	5,963.4	6,457.8	6,778.9	6,895.7	6,795.1	6,828.7	7,211.4	7,764.4	0.93	44.9
Alexandria	2,617.1	2,882.7	3,085.6	3,290.8	3,605.9	4,001.1	4,486.6	5,125.9	5,840.7	2.03	123.2
Giza	1,662.0	1,850.0	2,009.5	2,186.1	2,462.4	2,815.8	3,231.6	3,747.5	4,312.6	2.41	159.5
Shubra al-Khaymah	611.5	697.9	782.1	859.2	937.0	1,011.1	1,104.7	1,240.4	1,396.8	2.09	128.4
Port Said	352.7	393.8	429.2	463.7	508.5	559.9	623.4	708.8	805.1	2.08	128.3
Suez	273.3	318.5	366.3	410.8	453.5	492.4	540.3	608.5	686.5	2.33	151.2
El-Mansoura	279.3	311.7	339.5	365.5	397.3	432.2	476.3	538.0	608.2	1.96	117.8
Al-Mahallah al-Kubra	251.4	297.0	346.8	389.9	421.1	440.0	466.0	512.1	567.9	2.06	125.9
Tanta	303.5	332.0	351.9	368.7	391.5	417.5	453.0	506.2	568.1	1.58	87.2
Asyut	227.9	265.4	304.7	339.0	366.3	385.9	412.2	455.7	507.5	2.02	122.7

Chart 5.61 Population age shift 2000 and 2020, Each Column Represents a Single Age Group

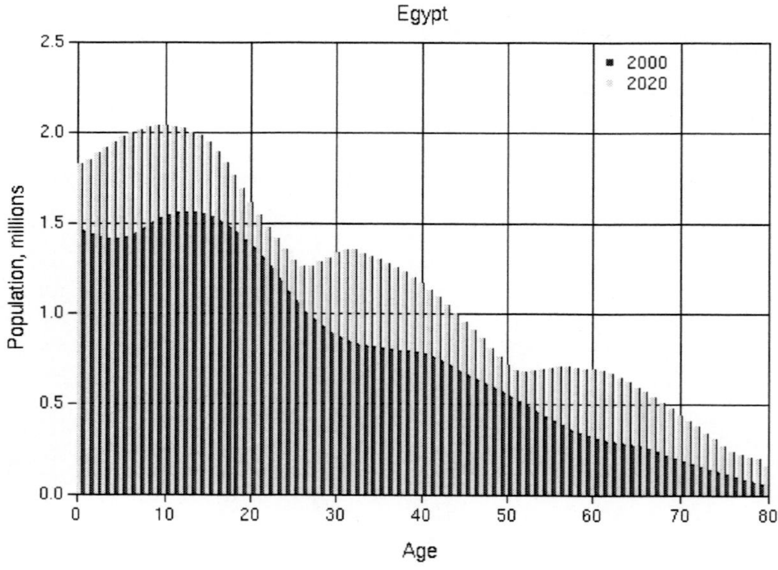

Chart 5.62 Population pyramids, 1980/2000/2010/2020

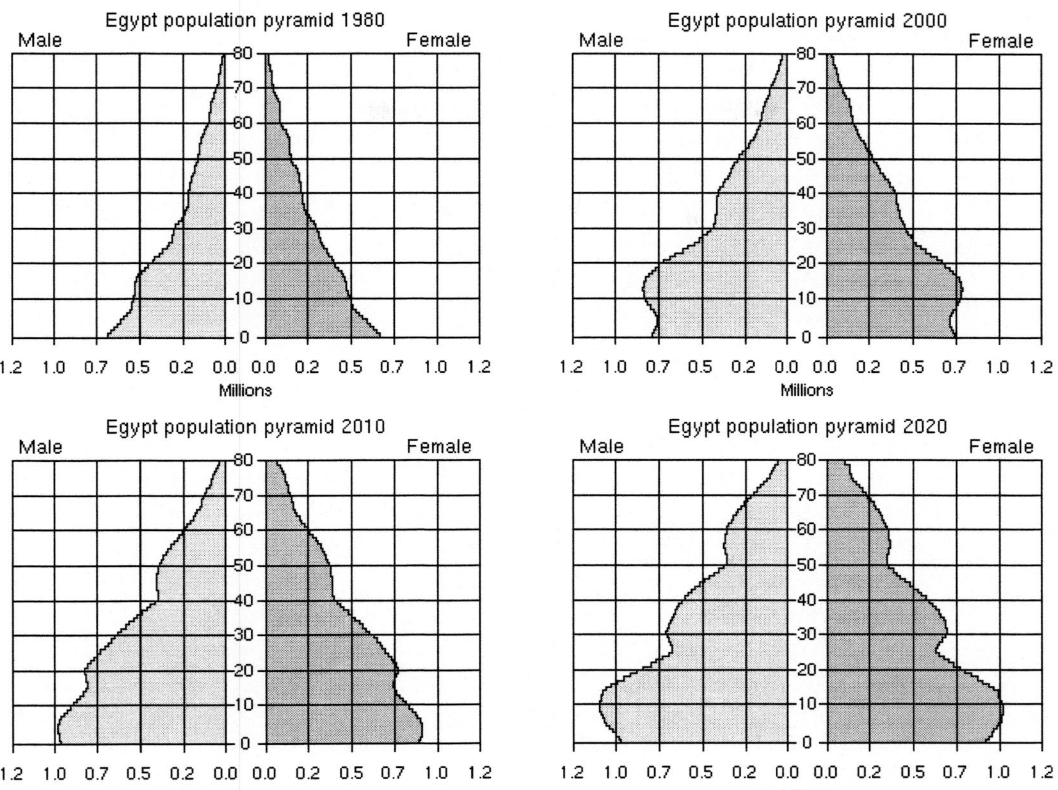

Chart 5.63 Major Cities: 1980, 2000 and 2020

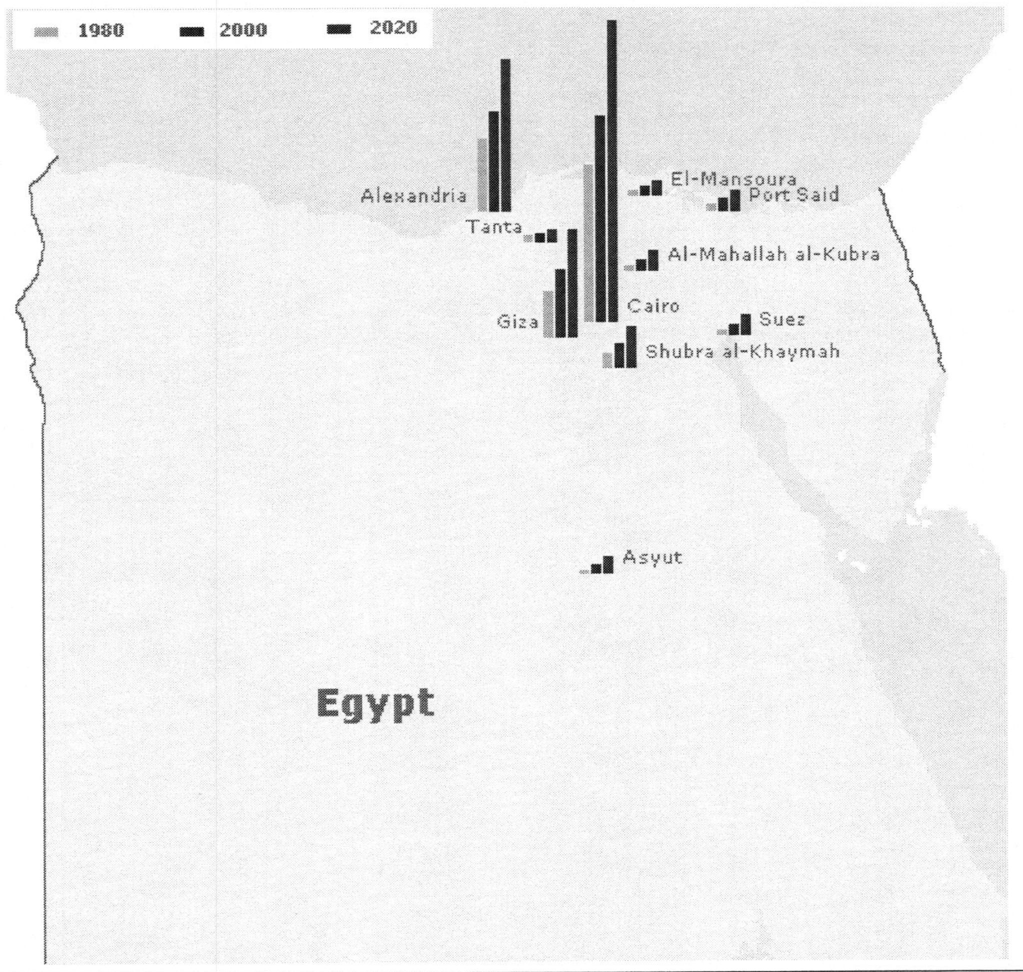

Estonia

Table 5.61 Key population trends

'000

	1980	1985	1990	1995	2000	2005	2010	2015	2020	CAGR	Period growth
Population at January 1st	1,472.2	1,523.5	1,570.6	1,448.1	1,372.1	1,347.5	1,326.1	1,302.2	1,282.0	-0.35	-12.92
Male	681.6	708.1	734.5	671.3	632.7	620.6	609.8	598.2	589.2	-0.36	-13.55
Female	790.6	815.4	836.1	776.8	739.4	726.9	716.2	704.1	692.8	-0.33	-12.38
0-4 yrs	110.5	117.1	121.2	83.9	61.5	65.2	73.2	76.2	74.4	-0.98	-32.64
5-9 yrs	110.7	111.2	117.5	111.1	81.7	61.3	65.0	72.9	76.1	-0.93	-31.29
10-14 yrs	105.1	111.4	111.4	107.5	107.4	81.6	61.1	64.6	72.7	-0.92	-30.84
15-19 yrs	111.1	103.7	109.7	100.0	103.4	107.2	81.2	60.5	64.2	-1.36	-42.22
20-24 yrs	116.6	113.8	105.7	99.6	94.6	102.8	106.2	80.0	59.7	-1.66	-48.75
25-29 yrs	115.2	120.7	117.3	93.3	94.7	93.9	101.5	104.3	78.8	-0.94	-31.56
30-34 yrs	103.2	115.8	120.8	103.8	89.1	93.8	92.4	99.2	102.5	-0.02	-0.67
35-39 yrs	92.7	102.5	114.9	106.7	97.5	88.0	92.2	90.3	97.4	0.12	5.06
40-44 yrs	105.2	91.7	101.2	102.4	99.6	95.6	85.9	89.6	88.2	-0.44	-16.19
45-49 yrs	98.1	104.6	90.2	91.8	94.8	96.5	92.3	82.7	86.7	-0.31	-11.60
50-54 yrs	96.6	95.5	101.6	82.6	84.4	90.5	92.1	88.0	79.1	-0.50	-18.07
55-59 yrs	77.2	93.0	91.2	91.9	75.7	79.3	85.2	86.8	83.2	0.19	7.90
60-64 yrs	54.5	70.6	86.3	80.8	82.3	69.4	73.3	79.1	81.1	1.00	48.91
65-69 yrs	58.2	46.6	62.7	73.2	70.1	73.4	62.0	66.1	71.8	0.53	23.47
70-74 yrs	46.5	51.3	38.9	50.5	60.5	59.4	62.7	53.1	57.6	0.53	23.76
75-79 yrs	34.4	36.2	40.5	28.3	38.5	47.5	46.8	50.2	43.0	0.56	25.22
80+ yrs	36.7	37.9	39.6	40.8	36.1	42.1	52.7	58.6	65.4	1.46	78.29
Median age of population (years)	33.0	33.6	34.2	36.2	37.8	38.8	39.5	40.2	40.8	0.53	23.71

Table 5.62 Key economic trends

As stated

	1990	1995	2000	2005	2010	2015	2020	CAGR	Period growth
Total GDP (EEK per capita)	98,166.7	75,075.8	109,413.5	163,179.8	157,883.5	188,129.6	226,630.6	2.83	130.9
Disposable income (EEK per capita)		40,425.1	56,889.8	81,007.7	82,095.3	97,012.6	116,996.7		
Disposable income (EEK per household)		102,340.2	134,097.8	185,689.2	185,197.6	216,807.1	260,043.9		
Number of households by annual household disposable income ('000)									
Over US$1,000		549.8	573.2	587.3	587.7	582.7	576.8		
Over US$10,000		28.0	58.2	295.3	452.9	531.9	559.7		
Over US$25,000		7.6	11.9	43.7	107.7	227.2	372.3		
Over US$75,000		1.9	3.0	8.2	13.6	23.2	46.9		
Over US$150,000		0.8	1.2	3.4	5.7	8.7	14.7		
Total households	521.0	572.0	582.1	587.9	587.8	582.7	576.8	0.34	10.7

Note: Per capita data is shown at constant 2010 prices. Household disposable income bands are shown at current prices.

Table 5.63 Young generation

'000

	1980	1985	1990	1995	2000	2005	2010	2015	2020	CAGR	Period growth
Babies under 12 months	22.1	24.2	24.0	13.8	12.1	13.9	15.0	15.3	14.4	-1.06	-34.78
Infants under 24 months	44.2	48.3	48.5	28.3	23.8	26.9	29.8	30.7	29.1	-1.04	-34.20
Toddlers aged 1-4	88.4	93.0	97.2	70.2	49.4	51.3	58.2	60.9	60.0	-0.96	-32.11
Children aged 2-9	177.0	180.0	190.2	166.7	119.4	99.7	108.4	118.5	121.4	-0.94	-31.41
Female	86.2	88.4	93.4	81.2	58.1	48.4	52.6	57.5	59.0	-0.94	-31.53
Male	90.8	91.7	96.8	85.4	61.3	51.3	55.8	61.0	62.4	-0.93	-31.30
Tweenagers aged 10-14	105.1	111.4	111.4	107.5	107.4	81.6	61.1	64.6	72.7	-0.92	-30.84
Female	49.7	54.1	54.6	52.7	52.4	39.8	29.7	31.4	35.2	-0.86	-29.17
Male	55.4	57.3	56.8	54.8	55.0	41.9	31.4	33.2	37.5	-0.97	-32.34
Teenagers aged 13-19	151.6	148.9	154.1	141.7	145.4	144.5	106.6	85.7	92.7	-1.22	-38.86
Female	73.8	70.7	75.0	69.3	71.3	70.5	52.0	41.5	44.9	-1.23	-39.06
Male	77.8	78.3	79.0	72.4	74.2	74.0	54.6	44.2	47.7	-1.21	-38.67
Studying age 18-22	115.2	105.1	108.5	98.9	97.1	105.1	101.9	68.6	60.0	-1.62	-47.93
Female	57.0	51.3	51.3	48.8	47.4	51.7	49.7	33.5	28.9	-1.68	-49.23
Male	58.2	53.9	57.2	50.1	49.7	53.4	52.2	35.1	31.0	-1.56	-46.65
Young adults aged 15-29	342.9	338.2	332.7	292.8	292.7	303.9	288.9	244.8	202.8	-1.30	-40.86
Female	169.7	165.5	161.9	145.4	144.5	149.2	141.8	119.9	99.0	-1.34	-41.68
Male	173.1	172.7	170.8	147.3	148.2	154.6	147.1	124.9	103.8	-1.27	-40.06

Table 5.64 Middle-aged generation

'000

	1980	1985	1990	1995	2000	2005	2010	2015	2020	CAGR	Period growth
Middle-aged adults 30-59	572.9	603.0	619.9	579.1	541.2	543.6	540.2	536.5	537.1	-0.16	-6.24
Female	307.5	319.0	324.4	304.9	286.7	287.4	284.6	281.6	279.9	-0.23	-8.98
Male	265.4	284.0	295.5	274.2	254.5	256.2	255.6	254.9	257.2	-0.08	-3.08
Baby boomers aged 40-59	377.0	384.8	384.2	368.7	354.5	361.8	355.6	347.1	337.2	-0.28	-10.55
Female	207.8	207.8	204.9	197.6	190.9	195.0	191.8	186.4	179.6	-0.36	-13.58
Male	169.2	176.9	179.3	171.1	163.6	166.8	163.9	160.7	157.6	-0.18	-6.82

Table 5.65 Elderly population

'000

	1980	1985	1990	1995	2000	2005	2010	2015	2020	CAGR	Period growth
Elderly population (60+)	230.2	242.6	267.9	273.7	287.6	291.9	297.6	307.1	319.0	0.82	38.5
Female	155.8	164.6	178.0	178.7	186.1	189.0	193.0	198.8	205.5	0.69	31.9
Male	74.4	78.0	89.9	94.9	101.4	102.9	104.6	108.3	113.4	1.06	52.5

Table 5.66 Population of biggest cities 1980-2020

'000

	1980	1985	1990	1995	2000	2005	2010	2015	2020	CAGR	Period growth
Tallinn	445.9	466.3	479.5	430.7	400.4	396.0	398.5	400.9	408.6	-0.22	-8.36
Tartu	105.0	109.1	114.3	105.6	101.2	101.5	102.9	104.1	106.5	0.03	1.40
Narva	76.4	79.0	81.5	73.5	68.7	67.1	66.0	65.2	65.6	-0.38	-14.15
Kohtla-Jarve	75.3	65.8	61.7	53.3	47.7	46.0	44.5	43.5	43.4	-1.37	-42.38
Parnu	53.6	52.0	52.7	48.1	45.5	44.4	43.8	43.5	43.9	-0.50	-18.07
Viljandi	22.4	22.5	23.3	21.6	20.8	20.4	20.0	19.7	19.8	-0.30	-11.30
Maardu	13.3	14.8	16.3	15.8	16.7	16.6	16.5	16.5	16.7	0.57	25.78
Rakvere	19.1	19.5	19.8	17.4	17.1	16.8	16.5	16.4	16.5	-0.36	-13.59
Sillamae	16.8	19.5	20.5	17.8	17.2	16.7	16.2	15.9	16.0	-0.13	-4.94
Kuressaare	14.4	15.4	16.3	14.7	14.9	14.9	15.0	15.0	15.3	0.16	6.51

Chart 5.64 Population age shift 2000 and 2020, Each Column Represents a Single Age Group

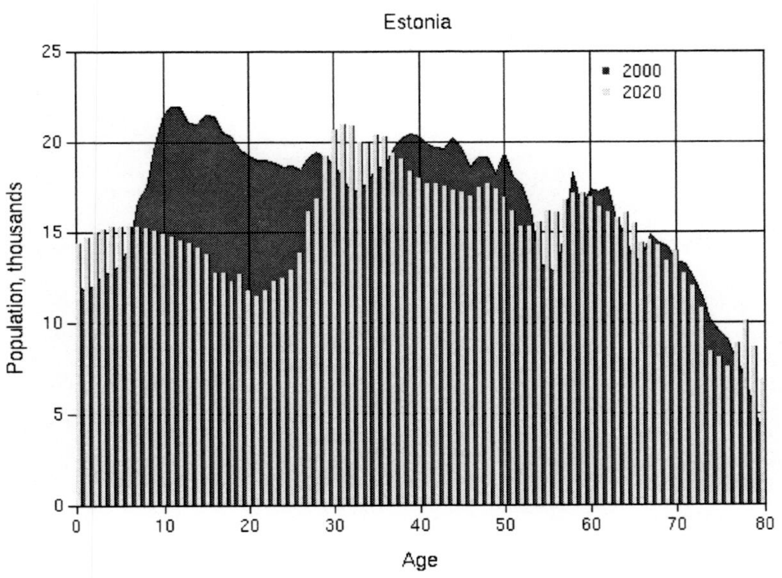

Chart 5.65 Population pyramids, 1980/2000/2010/2020

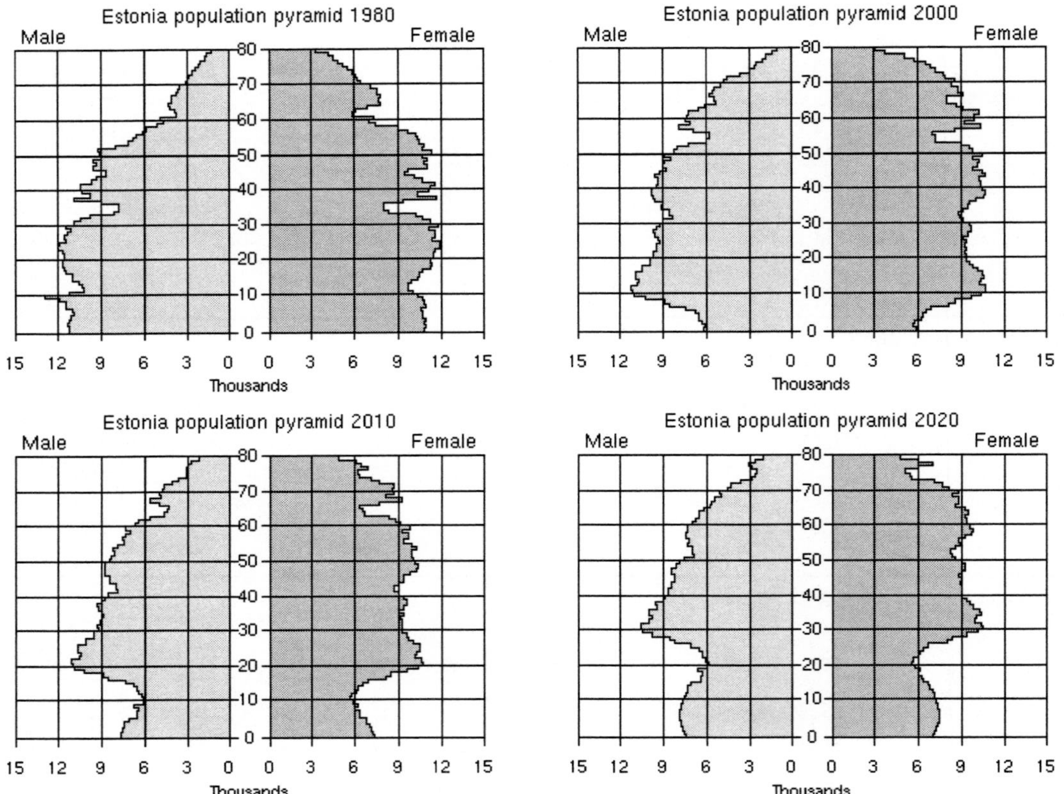

Chart 5.66 Major Cities: 1980, 2000 and 2020

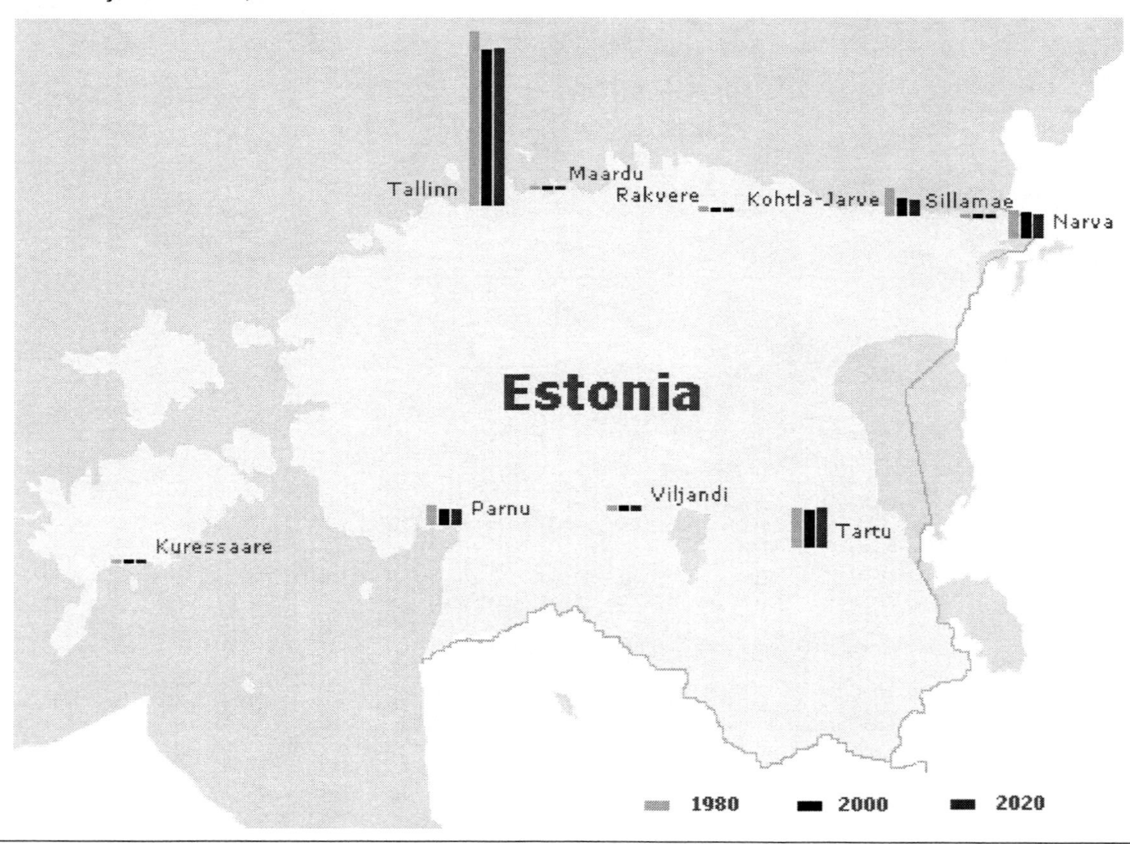

Finland

Table 5.67 Key population trends

'000

	1980	1985	1990	1995	2000	2005	2010	2015	2020	CAGR	Period growth
Population at January 1st	4,771.3	4,893.7	4,974.4	5,098.8	5,171.3	5,236.6	5,347.6	5,444.0	5,520.0	0.37	15.69
Male	2,306.8	2,369.2	2,412.8	2,481.6	2,523.0	2,562.1	2,621.4	2,671.9	2,710.8	0.40	17.51
Female	2,464.5	2,524.5	2,561.6	2,617.1	2,648.3	2,674.5	2,726.3	2,772.2	2,809.2	0.33	13.99
0-4 yrs	321.0	325.3	309.4	327.7	297.5	283.7	296.7	304.1	307.5	-0.11	-4.19
5-9 yrs	298.8	324.7	327.1	313.9	329.4	299.4	287.6	300.7	307.6	0.07	2.95
10-14 yrs	356.3	301.5	325.8	330.6	316.1	331.4	302.3	290.4	303.1	-0.40	-14.92
15-19 yrs	383.4	356.3	301.3	327.9	332.2	318.1	334.4	304.7	292.4	-0.68	-23.73
20-24 yrs	386.9	379.5	353.4	303.2	328.1	333.4	323.5	340.1	309.6	-0.56	-19.99
25-29 yrs	409.7	386.7	377.9	357.7	304.4	330.9	342.4	331.2	346.4	-0.42	-15.45
30-34 yrs	439.9	411.4	386.9	382.0	357.6	306.4	337.2	348.3	335.9	-0.67	-23.63
35-39 yrs	304.2	440.0	410.2	388.7	380.9	357.3	310.2	340.7	350.9	0.36	15.36
40-44 yrs	288.9	302.2	436.4	409.3	386.5	379.5	358.7	311.7	341.4	0.42	18.18
45-49 yrs	271.4	284.8	297.9	431.8	404.4	382.7	378.3	357.4	310.5	0.34	14.40
50-54 yrs	279.5	264.9	278.2	292.4	423.6	397.5	378.1	373.7	353.2	0.59	26.38
55-59 yrs	257.4	268.3	255.3	270.5	284.2	412.3	388.5	369.9	366.2	0.88	42.25
60-64 yrs	206.4	241.9	253.0	243.3	259.2	273.1	397.8	375.8	358.7	1.39	73.82
65-69 yrs	209.5	187.1	220.8	233.7	227.2	244.2	259.0	378.8	359.1	1.36	71.46
70-74 yrs	168.9	179.1	161.7	194.0	208.6	206.3	225.3	240.2	352.9	1.86	108.91
75-79 yrs	107.2	131.1	140.9	130.3	160.3	177.1	179.7	198.3	213.1	1.73	98.80
80+ yrs	82.0	109.0	138.3	161.8	171.1	203.3	247.9	278.2	311.3	3.39	279.59
Median age of population (years)	32.6	34.5	36.3	37.7	39.2	40.8	42.0	42.6	43.0	0.70	32.15

Table 5.68 Key economic trends

As stated

	1990	1995	2000	2005	2010	2015	2020	CAGR	Period growth
Total GDP (EUR per capita)	25,067.0	23,548.1	29,374.5	32,832.6	33,571.2	37,318.1	42,656.1	1.79	70.2
Disposable income (EUR per capita)	13,627.8	13,181.1	14,886.4	17,428.2	18,147.3	20,929.9	24,143.2	1.92	77.2
Disposable income (EUR per household)	33,284.2	30,816.3	33,537.4	37,565.1	38,010.0	43,080.6	49,119.6	1.31	47.6
Number of households by annual household disposable income ('000)									
Over US$1,000	2,036.7	2,180.9	2,295.4	2,429.5	2,553.1	2,644.9	2,713.2	0.96	33.2
Over US$10,000	2,014.9	2,156.6	2,194.3	2,406.6	2,529.4	2,631.7	2,708.0	0.99	34.4
Over US$25,000	1,358.6	1,496.3	1,020.7	1,968.5	2,167.0	2,418.3	2,613.8	2.21	92.4
Over US$75,000	85.6	104.6	84.8	238.9	364.8	636.5	1,143.5	9.03	1,236.2
Over US$150,000	34.7	42.4	34.8	68.0	83.7	117.0	187.1	5.78	439.8
Total households	2,036.7	2,180.9	2,295.4	2,429.5	2,553.2	2,644.9	2,713.2	0.96	33.2

Note: Per capita data is shown at constant 2010 prices. Household disposable income bands are shown at current prices.

Table 5.69 Young generation

'000

	1980	1985	1990	1995	2000	2005	2010	2015	2020	CAGR	Period growth
Babies under 12 months	63.0	65.0	63.0	64.9	57.4	57.6	59.6	60.9	61.2	-0.07	-2.91
Infants under 24 months	126.3	131.7	126.1	129.5	114.3	114.4	119.2	121.8	122.5	-0.08	-3.00
Toddlers aged 1-4	258.0	260.3	246.4	262.8	240.1	226.1	237.1	243.2	246.4	-0.12	-4.50
Children aged 2-9	493.4	518.2	510.4	512.1	512.6	468.7	465.1	483.0	492.6	0.00	-0.17
Female	241.0	253.1	249.4	250.5	251.3	229.2	227.3	235.6	239.6	-0.01	-0.57
Male	252.5	265.2	261.0	261.6	261.3	239.5	237.8	247.4	253.0	0.01	0.21
Tweenagers aged 10-14	356.3	301.5	325.8	330.6	316.1	331.4	302.3	290.4	303.1	-0.40	-14.92
Female	174.5	147.4	159.3	161.4	154.6	162.6	148.2	141.8	148.2	-0.41	-15.09
Male	181.7	154.1	166.5	169.2	161.6	168.9	154.1	148.6	154.9	-0.40	-14.76
Teenagers aged 13-19	531.5	480.7	432.9	457.2	458.4	451.2	460.1	420.4	412.9	-0.63	-22.31
Female	260.4	235.7	211.5	223.5	223.9	220.8	225.5	205.8	202.0	-0.63	-22.42
Male	271.1	245.0	221.4	233.6	234.5	230.5	234.6	214.6	210.9	-0.63	-22.21
Studying age 18-22	380.1	376.1	331.0	310.5	325.4	329.9	328.5	329.6	297.1	-0.61	-21.85
Female	185.7	184.2	162.3	151.4	159.3	161.1	160.8	161.7	145.6	-0.61	-21.61
Male	194.4	191.9	168.7	159.1	166.1	168.8	167.7	167.9	151.5	-0.62	-22.07
Young adults aged 15-29	1,180.0	1,122.6	1,032.6	988.8	964.7	982.3	1,000.2	975.9	948.4	-0.54	-19.63
Female	575.5	548.6	505.5	484.0	471.5	480.0	489.1	478.3	464.9	-0.53	-19.23
Male	604.5	574.1	527.1	504.9	493.2	502.4	511.1	497.6	483.5	-0.56	-20.01

Table 5.70 Middle-aged generation

'000

	1980	1985	1990	1995	2000	2005	2010	2015	2020	CAGR	Period growth
Middle-aged adults 30-59	1,841.3	1,971.5	2,064.8	2,174.7	2,237.2	2,235.7	2,151.1	2,101.7	2,058.2	0.28	11.78
Female	929.2	979.6	1,020.9	1,073.8	1,105.4	1,106.3	1,064.8	1,039.2	1,016.7	0.23	9.42
Male	912.2	991.9	1,043.9	1,100.8	1,131.8	1,129.4	1,086.3	1,062.5	1,041.5	0.33	14.18
Baby boomers aged 40-59	1,097.3	1,120.2	1,267.7	1,404.0	1,498.7	1,572.0	1,503.7	1,412.7	1,371.4	0.56	24.98
Female	567.2	566.1	631.7	696.7	743.4	781.0	748.9	703.3	681.3	0.46	20.12
Male	530.1	554.1	636.1	707.2	755.3	791.0	754.8	709.4	690.0	0.66	30.18

Table 5.71 Elderly population

'000

	1980	1985	1990	1995	2000	2005	2010	2015	2020	CAGR	Period growth
Elderly population (60+)	773.9	848.1	914.7	963.0	1,026.4	1,104.0	1,309.8	1,471.2	1,595.2	1.82	106.1
Female	482.5	531.5	564.9	583.7	609.5	640.6	738.9	818.0	880.3	1.51	82.5
Male	291.5	316.6	349.8	379.3	416.9	463.4	570.8	653.2	714.8	2.27	145.3

Table 5.72 Population of biggest cities 1980-2020

'000

	1980	1985	1990	1995	2000	2005	2010	2015	2020	CAGR	Period growth
Helsinki	483.4	485.2	489.6	517.4	551.1	560.2	569.3	577.2	584.3	0.48	20.88
Espoo	134.1	153.5	168.9	187.1	209.7	228.2	248.4	263.1	275.5	1.82	105.48
Tampere	166.0	168.5	171.3	180.5	193.2	202.7	211.7	217.7	222.2	0.73	33.87
Vantaa	130.2	141.7	152.0	163.9	176.4	185.4	197.8	206.9	214.9	1.26	65.07
Turku	164.3	161.9	159.1	163.5	172.1	174.7	176.0	177.6	178.6	0.21	8.72
Oulu	93.4	96.6	100.3	107.3	117.7	127.4	135.3	140.8	144.9	1.11	55.21
Lahti	94.9	94.7	93.1	94.6	96.7	98.2	99.8	101.3	102.6	0.19	8.08
Kuopio	77.0	77.8	79.9	83.8	86.6	89.7	91.5	92.0	92.3	0.45	19.77
Jyvaskyla	67.2	68.4	69.5	73.1	77.9	83.3	87.5	90.3	92.0	0.79	36.89
Pori	79.7	78.7	76.5	76.5	76.2	76.0	76.3	76.5	76.6	-0.10	-3.83

Chart 5.67 Population age shift 2000 and 2020, Each Column Represents a Single Age Group

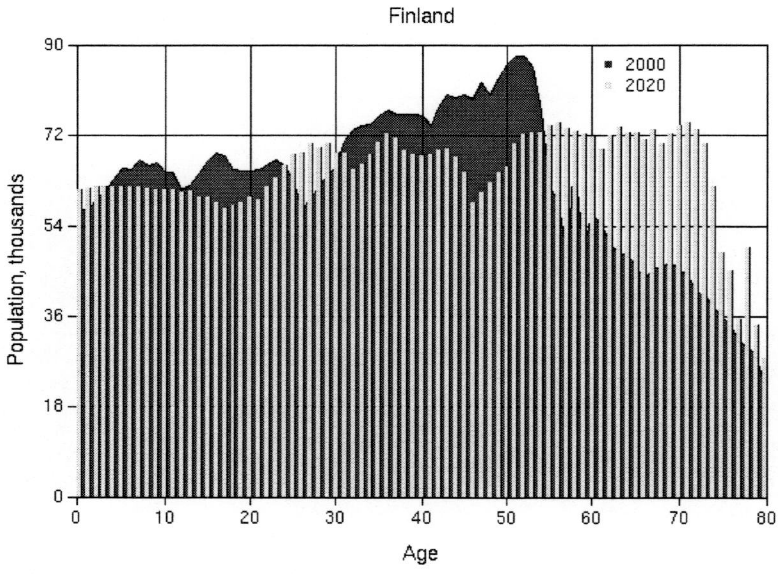

Chart 5.68 Population pyramids, 1980/2000/2010/2020

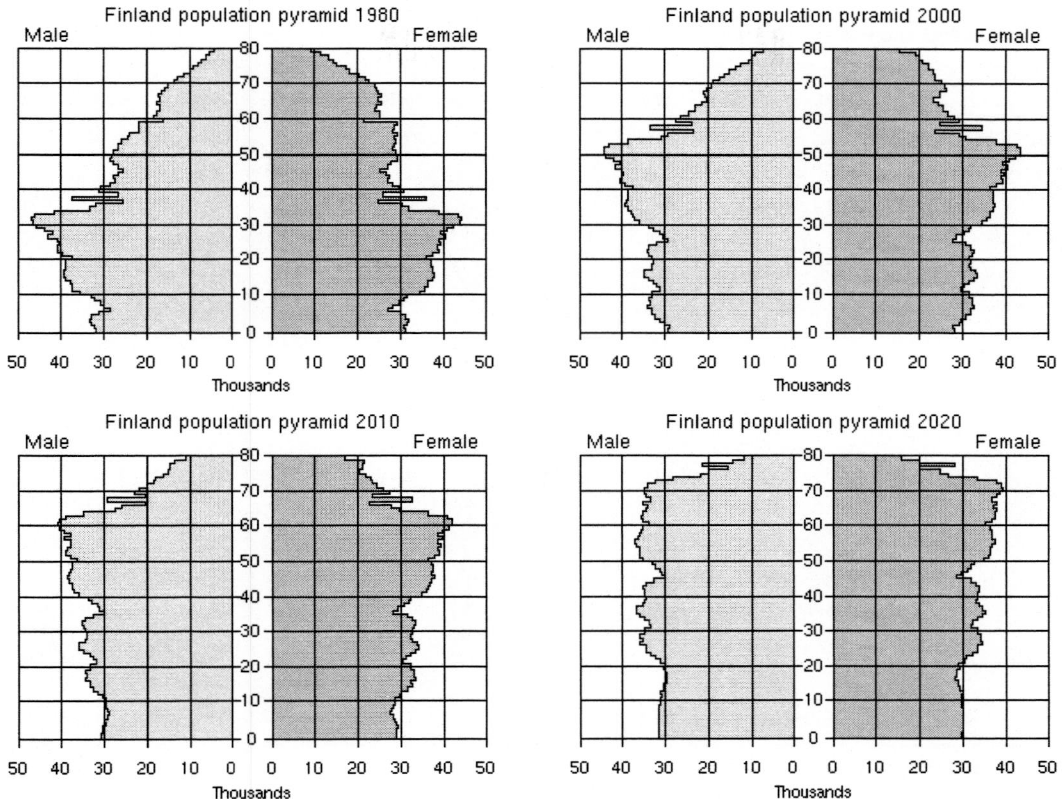

Chart 5.69 Major Cities: 1980, 2000 and 2020

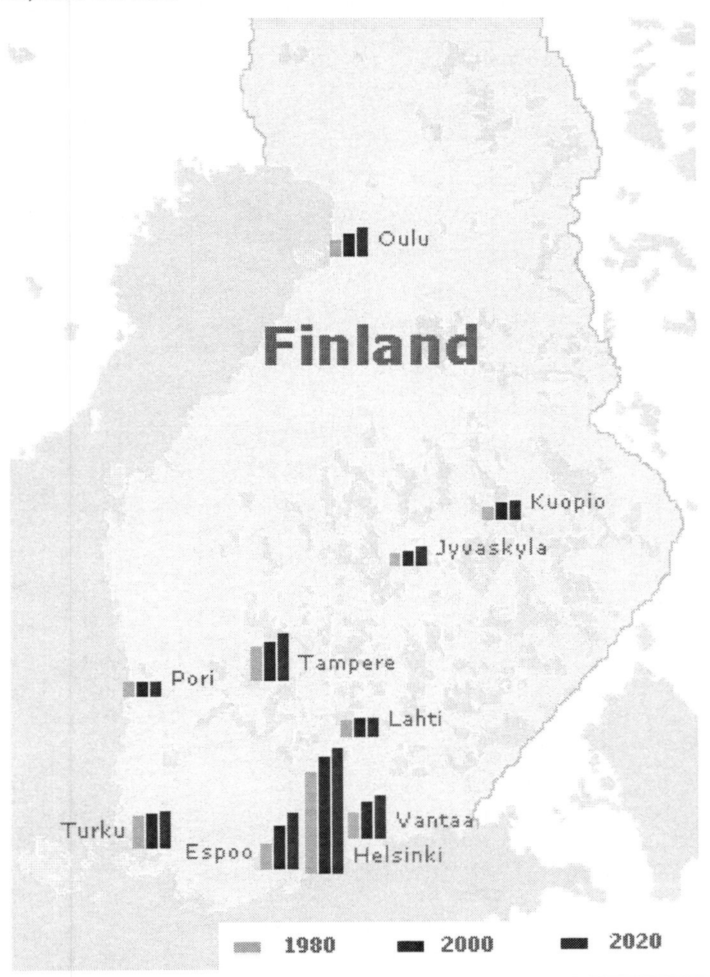

France

Table 5.73 Key population trends

'000

	1980	1985	1990	1995	2000	2005	2010	2015	2020	CAGR	Period growth
Population at January 1st	53,731.4	55,157.3	56,577.0	57,752.5	58,849.5	60,825.0	62,772.0	64,153.0	65,378.6	0.49	21.68
Male	26,243.8	26,890.1	27,544.0	28,078.1	28,579.5	29,555.0	30,405.6	31,122.1	31,769.3	0.48	21.05
Female	27,487.6	28,267.2	29,033.0	29,674.5	30,270.0	31,270.0	32,366.3	33,030.9	33,609.3	0.50	22.27
0-4 yrs	3,604.2	3,822.9	3,783.4	3,609.4	3,610.5	3,838.1	3,953.8	3,909.1	3,872.0	0.18	7.43
5-9 yrs	4,231.4	3,685.6	3,878.9	3,817.2	3,641.1	3,671.1	3,881.9	3,982.3	3,939.8	-0.18	-6.89
10-14 yrs	4,252.6	4,274.1	3,726.5	3,903.0	3,849.1	3,713.9	3,725.0	3,904.0	4,006.8	-0.15	-5.78
15-19 yrs	4,330.4	4,309.2	4,330.9	3,754.7	3,943.1	3,927.8	3,772.7	3,747.9	3,928.9	-0.24	-9.27
20-24 yrs	4,213.1	4,298.4	4,271.8	4,238.8	3,711.6	3,958.5	3,980.2	3,841.0	3,816.9	-0.25	-9.40
25-29 yrs	4,269.3	4,232.8	4,304.1	4,231.5	4,187.3	3,766.3	4,014.2	4,054.2	3,915.2	-0.22	-8.29
30-34 yrs	4,158.3	4,310.6	4,272.9	4,357.8	4,254.8	4,305.0	3,857.9	4,054.2	4,094.7	-0.04	-1.53
35-39 yrs	2,953.5	4,139.1	4,304.4	4,280.1	4,346.8	4,327.9	4,359.7	3,869.3	4,066.4	0.80	37.68
40-44 yrs	3,054.5	2,922.6	4,104.5	4,277.4	4,245.8	4,370.1	4,341.3	4,341.2	3,859.5	0.59	26.35
45-49 yrs	3,253.9	2,992.9	2,871.1	4,042.1	4,217.4	4,227.5	4,347.4	4,295.3	4,301.5	0.70	32.20
50-54 yrs	3,170.8	3,155.9	2,913.0	2,816.4	3,961.5	4,168.5	4,172.5	4,271.0	4,228.7	0.72	33.36
55-59 yrs	3,081.9	3,046.8	3,052.0	2,824.5	2,748.5	3,889.4	4,083.6	4,069.8	4,177.4	0.76	35.55
60-64 yrs	1,616.6	2,914.3	2,892.1	2,913.0	2,709.7	2,669.7	3,771.4	3,944.9	3,946.5	2.26	144.12
65-69 yrs	2,389.0	1,488.6	2,709.4	2,698.9	2,729.8	2,578.7	2,548.7	3,595.3	3,777.0	1.15	58.10
70-74 yrs	2,073.4	2,103.2	1,323.7	2,452.0	2,447.3	2,514.7	2,395.5	2,371.8	3,367.6	1.22	62.42
75-79 yrs	1,583.7	1,675.2	1,753.7	1,125.9	2,106.7	2,137.9	2,229.7	2,131.0	2,130.4	0.74	34.52
80+ yrs	1,495.0	1,784.9	2,084.7	2,409.6	2,138.4	2,760.0	3,336.5	3,770.6	3,949.5	2.46	164.19
Median age of population (years)	32.2	33.5	34.7	36.1	37.5	38.8	39.8	40.9	41.3	0.63	28.35

Table 5.74 Key economic trends

As stated

	1990	1995	2000	2005	2010	2015	2020	CAGR	Period growth
Total GDP (EUR per capita)	25,284.2	26,209.0	29,539.3	31,040.3	31,079.3	33,762.2	37,321.9	1.31	47.6
Disposable income (EUR per capita)	15,639.9	17,207.5	18,564.2	19,928.5	20,983.7	22,726.3	24,933.3	1.57	59.4
Disposable income (EUR per household)	41,076.1	43,529.5	45,317.2	47,185.5	48,487.3	51,218.8	55,100.2	0.98	34.1
Number of households by annual household disposable income ('000)									
Over US$1,000	21,539.0	22,827.7	24,104.5	25,689.0	27,164.6	28,464.4	29,583.8	1.06	37.3
Over US$10,000	20,849.0	22,296.2	23,163.3	25,580.7	26,875.5	28,242.1	29,428.1	1.16	41.1
Over US$25,000	16,293.6	18,618.9	16,738.1	23,278.8	24,643.0	26,521.1	28,220.1	1.85	73.2
Over US$75,000	1,814.9	2,971.2	1,458.5	4,754.3	8,657.3	11,983.2	16,247.1	7.58	795.2
Over US$150,000	542.0	700.4	502.6	999.7	1,229.6	1,676.7	2,861.1	5.70	427.9
Total households	21,542.0	22,830.0	24,107.7	25,689.0	27,165.7	28,465.3	29,584.4	1.06	37.3

Note: Per capita data is shown at constant 2010 prices. Household disposable income bands are shown at current prices.

Table 5.75 Young generation

'000

	1980	1985	1990	1995	2000	2005	2010	2015	2020	CAGR	Period growth
Babies under 12 months	735.8	744.3	751.4	698.6	742.5	764.1	799.4	776.2	768.4	0.11	4.43
Infants under 24 months	1,445.7	1,470.8	1,503.7	1,390.3	1,464.5	1,525.6	1,598.0	1,554.9	1,540.0	0.16	6.53
Toddlers aged 1-4	2,868.4	3,078.6	3,032.0	2,910.8	2,868.0	3,074.0	3,154.4	3,132.9	3,103.6	0.20	8.20
Children aged 2-9	6,389.9	6,037.7	6,158.6	6,036.3	5,787.2	5,983.6	6,237.7	6,336.5	6,271.8	-0.05	-1.85
Female	3,119.4	2,947.9	3,008.2	2,947.8	2,823.1	2,921.4	3,062.0	3,107.8	3,072.6	-0.04	-1.50
Male	3,270.5	3,089.7	3,150.4	3,088.5	2,964.1	3,062.3	3,175.7	3,228.7	3,199.2	-0.06	-2.18
Tweenagers aged 10-14	4,252.6	4,274.1	3,726.5	3,903.0	3,849.1	3,713.9	3,725.0	3,904.0	4,006.8	-0.15	-5.78
Female	2,069.9	2,081.1	1,819.5	1,905.1	1,881.3	1,811.7	1,825.0	1,918.1	1,968.2	-0.13	-4.92
Male	2,182.7	2,193.0	1,907.0	1,998.0	1,967.8	1,902.2	1,899.9	1,985.9	2,038.6	-0.17	-6.60
Teenagers aged 13-19	6,064.5	6,050.8	5,812.0	5,365.3	5,491.3	5,465.3	5,257.8	5,327.1	5,519.2	-0.24	-8.99
Female	2,974.1	2,955.9	2,840.6	2,622.7	2,686.0	2,675.0	2,577.7	2,613.2	2,713.5	-0.23	-8.76
Male	3,090.4	3,095.0	2,971.5	2,742.6	2,805.4	2,790.2	2,680.1	2,713.9	2,805.7	-0.24	-9.21
Studying age 18-22	4,247.9	4,350.6	4,319.1	4,009.9	3,878.3	3,911.6	3,951.8	3,742.4	3,878.7	-0.23	-8.69
Female	2,100.8	2,151.2	2,126.7	1,978.8	1,909.0	1,929.2	1,947.5	1,836.6	1,905.4	-0.24	-9.30
Male	2,147.1	2,199.4	2,192.3	2,031.1	1,969.3	1,982.3	2,004.3	1,905.8	1,973.3	-0.21	-8.09
Young adults aged 15-29	12,812.8	12,840.4	12,906.8	12,225.0	11,842.1	11,652.6	11,767.1	11,643.1	11,660.9	-0.24	-8.99
Female	6,326.2	6,361.3	6,389.8	6,059.4	5,860.0	5,758.7	5,826.2	5,735.3	5,731.2	-0.25	-9.41
Male	6,486.6	6,479.1	6,517.0	6,165.7	5,982.1	5,893.9	5,941.0	5,907.8	5,929.8	-0.22	-8.58

Table 5.76 Middle-aged generation

'000

	1980	1985	1990	1995	2000	2005	2010	2015	2020	CAGR	Period growth
Middle-aged adults 30-59	19,673	20,568	21,518	22,598	23,775	25,288	25,162	24,901	24,728	0.57	25.7
Female	9,800	10,258	10,765	11,331	11,975	12,776	12,775	12,622	12,481	0.61	27.4
Male	9,873	10,310	10,753	11,267	11,800	12,513	12,388	12,279	12,247	0.54	24.1
Baby boomers aged 40-59	12,561	12,118	12,941	13,960	15,173	16,656	16,945	16,977	16,567	0.69	31.9
Female	6,339	6,091	6,476	6,990	7,644	8,452	8,667	8,668	8,420	0.71	32.8
Male	6,222	6,027	6,465	6,971	7,529	8,204	8,278	8,309	8,147	0.68	30.9

Table 5.77 Elderly population

'000

	1980	1985	1990	1995	2000	2005	2010	2015	2020	CAGR	Period growth
Elderly population (60+)	9,158	9,966	10,764	11,599	12,132	12,661	14,282	15,814	17,171	1.58	87.5
Female	5,467	5,900	6,315	6,752	7,016	7,257	8,096	8,887	9,603	1.42	75.7
Male	3,691	4,066	4,448	4,848	5,116	5,404	6,186	6,926	7,568	1.81	105.0

Table 5.78 Population of biggest cities 1980-2020

'000

	1980	1985	1990	1995	2000	2005	2010	2015	2020	CAGR	Period growth
Paris	2,176.9	2,166.9	2,152.4	2,139.0	2,127.7	2,153.6	2,196.7	2,249.6	2,311.4	0.15	6.18
Marseille	896.0	835.7	800.6	797.0	801.2	826.7	858.8	891.3	924.5	0.08	3.18
Lyon	413.9	410.4	415.5	432.6	448.9	467.4	486.8	506.0	525.4	0.60	26.95
Toulouse	346.3	349.6	358.7	375.6	396.2	437.1	474.5	507.2	536.8	1.10	55.04
Nice	334.8	339.6	342.4	343.9	343.3	346.9	353.3	361.4	371.0	0.26	10.82
Nantes	240.4	240.0	245.0	259.6	272.8	281.8	289.6	298.4	307.9	0.62	28.08
Strasbourg	247.9	249.0	252.3	259.2	265.8	272.5	277.9	284.6	292.5	0.41	17.98
Montpellier	195.0	200.2	208.0	217.7	228.3	248.0	266.5	283.0	298.3	1.07	52.97
Bordeaux	207.6	208.3	210.3	213.1	217.1	229.5	243.3	255.9	268.0	0.64	29.08
Lille	196.9	195.7	198.7	206.4	214.7	224.9	235.7	246.1	256.3	0.66	30.16

Chart 5.70 Population age shift 2000 and 2020, Each Column Represents a Single Age Group

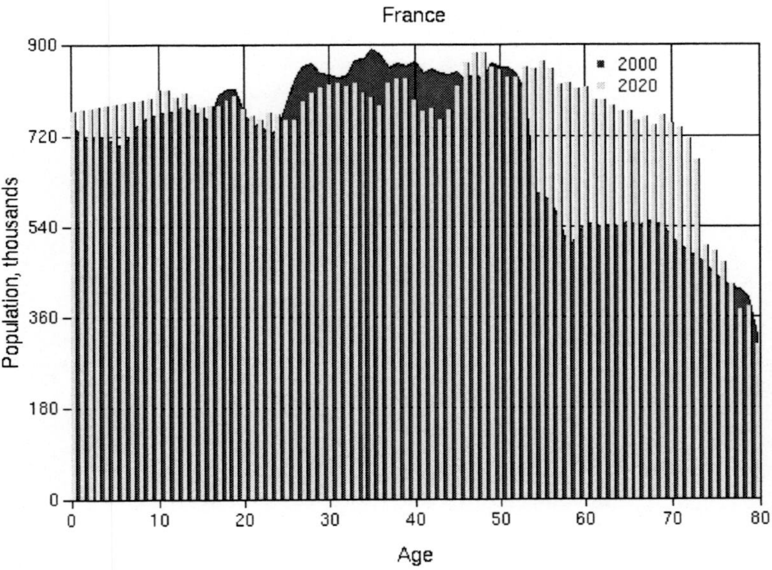

Chart 5.71 Population pyramids, 1980/2000/2010/2020

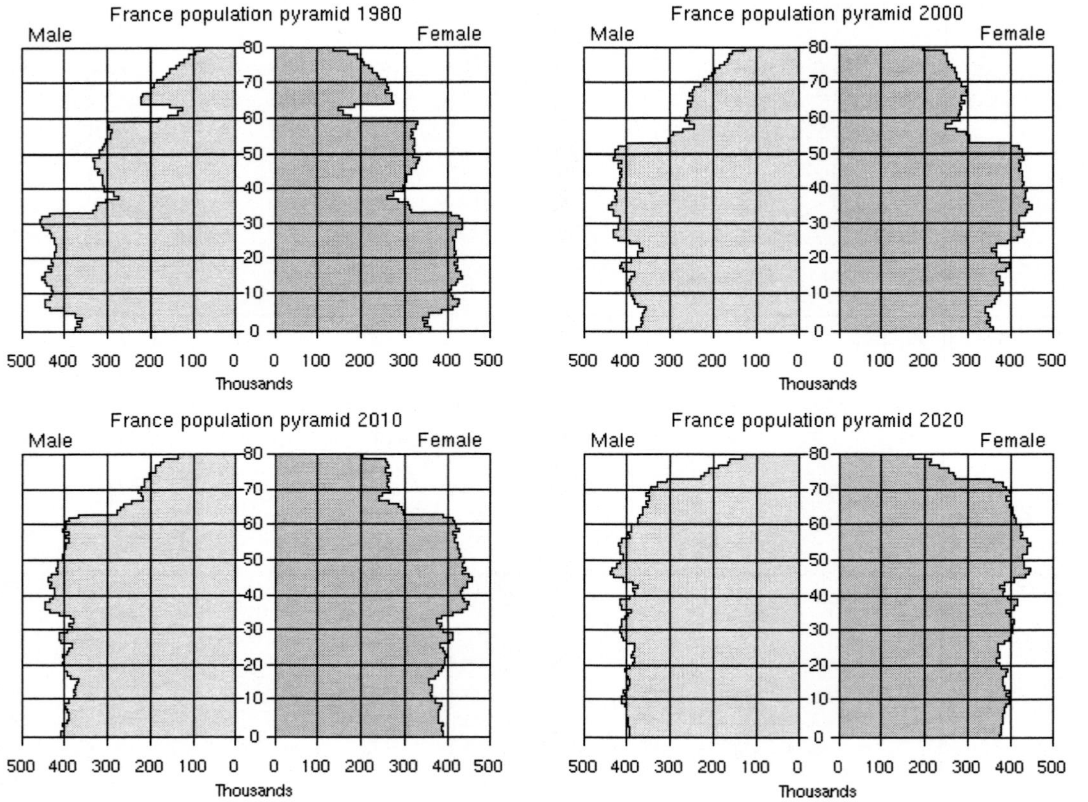

Chart 5.72 Major Cities: 1980, 2000 and 2020

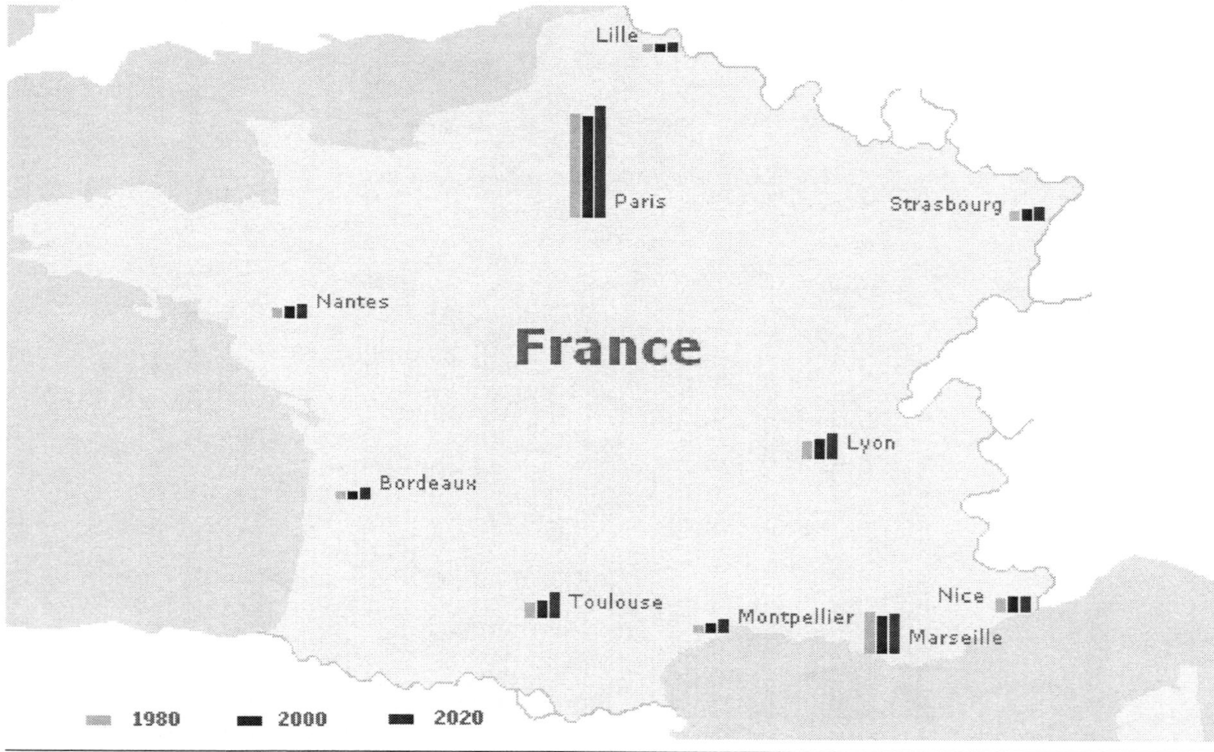

Germany

Table 5.79 Key population trends

'000

	1980	1985	1990	1995	2000	2005	2010	2015	2020	CAGR	Period growth
Population at January 1st	78,179.7	77,709.2	79,112.8	81,538.6	82,163.5	82,500.8	81,721.5	80,373.5	79,003.0	0.03	1.05
Male	37,156.6	37,048.1	38,109.7	39,645.0	40,090.8	40,353.6	40,087.0	39,526.4	38,908.1	0.12	4.71
Female	41,023.1	40,661.1	41,003.1	41,893.6	42,072.7	42,147.2	41,634.5	40,847.2	40,094.9	-0.06	-2.26
0-4 yrs	3,959.1	4,160.9	4,372.6	4,190.6	3,947.6	3,656.3	3,397.2	3,034.1	3,016.1	-0.68	-23.82
5-9 yrs	4,488.6	3,905.3	4,266.6	4,609.1	4,251.6	3,975.0	3,645.6	3,401.0	3,046.6	-0.96	-32.13
10-14 yrs	6,220.1	4,484.5	3,999.4	4,494.7	4,697.8	4,293.4	3,952.7	3,636.9	3,403.6	-1.50	-45.28
15-19 yrs	6,587.2	6,272.0	4,615.1	4,257.3	4,633.1	4,787.9	4,300.2	3,953.8	3,650.0	-1.47	-44.59
20-24 yrs	5,880.7	6,674.7	6,524.5	5,040.8	4,526.4	4,890.2	4,961.2	4,491.4	4,162.5	-0.86	-29.22
25-29 yrs	5,581.8	5,901.9	6,867.7	6,923.5	5,219.6	4,745.2	5,020.8	5,129.3	4,682.7	-0.44	-16.11
30-34 yrs	4,695.1	5,531.7	6,022.5	7,146.2	6,947.7	5,288.8	4,755.9	5,056.0	5,180.2	0.25	10.33
35-39 yrs	5,733.2	4,606.5	5,585.3	6,225.9	7,144.0	6,937.7	5,250.0	4,733.4	5,043.3	-0.32	-12.03
40-44 yrs	6,079.9	5,630.8	4,678.0	5,704.6	6,213.7	7,117.0	6,852.8	5,189.2	4,692.3	-0.65	-22.82
45-49 yrs	4,789.6	5,953.4	5,657.2	4,698.1	5,660.8	6,167.5	7,005.2	6,733.6	5,112.7	0.16	6.75
50-54 yrs	4,678.1	4,649.3	5,908.8	5,592.1	4,615.2	5,578.2	6,034.8	6,838.5	6,589.2	0.86	40.85
55-59 yrs	4,456.7	4,493.3	4,532.7	5,782.2	5,424.9	4,498.4	5,407.1	5,842.0	6,640.3	1.00	49.00
60-64 yrs	2,764.7	4,197.9	4,288.2	4,331.8	5,529.9	5,197.8	4,301.0	5,174.7	5,614.2	1.79	103.07
65-69 yrs	4,098.9	2,516.1	3,879.9	3,986.7	4,012.9	5,191.4	4,866.9	4,048.2	4,894.6	0.44	19.41
70-74 yrs	3,611.2	3,514.9	2,190.5	3,436.4	3,553.0	3,611.9	4,715.6	4,431.6	3,725.2	0.08	3.16
75-79 yrs	2,546.3	2,758.7	2,790.4	1,785.7	2,850.5	3,007.2	3,086.1	4,064.2	3,852.9	1.04	51.31
80+ yrs	2,008.7	2,457.4	2,933.4	3,333.0	2,934.8	3,557.0	4,168.5	4,615.5	5,696.5	2.64	183.60
Median age of population (years)	36.6	36.9	37.6	38.2	39.8	41.8	44.1	46.2	47.8	0.67	30.52

Table 5.80 Key economic trends

As stated

	1990	1995	2000	2005	2010	2015	2020	CAGR	Period growth
Total GDP (EUR per capita)	23,270.3	25,140.8	27,488.0	28,163.5	28,887.9	32,027.7	35,720.6	1.44	53.5
Disposable income (EUR per capita)	16,352.4	18,760.1	19,432.6	19,832.9	19,990.3	22,157.7	24,759.3	1.39	51.4
Disposable income (EUR per household)	37,201.5	41,412.0	41,880.4	41,764.1	40,859.2	44,552.7	49,279.9	0.94	32.5
Number of households by annual household disposable income ('000)									
Over US$1,000	34,759.2	36,929.4	38,106.7	39,169.9	39,974.3	39,966.3	39,688.6	0.44	14.2
Over US$10,000	32,121.6	35,464.2	35,317.6	37,851.7	38,703.7	38,962.4	39,019.3	0.65	21.5
Over US$25,000	20,107.6	27,432.5	22,596.4	30,512.7	31,598.1	33,203.4	35,031.4	1.87	74.2
Over US$75,000	2,128.9	4,943.3	2,557.1	6,581.0	7,266.6	9,431.2	13,462.9	6.34	532.4
Over US$150,000	686.1	1,080.1	797.6	1,244.4	1,374.8	1,622.2	2,207.2	3.97	221.7
Total households	34,775.0	36,938.0	38,124.0	39,178.0	39,982.2	39,972.6	39,692.9	0.44	14.1

Note: Per capita data is shown at constant 2010 prices. Household disposable income bands are shown at current prices.

Table 5.81 Young generation

'000

	1980	1985	1990	1995	2000	2005	2010	2015	2020	CAGR	Period growth
Babies under 12 months	811.0	806.4	882.3	769.6	771.2	705.0	666.0	599.7	602.3	-0.74	-25.73
Infants under 24 months	1,612.3	1,624.3	1,787.7	1,572.4	1,560.1	1,415.0	1,348.5	1,199.6	1,205.7	-0.72	-25.22
Toddlers aged 1-4	3,148.1	3,354.5	3,490.3	3,421.0	3,176.4	2,951.3	2,731.2	2,434.4	2,413.8	-0.66	-23.33
Children aged 2-9	6,835.4	6,441.9	6,851.4	7,227.2	6,639.1	6,216.3	5,694.3	5,235.5	4,857.0	-0.85	-28.94
Female	3,339.1	3,147.0	3,337.9	3,519.6	3,232.1	3,028.0	2,771.7	2,538.9	2,354.0	-0.87	-29.50
Male	3,496.2	3,294.9	3,513.6	3,707.6	3,407.0	3,188.3	2,922.6	2,696.6	2,503.1	-0.83	-28.41
Tweenagers aged 10-14	6,220.1	4,484.5	3,999.4	4,494.7	4,697.8	4,293.4	3,952.7	3,636.9	3,403.6	-1.50	-45.28
Female	3,031.8	2,194.8	1,945.4	2,189.3	2,286.8	2,090.3	1,925.3	1,773.3	1,652.4	-1.51	-45.50
Male	3,188.3	2,289.6	2,053.9	2,305.4	2,411.0	2,203.0	2,027.4	1,863.6	1,751.2	-1.49	-45.07
Teenagers aged 13-19	9,208.1	8,311.5	6,179.0	6,077.0	6,468.2	6,628.5	5,876.5	5,456.7	5,013.9	-1.51	-45.55
Female	4,481.5	4,045.3	3,008.2	2,954.9	3,150.1	3,228.6	2,866.6	2,666.0	2,449.1	-1.50	-45.35
Male	4,726.6	4,266.2	3,170.8	3,122.1	3,318.1	3,400.0	3,009.9	2,790.6	2,564.8	-1.52	-45.74
Studying age 18-22	6,175.6	6,720.6	5,884.7	4,421.3	4,618.1	4,766.8	4,846.7	4,126.6	3,986.5	-1.09	-35.45
Female	2,999.8	3,264.1	2,873.9	2,154.6	2,258.6	2,337.1	2,375.9	2,029.8	1,964.3	-1.05	-34.52
Male	3,175.8	3,456.5	3,010.8	2,266.7	2,359.5	2,429.6	2,470.8	2,096.8	2,022.2	-1.12	-36.33
Young adults aged 15-29	18,049.7	18,848.6	18,007.3	16,221.6	14,379.1	14,423.3	14,282.2	13,574.6	12,495.2	-0.92	-30.77
Female	8,791.2	9,155.1	8,756.0	7,853.5	7,016.3	7,076.9	7,021.2	6,686.2	6,170.4	-0.88	-29.81
Male	9,258.5	9,693.6	9,251.3	8,368.1	7,362.8	7,346.4	7,261.0	6,888.3	6,324.8	-0.95	-31.69

Table 5.82 Middle-aged generation

'000

	1980	1985	1990	1995	2000	2005	2010	2015	2020	CAGR	Period growth
Middle-aged adults 30-59	30,432	30,865	32,385	35,149	36,006	35,588	35,306	34,393	33,258	0.22	9.28
Female	15,533	15,406	15,931	17,245	17,678	17,525	17,409	16,919	16,353	0.13	5.28
Male	14,899	15,459	16,454	17,905	18,328	18,063	17,897	17,473	16,905	0.32	13.46
Baby boomers aged 40-59	20,004	20,727	20,777	21,777	21,915	23,361	25,300	24,603	23,035	0.35	15.15
Female	10,456	10,434	10,254	10,778	10,849	11,557	12,490	12,102	11,317	0.20	8.23
Male	9,548	10,293	10,522	10,999	11,066	11,804	12,810	12,501	11,717	0.51	22.72

Table 5.83 Elderly population

'000

	1980	1985	1990	1995	2000	2005	2010	2015	2020	CAGR	Period growth
Elderly population (60+)	15,030	15,445	16,082	16,874	18,881	20,565	21,138	22,334	23,783	1.15	58.2
Female	9,543	9,968	10,162	10,322	11,100	11,738	11,852	12,347	12,979	0.77	36.0
Male	5,487	5,478	5,920	6,552	7,781	8,827	9,286	9,988	10,804	1.71	96.9

Table 5.84 Population of biggest cities 1980-2020

'000

	1980	1985	1990	1995	2000	2005	2010	2015	2020	CAGR	Period growth
Berlin	3,306.0	3,266.4	3,352.1	3,471.4	3,398.6	3,395.2	3,432.1	3,445.9	3,459.9	0.11	4.66
Hamburg	1,624.5	1,598.5	1,633.9	1,707.9	1,724.6	1,743.6	1,790.3	1,804.4	1,813.5	0.28	11.63
Munchen	1,235.2	1,197.8	1,202.3	1,236.4	1,229.1	1,259.7	1,343.9	1,364.7	1,374.1	0.27	11.24
Koln	972.0	939.4	939.2	965.7	968.3	983.3	1,007.4	1,015.4	1,020.5	0.12	4.99
Frankfurt am Main	637.2	622.6	630.6	650.1	642.5	651.9	666.3	671.4	674.7	0.14	5.88
Stuttgart	565.9	554.9	564.3	585.6	587.6	592.6	601.2	604.3	607.0	0.18	7.27
Dortmund	616.6	592.6	588.4	598.8	590.4	588.2	586.0	586.2	588.0	-0.12	-4.63
Duesseldorf	604.8	574.9	562.3	571.0	571.3	574.5	585.8	589.4	592.1	-0.05	-2.10
Essen	677.4	638.6	617.8	614.9	595.1	585.4	579.5	578.7	580.3	-0.39	-14.34
Bremen	559.5	540.2	539.0	549.4	541.4	546.9	549.0	550.2	552.2	-0.03	-1.31

Chart 5.73 Population age shift 2000 and 2020, Each Column Represents a Single Age Group

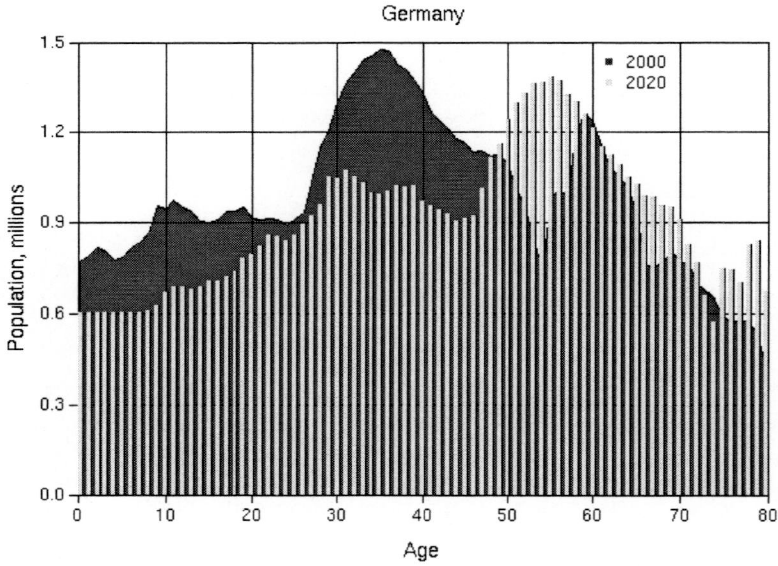

Chart 5.74 Population pyramids, 1980/2000/2010/2020

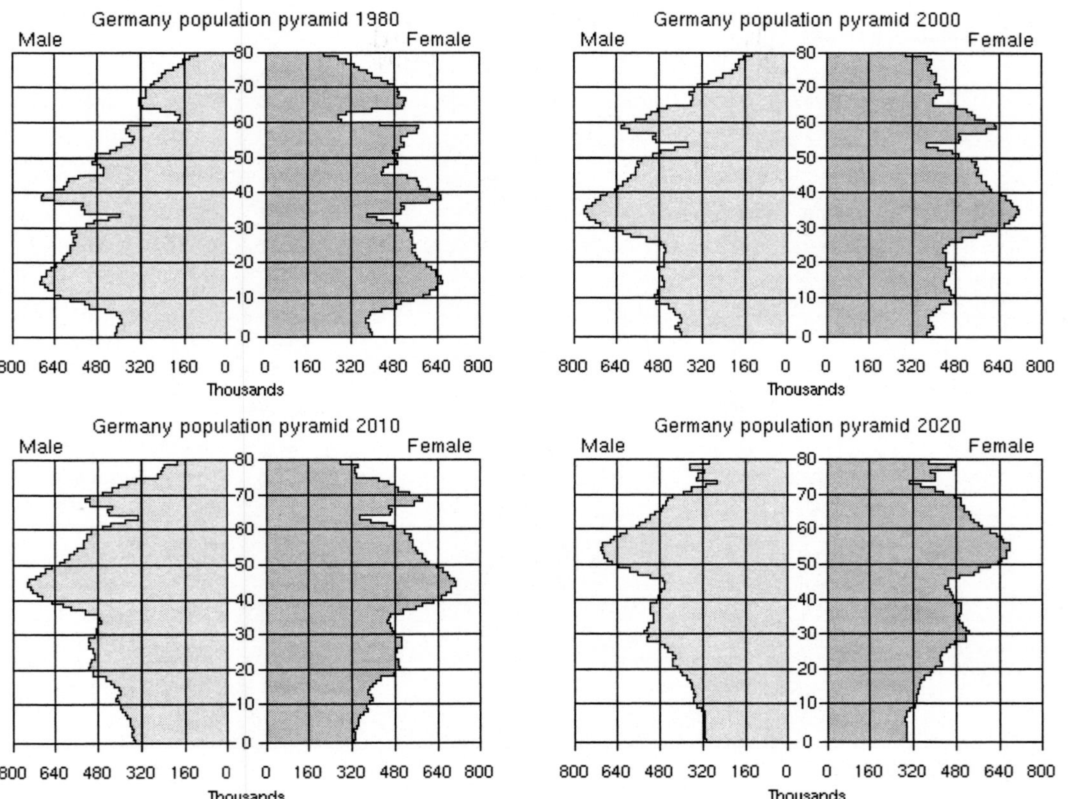

Chart 5.75 Major Cities: 1980, 2000 and 2020

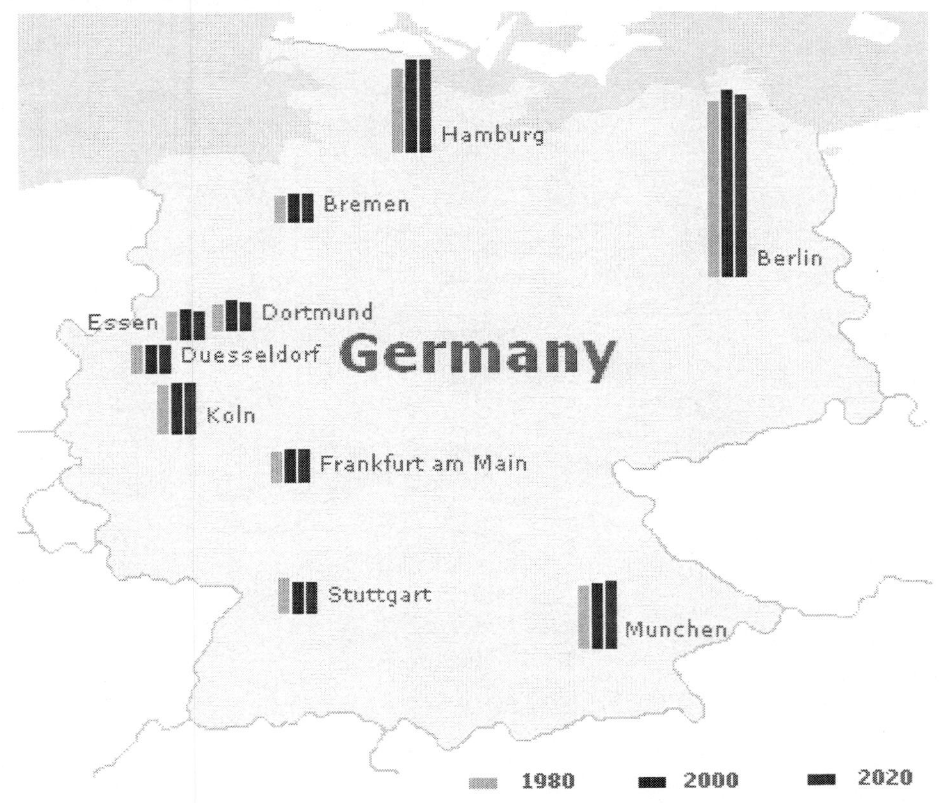

Greece

Table 5.85 Key population trends

'000

	1980	1985	1990	1995	2000	2005	2010	2015	2020	CAGR	Period growth
Population at January 1st	9,584.2	9,919.5	10,120.9	10,595.1	10,903.8	11,082.8	11,290.0	11,437.0	11,501.2	0.46	20.00
Male	4,702.3	4,879.4	4,982.0	5,243.2	5,399.9	5,486.6	5,586.0	5,658.0	5,692.2	0.48	21.05
Female	4,881.9	5,040.1	5,138.9	5,351.9	5,503.8	5,596.1	5,704.0	5,779.1	5,809.0	0.44	18.99
0-4 yrs	716.8	664.4	544.4	533.4	521.7	517.9	546.6	539.4	505.6	-0.87	-29.47
5-9 yrs	712.4	728.1	691.0	581.7	555.5	519.2	528.0	556.9	549.7	-0.65	-22.84
10-14 yrs	783.3	732.4	748.7	735.2	604.7	561.1	531.2	540.2	569.3	-0.79	-27.33
15-19 yrs	725.2	776.6	758.6	798.1	763.2	609.9	574.7	545.2	554.1	-0.67	-23.59
20-24 yrs	695.0	724.6	777.3	812.2	831.6	767.2	624.7	589.9	560.3	-0.54	-19.39
25-29 yrs	631.2	695.2	714.7	820.2	847.9	844.7	784.6	642.6	607.8	-0.09	-3.70
30-34 yrs	653.8	667.0	705.9	755.6	850.3	868.0	862.1	802.3	660.4	0.03	1.01
35-39 yrs	548.6	665.4	670.0	741.8	783.3	870.1	882.6	876.9	817.3	1.00	48.98
40-44 yrs	659.7	565.8	662.6	697.8	761.9	799.0	882.1	894.7	889.1	0.75	34.76
45-49 yrs	672.1	662.3	561.1	679.1	707.0	772.8	807.0	889.7	902.3	0.74	34.26
50-54 yrs	633.7	678.5	651.7	573.9	676.7	712.3	775.3	809.4	891.4	0.86	40.65
55-59 yrs	478.1	630.5	668.2	653.9	570.8	672.7	707.6	770.3	804.4	1.31	68.24
60-64 yrs	417.4	462.3	610.5	664.6	638.7	560.9	661.4	697.3	759.9	1.51	82.03
65-69 yrs	439.0	370.3	438.9	573.8	635.3	609.9	543.4	641.2	677.3	1.09	54.26
70-74 yrs	350.1	372.2	323.6	384.5	510.9	585.9	569.1	511.3	605.2	1.38	72.90
75-79 yrs	251.8	262.1	287.1	258.5	306.2	434.9	507.2	498.1	452.4	1.48	79.68
80+ yrs	215.9	261.9	306.6	330.8	337.9	376.3	502.5	631.6	694.8	2.97	221.80
Median age of population (years)	34.0	34.8	35.9	36.7	38.1	39.9	41.7	43.5	45.2	0.71	32.78

Table 5.86 Key economic trends

As stated

	1990	1995	2000	2005	2010	2015	2020	CAGR	Period growth
Total GDP (EUR per capita)	14,374.3	14,619.7	16,830.6	20,342.7	22,163.5	23,500.2	25,911.5	1.98	80.3
Disposable income (EUR per capita)	11,015.0	11,131.1	11,472.8	13,485.6	15,163.4	16,437.6	18,295.1	1.71	66.1
Disposable income (EUR per household)	35,187.9	34,656.9	34,485.6	39,049.3	42,337.9	44,295.7	47,627.1	1.01	35.4
Number of households by annual household disposable income ('000)									
Over US$1,000	3,128.8	3,398.3	3,619.4	3,826.2	4,042.7	4,243.5	4,417.6	1.16	41.2
Over US$10,000	1,780.4	2,904.8	2,918.9	3,635.3	3,913.8	4,149.1	4,363.2	3.03	145.1
Over US$25,000	421.8	1,444.9	1,265.0	2,681.3	3,220.3	3,621.6	4,033.5	7.82	856.3
Over US$75,000	49.2	152.8	122.7	479.0	855.2	1,291.3	2,007.7	13.16	3,979.7
Over US$150,000	20.7	55.4	45.4	107.4	157.8	265.2	536.3	11.46	2,493.0
Total households	3,168.2	3,402.9	3,627.5	3,827.4	4,043.5	4,244.1	4,418.0	1.11	39.4

Note: Per capita data is shown at constant 2010 prices. Household disposable income bands are shown at current prices.

Table 5.87 Young generation

'000

	1980	1985	1990	1995	2000	2005	2010	2015	2020	CAGR	Period growth
Babies under 12 months	146.9	118.7	102.3	104.7	103.4	105.4	109.3	105.1	97.3	-1.03	-33.78
Infants under 24 months	291.9	244.3	207.6	208.7	205.3	210.0	218.9	211.7	196.4	-0.99	-32.70
Toddlers aged 1-4	569.9	545.7	442.1	428.7	418.3	412.5	437.3	434.3	408.3	-0.83	-28.36
Children aged 2-9	1,137.4	1,148.2	1,027.8	906.5	872.0	827.2	855.7	884.7	858.9	-0.70	-24.48
Female	549.1	557.7	500.6	438.0	423.1	402.2	413.8	427.6	415.2	-0.70	-24.38
Male	588.2	590.5	527.1	468.5	448.8	425.0	441.8	457.0	443.7	-0.70	-24.58
Tweenagers aged 10-14	783.3	732.4	748.7	735.2	604.7	561.1	531.2	540.2	569.3	-0.79	-27.33
Female	379.8	356.5	364.3	354.0	289.9	272.2	258.7	261.2	274.9	-0.80	-27.62
Male	403.5	376.0	384.4	381.1	314.8	288.9	272.6	279.0	294.4	-0.79	-27.05
Teenagers aged 13-19	1,036.8	1,076.1	1,060.2	1,112.9	1,020.1	841.2	794.6	759.0	781.9	-0.70	-24.59
Female	502.6	525.2	515.6	537.2	487.2	404.9	385.6	368.4	377.8	-0.71	-24.83
Male	534.2	550.9	544.6	575.7	533.0	436.4	409.0	390.6	404.1	-0.70	-24.36
Studying age 18-22	714.1	738.7	780.9	807.8	820.7	696.7	597.7	572.2	547.9	-0.66	-23.27
Female	346.1	363.6	383.2	393.0	391.8	333.8	288.2	278.2	265.9	-0.66	-23.19
Male	367.9	375.1	397.7	414.7	428.9	362.9	309.5	294.0	282.0	-0.66	-23.34
Young adults aged 15-29	2,051.4	2,196.4	2,250.6	2,430.6	2,442.7	2,221.8	1,984.0	1,777.7	1,722.2	-0.44	-16.05
Female	1,002.6	1,083.3	1,114.7	1,188.3	1,175.3	1,064.7	955.4	862.2	837.2	-0.45	-16.49
Male	1,048.8	1,113.0	1,135.9	1,242.2	1,267.4	1,157.1	1,028.6	915.5	885.0	-0.42	-15.62

Table 5.88 Middle-aged generation

'000

	1980	1985	1990	1995	2000	2005	2010	2015	2020	CAGR	Period growth
Middle-aged adults 30-59	3,646	3,869	3,920	4,102	4,350	4,695	4,917	5,043	4,965	0.77	36.2
Female	1,887	1,977	1,984	2,079	2,192	2,345	2,438	2,490	2,441	0.65	29.4
Male	1,759	1,893	1,935	2,023	2,158	2,350	2,478	2,554	2,523	0.91	43.5
Baby boomers aged 40-59	2,444	2,537	2,544	2,605	2,716	2,957	3,172	3,364	3,487	0.89	42.7
Female	1,267	1,311	1,295	1,325	1,379	1,494	1,594	1,681	1,727	0.78	36.3
Male	1,176	1,226	1,249	1,279	1,338	1,463	1,578	1,684	1,761	1.01	49.6

Table 5.89 Elderly population

'000

	1980	1985	1990	1995	2000	2005	2010	2015	2020	CAGR	Period growth
Elderly population (60+)	1,674.2	1,728.8	1,966.7	2,212.2	2,429.0	2,567.9	2,783.5	2,979.4	3,189.6	1.62	90.5
Female	922.4	946.5	1,073.9	1,191.2	1,323.8	1,410.2	1,532.0	1,635.8	1,745.2	1.61	89.2
Male	751.8	782.2	892.8	1,021.0	1,105.2	1,157.7	1,251.5	1,343.7	1,444.3	1.65	92.1

Table 5.90 Population of biggest cities 1980-2020

'000

	1980	1985	1990	1995	2000	2005	2010	2015	2020	CAGR	Period growth
Athens	765.6	782.7	773.5	767.8	750.9	728.2	717.1	722.2	735.1	-0.10	-3.98
Thessaloniki	385.4	392.3	385.3	379.1	367.3	353.5	345.7	346.4	351.4	-0.23	-8.83
Piraeus	181.6	185.5	183.1	181.4	177.0	172.2	170.1	171.8	175.2	-0.09	-3.53
Patras	142.3	148.8	151.7	157.0	160.2	163.1	167.9	174.5	181.6	0.61	27.65
Heraklion	100.8	108.0	113.8	122.6	129.8	137.1	145.4	154.2	162.6	1.20	61.36
Peristeri	132.4	136.8	137.1	138.7	138.4	137.5	138.5	141.7	146.0	0.24	10.21
Larissa	101.1	107.3	111.6	118.4	123.7	128.6	134.8	141.7	148.6	0.97	46.93
Kallithea	113.7	116.1	114.5	113.3	110.5	107.6	106.5	107.7	109.9	-0.09	-3.37
Kalamaria	73.6	77.6	80.0	84.0	86.9	91.4	97.0	102.8	108.4	0.97	47.40
Nikaia	79.4	83.9	86.8	91.5	95.0	94.8	95.1	97.1	99.8	0.57	25.69

Chart 5.76 Population age shift 2000 and 2020, Each Column Represents a Single Age Group

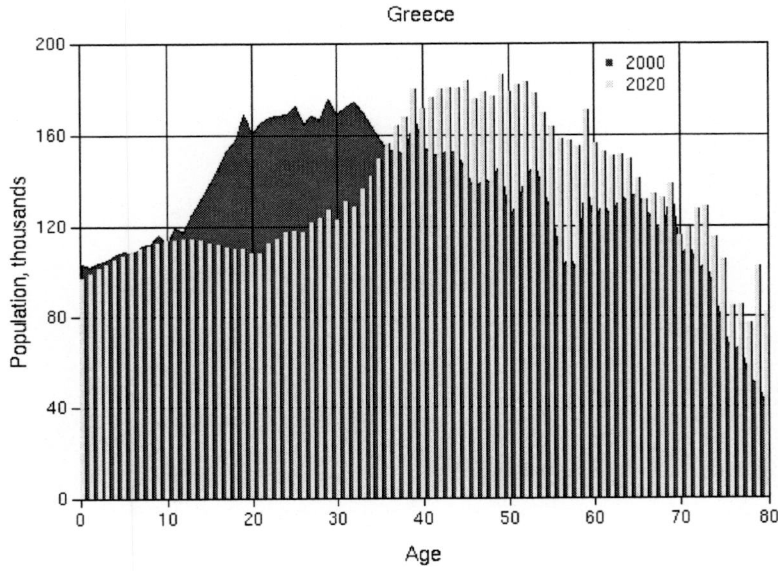

Chart 5.77 Population pyramids, 1980/2000/2010/2020

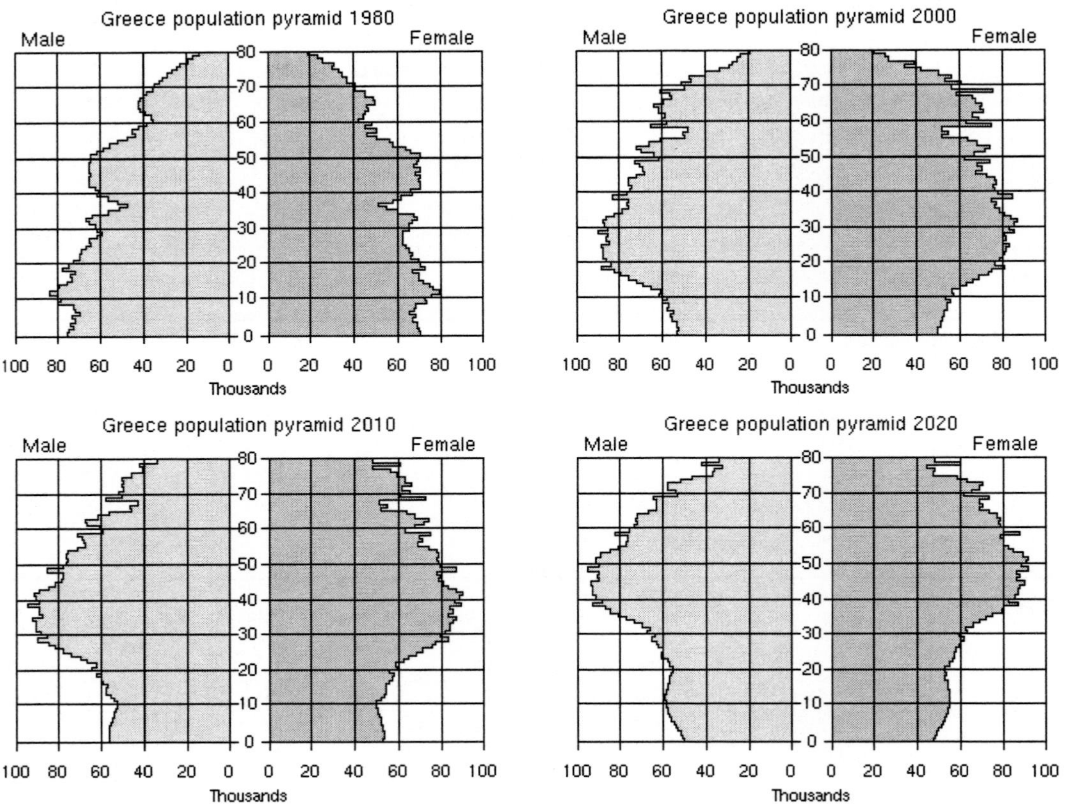

Chart 5.78 Major Cities: 1980, 2000 and 2020

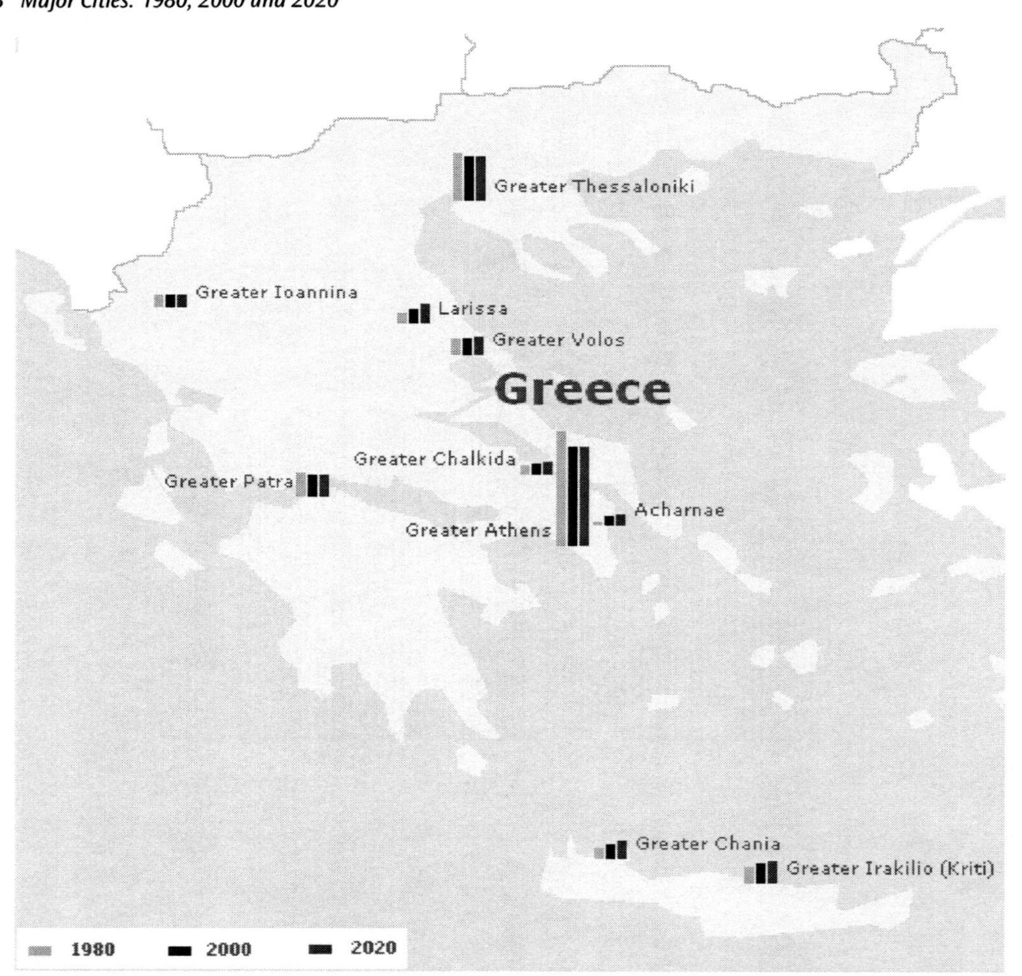

Hong Kong, China

Table 5.91 Key population trends

'000

	1980	1985	1990	1995	2000	2005	2010	2015	2020	CAGR	Period growth
Population at January 1st	5,063.1	5,456.2	5,704.5	6,156.1	6,665.0	6,813.2	7,130.9	7,443.2	7,727.6	1.06	52.63
Male	2,629.0	2,815.6	2,922.1	3,084.3	3,276.5	3,264.0	3,328.4	3,390.3	3,439.8	0.67	30.84
Female	2,434.1	2,640.6	2,782.4	3,071.8	3,388.5	3,549.2	3,802.6	4,052.9	4,287.7	1.43	76.15
0-4 yrs	408.2	422.1	375.7	377.6	294.7	221.1	243.3	253.7	274.0	-0.99	-32.87
5-9 yrs	422.2	418.1	426.2	385.0	401.5	332.8	270.1	324.4	332.3	-0.60	-21.29
10-14 yrs	462.7	438.1	424.4	432.5	431.9	415.0	362.1	298.8	356.6	-0.65	-22.93
15-19 yrs	584.8	471.0	434.2	421.2	459.0	434.2	434.4	376.7	315.0	-1.54	-46.14
20-24 yrs	581.0	581.0	461.9	450.6	466.8	470.9	503.7	496.2	444.9	-0.66	-23.42
25-29 yrs	477.6	599.9	607.3	538.8	533.2	486.7	568.3	601.5	583.6	0.50	22.19
30-34 yrs	381.5	490.7	608.2	654.6	585.3	556.4	550.9	629.2	650.1	1.34	70.42
35-39 yrs	231.2	391.1	494.7	636.8	689.6	590.9	561.5	553.1	633.6	2.55	174.03
40-44 yrs	260.9	241.2	390.4	506.5	658.8	689.2	564.6	532.5	526.9	1.77	101.97
45-49 yrs	269.9	265.9	239.7	398.9	514.6	648.2	658.9	534.4	505.2	1.58	87.18
50-54 yrs	260.2	273.0	259.4	240.8	401.2	509.9	632.1	644.3	518.8	1.74	99.37
55-59 yrs	216.8	249.9	263.2	256.2	241.8	388.1	500.7	624.4	635.5	2.73	193.14
60-64 yrs	181.0	207.8	236.4	254.8	257.4	235.1	378.2	488.8	609.3	3.08	236.63
65-69 yrs	137.5	161.5	185.5	221.7	251.6	246.2	227.6	365.9	470.8	3.12	242.40
70-74 yrs	90.1	118.7	135.5	165.1	202.4	228.3	232.1	214.9	344.3	3.41	282.16
75-79 yrs	54.6	67.2	89.6	111.3	139.3	169.8	200.1	205.5	191.1	3.18	249.93
80+ yrs	42.9	59.0	72.2	103.7	135.9	190.4	242.2	299.2	335.5	5.28	682.00
Median age of population (years)	25.7	28.2	31.0	33.6	36.2	39.2	40.6	41.7	42.5	1.27	65.35

Table 5.92 Key economic trends

As stated

	1990	1995	2000	2005	2010	2015	2020	CAGR	Period growth
Total GDP (HK$ per capita)	143,578.1	171,505.0	180,400.2	216,091.9	240,010.1	282,905.4	338,386.7	2.90	135.7
Disposable income (HK$ per capita)	134,125.5	158,335.0	158,585.8	174,348.3	194,403.5	227,825.8	270,583.2	2.37	101.7
Disposable income (HK$ per household)	490,775.5	542,386.2	523,074.6	542,233.6	586,207.2	670,738.4	779,532.9	1.55	58.8
Number of households by annual household disposable income ('000)									
Over US$1,000	1,558.6	1,796.6	2,016.3	2,186.0	2,361.7	2,526.4	2,681.3	1.82	72.0
Over US$10,000	1,440.2	1,732.7	1,880.8	2,016.3	2,249.1	2,456.4	2,638.6	2.04	83.2
Over US$25,000	867.5	1,429.2	1,530.1	1,572.4	1,927.4	2,238.7	2,496.1	3.59	187.7
Over US$75,000	125.3	467.1	605.8	568.3	944.0	1,385.5	1,822.2	9.33	1,354.1
Over US$150,000	25.7	118.1	163.7	168.9	349.3	638.0	1,020.6	13.06	3,878.2
Total households	1,559.0	1,797.1	2,020.7	2,190.7	2,364.8	2,528.2	2,682.3	1.83	72.1

Note: Per capita data is shown at constant 2010 prices. Household disposable income bands are shown at current prices.

Table 5.93 Young generation

'000

	1980	1985	1990	1995	2000	2005	2010	2015	2020	CAGR	Period growth
Babies under 12 months	83.6	78.2	71.5	73.9	49.5	39.4	42.7	46.4	48.9	-1.33	-41.48
Infants under 24 months	167.4	160.7	148.3	149.7	99.6	78.4	85.9	92.2	98.8	-1.31	-40.95
Toddlers aged 1-4	324.6	343.9	304.2	303.7	245.2	181.7	200.6	207.3	225.1	-0.91	-30.65
Children aged 2-9	663.0	679.5	653.6	612.9	596.6	475.5	427.5	485.9	507.5	-0.67	-23.45
Female	320.6	327.5	314.3	296.4	286.4	230.2	206.2	236.5	248.2	-0.64	-22.58
Male	342.4	352.0	339.3	316.5	310.2	245.3	221.3	249.5	259.3	-0.69	-24.26
Tweenagers aged 10-14	462.7	438.1	424.4	432.5	431.9	415.0	362.1	298.8	356.6	-0.65	-22.93
Female	224.6	209.3	203.3	210.0	210.0	201.9	176.6	144.8	173.0	-0.65	-22.98
Male	238.1	228.8	221.1	222.5	221.9	213.1	185.6	154.0	183.6	-0.65	-22.89
Teenagers aged 13-19	784.6	646.5	603.7	599.3	629.4	603.1	597.8	500.0	458.4	-1.33	-41.57
Female	380.4	310.2	289.0	288.7	305.7	295.9	291.9	244.3	223.3	-1.32	-41.29
Male	404.2	336.3	314.7	310.6	323.7	307.2	305.9	255.8	235.1	-1.35	-41.84
Studying age 18-22	601.3	541.6	432.2	433.8	463.6	450.4	474.9	452.8	366.7	-1.23	-39.02
Female	287.7	263.5	209.2	212.3	233.7	227.9	245.2	235.5	192.5	-1.00	-33.08
Male	313.6	278.1	223.0	221.5	229.9	222.5	229.7	217.3	174.2	-1.46	-44.46
Young adults aged 15-29	1,643.4	1,651.9	1,503.4	1,410.6	1,459.0	1,391.8	1,506.4	1,474.4	1,343.5	-0.50	-18.25
Female	781.7	800.2	740.0	716.3	755.3	724.7	821.2	830.9	766.3	-0.05	-1.97
Male	861.7	851.7	763.4	694.3	703.7	667.1	685.2	643.5	577.2	-1.00	-33.01

Table 5.94 Middle-aged generation

'000

	1980	1985	1990	1995	2000	2005	2010	2015	2020	CAGR	Period growth
Middle-aged adults 30-59	1,620.5	1,911.8	2,255.6	2,693.8	3,091.3	3,382.7	3,468.7	3,517.8	3,470.1	1.92	114.1
Female	739.3	886.9	1,067.1	1,322.4	1,574.6	1,794.5	1,883.5	1,962.8	2,015.6	2.54	172.6
Male	881.2	1,024.9	1,188.5	1,371.4	1,516.7	1,588.2	1,585.2	1,555.0	1,454.5	1.26	65.1
Baby boomers aged 40-59	1,007.8	1,030.0	1,152.7	1,402.4	1,816.4	2,235.4	2,356.4	2,335.5	2,186.4	1.96	117.0
Female	468.9	474.0	530.4	660.6	886.0	1,145.6	1,241.1	1,255.7	1,216.4	2.41	159.4
Male	538.9	556.0	622.3	741.8	930.4	1,089.8	1,115.3	1,079.8	970.1	1.48	80.0

Table 5.95 Elderly population

'000

	1980	1985	1990	1995	2000	2005	2010	2015	2020	CAGR	Period growth
Elderly population (60+)	506.1	614.2	719.2	856.6	986.6	1,069.8	1,280.3	1,574.2	1,951.0	3.43	285.5
Female	287.3	339.6	386.3	455.1	514.6	559.9	673.2	833.0	1,036.1	3.26	260.6
Male	218.8	274.6	332.9	401.5	472.0	509.9	607.1	741.2	914.8	3.64	318.1

Table 5.96 Population of biggest cities 1980-2020

'000

	1980	1985	1990	1995	2000	2005	2010	2015	2020	CAGR	Period growth
Hong Kong	4,633	5,077	5,603	6,156	6,665	7,040	7,448	7,827	8,164	1	76

Chart 5.79 Population age shift 2000 and 2020, Each Column Represents a Single Age Group

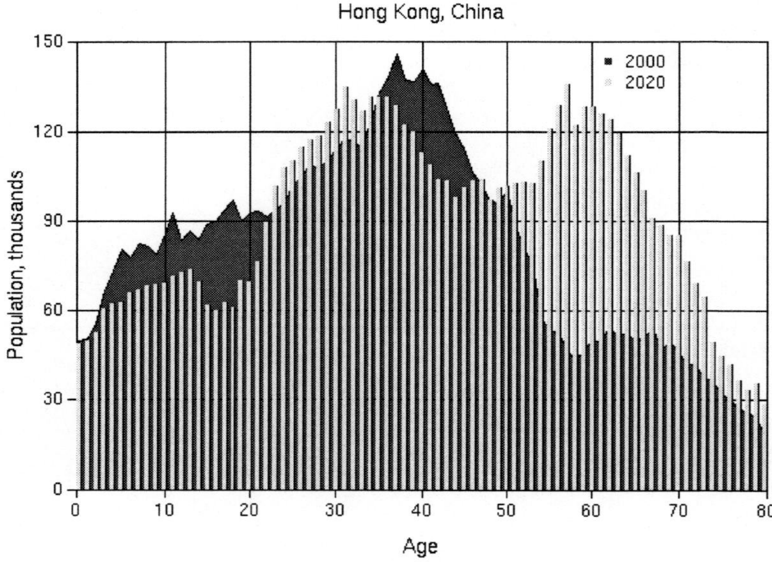

Chart 5.80 Population pyramids, 1980/2000/2010/2020

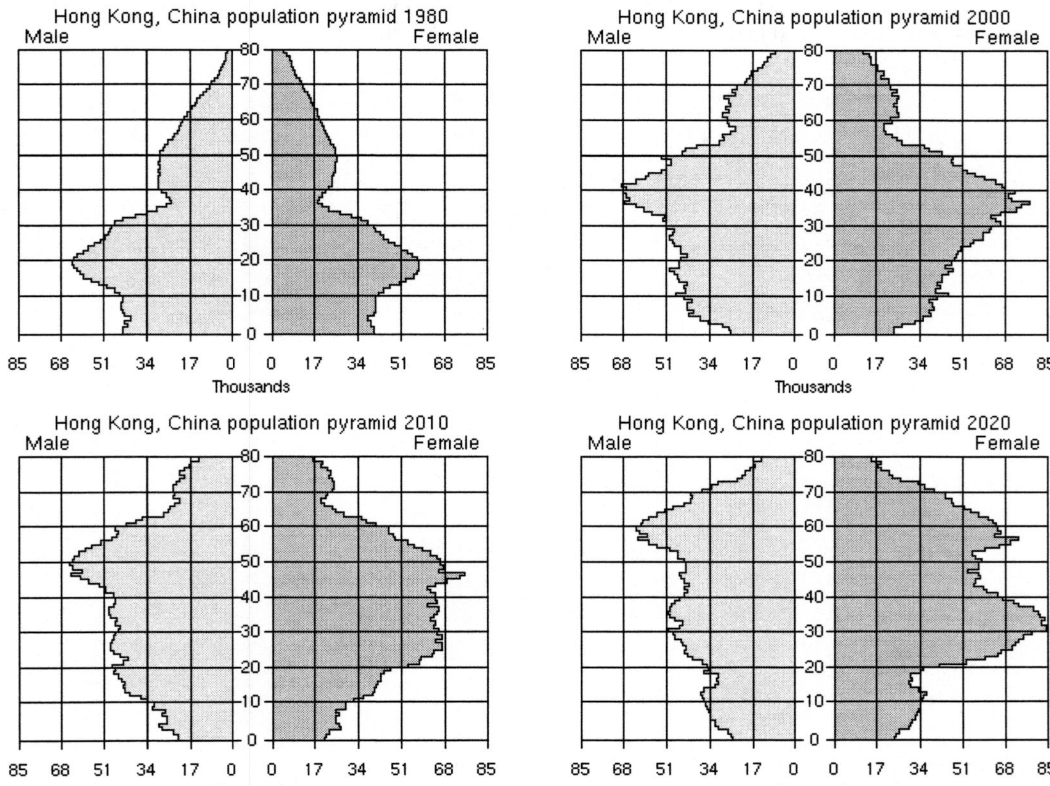

Chart 5.81 Major Cities: 1980, 2000 and 2020

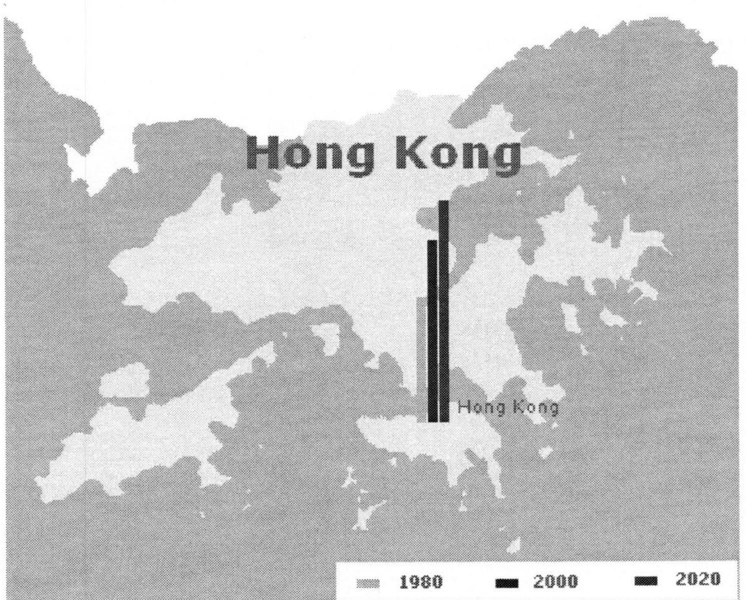

Hungary

Table 5.97 Key population trends

'000

	1980	1985	1990	1995	2000	2005	2010	2015	2020	CAGR	Period growth
Population at January 1st	10,709.5	10,657.4	10,374.8	10,336.7	10,221.6	10,097.5	9,999.7	9,870.7	9,748.0	-0.23	-8.98
Male	5,188.7	5,149.3	4,984.9	4,941.6	4,865.2	4,793.1	4,744.3	4,685.3	4,632.5	-0.28	-10.72
Female	5,520.8	5,508.1	5,389.9	5,395.1	5,356.5	5,304.4	5,255.3	5,185.4	5,115.5	-0.19	-7.34
0-4 yrs	864.9	662.5	617.2	598.8	501.7	477.8	492.2	480.4	471.8	-1.50	-45.45
5-9 yrs	772.7	863.9	656.2	623.6	596.9	503.1	482.8	495.9	483.9	-1.16	-37.38
10-14 yrs	702.8	771.6	857.2	669.3	630.6	598.7	505.6	484.7	497.5	-0.86	-29.22
15-19 yrs	650.5	701.1	766.9	851.2	682.3	634.3	602.4	509.4	488.3	-0.71	-24.94
20-24 yrs	814.0	647.5	678.7	759.0	844.3	687.7	645.3	612.1	519.7	-1.12	-36.16
25-29 yrs	891.6	809.3	620.3	679.3	751.4	846.2	703.7	658.9	625.5	-0.88	-29.84
30-34 yrs	756.0	884.8	774.4	621.6	679.5	752.7	852.7	710.7	665.6	-0.32	-11.96
35-39 yrs	720.6	747.3	847.3	768.4	621.0	678.9	753.5	850.8	709.3	-0.04	-1.58
40-44 yrs	652.0	707.2	716.7	833.1	757.3	614.2	674.2	746.8	842.5	0.64	29.22
45-49 yrs	685.5	633.3	675.0	697.9	811.3	738.1	601.0	659.4	730.8	0.16	6.61
50-54 yrs	694.3	656.3	597.7	650.3	670.9	779.0	707.6	571.2	629.0	-0.25	-9.40
55-59 yrs	674.0	650.5	607.5	566.3	617.6	634.6	739.0	668.1	538.7	-0.56	-20.08
60-64 yrs	380.7	614.3	585.9	559.9	525.8	574.5	590.7	692.9	625.9	1.25	64.41
65-69 yrs	547.4	332.3	529.7	516.4	501.8	473.7	520.3	535.9	631.1	0.36	15.29
70-74 yrs	416.3	442.5	267.8	439.0	433.9	428.1	404.0	450.3	466.2	0.28	11.99
75-79 yrs	274.7	295.5	316.6	200.4	335.3	337.9	334.6	313.5	364.7	0.71	32.76
80+ yrs	211.2	237.5	259.9	302.3	260.1	337.9	390.1	429.6	457.4	1.95	116.59
Median age of population (years)	34.3	34.9	36.1	37.6	38.5	38.9	39.7	40.8	42.5	0.54	24.10

Table 5.98 Key economic trends

As stated

	1990	1995	2000	2005	2010	2015	2020	CAGR	Period growth
Total GDP (HUF per capita)	2,420,128.7	2,032,370.0	2,436,687.9	3,039,700.3	2,630,133.1	3,307,003.8	3,966,623.9	1.66	63.9
Disposable income (HUF per capita)	962,713.7	934,444.8	1,073,160.0	1,348,689.4	1,297,764.8	1,633,678.0	1,992,555.2	2.45	107.0
Disposable income (HUF per household)	2,567,914.2	2,496,425.5	2,851,761.8	3,402,933.3	3,084,988.4	3,738,390.9	4,457,189.0	1.86	73.6
Number of households by annual household disposable income ('000)									
Over US$1,000	3,804.0	3,846.2	3,831.7	4,001.5	4,206.2	4,313.4	4,357.7	0.45	14.6
Over US$10,000	167.8	395.3	409.1	2,507.0	2,945.4	3,907.2	4,252.2	11.38	2,434.1
Over US$25,000	51.6	79.2	84.8	321.9	440.8	1,203.1	2,558.2	13.89	4,855.1
Over US$75,000	12.6	19.5	20.5	60.9	72.3	127.3	233.9	10.24	1,761.6
Over US$150,000	5.2	8.0	8.4	25.0	29.8	51.6	87.0	9.88	1,588.3
Total households	3,889.5	3,869.2	3,846.6	4,002.0	4,206.6	4,313.5	4,357.8	0.38	12.0

Note: Per capita data is shown at constant 2010 prices. Household disposable income bands are shown at current prices.

Table 5.99 Young generation

'000

	1980	1985	1990	1995	2000	2005	2010	2015	2020	CAGR	Period growth
Babies under 12 months	159.2	122.3	121.4	114.2	93.5	93.7	96.7	94.3	92.5	-1.35	-41.89
Infants under 24 months	324.6	247.1	243.2	229.6	189.2	187.5	195.0	189.7	186.4	-1.38	-42.56
Toddlers aged 1-4	705.7	540.2	495.9	484.5	408.3	384.1	395.5	386.1	379.3	-1.54	-46.26
Children aged 2-9	1,313.1	1,279.2	1,030.2	992.8	909.5	793.5	780.0	786.6	769.2	-1.33	-41.42
Female	637.9	622.8	503.6	485.3	443.6	386.4	379.8	382.7	374.6	-1.32	-41.27
Male	675.2	656.4	526.6	507.5	465.9	407.0	400.2	403.9	394.6	-1.33	-41.55
Tweenagers aged 10-14	702.8	771.6	857.2	669.3	630.6	598.7	505.6	484.7	497.5	-0.86	-29.22
Female	340.3	374.7	417.9	327.2	308.6	292.7	246.6	236.5	242.0	-0.85	-28.90
Male	362.5	396.9	439.3	342.2	322.0	306.1	259.1	248.2	255.5	-0.87	-29.52
Teenagers aged 13-19	912.5	993.3	1,135.5	1,138.5	943.9	885.0	818.3	705.7	687.8	-0.70	-24.62
Female	442.5	481.8	552.8	555.4	462.0	433.2	400.2	344.7	335.4	-0.69	-24.20
Male	470.0	511.5	582.7	583.2	481.8	451.7	418.1	361.0	352.4	-0.72	-25.02
Studying age 18-22	715.4	639.2	714.2	835.3	779.8	656.8	628.3	572.3	494.9	-0.92	-30.82
Female	350.0	309.7	348.7	407.7	380.2	322.7	308.1	280.5	242.4	-0.91	-30.75
Male	365.4	329.5	365.5	427.5	399.6	334.1	320.3	291.8	252.5	-0.92	-30.88
Young adults aged 15-29	2,356.1	2,158.0	2,065.8	2,289.4	2,277.9	2,168.2	1,951.4	1,780.4	1,633.5	-0.91	-30.67
Female	1,154.1	1,052.3	1,011.9	1,119.9	1,114.5	1,061.6	958.5	874.9	801.4	-0.91	-30.55
Male	1,202.1	1,105.6	1,053.9	1,169.5	1,163.4	1,106.6	992.9	905.5	832.1	-0.92	-30.78

Table 5.100 **Middle-aged generation**
'000

	1980	1985	1990	1995	2000	2005	2010	2015	2020	CAGR	Period growth
Middle-aged adults 30-59	4,183	4,279	4,219	4,138	4,158	4,198	4,328	4,207	4,116	-0.04	-1.59
Female	2,159	2,195	2,165	2,130	2,136	2,149	2,202	2,127	2,066	-0.11	-4.33
Male	2,023	2,085	2,053	2,008	2,021	2,048	2,126	2,080	2,050	0.03	1.33
Baby boomers aged 40-59	2,706	2,647	2,597	2,748	2,857	2,766	2,722	2,645	2,741	0.03	1.30
Female	1,422	1,385	1,356	1,435	1,490	1,442	1,413	1,361	1,389	-0.06	-2.37
Male	1,284	1,262	1,241	1,313	1,368	1,324	1,309	1,285	1,353	0.13	5.37

Table 5.101 **Elderly population**
'000

	1980	1985	1990	1995	2000	2005	2010	2015	2020	CAGR	Period growth
Elderly population (60+)	1,830.3	1,922.1	1,959.8	2,017.9	2,056.9	2,152.1	2,239.6	2,422.2	2,545.4	0.83	39.1
Female	1,072.5	1,142.7	1,172.5	1,221.0	1,261.3	1,323.1	1,374.0	1,471.7	1,541.0	0.91	43.7
Male	757.8	779.4	787.3	796.9	795.5	829.0	865.6	950.5	1,004.4	0.71	32.5

Table 5.102 **Population of biggest cities 1980-2020**
'000

	1980	1985	1990	1995	2000	2005	2010	2015	2020	CAGR	Period growth
Budapest	2,059.2	2,093.0	2,016.7	1,930.0	1,781.0	1,697.3	1,708.8	1,723.2	1,739.5	-0.42	-15.53
Debrecen	198.2	211.1	212.2	210.8	209.3	204.3	206.0	207.9	210.0	0.15	5.98
Szeged	164.4	170.7	169.9	169.7	166.6	162.9	169.2	172.6	174.8	0.15	6.28
Miskolc	208.1	208.0	196.4	182.1	182.5	175.7	168.5	162.6	158.2	-0.68	-23.98
Pecs	169.1	174.0	170.0	165.4	161.6	156.6	157.0	157.4	158.1	-0.17	-6.51
Gyor	124.1	130.1	129.3	127.2	127.8	127.6	129.8	131.7	133.5	0.18	7.54
Nyiregyhaza	108.2	114.0	114.2	114.1	117.2	116.3	117.4	118.2	119.1	0.24	10.06
Kecskemet	96.9	101.7	102.5	104.6	106.2	108.3	111.7	114.4	116.8	0.47	20.54
Szekesfehervar	103.6	109.2	109.0	108.1	105.5	101.5	102.2	103.0	104.0	0.01	0.42
Szombathely	82.9	86.6	85.6	83.7	81.3	80.5	79.0	78.7	79.0	-0.12	-4.64

Chart 5.82 Population age shift 2000 and 2020, Each Column Represents a Single Age Group

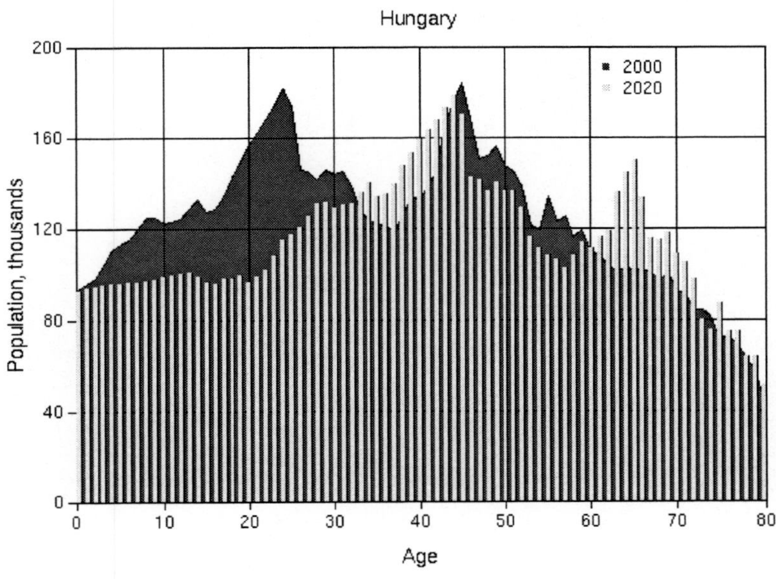

Chart 5.83 Population pyramids, 1980/2000/2010/2020

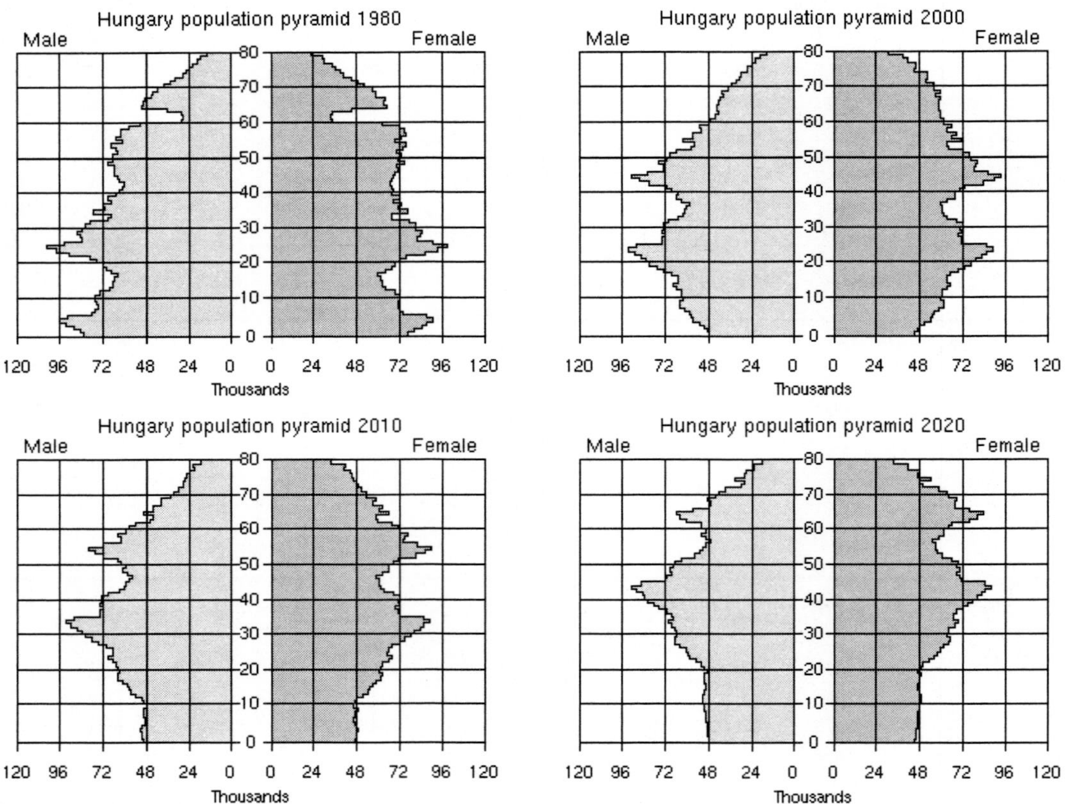

Chart 5.84 Major Cities: 1980, 2000 and 2020

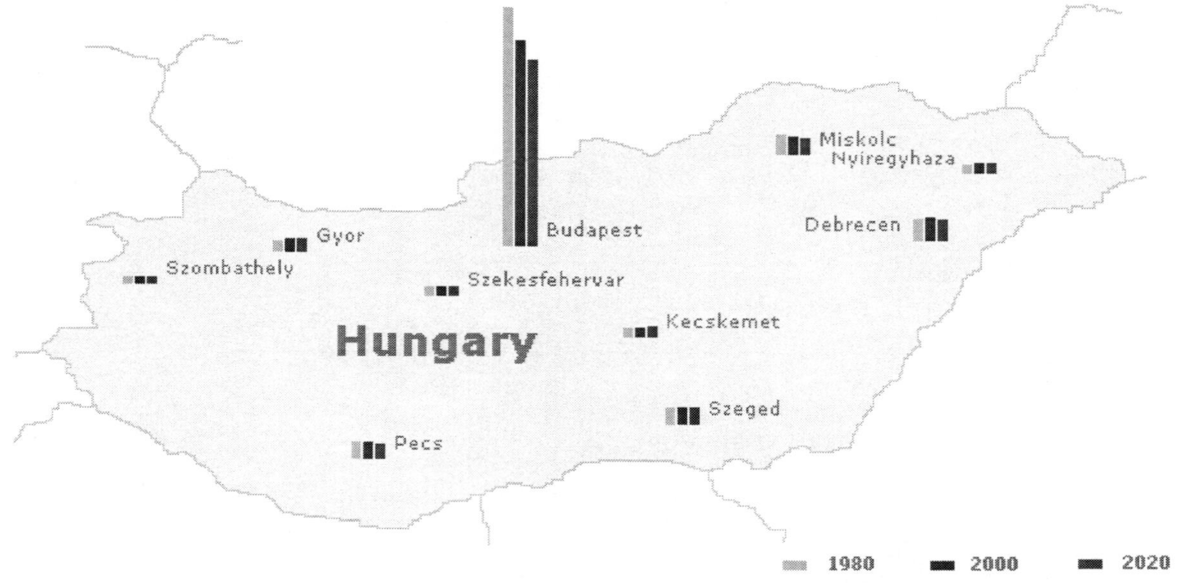

India

Table 5.103 Key population trends

'000

	1980	1985	1990	1995	2000	2005	2010	2015	2020	CAGR	Period growth
Population at January 1st	675,743.7	755,877.8	841,133.2	929,900.4	1,017,160.9	1,103,041.7	1,184,843.2	1,262,626.4	1,333,877.6	1.71	97.4
Male	351,723.4	393,037.1	437,098.8	482,741.8	527,302.1	570,804.7	611,900.9	650,860.1	686,307.6	1.69	95.1
Female	324,020.3	362,840.7	404,034.4	447,158.5	489,858.8	532,237.0	572,942.3	611,766.3	647,570.1	1.75	99.9
0-4 yrs	101,014.7	109,475.2	116,835.2	123,561.4	123,903.4	124,808.0	122,627.4	120,857.4	117,015.8	0.37	15.8
5-9 yrs	86,996.2	97,046.5	105,892.1	113,429.5	120,138.5	121,312.9	122,088.6	120,525.7	118,851.0	0.78	36.6
10-14 yrs	77,647.6	85,745.7	95,768.3	104,548.0	112,309.6	118,964.6	120,440.4	121,254.7	119,811.5	1.09	54.3
15-19 yrs	69,963.2	76,797.2	84,859.7	94,772.4	103,571.9	111,300.3	118,089.9	119,613.6	120,541.9	1.37	72.3
20-24 yrs	62,841.7	68,946.1	75,730.1	83,641.8	93,511.9	102,224.1	110,104.0	116,966.9	118,649.7	1.60	88.8
25-29 yrs	55,031.4	61,779.7	67,830.6	74,452.1	82,296.7	92,029.7	100,843.7	108,776.9	115,772.2	1.88	110.4
30-34 yrs	42,069.7	54,023.7	60,698.0	66,604.2	73,151.0	80,838.2	90,593.2	99,444.5	107,480.0	2.37	155.5
35-39 yrs	35,870.0	41,190.3	52,955.6	59,477.0	65,312.0	71,691.9	79,356.0	89,137.8	98,068.4	2.55	173.4
40-44 yrs	32,897.3	34,921.9	40,166.3	51,646.8	58,081.4	63,771.9	70,113.4	77,800.2	87,624.2	2.48	166.4
45-49 yrs	28,637.7	31,701.3	33,711.6	38,803.1	50,018.6	56,313.1	61,983.3	68,327.8	76,050.3	2.47	165.6
50-54 yrs	24,000.1	27,095.6	30,064.2	32,006.5	36,999.0	47,833.9	54,070.1	59,732.8	66,085.2	2.56	175.4
55-59 yrs	19,399.5	22,067.6	24,989.4	27,788.7	29,750.4	34,571.0	44,954.6	51,069.5	56,700.6	2.72	192.3
60-64 yrs	14,993.7	17,027.4	19,443.1	22,109.5	24,806.8	26,748.7	31,363.3	41,065.5	46,945.0	2.89	213.1
65-69 yrs	10,764.2	12,295.8	14,027.7	16,115.8	18,592.5	21,122.2	23,042.1	27,300.6	36,047.3	3.07	234.9
70-74 yrs	7,090.8	8,069.4	9,249.8	10,619.8	12,425.6	14,594.8	16,864.6	18,627.5	22,354.6	2.91	215.3
75-79 yrs	3,822.6	4,636.7	5,279.5	6,102.7	7,186.7	8,623.5	10,390.1	12,221.7	13,692.1	3.24	258.2
80+ yrs	2,703.2	3,057.7	3,632.0	4,221.0	5,104.9	6,292.7	7,918.5	9,903.1	12,187.7	3.84	350.9
Median age of population (years)	20.2	20.6	21.1	21.6	22.5	23.6	25.0	26.4	28.1	0.83	39.2

Table 5.104 Key economic trends

As stated

	1990	1995	2000	2005	2010	2015	2020	CAGR	Period growth
Total GDP (Rs per capita)	24,517.5	28,276.0	34,836.5	43,934.0	54,167.7	78,134.9	105,756.9	4.99	331.4
Disposable income (Rs per capita)	19,298.4	23,488.5	26,758.1	30,803.2	32,251.5	42,914.1	55,228.0	3.57	186.2
Disposable income (Rs per household)	109,357.4	130,230.9	144,708.9	163,948.8	169,224.7	222,475.2	283,317.8	3.22	159.1
Number of households by annual household disposable income ('000)									
Over US$1,000	105,910.6	120,030.5	141,797.1	173,955.4	201,138.3	227,591.3	252,046.7	2.93	138.0
Over US$10,000	1,737.6	2,418.2	2,943.8	4,996.2	8,434.5	18,402.7	41,803.6	11.18	2,305.9
Over US$25,000	540.3	755.3	926.5	1,556.6	2,300.4	3,820.5	6,911.5	8.87	1,179.1
Over US$75,000	133.2	187.2	231.7	393.1	586.4	970.4	1,642.1	8.73	1,133.0
Over US$150,000	55.0	77.6	96.6	165.0	247.6	408.7	696.6	8.83	1,165.6
Total households	148,435.3	167,717.5	188,083.1	207,242.7	225,811.8	243,552.9	260,017.0	1.89	75.2

Note: Per capita data is shown at constant 2010 prices. Household disposable income bands are shown at current prices.

Table 5.105 Young generation

'000

	1980	1985	1990	1995	2000	2005	2010	2015	2020	CAGR	Period growth
Babies under 12 months	21,602	22,856	24,343	25,605	24,751	25,553	24,418	24,391	23,135	0.17	7.09
Infants under 24 months	42,477	45,264	48,179	50,771	49,594	50,731	48,949	48,627	46,450	0.22	9.35
Toddlers aged 1-4	79,412	86,619	92,493	97,957	99,152	99,255	98,209	96,466	93,881	0.42	18.22
Children aged 2-9	145,534	161,258	174,548	186,220	194,448	195,389	195,767	192,756	189,417	0.66	30.15
Female	70,089	77,659	83,885	89,285	92,949	93,496	93,714	92,309	90,784	0.65	29.53
Male	75,446	83,599	90,663	96,935	101,499	101,894	102,053	100,447	98,633	0.67	30.73
Tweenagers aged 10-14	77,648	85,746	95,768	104,548	112,310	118,965	120,440	121,255	119,811	1.09	54.30
Female	37,229	41,162	46,005	50,164	53,812	56,812	57,570	58,013	57,353	1.09	54.05
Male	40,418	44,584	49,763	54,384	58,498	62,153	62,870	63,241	62,459	1.09	54.53
Teenagers aged 13-19	100,071	109,886	121,873	135,525	147,445	158,285	166,105	168,045	168,611	1.31	68.49
Female	47,891	52,641	58,452	65,041	70,694	75,754	79,318	80,341	80,685	1.31	68.48
Male	52,180	57,245	63,421	70,485	76,751	82,531	86,787	87,704	87,926	1.31	68.51
Studying age 18-22	65,539	72,042	79,141	88,022	97,785	105,891	113,782	118,502	119,537	1.51	82.39
Female	31,275	34,425	37,852	42,179	46,876	50,733	54,401	56,568	57,169	1.52	82.80
Male	34,264	37,618	41,288	45,843	50,909	55,158	59,381	61,934	62,368	1.51	82.02
Young adults aged 15-29	187,836	207,523	228,420	252,866	279,381	305,554	329,038	345,357	354,964	1.60	88.98
Female	89,484	98,999	109,129	121,015	133,825	146,393	157,444	165,135	169,721	1.61	89.67
Male	98,352	108,524	119,292	131,851	145,555	159,161	171,594	180,222	185,243	1.60	88.35

Table 5.106 Middle-aged generation

'000

	1980	1985	1990	1995	2000	2005	2010	2015	2020	CAGR	Period growth
Middle-aged adults 30-59	182,874	211,000	242,585	276,326	313,312	355,020	401,071	445,513	492,009	2.51	169.0
Female	87,433	101,126	116,403	132,698	150,567	171,062	193,904	216,010	238,921	2.54	173.3
Male	95,442	109,875	126,182	143,628	162,745	183,958	207,166	229,503	253,088	2.47	165.2
Baby boomers aged 40-59	104,935	115,786	128,932	150,245	174,849	202,490	231,121	256,930	286,460	2.54	173.0
Female	50,081	55,849	62,553	72,746	84,464	97,959	112,167	125,190	139,969	2.60	179.5
Male	54,854	59,937	66,379	77,499	90,386	104,531	118,954	131,740	146,491	2.49	167.1

Table 5.107 Elderly population

'000

	1980	1985	1990	1995	2000	2005	2010	2015	2020	CAGR	Period growth
Elderly population (60+)	39,375	45,087	51,632	59,169	68,116	77,382	89,579	109,118	131,227	3.06	233.3
Female	19,202	22,037	25,370	29,663	34,848	40,126	46,809	56,938	68,479	3.23	256.6
Male	20,173	23,050	26,262	29,506	33,269	37,256	42,770	52,180	62,747	2.88	211.1

Table 5.108 Population of biggest cities 1980-2020

'000

	1980	1985	1990	1995	2000	2005	2010	2015	2020	CAGR	Period growth
Bombay	7,396.4	8,527.1	9,710.5	10,839.0	11,854.3	12,915.2	14,199.7	15,699.2	17,551.0	2.18	137.3
Delhi	4,889.3	5,839.6	6,966.9	8,271.6	9,656.9	11,057.9	12,593.9	14,291.7	16,255.1	3.05	232.5
Bangalore	2,324.9	2,740.5	3,213.6	3,723.1	4,236.4	4,772.0	5,364.1	6,045.2	6,832.0	2.73	193.9
Calcutta	3,686.7	4,053.2	4,350.2	4,539.9	4,622.9	4,702.7	4,901.6	5,230.2	5,668.3	1.08	53.7
Madras	3,103.1	3,459.1	3,778.1	4,048.8	4,234.6	4,410.1	4,713.1	5,083.6	5,612.5	1.49	80.9
Ahmedabad	2,213.5	2,548.4	2,896.7	3,214.2	3,500.6	3,803.3	4,159.5	4,601.7	5,130.7	2.12	131.8
Hyderabad	2,534.7	2,830.9	3,099.6	3,314.5	3,459.3	3,622.5	3,842.0	4,169.3	4,567.2	1.48	80.2
Pune	814.0	1,103.5	1,486.3	1,947.1	2,452.7	2,982.8	3,525.5	4,108.1	4,737.9	4.50	482.1
Surat	784.0	1,065.9	1,428.5	1,868.3	2,354.0	2,856.1	3,376.6	3,933.7	4,531.1	4.48	477.9
Kanpur	1,286.1	1,531.5	1,822.8	2,148.9	2,490.6	2,844.5	3,231.0	3,656.0	4,152.2	2.97	222.8

Chart 5.85 Population age shift 2000 and 2020, Each Column Represents a Single Age Group

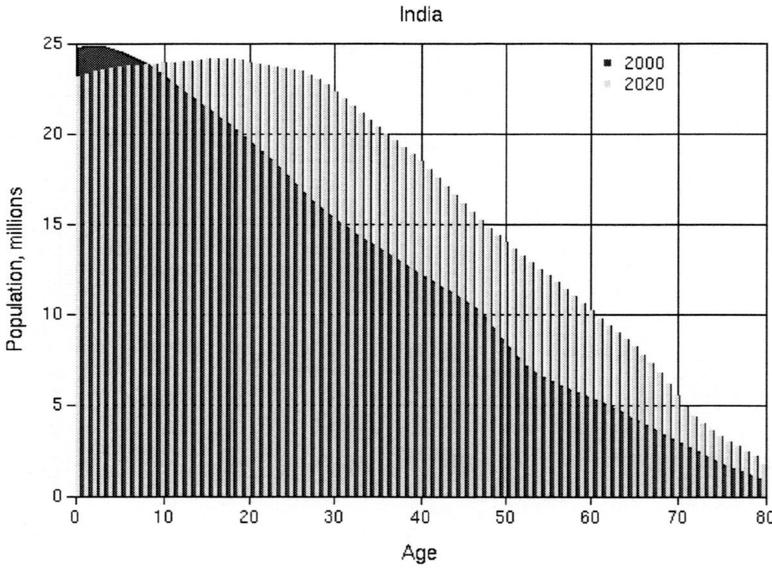

Chart 5.86 Population pyramids, 1980/2000/2010/2020

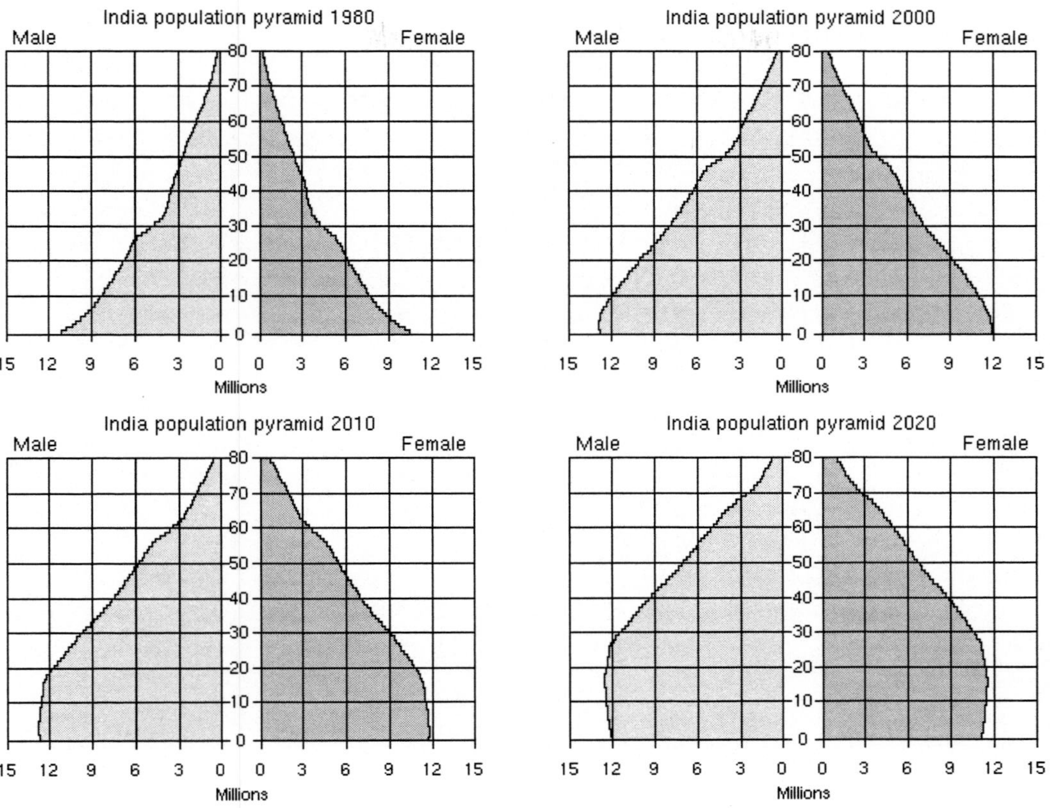

Chart 5.87 Major Cities: 1980, 2000 and 2020

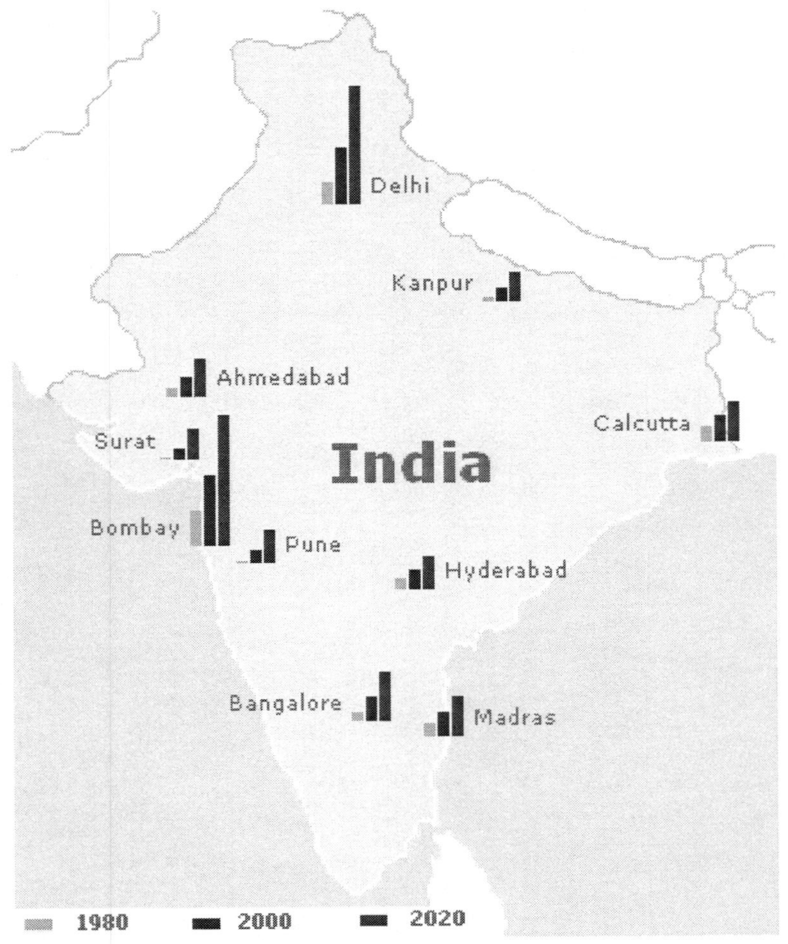

Indonesia

Table 5.109 Key population trends

'000

	1980	1985	1990	1995	2000	2005	2010	2015	2020	CAGR	Period growth
Population at January 1st	146,582.0	162,347.6	177,385.1	191,501.3	205,280.3	219,210.3	232,516.8	244,191.5	254,217.8	1.39	73.43
Male	73,472.4	81,371.4	88,886.0	95,909.6	102,675.3	109,513.4	116,062.3	121,790.4	126,724.3	1.37	72.48
Female	73,109.6	80,976.2	88,499.2	95,591.8	102,604.9	109,696.9	116,454.5	122,401.1	127,493.4	1.40	74.39
0-4 yrs	21,557.6	22,027.3	21,389.3	20,941.6	20,725.4	21,164.6	20,549.9	19,519.7	18,348.5	-0.40	-14.89
5-9 yrs	19,804.4	20,849.2	21,466.7	21,032.5	20,650.9	20,552.3	20,977.4	20,474.2	19,426.2	-0.05	-1.91
10-14 yrs	17,951.6	19,562.8	20,664.8	21,289.9	20,910.1	20,547.0	20,499.3	20,904.2	20,416.8	0.32	13.73
15-19 yrs	15,748.2	17,726.6	19,343.3	20,409.3	21,103.5	20,743.0	20,432.4	20,384.8	20,818.6	0.70	32.20
20-24 yrs	13,484.7	15,455.7	17,423.5	18,959.5	20,073.2	20,787.7	20,517.0	20,215.3	20,214.7	1.02	49.91
25-29 yrs	10,799.0	13,176.6	15,136.2	17,046.5	18,564.9	19,691.9	20,505.5	20,234.1	19,986.5	1.55	85.08
30-34 yrs	8,661.2	10,524.8	12,882.1	14,804.3	16,701.4	18,228.6	19,439.7	20,245.3	20,013.2	2.12	131.07
35-39 yrs	8,010.5	8,408.6	10,256.2	12,579.9	14,517.3	16,424.4	18,013.6	19,232.2	20,049.1	2.32	150.29
40-44 yrs	7,384.7	7,732.8	8,154.0	9,977.7	12,312.1	14,258.1	16,206.9	17,808.6	19,036.6	2.40	157.78
45-49 yrs	6,285.7	7,068.5	7,444.4	7,874.7	9,696.5	12,015.4	13,987.4	15,941.8	17,561.0	2.60	179.38
50-54 yrs	5,085.3	5,930.6	6,718.9	7,102.4	7,559.4	9,354.1	11,664.4	13,630.2	15,589.8	2.84	206.56
55-59 yrs	3,822.5	4,690.0	5,520.9	6,287.6	6,695.6	7,167.6	8,934.3	11,190.0	13,136.3	3.13	243.66
60-64 yrs	2,924.1	3,400.2	4,221.5	5,005.3	5,757.8	6,178.5	6,673.4	8,363.6	10,537.6	3.26	260.37
65-69 yrs	2,281.2	2,456.6	2,900.6	3,635.7	4,368.0	5,078.9	5,512.6	6,001.0	7,581.2	3.05	232.33
70-74 yrs	1,521.5	1,752.1	1,922.7	2,298.3	2,928.6	3,569.0	4,214.2	4,621.3	5,092.4	3.07	234.71
75-79 yrs	800.8	1,013.1	1,193.7	1,329.6	1,625.9	2,110.9	2,625.1	3,148.6	3,512.4	3.77	338.63
80+ yrs	459.2	572.3	746.4	926.6	1,089.6	1,338.4	1,763.7	2,276.8	2,897.0	4.71	530.90
Median age of population (years)	19.4	20.3	21.6	23.1	24.8	26.4	28.2	30.1	32.0	1.26	64.79

Table 5.110 Key economic trends

As stated

	1990	1995	2000	2005	2010	2015	2020	CAGR	Period growth
Total GDP (Rp per capita)	14,232,309.7	18,669,250.3	18,135,543.0	21,394,939.5	26,076,879.3	33,009,458.9	44,099,024.1	3.84	209.9
Disposable income (Rp per capita)	6,754,196.8	8,087,164.2	10,599,643.5	12,348,334.3	17,478,292.3	23,484,816.2	32,519,930.5	5.38	381.5
Disposable income (Rp per household)	29,858,300.7	34,387,344.0	42,173,030.4	44,869,892.7	58,778,684.6	73,922,644.7	96,824,330.9	4.00	224.3
Number of households by annual household disposable income ('000)									
Over US$1,000	30,364.4	39,898.8	45,725.9	55,343.9	66,825.1	76,278.8	84,723.0	3.48	179.0
Over US$10,000	710.6	1,247.5	1,118.0	2,081.4	6,375.5	16,374.9	33,864.4	13.75	4,665.7
Over US$25,000	225.1	396.3	343.4	595.3	1,274.2	2,389.3	5,278.7	11.09	2,245.2
Over US$75,000	56.7	100.2	83.4	148.4	320.3	548.7	967.0	9.92	1,605.0
Over US$150,000	23.8	42.1	34.1	61.8	134.0	229.9	405.8	9.92	1,607.1
Total households	40,126.0	45,037.0	51,594.5	60,327.4	69,140.6	77,578.3	85,382.9	2.55	112.8

Note: Per capita data is shown at constant 2010 prices. Household disposable income bands are shown at current prices.

Table 5.111 Young generation

'000

	1980	1985	1990	1995	2000	2005	2010	2015	2020	CAGR	Period growth
Babies under 12 months	4,452	4,500	4,212	4,241	4,168	4,322	3,978	3,832	3,591	-0.54	-19.34
Infants under 24 months	8,837	8,957	8,470	8,439	8,325	8,594	8,045	7,693	7,220	-0.50	-18.29
Toddlers aged 1-4	17,105	17,527	17,177	16,701	16,558	16,843	16,572	15,687	14,757	-0.37	-13.73
Children aged 2-9	32,525	33,919	34,386	33,535	33,052	33,123	33,482	32,301	30,555	-0.16	-6.06
Female	16,004	16,695	16,934	16,483	16,231	16,255	16,421	15,836	14,972	-0.17	-6.45
Male	16,522	17,224	17,451	17,052	16,820	16,867	17,061	16,465	15,583	-0.15	-5.68
Tweenagers aged 10-14	17,952	19,563	20,665	21,290	20,910	20,547	20,499	20,904	20,417	0.32	13.73
Female	8,827	9,630	10,179	10,502	10,293	10,101	10,071	10,261	10,017	0.32	13.48
Male	9,125	9,933	10,485	10,788	10,617	10,446	10,429	10,643	10,400	0.33	13.98
Teenagers aged 13-19	22,679	25,370	27,474	28,890	29,519	28,982	28,589	28,720	29,083	0.62	28.24
Female	11,145	12,481	13,537	14,254	14,571	14,277	14,066	14,118	14,284	0.62	28.16
Male	11,534	12,889	13,936	14,636	14,948	14,705	14,523	14,602	14,799	0.63	28.32
Studying age 18-22	14,428	16,373	18,264	19,585	20,603	20,872	20,469	20,232	20,485	0.88	41.98
Female	7,089	8,052	9,001	9,670	10,196	10,328	10,101	9,972	10,079	0.88	42.18
Male	7,340	8,321	9,263	9,915	10,407	10,544	10,367	10,260	10,407	0.88	41.78
Young adults aged 15-29	40,032	46,359	51,903	56,415	59,742	61,223	61,455	60,834	61,020	1.06	52.43
Female	19,662	22,797	25,579	27,862	29,610	30,373	30,446	30,083	30,082	1.07	53.00
Male	20,370	23,562	26,324	28,554	30,132	30,850	31,009	30,751	30,938	1.05	51.88

Table 5.112 Middle-aged generation

'000

	1980	1985	1990	1995	2000	2005	2010	2015	2020	CAGR	Period growth
Middle-aged adults 30-59	39,250	44,355	50,977	58,627	67,482	77,448	88,246	98,048	105,386	2.50	168.5
Female	20,012	22,540	25,780	29,494	33,825	38,748	44,157	49,193	52,941	2.46	164.5
Male	19,238	21,815	25,196	29,133	33,657	38,700	44,089	48,855	52,445	2.54	172.6
Baby boomers aged 40-59	22,578	25,422	27,838	31,242	36,264	42,795	50,793	58,571	65,324	2.69	189.3
Female	11,483	13,080	14,385	15,975	18,328	21,432	25,366	29,374	32,893	2.67	186.5
Male	11,095	12,342	13,453	15,268	17,936	21,363	25,427	29,197	32,431	2.72	192.3

Table 5.113 Elderly population

'000

	1980	1985	1990	1995	2000	2005	2010	2015	2020	CAGR	Period growth
Elderly population (60+)	7,987	9,194	10,985	13,195	15,770	18,276	20,789	24,411	29,621	3.33	270.9
Female	4,267	4,903	5,874	7,110	8,565	10,010	11,419	13,261	15,950	3.35	273.8
Male	3,720	4,291	5,111	6,086	7,205	8,266	9,370	11,151	13,671	3.31	267.5

Table 5.114 Population of biggest cities 1980-2020

'000

	1980	1985	1990	1995	2000	2005	2010	2015	2020	CAGR	Period growth
Jakarta	6,569.0	7,433.6	8,222.5	8,662.1	8,389.4	8,540.1	8,833.8	9,201.5	9,626.5	0.96	46.54
Surabaya	1,971.6	2,205.5	2,410.4	2,507.9	2,397.8	2,374.7	2,413.3	2,484.9	2,580.4	0.67	30.88
Medan	1,227.5	1,418.1	1,601.6	1,722.8	1,703.9	1,751.0	1,821.9	1,904.9	1,997.7	1.22	62.75
Bandung	1,811.9	1,942.0	2,025.2	2,000.8	1,806.1	1,699.7	1,668.0	1,676.9	1,713.8	-0.14	-5.42
Tangerang	568.5	750.0	950.5	1,131.8	1,225.7	1,372.1	1,500.1	1,616.7	1,727.8	2.82	203.91
Makasar	543.7	719.0	912.9	1,088.6	1,180.3	1,321.7	1,445.2	1,557.8	1,664.8	2.84	206.22
Semarang	992.8	1,126.4	1,249.2	1,319.6	1,281.5	1,288.1	1,321.7	1,369.5	1,428.0	0.91	43.83
Palembang	802.4	944.2	1,085.5	1,187.8	1,194.4	1,241.3	1,300.5	1,365.6	1,436.1	1.47	78.99
Bogor	333.8	434.3	544.6	642.9	691.4	769.3	838.3	901.7	962.4	2.68	188.36
Malang	538.8	617.7	692.4	739.3	725.8	746.7	778.0	814.1	854.2	1.16	58.54

Chart 5.88 Population age shift 2000 and 2020, Each Column Represents a Single Age Group

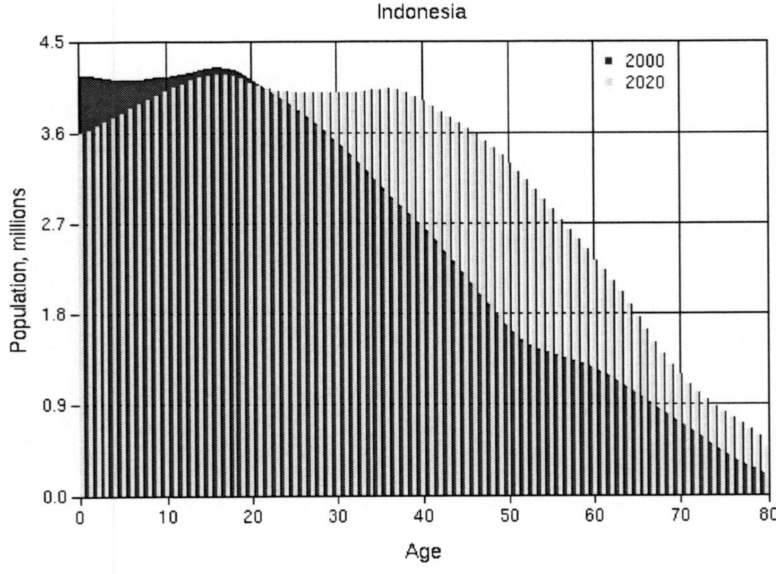

Chart 5.89 Population pyramids, 1980/2000/2010/2020

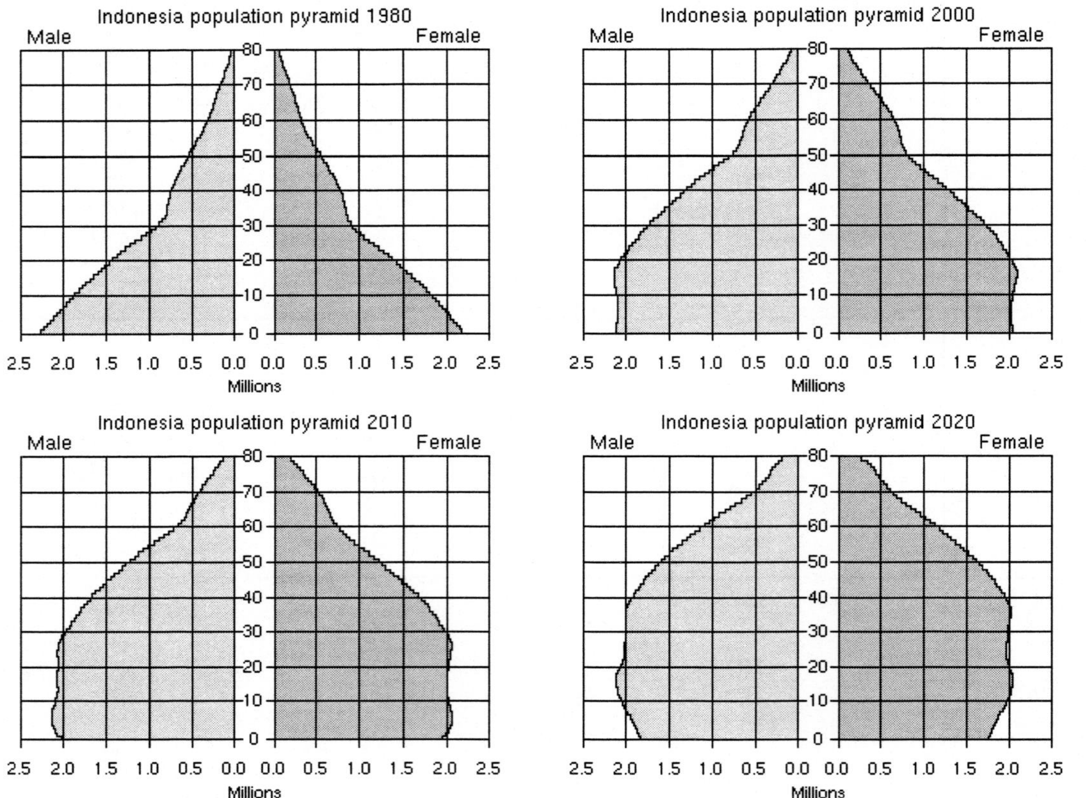

Chart 5.90 Major Cities: 1980, 2000 and 2020

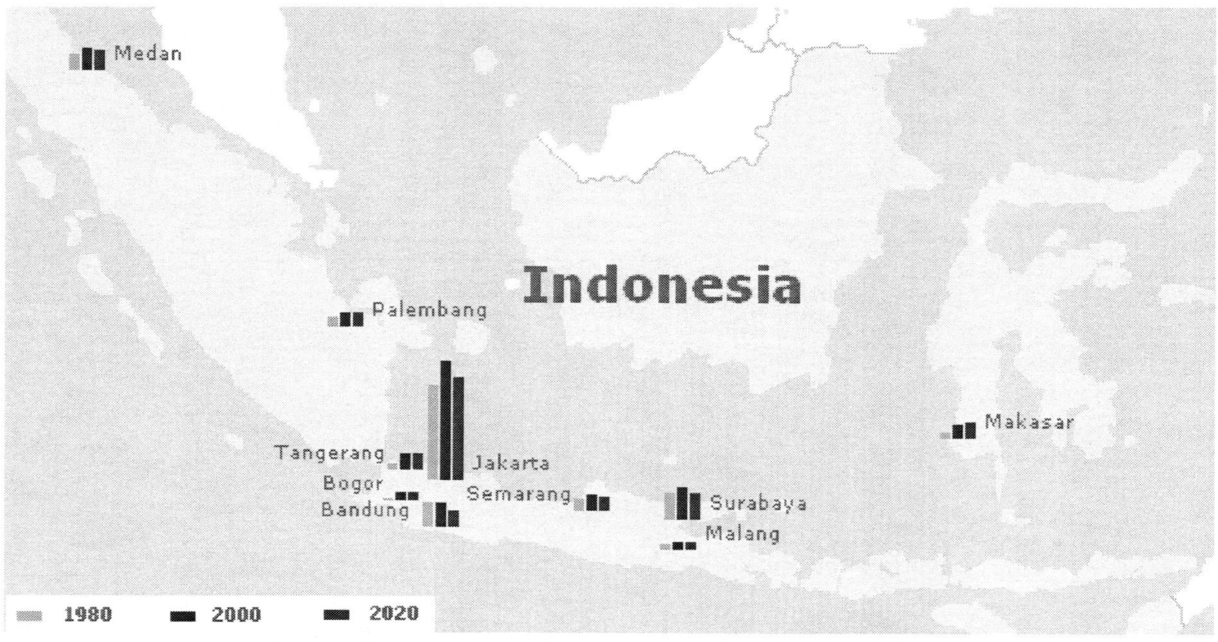

Iran

Table 5.115 Key population trends

'000

	1980	1985	1990	1995	2000	2005	2010	2015	2020	CAGR	Period growth
Population at January 1st	39,329.5	48,417.5	56,733.2	62,204.6	66,902.9	70,764.9	75,077.5	79,454.0	83,740.3	1.91	112.92
Male	20,117.6	24,846.6	29,218.1	31,632.9	34,048.4	36,057.7	38,153.8	40,289.3	42,370.9	1.88	110.62
Female	19,211.9	23,570.9	27,515.1	30,571.7	32,854.4	34,707.2	36,923.7	39,164.6	41,369.4	1.94	115.33
0-4 yrs	7,077.2	9,078.4	9,184.9	7,527.0	6,094.3	6,084.1	6,679.8	6,723.2	6,429.2	-0.24	-9.16
5-9 yrs	5,609.1	7,001.6	8,877.6	8,529.5	7,038.4	5,431.2	5,856.2	6,626.0	6,739.4	0.46	20.15
10-14 yrs	4,867.5	5,625.2	7,415.7	8,899.3	8,335.2	7,245.2	5,378.9	5,816.4	6,601.4	0.76	35.62
15-19 yrs	4,127.7	4,934.8	5,929.7	7,462.2	9,045.0	9,171.3	7,236.4	5,296.5	5,800.9	0.85	40.54
20-24 yrs	3,466.7	4,288.9	4,962.0	5,674.7	7,439.2	9,123.3	9,141.7	7,142.8	5,263.9	1.05	51.84
25-29 yrs	2,831.7	3,661.4	4,154.0	4,697.0	5,546.1	6,821.8	9,019.5	9,065.4	7,095.7	2.32	150.58
30-34 yrs	2,121.7	2,979.8	3,526.1	4,074.2	4,745.1	5,265.4	6,723.8	8,957.5	9,012.2	3.68	324.76
35-39 yrs	1,625.6	2,200.7	2,872.6	3,536.1	4,128.0	4,694.3	5,200.6	6,666.0	8,902.0	4.34	447.62
40-44 yrs	1,497.1	1,633.8	2,102.3	2,867.1	3,547.1	4,073.4	4,632.9	5,140.3	6,611.6	3.78	341.64
45-49 yrs	1,484.1	1,488.4	1,601.0	2,062.4	2,843.5	3,419.3	3,997.4	4,554.7	5,075.7	3.12	242.01
50-54 yrs	1,367.6	1,491.1	1,509.0	1,547.8	2,103.7	2,662.2	3,319.7	3,893.3	4,459.6	3.00	226.10
55-59 yrs	1,121.5	1,369.8	1,477.2	1,426.7	1,561.1	1,870.1	2,537.9	3,186.8	3,758.6	3.07	235.14
60-64 yrs	819.5	1,094.1	1,279.1	1,361.6	1,352.8	1,364.6	1,736.1	2,379.6	3,010.9	3.31	267.39
65-69 yrs	559.6	728.7	912.2	1,146.9	1,222.2	1,210.6	1,218.1	1,563.8	2,168.5	3.44	287.48
70-74 yrs	394.1	430.6	495.4	785.7	949.5	1,057.2	1,007.8	1,019.3	1,334.0	3.09	238.45
75-79 yrs	232.0	259.8	236.3	384.1	591.6	729.1	775.1	743.4	771.6	3.05	232.56
80+ yrs	126.7	150.5	198.1	222.1	360.0	541.8	615.7	679.0	705.1	4.39	456.59
Median age of population (years)	17.5	17.5	17.3	19.0	21.8	24.0	26.7	29.5	32.3	1.55	84.90

Table 5.116 Key economic trends

As stated

	1990	1995	2000	2005	2010	2015	2020	CAGR	Period growth
Total GDP (IRR per capita)	29,209,075	31,417,133	35,615,482	44,216,596	50,560,090	55,935,702	61,906,197	2.54	111.9
Disposable income (IRR per capita)	13,281,044	14,689,249	17,612,313	23,683,076	28,724,510	32,407,986			
Disposable income (IRR per household)	71,351,285	76,030,368	83,584,546	99,717,952	105,169,436	107,921,793			
Number of households by annual household disposable income ('000)									
Total households	10,560	12,018	14,097	16,807	20,506	23,859	26,561	3.12	151.5

Note: Per capita data is shown at constant 2010 prices. Household disposable income bands are shown at current prices.

Table 5.117 Young generation

'000

	1980	1985	1990	1995	2000	2005	2010	2015	2020	CAGR	Period growth
Babies under 12 months	1,595	2,002	1,764	1,439	1,191	1,454	1,323	1,306	1,247	-0.61	-21.80
Infants under 24 months	3,087	3,915	3,587	2,905	2,382	2,760	2,683	2,634	2,515	-0.51	-18.54
Toddlers aged 1-4	5,482	7,077	7,421	6,088	4,903	4,630	5,357	5,418	5,182	-0.14	-5.48
Children aged 2-9	9,599	12,165	14,476	13,152	10,751	8,755	9,853	10,715	10,654	0.26	10.99
Female	4,654	5,925	7,069	6,438	5,246	4,266	4,809	5,223	5,197	0.28	11.65
Male	4,945	6,241	7,406	6,714	5,505	4,489	5,045	5,492	5,457	0.25	10.36
Tweenagers aged 10-14	4,868	5,625	7,416	8,899	8,335	7,245	5,379	5,816	6,601	0.76	35.62
Female	2,355	2,721	3,597	4,384	4,083	3,525	2,618	2,837	3,218	0.78	36.64
Male	2,512	2,904	3,819	4,515	4,252	3,720	2,761	2,979	3,383	0.75	34.67
Teenagers aged 13-19	5,993	7,076	8,692	10,948	12,538	12,349	9,487	7,492	8,383	0.84	39.88
Female	2,902	3,419	4,208	5,410	6,177	6,053	4,616	3,646	4,091	0.86	40.95
Male	3,091	3,657	4,484	5,538	6,361	6,296	4,871	3,846	4,292	0.82	38.87
Studying age 18-22	3,718	4,553	5,309	6,315	8,275	9,473	8,541	6,209	5,252	0.87	41.25
Female	1,804	2,197	2,586	3,138	4,101	4,729	4,175	3,017	2,560	0.88	41.88
Male	1,914	2,356	2,723	3,177	4,174	4,744	4,366	3,192	2,692	0.86	40.65
Young adults aged 15-29	10,426	12,885	15,046	17,834	22,030	25,116	25,398	21,505	18,160	1.40	74.18
Female	5,145	6,230	7,344	8,875	10,899	12,447	12,571	10,519	8,851	1.37	72.03
Male	5,281	6,655	7,702	8,959	11,131	12,669	12,826	10,985	9,310	1.43	76.28

Table 5.118 Middle-aged generation

'000

	1980	1985	1990	1995	2000	2005	2010	2015	2020	CAGR	Period growth
Middle-aged adults 30-59	9,218	11,164	13,088	15,514	18,929	21,985	26,412	32,399	37,820	3.59	310.3
Female	4,482	5,512	6,379	7,661	9,353	10,761	12,943	16,023	18,720	3.64	317.7
Male	4,736	5,652	6,709	7,853	9,576	11,224	13,469	16,376	19,099	3.55	303.3
Baby boomers aged 40-59	5,470	5,983	6,689	7,904	10,056	12,025	14,488	16,775	19,906	3.28	263.9
Female	2,492	2,818	3,232	3,907	4,971	5,926	7,140	8,218	9,772	3.48	292.2
Male	2,978	3,165	3,457	3,997	5,085	6,099	7,348	8,557	10,133	3.11	240.2

Table 5.119 Elderly population

'000

	1980	1985	1990	1995	2000	2005	2010	2015	2020	CAGR	Period growth
Elderly population (60+)	2,132	2,664	3,121	3,900	4,476	4,903	5,353	6,385	7,990	3.36	274.8
Female	1,070	1,268	1,378	1,795	2,111	2,361	2,677	3,276	4,157	3.45	288.7
Male	1,062	1,395	1,743	2,105	2,365	2,543	2,676	3,110	3,833	3.26	260.8

Table 5.120 Population of biggest cities 1980-2020

'000

	1980	1985	1990	1995	2000	2005	2010	2015	2020	CAGR	Period growth
Tehran	5,007.6	5,886.9	6,412.5	6,712.7	6,942.2	7,054.2	7,358.1	7,794.7	8,248.2	1.26	64.7
Mashhad	916.5	1,368.8	1,710.0	1,862.2	2,090.5	2,363.1	2,654.9	2,882.2	3,074.6	3.07	235.5
Esfahan	768.5	953.2	1,100.1	1,237.8	1,394.4	1,562.3	1,745.6	1,891.8	2,016.9	2.44	162.4
Karaj	284.5	554.8	773.9	912.2	1,103.2	1,333.1	1,557.8	1,711.7	1,833.1	4.77	544.3
Tabriz	719.0	931.8	1,070.6	1,171.8	1,272.3	1,373.3	1,497.6	1,610.5	1,712.6	2.19	138.2
Shiraz	558.7	798.7	946.6	1,036.4	1,121.4	1,206.4	1,312.7	1,410.6	1,499.7	2.50	168.4
Ahvaz	411.3	549.6	699.9	790.5	874.1	964.1	1,066.4	1,152.0	1,226.9	2.77	198.3
Qom	339.8	507.9	657.5	760.0	850.3	942.7	1,046.1	1,131.3	1,205.3	3.22	254.7
Kermanshah	376.2	530.1	614.4	680.0	733.8	782.7	846.7	908.0	964.8	2.38	156.5
Orumiyeh	207.9	285.5	346.1	419.7	492.7	566.1	642.4	699.6	747.0	3.25	259.3

Chart 5.91 Population age shift 2000 and 2020, Each Column Represents a Single Age Group

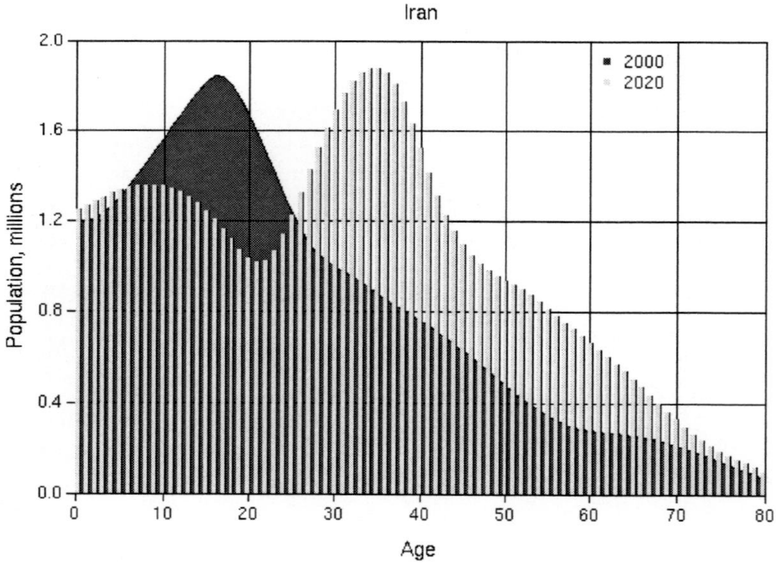

Chart 5.92 Population pyramids, 1980/2000/2010/2020

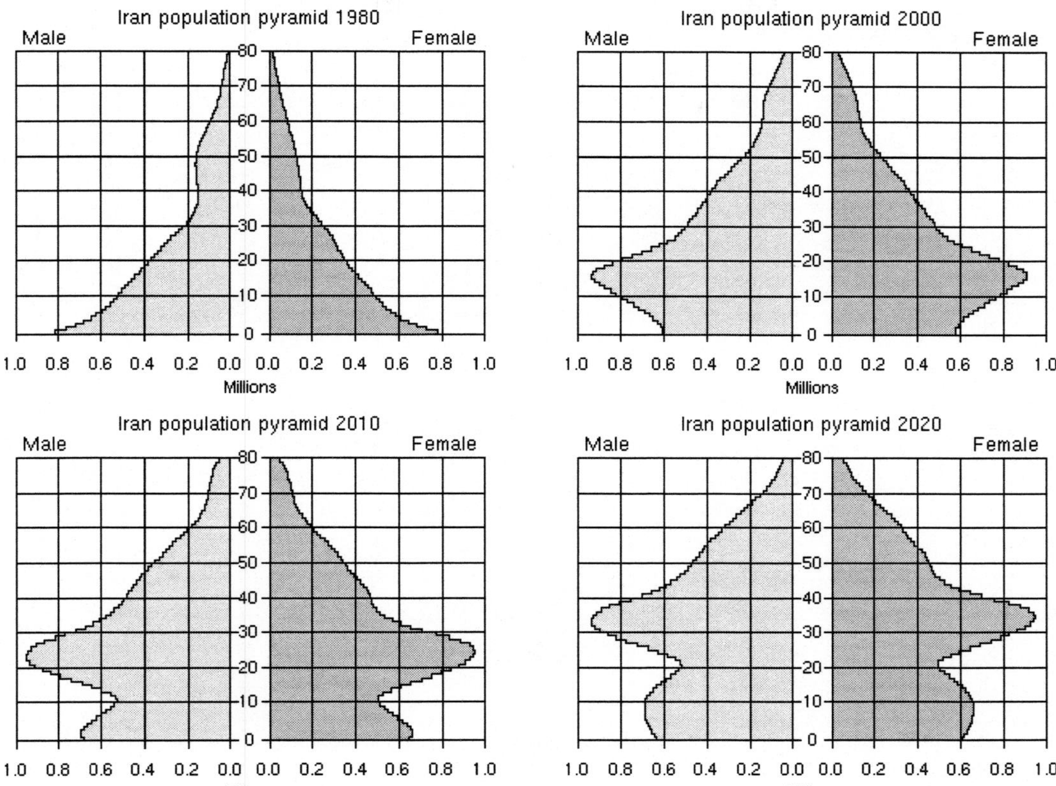

Chart 5.93 Major Cities: 1980, 2000 and 2020

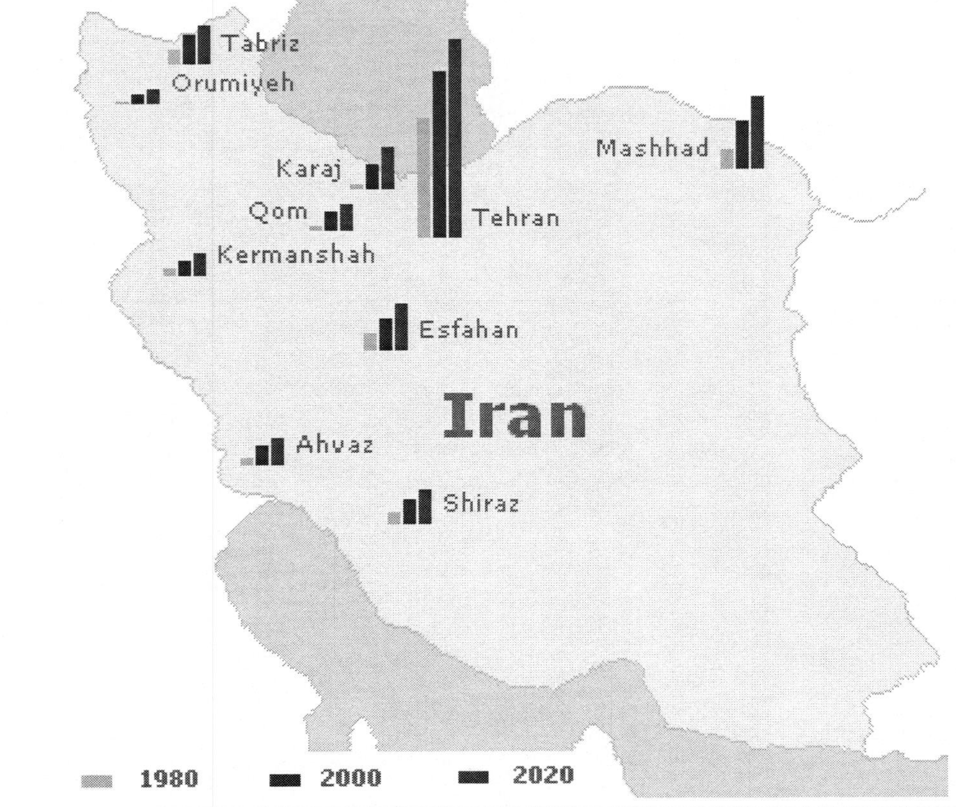

Ireland

Table 5.121 Key population trends

'000

	1980	1985	1990	1995	2000	2005	2010	2015	2020	CAGR	Period growth
Population at January 1st	3,392.8	3,544.3	3,507.0	3,597.6	3,777.8	4,109.2	4,506.6	4,766.3	4,996.2	0.97	47.26
Male	1,705.1	1,777.0	1,743.2	1,787.2	1,877.0	2,047.1	2,252.5	2,384.0	2,499.2	0.96	46.57
Female	1,687.7	1,767.3	1,763.8	1,810.4	1,900.8	2,062.1	2,254.1	2,382.3	2,497.0	0.98	47.95
0-4 yrs	346.7	334.2	284.7	256.7	264.6	295.8	315.4	308.3	286.9	-0.47	-17.25
5-9 yrs	349.5	353.4	332.0	288.8	267.7	279.6	311.9	321.7	314.3	-0.27	-10.07
10-14 yrs	337.8	350.6	342.7	337.6	296.4	275.4	291.2	314.8	324.3	-0.10	-4.01
15-19 yrs	320.5	332.7	328.1	334.2	331.7	297.2	279.1	287.1	310.7	-0.08	-3.07
20-24 yrs	269.7	286.3	266.9	290.3	309.9	340.7	310.8	283.4	292.1	0.20	8.30
25-29 yrs	241.6	257.5	246.2	251.2	287.0	345.9	393.9	342.2	315.4	0.67	30.55
30-34 yrs	224.3	242.1	242.9	259.3	276.1	327.9	396.0	427.0	375.0	1.29	67.19
35-39 yrs	184.0	222.4	237.5	249.1	278.5	304.8	352.6	410.1	441.2	2.21	139.75
40-44 yrs	161.6	186.7	220.5	236.8	259.3	288.9	318.3	356.4	413.5	2.38	155.86
45-49 yrs	152.1	160.6	176.4	220.7	238.0	262.4	296.6	317.6	355.2	2.14	133.48
50-54 yrs	150.7	149.2	153.6	174.9	223.1	241.3	266.7	294.9	315.8	1.87	109.52
55-59 yrs	152.2	145.3	141.4	150.8	172.7	220.2	240.2	263.1	291.2	1.64	91.31
60-64 yrs	138.1	140.9	134.7	136.5	148.6	170.8	216.5	235.1	258.2	1.58	86.92
65-69 yrs	133.7	131.6	132.6	126.7	129.2	140.5	163.6	206.8	225.8	1.32	68.85
70-74 yrs	100.0	109.8	107.8	113.5	111.3	116.5	129.6	149.4	190.4	1.62	90.36
75-79 yrs	68.6	74.0	84.2	82.3	88.9	90.9	99.3	109.2	127.6	1.56	85.92
80+ yrs	61.4	66.9	74.9	88.3	94.7	110.4	125.2	139.2	158.7	2.40	158.44
Median age of population (years)	26.4	27.2	29.1	30.8	32.4	33.3	34.4	36.1	38.2	0.93	44.71

Table 5.122 Key economic trends

As stated

	1990	1995	2000	2005	2010	2015	2020	CAGR	Period growth
Total GDP (EUR per capita)	18,537.7	22,602.9	34,064.1	40,861.0	35,647.6	37,639.0	40,941.2	2.68	120.9
Disposable income (EUR per capita)	11,213.0	12,473.6	18,592.2	21,310.2	17,239.9	17,558.7	18,995.6	1.77	69.4
Disposable income (EUR per household)	38,866.7	40,643.5	57,556.5	61,953.7	46,894.8	45,623.7	47,882.1	0.70	23.2
Number of households by annual household disposable income ('000)									
Over US$1,000	1,010.2	1,102.8	1,218.9	1,412.7	1,656.0	1,833.6	1,981.4	2.27	96.1
Over US$10,000	893.1	1,007.4	1,127.8	1,367.7	1,596.7	1,778.2	1,939.4	2.62	117.2
Over US$25,000	524.7	683.7	819.9	1,191.8	1,355.1	1,553.2	1,766.6	4.13	236.7
Over US$75,000	55.3	101.7	156.7	495.1	484.8	653.4	942.0	9.91	1,603.9
Over US$150,000	18.2	25.0	32.4	105.6	95.6	152.4	287.1	9.63	1,478.5
Total households	1,011.8	1,104.1	1,220.3	1,413.4	1,656.8	1,834.3	1,982.1	2.27	95.9

Note: Per capita data is shown at constant 2010 prices. Household disposable income bands are shown at current prices.

Table 5.123 Young generation

'000

	1980	1985	1990	1995	2000	2005	2010	2015	2020	CAGR	Period growth
Babies under 12 months	70.4	61.5	52.1	48.3	53.6	61.2	62.6	59.8	55.1	-0.61	-21.80
Infants under 24 months	139.7	125.4	107.5	97.9	107.4	123.1	125.5	120.5	111.1	-0.57	-20.46
Toddlers aged 1-4	276.3	272.7	232.6	208.3	211.0	234.6	252.7	248.5	231.8	-0.44	-16.10
Children aged 2-9	556.6	562.2	509.2	447.6	424.9	452.3	501.8	509.5	490.1	-0.32	-11.94
Female	272.6	273.4	247.8	217.8	206.6	220.3	245.0	248.2	238.7	-0.33	-12.43
Male	284.0	288.8	261.4	229.7	218.3	232.0	256.7	261.3	251.4	-0.30	-11.47
Tweenagers aged 10-14	337.8	350.6	342.7	337.6	296.4	275.4	291.2	314.8	324.3	-0.10	-4.01
Female	164.5	170.4	166.8	163.9	144.4	134.0	141.5	154.0	158.0	-0.10	-3.99
Male	173.3	180.2	175.8	173.8	152.0	141.4	149.7	160.9	166.3	-0.10	-4.03
Teenagers aged 13-19	459.1	474.6	464.0	477.2	456.2	412.0	391.7	406.5	440.4	-0.10	-4.08
Female	223.9	231.3	227.2	232.7	221.9	201.0	190.8	198.2	215.3	-0.10	-3.82
Male	235.2	243.3	236.8	244.5	234.3	211.0	200.9	208.3	225.0	-0.11	-4.34
Studying age 18-22	288.3	305.1	287.9	305.2	324.8	319.2	293.0	272.1	292.7	0.04	1.51
Female	142.0	149.4	141.2	149.2	160.2	157.7	144.3	133.5	144.1	0.04	1.45
Male	146.3	155.7	146.7	156.0	164.6	161.5	148.7	138.6	148.6	0.04	1.57
Young adults aged 15-29	831.9	876.4	841.2	875.7	928.5	983.8	983.7	912.6	918.2	0.25	10.38
Female	408.1	431.6	417.6	431.4	457.3	485.9	487.4	451.0	453.8	0.27	11.17
Male	423.7	444.8	423.6	444.3	471.2	497.9	496.3	461.6	464.5	0.23	9.62

Table 5.124 Middle-aged generation

'000

	1980	1985	1990	1995	2000	2005	2010	2015	2020	CAGR	Period growth
Middle-aged adults 30-59	1,025.0	1,106.4	1,172.3	1,291.5	1,447.8	1,645.4	1,870.4	2,069.1	2,191.9	1.92	113.8
Female	504.7	544.5	583.0	646.5	724.7	819.9	926.1	1,025.3	1,085.6	1.93	115.1
Male	520.3	561.8	589.3	645.0	723.1	825.5	944.3	1,043.9	1,106.3	1.90	112.6
Baby boomers aged 40-59	616.7	641.9	691.9	783.2	893.2	1,012.8	1,121.8	1,232.0	1,375.6	2.03	123.1
Female	305.5	315.9	341.7	388.0	444.1	505.6	557.8	610.8	677.7	2.01	121.8
Male	311.1	326.0	350.2	395.2	449.1	507.2	563.9	621.2	698.0	2.04	124.3

Table 5.125 Elderly population

'000

	1980	1985	1990	1995	2000	2005	2010	2015	2020	CAGR	Period growth
Elderly population (60+)	501.8	523.3	534.1	547.3	572.7	629.1	734.2	839.7	960.6	1.64	91.4
Female	270.5	286.6	296.0	303.4	315.6	342.2	393.1	445.3	507.0	1.58	87.4
Male	231.3	236.7	238.1	243.8	257.1	287.0	341.0	394.4	453.5	1.70	96.1

Table 5.126 Population of biggest cities 1980-2020

'000

	1980	1985	1990	1995	2000	2005	2010	2015	2020	CAGR	Period growth
Dublin	527.5	507.9	479.6	481.0	489.3	502.2	513.3	515.0	519.9	-0.04	-1.44
Cork	136.1	134.3	127.5	127.6	124.4	120.0	115.2	109.8	106.2	-0.62	-21.99
Galway	35.8	45.9	49.8	55.9	62.7	70.3	77.3	81.9	86.2	2.22	140.76
Limerick	61.2	57.3	52.5	52.0	53.3	53.1	50.5	47.7	45.8	-0.72	-25.12
Waterford	38.1	39.4	39.9	42.2	43.9	45.4	46.6	47.0	47.6	0.56	25.02
Swords	10.3	14.6	17.0	21.4	25.4	31.3	38.8	44.2	48.9	3.97	375.27
Dundalk	25.3	26.7	25.9	25.8	26.6	28.5	30.4	31.6	32.7	0.64	29.31
Drogheda	22.9	24.1	23.8	24.3	27.0	28.9	29.0	28.7	28.6	0.56	24.81
Bray	22.4	24.4	25.0	25.2	25.9	26.8	27.5	27.8	28.1	0.58	25.86
Tralee	16.3	17.1	17.1	18.7	20.0	20.3	19.9	19.4	19.0	0.39	16.86

Chart 5.94 Population age shift 2000 and 2020, Each Column Represents a Single Age Group

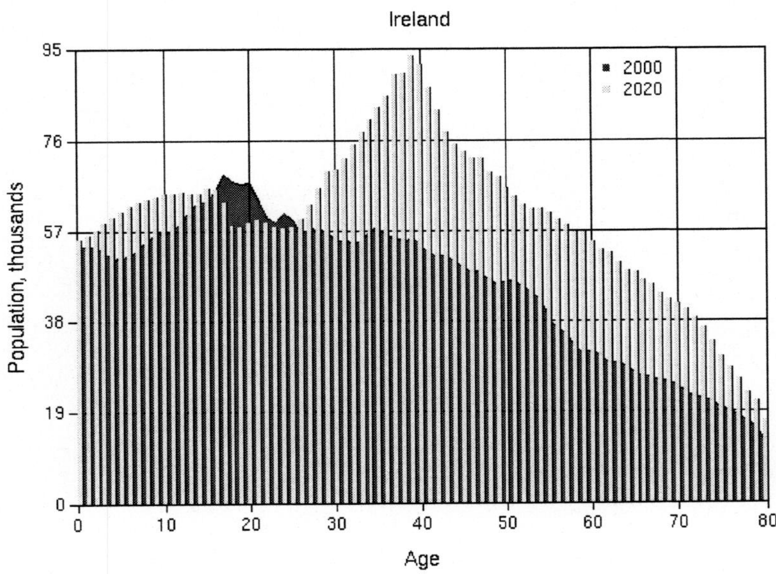

Chart 5.95 Population pyramids, 1980/2000/2010/2020

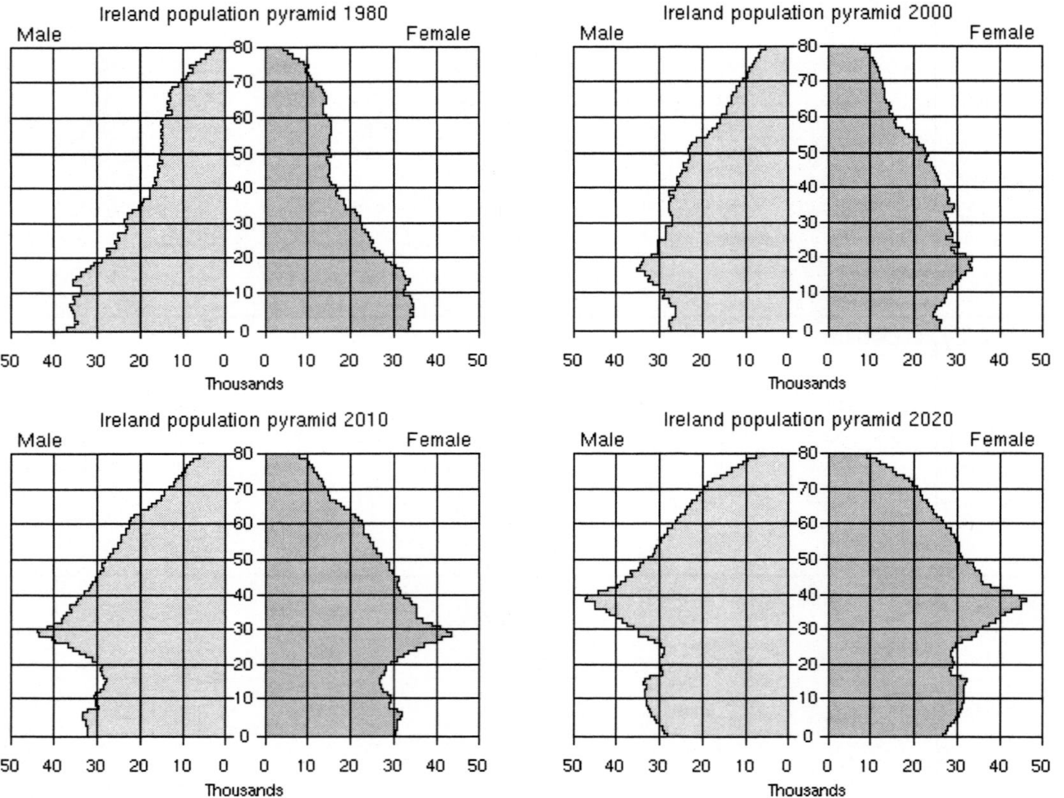

Chart 5.96 Major Cities: 1980, 2000 and 2020

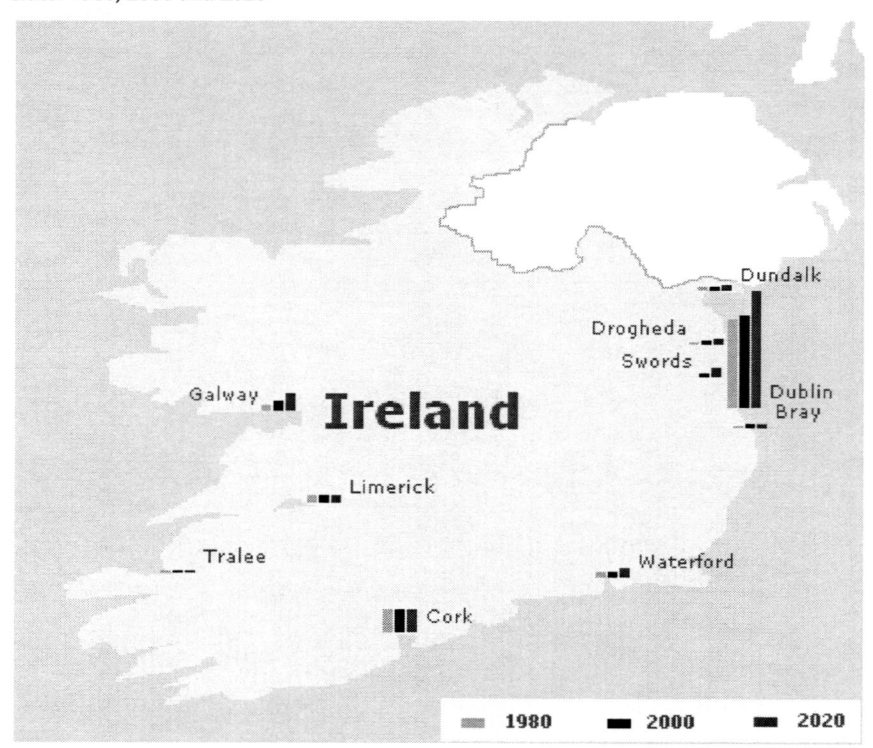

Israel

Table 5.127 Key population trends

'000

	1980	1985	1990	1995	2000	2005	2010	2015	2020	CAGR	Period growth
Population at January 1st	3,877.7	4,233.0	4,660.2	5,544.9	6,289.2	6,930.1	7,517.8	8,063.4	8,567.6	2.00	120.9
Male	1,937.4	2,112.3	2,321.0	2,746.5	3,102.4	3,423.1	3,722.5	4,003.7	4,265.2	1.99	120.2
Female	1,940.3	2,120.7	2,339.2	2,798.4	3,186.8	3,507.0	3,795.3	4,059.7	4,302.4	2.01	121.7
0-4 yrs	461.8	479.2	504.1	567.0	645.9	709.2	714.6	698.8	690.4	1.01	49.5
5-9 yrs	432.8	463.8	485.7	545.5	590.1	656.0	717.3	720.0	701.8	1.22	62.1
10-14 yrs	371.7	435.3	468.4	526.1	562.2	598.8	662.9	724.5	725.6	1.69	95.2
15-19 yrs	337.5	374.5	439.7	505.9	546.3	572.6	605.1	669.6	732.0	1.95	116.9
20-24 yrs	325.4	340.3	377.8	476.9	536.3	557.1	578.2	608.6	673.2	1.83	106.9
25-29 yrs	324.6	324.8	339.7	406.7	498.5	545.8	563.0	581.4	610.4	1.59	88.1
30-34 yrs	285.0	323.9	329.2	373.6	416.3	506.9	552.3	566.8	583.4	1.81	104.7
35-39 yrs	190.9	281.7	328.1	363.2	382.5	421.7	513.6	557.9	570.3	2.77	198.7
40-44 yrs	177.8	186.8	286.2	358.6	375.1	387.0	424.7	518.0	561.5	2.92	215.8
45-49 yrs	168.6	176.0	186.4	317.1	370.9	378.7	387.7	424.1	519.0	2.85	207.8
50-54 yrs	162.1	164.7	176.8	199.4	332.3	372.2	373.5	379.7	415.2	2.38	156.1
55-59 yrs	161.7	156.1	162.1	199.2	206.5	332.4	365.2	363.4	367.4	2.07	127.1
60-64 yrs	125.3	153.5	152.8	177.0	211.0	204.4	328.8	360.5	356.2	2.65	184.2
65-69 yrs	134.2	112.2	146.0	168.7	180.1	205.7	193.1	321.7	352.7	2.45	162.9
70-74 yrs	105.2	117.9	99.1	149.3	164.7	166.2	189.5	174.2	307.0	2.71	191.9
75-79 yrs	64.8	79.9	94.5	90.6	135.1	141.9	141.8	164.4	146.8	2.07	126.7
80+ yrs	48.3	62.1	83.9	120.0	135.3	173.6	206.5	229.7	254.8	4.25	427.6
Median age of population (years)	25.2	25.4	25.8	26.8	27.6	28.4	29.2	30.2	31.3	0.55	24.4

Table 5.128 Key economic trends

As stated

	1990	1995	2000	2005	2010	2015	2020	CAGR	Period growth
Total GDP (NIS per capita)	66,791.5	80,962.2	91,229.0	92,204.1	104,010.4	119,905.5	136,723.2	2.42	104.7
Disposable income (NIS per capita)	46,771.4	47,491.1	53,087.0	55,372.5	62,266.5	72,250.5	82,768.1	1.92	77.0
Disposable income (NIS per household)	177,567.4	174,485.6	192,158.3	192,910.2	214,401.3	246,078.8	279,142.5	1.52	57.2
Number of households by annual household disposable income ('000)									
Over US$1,000	1,226.2	1,507.4	1,735.4	1,985.9	2,181.4	2,365.8	2,539.0	2.46	107.1
Over US$10,000	1,087.0	1,361.4	1,583.3	1,791.3	2,063.6	2,267.4	2,460.0	2.76	126.3
Over US$25,000	603.5	871.9	1,079.6	1,206.0	1,644.6	1,911.6	2,170.7	4.36	259.7
Over US$75,000	57.3	122.4	183.5	206.1	473.9	714.9	1,023.9	10.08	1,685.8
Over US$150,000	19.4	32.5	41.9	45.7	82.5	154.2	282.1	9.32	1,350.6
Total households	1,227.5	1,509.2	1,737.5	1,989.2	2,183.3	2,367.5	2,540.4	2.45	107.0

Note: Per capita data is shown at constant 2010 prices. Household disposable income bands are shown at current prices.

Table 5.129 Young generation

'000

	1980	1985	1990	1995	2000	2005	2010	2015	2020	CAGR	Period growth
Babies under 12 months	92.6	98.5	101.5	115.7	133.9	143.5	141.3	138.1	137.8	1.00	48.8
Infants under 24 months	183.4	196.9	202.7	230.7	266.1	288.5	283.5	277.1	275.8	1.03	50.4
Toddlers aged 1-4	369.2	380.7	402.6	451.3	512.0	565.7	573.3	560.7	552.5	1.01	49.7
Children aged 2-9	711.2	746.2	787.1	881.8	969.9	1,076.7	1,148.3	1,141.8	1,116.3	1.13	57.0
Female	346.1	362.7	383.0	429.9	472.3	524.4	559.7	555.9	543.7	1.14	57.1
Male	365.2	383.5	404.0	451.9	497.6	552.3	588.7	585.9	572.7	1.13	56.8
Tweenagers aged 10-14	371.7	435.3	468.4	526.1	562.2	598.8	662.9	724.5	725.6	1.69	95.2
Female	179.3	212.2	228.1	255.7	274.2	291.9	322.9	353.3	353.3	1.71	97.0
Male	192.3	223.1	240.3	270.4	287.9	306.9	340.0	371.2	372.3	1.66	93.5
Teenagers aged 13-19	480.7	543.0	630.4	709.4	769.8	806.8	861.5	952.8	1,025.0	1.91	113.2
Female	230.0	263.7	307.5	345.3	375.0	393.9	420.2	464.3	499.7	1.96	117.2
Male	250.7	279.3	322.8	364.1	394.8	412.9	441.3	488.6	525.3	1.87	109.6
Studying age 18-22	327.3	354.0	403.0	499.1	533.5	568.5	585.2	630.2	699.9	1.92	113.8
Female	159.7	170.1	197.4	244.4	261.6	278.1	286.7	307.9	341.6	1.92	113.9
Male	167.6	183.9	205.6	254.7	271.9	290.4	298.5	322.3	358.3	1.92	113.8
Young adults aged 15-29	987.5	1,039.6	1,157.1	1,389.5	1,581.1	1,675.5	1,746.3	1,859.7	2,015.7	1.80	104.1
Female	484.1	508.5	566.1	683.0	777.1	824.8	857.8	911.7	986.5	1.80	103.8
Male	503.4	531.1	591.0	706.5	804.1	850.7	888.5	948.0	1,029.1	1.80	104.5

Table 5.130 Middle-aged generation

'000

	1980	1985	1990	1995	2000	2005	2010	2015	2020	CAGR	Period growth
Middle-aged adults 30-59	1,146.2	1,289.3	1,468.7	1,811.1	2,083.7	2,398.9	2,617.0	2,809.8	3,016.7	2.45	163.2
Female	589.6	659.8	746.5	920.9	1,067.0	1,223.9	1,328.3	1,416.6	1,510.9	2.38	156.3
Male	556.6	629.6	722.2	890.3	1,016.6	1,175.0	1,288.8	1,393.2	1,505.8	2.52	170.5
Baby boomers aged 40-59	670.3	683.8	811.4	1,074.3	1,284.8	1,470.3	1,551.1	1,685.2	1,863.0	2.59	178.0
Female	349.2	354.7	415.8	551.1	663.6	759.9	797.5	858.2	940.8	2.51	169.4
Male	321.1	329.0	395.6	523.2	621.2	710.4	753.6	827.0	922.3	2.67	187.3

Table 5.131 Elderly population

'000

	1980	1985	1990	1995	2000	2005	2010	2015	2020	CAGR	Period growth
Elderly population (60+)	477.7	525.7	576.3	705.6	826.2	891.8	1,059.8	1,250.5	1,417.5	2.76	196.7
Female	252.0	282.0	316.7	396.6	466.8	501.6	588.8	687.3	773.7	2.84	207.1
Male	225.7	243.7	259.5	309.0	359.5	390.2	471.0	563.2	643.8	2.65	185.2

Table 5.132 Population of biggest cities 1980-2020

'000

	1980	1985	1990	1995	2000	2005	2010	2015	2020	CAGR	Period growth
Jerusalem	393.4	456.7	520.8	617.0	657.5	713.5	784.9	852.1	914.2	2.13	132.4
Tel Aviv-Yafo	326.1	327.1	326.0	348.2	354.4	372.2	404.9	436.0	464.9	0.89	42.6
Haifa	222.7	227.6	232.1	255.9	270.5	270.3	261.9	254.9	249.9	0.29	12.2
Rishon LeZion	96.8	110.2	128.5	163.2	202.2	222.3	228.0	233.1	238.5	2.28	146.4
Ashdod	58.7	71.2	90.0	125.8	174.2	201.7	213.4	223.6	233.5	3.51	297.8
Petah Tiqwa	121.6	125.3	129.6	149.5	167.5	183.3	198.7	213.0	226.4	1.57	86.1
Be'er Sheva	105.9	114.4	125.1	149.4	172.9	184.6	188.2	191.7	195.6	1.54	84.6
Netanya	96.0	107.1	119.6	143.4	161.6	173.6	181.6	189.1	196.5	1.81	104.7
Holon	128.0	137.6	145.9	163.1	165.7	168.3	172.0	176.0	180.1	0.86	40.7
Bene Beraq	90.1	100.9	111.5	129.7	136.9	145.8	157.0	167.6	177.5	1.71	97.1

Chart 5.97 Population age shift 2000 and 2020, Each Column Represents a Single Age Group

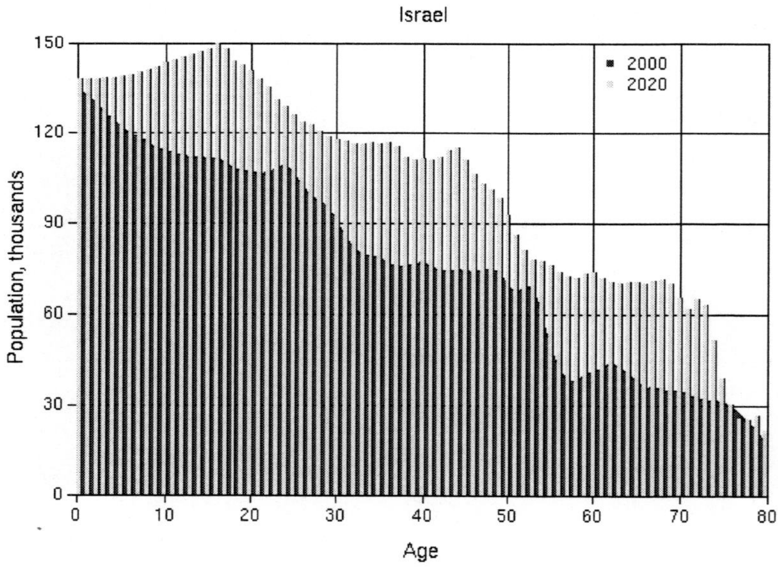

Chart 5.98 Population pyramids, 1980/2000/2010/2020

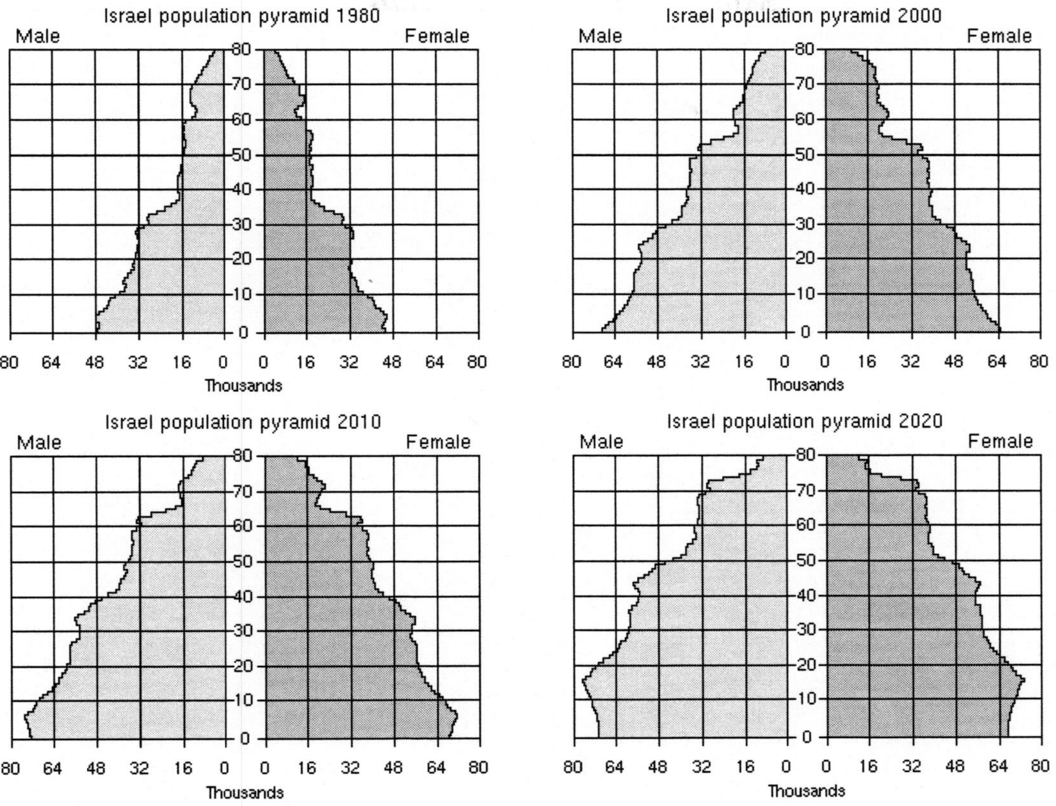

Chart 5.99 Major Cities: 1980, 2000 and 2020

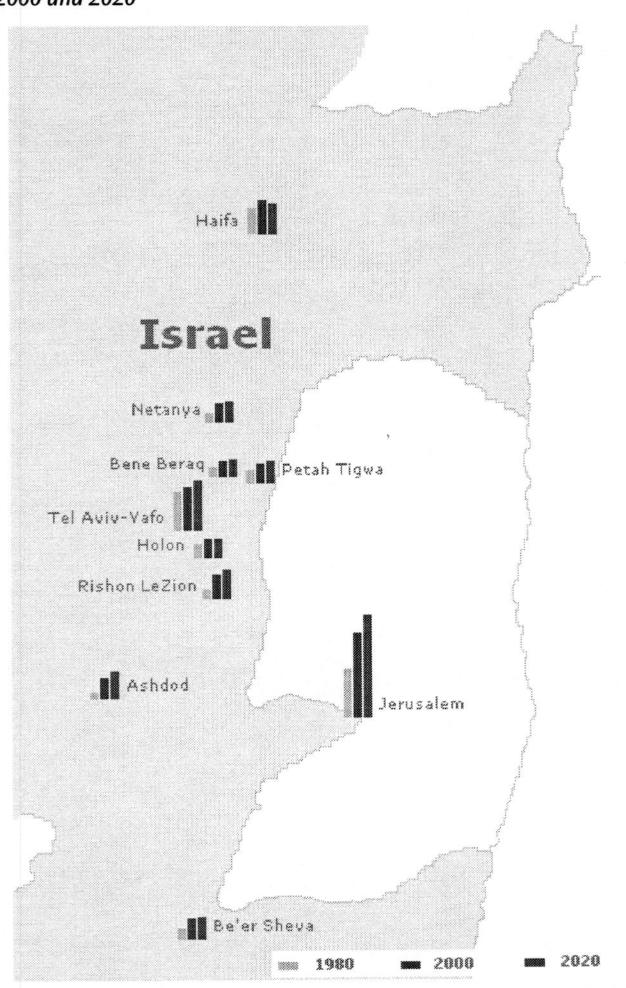

Italy

Table 5.133 Key population trends

'000

	1980	1985	1990	1995	2000	2005	2010	2015	2020	CAGR	Period growth
Population at January 1st	56,388.5	56,588.3	56,694.4	56,845.9	56,929.5	58,462.4	59,114.8	59,216.3	58,989.2	0.11	4.61
Male	27,459.2	27,501.1	27,527.8	27,569.8	27,566.2	28,376.8	28,744.7	28,841.5	28,779.2	0.12	4.81
Female	28,929.3	29,087.2	29,166.5	29,276.2	29,363.2	30,085.6	30,370.1	30,374.9	30,210.0	0.11	4.43
0-4 yrs	3,712.0	3,059.8	2,800.2	2,707.2	2,627.3	2,733.4	2,693.6	2,488.0	2,282.3	-1.21	-38.51
5-9 yrs	4,367.5	3,679.4	3,045.2	2,694.2	2,747.8	2,686.3	2,785.6	2,732.9	2,527.7	-1.36	-42.13
10-14 yrs	4,640.0	4,378.9	3,677.0	3,000.9	2,775.7	2,835.9	2,743.6	2,824.6	2,772.3	-1.28	-40.25
15-19 yrs	4,519.0	4,638.3	4,375.7	3,668.7	3,070.9	2,889.3	2,899.6	2,786.2	2,868.0	-1.13	-36.53
20-24 yrs	4,002.1	4,486.2	4,615.3	4,399.9	3,702.5	3,209.6	2,982.2	2,969.5	2,857.1	-0.84	-28.61
25-29 yrs	3,795.3	3,974.6	4,452.0	4,647.1	4,401.6	3,936.0	3,349.3	3,093.7	3,082.1	-0.52	-18.79
30-34 yrs	3,952.4	3,761.1	3,957.5	4,472.6	4,634.0	4,632.5	4,074.0	3,445.9	3,192.2	-0.53	-19.23
35-39 yrs	3,574.0	3,917.2	3,751.0	3,964.1	4,452.2	4,830.6	4,710.3	4,131.3	3,505.2	-0.05	-1.93
40-44 yrs	3,730.9	3,538.0	3,891.2	3,751.5	3,934.1	4,577.2	4,870.2	4,735.5	4,160.3	0.27	11.51
45-49 yrs	3,635.7	3,667.1	3,497.9	3,869.9	3,715.4	4,004.1	4,589.1	4,870.7	4,740.5	0.67	30.39
50-54 yrs	3,542.8	3,550.2	3,598.6	3,456.1	3,790.8	3,715.6	3,994.3	4,566.2	4,851.6	0.79	36.94
55-59 yrs	3,413.4	3,415.8	3,439.3	3,527.6	3,373.8	3,752.2	3,670.9	3,947.5	4,520.5	0.70	32.43
60-64 yrs	2,126.9	3,215.4	3,241.7	3,315.0	3,390.2	3,280.3	3,667.1	3,594.0	3,876.9	1.51	82.28
65-69 yrs	2,723.4	1,936.7	2,968.7	3,032.2	3,116.7	3,245.8	3,141.5	3,532.8	3,479.2	0.61	27.75
70-74 yrs	2,086.8	2,352.8	1,697.3	2,663.5	2,726.3	2,868.2	3,006.1	2,930.4	3,323.1	1.17	59.24
75-79 yrs	1,387.4	1,620.7	1,903.6	1,405.2	2,243.4	2,367.1	2,503.1	2,660.1	2,619.6	1.60	88.81
80+ yrs	1,178.8	1,396.2	1,782.3	2,270.1	2,226.7	2,898.2	3,434.2	3,907.0	4,330.7	3.31	267.37
Median age of population (years)	33.8	35.4	36.9	38.5	40.1	41.5	43.4	45.4	47.4	0.85	40.05

Table 5.134 Key economic trends

As stated

	1990	1995	2000	2005	2010	2015	2020	CAGR	Period growth
Total GDP (EUR per capita)	22,793.9	24,227.3	26,580.0	27,050.6	26,086.2	28,096.2	31,611.5	1.10	38.68
Disposable income (EUR per capita)	16,752.4	17,133.6	17,732.4	18,419.2	18,028.3	19,724.3	22,175.8	0.94	32.37
Disposable income (EUR per household)	48,241.8	46,776.3	46,638.7	46,280.1	43,414.4	46,178.7	50,970.7	0.18	5.66
Number of households by annual household disposable income ('000)									
Over US$1,000	19,674.3	20,815.0	21,634.2	23,267.2	24,547.5	25,292.8	25,664.2	0.89	30.45
Over US$10,000	18,039.9	19,811.9	20,002.2	22,863.1	24,176.7	25,040.3	25,535.3	1.16	41.55
Over US$25,000	11,532.8	14,895.1	12,883.9	18,694.4	20,234.9	22,142.5	23,931.6	2.46	107.51
Over US$75,000	1,515.1	2,809.8	1,664.4	3,922.9	4,573.0	6,280.7	9,796.2	6.42	546.59
Over US$150,000	416.3	598.2	469.7	851.2	947.3	1,309.8	2,317.3	5.89	456.68
Total households	19,687.6	20,822.0	21,645.0	23,267.7	24,548.0	25,293.1	25,664.4	0.89	30.36

Note: Per capita data is shown at constant 2010 prices. Household disposable income bands are shown at current prices.

Table 5.135 Young generation

'000

	1980	1985	1990	1995	2000	2005	2010	2015	2020	CAGR	Period growth
Babies under 12 months	671.9	590.5	561.7	532.6	532.1	555.0	522.2	476.8	441.2	-1.05	-34.33
Infants under 24 months	1,377.1	1,194.7	1,128.1	1,081.2	1,056.8	1,102.2	1,053.4	963.5	888.8	-1.09	-35.46
Toddlers aged 1-4	3,040.1	2,469.3	2,238.5	2,174.6	2,095.2	2,178.5	2,171.4	2,011.2	1,841.1	-1.25	-39.44
Children aged 2-9	6,702.4	5,544.5	4,717.3	4,320.2	4,318.3	4,317.6	4,425.8	4,257.5	3,921.2	-1.33	-41.50
Female	3,264.9	2,706.2	2,301.4	2,105.5	2,101.5	2,097.7	2,151.3	2,066.4	1,903.3	-1.34	-41.70
Male	3,437.5	2,838.2	2,415.9	2,214.7	2,216.7	2,219.9	2,274.6	2,191.0	2,017.8	-1.32	-41.30
Tweenagers aged 10-14	4,640.0	4,378.9	3,677.0	3,000.9	2,775.7	2,835.9	2,743.6	2,824.6	2,772.3	-1.28	-40.25
Female	2,272.2	2,138.8	1,800.0	1,466.1	1,352.9	1,379.0	1,331.3	1,373.4	1,344.4	-1.30	-40.83
Male	2,367.8	2,240.2	1,877.0	1,534.8	1,422.7	1,456.9	1,412.3	1,451.3	1,427.9	-1.26	-39.70
Teenagers aged 13-19	6,420.0	6,418.0	5,963.9	4,915.0	4,194.8	4,049.4	3,996.6	3,913.5	4,000.1	-1.18	-37.69
Female	3,147.3	3,146.6	2,920.4	2,410.5	2,049.9	1,968.8	1,941.1	1,897.8	1,941.2	-1.20	-38.32
Male	3,272.7	3,271.4	3,043.5	2,504.5	2,144.9	2,080.6	2,055.5	2,015.7	2,058.9	-1.15	-37.09
Studying age 18-22	4,175.5	4,663.4	4,509.1	4,195.2	3,376.8	3,041.7	2,961.7	2,865.3	2,853.8	-0.95	-31.65
Female	2,054.7	2,297.6	2,213.8	2,063.5	1,658.3	1,482.9	1,440.3	1,392.6	1,385.5	-0.98	-32.57
Male	2,120.8	2,365.7	2,295.3	2,131.7	1,718.5	1,558.8	1,521.4	1,472.7	1,468.4	-0.91	-30.76
Young adults aged 15-29	12,316.3	13,099.1	13,442.9	12,715.7	11,175.0	10,034.9	9,231.1	8,849.4	8,807.1	-0.83	-28.49
Female	6,084.3	6,467.2	6,629.4	6,269.0	5,508.5	4,913.0	4,514.8	4,315.4	4,293.1	-0.87	-29.44
Male	6,232.0	6,631.9	6,813.5	6,446.7	5,666.6	5,121.9	4,716.3	4,534.0	4,514.0	-0.80	-27.57

Table 5.136 Middle-aged generation
'000

	1980	1985	1990	1995	2000	2005	2010	2015	2020	CAGR	Period growth
Middle-aged adults 30-59	21,849	21,849	22,135	23,042	23,900	25,512	25,909	25,697	24,970	0.33	14.3
Female	11,157	11,102	11,204	11,626	12,040	12,789	12,948	12,803	12,400	0.26	11.1
Male	10,693	10,747	10,931	11,416	11,860	12,723	12,961	12,895	12,570	0.41	17.6
Baby boomers aged 40-59	14,323	14,171	14,427	14,605	14,814	16,049	17,124	18,120	18,273	0.61	27.6
Female	7,382	7,253	7,346	7,413	7,508	8,107	8,606	9,061	9,102	0.53	23.3
Male	6,941	6,918	7,081	7,192	7,306	7,942	8,518	9,059	9,171	0.70	32.1

Table 5.137 Elderly population
'000

	1980	1985	1990	1995	2000	2005	2010	2015	2020	CAGR	Period growth
Elderly population (60+)	9,503	10,522	11,594	12,686	13,703	14,660	15,752	16,624	17,629	1.56	85.5
Female	5,483	6,092	6,683	7,284	7,847	8,370	8,913	9,349	9,837	1.47	79.4
Male	4,021	4,429	4,911	5,402	5,857	6,290	6,839	7,275	7,792	1.67	93.8

Table 5.138 Population of biggest cities 1980-2020
'000

	1980	1985	1990	1995	2000	2005	2010	2015	2020	CAGR	Period growth
Roma	2,835.7	2,840.7	2,790.8	2,687.7	2,566.1	2,547.7	2,523.6	2,502.8	2,489.1	-0.33	-12.22
Milano	1,628.2	1,507.2	1,388.5	1,309.1	1,259.7	1,297.1	1,338.7	1,375.5	1,410.7	-0.36	-13.36
Napoli	1,228.4	1,146.6	1,076.8	1,040.4	1,011.6	990.1	954.8	923.9	898.3	-0.78	-26.87
Torino	1,131.9	1,055.1	976.8	909.4	867.9	892.4	921.4	947.0	971.5	-0.38	-14.18
Palermo	701.2	701.0	698.2	700.1	691.0	675.6	648.1	624.1	604.1	-0.37	-13.84
Genova	770.3	730.8	687.1	645.7	614.0	618.0	622.8	627.1	632.1	-0.49	-17.93
Firenze	451.6	433.0	408.6	380.3	358.2	364.2	372.9	380.6	388.2	-0.38	-14.05
Bologna	464.5	436.3	408.9	388.3	373.3	373.4	371.8	370.4	370.0	-0.57	-20.35
Bari	373.1	360.9	345.4	329.3	317.5	324.6	332.1	338.8	345.3	-0.19	-7.46
Catania	385.6	358.6	336.1	324.9	315.6	306.6	292.7	280.6	270.4	-0.88	-29.88

Chart 5.100 Population age shift 2000 and 2020, Each Column Represents a Single Age Group

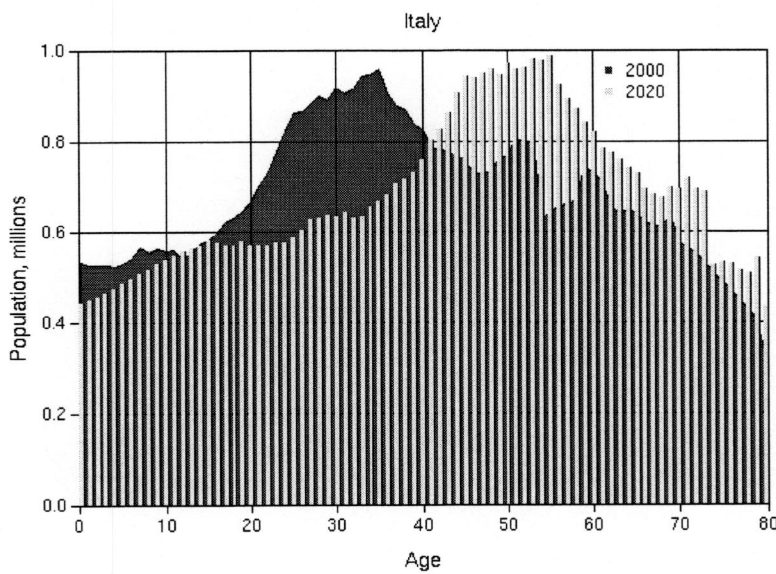

Chart 5.101 Population pyramids, 1980/2000/2010/2020

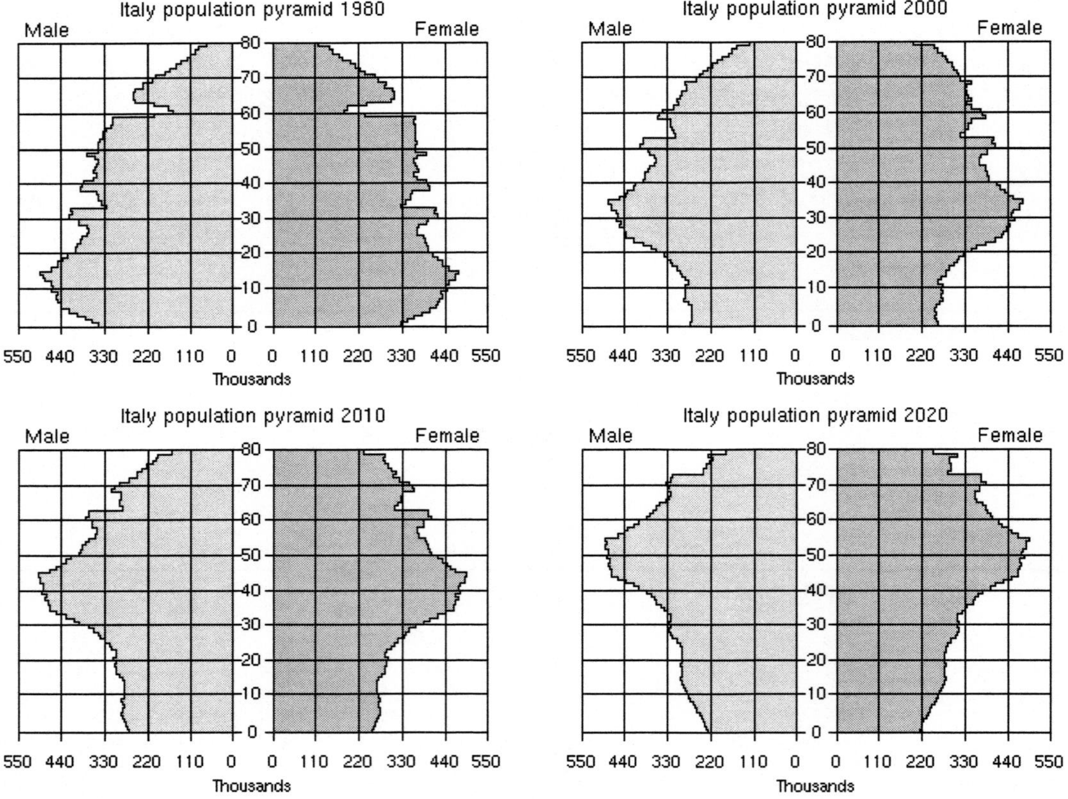

Chart 5.102 Major Cities: 1980, 2000 and 2020

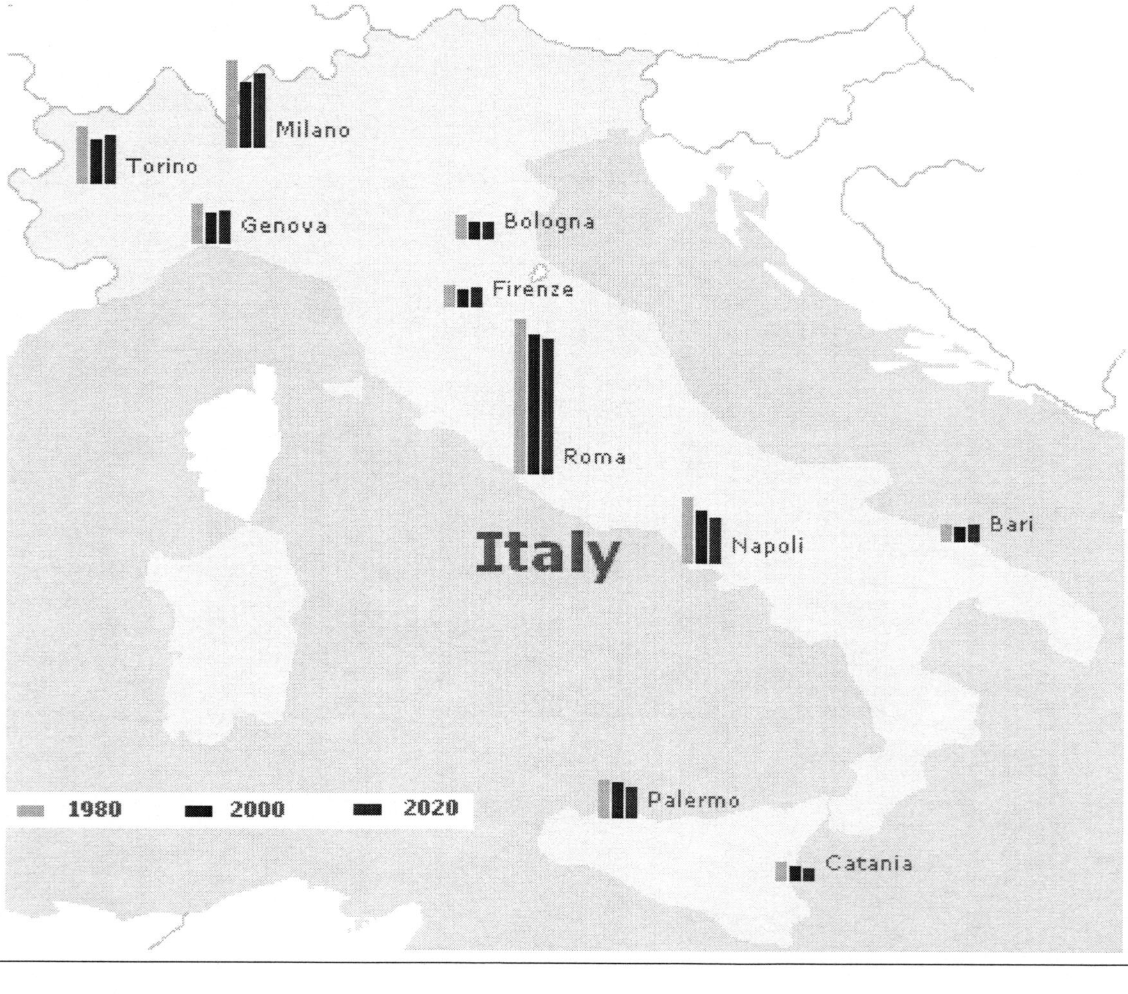

Milano
Torino
Genova
Bologna
Firenze
Roma
Italy
Napoli
Bari
Palermo
Catania
1980 2000 2020

Japan

Table 5.139 Key population trends

'000

	1980	1985	1990	1995	2000	2005	2010	2015	2020	CAGR	Period growth
Population at January 1st	117,061.0	121,049.0	123,611.0	125,570.0	126,926.0	127,768.0	127,363.0	125,846.0	123,463.5	0.13	5.47
Male	57,594.0	59,497.0	60,697.0	61,574.0	62,111.0	62,349.0	62,010.2	61,058.5	59,686.0	0.09	3.63
Female	59,467.0	61,552.0	62,914.0	63,996.0	64,815.0	65,419.0	65,352.9	64,787.5	63,777.5	0.18	7.25
0-4 yrs	8,520.8	7,461.8	6,509.7	6,000.9	5,914.9	5,599.5	5,411.0	4,875.9	4,417.8	-1.63	-48.15
5-9 yrs	10,038.7	8,534.7	7,485.7	6,546.9	6,032.9	5,951.2	5,553.2	5,374.0	4,848.9	-1.80	-51.70
10-14 yrs	8,965.8	10,043.7	8,548.7	7,485.9	6,557.9	6,037.7	5,925.1	5,540.2	5,368.0	-1.27	-40.13
15-19 yrs	8,277.8	8,983.7	10,034.6	8,565.8	7,501.8	6,593.6	6,037.5	5,939.7	5,564.3	-0.99	-32.78
20-24 yrs	7,846.8	8,202.7	8,826.6	9,906.8	8,438.8	7,378.8	6,721.9	6,150.3	6,072.0	-0.64	-22.62
25-29 yrs	9,046.8	7,825.7	8,093.7	8,798.8	9,808.8	8,311.7	7,439.7	6,775.0	6,221.7	-0.93	-31.23
30-34 yrs	10,777.7	9,056.7	7,808.7	8,135.9	8,792.8	9,792.1	8,278.9	7,418.6	6,768.6	-1.16	-37.20
35-39 yrs	9,207.8	10,742.7	9,025.6	7,831.9	8,129.8	8,769.1	9,710.2	8,220.7	7,376.3	-0.55	-19.89
40-44 yrs	8,343.8	9,138.7	10,686.6	9,013.8	7,813.8	8,111.4	8,687.5	9,630.8	8,164.4	-0.05	-2.15
45-49 yrs	8,094.8	8,238.7	9,042.6	10,630.8	8,930.8	7,755.3	8,016.8	8,593.0	9,539.6	0.41	17.85
50-54 yrs	7,204.8	7,935.7	8,110.7	8,930.9	10,461.8	8,830.0	7,628.3	7,889.7	8,472.7	0.41	17.60
55-59 yrs	5,615.9	7,002.8	7,745.7	7,961.9	8,750.8	10,294.2	8,624.0	7,456.7	7,729.8	0.80	37.64
60-64 yrs	4,467.9	5,407.8	6,761.7	7,482.9	7,749.8	8,577.0	9,966.8	8,360.4	7,247.0	1.22	62.20
65-69 yrs	3,964.9	4,194.8	5,114.8	6,402.9	7,118.8	7,460.6	8,198.6	9,560.7	8,039.7	1.78	102.77
70-74 yrs	3,024.9	3,565.9	3,826.9	4,700.0	5,910.9	6,662.3	6,961.1	7,675.4	9,010.5	2.77	197.87
75-79 yrs	2,037.9	2,492.9	3,025.9	3,292.0	4,157.9	5,282.2	5,948.3	6,252.8	6,945.8	3.11	240.82
80+ yrs	1,624.0	2,219.9	2,962.9	3,882.0	4,853.8	6,361.2	8,254.3	10,132.1	11,676.6	5.06	619.02
Median age of population (years)	32.5	35.2	37.7	39.7	41.5	43.3	44.9	46.6	48.6	1.01	49.57

Table 5.140 Key economic trends

As stated

	1990	1995	2000	2005	2010	2015	2020	CAGR	Period growth
Total GDP (¥ per capita)	3,243,479	3,443,866	3,577,257	3,791,289	3,794,405	4,249,474	4,761,372	1.29	46.80
Disposable income (¥ per capita)	2,438,126	2,566,033	2,474,246	2,426,206	2,454,485	2,695,911	2,995,363	0.69	22.86
Disposable income (¥ per household)	7,410,356	7,339,789	6,712,969	6,318,295	6,156,945	6,523,404	7,013,731	-0.18	-5.35
Number of households by annual household disposable income ('000)									
Over US$1,000	40,665	43,898	46,778	49,056	50,764	52,000	52,722	0.87	29.65
Over US$10,000	39,562	43,533	46,039	47,981	49,412	50,934	52,009	0.92	31.46
Over US$25,000	32,610	40,857	41,242	41,568	42,001	45,052	48,062	1.30	47.38
Over US$75,000	6,732	19,596	14,371	12,294	12,368	16,750	24,286	4.37	260.78
Over US$150,000	1,307	3,276	2,195	2,048	2,108	2,978	5,957	5.19	355.68
Total households	40,670	43,900	46,782	49,063	50,774	52,008	52,728	0.87	29.65

Note: Per capita data is shown at constant 2010 prices. Household disposable income bands are shown at current prices.

Table 5.141 Young generation

'000

	1980	1985	1990	1995	2000	2005	2010	2015	2020	CAGR	Period growth
Babies under 12 months	1,587.0	1,430.0	1,217.0	1,193.0	1,174.0	1,060.8	1,058.5	936.9	860.2	-1.52	-45.79
Infants under 24 months	3,223.9	2,918.9	2,480.9	2,395.0	2,341.9	2,156.3	2,167.4	1,889.7	1,730.0	-1.54	-46.34
Toddlers aged 1-4	6,933.8	6,031.8	5,292.8	4,807.9	4,740.9	4,538.6	4,352.5	3,939.0	3,557.5	-1.65	-48.69
Children aged 2-9	15,335.6	13,077.6	11,514.5	10,152.8	9,605.8	9,394.3	8,796.8	8,360.2	7,536.6	-1.76	-50.86
Female	7,473.7	6,376.6	5,612.8	4,950.2	4,685.8	4,578.3	4,289.1	4,072.1	3,672.5	-1.76	-50.86
Male	7,861.9	6,701.0	5,901.7	5,202.6	4,920.0	4,816.1	4,507.8	4,288.1	3,864.1	-1.76	-50.85
Tweenagers aged 10-14	8,965.8	10,043.7	8,548.7	7,485.9	6,557.9	6,037.7	5,925.1	5,540.2	5,368.0	-1.27	-40.13
Female	4,366.9	4,895.7	4,163.9	3,653.2	3,196.9	2,942.5	2,889.4	2,704.0	2,615.1	-1.27	-40.11
Male	4,598.9	5,148.0	4,384.8	3,832.7	3,361.0	3,095.2	3,035.7	2,836.2	2,752.9	-1.27	-40.14
Teenagers aged 13-19	11,578.7	12,995.6	13,634.4	11,609.8	10,236.8	9,020.0	8,410.2	8,240.4	7,705.3	-1.01	-33.45
Female	5,659.8	6,335.6	6,645.8	5,658.3	4,991.8	4,386.1	4,102.0	4,018.6	3,759.5	-1.02	-33.58
Male	5,918.9	6,660.0	6,988.7	5,951.5	5,245.0	4,633.9	4,308.1	4,221.9	3,945.8	-1.01	-33.34
Studying age 18-22	7,897.8	8,395.7	9,597.6	9,580.8	7,964.8	7,170.3	6,343.6	6,054.8	5,946.5	-0.71	-24.71
Female	3,889.9	4,117.7	4,699.9	4,683.2	3,879.8	3,488.0	3,099.6	2,960.5	2,905.9	-0.73	-25.30
Male	4,007.9	4,278.0	4,897.8	4,897.6	4,085.0	3,682.3	3,244.0	3,094.3	3,040.6	-0.69	-24.14
Young adults aged 15-29	25,171.4	25,012.2	26,954.9	27,271.5	25,749.4	22,284.0	20,199.1	18,865.1	17,857.9	-0.85	-29.05
Female	12,429.6	12,292.2	13,231.6	13,370.6	12,609.4	10,904.0	9,853.0	9,210.1	8,730.7	-0.88	-29.76
Male	12,741.8	12,720.0	13,723.3	13,900.9	13,140.0	11,380.1	10,346.1	9,655.0	9,127.2	-0.83	-28.37

Table 5.142 Middle-aged generation

'000

	1980	1985	1990	1995	2000	2005	2010	2015	2020	CAGR	Period growth
Middle-aged adults 30-59	49,245	52,115	52,420	52,505	52,880	53,552	50,946	49,210	48,051	-0.06	-2.42
Female	24,957	26,166	26,262	26,223	26,392	26,697	25,361	24,478	23,893	-0.11	-4.26
Male	24,288	25,949	26,158	26,282	26,488	26,855	25,584	24,731	24,158	-0.01	-0.53
Baby boomers aged 40-59	29,259	32,316	35,586	36,537	35,957	34,991	32,957	33,570	33,907	0.37	15.88
Female	14,996	16,328	17,908	18,329	18,023	17,516	16,488	16,790	16,963	0.31	13.11
Male	14,263	15,988	17,677	18,209	17,934	17,475	16,469	16,781	16,944	0.43	18.80

Table 5.143 Elderly population

'000

	1980	1985	1990	1995	2000	2005	2010	2015	2020	CAGR	Period growth
Elderly population (60+)	15,120	17,881	21,692	25,760	29,791	34,343	39,329	41,981	42,920	2.64	183.9
Female	8,670	10,396	12,434	14,630	16,789	19,244	21,905	23,403	24,023	2.58	177.1
Male	6,450	7,485	9,259	11,130	13,002	15,100	17,424	18,579	18,897	2.72	193.0

Table 5.144 Population of biggest cities 1980-2020

'000

	1980	1985	1990	1995	2000	2005	2010	2015	2020	CAGR	Period growth
Tokyo	8,351.9	8,354.6	8,163.6	7,967.6	8,134.7	8,489.7	8,750.4	8,912.6	9,015.0	0.19	7.94
Yokohama	2,773.7	2,992.9	3,220.3	3,307.1	3,426.7	3,579.6	3,682.5	3,743.7	3,780.6	0.78	36.30
Osaka	2,648.2	2,636.2	2,623.8	2,602.4	2,598.8	2,628.8	2,643.5	2,648.6	2,649.3	0.00	0.04
Nagoya	2,087.9	2,116.4	2,154.8	2,152.2	2,171.6	2,215.1	2,234.0	2,234.9	2,228.0	0.16	6.71
Sapporo	1,401.8	1,543.0	1,671.7	1,757.0	1,822.4	1,880.9	1,908.2	1,917.4	1,918.1	0.79	36.83
Kobe	1,367.4	1,410.8	1,477.4	1,423.8	1,493.4	1,525.4	1,529.6	1,522.1	1,510.6	0.25	10.47
Kyoto	1,473.1	1,479.2	1,461.1	1,463.8	1,467.8	1,474.8	1,475.3	1,472.9	1,469.6	-0.01	-0.24
Fukuoka	1,088.6	1,160.4	1,237.1	1,284.8	1,341.5	1,401.3	1,437.8	1,457.4	1,467.8	0.75	34.84
Kawasaki	1,040.8	1,088.6	1,173.6	1,202.8	1,249.9	1,327.0	1,386.7	1,425.9	1,452.2	0.84	39.53
Hiroshima	899.4	1,044.1	1,085.7	1,108.9	1,126.2	1,154.4	1,165.1	1,165.2	1,160.9	0.64	29.08

Chart 5.103 Population age shift 2000 and 2020, Each Column Represents a Single Age Group

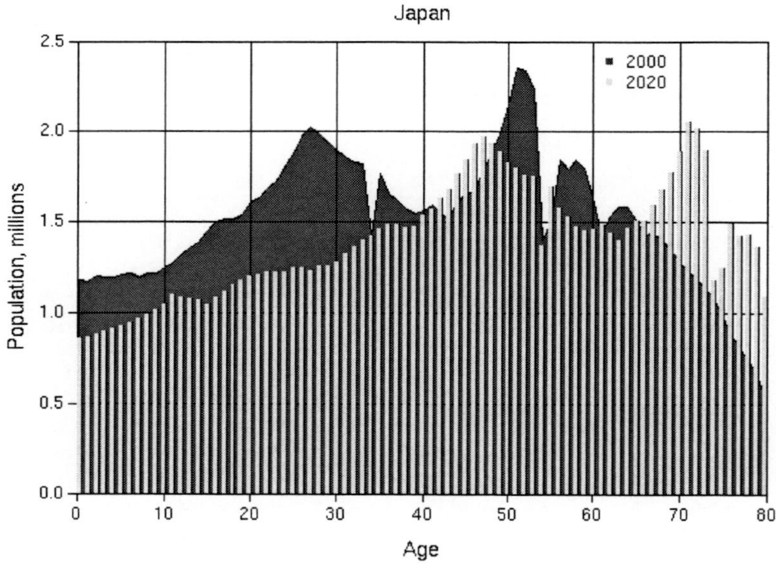

Chart 5.104 Population pyramids, 1980/2000/2010/2020

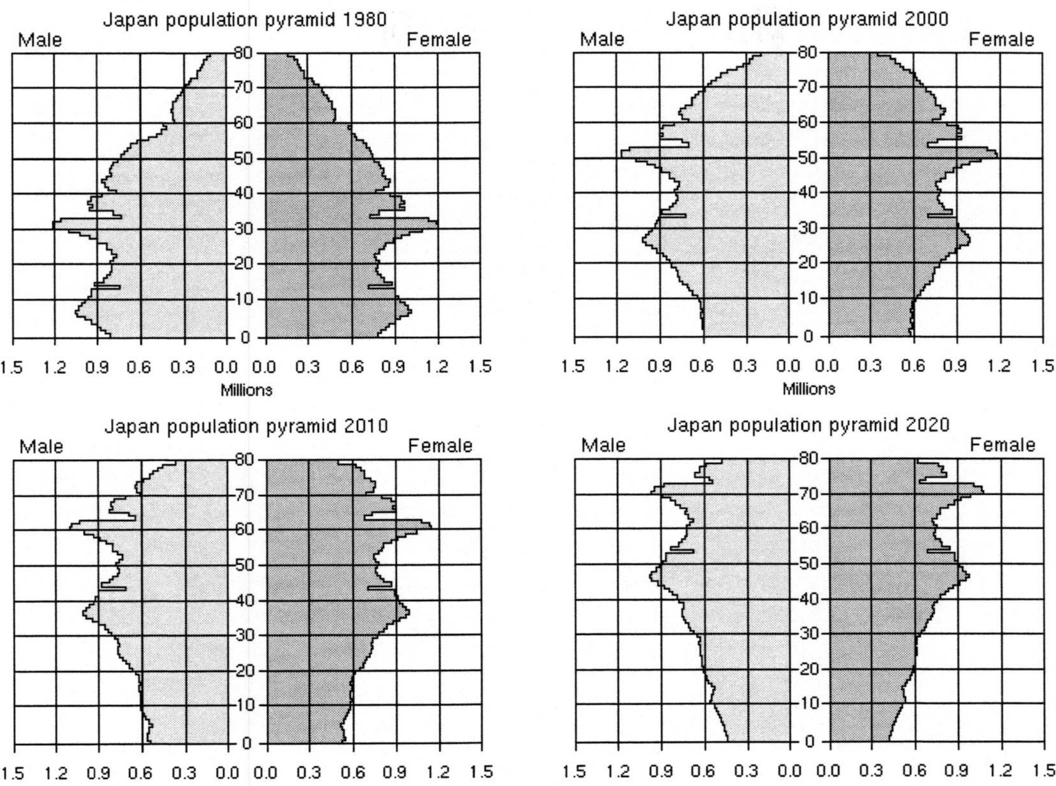

Chart 5.105 Major Cities: 1980, 2000 and 2020

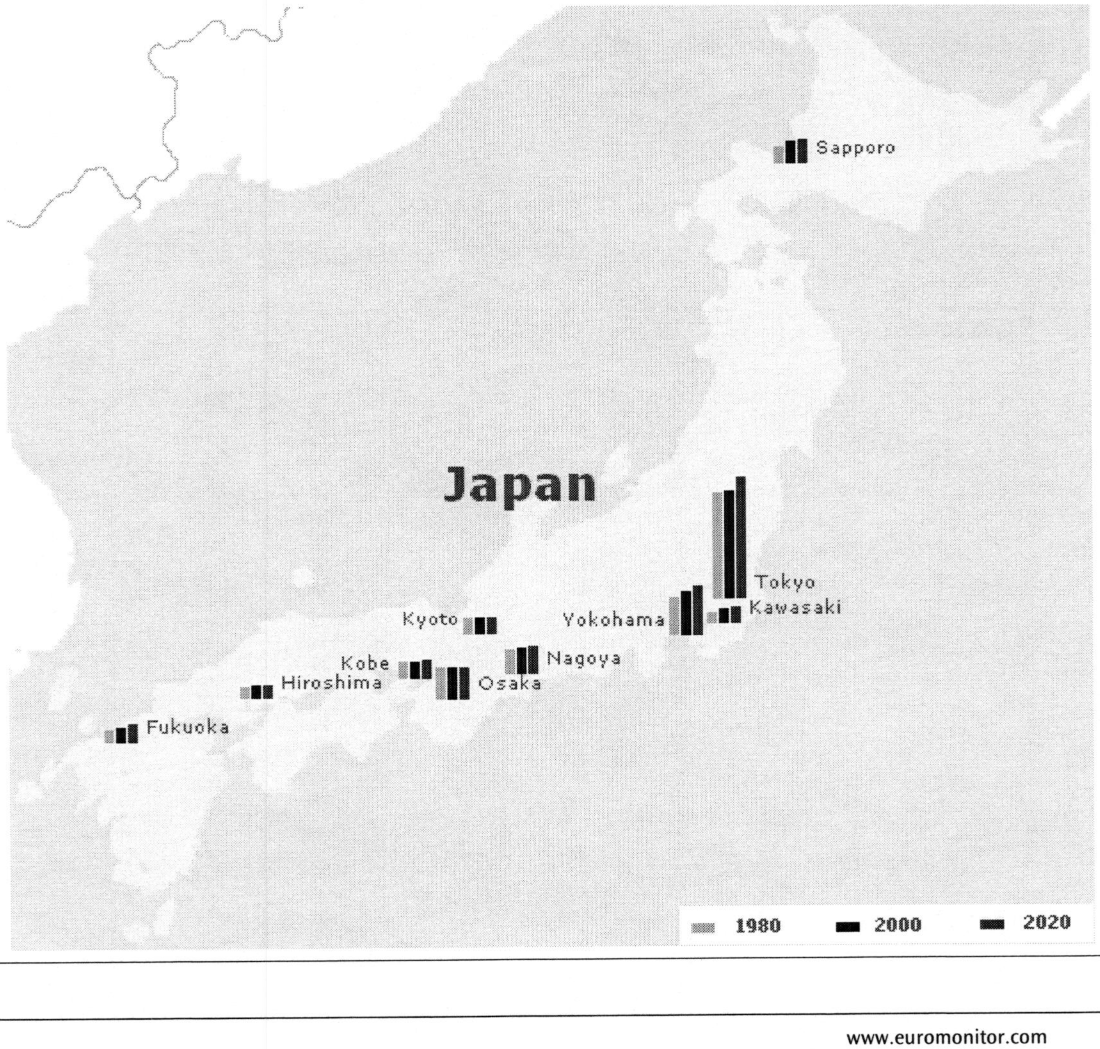

Japan
Sapporo
Tokyo
Kawasaki
Yokohama
Kyoto
Nagoya
Kobe
Osaka
Hiroshima
Fukuoka
1980
2000
2020

Jordan

Table 5.145 Key population trends

'000

	1980	1985	1990	1995	2000	2005	2010	2015	2020	CAGR	Period growth
Population at January 1st	2,225.2	2,706.4	3,254.0	4,304.1	4,853.4	5,565.9	6,472.4	6,957.0	7,518.6	3.09	237.9
Male	1,151.6	1,414.1	1,695.5	2,250.0	2,511.2	2,863.3	3,317.5	3,559.8	3,839.6	3.06	233.4
Female	1,073.6	1,292.3	1,558.5	2,054.0	2,342.1	2,702.6	3,154.9	3,397.2	3,679.0	3.13	242.7
0-4 yrs	415.7	481.9	576.5	646.9	692.8	706.7	778.0	774.9	742.2	1.46	78.6
5-9 yrs	366.3	419.0	499.8	591.2	629.2	697.0	720.1	763.6	772.4	1.88	110.9
10-14 yrs	313.6	376.9	440.2	544.6	592.9	661.1	705.4	712.5	762.4	2.25	143.1
15-19 yrs	250.9	320.9	391.1	498.6	543.9	610.1	677.1	690.4	708.9	2.63	182.5
20-24 yrs	178.5	237.3	319.6	470.2	515.0	585.7	645.2	649.1	681.3	3.41	281.8
25-29 yrs	126.1	175.4	226.4	396.4	437.1	502.0	626.6	612.8	636.8	4.13	405.0
30-34 yrs	109.2	133.9	165.2	287.2	354.5	433.2	535.9	598.5	601.4	4.36	450.7
35-39 yrs	99.9	111.1	125.6	198.4	271.0	353.6	457.5	514.2	589.0	4.53	489.5
40-44 yrs	90.7	102.6	106.2	146.8	200.6	263.9	368.1	440.8	506.0	4.39	458.1
45-49 yrs	72.9	87.0	100.2	130.5	154.7	187.5	270.9	354.4	432.5	4.55	492.9
50-54 yrs	56.6	67.4	84.8	118.1	126.0	140.7	189.3	259.1	345.3	4.62	510.1
55-59 yrs	42.3	54.2	65.0	95.7	108.0	123.7	139.8	178.5	249.1	4.53	489.4
60-64 yrs	32.5	41.3	51.1	70.8	87.5	107.3	119.6	128.8	167.8	4.19	416.5
65-69 yrs	23.4	28.4	36.6	44.5	60.5	78.7	98.5	106.3	116.7	4.10	399.0
70-74 yrs	22.2	31.6	24.0	30.0	38.2	51.6	67.3	82.1	90.7	3.58	307.9
75-79 yrs	14.5	22.1	23.7	15.7	22.2	28.0	39.8	50.9	63.7	3.77	338.7
80+ yrs	10.1	15.4	17.9	18.3	19.2	35.0	33.4	40.2	52.6	4.22	422.4
Median age of population (years)	15.3	16.1	16.4	18.7	19.7	20.9	22.7	24.1	25.7	1.30	67.9

Table 5.146 Key economic trends

As stated

	1990	1995	2000	2005	2010	2015	2020	CAGR	Period growth
Total GDP (JOD per capita)	1,812.2	1,855.5	1,926.7	2,287.8	2,674.1	3,202.0	3,809.9	2.51	110.2
Disposable income (JOD per capita)	1,401.9	1,272.7	1,526.4	1,927.6	2,041.0	2,322.3	2,673.4	2.18	90.7
Disposable income (JOD per household)	8,818.3	7,749.6	9,073.9	10,956.7	11,174.6	12,308.5	13,746.3	1.49	55.9
Number of households by annual household disposable income ('000)									
Over US$1,000	506.0	699.0	813.5	977.8	1,181.5	1,312.3	1,462.1	3.60	189.0
Over US$10,000	72.9	100.5	201.2	390.4	694.1	938.5	1,204.4	9.80	1,551.3
Over US$25,000	12.2	16.3	31.6	69.2	147.5	237.8	387.5	12.22	3,077.5
Over US$75,000	3.0	4.2	7.2	12.5	22.2	32.7	51.8	9.96	1,625.5
Over US$150,000	1.3	1.7	3.0	5.3	9.4	13.3	19.5	9.54	1,438.2
Total households	517.3	706.9	816.4	979.2	1,182.1	1,312.6	1,462.3	3.52	182.7

Note: Per capita data is shown at constant 2010 prices. Household disposable income bands are shown at current prices.

Table 5.147 Young generation

'000

	1980	1985	1990	1995	2000	2005	2010	2015	2020	CAGR	Period growth
Babies under 12 months	86.7	103.4	122.6	134.1	146.4	140.0	164.3	150.7	145.2	1.30	67.5
Infants under 24 months	171.8	202.9	241.2	266.1	288.4	281.3	323.4	305.0	291.8	1.33	69.8
Toddlers aged 1-4	329.0	378.5	453.9	512.8	546.5	566.7	613.7	624.2	597.1	1.50	81.5
Children aged 2-9	610.1	697.9	835.0	972.0	1,033.6	1,122.5	1,174.7	1,233.5	1,222.9	1.75	100.4
Female	292.9	337.2	406.3	474.0	504.6	548.7	573.8	603.3	597.7	1.80	104.1
Male	317.2	360.8	428.8	498.0	529.0	573.8	601.0	630.2	625.1	1.71	97.1
Tweenagers aged 10-14	313.6	376.9	440.2	544.6	592.9	661.1	705.4	712.5	762.4	2.25	143.1
Female	149.6	174.3	211.4	265.3	289.5	321.5	345.0	348.0	373.0	2.31	149.4
Male	164.1	202.6	228.8	279.3	303.4	339.6	360.4	364.5	389.5	2.18	137.4
Teenagers aged 13-19	369.6	466.4	561.1	710.4	775.6	868.5	957.4	971.1	1,008.5	2.54	172.9
Female	173.4	213.9	261.1	342.0	376.1	422.2	466.9	474.6	492.8	2.64	184.1
Male	196.2	252.5	300.0	368.3	399.5	446.3	490.5	496.5	515.7	2.45	162.9
Studying age 18-22	206.5	271.0	352.6	483.9	529.7	597.6	654.6	668.5	691.2	3.07	234.6
Female	98.0	126.0	160.7	227.4	253.8	289.9	319.4	325.8	337.9	3.14	244.9
Male	108.6	145.0	191.9	256.5	275.9	307.7	335.2	342.7	353.3	2.99	225.4
Young adults aged 15-29	555.5	733.7	937.1	1,365.2	1,495.9	1,697.8	1,948.9	1,952.4	2,026.9	3.29	264.9
Female	265.0	343.7	431.6	633.7	710.2	818.3	949.2	952.4	989.1	3.35	273.3
Male	290.5	390.0	505.5	731.5	785.7	879.6	999.7	1,000.0	1,037.8	3.23	257.3

Table 5.148 Middle-aged generation

'000

	1980	1985	1990	1995	2000	2005	2010	2015	2020	CAGR	Period growth
Middle-aged adults 30-59	471.6	556.2	647.1	976.7	1,214.8	1,502.5	1,961.4	2,345.4	2,723.2	4.48	477.5
Female	232.0	273.5	317.3	463.3	586.2	730.5	949.0	1,135.4	1,321.3	4.45	469.5
Male	239.6	282.7	329.8	513.4	628.6	772.1	1,012.4	1,210.0	1,401.9	4.52	485.2
Baby boomers aged 40-59	262.4	311.3	356.2	491.2	589.4	715.8	968.0	1,232.7	1,532.8	4.51	484.0
Female	130.1	151.6	175.6	236.0	288.2	352.4	472.3	599.3	742.0	4.45	470.5
Male	132.4	159.7	180.6	255.1	301.2	363.4	495.7	633.5	790.8	4.57	497.3

Table 5.149 Elderly population

'000

	1980	1985	1990	1995	2000	2005	2010	2015	2020	CAGR	Period growth
Elderly population (60+)	102.7	138.8	153.4	179.3	227.7	300.6	358.5	408.2	491.3	3.99	378.6
Female	50.9	65.5	75.6	88.1	110.4	146.9	179.4	209.2	255.3	4.12	402.0
Male	51.8	73.2	77.8	91.2	117.3	153.7	179.1	199.0	236.1	3.86	355.7

Table 5.150 Population of biggest cities 1980-2020

'000

	1980	1985	1990	1995	2000	2005	2010	2015	2020	CAGR	Period growth
Amman	647.62	767.77	855.04	1,010.03	1,000.97	1,053.51	1,172.50	1,194.89	1,233.91	1.62	90.5
Az-Zarqa'	223.96	264.72	296.68	358.63	369.20	405.08	470.62	499.07	533.90	2.20	138.4
Ar-Ru?ayfah	53.41	74.56	99.75	145.96	183.98	241.08	324.86	386.50	451.92	5.48	746.2
Irbid	118.36	146.55	171.33	214.15	227.77	258.65	311.06	339.81	372.63	2.91	214.8
Al-Quwaysimah	10.34	18.14	35.33	73.24	102.63	145.77	211.52	264.80	320.33	8.96	2,998.6
Tila' al-'Ali	6.15	10.44	19.07	42.71	76.96	124.10	193.62	252.62	313.51	10.33	5,001.4
Wadi as-Sir	27.78	47.07	66.84	93.07	105.14	127.80	166.82	194.98	225.12	5.37	710.2
Khuraybat as-Suq	3.52	5.97	10.83	26.63	56.01	93.33	143.64	185.15	228.11	10.99	6,385.8
Al-'Aqabah	28.88	39.51	49.70	64.77	71.10	83.09	102.76	114.98	128.50	3.80	345.0
As-Sal?	34.21	40.32	45.97	58.30	64.72	76.38	94.62	105.78	118.15	3.15	245.4

Chart 5.106 Population age shift 2000 and 2020, Each Column Represents a Single Age Group

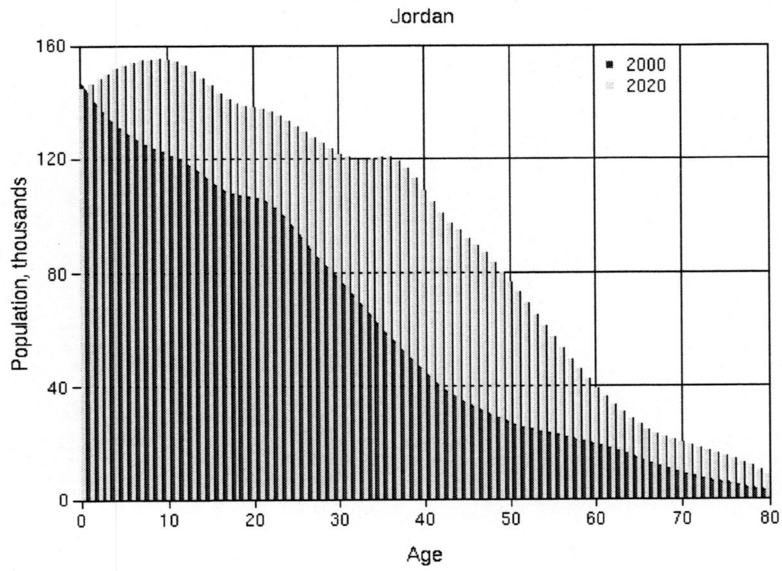

Chart 5.107 Population pyramids, 1980/2000/2010/2020

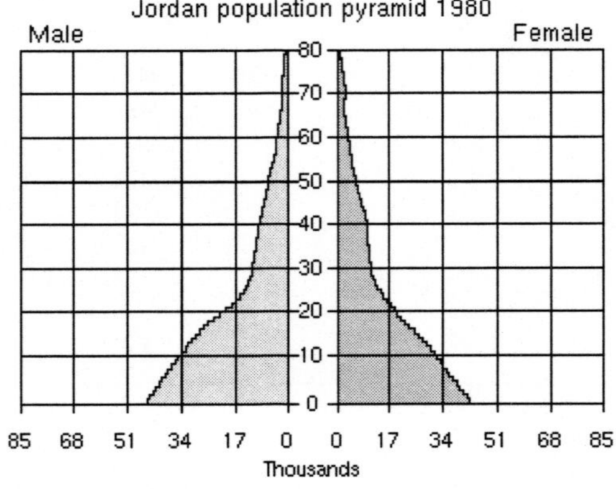

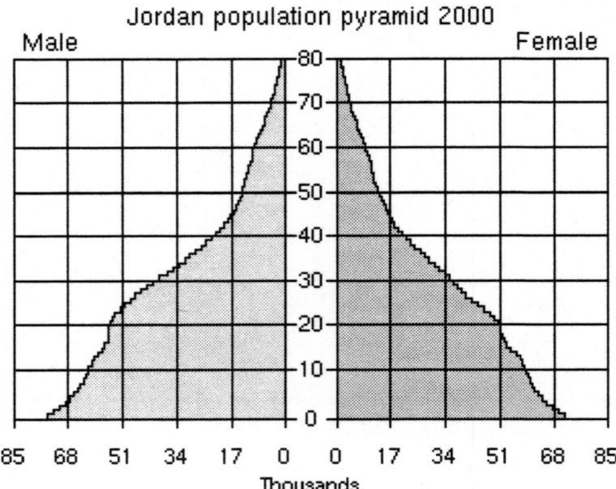

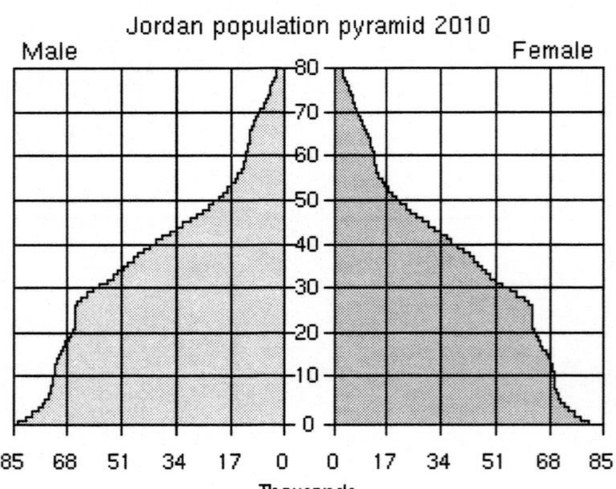

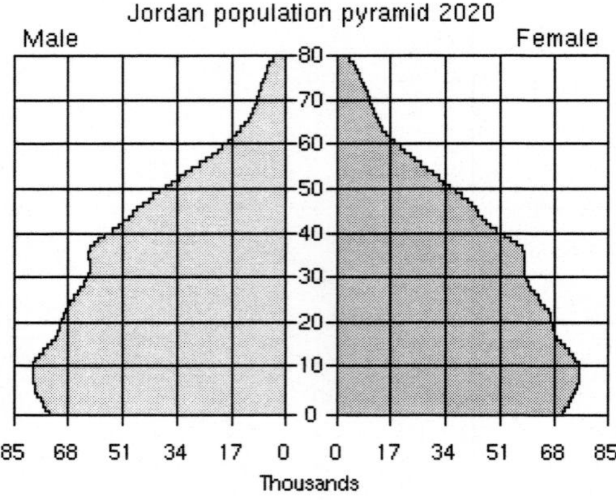

Chart 5.108 Major Cities: 1980, 2000 and 2020

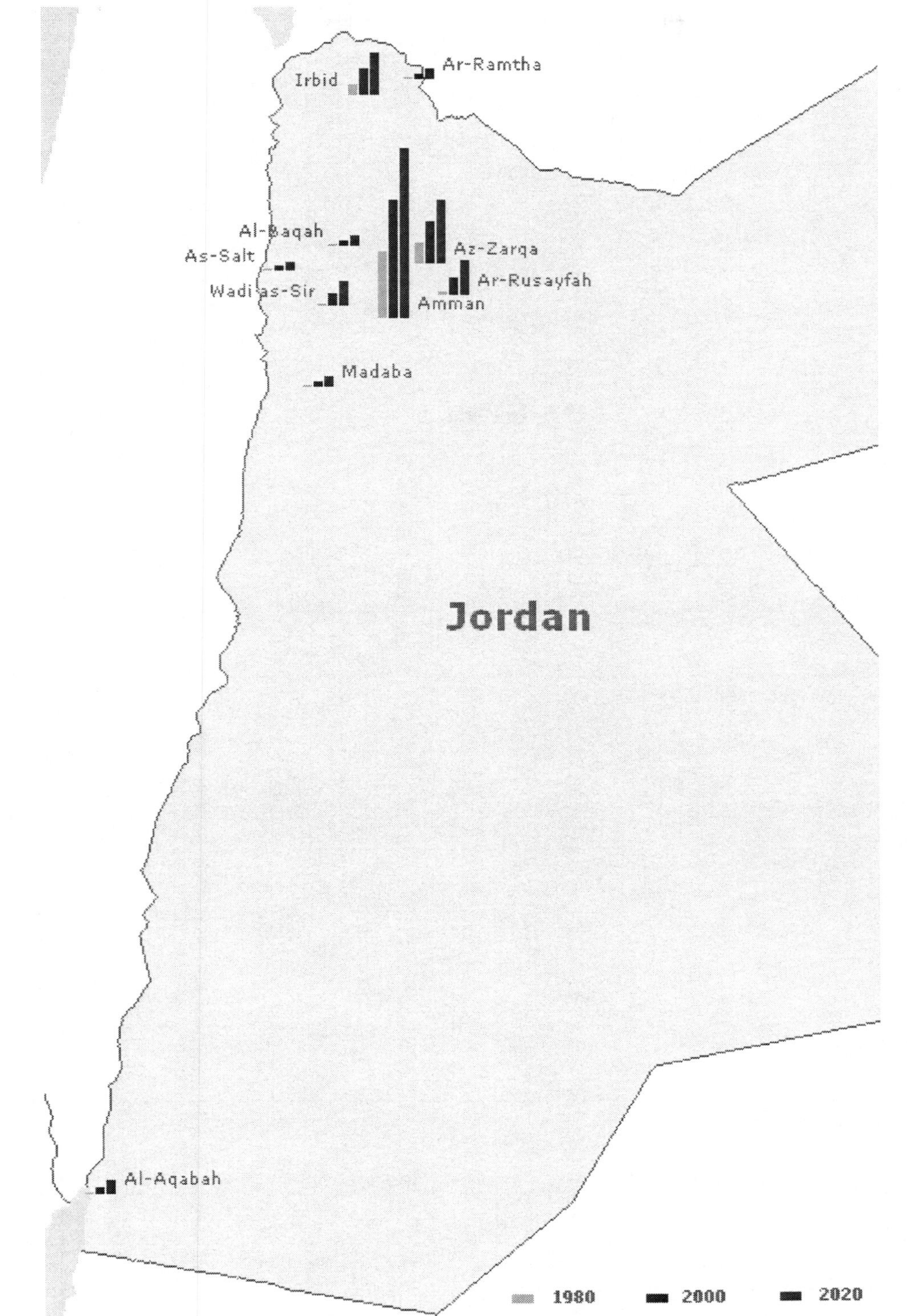

Kazakhstan

Table 5.151 Key population trends

'000

	1980	1985	1990	1995	2000	2005	2010	2015	2020	CAGR	Period growth
Population at January 1st	14,482.0	15,400.6	16,298.0	15,956.7	14,901.6	15,074.8	15,985.0	16,974.9	17,867.1	0.53	23.37
Male	6,975.0	7,428.7	7,892.0	7,710.2	7,145.5	7,204.0	7,606.9	8,057.4	8,470.8	0.49	21.44
Female	7,506.9	7,971.8	8,406.0	8,246.5	7,756.1	7,870.8	8,378.1	8,917.5	9,396.3	0.56	25.17
0-4 yrs	1,659.8	1,774.4	1,860.3	1,461.9	1,100.3	1,197.8	1,541.6	1,588.7	1,478.3	-0.29	-10.93
5-9 yrs	1,557.2	1,621.7	1,705.4	1,717.3	1,408.2	1,095.4	1,199.2	1,517.9	1,545.4	-0.02	-0.76
10-14 yrs	1,475.3	1,531.2	1,572.3	1,569.6	1,591.4	1,377.4	1,106.1	1,223.0	1,542.4	0.11	4.55
15-19 yrs	1,535.0	1,402.2	1,420.7	1,428.8	1,420.7	1,558.8	1,388.6	1,119.5	1,241.5	-0.53	-19.12
20-24 yrs	1,446.2	1,494.1	1,317.3	1,307.9	1,270.9	1,381.9	1,567.8	1,404.4	1,132.0	-0.61	-21.72
25-29 yrs	1,231.0	1,414.7	1,436.7	1,203.0	1,183.3	1,231.8	1,381.7	1,580.0	1,418.0	0.35	15.19
30-34 yrs	917.7	1,188.4	1,388.5	1,297.3	1,083.4	1,142.6	1,222.5	1,383.5	1,588.8	1.38	73.14
35-39 yrs	672.1	871.2	1,157.8	1,246.0	1,135.7	1,036.3	1,126.9	1,216.4	1,383.4	1.82	105.82
40-44 yrs	965.7	635.8	843.3	1,058.0	1,069.2	1,077.4	1,015.8	1,114.6	1,209.2	0.56	25.22
45-49 yrs	669.1	907.7	609.1	752.4	917.7	1,005.7	1,046.9	995.6	1,099.3	1.25	64.30
50-54 yrs	701.7	622.9	859.9	534.9	628.3	848.6	962.3	1,011.7	968.0	0.81	37.94
55-59 yrs	463.4	646.8	579.6	764.5	441.1	567.6	794.0	910.8	964.6	1.85	108.15
60-64 yrs	308.4	415.1	587.9	485.7	614.4	381.1	512.0	725.5	840.3	2.54	172.42
65-69 yrs	326.6	263.8	363.3	486.9	361.0	508.1	324.7	444.2	636.7	1.68	94.94
70-74 yrs	249.3	263.6	216.7	283.8	342.3	274.7	401.4	260.1	363.4	0.95	45.75
75-79 yrs	165.2	181.7	196.7	150.5	180.9	232.1	192.2	290.2	188.4	0.33	14.04
80+ yrs	138.2	165.3	182.5	208.2	152.8	157.7	201.3	188.5	267.4	1.66	93.46
Median age of population (years)	23.4	24.6	26.0	27.0	27.7	28.7	29.3	30.2	31.8	0.77	35.67

Table 5.152 Key economic trends

As stated

	1990	1995	2000	2005	2010	2015	2020	CAGR	Period growth
Total GDP (KZT per capita)	750,718.1	470,592.4	569,479.0	921,927.4	1,103,901.1	1,393,899.9	1,919,744.7	3.18	155.7
Disposable income (KZT per capita)		244,558.7	268,886.3	416,905.9	495,344.2	636,892.9	885,747.7		
Disposable income (KZT per household)		990,693.4	954,322.0	1,365,274.8	1,585,618.9	2,036,211.4	2,858,014.7		
Number of households by annual household disposable income ('000)									
Over US$1,000		3,538.3	3,845.1	4,573.6	4,987.2	5,308.4	5,537.2		
Over US$10,000		131.2	113.9	656.4	2,530.2	4,674.1	5,442.5		
Over US$25,000		41.5	39.8	115.9	333.2	1,855.3	4,427.1		
Over US$75,000		10.4	10.0	28.6	60.8	187.1	814.2		
Over US$150,000		4.4	4.2	11.8	25.1	72.1	184.4		
Total households	3,676.2	3,939.0	4,198.6	4,603.3	4,993.7	5,309.5	5,537.3	1.37	50.6

Note: Per capita data is shown at constant 2010 prices. Household disposable income bands are shown at current prices.

Table 5.153 Young generation

'000

	1980	1985	1990	1995	2000	2005	2010	2015	2020	CAGR	Period growth
Babies under 12 months	332.0	377.1	383.1	236.9	204.1	280.7	358.9	356.3	331.6	0.00	-0.14
Infants under 24 months	667.7	740.1	762.6	509.3	411.0	534.6	675.8	646.4	611.7	-0.22	-8.39
Toddlers aged 1-4	1,327.7	1,397.3	1,477.2	1,225.1	896.2	917.1	1,182.7	1,232.4	1,146.7	-0.37	-13.63
Children aged 2-9	2,549.3	2,656.0	2,803.1	2,669.9	2,097.5	1,758.5	2,065.0	2,460.2	2,412.0	-0.14	-5.39
Female	1,257.3	1,311.2	1,381.5	1,308.6	1,024.1	856.7	1,007.6	1,199.7	1,175.3	-0.17	-6.52
Male	1,292.0	1,344.7	1,421.7	1,361.3	1,073.4	901.8	1,057.4	1,260.5	1,236.7	-0.11	-4.28
Tweenagers aged 10-14	1,475.3	1,531.2	1,572.3	1,569.6	1,591.4	1,377.4	1,106.1	1,223.0	1,542.4	0.11	4.55
Female	729.6	755.8	778.5	774.0	780.2	673.1	538.8	597.3	752.1	0.08	3.09
Male	745.7	775.4	793.7	795.7	811.1	704.2	567.3	625.8	790.3	0.15	5.97
Teenagers aged 13-19	2,127.5	1,996.3	2,034.8	2,033.7	2,052.4	2,148.8	1,848.9	1,574.5	1,834.8	-0.37	-13.76
Female	1,050.2	984.1	998.5	1,010.2	1,009.5	1,053.4	903.5	768.1	895.8	-0.40	-14.70
Male	1,077.3	1,012.2	1,036.4	1,023.5	1,042.9	1,095.5	945.4	806.3	939.0	-0.34	-12.84
Studying age 18-22	1,504.7	1,453.7	1,331.2	1,361.6	1,315.9	1,473.1	1,542.0	1,269.2	1,121.9	-0.73	-25.44
Female	739.2	717.7	651.8	676.5	655.3	724.5	757.2	621.0	548.0	-0.75	-25.87
Male	765.4	736.0	679.4	685.1	660.7	748.5	784.8	648.2	574.0	-0.72	-25.01
Young adults aged 15-29	4,212.1	4,311.0	4,174.7	3,939.7	3,874.8	4,172.5	4,338.1	4,104.0	3,791.5	-0.26	-9.99
Female	2,082.3	2,136.2	2,060.1	1,959.5	1,937.2	2,071.2	2,139.6	2,019.7	1,860.2	-0.28	-10.66
Male	2,129.9	2,174.7	2,114.6	1,980.1	1,937.6	2,101.4	2,198.5	2,084.3	1,931.3	-0.24	-9.32

Table 5.154 Middle-aged generation

'000

	1980	1985	1990	1995	2000	2005	2010	2015	2020	CAGR	Period growth
Middle-aged adults 30-59	4,390	4,873	5,438	5,653	5,275	5,678	6,168	6,633	7,213	1.25	64.3
Female	2,309	2,531	2,795	2,928	2,780	3,013	3,290	3,526	3,801	1.25	64.6
Male	2,080	2,342	2,643	2,725	2,496	2,665	2,878	3,107	3,413	1.24	64.0
Baby boomers aged 40-59	2,800	2,813	2,892	3,110	3,056	3,499	3,819	4,033	4,241	1.04	51.5
Female	1,504	1,489	1,514	1,639	1,643	1,894	2,079	2,198	2,302	1.07	53.0
Male	1,296	1,324	1,378	1,470	1,413	1,605	1,740	1,835	1,939	1.01	49.7

Table 5.155 Elderly population

'000

	1980	1985	1990	1995	2000	2005	2010	2015	2020	CAGR	Period growth
Elderly population (60+)	1,187.8	1,289.6	1,547.1	1,615.0	1,651.4	1,553.6	1,631.6	1,908.5	2,296.2	1.66	93.3
Female	799.2	874.7	1,016.4	1,027.9	1,035.2	995.6	1,072.3	1,259.4	1,509.7	1.60	88.9
Male	388.6	414.9	530.7	587.2	616.2	558.0	559.3	649.0	786.5	1.78	102.4

Table 5.156 Population of biggest cities 1980-2020

'000

	1980	1985	1990	1995	2000	2005	2010	2015	2020	CAGR	Period growth
Almaty	963.6	1,008.6	1,093.1	1,097.7	1,141.5	1,227.4	1,328.6	1,429.4	1,521.0	1.15	57.84
Astana	233.0	257.1	279.6	274.1	334.1	506.4	707.4	877.0	1,017.3	3.75	336.55
Shymkent	325.1	358.7	382.5	350.5	372.8	494.1	640.9	767.4	873.6	2.50	168.75
Qaraghandy	558.4	521.7	505.5	455.3	435.9	443.7	456.3	469.7	481.4	-0.37	-13.80
Taraz	265.9	282.0	311.1	319.6	331.6	335.5	339.3	344.0	347.8	0.67	30.82
Pavlodar	277.4	306.3	334.2	313.3	299.5	303.4	310.7	318.5	325.3	0.40	17.25
Semey	275.3	300.3	319.3	287.2	268.5	278.4	295.0	311.8	326.9	0.43	18.77
Oskemen	278.1	298.9	328.4	320.0	308.6	292.9	273.1	255.2	237.9	-0.39	-14.46
Aqtobe	195.7	225.8	258.7	253.8	253.3	257.1	262.3	268.1	273.0	0.84	39.49
Qostanay	174.8	200.2	228.5	224.0	220.1	210.2	199.3	189.5	180.0	0.07	2.99

Chart 5.109 Population age shift 2000 and 2020, Each Column Represents a Single Age Group

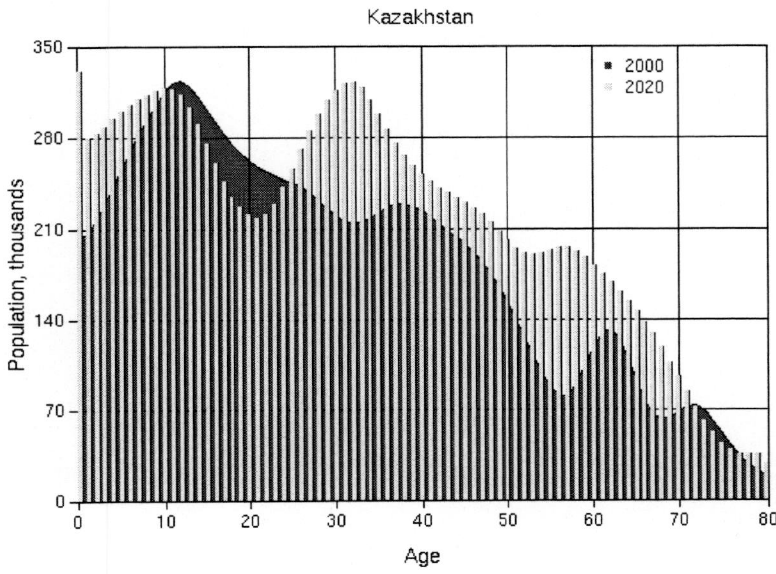

Chart 5.110 Population pyramids, 1980/2000/2010/2020

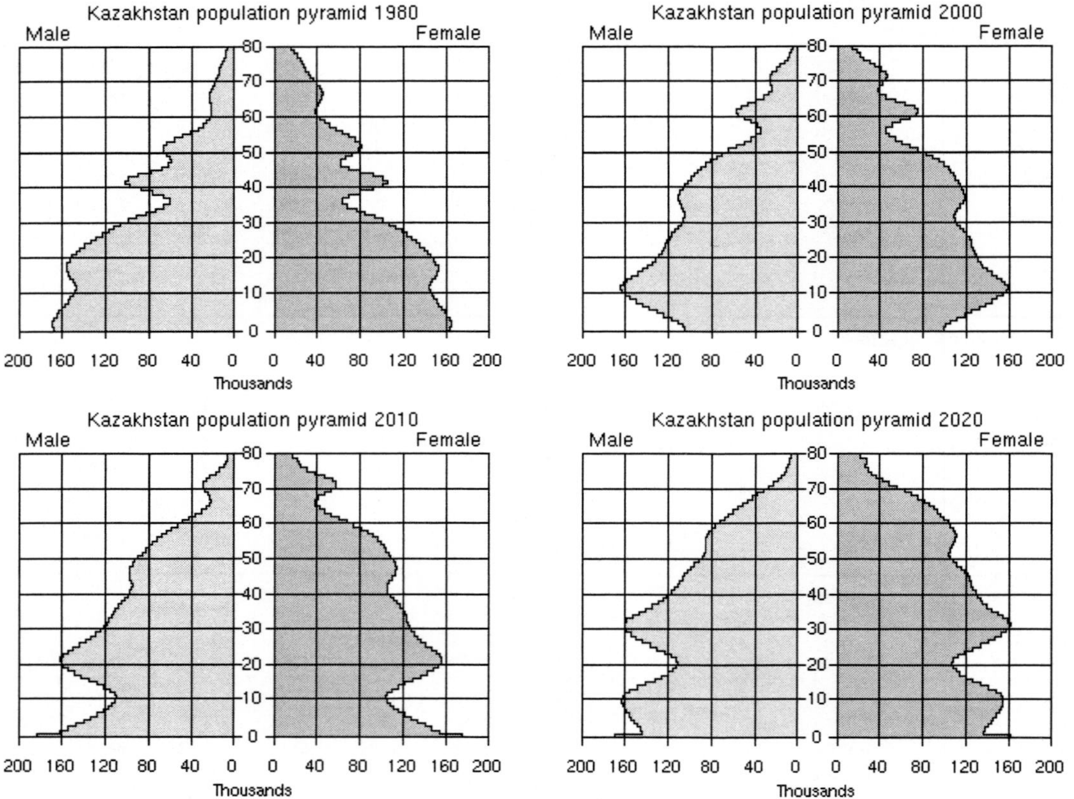

Chart 5.111 Major Cities: 1980, 2000 and 2020

Kuwait

Table 5.157 Key population trends

'000

	1980	1985	1990	1995	2000	2005	2010	2015	2020	CAGR	Period growth
Population at January 1st	1,357.95	1,697.30	2,067.88	1,575.57	1,883.44	2,213.40	2,498.76	2,766.83	3,022.44	2.02	122.57
Male	778.08	964.04	1,175.02	947.51	1,145.14	1,335.05	1,483.53	1,628.15	1,764.82	2.07	126.82
Female	579.87	733.27	892.87	628.06	738.30	878.36	1,015.22	1,138.68	1,257.62	1.95	116.88
0-4 yrs	212.31	246.93	291.32	166.81	176.29	189.02	211.64	213.78	210.18	-0.03	-1.00
5-9 yrs	183.92	211.57	253.15	158.72	162.69	176.34	192.54	213.18	216.73	0.41	17.84
10-14 yrs	150.33	173.65	207.70	132.92	149.64	161.64	177.88	194.27	214.62	0.89	42.77
15-19 yrs	120.85	145.09	176.32	114.20	132.08	156.74	167.87	182.92	198.99	1.25	64.66
20-24 yrs	124.35	149.71	184.35	145.81	152.66	196.86	194.35	197.32	206.87	1.28	66.37
25-29 yrs	137.53	183.90	228.94	207.92	221.82	267.51	267.72	245.54	241.32	1.42	75.47
30-34 yrs	120.71	171.80	213.94	198.82	257.02	294.20	316.88	297.17	277.34	2.10	129.76
35-39 yrs	96.75	136.13	169.98	162.08	211.34	257.24	290.89	312.37	299.00	2.86	209.04
40-44 yrs	76.30	98.15	120.82	114.14	162.62	183.73	231.44	276.24	300.02	3.48	293.19
45-49 yrs	50.92	71.26	87.76	70.24	107.33	132.73	163.03	220.52	265.58	4.22	421.53
50-54 yrs	34.12	46.04	56.53	42.15	62.73	80.30	115.17	154.85	212.08	4.67	521.65
55-59 yrs	18.95	27.35	33.52	27.39	37.35	47.68	68.05	108.18	147.54	5.26	678.38
60-64 yrs	11.97	15.16	18.48	15.29	23.98	30.30	42.68	63.86	102.82	5.52	759.01
65-69 yrs	8.56	8.81	10.73	8.18	12.86	19.75	27.75	39.74	59.67	4.97	596.84
70-74 yrs	4.77	5.45	6.74	5.11	6.46	10.69	17.10	24.40	35.14	5.12	636.06
75-79 yrs	3.15	3.06	3.68	2.83	3.64	4.93	8.51	13.77	19.88	4.71	530.58
80+ yrs	2.45	3.22	3.91	2.96	2.91	3.73	5.25	8.71	14.63	4.57	498.44
Median age of population (years)	20.49	22.50	22.99	26.78	28.91	29.28	30.61	32.38	34.05	1.28	66.19

Table 5.158 Key economic trends

As stated

	1990	1995	2000	2005	2010	2015	2020	CAGR	Period growth
Total GDP (KWD per capita)	7,479.1	12,855.9	11,817.6	14,854.6	15,343.2	17,410.8	20,338.6	3.39	171.9
Disposable income (KWD per capita)	3,341.3	4,575.1	4,814.5	5,655.9	6,100.0	6,955.8	8,010.7	2.96	139.8
Disposable income (KWD per household)	22,539.6	29,441.8	31,551.4	38,374.3	42,506.0	49,057.1	56,795.4	3.13	152.0
Number of households by annual household disposable income ('000)									
Over US$1,000	306.5	244.8	287.4	326.2	358.6	392.3	426.3	1.11	39.1
Over US$10,000	296.6	241.0	282.2	323.6	357.4	391.7	426.0	1.21	43.6
Over US$25,000	224.3	210.9	250.2	305.5	350.2	388.1	424.0	2.15	89.1
Over US$75,000	36.2	62.8	92.5	170.1	281.5	350.9	403.5	8.37	1,014.7
Over US$150,000	7.9	11.3	19.1	52.2	152.8	254.2	340.1	13.34	4,183.4
Total households	306.5	244.8	287.4	326.2	358.6	392.3	426.3	1.11	39.1

Note: Per capita data is shown at constant 2010 prices. Household disposable income bands are shown at current prices.

Table 5.159 Young generation

'000

	1980	1985	1990	1995	2000	2005	2010	2015	2020	CAGR	Period growth
Babies under 12 months	44.5	51.6	60.5	32.2	36.9	38.2	44.1	41.0	41.6	-0.17	-6.45
Infants under 24 months	87.9	102.3	120.0	65.5	72.7	76.4	87.3	83.2	83.3	-0.14	-5.27
Toddlers aged 1-4	167.9	195.4	230.8	134.6	139.4	150.8	167.5	172.8	168.6	0.01	0.44
Children aged 2-9	308.3	356.2	424.5	260.1	266.3	288.9	316.8	343.7	343.7	0.27	11.46
Female	150.7	175.7	209.3	126.4	129.4	142.3	156.4	169.5	169.5	0.29	12.45
Male	157.6	180.5	215.1	133.7	136.8	146.6	160.4	174.2	174.2	0.25	10.51
Tweenagers aged 10-14	150.3	173.7	207.7	132.9	149.6	161.6	177.9	194.3	214.6	0.89	42.77
Female	73.2	85.5	102.4	64.8	72.9	78.4	87.6	96.0	105.9	0.93	44.62
Male	77.1	88.1	105.3	68.1	76.8	83.2	90.3	98.3	108.7	0.86	41.01
Teenagers aged 13-19	176.6	210.3	254.2	163.8	189.6	219.7	237.2	258.3	283.2	1.19	60.36
Female	83.1	104.7	126.6	78.7	91.8	105.3	114.7	126.7	139.3	1.30	67.59
Male	93.5	105.5	127.7	85.1	97.8	114.4	122.5	131.7	143.9	1.08	53.93
Studying age 18-22	119.3	142.3	174.7	126.4	137.5	174.8	177.2	187.5	199.7	1.30	67.36
Female	52.3	70.6	86.7	56.7	64.4	78.7	83.4	88.4	97.2	1.56	86.10
Male	67.1	71.7	88.0	69.7	73.1	96.1	93.8	99.1	102.5	1.06	52.76
Young adults aged 15-29	382.7	478.7	589.6	467.9	506.6	621.1	629.9	625.8	647.2	1.32	69.10
Female	160.6	214.6	264.8	186.9	211.8	259.7	274.3	281.7	300.2	1.58	86.89
Male	222.1	264.1	324.9	281.1	294.7	361.4	355.7	344.1	347.0	1.12	56.24

Table 5.160 **Middle-aged generation**

'000

	1980	1985	1990	1995	2000	2005	2010	2015	2020	CAGR	Period growth
Middle-aged adults 30-59	397.8	550.7	682.6	614.8	838.4	995.9	1,185.5	1,369.3	1,501.6	3.38	277.5
Female	137.5	191.4	237.8	203.1	267.7	332.1	413.8	492.4	553.4	3.54	302.3
Male	260.2	359.4	444.8	411.7	570.7	663.7	771.6	876.9	948.2	3.29	264.4
Baby boomers aged 40-59	180.3	242.8	298.6	253.9	370.0	444.4	577.7	759.8	925.2	4.17	413.2
Female	59.1	80.5	99.3	82.6	115.6	149.7	199.9	264.8	329.1	4.38	456.5
Male	121.2	162.3	199.3	171.3	254.4	294.8	377.9	495.0	596.1	4.06	392.0

Table 5.161 **Elderly population**

'000

	1980	1985	1990	1995	2000	2005	2010	2015	2020	CAGR	Period growth
Elderly population (60+)	30.9	35.7	43.5	34.4	49.8	69.4	101.3	150.5	232.2	5.17	651.2
Female	14.5	16.0	19.6	15.2	20.3	28.2	40.0	57.9	87.6	4.60	504.5
Male	16.4	19.7	23.9	19.2	29.6	41.2	61.3	92.5	144.6	5.59	780.6

Table 5.162 **Population of biggest cities 1980-2020**

'000

	1980	1985	1990	1995	2000	2005	2010	2015	2020	CAGR	Period growth
Qalib ash-Shuyukh	71.6	96.4	120.5	102.2	154.8	179.3	208.6	235.5	257.9	3.26	260.27
As-Salimiyah	136.5	168.8	185.5	129.8	156.8	145.3	140.7	140.8	142.7	0.11	4.51
Hawalli	78.1	98.4	111.5	82.2	106.5	107.0	111.7	118.0	124.0	1.16	58.70
Janub Khitan	52.8	68.0	79.9	62.2	86.3	92.6	102.1	111.6	119.9	2.07	127.28
Al-Farwaniyah	42.2	55.2	66.1	52.9	75.7	83.5	94.0	104.1	112.7	2.48	166.75
Salwah	24.9	33.7	42.3	36.1	55.0	64.1	74.8	84.6	92.8	3.34	272.54
Abraq Khitan	16.9	23.9	31.9	29.2	47.5	57.9	69.6	80.0	88.5	4.23	424.53
Al-Fuhayhil	35.5	44.9	51.2	38.2	50.2	51.2	54.1	57.7	61.0	1.36	71.79
Sabah al-Salim	60.1	73.8	80.0	54.6	63.6	56.3	51.8	49.9	49.0	-0.51	-18.45
As-Sulaybiyah	59.3	72.7	78.8	53.6	62.2	54.8	50.2	48.1	47.1	-0.58	-20.63

Chart 5.112 Population age shift 2000 and 2020, Each Column Represents a Single Age Group

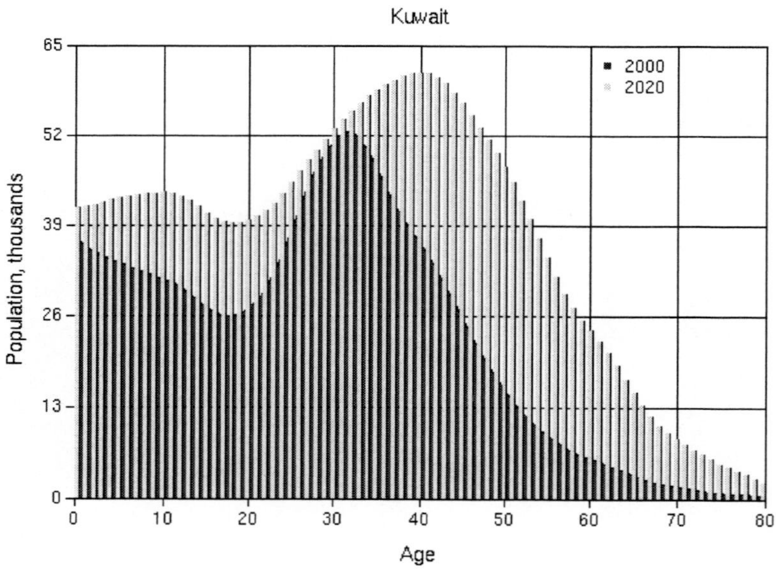

Chart 5.113 Population pyramids, 1980/2000/2010/2020

Kuwait population pyramid 1980
Male
Female
80
70
60
50
40
30
20
10
0
45 36 27 18 9 0 0 9 18 27 36 45
Thousands
Kuwait population pyramid 2000
Kuwait population pyramid 2010
Kuwait population pyramid 2020

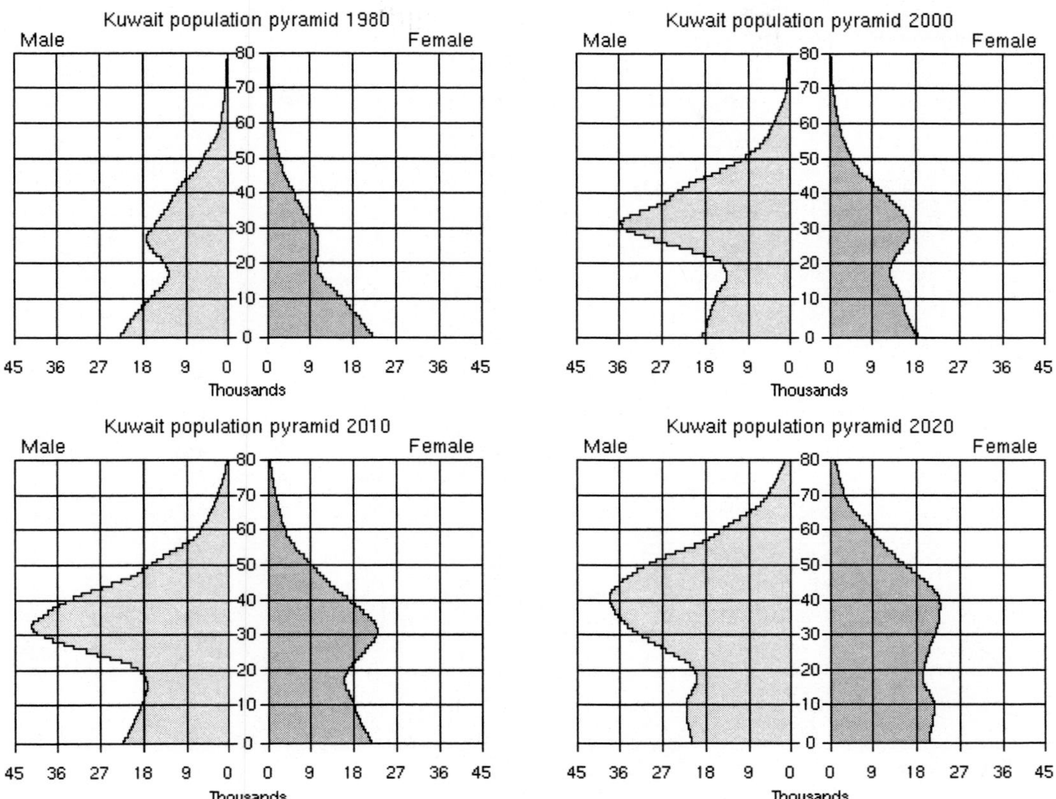

Chart 5.114 Major Cities: 1980, 2000 and 2020

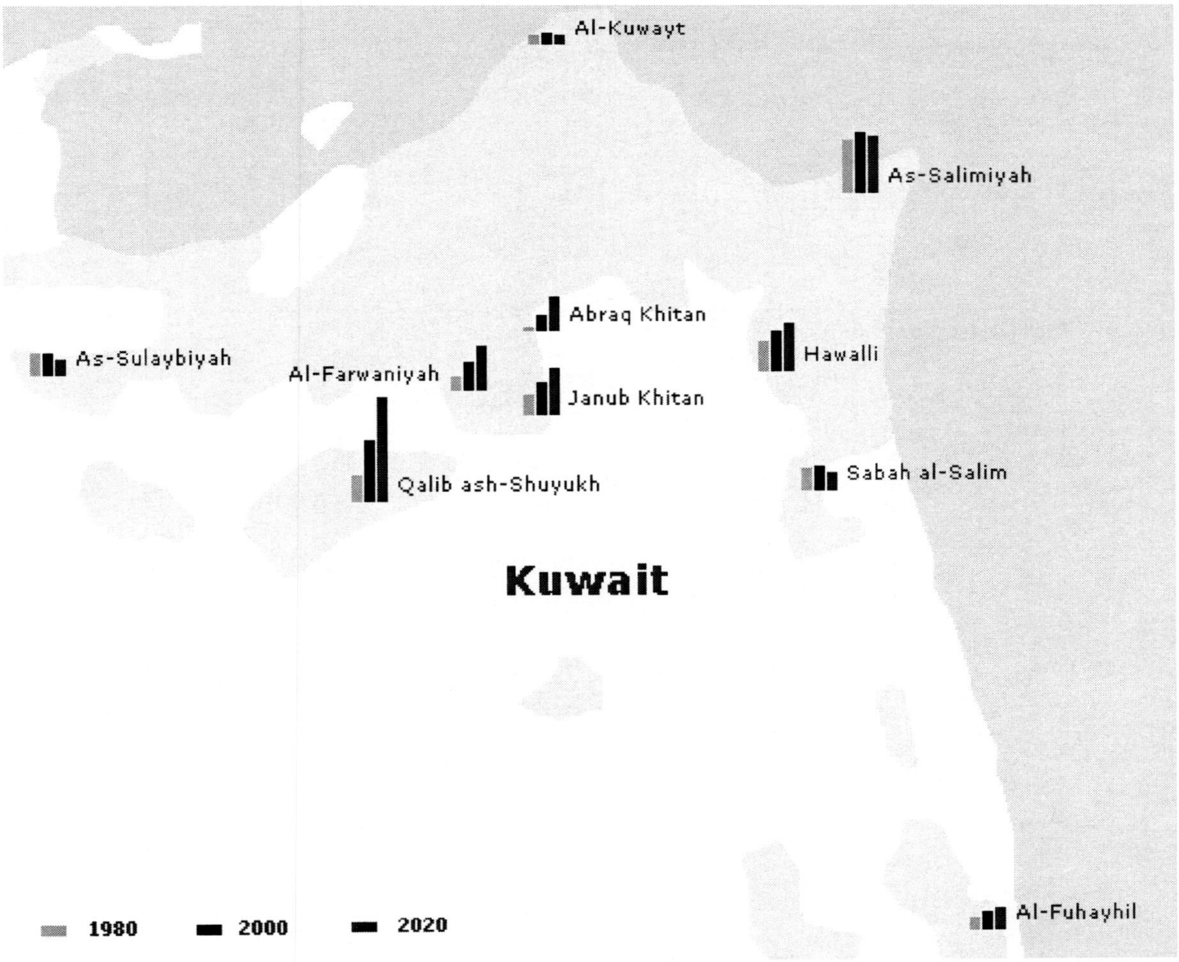

Al-Kuwayt
As-Salimiyah
Abraq Khitan
Hawalli
As-Sulaybiyah
Al-Farwaniyah
Janub Khitan
Qalib ash-Shuyukh
Sabah al-Salim
Kuwait
1980
2000
2020
Al-Fuhayhil

Latvia

Table 5.163 Key population trends

'000

	1980	1985	1990	1995	2000	2005	2010	2015	2020	CAGR	Period growth
Population at January 1st	2,508.8	2,570.0	2,668.1	2,500.6	2,381.7	2,306.4	2,240.3	2,171.8	2,109.9	-0.43	-15.90
Male	1,154.5	1,187.1	1,240.5	1,154.3	1,096.9	1,062.9	1,032.3	1,001.7	975.2	-0.42	-15.53
Female	1,354.3	1,382.9	1,427.6	1,346.3	1,284.8	1,243.5	1,208.1	1,170.0	1,134.7	-0.44	-16.21
0-4 yrs	172.4	191.0	208.5	148.0	95.9	100.6	111.5	117.3	112.0	-1.07	-35.04
5-9 yrs	176.8	174.2	188.7	192.4	145.3	95.8	99.9	110.1	116.4	-1.04	-34.16
10-14 yrs	163.4	179.0	174.6	181.5	186.8	145.1	94.8	98.6	109.2	-1.00	-33.15
15-19 yrs	187.5	169.8	184.7	164.0	178.1	184.5	143.3	93.3	97.6	-1.62	-47.95
20-24 yrs	199.1	196.9	185.6	174.5	161.5	175.1	182.1	140.9	92.3	-1.90	-53.65
25-29 yrs	185.7	201.0	208.9	168.5	165.0	158.8	172.7	179.1	139.3	-0.72	-24.97
30-34 yrs	168.4	184.1	199.5	182.5	159.3	162.2	156.4	169.5	176.8	0.12	5.02
35-39 yrs	175.6	165.4	183.0	181.7	176.9	156.2	159.3	153.1	166.8	-0.13	-4.96
40-44 yrs	191.9	170.8	156.7	164.8	175.3	172.2	152.3	154.7	149.6	-0.62	-22.06
45-49 yrs	171.9	185.8	178.1	148.4	155.5	168.3	165.9	146.3	149.5	-0.35	-13.04
50-54 yrs	169.5	165.3	173.6	155.0	139.7	147.2	159.9	157.0	139.3	-0.49	-17.85
55-59 yrs	131.8	161.3	161.9	163.0	142.5	129.1	137.2	148.5	146.6	0.27	11.22
60-64 yrs	87.8	122.1	148.8	140.0	146.6	130.3	117.6	124.5	135.5	1.09	54.38
65-69 yrs	109.9	77.8	103.1	129.2	120.9	128.3	114.6	103.4	109.8	0.00	-0.07
70-74 yrs	93.5	91.6	66.9	87.8	105.8	101.0	107.5	95.5	86.9	-0.18	-7.03
75-79 yrs	67.1	69.3	71.8	47.8	66.5	81.6	77.7	82.8	73.6	0.23	9.74
80+ yrs	56.5	64.6	73.6	71.5	60.1	70.3	87.5	97.1	108.6	1.65	92.20
Median age of population (years)	35.0	34.7	34.6	36.0	37.9	39.2	40.0	40.8	41.5	0.42	18.39

Table 5.164 Key economic trends

As stated

	1990	1995	2000	2005	2010	2015	2020	CAGR	Period growth
Total GDP (LVL per capita)	4,930.9	2,663.0	3,640.7	5,572.2	5,330.0	6,519.4	7,922.0	1.59	60.66
Disposable income (LVL per capita)		1,484.8	2,115.9	3,263.2	3,125.4	3,515.4	4,168.4		
Disposable income (LVL per household)		4,586.1	6,282.4	9,314.4	8,637.3	9,464.6	10,990.3		
Number of households by annual household disposable income ('000)									
Over US$1,000		789.4	788.6	803.0	807.1	804.2	798.8		
Over US$10,000		32.6	125.2	438.1	572.8	642.3	703.3		
Over US$25,000		9.5	18.5	75.0	183.5	284.6	425.1		
Over US$75,000		2.3	4.6	11.2	18.4	28.3	58.8		
Over US$150,000		1.0	1.9	4.7	7.7	10.6	16.0		
Total households	833.8	809.6	802.2	808.0	810.7	806.6	800.2	-0.14	-4.03

Note: Per capita data is shown at constant 2010 prices. Household disposable income bands are shown at current prices.

Table 5.165 Young generation

'000

	1980	1985	1990	1995	2000	2005	2010	2015	2020	CAGR	Period growth
Babies under 12 months	34.5	40.1	41.3	23.9	19.2	20.2	23.1	23.5	21.4	-1.19	-38.09
Infants under 24 months	68.4	80.4	83.5	50.3	37.5	41.2	45.8	47.2	43.4	-1.13	-36.58
Toddlers aged 1-4	137.9	150.9	167.2	124.1	76.7	80.3	88.4	93.7	90.7	-1.04	-34.27
Children aged 2-9	280.9	284.8	313.7	290.2	203.8	155.2	165.6	180.3	185.1	-1.04	-34.11
Female	137.5	139.4	153.8	141.9	99.5	75.7	81.0	87.9	90.1	-1.05	-34.47
Male	143.4	145.4	160.0	148.2	104.3	79.5	84.6	92.3	95.0	-1.02	-33.76
Tweenagers aged 10-14	163.4	179.0	174.6	181.5	186.8	145.1	94.8	98.6	109.2	-1.00	-33.15
Female	80.1	87.4	85.9	89.1	91.2	71.3	46.2	48.6	53.6	-1.00	-33.16
Male	83.3	91.6	88.7	92.4	95.6	73.8	48.6	50.0	55.7	-1.00	-33.15
Teenagers aged 13-19	251.8	242.1	255.1	232.0	253.9	250.8	183.1	131.9	140.0	-1.46	-44.40
Female	122.2	116.8	123.8	114.1	124.3	122.8	90.0	64.9	69.1	-1.42	-43.48
Male	129.6	125.2	131.3	117.9	129.5	128.0	93.1	67.1	70.9	-1.50	-45.27
Studying age 18-22	202.9	182.9	184.6	167.1	163.9	183.6	173.8	115.7	91.8	-1.96	-54.77
Female	97.7	89.4	88.8	81.7	80.5	90.2	85.4	57.0	45.4	-1.90	-53.52
Male	105.1	93.4	95.8	85.4	83.4	93.4	88.4	58.8	46.3	-2.03	-55.92
Young adults aged 15-29	572.3	567.7	579.2	507.0	504.6	518.4	498.1	413.4	329.2	-1.37	-42.48
Female	280.2	279.0	283.4	247.9	248.6	254.6	245.3	203.8	162.8	-1.35	-41.88
Male	292.2	288.7	295.8	259.1	256.0	263.8	252.8	209.5	166.4	-1.40	-43.05

Table 5.166 Middle-aged generation

'000

	1980	1985	1990	1995	2000	2005	2010	2015	2020	CAGR	Period growth
Middle-aged adults 30-59	1,009.1	1,032.7	1,052.9	995.4	949.1	935.1	931.0	929.2	928.6	-0.21	-7.97
Female	548.7	551.0	552.8	528.8	501.0	489.2	484.4	480.4	476.8	-0.35	-13.11
Male	460.3	481.7	500.1	466.7	448.1	445.9	446.6	448.8	451.8	-0.05	-1.86
Baby boomers aged 40-59	665.1	683.2	670.4	631.3	613.0	616.8	615.3	606.6	584.9	-0.32	-12.06
Female	372.4	372.3	358.3	340.9	330.1	329.4	327.0	320.0	306.2	-0.49	-17.78
Male	292.8	310.9	312.0	290.4	282.9	287.4	288.3	286.6	278.8	-0.12	-4.78

Table 5.167 Elderly population

'000

	1980	1985	1990	1995	2000	2005	2010	2015	2020	CAGR	Period growth
Elderly population (60+)	414.7	425.4	464.2	476.3	499.9	511.5	505.0	503.2	514.4	0.54	24.0
Female	274.5	286.9	311.0	313.9	326.0	332.8	328.9	326.4	330.4	0.46	20.4
Male	140.2	138.5	153.2	162.4	173.8	178.7	176.1	176.8	184.0	0.68	31.2

Table 5.168 Population of biggest cities 1980-2020

'000

	1980	1985	1990	1995	2000	2005	2010	2015	2020	CAGR	Period growth
Riga	835.2	872.3	905.9	827.4	764.3	728.3	706.1	686.3	669.7	-0.55	-19.81
Daugavpils	116.4	120.4	125.1	119.4	115.3	113.1	111.6	109.6	107.5	-0.20	-7.64
Liepaja	108.5	111.7	113.4	100.7	89.4	82.8	78.8	75.8	73.5	-0.97	-32.27
Jelgava	67.9	70.9	73.8	68.1	63.7	61.1	59.5	58.0	56.7	-0.45	-16.48
Jurmala	54.1	57.2	60.7	57.7	55.7	54.7	54.0	53.0	52.0	-0.10	-3.77
Ventspils	48.2	49.2	50.4	46.8	43.9	42.3	41.3	40.3	39.5	-0.50	-18.10
Rezekne	36.2	39.4	42.6	40.7	39.2	38.5	38.0	37.3	36.6	0.02	1.00
Valmiera	25.3	27.2	29.3	28.4	27.8	27.5	27.2	26.8	26.4	0.10	4.09
Jekabpils	26.4	28.7	30.9	29.2	27.9	27.2	26.7	26.1	25.6	-0.08	-3.06
Ogre	26.0	27.9	29.7	27.9	26.6	25.8	25.4	24.8	24.3	-0.17	-6.57

Chart 5.115 Population age shift 2000 and 2020, Each Column Represents a Single Age Group

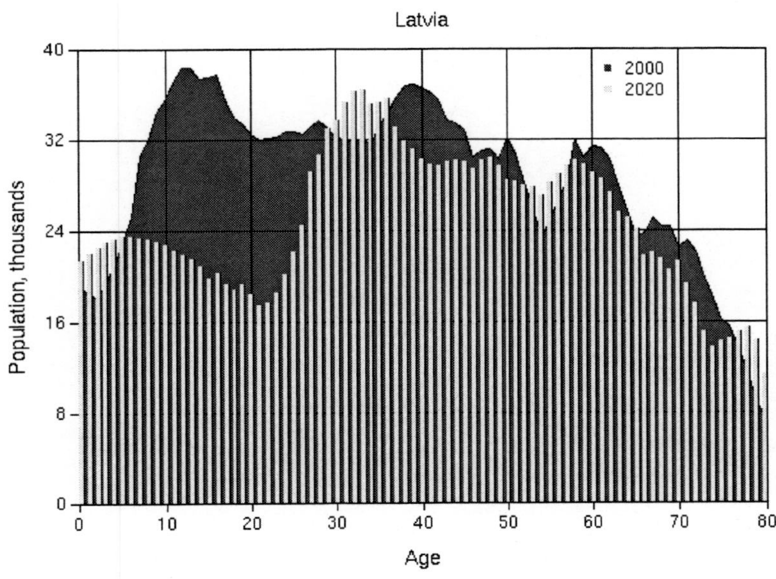

Chart 5.116 Population pyramids, 1980/2000/2010/2020

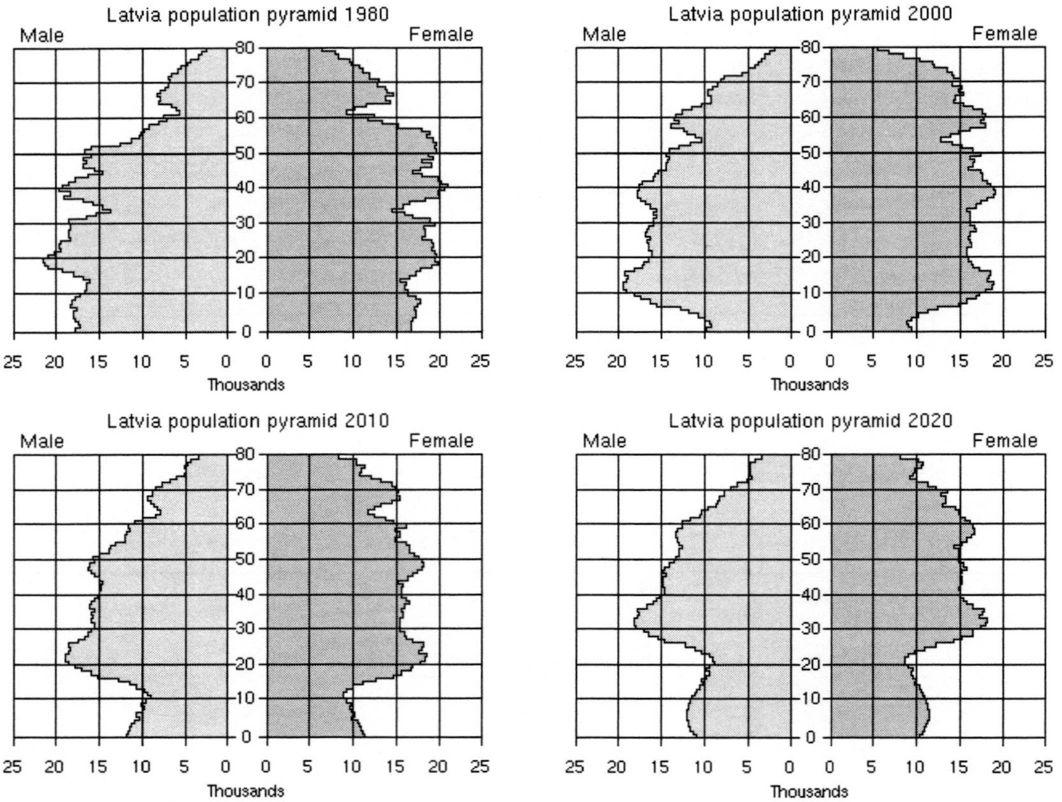

Chart 5.117 Major Cities: 1980, 2000 and 2020

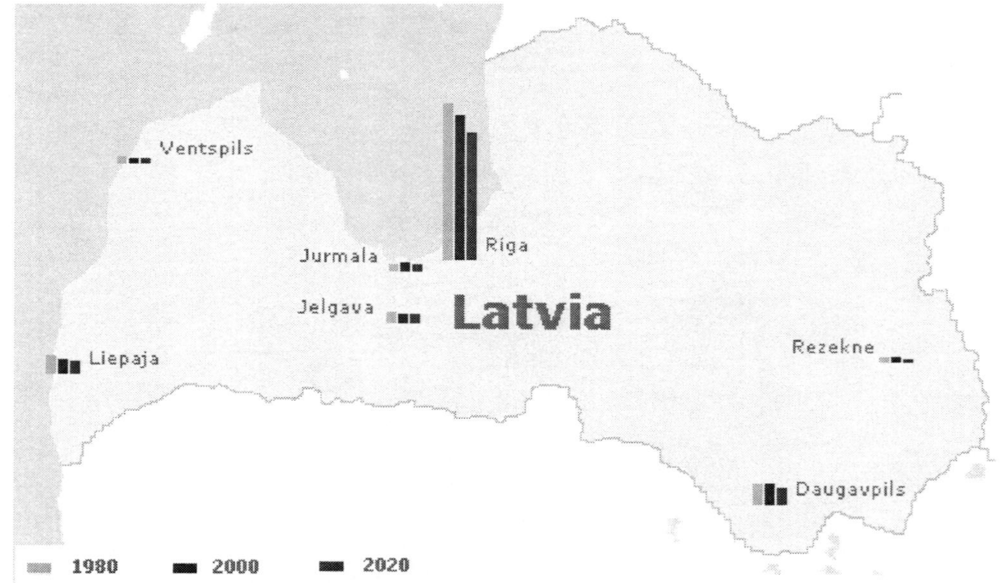

Lithuania

Table 5.169 Key population trends

'000

	1980	1985	1990	1995	2000	2005	2010	2015	2020	CAGR	Period growth
Population at January 1st	3,404.2	3,528.7	3,693.7	3,643.0	3,512.1	3,425.3	3,329.5	3,234.4	3,149.8	-0.19	-7.47
Male	1,602.3	1,662.0	1,747.5	1,717.2	1,644.3	1,598.2	1,548.1	1,499.8	1,459.6	-0.23	-8.91
Female	1,801.9	1,866.7	1,946.2	1,925.8	1,867.8	1,827.2	1,781.4	1,734.5	1,690.2	-0.16	-6.20
0-4 yrs	263.4	276.8	291.7	249.6	188.1	154.7	152.5	157.1	157.4	-1.28	-40.25
5-9 yrs	275.4	262.7	278.7	280.9	245.6	185.8	153.6	151.7	156.2	-1.41	-43.27
10-14 yrs	265.7	274.3	263.2	267.5	276.3	244.7	184.4	152.8	151.0	-1.40	-43.18
15-19 yrs	289.8	267.1	278.3	254.2	260.4	273.8	242.0	182.5	151.6	-1.61	-47.70
20-24 yrs	279.5	298.7	277.8	271.9	236.6	252.3	267.6	235.8	178.9	-1.11	-35.99
25-29 yrs	248.7	286.0	308.6	270.6	250.8	225.7	244.3	259.0	229.7	-0.20	-7.67
30-34 yrs	229.4	247.5	288.2	295.3	256.0	242.8	219.1	237.5	253.0	0.25	10.31
35-39 yrs	227.8	225.2	245.7	272.2	279.5	250.7	236.0	213.2	232.1	0.05	1.88
40-44 yrs	231.5	222.5	221.3	230.1	254.7	272.2	242.8	228.6	207.4	-0.27	-10.40
45-49 yrs	223.8	226.6	218.8	207.2	215.7	246.7	262.0	234.1	221.3	-0.03	-1.14
50-54 yrs	210.7	217.3	221.6	204.9	191.2	206.0	234.5	249.5	224.0	0.15	6.30
55-59 yrs	170.4	201.8	209.9	205.1	188.7	178.3	192.9	220.1	235.1	0.81	38.02
60-64 yrs	111.4	157.0	190.4	190.0	185.7	174.6	163.8	177.7	204.0	1.52	83.12
65-69 yrs	116.4	94.7	142.3	167.5	167.3	166.3	156.2	147.4	160.8	0.81	38.19
70-74 yrs	96.8	100.7	78.3	119.5	140.8	144.0	142.7	134.9	128.7	0.71	32.96
75-79 yrs	72.2	75.8	79.6	60.1	92.7	111.0	115.2	115.6	110.6	1.07	53.15
80+ yrs	91.2	94.2	99.2	96.4	81.8	95.7	119.8	136.8	148.0	1.22	62.21
Median age of population (years)	31.6	32.0	32.4	33.9	35.8	37.7	39.3	40.6	41.6	0.69	31.46

Table 5.170 Key economic trends

As stated

	1990	1995	2000	2005	2010	2015	2020	CAGR	Period growth
Total GDP (LTL per capita)	22,988.2	13,534.6	17,668.1	26,362.6	25,608.0	31,576.8	38,566.4	1.74	67.77
Disposable income (LTL per capita)		9,129.5	11,760.0	16,857.1	17,249.5	21,221.3	26,023.5		
Disposable income (LTL per household)		24,898.5	30,532.1	41,699.6	41,242.2	49,619.0	59,971.3		
Number of households by annual household disposable income ('000)									
Over US$1,000		1,273.9	1,349.2	1,384.6	1,392.5	1,383.3	1,366.8		
Over US$10,000		48.7	145.4	613.2	989.0	1,232.9	1,329.4		
Over US$25,000		14.3	29.8	101.0	203.4	346.7	629.1		
Over US$75,000		3.6	7.4	19.3	30.3	43.8	69.8		
Over US$150,000		1.5	3.1	8.0	12.7	17.7	25.4		
Total households	1,292.3	1,335.8	1,352.7	1,384.7	1,392.5	1,383.3	1,366.8	0.19	5.76

Note: Per capita data is shown at constant 2010 prices. Household disposable income bands are shown at current prices.

Table 5.171 Young generation

'000

	1980	1985	1990	1995	2000	2005	2010	2015	2020	CAGR	Period growth
Babies under 12 months	53.0	58.1	55.5	41.8	36.1	30.2	31.0	31.8	31.1	-1.32	-41.32
Infants under 24 months	105.8	116.1	112.2	88.1	72.6	60.6	61.6	63.4	62.5	-1.31	-40.93
Toddlers aged 1-4	210.4	218.7	236.3	207.8	152.0	124.5	121.6	125.3	126.3	-1.27	-39.98
Children aged 2-9	433.0	423.4	458.2	442.3	361.1	279.9	244.5	245.4	251.1	-1.35	-42.01
Female	211.2	208.5	224.9	216.7	176.2	136.0	119.2	120.0	122.8	-1.35	-41.86
Male	221.9	214.9	233.3	225.6	184.9	143.9	125.4	125.4	128.4	-1.36	-42.15
Tweenagers aged 10-14	265.7	274.3	263.2	267.5	276.3	244.7	184.4	152.8	151.0	-1.40	-43.18
Female	127.3	133.6	130.0	131.3	135.6	119.6	89.6	74.3	73.8	-1.35	-42.03
Male	138.4	140.7	133.3	136.2	140.7	125.1	94.7	78.5	77.2	-1.45	-44.23
Teenagers aged 13-19	396.0	379.9	383.2	356.8	374.3	379.7	319.1	246.1	211.4	-1.56	-46.61
Female	192.4	182.9	187.9	176.1	183.6	185.9	156.1	119.6	103.0	-1.55	-46.49
Male	203.6	196.9	195.4	180.7	190.7	193.8	163.0	126.4	108.5	-1.56	-46.73
Studying age 18-22	296.1	280.6	280.7	260.9	241.9	269.6	262.2	210.5	167.5	-1.41	-43.44
Female	147.1	136.5	135.7	129.1	119.0	132.3	128.6	103.1	81.3	-1.47	-44.76
Male	148.9	144.1	144.9	131.8	122.9	137.3	133.6	107.5	86.2	-1.36	-42.13
Young adults aged 15-29	818.1	851.8	864.7	796.7	747.9	751.9	753.9	677.3	560.1	-0.94	-31.53
Female	406.0	419.3	422.4	390.9	370.2	369.9	370.3	332.6	274.2	-0.98	-32.46
Male	412.1	432.6	442.3	405.9	377.7	382.0	383.6	344.7	285.9	-0.91	-30.61

Table 5.172 Middle-aged generation

'000

	1980	1985	1990	1995	2000	2005	2010	2015	2020	CAGR	Period growth
Middle-aged adults 30-59	1,293.6	1,340.8	1,405.5	1,414.8	1,385.9	1,396.7	1,387.3	1,383.1	1,373.0	0.15	6.13
Female	695.4	714.0	739.0	741.2	726.0	731.0	724.9	721.1	712.5	0.06	2.47
Male	598.2	626.8	666.5	673.6	659.9	665.7	662.5	662.1	660.4	0.25	10.39
Baby boomers aged 40-59	836.4	868.2	871.6	847.3	850.3	903.1	932.2	932.4	887.8	0.15	6.15
Female	461.0	472.4	468.7	455.6	455.5	481.1	494.8	494.3	469.0	0.04	1.72
Male	375.4	395.8	402.9	391.7	394.8	422.1	437.4	438.0	418.8	0.27	11.58

Table 5.173 Elderly population

'000

	1980	1985	1990	1995	2000	2005	2010	2015	2020	CAGR	Period growth
Elderly population (60+)	488.0	522.3	589.9	633.5	668.3	691.7	697.7	712.3	752.1	1.09	54.1
Female	310.4	334.6	375.2	402.8	424.7	441.2	447.3	455.6	476.4	1.08	53.5
Male	177.6	187.8	214.7	230.7	243.6	250.5	250.5	256.8	275.7	1.11	55.2

Table 5.174 Population of biggest cities 1980-2020

'000

	1980	1985	1990	1995	2000	2005	2010	2015	2020	CAGR	Period growth
Vilnius	492.0	539.3	593.6	571.9	547.1	541.3	546.9	551.9	554.5	0.30	12.69
Kaunas	376.8	403.2	433.9	416.6	385.6	364.1	351.9	345.1	340.6	-0.25	-9.61
Klaipeda	177.8	195.3	209.6	203.7	194.7	188.8	182.8	179.4	177.1	-0.01	-0.39
Siauliai	121.0	134.6	148.1	143.1	135.5	130.0	125.5	123.0	121.5	0.01	0.38
Panevezys	104.0	117.0	127.3	127.1	121.0	116.2	112.5	110.1	108.5	0.11	4.30
Alytus	57.4	68.2	75.1	75.8	72.0	69.9	67.7	66.4	65.4	0.33	13.98
Marijampole	39.8	47.3	52.1	51.2	48.9	47.7	46.8	46.3	45.9	0.36	15.38
Mazeikiai	28.2	37.1	44.1	45.0	42.8	41.4	40.3	39.7	39.2	0.83	39.14
Jonava	29.2	33.1	36.5	35.8	35.1	34.8	34.3	34.1	33.9	0.37	16.14
Utena	24.6	29.8	35.0	36.1	34.0	33.1	32.4	31.9	31.6	0.63	28.45

Chart 5.118 Population age shift 2000 and 2020, Each Column Represents a Single Age Group

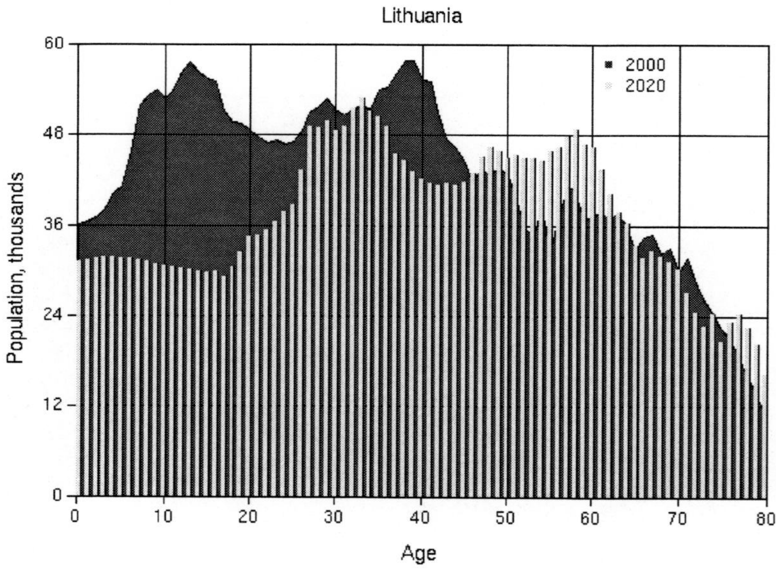

Chart 5.119 Population pyramids, 1980/2000/2010/2020

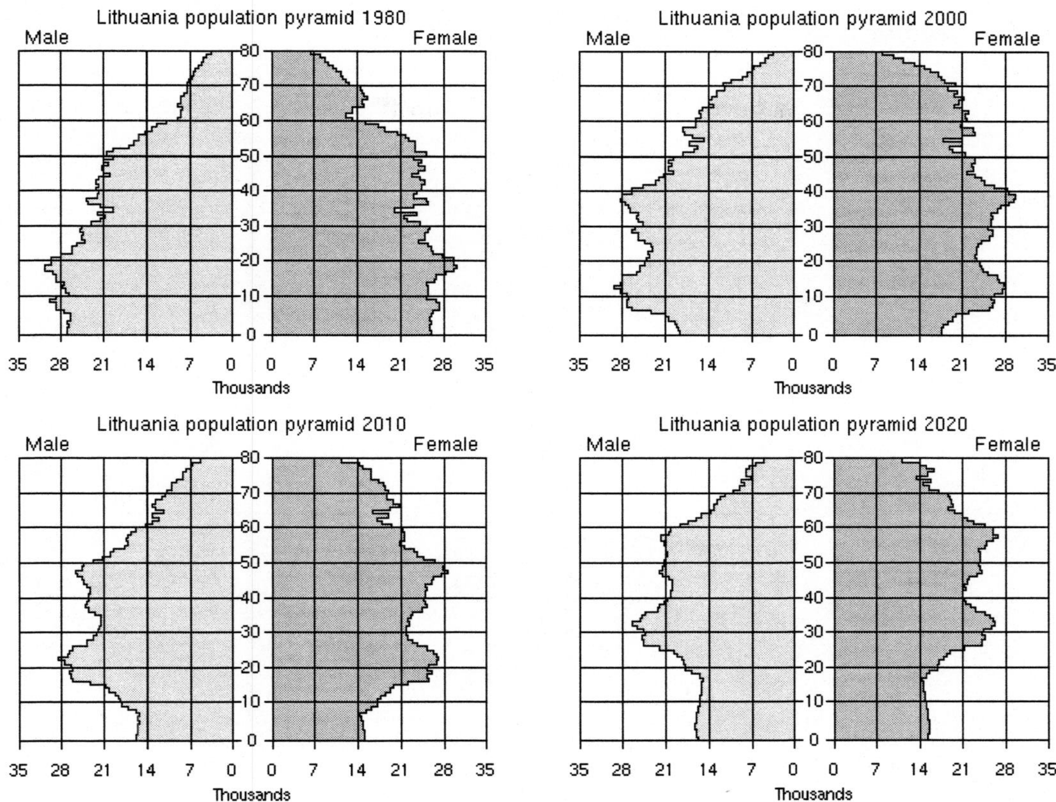

Chart 5.120 Major Cities: 1980, 2000 and 2020

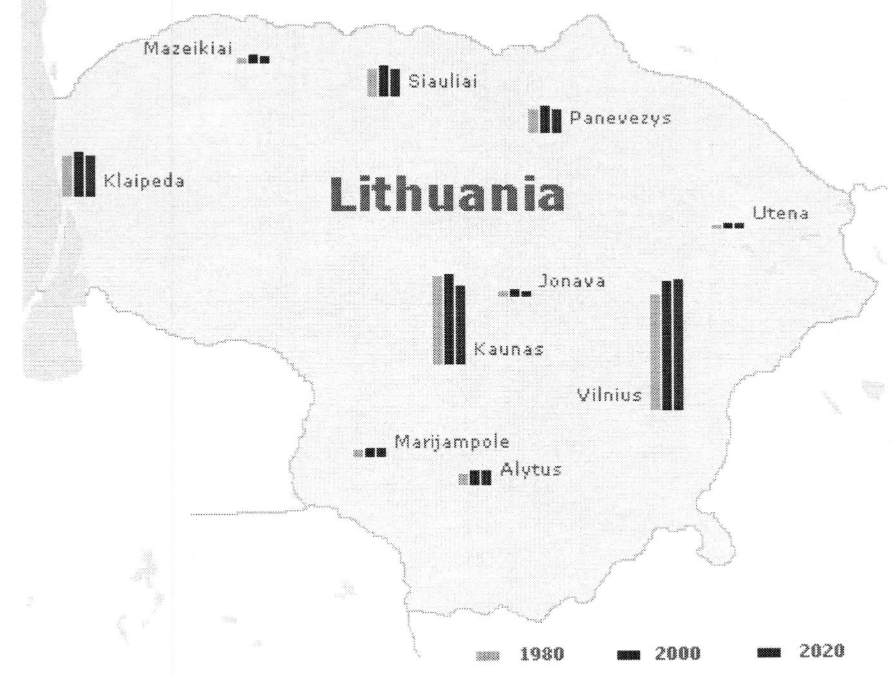

Malaysia

Table 5.175 Key population trends

'000

	1980	1985	1990	1995	2000	2005	2010	2015	2020	CAGR	Period growth
Population at January 1st	13,879.3	15,883.1	18,102.3	20,689.2	23,495.2	26,127.7	28,551.8	30,727.2	32,744.6	2.17	135.9
Male	6,991.9	8,033.5	9,185.0	10,563.9	11,965.7	13,302.7	14,523.5	15,606.4	16,603.7	2.19	137.5
Female	6,887.4	7,849.6	8,917.3	10,125.3	11,529.5	12,825.0	14,028.2	15,120.8	16,140.9	2.15	134.4
0-4 yrs	1,979.2	2,279.0	2,499.6	2,535.1	2,833.4	3,055.1	3,101.3	3,072.8	3,070.9	1.10	55.2
5-9 yrs	1,844.0	1,975.7	2,292.9	2,485.5	2,646.1	2,827.8	3,009.6	3,025.6	2,978.7	1.21	61.5
10-14 yrs	1,719.2	1,826.6	1,982.3	2,310.9	2,523.7	2,642.4	2,837.6	3,004.4	3,004.3	1.41	74.7
15-19 yrs	1,576.5	1,696.1	1,808.4	2,040.4	2,335.9	2,527.4	2,653.6	2,833.9	2,997.2	1.62	90.1
20-24 yrs	1,355.2	1,590.2	1,671.4	1,920.3	2,088.6	2,362.6	2,547.0	2,652.5	2,831.3	1.86	108.9
25-29 yrs	1,118.0	1,378.2	1,603.8	1,786.1	1,919.6	2,106.7	2,369.1	2,543.6	2,642.4	2.17	136.4
30-34 yrs	901.2	1,140.0	1,401.1	1,647.8	1,837.0	1,927.1	2,084.1	2,337.2	2,505.2	2.59	178.0
35-39 yrs	730.0	908.0	1,160.8	1,440.5	1,668.2	1,837.2	1,897.1	2,039.5	2,290.2	2.90	213.7
40-44 yrs	613.3	714.3	912.4	1,173.1	1,451.0	1,657.9	1,812.8	1,841.1	1,967.3	2.96	220.8
45-49 yrs	516.1	604.6	694.9	910.9	1,205.1	1,432.8	1,620.4	1,757.6	1,757.6	3.11	240.6
50-54 yrs	424.5	496.2	589.7	685.5	877.7	1,176.1	1,393.4	1,565.2	1,685.3	3.51	297.0
55-59 yrs	342.4	395.1	469.5	564.3	657.9	843.0	1,124.8	1,335.1	1,495.6	3.75	336.8
60-64 yrs	268.4	304.9	357.2	433.1	519.2	611.6	780.4	1,065.1	1,270.8	3.96	373.5
65-69 yrs	200.3	228.9	258.5	311.5	378.2	461.8	534.4	696.3	985.3	4.06	391.9
70-74 yrs	138.2	155.3	180.9	205.2	264.2	306.4	366.8	431.0	589.7	3.69	326.7
75-79 yrs	88.6	102.1	112.0	142.4	167.9	187.2	211.0	261.8	317.4	3.24	258.1
80+ yrs	64.2	87.9	106.9	96.6	121.5	164.2	208.3	264.5	355.3	4.37	453.9
Median age of population (years)	19.4	20.5	21.4	22.5	23.3	24.2	25.3	26.5	27.8	0.90	43.3

Table 5.176 Key economic trends

As stated

	1990	1995	2000	2005	2010	2015	2020	CAGR	Period growth
Total GDP (RM per capita)	14,242.1	19,590.9	21,763.6	24,669.7	26,227.8	31,913.6	40,147.6	3.51	181.9
Disposable income (RM per capita)	6,190.3	8,296.9	10,081.0	12,329.9	14,561.3	19,083.5	24,721.9	4.72	299.4
Disposable income (RM per household)	32,538.2	41,819.5	48,229.7	56,327.1	63,811.0	80,544.4	101,188.3	3.85	211.0
Number of households by annual household disposable income ('000)									
Over US$1,000	3,308.3	4,031.1	4,820.8	5,614.8	6,436.1	7,229.5	7,970.7	2.97	140.9
Over US$10,000	644.1	1,644.8	1,747.2	2,519.6	3,717.1	5,098.8	6,494.4	8.01	908.3
Over US$25,000	105.1	363.6	334.9	648.0	1,230.9	2,182.7	3,564.6	12.46	3,290.5
Over US$75,000	22.9	52.7	54.7	94.4	176.1	356.0	722.7	12.19	3,054.3
Over US$150,000	9.7	22.6	23.3	36.4	60.9	102.4	199.0	10.58	1,941.9
Total households	3,443.9	4,104.7	4,911.0	5,719.3	6,515.4	7,280.2	8,000.0	2.85	132.3

Note: Per capita data is shown at constant 2010 prices. Household disposable income bands are shown at current prices.

Table 5.177 Young generation

'000

	1980	1985	1990	1995	2000	2005	2010	2015	2020	CAGR	Period growth
Babies under 12 months	418.3	492.2	498.5	503.6	588.9	636.2	615.3	635.2	616.2	0.97	47.3
Infants under 24 months	821.7	950.1	998.2	1,011.1	1,165.2	1,257.6	1,231.0	1,261.6	1,231.1	1.02	49.8
Toddlers aged 1-4	1,560.9	1,786.8	2,001.1	2,031.5	2,244.5	2,418.9	2,486.0	2,437.6	2,454.7	1.14	57.3
Children aged 2-9	3,001.5	3,304.6	3,794.3	4,009.5	4,314.3	4,625.4	4,879.9	4,836.8	4,818.6	1.19	60.5
Female	1,465.6	1,610.2	1,844.4	1,940.6	2,087.5	2,242.2	2,358.0	2,332.7	2,322.3	1.16	58.5
Male	1,535.9	1,694.4	1,949.9	2,068.9	2,226.8	2,383.2	2,522.0	2,504.1	2,496.3	1.22	62.5
Tweenagers aged 10-14	1,719.2	1,826.6	1,982.3	2,310.9	2,523.7	2,642.4	2,837.6	3,004.4	3,004.3	1.41	74.7
Female	842.9	897.7	971.0	1,125.6	1,235.3	1,279.7	1,378.2	1,455.1	1,451.1	1.37	72.2
Male	876.3	928.9	1,011.3	1,185.3	1,288.4	1,362.8	1,459.5	1,549.3	1,553.2	1.44	77.2
Teenagers aged 13-19	2,253.6	2,411.1	2,583.2	2,933.9	3,327.1	3,569.1	3,761.4	4,023.6	4,228.0	1.59	87.6
Female	1,122.9	1,187.7	1,275.0	1,439.7	1,637.9	1,744.8	1,826.0	1,960.0	2,051.6	1.52	82.7
Male	1,130.7	1,223.4	1,308.2	1,494.2	1,689.2	1,824.3	1,935.3	2,063.6	2,176.4	1.65	92.5
Studying age 18-22	1,446.2	1,644.6	1,708.4	1,959.9	2,184.7	2,441.4	2,582.5	2,708.6	2,913.9	1.77	101.5
Female	739.0	814.5	847.5	960.9	1,080.2	1,201.4	1,260.4	1,316.1	1,422.2	1.65	92.4
Male	707.2	830.1	860.9	999.0	1,104.5	1,240.0	1,322.1	1,392.5	1,491.7	1.88	110.9
Young adults aged 15-29	4,049.7	4,664.5	5,083.6	5,746.8	6,344.1	6,996.8	7,569.7	8,030.0	8,471.0	1.86	109.2
Female	2,050.9	2,323.4	2,519.6	2,803.9	3,136.1	3,446.3	3,704.6	3,915.5	4,118.5	1.76	100.8
Male	1,998.8	2,341.1	2,564.0	2,942.9	3,208.0	3,550.5	3,865.1	4,114.6	4,352.4	1.96	117.8

Table 5.178 Middle-aged generation

'000

	1980	1985	1990	1995	2000	2005	2010	2015	2020	CAGR	Period growth
Middle-aged adults 30-59	3,527.5	4,258.2	5,228.4	6,422.1	7,696.9	8,874.2	9,932.6	10,875.7	11,701.1	3.04	231.7
Female	1,744.9	2,101.8	2,565.6	3,137.5	3,745.1	4,349.6	4,905.7	5,401.3	5,826.3	3.06	233.9
Male	1,782.6	2,156.4	2,662.8	3,284.6	3,951.8	4,524.7	5,027.0	5,474.4	5,874.9	3.03	229.6
Baby boomers aged 40-59	1,896.3	2,210.2	2,666.5	3,333.8	4,191.7	5,109.9	5,951.4	6,499.0	6,905.8	3.28	264.2
Female	944.3	1,090.1	1,303.8	1,627.6	2,021.9	2,491.4	2,934.0	3,234.9	3,466.0	3.30	267.0
Male	952.0	1,120.1	1,362.7	1,706.2	2,169.8	2,618.5	3,017.4	3,264.1	3,439.8	3.26	261.3

Table 5.179 Elderly population

'000

	1980	1985	1990	1995	2000	2005	2010	2015	2020	CAGR	Period growth
Elderly population (60+)	759.7	879.1	1,015.5	1,188.8	1,451.0	1,731.2	2,100.9	2,718.6	3,518.6	3.91	363.2
Female	383.3	455.0	533.5	629.6	758.1	898.6	1,085.6	1,405.4	1,826.8	3.98	376.6
Male	376.4	424.1	482.0	559.2	692.9	832.6	1,015.3	1,313.2	1,691.8	3.83	349.5

Table 5.180 Population of biggest cities 1980-2020

'000

	1980	1985	1990	1995	2000	2005	2010	2015	2020	CAGR	Period growth
Kuala Lumpur	817.2	972.2	1,122.6	1,233.6	1,297.5	1,356.0	1,437.3	1,533.8	1,636.7	1.75	100.3
Kelang	209.1	266.8	349.0	472.6	631.7	789.7	937.9	1,073.1	1,193.8	4.45	470.8
Johor Baharu	283.2	347.8	426.3	522.3	630.6	737.2	842.4	942.5	1,035.1	3.29	265.5
Subang Jaya	29.6	40.0	64.7	202.9	423.3	644.5	840.4	1,009.4	1,153.1	9.59	3,801.4
Ipoh	323.8	388.8	457.2	520.2	574.0	625.8	683.5	743.8	803.4	2.30	148.1
Kuching	170.5	212.1	265.8	337.6	423.9	509.2	591.3	667.9	737.6	3.73	332.6
Petaling Jaya	241.1	290.2	342.6	392.9	438.1	481.7	529.2	578.0	625.8	2.41	159.5
Shah Alam	77.7	104.2	147.2	220.0	319.6	418.9	510.1	591.6	663.2	5.51	753.6
Kota Kinabalu	83.3	109.5	150.1	216.4	305.4	394.0	476.0	549.6	614.7	5.12	638.2
Ampang	199.9	239.7	280.9	317.8	348.1	377.0	409.9	444.9	479.7	2.21	139.9

Chart 5.121 Population age shift 2000 and 2020, Each Column Represents a Single Age Group

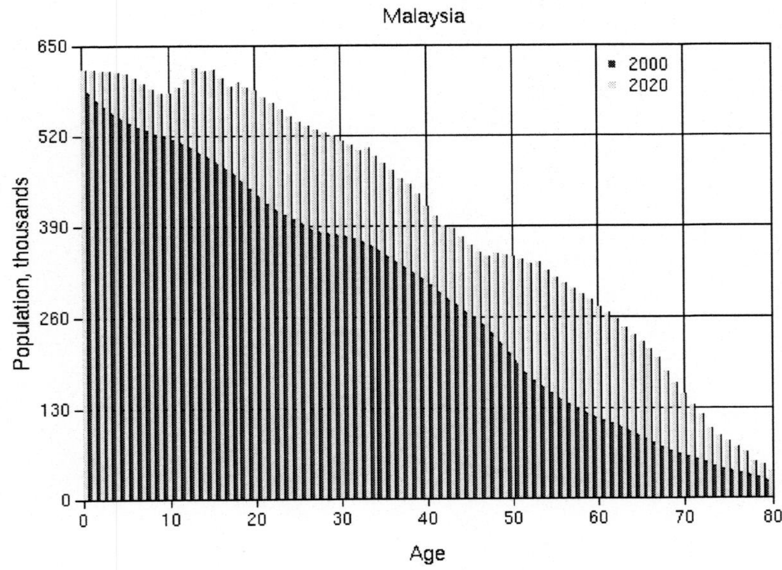

Chart 5.122 Population pyramids, 1980/2000/2010/2020

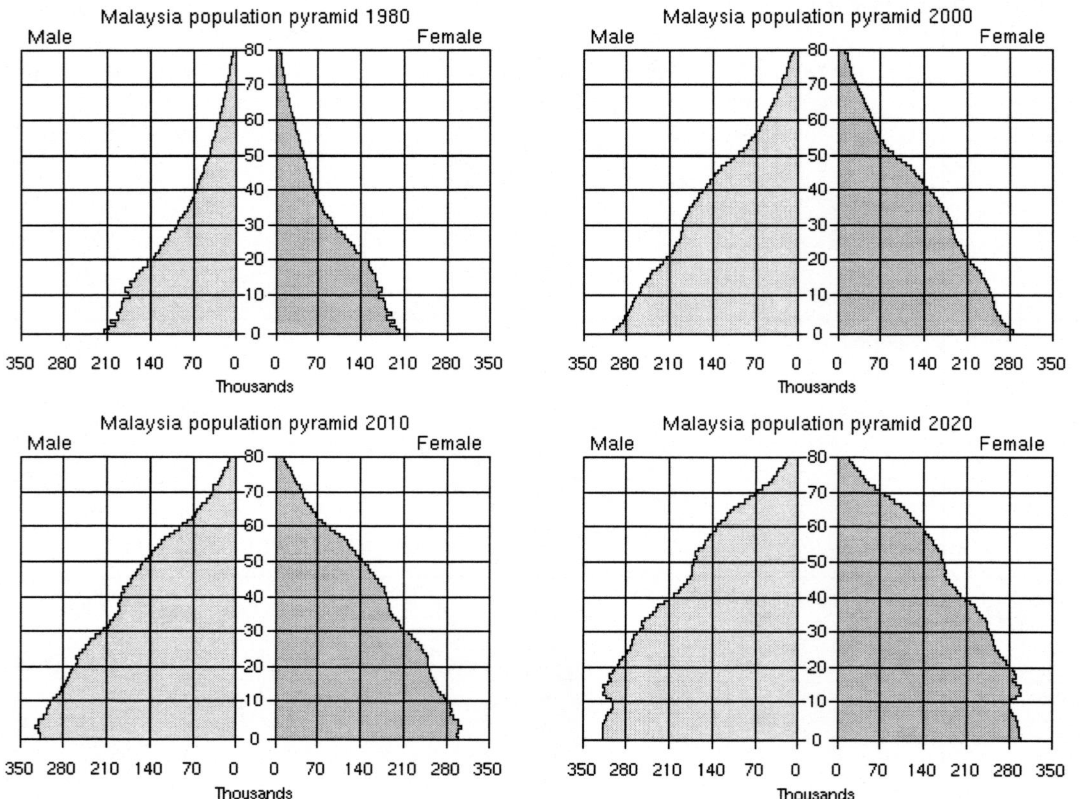

Chart 5.123 Major Cities: 1980, 2000 and 2020

Mexico

Table 5.181 Key population trends
'000

	1980	1985	1990	1995	2000	2005	2010	2015	2020	CAGR	Period growth
Population at January 1st	66,584.0	75,412.6	83,971.0	91,724.5	98,438.6	103,946.9	110,199.3	117,542.1	124,042.3	1.57	86.29
Male	33,249.6	37,607.4	41,839.9	45,622.2	48,722.4	51,238.4	54,169.9	57,741.3	60,911.5	1.52	83.20
Female	33,334.4	37,805.2	42,131.1	46,102.3	49,716.1	52,708.4	56,029.4	59,800.8	63,130.8	1.61	89.39
0-4 yrs	10,616.2	10,728.3	11,072.3	11,456.9	10,836.9	10,455.2	10,239.7	9,795.7	9,351.2	-0.32	-11.92
5-9 yrs	10,333.1	10,722.5	10,670.6	10,835.8	11,154.6	10,642.5	10,310.4	10,004.2	9,542.1	-0.20	-7.65
10-14 yrs	8,791.7	10,330.9	10,626.5	10,430.8	10,570.7	10,794.9	10,431.3	10,222.7	9,907.0	0.30	12.69
15-19 yrs	7,267.9	8,536.5	10,065.1	10,239.4	10,027.3	9,954.4	10,344.7	10,279.0	10,074.3	0.82	38.61
20-24 yrs	6,041.4	6,849.7	8,150.6	9,599.1	9,769.7	9,285.8	9,370.2	10,085.0	10,040.8	1.28	66.20
25-29 yrs	4,823.1	5,638.5	6,476.2	7,724.2	9,163.7	9,094.0	8,747.1	9,067.0	9,814.7	1.79	103.50
30-34 yrs	3,645.3	4,752.8	5,529.7	6,288.6	7,516.5	8,917.4	8,951.5	8,761.3	9,072.5	2.31	148.88
35-39 yrs	3,070.0	3,646.5	4,714.1	5,408.9	6,145.6	7,383.8	8,871.9	9,050.0	8,841.4	2.68	188.00
40-44 yrs	2,529.1	3,069.6	3,610.0	4,602.6	5,275.6	6,030.1	7,337.9	8,963.9	9,126.7	3.26	260.86
45-49 yrs	2,250.7	2,517.5	3,024.7	3,507.6	4,470.5	5,159.2	5,972.6	7,389.2	9,011.0	3.53	300.36
50-54 yrs	1,949.2	2,222.8	2,460.5	2,916.2	3,382.7	4,346.2	5,081.5	5,981.0	7,388.8	3.39	279.06
55-59 yrs	1,578.5	1,894.2	2,140.7	2,340.3	2,778.5	3,250.1	4,235.4	5,040.0	5,926.4	3.36	275.45
60-64 yrs	1,141.0	1,501.2	1,786.8	1,997.6	2,191.3	2,627.1	3,118.5	4,136.8	4,921.4	3.72	331.32
65-69 yrs	935.4	1,049.4	1,371.8	1,618.4	1,820.4	2,018.9	2,459.8	2,976.1	3,952.6	3.67	322.57
70-74 yrs	689.6	818.7	914.4	1,188.3	1,414.6	1,611.2	1,820.3	2,264.3	2,747.0	3.52	298.35
75-79 yrs	486.2	561.7	664.6	740.1	975.5	1,176.6	1,369.9	1,585.5	1,980.9	3.57	307.45
80+ yrs	435.7	571.7	692.3	829.8	944.5	1,199.4	1,536.7	1,940.5	2,343.6	4.30	437.84
Median age of population (years)	17.3	18.3	19.8	21.4	23.4	25.5	27.5	29.6	31.8	1.53	83.31

Table 5.182 Key economic trends
As stated

	1990	1995	2000	2005	2010	2015	2020	CAGR	Period growth
Total GDP (MX$ per capita)	92,721.9	91,494.5	111,190.2	115,696.1	114,952.3	137,899.8	160,416.3	1.84	73.0
Disposable income (MX$ per capita)	57,019.6	53,056.0	67,045.1	74,282.4	78,800.6	98,594.9	117,055.6	2.43	105.3
Disposable income (MX$ per household)	295,503.4	245,186.1	296,369.3	311,302.2	306,665.1	362,588.0	407,040.9	1.07	37.7
Number of households by annual household disposable income ('000)									
Over US$1,000	16,065.6	19,358.0	22,119.5	24,714.9	28,187.1	31,878.0	35,618.9	2.69	121.7
Over US$10,000	6,358.2	5,852.1	14,282.1	18,116.0	19,526.3	25,249.3	30,834.3	5.40	385.0
Over US$25,000	1,447.0	1,311.1	4,959.4	7,118.0	7,111.6	11,700.4	17,646.0	8.69	1,119.5
Over US$75,000	225.5	216.4	687.4	956.2	952.4	1,775.2	3,199.7	9.24	1,318.8
Over US$150,000	96.6	93.1	238.3	312.2	325.7	513.4	804.6	7.32	733.0
Total households	16,202.8	19,848.3	22,268.9	24,803.6	28,316.8	31,962.0	35,671.7	2.67	120.2

Note: Per capita data is shown at constant 2010 prices. Household disposable income bands are shown at current prices.

Table 5.183 Young generation
'000

	1980	1985	1990	1995	2000	2005	2010	2015	2020	CAGR	Period growth
Babies under 12 months	2,039	2,180	2,282	2,344	2,066	2,119	2,203	2,121	2,057	0.02	0.90
Infants under 24 months	4,143	4,327	4,526	4,666	4,199	4,210	4,184	4,004	3,851	-0.18	-7.05
Toddlers aged 1-4	8,577	8,548	8,790	9,113	8,771	8,336	8,037	7,675	7,294	-0.40	-14.96
Children aged 2-9	16,806	17,123	17,217	17,627	17,793	16,888	16,366	15,796	15,042	-0.28	-10.49
Female	8,264	8,407	8,429	8,617	8,728	8,305	8,051	7,757	7,376	-0.28	-10.74
Male	8,543	8,717	8,788	9,010	9,065	8,582	8,316	8,040	7,666	-0.27	-10.26
Tweenagers aged 10-14	8,792	10,331	10,627	10,431	10,571	10,795	10,431	10,223	9,907	0.30	12.69
Female	4,342	5,098	5,237	5,137	5,216	5,341	5,167	5,065	4,894	0.30	12.73
Male	4,450	5,233	5,389	5,294	5,355	5,454	5,264	5,158	5,013	0.30	12.64
Teenagers aged 13-19	10,578	12,521	14,307	14,384	14,169	14,222	14,535	14,379	14,070	0.72	33.01
Female	5,267	6,260	7,122	7,153	7,063	7,143	7,296	7,181	7,013	0.72	33.16
Male	5,311	6,261	7,185	7,230	7,106	7,079	7,239	7,198	7,057	0.71	32.87
Studying age 18-22	6,515	7,457	8,992	10,004	9,862	9,488	9,804	10,263	10,060	1.09	54.42
Female	3,267	3,767	4,536	5,021	4,961	4,815	4,993	5,176	5,046	1.09	54.45
Male	3,248	3,690	4,456	4,983	4,900	4,673	4,811	5,086	5,014	1.09	54.39
Young adults aged 15-29	18,132	21,025	24,692	27,563	28,961	28,334	28,462	29,431	29,930	1.26	65.06
Female	9,086	10,605	12,461	13,898	14,612	14,379	14,491	14,913	15,065	1.27	65.79
Male	9,046	10,420	12,231	13,665	14,349	13,955	13,971	14,518	14,865	1.25	64.33

Table 5.184 Middle-aged generation

'000

	1980	1985	1990	1995	2000	2005	2010	2015	2020	CAGR	Period growth
Middle-aged adults 30-59	15,023	18,103	21,480	25,064	29,569	35,087	40,451	45,185	49,367	3.02	228.6
Female	7,602	9,111	10,800	12,652	15,083	17,958	20,760	23,221	25,379	3.06	233.9
Male	7,421	8,992	10,679	12,412	14,486	17,129	19,691	21,965	23,987	2.98	223.2
Baby boomers aged 40-59	8,308	9,704	11,236	13,367	15,907	18,786	22,627	27,374	31,453	3.38	278.6
Female	4,295	4,949	5,656	6,706	8,067	9,624	11,690	14,143	16,226	3.38	277.8
Male	4,013	4,755	5,580	6,660	7,840	9,162	10,937	13,231	15,227	3.39	279.5

Table 5.185 Elderly population

'000

	1980	1985	1990	1995	2000	2005	2010	2015	2020	CAGR	Period growth
Elderly population (60+)	3,688	4,503	5,430	6,374	7,346	8,633	10,305	12,903	15,945	3.73	332.4
Female	2,009	2,472	3,001	3,526	4,023	4,665	5,514	6,885	8,532	3.68	324.6
Male	1,679	2,030	2,429	2,848	3,324	3,968	4,791	6,019	7,414	3.78	341.6

Table 5.186 Population of biggest cities 1980-2020

'000

	1980	1985	1990	1995	2000	2005	2010	2015	2020	CAGR	Period growth
Mexico City	6,870.7	7,615.6	8,092.4	8,270.4	8,391.5	8,463.9	8,796.5	9,188.4	9,594.3	0.84	39.64
Ecatepec	876.7	1,032.2	1,218.1	1,455.9	1,621.8	1,687.5	1,784.4	1,883.3	1,978.5	2.06	125.69
Guadalajara	1,448.3	1,587.0	1,650.0	1,633.1	1,646.2	1,600.9	1,610.2	1,647.4	1,698.7	0.40	17.29
Puebla	759.3	878.4	1,007.2	1,157.6	1,271.7	1,399.5	1,537.3	1,658.6	1,764.8	2.13	132.42
Tijuana	394.0	513.3	698.8	966.1	1,148.7	1,286.2	1,428.7	1,551.2	1,656.3	3.66	320.44
Juarez	529.2	640.7	789.5	995.8	1,187.3	1,301.5	1,418.7	1,524.1	1,617.6	2.83	205.68
Leon	519.8	623.8	758.3	941.6	1,020.8	1,137.5	1,259.5	1,365.1	1,456.1	2.61	180.12
Monterrey	912.4	1,009.4	1,069.0	1,088.0	1,110.9	1,133.1	1,187.3	1,246.3	1,305.3	0.90	43.06
Zapopan	443.0	538.8	668.3	850.3	910.7	1,026.5	1,144.9	1,245.9	1,332.0	2.79	200.68
Nezahualcoyotl	1,108.4	1,212.2	1,255.5	1,233.7	1,225.1	1,136.3	1,095.0	1,088.4	1,102.1	-0.01	-0.56

Chart 5.124 Population age shift 2000 and 2020, Each Column Represents a Single Age Group

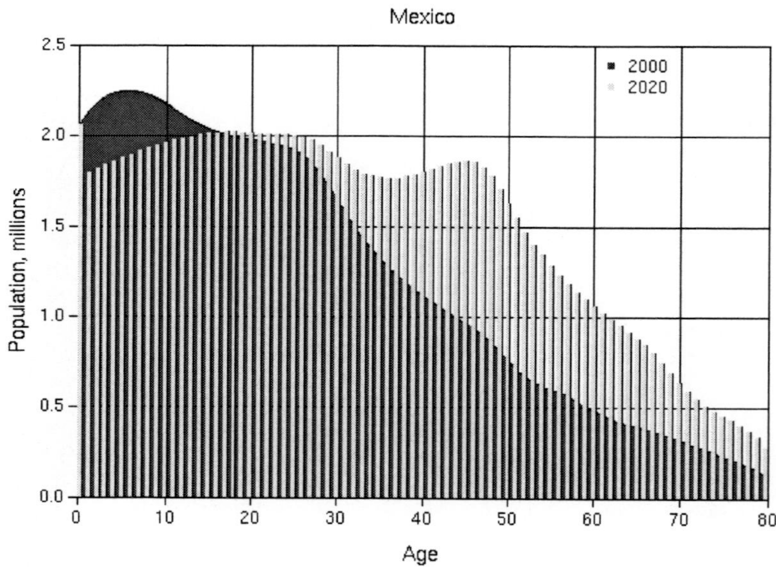

Chart 5.125 Population pyramids, 1980/2000/2010/2020

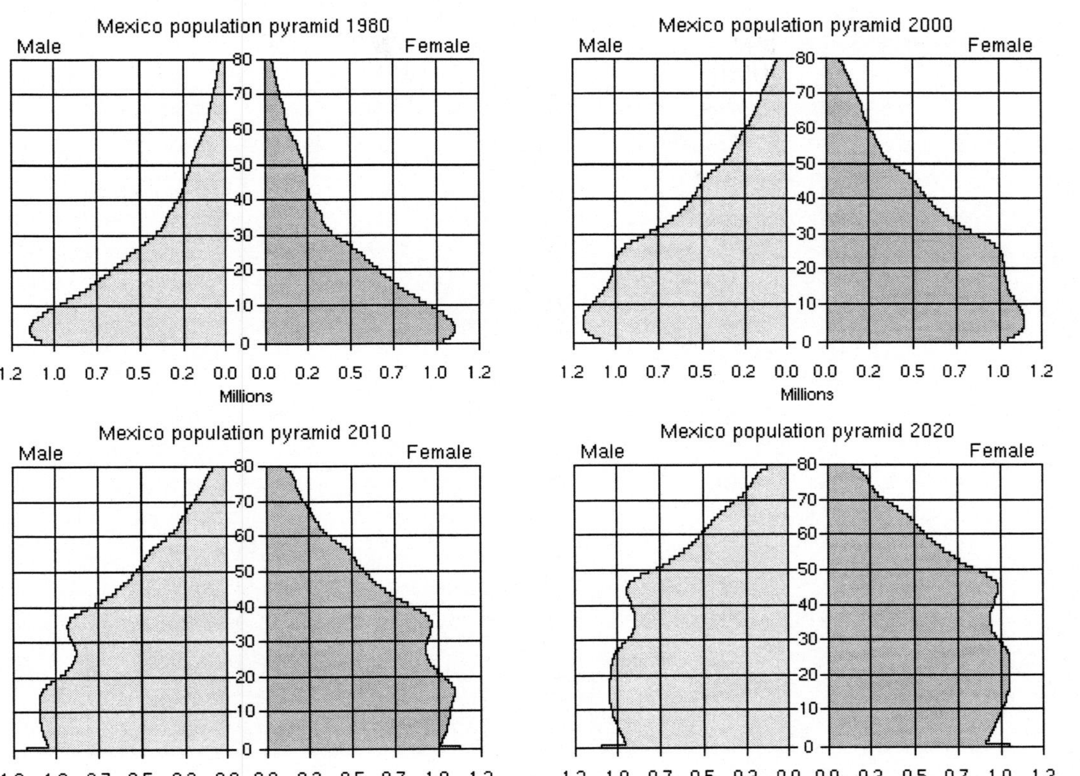

Chart 5.126 Major Cities: 1980, 2000 and 2020

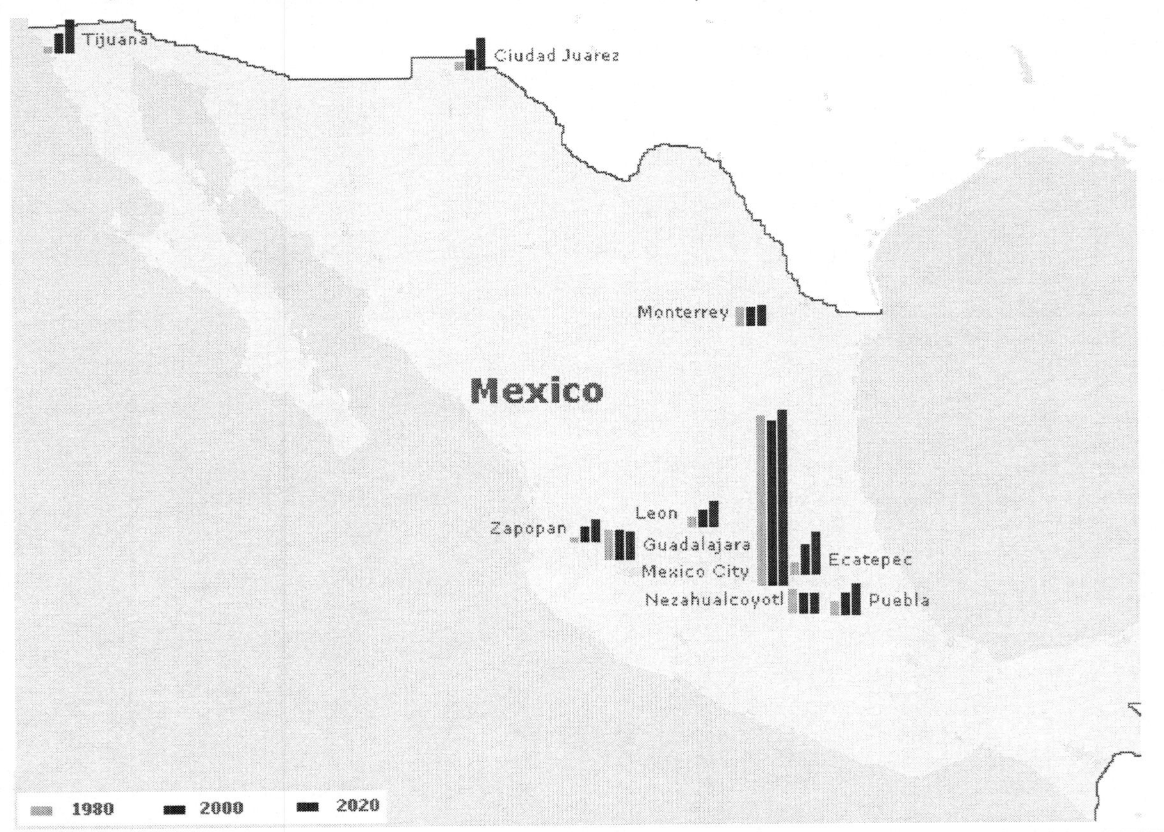

Morocco

Table 5.187 Key population trends

'000

	1980	1985	1990	1995	2000	2005	2010	2015	2020	CAGR	Period growth
Population at January 1st	19,566.9	22,299.1	24,807.7	26,950.6	28,827.1	30,495.0	32,381.3	34,330.5	36,199.8	1.55	85.01
Male	9,786.2	11,144.3	12,371.3	13,397.2	14,257.3	15,008.1	15,897.2	16,828.9	17,722.4	1.50	81.10
Female	9,780.7	11,154.7	12,436.5	13,553.4	14,569.8	15,486.9	16,484.1	17,501.6	18,477.5	1.60	88.92
0-4 yrs	3,142.0	3,502.7	3,459.3	3,289.2	3,090.3	2,963.8	3,120.2	3,199.4	3,143.4	0.00	0.05
5-9 yrs	2,777.6	3,034.6	3,401.0	3,403.5	3,238.1	3,047.1	2,936.4	3,081.2	3,178.5	0.34	14.43
10-14 yrs	2,423.8	2,739.6	3,015.5	3,371.5	3,376.0	3,219.3	3,028.1	2,926.1	3,069.9	0.59	26.66
15-19 yrs	2,119.7	2,383.2	2,697.1	2,956.6	3,296.4	3,300.3	3,174.2	2,989.9	2,891.0	0.78	36.39
20-24 yrs	1,916.4	2,076.5	2,302.8	2,579.9	2,796.3	3,134.1	3,202.1	3,092.5	2,915.4	1.05	52.13
25-29 yrs	1,447.9	1,877.0	1,990.4	2,170.1	2,404.0	2,621.5	3,018.5	3,106.1	3,005.7	1.84	107.59
30-34 yrs	1,060.6	1,419.4	1,804.3	1,888.4	2,054.3	2,284.1	2,529.0	2,939.4	3,034.4	2.66	186.10
35-39 yrs	828.4	1,034.9	1,368.3	1,727.7	1,829.7	1,985.5	2,216.3	2,471.0	2,885.5	3.17	248.33
40-44 yrs	829.2	810.0	999.6	1,310.7	1,699.5	1,796.4	1,932.6	2,169.3	2,427.4	2.72	192.75
45-49 yrs	700.5	805.4	784.7	964.2	1,295.4	1,680.6	1,756.6	1,896.8	2,135.4	2.83	204.85
50-54 yrs	661.8	681.1	783.0	761.2	945.4	1,268.8	1,639.5	1,720.5	1,862.7	2.62	181.47
55-59 yrs	447.2	632.2	657.3	752.9	736.1	913.8	1,219.9	1,583.8	1,667.8	3.35	272.96
60-64 yrs	403.8	413.7	590.5	613.4	706.6	693.7	857.7	1,151.0	1,500.5	3.34	271.61
65-69 yrs	320.4	358.9	364.3	524.9	547.8	636.2	625.0	777.8	1,049.5	3.01	227.60
70-74 yrs	218.8	258.5	288.7	297.7	432.2	455.2	533.8	528.7	663.7	2.81	203.39
75-79 yrs	158.7	152.2	180.6	203.3	213.6	316.1	335.6	401.2	401.2	2.35	152.76
80+ yrs	110.3	119.1	120.3	135.5	165.4	178.4	255.7	295.8	367.7	3.06	233.28
Median age of population (years)	18.3	18.9	19.7	20.8	22.4	24.3	26.2	28.0	29.8	1.22	62.59

Table 5.188 Key economic trends

As stated

	1990	1995	2000	2005	2010	2015	2020	CAGR	Period growth
Total GDP (Dh per capita)	15,005.1	14,464.2	16,315.9	19,664.8	23,456.5	28,117.4	33,875.6	2.75	125.8
Disposable income (Dh per capita)	10,945.2	10,342.9	10,808.5	12,197.4	16,894.8	21,953.5	27,223.9	3.08	148.7
Disposable income (Dh per household)	68,407.4	61,042.4	60,041.2	64,240.8	84,632.9	104,969.6	124,673.4	2.02	82.3
Number of households by annual household disposable income ('000)									
Over US$1,000	3,795.5	4,429.4	4,975.1	5,685.8	6,418.0	7,159.9	7,896.7	2.47	108.1
Over US$10,000	292.2	449.8	377.8	810.5	1,723.6	3,198.8	5,180.8	10.06	1,673.2
Over US$25,000	62.6	81.7	80.1	138.6	284.0	605.2	1,290.6	10.62	1,962.7
Over US$75,000	15.9	20.7	20.4	34.4	59.1	101.4	170.4	8.22	970.7
Over US$150,000	6.7	8.7	8.6	14.5	24.9	42.8	70.6	8.16	952.3
Total households	3,969.3	4,566.5	5,189.4	5,790.1	6,464.1	7,179.9	7,904.7	2.32	99.1

Note: Per capita data is shown at constant 2010 prices. Household disposable income bands are shown at current prices.

Table 5.189 Young generation

'000

	1980	1985	1990	1995	2000	2005	2010	2015	2020	CAGR	Period growth
Babies under 12 months	648.9	754.5	662.9	655.0	609.6	596.9	657.9	635.8	619.0	-0.12	-4.62
Infants under 24 months	1,293.1	1,479.0	1,348.8	1,307.8	1,223.4	1,189.3	1,295.9	1,278.0	1,243.4	-0.10	-3.84
Toddlers aged 1-4	2,493.1	2,748.2	2,796.4	2,634.2	2,480.7	2,366.9	2,462.3	2,563.6	2,524.5	0.03	1.26
Children aged 2-9	4,626.6	5,058.3	5,511.5	5,384.8	5,105.1	4,821.6	4,760.7	5,002.6	5,078.6	0.23	9.77
Female	2,275.4	2,481.4	2,708.2	2,646.9	2,510.4	2,371.2	2,339.4	2,457.7	2,493.5	0.23	9.59
Male	2,351.2	2,576.9	2,803.3	2,737.9	2,594.7	2,450.4	2,421.4	2,544.9	2,585.1	0.24	9.95
Tweenagers aged 10-14	2,423.8	2,739.6	3,015.5	3,371.5	3,376.0	3,219.3	3,028.1	2,926.1	3,069.9	0.59	26.66
Female	1,190.9	1,347.3	1,481.2	1,658.3	1,661.9	1,585.1	1,490.4	1,439.6	1,509.6	0.59	26.77
Male	1,232.9	1,392.2	1,534.4	1,713.2	1,714.1	1,634.2	1,537.7	1,486.6	1,560.2	0.59	26.55
Teenagers aged 13-19	3,048.7	3,442.3	3,858.7	4,272.2	4,657.1	4,605.3	4,405.7	4,155.0	4,095.7	0.74	34.34
Female	1,532.6	1,693.6	1,904.5	2,110.5	2,310.8	2,286.9	2,176.0	2,049.6	2,018.9	0.69	31.73
Male	1,516.1	1,748.7	1,954.2	2,161.7	2,346.2	2,318.5	2,229.7	2,105.4	2,076.8	0.79	36.98
Studying age 18-22	2,012.7	2,176.8	2,467.6	2,724.9	3,011.6	3,250.6	3,207.5	3,059.5	2,883.8	0.90	43.29
Female	1,014.9	1,096.4	1,221.4	1,362.4	1,516.5	1,640.1	1,600.4	1,517.6	1,429.4	0.86	40.83
Male	997.7	1,080.5	1,246.1	1,362.5	1,495.1	1,610.5	1,607.1	1,541.9	1,454.5	0.95	45.78
Young adults aged 15-29	5,483.9	6,336.6	6,990.4	7,706.6	8,496.7	9,055.9	9,394.8	9,188.5	8,812.1	1.19	60.69
Female	2,752.4	3,179.2	3,511.6	3,867.7	4,313.9	4,614.3	4,739.2	4,597.2	4,389.9	1.17	59.49
Male	2,731.5	3,157.4	3,478.8	3,838.9	4,182.8	4,441.6	4,655.6	4,591.3	4,422.2	1.21	61.90

Table 5.190 Middle-aged generation

'000

	1980	1985	1990	1995	2000	2005	2010	2015	2020	CAGR	Period growth
Middle-aged adults 30-59	4,528	5,383	6,397	7,405	8,560	9,929	11,294	12,781	14,013	2.86	209.5
Female	2,349	2,785	3,293	3,828	4,391	5,112	5,884	6,715	7,379	2.90	214.2
Male	2,179	2,599	3,104	3,577	4,169	4,817	5,409	6,066	6,634	2.82	204.5
Baby boomers aged 40-59	2,639	2,929	3,225	3,789	4,676	5,660	6,549	7,370	8,093	2.84	206.7
Female	1,370	1,549	1,687	1,960	2,359	2,857	3,359	3,868	4,316	2.91	215.0
Male	1,268	1,380	1,537	1,829	2,318	2,802	3,190	3,502	3,777	2.77	197.8

Table 5.191 Elderly population

'000

	1980	1985	1990	1995	2000	2005	2010	2015	2020	CAGR	Period growth
Elderly population (60+)	1,212.0	1,302.5	1,544.3	1,774.7	2,065.6	2,279.7	2,607.8	3,154.4	3,982.6	3.02	228.6
Female	583.8	635.3	781.7	910.8	1,092.9	1,221.7	1,395.1	1,665.5	2,096.4	3.25	259.1
Male	628.2	667.2	762.6	863.9	972.7	1,057.9	1,212.7	1,489.0	1,886.2	2.79	200.3

Table 5.192 Population of biggest cities 1980-2020

'000

	1980	1985	1990	1995	2000	2005	2010	2015	2020	CAGR	Period growth
Casablanca	2,082.5	2,229.8	2,377.6	2,540.1	2,738.6	2,981.0	3,215.5	3,428.4	3,610.4	1.39	73.4
Rabat	832.6	995.5	1,173.0	1,336.0	1,490.2	1,655.3	1,817.0	1,967.9	2,101.6	2.34	152.4
Fez	400.1	532.5	675.7	791.5	880.4	962.7	1,040.8	1,112.1	1,173.4	2.73	193.3
Marrakech	408.4	492.9	585.4	671.2	752.8	840.4	926.6	1,007.5	1,079.7	2.46	164.3
Agadir	283.5	356.6	439.7	521.9	605.0	696.9	789.5	878.4	960.0	3.10	238.6
Tangier	230.9	327.5	435.0	528.1	606.9	685.1	762.1	835.0	900.8	3.46	290.1
Meknes	305.0	344.4	387.8	434.4	486.9	548.4	609.9	668.0	720.4	2.17	136.2
Oujda	248.3	279.7	312.6	343.3	373.7	407.3	439.6	469.0	494.1	1.74	99.0
Kanitra	173.6	213.0	255.9	294.5	329.6	366.3	402.3	435.9	465.7	2.50	168.2
Tetouan	190.1	215.6	242.8	269.2	296.2	326.5	356.1	383.4	407.4	1.92	114.4

Chart 5.127 Population age shift 2000 and 2020, Each Column Represents a Single Age Group

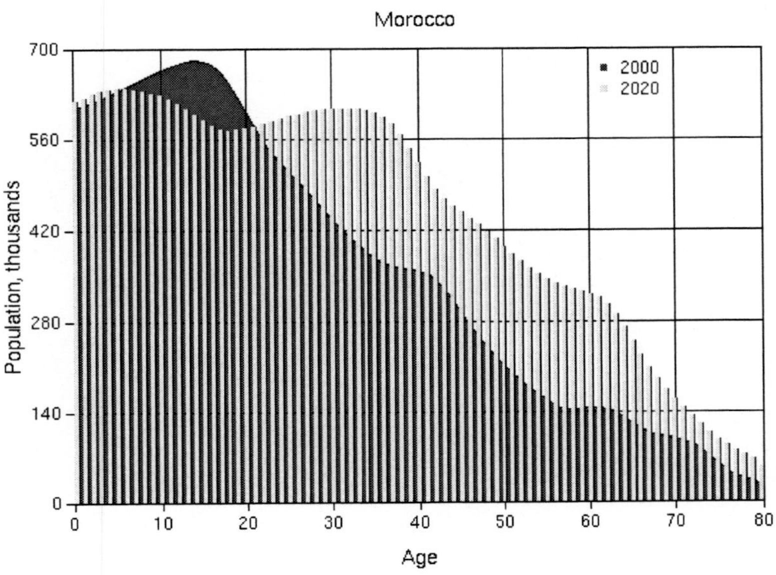

Chart 5.128 Population pyramids, 1980/2000/2010/2020

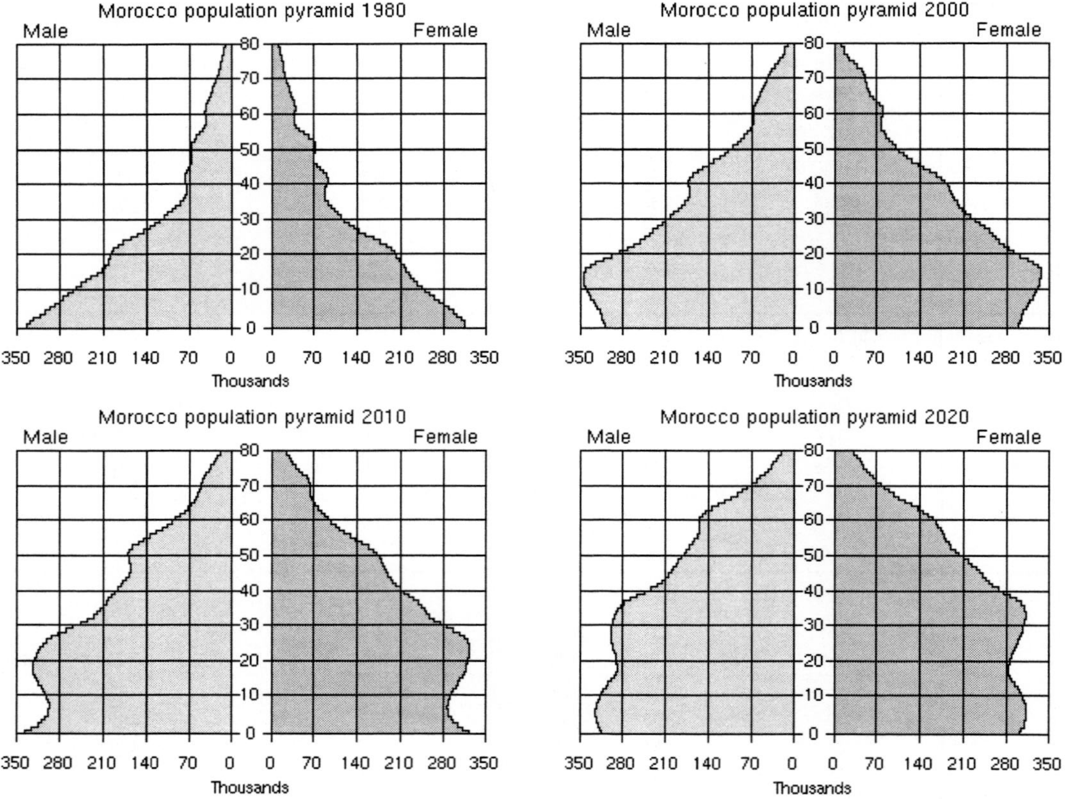

Chart 5.129 Major Cities: 1980, 2000 and 2020

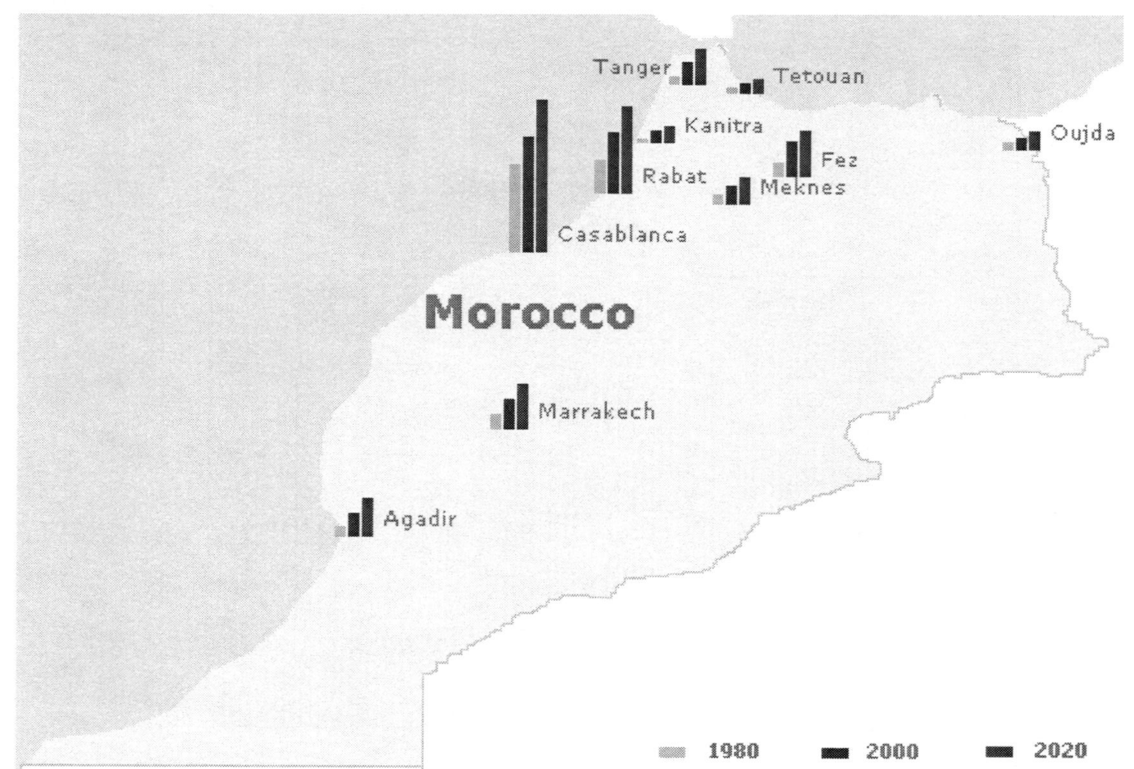

Netherlands

Table 5.193 Key population trends

'000

	1980	1985	1990	1995	2000	2005	2010	2015	2020	CAGR	Period growth
Population at January 1st	14,091.0	14,453.8	14,892.6	15,424.1	15,864.0	16,305.5	16,439.4	16,590.5	16,725.9	0.43	18.70
Male	6,994.3	7,149.6	7,358.5	7,627.5	7,846.3	8,066.0	8,133.3	8,213.8	8,284.0	0.42	18.44
Female	7,096.7	7,304.2	7,534.1	7,796.6	8,017.6	8,239.5	8,306.1	8,376.7	8,441.9	0.43	18.95
0-4 yrs	882.1	874.0	927.1	988.7	983.5	1,010.6	907.7	874.0	885.2	0.01	0.35
5-9 yrs	1,079.3	888.8	887.4	945.3	1,001.7	987.9	997.7	899.8	867.3	-0.55	-19.65
10-14 yrs	1,222.7	1,087.4	900.4	904.4	960.4	1,010.0	981.0	997.0	898.5	-0.77	-26.52
15-19 yrs	1,247.7	1,234.3	1,107.3	921.8	927.5	979.4	1,010.4	986.8	1,003.2	-0.54	-19.59
20-24 yrs	1,191.2	1,267.9	1,263.8	1,145.2	955.9	969.4	992.5	1,030.1	1,004.6	-0.43	-15.67
25-29 yrs	1,146.9	1,201.5	1,291.3	1,301.9	1,176.3	992.9	979.3	1,009.3	1,046.5	-0.23	-8.75
30-34 yrs	1,187.7	1,146.0	1,210.9	1,313.7	1,314.4	1,191.4	981.7	974.4	1,006.5	-0.41	-15.26
35-39 yrs	915.8	1,180.6	1,146.2	1,220.3	1,314.9	1,314.1	1,167.5	962.3	958.1	0.11	4.62
40-44 yrs	804.9	908.4	1,175.8	1,146.4	1,214.3	1,307.8	1,289.9	1,149.8	944.3	0.40	17.31
45-49 yrs	767.4	794.6	899.5	1,167.0	1,134.4	1,201.7	1,285.3	1,275.5	1,135.2	0.98	47.94
50-54 yrs	727.8	753.1	779.2	884.3	1,145.3	1,113.5	1,176.2	1,268.5	1,259.3	1.38	73.03
55-59 yrs	719.8	705.0	728.4	757.1	859.4	1,114.1	1,081.0	1,151.1	1,245.9	1.38	73.09
60-64 yrs	582.4	682.4	669.7	694.4	723.5	824.1	1,074.9	1,046.8	1,116.7	1.64	91.75
65-69 yrs	540.3	533.9	629.1	620.5	644.5	677.5	778.2	1,037.1	1,006.4	1.57	86.27
70-74 yrs	443.6	470.7	468.0	555.7	550.4	578.0	617.6	722.5	983.6	2.01	121.73
75-79 yrs	319.5	354.5	380.9	381.6	457.3	459.6	493.8	535.6	640.0	1.75	100.27
80+ yrs	311.9	370.7	427.7	475.8	500.3	573.6	624.7	670.1	724.7	2.13	132.36
Median age of population (years)	31.2	32.9	34.4	35.8	37.3	38.9	40.8	42.6	43.7	0.85	40.11

Table 5.194 Key economic trends

As stated

	1990	1995	2000	2005	2010	2015	2020	CAGR	Period growth
Total GDP (EUR per capita)	25,789.5	27,619.8	32,743.9	34,016.3	35,564.1	38,774.8	44,015.0	1.80	70.7
Disposable income (EUR per capita)	14,447.3	14,449.5	15,906.7	16,806.0	17,134.0	18,940.8	21,631.4	1.35	49.7
Disposable income (EUR per household)	35,498.7	34,203.6	37,005.9	38,645.0	38,473.5	41,816.5	47,179.5	0.95	32.9
Number of households by annual household disposable income ('000)									
Over US$1,000	6,060.9	6,515.9	6,818.9	7,090.9	7,321.2	7,514.7	7,668.7	0.79	26.5
Over US$10,000	5,793.4	6,338.8	6,562.1	7,032.6	7,268.8	7,484.6	7,655.6	0.93	32.1
Over US$25,000	3,147.6	4,108.5	3,384.4	5,913.6	6,287.8	6,883.7	7,367.6	2.88	134.1
Over US$75,000	266.7	361.7	271.4	792.4	1,052.5	1,666.5	2,792.7	8.14	947.1
Over US$150,000	104.6	131.8	114.1	210.5	247.0	322.1	457.8	5.05	337.8
Total households	6,061.0	6,516.0	6,819.0	7,091.0	7,321.2	7,514.7	7,668.7	0.79	26.5

Note: Per capita data is shown at constant 2010 prices. Household disposable income bands are shown at current prices.

Table 5.195 Young generation

'000

	1980	1985	1990	1995	2000	2005	2010	2015	2020	CAGR	Period growth
Babies under 12 months	174.4	173.7	187.5	195.9	201.7	193.8	177.0	174.5	179.0	0.06	2.61
Infants under 24 months	350.2	343.3	373.9	391.3	402.8	395.1	356.2	349.2	357.3	0.05	2.01
Toddlers aged 1-4	707.7	700.4	739.6	792.8	781.7	816.9	730.8	699.5	706.2	-0.01	-0.21
Children aged 2-9	1,611.2	1,419.5	1,440.6	1,542.7	1,582.4	1,603.5	1,549.2	1,424.6	1,395.2	-0.36	-13.41
Female	787.0	693.5	704.8	754.2	772.8	783.2	756.0	693.4	679.2	-0.37	-13.69
Male	824.2	726.0	735.8	788.5	809.6	820.3	793.2	731.1	715.9	-0.35	-13.14
Tweenagers aged 10-14	1,222.7	1,087.4	900.4	904.4	960.4	1,010.0	981.0	997.0	898.5	-0.77	-26.52
Female	597.2	531.8	439.5	442.0	470.0	493.2	478.1	485.4	435.8	-0.78	-27.03
Male	625.5	555.6	460.9	462.4	490.3	516.8	502.9	511.6	462.7	-0.75	-26.03
Teenagers aged 13-19	1,738.1	1,711.7	1,472.3	1,292.7	1,306.6	1,388.7	1,396.5	1,394.9	1,370.2	-0.59	-21.16
Female	849.1	836.2	720.1	632.1	638.5	678.8	681.2	679.1	665.7	-0.61	-21.60
Male	889.0	875.5	752.1	660.6	668.1	709.8	715.3	715.8	704.6	-0.58	-20.75
Studying age 18-22	1,216.5	1,263.5	1,243.2	1,016.3	947.9	961.0	1,006.5	999.2	1,018.4	-0.44	-16.28
Female	596.4	618.5	609.2	500.2	466.8	472.3	494.8	489.7	498.3	-0.45	-16.45
Male	620.1	645.0	634.0	516.1	481.1	488.7	511.6	509.5	520.1	-0.44	-16.12
Young adults aged 15-29	3,585.8	3,703.7	3,662.4	3,368.9	3,059.6	2,941.7	2,982.1	3,026.1	3,054.3	-0.40	-14.82
Female	1,754.0	1,816.0	1,792.3	1,649.6	1,506.7	1,453.3	1,472.7	1,491.3	1,500.5	-0.39	-14.45
Male	1,831.7	1,887.7	1,870.1	1,719.3	1,552.9	1,488.3	1,509.5	1,534.8	1,553.8	-0.41	-15.17

Table 5.196 Middle-aged generation

'000

	1980	1985	1990	1995	2000	2005	2010	2015	2020	CAGR	Period growth
Middle-aged adults 30-59	5,123	5,488	5,940	6,489	6,983	7,243	6,982	6,781	6,549	0.62	27.8
Female	2,529	2,699	2,917	3,185	3,434	3,582	3,475	3,390	3,282	0.65	29.8
Male	2,594	2,789	3,023	3,304	3,549	3,660	3,507	3,392	3,267	0.58	25.9
Baby boomers aged 40-59	3,020	3,161	3,583	3,955	4,354	4,737	4,832	4,845	4,585	1.05	51.8
Female	1,515	1,566	1,762	1,943	2,145	2,343	2,398	2,416	2,296	1.04	51.5
Male	1,505	1,595	1,821	2,012	2,208	2,394	2,434	2,429	2,289	1.05	52.1

Table 5.197 Elderly population

'000

	1980	1985	1990	1995	2000	2005	2010	2015	2020	CAGR	Period growth
Elderly population (60+)	2,197.7	2,412.2	2,575.3	2,728.0	2,875.9	3,112.8	3,589.2	4,012.1	4,471.3	1.79	103.5
Female	1,258.2	1,396.5	1,497.1	1,575.1	1,638.3	1,734.9	1,950.7	2,146.6	2,370.0	1.60	88.4
Male	939.5	1,015.6	1,078.2	1,152.9	1,237.6	1,377.9	1,638.5	1,865.5	2,101.3	2.03	123.7

Table 5.198 Population of biggest cities 1980-2020

'000

	1980	1985	1990	1995	2000	2005	2010	2015	2020	CAGR	Period growth
Amsterdam	716.9	704.0	695.2	714.7	731.3	748.0	749.0	756.3	765.7	0.16	6.80
Rotterdam	579.2	580.6	579.2	590.9	592.7	591.1	576.8	573.0	574.4	-0.02	-0.82
The Hague	456.9	451.5	441.5	439.6	441.1	462.9	483.9	501.6	515.5	0.30	12.84
Utrecht	253.3	249.9	245.7	249.0	253.8	279.8	303.4	321.0	333.7	0.69	31.75
Eindhoven	194.5	193.2	191.5	196.8	201.7	208.3	212.0	216.3	220.2	0.31	13.26
Tilburg	169.9	173.2	175.9	184.8	193.1	199.9	203.5	207.5	211.4	0.55	24.37
Breda	137.8	141.6	144.9	152.6	160.6	175.4	187.9	197.5	204.5	0.99	48.48
Groningen	161.3	165.2	167.9	170.8	173.1	180.1	184.9	189.5	193.6	0.46	20.00
Nijmegen	147.6	146.4	144.7	148.2	152.2	164.4	174.8	183.0	189.1	0.62	28.09
Apeldoorn	138.2	143.5	147.6	150.8	153.3	159.0	162.8	166.6	170.0	0.52	23.02

Chart 5.130 Population age shift 2000 and 2020, Each Column Represents a Single Age Group

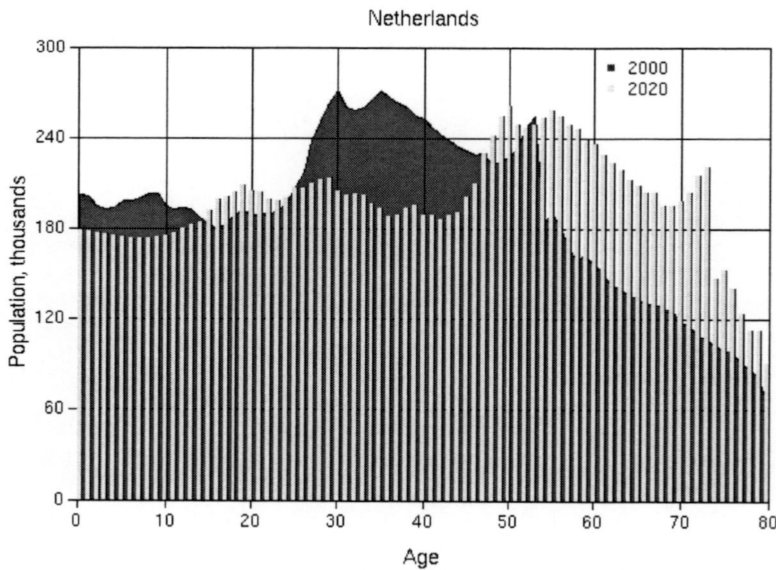

Chart 5.131 Population pyramids, 1980/2000/2010/2020

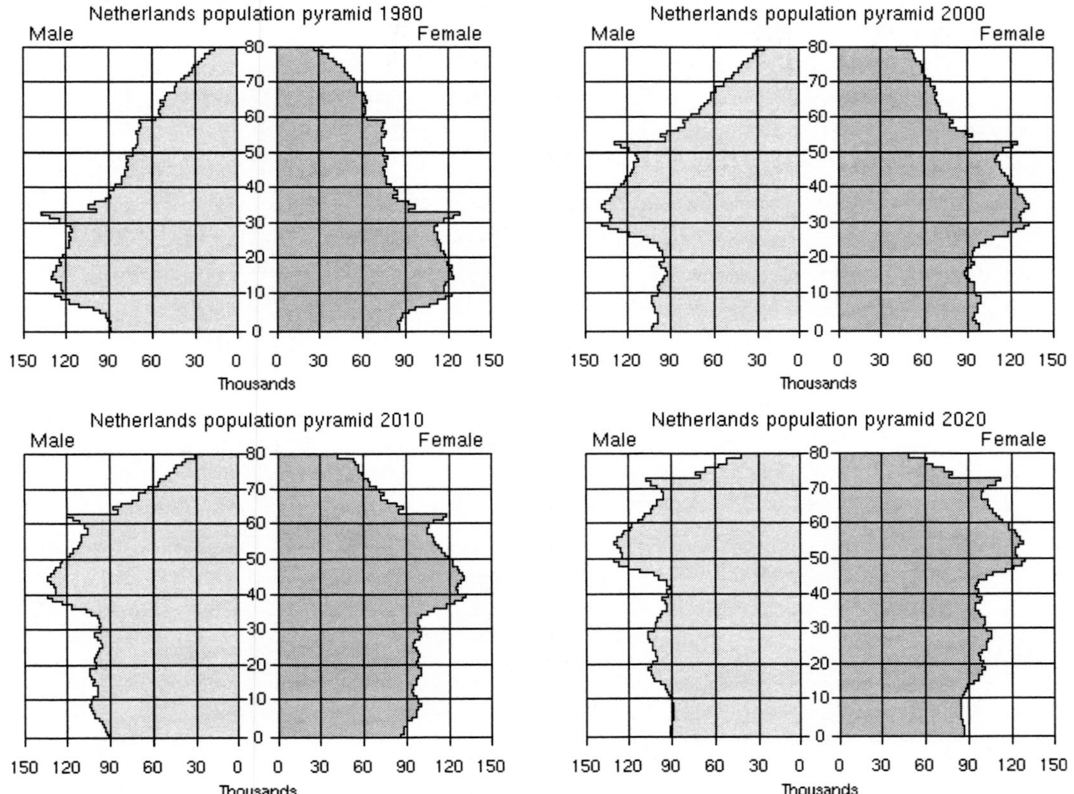

Chart 5.132 Major Cities: 1980, 2000 and 2020

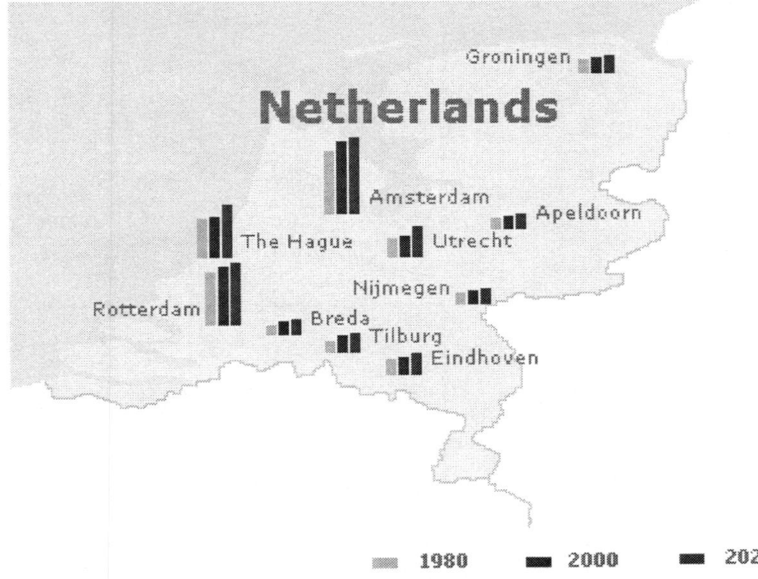

New Zealand

Table 5.199 Key population trends

'000

	1980	1985	1990	1995	2000	2005	2010	2015	2020	CAGR	Period growth
Population at January 1st	3,198.2	3,336.2	3,452.7	3,673.5	3,857.8	4,133.9	4,352.4	4,551.1	4,735.7	0.99	48.07
Male	1,587.1	1,648.6	1,698.8	1,810.9	1,893.8	2,025.2	2,134.9	2,235.8	2,328.5	0.96	46.72
Female	1,611.2	1,687.5	1,753.8	1,862.6	1,964.0	2,108.7	2,217.6	2,315.4	2,407.2	1.01	49.41
0-4 yrs	262.8	262.4	279.3	297.0	283.4	284.3	313.5	312.5	306.2	0.38	16.50
5-9 yrs	292.7	261.7	258.7	285.0	302.0	292.4	287.4	317.2	316.4	0.20	8.11
10-14 yrs	293.7	294.8	259.9	265.5	293.3	313.5	296.7	291.3	321.2	0.22	9.39
15-19 yrs	307.8	297.2	295.6	268.3	273.6	306.1	321.1	303.6	298.4	-0.08	-3.05
20-24 yrs	281.5	297.0	282.6	286.9	254.3	288.4	304.3	318.3	301.3	0.17	7.01
25-29 yrs	248.5	274.9	288.0	279.2	269.0	255.9	282.6	296.2	310.4	0.56	24.92
30-34 yrs	239.2	251.7	276.8	301.6	291.7	293.5	269.6	295.8	309.5	0.65	29.36
35-39 yrs	196.2	239.1	249.7	285.2	311.9	308.2	302.5	278.3	304.6	1.11	55.21
40-44 yrs	169.1	194.9	237.4	256.2	290.7	323.9	312.7	306.2	282.5	1.29	67.03
45-49 yrs	156.2	165.7	190.7	240.5	257.4	296.2	323.2	311.3	305.2	1.69	95.41
50-54 yrs	158.7	151.7	159.9	189.1	238.6	256.8	291.2	317.4	306.2	1.66	92.88
55-59 yrs	150.4	154.3	145.4	156.3	185.8	235.8	250.7	284.3	310.6	1.83	106.47
60-64 yrs	129.5	143.5	145.8	139.3	152.5	182.5	229.6	244.0	277.3	1.92	114.14
65-69 yrs	112.2	117.2	130.0	134.6	131.1	146.7	175.5	220.4	235.1	1.87	109.55
70-74 yrs	87.4	96.3	99.8	114.5	119.5	119.8	136.5	163.6	206.6	2.17	136.37
75-79 yrs	59.7	69.3	77.0	81.4	95.0	101.9	104.7	120.8	146.1	2.26	144.81
80+ yrs	52.5	64.3	75.9	93.0	107.8	127.9	150.6	170.0	198.1	3.38	277.39
Median age of population (years)	28.2	29.6	31.1	32.6	34.3	35.5	36.8	37.5	38.3	0.77	35.91

Table 5.200 Key economic trends

As stated

	1990	1995	2000	2005	2010	2015	2020	CAGR	Period growth
Total GDP (NZ$ per capita)	31,072.6	33,628.6	36,846.9	41,539.8	41,677.1	46,183.8	51,051.3	1.67	64.3
Disposable income (NZ$ per capita)	19,310.3	18,735.0	21,972.8	22,107.9	22,961.8	26,191.2	29,354.5	1.41	52.0
Disposable income (NZ$ per household)	58,127.3	54,993.5	63,947.5	63,766.9	65,379.6	73,664.5	81,645.8	1.14	40.5
Number of households by annual household disposable income ('000)									
Over US$1,000	1,145.4	1,249.4	1,320.5	1,429.3	1,513.4	1,601.7	1,687.1	1.30	47.3
Over US$10,000	932.9	1,038.6	974.5	1,255.6	1,195.2	1,288.9	1,399.7	1.36	50.0
Over US$25,000	379.1	490.1	379.1	821.6	681.9	783.8	915.5	2.98	141.5
Over US$75,000	37.5	57.8	45.4	166.0	114.2	156.3	218.0	6.05	482.1
Over US$150,000	14.7	19.4	16.0	35.4	26.6	33.1	43.2	3.67	194.5
Total households	1,147.0	1,251.5	1,325.6	1,433.2	1,528.6	1,618.1	1,702.7	1.33	48.4

Note: Per capita data is shown at constant 2010 prices. Household disposable income bands are shown at current prices.

Table 5.201 Young generation

'000

	1980	1985	1990	1995	2000	2005	2010	2015	2020	CAGR	Period growth
Babies under 12 months	52.9	53.4	59.3	58.0	56.8	57.8	63.9	61.5	60.8	0.35	15.05
Infants under 24 months	105.1	106.0	116.6	115.8	112.1	115.2	128.2	123.3	121.8	0.37	15.85
Toddlers aged 1-4	210.0	209.0	219.9	239.0	226.6	226.6	249.6	251.0	245.4	0.39	16.87
Children aged 2-9	450.4	418.1	421.3	466.2	473.3	461.5	472.7	506.4	500.9	0.27	11.20
Female	221.0	202.9	204.8	226.9	229.7	225.2	230.5	246.4	243.6	0.24	10.22
Male	229.4	215.3	216.5	239.3	243.6	236.3	242.2	260.0	257.3	0.29	12.14
Tweenagers aged 10-14	293.7	294.8	259.9	265.5	293.3	313.5	296.7	291.3	321.2	0.22	9.39
Female	146.1	146.9	127.8	129.0	143.3	152.5	144.6	141.9	156.1	0.17	6.83
Male	147.6	147.9	132.1	136.5	150.0	161.1	152.1	149.4	165.2	0.28	11.92
Teenagers aged 13-19	423.1	420.3	401.8	374.9	386.2	434.7	441.1	420.0	422.6	0.00	-0.13
Female	211.8	210.6	200.7	183.6	189.2	213.4	214.9	205.0	205.9	-0.07	-2.83
Male	211.3	209.7	201.1	191.3	197.0	221.3	226.2	215.1	216.8	0.06	2.58
Studying age 18-22	300.2	294.5	298.2	279.6	264.8	295.9	321.2	314.0	302.1	0.02	0.62
Female	149.7	147.9	149.7	139.0	131.4	146.5	156.9	152.4	146.9	-0.05	-1.88
Male	150.5	146.6	148.5	140.6	133.5	149.4	164.3	161.6	155.2	0.08	3.10
Young adults aged 15-29	837.8	869.1	866.3	834.3	796.9	850.4	907.9	918.2	910.0	0.21	8.63
Female	417.7	436.6	437.2	418.3	400.2	425.3	448.8	449.4	443.5	0.15	6.17
Male	420.1	432.5	429.1	416.0	396.7	425.1	459.1	468.7	466.6	0.26	11.06

Table 5.202 **Middle-aged generation**
'000

	1980	1985	1990	1995	2000	2005	2010	2015	2020	CAGR	Period growth
Middle-aged adults 30-59	1,069.9	1,157.5	1,259.9	1,428.9	1,576.1	1,714.4	1,749.9	1,793.2	1,818.5	1.33	70.0
Female	528.8	575.5	632.8	721.1	803.2	881.5	904.9	928.7	939.7	1.45	77.7
Male	541.2	582.0	627.1	707.8	772.9	832.9	845.0	864.5	878.8	1.22	62.4
Baby boomers aged 40-59	634.5	666.6	733.3	842.1	972.4	1,112.7	1,177.8	1,219.2	1,204.4	1.62	89.8
Female	312.6	329.7	366.6	422.4	491.2	567.1	605.8	632.0	627.4	1.76	100.7
Male	321.8	336.9	366.7	419.8	481.2	545.6	572.0	587.1	577.0	1.47	79.3

Table 5.203 **Elderly population**
'000

	1980	1985	1990	1995	2000	2005	2010	2015	2020	CAGR	Period growth
Elderly population (60+)	441.3	490.7	528.6	562.7	606.0	678.8	797.0	918.8	1,063.3	2.22	140.9
Female	247.1	274.7	294.2	311.1	333.0	368.0	426.3	488.8	565.0	2.09	128.7
Male	194.2	215.9	234.4	251.6	273.0	310.8	370.7	430.0	498.3	2.38	156.5

Table 5.204 **Population of biggest cities 1980-2020**
'000

	1980	1985	1990	1995	2000	2005	2010	2015	2020	CAGR	Period growth
Auckland	246.1	267.4	298.2	339.7	362.3	397.1	431.5	463.1	492.4	1.75	100.06
Christchurch	261.8	273.7	290.7	314.0	321.3	343.3	365.8	386.5	405.8	1.10	55.01
Manukau	187.0	200.8	220.7	249.0	275.9	319.4	364.2	405.5	443.4	2.18	137.17
North Shore	123.5	133.9	148.7	169.0	181.7	201.3	220.9	239.0	255.6	1.83	106.92
Waitakere	109.8	119.4	133.4	152.4	165.7	183.0	198.8	213.4	226.9	1.83	106.69
Wellington	134.5	139.4	146.5	156.4	161.8	176.2	191.0	204.6	217.2	1.21	61.54
Hamilton	83.8	89.3	97.3	108.2	114.5	126.5	139.0	150.6	161.2	1.65	92.40
Dunedin	106.4	109.3	113.4	118.3	114.6	117.6	121.8	125.5	129.2	0.49	21.41
Tauranga	51.8	57.0	64.5	75.4	88.1	101.3	112.3	122.3	131.6	2.36	154.06
Lower Hutt	93.2	93.8	94.5	96.0	95.2	97.4	98.2	98.8	99.6	0.17	6.84

Chart 5.133 Population age shift 2000 and 2020, Each Column Represents a Single Age Group

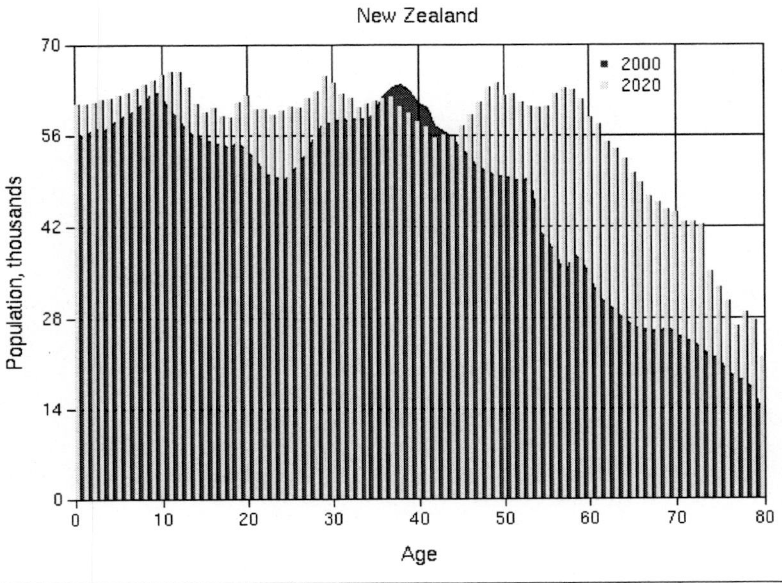

Chart 5.134 Population pyramids, 1980/2000/2010/2020

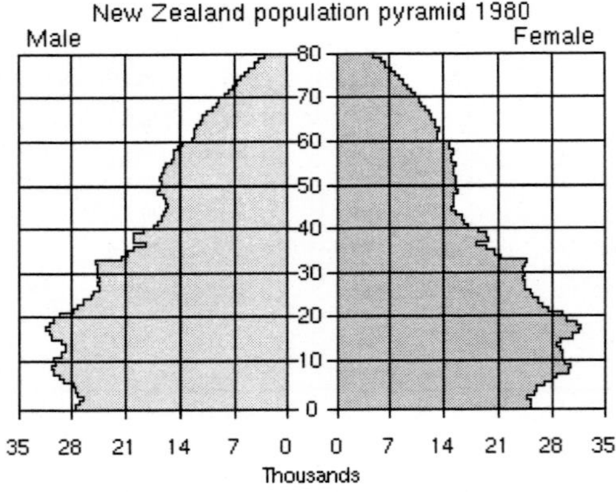

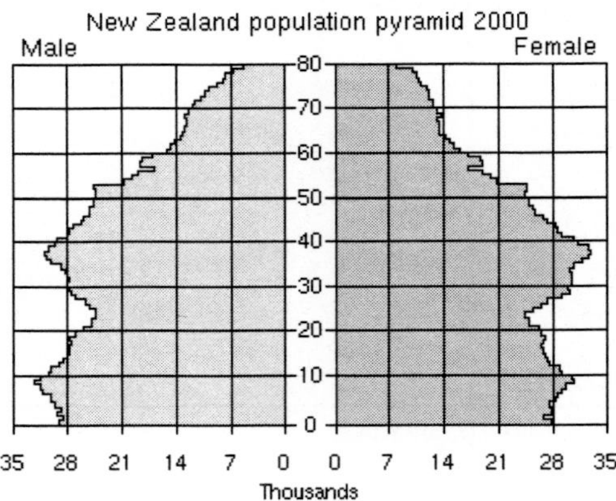

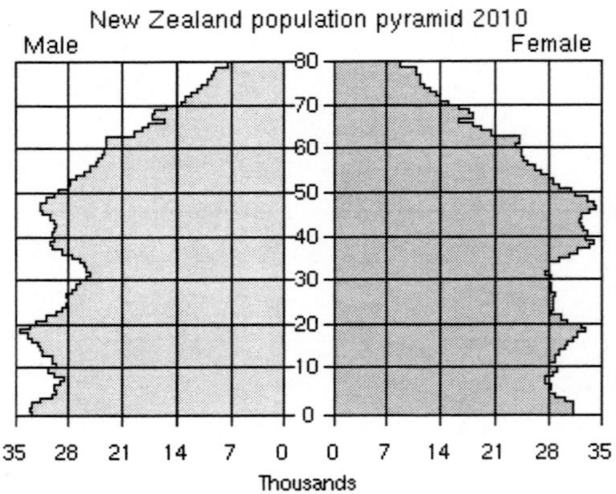

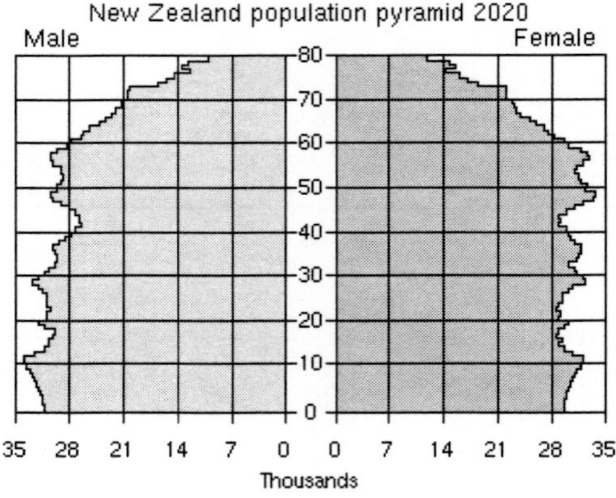

Chart 5.135 Major Cities: 1980, 2000 and 2020

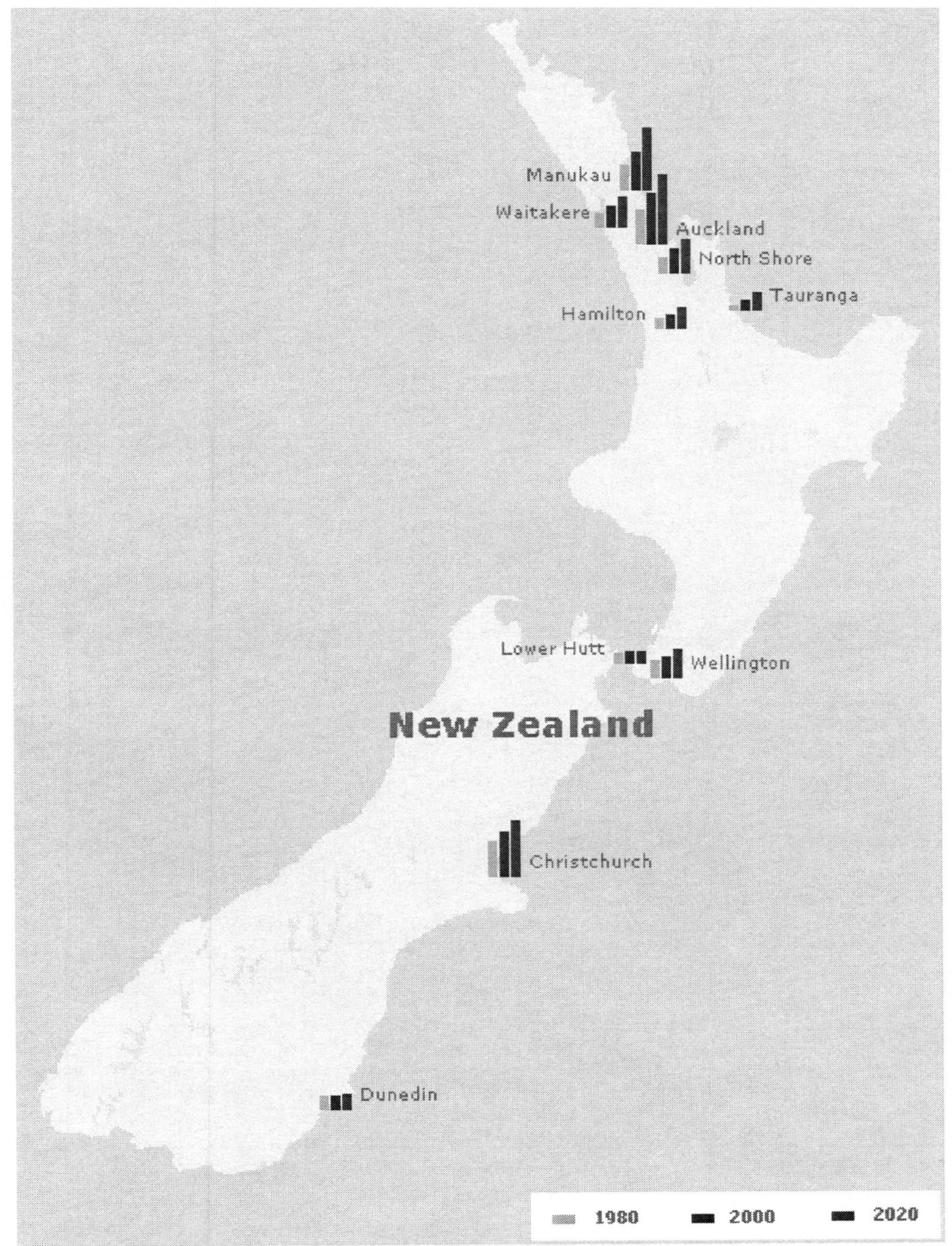

Nigeria

Table 5.205 Key population trends

'000

	1980	1985	1990	1995	2000	2005	2010	2015	2020	CAGR	Period growth
Population at January 1st	74,522.9	85,150.6	97,338.3	110,449.3	124,842.4	140,878.6	158,258.9	175,927.8	193,252.5	2.41	159.3
Male	37,014.8	42,271.9	48,388.9	55,019.5	62,326.3	70,497.6	79,343.4	88,329.3	97,137.4	2.44	162.4
Female	37,508.1	42,878.7	48,949.4	55,429.8	62,516.0	70,380.9	78,915.6	87,598.5	96,115.1	2.38	156.3
0-4 yrs	14,007.7	16,019.5	17,732.5	19,459.6	21,397.7	23,667.6	25,817.3	26,719.3	26,781.4	1.63	91.2
5-9 yrs	10,633.8	12,689.4	14,581.0	16,133.9	17,798.5	19,791.3	22,029.7	24,147.4	25,226.8	2.18	137.2
10-14 yrs	8,673.0	10,230.4	12,257.3	14,070.0	15,609.3	17,280.7	19,237.6	21,466.4	23,583.7	2.53	171.9
15-19 yrs	7,445.8	8,387.4	9,965.7	11,934.8	13,722.3	15,252.3	16,886.0	18,817.1	21,030.7	2.63	182.5
20-24 yrs	6,425.4	7,123.4	8,115.1	9,641.3	11,560.2	13,317.6	14,805.7	16,419.7	18,328.5	2.66	185.3
25-29 yrs	5,458.9	6,090.4	6,844.0	7,791.4	9,242.8	11,093.0	12,802.1	14,270.6	15,868.3	2.70	190.7
30-34 yrs	4,473.9	5,149.8	5,826.7	6,540.8	7,408.8	8,752.5	10,534.7	12,213.2	13,661.7	2.83	205.4
35-39 yrs	3,855.5	4,213.0	4,905.5	5,544.2	6,189.0	6,952.6	8,216.1	9,946.7	11,582.1	2.79	200.4
40-44 yrs	3,247.4	3,624.9	3,990.3	4,641.3	5,226.3	5,791.6	6,490.5	7,703.1	9,368.1	2.68	188.5
45-49 yrs	2,697.3	3,032.3	3,407.1	3,747.6	4,355.5	4,886.1	5,400.0	6,066.0	7,225.4	2.49	167.9
50-54 yrs	2,230.3	2,488.8	2,814.8	3,161.1	3,482.5	4,048.6	4,535.4	5,021.6	5,656.5	2.35	153.6
55-59 yrs	1,805.4	2,018.7	2,261.2	2,556.4	2,880.9	3,186.6	3,707.9	4,163.4	4,625.0	2.38	156.2
60-64 yrs	1,392.7	1,578.5	1,768.8	1,979.7	2,250.6	2,554.4	2,834.6	3,310.9	3,734.5	2.50	168.1
65-69 yrs	990.6	1,145.3	1,300.1	1,455.3	1,641.1	1,886.2	2,150.2	2,399.1	2,822.3	2.65	184.9
70-74 yrs	640.0	734.6	850.4	964.3	1,092.3	1,252.0	1,448.9	1,663.1	1,875.6	2.72	193.1
75-79 yrs	350.4	403.3	463.8	536.5	620.4	719.8	832.8	974.1	1,133.3	2.98	223.4
80+ yrs	194.8	221.0	254.0	291.0	364.1	445.6	529.6	625.8	748.6	3.42	284.3
Median age of population (years)	17.6	17.1	16.9	17.2	17.7	18.1	18.5	19.1	20.0	0.33	13.9

Table 5.206 Key economic trends

As stated

	1990	1995	2000	2005	2010	2015	2020	CAGR	Period growth
Total GDP (NGN per capita)	116,879.3	105,517.6	109,518.3	163,579.1	189,429.8	227,892.8	276,308.4	2.91	136.4
Disposable income (NGN per capita)	64,866.7	84,444.9	67,721.2	122,898.8	166,182.2	211,234.4	263,318.6	4.78	305.9
Disposable income (NGN per household)	364,804.7	455,141.7	351,109.2	617,792.5	815,576.2	1,011,229.1	1,227,966.6	4.13	236.6
Number of households by annual household disposable income ('000)									
Over US$1,000	6,291.2	8,361.6	6,836.0	20,692.2	28,313.9	33,970.5	40,085.0	6.37	537.2
Over US$10,000	160.0	188.8	192.5	921.8	1,995.2	3,243.2	6,514.1	13.15	3,971.2
Over US$25,000	52.1	61.1	63.9	235.2	479.0	763.2	1,523.4	11.91	2,822.5
Over US$75,000	13.6	15.8	17.1	62.1	117.1	172.7	309.1	10.98	2,175.4
Over US$150,000	5.8	6.7	7.4	27.1	51.1	75.8	132.5	10.98	2,178.8
Total households	17,307.9	20,492.3	24,079.3	28,025.3	32,246.9	36,749.3	41,440.0	2.95	139.4

Note: Per capita data is shown at constant 2010 prices. Household disposable income bands are shown at current prices.

Table 5.207 Young generation

'000

	1980	1985	1990	1995	2000	2005	2010	2015	2020	CAGR	Period growth
Babies under 12 months	3,150	3,513	3,862	4,255	4,659	5,128	5,518	5,527	5,504	1.41	74.7
Infants under 24 months	6,117	6,868	7,556	8,314	9,117	10,049	10,858	10,974	10,930	1.46	78.7
Toddlers aged 1-4	10,858	12,507	13,871	15,205	16,739	18,540	20,299	21,192	21,278	1.70	96.0
Children aged 2-9	18,524	21,841	24,757	27,280	30,079	33,410	36,989	39,893	41,079	2.01	121.8
Female	9,226	10,866	12,300	13,515	14,862	16,481	18,232	19,675	20,263	1.99	119.6
Male	9,299	10,975	12,458	13,764	15,217	16,930	18,757	20,218	20,816	2.04	123.9
Tweenagers aged 10-14	8,673	10,230	12,257	14,070	15,609	17,281	19,238	21,466	23,584	2.53	171.9
Female	4,328	5,102	6,100	6,989	7,730	8,530	9,480	10,570	11,622	2.50	168.5
Male	4,345	5,128	6,158	7,081	7,879	8,750	9,757	10,897	11,962	2.56	175.3
Teenagers aged 13-19	10,742	12,224	14,593	17,328	19,743	21,907	24,283	27,077	30,206	2.62	181.2
Female	5,357	6,108	7,274	8,618	9,798	10,839	11,982	13,342	14,879	2.59	177.7
Male	5,385	6,116	7,319	8,710	9,944	11,069	12,301	13,735	15,327	2.65	184.6
Studying age 18-22	6,821	7,583	8,779	10,540	12,468	14,110	15,613	17,346	19,387	2.65	184.2
Female	3,402	3,798	4,392	5,256	6,204	7,007	7,730	8,568	9,564	2.62	181.1
Male	3,418	3,785	4,387	5,283	6,264	7,103	7,883	8,779	9,823	2.67	187.4
Young adults aged 15-29	19,330	21,601	24,925	29,367	34,525	39,663	44,494	49,507	55,227	2.66	185.7
Female	9,660	10,830	12,486	14,677	17,203	19,708	22,062	24,494	27,279	2.63	182.4
Male	9,670	10,771	12,438	14,690	17,323	19,955	22,432	25,014	27,948	2.69	189.0

Table 5.208 Middle-aged generation

'000

	1980	1985	1990	1995	2000	2005	2010	2015	2020	CAGR	Period growth
Middle-aged adults 30-59	18,310	20,527	23,206	26,191	29,543	33,618	38,885	45,114	52,119	2.65	184.6
Female	9,296	10,440	11,799	13,311	15,010	17,039	19,619	22,645	26,035	2.61	180.1
Male	9,014	10,087	11,407	12,880	14,533	16,579	19,266	22,469	26,084	2.69	189.4
Baby boomers aged 40-59	9,980	11,165	12,473	14,106	15,945	17,913	20,134	22,954	26,875	2.51	169.3
Female	5,120	5,716	6,373	7,206	8,152	9,175	10,291	11,637	13,507	2.45	163.8
Male	4,861	5,449	6,101	6,900	7,793	8,738	9,843	11,317	13,368	2.56	175.0

Table 5.209 Elderly population

'000

	1980	1985	1990	1995	2000	2005	2010	2015	2020	CAGR	Period growth
Elderly population (60+)	3,569	4,083	4,637	5,227	5,969	6,858	7,796	8,973	10,314	2.69	189.0
Female	1,961	2,231	2,519	2,823	3,206	3,665	4,160	4,799	5,525	2.62	181.7
Male	1,607	1,852	2,118	2,404	2,763	3,193	3,636	4,174	4,790	2.77	198.0

Table 5.210 Population of biggest cities 1980-2020

'000

	1980	1985	1990	1995	2000	2005	2010	2015	2020	CAGR	Period growth
Lagos	2,033.1	3,322.2	4,874.1	6,306.4	7,547.3	8,749.0	9,925.5	11,129.0	12,365.2	4.62	508.2
Ibadan	1,091.9	1,374.2	1,746.5	2,205.2	2,798.0	3,527.5	4,330.9	5,155.3	5,984.0	4.34	448.0
Kano	821.6	1,381.4	2,036.0	2,593.7	3,051.8	3,592.4	4,227.0	4,876.6	5,535.6	4.88	573.7
Kaduna	392.0	641.8	934.8	1,186.9	1,384.1	1,574.3	1,764.7	1,959.2	2,160.1	4.36	451.1
Maiduguri	293.5	425.4	584.7	738.5	897.1	1,101.0	1,342.4	1,589.9	1,839.0	4.69	526.5
Port Harcourt	356.1	496.9	667.2	833.2	991.1	1,144.5	1,287.6	1,433.9	1,584.7	3.80	345.0
Benin City	340.4	518.7	722.7	888.4	1,007.6	1,120.5	1,232.2	1,346.0	1,465.0	3.72	330.4
Zaira	321.6	440.0	582.1	719.1	848.0	972.0	1,085.7	1,201.9	1,322.2	3.60	311.2
Ilorin	350.9	423.6	512.1	608.1	713.7	813.4	895.5	979.3	1,066.9	2.82	204.0
Abuja	426.4	459.8	499.7	556.2	645.6	756.4	866.1	978.4	1,093.4	2.38	156.4

Chart 5.136 Population age shift 2000 and 2020, Each Column Represents a Single Age Group

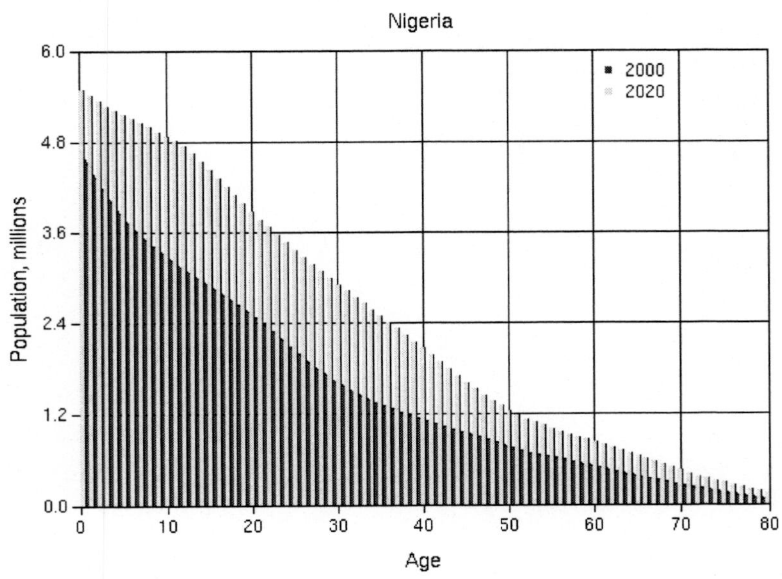

Chart 5.137 Population pyramids, 1980/2000/2010/2020

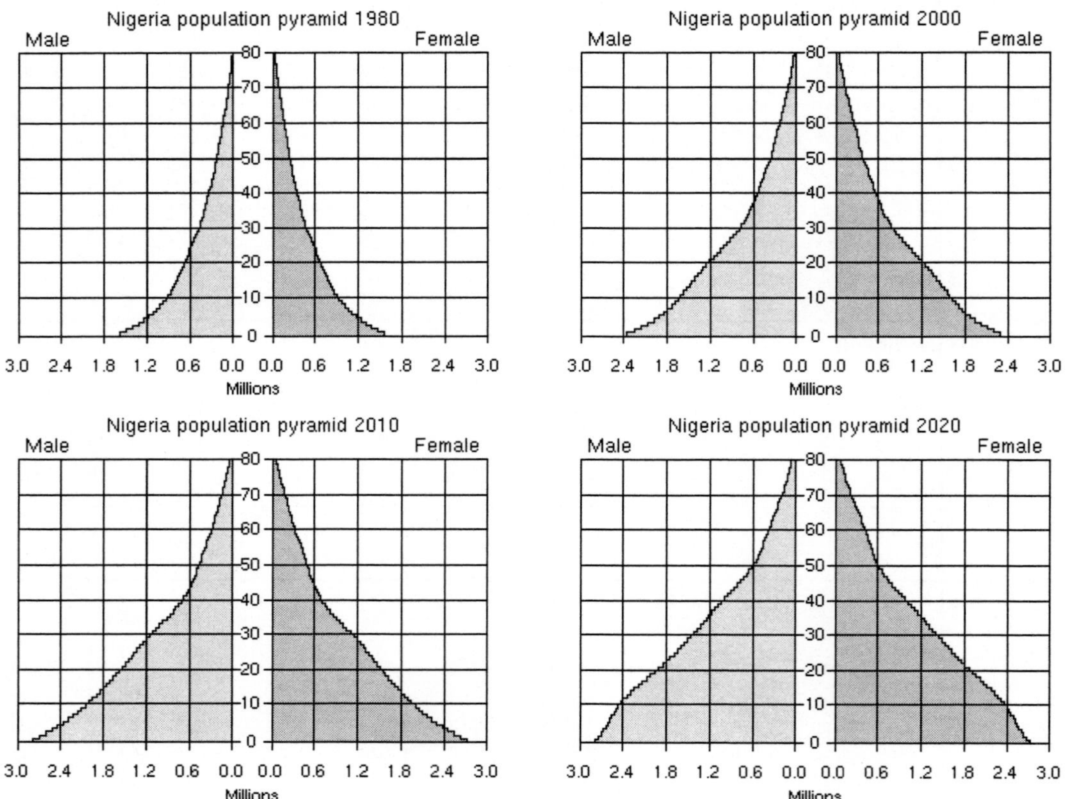

Chart 5.138 Major Cities: 1980, 2000 and 2020

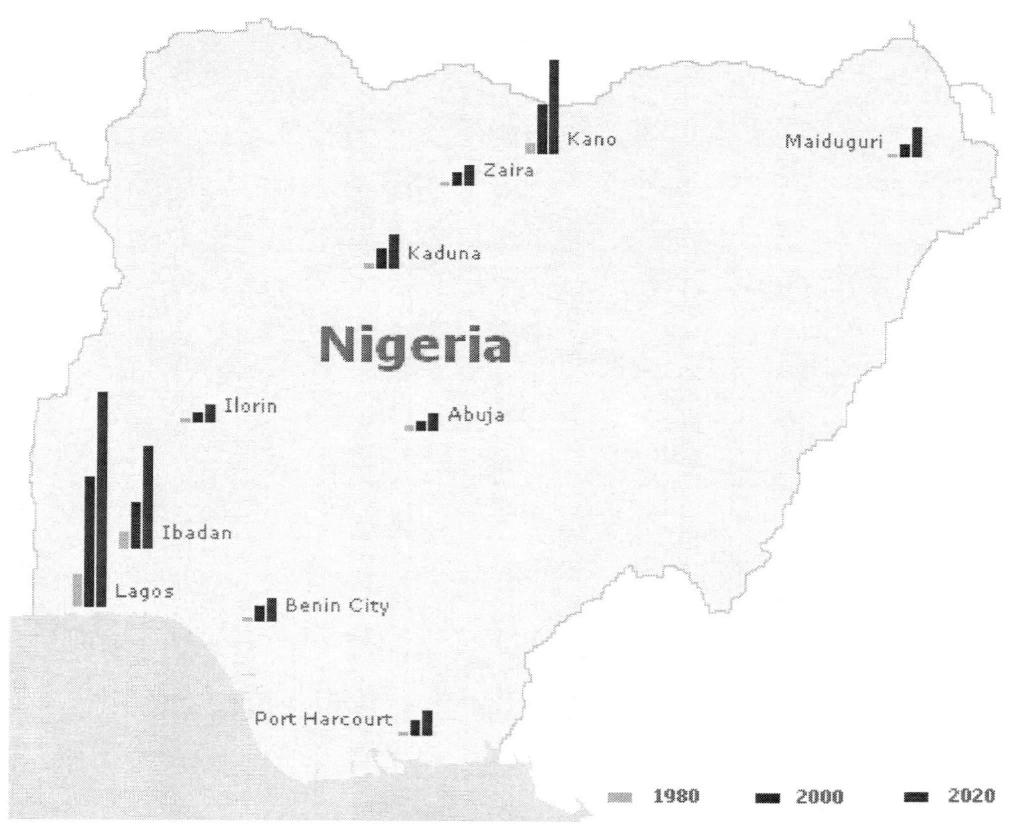

Norway

Table 5.211 Key population trends

'000

	1980	1985	1990	1995	2000	2005	2010	2015	2020	CAGR	Period growth
Population at January 1st	4,078.9	4,145.8	4,233.1	4,348.4	4,478.5	4,606.4	4,858.1	5,108.4	5,352.5	0.68	31.22
Male	2,021.9	2,050.1	2,093.3	2,150.3	2,217.1	2,284.1	2,427.8	2,566.1	2,697.0	0.72	33.39
Female	2,057.0	2,095.8	2,139.8	2,198.2	2,261.4	2,322.3	2,430.3	2,542.2	2,655.5	0.64	29.09
0-4 yrs	263.5	253.8	275.5	303.9	302.4	289.1	303.4	315.5	331.4	0.57	25.75
5-9 yrs	315.9	265.8	257.5	279.8	308.8	306.9	299.0	314.6	325.0	0.07	2.89
10-14 yrs	333.1	317.4	268.0	261.0	283.5	313.2	315.7	309.0	323.2	-0.07	-2.95
15-19 yrs	311.4	334.7	319.1	271.5	265.4	289.0	322.1	325.9	318.4	0.06	2.26
20-24 yrs	309.9	313.3	338.5	324.0	278.7	273.9	305.6	337.7	340.0	0.23	9.70
25-29 yrs	302.7	312.6	321.3	344.9	332.8	290.3	306.4	332.5	359.9	0.43	18.90
30-34 yrs	316.3	304.4	317.8	324.6	351.3	341.4	318.6	332.4	354.3	0.28	12.03
35-39 yrs	245.0	316.6	305.7	318.6	327.7	355.1	359.6	335.6	347.0	0.87	41.63
40-44 yrs	200.0	244.2	315.4	304.9	319.0	328.7	366.1	369.2	344.5	1.37	72.27
45-49 yrs	198.7	198.1	241.7	312.6	303.1	317.6	334.8	370.8	373.2	1.59	87.84
50-54 yrs	216.8	195.0	194.3	237.9	308.0	299.2	318.7	335.4	370.5	1.35	70.90
55-59 yrs	246.5	209.7	188.6	189.4	232.4	300.5	295.2	314.9	331.3	0.74	34.40
60-64 yrs	221.1	233.9	198.9	180.2	182.2	223.6	291.2	287.4	306.9	0.82	38.79
65-69 yrs	199.7	203.4	215.5	184.6	168.8	171.0	212.0	277.1	274.7	0.80	37.53
70-74 yrs	161.4	174.4	178.6	190.9	165.5	152.9	157.5	196.1	257.4	1.17	59.48
75-79 yrs	119.6	129.8	140.5	146.2	158.7	140.6	132.5	137.5	173.1	0.93	44.82
80+ yrs	117.4	138.6	156.3	173.5	190.0	213.2	219.8	216.8	221.6	1.60	88.75
Median age of population (years)	33.2	34.5	35.3	36.0	36.7	37.8	38.6	39.3	39.7	0.44	19.42

Table 5.212 Key economic trends

As stated

	1990	1995	2000	2005	2010	2015	2020	CAGR	Period growth
Total GDP (NOK per capita)	349,641.5	408,651.7	475,425.2	515,787.1	523,431.1	549,417.1	590,140.9	1.76	68.8
Disposable income (NOK per capita)	132,475.5	150,472.1	177,753.4	215,840.0	241,229.8	263,702.6	286,897.1	2.61	116.6
Disposable income (NOK per household)	320,198.7	351,907.6	408,747.6	494,400.9	547,291.2	604,372.4	662,789.0	2.45	107.0
Number of households by annual household disposable income ('000)									
Over US$1,000	1,751.4	1,859.3	1,947.6	2,011.0	2,141.3	2,228.9	2,316.9	0.94	32.3
Over US$10,000	1,731.3	1,846.9	1,932.2	2,007.6	2,138.6	2,227.1	2,315.7	0.97	33.7
Over US$25,000	1,284.2	1,550.1	1,471.7	1,916.1	2,065.7	2,176.9	2,282.1	1.94	77.7
Over US$75,000	84.3	148.3	141.1	599.5	800.9	1,053.4	1,328.9	9.63	1,475.8
Over US$150,000	34.2	49.7	48.0	104.1	154.3	235.1	337.6	7.93	887.0
Total households	1,751.4	1,859.3	1,947.6	2,011.0	2,141.3	2,228.9	2,316.9	0.94	32.3

Note: Per capita data is shown at constant 2010 prices. Household disposable income bands are shown at current prices.

Table 5.213 Young generation

'000

	1980	1985	1990	1995	2000	2005	2010	2015	2020	CAGR	Period growth
Babies under 12 months	51.2	50.0	59.1	59.9	59.4	57.1	61.1	62.8	66.5	0.65	29.74
Infants under 24 months	102.8	100.0	116.5	119.8	118.3	114.5	122.9	125.7	133.1	0.65	29.41
Toddlers aged 1-4	212.3	203.8	216.4	244.0	243.0	232.1	242.4	252.7	264.9	0.56	24.78
Children aged 2-9	476.6	419.7	416.5	463.9	493.0	481.6	479.5	504.3	523.3	0.23	9.81
Female	233.0	204.9	203.0	225.7	239.6	234.9	234.6	245.9	255.0	0.23	9.48
Male	243.6	214.8	213.5	238.2	253.3	246.7	245.0	258.4	268.3	0.24	10.12
Tweenagers aged 10-14	333.1	317.4	268.0	261.0	283.5	313.2	315.7	309.0	323.2	-0.07	-2.95
Female	161.9	155.1	130.8	127.1	138.2	152.3	153.6	151.3	157.7	-0.07	-2.60
Male	171.1	162.3	137.1	133.8	145.4	160.9	162.1	157.7	165.5	-0.08	-3.27
Teenagers aged 13-19	443.3	465.6	430.4	376.5	373.1	415.9	450.7	451.4	446.2	0.02	0.65
Female	215.6	226.8	210.5	184.1	181.8	202.4	219.1	220.0	218.3	0.03	1.26
Male	227.7	238.8	219.8	192.5	191.3	213.5	231.5	231.4	227.9	0.00	0.08
Studying age 18-22	307.8	322.9	335.0	303.3	270.1	273.5	317.6	332.7	330.2	0.18	7.27
Female	150.2	157.3	163.7	148.9	132.7	133.4	155.5	162.4	161.8	0.19	7.72
Male	157.6	165.5	171.4	154.4	137.4	140.0	162.1	170.4	168.4	0.17	6.85
Young adults aged 15-29	924.0	960.7	978.8	940.3	876.9	853.2	934.1	996.1	1,018.3	0.24	10.21
Female	450.3	468.9	476.9	460.1	431.1	419.8	457.4	488.2	499.8	0.26	10.99
Male	473.7	491.8	501.9	480.3	445.9	433.4	476.7	507.9	518.5	0.23	9.46

Table 5.214 **Middle-aged generation**
'000

	1980	1985	1990	1995	2000	2005	2010	2015	2020	CAGR	Period growth
Middle-aged adults 30-59	1,423.2	1,468.0	1,563.6	1,688.0	1,841.6	1,942.5	1,993.0	2,058.4	2,120.8	1.00	49.0
Female	703.0	721.9	766.8	827.9	902.5	955.2	973.9	1,003.4	1,032.3	0.97	46.9
Male	720.3	746.2	796.8	860.1	939.2	987.3	1,019.1	1,055.0	1,088.5	1.04	51.1
Baby boomers aged 40-59	861.9	847.1	940.1	1,044.8	1,162.6	1,246.0	1,314.9	1,390.4	1,419.5	1.25	64.7
Female	431.0	420.7	463.4	513.8	570.9	612.5	642.2	677.0	689.3	1.18	59.9
Male	430.9	426.4	476.7	530.9	591.7	633.5	672.6	713.4	730.1	1.33	69.4

Table 5.215 **Elderly population**
'000

	1980	1985	1990	1995	2000	2005	2010	2015	2020	CAGR	Period growth
Elderly population (60+)	819.2	880.0	889.8	875.4	865.2	901.3	1,012.9	1,114.9	1,233.7	1.03	50.6
Female	458.8	496.5	505.6	499.0	492.4	504.3	551.1	592.3	645.8	0.86	40.8
Male	360.4	383.6	384.2	376.3	372.8	397.1	461.8	522.6	587.9	1.23	63.1

Table 5.216 **Population of biggest cities 1980-2020**
'000

	1980	1985	1990	1995	2000	2005	2010	2015	2020	CAGR	Period growth
Oslo	643.0	666.3	685.5	721.6	773.5	827.5	878.5	937.1	999.6	1.11	55.5
Bergen	181.0	185.0	187.4	194.4	205.8	217.5	228.3	241.5	256.3	0.87	41.7
Stavanger/Sandnes	117.4	121.3	126.8	141.3	162.1	178.8	191.0	204.6	218.8	1.57	86.3
Trondheim	127.6	129.9	130.5	133.8	140.6	150.4	161.3	173.4	185.8	0.94	45.6
Fredrikstad/Skarpsborg	91.2	91.3	90.0	90.4	93.3	97.7	102.6	108.6	115.3	0.59	26.5
Drammen	56.9	58.5	58.7	71.5	86.7	93.3	96.3	100.7	106.0	1.57	86.5
Porsgrunn/Skien	63.5	63.4	64.5	72.3	83.4	87.6	86.0	86.4	88.5	0.84	39.5
Kristiansand	50.7	52.6	54.3	57.3	61.4	65.0	67.8	71.4	75.6	1.00	49.1
Tromso	36.3	38.9	41.7	45.3	49.4	52.7	55.2	58.3	61.8	1.34	70.4
Tonsberg	36.8	37.7	38.3	40.3	43.3	45.8	47.7	50.1	53.0	0.92	44.0

Chart 5.139 Population age shift 2000 and 2020, Each Column Represents a Single Age Group

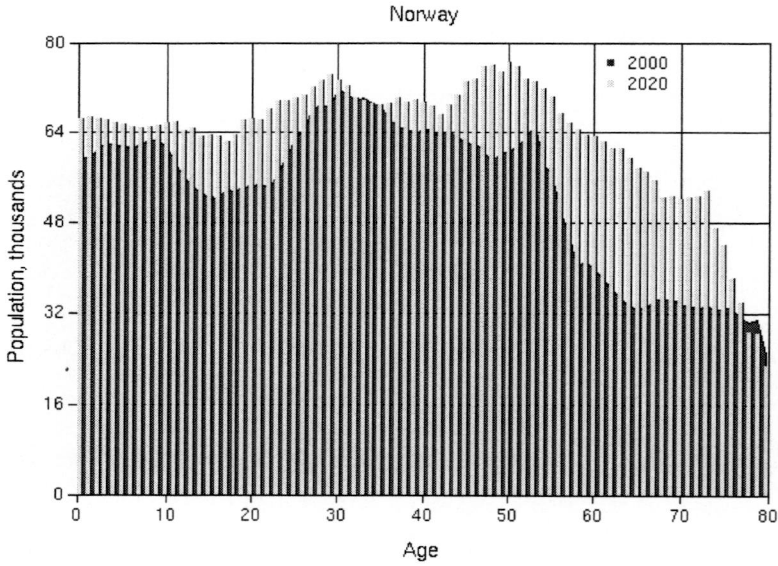

Chart 5.140 Population pyramids, 1980/2000/2010/2020

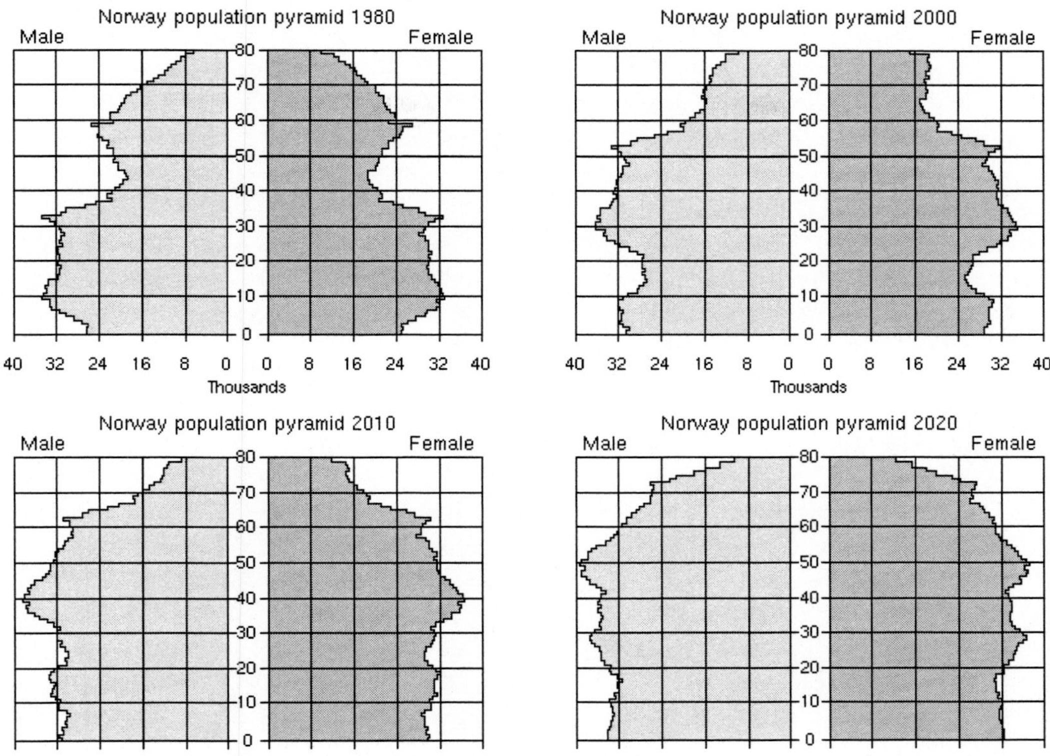

Chart 5.141 Major Cities: 1980, 2000 and 2020

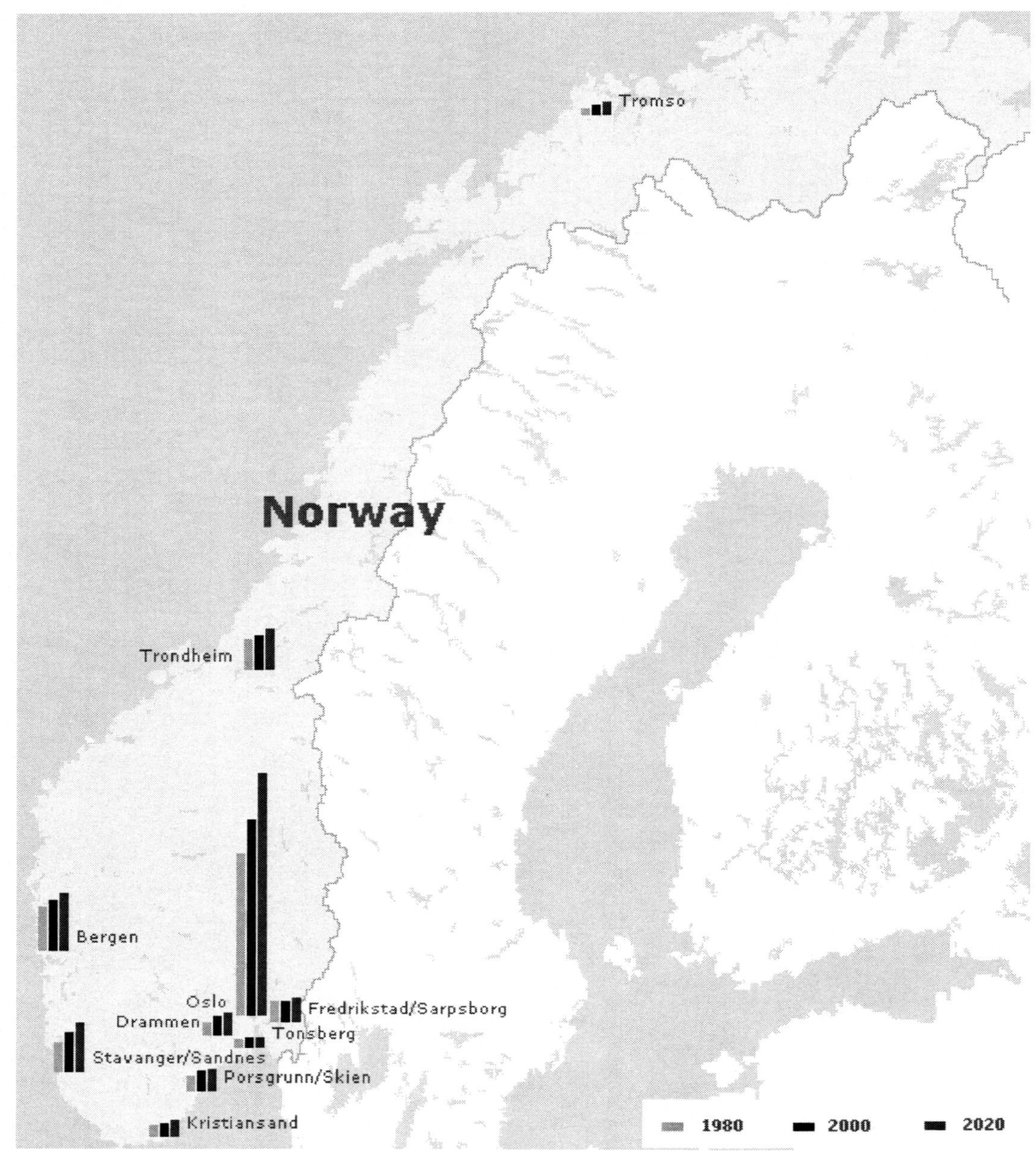

Pakistan

Table 5.217 Key population trends

'000

	1980	1985	1990	1995	2000	2005	2010	2015	2020	CAGR	Period growth
Population at January 1st	82,609.2	98,308.5	115,776.0	130,397.4	148,132.4	165,815.8	184,753.3	205,503.7	226,186.8	2.55	173.8
Male	43,430.0	51,337.1	60,185.4	67,557.1	76,505.3	85,476.4	95,115.1	105,743.5	116,325.1	2.49	167.8
Female	39,179.2	46,971.4	55,590.6	62,840.3	71,627.1	80,339.4	89,638.2	99,760.1	109,861.7	2.61	180.4
0-4 yrs	14,274.0	16,885.3	20,311.6	20,788.3	21,541.2	22,850.8	24,489.2	26,090.7	26,322.7	1.54	84.4
5-9 yrs	11,970.7	13,837.6	16,350.2	19,414.4	20,338.0	20,974.5	22,300.6	24,029.4	25,646.3	1.92	114.2
10-14 yrs	9,857.5	11,923.1	13,713.6	16,159.8	19,280.6	20,155.3	20,841.0	22,173.1	23,924.1	2.24	142.7
15-19 yrs	7,968.5	10,051.7	11,912.5	13,363.9	16,091.0	19,062.1	19,935.2	20,687.5	22,033.3	2.58	176.5
20-24 yrs	6,675.7	8,362.9	10,116.8	11,325.4	13,254.9	15,756.2	18,689.0	19,689.8	20,466.9	2.84	206.6
25-29 yrs	5,676.0	7,007.3	8,431.0	9,597.8	11,212.3	12,962.4	15,419.2	18,447.5	19,472.7	3.13	243.1
30-34 yrs	4,866.8	5,843.3	7,021.0	8,096.3	9,500.7	11,009.0	12,734.3	15,240.5	18,278.1	3.36	275.6
35-39 yrs	4,370.8	4,947.5	5,818.8	6,772.5	8,003.2	9,332.4	10,827.6	12,590.7	15,103.3	3.15	245.6
40-44 yrs	3,644.3	4,400.4	4,897.4	5,598.8	6,668.1	7,837.4	9,155.3	10,683.5	12,452.7	3.12	241.7
45-49 yrs	3,069.1	3,631.5	4,316.6	4,684.0	5,473.7	6,490.0	7,646.1	8,987.1	10,515.9	3.13	242.6
50-54 yrs	2,598.3	3,004.7	3,509.4	4,083.7	4,521.5	5,266.8	6,264.8	7,429.3	8,761.7	3.09	237.2
55-59 yrs	2,175.4	2,474.1	2,832.5	3,250.0	3,858.8	4,266.1	4,991.2	5,983.4	7,126.6	3.01	227.6
60-64 yrs	1,737.3	1,985.5	2,242.6	2,531.5	2,965.5	3,524.8	3,919.5	4,623.2	5,576.5	2.96	221.0
65-69 yrs	1,398.5	1,490.5	1,696.4	1,896.3	2,187.8	2,573.6	3,085.6	3,460.2	4,117.3	2.74	194.4
70-74 yrs	1,103.8	1,097.1	1,169.3	1,321.1	1,512.9	1,758.1	2,094.1	2,539.4	2,881.0	2.43	161.0
75-79 yrs	696.7	761.7	758.5	806.9	938.5	1,086.3	1,282.5	1,550.3	1,911.1	2.55	174.3
80+ yrs	525.9	604.2	677.7	706.8	783.7	910.3	1,077.9	1,298.0	1,596.4	2.81	203.5
Median age of population (years)	18.2	18.1	18.1	18.2	18.9	20.0	21.2	22.5	23.7	0.67	30.4

Table 5.218 Key economic trends

As stated

	1990	1995	2000	2005	2010	2015	2020	CAGR	Period growth
Total GDP (PKR per capita)	56,758.6	63,218.7	65,323.1	74,460.9	80,305.4	91,834.8	111,456.4	2.27	96.4
Disposable income (PKR per capita)	31,900.7	37,929.0	44,601.5	52,502.0	60,752.3	72,585.7	89,563.4	3.50	180.8
Disposable income (PKR per household)	236,777.7	280,715.3	322,556.2	379,330.7	436,939.4	518,279.3	633,546.1	3.34	167.6
Number of households by annual household disposable income ('000)									
Over US$1,000	14,093.9	17,318.5	19,669.8	22,844.0	25,682.8	28,780.7	31,975.7	2.77	126.9
Over US$10,000	292.6	483.3	536.0	972.4	2,176.2	4,972.5	14,605.4	13.92	4,891.0
Over US$25,000	89.2	149.0	167.3	277.8	521.3	1,061.4	3,039.8	12.48	3,308.2
Over US$75,000	21.5	36.4	41.4	69.7	131.3	241.8	564.4	11.51	2,529.9
Over US$150,000	8.7	14.9	17.2	29.1	55.0	102.0	233.6	11.58	2,574.1
Total households	15,598.3	17,618.7	20,483.0	22,950.0	25,688.2	28,781.1	31,975.7	2.42	105.0

Note: Per capita data is shown at constant 2010 prices. Household disposable income bands are shown at current prices.

Table 5.219 Young generation

'000

	1980	1985	1990	1995	2000	2005	2010	2015	2020	CAGR	Period growth
Babies under 12 months	3,049	3,713	4,435	4,088	4,518	4,788	5,108	5,378	5,235	1.36	71.7
Infants under 24 months	5,999	7,240	8,686	8,252	8,895	9,462	10,108	10,683	10,503	1.41	75.1
Toddlers aged 1-4	11,225	13,172	15,877	16,700	17,023	18,063	19,382	20,713	21,087	1.59	87.9
Children aged 2-9	20,246	23,483	27,976	31,951	32,984	34,363	36,681	39,437	41,466	1.81	104.8
Female	9,815	11,392	13,569	15,516	16,053	16,707	17,814	19,142	20,128	1.81	105.1
Male	10,431	12,091	14,407	16,435	16,931	17,656	18,868	20,295	21,338	1.81	104.6
Tweenagers aged 10-14	9,857	11,923	13,714	16,160	19,281	20,155	20,841	22,173	23,924	2.24	142.7
Female	4,764	5,774	6,644	7,829	9,354	9,803	10,132	10,764	11,608	2.25	143.6
Male	5,093	6,150	7,069	8,331	9,927	10,352	10,709	11,409	12,316	2.23	141.8
Teenagers aged 13-19	11,663	14,605	17,160	19,426	23,529	27,065	28,136	29,357	31,366	2.50	168.9
Female	5,627	7,070	8,311	9,401	11,401	13,133	13,679	14,260	15,219	2.52	170.4
Male	6,036	7,535	8,849	10,026	12,128	13,932	14,457	15,097	16,147	2.49	167.5
Studying age 18-22	7,134	8,997	10,839	12,090	14,257	17,197	19,408	20,027	21,036	2.74	194.9
Female	3,433	4,350	5,247	5,843	6,900	8,328	9,416	9,731	10,209	2.76	197.4
Male	3,701	4,647	5,591	6,247	7,357	8,868	9,992	10,296	10,827	2.72	192.5
Young adults aged 15-29	20,320	25,422	30,460	34,287	40,558	47,781	54,043	58,825	61,973	2.83	205.0
Female	9,762	12,263	14,733	16,585	19,624	23,140	26,213	28,548	30,082	2.85	208.1
Male	10,558	13,159	15,727	17,702	20,934	24,641	27,831	30,276	31,891	2.80	202.1

Table 5.220 Middle-aged generation

'000

	1980	1985	1990	1995	2000	2005	2010	2015	2020	CAGR	Period growth
Middle-aged adults 30-59	20,725	24,301	28,396	32,485	38,026	44,202	51,619	60,915	72,238	3.17	248.6
Female	9,589	11,448	13,531	15,591	18,351	21,358	24,953	29,474	34,986	3.29	264.9
Male	11,136	12,853	14,865	16,895	19,675	22,844	26,666	31,440	37,253	3.06	234.5
Baby boomers aged 40-59	11,487	13,511	15,556	17,617	20,522	23,860	28,057	33,083	38,857	3.09	238.3
Female	5,155	6,268	7,390	8,439	9,884	11,516	13,557	16,010	18,826	3.29	265.2
Male	6,332	7,243	8,166	9,178	10,638	12,344	14,501	17,074	20,031	2.92	216.4

Table 5.221 Elderly population

'000

	1980	1985	1990	1995	2000	2005	2010	2015	2020	CAGR	Period growth
Elderly population (60+)	5,462	5,939	6,544	7,263	8,388	9,853	11,460	13,471	16,082	2.74	194.4
Female	2,328	2,572	2,890	3,292	3,917	4,729	5,612	6,637	7,952	3.12	241.5
Male	3,134	3,367	3,654	3,970	4,471	5,124	5,848	6,834	8,130	2.41	159.4

Table 5.222 Population of biggest cities 1980-2020

'000

	1980	1985	1990	1995	2000	2005	2010	2015	2020	CAGR	Period growth
Karachi	4,990.7	6,151.4	7,463.9	8,580.8	9,871.5	11,207.5	12,941.8	15,168.7	17,823.4	3.23	257.1
Lahore	2,850.9	3,412.2	4,094.0	4,710.3	5,446.4	6,203.4	7,176.9	8,421.1	9,901.3	3.16	247.3
Faisalabad	1,066.9	1,298.7	1,584.2	1,835.7	2,129.5	2,430.2	2,814.7	3,304.9	3,887.3	3.29	264.4
Rawalpindi	770.8	928.3	1,124.6	1,293.9	1,491.0	1,694.5	1,957.9	2,295.6	2,697.9	3.18	250.0
Multan	707.6	839.3	990.0	1,113.5	1,257.6	1,411.4	1,618.6	1,889.5	2,214.9	2.89	213.0
Gujranwala	562.9	716.2	881.0	1,029.6	1,203.7	1,380.3	1,603.2	1,885.5	2,219.8	3.49	294.4
Hyderabad	735.5	829.7	958.4	1,078.7	1,229.5	1,388.2	1,597.7	1,869.0	2,193.6	2.77	198.2
Peshawar	525.8	663.3	796.4	907.6	1,036.1	1,170.7	1,348.1	1,577.4	1,851.7	3.20	252.1
Quetta	269.3	346.5	431.4	510.1	602.9	695.8	811.2	956.1	1,127.1	3.64	318.5
Islamabad	187.5	276.5	375.3	466.9	571.0	672.2	792.4	939.9	1,112.0	4.55	493.2

Chart 5.142 Population age shift 2000 and 2020, Each Column Represents a Single Age Group

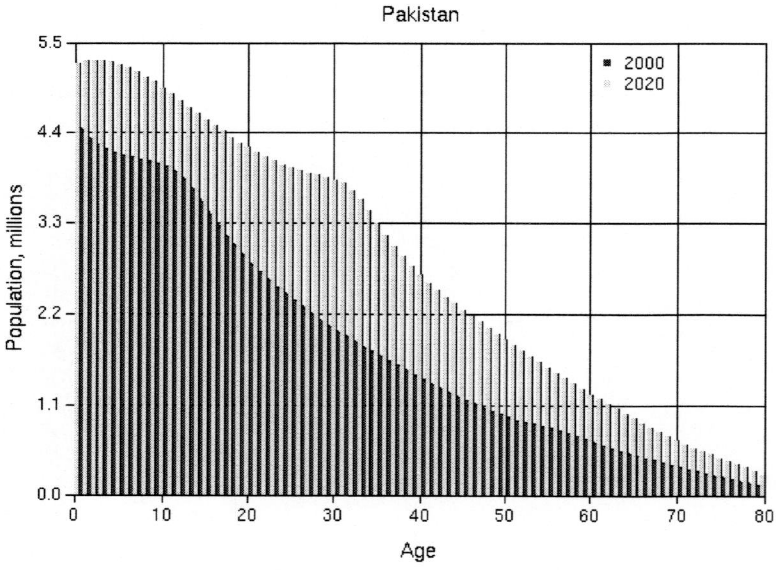

Chart 5.143 Population pyramids, 1980/2000/2010/2020

Pakistan population pyramid 1980
Male
Female
Millions
Pakistan population pyramid 2000
Male
Female
Millions
Pakistan population pyramid 2010
Male
Female
Millions
Pakistan population pyramid 2020
Male
Female
Millions

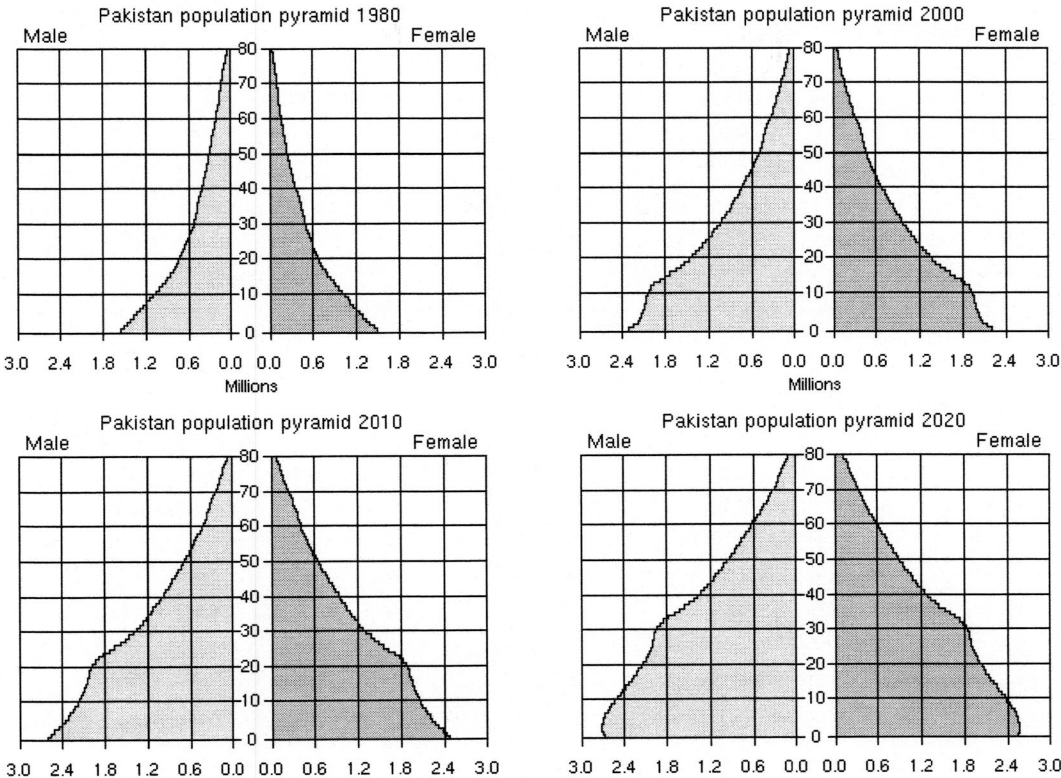

Chart 5.144 Major Cities: 1980, 2000 and 2020

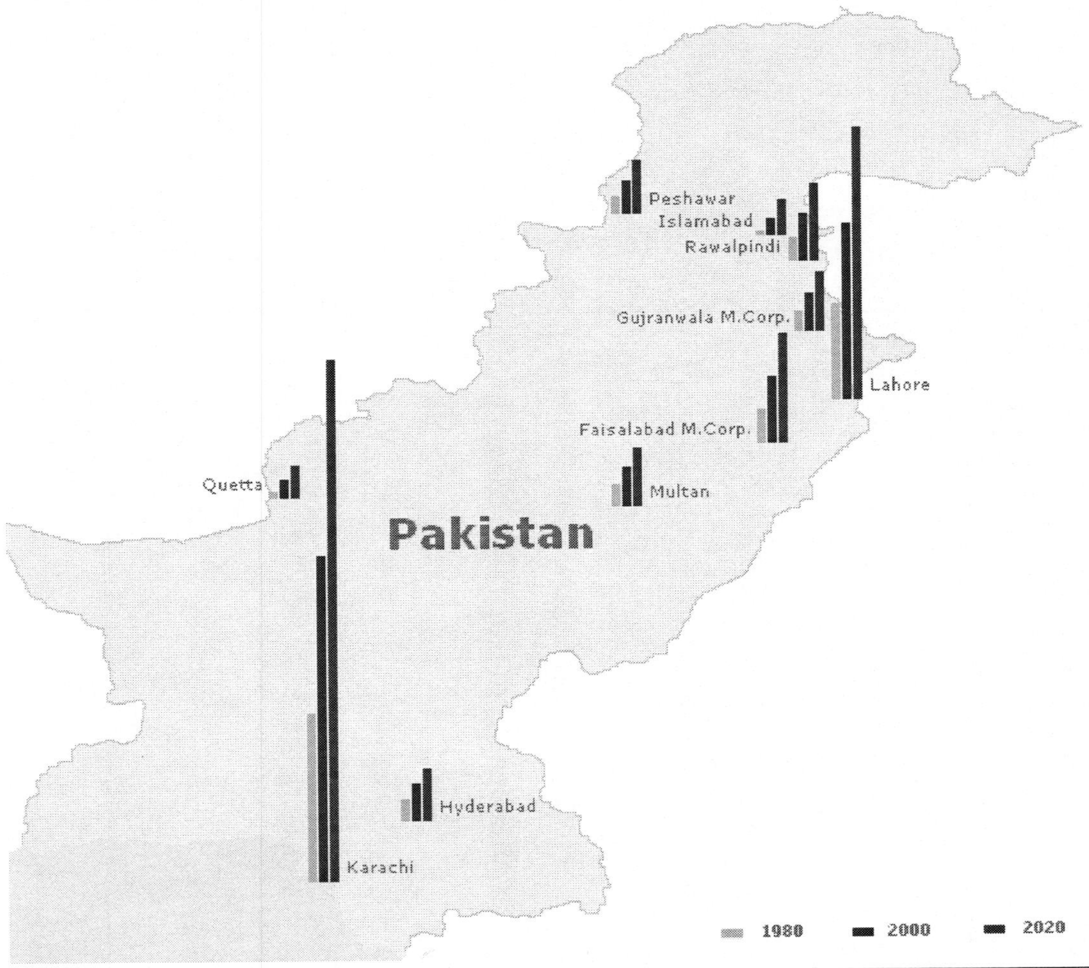

Peshawar
Islamabad
Rawalpindi
Gujranwala M.Corp.
Lahore
Faisalabad M.Corp.
Quetta
Multan
Pakistan
Hyderabad
Karachi
1980
2000
2020

Peru

Table 5.223 Key population trends

'000

	1980	1985	1990	1995	2000	2005	2010	2015	2020	CAGR	Period growth
Population at January 1st	17,356.3	19,390.2	21,425.0	23,444.4	25,442.7	27,428.1	29,402.9	31,328.6	33,159.8	1.63	91.05
Male	8,736.9	9,746.5	10,754.3	11,767.1	12,765.5	13,753.6	14,734.8	15,688.3	16,591.5	1.62	89.90
Female	8,619.4	9,643.7	10,670.7	11,677.3	12,677.2	13,674.5	14,668.0	15,640.2	16,568.3	1.65	92.22
0-4 yrs	2,733.9	2,789.1	2,930.6	2,971.3	2,939.6	2,940.7	2,951.1	2,872.5	2,814.6	0.07	2.95
5-9 yrs	2,402.8	2,624.1	2,704.4	2,844.7	2,918.0	2,918.7	2,928.5	2,933.7	2,859.6	0.44	19.01
10-14 yrs	2,144.3	2,363.5	2,570.4	2,661.1	2,814.5	2,905.6	2,918.3	2,927.6	2,926.3	0.78	36.47
15-19 yrs	1,888.4	2,107.2	2,314.1	2,523.7	2,621.8	2,784.8	2,883.1	2,901.2	2,911.5	1.09	54.18
20-24 yrs	1,579.8	1,844.4	2,046.1	2,250.0	2,462.1	2,559.4	2,724.4	2,839.3	2,866.1	1.50	81.43
25-29 yrs	1,309.4	1,533.0	1,777.1	1,973.8	2,179.6	2,388.4	2,485.1	2,669.9	2,796.1	1.91	113.54
30-34 yrs	1,063.9	1,268.2	1,473.5	1,710.7	1,906.8	2,106.2	2,313.8	2,429.4	2,625.6	2.28	146.79
35-39 yrs	883.2	1,029.3	1,218.4	1,417.5	1,651.5	1,839.8	2,038.1	2,261.6	2,386.9	2.52	170.27
40-44 yrs	767.9	852.6	986.7	1,168.8	1,364.8	1,591.8	1,779.5	1,989.9	2,219.7	2.69	189.07
45-49 yrs	656.5	737.6	814.2	943.6	1,121.7	1,311.0	1,537.1	1,733.0	1,947.2	2.76	196.61
50-54 yrs	533.6	624.5	698.4	772.5	899.6	1,072.3	1,260.7	1,490.5	1,687.1	2.92	216.15
55-59 yrs	424.4	499.6	582.8	654.2	728.4	853.1	1,024.2	1,212.5	1,438.6	3.10	238.94
60-64 yrs	337.2	387.0	454.8	533.5	604.8	679.6	802.6	970.0	1,152.3	3.12	241.75
65-69 yrs	267.8	293.6	337.5	400.0	476.3	547.6	621.6	739.6	898.0	3.07	235.32
70-74 yrs	189.2	215.8	238.9	278.6	337.7	410.7	478.7	548.3	656.6	3.16	247.07
75-79 yrs	107.9	134.2	157.8	180.4	216.7	270.1	335.0	395.0	456.6	3.67	323.23
80+ yrs	66.2	86.4	119.4	159.9	198.8	248.1	320.9	414.4	516.9	5.27	680.85
Median age of population (years)	18.6	19.5	20.4	21.5	22.8	24.2	25.6	27.2	28.9	1.11	55.28

Table 5.224 Key economic trends

As stated

	1990	1995	2000	2005	2010	2015	2020	CAGR	Period growth
Total GDP (PEN per capita)	7,828.9	9,378.4	9,771.3	11,129.2	14,354.1	17,612.0	21,791.1	3.47	178.3
Disposable income (PEN per capita)	5,943.9	6,593.1	6,628.7	7,300.9	9,067.3	10,889.8	13,337.9	2.73	124.4
Disposable income (PEN per household)	29,005.7	30,791.9	29,631.2	31,135.0	36,639.4	41,219.4	47,286.3	1.64	63.0
Number of households by annual household disposable income ('000)									
Over US$1,000	3,780.3	4,669.0	5,170.8	5,968.7	6,978.6	8,054.9	9,179.3	3.00	142.8
Over US$10,000	425.6	1,022.9	926.4	1,387.0	2,405.6	3,552.4	4,977.7	8.54	1,069.6
Over US$25,000	84.9	222.5	195.9	320.4	625.2	1,038.1	1,688.4	10.48	1,889.8
Over US$75,000	18.9	38.7	34.9	53.6	96.7	158.7	259.4	9.12	1,269.5
Over US$150,000	8.2	16.9	15.3	23.1	38.1	58.3	86.1	8.14	945.7
Total households	4,390.5	5,019.8	5,691.7	6,431.7	7,276.5	8,276.7	9,353.3	2.55	113.0

Note: Per capita data is shown at constant 2010 prices. Household disposable income bands are shown at current prices.

Table 5.225 Young generation

'000

	1980	1985	1990	1995	2000	2005	2010	2015	2020	CAGR	Period growth
Babies under 12 months	576.9	562.4	616.8	594.8	587.7	593.8	592.7	564.6	564.6	-0.05	-2.13
Infants under 24 months	1,139.1	1,124.5	1,215.4	1,192.6	1,175.3	1,184.0	1,184.5	1,135.2	1,127.0	-0.03	-1.07
Toddlers aged 1-4	2,157.0	2,226.7	2,313.8	2,376.5	2,351.9	2,346.9	2,358.4	2,307.9	2,250.0	0.11	4.31
Children aged 2-9	3,997.6	4,288.7	4,419.6	4,623.4	4,682.3	4,675.5	4,695.1	4,670.9	4,547.2	0.32	13.75
Female	1,966.2	2,109.7	2,175.4	2,275.0	2,302.3	2,296.3	2,303.1	2,289.3	2,227.6	0.31	13.29
Male	2,031.4	2,179.0	2,244.2	2,348.4	2,380.0	2,379.1	2,392.1	2,381.7	2,319.6	0.33	14.19
Tweenagers aged 10-14	2,144.3	2,363.5	2,570.4	2,661.1	2,814.5	2,905.6	2,918.3	2,927.6	2,926.3	0.78	36.47
Female	1,056.1	1,164.1	1,266.1	1,311.2	1,386.6	1,430.6	1,435.1	1,437.6	1,435.4	0.77	35.92
Male	1,088.2	1,199.4	1,304.3	1,349.9	1,427.9	1,475.0	1,483.2	1,490.0	1,490.9	0.79	37.00
Teenagers aged 13-19	2,717.7	3,019.7	3,319.6	3,571.2	3,726.5	3,940.8	4,049.5	4,069.4	4,085.4	1.02	50.32
Female	1,339.4	1,489.1	1,637.3	1,760.7	1,837.6	1,942.7	1,994.7	2,001.7	2,006.6	1.02	49.82
Male	1,378.4	1,530.6	1,682.3	1,810.5	1,888.8	1,998.0	2,054.8	2,067.7	2,078.8	1.03	50.82
Studying age 18-22	1,703.4	1,956.3	2,149.6	2,371.1	2,533.1	2,646.6	2,805.6	2,873.2	2,884.9	1.33	69.36
Female	840.5	966.5	1,062.7	1,170.9	1,250.8	1,307.3	1,385.2	1,416.7	1,419.9	1.32	68.93
Male	862.9	989.8	1,086.8	1,200.2	1,282.3	1,339.3	1,420.5	1,456.6	1,464.9	1.33	69.77
Young adults aged 15-29	4,777.5	5,484.7	6,137.3	6,747.5	7,263.6	7,732.6	8,092.6	8,410.4	8,573.7	1.47	79.46
Female	2,359.3	2,713.1	3,039.0	3,337.2	3,590.6	3,822.2	3,999.2	4,152.1	4,226.0	1.47	79.13
Male	2,418.3	2,771.5	3,098.2	3,410.3	3,673.0	3,910.3	4,093.4	4,258.3	4,347.7	1.48	79.78

Table 5.226 Middle-aged generation
'000

	1980	1985	1990	1995	2000	2005	2010	2015	2020	CAGR	Period growth
Middle-aged adults 30-59	4,329	5,012	5,774	6,667	7,673	8,774	9,953	11,117	12,305	2.65	184.2
Female	2,161	2,507	2,894	3,342	3,846	4,397	4,985	5,565	6,155	2.65	184.9
Male	2,169	2,505	2,880	3,326	3,827	4,377	4,969	5,552	6,150	2.64	183.6
Baby boomers aged 40-59	2,382	2,714	3,082	3,539	4,114	4,828	5,601	6,426	7,293	2.84	206.1
Female	1,195	1,363	1,549	1,780	2,072	2,433	2,821	3,233	3,664	2.84	206.6
Male	1,187	1,351	1,533	1,759	2,042	2,395	2,780	3,193	3,628	2.83	205.6

Table 5.227 Elderly population
'000

	1980	1985	1990	1995	2000	2005	2010	2015	2020	CAGR	Period growth
Elderly population (60+)	968.3	1,117.0	1,308.4	1,552.3	1,834.2	2,156.2	2,558.8	3,067.4	3,680.4	3.39	280.1
Female	518.0	597.8	699.2	826.6	975.9	1,148.5	1,365.9	1,641.1	1,972.8	3.40	280.9
Male	450.3	519.2	609.1	725.7	858.4	1,007.6	1,192.9	1,426.3	1,707.6	3.39	279.2

Table 5.228 Population of biggest cities 1980-2020
'000

	1980	1985	1990	1995	2000	2005	2010	2015	2020	CAGR	Period growth
Lima	4,440.8	5,135.0	5,957.0	6,647.7	7,379.9	8,161.5	8,947.6	9,733.3	10,505.7	2.18	136.6
Arequipa	433.3	505.2	587.0	646.0	694.8	735.7	771.0	811.0	854.3	1.71	97.2
Trujillo	342.7	404.2	476.7	537.1	597.4	658.8	719.5	780.6	840.9	2.27	145.3
Chiclayo	269.5	323.0	384.9	432.9	474.4	511.3	545.0	580.7	617.6	2.09	129.1
Piura	202.6	230.2	263.3	291.9	324.9	362.2	400.6	438.6	475.5	2.16	134.7
Iquitos	171.7	209.6	254.2	291.2	325.6	358.4	390.1	422.2	454.1	2.46	164.4
Cusco	179.2	207.1	240.5	269.2	300.7	335.0	370.0	404.7	438.4	2.26	144.6
Chimbote	212.1	234.3	259.7	278.9	300.7	325.0	349.3	374.5	400.1	1.60	88.6
Huancayo	158.0	195.8	239.4	272.4	297.6	316.9	332.9	350.9	370.2	2.15	134.3
Tacna	93.2	122.7	157.6	186.8	211.9	234.2	255.1	276.2	297.2	2.94	218.9

Chart 5.145 Population age shift 2000 and 2020, Each Column Represents a Single Age Group

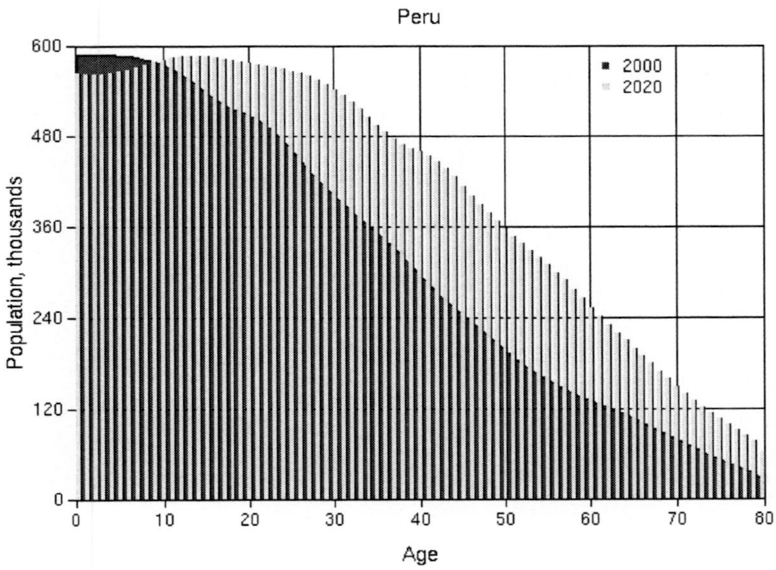

Chart 5.146 Population pyramids, 1980/2000/2010/2020

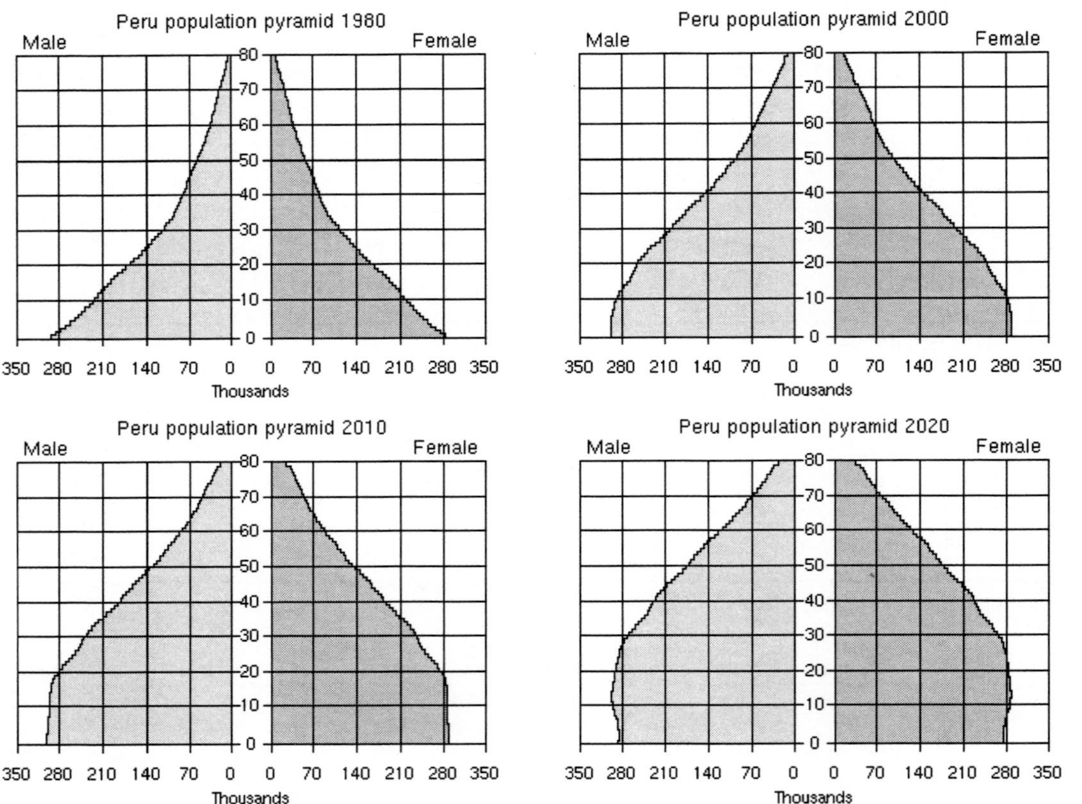

Chart 5.147 Major Cities: 1980, 2000 and 2020

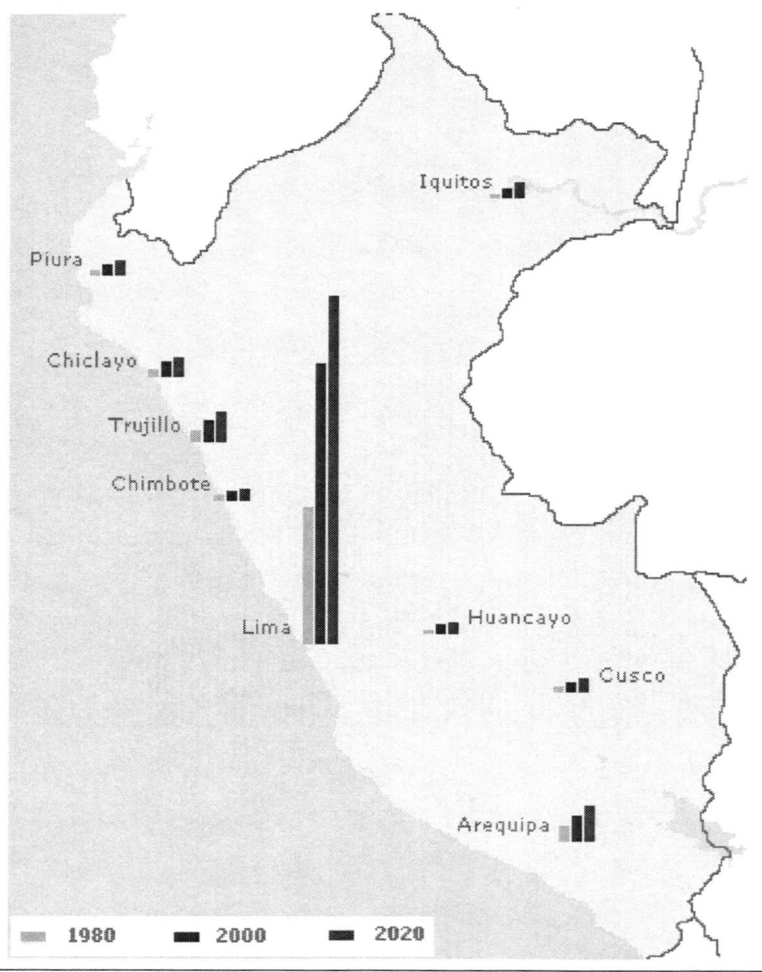

Philippines

Table 5.229 Key population trends

'000

	1980	1985	1990	1995	2000	2005	2010	2015	2020	CAGR	Period growth
Population at January 1st	48,098.5	53,828.7	60,559.1	68,616.5	76,504.1	85,028.7	93,923.4	102,895.7	112,189.8	2.14	133.3
Male	24,128.8	27,030.6	30,443.2	34,584.2	38,524.3	42,801.7	47,255.4	51,793.6	56,474.8	2.15	134.1
Female	23,969.7	26,798.1	30,115.9	34,032.4	37,979.8	42,227.0	46,668.1	51,102.0	55,715.0	2.13	132.4
0-4 yrs	7,822.1	8,363.6	9,111.4	9,803.8	10,082.2	10,353.6	10,906.6	11,254.1	11,508.3	0.97	47.1
5-9 yrs	6,828.1	7,493.4	8,166.8	9,072.1	9,735.6	10,100.4	10,380.8	10,899.7	11,197.2	1.24	64.0
10-14 yrs	6,088.6	6,635.0	7,373.6	8,198.4	9,061.4	9,783.4	10,142.9	10,416.9	10,977.2	1.48	80.3
15-19 yrs	5,340.5	5,901.9	6,503.8	7,356.6	8,141.1	9,062.8	9,784.8	10,135.8	10,454.9	1.69	95.8
20-24 yrs	4,571.1	5,139.7	5,723.2	6,390.3	7,206.8	8,044.8	8,968.8	9,699.2	10,091.2	2.00	120.8
25-29 yrs	3,816.8	4,376.7	4,948.5	5,565.7	6,199.9	7,064.7	7,904.0	8,827.4	9,595.2	2.33	151.4
30-34 yrs	2,928.7	3,647.6	4,208.6	4,809.0	5,397.3	6,073.5	6,940.5	7,771.8	8,729.4	2.77	198.1
35-39 yrs	2,413.3	2,791.8	3,506.6	4,098.5	4,674.9	5,299.6	5,979.0	6,850.1	7,716.8	2.95	219.8
40-44 yrs	1,995.0	2,292.0	2,676.1	3,416.1	3,987.1	4,594.6	5,222.3	5,912.3	6,818.1	3.12	241.8
45-49 yrs	1,634.4	1,881.9	2,185.6	2,594.9	3,312.8	3,907.3	4,516.2	5,153.9	5,873.2	3.25	259.4
50-54 yrs	1,234.8	1,523.3	1,776.0	2,101.0	2,492.6	3,220.8	3,812.1	4,427.8	5,088.1	3.60	312.1
55-59 yrs	1,050.4	1,128.5	1,411.8	1,680.0	1,987.2	2,386.1	3,098.5	3,680.9	4,309.2	3.59	310.3
60-64 yrs	838.8	930.5	1,015.1	1,298.8	1,547.8	1,855.1	2,239.8	2,921.6	3,502.3	3.64	317.5
65-69 yrs	669.2	706.3	797.6	891.3	1,144.3	1,385.0	1,671.7	2,028.4	2,679.0	3.53	300.4
70-74 yrs	462.9	517.9	558.7	648.1	728.2	951.9	1,163.8	1,410.9	1,739.8	3.37	275.8
75-79 yrs	246.7	313.3	358.2	399.4	467.5	536.8	712.1	877.8	1,087.2	3.78	340.7
80+ yrs	157.2	185.3	237.6	292.5	337.5	408.4	479.6	627.2	822.7	4.22	423.2
Median age of population (years)	18.0	18.7	19.3	19.9	20.8	21.9	23.1	24.5	25.9	0.92	44.1

Table 5.230 Key economic trends

As stated

	1990	1995	2000	2005	2010	2015	2020	CAGR	Period growth
Total GDP (Ps per capita)	65,696.3	64,588.1	70,257.2	78,709.0	86,994.4	98,261.1	112,368.7	1.81	71.0
Disposable income (Ps per capita)	47,959.0	49,211.2	51,988.6	57,266.2	63,855.8	73,389.3	84,243.8	1.90	75.7
Disposable income (Ps per household)	254,605.7	251,841.1	260,441.0	281,098.2	307,438.7	347,118.1	392,855.4	1.46	54.3
Number of households by annual household disposable income ('000)									
Over US$1,000	8,699.2	11,749.6	12,207.5	14,858.1	18,035.4	20,580.2	23,285.7	3.34	167.7
Over US$10,000	433.3	1,045.5	874.0	1,182.2	2,757.8	4,178.5	6,613.0	9.51	1,426.2
Over US$25,000	102.9	202.6	175.7	229.1	486.2	768.6	1,330.2	8.90	1,192.5
Over US$75,000	27.4	51.9	46.0	60.4	107.8	152.1	228.6	7.33	734.7
Over US$150,000	11.9	22.4	20.0	26.0	46.5	65.5	97.7	7.28	722.7
Total households	11,407.3	13,408.1	15,271.5	17,322.3	19,508.1	21,754.7	24,057.9	2.52	110.9

Note: Per capita data is shown at constant 2010 prices. Household disposable income bands are shown at current prices.

Table 5.231 Young generation

'000

	1980	1985	1990	1995	2000	2005	2010	2015	2020	CAGR	Period growth
Babies under 12 months	1,663	1,736	1,913	2,001	2,028	2,101	2,231	2,336	2,449	0.97	47.3
Infants under 24 months	3,274	3,443	3,778	3,988	4,052	4,183	4,449	4,563	4,727	0.92	44.4
Toddlers aged 1-4	6,159	6,628	7,198	7,803	8,055	8,253	8,675	8,918	9,059	0.97	47.1
Children aged 2-9	11,376	12,414	13,500	14,888	15,766	16,271	16,839	17,590	17,979	1.15	58.0
Female	5,600	6,109	6,636	7,289	7,717	7,958	8,232	8,594	8,776	1.13	56.7
Male	5,776	6,306	6,864	7,599	8,048	8,313	8,606	8,996	9,203	1.17	59.3
Tweenagers aged 10-14	6,089	6,635	7,374	8,198	9,061	9,783	10,143	10,417	10,977	1.48	80.3
Female	3,005	3,268	3,628	4,023	4,445	4,795	4,966	5,097	5,367	1.46	78.6
Male	3,084	3,367	3,745	4,176	4,616	4,989	5,177	5,320	5,610	1.51	81.9
Teenagers aged 13-19	7,691	8,461	9,353	10,535	11,663	12,915	13,817	14,256	14,795	1.65	92.4
Female	3,801	4,174	4,605	5,173	5,731	6,340	6,776	6,982	7,240	1.62	90.5
Male	3,890	4,287	4,748	5,362	5,932	6,575	7,041	7,274	7,555	1.67	94.2
Studying age 18-22	4,871	5,453	6,026	6,776	7,589	8,459	9,347	9,922	10,223	1.87	109.9
Female	2,413	2,696	2,973	3,332	3,736	4,163	4,595	4,868	5,009	1.84	107.6
Male	2,458	2,757	3,053	3,444	3,853	4,296	4,753	5,054	5,214	1.90	112.1
Young adults aged 15-29	13,728	15,418	17,176	19,313	21,548	24,172	26,658	28,662	30,141	1.99	119.6
Female	6,809	7,633	8,485	9,511	10,619	11,909	13,123	14,083	14,788	1.96	117.2
Male	6,920	7,786	8,690	9,801	10,929	12,263	13,534	14,579	15,354	2.01	121.9

Table 5.232 Middle-aged generation
'000

	1980	1985	1990	1995	2000	2005	2010	2015	2020	CAGR	Period growth
Middle-aged adults 30-59	11,257	13,265	15,765	18,700	21,852	25,482	29,569	33,797	38,535	3.12	242.3
Female	5,641	6,619	7,860	9,323	10,917	12,751	14,818	16,885	19,193	3.11	240.3
Male	5,616	6,646	7,905	9,377	10,935	12,731	14,751	16,912	19,342	3.14	244.4
Baby boomers aged 40-59	5,915	6,826	8,049	9,792	11,780	14,109	16,649	19,175	22,089	3.35	273.5
Female	3,019	3,435	4,013	4,893	5,906	7,096	8,400	9,641	11,064	3.30	266.4
Male	2,895	3,391	4,036	4,899	5,874	7,013	8,249	9,534	11,024	3.40	280.8

Table 5.233 Elderly population
'000

	1980	1985	1990	1995	2000	2005	2010	2015	2020	CAGR	Period growth
Elderly population (60+)	2,375	2,653	2,967	3,530	4,225	5,137	6,267	7,866	9,831	3.62	314.0
Female	1,307	1,479	1,655	1,938	2,302	2,772	3,356	4,216	5,288	3.56	304.8
Male	1,068	1,175	1,312	1,592	1,924	2,365	2,911	3,650	4,543	3.68	325.2

Table 5.234 Population of biggest cities 1980-2020
'000

	1980	1985	1990	1995	2000	2005	2010	2015	2020	CAGR	Period growth
Quezon City	1,165.9	1,392.1	1,669.8	1,989.4	2,173.8	2,506.0	2,935.3	3,355.7	3,760.7	2.97	222.6
Manila	1,630.5	1,623.1	1,601.2	1,654.8	1,581.1	1,618.6	1,716.2	1,813.9	1,916.3	0.40	17.5
Caloocan	467.8	593.3	763.4	1,023.2	1,177.6	1,322.6	1,460.4	1,596.9	1,732.3	3.33	270.3
Davao	408.8	462.9	521.5	593.2	666.8	751.8	834.9	917.0	998.3	2.26	144.2
Cebu	490.3	553.2	610.4	662.3	718.8	778.8	826.4	874.4	924.4	1.60	88.5
Antipolo	54.1	56.9	83.6	246.2	470.9	596.7	689.9	781.7	870.4	7.19	1,508.4
Tagig	134.1	186.2	266.6	381.3	467.4	567.4	681.9	793.9	901.0	4.88	571.7
Pasig	268.6	327.4	397.7	471.1	505.1	577.5	675.8	772.1	864.8	2.97	222.0
Valenzuela	212.4	265.4	340.2	437.2	485.4	542.1	607.8	672.6	736.3	3.16	246.7
Cagayan de Oro	170.4	204.9	252.5	349.7	461.9	532.7	584.9	636.8	688.5	3.55	304.0

Chart 5.148 Population age shift 2000 and 2020, Each Column Represents a Single Age Group

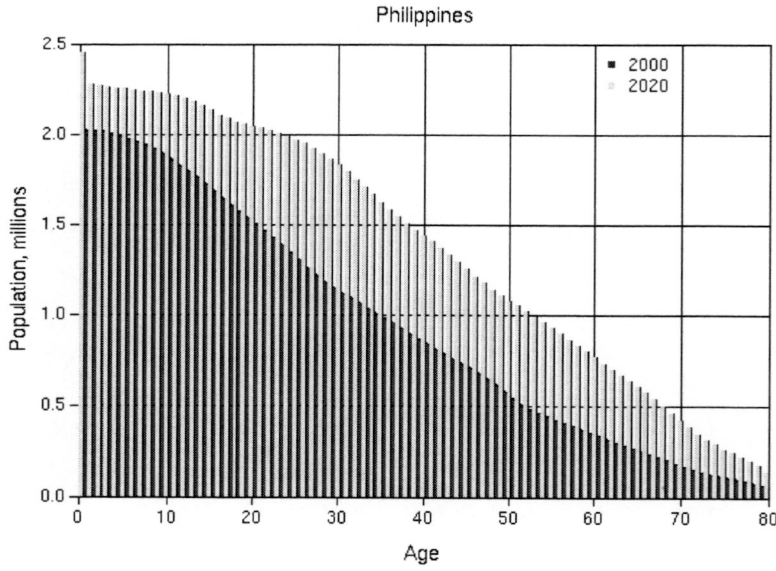

Chart 5.149 Population pyramids, 1980/2000/2010/2020

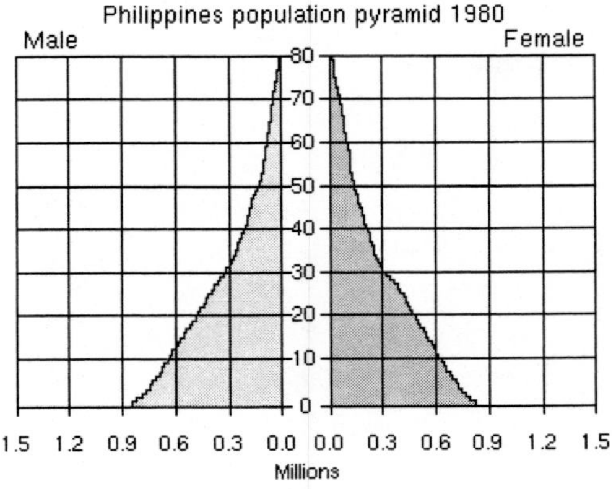

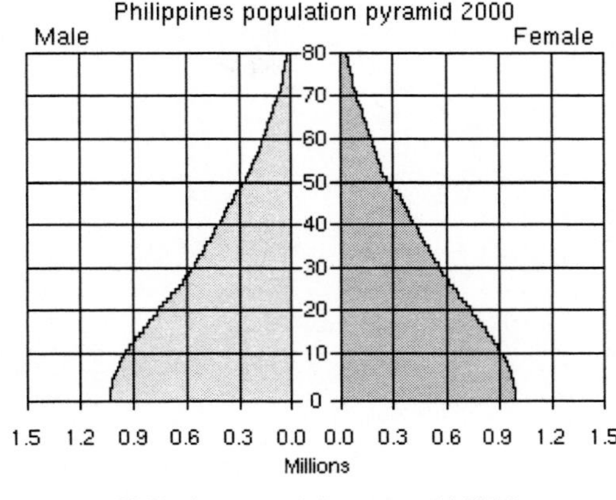

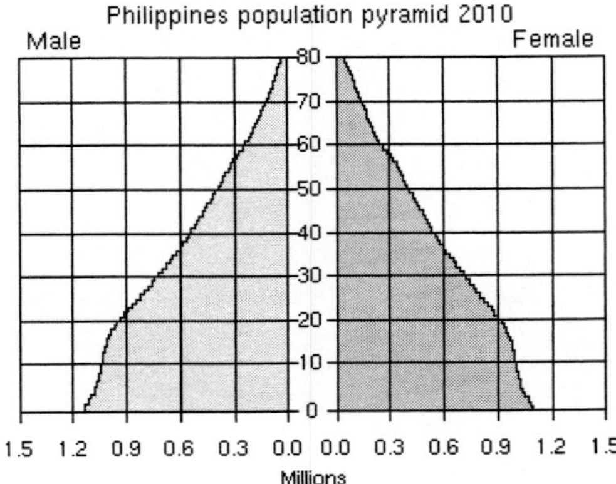

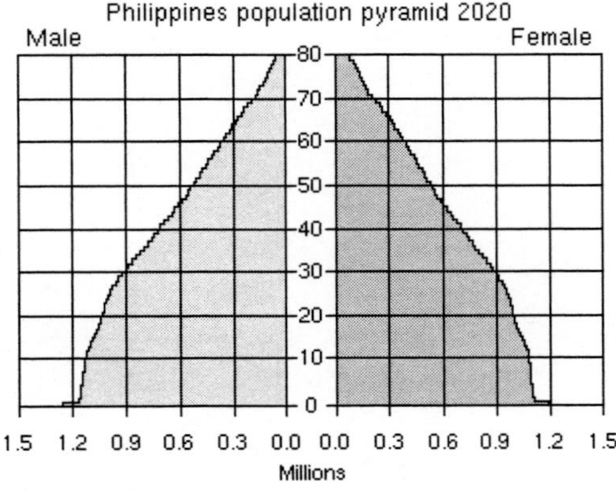

Chart 5.150 Major Cities: 1980, 2000 and 2020

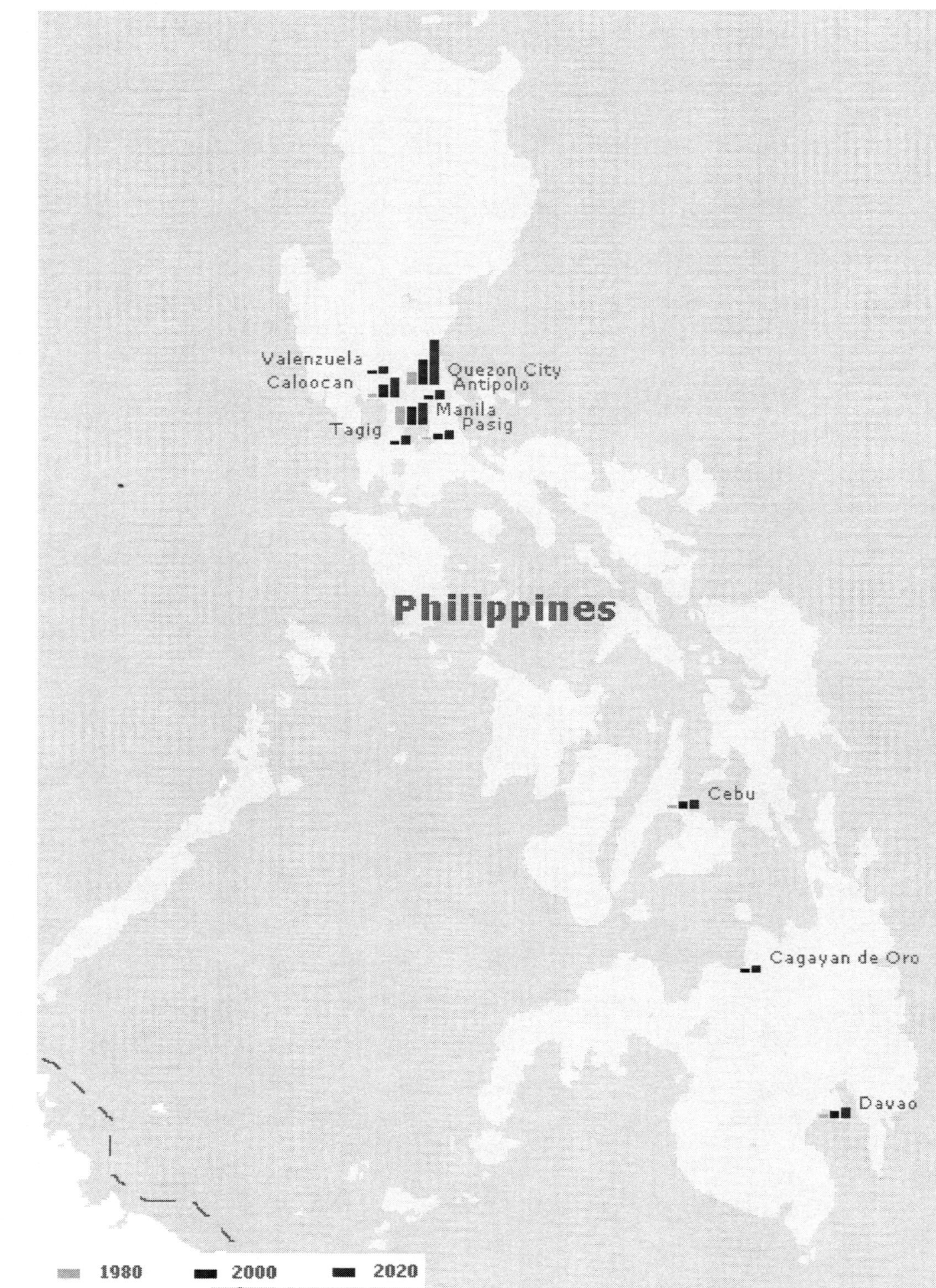

Poland

Table 5.235 Key population trends

'000

	1980	1985	1990	1995	2000	2005	2010	2015	2020	CAGR	Period growth
Population at January 1st	35,413.4	37,063.3	37,988.0	38,265.0	38,263.0	38,173.8	37,929.5	37,631.1	37,384.9	0.14	5.57
Male	17,253.8	18,073.8	18,515.9	18,601.7	18,549.5	18,470.3	18,325.9	18,163.8	18,043.8	0.11	4.58
Female	18,159.6	18,989.5	19,472.1	19,663.3	19,713.5	19,703.6	19,603.6	19,467.3	19,341.1	0.16	6.51
0-4 yrs	3,219.6	3,419.6	3,005.5	2,518.9	2,008.6	1,794.5	1,819.7	1,895.2	1,915.2	-1.29	-40.52
5-9 yrs	2,813.0	3,201.7	3,389.3	2,975.4	2,509.8	2,045.5	1,787.3	1,815.1	1,890.6	-0.99	-32.79
10-14 yrs	2,517.0	2,800.5	3,205.4	3,354.7	2,962.0	2,537.3	2,038.4	1,782.4	1,810.1	-0.82	-28.08
15-19 yrs	2,825.2	2,503.4	2,795.5	3,168.6	3,331.3	2,980.5	2,528.6	2,030.8	1,776.1	-1.15	-37.14
20-24 yrs	3,383.4	2,801.9	2,454.2	2,754.9	3,136.2	3,306.8	2,954.6	2,499.9	2,012.4	-1.29	-40.52
25-29 yrs	3,326.8	3,348.3	2,726.3	2,417.0	2,730.1	3,062.1	3,266.4	2,898.9	2,461.9	-0.75	-26.00
30-34 yrs	2,638.6	3,287.5	3,306.5	2,682.0	2,393.7	2,665.0	3,024.6	3,206.6	2,854.6	0.20	8.19
35-39 yrs	1,873.9	2,603.6	3,217.0	3,242.4	2,647.6	2,366.3	2,634.1	2,982.0	3,169.6	1.32	69.15
40-44 yrs	2,120.0	1,837.9	2,544.8	3,136.7	3,181.9	2,585.9	2,327.7	2,587.2	2,939.8	0.82	38.67
45-49 yrs	2,195.9	2,064.0	1,780.1	2,461.5	3,053.4	3,093.5	2,523.7	2,267.4	2,531.5	0.36	15.28
50-54 yrs	2,090.2	2,113.0	1,974.8	1,698.5	2,370.6	2,942.4	2,989.8	2,436.8	2,198.2	0.13	5.16
55-59 yrs	1,740.8	1,978.0	1,992.1	1,851.5	1,607.2	2,264.5	2,807.3	2,856.8	2,337.9	0.74	34.30
60-64 yrs	1,058.6	1,609.2	1,815.8	1,816.9	1,711.9	1,511.5	2,122.6	2,645.5	2,707.2	2.38	155.73
65-69 yrs	1,332.6	942.8	1,427.5	1,594.5	1,619.0	1,561.7	1,373.3	1,951.5	2,450.7	1.53	83.90
70-74 yrs	1,078.7	1,113.3	780.2	1,182.3	1,346.4	1,412.4	1,355.7	1,204.6	1,739.8	1.20	61.29
75-79 yrs	706.4	803.5	821.1	584.2	914.4	1,078.0	1,133.3	1,105.4	997.8	0.87	41.26
80+ yrs	492.7	635.2	751.9	825.0	739.0	966.2	1,242.4	1,464.8	1,591.6	2.97	223.02
Median age of population (years)	29.4	30.7	32.2	33.7	35.1	36.5	37.8	39.5	41.3	0.85	40.52

Table 5.236 Key economic trends

As stated

	1990	1995	2000	2005	2010	2015	2020	CAGR	Period growth
Total GDP (PLN per capita)	17,645.7	19,506.3	25,388.3	29,620.5	36,631.8	44,801.1	53,341.8	3.76	202.3
Disposable income (PLN per capita)	14,536.0	15,057.5	17,978.3	19,552.7	24,117.0	29,843.5	35,654.6	3.04	145.3
Disposable income (PLN per household)	45,588.6	46,090.2	52,789.4	53,981.7	62,781.9	74,628.0	87,530.4	2.20	92.0
Number of households by annual household disposable income ('000)									
Over US$1,000	11,891.2	12,489.5	13,015.0	13,822.0	14,567.3	15,047.2	15,227.6	0.83	28.1
Over US$10,000	423.3	2,908.0	4,045.1	8,517.2	10,853.3	12,895.0	14,042.5	12.38	3,217.5
Over US$25,000	129.2	405.3	558.8	1,574.5	2,584.4	4,299.9	6,394.6	13.89	4,851.1
Over US$75,000	31.1	98.5	126.1	241.6	339.2	497.1	758.9	11.23	2,338.6
Over US$150,000	12.7	40.3	52.3	100.9	141.2	194.6	263.2	10.64	1,976.0
Total households	12,112.6	12,501.0	13,031.1	13,827.0	14,570.2	15,048.6	15,228.3	0.77	25.7

Note: Per capita data is shown at constant 2010 prices. Household disposable income bands are shown at current prices.

Table 5.237 Young generation

'000

	1980	1985	1990	1995	2000	2005	2010	2015	2020	CAGR	Period growth
Babies under 12 months	675.5	687.8	553.2	470.9	375.3	354.2	369.7	384.2	380.5	-1.43	-43.68
Infants under 24 months	1,317.7	1,395.0	1,130.6	953.0	763.2	703.2	735.2	766.3	763.0	-1.36	-42.10
Toddlers aged 1-4	2,544.1	2,731.9	2,452.3	2,048.0	1,633.3	1,440.3	1,450.0	1,511.0	1,534.7	-1.26	-39.68
Children aged 2-9	4,714.9	5,226.3	5,264.2	4,541.3	3,755.2	3,136.8	2,871.8	2,944.0	3,042.8	-1.09	-35.47
Female	2,303.6	2,551.8	2,574.4	2,217.8	1,833.4	1,528.6	1,394.5	1,429.6	1,478.2	-1.10	-35.83
Male	2,411.3	2,674.5	2,689.8	2,323.5	1,921.8	1,608.1	1,477.3	1,514.4	1,564.5	-1.08	-35.12
Tweenagers aged 10-14	2,517.0	2,800.5	3,205.4	3,354.7	2,962.0	2,537.3	2,038.4	1,782.4	1,810.1	-0.82	-28.08
Female	1,230.1	1,368.1	1,566.3	1,643.9	1,449.3	1,239.9	992.6	864.2	876.9	-0.84	-28.71
Male	1,286.9	1,432.4	1,639.1	1,710.8	1,512.7	1,297.4	1,045.7	918.3	933.2	-0.80	-27.49
Teenagers aged 13-19	3,840.8	3,559.3	4,061.1	4,476.0	4,593.9	4,065.2	3,391.4	2,765.0	2,494.1	-1.07	-35.06
Female	1,868.7	1,740.2	1,984.4	2,193.3	2,257.0	1,985.7	1,656.9	1,345.8	1,208.5	-1.08	-35.33
Male	1,972.1	1,819.1	2,076.7	2,282.8	2,336.9	2,079.5	1,734.6	1,419.2	1,285.7	-1.06	-34.81
Studying age 18-22	3,189.8	2,633.1	2,529.7	2,960.1	3,195.0	3,301.6	2,777.5	2,293.8	1,894.4	-1.29	-40.61
Female	1,550.9	1,284.4	1,232.1	1,452.4	1,572.1	1,619.1	1,357.7	1,122.5	922.1	-1.29	-40.54
Male	1,638.9	1,348.8	1,297.6	1,507.7	1,622.9	1,682.5	1,419.8	1,171.2	972.3	-1.30	-40.68
Young adults aged 15-29	9,535.5	8,653.6	7,976.0	8,340.5	9,197.6	9,349.3	8,749.6	7,429.6	6,250.4	-1.05	-34.45
Female	4,665.4	4,228.4	3,905.9	4,087.9	4,524.5	4,591.2	4,294.0	3,638.1	3,051.9	-1.06	-34.58
Male	4,870.1	4,425.2	4,070.1	4,252.6	4,673.1	4,758.1	4,455.6	3,791.5	3,198.4	-1.05	-34.32

Table 5.238 **Middle-aged generation**
'000

	1980	1985	1990	1995	2000	2005	2010	2015	2020	CAGR	Period growth
Middle-aged adults 30-59	12,659	13,884	14,815	15,073	15,254	15,918	16,307	16,337	16,032	0.59	26.6
Female	6,508	7,067	7,501	7,639	7,725	8,053	8,240	8,230	8,048	0.53	23.7
Male	6,151	6,817	7,314	7,433	7,529	7,864	8,067	8,107	7,984	0.65	29.8
Baby boomers aged 40-59	8,147	7,993	8,292	9,148	10,213	10,886	10,649	10,148	10,007	0.52	22.8
Female	4,258	4,145	4,265	4,701	5,231	5,569	5,440	5,162	5,066	0.44	19.0
Male	3,889	3,848	4,027	4,448	4,982	5,317	5,208	4,986	4,941	0.60	27.1

Table 5.239 **Elderly population**
'000

	1980	1985	1990	1995	2000	2005	2010	2015	2020	CAGR	Period growth
Elderly population (60+)	4,669	5,104	5,596	6,003	6,331	6,530	7,227	8,372	9,487	1.79	103.2
Female	2,810	3,094	3,374	3,609	3,810	3,949	4,325	4,932	5,515	1.70	96.2
Male	1,859	2,010	2,222	2,394	2,521	2,581	2,902	3,439	3,972	1.92	113.7

Table 5.240 **Population of biggest cities 1980-2020**
'000

	1980	1985	1990	1995	2000	2005	2010	2015	2020	CAGR	Period growth
Warsaw	1,578.6	1,633.9	1,644.9	1,651.5	1,680.5	1,702.0	1,709.3	1,722.8	1,774.9	0.29	12.43
Krakow	706.9	741.5	750.0	748.3	756.7	762.7	765.1	770.7	793.7	0.29	12.29
Lodz	827.5	854.7	851.7	829.0	802.3	770.8	738.7	723.4	732.8	-0.30	-11.45
Wroclaw	610.1	639.7	646.5	641.9	641.7	637.0	630.0	629.3	644.9	0.14	5.71
Poznan	545.6	575.3	585.2	582.7	580.7	578.4	576.3	578.3	594.2	0.21	8.90
Gdansk	451.8	469.1	467.7	462.5	462.3	461.5	460.4	462.3	475.2	0.13	5.18
Szczecin	382.7	406.5	416.6	417.0	416.4	415.4	414.3	415.8	427.4	0.28	11.68
Bydgoszcz	343.0	368.1	381.4	382.3	376.7	371.6	368.1	368.1	377.5	0.24	10.06
Lublin	298.5	326.9	345.1	352.9	356.5	358.7	359.5	361.9	372.6	0.56	24.83
Katowice	351.0	366.5	367.1	353.5	334.7	318.8	307.0	301.6	306.1	-0.34	-12.80

Chart 5.151 Population age shift 2000 and 2020, Each Column Represents a Single Age Group

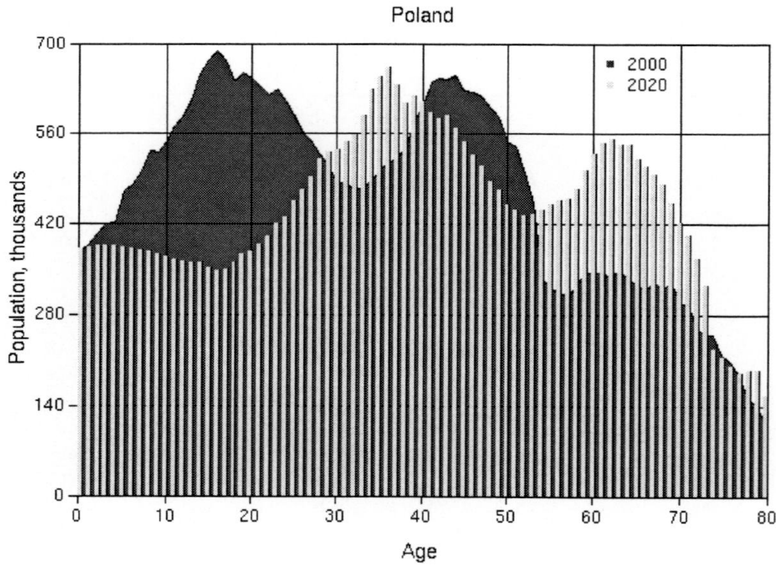

Chart 5.152 Population pyramids, 1980/2000/2010/2020

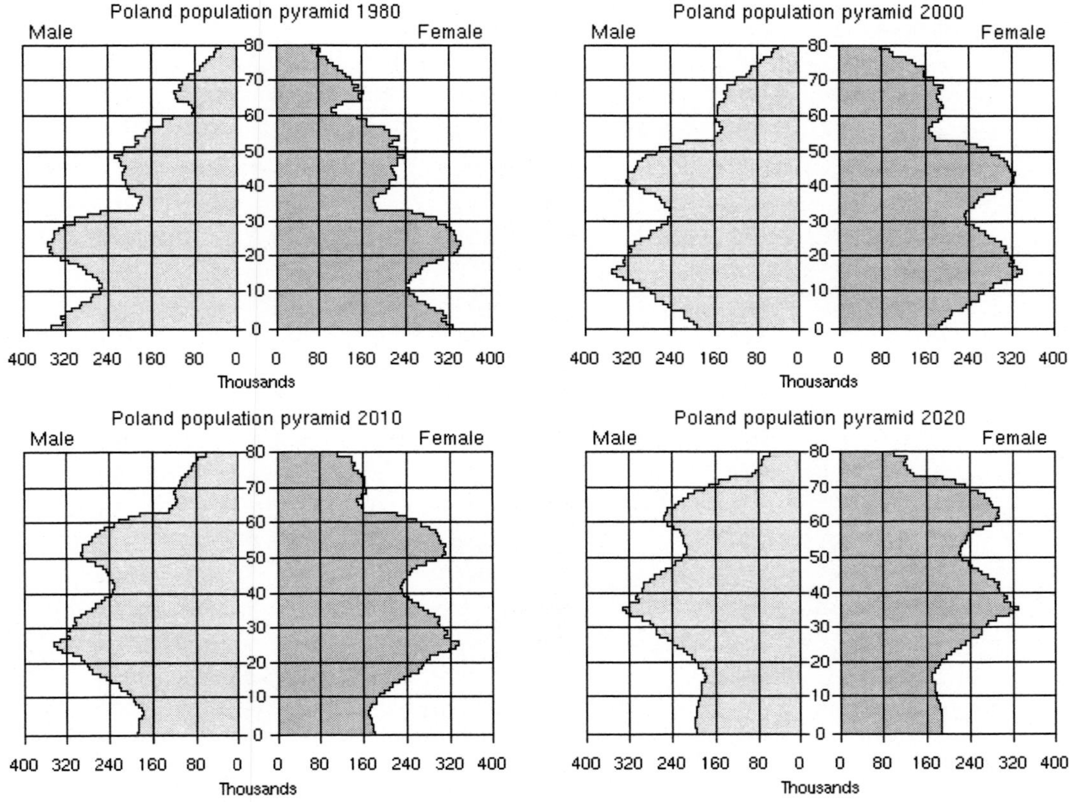

Chart 5.153 Major Cities: 1980, 2000 and 2020

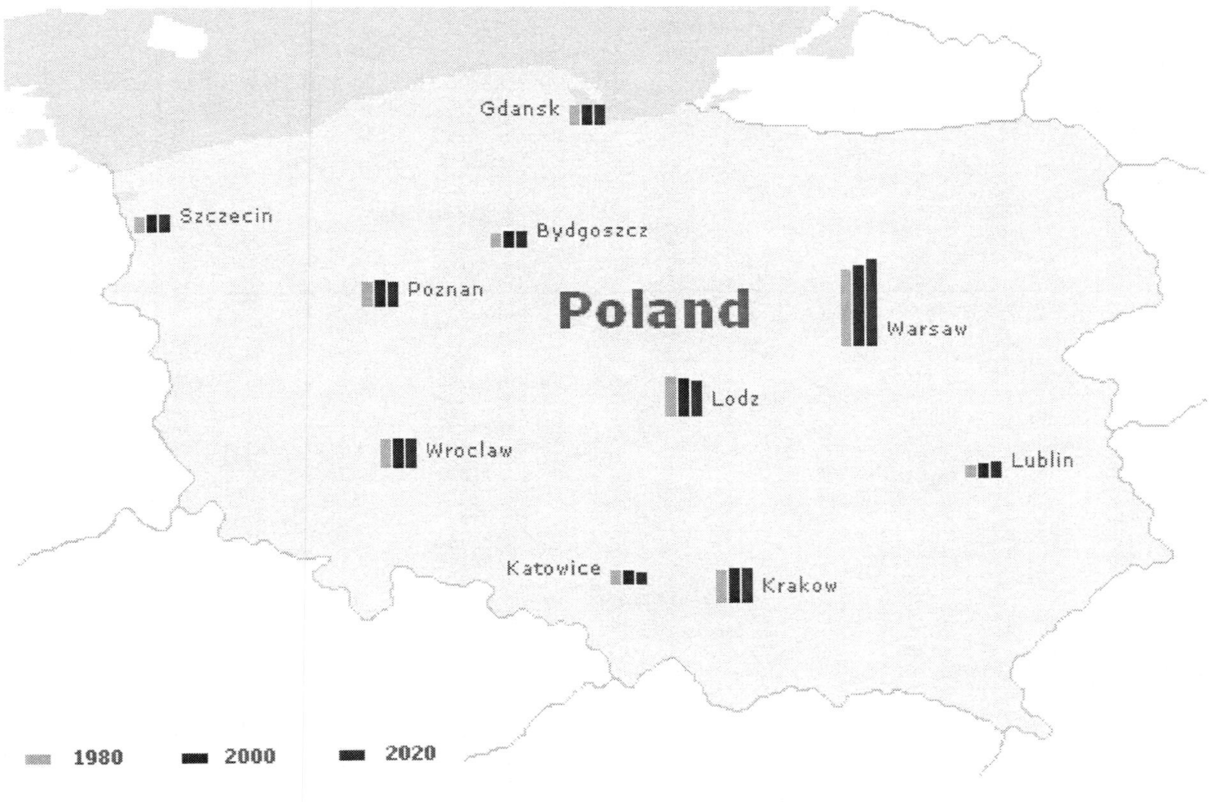

Portugal

Table 5.241 Key population trends

'000

	1980	1985	1990	1995	2000	2005	2010	2015	2020	CAGR	Period growth
Population at January 1st	9,713.6	10,016.6	9,996.0	10,017.6	10,195.0	10,529.3	10,694.5	10,778.9	10,799.2	0.27	11.18
Male	4,670.7	4,830.5	4,819.3	4,826.9	4,918.2	5,094.3	5,181.0	5,225.7	5,236.0	0.29	12.10
Female	5,042.9	5,186.1	5,176.7	5,190.7	5,276.8	5,434.9	5,513.5	5,553.1	5,563.2	0.25	10.32
0-4 yrs	829.7	720.8	574.9	548.3	535.9	553.7	544.9	522.9	481.9	-1.35	-41.91
5-9 yrs	853.0	817.5	688.3	561.0	539.6	537.3	557.4	548.6	526.5	-1.20	-38.28
10-14 yrs	851.4	855.4	818.3	686.6	579.2	556.5	547.2	564.6	555.2	-1.06	-34.79
15-19 yrs	849.2	848.5	842.7	803.6	703.9	598.7	565.4	553.7	570.7	-0.99	-32.79
20-24 yrs	749.6	838.3	777.0	809.6	798.6	728.9	609.5	573.1	560.9	-0.72	-25.17
25-29 yrs	673.7	738.9	751.1	745.6	793.1	825.2	742.2	618.5	581.5	-0.37	-13.68
30-34 yrs	616.4	665.4	701.7	733.5	749.3	817.8	838.5	750.7	626.6	0.04	1.67
35-39 yrs	547.9	616.2	663.8	694.2	755.1	776.9	829.9	845.5	757.4	0.81	38.24
40-44 yrs	578.3	548.2	630.5	664.7	706.6	780.3	785.5	833.6	848.7	0.96	46.75
45-49 yrs	582.6	575.8	556.0	629.6	670.5	719.5	782.2	784.5	832.3	0.90	42.85
50-54 yrs	560.6	572.8	573.4	553.0	626.5	675.7	716.5	777.2	780.2	0.83	39.19
55-59 yrs	521.8	545.7	565.1	564.2	548.2	624.7	667.6	707.4	768.1	0.97	47.21
60-64 yrs	414.0	497.5	531.7	548.6	553.6	543.5	611.0	652.7	693.1	1.30	67.42
65-69 yrs	409.4	382.0	465.6	496.3	525.4	536.0	522.0	586.6	628.8	1.08	53.59
70-74 yrs	314.1	354.4	333.4	411.9	442.0	482.6	493.7	484.8	548.9	1.41	74.75
75-79 yrs	211.0	244.4	277.2	267.5	337.3	370.9	412.5	428.6	427.8	1.78	102.75
80+ yrs	151.0	195.1	245.4	299.6	330.3	401.0	468.5	546.1	610.5	3.55	304.33
Median age of population (years)	30.4	31.4	33.9	35.9	37.6	39.2	40.7	42.4	44.4	0.95	46.02

Table 5.242 Key economic trends

As stated

	1990	1995	2000	2005	2010	2015	2020	CAGR	Period growth
Total GDP (EUR per capita)	11,512.5	12,632.1	15,162.3	15,334.2	15,190.2	16,021.4	17,215.5	1.35	49.5
Disposable income (EUR per capita)	7,766.1	8,875.6	10,323.0	10,526.3	11,123.2	11,933.8	12,825.5	1.69	65.1
Disposable income (EUR per household)	24,809.2	26,991.5	29,415.8	28,141.0	28,547.0	29,888.3	31,662.5	0.82	27.6
Number of households by annual household disposable income ('000)									
Over US$1,000	3,121.7	3,291.8	3,575.0	3,938.0	4,166.7	4,303.5	4,374.3	1.13	40.1
Over US$10,000	1,971.5	2,775.0	2,877.9	3,655.6	3,935.9	4,143.4	4,282.6	2.62	117.2
Over US$25,000	461.1	1,158.8	1,001.6	2,011.3	2,407.9	2,882.8	3,408.8	6.90	639.2
Over US$75,000	63.4	121.1	102.8	246.9	322.3	453.3	689.7	8.28	987.5
Over US$150,000	26.6	45.6	42.5	77.7	91.6	117.6	156.4	6.08	488.0
Total households	3,129.1	3,294.1	3,577.8	3,938.5	4,167.1	4,303.8	4,374.4	1.12	39.8

Note: Per capita data is shown at constant 2010 prices. Household disposable income bands are shown at current prices.

Table 5.243 Young generation

'000

	1980	1985	1990	1995	2000	2005	2010	2015	2020	CAGR	Period growth
Babies under 12 months	157.0	140.4	114.5	107.5	113.8	108.7	108.5	101.4	93.3	-1.29	-40.54
Infants under 24 months	313.8	281.0	225.9	218.1	221.4	220.3	217.5	204.5	188.0	-1.27	-40.07
Toddlers aged 1-4	672.7	580.4	460.4	440.8	422.1	445.0	436.4	421.5	388.6	-1.36	-42.23
Children aged 2-9	1,368.9	1,257.3	1,037.2	891.1	854.0	870.6	884.7	867.0	820.4	-1.27	-40.07
Female	670.7	614.0	505.1	434.9	416.8	423.8	427.8	418.2	395.9	-1.31	-40.97
Male	698.2	643.3	532.1	456.2	437.3	446.8	456.9	448.8	424.5	-1.24	-39.21
Tweenagers aged 10-14	851.4	855.4	818.3	686.6	579.2	556.5	547.2	564.6	555.2	-1.06	-34.79
Female	418.9	419.7	401.2	335.7	283.0	272.2	267.5	273.6	268.3	-1.11	-35.97
Male	432.5	435.7	417.0	350.9	296.2	284.2	279.7	290.9	287.0	-1.02	-33.65
Teenagers aged 13-19	1,195.4	1,189.3	1,191.3	1,092.9	944.7	829.1	783.5	779.5	793.7	-1.02	-33.61
Female	591.3	584.7	586.3	537.0	463.1	405.7	383.4	380.8	384.9	-1.07	-34.90
Male	604.2	604.6	605.0	555.8	481.6	423.4	400.1	398.8	408.8	-0.97	-32.35
Studying age 18-22	795.9	854.2	799.5	833.2	758.2	671.7	589.9	556.5	565.4	-0.85	-28.96
Female	394.8	424.1	394.4	411.9	374.1	329.4	289.1	272.7	276.8	-0.88	-29.89
Male	401.0	430.2	405.1	421.3	384.1	342.3	300.9	283.8	288.6	-0.82	-28.05
Young adults aged 15-29	2,272.5	2,425.7	2,370.8	2,358.8	2,295.6	2,152.8	1,917.0	1,745.3	1,713.2	-0.70	-24.61
Female	1,134.7	1,205.1	1,179.4	1,169.4	1,135.1	1,060.0	942.0	856.7	839.1	-0.75	-26.05
Male	1,137.8	1,220.5	1,191.5	1,189.4	1,160.6	1,092.8	975.0	888.6	874.0	-0.66	-23.18

Table 5.244 Middle-aged generation

'000

	1980	1985	1990	1995	2000	2005	2010	2015	2020	CAGR	Period growth
Middle-aged adults 30-59	3,408	3,524	3,691	3,839	4,056	4,395	4,620	4,699	4,613	0.76	35.4
Female	1,794	1,844	1,917	1,986	2,084	2,240	2,342	2,373	2,326	0.65	29.6
Male	1,613	1,680	1,774	1,853	1,972	2,155	2,279	2,325	2,288	0.88	41.8
Baby boomers aged 40-59	2,243	2,242	2,325	2,411	2,552	2,800	2,952	3,103	3,229	0.91	44.0
Female	1,187	1,188	1,220	1,258	1,323	1,441	1,510	1,581	1,640	0.81	38.2
Male	1,056	1,054	1,105	1,154	1,229	1,360	1,441	1,522	1,590	1.03	50.5

Table 5.245 Elderly population

'000

	1980	1985	1990	1995	2000	2005	2010	2015	2020	CAGR	Period growth
Elderly population (60+)	1,499.5	1,673.3	1,853.2	2,023.9	2,188.5	2,334.1	2,507.7	2,698.8	2,909.1	1.67	94.0
Female	871.8	967.9	1,063.9	1,158.6	1,250.0	1,332.2	1,429.7	1,532.7	1,643.5	1.60	88.5
Male	627.7	705.4	789.2	865.3	938.5	1,001.9	1,078.0	1,166.1	1,265.6	1.77	101.6

Table 5.246 Population of biggest cities 1980-2020

'000

	1980	1985	1990	1995	2000	2005	2010	2015	2020	CAGR	Period growth
Lisboa	786.7	783.1	690.9	589.5	564.5	573.8	587.9	605.1	623.4	-0.58	-20.76
Vila Nova de Gaia	217.6	247.0	253.6	265.0	284.2	307.9	327.8	345.3	360.5	1.27	65.66
Porto	319.0	330.5	311.2	276.9	264.1	264.6	268.6	274.9	282.2	-0.31	-11.52
Matosinhos	131.3	148.7	153.1	156.6	165.0	176.3	186.3	195.3	203.4	1.10	54.89
Amadora	158.0	176.7	183.5	176.6	175.4	180.3	186.1	192.4	198.7	0.58	25.81
Braga	109.4	125.9	131.8	139.1	150.1	163.4	174.4	184.0	192.3	1.42	75.69
Coimbra	125.0	136.1	132.2	131.7	137.2	145.3	152.6	159.5	165.9	0.71	32.69
Maia	78.4	90.1	94.2	103.3	117.0	131.8	143.5	153.0	160.9	1.81	105.28
Feira	88.1	99.5	101.4	105.5	113.1	122.5	130.4	137.3	143.3	1.22	62.68
Funchal	78.6	99.8	115.1	112.0	105.3	101.8	100.9	101.7	103.4	0.69	31.62

Chart 5.154 Population age shift 2000 and 2020, Each Column Represents a Single Age Group

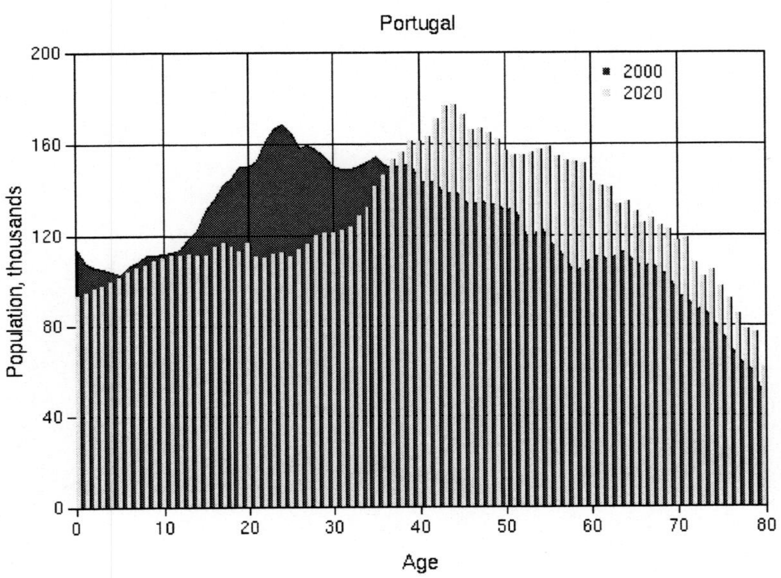

Chart 5.155 Population pyramids, 1980/2000/2010/2020

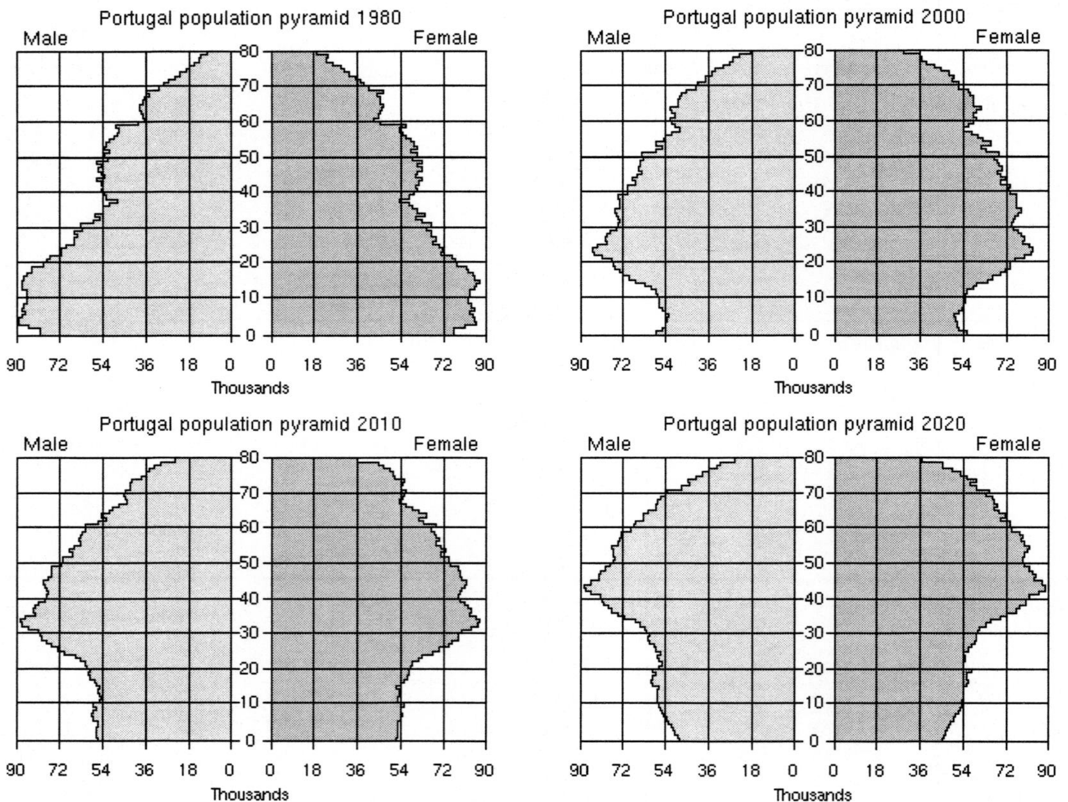

Chart 5.156 Major Cities: 1980, 2000 and 2020

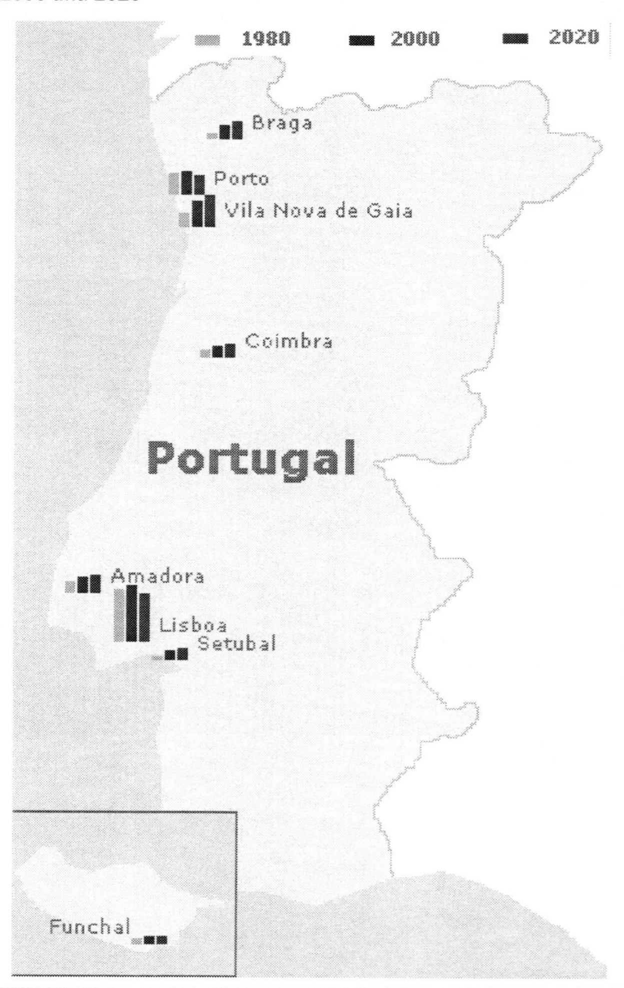

Romania

Table 5.247 Key population trends

'000

	1980	1985	1990	1995	2000	2005	2010	2015	2020	CAGR	Period growth
Population at January 1st	22,132.7	22,687.4	23,211.4	22,285.4	21,929.0	21,658.5	21,369.8	20,953.0	20,388.9	-0.20	-7.88
Male	10,918.1	11,195.3	11,450.8	10,938.5	10,724.4	10,561.7	10,400.6	10,195.7	9,925.6	-0.24	-9.09
Female	11,214.6	11,492.1	11,760.6	11,347.0	11,204.6	11,096.8	10,969.3	10,757.2	10,463.3	-0.17	-6.70
0-4 yrs	2,007.5	1,740.7	1,811.4	1,287.4	1,116.2	1,062.4	1,087.6	1,049.7	964.2	-1.82	-51.97
5-9 yrs	1,915.1	1,991.4	1,720.3	1,755.4	1,271.2	1,107.8	1,057.5	1,078.8	1,034.8	-1.53	-45.97
10-14 yrs	1,960.3	1,907.7	1,976.8	1,651.1	1,738.9	1,266.6	1,105.4	1,054.9	1,074.5	-1.49	-45.19
15-19 yrs	1,455.3	1,924.6	1,894.6	1,810.1	1,638.5	1,731.7	1,262.8	1,101.4	1,050.4	-0.81	-27.82
20-24 yrs	1,802.1	1,443.0	1,908.4	1,727.8	1,795.5	1,631.3	1,718.4	1,243.4	1,076.9	-1.28	-40.24
25-29 yrs	1,752.2	1,771.7	1,426.2	1,749.2	1,705.8	1,783.5	1,611.1	1,674.9	1,189.0	-0.96	-32.14
30-34 yrs	1,418.3	1,735.7	1,747.4	1,311.7	1,720.2	1,688.3	1,765.0	1,584.2	1,625.0	0.34	14.57
35-39 yrs	1,293.5	1,403.6	1,708.7	1,643.5	1,286.4	1,698.8	1,669.6	1,741.3	1,553.1	0.46	20.06
40-44 yrs	1,538.1	1,274.7	1,377.3	1,610.1	1,601.2	1,264.4	1,673.3	1,642.7	1,707.8	0.26	11.03
45-49 yrs	1,500.0	1,501.1	1,239.1	1,316.8	1,554.9	1,558.9	1,233.7	1,633.7	1,599.8	0.16	6.66
50-54 yrs	1,387.8	1,444.7	1,442.1	1,163.0	1,256.2	1,495.2	1,503.2	1,190.9	1,577.6	0.32	13.68
55-59 yrs	1,175.6	1,315.2	1,364.8	1,342.8	1,088.9	1,189.6	1,420.8	1,432.1	1,136.7	-0.08	-3.30
60-64 yrs	648.7	1,087.9	1,210.9	1,237.1	1,225.0	1,005.0	1,105.4	1,324.9	1,340.6	1.83	106.67
65-69 yrs	898.9	576.0	964.8	1,060.3	1,085.8	1,089.1	899.9	996.9	1,200.1	0.72	33.50
70-74 yrs	674.0	742.4	475.4	789.2	871.7	910.7	922.4	768.0	860.8	0.61	27.72
75-79 yrs	440.4	486.9	542.3	347.2	580.5	658.2	696.4	717.2	606.5	0.80	37.72
80+ yrs	264.9	340.2	400.9	482.6	392.1	517.0	637.3	718.0	791.2	2.77	198.68
Median age of population (years)	30.5	31.6	32.6	34.5	34.9	36.4	38.3	39.8	41.8	0.79	37.18

Table 5.248 Key economic trends

As stated

	1990	1995	2000	2005	2010	2015	2020	CAGR	Period growth
Total GDP (RON per capita)	17,374.7	16,738.9	16,208.1	21,471.0	24,574.9	32,832.4	40,720.7	2.88	134.4
Disposable income (RON per capita)	10,476.1	8,242.4	7,882.0	12,060.4	15,320.3	20,819.3	26,045.0	3.08	148.6
Disposable income (RON per household)	32,960.2	25,503.9	23,777.9	35,384.4	43,820.2	58,191.1	71,292.8	2.60	116.3
Number of households by annual household disposable income ('000)									
Over US$1,000	7,346.1	7,165.9	7,220.6	7,381.5	7,471.2	7,496.4	7,448.6	0.05	1.4
Over US$10,000	275.4	260.2	310.2	2,017.0	4,707.9	7,115.2	7,407.4	11.60	2,589.5
Over US$25,000	84.5	79.8	95.5	301.6	718.3	2,379.0	5,318.1	14.81	6,195.9
Over US$75,000	20.5	19.3	23.3	71.4	127.7	272.5	635.7	12.13	3,004.7
Over US$150,000	8.4	7.9	9.6	29.5	52.8	106.7	197.0	11.10	2,252.2
Total households	7,377.5	7,202.2	7,269.1	7,382.1	7,471.2	7,496.4	7,448.6	0.03	1.0

Note: Per capita data is shown at constant 2010 prices. Household disposable income bands are shown at current prices.

Table 5.249 Young generation

'000

	1980	1985	1990	1995	2000	2005	2010	2015	2020	CAGR	Period growth
Babies under 12 months	400.3	344.0	362.0	237.3	225.7	213.2	217.2	206.6	184.4	-1.92	-53.95
Infants under 24 months	803.3	657.1	731.2	475.7	452.1	422.0	435.1	414.9	373.3	-1.90	-53.53
Toddlers aged 1-4	1,607.2	1,396.7	1,449.4	1,050.1	890.5	849.2	870.4	843.0	779.9	-1.79	-51.48
Children aged 2-9	3,119.3	3,075.0	2,800.5	2,567.1	1,935.3	1,748.2	1,710.0	1,713.5	1,625.7	-1.62	-47.88
Female	1,522.0	1,502.2	1,369.5	1,254.4	944.1	851.6	831.6	833.4	791.0	-1.62	-48.03
Male	1,597.3	1,572.8	1,431.0	1,312.7	991.2	896.5	878.4	880.1	834.7	-1.61	-47.74
Tweenagers aged 10-14	1,960.3	1,907.7	1,976.8	1,651.1	1,738.9	1,266.6	1,105.4	1,054.9	1,074.5	-1.49	-45.19
Female	975.6	932.3	965.8	805.4	850.8	618.5	539.5	513.3	522.9	-1.55	-46.41
Male	984.8	975.3	1,010.9	845.6	888.1	648.2	566.0	541.7	551.6	-1.44	-43.99
Teenagers aged 13-19	1,993.3	2,698.2	2,683.6	2,511.6	2,332.6	2,281.9	1,702.7	1,533.2	1,481.4	-0.74	-25.68
Female	981.5	1,321.7	1,311.8	1,224.5	1,138.5	1,116.6	831.9	747.4	720.2	-0.77	-26.63
Male	1,011.8	1,376.4	1,371.7	1,287.1	1,194.1	1,165.4	870.8	785.8	761.2	-0.71	-24.77
Studying age 18-22	1,659.7	1,351.3	2,157.4	1,742.2	1,778.5	1,629.9	1,581.8	1,143.8	1,081.9	-1.06	-34.81
Female	812.5	660.4	1,058.1	850.5	868.4	795.0	775.6	558.7	526.3	-1.08	-35.22
Male	847.1	690.9	1,099.4	891.6	910.0	835.0	806.2	585.1	555.6	-1.05	-34.42
Young adults aged 15-29	5,009.5	5,139.3	5,229.1	5,287.1	5,139.8	5,146.5	4,592.4	4,019.7	3,316.3	-1.03	-33.80
Female	2,453.3	2,519.1	2,558.8	2,590.5	2,511.3	2,514.1	2,248.2	1,967.0	1,616.7	-1.04	-34.10
Male	2,556.3	2,620.2	2,670.4	2,696.6	2,628.5	2,632.5	2,344.2	2,052.7	1,699.6	-1.02	-33.51

Table 5.250 Middle-aged generation
'000

	1980	1985	1990	1995	2000	2005	2010	2015	2020	CAGR	Period growth
Middle-aged adults 30-59	8,313	8,675	8,879	8,388	8,508	8,895	9,266	9,225	9,200	0.25	10.67
Female	4,210	4,371	4,473	4,242	4,303	4,492	4,664	4,623	4,589	0.22	9.02
Male	4,104	4,304	4,407	4,146	4,204	4,403	4,601	4,602	4,611	0.29	12.36
Baby boomers aged 40-59	5,601	5,536	5,423	5,433	5,501	5,508	5,831	5,899	6,022	0.18	7.51
Female	2,864	2,814	2,764	2,774	2,815	2,823	2,980	2,994	3,028	0.14	5.73
Male	2,737	2,721	2,660	2,658	2,686	2,685	2,851	2,906	2,994	0.22	9.37

Table 5.251 Elderly population
'000

	1980	1985	1990	1995	2000	2005	2010	2015	2020	CAGR	Period growth
Elderly population (60+)	2,927	3,234	3,594	3,917	4,155	4,180	4,261	4,525	4,799	1.24	64.0
Female	1,662	1,847	2,036	2,222	2,375	2,416	2,474	2,619	2,762	1.28	66.2
Male	1,265	1,386	1,559	1,694	1,781	1,764	1,787	1,906	2,037	1.20	61.0

Table 5.252 Population of biggest cities 1980-2020
'000

	1980	1985	1990	1995	2000	2005	2010	2015	2020	CAGR	Period growth
Bucharest	2,020.7	2,122.1	2,134.8	2,013.5	1,937.4	1,903.1	1,874.0	1,843.3	1,810.4	-0.27	-10.40
Cluj-napoca	300.2	326.2	336.9	325.0	318.1	316.0	313.2	309.2	304.4	0.03	1.39
Iasi	305.1	335.9	351.7	337.2	323.3	317.2	312.7	307.7	302.3	-0.02	-0.90
Timisoara	306.6	331.7	342.2	328.3	318.7	314.8	310.9	306.4	301.3	-0.04	-1.75
Craiova	257.5	288.7	307.8	303.3	301.1	302.6	301.9	299.3	295.2	0.34	14.65
Constanta	298.8	334.3	355.8	338.3	316.2	306.5	301.5	296.4	291.0	-0.07	-2.60
Galati	277.2	310.7	331.0	317.9	302.2	293.4	287.0	281.1	275.5	-0.02	-0.64
Brasov	293.7	320.5	332.4	311.8	289.8	280.1	275.3	270.5	265.5	-0.25	-9.59
Ploiesti	229.1	250.4	259.3	246.7	235.3	228.2	223.0	218.4	214.0	-0.17	-6.59
Braila	221.3	236.6	241.1	228.1	218.3	212.9	208.8	204.8	200.9	-0.24	-9.21

Chart 5.157 Population age shift 2000 and 2020, Each Column Represents a Single Age Group

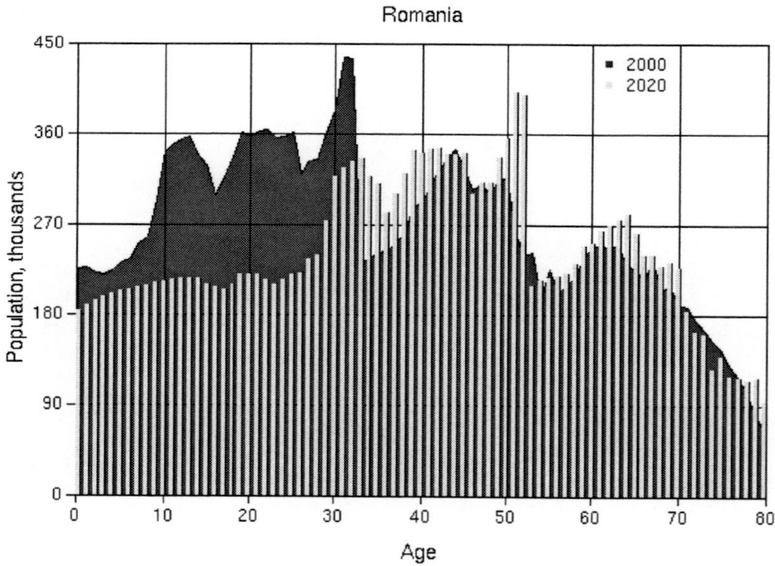

Chart 5.158 Population pyramids, 1980/2000/2010/2020

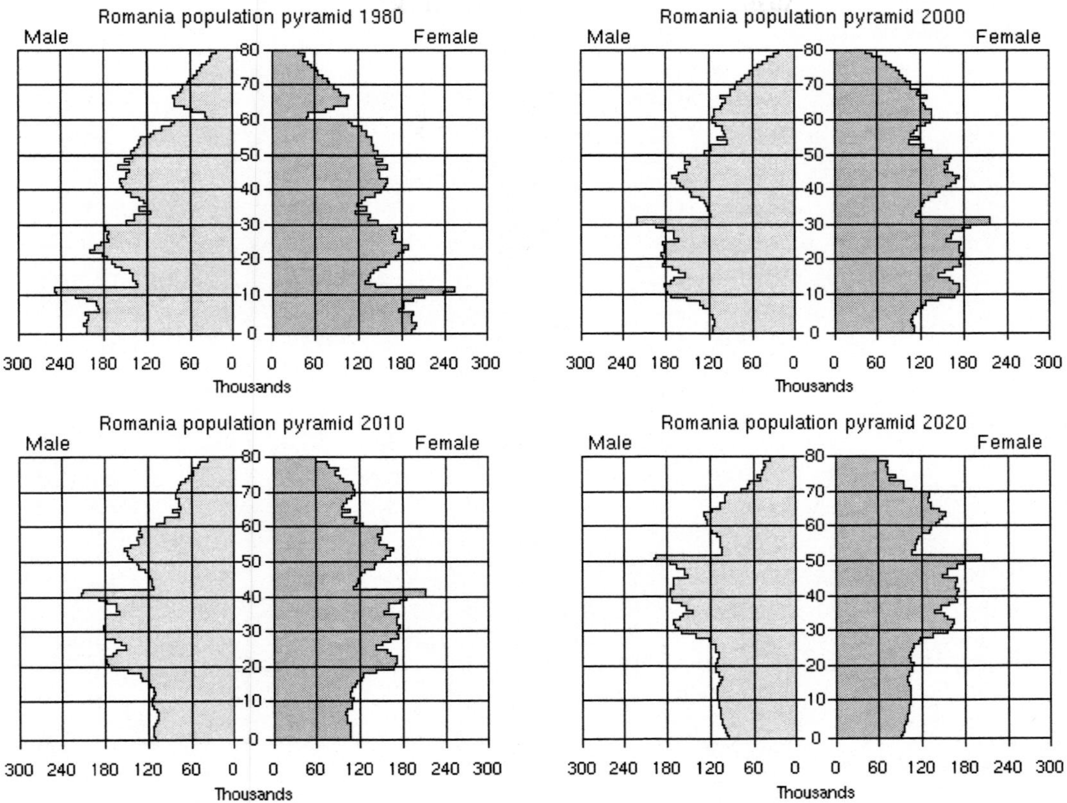

Chart 5.159 Major Cities: 1980, 2000 and 2020

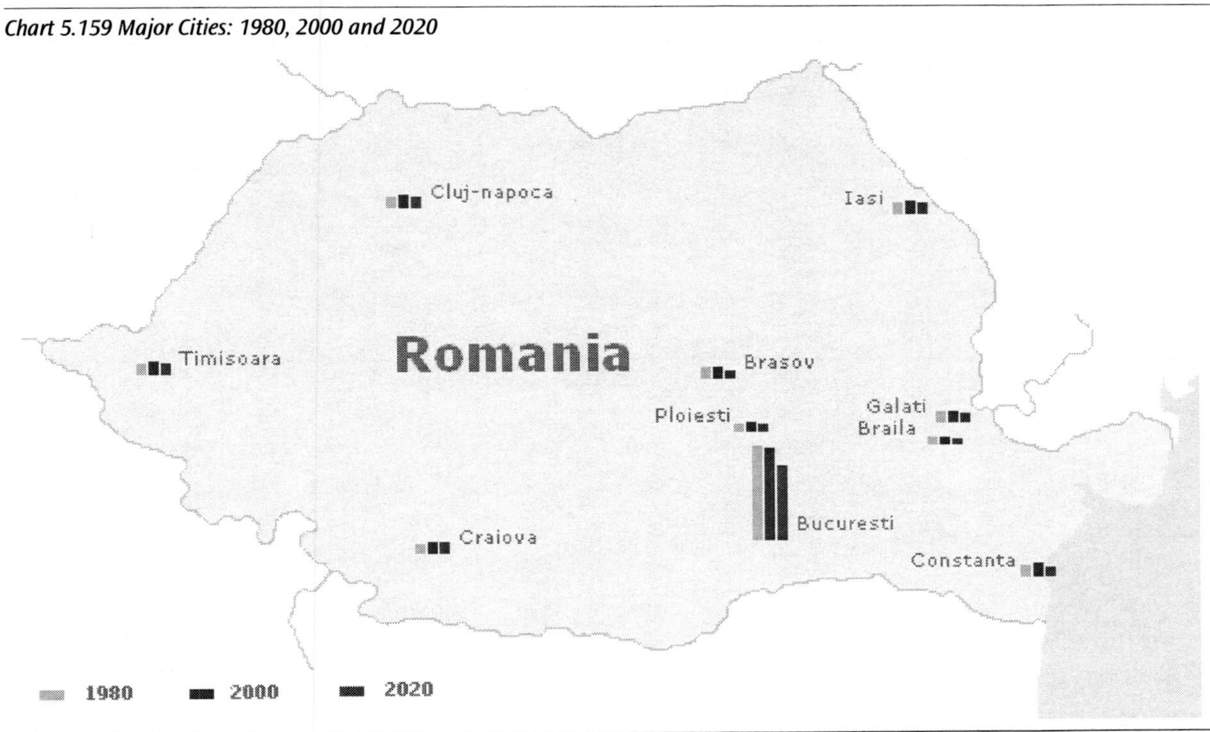

Russia

Table 5.253 Key population trends

'000

	1980	1985	1990	1995	2000	2005	2010	2015	2020	CAGR	Period growth
Population at January 1st	138,126.6	142,539.0	147,665.1	148,459.9	146,890.1	143,474.2	141,785.7	140,507.2	139,169.5	0.02	0.76
Male	63,609.6	66,078.7	69,115.5	69,659.2	68,698.3	66,602.8	65,544.3	64,789.4	64,081.8	0.02	0.74
Female	74,517.0	76,460.3	78,549.6	78,800.8	78,191.8	76,871.5	76,241.5	75,717.7	75,087.7	0.02	0.77
0-4 yrs	10,625.0	11,528.8	11,730.2	8,259.1	6,475.7	6,866.6	7,979.1	8,544.6	8,284.8	-0.62	-22.02
5-9 yrs	9,969.1	10,645.7	11,603.5	11,943.5	8,416.1	6,535.7	6,914.5	8,062.4	8,663.5	-0.35	-13.10
10-14 yrs	9,262.7	10,005.2	10,697.0	11,847.4	12,174.0	8,468.9	6,593.1	6,991.4	8,158.9	-0.32	-11.92
15-19 yrs	11,842.7	9,315.6	10,135.7	10,830.9	12,126.6	12,241.8	8,522.0	6,661.8	7,076.7	-1.28	-40.24
20-24 yrs	12,982.0	11,971.0	9,556.8	10,225.7	10,924.8	12,267.6	12,267.4	8,570.4	6,754.0	-1.62	-47.97
25-29 yrs	12,067.8	12,966.4	12,062.1	9,537.1	10,336.7	10,881.0	12,246.9	12,247.3	8,630.5	-0.83	-28.48
30-34 yrs	9,467.9	11,963.9	12,906.6	12,087.4	9,594.3	10,211.5	10,798.6	12,155.2	12,172.6	0.63	28.57
35-39 yrs	6,920.5	9,258.0	11,890.3	12,790.0	12,027.8	9,411.7	10,065.8	10,654.3	11,996.3	1.38	73.34
40-44 yrs	11,223.6	6,763.3	9,074.9	11,688.5	12,483.8	11,665.4	9,184.1	9,834.7	10,422.3	-0.19	-7.14
45-49 yrs	8,730.7	10,781.0	6,588.5	8,808.3	11,269.0	11,884.6	11,223.5	8,854.9	9,497.2	0.21	8.78
50-54 yrs	10,109.0	8,300.6	10,323.4	6,272.8	8,367.8	10,517.6	11,225.9	10,597.1	8,399.2	-0.46	-16.91
55-59 yrs	6,199.6	9,443.1	7,833.9	9,665.8	5,851.0	7,655.7	9,717.8	10,369.2	9,804.6	1.15	58.15
60-64 yrs	4,635.6	5,650.4	8,684.3	7,102.0	8,779.2	5,179.0	6,892.4	8,744.2	9,340.1	1.77	101.49
65-69 yrs	5,622.4	4,060.7	5,004.7	7,554.0	6,142.3	7,509.9	4,464.0	6,031.9	7,649.3	0.77	36.05
70-74 yrs	4,056.5	4,623.2	3,368.0	4,126.1	6,088.7	4,896.0	6,140.3	3,638.9	5,030.2	0.54	24.00
75-79 yrs	2,562.7	2,958.0	3,447.7	2,472.1	3,034.9	4,370.4	3,587.8	4,571.1	2,705.0	0.14	5.55
80+ yrs	1,848.8	2,304.1	2,757.6	3,249.6	2,797.5	2,910.9	3,962.5	3,977.8	4,584.3	2.30	147.96
Median age of population (years)	31.0	32.0	33.1	34.8	36.6	37.3	37.7	38.3	39.0	0.58	26.11

Table 5.254 Key economic trends

As stated

	1990	1995	2000	2005	2010	2015	2020	CAGR	Period growth
Total GDP (RUB per capita)	299,478.0	184,938.3	202,508.2	279,054.2	333,100.4	399,794.5	515,160.0	1.82	72.0
Disposable income (RUB per capita)		83,471.7	80,795.1	140,414.7	195,352.8	249,713.5	327,272.5		
Disposable income (RUB per household)		253,565.1	227,370.4	380,439.7	525,765.4	674,130.0	885,308.1		
Number of households by annual household disposable income ('000)									
Over US$1,000		44,466.0	42,387.5	52,086.2	52,512.7	52,013.1	51,437.3		
Over US$10,000		2,076.4	1,220.9	12,749.9	30,880.6	45,435.5	49,637.2		
Over US$25,000		580.9	422.9	2,057.0	7,362.4	23,036.4	39,593.3		
Over US$75,000		147.0	107.0	430.6	930.6	3,126.7	10,441.1		
Over US$150,000		61.7	44.9	182.4	394.1	944.1	2,374.6		
Total households	42,280.2	48,871.9	52,196.8	52,954.2	52,681.7	52,047.1	51,446.9	0.66	21.7

Note: Per capita data is shown at constant 2010 prices. Household disposable income bands are shown at current prices.

Table 5.255 Young generation

'000

	1980	1985	1990	1995	2000	2005	2010	2015	2020	CAGR	Period growth
Babies under 12 months	2,152	2,389	2,124	1,436	1,221	1,488	1,746	1,718	1,588	-0.76	-26.18
Infants under 24 months	4,289	4,841	4,434	2,838	2,508	2,946	3,451	3,447	3,213	-0.72	-25.09
Toddlers aged 1-4	8,473	9,139	9,607	6,823	5,254	5,379	6,233	6,826	6,696	-0.59	-20.97
Children aged 2-9	16,305	17,333	18,899	17,365	12,383	10,456	11,443	13,160	13,736	-0.43	-15.76
Female	8,027	8,525	9,290	8,494	6,045	5,106	5,570	6,390	6,662	-0.46	-17.00
Male	8,278	8,808	9,610	8,871	6,338	5,350	5,873	6,770	7,073	-0.39	-14.56
Tweenagers aged 10-14	9,263	10,005	10,697	11,847	12,174	8,469	6,593	6,991	8,159	-0.32	-11.92
Female	4,563	4,909	5,270	5,823	5,973	4,140	3,220	3,403	3,957	-0.36	-13.27
Male	4,700	5,096	5,427	6,024	6,201	4,329	3,373	3,589	4,202	-0.28	-10.60
Teenagers aged 13-19	15,664	13,201	14,383	15,338	17,155	16,151	11,260	9,263	10,066	-1.10	-35.74
Female	7,680	6,471	7,059	7,554	8,431	7,929	5,507	4,521	4,893	-1.12	-36.29
Male	7,985	6,730	7,324	7,784	8,724	8,222	5,753	4,742	5,173	-1.08	-35.21
Studying age 18-22	13,065	10,638	9,589	10,500	11,201	12,693	11,129	7,393	6,587	-1.70	-49.58
Female	6,331	5,254	4,661	5,169	5,534	6,258	5,463	3,618	3,215	-1.68	-49.22
Male	6,734	5,384	4,928	5,331	5,667	6,434	5,665	3,774	3,372	-1.71	-49.92
Young adults aged 15-29	36,892	34,253	31,755	30,594	33,388	35,390	33,036	27,480	22,461	-1.23	-39.12
Female	18,095	16,851	15,575	15,033	16,476	17,527	16,317	13,532	11,003	-1.24	-39.19
Male	18,798	17,402	16,180	15,561	16,912	17,863	16,719	13,947	11,458	-1.23	-39.04

Table 5.256 Middle-aged generation

'000

	1980	1985	1990	1995	2000	2005	2010	2015	2020	CAGR	Period growth
Middle-aged adults 30-59	52,651	56,510	58,618	61,313	59,594	61,346	62,216	62,465	62,292	0.42	18.31
Female	28,362	29,735	30,326	31,731	30,949	32,229	32,921	33,033	32,766	0.36	15.53
Male	24,290	26,775	28,292	29,582	28,645	29,117	29,295	29,432	29,526	0.49	21.56
Baby boomers aged 40-59	36,263	35,288	33,821	36,435	37,972	41,723	41,351	39,656	38,123	0.13	5.13
Female	20,117	19,118	17,959	19,279	20,077	22,319	22,344	21,486	20,603	0.06	2.41
Male	16,146	16,170	15,862	17,156	17,895	19,404	19,007	18,170	17,521	0.20	8.51

Table 5.257 Elderly population

'000

	1980	1985	1990	1995	2000	2005	2010	2015	2020	CAGR	Period growth
Elderly population (60+)	18,726	19,596	23,262	24,504	26,843	24,866	25,047	26,964	29,309	1.13	56.5
Female	13,366	14,064	15,921	16,338	17,528	16,436	16,537	17,685	19,140	0.90	43.2
Male	5,360	5,532	7,341	8,166	9,315	8,430	8,510	9,279	10,169	1.61	89.7

Table 5.258 Population of biggest cities 1980-2020

'000

	1980	1985	1990	1995	2000	2005	2010	2015	2020	CAGR	Period growth
Moscow	8,232.7	8,647.0	9,132.1	9,689.4	10,174.8	10,420.2	10,494.8	10,530.3	10,548.7	0.62	28.13
St Petersburg	4,639.4	4,869.2	5,036.8	4,905.0	4,723.2	4,548.6	4,421.1	4,344.4	4,299.9	-0.19	-7.32
Novosibirsk	1,326.5	1,389.9	1,445.8	1,441.4	1,427.4	1,409.8	1,390.7	1,378.4	1,371.2	0.08	3.37
Nizhniy Novgorod	1,355.9	1,405.2	1,438.6	1,387.5	1,328.1	1,289.6	1,267.1	1,253.0	1,244.7	-0.21	-8.20
Yekaterinburg	1,227.7	1,305.3	1,369.0	1,341.1	1,304.6	1,269.0	1,240.7	1,223.4	1,213.4	-0.03	-1.16
Omsk	1,028.4	1,095.6	1,156.9	1,159.4	1,155.3	1,147.4	1,135.4	1,127.5	1,122.8	0.22	9.18
Samara	1,221.4	1,240.2	1,253.4	1,211.4	1,170.2	1,133.2	1,105.1	1,088.0	1,078.1	-0.31	-11.73
Kazan	1,003.8	1,054.7	1,101.8	1,106.0	1,103.5	1,096.7	1,085.7	1,078.3	1,074.0	0.17	6.99
Chelyabinsk	1,042.0	1,099.3	1,147.2	1,133.0	1,110.7	1,087.4	1,067.2	1,054.7	1,047.4	0.01	0.52
Rostov-na-Donu	943.4	985.2	1,028.0	1,047.1	1,060.3	1,066.7	1,063.3	1,060.3	1,058.4	0.29	12.19

Chart 5.160 Population age shift 2000 and 2020, Each Column Represents a Single Age Group

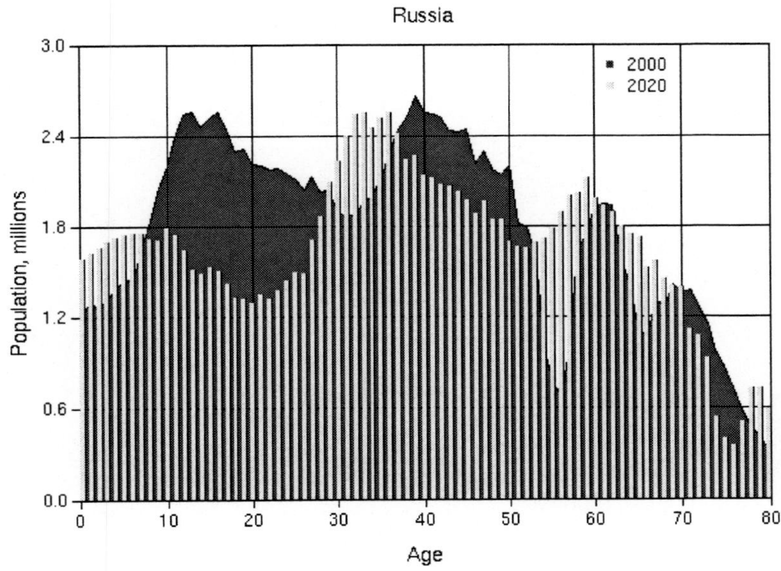

Chart 5.161 Population pyramids, 1980/2000/2010/2020

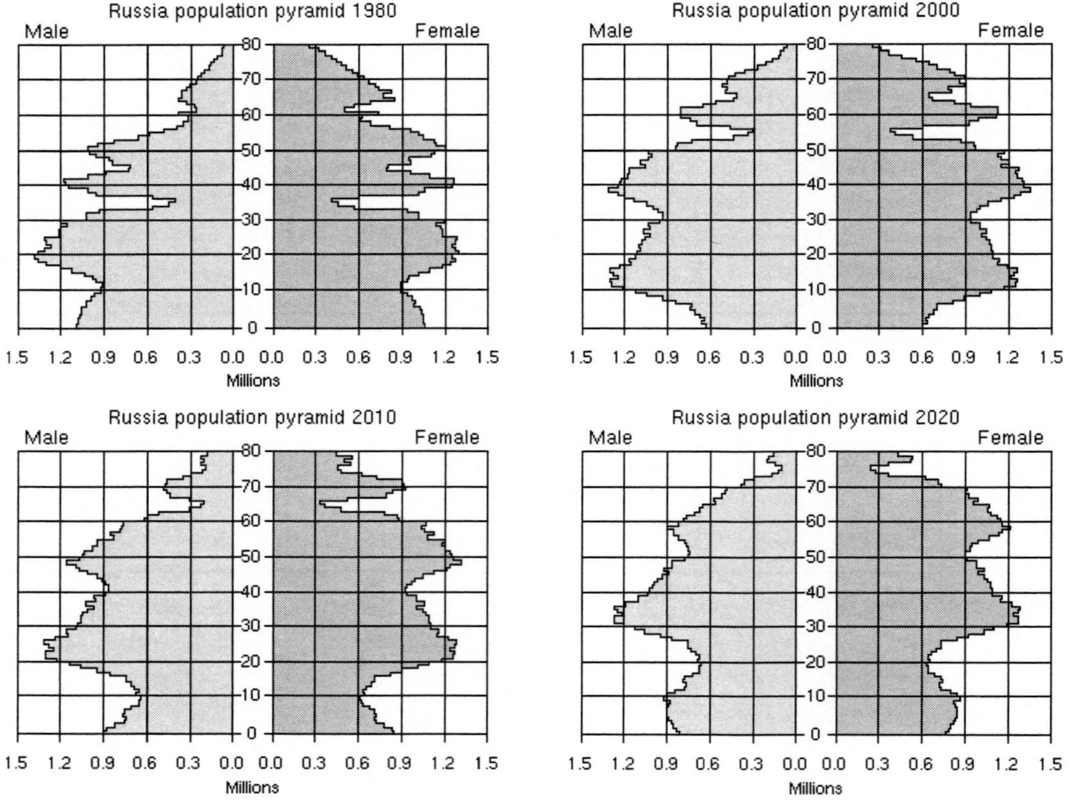

Chart 5.162 Major Cities: 1980, 2000 and 2020

Saudi Arabia

Table 5.259 Key population trends

'000

	1980	1985	1990	1995	2000	2005	2010	2015	2020	CAGR	Period growth
Population at January 1st	9,604.4	12,866.9	16,258.9	18,254.6	20,808.0	23,612.7	26,246.0	28,932.5	31,607.8	3.02	229.1
Male	5,188.2	7,115.1	9,028.6	10,190.1	11,520.1	13,045.9	14,355.0	15,682.7	16,994.3	3.01	227.6
Female	4,416.2	5,751.8	7,230.3	8,064.5	9,287.9	10,566.8	11,891.0	13,249.8	14,613.5	3.04	230.9
0-4 yrs	1,823.4	2,171.8	2,669.5	2,769.4	2,756.9	2,850.8	2,872.8	2,981.9	3,041.0	1.29	66.8
5-9 yrs	1,350.6	1,858.8	2,245.8	2,597.5	2,699.5	2,704.9	2,819.6	2,862.9	2,961.1	1.98	119.2
10-14 yrs	1,085.4	1,419.1	1,908.7	2,187.9	2,442.7	2,608.7	2,689.4	2,802.9	2,847.9	2.44	162.4
15-19 yrs	917.9	1,233.4	1,513.8	1,758.8	2,010.9	2,293.7	2,562.9	2,648.6	2,762.2	2.79	200.9
20-24 yrs	874.9	1,255.0	1,482.9	1,436.4	1,924.6	2,095.7	2,385.5	2,660.3	2,738.3	2.89	213.0
25-29 yrs	815.0	1,233.8	1,552.3	1,690.4	1,890.8	2,311.6	2,335.6	2,622.3	2,895.2	3.22	255.2
30-34 yrs	652.5	1,057.8	1,425.0	1,691.0	1,909.1	2,171.0	2,432.1	2,444.8	2,743.7	3.66	320.5
35-39 yrs	500.0	770.4	1,119.1	1,281.2	1,606.9	1,928.8	2,131.4	2,381.6	2,403.4	4.00	380.7
40-44 yrs	393.9	505.0	740.1	890.6	1,140.3	1,490.6	1,829.7	2,031.0	2,282.8	4.49	479.6
45-49 yrs	317.0	364.2	461.7	581.6	764.3	1,032.9	1,390.1	1,728.8	1,931.0	4.62	509.2
50-54 yrs	251.9	277.9	319.4	405.8	482.9	692.0	941.4	1,292.2	1,627.8	4.78	546.1
55-59 yrs	202.6	220.7	243.9	298.4	340.9	447.7	644.9	885.0	1,227.7	4.61	506.1
60-64 yrs	152.1	183.1	200.7	225.2	275.2	327.3	434.0	620.1	849.4	4.39	458.5
65-69 yrs	116.4	132.2	159.8	178.1	225.4	252.5	305.0	403.9	575.0	4.07	394.1
70-74 yrs	78.9	93.1	106.5	130.9	167.9	191.4	216.5	264.1	351.2	3.80	345.3
75-79 yrs	46.6	55.2	65.9	76.6	103.4	125.3	143.5	165.6	205.1	3.77	340.0
80+ yrs	25.4	35.1	43.9	54.8	66.1	87.8	111.6	136.4	165.0	4.79	550.1
Median age of population (years)	17.9	19.0	19.3	19.4	21.3	23.2	24.6	26.0	27.5	1.08	53.8

Table 5.260 Key economic trends

As stated

	1990	1995	2000	2005	2010	2015	2020	CAGR	Period growth
Total GDP (SR per capita)	56,428.2	57,877.4	57,640.8	61,172.5	63,177.5	72,564.9	86,574.6	1.44	53.4
Disposable income (SR per capita)	15,470.7	20,172.0	17,773.9	18,666.6	24,102.6	29,296.1	35,924.5	2.85	132.2
Disposable income (SR per household)	93,371.9	126,652.2	107,887.4	106,280.8	129,752.9	151,293.9	179,966.0	2.21	92.7
Number of households by annual household disposable income ('000)									
Over US$1,000	2,691.4	2,906.4	3,424.5	4,143.4	4,873.2	5,601.1	6,308.7	2.88	134.4
Over US$10,000	1,987.4	2,579.8	2,806.2	3,363.5	4,474.4	5,364.3	6,164.8	3.85	210.2
Over US$25,000	513.7	1,213.4	1,086.6	1,254.5	2,745.0	4,102.7	5,307.1	8.09	933.1
Over US$75,000	58.1	124.0	110.2	126.8	375.1	878.3	1,752.8	12.02	2,915.1
Over US$150,000	24.3	46.3	45.6	50.3	104.0	189.8	379.4	9.59	1,461.1
Total households	2,693.9	2,907.4	3,428.0	4,147.2	4,875.4	5,602.4	6,309.5	2.88	134.2

Note: Per capita data is shown at constant 2010 prices. Household disposable income bands are shown at current prices.

Table 5.261 Young generation

'000

	1980	1985	1990	1995	2000	2005	2010	2015	2020	CAGR	Period growth
Babies under 12 months	414.7	438.5	580.0	545.1	551.0	592.6	570.3	616.0	608.6	0.96	46.8
Infants under 24 months	803.1	880.1	1,133.9	1,100.5	1,101.1	1,172.0	1,145.2	1,219.6	1,219.2	1.05	51.8
Toddlers aged 1-4	1,408.6	1,733.3	2,089.5	2,224.3	2,205.9	2,258.2	2,302.5	2,365.8	2,432.3	1.37	72.7
Children aged 2-9	2,370.8	3,150.5	3,781.3	4,266.4	4,355.3	4,383.7	4,547.2	4,625.1	4,782.9	1.77	101.7
Female	1,170.9	1,566.7	1,869.9	2,109.4	2,157.0	2,171.3	2,251.3	2,288.7	2,363.9	1.77	101.9
Male	1,200.0	1,583.8	1,911.4	2,157.0	2,198.3	2,212.4	2,295.8	2,336.5	2,419.0	1.77	101.6
Tweenagers aged 10-14	1,085.4	1,419.1	1,908.7	2,187.9	2,442.7	2,608.7	2,689.4	2,802.9	2,847.9	2.44	162.4
Female	530.8	698.2	950.2	1,083.4	1,220.1	1,304.5	1,336.2	1,388.8	1,410.6	2.47	165.7
Male	554.6	720.9	958.5	1,104.5	1,222.7	1,304.2	1,353.2	1,414.1	1,437.3	2.41	159.2
Teenagers aged 13-19	1,328.1	1,759.8	2,228.4	2,580.9	2,935.9	3,312.6	3,623.0	3,753.8	3,889.4	2.72	192.9
Female	634.7	848.7	1,088.1	1,288.8	1,441.5	1,663.2	1,816.8	1,869.6	1,933.2	2.82	204.6
Male	693.4	911.1	1,140.2	1,292.0	1,494.4	1,649.4	1,806.2	1,884.2	1,956.2	2.63	182.1
Studying age 18-22	884.3	1,239.6	1,453.0	1,509.2	1,933.9	2,118.4	2,458.4	2,642.1	2,724.0	2.85	208.0
Female	383.3	561.9	671.2	716.4	904.7	1,025.6	1,223.6	1,307.3	1,343.0	3.18	250.4
Male	501.0	677.7	781.8	792.8	1,029.2	1,092.8	1,234.9	1,334.8	1,381.0	2.57	175.7
Young adults aged 15-29	2,607.8	3,722.2	4,549.0	4,885.6	5,826.4	6,701.1	7,284.0	7,931.2	8,395.6	2.97	221.9
Female	1,090.8	1,574.0	1,999.7	2,143.7	2,567.8	3,103.0	3,495.4	3,852.4	4,077.9	3.35	273.9
Male	1,517.1	2,148.3	2,549.3	2,741.9	3,258.6	3,598.0	3,788.6	4,078.8	4,317.7	2.65	184.6

Table 5.262 Middle-aged generation

'000

	1980	1985	1990	1995	2000	2005	2010	2015	2020	CAGR	Period growth
Middle-aged adults 30-59	2,317.9	3,196.1	4,309.1	5,148.6	6,244.5	7,762.9	9,369.6	10,763.4	12,216.5	4.24	427.0
Female	1,004.4	1,224.2	1,557.2	1,862.6	2,400.3	2,935.2	3,664.2	4,396.3	5,237.9	4.22	421.5
Male	1,313.5	1,971.9	2,751.9	3,286.1	3,844.2	4,827.7	5,705.3	6,367.2	6,978.6	4.26	431.3
Baby boomers aged 40-59	1,165.4	1,367.9	1,765.1	2,176.4	2,728.4	3,663.2	4,806.1	5,937.0	7,069.3	4.61	506.6
Female	533.8	569.1	667.9	765.3	1,067.4	1,360.0	1,771.7	2,263.1	2,855.2	4.28	434.9
Male	631.6	798.7	1,097.2	1,411.1	1,661.0	2,303.2	3,034.4	3,673.9	4,214.2	4.86	567.3

Table 5.263 Elderly population

'000

	1980	1985	1990	1995	2000	2005	2010	2015	2020	CAGR	Period growth
Elderly population (60+)	419.3	498.8	576.9	665.6	838.0	984.3	1,210.7	1,590.2	2,145.7	4.17	411.7
Female	216.2	256.7	290.9	322.4	395.8	472.6	577.7	721.8	921.8	3.69	326.3
Male	203.1	242.1	286.0	343.2	442.2	511.7	633.0	868.4	1,223.9	4.59	502.7

Table 5.264 Population of biggest cities 1980-2020

'000

	1980	1985	1990	1995	2000	2005	2010	2015	2020	CAGR	Period growth
Riyadh	1,351.0	1,925.7	2,567.1	2,999.2	3,624.1	4,201.6	4,740.5	5,272.1	5,791.9	3.71	328.7
Jidda	1,028.5	1,453.5	1,908.7	2,172.8	2,547.7	2,865.0	3,168.0	3,481.4	3,797.8	3.32	269.3
Mecca	489.7	690.5	903.0	1,020.4	1,186.0	1,321.4	1,451.9	1,589.4	1,729.9	3.21	253.3
Medina	292.4	418.2	560.7	661.4	807.8	946.3	1,074.8	1,199.9	1,321.2	3.84	351.8
Dammam	229.4	329.0	443.3	527.2	649.7	767.6	876.5	981.6	1,082.7	3.96	371.9
Taif	216.6	303.4	392.0	433.2	489.7	529.4	569.4	615.1	664.2	2.84	206.6
Tabouk	140.7	201.2	269.7	318.0	388.1	454.5	516.0	576.0	634.1	3.84	350.6
Khamis Mushayt	98.0	142.7	197.4	244.7	314.8	386.8	452.3	513.3	570.5	4.50	482.1
Buraidah	119.1	170.5	228.9	270.8	331.8	389.9	443.7	495.9	546.3	3.88	358.7
Al Hofuf	116.8	163.9	212.3	236.0	268.7	292.8	316.6	343.3	371.5	2.93	218.0

Chart 5.163 Population age shift 2000 and 2020, Each Column Represents a Single Age Group

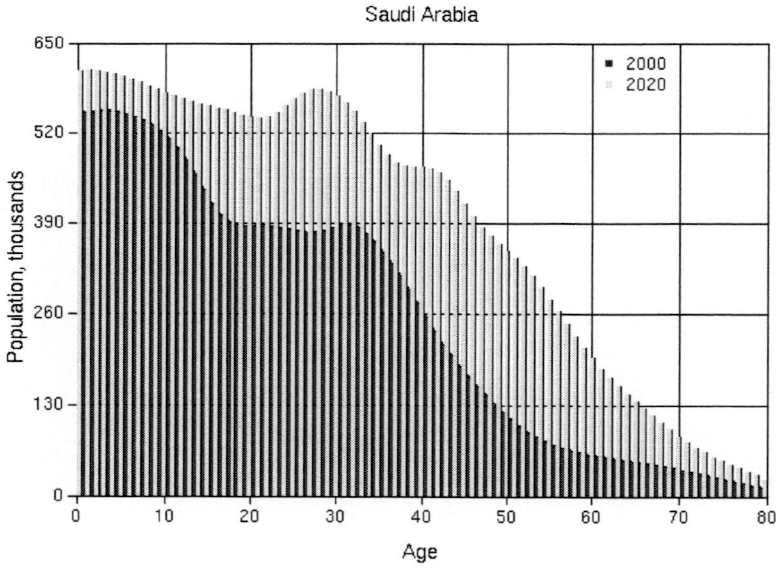

Chart 5.164 Population pyramids, 1980/2000/2010/2020

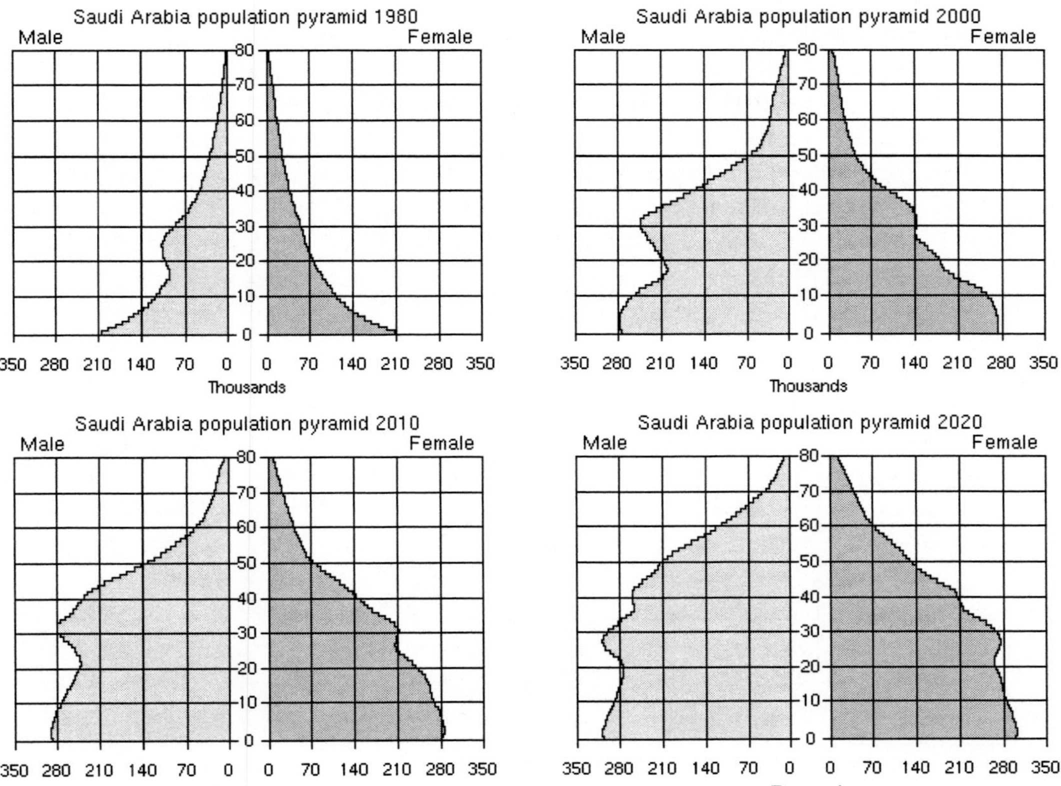

Chart 5.165 Major Cities: 1980, 2000 and 2020

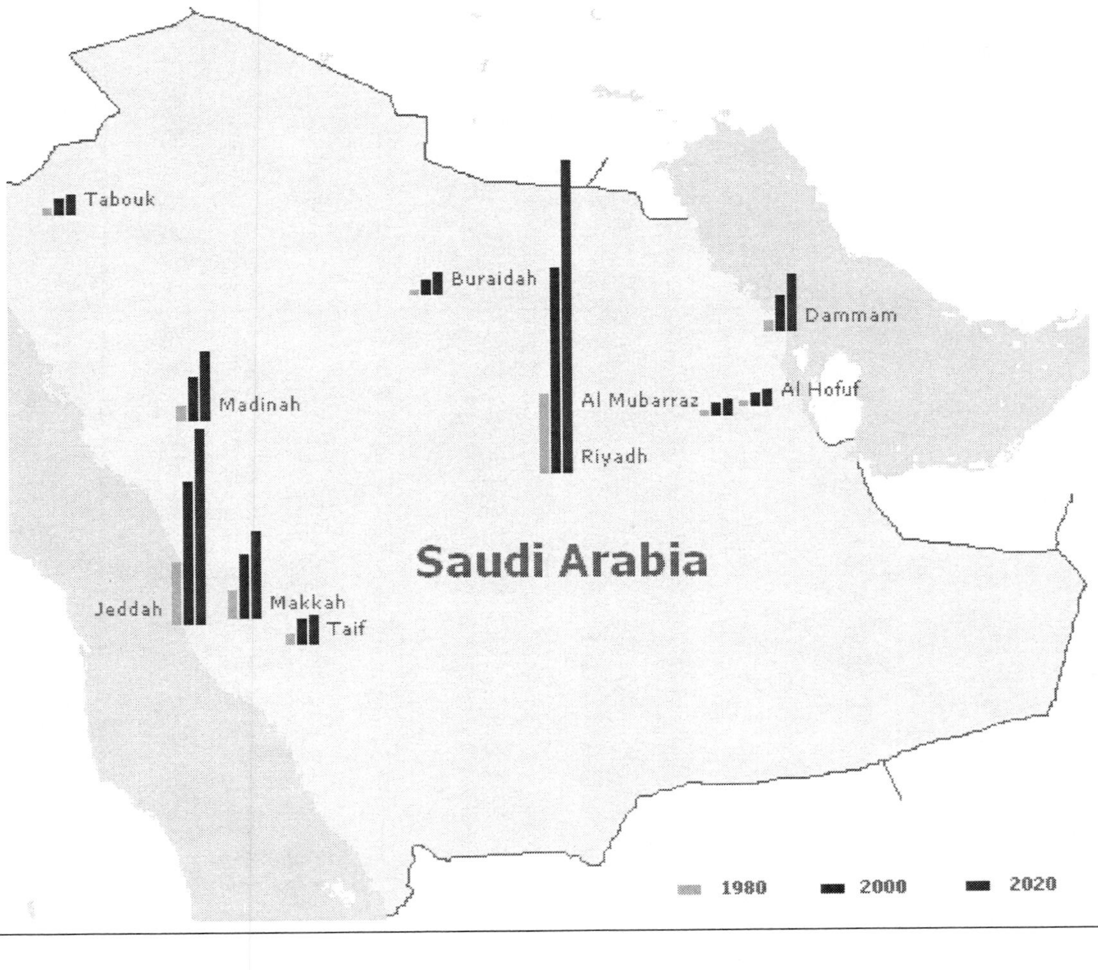

Singapore

Table 5.265 Key population trends

'000

	1980	1985	1990	1995	2000	2005	2010	2015	2020	CAGR	Period growth
Population at January 1st	2,413.9	2,736.0	3,047.1	3,524.5	4,027.9	4,341.8	4,772.3	5,054.8	5,276.1	1.97	118.57
Male	1,225.9	1,386.7	1,544.0	1,770.7	2,011.3	2,153.9	2,356.5	2,489.0	2,592.9	1.89	111.50
Female	1,188.0	1,349.3	1,503.1	1,753.8	2,016.6	2,187.9	2,415.8	2,565.8	2,683.2	2.06	125.87
0-4 yrs	196.6	223.0	249.5	288.7	277.7	247.5	241.7	252.0	267.1	0.77	35.90
5-9 yrs	229.1	212.6	229.0	271.0	315.8	295.9	271.2	254.4	261.1	0.33	13.96
10-14 yrs	241.3	241.5	221.1	244.6	289.5	321.9	310.3	273.0	252.2	0.11	4.49
15-19 yrs	286.2	251.4	248.7	234.3	260.0	291.0	336.6	312.9	270.0	-0.15	-5.65
20-24 yrs	287.9	300.2	266.2	278.7	261.1	273.4	316.2	354.0	323.2	0.29	12.27
25-29 yrs	246.2	313.5	324.0	311.6	328.8	307.1	325.9	358.7	390.7	1.16	58.65
30-34 yrs	205.5	269.5	332.3	361.3	357.2	371.3	355.3	360.6	388.4	1.60	89.02
35-39 yrs	131.9	220.6	285.1	359.6	397.0	377.5	409.7	374.0	374.0	2.64	183.58
40-44 yrs	131.3	139.9	229.5	305.2	384.4	403.5	397.5	419.7	378.4	2.68	188.33
45-49 yrs	108.9	133.8	143.1	243.3	322.6	383.6	417.1	399.2	419.2	3.43	284.93
50-54 yrs	95.4	112.3	131.5	149.6	254.4	317.7	391.3	413.1	387.6	3.57	306.35
55-59 yrs	73.5	96.1	111.5	135.1	153.8	248.2	319.1	383.8	398.1	4.32	441.97
60-64 yrs	61.8	71.9	92.5	111.5	136.0	146.7	249.4	313.5	374.4	4.61	505.63
65-69 yrs	51.2	57.6	66.7	88.9	108.8	126.9	139.9	241.6	303.3	4.55	492.24
70-74 yrs	34.6	44.6	50.2	59.6	82.3	96.7	117.1	124.6	227.6	4.82	556.94
75-79 yrs	19.4	27.0	36.0	39.6	48.7	68.0	84.5	100.8	105.4	4.32	443.78
80+ yrs	13.2	20.3	30.3	41.9	49.7	65.0	89.5	119.0	155.3	6.37	1,080.70
Median age of population (years)	24.4	27.2	29.8	31.9	34.0	35.9	37.8	39.8	41.5	1.34	70.15

Table 5.266 Key economic trends

As stated

	1990	1995	2000	2005	2010	2015	2020	CAGR	Period growth
Total GDP (S$ per capita)	28,362.7	37,464.0	44,546.8	51,120.1	55,277.9	64,930.4	79,159.1	3.48	179.1
Disposable income (S$ per capita)	18,197.5	21,210.4	28,322.3	30,788.2	31,753.9	34,691.1	41,030.0	2.75	125.5
Disposable income (S$ per household)	74,509.3	89,557.5	123,556.1	127,430.6	125,075.6	133,194.9	155,504.0	2.48	108.7
Number of households by annual household disposable income ('000)									
Over US$1,000	741.8	833.0	919.8	1,048.1	1,210.4	1,315.7	1,391.6	2.12	87.6
Over US$10,000	617.7	768.6	845.5	993.9	1,155.3	1,272.9	1,365.0	2.68	121.0
Over US$25,000	335.8	591.3	682.6	810.2	976.7	1,128.1	1,267.3	4.53	277.4
Over US$75,000	48.5	172.7	269.8	299.6	427.7	596.0	816.8	9.87	1,585.7
Over US$150,000	13.4	31.4	62.6	85.4	139.9	229.0	381.8	11.82	2,752.1
Total households	744.2	834.7	923.3	1,049.0	1,211.6	1,316.5	1,392.1	2.11	87.1

Note: Per capita data is shown at constant 2010 prices. Household disposable income bands are shown at current prices.

Table 5.267 Young generation

'000

	1980	1985	1990	1995	2000	2005	2010	2015	2020	CAGR	Period growth
Babies under 12 months	37.4	46.4	52.0	54.6	51.2	44.1	46.8	49.8	53.5	0.90	42.96
Infants under 24 months	76.9	91.1	109.3	111.1	103.6	90.6	94.5	100.0	107.1	0.83	39.28
Toddlers aged 1-4	159.1	176.6	197.6	234.0	226.5	203.4	195.0	202.2	213.6	0.74	34.24
Children aged 2-9	348.8	344.4	369.3	448.6	489.9	452.7	418.4	406.4	421.1	0.47	20.74
Female	168.3	165.7	177.7	216.9	237.3	219.5	205.4	199.1	205.2	0.50	21.93
Male	180.5	178.8	191.5	231.7	252.6	233.2	213.0	207.3	215.9	0.45	19.64
Tweenagers aged 10-14	241.3	241.5	221.1	244.6	289.5	321.9	310.3	273.0	252.2	0.11	4.49
Female	117.7	116.5	106.7	117.7	139.9	156.4	151.4	137.0	127.6	0.20	8.41
Male	123.6	125.0	114.3	126.9	149.6	165.5	158.9	136.1	124.5	0.02	0.76
Teenagers aged 13-19	391.1	349.8	338.2	331.8	361.6	421.5	465.6	428.7	370.1	-0.14	-5.36
Female	190.3	170.1	163.6	160.6	174.8	205.2	227.8	213.0	190.8	0.01	0.27
Male	200.8	179.7	174.6	171.3	186.8	216.3	237.9	215.8	179.4	-0.28	-10.69
Studying age 18-22	292.5	286.7	250.5	259.4	254.9	263.9	339.6	338.2	300.9	0.07	2.85
Female	141.4	140.6	122.2	128.2	125.0	129.4	167.9	167.8	153.2	0.20	8.35
Male	151.1	146.1	128.3	131.2	129.8	134.5	171.8	170.3	147.7	-0.06	-2.28
Young adults aged 15-29	820.3	865.2	838.9	824.5	849.9	871.5	978.7	1,025.6	983.9	0.46	19.94
Female	400.2	423.1	410.6	410.9	426.0	437.7	489.2	513.7	499.8	0.56	24.89
Male	420.1	442.1	428.3	413.6	423.9	433.9	489.5	511.9	484.0	0.35	15.23

Table 5.268 Middle-aged generation

'000

	1980	1985	1990	1995	2000	2005	2010	2015	2020	CAGR	Period growth
Middle-aged adults 30-59	746.4	972.2	1,232.9	1,554.2	1,869.4	2,101.8	2,290.1	2,350.3	2,345.8	2.90	214.3
Female	369.0	481.7	607.9	771.3	934.8	1,058.1	1,161.2	1,198.4	1,202.1	3.00	225.7
Male	377.3	490.5	625.1	782.9	934.6	1,043.7	1,128.9	1,151.9	1,143.6	2.81	203.1
Baby boomers aged 40-59	409.0	482.1	615.6	833.3	1,115.2	1,353.0	1,525.1	1,615.7	1,583.4	3.44	287.1
Female	201.1	239.4	305.2	413.6	554.5	672.3	761.0	817.5	816.2	3.56	306.0
Male	207.9	242.7	310.4	419.7	560.8	680.7	764.1	798.2	767.1	3.32	268.9

Table 5.269 Elderly population

'000

	1980	1985	1990	1995	2000	2005	2010	2015	2020	CAGR	Period growth
Elderly population (60+)	180.2	221.5	275.6	341.5	425.5	503.3	680.3	899.5	1,166.1	4.78	547.0
Female	96.0	118.3	147.4	183.4	228.8	272.3	362.9	469.3	596.8	4.67	521.4
Male	84.2	103.1	128.2	158.1	196.8	230.9	317.3	430.1	569.3	4.89	576.2

Table 5.270 Population of biggest cities 1980-2020

'000

	1980	1985	1990	1995	2000	2005	2010	2015	2020	CAGR	Period growth
Singapore	2,414	2,736	3,047	3,525	4,028	4,342	4,772	5,055	5,276	2	119

Chart 5.166 Population age shift 2000 and 2020, Each Column Represents a Single Age Group

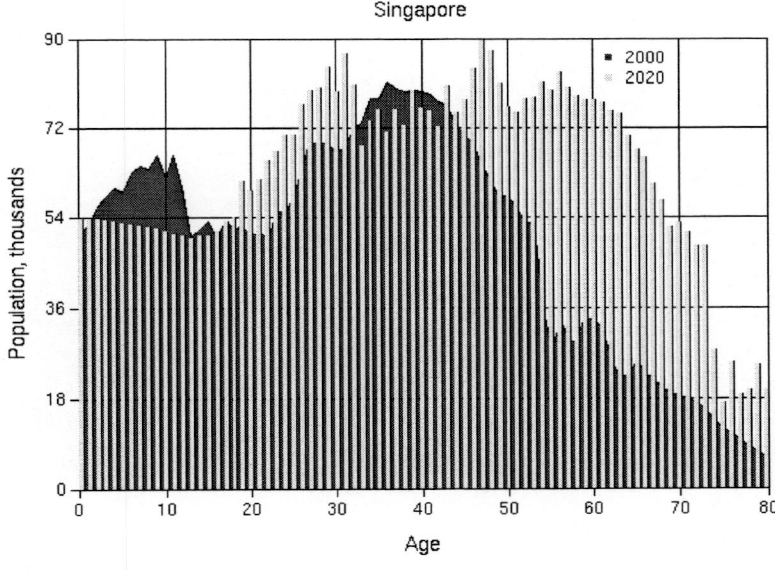

Chart 5.167 Population pyramids, 1980/2000/2010/2020

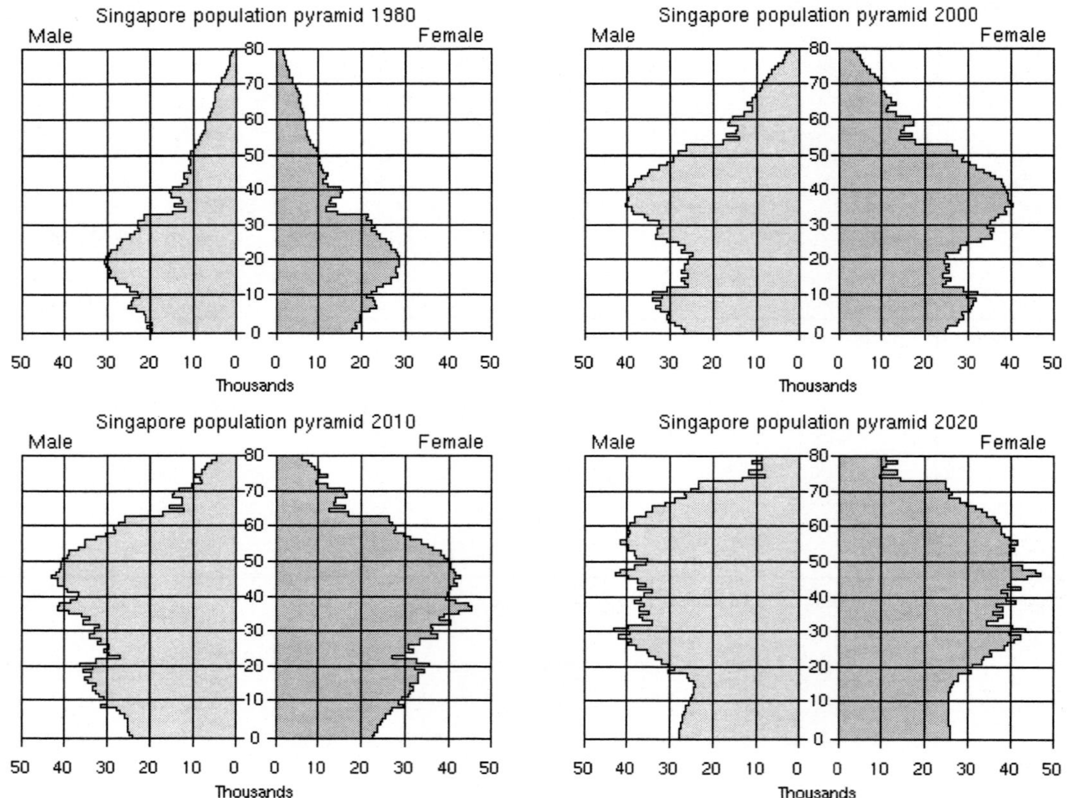

Chart 5.168 Major Cities: 1980, 2000 and 2020

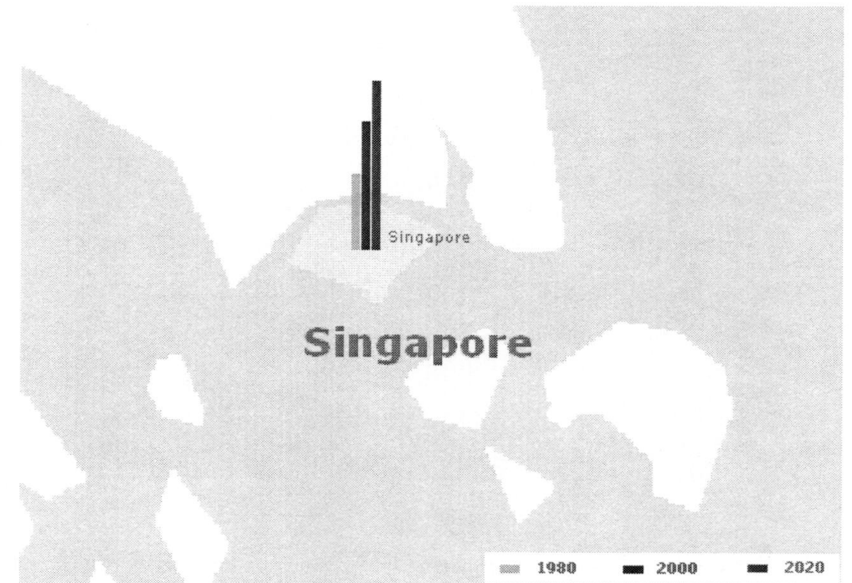

Slovakia

Table 5.271 Key population trends

'000

	1980	1985	1990	1995	2000	2005	2010	2015	2020	CAGR	Period growth
Population at January 1st	4,963.3	5,139.6	5,269.7	5,348.7	5,378.7	5,384.8	5,396.7	5,397.8	5,390.2	0.21	8.60
Male	2,441.7	2,521.1	2,577.7	2,605.2	2,614.4	2,613.5	2,621.8	2,624.2	2,621.4	0.18	7.36
Female	2,521.6	2,618.5	2,692.0	2,743.5	2,764.3	2,771.3	2,775.0	2,773.6	2,768.8	0.23	9.81
0-4 yrs	483.9	452.2	415.1	366.1	290.5	260.0	269.6	270.0	267.1	-1.47	-44.80
5-9 yrs	431.3	479.7	448.9	410.9	365.0	290.9	259.9	269.4	269.2	-1.17	-37.58
10-14 yrs	380.9	425.3	477.4	447.3	409.8	368.0	290.9	259.6	268.6	-0.87	-29.49
15-19 yrs	412.1	380.0	422.8	475.8	446.1	417.9	367.7	290.3	258.4	-1.16	-37.30
20-24 yrs	442.2	405.9	373.6	419.2	473.7	450.9	417.2	366.6	288.4	-1.06	-34.78
25-29 yrs	437.5	431.1	397.2	368.5	417.7	471.6	450.2	415.9	364.5	-0.46	-16.69
30-34 yrs	343.1	430.1	425.8	393.2	367.1	412.0	471.0	449.1	414.0	0.47	20.64
35-39 yrs	289.4	339.9	424.6	420.1	390.7	363.3	411.2	470.0	447.2	1.09	54.55
40-44 yrs	262.4	284.0	334.0	416.2	414.9	385.6	360.7	408.4	466.4	1.45	77.73
45-49 yrs	277.3	256.2	276.3	324.9	407.8	406.6	379.4	354.1	401.0	0.93	44.59
50-54 yrs	273.2	266.4	245.8	266.2	314.4	394.5	395.4	367.8	341.8	0.56	25.11
55-59 yrs	269.9	258.5	250.7	232.3	253.0	301.0	379.7	380.3	352.0	0.67	30.42
60-64 yrs	136.1	247.1	236.3	230.3	214.9	236.6	283.9	362.6	362.6	2.48	166.45
65-69 yrs	194.4	121.2	216.6	208.5	204.5	192.1	215.4	262.7	340.9	1.41	75.32
70-74 yrs	154.4	160.1	99.7	178.8	174.2	172.8	163.4	186.4	233.3	1.04	51.11
75-79 yrs	102.6	112.6	118.5	74.7	134.8	133.6	134.3	124.5	147.3	0.91	43.61
80+ yrs	72.5	89.4	106.3	115.6	99.4	127.4	146.8	160.0	167.6	2.12	131.21
Median age of population (years)	28.7	30.0	31.2	32.4	33.9	35.3	36.9	39.0	41.2	0.91	43.50

Table 5.272 Key economic trends

As stated

	1990	1995	2000	2005	2010	2015	2020	CAGR	Period growth
Total GDP (EUR per capita)	5,513.2	8,445.1	10,820.6	12,446.6	12,675.1	15,751.5	19,213.8	4.25	248.5
Disposable income (EUR per capita)		3,662.7	3,990.1	6,403.1	8,158.6	9,841.0	11,859.0		
Disposable income (EUR per household)		10,209.3	10,492.8	15,849.7	19,348.3	22,685.6	26,835.7		
Number of households by annual household disposable income ('000)									
Over US$1,000		1,917.3	2,044.8	2,175.4	2,275.6	2,341.6	2,382.0		
Over US$10,000		177.2	226.9	1,416.6	2,160.2	2,317.6	2,376.6		
Over US$25,000		38.3	49.6	168.1	810.1	1,699.4	2,190.5		
Over US$75,000		9.3	12.0	33.3	73.8	153.0	382.1		
Over US$150,000		3.8	4.9	13.6	30.1	53.3	88.3		
Total households	1,814.9	1,918.9	2,045.3	2,175.4	2,275.6	2,341.6	2,382.0	0.91	31.2

Note: Per capita data is shown at constant 2010 prices. Household disposable income bands are shown at current prices.

Table 5.273 Young generation

'000

	1980	1985	1990	1995	2000	2005	2010	2015	2020	CAGR	Period growth
Babies under 12 months	98.3	89.3	78.8	65.7	55.6	53.5	54.0	54.0	52.9	-1.53	-46.14
Infants under 24 months	195.8	179.2	160.4	138.1	112.5	104.8	107.8	108.1	106.2	-1.52	-45.78
Toddlers aged 1-4	385.7	362.9	336.2	300.4	234.9	206.5	215.7	216.0	214.2	-1.46	-44.46
Children aged 2-9	719.5	752.7	703.5	638.9	543.1	446.1	421.7	431.3	430.2	-1.28	-40.20
Female	351.9	368.6	344.2	312.4	264.8	217.4	205.2	209.7	209.2	-1.29	-40.54
Male	367.5	384.1	359.3	326.5	278.3	228.7	216.5	221.6	221.0	-1.26	-39.88
Tweenagers aged 10-14	380.9	425.3	477.4	447.3	409.8	368.0	290.9	259.6	268.6	-0.87	-29.49
Female	186.2	208.2	234.1	218.7	200.8	179.8	141.8	126.5	130.9	-0.88	-29.72
Male	194.7	217.1	243.4	228.6	209.0	188.2	149.1	133.1	137.7	-0.86	-29.28
Teenagers aged 13-19	569.7	537.3	612.2	656.9	617.3	574.0	488.7	394.8	365.9	-1.10	-35.76
Female	278.5	262.8	300.0	322.1	302.1	280.9	238.7	192.6	178.6	-1.10	-35.88
Male	291.2	274.5	312.2	334.9	315.2	293.1	250.1	202.3	187.4	-1.10	-35.65
Studying age 18-22	426.3	399.2	376.4	453.1	466.5	442.8	398.9	331.8	272.5	-1.11	-36.07
Female	207.8	195.3	184.1	222.5	229.1	216.7	195.3	162.3	133.3	-1.11	-35.88
Male	218.4	204.0	192.2	230.6	237.4	226.1	203.5	169.5	139.3	-1.12	-36.25
Young adults aged 15-29	1,291.8	1,217.0	1,193.6	1,263.5	1,337.4	1,340.4	1,235.1	1,072.8	911.3	-0.87	-29.46
Female	631.8	594.9	585.1	621.2	656.8	656.9	604.4	525.1	445.9	-0.87	-29.42
Male	660.0	622.1	608.5	642.3	680.7	683.5	630.6	547.6	465.4	-0.87	-29.49

Table 5.274 Middle-aged generation

'000

	1980	1985	1990	1995	2000	2005	2010	2015	2020	CAGR	Period growth
Middle-aged adults 30-59	1,715.3	1,835.0	1,957.2	2,053.0	2,148.0	2,263.0	2,397.4	2,429.7	2,422.3	0.87	41.2
Female	880.4	937.8	995.1	1,042.9	1,087.2	1,142.5	1,203.5	1,215.1	1,209.5	0.80	37.4
Male	834.9	897.2	962.1	1,010.0	1,060.7	1,120.4	1,193.9	1,214.6	1,212.8	0.94	45.3
Baby boomers aged 40-59	1,082.8	1,065.0	1,106.8	1,239.6	1,390.1	1,487.7	1,515.2	1,510.6	1,561.2	0.92	44.2
Female	562.5	555.7	576.0	640.8	712.3	758.9	769.6	764.5	787.0	0.84	39.9
Male	520.3	509.4	530.8	598.8	677.8	728.8	745.6	746.1	774.1	1.00	48.8

Table 5.275 Elderly population

'000

	1980	1985	1990	1995	2000	2005	2010	2015	2020	CAGR	Period growth
Elderly population (60+)	660.0	730.4	777.4	808.0	827.9	862.5	943.8	1,096.3	1,251.6	1.61	89.7
Female	375.0	421.4	455.0	480.9	499.6	523.7	567.6	644.6	721.7	1.65	92.4
Male	284.9	309.0	322.4	327.1	328.2	338.9	376.1	451.6	530.0	1.56	86.0

Table 5.276 Population of biggest cities 1980-2020

'000

	1980	1985	1990	1995	2000	2005	2010	2015	2020	CAGR	Period growth
Bratislava	380.3	421.3	441.5	439.0	429.9	430.0	435.7	441.4	446.5	0.40	17.4
Kosice	202.4	224.0	234.6	236.6	235.9	239.3	244.4	248.7	252.3	0.55	24.7
Presov	68.5	79.5	86.9	90.3	92.3	95.3	98.3	100.6	102.4	1.01	49.4
Nitra	68.9	78.8	84.9	86.8	87.1	88.7	90.9	92.6	94.0	0.78	36.5
Zilina	70.0	78.6	83.5	84.9	85.2	86.9	89.0	90.7	92.1	0.69	31.6
Banska Bystrica	62.7	74.1	82.5	83.8	83.1	83.9	85.5	86.9	88.0	0.85	40.4
Trnava	60.8	66.0	68.6	69.3	70.0	71.8	73.9	75.5	76.7	0.59	26.3
Martin	47.5	54.0	58.0	59.4	59.9	61.3	63.0	64.3	65.3	0.80	37.5
Trencin	50.0	54.5	56.7	57.2	57.7	59.0	60.6	61.9	62.9	0.58	25.8
Poprad	38.1	46.3	52.2	54.8	55.9	57.5	59.2	60.5	61.6	1.21	61.7

Chart 5.169 Population age shift 2000 and 2020, Each Column Represents a Single Age Group

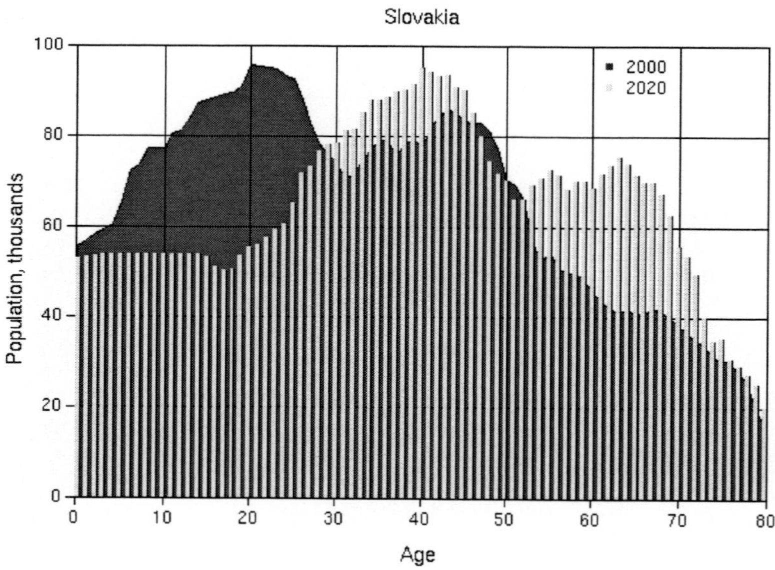

Chart 5.170 Population pyramids, 1980/2000/2010/2020

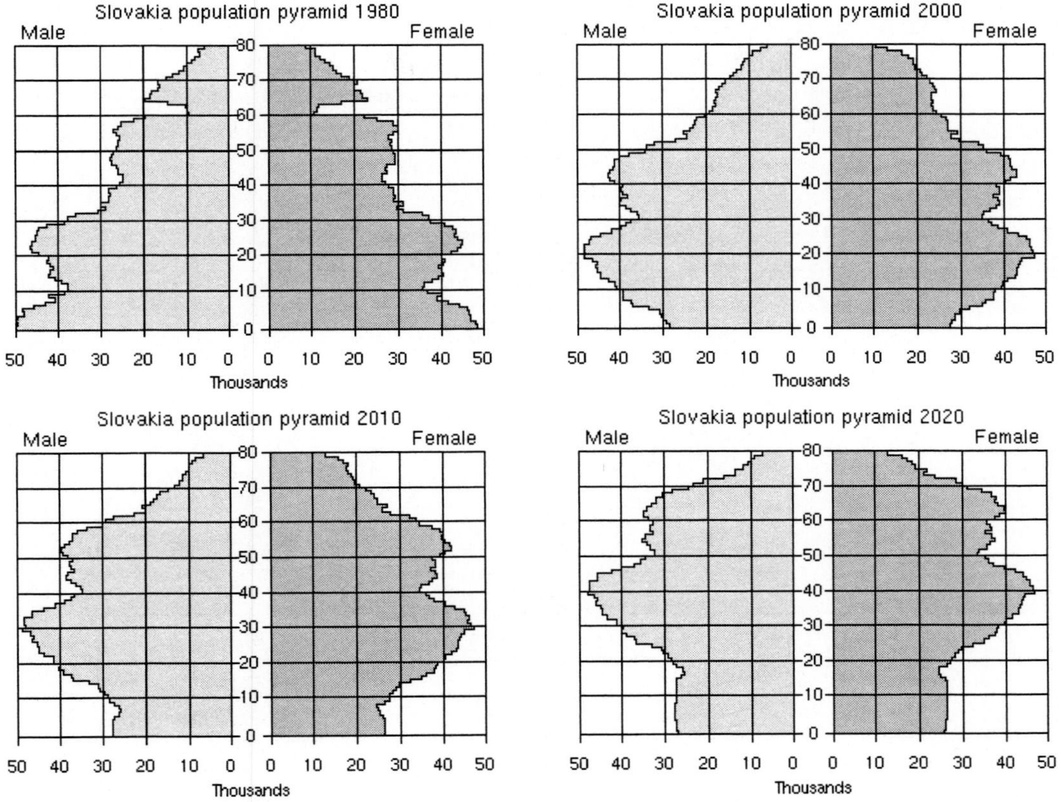

Chart 5.171 Major Cities: 1980, 2000 and 2020

Slovenia

Table 5.277 Key population trends

'000

	1980	1985	1990	1995	2000	2005	2010	2015	2020	CAGR	Period growth
Population at January 1st	1,893.1	1,948.6	1,996.4	1,989.5	1,987.8	1,997.6	2,028.9	2,048.0	2,061.0	0.21	8.87
Male	918.9	945.7	968.3	964.4	970.8	977.1	998.3	1,011.6	1,021.4	0.26	11.15
Female	974.1	1,002.9	1,028.1	1,025.1	1,016.9	1,020.5	1,030.6	1,036.5	1,039.6	0.16	6.72
0-4 yrs	151.5	141.7	125.1	102.4	92.0	89.5	94.3	98.7	97.3	-1.10	-35.81
5-9 yrs	143.3	151.9	141.6	124.8	103.6	92.8	91.6	96.1	100.6	-0.88	-29.79
10-14 yrs	144.7	143.1	151.5	141.4	124.8	104.4	94.2	92.6	97.4	-0.99	-32.73
15-19 yrs	143.6	146.0	143.9	150.9	140.9	125.7	105.9	95.2	93.9	-1.06	-34.65
20-24 yrs	154.8	150.1	150.9	142.4	151.2	142.4	129.0	107.7	97.1	-1.16	-37.26
25-29 yrs	166.3	159.3	156.1	149.1	143.7	152.4	146.9	131.8	110.2	-1.02	-33.74
30-34 yrs	134.1	165.6	162.1	153.1	151.4	144.4	155.8	149.3	134.1	0.00	-0.05
35-39 yrs	127.5	131.6	166.2	158.1	154.7	151.8	147.2	157.8	151.4	0.43	18.67
40-44 yrs	124.0	125.2	131.5	161.8	158.1	154.9	154.2	148.8	159.6	0.63	28.71
45-49 yrs	127.7	120.5	123.4	127.5	157.4	156.7	155.9	154.8	149.5	0.39	17.06
50-54 yrs	114.0	122.4	116.7	118.9	120.4	154.0	155.6	154.7	153.9	0.75	34.92
55-59 yrs	94.2	107.3	116.3	110.9	111.2	116.5	150.7	152.4	152.0	1.20	61.27
60-64 yrs	52.2	87.2	99.5	108.0	102.9	105.7	112.2	145.3	147.6	2.63	182.88
65-69 yrs	78.0	46.1	78.3	90.2	97.4	95.4	99.3	106.0	138.0	1.44	76.96
70-74 yrs	63.1	65.5	39.0	67.6	78.4	86.0	85.6	89.6	96.8	1.08	53.42
75-79 yrs	41.5	46.2	50.1	30.4	54.7	64.6	71.9	72.3	76.8	1.55	85.18
80+ yrs	32.4	39.0	44.2	52.0	44.9	60.5	78.5	94.9	105.0	2.98	223.85
Median age of population (years)	31.4	32.5	34.0	36.0	37.8	39.9	41.7	43.1	44.7	0.88	42.20

Table 5.278 Key economic trends

As stated

	1990	1995	2000	2005	2010	2015	2020	CAGR	Period growth
Total GDP (EUR per capita)	1,595.9	7,147.7	11,815.6	16,340.4	18,029.9	21,187.8	24,735.1	9.57	1,449.9
Disposable income (EUR per capita)		10,299.9	8,937.6	10,492.4	11,464.3	13,719.6	16,151.6		
Disposable income (EUR per household)		31,454.8	26,302.4	29,674.6	31,362.1	36,529.5	42,073.4		
Number of households by annual household disposable income ('000)									
Over US$1,000	635.8	651.4	675.4	706.3	741.6	769.2	791.2	0.73	24.4
Over US$10,000	109.1	585.9	579.5	695.3	736.5	767.2	790.4	6.82	624.6
Over US$25,000	18.3	129.0	85.4	459.7	608.1	713.7	771.0	13.28	4,111.9
Over US$75,000	4.4	15.3	13.6	34.5	59.3	141.9	330.7	15.48	7,405.7
Over US$150,000	1.8	6.2	5.5	13.2	19.8	29.4	48.6	11.63	2,611.7
Total households	636.3	651.5	675.4	706.3	741.6	769.2	791.2	0.73	24.3

Note: Per capita data is shown at constant 2010 prices. Household disposable income bands are shown at current prices.

Table 5.279 Young generation

'000

	1980	1985	1990	1995	2000	2005	2010	2015	2020	CAGR	Period growth
Babies under 12 months	30.5	26.2	23.2	19.3	17.5	17.9	19.1	19.7	18.8	-1.21	-38.45
Infants under 24 months	60.8	53.3	48.3	39.0	35.5	35.3	38.0	39.4	38.0	-1.17	-37.54
Toddlers aged 1-4	121.0	115.5	101.9	83.1	74.5	71.6	75.2	79.0	78.5	-1.08	-35.15
Children aged 2-9	234.0	240.3	218.4	188.3	160.0	147.0	147.9	155.4	159.9	-0.95	-31.68
Female	113.3	116.2	106.7	91.7	77.9	71.3	71.9	75.4	77.6	-0.94	-31.53
Male	120.7	124.2	111.7	96.6	82.1	75.7	76.0	80.0	82.3	-0.95	-31.81
Tweenagers aged 10-14	144.7	143.1	151.5	141.4	124.8	104.4	94.2	92.6	97.4	-0.99	-32.73
Female	70.5	69.3	73.6	69.1	60.9	50.9	45.6	45.0	47.2	-1.00	-32.97
Male	74.2	73.8	77.9	72.2	64.0	53.5	48.5	47.6	50.1	-0.98	-32.50
Teenagers aged 13-19	203.4	201.5	204.3	210.4	191.8	170.0	144.8	132.5	132.4	-1.07	-34.91
Female	100.3	98.6	100.1	102.4	93.7	82.9	70.4	64.2	64.3	-1.10	-35.84
Male	103.1	102.9	104.2	108.0	98.1	87.1	74.4	68.3	68.0	-1.03	-34.01
Studying age 18-22	147.0	150.2	143.6	147.2	150.0	133.6	121.1	101.2	94.8	-1.09	-35.55
Female	73.7	74.7	71.6	72.1	72.5	65.3	58.8	49.2	45.9	-1.18	-37.70
Male	73.3	75.5	72.0	75.1	77.6	68.3	62.2	52.0	48.9	-1.01	-33.39
Young adults aged 15-29	464.7	455.4	451.0	442.4	435.8	420.5	381.8	334.7	301.2	-1.08	-35.19
Female	228.4	225.4	224.5	218.2	211.8	204.6	185.3	162.1	146.0	-1.11	-36.06
Male	236.3	230.0	226.5	224.2	224.0	215.9	196.5	172.5	155.1	-1.05	-34.36

Table 5.280 Middle-aged generation

'000

	1980	1985	1990	1995	2000	2005	2010	2015	2020	CAGR	Period growth
Middle-aged adults 30-59	721.7	772.5	816.1	830.3	853.3	878.2	919.5	917.8	900.4	0.55	24.8
Female	369.8	388.0	404.7	412.6	420.0	431.0	448.0	446.2	436.2	0.41	17.9
Male	351.9	384.5	411.4	417.8	433.3	447.3	471.5	471.6	464.2	0.69	31.9
Baby boomers aged 40-59	460.0	475.3	487.8	519.1	547.2	582.1	616.5	610.7	615.0	0.73	33.7
Female	243.4	244.1	244.7	258.0	268.6	285.7	302.0	298.5	298.7	0.51	22.7
Male	216.6	231.2	243.1	261.2	278.6	296.4	314.5	312.2	316.2	0.95	46.0

Table 5.281 Elderly population

'000

	1980	1985	1990	1995	2000	2005	2010	2015	2020	CAGR	Period growth
Elderly population (60+)	267.2	284.0	311.1	348.1	378.3	412.2	447.5	508.3	564.3	1.89	111.2
Female	163.2	177.9	195.3	214.5	229.2	245.6	261.3	288.6	314.2	1.65	92.6
Male	104.0	106.0	115.8	133.6	149.1	166.6	186.2	219.6	250.0	2.22	140.4

Table 5.282 Population of biggest cities 1980-2020

'000

	1980	1985	1990	1995	2000	2005	2010	2015	2020	CAGR	Period growth
Ljubljana	218.7	245.0	272.3	268.9	260.9	256.6	259.1	263.6	273.6	0.56	25.09
Maribor	104.7	107.8	108.8	102.1	95.3	92.1	92.0	93.0	96.2	-0.21	-8.17
Celje	32.1	36.3	40.7	39.9	38.3	37.3	37.4	37.9	39.3	0.51	22.38
Kranj	32.9	35.2	37.2	36.8	35.9	35.2	35.6	36.2	37.5	0.33	14.24
Velenje	22.2	24.7	27.3	27.2	26.8	26.7	27.1	27.7	28.8	0.66	29.93
Koper/Capodistria	23.2	24.3	25.2	24.6	23.9	23.5	23.7	24.2	25.1	0.19	8.04
Novo mesto	19.3	20.9	22.5	22.5	22.4	22.4	22.9	23.5	24.5	0.59	26.65
Ptuj	11.7	11.5	11.2	13.7	17.0	19.9	22.0	23.6	25.2	1.93	114.99
Trbovlje	17.0	17.3	17.4	16.9	16.4	16.1	16.3	16.6	17.2	0.04	1.41
Nova Gorica	17.6	16.1	14.8	13.8	13.5	13.4	13.7	13.9	14.5	-0.48	-17.48

Chart 5.172 Population age shift 2000 and 2020, Each Column Represents a Single Age Group

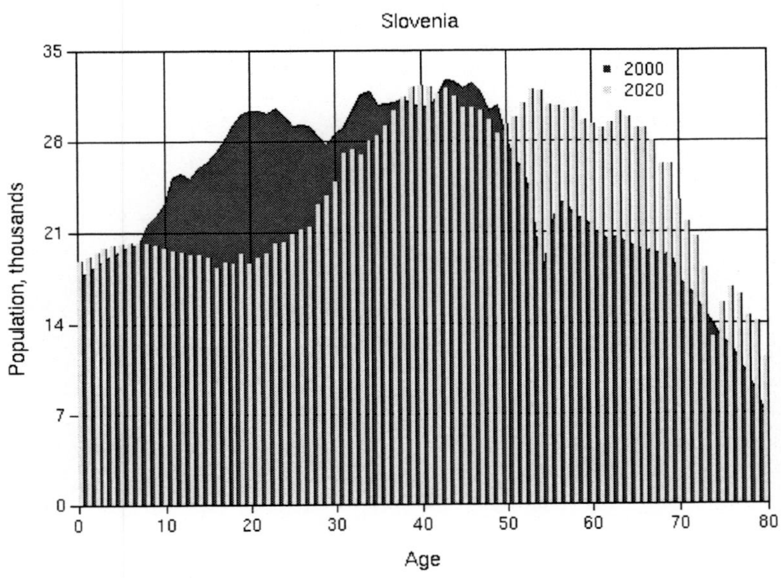

Chart 5.173 Population pyramids, 1980/2000/2010/2020

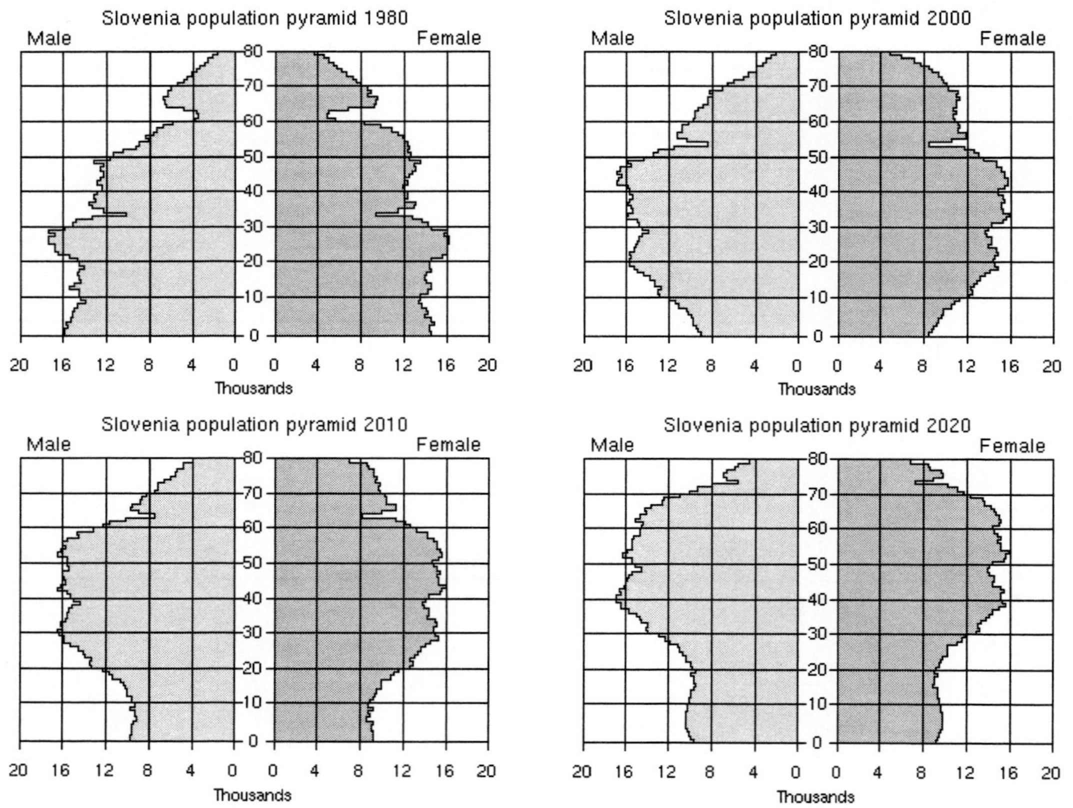

Chart 5.174 Major Cities: 1980, 2000 and 2020

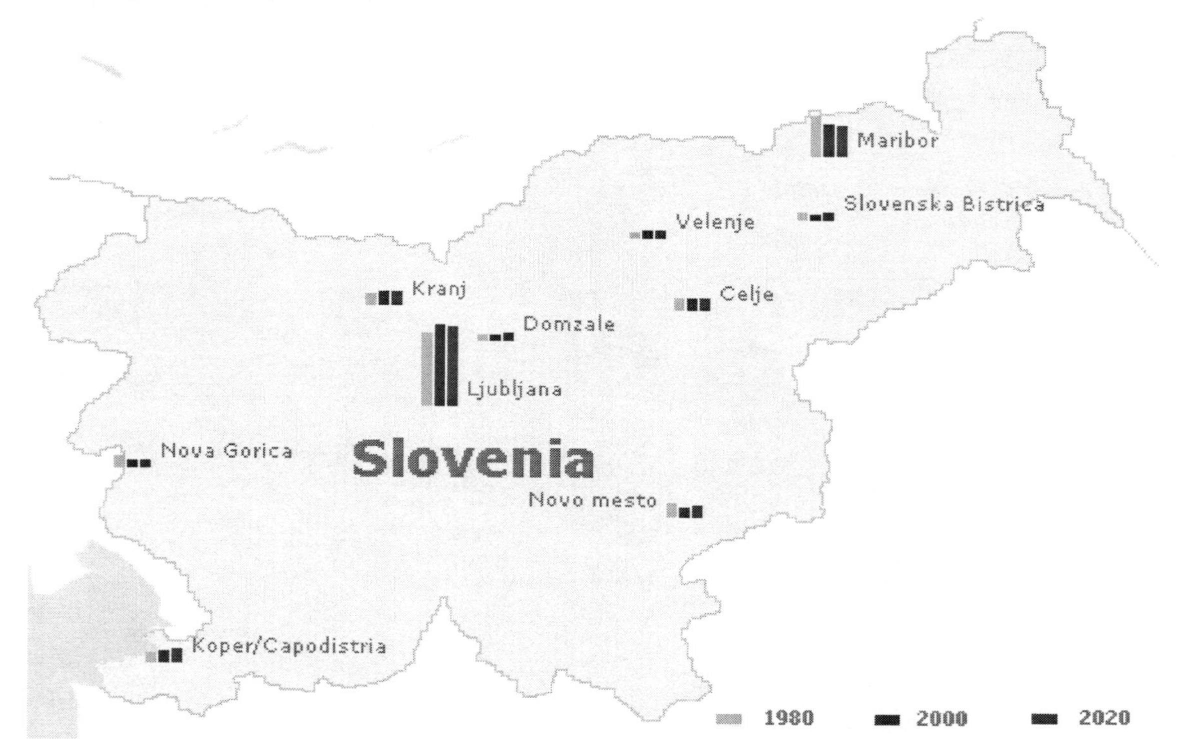

South Africa

Table 5.283 Key population trends

'000

	1980	1985	1990	1995	2000	2005	2010	2015	2020	CAGR	Period growth
Population at January 1st	29,075.3	32,959.0	36,745.3	41,374.8	44,871.9	48,073.4	50,492.4	51,684.4	52,671.4	1.50	81.16
Male	14,462.7	16,384.7	18,181.9	20,382.0	22,058.6	23,660.8	24,902.6	25,522.1	26,068.8	1.48	80.25
Female	14,612.6	16,574.3	18,563.4	20,992.9	22,813.3	24,412.6	25,589.8	26,162.4	26,602.6	1.51	82.05
0-4 yrs	4,500.6	4,902.1	5,092.4	5,057.5	5,076.0	5,249.3	5,154.7	5,113.6	4,928.2	0.23	9.50
5-9 yrs	4,047.1	4,430.5	4,806.2	5,039.9	4,996.2	5,011.1	5,158.2	5,094.3	5,056.8	0.56	24.95
10-14 yrs	3,528.2	4,019.2	4,390.0	4,799.5	5,007.5	4,982.6	4,993.9	5,094.3	5,058.7	0.90	43.38
15-19 yrs	3,035.2	3,509.7	3,979.3	4,409.8	4,780.1	5,026.4	4,996.5	4,920.6	5,019.3	1.27	65.37
20-24 yrs	2,672.9	3,017.8	3,457.8	4,041.1	4,376.9	4,813.1	5,067.6	4,895.4	4,820.4	1.49	80.35
25-29 yrs	2,286.5	2,655.9	2,963.5	3,526.7	3,962.8	4,301.9	4,748.0	4,852.7	4,701.8	1.82	105.64
30-34 yrs	1,860.8	2,264.4	2,605.1	3,013.4	3,423.5	3,745.6	4,020.4	4,346.2	4,490.2	2.23	141.30
35-39 yrs	1,580.7	1,829.9	2,208.0	2,637.7	2,914.6	3,174.2	3,350.5	3,504.0	3,859.3	2.26	144.15
40-44 yrs	1,331.2	1,536.1	1,763.9	2,218.2	2,543.5	2,710.3	2,822.7	2,864.3	3,033.2	2.08	127.86
45-49 yrs	1,124.1	1,272.8	1,459.1	1,768.5	2,126.5	2,386.7	2,456.9	2,454.3	2,489.1	2.01	121.43
50-54 yrs	914.9	1,048.7	1,184.5	1,450.4	1,671.7	1,993.2	2,196.3	2,193.1	2,178.2	2.19	138.07
55-59 yrs	722.3	825.8	949.3	1,144.7	1,336.6	1,541.0	1,827.3	1,980.1	1,974.1	2.55	173.32
60-64 yrs	566.0	621.4	717.0	871.7	1,010.2	1,186.7	1,372.0	1,616.8	1,761.2	2.88	211.14
65-69 yrs	396.7	453.6	505.6	612.3	719.6	843.8	998.5	1,155.2	1,377.7	3.16	247.31
70-74 yrs	260.5	289.5	337.8	392.5	463.2	552.4	655.6	780.2	917.5	3.20	252.25
75-79 yrs	143.2	168.1	191.5	231.5	265.4	318.1	385.2	463.3	562.2	3.48	292.61
80+ yrs	104.5	113.6	134.3	159.2	197.5	236.9	288.3	356.1	443.5	3.68	324.43
Median age of population (years)	19.0	19.4	20.1	21.7	22.9	23.9	24.9	25.7	26.5	0.84	39.63

Table 5.284 Key economic trends

As stated

	1990	1995	2000	2005	2010	2015	2020	CAGR	Period growth
Total GDP (R per capita)	42,613.5	39,508.4	41,797.7	47,251.7	50,984.8	61,502.5	74,710.5	1.89	75.3
Disposable income (R per capita)	18,623.4	18,762.8	21,160.0	26,573.1	30,919.9	38,117.9	46,468.7	3.09	149.5
Disposable income (R per household)	101,649.9	86,464.5	84,668.1	100,770.1	112,306.0	128,976.7	144,064.4	1.17	41.7
Number of households by annual household disposable income ('000)									
Over US$1,000	5,910.0	7,760.5	8,973.1	10,888.8	11,625.9	13,051.0	14,900.2	3.13	152.1
Over US$10,000	1,695.5	2,671.8	2,274.6	3,881.0	3,837.4	4,747.9	6,172.7	4.40	264.1
Over US$25,000	499.2	854.6	630.8	1,313.1	1,236.9	1,631.8	2,331.8	5.27	367.1
Over US$75,000	84.2	130.8	94.8	211.2	190.3	259.7	400.1	5.33	375.0
Over US$150,000	29.1	43.3	36.5	63.9	62.3	78.2	112.0	4.59	284.3
Total households	6,732.1	8,978.3	11,214.3	12,677.0	13,901.5	15,274.9	16,989.4	3.13	152.4

Note: Per capita data is shown at constant 2010 prices. Household disposable income bands are shown at current prices.

Table 5.285 Young generation

'000

	1980	1985	1990	1995	2000	2005	2010	2015	2020	CAGR	Period growth
Babies under 12 months	930.8	1,025.9	1,027.7	1,001.3	1,038.4	1,079.6	1,009.4	1,035.4	963.2	0.09	3.48
Infants under 24 months	1,847.3	2,027.9	2,054.7	2,009.3	2,061.0	2,144.0	2,035.0	2,060.8	1,941.0	0.12	5.07
Toddlers aged 1-4	3,569.8	3,876.2	4,064.6	4,056.3	4,037.6	4,169.8	4,145.3	4,078.2	3,965.0	0.26	11.07
Children aged 2-9	6,700.4	7,304.7	7,843.9	8,088.1	8,011.3	8,116.5	8,277.9	8,147.1	8,044.0	0.46	20.05
Female	3,338.0	3,637.5	3,903.3	4,022.1	3,982.3	4,032.7	4,111.6	4,045.8	3,988.7	0.45	19.49
Male	3,362.3	3,667.2	3,940.6	4,066.0	4,028.9	4,083.7	4,166.3	4,101.2	4,055.3	0.47	20.61
Tweenagers aged 10-14	3,528.2	4,019.2	4,390.0	4,799.5	5,007.5	4,982.6	4,993.9	5,094.3	5,058.7	0.90	43.38
Female	1,761.8	2,008.0	2,193.1	2,395.0	2,496.5	2,482.1	2,486.4	2,535.3	2,516.6	0.90	42.84
Male	1,766.3	2,011.2	2,197.0	2,404.5	2,511.1	2,500.6	2,507.4	2,559.0	2,542.0	0.91	43.92
Teenagers aged 13-19	4,382.1	5,062.9	5,686.4	6,286.3	6,772.7	7,028.0	6,980.4	6,944.6	7,042.3	1.19	60.70
Female	2,177.4	2,531.1	2,847.7	3,145.8	3,381.8	3,505.0	3,479.0	3,461.6	3,507.7	1.20	61.09
Male	2,204.7	2,531.9	2,838.6	3,140.5	3,390.8	3,523.1	3,501.4	3,483.0	3,534.6	1.19	60.32
Studying age 18-22	2,809.8	3,199.2	3,676.4	4,197.0	4,543.1	4,941.9	5,062.9	4,884.2	4,904.0	1.40	74.53
Female	1,393.1	1,592.2	1,848.6	2,110.2	2,271.7	2,464.3	2,523.8	2,437.7	2,446.0	1.42	75.58
Male	1,416.8	1,607.0	1,827.8	2,086.9	2,271.3	2,477.6	2,539.1	2,446.6	2,458.0	1.39	73.49
Young adults aged 15-29	7,994.6	9,183.4	10,400.6	11,977.6	13,119.8	14,141.4	14,812.0	14,668.7	14,541.6	1.51	81.89
Female	3,960.9	4,568.0	5,217.8	6,039.3	6,571.4	7,024.7	7,344.1	7,293.0	7,235.2	1.52	82.67
Male	4,033.7	4,615.3	5,182.8	5,938.3	6,548.5	7,116.8	7,467.9	7,375.7	7,306.4	1.50	81.14

Table 5.286 Middle-aged generation

'000

	1980	1985	1990	1995	2000	2005	2010	2015	2020	CAGR	Period growth
Middle-aged adults 30-59	7,534	8,778	10,170	12,233	14,016	15,551	16,674	17,342	18,024	2.20	139.2
Female	3,773	4,392	5,135	6,234	7,196	7,975	8,456	8,648	8,810	2.14	133.5
Male	3,761	4,386	5,035	5,999	6,820	7,576	8,218	8,694	9,214	2.26	144.9
Baby boomers aged 40-59	4,092	4,683	5,357	6,582	7,678	8,631	9,303	9,492	9,675	2.17	136.4
Female	2,066	2,371	2,733	3,374	3,974	4,519	4,906	4,926	4,824	2.14	133.5
Male	2,027	2,313	2,624	3,208	3,705	4,112	4,397	4,566	4,851	2.21	139.3

Table 5.287 Elderly population

'000

	1980	1985	1990	1995	2000	2005	2010	2015	2020	CAGR	Period growth
Elderly population (60+)	1,470.9	1,646.2	1,886.2	2,267.3	2,655.9	3,138.0	3,699.6	4,371.6	5,062.1	3.14	244.2
Female	861.6	963.0	1,095.8	1,306.2	1,545.1	1,836.0	2,183.1	2,621.1	3,091.7	3.25	258.8
Male	609.3	683.2	790.4	961.0	1,110.8	1,302.0	1,516.5	1,750.6	1,970.3	2.98	223.4

Table 5.288 Population of biggest cities 1980-2020

'000

	1980	1985	1990	1995	2000	2005	2010	2015	2020	CAGR	Period growth
CapeTown	1,367.7	1,554.8	1,802.2	2,345.9	2,723.6	3,202.1	3,667.9	4,237.0	4,989.4	3.29	264.8
Durban	1,310.3	1,484.3	1,692.6	2,082.8	2,450.4	2,977.3	3,523.1	4,163.2	4,974.8	3.39	279.7
Johannesburg	803.0	914.5	1,068.8	1,429.6	1,632.7	1,862.8	2,067.7	2,333.5	2,705.4	3.08	236.9
Soweto	648.6	736.0	846.4	1,072.8	1,267.8	1,536.3	1,813.1	2,138.8	2,552.8	3.48	293.6
Pretoria	700.2	792.4	899.7	1,090.2	1,255.9	1,492.8	1,728.9	2,012.8	2,382.4	3.11	240.3
PortElizabeth	472.9	535.3	608.4	739.6	854.1	1,017.3	1,180.7	1,376.7	1,631.1	3.14	244.9
Pietermaritzburg	177.2	203.3	245.6	362.7	504.6	705.5	939.3	1,194.0	1,490.3	5.47	740.8
Benoni	207.1	235.4	272.8	355.0	437.7	554.0	680.7	824.6	1,000.6	4.02	383.2
Welkom	104.4	120.1	146.4	222.1	318.6	456.1	617.7	792.5	994.4	5.80	852.4
Bloemfontein	206.7	234.1	267.0	328.6	396.8	497.3	605.7	729.6	882.3	3.70	326.9

Chart 5.175 Population age shift 2000 and 2020, Each Column Represents a Single Age Group

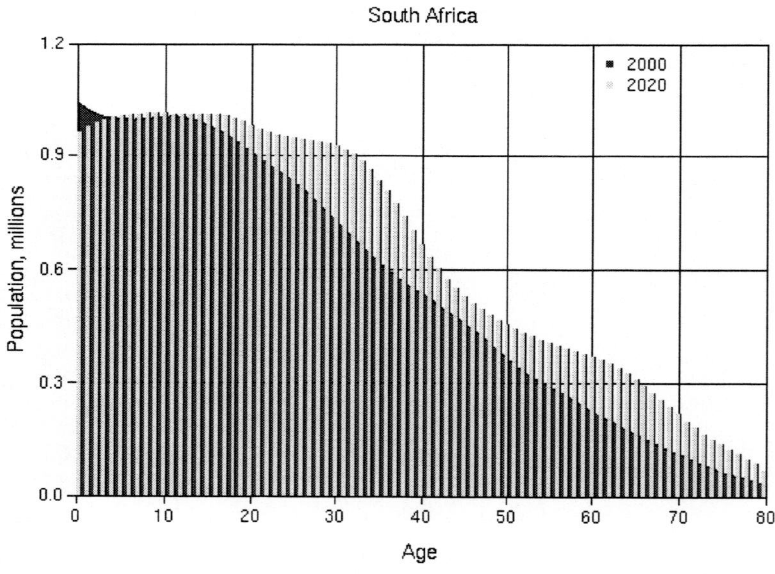

Chart 5.176 Population pyramids, 1980/2000/2010/2020

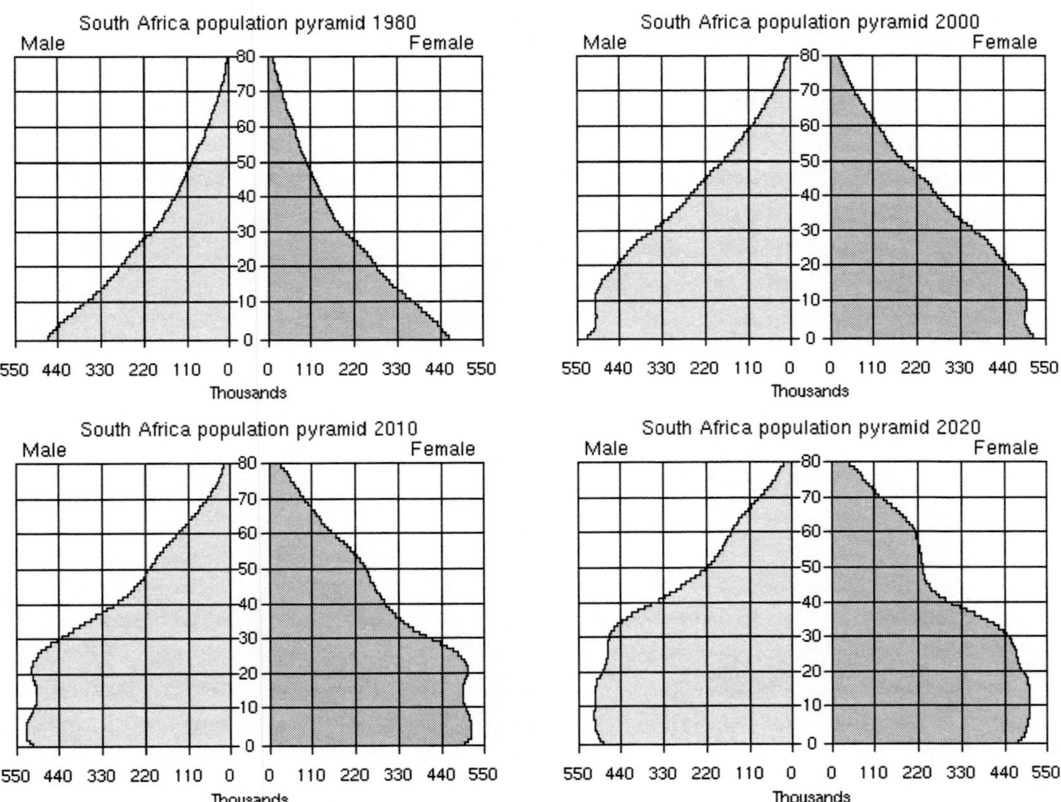

Chart 5.177 Major Cities: 1980, 2000 and 2020

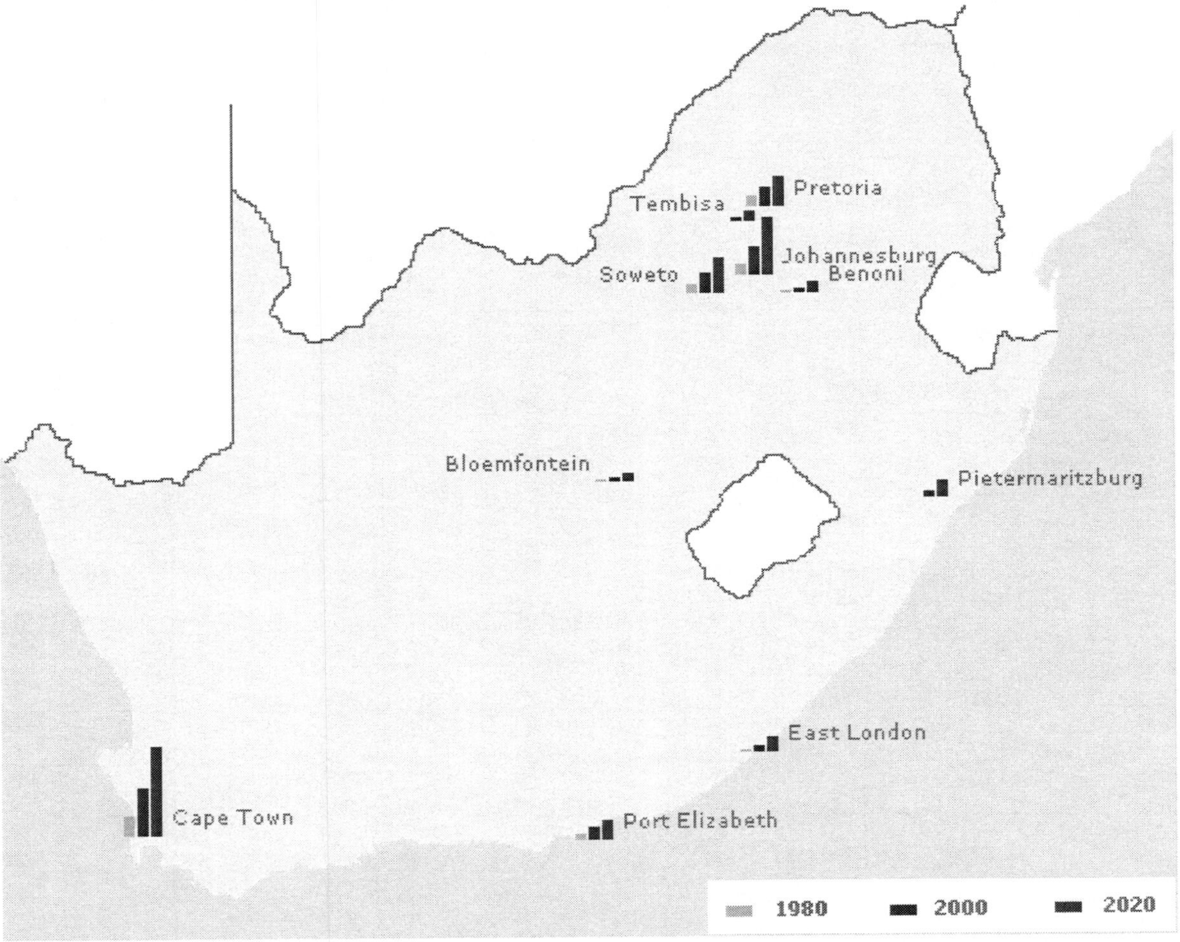

Pretoria
Tembisa
Johannesburg
Soweto
Benoni
Bloemfontein
Pietermaritzburg
East London
Cape Town
Port Elizabeth
1980 2000 2020

South Korea

Table 5.289 Key population trends

'000

	1980	1985	1990	1995	2000	2005	2010	2015	2020	CAGR	Period growth
Population at January 1st	38,123.8	40,805.7	42,869.3	45,093.0	47,008.1	48,138.1	48,874.5	49,277.1	49,325.7	0.65	29.38
Male	19,235.7	20,575.6	21,568.2	22,705.3	23,666.8	24,190.9	24,540.3	24,706.8	24,679.8	0.62	28.30
Female	18,888.0	20,230.1	21,301.1	22,387.7	23,341.3	23,947.2	24,334.2	24,570.2	24,645.9	0.67	30.48
0-4 yrs	4,033.7	3,845.5	3,203.2	3,545.7	3,259.8	2,544.8	2,201.5	2,072.8	1,919.3	-1.84	-52.42
5-9 yrs	4,458.4	3,967.7	3,843.5	3,166.8	3,521.5	3,233.5	2,517.3	2,177.9	2,050.8	-1.92	-54.00
10-14 yrs	4,458.6	4,491.3	3,926.9	3,824.4	3,130.0	3,462.8	3,188.1	2,482.2	2,148.0	-1.81	-51.82
15-19 yrs	4,519.7	4,407.8	4,442.0	3,896.9	3,842.4	3,136.5	3,402.3	3,133.3	2,440.0	-1.53	-46.01
20-24 yrs	4,093.4	4,274.3	4,342.4	4,391.6	3,854.4	3,742.6	3,113.2	3,378.0	3,111.6	-0.68	-23.99
25-29 yrs	3,072.8	4,097.9	4,326.7	4,300.7	4,352.9	3,844.0	3,720.6	3,095.6	3,359.8	0.22	9.34
30-34 yrs	2,525.2	3,089.3	4,134.7	4,296.7	4,248.0	4,301.0	3,828.4	3,706.7	3,085.6	0.50	22.19
35-39 yrs	2,279.6	2,552.2	3,042.3	4,092.1	4,273.1	4,233.4	4,270.2	3,803.7	3,684.4	1.21	61.63
40-44 yrs	2,178.6	2,262.9	2,477.7	2,995.4	4,020.4	4,248.4	4,184.4	4,225.3	3,767.0	1.38	72.91
45-49 yrs	1,756.1	2,119.3	2,166.7	2,418.9	2,921.4	3,960.4	4,192.0	4,135.1	4,180.8	2.19	138.07
50-54 yrs	1,324.9	1,686.8	2,021.7	2,090.7	2,365.9	2,867.9	3,907.7	4,144.6	4,095.8	2.86	209.14
55-59 yrs	1,130.8	1,258.6	1,589.5	1,927.9	2,006.4	2,269.6	2,805.2	3,830.2	4,069.9	3.25	259.91
60-64 yrs	835.9	1,010.3	1,156.7	1,488.5	1,817.1	1,926.5	2,186.7	2,710.9	3,711.5	3.80	344.02
65-69 yrs	624.0	712.2	900.9	1,048.2	1,381.2	1,682.5	1,811.3	2,071.4	2,580.8	3.61	313.61
70-74 yrs	426.0	506.4	598.9	766.8	922.2	1,246.2	1,526.9	1,653.7	1,908.1	3.82	347.91
75-79 yrs	227.9	308.1	393.1	459.4	608.1	761.7	1,066.9	1,305.8	1,429.5	4.70	527.35
80+ yrs	178.2	215.2	302.3	382.2	483.4	676.2	951.7	1,349.9	1,782.8	5.93	900.33
Median age of population (years)	21.8	24.3	27.0	29.3	31.8	34.8	38.0	41.0	43.8	1.76	101.03

Table 5.290 Key economic trends

As stated

	1990	1995	2000	2005	2010	2015	2020	CAGR	Period growth
Total GDP (Won per capita)	9,816,878.9	13,597,781.0	16,159,349.8	19,653,820.1	22,430,925.7	28,110,439.2	35,476,065.1	4.38	261.4
Disposable income (Won per capita)	5,510,764.6	8,275,995.5	10,339,463.2	13,025,247.8	14,059,896.5	17,165,786.7	21,255,293.7	4.60	285.7
Disposable income (Won per household)	20,805,154.2	28,799,519.9	33,960,675.6	38,678,081.6	37,937,140.7	44,060,983.1	53,181,690.6	3.18	155.6
Number of households by annual household disposable income ('000)									
Over US$1,000	11,326.6	12,951.7	14,293.6	16,200.0	18,079.1	19,164.9	19,688.9	1.86	73.8
Over US$10,000	7,000.3	11,333.0	11,914.3	14,834.5	15,055.3	16,755.5	18,028.1	3.20	157.5
Over US$25,000	1,086.5	4,719.9	4,866.5	9,333.7	6,983.1	9,714.6	12,622.1	8.52	1,061.7
Over US$75,000	176.6	395.2	424.8	1,084.7	642.6	1,207.6	2,419.6	9.12	1,269.9
Over US$150,000	73.1	162.6	175.9	317.0	249.4	352.0	524.0	6.78	616.5
Total households	11,355.0	12,958.2	14,311.8	16,211.0	18,113.4	19,197.9	19,714.2	1.86	73.6

Note: Per capita data is shown at constant 2010 prices. Household disposable income bands are shown at current prices.

Table 5.291 Young generation

'000

	1980	1985	1990	1995	2000	2005	2010	2015	2020	CAGR	Period growth
Babies under 12 months	870.0	668.1	656.4	720.2	622.1	453.8	438.2	403.5	380.7	-2.04	-56.24
Infants under 24 months	1,691.0	1,387.4	1,295.2	1,441.2	1,248.2	932.1	878.0	811.3	760.7	-1.98	-55.02
Toddlers aged 1-4	3,163.8	3,177.4	2,546.8	2,825.5	2,637.7	2,091.0	1,763.3	1,669.3	1,538.6	-1.79	-51.37
Children aged 2-9	6,801.1	6,425.8	5,751.5	5,271.3	5,533.0	4,846.2	3,840.8	3,439.3	3,209.5	-1.86	-52.81
Female	3,274.1	3,103.4	2,761.0	2,484.2	2,596.5	2,309.5	1,844.2	1,657.0	1,549.8	-1.85	-52.66
Male	3,527.1	3,322.4	2,990.5	2,787.1	2,936.6	2,536.7	1,996.5	1,782.3	1,659.6	-1.87	-52.95
Tweenagers aged 10-14	4,458.6	4,491.3	3,926.9	3,824.4	3,130.0	3,462.8	3,188.1	2,482.2	2,148.0	-1.81	-51.82
Female	2,152.8	2,174.9	1,897.9	1,845.7	1,478.7	1,621.0	1,517.3	1,190.8	1,035.5	-1.81	-51.90
Male	2,305.8	2,316.4	2,029.1	1,978.7	1,651.3	1,841.8	1,670.8	1,291.3	1,112.5	-1.81	-51.75
Teenagers aged 13-19	6,235.7	6,279.2	5,998.1	5,558.3	5,095.7	4,490.4	4,732.5	4,225.5	3,298.9	-1.58	-47.10
Female	3,002.8	3,043.2	2,904.4	2,691.4	2,452.5	2,128.1	2,225.5	2,015.5	1,585.7	-1.58	-47.19
Male	3,232.9	3,236.0	3,093.7	2,866.9	2,643.3	2,362.3	2,507.0	2,209.9	1,713.2	-1.58	-47.01
Studying age 18-22	4,443.8	4,251.8	4,522.7	4,113.3	4,021.3	3,393.7	3,180.9	3,362.3	2,884.2	-1.07	-35.10
Female	2,152.9	2,057.7	2,191.0	1,993.7	1,952.5	1,634.7	1,496.0	1,575.8	1,373.9	-1.12	-36.18
Male	2,290.8	2,194.1	2,331.7	2,119.6	2,068.8	1,759.0	1,684.9	1,786.4	1,510.3	-1.04	-34.07
Young adults aged 15-29	11,685.9	12,780.0	13,111.2	12,589.3	12,049.7	10,723.1	10,236.1	9,606.9	8,911.4	-0.68	-23.74
Female	5,679.4	6,229.4	6,361.6	6,109.3	5,840.7	5,165.2	4,865.3	4,529.5	4,209.8	-0.75	-25.88
Male	6,006.4	6,550.6	6,749.5	6,479.9	6,209.0	5,557.9	5,370.8	5,077.4	4,701.6	-0.61	-21.72

Table 5.292 Middle-aged generation

'000

	1980	1985	1990	1995	2000	2005	2010	2015	2020	CAGR	Period growth
Middle-aged adults 30-59	11,195	12,969	15,433	17,822	19,835	21,881	23,188	23,846	22,884	1.80	104.4
Female	5,600	6,409	7,637	8,790	9,774	10,757	11,398	11,714	11,190	1.75	99.8
Male	5,595	6,560	7,796	9,031	10,061	11,123	11,790	12,132	11,694	1.86	109.0
Baby boomers aged 40-59	6,390	7,328	8,256	9,433	11,314	13,346	15,089	16,335	16,114	2.34	152.2
Female	3,285	3,709	4,146	4,702	5,611	6,594	7,471	8,087	7,959	2.24	142.3
Male	3,106	3,618	4,110	4,731	5,704	6,752	7,618	8,248	8,154	2.44	162.5

Table 5.293 Elderly population

'000

	1980	1985	1990	1995	2000	2005	2010	2015	2020	CAGR	Period growth
Elderly population (60+)	2,291.9	2,752.2	3,351.8	4,145.2	5,212.0	6,293.2	7,543.6	9,091.8	11,412.6	4.09	398.0
Female	1,365.1	1,645.2	2,036.9	2,488.1	3,059.9	3,645.9	4,285.8	5,087.9	6,292.8	3.89	361.0
Male	926.8	1,106.9	1,315.0	1,657.0	2,152.1	2,647.2	3,257.7	4,003.9	5,119.8	4.37	452.4

Table 5.294 Population of biggest cities 1980-2020

'000

	1980	1985	1990	1995	2000	2005	2010	2015	2020	CAGR	Period growth
Seoul	7,046.2	8,461.9	9,778.8	10,231.2	9,895.2	9,820.2	9,878.1	9,958.3	10,025.6	0.89	42.3
Busan	2,635.2	3,163.1	3,652.1	3,814.3	3,662.9	3,523.6	3,453.8	3,426.2	3,416.2	0.65	29.6
Incheon	1,382.2	1,699.7	2,048.3	2,308.2	2,475.1	2,531.3	2,574.1	2,611.5	2,639.0	1.63	90.9
Daegu	1,587.2	1,925.3	2,265.3	2,449.4	2,480.6	2,464.5	2,465.1	2,476.2	2,487.7	1.13	56.7
Daejeon	764.1	939.1	1,130.6	1,272.1	1,368.2	1,442.9	1,503.2	1,546.9	1,576.1	1.83	106.3
Gwangju	754.0	927.0	1,116.7	1,257.6	1,352.8	1,417.7	1,469.8	1,508.2	1,534.1	1.79	103.5
Suweon	378.0	480.0	610.0	755.6	946.7	1,044.1	1,107.2	1,150.6	1,178.9	2.88	211.9
Ulsan	601.4	734.7	875.3	967.4	1,014.4	1,049.2	1,079.8	1,103.3	1,119.6	1.57	86.2
Seongnam	535.9	655.6	783.0	869.1	914.6	935.0	952.8	967.9	978.8	1.52	82.7
Goyang	234.2	296.1	383.8	518.3	764.0	866.8	925.5	965.2	991.0	3.67	323.1

Chart 5.178 Population age shift 2000 and 2020, Each Column Represents a Single Age Group

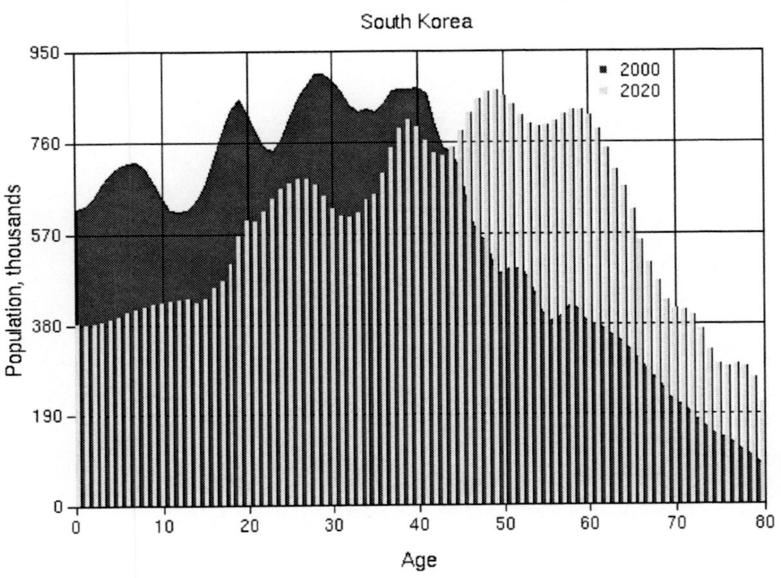

Chart 5.179 Population pyramids, 1980/2000/2010/2020

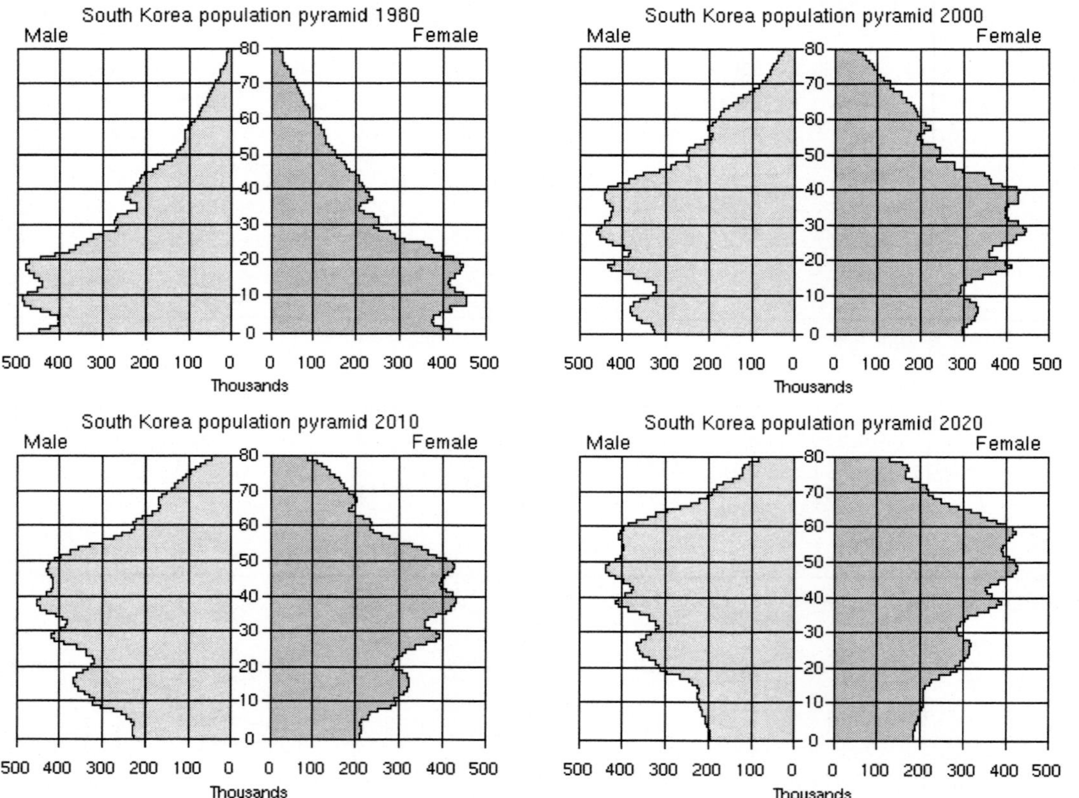

Chart 5.180 Major Cities: 1980, 2000 and 2020

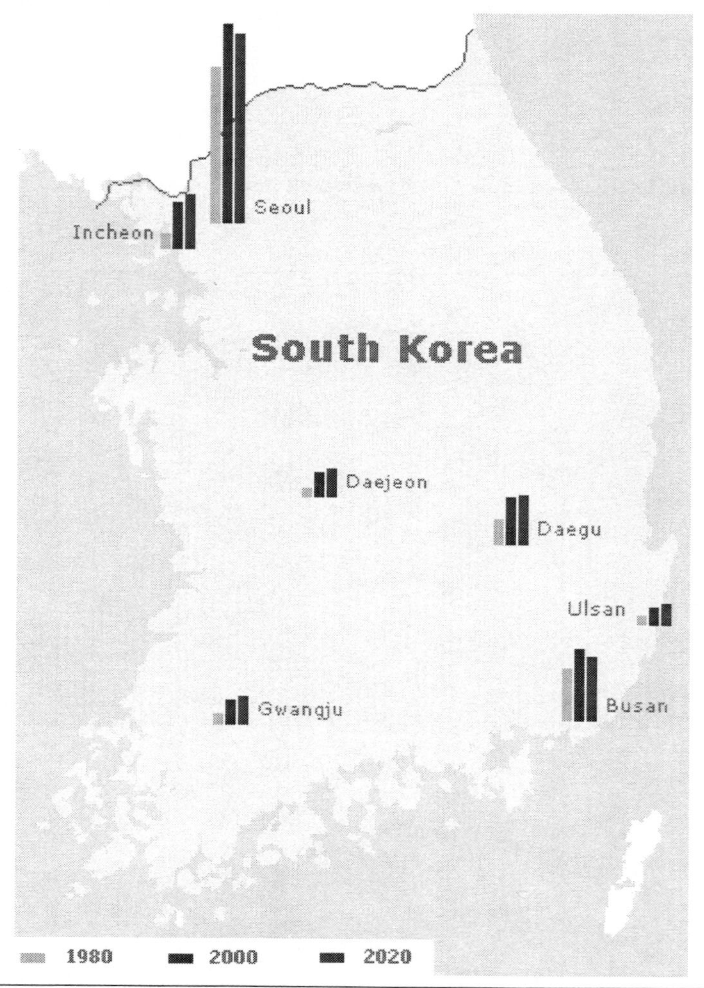

Spain

Table 5.295 Key population trends

'000

	1980	1985	1990	1995	2000	2005	2010	2015	2020	CAGR	Period growth
Population at January 1st	37,241.9	38,353.0	38,826.3	39,343.1	40,049.7	43,038.0	45,928.3	47,732.3	49,268.0	0.70	32.29
Male	18,273.1	18,820.2	19,024.6	19,268.6	19,606.8	21,173.3	22,669.2	23,595.3	24,385.8	0.72	33.45
Female	18,968.8	19,532.8	19,801.7	20,074.5	20,442.9	21,864.7	23,259.1	24,137.0	24,882.2	0.68	31.17
0-4 yrs	3,190.2	2,556.5	2,095.6	1,931.3	1,840.2	2,171.5	2,450.6	2,490.9	2,355.8	-0.76	-26.16
5-9 yrs	3,275.0	3,163.8	2,580.4	2,110.1	1,954.6	1,978.7	2,299.4	2,534.4	2,573.6	-0.60	-21.42
10-14 yrs	3,227.4	3,305.1	3,180.1	2,615.8	2,169.8	2,090.3	2,101.2	2,375.8	2,611.6	-0.53	-19.08
15-19 yrs	3,170.2	3,285.5	3,314.3	3,201.4	2,669.7	2,323.1	2,214.7	2,178.9	2,452.3	-0.64	-22.65
20-24 yrs	2,957.4	3,138.5	3,237.0	3,302.6	3,248.0	2,961.8	2,549.5	2,360.9	2,324.1	-0.60	-21.41
25-29 yrs	2,538.3	2,810.6	3,066.7	3,227.7	3,333.7	3,685.3	3,320.5	2,767.8	2,576.6	0.04	1.51
30-34 yrs	2,465.2	2,500.7	2,778.6	3,073.0	3,271.5	3,708.4	4,008.8	3,505.5	2,951.8	0.45	19.74
35-39 yrs	2,230.4	2,429.2	2,483.6	2,791.6	3,124.7	3,553.1	3,944.7	4,134.3	3,634.0	1.23	62.93
40-44 yrs	2,063.6	2,139.3	2,403.9	2,488.7	2,828.6	3,324.8	3,716.0	4,020.1	4,209.1	1.80	103.97
45-49 yrs	2,371.2	2,093.3	2,108.3	2,393.6	2,503.9	2,960.4	3,432.8	3,754.4	4,056.4	1.35	71.07
50-54 yrs	2,205.9	2,323.3	2,045.6	2,084.1	2,386.9	2,575.2	3,023.5	3,437.7	3,756.3	1.34	70.28
55-59 yrs	1,963.9	2,152.2	2,253.0	2,001.3	2,060.4	2,417.3	2,605.6	3,004.6	3,412.7	1.39	73.77
60-64 yrs	1,553.9	1,881.5	2,063.8	2,175.5	1,952.0	2,059.8	2,417.6	2,565.8	2,957.0	1.62	90.30
65-69 yrs	1,409.6	1,459.4	1,763.3	1,942.6	2,075.8	1,902.0	2,020.3	2,335.3	2,482.3	1.42	76.09
70-74 yrs	1,164.9	1,268.0	1,305.1	1,588.9	1,776.2	1,934.1	1,794.9	1,892.3	2,193.3	1.59	88.28
75-79 yrs	813.8	950.8	1,040.7	1,095.6	1,351.2	1,547.6	1,719.5	1,594.9	1,698.9	1.86	108.76
80+ yrs	640.7	895.3	1,106.2	1,319.1	1,502.4	1,844.7	2,308.8	2,778.6	3,022.1	3.95	371.67
Median age of population (years)	30.5	31.8	33.4	35.4	37.4	38.6	40.1	41.8	43.8	0.90	43.37

Table 5.296 Key economic trends

As stated

	1990	1995	2000	2005	2010	2015	2020	CAGR	Period growth
Total GDP (EUR per capita)	16,755.5	17,972.8	21,590.9	23,593.3	22,804.2	23,798.5	25,558.4	1.42	52.5
Disposable income (EUR per capita)	10,691.2	11,345.6	12,913.9	15,030.4	14,517.5	15,017.9	15,983.0	1.35	49.5
Disposable income (EUR per household)	35,701.7	34,913.8	37,117.3	40,669.3	37,794.6	38,207.2	40,114.6	0.39	12.4
Number of households by annual household disposable income ('000)									
Over US$1,000	11,616.6	12,780.0	13,929.5	15,904.8	17,640.9	18,761.3	19,629.6	1.76	69.0
Over US$10,000	9,857.1	11,728.8	12,520.2	15,535.2	17,331.6	18,503.6	19,460.7	2.29	97.4
Over US$25,000	4,235.4	6,825.8	6,060.7	12,570.9	14,702.1	16,230.9	17,916.8	4.92	323.0
Over US$75,000	378.4	692.4	517.1	2,123.5	3,012.1	4,001.0	6,317.0	9.84	1,569.4
Over US$150,000	153.7	237.0	207.4	478.8	591.7	727.0	1,008.3	6.47	556.1
Total households	11,626.9	12,784.9	13,934.1	15,905.8	17,641.7	18,761.9	19,630.0	1.76	68.8

Note: Per capita data is shown at constant 2010 prices. Household disposable income bands are shown at current prices.

Table 5.297 Young generation

'000

	1980	1985	1990	1995	2000	2005	2010	2015	2020	CAGR	Period growth
Babies under 12 months	591.3	467.2	401.8	368.2	379.2	450.7	491.9	484.9	446.5	-0.70	-24.50
Infants under 24 months	1,214.6	947.3	806.4	750.7	744.9	896.3	985.7	978.3	905.1	-0.73	-25.48
Toddlers aged 1-4	2,598.9	2,089.3	1,693.9	1,563.1	1,461.0	1,720.8	1,958.7	2,006.0	1,909.3	-0.77	-26.53
Children aged 2-9	5,250.7	4,773.1	3,869.6	3,290.7	3,049.9	3,254.0	3,764.3	4,047.0	4,024.3	-0.66	-23.36
Female	2,557.9	2,316.5	1,882.7	1,599.7	1,482.5	1,583.5	1,827.6	1,965.0	1,957.4	-0.67	-23.47
Male	2,692.8	2,456.6	1,986.9	1,691.0	1,567.5	1,670.5	1,936.7	2,082.0	2,066.8	-0.66	-23.25
Tweenagers aged 10-14	3,227.4	3,305.1	3,180.1	2,615.8	2,169.8	2,090.3	2,101.2	2,375.8	2,611.6	-0.53	-19.08
Female	1,574.4	1,607.5	1,551.3	1,275.3	1,055.7	1,016.4	1,022.9	1,154.2	1,267.5	-0.54	-19.49
Male	1,653.0	1,697.6	1,628.8	1,340.5	1,114.1	1,074.0	1,078.2	1,221.6	1,344.1	-0.52	-18.69
Teenagers aged 13-19	4,453.3	4,599.6	4,635.7	4,325.3	3,577.7	3,184.1	3,050.9	3,106.9	3,485.8	-0.61	-21.73
Female	2,174.6	2,243.9	2,262.4	2,110.8	1,743.7	1,549.0	1,484.6	1,513.2	1,693.4	-0.62	-22.13
Male	2,278.7	2,355.7	2,373.4	2,214.5	1,834.0	1,635.0	1,566.3	1,593.7	1,792.3	-0.60	-21.34
Studying age 18-22	3,088.5	3,238.4	3,260.3	3,321.6	3,051.3	2,645.5	2,377.3	2,245.0	2,344.2	-0.69	-24.10
Female	1,519.7	1,588.5	1,593.8	1,624.4	1,489.7	1,291.8	1,158.9	1,095.3	1,143.9	-0.71	-24.72
Male	1,568.8	1,649.9	1,666.4	1,697.2	1,561.7	1,353.7	1,218.5	1,149.8	1,200.2	-0.67	-23.50
Young adults aged 15-29	8,666.0	9,234.5	9,618.0	9,731.7	9,251.4	8,970.2	8,084.7	7,307.6	7,353.1	-0.41	-15.15
Female	4,263.6	4,547.8	4,720.9	4,769.3	4,527.3	4,366.5	3,939.8	3,564.5	3,584.8	-0.43	-15.92
Male	4,402.3	4,686.7	4,897.2	4,962.4	4,724.1	4,603.7	4,144.9	3,743.2	3,768.2	-0.39	-14.40

Table 5.298 Middle-aged generation

'000

	1980	1985	1990	1995	2000	2005	2010	2015	2020	CAGR	Period growth
Middle-aged adults 30-59	13,300	13,638	14,073	14,832	16,176	18,539	20,731	21,857	22,020	1.27	65.6
Female	6,744	6,886	7,097	7,457	8,113	9,222	10,228	10,737	10,775	1.18	59.8
Male	6,556	6,752	6,976	7,375	8,063	9,317	10,504	11,120	11,246	1.36	71.5
Baby boomers aged 40-59	8,605	8,708	8,811	8,968	9,780	11,278	12,778	14,217	15,435	1.47	79.4
Female	4,394	4,428	4,474	4,537	4,935	5,676	6,389	7,045	7,580	1.37	72.5
Male	4,211	4,280	4,337	4,431	4,845	5,602	6,389	7,172	7,854	1.57	86.5

Table 5.299 Elderly population

'000

	1980	1985	1990	1995	2000	2005	2010	2015	2020	CAGR	Period growth
Elderly population (60+)	5,583	6,455	7,279	8,122	8,658	9,288	10,261	11,167	12,354	2.01	121.3
Female	3,235	3,718	4,159	4,610	4,903	5,242	5,763	6,241	6,857	1.90	112.0
Male	2,348	2,737	3,120	3,512	3,754	4,047	4,498	4,926	5,497	2.15	134.1

Table 5.300 Population of biggest cities 1980-2020

'000

	1980	1985	1990	1995	2000	2005	2010	2015	2020	CAGR	Period growth
Madrid	2,911.6	3,012.2	3,020.4	2,961.3	2,922.0	3,085.3	3,271.6	3,406.3	3,547.7	0.50	21.85
Barcelona	1,648.1	1,686.6	1,657.9	1,571.4	1,502.4	1,559.5	1,640.9	1,700.6	1,766.4	0.17	7.18
Valencia	725.9	751.7	755.1	742.3	734.1	775.4	821.7	855.2	890.5	0.51	22.66
Sevilla	640.9	669.2	682.3	686.5	682.9	696.6	698.6	701.6	714.9	0.27	11.55
Zaragoza	551.9	578.2	592.8	602.3	610.0	644.6	675.4	697.8	723.5	0.68	31.09
Malaga	494.4	514.8	522.2	521.6	521.1	548.1	574.3	593.5	615.4	0.55	24.47
Murcia	289.8	308.5	325.0	344.2	364.4	404.1	443.5	471.2	496.6	1.36	71.34
Palma de Mallorca	264.6	280.8	294.3	309.5	327.6	368.0	410.8	440.9	467.1	1.43	76.55
Palmas de las Gran Canaria	336.7	350.4	355.1	354.0	352.8	369.8	385.9	397.7	411.8	0.50	22.30
Bilbao	359.6	371.4	371.4	362.0	350.4	352.9	352.2	352.6	358.6	-0.01	-0.28

Chart 5.181 Population age shift 2000 and 2020, Each Column Represents a Single Age Group

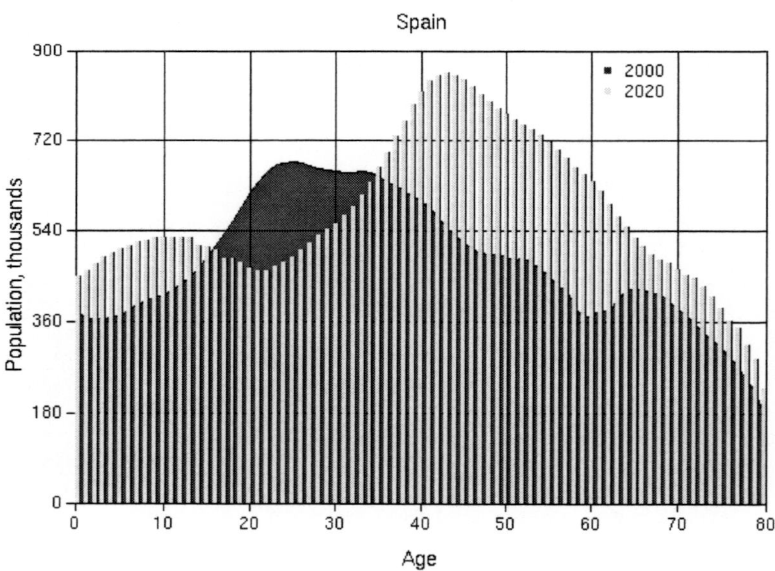

Chart 5.182 Population pyramids, 1980/2000/2010/2020

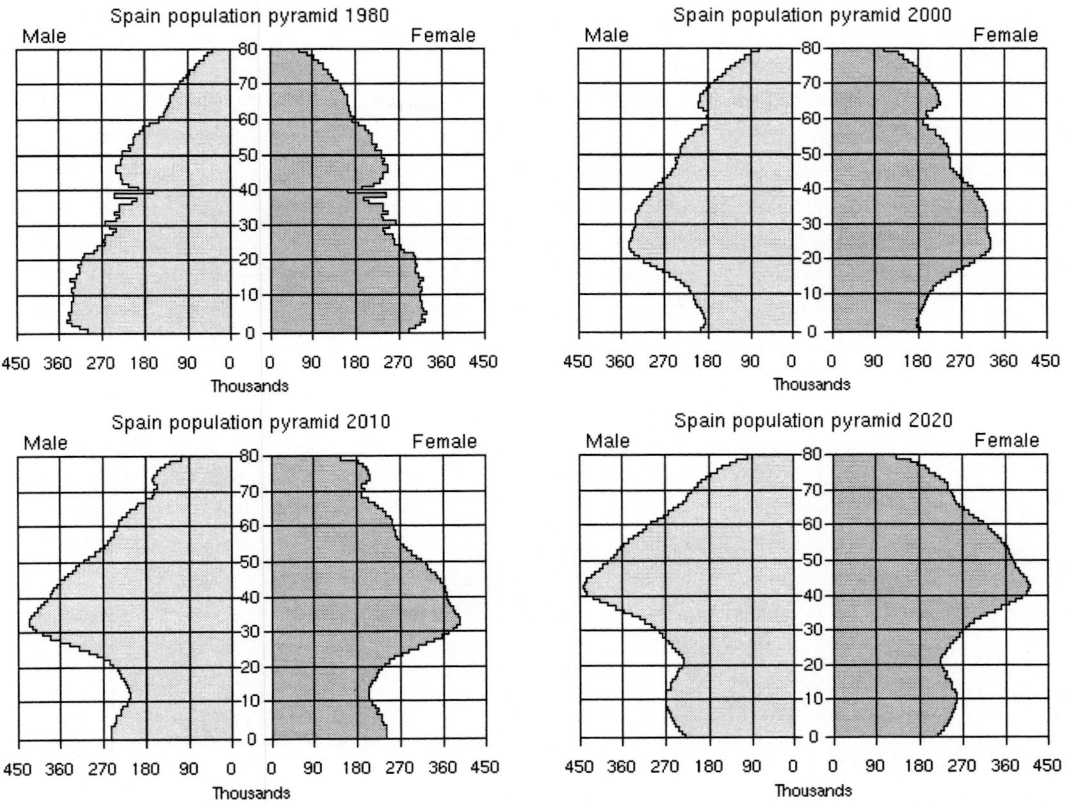

Chart 5.183 Major Cities: 1980, 2000 and 2020

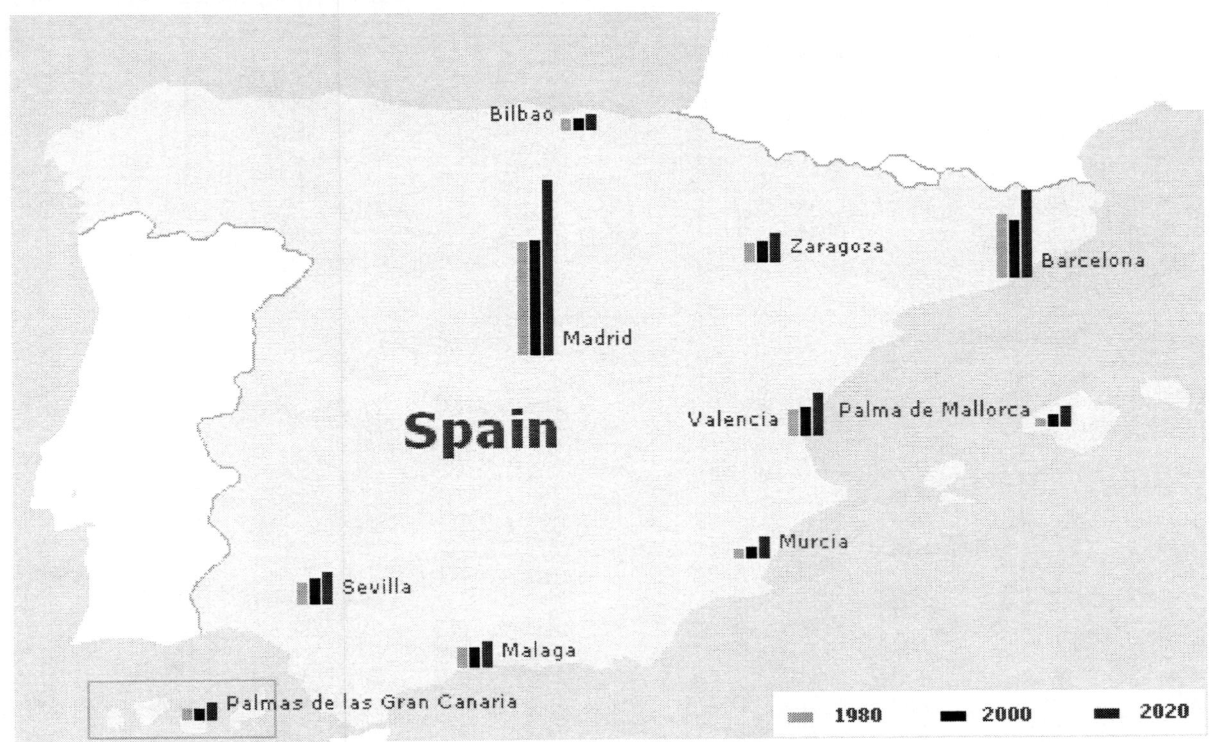

Sweden

Table 5.301 Key population trends

'000

	1980	1985	1990	1995	2000	2005	2010	2015	2020	CAGR	Period growth
Population at January 1st	8,303.0	8,342.6	8,527.0	8,816.4	8,861.4	9,011.4	9,244.3	9,466.2	9,706.0	0.39	16.90
Male	4,115.5	4,120.5	4,212.1	4,356.3	4,380.1	4,466.3	4,591.6	4,711.7	4,839.0	0.41	17.58
Female	4,187.5	4,222.1	4,315.0	4,460.1	4,481.3	4,545.1	4,652.8	4,754.5	4,866.9	0.38	16.23
0-4 yrs	491.1	471.5	539.8	605.7	468.7	485.6	520.5	534.1	555.8	0.31	13.17
5-9 yrs	559.3	491.5	483.2	558.0	608.0	479.9	498.6	531.9	544.9	-0.07	-2.58
10-14 yrs	590.9	558.2	498.9	499.0	563.0	618.1	493.8	511.1	543.9	-0.21	-7.95
15-19 yrs	558.9	592.2	566.5	512.2	504.7	574.7	633.5	508.9	525.0	-0.16	-6.06
20-24 yrs	558.3	568.3	612.5	585.1	520.4	522.3	593.1	653.6	529.6	-0.13	-5.14
25-29 yrs	587.4	565.0	592.1	636.7	595.2	545.7	550.6	617.2	680.9	0.37	15.92
30-34 yrs	675.3	585.9	577.8	611.8	641.4	612.6	568.0	568.9	633.3	-0.16	-6.22
35-39 yrs	585.1	669.3	590.1	589.7	611.6	651.2	627.6	580.4	579.6	-0.02	-0.95
40-44 yrs	468.4	579.5	667.8	593.9	586.4	615.8	659.1	634.2	585.7	0.56	25.05
45-49 yrs	438.8	462.3	575.3	664.3	588.4	586.4	618.6	661.2	635.9	0.93	44.90
50-54 yrs	463.1	430.2	455.8	568.4	654.4	583.6	585.1	615.7	658.2	0.88	42.13
55-59 yrs	520.0	449.3	419.5	446.7	555.4	642.7	576.9	577.8	607.7	0.39	16.87
60-64 yrs	460.9	495.0	430.1	404.8	431.4	538.5	627.6	563.5	564.7	0.51	22.52
65-69 yrs	446.6	425.7	460.1	404.0	381.2	409.2	516.0	601.9	541.8	0.48	21.30
70-74 yrs	375.9	392.4	377.8	413.3	366.0	348.2	379.1	480.6	562.2	1.01	49.55
75-79 yrs	268.5	302.4	320.8	314.7	348.9	314.6	304.6	334.9	428.5	1.18	59.58
80+ yrs	254.3	304.1	358.9	408.1	436.5	482.3	491.6	490.3	528.3	1.84	107.72
Median age of population (years)	36.0	37.6	38.4	38.4	39.3	40.1	41.1	41.8	42.3	0.40	17.54

Table 5.302 Key economic trends

As stated

	1990	1995	2000	2005	2010	2015	2020	CAGR	Period growth
Total GDP (SEK per capita)	260,753.3	262,985.3	308,343.6	343,992.4	344,666.6	397,234.3	475,526.5	2.02	82.4
Disposable income (SEK per capita)	132,074.6	127,176.6	142,674.0	161,007.6	166,787.4	193,847.5	232,120.0	1.90	75.7
Disposable income (SEK per household)	294,048.4	264,813.5	289,776.6	326,383.5	337,316.3	390,884.3	466,293.7	1.55	58.6
Number of households by annual household disposable income ('000)									
Over US$1,000	3,830.0	4,234.1	4,363.0	4,445.4	4,570.9	4,694.5	4,831.6	0.78	26.2
Over US$10,000	3,811.0	4,179.4	4,267.5	4,422.4	4,545.3	4,688.0	4,829.9	0.79	26.7
Over US$25,000	2,832.6	2,770.3	1,732.7	3,540.3	3,268.3	4,233.1	4,694.8	1.70	65.7
Over US$75,000	197.3	194.6	168.7	362.0	328.6	645.1	1,276.6	6.42	547.0
Over US$150,000	79.8	78.9	69.5	118.2	111.7	164.4	259.6	4.01	225.4
Total households	3,830.0	4,234.1	4,363.0	4,445.4	4,570.9	4,694.5	4,831.6	0.78	26.2

Note: Per capita data is shown at constant 2010 prices. Household disposable income bands are shown at current prices.

Table 5.303 Young generation

'000

	1980	1985	1990	1995	2000	2005	2010	2015	2020	CAGR	Period growth
Babies under 12 months	95.9	93.6	115.8	112.0	88.4	101.1	104.2	107.2	111.7	0.38	16.44
Infants under 24 months	189.6	185.9	228.7	229.6	178.3	201.4	208.4	214.3	223.4	0.41	17.86
Toddlers aged 1-4	395.2	377.9	423.9	493.7	380.3	384.5	416.4	426.9	444.1	0.29	12.38
Children aged 2-9	860.8	777.1	794.2	934.1	898.5	764.1	810.8	851.7	877.2	0.05	1.90
Female	420.1	379.2	386.8	454.4	437.9	372.1	395.2	415.7	428.1	0.05	1.90
Male	440.8	397.9	407.4	479.7	460.5	392.0	415.6	436.0	449.2	0.05	1.91
Tweenagers aged 10-14	590.9	558.2	498.9	499.0	563.0	618.1	493.8	511.1	543.9	-0.21	-7.95
Female	287.6	272.7	243.3	242.8	273.8	301.3	240.5	248.7	265.2	-0.20	-7.77
Male	303.3	285.5	255.6	256.2	289.2	316.9	253.3	262.4	278.7	-0.21	-8.13
Teenagers aged 13-19	805.7	815.8	773.6	714.1	718.9	832.8	842.9	705.7	742.5	-0.20	-7.84
Female	393.1	397.7	377.7	348.3	349.6	405.0	411.0	343.4	361.5	-0.21	-8.04
Male	412.6	418.1	395.9	365.9	369.3	427.9	431.9	362.2	381.0	-0.20	-7.66
Studying age 18-22	542.5	599.7	582.6	561.8	508.1	528.5	629.6	596.3	506.0	-0.17	-6.72
Female	265.8	292.8	284.2	274.9	248.7	257.5	307.6	292.4	247.1	-0.18	-7.03
Male	276.7	306.9	298.4	286.9	259.4	271.0	322.0	303.9	258.9	-0.17	-6.43
Young adults aged 15-29	1,704.5	1,725.5	1,771.0	1,734.0	1,620.2	1,642.7	1,777.2	1,779.7	1,735.5	0.05	1.82
Female	832.7	842.8	862.3	847.2	793.4	803.3	869.5	871.6	850.2	0.05	2.10
Male	871.8	882.7	908.7	886.8	826.8	839.5	907.6	908.1	885.3	0.04	1.55

Table 5.304 Middle-aged generation

'000

	1980	1985	1990	1995	2000	2005	2010	2015	2020	CAGR	Period growth
Middle-aged adults 30-59	3,150.8	3,176.5	3,286.4	3,474.7	3,637.6	3,692.3	3,635.2	3,638.2	3,700.4	0.40	17.4
Female	1,557.9	1,568.6	1,617.9	1,706.7	1,787.5	1,819.0	1,792.8	1,795.9	1,827.1	0.40	17.3
Male	1,592.9	1,607.9	1,668.5	1,768.1	1,850.1	1,873.2	1,842.4	1,842.3	1,873.3	0.41	17.6
Baby boomers aged 40-59	1,890.4	1,921.3	2,118.5	2,273.3	2,384.6	2,428.5	2,439.7	2,488.9	2,487.5	0.69	31.6
Female	946.0	954.6	1,047.3	1,120.7	1,176.0	1,199.2	1,204.0	1,230.1	1,230.8	0.66	30.1
Male	944.4	966.6	1,071.2	1,152.6	1,208.5	1,229.2	1,235.6	1,258.8	1,256.8	0.72	33.1

Table 5.305 Elderly population

'000

	1980	1985	1990	1995	2000	2005	2010	2015	2020	CAGR	Period growth
Elderly population (60+)	1,806.3	1,919.6	1,947.7	1,945.0	1,963.9	2,092.8	2,318.9	2,471.2	2,625.5	0.94	45.4
Female	996.6	1,068.6	1,093.6	1,096.8	1,102.0	1,151.6	1,253.1	1,318.1	1,387.5	0.83	39.2
Male	809.7	851.0	854.2	848.2	861.9	941.3	1,065.8	1,153.1	1,238.0	1.07	52.9

Table 5.306 Population of biggest cities 1980-2020

'000

	1980	1985	1990	1995	2000	2005	2010	2015	2020	CAGR	Period growth
Stockholm	645.8	650.4	667.3	712.3	743.9	773.4	808.1	839.3	870.7	0.75	34.8
Gothenburg	431.6	427.0	430.0	451.2	464.0	480.3	501.4	520.5	539.8	0.56	25.1
Malmo	234.1	231.0	232.1	246.3	257.1	270.6	286.7	300.2	312.9	0.73	33.7
Uppsala	144.8	152.4	164.3	180.6	188.8	189.3	186.9	187.4	190.5	0.69	31.6
Linkoping	112.0	115.1	120.7	128.4	132.3	136.9	142.5	147.6	152.9	0.78	36.6
Vasteras	117.5	116.9	118.9	123.5	125.7	130.0	136.0	141.3	146.7	0.56	24.9
Orebro	116.8	117.4	120.0	123.8	124.0	125.9	129.4	133.2	137.4	0.41	17.7
Helsingborg	101.5	103.7	108.0	114.0	117.0	121.4	127.1	132.2	137.2	0.76	35.2
Norrkoping	119.2	118.6	119.9	122.7	122.2	123.4	126.5	130.0	134.0	0.29	12.4
Jonkoping	107.4	108.0	110.6	114.9	116.5	120.3	125.8	130.6	135.6	0.59	26.3

Chart 5.184 Population age shift 2000 and 2020, Each Column Represents a Single Age Group

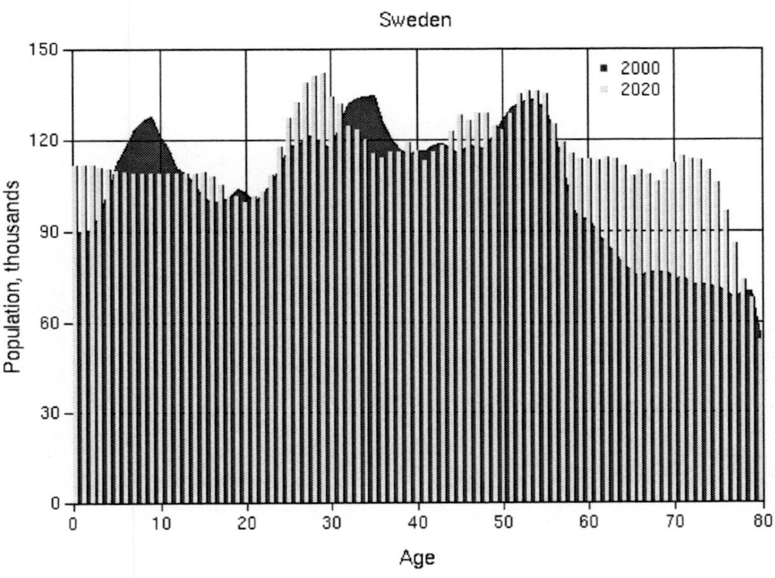

Chart 5.185 Population pyramids, 1980/2000/2010/2020

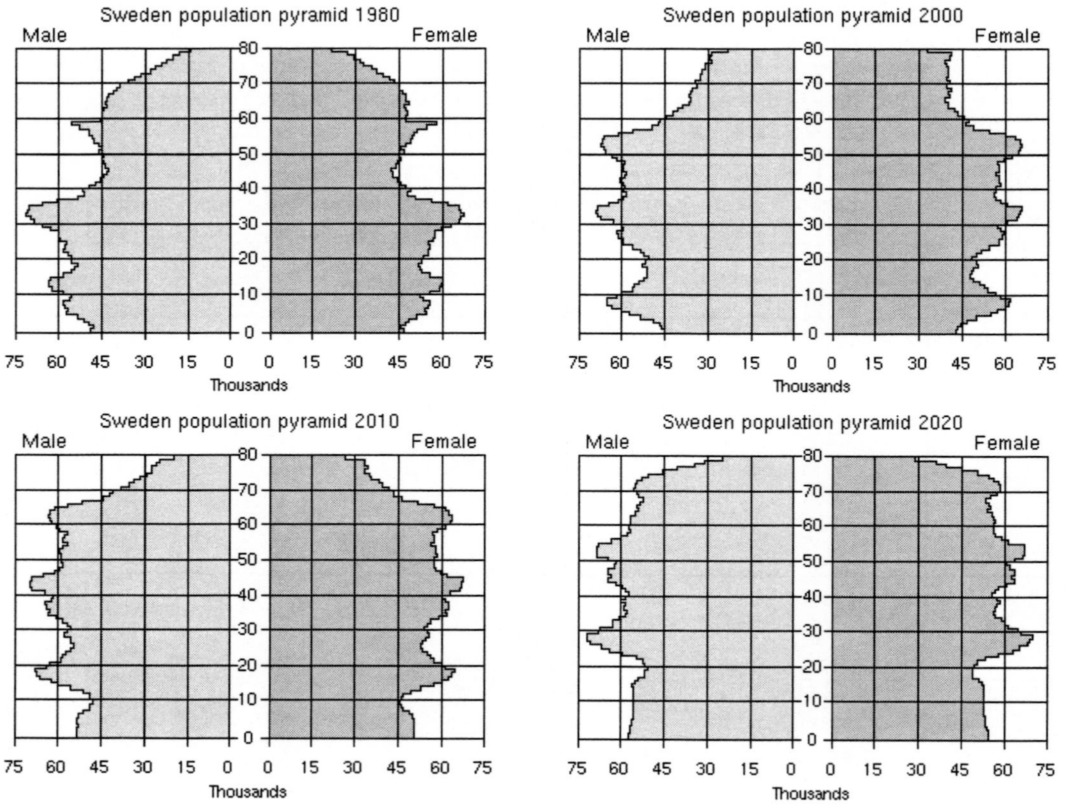

Chart 5.186 Major Cities: 1980, 2000 and 2020

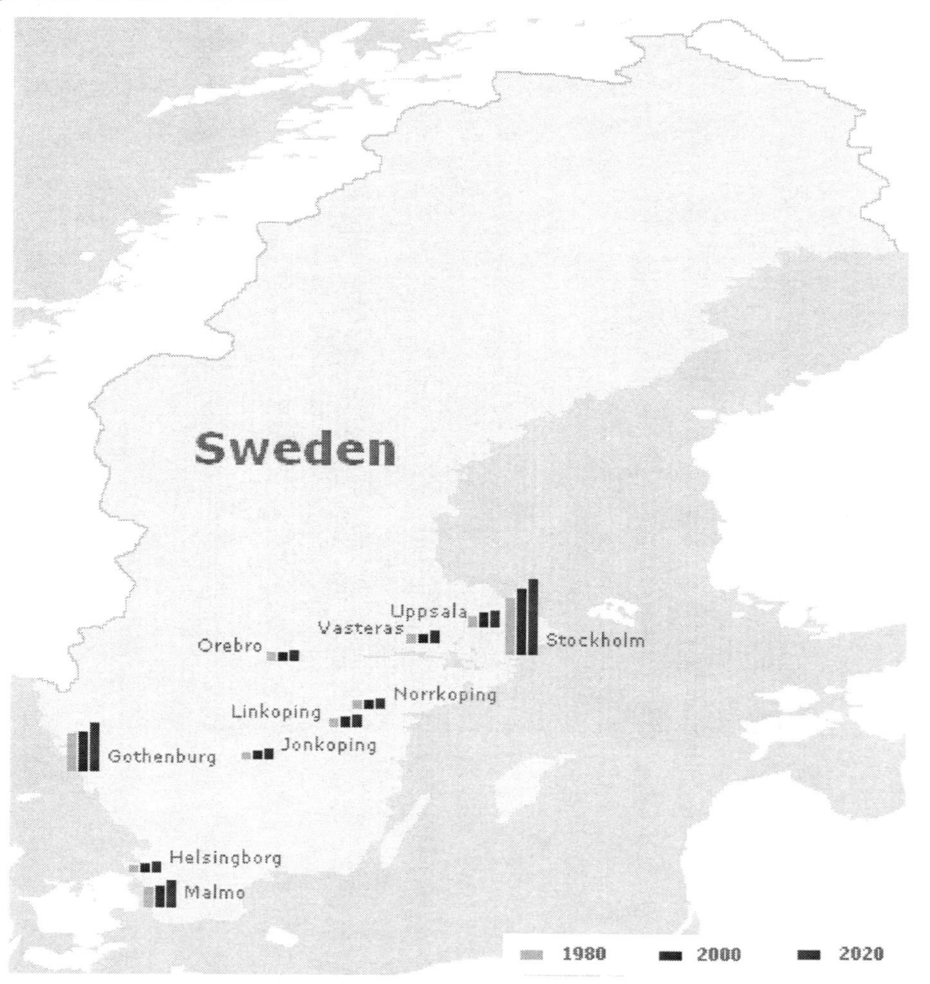

Switzerland

Table 5.307 Key population trends

'000

	1980	1985	1990	1995	2000	2005	2010	2015	2020	CAGR	Period growth
Population at January 1st	6,303.6	6,455.9	6,673.9	7,019.0	7,164.4	7,415.1	7,589.1	7,732.1	7,879.3	0.56	25.00
Male	3,066.2	3,145.3	3,257.5	3,428.4	3,500.7	3,628.7	3,706.5	3,763.0	3,820.5	0.55	24.60
Female	3,237.3	3,310.6	3,416.3	3,590.7	3,663.7	3,786.4	3,882.6	3,969.1	4,058.8	0.57	25.37
0-4 yrs	355.5	368.2	384.6	424.7	400.7	365.4	364.6	370.0	396.2	0.27	11.47
5-9 yrs	415.2	362.0	379.5	410.9	427.6	402.5	371.7	369.3	374.1	-0.26	-9.90
10-14 yrs	490.1	418.3	372.4	401.8	420.6	437.5	409.1	376.1	372.9	-0.68	-23.92
15-19 yrs	499.0	495.8	433.4	396.0	414.9	433.6	448.4	417.8	383.4	-0.66	-23.17
20-24 yrs	461.3	511.4	513.5	457.8	411.6	441.4	458.0	471.5	439.7	-0.12	-4.67
25-29 yrs	463.7	488.5	545.9	566.6	482.8	463.6	480.7	497.0	510.5	0.24	10.09
30-34 yrs	503.7	482.3	521.1	605.6	588.2	532.9	499.0	515.1	531.3	0.13	5.47
35-39 yrs	465.7	508.1	498.1	551.5	610.4	618.1	550.3	513.9	529.4	0.32	13.68
40-44 yrs	406.0	464.1	511.0	506.5	546.5	621.2	624.4	552.6	514.3	0.59	26.68
45-49 yrs	388.4	400.8	460.5	506.7	498.1	549.3	620.3	620.7	546.0	0.85	40.56
50-54 yrs	363.2	379.3	391.9	448.7	492.0	491.6	540.7	610.4	609.3	1.30	67.74
55-59 yrs	346.1	349.0	363.1	372.0	428.4	477.2	474.6	522.0	591.4	1.35	70.91
60-64 yrs	274.7	324.9	326.4	338.4	348.4	406.4	452.9	447.7	494.4	1.48	79.94
65-69 yrs	285.4	251.8	297.1	298.7	312.4	323.7	380.9	426.1	419.2	0.97	46.90
70-74 yrs	245.5	251.5	223.4	266.5	271.0	285.6	296.8	352.9	397.5	1.21	61.90
75-79 yrs	178.8	199.3	208.2	188.0	227.4	237.0	250.8	260.0	315.9	1.43	76.66
80+ yrs	161.3	200.3	243.7	278.5	283.5	328.1	365.8	409.1	453.8	2.62	181.40
Median age of population (years)	34.6	36.0	36.9	37.2	38.5	40.1	41.8	43.1	43.9	0.59	26.76

Table 5.308 Key economic trends

As stated

	1990	1995	2000	2005	2010	2015	2020	CAGR	Period growth
Total GDP (CHF per capita)	63,571.8	60,733.8	65,829.5	67,874.0	71,394.1	74,951.2	80,694.6	0.80	26.9
Disposable income (CHF per capita)	40,265.9	39,296.6	41,889.1	41,818.6	44,594.0	49,039.5	53,518.8	0.95	32.9
Disposable income (CHF per household)	93,967.7	89,033.4	94,328.5	93,402.2	98,791.5	107,747.8	116,615.9	0.72	24.1
Number of households by annual household disposable income ('000)									
Over US$1,000	2,859.7	3,097.9	3,181.5	3,319.8	3,425.5	3,518.9	3,615.8	0.79	26.4
Over US$10,000	2,820.3	3,074.3	3,135.2	3,288.4	3,390.5	3,476.6	3,575.5	0.79	26.8
Over US$25,000	2,444.8	2,848.9	2,700.4	3,053.3	3,157.6	3,206.9	3,320.7	1.03	35.8
Over US$75,000	516.2	1,033.0	576.4	1,296.0	1,469.5	1,402.8	1,557.1	3.75	201.7
Over US$150,000	99.6	153.9	115.5	191.5	224.7	202.7	253.0	3.16	154.1
Total households	2,859.8	3,098.0	3,181.6	3,319.9	3,425.7	3,519.1	3,616.1	0.79	26.4

Note: Per capita data is shown at constant 2010 prices. Household disposable income bands are shown at current prices.

Table 5.309 Young generation

'000

	1980	1985	1990	1995	2000	2005	2010	2015	2020	CAGR	Period growth
Babies under 12 months	70.7	74.0	80.6	82.0	77.8	72.9	72.3	75.2	81.5	0.36	15.24
Infants under 24 months	140.6	147.3	159.9	165.1	156.7	144.6	144.8	149.5	161.9	0.35	15.15
Toddlers aged 1-4	284.8	294.2	304.0	342.6	322.9	292.5	292.2	294.8	314.8	0.25	10.53
Children aged 2-9	630.1	583.0	604.2	670.5	671.7	623.3	591.5	589.7	608.4	-0.09	-3.43
Female	306.8	284.9	295.5	326.7	326.1	302.6	288.7	288.2	296.8	-0.08	-3.26
Male	323.2	298.1	308.7	343.7	345.6	320.7	302.8	301.5	311.6	-0.09	-3.60
Tweenagers aged 10-14	490.1	418.3	372.4	401.8	420.6	437.5	409.1	376.1	372.9	-0.68	-23.92
Female	239.5	203.3	181.8	195.1	204.6	212.9	199.6	184.4	183.5	-0.66	-23.38
Male	250.6	215.0	190.6	206.8	216.0	224.6	209.5	191.8	189.4	-0.70	-24.43
Teenagers aged 13-19	703.0	674.0	583.7	556.7	581.0	612.7	616.8	569.8	533.6	-0.69	-24.09
Female	344.0	328.6	284.5	271.0	282.1	298.6	301.8	279.7	263.4	-0.67	-23.43
Male	359.0	345.4	299.2	285.7	298.9	314.1	315.0	290.1	270.2	-0.71	-24.73
Studying age 18-22	470.0	519.5	483.5	422.7	411.4	433.7	458.9	448.5	411.7	-0.33	-12.40
Female	233.9	255.0	237.9	208.8	201.6	213.7	226.3	222.7	205.0	-0.33	-12.34
Male	236.1	264.5	245.5	213.9	209.8	220.0	232.6	225.8	206.7	-0.33	-12.46
Young adults aged 15-29	1,424.0	1,495.8	1,492.8	1,420.4	1,309.3	1,338.6	1,387.1	1,386.3	1,333.6	-0.16	-6.35
Female	710.8	739.1	736.0	706.6	649.9	664.4	689.5	691.8	668.5	-0.15	-5.95
Male	713.2	756.7	756.8	713.8	659.3	674.3	697.6	694.5	665.1	-0.17	-6.74

Table 5.310 Middle-aged generation

'000

	1980	1985	1990	1995	2000	2005	2010	2015	2020	CAGR	Period growth
Middle-aged adults 30-59	2,473.1	2,583.6	2,745.7	2,991.1	3,163.6	3,290.3	3,309.3	3,334.6	3,321.7	0.74	34.3
Female	1,245.2	1,295.8	1,365.3	1,483.2	1,575.5	1,640.8	1,660.3	1,681.9	1,685.8	0.76	35.4
Male	1,227.9	1,287.8	1,380.3	1,507.9	1,588.1	1,649.5	1,649.0	1,652.7	1,635.9	0.72	33.2
Baby boomers aged 40-59	1,503.7	1,593.2	1,726.5	1,833.9	1,965.0	2,139.3	2,260.0	2,305.6	2,261.1	1.02	50.4
Female	767.1	804.7	862.5	913.8	977.2	1,063.9	1,130.5	1,160.3	1,147.5	1.01	49.6
Male	736.6	788.5	863.9	920.1	987.8	1,075.4	1,129.5	1,145.4	1,113.6	1.04	51.2

Table 5.311 Elderly population

'000

	1980	1985	1990	1995	2000	2005	2010	2015	2020	CAGR	Period growth
Elderly population (60+)	1,145.7	1,227.9	1,298.9	1,370.1	1,442.6	1,580.8	1,747.2	1,895.8	2,080.8	1.50	81.6
Female	666.5	716.0	759.7	798.6	831.3	895.3	974.1	1,050.2	1,145.6	1.36	71.9
Male	479.2	511.9	539.2	571.5	611.3	685.5	773.2	845.7	935.1	1.69	95.2

Table 5.312 Population of biggest cities 1980-2020

'000

	1980	1985	1990	1995	2000	2005	2010	2015	2020	CAGR	Period growth
Zurich	292.3	319.4	341.3	342.3	337.9	351.7	367.6	382.2	396.8	0.77	35.78
Geneva	138.0	152.7	167.2	174.0	175.0	178.9	181.9	186.1	191.4	0.82	38.78
Basel	146.4	160.0	171.0	171.3	166.0	164.5	162.8	163.7	166.7	0.33	13.87
Bern	119.4	128.9	134.6	129.7	122.5	122.3	123.4	125.6	128.8	0.19	7.85
Lausanne	108.4	117.3	123.2	119.8	114.9	117.5	121.4	125.3	129.6	0.45	19.54
Winterthur	70.9	78.4	85.7	88.9	88.8	91.0	93.4	96.0	99.1	0.84	39.81
St. Gallen	63.7	69.3	73.4	72.4	69.8	70.6	71.9	73.5	75.6	0.43	18.56
Luzern	51.4	55.9	59.4	58.8	57.0	57.9	59.2	60.7	62.6	0.49	21.79
Lugano	37.0	41.0	45.0	47.0	47.8	49.8	51.6	53.4	55.2	1.01	49.45
Biel	46.3	50.2	52.7	51.2	48.8	49.1	49.8	50.8	52.2	0.30	12.65

Chart 5.187 Population age shift 2000 and 2020, Each Column Represents a Single Age Group

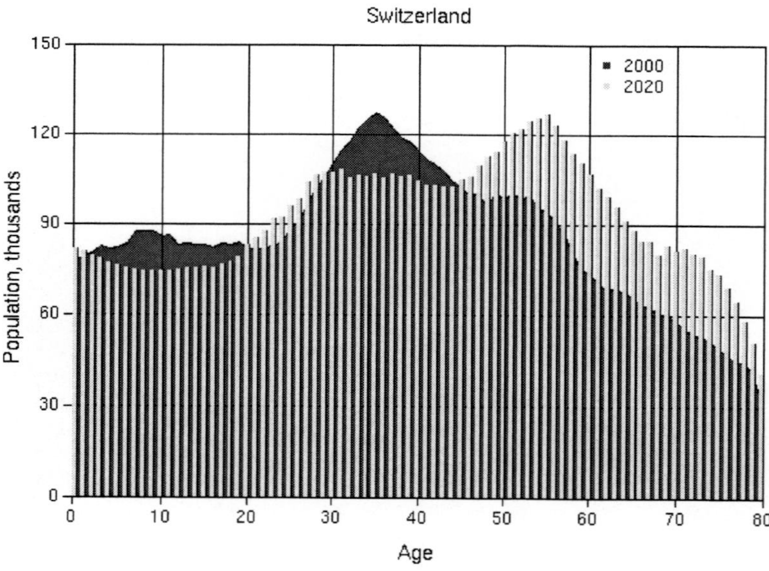

Chart 5.188 Population pyramids, 1980/2000/2010/2020

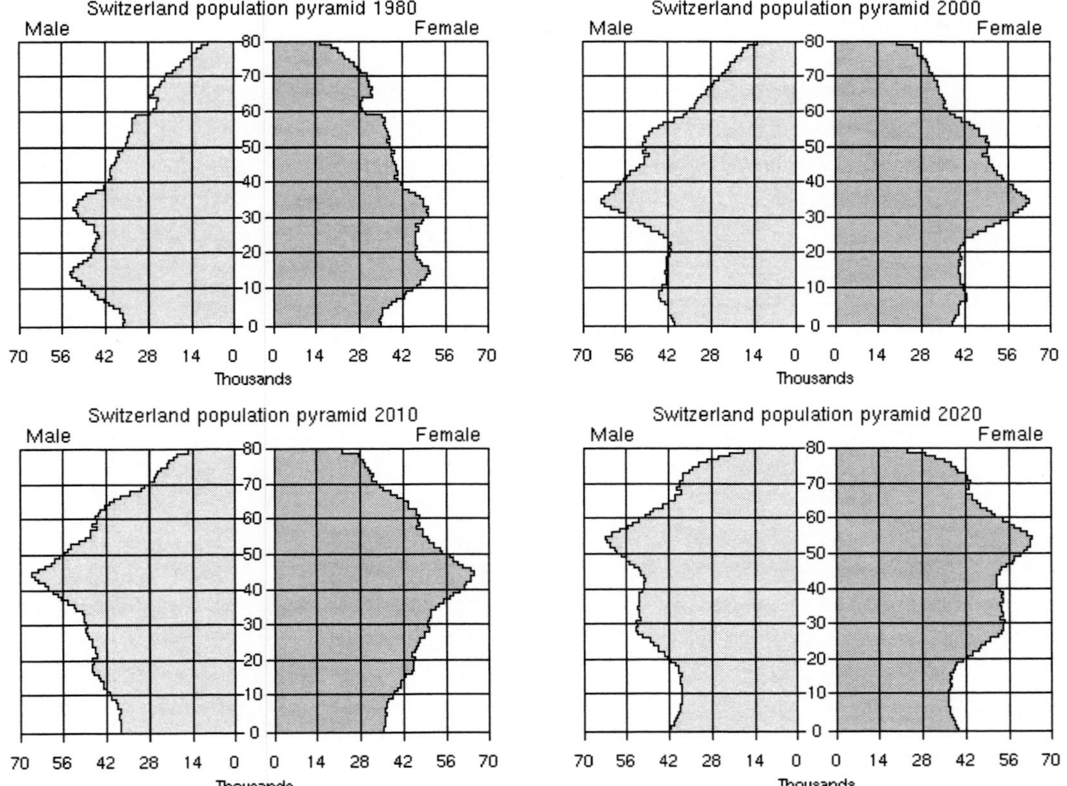

Chart 5.189 Major Cities: 1980, 2000 and 2020

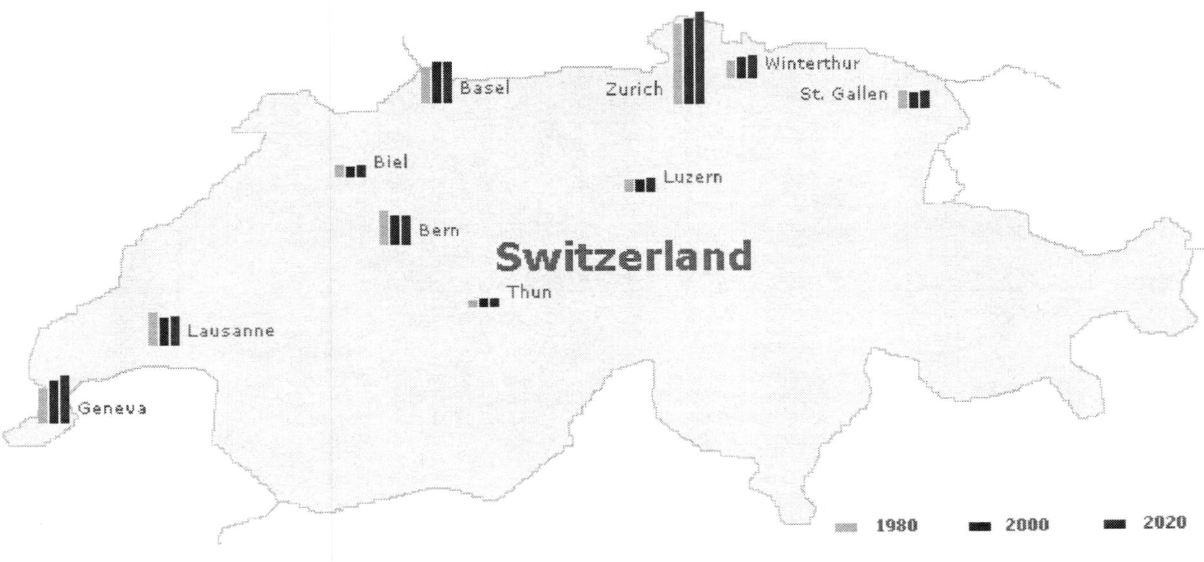

Taiwan

Table 5.313 Key population trends

'000

	1980	1985	1990	1995	2000	2005	2010	2015	2020	CAGR	Period growth
Population at January 1st	17,543.1	19,069.2	20,156.6	21,177.9	22,092.4	22,689.1	23,105.1	23,376.0	23,485.1	0.73	33.87
Male	9,160.2	9,904.9	10,424.1	10,907.0	11,312.7	11,541.6	11,639.2	11,679.4	11,654.1	0.60	27.22
Female	8,382.8	9,164.3	9,732.5	10,270.8	10,779.7	11,147.5	11,465.8	11,696.5	11,831.0	0.87	41.13
0-4 yrs	1,965.8	1,929.4	1,606.6	1,601.6	1,507.2	1,243.9	1,015.6	987.1	937.3	-1.83	-52.32
5-9 yrs	1,838.2	1,996.9	1,955.6	1,615.5	1,625.3	1,521.0	1,255.3	1,027.5	997.9	-1.52	-45.71
10-14 yrs	1,936.7	1,832.0	1,981.0	1,952.4	1,602.1	1,622.1	1,519.2	1,253.0	1,025.1	-1.58	-47.07
15-19 yrs	2,013.8	1,926.1	1,818.7	1,968.6	1,940.3	1,592.7	1,617.5	1,514.0	1,248.0	-1.19	-38.03
20-24 yrs	1,899.5	2,006.2	1,918.8	1,800.7	1,958.8	1,928.1	1,589.8	1,613.7	1,509.7	-0.57	-20.52
25-29 yrs	1,658.2	1,878.5	1,975.4	1,892.3	1,796.1	1,958.6	1,948.6	1,604.8	1,627.8	-0.05	-1.84
30-34 yrs	1,047.0	1,639.9	1,846.1	1,959.6	1,889.7	1,796.9	1,978.5	1,968.0	1,619.6	1.10	54.69
35-39 yrs	939.0	1,036.7	1,606.6	1,834.6	1,951.1	1,877.7	1,801.8	1,982.8	1,970.7	1.87	109.88
40-44 yrs	860.7	926.4	1,022.3	1,594.5	1,815.9	1,926.4	1,867.3	1,791.0	1,969.9	2.09	128.88
45-49 yrs	823.1	844.2	915.5	1,000.7	1,567.8	1,783.7	1,905.3	1,845.9	1,769.4	1.93	114.97
50-54 yrs	790.9	800.2	827.5	883.7	974.5	1,532.4	1,755.7	1,874.2	1,814.6	2.10	129.43
55-59 yrs	612.0	756.4	771.4	789.2	850.8	943.9	1,497.4	1,714.1	1,828.5	2.77	198.78
60-64 yrs	430.4	570.7	709.9	722.0	747.5	811.1	909.6	1,441.0	1,648.1	3.41	282.94
65-69 yrs	338.6	386.0	515.0	647.1	663.4	694.4	761.9	855.6	1,352.8	3.52	299.60
70-74 yrs	207.1	284.3	328.5	444.5	565.9	588.1	625.7	685.5	771.5	3.34	272.54
75-79 yrs	110.6	153.9	214.1	256.0	354.4	464.8	494.2	527.8	577.0	4.22	421.75
80+ yrs	71.6	101.4	143.7	214.7	281.7	403.1	561.5	689.9	817.1	6.28	1,042.02
Median age of population (years)	22.6	24.6	27.0	29.4	31.6	34.1	36.8	39.3	42.0	1.55	85.36

Table 5.314 Key economic trends

As stated

	1990	1995	2000	2005	2010	2015	2020	CAGR	Period growth
Total GDP (NT$ per capita)	258,898.4	349,456.7	443,826.0	506,253.8	547,717.8	683,838.1	863,780.3	4.10	233.6
Disposable income (NT$ per capita)	205,816.9	266,222.8	344,687.3	367,399.3	381,048.6	483,378.2	611,224.0	3.69	197.0
Disposable income (NT$ per household)	825,347.2	983,747.6	1,155,771.4	1,156,667.7	1,141,528.9	1,378,876.2	1,666,015.2	2.37	101.9
Number of households by annual household disposable income ('000)									
Over US$1,000	5,020.6	5,728.0	6,584.8	7,200.8	7,702.9	8,189.2	8,613.4	1.82	71.6
Over US$10,000	4,208.6	5,290.2	6,108.0	6,611.4	6,791.1	7,661.9	8,342.2	2.31	98.2
Over US$25,000	1,646.5	3,350.3	4,048.4	4,348.1	3,761.5	5,511.6	7,071.7	4.98	329.5
Over US$75,000	133.9	304.4	423.0	490.6	335.8	837.8	2,122.8	9.65	1,485.0
Over US$150,000	55.5	109.6	135.3	146.8	125.2	202.0	343.3	6.26	518.3
Total households	5,026.5	5,731.2	6,588.6	7,206.9	7,712.6	8,194.7	8,616.2	1.81	71.4

Note: Per capita data is shown at constant 2010 prices. Household disposable income bands are shown at current prices.

Table 5.315 Young generation

'000

	1980	1985	1990	1995	2000	2005	2010	2015	2020	CAGR	Period growth
Babies under 12 months	381.0	338.0	296.4	293.7	270.2	206.9	192.5	183.5	174.3	-1.94	-54.25
Infants under 24 months	787.0	714.8	635.3	618.9	537.0	434.3	396.4	381.9	361.8	-1.92	-54.03
Toddlers aged 1-4	1,584.8	1,591.4	1,310.2	1,307.9	1,237.0	1,037.0	823.1	803.6	763.0	-1.81	-51.86
Children aged 2-9	3,017.1	3,211.5	2,926.9	2,598.3	2,595.5	2,330.7	1,874.5	1,632.7	1,573.5	-1.61	-47.85
Female	1,463.7	1,557.6	1,416.9	1,247.6	1,241.9	1,116.4	894.8	778.9	749.0	-1.66	-48.82
Male	1,553.4	1,653.9	1,510.0	1,350.7	1,353.6	1,214.3	979.6	853.8	824.4	-1.57	-46.93
Tweenagers aged 10-14	1,936.7	1,832.0	1,981.0	1,952.4	1,602.1	1,622.1	1,519.2	1,253.0	1,025.1	-1.58	-47.07
Female	940.9	890.6	961.4	945.8	772.0	775.3	728.3	596.8	487.4	-1.63	-48.20
Male	995.8	941.5	1,019.6	1,006.6	830.1	846.8	790.9	656.3	537.7	-1.53	-46.00
Teenagers aged 13-19	2,807.3	2,679.7	2,597.3	2,780.6	2,579.6	2,245.6	2,263.8	2,075.8	1,661.4	-1.30	-40.82
Female	1,366.8	1,304.5	1,265.4	1,350.9	1,252.1	1,079.7	1,084.4	993.4	789.6	-1.36	-42.24
Male	1,440.5	1,375.3	1,331.9	1,429.7	1,327.5	1,165.9	1,179.4	1,082.4	871.9	-1.25	-39.48
Studying age 18-22	1,945.5	2,000.0	1,883.1	1,833.5	1,993.8	1,760.1	1,605.7	1,606.8	1,425.9	-0.77	-26.71
Female	949.7	975.8	917.4	894.0	972.0	855.7	770.9	771.2	680.7	-0.83	-28.32
Male	995.8	1,024.2	965.7	939.6	1,021.8	904.4	834.9	835.5	745.1	-0.72	-25.17
Young adults aged 15-29	5,571.5	5,810.8	5,712.8	5,661.6	5,695.1	5,479.4	5,156.0	4,732.5	4,385.4	-0.60	-21.29
Female	2,718.8	2,836.2	2,785.3	2,760.1	2,780.0	2,670.5	2,506.4	2,283.6	2,103.4	-0.64	-22.64
Male	2,852.7	2,974.6	2,927.4	2,901.5	2,915.1	2,808.8	2,649.6	2,448.9	2,282.1	-0.56	-20.00

Table 5.316 Middle-aged generation

'000

	1980	1985	1990	1995	2000	2005	2010	2015	2020	CAGR	Period growth
Middle-aged adults 30-59	5,073	6,004	6,989	8,062	9,050	9,861	10,806	11,176	10,973	1.95	116.3
Female	2,324	2,845	3,406	3,976	4,472	4,896	5,410	5,628	5,540	2.20	138.4
Male	2,748	3,159	3,584	4,086	4,578	4,965	5,396	5,548	5,432	1.72	97.7
Baby boomers aged 40-59	3,087	3,327	3,537	4,268	5,209	6,186	7,026	7,225	7,382	2.20	139.2
Female	1,358	1,537	1,715	2,114	2,587	3,080	3,521	3,643	3,742	2.57	175.5
Male	1,728	1,790	1,822	2,154	2,622	3,106	3,504	3,582	3,641	1.88	110.7

Table 5.317 Elderly population

'000

	1980	1985	1990	1995	2000	2005	2010	2015	2020	CAGR	Period growth
Elderly population (60+)	1,158.2	1,496.3	1,911.2	2,284.4	2,612.9	2,961.5	3,353.0	4,199.8	5,166.6	3.81	346.1
Female	555.7	689.8	857.9	1,045.0	1,256.8	1,482.7	1,736.3	2,227.1	2,778.2	4.11	400.0
Male	602.5	806.5	1,053.3	1,239.3	1,356.2	1,478.8	1,616.7	1,972.6	2,388.4	3.50	296.4

Table 5.318 Population of biggest cities 1980-2020

'000

	1980	1985	1990	1995	2000	2005	2010	2015	2020	CAGR	Period growth
Taipei	2,311.6	2,563.8	2,719.7	2,722.3	2,646.5	2,594.2	2,590.2	2,611.5	2,641.1	0.33	14.3
Kaohsiung	1,129.5	1,271.7	1,386.7	1,453.5	1,490.6	1,522.1	1,559.9	1,597.9	1,631.5	0.92	44.4
Taichung	569.3	661.5	761.8	866.7	965.8	1,043.7	1,105.9	1,155.1	1,192.8	1.87	109.5
Tainan	556.4	626.5	683.3	716.3	734.7	750.3	769.0	787.8	804.3	0.93	44.6
Banciao	456.5	506.9	539.0	541.6	529.1	520.6	521.1	526.2	532.7	0.39	16.7
Sinjhuang	226.0	261.6	299.2	337.1	372.2	399.8	422.3	440.2	454.1	1.76	100.9
Yonghe	306.4	344.4	374.3	390.4	398.1	404.9	413.9	423.3	431.8	0.86	41.0
Keelung	284.3	321.3	352.9	374.1	388.4	400.2	412.4	423.8	433.5	1.06	52.5
Hsinchu	257.4	292.5	324.4	349.2	368.4	383.9	398.4	411.0	421.5	1.24	63.8
Sanchong	313.9	350.3	376.0	384.0	382.3	381.8	385.9	392.0	398.2	0.60	26.9

Chart 5.190 Population age shift 2000 and 2020, Each Column Represents a Single Age Group

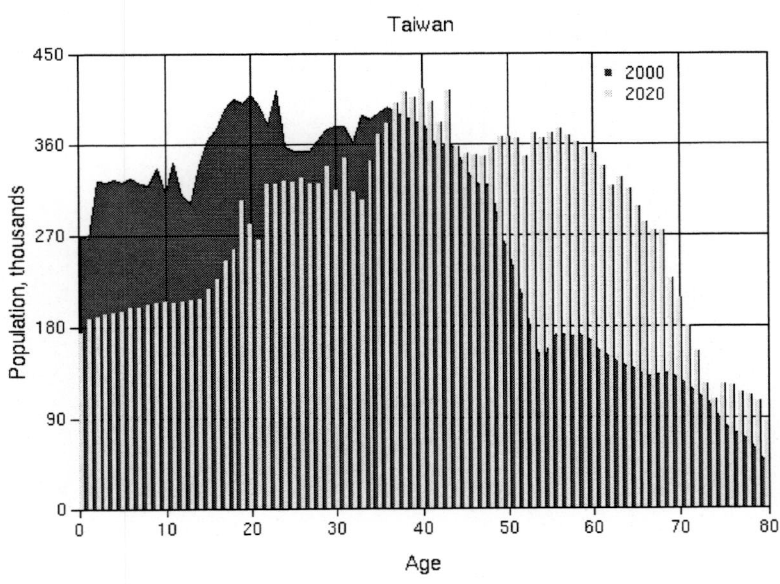

Chart 5.191 Population pyramids, 1980/2000/2010/2020

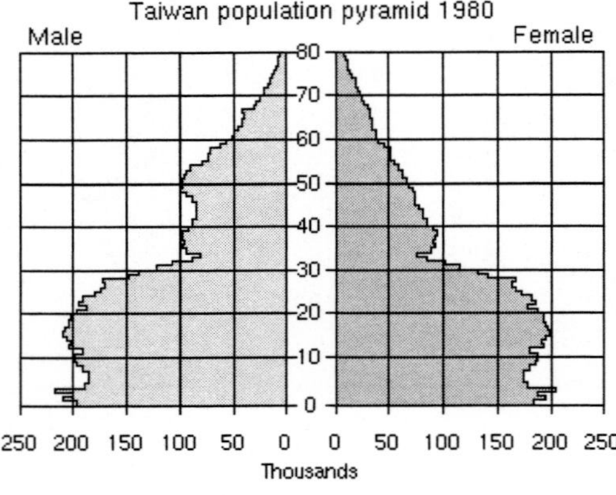

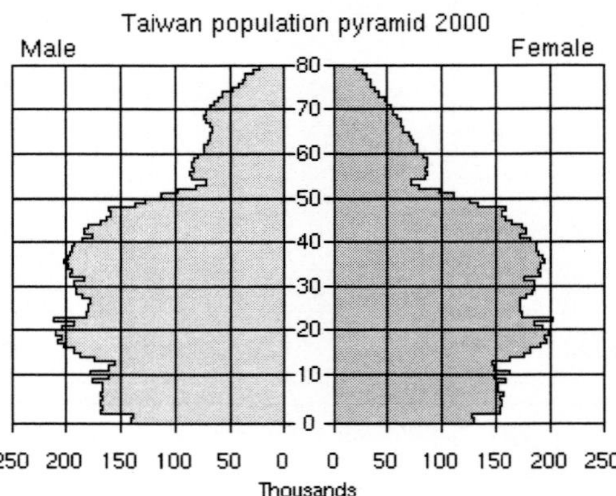

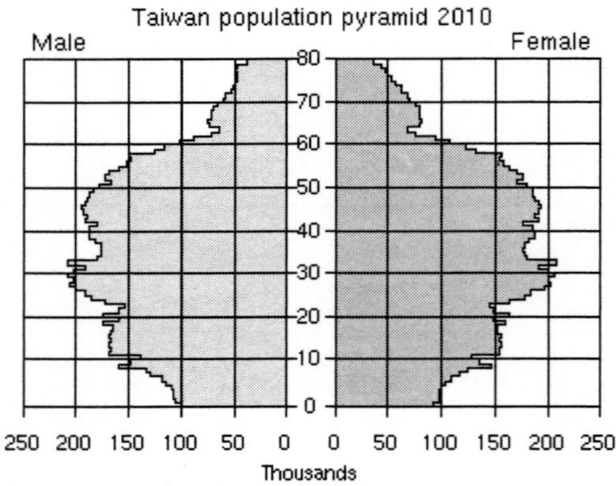

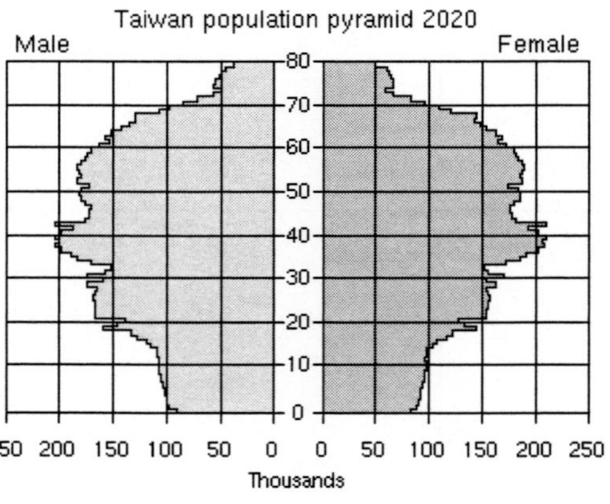

Chart 5.192 Major Cities: 1980, 2000 and 2020

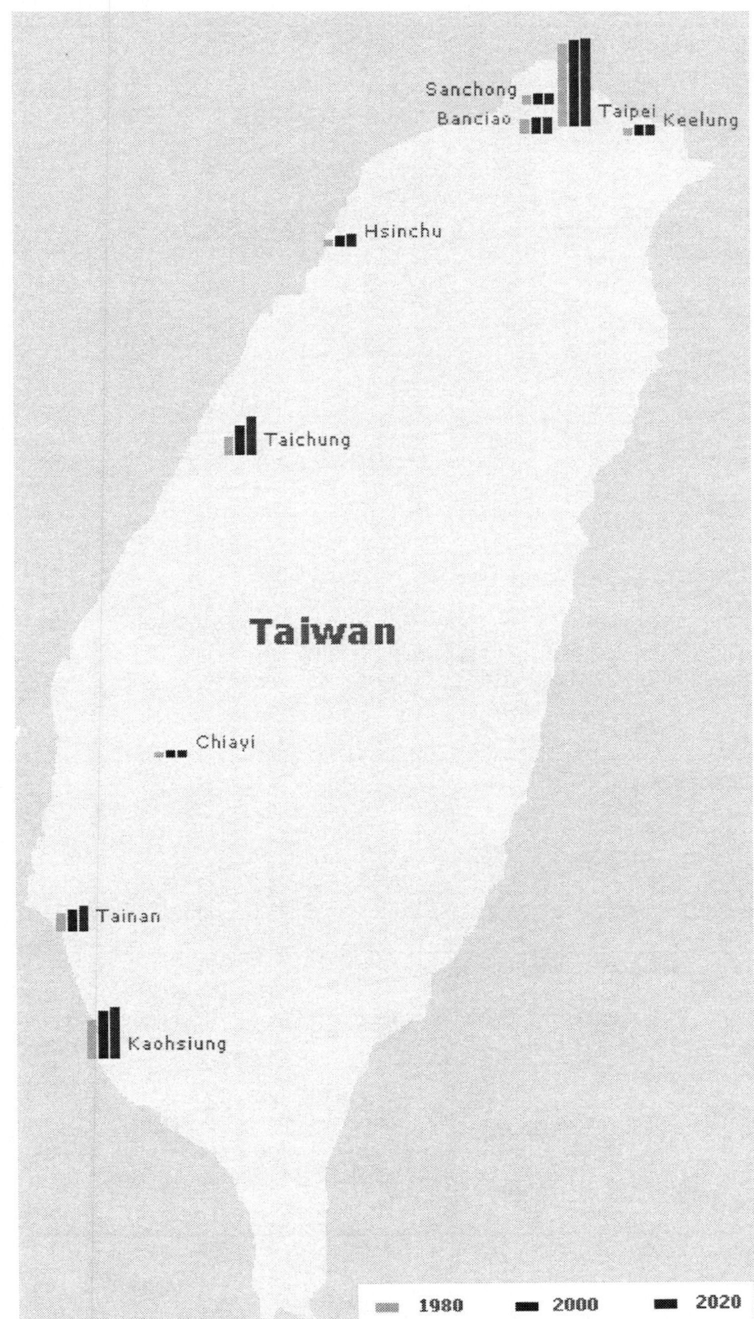

Thailand

Table 5.319 Key population trends
'000

	1980	1985	1990	1995	2000	2005	2010	2015	2020	CAGR	Period growth
Population at January 1st	46,808.6	50,819.7	54,291.3	57,522.7	60,665.6	63,002.9	65,124.7	66,763.3	67,990.0	0.94	45.25
Male	23,414.8	25,297.6	26,925.9	28,445.3	29,808.3	30,736.6	31,640.6	32,334.5	32,840.2	0.85	40.25
Female	23,393.8	25,522.2	27,365.4	29,077.5	30,857.3	32,266.3	33,484.1	34,428.8	35,149.8	1.02	50.25
0-4 yrs	4,742.5	4,404.9	4,109.9	4,729.4	4,493.7	4,050.1	4,049.9	3,834.8	3,650.3	-0.65	-23.03
5-9 yrs	5,501.2	5,253.2	4,908.9	4,569.4	4,930.0	4,665.9	4,176.8	4,161.7	3,942.3	-0.83	-28.34
10-14 yrs	5,948.6	5,829.9	5,552.1	5,119.8	4,701.5	4,975.8	4,746.7	4,243.6	4,227.6	-0.85	-28.93
15-19 yrs	5,786.7	6,146.8	5,987.0	5,629.6	5,199.1	4,743.1	5,050.8	4,812.2	4,296.8	-0.74	-25.75
20-24 yrs	5,080.3	5,805.8	6,135.7	5,852.9	5,580.2	5,159.6	4,749.5	5,062.1	4,815.9	-0.13	-5.20
25-29 yrs	4,090.6	4,997.9	5,711.3	5,935.4	5,756.1	5,510.7	5,136.9	4,706.3	5,022.8	0.51	22.79
30-34 yrs	3,230.9	3,984.3	4,897.7	5,533.8	5,794.8	5,634.0	5,457.4	5,066.7	4,622.2	0.90	43.06
35-39 yrs	2,527.7	3,117.3	3,874.5	4,740.7	5,410.7	5,653.8	5,526.9	5,337.1	4,932.2	1.69	95.13
40-44 yrs	2,315.5	2,432.4	3,024.4	3,755.1	4,633.9	5,276.2	5,505.9	5,364.2	5,163.6	2.03	123.00
45-49 yrs	1,992.3	2,231.2	2,323.4	2,893.0	3,688.1	4,504.5	5,117.4	5,340.1	5,188.7	2.42	160.44
50-54 yrs	1,616.5	1,911.0	2,136.4	2,180.1	2,801.6	3,589.5	4,337.0	4,954.9	5,176.8	2.95	220.25
55-59 yrs	1,216.4	1,503.9	1,788.6	1,975.1	2,085.5	2,688.9	3,422.2	4,177.4	4,804.0	3.49	294.95
60-64 yrs	924.2	1,076.3	1,354.1	1,616.8	1,858.4	1,961.8	2,526.2	3,271.5	4,039.3	3.76	337.06
65-69 yrs	697.6	783.3	919.6	1,180.5	1,462.4	1,702.1	1,779.6	2,356.9	3,114.6	3.81	346.48
70-74 yrs	496.8	564.7	633.5	750.8	1,024.4	1,279.5	1,488.7	1,571.8	2,156.9	3.74	334.17
75-79 yrs	317.7	375.4	428.5	476.9	599.8	835.8	1,067.3	1,287.9	1,367.5	3.72	330.44
80+ yrs	323.2	401.4	505.5	583.3	645.6	771.7	985.3	1,214.2	1,468.5	3.86	354.34
Median age of population (years)	21.3	23.2	25.4	27.4	29.7	32.2	34.3	36.4	38.5	1.49	80.70

Table 5.320 Key economic trends
As stated

	1990	1995	2000	2005	2010	2015	2020	CAGR	Period growth
Total GDP (Bt per capita)	77,351.1	109,911.3	106,579.3	131,608.8	144,396.7	183,895.5	238,540.0	3.83	208.4
Disposable income (Bt per capita)	47,996.0	63,582.6	59,637.1	74,421.7	80,832.8	102,171.2	132,309.5	3.44	175.7
Disposable income (Bt per household)	211,544.6	260,196.5	230,995.4	274,046.0	283,833.7	343,288.3	426,807.9	2.37	101.8
Number of households by annual household disposable income ('000)									
Over US$1,000	10,354.9	12,911.8	13,369.8	15,725.5	17,604.8	19,217.1	20,679.4	2.33	99.7
Over US$10,000	1,043.3	2,804.3	1,545.2	2,770.4	4,903.3	7,583.6	11,370.8	8.29	989.9
Over US$25,000	177.0	438.3	231.5	433.9	816.0	1,556.0	3,252.8	10.19	1,737.7
Over US$75,000	44.4	89.7	60.2	98.1	149.4	225.4	367.3	7.30	727.8
Over US$150,000	19.1	38.7	25.9	42.1	64.0	96.1	154.5	7.22	710.0
Total households	12,317.8	14,056.5	15,662.3	17,109.5	18,546.8	19,870.4	21,076.8	1.81	71.1

Note: Per capita data is shown at constant 2010 prices. Household disposable income bands are shown at current prices.

Table 5.321 Young generation
'000

	1980	1985	1990	1995	2000	2005	2010	2015	2020	CAGR	Period growth
Babies under 12 months	853.6	763.2	823.8	886.5	765.1	788.5	783.7	717.4	705.2	-0.48	-17.39
Infants under 24 months	1,804.1	1,629.1	1,684.0	1,829.1	1,607.5	1,617.8	1,593.3	1,467.5	1,434.1	-0.57	-20.51
Toddlers aged 1-4	3,888.9	3,641.8	3,286.0	3,842.9	3,728.5	3,261.5	3,266.2	3,117.4	2,945.1	-0.69	-24.27
Children aged 2-9	8,439.6	8,029.0	7,334.8	7,469.8	7,816.2	7,098.1	6,633.4	6,529.0	6,158.5	-0.78	-27.03
Female	4,154.0	3,955.1	3,615.6	3,665.8	3,831.3	3,484.5	3,246.0	3,191.0	3,012.5	-0.80	-27.48
Male	4,285.6	4,073.9	3,719.2	3,803.9	3,984.9	3,613.6	3,387.4	3,337.9	3,146.0	-0.77	-26.59
Tweenagers aged 10-14	5,948.6	5,829.9	5,552.1	5,119.8	4,701.5	4,975.8	4,746.7	4,243.6	4,227.6	-0.85	-28.93
Female	2,930.1	2,879.2	2,736.8	2,524.3	2,311.7	2,448.2	2,330.0	2,072.6	2,056.7	-0.88	-29.81
Male	3,018.5	2,950.7	2,815.4	2,595.5	2,389.7	2,527.6	2,416.7	2,171.1	2,170.8	-0.82	-28.08
Teenagers aged 13-19	8,162.3	8,573.5	8,287.0	7,765.7	7,066.5	6,743.9	7,105.7	6,498.4	5,997.6	-0.77	-26.52
Female	4,040.3	4,246.4	4,107.7	3,850.9	3,492.4	3,329.2	3,497.9	3,186.6	2,923.5	-0.81	-27.64
Male	4,121.9	4,327.2	4,179.3	3,914.8	3,574.1	3,414.8	3,607.9	3,311.8	3,074.1	-0.73	-25.42
Studying age 18-22	5,364.1	6,020.9	6,188.5	5,738.0	5,454.8	4,903.8	4,902.1	5,120.0	4,442.6	-0.47	-17.18
Female	2,666.1	2,999.3	3,078.9	2,855.7	2,712.1	2,443.2	2,428.6	2,528.8	2,184.0	-0.50	-18.08
Male	2,698.0	3,021.6	3,109.6	2,882.3	2,742.8	2,460.6	2,473.5	2,591.2	2,258.6	-0.44	-16.29
Young adults aged 15-29	14,957.6	16,950.5	17,834.1	17,417.9	16,535.4	15,413.4	14,937.3	14,580.6	14,135.5	-0.14	-5.50
Female	7,470.4	8,464.0	8,904.5	8,702.0	8,258.3	7,694.9	7,441.6	7,236.8	6,986.4	-0.17	-6.48
Male	7,487.1	8,486.5	8,929.6	8,715.9	8,277.0	7,718.5	7,495.7	7,343.8	7,149.1	-0.12	-4.51

Table 5.322 Middle-aged generation

'000

	1980	1985	1990	1995	2000	2005	2010	2015	2020	CAGR	Period growth
Middle-aged adults 30-59	12,899	15,180	18,045	21,078	24,414	27,347	29,367	30,240	29,887	2.12	131.7
Female	6,489	7,700	9,192	10,761	12,579	14,193	15,267	15,717	15,516	2.20	139.1
Male	6,410	7,480	8,853	10,317	11,835	13,154	14,100	14,524	14,371	2.04	124.2
Baby boomers aged 40-59	7,141	8,079	9,273	10,803	13,209	16,059	18,382	19,837	20,333	2.65	184.8
Female	3,596	4,097	4,735	5,549	6,854	8,406	9,669	10,436	10,673	2.76	196.8
Male	3,545	3,982	4,538	5,254	6,355	7,653	8,713	9,401	9,660	2.54	172.5

Table 5.323 Elderly population

'000

	1980	1985	1990	1995	2000	2005	2010	2015	2020	CAGR	Period growth
Elderly population (60+)	2,759	3,201	3,841	4,608	5,591	6,551	7,847	9,702	12,147	3.77	340.2
Female	1,466	1,722	2,090	2,529	3,091	3,652	4,418	5,491	6,874	3.94	368.9
Male	1,293	1,479	1,751	2,079	2,500	2,899	3,429	4,211	5,273	3.58	307.7

Table 5.324 Population of biggest cities 1980-2020

'000

	1980	1985	1990	1995	2000	2005	2010	2015	2020	CAGR	Period growth
Bangkok	4,697.1	5,373.3	5,882.4	6,131.1	6,320.2	6,642.6	7,064.5	7,550.8	8,114.7	1.38	72.8
Samut Prakan	281.6	313.3	341.0	360.6	378.7	394.9	416.2	441.4	471.2	1.29	67.3
Nonthaburi	210.5	235.8	258.6	275.5	291.6	306.1	324.5	346.0	371.0	1.43	76.2
Udon Thani	78.9	109.3	145.8	183.2	222.4	261.2	302.2	345.5	392.0	4.09	396.6
Hat Yai	95.3	117.4	141.5	164.4	187.9	210.8	235.9	262.9	292.5	2.84	206.8
Nakhon Ratchasima	184.0	196.5	204.1	205.2	204.6	202.7	203.8	207.0	212.5	0.36	15.5
Chon Buri	149.7	163.1	173.4	178.9	183.3	186.6	192.6	200.4	210.4	0.85	40.5
Phra Pradaeng	131.9	145.6	157.2	164.7	171.5	177.4	185.6	195.6	207.6	1.14	57.3
Chiang Mai	142.3	155.1	164.9	170.2	174.4	177.6	183.3	190.8	200.4	0.86	40.8
Lampang	118.2	129.4	138.4	143.7	148.2	151.8	157.5	164.8	173.8	0.97	47.0

Chart 5.193 Population age shift 2000 and 2020, Each Column Represents a Single Age Group

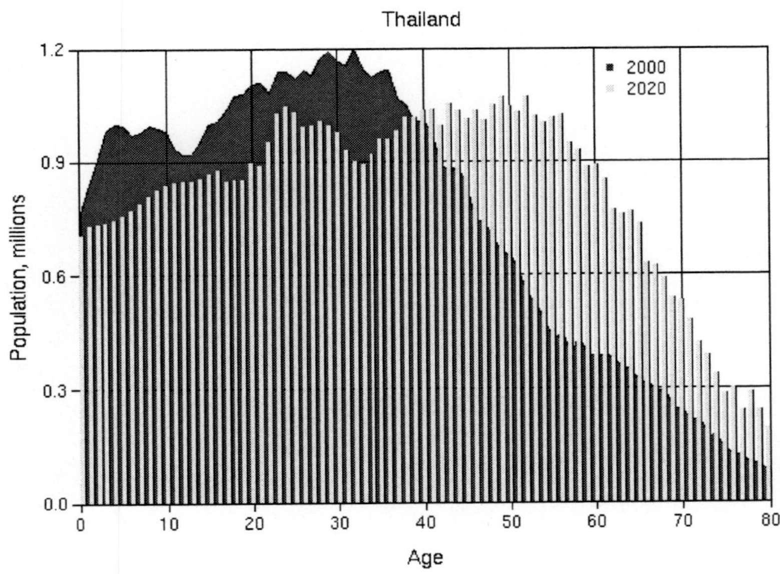

Chart 5.194 Population pyramids, 1980/2000/2010/2020

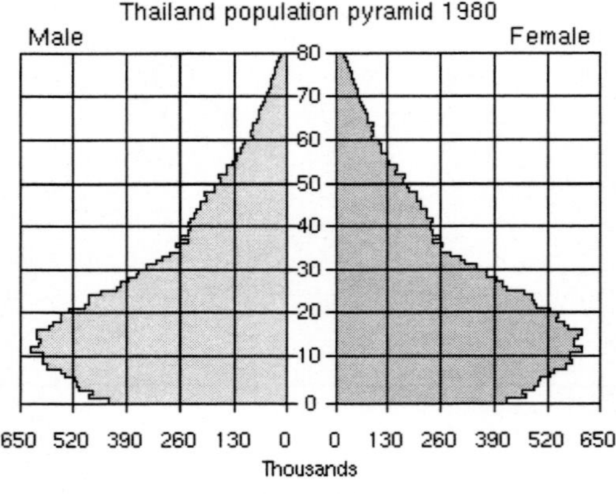

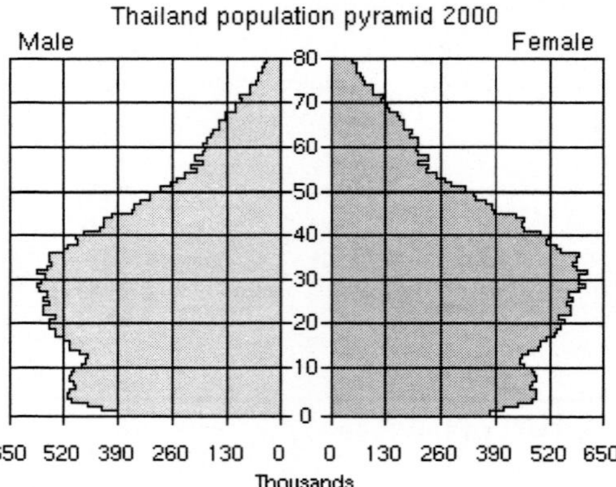

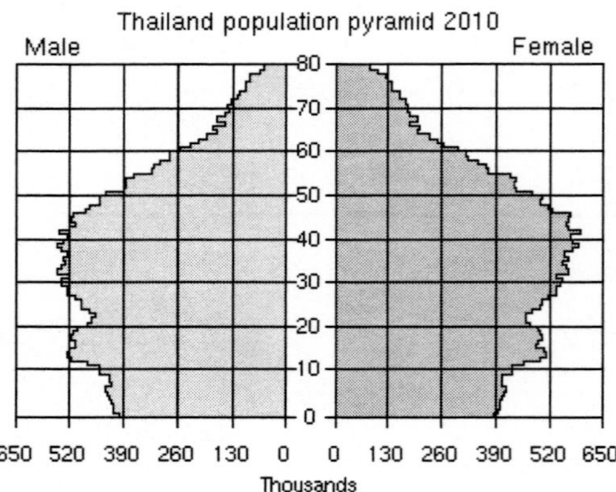

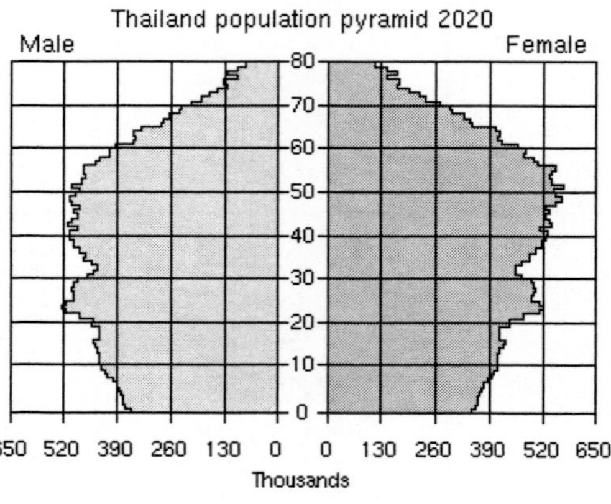

Chart 5.195 Major Cities: 1980, 2000 and 2020

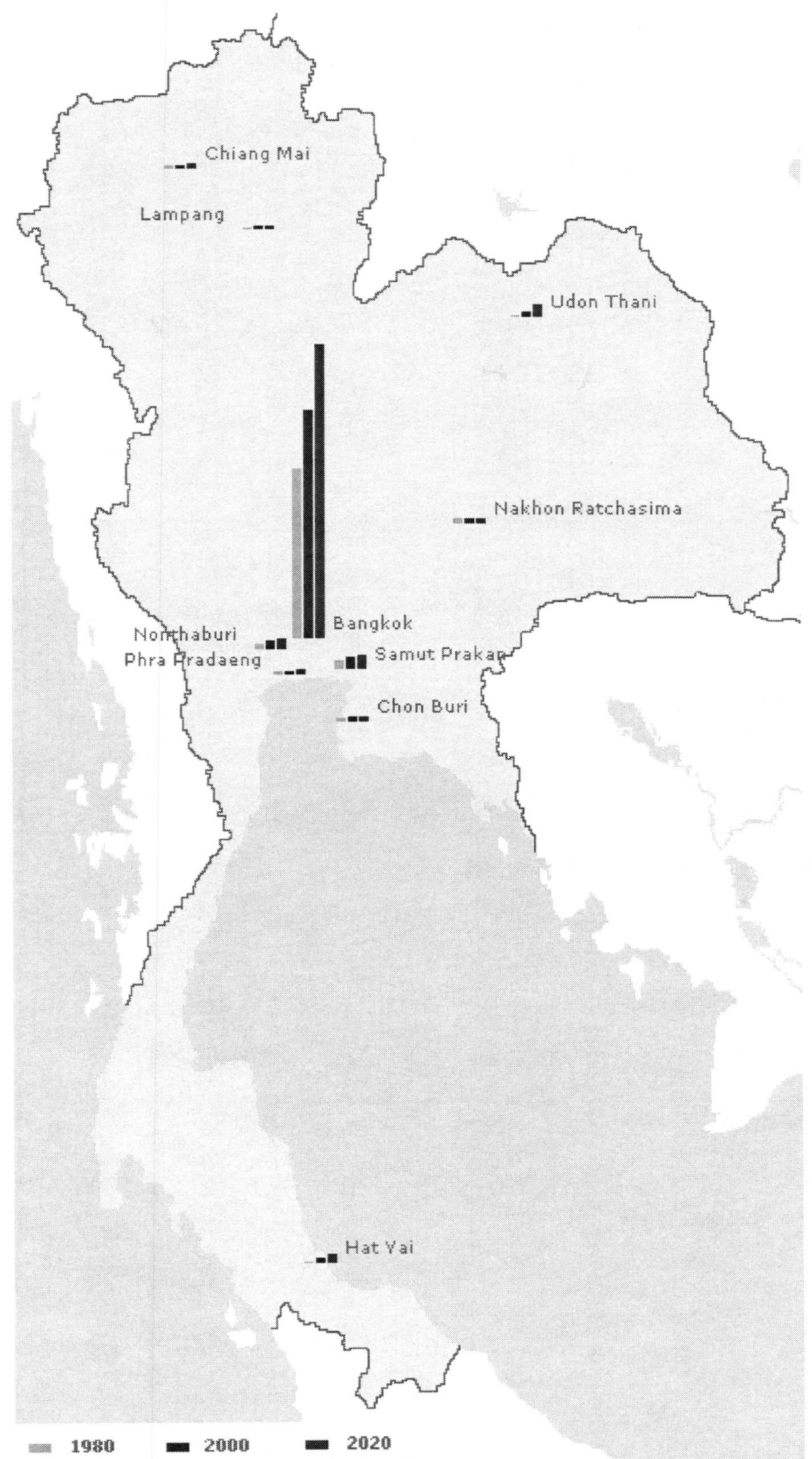

Tunisia

Table 5.325 Key population trends

'000

	1980	1985	1990	1995	2000	2005	2010	2015	2020	CAGR	Period growth
Population at January 1st	6,457.1	7,330.2	8,214.9	8,935.0	9,452.0	9,878.4	10,374.0	10,884.0	11,366.2	1.42	76.03
Male	3,271.7	3,709.7	4,151.7	4,512.1	4,770.4	4,973.2	5,215.7	5,465.6	5,701.9	1.40	74.28
Female	3,185.4	3,620.5	4,063.2	4,422.9	4,681.6	4,905.3	5,158.2	5,418.4	5,664.3	1.45	77.82
0-4 yrs	1,004.8	1,086.2	1,105.3	968.5	816.4	768.0	799.4	834.2	829.5	-0.48	-17.44
5-9 yrs	886.2	982.2	1,056.8	1,063.2	963.6	811.8	762.4	795.3	832.1	-0.16	-6.11
10-14 yrs	820.7	875.2	966.7	1,032.4	1,058.5	956.8	810.9	762.2	794.3	-0.08	-3.22
15-19 yrs	736.8	806.9	860.9	945.1	1,025.3	1,050.1	953.9	808.4	760.0	0.08	3.15
20-24 yrs	624.4	716.5	782.4	825.4	929.8	1,010.1	1,044.2	948.7	803.6	0.63	28.70
25-29 yrs	473.3	599.7	687.5	729.9	805.2	911.9	1,002.6	1,037.4	942.3	1.74	99.10
30-34 yrs	313.0	460.9	578.9	649.2	710.7	789.4	904.9	996.1	1,030.9	3.02	229.36
35-39 yrs	257.7	313.5	456.2	582.2	633.9	697.3	783.1	898.9	989.9	3.42	284.15
40-44 yrs	289.8	258.8	324.3	483.6	571.2	622.8	691.1	776.9	892.4	2.85	207.87
45-49 yrs	270.3	286.5	268.6	344.2	477.1	560.4	615.1	683.3	768.8	2.65	184.42
50-54 yrs	226.3	265.3	283.9	271.8	340.2	464.7	548.9	603.6	671.4	2.76	196.64
55-59 yrs	175.2	218.9	255.7	273.0	265.3	327.4	449.0	531.7	586.1	3.07	234.56
60-64 yrs	137.4	164.7	210.0	252.5	260.8	250.2	309.8	426.0	506.2	3.31	268.36
65-69 yrs	112.0	123.0	152.5	208.7	231.8	236.7	228.5	284.2	392.5	3.18	250.43
70-74 yrs	69.5	93.1	106.8	142.1	177.2	196.0	202.7	197.2	247.3	3.22	255.56
75-79 yrs	38.4	50.4	71.4	87.3	106.1	133.0	149.5	157.0	154.8	3.55	303.13
80+ yrs	21.3	28.6	47.2	76.0	78.8	91.8	117.9	143.0	164.3	5.24	672.26
Median age of population (years)	18.4	19.5	20.7	22.7	24.6	26.8	29.0	31.2	33.5	1.50	81.70

Table 5.326 Key economic trends

As stated

	1990	1995	2000	2005	2010	2015	2020	CAGR	Period growth
Total GDP (TND per capita)	2,793.8	3,106.1	3,858.6	4,595.3	5,493.2	6,901.6	8,760.2	3.88	213.6
Disposable income (TND per capita)	1,788.3	1,937.8	2,384.5	2,937.4	3,363.9	4,144.7	5,212.6	3.63	191.5
Disposable income (TND per household)	9,566.0	9,846.8	11,261.8	12,955.3	13,948.0	16,283.3	19,478.3	2.40	103.6
Number of households by annual household disposable income ('000)									
Over US$1,000	1,523.2	1,751.0	1,991.1	2,236.4	2,499.9	2,769.4	3,041.4	2.33	99.7
Over US$10,000	124.8	218.9	219.7	455.4	720.8	1,234.7	2,021.5	9.73	1,520.1
Over US$25,000	28.7	45.4	45.8	83.5	129.6	229.7	445.9	9.57	1,452.7
Over US$75,000	7.3	10.9	11.5	18.8	26.9	40.8	66.8	7.64	809.5
Over US$150,000	3.1	4.6	4.8	7.9	11.3	17.2	27.6	7.56	790.0
Total households	1,535.7	1,758.4	2,001.3	2,239.8	2,501.9	2,770.4	3,041.7	2.30	98.1

Note: Per capita data is shown at constant 2010 prices. Household disposable income bands are shown at current prices.

Table 5.327 Young generation

'000

	1980	1985	1990	1995	2000	2005	2010	2015	2020	CAGR	Period growth
Babies under 12 months	215.0	223.0	222.1	177.2	152.9	159.8	165.3	167.8	162.6	-0.70	-24.37
Infants under 24 months	422.3	444.1	444.3	364.6	310.0	314.5	328.0	335.7	327.4	-0.63	-22.48
Toddlers aged 1-4	789.7	863.1	883.2	791.2	663.5	608.2	634.1	666.4	666.9	-0.42	-15.56
Children aged 2-9	1,468.7	1,624.3	1,717.8	1,667.1	1,470.1	1,265.3	1,233.7	1,293.7	1,334.2	-0.24	-9.16
Female	716.6	786.5	834.7	811.6	712.8	612.4	597.1	625.8	645.1	-0.26	-9.98
Male	752.1	837.7	883.2	855.4	757.3	652.9	636.7	667.9	689.1	-0.22	-8.38
Tweenagers aged 10-14	820.7	875.2	966.7	1,032.4	1,058.5	956.8	810.9	762.2	794.3	-0.08	-3.22
Female	401.3	429.7	470.3	505.0	516.4	464.5	392.6	369.0	384.3	-0.11	-4.23
Male	419.4	445.4	496.3	527.5	542.1	492.3	418.3	393.2	410.0	-0.06	-2.25
Teenagers aged 13-19	1,057.1	1,147.0	1,234.8	1,349.7	1,451.4	1,450.4	1,292.0	1,112.9	1,071.9	0.03	1.40
Female	515.1	564.6	606.5	659.4	710.1	707.3	627.0	539.0	518.9	0.02	0.74
Male	542.0	582.4	628.3	690.3	741.4	743.1	665.0	573.9	552.9	0.05	2.02
Studying age 18-22	673.2	756.8	812.9	872.9	973.3	1,037.9	1,023.7	889.2	772.3	0.34	14.71
Female	328.7	372.3	402.2	430.1	475.8	508.5	498.9	431.4	374.1	0.32	13.80
Male	344.5	384.4	410.7	442.8	497.5	529.5	524.8	457.8	398.2	0.36	15.58
Young adults aged 15-29	1,834.4	2,123.1	2,330.7	2,500.3	2,760.3	2,972.2	3,000.8	2,794.5	2,505.8	0.78	36.60
Female	906.8	1,050.8	1,155.5	1,247.5	1,360.1	1,455.9	1,465.7	1,360.1	1,215.8	0.74	34.07
Male	927.6	1,072.3	1,175.3	1,252.8	1,400.2	1,516.3	1,535.1	1,434.4	1,290.0	0.83	39.08

Table 5.328 Middle-aged generation

'000

	1980	1985	1990	1995	2000	2005	2010	2015	2020	CAGR	Period growth
Middle-aged adults 30-59	1,532.4	1,803.9	2,167.5	2,604.0	2,998.4	3,462.0	3,992.1	4,490.4	4,939.5	2.97	222.3
Female	786.8	927.9	1,106.4	1,305.4	1,510.1	1,749.7	2,015.2	2,265.2	2,479.7	2.91	215.2
Male	745.6	875.9	1,061.2	1,298.6	1,488.2	1,712.3	1,976.9	2,225.2	2,459.9	3.03	229.9
Baby boomers aged 40-59	961.7	1,029.5	1,132.4	1,372.5	1,653.8	1,975.3	2,304.1	2,595.5	2,918.7	2.81	203.5
Female	483.3	527.9	579.2	680.4	814.4	990.9	1,176.3	1,333.6	1,488.4	2.85	208.0
Male	478.4	501.6	553.3	692.2	839.4	984.4	1,127.8	1,261.9	1,430.3	2.78	199.0

Table 5.329 Elderly population

'000

	1980	1985	1990	1995	2000	2005	2010	2015	2020	CAGR	Period growth
Elderly population (60+)	378.6	459.7	587.8	766.5	854.8	907.7	1,008.4	1,207.4	1,465.1	3.44	286.9
Female	170.5	209.5	281.4	376.7	432.0	470.5	529.0	635.9	781.3	3.88	358.4
Male	208.2	250.2	306.4	389.8	422.7	437.1	479.3	571.5	683.7	3.02	228.4

Table 5.330 Population of biggest cities 1980-2020

'000

	1980	1985	1990	1995	2000	2005	2010	2015	2020	CAGR	Period growth
Tunis	544.2	615.3	704.0	731.0	735.2	728.8	742.8	772.5	811.6	1.00	49.14
Safaqis	212.8	238.6	269.5	275.7	272.3	264.2	265.0	272.7	284.7	0.73	33.77
Susah	71.0	88.3	114.6	135.6	156.0	177.2	197.6	216.8	235.0	3.04	230.90
al-Qayrawan	63.8	75.4	92.0	102.4	111.2	119.7	129.0	138.9	149.0	2.14	133.70
at-Tadaman Dawwar Hishar	82.4	94.0	109.0	114.9	117.6	119.0	123.0	129.2	136.5	1.27	65.64
Qabis	83.9	95.3	109.7	114.7	116.4	116.6	119.7	125.1	131.8	1.14	57.12
Binzart	86.3	97.4	111.3	115.3	115.7	114.4	116.3	120.8	126.8	0.97	47.00
Aryanah	91.6	101.0	111.2	110.2	104.5	96.4	92.9	93.0	95.3	0.10	4.03
Sukrah	62.0	70.7	82.0	86.4	88.5	89.5	92.6	97.2	102.7	1.27	65.64
Qafsah	54.9	63.2	74.3	79.5	82.8	85.3	89.4	94.6	100.4	1.52	83.02

Chart 5.196 Population age shift 2000 and 2020, Each Column Represents a Single Age Group

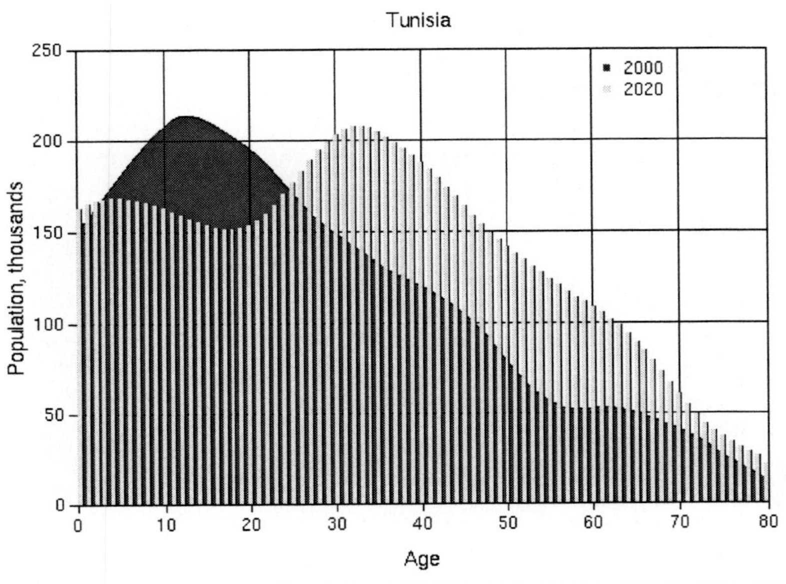

Chart 5.197 Population pyramids, 1980/2000/2010/2020

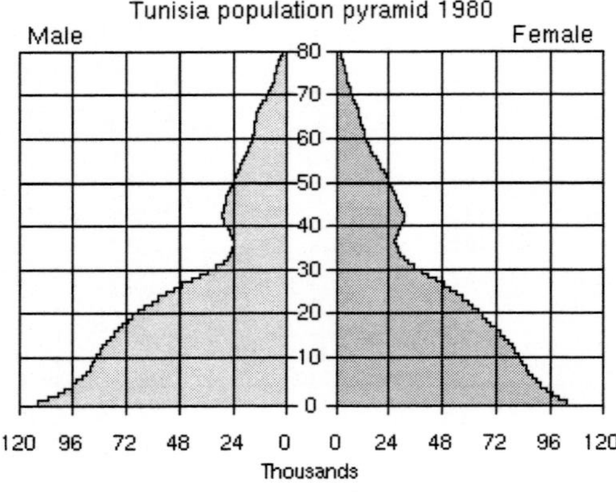

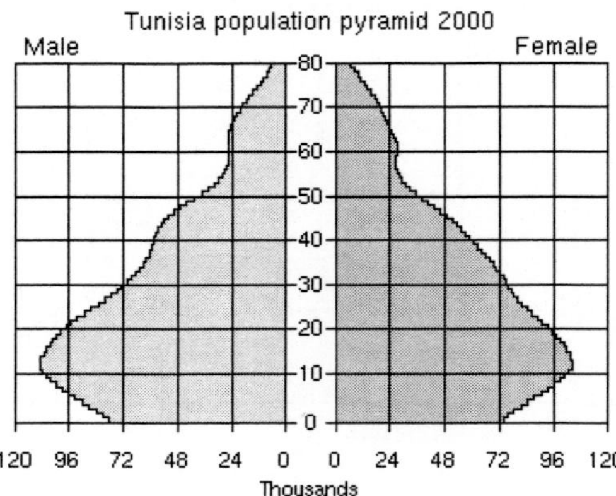

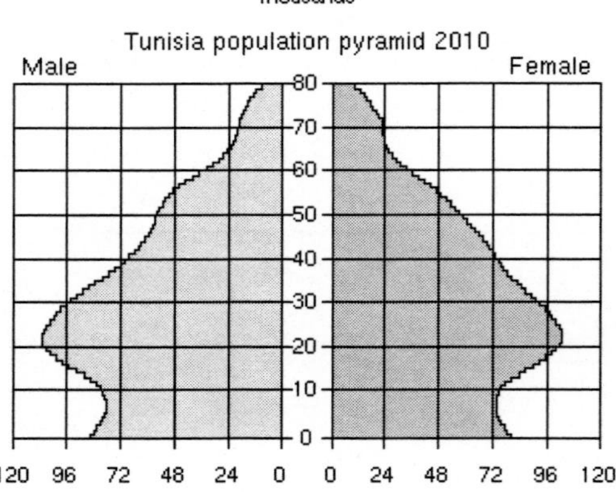

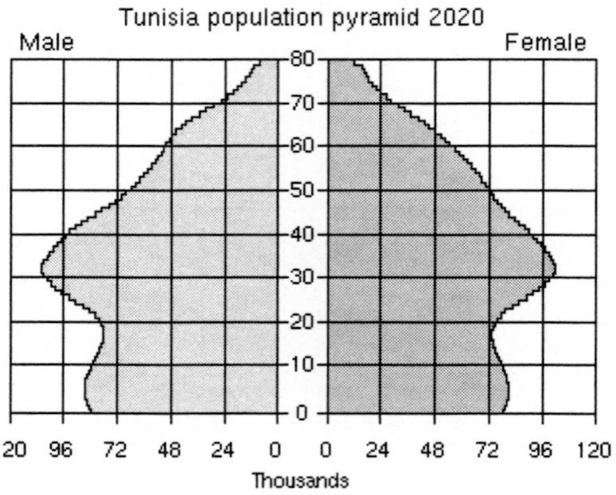

Chart 5.198 Major Cities: 1980, 2000 and 2020

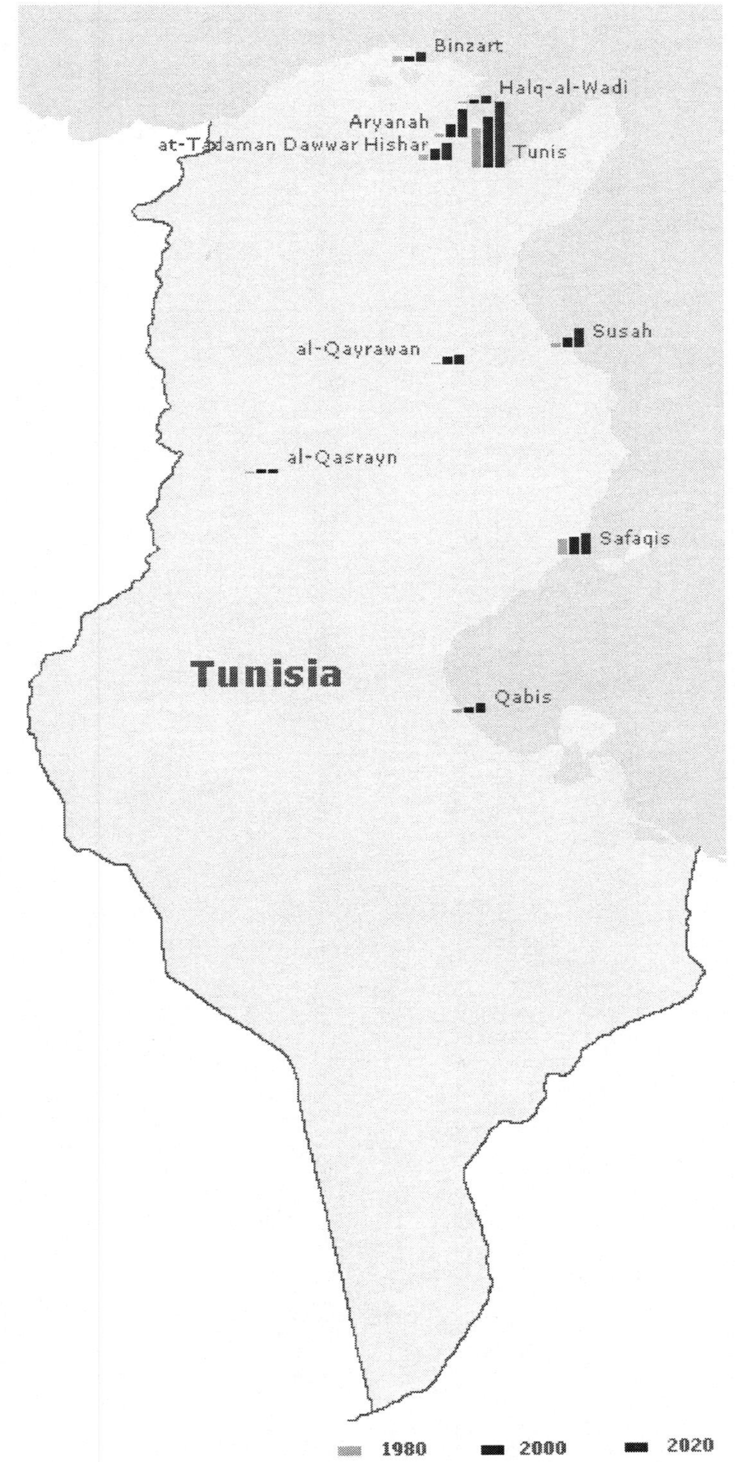

Turkey

Table 5.331 Key population trends

'000

	1980	1985	1990	1995	2000	2005	2010	2015	2020	CAGR	Period growth
Population at January 1st	44,021.1	49,663.0	55,494.7	61,203.6	66,889.4	71,610.0	76,156.6	80,431.7	84,303.5	1.64	91.51
Male	22,696.4	25,230.6	27,539.1	29,816.4	32,024.1	34,127.5	36,372.0	38,201.4	39,798.6	1.41	75.35
Female	22,335.3	24,803.2	27,136.3	29,457.6	31,716.6	33,901.2	36,101.6	38,007.6	39,704.3	1.45	77.76
0-4 yrs	5,489.9	6,114.3	6,019.9	6,112.4	6,380.8	6,055.1	5,942.4	5,560.7	5,436.1	-0.02	-0.98
5-9 yrs	5,294.7	5,649.8	6,222.5	6,110.8	6,105.3	6,436.6	6,176.0	5,956.1	5,586.0	0.13	5.50
10-14 yrs	4,643.0	5,422.2	5,762.1	6,364.9	6,132.8	6,161.4	6,520.9	6,222.6	6,009.9	0.65	29.44
15-19 yrs	4,466.6	4,659.3	5,464.3	5,829.8	6,382.9	6,185.7	6,232.5	6,557.4	6,260.8	0.85	40.17
20-24 yrs	3,800.8	4,458.3	4,651.9	5,447.5	5,826.7	6,426.5	6,256.7	6,256.3	6,584.7	1.38	73.24
25-29 yrs	3,174.4	3,815.0	4,470.9	4,636.4	5,446.2	5,860.6	6,483.8	6,276.6	6,278.6	1.72	97.79
30-34 yrs	2,768.9	3,183.0	3,836.4	4,481.0	4,642.8	5,474.1	5,922.0	6,502.2	6,297.7	2.08	127.44
35-39 yrs	2,278.6	2,737.2	3,183.4	3,832.2	4,481.8	4,659.6	5,520.1	5,927.2	6,510.3	2.66	185.71
40-44 yrs	1,996.0	2,246.5	2,703.0	3,136.5	3,812.3	4,483.4	4,679.0	5,504.0	5,913.6	2.75	196.27
45-49 yrs	2,477.3	1,990.1	2,222.1	2,647.8	3,096.4	3,789.0	4,471.3	4,631.1	5,454.0	1.99	120.16
50-54 yrs	2,388.2	2,441.8	1,961.5	2,179.3	2,585.7	3,042.9	3,737.6	4,376.7	4,538.7	1.62	90.04
55-59 yrs	2,103.3	2,294.9	2,348.7	1,891.9	2,092.6	2,500.5	2,957.9	3,596.2	4,222.4	1.76	100.75
60-64 yrs	1,756.0	1,946.2	2,111.6	2,180.2	1,769.8	1,966.2	2,375.1	2,774.2	3,376.5	1.65	92.28
65-69 yrs	1,250.8	1,510.6	1,668.9	1,855.7	1,944.3	1,589.2	1,761.9	2,136.6	2,506.4	1.75	100.39
70-74 yrs	770.0	994.4	1,236.2	1,374.4	1,548.6	1,607.3	1,312.9	1,480.0	1,812.6	2.16	135.40
75-79 yrs	338.9	508.8	718.1	945.6	1,065.8	1,063.5	1,138.0	1,149.3	1,220.6	3.26	260.19
80+ yrs	28.2	48.8	74.1	192.6	330.6	563.1	628.8	543.5	765.0	8.60	2,614.22
Median age of population (years)	20.1	20.8	21.9	23.3	24.9	26.7	28.6	30.4	31.8	1.16	58.47

Table 5.332 Key economic trends

As stated

	1990	1995	2000	2005	2010	2015	2020	CAGR	Period growth
Total GDP (TL per capita)	9,342.6	9,921.3	11,110.8	12,966.5	13,501.6	15,145.5	17,322.8	2.08	85.4
Disposable income (TL per capita)	7,217.8	7,249.4	9,204.9	10,147.1	10,170.0	11,552.5	13,246.0	2.04	83.5
Disposable income (TL per household)	35,799.5	33,530.7	40,856.3	43,328.7	41,717.8	45,447.5	49,884.4	1.11	39.3
Number of households by annual household disposable income ('000)									
Over US$1,000	10,976.5	13,019.2	14,915.0	16,748.2	18,548.1	20,431.9	22,379.0	2.40	103.9
Over US$10,000	2,821.4	3,370.8	6,786.6	13,177.8	14,948.3	17,465.9	20,440.9	6.82	624.5
Over US$25,000	603.9	658.6	1,516.5	4,736.7	5,319.1	7,458.4	11,143.8	10.21	1,745.3
Over US$75,000	109.3	121.0	214.5	492.2	523.3	722.2	1,221.1	8.38	1,017.2
Over US$150,000	47.3	51.7	91.5	197.8	220.1	288.9	440.5	7.72	831.5
Total households	11,188.6	13,232.3	15,070.1	16,770.3	18,565.6	20,445.2	22,385.5	2.34	100.1

Note: Per capita data is shown at constant 2010 prices. Household disposable income bands are shown at current prices.

Table 5.333 Young generation

'000

	1980	1985	1990	1995	2000	2005	2010	2015	2020	CAGR	Period growth
Babies under 12 months	1,285	1,262	1,262	1,447	1,460	1,300	1,304	1,288	1,268	-0.03	-1.33
Infants under 24 months	2,564	2,519	2,506	2,831	2,895	2,619	2,587	2,576	2,539	-0.02	-0.97
Toddlers aged 1-4	5,067	5,081	4,911	5,287	5,668	5,385	5,112	5,095	5,108	0.02	0.80
Children aged 2-9	9,755	10,351	10,187	10,166	10,954	11,176	10,531	10,241	10,227	0.12	4.84
Female	4,738	5,034	4,960	4,967	5,375	5,482	5,156	5,010	5,000	0.13	5.53
Male	5,017	5,317	5,228	5,199	5,579	5,694	5,375	5,231	5,227	0.10	4.19
Tweenagers aged 10-14	4,643	5,422	5,762	6,365	6,133	6,161	6,521	6,223	6,010	0.65	29.44
Female	2,231	2,647	2,799	3,099	2,986	2,994	3,172	3,025	2,917	0.67	30.77
Male	2,412	2,775	2,964	3,266	3,147	3,167	3,349	3,198	3,093	0.62	28.21
Teenagers aged 13-19	6,459	7,483	8,877	9,508	9,218	8,873	9,573	9,953	9,352	0.93	44.79
Female	3,166	3,674	4,325	4,628	4,494	4,339	4,706	4,890	4,585	0.93	44.82
Male	3,293	3,810	4,552	4,880	4,724	4,534	4,867	5,062	4,767	0.93	44.75
Studying age 18-22	4,169	4,712	5,589	6,512	6,823	6,480	6,357	6,976	7,104	1.34	70.39
Female	2,032	2,324	2,746	3,179	3,328	3,164	3,119	3,437	3,494	1.36	71.92
Male	2,137	2,388	2,843	3,334	3,494	3,316	3,238	3,539	3,610	1.32	68.94
Young adults aged 15-29	11,823	13,585	15,934	18,148	19,648	19,669	19,657	20,194	20,659	1.41	74.74
Female	5,763	6,670	7,830	8,896	9,606	9,614	9,643	9,932	10,170	1.43	76.49
Male	6,060	6,915	8,104	9,252	10,042	10,054	10,014	10,261	10,488	1.38	73.07

Table 5.334 Middle-aged generation

'000

	1980	1985	1990	1995	2000	2005	2010	2015	2020	CAGR	Period growth
Middle-aged adults 30-59	11,967	13,752	16,200	18,716	21,644	25,306	29,343	32,561	34,720	2.70	190.1
Female	5,906	6,789	7,978	9,232	10,705	12,521	14,519	16,121	17,213	2.71	191.4
Male	6,060	6,963	8,221	9,484	10,939	12,785	14,824	16,440	17,507	2.69	188.9
Baby boomers aged 40-59	7,009	7,747	8,768	10,151	11,929	14,034	16,460	19,158	21,805	2.88	211.1
Female	3,478	3,854	4,355	5,026	5,893	6,951	8,188	9,543	10,864	2.89	212.4
Male	3,531	3,893	4,413	5,124	6,036	7,083	8,272	9,615	10,940	2.87	209.8

Table 5.335 Elderly population

'000

	1980	1985	1990	1995	2000	2005	2010	2015	2020	CAGR	Period growth
Elderly population (60+)	2,779	3,358	3,944	4,676	5,466	6,133	6,891	8,122	9,702	3.17	249.1
Female	1,477	1,805	2,125	2,513	2,930	3,295	3,699	4,343	5,172	3.18	250.1
Male	1,302	1,552	1,820	2,162	2,536	2,838	3,192	3,780	4,530	3.17	247.9

Table 5.336 Population of biggest cities 1980-2020

'000

	1980	1985	1990	1995	2000	2005	2010	2015	2020	CAGR	Period growth
Istanbul	4,239.6	5,476.0	6,629.4	7,664.6	8,803.5	9,992.4	11,251.6	12,388.1	13,412.9	2.92	216.4
Ankara	1,786.7	2,235.0	2,584.0	2,884.8	3,203.4	3,551.6	3,904.8	4,238.7	4,552.3	2.37	154.8
Izmir	1,173.7	1,489.8	1,758.8	1,989.1	2,232.3	2,464.3	2,701.4	2,927.5	3,141.0	2.49	167.6
Bursa	430.2	612.5	834.6	1,023.8	1,194.7	1,343.7	1,488.7	1,623.4	1,748.1	3.57	306.3
Adana	613.6	777.6	916.2	1,021.8	1,130.7	1,276.5	1,424.4	1,559.9	1,683.8	2.56	174.4
Gaziantep	359.2	478.6	603.4	715.3	853.5	1,040.2	1,258.2	1,441.0	1,594.2	3.80	343.9
Konya	350.6	439.2	513.3	610.5	742.7	880.4	1,021.6	1,143.8	1,250.1	3.23	256.6
Antalya	173.7	261.1	378.2	490.5	603.2	709.9	816.5	909.6	991.4	4.45	470.8
Kayseri	301.9	373.9	425.8	473.9	536.4	627.8	739.7	833.8	914.7	2.81	203.0
Icel	215.1	314.4	422.4	478.1	537.8	592.0	645.4	697.1	746.5	3.16	247.1

Chart 5.199 Population age shift 2000 and 2020, Each Column Represents a Single Age Group

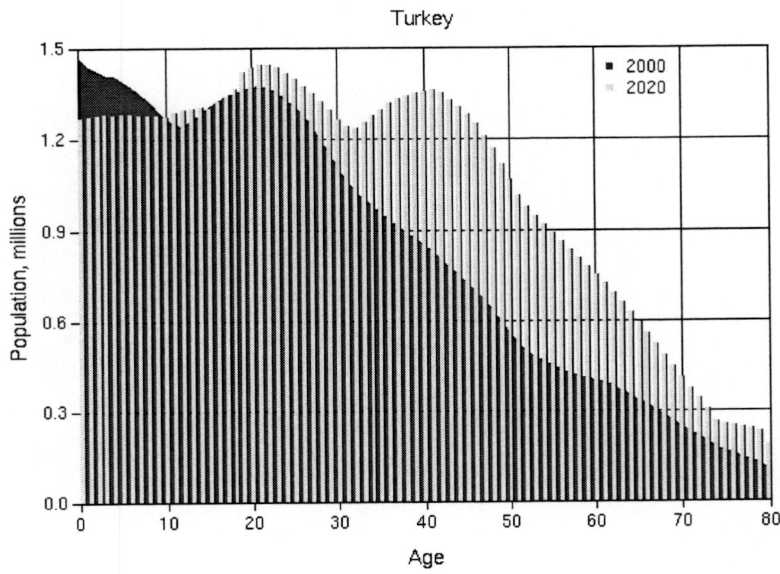

Chart 5.200 Population pyramids, 1980/2000/2010/2020

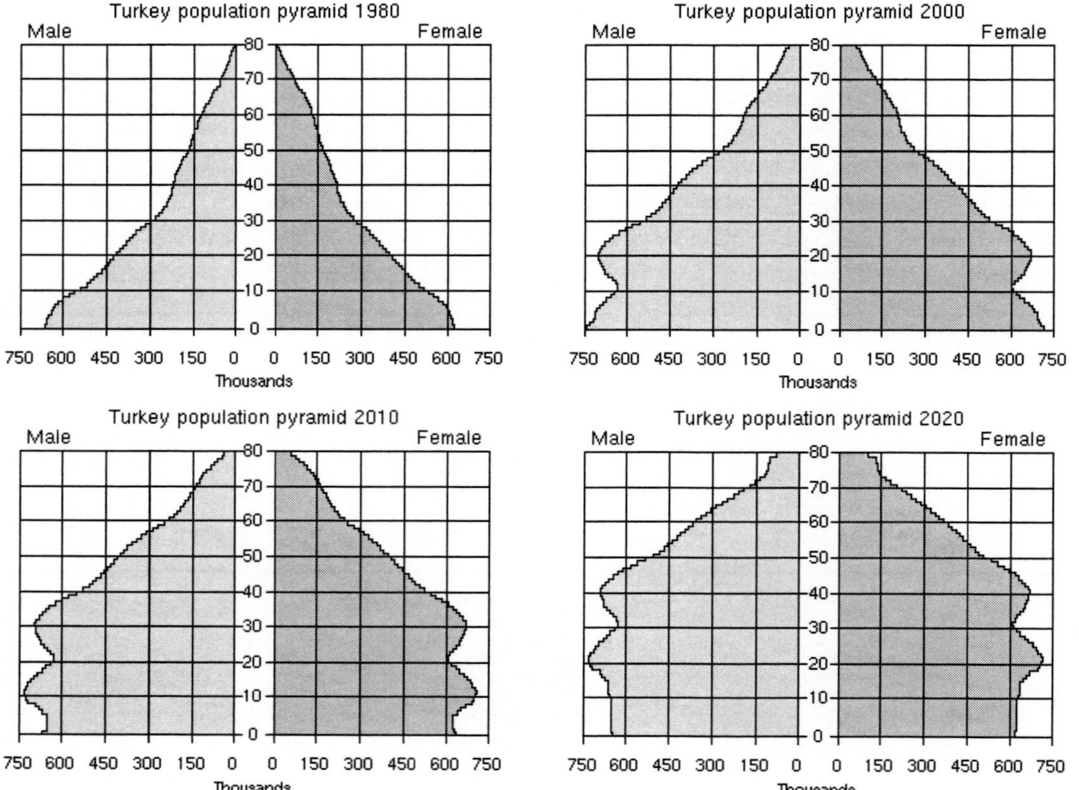

Chart 5.201 Major Cities: 1980, 2000 and 2020

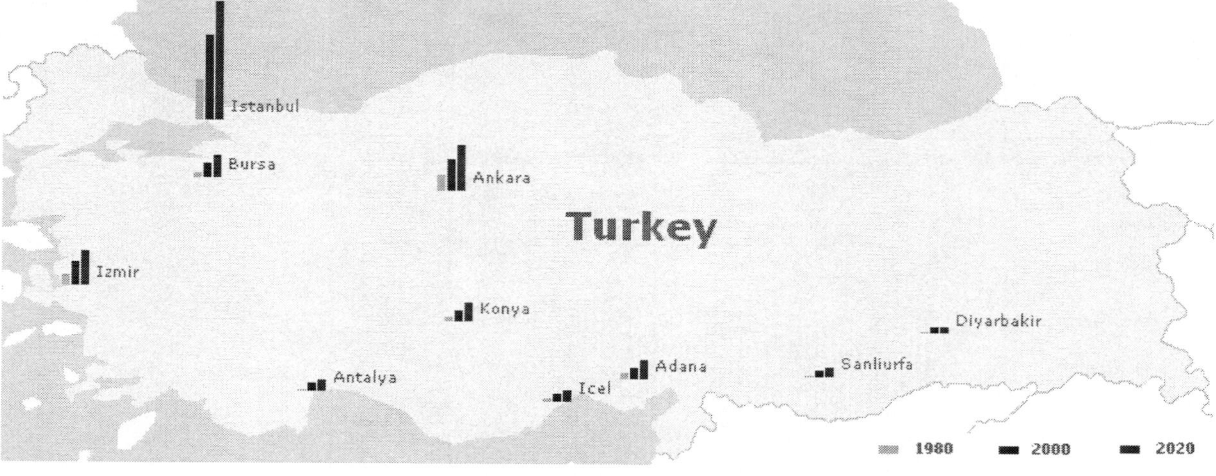

Turkmenistan

Table 5.337 Key population trends

'000

	1980	1985	1990	1995	2000	2005	2010	2015	2020	CAGR	Period growth
Population at January 1st	2,861.0	3,229.5	3,668.0	4,187.4	4,501.7	4,843.2	5,176.5	5,509.0	5,816.4	1.79	103.3
Male	1,406.1	1,587.3	1,808.6	2,067.4	2,222.3	2,389.5	2,550.1	2,711.0	2,858.7	1.79	103.3
Female	1,454.9	1,642.2	1,859.4	2,120.0	2,279.4	2,453.6	2,626.4	2,798.1	2,957.7	1.79	103.3
0-4 yrs	437.2	497.1	580.8	590.9	489.6	515.8	520.2	525.3	509.3	0.38	16.5
5-9 yrs	390.4	425.7	484.3	574.4	574.7	487.6	499.9	513.5	518.2	0.71	32.7
10-14 yrs	355.1	385.1	420.9	489.2	566.2	565.4	483.9	496.0	508.8	0.90	43.3
15-19 yrs	332.4	345.0	374.4	424.9	482.3	560.2	560.9	479.9	492.4	0.99	48.1
20-24 yrs	288.3	331.9	339.4	376.8	417.4	475.2	554.2	555.0	475.1	1.26	64.8
25-29 yrs	213.9	283.8	323.9	340.5	368.9	409.7	468.3	546.7	548.3	2.38	156.3
30-34 yrs	145.6	207.2	275.8	323.7	332.1	360.7	402.4	460.5	538.6	3.33	270.0
35-39 yrs	104.1	137.6	200.9	274.7	314.6	323.5	353.0	394.3	452.3	3.74	334.6
40-44 yrs	132.8	98.5	131.9	198.8	265.3	304.7	314.5	343.9	385.2	2.70	190.0
45-49 yrs	111.6	125.1	94.3	129.4	189.9	254.2	293.4	303.5	333.1	2.77	198.6
50-54 yrs	105.2	105.0	117.7	91.3	121.7	179.4	241.4	279.6	290.3	2.57	176.0
55-59 yrs	72.0	97.4	97.2	111.4	84.0	112.7	167.0	225.9	263.1	3.29	265.5
60-64 yrs	50.2	64.3	86.9	89.5	99.9	75.1	101.7	151.7	206.6	3.60	311.6
65-69 yrs	46.7	42.5	55.0	76.3	76.7	85.5	64.6	88.4	133.0	2.65	184.4
70-74 yrs	34.2	37.0	33.9	45.2	60.9	61.1	68.6	52.3	72.7	1.91	112.7
75-79 yrs	22.4	24.0	26.7	24.6	32.5	43.2	43.8	50.0	38.4	1.35	71.1
80+ yrs	18.9	22.2	23.8	25.7	25.1	29.0	38.7	42.7	51.1	2.52	170.5
Median age of population (years)	18.7	19.4	19.6	20.2	21.6	23.0	24.7	26.6	28.7	1.08	53.7

Table 5.338 Key economic trends

As stated

	1990	1995	2000	2005	2010	2015	2020	CAGR	Period growth
Total GDP (TMM per capita)	112,141,145	55,080,041	62,501,461	122,927,009	189,378,033	265,539,662	364,681,510	4.01	225.2
Disposable income (TMM per capita)	12,113,776	7,159,949	5,217,501	12,855,281	20,704,120	27,807,910	37,737,129	3.86	211.5
Disposable income (TMM per household)	76,477,333	48,279,685	35,161,327	86,233,419	136,877,292	180,017,495	237,034,949	3.84	209.9
Number of households by annual household disposable income ('000)									
Over US$1,000		606	572	707	759	839	920		
Over US$10,000		120	28	319	284	523	746		
Over US$25,000		17	8	75	60	187	431		
Over US$75,000		4	2	10	9	24	80		
Over US$150,000		2	1	4	4	8	18		
Total households	581	621	668	722	783	851	926	1.57	59.4

Note: Per capita data is shown at constant 2010 prices. Household disposable income bands are shown at current prices.

Table 5.339 Young generation

'000

	1980	1985	1990	1995	2000	2005	2010	2015	2020	CAGR	Period growth
Babies under 12 months	91.1	108.1	125.3	112.5	87.3	117.2	100.7	106.8	99.3	0.22	9.02
Infants under 24 months	180.6	211.1	246.1	229.6	180.0	224.8	205.0	212.3	200.4	0.26	10.96
Toddlers aged 1-4	346.1	389.1	455.6	478.4	402.3	398.6	419.5	418.5	410.0	0.42	18.46
Children aged 2-9	647.0	711.7	819.0	935.8	884.3	778.6	815.1	826.5	827.1	0.62	27.84
Female	322.1	352.9	404.8	461.6	436.6	383.8	401.7	407.2	406.8	0.59	26.30
Male	324.9	358.8	414.3	474.2	447.7	394.9	413.5	419.4	420.3	0.65	29.37
Tweenagers aged 10-14	355.1	385.1	420.9	489.2	566.2	565.4	483.9	496.0	508.8	0.90	43.25
Female	175.9	191.7	209.1	242.5	279.8	279.7	239.0	244.8	251.0	0.89	42.75
Male	179.3	193.4	211.9	246.8	286.4	285.7	244.8	251.2	257.7	0.91	43.75
Teenagers aged 13-19	471.5	493.9	537.0	610.7	700.8	793.2	760.1	674.0	694.8	0.97	47.35
Female	233.3	244.0	266.4	303.4	347.3	392.4	376.2	333.1	343.1	0.97	47.07
Male	238.2	249.8	270.6	307.3	353.5	400.8	383.8	340.9	351.7	0.98	47.61
Studying age 18-22	310.3	337.6	350.3	395.4	439.8	511.0	572.0	523.9	472.5	1.06	52.27
Female	153.7	167.9	172.2	196.7	218.7	253.4	283.3	259.6	233.6	1.05	52.05
Male	156.6	169.7	178.0	198.7	221.1	257.6	288.7	264.2	238.8	1.06	52.49
Young adults aged 15-29	834.6	960.8	1,037.8	1,142.2	1,268.6	1,445.1	1,583.4	1,581.5	1,515.8	1.50	81.62
Female	415.9	480.2	518.4	566.5	630.9	718.1	786.1	784.5	751.3	1.49	80.63
Male	418.7	480.6	519.4	575.7	637.7	727.0	797.3	797.1	764.5	1.52	82.59

Table 5.340 Middle-aged generation

'000

	1980	1985	1990	1995	2000	2005	2010	2015	2020	CAGR	Period growth
Middle-aged adults 30-59	671.2	770.8	917.8	1,129.3	1,307.6	1,535.2	1,771.7	2,007.7	2,262.6	3.08	237.1
Female	343.9	393.0	468.0	580.8	671.6	790.2	913.3	1,032.7	1,157.7	3.08	236.7
Male	327.3	377.7	449.9	548.5	636.0	745.0	858.4	975.0	1,104.9	3.09	237.5
Baby boomers aged 40-59	421.6	425.9	441.2	530.9	660.9	851.0	1,016.3	1,152.9	1,271.7	2.80	201.7
Female	219.9	217.4	224.6	273.4	343.8	447.9	533.3	602.6	661.0	2.79	200.6
Male	201.7	208.5	216.6	257.5	317.1	403.1	483.1	550.3	610.7	2.81	202.8

Table 5.341 Elderly population

'000

	1980	1985	1990	1995	2000	2005	2010	2015	2020	CAGR	Period growth
Elderly population (60+)	172.4	190.0	226.3	261.3	295.1	294.0	317.4	385.0	501.7	2.71	191.0
Female	107.6	120.3	138.3	155.2	172.2	171.3	185.4	224.7	292.5	2.53	171.8
Male	64.8	69.8	88.0	106.1	122.9	122.7	131.9	160.3	209.2	2.97	222.9

Table 5.342 Population of biggest cities 1980-2020

'000

	1980	1985	1990	1995	2000	2005	2010	2015	2020	CAGR	Period growth
Asgabat	292.2	343.1	422.8	540.6	629.7	721.4	820.3	933.2	1,053.9	3.26	260.7
Turkmenabat	133.4	147.6	165.3	189.2	206.1	227.5	253.4	285.0	319.7	2.21	139.7
Dasoguz	86.7	98.9	116.5	141.8	160.5	181.2	204.3	231.3	260.6	2.79	200.6
Mari	80.9	87.4	93.7	101.0	105.5	113.6	124.8	139.1	155.3	1.64	91.8
Balkanabat	79.7	84.2	86.6	87.8	87.5	91.3	98.4	108.5	120.3	1.04	51.0
Bayramali	34.6	39.1	45.4	54.3	60.8	68.3	76.7	86.7	97.6	2.63	182.1
Turkmenbasi	52.5	56.3	59.6	63.0	64.9	69.3	75.6	84.0	93.6	1.46	78.3
Serdar	23.9	28.3	35.2	45.5	53.3	61.2	69.8	79.4	89.8	3.36	275.1
Tecen	31.9	35.9	41.5	49.3	55.0	61.6	69.1	78.1	87.8	2.56	175.0
Buzmeyin	27.6	29.9	32.1	34.7	36.3	39.2	43.0	48.0	53.6	1.67	94.0

Chart 5.202 Population age shift 2000 and 2020, Each Column Represents a Single Age Group

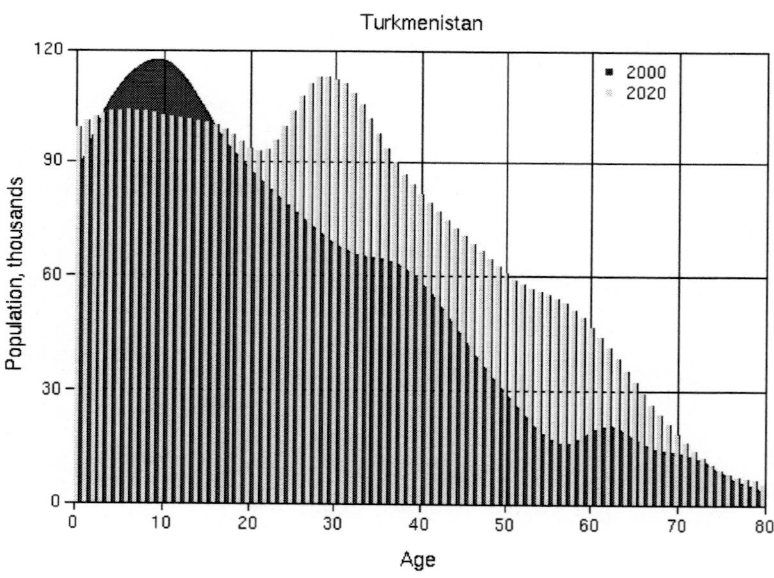

Chart 5.203 Population pyramids, 1980/2000/2010/2020

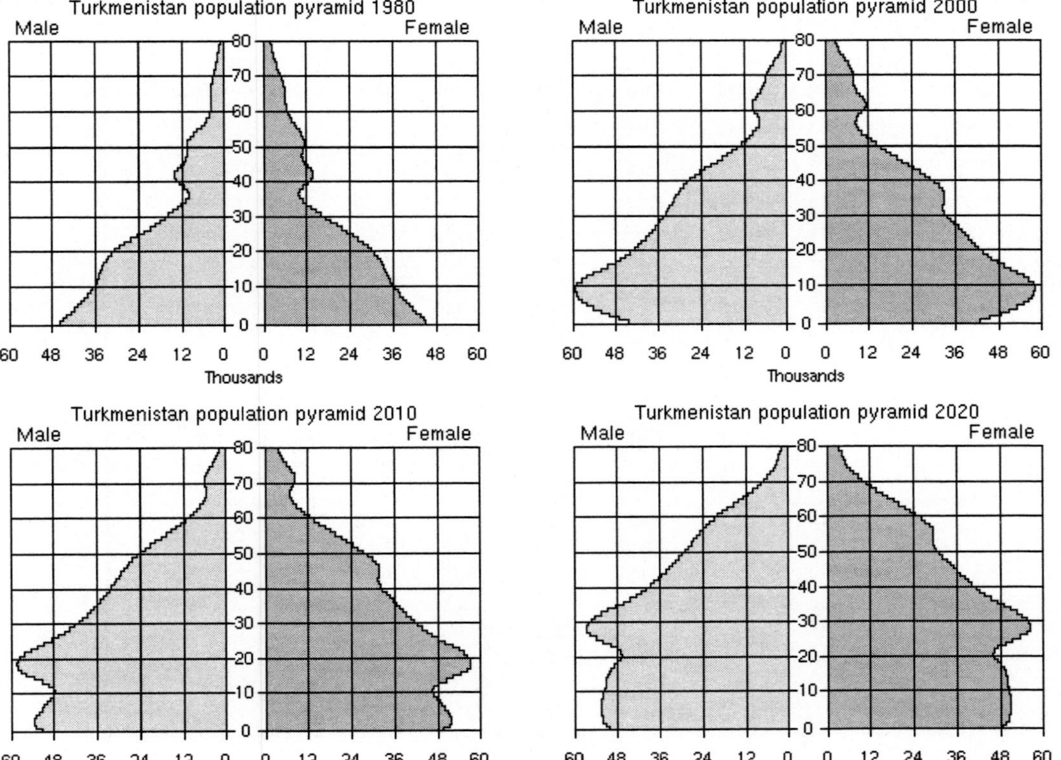

Chart 5.204 Major Cities: 1980, 2000 and 2020

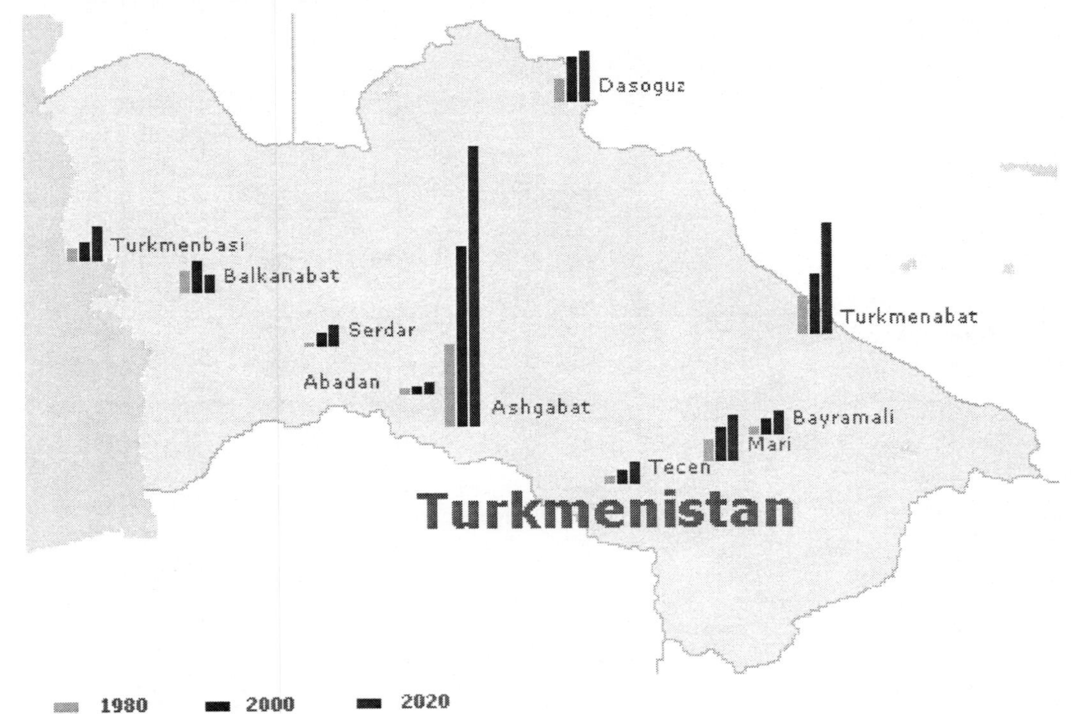

Ukraine

Table 5.343 Key population trends

'000

	1980	1985	1990	1995	2000	2005	2010	2015	2020	CAGR	Period growth
Population at January 1st	49,780.7	50,648.1	51,556.5	51,300.4	49,115.0	47,100.5	45,640.9	44,187.2	42,692.9	-0.38	-14.24
Male	22,720.3	23,252.3	23,826.2	23,792.4	22,754.7	21,754.0	21,011.6	20,283.2	19,567.0	-0.37	-13.88
Female	27,060.4	27,395.8	27,730.3	27,508.1	26,360.3	25,346.5	24,629.3	23,904.0	23,125.9	-0.39	-14.54
0-4 yrs	3,526.9	3,703.3	3,714.1	2,941.6	2,176.5	1,966.0	2,221.8	2,042.6	1,868.2	-1.58	-47.03
5-9 yrs	3,624.0	3,581.5	3,760.1	3,768.5	2,881.7	2,167.7	1,955.5	2,187.9	2,011.1	-1.46	-44.51
10-14 yrs	3,346.5	3,651.2	3,610.0	3,818.6	3,722.8	2,856.1	2,162.4	1,938.6	2,157.6	-1.09	-35.53
15-19 yrs	3,862.1	3,326.9	3,634.0	3,598.5	3,785.5	3,699.6	2,849.8	2,154.1	1,925.3	-1.73	-50.15
20-24 yrs	3,905.3	3,837.5	3,301.2	3,561.1	3,490.3	3,756.1	3,684.0	2,832.0	2,144.3	-1.49	-45.09
25-29 yrs	3,747.6	3,919.6	3,852.9	3,293.6	3,408.9	3,414.7	3,714.0	3,620.6	2,791.1	-0.73	-25.52
30-34 yrs	3,083.8	3,751.2	3,925.1	3,861.1	3,191.8	3,314.2	3,356.2	3,627.8	3,541.9	0.35	14.86
35-39 yrs	2,955.0	3,055.3	3,726.2	3,900.6	3,742.3	3,108.9	3,241.8	3,267.9	3,539.4	0.45	19.77
40-44 yrs	4,142.7	2,907.7	3,009.0	3,671.7	3,749.3	3,622.8	3,018.7	3,138.7	3,176.7	-0.66	-23.32
45-49 yrs	3,026.5	4,093.7	2,854.7	2,932.6	3,492.3	3,586.3	3,481.9	2,894.8	3,031.8	0.00	0.17
50-54 yrs	3,693.8	2,910.9	3,982.5	2,743.2	2,751.4	3,285.8	3,399.8	3,306.6	2,769.7	-0.72	-25.02
55-59 yrs	2,804.7	3,521.5	2,736.0	3,753.0	2,532.5	2,542.9	3,056.7	3,187.8	3,143.8	0.29	12.09
60-64 yrs	1,992.2	2,557.2	3,276.2	2,495.2	3,370.8	2,272.2	2,323.3	2,844.5	3,020.3	1.05	51.60
65-69 yrs	2,156.7	1,638.4	2,203.4	2,850.8	2,143.6	2,912.5	1,944.8	2,047.1	2,633.6	0.50	22.11
70-74 yrs	1,605.0	1,836.1	1,314.9	1,803.9	2,287.1	1,730.5	2,455.9	1,597.6	1,795.6	0.28	11.87
75-79 yrs	1,182.4	1,225.6	1,455.7	957.6	1,308.7	1,666.2	1,262.8	2,056.0	1,346.4	0.33	13.87
80+ yrs	1,125.3	1,130.5	1,200.5	1,348.7	1,079.4	1,197.9	1,511.4	1,442.7	1,796.1	1.18	59.61
Median age of population (years)	34.5	34.4	35.0	36.0	37.7	38.8	39.4	40.7	42.1	0.50	22.20

Table 5.344 Key economic trends

As stated

	1990	1995	2000	2005	2010	2015	2020	CAGR	Period growth
Total GDP (UAH per capita)	31,686.1	15,214.7	14,361.4	21,751.8	22,954.6	30,023.6	41,092.5	0.87	29.7
Disposable income (UAH per capita)		5,146.3	6,230.8	10,520.2	13,748.7	18,777.0	26,449.4		
Disposable income (UAH per household)		16,736.1	17,305.0	25,188.1	31,362.8	42,261.0	59,312.2		
Number of households by annual household disposable income ('000)									
Over US$1,000		7,159.3	8,150.4	17,199.0	19,178.4	19,477.0	19,009.4		
Over US$10,000		129.5	147.2	461.5	1,069.3	5,086.5	11,711.5		
Over US$25,000		40.5	45.9	144.5	266.0	769.4	2,216.2		
Over US$75,000		10.0	11.4	35.9	66.4	156.7	318.4		
Over US$150,000		4.2	4.7	14.9	27.7	65.3	132.5		
Total households	14,559.0	15,774.7	17,684.2	19,672.2	20,007.8	19,632.8	19,038.2	0.90	30.8

Note: Per capita data is shown at constant 2010 prices. Household disposable income bands are shown at current prices.

Table 5.345 Young generation

'000

	1980	1985	1990	1995	2000	2005	2010	2015	2020	CAGR	Period growth
Babies under 12 months	701.1	771.3	688.1	515.9	385.0	423.9	445.6	387.8	369.8	-1.59	-47.25
Infants under 24 months	1,400.3	1,556.2	1,430.4	1,067.7	798.1	828.1	895.8	784.1	742.8	-1.57	-46.96
Toddlers aged 1-4	2,825.8	2,931.9	3,026.0	2,425.7	1,791.5	1,542.1	1,776.2	1,654.7	1,498.4	-1.57	-46.97
Children aged 2-9	5,750.6	5,728.5	6,043.8	5,642.4	4,260.1	3,305.6	3,281.5	3,446.3	3,136.5	-1.50	-45.46
Female	2,803.1	2,814.3	2,965.9	2,757.4	2,075.1	1,609.3	1,595.1	1,678.9	1,527.1	-1.51	-45.52
Male	2,947.5	2,914.2	3,077.9	2,885.0	2,185.0	1,696.3	1,686.4	1,767.5	1,609.4	-1.50	-45.40
Tweenagers aged 10-14	3,346.5	3,651.2	3,610.0	3,818.6	3,722.8	2,856.1	2,162.4	1,938.6	2,157.6	-1.09	-35.53
Female	1,626.8	1,776.9	1,777.4	1,873.2	1,819.5	1,392.0	1,054.9	942.7	1,053.9	-1.08	-35.22
Male	1,719.7	1,874.4	1,832.6	1,945.4	1,903.3	1,464.1	1,107.5	995.9	1,103.7	-1.10	-35.82
Teenagers aged 13-19	5,215.5	4,759.0	5,099.5	5,065.9	5,351.3	4,955.6	3,790.3	2,899.4	2,775.1	-1.56	-46.79
Female	2,562.3	2,330.5	2,507.4	2,502.3	2,621.3	2,419.8	1,848.1	1,413.5	1,351.7	-1.59	-47.25
Male	2,653.2	2,428.5	2,592.1	2,563.6	2,730.0	2,535.8	1,942.3	1,485.9	1,423.4	-1.54	-46.35
Studying age 18-22	4,001.1	3,555.2	3,375.9	3,621.7	3,527.1	3,881.0	3,386.9	2,527.2	1,955.8	-1.77	-51.12
Female	1,986.0	1,767.3	1,671.3	1,793.7	1,738.3	1,898.1	1,652.9	1,233.1	952.9	-1.82	-52.02
Male	2,015.1	1,787.8	1,704.6	1,828.0	1,788.8	1,982.9	1,733.9	1,294.2	1,002.8	-1.73	-50.23
Young adults aged 15-29	11,515.0	11,084.0	10,788.1	10,453.2	10,684.7	10,870.4	10,247.8	8,606.7	6,860.7	-1.29	-40.42
Female	5,720.1	5,514.8	5,361.9	5,191.3	5,281.3	5,349.5	5,019.8	4,212.1	3,351.6	-1.33	-41.41
Male	5,794.8	5,569.2	5,426.2	5,261.9	5,403.5	5,520.9	5,228.0	4,394.6	3,509.1	-1.25	-39.44

Table 5.346 Middle-aged generation

'000

	1980	1985	1990	1995	2000	2005	2010	2015	2020	CAGR	Period growth
Middle-aged adults 30-59	19,707	20,240	20,233	20,862	19,460	19,461	19,555	19,424	19,203	-0.06	-2.55
Female	10,662	10,757	10,628	10,990	10,271	10,292	10,355	10,223	10,011	-0.16	-6.11
Male	9,045	9,484	9,606	9,872	9,189	9,169	9,200	9,201	9,192	0.04	1.63
Baby boomers aged 40-59	13,668	13,434	12,582	13,101	12,526	13,038	12,957	12,528	12,122	-0.30	-11.31
Female	7,574	7,290	6,733	7,031	6,735	7,029	7,019	6,768	6,488	-0.39	-14.33
Male	6,094	6,144	5,850	6,069	5,791	6,009	5,938	5,760	5,633	-0.20	-7.55

Table 5.347 Elderly population

'000

	1980	1985	1990	1995	2000	2005	2010	2015	2020	CAGR	Period growth
Elderly population (60+)	8,062	8,388	9,451	9,456	10,190	9,779	9,498	9,988	10,592	0.68	31.4
Female	5,563	5,770	6,300	6,176	6,526	6,301	6,169	6,467	6,821	0.51	22.6
Male	2,499	2,618	3,151	3,280	3,664	3,479	3,329	3,521	3,771	1.03	50.9

Table 5.348 Population of biggest cities 1980-2020

'000

	1980	1985	1990	1995	2000	2005	2010	2015	2020	CAGR	Period growth
Kiev	2,195.3	2,429.8	2,613.8	2,668.8	2,616.6	2,666.7	2,776.1	2,821.6	2,831.2	0.64	28.97
Kharkov	1,465.1	1,555.0	1,616.0	1,598.2	1,493.4	1,409.0	1,357.5	1,319.5	1,291.0	-0.32	-11.88
Dnepropetrovsk	1,079.6	1,137.5	1,180.5	1,158.1	1,080.1	1,030.3	1,005.8	985.3	968.5	-0.27	-10.30
Odessa	1,055.6	1,091.7	1,117.6	1,105.3	1,042.4	996.5	970.4	949.2	932.1	-0.31	-11.69
Donetsk	1,032.1	1,078.5	1,111.6	1,096.6	1,030.2	981.7	954.3	932.5	915.1	-0.30	-11.34
Zaporizhzhya	793.6	849.2	887.2	877.5	826.2	788.6	767.3	750.1	736.4	-0.19	-7.21
L'viv	682.3	749.2	793.7	786.4	742.2	709.9	691.5	676.5	664.4	-0.07	-2.62
Kryvyy Rih	658.0	690.9	715.8	713.1	676.8	650.1	634.8	621.9	611.3	-0.18	-7.10
Mykolayiv	446.7	477.4	508.1	525.7	517.1	508.9	504.9	499.2	493.3	0.25	10.45
Mariupol' (Zdanov)	504.9	512.0	521.2	521.6	497.5	480.8	471.4	462.9	455.6	-0.26	-9.77

Chart 5.205 Population age shift 2000 and 2020, Each Column Represents a Single Age Group

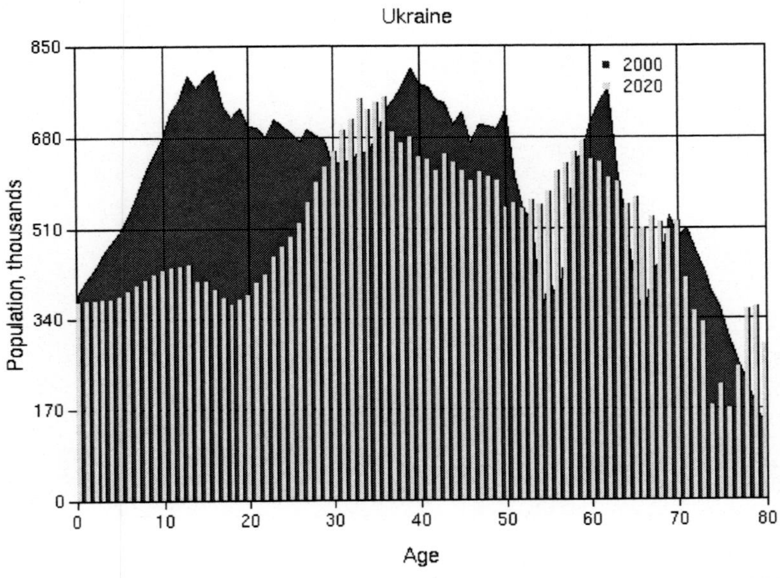

Chart 5.206 Population pyramids, 1980/2000/2010/2020

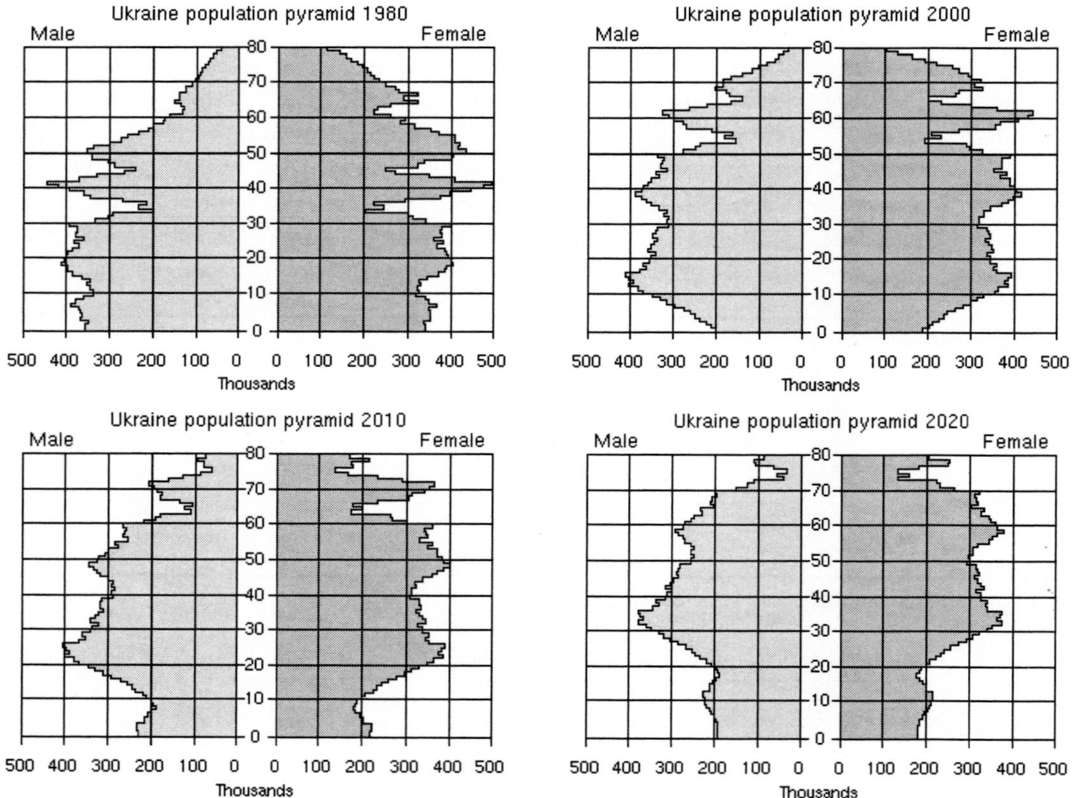

Chart 5.207 Major Cities: 1980, 2000 and 2020

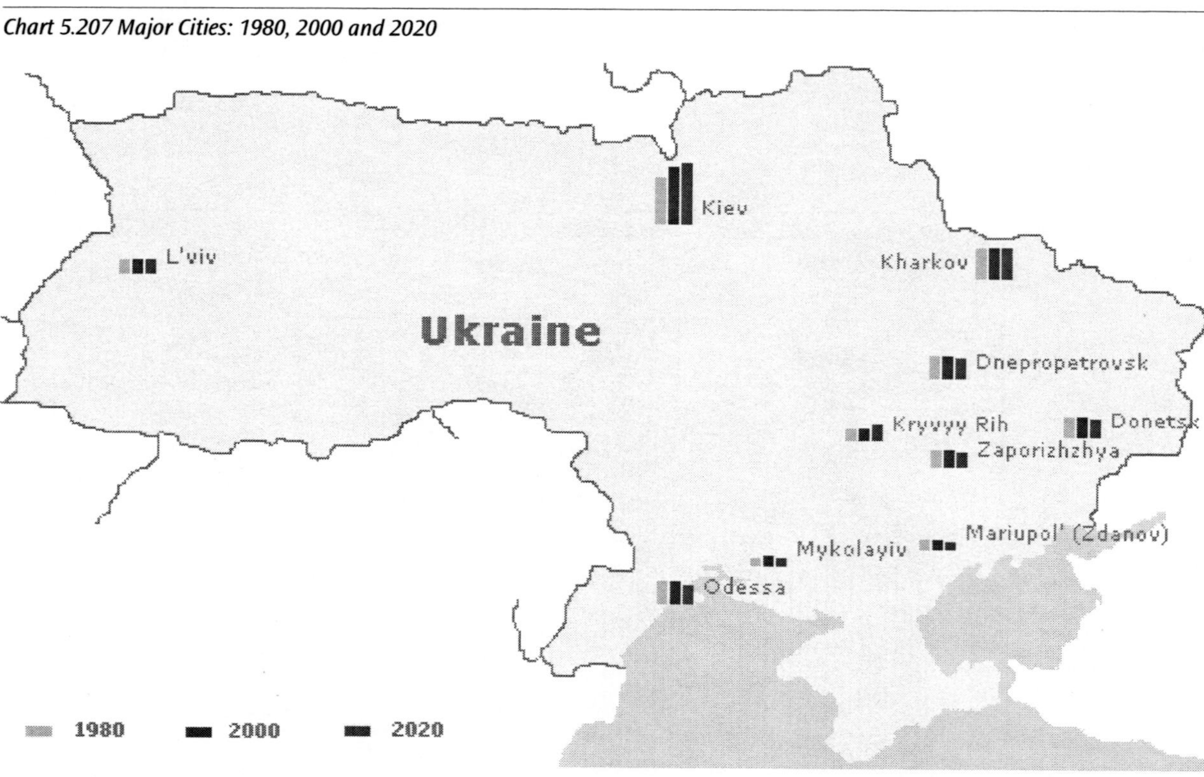

United Arab Emirates

Table 5.349 Key population trends

'000

	1980	1985	1990	1995	2000	2005	2010	2015	2020	CAGR	Period growth
Population at January 1st	1,042.10	1,379.30	1,839.14	2,411.04	3,236.21	4,104.70	4,725.34	5,213.32	5,681.42	4.33	445.2
Male	719.68	895.12	1,203.37	1,593.43	2,184.47	2,792.78	3,169.06	3,465.37	3,764.72	4.22	423.1
Female	322.42	484.19	635.77	817.61	1,051.74	1,311.92	1,556.28	1,747.95	1,916.70	4.56	494.5
0-4 yrs	136.75	177.63	234.13	242.14	255.28	301.91	308.95	325.10	312.27	2.09	128.4
5-9 yrs	97.61	129.06	179.43	234.98	254.61	263.48	315.66	319.45	331.26	3.10	239.4
10-14 yrs	63.53	103.45	137.69	193.48	257.28	244.74	277.77	323.71	327.05	4.18	414.8
15-19 yrs	58.97	76.91	129.83	167.69	235.56	255.00	244.02	322.03	368.60	4.69	525.0
20-24 yrs	125.40	125.47	145.31	221.14	309.17	413.44	330.37	368.87	444.22	3.21	254.3
25-29 yrs	178.32	201.47	207.02	303.52	438.84	635.96	615.83	499.86	525.52	2.74	194.7
30-34 yrs	137.98	185.94	247.21	306.58	435.46	639.68	823.37	726.45	606.23	3.77	339.4
35-39 yrs	92.61	139.49	205.80	269.51	373.21	484.15	728.12	815.21	724.38	5.28	682.2
40-44 yrs	59.86	95.63	147.12	204.96	295.52	341.20	441.30	659.43	749.60	6.52	1,152.2
45-49 yrs	36.27	61.60	90.37	123.64	179.19	232.43	243.20	374.95	593.55	7.24	1,536.4
50-54 yrs	22.47	34.39	50.83	63.89	97.87	143.20	187.86	184.42	316.74	6.84	1,309.8
55-59 yrs	10.92	17.77	26.60	33.28	44.00	74.36	111.38	140.59	144.55	6.67	1,224.0
60-64 yrs	8.01	11.06	14.39	18.22	24.78	30.91	48.95	81.62	114.78	6.88	1,332.2
65-69 yrs	5.58	7.76	9.66	11.03	14.82	18.70	19.61	36.13	66.32	6.38	1,088.5
70-74 yrs	4.02	5.67	6.63	8.20	9.06	11.64	13.44	16.04	30.86	5.23	668.4
75-79 yrs	1.66	2.57	4.24	5.10	6.54	7.07	7.00	10.76	13.27	5.34	701.2
80+ yrs	2.15	3.43	2.87	3.68	5.00	6.82	8.51	8.71	12.25	4.44	469.3
Median age of population (years)	26.13	27.05	27.44	27.50	28.55	29.54	31.70	33.23	34.43	0.69	31.8

Table 5.350 Key economic trends

As stated

	1990	1995	2000	2005	2010	2015	2020	CAGR	Period growth
Total GDP (AED per capita)	182,250.0	161,268.5	158,595.8	173,316.5	192,204.9	217,906.5	255,947.9	1.14	40.4
Disposable income (AED per capita)	73,283.1	66,824.6	70,100.6	111,827.4	122,890.0	141,965.9	167,591.3	2.80	128.7
Disposable income (AED per household)	400,290.2	389,945.4	425,546.5	694,770.4	775,338.3	902,378.3	1,073,516.4	3.34	168.2
Number of households by annual household disposable income ('000)									
Over US$1,000	336.7	413.1	533.0	660.7	748.9	820.2	886.9	3.28	163.5
Over US$10,000	324.2	403.6	522.7	656.6	746.0	818.2	885.9	3.41	173.2
Over US$25,000	240.9	333.5	457.7	626.6	725.9	805.3	878.7	4.41	264.7
Over US$75,000	41.2	79.3	155.4	373.0	536.9	673.0	799.4	10.39	1,839.7
Over US$150,000	10.0	15.6	29.9	118.4	240.0	390.6	579.8	14.49	5,701.3
Total households	336.7	413.2	533.1	660.7	749.0	820.2	887.0	3.28	163.4

Note: Per capita data is shown at constant 2010 prices. Household disposable income bands are shown at current prices.

Table 5.351 Young generation

'000

	1980	1985	1990	1995	2000	2005	2010	2015	2020	CAGR	Period growth
Babies under 12 months	30.6	41.1	50.6	46.0	52.8	63.9	57.4	66.9	57.1	1.57	86.5
Infants under 24 months	59.4	79.3	99.7	93.7	104.3	126.2	117.8	132.5	117.8	1.73	98.5
Toddlers aged 1-4	106.1	136.5	183.5	196.2	202.5	238.0	251.5	258.2	255.2	2.22	140.4
Children aged 2-9	175.0	227.4	313.8	383.4	405.6	439.2	506.8	512.1	525.7	2.79	200.4
Female	84.8	111.2	152.6	187.9	198.2	213.4	247.0	252.3	259.3	2.83	205.6
Male	90.1	116.2	161.3	195.5	207.5	225.8	259.8	259.8	266.4	2.75	195.6
Tweenagers aged 10-14	63.5	103.4	137.7	193.5	257.3	244.7	277.8	323.7	327.1	4.18	414.8
Female	29.8	49.6	66.7	93.5	125.0	118.5	134.1	158.5	163.2	4.34	447.3
Male	33.7	53.8	71.0	100.0	132.3	126.2	143.7	165.2	163.8	4.03	386.0
Teenagers aged 13-19	81.0	114.5	182.3	239.2	335.7	351.0	349.0	451.3	501.2	4.66	519.1
Female	36.1	55.1	81.0	112.1	158.4	164.5	166.3	201.2	229.2	4.73	535.2
Male	44.9	59.4	101.3	127.1	177.2	186.5	182.6	250.1	272.0	4.61	506.1
Studying age 18-22	94.0	96.8	133.9	191.4	266.2	331.2	271.3	342.4	411.9	3.76	338.1
Female	31.1	41.9	49.9	75.4	108.6	134.4	120.5	130.4	158.9	4.16	411.1
Male	62.9	54.9	83.9	116.0	157.6	196.8	150.7	212.0	253.0	3.54	302.0
Young adults aged 15-29	362.7	403.8	482.2	692.3	983.6	1,304.4	1,190.2	1,190.8	1,338.3	3.32	269.0
Female	98.1	145.4	167.4	236.6	338.0	451.3	444.2	419.7	464.2	3.96	373.0
Male	264.5	258.5	314.7	455.8	645.5	853.1	746.1	771.0	874.1	3.03	230.4

Table 5.352 Middle-aged generation

'000

	1980	1985	1990	1995	2000	2005	2010	2015	2020	CAGR	Period growth
Middle-aged adults 30-59	360.1	534.8	767.9	1,001.9	1,425.3	1,915.0	2,535.2	2,901.0	3,135.0	5.56	770.6
Female	71.8	126.0	183.6	235.3	315.9	440.3	639.7	804.9	897.1	6.52	1,149.0
Male	288.3	408.8	584.4	766.6	1,109.4	1,474.8	1,895.5	2,096.1	2,237.9	5.26	676.3
Baby boomers aged 40-59	129.5	209.4	314.9	425.8	616.6	791.2	983.7	1,359.4	1,804.4	6.81	1,293.2
Female	28.7	47.6	69.1	89.0	122.5	177.2	251.7	373.6	524.8	7.53	1,727.9
Male	100.8	161.8	245.8	336.8	494.1	614.0	732.1	985.7	1,279.7	6.56	1,169.4

Table 5.353 Elderly population

'000

	1980	1985	1990	1995	2000	2005	2010	2015	2020	CAGR	Period growth
Elderly population (60+)	21.42	30.49	37.79	46.23	60.20	75.15	97.51	153.26	237.48	6.20	1,008.7
Female	9.04	13.65	16.27	18.71	23.87	26.84	33.92	47.59	74.81	5.43	727.7
Male	12.38	16.85	21.53	27.53	36.33	48.31	63.59	105.67	162.66	6.65	1,213.9

Table 5.354 Population of biggest cities 1980-2020

'000

	1980	1985	1990	1995	2000	2005	2010	2015	2020	CAGR	Period growth
Dubai	263.45	354.18	484.96	669.18	961.60	1,305.06	1,591.84	1,834.38	2,058.10	5.27	681.2
Ash-Shariqa	125.19	173.79	234.75	320.10	476.05	685.00	875.23	1,039.65	1,190.41	5.79	850.9
Abu Dhabi	243.26	283.36	332.90	398.70	511.39	630.00	708.52	769.71	827.52	3.11	240.2
Al-Ayn	102.33	133.02	174.65	225.97	293.59	350.00	379.21	399.69	419.68	3.59	310.1
Ajman	33.65	49.11	76.56	114.40	159.78	197.47	220.57	238.28	255.09	5.19	658.0
Ras al-Khaymah	41.44	54.43	66.46	77.55	95.15	111.26	118.85	123.79	128.74	2.87	210.7
Al-Fujayrah	12.66	17.93	24.33	33.18	49.58	71.87	92.34	110.06	126.30	5.92	897.7
Khawr Fakkan	10.79	15.33	18.74	22.59	32.21	45.00	56.21	65.81	74.63	4.95	591.7
Umm al-Qaywayn	9.65	17.93	23.19	25.05	28.83	32.80	34.25	34.98	35.79	3.33	270.8

Chart 5.208 Population age shift 2000 and 2020, Each Column Represents a Single Age Group

Chart 5.209 Population pyramids, 1980/2000/2010/2020

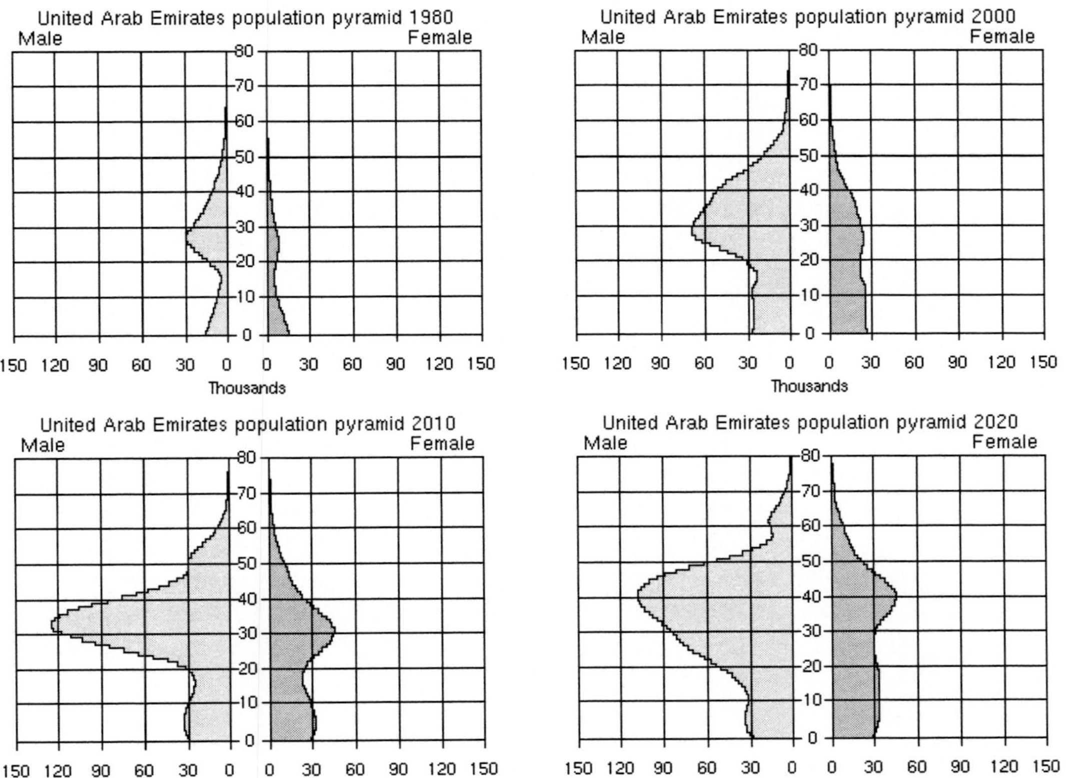

Chart 5.210 Major Cities: 1980, 2000 and 2020

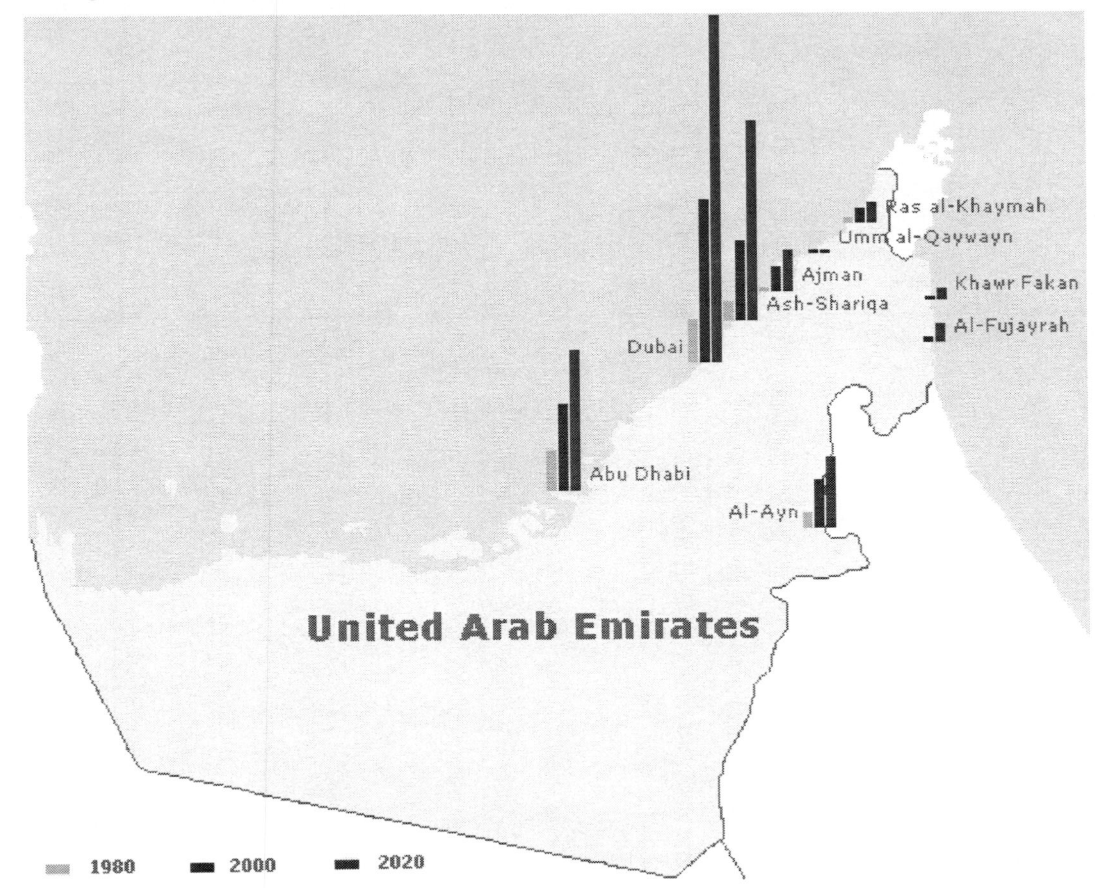

United Kingdom

Table 5.355 Key population trends

'000

	1980	1985	1990	1995	2000	2005	2010	2015	2020	CAGR	Period growth
Population at January 1st	56,284.9	56,481.6	57,157.0	57,943.5	58,785.2	60,059.9	61,965.7	63,717.3	65,730.5	0.39	16.78
Male	27,392.2	27,454.7	27,773.7	28,156.0	28,634.5	29,395.0	30,440.2	31,411.9	32,480.1	0.43	18.57
Female	28,892.7	29,026.9	29,383.3	29,787.5	30,150.8	30,664.9	31,525.6	32,305.4	33,250.3	0.35	15.08
0-4 yrs	3,389.0	3,597.7	3,808.9	3,831.2	3,576.0	3,414.6	3,833.7	3,965.3	4,133.8	0.50	21.98
5-9 yrs	3,978.5	3,372.4	3,624.7	3,819.3	3,830.0	3,586.5	3,414.6	3,820.6	3,965.4	-0.01	-0.33
10-14 yrs	4,580.5	3,954.7	3,399.4	3,641.1	3,838.2	3,846.9	3,582.7	3,402.5	3,819.8	-0.45	-16.61
15-19 yrs	4,643.9	4,579.7	3,974.2	3,405.3	3,629.1	3,958.4	3,927.4	3,634.2	3,463.3	-0.73	-25.42
20-24 yrs	4,109.0	4,663.1	4,567.8	4,001.7	3,485.4	3,874.2	4,337.1	4,311.8	4,014.1	-0.06	-2.31
25-29 yrs	3,852.7	4,033.7	4,613.6	4,562.6	4,104.7	3,710.0	4,269.0	4,716.2	4,685.0	0.49	21.60
30-34 yrs	4,157.9	3,781.3	4,023.6	4,568.1	4,615.7	4,217.2	3,858.9	4,411.2	4,859.7	0.39	16.88
35-39 yrs	3,417.6	4,115.5	3,778.5	4,022.2	4,553.8	4,665.5	4,250.3	3,869.6	4,428.2	0.65	29.57
40-44 yrs	3,212.1	3,373.6	4,094.3	3,768.3	4,022.3	4,550.0	4,657.2	4,202.6	3,836.6	0.45	19.44
45-49 yrs	3,131.2	3,156.7	3,331.3	4,056.2	3,745.5	3,987.1	4,494.9	4,577.0	4,141.6	0.70	32.27
50-54 yrs	3,221.2	3,055.8	3,091.0	3,280.3	3,999.8	3,678.6	3,915.3	4,392.6	4,490.2	0.83	39.39
55-59 yrs	3,438.6	3,094.9	2,950.4	3,008.1	3,203.4	3,890.0	3,575.8	3,796.8	4,282.2	0.55	24.53
60-64 yrs	2,782.3	3,214.8	2,915.5	2,804.2	2,888.7	3,063.6	3,722.4	3,426.7	3,661.4	0.69	31.60
65-69 yrs	2,849.4	2,497.6	2,913.2	2,665.7	2,605.3	2,702.1	2,865.2	3,496.8	3,241.8	0.32	13.77
70-74 yrs	2,369.3	2,405.8	2,134.2	2,515.8	2,338.5	2,338.1	2,438.5	2,599.8	3,207.8	0.76	35.39
75-79 yrs	1,657.5	1,812.8	1,878.1	1,697.9	2,029.8	1,941.5	1,974.7	2,074.7	2,250.7	0.77	35.79
80+ yrs	1,494.2	1,771.6	2,058.3	2,295.6	2,319.1	2,635.7	2,848.0	3,018.8	3,248.9	1.96	117.44
Median age of population (years)	34.2	35.3	35.8	36.4	37.5	38.7	39.5	39.6	39.4	0.35	15.11

Table 5.356 Key economic trends

As stated

	1990	1995	2000	2005	2010	2015	2020	CAGR	Period growth
Total GDP (£ per capita)	16,763.8	17,945.3	20,942.8	23,189.3	23,076.0	25,759.2	28,819.8	1.82	71.9
Disposable income (£ per capita)	10,041.5	11,354.5	13,306.8	15,216.8	15,091.1	16,610.2	18,557.6	2.07	84.8
Disposable income (£ per household)	24,731.7	27,095.2	31,049.9	34,821.5	34,122.0	37,108.2	41,197.4	1.72	66.6
Number of households by annual household disposable income ('000)									
Over US$1,000	23,129.9	24,226.4	25,139.4	26,215.2	27,357.9	28,484.9	29,582.1	0.82	27.9
Over US$10,000	19,523.4	21,366.6	22,689.6	24,767.0	25,267.6	26,866.8	28,358.2	1.25	45.3
Over US$25,000	10,826.6	13,447.4	15,804.9	20,122.5	19,133.0	21,799.7	24,315.6	2.73	124.6
Over US$75,000	1,156.0	1,787.6	2,948.1	6,432.1	4,781.3	7,052.9	10,065.3	7.48	770.7
Over US$150,000	377.3	482.2	621.9	1,102.2	841.6	1,219.2	2,148.4	5.97	469.3
Total households	23,206.6	24,281.8	25,193.1	26,245.9	27,405.6	28,520.9	29,608.7	0.82	27.6

Note: Per capita data is shown at constant 2010 prices. Household disposable income bands are shown at current prices.

Table 5.357 Young generation

'000

	1980	1985	1990	1995	2000	2005	2010	2015	2020	CAGR	Period growth
Babies under 12 months	721.9	727.0	771.4	743.5	693.4	717.9	802.4	807.0	836.9	0.37	15.93
Infants under 24 months	1,401.7	1,439.9	1,543.6	1,497.5	1,400.8	1,409.3	1,596.2	1,606.4	1,669.9	0.44	19.13
Toddlers aged 1-4	2,667.1	2,870.6	3,037.6	3,087.7	2,882.5	2,696.7	3,031.3	3,158.4	3,297.0	0.53	23.62
Children aged 2-9	5,965.8	5,530.2	5,890.1	6,152.9	6,005.2	5,591.8	5,652.1	6,179.5	6,429.4	0.19	7.77
Female	2,900.8	2,694.6	2,877.1	3,007.3	2,928.2	2,728.3	2,758.6	3,003.3	3,118.2	0.18	7.49
Male	3,065.0	2,835.6	3,012.9	3,145.6	3,076.9	2,863.5	2,893.5	3,176.2	3,311.1	0.19	8.03
Tweenagers aged 10-14	4,580.5	3,954.7	3,399.4	3,641.1	3,838.2	3,846.9	3,582.7	3,402.5	3,819.8	-0.45	-16.61
Female	2,229.2	1,927.2	1,657.2	1,781.4	1,873.2	1,871.4	1,749.5	1,654.8	1,850.8	-0.46	-16.98
Male	2,351.3	2,027.5	1,742.1	1,859.7	1,965.0	1,975.5	1,833.2	1,747.7	1,969.0	-0.44	-16.26
Teenagers aged 13-19	6,528.0	6,287.6	5,320.0	4,869.6	5,143.5	5,537.9	5,389.1	4,966.2	4,924.8	-0.70	-24.56
Female	3,187.6	3,075.7	2,599.9	2,393.7	2,523.6	2,687.9	2,617.3	2,409.3	2,379.6	-0.73	-25.35
Male	3,340.3	3,211.9	2,720.1	2,475.9	2,619.9	2,850.0	2,771.7	2,556.9	2,545.2	-0.68	-23.80
Studying age 18-22	4,332.4	4,752.0	4,398.4	3,628.8	3,528.2	3,897.9	4,216.9	3,988.4	3,703.2	-0.39	-14.52
Female	2,130.4	2,341.1	2,169.9	1,796.0	1,754.2	1,902.9	2,059.6	1,946.9	1,805.6	-0.41	-15.25
Male	2,202.0	2,410.9	2,228.5	1,832.7	1,774.0	1,995.0	2,157.3	2,041.5	1,897.6	-0.37	-13.82
Young adults aged 15-29	12,605.5	13,276.5	13,155.6	11,969.6	11,219.3	11,542.6	12,533.5	12,662.1	12,162.4	-0.09	-3.52
Female	6,195.2	6,550.0	6,514.1	5,952.5	5,587.2	5,686.4	6,132.0	6,222.2	5,976.2	-0.09	-3.54
Male	6,410.3	6,726.5	6,641.4	6,017.2	5,632.1	5,856.2	6,401.5	6,439.9	6,186.3	-0.09	-3.50

Table 5.358 Middle-aged generation

'000

	1980	1985	1990	1995	2000	2005	2010	2015	2020	CAGR	Period growth
Middle-aged adults 30-59	20,579	20,578	21,269	22,703	24,140	24,988	24,752	25,250	26,038	0.59	26.5
Female	10,313	10,301	10,662	11,421	12,174	12,623	12,524	12,739	13,108	0.60	27.1
Male	10,265	10,277	10,607	11,282	11,967	12,365	12,228	12,511	12,930	0.58	26.0
Baby boomers aged 40-59	13,003	12,681	13,467	14,113	14,971	16,106	16,643	16,969	16,750	0.64	28.8
Female	6,561	6,368	6,756	7,095	7,547	8,146	8,455	8,660	8,557	0.67	30.4
Male	6,442	6,313	6,711	7,018	7,424	7,960	8,188	8,309	8,194	0.60	27.2

Table 5.359 Elderly population

'000

	1980	1985	1990	1995	2000	2005	2010	2015	2020	CAGR	Period growth
Elderly population (60+)	11,153	11,703	11,899	11,979	12,181	12,681	13,849	14,617	15,611	0.84	40.0
Female	6,571	6,852	6,918	6,895	6,905	7,069	7,584	7,905	8,386	0.61	27.6
Male	4,581	4,851	4,981	5,084	5,276	5,612	6,265	6,712	7,224	1.15	57.7

Table 5.360 Population of biggest cities 1980-2020

'000

	1980	1985	1990	1995	2000	2005	2010	2015	2020	CAGR	Period growth
London	6,319.7	6,429.3	6,595.3	6,817.5	7,100.5	7,517.7	7,929.1	8,271.5	8,583.7	0.77	35.82
Birmingham	954.0	959.4	964.8	966.2	969.4	983.8	1,008.9	1,035.6	1,064.8	0.28	11.61
Glasgow	671.4	668.6	660.7	643.1	630.4	632.0	643.4	657.6	674.4	0.01	0.45
Liverpool	484.7	484.7	482.5	475.4	469.0	477.6	492.4	507.1	522.3	0.19	7.77
Leeds	410.0	415.1	422.4	430.9	440.8	454.1	469.7	484.6	499.6	0.50	21.86
Edinburgh	381.2	387.9	398.0	411.5	426.6	443.9	461.7	477.9	493.7	0.65	29.50
Sheffield	423.1	426.5	430.6	434.1	438.6	447.5	460.4	473.4	487.2	0.35	15.17
Bristol	397.4	401.4	406.7	412.2	418.8	429.2	442.7	455.9	469.6	0.42	18.17
Manchester	403.5	404.1	403.2	398.8	394.8	396.3	403.9	413.1	423.8	0.12	5.02
Leicester	309.1	312.5	317.3	322.7	329.0	338.0	349.2	359.9	370.9	0.46	20.00

Chart 5.211 Population age shift 2000 and 2020, Each Column Represents a Single Age Group

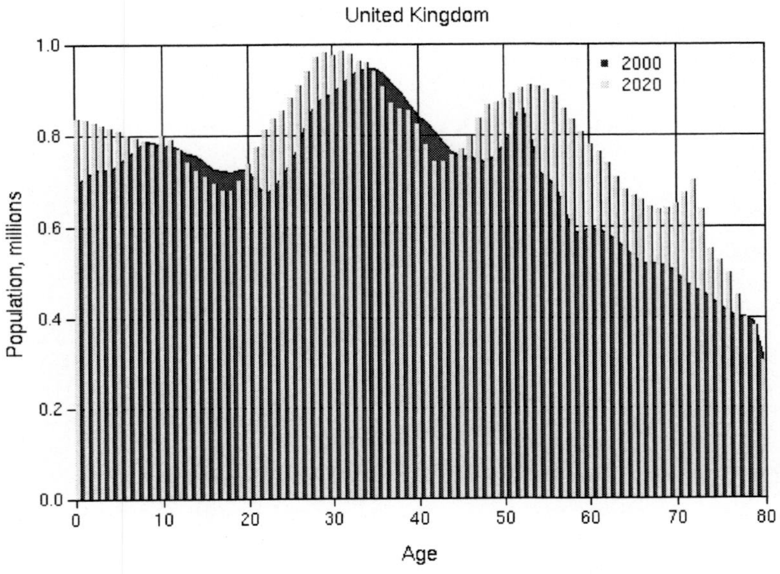

Chart 5.212 Population pyramids, 1980/2000/2010/2020

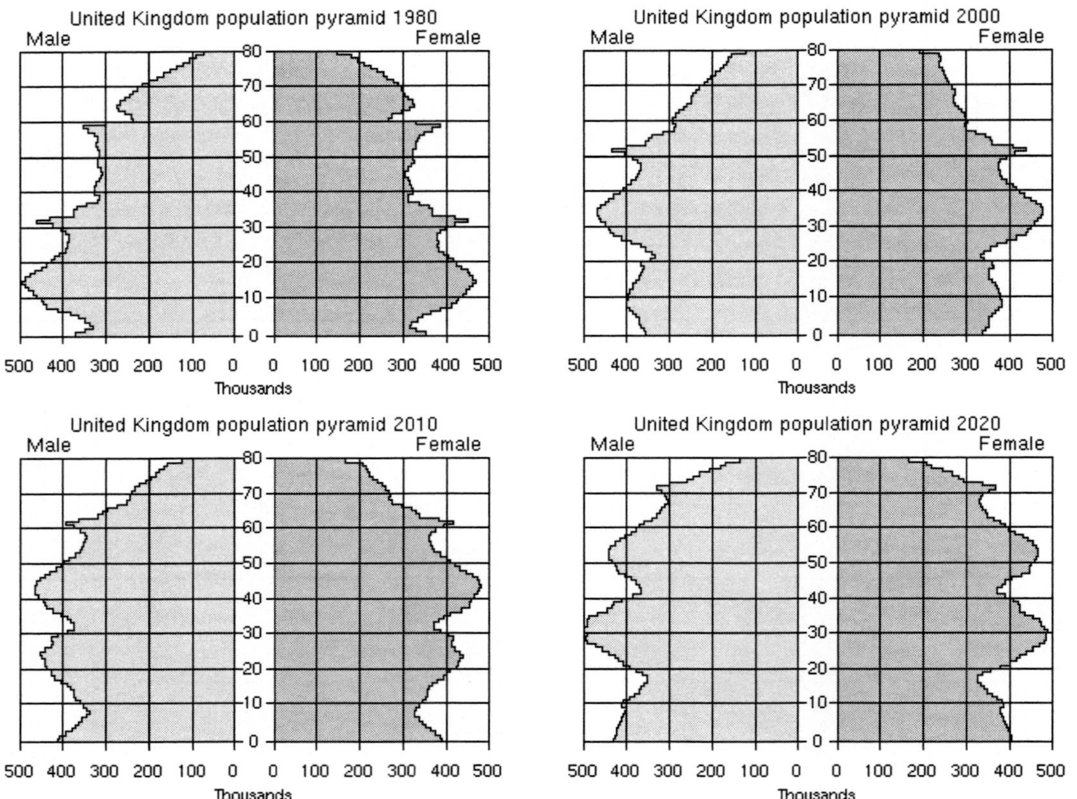

Chart 5.213 Major Cities: 1980, 2000 and 2020

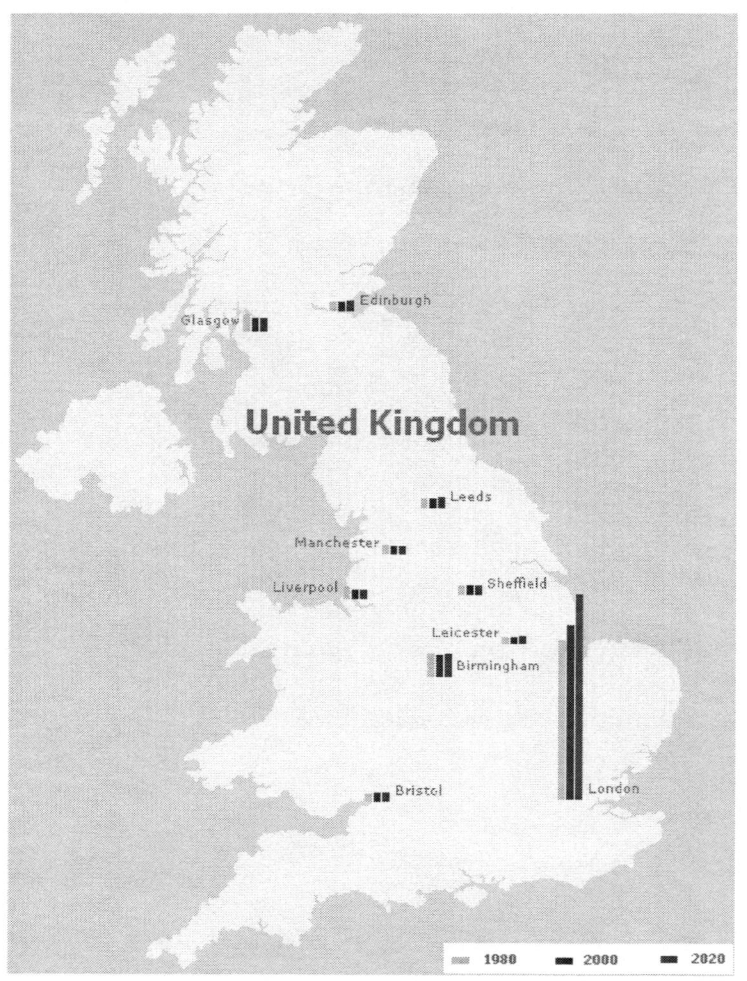

USA

Table 5.361 Key population trends

'000

	1980	1985	1990	1995	2000	2005	2010	2015	2020	CAGR	Period growth
Population at January 1st	227,726.5	237,923.8	249,622.8	266,278.4	282,171.9	295,560.5	308,862.2	319,441.3	330,205.7	0.93	45.00
Male	110,859.1	115,729.6	121,713.8	130,215.4	138,458.2	145,464.7	152,419.5	157,771.2	163,112.2	0.97	47.13
Female	116,867.4	122,194.2	127,909.1	136,063.0	143,713.8	150,095.9	156,442.7	161,670.2	167,093.4	0.90	42.98
0-4 yrs	16,451.2	17,841.7	18,856.4	19,626.5	19,186.4	20,301.4	21,405.4	21,074.1	21,494.8	0.67	30.66
5-9 yrs	16,602.4	16,664.9	18,076.7	19,438.2	20,475.0	19,505.8	20,623.7	21,743.1	21,429.7	0.64	29.08
10-14 yrs	18,236.3	17,027.5	17,212.9	19,207.0	20,618.7	20,823.3	19,905.9	21,115.0	22,326.0	0.51	22.43
15-19 yrs	21,165.4	18,727.3	17,771.6	18,374.0	20,259.3	20,993.8	21,207.8	20,437.5	21,715.2	0.06	2.60
20-24 yrs	21,589.9	21,264.6	19,150.4	18,300.2	19,123.8	20,888.3	21,460.3	21,505.1	20,759.4	-0.10	-3.85
25-29 yrs	19,792.5	21,671.1	21,277.0	19,679.9	19,302.2	19,868.9	21,546.0	21,799.1	21,820.7	0.24	10.25
30-34 yrs	17,810.4	20,025.4	21,938.8	22,372.2	20,538.1	19,947.7	20,421.5	21,948.4	22,210.4	0.55	24.70
35-39 yrs	14,120.5	17,603.6	19,990.3	22,491.6	22,658.2	20,912.8	20,241.3	20,598.9	22,151.4	1.13	56.87
40-44 yrs	11,746.8	14,087.4	17,792.9	20,219.1	22,522.8	22,801.0	20,989.7	20,175.1	20,573.0	1.41	75.14
45-49 yrs	11,053.4	11,605.6	13,829.0	17,623.7	20,221.0	22,451.0	22,648.0	20,714.8	19,963.7	1.49	80.61
50-54 yrs	11,696.0	10,853.6	11,377.8	13,856.5	17,774.1	19,980.8	22,101.3	22,134.5	20,311.3	1.39	73.66
55-59 yrs	11,611.6	11,228.6	10,478.2	11,182.3	13,558.8	17,340.5	19,465.4	21,400.1	21,493.6	1.55	85.11
60-64 yrs	10,142.7	10,906.4	10,623.5	10,137.7	10,856.5	12,993.1	16,623.8	18,573.0	20,476.5	1.77	101.88
65-69 yrs	8,809.5	9,343.1	10,078.9	9,976.5	9,517.4	10,127.0	12,154.2	15,488.1	17,367.6	1.71	97.15
70-74 yrs	6,841.2	7,515.4	8,025.1	8,889.6	8,851.6	8,512.8	9,118.1	10,918.6	13,979.8	1.80	104.35
75-79 yrs	4,829.8	5,510.8	6,147.0	6,707.9	7,435.5	7,417.6	7,204.5	7,731.5	9,334.7	1.66	93.27
80+ yrs	5,226.9	6,046.7	6,996.3	8,195.3	9,272.4	10,694.7	11,745.2	12,084.5	12,797.8	2.26	144.85
Median age of population (years)	30.0	31.4	32.8	34.2	35.4	36.3	37.0	37.4	38.0	0.59	26.71

Table 5.362 Key economic trends

As stated

	1990	1995	2000	2005	2010	2015	2020	CAGR	Period growth
Total GDP (US$ per capita)	35,597	37,776	44,007	47,299	47,078	51,167	54,125	1.41	52.0
Disposable income (US$ per capita)	28,798	28,694	31,404	33,805	34,278	37,260	39,417	1.05	36.9
Disposable income (US$ per household)	77,011	77,185	84,633	88,152	88,328	94,130	97,749	0.80	26.9
Number of households by annual household disposable income ('000)									
Over US$1,000	92,862	98,505	104,267	112,958	119,485	126,086	132,814	1.20	43.0
Over US$10,000	82,516	88,574	95,691	105,267	111,786	119,131	126,485	1.43	53.3
Over US$25,000	60,995	68,058	77,719	88,593	94,818	103,954	112,708	2.07	84.8
Over US$75,000	16,452	22,954	33,027	43,171	47,580	59,005	69,872	4.94	324.7
Over US$150,000	2,124	4,660	9,167	14,451	16,712	24,577	32,949	9.57	1,451.2
Total households	93,347	98,990	104,705	113,343	119,860	126,447	133,155	1.19	42.6

Note: Per capita data is shown at constant 2010 prices. Household disposable income bands are shown at current prices.

Table 5.363 Young generation

'000

	1980	1985	1990	1995	2000	2005	2010	2015	2020	CAGR	Period growth
Babies under 12 months	3,560	3,679	3,986	3,791	3,856	4,102	4,273	4,238	4,312	0.48	21.14
Infants under 24 months	6,875	7,155	7,785	7,624	7,655	8,197	8,586	8,462	8,617	0.57	25.33
Toddlers aged 1-4	12,891	14,163	14,870	15,835	15,331	16,200	17,132	16,836	17,183	0.72	33.29
Children aged 2-9	26,178	27,351	29,149	31,441	32,006	31,610	33,443	34,355	34,307	0.68	31.05
Female	12,789	13,358	14,228	15,345	15,623	15,447	16,350	16,809	16,794	0.68	31.31
Male	13,389	13,994	14,921	16,096	16,383	16,164	17,093	17,547	17,513	0.67	30.81
Tweenagers aged 10-14	18,236	17,027	17,213	19,207	20,619	20,823	19,906	21,115	22,326	0.51	22.43
Female	8,923	8,309	8,396	9,366	10,054	10,159	9,720	10,327	10,926	0.51	22.45
Male	9,313	8,719	8,817	9,841	10,565	10,664	10,186	10,788	11,400	0.51	22.41
Teenagers aged 13-19	28,541	26,001	24,417	26,069	28,335	29,531	29,243	28,860	30,615	0.18	7.27
Female	13,998	12,726	11,897	12,681	13,779	14,396	14,273	14,091	14,965	0.17	6.90
Male	14,543	13,275	12,520	13,388	14,556	15,135	14,970	14,769	15,650	0.18	7.61
Studying age 18-22	21,856	20,219	19,262	17,777	19,951	20,679	21,670	20,964	21,072	-0.09	-3.59
Female	10,796	9,989	9,423	8,690	9,732	10,024	10,587	10,266	10,325	-0.11	-4.36
Male	11,061	10,230	9,838	9,087	10,220	10,655	11,083	10,698	10,748	-0.07	-2.83
Young adults aged 15-29	62,548	61,663	58,199	56,354	58,685	61,751	64,214	63,742	64,295	0.07	2.79
Female	30,995	30,538	28,647	27,688	28,726	30,090	31,269	31,222	31,582	0.05	1.89
Male	31,553	31,125	29,552	28,666	29,959	31,661	32,945	32,519	32,713	0.09	3.68

Table 5.364 Middle-aged generation
'000

	1980	1985	1990	1995	2000	2005	2010	2015	2020	CAGR	Period growth
Middle-aged adults 30-59	78,039	85,404	95,407	107,745	117,273	123,434	125,867	126,972	126,703	1.22	62.4
Female	40,013	43,622	48,482	54,551	59,257	62,244	63,231	63,502	63,177	1.15	57.9
Male	38,026	41,782	46,925	53,195	58,016	61,189	62,637	63,470	63,527	1.29	67.1
Baby boomers aged 40-59	46,108	47,775	53,478	62,882	74,077	82,573	85,204	84,425	82,342	1.46	78.6
Female	23,878	24,616	27,384	32,100	37,699	41,959	43,181	42,682	41,434	1.39	73.5
Male	22,229	23,160	26,094	30,781	36,378	40,615	42,024	41,742	40,908	1.54	84.0

Table 5.365 Elderly population
'000

	1980	1985	1990	1995	2000	2005	2010	2015	2020	CAGR	Period growth
Elderly population (60+)	35,850	39,322	41,871	43,907	45,933	49,745	56,846	64,796	73,956	1.83	106.3
Female	20,788	22,873	24,355	25,391	26,316	28,154	31,679	35,674	40,401	1.68	94.3
Male	15,062	16,449	17,516	18,516	19,618	21,592	25,167	29,121	33,555	2.02	122.8

Table 5.366 Population of biggest cities 1980-2020
'000

	1980	1985	1990	1995	2000	2005	2010	2015	2020	CAGR	Period growth
New York	7,071.6	7,157.0	7,322.6	7,683.4	8,008.7	8,238.8	8,468.9	8,794.1	9,188.4	0.66	29.93
Los Angeles	2,968.5	3,202.4	3,485.4	3,638.9	3,694.6	3,768.9	3,886.9	4,045.4	4,232.6	0.89	42.58
Chicago	3,005.1	2,865.3	2,783.7	2,836.5	2,896.1	2,883.0	2,849.0	2,882.3	2,963.8	-0.03	-1.37
Houston	1,595.1	1,587.1	1,630.6	1,799.3	1,974.2	2,143.2	2,306.4	2,463.2	2,616.3	1.24	64.02
Phoenix	789.7	872.9	983.4	1,147.5	1,322.0	1,476.8	1,624.9	1,757.7	1,880.7	2.19	138.15
Philadelphia	1,688.2	1,634.8	1,585.6	1,558.2	1,517.6	1,473.2	1,439.6	1,445.7	1,479.7	-0.33	-12.35
San Antonio	785.9	854.5	935.9	1,045.5	1,160.0	1,276.4	1,398.5	1,509.4	1,612.9	1.81	105.22
Dallas	904.6	948.5	1,006.9	1,097.3	1,188.6	1,271.9	1,356.9	1,441.9	1,527.0	1.32	68.81
San Diego	875.5	1,001.6	1,110.5	1,176.0	1,223.4	1,255.9	1,297.9	1,352.5	1,416.1	1.21	61.74
Detroit	1,203.4	1,109.3	1,028.0	984.3	951.3	925.2	908.9	916.2	939.9	-0.62	-21.89

Chart 5.214 Population age shift 2000 and 2020, Each Column Represents a Single Age Group

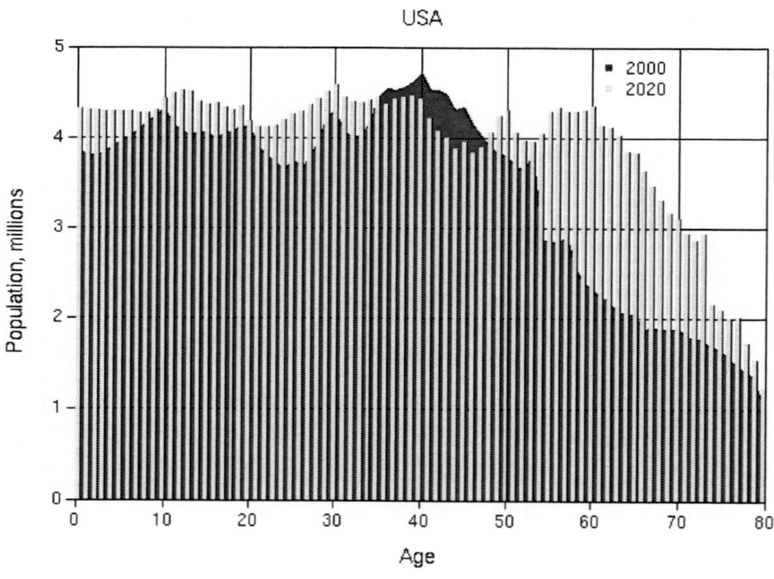

Chart 5.215 Population pyramids, 1980/2000/2010/2020

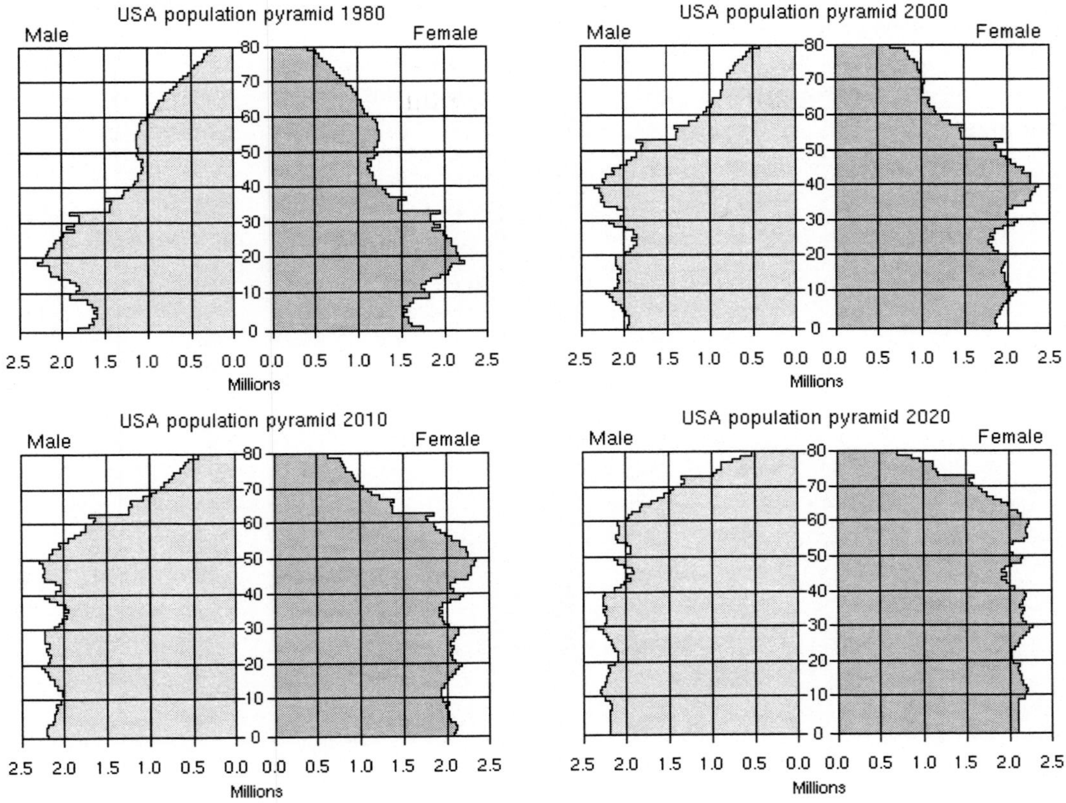

Chart 5.216 Major Cities: 1980, 2000 and 2020

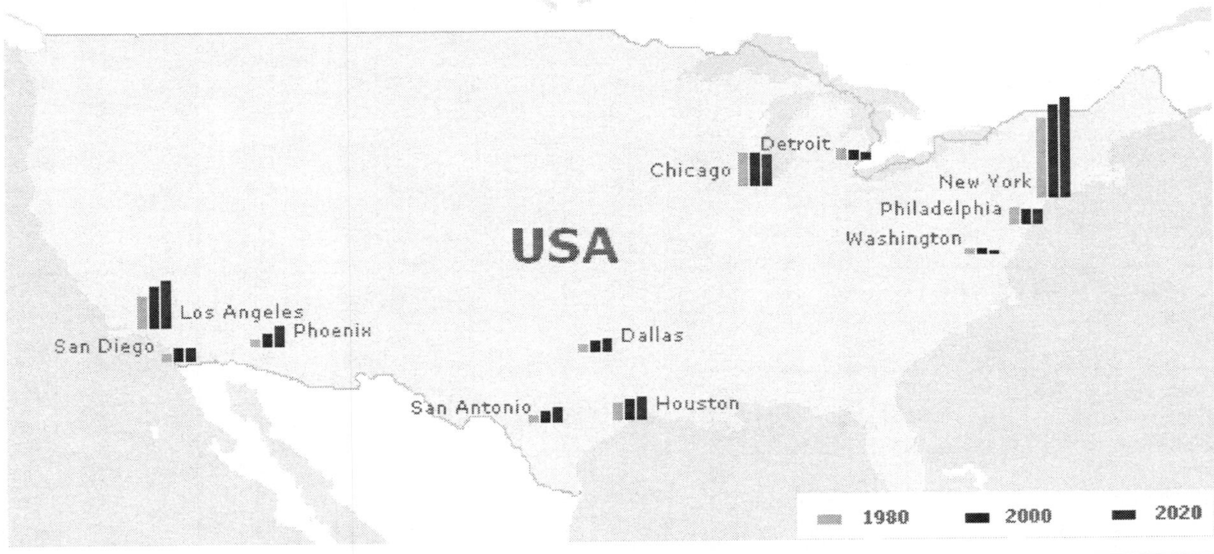

Venezuela

Table 5.367 Key population trends

'000

	1980	1985	1990	1995	2000	2005	2010	2015	2020	CAGR	Period growth
Population at January 1st	15,096.5	17,322.8	19,740.8	22,092.2	24,407.7	26,726.1	29,043.6	31,291.6	33,412.2	2.01	121.3
Male	7,640.9	8,751.0	9,958.4	11,132.6	12,283.9	13,432.3	14,575.6	15,680.0	16,715.3	1.98	118.8
Female	7,455.6	8,571.8	9,782.4	10,959.7	12,123.8	13,293.8	14,467.9	15,611.6	16,696.9	2.04	124.0
0-4 yrs	2,302.2	2,504.8	2,727.6	2,743.9	2,781.2	2,866.1	2,934.6	2,948.0	2,914.7	0.59	26.6
5-9 yrs	1,975.9	2,274.3	2,504.0	2,710.7	2,742.4	2,771.8	2,855.0	2,926.9	2,942.6	1.00	48.9
10-14 yrs	1,871.8	1,979.6	2,272.3	2,502.0	2,705.6	2,738.1	2,770.5	2,852.9	2,924.5	1.12	56.2
15-19 yrs	1,726.0	1,873.1	1,980.0	2,267.8	2,494.1	2,697.7	2,731.1	2,764.5	2,847.6	1.26	65.0
20-24 yrs	1,440.1	1,728.0	1,872.1	1,973.7	2,254.9	2,480.0	2,684.1	2,719.1	2,753.9	1.63	91.2
25-29 yrs	1,241.4	1,441.9	1,723.9	1,865.2	1,961.4	2,240.1	2,465.4	2,669.8	2,706.4	1.97	118.0
30-34 yrs	1,023.7	1,239.7	1,434.6	1,715.2	1,852.1	1,947.9	2,225.9	2,450.9	2,655.4	2.41	159.4
35-39 yrs	787.4	1,018.1	1,229.9	1,423.7	1,699.4	1,835.7	1,932.4	2,209.1	2,433.7	2.86	209.1
40-44 yrs	618.3	778.7	1,005.9	1,215.5	1,406.0	1,679.2	1,815.5	1,912.5	2,187.8	3.21	253.9
45-49 yrs	532.7	606.6	764.3	987.9	1,193.6	1,382.2	1,652.7	1,788.5	1,885.8	3.21	254.0
50-54 yrs	459.7	516.3	589.2	743.1	961.1	1,163.1	1,349.1	1,615.4	1,750.4	3.40	280.8
55-59 yrs	353.0	437.7	493.0	563.5	712.3	923.5	1,120.4	1,302.6	1,562.9	3.79	342.7
60-64 yrs	269.4	327.1	407.6	460.5	528.7	670.8	872.9	1,062.3	1,239.0	3.89	359.8
65-69 yrs	200.9	239.6	293.3	367.5	417.8	482.2	615.2	804.4	983.4	4.05	389.6
70-74 yrs	143.4	168.9	203.6	251.1	317.3	363.3	422.9	543.3	715.2	4.10	398.7
75-79 yrs	86.5	109.5	131.4	160.6	201.2	256.9	297.2	350.0	454.5	4.24	425.5
80+ yrs	64.2	78.8	108.2	140.5	178.8	227.5	298.8	371.4	454.3	5.01	608.0
Median age of population (years)	19.0	20.1	21.0	22.0	23.2	24.6	26.1	27.7	29.3	1.09	54.3

Table 5.368 Key economic trends

As stated

	1990	1995	2000	2005	2010	2015	2020	CAGR	Period growth
Total GDP (BsF per capita)	30,183.0	31,902.2	29,975.1	31,052.9	34,968.8	33,129.6	31,569.6	0.15	4.59
Disposable income (BsF per capita)	22,105.5	21,850.0	15,231.1	19,804.5	25,119.2	24,485.8	23,589.0	0.22	6.71
Disposable income (BsF per household)	116,339.4	109,727.8	72,657.5	91,606.7	111,719.3	104,732.3	96,886.8	-0.61	-16.72
Number of households by annual household disposable income ('000)									
Over US$1,000	3,681.2	4,362.3	5,056.6	5,691.7	6,513.9	7,296.1	8,110.5	2.67	120.32
Over US$10,000	1,132.5	2,345.3	2,599.7	3,153.6	5,774.7	6,467.5	7,142.6	6.33	530.72
Over US$25,000	181.0	557.9	660.9	875.9	3,840.1	4,356.8	4,766.5	11.52	2,533.03
Over US$75,000	34.1	72.5	83.6	98.6	734.4	889.0	973.2	11.82	2,756.25
Over US$150,000	14.4	30.8	35.7	42.1	156.3	184.7	203.0	9.22	1,308.42
Total households	3,750.9	4,399.2	5,116.6	5,777.9	6,530.2	7,315.8	8,134.9	2.61	116.88

Note: Per capita data is shown at constant 2010 prices. Household disposable income bands are shown at current prices.

Table 5.369 Young generation

'000

	1980	1985	1990	1995	2000	2005	2010	2015	2020	CAGR	Period growth
Babies under 12 months	504.0	504.9	567.2	536.0	568.1	583.5	591.0	587.6	579.1	0.35	14.9
Infants under 24 months	983.6	1,012.1	1,122.2	1,082.0	1,127.3	1,162.2	1,180.8	1,176.9	1,160.3	0.41	18.0
Toddlers aged 1-4	1,798.2	1,999.9	2,160.5	2,207.9	2,213.1	2,282.6	2,343.6	2,360.4	2,335.6	0.66	29.9
Children aged 2-9	3,294.5	3,767.0	4,109.4	4,372.6	4,396.3	4,475.8	4,608.8	4,698.0	4,697.0	0.89	42.6
Female	1,614.1	1,846.2	2,014.3	2,141.8	2,151.7	2,189.8	2,255.1	2,297.9	2,296.7	0.89	42.3
Male	1,680.4	1,920.8	2,095.2	2,230.8	2,244.6	2,285.9	2,353.7	2,400.1	2,400.3	0.90	42.8
Tweenagers aged 10-14	1,871.8	1,979.6	2,272.3	2,502.0	2,705.6	2,738.1	2,770.5	2,852.9	2,924.5	1.12	56.2
Female	918.3	970.9	1,114.4	1,227.3	1,326.3	1,341.1	1,356.2	1,396.6	1,431.3	1.12	55.9
Male	953.5	1,008.7	1,157.9	1,274.8	1,379.2	1,397.0	1,414.3	1,456.3	1,493.3	1.13	56.6
Teenagers aged 13-19	2,466.2	2,641.0	2,853.8	3,241.6	3,559.8	3,792.9	3,831.3	3,894.6	4,011.1	1.22	62.6
Female	1,211.4	1,297.6	1,401.4	1,591.5	1,748.3	1,861.6	1,878.6	1,908.6	1,965.5	1.22	62.2
Male	1,254.8	1,343.3	1,452.4	1,650.1	1,811.5	1,931.3	1,952.7	1,986.0	2,045.6	1.23	63.0
Studying age 18-22	1,554.0	1,807.9	1,900.1	2,080.0	2,358.4	2,577.9	2,719.9	2,729.8	2,788.8	1.47	79.5
Female	764.6	890.4	935.6	1,023.4	1,161.5	1,269.9	1,338.4	1,341.5	1,369.6	1.47	79.1
Male	789.4	917.5	964.5	1,056.6	1,196.9	1,308.0	1,381.6	1,388.4	1,419.2	1.48	79.8
Young adults aged 15-29	4,407.5	5,042.9	5,576.0	6,106.7	6,710.4	7,417.8	7,880.6	8,153.3	8,307.9	1.60	88.5
Female	2,168.5	2,485.7	2,749.1	3,010.1	3,310.0	3,660.9	3,887.5	4,017.5	4,089.3	1.60	88.6
Male	2,239.1	2,557.2	2,826.9	3,096.7	3,400.3	3,756.9	3,993.0	4,135.7	4,218.7	1.60	88.4

Table 5.370 Middle-aged generation

'000

	1980	1985	1990	1995	2000	2005	2010	2015	2020	CAGR	Period growth
Middle-aged adults 30-59	3,774.8	4,597.1	5,516.8	6,648.8	7,824.4	8,931.6	10,096.0	11,279.1	12,476.0	3.03	230.5
Female	1,866.5	2,280.1	2,744.7	3,314.7	3,908.7	4,472.3	5,066.2	5,666.4	6,268.9	3.08	235.9
Male	1,908.3	2,317.0	2,772.1	3,334.1	3,915.7	4,459.3	5,029.8	5,612.6	6,207.0	2.99	225.3
Baby boomers aged 40-59	1,963.7	2,339.3	2,852.3	3,510.0	4,273.0	5,147.9	5,937.7	6,619.0	7,386.9	3.37	276.2
Female	976.1	1,165.9	1,422.8	1,753.8	2,139.7	2,584.8	2,990.2	3,339.4	3,730.5	3.41	282.2
Male	987.6	1,173.4	1,429.5	1,756.1	2,133.3	2,563.2	2,947.6	3,279.7	3,656.4	3.33	270.2

Table 5.371 Elderly population

'000

	1980	1985	1990	1995	2000	2005	2010	2015	2020	CAGR	Period growth
Elderly population (60+)	764.4	924.0	1,144.1	1,380.1	1,643.7	2,000.7	2,506.9	3,131.4	3,846.4	4.12	403.2
Female	406.5	493.0	610.7	736.8	876.0	1,061.4	1,325.9	1,658.1	2,043.8	4.12	402.8
Male	357.9	431.0	533.3	643.3	767.8	939.3	1,181.0	1,473.4	1,802.5	4.12	403.7

Table 5.372 Population of biggest cities 1980-2020

'000

	1980	1985	1990	1995	2000	2005	2010	2015	2020	CAGR	Period growth
Caracas	1,803.8	1,814.7	1,822.5	1,834.5	1,837.8	1,845.4	1,906.9	1,996.5	2,097.5	0.38	16.3
Maracaibo	850.5	1,045.1	1,249.7	1,428.1	1,580.0	1,722.1	1,857.5	1,986.6	2,108.7	2.30	147.9
Valencia	584.8	739.9	903.6	1,047.6	1,172.0	1,290.4	1,406.0	1,517.7	1,624.3	2.59	177.7
Barquisimeto	510.7	562.5	625.5	703.4	792.4	883.2	968.9	1,049.5	1,124.5	1.99	120.2
Ciudad Guayana	299.6	372.4	453.0	533.5	612.9	691.3	764.7	833.1	896.3	2.78	199.1
Maturin	149.8	173.9	206.7	253.3	312.2	374.0	430.3	481.3	527.3	3.20	252.1
Maracay	317.4	335.2	354.2	373.4	390.8	407.0	424.7	443.3	462.2	0.94	45.6
Turmero	105.2	135.1	174.3	227.0	291.9	359.9	421.3	476.5	526.0	4.10	399.8
Petare	399.4	365.6	338.4	339.5	363.1	391.8	419.7	446.6	472.1	0.42	18.2
Barcelona	149.7	182.6	221.8	267.0	317.4	368.8	416.1	459.5	499.0	3.06	233.4

Chart 5.217 Population age shift 2000 and 2020, Each Column Represents a Single Age Group

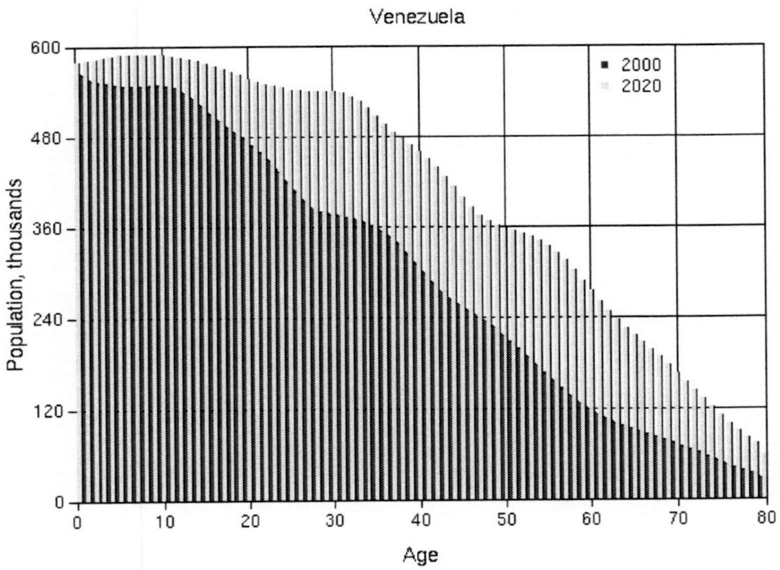

Chart 5.218 Population pyramids, 1980/2000/2010/2020

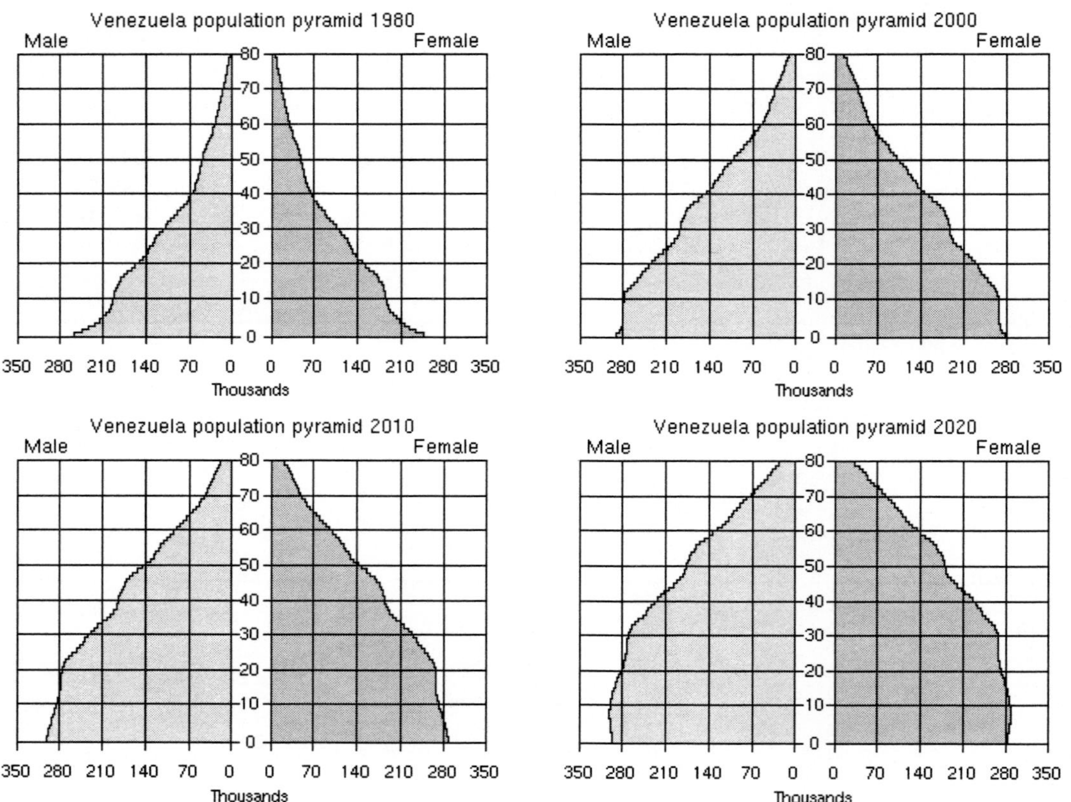

Chart 5.219 Major Cities: 1980, 2000 and 2020

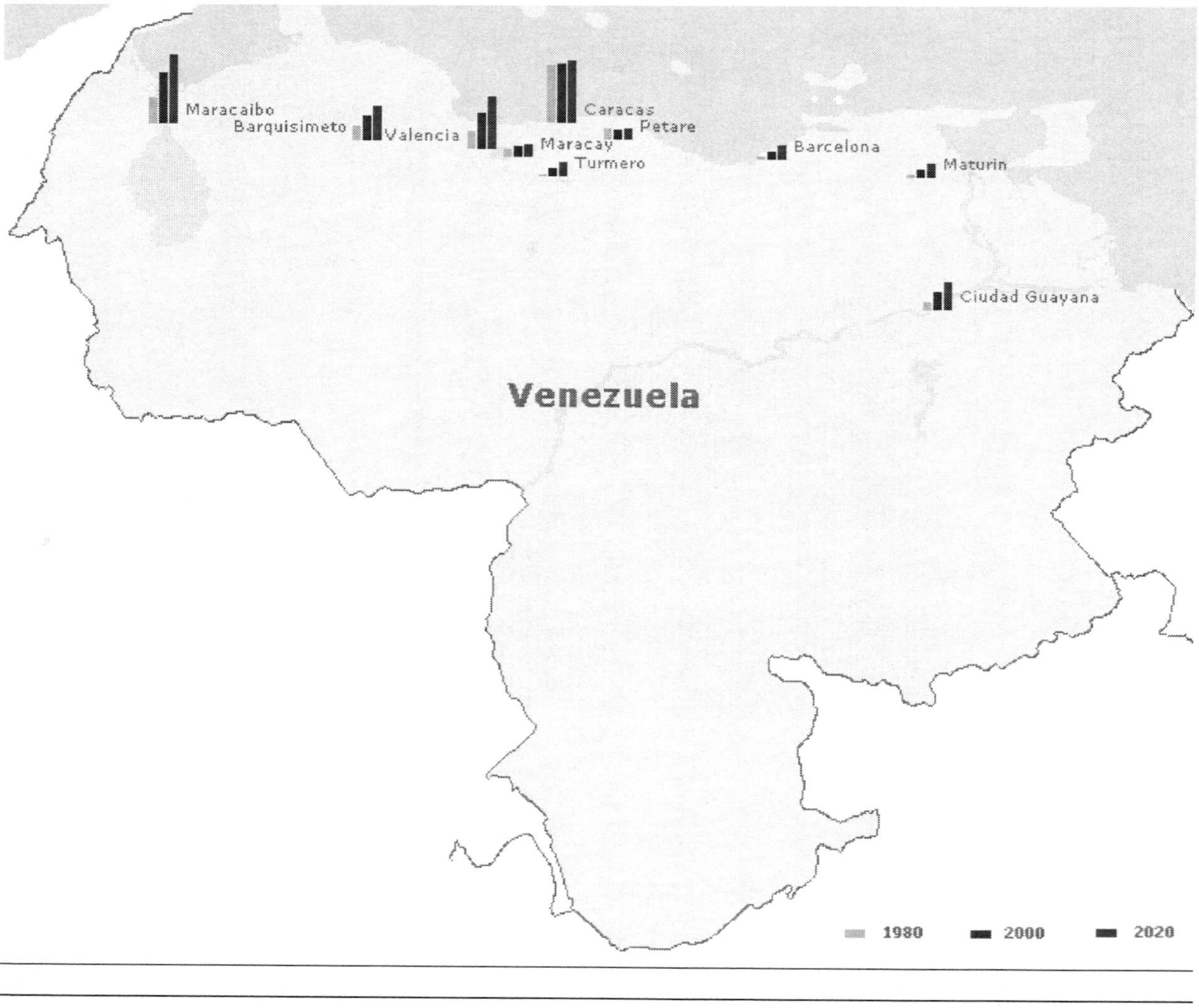

Maracaibo
Barquisimeto
Valencia
Caracas
Petare
Maracay
Turmero
Barcelona
Maturin
Ciudad Guayana
Venezuela
1980 2000 2020

Vietnam

Table 5.373 Key population trends

'000

	1980	1985	1990	1995	2000	2005	2010	2015	2020	CAGR	Period growth
Population at January 1st	52,576.1	58,546.4	65,493.8	72,363.0	77,775.6	83,198.1	88,744.5	94,372.5	99,768.9	1.61	89.76
Male	26,129.2	29,122.4	32,633.0	36,117.0	38,857.8	41,593.4	44,376.7	47,191.3	49,878.9	1.63	90.89
Female	26,446.9	29,423.9	32,860.8	36,246.0	38,917.8	41,604.8	44,367.8	47,181.2	49,890.0	1.60	88.64
0-4 yrs	8,109.0	8,599.5	9,405.3	9,279.9	7,758.0	7,893.7	7,888.4	7,856.5	7,639.8	-0.15	-5.79
5-9 yrs	7,226.1	7,792.8	8,367.8	9,240.0	9,167.1	7,675.6	7,844.0	7,868.8	7,855.3	0.21	8.71
10-14 yrs	6,606.2	7,097.7	7,693.4	8,277.7	9,160.1	9,085.9	7,634.3	7,828.8	7,869.6	0.44	19.13
15-19 yrs	5,956.2	6,482.8	6,995.2	7,591.9	8,186.5	9,060.5	9,021.7	7,603.4	7,814.0	0.68	31.19
20-24 yrs	4,902.5	5,812.7	6,357.4	6,872.3	7,479.9	8,072.1	8,973.8	8,968.7	7,571.8	1.09	54.45
25-29 yrs	3,839.4	4,761.0	5,679.8	6,228.7	6,756.3	7,363.1	7,982.8	8,911.6	8,927.6	2.13	132.53
30-34 yrs	2,483.6	3,715.7	4,640.6	5,557.0	6,117.7	6,645.4	7,276.3	7,921.5	8,867.5	3.23	257.04
35-39 yrs	2,108.8	2,389.9	3,611.2	4,532.1	5,452.7	6,012.0	6,561.4	7,214.8	7,876.0	3.35	273.48
40-44 yrs	2,024.6	2,020.7	2,308.6	3,514.5	4,434.7	5,347.3	5,925.1	6,495.1	7,162.6	3.21	253.78
45-49 yrs	2,112.3	1,935.3	1,945.9	2,236.1	3,426.0	4,334.4	5,254.8	5,850.0	6,432.6	2.82	204.53
50-54 yrs	1,761.1	2,002.5	1,848.8	1,869.9	2,160.8	3,323.2	4,229.7	5,155.0	5,758.9	3.01	227.01
55-59 yrs	1,567.6	1,643.2	1,887.7	1,755.6	1,786.0	2,072.3	3,210.0	4,110.0	5,029.9	2.96	220.86
60-64 yrs	1,275.5	1,426.4	1,514.0	1,759.3	1,647.5	1,685.0	1,969.8	3,072.9	3,953.9	2.87	209.99
65-69 yrs	1,068.1	1,106.9	1,258.6	1,357.3	1,592.8	1,503.9	1,552.2	1,829.9	2,873.9	2.51	169.06
70-74 yrs	741.0	857.6	909.1	1,058.2	1,157.0	1,375.8	1,315.1	1,372.7	1,633.2	2.00	120.41
75-79 yrs	503.6	525.1	627.1	687.2	815.6	909.2	1,100.7	1,068.8	1,130.7	2.04	124.50
80+ yrs	290.5	376.8	443.0	545.3	677.2	838.7	1,004.5	1,243.9	1,371.5	3.96	372.08
Median age of population (years)	18.6	19.4	20.2	21.3	23.0	24.9	26.8	28.9	31.2	1.31	68.06

Table 5.374 Key economic trends

As stated

	1990	1995	2000	2005	2010	2015	2020	CAGR	Period growth
Total GDP (VND per capita)	7,014,537	9,421,027	12,265,897	16,467,675	21,198,237	27,563,338	36,701,229	5.67	423.2
Disposable income (VND per capita)	5,021,414	6,168,970	8,401,403	11,432,163	15,543,773	20,874,173	28,220,885	5.92	462.0
Disposable income (VND per household)	24,535,324	28,962,913	38,550,176	51,404,597	68,464,676	90,025,887	119,118,630	5.41	385.5
Number of households by annual household disposable income ('000)									
Over US$1,000	675	6,716	8,976	12,696	17,628	20,480	23,098	12.50	3,322.3
Over US$10,000	33	111	172	304	806	1,736	4,294	17.57	12,734.9
Over US$25,000	10	35	55	98	211	347	728	15.21	6,894.6
Over US$75,000	3	9	14	25	54	89	164	14.87	6,302.4
Over US$150,000	1	4	6	11	23	38	70	14.97	6,468.6
Total households	13,404	15,413	16,950	18,503	20,148	21,882	23,637	1.91	76.3

Note: Per capita data is shown at constant 2010 prices. Household disposable income bands are shown at current prices.

Table 5.375 Young generation

'000

	1980	1985	1990	1995	2000	2005	2010	2015	2020	CAGR	Period growth
Babies under 12 months	1,715	1,791	1,995	1,775	1,356	1,777	1,514	1,572	1,497	-0.34	-12.73
Infants under 24 months	3,379	3,545	3,926	3,608	2,825	3,415	3,077	3,143	3,012	-0.29	-10.86
Toddlers aged 1-4	6,394	6,809	7,411	7,505	6,402	6,116	6,374	6,284	6,143	-0.10	-3.93
Children aged 2-9	11,956	12,847	13,847	14,912	14,100	12,154	12,656	12,582	12,483	0.11	4.41
Female	5,940	6,343	6,822	7,322	6,912	5,954	6,199	6,159	6,108	0.07	2.82
Male	6,016	6,504	7,025	7,590	7,188	6,199	6,457	6,423	6,376	0.15	5.97
Tweenagers aged 10-14	6,606	7,098	7,693	8,278	9,160	9,086	7,634	7,829	7,870	0.44	19.13
Female	3,301	3,541	3,809	4,087	4,506	4,460	3,744	3,838	3,855	0.39	16.79
Male	3,305	3,557	3,885	4,191	4,654	4,626	3,891	3,991	4,014	0.49	21.45
Teenagers aged 13-19	8,530	9,246	9,992	10,800	11,766	12,790	12,182	10,694	10,960	0.63	28.48
Female	4,264	4,625	4,981	5,349	5,810	6,294	5,983	5,248	5,376	0.58	26.09
Male	4,266	4,621	5,011	5,451	5,957	6,496	6,199	5,446	5,584	0.68	30.88
Studying age 18-22	5,344	6,117	6,607	7,157	7,742	8,488	9,173	8,437	7,523	0.86	40.79
Female	2,674	3,066	3,312	3,570	3,837	4,195	4,518	4,149	3,696	0.81	38.25
Male	2,670	3,051	3,295	3,588	3,905	4,293	4,654	4,288	3,827	0.90	43.33
Young adults aged 15-29	14,698	17,056	19,032	20,693	22,423	24,496	25,978	25,484	24,313	1.27	65.42
Female	7,358	8,554	9,545	10,341	11,155	12,129	12,826	12,557	11,964	1.22	62.60
Male	7,340	8,502	9,488	10,352	11,268	12,367	13,152	12,927	12,350	1.31	68.24

Table 5.376 Middle-aged generation

'000

	1980	1985	1990	1995	2000	2005	2010	2015	2020	CAGR	Period growth
Middle-aged adults 30-59	12,058	13,707	16,243	19,465	23,378	27,735	32,457	36,746	41,127	3.11	241.1
Female	6,107	6,944	8,229	9,859	11,842	14,047	16,407	18,533	20,675	3.10	238.5
Male	5,951	6,763	8,014	9,606	11,536	13,688	16,051	18,213	20,453	3.13	243.7
Baby boomers aged 40-59	7,466	7,602	7,991	9,376	11,807	15,077	18,620	21,610	24,384	3.00	226.6
Female	3,790	3,864	4,066	4,763	5,997	7,662	9,465	10,984	12,355	3.00	226.0
Male	3,676	3,737	3,925	4,613	5,811	7,416	9,154	10,627	12,029	3.01	227.2

Table 5.377 Elderly population

'000

	1980	1985	1990	1995	2000	2005	2010	2015	2020	CAGR	Period growth
Elderly population (60+)	3,879	4,293	4,752	5,407	5,890	6,313	6,942	8,588	10,963	2.63	182.6
Female	2,083	2,297	2,533	2,871	3,120	3,344	3,688	4,558	5,817	2.60	179.2
Male	1,795	1,996	2,218	2,536	2,770	2,969	3,254	4,031	5,147	2.67	186.7

Table 5.378 Population of biggest cities 1980-2020

'000

	1980	1985	1990	1995	2000	2005	2010	2015	2020	CAGR	Period growth
Ho Chi Minh City	2,703.5	2,758.1	2,981.5	3,493.7	4,365.8	5,114.6	5,941.0	6,818.0	7,750.1	2.67	186.7
Hanoi	895.4	992.1	1,118.2	1,285.1	1,576.2	1,824.5	2,104.4	2,405.2	2,727.6	2.82	204.6
Da Nang	321.6	342.2	381.2	449.4	564.6	663.6	772.4	887.4	1,009.4	2.90	213.9
Bien Hoa	194.1	234.3	285.1	349.8	454.7	545.6	642.4	743.0	848.4	3.76	337.1
Haiphong	391.4	425.7	454.4	466.0	487.6	499.8	532.5	579.3	637.5	1.23	62.9
Nha Trang	176.2	196.7	217.5	235.7	266.1	290.3	322.9	361.0	404.0	2.10	129.2
Can Tho	184.9	197.4	210.8	223.9	249.5	269.6	297.9	331.7	370.4	1.75	100.3
Qui Nhon	129.8	145.2	163.9	186.6	225.4	258.2	296.0	337.0	381.4	2.73	193.8
Vung Tau	85.1	104.7	128.8	158.3	205.4	246.2	289.7	334.9	382.3	3.83	349.4
Hue	169.4	191.6	215.0	223.7	235.0	241.5	257.9	280.9	309.4	1.52	82.6

Chart 5.220 Population age shift 2000 and 2020, Each Column Represents a Single Age Group

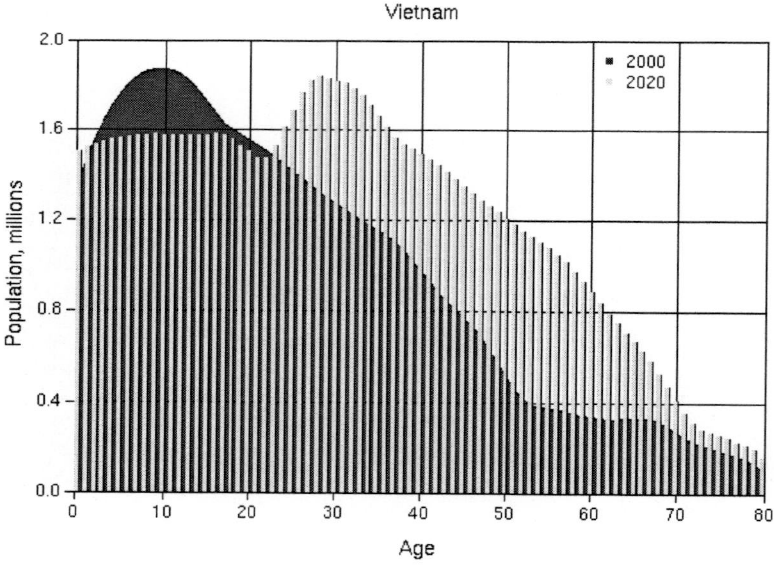

Chart 5.221 Population pyramids, 1980/2000/2010/2020

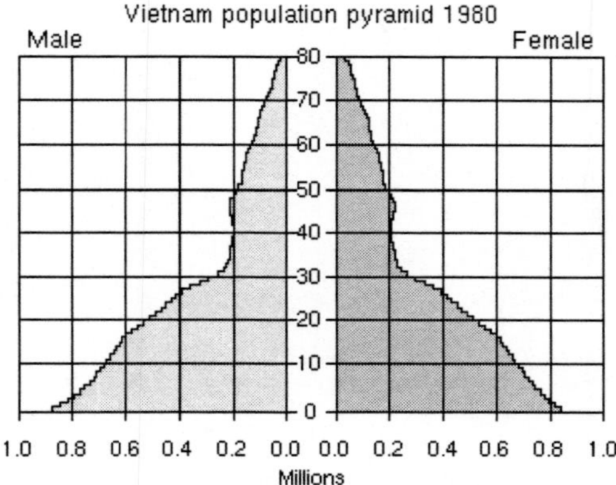

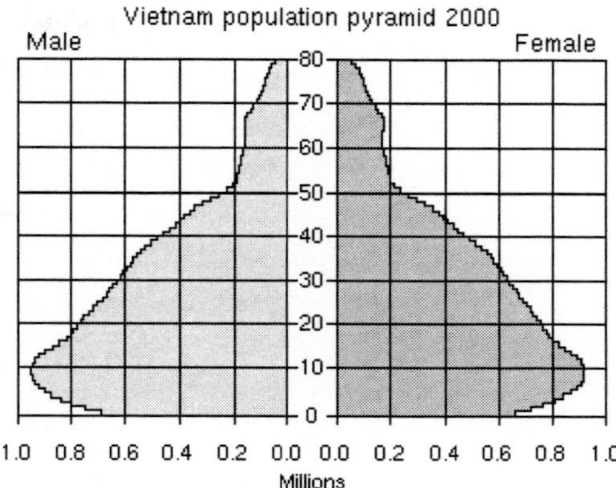

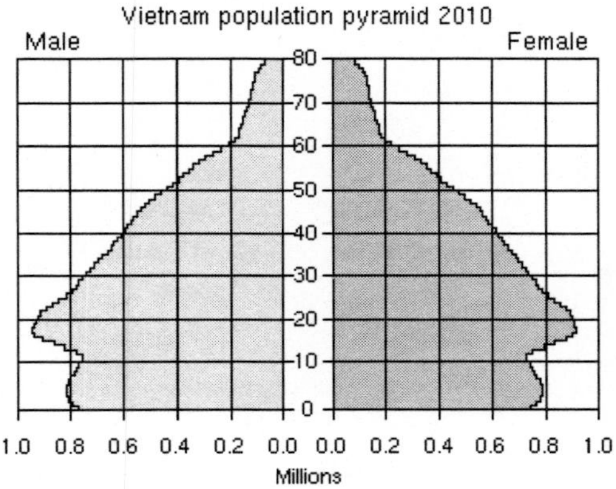

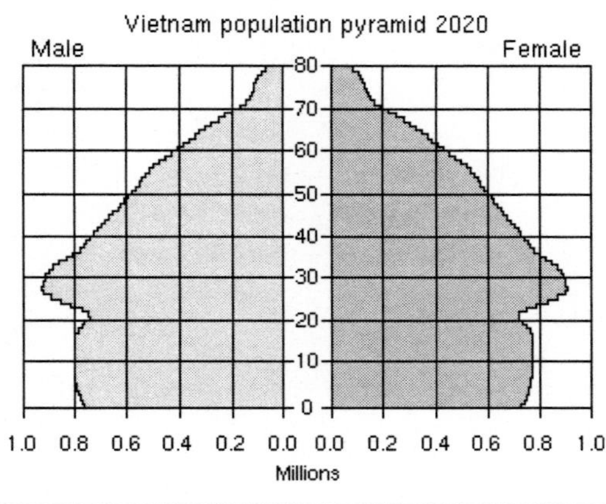

Chart 5.222 Major Cities: 1980, 2000 and 2020

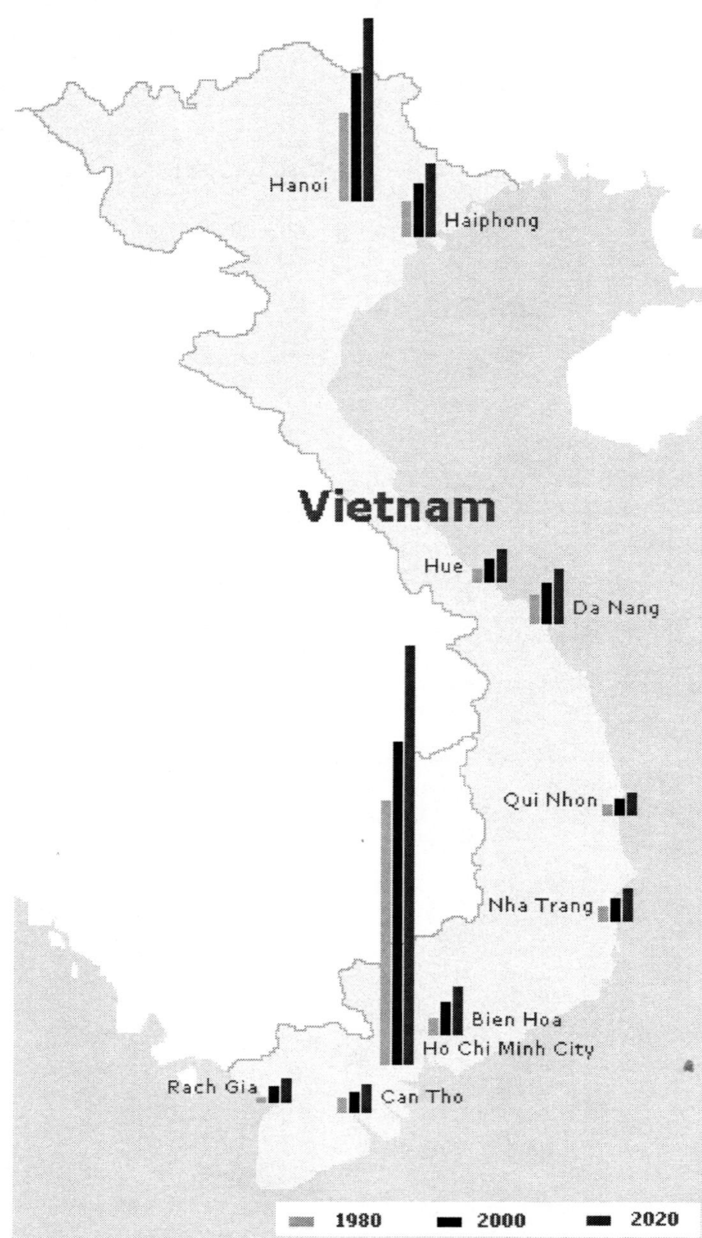

